Australia

written and researched by

Margo Daly, Anne Dehne, David Leffman
and **Chris Scott**

with additional contributions by

Nicky Agate, Tim Dub, Matthew Hall, Ian Osborn,

Stephen Townshend and Rosie Waitt

**ROUGH
GUIDES**

www.roughguides.com

INDONESIA

*TIMOR
SEA*

Darwin

Katherine

*INDIAN
OCEAN*

Kununurra

Halls
Creek

*TANAMI
DESERT*

Broome

NORTHERN

Port Hedland

*GREAT SANDY
DESERT*

Newman

GIBSON DESERT

Uluru
(Ayers Rock)

Carnarvon

**WESTERN
AUSTRALIA**

Meekatharra

SOUTH

Geraldton

*GREAT VICTORIA
DESERT*

Kalgoorlie
Boulder

Perth   Northam

*Great Australian
Bight*

Bunbury

Esperance

Albany

SOUTHERN OCEAN

N

| 0 | 800 km |

PAPUA
NEW GUINEA

ARAFURA SEA

*Cape
York
Peninsula*

*Gulf of
Carpentaria*

*CORAL
SEA*

Cairns

Great Barrier Reef

Tennant
Creek

Mount
Isa

Townsville

*PACIFIC
OCEAN*

TERRITORY

Charters
Towers

Mackay

Alice Springs

Rockhampton

QUEENSLAND

GREAT DIVIDING RANGE

SIMPSON

DESERT

AUSTRALIA

Coober
Pedy

Brisbane
Toowoomba

NEW SOUTH WALES

Grafton

Port
Augusta

Broken Hill

Tamworth

Dubbo

Newcastle

Mildura

Adelaide

*Kangaroo
Island*

VICTORIA

Bendigo

ACT Canberra

Albury

Sydney

Ballarat

Melbourne

Mount
Gambier

Geelong

King Is *Bass Strait* *Flinders Is*

*TASMAN
SEA*

Launceston

TASMANIA

Hobart

iii

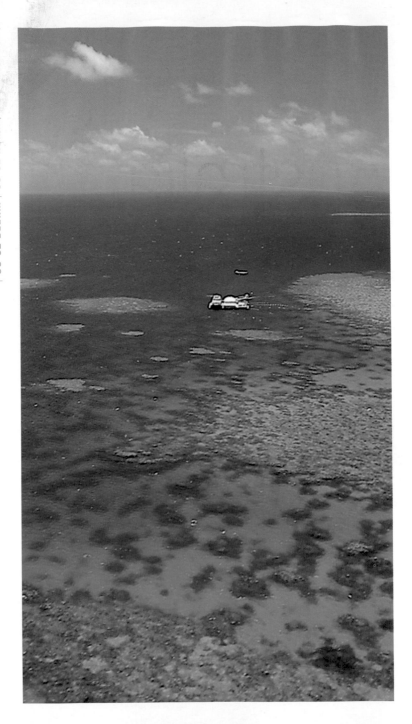

Introduction to

Australia

Australia is massive, and very sparsely peopled: in size it rivals the USA, yet its population is just over eighteen million – little more than that of the Netherlands. This is an ancient land, and often looks it: in places, it's the most eroded, denuded and driest of continents, with much of central and western Australia – the bulk of the country – overwhelmingly arid and flat. In contrast, its cities – most of which were founded as recently as the mid-nineteenth century – express a youthful energy.

The most memorable scenery is in the Outback, the vast desert in the interior of the country west of the Great Dividing Range. Here, vivid blue skies, cinnamon-red earth, deserted gorges and other striking geological features as well as bizarre wildlife comprise a unique ecology – one that has played host to the oldest surviving human culture for at least fifty thousand years.

The harshness of the interior has forced modern Australia to become a coastal country. Most of the population lives within 20km of the ocean, occupying a suburban, southeastern arc extending from southern Queensland to Adelaide. These urban Australians celebrate the typical New World values of material self-improvement through hard work and hard play, with an easy-going vitality that visitors, especially Europeans, often find refreshingly hedonistic. A sunny climate also contributes to this exuberance, with an outdoor life in which a thriving beach culture and the congenial backyard "barbie" are central.

While visitors might eventually find this *Home and Away* lifestyle rather prosaic, there are opportunities – particularly in the Northern Territory – to

Fact file

● With an area of eight million square kilometres, Australia is the sixth **largest country** in the world.

● The **population** stands at just over 18 million, of whom some 85% live in urban areas, mainly along the coast. 95.2% of the population are of European origin, 2% Aboriginal and 1.3% Asian.

● Much of Australia is arid and flat. One-third of the country is **desert** and another third is steppe or semi-desert. Only six percent of the country rises above 600m in elevation, and its tallest peak, Mount Kosciusko, is just 2228m high.

● Australia's main **exports** are food, live animals, minerals, metals and fossil fuels, and its main **trading partners** are Japan and the US.

● Australia is a **federal parliamentary state** (formally a constitutional monarchy) with two legislative houses, the Senate and the House of Representatives. The chief of state is the British Monarch, represented by the Governor-General, while the head of government is the Prime Minister.

gain some experience of Australia's indigenous peoples and their culture, through visiting ancient art sites, taking tours and, less easily, making personal contact. Many Aboriginal people – especially in central Australia – have managed to maintain their traditional way of life (albeit with some modern accoutrements), speaking their own languages and living according to their law (the *tjukurpa*). Conversely, most Aboriginal people you'll come across in country towns and cities are victims of what is scathingly referred to as "welfare colonialism" – a disempowering system in which, supported by dole cheques and other subsidies, they often fall prey to a destructive cycle of poverty, ill-health and alcoholism. There's still a long way to go before black and white people in Australia can exist on genuinely equal terms.

The Outback has played host to the oldest surviving human culture for at least fifty thousand years

Where to go

For visitors, deciding where to go can mean juggling with distance, money and time. You could spend months driving around the Outback, exploring the national parks, or just hanging out at beaches; or you could take an all-in two-week "Reef, Rock and Harbour" package, encompassing Australia's outstanding trinity of "must sees".

Both options provide thoroughly Australian experiences, but neither will leave you with a feeling of having more than scraped the surface of this vast country. The two big natural attractions are the two-thousand-kilometre-long Great Barrier Reef off the Queensland coast, with its complex of islands and underwater splendour, and the brooding monolith of Uluru (Ayers Rock), in the Northern Territory's Red Centre. You should certainly try to see them, although exploration of other parts of the country will bring you into contact with more subtle but equally rewarding sights and opportunities.

The cities are surprisingly cosmopolitan: waves of postwar immigrants from southern Europe and, more recently, Southeast Asia have done much to erode Australia's Anglocentrism. Each Australian state has a capital

Outdoor Activities

Though there's fun to be had in the cities, it's really the great outdoors that makes Australia such a special place. Its multitude of national parks – around a thousand in total – embrace everything from isolated beaches and tropical rainforest, to the vast wildernesses of the bush and the Outback. Visitors are spoilt for choice when it comes to getting out and about, with a huge range of outdoor pursuits on offer – everything from diving off the Great Barrier Reef or white-water rafting Tasmania's Franklin River, to hot-air ballooning over Alice or even skiing in the Australian Alps. Perhaps the best way to see something of the great outdoors, and certainly the cheapest, is bushwalking. Extremely popular nationwide, you'll find trails marked in almost every national park. For more see p.61.

Big Things

Don't be surprised if, on a long, hot stretch of Queensland highway, you find yourself hitchhiking next to Captain Cook ... and no, that enormous pineapple on the horizon isn't an alien spacecraft – it's real. Real fibreglass, that is. Big Things are an Australian obsession, and a way for a small town to make a mark on the tourist map. As you travel around the country you'll find giant fruit – the Big Apple, the Big Banana, the Big Strawberry; animals – the Big Lobster, the Big Penguin, the Big Cow; and tourist attractions – the Big Gold Panner and even Big Ayers Rock. They're places to stop and get a drink or a bite, buy joyously tacky souvenirs and look at an exhibition – but above all they're places to take a photo. No Australian holiday is complete without at least one Big Thing in your album.

stamped with its own personality, and nowhere is this more apparent than in New South Wales where glamorous Sydney has the iconic landmarks of the Opera House and Harbour Bridge. Elsewhere, the sophisticated café society of Melbourne (Victoria) contrasts with the vitality of Brisbane (Queensland). Adelaide, in South Australia, has a human-scale and old-fashioned charm, while Perth, in Western Australia, camouflages its isolation with a leisure-oriented urbanity. In Hobart, capital of Tasmania, you'll encounter fine heritage streetscapes and get a distinct maritime feel. The purpose-built administrative centre of Canberra, in the Australian Capital Territory, often fails to grip visitors, but Darwin's continuing revival enlivens an exploration of the distinctive "Territory".

Away from the suburbs, with their satellite shopping malls and quarter-acre residential blocks, is the transitional "bush", and beyond that the wilderness of the Outback – the quintessential Australian experience. Protected from the arid interior, the East Coast has the pick of the country's greenery and scenery, from the north's tropical rainforests and the Great Barrier Reef to the surf-lined beaches further south. The east coast is backed by the Great Dividing Range, which steadily decreases in elevation as it extends from Mount Kosciusko (2228m) in New South Wales north into tropical Queensland. If you have

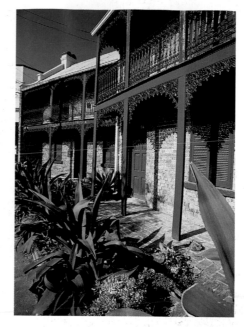

time to spare, a trip to often-overlooked Tasmania, across the Bass Strait, is worthwhile: you'll be rewarded with vast tracts of wilderness as well as landscapes almost English in their bucolic qualities.

Wildlife

Millions of years of isolation has meant that Australia's wildlife has evolved along different lines from the rest of the world, and despite forty thousand years of human pressure, it remains among the most distinctive on earth. Although marsupials and

monotremes – pouched and egg-laying mammals – are found elsewhere in the world (in New Guinea and South America), it is Australia with which they are most closely associated. In the last two hundred years, more native mammals have become extinct in Australia than on any other continent, and land clearing – which kills an estimated 7.5 million birds a year, bringing several species to the edge of extinction – has also placed the wombat and the koala on the endangered list. See p.1159 for more on Australian wildlife.

When to go

Australia's climate has become less predictable in recent times, although like the rest of the planet the country has rarely had stable weather patterns over the last few thousand years. Recently observed phenomena, such as an extended drought in the eastern Outback, the cyclic El Niño effect, and even the hole in the ozone layer – which is disturbingly close to the country – are probably part of a long-term pattern.

Visitors from the northern hemisphere should remember that, as early colonials observed, in Australia "nature is horribly reversed": when it's winter or summer in the northern hemisphere, the opposite season prevails Down Under. Although this is easy to remember, the principle becomes harder to apply to the transitional seasons of spring and autumn. To confuse things further, the four seasons only really exist outside of the

Aboriginal Art

Aboriginal art has grown into a million-dollar industry since the first canvas dot paintings of the central deserts emerged in the 1970s. Though seemingly abstract, early canvases are said to replicate ceremonial sand paintings – maps illustrating sacred Dreaming trails. In the tropics figurative bark and cave paintings are less enigmatic but much older, though until recently they were ceremonially repainted. The unusual x-ray style found in the Top End details the internal structure of animals. The Northern Territory – and Alice Springs in particular – are the best places to look; for tips on buying Aboriginal art as well as didgeridoos, see p.663.

tropics in the southern half of the country. Here, you'll find reliably warm summers at the coast with regular, but thankfully brief, heatwaves in excess of 40°C. Head inland, and the temperatures rise further. Winters, on the other hand, can be miserable, particularly in Victoria, where the short days add to the gloom. Tasmania's highlands make for unpredictable weather all year round, although summer is the best time to explore the island's outdoor attractions.

In the coastal tropics, weather basically falls into two seasons. The best time to visit is during the hot and cloudless Dry (from April to November), with moderate coastal humidity maintaining a pleasant temperature day and night and cooler nights inland. In contrast, the Wet – particularly the "Build Up" in November or December before the rains – is very uncomfortable, marked by stifling, near-total humidity. As storm clouds gather, rising temperatures, humidity and tension can provoke irrational behaviour in the psycholog-

ically unacclimatized – something known as "going troppo". Nevertheless, the mid-Wet's daily downpours and enervating mugginess can be quite intoxicating, compelling a hyper-relaxed inactivity for which these regions are known; furthermore the countryside – if you can reach it – looks its best at this time.

Aussie Rules

Once the summer cricket season comes to a close sports-mad Australians turn their attention to the winter football (footy) season. Though soccer, rugby union and rugby league all have their followers, there is nothing more quintessentially Australian than Australian Rules ("Aussie Rules") football, which dominates Victoria, South Australia, Tasmania and Western Australia. A no-holds-barred, eighteen-a-side brawl, Aussie Rules is most closely related to Gaelic football and is cheerfully derided north of the Victorian border. Victoria is the traditional home of the game, and Melbourne's venerable MCG, home of Australian sport, is the best place to take in a match. For more, see p.64.

If you want to tour extensively, keep to the southern coasts in summer and head north for the winter

Australia's interior is an arid semi-desert with very little rain, high summer temperatures and occasionally freezing winter nights. Unless you're properly equipped to cope with these extremes, you'd be better off coming here during the transitional seasons between April and June, or October and November.

In general, the best time to visit the south is during the Australian summer, from December to March, though long summer holidays from Christmas through January mean that prices are higher and beaches more crowded at this time. In the tropical north the best months are from May to October, while in the Centre they are from October to November and from March to May. If you want to tour extensively, keep to the southern coasts in summer and head north for the winter.

Average Temperatures (°C) and Rainfall (mm)

		Jan/Feb		Mar/Apr		May/Jun		July/Aug		Sept/Oct		Nov/Dec	
Sydney	c°	25	25	24	23	20	17	16	17	19	22	23	24
	mm	100	105	125	130	125	130	110	75	60	75	70	75
Canberra	c°	27	25	23	20	15	13	12	13	15	18	22	25
	mm	55	50	50	45	50	30	30	50	50	70	65	65
Brisbane	c°	27	27	26	25	23	21	23	22	24	25	26	27
	mm	160	160	150	80	70	60	55	50	50	75	100	140
Cairns	c°	31	31	30	29	28	25	25	27	27	28	30	31
	mm	400	440	450	180	100	50	30	25	35	35	90	160
Darwin	c°	31	30	31	32	31	30	30	31	32	32	33	32
	mm	400	430	435	75	50	10	5	10	15	70	110	310
Alice Springs	c°	36	35	32	27	22	21	19	21	25	30	32	35
	mm	35	40	25	20	25	25	20	20	10	25	30	35
Perth	c°	30	30	28	25	22	20	19	19	20	22	25	28
	mm	10	15	25	50	125	185	175	145	80	75	25	20
Adelaide	c°	28	27	25	22	18	16	14	15	17	21	22	25
	mm	20	20	25	45	65	70	65	60	55	40	25	20
Melbourne	c°	26	26	24	21	16	15	14	15	17	19	21	20
	mm	45	50	55	60	55	50	50	50	55	65	55	55
Hobart	c°	21	21	20	17	14	12	11	12	15	18	19	20
	mm	50	45	50	55	50	45	50	50	55	55	50	50

50

things not to miss

It's not possible to see everything that Australia has to offer in one trip – and we don't suggest you try. What follows is a selective taste of the country's highlights: great places to stay, outstanding national parks, spectacular wildlife – and even good things to eat and drink. Arranged in five colour-coded categories, you can browse through to find the very best things to see, do and experience. All highlights have a page reference to take you straight into the guide, where you can find out more.

01 Atherton Tablelands (Qld) Page **524** • With its majestic rainforest, crater lakes and abundant wildlife, you could spend days exploring the Atherton Tablelands.

02 Adelaide Festival of Arts and Womadelaide (SA) Page **805** • Australia's "Festival City" comes to life every year with the huge Festival of Arts (held on even years) and the world-music event, Womadelaide (odd years).

04 Dolphins at Monkey Mia (WA)
Page **746** • Scores of day-trippers flock to witness the almost daily dolphin visits at Monkey Mia.

03 Climbing Sydney Harbour Bridge (Syd)
Page **110** • Scale the bridge for adrenaline thrills and great vistas – or walk or cycle across it for free.

05 Birdsville Races (Qld)
Page **568** • Birdsville Hotel is the focus for the annual Birdsville Races, where 5000 people descend on the tiny desert township in Queensland's Outback for a weekend of drinking, horse racing, and mayhem.

06 Bush tucker
Page **52** • Witchetty grubs and wattle seeds, possum-tail soup and rooburgers – a good few restaurants around the country are now experimenting with bush tucker.

07 Bondi Beach (Syd)
Page **148** • Beach, surf and café culture. The stunning coastal walk around the headlands to Bronte Beach via Tamarama is a must.

08 **Uluru (NT)** Page **679** • Uluru, otherwise known as Ayers Rock, represents a sacred landmark for Aboriginal peoples, and a magnet to tourists the world over.

09 **Four-wheel-driving on Cape York (Qld)** Page **536**
• The creeks and savannah of the Cape York Peninsula provide the setting for what is widely regarded as the most rugged 4WD adventure in the country.

10 **Whale sharks at Ningaloo Reef (WA)**
Page **748** • In places accessible right off the beach, the 250-kilometre-long Ningaloo Reef is home to a huge variety of marine life, including whale sharks in autumn.

11 **Chambers Pillar (NT)** Page **676** • A historic dead-end 165km from Alice, this eighty-metre-high sandstone pillar was used as a landmark by early overlanders.

12 **Aussie Rules match at the MCG (Melb)** Page **909** • Taking in a game at the venerable Melbourne Cricket Ground (MCG) is a must for sports fans.

14 **Coober Pedy (SA)** Page **867** • The underground homes, shops and churches of Coober Pedy – where temperatures soar to over 50°C in summer – are the most enduring symbol of the harshness of Australia's Outback.

13 **Diving at the Great Barrier Reef (Qld)** Page **464** • Come face-to-face with stunning coral and shoals of curious fish.

15 **Melbourne Cup (Melb)** Page **60** • Melbourne's 130-year-old horse race brings the entire country to a standstill round the radio or TV.

16 **Henley on Todd Regatta in Alice Springs (NT)** Page **663** • Bottomless boats are run down the dry riverbed in Alice's most famous – and wackiest – event, held every year in early October.

17 The Kimberley (WA)

Page **768** • Regarded as Australia's last frontier, the Kimberley's inaccessible coasts are washed by enormous tides and inhabited only by isolated Aboriginal communities and crocodiles.

18 The Sanctuary at Mission Beach (Qld)

Page **510** • Rainforest retreat par excellence, with stilt cabins at tree level surrounded by fifty acres of steamy coastal jungle.

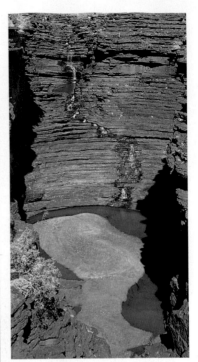

19 Karijini National Park (WA)

Page **758** • The dramatic water-carved gorges of the Karijini National Park remain one of WA's undiscovered gems.

20 Kakadu National Park (NT)

Page **623** • Australia's largest national park is a vast World Heritage-listed wilderness with an amazing diversity of wildlife.

21 Lake Eyre (SA)

Page **878** • This massive saline lake, topped by a glaring salt crust and walled by red dunes, creates a harsh, unforgettable landscape.

22 Wilpena Pound (SA)
Page **874** • Fantastic hikes amid spectacular scenery at the famous elevated basin of Wilpena Pound in the Flinders Ranges National Park.

23 The Franklin River (Tas) Page **1135** • White-water rafting is the only way to explore the wild Franklin River, one of the great rivers of Australia.

24 Gunnedah (NSW) Page **353** • Home to one of the healthiest koala populations in the state, Gunnedah state forest is the perfect place to spot mothers with their babies in the wild.

25 Barossa Valley wineries (SA) Page **816** • Australia's premier wine-producing region, just 50km from Adelaide, is a great place to stop over and unwind.

26 Fraser Island (Qld) Page **450** • The giant dunes, freshwater lakes and sculpted coloured sands of the world's largest sand island form the backdrop to exciting 4WD safaris.

27 Humpback Whales (Qld) Page **447** •
Saved from extinction by a ban on whaling, Humpback whales migrate up the Queensland coast each June–October to calve around the Whitsundays' warm tropical waters.

28 Boating on the Murray River (SA)
Page **846** • By far the best way to see the great brown Murray River is to get out on the water – hop on a paddlesteamer, splash about in a canoe or rent a houseboat.

29 The Strzelecki, Birdsville and Oodnadatta tracks (SA)
Pages **876, 878 & 879** • Making the most of the journey is what counts – the fabled Outback routes to Oodnadatta, Birdsville and Innamincka are still real adventures.

30 The Great Ocean Road (Vic) Page **962** •
On two wheels or four, the 280km-ride along the rugged, surf-battered cliffs bordering Great Ocean Road comes straight out of a road movie.

31 Hot-air ballooning around Alice (NT)
Page **665** • Watch the sun rise from a thousand feet up in Australia's ballooning capital.

32 Manly Ferry (Syd) Page **106** • The short ferry trip from Circular Quay to the surfing Mecca of Manly takes in picture postcard views of Sydney Opera House and the Harbour Bridge.

33 Wilson's Promontory National Park (Vic) Page **1018** • Victoria's most popular national park, "The Prom" boasts some superb coastal scenery and bushwalks.

35 Blue Mountains (NSW) Page **213** • Now World Heritage listed, the Blue Mountains, just west of Sydney, get their name from the blue mist of fragrant eucalyptus oil hanging in the air all year round.

34 Giant termite mounds (NT) Page **634** • These impressively huge towers – up to four metres tall – are a regular feature of the Top End.

36 Sailing in the Whitsundays (Qld) Page **488** • There's fantastic sailing and diving – and whale-watching in season – in the idyllic white-sand Whitsunday Islands.

37 Overland Track in Cradle Mountain/Lake St Clair National Park (Tas)

Page **1132** • The eighty-kilometre Overland Track, attracting walkers from all over the world, is Australia's greatest extended bushwalk, spread over five or more mud- and leech-filled days of physical, exhilarating exhaustion.

38 Salamanca market on Hobart waterfront (Tas) Page **1061** •

Small, friendly and beautifully situated, the capital of Tasmania is a city built around water – don't miss the lively Saturday market on Salamanca Place.

39 Mutawintje National Park (NSW) Page **383** • Red,

barren earth laced with ancient galleries of Aboriginal rock art, secluded gorges and quiet waterholes.

40 Aboriginal Dance Festival at Laura (Qld) Page **540** •

Electrifying celebration of Aboriginal culture, held in June in odd-numbered years.

41 Tree kangaroo (Qld)

Page **529** • North Queensland's tropical rainforest is home to two species of tree kangaroo, which forage at night on the forest floor but spend the days crashed out in the canopy. Spot them at Yungaburra in the Atherton Tablelands.

42 Hiking through Carnarvon Gorge

(Qld) Page **562** • With its Aboriginal art sites and magical scenery, a day-hike into the Carnarvon gorge takes some beating.

43 Broken Hill

(NSW) Page **372** • Historic Outback mining town and thriving arts centre.

44 Sydney Opera House performance (Syd)

Page **109** • Take in a performance at one of the world's busiest performing arts centres – interval drinks certainly don't have as spectacular harbour views anywhere else in the world.

45 Tall Timber Country (WA)

Page **717** • The brooding, primeval karri forests of the so-called Tall Timber Country are one of WA's greatest natural sights.

46 Kings Canyon in Watarrka National Park (NT) Page **677** • The hike around the canyon's rim takes you past exposed lookouts, domed outcrops and a secluded waterhole that's great for a dip on a hot day.

47 Kangaroo Island (SA) Page **831** • Unspoilt Kangaroo Island boasts fantastic coastal scenery and excellent wildlife-spotting opportunities.

49 Skiing in the Snowy Mountains (NSW) Page **264** • The Snowy Mountains have the best skiing in Australia.

48 Mardi Gras (Syd) Page **175** • The irreverent Oxford Street parade, from dykes on bikes to the Melbourne marching boys, ends the summer season.

50 Canoeing up the Katherine Gorge (NT) Page **641** • Hop on a cruise or paddle a canoe through the dramatic orange cliffs of the Katherine Gorge – you won't have it to yourself, but it's still hugely enjoyable.

contents

using the Rough Guide

We've tried to make this Rough Guide a good read and easy to use. The book is divided into five main sections, and you should be able to find whatever you want in one of them.

front section

The front colour section offers a quick tour of Australia. The **introduction** aims to give you a feel for the place, with suggestions on where to go. We also tell you what the weather is like and include a basic country fact file. Next, our authors round up their favourite aspects of Australia in the **things not to miss** section – whether it's great festivals, amazing sights or a special hotel. Right after this comes the Rough Guide's full **contents** list.

basics

You've decided to go and the basics section covers all the **pre-departure** nitty-gritty to help you plan your trip. This is where to find out which airlines fly to your destination, what paperwork you'll need, what to do about money and insurance, about internet access, food, security, public transport, car rental – in fact just about every piece of **general practical information** you might need.

guide

This is the heart of the Rough Guide, divided into user-friendly chapters, each of which covers a specific region. Every chapter starts with a list of **highlights** and an **introduction** that helps you to decide where to go, depending on your time and budget. Likewise, introductions to the various towns and smaller regions within each chapter should help you plan your itinerary. We start most town accounts with information on arrival and accommodation, followed by a tour of the sights, and finally reviews of places to eat and drink, and details of nightlife. Longer accounts also have a directory of practical listings. Each chapter concludes with **public transport** details for that region.

contexts

Read Contexts to get a deeper understanding of how Australia ticks. We include a brief **history**, articles about **indigenous peoples** and **wildlife**, together with a detailed further reading section that reviews dozens of **books** relating to the country.

index + small print

Apart from a **full index**, which includes maps as well as places, this section covers publishing information, credits and acknowledgements, and also has our contact details in case you want to send in updates and corrections to the book – or suggestions as to how we might improve it.

chapter map of **Australia**

contents

colour section

basics

guide

contexts   1141–1189

index + small print   1191–1205

map symbols

symbols

maps are listed in the full index using coloured text

═══	Main road	⌂	Cave
═══	Minor road	♠	Conservation hut
⋯⋯	Unpaved road	♦	Museum
▬▬	Pedestrianized street (town maps)	⚲	Lighthouse
‐‐‐‐‐	Tunnel	⚑	Golf course
‐ ‐ ‐	Path	★	Bus stop
───	Track	ⓘ	Tourist information
━━	Railway	⊠	Post office
─ ─	Ferry route	◉	Hotel
───	River	▣	Restaurant
▬▪	State/territorial boundary	▬▬	Building
‐‐‐	Chapter division boundary	▬╪▬	Church/cathedral
▲	Mountain peak	▬▬	Built-up area
⌃⌃	Mountain range	▨	Aboriginal land
	Gorge	▨	Beach
�nk	Viewpoint	▣	Cemetery
爪	Waterfall	▭	Marsh
	Reef	▨	National Park
♦	Point of interest	▨	Park
✈	Airport		

basics

basics

Getting there from
Britain and Ireland

The market for flights between Britain and Australia is one of the most competitive in the world, and in real terms prices have never been lower. Modern aircraft can now reach the north Australian coast from London in just fifteen hours' flying time, though in practice the journey to Sydney or the other eastern cities takes a minimum of 21 hours by the time you've stopped and refuelled. If you take a bit longer – breaking the journey in Southeast Asia or North America – it need not be the tedious, seat-bound slog you may have imagined. There are no direct flights from Ireland.

A word of warning: don't actually buy your ticket until you're sure that you've been granted a visa (see p.22 for more details). Visa in hand, you'll next need to decide where you want to fly to in Australia, where you would like to stop en route (or on the way back) and whether you want to use flights to get around once you're there. Sydney and Melbourne are served by the greatest number of airlines, and carriers such as Qantas offer the same price to fly to any east-coast city between Cairns and Adelaide; flights to Darwin and Perth are around £100 cheaper, but you need to consider the expense of the overland journey from here. An **open-jaw ticket** (flying into one city and out from another) usually costs no more than an ordinary return.

Direct scheduled flights depart from London's two main airports, Gatwick and Heathrow, although Singapore Airlines has daily flights from Manchester to Singapore which connect with onward flights to Sydney.

Fares

Note that all the fares quoted below are exclusive of **airport tax** – this is usually an extra £40–60.

The cheapest fare you're likely to find is around £550 return, available during the **low-season** months of April to June, though special offers can go as low as £450; if you insist on flying with Qantas, BA or Singapore Airlines, expect to pay from around £800 for a flight in this off-peak period with special

offers sometimes taking prices down to £600. The **most expensive time to fly** is in the two weeks before Christmas, when you'd be lucky to find anything for less than £1000 return: to stand a chance of getting one of the cheaper tickets, aim to book at least six months in advance. Prices also go up from mid-June or the beginning of July to the middle of August coinciding with the peak European holiday times. In between times (the **shoulder seasons** of mid-Aug to Nov and mid-Jan to March) you should expect to pay around £700 (around £950 with one of the prestige airlines).

With Qantas you can fly from **regional airports** at Aberdeen, Belfast, Edinburgh, Glasgow, Manchester or Newcastle to connect with your international flight at Heathrow. There is no extra charge from Manchester, but you'll pay a **supplement** of £25 each way from the others.

An excellent alternative to a long direct flight is a **multi-stopover ticket**, which can cost the same or just a little more than the price of an ordinary return; check out the routing of the airlines detailed on pp.12–13 for some ideas. Unusual routes are inevitably more expensive, but it's possible to fly **via South America** with Aerolineas Argentinas, which offers stops in Buenos Aires and Auckland – at least £925 return – or **via Africa** with South African Airways, which offers return fares via Johannesburg to Perth and Sydney from around £1000, with the added bonus of discounted internal flights to Harare (Botswana), Victoria Falls, Nairobi and many other African destinations. You can also often get good deals **via Japan** on All Nippon Airlines and Japan Airlines.

More expensive, but still good value, **round-the-world (RTW) tickets** incorporating Australia provide a chance to see the world on your way to and from down under. RTW flights come prepackaged in a tantalizing variety of permutations, with stopovers chiefly in Asia, the Pacific and North America, but you can pretty much devise your fantasy itinerary and get it priced. A good agent should be able to piece together sector fares from various airlines: prices range from around £840 for a simple London–Bangkok–Sydney–LA–London deal to well over £1000 for more complicated routings. It's also possible to incorporate substantial overland segments for variety. A sample itinerary London–Nairobi–overland to Johannesburg–Perth overland to Broome–Alice Springs overland to Melbourne–Bali–Hong Kong–Bangkok–London costs from around £860.

Shopping for tickets

You'll see eye-catching low fares in the masses of small ads in **newspapers** (the quality Sunday papers are the best place to start your search), or, in London, in the **listings magazine** *Time Out* or the free travellers' magazine *TNT*, but in practice these are often unavailable by the time you call. Booking ahead as far as possible is the best way to secure the most reasonable prices: it is almost invariably cheaper to buy tickets through **discount travel agents** (see opposite), but we've also listed a selection of **airlines** along with the variety of routes available. We've also included **airline websites** where available – it's worth checking out these sites for last-minute cheap offers. Lauda Air and Malaysian Airlines both have good-value deals, as do the prestige airlines, in particular Qantas and British Airways, which often offer two extra stopovers if you book before a certain date. There is also a growing number of **flight agents' websites** which display the latest timetables and fares, and increasingly, provide an online booking service. We've listed some of these on p.14; others can be found through the online service Cheapflights (ⓦwww.cheapflights.co.uk), which will signpost you to the booking agent or airline offering the lowest prices.

In the end, you'll find the available flights at much the same price everywhere, the main difference being between the plusher airlines such as Qantas, British Airways (BA) and Singapore Airlines – which offer more leg room, better-quality inflight entertainment, service and meals and more drinks – and the cheaper ones such as Garuda Indonesia Airlines and Royal Brunei (to Brisbane and Perth only).

Tourists and those on one-year working visas (see p.22 for the lowdown on visas) are generally required by Australian immigration to arrive with a ticket out of the country, so **one-way tickets** are really only viable for Australian and New Zealand residents. If you've purchased a return ticket and find you want to stay longer or head off on a totally different route, it's sometimes possible to cash in the return half of your ticket (though you'll make a loss on the deal) at the travel agent where you bought it: either post it back to them or arrange for someone in the UK to do it on your behalf.

With any international ticket, you can buy a Qantas Boomerang Pass or an Ansett G'Day Pass, both of which entitle you to cheap **internal flights**, but these must be purchased before you leave the UK (see p.36).

Airlines

Aerolíneas Argentinas (☏0845/601 1915, ⓦwww.aerolineas.com.ar). London Heathrow to Madrid, changing planes for Buenos Aires and changing again for Sydney.
Air New Zealand (☏020/8741 2299, ⓦwww.airnz.co.uk). Daily scheduled flights from London Heathrow to all major Australian airports via Los Angeles. Their popular Pacific routing gives you a choice of stopovers in Fiji, Western Samoa, the Cook Islands, Tahiti and New Zealand.
All Nippon Airways (ANA) (☏020/7224 8866, ⓦwww.ana.co.jp). From London Heathrow to Tokyo, then on to Osaka, with connecting flights daily to Sydney.
British Airways (☏0845/773 3377, ⓦwww.britishairways.com). Daily scheduled flights from London Heathrow to all major Australian airports via Bangkok, Kuala Lumpur, Singapore or Hong Kong.
Emirates Airlines (☏0870/243 2222, ⓦwww.emirates.com). Daily from London Heathrow and Manchester to Melbourne and every other day to Sydney. All flights via Dubai.

Garuda Indonesia (℡020/7486 3011 or 0161/834 3747 in Manchester, ⓦwww.garuda-indonesia.co.uk). Three flights weekly from London Gatwick via Frankfurt flying into all the main Australian airports.

Japan Airlines (℡0845/774 7700 or 020/7408 1000, ⓦwww.jal.co.jp). From London Heathrow, daily nonstop flights to Tokyo and five times weekly to Osaka, with connecting flights to Sydney from both airports. Connecting flights to Brisbane and Cairns daily from Tokyo, three times weekly from Osaka.

KLM Royal Dutch Airlines (℡0990/750900, ⓦwww.klm.nl). Daily flights to Amsterdam from just about every British airport except Gatwick and Luton but including London Heathrow, London City, Edinburgh, Manchester, Glasgow and Bristol, with connecting flights to Sydney via Kuala Lumpur.

Lauda Air (℡0845/601 0934, ⓦwww.laudaair.co.uk). Three flights weekly from Heathrow via Vienna and Kuala Lumpur to Sydney and two flights weekly to Melbourne.

Malaysia Airlines (℡0870/607 9090, ⓦwww.malaysiaair.com). Daily flights from London Heathrow to Kuala Lumpur connecting daily to Sydney and Perth, four times weekly to Melbourne, five times weekly to Brisbane and twice weekly to Darwin and Cairns.

Olympic Airways (℡0870/606 0460, ⓦwww.olympic-airways.gr). Twice-daily flights from London Heathrow to Athens with three-times-weekly connecting flights to Sydney and Melbourne.

Qantas (℡0845/774 7767, ⓦwww.qantas.co.uk). Numerous flights daily from London Heathrow to all the mainland Australian state capitals and Cairns, via Singapore or Bangkok.

Royal Brunei Airlines (℡020/7584 6660, ℻581 9279). London Heathrow to Perth and Brisbane via Brunei.

Singapore Airlines (℡0870/608 8886 or 0161/830 8888 in Manchester, ⓦwww.singaporeair.com). Three-times-daily flights from London Heathrow, and once-daily flights from Manchester to Singapore, with connections to Adelaide, Brisbane, Melbourne, Perth and Sydney.

South African Airways (℡020/7312 5000, ⓦwww.saa.co.za). Daily flights to Johannesburg, with connecting flights three times weekly to Perth and Sydney.

Thai Airways (℡0870/606 0911, ⓦwww.thaiair.com). Daily flights to Bangkok from London Heathrow, with connections to Sydney, Melbourne and Perth.

United Airlines (℡0845/844 4777, ⓦwww.unitedairlines.co.uk). Daily flights from London Heathrow to Los Angeles or San Francisco with a six-hour wait for connections to Sydney and Melbourne.

Discount travel agents

Austravel, 50–51 Conduit St, London W1R 9FB (℡020/7734 7755, ⓦwww.austravel.net), and two other London sites, plus branches in Bournemouth, Bristol, Edinburgh, Leeds and Manchester. Specialists for flights and tours to Australia. Austravel also lays on audiovisual presentations all over the UK to help you make up your mind, aimed at independent travellers heading round the world via Australia. Issues ETAs and traditional visas for an administration fee of £16.

Bridge the World, 47 Chalk Farm Rd, London NW1 8AN (℡020/7916 0990, ⓦwww.bridgetheworld.com). Specialists in RTW tickets, many with Australian components, with good deals aimed at the backpacker market.

Flightbookers (ⓦwww.ebookers.com), 177–178 Tottenham Court Rd, London W1P 0LX (℡020/7757 2000); 34 Argyle Arcade, off Buchanan St, Glasgow G1 1RS (℡0141/204 1919). Low fares on an extensive range of scheduled flights.

Flynow.com (ⓦwww.flynow.com), 125A Gloucester Rd, London SW7 4SF (℡020/7835 2000); 597 Cheetham Hill Rd, Manchester M8 5EJ (℡0161/721 4000). Large range of discounted tickets.

The London Flight Centre, 131 Earls Court Rd, London SW5 9RH (℡020/7244 6411, ⓦwww.topdecktravel.co.uk), and two other London sites. Long-established agent dealing in discount flights; vaccinations and Australian visas arranged at the Earls Court office.

North South Travel, Moulsham Mill Centre, Parkway, Chelmsford, Essex CM2 7PX (℡01245/492882, ℻356612, ⓦwww.northsouthtravel.co.uk). Friendly, competitive travel agency, offering discounted fares worldwide – profits are used to support projects in the developing world, especially the promotion of sustainable tourism.

Quest Worldwide, 10 Richmond Rd, Kingston, Surrey KT2 5HL (℡020/8547 3322, ⓦwww.questtravel.co.uk). Specialists in RTW and Australian discount fares.

STA Travel, 86 Old Brompton Rd, London SW7 3LH (℡020/7361 6144, ⓦwww.statravel.co.uk), and five other London sites, plus branches in Aberdeen, Brighton, Bristol, Cambridge, Edinburgh, Glasgow, Liverpool, Manchester, Newcastle-upon-

Tyne, Oxford, and university campuses. Worldwide specialists in low-cost flights and tours for students and under-26s, though other customers welcome. Also has offices in Australia.

Trailfinders, 215 Kensington High St, London W6 6BD (☎020/7937 5400, �🖥www.trailfinders.co.uk), and three other London sites, plus branches in Birmingham, Bristol, Cambridge, Dublin, Glasgow, Manchester and Newcastle. Excellent for multistop and RTW tickets, including some unusual routings via South Africa, the Pacific and the US. Well-informed and efficient – visa service available at the Kensington High St branch. Also has branches in Brisbane, Cairns, Melbourne, Perth and Sydney.

Travel Bag, 52 Regent St, London W1R 6DX (☎020/7287 5559, �🖥www.travelbag.co.uk), and other branches in Alton, Knutsford and Solihull. Well-established long-haul travel agent with a good reputation for Australian coverage. Direct and RTW flights on all the best airlines like Qantas, British Airways and Singapore, plus packages (see opposite).

Travelmood (call centre ☎0870/500 1002), 246 Edgware Rd, London W2 1DS; 1 Reform St, Dundee DD1 1SP. Direct and RTW flights.

Usit CAMPUS, 52 Grosvenor Gardens, London SW1W 0AG (☎020/7730 2101, national call centre ☎0870/240 1010, �🖥www.usitcampus.co.uk), and three other London sites, plus branches in Birmingham, Brighton, Bristol, Cambridge, Edinburgh, Glasgow, Manchester and Oxford. Student/youth travel specialists, with further branches in YHA shops and on university campuses all over Britain.

Discount travel websites

�🖥**www.dialaflight.co.uk** Website useful for tracking down bargains, plus telephone sales for scheduled flights (☎0870/333 4488).

�🖥**www.expedia.co.uk** Microsoft's venture into the internet travel market, offering special fares and an online booking service.

�🖥**www.flightline.co.uk** A telephone-based outfit (☎0800/036 0777), also offering online searches for cheap scheduled flights.

�🖥**www.lastminute.com** Website selling everything from holidays to mobile phones, but with a particular emphasis on cheap travel.

Packages and organized tours

There are relatively few traditional **package holidays** available – nobody's going to fly all the way to Australia just to spend a couple of

weeks on the beach – but if your time is short and you're reasonably sure of what you want to do, it may not be a bad idea to prebook some of your accommodation, tours and vehicle rental. Many companies offer minimal packages, consisting of a flight with some accommodation and a couple of tours. Full "see-it-all" packages can work out quite expensive and the pace can be rather tiring, but they aren't bad value, considering what you'd be spending anyway. The ultimate package must be the sea trip to Australia from Southampton in England or Los Angeles in the US on either P&O or Cunard Line (see below).

Many of the Australian specialists also offer such things as bus and train passes (see pp.36–40), discounted hotel vouchers and the like – all of which are worth considering. Some discount flight agents also arrange tours and accommodation – check out Austravel and Trailfinders, among others.

Package tours and specialist operators

Contiki (☎020/8290 6777, �🖥www.contiki.com). Big-group, countrywide bus and four-wheel-drive tours for 18- to 35-year-olds "thriving on good times and loads of fun". All transport (excluding flights to Australia) and most meals covered; plenty of additional excursions (mountain climbing, diving, etc) at extra cost. From £460 for an 11-day Brisbane-to-Cairns trip; 25-day Sydney to Darwin via the east coast from £1200.

Cunard Line (☎023/8071 6605, ☏8022 5843, �🖥www.cunardline.com). Their annual four-month "World Cruise" on the flagship *QE2* takes in Australia in February, visiting Sydney, Melbourne, Perth and Adelaide. The whole package costs from £16,660.

Explore Worldwide (☎01252/760000 in UK; ☎01/677 9479 in Eire; �🖥www.exploreworldwide.com). Bus and 4WD tours through Western Australia and the Northern Territory, ranging from an 18-day trip from Darwin to Alice Springs (£1375), to a 36-day "Western Half Explorer" (£2495) all the way up the coast from Perth to Darwin and Kakadu then down to Alice Springs; all including flights from the UK.

Jetabout (☎020/8741 3111, ☏8748 7505, �🖥www.jetabout.com). Qantas' holiday arm, specializing in tailor-made itineraries, as well as vehicle rentals and a couple of see-it-all deals.

Newmans Holidays (☎020/8879 1999, �🖥www.newmans.com). New Zealand-based company offering self-drive tours of Australia; the smallest two-berth motorhome starts from £26 per day.

P&O (☎020/7800 2222, ⓦwww.pocruises.com). Once-yearly cruises to Sydney westbound on the *Aurora* (via Rio de Janeiro) or eastbound on the *Oriana* (via San Francisco). P&O's own price is £5500 on the *Aurora* and £3380 on the *Oriana*, but you can get a cheaper price from a travel agent.

Qantas Holidays (☎0990/673464, ⓦwww.qantas.com.au/qantasholidays). Quality packages from undoubted Australian experts. Car and campervan rental, accommodation and sightseeing passes, rail holidays, cruises, coach transport, city packages and tours can all be priced in.

Travelbag (☎020/7497 0515, ⓦwww.travelbag.co.uk). Everything from flights to car and campervan rental, farmstays and coach and 4WD tours all over the country, including a 6-day "Islands of Tropical North Queensland" tour for £820 including airport transfers, 5 nights' accommodation and a Barrier Reef cruise. Several action and eco-oriented trips including Barrier Reef dive packages. Flights extra.

Travelmarvel (☎020/8879 3003, ⓦwww.aptours.com). Offers major bus tours Australia-wide, from 7 days in Tasmania (£635) through to the 26-day "Grand Australian Discovery" tour (£2525). Accommodation and meals included; flights extra.

Travelmood (☎0870/500 1002, ⓦwww.travelmood.com). Flights, quality accommodation, car and campervan rental; tailor-made itineraries, bus passes, tickets and package tours.

Wildlife Worldwide (☎020/8667 9158, ⓦwww.wildlifeworldwide.co.uk). Tailor-made trips for wildlife and wilderness enthusiasts: includes a 5-day "Jabiru Safari" ex-Darwin for £1055, a 5-day "Kimberley Wildlife" ex-Broome for £655, and a 16-day London-to-London "Wilderness Queensland" trip for £1895.

World Expeditions (☎0800/074 4135, ⓦwww.worldexpeditions.co.uk). Australian-owned adventure company; small-group active wilderness holidays; cycling, canoeing, rafting, 4WD excursions, walking and camping. All expeditions are graded according to difficulty.

Flights from Ireland

Flying **from Ireland**, prices are rather higher, but since you can't fly direct anyway, the choice of routes and airlines is if anything even wider.

Although most of the cheaper routings involve a stopover in London and transfer to one of the airlines listed on pp.12–13, there are often good deals on Olympic Airways (☎01/608 0090) **from Dublin** via Greece. Singapore Airlines (☎01/671 0722) has flights ticketed through from Dublin, Shannon or Cork via London to Singapore and Sydney, while Malaysian Airlines (☎01/676 1561) also goes from all three Irish airports via Kuala Lumpur. The three airports are also served by the affiliated British Airways and Qantas (both ☎01/874 7747); all their flights to Australia have a Dublin–London add-on included in the price. Malaysian Airlines fares start from around IR£770 for an open one-year return in low season, up to IR£1300 in the Christmas period, while a Singapore Airlines ticket would cost around IR£910 in the shoulder season. A low-season fare **from Belfast** with British Airways starts at £610, going up to £720 in the shoulder season. In high season fares average at around £1000. For youth and student discount fares, the best first stop is Usit (see below).

When it comes to **packages**, you're best off contacting one of the UK-based companies listed on pp.13–14, or booking through one of the agents listed opposite.

Irish operators

Australia Travel Centre, 43 Middle Abbey St, Dublin 1 (☎01/804 7188). Specialists in long-haul flights.

Thomas Cook (ⓦwww.tcholidays.com), 118 Grafton St, Dublin (☎01/677 1721); 11 Donegall Place, Belfast (☎028/9055 0232). Mainstream package-holiday and flight agent, with occasional discount offers.

Trailfinders, 4–5 Dawson St, Dublin 2 (☎01/677 7888, ⓦwww.trailfinder.com). Excellent for multistop and RTW tickets.

Travel Care, 35 Belmont Rd, Belfast 4 (☎028/9047 1717, 🖷9047 1339, ⓦwww.travelcare.ie). Discount flight specialists.

Unijet, Parkwood House, Newforge Lane, Belfast BT9 5NW (☎028/9031 4656, ⓦwww.unijet.com). Discount scheduled fares to major Australian cities; the best agent to contact for Malaysian Airline ticket deals.

UsitNOW (ⓦwww.usitnow.ie), Fountain Centre, College St, Belfast BT1 6ET (☎028/9032 4073); 19 Aston Quay, Dublin 2 (☎01/602 1700). Also branches in Athlone, Coleraine, Cork, Derry, Galway, Jordanstown, Limerick, Maynooth and Waterford. Student and youth specialist.

Getting there from
the US and Canada

From Los Angeles it's possible to fly nonstop to Sydney in fourteen and a half hours. Qantas, United, Air Canada Airlines and Air New Zealand all operate direct to the east coast of Australia. Flying on an Asian airline will most likely involve a stop in their capital city (Singapore, Tokyo, Hong Kong, etc) and if you're travelling from the west coast of North America to the east coast of Australia you'll probably find their fares on the Pacific route somewhat higher than their American or Australian competitors. However, if you're travelling from the east coast of North America with Perth, say, as your destination, a carrier such as Singapore Airlines or Malaysia Airlines with a transatlantic routing may offer the best value. Flights leave the west coast of the US in the evening, and there are good connections from most North American cities.

Many of the major airlines offer deals whereby you can make **stopovers** either at Pacific Rim destinations such as Tokyo, Honolulu or Kuala Lumpur or at a number of exotic South Pacific locations. Either there will be a flat surcharge on your ticket or they may offer you a higher priced ticket allowing you to make as many stops as you like, within certain parameters, over a fixed period of time.

But the best deal, if you don't mind planning your itinerary in advance, will most likely be a **Circle Pacific** or a **Round-the-world** (RTW) ticket from a discount outfit (see opposite).

Fares

Fares vary significantly according to **season** – most airlines regard December through February as the high season, April to August as the low season, and other times as shoulder. These boundaries are by no means fixed and can differ radically from airline to airline, so if you want to make sure you're getting the best deal available, always double check. However, you can be sure that fares will be at their highest over Christmas and New Year, when seats are at a premium and booking as far in advance as possible is highly recommended. Note also that **midweek fares** tend to be cheaper (US$60–100) than weekend departures.

Sample lowest standard **scheduled fares** for low/high seasons are approximately as follows: **to Sydney or Melbourne** from

Chicago or New York (US$1160/1890); Los Angeles or San Francisco (US$860/1470); Montréal or Toronto (CDN$1850/2490); Vancouver (CDN$1770/1960); **to Perth** from New York, Los Angeles or San Francisco (US$1250/1800); Vancouver, Toronto or Montréal (CDN$2480/3945). The price of an **open-jaw ticket** (flying into one city and returning from another) should be approximately the average of the return fares to the two cities. If your destination is on the west coast you might also want to check out Qantas' "Boomerang Pass" which offers coast-to-coast return flights in Australia for US$390 (US$195 one-way); see "Getting Around", p.36, for more on these and other **internal air passes**.

Round-the-World (RTW) and **Circle Pacific** tickets can be very good value. A sample **RTW** itinerary would be: Los Angeles–Sydney–Bangkok–Delhi–Mumbai (Bombay)–London–Los Angeles (US$2480); or New York–Tokyo–Hong Kong–Bangkok–Singapore–Jakarta–Yogyakarta–Denpasar (Bali)–Darwin, overland through Australia, Sydney–Kuala Lumpur–Amsterdam–New York (US$2700). Sample **Circle Pacific** routes are: Los Angeles–Tokyo–Kuala Lumpur–Singapore–Perth–Sydney–Los Angeles (US$1880); and New York–Hong Kong–Bangkok–Bandar Seri Begawan (Brunei)–Perth, overland through Australia, Sydney–Kuala Lumpur–Tokyo–Los Angeles/ New York (US$2090).

Charter flights to Australia, a more recent arrival on the scene, are offered by companies such as Jetset (who will only take bookings through a travel agent). Fares may slightly undercut those on scheduled flights, but this is offset by more restrictions to contend with, so check conditions carefully.

Shopping for tickets

A specialist flight agent is generally the best starting point – either a **consolidator**, who buys up blocks of tickets from the airlines and sells them at a discount, or a **discount agent**, who wheels and deals in blocks of tickets offloaded by the airlines, and often offers special student and youth fares and a range of other travel-related services such as travel insurance, bus and train passes, car rentals, tours and the like. Bear in mind, though, that penalties for changing your plans can be stiff. Remember, too, that these companies make their money by dealing in bulk – don't expect them to answer lots of questions.

If you travel a lot, **discount travel clubs** are another option – the annual membership fee may be worth it for benefits such as cut-price air tickets and car rental. Many airlines offer **youth or student fares** to under-26s; a passport or driving licence is sufficient proof of age, though these tickets are subject to availability and can have eccentric booking conditions. A further possibility is to see if you can arrange a **courier flight**, although the hit-or-miss nature of these makes them most suitable for the single traveller who travels light and has a very flexible schedule. In return for shepherding a parcel through customs and possibly giving up your baggage allowance, you can expect to get a heavily discounted ticket. You'll probably also be restricted in the duration of your stay. Courier flights are generally available to Sydney, Brisbane, Melbourne and Cairns.

Don't automatically assume that tickets purchased through a travel specialist will be cheapest – once you get a quote, check with the **airlines** and you may turn up an even better deal. Be advised also that the pool of travel companies is swimming with sharks – exercise caution and never deal with a company that demands cash up front or refuses to accept payment by credit card.

Many airlines' and **discount travel websites** offer you the opportunity to book your tickets online, cutting out the costs of agents and middlemen. Good deals can often be found – whether it be through discount or **auction sites** – but travellers should remember that most low-fare airlines don't appear in the reservations systems listings. Always check the airlines' sites, too, for special Web-only deals.

Airlines

Air Canada (℡1-888/247-2262, Ⓦwww.aircanada.ca). Daily flights to Sydney from Vancouver and Toronto via Honolulu; and from Montréal, via Toronto and Honolulu, or Chicago and Los Angeles, or Newark and San Francisco.

Air New Zealand (US ℡1-800/262-1234; Canada ℡1-800/563-5494; Ⓦwww.airnz.com). Daily nonstop flights from Los Angeles to Sydney plus sporadic service from Vancouver.

Cathay Pacific (℡1-800/233-2742, Ⓦwww.cathaypacific.com). Daily flights to Sydney via Hong Kong from Los Angeles, San Francisco, Vancouver and Toronto; from New York via Vancouver and Hong Kong.

Japan Airlines (℡1-800/525-3663, Ⓦwww.japanair.com). Daily flights via Tokyo to Sydney, Melbourne or Cairns from New York, Chicago, Los Angeles, San Francisco and Vancouver plus a few flights a week from Dallas and Las Vegas.

Malaysia Airlines (℡1-800/552-9264, Ⓦwww.malaysiaair.com). Pacific and Atlantic route daily flights from Los Angeles and New York to Sydney or Perth, all via Kuala Lumpur.

Qantas (℡1-800/227-4500, Ⓦwww.qantas.com.au). Two or three nonstop flights daily from Los Angeles to Sydney, and one daily to Melbourne, with connections available from other major cities. Special fares and Boomerang Passes available for travel within Australia – check Web fares too.

Singapore Airlines (℡1-800/742-3333, Ⓦwww.singaporeair.com). Daily flights via Singapore to Sydney and Perth from Los Angeles, San Francisco (both Pacific routes) and New York (via the Atlantic).

United Airlines (℡1-800/538-2929, Ⓦwww.ual.com). Daily nonstop flights to Sydney from Los Angeles and San Francisco, with connections from many other cities.

Discount flight agents, travel clubs, courier brokers and consolidators

Air Brokers International, 150 Post St, Suite 620, San Francisco, CA 94108 (℡1-800/883-3273 or 415/397-1383, ⓦwww.airbrokers.com). Consolidator and specialist in RTW tickets.

Air Courier Association, 15000 W 6th Ave, Suite 203, Golden, CO 80206 (ⓣ1-800/282-1202 or 303/215-0900, ⓦwww.aircourier.org). Courier flight broker.

Air Treks, 442 Post St, 4th floor, San Francisco, CA 94102 (ⓣ1-800/350-0612 or 415/912-5600, ⓦwww.airtreks.com). RTW and Circle Pacific tickets. The website features an interactive database that lets you build and price your own RTW itinerary.

Airtech, 588 Broadway, Suite 204, New York, NY 10017 (ⓣ1-800/575-8324 or 212/219-7000, ⓦwww.airtech.com). Courier flight broker.

Austravel, 51 E 42nd St, Suite 616, New York, NY 10017 (ⓣ1-800/633-3404, ⓕ212/983-8376, ⓔusinfo@austravel.com). Flights and customized tours. Other locations in Chicago, Houston and San Francisco.

Council Travel, 205 E 42nd St, New York, NY 10017 (ⓣ1-800/226-8624, 1-888/COUNCIL or 212/822-2700, ⓦwww.counciltravel.com). Other branches in San Francisco, Los Angeles, Boston, Chicago and Washington DC, amongst others. Nationwide specialists in student travel.

Educational Travel Center, 438 N Frances St, Madison, WI 53703 (ⓣ1-800/747-5551 or 608/256-5551, ⓦwww.edtrav.com). Student/youth and consolidator fares.

International Association of Air Travel Couriers, PO Box 1349, Lake Worth, FL 33460 (ⓣ561/582-8320, ⓦwww.courier.org). Courier flight broker; membership $45 a year.

Moment's Notice, 7301 New Utrecht Ave, Brooklyn, NY 11204 (ⓣ718/234-6295, ⓦwww.moments-notice.com). Discount travel club.

Now Voyager, 74 Varick St, Suite 307, New York, NY 10013 (ⓣ212/431-1616, ⓦwww.nowvoyagertravel.com). Courier flight broker and consolidator.

Pacific Experience, 181 Spring St, Newport, RI 02840 (ⓣ1-800/233-4255, ⓦwww.pacificexperience.com). Good deals on flights made in conjunction with land bookings.

STA Travel (central booking ⓣ1-800/781-4040, telesales ⓣ1-800/777-0112, ⓦwww.statravel.com). Other branches in Los Angeles, Chicago, San Francisco, Philadelphia and Boston, amongst others. Worldwide discount travel firm specializing in student/youth fares; also student IDs, travel insurance, car rental and train passes.

Travel Avenue, 10 S Riverside, Suite 1404, Chicago, IL 60606 (ⓣ1-800/333-3335 or

312/876-6866, ⓦwww.travelavenue.com). Travel company offering discounted fares.

Travel Cuts (ⓣ1-800/667-2887 from Ontario, or ⓣ604/717-7800, ⓦwww.travelcuts.com). Canadian youth and discount travel agency with branches in Toronto, Vancouver, Halifax, Montréal, Calgary and Ottawa, amongst others.

Discount travel and auction websites

ⓦ**www.expedia.com** Discount airfares, all-airline search engine and daily deals.

ⓦ**www.hotwire.com** Last-minute savings of up to 40 percent on regular published fares. Travellers must be at least 18 and there are no refunds, transfers or changes allowed.

ⓦ**www.priceline.com** Name-your-own-price website that has deals at around 40 percent off standard fares. You cannot specify flight times (although you can specify dates) and the tickets are non-refundable, non-transferable and non-changeable.

ⓦ**www.skyauction.com** Auctions off tickets and travel packages using a "second bid" scheme similar to the system used by eBay and other online auctioneers. The best strategy is to bid the maximum you're willing to pay, since if you win you'll pay just enough to beat the runner up regardless of your maximum bid.

ⓦ**www.travelocity.com** Destination guides, hot Web fares and best deals for car hire, accommodation and lodging as well as fares. Provides access to the travel-agent system SABRE, the most comprehensive central reservations system in the US.

Package tours

Organized tours of Australia are usually tailored for those short on time and long on funds; that said, even independent travellers may want to build their stay around one or two planned activities arranged through a tour company. Several of the operators listed opposite offer so-called **city stopovers/city modules**, providing, for instance, two nights' accommodation, and perhaps a day-tour, costing from US$180 to US$450 depending on the location and time of year. Though **fly-drive deals** don't always make sense in sprawling Australia, they're worth considering if you plan to explore just one part of the country closely. Typical prices for the smallest class of car work out at about US$75 a day. And even if a package tour is the furthest thing from your mind, before you leave home you may want to check out tour or specialist operators for **rail or bus passes** (see pp.36–40 for some of the options).

Tour operators

AAT King's (℡1-800/353-4525, ⓦwww.aatkings.com). Offers a wide selection of escorted, independent tours and city stopovers.
Abercrombie and Kent (℡1-800/323-7308 or 630/954-2944, ℱ954-3324, ⓦwww.abercrombiekent.com). Offers 12- to 20-day tours, ranging from basic tours (including Sydney, Melbourne and the Great Barrier Reef) to more extensive ones (including Kangaroo Island and the Outback). Also specializes in family tours and customized itineraries. Extensions available to Papua New Guinea, New Zealand and Fiji (US$3150–5995, land only).
Adventure Center (℡1-800/227-8747 or 510/654-1879, ℱ654-4200, ⓦwww.adventure-center.com). Customized tour service, 4WD safaris, nature and wildlife tours, Aboriginal culture tours, Harley Davidson tours, 18 to 35 group tours, car rentals, camel safaris and rainforest lodges.
Adventures Abroad (℡1-800/665-3998, ℱ604/303-1076, ⓦwww.adventures-abroad.com). Small-group cultural/historical/nature interest tours. A choice of multi-country South Pacific and Australia specific tours. Two weeks in Australia from US$3108 (land only).
Asia Transpacific Journeys (℡1-800/642-2742, ℱ303/443-7078, ⓦwww.southeastasia.com). Wide range of customized itineraries and group tours including nature, adventure and Aboriginal rock art.
ATS Tours (℡1-800/423-2880, ℱ310/643-0032, ⓦwww.atstours.com). Huge Australian and New Zealand specialist; dive deals, fly-drives, city stopovers, rail/bus passes, motel vouchers and other add-ons.
Australian Pacific Tours (℡1-800/290-8687 or 416/234-9676, ℱ234-8385, ⓦwww.aptours.com). General interest escorted tours (eg 15-day "Classic South Pacific" from US$4750 land/air) and safaris; specializes in coach tours (US$1500–4000 land only) and fully independent travel.
Austravel (℡1-800/633-3404, ℱ212/983-8376, ⓦwww.austravel.com). Escorted tours and customized itineraries to Australia, New Zealand and the South Pacific.
Brendan Tours (℡1-818/785-9696, ⓦwww.brendantours.com). Fully escorted tours, city stopovers, fly-drives and custom-designed itineraries.

Destination World (℡1-888/345-4669, ℱ805/685-3385, ⓦwww.destinationworld.com). Offers a wide variety of tours, from budget to expensive. Off-the-beaten-track tours include a pub-crawl on horseback and motorcycle tours. Also offers a wheelchair-accessible bus for disabled groups.
Down Under Answers (℡1-800/788-6685, ℱ425/895-8929, ⓦwww2.gorp.com/downunder). Great Ocean Road cycling tours, hiking, kayaking and white-water rafting trips.
Down Under Direct/Swain Australia Tours (℡1-800/227-9246 or 610/896-9595, ℱ896-9592, ⓦwww.swainaustralia.com). Customized tours to meet individual travel needs and budgets.
Esplanade Tours (℡1-800/426-5492 or 617/266-7465). Customized itineraries from Sydney to the Outback, Qantas air deals and much more.
Goway Travel (℡1-800/387-8850, ℱ665-4432, ⓦwww.goway.com). Airfare deals, independent land bookings, fully escorted tours, over-50s vacations, bus tours, hostel passes, camping safaris, cruises, rail, fly-drives and group arrangements.
International Gay and Lesbian Travel Association (℡1-800/448-8550, ⓦwww.iglta.org). Trade group with lists of gay-owned or gay-friendly travel agents, accommodation and other travel businesses.
Maupintour (℡1-800/255-4266, ℱ785/331-1057, ⓦwww.maupintour.com). Variety of South Pacific tours, including 15 days in Australia (US$4525–5125 land/air).
Nature Expeditions International (℡1-800/869-0639, ℱ520/721-6719, ⓦwww.naturexp.com). 16-day educational/nature-focused tour including Sydney, Ayers Rock, Great Ocean Road, Blue Mountains National Park, Alice Springs and the Great Barrier Reef, led by professional guides (US$3450 land only).
Newmans Vacations (℡1-800/468-2665, ℱ310/648-7066, ⓦwww.newmans.com). New Zealand-based company that also offers city modules and tours in Australia.
Qantas Vacations (US ℡1-800/348-8139, Canada ℡1-800/268-7525, ⓦwww.qantasvacations.com). Offers a variety of special travel deals to cities (Sydney/Melbourne), the Great Barrier Reef and the Outback, plus Fiji or New Zealand extensions.
Saga Holidays (℡1-877/265-6862, ⓦwww.sagaholidays.com). Specialists in group travel for seniors. Their "Australian Adventure" 19-night escorted coach and rail tour is available from US$4199 (land/air).

Tauck World Discovery (☎1-800/788-7885, ⓦwww.tauck.com). Upmarket guided group tours of varying duration, with optional extensions to Fiji.
Tropical Adventures (☎1-888/250-1799 or 348-9778, ⓕ206/441-5431, ⓦwww.divetropical.com). Independent dive excursions to Australia and neighbouring islands.
United Vacations (☎1-800/917-9246, ⓦwww.unitedvacations.com). Varied assortment of individual tours, city-break packages, and multi-city excursions.

Getting there from New Zealand

New Zealand–Australia routes are busy and competition is fierce, resulting in an ever-changing range of deals and special offers; your best bet is to check the latest with a specialist travel agent (see opposite). It's a relatively short hop across the Tasman Sea: flying time from Auckland to Sydney is around three and a half hours.

All the **fares** quoted below are for travel during low or shoulder seasons; flying at peak times (primarily Dec to mid-Jan) can add substantially to these prices. Ultimately, the price you pay for your flight will depend on how much flexibility you want; many of the cheapest deals are hedged with restrictions – typically a maximum stay of thirty days and an advance-purchase requirement. The cheapest return fare from Auckland is to Sydney with Thai (NZ$510 for a maximum stay of thirty days; NZ$590 for a ticket valid for six months), but flights tend to be heavily booked. Qantas and Air New Zealand each have daily direct flights to Sydney, Brisbane (both NZ$690), Cairns and Perth (both NZ$825); and Malaysian Airlines fly regularly to Brisbane (NZ$695). Flying from Wellington or Christchurch adds an extra NZ$175. Outside peak season, when the airlines often have surplus capacity, they may offer promotional fares, which can bring down prices to as low as NZ$660 for a thirty-day return from Auckland to Cairns.

Open-jaw tickets – which let you fly into one city and out of another, making your own way between – can save a lot of backtracking and don't add hugely to the total fare. For example, flying into Cairns and out of Sydney, or vice versa, with Qantas or Air New Zealand costs from NZ$780. There are also various internal flight deals available to buy with your main ticket (see "Getting Around", p.36, for details).

If you're taking in Australia at the beginning (or end) of your grand tour, you can usually add one or two Australian stops at negligible extra cost, since many airlines go via Australian gateway airports anyway. There's a vast range of **RTW routes** and your choice will largely depend on where you plan to travel after the Antipodes: sample routes from Auckland might take in Sydney–Bangkok–London–Johannesburg–Perth, and back to Auckland (from NZ$3100); or Los Angeles–Rome–London–Bangkok–Melbourne, returning to Auckland (from NZ$2895).

Airlines

Air New Zealand (☎09/357 3000, ⓦwww.airnz.co.nz).
Ansett Australia (☎09/796 409, ⓦwww.ansett.com.au).
Malaysia Airlines (☎09/373 2741, ⓦwww.malaysiaair.com).

Qantas (☎09/357 8900, ⓦwww.qantas.com).
Thai Airways (☎1300/651 960,
ⓦwww.thaiair.com).
United Airlines (☎09/379 3800,
ⓦwww.unitedairlines.com).

Specialist travel agents

Budget Travel, 16 Fort St, Auckland, plus other branches around the city (☎09/366 0061 or free call 0800/808 040). Long-established agent with budget airfares and accommodation packages.
Destinations Unlimited, 220 Queen St, Auckland (☎09/373 4033). Discount fares, plus a good selection of tours and holiday packages.
Flight Centres, 350 Queen St, Auckland (☎09/358 4310, ⓦwww.flightcentre.co.nz), plus branches nationwide. Competetive discounts on airfares and a wide range of package holidays and adventure tours.
STA Travel, Travellers' Centre, 10 High St, Auckland (☎09/309 0458, fastfare telesales ☎09/366 6673), plus branches nationwide. Fare discounts for students and those under 26, as well as visas, student cards and travel insurance.
Thomas Cook, 191 Queen St, Auckland (☎09/379 3920, ⓦwww.thomascook.co.nz). Low cost flights, tours and accommodation; also issues travellers' cheques and bus and rail passes.
Usit Beyond, cnr Shortland St and Jean Batten Place, Auckland (☎09/379 4224,

ⓦwww.usitbeyond.co.nz). Student/youth travel specialists.

Packages and tours

There's a huge variety of holidays and tours to Australia available in New Zealand; call any of the travel agents listed here. The holiday subsidiaries of airlines such as Air New Zealand, Ansett and Qantas package short **city-breaks** (flight and accommodation) and **fly-drive deals** for little more than the cost of the regular airfare. On the other hand, if romping around the Outback is a high priority, check out any available **adventure tours** as they can be a good way of covering a lot of ground in a short time and getting you to remote places that would otherwise be inaccessible without your own transport. Itineraries range from 14 to 39 days and concentrate on exploring remoter regions, as well as classic rainforest-and-reef trips; prices (not including airfare from New Zealand) start at NZ$1500 and go up to NZ$4250 for extended journeys. A more economical option is offered by backpacker-oriented companies based in Australia, such as Oz Experience and Wayward Bus (see "Getting Around", pp.39–40), whose tours can be booked through STA offices in New Zealand if you want to plan ahead.

Getting there from
Southeast Asia

A satisfying way of reaching Australia and really getting some impression of the distance you've come is to travel overland through Southeast Asia. Plenty of people make this journey, especially Australian backpackers heading in the other direction at the start of their trip. Southeast Asia isn't as straightforward or relaxing as Australia (and you'll need to take appropriate health precautions), but it's a fascinating region and is unlikely to make a big dent in your budget.

Bangkok, in Thailand, is a popular starting point, with return flights available from around £450 in the UK and US$800 in the US. From Bangkok an inexpensive bus serv-

ice leaves twice daily for the 2000km ride to **Singapore**, though it's a gruelling 48-hour trip unless you make a stop or two along the way; a more comfortable option is the train

21

to Singapore via Padang Besar (at least one daily; 30hr; £60/US$90) – book a day or two in advance to be sure of a seat.

From Singapore, you can cross to the **Indonesian islands** of Sumatra or Kalimantan (Indonesian Borneo) and from there island-hop via local buses and ferries southeast through to Java and Bali, from where there are several direct flights a week to Darwin, Brisbane or Sydney (around A$600). Allow at least a month from Bangkok to Bali, and count on minimum living expenses of £7/US$10 a day, not including flights. Be aware, however, that there is political and social unrest right through Indonesia at present, and travel through some of these regions may not be possible.

Visas and red tape

All visitors to Australia, except New Zealanders, require a visa or Electronic Travel Authority (ETA) to enter the country; if you're heading overland, you'll obviously need to check visa requirements for countries en route. You can get visa application forms from the Australian High Commissions, embassies or consulates listed opposite. Citizens of the US can get visa application forms from the Washington, Los Angeles and Ottawa offices and from the embassy internet sites.

Nationals of the UK, Ireland, the US, Canada, Malaysia, Singapore, Japan and several European and Scandinavian countries who intend to stay for **less than three months**, can apply for an **ETA** (Electronic Travel Authority), valid for multiple entry over one year. This replaces a visa – all the information is stored on computer – and saves you the hassle of having to queue or send off your passport. ETAs are available from travel agents and airlines and can be applied for at the same time as you book your flight. A fee may be levied for this service – in the UK around £16.

Citizens of other countries or visitors who intend to stay for longer than three months should apply for a **visitor visa**, valid for **three to six months**. You'll need to complete an application form and lodge it either in person or by post to the embassy or consulate. It costs £25 in the UK, US$36 in the US, CDN$55 in Canada, and takes around three weeks to process. If you think you might stay more than three months, it's best to get the longer visa before departure, because once you get to Australia extensions cost A$145. Once issued, a visa usually allows multiple entries, so long as your passport is valid.

An important condition for all holiday visa applications is that you have **adequate funds** both to support yourself during your stay – at least A$1000 a month – and eventually to get yourself home again. If you're visiting immediate family who live in Australia – parent, spouse, child, brother or sister – you can apply for a **Close Family Visa**, which has fewer restrictions.

Twelve-month **working holiday visas** are easily available to British, Irish, Canadian, Dutch, German, Japanese and Korean single people aged 18–30, though exceptions are made for young married couples without children. It is not normally a chance to further your career, since the stress is on casual employment: you are meant to work for no more than three months at any one job. You must arrange the visa before you arrive in Australia, and several months in advance. Working visas cost £65 in the UK and

CDN$140 in Canada; some travel agents such as Trailfinders in the UK (see p.14) can arrange them for you.

Young American citizens wishing to work in Australia might consider the **Special Youth Program**, designed to allow young people (aged 18–30) to holiday while working in short-term employment over a four-month period. Membership of the scheme costs US$365, which includes two nights' accommodation in Sydney and work support once you arrive; flights out to Australia are specially arranged by the programme and leave Los Angeles twice a month. Applications can be made through BUNAC (☏1-800/GO-BUNAC or 203/264-0901, ⍈www.bunac.com), Work Experience Down Under (☏1-800/999-2267, ⍈www.campcounselors.com) or Council/CIEE (☏1-888/COUNCIL, ⍈www.ciee.org).

Note that having a visa is not an absolute guarantee that you'll be allowed into Australia – immigration officials may well check again that you have enough money to cover you during your stay, and that you have a return or onward ticket. In extreme cases they may refuse entry, or more likely restrict your visit to a shorter period.

Australia has strict **quarantine** laws that apply to fruit, vegetables, fresh and packaged food, seed and some animal products, among other things; there are also strict laws prohibiting drugs, steroids, firearms, protected wildlife and associated products. Those over 18 can take advantage of a **duty-free allowance** on entry of 1 litre of alcohol and 250 cigarettes or 250g of tobacco.

Australian embassies and consulates abroad

UK

LondonAustralian High Commission, Australia House, Strand, London WC2B 4LA (☏020/7379 4334, ☏7240 5333, ⍈www.australia.org.uk). **Manchester**Australian Consulate, Chatsworth House, Lever St, Manchester M1 2DL (☏09065/508900, ☏061/236 4074).

Ireland

DublinAustralian Embassy, Fitzwilton House, Wilton Terrace, Dublin 2 (☏01/676 1517, ☏678 5185, ⍈www.australianembassy.ie).

US

AtlantaAustralian Consulate-General, 1 Buckhead Plaza, Suite #970, 3060 Peachtree Rd NW, Atlanta, GA 30305 (☏404/760-3400, ☏760-3401). **Honolulu**Australian Consulate-General, 1000 Bishop St, Honolulu, HI 96813 (☏808/524-5050, ☏531-5142). **Los Angeles**Australian Consulate-General, Century Plaza Towers, 19th floor, 2049 Century Park E, Los Angeles, CA 90067 (☏310/229-4800, ☏277-2258). **New York**Australian Consulate-General, 34th Floor, 150 E 42nd St, New York, NY 10017-5612 (☏212/351-6500, ☏351-6501). **San Francisco**Australian Consulate-General, 7th floor, 1 Bush St, San Francisco, CA 94104-4413 (☏415/362-6160, ☏986-2775). **Washington**Australian Embassy, 1601 Massachusetts Ave NW, Washington, DC 20036 (☏202/797-3000, ☏797-3168, ⍈www.austemb.org).

Canada

OttawaAustralian High Commission, Suite 710, 50 O'Connor St, Ottawa, ON K1P 6L2 (☏613/236-0841, ☏236-4376, ⍈www.ahc-ottawa.org/). **Toronto**Australian Consulate-General, Suite 314, 175 Bloor St E, Toronto, ON M4W 3R8 (☏416/323-1155, ☏323-3910). **Vancouver**Australian Consulate, Suite 1225, 888 Dunsmuir St, Vancouver, BC V6C 3K4 (☏604/684-1177, ☏684-1856).

New Zealand

AucklandAustralian Consulate-General, 8th floor, Union House, 32–38 Quay St, Auckland 1 (☏09/303 2429, ☏377 0798). **Wellington**Australian High Commission, 72–78 Hobson St, Thorndon, Wellington (☏04/473 6411, ☏498 7135).

Indonesia

BaliAustralian Consulate, Jalan Prof Moh Yamin 51, Renon, Denpasar, Bali (☏0361/23 5092, ☏23 1990). **Jakarta**Australian Embassy, Jalan HR Rasuna Said Kav C15–16, Kuningan, Jakarta Selatan 12940 (☏021/2550 5555, ☏522 7101).

Malaysia

Kuala Lumpur Australian High Commission, 6 Jalan Yap Kwan Seng, Kuala Lumpur 50450 (☏246 5555, ☏241 5773).

Singapore

Singapore Australian High Commission, 25 Napier Rd, Singapore 258507 (℡ 065/836 4150, ℻ 737 7465).

Thailand

Bangkok Australian Embassy, 37 South Sathorn Rd, Bangkok 10120 (℡ 02/287 2680, ℻ 287 2029).

Insurance

If you're entitled to free emergency healthcare from Medicare (see p.30 for details of reciprocal arrangements), you may feel that the need for the health element of travel insurance is reduced, but check carefully what is included (ambulance trips, among other things, will not be reimbursed). In any case, some form of travel insurance can help plug the gaps and will cover you in the event of losing your baggage, missing a plane and the like.

A typical travel insurance policy usually provides cover for the loss of baggage, tickets and – up to a certain limit – cash or cheques, as well as cancellation or curtailment of your journey. Most of them exclude **"high-risk" activities** unless an extra premium is paid: depending on the insurer, these can include water sports (especially diving), skiing or even just hiking; check carefully that any policy you are considering will cover you in case of an accident. Many policies can be chopped and changed to exclude

coverage you don't need – for example, sickness and accident benefits can often be excluded or included at will. If you do take medical coverage, ascertain whether benefits will be paid as treatment proceeds or only after return home, and whether there is a 24-hour medical emergency number. When securing baggage cover, make sure that the per-article limit – typically under £500 – will cover your most valuable possession. If you need to make a claim, you should keep receipts for medicines and

Rough Guides travel insurance

Rough Guides now offers its own **travel insurance**, customized for our readers by a leading UK broker and backed by a Lloyds underwriter. It's available for anyone, of any nationality, travelling anywhere in the world.

There are two main Rough Guide insurance plans: **Essential**, for basic, no-frills cover; and **Premier** – with more generous and extensive benefits. Alternatively, you can take out annual **multitrip insurance**, which covers you for any number of trips throughout the year (with a maximum of 60 days for any one trip). Unlike many policies, the Rough Guides schemes are calculated by the day, so if you're travelling for 27 days rather than a month, that's all you pay for. If you intend to be away for the whole year, the **Adventurer** policy will cover you for 365 days. Each plan can be supplemented with a "Hazardous Activities Premium" if you plan to indulge in sports considered dangerous, such as skiing, scuba-diving or trekking. Rough Guides also does good deals for older travellers, and will insure you up to any age, at prices comparable to SAGA's.

For a **policy quote**, call the Rough Guides Insurance Line on UK freefone ℡ 0800/015 0906, or, if you're calling from outside Britain on (+44) 1243/621046. Alternatively, get an online quote, or buy your policy online, at ⊛ www.roughguides.com/insurance

medical treatment, and in the event you have anything stolen, you must obtain an official statement from the police.

Before spending out on a new policy it's worth checking whether you are already covered: some all-risks home insurance policies, for example, may cover your possessions against loss or theft when overseas, and many private medical schemes such as BUPA or PPP include cover when abroad, including baggage loss, cancellation or curtailment and cash replacement as well as sickness or accident. Bank and credit cards often have certain levels of medical or other insurance included

and you may automatically get travel insurance if you use a major credit card to pay for your trip (check the small print on this, though, as it may not be of much use).

In Canada, provincial health plans usually provide partial cover for medical mishaps overseas, while holders of official student/teacher/youth cards in Canada and the US are entitled to meagre accident coverage and hospital inpatient benefits. Students will often find that their student health coverage extends during the vacations and for one term beyond the date of last enrolment.

 # Travellers with disabilities

The vast distances between Australia's cities and popular tourist resorts present visitors with mobility difficulties with a unique challenge, but, overall, travel in Australia for people with disabilities is rather easier than it would be in the UK and Europe.

The federal government provides information and various nationwide services through the **National Information Communication Awareness Network** (NICAN) and the **Australian Council for the Rehabilitation of the Disabled** (ACROD) – see overleaf for contact details. The **Australian Tourist Commission** offices provide a helpline service and publish a factsheet, *Travelling in Australia for People with Disabilities*, available from its offices worldwide (see p.33 for addresses and phone numbers).

Disability needn't interfere with your sight-seeing: the attitude of the management at Australia's major tourist attractions is excellent, and they will provide assistance where they can. For example, you'll find you can view the rock art at Kakadu National Park, do a tour around the base of Uluru (Ayers Rock), snorkel unhindered on the Great Barrier Reef, go on a cruise around Sydney Harbour, and see the penguins at Phillip Island.

Planning a holiday

There are **organized tours and holidays** specifically for people with disabilities (including mobility, hearing, vision and intellectual restrictions). Some arrange travel only, some organize travel and accommodation, and others provide a complete package – travel, accommodation, meals and carer support. This last type, as well as catering fully for special needs, provides company for the trip. The contacts overleaf will be able to put you in touch with any specialists for trips to Australia; several are listed in the Australian Tourist Commission factsheet. If you want to be more independent, it's important to become an authority on where you must be self-reliant and where you may expect help, especially regarding transport and accommodation. It is also vital to be honest – with travel agencies, insurance companies and travel companions. Know your limitations and make sure others know them. If you do not use a wheelchair all the time but your walking capabilities are limited, remember that you are likely to need to cover greater distances while travelling (often over rougher terrain and in hotter temperatures) than you are used to. If you use a wheelchair, have it serviced before you go and carry a repair kit.

Read your **travel insurance** small print carefully to make sure that people with a pre-existing medical condition are not excluded. And use your travel agent to make your journey simpler: airline or bus companies can cope better if they are expecting you, with a wheelchair provided at airports and staff primed to help. A **medical certificate** of your fitness to travel (provided by your doctor) is also extremely useful; some airlines or insurance companies may insist on it. Make sure that you have extra supplies of medication – carried with you if you fly – and a prescription including the generic name in case of emergency.

Several **books** give a good overview of accessible travel in Australia, and include: *Smooth Ride Guides: Australia and New Zealand*, *Freewheeling Made Easy* (FT Publishing), which lists support organizations, airports and transport, specialist tour operators and places to visit and stay; *Easy Access Australia* (Easy Access Australia Publishing), which has information on all the states, with maps, and a separate section with floor plans of hotel rooms; and *A Wheelie's Handbook of Australia* (Program Print).

Useful organizations

Australia

ACROD (Australian Council for the Rehabilitation of the Disabled), PO Box 60, Curtin, ACT 2605 (☎ 02/6282 4333, ⓦ www.acrod.org.au). Regional offices provide lists of state-based help organizations, accommodation, travel agencies and tour operators.
Aged and Disability Care Information Service, "Westella", 181 Elizabeth St, Hobart, TAS 7000 (☎ 03/6234 7448).
DIRC (Disability Information Resource Centre), 195 Gilles St, Adelaide, SA 5000 (☎ 08/8223 7522).
Disability Information Victoria, PO Box 295, Malvern, Victoria (☎ 1300/650 865).
Disability Services and Liaison, PO Box 721, Alice Springs, NT 0871 (☎ 08/8951 5177).

NICAN (National Information Communication Awareness Network), PO Box 407, Curtin, ACT 2605 (☎ 02/6285 3713 or free call 1800 806 769, ⓕ 6285 3714, ⓦ www.nican.com.au). A national, nonprofit, free information service on recreation, sport, tourism, the arts, and much more, for people with disabilities. Has a database of 4500 organizations – such as wheelchair-accessible tourist accommodation venues, sports and recreation organizations, and rental companies who have accessible buses and vans.
Paraplegic and Quadriplegic Association of NSW, 33–35 Burlington Rd, Homebush, NSW 2140 (☎ 02/9764 4166). Serves the interests of the spinally injured; offices also in each state capital.
Travellers Aid Support Centre, 2nd floor, 169 Swanston St, Melbourne, VIC 3000 (☎ 03/9654 7690).

UK

Holiday Care Service, 2nd floor, Imperial Building, Victoria Rd, Horley, Surrey RH6 7PZ (☎ 01293/774535, ⓕ 784647, minicom 776943, ⓦ www.holidaycare.org.uk).
RADAR (Royal Association for Disability and Rehabilitation), 12 City Forum, 250 City Rd, London EC1V 8AF (☎ 020/7250 3222, ⓦ www.radar.org.uk).
Tripscope, The Courtyard, Evelyn Rd, London W4 5JL (☎ 020/8994 9294, ⓕ 994 3618, ⓦ www.justmobility.co.uk/tripscope). National telephone information service offering free advice on transport and travel.

Ireland

Disability Action Group, 2 Annadale Ave, Belfast BT7 3JH (☎ 028/9029 7880, ⓦ www.disabilityaction.org).
Irish Wheelchair Association, Blackheath Drive, Clontarf, Dublin 3 (☎ 01/833 8241, ⓕ 833 3873, ⓔ iwa@iol.ie).

US

Directions Unlimited, 720 N Bedford Rd, Bedford Hills, NY 10507 (☎ 1-800/533-5343). Tour operator specializing in custom tours for people with disabilities.
Mobility International US, PO Box 10767, Eugene, OR 97440 (voice and TDD ☎ 503/343-1284, ⓦ www.miusa.com). Information and referral services, access guides, tours and exchange programmes. Annual membership $35 (including a quarterly newsletter).
Society for the Advancement of Travel for the Handicapped (SATH), 347 5th Ave, New York, NY 10016 (☎ 212/447-7284,

Ⓦ www.sath.org). Nonprofit travel-industry referral service; allow plenty of time for a response.

Travel Information Service, Moss Rehabilitation Hospital, 1200 W Tabor Rd, Philadelphia, PA 19141 (☎ 215/456-9900, Ⓦ www.mossresourcenet.org). Internet and telephone information and referral service.

Twin Peaks Press, Box 129, Vancouver, WA 98666 (☎ 1-800/637-2256 or 206/694-2462, Ⓦ http://home.pacifier.com/~twinpeak/). Publisher of the *Directory of Travel Agencies for the Disabled* ($19.95), listing more than 370 agencies worldwide; *Travel for the Disabled* ($19.95); the *Directory of Accessible Van Rentals* ($9.95); and *Wheelchair Vagabond* ($14.95), loaded with personal tips.

Canada

Jewish Rehabilitation Hospital, 3205 Place Alton Goldbloom, Montréal, PQ H7V 1R2 (☎ 514/688-9550 ext 226). Guidebooks and travel information.

Accommodation

Much of Australia's tourist accommodation is well set up for people with disabilities, because buildings tend to be built outwards rather than upwards. New buildings in Australia must comply with a legal minimum **accessibility standard**, requiring that bathrooms contain toilets at the appropriate height, proper circulation and transfer space, wheel-in showers (sometimes with fold-down seat, but if this is lacking, proprietors will provide a plastic chair), grab rails, adequate doorways, and space next to toilets and beds for transfer. There are, of course, many older hotels which may have no wheelchair access at all or perhaps just one or two rooms with full wheelchair access. Most hotels also have refrigerators for medication which needs to be kept cool.

The best place to start looking for accommodation is the *A–Z Australian Accommodation Guide* published by the Australian Automobile Association (AAA) – the umbrella organization for state- and territory-based motoring associations that rate accommodation. They also offer some specialized services, a centralized **booking service** and a repair service for motorized wheelchairs, with reciprocal rights if you are a member of an affiliated overseas motoring organization. The guide is available from any

of the state organizations; NICAN also has access to their database via computer, so you can choose your accommodation over the phone. Many travel shops and bookshops have accommodation guides which detail places that have wheelchair access.

The greatest range of accessible accommodation is found in the more densely populated areas of Australia – especially the east coast. In the **cities**, the big chain hotels have rooms with wheelchair access. Some of the smaller hotels do provide accessible accommodation, and a large proportion of suburban motels will have one or two suitable rooms. In the **country** there are fewer specially equipped hotels, but many motels have accessible units; this is particularly true of those that belong to a chain such as Flag – consult their directories for locations. The newest YHA **hostels** are all accessible, and there has been an effort to improve facilities throughout; accessible hostels are detailed in the YHA *Handbook*, or contact them direct (see p.48). **Caravan parks** are also worth considering, since some have accessible cabins. Others may have accessible toilets and washing facilities. Many **resorts** are also fully designed and equipped for wheelchair travellers, though in all cases, it's best to check in advance what facilities are available.

Transport

Interstate **buses** are generally not an option, though interstate **trains** can accommodate wheelchairs and give assistance for other disabilities; for enquiries about services in Queensland, New South Wales and Victoria call ☎ 13 2232; for elsewhere phone free call ☎ 1800 888 480. However, the most convenient ways of getting around are by **plane** and car. The three major airlines – Ansett, Qantas and Virgin Blue – have services to help people with disabilities; Qantas staff undergo special disability-awareness training and on international flights their aircraft carry the sky chair and are equipped with a larger toilet cubicle.

Of the major car-rental agencies, Hertz and Avis offer **vehicles with hand controls** at no extra cost, but advance notice is required. Reserved **parking** is available for vehicles displaying the wheelchair symbol (available from local council offices) in all major centres. There is no formal acceptance of overseas parking permits, but states will generally accept most home-country permits as sufficient evidence to obtain a temporary countrywide permit in Australia. Parking charges and designated spaces differ from state to state (call NICAN for further information). A specially adapted **taxi service** operates from all the major national airports, booked in advance on freecall ☎ 1800 043 187; in addition every capital city has wheelchair-accessible taxis. Some **suburban rail services** can be used with a wheelchair: Melbourne's MET leads the way – call Disability Services (☎ 03/9619 2355). Minibuses in some cities have either a hoist or a ramp for rental (call NICAN for further information – see p.26).

All capital cities and most regional centres produce **mobility maps** showing accessible paths, car parking, toilets, etc, which can be obtained from local councils. Other cities have gone further and their tourist authorities produce comprehensive books such as *Access Brisbane* and *Darwin City without Steps*, while ACROD in New South Wales publishes *Accessing Sydney* (available from them at 55 Ryde St, Ryde, NSW 2112). *Easy Access Australia – A Travel Guide to Australia* is a comprehensive guide written by wheelchair-users for anyone with a mobility difficulty and is available for £11.95 in the UK from the following address: c/o Prawles Oast, Ewhurst Green, near Robertsbridge, E. Sussex TN32 5RG.

Costs, money and banks

If you've travelled down from Southeast Asia you'll find Australia expensive on a day-to-day basis, but fresh from Europe or the US you'll find prices comparable or cheaper. Australia is well set up for independent travellers, and with a student, YHA or a backpackers' card (see p.48) you can get discounts on a wide range of travel and entertainment.

Australia's currency is the Australian dollar, or "buck", divided into 100 cents. Plastic notes with forgery-proof clear windows come in $100, $50, $20, $10 and $5 denominations, along with $2, $1, 50¢, 20¢, 10¢ and 5¢ coins. There are no longer 1¢ or 2¢ coins, but prices are regularly advertised at $1.99 etc and an irregular bill will be rounded up or down to the closest denomination.

Exchange rates fluctuate around an over-the-counter rate of A$2.90 for £1; A$2 for US$1; A$1.20 for CDN$1; and A$0.80 for NZ$1.

Some basic costs

If you're prepared to camp you might get by on as little as $40 a day, but you should count on around $60 a day for food, board

and transport if you stay in hostels, travel on buses and eat and drink carefully. Stay in motels and B&Bs, and eat out regularly, and you'll need to budget $100 or more: extras such as scuba-diving courses, clubbing, car rental and tours will all add to your costs.

Hostel **accommodation** will set you back $15–25 a person, while a double room in a motel costs between $45 and $100. **Food**, on the whole, is good value: counter meals in hotels rarely cost more than $12; restaurants cost upwards of $25 for a reasonable three-course feed, and many let you BYO (Bring Your Own) wine or beer. Buying your own ingredients is not always the cheapest way to eat in the bigger cities, where there's sure to be a range of budget diners and food halls, but overall you'll save; meat and fresh seasonal produce are generally inexpensive. For a nation of sociable boozers, **drinking** out is surprisingly costly, at around $2.75 or more for a beer in a bar – it's cheaper bought in bulk from a bottle shop.

Given the size of the country, **transport** can make a major dent in your budget and is perhaps the area in which you're most likely to overspend. **Pre-planning** helps – an open-jaw plane ticket, for example, saves you having to get back to where you started; or pay a little extra for an international flight that gives you some discounted internal fares. There are also a huge variety of **bus and train passes** available overseas (see "Getting Around", pp.36–40, for more on the options available). **Driving** yourself may not always save money, but it does give you a great deal more flexibility. Finding passengers willing to share costs is one way to minimize expenses and is usually not too difficult – try the notice boards at hostels and other meeting places. Buying a used car will, realistically, set you back $4000 or more for a mechanically sound vehicle with a reasonable resale value (see p.42 for more advice), but even $1500 should buy something that will get you around – if not in the greatest of style. Renting a car starts at $29 a day for local rental to at least $65 a day for longer distances. Fuel averages 95¢ a litre, but with substantial local variations.

Travellers' cheques, credit and cash cards

Travellers' cheques are the best way to bring your funds into Australia, as they can be replaced if lost or stolen (remember to keep a list of the serial numbers separate from the cheques). Australian dollar travellers' cheques are ideal as theoretically they're valid as cash and so shouldn't attract exchange fees, though smaller businesses may be unwilling to take them, and some banks do try to charge commission when exchanging them. Cheques in US dollars and pounds sterling are also widely accepted, and banks should be able to handle all major currencies. It's worth checking both the rate and the commission when you change your cheques (as well as when you buy them), as these can vary quite widely – many places charge a set amount for every cheque, in which case you're better off changing relatively large denominations. You'll need a passport to cash travellers' cheques.

Credit cards can come in very handy as a backup source of funds, and they can even save on exchange-rate commissions. They can also be used to leave a deposit – for example, for a rental car or a hotel booking – even if you settle the final bill with cash. MasterCard and Visa are the most widely recognized; you can also use Amex, Bankcard and Diners Club. In addition, with an **international debit card** you may be able to pay for goods via EFTPOS (see overleaf) and gain direct access to your home funds via ATM machines displaying the Cirrus-Maestro symbol. As a flat rate is charged for these transactions, this can work out to be cheaper than travellers' cheques for large sums – check with your bank before leaving.

Banks and exchange

Closures of local banks throughout much of Australia means you will no longer necessarily find a branch of one of the main **banks** in every town, though there will be a local agency which handles bank business – usually based at the general store, post office or roadhouse – though not necessarily a 24hr ATM machine. The best policy is always make sure you have some cash on you before leaving the bigger towns, especially at weekends. The major banks, with branches countrywide, are Westpac, ANZ, the Commonwealth and the National.

Banking hours are Monday to Thursday 9.30am to 4pm, Friday 9.30am to 5pm, though in country areas some agencies will be open later, and some big-city branches might also have extended hours; autotellers or **ATMs** are generally open 24 hours. **Bureaux de change** are only found in major tourist centres and airports, so make sure you exchange your currency during banking hours. All **post offices** act as Commonwealth Bank agents, which means there's a fair chance of changing money even in the smallest Outback settlements – withdrawals at these places are often limited by a lack of ready cash, however, though less remote post offices may have EFTPOS facilities (see overleaf).

If you're spending some time in Australia, and plan to work or move around, it makes life a great deal easier if you **open a bank account**. To do this you'll need to take along every piece of ID documentation you own –

a passport may not be enough, though a letter from your bank manager at home may help – but it's otherwise a fairly straightforward process. The Commonwealth Bank and Westpac are the most widespread options, and their **keycards** give you access not only to ATM machines but also anywhere that offers **EFTPOS** facilities (Electronic Funds Transfer at Point of Sale). This includes many Outback service stations and supermarkets, where you can use your card to pay directly for goods; some of them will also give you cash (ask for "cash back"). However, bear in mind that **bank fees and charges** are exorbitant in Australia; most banks allow only a few free withdrawal transactions per month (depending on who you bank with – it's well worth shopping around before you open an account), and there are even bigger charges for using a competitor's ATM machine, as well as monthly fees.

International money transfers can be made from any bank in Australia to a nominated bank abroad and cost approximately A$25. Transfers can take anywhere from a few days to several months. For **moneygrams**, you can make arrangements with either American Express Moneygram (within Sydney ☎ 02/9886 0666; elsewhere free call ☎ 1800 230 100) or Western Union (within Sydney ☎ 02/9241 5722; elsewhere free call ☎ 1800 649 565).

Health

Australia has high standards of hygiene, and there are few exceptional health hazards – at least in terms of disease. No vaccination certificates are required unless you've come from a yellow-fever zone within the past week. Standards in Australia's hospitals are also very high, and medical costs are reasonable by world standards. For general health information while in Australia, check out the website ⓦ www.travmed.com.au.

The national healthcare scheme, **Medicare**, offers a reciprocal arrangement – free essential healthcare – for citizens of the UK, New Zealand, Italy, Malta, Finland, the Netherlands and Sweden. This free treatment is limited to public hospitals and casualty departments (though the **ambulance** ride to get you there isn't covered); at GPs you pay up front (about $40 minimum) with two-thirds of your fee reimbursed by Medicare.

The whole process is made easier by the production of a **Medicare Card**, available from any Medicare Centre. Anyone eligible who's staying in Australia for a while – particularly those on extended working holidays – is advised to obtain one. Dental treatment is not included: if you find yourself in need of dental treatment in one of the larger cities, try the dental hospital, where dental students may treat you cheaply or for free.

The sun

Australia's biggest health problem for fair-skinned visitors is also one of its chief attractions: **sunshine**. A sunny day in London, Toronto, or even Miami, is not the same as a cloudless day in Cairns, and the intensity of the Australian sun's damaging ultraviolet rays is far greater. Whether this is because of Australia's proximity to the reputed **ozone hole** is a matter of debate, but there's absolutely no doubt that the southern sun burns more fiercely than anything in the northern hemisphere, and you need to take extra care.

Australians of European origin, especially those of Anglo-Saxon or Celtic decent, could not be less suited to Australia's outdoor lifestyle, which is why two out of three Australians are statistically likely to develop **skin cancer** in their lifetime, the world's worst record. About five percent of these will develop potentially fatal **melanomas**, and about a thousand die each year. Looking at the ravaged complexions of some older Australians (who had prolonged exposure to the sun in the days before there was an awareness of the great dangers of skin cancer) should be enough to make you want to cover yourself with lashings of the highest factor (SPF 35+) sun block, widely used and sold just about everywhere. Sunscreen should not be used on babies less than six months old: instead, keep them out of direct sunlight. What looks like war paint on the noses of surfers and small children is actually **zinc cream**; the thick, sticky waterproof cream, which comes in fun colours, provides a total blockout and is particularly useful when applied to protruding parts of the body, such as noses and shoulders.

These days, Australians are fully aware of the sun's dangers, and you're constantly reminded to **"Slip, Slop, Slap"**, the government-approved catch phrase reminding you to slip on a T-shirt, slop on some sun block and slap on a hat – sound advice. Pay attention to any moles on your body: if you notice any changes, either during or after your trip, see a doctor; cancerous melanomas are generally easily removed if caught early. To prevent headaches and – in the long term – cataracts, it's a good idea to wear **sunglasses**; look for "UV block" ratings when you buy a pair.

The sun can also cause **heat exhaustion** and **sunstroke**, so as well as keeping well covered up, stay in the shade if you can. Drink plenty of liquids: on hot days when walking, experts advise drinking a litre of water an hour – which is a lot to carry. Alcohol and sun don't mix well; when you're feeling particularly hot and thirsty, remember that a cold beer will actually dehydrate you.

Wildlife dangers

Although **mosquitoes** are found across the whole of the country, malaria is not endemic; however, in the tropical north there are regular outbreaks of similarly transmitted Ross River Fever and Dengue Fever, chronically debilitating viruses which are potentially fatal to children and the elderly. Medical researchers believe that mosquitoes as far south as Sydney may be carrying the Ross River virus, which is reason enough not to be too blasé about mozzie bites. Aeroguard and Rid are the popular brands of insect repellent.

The danger from other **wildlife** is much overrated: snake and spider bites, and crocodile and shark attacks are widely publicized and an essential part of the perilous Outback myth – nonetheless, all are extremely rare. There are always scares, such as when a couple of people died from being bitten by flying foxes infected with the rabies-like lyssa virus in Queensland in 1996 – it's best not to handle bats, should you have the opportunity. Rabies itself is unknown in Australia.

The way to minimize danger from **saltwater crocodiles** (which actually range far inland) is to keep your distance. If you're camping in the bush within 100km of the northern coast between Broome (WA) and Rockhampton (QLD), make sure your tent is at least 50m from waterholes or creeks, don't collect water at the same spot every day or leave any rubbish around, and always seek local advice. Four-wheel drivers should take extra care when walking creeks prior to driving across.

Snakes almost always do their best to avoid people and you'll probably never see one. They're more likely to be active in hot weather, when you should be more careful. Treat them with respect, and it's unlikely you'll be bitten: most bites occur when people try to catch or kill snakes. Wear boots and long trousers when hiking through undergrowth, collect firewood carefully, and, in the event of a confrontation, back off. **Sea snakes** sometimes find divers intriguing, wrapping themselves around limbs or staring into masks, but they're seldom aggressive. If **bitten** by a snake, use a crepe bandage to bind the entire limb firmly and splint it, as if for a sprain; this slows the distribution of venom into the lymphatic system. Don't clean the bite area (venom around the bite can identify the species, making treatment easier), and don't slash the bite or apply a tourniquet. Treat all bites as if they were serious and always seek immediate medical attention, but remember: not all snakes are poisonous, not all poisonous snakes inject a lethal dose of venom every time they bite, and death from snakebite is rare.

Two **spiders** whose bites can be fatal are the **Sydney funnel-web**, a black, stocky creature found in the Sydney area, and the small **redback**, a relative of the notorious black widow of the Americas, usually found in dark, dry locations. January and February are the months in which there is the greatest danger of bites by both. Treat funnel-web bites as for snakebite, and apply ice to redback wounds to relieve pain; if bitten by either, get to a hospital – antivenins are available. **Other spiders, centipedes** and **scorpions** can deliver painful wounds but generally only cause serious problems if you have allergies.

Ticks, mites and **leeches** are the bane of bushwalkers, though spraying **repellent** over shoes and leggings will help keep these pests away in the first instance. Ticks are poisonous and you may want to check yourself over after a hike, but you'll probably feel them – look for local stinging and swelling (usually just inside hairlines) and you'll find either a tiny black dot, or a pea-sized animal attached, depending on which species has bitten you. Kill the tick with kerosene and then, using tweezers, pull it off, while trying to avoid squeezing the animal's body, which will inject more venom. Some mites cause an infuriating rash known as "scrub itch", which characteristically appears wherever your clothes are tightest, such as around the hips and ankles. Unfortunately, there's not much you can do except dab on more kerosene to kill the mites, take antihistamines and wait a day or two for the itching to stop. Leeches are gruesome but harmless; insect repellent, fire or salt gets them off the skin, though bites will bleed heavily for some time.

More serious is the threat from various types of **jellyfish** (also known as stingers or sea wasps), which occur in coastal tropical waters through the summer months. Two to watch out for are the tiny irukanji and saucer-sized box jellyfish, though both are virtually invisible in water. Irukanji have painless stings, but their venom causes cramping and severe abdominal pain, and side-affects which can continue for months. Box jellyfish stings leave permanent red weals, and the venom can cause rapid unconciousness and even kill if the weals cover more than half a limb. Treat stinger victims by dousing the sting area (front and back) with liberal amounts of **vinegar** (never rub with sand or towels, or attempt to remove tentacles from the skin – both could trigger the release of more venom); apply mouth-to-mouth resuscitation if needed, and get the victim to hospital for treatment. Whatever the locals are doing, don't risk swimming on tropical beaches during the **stinger season** (roughly Oct to May). Specific reef hazards are covered at the start of the chapter on Queensland's tropical coast (p.465).

For more background on Australian fauna, see "Wildlife" on p.1159.

Other health hazards

Australia has one of the lowest rates of **AIDS** infection in the world, largely because the population caught on very early to the need for safe sex, which has been promoted heavily. Infected needles are also a danger, not only among intravenous drug users but also from ear-piercing and tattooing. The Australian National Council on AIDS (ANCA) has centres all over the country, and you'll find AIDS helplines listed in the major cities in this guide.

Other health hazards are far less pressing. **Tap water** is safe to drink everywhere. It doesn't always taste good, but bottled water is commonly available. One thing to watch out for in the hot and humid north is **tropical ear**, a very painful fungal infection of the ear canal. Treatment is with ear drops and if you think you might be susceptible, use them anyway after getting wet.

Although you're unlikely to find yourself in the path of a raging **bushfire**, it helps to know how to survive one. If you're in a car, don't attempt to drive through smoke but park at the side of the road in the clearest spot, put on your headlights, wind up the windows and close the air vents. Although it seems to go against common sense – and your natural instincts – it's safer to **stay inside the car**. Lie on the floor and cover all exposed skin with a blanket or any covering at hand. The car won't explode or catch on fire, and a fast-moving wildfire will pass quickly overhead. If you smell or see smoke and fire while **walking**, find a cleared rocky outcrop or an open space: if the terrain and time permits, dig a shallow trench – but in any event, lie face down and cover all exposed skin.

AIDS organizations ACON (AIDS Council of NSW), PO Box 350, Darlinghurst, NSW 2010 (℡02/9206 2000 or free call 1800 063 060, ⊚www.acon.org.au); AIDS Trust of Australia, PO Box 1030, Darlinghurst, NSW 2010 (℡02/9310 1066).

Information and maps

Australian tourism abroad is represented by the Australian Tourist Commission, who produce an annual, glossy *Australia, A Traveller's Guide* which gives an excellent introduction. It details the country region by region, offers travel tips and ways of getting around, and has a useful directory of addresses. You can also get information on the internet at the Tourist Commission's website (ⓦwww.australia.com) and at the Gateway to Australias site (ⓦwww.aussie.net.au).

More detailed information is available by the sackful once you're in the country. Each state or territory has its own **tourist authority**, which operates information offices throughout its own area and in major cities in other parts of Australia – some are even represented abroad (almost all have London offices, detailed below). A level below this are a host of regional and community-run **visitors centres** and **information kiosks**. Even the smallest Outback town seems to have one – or at the very least a pamphlet rack at the local service station – while larger places will often have two or more rival offices. Remember though, most of these associations only promote subscribing or advertising members – the information they supply is not comprehensive or impartial, as anyone in the tourist business is likely to be involved with a tourism association.

It's also worthwhile asking **fellow travellers** about places they've been to. **Hostels** tend to act as information points, with **notice boards** where you'll find local bus schedules, offers of cheap excursions or ride shares, and comments and advice from people who've already passed this way.

Another thing that has cropped up in recent years are **travellers centres**, countrywide networks with branches in tourist hotspots. The most widespread of these organizations are Backpackers' World (ⓦwww.backpackers-world.com.au), Backpackers' Travel Centre (ⓦwww.backpackerstravel.net.au), World Wide Workers (ⓦwww.worldwideworkers.com), and Travellers Contact Point (ⓦwww.travellers.com.au); all have branches in New South Wales, Victoria and Queensland. Once signed up with them, they can help find work and prebook travel and accommodation as you move around; you also get discounted phone and internet rates, cheap drinks at selected pubs, and use of mail services and notice boards. At around $40 a year, this sounds like a bargain, and they can certainly help streamline a trip, but you'd be wise not to book everything in advance and lose your flexibility – you won't be able to get refunds if you change your plans.

Australian Tourist Commission offices

United Kingdom, Gemini House, 10–18 Putney Hill, Putney, London SW15 6AA ("Aussie Helpline" charged at 50p a minute: ☏0990/022000, ⓦwww.tourism.gov.au).
US, Visitors should contact the "Aussie Helpline" for tour information (☏805/775-2000), or alternatively check out the tourist commission's website (ⓦwww.australia.com).
New Zealand, Level 13, 44–48 Emily Place, Auckland 1 (☏09/379 9594).

State tourist offices in London

Northern Territory Tourist Commission, 1st floor, Beaumont House, Lambton Rd, London SW20 0LW (☏020/8944 2992, ⓦwww.ntholidays.com).
Queensland Tourist & Travel Corporation, 392 Strand, London WC2R 0LZ (☏020/7836 7142, ⓦwww.qttc.com.au).
South Australian Tourist Commission, 1st floor, Beaumont House, Lambton Rd, London SW20 0LW (☏020/8944 5375).
Tourism New South Wales, 2nd floor, Australia Centre, Strand, London WC2B 4LG (☏020/7887 5003, ⓦwww.tourism.nsw.gov.au).

33

Tourism Victoria, 4th floor, Victoria House, Melbourne Place, Strand, London WC2B 4LG (ⓣ 020/7240 7176, ⓦ www.visitmelbourne.com). **Western Australian Tourist Commission**, 4th floor, Australia Centre, Strand, London WC2B 4LC (ⓣ 020/7240 2881, ⓦ www.westernaustralia.net).

Australia online

General

ⓦ **www.ozemail.com.au/atie/index.html**
The site of the Australian Travel Information Exchange gives an easy-to-read overview of key destinations, resorts, tour operators and transport services.
ⓦ **www.infoaustralia.com.au/**
This answers your questions, has history and photo gallery pages, and links to travel, recreation, government, weather and radio.
ⓦ **www.travel.com.au**
Book flights, get the basics on destinations, and read all about others' experiences.
ⓦ **www.oztravel.com.au**
Online database of hotels, tours, car rental and other travel services.
ⓦ **www.walkabout.fairfax.com.au/**
Better than average directory including travellers' tales, links and not too much commerce.
ⓦ**www.ozramp.net.au/~senani/mainpage.htm**
Colourful site that's good for kids.

Newspapers

Try these sites for online versions of today's news – in fact, tomorrow's news if you're in Western Australia.
ⓦ **www.theage.com.au** – *The Age*
ⓦ **www.smh.com.au** – *Sydney Morning Herald*
ⓦ **www.news.com.au** – *The Australian*

Weather

Two sites for nationwide views of this timeless topic.
ⓦ **www.abc.net.au/news/weather**
ⓦ **www.bom.gov.au/weather**

Gay and Lesbian

All the info for a carefree holiday.
ⓦ **www.galta.com.au** – Gay and Lesbian Tourism Association
ⓦ **www.gaytravel.com** – Gay Travel
ⓦ **www.pinkstay.com** – Pink Stay

Surfing

Access to real rather than virtual surfing. Much more fun.

ⓦ **www.surfaris.com**
ⓦ **www.surfadventures.com.au**

Maps

If you want to obtain maps before you go, the GeoCenter (including NZ) and Nelles **maps of Australia**, both 1:4,000,000, are finely produced, with good topographical detail: the Nelles (printed in northern and southern halves on both sides of the sheet) includes additional detail of major city environs. The Bartholomew and the new Globetrotter (both 1:5,000,000) are the best of the rest. Any of the specialist map shops listed opposite should have all of these, together with a reasonable selection of more detailed local maps.

In Australia UBD, Gregory's and AusMap produce national, state, regional and city maps of varying sizes and quality: the first two are the most widely available. BP and the state motoring organizations have regularly updated **touring guides** to Australia, with regional maps, listings and details of things to see and do – something for the back shelf of the car rather than a backpack.

If you're a member of a **motoring organization** or automobile association, there's a chance you'll have reciprocal rights with the Australian equivalent and be entitled to **free maps** and other discounted services. Each state has its own organization (they're listed in the Australian Tourist Commission's guide) and most are excellent – you'll need to bring proof of membership along to take advantage.

The whole country is now covered by 1:50,000 topographical sheets, suitable for hiking or travel in remote areas. You can get them at government mapping agency offices or official government bookshops (in major cities) or take a look at them at a library in the nearest major town; they're also available by mail from the **National Mapping Agency**, PO Box 31, Belconnen, ACT 2616.

Specialist book and map suppliers

UK

Blackwells (ⓦ www.bookshop.blackwell.co.uk), 13–17 Royal Arcade, Cardiff CF1 2PR (ⓣ 029/2039 5036); 50 Broad St, Oxford OX1 3BQ (ⓣ 01865/792792). General bookshop with good range of foreign maps. Mail order available.

Heffers Map and Travel, 20 Trinity St, Cambridge CB2 1TJ (℡ 01223/586586, ⓦ www.heffers.co.uk). Mail order available.

James Thin Melven's Bookshop, 29 Union St, Inverness IV1 1QA (℡ 01463/233500, ⓦ www.jthin.co.uk). Map department with all foreign maps; mail order specialist.

John Smith and Son, 50 Crouper St, Townhead, Glasgow G4 ODL (℡ 0141/552 4394, ⓦ www.johnsmith.co.uk).

The Map Shop, 30a Belvoir St, Leicester LE1 6QH (℡ 0116/247 1400). Mail order available.

National Map Centre, 22–24 Caxton St, London SW1H 0QU (℡ 020/7222 2466, ⓦ www.mapsnmc.co.uk).

Stanfords (ⓦ www.stanfords.co.uk), 12–14 Long Acre, London WC2E 9LP (℡ 020/7836 1321); 29 Corn St, Bristol BS1 1HT (℡ 0117/929 9966). Mail order service available.

Thomas Nelson and Sons Ltd, 51 York Place, Edinburgh EH1 3JD (℡ 0131/557 3011).

The Travel Bookshop, 13–15 Blenheim Crescent, London W11 2EE (℡ 020/7229 5260, ⓦ www.thetravelbookshop.co.uk).

Ireland

Easons Bookshop, 40 O'Connell St, Dublin 1 (℡ 01/873 3811, ⓦ www.eason.ie).

Fred Hanna's Bookshop, 27–29 Nassau St, Dublin 2 (℡ 01/677 1255).

Hodges Figgis Bookshop, 56–58 Dawson St, Dublin 2 (℡ 01/677 4754, ⓦ www.hodgesfiggis.com.).

Waterstone's, Queens Building, 8 Royal Ave, Belfast BT1 1DA (℡ 028/9024 7355); 69 Patrick St, Cork (℡ 021/276522); 7 Dawson St, Dublin 2 (℡ 01/679 1415).

US

ADC Map and Travel Centre, 1636 I St, NW, Washington, DC 20006 (℡ 1-800/544-2659 or 202/628-2608).

Blue Dog Travel (ⓦ www.bluedogtravel.com). Online travel bookstore selling guidebooks, maps and accessories at discounted rates.

Book Passage, 51 Tamal Vista Blvd, Corte Madera, CA 94925 (℡ 1-800/999-7909 or 415/927-0960, ⓦ www.bookpassage.com/travel).

Elliot Bay Book Company, 101 S Main St, Seattle, WA 98104 (℡ 1-800/962-5311 or 206/624-6600, ⓦ www.elliotbaybook.com).

Forsyth Travel Library, 226 Westchester Ave, White Plains, NY 10604 (℡ 1-800/367-7984, ⓦ www.forsyth.com).

The Literate Traveler, 8306 Wilshire Blvd, Suite 591, Beverly Hills, CA 90211 (℡ 1-800/850-2665 or 310/398-8781, ⓦ www.literatetraveler.com).

Map Link Inc, 30 S La Patera Lane, Unit #5, Santa Barbara, CA 93117 (℡ 805/692-6777, ⓦ www.maplink.com).

Phileas Fogg's Books & Maps, #240 Stanford Shopping Center, Palo Alto, CA 94304 (℡ 1-800/533-3644 or 650/327-1754, ⓦ www.foggs.com).

Rand McNally (ⓦ www.randmcnally.com), 444 N Michigan Ave, Chicago, IL 60611 (℡ 312/321-1751); 150 E 52nd St, New York, NY 10022 (℡ 212/758-7488); 595 Market St, San Francisco, CA 94105 (℡ 415/777-3131). Note: Rand McNally now has almost 30 stores across the US; call (℡ 1-800/234-0679) for the address of your nearest store, or for direct mail maps.

Sierra Club Bookstore, 6014 College Ave, Oakland, CA 94618 (℡ 510/658-7470, ⓦ www.sierraclubbookstore.com).

Travel Books & Language Center, 4437 Wisconsin Ave, Washington, DC 20016 (℡ 1-800/220-2665).

Canada

International Travel Maps & Books, 530 W Broadway, Vancouver, BC V5Z 1E9 (℡ 604/879-3621, ⓦ www.itmb.com).

Open Air Books and Maps, 25 Toronto St, Toronto, ON M5C 2R1 (℡ 416/363-0719).

The Travel Bug, 2667 W Broadway, Vancouver, BC V6K 2G2 (℡ 604/737-1122, ⓦ www.swifty.com/tbug).

Ulysses Travel Bookshop, 4176 St Denis, Montréal, PQ H2W 2M5 (℡ 1-877/542-7247 or 514/843-9447, ⓦ www.ulysses.ca).

New Zealand

Specialty Maps, 58 Albert St, Auckland (℡ 09/307 2217).

Getting around

Australia's huge scale makes the distances, and how you conquer them, a major feature of any stay in the country. In general, public transport will take you only along the major highways to capital cities, the bigger towns between them, and popular tourist destinations; to get off the beaten track you'll have to consider driving, either by buying or renting your own vehicle. Regular long-distance bus, train and plane services can be found under "Travel details" at the end of each chapter, with local buses and trains covered in the main text.

However you decide to travel, check out the route on a map first, as it's very easy to underestimate **distances and conditions** – you may well be letting yourself in for a three-day bus journey, or planning to drive 500km on bad roads. Bear in mind what the **weather** will be doing too; you don't want to head into central Australia in a battered old car during the summer, or into the northern Outback in the wet season.

Planes

Flying, at least between major destinations around the **east coast** between Melbourne and Cairns, is undergoing a revolution at the moment, with newcomer Virgin Blue seriously undercutting prices and grabbing a good part of the market away from one-time monopolists Ansett and Qantas. Elsewhere, **regional routes** are served by smaller airlines such as Kendell (an Ansett subsidiary), who cover New South Wales, Victoria, South Australia and Queensland; and state-based companies such as Airlines of South Australia, Hazelton in NSW, and Sunstate in Queensland. While these smaller airlines' fares remain relatively costly, they can begin to seem a bargain when you take into account the time saved, and the money you'll spend on incidentals during a long bus or train journey.

If you expect to be flying a fair amount, you may be able to save costs **before you leave** home. Some airfares to Australia allow you to buy a set number of internal flights at a substantial discount if booked with your international ticket; otherwise, various **passes** are offered by Ansett and Qantas, which

have to be purchased before arrival in Australia. All of them divide the country into **zones** – for instance, "Western Australia", "the Centre" or "East Coast" – and you pay according to how many zones your flight crosses. With Ansett's **G'Day Pass**, you book a minimum of three flights (and a maximum of ten) at £79/US$160 for each flight within the same zone – for example, Sydney–Hobart – and £99/US$200 for longer flights such as Sydney–Perth. Similarly, Qantas' **Boomerang Pass** requires you book at least two flights (and a maximum of ten) at £95/US$155 for single-zone fares, and £120/US$195 for multiple-zone journeys. In both cases, as long as you have purchased the minimum number of flights before arriving in Australia, you can purchase additional flights at the same rates, up to the maximum allowed.

Once **in Australia**, Qantas also offers the **Discover Australia** fare which gives you around a thirty percent discount on the full fare on all domestic Qantas routes on production of your international air ticket (which need not be with Qantas). Often however, it's cheaper to simply **buy your ticket in advance**; Qantas and Ansett offer 21-day advance purchase discount fares (APEX), while Virgin Blue offers by far the best prices on their cheapest seats – though as these are sold on a first-come, first-served basis, you still need to get in early. Savings can be substantial: a Brisbane–Sydney return with Ansett or Qantas costs around $410 on the day, $290 with a Discover Australia fare, or $280 as an APEX; with Virgin Blue you pay just $240.

Domestic airlines

Ansett (☎ 13 1300, ⓦ www.ansett.com.au)
Qantas (☎ 13 1313, ⓦ www.qantas.com.au)
Virgin Blue (☎ 13 6789,
ⓦ www.virginblue.com.au)

You may also be able to get further **student and pensioner reductions**. Qantas and Ansett's **backpacker fares** are available to anyone with a YHA or VIP card (see p.48); you buy a minimum of three flights and get a substantial discount – a useful adjunct to an open-jaw ticket.

Another type of flight offered all over Australia is brief **sightseeing** or joyrides. Everything is covered, from biplane spins above cities to excursions to the Great Barrier Reef and flights over well-known landscapes. The last, especially, can be worthwhile, enabling you to see things that are inaccessible or impractical to reach overland. **Aircruising Australia** (☎ 02/9693 2233, ⓦ www.aircruising.com.au) offers a twelve-day tour by air which takes in the main sights; the price of around A$9400 includes absolutely everything accommodation, all meals and guides. Primarily a bus company, **Oz Experience** (Sydney ☎ 02/9221 4711, rest of Australia ☎ 1300/301 359, ⓦ www.ozexperience.com) offer an Air-Bus Pass where you fly one-way around Australia with Qantas and bus the other in off-the-beaten-track routes with driver-guides; for example, the cheapest tour ("Cobber Rama"; A$630) allows you to fly from Sydney to Cairns and then bus down the coast from Cairns to Sydney with unlimited stops (minimum nine days, maximum six months), while the priciest tour ("Devil's Bollocks"; A$1370) lets you fly Sydney to Darwin, bus Darwin to Alice, fly Alice to Cairns and then bus Cairns to Sydney (minimum thirteen days, maximum one year).

Trains

Trains are not the most obvious way to get around Australia, which has a limited network, but there are a couple of wonderful, epic journeys to be made. The populous southeast, at least, does have a reasonably comprehensive service: **interstate railways** link the entire east coast from Cairns to Sydney, and on to Melbourne and Adelaide. The two great journeys, though, are the coast-to-coast **Indian Pacific** (Sydney–Perth; 65hr; seat only $466, sleeper $976, first class with meals $1485) and the **Ghan** (Adelaide–Alice Springs; 20hr; seat $200, sleeper $411, first class with meals $631). Like much of the national network, both these routes have been losing money for years, and the plan now is to make these journeys unapologetically upmarket (and therefore expensive) – a down-under answer to the Orient Express. A real partnership between the Venice-Simplon-Orient-Express has created the **Great South Pacific Express** (in Australia free call Abercrombie and Kent on ☎ 1800 677 777, or check out the Orient-Express website, ⓦ www.orient-express.com), which runs year-round from Sydney up the east coast to Cairns. The entire journey takes four nights or can be done in components (the three-day Brisbane to Cairns component, with all meals and sightseeing, costs from $2830, while the entire trip will set you back $3930). Other than these, there are a couple of inland tracks in Queensland – to Mount Isa, Longreach and Charleville, plus the rustic Cairns–Forsayth run and isolated Croydon–Normanton stretch – and suburban networks around some of the major cities. Only around Sydney does this amount to much, with decent services to much of New South Wales. There are no passenger trains in Tasmania.

The advantages of travelling by train rather than bus are comfort and (usually) a bar; disadvantages are the slower pace, higher price and potential booking problems – Queensland trains, for instance, travel at about 60kph and require a month's advance booking during the holiday season. The famous long-distance journeys can also be booked solid, so you'd be wise to reserve a place before you leave home if this is a major part of your plans (Rail Australia agents are listed overleaf). Sample one-way fares from Sydney are: Adelaide $207 (sleeper $414); Alice Springs $439 (sleeper $895); Brisbane $131 (sleeper $313); Cairns $184 (sleeper $225); Melbourne $131 (sleeper $313); and Perth $466 (sleeper $976).

Rail passes include the **Austrailpass**, which must be bought before you arrive in Australia, and gives unlimited travel for fourteen, twenty-one or thirty consecutive days on all state-owned railways, including suburban links around state capitals; prices cost

£264 (US$431) for fourteen days, £344 (US$560) for twenty-one days and £414 (US$672) for thirty days. You can also buy a seven-day extension for £138 (US$197). The **Austrail Flexipass** – which must also be bought before you arrive in Australia – lets you linger without wasting your ticket: eight days of travel within a six-month period, for example, costs around £220 (US$357); you can also choose 15, 22 or 29 days. To be sure that you can make full use of your pass, it's advisable to book your route when you buy it. Western Australia, Victoria, New South Wales and Queensland also have their own passes available through main stations, but check any travel restrictions before buying – interstate routes do not overlap as far as passes are concerned.

Buses

Travelling by **bus** is almost certainly the cheapest way to get around, although it's rarely a very satisfactory one – there's a lot to be said against spending much of your trip staring at the passing landscape from a cramped seat. And even though the bus network is far more comprehensive than the train network, it will still let you down if you hope to escape the tourist trail: routes follow the main highways between cities, and may mean arriving at smaller places in the middle of the night. On the other hand, bus services are regular and good value, and vehicles are about as comfortable as they could be, with reclining seats, air-conditioning, toilets and videos: the real problem is having all these things work for the entire duration of your trip. If possible, try and plan for a stopover after every twenty hours – if you try stoically to sit out a two-day trip, you'll be in a foul mood when you reach your destination. Substantial **discounts** (ten percent, or fifteen percent if you buy your ticket before entering Australia) are available on many fares if you have a YHA, ISIC or recognized backpacker card such as VIP (see p.48), or if you are a pensioner.

The major **interstate bus companies** on the mainland are **McCafferty's** (℡ 13 1499, ⓦ www.mccaffertys.com.au) and **Greyhound Pioneer** (℡ 13 2030, ⓦ www .grehound.com.au) – both of which are actually owned by McCafferty's – which between them circuit the entire country. Along the east coast, there's also the newcomer **Premier** (℡ 13 3410, ⓦ www.premierms .com.au), which calls in everywhere along the highway between Melbourne and Cairns. **Tasmania** is thoroughly covered by

---

Train and bus representatives abroad

RAIL AUSTRALIA
UK and Ireland Leisurail, PO Box 113, Peterborough PE1 1LE (℡ 0870/750 0222).
US ATS Tours, Suite 325, 2381 Rosecrans Ave, El Segundo, CA 90245 (℡ 1-800/423-2880, ⓦ www.atstours.com).
Canada Goway Travel Ltd, Suite 300, 3284 Yonge St, Toronto, ON M4N 3M7; Suite 1050, 1200 W 73rd Ave, Vancouver, BC V6P 6G5 (℡ 1-800/387-8850, ⓦ www.goway.com).

GREAT SOUTH PACIFIC EXPRESS
UK and Ireland Abercrombie and Kent, Sloane Square House, Holbein Place, London SW1W 8NS (℡ 0845/070 0615, ⓦ www.abercrombiekent.co.uk).
US Abercrombie and Kent, 1520 Kensington Rd, Suite 201, Oakbrook, IL (℡ 1-800/323-7308, ⓦ www.abercrombiekent.com).

AUSTRALIAN COACHLINES
UK and Ireland Contact one of the travel agents listed on pp.13–14, such as STA, Usit CAMPUS or Trailfinders.
US Austravel, 51 E 42nd St, Suite 616, New York, NY 10017 (℡ 1-800/633-3404, ℻ 212/983-8376, Ⓔ usinfo@austravel.com), with branches also in Boston, San Francisco, Los Angeles, Seattle, Chicago and Denver. Swain Australia Tours, 6 W Lancaster Ave, Ardmore, PA 19003 (℡ 1-800/227-9246, ⓦ www.swaintours.com).
Canada Goway Travel Ltd, Suite 300, 3284 Yonge St, Toronto, ON M4N 3M7; Suite 1050, 1200 W 73rd Ave, Vancouver, BC V6P 6G5 (℡ 1-800/387-8850, ⓦ www.goway.com).

Tasmanian Redline Coaches and Tassie Link.

Fares vary according to the popularity of the route and quality and speed of the road, and, though competing companies offer similar rates, special offers can slash prices – it's always worth shopping around. Sample one-way fares from Sydney are: Adelaide $104, Alice Springs $251, Brisbane $77, Cairns $233, Darwin $383, Melbourne $54 and Perth $300. Return fares are, at best, only marginally cheaper than two singles.

A popular option for many travellers is to buy a **bus pass**, though bear in mind that you won't save money over shorter routes, and that passes are **nonrefundable** – tie yourself into a specific schedule and you'll be unable to change your plans. Both McCafferty's and Greyhound offer a range of passes lasting between one and twelve months covering **preset routes**, on which you can break your journey as often as you like and travel in any direction, but are not allowed to backtrack. Sample fares include the Melbourne–Cairns "Follow the Sun" pass for $300; a "Best of the East" pass which circuits via everywhere between Adelaide, Uluru, Alice Springs, Mount Isa, Cairns, Sydney and Melbourne for $864; and the "All Australian" pass which covers Australia's east, west, north, south and centre for $1772. Year-long **kilometre passes** are more flexible, giving you unlimited travel in any direction until you have used up the distance paid for – these work out upwards of 8¢ per kilometre. Premier's range of passes are all valid for three months, allow unlimited stopovers, and include the Melbourne–Cairns "Eastcoaster" ($300), and the Sydney–Melbourne "Getaway" ($80). Tasmania has its own passes offered by Tassie Link (ⓦ www.tassie.net.au/wildtour). Their coverage is not comprehensive, but the passes do also give a third off Tasmanian Redline Coaches' services; passes cost from $99 for five days' travel within a seven-day period, to $220 for thirty days' of travel within a forty-day period.

One-way tours

The big bus companies exist to transport as many passengers as quickly as possible from A to B. If you want more than a fleeting look at what you're passing, a **one-way tour** may be a lot more fun, and operators such as **Oz Experience** and **Wayward Bus** have routes that visit offbeat locations well outside the major bus companies' schedules. Some tours are quite small (ten to eighteen people) and the driver/guide might be a knowledgeable local. Some of these tour companies offer **passes** too, but – more so than the blander major companies – these tours project a character which might either suit you or drive you mad, and you'd be well advised to make sample excursions before plumping for a long-distance commitment. More conventional tours, starting from and returning to the same place, are mentioned in the "Listings" sections of the relevant accounts and in other interest boxes throughout the *Guide*.

Safari and one-way tour operators

Autopia Tours (ⓦ www.netspace.net.au/~autopia). Melbourne-based company offering one- to three-day tours along the Great Ocean Road ($54), Phillip Island ($60) and an inland cruise to the Grampians and Snowy Mountains ($170).

Heading Bush (free call ☎ 1800 639 933, ℗ 08/8648 6655, ⓦ www.headbush.mtx.net). Adelaide–Alice Springs in ten days, via Flinders Ranges, Oodnadatta Track, the Simpson Desert, Ayers Rock, the Olgas, Kings Canyon and Alice ($750). The tour is operated by *Andu Lodge* in Quorn (see p.871) and emphasizes Aboriginal heritage. All buses are 4WD, with seating for a maximum of ten people, and all meals are vegetarian; departures every Mon. They also offer shorter excursions to Lake Eyre ($769) and the Flinders ($199–299).

Groovy Grape Tours (ⓦ www.groovygrape .com.au). Week-long tours from Adelaide to Alice, via the Flinders, Coober Pedy and Yulara ($650). Also three days on the Great Ocean Road ($245), and a two-day transfer between Alice and Adelaide ($95).

Oz Experience (☎ 1300/300 028, ⓦ www. ozexperience.com). Oz Experience are strictly for the party crowd; numerous reports of breakdowns and strandings suggest that you check out their current reputation with fellow travellers before committing yourself to any long-term deals. Various unlimited-stop routes, which often follow minor roads, include: Sydney–Cairns ($299), Cairns–Adelaide ($480), Sydney–Melbourne ($185), Melbourne–Adelaide ($185) and Adelaide–Alice ($225), with plenty of pauses at wineries, beaches, national parks and cattle stations. There are also four twelve-month passes, ranging from $997 (for Sydney up the north coast to Cairns then inland to Alice and up to Darwin) to $1640 (for a complete circuit from Melbourne to Darwin). Passes are valid for six months. **Wayward Bus** (free call ☎ 1800 882 823, ⓦ www.waywardbus.com.au). The excellent long-established Wayward Bus, based in Adelaide, does a series of one-way and circuit trips in eastern, central Australia and Western Australia. The bus seats twenty people, with the driver acting as your guide, and the price includes transport only – you can choose to stay at hostels, campgrounds or motels en route, depending on your budget. You can hop on and off where you like over a six-month period. Routes include Melbourne–Adelaide via the Great Ocean Road and the Coorong (three to four days for $265), Adelaide–Perth (eight days for $730), two days on Kangaroo Island, including accommodation ($265), and a quickie through central Australia in four days ($370).

Driving

Having **your own vehicle** really allows you to explore Australia, filling the public transport void away from the cities and allowing you to get to the national parks, the isolated beaches and the ghost towns that make the country such a special place. If your trip is a long one – three months or more – then **buying a vehicle** may well be the cheapest way of seeing Australia. On shorter trips you should consider **renting** – if not for the whole time, then at least for short periods between bus rides, thereby allowing you to explore an area in depth.

Most foreign **licences** are valid for a year in Australia. An International Driving Permit (available from national motoring organizations) may be useful if you come from a non-English-speaking country. **Fuel** prices start at around 66¢ per litre for "super" (standard) or unleaded, with diesel slightly cheaper: prices can double at remote roadhouses, and you can expect a ten to fifteen percent increase in Outback areas. The **rules of the road** are similar to those in the US and UK. Most importantly, **drive on the left** (as in Britain), remember that seatbelts are compulsory for all, and that the **speed limit** in all built-up areas is 60kph or less. Outside built-up areas, maximums are around 100kph – often 110kph on long, isolated stretches – except in the Northern Territory, where common sense and horsepower are your only limits between towns. Whatever else you do in a vehicle, avoid **drinking and driving**;

random breath tests are common even in rural areas, especially during the Christmas season and on Friday and Saturday nights. The Australian media are lovingly obsessed with comparing annual figures from road deaths.

Main **hazards** are fatigue, losing control on dirt roads, and the presence of animals on the road – a serious problem everywhere (not just in the Outback) at dawn, dusk and night-time. Beware of fifty-metre-long **road trains**: these colossal trucks can't stop quickly or pull off the road safely, so if there's the slightest doubt, get out of the way; only overtake a road train if you can see well ahead and are certain that your vehicle can manage it. On dirt roads be doubly cautious, or just pull over for a rest and let the road train get ahead.

Roads, outback driving and breakdowns

Around the cities the only problem you'll face is inept signposting, but interstate main roads – even Highway 1, which circles the country – aren't always great, and some of the minor routes are awful. **Conditions**, especially on unsealed roads, are unpredictable and some roads can be impassable after a storm, so always seek reliable advice (from the local police or a roadhouse) before starting out. Make it clear what sort of vehicle you're driving and remember that their idea of a "good" or "bad" road may be radically different from yours. Some "4WD only" tracks *might* be navigable in lesser transport with a skilled driver – high ground clearance, rather than four driven wheels, is often the crucial factor.

Rain and floods – particularly in the tropics and central Australia – can close roads to all vehicles within minutes, so driving through remote regions in the wet season – or even along the coastal highway – can be prone to delays. The stretch of highway between Cairns and Townsville is notorious for being cut by floods during the summer cyclone season, and in late 2000 dozens of vehicles were stranded for several weeks on the main Queensland–Territory road waiting for floods to recede in western Queensland. Several remote and unsealed roads through central Australia (the Sandover and Plenty highways, the Oodnadatta, Birdsville and Tanami tracks, and others) are theoretically open to all vehicles in dry winter weather, but unless you're well equipped with a tough car, don't attempt a crossing during the summer, when extreme temperatures place extra strain on both driver and vehicle.

On **poor roads and dirt tracks**, the rules are to keep your speed down to a maximum of 80kph, stick to the best section and never assume that the road is free from potholes, eroded cattle grids, sand, rocks or oncoming traffic. Long corrugated stretches are a major bugbear and can literally shake the vehicle apart – check radiators and fuel tanks for cracks afterwards; reducing tyre pressures slightly softens the ride but can cause the tyres to overheat at high speeds, making them more prone to punctures. Windscreens are often shattered by flying stones from passing traffic, so slow down and pull over to the left. Fine "bulldust" obscures potholes and other hazards and invades the car. Dirt tracks are often deeply rutted, and exposed tree roots can burst tyres if you drive over them too fast.

At all times carry plenty of **drinking water**, food and **fuel**, and tell someone reliable your timetable, route and destination, so that a rescue can be organized if you don't report in. Carry a detailed, recent **map** and don't count on finding regular signposts. In the event of a **breakdown** in the Outback, always **stay with your vehicle**: it's visible to potential rescuers and you can use it for shade; in any case, you risk finding it stripped when you return with a tow truck if you're stranded on an isolated road. As a last resort, burn a tyre – the black smoke will be distinctive from the average bushfire.

Car rental

To **rent** a car you need a full, clean driver's licence; usually, a minimum age of 21 is stipulated by the major car-rental companies, rising to 25 for 4WDs. Check on any mileage limits or other restrictions, extras, and what you're covered for in an accident, before signing. The multinational operators Hertz, Budget, Avis and Thrifty have offices in the major cities, but outside the big cities lack of competition makes their **standard rates** expensive at $70–90 a day for a sedan; long-term rental, specials and even plain bargaining can bring this down to a more affordable level.

National has offices in Melbourne, Brisbane, Cairns, the Gold Coast and Surfers Paradise, and Holiday has several branches throughout the country. **Local firms** – of which there are many in the cities – are almost always better value, and the bottom-line "rent-a-bomb" agencies go as low as $29 a day; however, these places often have restrictions on how far away from base you're allowed to go.

One-way rental might appear handy, but is usually very expensive: at least $200 extra for the drop-off fee. If you're simply trying to get from one place to another, you could try offering to relocate any vehicles they may have from other cities (ie returning someone else's one-way). They'll have regular drivers to do this, but being politely persuasive and claiming previous experience might get you massive reductions. As a rule, cars are needed in the southern cities as the Wet hits the tropics towards the end of the year. From New Zealand, prebooking a rental car will cost you at least NZ$280 per week, including insurance and tax – though rates will be considerably higher than this away from the main cities. However, you may get a cheaper deal during slack periods or as part of a fly-drive package. To reserve a rental car from the UK, USA or Canada, contact the companies listed overleaf.

Four-wheel drives are best used for specific areas rather than long term, as rental costs are steep, starting at around $120 a day. Many 4WD agents actually don't allow their vehicles to be driven off sealed roads, so check the fine print first. An increasing number of places offer **campervans** and **motor homes** to rent, and with fierce competition prices start at around $80 a day with unlimited kilometres – amazing value when you consider the independence, comfort and the saving on accommodation charges. Although, like cars, they are limited to sealed roads, campervans give you the chance to create your own tour of a lifetime across Australia. Their only drawback is that you can get pretty cranky spending all day *and* all night in the same compact vehicle; raised-roof or pop-top models are more tolerable (as is the occasional night in a motel). Remember, too, that the sleeping capacity stated in the adverts (especially on the larger vehicles) is an absolute maximum, which you wouldn't want to endure for too long.

Branches of the big rental chains and local firms are detailed in "Listings" sections throughout the *guide*.

Car reservations

Autos Abroad, ⓦ www.autosabroad.co.uk – in the UK (ⓣ 020 7287 6000).

Avis, ⓦ www.avis.com – in the UK (ⓣ 0870/606 0100); in Eire (ⓣ 01/874 5844); in the US (ⓣ 1-800/230-4898); in Canada (ⓣ 1-800/272-5871); in New Zealand (ⓣ 09/526 2847).

Budget, ⓦ www.budget.com – in the UK (ⓣ 0800/181181); in Eire (ⓣ 0800/973159); in the US (ⓣ 1-800/527-0700); in New Zealand (ⓣ 09/375 2222).

Hertz, ⓦ www.hertz.com – in the UK (ⓣ 0870/844 8844); in Eire (ⓣ 01/676 7476); in the US (ⓣ 1-800/654-3001); in Canada (ⓣ 1-800/263-0600 or 416/620-9620 from Toronto).

Holiday Autos, ⓦ www.holidayautos.com – in the UK (ⓣ 0870/400 0011); in Eire (ⓣ 01/872 9366).

Kemwel Holiday Autos, ⓦ www.kemwel.com – in the US (ⓣ 1-800/678-0678).

National, ⓦ www.nationalcar.com – in the US (ⓣ 1-800/CAR-RENT).

Campervan and motor homes reservations

Britz Australia (in the UK ⓣ 0990/143609, ⓕ 168309, ⓔ info@britz.com.au; in Australia ⓣ 03/9483 1888, ⓕ 9416 2933, ⓦ www.britz.com). Long-established, German-

owned company whose high-roofed Land Cruisers are a common sight all around the country. Their 4WD models are well equipped, with long-range tanks and even a kitchen sink, but leaf-sprung suspension can be tiring. Also rents out Koala campervans and motor homes holding from two to six people.

Budget Campervan Rentals (in Australia ⓣ 03/9483 1849, ⓕ 9416 2933, ⓦ www.budget.com.au). Chasing Britz Australia's lead with a similar range of well-equipped vehicles.

NQ Rentals (in the UK ⓣ 020 8715 1590, ⓕ 715 1591; in Australia ⓣ 07/7053 1875 or free call 1800 899 558, ⓕ 7032 2068, ⓦ www.campervansaust.com.au). A Cairns-based campervan company with agents in all major mainland cities. Vans from $80 a day, motor homes $150 a day.

Buying a car

Buying a used vehicle needn't be an expensive business and a well-kept car should resell at about two-thirds of the purchase price at the end of your trip – if you're lucky, or a skilful negotiator, you might even make a profit.

If you don't know your axle from your big end, **car yards** can save you a lot of hassle and provide welcome advice: in Sydney, they're the most common place to buy a

Best secondhand buys

Big-engined, mid-1970s or later, Holden Kingswood or Ford Falcon station wagons are the ideal travellers' cars: roomy, reliable, mechanically simple and durable, with spares available in just about any city supermarket, roadhouse or wrecker's yard. At the bottom end, $1500 plus some luck should find you some kind of old car that runs reliably. Chances are, if a vehicle has survived this long, there's nothing seriously wrong with it and you should be able to nurse it through a bit further. Also, real bargains can be secured from travellers desperate to get rid of their vehicle before flying out. Ideally, though, you should plan to pay at least $4000 in total for a sound, fully prepared and equipped vehicle. Manual transmission models are more economical than automatic, with the four-speed versions superior to the awkward, three-speed, steering-column-mounted models. Smaller and less robust, but much more economical to run, are old Toyota Corollas or other Japanese station wagons, suitable for one or two people travelling light.

Four-wheel drives are expensive, and, with poor fuel economy and higher running costs, worth it only if you have some serious off-roading planned. Toyota FJ or HJ Land Cruisers are Outback legends, especially the long-wheelbase (LWB) models: tough, reliable and with plenty of new and used spares all over the country. If nothing goes wrong, a diesel (HJ) is preferable to a petrol (FJ) engine, being sturdier and more economical – although all Toyota engines, particularly the six-cylinder FJs, seem to keep on running, even if totally clapped-out. The trouble with diesels is that problems, when they occur, tend to be serious and repairs expensive; also, lower revs mean slower acceleration which can cause a problem in mud or sand, or going up hills. Generally, you're looking at $8000–16,000 for a reliable fifteen-year-old model.

used vehicle, and some even cater specifically to travellers (see p.188). Assuming you have a little time and some mechanical knowledge, however, you'll save money by buying **privately**; a **buy-back guarantee** offered by some car yards and dealers is usually a guarantee to pay you a fraction of the car's potential value. Adverts in the local newspapers and hostel notice boards in main exit points from Australia are the best places to start. One of the great advantages of buying from a **fellow traveller** is that you might get all sorts of gear thrown in – jerrycans, camping gear and many of the spares listed below. The disadvantage is that the car may have already been thrashed to death circumnavigating the country while being maintained on a backpacker's budget.

A thorough **inspection** is essential. **Rust** is one thing to watch for, especially in the tropics where humidity and salt air will turn scratches to holes within weeks – look out for poorly patched bodywork. Take cars for a spin and check the engine, gearbox, clutch and brakes for operation, unusual noises, vibration and leaks; repairs on some of these parts can be costly. Don't expect perfection, though: worn brake pads and tyres, grating wheel bearings and defective batteries can be fixed inexpensively, and if repairs are needed, it gives you a good excuse to haggle over the price. All tyres should be the same type and size, especially on 4WDs. If you lack faith in your own abilities, the various state automobile associations offer rigorous **pre-purchase inspections** for about $90, which isn't much to pay if it saves you from buying a wreck – and plenty of people do.

If you're buying privately (or from an unscrupulous dealer) you should also check the requirements of the state transport department: in most states you'll need a **roadworthiness certificate** to have the vehicle transferred from its previous owner's name to yours. This means having a garage check it over; legally, the previous owner should do this, and theoretically it guarantees that the car is mechanically sound – but don't rely on it. You then proceed to the local Department of Transport with the certificate, a receipt, your driver's licence and passport; they charge a percentage of the price as stated on the receipt to register the vehicle in your name.

If the annual **vehicle registration** is due, or you bought an interstate or deregistered vehicle ("as is", without number plates), you'll have to pay extra for registration, which is dependent on the engine size and runs into hundreds of dollars. Note that cars with interstate registration can be difficult to sell: if possible, go for a car with the registration of the state where you anticipate selling. Registration includes the legal minimum third-party personal **insurance**, but you might want to increase this cover to protect you against theft of the vehicle (for around $95), or if you've bought something more flash go the whole way with comprehensive motor insurance. Joining one of the **automobile clubs** for another $60 or so is well worth considering, as you'll get free roadside assistance (within certain limits), and discounts on road maps and other products. Each state has their own, but membership is reciprocal with overseas equivalents.

Equipping your car

Even if you expect to stick mostly to the main highways, you'll need to carry a fair number of **spares**: there are plenty of very isolated spots, even between Sydney and Melbourne. For ordinary cars, the cheapest place to **buy spares** is at a supermarket – head for the racks of any branch of K-Mart or Coles. A proper tow rope is vital; passing motorists are far cheaper than tow trucks. In addition – and especially if your vehicle is past its prime – you should have a set of spark plugs, points, fuses, fuel filters (for diesels), fuel lines, fan belt and radiator hoses – you need to check all these anyway and might want to replace them as a matter of course and keep the originals as backups. A selection of hose clamps, radiator sealant, putty for leaking tanks, water-dispersing spray, jump leads and a board to support the jack on soft ground may also come in handy. Again, if the car is old, establish its engine oil consumption early on; a car can carry on for thousands of kilometres guzzling oil at an alarming rate, and if the level drops too much the engine is ruined. If you're confident, get a *Gregory's* workshop manual for your vehicle; even if you're not, carry these spares anyway – someone who knows how to use them might stop. Whatever else, always carry jerrycans with enough water and fuel to get you to the next garage after a mishap.

Before you set off, check battery terminals for corrosion, and the battery for charge – buy a new one if necessary, and don't risk money on a secondhand item. Carry two spare tyres; **off-road drivers** in remote regions should add to the list a puncture repair kit, bead breaker and tubes – and know how to use them. Keeping tyres at the correct pressure and having a wheel balance/alignment will cut down wear. Change the oil and filter, clean or replace the air filter and check the radiator for coolant/antifreeze.

Motorbiking

Motorbikes, especially large-capacity trail bikes, are perfect for the Australian climate and an inexpensive compromise between conventional vehicles and 4WDs, although long distances place a premium on their comfort and fuel range. Mid-1980s 600cc Japanese trail bikes, such as **Yamaha**'s trendsetting XT600 Ténéré, sell for around $3000 and allow 100kph on-road cruising with adequate off-road agility and readily available spares. A **Honda** XL600V Transalp is much more comfortable on the road and OK on gravel. The choice of tyres is crucial to off-road performance. Pirelli MT21 tyres are widely regarded as the best-compromise tyre for road and track, but always carry a complete puncture repair kit and a spare tube – and know how to use them. The *Adventure Motorbiking Handbook* (Compass Star) is a definitive manual to motorbiking off the beaten track and includes a regional rundown of Australia's Outback biking highlights.

If it's likely that you'll return to your starting point, look out for dealers offering **buy-back** options, which guarantee a resale at the end of your trip; bikes can be more difficult to sell than cars. You're going to need a helmet and, especially if you're heading **off-road**, plenty of water-carrying capacity. It's also essential that you know what you're doing: the Outback is not somewhere you can afford to have things go wrong. Travelling alone can be risky, and **night-riding** is plain dangerous, with poor surfaces hard to judge and kangaroos liable to bounce out of nowhere.

Motorbike **rental** – usually available only in the cities – is expensive: at least the same price as a car. A better alternative is a

Four-wheel driving: some hints

The Outback is not the place to learn how to handle a 4WD, and you should know what you're doing before disappearing off the map. Many novice four-wheel drivers assume that their vehicles are unstoppable, all-terrain machines and soon get stuck through lack of technique and experience. Take all the spares listed on p.43, plus a shovel, hi-lift jack and gloves. In addition to the many "how to" manuals easily found in bookshops, try and get a copy of *Off Road Sense* produced by Dunlop (Dunlop Tyres, PO Box 100, Port Melbourne, VIC 3207). This illustrated booklet clearly spells out the practicalities of off-road driving without confusing the beginner with technical jargon. If you're planning a long off-road tour, *Explore Australia by Four-Wheel Drive* (Viking) will suit recreational drivers. In remote areas you may want to rent a two-way HF radio tuned to the Royal Flying Doctor Service – contact the state motoring association or National Parks and Wildlife Service for details. The following basic hints should help; see also the advice on creek crossings on p.543.

❑ Be aware of your limitations, and those of your vehicle.

❑ Know how to operate everything – including how to change a tyre – before you need it.

❑ Always cross rivers and very sandy or muddy sections on foot first.

❑ Don't persevere if you're stuck – avoid wheel spin (which will only dig you further in) and reverse out. Momentum is key on slippery surfaces such as mud, sand and snow – as long as you're moving forward, however slowly, resist the temptation to change gear, and so lose traction.

❑ Reducing tyre pressure by up to seventy per cent dramatically increases traction in mud or sand, but risks punctures and causes over-heating at higher road speeds.

❑ If stuck, clear all the wheels with a shovel, create a shallow ramp (again, for all wheels), engage four-wheel-drive and lower tyre pressures if necessary, and drive out in low-range second or third gear.

❑ Keep to tracks – avoid unnecessary damage to the environment.

❑ Driving on beaches can be great fun, but treacherous – observe other vehicles' tracks and be aware of tidal patterns.

Useful motorcycling websites

Adventure Motorbiking –
Ⓦ www.adventure-motorcycling.com.
Complements the *Adventure Motorbiking Handbook* with regular updates and many links, but not Australia specific.
Drop Bear – Ⓦ www.dropbear.com.
Links to bike sites and events Australia-wide.
Honda V-twins Adventure Club –
Ⓦ www.geocities.com/MotorCity/Track/4459/.
Australian-based club dealing with Africa Twins, Transalps and the little known 750 XLVs. If you own or are interested in these Hondas – a good choice for smooth adventuring, the way singles never are – pay them a visit. Plenty of links to other Australian sites too.
Net Bikes – Ⓦ www.netbikes.com.au.
Check out bike prices and availability in Australia before you go with this "classified ads" site.

motorbike **tour**: these take various forms, from ones where you provide the bike and the tour consists of an itinerary, company on the road and a support vehicle (check out the bimonthly *Side Track* magazine once in Australia), to a quick blast on the back of a Harley Davidson (see "Listings" sections throughout the *Guide* for details of operators).

Cycling

Cycling is popular in Australia, and even if you're not a triathlete bent on pedalling between Sydney and Perth, bicycles are easily ferried between the places where you'd want to use them. Mountain bikes are ideal for rougher country, but lighter and more efficient tourers are better if you're attempting any long-distance travel on main roads. Most cities have well-defined cycle routes and bike lanes; helmets are compulsory, though the law is not always enforced in rural areas. **Renting** and finding **spares** is no trouble in capital cities and larger country towns.

If you're **bringing your own** bike, international airlines usually overlook the odd extra kilo if the bike is properly packaged; ask first – though it's often the airport check-in counter which has the last word. On **internal flights** you'll need to have the handlebars and pedals turned in, the front wheel removed and strapped to the back, and the tyres deflated; some airlines consider bikes as two pieces of excess baggage and charge accordingly (excess baggage is usually insured against damage up to a maximum of $1600 damages, so you might want to extend this). **Trains** have fixed rates for carrying bikes (depending on the route) and you'll save on bus charges by disassembling and packing your bike flat. See "Books" (p.1186) for specialist guides to cycling in Australia.

Hitching

The gruesome 1992 "backpacker murders" drastically changed Australian attitudes to hitching. What proved most shocking was the seemingly indiscriminate choice of victims: men and couples seemed as likely a target as lone women, allaying several hitch-hiking myths. The official advice is **don't**: with so many affordable forms of transport available, there's no real need to take the risk.

If you must do it, never hitch **alone**, and always avoid being dropped in the middle of nowhere between settlements. In rural areas people seem more willing to stop, but long, isolated stretches of road don't make this the safest country to hitch in; as usual, **women** are at greatest risk. Remember that you don't have to get into a vehicle just because it stops: choose who to get in with and don't be afraid to ask questions before you do get in, making the arrangement clear from the start. Ask the driver where he or she is going rather than saying where you want to go. Try to keep your pack with you; having it locked in the boot makes a quick escape more difficult.

A much better method is lining up lifts through **hostel notice boards** (though this means sharing fuel costs). This option gives you the chance to meet the driver in advance, and – as a fellow traveller – they will most likely be stopping to see many of the same sights along the way. In out-of-the-way locations, roadhouses are a good place to head, as the owners often know of people who'll be heading your way.

The best way to ensure your **safety**, apart from exercising your judgement and common sense, is to make concrete arrangements before your departure and stick to them. Hostel managers are well aware of the possible danger to young women departing across the Outback with new acquaintances or undertaking work on remote stations, and will gladly receive – or better still – make calls to ensure your safe arrival.

Accommodation

Australians love to move around, and finding somewhere to bed down is rarely a problem, even in the smallest of places. However, on the east coast it's a good idea to book ahead for Christmas and Easter holidays, and in some places (the Gold Coast for instance) there are price rises and room shortages even at weekends.

Watch out for the term **"hotel"**, which in Australia generally means a pub or bar. Although they were once legally required to provide somewhere for customers to sleep off a skinful – and many still do provide accommodation – the facilities are not necessarily luxurious. Those highlighted in this *Guide* do offer decent rooms, though the majority of them are still primarily places to drink, can be loud and drunken, and are not necessarily enticing places to stay.

The other side of this coin is that many places that would call themselves hotels anywhere else prefer to use another name – hence the reason for so many **motels** and **resorts**, and in the cities "**private**

hotels" or (especially in Sydney) "**boutique hotels**" that tend to be smaller and more characterful places to stay, run along guesthouse lines. There are also a growing number of **bed and breakfast** places (B&Bs) and **farmstays** where you can join in with farm life.

Other categories of accommodation worth looking into are the huge array of excellent **hostels** and "**backpackers**", **caravan parks** that offer accommodation in the form of permanent on-site vans and cabins or chalets as well as campervan facilities and tent spaces, and self-catering **apartments** or, in country areas, cabins and cottages.

Accommodation price codes

All the accommodation listed in this book has been categorized into one of eight price bands, as set out below. Apart from band ❶, these represent the cost of the cheapest available double or twin room in high season; single rooms are generally about two-thirds the price of doubles. However, there's a variety of different types of accommodation on offer – sometimes under the same roof: band ❶ is used only for hostels and backpackers' accommodation, where it refers to a bed in a dorm; for units, cabins and vans the code covers the cost of the entire unit, which may sleep as many as six people.

In the lower categories, most rooms will be without private bath, though there's usually a washbasin in the room. From band ❺ upwards you'll probably have private facilities. Remember that many of the cheaper places may also have more expensive rooms with en-suite facilities.

❶ Under $20	❸ $35–50	❺ $70–90	❼ $115–150
❷ $20–35	❹ $50–70	❻ $90–115	❽ $150 and upwards

Hotels and motels

Cheaper Australian **hotels** tend to be basic – no TV, and shared bathrooms and plain furnishings – and aren't always the best choice for peace and quiet. In country areas hotels are often the social centre of town, especially on Friday and Saturday nights. But with double rooms at around $45–65 and singles from $30 (often with breakfast included), for two or more people sharing they can be better value – and more private – than hostel accommodation. **Motels** are typically a comfortable, bland choice, often found en masse at the edge of town to catch weary drivers, and priced on average upwards of $50 for a double room with TV and bath, not including breakfast. They rarely have single rooms, but they may have larger units for families, often with basic cooking facilities.

In **cities**, you're far more likely to come across a hotel in the conventional sense. The cheaper of these may well describe themselves as **"private hotels"** to distinguish themselves from pubs, the decisive factor being the absence of a public bar. Some of these, especially in inner cities, can be rather sleazy, but others are very pleasant, family-run guesthouses. Double rooms might cost anything from $50 and up, and there are often singles available at about two-thirds of the price. More expensive hotels are much as you'd expect: in the cities most of them are standard places with all the usual facilities, aimed at the business community; in resorts and tourist areas they're more like upmarket motels. Prices might be anything from $90 to $300 or more in five-star establishments: a typical city three-star will probably cost you above $120. Similar places in a resort or country area charge $100 or more.

There are numerous nationwide hotel and motel **chains** that give certain guarantees of standards, among them familiar names such as Best Western and Travelodge, as well as Australian ones such as Budget, Golden Chain and Flag. All have directories of their members, which you can use to plan ahead. While you might find it rather restrictive to use them for your whole stay, they offer dependable facilities and can be used to ensure that you have a reservation on arrival, or at anywhere else you know you'll be spending some time.

Resorts and self-catering units

You'll find establishments calling themselves **resorts** all over Australia, but the term is not a very clearly defined one. At the bottom end, price, appearance and facilities may be little different to those of a motel, while top-flight places can be exclusive hideaways costing hundreds of dollars a night. Originally the name implied that the price was all-inclusive of accommodation, drinks, meals, sports and anything else on offer, but this isn't always the case. These places tend to be set in picturesque locations – the Barrier Reef islands swarm with them – and are often brilliant value if you can wangle a stand-by or off-season price.

Self-catering or self-contained **units**, **apartments** or country **cabins** can be a very good deal for families and larger groups. The places themselves range from larger units at a motel to purpose-built apartment hotels, but are usually excellent value. Cooking facilities are variable, but there'll always be a TV and fridge; linen (generally not included) can sometimes be rented for a small extra charge.

Farmstays and bed & breakfasts

Another option in rural areas are **farmstays** on working farms and **B&Bs** or **guesthouses**, the last two predominantly in the south and east. Both offer a more homely atmosphere, though B&Bs especially can be anything from someone's large home to your own colonial cottage – ask what the "breakfast" actually includes. Farmstays are even more variable, with some offering very upmarket comforts while at others you make do with the basic facilities in vacant shearers' quarters; their attraction is that they are always in out-of-the-way locations, and you'll often get a chance to participate in the working of the farm, or take advantage of guided tours around the property on horseback or 4WD.

Hostels

There's a huge amount of **budget accommodation** in Australia, and though the more shambolic operations don't survive for long, standards are still variable. Official **YHA**

youth hostels are pretty dependable – if often relatively expensive – and many of their depressingly regimented rules and regulations have been dropped in the face of competition, especially from the firmly established **Backpacker Resorts/VIP** network, whose membership card is as useful and widely known as the YHA equivalent.

At their best, hostels and backpackers' accommodation – both names are widely used, and don't necessarily imply membership of an organization – are excellent value and are good places to meet other travellers and plug into the grapevine. There's often a choice of dormitories, double or family rooms, plus bike rental, kitchen, games room, TV, internet access, a pool and help with finding work or organizing trips. Many have useful notice boards, organized activities and tours. At their worst, their double rooms might be poorer value than local hotel accommodation, and some are simply grubby, rapid-turnover dives – affiliation to an organization does not ensure quality. Hostels charge between $15 and $22 or more for a dormitory bed, with doubles – if available – from around $40.

While it's a good idea to carry at least a **sheet sleeping bag** for hostels which don't provide linen, some hygienically minded establishments now prohibit the use of personal sleeping bags and instead provide all bedding needs.

Youth hostel associations

England and Wales Youth Hostel Association (YHA), Trevelyan House, 8 St Stephen's Hill, St Albans, Herts AL1 2DY (℡01727/855215, ⓦwww.yha/england/wales.org.uk); London membership desk and booking office: 14 Southampton St, London WC2 7HY (℡020/7836 8541).
Northern Ireland Belfast International Youth Hostel, 22–33 Donegall Rd, Belfast BT12 5JN (℡028/9032 4733, ⓦwww.hini.org.uk).
Scotland Scottish Youth Hostel Association, 7 Glebe Crescent, Stirling, FK8 2JA (℡01786/451181, ⓦwww.syha.org.uk).
Ireland An Óige, 61 Mountjoy Square, Dublin 1 (℡01/830 4555, ⓦwww.irelandyha.org).
US Hostelling International-American Youth Hostels (HI-AYH), 733 15th St NW, Suite 840, PO Box 37613, Washington, DC 20005 (℡202/783-6161, ⓦwww.hiayh.org).
Canada Hostelling International/Canadian Hostelling Association, Room 400, 205 Catherine St, Ottawa, ON K2P 1C3 (℡1-800/663-5777 or 613/237-7884, ⓦwww.hostellingintl.ca).
Australia Australian Youth Hostels Association, Level 3, 10 Mallet St, Camperdown, NSW 2050 (℡02/9565 1325, ⓦwww.yha.com.au).
New Zealand Youth Hostels Association of New Zealand, PO Box 436, Christchurch 1 (℡03/379 9970, ⓦwww.yha.co.nz).

Camping, caravan parks and roadhouses

Perhaps because Australian hostels are so widespread and inexpensive, simple tent **camping** is an option little-used by foreign travellers. Australia has some remarkably hard ground, as well as lots of sand, so vital **equipment** includes ground mats and a range of pegs – some wide for sand, others narrow for soil. A hatchet for splitting firewood is light to carry and doubles

---

Hostel passes

If you're travelling on a budget, it's well worth laying your hands on at least one of the following hostel passes, which give you cheaper rates – around ten percent off – on accommodation at member hostels, and also entitle you to a wide range of other discounts on everything from bus tickets and tours to phone calls, museum entry fees and meals.

Probably of most use in Australia is a Backpacker Resorts VIP card, which anyone can obtain from member hostels in Australia for $29, or over the net at ⓦwww.backpackers.com.au. At present there are around 100 member hostels around the country, and your card will also be valid at a score more in New Zealand and Fiji, if you're heading in those directions.

The alternative is an International YHA card, available through your national youth hostel association before you leave home. Australian residents can join in Australia for $52, either through YHA offices in Sydney, Darwin, Brisbane, Adelaide, Hobart, Melbourne and Perth, or on their website ⓦwww.yha.com.au. Australian YHA hostels also number around a hundred, with thousands more worldwide.

B

as a hammer. Fuel stoves are recommended, but if you do build a fire, make sure it doesn't get out of control – and always observe any fire bans. In national parks, **bushcamping** is often the only option for staying overnight: some park sites have hot showers, drinking water and toilets; others provide absolutely nothing. Prices depend on state policy and site facilities, and you'll usually need a permit from the local NPWS (National Parks and Wildlife Service) office, details of which are given throughout the *Guide*.

Camping rough by the road is not a good idea, even if you take the usual precautions of setting up away from the roadside and avoiding dry riverbeds. If you have to do it, try and ensure you're not too visible: having a group of drunks pitch into your camp at midnight is not an enjoyable experience. Animals are unlikely to pose a threat, except to your food – keep it in your tent or a secure container,

or be prepared to be woken by their nocturnal shenanigans.

In towns, there's often a choice between basic **council campsites** and better-equipped private **caravan parks**, which will not only have space to pitch a tent but will also have hook-up facilities for campervans and probably a store; some even offer pools and all the facilities of a mini-resort. Many have **on-site vans** (caravans with cooking facilities but no toilet) or **cabins** (with bath or shower and often a TV): these can be very good value and are often available even when all the hotel and motel rooms have been filled up. The main problem is that linen – sheets, towels, etc – is usually not included, though you may be able to rent it. Expect to pay between $3–15 per tent for an unpowered site, or upwards of $15 per person for a van or cabin. Highway **road-houses** are similar, combining a range of accommodation with fuel and restaurants for long-distance travellers.

Food and drink

Australia is almost two separate nations when it comes to food. In the cities of the southeast – especially Melbourne – there's a range of cosmopolitan and inexpensive restaurants and cafés featuring almost every imaginable cuisine. Here there's an exceptionally high ratio of eating places to people, and they survive because people eat out so much – three times a week is not unusual. Remote country areas are the complete antithesis of this, where the only thing better than meat pies and microwaveable fast food are the plain, straightforward counter meals served at the local hotel, or a slightly more upmarket bistro or basic Chinese restaurant.

Traditionally, Australian food found its roots in the English overcooked-meat-and-three-veg "common-sense cookery" mould. Two things have rescued the country from its culinary destitution: immigration and an extraordinary range of superb, locally produced fresh ingredients that not even the most ham-fisted chef could ruin. Various ethnic cuisines are briefly discussed below, but in addition to introducing their own cuisine, immigrants have had at least as profound an effect on mainstream Australian food. "Contemporary Australian" cuisine is an exciting blend of tastes and influences from around the world – particularly Asia and the Mediterranean – and many not specifically "ethnic" restaurants will have a menu that includes properly prepared curry, dolmades and fettucine alongside steak and prawns. This healthy, eclectic – and above all, fresh – modern Australian cuisine has a lot in common with Californian cooking styles, and both go under the latest trendy banner of "Pacific Rim cuisine".

Australian food

Meat is plentiful, cheap and excellent: steak forms the mainstay of the pub counter meal and of the ubiquitous **barbie**, or barbecue – as Australian an institution as you could hope to find. Even if no one invites you along to one, you can still enjoy a barbie: free or coin-operated electric barbecues can be found in car parks, campsites and beauty spots all over the country. As well as beef and lamb, you may also find **exotic meats**, especially in the more upmarket restaurants. Emu, buffalo, camel and witchetty grubs are all served, but the two most common are kangaroo, a rich, tender and virtually fat-free meat, and crocodile, which tastes like a mix of chicken and pork and is at its best when simply grilled. At the coast, and elsewhere in specialist restaurants, there's tremendous **seafood** too: prawns and oysters, mud crabs, Moreton Bay bugs and yabbies (sea- and freshwater crayfish), lobsters, and a wide variety of fresh- and seawater fish – barramundi has a reputation as one of the finest, but is easily beaten by sweetlips or coral trout.

Fruit is good, too, from Tasmanian apples and pears to tropical bananas, pawpaw (papaya), mangoes, avocados, citrus fruits, custard apples, lychees, pineapples, passion fruit, star fruit and coconuts – few of them native, but delicious nonetheless. **Vegetables** are also fresh, cheap and good, and include everything from European cauliflowers and potatoes to Chinese choi sam and Indian bitter gourds. Note that aubergine is known as eggplant, courgettes as zucchini and red or green peppers as capsicums.

Vegetarians might assume that they'll face a narrow choice of food in "meatocentric" Australia, and in the country areas that's probably true. But elsewhere most restaurants will have one vegetarian option at least, and in the cities veggie cafés have cultivated a wholesome, trendy image that suits Australians' active, health-conscious nature.

Infamous Australian foods and "Esky"

Chicko Roll Imagine a wrapper of stodgy dough covered in breadcrumbs, filled with a neutered mess of chicken, cabbage, thickeners and flavourings, and then deep fried. You could only get away with it in Australia.

Damper Sounding positively wholesome in this company, "damper" is the swagman's staple – soda bread baked in a pot buried in the ashes of a fire. It's not hard to make after a few attempts – the secret is in the heat of the coals and a splash of beer.

Lamington A chocolate-coated sponge cube rolled in shredded coconut.

Pavlova (pav) A dessert concoction of meringue with layers of cream and fruit; named after the eminent Russian ballerina. Made properly with fresh fruit and minimum quantities of cream and sugar, it's not bad at all.

Pie floater The apotheosis of the meat pie; a "pie floater" is an inverted meat pie swamped in mashed green peas and tomato sauce; found especially in South Australia. Floaters can be surprisingly good, or horrible enough to put you off both pies and peas for life.

Vegemite Regarded by the English as an inferior form of Marmite and by almost every other nationality with total disgust, Vegemite is an Australian institution – a strong, dark, yeast spread for bread and toast.

Witchetty grubs (witjuti) About the size of your little finger, witchetty grubs are dug from the roots of mulga trees and are a well-known Australian bush delicacy. Eating the plump, fawn-coloured caterpillars live (as is traditional) takes some nerve, so try giving them a brief roasting in embers. They're very tasty either way – reminiscent of peanut butter.

Esky Eskies are insulated food containers varying from handy "six-pack" sizes to cavernous sixty-litre trunks capable of refrigerating a weekend's worth of food or beer. No barbie or camping trip is complete without a couple of eskies. The brand name "Esky" has been adopted to describe all similar products.

Ethnic food

Since World War II wave after wave of immigrants have brought a huge variety of **ethnic cuisines** to Australia: first North European, then Mediterranean and most recently Asian.

Chinese

Chinese restaurants were on the scene early in Australia – a result of post-goldrush Chinese enterprise – and Sydney, Melbourne and Darwin have Chinese connections dating back to the 1850s. The Chinese restaurants you'll find in most of the country tend to be rather old-fashioned and heavily reliant on MSG, but they're often the only alternative to Australian food. In contrast, the Chinatown area of big cities will provide a chance to sample some regional Chinese dishes as well as the usual Cantonese fare.

Two specialities served in Chinese restaurants are **yum cha** (or dim sum), lots of little titbits such as steamed buns and dumplings served from trolleys; and **steamboat**, an Asian version of fondue. Both are tasty and extremely good value for money – especially for a group.

Other Asian cuisines

Since the 1970s a new wave of immigrants from Southeast Asia has further energized Australian cuisine. **Vietnamese** restaurants not only offer some of the cheapest meals anywhere but also combine fresh ingredients with sophisticated French influences from colonial days; with your meal comes a plate of red chillies, lemon wedges and crunchy beansprouts.

There are numerous **Malaysian** and **Indonesian** restaurants and market stalls, where hearty noodle soups and satays with hot peanut sauce are served up. Hawker-style stalls in city food courts often serve laksa, a huge bowl of hot and spicy coconut-milk-based soup full of noodles, tofu and chicken or prawns.

The biggest success of them all, however, are the **Thai** restaurants, and it's hard to believe that they've been around for less than twenty years. Dishes can be fiery, yet subtly flavoured, with ingredients such as basil, lemongrass, garlic, chilli and coriander.

Because so much fresh seafood is available in Australia, **Japanese** food is more accessible – and less expensive – that it is in many other countries. There may not be a large Japanese population, but there are a huge number of Japanese visitors, and plenty of places catering for them (you'll find lots on the Gold Coast and in Cairns, for example).

Mongolian barbecues sound like a short-lived novelty but in fact are quite good: an unusual, fast and inexpensive complement to the already diverse Asian food culture. Thinly sliced meat or seafood is added to a selection of sliced vegetables and stir-fried in a soy-type sauce before your eyes on a giant wok – a Mongol warrior's shield is said to have been the original cooking utensil.

Italian – and coffee

The **Italian** influence on Australian cooking has been enormous. Second in number only to the English as an ethnic group, the Italians brought with them their love of food, which was a perfect complement to the Australian climate and way of life, and from the 1950s pizzerias, espresso and *gelati* bars, and the then-exotic taste of garlic, were conquering palates countrywide. One particularly Australian metamorphosis is **focaccia**, now a staple of every city café and even begin-

Bush tucker

The first European colonists decided that the country was not "owned" by the Aborigines because they didn't systematically farm the land. As many frustrated pastoralists later came to realize, this was a direct response to Australia's erratic seasons, which don't lend themselves to European farming methods with any degree of long-term security. Instead, Aborigines followed a nomadic lifestyle within extensive tribal boundaries, following seasonal game and plants and promoting both by annually burning off grassland.

Along the coast people speared turtles and dugong from outrigger canoes, caught fish in stone traps, piled emptied oyster shells into giant middens, and even co-operated with dolphins to herd fish into shallows. Other **animals** caught all over the country were possums, snakes (highly prized), goannas, emus and kangaroos. These animals were thrown straight onto a fire and cooked in their own juices, and their skins, bones and fat were sometimes used as clothing, tools and ointment respectively. More meagre pickings were provided by honey and green ants, water-holding frogs, moths and various grubs – the witchetty (or witjuti) being the best known. Foot-long ooli worms were drawn out of rotten mangrove trunks and tiny native bees were tagged with strands of spider web and then followed to their hives for honey; another sweet treat was mulga resin, picked off the tree trunk.

Plants, usually gathered by women, were used extensively and formed the bulk of the diet. The cabbage palm, sea almond, mangrove seeds, pandanus and dozens of fruits, including tropical coconuts, plums and figs, all grew along the coast. Inland were samphire bush, wild tomatoes and "citrus", grasstree hearts, cycad nuts (very toxic until washed, but high in starch), native millet, wattle seeds, waterlily tubers, nardoo seeds (a water fern), fungi, macadamia nuts, quandongs, and bunya pine nuts – the last had great social importance in southern Queensland, where they were eaten at huge feasts. In Queensland's far north you'll find one of the few surviving traditional styles of cooking, the Torres Strait Islander *kup maori* – meat and vegetables wrapped in banana leaves and roasted in an underground oven.

It's tempting to **taste** some bush foods, and a good few city restaurants, as well as the *Bushtucker Café* in the Grampians (see p.1002), are now experimenting with them as ingredients; otherwise you'll need expert guidance, as many plants are poisonous. A few tours and safaris (particularly in the Northern Territory) give an introduction to living off the land; for further reading, try *Bush Tucker: Australia's Wild Food Harvest* by Tim Low (Angus & Robertson Aus).

ning to make an appearance in country towns.

Australia can also thank the Italians for elevating **coffee** to a pastime rather than just a hot drink. Nowadays every suburban café has an espresso machine, and it's not just used to make cappuccino. Other **styles of coffee** have adopted uniquely Australian names: a "flat white" is a plain white coffee, a "cafe latte" is a milkier version usually served in a glass (like cappuccino without the froth), a "long black" is a regular cup of black coffee, and a "short black" is an espresso – transformed by a splash of milk into a macchiato. ("Espresso" is also a brand of instant coffee, so ask for a short black if you're after the genuine article.) A cappuccino costs around $2.50.

Other European and Middle Eastern

Melbourne is Australia's food capital, with its legendary **Greek** population among the many European influences in the city. As well as taverna-style Greek restaurants, souvlakia bars, with spiced lamb rotating on a spit, abound. **Turkish** and **Lebanese** takeaways use a similar ingredient for their spicy filled rolls, while some Turkish places also offer pides, small, simple but spicy variants on a pizza. Lebanese restaurants are especially good for vegetarians, with falafel rolls (pitta bread stuffed with chickpea patties, hummus and tabbouleh) making an inexpensive, filling meal.

Central European influences are most obvious in baking, particularly in Melbourne, where there is a large **Jewish** community made up of immigrants from prewar Poland, and there are also a few **Polish** restaurants serving solid, peasant-style dishes. **German** influences are most prominent around Adelaide – as well as at deli counters throughout the country, where you'll find an abundance of Australian-made salamis and sausages.

Places to eat

Restaurants are astonishingly good value compared with Britain and North America, particularly as many restaurants are **BYO** (bring your own): you buy your own wine or beer and bring it with you – you're rarely far from a **bottle shop** (the Australian term for an off-licence or liquor store). There may be a small corkage fee, but it's still better than paying inflated restaurant prices for your drink: even many licensed restaurants also allow you to BYO. You should have no problem finding an excellent two- or three-course meal in a BYO restaurant for $22 or less, though a main course at a moderate restaurant is around $15–19. There are also lots of excellent **cafés and coffee shops** – Italian ones (see above), continental patisseries/bakeries, and places that serve English-style Devonshire (cream) teas and cakes. In the cities and resorts, cafés will be open from early in the morning until late at night, serving food all day; in the country, they may stick more or less to shop hours.

The hotel **counter meal** is another mainstay, and at times may be all that's available: if it is, make sure you get there in time – meals in pubs are generally served only from noon to 2pm and again from 6 to 8pm, and rarely at all on Sunday evening. The food – served at the bar – will be simple but substantial and inexpensive (usually around $10 or less): steak, salad and chips, and variations on this theme. Slightly upmarket from this is the hotel **bistro** or restaurant in a motel, where you sit down to be served much the same food; these places often have a help-yourself salad bar, too, which is always a good alternative for vegetarians. Usually the most expensive thing on the menu is a huge steak for $12–15.

Fast food is widely available, with all the usual burger, pizza and chicken places offering a quick bite for as little as $5. Fish (usually shark or snapper) and chips can be excellent in coastal regions. In cities and bigger resorts you'll find fantastic fast food in **food courts**, often in the basements of office buildings or in shopping malls, where dozens of small stalls compete to offer Thai, Chinese, Japanese or Italian food as well as burgers, steaks and sandwiches. On the road, you may be reduced to what's available at the roadhouse, usually the lowest common denominator of reheated meat pies and microwaved ready meals.

Drinking

Australians have a reputation for enjoying a drink, and **hotels** (also sometimes called taverns, inns, pubs and bars) are where it mostly takes place. Traditionally, public bars are male enclaves, the place where mates meet after work on their way home, with the emphasis more on the beer and banter than the surroundings (see also "Women and sexual harassment", p.66). While changing attitudes have converted many city hotels into comfortable, relaxed bars, many Outback pubs are still pretty spartan and daunting for strangers of either sex, but you'll find barriers will come down if you're prepared to join in the conversation.

Friday and Saturday are the serious **party nights**, when there's likely to be a band and – in the case of some Outback establishments – literally everybody for a hundred kilometres around jammed into the building. **Opening hours** vary from state to state; they're usually 11am to 11pm, but are often much later, with early closing on Sunday. Some places are also "early openers", with hours ranging from 6am to 6pm.

For take-out sales, liquor stores or off-licenses are known as **bottle shops**. These are usually in a separate section attached to a pub or supermarket – in some states, you can't buy alcohol from supermarkets or grocery stores. There are also **drive-in bottle shops** attached to pubs where locals can load bulk purchases directly into the boot of their car; these solve the question of parking, though aren't totally the lazy option as you normally have to get out of the car to make your selection.

Beer

As anyone you ask will tell you, the proper way to drink **beer** in a hot country such as Australia is ice cold (the English can expect to be constantly berated for their warm beer preferences) and fast, from a small container so it doesn't heat up before you can down the contents. Tubular foam or polystyrene **coolers** are often supplied for **tinnies** (cans) or **stubbies** (short-necked bottles) to make sure they stay icy. Glasses are always on the small side, and are given confusingly different names state by state. The standard ten-ounce (half-pint) serving is known as a **pot** in Victoria and Queensland, and a **middie** in NSW and WA, where the situation is further complicated by the presence of fifteen-ounce **schooners**. A **carton** or **slab** is a box of 24–30 tinnies or stubbies, bought in bulk from a bottle shop and always cheaper when not chilled (a "Darwin stubby", with

typically Territorian eccentricity, is two litres of beer in an oversized bottle).

Australian beers are lager- or pilsner-style, and even the big mass-produced ones are pretty good – at least once you've worked up a thirst. They're considerably stronger than their US equivalents, and marginally stronger than the average British lager at just under five percent alcohol. Each state has its **own label** and there are fierce local loyalties, even though most are sold nationwide: Fourex (XXXX) (see p.402) and Powers in Queensland; Swan in Western Australia; Coopers in South Australia; VB in Victoria; Tooheys in New South Wales; and Bogues in Tasmania. Almost all of these companies produce more than one beer – usually a light low-alcohol version and a premium "gold" or bitter brew. There are also a number of smaller "boutique" breweries and specialist beermakers: Tasmania's Cascade, WA's Redback or Matilda Bay, Cairns' Draught and Eumundi from Queensland are more distinctive but harder to find. Fosters is treated as a joke in Australia, something that's fit only for export. Larger bottle shops might have imported beers, but outside cities (where Irish pubs serve surprisingly authentic-tasting Guinness) it's rare that you'll find anything foreign on tap.

Wines and spirits

Australian **wines** have long been appreciated at home, and it's not hard to see why; even an inexpensive bottle (around $12) will be better than just drinkable, while pricier varieties compare favourably with fine French wines – though some critics complain that Australian reds have become a bit too "woody" in recent years. If you're new to Australian wines, you'll always find Yalumba (for whites), Lindeman's, Hardy's and Wolfblass (for blended wines) will give satisfaction, but the secret is to be adventurous: you're extremely unlikely to be disappointed. Even the "chateau cardboard" four-litre bladders or wine casks that prevail at parties and barbecues are perfectly palatable. Whatever the colour, a mid-range bottle of wine will set you back about $16.

The biggest wine-producing regions are the Hunter Valley in New South Wales (see p.206) and the Barossa Valley in South Australia (see p.816), but you'll find smaller commercial vineyards as far north as

Kingaroy in Queensland and in southwest Western Australia; all are detailed in the text of the *Guide*. If you **buy** at these places you'll be able to sample in advance, though there's occasionally a charge for tasting to discourage overly enthusiastic visitors from just trying everything and then moving on elsewhere (see the box "Wine tasting tips" on p.818). Most bottle shops will in any case have a good range of very reasonably priced options.

(see the box "Wine tasting tips" on p.818)

Aussie Wine on the Net

Boutique Wines –
Ⓦ www.boutiquewines.com.au
Links to all those vineyards you've probably never heard of.
Hardy's – Ⓦ www.hardys.com.au
Lindeman's – Ⓦ www.lindemans.com
Penfolds – Ⓦ www.penfolds.com.au
Wine Planet – Ⓦ www.wineplanet.com.au
Staid but comprehensive rundown on tastes, or lack of them, in the Australian wine industry.
Wines of Distinction –
Ⓦ www.australianwines.com.au
Where to go and what to look for when making a selection.
Yalumba – Ⓦ www.yalumba.com

The Australian wine industry also makes **port** and **brandy** as a sideline, though these are not up to international standards. Two excellent dark **rums** from Queensland's sugar belt are well worth tasting, however: the sweet, deliciously smoky Bundaberg (see p.462) and the more conventionally flavoured Beenleigh. They're of average strength, normally 33 percent alcohol, but beware of "overproof" variations, which will have you flat on your back if you try to drink them like ordinary spirits.

Soft drinks

Various colas, Sprite, 7-Up, Fanta and a couple of home-produced brands – Bundaberg ginger beer and Cascade's Tasmanian apple juice – are the **soft** alternatives to alcohol. Bottled **fruit juices** come in every style, and in the tropics (and trendy city cafés) you can often get freshly squeezed juices made from familiar and not-so-familiar fruits. There's also a range of **spring waters** from several sources along the Great Dividing Range – a relief at times from the heavily chlorinated tap water. Sickly **flavoured milk** is another national institution: every store's fridge will be packed with different flavoured cartons.

Mail, phones and the internet

Australia may be far away to some but efficient international communication has enabled the visitor from abroad to be in contact wherever they are. To ensure you're not waking somebody up when phoning, see p.75 for the relevant time zone.

see p.75 for the relevant time zone

Mail

Every town of any size will have a **post office**, and where there isn't one there'll be an **Australia Post agency**, usually at the general store. Post offices and agencies are officially open Monday to Friday 9am to 5pm. Agencies might have an hour off during the day for lunch or close early, and big city GPOs sometimes open late or on Saturday morning. Out in the country it's rare to see postboxes, so you'll usually have to take your mail to the nearest post office or agency.

Domestically, the mail service has a poor reputation, at least for long distances: it can take a week for a letter to get from Wittenoom (WA) to Wagga Wagga (NSW), though major cities have a guaranteed express delivery service to other major cities – worth the expense for important packages. On the other hand **international mail** is extremely efficient, taking five to ten days to reach Europe, Asia and the US, depending on where it's posted. **Stamps** are sold at some newsagents and general stores, as well as post offices and agencies. A standard letter or postcard within Australia costs 45¢; printed aerogrammes for international letters anywhere in the world cost 70¢; postcards cost 95¢ to the US and Canada, $1 to Europe; regular letters start at $1.05 to the US and Canada, $1.20 to Europe. If you're sending anything bigger in or outside Australia, there are many different ways to do it, all at different prices; get some advice from the post office. Large **parcels** are reasonably cheap to send home by surface mail, but it will take up to three months for them to get there.

You can receive mail at any post office or agency: address the letter to **Poste Restante** (add "GPO" or "Central Post Office" for cities, unless you have the address of a particular branch), followed by the town, state and post code. You need a passport or other ID to collect mail, which is kept for a month and then returned; it's possible to get mail redirected if you change your plans – ask for a form at any post office. Some smaller post offices will allow you to phone and check if you have any mail waiting.

Most **hostels** and **hotels** will also hold mail for you if it's clearly marked, preferably with a date of arrival, or holders of Amex cards or travellers' cheques can have it sent to American Express offices.

Phones

The two major phone operators in Australia are Telstra and Optus, though all public phones are Telstra-operated and their rates, on a day-to-day basis, are pretty similar. Post offices (but not agencies) always have a bank of **telephones** outside; otherwise head for the nearest bar or service station – you'll even find solar-powered, satellite-connected booths in the Outback. Public telephones take coins or **Telstra phonecards**, which are sold through newsagents and other stores for $5, $10, $20 or $50. You can make **international calls** from virtually any of them as from a private phone. Many bars, shops and restaurants have orange or blue **payphones**, but these cost more than a regular call box, and international dialling is not advised because they'll start to gobble money the moment you're connected, even if the call goes unanswered. Whatever their type, payphones do not accept incoming calls.

Crediphones accept most major credit cards such as Amex, Visa and Diners International, and can be found at international and domestic airports, central locations in major cities, and many hotels.

You can make **reverse charge** calls through the operator, but it's easier with **Country Direct** which, for the price of a local call, will connect you directly to an operator in the country you're calling (numbers are listed in the box opposite). Cash is not needed, as the call is charged to the receiving number or to your own phone credit card. Country Direct calling cards are available through hotels, travel agents and tour operators.

Rates for calls within Australia are cheapest in the evenings from Monday to Saturday, and all day Sunday. **Local calls** are untimed, allowing you to talk for as long as you like; this costs around 17¢ on a domestic phone, though public phones may charge 50¢. Many businesses and services operate **free call numbers**, prefixed ☎1800, while others have six-digit numbers beginning ☎13 that are charged at the local-call rate. Numbers starting ☎0055 are private information services (often recorded), costing between 35¢ and 70¢ a minute, but with a minimum charge of 40¢ from public phones.

International calls are charged at a flat per minute rate depending on the country called, whatever the hour or day of the week that the call is made. All incur a connection fee of 22¢, then it costs 37.4¢ per minute to the UK; 31¢ to the US; 44¢ for Canada; and 31¢ for New Zealand. If you plan to speak for a while, you can save money by buying half-hour blocks to all the above countries for $6.60 by dialling ☎0018 (instead of ☎0011), then the country code and number. Hang up within the first minute and you only pay a $2 connection fee, otherwise you'll be charged for the full half hour; speak for over thirty minutes and you'll pay double.

Operators and international codes

OPERATOR SERVICES

Local Directory Assistance ☏1223
National Directory Assistance ☏12 455
International Directory Assistance ☏12 455

Operator ☏1234
International Operator ☏1234

INTERNATIONAL CALLS

To call Australia from overseas dial the international access code (☏00 from the UK or New Zealand, ☏011 from the US and Canada), followed by ☏61, the area code minus its initial zero, and the number. To dial out of Australia it's ☏0011, followed by the country code, then the area code (without the zero, if there is one), followed by the number:

| Ireland ☏0011 353 | New Zealand ☏0011 64 | UK ☏0011 44 | US and Canada ☏0011 1 |

COUNTRY DIRECT

Ireland		UK	
Telecom	free call ☏1800 881 353	BT operator	free call ☏1800 881 440
		BT automatic	free call ☏1800 881 441
Canada		Mercury	free call ☏1800 881 417
Teleglobe	free call ☏1800 881 490		
		US	
New Zealand		AT&T	free call ☏1800 881 011
Clear	free call ☏1800 124 333	LDDS Worldcom	free call ☏1800 881 212
Telecom	free call ☏1800 881 640	MCI	free call ☏1800 881 100
		Sprint	free call ☏1800 881 877

The internet

Like everywhere else, internet availability has boomed over the last few years in Australia. Larger cities have **internet cafés**, typically charging around $4 to $6 an hour (though they sometimes offer half-price discounts early in the morning); and many places to stay – especially **hostels** – also provide terminals for their guests at similar rates. Otherwise, try **local libraries**, who almost always provide free access, though time is generally limited to one hour and you'll generally have to sign up in advance on a waiting list. In Tasmania, most towns now have an **Online Access Centre** (see p.1052), which provide internet access and word processing facilities for $5 per half hour, with a volunteer to help you out if needed.

The media

The Murdoch-owned *Australian* is Australia's only national daily newspaper; aimed mainly at the business community, it has good overseas coverage but local news is often built around statistics. Each state (or more properly, each state capital) has its own daily paper, the best of which are the *Sydney Morning Herald* and Melbourne's venerable *The Age* – both available across the southeast.

Local papers are always a good source of listings, if not news. You should be able to track down some **international papers**, or their overseas editions – British, American, Asian and European – in the state capitals. The weekly *Time Australia* and *Newsweek/Bulletin* are the current affairs **magazines**. The monthly *HQ* focuses on literature, the arts and current affairs from a younger but sophisticated international and Australian perspective, while *Juice* is an intelligent and amusing music/popular culture mag. If you're interested in wildlife, pick up a copy of *Geo* or the bimonthly *Australian Geographic* (related only in name to the US magazine) for some excellent photography and in-depth coverage of Australia's remoter corners. There are some excellent glossy Australian-focused adventure travel magazines, too, like the Victorian based monthly *Expanse* and the quarterly *Wild*. You'll find Australian versions of all the fashion mags, from *Vogue* to *Elle*, plus enduring publications like the *Australian Women's Weekly* (now monthly) which is well-known for its excellent recipes, and gossipy magazines like *Who Weekly* featuring the lowdown on the antics of international and Australian celebs. On a different note, the Australian version of *The Big Issue*, produced out of Melbourne, is called *The Big Issue Australia* and has been operating since 1996. Vendors are homeless, ex-homeless or long-term unemployed and make half of the $2 cover price.

Australia's first **television station** opened in 1956 and the country didn't get colour television until 1974 – both much later than other westernized countries. Australian television isn't particularly exciting unless you're into sport, of which there's plenty, and commercial stations put on frequent commercial breaks – with often annoyingly unsophisticated advertisements – throughout films. There are Australian content rulings which mean that there are a good amount of Australian dramas, series and soap operas, many of which go on to make it big overseas, from *Neighbours* and *Home and Away* to *Blue Heelers*. However, there's a predominance of American programmes and lots of repeats. Australian TV is also fairly permissive in terms of sexual content compared to the programming of Britain or North America. There are three predictable commercial stations: Channel Seven; Channel Nine, which aims for an older market with more conservative programming; and Channel Ten, which tries to grab the younger market with some good comedy programmes including *Good News Week* and the irreverent talk show *The Panel*. In addition, there is also the more serious ABC – a national, advertisement-free station still with a British bias, showing all the best British sitcoms and mini-series – and the livelier SBS, a government-sponsored, multicultural station, which has the best coverage of world news, as well as interesting current affairs programmes and plenty of foreign-language films (and carefully timed advertisements which fit into the upmarket end of the scale). In more remote areas you will not be able to access all five channels and often only ABC and one commercial offering are receivable. There are two **pay TV** stations, Optus and the Murdoch-owned Foxtel, though the pay-TV culture is not firmly established yet as in other countries, and even expensive hotels often still only have terrestrial TV.

The best **radio** is on the various ABC stations, both local and national. ABC Radio National – broadcast all over Australia – offers a popular mix of arty intellectual topics, and another ABC station, 2JJJ ("Triple J"), a former Sydney-based alternative rock station, is aimed at the nation's youth and is available across the country in watered-down form.

Opening hours, holidays and festivals

Shops and services are generally open Monday to Friday 9am to 5pm and until lunchtime on Saturday. In cities and larger towns, many shops stay open late on Thursday or Friday evening – usually until 9pm – and all day on Saturday.

In remote country areas, **roadhouses** provide all the essential services for the traveller and, on the major highways, are generally open 24 hours a day. In tourist areas, even ones well off the beaten track, **tourist offices** are often open every day or at least through the week plus weekend mornings; urban information centres are more likely to conform to normal shopping hours.

Tourist attractions such as museums, galleries and attended historic monuments, are often open daily, though those in rural communities may have erratic opening hours. Specific opening hours are given throughout the *Guide*.

Holidays

Contrary to popular opinion and Australia's commendably relaxed interpretation of the work ethic, there are surprisingly few nationwide **public holidays** – and even when you add in the state ones (two or three per state, about eight in the Northern Territory), Australia lags behind most European countries in having official days off.

Watch out for **school holidays**, when seaside resorts can be transformed into bucket-and-spade war zones, national park campsites are full to overflowing, and the roads are jammed with station wagons full of holidaying families. Dates vary from year to year and state to state, but generally people are on the move for six weeks from mid-December (January is worst, as many people stay home until after Christmas), two weeks around Easter, and another couple of weeks in June or July.

Festivals

The nationwide selection of festivals listed opposite all include, necessitate and are in some cases the imaginative product of, prolonged beer-swilling. Why else would you drive to the edge of the Simpson Desert to watch a horse race? (See "Birdsville".) Also, all cities and towns have their own agricultural festivals ("shows") which are high points of the local calendar.

More seriously, each mainland capital tries to elevate its sophistication quotient with a regular celebration and showcase of art and culture, of which the biennial Adelaide Arts Festival is the best known.

Besides the major events listed below, there's a host of smaller, local events many of which are detailed throughout the *Guide*. The Christmas and Easter holiday periods, especially, are marked by celebrations at every turn, all over the country.

January

Festival of Sydney, NSW. A month of festivities, with something for absolutely everyone.

Montsalvat Jazz Festival, Eltham, VIC. Australia's premier jazz festival, which takes place on the Montsalvat Estate over Australia Day weekend; book well ahead.

Tamworth Country Music Festival, Tamworth, NSW. A week of Slim Dusty and his ilk, culminating in the Australian Country Music Awards.

February

Sydney Gay and Lesbian Mardi Gras, NSW. Sydney's proud gay community's festival begins at the end of February and lasts three weeks, ending with an extravagant parade and an all-night dance party.

Festival of Perth, WA. A month of "low-brow arts" at venues all over the city.

Bindoon Rock Festival, Bindoon, WA. WA's answer to Woodstock or Reading, with some visiting overseas bands.

March

Adelaide Arts Festival, SA. The country's best-known and most innovative arts festival (biennial, in even years); not to be missed.

Melbourne Moomba Festival, VIC. Eleven days of partying, beginning and ending with fireworks and lots of fun in between.

April

Barossa Valley Vintage Festival, SA. Biennial (odd years) Germanic festival set in the country's viticultural heart.

Melbourne International Comedy Festival, VIC. Opening on April Fools' Day, comics from around the world gather for three weeks.

May

Bangtail Muster, Alice Springs, NT. Nutty parades and Outback silliness.

June

Melbourne International Film Festival, VIC. The country's largest and most prestigious film festival, lasting two weeks.

Sydney International Film Festival, NSW. Also an important film festival, running for over two weeks in June and based at the glorious State Theatre.

Barunga Sports Festival, Beswick Aboriginal Land, NT. A rare and enjoyable chance to encounter Aboriginal culture in the NT. No alcohol.

Cape York Aboriginal Dance Festival, QLD. Three-day, alcohol-free celebration of authentic Aboriginal culture. Biennial in odd-numbered years.

July

Camel Cup, Alice Springs, NT. Camel-racing down the dry Todd River.

Darwin Beer Can Regatta, NT. Mindil Beach is the venue for the recycling of copious empties into a variety of nutty seacraft. Also a thong-throwing contest; Territorian eccentricity personified.

August

Shinju Matsuri Festival, Broome, WA. Probably the most remote big festival, which doesn't stop the town being packed for this Oriental-themed pearl festival.

Mount Isa Rodeo, Mount Isa, QLD. Australia's largest rodeo – a gritty, down-to-earth encounter with bulls, horses and their riders.

September

Bathurst 1000 Road Races, Bathurst, NSW. Australia's premier weekend of car and bike street racing.

Birdsville Races, QLD. Once a year the remote Outback town of Birdsville (population 120) comes alive for a weekend of drinking and horse-racing – a well-known and definitive Australian oddity.

Warana, Brisbane, QLD. Huge, two-week arts festival centred in the city's Botanic Gardens with food, wine, beer, music, writing and children's events topped off with fireworks and a wacky Concours de Decadence.

Melbourne International Festival of the Arts, VIC. Two-week celebration of visual, performing and written arts in venues all over the city.

October

Henley-on-Todd Regatta, Alice Springs, NT. Wacky races in bottomless boats running down the dry Todd riverbed; the event is heavily insured against the river actually flowing.

Manly Jazz Festival, Sydney, NSW. Three-day jazz festival with artists from all over the world.

November

Australian Grand Prix, Melbourne, VIC. Formula One street-racing which follows a week of partying; formerly held in Adelaide, now relocated to Albert Park in Melbourne.

Melbourne Cup, Flemington Racecourse, VIC. Australia's Ascot, a 130-year-old horse race which brings the entire country to a standstill around the radio or TV.

December

Sydney to Hobart Yacht Race, Sydney, NSW. Crowds flock to the harbour to witness the start of this classic regatta which departs Sydney on Boxing Day and arrives in Hobart three days later. The Christmas holidays and New Year's Eve are celebrated with gusto everywhere.

Outdoor activities

Though the cities are fun, what really makes Australia special is the great outdoors: the vast and remote wilderness of the bush, the legendary Outback, and the thousands of kilometres of unspoilt coastline. There's tremendous potential here to indulge in a huge range of outdoor pursuits – hiking, fishing, surfing, diving, even skiing – especially in the multitude of national parks that cover the country. Further information on all of these is available from local tourist offices, which publicize what's available in their area; from the National Parks and Wildlife Service (NPWS), who have detailed maps of parks with walking trails, climbs, swimming holes and other activities; and from specialist books. In addition, virtually any activity can be done as part of an organized excursion, often with all the gear supplied. If you want to go it alone you'll find plenty of places ready to rent or sell you the necessary equipment, along with some friendly advice. Before indulging in adventure activities, check your insurance cover (see pp.24–25).

As with any wilderness area, the Australian interior does not suffer fools, and the coast conceals **dangers** too: sunstroke and dehydration are risks everywhere, with riptides, currents and unexpectedly strong waves to be wary of on exposed coasts. In the more remote regions isolation and lack of surface water compromise energetic outdoor activities such as bushwalking or mountain biking, which are probably better indulged in the cooler climes and more populated locations of the south.

Bushwalking

Bushwalking in Australia doesn't mean just a stroll in the bush, but refers to self-sufficient hikes, from a day to a week or longer. It's an extremely popular activity nationwide, and you'll find trails marked in almost every national park, as well as local bushwalking **clubs** whose trips you may be able to join. In any tourist area you'll also find experienced **guides**.

It's essential to be **properly equipped** for the conditions you'll encounter – and to know what those conditions are likely to be. Carry a **map** (often on hand at the ranger station in popular national parks), know how the trail is marked, and stay on the route. If your trip is a long one, let someone know

where you're going, and confirm to them that you've arrived back safely – park rangers are useful contacts for this, and some will insist on it anyway. The essentials, even for a short walk, are adequate clothing including a wide-brimmed hat, enough food, and, above all, **water**. Other things you really shouldn't be without are a torch, matches or lighter, penknife, sun block, insect repellent, toilet paper, first-aid kit, and a whistle or mirror to attract attention if you get lost. A lot of this gear can be rented, or bought cheaply at disposal stores, which can often also put you in touch with local clubs or specialists.

Long-distance tracks exist mostly in the south of the country, with Tasmania's wilderness areas being perhaps the most rewarding bushwalking location; the eighty-kilometre **Overland Track** from Cradle Mountain to Lake St Clair is one of the country's best-known trails. On the mainland, the **Blue Mountains**, a two-hour train ride from Sydney, the **Snowy Mountains** further south, and Victoria's spectacular **Grampians** are all popular regions for longer, marked walks.

South Australia's **Flinders Ranges**, 300km north of Adelaide, are accessible along the **Heysen Trail** from the Fleurieu Peninsula, the walk into the thousand-metre-high natural basin of Wilpena Pound being

Bush essentials

Three things above all:

Fire: the driest continent on earth is covered by vegetation specifically evolved to make use of regular conflagrations, and is always at risk from bushfires. Sydney's Black Friday fires of 1994 saw the city ringed with burning bushland and, even in wet years, there's a constant red alert during summer months. Always use an established fireplace where available, or ideally dig a shallow pit and ring it with stones. Keep fires as small as practicable, and make absolutely sure that even embers are smothered before going to sleep or moving on. Never discard burning cigarette butts from cars. Periodic total fire bans – announced in the local media when in effect – prohibit any fire in the open, including wood, gas or electric barbecues, with heavy fines for offenders. Check on the local fire danger before you go bushwalking – some walking trails are closed in the riskiest periods (summer in the south; the end of the dry season – Sept/Oct – in the north). If driving, carry blankets and a filled water container, listen to your car radio and watch out for roadside fire danger indicators. If the worst happens, there are practical ways of surviving a bushfire.*

Water: carry plenty with you and do not contaminate local water resources. In particular, soaps and detergents can render water undrinkable and kill livestock and wild animals. Avoid washing in standing water, especially tanks and small lakes or reservoirs.

Waste: take only photographs, leave only footprints. That means carrying all your rubbish out with you – never burn or bury it – and making sure you urinate (and bury your excrement) at least 50m from a campsite or water source.

*See "Health", pp.30–32, for potential bushwalking hazards and advice on how to deal with them – including ways to survive if caught in a bushfire.

---

the highlight. In vast Western Australia, only the southwestern corner can offer extended walks: the 640-kilometre **Bibulman Track**, an old Aboriginal trail passing through the region's giant eucalypt forests, is signed all the way from Walpole to Perth. An hour's drive north of Albany, the peaks of the **Stirling Ranges**, almost a thousand metres high, also offer some spectacular trails. In the Northern Territory, **Litchfield Park**, two hours south of Darwin in a croc-free tableland fringed with perennial springs, has some satisfying bushwalks in the dry season; while the **Larapinta Trail**, along the MacDonnell Ranges west of Alice Springs, is being extended each year. Queensland's rainforested coastal strip offers plenty more opportunities for walks, including the **Lamington** area in the south, and around northern **Atherton Tablelands** and **Hinchinbrook Island**.

Water sports

The oceans and seas around Australia are a national playground and are not just for tanning or playing volleyball on the beach. Always take local advice on the waves, which must be treated with respect. If possible, **swim** from a patrolled beach, between the flags: raise one hand if you get into difficulty, and clear the water if a siren sounds – it could signal dangerous waves, a shark sighting or a swarm of bluebottles (stinging jellyfish).

Enjoying the water doesn't necessarily involve any special effort or equipment, but if you want it, there are plenty of activities on offer. Probably the easiest to get into is **surfing**, starting with body-surfing and progressing to boogie-boards (small boards that you lie on) and then on to full-scale surfboards. Surfing is popular everywhere, but don't expect the local surfie community to be too friendly at first – they're often very cliquey. Seaside hostels often have boards which they loan out free. **Windsurfing** and **sailing** are also extremely popular, and you'll be able to rent equipment and get instruction in almost any resort, though some of the best sailing in the country can be found around Queensland's Whitsunday Islands. Other water sports include **white-water rafting**, **sea-kayaking** and **canoeing**.

The Great Barrier Reef is one of the world's great **scuba-diving** meccas, with some other lesser-known but excellent sites around the country – such as West Australia's Ningaloo Reef – beginning to attract attention. Dive facilities in Australia are of a high standard, and scuba courses are not that expensive, though if you simply want to try it once there are plenty of people offering closely supervised "resort dives". Good **rental gear** is widely available, but if you're bringing your own, check for compatibility problems; yokes are the Australian norm, so if your first-stage fitting is DIN (likely in Europe and the UK), you'll need an adaptor. **Snorkelling** is the low-tech alternative, and still allows you to get dramatically close to the aquatic life around the Reef.

Fishing is an Australian obsession, conducted on rivers and lakes, off piers or small boats ("tinnies"), or out at sea where – if your cheque book is up to the challenge – marlin and other game fish are caught. Again, all the equipment – even boats – can be rented in most good fishing areas. Barramundi, renowned for its fighting qualities, is the thing to go for up north.

Australia's top dive sites

Bougainville Reef , Coral Sea, QLD (see p.524). Exceptional in every way: kilometre-deep coral walls, clear water, and both reef and pelagic life in abundance. Live-aboard trips from Cairns and Port Douglas.

Cod Hole , Great Barrier Reef, QLD (see p.524). Where the giant potato cod and divers meet. Live-aboard trips from Cairns.

Lord Howe Island , NSW (see p.328). The world's southernmost reef surrounds one of the world's most beautiful islands. Flights from Brisbane and Sydney.

Ningaloo , WA (see p.751). Late March or April sees scores of whale sharks – the world's largest fish – assembling at Ningaloo Reef off Exmouth for a free feed of coral spawn. Tours from Exmouth.

Port Lincoln , SA (p.863). South Australian waters are one of the last bastions for the poorly-understood Great White shark. Trips out from Port Lincoln use shark cages.

Seal Rocks , NSW (see p.282). Hosts a great grey nurse convergence every so often, a chance to be surrounded by these fierce looking but largely harmless sharks. Trips from Foster or Tuncurry.

Yongala Shipwreck , QLD (see p.497). Huge fish and the remains of a 100m-long passenger liner which went down in an early-twentieth-century cyclone. Trips from Townsville and Cairns.

Other pursuits

The craze for **bungee jumping** has, not surprisingly, caught on with Australia's hardcore thrill-seekers, though it's on the wane nowadays: Cairns in northern Queensland is a good place to try it in a spectacular setting. **Rap jumping** essentially involves abseiling headfirst at very high speed down sheer cliff faces. Alice Springs' wide-open spaces make it the country's **hot-air-ballooning** centre and also a base for **camel treks** through the surrounding desert.

More regular riding, on **horseback**, is offered all over the country – anything from a gentle hour at walking pace to a serious cattle roundup. **Cycling** and **mountain biking** are tremendously popular too, as well as being a good way of getting around resorts; many hostels rent out bikes, and we've listed other outlets throughout the text.

Australia's wilderness is an ideal venue for extended **off-road driving** or **dirt-bike riding**, although permission may be needed to cross station- and Aboriginal-owned lands, and the fragile desert ecology should be respected at all times. Northern Queensland's Cape York and WA's Kimberley are the most adventurous destinations, 4WD-accessible in the dry season only. The great **Outback tracks** pushed out by explorers or drovers, such as the Gunbarrel and Sandover highways and the Tanami, Birdsville and Oodnadatta tracks, are technically mostly two-wheel driveable in dry conditions, but can be hard on poorly prepared vehicles. Getting right to the tip of Queensland's eight-hundred-kilometre-long Cape York Peninsula will definitely require a 4WD or off-road bike; while Western Australia's two-thousand-kilometre-long Canning Stock Route demands a 4WD with an enormous fuel range, effectively ruling out motorbikes.

Finally, you may not associate Australia with **skiing**, but there's plenty of it in the 1500-metre-high Australian Alps on the border of Victoria and New South Wales, based around the winter resorts of Thredbo, Mount Hotham and Perisher. Europeans tend to be sniffy about Australian skiing, and certainly it's limited, with a season that lasts barely two months – July and August – and very few challenging runs. The one area where it does match up to Europe is in the prices. On the other hand it's fun if you're here, and the relatively gentle slopes of the mountains are ideal **for cross-country skiing**, which is increasingly being developed alongside downhill.

National parks

The Australian **Environmental Protection Agency** is split into federal and state bodies, the federal organization dealing with international problems such as whaling and how to make use of Antarctica, and occasionally arbitrating between the state-run **National Parks and Wildlife Service** departments. These run the national parks themselves, and, though the departmental names vary from state to state, throughout the *Guide* we've usually referred to them as **NPWS**.

The thousand-odd national parks range from suburban commons to the Great Barrier Reef, and from popular hiking areas within striking distance of the big cities to wilderness regions which require days in a 4WD simply to reach. They protect everything within their boundaries: flora, fauna and landforms as well as Aboriginal art and sacred sites.

Fees are variable. Some parks or states have no fees at all, some charge for use of camping facilities, while others require permits bought in advance. If you're camping you can usually pay on site, but booking ahead might be a good idea during the Christmas and Easter holidays. Nearby resorts or alternative accommodation are always independently run, rather than by the NPWS.

Sport

Australians are sports mad, especially for the ostensibly passive spectator sports of cricket, Aussie Rules football, rugby (league or union), tennis or any type of racing, from cockroach to camel. No matter what it is, it'll draw a crowd – with thousands more watching on TV – and a crowd means a party. Even unpromising-sounding activities such as surf lifesaving and yacht racing (the start of the Sydney to Hobart race just after Christmas is a massive social event) are tremendously popular.

It's hard to escape sport in Australia: people talk about it all the time; sporting news fills up the newspapers; events and commentary are constantly broadcast on TV and radio; and it's a huge source of national pride. The wintertime **football** (footy) season in Australia lasts from March to September; in summer **cricket** is played from October to March.

Footy comes in several varieties. Before World War II, **soccer** was played by British immigrants but with postwar immigration it was branded as "ethnic", as new clubs became based on the country of origin of the players: **Australian Rules** (see opposite) was considered the game "real Australians"

played. More than fifty percent of Australia's twelve league soccer clubs evolved from communities of postwar immigrants – mainly Italians, Greeks and Yugoslavs – and the former chairman of Soccer Australia, David Hill, believed that their fervent nationalism marginalized the game; his mid-1990s ban on clubs that included national flags in their logos won support as well as accusations of the pursuance of a policy of "ethnic cleansing". Getting the national team, the Socceroos, to play for the World Cup is seen as the best way to create interest in the sport on a national level. To this end, the once-famous English footballer Terry Venables was appointed coach in the wake of his success in managing England to the semi-finals of the European Championships (Euro '96), training the Socceroos for their qualifying rounds to enter the 1998 World Cup in France. **Rugby union**, despite the huge success of the Wallabies national team, is also very much a minority interest domestically. The introduction of a Super 12 competition, involving teams from Australia, New Zealand and South Africa, has generated a much greater interest in what was formerly an elitist sport.

Australian Rules ("Aussie Rules") football dominates Victoria, South Australia and Western Australia. It's an extraordinary, anarchic, no-holds-barred, eighteen-a-side brawl, most closely related to Gaelic football and known dismissively north of the Victorian border as "aerial ping pong". The ball can be propelled by any means necessary, and the fact that players aren't sent off for misconduct ensures a lively, skilful and, above all, gladiatorial confrontation. Aussie Rules stars have delightful sobriquets such as "Tugger" and "Crackers", and their macho garb consists of tiny butt-hugging shorts and a biceps-revealing tank top. The game is mostly played on cricket grounds, with a ball similar to that used in rugby or American football. The aim is to get the ball through the central uprights for a goal (six points). There are four 25-minute quarters, plus lots of time added on for injury. Despite the violence on the pitch (or perhaps because of it), Aussie Rules fans tend to be loyal and well behaved. Victoria has traditionally been the home of the game, and Victorian sides are expected to win the AFL Flag, decided at the Grand Final in September, as a matter of course.

In New South Wales and Queensland **Rugby League** attracts the fanatics, especially for the hard-fought **State of Origin** matches. The thirteen-a-side game is one of which the Australians seem permanent world champions, despite having a relatively small professional league. Recently, the game has been split down the middle – there are now two rival competitions – the traditional Australian Rugby League (ARL) and the Murdoch-owned Super League. One of the sadder consequences of this media-inspired revolution has been the loss of some of the traditional inner-city clubs through mergers. The common view is that the game cannot support the number of teams required for two competitions. Many people also resent the way in which this one-time bastion of working-class culture has been co-opted by pay TV.

Summertime **cricket** is a great spectator sport – for the crowd, the sunshine and the beer as much as the play. Every state is involved, and the three- or four-day Sheffield Shield matches of the interstate series are interspersed with one-day games and internationals, as well as full five-day international test matches. Interest in the five-day matches has been revitalized by Australia's recent victories against all-comers: the 1996–97 cricket season saw the home side convincingly defeat the West Indies, who had reigned supreme in world cricket for the best part of twenty years. In 1998 they beat South Africa and England, but really consolidated their position of World Champion when they beat Pakistan in Pakistan itself in 2001.

The international competition that still arouses greatest interest is that between Australia and England – **The Ashes**. Having been around for 120 years, this is perhaps the oldest rivalry between nations in international sport. The "trophy" competed for has an interesting provenance: in 1882 an Australian touring side defeated England at the Oval in Surrey by seven runs, and the *Sporting Times* was moved to report, in a mock obituary, that English cricket had "died at the Oval… deeply lamented by a large circle of sorrowing friends". The funeral ceremony involved the cremation of a set of bails, which were then preserved in a funerary urn. Each time the two countries compete, this is the trophy that is up for grabs (though the urn itself never actually leaves Lord's cricket ground in London) and a new crystal trophy actually goes to the winners.

Minor sports are followed with no less avid attention, and there are plenty of them, including horse-racing and trotting, motor-racing, swimming, athletics, tennis – you name it. One peculiarly Australian institution is the **surf carnival**, when teams of volunteer lifesavers demonstrate their skills – this makes for a great day out on the beach. **Surfing** itself can also be a competitive sport, with the Eastertime World Championships held at Bell's Beach, southwest of Melbourne, and November's Margaret River Classic, south of Perth, both good opportunities to catch some hot wave-riding action. Inland, many rural towns have a **speedway track** occupying a tract of wasteland, where at weekends motor-headed hoons demonstrate their dirt-tracking skills in souped-up utes or motorbikes; a dusty, noisy and merry focus for the entire community and passers-by.

Women and sexual harassment

The stereotyped image of the Aussie male is of a boozy bloke interested in sport, his car and his mates, with his girlfriend a poor fourth. And it's not far wrong: the Australian ethos of mateship has traditionally excluded women – the hard, tough life of the early days of white settlement, when women were scarce, fostered a male culture that's to some extent still current. Another legacy of pioneering times is the reputation of Australian women for being robust and practical.

In the main **cities**, attitudes are generally enlightened and "new men" are gaining ground, but in the more remote **country and Outback** areas, the older attitudes are more tenacious and sexual harassment can be commonplace – if rarely threatening. Men driving by in cars, in particular, are notorious for shouting out crude comments and sexual remarks as a woman walks by, and catcalling from groups of men in the street can be intimidating.

Meeting Australian men **socially**, as individuals, you'll often find that their brusque, offhand exterior conceals a surprisingly helpful and kind nature; they're also, on the whole, honest and upfront.

Sexual equality and attitudes

In public life, Australia has one of the best records for **sexual equality** in the world. It was the second country to give women the vote (after New Zealand in 1893), and the fact that this happened a year after federation in 1901 shows that the intention was for women to take a full role in the new nation. In the 1970s and 1980s Australia kept pace with the worldwide **feminist movement** (indeed, with Germaine Greer, it helped lead it): the first big milestone – equal pay for equal work – was finally achieved in 1974.

Equal opportunities legislation and affirmative action schemes for employment have been widely adopted: today, nonsexist language is the norm for newspapers and officialdom.

However, corresponding changes in attitudes have not always kept pace with all of this. At about the same time that women achieved equal pay, the **public bars** of hotels, which had traditionally refused to serve women, were being stormed by women's groups. Today, a woman can be served a drink anywhere in the country, but the way that Australian pubs are set up – with two separate bars – continues to reflect the old bias; you'll still see signs saying "Ladies' Lounge", and if you want to go to the women's toilets you'll have to walk a long way from the public bar. **Outback and country pubs** are still very much male bastions, and any woman travelling on her own would do well to avoid them, thus escaping the full blast of misogyny.

Travelling solo

Avoiding pubs is all very well, but **hotels** are often the cheapest and sometimes the only places to stay in **small towns**. The major drawback is that pub accommodation is often full of single male workers from other towns, or old men who are permanent boarders, so roaming corridors late at night in search of the toilet can be an unpleasant experience. That said, the management is usually friendly, and most country pubs are family-run. **Bed and breakfast** establishments and **guesthouses** provide a more homelike, friendly environment, unlike the inevitably impersonal **motels** where a stay can be a potentially lonely experience. **Caravan parks** and **campsites** tend to be safe, family-dominated environments and are a good bet if you have your own transport – and sleeping bag. In larger towns and cities, **hostels** are where you're most likely to meet like-minded women travelling alone. Easy-going Australian attitudes mean that dorms in backpackers' hostels (never YHA hostels) are often mixed sex. There's usually at least one female-only dorm and if this is really important to you, you should ask about it in advance or when you check in.

Best of all for making contact with locals and generally getting involved are **farmstays** (which needn't be expensive if you stay in shearers' quarters and the like) or the experience of being a WWOOF (Willing Workers on Organic Farms; see p.73). Before going to work or to stay on remote **Outback stations**, try to find out as much about the setup as possible, for you could end up being the only woman among a group of men – which could create potentially uncomfortable situations.

Rape and serious trouble

If the worst happens, it's best to contact a **Rape Crisis Line** before going straight to the police; all major cities have them and there's always a free-call line if you're in the country. Women police officers form a large part of the force, and in general the police deal sensitively with sexual assault cases.

To **avoid** physical attack, don't get too relaxed about Australia's friendly, easy-going attitude. The usual defensive tactics apply. In the cities at night, buses or trams are gener-

ally safer than trains – on the train, always sit next to the guard in the carriage. Pick somewhere to stay that's close to public transport so you don't have to walk far at night – an area with busy nightlife may well be safer than a dead suburban backstreet. If you're going to have to walk for long stretches at night, take a cab unless the streets are busy with traffic, restaurants and people.

The 1992 "backpacker murders" of hitching travellers just outside Sydney prove that it's not only in remote areas or when travelling alone that **hitchhiking** is dangerous – and that even male company is no safeguard. Hitching is doubly inadvisable for women and, with the wide variety of inexpensive transport options available, is hard to justify. If you must do it, never do it alone – and heed the general advice and warnings given on pp.45–46.

Women's contacts

All the major cities have good **women's contacts**, from resource centres and information lines to health centres where you can often get free pregnancy testing and other help. There's also a lively culture of women's galleries and bookshops; as well as stocking the works of the hundreds of great Australian women writers (see "Books" in Contexts for suggested reading), they'll have copies of feminist journals and good notice boards which often have information about **women-only accommodation**. Lesbian magazines also carry ads for women's bed and breakfasts and the like – you don't have to be gay to stay. In March, **International Women's Day** provides an excuse for a month-long series of women's events in the cities, culminating in enthusiastically attended street marches.

Specific women's contacts are listed in the city accounts of this *Guide*. For more, check out the White Pages under "Women"; alternatively, the Citizen's Advice Bureau in each city should be able to refer you to relevant organizations.

Gay and lesbian Australia

Year by year Australia grows in popularity as a Queer destination. Even as far back as 1832 a Select Committee of the British Parliament noted the popularity of "alternative lifestyles" among the colonists. Today, the beautiful people flock down under, lured by the conducive climate and laid-back lifestyle and eager to hang out with the homeboys on balmy beaches and sun-kissed city streets.

Despite its reputation as a macho culture, Australia revels in a large and active **scene**: you'll find an air of confidence and a sense of community that is often missing in other countries – and, what's more, it's friendly and accessible.

The colonists transported English **law** to Australia, but in 1972 South Australia was the first state to enact **decriminalization**, followed the next year by the ACT and Northern Territory. Surprisingly, Victoria and New South Wales (generally thought of as liberal states) delayed similar legislation until the 1980s. Less surprisingly, Queensland took the plunge only in 1991, while it took a decade of constant petitioning from the Tasmanian Gay and Lesbian Rights Group, and pressure from the Federal Government and the UN Human Rights Committee for the law to change in Tasmania in 1997. In Western Australia there's still an age of consent of 21, whereas the ages of consent in ACT and Victoria (both 16), SA and Tasmania (both 17), are the same as the heterosexual age. In the Northern Territory and NSW, the homosexual age of consent is 18. In Queensland, the age of consent for homosexuals depends on the sexual act practised, with anal sex outlawed until 18 but otherwise 16. Sex between women is either not mentioned in state laws or is covered by the heterosexual age. The foreign partner in a de facto gay relationship can apply to immigrate to or permanently reside in Australia, a much better situation than in many countries, but the current battle Australian gay and lesbian lobby groups are waging is to make same-sex relationships completely equal in the eyes of the law as heterosexual ones, in terms of marriage,

next of kin rights, superannuation and age of consent.

Today, Australia is testimony to the power of the pink dollar, and there's an abundance of gay venues, services, businesses, travel clubs, country retreats and the like.

Australia is definitely the place to watch Men At Work – and at play. **Aussie boys** get a lot of sun and sport – although the scene is a lot more diverse than simply tan and toned muscle, and the community is so large that there's bound to be something for everyone. One thing's for certain: you won't be bored. Just remember to pack your trunks, snorkel and fins, your clubbing gear and some barbecue tongs.

Australian **dykes** are refreshingly open and self-possessed – a relief after the more closed and cliquey scene in Europe. The flip side of their fearlessness is the predominance of S&M on the scene. Maybe the climate has something to do with it, but you'll see a good deal of tattoos and pierced flesh around.

Dyke **scenes** are nothing if not mercurial, and Australia is no exception. We've done our best to list bars, clubs and meeting places, but be warned that venues open, change their names, change hands, shut for refurbishment, get relaunched at a new address and finally go out of business with frightening rapidity.

Where and how to go

Sydney is the jewel in Australia's luscious navel. Firmly established as one of the world's great gay cities – only San Francisco can really rival it – it attracts lesbian and gay visitors from around the world. And if this can be overwhelming at times (the gossip alone has been known to drive people to the other side of the continent), Australia has plenty more to offer. Melbourne closely follows the scene in Sydney, but for a change of pace, take a trip to Brisbane and the Gold Coast. Perth, Adelaide and Darwin all have smaller, quieter scenes.

Away from the cities, things get more discreet, but a lot of **country areas** do have very friendly local scenes – impossible to pinpoint, but easy to stumble across. Australians on the city scene are a friendly bunch, but in a small country town they get really friendly, so if there's anything going on you'll probably get invited along.

The **Outback** covers the vast majority of the Australian continent and is, in European terms, sparsely populated. Mining and cattle ranching are the primary employers and they help to create a culture not famed for its tolerance of homosexuality. Tread carefully: bear in mind that Ayers Rock may be 2000km from Sydney as the crow flies, but in many ways it's a million miles away in terms of attitudes.

The **Australian Gay and Lesbian Tourism Association** (AGLTA, see below for details) is a dynamic organization dedicated to turning Australia into the premier destination for gay and lesbian tourists from all over the world. They give their seal of approval to accommodation, resorts, travel agents and promoters that provide the attitude or atmosphere that today's gay globetrotter demands – and their *Gay and Lesbian Tourism Services Directory* covers retreats, guesthouses and country lodges across Australia, not just in the cities.

Each chapter of this guide has specific gay and lesbian listings, with a wealth of information – see in particular the box on pp.175–176, which has all you need to know to join in Sydney's Mardi Gras celebrations. Check out too **The Rough Guide to**

Gay and Lesbian Australia, reviewed in our "Books" section on p.1177.

Gay and lesbian contacts

Personal contacts Country Network (or just "CN"), PO Box 192, Subiaco, WA 6904 (℡ 08/9385 1366, ⊛ www.pinkboard.com.au~countrynetwork), is a friendship network linking gay guys in rural Australia.

Press and multimedia Two monthly national gay and lesbian glossy magazines are widely available at newsagents: *Campaign* and *Outrage*. *LOTL* (*Lesbians on the Loose*) is a monthly publication available at lesbian and gay venues. Each major capital has excellent free gay newspapers, like the *Sydney Star Observer* or Melbourne's *Brother Sister* (now available in a Brisbane edition too) that give the local lowdown. There are also some very useful websites, the best of which is ⊛ www.outbiz.com.au for online gay and lesbian business, community information and links to other sites, including that of the Gay and Lesbian Mardi Gras. The ALSO Foundation, based in Victoria (see p.933), also have a good website containing their directory: ⊛ www.also.org.au

Tour operator Destination Downunder, Level 10, 130 Elizabeth St, Sydney, NSW 2000 (℡ 02/9268 2188), is a gay tour operator that can arrange packages for the Gay and Lesbian Mardi Gras.

Tourist services AGLTA (Australian Gay and Lesbian Tourism Association), PO Box 208, Darlinghurst, NSW 2010 (℡ 02/8379 7498, ℱ 8379 2483) produces the *Gay and Lesbian Tourism Services Directory*. It's free, but there's a small charge for overseas postage.

Travel agents Parkside Travel, 70 Glen Osmond Rd, Parkside, SA 5063 (℡ 08/8274 1222 or free call 1800 888 501); Silke's Travel, 263 Oxford St, Darlinghurst, NSW 2010 (℡ 02/9380 6244 or free call 1800 807 860, ℮ silba@magna.com.au); Tearaway Travel, 52 Porter St, Prahan, VIC 3181 (℡ 03/9510 6344, ℮ tearaway@bigpond.com).

Police, prejudice and trouble

"Transportation across the seas", to which judges condemned the petty criminals of two centuries ago, seems to have been a successful policy; Australia today can pride itself on being a relatively crime-free country, although increasingly it is following the American trend in gun-related incidents.

This is not to say there's no petty crime, or that you can leave normal caution behind, but there is less violent crime and theft in Australia, even in the big cities, than in most of Europe or North America, and even so-called "heavy" downtown areas can appear pretty tame. One place where **violence** is commonplace is at the ritual pub "blue" (fight) among known protagonists on a Friday or Saturday night, but strangers are seldom involved without at least some apparent provocation.

You're perhaps more likely to fall victim to a fellow traveller or an opportunist: **theft** is fairly common in some hostels, while if you leave valuables lying around, or on view in cars, you can expect them to be stolen. Exercise caution, don't forget your normal streetwise precautions, and you should be fine; in cities at night stay in areas that are well-lit and full of people, look like you know where you are going and don't carry excess cash or anything else you can't afford to lose.

Police and the law

Australia's **police** – all armed – have a thoroughly poor public image and perhaps as a result tend to keep a low profile; you should have no trouble in your dealings with them. Indeed you'll hardly see them, unless you're out on a Friday or Saturday night when they cruise in search of drink-related brawls.

Things to watch out for, most of all, are drugs. A lot of marijuana is grown and its use is widespread, but you'd be foolish to carry it when you travel, and crazy to carry any other illicit narcotic. Each state has its own penalties, and though a small amount of grass may mean no more than confiscation or an on-the-spot fine, they're generally pretty tough – especially in Queensland. When you **cross state borders** you may find that your vehicle will be **searched** – not just for "firearms, pornography or drugs" but also for fruit and fresh produce, which often cannot be carried from one state to the next, to minimize the spread of plant pests and viruses. Driving in general makes you more likely to have a confrontation of some kind, if only for a minor traffic infringement: **drunk driving** is regarded extremely seriously, so don't risk it – random breath tests are common around all cities and larger towns.

Lesser potential problems are **alcohol** – there are all sorts of controls on where and when you can drink, and taking alcohol onto Aboriginal lands can be a serious offence – **smoking**, which is increasingly being banned in public places; and nude or **topless** sunbathing, which is quite acceptable in many places, but absolutely not in others – follow the locals' lead.

If for any reason you are **arrested** or need help (and you can be arrested merely on suspicion of committing an offence), you are entitled to contact a friend or lawyer before answering any questions. You could call your consulate, but don't expect much sympathy. If necessary, the police will provide a lawyer, and you can usually get legal aid to settle the bill.

Emergencies

☏ 000 is the free emergency telephone number which summons the police, ambulance or fire service.

Prejudice, police and the traveller

Given Australia's record on its treatment of the Aboriginal population, the history of the

White Australia policy, and the recent rise of Pauline Hanson's One Nation party on a partly racist agenda, it comes as little surprise to find that this is a nation where **racial prejudice** is ingrained. As a **black traveller** you're likely to attract attention when you don't particularly want it, and be unable to get it when you do – even to the extent of being refused service in an Outback bar or being unable to flag down a cab in a city. Certainly in remote areas, where Aboriginal people are still often treated as second-class citizens at best, black travellers may have an uncomfortable time.

Asians are generally more accepted (in Australia, "Asian" usually means Southeast Asian – the Indian and Pakistani populations are negligible). However, a strong undercurrent of anti-Asian feeling – never too far below the surface in Australia's European history – has recently come out into the open, encouraged by Pauline Hanson's many infamous remarks since her maiden speech in parliament in September 1996. Cliché-ridden, uninformed and simplistic as they are, her statements have struck a chord with some Australians, who feel bewildered and marginalized by the massive socioeconomic changes their country has gone through in the last 25 years. In hard times it's handy to have a scapegoat, and Asians have always been a target for criticism in Australia.

Nevertheless, Australia does have powerful anti-discrimination laws. Any racial discrimination can be reported to the **Human Rights and Equal Opportunities Commission**, who have offices in each state capital (listed in the "Government" section at the front of the White Pages phone book). Although you might not have time (or the desire) to go through the lengthy complaints process, the threat is a useful one, as their powers are considerable. Just don't expect a country policeman to help you – many are part of the problem rather than its solution.

Work

Most visitors' visas clearly state that no employment of any kind is to be undertaken during a visit to Australia. However, if you've succeeded in getting a Working Holiday Visa (see "Visas and red tape", pp.22–24) and are prepared to try anything – officially for no more than three months at a time – there are plenty of possibilities for finding work. There are also organized work programmes – both paid and voluntary.

In practice this means that the only jobs officially open to you are unskilled, temporary ones. The former Commonwealth Employment Service (CES) has been broken up into competing, semi-privatized employment agencies. One of the largest ones is **Employment National** (Mon–Fri 9am–5pm; ☏ 13 3444, ⓦ www.employmentnational.com.au). They will usually ask you to come in and register, or send a fax with all your details and a resumé. There are 209 branches all over Australia, including rural areas where there's a lot of seasonal work.

What they offer will usually be either **harvesting or farm-labouring jobs** (see overleaf), or in the cities **clerical**, **bar** or **restaurant** jobs, or occasional **factory** work.

Aimed at backpackers with work visas, **travellers centres** are scattered around eastern Australia, and can sort out all aspects of working, from organizing tax file numbers to actually getting you jobs. Each has links between their various branches, so you can check in advance about the likelihood of finding work where you are heading.

Membership costs around $40 a year. See under "Information and maps" on p.33 for travellers centres' contact details.

In addition, more specialized **employment agencies** are worth a try in the cities if you have a marketable skill (computer training, accountancy, nursing, cooking and the like). They might have better, higher-paid jobs on their books, though they may be looking for full-time or at least longer-term commitment. Newspaper **job ads** are also worth checking out, especially in smaller local papers. And finally, fellow travellers, **hostel staff** in smaller hostels, and notice boards may be the best source of all, especially in remote areas, some even run their own employment agency or have a permanently staffed employment desk. This is where you'll find out about local opportunities, and the hostels themselves may occasionally offer free nights in lieu of cleaning work – or even pay you for jobs that involve a bit more skill. Some of the hostels in the big cities or in country towns where there is a lot of harvesting work also arrange employment.

Significant long-term **unemployment** is prevalent in Australia, and the days of legendary wages for relentless hard work in mines, on the roads or on prawn trawlers are long gone. Nonetheless, plenty of people still manage to work illegally, though visa checks in the major harvest areas (they really do happen!) and tax reforms have made this much harder than it used to be.

Seasonal picking and harvesting work

Listed below are the major **harvest seasons** around the country. Once you're into the harvest season it's possible to move with it around the country, from one product to another, as many people do. There may be lesser harvests and other work in all of these places at any time. Just remember that crop picking is hard work for low wages (which are paid on a commission basis) – if you're bad at it and don't pick much, you'll put in a lot of effort for virtually nothing.

New South Wales

Summer November–April, peaking in February, in the central eastern district around Bathurst, Dubbo and Orange; orchard and other fruits, cotton, onions and asparagus.
Year-round The north coast around Coffs Harbour; bananas.

Victoria

Summer November–April, peaking in February, in central northern areas around Shepparton, and also along the Murray River (Mildura, Swan Hill and, to a lesser extent, Echuca); orchard fruits, tomatoes, tobacco, grapes and soft fruits.

Queensland

Summer December–March, around Warwick, inland on the NSW border; stone and orchard fruits, grapes.
Year-round The southern central coast around Bundaberg and Childers; all kinds of fruit and vegetables.
May–December The central coast around Bowen; fruit and vegetables, especially mangoes at the end of the year.
May–November The northern coast around Ayr, Tully and Innisfail; sugar cane, bananas and tobacco.

Tasmania

Summer December–March; orchard and soft fruits, grapes.

South Australia

February–April The Barossa Valley; grapes.
Year-round The Riverland; picking, pruning and packaging citrus and soft fruits.

Western Australia

October–June The southwest; grapes and orchard fruits (February–April), plus tractor-driven grain harvesting.
March–November The west coast from Fremantle to Carnarvon; crayfish, prawn and scallop fishing and processing.
May–October The northeast around Kununurra; fruit and vegetable picking and packing.

Organized work programmes

To streamline the process of procuring a working visa, getting to Australia and orienting yourself on arrival, there are several packages aimed at working travellers. BUNAC organizes a **Work Australia** programme that can be combined with their North American programmes, with departures from London between August and December and from Los Angeles in September and October. See opposite for contact details of this and other organizations.

Contacts

ATCV (Australian Trust for Conservation Volunteers), PO Box 423, Ballarat, VIC 3353 (T 03/5333 1483 or free call 1800 032 501, F 5333 2166, W www.atcv.com.au). Volunteer work (unpaid) on conservation projects across Australia; $20 a day charged for food and accommodation.

BUNAC (British Universities North America Club). In the UK: 16 Bowling Green Lane, London EC1R 0QH (T 020/7251 3472, F 7251 0215, W www.bunac.org). In the US: PO Box 430, Southbury, CT 06488 (T 1-800/GO-BUNAC, F 203/264-0251, W www.bunac.com).

Earthwatch (T 1-800/776-0188 or 978/461-0081, F 461-2332, W www.earthwatch.org). International non profit organization, with offices in Boston (US), Oxford (UK), Melbourne (Australia) and Tokyo (Japan). Arranges placements for paying volunteers in scientific projects around the country.

Visitoz, Springbrook Farm, MS 188 via Goomeri, 4601, Queensland (T 07/4168 6106, E VISITOZSCHEME@onaustralia.com.au). This long-established organization is useful for those wanting to work on farms or in rural hospitality, with links to 700 employers right around Australia. They sort out all tax and Medicare paperwork, and give you a week or so relevant job training before packing you off to your employer. Those completing this one-week course are guaranteed work; you'll also need a driving licence.

WWOOF (Willing Workers on Organic Farms), Mount Murrindal Reserve, Buchan, VIC 3885 (T & F 03/5155 0218, E woof@ozemail.com.au). More unpaid volunteer projects for good causes. Their listings book *The Australian Farm and Cultural Experience* is available direct or from agents (eg Backpackers' Travel Centres; branches of Student Uni Travel) in the capital cities of the Australian states and some other cities in the eastern states (eg Byron Bay, Surfers Paradise, Cairns). The price ($35 single, $40 for a couple) includes work insurance.

Tax

In recent years employers have been threatened with huge fines for offering cash-in-hand labour and, as a result, it's difficult to avoid paying **income tax**, which is levied at 29 percent for earnings under about $26,000 per annum and deducted at source. To become part of the system you'll need a **tax file number** (form available at post offices or taxation offices), which is pretty easy to obtain on presentation of a passport with relevant visa. Your employer will give you a couple of weeks' grace, but not much more – if you don't have a number, after that you'll be taxed at 49 percent. Nowadays it's hard to claim a tax **rebate**, no matter how little you earn; however, it's worth a try, and possibly a visit to a tax adviser.

Directory

CHILDREN Children are well catered for in Australia, and are welcome in the bistros of hotels, with kids' menus and often a children's playroom. Nearly every park has a playground. Many attractions have reduced rates for children or families, and most motels and self-catering accommodation can provide family rooms and special rates.

ELECTRICITY Australia's electrical current is 240/250v, 50Hz AC. British appliances will work with an adaptor for the Australian three-pin plug. American and Canadian 110v appliances will also need a transformer.

EMERGENCIES Dial ☏000.

GAMBLING Australians are obsessive about gambling, though legalities vary from state to state. Even small towns have their own racetracks and there are government

Metric conversion table

1 inch (in) = 2.54cm
1 foot (ft) = 30.48cm
1 yard (yd) = 0.91m
1 mile = 1.610km
1 centimetre (cm) = 0.394in
1 metre = 39.37in
1 kilometre = 0.621 miles
1 metre (m) = 100cm
1 kilometre (km) = 1000m
1 acre = 0.4 hectares
1 hectare = 2.471 acres
1 hectare = 10,000 square metres
1 UK gallon (gal) = 4.55 litres
1 US gallon (gal) = 5.46 litres
1 litre = 0.22 UK gal
1 litre = 0.26 US gal
1 kilometre (km) = 1000m
1 gram (g) = 0.035oz
1 kilogram = 2.2lb
1 ounce (oz) = 28.57g
1 pound (lb) = 454g

TAB betting agencies everywhere; you can often bet in pubs too. Many states have huge "casinos" and clubs, open to anyone, with wall-to-wall one-armed bandits (poker machines or "pokies"); there are also big state lotteries.

LAUNDRIES Known as laundromats, these are rare outside urban centres. Hostels, motels and caravan parks will often have a laundry area with a washing machine (coin-op). Fancy hotels, of course, will do it for you.

PUBLIC TOILETS Towns and cities are very well supplied with public facilities in civic-minded Australia. They're found in parks and at council and tourist offices in country areas, and in shopping arcades, train stations and department stores in the cities. Most roadhouses offer showers as well as toilets, usually for a small payment.

SEASONS Don't forget that in the southern hemisphere the seasons are reversed. Summer lasts from November to February, winter from June to September. But of course it's not that simple: in the tropical north the important seasonal distinction is between the Wet (effectively summer) and the Dry (winter) – for more on their significance to travellers, (see p.xiii).

STUDENT CARDS These are well worth having (if you're eligible) for discounts on travel, tours, museum entry, etc. Backpackers of any age or status who can produce a YHA or VIP membership card (see p.48) are entitled to many of these discounts.

TAX A Goods and Services Tax (GST) of ten percent was introduced in 2000, and caused a general across-the-board price hike. Visitors can claim GST refunds for goods purchased in Australia as they clear customs, providing individual reciepts exceed $300 and the claim is made within thirty days of purchase.

TIME ZONES Australia has three time zones: Eastern Standard Time (TAS, VIC, NSW, QLD), Central Standard Time (SA, NT) and Western Standard Time (WA). Eastern Standard Time is ten hours ahead of GMT (Greenwich Mean Time) and fifteen hours ahead of US Eastern Time. (When it's 10pm in Sydney, it's noon in London, 7am in New York and 4am in Los Angeles – but don't forget daylight saving, which can affect this by one hour either way.) Central Standard Time is thirty minutes behind Eastern Standard, and Western Standard two hours behind Eastern. Daylight saving (Oct–March) is adopted everywhere except QLD, NT and WA; clocks are put forward one hour.

TIPS Tipping is not customary in Australia, and cab drivers and bar staff don't generally expect anything. In fact, cab drivers often round the fare down rather than bother with change. In cafés and restaurants you might leave the change – only very fancy establishments expect ten percent.

WEIGHTS AND MEASURES Australia has been fully metric since the early 1970s and is thoroughly adapted to kilometres, kilograms, litres and degrees Celsius. Shoe sizes are unique to Australia, while dress sizes are the same as in the UK (US 8 is equivalent to Australian 10). See the conversion table opposite.

guide

guide

Sydney and around

CHAPTER 1 # Highlights

✳ **Manly Ferry** – The ferry trip out to Manly, with its unbeatable views of the harbour, is a must. **p.106**.

✳ **Opera House performance** – Admire the stunning exterior of this Australian icon, or better still, take in a performance. **p.109**.

✳ **Climbing Sydney Harbour Bridge** – Climb the famous coathanger for great harbour views, or simply walk across and save $100. **p.110**.

✳ **Oxford Street** – Crammed with bars, clubs and restaurants, a night out on Oxford Street is essential. **p.137**.

✳ **Paddington Market** – Visit Paddington, with its gorgeous colonial-style houses, on Saturday, when the famous market is in full swing. **p.138**.

✳ **Bondi Beach** – One of the best-known beaches in the world, big, brash Bondi is synonymous with Australian beach culture. **p.148**.

✳ **Mardi Gras** – The biggest celebration of gay and lesbian culture in the world. **p.175**.

✳ **Cruising on the Hawkesbury River** – The best way to explore the pretty Hawkesbury River is to take a leisurely cruise. **p.195**.

✳ **Hunter Valley wineries** – One of Australia's most famous wine-growing regions. **p.208**.

✳ **Blue Mountains** – The World Heritage-listed Blue Mountains make a great weekend break from Sydney. **p.213**.

Sydney and around

Flying into Sydney provides the first snapshot of Australia for most overseas visitors: toy-sized images of the Harbour Bridge and the Opera House, tilting in a glittering expanse of blue water. The Aussie city par excellence, Sydney stands head and shoulders above any other in Australia. Taken together with its surrounds, it's in many ways a microcosm of Australia as a whole – if only in its ability to defy your expectations and prejudices as often as it confirms them. A thrusting, high-rise business centre, a high-profile gay community and inner-city deprivation of unexpected harshness are as much part of the scene as the beaches, the bodies and the sparkling harbour. The sophistication, cosmopolitan population and exuberant nightlife of Sydney are a long way from the Outback, and yet Sydney has the highest Aboriginal population of any Australian city.

The area around – everything in this chapter is within day-trip distance – offers a taste of virtually everything you'll find in the rest of the country, with the exception of desert. There are magnificent **national parks** and native wildlife – Ku-Ring-Gai Chase and Royal being the best known of the parks, each a mere hour's drive from the centre of town – and beyond them stretch endless ocean **beaches**, great for surfers, and more enclosed waters for safer swimming and sailing. Inland the **Blue Mountains**, with three more national parks, offer isolated bushwalking and scenic viewpoints. On the way are historic colonial towns that were among the earliest foundations in the country – Sydney itself, of course, was the very first. The commercial and industrial heart of the state of New South Wales, especially the central coastal region, is bordered by **Wollongong** in the south and **Newcastle** in the north. Both are synonymous with coal and steel, but the smokestack industries that supported them for decades are now in severe decline. This is far from an industrial wasteland, though: the heart of the coal-mining country is the **Hunter**

Accommodation price codes

All the accommodation listed in this book has been categorized into one of eight price bands, as set out below. The rates quoted represent the cheapest available double or twin room in high season – except for category ❶, which indicates per-person rates for a dorm bed, and the categories given for units, cabins and vans, which represent the daily charge for the whole unit.

❶ Under $20	❸ $35–50	❺ $70–90	❼ $115–150
❷ $20–35	❹ $50–70	❻ $90–115	❽ $150 upwards

For more accommodation details, see pp.46–49.

Valley, northwest of Newcastle, but to visit it you'd never guess, because this is also Australia's oldest and arguably its best-known wine-growing region.

Sydney

The 2000 Olympics were a coming-of-age ceremony for **SYDNEY**. The impact on the city was all-embracing, with fifty years' worth of development compressed into four years under the pressure of intense international scrutiny. Transport infrastructure was greatly improved and a rash of luxury hotels and waterside apartments added themselves to the skyline. The City of Sydney Council spent $200 million to improve and beautify the city streets, public squares and parks, with everything from sculpture walks to smartly designed new street furniture, and licensing laws changed too, creating a European-style bar culture. Sydney now has all the vigour of a world-class city, with the reputation of its restaurants in particular turning the lingering cultural sneers to swoons. It seems to have the best of both worlds – twenty minutes from Circular Quay by bus, the high-rise office buildings and skyscrapers give way to colourful inner-city suburbs where you can get an eyeful of sky and watch the lemons ripening above the sidewalk, while to the centre's north and south are corridors of largely intact bushland where many have built their dream homes. In the summer the city's hot offices are abandoned for the remarkably unspoilt beaches strung around the eastern and northern suburbs.

It's also as beautiful a city as any in the world, with a **setting** that perhaps only Rio de Janeiro can rival: the water is what makes it so special, and no introduction to Sydney would be complete without paying tribute to one of the world's great **harbours**. Port Jackson is a sunken valley which twists inland to meet the fresh water of the Parramatta River; in the process it washes into a hundred coves and bays, winds around rocky points, flows past the small harbour islands, slips under bridges and laps at the foot of the Opera House. If Sydney is seen at its gleaming best from the deck of a harbour ferry, especially at weekends when the harbour's jagged jaws fill with a flotilla of small vessels, racing yachts and cabin cruisers, it's seen at its most varied in its lively neighbourhoods. Getting away from the city centre and exploring them is an essential part of Sydney's pleasures.

It might seem surprising that Sydney is not Australia's capital: the creation of Canberra in 1927 – intended to stem the intense rivalry between Sydney and Melbourne – has not affected the view of many Sydneysiders that their city remains the *true* capital of Australia, and certainly in many ways it feels like it. The city has a tangible sense of history: the old stone walls and well-worn steps in the backstreets around The Rocks are an evocative reminder that Sydney has more than two hundred years of white history behind it.

Some history

The early history of Sydney is very much the history of white Australia, right from its founding as a penal colony, amid brutality, deprivation and despair. In January 1788 the **First Fleet**, carrying over a thousand people, 736 of them convicts, arrived at **Botany Bay** expecting the "fine meadows" that Captain James Cook had described eight years earlier. In fact what greeted them was mostly swamp, scrub and sand dunes: a desolate sight even for sea-weary eyes. An unsuccessful scouting expedition prompted Commander Arthur Phillip to move the fleet a few kilometres north, to the well-wooded Port Jackson, where a stream of fresh water was found. Based around the less than satisfactory Tank Stream, the settlement was named **Sydney Cove** after Viscount Sydney, then Secretary of State in Great Britain. In the first three years of settlement, the new colony nearly starved to death several times; the land around Sydney Cove proved to be barren. When supply ships did arrive, they inevitably came with hundreds more convicts to further burden the colony. It was not until 1790, when land was successfully farmed further west at **Parramatta**, that the hunger began to abate. Measure this suffering with that of the **Eora Aborigines**: their land had been invaded, their people virtually wiped out by smallpox, and now they were stricken by hunger as the settlers shot at their game – and even, as they moved further inland, at the Eora themselves.

By the early 1800s Sydney had become a stable colony and busy trading post. Army officers in charge of the colony, exploiting their access to free land and cheap labour, became rich farm-owners and virtually established a currency based on rum. The **military**, known as the New South Wales Corps (or more familiarly as "the rum corps"), became the supreme political force in the colony in 1809, even overthrowing the governor (mutiny-plagued Captain Bligh himself). This was the last straw for the government back home, and the rebellious officers were finally brought to heel when the reformist Governor **Lachlan Macquarie** arrived from England with forces of his own. He liberalized conditions, supported the prisoners' right to become citizens after they had served their time, and appointed several to public offices.

By the 1840s the transportation of convicts to New South Wales had ended, the explorers Lawson and Blaxland had found a way through the Blue Mountains to the Western Plains and gold had been struck in Bathurst. The population soared as free settlers arrived in ever-increasing numbers. In the Victorian era Sydney's population became even more starkly divided into the **haves** and the **have-nots**: while the poor lived in slums where disease, crime, prostitution and alcoholism were rife, the genteel classes – self-consciously replicating life in the mother country – took tea on their verandahs and erected grandiloquent monuments such as the Town Hall, the Strand Arcade and the Queen Victoria Building in homage to English architecture of the time. An outbreak of the plague in The Rocks at the beginning of the twentieth century made wholesale slum clearances inevitable, and with the demolitions came a change in attitudes. Strict new vice laws meant the end of the bad old days of backstreet knifings, drunken taverns and makeshift brothels.

Over the next few decades, Sydney settled into comfortable suburban living. The metropolis sprawled westwards, creating a flat, unremarkable city with no real centre, an appropriate symbol for the era of shorts and knee socks and the stereotypical, barbecue-loving Bruce and Sheila – an international image which still plagues Australians. Sydney has come a long way since the parochialism of the 1950s, however: the cultural clichés of cold tinnies of beer and meat pies with sauce have at last been tossed out, giving way to a city confident in itself and its culinary attractions too. Skyscrapers at the city's centre have rocketed heavenward and constructions such as the Opera House and Renzo Piano's Aurora Place reflect the city's dynamism. Today, Sydney's citizens don't look inward – or even to England. Thousands of immigrants from around the globe have given Sydney a truly cosmopolitan air and it's a city as thrilling and alive as any.

Arrival and information

The classic way to **arrive** in Sydney is, of course, by ship, cruising in under the great coathanger of the Harbour Bridge to tie up at the docks alongside Circular Quay. Unfortunately you're not likely to be doing that, and the reality of the functional airport, bus and train stations is a good deal less romantic.

By air

Sydney's **Kingsford Smith Airport**, commonly referred to as "Mascot" after the suburb where it's located, near Botany Bay, is barely 8km south of the city (international flight times ☏13 1223). Domestic and international terminals are on opposite sides of the airport, linked by the free Long-Term Car Park Shuttle Bus (every 30min), or you can take the Airport Express bus for $2.50; see box opposite for details of this and other **bus services** into the city.

Travellers can also now take a train right into the city centre: the new $365-million **Airport Link** underground railway, which opened in May 2000, connects the airport to the City Circle train line in just over ten minutes (every 15min; one-way $9, return $12). However, the train has not been as popular as expected: as a suburban commuter service it can be crowded at peak hours, there is no dedicated space for luggage and it is more expensive than Airport Express buses, which will drop you off near your hotel. If there are three or

Airport buses

State Transit
Airport Express (☎13 1500) buses (green-and-yellow) link the domestic and international terminals ($2.50), and shuttle to and from the city centre, and Kings Cross and Glebe on three different routes, picking up and setting down at various stops. Fares on all routes are $7 one-way and $12 return (return valid for two months). The #300 runs to Circular Quay via Central Station and George Street (daily 5am–11pm; every 10min); the #350 runs to Central Station and Kings Cross (daily 5am–11pm; every 20min); and the #352 runs to Glebe (daily 7am–9pm; every 30min). Tickets can be bought on board and at the **Sydney Visitor Centre** in the international terminal (see p.86), where you can also buy tourist bus passes – the Sydney Pass (see p.91) includes return airport–city transfer.

State Transit also has some ordinary commuter routes serving the airport that may be useful: the only daily service is the Metroline #400 which goes frequently to Bondi Junction via Maroubra and Randwick in one direction, and to Burwood in the other; the #100 route heads out to the northern beach suburb of Dee Why via the city, North Sydney, Neutral Bay and Cremorne Junction (Mon–Fri only 6.25am–6.30pm). Tickets on these routes cost a maximum of $4.40; regular weekly travel passes can be used but these cannot be purchased at the airport.

Shuttle services – Sydney area
Eastern Suburbs Airport Shuttle (☎0500/88113 to book a pick-up from the airport or accommodation). Minibus service operating from the airport (quick call out service) to and from the eastern beaches – Bondi, Coogee, Randwick, Clovelly and Bronte – and dropping off at all hostels, motels and hotels ($10 one-way).

Kingsford Smith Transport/Sydney Airporter (☎02/9667 3221 or 9667 0663 to book a pick-up from your accommodation). This private bus service will drop you right at the door of your hotel or hostel in the area bounded by Kings Cross and Darling Harbour. Service leaves when the bus is full ($7 one-way, $11 return).

Northern Beaches Airport Shuttle (☎02/9913 9912 or 0414 66 626, ℱ9970 5248). Minibus service from the international and domestic terminals to the northern beaches – including Manly, Whale Beach and Palm Beach – dropping off at your chosen accommodation. You must book in advance giving the day, time and flight and they will designate a waiting point. Manly $27.50, Palm Beach $44 (cheaper rates for couples and groups).

Coach services – central coast and south coast
Central Coast Airbus (☎02/4332 8655). Scheduled #747 service that runs to the Central Coast (Terrigal and Bateau Bay; 2hr 15min–2hr 30min; $20) via the northern suburbs, taking in Pymble, Turramurra, Hornsby, Asquith, Mount Colah, Mount Ku-Ring-Gai and Berowra (Mon–Fri 8am, 9.30am, 11.30am, 2.30pm, 3pm, 3.30pm, 4pm, 4.45pm & 5.45pm, Sat & Sun 9.30am & 4pm).

Premier Motor Service (☎13 3410). Departs daily at 9.45am & 3.30pm, plus Mon–Fri at 7.45am from the domestic terminal, 15min later from the international terminal, to south coast towns as far as Bega ($44), the 9.45am and 3.30pm service continuing on to Eden ($49).

more of you it can be cheaper to share a **taxi**: a taxi from the airport to the city centre or Kings Cross costs $25–30, depending on traffic.

Bureau de change offices at both terminals are open daily from 5am until last arrival with rates comparable to major banks. On the ground floor (arrivals) of the international terminal, the **Sydney Visitor Centre** (daily 5am until last arrival; ☎02/9667 6050) can arrange car rental and onward travel – it's licensed to sell train and bus tickets – and **book hotels** (but not hostels) anywhere in Sydney and NSW free of charge (accommodation bookings here are at stand-by rates). Most hostels do, however, advertise on an adjacent notice board, the "Backpacker Accommodation Directory"; there's a freephone line for reservations, and many of them will refund your bus fare.

By train and bus

All local and interstate **trains** arrive at **Central Station** on Eddy Avenue, just south of the city centre. From here, and neighbouring **Railway Square** you can hop onto nearly every major bus route, and from within Central Station you can take a CityRail train to any city or suburban station. See "City transport" opposite for more details.

All **buses** to Sydney arrive and depart from Eddy Avenue and Pitt Street, bordering Central Station. The area is well set up with decent cafés, a 24-hour police station and a huge YHA hostel (see p.98), as well as the **Sydney Coach Terminal** (daily 6am–10pm), which also has luggage lockers ($6–11 per 24hr, depending on size). The **Traveller's Information Service** (☎02/9281 9366) in the coach terminal can make hotel **accommodation bookings** at stand-by rates while a range of hostels advertise on an adjacent notice board with free phones for direct reservations; many of them will also provide free pick-ups (usually from Bay 14). You can purchase coach tickets and passes from the Information Service as well as Sydney Passes (see p.91), and arrange harbour cruises and other tours. Greyhound Pioneer and McCafferty's also have separate ticket offices/departure lounges on Eddy Avenue.

Information

There's no shortage of places offering **information** about Sydney. The Sydney Visitor Centre at the international airport terminal (see above) offers the most comprehensive service, with free maps and brochures – including *Sydney: The Official Guide* which is packed with useful maps, and the *Hip Guide to Sydney* – on-the-spot accommodation reservations at stand-by rates and transport bookings for Sydney and the rest of New South Wales. The main central tourist office is the **Sydney Visitor Centre** in The Rocks at 106 George St near Circular Quay (daily 9am–6pm; ☎02/9255 1788 or free call 1800 067 676, ⓦwww.sydneyvisitorcentre.com; also see p.112), offering a similar range of literature; they also have a self-service budget accommodation booking board with free phones directly linked to the listed hotels. Tourism NSW run the **City Host Programme** with three green-coloured information kiosks at Circular Quay, Martin Place and Town Hall (all daily 9am–5pm; no phone) providing brochures, maps and information. Otherwise, tourist information is supplied by the **Darling Harbour Visitor Information Centre** (see p.127), or the tourist office at Manly (see p.152).

Several free monthly **listings magazines** are worth picking up at tourist offices: the weekly *Where Magazine* is probably the best for general information, and *This Month in Sydney* is also worth consulting. The City of Sydney Council distributes a basic photocopied guide, *City Life*, every Wednesday to all visitor centres and infomation booths, and also publishes the bimonthly *Official Sydney Events Guide* (free from the Town Hall, $3.25 from newsagents); similar information is available on their website, Ⓦwww.cityofsydney.nsw .gov.au. *TNT Magazine* is the best of an array of publications aimed at **backpackers**, giving the lowdown on Sydney on the cheap, while **hostel notice boards** themselves act as an informal network, advertising everything from cars and international plane tickets to backpacks, camping gear and rides to other cities.

City transport

Sydney's public transport network is reasonably good, though the system relies heavily on buses and traffic jams can be a problem. There are buses, trains, ferries, a light rail system and the city monorail to choose from, plus plenty of licensed taxis. Trains stop running around midnight, as do most regular buses, though several services towards the eastern and northern beaches, such as the #380 to Bondi Beach, the #372 and #373 to Coogee and the #151 to Manly, run through the night. Otherwise a pretty good network of **Nightride buses** follow the train routes to the suburbs, departing from Town Hall Station (outside the Sydney Electricity Building on George St) and stopping at train stations (where taxi ranks fine-tune the getting home process). You can use return train tickets, Railpasses and Travelpasses on board the nightbuses or else buy a ticket from the driver. If you're staying for more than a few days, a weekly **Travelpass** is a worthwhile investment (see box on p.91). For public transport information, routes and timetables call ☏13 1500 (daily 6am–10pm; Ⓦwww.131500.com.au).

Buses

Within the central area, **buses**, hailed from yellow-signed bus stops, are much the most convenient and widespread mode of transport, and in general they cover more of the city than the trains. With few exceptions buses radiate from the centre: major interchanges are located at Railway Square near Central Station, especially for the southwest routes; at Circular Quay for a range of routes; from York and Carrington streets outside Wynyard Station for the North Shore; and Bondi Junction Station for the eastern suburbs and beaches. **Tickets**, costing from $1.40 for up to two sections, $2.50 (the most typical fare) for up to five sections and rising to $4.40 according to the distance travelled, can be bought on board from the driver. If you're going to use the bus network more than occasionally, substantial discounts are available with TravelTen tickets and other travel passes (see box on pp.91–92). These must be validated in the green ticket reader by the front door. You can get bus **information**, **timetables** and **passes** from a few handy booths: at Carrington Street, Wynyard (Mon–Fri 8am–6pm, Sat 9am–2pm); at Circular Quay on the corner of Loftus and Alfred streets (Mon–Fri 8am–8pm, Sat & Sun 9am–6pm); at the Queen Victoria Building on York Street (Mon–Fri 8am–6pm, Sat 9am–2pm); at Bondi Junction bus interchange (Mon–Fri 7.15am–5pm, Sat 7.30am–2.30pm); and at Manly Wharf (Mon–Fri 7am–6pm, Sat & Sun 8am–4pm).

Trains

Trains, operated by **CityRail** (see map overleaf), will get you where you're going faster than buses, especially at rush hour and when heading out to the

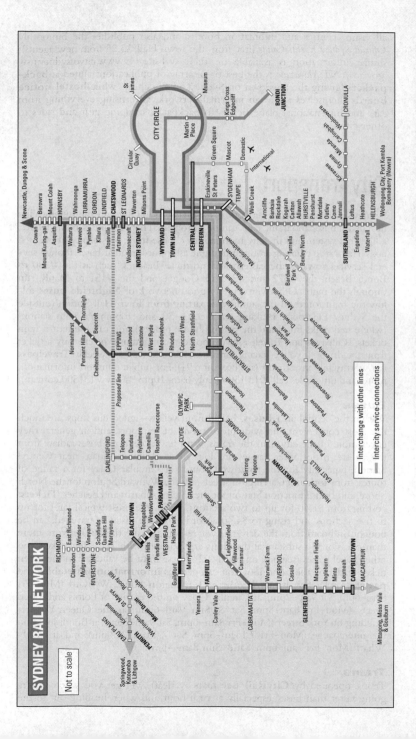

SYDNEY RAIL NETWORK

Not to scale

Interchange with other lines

Intercity service connections

Proposed line

suburbs, but you need to transfer to a bus or ferry to get to most harbourside or beach destinations. There are six train lines, each of which stops at Central and Town Hall stations. The underground City Loop is very useful, linking Central Station, Town Hall, Wynyard, Circular Quay, St James and Museum, and allowing you to connect with the rail system from almost anywhere in the centre. The only other underground route, running from Bondi Junction, through Edgecliff, Kings Cross, Martin Place, Town Hall, Central and Redfern, then overland to the beach at Cronulla, is handy for tourists. Trains run from around 5am to midnight, with **tickets** starting at around $2.20 on the City Loop and for short hops; you can save money by buying off-peak returns after 9am and all weekend.

Automatic ticket machines (which give change) and barriers (if you have a magnetic ticket insert it, otherwise show your ticket at the gate) have been introduced just about everywhere. No excuses will be accepted if you don't have a ticket or have overridden your fare, with fines of $150. All platforms are painted with designated "nightsafe" waiting areas and all but two or three train carriages are closed after about 8pm, enforcing a cattle-like safety in numbers. Security guards also patrol trains at night. At other times, if the train is deserted, sit in the carriage nearest the guard, marked by a blue light.

Ferries

Sydney's distinctive green-and-yellow **ferries** are the fastest means of transport from Circular Quay to the North Shore, and indeed to most places around the harbour. Even if you don't want to go anywhere, a ferry ride is a must, for it gives you a chance to get out on the water and see the city from the harbour. There's also a speedy **hydrofoil**, the JetCat, which gets you to Manly in half the time, but with less charm.

There are ferries going off in various directions from the wharves at Circular Quay (see map overleaf); cruises depart from Wharf 6. The last ferry service from Circular Quay to Manly is at 7pm after which time the faster JetCats operate until midnight, 11pm on Saturdays. Other ferry routes, such as those to Parramatta and Pyrmont Bay, also operate only until early evening, while ferries to locations including Neutral Bay and Balmain continue to around 11.30pm. Except for the Manly ferry, services on Sunday are greatly reduced and often finish earlier. Timetables for each route are available at Circular Quay.

One-way **fares** are $4 ($5 for the Manly Ferry); return fares are doubled. The pricier JetCat to Manly and RiverCat to Parramatta are $6.10. Once again, the various Travelpasses and FerryTen tickets can be a good deal – see box on pp.91–92 for details. A private company, Hegarty's Ferries (☏ 02/9206 1167), also operates its own blue-and-white boats to Milsons Point, Lavender Bay and McMahons Point from Wharf 6 ($3; ten trips $23).

Monorail and Light Rail

The **Metro Monorail** (☏ 02/9552 2288, ⓦ www.metromonorail.com.au) is essentially a tourist shuttle designed to loop around Darling Harbour every 3–5 minutes, connecting it with the city centre. Thundering along tracks set above the older city streets, the monster rail – as many locals know it – doesn't exactly blend in with its surroundings. Still, the elevated view of the city, particularly from Pyrmont Bridge, makes it worth investing $3.50 (day-pass $7) and ten minutes to do the whole circuit with its seven stops (see "Central Sydney" map on pp.96–97; Mon–Wed 7am–10pm, Thurs–Sat 7am–midnight, Sun 8am–10pm).

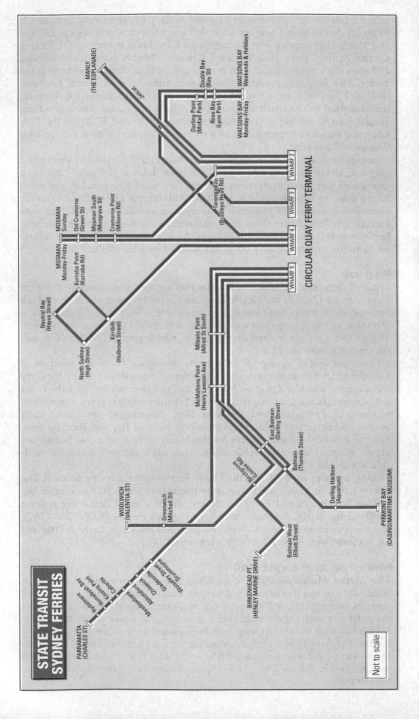

STATE TRANSIT
SYDNEY FERRIES

MANLY
(THE ESPLANADE)

Jetcat

Darling Point
(McKell Park)

Rose Bay
(Lyne Park)

Double Bay
(Bay St)

WATSONS BAY
Weekends & Holidays

WATSONS BAY
Monday-Friday

WHARF 2

WHARF 3

WHARF 4

WHARF 5

CIRCULAR QUAY FERRY TERMINAL

Taronga Zoo
(Bradleys Head Rd)

MOSMAN
Sunday

Old Cremorne
(Green St)

Mosman South
(Musgrave St)

Cremorne Point
(Milsons Rd)

MOSMAN
Monday-Friday

Kurraba Point
(Kurraba Rd)

Neutral Bay
(Hayes Street)

North Sydney
(High Street)

Kirribilli
(Holbrook Street)

Milsons Point
(Alfred St South)

McMahons Point
(Henry Lawson Ave)

East Balmain
(Darling Street)

Balmain
(Thames Street)

Birchgrove
(Louisa Rd)

Darling Harbour
(Aquarium)

PYRMONT BAY
(CASINO/MARITIME MUSEUM)

WOOLWICH
(VALENTIA ST)

Greenwich
(Mitchell St)

Balmain West
(Elliott Street)

BIRKENHEAD PT
(HENLEY MARINE DRIVE)

PARRAMATTA
(CHARLES ST)

Rydalmere

Meadowbank

Homebush Bay

Abbotsford

Kissing Point

Chiswick

Cabarita

Gladesville

Wolseley Street

Drummoyne

Not to scale

Travel passes

In addition to single-journey tickets, there's a vast array of **travel passes** available. The most useful for visitors are outlined below; for more **information** on the full range of tickets and timetables, phone the Bus, Train, Ferry InfoLine or check out their website (daily 6am–10pm; ⊕13 1500, ⓦwww.131500.com.au).

Passes are sold at most **newsagents** and at **train stations**; the more tourist-oriented Sydney Passes and Sydney Explorer Passes can be bought on board the Explorer buses, at the airport (from the NSW Travel Centre and the STA booth in the international terminal and from State Transit ground staff in the domestic), at State Transit Info booths, from the Sydney Visitor Centre in The Rocks (see p.112) and at some Countrylink offices as well as at train stations.

Tourist passes

Sydney Explorer Pass (one-day $30, child $15, family pass $75) comes with a map and description of the sights, and includes free travel on any State Transit bus within the same zones as the Explorer routes. The red **Sydney Explorer** (daily 8.15am–5.25pm; every 15min) takes in all the important sights in the city and inner suburbs, and you can hop on and off at any of the 24 stops. The blue **Bondi & Bay Explorer** (daily 9.15am–4.20pm; every 25min) covers the waterside eastern suburbs; nineteen stops en route include Kings Cross, Paddington, Double Bay, Vaucluse and the beaches of Bondi, Bronte, Clovelly and Coogee. A two-day **Twin Ticket** ($55, child $30, family $140) allows you to use both bus services over two days in a seven-day period.

Sydney Pass (three-, five- or seven-days' travel within a seven-day period for $85, $115 and $135 respectively; children $45/$60/$70, family rates $215/$290/$340) is valid for all buses and ferries including the above Explorer services, the ferry and JetCat to Manly, the RiverCat to Parramatta and a return trip to the airport valid for two months with the Airport Express bus (make sure you buy it at the airport). It also includes four narrated harbour cruises, one of them in the evening, and travel on trains within a central area.

Buses, trains and ferries

Travelpasses allow unlimited use of buses, trains and ferries and can begin on any day of the week. Most useful are the **Red Travelpass** ($28 a week), valid for the city and inner suburbs, and inner harbour ferries (not the Manly Ferry or the RiverCat beyond Meadowbank); and the **Green Travelpass** ($36), which allows use of all ferries – except JetCats before 7pm. Passes covering a wider area cost between $39 and $56 a week, and monthly passes are also available.

DayRover tickets ($17.60 off-peak to $22 peak) are also available for unlimited travel on all services offered by CityRail and State Transit.

Buses and trains

Cityhopper tickets give one-day's unlimited train and bus travel in the area between Central Station, Darling Harbour, Redfern, Moore Park, Kings Cross and North Sydney for $8; the off-peak fare is $6.20 (Mon–Fri after 9am and any time at weekends and public holidays).

Buses and ferries

DayPass provides all-day bus and ferry transport as far afield as you like for $13. The **Blue Travelpass** ($25 a week) gives you unlimited travel on buses in the inner-city area and on inner-harbour ferries but cannot be used for Manly or beyond Meadowbank; the **Orange Travelpass** ($31 a week), which gets you further on the buses and is valid on all ferries; and the **Pittwater Travelpass** ($44 a week) which

continued overleaf

Buses and ferries continued

gives unlimited travel on all buses and ferries. These travelpasses start with first use rather than on the day of purchase.

Buses

TravelTen tickets represent a 45 percent saving over single fares by buying ten trips at once; they can be used over a space of time and for more than one person. The blue version ($10.40) lets you ride up to two sections per validation (it's one section from Central Station to Circular Quay, for example), while a Red TravelTen ($22) allows you to travel up to five sections per ride, and there are three other colour-coded TravelTens for greater distances.

Two Zone Travelpass comes in a bus-only variant for $25 a week for adjacent bus zones.

BusTripper offers a day's unlimited bus travel for $9.

Ferries

FerryTen tickets, valid for ten single trips, start at $25.30 for Inner Harbour Services, go up to $37.40 for the Manly Ferry, and peak at $52 for the JetCat services.

Trains

Rail Weekly tickets allow unlimited travel between any two nominated stations and those in between, with savings of about twenty percent on the price of five return trips.

Metro Light Rail (T02/8584 5288, Wwww.metrolightrail.com.au) runs from Central Station to the Pyrmont peninsula (see "Central Sydney" map on pp.96–97) and on to Lilyfield in the inner west. There are fourteen stops on the route, which links Central Station with Chinatown, Darling Harbour, Star City Casino, the fish markets at Pyrmont, Wentworth Park's greyhound racecourse, Glebe (with stops near Pyrmont Bridge Road, at Jubilee Park and Rozelle Bay by Bicentennial Park) and Lilyfield, not far from Darling Street, Rozelle. The air-conditioned light rail vehicles can carry two hundred passengers, and are fully accessible to disabled commuters. The service operates 24 hours to the casino (daily: 6am–midnight every 10–15min; midnight–6am every 30min) with reduced hours for stops beyond to Lilyfield (Mon–Thurs & Sun 6am–11pm, Fri & Sat 6am–midnight; every 10–15min). Tickets can be purchased at vending machines by the stops and range from $2.20 to $4.40 (day-pass $7, weekly pass $18). You can buy a TramLink ticket from any CityRail station and this combines a rail ticket to Central Station with an MLR ticket; price depends on which train station you buy your ticket from.

Taxis

Taxis are vacant if the rooftop light is on, though they are notoriously difficult to find at 3pm, when the shifts change over. The four major city cab ranks are outside the *Regent Hotel* on George Street, The Rocks; on Park Street outside Woolworths, opposite the Town Hall; outside David Jones department store on Market Street; and at the Pitt Street entrance to Central Station. Drivers never expect a tip but often need directions – try to have some idea of where you're going. Check the correct tariff rate is displayed: tariff 2 (10pm–6am) is twenty percent more than tariff 1 (6am–10pm). See "Listings", p.190, for phone numbers.

Accommodation

There are a tremendous number of places to stay in Sydney, and fierce competition helps keep prices down. Finding somewhere to stay is usually only a problem just before Christmas and throughout January, and in late February/early March during the Gay Mardi Gras: at these times you'll definitely need to **book ahead**. All types of accommodation offer a (sometimes substantial) discount for **weekly bookings**, and may also cut prices considerably during the **low season** (from autumn to spring, school holidays excepted); it's always worth asking.

The larger **international hotels** in The Rocks and the Central Business District (CBD) charge around $150–220 for a double room but if you head downtown to the area around Central Station you can find a four-star for $140; if you have a car even the five-star hotels seem to charge around $15 a day for parking. The least expensive hotels in the city centre, often above **pubs** and sharing bathrooms, start from $95. Rates in Kings Cross are much cheaper than in the city centre, with rooms in **private hotels** available for $55 (sharing a bathroom) and in three- or four-star hotels at around $110–130. **Motels**, such as ones we've listed in Glebe, Surry Hills and Bondi, charge $90–100. There is now an increasing number of mid-range "boutique" hotels and **guesthouses**, mostly away from the centre, which tend to be smaller, more characterful places to stay, charging upwards of $100. **Serviced holiday apartments** can be very good value for a group, but are generally heavily booked.

Despite the number of **hostels** all over Sydney and the rivalry between them, standards are very variable and, in Kings Cross especially, can be very low. As the scene changes rapidly, it's worth getting the latest news from other travellers. Rates (which include bedding) are pretty standard – in summer about $20–25 for a dorm bed ($22–26 all year at YHAs) and $50 for a double (around $65 for an en suite), with rates dropping to around $18–20 for a dorm bed in winter. If you're staying longer, weekly rates can often save you the cost of a night's stay. All hostels have a laundry, kitchen and common room with TV unless stated otherwise. Office hours are generally restricted, so it's best to call first and arrange an arrival time.

If you're staying for any length of time, you might want to consider a **flatshare** as an alternative to hotels or hostels. The best place to look is in Saturday's real-estate section of the *Sydney Morning Herald* or on café notice boards, especially in King Street in Newtown, Glebe Pt Road in Glebe and Hall Street in Bondi; the window of the Health Food store at 29 Hall St is crammed with house-share notices aimed at travellers. The average room price in a shared house in these areas is $150 a week (rent is usually two weeks in advance, plus a deposit of four weeks' rent and you'll need to provide at least your own bedroom furniture and linen). **Homeshare Flatmates**, 127 York St, City (℡02/9261 3146, ⓦwww.homeshare.com.au), is a reliable agency that can help you find a flatshare for a $80 fee. It's now become easier to rent regular (as opposed to holiday) **apartments** on a short-term basis: the minimum lease is usually six months, but a two- or three-month lease can usually be secured by offering the real estate agent the total rent up front. Note, however, that furnished places are not the norm.

There are no **campsites** or caravan parks close to the centre; the nearest are in the suburbs of Rockdale, 13km south of the city, and North Ryde, 14km northwest (see box overleaf).

Campsites around Sydney

It's possible to camp in one of several well-equipped caravan parks around Sydney. The three listed below are the closest sites to the centre. Camping will cost around $20 for two people in an unpowered site.

Lakeside Caravan Park, Lake Park Rd, Narrabeen, 26km north of the city (ⓣ02/9913 7845, ⓕ9970 6385, ⓦwww.sydneylakeside.com.au). Bus #190 or #L90 from Wynyard and then a 10min walk. Great spot by Narrabeen Lakes on Sydney's northern beaches. Free gas BBQs, camp kitchen and a nearby shop. Minimum two-night stay in cabins. Cabins ⑥

Lane Cove River Caravan Park, Plassey Rd, North Ryde, 14km northwest of the city (ⓣ02/9888 9133, ⓕ9888 9322, ⓦwww.caravanparksnsw.com/parks/lanecove). Wonderful bush location beside Lane Cove National Park, right on the river, in Sydney's northern suburbs. Facilities include a bush kitchen (with fridge) and swimming pool. Train to Chatswood then bus #550 or #551. En-suite cabins ⑥

Sheralee Tourist Caravan Park, 88 Bryant St, Rockdale, 13km south of the city (ⓣ02/9567 7161). Train to Rockdale station, then a 10min walk. Small park with camp kitchen; on-site vans ❸

Where to stay

The listings below are arranged by area. For short visits, you'll want to stay in the **city centre** or the immediate vicinity: The Rocks, the CBD and Darling Harbour have the greatest concentration of expensive hotels while the area around Central Station and Chinatown, known as Haymarket, has a glut of cheaper, more downmarket places. **Kings Cross** is still very much the travellers' centre, with more backpackers' accommodation and cheaper hotels than elsewhere – it's a ten-minute walk from the city, has its own train station, and makes a convenient base if you don't mind the sleaze and the all-night partying. The adjacent suburbs of **Woolloomooloo**, **Potts Point** and **Elizabeth Bay** move gradually upmarket, and what little you lose in terms of accessibility, you gain in peace and quiet. To the west, **Glebe** is another slice of prime backpackers' territory, featuring a large YHA hostel, as well as several other backpackers' places and a number of small guesthouses.

If you're staying longer, consider somewhere further out, on the **North Shore**, where you'll get more for your money and more of a feel for Sydney as a city. **Kirribilli**, **Neutral Bay** or **Cremorne Point** offer some serenity and maybe an affordable water view as well: they're only a short ferry ride from Circular Quay. Large old private hotels out this way are increasingly being converted into hostels, particularly on Carabella Street in Kirribilli. **Manly**, tucked away in the northeast corner of the harbour, is a seaside suburb with ocean and harbour beaches, just thirty minutes from Circular Quay by ferry. The **eastern suburbs** also have a couple of great beachside locations close to the city – **Bondi** and **Coogee Beach** – both with concentrations of hostels and budget accommodation.

The CBD and The Rocks

Grand Hotel, 30 Hunter St, City (ⓣ02/9232 3755, ⓕ9232 1073, ⓦwww.grandhotel.com.au). Close to Wynyard Station, with several floors of accommodation above one of Sydney's oldest, but not necessarily nicest, pubs (open until 3am Thurs–Sat). Rooms, sharing bathrooms, are fine – all brightly painted, with colourful bed covers, lamps, fridge, TV, fan, heating and ceiling fans. ⑥

Hotel Intercontinental, 117 Macquarie St (ⓣ02/9230 0200, ⓕ9240 1240, ⓦwww.interconti.com). The old sandstone Treasury building forms the lower floors of this 31-storey five-star property, with stunning views of the Botanic Gardens, Opera House and harbour. The café/bar is the perfect place for everything from champagne to afternoon tea, and there are three other eateries, a cigar divan, and a pool and gym on the top floor. All this comes at a price, of course: $299 city view and $343 harbour view. Rates include breakfast and parking. ⑧

Lord Nelson Brewery Hotel, cnr Argyle and Kent streets, The Rocks (☎02/9251 4044, ⓕ9251 1532, ⓦwww.lordnelson.com.au). B&B in a historic pub. The ten very smart Colonial-style rooms are mostly en suite and come with all mod-cons. Price varies according to size and position ($150–180): best is the corner room with views of Argyle St. Meals served in the upmarket brasserie. Breakfast included. ⑥

Mercantile Hotel, 25 George St (☎02/9247 3570, ⓕ9247 7047, ⓦwww.merctpg.com.au). Sydney's best-known Irish pub, right on the edge of The Rocks near the Harbour Bridge, has a stash of fab rooms upstairs. Original features include huge fireplaces in several rooms, which are all furnished in Colonial style. Several have bathrooms complete with spa baths. Breakfast included. ⑥–⑦

Old Sydney Holiday Inn, 55 George St, The Rocks (☎02/9252 0524, ⓕ9251 2093, ⓦwww.holiday-inn.com). Four-star in a great location right in the heart of The Rocks, with impressive architecture: eight levels of rooms around a central atrium creates a remarkable feeling of space. The best rooms have harbour views but the rooftop swimming pool (plus spa and sauna) also gives fantastic vistas. 24hr room service. ⑧

Palisade Hotel, 35 Bettington St, Millers Point (☎02/9247 2272, ⓕ9247 2272, ⓦwww.palisadehotel.com). Magnificent tiled pub which manages to retain both old-style charm and simplicity – the bar downstairs is very down to earth, but there's a stylish contemporary restaurant upstairs. Clean, cute, shared-bath rooms have a bright old-fashioned feel. Some have fantastic views over the inner harbour and Harbour Bridge. ⑥

The Russell, 143a George St, The Rocks (☎02/9241 3543, ⓕ9252 1652, ⓦwww.therussel.com.au). Charming, small National Trust-listed hotel. Rooms have Colonial-style decor; some are en suite but the small shared bathroom options are very popular – and at $110 are a great price for the area. Other rooms range from $150 to $220, the best with views of the Quay. Sunny central courtyard and a rooftop garden, sitting room and bar, and downstairs restaurant for continental breakfast. B&B ⑦–⑧

Wynyard Vista Hotel, 7–9 York St, City (☎02/9274 1222, ⓕ9274 1230, ⓦwww.sydneyvista.citysearch.com.au). Central position for both the CBD and The Rocks. This 22-storey highrise hotel has the usual motel-style rooms but it excels with its spacious studios, which come with kitchen area, CD player, voicemail and a safe. Small gym; 24hr room service; pleasant café-brasserie. Cheaper weekend packages available. Rooms ⑦, studios ⑧

Darling Harbour, Haymarket and Ultimo

Aarons Hotel, 37 Ultimo Rd, Haymarket (☎02/9281 5555, ⓕ9281 2666, ⓦwww.aaronshotel.citysearch.com.au). Large, three-star hotel right in the heart of Chinatown, with its own modern café downstairs where a light breakfast is available. Comfortable en suites, all with TV and air-con. The least expensive are internal, small and box-like, with skylight only, while the pricier courtyard rooms have their own balconies. Rates are cheaper midweek. Parking $15 per day. ⑥–⑦

Hotel Bakpak, 412 Pitt St, City (☎02/9571 9049 or free call 1800 013 186, ⓕ9571 9048, ⓦwww.hotelbakpak.com). Two related hostels, across the street from each other in renovated big, old private hotels. In *Hotel Bakpak West End*, all rooms and dorms are air-con and en suite. Rooms have TV and/or minifridge and dorms (four- and six-bed) come with lockers. Common areas are spic-and-span – with a good modern kitchen and a cute little espresso bar downstairs – and staff are very clued-up. Opposite is *Hotel Bakpak CB*, with charming original features and bright funky furniture. Since there are no en suites, it's cheaper than *West End*, but *CB* is actually the better choice, particularly if you're after a single room ($45), as it has 60 of them. *West End* dorms ②, rooms ⑤. *CB* dorms ②, rooms ④

Capitol Square Hotel, Capitol Square, Campbell and George streets, Haymarket (☎02/9211 8633, ⓕ9211 8733, ⓦwww.goldspear.com.au). One of the centre's most affordable four-stars (rooms from $150), and small enough not to feel impersonal. Decor in the rooms is modern if a little chintzy. In an excellent location right next to the Capitol Theatre and cafés; it also has its own restaurant serving Asian and European food. Price includes buffet breakfast. ⑦

The George, 700A George St, Haymarket (☎ & ⓕ 02/9211 1800). Budget private hotel on three floors opposite Chinatown. Though the key deposit and payment-in-advance are off-putting, the bargain-priced rooms – all but two sharing bathrooms

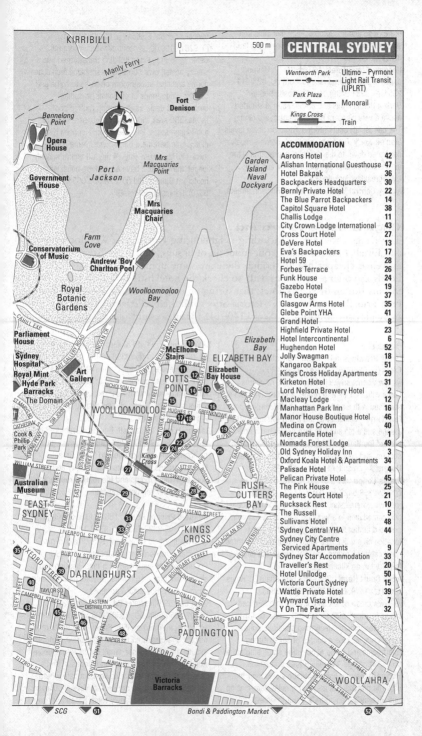

– are clean and acceptable. Facilities include a small combined kitchen and TV room and a laundry.**④**

Glasgow Arms Hotel , 527 Harris St, Ultimo, opposite the Powerhouse Museum Ⓣ 02/9211 2354,Ⓕ 9281 9439). Handily positioned for Darling Harbour, this accommodation is situated above a very pleasant pub with courtyard dining. The bar usually shuts around 10pm so noise levels aren't a worry. The high-ceilinged rooms – nicely decorated down to the polished floorboards – are air-conditioned and en suite with TV and radio. Light breakfast included.**⑥**

Sydney Central YHA , cnr Pitt and Rawson streets,

opposite Central Station Ⓣ 02/9281 9111, Ⓕ 9281 9199,Ⓔ sydcentral@yhansw.org.au). Centrally located listed building transformed into a snazzy hostel; over 500 beds – spacious four-share dorms and shared bathroom or en-suite twins and doubles. Wide range of amenities, including employment desk, travel agency, rooftop pool, sauna, BBQ area, video and TV lounges, kitchens and lounge areas. 24hr reception. Licensed bistro plus a cute basement bar, *Scubar*. Some parking available. Maximum stay 14 days. If you're staying longer, the YHA also have a "working holidaymaker hostel" at Dulwich Hill Ⓣ 02/9550 0054,Ⓕ 9550 0570). Rooms**⑤** , dorms**②**

Kings Cross and around

The Kings Cross area – including neighbouring Potts Point, Woolloomooloo and Elizabeth Bay – has a concentration of hostels, which are listed separately, as well as cheaper hotels, though there are some upmarket choices too. Some hotels also offer a few dorm beds, so check the hotel listings too. It's best avoiding any hostels or cheap hotels that spring up on Darlinghurst Road, the hardcore strip; the parallel, leafy Victoria Street and the backstreets have a contrastingly pleasant atmosphere. See p.140–141 for an account of the area.

Hotels

Bernly Private Hotel , 15 Springfield Ave, Kings Cross Ⓣ 02/9358 3122,Ⓕ 9356 4405, Ⓦ www.bernlyprivatehotel.com.au). All rooms come with TV, sink and fridge, and are available en suite and with air-con or share bathroom; also a few dorms. Facilities include a tidy kitchen and TV lounge and a big sunroom with deck chairs and a view of the Harbour Bridge. 24hr reception, good security and courteous service. Good single rates. Rooms**④** , en suite**⑥** , dorms**①** **②**

Challis Lodge , 21–23 Challis Ave, Potts Point Ⓣ 02/9358 5422,Ⓕ 9357 4742, Ⓦ www.wheretostay.com.au/challislodge). Budget accommodation in a wonderful old mansion with polished timber floors throughout. In a great location on a quiet, tree-filled street that has three good cafés. All rooms have TV, fridge and sink; laundry but no kitchen.**④**

Cross Court Hotel , 201–203 Brougham St, Kings Cross Ⓣ 02/9368 1822,Ⓕ 9358 2595, Ⓦ www.crosscourthotel.com.au). In a terraced house in a leafy side street, this small, well-run hotel offers smartly decorated spacious doubles, some en suite, plus a couple of self-catering apartments and some good-value small singles; all come with fridge, TV, ceiling fans and lamps. Rooms at the rear have fantastic views over the city. The drawback is it's near a noisy, late-closing pub. Rooms**④** , en suite**⑤** , apartments**⑥**

DeVere Hotel , 44–46 Macleay St, Potts Point Ⓣ 02/9358 1211,Ⓕ 9358 4685, Ⓦ www.devere.com.au). Comfortable three-star hotel in a great position, close to cafés and restaurants. Third- and fourth-floor rooms have stunning views of Elizabeth Bay; studios with kitchenette are also available.**⑥**

Gazebo Hotel , 2 Elizabeth Bay Rd, Elizabeth Bay Ⓣ 02/9358 1999,Ⓕ 9356 2951,Ⓦ www.gazebo.hotels.com.au). Right next to Kings Cross' Fitzroy Gardens, with views over the city and harbour from most rooms and the rooftop restaurant and bar. Swimming pool and sauna, free parking. **⑦**

Highfield Private Hotel , 166 Victoria St, Kings Cross Ⓣ 02/9326 9539,Ⓕ 9358 1552, Ⓦ www.highfield.hotel.com). Scandinavian-run, very clean, modern and secure budget hotel. Rooms are well-equipped with fans, heating and sinks. Also three-bed dorms. Tiny kitchen/common room with TV. Rooms**④** , dorms**②**

Hotel 59 , 59 Bayswater Rd, Kings Cross Ⓣ 02/9360 5900,Ⓕ 9360 1828,Ⓦ www.interspace.net.au/inns/hotel59). Small hotel that's reminiscent of a pleasant European *pensione*; benefits include a friendly owner, small but tastefully decorated air-con rooms, a quiet leafy location that's close to the bustle, and a downstairs café where full cooked breakfasts are served. Very popular, so book in advance. One family room (sleeps 4) has a

small kitchenette. Outdoor courtyard. B&B ❼
Macleay Lodge, 71 Macleay St, Potts Point
(Ⓣ02/9368 0660, Ⓕ9357 4742). Don't expect
anything fancy from this budget option on four
floors, but it's perfectly fine and in a fab spot in the
midst of Potts Point's café and restaurant scene.
All rooms (bar one) share bathroom and come with
sink, plates, cutlery, kettle, fridge, cheap furniture
and wonky colour TV. Best rooms have access to
the balcony area. ❹
Manhattan Park Inn, 8 Greeknowe Ave, Elizabeth
Bay (Ⓣ02/9358 1288, Ⓕ9357 3696,
Ⓦwww.parkplaza.com.au). The foyer and restaurant of this hotel dating from 1926 are Art Deco. In
the rooms, decorative ceiling mouldings and windows you can actually open are a civilized touch.
Bathrooms are colourful, and have tubs you can
soak in. "Superior" rooms are large, with views
over Elizabeth Bay. Some rooms have attached
kitchenettes. ❺–❻
Regents Court Hotel, 18 Springfield Ave, Potts
Point (Ⓣ02/9358 1533, Ⓕ9358 1833,
Ⓦwww.regentscourt.com.au). Small hotel raved
about by international style mags, from *Wallpaper*
to *British Vogue* – yet despite lots of arty guests,
the place is very friendly and homey. Classic
designer furniture, and each room has a sleek
kitchen area. Instead of a bar downstairs, you'll
find a well-chosen wine-list (at bottle-shop prices),
and you can help yourself to coffee and *biscotti*. A
small kitchen and BBQ area is located on the
rooftop, amongst citrus trees growing in pots. A
breakfast of fresh, baked goodies and just-
squeezed juice costs extra. Expect to pay between
$180 and $250 for all this. ❽
Sydney Star Accommodation, 275 Darlinghurst
Rd, Darlinghurst (Ⓣ02/9232 4455, Ⓕ9233 6399,
Ⓔstay@sydneystar.com.au). Individually styled
and nicely painted self-catering rooms in two
adjoining terraces. Rooms in the first terrace, with
a rather camp film-star theme, share bathrooms,
while in the second they're stylish en suites with
air-con. Each room has a microwave, sink, kettle,
fridge, plates and cutlery, plus TV. Some dorm
rooms available. Rooms ❹, en suite ❺, dorms ❷
Victoria Court Sydney, 122 Victoria St, Kings
Cross (Ⓣ02/9357 3200, Ⓕ9357 7606,
Ⓦwww.victoriacourt.com.au). Boutique hotel in
two interlinked Victorian terraced houses; very
tasteful and quiet. En-suite rooms with all mod
cons, some with balconies; buffet breakfast included and served in the conservatory. Secure parking
a bonus. ❼–❽

Hostels
Backpackers Headquarters, 79 Bayswater Rd,

Kings Cross (Ⓣ & Ⓕ 02/9331 6180,
Ⓦwww.backpackershqhostel.com.au). Modern,
light and clean hostel well-run by very courteous
management. Large, partitioned dorms with firm
mattresses, fans, heaters and mirrors; only two
doubles. Usual amenities plus sun deck and BBQ
area on the rooftop. Excellent security. Rooms ❹,
dorms ❷
The Blue Parrot Backpackers, 87 Macleay St,
Potts Point (Ⓣ02/9356 4888). In a great position
in the trendy part of Potts Point, this converted
mansion is sunny, airy, brightly painted and tastefully furnished. One of the best points is the huge
courtyard garden out back with wooden furniture
and big shady trees, looking onto a heritage building. Mostly six- and eight-bed dorms; one four-bed
dorm but no doubles. Common room has cable TV
and gas fire. ❷
Eva's Backpackers, 6–8 Orwell St, Potts Point
(Ⓣ02/9358 2185, Ⓕ9358 3259). Recommended
family-run hostel with colourfully painted, clean
rooms, well-set-up with fans, mirrors and lamps.
Dorms are four-, six-, eight- and ten-bed; four-bed
dorms are en suite. Peaceful rooftop garden with
table umbrellas, greenery, BBQ area and fantastic
views over The Domain. 24hr reception. Great
kitchen/diner on corner at street level. Rooms
❷–❸
Forbes Terrace, 153 Forbes St, Woolloomooloo
(Ⓣ02/9358 4327, Ⓕ9357 3652, Ⓦwww.alfred-
park.com.au). Well-run and clean hostel; well-positioned just off William St. Dorms are four- to ten-
bed and rooms come with TV and fridge. Rooms
❺, dorms ❷
Funk House, 23 Darlinghurst Rd, Kings Cross
(Ⓣ02/9358 6455, Ⓕ9358 3506,
Ⓦwww.funkhouse.com.au). With different murals
on every door – Acid art, Aboriginal and cartoons –
and upbeat music playing in the corridors and
showers, this very colourful place has a relaxed
vibe. Not too squeezy either, with three- and four-
bed dorms, all with fans. Doubles and twins also
come with fridge and TV. Rooftop garden with BBQ.
Also licensed travel agents; reception 7am–10pm.
Rooms ❹, dorms ❷
Jolly Swagman, 27 Orwell St (Ⓣ02/9358 6400,
Ⓕ9331 0125, Ⓦwww.jollyswagman.com.au).
Colourful, clean and lively, with good notice
boards and work connections. They run their
own events from sporting teams to pub crawls
plus tours. Along with the usual communal
facilities, every room has its own fridge and
lockers; four- to six-bed dorms. A cheap café
with internet access out front. Rooms ❹,
dorms ❷
The Pink House, 6–8 Barncleuth Square, Kings

Cross ⓣ &Ⓕ 02/9358 1689, free callⓣ 1800 806 384,Ⓦ www.qd.com.au/~theglobe). Attractive Art Deco mansion with big dorms and a few doubles, and all the expected amenities plus cable TV in the common room and a café. Friendly, very peaceful place but close to the action. YHA-associated. Rooms❹ , dorms❷

Rucksack Rest , 9 McDonald St, Potts Point ⓣ & Ⓕ 02/9358 2348). Small (thirty-bed) and well-run private hostel in a lovely old terrace house, exuding a shabby charm, which benefits from a friendly atmosphere, quiet leafy location and on-site local owner-manager. Facilities include a BBQ area and an outdoor kitchen perfect for summer. Dorms are maximum three-bed. Not a party hostel. Rooms ❸ -❹ , dorms❷

Traveller's Rest , 156 Victoria St, Kings Cross ⓣ 02/9358 4606,Ⓕ 9358 4531). Efficiently run by the helpful owner, this place is very popular with long-stayers who are well provided for and given good-value weekly rates. Decent twins and doubles; triple rooms available on a share basis as dorms – all with TV, fan, phone with voicemail, fridge, kettle, sink, wardrobe and table and chairs. Some en suites. Usual shared facilities plus a yard for smokers. No advance bookings. Rooms❸ -❹ , dorms❶

Surry Hills, Darlinghurst, Paddington and Woollahra

City Crown Lodge International , 289 Crown St, cnr of Reservoir St, Surry Hills ⓣ 02/9331 2433, Ⓕ 9360 7760,Ⓦ www.citycrownlodge.com.au). A fairly typical motel but well-located offering en-suite units with heating and fan. One self-catering unit is available. Free in-house movies. Some parking space: enter on Reservoir St.❻

Hughendon Hotel , 14 Queen St, Woollahra ⓣ 02/9363 4863,Ⓕ 9362 0398,Ⓦ www.hughendonhotel.com.au). Old-fashioned guesthouse, built in 1876, situated opposite Centennial Park. Expensive en-suite singles and doubles with rates ranging from $174 to $218, depending on size of room. Hot breakfast included.❽

Kangaroo Bakpak , 665 South Dowling St, Surry Hills ⓣ 02/9319 5915,Ⓕ 9318 0902, Ⓦ www.kangaroobakpak.com.au). Small, clean and very friendly family-run backpackers' hostel in a terraced house on a major traffic artery – though it's surprisingly calm inside. Spacious dorms (three-, four- or six-bed) are well furnished and most have lockers. There's a BBQ area with lots of greenery out back. The owners also run *Gracelands Budget Accommodation* on nearby Cleveland St, which is aimed more at long-stayers,

with more twins and doubles; rooms are brightly painted and there's a great common room downstairs. Rooms❸ , dorms❶ -❷

Kirketon Hotel , 229–231 Darlinghurst Rd, Darlinghurst ⓣ 02/9332 2011,Ⓕ 9332 2499, Ⓦ www.kirketon.com.au). Top in the fashion stakes, thanks to the big name Australian designers who created the swish interiors. Stylish bars and a restaurant beckon on the ground level, while the forty rooms (costing from $240 to $295) boast luxuries such as toiletries by Aveda, mohair throw rugs and CD players. You may feel less beautiful than the staff, but service is slick. Room service.❽

Medina on Crown , 359 Crown St, Surry Hills ⓣ 02/9360 6666,Ⓕ 9361 5965, Ⓦ www.medinaapartments.com.au). Stylishly decorated one- or two-bedroom serviced apartments, with air-con, lounge suite, dining area, TV, video and telephone – all from $209 nightly. Well-equipped kitchen, laundry and balcony, and a café, gym, sauna and swimming pool downstairs. 24hr reception and free undercover parking.❽

Oxford Koala Hotel & Apartments , cnr Oxford and Pelican streets, Darlinghurst ⓣ 02/9269 0645,Ⓕ 9283 2741, Ⓦ www.oxfordkoala.com.au). Multistorey motel overlooking Hyde Park. The fully equipped apartments ($185) are good for families, and the complex has a swimming pool. Room service. Rooms ❼ , apartments❽

Sullivans Hotel , 21 Oxford St, Paddington ⓣ 02/9361 0211,Ⓕ 9360 3735,Ⓦ www.sullivans.com.au). Medium-sized (64-bed) contemporary-style private hotel in a trendy location, run by staff tuned into the local scene. Comfortable, modern en-suite rooms with TV and telephones. Free (but limited) parking, swimming pool, in-house movies, 24hr reception and a café open for breakfast.❼

Y On The Park , 5–11 Wentworth Ave, Darlinghurst ⓣ 02/9264 2451,Ⓕ 9285 6288,Ⓦ www.ywca-sydney.com.au). Great location just off Oxford St near Hyde Park for this YWCA (both sexes welcome). Double or twin rooms with en-suite or shared bathrooms, plus singles sharing bathrooms ($68) and four-bed dorms. En-suite rooms come with TV, or there are TV lounges. There's no kitchen, but facilities include a café (open 7am–8pm), and a laundry. Rooms❻ -❼ , dorms❷

Inner west: Glebe, Newtown and Dulwich Hill

Alishan International Guesthouse , 100 Glebe Point Rd, Glebe ⓣ 02/9566 4048,Ⓕ 9525 4686, Ⓦ www.alishan.com.au). Beautifully restored old villa offering rather chintzy double en-suite rooms plus one furnished contrastingly in Japanese fashion, as well as spotless four-bed dorms. Facilities include a kitchen, spa, an airy common room, garden and BBQ area. Rooms ❻, dorms ❷

Australian Sunrise Lodge, 485 King St, Newtown (T 02/9550 4999, F 9550 4457). Inexpensive, tastefully furnished and well-managed small, private hotel with kitchen. Sunny single and double rooms, all with TV, fridge and toaster, most with bath and balcony. Family rooms available. Rooms ❹–❺

Billabong Gardens, 5–11 Egan St, off King St, Newtown (T 02/9550 3236, F 9550 4352, W www.billabonggardens.com.au). In a quiet street but close to the action, and run by a friendly team, this purpose-built hostel is arranged around a peaceful inner courtyard with swimming pool. It offers clean dorms (up to six-bed; some en suite), and rooms and motel-style en suites. Communal facilities include internet access. Undercover car park $5 per night. Rooms ❹–❺, dorms ❷

Glebe Point YHA, 262 Glebe Point Rd, Glebe (T 02/9692 8418, F 9660 0431, E glebe@yhansw.org.au). Reliable YHA standard with impeccably helpful, patient staff. Private rooms as well as four-bed dorms. Facilities include a roof terrace with city views, pool table, TV and video lounge, and luggage storage. Lots of activities organized. Reception 7am–11pm. Rooms ❹, dorms ❷

Glebe Village Backpackers, 256 Glebe Point Rd, Glebe (T 02/9660 8133 or free call T 1800 801 983, F 9552 3707, W www.bacpakgroup.com.au/glebevillage). Three large old houses with a mellow atmosphere, feeling more like a guesthouse than a hostel, and staffed by young locals who know what's going on around town. Double and twin rooms as well as four-, six- and eight-bed dorms. Alfresco café overlooking the street, shady courtyard and a travel agency. Rooms ❹, dorms ❷

Nomads Forest Lodge Hotel, 117 Arundel St, Forest Lodge, near Glebe (T 02/9660 1872, F 9552 1053, W www.nomads-backpackers.com). Hostels above pubs can be dodgy but this one is clean and well-run. Mostly two- or four-bunk dorms, plus two doubles, all with lockers and linen; small all-in-one kitchen/TV/common room. No laundry. The pleasant pub, with a laid-back café attached, is in a quiet street, and closes at 11pm. Bus #470 from Central. Rooms ❹, dorms ❶

Rooftop Motel, 146 Glebe Point Rd, Glebe (T 02/9660 7777, F 9660 7155, E davidpetrie@bigpond.com). Reasonably priced motel with 24hr reception, right in the heart of Glebe; BBQ and swimming pool. Parking included. ❻

Tricketts Bed and Breakfast, 270 Glebe Point Rd, Glebe (T 02/9552 1141, F 9692 9462, W www.citysearch.com.au/syd/trickettsbandb). Luxury B&B in an 1880 mansion. En-suite rooms are furnished with antiques and Persian rugs, and

Gay and lesbian accommodation

You won't encounter any problems booking into a regular hotel as gay men or lesbians, but here are several places that are particularly gay friendly or close to Oxford Street in Darlinghurst. For **flat shares** check the community press and café notice boards or try an agency: Share-A-Home, 127 York St, City (T 02/9267 9824, W www.gayshare.xrs.net), deals with gay and lesbian shares for a $65 fee.

Manor House Boutique Hotel, 86 Flinders St, Darlinghurst (T 02/9380 6633, F 9380 5016, W www.manorhouse.com.au). This was the residence of Sydney's first Lord Mayor, now gay-owned and run mostly for men. Rooms have decks overlooking the courtyard, where there's a heated pool and a spa. Licensed restaurant and bar. Continental breakfast included. ❼–❽

Pelican Private Hotel, 411 Bourke St, Darlinghurst (T & F 9331 5344, W www.rainbow.net.au/-pelican). Comfortable budget accommodation in one of Sydney's oldest gay guesthouses. Appealing rooms have TV and fridge, but share facilities; some rooms with kitchenettes. Communal kitchen and garden courtyard. Rate includes continental breakfast. ❹

Wattle Private Hotel, 108 Oxford St, cnr Palmer St, Darlinghurst (T 02/9332 4118, F 9331 2074, W www.sydneyhotel.com.au). You can't get any closer to the action, and although the rooms aren't flash, they're clean. Ask for the room on the roof, which opens out to the garden with spectacular city and harbour views. Continental breakfast included. ❻ the lounge, complete with a billiard table and leather armchairs, was originally a small ballroom. There's also a fully self-contained one-bedroom garden apartment with its own verandah. Delicious, generous and sociable breakfast. ❽

Hotel Unilodge , cnr Broadway and Bay streets, near Glebe Ⓣ 02/9338 5000, Ⓕ 9338 5111, Ⓦ www.unilodge.com.au). Converted from a former department store and retaining some striking original fixtures, this hotel has a luxury feel, but rates can be reasonable. Split-level self-catering rooms, some sleeping up to five, are comfortably furnished, with kitchenettes. There's a small gym, lap-pool, spa and sauna, rooftop running track and BBQ. 24hr reception, and 24hr convenience store and food court in the foyer. Children under 12 free. Parking extra. ❽

Wattle House Hostel , 44 Hereford St, Glebe Ⓣ 02/9552 4997, Ⓕ 9660 2528, Ⓦ www.wattle-house.com.au). Top-class small, cosy and clean privately owned hostel in a restored terrace house on a quiet street. Four-bed dorms and well-furnished doubles. Pretty gardens and an outdoor eating area make staying here extra pleasant, and there's even a library room. Rates include linen and towels. Very popular, so book in advance; generally minimum three-night stay. Rooms ❺ , dorms ❷

Bondi Beach

Bondi Beach House Accommodation , 28 Sir Thomas Mitchell Rd Ⓣ 02/9300 0250, Ⓕ 9300 0369, Ⓦ www.bondibeachhouse.com.au). You could almost imagine you are staying in a friend's beach house here, with its friendly informal atmosphere and communal kitchen and lounge areas, all polished floors and summery furniture. There's a big deck area with BBQ out the front, and a shady private garden out back. Doubles and dorms (five-bed) are pleasantly furnished and decorated. Just back from the beach and the action, this is the best budget accommodation in Bondi – if you can get a room. Rooms ❹ , dorms ❷

Bondi Lodge , 63 Fletcher St Ⓣ 02/9365 2088, Ⓕ 9365 2177, Ⓦ www.sydney_accom_group.com). Handily located between Bondi and Tamarama beaches, this nicely decorated family-run guesthouse is popular with budget travellers and international students: even dorm rates include a buffet breakfast and three-course dinner, and it has plenty of singles and twins (all share bathrooms), though no doubles. Facilities include a laundry, rooftop terrace with ocean views and spa, and courtyard with BBQ. 24hr reception. Rooms ❻ , dorms ❸

Indy's at Bondi , 35a Hall St Ⓣ 02/9365 4900, 24hr 0413/836681, Ⓕ 9365 4994, Ⓦ www.indys-backpackers.com). Justifiably popular, this spacious hostel feels like a friendly student house-share – except it's well-organized and there's every amenity, including a pool table, outdoor area with seating, excellent security and free use of surfboards and bike. Social events and trips organized; also travel bookings. Dorms only here (four-to eight-bed) – couples and families can stay at their annexe, *Couples on the Beach*, opposite the beach at North Bondi, where all rooms have TV, and there's a small kitchen but no common room – you can sit out on the roof. Rooms ❹ , dorms ❷

Lamrock Lodge , 19 Lamrock Ave, cnr Consett Ave Ⓣ 02/9130 5063, Ⓕ 9300 9582, Ⓦ www.lamrocklodge). This bright yellow-painted hostel on a pleasant residential street close to the beach and shops is friendly, well-run, secure and clean. The doubles, twins, singles and four-bed dorms are all very well set-up with sink, fridge, microwave, fans and TV with cable and Foxtel. However, compared to other hostels it's lacking in communal facilities: outside tables at the front of the building provide the only common area, and the tiny kitchen has only one stovetop, and no kettle, crockery or cutlery. Rooms ❹ , dorms ❷

Plage Bondi , 212 Bondi Rd Ⓣ 02/9387 1122, Ⓕ 9389 1266, Ⓦ www.ozemail.com.au/~theplage). Excellent-value serviced motel studio apartments. Air-conditioned units all have clean modern furniture, TV, telephone, kitchen and a balcony with sea view. Mostly recently decorated, but some older-style apartments without views are cheaper. Best of all is the rooftop pool. Cheaper rates if you stay a week or more. Parking included. ❹ –❻

Ravesi's , cnr Campbell Parade and Hall St Ⓣ 02/9365 4422, Ⓕ 9365 1481, Ⓦ www.ravesis.com.au). The first-floor restaurant/bar and most rooms at this boutique hotel have glorious ocean views. The facade is pure 1914, but interiors are totally modern: well thought-out rooms (16 in all) have a relaxing by-the-beach feel with cane furniture and ceiling fans (in addition to air-con). Most of the second-floor rooms have French windows opening onto small balconies; split-level and penthouse suites on the top floor have spacious ones. Smaller standard rooms don't have views, but offer great value. ❻ –❽

Coogee and Randwick

Coogee Bay Boutique Hotel , 9 Vicar St, Coogee Ⓣ 02/9665 0000, Ⓕ 9664 2103, Ⓦ www.coogeebayhotel.com.au). New hotel attached to the rear of a pub, the older, sprawling *Coogee Bay Hotel*. Rooms – all with balconies, half with ocean views – look like something from *Vogue Interior*; luxurious touches include marble floors in the bathrooms, minibars, in-room safes and data ports. Cheaper rooms in the old hotel are noisy on weekends but are just as stylish; several offer splendid water views. Parking included. 24hr reception. The pub has an excellent brasserie, sev-

eral bars and a nightclub. **⑥ –⑧**

Coogee Beach Wizard of Oz , 172 Coogee Bay Rd (ⓣ 02/9315 7876, ⓕ 9315 8974, ⓦ www .wizardofoz.com.au). Top-class hostel run by a friendly local couple in a big and beautiful Californian-style house with a huge verandah and polished wooden floors. Spacious, vibrantly painted dorms with ceiling fans, and some well set-up doubles. TV/video room, dining area, modern

Holiday apartments

The following places rent out apartments, generally for a minimum of a week. Expect to pay between $350 and $600 per week, depending on the size and the season; all are completely furnished and equipped – though occasionally you're expected to provide linen and towels: check first. Many hotels (some called apartment hotels) and all hostels also have self-catering facilities – see main listings for details.

Enochs Holiday Flats (ⓣ 02/9388 1477, ⓕ 9388 1353). One-, two- or three-bedroom apartments, all close to Bondi Beach, sleeping four to six people. $500–2000 weekly, depending on the size and season.

Kings Cross Holiday Apartments , 169 William St, Kings Cross, Sydney, NSW 2011 (ⓣ 02/9361 0637, ⓕ 9331 1366, ⓦ www.kxr.com.au). One-bedroom apartments in this very central location, with accommodation for up to five. Linen and towels included, and though the apartments aren't serviced, a washing-machine and dryer are provided in the kitchen. $570 weekly (for two adults and two children; extra guests $10 each per day), cheaper in winter and longer-term rates are negotiable. One "backpacker" apartment can sleep ten in dorm accommodation, which works out at $120 per week per person.

Manly National , 22 Central Ave, Manly, NSW 2095 (ⓣ 02/9977 6469, ⓕ 9977 3760, ⓦ www.property.com.au). One- and two-bedroom apartments accommodate up to four people; swimming pool; linen not supplied. One-bedroom $550–700 weekly, two-bedroom $700–850.

Medina Executive Apartments , Head office, Level 1, 355 Crown St, Surry Hills, Sydney, NSW 2010 (ⓣ 02/9360 1699, ⓕ 9332 4813, ⓦ www.medinaapartments .com.au). Upmarket studio or one-, two- and three-bedroom serviced apartments with resident managers and reception in salubrious locales. Various locations in the city include Lee St near Central Station, Kent St in the CBD and Martin Place; eastern suburbs include Double Bay, Paddington, Randwick and Coogee, on the lower North Shore at Crows Nest, and at North Ryde handy for Macquarie University. All include undercover parking. From $1000 weekly upwards. See also *Medina on Crown*, p.100.

The Park Agency , 190 Arden St, Coogee, NSW 2034 (ⓣ 02/9315 7777, ⓕ 9665 7777, ⓦ www.parkagency.com.au). Very friendly staff who offer several spacious well set-up one-, two- and three-bedroom apartments near the beach from $480, $650 and $800 per week respectively. All fully furnished including linen, blankets and washing-machine.

Raine and Horne , 255 Miller St, North Sydney, NSW 2060 (ⓣ 02/9959 5906, ⓕ 9929 0772, ⓦ www.raineandhorne.com.au/northsydney). Modern executive/upmarket fully furnished apartments fitted out by interior designers, on the leafy North Shore: North Sydney, Kirribilli, Milsons Point and McMahons Point. Studios $495–595, one-bed $600–750, two-bed $750–1000, three-bed $1500 per week. All have TV, video, CD player, telephone; several have spas, pools or gyms. One-off cleaning fee of $110.

Sydney City Centre Serviced Apartments , 7 Elizabeth St, Martin Place (ⓣ 02/9233 6677, ⓕ 9235 3432). Fully equipped apartments with kitchenette, TV, video, fans; basic, but in an excellent location. $420 weekly (or $60 per night).

kitchen and big pleasant backyard with BBQ. Rooms ❹, dorms ❷

Coogee Beachside, 178 Coogee Bay Rd, Coogee (☎ 02/9315 8511, ⓕ 9315 8974, ⓦ www.sydneybeachside.com.au). Run by the same management as *Wizard of Oz* (below), this airy old two-storey house has been pleasantly renovated, with wooden floors. All rooms and dorms (four- and six-bed) come with TV and fans but share bathrooms. Doubles and family rooms also have fridge. Small kitchen but no common room – everyone hangs out in the big sunny back garden. Up the hill from the beach but handy for shops and the supermarket. Rooms ❹, dorms ❷

Indy's Beachside Backpackers, 302 Arden St, Coogee (☎ 02/9315 7644, ⓕ 9365 4994, ⓦ www.indysbackpackers.com). Owned and run by a friendly young local, this small laid-back hostel feels more like a house-share, complete with a sociable dining table and leather armchairs and big-screen TV in the lounge. Mostly four-bed dorms, all brightly painted and with duvets; no doubles. Day-trips booked. ❷

The Royal, cnr Perouse Rd and Cuthill St, Randwick (☎ 02/9399 3006 or 9399 5659, ⓕ 9399 8181, ⓦ www.royalhotel-sydney.com). Big, historic pub (listed by the National Trust), with fairly upmarket rooms, all sharing bathrooms except for one en suite. Good transport to the city and beaches. ❺

Surfside Backpackers Coogee, 186 Arden St, Coogee (☎ 02/9315 7888, ⓕ 9315 7892, ⓦ www.surfsidebackpackers.com). On Coogee's main drag, above *McDonald's* and opposite the beach, Coogee's largest hostel tends to attract a drinking, party crowd – try elsewhere for quiet. Modern facilities and great views from its high balconies, but a bit of a tower-block feel and dorms are mostly ten-, twelve- and sixteen-bed, though some four-beds are available. No doubles or twins. ❷

North Shore

Cremorne Point Manor, 6 Cremorne Rd, Cremorne Point (☎ 02/9953 7899, ⓕ 9904 1265, ⓦ www.cremornepointmanor.com.au). Huge restored Federation-style villa with very cheap singles and good-value doubles run by a friendly couple. Most rooms are en suite with TV and fridge and some have harbour views. There's a communal kitchen and a laundry. Rate includes continental breakfast. ❻

Elite Private Hotel, 133 Carabella St, Kirribilli (☎ 02/9929 6365, ⓕ 9925 0999, ⓦ www.citysearch.com.au/syd/elite). Bright place surrounded by plants offering good rooms with sink, TV, fridge and kettle; some have a harbour view and most share bathrooms. Small communal cooking facility but no laundry. Only minutes by ferry from the city (to Kirribilli Wharf) and near Milsons Point train station. Cheaper weekly rates. Rooms ❹–❺

Glenferrie Lodge, 12a Carabella St, Kirribilli (☎ 02/9955 1685, ⓕ 9929 9439, ⓦ www.sydney.accom.group.com). Another made-over Kirribilli mansion, clean, light and secure with 24hr reception. Rates include a buffet breakfast and three-course dinner, whether you're in a four-share dorm, single, double or family room (all share bathroom). Facilities include a TV lounge and laundry. Ferry to Kirribilli Wharf or train to Milsons Point. Rooms ❻, dorms ❸

North Shore Hotel, 310 Miller St, North Sydney (☎ 02/9955 1012, ⓕ 9955 4212, ⓔ sales@pacrimhotels.com.au). Two-storey mansion with balconies in a quiet location opposite a park. En-suite rooms or family studios sleeping four, all with air-con, TV, hot drinks and telephone. Shared kitchen and laundry facilities; breakfast available. ❻

Manly and the northern beaches

Avalon Beach Hostel, 59 Avalon Parade, Avalon (☎ 02/9918 9709, ⓕ 9973 1322). Located at one of Sydney's best – and most beautiful – surf beaches, this owner-managed hostel is certainly conducive to year-round relaxation, with warming fireplaces, breezy balconies and plenty of greenery and rainbow lorikeets to gaze at. Built mainly of timber, it has a real airy beachhouse feel. Boat trips on Pittwater organized, and the hostel has its own minibus, offering tours up the Central Coast. Dorms (four- and six-bed) and rooms have storage area and fans. Surfboard rental available. Excellent local work contacts. Rooms ❸, dorms ❷

Chateau Sur Mer, 124 Pacific Palm Rd, Palm Beach (☎ 02/9974 4220, ⓕ 9974 1147, ⓦ www.palmbeachchateau.com.au). "Chateau" is not too grand a description for this Mediterranean-style mansion perched on a hilltop with ocean views. The three guestrooms – the Riveria Suite, St Tropez Suite and Parisian Room – are within the family home, much like a British B&B, but the friendly English couple who run it don't intrude on their guests' privacy, and rooms have their own bathroom and balcony. A fridge comes stocked with breakfast things and more goodies arrive on a tray in the morning. ❽

Manly Backpackers Beachside, 28 Raglan St, Manly (☎ 02/9977 3411, ⓕ 9977 4079, ⓦ www.manlybackpackers.com.au). Well-run modern purpose-built two-storey hostel one block from the surf. Clean twin and double rooms – some en suite – plus small three-bed dorms (six-bed is largest) which are pricier than others in the area. The best dorm is at the front with a balcony. Outside terrace with BBQ; free boogie-boards. No weekly rates on private rooms. Rooms ❹–❺, dorms ❷

Manly Beach Resort Backpackers, 6 Carlton St, Manly (Ⓣ02/9977 4188, Ⓕ9977 0524). Located one block from the beach. Clean, four- to six-bed en-suite dorms and a few very reasonable doubles. There is also a more upmarket motel section. The attached café is good for breakfast. 24hr reception. Rooms ❹–❼, dorms ❷

Manly Pacific Park Royal, 55 North Steyne, Manly (Ⓣ02/9977 7666, Ⓕ9977 7822, Ⓦwww.parkroyal.com.au). Beachfront multistorey four-star hotel with 24hr reception, room service, spa, sauna, gym and heated rooftop pool – all at a price: over $200, and more for an ocean view ($235). ❽

Periwinkle Guesthouse, 18–19 East Esplanade, cnr Ashburner St, Manly (Ⓣ02/9977 4668, Ⓕ9977 6308, Ⓦwww.periwinkle.citysearch .com.au). Pleasant B&B near Manly Cove, close to the ferry terminal and shops. Rooms have fridge and fans and facilities include a communal kitchen and car park. Several en suites available, with larger rooms suitable for families or groups. ❼–❽

Sydney Beachhouse YHA, 4 Collaroy St, Collaroy Beach (Ⓣ02/9981 1177, Ⓕ9981 1114, Ⓦwww.sydneybeachhouse.com.au). Purpose-built YHA hostel with a heated swimming pool, open

fireplaces, video lounge and games and pool rooms. Four- to six-bed dorms plus several doubles (some en suite) and family rooms. Free use of surfboards, boogie-boards and bikes, and surfing lessons for weekly guests – the beach is just across very busy Pittwater Rd. Trips organized include the popular jaunt to the *Home and Away* filming location. Free car parking. Rooms ❹, dorms ❷

Wharf Backpackers, 48 East Esplanade, Manly (Ⓣ02/9977 2800, Ⓕ9977 2820). Quirky but well-run hostel, directly opposite the ferry terminal, that really gets into the concept of outdoor living. The big back garden becomes another living area, with a kitchen and TV, tables and oversized chess set. Though there's room for 60 guests, there are several kitchens and TV rooms so it never feels too crowded. Colourfully painted dorms – four-, six- and eight-bed – have ceiling fans and heaters. Doubles and twins come with TV. Good local work contacts. Rooms ❹, dorms ❷

Cronulla Beach

Cronulla Beach YHA, 40 Kingsway, Cronulla (Ⓣ02/9527 7772, Ⓕ9527 0533, Ⓦwww .cronullabeachyha.com.au). Brand-new hostel in this unpretentious, surf-oriented suburb that's well-situated for trips to the Royal National Park; the friendly live-in manager offers surf trips to Garie and drop-offs to Wattamolla. Surfboards, kayaks and bicycles for rent. Private rooms are en suite and there are four- and six-bed dorms, all with fans and lockers. Rooms ❹, dorms ❷

The City

Port Jackson carves Sydney in two halves, linked by the Harbour Bridge and Harbour Tunnel. The **South Shore** is the hub of activity, and it's here that you'll find the **city centre** and most of the things to see and do. Many of the classic images of Sydney are within sight of **Circular Quay**, making this busy waterfront area on Sydney Cove a logical – and pleasurable – point to start discovering the city, with the **Opera House** and the expanse of the Royal Botanic Gardens to the east of Sydney Cove and the historic area of **The Rocks** to the west. By contrast, **Darling Harbour**, at the centre's western edge, was redeveloped in the late 1980s as a tourist and entertainment area and is a gleaming, if slightly tawdry, showcase for the new Sydney.

Circular Quay

At the southern end of Sydney Cove, **Circular Quay** is the launching pad for harbour and river ferries and sightseeing boats, the terminal for buses from the eastern and southern suburbs, and a major suburban train station to boot. Circular Quay itself is always bustling with commuters during the week, and with people simply out to enjoy themselves at the weekend. Restaurants, cafés and fast-food outlets stay open until late at night and buskers entertain the crowds, while vendors of newspapers and trinkets add to the general hubbub. The sun reflecting on the water and its heave and splash as the ferries come and go make for a dreamy setting – best appreciated over an expensive beer and some oysters at a waterfront bar. For intellectual stimulation, you need only look beneath your feet as you stroll along: the inscribed bronze pavement plaques of **Writers' Walk** provide an introduction to the Australian literary canon. There are short biographies of writers ranging from Miles Franklin, author of *My Brilliant Career*, through Booker Prize winner Peter Carey and Nobel Prize awardee Patrick White, to the feminist Germaine Greer, and quotable quotes on what it means to be Australian. Notable literati who've vis-

Harbour cruises

There's a wide choice of **harbour cruises** , almost all of them leaving from Jetty 6, Circular Quay and the rest from Darling Harbour. Before you part with your cash, however, bear in mind that apart from the running commentary (which can be rather annoying), most offer nothing that you won't get on a regular harbour **ferry** for a lot less. The best of the ordinary trips is the thirty-minute ride to **Manly** , but there's a ferry going somewhere at almost any time throughout the day. If you really want to splash out, you could take a **water taxi** ride – Circular Quay to Watsons Bay, for example, costs $45 for the first passenger and then an additional $6 for each extra person. Pick-ups are available from any wharf if booked in advance (try Taxis Afloat on℡ 02/9955 3222). One water taxi company, **Watertour** , located on Cockle Bay wharf in Darling Harbour (℡ 02/9267 0099, ⊛ www.watertours.com.au), has even started to offer tours on their latest model, bright yellow taxis looking like New York cabs on the water, from $10 for a half-hour spin.

The **Australian Travel Specialists (ATS)** at Jetty 2 and 6, Circular Quay, the Harbourside Shopping Centre at Darling Harbour and Manly Wharf (℡ 02/9247 5151 or 9555 2700) book all cruises. Those offered by State Transit – **Sydney Harbour Ferry Cruises** – seem to offer the best value: choose between the Morning River Cruise (daily 10am & 11.15am; 1hr; $14), the recommended Afternoon Harbour Cruise to Middle Harbour and back (Mon–Fri 1pm, Sat & Sun 1.30pm; 2hr 30min; $21), or the Evening Cruise (Mon–Sat 8pm; 1hr 30min; $18).

Captain Cook Cruises at Jetty 6 (℡ 02/9206 1111,⊛ www.captaincook.com.au), the big commercial operator, offers a vast range of cruises on their very large boats including morning and afternoon "Coffee" Cruises into Middle Harbour (daily 10am & 2.15pm; 2hr 20min; $36), a lunch cruise (daily 12.30pm; $52), a daily range of rather expensive dinner cruises (including three-course meal with drinks from $69; Opera Afloat with opera singers accompanying a four-course dinner for $95), and a Harbour Highlights Cruise (daily 9.30am, 11am, 12.45pm, 2.30pm, 4pm; 1hr 15min; $20; option of getting off at Darling Harbour on the 11am, 2.30pm and 4pm trips). They also have a hop-on, hop-off Sydney Harbour Explorer (daily 9.30am–5.30pm; $22; combined ticket with the zoo or the aquarium is $36.50) circuiting between Circular Quay, the Man O' War jetty at the Opera House, Watsons Bay, Taronga Zoo and Darling Harbour.

Matilda Cruises , based in Darling Harbour (Aquarium Wharf, Pier 26;℡ 02/9264 7377,⊛ www.matilda.com.au), offer various smaller-scale cruises on sailing catamarans (engines mostly used), with big foredecks providing great views. Departures are from Darling Harbour, with pick ups from Circular Quay twenty minutes later. Morning and afternoon cruises include a cappuccino, cake and pastries (10am & 3.05pm; 1hr 30min; $26); there's a buffet on the Lunch Cruise (12.15pm; 2hr;

106

ited Australia – including Joseph Conrad, Charles Darwin and Mark Twain – also feature.

Having dallied, read, and taken in the view and the crush of people, the next thing to do is to embark on a sightseeing **cruise** or enjoy a ferry ride on the harbour (see box below). Staying on dry land, you're only a short walk from most of the city-centre sights, along part of a continuous foreshore walkway beginning under the Harbour Bridge and passing through the historic area of Sydney's first settlement The Rocks, and extending beyond the Opera House to the Royal Botanic Gardens. The Gardens boast some wonderfully pictur-esque picnic spots – all the necessaries, including bubbly and fresh prawns, can be purchased at the quay. Besides ferries, Circular Quay still acts as a passenger terminal for ocean liners; head in the opposite direction past the Museum of Contemporary Art to Circular Quay West. It's a long time since the crowds waved their hankies regularly from the rust-coloured **Sydney Cove**

$53.50), while the pricey Dinner Cruise allows you to dine on the foredeck (Darling Harbour 7pm, Circular Quay 7.30pm; 3hr 30min; $103). They also offer the Rocket Harbour Express Cruise, a one-hour trip stopping at the Aquarium wharf at Darling Harbour, Man O' War jetty at the Opera House, Commissioners Steps at Circular Quay West, Taronga Zoo and Watsons Bay; you can get off at the stops and rejoin later cruises (every 30min 9.30am–4.30pm; $19.50 includes refreshment). There is also a straight Matilda Ferry service, the Rocket Express, shuttling between Darling Harbour, the Star City casino and Circular Quay ($4 one-way).

If you're feeling romantically inclined, or mutinous, you might fancy sailing with the Bounty (office at 29 George St, The Rocks; ℡02/9247 1789, ℠www.bounty.com), a replica of Captain Bligh's ship made for the film starring Mel Gibson. It embarks at Campbells Cove, The Rocks, for various cruises daily; cheapest is the Sunday brunch (10–11.30am; $53) while the splurge is the nightly dinner cruise (7–9.30pm; three-course buffet and entertainment, drinks extra; $99). A similar sailing experi-ence is offered by Sail Svanen (℡02/9698 4456, ℠www.sailsvanen.com), moored at Campbells Cove next to the *Bounty*: this sailing ship, built in 1922, offers day-sails on the harbour for $83.50, including morning tea and lunch, or longer overnight sails to Broken Bay ($275).

With Sydney by Sail (bookings ℡02/9280 1110, ℠www.sydneybysail.com), you can enjoy the harbour from on board a luxury Beneteau yacht. Groups are small (up to 12) and if you're interested the skipper will even show you some sailing techniques. There are shorter sails to Port Jackson ($54; 1hr 30min) and longer ones going fur-ther into surrounding inlets ($98; 3hr); call for times. Departures are from the National Maritime Museum at Darling Harbour, with free entry to the museum thrown in. Experienced sailors can charter the yachts (from $345 half-day to $945 for a week-end).

For something completely different, Aussie Duck (bookings ℡13 1007, ℠www.aussieduck.com) combines a land and a sea tour in an amphibious vehicle (1hr 45min; $49.50, child $27.50, family pass $132). The 50-seater brightly painted "coach" departs from Clocktower Square in The Rocks and spends 45min touring around the city centre until a startling "splash-down" into Walsh Bay when it's trans-formed into a jet-powered boat zooming around Darling Harbour and the Opera House. This is strictly a "fun" tour, with everyone given duck quackers and pumping themed music accompanying the different sights. Another alternative to the sedate cruises listed above is offered by Ocean Extreme (℡0414 800 046 or 0418 213 145, ℠www.oceanextreme.com.au) on *Extreme 1*, an RIB (Rigid Inflatable Boat), with small groups of ten passengers taken on a hair-raising 40min "Adrenaline Tour" (daily 11am & 1pm; bookings necessary; $60) at speeds of more than 100km an hour, making the harbour scenery mostly a blur but great fun.

Passenger Terminal, looking for all the world like the deck of a ship itself, but you may still see an ocean liner docked here; even if there's no ship, take the escalator and the flight of stairs up for excellent views of the harbour. The rest of the terminal is now given over to swanky restaurants.

Leading up to the Opera House is the once-controversial **Opera Quays** development which runs the length of **East Circular Quay**. Locals and tourists have flocked to promenade along the pleasant collonnaded lower level with its outdoor cafés, bars and bistros, upmarket shops and Dendy Cinema, all looking out to sublime harbour views. The ugly apartment building above, dubbed "The Toaster" by locals and described by Robert Hughes, the famous expat Australian art critic and historian, as "that dull brash, intrusive apartment block which now obscures the Opera House from three directions", caused massive protests, but went up anyway, opening in 1999.

Customs House and the Justice and Police Museum

The railway and the ugly Cahill Expressway block views to the city from Circular Quay, cutting it off from Alfred Street immediately opposite, with its architectural gem, the sandstone and granite **Customs House**. First constructed in 1845, it was redesigned in 1885 by the colonial architect James Barnet to give it its current Classical Revival-style facade. On the fourth floor, the **City Exhibition Space** (daily 10am–5pm; free) keeps pace with the sometimes bewildering development of Sydney with an up-to-the-minute detailed 500:1 scale model of the city accompanied by history boards and video screens. If you're really interested in the city's modern architecture, the Sydney Architecture Walk leaves from here every Wednesday and Saturday (10am; 2hr 30min; $20; enquiries ☎ 02/9565 2344). The building is blessed with eateries too: on the top floor, a contemporary brasserie, *Cafe Sydney*, comes with wonderful Harbour Bridge views, while on the ground floor, take a coffee at *Caffe Bianchi*, or eat oysters and have a beer at *Quay Bar*, both with alfresco seating on Customs House Square out front. On the third floor, the **Centre for Contemporary Craft** shows free changing exhibitions of Australia's best artisans in the **Object Galleries** (daily 10am–5pm); Object Stores is the retail outlet on the ground floor (Mon–Fri 10am–5.30pm, Sat & Sun noon–5pm), selling beautifully designed glass, ceramics, woodwork and jewellery.

A block east of Customs House, on the corner of Phillip Street, the **Justice and Police Museum** is housed in the former Water Police station (Jan daily except Fri 10am–5pm, Feb–Dec Sat & Sun 10am–5pm; $7; Ⓦ www.hht.nsw.gov.au), an 1858 sandstone building with a particularly fine ironwork verandah. This social history museum focuses on law, policing and crime in NSW. The crime displays, including some truly macabre death masks and gruesome confiscated weapons, some of them murder implements, are shown within the context of a late nineteenth-century police station and courtroom. There's also an interesting display on bushrangers.

Museum of Contemporary Art

The **Museum of Contemporary Art** (daily 10am–6pm; free; free tours Mon–Fri 11am & 2pm, Sat & Sun noon & 1.30pm; ☎ 02/9252 4033 for details of special exhibitions and events; Ⓦ www.mca.com.au), on the western side of Circular Quay with another entrance on George Street (no. 140), was developed out of a bequest by the art collector John Power in the 1940s to Sydney University to purchase international contemporary art. The growing collection finally found a permanent home in 1991 in the former Maritime Services

Building, provided for peppercorn rent by the State Government. The striking Deco-style 1950s building is now dedicated to international twentieth-century art, with an eclectic approach encompassing lithographs, sculpture, film, video, drawings, paintings and Aboriginal art, mostly shown in themed exhibitions. Surprisingly, the permanent collection of 1600 works, including pieces by Julian Schnabel, Keith Haring, Bridget Riley, Jasper Johns, Beuys, Hockney, Duchamp, Tinguely and Rauchenberg, is mostly kept in storage, though a selection is shown in special exhibitions twice a year. The museum's superbly sited, if expensive, café (Mon–Fri 11am–4.30pm, Sat & Sun 9am–4.30pm) has outdoor tables overlooking the waterfront. Since John Power left no recurrent funding, the museum now has to raise ninety percent of its own funding and has been financially troubled since opening; the free entry is courtesy of corporate sponsorship. Sydney Council is considering a A$59 million rescue package for the redevelopment of the museum; part of the plan involves the addition of a new wing to house a Moving Images Centre. If the plan goes ahead, the museum will close for two years.

The Opera House

The **Sydney Opera House**, such an icon of Australiana that it almost seems kitsch, is just a short stroll from Circular Quay, by the water's edge on Bennelong Point. It's best seen in profile, when its high white roofs, at the same time evocative of full sails and white shells, give the building an almost ethereal quality. Some say the inspiration for the distinctive design came from the simple peeling of an orange into segments, though perhaps Danish architect **Jørn Utzon**'s childhood as the son of a yacht designer had something to do with their sail-like shape – he certainly envisaged a building which would appear to "float" on water. Despite its familiarity, or perhaps precisely because you already feel you know it so well, it's quite breathtaking at first sight. Close-up, you can see that the shimmering effect is created by thousands of white tiles.

The feat of structural engineering required to bring to life Utzon's "sculpture", which he compared to a Gothic church and a Mayan temple, made the final price tag A$102 million, ten times original estimates. Now almost universally loved and admired, it's hard to believe quite how controversial a project this was during its long haul from plan, as a result of an international competition in the late 1950s, to completion in 1973. For sixteen years, construction was plagued by quarrels and scandal, so much so that Utzon, who won the competition in 1957, was forced to resign in 1966. Some put it less kindly and say he was hounded out of the country by politicians – the newly elected Askin government disagreeing over his plans for the completion of the interior – and xenophobic local architects. Seven years and three Australian architects later the interior, which never matched Utzon's vision, was finished: the focal Concert Hall, for instance, was completely designed by **Peter Hall** and his team. However, Utzon will now have a chance to have final say: in 1999 he was appointed as a design consultant to prepare a Statement of Design Principles for the building, which will become the permanent reference for its conservation and development.

"Opera House" is actually a misnomer: it's really a performing arts centre, one of the busiest in the world, with five performance venues inside its shells, plus two restaurants, several popular cafés and bars, an Aboriginal artists' gallery, and a stash of upmarket souvenir shops on the lower concourse. The building's initial impetus, in fact, was as a home for the Sydney Symphony Orchestra, and it was designed with the huge **Concert Hall**, seating 2690, as the focal point;

the smaller **Opera Theatre** (1547 seats), is used as the Sydney performance base for Opera Australia (seasons June–Nov & Feb–March), the Australian Ballet (mid-March to May & Nov–Dec) and the Sydney Dance Company. There are three theatrical venues: the **Drama Theatre** and **The Playhouse**, both used primarily by the Sydney Theatre Company, and the more intimate **Studio**. The last was added in 1999 as part of the ten-year plan, and aims to draw in a younger audience, offering mainly contemporary Australian work and cabaret, with an adaptable theatre-in-the-round format. There's plenty of action outside the Opera House too, with the use of the Mayan temple-inspired **Forecourt** and Monumental Steps as an amphitheatre; the steps provide seating for everything from free rock concerts to outdoor films. Sunday is the liveliest day, when the **Tarpeian Markets** (10am–4pm), with an emphasis on Australian crafts, are held, further enlivened by a programme of "Sundays 'Round the House": free outdoor concerts ranging from jazz, classical and folk to rock.

If you're not content with gazing at the outside – much the building's best feature – and can't attend a performance, there are **guided tours** available: the Front-of-House tour gives an overview of the site, looking at the public areas and discussing the unique architecture (daily 8.30am–5pm, every 30–40min; 45min; $14.70). Backstage tours run less frequently, about once or twice a week, and include access to the scenery docks, rehearsal rooms and technical areas (1hr 30min; $24; bookings on ☎ 02/9250 7250). It's only on these tours that you can see the small exhibition area in the foyer of The Playhouse where two original Utzon models of the Opera House are displayed, alongside a series of small oil paintings depicting the life of **Bennelong**, the Iora tribesman who was initially kidnapped as little more than an Aboriginal "specimen" but later became a much-loved addition to Governor Arthur Phillip's household; Phillip later built a hut for him on what is now the site of the Opera House. History buffs who would like to learn more can go on Bennelong Point history tours, offered by arrangement on the booking number above.

The best way to appreciate the Opera House, of course, is to attend an evening **performance**: the building is particularly stunning when floodlit and, once you're inside, the huge windows come into their own as the dark harbour waters reflect a shimmering image of the night-time city – interval drinks certainly aren't like this anywhere else in the world. You could choose to **eat** at what is considered to be one of Sydney's best restaurants, *Bennelong* (☎ 02/9250 7548), overlooking the city skyline, or take a drink at its stylish cocktail bar. For fish and chips head for *Harbour*, located on the Northern Boardwalk with uninterrupted views of the Bridge, Manly and the Heads, or go down to the Lower Concourse to the cheaper, and very lively, *Concourse Cafe and Bar*. **Packages** which include tours, meals, drinks and performances can be purchased over the internet or on-site (☎ 02/9250 7250, ⓦ www.soh.nsw.gov.au), and can be good value.

The Harbour Bridge

The charismatic **Harbour Bridge**, in the opposite direction from Circular Quay, has straddled the channel dividing North and South Sydney since 1932; today it makes the view from Circular Quay complete. The largest arch bridge in the world when it was built, its construction costs weren't paid off until 1988. There's still a $2 toll to drive across, payable only when heading south; you can walk or cycle it for free. Pedestrians should head up the steps to the bridge from Cumberland Street, reached from The Rocks via the Argyle Steps off Argyle Street (see p.114), and walk on the eastern side (the western side is the preserve of cyclists). The ever-increasing volume of traffic in recent years proved too much for the bridge to bear, and a harbour **tunnel** (also $2 heading south) now crosses the river, starting south of the Opera House.

The bridge demands full-time maintenance, protected from rust by continuous painting in trademark steel-grey. One of Australia's best-known comedians, Paul Hogan of *Crocodile Dundee* fame, worked as a rigger on "the coathanger" before being rescued by a *New Faces* talent quest in the 1970s. To check out Hoge's vista, you can follow a rigger's route and climb the bridge with **Bridge Climb**, who take small, specially equipped groups (maximum ten) to the top of the bridge (tours every 10–20min; daily 7.45am–3.05pm, or until 4.25pm during Daylight Saving, plus pricier night-time climbs available; minimum age 12; Mon–Fri $117, Sat & Sun $142; booking advised, particularly on weekends on ☎ 02/8274 7777 or through ATS on ☎ 02/9247 5151; ⓦ www.bridge-climb.com). Though the experience takes three hours, only two hours is spent on the bridge, gradually ascending and pausing while the guide points out landmarks and offers interesting background snippets. The hour spent checking in and getting kitted up at the "Base" at 5 Cumberland St, The Rocks, makes you feel as if you are preparing to go into outer space, as do the grey *Star Trek*-style suits specially designed so that you blend in with the bridge and don't spoil the view at ground level. It's really not as scary as it looks – there's no way you can fall off, harnessed as you are into a cable system, though phobics beware. The only thing of your own you can take up are your glasses, attached to your suit by special cords so that nothing be dropped onto cars or people below. Annoyingly, since this has to be one of the world's greatest **photo opportunities**, this precaution means you can't take your camera with you, and although you get one group photo on top of the bridge free with the price of the climb, the group – of jolly strangers, arms akimbo – crowds out the background. To get a good shot showing yourself with the splendours of the harbour behind, you'll need to fork out $14.95 for one large photo or $24.95 for four different small ones, taken by the guide.

If you can't stomach (or afford) the climb, there's a **lookout point** (daily 10am–5pm; $5; 5min walk from Cumberland St then 200 steps) actually inside the bridge's southern pylon where, as well as gazing out across the harbour, you can study a photo exhibition on the bridge's history.

The Rocks

The Rocks, immediately beneath the bridge, is the heart of historic Sydney. On this rocky outcrop between Sydney Cove and Walsh Bay, Captain Arthur Phillip proclaimed the establishment of Sydney Town in 1788, the first permanent European settlement in Australia. Within decades, the area had become little more than a slum of dingy dwellings, narrow alleys and dubious taverns and brothels. In the 1830s and 1840s, merchants began building fine stone warehouses here, but as the focus for Sydney's shipping industry moved from Circular Quay, the area fell into decline. By the 1870s and 1880s, the notorious Rocks "pushes", gangs of "larrikins" (louts), mugged passers-by and brawled with each other: the narrow street named **Suez Canal** was a favourite place to hide in wait. Some say the name is a shortening of Sewers' Canal, and indeed the area was so filthy that whole streetfronts had to be torn down in 1900 to contain an outbreak of the bubonic plague. It remained a run-down, depressed and depressing quarter until the 1970s, when there were plans to raze the historic cottages, terraces and warehouses to make way for office towers.

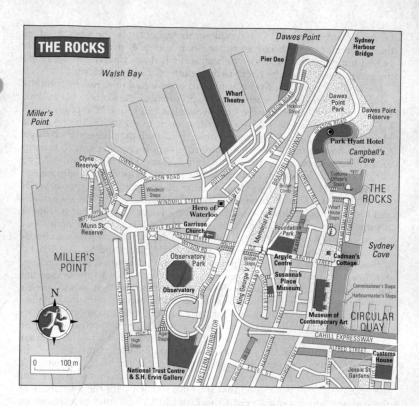

However, due to the foresight of a radical building workers' union which opposed the demolition, the restored and renovated **historic quarter** is now one of Sydney's major tourist attractions and, despite a passing resemblance to a historic theme park, it's worth exploring. It's also the best place, apart from the airport, to do tax-free shopping.

There are times, though, when the old atmosphere still seems to prevail: Friday and Saturday nights in The Rocks can be thoroughly drunken, and there's frequently **trouble** – so much so that police often patrol on horseback and CCTV has been installed. New Year's Eve is also riotously celebrated here, to the backdrop of fireworks over the harbour. The best time to come for a drink is Sunday afternoon when many of the pubs here offer live jazz or folk music.

Information, tours and transport

The best place to start your tour of The Rocks is the **Sailors' Home**, at 106 George St, built in 1864 to provide decent lodgings for visiting sailors as an alternative to the brothels and inns in the area. The building housed sailors until the early 1980s but now contains the **Sydney Visitor Centre** (daily 9am–6pm; ☏ 02/9255 1788, ⓦ www.sydneyvisitorcentre.com), which at street level supplies tourist information (including a guided tour leaflet for $2.20), and also has a budget accommodation booking board, with direct freephone access to the establishments listed. On the two galleried levels, information is provided about the history and sights of The Rocks along with a re-creation of the original sailors' sleeping quarters. The centre can also book you on **The Rocks Walking Tours**, which start from the tour operator's offices at Shop 4, Kendall Lane (tours Mon–Fri 10.30am, 12.30pm & 2.30pm, Sat & Sun 11.30am & 2pm; Jan 10.30am & 2.30pm only; 1hr 30min; $14.85; ℡02/9247 6678, ⓦwww.rockswalkingtours.com.au). Well worth the money is the night-time **Ghost tour** offered by Unseen Sydney Walking Tours (Tues & Thurs–Sun at 6.30pm at an appointed place in Circular Quay; 1hr 30min; $19.80; book through ATS on ℡02/9555 2700; ⓦwww.unseensydney.com.au), a history tour with a chilling angle, led by a funny, theatrical storyteller; highlight is the final drink in the *Hero of Waterloo* pub. For a cyber tour of the area, the ⓦwww.rocksvillage.com website focuses on The Rocks precinct.

The small sandstone house next to the information centre, at 110 George St, is **Cadman's Cottage**, the oldest private house still standing in Sydney, built in 1816 for John Cadman, ex-convict and Government coxswain. It's now the **National Parks and Wildlife Service** bookshop and information centre (Mon–Fri 9.30am–4.30pm, Sat & Sun 10am–4.30pm; ℡02/9247 5033, ⓦwww.npws.nsw.gov.au), providing information about Sydney's national parks and taking bookings for trips to Fort Denison and other har-bour islands.

The corner of Argyle and Kent streets, Millers Point is a terminus for sever-al useful **bus routes** so you can aim to walk here through The Rocks and then catch a bus back: routes #431–434 go along George Street to Railway Square and from there to varying locations including Glebe and Balmain, while #339 goes to the eastern beaches suburb of Clovelly via George Street in the City and Elizabeth and Albion streets in Surry Hills.

Exploring The Rocks: from Campbells Cove to the Argyle Cut

Just exploring the narrow alleys and streets hewn out of the original rocky spur is the chief delight of The Rocks, a voyage of discovery that involves climbing and descending several stairs and cuts to different levels. A set of steps alongside The Sydney Visitor Centre leads down to the waterfront and the Overseas Passenger Terminal (see p.108). Head north from here along the waterfront walkway to **Campbells Cove**, where the beautifully restored 1830s **Campbell's Storehouses**, once part of the private wharf of the merchant Robert Campbell, now house a shopping and eating complex (for details of restaurants, see "Eating and Drinking", beginning on p.158). A replica of Captain Bligh's ship, the *Bounty*, is moored here between cruises (see box p.107), adding a Disneyish atmosphere, while a luxury hotel, the *Park Hyatt*, overlooks the whole area. Climb the **Customs Officer's Stairs** from Campbells Cove to Hickson Road, from where it's a short walk to Dawes Point (see overleaf) beneath the Harbour Bridge, or browse in the road's **Metcalfe Stores**, anoth-er storehouses-turned-shopping complex, this time dating from around 1912. Exit onto George Street, where at weekends you can further satisfy your shop-ping urge at **The Rocks Market** (Sat & Sun 10am–5pm), which takes over the entire Harbour Bridge end of the street with more than a hundred stalls selling bric-a-brac and arts and crafts mostly with an Australiana/souvenir slant.

There's more shopping at the **Argyle Stores**, on the corner of Argyle and Playfair streets, a complex of decidedly more tasteful and upmarket boutiques (including an outlet of the fashionable Australian jewellery-makers Dinosaur Designs) in a beautifully restored set of former bond stores arranged around an inner courtyard; on the top floor you can take in great views from the bar of *Bel Mondo* (see p.160), a pricey Italian restaurant (also accesses from Gloucester

1

> ## Just for kids
>
> There are two attractions in The Rocks aimed at children:**The Rocks Toy Museum** , just off Argyle Street on Kendall Lane (daily 10am–6pm; $6, child $4, family $12), has two floors of collectable toys from the nineteenth through to the twentieth century, housed in a sandstone 1850s coachhouse; while next door, the**Rocks Puppet Cottage** puts on free weekend and school holiday puppet shows (11am, 12.30pm & 2pm).

Walk, see below). The Argyle Stores is just near the impressive **Argyle Cut**, which slices through solid stone to The Rocks' other half, Millers Point (see opposite). The cut took eighteen years to complete, carved first with chisel and hammer by convict chain gangs who began the work in 1843; when transportation ended ten years later the tunnel was still unfinished, and it took hired hands to complete it in 1859. Walk up the **Argyle Steps** and along the narrow, brick pedestrian walkway of peaceful **Gloucester Walk** – this was the very rocky spur the area was named after – peep through greenery to gardens below. There's also a tiny sculpture park, **Foundation Park**, which is a delight to stumble across: remains of cottage foundations were recently discovered here and they have been used as the basis for installations of sculptures of Victorian furniture. En route back to the northern end of George Street have a drink at *The Mercantile*, one of Sydney's best-known Irish hotels (see p.170). Gloucester Walk also leads to the pedestrian entrance of the Harbour Bridge on **Cumberland Street**, the location of a couple of fine old boozers, the *Glenmore* and the *Australian* (see p.169). From the latter, head down **Gloucester Street**; at nos. 58–64 is the **Susannah Place Museum** (Jan daily 10am–5pm, Feb–Dec Sat & Sun 10am–5pm; $7; Ⓦ www.hht.nsw.gov.au), a row of four brick terraces built in 1844 and occupied by householders until 1990; it's now a "house museum" (including a re-created corner store), which conserves the domestic history of Sydney's working class.

The old wharves and Fort Denison

At the end of George Street, under the Harbour Bridge, **Dawes Point** separates Sydney Cove, on the Circular Quay side, from **Walsh Bay** and the old piers; the park here is a favourite spot for photographers. Looking out past the Opera House, you can see **Fort Denison** on a small island in the harbour: "Pinchgut", as the island is still known, was originally used as a special prison for the tough nuts the penal colony couldn't crack. During the Crimean Wars in the mid-nineteenth century, however, old fears of a Russian invasion were rekindled and the fort was built as part of a defence ring around the harbour. For those interested in Australian history, there are tours organized by the NPWS from Circular Quay. Tours are booked through and meet up at Cadman's Cottage (see overleaf; ☎ 02/9247 5033). There are daytime tours (Mon–Fri 11.30am & 2pm, Sat 9am, 11.30am & 2pm, Sun 11.30am & 1.30pm; 2hr 30min; $22) and for early birds, breakfast tours with a cooked meal in the fort's new café included (Tues & Thurs 6.50am, Sat 6.40am; 2hr; $37).

Go a bit further along Hickson Road to the **Wharf Theatre** (Pier 4/5), home to the Sydney Theatre Company and the Sydney Dance Company as well as about twenty other smaller arts organizations. From the restaurant and its bar you can revel in the sublime view across Walsh Bay to Balmain, Goat Island and the North Shore, or get closer to the water (and the arts workers) at the cute little *Dance Cafe* on the ground floor. The exhibition of posters of past productions in the hallway leading to the restaurant might even tempt you to come back for a performance (see 8). Guided tours of the theatre, including the costume department and a set construction, are also available (Thurs 10am; 1hr–1hr 30min; $5; kings on ☎02/9250 1777).

Millers Point and Observatory Park

Beyond the wharves, looking towards Darling Harbour, **Millers Point** is a reminder of how The Rocks used to be – with a surprisingly real community feel so close to the tourist hype of The Rocks, as much of the housing is government or housing association-owned. Of course the area has its upmarket pockets, like the very swish *Observatory Hotel* (see Kent Street, but for the moment, the traditional street-corner pubs and shabby terraced houses on the hill are reminiscent of the raffish atmosphere typical of the whole area, and the mostly peaceful residential streets, a delight to wander in.

Reach the area through the Argyle Cut (see opposite) or from the end of George Street, heading onto **Lower Fort Street**. The **Colonial House Museum**, 53 Lower Fort St (daily 10am–5pm; $1), takes up the bottom two floors of a residential terrace house (1883) where local character Shirley Ball has lived for over 50 years; her collection – a labour of love rather than a commercial enterprise – is crammed into six rooms, and includes period furnishings, hundreds of photographs of the area, etchings, artefacts and models. Continue to wander up Lower Fort Street and stop for a drink at the **Hero of Waterloo** at no. 81 (see p.169), built from sandstone excavated from the Argyle Cut in 1844, then peek in at the place of worship for the military stationed at Dawes Point fort from the 1840s, the **Garrison Church** (officially Holy Trinity Church; daily 9am–5pm) on the corner of Argyle Street. Next to the church, the volunteer-run **Garrison Gallery Museum** (Tues, Wed, Fri & Sat 11am–3pm, Sun noon–4pm; free) is housed in what was once the parish schoolhouse – Australia's first Prime Minister, Edmund Barton, was educated here and the collection of turn-of-the-century photographs, complete with images of ragged barefoot children and muddy dirt roads, gives a good indication of the conditions of his tutelage. Beside the church, Argyle Place has some of the area's prettiest old terrace houses.

From here, walk up the steps on Argyle Street opposite the church to **Observatory Park** with its shady Moreton Bay figs, park benches and lawns, for a marvellous hilltop view over the architecture below and the whole harbour in all its different aspects – glitzy Darling Harbour, the new Anzac Bridge in one direction and the old Harbour Bridge in the other, gritty container terminals, ferries gliding by – and on a rainy day enjoy it from the bandstand which dominates the park. It's also easy to reach the park from the **Bridge Stairs** off Cumberland Street by the Argyle Cut.

The Italianate-style **Sydney Observatory** from which the park takes its name marked the beginning of an accurate time standard for the city when it opened in 1858, calculating the correct time from the stars and signalling it to ships in the harbour and Martin Place's GPO by the dropping of a time ball in its tower at 1pm every day – a custom which still continues. Set amongst some very pretty gardens, the Observatory has been a **museum of astronomy** (daily 10am–5pm; free; ⓦwww.phm.gov.au) since 1982 when it became an offshoot of the Powerhouse Museum (see p.128). A large section is devoted to the Transit of Venus, a rare astronomical event which occurs about twice every century; it was the observation of this which prompted Captain Cook's 1769 voyage. The extensive ... ition of astronomical equipment, both obselete and high-tech, includes ...till working) telescope installed under the copper dome to observe th... 4 Transit of Venus. Another highlight, in the "Stars of the Southern Sky"... on, are three animated videos of Aboriginal creation stories, retellings o... v the stars came to be, from the Milky Way to Orion. Every evening yo... n view the southern sky through telescopes and learn about the South... ross and other southern constellations (times vary with season; 2hr tour... ude a lecture, film, exhibition, guided view of the telescopes and a ... at the sky, weather permitting; booking essential on ☎ 02/9217 04... usually up to a week in advance; $10); there's also a small planetarium w... is only used during night visits when the sky is not clear enough for o... vation.

Also in the ... k is the **National Trust Centre**, located in the former military hospital ...315) south of the Observatory. The rear of the building, purpose-built a... school in 1850 in neo-Regency style, houses the **S. H. Ervin Gallery** (T...–Fri 11am–5pm, Sat & Sun noon–5pm; free; entry to special exhibitions ... $6; ☎ 02/9258 0123 for details of special exhibitions; Ⓦ www.nsw... tionaltrust.org.au), the result of a million-dollar bequest by Ervin in 19...; the changing thematic exhibitions, around eight each year, are of scholarly ... non-mainstream Australian art, focusing on subjects such as Aboriginal ... r women artists. There's also a café (Tues–Fri 11am–3pm, Sat & Sun 1–5pm), and a specialist bookshop (Tues–Fri 9am–5pm, Sat & Sun noon–5pm) where you can pick up leaflets about other historic buildings and settlements in New South Wales.

City Centre

From Circular Quay south as far as King Street is Sydney's **Central Business District**, often referred to as the **CBD**, with **Martin Place** as its commercial nerve centre. A pedestrian mall lined with imposing banks and investment companies (check out the splendid marbled interior of the National Australia Bank), Martin Place has its less serious moments at summer lunchtimes, when street performances are held at the little amphitheatre, and all year round stalls of flower- and fruit-sellers add some colour. The vast **General Post Office**, built between 1865 and 1887 with its landmark clock tower added in 1900, broods over the George Street end of the place in all its Victorian-era pomp. The upper floors have been incorporated into part of a five-star luxury hotel, the *Westin Sydney*, which opened in late 1999; the rest of the hotel resides in the 31-storey tower behind. The old building and the new tower meet in the grand Atrium Courtyard, with its restaurants, bars, classy designer stores and the **GPO Store**, a gastronome's delight featuring a butcher, fish shop, deli, cheese room, wine merchant and greengrocer. The other end of Martin Place emerges opposite the old civic buildings on lower Macquarie Street (see p.122). The cramped streets of the CBD itself, overshadowed by office buildings, have little to offer as you stroll through, though a crowd often gathers outside the **Australian Stock Exchange** opposite Australia Square at 20 Bond St to gaze at the computerized display of stocks and shares through the glass of the ground floor. For a glimpse at how all this wealth might be spent, stroll over to Sydney's most upmarket shopping centre, **Chifley Plaza**, on the corner of Hunter and Phillip streets, where you'll find Kenzo, Max Mara and other exclusive labels; a huge stencil-like sculpture of former Australian Prime Minister Ben Chifley, by artist Simeon Nelson, stands on the pleasant palm-filled square outside.

Sydney Sculpture Walk

The specially commissioned artworks of the **Sydney Sculpture Walk** – a City of Sydney Council initiative for the 2000 Olympics and the 2001 Centenary of Federation – form a circuit from the the Royal Botanic Gardens, through the Domain, Cook and Phillip Park, the streets of the CBD, Hyde Park and East Circular Quay. One of the most striking of the twenty site-specific pieces is Anne Graham's *Passage*, at the eastern end of Martin Place. At timed intervals, a fine mist emerges from grilles marking the outlines of an early colonial home which once stood here, creating a ghostly house on still days. A map showing the sculpture sites is available from Sydney Town Hall (p.118) or the City Exhibition Space (p.108).

Museum of Sydney

North of Martin Place, on the corner of Bridge and Phillip streets, stands the **Museum of Sydney** (daily 9.30am–5pm; $7; ℡ 02/9251 5988 for exhibition details). The site itself is the reason for the museum's existence, for here from 1983 a ten-year archeological dig unearthed the foundations of the first Government House built by Governor Phillip in 1788 which was home to eight subsequent governors of NSW before it was demolished in 1846. The museum is totally original in its approach, presenting history in an interactive manner, through exhibitions, film, photography and multimedia, though you may come away feeling less well informed than you expected. A key feature of the museum are the special exhibitions – about four each year – so it's worth finding out what's on before you go.

First Government Place, a public square in front of the museum, preserves the site of the original Government House: its foundations are marked out in different coloured sandstone on the pavement. The museum itself is built of honey-coloured sandstone blocks, using the different types of tooling available from the earliest days of the colony right up to modern times: you can trace this development from the bottom to the top of the facade. Near the entrance, **Edge of the Trees**, an emotive sculptural installation which was a collaboration between a European and an Aboriginal artist, conveys the complexity of a shared history that began in 1788.

If you decide to pay to get into the rest of the museum, it's best first to go upstairs to the **auditorium** on level 2 and watch the fifteen-minute video explaining the background and aims of the museum. Back on level 1 a video screen shows images of the bush, sea and sandstone Sydney as it was before the arrival of Europeans, while on level 2, recordings of Sydney Kooris (Aboriginal people) are combined with video images to help the viewer reflect on contemporary experience. At the dark and creepy **Bond Store** on level 3, holographic "ghosts" relate tales of old Sydney as an ocean port. On the same level, a whole area is devoted to some rather wonderful **panoramas** of Sydney Harbour with views of the harbour itself from the windows.

There is also an excellent **gift shop** with a wide range of photos, artworks and books on Sydney. Quite separate from the museum is the expensive, licensed *MOS* **café**, on First Government Place; usually filled with lawyers at lunchtime, it's agreeably peaceful for a (reasonably priced) coffee at other times.

King Street to Liverpool Street

Further south from Martin Place, the streets get a little more interesting. The rectangle between Elizabeth, King, George and Park streets is Sydney's prime shopping area, with a number of beautifully restored **Victorian arcades** (the

Imperial Arcade, Strand Arcade and Queen Victoria Building are all worth a look) and Sydney's two **department stores**, the very upmarket David Jones on the corner of Market and Elizabeth streets, established over 160 years ago, and the more populist but still quality-focused Grace Bros on Pitt Street Mall.

The landmark **AMP Centrepoint Tower** (daily 9am–10.30pm, Sat until 11.30pm; viewing gallery and skyride $19.80, child $13.20; ⓦ www.centre-point.com.au), on the corner of Market and Pitt streets, a giant golden gear-stick thrusting up 305m, is the tallest poppy in the Sydney skyline – and its observation level is the highest in the entire southern hemisphere, though management must ruefully admit the tower's height is just beaten by the spire of the Sky Tower in Auckland, New Zealand, which is 23m taller. The 360° view from the observation level is especially fine at sunset, and on clear days you can even see the Blue Mountains, 100km away. It can get crowded on the observation level and to see the view in more peace, head down the stairs to the café, where you can enjoy floor-to-ceiling views along with a cup of tea. The observation deck is now packaged with the new **Skytour** on entry lift level, a tacky "virtual ride" introduction to a clichéd Australia that lasts forty long minutes. Unfortunately the addition of Skytour has doubled the entry price to Centrepoint Tower and no single ticket is available.

Nearby, several fine old buildings – the State Theatre, the Queen Victoria Building and the Town Hall – provide a pointed contrast. If heaven has a hall-way, it surely must resemble that of the restored **State Theatre**, just across from the Pitt Street Mall at 49 Market St, host to the Sydney Film Festival (see p.179). Step inside and take a look at the ornate and glorious interior of this picture palace opened in 1929 – a lavishly painted, gilded and sculpted corri-dor leads to the lush, red and wood-panelled foyer. To see more of the interi-or, you'll need to attend the film festival or other events held here, such as con-certs and drama, or if you're really keen you can go on a self-guided tour (Mon–Fri 10am–5pm, Sat 10am–2pm; 1hr; $12). Otherwise, pop into the beautiful little *Retro Cafe*, attached, for a coffee.

The stately **Queen Victoria Building**, taking up the block bounded by Market, Druitt, George and York streets, is another of Sydney's finest – but this hasn't stopped Sydneysiders, with characteristic disrespect, from abbreviating it to the QVB. Stern and matronly, a huge statue of Queen Victoria herself sits outside the magnificent building. Built as a market hall in 1898, two years before her death, the long-neglected building was beautifully restored and reborn in 1986 as an upmarket shopping mall (shopping hours Mon–Sat 9am–6pm, Thurs until 9pm, Sun 11am–5pm but you can walk through the building 24hr). The interior is magnificent, with its beautiful woodwork, gallery levels and antique lifts; Charles I is beheaded on the hour, every hour, by figurines on the ground-floor mechanical clock. From Town Hall Station you can walk right through the basement level (mainly bustling food stalls) and continue via the Sydney Central Plaza to Grace Bros Department Store, emerging on Pitt Street without having to go outside – very cooling on a hot day. From the basement up, the four levels of the QVB become progressively upmarket; the third level is worth visiting for its boutiques featuring the work of new young Australian designers. There's also a guided **tour** of the building from the tour desk on the ground floor (Mon–Sat 11.30am & 2.30pm, Sun noon & 2.30pm; 1hr; $5) which delves into its architecture and history.

In the realm of architectural excess, however, the **Town Hall** is king – you'll find it across from the QVB on the corner of George and Druitt streets. It was built during the boom years of the 1870s and 1880s as a homage to Victorian England, and has a huge organ inside its Centennial Hall, giving it the air of a sec-

ular cathedral. Throughout the ~~rior~~ different styles of ornamentation compete for attention in a riot of colo~~~~nd detail; the splendidly dignified toilets are a must-see. Concerts and the~~~~ performances (details on the City Infoline Mon–Fri 9am–6pm; ℡ 02/9~~~~ 9007) set off the splendiferous interior perfectly.

Down to Chinatow~~~~

Between Town Hall and ~~~~ntral Station, **George Street** becomes increasingly downmarket but alon~~~~he way you'll pass Chinatown and Paddy's Market, both in the area know~~~~ **Haymarket**, and just beyond is Darling Harbour (see p.125). The short ~~~~tch between the Town Hall and Liverpool Street is for the most part teen~~~~ territory, a frenetic zone of **multiscreen cinemas**, pinball halls and fast-f~~~~d joints; *Planet Hollywood* also attracts a keen stream of youngsters. The stretc~~~~ i~~~~ trouble-prone on Friday and Saturday nights when there are pleasanter p~~~~es to choose to catch a film (see cinema listings, p.178). Things change pace ~~~~ Liverpool Street, where Sydney's **Spanish corner** consists basically of a ~~~~tch of Spanish restaurants (see pp.160–161 for recommendations) and th~~~~ *Spanish Club*.

Sydney's **Chinatown** is a more full-blooded affair than Spanish corner. Through the Chinese gates, **Dixon Street Mall** is the main drag, buzzing day and night as people crowd into numerous restaurants, pubs, cafés, cinemas, food stalls and Asian grocery stores. Towards the end of January or in the first weeks of February, Chinese New Year is celebrated here with gusto: dragon and lion dances, food festivals and musical entertainment compete with the noise and smoke from strings of Chinese crackers. The return of Hong Kong to China in 1997 has resulted in massive investments of Hong Kong money in Australian enterprises, including Australia's biggest restaurant, the *Kam Fook* in Chinatown (see p.161). Just on the edge of Chinatown at the southern fringes of Darling Harbour, is the serene **Chinese Garden** (see p.127).

The area immediately south of Chinatown is enlivened every Saturday and Sunday by Sydney's oldest market, frenetic **Paddy's Market** (Fri, Sat & Sun 9am–4.30pm), in its undercover home at the corner of Thomas and Quay streets, next door to the Entertainment Centre. It's a good place to buy cheap vegetables, seafood, plants, clothes and bric-a-brac. Above the old market, a new multilevel shopping mall has been built, the **Market City Shopping Centre**, which has a very Asian feel – you could easily imagine yourself in one of the air-conditioned centres of Bangkok or Kuala Lumpur; there's an excellent Asian food court (see p.160) on the top floor next to the Reading multiscreen cinema.

The historic precinct: Hyde Park, College Street and Macquarie Street

Lachlan Macquarie, reformist governor of New South Wales between 1809 and 1821, gave the early settlement its first imposing public buildings, clustered on the southern half of his namesake Macquarie Street. He had a vision of an elegant, prosperous city – although the Imperial Office in London didn't share his enthusiasm for expensive civic projects. Refused both money and expertise, Macquarie was forced to be resourceful: many of the the city's finest buildings were designed by the ex-convict architect Francis Greenway and paid for with rum money, the proceeds of a monopoly on liquor sales. Hyde Park was fenced off by Governor Macquarie in 1810 to mark the outskirts of his township, and with its war memorials and church, and peripheral museum and Catholic cathedral, is still very much a formal city park.

Hyde Park

From the Town Hall, it's a short walk east to **Hyde Park** along Park Street, which divides the park into two sections, with the Anzac Memorial in the southern half, and the Sandringham Memorial Gardens and Archibald Fountain in the north, overlooked by St James's Church across the northern boundary. From Queens Square, **St James's Church** (daily 9am–5pm) marks the entry to the park – the Anglican church, completed in 1824, is Sydney's oldest place of worship. It was one of Macquarie's schemes built to ex-convict Greenway's design, and the architect originally planned it as a courthouse – you can see how the simple design has been converted into a graceful church. It's worth popping into the crypt to see the richly coloured Children's Chapel mural painted in the 1930s. Behind St James train station, the **Archibald Fountain** commemorates the association of Australia and France during World War I and near here is a **giant chess set** where you can challenge the locals to a match. Further south near Park Street, the Sandringham Memorial Gardens also commemorate Australia's war dead, but the most potent of these monuments is the famous **Anzac Memorial** at the southern end of the park. Fronted by the tree-lined Pool of Remembrance, the thirty-metre-high cenotaph, unveiled in 1934, is classic Art Deco right down to the detail of Raynor Hoff's stylized soldier figures solemnly decorating the exterior.

College Street: the Australian Museum and St Mary's Cathedral

Facing Hyde Park across College Street, at the junction of William Street as it heads up to Kings Cross, the **Australian Museum** (daily 9.30am–5pm; 30min tours 10am–3pm on the hour; $8; ⓦwww.austmus.gov.au) is primarily a museum of natural history, with an interest in human evolution and Aboriginal culture and history. The collection was founded in 1827, but the actual building, a grand sandstone affair with a facade of Corinthian pillars, wasn't fully finished until the 1860s and was extended in the 1980s. The core of the old museum are the three levels of the **Long Gallery**, Australia's first exhibition gallery, opened in 1855 to a public keen to gawk at the colony's curiosities. Many of the classic displays of the following hundred years remain here, Heritage-listed, contrasting with a very modern approach in the rest of the museum.

On the **ground floor**, the impressive **Indigenous Australian** exhibition looks at the history of Australia's Aboriginal people from the Dreamtime to more contemporary issues of the "stolen generation" and the freedom rides. The ground-floor level of the Long Gallery houses the **Skeletons** exhibit, where you can see a skeletal human going through the motions of riding a bicycle, for example. Level 1 is devoted to **minerals**, but far more exciting are the disparate collections on level 2 – especially the Long Gallery's **Birds and Insects** exhibit, which includes chilling contextual displays of dangerous spiders such as redbacks and funnelwebs. Past this section is the **Biodiversity: life supporting life** exhibition, which looks at the impact of environmental change on the ecosystems of Australian animals, plants, and micro-organisms, around eighty percent of which do not naturally occur elsewhere, giving the country one of the highest levels of so-called biodiversity. In the newer section, the **Discovery Centre** is a hands-on hive of activity for children, while the **Human Evolution** gallery traces the development of fossil evidence worldwide and ends with an exploration of archeological evidence of Aboriginal occupation of Australia. A separate section deals with fossil skeletons of dinosaurs and giant marsupials: best of all is the model of the largest of

Australia's megafauna, the wombat-like Diprotodon, which may have roamed the mainland as recently as ten thousand years ago.

Stanley Street, off College Street just south of the museum, has a cluster of cheap Italian cafés and restaurants (see pp.164–165), and nearby Crown Street features Sydney's version of the *Hard Rock Cafe*. North up College Street is Catholic **St Mary's Cathedral**, overlooking the northeast corner of Hyde Park. The huge Gothic-style church opened in 1882, though the foundation stone was laid in 1821. In 1999 the cathedral at last gained the twin stone spires originally planned for the two southern towers by architect William Wardell in 1865, with $8 million of the project funded by State and Federal governments. The cathedral also gained an impressive new forecourt – a pedestrianized terrace with fountains and pools – with the consolidation of two traffic-isolated parks into the large **Cook and Phillip Park**, which includes a recreation centre (see p.190) with a 50m swimming pool, gym and vegetarian restaurant, *Bodhi on the Park*. The remodelling also created a green link to The Domain.

Macquarie Street

The southern end of Governor Macquarie's namesake street is lined with the grand edifices that were the result of his dreams for a stately city: Hyde Park Barracks, Parliament House, the State Library and the hospital he and his wife designed. The new Sydney – wealthy and international – shows itself on the corner of Bent and Macquarie streets in the curved glass sails of the 41-floor Aurora Place tower, designed by Italian architect Renzo Piano, co-creator of the extraordinary Georges Pompidou Centre in Paris. Macquarie Street neatly divides business from pleasure, separating the office towers and cramped streets of the CBD from the open spaces of The Domain and the Royal Botanic Gardens (see opposite).

Sandstone **Sydney Hospital**, the so-called "Rum Hospital", funded by liquor-trade profits, was Macquarie's first enterprise, commissioned in 1814 and therefore one of the oldest buildings in Australia – apart from the central section, which collapsed and was rebuilt at the end of the century. You can take a short cut through the grounds to The Domain and across to the Art Gallery of NSW (see opposite). One of the original wings of the hospital is now **NSW Parliament House** (Mon–Fri 9.30am–4pm; free guided tours Mon & Fri at 10am, 11am & 2pm; question time Tues–Thurs at 2.15pm; call ☎02/9230 2111 to check), where as early as 1829 local councils called by the governor started to meet, making it by some way the oldest parliament building in Australia. Varied exhibitions in the foyer change about every fortnight – all represent community or public sector interests and range from painting, craft and sculpture to excellent photographic displays. You can listen in on question time when the Parliament is sitting. The other wing was converted into a branch of the **Royal Mint** in response to the first Australian goldrush, and for some time served as a museum of gold mining; since the museum closed in 1997, most of the building has been taken over by NSW Historic Trust offices, but a café (Mon–Fri 9am–5pm) extends onto the verandah looking over Macquarie Street, and some interpretive boards detail the Mint's history.

Next door, the **Hyde Park Barracks** (daily 9.30am–5pm; $6.50), designed by convict-architect Francis Greenway, was built in 1816, again without permission from London, to house 600 male convicts. Now a museum of the social and architectural history of Sydney, it's a great place to visit for a taste of convict life during the early years of the colony: start at the top floor, where you can swing in recreations of the prisoners' rough hammocks. Computer terminals allow you to search for information on a selection of convicts' history and background – several of those logged were American sailors nabbed for misdeeds while in Dublin or English ports (look up poor William Pink). Later the Barracks took in single immigrant women, many of them Irish, escaping the potato famine; an exhibition looks at their lives, and there's a moving monument in the grounds erected by the local Irish community. Look out too for the excellent temporary historical exhibitions (℡02/9223 8922 for details).

The **State Library of New South Wales** (Mon–Fri 9am–9pm, Sat & Sun 11am–5pm; Mitchell Library closed Sun) completes the row of public buildings on the eastern side of Macquarie Street. This complex of old and new buildings includes the 1906 sandstone **Mitchell Library**, with an imposing Neoclassical facade gazing across to the greenness of the Botanic Gardens. Its archive of old maps, illustrations and records relating to the early days of white settlement and exploration in Australia includes the **Tasman Map**, drawn by the Dutch explorer Abel Tasman in the 1640s. The floor-mosaic in the foyer replicates his curious map of the continent, still without an east coast, and its northern extremity joined to Papua New Guinea. A glass walkway links the library with the modern building housing the General Reference Library. Free exhibitions relating to Australian history and literature are a regular feature of its vestibules while lectures, films and video shows take place regularly in the **Metcalfe Auditorium** (call ℡02/9273 1414 for details). You can refresh yourself at the glass-roofed **café** on Level 7 (Mon–Fri 10am–4.30pm, Sat & Sun 11am–3.30pm); airy and with masses of plants, it's a relaxing, inexpensive spot for lunch or just coffee and cake. It's also worth browsing in the library's bookshop on the ground floor, which has the best collection of Australia-related books in Sydney.

The Domain and the Royal Botanic Gardens

The Cook and Phillip Park fills in the gap between Hyde Park and **The Domain**, a much larger, plainer open space that stretches from behind the historic precinct on Macquarie Street to the waterfront, divided from the Botanic Gardens by the ugly Cahill Expressway and Mrs Macquaries Road. In the early days of the settlement, The Domain was the governor's private park; now it's a popular place for a stroll or a picnic, with the Art Gallery of New South Wales, an outdoor swimming pool and Mrs Macquaries Chair to provide distraction. The park has lots of shady trees and during the week it's very busy, with city workers sprawling on the grass eating their sandwiches while more energetic types jog, kick around a football or play lunch-time volleyball. On Sundays, assorted cranks and revolutionaries assemble here for **Speakers' Corner**, and every January thousands of people gather on the lawns to enjoy the free openair opera and concerts of the Sydney Festival (see p.181).

Art Gallery of New South Wales

Beyond St Mary's Cathedral, Art Gallery Road runs through The Domain to the **Art Gallery of New South Wales** (daily 10am–5pm; free except for special exhibitions; free tours Tues–Fri 11am, noon, 1pm & 2pm; ⓦwww.artgallery.nsw.gov.au), whose collection was established in 1874. The original part of the building (1897) is an imposing Neoclassical structure with a facade inscribed with the names of important Renaissance artists, and principally contains the large collection of European art dating from the eleventh century to the twentieth; extensions were added in 1988 which doubled the gallery space and provided a home for mainly Australian art. On level 1, the **Yiribana**

1

Gallery was opened in 1994, devoted to the art and cultural artefacts of Aboriginal and Torres Strait Islanders; one of the most striking exhibits is the **Pukumani Grave Posts**, carved by the Tiwi people of Melville Island. There is a highly recommended half-hour performance in this gallery (Tues–Sat noon) of dance and didgeridoo by an indigenous Australian who also gives a talk about his people, best combined with the free one-hour tour of the indigenous collection (Tues–Fri 11am, Sat & Sun 1pm). Other highlights include some classic **Australian paintings** on level 4: Tom Roberts' romanticized shearing-shed scene *The Golden Fleece* (1894) and an altogether less idyllic look at rural Australia in Russell Drysdale's *Sofala* (1947), a depressing vision of a drought-stricken town. On level 5, the **photographic collection** includes Max Dupain's iconic *Sunbaker* (1939), an early study of Australian hedonism that looks as if it could have been taken in the 1990s.

In addition to the galleries, there is also an auditorium (used for art lectures), an excellent bookshop, a coffee shop on level 2, and a restaurant on level 5 that attracts Sydneysiders for its food and atmosphere.

Mrs Macquaries Chair and "the Boy"

Beyond the Art Gallery, an overpass used to give a good view of the speeding traffic of the ugly 1960s Cahill Expressway but largely as the result of lobbying by the Art Gallery itself, a large section of the expressway has been covered over and grassed. The landscaping greatly reduces the problem of noise and fumes, and no longer disgraces the beginning of one of Sydney's most scenic routes – Mrs Macquaries Road, built in 1816 at the urging of the governor's wife, Elizabeth. The road curves down from Art Gallery Road to Mrs Macquaries Point, which separates idyllic Farm Cove from the grittier Woolloomooloo Bay. At the end is the celebrated lookout point known as **Mrs Macquaries Chair**, a seat fashioned out of the rock, from which Elizabeth could admire her favourite view of the harbour on her daily walk in what was then the governor's private park. On the route down to the point, the **Andrew "Boy" Charlton Pool** is an open-air, saltwater swimming pool safely isolated from the harbour waters (daily Sept–April 6.30am–8pm; $2.75) on the Woolloomooloo side of the promontory, with excellent views across to the engrossingly functional Garden Island Naval Depot; "the Boy", as the locals fondly call it, is a popular hangout for groovy Darlinghurst types and sun-worshipping gays. To get here from King's Cross, descend the McElhone Stairs from Victoria Street (via Woolloomooloo).

The Royal Botanic Gardens

The **Royal Botanic Gardens** (daily 7am–sunset; free), established in 1816, occupy the area between this strip of The Domain and the Opera House, around the headland on Farm Cove where the first white settlers struggled to grow vegetables for the hungry colony. Today's gardeners are much more successful, judging by the well-tended flower beds. While duckponds, a romantic rose garden and fragrant herb garden strike a very English air, look out for native birds and, at dusk, the fruit bats which fly overhead as the nocturnal possums begin to stir (you can also see hundreds of the giant bats hanging by day in the Palm Grove area near the restaurant). There are examples of trees and plants from all over the world, although it's the huge, gnarled native Moreton Bay figs that stand out. The gardens provide some of the most stunning **views** of Sydney Harbour and are always crowded with workers at lunch time, picnickers on fine weekends, and lovers entwined beneath the trees or in the popular café/restaurant.

Many **paths** run through the gardens. A popular and speedy route (roughly 15min) is to start at the northern gates near the Opera House and stroll along the waterfront path to the gates which separate it from The Domain, through here and up the **Fleet Steps** to Mrs Macquaries Chair (see opposite). Within the northern boundaries of the park, the sandstone mansion glimpsed through a garden and enclosure is the Gothic Revival **Government House** (built 1837–45), seat of the governor of New South Wales, and still used for official engagements by the governor, who now lives in a private residence. The stately interior has limited opening hours (Fri–Sun 10am–3pm; free guided tour 45min; ℡02/9931 5222 for more details) but you are free to roam the grounds (daily 10am–4pm). Further south, just inside the gardens at the end of Bridge Street, the **Conservatorium of Music** is housed in what was intended to be the servants' quarters and stables of Government House. Public opinion in 1821, however, deemed the imposing castellated building far too grand for such a purpose and a complete conversion, including the addition of a concert hall, gave it a loftier aim of training the colony's future musicians. Conservatorium students have traditionally given free lunch-time recitals every Tuesday and Friday at 1.10pm during term time. A two-year renovation project, finished in 2000, uncovered an earlier convict-era site which led to an archeological dig being incorporated into the final redesign.

Below the Conservatorium, the remaining southern area of the gardens has a Herb Garden, a cooling Palm Grove, a popular café by the duckponds, and the **Sydney Tropical Centre** (daily 10am–4pm; $2.20), where a striking glass pyramid and adjacent glass arc respectively house native tropical plants and exotics. At an entrance to the park in the southeast corner you'll find the **visitors centre** (daily 9.30am–4.30pm), where free **guided tours** of the gardens commence (daily 10.30am; 1hr–1hr 30min; no bookings required). If you're short of time, a **trackless train** runs through the gardens every twenty minutes (daily 9am–5pm, summer until 6pm; all-day hop-on hop-off service $10, child $5); the main pick-up point is near the Opera House, with stops along the way, including near the visitors centre.

Darling Harbour and around

Darling Harbour, once a grimy industrial docks area, lay moribund until the 1980s, when the State Government chose to pump millions of dollars into the regeneration of this prime city real estate as part of the Bicentenary Project. The huge redevelopment scheme around Cockle Bay included the building of the above-ground monorail, which particularly irked environmentalists, and despite bitter protests a new shopping and entertainment precinct opened in 1988. In many ways it's a thoroughly stylish redevelopment of the old wharves around Cockle Bay – the glistening water channels that run along Palm Avenue are a great piece of modern design – and Darling Harbour and the surrounding areas of **Haymarket**, **Ultimo** and **Pyrmont** have plenty else to offer: museums, an aquarium, entertainment areas, a shopping mall, an IMAX cinema, a children's playground, gardens, a casino, and a convention and exhibition centre. However, it's only recently that Sydneysiders themselves have embraced it. Sneered at for years by locals as tacky and touristy, it took the 1999–2000 Cockle Bay and King Street Wharf development – an upmarket café and restaurant precinct on the eastern side of the waterfront, with several lively bars and a huge 2000-capacity nightclub (*Home*, see p.174) – to finally lure locals in to the much-maligned area.

Behind the development, and accessible from it, is **Darling Park**, with paths laid out in the shape of a waratah flower. The western side of Darling Harbour

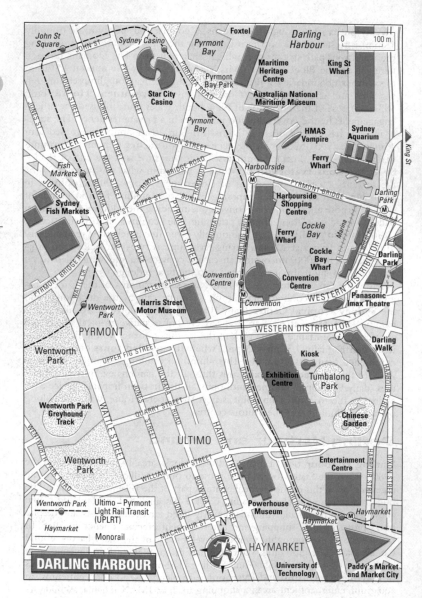

John St
Square
JOHN ST
Sydney Casino
Foxtel
Pyrmont
Bay
Darling
Harbour
0   100 m

Maritime
Heritage
Centre
King St
Wharf

Pyrmont
Bay Park
Star City
Casino
PIRRAMA ROAD
Australian National
Maritime Museum

Pyrmont
Bay
HMAS
Vampire
Sydney
Aquarium

MILLER STREET
UNION STREET
Ferry
Wharf

King St

MOUNT STREET
JONES ST
BULWARA
MT MOUNT STREET
PYRMONT STREET
HARRIS STREET
BRIDGE ROAD
Harbourside

Fish
Markets

PYRMONT BRIDGE

Darling
Park

Sydney
Fish Markets
GIPPS ST
GIPPS ST
PYRMONT
BUNN ST
MURRAY STREET
Harbourside
Shopping
Centre

ADA PLACE
ALLEN STREET
DARLING DRIVE

Cockle
Bay

Marina

Darling
Park

PYRMONT BRIDGE RD
WATTLE ST
Wentworth
Park

Ferry
Wharf
Cockle
Bay
Wharf

PYRMONT

Convention
Centre
Convention
Centre
WESTERN DISTRIBUTOR

Harris Street
Motor Museum
Convention
Panasonic
Imax Theatre

Wentworth
Park
UPPER FIG STREET
WESTERN DISTRIBUTOR
Darling
Walk

Kiosk

Wentworth Park
Greyhound
Track
QUARRY STREET
JONES STREET
BULWARA ROAD
Exhibition
Centre
Tumbalong
Park

DARLING DRIVE
HARBOUR STREET

Wentworth
Park
ULTIMO

HARRIS STREET
Chinese
Garden

WILLIAM HENRY STREET

Entertainment
Centre

WENTWORTH PARK ROAD
WATTLE STREET
HACKETT STREET
DIXON STREET

Powerhouse
Museum
HAY ST
Haymarket

MACARTHUR ST
N
Haymarket
Haymarket

Wentworth Park
Haymarket
Ultimo – Pyrmont
Light Rail Transit
(UPLRT)

Monorail

DARLING HARBOUR
HAYMARKET

University of
Technology
Paddy's Market
and Market City

is dominated by rather ugly modern chain hotels – the *Novotel*, *Hotel Ibis* and *Grand Mercure* – providing the view for the stylish Cockle Bay wharf diners.

To **get to Darling Harbour** you could walk – it's only ten minutes on foot from the Town Hall; from the Queen Victoria Building, walk down Market Street and along the overhead walkway. Further south there's a pedestrian bridge from Bathurst Street or you can cut through on Liverpool Street to Tumbalong Park, both bringing you out near the Chinese Garden.

Alternatively, the **monorail** (see p.89) runs from the city centre to one of three stops around Darling Harbour, and has the views to recommend it. Getting there by **ferry** from Circular Quay, to the wharf outside the Sydney Aquarium, gives you a chance to see a bit of the harbour. State Transit ferries leave from Wharf 5, and stop at McMahons Point and Balmain en route. The Matilda Ferry runs from the Commissioners Steps, outside the Museum of Contemporary Art, and goes via the casino at Pyrmont. By **bus**, the #456 goes from Circular Quay to Darling Harbour, the casino and the Powerhouse Museum. There's actually quite a bit of walking involved getting around the large site and if you're exhausted, or just for fun, you might consider hopping on board the dinky Darling Harbour People Mover Train (daily: summer 10am–6pm, winter 10am–5pm; full circuit 20min; $3) leaving every fifteen minutes from various points around Darling Harbour. The **Darling Harbour Super Ticket** ($48, child $35) includes rides on the monorail, a one-hour cruise on the *Matilda Rocket*, entry to the Aquarium and the Chinese Garden, a meal at the Aquarium's café and discounts at the IMAX Cinema, the Powerhouse Museum and on the People Mover train.

There are always festivals and events, particularly during school holidays. To find out what's on, visit the **Darling Harbour Visitor Information Centre** (daily 9.30am–5.30pm; ℡02/9281 0788, Ⓦwww.darlingharbour.com.au), next door to the IMAX cinema.

Tumbalong Park and around

The southern half of Darling Harbour, just beyond Chinatown and the Entertainment Centre, is focused around **Tumbalong Park**, reached from the city via Liverpool Street. Backed by the Exhibition Centre, this is the "village green" of Darling Harbour and serves as a venue for open-air concerts and free public entertainment. The area surrounding it is perhaps Darling Harbour's most frenetic – at least on weekends during school holidays – as most of the attractions, including a free playground and a stage for holiday concerts, are aimed at children. For some peace and quiet head for the adjacent **Chinese Garden** (Mon–Fri 9.30am–5.30pm, Sat & Sun 9.30am–6pm; closes 1hr earlier in winter; $4.50), which was completed for the Bicentenary Festival in 1988 as a gift from Sydney's sister city Guangdong; the "Garden of Friendship" is designed in the traditional southern Chinese style. Although not large, it feels remarkably calm and spacious – a great place to retreat from the commercial hubbub to read a book, smell the fragrant flowers that attract birds and listen to the lilting Chinese music that fills the air. The balcony of the traditional tea-room offers a bird's-eye view of the dragon wall, waterfalls, a pagoda on a hill and carp swimming in winding lakes.

Beyond the children's playground, the Southern Promenade of Darling Harbour is dominated by the **Panasonic IMAX Theatre** (℡02/9281 3300; $16.20). Its giant cinema screen – which at eight storeys high is said to be the world's largest – shows a constantly changing programme from their 100-film library, with an emphasis on scenic wonders. Other Darling Harbour visual onslaughts include **Aquamagic**, a free night-time laser show projected onto a semicircular water screen on Cockle Bay (Wed–Sun: summer 9pm, 9.30pm & 10pm; winter 7pm & 8pm; 25min).

Sydney Aquarium

Beside the eastern side of **Pyrmont Bridge** – a pedestrian walkway across Cockle Bay, linking the two sides of the harbour – is the impressive **Sydney Aquarium** (daily 9.30am–10pm; $19.50, child $8.50; also an Aquarium Pass including STA ferry from Circular Quay $23.40, child $10.70; also see Darling Harbour Super Ticket, p.127; Ⓦ www.sydneyaquarium.com.au). You can also visit the aquarium with Captain Cook Cruises from Wharf 6 at Circular Quay (for details see box on pp.106–107). If you're not going to get the chance to explore the Barrier Reef, the aquarium makes a surprisingly passable substitute.

The entry level exhibits freshwater fish from the Murray–Darling basin, Australia's biggest river system, but speed past these to get to the two underwater walkways, where you can wander in complete safety among sharks and gigantic stingrays. Another area features exotic species from the Great Barrier Reef, including a mass of glowing, undulating Moon Jellyfish. The Great Barrier Reef Oceanarium finishes with a huge floor-to-ceiling tank where you can sit and be mesmerized by the movement and colour of the underwater world while classical music plays. Alongside all the fish, there are also platypus, seals and fairy penguins on display. Removed here after becoming lost or injured, the seals at least seem to be enjoying themselves in their glass-walled outdoor pool, but the sad looking Fairy penguins appear most out of place.

The National Maritime Museum and around

On the western side of Pyrmont Bridge the **National Maritime Museum** (daily 9.30am–5pm; $10, or with a guided tour of HMAS *Vampire* and HMAS *Onslow* $14; Ⓦ www.anmm.gov.au), with its distinctive modern architecture topped by a wave-shaped roof, highlights the history of Australia as a seafaring nation. However, it goes beyond maritime interests to look at how the sea has shaped Australian life, covering everything from immigration to beach culture and Aboriginal fishing methods. Highlights include the "Merana Eora Nora – First People" exhibition which delves into indigenous culture, and "Navigators – Defining Australia" which focuses on the seventeenth-century Dutch explorers. Outside are its own wharfs, with several vessels moored: the navy destroyer, the *Vampire* and a submarine, the *Onslow* are permanently on display, while a collection of historic vessels, including a 1970s Vietnamese refugee boat, are rotated. There is a pleasant alfresco café here, which you don't have to enter the museum to use, with views of the boats. The bronze **Welcome Wall** outside the museum, unveiled in mid-2000, pays honour to Australia's six million immigrants; over 30,000 names will eventually be added to the wall – members of the public pay $100 to have the name of their immigrant forebear inscribed.

Included in the museum entry charge is a behind-the-scenes tour of the **Maritime Heritage Centre** at Wharf 7 (same hours as museum), just beyond the museum off Pirrama Road and beside Pyrmont Bay Park, where conservation and model-making work takes place and some of the collection is stored. Just nearby, the two-level **Harbourside Shopping Centre** has undergone a A$60 million refurbishment and though it still provides opportunities for souvenir shopping, the range on the first floor is certainly more stylish than it used to be; the ground level, one end of which remains dominated by a noisy video-game parlour, has a more mainstream selection. Amongst the highlights, the first-floor **Gavala: Aboriginal Owned Cultural Centre** (daily 10am–7pm) is a very spacious and relaxed store selling Aboriginal art, clothing, accessories and music – where you can be sure all the profits will go back to the Aboriginal community.

Ultimo: the Powerhouse Museum and around

From Tumbalong Park, a signposted walkway leads to **Ultimo** and its **Powerhouse Museum** on Harris Street (daily 9.30am–5pm; $9, child $2; free first Sat in month; free 45min tour daily 11.30am & 1.30pm; monorail to Haymarket; Ⓦwww.phm.gov.au). Located, as the name suggests, in a former power station, this is arguably the best museum in Sydney, an exciting place with fresh ideas, combining arts and sciences, design, sociology and technology under the same roof – and even fashion, with the much-anticipated "Fashion of the Year" display every November. The displays are varied, presented with an interactive approach that means you'll need hours, or several trips, to investigate the five-level museum properly. The entrance level is dominated by the huge **Boulton and Watt Steam Engine**, first put to use in 1875 in a British brewery; still operational, the engine is often loudly demonstrated. The **Kings Cinema** on level 3, with its original Art Deco fittings, suitably shows the sorts of newsreels and films a Sydneysider would have watched in the 1930s. Judging by the tears at closing time, the **special children's areas** have proved a great success. On level 5, there's a licensed restaurant, colourfully painted with bright Ken Done flower shapes, with a more inexpensive courtyard cafeteria downstairs. The souvenir shop is also worth a browse for some unusual gifts.

Three blocks north, at 320 Harris St, the **Motor World Museum** (Wed–Sun, public holidays & daily during school holidays 10am–5pm; $11; monorail to Convention) houses around two hundred vehicles on three levels. There's the usual mix of vintage cars and 1950s American-style cruisers, a comprehensive collection of Australian automobilia, plus the latest model cars, rally cars and motorcycles.

Pyrmont: Star City and the Sydney Fish Market

Frantic redevelopment is taking place at **Pyrmont**, which juts out into the water between Darling Harbour and Blackwattle Bay. The once dilapidated suburb was Sydney's answer to Ellis Island in the 1950s when thousands of immigrants disembarked at the city's main overseas passenger terminal, Pier 13. Today the former industrial suburb, which had a population of only nine hundred in 1988, is in the process of being transformed into a residential suburb of twenty thousand with A$2 billion worth of investment. With the NSW government selling A$97 million worth of property, this is one of the biggest concentrated sell-offs of land in Australia. The area has certainly become glitzier, with Sydney's casino, Star City, and two TV companies – Channel Ten and Foxtel – now based here. Harris Street has filled up with new shops and cafés, and the area's old pubs have been given a new lease of life. The approach to the spectacularly cabled **Anzac Bridge** (complete with statue of an Australian and New Zealand Army Corps soldier) – Sydney's newest – cuts through Pyrmont and saves between fifteen and twenty minutes' travelling time to Sydney's inner west.

Beyond the Maritime Museum, on Pyrmont Bay is the palm-fronted **Star City**, the spectacularly tasteless Sydney casino (Ⓣ1300/300 711 for more information), open 24 hours a day. As well as the casino, the building houses two theatres, fourteen restaurants, cafés and theme bars, souvenir shops, small supermarkets and a nightclub. It's certainly a place to come for late-night eats, with some quite good-value places like the *City Noodle Cafe* staying open until 2am. The casino interior itself is a riot of giant palm sculptures, prize cars spinning on rotating bases, Aboriginal painting motifs on the ceiling, Australian critters scurrying across a red desert-coloured carpet and an endless array of flashing poker machines. Nearby **Pyrmont Bay Park** is a shady spot to rest, and on the first Saturday of the month it hosts an early morning **Growers Market** (7–11am). To **get to the casino** by bus, you can take the #888

The Olympic legacy

Sydney proudly beat Beijing and Manchester in the chase for the **Olympics** in the year 2000, but no one would have guessed that Juan Antonio Samaranch, Olympic Chairman, would pronounce it the "best games ever". Unseasonably fine spring weather, a public transport system that held up to the job, cheerful volunteers who gave it their all and a public who at the last minute pulled out the stops to buy tickets (91 percent of seats were sold) and party hard in the Live Sites dotted around town, all added up to a hitch-free three-week sporting fiesta. Cries of "Aussie Aussie Aussie Oi Oi Oi" filled the air as Australia won its biggest pile of gold medals ever, 16 in all (plus 25 silver and 17 bronze), putting it fourth on the list (behind the US, Russia and China), an amazing achievement for its population size. Cathy Freeman's lighting of the Olympic flame, and then her gold medal run in the women's 400m, became symbolic of the hopes for reconciliation between Aboriginal and white Australia.

It was all over too soon as far as Sydney was concerned, though the 11th summer **Paralympics** a few weeks later, extended the excitement somewhat as ticket sales far outran expectations, and tested the city's disabled access. Now there's the **Gay Games** (see box pp.175–176) to look forward to in November 2002.

A new body, the **Sydney Olympic Park Authority** which came into existence on 1 January 2001, has the task of turning Sydney Olympic Park into an entertainment and sporting complex with family-oriented recreation in mind.

Sydney Olympic Park

The main focus of Olympic events was **Homebush Bay**, a down-at-heel working-class area in the city's west, far removed from the glamour of Sydney's harbour. There was a certain logic to the choice, as Homebush Bay is virtually the geographical heart of the city, and some heavy-duty sporting facilities – the State Sports Centre and the Aquatic Centre (see opposite) – were already in place. The A$470 million Olympic site was centred around the **Stadium Australia** the venue for the opening and closing ceremonies, track and field events, and marathon and soccer finals. With 110,000 seats, it was the largest ever outdoor Olympic venue, although at the time of writing a A$68 million overhaul is underway to reduce the number of seats to 80,000, a more realistic number for its planned use as a Australian Rules football, cricket, rugby league, rugby union and soccer venue. Tours of the stadium, with commentary, are available daily (hourly 9.30am–5.30pm; 1hr; $26, children $13, family pass $60; turn up at Gate C or book on ☏02/8765 2300, ⓦwww.stadiumaustralia.com).

from Circular Quay via George Street and Town Hall and Darling Habour, #443 from Circular Quay via Phillip and Market streets and the QVB on York street. The Light Rail (see p.89) pulls in underneath the building.

The main reason to visit this area, though, is the **Sydney Fish Market**, on the corner of Pyrmont Bridge Road and Bank Street (daily 7am–4pm; ⓦwww.sydneyfishmarket.com.au), only a ten-minute walk via Pyrmont Bridge Road from Darling Harbour. Now a popular tourist attraction, it's a frenetic, early-morning spectacular. The market is the second-largest seafood market in the world for variety of fish, after the massive Tsukiji market in Tokyo. You need to visit early to see the **auctions** (Mon–Fri only, with the biggest auction floor on Friday; the buyers begin viewing the fish at 4.30am and auctions begin 5.30am but public viewing platform opens 7am); buyers log into computer terminals to register their bids.

You can take away oysters, prawns and cooked seafood and eat picnic-style on waterfront tables. Everything is set up for throwing together an impromptu meal – there's a nearby bakery, a deli, a bottle shop and a grocer. Alternatively, you can eat in at the fish restaurant, *Doyles*, an excellent sushi bar, or have dirt-cheap fish

Just south of the stadium is the **State Sports Centre** (daily 9am–5pm; ☏02/9763 0111), where you can visit the **NSW Hall of Champions**, devoted to the state's sporting heroes (same hours as centre; free; the Hall of Champions is closed when events are being held at the the State Sports Centre, so call the latter before setting out); and the **Sydney International Aquatic Centre** (Mon–Fri 5am–10pm, Sat & Sun 6am–7pm; $5.50; ☏02/9752 3666), where you can hop in the water and try out the facilities, from the competition pools to the landscaped leisure pools with their fountains and slides. On the south side of the site, you can play tennis on the 16-court **Tennis Centre** (enquiries ☏02/8746 0777; tours are also planned), while on the north side, the **Sydney Superdome** (tours daily 10am–4pm on the hour; 45min; $15.40; ☏02/8765 4321, ⊛www.superdome.com.au), which hosted the basketball, rythmic gymnastics and paralympic basketball, is now home to the Sydney Kings (men's team) and Paragon Panthers (women's team) who train and play home games here – basketball season runs between October and April. Further north, the green-friendly Athlete's Village consisted mostly of modular dwellings, which have been moved and reused elsewhere; it is now incorporated into a new solar-powered suburb, **Newington**.

Opposite the Olympic site, the **Bicentennial Park**, opened in 1988, is huge; more than half of the expanse is conservation wetlands. The Visitor Centre (☏02/9763 1844) at the park can give details of around 8km of cycling and walking tracks, and on weekdays at 1.30pm an "Explorer Train" tours the wetlands.

To get an overview of the site, there is an **observation centre** on the 17th floor of the *Novotel Hotel* (daily 10am–4pm; $4), on Olympic Boulevard between Stadium Australia and the Aquatic Centre. **Bus tours**, with commentary, offer a hop-on, hop-off circuit of the venues detailed above, picking up from Olympic Park train station and Homebush Bay ferry wharf (daily 9am–5pm; every 15min; $10); note that entry fees to the venues themselves are not included in the price of the tour, though there is a twenty-percent discount on entry to Stadium Australia.

The nicest way to get out to the Olympic Park is to take the **RiverCat** from Circular Quay which stops off frequently en route to Parramatta; second best option is the direct **train** from Central to Olympic Park Station which runs four times daily on weekdays (otherwise and at weekends change at Lidcombe station from where trains depart every 10min). You can also take a more direct route to some of the venues: **buses** #401–404 run regularly from Strathfield station to the Homebush Bay Olympic Centre, the State Sports Centre and the Athletic Centre.

and chips at the *Italian Fish Market Cafe* (Mon–Fri 4am–4pm, Sat & Sun 5am–5pm); retail shops open at 7am. The **Sydney Seafood School** (☏02/9552 2180) offers seafood cookery lessons, from Thai-style to French provincial, under the expert tuition of well-known local chefs, and also runs a two-hour early morning tour of the selling floor followed by a hands-on cookery class – making yourself a fishy breakfast (held about once a month; $49.50).

To **get to** the fish market by public transport, take the Light Rail service from Central to Fish Market station on Miller Street, near the entrance to the market. Bus #501 runs from outside the Sydney Electricity Building, on the corner of George and Bathurst streets opposite the Town Hall, to right outside the market on Bank Street; otherwise take bus #443 from the Queen Victoria Building, and it's a five-minute walk from the corner of Harris Street and Pyrmont Bridge Road.

Inner western suburbs

West of the centre, immediately beyond Darling Harbour, the inner-city areas of **Glebe** and **Newtown** surround Sydney University, their vibrant cultural mix enlivened by large student populations. On a peninsula north of Glebe and west of The Rocks, **Balmain** is a gentrified working-class dock area popular for its village atmosphere, while en route **Leichhardt** is the focus of Sydney's Italian community.

Glebe

Glebe, right by Australia's oldest university, has gradually been evolving from a café-oriented student quarter to more upmarket thirtysomething territory with a New Age slant. Indeed, it's very much the centre of alternative culture in Sydney, with its yoga schools, healing centres and places selling organic vegetables. **Glebe Point Road**, the focal point of the area, is filled with a mix of cafés with trademark leafy courtyards, restaurants, bookshops and secondhand and speciality shops as it runs uphill from **Broadway**, becoming quietly residential as it slopes down towards the water of Rozelle Bay. The side streets are fringed with renovated two-storey terraced houses with white-iron lacework verandahs. Not surprisingly, Glebe is popular with backpackers, with several hostels (see "Accommodation", p.100); for **longer stays**, check the many café notice boards for flat shares. The new **Broadway Shopping Centre** on nearby Broadway is altering Glebe's laid-back, almost villagey feel, though it certainly is handy if you're staying in the area, with its supermarkets, speciality food shops, huge food court, record, book and clothes shops and twelve-screen cinema. It's linked to Glebe by an overhead walkway from Glebe Point Road opposite one of the street's favourite cafés, *Badde Mannors* (see p.162).

Just before the beginning of Glebe Point Road, on Broadway, **Victoria Park** has a very pleasant, heated outdoor swimming pool and attached gym with a sophisticated café. Next door to the park, as Broadway turns into **Parramatta Road**, is one of the main gates to **Sydney University**, Australia's oldest tertiary educational institution, inaugurated in 1850. You can freely walk through the gates and wander through the pleasant grounds which take up a suburb-sized area between Parramatta Road, and City Road running up to King Street, Newtown (see p.134).

Glebe itself is at its best on Saturday, when **Glebe Market**, which takes place on the shady primary school playground a couple of blocks up from Broadway, is in full swing. On sale are mainly clothes and accessories, plus plants, CDs, the inevitable crystals and a bit of bric-a-brac, but the food stalls are disappointing. At no. 49 Glebe Point Rd, you'll find the excellent **Gleebooks** – one of Sydney's best-loved bookshops (see "Shopping", p.184). The original Gleebooks, now selling secondhand and children's books only, is worth the trek further up at 191 Glebe Point Rd, past St Johns Road and Glebe's pretty park. Across the street and a couple of blocks further on is one of Sydney's best independent cinemas, the Valhalla (see p.180), established in 1976; stop for a coffee next door in the relaxed and very popular *Craven Cafe*. A few blocks on from here, the action stops and Glebe Point Road trails off into a more residential area, petering out at **Jubilee Park** with characterful views across the water to boats and Rozelle Bay's container terminal. The pleasantly landscaped waterfront park, complete with huge, shady Moreton Bay fig trees and a children's playground, offers an unusual view of far-off Sydney Harbour Bridge framed within Sydney's newest, the fanciful Anzac Bridge.

Buses #431, #433 and #434 run to Glebe from Millers Point, George Street and Central Station; #431 and #434 run right down the length of Glebe Point Road to Jubilee Park, with the #434 continuing on to Balmain, while the #433 runs half-way turning at Wigram Road and heads on to Balmain.

Otherwise it's a fifteen-minute **walk** from Central up Broadway to the beginning of Glebe Point Road.

Newtown and around

Newtown, separated from Glebe by Sydney University and easily reached by train (to Newtown Station), is another up-and-coming inner-city neighbourhood. What was once a working-class district – a hotchpotch of derelict factories, junkyards and cheap accommodation – has been transformed into a trendy, offbeat area where body piercing, shaved heads and weird fashions rule. Newtown is characterized by a large gay and lesbian population, a rich cultural mix and a healthy dose of students and lecturers from the nearby university. It also has an enviable number of great cafés and diverse restaurants, especially Thai. A big part of its changing face is no doubt due to the Dendy Cinema complex (see p.180), more like a cultural centre than just a film theatre, with its attached bookshop, excellent record store, and streetfront café, all open daily and into the night.

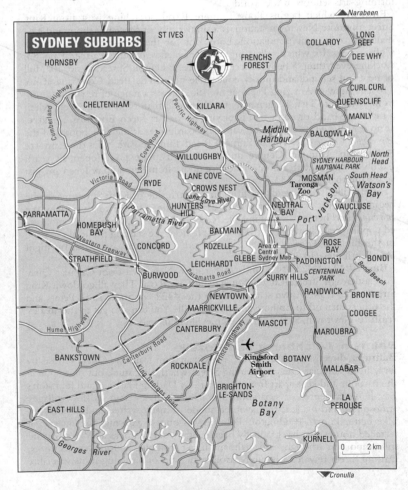

The main drag, **King Street**, is filled with unusual secondhand, funky fashion and speciality shops; during the **Newtown Festival** (early Oct to early Nov; ⓦ www.newtownfestival.org.au) various shop windows let themselves be taken over by young, irreverent and in-your-face art. On the book front, check out Gould's Book Arcade at no. 32, a vast and chaotic secondhand book warehouse that is a Sydney institution, browsable until midnight. Veer off King Street for Pretty Dog, at 1 Brown St, which is open daily for a good range of retro secondhand gear and over-the-top club and streetwear.

King Street becomes less crowded south of Newtown train station as it heads for a kilometre towards **St Peters** train station, but it's well worth strolling down to look at the more unusual speciality shops (buttons, ribbons, cacti, Chinese medicine amongst them), as well as several small art galleries and yet more retro clothes shops. It's also stacked with culturally diverse restaurants through Turkish to African, and closer to St Peters station are several businesses aimed at the local Indian community. You'll also find a couple of theatres and a High School for the Performing Arts, reputed to be one of the top-five performing-arts schools in the world.

Enmore, which begins along Enmore Road, stretching west from King Street, opposite Newtown station, is a similar mix of speciality shops and evidence of a migrant population. Look out for the long-established Mocha Coffee at no. 16, which sells a big range of blends; Amera's Palace, at no. 83, stocking everything a belly dancer might need; Lemon Spread at no. 101, full of new and secondhand quirky collectable items; The Bead Company at no. 116; and Artwise Amazing Paper at no. 186. There's a range of restaurants, too, from Swedish to Thai. It's generally much quieter than Newtown, except when a big-name band or comedian is playing at the Art Deco **Enmore Theatre**, at no. 130. When its closed, you can play boardgames at the cosy booths of the *Box Office Cafe*. At the end of Enmore Road, Enmore Park hides the **Annette Kellerman Aquatic Centre** and its tiny 33-metre pool (open all year). Combine a swim with a home-made ice cream from Serendipity Icecream, just across the road at no. 333.

Erskineville Road, stretching from the eastern side of King Street marks the beginning of the adjoining suburb of **Erskineville**, a favourite gay address; the *Imperial Hotel* here at 35 Erskineville Rd (see also p.174), which has long hosted popular drag shows, now trades on its fame as the starting point of the gang in the hit film *Priscilla, Queen of the Desert* with Friday and Saturday night *Priscilla* tributes (10.30–11.30pm).

Buses #422, #423, #426 and #428 run to Newtown from Circular Quay via Castlereagh Street, Railway Square and City Road. They all go down King Street as far as Newtown station, where the #422 continues to St Peters and the others turn off to Enmore and Marrickville. You can also get to the area by **train** to Newtown, St Peters or Erskineville train stations.

Balmain, Leichhardt and Rozelle

Balmain, directly north of Glebe, is less than 2km from the Opera House, by ferry from Circular Quay to Darling Street wharf. But, stuck out on a spur in the harbour and kept apart from the centre by Darling Harbour and Johnston's Bay, it has a degree of separation that has helped it retain its slow, villagey atmosphere and made it the favoured abode of many writers and filmmakers. Like better-known Paddington, Balmain was once a working-class quarter of terraced houses that has gradually been gentrified. The docks at White Bay are still important, though, and Balmain hasn't completely forsaken its roots. Darling Street rewards a leisurely stroll, with a bit of browsing in its speciality

Goat Island

Just across the water from Balmain East, **Goat Island** is the site of a well-preserved gunpowder magazine complex. The sandstone buildings, including a barracks, were built by two hundred convicts between 1833 and 1839. Treatment of the convicts was harsh: 18-year-old Charles Anderson, a mentally impaired convict with a wild, seemingly untameable temper who made several attempts to escape, received over twelve hundred lashes in 1835 – and if that wasn't enough, he was sentenced to be chained to a rock for two years in an attempt to control him, a cruel punishment even by the standards of the day. Tethered to the rock, which you can still see, his unhealed back crawling with maggots, he slept in a cavity hewn into the sandstone "couch". Sydneysiders would row up and tease him for entertainment. Eventually Anderson ended up on Norfolk Island (see p.335), where under the humane prisoner reform experiments of Alexander Maconochie, the feral, abused 24-year-old made a startling transformation. The island is looked after by the NPWS, who run various **tours** with Sydney Ferries (bookings essential, call ☎02/9247 5033; meet at Cadman's Cottage see p.113), making the most of the island's gruesome history and its present use as the shooting location for the popular TV series *Water Rats* about the water police. Tours range from a Heritage Tour (Mon & Fri–Sun 12.30pm; $19.80), and a *Water Rats* tour checking out film sets (Wed 11.45am; $19.80). There are also night-time **gruesome tales tours** for over-12s only (Sat 5.45–6.45pm depending on sunset; 3hr; $24.20 child or adult; supper included).

shops (focused on clothes and gifts), and grazing in its restaurants and cafés. It, and the surrounding backstreets, are also blessed with enough watering holes to warrant a pub crawl – two classics are the *London Hotel* on Darling Street and the *Exchange Hotel* on Beattie Street (see p.170). The best time to come is on Saturday, when the lively **Balmain Market** occupies the shady grounds of St Andrews Church (7.30am–4pm), on the corner opposite the *London Hotel*. An assortment of books, handmade jewellery, clothing and ceramics, antiques, home-made chocolates, cakes and gourmet foods and organic produce are sold. The highlight is an eclectic array of food stalls in the church hall where you can snack your way from the Himalayas to Southern India.

For long, stunning sunsets and wow-worthy real estate, meander down the backstreets towards water-surrounded **Birchgrove** on its finger of land, where Louisa Road leads to Birchgrove wharf; from here you can catch a ferry back to Circular Quay, or stay and relax in the small park on Yurulbin Point. For a **self-guided tour** of Balmain and Birchgrove, you can buy a *Balmain Walks* leaflet ($2) from Balmain Library, 370 Darling St, or the well-stocked Pentimento Bookshop, at no. 275.

It's almost an hour from The Rocks to Balmain by the #440 bus, via **Leichhardt**, Sydney's "Little Italy", where the famous **Norton Street** strip of cafés and restaurants runs off ugly **Parramatta Road**. Leichhardt is very much up and coming – shiny, trendy, Italian cafés keep popping up all along the strip, in the wake of the new upmarket cinema complex, The Palace (which hosts an Italian film festival in early Dec), with its attached record store, bookshop and internet café, the new Beurkelow's bookstore, a new shopping centre and, showcase for the Italian community, the **Italian Forum**. The Forum is arranged around a central square, with two collonnaded levels surrounding it, there's a load of upmarket fashion shops on the top level, several featuring Italian fashion, of course, while downstairs are hosts of mostly Italian eateries, with alfresco tables on the square – huge for lunch on a Sunday. There's also the Italian Cultural Centre and the local library branch down here, and attached apartments. However, the lively, much-loved and enduring *Bar Italia* (see p.163), a fifteen-minute walk further down Norton at the extent of the tempting array of eateries, is still the best Italian café in Leichhardt.

From Leichhardt, the #440 bus continues to Darling Street, which runs from **Rozelle** right down to Balmain's waterfront. Rozelle, once very much the down-at-heel, poorer sister to Balmain is now emergently trendy with the Sydney College of the Arts and the Sydney Writers' Centre based here as well as lots of cafés, bookshops, speciality shops, gourmet grocers, restaurants, made-over pubs, and designer home-goods stores. There's also the new, very ritzy Rozelle Bay Super Yacht Marina on James Craig Road; enjoy the views with a glass of wine at the bar-restaurant *Liquidity*, with its huge glassfront overlooking the water. A weekend flea market takes place in the grounds of Rozelle Primary School on Darling Street, Rozelle, near Victoria Road (Sat & Sun 9am–4pm). Further on towards Balmain, Elkington Park has the quaint **Dawn Fraser Swimming Pool** (Oct–April daily 7.15am–5.30pm; $2.40), an old-fashioned harbour pool named after the famous Australian Olympic swimmer.

To **get to** Balmain, you can catch a ferry from Circular Quay to Darling Street wharf in Balmain East, where buses wait to take you up Darling Street to Balmain proper. Buses #433 and #434 run out to Balmain via George Street, Railway Square and Glebe Point Road and down Darling Street; faster is the #442 from the QVB, which crosses Anzac Bridge and heads to Balmain wharf. Birchgrove can be reached via ferry from Circular Quay or on the #441 from the QVB. To get to Leichhardt you can take bus #436, #437, #438 or #440 from George Street in the city; the #440 continues to Rozelle.

Inner eastern suburbs

To the east, **Surry Hills**, **Darlinghurst** and **Paddington** were once rather scruffy working-class suburbs, but they have been taken over and revamped by the young, arty and upwardly mobile. **Kings Cross** is home to Sydney's red-light district as well as many of its tourists, while in adjacent **Woolloomooloo** container ships tie up at the docks. Further east, the "Cross" fades into the more elegant suburbs of **Potts Point** and **Elizabeth Bay**, which trade on their harbour views.

Surry Hills

Surry Hills, directly east of Central Station from Elizabeth Street, was traditionally the centre of the rag trade, which still finds its focus on Devonshire Street. Rows of tiny terraces once housed its original poor, working-class population, many of them of Irish origin. Considered a slum by the rest of Sydney, the dire and overcrowded conditions were given fictional life in Ruth Park's *The Harp in the South* trilogy (see "Books", p.1183), set in the Surry Hills of the 1940s. The area became something of a cultural melting pot with European postwar immigration, and doubled as a grungy, studenty, muso heartland in the 1980s. By the mid-1990s, however, the slickly fashionable scene of neighbouring Darlinghurst and Paddington had finally taken over Surry Hills' twin focal points of parallel **Crown Street**, filled with cafés, swanky restaurants, funky clothes shops and designer galleries, and leafy **Bourke Street**, where a couple of Sydney's best cafés lurk among the trees. As rents have gone up, only **Cleveland Street**, running west to Redfern and east towards Moore Park and the Sydney Cricket Ground (see p.139), traffic-snarled and lined with cheap Lebanese and Turkish restaurants, retains its ethnically varied population.

Aboriginal Sydney

Just beyond Surry Hills, and only 2km from the glitter and sparkle of Darling Harbour, **Redfern** is Sydney's underbelly. Around the **Eveleigh Street** area, Australia's biggest urban Aboriginal community lives in "**the Block**", a squalid streetscape of derelict terraced houses and rubbish-strewn streets not far from Redfern train station – the closest Sydney has to a no-go zone. The Aboriginal Housing Company, set up as a co-operative in 1973, has been unable to pay for repairs and renovation work, in shocking contrast to Paddington's cutesy restored terraces and the harbourview mansions of Sydney's rich and beautiful. Recently the Company began knocking down derelict houses and relocating people, which has upset many residents who want to keep the community together.

A good time to visit Surry Hills is the first Saturday of the month when a lively **flea market**, complete with tempting food stalls, takes over the small Shannon Reserve, on the corner of Crown and Fouveaux streets, overlooked by the **Clock Hotel**. The hotel, which has expanded out of all recognition from its 1840s roots, is emblematic of the new Surry Hills, and its swish restaurant and cocktail bar attract a very different crowd from the rough and ready pool-playing crew of recent years. The artistic side of Surry Hills can be experienced nearby at the **Brett Whitely Studio** at 2 Raper St (Sat & Sun 10am–4pm; by appointment Thurs & Fri ☏02/9225 1881; $7); walk about three blocks further south down Crown Street, and it's off Davies Street. Whitely was one of Australia's best-known contemporary painters with an international reputation by the time he died of a heroin overdose at the age of 53; wild self-portraits and expressive female nudes were some of his subjects, but it is his sensual paintings of Sydney Harbour for which he is best known, painted from his home in Lavender Bay. In 1986 Whitely converted this one-time factory into a studio and living space, and since his death it has become a museum and gallery showing his paintings and memorabilia.

Surry Hills is a short **walk** uphill from Central (Devonshire St or Elizabeth St exit); take Fouveax or Devonshire Street and you'll soon hit Crown, or it's an even quicker stroll from Oxford Street, Darlinghurst, heading south along Crown or Bourke streets.

Darlinghurst, Paddington and Woollahra

Oxford Street, from Hyde Park to Paddington and beyond, is a major amusement strip. Waiting to be discovered, here and in the side streets, is an array of nightclubs, restaurants, cafés and pubs. Around **Darlinghurst**, Oxford Street is the focus of Sydney's very active gay and lesbian movement. Hip and bohemian, Darlinghurst mingles seediness with a certain hedonistic style: some art students and clubbers never leave the district – save for a coffee at the Cross or a swim at "the Boy" in The Domain (see p.124). There's another concentration of cafés, restaurants and fashion on Liverpool Street, while Victoria Street is a classic pose strip with the legendary, street-smart *Bar Coluzzi* (see p.164). At 148 Darlinghurst Rd, the impressive **Sydney Jewish Museum** (Mon–Thurs 10am–4pm, Fri 10am–2pm, Sun 11am–5pm; $7) is housed in the old Maccabean Hall, which has been a Jewish meeting point for over seventy years. Sixteen Jews were among the convicts who arrived with the First Fleet, and the high-tech, interactive museum explores over two hundred years of Australian Jewish experience. An introductory fifteen-minute film discusses anti-Semitism through the ages, and the Holocaust is covered in harrowing detail with Australian survivors' videotaped testimony. You can pick up the pamphlet *Guide to Jewish Sydney* from the museum.

Paddington, a slum at the turn of the century, became a popular hangout for hipsters during the late 1960s and 1970s. Since then, yuppies have taken over and turned Paddington into the smart and fashionable suburb it is today: the Victorian-era terraced houses, with their iron-lace verandahs reminiscent of New Orleans, have been beautifully restored. Many of the terraces were originally built in the 1840s to house the artisans who worked on the graceful, sandstone **Victoria Barracks** on the southern side of Oxford Street, its walls stretching seven blocks, from Greens Road to just before the Paddington Town Hall on Oatley Road. **Shadforth Street**, opposite the entrance gates, has many examples of the original artisans' homes. Though the barracks are still used by the army, there are free guided tours (Thurs 10am) – complete with army band – while a small **museum** is open to visitors (Sun 10am–3pm). On the other side of Oxford Street the small, winding, tree-lined streets are a pleasant place for a stroll, and offer a chance to wander into the many small art galleries or to take some liquid refreshment. Head via Underwood and Heeley streets to **Five Ways**, where you'll find cafés, speciality shops and a typically gracious old boozer, the *Royal Hotel* (see p.166). There are more shops on Elizabeth Street running off Oxford Street, but the main action is, of course, on Oxford Street itself, most lively on Saturday from 10am to around 4pm, when the crowds descend on **Paddington Market** in the church grounds at no. 395. As well as being a prime spot to show off and hang out, it's a sure-fire source of great presents, with leather goods, jewellery and clothes – old and new – at the top of the list, and an emphasis on Australian-made products.

Woollahra, along Oxford Street from Paddington, is even more moneyed but contrastingly staid, with expensive **antique shops** and **art galleries** along **Queen Street** replacing the fashion and trendy lifestyle focus of Paddington's shops. Leafy Moncur Street hides *jones the grocer* (at no. 68), where Woollahra locals gather for coffee at the long central table; it sells stylishly packaged, outlandishly priced and utterly delicious groceries and gourmet treats to eat in or take away.

Transport heading in this direction includes **buses** #380 and #382 from Circular Quay which both run up Elizabeth Street and along Oxford Street. The #378, from Central Station, also heads along Oxford Street. Bus #389 from Circular Quay runs via Elizabeth and William streets in the city and along Glenmore Road and Hargrave Street, Paddington, to emerge on Oxford Street.

Centennial and Moore parks

South of Paddington and Woollahra lies the green expanse of **Centennial Park**, opened to the citizens of Sydney at the Centennial Festival in 1888 (the bicentennial version was opened at Homebush in 1988 – see box pp.130–131). With its vast lawns, rose gardens and extensive network of ponds it resembles an English country park, but is reclaimed at dawn and dusk by distinctly antipodean residents, including possums and flying foxes. The park is criss-crossed by walking paths and tracks for cycling, rollerblading, jogging and horse-riding: you can rent a bike or rollerblades or hire a horse and then recover from your exertions in the café or, in the finer months, stay on until dark and catch an outdoor film with the Moonlight Cinema (see p.180).

Adjoining **Moore Park** has facilities for tennis, golf, grass-skiing, bowling, cricket and hockey; it is also home to the Sydney Cricket Ground and the Fox

Studios (see below). To get to the park you can take a **bus** from Central Station (#372, #393 or 395) or from Elizabeth Street in City, before Museum Station (#390, #391, #394, #396 or #398). Alternatively you could take a bus to Oxford Street, Paddington (see opposite) and then walk. If you have a car there is plenty of parking (first two hours free).

The Sydney Cricket Ground (SCG)

The venerated institution of the **Sydney Cricket Ground (SCG)** earned its place in cricketing history for Don Bradman's score of 452 not out in 1929, and for the controversy over England's bodyline bowling techniques in 1932. Ideally, proceedings are observed from the lovely 1886 Members Stand, while sipping an icy gin and tonic – but unless you're invited by a member, you'll end up elsewhere, probably drinking beer from a plastic cup. Cricket spectators aren't a sedate lot in Sydney, and the noisiest barrackers will probably come from "the Hill" – or the Doug Walters stand, as it's officially known. Still the cheapest spot to sit, the concreted area was once a grassy hill where rowdy supporters threw empty beer cans at players and each other, but beer is now strictly rationed. The Bill O'Reilly Stand gives comfortable viewing until the afternoon, when you'll be blinded by the sun, whereas the Brewongle Stand provides consistently good viewing. Best of all is the Bradman Stand, with a view directly behind the bowler's arm, and adjacent to the exclusive stand occupied by members, commentators and ex-players. The Test to see here is, of course, **The Ashes** (see p.65); the Sydney leg of the five tests, each for five days, begins on New Year's Day. For information, scores, prices and times, call ✆02/9360 6601. You can buy tickets at the gates on the day subject to availability, or purchase them in advance from Ticketek (✆02/9266 4800). Die-hard cricket fans can actually go on a **tour** of the SCG on non-match days (Mon–Sat 10am, 1pm & 3pm; 1hr 30min; $19.50; ✆02/9380 0383). The tour also covers the **Sydney Football Stadium** next door, where **State of Origin** Rugby League is played, coverage of which consistently produces the highest ratings on Australian television.

Fox Studios

Also within Moore Park, immediately southeast of the SCG, are the Murdoch-owned **Fox Studios**, constructed at a cost of $A300 million within the old Showgrounds site, where the Royal Agricultural Society held its annual Royal Easter Show from 1882 until 1997; in 1998 the huge show took place for the first time at the new A$380 million Sydney Showground at the Olympic site at Homebush Bay. The **Professional Studio**, opened in May 1998, takes up over half the site and has facilities for both film and television production, with six high-tech stages and industry tenants on-site providing everything from casting services to stunt professionals. Films made here so far include *The Matrix* for Warner Bros, *Mission Impossible II* for Paramount, Baz Luhrmann's *Moulin Rouge*, and Episode I and II of the *Star Wars* saga. The **public areas** of the site opened in late 1999, focused around a mega state-of-the-art sixteen-screen **cinema complex** – a world-class centre for international film premieres. The old **Show Ring**, once the preserve of wood-chopping competitions and rodeo events, is now used for everything from open-air cinema and circuses, to the weekend market (Sat & Sun 10am–6pm) and the midweek Farmers Market (Wed noon–7pm). The Show Ring is surrounded by the shops, cafés, restaurants and bars of Bent Street; there's also a stand-up comedy venue, the *Comedy Store* (see p.178).

The theme park area of Fox Studios, **The Backlot** (daily 10am–5pm; self-guided tour $24.95, child $14.95; ✆02/9383 4000, ⊛www.foxstudios.com.au), is sandwiched between the professional studio and the public areas: if there is something in production, Backlot visitors may be able to take a peek at film or television sets in action from an elevated walkway running from the Backlot to the Professional Studio. There are eight areas to visit and 4–5 hours is recommended to experience them properly: the Hall of Cool Stuff shows Fox Studio movie memorablia, including a reproduced set from *The Titanic*; the Star Dressing Room has Fox props and costumes and an in-house make-up artist; Titanic – The Experience is a 20-minute "heightened reality" experience where the audience re-enact scenes from the film; The TV Tour shows how television shows are made; Lights! Camera! Chaos is a 25-minute live show recreating a movie shoot; Sound Stage demonstrates audio effects; The Babe Set is focused around *Babe 2: Pig in the City*, filmed here; and The Simpsons Down Under demonstrates animation.

Kings Cross and Potts Point

The preserve of Sydney's bohemians in the 1950s, **Kings Cross** became an R&R spot for American soldiers during the Vietnam war, and is now Sydney's red-light district, its streets prowled by prostitutes, junkies, drunks, strippers and homeless teenagers. It is also a bustling centre for backpackers and other travellers, especially around leafy and quieter Victoria Street; the two sides of "the Cross" (as locals call it) coexist with little trouble, though some of the tourists seem a little surprised at where they've ended up, and it can be rather intimidating for lone women. However, the constant flow of people makes it relatively safe, and it's always lively, with places to eat and drink that stay open all hours.

Climbing up William Street from Hyde Park, **Darlinghurst Road** beckons with its giant neon Coca-Cola sign. At weekends, an endless stream of ice-cream-licking suburban voyeurs trawl along the Darlinghurst Road strip past the El Alamein fountain in Fitzroy Gardens to **Macleay Street**, as touts try their best to haul them into tacky strip-joints and sleazy nightclubs. Kings Cross is much more subdued during the day, with a slightly hung-over feel to it: local residents emerge and it's a good time to hang out in the cafés. Every Sunday there's a small art and crafts market in the Fitzroy Gardens by the fountain. South Sydney Council has produced a free **Kings Cross Walking Tour** map available from the library off Fitzroy Gardens (or download it from Ⓦwww.kingscross.nsw.gov.au), which points out some of the Art Deco architecture the area is known for and provides some background history.

All around the Cross, and indeed very close by, are quiet, upmarket pockets. Towards the harbour, **Potts Point** becomes more peaceful and more expensive the closer you get to exclusive Elizabeth Bay (see opposite). You can get to Kings Cross by **train** (Eastern Suburbs line) or **bus** (#311, #324, #325 or #327 from Circular Quay; many others from the city to Darlinghurst Rd), or it's not too far to walk: an uphill walk straight up William Street from Hyde Park. For a quieter route, you could head up from The Domain via Cowper Wharf Road in Woolloomooloo, and then up the McElhone Stairs to Victoria Street.

Woolloomooloo

North of William Street just below Kings Cross, **Woolloomooloo** occupies the old harbourside quarter between The Domain and the grey-painted fleet of the **Garden Island Naval Depot**. Once a narrow-streeted slum, Woolloomooloo is quickly being transformed, though its upmarket apartment developments sit uneasily side by side with problematic community housing, and you should still be careful at night in the backstreets. There are some lively pubs and some old-fashioned quiet locals – such as the *Tilbury* and the *Woolloomooloo Hotel*, which both serve good meals – as well as the legendary **Harry's Café de Wheels** on Cowper Road, a 24-hour pie-cart operating since 1945 and popular nowadays with Sydney cabbies and hungry clubbers in the small hours.

Next door, the once picturesquely dilapidated **Woolloomooloo Finger Wharf**, dating from 1917, has been redeveloped into an upmarket complex comprising a marina, luxury residential apartments, the cool *W Hotel*, and some slick new restaurants with alfresco dining – *Otto Ristorante Italiano*, *Man Ray* and *Shimbashi* are the swankiest. The general public are free to wander along the wharf and even go inside: there's a free exhibition space with a changing theme in the centre. Anyone can afford a cake and pastry at the Parisian-feel *Laurent Patissier* (see p.165), or you can grab a pie from *Harry's* and sit for free on the other side of the wharf.

Woolloomooloo is best reached by foot from Kings Cross by taking the **McElhone Stairs** or the **Butlers Stairs** from Victoria Street; alternatively take bus #311 from Kings Cross, Circular Quay or Central Station.

The Harbour

Loftily flanking the mouth of Sydney Harbour are the rugged sandstone cliffs of North Head and South Head, providing spectacular viewing points across the calm water to the city 11km away, where the Harbour Bridge spans the sunken valley at its deepest point. The many coves, bays, points and headlands of Sydney Harbour, and their parks, bushland and swimmable beaches are rewarding to explore. However, harbour beaches are not as clean as ocean ones, and after storms are often closed to swimmers (see pp.146–147). Finding your way by ferry is the most pleasurable method: services run to much of the **North Shore** and to harbourfront areas of the **eastern suburbs**. The eastern shores are characterized by a certain glitziness and are the haunt of the nouveaux riches, while the leafy North Shore is very much old money. Both sides of the harbour have pockets of bushland which have been incorporated into **Sydney Harbour National Park**, along with five islands, two of which – Goat Island and Fort Denison – can be visited on tours; the other three – Shark Island, Clark Island and Rodd Island – are bookable for picnics but you must provide your own transport. The NPWS publish an excellent free map detailing the areas of the national park and its many walking tracks (℡02/9337 5511 for general information or visit Cadman's Cottage in The Rocks or NPWS office in Nielson Park – see p.113 and p.142 respectively).

Elizabeth Bay to South Head

The suburbs on the hilly southeast shores of the harbour are rich and exclusive. A couple of early nineteenth-century mansions, Elizabeth Bay House and Vaucluse House, are open to visitors, giving an insight into the lifestyle of the pioneering upper crust. **Buses** #324 and #325 from Circular Quay via Pitt Street, Kings Cross and Edgecliff cover the places listed below, heading to Watsons Bay via New South Head Road; #325 detours at Vaucluse for Nielson Park.

Elizabeth Bay and Rushcutters Bay

Barely five minutes' walk northwest of Kings Cross, **Elizabeth Bay** is nevertheless a well-heeled residential area, centred on **Elizabeth Bay House**, at 7

Onslow Ave (Tues–Sun 10am–4.30pm; $6.50; bus #311 from either Railway Square or Circular Quay, or walk from Kings Cross Station), a grand Regency residence with fine harbour views, built in 1832. Heading southeast, you're only a few minutes' walk from **Rushcutters Bay Park**, wonderfully set against a backdrop of the yacht- and cruiser-packed marina in the bay; the marina was recently revamped for the 2000 Olympics sailing competition. Gangs of picnickers book out the **tennis** courts at Rushcutters Bay Tennis Centre (daily 8am–9pm or 10pm; courts $14 per hour, $16 after 4pm and on Sat & Sun; racket rental $3; ℡ 02/9357 1675 for bookings). If you don't have anyone to play, the friendly managers promise a hitting partner thrown in with the court; there's a nice little coffee bar too (open Mon–Fri 9am–6pm, Sat & Sun 8am–6pm).

Double Bay and Rose Bay

Continuing northeast to **Darling Point**, McKell Park provides a wonderful view across to **Clarke Island** and **Bradleys Head**, both part of Sydney Harbour National Park; follow Darling Point Road (or take bus #327 from Edgecliff Station). The next port of call is **Double Bay**, dubbed "Double Pay" for obvious reasons. The noise and traffic of New South Head Road are redeemed by several excellent antiquarian and secondhand bookshops (see p.184), while in the quieter "village" are some of the most exclusive shops in Sydney, full of imported designer labels and expensive jewellery. The eastern suburbs' socialites meet on Cross Street, where the swanky pavement cafés are filled with well-groomed women in Armani outfits sipping coffee. If all this sounds like a turn-off, Double Bay's real delight is **Redleaf Pool** (daily Sept–May dawn–dusk; free), a peaceful, shady harbour beach – one of the cleanest – enclosed by a wooden pier you can wander around, dive off or just laze on; there's also an excellent café famed for its fruit salad and cappuccino. A ferry from Circular Quay (Wharf 2) stops at both Darling Point and Double Bay; otherwise catch bus #324 or #325, also from Circular Quay.

The ferry to **Rose Bay** (Circular Quay, Wharf 2) gives you a chance to check out the waterfront mansions of **Point Piper** as you skim past. Rose Bay itself is quite a haven of exclusivity, with the verdant expanse of the members-only Royal Sydney Golf Course. Directly across New South Head Road from the course, waterfront **Lyne Park** provides welcome distraction in the form of a **seaplane** service, based here since the 1930s (see "Listings", p.189). Rose Bay is also a popular **windsurfing** spot, and you can rent equipment to join in from Rose Bay Aquatic Hire (see p.190).

Nielson Park and Vaucluse

Sydney Harbour National Park emerges onto the waterfront at Bay View Hill, where the 1.5km **Hermitage walking track** to Nielson Park begins; the starting point, Bay View Hill Road, is off South Head Road between the Kambala School and the Rose Bay Convent (on bus routes #324 and #325). The walk takes about an hour, with great views of the Opera House and Harbour Bridge, some lovely little coves to swim in and a picnic ground and sandy beach at yacht-filled **Hermit Point**. Extensive, tree-filled **Nielson Park**, on Shark Bay, is one of Sydney's delights (don't worry about Shark Bay's ominous name – it's netted), a great place for a daytime swim, a night-time skinny-dip, a picnic, or refreshment at the popular café. Within the park, the decorative Victorian-era mansion, **Greycliffe House**, built for William Wentworth's daughter in 1852 (see opposite), is now the headquarters of Sydney Harbour National Park; if it's open (no regular hours) pop in for information on other waterfront walks.

Beyond Shark Bay, Vaucluse Bay shelters the magnificent **Vaucluse House** and its large estate on Wentworth Road (Tues–Sun 10am–4.30pm and public holiday Mondays; $6.50), with tearooms in the grounds for refreshment. The house's original owner was the explorer and reformer William Wentworth, who was a member of the first party to cross the Blue Mountains. In 1831 he invited four thousand guests to Vaucluse House to celebrate the departure of the hated Governor Darling – the climax of the evening was a fireworks display which burned "Down with the Tyrant" into the night sky. To get there, walk from Nielson Park along Coolong Road, or take bus #325 right to the door.

Watsons Bay to South Head

Narrow **Parsley Bay**, crossed by a pedestrian suspension bridge, follows Vaucluse Bay to **Watsons Bay** (accessible by ferry from Wharf 4 at Circular Quay), on the now narrow finger of land culminating in South Head. Once a fishing village, the suburb has retained a villagey feel with old fishermen's cottages still found on the narrow streets. These associations make an appropriate location for one of Sydney's most popular fish restaurants, *Doyles*, right out on the bay by the old Fishermans Wharf, with superb views and food (see p.166). For less expensive views, settle in at the bayfront beer garden of the adjacent *Watsons Bay Hotel*. More spectacular views from the ocean cliffs are just a two-minute walk away through grassy Robertson Park, across Gap Road to **The Gap**, whose high cliffs are a well-known place to commit suicide. This is where bus #325 terminates, but a **walking track** leads from here to South Head through another chunk of **Sydney Harbour National Park**. From The Gap the track heads back to the bay side, past **Camp Cove**, a tiny palm-fronted beach popular with families. If you'd prefer to swim *au naturel*, continue on the track to the next bay just on the harbour side of South Head, to reach Sydney's best-known **nude beach**, Lady Jane (officially "Lady Bay" on maps). Unfortunately tour boats cruise past all weekend – Cobblers Beach in Middle Harbour (see p.146) is a better bet for privacy. From Lady Bay, it's about a fifteen-minute walk along the track to **South Head**, the lower jaw of the harbour mouth affording fantastic views of Port Jackson and the city.

The North Shore

The **North Shore** is generally more affluent than the South. **Mosman** and **Neutral Bay** in particular have some stunning waterfront real estate, priced to match. It's surprising just how much harbourside bushland remains intact here – "leafy" just doesn't do it justice – and superbly sited amongst it all is **Taronga Zoo**. A ride on any ferry lets you gaze at beaches, bush, yachts and swish harbourfront houses and is one of the chief joys of this area.

North Sydney and around

North Sydney has been associated with pure fun since the 1930s – beside the Bridge on Lavender Bay at **Milsons Point**, you can't miss the huge laughing clown's face that belongs to **Luna Park**. Generations of Sydneysiders have walked through the grinning mouth, and the park's old rides and conserved 1930s fun hall, complete with period wall murals, slot machines, silly mirrors and giant slippery dips, have great nostalgia value for locals. Luna Park was closed down for several years from the late 1980s until a grand reopening in January 1995 with a new clown's face – the eighth since the park began – closely resembling the 1950s model. Unfortunately, the amusement park noise upset nearby residents who'd grown used to peace and quiet, and the park promptly closed again, losing developers millions of dollars. Back in business in 2000, it shut down again in early 2001 for yet another bout of redevelopment, which will include the dismantling of its classic old rollercoaster, the Big Dipper; the park should reopen some time between February and July 2002 (call ☎ 02/9922 6644 or check ⓦ www.lunaparksydney.com for the latest information). The water views from the park's rides, particulary the Ferris wheel, with the Harbour Bridge as a backdrop, are just sensational, and it's worth coming for these alone. Getting here can be pleasant too: the ferry to Milsons Point wharf from Circular Quay or Darling Harbour pulls up right outside (or catch a train from Circular Quay to Milsons Point Station). Beyond the park there's a boardwalk right around Lavender Bay.

Right next door to the amusement park is Sydney's most picturesquely sited public swimming pool, with terrific views of the Harbour Bridge – the heated **North Sydney Olympic Pool**, Alfred South Street (Mon–Fri 6am–9pm, Sat & Sun 7am–7pm; $3.50), is open year round. At the time of writing the pool was in the process of being revamped – indoor pools, a gym and a café are being added – and a slick new restaurant, *Aqua*, has already opened overlooking the pool, so be prepared to be ogled by diners as you swim your laps.

Beyond Luna Park and the pool, worth visiting in amongst North Sydney's impersonal corporate zone, is the Catholic church-run **Mary McKillop Place Museum**, 7 Mount St (daily 10am–4pm; $8.25). Housed in a former convent, it provides a surprisingly broadminded look at the life and times of Australia's first would-be saint (McKillop was beatified in 1995 and is entombed here) and sainthood itself. For the full story, see the account in Coonawarra (on p.843), where the nun's charitable educational work began. The best way to get here directly is to take the train to North Sydney station and head north along Miller Street for about five minutes.

Just east of the Harbour Bridge and immediately opposite the Opera House, **Kirribilli** and adjacent **Neutral Bay** are mainly residential areas, although Kirribilli hosts a great **market** on the last Saturday of the month in Bradfield Park (7am–3.30pm), the best and biggest of several rotating markets on the North Shore (see "Markets" p.185). On Kirribilli Point, the current Prime Minister, John Howard, lives in an official residence, **Kirribilli House**. Admiralty House, next door, is the Sydney home of the Governor General. The highlight of North Shore drinking is the shady **beer garden** at Neutral Bay's *Oaks Hotel* on Military Road. Bush-covered **Cremorne Point**, which juts into the harbour here, is also worth a jaunt. Catch the ferry from Circular Quay and you'll find a quaint open-access sea pool to swim in by the wharf; from here, you can walk right around the point to Mosman Bay (just under 2km; see below), or in the other direction, past the pool, there's a very pretty walk along **Shell Cove** (1km).

Mosman Bay: Taronga Zoo

Mosman Bay's seclusion was first recognized as a virtue during its early days as a whaling station, since it kept the stench of rotting whale flesh from the Sydney Cove settlement. Now the seclusion is a corollary of wealth. The ferry ride into the narrow, yacht-filled bay is a choice one – get off at Mosman Wharf, not South Mosman (Musgrave St) – and fittingly finished off with a beer at the unpretentious *Mosman Rowers' Club* (visitors welcome).

What Mosman is most famous for, though, is **Taronga Zoological Park** on Bradleys Head Road, with its superb hilltop position overlooking the city (daily: Jan 9am–9pm; Feb–Dec 9am–5pm; $21, child $11.50, family $55, Zoo Pass from Circular Quay including return ferry and entry $25, child pass

$12.50; Ⓦ www.zoo.nsw.gov.au). The wonderful views and the natural bush surrounds are as much an attraction as the chance to get up close to some animals. The zoo houses bounding Australian marsupials, native birds (including kookaburras, galahs and cockatoos), reptiles, and sea lions and seals from the sub-Antarctic region. You'll also find exotic beasts from around the world, including those frequently photographed giraffes, sticking their necks out across a sublime harbour view. Established in 1916, the zoo has come a long way from its Victorian roots, and the animals now live in more natural habitats, rather than cages. You can get close to kangaroos and wallabies in the **Australian Walkabout** area, and the **koala house** gives you eye-level views; you can get closer by arranging to have your photo taken patting a koala, but for a guaranteed **hands-on experience** with a native animal, a VIP Gold Tour (daily 9.15am & 1.30pm; 1hr 30min; $33; book 24hr in advance on ⓣ 02/9969 2777) will give you and a small group a session with a zookeeper, guiding you through the Australian animals.

The zoo is best reached by taking the ferry from Wharf 2 at Circular Quay to the Taronga Zoo wharf (every half-hour). Though there's a lower entrance near the wharf on Athol Road, it's best to start your zoo visit from the upper entrance so you can spend several leisurely hours winding your way downhill and exit for the ferry: State Transit buses still meet the ferries for the trip uphill, or take the **Sky Safari** cable car (the cable car is included in the entry price and can be taken as often as you want). You can also get to the zoo on bus #247 from Wynyard.

Bradleys Head

Beyond the zoo, at the termination of Bradleys Head Road, **Bradleys Head** itself is marked by an enormous mast that towers over the rocky point. The mast once belonged to HMS *Sydney*, a victorious World War II battleship, long since gone to the wrecker's yard. It's a peaceful spot with a dinky lighthouse and, of course, a fabulous view back over the south shore. A colony of ring-tailed possums nests here, and boisterous flocks of rainbow lorikeets visit. The headland comprises another large chunk of **Sydney Harbour National Park** and you can walk to Bradleys Head via the six-kilometre Ashton Park **walking track** which starts near the ferry wharf, opposite the zoo entrance, and continues beyond the headland to Taylors Bay and Chowder Head, finishing at **Clifton Gardens**, where there's a jetty and sea baths on **Chowder Bay**. The now defunct military reserve which separates Chowder Bay from another chunk of Sydney Harbour National Park on Middle Head is now open to the public (see overleaf) and reached by a brand-new boardwalk from the northern end of Clifton Gardens. The NPWS offer **bush tucker tours** of Bradleys Head on the first and third Sunday of the month (1.30pm; $13.20; ⓣ 02/9247 5033), departing from the rear entrance of the zoo.

Middle Harbour

Middle Harbour is the largest inlet of Port Jackson, its two sides joined across the narrowest point at **The Spit**. The Spit Bridge opens regularly to let tall-masted yachts through – much the best way to explore its pretty, quiet coves and bays; several cruises pass by (see box on pp.106–107). The area also hides some architectural gems: the mock-Gothic 1889 bridge leading to **Northbridge**, and the idyllic enclave of **Castlecrag**, which was designed in 1924 by **Walter Burley Griffin**, fresh from planning Canberra and intent on building an environmentally friendly suburb – free of the fences and the red-tiled roofs he hated – that would be "for ever part of the bush".

Between Clifton Gardens and Balmoral Beach, a military reserve and naval depot at **Chowder Bay** blocked coastal access to both **Georges Head** and the more spectacular **Middle Head** by foot for over a century, although they could always be reached by road. However, since the military's recent withdrawal from the site, walkers can now trek all the way between Bradleys Head and Middle Head. The 1890s military settlement itself is now open to visitors as a reserve, and NPWS offer tours exploring its underground fortifications (second & fourth Sun of each month; 10.30am; 2hr; $13.20). You can reach the military reserve entrance from the northern end of Clifton Gardens (see overleaf). On the Hunters Bay side of Middle Head, tiny **Cobblers Beach** (ferry to Cremorne, then bus #204, or bus #206 direct from outside the Queen Victoria Building) is officially nude, and is a much more peaceful, secluded option than the more famous Lady Jane at South Head (see p.143).

The bush setting provided by Middle Head helps lend **Balmoral**, on Hunters Bay, the peaceful secluded air that makes it so popular with families (it's netted, too, which helps). There's something very Edwardian and genteel about palm-filled, grassy Hunters Park and its bandstand, which is still used for Sunday jazz concerts or even Shakespeare recitals in summer. The antiquated air is added to by the pretty white-painted **Bathers Pavilion** at the northern end, now converted into a restaurant and café (see p.168). There are really two beaches at Balmoral, separated by **Rocky Point**, a noted picnicking spot. South of Rocky Point, the "baths" – actually a netted bit of beach with a boardwalk and lanes for swimming laps – have been here in one form or another since 1899; you can rent sailboards, catamarans and take lessons from the neighbouring boat shed (see p.190). The hillside houses overlooking Balmoral have some of the highest price tags in Sydney: for a stroll through some prime real estate, head for **Chinamans Beach**, via Hopetoun Avenue and Rosherville Road. Famous residents include Ken Done, the artist who found fame with colourful impressionistic harbour scenes that now adorn duvet covers and wine bottles – and every souvenir shop in town. To get to Balmoral, catch a ferry from Circular Quay to Athol Wharf and then bus #238 via Bradleys Head Road, or the ferry to Musgrave Street wharf, Mosman, then bus #233 or #257 via Military Road.

Crossing the Spit Bridge, you can walk all the way to Manly Beach along the ten-kilometre Manly Scenic Walkway (see p.154), while bus #144 runs from Spit Road to Manly Wharf, taking in a scenic route uphill overlooking the Spit marina.

Ocean beaches

Sydney's **beaches** are among its great natural joys, key elements in the equation that makes the city special. The water and sand seem remarkably clean – people actually fish in the harbour, and don't just catch old condoms and plimsolls – and at Long Reef, just north of Manly, you can find rock pools teeming with starfish, anemones, sea-snails and crabs, and even a few shy moray eels. In recent years, humpback whales have even made an occasional appearance between May and November on their migratory path from the Antarctic to the tropical waters of Queensland (for more information consult the Oceania Project website – Ⓦwww.oceania.org.au).

Don't be lulled into a false sense of security, however beaches do have **perils** as well as pleasures. Some beaches are protected [by] special shark nets, but they don't keep out stingers such as bluebottles, which [can] suddenly swamp an entire beach; listen for loudspeaker announcements [that] will summon you from the water in the event of shark sightings or other dangers. Pacific **currents** can be very strong indeed – inexperienced swimmers and those with small children would do better sticking to the sheltered **harbour beaches** or **sea pools** at the ocean beaches. Ocean beaches are generally patrolled by **surf lifesavers** during the day between October and April (all year at Bondi): red and yellow flags (generally up from 6am until 6pm or 7pm) indicate the safe areas to swim, avoiding dangerous rips and undertows. [It] can't be stressed strongly enough that you must try to swim between the [flags] – people have drowned in strong surf. If you do get into difficulty, stay calm [and] raise one arm above your head as a signal to be rescued. It's hard not to [be] impressed as **surfers** paddle out on a seething ocean that you wouldn't dip your big toe in, but don't follow them unless you're confident you know what you're doing. Surf schools can teach you the basic skills and enlighten you [in] surfing etiquette and lingo; Let's Go Surfing (②02/9365 1800) is based at Bondi, while Manly Surf School (②02/9977 6977, ⑩www.manlysurfschool.com) covers the northern beaches. Listen to radio station 2MMM (104.9 FM) for the **surf report** at 7am, 9am and 3.40pm on weekdays and 7am, 9am and noon on weekends.

It's easy to underestimate the strength of the southern **sun**: follow the local slogan and Slip (on a shirt), Slop (on the sun block), Slap (on a hat). The final hazard, despite the apparent cleanliness, is **pollution**. After storms, currents and onshore breezes wash up sewage and other rubbish onto certain beaches making them (as signs will indicate) unsuitable for swimming and surfing. Harbour swimming spots in Port Jackson, Botany Bay and Pittwater and southern ocean beaches are the worst performers. South Sydney beaches suffer from the cliff-face sewage outfall on the Kurnell Peninsula with deceptively pretty Boat Harbour Beach consistently the most polluted. A recent pollution survey rating Sydney's cleanest beaches had Bondi coming out on top, but all the others were northern beaches including Palm, Whale, Bilgola, Newport, Bungan, Mona Vale, North Narabeen, Long Reef, North and South Curl Curl, Freshwater and North Steyne. To check pollution levels, call the Beachwatch Info Line on ②02/9901 7996.

A final note: topless bathing for women is accepted on many beaches but frowned on in others, so if in doubt, do as the locals do. There are two official nude beaches around the harbour (see pp.143 and 146).

Bondi and the eastern beaches

With brash **Bondi Beach** as their epicentre, Sydney's eastern beaches stretch from South Head down to Maroubra. North of Bondi, **Watsons Bay** (see p.143), once a fishing village, harbours Sydney's most famous seafood restaurant and there are spectacular views from **The Gap** in another chunk of Sydney Harbour National Park. Heading south from Bondi, you can walk right along the coast to its smaller, less brazen but very lively cousin **Coogee**, passing through gay favourite **Tamarama**, family-focused, café-cultured **Bronte**, narrow **Clovelly** and **Gordons Bay**, the latter with an underwater nature trail. Randwick Council have designed the "Eastern Beaches Coast Walk" from Clovelly to Coogee and beyond to more downmarket **Maroubra**, with stretches of boardwalk and interpretive boards detailing environmental features.

①

A free guide-mailing the walk can be picked up from the council's Customer Service, 30 Francis St, Randwick (☎02/9399 0999), or from Coogee at the front Coogee Kiosk, Goldstein Reserve, Arden Street opposite McDo

Bondi Bea

Bondi Beach nonymous with Australian beach culture, and indeed the mile-long cur golden sand (once again free of the controversial Olympic beach-volleyb dium) must be one of the best-known beaches in the world. It's the closes an beach to the city centre; you can take a train to Bondi Junction and a ten-minute bus ride, or drive there in twenty minutes (parking is a er story). Big, brash and action-packed, it's probably not the best place fo uiet sunbathe and swim, but the sprawling sandy crescent really is spectac Red-tiled houses and apartment buildings crowd in to catch the view, m of them erected in the 1920s when Bondi was a working-class suburb. Alt gh still residential, it has long since become a popular gathering place for kpackers from around the world (see box below), though the charm has gun to wear off and many have headed south to Coogee or north to Manly, pecially as it is now an alternative to the city centre for suburban teenagers make weekend whoopee, sometimes a little too aggressively.

The beahfront **Campbell Parade** is both cosmopolitan and highly commercialized, ined with cafés and shops. Future developments to the parade may include an nderground train line extending from Bondi Junction. For a gentler experince, explore some of the side streets, such as **Hall Street**, where you'll find an assortment of kosher bakeries and delis that serve the area's Jewish community, as well as some of Bondi's best cafés. On Sunday the **Bondi Beach markets** (10am–5pm), in the grounds of the primary school on the corner of Campbell Parade and Warners Avenue facing the northern end of the beach, place great emphasis on groovy fashion and jewellery. Between Campbell Parade and the beach, **Bondi Park** slopes down to the promenade, and is always full of sprawling bodies. Along the promenade there are two board ramps for **rollerblading** and **skateboarding**. The focus of the promenade is the arcaded, Spanish-style **Bondi Pavilion**, built in 1928 as a deluxe changing-room complex and now converted to a community centre hosting an array of workshops, classes and events, from drama and comedy in the theatre and the Seagull Room

Christmas Day on Bondi

For years backpackers and Bondi Beach on **Christmas Day** were synonymous. The beach was transformed into a drunken party scene, as those from colder climates lived out their fantasy of spending Christmas on the beach under a scorching sun. The behaviour and litter had been getting out of control over several years, and after riots in 1995, and a rubbish-strewn beach to clean up, the local council has begun strictly controlling the whole performance – but with the idea of trying to keep a spirit of goodwill towards the travellers while also tempting local families back to the beach on what is regarded as a family day. Nowadays alcohol is banned from the beach on Christmas Day, and police enforce the rule with on-the-spot confiscations – even locals can't enjoy a bottle of beachfront bubbly. However, a big **beach party** is organized for backpackers: a large area of sand is fenced off, with a bar, bands, food and entertainment running from 11am to 8pm. Around 3000 revellers cram into "the cage", while around 30,000 others – including a greater proportion of the desired family groups – enjoy the alcohol-free beach outside. In 2000, tickets for what is now called **Sunburnt Christmas** were $28 in advance from the Bondi Pavilion (☎02/9130 3325) or Ticketek (☎02/9266 4800), or $38 on the day.

Bondi's surf lifesavers

Surf lifesavers are what made Bondi famous; there's a the sculpture of one outside the Bondi Pavilion. The surf lifesaving movement beg 1906 with the founding of the Bondi Surf Life Bathers' Lifesaving Club in resp to the drownings that
accompanied the increasing popularity of swimming. Fr he beginning of the
colony, swimming was harshly discouraged as an unsuita bare-fleshed activity.
However, by the 1890s swimming in the ocean had become th test fad, and a Pacific
Islander introduced the concept of catching waves or bo urfing that was to
become an enduring national craze. Although "wowsers" (tee puritanical types)
attempted to put a stop to it, by 1903 all-day swimming was eve ydneysider's right.

The bronzed and muscled surf lifesavers in their distinctive and yellow caps
are a highly photographed, world-famous Australian image. Su lifesavers (members of what are now called Surf Life Saving Clubs, abbreviated SLSC) are volunteers working the beach at weekends, so come then to watch ir exploits – or
look out for a surf carnival; lifeguards, on the other hand, are ployed by the
council and work all week during swimming season (year-round a Bondi).

(the former ballroom) to daytime dance parties and outdoor film festivals in the
courtyard (programme details on ☎02/9130 3325 Mon–Fri, ☎02/9368 1253
Sat & Sun; ⓦwww.waverley.nsw.gov.au/info/pavilion.htm). The pavilion is now
also the base for the Sydney Fringe Festival in January. Downstairs in the foyer,
photos of Bondi's past are worth checking out, with some classic beach images
of men in 1930s bathing suits, and there's an excellent **souvenir shop** (daily
9.30am–5.30am) which utilizes lots of old-fashioned Bondi imagery. There's
even a community-access **art gallery** (daily 10am–5pm) featuring changing
exhibitions by local artists. In September, the Festival of the Winds, Australia's
largest **kite festival**, takes over the beach.

Surfing is part of the Bondi legend, the big waves ensuring that there's always
a pack of damp young things hanging around, bristling with surfboards. However,
the beach is carefully delineated, with surfers using the southern end of the beach
– so you shouldn't have to fear catapulting surfboards. There are two sets of flags
for swimmers and boogie-boarders, with families congregating at the northern
end near the sheltered saltwater pool (free), and everybody else using the middle
flags. The beach is netted and there hasn't been a shark attack for over forty years.
If the sea is too rough, or if you want to swim laps, there is a seawater swimming
pool at the southern end of the beach under the **Bondi Icebergs Club** building entrance on Notts Avenue. The Icebergs Club has been part of the Bondi legend since 1929. Members swim throughout the winter, and media coverage of
their plunge, made truly wintry with the addition of chunks of ice, heralds the
first day of winter. The unpretentious club, which has stunning surf views from its
bar area, is closed for renovations – an upgraded swimming pool, the addition of
a sauna and spa and even a surf lifesaving museum – until 2001/2002.

Topless bathing is condoned at Bondi – a long way from conditions right
up to the late 1960s when stern beach inspectors were constantly on the lookout for indecent exposure. If you want to join in the sun and splash but don't
have the gear, Beached at Bondi, below the lifeguard lookout tower, rents out
everything from umbrellas, wetsuits, cozzies and towels to surfboards and body-
boards. They also sell hats and sun block and have lockers for valuables.

You can reach Bondi on **bus** #380, #382 and #389 from Circular Quay via
Oxford Street and Bondi Junction, or take the train directly to Bondi Junction,
then transfer to these buses or to the #361 or the #365.

Tamarama to Gordons Bay

Many people find the smaller, quieter beaches to the south of Bondi more enticing, and it's a pleasant walk or jog right around the oceanfront and clifftop **walking track** to Clovelly (about 2hr) – the track also includes a fitness circuit, so you'll see plenty of joggers en route. Walk past the Bondi Icebergs Club on Notts Avenue (see overleaf) round Mackenzies Point, through Marks Park, until you reach a modest and secluded **Mackenzies Bay**. Next is **Tamarama Bay**, a deep, narrow beach favoured by the smart set and a hedonistic gay crowd ("Glamarama" to the locals), as well as surfers. Topless bathing is the norm for women here. The beach has its own small Surf Life Saving Club (SLSC), as well as a popular café. Tamarama Bay is a fifteen-minute walk from Bondi, or if you want to come here directly, it's a 300-metre walk from the #380 bus stop on Fletcher Street (from Circular Quay or Oxford St), or hop on bus #360 or 361 from Bondi Junction.

Walk through Tamarama's small park and follow the oceanfront road for five minutes to the next beach along, **Bronte Beach** on Nelson Bay, where the Olympic road cycling races picturesquely terminated. More of a family affair with a large green park, a popular café strip and sea baths, it's also easily reached on bus #378 from Central Station via Oxford Street and Bondi Junction. The **northern end** as you arrive from Tamarama has inviting flat-rock platforms, popular as fishing and relaxation spots, and the beach here is cliff-backed, providing some shade. The valley-like **park** beyond is extensive and shady; a **mini-train ride** for small children ($1.50) has been operating here since 1947, while further back there's an imaginative children's playground. At the **southern end** of the beach, palm trees give a suitably holiday feel as you relax at one of the outside tables of Bronte Road's wonderful café strip, with a clutch of eight to choose from, plus a fish-and-chip shop. Back on the water at this end, a natural rock enclosure makes a calm area for kids to swim in, and there are rock ledges to lie on around the enclosed sea swimming pool known as **Bronte Baths** (open access; free).

From Bronte, it's a pleasant five-minute walk past the baths to **Waverly Cemetery**, a fantastic spot to spend eternity. Established in 1877, it contains the graves of many famous Australians, with the bush poet contingent well represented. **Henry Lawson**, described on his headstone as poet, journalist and patriot, languishes in section 3G 516, while **Dorothea Mackeller**, who penned the famous poem "I love a sunburnt country", is in section 6 832–833. Beyond here – another five-minute walk – on the other side of the ominously named Shark Point, is the channel-like **Clovelly Bay**, with concrete platforms on either side and several sets of steps leading into the very deep water. Rocks at the far end keep out the waves and the sheltered bay is popular with lap-swimmers. On Sunday afternoons and evenings, the nearby *Clovelly Hotel* is a popular hangout for locals and travellers, with free live music. To get to Clovelly directly, take bus #339 from Millers Point via Central Station and Albion Street, Surry Hills; #340 from Millers Point via Taylor Square in Darlinghurst; #329 from Bondi Junction; or the weekday peak-hour X39 from Wynyard.

From Clovelly you can rock-hop around to equally narrow **Gordon's Bay**, though this can be a little tricky – backed by high sandstone cliffs with some rocky tunnels to pass through – and without local knowledge you're probably better off sticking to the road route along Cliffbrook Parade. The secluded rocks are popular with locals for peaceful fishing or sunbathing, and rescuing stranded tourists tends to shatter the equilibrium. Unsupervised, undeveloped Gordons Bay itself is not a pretty beach, but another world exists beneath the sheltered water: the protected **underwater nature trail** makes it diving and snorkelling heaven (see "Listings", p.187 for diving operators). From here, a walkway leads around the waterfront to Major Street and then onto **Dunningham Reserve** overlooking the northern end of Coogee Beach; the walk to Coogee proper takes about fifteen minutes in all.

Coogee

You could say that the battle for Bondi to keep its local feel has already been lost when you compare it to **Coogee**, another popular seaside resort. The hustle, bustle and aggro of the city has already truly arrived at Bondi, and while Coogee has a lively bar, café, restaurant and backpacker scene, and some big hotels, there's just something more laid-back, community-oriented and friendly about it – and it's not teeming with pseudo-trendy people. With its hilly streets of Californian-style apartment blocks looking onto a compact, pretty beach enclosed by two cliffy, green-covered headlands, Coogee has a snugness that Bondi just can't match. Everything is close to hand: beachfront Arden Street has a down-to-earth strip of cafés that compete with each other to sell the cheapest cooked breakfast (about $5), while the main shopping street, Coogee Bay Road, running uphill from the beach, has a choice selection of coffee spots and eateries, plus a big supermarket.

The ugly high-rise *Holiday Inn* has spoilt the southern end of the beach, though its *Pier Bar* does have fabulous views over the water. Other 1990s developments were more aesthetically successful: the imaginatively modernized promenade is a great place to stroll and hang out. Between it and the medium-sized beach is a grassy park with free electric barbecues, picnic tables and shelters. The beach is popular with families (there's an excellent children's playground at the southern end) and young travellers, as there's a stack of backpackers' hostels here (see "Accommodation", p.102–104). However, one of Coogee's chief pleasures are its baths, beyond the southern end of the beach. The first, McIvers Baths, for women and children only, is known by locals as **Coogee Women's Pool** (noon–5pm; 50¢); it's suitably secluded for nude sunbathing if you prefer. Opposite the entrance to the women's pool Grant Reserve has a full-on adventure playground. Just south of the women's pool, the unisex **Wylie's Baths**, a saltwater pool on the edge of the sea, is at the end of Neptune Street (7am–7pm; $2.40) with big decks to lie on, and solar heated showers; a fine spot for the excellent coffee made at its kiosk.

You can reach Coogee on **bus** #373 from Circular Quay via Randwick, or #372 from Eddy Avenue, outside Central Station; journey time from Central is about 25min. There are also buses from Bondi Junction via Randwick: #314 and #315.

Immediately south of Wylie's, **Trenerry Reserve** is a huge green park jutting out into the ocean; its spread of big, flat rocks offer tremendous views and make a great place to chill out. Probably the most impressive section of Randwick Council's **Eastern Beaches Coast Walk** commences here. The council is attempting to regenerate the native flora, and the walk, sometimes on boards, is accompanied by interpretive panels detailing the surrounding plant- and birdlife. Steps lead down to a rock platform full of small pools – you can wander down and look at the life within, and there is a large tear-shaped pool you can swim in. It's quite thrilling with the waves crashing over – but be careful of both the waves and the blue-ringed octopus found here. At low tide you can continue walking along the rocks around Lurline Bay – otherwise you must follow the streets inland for a bit, rejoining the waterfront from Mermaid Avenue. Jack Vanny Memorial Park is fronted by the great cliffy rocks of Mistral

Point, a great spot to sit and look at the water, and down by the water the **Mahon Pool**, a small, pleasant sea pool (free; open access), with waves crashing at the edge and surrounded by great boulders, has an unspoilt secluded feel. The isolated *Pool Caffe* across the road makes a wonderful lunch or coffee spot (see p.167).

Manly and the northern beaches

Manly, just above North Head at the northern mouth of the harbour, is doubly blessed with both ocean and harbour beaches. When Captain Arthur Phillip, the commander of the First Fleet, was exploring Sydney Harbour in 1788, he saw a group of well-built Aboriginal men onshore, proclaimed them to be "manly" and named the cove in the process. During the Edwardian era it became fashionable as a recreational retreat from the city, and the promotional slogan of the time "Manly – seven miles from Sydney, but a thousand miles from care" still holds true today. The area has become quite a travellers' centre in recent years with some of Sydney's best backpackers' hostels. An excellent time to visit is over the Labour Day long weekend in early October, when there is a **Jazz Festival** with free outdoor concerts featuring musicians from around the world. Beyond Manly, the **northern beaches** continue for 30km up to Barrenjoey Heads and **Palm Beach**.

Manly

A day-trip to Manly, rounded off with a dinner of fish and chips, offers a classic taste of Sydney life. The ferry trip out here has always been half the fun: the legendary Manly Ferry service has been running from Circular Quay since 1854, and the huge old boats come complete with snack bars selling the ubiquitous meat pie. Ferries terminate at Manly Wharf in Manly Cove, near a small section of harbour beach with a netted-off swimming area popular with families. Like a typical English seaside resort, Manly Wharf has always had a **funfair**: although it's been modernized into a sort of two-storey shopping mall, a colourful Ferris wheel and merry-go-round still light up the waterfront. From the wharf, walk west, either along the beach with the pool or along West Esplanade to **Oceanworld** (daily 10am–5.30pm; $15.90, child $8, family ticket $39.90), where clear acrylic walls hold back the water so you can saunter along the harbour floor, gazing at sharks and stingrays. Divers hand-feed sharks every Monday, Wednesday and Friday at 11am and there's also a thirty-minute Shark Tunnel Tour (Tues, Thurs, Sat & Sun 11am) when a guide can answer all your shark questions. The original vividly painted aquarium now houses an art gallery. **Belgrave Street**, running north from Manly Wharf, is Manly's alternative strip, where you'll find some good cafés tucked away, interesting shops to browse, yoga schools and the Manly Environment Centre.

Many visitors mistake Manly Cove for the ocean beach, which in fact lies on the other side of the isthmus, 500m down The Corso, Manly's busy pedestrianized main drag. The ocean beach, **South Steyne**, is characterized by the stands of Norfolk pine which line the shore. Here you'll find the **Manly Visitor Information Centre** (daily 10am–4pm; ☎02/9977 1088). A six-kilometre-long cycle path (shared with pedestrians) begins at the visitor centre and runs north to Seaforth, past North Steyne Beach and Queenscliff. You can rent bikes from Manly Beach & Surf Hire, Shop 8, 1–15 Central Ave, off The Corso (mountain bikes $25 half-day, $35 full-day; basic bikes $20/$28), plus just about anything to make the beach more fun, from surfboards to

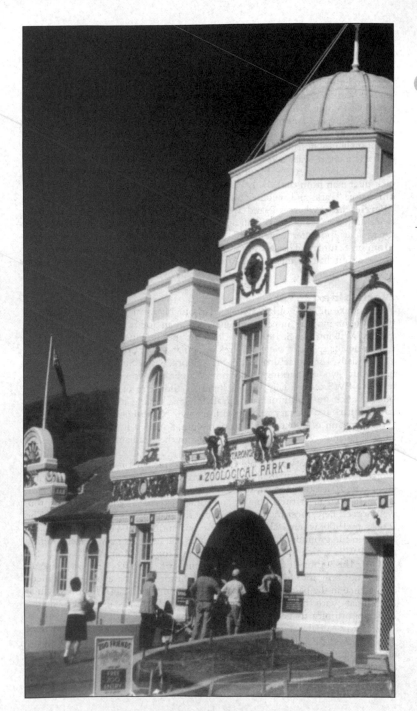

snorkel sets. For a more idyllic beach than the long stretch of South Steyne, follow the footpath from the southern end of the beach around the headland to Cabbage Tree Bay, with two very pretty, green-backed beaches at either end – **Fairy Bower** to the west and **Shelley Beach** to the east.

A wonderful long-distance seaside walk starts at Manly Cove. The **Manly Scenic Walkway** follows the harbour shore inland from Manly Cove all the way back to Spit Bridge on Middle Harbour, where you can catch bus #180 back to Wynyard Station in the city centre (20min). The eight-kilometre walk takes you through a section of **Sydney Harbour National Park**, past a number of small beaches and coves, Aboriginal middens and some subtropical rainforest. The entire walk takes three to four hours but is broken up into six sections with obvious exit/entry points if you're not up to doing the whole thing; pick up a map from the Manly Visitor Information Centre (above) or NPWS offices (see "Parks and wildlife" on p.189).

Ferries leave wharves 2 and 3 at Circular Quay for Manly approximately twice an hour ($5) and take half an hour. The last ferry service from Circular Quay is at 7pm after which time the faster JetCats operate until midnight, 11pm on Saturdays. The JetCat ($6.10) goes twice as fast as the regular ferries but is about half as much fun. After if finishes, night bus #150 runs from Wynyard Terminal.

North Head

You can take in more of the Sydney Harbour National Park at **North Head**, the harbour mouth's upper jaw, where you can follow the short circuitous Fairfax Walking Track to three lookout points, including the **Fairfax Lookout**, for splendid views. There's a regular #135 **bus** from Manly Wharf (10–14 daily; last bus returns Mon–Fri 3.56pm, Sat & Sun 4.26pm), or if you have your own car (parking $3 per hour, $5 per day) you can drop in en route to the NPWS office (daily 9am–4.30pm), a kilometre of so before the lookouts, to pick up free information leaflets. Smack bang in the middle of this national park is a military reserve with its own **National Artillery Museum** (Wed, Sat, Sun & public holidays noon–4pm; $6) sited in the historic **North Fort**; a curious system of tunnels is built into the headland here – it takes up to two hours to wander through them.

There's more history at the old **Quarantine Station**, on the harbour side of North Head, used from 1828 until 1984: arriving passengers or crew who had a contagious disease were set down at Spring Cove to serve a spell of isolation at the station, all at the shipping companies' expense. Sydney residents, too, were forced here, most memorably during the plague which broke out in The Rocks in 1900, when 1832 people were quarantined (104 plague victims are buried in the grounds). The site, its buildings still intact, is now looked after by the NPWS, which offers **guided history tours** (Mon, Wed & Fri–Sat 1.10pm; 1hr 30min–2hr; $11; booking essential on ☎02/9247 5033), giving an insight not only into Sydney's immigration history but the evolution of medical science in the past century and a half, often in gory detail. The tours, which co-ordinate with the #135 bus from Manly Wharf (bus fare extra), provide the only opportunity to get out to this beautiful isolated harbour spot with its views across to Balmoral Beach. The night-time **ghost tours** (Wed & Fri–Sun; 3hr; $22 Wed, $27.50 Fri–Sun, including tea and damper) are very popular; children under 12 have a Friday-night, less hair-raising, Kids Ghost Tour (Fri $13.20 child or adult; 2hr; no supper). Unfortunately, no public transport is available for the night-time visits, so without your own vehicle you'll have to catch a taxi.

Freshwater to Bilgola Beach

Freshwater, just beyond Manly, sits snugly between two rocky headlands on Queenscliff Bay, and is one of the most picturesque of the northern beaches. There's plenty of surf culture around the headland at Curl Curl, and a walking track at its northern end, commencing from Huston Parade, will take you above the rocky coastline to the curve of **Dee Why Beach**. Dee Why provides consistently good surf, while its sheltered lagoon makes it popular with families. Beyond the lagoon, windsurfers gather around **Long Reef**, where the point is surrounded by a wide rock shelf creviced with rock pools and protected as an aquatic reserve – well worth a wander to peek at the creatures within. The long, beautiful sweep of **Collaroy Beach**, now with a popular YHA (see p.105), shades into **Narrabeen Beach**, an idyllic spot backed by the extensive, swimmable and fishable **Narrabeen Lakes**, popular with anglers and families; there's also a good campsite here (see box on p.94). Beyond Narrabeen, **Mona Vale** is a long, straight stretch of beach with a large park behind and a sea pool dividing it from sheltered **Bongin Bongin Bay**, whose headland reserve, and rocks to clamber on, make it ideal for children. Inland from Mona Vale at Ingleside, the domed **Bahá'i Temple** on Mona Vale Road (daily 9am–5pm; ⓦwww.bahai.org) is one of only seven in the world; the Bahá'i faith teaches the unity of religion, and Sunday services (11am) read from texts of the world's main religions.

After Bongin Bongin Bay the Barrenjoey Peninsula begins, with calm Pittwater (see p.194) on its western side and ocean beaches running up its eastern side until it spears into Broken Bay. **Newport** boasts a fine stretch of ocean beach between two rocky headlands; on Sunday crowds gather to listen to live jazz in the beer garden of the *Newport Arms* on Kalinya Street, overlooking Heron Cove on Pittwater. Unassuming **Bilgola Beach**, next door to Newport, is one of the prettiest of the northern beaches.

Avalon, Whale and Palm Beach

From Bilgola Beach, a trio of Sydney's best beaches, for both surf and scenery, run up the eastern fringe of the mushroom-shaped peninsula: Avalon and Whale Beach are less fashionable than Palm Beach, and are popular surfie territory.

Backed by bush-covered hills, and reached by three kilometres of winding road, small **Avalon Beach** has a suitably secluded feel and is a slice of paradise on a summer's day. A pleasing set of shops and eateries run perpendicular from the beach on Avalon Parade; *Macabar* at no. 23 is a good licensed café with a very contemporary feel and live music on Saturday nights – it's popular with the travellers who stay nearby at the marvellous hostel (see p.104). The people of Avalon memorably rejected the proposed filming of a series of *Baywatch* in early 1999, though the beach did feature in a tacky *Baywatch* special.

Whale Beach, 8km further north via Barrenjoey Road and Whale Beach Road, is much less of a settlement, with the beach fronted by the inevitable Surf Life Saving Club and the classy *De Beers Restaurant*. You can continue following Whale Beach Road north to reach **Palm Beach** which, living up to its name, is a hangout for the rich and famous: you can even get here by Hollywood-style seaplane from Rose Bay (see p.142). Palm Beach residents aren't as concerned about the film cameras as their Avalon neighbours: the ocean beach, on the western side of the peninsula, leads a double life as "Summer Bay" in the famous Aussie soap *Home and Away*, with the Barrenjoey Lighthouse and headland regularly in shot; *Collaroy YHA* (see p.105) offer a phenomenally popular "Summer Bay" location tour. The bush-covered headland where the lighthouse sits is actually an outpost of Ku-Ring-Gai Chase National Park (see p.194), the bulk of which is across Pittwater, and can be visited courtesy of Palm Beach and Hawkesbury River Ferries (☎02/9997 4815, ⓦwww.pbhrc.bizland.com). The **ferries** leave from the wharf on the eastern, Pittwater side of the peninsula (leaving at 11am, back at 3pm, with a 1hr lunch break at Bobbin Head; cruise $30; general transport to Patonga $6.50 one-way, $13 return). Alternatively, the Palm Beach Ferry Service (☎02/9918 2747 or 9973 2704, ⓦwww.palmbeachferry.com.au) runs from Palm Beach wharf via The Basin to Mackeral Beach reaching picnicking and camping spots on Pittwater (departing hourly 9–11am & 1–5pm, Sat & Sun until 6pm; $4 one-way, $8 return). Beside the wharf is calm Snapperman Beach, fronted by yachts and a shady park, while across the road is the *Barrenjoey Boathouse*, an upmarket guesthouse and restaurant. You can also dine well at *Ancora* here, but for less cash, try the excellent milk bar serving cheap fish and chips, hamburgers and good sandwiches. There's a few interesting shops to browse in too, offering Indian clothes and accessories, funky secondhand furniture and women's clothing.

The northern beaches can be reached by regular **bus** from Wynyard in the city or from Manly. Bus #190 and #L90 run up the peninsula from Wynyard to Avalon, continuing to Palm Beach via the Pittwater side; change at Avalon for bus #193 to Whale Beach.

Botany Bay

The southern suburbs of Sydney, arranged around huge **Botany Bay**, are seen as the heartland of red-tiled-roof suburbia, a terracotta sea spied from above as the planes land at **Mascot**. Clive James, the area's most famous son, hails from Kogarah – described as a 1950s suburban wasteland in his tongue-in-cheek *Unreliable Memoirs*. The popular perception of Botany Bay is coloured by its proximity to an airport, a high-security prison (Long Bay), an oil refinery, a container terminal and a sewerage outlet (pollution levels are high). Yet the surprisingly clean-looking water is fringed by quiet, sandy beaches and the marshlands shelter a profusion of birdlife. Whole areas of the waterfront, at **La Perouse**, with its associations with eighteenth-century French exploration, and on the **Kurnell Peninsula** where Captain Cook first put anchor, are designated as part of **Botany Bay National Park**, and large stretches on either side of the Georges River form a State Recreation Area.

La Perouse

At least, is there any news of Monsieur de Laperouse?

Louis XVI, about to be guillotined, 1793

La Perouse, tucked into the northern shore of Botany Bay where it meets the Pacific Ocean, contains Sydney's oldest Aboriginal settlement, the legacy of a mission. The suburb took its name from the eighteenth-century French explorer, **Laperouse**, who set up camp here for six weeks, briefly and cordially meeting Captain Arthur Phillip, who was making his historic decision to forgo swampy Botany Bay and move on to Port Jackson; after leaving Botany Bay, the Laperouse expedition was never seen again.

A monument erected in 1825 and the excellent NPWS-run **Laperouse Museum** (Wed–Sun 10am–4pm; $5.50), which sits on a grassy headland between the pretty beaches of Congwong Bay and Frenchmans Bay, tell the whole fascinating story. Tracing Laperouse's voyage in great detail, the museum displays are enlivened by relics from the wrecks, exhibits of antique French maps and copies of etchings by the naturalists on board. The voyage was commissioned by the French king Louis XVI in 1785 as a purely scientific exploration of the Pacific to rival Cook's voyages, and strict instructions were given for Laperouse to "act with great gentleness and humanity towards the different people whom he will visit". After an astonishing three-and-a-half-year journey through South America, the Easter Islands, Hawaii, the northwest coast of America, and past China and Japan to Russia, the *Astrolabe* and the *Boussole* struck disaster – first encountering hostility in the Solomon Islands and then in their doomed sailing from Botany Bay, on March 10, 1788. Their disappearance remained a mystery until 1828, when relics were discovered on Vanikoro in the Solomon Islands; the wrecks themselves were found only in 1958 and 1964. A recent addition to the museum is a new exhibition which looks at the Aboriginal history and culture of the area.

The surrounding headlands and foreshore have been incorporated into the northern half of **Botany Bay National Park** (no entry fee; the other half is across Botany Bay on the Kurnell Peninsula, see below). A **visitor centre** (☎02/9311 3379), in the same building as the Laperouse Museum, can give details of walks including a fine one past Congwong Bay Beach to Henry Head and its lighthouse (5km round trip). The idyllic verandah of the *Boatshed Cafe*, on the small headland between Congwong and Frenchmans bays, sits right over the water with pelicans floating about below. La Perouse is at its most lively on **Sunday** (and public holidays) when, following a tradition established at the turn of the twentieth century, Aboriginal people come down to sell boomerangs and other crafts, and demonstrate snake-handling skills (from 1.30pm) and boomerang throwing. There are also tours of the nineteenth-century fortifications on **Bare Island** (Sat, Sun & public holidays 12.30pm, 1.30pm, 2.30pm & 3.30pm; $7; no booking required, wait at the gate to the island), joined to La Perouse by a walkway. The island featured in the 2000 film *Mission Impossible 2*, starring Tom Cruise.

To **get to** La Perouse, catch bus #394 from Circular Quay or #393 from Railway Square (Sun only), or take the #L94 express from Circular Quay.

The Kurnell Peninsula and Cronulla

From La Perouse, you can see across Botany Bay to Kurnell and the red buoy marking the spot where Captain James Cook and the crew of the *Endeavour* anchored on April 29, 1770 for an eight-day exploration. Back in England, many refused to believe that the uniquely Australian plants and animals they had recorded actually existed – the kangaroo in particular was thought to be a hoax. **Captain Cook's Landing Place** is now the south head of **Botany Bay National Park**, where the informative **Discovery Centre** (Mon–Fri 10am–4pm, Sat & Sun 9.30am–4.30pm; $7.50 fee per car; ☎02/9668 9111) looks at the wetlands ecology of the park and tells the story of Cook's visit and its implications for Aboriginal people. Indeed the political sensitivity of the spot which effectively marks the beginning of the decline of an ancient culture has led for a search for an Aboriginal name for the park: one suggestion was "Gillingarie" from the language of the original Dharawal people of the area, which means "land that belongs to us all", but the name which has been settled on (though the park has not yet been officially renamed) is Kamay-Botany Bay National Park – "Kamay" being the Dharawal name for the bay. Set aside as a public recreation area in 1899, the heath and woodland is unspoilt and there are some secluded beaches for swimming; you may even spot parrots and honeyeaters if you keep your eyes peeled. To get here by **public transport**, take the train to Cronulla and then Kurnell Bus Services route #987 (☎02/9524 8977).

On the ocean side of the **Kurnell Peninsula** is Sydney's longest beach: the ten-kilometre stretch begins at **CRONULLA** and continues as deserted, dune-backed **Wanda Beach**. This is prime surfing territory – and the only Sydney beach accessible by train (Sutherland line from Bondi Junction; surfboards carried free). Like Manly, Cronulla has both sheltered bay beaches and ocean frontage, situated as it is on a finger of land jutting into **Port Hacking**. Its modern residential and commerical developments can give it the feel of a Gold Coast resort but at heart it's just a down-to-earth outer suburb. There are no trendies here, though with the recent opening of a purpose-built YHA hostel (see p.105), travellers will soon be added into the mix. Life revolves around the beaches and the shopping strip on **Cronulla Street**, which becomes a pedestrianized mall between Kingsway and Purley Place. The train station is at the southern end of this street, along with Cronulla's more interesting shops and two hip young café-bars, *Voodoo Lounge* and *Nulla Nulla*, the latter with cheaper drinks and internet access.

Serious surfing is done at the main beach, **North Cronulla**, straight down Kingsway. It's fronted by a commercial-looking eating precinct and the all-new *Northies* pub across the road, with outdoor tables. Follow the concreted walkway, **The Esplanade**, south along the rock platform and past a couple of delightful sea pools to reach the smaller, more sheltered and less developed **South Cronulla** beach. Above, shady Cronulla Park, popular with families, slopes down to the water while the Cronulla Sports Complex on The Esplanade has indoor heated pools and a gym (Mon–Fri 7am–3.45pm, Sat 7am–4.45pm, Sun 8am–4.45pm; swim $2.75, gym $5.50, sauna and spa $8.80) and next door the *Cronulla Kiosk* is a magic spot for breakfast or lunch. Behind the Sports Centre, the unpretentious *Cronulla RSL Memorial Club* has stunning ocean views from its wall-to-ceiling windows, which can be enjoyed with a cheap drink or meal. Keep following The Esplanade right around to Darook Park on sheltered **Gunnamatta Bay**, where you can catch a ferry to Bundeena in the Royal National Park (see pp.225–227) from the Tonkin Street wharf (Tonkin St is just behind the train station).

Eating and drinking

Sydney boasts an extraordinary number of food stalls, cafés, takeaways and restaurants, only a fraction of which are listed here. Check out too the "Pubs and bars" listings starting on p.169, as many have eateries attached. Be adventurous, as quality is uniformly high, with fresh ingredients and imaginative cuisine on offer. The restaurant scene is highly fashionable, and with more than 3000 restaurants, businesses rise in favour, fall in popularity and close down or change names and style at an astonishing rate. Since 2000, all New South Wales' restaurants have been **non-smoking**, except for reception areas and outside tables.

Most of the inner suburbs are just a few minutes away by , train, ferry or taxi, and there you'll generally find better, less expensive a more enjoyable places to eat and drink. Sydney's fully fledged café culture c be found most notably in Darlinghurst, Glebe, Newtown and the eastern beaches of Bondi, Bronte and Coogee. There are also fantastic places to eat out in the suburbs: one of the best is **Cabramatta**, where Sydney's Vietnamese community makes its home. To get there, take the train from Central Station (fourteen stops) and you'll find a glut of excellent restaurants on Road and John Street, just west of Cabramatta Station.

All restaurants in the following listings are open daily for nch and dinner, unless otherwise stated, and the more specific café times are given (most are open for breakfast, one of Sydney's most popular meals).

The city centre and The Rocks

The cafés and food stalls in the business and shopping districts of the city centre cater mainly for lunchtime crowds, and there are lots of **food courts** and stalls serving fast food and snacks. Check out the selection in the basements of the **Queen Victoria Building** (see p.118), **Grace Bros Department Store** (see p.118) and the **MLC Centre** near Martin Place, in the first floor of the **Hunter Connection** shopping arcade, 310 George St, opposite Wynyard Station, and the ground floor of the **Quayside Shopping Centre** at Circular Quay, off Alfred Street. The classiest of them is probably the foodie's paradise in the basement of the **David Jones** department store on Market Street, where a number of counters serve rather pricey snacks and titbits. Many museums and tourist attractions also have surprisingly good **cafés** – notably the Museum of Contemporary Art, the Australian Museum, the Hyde Park Barracks and the Art Gallery of New South Wales.

There are several good **pubs** in The Rocks (see pp.169–170), many of which serve some kind of food, but for the most part the area around the harbour has a choice of expensive restaurants and upmarket cafés or average fast food.

Cafés and brasseries

Café Opera *Hotel Intercontinental*, 117 Macquarie St (☎02/9240 1260). The five-star *Intercontinental* (see p.94) has long been a hit with the locals, not just tourists, and the buffet offered by its *Café Opera*, groaning under the display of seafood, is legendary. You can stuff yourself silly for $37 at lunchtime ($42.50 Sun, with live jazz), $43.50 at dinner ($49 Fri & Sat) or $28.50 at supper from 10pm (except Sun).

Obelisk Café Shop 1, 7 Macquarie Place. Stylish outdoor café close to Circular Quay. Fab spot on an historic square with big shady trees, or sit inside on stools and listen to jazzy music on a wet day. Attracts a working crowd who plunge in for great coffee, *pizzetta, focaccia*, pasta, steak sandwiches and healthy filled wraps. Mon–Fri 6am–5pm.

Pavilion on the Park 1 Art Gallery Rd (☎02/9232 1322). On the edge of The Domain, this totally round building (circa 1960s with a stylish contemporary interior refit) has great views of the city. Right opposite the Art Gallery of NSW and just by the Botanical Gardens entrance, it's a great place to take a break from sightseeing – with an outdoor kiosk, a café section and an upmarket well-reviewed restaurant, it has something for everyone. Licensed. Café daily 9am–5pm; restaurant closed Sat lunch and Sun–Wed dinner.

QVB Jet cnr York and Druitt streets, City. On the corner of the QVB building looking across to the Town Hall, with big, glass windows and outdoor seating providing people-watching opportunites, this is a very lively Italian café/bar. The coffee is predictably excellent, and the menu is big on breakfast. The rest of the day choose from pasta, risotto and soups, salads and sandwiches. Licensed. Mon–Fri 8am–10pm, Sat 9am–10pm.

Rossini between wharves 5 and 6, Circular Quay. Quality Italian fast food alfresco while you're waiting for a ferry or just watching the Quay. *Panzerotto* – big, cinnamon-flavoured and ricotta-filled doughnuts – are a speciality. Pricey but excellent coffee. Licensed. Daily 7am–11pm.

Sailors Thai Canteen, 106 George St, The Rocks. The cheaper version of the much-praised, pricey downstairs restaurant (☎02/9251 2466 for bookings), housed in the restored Sailors' Home. Its ground-level canteen with a long stainless-steel communal table looks onto an open kitchen, where the chefs chop away to provide simple one-bowl meals. Come early for lunch in the canteen. Licensed. Daily noon–6pm.

Sydney Cove Oyster Bar, Circular Quay East. It's hard not to be lured into this place on a stroll to the Opera House. The quaint little building housing the bar and kitchen was once a public toilet, but don't let that put you off. The outdoor tables provide a magical locale to sample Sydney Rock Pacific oysters (around $14.50 for half a dozen). There's other seafood as well, or just come for coffee, cake and the view.

Restaurants

bel mondo, Level 3, the Argyle Stores, 12–24 Argyle St, The Rocks (☎02/9241 3700). With fabulous views over The Rocks and the harbour, the North Italian food served here is probably the best of its kind in Sydney. A sophisticated crowd eats here, but for less cash you can get views and similar food at the fashionable *Anti-Bar* at the front. Very expensive; licensed. Restaurant closed Sat & Sun lunch.

Doyles on the Quay, Overseas Passenger Terminal, Circular Quay West (☎02/9252 3400). Downtown branch of a Sydney seafood institution; pricey but excellent, with great harbour views from the outdoor waterfront tables. You'll probably need to book. Licensed.

Quay, Sydney Cove Passenger Terminal, Circular Quay West (☎02/9251 5600). Fabulous views and a French chef means it's posh and very pricey. Bookings essential; licensed. Closed Sat & Sun lunch.

Rockpool, 109 George St, The Rocks (☎02/9252 1888). Rated as one of Sydney's most glamorous dining spots, owned by top chef Neil Perry, with celebrities filing in to eat the raved-about seafood and other contemporary creations. With mains around $45, this is definitely splurge material. Licensed. Closed Sat lunch & Sun.

Tetsuya's, 529 Kent St, City (☎02/9267 2900). Stylish new city premises – all Japanese timber interior, and a beautiful Japanese garden outside – of one of Sydney's star chefs, Tetsuya Wakuda. The waiting list is a month ahead – worth it to sample the twelve-course *dégustation* dinner menu ($143; also available Sat lunch), or the eight-course Fri lunch ($93.50); wine teamed with each course is $60 dinner, $40 lunch. Licensed and BYO. Lunch Fri & Sat, dinner Tues–Sat.

The Wharf Restaurant, Pier 4, Hickson Rd, The Rocks (☎02/9250 1761), next to the Wharf Theatre. Enterprising modern food (lots of seafood), served up in an old dock building with heaps of raw charm and a harbour vista; bag the outside tables for the best views. Cocktail bar open from noon until end of evening performance. Expensive. Closed Sun.

Haymarket, Chinatown, Darling Harbour and around

The southern end of George Street has plenty of very cheap restaurants, of variable quality. Chinatown around the corner is a better bet: many places here specialize in *yum cha* (or dim sum as it's also known), and there are several late-night and all-night eating options. Inexpensive licensed Asian **food courts**, serving everything from Japanese to Vietnamese, and of course Chinese food, can be found in the Sussex Centre (1st floor, 401 Sussex St, daily 10am–9pm); Dixon House (basement level, corner Little Hay and Dixon streets; daily 10.30am–8.30pm); the Harbour Plaza (basement level, corner Factory and Dixon streets; daily 10am–10pm); but the best is on the top floor of the Market City Shopping Centre, above Paddy's Market at the corner of Quay and Thomas streets (daily 8am–10pm). A few blocks from Chinatown back toward the city centre, there's a good array of Spanish eateries on Liverpool Street, while the new Cockle Bay Wharf restaurant precinct harbours some gems. Beyond Darling Harbour, you can eat fantastically well at the Sydney Fish Market (see p.130).

Cafés, pubs and cheap eats

Glasgow Arms Hotel, 527 Harris St, Ultimo, opposite the Powerhouse Museum. Very pleasant pub with leafy courtyard dining. Sat dinner only and Sun restaurant is closed.

Grand Taverna, *Sir John Young Hotel*, cnr Liverpool and George streets, Haymarket. Spanish food, including tapas, at the heart of the Spanish quarter. Authentically lively atmosphere and no-frills setting for some of the best paella and sangria in town. Closed Sun.

Ippon Sushi, 404 Sussex St, Haymarket. Fun, inexpensive Japanese sushi train downstairs, with a revolving choice of delectables from $2 to $5.50. Licensed and BYO. Daily 11am–11pm.

Roma Caffe, 191 Hay St, Haymarket. The *Roma* has been in the area for over 35 years offering fabulous coffee, great breakfasts and a huge gleaming display of wicked Italian desserts, plus delicious *focaccia* and fresh pasta – try the home-made pumpkin tortellini. Mon–Sat 8am–6pm.

Tai Pei, Shop 2, Prince Centre, 8 Quay St, Haymarket. Tiny, congenial and cheap Taiwanese eatery offering generous servings; great dumplings, and very tasty Mama Pho's tofu (with pork – like most things on the menu). Daily 11am–9pm.

Restaurants

BBQ King, 18–20 Goulburn St, Haymarket (⊤ 02/9267 2433). Unprepossessing but perpetually crowded Chinese restaurant specializing in barbecued meat. There is also, surprisingly, a big vegetarian list on the menu. Inexpensive to moderate; licensed. Daily 11.30am–2am.

Blackbird, Cockle Bay Wharf, Darling Harbour (⊤ 02/9283 7835). This place has the feel of a funky American diner; sit on stools at the bar or couches out the back, or enjoy the water views from the terrace. Generous, good-value meals – from *dahl* to spaghetti, T-bone steaks, noodles, salads, pizzas from a hot-stone oven, and breakfast until 4pm. Licensed. Daily 7am–1am.

Bodhi, Capitol Square, 730–742 George St, Haymarket (⊤ 02/9281 6162; another branch attached to Cook and Philip Park Pool). In a smart modern "Eat Street" arcade attached to the Capitol Theatre, *Bodhi* is the vegetarian/vegan option, but there's not a hint of quiche on the menu: this is top-notch Chinese vegetarian food, with the focus on delicious *yum cha*. Organic and biodynamic produce is used. Licensed.

Capitan Torres, 73 Liverpool St (⊤ 02/9264 5574). An atmospheric and enduring Spanish place, specializing in seafood – a fresh display helps you choose – and paella; licensed. Sit downstairs at the bar or upstairs in the restaurant.

Chinta Ria ~ Temple of Love, Roof Terrace, 201 Sussex St, Cockle Bay Wharf development, Darling Harbour (⊤ 02/9264 3211). People queue to get in here (bookings lunch only) as much for the fun atmosphere – a blues and jazz soundtrack and decor which mixes a giant Buddha, a lotus pond and 50s-style furniture – as for the yummy Malaysian food. The latter is cooked up in the frenzied open kitchen; popular dishes include *lohbak*, a starter of bean-curd skin wrapped around minced chicken and deep fried, and the coconut milk-based noodle soup, Curry Laksa. Licensed.

Kam Fook Sharks Fin Seafood Restaurant, Level 3, Market City complex, cnr Quay and Haymarket streets, Haymarket (⊤ 02/9211 8988). The long name matches the size of this Cantonese establishment, officially Australia's largest restaurant, seating 800. You can eat some of the best *yum cha* in Sydney here, and you'll still have to queue for it if you haven't booked, despite the restaurant's size. Moderate to expensive; licensed. *Yum cha* Mon–Fri 10am–5.30pm, Sat & Sun 9am–5.30pm, dinner nightly.

The Malaya, 761 George St, Haymarket, near Railway Square (⊤ 02/9211 0946). Popular, veteran Chinese–Malaysian place, serving some of the best, most authentic and spicy *laksa* in town. Moderately priced; licensed. Closed Sun.

Glebe

In Glebe you'll find both cheap and upmarket restaurants, ethnic takeaways, delis and a string of good cafés. **Glebe Point Road** is dominated by bookshops and cafés – with a cluster of particularly good cafés at the Broadway end. No one cuisine dominates: café fare is eclectic with plenty of choice for vegetarians, and Indian, Lebanese and Thai eateries rub shoulders. A delightful feature of Glebe cafés are their leafy courtyards and gardens.

Vegetarian eating

Vegetarians are well catered for on just about every café menu, and most contemporary restaurant menus too. The following are specifically vegetarian: *Badde Manors* (below), *Bodhi* (overleaf), *Green Gourmet* (below), *Harvest* (opposite), *Iku* (below), *Sloanes* (p.166) and *Red Kite* (p.167).

Badde Manors 37 Glebe Point Rd. Vegetarian corner café with a wonderful light-and-airy ambience, eclectic decor and laid-back staff; always packed, especially for weekend brunch. One of the best cafés on this strip, with yummy cakes and ice cream, and inexpensive and generous servings. Mon–Fri 8am until midnight, Sat & Sun 9am–1am.

The Boathouse on Blackwattle Bay end of Ferry Rd, Glebe (☎02/9518 9011). Atmospheric restaurant located in a former boatshed, with fantastic views across the bay to Anzac Bridge and the fishmarkets, opposite. Fittingly, seafood is the thing here, from the six different kinds of oysters to the raved-about fish pie made from snapper. Expensive. Closed Mon.

Borobudur 123–125 Glebe Point Rd (☎02/9660 5611). Value-for-money Indonesian with an outdoor courtyard and courteous service. Dinner only Mon–Sat. Licensed and BYO.

The Craven 166 Glebe Point Rd, next door to the Valhalla Cinema. At the other end of the street to *Badde Manors* and just as popular, this café is a great place to devour tasty titbits before or after the pictures, or plough into more substantial North African and Mediterranean-style fare from the daily blackboard specials. The atmosphere is friendly and relaxed, and there's plenty of space, light and air in the split-level shopfront building with big ceiling fans; on-street tables too. Mon–Fri 8am–10.30pm, Sat & Sun 9am–10.30pm.

Dakhni 65 Glebe Point Rd (☎02/9660 4887). A range of Indian dishes from tandoori through to delicious South Indian vegetarian *masala dosai* (filled pancakes). A meat or vegetarian *thali* costs around $18.50, plus it's BYO. A popular spot, so book. Closed Mon lunch.

Darling Mills 134 Glebe Point Rd (☎02/9660 5666). Innovative modern Australian cuisine with fresh herbs and floral ingredients grown on the premises, served in an old sandstone building in a leafy garden. Fireplaces give a cosy feel in winter. Very posh – an expensive treat. Licensed. Lunch Fri only, dinner nightly.

Iku 25a Glebe Point Rd (also at 168 Military Rd, Neutral Bay; 279 Bronte Rd, Waverly; and 62 Oxford St, Darlinghurst). The original *Iku* at Glebe proved so popular it keeps branching out. Healthy – but delicious – macrobiotic meals and snacks, all vegetarian or vegan. Organic, pesticide-free coffee too. Meditative interior and outdoor dining area. Mon–Sat 11am–9pm, Sun 12.30–8pm.

Newtown

On the other side of Sydney University from Glebe, **King Street** in **Newtown** is lined with cafés, takeaways and restaurants of every ethnic persuasion, particularly Thai.

El Bahsa Sweets 233 King St. Lebanese coffee lounge with some of the best coffee on King St: try it with some Lebanese sweets, all home-made. Daily until 11pm, later at weekends.

George's Café 222 King St. *George's* is late-night – or all-night – cake heaven with such delights as mango and passionfruit coconut cake to choose from. Lots of cheesecakes and pancakes also feature. Enjoy the generous servings from comfy booth-style seating. Mon–Thurs & Sat 10am–midnight, Fri & Sat 24hr.

Green Gourmet 115 King St (☎02/9519 5330). This loud and busy Chinese vegetarian restaurant always has plenty of Asian customers, including the odd Buddhist monk. Buffet meals are sold per 100g weight at dinner, or by the plate (around $9) at lunch; you can also order off the menu. Closed Sun.

Kilimanjaro African Fast Food Eatery 280 King St. Senegalese-run place, but the authentic and simple dishes span Africa – from West African marinated chicken to North African couscous. Casual and friendly atmosphere. BYO.

The Old Fish Shop 239 King St. This little corner place, decorated with strands of dried garlic and chilli, is pure Newtown: lots of shaven heads, body piercings, tattoos and bizarre fashions. Food is simple – mainly *focaccia* and mini pizzas – and the excellent raisin loaf goes well with a coffee. Daily 6am–11pm.

Steki Taverna 2 O'Connell St, off King St (☎02/9516 2191). Atmospheric and moderately priced Greek taverna, with live music and dancing at weekends – when you'll need to book. Dinner Wed–Sun.

Sumalee, courtyard of the *Bank Hotel*, 324 King St, next to Newtown Station (☎02/9565 1730). Great Thai restaurant in a pub. Eat in the leafy beer garden. Closed Mon.

Tamana's North Indian Diner, 196 and 236 King St. Very cheap, absolutely delicious fast meals to eat in or take away. Licensed and BYO.

Thai Pothong, 294 King St (☎02/9550 6277). King St's best Thai; excellent service and moderate prices. Essential to book on the weekend. Closed Mon lunch.

Thanh Binh, 111 King St (☎02/9557 1175). With a celebrated original in Cabramatta (see p.159), the Vietnamese food at this Newtown offspring is just as fresh, delicious and inexpensive. There are a huge range of noodles to choose from. Licensed and BYO. Closed lunch Mon–Wed.

Balmain, Rozelle and Leichhardt

Further west is **Leichhardt**, Sydney's "Little Italy", which has a concentration of cafés and restaurants on **Norton Street**, while the **Darling Street** strip of restaurants runs from up-and-coming **Rozelle** to upmarket **Balmain**.

Bar Italia, 169 Norton St, Leichhardt. Like a community centre with the day-long comings and goings of Leichhardt locals, positively packed at night. The *focaccia,* served during the day, comes big and tasty, and coffee is spot-on. Best ice cream in Sydney; pasta from $8, and the extra night-time menu includes more substantial meat dishes (nothing over $15). BYO. Sun & Mon 10am–midnight, Tues–Thurs 9am–midnight, Fri 9am–1am, Sat 10am–1am.

Canteen, 332 Darling St, Balmain. Airy, high-ceilinged café with whitewashed walls inside the old Working Men's Institute. Simple fare: generous baguettes, burgers and salads, and big cooked breakfasts particularly popular on weekends when customers spill onto the sunny outside tables. Order and pay at the counter. Mon–Fri & Sun 7am–5pm, Sat 6am–5pm.

Harvest, 71 Evans St, Rozelle (☎02/9818 4201), also a branch at 152 Jersey Rd, Woollahra (☎02/9328 1939; Sunday lunch, dinner Wed–Sat). Established for over 30 years, this vegan and vegetarian restaurant has kept up with the times, dipping into Vietnamese, Japanese, Italian and a whole range of cuisines. The moderately priced food is delicious, desserts decadent and the coffee gets the thumbs up. BYO. Dinner only; closed Sun.

Tutto, Shop 20, The Italian Forum, 39 Norton St, Leichhardt (☎02/9568 4242). One of a stash of excellent Italian restaurants set around the central square of the new Italian Forum (see p.135). Book a table for Sunday lunch, when the whole Forum is abuzz with Italian families enjoying alfresco dining. Licensed. Expensive.

Surry Hills and Redfern

Just east of Central Station, **Elizabeth and Cleveland streets** in Surry Hills, running down to Redfern, are traditionally the domain of Turkish and Lebanese restaurants, which are among the cheapest in Sydney, and almost all BYO. Several Indian restaurants have recently made an appearance too. **Crown Street** in Surry Hills harbours several interesting cafés and some upmarket restaurants.

Abdul's, cnr Cleveland and Elizabeth streets, Surry Hills. Good-value, somewhat grungy Lebanese place. A late-night after-pub institution; eat in or takeaway.

Café Niki, 544 Bourke St, Surry Hills. Corner café with a relaxed ambience, which manages to feel groovy but not pretentious. Cheap and delicious food: best are their soups and *focaccia* plus excellent coffee. Mon–Fri 7am–10pm, Sat 8am–10pm, Sun 8am–6pm.

Chu Bay, 312a Bourke St, Darlinghurst (☎02/9331 3386). Tiny, cheap Vietnamese restaurant that's authentic and very popular. BYO. Cheap. Dinner nightly.

Dhaba House, 466 Cleveland St, Surry Hills (☎02/9319 6260). Downmarket decor matches the cheap prices at this invariably crowded Indian restaurant, but the dishes are above average in quality. If it's full, try the superb South Indian vegetarian fare a few doors up at *Maya Masala*. BYO. Lunch Wed–Sun, dinner nightly.

Erciyes, 409 Cleveland St, Redfern (☎02/9319 1309). Among the offerings of this busy Turkish restaurant is delicious *pide* – a bit like pizza – available with a range of toppings, many vegetarian; take-out section too. Belly dancing Fri & Sat nights. BYO. Daily 10am–midnight.

La Passion du Fruit 633 Bourke St, cnr Devonshire St, Surry Hills. One of the best brunches in town is served at this bright and friendly place with interesting salads, sandwiches and light meals. Mon–Sat 8am–5pm.

Maltese Cafe 310 Crown St, Surry Hills. Café known for its delicious Maltese *pastizzi* – flaky pastry pockets of ricotta cheese, plain or with meat, spinach or peas – to eat in or take away; ridiculously cheap and satisfying. Mon 10am–4pm, Tues–Sun 8am–6pm.

MG Garage 490 Crown St, Surry Hills (☎02/9383 9383). Flash restaurant which doubles as a car showroom with MG cars sharing the dining room. The modern Australian fare on offer is superb, and if you can afford it, this makes a fun night out; licensed. Next door, *Fuel* is the cheaper café/bistro version, with an attached gourmet supermarket, and is phenomenally popular for weekend brunch. *MG Garage* closed Sun & lunch Sat; *Fuel* open Mon–Fri 10am–10.30pm, Sat 8am–10.30pm, Sun 8am–8.30pm.

Mohr Fish 202 Devonshire St, Surry Hills. This tiny but stylish fish-and-chip bar, with stools and tiled walls, packs in the customers. BYO. Daily 10am–10pm.

Nepalese Kitchen 481 Crown St, Surry Hills (☎02/9319 4264). The speciality here is goat curry, served with some *achars*, freshly cooked relishes which traditionally accompany the mild Nepalese dishes. There's also a whole range of vegetarian options. Cosy, calming atmosphere, with traditional music playing, or sit outside in the courtyard on a fine night. Dinner nightly. BYO.

Prasit's Northside Take-away 395 Crown St, and **Prasit's Northside on Crown** 415 Crown St, Surry Hills (☎02/9319 0748). Be prepared for some great Thai taste sensations amongst the bold purple colour scheme. Since entrees are available cheaply by the piece, you can attempt to work your way through their delicious repertoire; plenty of vegetarian options too. The takeaway branch can squeeze diners out front on stools, with a few more places upstairs. Both BYO. Takeaway closed Mon; restaurant open lunch Thurs & Fri, dinner Mon–Sat.

Sushi-Suma 419 Cleveland St, Surry Hills (☎02/9698 8873). That this small, noisy Japanese restaurant is extremely popular with Japanese locals and visitors says it all. You'll need to book a table to avoid disappointment. Moderate. BYO. Closed Mon & lunch Sat & Sun.

Darlinghurst and East Sydney

Oxford Street is lined with restaurants and cafés from one end to the other. **Taylor Square** and its surround is a particularly busy area, with lots of ethnic restaurants and several pubs. **Victoria Street** in Darlinghurst has a thriving café scene. East Sydney, where Crown Street heads downhill from Oxford Street towards William Street, has some excellent Italian restaurants and coffee bars – particularly on **Stanley Street**.

Balkan Seafood Restaurant 215 Oxford St, Darlinghurst (☎02/9331 7670). This Croatian/Italian place is a Darlinghurst institution: fish and seafood is the best choice, but you can also get huge schnitzels and other continental meat dishes. Bustling atmosphere, moderate prices. BYO. Tues–Sun dinner.

Bar Coluzzi 322 Victoria St, Darlinghurst. Famous Italian café: tiny and always packed with a characterful crew of regulars spilling out onto stools on the pavement. You can watch from a safe distance at the trendier, though equally tiny and very popular *Latteria* next door. Daily 5am–7.30pm.

Betty's Soup Kitchen 269 Crown St, Darlinghurst. Soup is the speciality ($6), and makes for a cheap meal, served with damper, but there's also all the simple things your granny might serve: stews, sausages or fish fingers with mash, pasta, salads and desserts too. Yummy home-made ginger beer or lemonade. Nothing

over $10. Daily noon to 11pm (midnight Fri & Sat). BYO.

Bill and Toni 72–74 Stanley St, East Sydney. Atmospheric, cheap Italian restaurant with balcony tables. Queue to get in. The café downstairs is a popular Stanley St local (daily 7am–midnight) and serves tasty Italian sandwiches. BYO.

Bills 433 Liverpool St, Darlinghurst. This small corner café is one of Sydney's favourite breakfast spots, and top three on the list are the ricotta hotcakes, the huge muffins and the deliciously creamy scrambled eggs. There's lunch too, or queue to get in for dinner (or breakfast) at *Bills 2*, 359 Crown St, Surry Hills.

Fez Cafe 247 Victoria St, cnr of Liverpool St, Darlinghurst (☎02/9360 9581). With its corner position and cushioned window seats, this Middle Eastern and North African café-by-day, restaurant-by-night, is a favoured Darlinghurst hangout. You can start the day with a breakfast of sweet couscous here and end it with a spicy lamb *tagine*. Licensed and BYO. Daily 8am–10.30pm.

Fishface 132 Darlinghurst Rd, Darlinghurst. Best market buys of fish, and a chance to taste some unusual varieties (imaginatively cooked), served at fish-shop-style, stool-height tables and benches. BYO. Dinner nightly.

fu-manchu 249 Victoria St, Darlinghurst (also a branch at Level 1, 80 Campbell Parade, Bondi Beach). Perch yourself on red stools at stainless-steel counters and enjoy stylish but inexpensive Chinese and Malaysian noodles. BYO.

Govinda's 112 Darlinghurst Rd, Darlinghurst. Excellent, cheap Indian vegetarian restaurant, in the Hare Krishna centre. All-you-can-eat specials cost $15.90 with a film thrown in – they have their own cinema (see p.180). Dinner nightly from 6pm.

Le Petit Crème 118 Darlinghurst Rd, Darlinghurst. Friendly and thriving French café whose speciality is huge, good-value filled baguettes. Also steak and *frites*, omelettes, home-made paté, *pain au chocolat* and big bowls of *café au lait*; bread and pastries are baked on the premises. Mon–Sat 7am–3pm, Sun 8am–3pm.

Oh! Calcutta! 252 Victoria St, Darlinghurst (℡02/9360 3650). This is not your grungy neighbourhood Indian: the interior was fitted out by Australia's star interior decorator Iain Halliday. *Oh! Calcutta!* keeps getting suitably exclamatory reviews for its authentic – and occasionally inventive – food, and despite the decor, prices remain moderate. Licensed. Lunch Fri only, dinner nightly.

Onde 346 Liverpool St, Darlinghurst (℡02/9331 8749). The French owner is on to a winner with this popular restaurant that offers very good-value authentic bistro food: soups and patés to start, mains like steak and *frites* or *confit* of duck, and decadent desserts. Serves are generous, service excellent, and it's invariably squeezed full of happy diners. Licensed, and all wine is available by the glass. Dinner nightly. No bookings, so be prepared to queue.

Tropicana Café 227b Victoria St, Darlinghurst. The birthplace of the Tropfest film festival (see box p.179). Still a hugely popular place to hang out and pose, on the weekend especially. For $7.70 the huge Trop salad could fuel you all day. Daily 5am–11pm (Fri & Sat until midnight).

Una's Coffee Lounge 340 Victoria St, Darlinghurst. Cosy café that's been here for years dishing up schnitzel and other German dishes that are cheap, plentiful and tasty. The big breakfasts are very popular. BYO. Mon–Sat 6.30am–11pm, Sun 8am–11pm.

Kings Cross, Potts Point and Woolloomooloo

Many of the coffee shops and eateries in the Cross cater for the tastes (and wallets) of the area's backpackers, though there are also several stylish restaurants particularly in Potts Point. Most are also open late.

Bayswater Brasserie 32 Bayswater Rd, Kings Cross (℡02/9357 2177). Busy, lively, upmarket brasserie consistently rated for its interesting modern food and long-time hang out for Sydney's media types. Expensive; licensed. Closed Sun.

Cafe Hernandez 60 Kings Cross Rd, Potts Point. This Argentinian-run 24hr coffee shop, open daily, is relaxed and friendly: you can dawdle here for ages and no one will make you feel unwelcome. Popular with taxi drivers and a mixed clientele of locals. Spanish food is served –*churros*, tortilla, *empanadas* and good pastries – but the coffee is really the focus.

Laurent Boulangerie Pâtisserie 3 The Wharf, Cowper Wharf Rd, Woolloomooloo. Paris meets Sydney at this bakery café: the gleaming glass counters hold a tempting array of pastries plus filled baguettes and *croque monsieurs*, while the woven outdoor seats could have been stolen from the nearest *boulevarde*. The most affordable of the eight eateries in the new upmarket Woolloomooloo restaurant precinct, with nothing over $10. Order at the counter. Daily 7.30am–8pm.

Macleay's Pizza Bar 101 Macleay St, Kings Cross. Unassuming, inexpensive pizza bar. Open late, it's the perfect place to stuff your face post-pubbing or clubbing. Daily noon–2.30am, Fri & Sat until 4.30am.

Minami 87c Macleay St, Potts Point. Tiny, authentic Japanese noodle bar – with popular dishes like *ramen*, *yakisoba* and *kushikatsu* – where Japanese residents and visitors alike are squeezed around one large counter. Very cheap. BYO. Mon–Sat noon–1am, Sun noon–midnight.

A Touch of Thai 230 William St, Kings Cross. Tiny frenetic Thai café with friendly young staff cooking in the open kitchen to the sugary strains of Thai pop music. Food is inexpensive and delicious with an inventive line in daily specials.

Venice Beach Restaurant, 3 Kellet St, Kings Cross (℡02/9326 9928). In a big Victorian terrace house with a courtyard and a cushion room, this is a seriously stylish cheap eat. All entrees are $6.60 except for half-dozen oysters ($7.15), and mains range from pasta ($10.90) to steak ($14.25). A giant chargrilled seafood platter feeding two costs $42.50. Daily 5pm until late.

Paddington

As **Oxford Street** continues through Paddington, it becomes gradually more upmarket; the majority of restaurants here are attached to gracious old pubs.

Grand National Hotel, 161 Underwood St, cnr of Elizabeth St (℡02/9963 4557). One of the best pub-restaurants in Sydney dishing up imaginative fare, but with old-fashioned attentive service. Booking essential at weekends. Expensive. Lunch Tues–Sun, dinner Tues–Sat.

Paddington Inn Bistro, 338 Oxford St. Busy upmarket pub-bistro with an extensive and eclectic menu. Interior decor of textured glass, cushioned booths, polished concrete floors and fabric-lined walls. Packed on Saturdays, as it's opposite the market.

Royal Hotel Restaurant, Royal Hotel, 237 Glenmore Rd, off Five Ways. Pub-restaurant serving some of the best steaks in Sydney, nonstop from noon to 11pm (9pm Sun). Smart interior and staff. Eating on the verandah is a real treat, with views over the art gallery and Five Ways action below, but places fill fast – and they don't take bookings. Wait to be called in the charming top floor *Elephant Bar* (from 4.30pm daily).

Sloanes Cafe, 312 Oxford St (℡02/9331 6717). The emphasis here is on good, unusual vegetarian food, moderately priced, but some meatier dishes have slipped onto the menu. The stone-floored dining room opens onto the street to check out all the Saturday market action, or for more peace eat out back under vines in the delightful courtyard. Breakfast served all day. BYO. Daily 7am–6pm.

Bondi and Watsons Bay

Bondi is a cosmopolitan centre with the many Eastern European and Jewish people giving its cafés a continental flair; there are also some fantastic kosher restaurants, delis and cake shops. The Bondi Beach area is full of cheap take-aways, fish-and-chip shops and beer gardens, as well as some seriously trendy cafés and restaurants, several of them at the quieter northern end of Campbell Parade. Also try the Bondi branch of *fu-manchu* (see overleaf). To the north, **Watsons Bay** is known for its famous seafood restaurant.

Bondi Tratt, 34b Campbell Parade, Bondi Beach (℡02/9365 4303). Considering the setting, with outdoor seating overlooking the beach, not at all expensive. Come here to take in the view and the invariably buzzing atmosphere over breakfast, lunch and dinner, or just a coffee. Serves contemporary Australian and Italian food. Daily from 7am–11pm. Licensed and BYO.

Burgerman, 249 Bondi Rd, Bondi. Gourmet burgers to slaver over, at bargain prices. Vegetarian options, too. Busy takeaway service and small eat-in area. Daily noon–10pm. There's a newer branch at 116 Surrey St, off Victoria St, Darlinghurst.

Doyles on the Beach, 11 Marine Parade, Watsons Bay (℡02/9337 1350); also **Doyles Wharf Restaurant** (℡02/9337 1572). The original of the long-running Sydney institution is the first of these, but both serve great seafood and have views of the city across the water. A water taxi can transport you from Circular Quay to Watsons Bay. Expensive. Daily lunch and dinner.

Gelato Bar, 140 Campbell Parade, Bondi Beach. The gleaming window display of indulgent creamy continental cakes and strudels lure in the beach-goers to this Hungarian-run place that's been serving up Eastern European dishes and huge portions of cake for over thirty years – and *gelato* too, of course. The coffee is among the best in Bondi. Smart coffee-lounge decor. Daily 8am–midnight.

Gusto, 16 Hall St, Bondi Beach. Deli-café which creates quite a Bondi scene, with its cosmopolitan crew of regulars and travellers blocking the pavement outside. Excellent coffee, delicious edibles piled high on platters and a separate deli counter too. There's just enough room for a few more people to perch on stools inside and along the front.

Good notice board. Daily 6.15am–7.30pm.

Hugo's 70 Campbell Parade, Bondi Beach (☎02/9300 0900). Set smack amongst the parade of posers, surfers and travellers, this is contemporary Bondi – part café, part fine dining – with a casual, young and friendly flair. On weekends it opens for all-day brunch (9am–4pm; no bookings); while every night white tablecloths and softly glowing lamps appear and everyone seems to be having noisy fun. Service is wonderful and honed for your comfort, including blankets for those chilly sea breezes if you sit outside. Portions are generous modern Asian and Mediterranean-slanted creations. Expensive; licensed.

Lamrock Cafe 72 Campbell Parade, cnr Lamrock Ave. Stalwart Bondi café, always lively. The unpretentious local crowd come for the magnificent ocean views, the uncomplicated food – *panini* sandwiches, salads, pasta, burgers and fish and chips – and the breakfasts. You can even have a cocktail with your brunch – try the scarily named "Shark Attack", their version of a Bloody Mary. Umbrella-covered sidewalk tables outside, or cosy-up to cushions inside. Licensed. Daily 7am–midnight.

The Red Kite 95 Roscoe St, Bondi Beach. Funky

vegetarian café just back from Campbell Parade. Outside tables to catch the breeze. Fresh, imaginative food and freshly squeezed juices; yummy spiced Indian tea. Nothing over $10. Daily 8am–6pm.

Speedo's 126 Ramsgate Ave, North Bondi. Totally casual café bang opposite the north end of the beach, where the locals and their kids and dogs hang out, with no busy road in between you and the view. The walls are covered with vintage Speedo paraphernalia (the Australian cossie in every surf lifesaver's wardrobe). The breakfast specials ($6) are very popular. It gets so crowded expect long waits for your order, but there's always the big blue to gaze at. Daily 6am–6pm.

Yulla 1st Floor, 38 Campbell Parade, Bondi Beach (☎02/9365 1788). You could almost miss the discreet orange sign for *Yulla*, but this is no exclusive restaurant, though the beach views from the balcony are certainly million dollar. Instead, you'll find a relaxed café atmosphere – glowing orange walls, shining wooden floors and a window of blue sea – and very affordable contemporary Israeli food, which means a mix of Middle Eastern and North African dishes. Licensed. Mon–Fri 11am–10.30pm, Sat & Sun 7am–10.30pm.

Bronte, Coogee and Maroubra

South of Bondi, **Bronte**'s beachfront café strip is wonderfully laid-back, and **Coogee** has a thriving café scene.

Barzura 62 Carr St, Coogee (☎02/9665 5546). Fantastic spot providing up-close ocean views. Both a café and a fully fledged restaurant, with wholesome breakfast until 1pm, snacks until 7pm, and restaurant meals – like seafood spaghetti or kangaroo fillets – served at lunch and dinner. Unpretentious though stylish service encourages a local crowd. Moderate; licensed and BYO. Daily 7am–11pm.

The Beach Pit 211 Coogee Bay Rd, Coogee (☎02/9665 0068). Really enjoyable café-restaurant with Coogee's trademark informality and friendliness. Small but succulent menu has European and Asian influences and plenty of fish and seafood on offer; dishes are generous, well-priced and presented. You can breakfast here at the weekend too. BYO.

The Pool Caffe 94 Marine Parade, Maroubra (☎02/9314 0364). In a quiet residential spot opposite the Mahon sea pool on the Coogee to Maroubra coastal walk, this café has a relaxed holiday feel. Breakfast on organic porridge and fresh fruit plates on the weekend, have a coffee

with fresh muffins, biscuits and cakes, or tuck into more expensive restaurant-style meaty modern food (bookings recommended weekends). Breakfast Sat & Sun, lunch Fri–Sun, dinner Wed–Sun. Inexpensive to moderate. Bus #376, #377.

Sari Rasa 186 Arden St, above *McDonald's*, Coogee Beach (☎02/9665 5649). A mostly Indonesian menu, plus delicious Malaysian and Indian specialities, accompanied by ocean views – some tables outside on the balcony. Generous servings and low prices; BYO. Daily noon–3pm & 6pm–late.

Sejuiced 487 Bronte Rd, Bronte. Delicious fresh juices, smoothies and frappés, combined with ocean and palm-tree views, make this tiny place a beauty to kick-start a summer's day. The "Morning Energiser" (beetroot, apple, ginger and carrot juice) ought to get you going, or there's all manner of other breakfast foods. Salads, soups and pasta are terrific too. If it's full, choose from several other great options on this café strip. Daily 6.30am–6pm.

North Shore and Manly

Military Road, running from Neutral Bay to Mosman, rivals and perhaps outdoes all the gourmet streets south of the harbour. The string of excellent restaurants tends to be expensive, but there are a number of bakeries, tempting pastry shops and well-stocked delis. **Manly** offers something for every taste and budget, though cheap and cheerful is its forte; there are some good cafés tucked away on **Belgrave Street**. **Miller Street**, which runs from North Sydney, has a great range of eateries around **Cammeray**.

The Bathers Pavilion, 4 The Esplanade, Balmoral Beach (ⓣ02/9969 5050). Indulgent beach-house-style dining in the former changing rooms on Balmoral Beach, now a very pricey restaurant and café double act, presided over by one of Sydney's top chefs, Serge Danserau. The fixed-price dinner menu is $95 (cheaper lunches). Weekend breakfast in the café is a North Shore ritual – expect to queue to get in – while the wood-fired pizzas are popular later in the day. Licensed.

Brazil Cafe, 46 North Steyne, Manly (ⓣ02/9977 3825). A classy surf-front café that's more Italian/eclectic than Brazilian, and transforms into a pricey restaurant in the evenings. A popular local hangout, particularly for the breakfasts and famed Sunday brunch. Daily 8am–10pm.

Cafe Tunis, 30 South Steyne, Manly (ⓣ02/9976 2805). Airy and cool beachfront restaurant with tiled floors. The Cous Cous Royale is the main dish here, or you could opt for the tasty toasted *pide* sandwiches; servings are filling. Delicious drinks like lime and rosewater go well, or there's wine by the glass. Moderate. Licensed and BYO. Daily 7am–9pm.

Gourmet Pizza Kitchen, 199–207 Military Rd, Neutral Bay (ⓣ02/9953 9000). Spacious, busy place that's especially popular with families – how many other pizza joints provide pizza dough for the kids to play with? Pizzas $11–18. Licensed.

Jipang, 37 The Corso, Manly (ⓣ02/9977 4436).

Excellent Japanese noodle house; very inexpensive. BYO. Closed Mon.

Just Hooked, 236 Military Rd, Neutral Bay (ⓣ02/9904 0428). A small range of delicious fresh fish (five starters, five main courses) in a classy version of a classic fish shop, with white-tiled walls and high stools. Stand-out dish is the seafood paella featuring blue swimmer crab, but the simple fish and chips is just as popular. BYO. Dinner nightly.

Maisys Cafe, 164 Military Rd, Neutral Bay. Cool hangout on a hot day or night (open 24hr), with funky interior and music. Good for breakfast – from croissants to bacon and eggs – or delicious Maltese *pastizzi* plus soups, burgers, pasta and cakes. Not cheap but servings are generous. BYO.

Somi's, 48 Victoria Parade, cnr South Steyne, Manly (ⓣ02/9977 7511). Inexpensive Thai restaurant across from the beach with an appropriately fresh and delicious range of spicy seafood dishes on the menu, and quite a few vegetarian dishes too. Licensed and BYO.

Watermark, 2a The Esplanade, Balmoral Beach (ⓣ02/9968 3433). For a memorable Sydney meal, both for location and food, you can't go wrong here. Chef Kenneth Leung is well-known for his fusion of Eastern and Western cooking styles and ingredients, plus there are views right across the water, a terrace to dine on under the sun or stars (or sit by the fireplace in winter), a stylish interior and fabulous service. Very expensive; licensed.

Entertainment, nightlife and culture

To find out exactly **what's on** in Sydney, Sunday's *Sun-Herald* offers "Time Out", a weekly entertainment lift-out, and the *Daily Telegraph* has the "Seven Days" pull-out every Thursday. In addition to these and the rather bland monthly programmes distributed by various tourist organizations (see p.86), there is a plethora of **free listings magazines** for more alternative goings-on – clubbing, bands, fashion, music and the like – which can be found lying around in the cafés, record shops and boutiques of Paddington, Glebe and Kings Cross: these include *On the Street*, *Revolver* and *Drum Media* with their weekly band listings and reviews, and *3D World* and *Beat* covering the dance scene. *City Hub*, a politically aware free weekly newspaper, also has an excellent events listing section, and the *Sydney Morning Herald*'s "Metro" **website** (Ⓦ www.metro.citysearch.com.au) has comprehensive listings of film, theatre and music events.

Ticketek is the main **booking agency**, with branches located at 195 Elizabeth St, inside Grace Bros department store at the corner of George and Market streets, and within the Entertainment Centre (bookings ☎ 02/9266 4800, Ⓦ www.ticketek.com.au). There's also Ticketmaster, 1st floor, 66 Hunter St (☎ 13 6166, Ⓦ www.ticketmaster.com.au). For theatre, concerts, opera and ballet you can always try for cheap, same-day tickets at the **Halftix** office at 201 Sussex St, near the corner of Market Street (Mon–Fri 9am–5pm, Sat 10am–3pm; Ⓦ www.halftix.com.au); they also sell regular tickets.

Pubs and bars

The differences between a restaurant, bar, pub and nightclub are often blurred in Sydney, and one establishment may be a combination of all these under one roof. The list below consists mainly of traditional old **hotels**, though at most of these there'll be some kind of food available, and they may even occasionally lay on entertainment. Sydney has many Art Deco pubs, a classic 1930s style notably seen in the tilework; we've mentioned some of the best below. For a guaranteed drink any time, head for Kings Cross. A recent relaxing of licensing laws also means many restaurants now serve drinks to non-diners.

The Rocks, city centre and Darling Harbour

Aqualuna Bar, Shop 18, East Circular Quay. Slick new ground-floor bar near the Opera House, with fantastic views of the harbour from the terrace. Expensive.

Australian Hotel, 100 Cumberland St, The Rocks. Convivial corner hotel with crowded outside tables facing across to the lively basketball courts tucked beneath the Harbour Bridge. Inside, original fittings give a lovely old-pub feel. Known for its Bavarian-style draught beer brewed in Picton (see p.230), plus gourmet pizzas.

Customs House Bar, Macquarie Place, off Bridge St, City. A nice spot on a square with palm trees and statues. Customers have been enjoying a drink here since 1826. Very popular with city workers, with tables outside on the square. Cheap lunches. Closed Sat & Sun.

Establishment, 252 George St. Another of the new breed of deluxe bars opening in Sydney aimed at twenty-somethings with a yearning for some old-school glamour. The huge main room boasts an extraordinarily long marble bar, white pillars, high decorative ceilings, and an atrium and fountain at the back. Despite the size, it gets jam-packed, particularly on Fri nights, and the door policy is very strict, so prepare for humiliation. On site there's a ballroom, restaurants, the *Tank* night-

club, and 30-odd luxurious hotel rooms.

Forbes Hotel, cnr King and York streets, City. Atmospheric, turn-of-the-twentieth-century corner hotel with a lively downstairs bar. Upstairs is more sedate, with a pool table and plenty of window seating – the best spot is the tiny cast-iron balcony, with just enough room for two. Very popular Thurs & Fri nights. Fri & Sat to 3am.

Glenmore Hotel, 96 Cumberland St, The Rocks. Unpretentious, inexpensive breezy pub perched over The Rocks, with great views from large windows in the public bar and spectacular ones from the rooftop beer garden (not always open). A handy refresher before or after the Harbour Bridge walk – it's opposite the pedestrian walkway entrance – and serving up reasonably priced pub grub.

Hero of Waterloo, 81 Lower Fort St, Millers Point, The Rocks. One of Sydney's oldest pubs, built in 1843 from sandstone dug out from the Argyle Cut (see p.114), this place has plenty of atmosphere. Open fireplaces make it a good choice for a winter drink, and it serves simple meals.

Lord Nelson Brewery Hotel, cnr Argyle and Kent streets, Millers Point, The Rocks. Licensed in 1841, this very old pub serves beer brewed on the premises, plus bar food daily and upmarket meals from its first-floor brasserie (lunch Mon–Fri, dinner Mon–Sat). Ask for a tour of the brewery.

The Marble Bar, *Hilton Hotel*, 259 Pitt St, City. As much a sightseeing stop-off as a good spot for a drink amongst high Victorian decor featuring Italian marble. This was the original 1893 basement bar of the *Tattersalls Hotel*, which was replaced by the *Hilton* in 1973. Pricey drinks but happy hour 5–7pm. Free jazz or blues Tues–Sat. Mon–Fri 3pm–1am, Sat 5pm–2am.

Mercantile Hotel , 25 George St, The Rocks. High-spirited Irish pub where you can get Sydney's best-poured Guinness; bistro meals and outdoor tables are a fine spot to watch the weekend market crowds.

One World Sports Bar , 25 Harbour St, Darling Harbour. The place to come to catch televised sport, with 73 TVs plus three megascreens on the go, showing everything from Fox Sports to SBS football coverage. There are even TVs in the toilets, and some booths at the back where you can control your viewing. Sporting paraphernalia cover the walls, and bar snacks are suitably unfancy burgers and pizzas.

Pontoon , Cockle Bay Wharf, Darling Harbour. This open-fronted bar with outside tables feels like one big lively beer garden, right on the water opposite the new marina. Big umbrellas shade you from the sun for a daytime drink, and there are pool tables inside. Attracts a young casual crowd, despite the upmarket restaurants surrounding it.

Scruffy Murphy's , 43 Goulburn St. Rowdy, late-opening Irish pub with Guinness on tap, of course; phenomenally popular, particularly with travellers. Just around the corner from Central Station. Closes around 3.30 or 4.30am most nights.

Slip Inn , 111 Sussex St Ⓣ 02/9299 4777). On three levels overlooking Darling Harbour, this huge place has several bars, a bistro and a nightclub, *The Chinese Laundry* (Fri & Sat night; $10–15). Weekdays it attracts a young, style-conscious after-work crowd, but it's popular on Saturday too. The front bars have a pool room, while downstairs a boisterous beer garden fills up on sultry nights, with the quieter, more sophisticated *Sand Bar* beside it. Excellent wine list, with lots available by the glass. Expensive pub food and gourmet pizzas by day, tasty contemporary fare in the bistro by night. Live jazz Thurs night, DJs Fri night. Closed Sun.

Inner west: Glebe, Newtown and Balmain

Bank Hotel , 324 King St, next to Newtown Station. Smart-looking pub that's always packed and open late. Pool table out front, cocktail bar out back and a big beer garden downstairs (with Thai restaurant).

Exchange Hotel , cnr Beattie and Mullens streets, Balmain. Classic Balmain boozer built in 1885, a backstreet corner pub with a large iron-lace bal-

cony, perfect for sitting out at and drinking the weekend early morning Bloody Mary specials.

Friend in Hand , 58 Cowper St, Glebe. This characterful pub, with all manner of curious objects dangling from the walls and ceilings, is a popular haunt for backpackers. Diverse entertainment includes poetry nights (Tues), crab racing (Wed), quizzes (Thurs), live music (Fri) and sometimes DJs on Sat. Excellent, inexpensive Italian restaurant, *No Names* (closed Sun lunch), is hidden out the back with pasta from $8. Upstairs bar with pool tables offers half-price cocktails Fri & Sat 7.30–8.30pm.

London Hotel, 234 Darling St, Balmain. Convivial British-style pub, with a high verandah overlooking the Saturday market. Attracts a typically mixed Balmain crowd.

Nag's Head , cnr Lodge St and St Johns Rd, off Glebe Point Rd. Calling itself a "posh pub", this is a good place for a quiet drink – definitely no pokies. With several imported beers on tap – Guinness, Boddingtons, Stella and Becks – and pints and half-pints available, decor and atmosphere is very much that of a British pub. Its bistro also dishes up excellent steaks and other grills, and there's an extensive bar menu. For more action, there's a new loft area upstairs with pool tables.

The Rose , 54 Cleveland St, Chippendale. This funkily decorated pub is a real treasure, despite the unpromising location at the traffic-laden end of Cleveland St (very handy, however, for a Glebe or Newtown base, being just near Victoria Park). A mock-Renaissance ceiling mural overlooks a popular pool table, while a bizarrely decorated rocking horse is suspended over the partly covered beer garden out back (doubling as a modern Australian eatery with a huge blackboard menu). Good wine list, available by the glass.

Kings Cross, Darlinghurst and Potts Point

Bourbon and Beefsteak Bar , 24 Darlinghurst Rd, Kings Cross. Infamous – and outrageously tacky – 24hr Kings Cross drinking hole, which opened in 1968 to attract US soldiers on R&R. Come here for a steak breakfast and a Bloody Mary after a night out – breakfast served around the clock. Live music – very middle-of-the-road jazz or rock'n'roll – all week from 5pm until 2 or 3am (Fri & Sat until 5.30am). $5 cover charge Fri & Sat 10pm–5.30am.

Burdekin , 2 Oxford St. This well-preserved Art Deco pub has several trendy bars on four levels. The basement *Dug Out Bar* (from 5pm) is tiny and beautifully tiled, and has table service and generous cocktails; while the spacious, ground-level

Main Bar sports dramatic columns and a huge round bar.

Darlo Bar , *Royal Sovereign Hotel*, cnr Darlinghurst Rd and Liverpool St. Popular Darlinghurst meeting place, with a lounge-room atmosphere. Comfy colourful chairs, sofas and lamps have a 1950s feel, the crowd is mixed and unpretentious and drinks aren't expensive (house wines from $4 a glass). At night you can order from the menu of nearby *Fishface* (see p.165) and a local Thai restaurant, and from neighbouring *Eca Bar* during the day, and they'll fetch the food for you.

First Floor , *Exchange Hotel*, 34 Oxford St. Stylish, straight bar in a gay strip – spacious interior, wooden floorboards, changing art exhibitions on the walls and comfy leather couches in the corner (bag one of these early). Happy hour (5–8pm) gets them in, and as the crowd gathers and the music cranks up, posing becomes the main game. Mon–Sat 5pm to around 3am.

Green Park Hotel , 360 Victoria St, Darlinghurst. A Darlinghurst stalwart. Always lively, packed and cruisy at night with a crowd of young regulars. The stash of pool tables out back are a big part of the attraction.

International Bar , 14th floor, *Top of the Town Hotel*, 227 Victoria St, Darlinghurst. Try to come here for just one drink to admire the fantastic view of the Sydney skyline. Get dressed up in your most stylish gear, but don't be disappointed if you're turned away from this beautiful people's bar, which opened in the 1960s and is now trendy again after several cheesy years. The price of beer here is steep and the bar snacks include Russian caviar.

Judgement Bar , *Courthouse Hotel*, 189 Oxford St, Darlinghurst. Overlooking Taylor Square, the upstairs bar of this pub is often open 24hr. Totally undiscriminating – you may find yourself here in the wee hours among an assortment of young clubbers and old drunks – and drinks aren't pricey. Wakes up around 1am.

Middle Bar , 1st floor, *Kinsela's*, 383 Bourke St, Darlinghurst. Once a deluxe Art Deco funeral parlour, *Kinsela's* has long been transformed into an altogether lively drinking and dancing spot spread across three levels. The *Middle Bar* (Tues, Wed & Sun 5pm–1am, Thurs 5pm–3am, Fri–Sat 5p,–4am) is seriously sexy, from its lush decor and sunken seating area to the the young good-looking crowd who drink here. You can gaze at the action in Taylor Square from the glass balcony.

Palace Hotel , cnr Flinders and South Dowling streets, Darlinghurst. Tastefully distressed decor in the noisy smart-set hangout downstairs, with a tiny eating area for the recommended Thai kitchen. Several rooms of pool tables upstairs are

the star attra...

Soho Bar , *Pi. Hotel*, 171 Victoria St, Potts Point. This tren Deco pub, popular with travellers, is a good for a chat. Most locals head for the upstairs le bar (Tues–Sun nights only) to hang out on th ck balcony and play pool.

Surry ills Paddington and Wo hra

Bar Cleveland , Cleveland and Bourke streets, Surry Hills. Huge glass windows have opened this pub o e busy, gritty street of traffic, Turkish and Indi keaways – and punters have packed it ever s for an authentic urban brew. There's a pool ta the main bar, or head for the cosier rear bar. S. open until 2am most nights.

Clock Hotel , 470 Crown S urry Hills. This huge hotel has expanded out of buch with its 1840s roots (the landmark clock we was only added in the 1960s). Upstairs, a swi restaurant and cocktail bar runs off the huge bal ny – a great place to hang out. There's a popula olhall and basement gaming room.

Cricketers Arms , 106 Fitzroy St, urry Hills. Just down the road from the live music s ne at the *Hopetoun* (p.173), the *Cricketers* has equally dedicated clientele. A young, offbeat crowd – plenty of piercings and shaved heads – cram in and fall about the bar, pool room, and tiny beer garden, and yell at each other over a funky soundtrack. Hearty bar snacks and a bistro (Tues–Sun 3–10pm).

Elephant Bar , *Royal Hotel*, 237 Glenmore Rd, Paddington. The top-floor bar of this beautifully renovated, Victorian-era hotel has knockout views of the city, best appreciated at sunset (happy hour 6–7pm). The small interior is great too, with its fireplaces, paintings and elephant prints. As it gets crowded later on, people cram onto the stairwell and it feels like a party.

Lord Dudley , 236 Jersey Rd, Woollahra. Sydney's most British pub, complete wtih fireplaces, fox-hunting pictures, dark wood furniture – and a dartboard. Thirty-six beers on tap, many imported, including Newcastle Brown Ale. The bistro serves up hearty British fare.

Bondi

BB's Bar , 157 Curlewis St, Bondi Beach. This welcoming, unpretentious local wine bar, with beer on tap, attracts an older crowd. Free live music Wed–Sun from 8.30pm. The bands are of varied quality – through Irish, acoustic duos, soft rock, grunge – but unvarying enthusiasm. Daily from 5pm, happy hour 5–7pm.

Legendary beer ...ens

Many Sydney pubs an outdoor drinking area, perfect for enjoying the sunny weather – the three below, however, are outright legends.

Newport Arms Hot Kalinya St, Newport. Overlooking Pittwater; Sunday is the big day, with free ja utside (1-5pn), and the bistro serving food from noon right through until closing e.

The Oaks Hotel, 11 Ailitary d, Neutral Bay. The North Shore's most popular pub takes its name from e hu oak that shades the entire beer garden. Make use of the BBQ and cook ur (expensive) steak, or if you're feeling lazy, there's a gourmet pizza restaurant de.

Watsons Bay Hotel, 1 arine Parade, Watsons Bay. Relaxing beer garden with views over Watsons B and good-value bistro meals, crowded on weekends with people enjoying a be ith their fish and chips.

Beach Road Hotel, 71 ach Rd, Bondi Beach. Huge, stylishly decora pub with a bewildering range of bars on two els and a beer garden. Popular with both tr lers and locals for its good vibe. Entertain nt, mostly free, comes from rock bands, D and a jazz supper club. The hotel also ha cheap Italian bistro, No

Names, and an upmarket contemporary Australian restaurant.

Bondi Hotel, 178 Campbell Parade, Bondi Beach. Huge pub dating from the 1920s, with many of its original features intact. Sedate during the day but at night an over-the-top, late-night backpackers' hangout. Mon–Sat until 4am.

Live music: jazz, blues and rock

The live music scene in Sydney has passed its boom time, and pub venues keep closing down to make way for the dreaded poker machines. However, there are still enough venues to nourish a steady stream of local, interstate and overseas acts passing through every month, peaking in summer with a well-established open-air festival circuit. Pub bands and clubs are often free, especially if you arrive early; if there is a charge, it's usually from $6, with $15 the uppermost price for smaller international acts or the latest interstate sensation. Early Sunday evenings (6–10pm) are a mellow time to catch some music, particularly jazz, around town.

The **venues for major events**, with bookings direct or through Ticketek or Ticketmaster (see p.169), are the Entertainment Centre at Haymarket near Darling Harbour (enquiries and credit-card sales ☏ 02/9266 4800); the Capitol Theatre, 13 Campbell St, Haymarket (☏ 02/9266 4800); the Enmore Theatre, 130 Enmore Rd, just up from Newtown (☏ 02/9550 3666); the centrally located Metro Theatre, 624 George St (☏ 02/9264 2666); and *Selina's*, at the *Coogee Bay Hotel*, 212 Arden St, Coogee (☏ 02/9665 0000).

There are several big outdoor rock concerts through the year. **Homebake** (around $50; ☻ www.whammo.com.au/homebake) is a huge annual open-air festival in The Domain in early December with food and market stalls, rides and a line-up of around forty underground Australian bands. The **Big Day Out** on Australia Day (Jan 26; around $80), at the showground at Homebush Bay, features big international names like the Manic Street Preachers and Marilyn Manson as well as local talent. Also see Festivals, p.181, for other music events, including the Manly Jazz Festival.

Annandale Hotel, cnr Nelson St and Parramatta Rd, Annandale (☏ 02/9550 1078). One of Sydney's best showcases for local and interstate indie bands, and the closest thing the city has to a beer

barn for mid-sized bands who aren't quite charting but have a good following. Music Fri & Sat nights (door $8–12).

The Basement, 29 Reiby Place, Circular Quay

02/9251 2797). A great place to see jazz, acoustic and world music as well as a roster of the world's most renowned blues performers. The best way to take in a performance is to book a table and dine in front of the low stage.

Bridge Hotel , 135 Victoria Rd, Rozelle Ⓣ 02/9810 1260). A legendary inner west venue specializing in blues and pub rock, with some international but mostly local acts. Also has a good pub theatre and comedy nights.

Harbourside Brasserie , Pier One, Hickson Rd, Millers Point Ⓣ 02/9252 3000). Great location on the harbour near The Rocks; jazz, blues, soul, fusion, world music or cabaret Mon–Sat from 10pm. Sunday's Club Salsa (7.30pm) is also popular. Discriminating crowd, mellow atmosphere.

Hopetoun Hotel , 416 Bourke St, cnr of Fitzroy St, Surry Hills Ⓣ 02/9361 5257). "The Hoey" is one of Sydney's best venues for the indie band scene, focusing on new, young bands: local, interstate and international all play in the small and inevitably packed front bar Mon–Sat (from 8.30/9.30pm; $7–10 cover charge, sometimes free), and on Sun there are DJs (5–10pm; $4). There's also a popular pool room, a drinking pit in the basement, and an ambitious little restaurant upstairs. Closes midnight.

Newtown RSL , 52 Enmore Rd, Enmore Ⓣ 02/9516 1911). The only remaining music venue in the Newtown area, in the unpretentious Returned Servicemen's Leagues club (drinks at RSL prices). The cream of the Australian live music circuit and alternative scene play here, from hip hop to rock. Music Thurs–Sat nights (door $8–15).

Side On Cafe , 83 Parramatta Rd, Annandale Ⓣ 02/9519 0055). Sydney's most interesting venue calls itself a "multi-arts complex", and on Wed–Sun nights you can hear jazz here in an intimate café atmosphere – everything from popular trios to the latest experimental fusions. Wed night is a jam session where anyone can join in. Book if you want to dine Ⓣ 02/9516 3077); mains like steak with roasted vegetables cost around $20. The venue also offers Sun night cabaret and short film screenings on Mon. Door charge for jazz $6–11.50.

Soup Plus , 383 George St Ⓣ 02/9299 7728). This simple restaurant, in a basement near the Strand Arcade, has been serving up live jazz with its bowls of soup ($5) for over 25 years; other simple meals, from fish through to pasta, are also served. Music Mon–Sat 7pm–11.30pm. Fri & Sat nights there's a cover charge of $25 which includes a two-course meal. Closed Sun.

Clubs

Many of Sydney's best clubs are at **gay** or **lesbian** venues, and although we've listed these separately overleaf, the divisions are not always clear – many places have specific gay, lesbian and straight nights scheduled each week. A long strip of thriving clubs stretches from Kings Cross to Oxford Street and down towards Hyde Park, with *D.C.M.* (see overleaf) perhaps the most popular. The scene can be pretty snobby, with door gorillas frequently vetting your style. Admission ranges from $5 to $20, depending on the club; many stay open until 5am Saturday morning and until 6am Sunday morning. The year's big dance party is **Vibes on a Summers Day**, a sweltering weekend of sultry beats, trip-hop, reggae flavours and excruciatingly beautiful bodies in the Bondi Pavilion at the end of January (noon–9pm; around $75 for either Sat or Sun).

BJs , 195 Oxford St Mall, Bondi Junction. Lively club for lovers of South American sounds and salsa. A Latino band plays three sets through the night, while DJs offer up merengue plus house and techno in two different club rooms. Sat 8pm–3am only. Entry $15.

Club 77 , 77 William St, Kings Cross. Retro and indie alternative nights, techno beats, progressive trance and house sounds produce a hands-in-the-air rave atmosphere. You may have to queue, but without too much anxiety. Mood is largely all-night party and the drinks are only a little above pub prices. Closed Mon. Entry $5–8.

Gas , 467 Pitt St, Haymarket. Newish club, entered through the foyer of an office building. There's one huge cutting-edge room downstairs – where international DJs occasionally appear – and a mezzanine level which acts as a viewing area over the dance floor, with chill-out lounges attached. Two bar areas. Thurs–Sun 10pm–5am. Entry $10–20.

Globe , 60 Park St, City. *Globe*'s cocktail bar lounge is open 24 hours, and on Thursday to Saturday nights it's linked to a downstairs club – you'll have to dress very cool to get past the door then. The music is energetic house, hip-hop and big beats; beers are pricey. Club Thurs 11pm–4am, Fri & Sat

11pm–7am. Entry $10–15.

Home, Cockle Bay Wharf, Darling Harbour. The first *really* big club venture in Sydney can cram 2000 punters into its cool, cavernous interior; there's also a mezzanine, a chill-out room, and outdoor balconies if you want some air. The decks are often manned by name DJs, drinks are expensive and staff beautiful. Thurs–Sat 11pm–7am. Entry $10–20.

Kings Cross Hotel, cnr William St and Darlinghurst Rd, Kings Cross. Popular with backpackers, a brash in-your-face pub section at ground level has nightly dance music. Thursday is very big with the British crowd, or homesick Brits can watch *Eastenders* on Monday nights. Daily 10pm until 4am or 5am. Entry

$5 after midnight Thurs, Fri and Sat.

Sugareef, 20 Bayswater Rd, Kings Cross. After the sweaty writhing of *The World*, nearby *Sugareef* presents a more chilled, sophisticated atmosphere with funky vocal house music. Two rooms, two DJs and a popular pool table too. Good on Tuesday nights. Free Wednesday, otherwise entry $5–15.

The World, 24 Bayswater Rd, Kings Cross. With cheap drinks on Fri and Sat nights and a relatively relaxed door policy, *The World* is popular with a fun party-loving crowd of travellers, who jive to a pleasing mix of dub and house grooves. The atmosphere throughout is lively, if a little beery in the front bar. Fri & Sat noon–6am, Sun–Thurs noon–4am. Entry $5 after 10pm Fri & Sat.

Gay and lesbian bars and clubs

One of the best things about Sydney's gay and lesbian scene is that, apart from a few pubs in the inner west, it's all concentrated in one area, so it's easy to bar-hop – start at the *Albury* and keep on going. Sydney never closes – there's always somewhere else to move on to. Entry is free unless otherwise indicated.

Albury Hotel, 6 Oxford St, Paddington. Sydney's most entertaining drag performances behind the huge, horseshoe bar of this stylish, Art Deco hotel. Regulars get here in time for the show, then move on to the other pubs and clubs. The *Albury* attracts a lively and very mixed crowd – gay or straight, you'll feel pretty welcome. Shows nightly from 10.30pm and midnight (amateur version Sun 7pm); $5 Fri & Sat otherwise free.

Arq, 16 Flinders St, Darlinghurst. The newest club on the scene is huge (900-person capacity) and state-of-the-art, with something on every night of the week, from DJs and drag shows to pool com-petitions. There are two levels each with a very different scene: the *Arena*, on the top floor, is strictly gay, while the ground-floor *Vortex* is a qui-eter, less crowded mix of gay and straights, with pool tables. Chilling out booths, laser lighting on the dance floors, viewing decks and fishtanks add to the fun and friendly atmosphere. The attached gaming lounge is open 24hr. Mon–Thurs free, Fri & Sat $15–20, Sun $5.

Bank Hotel, 324 King St, next to Newtown Station. This stylish bar has become a dyke favourite. The Wed night women's pool competition (8pm) draws large crowds.

The Barracks, cnr Bourke and Flinders streets (enter from rear door in Patterson Lane), Surry Hills. Strictly for men, this venue started off being a haunt for leather men and "bears", but its appeal is broadening. No point getting here until after 11pm. The focus is the pool tables at the back, which are free until 9pm. Daily 5pm–3am.

Beaucamp Hotel, 267 Oxford St, Darlinghurst. Traditional Aussie pub decor with a mainly male, rough trade crowd. Especially worth visiting on Sunday afternoons. Daily noon till midnight.

D.C.M. Nightclub, 33 Oxford St, Darlinghurst. Young, fast, mixed gay, lesbian and straight venue. Like most Sydney clubs, this doesn't really liven up till after midnight when you can be assured of a wild night of dancing. Thurs, Fri & Sun 10pm–6am, Sat 10pm–noon. Entry $15–22.

Exchange Hotel, 34 Oxford St, Darlinghurst. In the downstairs *Phoenix* bar, Fri night *Sirens* is strictly for girls, a lesbian club night which aims for a little sophistication with cabaret, half-price cocktails and free canapés 9–11pm, and DJs 11pm–5am (entry $7). Sat night's *Lowlife* under-ground "alternative" dance club is strictly for gay men, but on Sun nights there's a happy mix of gays and dykes who go wild to some groovy music (Sat & Sun from 10pm; free).

Gurlesque, *Imperial Hotel*, 35 Erskineville Rd, Erskineville. Sydney's first and only lesbian strip club (women-only), disapproved by some, but loads of fun and wildly popular. Sun nights 6–11pm. Entry $10.

Imperial Hotel, 35 Erskineville Rd, Erskineville. A notorious late-night gay venue, with a popular, hot and sweaty dance floor. This is where the film *Priscilla, Queen of the Desert* both started and ended. It was the *Imperial's* finest hour, and the theme is revived with free *Priscilla* drag shows on Thursday (after midnight & 1.30am), Friday and Saturday nights (10.30pm, 11.30pm, 1.15am & 2.15am).

Gay and lesbian Sydney

Sydney is undisputably one of the world's great gay cities – indeed, many people think it capable of snatching San Francisco's crown as the Queen of them all. There's something for everyone – whether you want to lie on a beach during the warmer months (April–Oct) or party hard all year round. Gays and lesbians are pretty much accepted – particularly in the inner-city and eastern areas. They have to be – there's too many of them for anyone to argue. A big drawcard is the month-long Sydney **Gay and Lesbian Mardi Gras Festival** ; the first was held in 1978 as a gay-rights protest. Today, it's the biggest celebration of gay and lesbian culture in the world. The festival goes for four weeks, starting the first week of **February** and after hundreds of arts and community events, culminates in the parade and party on the last weekend of February or the first weekend of March.

But don't despair if you can't be here for Mardi Gras. The city has much more to offer. **Oxford Street** is Sydney's official "pink strip" of gay restaurants, coffee shops, bookshops and bars, and here you'll find countless pairs of tight-T-shirted guys strolling hand-in-hand, or checking out the passing talent from a hip, streetside café. **King Street** , Newtown, is another burgeoning centre of gay culture, while lesbian communities have carved out territory of their own in **Erskineville** and **Leichhardt** (known affectionately as "Dykehart"). Although the bar and club listings below have been split into separate gay and lesbian listings, the scene thankfully doesn't split so neatly into "them and us".

If you've come for the sun, popular **gay beaches** are Tamarama (see p.150), Bondi (p.148), and "clothing optional" Lady Jane, at Watsons Bay (p.143), while pools of choice are Red Leaf harbour pool at Double Bay (p.142) and the appropriately named Andrew "Boy" Charlton pool in The Domain (p.124). The Coogee Women's Baths, at the southern end of Coogee Beach (p.151) is popular with lesbians.

Mardi Gras, sleaze and the Gay Games

From a Queer perspective the best time of year to visit Sydney is February, when the **Sydney Gay and Lesbian Mardi Gras** takes over the city. Four weeks of exhibitions, performances and other events – including a two-week **Gay and Lesbian Film Festival** in mid-February – represent the largest lesbian and gay arts festival in the world, paving the way for the main event, an exuberant night-time **parade** down Oxford Street, when up to a million gays and straights jostle for the best viewing positions, before the Dykes on Bikes, traditional leaders of the parade, roar into view. Participants devote months to the preparation of outlandish floats and outrageous costumes at Mardi Gras workshops, and even longer is devoted to the preparation of beautiful bodies in Sydney's packed gyms. The parade begins at 7.30pm (finishing around 10.30pm), but people line the barricades along Oxford Street from mid-morning. If you can't get to Oxford Street until late afternoon, your best chance of finding a spot is along Flinders Street near Moore Park Road, where the parade ends. Otherwise, AIDS charity The Bobby Goldsmith Foundation (⊕ 02/9283 8666) has 7000 grandstand seats on Moore Park Road, at around $75 each.

The all-night **dance party** which follows the parade is held in several differently themed dance spaces at the old Showgrounds at Moore Park. You have to plan ahead if you want to get a **ticket** : party tickets (around $110) often sell out by the end of January, and the purchase of tickets is restricted to "Mardi Gras members". The annual membership fee is $44; cheaper associate membership for those who live 150km outside Sydney costs $35, and international membership costs $60. Membership forms – and tickets – are available from the **Mardi Gras office** , 21 Erskineville Rd, Erskineville, NSW 2043 (Mon–Fri 10am–6pm; ⊕ 02/9557 4332, or ⊕ 9516 4446, ⊛ www.mardigras.com.au); forms can be downloaded from the website. There are special provisions for overseas visitors:

continued overleaf

Mardi gras, sleaze and the Gay Games continued

to be sure of a ticket (international and associate members are entitled to only one per person), order one at the same time you apply for membership. Once you've given your credit card details, they'll post the ticket to you, or hold it for collection. Full members can buy three tickets so, if all else fails, once you're on the ground ask around and you may find someone with a spare ticket. For credit card bookings for festival events visit ⓦwww.ticketek.com.au. The Mardi Gras Guide, available from mid-December, can be picked up from bookshops, cafés and restaurants around Oxford Street or at the Mardi Gras office. Also look out for the *Sydney Morning Herald*'s "Gay and Lesbian Mardi Gras Guide" in the first week of February.

Sydney just can't wait all year for Mardi Gras, so the Sleaze Ball is a very welcome stopgap in late September or early October. Similar to the Mardi Gras party, it's held at the former Showground site, and goes on through the night. Tickets, which cost $82.50 in 2000, are organized by Mardi Gras Ltd and are likewise restricted to members.

The 6th International Gay Games and Cultural Festival will be held in Sydney on 2–9 November 2002. For more information consult their website (ⓦwww.gaygamesvi.org.au). Gay Games packages are offered by FOD travel (see below).

Groups and information

Information The Bookshop, 207 Oxford St, Darlinghurst (℡02/9331 1103), is a good starting point for getting to know gay Sydney, with a complete stock of gay and lesbian-related books, cards and magazines. The staff are friendly and ready to help in any way they can. You can pick up the free gay and lesbian weekly, *Sydney Star Observer* (PO Box 939, Darlinghurst NSW 1300; ℡02/9380 5577), from venues and gay-friendly businesses in the eastern suburbs and inner west, while the Lesbian-specific *LOTL* (*Lesbians on the Loose*; PO Box 1099, Darlinghurst, NSW 1300; ℡02/8347 1033, ⓦwww.lotl.com), another free monthly magazine, is available in The Bookshop and cafés of Newtown and Glebe. These magazines will tell you where and when the weekly dance parties are being held, and where you can buy tickets.

Support networks Gay & Lesbian Counselling Service of New South Wales, GLCS Centre, 197 Albion St, Surry Hills (daily 4pm–midnight; ℡02/9207 2800). AIDS Council of NSW (ACON), 9 Commonwealth St, Surry Hills (℡02/9206 2000). Bobby Goldsmith Foundation for AIDS and AIDS Related Diseases, Level 2, 9 Commonwealth St, Surry Hills (℡02/9283 8666). Sydney AIDS Hotline/NSW AIDS line (℡02/9332 4000 or free call 1800 451 600). Albion Street Centre, 150–154 Albion St, Surry Hills (℡02/9332 1090); counselling, testing clinic, information and library.

Travel agents

FOD Travel, Level 2, 77 Oxford St, Darlinghurst (℡02/9360 3616, ℻9332 3326, ⓦwww.fod.com.au), and 96 Crystal St, Petersham (℡02/9569 5331). Offers special tours designed for gay men and lesbians, and can advise about travel during Mardi Gras. Gay Games packages available.

Silke's Travel, PO Box 1099, Darlinghurst, NSW 1300 (℡02/8347 2000 or free call 1800 807 860, ℻8347 2022, ⓦwww.silkes.com.au). Offers advice and bookings for domestic and international travel, and accommodation from a gay and lesbian perspective. Lots of experience with backpacker tours.

See also p.101 for gay- and lesbian-friendly places to stay, and pp.174 and 177 for a lowdown on the club scene and listings of specifically gay and lesbian venues.

Leichhardt Hotel, cnr Short and Balmain roads, Leichhardt. Popular lesbian watering hole; pool competition Thurs from 8pm. Wed–Sat 10am–midnight, Mon, Tues & Sun noon–10pm.

Midnight Shift, 85 Oxford St, Darlinghurst. A large drinking and cruising space for (mainly) gay men, and a "locker room" out the back. Commonly known as "The Shift", this is the mainstream club for gay men. In the early hours of Sun you can hardly move on a dance floor full of gym-pumped men, sweating it out with their shirts off. Daily noon–6am.

Newtown Hotel, 174 King St, Newtown. A stalwart of the Sydney scene that's a 20-minute taxi ride but a thousand miles from Oxford St. Laid-back mix of Newtown lesbians and gays, drag shows Tues–Sun, and pool tables. Mon–Sat 11am–midnight, Sun 11am–10pm.

On the Other Side, *NV Nightclub*, 163 Oxford St, Darlinghurst. Mainly lesbian party night Sun 8pm–2am. Happy hour 9–10pm. Entry $5.

Oxford Hotel, 134 Oxford St, Darlinghurst. The ground-floor bar, open 24 hours, is the macho pillar of the Sydney gay community, with dim lights, hard music and a packed crowd after 11pm – particularly busy on Fri and Sat nights. On the first floor, *Gilligans* is a very different scene from below, a very popular cocktail bar which attracts a mixed crowd of gay boys, lesbians and the straight party set; happy hour 5–7pm. Daily 5pm–3am.

Spicy Friday, *Lansdowne Hotel*, 2–6 City Rd, Chippendale, just off Broadway. The crowd is about 80 percent lesbian at this funky soul and cabaret Fri theme night (8pm–3am). Pool tables and upstairs chill-out lounge. Entry $5.

Stonewall Hotel, 175 Oxford St, Darlinghurst. A big hit with young gays and lesbians and their straight friends. You can expect theme nights like karaoke, celebrity drag, or Mailbox (a dating game), and there are DJs in the various different bars Wed–Sat. There's also a cocktail bar, and a nightclub complete with go-go dancers (Fri & Sat 11pm–5am; $2). "Girls Night Out" is for lesbians on Thurs nights from 9pm in the VIP Bar (free). Tues–Sun noon–5am.

Taxi Club, 40 Flinders St, Surry Hills. Last stop. If you've made it here, congratulations, you're a true bar hopper. It's a Sydney legend, but don't bother before 2 or 3am, and you'll need to be suitably intoxicated to appreciate it fully. There's a strange blend of drag queens, taxi drivers, lesbians and boys (straight and gay) to observe, and the cheapest drinks in gay Sydney. You have to be a member, but simply ask to join at the door.

Classical music, theatre and dance

Sydney's **arts scene** is vibrant and extensive. **Prices** for mainstream theatre and music performances are fairly high, upwards of $25, with tickets in smaller, fringe venues costing from around $22. Half-price same-day tickets are available from Halftix (see p.169). The Sydney Symphony Orchestra plays at the Town Hall, St James's Church or the Opera House while the Australian Ballet (prices $49–75) performs at the Opera House and the Capitol Theatre. The free outdoor performances in The Domain, under the auspices of the Sydney Festival, are a highlight of the year, as crowds gather to enjoy the music with a picnic.

Concert halls

Conservatorium of Music, Royal Botanic Gardens, off Macquarie St (concert department ℡ 02/9351 1263). Conservatorium students have traditionally given free lunch-time recitals every Tuesday and Friday at 1.10pm during term time. Staff and students also give other concerts, both free and ticketed (up to $27.50) at various venues around town; a programme is available from the concert department. See p.125 for more details.

Sydney Opera House, Bennelong Point (℡ 02/9250 7777, 🔊 www.soh.com.au). The Opera House is, of course, *the* place for the most prestigious performances in Sydney, hosting not just opera and classical music but also theatre and ballet in its many auditoriums. Forget quibbles about ticket prices (classical concerts from $40, opera from $90) – it's worth going just to say you've been. See pp.109–110 for more details.

Town Hall, cnr Druitt and George streets (℡ 02/9265 9230). Centrally located concert hall. See p.118 for more details.

Theatre and dance

Aboriginal and Islander Dance Theatre (℡ 02/9252 0199). Established in 1976, this famous training company for young Aboriginal and Islander dancers, based in The Rocks, puts on about three productions per year at various venues; call for times and locations.

Bangarra Dance Theatre , Pier 4, Hickson Rd, Millers Point, The Rocks Ⓣ 02/9251 5333, Ⓦ www.bangarra.com). Formed in 1989, Bangarra's innovative style fuses contemporary movement with the traditional dances and culture of the Yirrkala Community in Arnhemland. Based at the same pier as the Wharf Theatre but performing at other venues in Sydney and touring nationally and internationally – check their website for the latest details.

Belvoir St Theatre , 25 Belvoir St, Surry Hills Ⓣ 02/9699 3444). Highly regarded two-stage venue for a wide range of contemporary Australian and international theatre.

Capitol Theatre , 13 Campbell St, Haymarket Ⓣ 02/9266 4800). Built as a deluxe picture theatre in the 1920s, the theatre was saved from demolition and beautifully restored in the mid-1990s. The 2000-seater now hosts big-budget musicals and ballet, watched from beneath its best feature, the deep-blue ceiling spangled with the stars of the southern skies.

Ensemble Theatre , 78 McDougall St, Milsons Point Ⓣ 02/9929 0644, Ⓦ www.ensemble.com.au). Australian contemporary and classic plays.

The Footbridge Theatre , Parramatta Rd, University of Sydney, Glebe Ⓣ 02/9692 9955). Rich and varied repertoire, from *Cabaret* to Shakespeare.

Lyric Theatre , Star City Casino, Pirrama Rd, Pyrmont Ⓣ 02/9657 9657). The place to see those big musical extravaganzas imported from the West End and Broadway. The casino's smaller theatre, the Star City Showroom, puts on more off-beat musicals and comedy, from the *Rocky Horror Picture Show* to *Girls Night Out.*

Marion Street Theatre , 2 Marian St, Killara Ⓣ 02/9498 3166, Ⓦ www.marianst.com.au). Broadway, West End and Australian comedies and popular drama. Bookings are essential for the popular 1pm Saturday matinee for kids (aged 3–10; also school holidays Mon–Fri 10.30am & 1pm).

The Playhouse and **Drama Theatre** , both at the Sydney Opera House, Bennelong Point Ⓣ 02/9250 7777, Ⓦ www.soh.com.au). Modern and traditional plays mostly put on by the Sydney Theatre Company.

Theatre Royal , MLC Centre, King St, City Ⓣ 02/9320 9191). Imported musicals and blockbuster plays.

Wharf Theatre , Pier 4, Hickson Rd, Millers Point, The Rocks Ⓣ 02/9250 1777). Home to the highly regarded Sydney Theatre Company, producing Shakespeare and modern pieces, and to the Sydney Dance Company. Atmospheric waterfront location, and a well-regarded restaurant, bar and café.

Fringe theatre, comedy and cabaret

As well as the venues listed below, also see the *Bridge Hotel* (p.173) which has Monday comedy nights and Tuesday improv and cabaret runs, and *The Albury* (p.174) and *The Imperial* (p.174) for their brilliant free drag shows.

Comedy Store , Fox Studios, Driver Ave, Moore Park Ⓣ 02/9357 1419; bookings recommended). Sydney's longest running stand-up comedy venue has now moved from gritty Petersham to upmarket Fox Studios. International (often American) and Australian stand-up comics Tues–Sun. Bar open 6–11pm, show 9pm. Entry Tues–Thurs $15, Fri & Sat $27.50.

New Theatre , 542 King St, Newtown Ⓣ 02/9873 3575). Professional and amateur actors (all unpaid) perform contemporary dramas with socially relevant themes. Entry $25.

NIDA Studio , 215 Anzac Parade, Kensington Ⓣ 02/9697 7613). Australia's premier dramatic training ground – the National Institute of Dramatic Art – where the likes of Mel Gibson, Judy Davis and Colin Friels started out, also offers student productions for talent-spotting. Tickets $22.

The Performance Space , 199 Cleveland St, Redfern, opposite Prince Alfred Park Ⓣ 02/9319 5091). Experimental performances.

Stables Theatre , 10 Nimrod St, Darlinghurst Ⓣ 02/9361 3817). Theatre with a mission to develop and foster new Australian playwrights.

Theatresports Ⓣ 02/9281 7666; bookings Ⓣ 02/9699 3444). Improvised genius with teams competing against each other. The theatrical games are at Belvoir St Theatre most Sun evenings (see above), or occasionally at other venues around town.

Cinemas

The commercial movie centre of Sydney is on George Street, south of the Town Hall, where you'll find Hoyts at no. 505 Ⓣ 02/9273 7431, Ⓦ www.hoyts.com.au) and Greater Union at no. 525 Ⓣ 02/9267 8666, Ⓦ www.greaterunion.com.au). Other Hoyts can be found at the Broadway

Shopping Centre, on Broadway near Glebe (ⓣ 02/9211 1911), and at Fox Studios (ⓣ 02/9332 1300), which incorporates the less mainstream Cinema Paris (ⓣ 02/9332 1633) and upmarket screening room La Premiere (ⓣ 02/9266 4887). There's another mainstream multiplex, Reading Cinemas, at Level 3, Market City Shopping Centre, Haymarket (ⓣ 02/9280 1202, ⓦ www.readingcinemas.com.au). Standard tickets cost around $12, but

Film festivals

The **Sydney Film Festival**, held annually for two weeks in **early June**, is an exciting programme of features, shorts, documentaries and retrospective screenings from Australia and around the world. Founded in 1954 by a group of film enthusiasts at Sydney University, the festival struggled with prudish censors and parochial attitudes until freedom from censorship for festival films was introduced in 1971. From the early, relaxed atmosphere of picnics on the lawns between screenings and hardy film-lovers crouching under blankets in freezing prefabricated sheds, it has gradually moved off-campus, to find a home from 1974 in the magnificent State Theatre (see p.118). Films are also shown at the three-screen Dendy Quays in Circular Quay. The festival was once mainly sold on a subscription basis, but subscriptions now only apply to screenings at the State Theatre; the more provocative line-up of films at the Dendy Quays aims to attract a new, under-35 audience to the festival on a single or packaged ticket basis. Single **tickets** cost around $12, packages of four around $44 or ten around $100; **subscriptions** for the State programme start from $110 for one week daytime only unreserved stalls seating, and go up to $250 for two weeks reserved dress circle night-time screenings. For more information, call or drop into the Festival office at 405 Glebe Point Rd, Glebe (Mon–Fri 9am–5pm; ⓣ 02/9660 3844 or 9660 0252, ⓕ 9692 8793, ⓦ www.sydfilm-fest.com.au), or write to PO Box 950, Glebe, NSW 2037.

There are also two short film festivals in the summer with the sort of irreverent approach which once fuelled the Sydney Film Festival. Stars above and the sound of waves accompany the week-long **Flickerfest International Short Film Festival** (ⓣ 02/9365 6888, ⓔ flickerfest@bigpond.com), held in the amphitheatre of the Bondi Pavilion in early January, and showcasing foreign and Australian productions, including documentaries. The **Tropfest** is a competition festival for short films held annually around the end of February; its name comes from the *Tropicana Cafe* (see p.165) on Victoria Street, Darlinghurst, where the festival began almost by chance in 1993 when young actor, John Polsen, forced his local coffee spot to show the short film he had made. He pushed other filmmakers to follow suit, and the following year a huge crowd of punters packed themselves into the café to watch around twenty films. These days the entire street is closed to traffic to enable an outdoor screening, while cafés along the strip also screen films on TVs inside. The festival has grown enormously over the years, and the focus of the event has now been moved to The Domain, with huge crowds turning up to picnic and watch the free 8pm screening, and live entertainment from 3pm. Each state capital also screens the event simultaneously in venues ranging from cafés to parks. Films must be specifically produced for the festival and be up-to-the-minute. To this end, an item is announced a few months in advance of the entry date which must feature in the shorts – in 2001 it was a horn – however you wanted to interpret it. For more details, contact Tropfest, Suite 24, 2A Bayswater Rd, Kings Cross, NSW 2011 (ⓣ 02/9368 0434, ⓕ 9356 4531, ⓦ www.tropfest.com.au).

There's also a **Women on Women Film Festival** held over three days in late September at the Chauvel Cinema, Paddington (see overleaf); a **gay and lesbian film festival** in late February; and the latest, and quirkiest, addition to the scene, the week-long **Goat Island Film Festival** (late Nov or early Dec), an outdoor event with a different theme each year.

Tuesdays are reduced-price (around $8.50) at all of these cinemas and their suburban outlets.

In the summer, two open-air cinemas open up: from November to mid-February the **Epson Moonlight Cinema**, in the Centennial Park Amphitheatre (Oxford St, Woollahra entrance; Tues–Sun, films start 8.45pm, tickets from 7.30pm or via Ticketmaster on ☏ 13 6100; $12.50; ⓦ www.moonlight.com.au), shows classic, art house and cult films; and throughout January as part of the Sydney Festival, the **Open Air Cinema** (tickets from 6.30pm or bookings on ☏ 1300/366 649; $15) is put up at Mrs Macquaries Point in the Royal Botanic Gardens for a very picturesque film screening – mainly mainstream recent releases and some classics. See p.179 for details of Sydney's annual film festivals.

Chauvel Twin Cinema , Paddington Town Hall, cnr Oatley Rd and Oxford St, Paddington ☏ 02/9361 5398). Varied programme of Australian and foreign films plus classics at this Australian Film Institute Cinema. $8 on Mon and Tues.

Cremorne Orpheum , 380 Military Rd, Cremorne ☏ 02/9908 4344, ⓦ www.orpheum.com.au). Charming heritage-listed, four-screen cinema built in 1935 with a splendid Art Deco interior and old-fashioned friendly service. The main cinema has never dispensed with its Wurlitzer organ recitals preceding Sat and Sun night films. Mainstream, and foreign new releases. $8.50 on Tues.

The Dendy , MLC Centre, 19 Martin Place ☏ 02/9233 8166, ⓦ www.dendy.com.au). Trendy single-screen cinema, café, bar and pool room complex (daily noon–midnight). Also the four-screen Dendy Newtown, 261 King St ☏ 02/9550 5699), with attached café, bar and bookshop; and the newest, superbly sited, addition – the three-screen Dendy Opera Quays, 2 East Circular Quay ☏ 02/9247 3800). All showing prestige new-release films. $9 on Mon.

Govinda's Movie Room , 112 Darlinghurst Rd, Darlinghurst ☏ 02/9380 5162 for bookings or 9360 7853 for recorded programme information). Run by the Hare Krishnas (but definitely no indoctrination), it shows two films every night from a

range of classics and recent releases. The $15.90 movie and dinner deal (all-you-can-eat vegetarian buffet) is popular and you may need to book (see p.165).

Palace Cinemas . Chain of four inner-city cinemas showing foreign-language, arthouse and new releases: Academy, 3a Oxford St, cnr South Dowling St, Paddington ☏ 02/9361 4453); Verona, 17 Oxford St, cnr Verona St, Paddington ☏ 02/9360 6099), with a groovy bar/café; Norton, 99 Norton St, Leichhardt ☏ 02/9550 0122), the newest with a bookshop and cybercafé; and Walker, 121 Walker St, North Sydney ☏ 02/9959 4222). All $8.70 on Mon.

Panasonic Imax Theatre , Southern Promenade, Darling Harbour ☏ 02/9281 3300, ⓦ www.imax.com.au). State-of-the-art giant cinema screen showing a choice of four films designed to thrill your senses, at $16.20 a go.

Valhalla , 166 Glebe Point Rd, Glebe ☏ 02/9660 8050). The beloved Valhalla, Sydney's first alternative cinema (established in 1976), nearly closed down in 1999 but is now back to life showing documentaries, foreign films, new-release independents and Australian film. Also hosts specialist evenings which draw in local filmmakers for screenings and discussions. The $35 four-film pass can also be used at the Chauvel.

Art galleries and exhibitions

The *Sydney Morning Herald*'s "Metro" website (ⓦ www.metro.citysearch.com.au) has comprehensive listings of art galleries and current exhibitions, while Friday's printed version offers reviews of recently opened shows. Galleries tend to be concentrated in Paddington and there are several small ones on King Street, Newtown.

Artspace , The Gunnery Arts Centre, 43–51 Cowper Wharf Rd, Woolloomooloo ☏ 02/9368 1899). In a wonderful location, showing provocative young artists. Tues–Sat 11am–6pm.

Australian Centre for Photography , 257 Oxford St, Paddington ☏ 02/9332 1455). Photographic

exhibitions. Tues–Sat 11am–6pm.

Australian Galleries: Painting & Sculpture , 15 Roylston St, Paddington ☏ 02/9360 5177). Serene gallery exhibiting and selling contemporary Australian art, including works by Margaret Olley, Jeffrey Smart and John Coburn. Tues–Sat 10am–6pm.

Australian Galleries: Works on Paper , 24 Glenmore Rd, Paddington ☏ 02/9380 8744). Works for sale here include drawings by Brett Whiteley and Arthur Boyd, as well as prints and sketches by young Australian artists. Daily 10am–6pm.

Hogarth Aboriginal Art Gallery , 7 Walker Lane, Paddington ☏ 02/9360 6839). Extensive collection of work by contemporary Aboriginal artists, both tribal and urban, and special exhibitions. Tues–Sat 11am–5pm.

Ivan Dougherty Gallery , cnr Albion Ave and Selwyn St, Paddington ☏ 02/9385 0726). National and international contemporary art; forums and performances sponsored by the College of Fine Arts, University of NSW. Mon–Sat 10am–5pm.

Josef Lebovic Gallery , 34 Paddington St, Paddington ☏ 02/9332 1840). Renowned print and graphic gallery specializing in Australian and international prints from the nineteenth and twentieth centuries, as well as vintage photography. Tues–Fri 1–6pm, Sat 11am–5pm.

The Performance Space , 199 Cleveland St, Redfern, opposite Prince Alfred Park ☏ 02/9698 7235). Experimental multimedia and plastic arts: installations, sculpture, photography and painting. Wed–Fri noon–6pm, Sat noon–5pm.

Ray Hughes Gallery , 270 Devonshire St, Surry Hills ☏ 02/9698 3200). Has a stable of high-profile contemporary Australian and New Zealand artists. Openings monthly, with two artists per show. Tues–Sat 10am–6pm.

Roslyn Oxley , 8 Soudan Lane, Paddington ☏ 02/9331 1919). Avant-garde videos and installations among the Australian and international offerings. Tues–Fri 10am–6pm, Sat 11am–6pm.

Festivals and events

The Sydney year is interspersed with festivals and events of various sorts that reach their peak in the summer. The City of Sydney Council has a **City Infoline** ☏ 02/9265 9007; Mon–Fri 9am–5pm) for details of events year round or you can consult their website ⓦ www.cityofsydney.nsw.gov.au).

The **New Year** begins with a spectacular **fireworks** display from the Harbour Bridge and Darling Harbour. There's a brief hiatus of a week or so until the annual **Festival of Sydney**, an exhaustive and exhausting arts event that lasts for most of **January** and ranges from opera-in-the-park, concerts, plays and outdoor art installations to circus performances. About fifty percent of the events are free and are based around urban public spaces, focusing on Circular Quay, The Domain and Darling Harbour; the remainder – mostly international performances – can cost a packet. The general programme is usually printed in the *Sydney Morning Herald* in October while a full eighty-plus-page programme is available nearer the time. There's also a **fringe festival** based at the Bondi Pavilion. From Boxing Day to the end of January, Darling Harbour hosts its own festival, linked with the Festival of Sydney. Most of the attractions are aimed at children, but there's also a free promenade jazz festival.

Horse-racing in Sydney

There are horse-racing meetings on Wednesday, Saturday and most public holidays throughout the year, but the best times to hit the track are during the **Spring and Autumn Carnivals** (respectively Aug–Sept and March–April), when prize money rockets, and the quality of racing rivals the best in the world. The venues are well maintained, peopled with colourful racing characters, and often massive crowds. Principal **racecourses** are: Royal Randwick (Alison Rd, Randwick), which featured in *Mission Impossible 2*; Rosehill Gardens (James Ruse Drive, Rosehill); and Canterbury Park (King St, Canterbury), which has midweek racing, plus floodlit night racing from September to March. Entry is around $8, or $15–20 on carnival days. There are also plenty of picturesque country venues to choose from; contact the Australian Jockey Club for more details on ☏ 02/9663 8400. Every Friday the *Sydney Morning Herald* publishes its racing guide, "The Form". Bets are placed at TAB shops; these are scattered throughout the city, and most pubs also have TAB access.

Australia Day on January 26 is a huge celebration in Sydney, with activities focused on the water. There's the Coca-Cola Amatil Marathon, where Sydney's passenger ferries race from Fort Denison to the Harbour Bridge, the Tall Ships Race from Bradley's Head to the Harbour Bridge, a 21-gun salute fired from the Man O'War steps at the Opera House, and an aerial display of military planes. The **Australia Day Regatta** takes place in the afternoon, with hundreds of yachts racing all over the water, from Botany Bay to the Parramatta River. There are also events at The Rocks and Hyde Park, and at Darling Harbour, where the day culminates at around 9pm with a fireworks display. In addition, many museums let visitors in for free. Besides all this, there are at least two outdoor rock concerts to choose from: **Survival**, which celebrates Aboriginal culture and acts as an antidote to the mainstream white Australia Day festivities, is held at Waverly Oval near Bondi; while the **Big Day Out** is held at the Showground at Homebush Bay, featuring around fifty local and international acts.

An entirely different side of Sydney life is on view at the impressive summer **surf carnivals**, staged regularly by local surf lifesaving clubs; check the newspapers for details.

At the end of **February** the city is engulfed by the **Sydney Gay and Lesbian Mardi Gras** (see box on pp.175–176). Another big event is the **Royal Easter Show**, an agricultural and garden show in late **March/early April**, based at the Sydney Showground at Homebush Bay. For twelve consecutive days (with the second weekend always the Easter weekend) there is a frantic array of amusement-park rides, fireworks, parades of prize animals, a rodeo and wood-chopping displays – it's when the country comes to the city.

The **International Film Festival** takes over many of the city's screens in **June** (see box on p.179); and the **City to Surf Race**, an eight-kilometre fun run from the city to Bondi, happens every **August**. In spring, from September to early October, **Carnivale** celebrates ethnic diversity and "vibrant collaborations in the fields of theatre, music and dance". The Labour Day weekend in early **October** is marked by the **Manly International Jazz Festival**, with several free outdoor, waterfront events and a few indoor concerts charging entry. In mid-October there's the weekend **Erskineville Music Festival**, featuring a wide variety of sounds, from world music and jazz through to hip hop and rock. This is followed by the very Italian **Blessing of the Fleet** at Darling Harbour. Every alternate (even-numbered) year, the **Biennale of Sydney** takes place over six weeks from mid-September until early November, with provocative contemporary art exhibitions at various venues and public spaces around town.

The year is brought to a close by the **Sydney to Hobart Yacht Race**, when it seems that half of Sydney turns up at or on the harbour on December 26 to cheer the start of this classic regatta and watch the colourful spectacle of two hundred or so yachts setting sail for a 630-nautical-mile slog.

Shopping

Sydney's main shopping focus is the city centre, in the stretch between Martin Place and the Queen Victoria Building. Apart from its charming old nineteenth-century arcades and two **department stores**, David Jones and Grace Bros (see p.118), the city centre also has several modern multilevel **shopping complexes** where you can hunt down clothes and accessories without raising a sweat, among them Skygarden (between Pitt and Castlereagh streets) and Centrepoint on Pitt

Street Mall, on the corner of Market Street. Much of the area from the QVB to the mall is linked by underground arcades which will also keep you cool.

Most stores are **open** Monday to Saturday 8.30am–5.30pm, with Thursday late-night shopping until 9pm. Many of the larger shops and department stores in the city are also open on Sunday 10am–5pm, as are shopping centres at tourist centres such as Darling Harbour. If you've run out of time to buy presents and souvenirs, don't worry: the revamped **Sydney Airport** is attached to one of the biggest shopping malls in Sydney, with outlets for everything from surfwear to R.M. Williams bush outfitters, at the same prices as the downtown stores. The Rocks is the best place for souvenir and tax-free shopping.

Fashion

Oxford Street in Paddington (see p.138) is the place to go for interesting fashion, along with the Strand Arcade (see p.118) in the city; for striking street fashion check out Crown Street in Surry Hills, with places such as Wheels & Doll Baby at no. 259 and Dangerfield at no. 330; and for cheaper styles, retro clothes and other interesting junk, try King Street in Newtown (see p.133). If you want to peek at expensive Australian **designer fashion**, head for the two upper levels of the Queen Victoria Building (see p.118); or go to the shops of the designers themselves, such as Bettina Lliano at 440 Oxford St, Paddington; Morrisey at 76a Oxford St, Darlinghurst; Alannah Hill at 118 Oxford St, Darlinghurst; and Colette Dinnigan at 33 William St, Paddington. There are several outlets for samples and seconds of Australian-made fashions, such as Country Road, on Regent Street in Redfern. To go with the outfits, funky Australian **jewellery** can be found in the Strand Arcade at Dinosaur Designs (also at Argyle Stores, The Rocks, see p.113, and 330 Oxford St, Paddington), and at Love and Hatred, both on Level 1. For **beauty** products, Jurlique, also in the Strand Arcade, sells its own pure, hypoallergenic Australian-made skin and hair products; check the department stores for home-grown Poppy Lipsticks. The city centre's most glamorous shopping centre is Chifley Plaza on the corner of Hunter and Phillip streets in the Chifley Tower, which sells expensive labels from around the world such as Bruno Magli and MaxMara. Otherwise head for the exclusive boutiques of Double Bay (see p.142).

For Australian **workwear** the place to head for is Gowings, on the corner of Market and George streets – a beloved Sydney institution for 125 years and a delightfully old-fashioned **menswear** department store. It has everything a bloke (and often a sheila) could want, from Bonds T-shirts to Speedo swimwear, Blundestone boots and a range of felt hats at the best prices in town – plus cheap haircuts. Three other branches are at 319 George St, Wynyard (with a rooftop café); 82 Oxford St, Darlinghurst; and at the airport. The quality **bush outfitters** R.M. Williams, 389 George St (also at Chifley Plaza, at Darling Walk, Darling Harbour, and at the airport), are great for moleskins and Drizabones and superb leather riding boots. For the widest range of Akubra hats, check out Strand Hatters in the Strand Arcade. If it's **surfwear** you're after, head for Hot Tuna at 180 Oxford St, Paddington, or Mambo, 17 Oxford St, Paddington and 80 Campbell Parade, Bondi Beach. Campbell Parade is, of course, bursting with **swimwear** shops: Bikini Island at no. 38 has a huge range of women's styles, while its store at no. 30 has bargain remaindered lines.

Arts and crafts

The Rocks is heaving with **Australiana** and **arts and crafts** souvenirs, from opals to sheepskin. It's the best place to do duty- and GST-free shopping; many Rocks' stores have a "sealed bag" system which lets you buy goods without paying the ten percent goods and services tax, and waive the minimum of $300. Tourists flock to Ken Done's emporium here at 123 George St and 1–5 Hickson Rd (in the restored Australian Steam and Navigation Building) to buy his colourful designs, which feature Sydney's harbour, boats and flowers on such items as duvet covers.

The Rocks is also a focus for **Aboriginal art** (see also "Art Galleries and exhibitions", p.180): the Aboriginal and Tribal Art Centre, 1st floor, 117 George St, has a huge collection of traditional Aboriginal art from around Australia; the Dreamtime Gallery, Shop 35, The Rocks Centre, 12–26 Playfair St (also a branch at the Opera House), sells traditional Aboriginal art including didgeridoos (live didj played weekends); and Balarinji, 1st floor, Argyle Stores, Argyle St, is an Aboriginal-owned clothing and accessory company. However, the best place to buy Aboriginal art and craft is Gavala, in the Harbourside Shopping Centre in Darling Harbour (see p.128). A great place to buy **boomerangs** is Duncan MacLennon's Boomerang School, 200 William St; the boomerangs sold here are mostly authentic, made by Aboriginal artisans from around Australia. Duncan has been giving free boomerang-throwing lessons every Sun in Yarranabbe Park near Rushcutters Bay (10am–noon) since 1958.

Music and books

For a take-home sample of the **Australian music** scene in all its variety, from Aboriginal through to indie and jazz, head for Sounds Australian, Shop 33, The Rocks Centre, 12–26 Playfair St, The Rocks – the retail arm of the Australian Music Centre with very knowledgeable staff. You can listen before you buy.

One of the biggest **bookshops** in the city is Dymocks, 428 George St, open daily, on several floors with an impressive Australian selection and a café. Collins Superstore, Level 2, Broadway Shopping Centre, is a vast bookstore based on the Barnes & Noble model, with curving bookshelves, soft lighting and comfy sofas and window seats; there's also an in-store coffee shop. Nearby, Gleebooks, 49 Glebe Point Rd, Glebe, is one of Australia's best bookshops, specializing in academic and alternative books, contemporary Australian and international literature, and is open daily until 9pm; book launches and other literary events are regularly held upstairs and the website has excellent reviews (for details of events call ☎02/9660 2333; ⓦwww.gleebooks.com.au). Ariel has two large, lively and hip branches, one at 103 George St, The Rocks and the other at 42 Oxford St, Paddington; both branches are open daily until midnight. When you're sick of all the bigger stores, Macleay Bookshop, 103 Macleay St, Potts Point (daily until 9pm), is a tiny and peaceful choice. **The Travel Bookshop** at 175 Liverpool St (closed Sun) is the place to head for maps, guides and travel journals, plus a good selection of Australiana. **Secondhand books** can be found at Glebe and Paddington markets, at Gleebooks Second Hand Books, 191 Glebe Point Rd (daily until 9pm); upstairs at Lesley McKays Bookshop, 346 New South Head Rd, Double Bay (the ground level, for new books, is open until midnight); and in the secondhand bookshops on King Street, Newtown – in particular check out the amazingly chaotic piles of books at Gould's Book Arcade, 32–38 King St, Newtown (daily 7am–midnight).

Food and drink

There are two handy **supermarkets** in the city centre with extended opening hours: one is in the basement of Woolworths on the corner of Park and George streets, above Town Hall Station (Mon–Wed 7am–8pm, Thurs & Fri 7am–9pm, Sat 9am–6.30pm, Sun 10am–5.30pm); and the other, Coles Express, is on Level 2, Wynyard Station (daily 6am–midnight). The Coles Express in Kings Cross, at 88 Darlinghurst Rd, is also handy for travellers (daily 6am–midnight). In the suburbs, large supermarkets such as Coles stay open daily until about 10pm, and there are plenty of 24-hour 7-Eleven convenience stores in the inner city and suburbs. For **delicatessen** items, look no further than the splendid food hall at David Jones (see p.118). The **Australian Wine Centre**, cnr George and Alfred streets, Circular Quay (Mon–Sat 9.30am–6pm, Sun 11am–5pm), sells more than a thousand **wines** from around Australia.

Markets

The two best **markets** are the Paddington Market and Balmain Market, both on Saturday (see p.138 and p.135, respectively), while the relaxed Glebe Market (see p.132), also on a Saturday, and flea market at Rozelle (Sat & Sun 9am–4pm; see p.136) are also worth a look. The Rocks Market on George Street (Sat & Sun 10am–5pm; see p.113), is more touristy but worth a browse, while Paddy's Market (Thurs 10am–6pm, Fri–Sun 9am–4.30pm; see p.120), in Haymarket near the Entertainment Centre and Chinatown, is Sydney's oldest, selling fruit and veg, deli products, meat and fish, plus large quantities of bargain-basement clothes and toys. There's also a series of alternating Saturday markets on the North Shore; Kirribilli Market (fourth Sat of month; see p.144) is the most well known – call ☎02/9936 8197 for details of the others. The latest addition to Sydney's market scene is a series of **produce markets**: at Pyrmont Bay Park in front of the Star City Casino (first Sat of month 7–11am); at Fox Studios on Bent St (Wed noon–7pm); and at Northside Produce Market at the Civic Centre, Miller St, North Sydney, between Ridge and McClaren streets (third Sat of month 8am–noon).

Listings

Airlines (domestic) Aeropelican (☎ 02/4945 0988), to Belmont, nr Newcastle; Ansett Australia (32 Martin Place; ☎ 13 1300, ⓦ www.ansett.com.au), Australia-wide; Eastern Australia Airlines (☎ 13 1313), to Albury, Armidale, Ballina, Canberra, Coffs Harbour, Dubbo, Grafton, Kempsey, Lord Howe Island, Moree, Narrabri, Newcastle, Port Macquarie, Tamworth and Taree; Hazelton Airlines (☎ 13 1713, ⓦ www.hazelton.com.au), in NSW to Albury, Armidale, Bathurst, Broken Hill, Casino, Dubbo, Griffith, Lismore, Merimbula, Moruya, Mudgee, Narrandera, Orange, Parkes, Tamworth and Wagga Wagga, and to Traralgon in Victoria; Kendell Airlines (☎ 13 1300), to Albury, Ballina, Canberra, Coffs Harbour and Wagga Wagga; Qantas (70 Hunter St, cnr Phillip St; ☎ 13 1313), Australia-wide; Sydney Harbour Seaplanes (Lyne Park, Rose Bay; ☎ 02/9388 1878), to Newcastle and Port Stephens.

Airlines (international) Aeroflot, 44 Market St (☎ 02/9262 2233); Aerolineas Argentinas, Level 2, 580 George St (☎ 02/9283 3660); Air Canada, Level 12, 92 Pitt St (☎ 02/9232 5222); Air New Zealand, 5 Elizabeth St (☎ 13 2476); Alitalia, 115 Pitt St (☎ 02/9922 1555); All Nippon (ANA), Level 32, Chifley Tower, 2 Chifley Square (☎ 02/9367 6700); British Airways, Chifley Square, 70 Hunter St (☎ 02/9258 3200); Canadian Airlines, Level 8, 80 Clarence St (☎ 1300/655 757); Cathay Pacific (☎ 13 1747); Continental, 64 York St (☎ 02/9244 2242); Delta, Level 9, 189 Kent St (☎ 02/9251 3211); Finnair, 64 York St (☎ 02/9244 2299); Garuda, 55 Hunter St (☎ 02/9334 9900); Gulf Air, 64 York St (☎ 02/9244 2199); Japan Airlines, Level 14, 201 Sussex St (☎ 02/9272 1111); KLM, 115 Pitt St (☎ 02/9231 6333); Lauda Air, Level 11, 143 Macquarie St (☎ 02/9251 6155); Malaysia Airlines, 16 Spring St (☎ 13 2627); Olympic, 3rd floor, 37–49 Pitt St (☎ 02/9251 1048); Qantas, 70 Hunter St, cnr Phillip St, and 468 Oxford St, Bondi Junction (☎ 13 1211); Sabena, 64 York St (☎ 02/9344 2135); Scandinavian Airlines, Level 15, 31 Market St (☎ 02/9299 9800); Singapore

Airlines, 17–19 Bridge St ⊤ 02/9350 0100);
Swissair, 33 Pitt St ⊤ 02/9232 1744); Thai
International, 75 Pitt St ⊤ 02/9251 1922); United,
Level 5, 10 Barrack St ⊤ 13 1777).

American Express , Level 1, 124–130 Pitt St
(Mon–Fri 9am–5.30pm, Sat 9am–noon;
⊤ 1300/139 060). Lost or stolen travellers'
cheques ⊤ 02/9271 8689.

Banks and foreign exchange Head offices of
banks are mostly in the CBD, around Martin Place;
hours are Mon–Thurs 9am–4pm, Fri 9am–5pm,
with some suburban branches open later and on
Saturday. ANZ, 20 Martin Place ⊤ 02/9227 1911);
Commonwealth Bank, 48 Martin Place
⊤ 02/9378 2000); National Australia Bank, 255
George St ⊤ 02/9237 9799); Westpac, AMP
Centre, 50 Pitt St, cnr Bridge St ⊤ 13 2032).
Money can also be exchanged at the airport;
American Express (see above); Thomas Cook, 175
Pitt St (Mon–Fri 8.45am–5.15pm, Sat 10am–2pm;
⊤ 02/9231 2523) with longer weekend hours at
the Queen Victoria Building outlet at Shop 64,
Lower Ground Floor (Sat 9am–6pm, Sun
11am–5pm); Singapore Money Exchange, Eddy
Ave (Mon–Fri 8am–8pm, Sat & Sun 9am–6pm;
⊤ 02/9281 4118); Travelex Australia, 37–49 Pitt
St (daily 8am–7pm; ⊤ 02/9241 5722) with
branches at 182 George St, 32 Martin Place and
Darling Walk, Darling Harbour (all open daily
8.30am–5pm).

Bus companies Central Coast Airbus ⊤ 02/4332
8655), to Terrigal and Bateau Bay via Mount Ku-
Ring-Gai and Berowra; Firefly Express ⊤ 02/9211
1644, Ⓦ www.fireflyexpress.com.au), to
Melbourne and Adelaide; Great Lakes Coaches
⊤ 02/4983 1560), daily to Forster via Newcastle;
Greyhound Pioneer (ticket office at Eddy Ave,
Central Station; ⊤ 02/9212 1500, nationwide
reservations ⊤ 13 2030,
Ⓦ www.greyhound.com.au), Australia-wide; Keans
Travel Express (Sydney ⊤ 02/9211 3387,
Muswellbrook ⊤ 02/6543 1322), daily Sydney to
Hunter Valley including Cessnock, Muswellbrook
and Scone; McCafferty's (ticket office at Eddy Ave,
Central Station; ⊤ 02/9212 3433, nationwide
reservations ⊤ 13 1499,
Ⓦ www.mccaffertys.com.au), to Melbourne and
Adelaide, Brisbane and Queensland; Murray's
⊤ 13 2251), to Canberra three times daily from
Central or Strathfield; Pioneer Motor Service (Shop
1, Sydney Coach Terminal, Eddy Ave; ⊤ 1300/368
100), Sydney to Brisbane via the north coast with
stops including Byron Bay (a pass is available –
see p.39); Port Stephens Coaches ⊤ 02/9281
9366), daily to Port Stephens at 2pm from Central
via Newcastle outskirts; Premier Motor Service

⊤ 1300/368 100), daily to Bega via the south
coast, with one service daily continuing on to Eden
(a pass is available – see Basics p.39); the service
is also available from the airport, both domestic
and international terminals. Prior's Scenic Express
⊤ 02/4472 4040 or free call 1800 816 234), five
times weekly from Campbelltown train station to
the Southern Highlands including Kangaroo Valley,
thence to Moruya or Narooma via the south coast.
Selwoods ⊤ 02/9281 9366) once daily to Orange
via the Blue Mountains, Lithgow and Bathurst.

Bus terminal Sydney Coach Terminal, cnr Eddy
Ave and Pitt St, next to Central Station (daily
6am–9.30pm; ⊤ 02/9281 9366).

Bus tickets Make bookings at the Traveller's
Information Service at the bus terminal
⊤ 02/9281 9366), at Backpackers Travel Centres
listed under "Travel agents" p.190, or direct with
the bus companies listed above.

Campervans and 4WD rental Australian Outback
4 Wheel Drive Hire Co. (184 Elizabeth St, City;
⊤ 02/9281 9676); Britz Australia (263 Coward St,
Mascot; ⊤ 02/9667 0402 or free call 1800 331
454, Ⓦ www.britz.com), campervans, 4WDs and
camping gear, available one-way to Adelaide, Alice
Springs, Brisbane, Cairns, Darwin, Melbourne and
Perth; Daytona Rentals (191 William St, Kings
Cross and 164 Parramatta Rd, Ashfield;
⊤ 02/9716 8777), affordable 4WD rates; Jay &
Jay Campervan Rentals (94 Bryant St, Padstow;
⊤ 02/9773 4349), campervans and motor homes;
Koala Campervan Rentals (263 Coward St, Mascot;
⊤ 02/9599 3533,
Ⓦ www.koalacampervans.com), campervans and
4WDs, one-way deals to Adelaide, Alice Springs,
Brisbane, Broome, Cairns, Darwin, Melbourne and
Perth; Maui (9 Wollongong Rd, Arncliffe;
⊤ 02/9597 6155 or 1300/363 800,
Ⓦ www.maui-rentals.com), two-, four- and six-
berth campervans and converted 4WDs with one-
way rentals available between Sydney and
Adelaide, Alice Springs, Brisbane, Cairns, Darwin,
Melbourne and Perth; Travel Car Centre (54
Orchard Rd, Brookvale; ⊤ 02/9905 6928,
Ⓦ www.travelcar.com.au), hatchbacks, station-
wagons, campervans and 4WDs available for long-
term rental; Travellers Auto Barn ⊤ 02/9360
1500; see "Cars – buying and selling" box on
p.188), budget campervan rental.

Camping equipment and rental Kent St in the
city behind the Town Hall is nicknamed "adventure
alley" for its preponderance of outdoor equipment
stores; the best-known is Paddy Pallin at no. 507.
Cheaper options include disposal stores at the
downtown ends of George and Pitt streets (try

Boss Disposals, 708 George St, or Mitchell King Disposals, 323 and 327 Pitt St) and suburban K-Mart stores (closest stores to the city are at Spring St, Bondi Junction and at the Broadway shopping centre, Bay St) or hostel notice boards. Only a few places rent gear, mostly based in the suburbs, with weekend rent of a backpack for around $29, sleeping bag from $24, and tent from $25: try Alpsport, 1045 Victoria Rd, West Ryde (T 02/9858 5844), or Tramping 'n' Camping, 30 Bronte Rd, Bondi Junction (T 02/9387 4095).

Car rental The big four car-rental firms, with expensive new model cars, charge from around $50–70 for a small manual: Avis, airport (T 02/9353 9000, W www.avis.com) and 220 William St, Kings Cross (T 02/9357 2000); Budget, airport (T 13 2727, W www.budget.com.au), and 93 William St, Kings Cross (T 02/9339 8888); Hertz (T 13 3039, W www.hertz.com), airport and elsewhere including cnr William and Riley streets, Kings Cross; Thrifty, airport (T 1300/367 227, W www.thrifty.com.au) and elsewhere, including 75 William St, Kings Cross. Also at the airport, Network (T 02/9317 3223, W www.networkrentals.com.au), offer good-value one-way rentals. There are cheaper deals with Bayswater, 180 William St, Kings Cross (T 02/9360 3622, W www.bayswater.com.au), which has low rates but limited km; Kings Cross Rent-a-Car, 169 William St, Kings Cross (T 02/9361 0637, W www.kxr.com.au), which is open daily and has low rates; and Apollo Car Rental, 33 Pittwater Rd, Manly (T 02/9977 5777, W www.apollo-car-rental.com), which has new model cars and also incorporates Rent-a-Ruffy, for cheap, older-model cars; both have limited km. Bondi Car Rentals, 4a Campbell Parade, Bondi Beach (T 02/9130 7660), has good deals on older model cars, wagons, and 4WD; discounts offered with a copy of *Rough Guide*. Travellers Auto Barn, 177 William St, Kings Cross (T 02/9360 1500, W www.travellers-autobarn.com.au), does cheap one-way rentals to Brisbane or Cairns; The Jalopy Shoppe, 690 Parramatta Rd, Croydon (T 02/9798 8666, E jalopy@ozemail.com.au), rents and sells older model cars.

Consulates Embassies are all in Canberra (see p.257), and it's usually easier to call them when in difficulty than to go to the consulates in Sydney: Canadian, Level 5, 111 Harrington St (T 02/9364 3000); New Zealand, 55 Hunter St (T 02/8256 2000); and UK, Level 16, Gateway Building, 1 Macquarie Place (T 02/9247 7521); US, Level 59, MLC Centre, 19–29 Martin Place (T 02/9373 9200). For visas for onward travel, consult "Consulates and Legations" in the *Yellow Pages*.

Cycling Bicycles are carried free on trains outside of peak hours (Mon–Fri 6–9am & 3.30–7.30pm) and on ferries at all times if there is room in the bicycle racks. The Roads and Traffic Authority (RTA; T 13 2213) has some brochures listing bicycle routes which they will post out, but the best source of information is Bicycle NSW at Level 2, 209 Castlereagh St, cnr Bathurst St (Mon–Fri 9am–5.30pm; T 02/9283 5200). Two of their useful publications are *Cycling Around Sydney* ($11) and *Discovering NSW and Canberra Bike and Walking Paths* ($18.65). Recommended central bicycle shops include Clarence Street Cyclery, 104 Clarence St (T 02/9299 4962); Wooleys Wheels, 82 Oxford St, Paddington (T 02/9331 2671); and Inner City Cycles, 31 Glebe Point Rd, Glebe (T 02/9660 6605). The cheapest **bike rental** is at Cheeky Monkey Cycle Co, 456 Pitt St, City (open daily; T 02/9212 446); mountain bikes cost $25 per day, and they also sell bikes. Clarence Street Cyclery also hire mountain bikes ($65 per day, $110 per weekend), as do Inner City Cycles ($33 per 24hr, $55 per weekend; open daily). For a leisurely ride in the park, Centennial Park Cycles, 50 Clovelly Rd, Randwick (open daily; T 02/9398 5027) hire bikes at hourly rates (mountain bikes $9 per hour, bikes for kids $7 per hour).

Disabled travellers ACROD NSW, 24 Cabarita Rd, Cabarita, NSW 2137 (T 02/9743 2699, F 9743 2899); People with Disabilities NSW, 52 Pitt St, Redfern, NSW 2016 (T 02/9319 6622). Randwick Council (Customer Services, 30 Francis St, Randwick, NSW 2031; T 02/9399 0999) have installed wheelchair accessible ramps at Clovelly and Malabar beaches; they also publish a series of mobility maps which they will post out. For taxis, try Wheelchair Accessible Taxis (T 02/8332 0200) or ABC (T 13 2522).

Diving One of the best places to dive is at Gordon's Bay in Clovelly, and off the North and South Heads. Prodive Coogee, 27 Alfreda St, Coogee (T 02/9665 6333, W www.prodive.com.au), offer boat and shore dives anywhere between Camp Cove and La Perouse (double boat dive with gear $135, double shore dive $105). If you plan to dive a lot, joining the Prodive Club for $50 will save you around 30 percent on dives. Cronulla Dive Centre, 40 Kingsway, Cronulla (T 02/9523 7222, W www.cronulladive.com.au), do local shore dives (free but gear rental costs $55 per day) and also organize dives and weekends away up and down the NSW coast. Dive Centre, 10 Belgrave St, Manly (T 02/9977 4355, W www.divesydney.com), offer shore dives to Shelley Beach, Fairlight, Little Manly and Harbord plus boat dives off North and South Head and Long Reef (boat dive with full gear $80, shore dive with gear $60).

Cars – buying and selling

Sydney is the most popular place to buy a car or campervan in which to travel around Australia; the information below is specific to buying a car in NSW – for general background on buying and selling a car, see Basics p.42.

Before you start looking for wheels, pick up the NRMA's complimentary *Worry Free Guide to Buying a Car* from the NRMA offices at 388 George St, City, or 17 Newland St, Bondi Junction (☎ 13 2132). If you're a member of a motoring association overseas, you'll have reciprocal membership of the NRMA (otherwise there's a $94.60 initial joining fee then the annual charge is $50.60), which entitles you to roadside assistance and a $120 inspection and appraisal of a potential purchase (call ☎ 02/9892 0355 to book a vehicle inspection). The *Weekly Trading Post*, out every Thursday, has a big secondhand car section and it's worth checking through this to get a general idea of prices of cars bought direct from sellers; it's good also if you know a fair bit about cars and want to go it alone (see "Getting around" in Basics for general advice), though you would probably need to rent a car to get to most of the far-flung suburban locations. The *Sydney Morning Herald*'s Friday edition has a "Drive" supplement which has full-page ads for secondhand dealers and private used cars for sale at the pricier end of the secondhand market. Demand to see the pink slip (certificate of roadworthiness), as it proves the car is safe. In NSW the seller is under no obligation to show a certificate of roadworthiness but the buyer is entitled to ask to see one. If you're seriously thinking about buying, call REVS on ☎ 02/9600 0022 to check the validity of NSW-registered cars; quote registration, engine and chassis numbers and they will inform you of any payments owing or unpaid parking fines. Call the Roads and Traffic Authority (RTA; ☎ 13 2213) to double-check that the registration has not been cancelled.

As Sydney is the first place where most tourists arrive, the city is well-equipped with dealerships who will arrange to **buy back** the vehicle they've sold you at the end of your trip for a 30–50 percent buy-back if you provide a roadworthy certificate (see "Getting around" in Basics for general advice). One of the longest running is **Travellers Auto Barn**, 177 William St, Kings Cross (☎ 02/9360 1500, ⊛ www.travellers-autobarn.com.au), who also have offices in Brisbane and Cairns. Others include **Auto Becker**, 752 Parramatta Rd, Lewisham, NSW 2049 (☎ 02/9568 4455, ⓕ 9337 4202), who also offer a 12-month warranty on cars purchased for over $4000 (payout of $1000 only); and **Jalopy Shoppe**, 690 Parramatta Rd, Croydon, NSW 2132 (☎ 02/9798 8666, ⓕ 9797 9604, ⓔ jalopy@ozemail.com.au).

The Backpackers Car Market, Kings Cross Car Park, Level 2, Ward Ave (daily 9am–6pm; ☎ 02/9358 5000 or free call 1800 808 188, ⓕ 9358 5102, ⊛ www.carmarket.com.au) is the only place where it's legal for travellers to resell their cars at the Cross – selling on the street is not allowed. Dealers are barred, and fees for sellers (if you have a pink slip) are set at $15 per day or $40 per week; inspection reports for the seller cost around $25 – call the car market for recommended mechanics. One of the advantages of the **car market** for sellers is that it's one of the few places where you will be able to sell a car registered in another state. If you're thinking of buying here, get here early for the best choice: many of the vehicles come ready equipped with camping gear and other extras at good prices. But think carefully about whether you really want to buy a car that's already done the rounds of Australia. The guys will advise you and help with the paperwork, and they'll even oversee the exchanging of the contract to make sure everything's done properly, and arrange third-party property **insurance** ($210 for 3 months, $375 for 12 months) – the NRMA refuses to provide cover for overseas travellers. Another car market is held on Sunday at Flemington Market opposite Flemington Station, Austen Avenue entrance (8am–4pm; ☎ 02/9818 3085), but is better for buying than selling: if you're trying to sell a vehicle that's travelled around Australia, particularly if the clock is past 200,000km, local buyers won't be interested; besides, fees for sellers are steep at around $60 per day (no bookings required).

Emergency T 000 for fire, police or ambulance.

Hospitals Sydney Hospital, Macquarie St
(T 02/9382 7111); St Vincents Hospital, cnr
Victoria and Burton streets, Darlinghurst
(T 02/9339 1111).

Immigration Department of Immigration and
Multicultural Affairs, 88 Cumberland St, The Rocks
(T 02/9258 4555).

Internet access You can surf the Net for free at the
State Library, Macquarie St (see p.123), but can't
send emails. Many backpackers hostels have internet terminals, and dedicated internet places have
sprung up all over Sydney, with a glut of cheap
places around Kings Cross. Global Gossip has six
offices (all daily 9am–midnight; $3.95 for 30min,
$4.95 for 1hr), including 770 George St, City; 111
Darlinghurst Rd, Kings Cross; 317 Glebe Pt Rd,
Glebe; 37 Hall St, Bondi; and 108 Oxford St,
Darlinghurst; they also offer cut-rate international
calls and postage. Phone.Net Cafe, 73–75 Hall St,
Bondi (daily 9am–9pm; from $1.10 for 10min, $2.20
for 45min) is a lively café haunt in its own right, as is
the Well Connected Cafe, 35 Glebe Point Rd, Glebe
(daily 7am–midnight; $6 per hour, $1 per 15min).

Left luggage Cloakrooms at Town Hall Station
and Central Station (country trains) are both open
Mon–Sat 9am–4.40pm ($1.50 per 24hr); also
lockers at the airport and the Sydney Coach
Terminal ($6, $9 or $11 per 24hr).

Libraries City of Sydney Public Library, just
behind the Town Hall on Sydney Square
(Mon–Thurs 9am–7pm, Fri 9am–6pm, Sat
9am–noon; T 02/9265 9470). Also see the State
Library, p.123.

Maps Map World, 371 Pitt St, City T 02/9261
3601); also see "Parks and wildlife", below.

Medical centres Broadway Medical Centre
(185–211 Broadway near Glebe; T 02/9212
2733), general practitioners open Mon–Sat, no
appointment necessary; Skin Cancer Centre,
ground floor, 403 George St T 02/9262 4877);
Sydney Sexual Health Centre, Nightingale Wing,
Sydney Hospital, Macquarie St T 02/9382 7440),
free tests, counselling and condoms; Travellers
Medical and Vaccination Centre, 7th floor, 428
George St T 02/9221 7133,
W www.tmvc.com.au).

Motorbikes Wentworth Ave in the city has a con-
centration of motorbike salerooms for new models.
For secondhand motorbikes there's Bikescape, 154
Abercrombie St, cnr Cleveland St, Chippendale
(T 02/9699 4722, W www.bikescape.com.au),
with scooters from $65 per day and motorbikes
from $90. Maverick Motorcycles, 133 Parramatta
Rd, Homebush, NSW 2140 T 02/9746 2005,
(F) 9746 2006,

W www.maverickmotorcycles.com.au), specializes
in selling and exchanging travellers' motorbikes.

NRMA Head office, 388 George St T 13 2132,
W www.nrma.com.au). Road maps of NSW and
other states, a useful map of Sydney and other
cities, comprehensive accommodation directories
and lots more information, much of it free to members of associated organizations.

Parks and wildlife information The NPWS
(Cadman's Cottage, 110 George St, The Rocks;
T 02/9247 8861, W www.npws.nsw.gov.au) has
details on Sydney Harbour National Park and
books tours to its islands; they do not arrange
camping permits. There are also NPWS offices at
Nielson Park (see p.142), North Head (see p.154),
La Perouse (see p.156) and Botany Bay National
Park (see p.157). The Sydney Map Shop, part of
the Surveyor-General's Department (23–33 Bridge
St; T 02/9228 6111) sells detailed National Park
and bushwalking maps of NSW.

Pharmacy Crest Hotel Pharmacy, 60a Darlinghurst
Rd, Kings Cross (Tues–Sat 8.30am–2am, Sun &
Mon 8.30am–midnight; T 02/9358 1822).

Police Headquarters at 14 College St T 02/9339
0277); emergency T 000.

Post office The General Post Office (GPO) is in
Martin Place (Mon–Fri 8.15am–5.30pm, Sat
9am–1pm). Poste restante is located at the post
office in the Hunter Connection shopping mall at
310 George St (Mon–Fri 8.15am–6pm), opposite
Wynyard Station. Log your name in the computer
to see if there is any post for you before queueing.
Poste Restante, Sydney GPO, Sydney, NSW 2000.

Public holidays In addition to the Australia-wide
public holidays (see Basics, p.59), the following
are celebrated only in NSW: Bank Holiday – first
Monday in August; Labour Day – first Monday in
October; Queen's Birthday – first Monday in June.

Scenic flights Sydney Harbour Seaplanes, Rose
Bay (T 02/9388 1978) can take you on a 15min
scenic flight over Sydney Harbour and Bondi Beach,
or drop you off to lunch at Palm Beach or one of the
Hawkesbury River restaurants. The price, $220, is
for the whole six-seater plane, so it's very affordable if you can get a party together. They can also
take people to destinations such as Palm Beach and
the Hawkesbury River; price on application.

Swimming pools Most pools are outdoors and
unheated, and open from the long weekend in
October until Easter. The best pool, open all year, is
the heated outdoor North Sydney Olympic Pool, near
the water's edge on Alfred South St, Milsons Point
(Mon–Fri 6am–9pm, Sat & Sun 7am–7pm; $3.50).
There's another heated outdoor pool at Victoria Park,
City Rd, next to Sydney University (Mon–Fri
6am–7.15pm, Sat & Sun 7am–5.45pm; $3; pool and

gym $7). The heated 33-metre indoor pool of the Annette Kellerman Aquatic Centre in Enmore Park off Enmore Rd stays open all year (daily 6am–8pm, April–Sept weekends closes 6pm; $3.20). Inner-city outdoor pools are at Prince Alfred Park, Chalmers St, Surry Hills (daily 6.30am–8pm) and the Andrew "Boy" Charlton in The Domain (see p.124). The Cook and Phillip Park Aquatic and Leisure Centre, cnr William and College streets, has a 50-metre heated indoor pool (Mon–Fri 6am–10pm, Sat & Sun 7am–8pm; $4.50, pool and gym $11). For the ultimate swimming experience, head out west to the Olympic site for the Sydney International Aquatic Centre (see pp.130–131).

Taxis ABC (T 13 2522); Legion (T 13 1451); Premier (T 13 1017); RSL (T 13 1581); St George (T 13 2166); Taxis Combined (T 02/8332 8888). For harbour water taxis call Taxis Afloat (T 02/9955 3222).

Telephones The unattended Telstra Pay Phone Centre, 231 Elizabeth St, City (Mon–Fri 7am–11pm, Sat & Sun 7am–5pm) has private booths. Global Gossip (see "Internet access" overleaf) offer discount-rate international calls.

Trains All out-of-town trains depart from the country trains terminal of Central Station (information and booking 6.30am–10pm; T 13 2232). There are Countrylink Travel Centres (W www.countrylink.nsw.gov.au) at Central Station (T 02/9379 3800); Wynyard Station (T 02/9224 4744); in the Queen Victoria Building Arcade at Town Hall Station (T 02/9379 3600); and at Circular Quay (T 02/9224 3400) and Bondi Junction Station (T 02/9379 3777). Interstate trains should be booked as early as possible, especially the Indian Pacific and Brisbane–Cairns trains.

Travel agents Backpackers Travel Centre, Shop 33, Imperial Arcade, near Centrepoint, Pitt St (T 02/9231 3699, W www.backpackerstravel.net.au), do everything from international flights to bus passes; offices also at 87 Glebe Point Rd, Glebe (T 02/9552 4544), Bronka Arcade, 157 Oxford St, Bondi Junction (T 02/9369 1331), and 37 Hall St, Bondi Beach (T 02/9369 1331). Flight Centre, 52 Martin Place (T 02/9235 0166, W www.flightcentre.com), also at several other locations, offer cheap domestic and international air tickets. STA Travel has many branches, including Shop 205, Broadway Shopping Centre, Bay St, Broadway (T 02/9211 2563, W www.statravelaus.com.au). The British travel agency, Trailfinders, have a branch in Sydney at 8 Spring St (T 02/9247 7666, W www.trailfinders.com). YHA Travel, 422 Kent St, behind the Town Hall (T 02/9261 1111, W www.yha.com.au) also has a branch at Sydney

Central YHA, 11 Rawson Place off Eddy Ave (T 02/9281 9444), and offer excellent Sydney tours. For details of tours from Sydney see p.192.

Water sports Rose Bay Aquatic Hire, just near the waterfront at 1 Vickery Ave, Rose Bay (T 02/9371 7036), rents out catamarans ($25 first hour, $15 thereafter), windsurfers ($15 per hour), surf skis and kayaks ($10 per hour) and motorboats (weekends $50 for the first two hours, $15 for each subsequent hour; cheaper deals midweek). Balmoral Windsurf, Sail and Kayak School is open all year at the Balmoral boatshed, southern end of the Esplanade, Balmoral (T 02/9960 5344, W www.balmoralwindsurfing.net.au), and rents out sailboards (from $27 per hour for beginners, $38 per hour for intermediate and advanced), as well as giving sailboarding lessons (beginners $175 per 5hr lesson; improving techniques $195 per 6hr lesson) and offering a Hobiecat sailing course (6hr; $195). Northside Sailing School, Spit Bridge, Mosman (T 02/9969 3972, W www.northsidesailing.com.au) specializes in weekend dinghy sailing courses on Middle Harbour during the sailing season (Sept–April); tuition is one-on-one ($110 per 3hr lesson). They also offer boats for rent for $30 for the first hour and $20 for subsequent hours. Teamsail, based at the Royal Prince Alfred Yacht Club, Mitala St, Newport (T 02/9999 3047, W www.yachtcharter.com.au), offer all-year yachting courses on Pittwater. The two-day course costs $345 (maximum five participants), and you can develop your skills at follow-up twilight sails (summer Mon & Thurs; 2hr) and Sunday sails (last Sun of month; 4hr), both $35. For other sailing courses and yacht hire contact the NSW Yachting Association (T 02/9660 1266, W www.nsw.yachting.org.au). Experienced sailors can charter yachts from Sydney by Sail (T 02/9280 1110; see box on pp.106–107 for details). Natural Wanders Sea Kayak Adventures (T 02/9899 1001, W www.kayaksydney.com or W www.naturalwanders.com.au) arrange sea-kayaking in the harbour: their most popular trip is the Bridge Paddle ($65; 4hr; suitable for beginners) which starts from Lavender Bay near Luna Park, goes under the Harbour Bridge and explores the North Shore, with a picnic included. For scuba-diving, see "Diving", p.187.

Western Union, office in Travelex, 37–49 Pitt St (daily 8.30am–6.30pm; T 02/9241 5722).

Women The big events are the Reclaim the Night march in late October and events around International Women's Day in March. Contact the Women's Information and Referral Service (Mon–Fri 9am–5pm; free call T 1800 817 227) for information on this and women's organizations, services and referrals, or try The Women's Library, 8–10 Brown St, Newtown (Tues–Fri 11am–8pm, Sat & Sun

11am–5pm), which lends feminist and lesbian literature. Jesse Street National Women's Library, housed in the Town Hall, 456 Kent St (Mon–Fri 10am–2pm), is an archive collecting literature detailing Australian women's history and writing. The Feminist Bookshop is in Orange Grove Plaza on Balmain Rd, Lilyfield (T) 02/9810 2666). For medical advice, contact the Women's Health Clinic, 139 Macquarie St, City (T) 02/9247 1555).

Work If you have a working holiday visa, you shouldn't have too much trouble finding some sort of work in Sydney, particularly in hospitality or retail. Offices of the government-run Centrelink (T) 13 2850) have a database of jobs; the most central offices are at George and Redfern streets, Redfern; 151 Crown St, Darlinghurst; and Level 6, Carousel Centre, Bondi Junction. Centrelink also refer job-seekers to several private "Job Network" agencies, including Employment National (T) 13 3444). The private agency Troy's (Level 1, 89 York St; (T) 02/9290 2955), specializes in the hospitality industry. If you have some office or professional skills, there are plenty of temp agencies that are more than keen to take on travellers: flick through "Employment agencies" in the *Yellow Pages*. For a whole range of work, from unskilled to professional, the multinational Manpower is a good bet (T) 13 2502). Otherwise, scour hostel notice boards and the *Sydney Morning Herald*'s employment pages – Saturday's bumper edition is best.

YHA New South Wales , 422 Kent St, behind the Town Hall (Mon–Fri 9am–5pm, Thurs until 6pm, Sat 9am–noon;(T) 02/9261 1111). Membership and travel centre.

Around Sydney

If life in the fast lane is taking its toll, Sydney's residents can easily get away from it all. Right on their doorstep, golden beaches and magnificent national parks beckon, interwoven with intricate waterways. Everything in this part of the chapter can be done as a day-trip from the city, although some require an overnight stay to explore more fully. See the box overleaf for some of the huge variety of tours on offer.

North of Sydney the Hawkesbury River flows into the jagged jaws of the aptly named **Broken Bay**, which streaks across the map like a bolt of lightning. The entire area is surrounded by bush, with the huge spaces of the **Ku-Ring-Gai Chase National Park** in the south and the **Brisbane Waters National Park** in the north. Beyond Broken Bay, the **Central Coast** between Gosford and Newcastle is an ideal spot for a bit of fishing, sailing and lazing around. **Newcastle** is more attractive than its reputation as a coal and steel city might suggest. Immediately beyond, however, are the bountiful vineyards of the **Hunter Valley**, which make a great day out, with visits to wineries interspersed with some gentle driving on country roads.

To the **west**, you escape suburbia to emerge at the foot of the beautiful World Heritage-listed **Blue Mountains**, while the scenic Hawkesbury–Nepean river valley is home to historic rural towns such as **Richmond** and **Windsor**.

Heading **south**, the **Royal National Park** is an hour's drive away, while on the coast beyond are a string of small, laid-back towns – Waterfall, Stanwell Park, Wombarra – with beautiful, unspoilt **beaches**. The industrial city of **Wollongong** and neighbouring Port Kembla are impressively located between the Illawarra Escarpment and the sea, but of paltry interest to visitors, although more interesting spots cluster around. Inland, the **Southern Highlands** are covered with yet more national parks, punctuated by pleasing little towns such as **Bundanoon** and **Berrima**.

Tours from Sydney span the range from a day spent staring out the window of a bus to two days canyoning in the Blue Mountains. Listed below are a couple of regular bus-tour operators, but you'll almost certainly have a better time with one of the outfits who specialize in small-group tours, quite often with an emphasis on physical activities such as bushwalking, horseriding, white-water rafting or abseiling. Many hostels organize their own trips – most often to the beach – which are usually fun and tremendously good value. YHA and VIP cardholders are offered substantial discounts on many tours – we have quoted full prices only.

One-way tours can be the next best thing to going by car: small groups in minibuses travel from Sydney to Melbourne (for example), taking detours to attractions along the way that you'd never be able to reach on public transport.

As well as booking direct on the numbers given, most of the tours listed below can be booked through YHA Travel (⊕02/9261 1111 or 9281 9444, ⊜travel@yhansw.org.au).

Return tours

AAT Kings (⊕02/9518 6095, ⊛www.aatkings.com.au). One of the largest operators, its big-group bus tours cover city sights, wildlife parks, the Blue Mountains, Jenolan Caves, the Hawkesbury River and the Hunter Valley. Admissions and hotel pick-ups and drop-offs included in price.

Blue Mountains Canyon Tours (⊕ & ⊕ 02/9371 5859, ⊛www.canyontours.com.au). Exploring the Blue Mountains' deep canyons requires a thrilling mixture of abseiling down waterfalls, swimming through cave slots, bushwalking and rock climbing. Wet canyoning is offered Oct–April, dry canyoning is available all year. Depending on the area or the number of abseils, trips range from $95 to $149. The most popular canyoning trip is to Fortress Canyon (grade 2), near Leura, picking up Sydney 7am and returning 7pm.

CityRail (⊕13 1500). Day-trips by rail can be very good value, generally covering all transport and entry fees – trips include the Blue Mountains, and the Hawkesbury River (which includes a cruise). Details and tickets from CityRail at Circular Quay or Central Station.

East Coast Motorcycle Tours (⊕0408 618 982, ⊛www.eastcoast-mc-tours.com.au). Trips to anywhere you fancy around Sydney on Harley-Davidsons; from 1hr ($90) to a full day ($345).

Oz Trek (⊕02/9360 3444, ⊛www.oztrek.com.au). Highly recommended active full-day tours to the Blue Mountains ($54), with a choice of three bushwalks (30min–1hr 30min). Small groups (max 21). The trip can be extended to overnight packages with three options to choose from: horse riding ($189), abseiling ($179), or a visit to Jenolan Caves ($165–189).

Waves Surf School (⊕0414 682 228 or free call 1800 851 101). One- or two-day "Learn To Surf" trips in the Royal National Park (1 day including lunch $55; 2 days including meals, bushwalking and camping or beachhouse accommodation $129; both include tuition, unlimited use of gear and park fees). Pick-ups and drop-offs from Bondi, Coogee, Kings Cross and the City.

North

The **Hawkesbury River** widens and slows as it approaches the South Pacific, joining Berowra Creek, Cowan Creek, Pittwater and Brisbane Water in the system of flooded valleys that form **Broken Bay**. The bay and its surrounding inlets are a haven for anglers, sailors and windsurfers, while the surrounding bushland is virtually untouched. Three major national parks surround the

Wildframe Ecotours (☎02/9314 0658, ⊛www.wildframe.com.au). Two full-day tours to the Blue Mountains, the first for fit walkers, the second for lazier types. The Grand Canyon Eco-tour ($72) is a small group bushwalk (max 16) through the Grand Canyon, on which you'll see kangaroos and learn how to throw a boomerang. The Blue Mountains Bush Tour ($84) is a more relaxed day with short bushwalks and lunch at a mountain lodge, plus the kangaroos and boomerang throwing. The same company offers a tour to the Hunter Valley via the Hawkesbury River and Wattagans National Park, stopping at four vineyards, with a BBQ lunch at one of them, and returning via the Central Coast, with a pelican-feeding stop at The Entrance ($95 including lunch). Pick-ups from Kings Cross and city accommodation.

Wonderbus (☎02/9555 9800 or free call 1800 669 800, ⊛www.wonderbus.com.au). Good-value day-tours to the Blue Mountains, including a drive through the Olympic site, wildlife-watching at morning or dusk and 2–3hr bushwalk ($70). The day-trip can be extended into an overnight package including abseiling ($230), a trip to the Jenolan Caves ($215) or an off-road 4WD trip ($300). Another pricey day-tour goes to the Hunter Valley and Port Stephens – wine tasting followed by a dolphin cruise ($185).

One-way tours

Ando's Outback Tours (☎02/9559 2901 or free call 1800 228 828, ⊛www .outbacktours.com.au). Popular five-day tour from Sydney to Byron Bay but taking an inland route, getting well off the beaten track via Coonabarabran and Lightning Ridge ($460 all inclusive). Tours leave every Sun; you can return to Sydney on Sat for $35. Book well in advance.

Autopia Tours (free call ☎1800 000 507, ⊛www.autopiatours.com.au). Run by the excellent long-established Autopia Tours, this three-day Highland Explorer tour ($170) from Sydney to Melbourne goes via the Blue Mountains, Jenolan Caves, Canberra, the Snowy Mountains and Victoria's Alpine Way. Buses are small-seaters, with the driver acting as your guide; price includes transport only – you can choose to stay at hostels, campsites or motels en route (Katoomba and Canberra), depending on your budget. Entry fees also extra. You can also take a shortened version to Canberra ($70).

Oz Experience, 88–96 Darlinghurst Rd, Kings Cross (Australia-wide ☎1300/300 028, Sydney ☎02/9368 1766, ⊛www.ozexperience.com.au). A cross between transport and tours that go a little off the beaten track, with a hop-on, hop-off component lasting six months aimed at young independent travellers. Their scheduled routes include Sydney to Cairns in nine days ($365), and Sydney to Melbourne in four days via the south coast, Canberra, the Snowy Mountains and Phillip Island ($240).

Pioneering Spirit (free call ☎1800 672 422, ⊛www.pioneeringspirit.com.au). Another tour that heads to beach-heaven Byron, this three-day excursion goes via the Hunter Valley for a spot of wine-tasting; $235 including meals, accommodation and entry fees (or $270 if you want to return to Sydney afterwards). Tours leave every Fri.

Surfaris (free call ☎1800 634 951, Byron Bay ☎02/4845 9193, ⊛www.surfaris.com). Excellent five-day surfing trip, Sydney to Byron Bay; you're taught how to surf and judge the waves and more experienced folk often come along for the ride. Price ($449) includes gear, lessons, meals, and secluded camping by the beach with a chance to spot wildlife.

Hawkesbury River: **Ku-Ring-Gai Chase** in the south, **Brisbane Waters** facing it across the bay, and **Dharug**, inland to the west.

The **Pacific Highway** up here, partly supplanted by the Sydney–Newcastle Freeway, is fast and efficient, though not particularly attractive until you're approaching Ku-Ring-Gai Chase; if you want to detour into the park or towards Brooklyn, don't take the freeway. The **rail** lines follow the road almost as far as Broken Bay, before they take a scenic diversion through Brooklyn and Brisbane Waters to Woy Woy and Gosford.

Ku-Ring-Gai Chase National Park

Ku-Ring-Gai Chase is much the best known of New South Wales' national parks and, with the Pacific Highway running all the way up one side, is also the easiest to get to. The bushland scenery is crisscrossed by walking tracks, which you can explore to seek out Aboriginal rock paintings, or just to get away from it all and see the forest and its wildlife. Only 24km from the city centre, the huge park's unspoilt beauty is enhanced by the presence of water on three sides: the Hawkesbury, its inlet Cowan Creek, and the expanse of **Pittwater**, an inlet of Broken Bay. From Palm Beach you can take a boat cruise (see p.196) through all these waters to the park's most popular picnic spot at **Bobbin Head**, with a colourful marina. At the **Kalkari Visitor Centre** (daily 9am–5pm), on the Ku-Ring-Gai Chase Road, you can watch videos about the area's Aboriginal heritage and the wildlife you might encounter, pick up information about walks in the park or take a guided walk led by volunteers. The Birrawanna Walking Track leads from here for 1.5km to the park headquarters, which can also be approached by car further along Ku-Ring-Gai Chase Road. The NPWS **Bobbin Head Information Centre** (daily 9am–4pm; ☎02/9472 8949) is located inside the Art Deco *Bobbin Inn* which also has a very pleasant restaurant, popular for weekend breakfasts and Sunday afternoon jazz. There are four road entrances to the park and a $10 entrance fee for cars. Without your own transport, the best means of getting here are the ferries to the Pittwater side, or by train to Turramurra Station and then a private Hornsby Bus #577 (☎02/9457 8888 for times) to the Bobbin Head Road entrance; some buses continue down to Bobbin Head itself.

Waratah Park and Pittwater

One of Sydney's oldest wildlife reserves, **Waratah Park** (daily 10am–5pm; $14.50, child $7.30, family $39; koala patting hourly 11am–4pm & 4.30pm; ☎02/9968 1111) sits in the middle of this stunning scenery on Namba Road, off Mona Vale Road. Waratah is most famous as the home of **Skippy**, the bush kangaroo, television's first marsupial star: you can still see Skippy (or at least her fifth- or sixth-generation descendant) amongst the free-ranging kangaroos (which can be fed with special food purchased here), and visit the Ranger Station where most of the filming was done. To get here, take the train to Chatswood (North Shore line) and then bus #284 from stand "S" of the interchange (☎02/9450 1236 for times).

From West Head at the northeastern corner of Ku-Ring-Gai Chase, there are superb views across Pittwater to the Barrenjoey Lighthouse at Palm Beach (see p.155). The **Garigal Aboriginal Heritage Walk** (3.5km circuit) heads from West Head Road to the Aboriginal rock engravings and hand art, the most accessible Aboriginal art site in the park. The only place to **camp** is The Basin (☎02/9451 8124 for bookings) on Pittwater, reached via the Palm Beach Ferry Service (see p.156). Facilities at the site are minimal so bring everything with you.

If you want to stay in the park in rather more comfort, there's a very popular **YHA hostel** (☎02/9999 2196, ℱ9997 4296, ℮pittwater@rivernet.com.au; rooms ❹, dorms ❶–❷; phone bookings essential and well in advance for weekends) at **Halls Wharf**. It's one of New South Wales' most scenically sited – a rambling old house surrounded by bush and with a verandah where you can feed rainbow lorikeets and look down onto the water; sailing lessons can also be arranged. You must bring everything with you – the last food (and bottle) shop is at Church Point where the **ferry** departs to Halls Wharf (last departure Mon–Fri 7pm, Sat & Sun 6.30pm; call ☎02/9999 3492 for times; $6.50 return).

Cuddly koalas

It is no longer legal to physically pick up and hold a koala in NSW wildlife parks but photo-opportunity "patting" sessions are still on offer. If meeting Skippy and cuddling up close to the koalas at Waratah is your kind of thing – and who could resist – there are several other hands-on wildlife experiences around Sydney you might like to try.

The **Koala Park Sanctuary** (daily 9am–5pm; adults $12.50, children $7, family pass $35; ☏02/9481 3141, ⓦwww.koalaparksanctuary.com.au) was established as a safe haven for koalas in 1935 and has since opened its gates to many other Australian natives – wombats, possums, kangaroos and birds of all kinds. Koala patting sessions are held daily at 10.20am, 11.45am, 2pm and 3pm. It's around 25km north of Sydney, not far from the Pacific Highway on Castle Hill Road, West Pennant Hills. To get here on public transport take the train from Central Station to Pennant Hills and then bus #651 or #655 towards Glenorie (Mon–Sat).

At **Featherdale Wildlife Park** (daily 9am–5pm; $14, children $7, family $36; ☏02/9622 1644, ⓦwww.featherdale.com.au), patting koalas is the special attraction (available all day). Featherdale is at 217 Kildare Rd, Doonside, 30km west of Sydney off the Western Highway between Parramatta and Penrith; take the train to Blacktown Station (Emu Plains line) and then bus #725.

Wonderland Sydney (daily 10am–5pm, wildlife park from 9am; $16.50, children $9.90, family $47.50; or $42.90, children $29.70 for the whole complex, including all rides and events; ☏02/9830 9100, ⓦwww.wonderland.com.au) is not far away from Featherdale Wildlife Park. It's a huge family entertainment complex encompassing shows, giant waterslides, three roller coasters (including *The Demon*, one of the fastest in the southern hemisphere) and other theme park rides (queues of up to an hour on a busy day), plus the **Australian Wildlife Park** (☏02/9830 9187), where the "meet the animals" experience includes koalas, kangaroos, echidnas, wombats, emus, goannas, saltwater crocodiles (from a discreet distance) and forest birds in simulated natural habitats – it's wildly popular with children. Wonderland Sydney is on Wallgrove Road, Rooty Hill, not far off the M4 approaching Penrith. To get there by public transport, take a train to Rooty Hill Station (on the Emu Plains line) and then a special Busways service (☏02/9625 8900 for times) from outside the Commonwealth Bank. Alternatively, AAT Kings (☏02/9252 2788) offers a bus transfer and admission package.

There are two direct buses to Church Point: #E86 from Central Station or #156 from Manly Wharf; it's then a ten-minute uphill walk. Alternatively there's a 24-hour water-taxi service from Newport with Pink Water Taxi (☏0428 238 190); bus #190 from Wynyard runs up the coast to Newport.

The Church Point–Halls Wharf ferry service can also get you to and from **Scotland Island** at the southern end of Pittwater, which it stops at on the forty-minute round trip from Church Point. The bush-clad island is residential only with no sealed roads or shops, just a school, a kindergarten and a bush fire brigade.

The Hawkesbury River

One of New South Wales' prettiest rivers, with bush covering its banks for much of its course and some interesting old settlements alongside, the **Hawkesbury River** has its source in the Great Dividing Range and flows out to sea at Broken Bay. For information about the many national parks along the river, contact the the NPWS in Sydney (☏02/9247 8861) or at 370 Windsor Rd in Richmond (☏02/4588 5247). Short of chartering your own boat, the best way to explore the river system is to take a cruise (see box overleaf); the River Boat Mail Run is probably the most interesting.

Exploring the Hawkesbury River system

Brooklyn, just above the western mass of Ku-Ring-Gai Chase National Park, and easily reached by train from Central, is the base for Hawkesbury River Ferries (☏02/9985 7566), whose River Boat Mail Run still takes letters, as well as tourists, up and down the river. Departures are from Brooklyn Wharf on Dangar Road (Mon–Fri 9.30am excluding public holidays, connecting with the 8.16am train from Central Station in Sydney and the 8.16am from Gosford; 4hr; $33 including morning tea, or good-value combined train-boat ticket available; booking essential). Hawkesbury River Ferries also offers two-hour coffee cruises towards the mouth of the river (Mon–Fri 1.30pm, Sun 11am & 1.30pm; $20); you can get to Patonga at the edge of Brisbane Waters National Park on this service ($8 single, $16 return).

Gosford's Public Wharf is the starting point for the MV *Lady Kendall* (☏02/4323 1655, ⊛www.ozemail.com.au/~starshp), which cruises both Brisbane Water and Broken Bay (Mon–Wed, Sat & Sun, daily during school & public holidays, 10.15am & 1pm; 2hr 30min; $18; bookings essential).

Windsor is the base for Windsor River Cruises (☏02/9831 6630, ⊛www.hawkesburyvalley.com.au), with cruises Sun & Wed only: coffee cruise (2hr 15min; $20), Bridge to Bridge cruise from Windsor to Kangaroo Point in Brooklyn ($65 includes lunch at Wisemans Ferry; 9hr), and the Tizzana Winery cruise including wine tasting and a smorgasboard lunch ($60; 6hr).

Woy Woy is also a port of call for the MV *Lady Kendall* (see above) at 10.35am and 12.10pm.

Boat and houseboat rentals

The Hawkesbury Boating Centre, on Dangar Road, opposite the railway station in Brooklyn (☏02/9985 7252) hires out **boats** which seat up to eight people (from $60.50 half-day, $82.50 full day, more at weekends) and are perfect for fishing expeditions around the mouth of the Hawkesbury or Dangar Island. The centre has a fishing shop and sells bait supplies; you'd need to buy rather than hire rods here. **Houseboats** can be good value if you can get a group together. The Sydney Visitor Centre in Sydney (☏02/9667 6050) has details of operators, or try Able Hawkesbury River Houseboats, on River Road in Wisemans Ferry (☏02/4566 4308 or free call 1800 024 979, ⊛www.hawkesburyhouseboats.com.au), with prices starting from $1230 per week for six people, or Ripples Houseboats, 87 Brooklyn Rd, Brooklyn (☏02/9985 7788, ⊛www.ripples.com.au), which has boats sleeping two to ten people; a six-berther costs around $700–990 for a weekend (Fri 2pm to Mon 9am), or $750–1190 during the week (Mon 11am to Fri 9am), depending on the season.

Upstream: Wisemans Ferry

The first ferry across the Hawkesbury River was opened by ex-convict Solomon Wiseman ten years after he was granted 200 acres of river frontage in 1817, at the spot now known as **WISEMANS FERRY**. The crossing forged an inland connection between Sydney and the Hunter Valley via the convict-built Great North Road. Unfortunately, travellers on this isolated route were easy prey for marauding bushrangers and it was largely abandoned for the longer but safer coastal route. Today it's a popular recreational spot for day-trippers – just a little over an hour from Sydney by car, and with access to the **Dharug National Park** over the river by a free 24-hour car ferry. Dharug's rugged sandstone cliffs and gullies shelter Aboriginal rock engravings which can be visited only on ranger-led trips during school holidays; there's a camping area at Mill Creek (call Gosford NPWS on ☏02/4324 4911 for details of walks and camping; bookings for both essential at weekends and holiday periods). Open to walkers, cyclists and horse-riders but not vehicles, the **Old**

Great North Road was literally carved out of the rock by hundreds of convicts from 1829; you can camp en route at the Ten Mile Hollow camping area.

The settlement of Wisemans Ferry was based around Wisemans home, Cobham Hall, built in 1826. Much of the original building still exists in the blue-painted *Wisemans Ferry Inn* on the Old Great North Road (℡02/4566 4301, ℻9629 1757; pub ❺, motel ❹), with characterful **rooms** upstairs sharing bathrooms, and en-suite motel-style rooms outside at the back. Bistro meals are served daily and there's entertainment on Sunday afternoons. Just across the road, with extensive grounds fronting onto the river, is the contrastingly modern *Retreat at Wisemans* (℡02/4566 4422, ℻4566 4613, ⓦwww.wisemans.com.au; B&B ❽), a 54-room resort. The upmarket motel rooms can't compete with the inn's colonial charm, but the location is suberbly scenic and facilities include a restaurant, golf course, tennis courts, swimming pool, in-house masseuse and bike hire; cheaper rates are available during the week. Other accommodation in the surrounding area includes *Del Rio Riverside Resort* (℡02/4566 4330, ℻4566 4358, ⓦwww.delrioresort.com.au; en-suite cabins ❻), a campsite in Webbs Creek across the Webbs Creek ferry, 3km south of Wisemans Ferry; facilities include a Chinese restaurant, swimming pool, tennis court and golf course. Better still is *Rosevale Farm Resort*, 3km along Wisemans Ferry Road en route to Gosford (℡ & ℻ 02/4566 4207; on-site vans ❸, en-suite cabins ❹–❺), with inexpensive camping and cabins – cheaper weekdays – in extensive bushland close to Dharug National Park. For considerably more luxury, check out houseboat rentals (see box opposite).

Taking the ferry across the river from Wisemans Ferry, it's a scenic nineteen-kilometre river drive north along Settlers Road, another convict-built route, to **ST ALBANS**, where you can partake of a cooling brew (or stay a while) at a pub built in 1836, the hewn sandstone *Settlers Arms Inn* (℡02/4568 2111, ℻4568 2046, ⓔsettlersarms@ozemail.com.au; all rooms en suite; ❻). The pub is set on two-and-a-half acres and much of the fruit and vegetables for the delicious home-cooked food is organically grown on site.

The Upper Hawkesbury: Windsor and Richmond

About 50km inland from Sydney and just a few kilometres apart, Windsor and Richmond are two of five towns founded by Governor Macquarie in the early nineteenth century to capitalize on the fertile, well-watered soil of the Upper Hawkesbury River area. You can take a train to Windsor and Richmond from Central Station in Sydney via Blacktown. **WINDSOR** is probably the best preserved of all the historic towns in the riverlands, with a lively centre of narrow streets, spacious old pubs and numerous historic colonial buildings. The **Hawkesbury River Museum and Tourist Information Centre** on Thompson Square (daily 10am–4pm; museum $2.50; ℡02/4577 2310, ⓦwww.hawkesburycitycouncil.com.au) is a good place to start exploring, and the *Macquarie Arms Hotel,* claimed to be the oldest in Australia, is the best place to end up for a cool beer. From Windsor, Putty Road (route 69) heads north through beautiful forest country, along the eastern edge of the Wollemi National Park, to Singleton in the Hunter Valley (see p.209).

RICHMOND's attractions include an old graveyard and settlers' dwellings, plus its unspoilt riverside setting. Cinema buffs could take in a bargain-priced film at the Regent Twin Cinema (Mon–Thurs and daytime Fri & Sat $8, Sun $7; ℡02/4578 1800), a classic, beautifully decorated old theatre. Moving on, the Bells Line of Road (Route 40), from Richmond to Lithgow via Kurrajong, is a great scenic drive; all along the way are fruit stalls stacked with produce from the valley. There's a wonderful view of the Upper Hawkesbury Valley

from the lookout point at **Kurrajong Heights**, on the edge of the Blue Mountains, and you can take it all in from the *Corkscrew Cafe* (Mon–Fri 11am–4pm, Sat & Sun 9am–5pm). Another scenic drive from Richmond to the Blue Mountains, emerging near Springwood (see p.215), is south along the Hawkesbury Road, with the **Hawkesbury Heights Lookout** halfway along providing panoramic views. Not far from the lookout is the modern solar-powered *Hawkesbury Heights YHA Hostel* (℡02/4754 5621; ❶), with more views from its secluded bush setting, and no chance of overcrowding with only two beds in each of the six rooms.

The Central Coast

The shoreline between Broken Bay and Newcastle, known as the **Central Coast**, is characterized by large **coastal lakes** – saltwater lagoons almost entirely enclosed, but connected to the ocean by small waterways. The northernmost, **Lake Macquarie**, is the biggest saltwater lake in New South Wales. People in a hurry can bypass the Central Coast altogether on the Sydney–Newcastle Freeway, which runs some way inland, but to see a bit more of the coastal scenery and the lakes, stay on the old Pacific Highway. A further detour would take you from Gosford to **Terrigal** and then right along the narrow coastal strip via **The Entrance** and **Budgewoi** to rejoin the Pacific Highway at **Elizabeth Bay**. The fit and intrepid can get here by bike: from Manly, head up the northern beaches, hop on a ferry service from Palm Beach (see p.156) to **Patonga** (Sat, Sun & holidays departs Palm Beach 9am, 11am & 3.45pm, returns 9.30am, 3pm & 4.15pm; Mon–Fri departs 11am, returns 3pm; $6.50 one-way; ℡02/9997 4815), then continue up through Woy Woy and Gosford to the coast. You can also reach Patonga by ferry from Brooklyn (see box p.196) with Hawkesbury River Ferries (℡02/9985 7566; $8, bike free). Otherwise you can take the **train** to Gosford or Woy Woy, following a very scenic route. You can also get to the area direct from Sydney airport: the Central Coast Airbus (℡02/4332 8655) provides several services daily (also picking up in the city centre): stops include Gosford, Erina, Terrigal and The Entrance.

For **tourist information** on the whole region, and accommodation bookings, call Central Coast Tourism (free call ℡1800 806 258, ⓦwww.cctourism.com.au). Within the Central Coast area there is a well-developed **bus service**, run by a collection of operators: Busways Peninsula (℡02/4392 6666), Busways Central Coast (℡02/4368 2277), Gosford Bus Service (℡02/4325 1781), and The Entrance Red Bus Services (℡02/4332 8655). For **taxis**, call Central Coast Taxis (℡13 1008).

Gosford and around

To get anywhere on the Central Coast, you need to go through **GOSFORD**, perched on the north shore of Brisbane Water and just about within commuting distance of Sydney. Its proximity to the city has resulted in uncontrolled residential sprawl along much of the Central Coast, which has put a great strain on the once-unspoilt lakes. Although there's plenty of accommodation in and around Gosford – details from **Central Coast Tourism**, near the train station at 200 Mann St (Mon–Sat 9am–5pm & Sun 9am–3pm school holidays and long weekends only; ℡02/4385 4074, ⓦwww.cctourism.com.au) – there's not much incentive to stay. Gosford's main appeal though is as a gateway to two excellent national parks, beyond which are two idyllic beach retreats – Pearl Beach and nearby Patonga.

Old Sydney Town (daily 10am–4pm; $22), southwest of Gosford just off the Pacific Highway, is a reconstruction of Sydney as it looked in the early years of the penal settlement. "Everyday" scenes, such as a convict's escape or a flogging, are acted out, and a token gesture towards Aboriginal culture has been made in the form of a Koorie Trading Post, which sells souvenirs. Most tour buses include Old Sydney Town in their itineraries. Take Peninsula Bus Lines #38 to Old Sydney Town from Gosford.

Brisbane Waters National Park, immediately south of Gosford, is the site of the **Bulgandry Aboriginal engravings**, which are of a style unique to the Sydney region, with figurative outlines scratched boldly into sandstone. The site, no longer frequented by the Guringgai people – whose territory ranged south as far as Sydney Harbour and north to Lake Macquarie – is 7km southwest of Gosford off the Woy Woy Road. Tiny **Bouddi National Park** is 20km southeast along the coast, at the northern mouth of Broken Bay, and is a great spot for bushwalking, with camping facilities at Putty Beach, Little Beach and Tallow Beach: book through the NPWS office at 207 Albury St, Gosford (☎02/4324 4911), which also has information on both parks.

Surrounded by Brisbane Waters National Park, friendly, undeveloped **PEARL BEACH** is a small community which expands on weekends. There are holiday houses to rent, but no other accommodation. Besides a popular café and a beachfront restaurant, *Pearls on the Beach* (licensed and BYO; bookings advised on ☎02/4342 4400; closed Mon–Wed, no dinner Sun), there's a general store (daily 8am–6pm) also selling petrol, a real estate agent who can arrange holiday lets (☎02/4341 7555, ℻4341 9665, ⓦwww.pearl-beachrealestate.com.au; from $550 per week in peak season), and some tennis courts. The very pretty, sheltered beach, popular with families, has a relaxing open-access saltwater pool at one end. You can walk from the end of Crystal Avenue to the neighbouring beach settlement of **PATONGA** visiting a lookout and the **Crommelin Native Arboretum** en route. The walk takes about 45 minutes and is best undertaken on the last Sunday of the month when the **Patonga Beach market** is held (8am–4pm), with arts and crafts, food stalls and buskers. Central Coast Kayak Tours, 25 Broken Bay Rd, Ettalong Beach (☎02/4342 2222, ⓦwww.kayaktours.com), does **kayaking trips** on Patonga Creek for $88 with pick-ups from Woy Woy train station. They also hire out kayaks (single kayak $30 half-day, $49.50 full day).

To get to Pearl Beach or Patonga, you can take the Busways Peninsula **bus** (☎02/4392 6666) from Woy Woy train station; or take the Palm Beach ferry (see overleaf).

Terrigal, Avoca Beach and The Entrance

Twelve kilometres southeast of Gosford, **TERRIGAL** is one of the most enjoyable spots on the Central Coast, a family-oriented beach resort with foodie and New Age inclinations. **Central Coast Tourism** at Rotary Park, Terrigal Drive (summer daily 9am–5pm, winter closed Sun; ☎02/4385 4074, ⓦwww.cctourism.com.au), is a good source of information on the whole region, and can make free **accommodation** bookings. If you're after a holiday unit (from around $400 weekly) contact Hunters Real Estate, 104 Terrigal Esplanade (☎02/4384 1444, ℮hunters@ozemail.com.au). The deluxe YHA-affiliated *Terrigal Beach Backpackers Lodge*, at 12 Campbell Crescent (☎ & ℻ 02/4385 3330, ℮yha@terrigalbeachlodge.com.au; rooms ❸, dorms ❶), is only one minute's walk from the beach, and is run by a friendly, well-travelled Canadian. Bikes and boogie-boards are provided free. Terrigal is a popular spot for sailboarding: contact Erina Sail 'n' Ski (☎02/4365 2355) for lessons and hire if you want to join in. For eating, there are plenty of adventurous **cafés** along the Esplanade, though the nicest, *Patcino's*, is tucked away in Church Street near the hostel. The best **restaurant** meal – with a contemporary Mediterranean/Middle Eastern twist and fabulous balcony views – is at the eastern end of the beach at *The Gallery Beach House* (BYO; T02/4385 3222; lunch daily, dinner Wed–Sat). If it's beyond your budget (mains around $26), then *Haven Seafood* is just nearby for fish and chips. To get to Terrigal, take Peninsula Bus Lines #80, #81 or #82 from Gosford; #81 also links Terrigal and Avoca Beach.

Six kilometres to the south, and altogether quieter, **AVOCA BEACH** is especially popular with surfers. A large, crescent-shaped and sandy beach between two headlands, it has its own surf lifesaving club and a safe children's rock pool. Its pleasant small-town atmosphere is enhanced by the Avoca Beach Theatre on Avoca Drive (T02/4382 2156), a surviving early-1950s cinema that has changed little. You can **learn to surf** here and at other local beaches with Central Coast Surf School (T02/4382 1020; 1hr group lesson $20, including gear). **Accommodation** includes a caravan park, *The Palms*, at 160 The Round Drive (T02/4382 1227; cabins ⑤), but the best bet is to rent a holiday unit (from $450 per week) – call George Brand Real Estate (T02/4382 1311) for listings. For **eating**, grab fish and chips from the *Prawn Star Cafe*, across from the beach at 168 Avoca Drive (eat-in or take-away), or there's fine dining at the expensive French-run *Feast* at no. 200 (T02/4381 0707), teamed with fabulous beach views. **To get here**, take Peninsula Bus Lines #79 from Gosford.

Further north, Tuggerah and Munmorah lakes meet the sea at **THE ENTRANCE**, a beautiful spot with water extending as far as the eye can see. It's a favourite fishing spot with anglers – and with swarms of **pelicans**, which turn up for the afternoon fish-feeds daily at 3.30pm (free) at Memorial Park, near the visitor centre (see below). The beaches and lakes along the coast from here to Newcastle are crowded with caravan parks, motels and outfits offering the opportunity to fish, windsurf, sail or waterski: although less attractive than places further north, they make a great day-trip or weekend escape from Sydney. Pro Dive Central Coast, 96 The Entrance Rd (T02/4334 1559), arranges **scuba-diving** lessons, daily boat dives and rents out snorkelling and dive gear. The **Entrance Visitors Centre**, Marine Parade (daily 9am–5pm; T02/4385 4074 or T1300/13 0708, Wwww.cctourism.com.au), has a free **accommodation** booking service.

Newcastle

NEWCASTLE is a blue-collar town enlivened by its waterside location, and with an alternative feel provided by a big dose of surf culture and a large student community. New South Wales' second city, with a population of around a quarter of a million, it suffers from comparison with nearby Sydney but in fact it has plenty going for it, especially as it's recently had a much-needed facelift: years of accumulated soot has been scraped off its stately buildings, riverside gardens have been created in front of the city centre, and an old wharf has been converted into a waterside entertainment venue. Heavy industry is a thing of the past in Newcastle – the production of steel here ceased in late 2000 and most of the slag heaps have been worked over – but the docks are still functional, particularly with the through traffic of coal from the Hunter Valley. However, for a former major industrial city, Newcastle is surprisingly attractive. You might not choose to spend your entire holiday here, but it can be a good base for excursions, particularly for the wineries of the nearby

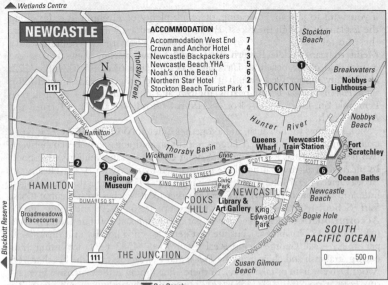

▲ Wetlands Centre

NEWCASTLE

ACCOMMODATION	
Accommodation West End	7
Crown and Anchor Hotel	4
Newcastle Backpackers	3
Newcastle Beach YHA	5
Noah's on the Beach	6
Northern Star Hotel	2
Stockton Beach Tourist Park	1

▼ Bar Beach

Hunter Valley. The surf beaches are wonderful, and there are some more sheltered sandy beaches around the rocky promontory at the mouth of the Hunter.

Newcastle was founded in 1804 for convicts too hard even for Sydney to
cope with, but the river is the real reason for the city's existence. Coal was
brought down it from the fields of the Hunter Valley, to be exported around
the country and the world, and the proximity of the mines encouraged the
establishment of other heavy industries. In more recent years Newcastle
made world headlines when Australia's worst earthquake struck the area two
days after Christmas in 1989, killing twelve people and destroying several
buildings. Rebuilding was imaginative – for example, the use of colourful
mosaics in the pavement of Beaumont Street in Hamilton, one of the hard-
est-hit areas.

Arrival, public transport and information

If you're not driving, you'll arrive by train at Newcastle **train station**, right in
the heart of the city on Scott Street, or by bus at nearby Watt Street. A novel
way to arrive (or depart) right on Newcastle Harbour is by **seaplane** (see
p.185).

Heading west from Newcastle train station, Scott Street eventually becomes
Hunter Street, the city's main street. Newcastle's hub is the pedestrianized
Hunter Street Mall, with its large department stores and shops. Continuing
west along Hunter Street, the Civic train station marks the city's cultural and
administrative district focused around City Hall and Civic Park. A short walk
south of here is an area called Cooks Hill, focused on café- and restaurant-lined
Darby Street; the other eat street is Beaumont Street in Italian-dominated
Hamilton, 3km west of the centre.

It's easy to get around using Newcastle's **public transport** system. Newcastle
Bus and Ferry Services (☏02/4961 8933) has an information booth at the west
end of Hunter Street Mall on the corner of Perkins Street. Bus fares are time-
based with a one-hour ticket, allowing transfers, costing $2.40; an all-day bus

and ferry ticket costs $7. All tickets can be bought on board. The one ferry operating goes to Stockton, departing from Queens Wharf (Mon–Sat 5.15am–11pm or midnight, Sun 8.30am–8.30pm; $1.70 one-way). Two passenger train lines have several suburban stops, the most useful heading southwest from Newcastle Station (towards Sydney), with handy stops at Civic (for Darby St) and Hamilton (for Beaumont St), the other line runs northeast (towards Maitland). Weekly passes, combining bus and ferry ($31) or bus, ferry and train ($39) are available from selected newsagencies.

The helpful **Newcastle Tourist Information** (Mon–Fri 9am–5pm, Sat & Sun 10am–3.30pm; ⓣ02/4974 2999 or free call 1800 654 558, Ⓦwww.new-castletourism.ncc.gov.au) is at 363 Hunter St, right next to the Civic Theatre. Disabled travellers can pick up the useful *Newcastle Mobility Map* from here.

Accommodation

Accommodation West End, 775 Hunter, cnr Stewart St (ⓣ02/4961 4446, Ⓕ4961 0766). Clean budget accommodation – singles, doubles, twins and dorms – in a former hotel. Small enough to have a personal touch (max 30 guests) and lots of advice provided. TV lounge, kitchen, rooftop terrace and BBQ. Rooms ❹, dorms ❷

Crown and Anchor Hotel, cnr Hunter and Perkins streets, next to David Jones department store (ⓣ02/4929 1027, Ⓕ4927 0161). Inexpensive, central rooms in a pub. Good single rates ($30). ❸

Newcastle Backpackers, 42 and 44 Denison St, Hamilton (ⓣ02/4969 3436 or free call 1800 333 436, Ⓦwww.newcastlebackpackers.com.au). A home-style hostel in two houses run by a friendly young family. No. 44 is the more upmarket option, with double rooms, while no. 42 has dorms and one small double. Located 3km from the city centre and beach but only a few minutes' walk from lively Beaumont St. Take bus #260 from the city centre, or call for a free pick-up. The owner runs people down to the beach most days and offers free surfing lessons too (boogie boards free, surfboards $7 per day). Rooms ❸, dorms ❶

Newcastle Beach YHA, 30 Pacific St, cnr King St (ⓣ02/4925 3544, Ⓕ4295 3944, Ⓔyhanewcastle@hunterlink.net.au). Newish hostel in an impressively restored, spacious Queen Anne-style building complete with ballroom, but with very modern facilities. There are four-bed dorms, doubles, twins and family rooms, plus a pool table and courtyard with BBQ. Just 50m from the surf and right in the centre of town. Rooms ❹, dorms ❷

Noah's on the Beach, cnr Shortland Esplanade and Zaara St (ⓣ02/4929 5181, Ⓕ4926 5208, Ⓦwww.noahsonthebeach.com.au). Most rooms in this upmarket, modern motel have ocean views, and there's room service. ❼

Northern Star Hotel, 112 Beaumont St, Hamilton (ⓣ02/4961 1087, Ⓕ4961 2944, Ⓦwww.northernstarhotel.com.au). Pub accommodation in a great location on this restaurant- and café-lined street northwest of the centre – though with bands downstairs until 1am Wed–Sun this is not the place for light sleepers. All double rooms are en suite, spacious, clean and have fridges, TV, tea and coffee facilities and ceiling fans; cheaper shared-bath singles available. ❺

Stockton Beach Tourist Park, Stockton Beach (ⓣ02/4928 1393). Picturesquely sited campground on an extensive beach, just a ferry ride from the centre (but a much longer car ride). Cabins ❷–❹

The City

Newcastle has whole streetscapes of beautiful **Victorian terraces** that would put Sydney's to shame – pick up a free *Newcastle City of Heritage and Enterprise* map from the tourist office, or the *Newcastle Town Walk*, to guide you around some of the old buildings. A couple of buildings in **Newcastle Harbour Foreshore Park** show the trend for the city's wealth of disused public architecture: on one corner of the park stands the beautiful Italianate brick **Customs House**, now a popular pub. Nearby is the wooden two-storey **Paymasters House**, where you can sit with a coffee in its fine verandah café and contemplate the water.

The restored **Queens Wharf**, a landmark with its distinctive observation tower, is located on the south bank of the Hunter River. It's linked to the city centre by an elevated walkway from Hunter Street Mall and boasts *The Brewery*, a popular and stylish waterfront drinking spot. From the nearby Merewether Street Wharf you can take a cruise on *William the Fourth*, a reproduction of the first Australian-built coastal **paddlewheel steamship** (third Sun of month 11am & 2pm; 1hr 30min; $11; ☎02/4926 1200). It's also quite a sight to watch the **seaplanes** from Sydney land nearby the two wharfs.

Besides Newcastle's waterside attractions, there are a few other places that might be of interest. The **Newcastle Regional Museum**, 787 Hunter St (Tues–Sun 10am–5pm, daily during school holidays; free), housed in what began as a brewery in the 1870s, focuses on the history of the mining and steel industries of the area; attached is the Supernova hands-on science centre, much the best thing about the museum. If you're at a loose end, the **Newcastle Regional Art Gallery**, on Laman Street near Civic Park (Tues–Sun 10am–5pm; free), usually has an interesting temporary exhibition in addition to its permanent display.

Beaches and wildlife reserves

The city centre, positioned on a narrow length of land between the Hunter River to the west and the Pacific Ocean to the east, has several popular and pleasantly low-key beaches close by. **Newcastle Beach**, only a few hundred metres from the city on Shortland Esplanade, has patrolled swimming between flags, a sandy saltwater pool perfect for children, shaded picnic tables and good surfing at its southern end. At the northern end, the beautifully painted Art Deco-style **Ocean Baths** (daily 6am–2pm, until 6pm in spring and 10pm in summer; closed in winter; free) houses the changing pavilions for the huge saltwater pool, which has its own diving board.

Overlooking the water north of Newcastle Beach, **Fort Scratchley**, built in the 1880s, houses a maritime and military museum (generally Tues–Sun noon–4pm but check on ☎02/4929 2588 as it's volunteer-run; free). Beyond the fort is the long, uncrowded stretch of **Nobbys Beach**, with a lovely old beach pavilion. A walkway leads to Nobbys Head and its nineteenth-century lighthouse.

If you follow Shortland Esplanade south from Newcastle Beach, you'll come to the huge expanse of King Edward Park, with good walking paths and cliff views over this rocky stretch of waterfront. One section of the rock ledge holds Australia's first man-made ocean pool, the **Bogie Hole**. Chiselled out of the rock by convicts in the early nineteenth century for the Military Commandant's personal bathing pleasure, it's still a fine spot for a swim. The cliffs are momentarily intercepted by **Susan Gilmore Beach** – secluded enough to indulge in some nude bathing – then further around the rocks is **Bar Beach**, a popular surfing spot that's floodlit at night. The longer **Merewether Beach** next door has a fabulous ocean baths at its southern end and a separate children's pool; overlooking the beach is the *Merewether Hotel*, a fine place for a drink.

Blackbutt Reserve is a large slab of bushland in the middle of Newcastle suburbia in New Lambton Heights about 10km southwest of the city (daily 9am–5pm; free); consisting of four valleys, it includes a remnant of rainforest, creeks, lakes and ponds and 20km of walking tracks to explore them. En route you'll see kangaroos, koalas, wombats, emus and other native animals in the reserve's wildlife enclosures. To get there, take the **train** to Kotara and walk to the Carnley Avenue entrance or take **bus** #216 or #217 via Kotara; for the entrances on Lookout Road you can take bus #363. As it's a little hard to find the tourist office produces a helpful free map which you might like to get a copy of first. Northwest of the city, the **Wetlands Centre**, Sandgate Road, Shortland (daily 9am–5pm; donation), is situated on the wetlands of Hexham Swamp by Ironbark Creek and is home to a mass of birdlife. There are walking and cycling trails here, and the more intrepid can rent canoes from tourist information. You can reach the Wetlands Centre by train from Newcastle to Sandgate, from where it's a ten-minute walk.

Cafés and restaurants

The two streets to head for are **Darby Street**, close to the city centre, which has a multicultural mix of restaurants and some fairly hip cafés as well as some secondhand bookshops and retro clothes stores to browse in between coffees; and **Beaumont Street** in Hamilton, northeast of the city centre (take the train to Hamilton Station or bus #260), where there is a concentration of Italian places, as well as Turkish, Lebanese, Dutch and Indian.

Al-Oi-Thai, Shop 2, 50 Beaumont St, Hamilton (☎02/4969 1434). Delicious traditional Thai food served in stylish surrounds that's justifiably popular. Lunch Wed–Sat, dinner Tues–Sun; BYO. Fronted by a cheaper express noodle bar serving superb noodle soups and fried noodles. There's another Al-Oi-Thai at 133 Darby St (☎02/4929 3610).

Dolomiti Gelato, 20 Beaumont St, Hamilton. Great home-made *gelati*, plus pasta and *focaccia* in a typically casual Italian café. Closed Sun.

Goldbergs Coffee House, 137 Darby St. This popular, buzzy café is big and airy with modish green walls and polished wooden floors. The emphasis is on the excellent coffee, plus very reasonably priced eclectically modern meals. Daily 8am–midnight. Licensed.

Italian Centre Restaurant, Upstairs, 44 Beaumont St, Hamilton (☎02/4961 4656). Good, authentic food in a homely restaurant above the Italian community centre. Balcony to sit out on. Licensed. Closed Mon.

Little Swallows Café Restaurant, 54 Beaumont St, Hamilton (☎02/4969 2135). Simple place, a favourite daytime coffee hangout for Italian locals presided over by the friendly owner Paolo. Captures the earthy feel of a traditional Italian trattoria, with suitably generous portions. BYO. Daily 9am–10pm.

Market Square Foodcourt, upstairs in the Hunter Street Mall. Best place in the city centre, with a good range of food bars – Italian, Chinese, kebabs, roasts – and mightily generous salad sandwiches and fresh juices at the *Oak Dairy Bar*. Mon–Sat 8am–5pm, Thurs until 9pm.

Scott Street Café Restaurant, 19 Scott St (☎02/4927 0107). Smart, minimalist restaurant close to Newcastle Beach. The small seasonal dinner changes every six weeks, with contemporary-style dishes like King Prawn risotto with coriander and chilli to slaver over. BYO. Brunch Sat & Sun 10am–3pm, dinner Mon–Sat from 6pm.

Splash, 126 Darby St. Freshly cooked budget takeaway seafood; tempura prawns and crumbed calamari are among the offerings. Mon–Thurs 4.30–8.30pm, Fri–Sun 11am–9pm.

Taj Takeaway, 120 Darby St. Quick and tasty Indian takeaway – and also a grocery. Daily 7am–11pm.

View Factory, cnr Scott and Telford streets (☎02/4929 4580). Calling itself an "arts café", this airy, slickly decorated brasserie/café/gallery near the waterfront serves all the café favourites – from big breakfasts to *focaccia* and nachos – plus a pricier restaurant menu (nightly from 6pm) which makes creative use of seafood and fine ingredients. There's even a pool table. Licensed. Daily 11am–10pm/midnight.

Drinking and nightlife

For listings, check out the "That's Entertainment" in Wednesday's *Post*. During term time, the students of Newcastle University add a lot of life to the city, but there is always a thriving **live music** scene. On Friday and Saturday nights the city pubs on Hunter Street, parallel King Street and perpendicular Watt Street all have bands, many of them free.

The Bar on the Hill, Newcastle University campus at Callaghan (☎02/4921 5000). Hosts live bands; all welcome. Take bus #260.

Beaches Hotel, opposite Merewether Beach

(☎02/4963 1574). The only place to go on Sun night; live bands.

The Brewery, 150 Wharf Rd. Popular waterfront drinking hole which has a crowded bistro.

The Kent, cnr Cleary and Beaumont streets, Hamilton (℡02/4961 3303). Beautifully renovated old pub and music venue (rock Wed, Fri & Sun nights; jazz Sat & Sun afternoon; no cover charge). Busy every night, but with several refuges, including a wonderful plant-filled beer garden and a great bistro. Pool competition Mon night, quiz Tues.

Newcastle Workers Club, cnr King and Union streets (℡02/4926 2700). Big gigs by touring bands Fri & Sat nights.
Northern Star Hotel, 112 Beaumont St, Hamilton (℡02/4961 1087). Music in the back bar Wed–Sun from folk to jazz, blues and rock; mostly free.

Entertainment and culture

The area known as "the cultural precinct", near Civic Park on King, Hunter and Auckland streets, is the location for three refurbished Art Deco venues; pick up a monthly calendar from the tourist office for details of what's on. The **Civic Theatre**, 375 Hunter St (℡02/4929 1977) hosts mainly big-budget musicals and theatre productions. At the **University Conservatorium of Music** on Auckland Street (℡02/4921 8900), there are often free lunchtime concerts as well as evening performances, while the grand **City Hall**, 290 King St (℡02/4974 2948) has occasional classical music events such as the Australian Chamber Orchestra. **Film** buffs should head for the small, single-screen Kensington Cinema, 299 Hunter St, opposite Civic Station (℡02/4929 3893), or the three-screen Showcase City Cinemas, 31–33 Wolfe St, off Hunter Street Mall (℡02/4929 5019); both show arthouse and mainstream releases.

Listings

Banks and exchange The Commonwealth Bank, 136 Hunter Street Mall (℡02/4927 2777), has foreign exchange. American Express, 25 Bolton St (℡02/4929 5500).
Car Hire A.R.A (℡02/4962 2488), from $48.50 including standard insurance, with 100km mileage; Thrifty (℡02/4942 2266).
Environment The Wilderness Society, 90 Hunter St (℡02/4929 4395).
Left luggage The train station has a luggage room (daily 8am–5pm; $1.50 per article).
Post office Newcastle GPO, 96 Hunter St, NSW 2300 (Mon–Fri 8am–5pm).

Taxi Taxi Services Co-Op (℡02/4979 3000).
Tours Shadows Wine Tours (℡02/4990 7002) do good-value wine tours of the Hunter Valley, visiting five wineries, with free pick-ups from Newcastle ($35 or $55 with restaurant lunch). Hunter Vineyard Tours (℡02/4991 1659) and Hunter Valley Day Tours (℡02/4938 5031) also do Newcastle pick-ups, for an extra charge; see p.209 for both.
Trains Newcastle Station enquiries ℡02/4962 9696.
Travel Agent Newcastle Travel, 68 Hunter St, cnr Watt St (℡02/4926 1855). Sells bus tickets for coaches going up the North Coast.

The Lower Hunter Valley

In Australia (and, increasingly, worldwide) the **Hunter Valley** is synonymous with fine **wine**. The first vines were planted 150 years ago and are mainly the two classic white-wine varieties of Semillon and Chardonnay, with Pinot Noir and Shiraz dominating the reds. In what seems a bizarre juxtaposition, this is also a very important **coal-mining region**: in the upper part of the valley especially, the two often go hand-in-hand. By far the best-known area, however, is in the Lower Hunter Valley around the old country town of Cessnock. Even the town's jail has its own vineyard, and the prisoners have produced some prize-winning wines. One of the appeals of the Hunter Valley wine country is the bush and farming feel of the place with the vast plantings of vineyards seemingly lost among bushland, forested ridges, red-soiled dirt tracks, and paddocks with grazing cattle.

    CESSNOCK itself is much the best place to base yourself if you plan to stay overnight, while most of the vineyards are clustered around nearby **Pokolbin**.

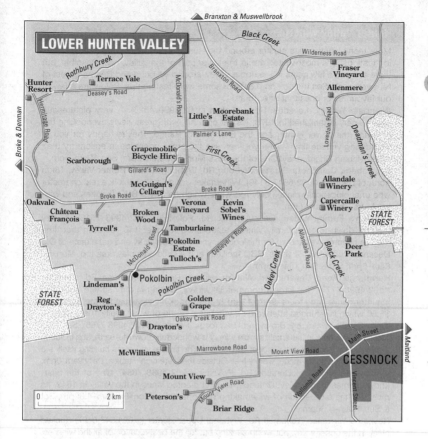

Pick up the excellent free fold-up maps and brochures on the Hunter Valley from the NSW Travel Centre in Sydney or **Wine Country Tourism**, at Turner Park, Abedare Road in Cessnock (Mon–Fri 9am–5pm, Sat 9.30am–5pm, Sun 9.30am–3.30pm; ☎02/4990 4477, ⓦwww.winecountry.com.au); the latter can also book accommodation. If you're going to tour the wineries, try and do so during the week; at weekends both the number of visitors and the prices go up. In February, when the place is flooded with wine-lovers enjoying the Dionysian delights of the **Hunter Valley Vintage Festival**, accommodation is impossible to find. Another lively time is October, when Wyndham Estate hosts **Opera in the Vineyards** (☎02/4938 3444), followed by the **Jazz in the Vines Festival** (☎02/4993 7000) based at Tyrell's.

Getting there and around

To get to Cessnock, catch a train from Central to Maitland or Newcastle and then a bus to Cessnock with Rover Motors (☎02/4990 1699). Alternatively, Keans Travel Express (Sydney ☎02/9211 3387; Muswellbrook ☎02/6543 1322) goes direct from Sydney to the Hunter Valley once daily (terminating at Scone), taking just over two hours with stops including Kurri Kurri, Neath, Cessnock, Pokolbin and Muswellbrook.

Hunter Valley wineries

More than sixty wineries cluster around the Hunter Valley, almost all of them offering tastings. The most-visited are in the lower part of the valley, near Pokolbin, but there are also a few gems in the upper valley, around Wybong and Denman, west of Muswellbrook. See the box on p.818 for some wine-tasting tips. Below are a few of our favourites or ones that offer tours.

Allandale Winery, Lovedale Rd, Pokolbin (℡ 02/4990 4526). A very picturesque small winery established in 1978; it's set on a hill, with great views overlooking the vineyard, the Lower Hunter and the Brokenback Range. They're happy for you to visit during vintage time, when you can see the small operation in action; try their prize-winning Chardonnay. One of the best. Mon–Sat 9am–5pm, Sun 10am–5pm.

Cruikshank Callatoota Estate, Wybong Rd, Wybong, Upper Hunter Valley, 18km north of Denman (℡ 02/6547 8149). Winemaker John Cruikshank is a real character who unapologetically makes only red wine, which he loves. BBQ facilities and winery tours. Daily 9am–5pm.

Drayton's Family Wines, Oakey Creek Rd, Pokolbin (℡ 02/4998 7513). A very friendly, down-to-earth family winery, established for over 140 years. In that time they've become well known for their ports; you might be lucky and get a taste of Old Decanter Port, aged 21 years. BBQ facilities and a children's play area too. Mon–Fri 8am–5pm, Sat & Sun 10am–5pm.

Hermitage Road Cellars and Winery, Hunter Resort, Hermitage Rd, Pokolbin (℡ 02/4998 7777). The largest commercial winery, lacking in atmosphere but offering informative wine tours (9am, 11am & 2pm; booking essential for the 9am tour; $5.50 which is refunded afterwards if you buy a bottle of wine). Daily 10am–5pm.

Kevin Sobels Wines, cnr Broke and Halls roads, Pokolbin (℡ 02/4998 7766). Set up in 1992, the welcome at this small, simple winery is wonderfully down-to-earth, and includes a greeting by Bacchas, the resident St Bernard. The timber-and-glass building itself is a real treat, with a home-made, wonky feel. Outside there are picnic tables. Daily 9am–5pm.

Lindemans Wines, McDonalds Rd, Pokolbin (℡ 02/4998 7684). One of the best-known names in the valley; Dr Lindeman first planted vines in the valley in 1842. Its museum has a collection of winemaking paraphernalia. Mon–Fri 9am–4.30pm, Sat & Sun 10am–4.30pm.

Reynolds Yarraman, Yarraman Rd, Wybong, Upper Hunter (℡ 02/6547 8127). Tucked away in the upper valley, but worth seeking out for the best location of all the wineries. Convict-constructed sandstone buildings, circa 1837, and excellent, prize-winning wines. There's also a café open weekends. Mon–Sat 10am–4pm, Sun 11am–4pm.

Rosemount Estate, Rosemount Rd, Denman, Upper Hunter (℡ 02/6549 6400). Producer of some of Australia's best-known, award-winning wines, and with an excellent vineyard brasserie (Tues–Sun 10am–3pm). Mon–Sat 10am–4pm, Sun 10.30am–4pm.

Scarborough Wine Co, Gilliards Rd, Pokolbin (℡ 02/4998 7563). Small, friendly winery specializing in Chardonnay. Pleasantly relaxed sit-down tastings are held in a small cottage on Hungerford Hill with wonderful valley views. Daily 9am–5pm.

Tamburlaine Wines, McDonalds Rd, Pokolbin (℡ 02/4998 7570). The jasmine-scented garden outside gives a hint of the flowery, elegant wines within. Only a small range of wines – too small even for the domestic market, so you must buy here. Tastings are well orchestrated and delivered with a heap of experience. Daily 9.30am–5pm.

Tyrrell's Family Vineyard, Broke Rd, Pokolbin (℡ 02/4998 7509). The oldest independent family vineyards, producing consistently good wines. The tiny ironbark slab hut, where Edward Tyrrell lived when he began the winery in 1858, is still in the grounds, and the old winery with its cool earth floor is much as it was. Beautiful setting against the Brokenback Range. Mon–Sat 8am–5pm, with free tour 1.30pm.

Verona Vineyard & The Small Winemakers Centre, McDonalds Rd, Pokolbin (℡ 02/4998 7668). Sells wines produced by eight other small vineyards; the tasting charge levied on some wines is usually refunded on purchases. Excellent café, *Cafe Max*, attached (see p.211). Daily 10am–5pm.

If you're without transport (there's no public transport to the wineries) – or don't want to meander unintentionally off-road after excessive wine-tasting – **vineyard tours** are a good option. Most are exhausting return trips from Sydney (see box pp.192–193), but a local operator, Hunter Vineyard Tours (☎02/4991 1659, 🌐www.huntervineyardtours.com.au) runs small-group bus tours visiting five well-chosen wineries over six hours, all offering tastings ($38, including pick-up from Cessnock; with Newcastle or Maitland pick-ups $5 extra; restaurant lunch $17 extra or BYO). The more expensive Hunter Valley Day Tours (☎02/4938 5031, 📧daytours@hunter-region.org.au) offers tailor-made tours which can include surrounding scenic areas such as Barrington Tops. Pedal power is also popular: either **rent bikes** from Grapemobile, on the corner of McDonalds and Gilliards roads, Pokolbin (☎ & 📠 02/4991 2339, 🌐www.grapemobile.com.au; $25 per day, $15 half-day), or go on their day-long **bicycle tour**, which takes in four wineries and includes morning tea and a restaurant lunch (around $100).

Around Cessnock

Cessnock lies more or less due west of Newcastle, in an area of small creeks and tributaries of the Hunter River. But even in the main valley of the Hunter, followed by the New England Highway as it heads up towards the mountains of the Great Dividing Range and the New England Plateau, the impression is overwhelmingly rural, with green meadows and pastures interspersed with cornfields, vegetable patches and, of course, vineyards. Old mansions and sleepy hamlets, dating back to colonial times, complete the seemingly idyllic pastoral scene – though coal is extracted nearby from several enormous open-cast mines to feed Newcastle's power stations.

The area is dotted with interesting old country towns: even **MAITLAND** and **SINGLETON**, two of the main centres of the coal industry, boast historic buildings that help retain a beguilingly colonial flavour. Maitland, 25km northwest of Cessnock, is in fact a throughly historic place – an early convict foundation that in the nineteenth century became one of the most important towns in early Australia. There's an excellent state-of-the-art **tourist information centre** in Ministers Park on the corner of the New England Highway and High Street (☎02/4933 2611, 🌐www.maitlandtourism.nsw.gov.au), and in both towns the old jails have been converted into local history museums. Only 6km from Maitland, **MORPETH** is a picturesque river town that was an important Hunter Valley river port 150 years ago; today the old buildings house art galleries and craft shops.

WOLLOMBI, a historic homestead some 30km south of Cessnock, is the gateway to the Hunter Valley on the scenic inland route from Sydney, which involves leaving the freeway at Calga and heading north via Mangrove and Bucketty. The *Wollombi Tavern* makes a fine refreshment stop – sitting out on the wooden verandah looking over the creek to trees, fields and hills beyond is a real pleasure. Wollombi was once a ceremonial meeting place, and there are **Aboriginal rock carvings** and cave paintings throughout the area, some of which can be visited on horseback with the Wollombi Horse Riding Centre (☎02/4998 3221; 1hr 30min–2hr; $30), 4km past the *Wollombi Tavern* on the Singleton Road. The **New Gokula Farm**, halfway between Cessnock and Wollombi on the Wollombi Road (☎02/4998 1800), is a Hare Krishna farming community that puts on a free vegetarian feast at 12.30pm on Sunday; ask about staying in their guesthouse (☎02/4998 1973 for details) – a very peaceful spot flanked by bush-covered hills.

Moving on from the valley, it's an easy detour to **Barrington Tops National Park** (see p.284), north from Singleton and Maitland, or to the **Chichester Dam**, slightly closer in the same direction, surrounded by beautiful mountain and forest scenery and inhabited by melodic bellbirds.

Accommodation

Since the Hunter Valley is a popular weekend trip for Sydneysiders, accommodation **prices** invariably rise on Friday and Saturday nights when many places only offer two-night deals. Prices given below are for the cheapest doubles available on weekdays in high season; expect higher prices at weekends. If you're going to be here at a weekend, or during the February vintage festival, advance **booking** is essential. Most of the accommodation is around Pokolbin, at the centre of the vineyards, 12–15km northwest of Cessnock.

Belford Country Cabins, 659 Hermitage Rd, Pokolbin (T & 02/6574 7100, W www.belfordcabins.com.au). Family-run, fully equipped wooden bungalows for up to eight people. Great bushland location, small pool and playground. ⑤

Bellbird Hotel, 388 Wollombi Rd, 5km southwest from the centre of Cessnock (T 02/4990 1094, F 4991 5475, W www.bellbirdhotel.com.au). Great classic country pub, circa 1908, with wide iron-lace. Bistro, pretty beer garden and children's playground. Rates include a generous cooked breakfast. ④

Black Opal Hotel, 216 Vincent St, Cessnock (T 02/4990 1070, W www.huntervalleyhotels.com.au). Good standard of inexpensive pub accommodation. Bistro meals daily. ④

Elfin Hill Motel, Marrowbone Rd, Pokolbin (T 02/4998 7543, F 4998 7817, W www.hunterweb.com.au/elfinhill). Friendly, family-run hilltop motel with extensive views. Comfortable air-con units in timber cabins, plus a saltwater pool and BBQ area. ⑤

Hunter Valley Gardens, Broke Rd, Pokolbin (T 02/4998 7854, F 4998 7845, W www.hvg.com.au). Modern combined motel and hotel complex overlooking the vineyards, complete with an Irish pub, *Harrigan's*, bistro, pool, spa, tennis courts and three standards of accommodation: four-star in the *Lodge* ($220, $280 weekend); motel-style in *Harrigan's* ($160, $240 weekends); or in self-contained cabins at *Grapeview Villas* ⑤, two-day minimum at weekends. One room is accessible to disabled guests.

Neath Hotel, Cessnock Rd, Neath, 6km east of Cessnock (T 02/4930 4270, F 4930 4195, W www.huntervalleyhotels.com.au). B&B in a nicely furnished historic pub, listed by the National Trust. Fri and Sat night rates include a cooked breakfast and a three-course meal in the bistro or restaurant. ④

Peppers Convent, Halls Rd, Pokolbin (T 02/4998 7764, F 4998 7323, W www.peppers.com.au).

The swankiest place to stay in the Hunter Valley, with a price to match (from $290 per night). The guesthouse, converted from an old convent, has heaps of cosy cachet, fireplaces and low beams, and is part of the Peppertree winery. Attached is the fine-dining restaurant, *Roberts at Pepper Tree*. ⑧

Pokolbin Cabins, Palmers Lane, Pokolbin (T 02/4998 7611, F 4998 7873, W www.touristvision.com.au). In the midst of the wineries, this extensive complex has two- and three-bedroom log cabins and five-bedroom homesteads, fully equipped with everything from linen to firewood. Swimming pool and tennis court in the shady grounds. ④

Sussex Ridge, off Deaseys Rd, Pokolbin (T 02/4998 7753, F 4998 7359, W www.sussexridge.com.au). Guesthouse in a classic two-storey, tin-roofed homestead among extensive bushland, with great views from the balcony. All rooms are en suite and facilities include two communal lounge areas with open fires, an outdoor BBQ area and a swimming pool. B&B ⑦

Valley Vineyards Tourist Park, Mount View Rd, 2km northwest of Cessnock (T & F 02/4990 2573, W www.users.hunterlink.net.au/vvtp). High-standard camping site with camp kitchen, portable BBQs and pool. Cabins have external en suites, cottages internal. Cabins ④, cottages ⑤

Wentworth Hotel, 36 Vincent St, Cessnock (T 02/4990 1364). Large old country pub with original wooden fixtures circa 1914. Rooms are clean and spacious with washbasin, fan and heating, and rates include a continental breakfast. B&B ⑤

Wollombi Horse Riding Centre, Singleton Rd, 4km past the *Wollombi Tavern* (T 02/4998 3221, F 4998 3231). Barnstay accommodation in bunks, with semi-stocked kitchen, cosy lounge area set up with a combustion stove, sound system, library and games; verandah and BBQ area. Rates include linen. Also riverside camping for $5 per person. ④–⑤

Eating and drinking

Most of the many excellent (and pricey) Hunter Valley restaurants are attached to the various wineries or are among the vineyards, rather than in the towns, while the Hunter's large old pubs dish out less fancy but more affordable grub. Every year over a mid-May weekend seven wineries along and around Lovedale Road team up with local restaurants to host the **Lovedale Long Lunch** (℡02/4930 7611), with wine and gourmet food served amongst the vines. You can taste free samples of The Hunter Valley Cheese Company's handmade wares, or buy some to accompany a picnic, at the McGuigan Bros Winery, Broke Road, Pokolbin.

Amicos, 138 Wollombi Rd, Cessnock (℡02/4991 1995). A popular cheap eat, this BYO restaurant serves Italian and Mexican food in a casual atmosphere. Daily from 6pm.

Baron's Restaurant, at the *Neath Hotel* (℡02/4930 4270). Antique-filled restaurant in a historic pub. Sat nights only; cheaper bistro restaurant available all week.

Bellbird Hotel, 388 Wollombi Rd, 5km from the centre of Cessnock. Vast old-fashioned pub full of country characters. Eat inexpensive no-frills bistro food in the very pleasant vine-covered and flower-filled beer garden with adjacent children's playground.

Bimbadgen Estate, Lot 21, McDonalds Rd, Pokolbin (℡02/4998 7585). With a squint this winery, complete with bell tower, could be in Europe. Its modern restaurant, however, is all timber and glass, reached via the working winery, and with vineyard views from the balcony. Food, with mains around the $25 mark, is contemporary European, with rabbit, spatchcock and roast duck all on the menu. Licensed. Lunch daily, dinner Wed–Sat.

Blaxlands Restaurant, Broke Rd, Pokolbin (℡02/4998 7550). More than a hundred wines from the Hunter Valley are available at this well-regarded restaurant in an 1829 sandstone cottage. You can eat outside on the verandah. Expensive. Booking advised.

Café Enzo, Peppers Creek Antiques, Broke Rd, Pokolbin (℡02/4998 7233). Courtyard café with a light Mediterranean menu and excellent Italian-style coffee. Wed–Sun 10am–5pm.

Café Max, McDonalds Rd, Pokolbin (℡02/4998 7899). Above The Small Winemakers Centre (see box on p.208), with balcony views of vineyards and far-off hills. An eclectic menu to team with your BYO wine. Lunch Wed–Sun 11am–4pm.

Chez Pok, *Pepper's Guesthouse*, Ekerts Rd, Pokolbin (℡02/4998 7596). Highly regarded restaurant stylishly using local produce. The views overlooking vineyards are very pretty as is the antique-filled cottage interior. Expensive. Daily breakfast to dinner.

The Hoot Café, 115 Vincent St, Cessnock. Sydney style and prices in this bright and airy café with ceiling fans whirring and soul music playing. Gourmet sandwiches, croissants, tasty cakes, good coffee and delicious stuffed potatoes. Mon–Fri 8am–4pm, Sat 8am–1pm.

Il Cacciatore, Hermitage Lodge, cnr McDonalds and Gilliards roads, Pokolbin (℡02/4998 7639). Excellent upmarket Italian restaurant with a wide choice, including fish dishes. Desserts like chocolate pasta ensure that the place is packed. Licensed and BYO.

Mulligans Brasserie, Cypress Lakes Resort, McDonalds Rd, Pokolbin (℡02/4993 1835). Gourmet sandwiches, salads, tortillas and burgers accompanied by pleasant courtyard views looking out over the resort's pool and verdant golf course. Licensed. Daily 7am–10pm.

Roberts at Pepper Tree, Halls Rd, Pokolbin (℡02/4998 7330). Attached to *Peppers Convent* (see "Accommodation", opposite), this is the place to head for a treat, in a charming 1876 wooden farmhouse filled with flowers. French rustic-style food emerges from wood-fired ovens. Expensive; licensed.

West

For fifty years, Sydney has been sliding ever westwards in a monotonous sprawl of shopping centres, brick-veneer homes and fast-food chains, along the way swallowing up towns and villages, some of which date back to colonial times. The first settlers to explore inland found well-watered, fertile river flats, and quickly established agricultural outposts to support the fledgling colony. **Parramatta**, **Liverpool**, **Penrith** and **Campbelltown**, once separate communities, have now become satellite towns inside Sydney's commuter belt. Yet, despite Sydney's advance, bushwalkers will find there's still plenty of wild west to explore. Three wildlife parks keep suburbia at bay, and the beauty of the **Blue Mountains** are a far cry from the modernity of Sydney.

Parramatta and Penrith

Situated on the Parramatta River, a little over 20km upstream from the harbour mouth, **PARRAMATTA** was the first of Sydney's rural satellites – the first farm settlement in Australia, in fact. The fertile soil of "Rosehill", as it was originally called, saved the fledgling colony from starvation with its first wheat crop of 1789. It's hard to believe today, but dotted here and there among the malls and busy roads are a few remnants from that time – eighteenth-century public buildings and original settlers' dwellings that warrant a visit if you're interested in Australian history.

You can call in to Parramatta on your way out of Sydney – a rather depressing drive along the ugly and congested Parramatta Road – or endure the dreary thirty-minute suburban train ride from Central Station. But much the most enjoyable way to get here is on the sleek RiverCat ferry from Circular Quay up the Parramatta River (1hr; $6.10 one-way). The wharf at Parramatta is on Phillip Street, a couple of blocks away from the helpful **Parramatta Visitors Centre** on the corner of Church and Market streets (Mon–Fri 10am–4pm, Sat 9am–1pm, Sun 10.30am–3.30pm; ℡ 02/9630 3703, ⓦ www.parracity.nsw .gov.au), which hands out free walking route maps.

Parramatta's most important historic feature is the National Trust-owned **Old Government House** (Tues–Fri 10am–4pm, Sat & Sun 11am–4pm; last admission 3.30pm; $6.60, joint ticket with Experiment Farm $10) in **Parramatta Park** by the river. Turn left onto Marsden Street from the visitors centre, cross the river, then go right onto George Street. Entered through the 1885 gatehouse on O'Connell Street, the park – filled with native trees – rises up to the gracious old Georgian-style building, the oldest remaining public edifice in Australia. It was built between 1799 and 1816 and used as the Viceregal residence until 1855; one wing has been converted into a pleasant teahouse. The three other main historic attractions are close together: from Parramatta Park, follow Macquarie Street and turn right at its end onto Harris Street. Running off here is Ruse Street, where the aptly named **Experiment Farm Cottage** at no. 9 (Tues–Thurs 10am–4pm, Sun 11am–4pm; $6.60, free for National Trust members, joint ticket with Old Government House $10) was built on the site of the first land grant, given in 1790 to reformed convict James Ruse. On parallel Alice Street, at no. 70, **Elizabeth Farm** (daily 10am–5pm; $7) dates from 1793 and claims to be the oldest surviving home in the country. The farm was built and run by the Macarthurs, who bred the first of the merino sheep that made Australian wealth "ride on a sheep's back"; a small café here serves refreshments. Nearby **Hambledon Cottage**, 63 Hassel St (Wed, Thurs, Sat & Sun 11am–4pm; $3), built in 1824, was part of the Macarthur estate.

Continuing west, the Western Highway and the rail lines head on to **PENRITH**, the most westerly of Sydney's satellite towns, in a curve of the Nepean River at the foot of the Blue Mountains (on the way out here you pass a couple of wildlife parks; see box on p.195). Penrith has an old-fashioned Aussie feel about it – a tight community that is immensely proud of the Panthers, its boisterous rugby league team. From Penrith Station, you can't miss the huge lettering announcing the **Museum of Fire** on Castlereagh Road (daily 10am–3pm; $6), with its extensive collection of fire-fighting vehicles (fifty in all).You can take in the splendour of the spectacular **Nepean Gorge** from the decks of the paddle steamer *Nepean Belle* (range of cruises from $13 for 1hr 30min, morning or afternoon tea $5 extra; bookings ⊕02/4733 1274, ⓦwww.neapeanbelle.com.au), or head 24km south to the **Warragamba Dam**.The dam has created the huge reservoir of **Lake Burragorang**, a popular picnic spot with barbecues and a kiosk, and some easy walking trails through the bush.

The Blue Mountains region

The section of the Great Dividing Range nearest Sydney gets its name from the blue mist that rises from millions of eucalyptus trees and hangs in the mountain air, tinting the sky and the range alike. In the early days of the colony, the **Blue Mountains** were believed to be an insurmountable barrier to the west.The first expeditions followed the streams in the valleys until they were defeated by cliff faces rising vertically above them. Only in 1813, when the explorers Wentworth, Blaxland and Lawson followed the ridges instead of the valleys, were the mountains finally conquered, allowing the western plains to be opened up for settlement.The range is surmounted by a plateau at an altitude of more than 1000m where, over millions of years, rivers have carved deep valleys into the sandstone, and winds and driving rain have helped to deepen the ravines, creating a spectacular scenery of sheer precipices and walled canyons. Before white settlement, the Daruk Aborigines lived here, dressed in animal-skin cloaks to ward off the cold. An early coal-mining industry, based in Katoomba, was followed by tourism which snowballed after the arrival of the railway in 1868; by 1900 the first three mountain stations of Wentworth Falls, Katoomba and Mount Victoria had been established as fashionable resorts, extolling the health-giving benefits of eucalyptus-tinged mountain air. In 2000 the Blue Mountains became a **World Heritage Listed** site, joining the Great Barrier Reef; the listing came after abseiling was finally banned on the mountains' most famous scenic wonder, the **Three Sisters**, after forty years of clambering had caused significant erosion. The Blue Mountains stand out from other Australian forests, in particular for the recently discovered **Wollemi Pine** (see p.217), a "living fossil" which dates back to the dinosaur era.

All the villages and towns of the romantically dubbed "**City of the Blue Mountains**" – Glenbrook, Springwood, Wentworth Falls, Katoomba and Blackheath – lie on a ridge, connected by the Great Western Highway. Around them is the **Blue Mountains National Park**, the fourth-largest national park in the state and to many minds the best. The region makes a great weekend break from the city, with stunning views and clean air complemented by a wide range of accommodation, cafés and restaurants. But be warned: at weekends, and during the summer holidays, Katoomba is thronged with escapees from the city, and prices escalate accordingly. Even at their most crowded, though, the Blue Mountains always offer somewhere where you can find peace and quiet, and even solitude – the deep gorges and high rocks make much of the terrain inaccessible except to bushwalkers and mountaineers. Climbing schools offer courses in rock-climbing, abseiling and canyoning for both beginners and experienced climbers.

Transport, tours and information

Public transport to the mountains is quite good but your own vehicle will give you much greater flexibility once you've arrived, allowing you to take detours to old mansions, cottage gardens and the lookout points scattered along the ridge. **Trains** leave from Central Station to Mount Victoria and follow the highway, stopping at all the major towns en route (frequent departures until about midnight; 2hr; $11 one-way to Katoomba, $12.80 off-peak day return). If you're dependent on public transport, Katoomba makes the best base: facilities and services are concentrated here, and there are **local buses** to attractions in the vicinity and to other centres. The Blue Mountains Bus Co (☎02/4782 4213) links Katoomba with the new Katoomba Aquatic Centre, the scenic railway, Leura, Wentworth Falls, Bullaburra, Lawson, Hazelbrook and Woodford; buses run daily between about 7am and 6pm, roughly half-hourly, and an all-day bus pass costs $7.50. Mountainlink (☎02/4782 3333) has four commuter routes from Katoomba: to Medlow Bath, Blackheath and Mount Victoria; to Echo Point; to Leura and Gordon Falls; and to North Katoomba. Buses run daily between about 7.30am and 5.30pm, and fares are cheap ($2 to Echo Point for example); Mountainlink also offer an $8 all-day pass to travellers with a VIP or YHA pass, valid on all routes, including the tour bus detailed below. All buses leave town from Katoomba Street outside the *Carrington Hotel*.

There are also a couple of Katoomba-based hop-on hop-off **tours**. Mountainlink (see above) also run **Trolley Tours** (Ⓦ www.trolleytours .com.au), a minibus decked out like a tram, which takes the scenic route from Katoomba to Leura around Cliff Drive, and continues to the Three Sisters and the Skyway cable car (hourly 10am–5pm; $9 all-day pass). The **Blue Mountains Explorer Bus**, run by Fantastic Aussie Tours, 283 Main St, Katoomba, by the train station (☎02/4782 1866 or 1300 300 915, Ⓦ www.fantastic-aussie-tours.com.au), links Katoomba and Leura with all attractions, including the Edge Maxvision Cinema, Three Sisters, the Skyway and other lookouts, in a red London double-decker bus (departs Katoomba hourly 9.30am–4.30pm; $22 all-day pass, discounts for YHA/VIP/student card holders). Although the Explorer Bus is pricier, it comes with a forty-page guidebook, includes entry to the Edge Maxvision Cinema (worth $12.50) and offers substantial discounts on entry fees to other attractions.

The **Blue Mountains Information Centre** (Mon–Fri 9am–5pm, 8.30am–4.30pm; ☏1300/653 408, ⓦwww.bluemts.com.au) is on the Great Western Highway at **GLENBROOK**, the gateway to the Blue Mountains. The centre has a huge amount of information on the area, including a couple of useful free publications: the *Blue Mountains Wonderland Visitors Guide*, which has several detailed colour maps, and *This Month in the Blue Mountains*. The other official tourist information centre is at **Echo Point**, near Katoomba (see p.218); both offices have vacancy listings and can **book accommodation**. The **NPWS** has ranger stations at Wentworth Falls (see overleaf) and Blackheath (see p.218) where you can get comprehensive walking information.

Springwood to Wentworth Falls

Eleven kilometres west of Glenbrook, **SPRINGWOOD** is home to many of the artists who have settled in the mountains, and there are numerous shops selling antiques and arts and crafts. Further west is **FAULCONBRIDGE**, where it's well worth visiting the exhibition of paintings and drawings at the **Norman Lindsay Gallery**, 14 Norman Lindsay Crescent (daily 10am–4pm;

$7.70). The controversial artist and poet (1879–1969), whose nude studies scandalized Australia in the 1930s and whose story was told in the 1994 film *Sirens* (with Elle McPherson as one of the life models), spent the last part of his life here. He is also famous for his humorous children's tale, *The Magic Pudding*, made into a film in 2001; some of the streets around the gallery, such as Bill Barnacle Avenue, are named after its characters.

The small village of **WENTWORTH FALLS** was named after William Wentworth, one of the famous trio who conquered the mountains in 1813. A signposted road leads from the Great Western Highway to the **Wentworth Falls Reserve**, with superb views of the waterfall tumbling down into the Jamison Valley. You can reach this picnic area from Wentworth train station by following **Darwin's Walk** – the route followed by the famous naturalist in 1836. Of the view, which has changed little, Charles Darwin wrote, "If we imagine a winding harbour, with its deep water surrounded by bold cliff-like shores, laid dry, and a forest sprung up on its sandy bottom, we should then have the appearance and structure here exhibited. This kind of view was to me quite novel, and extremely magnificent." Most of the other bushwalks in the area start from the NPWS **Valley of the Waters Conservation Hut** (daily 9am–5pm; ☏ 02/4757 3827), about 3km from the station at the end of Fletcher Street. Bus services are infrequent; a taxi from the station costs about $7. The hut is in a fantastic location overlooking the Jamison Valley, and from its wonderful *Conservation Hut Cafe* you can take full advantage of the stupendous views through the big windows or from the deck outside; in winter an open fire crackles in the grate. A wide selection of bushwalks, detailed on boards outside, ranges from the two-hour **Valley of the Waters track**, which descends into the valley, to an extended two-day walk to **Mount Solitary**. One of the most rewarding is the quite strenuous, six-kilometre **National Pass**, a one-way walk which will conveniently get you back to the train station and takes in Wentworth Falls en route.

Leura

Just two kilometres east of Katoomba, the more upmarket **LEURA**, packed with great cafés, art galleries and small boutiques, retains its own distinct identity and a real village atmosphere. It helps that the main street – The Mall – is quite secluded from the highway and its green median strip practically qualifies as a small park. Even the flower-filled station manages to look pretty, and indeed Leura is renowned for its beautiful **gardens**, some of which are open to the public during the **Leura Gardens Festival** (early to mid-Oct; $12 for visits to around eight gardens, or $3 per garden; more details from the tourist office). Open all year round, though, is the beautiful **Everglades Gardens** (daily 9am–sunset; $6), situated in the grounds of an elegant mansion at 37 Everglades Ave. There are enjoyable views from its formal terraces, with a colourful display of azaleas and rhododendrons, an aboretum, and peacocks strutting among it all. Not far from the village, the flowers give way to the bush: less tame scenery, such as **Leura Cascades**, can be viewed from the picnic area on Cliff Drive; to see it at closer quarters, take the two- to three-hour walk to the base and back. Other waterfalls in the area include the much-photographed **Bridal Veil Falls**, accessible from the Cascades picnic area, and **Gordon Falls**, which you can walk to from Lone Pine Avenue. To the east of Gordon Falls, Sublime Point Road leads to the aptly named **Sublime Point** lookout, with panoramic views of the Jamison Valley. A popular walking track from Leura Falls is the Federal Pass, which skirts the cliffs between here and **Katoomba Falls** (6km one-way; 2hr 30min).

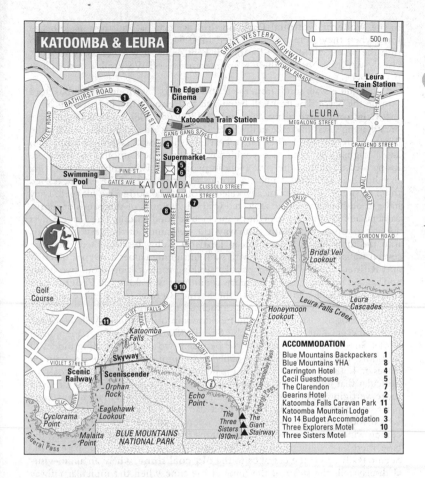

Katoomba and around

KATOOMBA, the biggest town in the Blue Mountains and the area's commercial heart, is also the best located, though for all its surrounding charms, café culture and vintage clothes shops, it can still seem a little raw and characterless. When the town was discovered by fashionable city dwellers in the late nineteenth century, the grandiose *Carrington Hotel*, prominently located in lands near the train station, was the height of elegance, with its leadlighting and wood panelling. After sitting empty and derelict for years, it has finally been renovated and now has accommodation, a restaurant and two cocktail bars.

A stunning introduction to the ecology of the Blue Mountains can be had at the **Edge Maxvision Cinema**, at 225–237 Great Western Highway (℡02/4782 8928), a huge six-storey cinema screen created as a venue to show *The Edge – The Movie* (daily 10.30am, 11.20am, noon, 1.30pm, 2.25pm & 5.30pm; $12.50). The highlight of the forty-minute film is the segment about the "dinosaur trees", a stand of thirty-metre-high **Wollemi Pine**, previously known only from fossil material over sixty million years old. The trees – miraculously still existing – survive deep within a sheltered rainforest gully in the **Wollemi National Park**, north of Katoomba, and they made headlines when they were first discovered in 1994 by a group of canyoners. To film the pines, whose exact location is kept secret, it was necessary to work closely with the NPWS; there is an informative NPWS display in the cinema lobby.

A 25-minute walk south from the train station (or by Mountainlink bus from outside the Savoy Theatre) will bring you to **Echo Point**, the location of an **information centre** (daily 9am–5pm; ☎ 1300/653 408). From here you have breathtaking vistas that take in the Blue Mountains' most famous landmark, the **Three Sisters** (910m). These three gnarled rocky points take their name from an Aboriginal Dreamtime story which relates how the Katoomba people were losing a battle against the rival Nepean people: the Katoomba leader, fearing that his three beautiful daughters would be carried off by the enemy, turned them to stone, but was tragically killed before he could reverse his spell. They have stood here ever since, subjected to the indignities of thousands of tourist cameras and kept awake at night by spectacular floodlighting. The Three Sisters are at the top of the **Giant Stairway**, the beginning of the very steep stairs into the three-hundred-metre-deep **Jamison Valley** below, where there are several walking tracks to places with such intriguing names as **Orphan Rock** and **Ruined Castle**. There's a popular walking route, taking about two hours and graded medium, down the stairway and part way along the **Federal Pass** to the **Landslide**, and then on to the Scenic Railway and Sceniscender (see below), either of which you can take back up to the ridge.

If you want to spare yourself the trek down into the Jamison Valley – or the walk back up – head for the tacky **Scenic World complex** at the end of Violet Street, where you can choose between two equally thrilling modes of transport. The **Scenic Railway** (daily 9am–5pm; every 10min; last train up leaves at 4.50pm; $5 one-way), originally built in the 1880s to carry coal, is a funicular that glides down an impossibly steep gorge to the valley floor. Even more vertiginous, but not as nail-bitingly thrilling, is **Sceniscender** (same price and hours), a new high-tech cable car (pram and wheelchair accessible) which took A$8 million to construct, opening in late 2000. With floor-to-ceiling windows, the views as the car drops 545m are really spectacular. At the base, there's a 330-metre elevated boardwalk through forest to the base of the Scenic Railway via the entrance to the **old coal mine**, where an audio-visual display tells the story of the mine at the time when the funicular railway still hauled coal.

Back up on the ridge, you can get your legs trembling again with **Skyway** (daily 9am–5pm; $8), a rickety-looking cable-car contraption that starts inside the Scenic World complex next to the Scenic Railway and travels 350m across to the other side of the gorge and back again – you can't actually get off – giving those who can bear to look a bird's-eye view of Orphan Rock, Katoomba Falls and the Jamison Valley. The **Scenic World** complex also features a new **Scenic Cinema** which shows a seventeen-minute film, *Rapture in Blue* ($3.30), of the mountain sights, designed to satisfy visitors who have missed the fabulous views on wet and misty days. There are more views at the complex's overpriced cafeteria-style **revolving restaurant** (9am–5pm daily), with a souvenir shop next door.

Blackheath

North of Katoomba, there are more lookout points at **BLACKHEATH** – just as impressive as Echo Point and much less busy. One of the best is **Govetts Leap**, near the NPWS **Blackheath Heritage Centre** (daily 9am–4.30pm;

☎02/4787 8877).The centre has good interpretive material on history, flora and fauna, as well as practical information (with plenty on the adjacent Wollemi and Kanangra Boyd parks too).The two-kilometre **Fairfax Heritage Track** from the NPWS Centre is wheelchair- and pram-accessible and takes in the Govett's Leap Lookout with its marvellous panorama of the Grose Valley and Bridal Veil Falls. Although many walks start from the centre, one of the most popular, **The Grand Canyon**, begins from Evans Lookout Road at the south end of town, west of the Great Western Highway.The village of Blackheath itself is quiet and unspoilt, offering some good browsing in antique shops. Southwest of Blackheath, the beautiful **Megalong Valley** is popular for **horseriding**, with two recommended operators taking people out (see "Listings" p.223).

Mount Victoria and around

Secluded and homely **MOUNT VICTORIA**, 6km from Blackheath and the last mountain settlement proper, is the only one with an authentic, unspoilt village feel.There's a great old pub, the *Imperial*, and the best scones on the mountain at the *Bay Tree Tea Shop*. Mount Victoria is also fondly regarded for its tiny cinema in the public hall (see p.223), where the patron introduces the varied films and defends his choice. Worth a browse are several antique shops and a cluttered antiquarian and secondhand bookshop. Some short **walks** start from the Fairy Bower Picnic area, a ten-minute walk from the Great Western Highway via Mount Piddington Road: get details from any Blue Mountains tourist office, or ask at the *Victoria and Albert Guesthouse* (overleaf).

The **Hartley Historic Site** (daily 10am–1pm & 2–4.30pm; ☎02/6355 2117) lies at the foot of the scenic Victoria Pass in the small valley of the River Lett, 11km from Mount Victoria. It's a well-preserved nineteenth-century village, which began to develop as settlers headed west and forged roads through the mountains.The need for a police centre led to the building of a courthouse here in 1837, and the village of Hartley developed around it until it was bypassed by the Great Western Highway in 1887. It's free to look at the site, and a map is provided in the NPWS information centre and shop (daily 10am–4.30pm) but to enter the buildings – only the courthouse is currently visitable – you have to take a guided tour (10am, 11am, noon, 2pm & 3pm; 30min; $4.40).There is no transport to the site.

Beyond Mount Victoria, drivers can circle back towards Sydney via the scenic **Bells Line of Road**, which heads back east through the fruit- and vegetable-growing areas of Bilpin and Kurrajong to Richmond, with growers selling their produce at roadside stalls. On the way you'll pass **Mount Tomah Botanic Garden** (daily 10am–4pm; $4.40; ☎02/4567 2154 for details of free guided tours), an outpost of Sydney's Royal Botanic Gardens since 1987. There's a rhododendron garden, a display of conifers and a collection of southern hemisphere cool-climate species.The popular *Garden Restaurant* at the visitors centre (lunch daily, dinner Sat only; BYO; ☎02/4567 2060) has fantastic north-facing views over the gardens, Wollemi National Park and the orchards of Bilpin. If you spend more than $12.50 here, the garden entry fee is deducted. You can continue west along the Bells Line of Road to the Zig Zag Railway at Clarence, just over 35km away (see p.223).

Accommodation

Accommodation rates rise on Friday and Saturday nights, so you should aim to visit on weekdays when it's quieter and cheaper. Prices given below are for the cheapest double room available on a weekday in the high season. The tourist offices at Glenbrook and Echo Point (opposite) can both book accommodation. **Katoomba** is the obvious choice if arriving by train, particularly for those on a budget since it has five **hostels** to choose from, but if you have your own transport you can indulge in some of the more unusual and characterful guesthouses in **Blackheath** and **Mount Victoria**.

Hotels, motels and guesthouses

Carrington Hotel, 15–47 Katoomba St, Katoomba (℡ 02/4782 1111, 𝔽 4782 1421, 𝕎 www.thecarrington.com.au). Fronted by a green lawn, the restored *Carrington* is a gracious sight on Katooma's main street. When it opened in 1882 it was one of the region's finest hotels, with British royalty and a roll-call of Australian Prime Ministers amongst its guests. Original features include stained-glass windows and open fireplaces, and there's a snooker and games room and guest lounges to add to the old-fashioned hotel atmosphere. Ten of the 43 rooms share bathrooms. If you can't afford to stay, just come and have a cream tea in the dining room, with old silver on display and its own wine cellar. 24-hour reception. ➐–➑

Cecil Guesthouse, 108 Katoomba St, Katoomba (℡ 02/4782 1411, 𝔽 4728 5364, 𝕎 www.our-guest.com.au). Very central choice, set back from the main drag so very peaceful. Has an old-fashioned 1940s atmosphere, with log fires, games room and tennis courts, plus modern touches such as a spa. Some en-suite rooms. Meals served. ➍

The Clarendon, cnr Lurline and Waratah streets, Katoomba (℡ 02/4782 1322, 𝔽 4782 2564, 𝕎 www.clarendonguesthouse.com.au). Classic 1920s guesthouse with its own bar and restaurant, and cabaret weekends. Nice firm beds and mostly en suites. The guesthouse rooms are best – avoid the fairly unattractive, 1970s-style motel rooms. Budget rooms without bathroom are also available. ➎–➏

Glenella, 56 Govett's Leap Rd, Blackheath (℡ 02/4787 8352, 𝔽 4787 6114). Guesthouse in a charming 1905 homestead with a well-regarded restaurant. Rooms are furnished with antiques. Rates vary with size of room. Breakfast extra. ➐–➑

Hydro-Majestic Hotel, Great Western Highway, opposite Medlow Bath train station, 7km west of Katoomba (℡ 02/4788 1002, 𝔽 4788 1063, 𝕎 www.hydromajestic.com.au). Luxurious, Art Deco hotel restored to its former glory, with en-suite rooms from $220 to $330. Breakfast included; bar and restaurant. Magnificent views. ➑

Hotel Imperial, Station St, Mount Victoria (℡ 02/4787 1233, 𝔽 4787 1461, 𝕎 www.bluemts.com.au/hotelimperial). Nicely restored country pub with beautiful leadlighting and good food. B&B, with some en-suite rooms. ➏

Jemby-Rinjah Lodge, 336 Evans Lookout Rd, Blackheath (℡ 02/4787 7622, 𝔽 4787 6230, 𝕎 www.jemby-rinjah.com.au). Award-winning accommodation, calling itself an "eco-lodge", with accommodation in distinctive timber cabins with wood fires, in bushland near the Grose Valley. Good links with National Park rangers, and bushwalks organized for guests. Cabins sleep up to six people; linen extra but duvets supplied. Minimum two-night stay at weekends. ➐

Kanangra Lodge, 9 Belvedere Ave, Blackheath (℡ 02/4787 8715, 𝔽 4787 7563, 𝕎 www.kanlodge.com.au). Small, peaceful B&B with four rooms, all en suite. Open fireplaces in its cosy lounges, and a large garden outside. Full hot breakfast. ➑

Peppers Fairmont Resort, 1 Sublime Point Rd, 2km southeast of Leura (℡ 02/4782 5222, 𝔽 4784 1685, 𝕎 www.fairmont.com). Huge four-and-a-half-star resort (over 200 rooms) in peaceful grounds with fantastic recreational facilities. There's a large indoor pool and spa, but a wintry swim in the heated outdoor pool and a dip in the steaming spa is quite magical. Also a gym, and squash and tennis courts. Room service. ➑

Three Explorers Motel, 197 Lurline St, Katoomba (℡ 02/4782 1733, 𝔽 4782 1146, 𝕎 www.3explorers.com.au). Well-run, three-star place a cut above the usual charmless motel, on two levels with tastefully decorated units. Spa rooms plus large family suites. Great spot near Echo Point. Minimum two-night stay at weekends. ➏

Three Sisters Motel, 348 Katoomba St, Katoomba (℡ 02/4782 2911, 𝔽 4782 6263). Small, old-style red-brick motel units, but clean, well-equipped and run by an amiable couple. Continental breakfast included. Excellent location near Echo Point. ➎

Victoria and Albert Guesthouse, Station St, Mount Victoria (℡ 02/4787 1241, 𝔽 4787 1588). Classy but friendly place with Art Deco features. Rooms are large and there's a bar, café, restaurant, pool, spa and sauna. Cheaper rooms share bathroom. Breakfast included. ➏–➐

Hostels and camping

Blue Mountains Backpackers, 190 and 194 Bathurst Rd, Katoomba (℡ 02/4782 4226, 𝔽 4782 4236). Two shabby but comfortable bungalows near the station, one with dorms sleeping six to ten. Separate TV/video rooms, a small kitchen, free tea and coffee and lifts to bushwalks. The owners also have an adventure company offering tours and activities. Rooms ❸, dorms ❶

Blue Mountains YHA, 207 Katoomba St, Katoomba (Ⓣ02/4782 1416, Ⓕ4782 6203, Ⓔbluemountains@yhansw.org.au). This larger 22-room YHA hostel, opened in April 2001, is right in the town centre. The former 1930s guesthouse has been modernized but retains its charming Art Deco decor and an old-fashioned mountain retreat ambience, with an open fire in the reading room and a separate games room (with pool table). Most rooms and some of the four-bed dorms are en suite. Mountain-bike rental for guests and abseiling and Jenolan Caves trips can be arranged. Internet access. Reception open 24hr. Rooms ❹–❺, dorms ❶

Gearins Hotel, 273 Great Western Highway, Katoomba (Ⓣ02/4782 4395, Ⓕ4782 4730, Ⓦwww.gearinhotel.com). A large Victorian-era hotel with a 1930s facade. Plenty of rooms upstairs, many converted into clean, four-bed dorms with lockers. Linen and bedding included, and free tea and coffee in the TV lounge. There's no kitchen, though, and the music from the pub below, on Fri & Sat nights, might bother you. Rooms ❹, dorms ❶

Katoomba Falls Caravan Park, Katoomba Falls Rd, Katoomba (Ⓣ & Ⓕ 02/4782 1835). A good location to camp, near the falls. En-suite cabins ❻

Katoomba Mountain Lodge, Church Lane, off Katoomba St, Katoomba (Ⓣ & Ⓕ 02/4782 3933). Central budget accommodation with great views over the town from its verandah, TV room and some bedrooms. Four-bed dorms and attractive doubles (all share bathrooms) with window seats. Small kitchen, and large dining room with free tea and coffee. Breakfast and dinner available. Rooms ❹, dorms ❶

No 14 Budget Accommodation, 14 Lovel St, Katoomba (Ⓣ02/4782 7104, Ⓔno14@lisp.com.au). This relaxed hostel in a charming restored former guesthouse – polished floors, cosy fire, and original features – is like a home away from home, run by an informative, friendly young couple who put in a lot of effort. Mostly twin and double rooms, plus dorms with comfy beds instead of bunks; all centrally heated. Peaceful verandah surrounded by pretty plants and valley views. Rooms ❸, dorms ❶

Eating and drinking

Cuisine in the Blue Mountains has gone way beyond the ubiquitous "Devonshire teas", with some well-regarded restaurants, and a real café culture in Katoomba and Leura; don't forget the NPWS-run *Conservation Hut Cafe* (see 216), with tremendous views over the Jamison Valley. The best place for a civilized **drink** is the *Carrington Bar,* the modern annexe of the grand old *Carrington Hotel* on Katoomba Street, which features a piano player on Friday nights and jazz on Saturday; or you could try your luck at *The Clarendon*'s salubrious little bar, mostly reserved for guests, where there are also cabaret acts. On the other side of the railway line, the huge *Gearins Hotel* is a hive of activity, with several bars where you can play pool and see bands, and it stays open very late.

Arjuna, 16 Valley Rd, just off the Great Western Highway, Katoomba (Ⓣ02/4782 4662). Excellent, authentic Indian restaurant. A bit out of the way, but positioned for spectacular sunset views, so get there early. Good veggie choices too. BYO. Evenings from 6pm; closed Tues & Wed.

Avalon Restaurant, upstairs at 18 Katoomba St (Ⓣ02/4782 5532). Stylish restaurant with the ambience of a quirky café, located in the dress circle of the old Savoy Theatre, with many Art Deco features intact. There are beautiful views down the valley too, which puts coming here for lunch high on the agenda. Moderately expensive menu, and generous servings and huge desserts to die for. BYO & Licensed. There's a separate bar, so you can come here just for a drink and soak up the atmosphere. Lunch & dinner Wed–Sun.

Barcode 6ix, 6 Katoomba St, Katoomba, opposite the station. The mountains' internet café (see "Listings") is colourful and light, attracting a young local crowd. During the week, there's only coffee, drinks and cake, but hot food emerges on the weekend: breakfasts, soups, burgers, Italian sandwiches, steaks and chicken dishes. Daily 9am–9pm.

Bay Tree Tea Shop, 26 Station St, Mount Victoria. A family-run place in a converted Victorian cottage, and the best place in the mountains for scones and pots of real leaf tea. Daily 10am–5pm.

Blues Café, 57 Katoomba St, Katoomba. Bakery and cosy vegetarian café – this place has been going for years and is as popular as ever. Daily 9am–9pm.

Cleopatra, 118 Cleopatra St, Blackheath (☎ 02/4287 8456). This elegant guesthouse restaurant is the place for a splurge. Food is French provincial, the mood is classy and the staff amiable but professional. Set-price menu is around $95. Licensed. Dinner nightly, lunch Sun only.

Conditorei Patisserie Schwarz, Renae Arcade, 30 Station St, Wentworth Falls. German-style pastries to eat in or take away. Ideal to replenish your energies after a bushwalk. Daily except Tues 7.30am–5.30pm.

House of Penang, 183 Katoomba St, Katoomba. Chinese and Malaysian fast-food joint with a few eat-in tables. Delicious laksa noodle soups for around $7. Daily 10am–10pm.

Hydro-Majestic Hotel, Great Western Highway, opposite Medlow Bath train station, 7km west of Katoomba (☎ 02/4788 1002). Turn-of-the-century spa atmosphere, and scintillating views of the Megalong Valley, especially from the Megalong Room – beer, cocktails, coffee, cakes – and beer-garden balcony.

Hotel Imperial, Station St, Mount Victoria, opposite the post office. Good-value, filling and tasty bistro meals can be eaten in the foyer, ballroom, verandah or garden of this classic, old-fashioned, country-style pub, and the dining-room restaurant is open Sat for dinner. Also serves coffee and cakes. Food served daily 8am–8.30pm.

Landseers, 178 The Mall, Leura. Tiny café with a very striking, cosily dark interior – or you can sit outside in the courtyard. Substantial sandwiches, soups and lasagne, plus delicious home-made cakes and puddings. Daily 7.30am–5pm.

The Mountain Deli, 134 The Mall, Leura. A big range of food at reasonable prices makes this a popular one with the locals, and the big window overlooking the street means all-day people-watching. Good-value sandwiches, yummy home-baked cakes, and friendly staff. Mon–Fri & Sun 9am–6pm, Sat 8am–6pm.

The Paragon Café, 65 Katoomba St, Katoomba. Known for its fabulous handmade chocolates and sweets – check out the window and the counter display – and its wonderful National Trust-listed Art Deco interior complete with cocktail bar. They do meals, but you're better off buying chocolate or having a coffee and a gawk. Licensed. Tues–Sun 10am–4pm.

Parakeet Café, 195b Katoomba St, Katoomba. Eclectic, colourful café, its walls covered with paintings by local artists. Simple, inexpensive food and hearty soups are the favourite here. Daily 7am–9pm, later Sat night when there's live music.

Siam Cuisine, 172 Katoomba St, Katoomba (☎ 02/4782 5671). Crowded, inexpensive Thai restaurant with $6.60 lunchtime specials. BYO. Tues–Sun 11.30am–2.30pm & 5.30–10pm.

Victoria and Albert, Station St, Mount Victoria (☎ 02/4787 1241). Civilized verandah café (Fri–Sun 10am–5pm), plus a highly recommended restaurant in a wonderful old dining room, open nightly. Bookings preferred for non-residents.

Zuppa, 36 Katoomba St, Katoomba (☎ 02/4782 9247). Katoomba's trendiest café – amiable staff, Art Deco interior, generous servings and affordable prices. Though it gets crowded, they claim they'll always fit you in somewhere. Prices range from $6.50 for a sandwich to $17.50 for a steak. The DVD player gets fired up occasionally to show music concerts. BYO. Daily 7am–11pm.

Listings

Adventure activities Australian School of Mountaineering (at Paddy Pallin, 166b Katoomba St; ☎ 02/4782 2014, ⓦ www.asmguides.com), Katoomba's original abseiling outfit, offers daily courses ($99 including lunch), plus canyoning, rock-climbing and bush-survival courses. Canyoning is the big thing with Blue Mountains Adventure Company (1 Katoomba St; ☎ 02/4782 4009), with beginners' full-day canyoning and abseiling trips in the Grand Canyon or Empress Canyon (respectively $119 and $125, includes lunch), rock-climbing and mountain-biking. High 'n' Wild Mountain Adventures (3/5 Katoomba St; ☎ 02/4782 6224, ⓦ www.high-n-wild.com.au) has a consistently good reputation for its beginners' abseiling courses (full day $119 including lunch, half-day $69), plus half-day canyoning ($85), rock-climbing ($85) and mountain biking ($75).

Bike rental Cycle Tech, 182 Katoomba St, Katoomba (☎ 02/4782 2800), has mountain bikes from $19 half-day, $27.50 full day. The YHA also rents bikes to guests ($26 full day, $16.50 half-day).

Bookshops There are several interesting second-hand bookshops on Katoomba St, Katoomba, and in the other villages. New books can be bought at Megalong Books, 183 The Mall, Leura.

Bus services Blue Mountains Bus Co (☎ 02/4782 3333); Mountainlink (☎ 02/4782 4213).

Camping equipment If you haven't got your own gear, you must rent it in Sydney before you come up (see Sydney "Listings", p.186). Alternatively, Paddy Pallin, 166b Katoomba St (☎ 02/4782 4466), sells camping gear and a good range of topographic maps and bushwalking guides.

Car rental Thrifty, 80 Megalong St, Leura (⊤02/4784 2888).

Cinemas The Edge Maxvision Cinema, 225–237 Great Western Highway, Katoomba (⊤02/4782 8928), shows new-release feature films on a giant screen at 3.15pm, 7pm & 9.15pm ($9.50; cheap tickets $7.50 at 3.15pm and all day Tues), as well as *The Edge – The Movie* (see p.217) and a changing programme of other Maxvision films (9.45am, 12.45pm & 6.15pm). Mount Vic Flicks, Harley Ave, off Station St, Mount Victoria (⊤02/4787 1577), is a quaint local cinema in an old hall showing a fine programme of prestige new releases and independent films (Thurs–Sun, daily during school holidays; cheap tickets Thurs).

Horseriding The Packsaddlers, Green Gully, Megalong Rd, Megalong Valley (⊤02/4787 9150), offers one-hour rides up to the mountains ($25) or fully catered one-day ($100) or overnight (with camping; $140) excursions down to the Coxs River; accommodation available on-site in well-equipped cabins. Werriberri Trail Rides, Megalong Rd, Megalong Valley (⊤02/4787 9171), offers horseriding for all abilities and pony rides for children. Their two-hour ride, including pick-up from Katoomba, is $41.80.

Hospital Blue Mountains District Anzac Memorial, Katoomba (⊤02/4782 2111).

Internet access, *Barcode 6ix*, 6 Katoomba St, Katoomba, opposite the station, has 12 terminals ($2.50 15min, $5.50 1hr). See also "Eating and drinking", p.221.

Laundry The Washing Well, K-Mart car park, Katoomba. Daily 7am–7pm.

Pharmacies Blooms Springwood Pharmacy, 161 Macquarie Rd, Springwood (Mon–Fri 8.30am–9pm, Sat 8.30am–7pm, Sun 9am–7pm; ⊤02/4751 2963); Greenwell & Thomas, 145 Katoomba St, Katoomba (Mon–Fri 8.30am–7pm, Sat & Sun 8.30am–6pm; deliveries available; ⊤02/4782 1066).

Post office Katoomba Post Office, Pioneer Place opposite Coles supermarket, off Katoomba St, Katoomba, NSW 2780.

Supermarket Coles, Pioneer Place off Katoomba St, Katoomba (daily 6am–midnight).

Swimming pool Katoomba Aquatic Centre, Gates Ave, Katoomba (Mon–Fri 6am–8pm, Sat & Sun 8am–8pm, winter weekends closes 6.30pm; ⊤02/4782 1748), has outdoor heated Olympic-sized and children's pools, plus an attached complex which is open all year with heated indoor pool, sauna, spa and gym. Entry is $3.30 (plus sauna and spa $6; gym $7; gym, sauna and spa $10).

Taxis Taxis wait outside the main Blue Mountains train stations to meet arrivals; otherwise call Katoomba Radio Cabs (⊤02/4782 1311) or Blue Mountains Taxis (⊤02/4759 3000).

Tours Most tours of the Blue Mountains start from Sydney; see box on pp.192–193. There are two hop-on hop-off tour services offered from Katoomba of the immediate area, run by Mountainlink and Fantastic Aussie Tours (see p.214). Fantastic Aussie Tours also do large-group coach tours: there's a day-tour to the Jenolan Caves (daily from $64) and a combined bushwalk and cave visit ($99), plus adventure caving ($107), while a full-day tour of the local area takes in Mount Tomah Botanic Gardens (see p.219) and the Zig Zag Railway (see below) for $65. A small-group half-day 4WD tour takes in the Blue Mountains National Park ($81). All prices include entry fees.

Trains Katoomba Station general enquiries ⊤02/4782 1902.

The Zig Zag Railway

LITHGOW, on the Great Western Highway 11km northwest of Hartley, is a charming coal-mining town nestled under bush-clad hills, with wide leafy streets and some imposing old buildings. Situated about 13km east of the town on the Bells Line of Road, by the small settlement of Clarence, is the **Zig Zag Railway**. In the 1860s engineers were faced with the problem of how to get the main western railway line from the top of the Blue Mountains down the steep drop to the Lithgow Valley, so they came up with a series of zigzag ramps. These fell into disuse in the early twentieth century, but tracks were relaid by rail enthusiasts in the 1970s. Served by old steam trains, the picturesque line passes through two tunnels and over three viaducts. You can stop at points along the way and rejoin a later train. The Zig Zag Railway can be reached by ordinary State Rail train on the regular service between Sydney and Lithgow, by requesting the guard in advance to stop at the Zig Zag platform; you then walk across the line to Bottom Point platform at the base of the Lithgow Valley. To catch the Zig Zag Railway from Clarence, which is at the top of the valley, you'll need to have your own transport, or take the Fantastic Aussie Tour (see above). Zig Zag trains depart from Clarence daily (11am, 1pm & 3pm; from the Zig Zag platform add 40min to these times; $15; no bookings required but to check times call ☎02/6353 1795). There are plenty of **motels** in and around Lithgow – and the helpful **Lithgow Visitors Centre**, 184 Mort St (daily 9am–5pm; ☎02/6353 1859) can advise on accommodation.

Kanangra Boyd National Park and the Jenolan Caves

Kanangra Boyd National Park shares a boundary with the Blue Mountains National Park. Further south than the latter, much of it is inaccessible but you can explore the rugged beauty of **Kanangra Walls**, where the Boyd Plateau falls away to reveal a wilderness area of creeks, deep gorges and rivers below. Reached via Jenolan Caves, there are three walks from the car park at Kanangra Walls: a short lookout walk, a waterfall stroll and a longer plateau walk – contact the NPWS in Oberon for details (☎02/6336 1972). You can get to **Oberon**, a timber-milling town and the closest settlement to Kanangra, by Countrylink bus from Mount Victoria (3 weekly).

The **Jenolan Caves** lie 30km southwest across the mountains from Katoomba on the far edge of the Kanangra Boyd National Park – over 80km by road – and contain New South Wales' most spectacular limestone formations. There are nine "show" caves with prices for a guided tour of each cave ranging from $13.20 to $22 depending on the cave (guided tours various times daily 10am–5pm; 1hr 30min–2hr). If you're coming for just a day, plan to see one or two caves: the best general cave is the Lucas Cave ($13.20), and a more spectacular one is the Temple of Baal ($17.60); the Lucas combined with the Temple of Baal is $22. The system of caves is surrounded by the **Jenolan Caves Reserve**, a fauna and flora sanctuary with picnic facilities and walking trails to small waterfalls and lookout points. It and the caves are looked after by The Jenolan Caves Trust (☎02/6359 3311, ⓦ www.jenolancaves.org.au), who also offer adventure caving. There's no public transport to the caves but you can get here from Katoomba with Fantastic Aussie Tours (see p.214) or many other tours are available from Sydney.

You can actually **walk** from Katoomba to the Jenolan Caves; the 42-kilometre-long **Six Foot Track** through the bush begins at the Explorers Tree next to the Great Western Highway about 2.5km west of Katoomba train station; you'll need to allow two to three days for the walk, and you're advised to carry plenty of water. The track, which finishes near *Jenolan Caves House* (see opposite), was originally cut as a bridle path in 1884 to provide access to the caves from Katoomba. There are four basic **campsites** along the way, plus well-equipped cabins at Binda Flats reached by car from Jenolan Caves Road, sleeping six to eight people, with a minimum two-night stay at weekends (❺, weekends ❼). Book the cabins through Jenolan Caves Trust (see above), who will also supply details and **information** on the walk. Glenbrook NPWS information centre (see p.215) can provide more information on camping. Great Australian Walks (☎02/9555 7580, ⓦ www.walkaustralia.com), offer three-day fully catered and supported **guided walks** along the Six Foot Track ($480) during spring and autumn, camping one night and staying in a lodge the next. If you're going it alone, Fantastic Aussie Tours (see p.214) provides a daily transfer service ($44) for bushwalkers to the start of the track; you can leave your car in their depot. The same service will get you from Katoomba to the Jenolan

Caves (2hr; departs Katoomba 10.30am; departs Jenolan Caves 3.45pm), designed as an overnight rather than a day-return service; otherwise the same company offers day-tours from Katoomba, as do several other operators (see "Listings" p.223), or there are many tours from Sydney (see pp.192–193).

The focus of the area, apart from the caves themselves, is the rather romantic *Jenolan Caves House*, a beautiful old hotel (℡02/6359 3322, ℻6359 3388; ➏–➐) which found fame as a honeymoon destination in the 1920s. If you decide to indulge, make sure you get one of the characterful older rooms (though most share bathroom) rather than the motel-style ones in the newer annexe; food in the restaurant is good and plentiful, and dinner plus bed and breakfast packages are available. Other **places to stay** in the area include *Jenolan Cabins*, Edith Road, 4km west of Jenolan Caves on Porcupine Hill (℡ & ℻ 02/6335 6239, ⓦwww.bluemts.com.au/JenolanCaves; ➏), whose very reasonably priced, well-equipped, modern, two-bedroom timber cabins with wood-fires accommodate six (bring your own linen) – all with magnificent views over the Blue Mountains National Park, Kanangra Boyd National Park and the Jenolan Caves Reserve.

South

Once you escape Sydney's uninspiring outer suburbs, the journey south is very enjoyable. Beyond Botany Bay and Port Hacking, the Princes Highway and the Illawarra railway hug the edge of the **Royal National Park** for more than 20km. South of the park, the railway and the scenic Lawrence Hargrave Drive (Route 68) follow the coast to **Wollongong**. Between here and Nowra, the ocean beaches of the Leisure Coast are popular with local holiday-makers, while fishermen, windsurfers and yachtsmen gather at **Lake Illawarra**, a huge coastal lake near Port Kembla. A few kilometres further down the coast is the famous, and often lethal, blowhole at **Kiama**.

Inland, west of Wollongong, Sydney's drinking water is stored in the Cataract and Cordeaux **reservoirs**, surrounded by picnic and leisure areas. Further southwest, past **Kangaroo Valley**, the softly rolling hills of the **Southern Highlands** are dotted with old country towns such as **Berrima** and **Bundanoon**, the latter overlooking the wild and windswept crags of **Morton National Park**.

Transport down south is good, with a frequent train service operating between Sydney and Nowra, stopping at most of the coastal locations detailed below. The main bus service is Pioneer Motor Service, which stops at Wollongong and Kiama en route to Bega and Eden (℡02/4423 5233; 3–4 daily Mon–Fri, 1 daily Sat & Sun). Greyhound Pioneer (℡13 2030) has a daily Sydney–Melbourne coastal route (departing 11.30am) which also stops at Wollongong and Kiama. There are also several local bus companies in the region; these are detailed in the accounts below.

The Royal and Heathcote national parks

The **Royal National Park** is a huge nature reserve right on Sydney's doorstep, only 36km south of the city. Established in 1879, it was the second national park in the world (after Yellowstone in the USA). The railway between Sydney and Wollongong marks its western border, and from the train the scenery is fantastic – streams, waterfalls, rock formations and rainforest flora fly past the window. If you want to explore more closely, get off at one of the stations along the way – Loftus, Engadine, Heathcote, Waterfall or Otford – all starting points for walking trails into the park. On the eastern side, from Jibbon Head to Garie Beach, the park falls away abruptly to the ocean, creating a spectacular coastline of steep cliffs broken here and there by creeks cascading into the seas and little coves with fine sandy beaches; the remains of **Aboriginal rock carvings** are the only traces of the original Dharawal people. The ultimate trek is the spectacular 26km **Coastal Walk**, taking in the entire coastal length of the park. Give yourself two days to complete it, beginning at either Otford or Bundeena, camping overnight at one of several bush camps en route. Undertaking part of the route is also satisfying, such as the popular trail from **Otford** down to beachfront **Burning Palms** (2hr one-way; no camping). A good book to buy is the *Royal National Park on Foot* by Alan Fairley, and try to get a copy of the *Royal National Park* map; both are available at the NPWS Visitor Centre (see below).

You can also drive in at various points ($10 entry per car, bike and pedestrians free; gates open 24hr except at Garie Beach, where they shut at 8.30pm). Coming in at the northern end, turning off the Princes Highway south of Loftus, you can visit the **NPWS Visitor Centre** (daily 8.30am–4.30pm; ☎02/9542 0648), 2km from Loftus train station. The easy one-kilometre track from here to the Bungoona Lookout boasts panoramic views and is wheelchair-accessible. Cars are allowed right through the park, exiting at **Waterfall** on the Princes Highway or **Stanwell Park** on Lawrence Hargrave Drive. Not far south of the NPWS centre, **Audley** is a picturesque picnic ground on the Hacking River, where you can rent a boat or canoe for a leisurely paddle. Deeper into the park, on the ocean shore, **Wattamolla** and **Garie beaches** have good surfing waves; the two beaches are connected by a walking track. There are **kiosks** at Audley, Wattamolla and Garie Beach.

There's a small, very basic but secluded YHA **youth hostel** inside the park 1km from Garie Beach (book in advance at any YHA hostel; key must be collected in advance; ❶), with no electricity or showers. There are also a number of **bushcamps** which require a permit (free) from the visitor centre; you'll need to telephone in advance so that the permit can be posted out to you (which can take up to five days), or they can tell you if there are any spaces and give you a permit number over the phone. You can of course just sidestep bureaucracy but you may not be able to find a space at a site.

An interesting alternative way to get here is by **ferry** from the southern beachside suburb of Cronulla (see p.158) at the Tonkin Street wharf just below the train station: Cronulla National Park Ferries (hourly: April–Oct Mon–Fri 8.30am–5.30pm; Nov–March Mon–Fri 5.30am–6.30pm except 12.30pm, Sat & Sun 8.30am–6.30pm; returns from Bundeena on the hour; $3.10; also narrated cruises Mon, Wed, Fri & Sun 10.30am; 3hr; $14; ☎02/9523 2990) take half an hour to cross Port Hacking to the small town of **BUNDEENA** at the park's northeast tip. To begin the Coastal Walk from Bundeena, follow The Avenue and Lambeth Walk 1km to the national park gate. A shorter option is the pleasant half-day walk to pretty sheltered **Little Marley Beach** for a swim and a picnic (2hr one-way) – or head down a pathway to **Jibbons Beach**, a thirty-minute stroll which will take you past some Dharawal rock engravings, where faint outlines of a kangaroo, stingrays, whales and a six-fingered man can be seen (pick up the *Jibbon Aboriginal Rock Engravings Walk* map and leaflet from the café near the wharf). Just west of the town on the shores of the Hacking River is a NPWS **campsite**, the *Bonnie Vale Camping Ground*, but for more comfort, *Bundeena Caravan Park*, south of the wharf on Scarborough Street (℡02/9523 9520; cabins ❸, en suite ❹), has en-suite cabins.

Heathcote National Park, across the Princes Highway from the Royal National Park, is much smaller and quieter. This is a serious bushwalkers' park with no roads and a ban on trail bikes. The best **train** station for the park is Waterfall, from where you can follow a twelve-kilometre trail through the park, before catching a train back from Heathcote. On the way you pass through quite a variety of vegetation and alongside several swimmable pools, the carved sandstone of the **Kingfisher Pool** making it the most picturesque. By **car**, you can reach the picnic area at Woronora Dam on the western edge of the park: turn east off the Princes Highway onto Woronora Road. **Camping** permits are available from the NPWS Visitor Centre (see opposite).

Wollongong and around

Although it's New South Wales' third-largest city, **WOLLONGONG** has more of a country-town feel, with the students of Wollongong University giving it extra life in term time. Eighty kilometres south of Sydney, it's essentially an industrial centre (Australia's largest steelworks is at nearby Port Kembla) but there are a few natural attractions to make it worth visiting – such as the **Illawarra Escarpment**, which rises dramatically beyond and provides a lush backdrop to the city.

The highlight of the city itself is **Wollongong Harbour**, with its maritime feel enhanced by a fishing fleet in Belmore Basin, a fish market, a few seafood restaurants, and a picturesque nineteenth-century lighthouse on the breakwater. On either side are Wollongong's central **surf beaches**: choose North Beach for the best surf, the harbour beaches for more gentle swimming. There's not really much to see in the **city centre**, which has been swallowed up by a giant shopping mall on Crown Street, but if you want to kill a few hours, visit the **City Gallery**, on the corner of Kembla and Burelli streets (Tues–Fri 10am–5pm, Sat & Sun noon–4pm; free), a regional art centre showing changing exhibitions plus a permanent collection with an emphasis on contemporary Aboriginal and colonial Illawarra artists. Wollongong is also home to the vast **Nan Tien Buddhist Temple**, the largest in Australia, on Berkeley Road, Berkeley, south of the centre and reached from Wollongong by train. The temple offers monthly two-day meditation retreats (℡02/4272 0600 for details).

If you're **driving from Sydney**, the quickest route to take is the Princes Highway past Heathcote and the Royal National Park, avoiding the coast. However, a more scenic coastal and bush route involves driving through the Royal National Park, emerging above the cliffs at **Otford**. A few kilometres on is the impressive clifftop lookout on **Bald Hill** above Stanwell Park – you'll see not only the vista but also the breathtaking sight of **hang-gliders** taking off and soaring down. You can join in with the Sydney Hang Gliding Centre (℡02/4294 4294, ⓦ www.hanggliding.com.au), which offers tandem flights with an instructor for around $180 during the week, $195 weekends (available daily depending on the weather); the centre also runs courses. At **Coalcliff** the *Imperial Hotel* is a must for an en-route drink, as it sits right on the cliff's edge. By the time you get to **Austinmer** you're at the base of the stunning cliffs and into some heavy surf territory; another drinking hole here is the legendary *Headlands Hotel*, which also offers budget accommodation (see p.228). There's impressive cliff scenery as you pass through **Scarborough**, **Wombarra** and **Thirroul**, tiny seaside villages with a station, lovely local beaches and not much else; Thirroul is the spot where the English novelist D.H. Lawrence wrote *Kangaroo* during his short Australian interlude. The appropriately named **Sublime Point**, on the Bulli Pass at the Illawarra Escarpment, is a place to stop for fantastic views. If you have your own transport you can explore the escarpment using the **walking tracks** on Mount Kembla and Mount Keira, about 10km from Wollongong.

Practicalities

The best and cheapest way to get to Wollongong from Sydney is by **train** (departs Sydney Central Station or Redfern every 30min), which hugs the coast and stops at most of the small towns en route; Wollongong Station is right in the centre just off Crown Street. Pioneer Motor Service has three to four services on weekdays and two a day at weekends, while Greyhound Pioneer runs one daily bus service, leaving Sydney at 11.30am and returning from Wollongong at 11.50am. **Tourism Wollongong**, near the mall at 93 Crown St (Mon–Fri 9am–5pm, Sat & Sun 10am–4pm; ☎02/4228 0300), provides information and can advise on **accommodation**. The *Boat Harbour Motel,* on the corner of Campbell and Wilson streets (☎02/4228 9166, ℱ4226 4878; ❼–❻), has comfortable and spacious rooms with balconies, some with sea views; more upmarket, and also with ocean views, is Wollongong's five-star *Novotel Northbeach*, 2–14 Cliff Rd, North Wollongong (☎02/4226 3555, ℱ4229 1705, Ⓦ www.novotel.northbeach.com.au; ❽). Dorm rooms as well as singles and twins, some en suite, are available at *Keiraleagh House*, 60 Kembla St (☎02/4228 6765; rooms ❸, dorms ❶), in an old converted mansion a few blocks back from the beach. A garden with a barbecue area makes for happy mingling between students and travellers. There's nowhere central to **camp** in Wollongong, but the two caravan parks to the north are right on the beach: *Corrimal Beach Tourist Park* is on Lake Parade in Corrimal, 6km north at the mouth of Towradgi Lagoon (☎02/4285 5688; cabins ❹–❻); while *Bulli Beach Tourist Park* is 11km north of town on Farrell Road, Bulli (☎02/4285 5677; cabins ❻–❼, bungalows ❸–❹). In Austinmer the *Headlands Hotel*, on Headlands Avenue (☎02/4267 1146; ❹), has inexpensive – dilapidated, but clean – en-suite rooms with stunning views overlooking the water. Food is available from the cheap pub bistro at lunchtime.

Wollongong isn't really renowned for its **food**. There is a concentration of cafés on Crown Street and intersecting Corrimal Street, just around the corner from *Keiraleagh House*. *Tannous*, on the corner of Crown and Corrimal streets, serves cheap and generous Lebanese food including falafel rolls and plenty of Lebanese sweets (daily 8am–midnight). Wollongong's most well-regarded restaurant is *Sweetlips Cafe*, 50 Crown St (lunch Tues–Fri, dinner Wed–Sat; ☎02/4225 9542), with a vivid colour scheme, outdoor seating and a Mediterranean menu.

Kiama and around

Of the coastal resorts south of Sydney, **KIAMA** is probably the most attractive – though if you want more than a day- or overnight trip to the beach, you'd be better off continuing down to Nowra and beyond (see p.269). A small resort and fishing town, Kiama is famous for its star attraction, the **Blowhole**, a five-minute walk from the **railway station** on Blowhole Point. Stemming from a natural fault in the cliffs, the blowhole explodes into a waterspout when a wave hits with sufficient force. It's impressive, but also potentially dangerous: freak waves can be thrown over 60m into the air and have swept several over-curious bystanders into the raging sea – so stand well back. The **Kiama Visitor Information Centre**, nearby on Blowhole Point Road (daily 9am–5pm; ☎02/4232 3322 or free call 1800 803 897, Ⓦ www.kiama.com.au), supplies details of other local attractions such as **Cathedral Rocks**, a few kilometres to the north, whose rocky outcrops drop abruptly to the ocean. About 15km south of Kiama is **Seven Mile Beach**, a good sandy beach with its own small oceanfront **national park**.

West of Kiama, a steep road leads to **Mount Saddleback Lookout**, from where on a clear day you can get an incredible view of the entire coast – from the Royal National Park in the north to Jervis Bay in the south. Further west, about 14km from Kiama, is the **Jamberoo Recreation Park** (Sat, Sun & holidays 10am–5pm; $24), a mixed bag of offerings including chairlifts, bobsleds, giant waterslides and a barbecue area. Beyond Jamberoo you can head north to join the Illawarra Highway, and follow that inland to **Macquarie Pass**, the gateway to the Southern Highlands. The **Macquarie Pass National Park** is one of the southernmost stands of Australia's sub tropical rainforest; there's a car park on the road from where the Cascades Walk takes you on a 2km loop through the forest. Alternatively, Jamberoo Mountain Pass Road heads to Robertson on the Illawarra Highway via the **Budderoo National Park** where the **Minnamurra Rainforest Centre** (daily 9am–5pm, boardwalk and track closes 4pm; ℡02/4236 0469), offers an elevated boardwalk and walking track through cabbage tree palms, staghorn ferns and impressive Illawarra fig trees to the upper **Carrington Falls**. The impressive falls are 8km east of Robertson by road, and are worth a detour: a turn-off from the Jamberoo Mountain Pass Road leads to lookout points over the waterfalls.

If you want to **stay** in this area you'll find plenty of motels strung out along the highway. Alternatives in Kiama include *Kiama Backpackers*, 31 Bong Bong St, very close to the train station and right near the beach (℡ & Ⓕ 02/4233 1881, Ⓦwww.suresite.com/oh/k/kiama; rooms ❷, weekends ❸, dorms ❶), a hostel whose owner sometimes offers free trips to the surrounding areas on a quiet day; and the *Grand Hotel*, on the corner of Manning and Bong Bong streets (℡02/4232 1037; ❸, weekends ❹), which has budget-priced, old-fashioned pub accommodation – the pub restaurant serves decent filling meals lunch and dinner daily. The closest campsite to the centre is at *Blowhole Point Holiday Park* right near the Blowhole (℡02/4232 2707; on-site vans ❹, cabins ❺–❻), while *Easts Beach Caravan Park*, on Easts Beach a couple of kilometres south of Kiama (℡02/4232 2124, Ⓕ4233 1009, Ⓔeastpark@ozemail.com.au; cabins ❹, en-suite ❺), is handy for the beach with safe, sheltered swimming; there's a two-night minimum stay at weekends.

In **GERRINGONG**, 10km south of Kiama, there's a YHA hostel, *Nestor House*, on Fern Street, just 250m from Werri Beach (℡ & Ⓕ 02/4234 1249; dorms ❶, rooms ❸), or there's the *Werri Beach Holiday Park* (℡02/4234 1285; on-site vans ❹, cabins ❺–❻), which benefits from a great location at the northern end of Seven Mile Beach, between Crooked River and the sand. A further 10km south, easily reached by train on the Sydney–Nowra route, **BERRY** is a charming little town which has become a magnet for gay-owned cafés and restaurants and a popular **gay and lesbian** weekend destination. Three kilometres out of town, the gay-and-lesbian-friendly *Spotted Gums Cottage* (℡02/4464 1779, Ⓔspotgum@shoalhaven.net.au; ❼) is a one-bedroom self-contained retreat with its own spa and five acres of native gardens; expect champagne when you arrive, and bikes to explore the area.

Inland: the road to Canberra

If you want to take your time getting to Canberra, there are a number of worthwhile diversions off the speedy South Western Freeway (Route 31), the main road inland which eventually joins up with the Hume Highway. Camden

Valley Way heads west from the freeway to **CAMDEN** on the Nepean River, where John Macarthur pioneered the breeding of Merino sheep in 1805. The town still has a rural feel and several well-preserved nineteenth-century buildings, the oldest of which dates from 1816. En route, you'll pass **Mount Annan Botanical Garden** (daily: April–Sept 10am–4pm; Oct–March 10am–6pm; $4.40). Actually the native-plant section of the Royal Botanic Gardens in Sydney, this outstanding collection of flora is the largest of its kind in Australia. Within the grounds, you can eat well at idyllically-sited *Kylie's Kitchen*, from sandwiches to a fillet steak, at outside tables surrounded by trees; if you spend over $12.50 they'll refund the entry fee to the gardens. The garden is 57km southwest of Sydney and can be reached by a combination of CityRail train to Campbelltown, and then Busways (℡ 02/4625 8922).

From Camden, Remembrance Drive leads to **PICTON**, a small farming town cradled by hills; you can get here by train from Sydney or with Picton Coaches (℡ 02/4677 1564) from Campbelltown or Wollongong, via Bargo, Tahmoor and Thirlmere. Picton is a good spot for a drink at the 1839 sandstone *George IV Inn*, which brews its own beer by a traditional German method; you can imbibe in the shady beer garden and indulge in one of their legendary seafood platters. Eleven kilometres south of Picton, the five connected freshwater lakes that make up **Thirlmere Lakes National Park** are named in the language of the Gandangarra Aborigines. Lake Couridjah is best for swimming, surrounded by unspoilt bushland and plenty of birdlife. Continuing along Remembrance Drive, it's 8km to the **Wirrimbirra Sanctuary** at **Bargo** (daily 8am–5pm; free), a peaceful bushland spot run by the National Trust, with a field studies centre, a native nursery, bushwalking trails, and pools to swim in and engage in a bit of platypus-spotting at dawn or dusk. You might also see wallabies, kangaroos, wombats, brush-tailed possums and goannas, along with 150 different species of birds. There are basic **cabins** with bunk-style accommodation (℡ 02/4684 1112; ❶), and outside there's a big open fireplace to sit around, which comes into its own in August when local musicians gather for the annual Brush with the Bush weekend. If you don't have your own **transport**, you can get here by taking the train from Sydney to Bargo and then walking a couple of kilometres.

The Southern Highlands

From Bargo, there are a couple of detours worth taking on the old road south, the Hume Highway, through the picturesque Southern Highlands which have been a favourite weekend retreat for Sydneysiders since the 1920s. Marking the beginning of the Highlands is **MITTAGONG**, a small agricultural and tourist town 110km south of Sydney, mostly visited on the way to the limestone **Wombeyan Caves** (daily 8.30am–5pm; $14.50 guided tour of one cave, $25 for two caves; 1hr 30min for each cave) in the nearby hills. The route to the five caves begins 4km south of the town off the highway and winds upwards for 65km; high-country scenery helps to distract you from the bumpiness of the partly unsealed road. There's a well-run **campsite** near the caves (℡ 02/4843 5976, ℻ 4843 5988, ⓦ www.goulburn.net.au/wombeyan; cottages ❻, cabins ❹, on-site vans ❸). For more on accommodation in the area – and a free booking service – contact **Tourism Southern Highlands** (daily 8am–5.30pm; ℡ 02/4871 2888, accommodation bookings on ℡ 1300/657 559, ⓦ www.highlandsnsw.com.au) in Winifred West Park on the Hume Highway; they also have masses of information on bushwalks of varying lengths. The Southern Highlands is well served by **transport**, with a frequent train service between Sydney and Canberra stopping at Picton, Mittagong,

Bowral, Moss Vale, Bundanoon and Goulburn. Priors Scenic Express (℡02/4472 4040) from Campbelltown train station on Sydney's western fringes also goes to Mittagong, Bowral and Moss Vale (daily during school holidays, otherwise Mon, Tues & Thurs–Sat) while Berrima Coaches provides a local bus service (℡02/4871 3211).

Mittagong and neighbouring **BOWRAL**, 6km southwest, while less pretty than other Highland bases such as Berrima and Bundanoon, share a stash of impressive **restaurants**. At Mittagong, *Thonburi*, 60 Bowral Rd (lunch Tues–Sun, dinner daily; BYO and licensed; ℡02/4872 1511), serves delicious traditional Thai meals in an elegant setting, while *The Blue Cockerel*, 95 Hume Highway (dinner Tues–Sat; licensed and BYO; ℡02/4872 1677), is a busy bistro serving modern Australian food with a French twist. In Bowral, *The Catch*, 250 Bong Bong St (lunch Fri–Sun, dinner Wed–Mon; licensed and BYO; ℡02/4862 2677), is a city-style brasserie focusing on fish, plus wood-fired gourmet pizzas; further down the same street, in the Empire Cinema complex, you can have the best coffee in town at *Coffee Culture* (Mon–Thurs 8.30am–5.30pm, Fri & Sat 8.30am–9.30pm). After scoffing in Bowral, cricket fans might like to check out the **Bradman Museum** on Jude Street (daily 10am–5pm; $8), which details the career of the legendary Australian cricketer Don Bradman, who died in March 2001, and the history of The Ashes.

The picturesque village of **BERRIMA** is 7km on from Mittagong. The *Surveyor General Inn*, one of an excellent complement of well-preserved and restored old buildings, has been serving beer here since 1835 – making it a good enough reason to indulge. Suitably refreshed, you can check out some of the other sights: inside the 1838 sandstone **courthouse**, on the corner of Argyle and Wiltshire streets (daily 10am–4pm; $5.50), is the **Berrima Visitor Centre** (same hours; ℡02/4877 1505), while across the road is the still-operational **Berrima Gaol**, which once held the infamous bushranger Thunderbolt – and also has the dubious distinction of being the first place in Australia where a woman was executed. The quality of the craftwork made by the prisoners is so high that it's sold in a weekend-opening shop attached to the gaol (Sat & Sun 9.30am–4.30pm). Continue up Wiltshire Street from the courthouse to get to the **River Walk**, the end of which is marked by a fine reserve with picnic tables – and camping too. Other **accommodation** includes a slather of B&Bs in pretty, old stone cottages such as *Waldon Wood* (℡02/4877 1164; ⑥–⑧). Motels here are also fairly salubrious: the *Berrima Bakehouse Motel* (℡02/4877 1381, ⑥4877 1047; ⑤, Sat ⑦), on the highway at the corner of Wingecarribee Street, is a modern brick building but with the bonus of a peaceful, pleasant garden leading down to the river and a saltwater pool; the *White Horse Inn* in Market Place (℡02/4877 1204, ⑥4877 2185, ⓦwww.highlandsnsw.com.au/whitehorseinn; ⑥, Sat ⑦) is a large, old 1832 sandstone hotel with accommodation in modern motel units in the garden.

Five kilometres from Moss Vale on the Hume Highway is the turn-off south to **BUNDANOON**, famous for its annual April celebration of its Scottish heritage. Exploiting the autumnal atmosphere of mist and turning leaves, Bundanoon becomes Brigadoon for a day, overtaken by Highland Games – Aussie-style. Even if you miss the frivolity, it's an attractive spot set in hilly countryside scarred by deep gullies and with splendid views over the gorges and mountains of the huge **Morton National Park**. The park, and Bundanoon, have traditionally been a mecca for cyclists, with the long-established Ye Olde Bicycle Shop renting out bikes at very reasonable rates (Mon–Fri 10am–4.30pm, Sat & Sun 9.30am–5pm; $8.80 per hour, $16.50 half-day, $22 full-day; ℡02/4883 6043). A recommended evening activity is a visit to **Glow Worm Glen**; after dark the small sandstone grotto is transformed by the naturally flickering lights of these creatures. It's a 25-minute walk from town via the end of William Street, or an easy forty-minute signposted trek from Riverview Road in the park. Set off at sunset, armed with a torch.

The *Bundanoon YHA* **hostel**, Railway Avenue (Ⓣ & Ⓕ 02/4883 6010; rooms ❸, dorms ❶), is a spacious Edwardian-era guesthouse complete with open fireplaces, and set on extensive grounds. A good-value **motel** is the central *The Highlander*, on the corner of Penrose Road and Anzac Parade (Ⓣ & Ⓕ 02/4883 6242; ❺); breakfast is included, served in the attached restaurant. For more style, there are several pricy guesthouses including *Tree Tops Country Guesthouse*, 101 Railway Ave (Ⓣ 02/4883 6372, Ⓕ 4883 6176, Ⓦ www.highlandsnsw.com .au/treetops; B&B ❼–❽), dating from 1910 and set in pretty gardens; there are log fires in the sitting room, billiard room and beautiful dining room, and the rooms (all en suite) are furnished with Victorian antiques. Recommended **places to eat** are the *Post Office Restaurant*, on Railway Parade opposite the classic, well-preserved train station (Ⓣ 02/4883 6354), dishing up modern Australian cuisine by night (dinner Wed–Sat) and doubling as a café during the day (Wed–Sun 10am–3pm). The best coffee in town is rather incongruously served at Ye Olde Bicycle Shop (see overleaf), together with sandwiches and cakes. The *Bundanoon Hotel*, on Erith Street near the train station, is a quaint little country pub which serves up plain, affordable food and is a friendly spot for a drink. There's a supermarket on Railway Terrace open daily until 9pm.

Kangaroo Valley

Between Nowra on the coast and Moss Vale on the inland road, **Kangaroo Valley** is a popular spot for weekenders from Sydney – a lovely, hidden valley situated between the lush dairy country of Nowra and the Southern Highlands. Coming from the coastal end, a narrow, winding country road climbs 700m up Cambewarra Mountain, with superb coastal panoramas along the way. In **KANGAROO VALLEY** village itself you'll find tearooms and a **Pioneer Settlement Museum** (daily 9.30am–4.30pm; $3.50) with an attached bushwalk and a **market** held in the grounds on the last Sunday of the month. From here the drive continues across the old sandstone Hampden Suspension Bridge over the Kangaroo River, to the Barrengarry plateau. Allow yourself to be waylaid at **Fitzroy Falls**, at the northeast edge of **Morton National Park**, where a short walk from the car park takes you to a waterfall plunging 80m into the valley below. The **NPWS Visitor Centre** here (daily 8.30am–5pm; Ⓣ 02/4887 7270) includes an excellent café, and there's disabled access to the falls. Detailed information about walking tracks in the surrounding area is available, and the office issues **camping** permits for the nearby bushcamp at Yarrunga Creek. If you want to camp in rather more comfort, try the very pleasant *Kangaroo Valley Tourist Park*, Moss Vale Road (Ⓣ & Ⓕ 02/4465 1310, Ⓦ www.holidayhaven.com.au; cabins ❸–❺), on the banks of the Kangaroo River about a kilometre from the village centre, complete with camp kitchen, and canoes and kayaks for hire. This is above all **B&B** territory: *Tall Trees Bed and Breakfast*, 8 Nugents Creek Rd, 1km east from the Kangaroo Valley village (Ⓣ & Ⓕ 02/4465 1208, Ⓦ www.babs.com.au/nsw/tall_trees .htm; ❻, weekend ❼), boasts a guest lounge with log fires and serves a full country breakfast on a patio with views across the valley; there's also a self-contained studio with a spa, wood fire and kitchen (breakfast basket supplied; minimum two-night stay at weekends).

You can get to Kangaroo Valley from Campbelltown train station on the outskirts of Sydney on Priors Scenic Express (Ⓣ 02/4472 4040 or free call 1800

816 234; daily during school holidays, otherwise Mon, Tues & Thurs–Sat); a half-hour stop is scheduled at Fitzroy Falls.

Travel details

Sydney is very much the centre of the Australian transport network, and you can get to virtually anywhere in the country from there on a variety of competing services. The following list represents a minimum; as well as the dedicated services listed below, many places will also be served by long-distance services stopping en route.

Trains

Sydney to: Adelaide (Indian Pacific 2 weekly, Mon & Thurs 2.40pm; 27hr 30min); Brisbane (1 daily; 16hr); Canberra (3 daily; 5hr); Dubbo (1 daily; 6hr 40min); Goulburn (8–10 daily; 3hr); Katoomba (22–30 daily; 2hr); Maitland (1 daily; 2hr 30min); Melbourne (1 daily; 10hr 20min; plus daily bus/train Speedlink via Albury; 12–13hr); Murwillumbah (1 daily; 13hr 35min); Newcastle (20–25 daily; 2hr 30min); Perth (2 weekly, Mon & Thurs 2.40pm; 60hr); Richmond (18–25 daily; 1hr 15min); Windsor (18–25 daily; 1hr 15min); Wollongong (15–25 daily; 1hr 40min).

Buses

Sydney to: Adelaide (2–3 daily; 20hr); Albury (2 daily; 8hr 30min); Armidale (2 daily; 8hr 30min); Batemans Bay (3 daily; 5hr 20min); Bathurst (2–3 daily; 4hr); Bega (2–3 daily; 8hr); Bowral (5 weekly; 2hr 35min); Brisbane (8–12 daily; 15–17hr, with connections to Cairns and Darwin); Broken Hill (2–3 daily; 15hr 30min); Byron Bay (8 daily; 12hr 30min); Canberra (3 daily; 4hr); Cessnock (1 daily; 2hr 20min); Coffs Harbour (8 daily; 8hr 30min); Eden (4 daily; 8hr 30min–9hr 30min); Forster (1 daily; 5hr 30min); Glen Innes (2 daily; 10hr); Grafton (2 daily; 10hr); Melbourne (5 daily; 12–18hr); Mildura (2–3 daily; 16hr); Mittagong (5 weekly; 2hr 30min); Moss Vale (5 weekly; 2hr 45min); Muswellbrook (1 daily; 3hr 30min); Narooma (4 weekly; 8hr); Newcastle (8 daily; 3hr); Nowra (3 daily; 3hr–4hr 20min); Orange (1 daily; 4hr 15min); Perth (2–3 daily; 52–56hr); Port Macquarie (8 daily; 7hr); Port Stephens (1 daily; 4hr); Scone (1 daily; 3hr 50min); Tamworth (2 daily; 7hr); Taree (5 daily; 6hr); Tenterfield (2 daily; 11hr 30min).

Flights

Sydney to: Adelaide (20 daily; 2hr 30min); Albury (4–6 daily; 1hr 20min); Alice Springs (4 daily; 2hr 40min); Armidale (4–8 daily; 1hr 10min); Ayers Rock Resort (2 daily; 3hr); Ballina (1–7 daily; 1hr 35min); Bathurst (2–4 daily; 40min); Brisbane (20 daily; 1hr 15min); Broken Hill (6 weekly; 2hr 30min); Cairns (15 daily; 2hr 40min); Canberra (15–20 daily; 1hr 20min); Coffs Harbour (4–6 daily; 1hr 15min); Cooma (1–2 daily; 1hr); Darwin (3 daily; 4hr); Dubbo (4–7 daily; 1hr); Glen Innes (1–3 daily; 1hr 25min); Grafton (4–6 daily; 1hr 45min); Griffith (3–4 daily; 1hr 40min); Hobart (8 daily; 1hr 30min); Inverell (1–3 daily; 2hr 15min); Lismore (2–3 daily; 1hr 35min); Lord Howe Island (6 weekly; 2hr 20min); Melbourne (20 daily; 1hr 10min); Mudgee (2–3 daily; 1hr); Newcastle (Mon–Fri 4 daily; 40min); Orange (3–4 daily; 45min); Parkes (1–4 daily; 1hr); Perth (10 daily; 4hr); Port Macquarie (3–4 daily; 1hr 25min); Port Stephens (Mon–Fri 1 daily; 1hr); Tamworth (4–6 daily; 1hr); Taree (3–4 daily; 1hr); Wagga Wagga (2–4 daily; 1hr 5min).

New South Wales and ACT

CHAPTER 2   # Highlights

* **New Parliament House**, Canberra – The angular contours of the New Parliament House show contemporary Australian design at its best. **p.249**.

* **Snowy Mountains** – Fine bushwalking in summer, and the best skiing in Australia in winter. **p.264**.

* **Byron Bay** – New Age mecca with 30km of sandy beaches and fantastic diving – an essential stop on the backpacker circuit. **p.304**.

* **Tamworth Country Music festival** – Fans from all over the country descend on Tamworth for its famous annual festival. **p.320**.

* **Bald Rock** – Climb the largest granite monolith in the world for unbeatable views. **p.326**.

* **Warrumbungle National Park** – The rugged Warrumbungle National Park is especially beautiful in spring, when the wild flowers are in bloom. **p.351**.

* **Gunnedah** – You stand a good chance of spotting koalas in the wild at Gunnedah. **p.353**.

* **Broken Hill** – Take a mine tour, visit the Flying Doctors Service or browse in the art galleries of this gracious Outback town. **p.372**.

* **Mutawintje National Park** – Aboriginal rock art is the main draw of the remarkable, red-earth Mutawintje National Park. **p.383**.

New South Wales and ACT

N ew South Wales is Australia's premier state in more ways than one: it's not only the oldest of the five states, but it's the most densely populated too. Including Sydney, New South Wales covers an area about twice the size of Britain, with roughly a tenth of its population; not a very big state by antipodean standards, but its six and a quarter million residents constitute one-third of the country's population. Their distribution is wildly uneven: few live in the Outback or the rural regions, and the vast majority are absorbed by the urban and suburban sprawl on the coast. The state's Aboriginal population is about forty thousand, approximately one-fifth of the total living in Australia. This chapter also covers the Australian Capital Territory (ACT), which was carved out of NSW at the beginning of the twentieth century as an independent base for the new national capital, Canberra.

When Lieutenant James Cook claimed New South Wales for Great Britain in 1770, naming it after a land that he'd apparently never visited – and to which it bears strikingly little resemblance – he could have hardly foreseen what would become of it. And indeed the early years, of penal settlement and timid encroachment into the fringes of the coastal area around Sydney, were hardly a promising start. But with the discovery of a passage through the Blue Mountains in 1813 (see p.213), the rolling plains of the west were opened up. Free (non-convict) settlers – **squatters** – appropriated vast areas of this rich pastureland, making immense fortunes off the backs of sheep. When **gold** was discovered near Bathurst in 1851, and the first goldrush

Accommodation price codes

All the accommodation listed in this book has been categorized into one of eight price bands, as set out below. The rates quoted represent the cheapest available double or twin room in high season – except for category ❶, which indicates per-person rates for a dorm bed, and the categories given for units, cabins and vans, which represent the daily charge for the whole unit.

❶ Under $20
❷ $20–35
❸ $35–50
❹ $50–70
❺ $70–90
❻ $90–115
❼ $115–150
❽ $150 upwards

For more accommodation details, see pp.46–49.

began, New South Wales' fortunes were assured. Although penal transport ceased the following year, the population continued to increase rapidly and the economy boomed as fortune-seekers arrived in droves. At much the same time, Victoria broke off to form a separate colony, followed by Queensland in 1859. The much-reduced borders that New South Wales has today were defined in 1863.

There are over a thousand kilometres of **Pacific coastline** in New South Wales, from subtropical **Tweed Heads** in the north to temperate **Eden** in the south. The year-round mild climate, together with the ocean and the **beaches**, draws visitors pretty much all the time – though it's the summer holiday season that brings thousands of Australians to the coast to enjoy the extensive surf beaches and the numerous more sheltered waters, in bays, river mouths and inlets, and in a series of salt lagoons or "coastal lakes", protected behind a narrow spit from the force of the ocean waves. **South of Sydney** the coast is relatively undeveloped, and there's a string of low-key family resorts and fishing ports, great for water sports and fishing. To the **north** the climate gradually becomes warmer, and the coastline more popular – the series of big resorts up here includes **Port Macquarie** and **Coffs Harbour**, but there are also less-developed places where you can escape it all. One of the most enjoyable beach resorts in Australia is **Byron Bay**, which is just about managing to retain its slightly offbeat, alternative appeal, which radiates from the still-thriving hippie communes of the lush, hilly **North Coast Hinterland**. We've also included in this chapter the Pacific islands far off the north coast of New South Wales: subtropical **Lord Howe Island**, 700km northeast of Sydney and roughly parallel to Port Macquarie, and **Norfolk Island**, 900km further northeast and actually closer to New Zealand, inhabited by the descendants of the mutiny on the *Bounty*.

The **Great Dividing Range** runs parallel to the coastline – often very close – splitting the state in two. In the north, the gentle **New England** stretch of the range comprises tablelands ideal for sheep- and cattle-farming; where this plateau falls away steeply towards the coast are some of the few remaining pockets of dense – at times impenetrable – primeval **forest**: the Big Scrub that drove the early settlers to despair. To the south is the Australian Capital Territory where **Canberra**, the nation's capital and a city struggling to shed its dull image, is the gateway to the **Snowy Mountains**. Here the range builds to a crescendo as **Mount Kosciuszko** (Australia's highest at 2228m) marks the peak of the Australian Alps. In winter there's skiing here, but the mountains are perhaps even better in summer, when the national park that covers most of them offers some unbeatable hiking. Unsurprisingly, it's not so warm up in the mountains of the Great Dividing Range: in summer the cooler days and the drop in temperature at night offer a welcome respite from the coastal heat and humidity. In winter, however, it can be genuinely freezing, with snow even falling near the Queensland border in Tenterfield.

West of the range, rich agricultural country gradually fades into desert-like **Outback** regions where the mercury can climb well above the 40°C mark in summer, while mild winter days are followed by very cold, frosty nights. West of Canberra, between the three rivers of the Murrumbidgee, the Darling and the Murray (the last dividing NSW from Victoria), is the fertile **Riverina**. Beyond New England, the flat, black-soiled plains of the **northwest** head through cotton country to the opal-mining town of **Lightning Ridge**. It's a uniquely Australian experience to leave Sydney, cross the extraordinarily scenic Blue Mountains and be gradually sucked into this vast emptiness, where the **"back o' Bourke"** is synonymous with the Outback. The mining settlement of **Broken Hill**, almost at the South Australian border, is the obvious destination, a gracious city surrounded by the desert landscape of *Mad Max* and home to the classic Outback institutions of the School of the Air and the Flying Doctor Service.

New South Wales still has a fairly extensive **rail** network, although Countrylink (Ⓦ www.countrylink.nsw.gov.au), as it's called, has replaced many services with buses. A one-month $274 unlimited NSW Discovery Pass will get you just about anywhere in the state on this system (call Ⓣ 13 2829 for reservations).

Parks and wildlife

Throughout the state there are magnificent **national parks** and wilderness areas. Before European settlement, the **northeastern** corner of New South Wales was covered by dense subtropical rainforest. It's this that you can visit along the escarpment of the Great Dividing Range, though often only the very edge of these national parks or forests can be reached by road or track, while the interior is accessible only to hardy bushwalkers. These forests are inhabited by many types of parrots, and occasionally by bell birds and bower birds, brush turkeys, and marsupials such as ringtail possums, bandicoots and padimelons. **Further south**, the slightly higher altitudes and the plateaus are dominated by eucalypt forest with a more open canopy, and by less-dense eucalypt woodland – the preferred habitat of wombats, wallabies, other types of possum, koalas and a few small marsupials, as well as echidnas and platypuses, kookaburras, magpies and parrots. The **Snowy Mountains** are covered by snow gums, a slow-growing, cold-resistant eucalypt, and in the summer clusters of delicate wild flowers cover the mountain hillsides and meadows. Where the forest is not protected, lumber is still big business in NSW, and is the source of fierce clashes between environmentalists and the towns that make their living from the timber trade. To the **west**, kangaroos, wallabies and emus roam the wide plains, and with a bit of luck a wedge-tailed eagle can be sighted. Parks here tend to encompass vast areas of desert or places marked out by extraordinary geological formations. The far southwest corner is part of the **Mallee** – a sandy, semi-arid area covered by the eucalypt shrubs that lend the area its name. Here the mallee fowl build the incubation mounds for their eggs in the sand.

The **National Parks and Wildlife Service** (NPWS) has **entrance fees** to many of its parks – usually $6–15 per car and $4 for motorcyles (often on an honour system when there is no ranger station). If you intend to go bush often in NSW you can buy an **annual pass** for $60 ($30 for motorbikes), which includes all parks except Kosciuszko. Because of its popularity as a skiing destination, entrance to Kosciuszko is a steep $15 per car per day, perversely levied in summer too – so if you plan on spending any length of time here, or are going to visit other parks as well, consider the $80 annual pass which covers entry to all parks, including Kosciuszko. Passes can be bought in person at NPWS offices and some park entry stations, over the phone using a credit card (℡ 02/9253 4600 or 1300/361 967) or online at Ⓦ www.npws.nsw.gov.au; you can also download an order form at this site and send it by fax (Ⓕ 02/9251 9192) or by mail (include your vehicle type and its registration number) to the National Parks Centre, PO Box N429, Grosvenor Place, NSW 1220.

You can **camp** in most national parks. Bush camping is generally free, but where there is a ranger station and a designated campsite with facilities, fees are charged, usually around $6 per site. If the amenities are of a high standard, including hot showers and the like, or if the spot is just plain popular, fees can be as high as $18 per tent. Open fires are banned in most parks and forbidden everywhere on days when there is high danger of fire, and while there are often electric or gas barbecues in picnic areas, you'll need a fuel stove for bush camping.

Australian Capital Territory

In the 1820s the first European squatters settled in the valleys and plains north of the Snowy Mountains and established family dynasties on their prosperous grazing properties. Until 1900, however, this remained a remote rural area. When the Australian colonies united in the **Commonwealth of Australia** in 1901, a capital city had to be chosen, with Melbourne and Sydney the two obvious and eager rivals. After much wrangling, and partly in order to avoid having to decide on one of the two, it was agreed to establish a brand-new capital instead: Melbourne was to be the seat of the provisional government until the new capital was completed and the government departments had moved there. A provision in the Constitution Act decreed that the seat of government was to be in the state of New South Wales and not less than one hundred miles from Sydney. In 1909 Limestone Plains, a plain south of Yass surrounded by mountain ranges, was chosen out of several possible sites as the future seat of the Australian government. An area of 2368 square kilometres was excised from the state of New South Wales and named the **Australian Capital Territory** (ACT). The ACT officially included an adjunct at Jervis Bay (see p.270), on the coast south of Nowra, to give Australia's capital its own access to the sea and a naval base. The name for the future capital was supposedly taken from the language of local Aborigines: **Canberra** – the meeting place.

Canberra is situated on a high plain (600m above sea level) and, unlike the coastal cities, experiences four distinct **seasons**. In summer, the average temperatures are 27°C maximum during the day and 12°C minimum at night; in winter they drop from an average of 12°C maximum during the day to freezing point (and below) at night. Spring and autumn can be really delightful, though. The mountain ranges to the west and south of the city rise up to 1900m and are snow-covered in winter.

Canberra

In 1912 Walter Burley Griffin, an American landscape architect from Chicago, won the international competition for the design of the future Australian capital: his plan envisaged a garden city for about 25,000 people, which took into account the natural features of the landscape. There were to be five main centres, each with separate city functions, located on three axes: land, water and municipal. Roads were to be in concentric circles, with arcs linking the radiating design. Construction started in 1913, but political squabbling and the effects of World War I prevented any real progress being made. Little building had been done, in fact, by the time Griffin left the site in 1920, and only in 1927 was the provisional parliament building officially opened. By 1930 some one thousand families had settled in the capital. Then the Depression set in, World War II broke out and development slowed again. After more years of stagnation, the National Capital Development Commission (NCDC) was finally established in 1958, and at last growth began in earnest.

In 1963 the Molonglo River was dammed to form a lake 11km wide, the artificial **Lake Burley Griffin** that is the centrepiece of modern **CANBERRA**. Numerous open spaces and public buildings came into existence, as a real city started to emerge. Slowly, the **Civic Centre** near London Circuit began to live up to its name. The **population** grew rapidly, from fifteen thousand in 1947 to over one hundred thousand in 1967; today, it is more than three hundred thousand. This population growth has been accommodated in satellite towns with their own centres: **Woden**, 12km south of the Civic Centre, was built in the mid-1960s; five years later **Belconnen** was added in the northwest; and in the mid-1970s **Tuggeranong** in the south. It was this sprawl that fostered Canberra's image as "a cluster of suburbs in search of a centre".

Inevitably, modern Canberra is mainly a city of civil servants and administrators. There are plenty of service industries – especially ones aimed at feeding and watering all those politicians and visitors – but little real industrial activity. Canberra recently gained self-government, with only the Parliamentary Triangle remaining under federal control; the self-financing responsibilities that this entails have placed a premium on tourism revenues. And indeed, the main reason to come to Canberra is for the **national museums and institutions** you can visit – top of the list is the **National Gallery**, and the stunning **New Parliament House**, opened in 1988 and certainly one of the principal tourist sights, with its original architecture intended to blend into the landscape.

CANBERRA

& O'Conner

Dickson & (i)

BELCONNEN WAY

MACARTHUR AVE

AINSLIE

Canberra
Nature Park

Canberra
Nature Park

Black
Mountain

Mount
Ainslie

TURNER

BRADDON

Australian
National
Botanic
Gardens

Jolimont
Centre

Melbourne
Building

Australian
War Memorial

Australian National
University

Canberra Centre

ACTON

CIVIC

REID

FAIRBAIRN AVE

Film & Sound
Archive

CAMPBELL

National
Capital
Exhibition

Acton
Peninsula

Captain Cook
Memorial Jet

National
Library

Blundells
Farmhouse

Lake Burley Griffin

National
Museum of
Australia

Questacon

Carillon

High Court

National
Gallery

MORSHEAD DR

Airport

Old
Parliament
House

YARRALUMLA

Lake
Burley Griffin

Capital Hill

Canberra
Nature
Park

New Parliament
House

BRISBANE AVE

Queanbeyan

DEAKIN

BARTON

FORREST

KINGSTON

Train
Station

Canberra
Nature
Park

Golf
Course Red
Hill

Zoo

ACCOMMODATION

Acacia Motor Lodge	6
Bruce Hall	4
Burton Hall	5
Capital Parkroyal	8
Canberra City VIP/ Backpackers	9
Canberra YHA Hostel	1
City Walk Hotel	7
Forrest Inn	11
Kythera Motel	3
Macquarie Hotel	10
Medina Classic	13
Tall Trees Motel	2
Victor Lodge	12

Canberra is also trying very hard to present an image to counter its reputation as the domain of dull bureaucrats. It hasn't succeeded yet: most Australians still regard Canberra as "pollie city" – a frosty, boring place where politicians and public servants live it up at the expense of the hard-done-by Australian tax-payer. They also complain about its concentric circular streets, which can make driving here seem like a Kafkaesque nightmare, and about the contrived, neat-as-a-pin nature of the place.

But the image-makers have a point, and Canberra is a far more pleasant place than it's usually given credit for. The city has wide open spaces and many **parks** and gardens, with the impressive architecture housing the national institutions set in astonishingly well-groomed surroundings, so that you can pad barefoot through the grass from the National Gallery to the National Library, peacefully admiring the gum trees. Right on its doorstep are forests and **bushland**, with unspoilt wilderness just a bit further afield in the Brindabella Ranges and the Namadgi National Park; skiing in the Snowy Mountains or surfing on the coast are only a few hours away.

Canberra's **nightlife** is also a great deal better than you might expect considering its reputation, in term time at least: the two universities here (and the Duntroon Military Academy for officer material) means there's a large and lively **student population** (good news for those who have student cards, as most attractions offer hefty discounts). The city is said to have more **restaurants** per capita than any other in Australia – which is saying something – and there are plenty of pubs and nightclubs to choose from, too. Many of them, though, are tucked away in hidden corners of the city or in the satellite towns. Surprisingly perhaps, Canberra also holds the dubious title of Australia's **porn** capital, due to its liberal licensing laws which legalize and regulate the sex industry.

Arrival and information

Canberra's **airport**, about 7km east of the city, handles domestic flights only. Despite recent efforts to welcome the backpacker market, the city has ceased its bus service between the airport and the city centre, leaving air passengers no choice but to catch a taxi (roughly $12–14). The main **train station** is located southeast of the centre, on Wentworth Avenue in Kingston, and from here taxis are again the easiest way to get where you're going; trains also stop at the suburb of Queanbeyan, in NSW, where there's some cheap accommodation. Most interstate **buses** drop and pick up at the handy **Jolimont Centre**, downtown at 67 Northbourne Ave; the modern centre has showers, lockers (free if you can find one that works), a TV room, snack bar, post office, internet kiosk and a travel bookshop, which also offers everything from Australia-wide tours to Canberra city bus tickets, as well as some tourist information and maps. Additionally, the centre has ticket offices for the train, airline and bus companies. There is a free direct telephone line to the tourist office (see below), to taxi companies and to accommodation.

The **Canberra Visitor Information Centre**, the main tourist office, is inconveniently located about 2km north of the centre, on Northbourne Avenue in Dickson (Mon–Fri 9am–5pm, Sat & Sun 9am–4pm; ☎ 02/6205 0044 or free call 1800 026 166, ⓦ www.canberratourism.com.au), reached by bus #380; it books tours, transport and accommodation. More central is the **tourist information booth** on the ground floor of the Canberra Centre, a shopping mall on Bunda Street (Mon–Thurs & Sat 9am–5.30pm, Fri 9am–7.30pm, Sun 10am–4pm); it provides maps and information but doesn't make bookings.

City transport

To appreciate the city, you ideally need a vehicle of some kind – things are very spread out, and at the weekend especially (when many residents leave and the city is quite dead) public transport is extremely limited. You'll find that the dispersed nature of Canberra means that you can easily park your car, often for free, at the main sights. Cycling is very popular and renting a bike – to take advantage of the excellent network of bike paths – is strongly recommended (see "Listings" on p.257). An alternative to your own transport is the tourist office's handy **hop-on, hop-off double-decker bus**, which serves eleven major sights and routes; buses depart from 9am until 5pm (every 40min) at the Melbourne Building on Northbourne Avenue. Your $25 ticket is valid for 24 hours, and includes obligatory running commentary from the driver; call ☎0500/505 012 for further information. Note, however, that unless you are planning a relentless sightseeing spree, municipal route #34 (see below) actually covers many of the major tourist haunts for a fraction of the cost.

Municipal buses are run by Action. The **day-trip ticket**, purchased from the driver, offers enormous savings; it's valid for as many journeys as you like and costs $8.40 (or $4.40 off-peak – Mon–Fri 9am–4.30pm and after 6pm, Sat & Sun all day). Other buses cover all of Canberra, including the satellite towns: for details, contact Action **timetable information** (Mon–Sat 6am–11pm, Sun 8am–5.30pm; ☎02/6207 7611 or 13 1710, ⓦwww.action.act.gov.au).

Most Action buses start at the City Bus Interchange, at East Row just across Northbourne Avenue from the Jolimont Centre; you can buy tickets at the Newslink shop behind stance 9, or at most other newsagents. For ticketing purposes, the city is divided into three zones: North, South and Central – most sights are situated within the central zone. Besides the day-trip ticket (valid for all zones), you can pay a single zone, flat-rate fare ($2.30) or a single, all-zone fare ($4.40), both of which can also be bought on board; a ten-journey Faresaver ticket costs $18.40 one zone ($36.80 all zones), or a weekly ticket costs $19.80 ($38).

Accommodation

Staying in Canberra, on the whole, is not cheap, but most places are modern and clean. Location is problematic, as most accommodation is in the nearby suburbs rather than the centre. One of the best locations is **Kingston**, a salubrious, café-filled suburb close to the train station, and also within walking distance of the Parliamentary Triangle attractions. **Hotels** and **motels** rarely charge less than $65 for a double, although guesthouses often have more reasonable rates. Canberra has a couple of excellent, modern **youth hostels**, and out-of-term inexpensive B&B is available in several student halls of residence. Accommodation in the neighbouring city of **Queanbeyan**, 14km away, costs on average $10–20 less, so we've listed a couple of suggestions there, too.

Hotels, motels and guesthouses

Acacia Motor Lodge, 65 Ainslie Ave, Braddon (☎02/6249 6955, ⓕ6247 7058). Very central motel in a leafy street near the war memorial. A light breakfast is included. Bus #33 or #38. ❺

Blue & White Lodge, 524 Northbourne Ave, Downer, 5km north of the city (☎02/6248 0498, ⓕ6248 8277). B&B with well-equipped rooms – TV, fridge, heating, air-con and tea-making facilities; mostly shared bathrooms, and discounts for longer stays. Bus #39 or #50. ❻

Capital Parkroyal, 1 Binara St, Civic (☎02/6247 8999, ⓕ6257 4903). Central, four-star hotel with all the conveniences you'd expect, including room service, swimming pool, sauna and gym. ❽

Forrest Inn, 30 National Circuit, Forrest (☎02/6295 3433, ⓕ6295 2119). Modern motel in

the embassy area next to the pretty Serbian Church offering air-con units. Bus #35 or #36. ❻

Kythera Motel, 98 Northbourne Ave, Braddon (☎02/6248 7611, ⓕ6248 0419). Well-equipped rooms with heating and air-con and a swimming pool to cool off even further. Bus #33 or #72. ❺

Macquarie Hotel, 18 National Circuit, Barton, 6km southeast (☎02/6273 2325, ⓕ6273 4241). Comfortable place with heating; all rooms share bathroom. Includes a cooked breakfast, with dinner available. Weekly rates offered. Bus #310, #311 or #360. ❸

Medina Classic, 11 Giles St, Kingston (☎02/6239 8100, ⓕ6239 7226). Upmarket one-, two- or three-bedroom self-catering serviced apartments with fully equipped kitchens (except for a couple of smaller apartments), popular with families. Facilities include reception, swimming pool, spa, gym and undercover parking; bike rental available. Bus #39 or #84. ⑧

Parkview Lodge, 526 Northbourne Ave, Downer, 4km north (℡ 02/6248 0655, 🄵 6247 6166). A recommended nonsmoking B&B near Southall Park; rooms with TV, fridge, heating and tea-making facilities, all en suite and some with whirlpool. Bus #39 or #50. ⑥

Sunrise Motel, 9 Uriarra Rd, Queanbeyan (℡ 02/6297 2822, 🄵 6297 2978). Value-for-money motel with lots of extras: air-con, videos and swimming pool. ④

Tall Trees Motel, 21 Stephen St, Ainslie (℡ 02/6247 9200, 🄵 6257 4479). Pleasant, upmarket motel in quiet shady grounds. Laundry. Bus #38. ⑥

Hostels and college accommodation

ANU student accommodation: Bruce Hall (℡ 02/6267 4000), Burton & Garran Hall (℡ 02/6267 4333), Fenner Hall (℡ 02/6279 9000), Ursula College (℡ 02/6279 4300). Located around the Australian National University campus in Acton, just west of the city centre; most rooms are singles, but there are also a few twins. ②–③

Canberra City VIP/Backpackers, 7 Akuna St, Civic (℡ 02/6229 0888 or free call 1800 300 488, 🄵 6229 0777, 🆆 www.canberrabackpackers.com.au). With facilities that would put many a palace to shame, Canberra's latest and most central hostel heralds a new backpacking dawn. The megalith could be daunting to lone travellers, but boasts TV-chef kitchens, licensed bar, rooftop BBQ garden, laundry, internet café, sauna, bike hire, cable TV and lockers in every room. Oh, and 24hr check-in. Rooms ⑤, dorms ②

Canberra YHA Hostel, 191 Dryandra St, O'Connor (℡ 02/6248 9155, 🄵 6249 1731, 🄴 canberra@yhansw.org.au). Canberra's YHA is a friendly, modern hostel with excellent facilities, situated about 4km out of town in a gorgeous bush setting. There's a small shop, internet access and super-cheap bike rental; rates include linen. The congenial staff at reception (7am–10pm) run regular minibus pick-ups from town (call beforehand); otherwise it's a ten-minute trip on bus #35. Rooms ③, dorms ①

City Walk Hotel, 2 Mort St, City (℡ 02/6257 0124, 🆆 www.citywalkhotel.citysearch.com.au). Just across the road from the bus station, this passable establishment is clean and relatively safe. Its biggest draws are location and the excellent Irish bar downstairs; guests often get discounted beer. Facilities include kitchen, internet access and a common room with TV. Rooms ④–⑤, dorms ②

Victor Lodge, 29 Dawes St, Kingston, 4km southwest (℡ 02/6295 7777, 🄵 6295 2466, 🆆 www.victorlodge.com.au). A small, friendly, very popular family-run hostel/guesthouse, situated in a lovely area and affiliated to the VIP network. Clean, bright rooms with heating, washbasin, and desks in the singles; rates include linen and duvets. There's also a well-equipped kitchen and outside BBQ area, laundry, TV room with internet station and the opportunity to soak in a long, hot bath. Very reasonable bike rental; city pick-ups and drop-offs. Bus #39, #80 or #84. Rooms ④, dorms ②

Camping and caravan parks

Blue Gums, Stromlo Observatory Rd, off Cotter Road (ACT Forests ℡ 02/6207 2486). One of several state-owned campsites, this one in a magic location at the base of Mount Stromlo, with toilet facilities and BBQs (wood provided). ①

Canberra Carotel, Federal Highway, Watson, 6km north (℡ 02/6241 1377). Park with a swimming pool and café. Campsites and holiday apartments (for up to six people). Bus #36. Cabins ④, on-site vans ③

Canberra Holiday Retreat, Federal Highway, Sutton, NSW, 12km northeast (℡ 02/6241 6411). Good facilities – swimming pool, tennis courts, licensed bistro and supermarket. Cabins ⑤

Crestview Tourist Park, 81 Donald Rd, Queanbeyan (℡ 02/6297 2443). Facilities include a swimming pool and shop. Camping space, plus cabins. ③

White Ibis Tourist Village and Caravan Park, Bidges Rd, off the Federal Highway, Sutton, NSW, 12km northeast (℡ 02/6230 3433, 🄵 6230 3483, 🆆 www.sydneycaravanparks.com.au). Good site with pool, tennis court and kiosk selling the essentials. Cabins ⑤

The City

Strictly planned as it is, Canberra is a straightforward place to find your way around – though distances are such that only in the very centre will you want to do much walking, and even there it can be something of a test of fitness.

The eleven-kilometre-wide **Lake Burley Griffin** pretty much marks the heart of the city, with several lakeside places of interest both north and south. North of the lake is the city centre proper, the **Civic Centre**, or "Civic" for short, which houses shops, restaurants, cafés, pubs, cinemas and theatres, as well as the GPO. Like many Australian cities, drug use is on the increase here, and Civic can get a little dangerous at night. The campus of the **Australian National University** (ANU) is just to the west of the centre in the suburb of Acton, as is **Screensound Australia**, the old National Film and Sound Archive. Beyond Acton, the **National Botanic Gardens** sit at the flanks of the 806-metre **Black Mountain**, topped by the distinctive Telecom Tower and just one of many scattered sections of the **Canberra Nature Park**. East of the centre is the **Australian War Memorial**, solemnly gazing back along monument-lined **Anzac Parade** to the **Parliamentary Triangle**, south of the lake, with the old Parliament House overlooked by the New Parliament House on Capital Hill. This political quarter, linked to the city centre by the **Commonwealth Avenue Bridge**, is where you'll find the government offices and national cultural institutions, and is the part of Canberra that is of most architectural interest. Fronting the lake, strung along King Edward Terrace, are four impressive modern public buildings: the **National Library**, **Questacon** (the National Science and Technology Centre), the **National Gallery** and the **High Court**. The prime minister himself resides at The Lodge in **Yarralumla**, at the foot of Capital Hill, while most of the foreign embassies – intended to resemble the vernacular architecture of their home countries – cluster around Yarralumla and Forrest.

Questacon and the National Library

Crossing the Commonwealth Avenue Bridge from the city centre, you turn left onto King Edward Terrace. Immediately before you is **Questacon – the National Science and Technology Centre** (daily 9am–5pm; $10; Ⓦ www.questacon.edu.au), a "hands-on" museum opened in 1988 as a joint Australian/Japanese bicentennial project. The centre's six galleries are arranged around a 27-metre-high drum at the core of the building, and are linked by a continuous spiral walkway. There are some free interactive exhibits in the foyer if you just want a taste, but it's a good place to keep children occupied.

Looming behind the science centre is one of the country's most important institutions, the **National Library** (Mon–Thurs 9am–9pm, Fri & Sat 9am–5pm, Sun 1.30–5pm; Ⓦ www.nla.gov.au), whose Reading Room has a comprehensive selection of overseas newspapers and magazines. There are also exhibitions of rare books in the foyer, and usually some kind of interesting temporary display, including items from the pictorial collection comprising about forty thousand items; you can view any of those not on display via an interactive touch-screen system in the foyer. The library's *Brindabella Bistro* is a good place to stop for a cappuccino and a snack – it's open until half an hour before the library closes.

The High Court of Australia

From the library, it's a pleasant walk about 500m east along lakefront Parkes Place to the **High Court of Australia** (daily 9.45am–4.30pm), the highest authority in the Australian judicial system, set in an appropriately grandiose, glass-fronted edifice with a stylized waterfall running alongside the walkway up to the entrance. Its functions are to uphold and interpret the constitution and to hear cases referred from the lower courts, which involves delivering about seventy judgments a year. Visitors can watch a short video that explains the court's function and examines two of its landmark cases: its 1983 ruling that saved Tasmania's wild Franklin River from damming as part of a hydroelectric scheme; and its finding on the 1992 land rights case Mabo versus Queensland – a momentous decision that overturned the British legal concept of *terra nullius* whereby Australia was considered uninhabited prior to white settlement in 1788. The Great Hall and three courtrooms are also worth looking at – and there's a licensed café upstairs.

The National Gallery

One of the major attractions in Canberra is the **National Gallery** (daily 10am–5pm; free; 1hr guided tours of Australian art daily 11am & 2pm, international art same hours, Aboriginal and Torres Strait Islands art Thurs & Sun 11am), situated on Parkes Place immediately east of the High Court, to which it is linked by a footbridge. Occupying twelve galleries spread over three floors, the collection explores the art of Africa and the Americas, Asia and Europe from ancient to modern (with a fairly good collection of modern European and North American art, including works by Monet, de Chirico, Magritte and Tanguy), but the core of the national collection is Australian. There are also regular special exhibitions and international touring shows (admission charge).

For most visitors, the highlight is the **Art of Aboriginal Australia and Torres Strait Islands** gallery on the entrance level; the collection is extensive and every six months a new display is mounted, ranging from traditional bark paintings from the Northern Territory to politically aware contemporary work in different media. On permanent display is the **Aboriginal Memorial 1988**, which pays homage to the Aboriginal people who since 1788 have lost life, land and culture; the memorial comprises two hundred termite-hollowed logs representative of the culture's log coffins, painted with totemic designs by over forty artists from around Ramingining in Central Arnhemland.

On the upper level, the **Australian Art** gallery explores the country's visual arts, from colonial to contemporary. Most striking are the 25 bushranger paintings in Sidney Nolan's celebrated *Ned Kelly* series, painted in the 1940s. Other works on permanent display include Russell Drysdale's *The Drover's Wife* (1945), probably his best-known painting. Along with Jackson Pollack's Blue Poles (see box on below) these are probably the only permanent features of an ever-changing "permanent" collection, only three percent of which is on show at any one time.

Outside is a living fern-tree sculpture by Australian artist Fiona Hall, and a **Sculpture Garden** overlooking Lake Burley Griffin. Also visible and audible

Blue Poles

The National Gallery's most valuable foreign work of art is Blue Poles by the American painter Jackson Pollack. The monumental abstract painting was bought by the Labor government in 1973 for A$1.3 million, which at the time was a world-record price for a contemporary American painting. The Australian press immediately vilified the painting as the work of drunks and an emblem of the liberal excesses of the Whitlam era (see "History" on p.1151). Yet when the painting was recently loaned to MoMA in New York to feature in a Pollack retrospective as one of the artist's most significant works, the museum's chief curator, Kirk Varnedoe, expressed that he would love to have this masterpiece as part of the permanent collection. Despite recent offers touching $70 million, *Blue Poles* is resolutely not for sale.

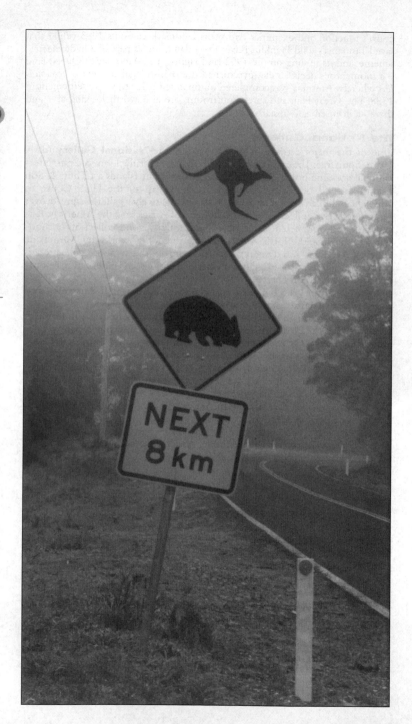

from here is the **Carillon** stranded on Aspen Island, whose three bell towers with 53 bronze bells were a gift from the British government to mark Canberra's fiftieth birthday. It's pleasant to sit on the lawns under a shady tree by the lake and listen to the recitals (Wed 12.30–1.30pm & Sun 2.45–3.30pm). On summer evenings, concerts and other events, such as open-air film screenings, sometimes take place here to coincide with special exhibitions.

The Old and New Parliament houses

Away from the lake, on King George Terrace at the foot of Capital Hill, is the **Old Parliament House** (daily 9am–5pm; tours every 30min; $2; ⓦ www.dcita.gov.au/oph.html), whose grounds became the site of a live-in Aboriginal protest for land rights (dubbed the **Tent Embassy**) for over six months in 1972. Twenty years later a second tent embassy was erected, to protest the fact that Aboriginal land rights had still not been achieved, and it remains there still, flying the Aboriginal flag.

The simple white Neoclassical building was the seat of government from 1927 until 1988, but it was only ever meant to be a provisional parliament house for fifty years; a **tour** of the "wedding cake" – either before or after seeing the New Parliament House to allow comparisions – provides a fascinating insight into how crowded and inconvenient the building actually was. Presently, the **National Portrait Gallery** (ⓦ www.portrait.gov.au) uses the building for exhibitions, making it something of a treasure trove to visit. Outside, you can wander in the **Senate Rose Garden** or visit the National Archives of Australia on Queen Victoria Terrace which has socio-historical exhibitions (daily 9am–4pm; free).

Merging onto Capital Hill itself is the **New Parliament House**, with its grass-covered contours (daily 9am–5pm, extended hours for Parliamentary evening sessions; free guided tours 9am–4.30pm every 30min; information line ⓣ 02/6277 5399). The stunning angular design of the exterior, topped by a sputnik-like flagpole, is matched by the interior, which represents the best in Australian art and design. You can wander about inside unattended but the excellent guided tour is recommended, helping you to come to grips with the amount of work that went into a building which employs three people just to change the lightbulbs. The first-floor theatre screens hourly films about the construction of the building, including interviews with architects and artisans. There's an excellent café (daily 10am–4.30pm) with an outdoor area with views across to Old Parliament House.

An **international competition** for a new Parliament House was launched in 1980, the brief being to create a building true to Walter Burley Griffin's vision of a city nestling in the natural folds of the land. The resulting building (opened in May 1988) was the startling design of Romaldo Giurgola, an American-based Italian architect. Visitors and locals are generally impressed, but the unnecessarily large edifice still causes many an Aussie cheek to burn, not least that of former president Malcolm Fraser, who in 1997 described the building as "an unmitigated disaster" and "my one very serious political mistake." Whatever your views on the architecture and scope of the thing, you're free to walk over, loll on, and even roll down the grassy ramps covering the building. Outside the ground-floor entrance level is a **mosaic** by the Aboriginal artist Michael Tjakamarra Nelson – a piece that conveys the idea of a sacred meeting place. Inside, the impressive **foyer** is dominated by grand marble staircases and over forty columns speckled grey-green and brown representing both a eucalypt forest and the marble columns used by European settlers when they built. The floors are made of native woods, and the walls feature marquetry panels detailing native plants.

Beyond the foyer, the **Great Hall** is dominated by a vast twenty-metre-high tapestry based on a painting of the same dimensions by **Arthur Boyd**; in a richly symbolic landscape, the opposing forces of life and death meet in blackened trees set against a powerful sky. Other chambers are adorned with paintings by artists such as Albert Tucker, Sidney Nolan and Ian Fairweather, as well as portraits of political figures, photographs and ceramics. Important documents in the country's political history are also on display, as is an exhibition on Federation and a display outlining the Australian political system.

When Parliament is in session – usually from seventy to eighty days a year – you can sit in the public gallery and watch the proceedings in the House of Representatives (the lower chamber of Parliament) or the Senate (the upper chamber of the legislature); **Question Time** in both chambers starts at 2pm, with the House of Representatives making for better (and therefore more popular) viewing; to guarantee a seat, book in advance on ⊤02/6277 4889.

The diplomatic quarters and the mint

After visiting the New Parliament House, a trip among the upmarket suburban homes in Canberra's diplomatic quarters – **Yarralumla** and **Forrest** – completes the political sightseeing tour. The consuls and high commissions were asked to construct buildings that deployed the typical architecture of the countries they represent. The result is an international compendium of architectural styles. Some of the eye-catching national designs worth looking out for include the American Embassy's plantation-style mansion, and the embassies of Thailand, Indonesia (with a small cultural centre), the People's Republic of China and Papua New Guinea.

At the **Royal Australian Mint**, a few kilometres to the southwest on Denison Street, Deakin (Mon–Fri 9am–4pm, Sat & Sun 10am–3pm; free), you can watch money being "made" on weekdays and acquire a few items for your coin collection at the Collectors' Shop.

Lake Burley Griffin

Back across the Commonwealth Avenue Bridge, the northern shores of Lake Burley Griffin have plenty to offer. At the furthest western end of the lake, by the Scrivener Dam on Lady Denman Drive, is the **Zooquarium**, Australia's only National Aquarium and Wildlife Park (daily 9am–5pm; $10; Ⓦ www.zooquarium.com.au). Visitors walk through tunnels of acrylic glass while sharks, stingrays and other creatures glide past, only an arm's-length away; outside there's a bear park, a monkey island, and kangaroos, emus and dingoes.

On the Acton Peninsula, the prime lakefront site of the old Royal Canberra Hospital is now home to the **National Museum of Australia** (daily 9am–5pm; free; three "blockbuster" exhibitions per year $15; Ⓦ www.nma.gov.au). The $100 million museum finally opened in March 2001 – twenty-five years after it was first proposed – to coincide with celebrations for the centenary of the Federation. Melbourne architectural firm Ashton Raggat McDougall won the competion to design the building, given the brief that it was to be "anti-monumental". The controversial result, a postmodern riot of differing colours, building materials and quirky features such as the orange metal structure looping above, is considered vibrant and playful by some, mediocre and crass by others. The exhibitions, which range over five permanent galleries (plus an outdoor section and three temporary exhibition halls), have been similarly controversial, with claims that white Australia has been trivialized and Australian kitsch celebrated: the **Nation: Symbols of Australia gallery** features Victa lawnmowers and Hills Hoists, while the bleak symbolism of an arid, treeless country is presented in the concrete **Garden of Australian Dreams**. There has been discomfort, too, at the **First Australians gallery** which goes beyond boomerangs and canoes to tell the story of the "massacre" of Aboriginal people, the reserve system, black deaths in custody, and the "stolen generations". In the **Eternity gallery**, the inclusion of an outfit worn by baby Azaria Chamberlain has been considered bad taste by some, though without doubt her disappearance at Ayers Rock in the 1980s and the subsequent miscarriage of justice suffered by her mother, Lindy, live deep in the national psyche. The **Tangled Destinies gallery**, focusing on the environment, explores the relationship between land and people in Australia, while the **Horizons gallery**, subtitled "The Peopling of Australia since 1788" looks at the nation's migrant history.

Just east of the Commonwealth Avenue Bridge, you'll pass the **National Capital Exhibition** at Regatta Point (daily 9am–5pm, until 6pm in summer; free), comprising a small theatre, displays and models depicting Canberra's development from the cattle and sheep pastures of the nineteenth century to its modern incarnation as capital city. There's a great view from the terrace, though on windy days you have to beware of the spray from the **Captain Cook Memorial Jet** (10am–noon & 2–4pm, also 7–9pm during daylight saving), which spurts a column of water 140m into the air. The jet, built in 1970 to mark the bicentenary of Captain Cook's "discovery" of Australia, costs over $130 an hour to run – hence the limited operating times.

Further east is one of the few historic buildings in the city: **Blundells Cottage**, on Wendouree Drive in Kings Park (daily 10am–3.30pm; $2), serves as a reminder of the farming industry that flourished here before Canberra became the capital. Built in 1860, this simple farmhouse once housed workers from a sheep station, and has been preserved as a small museum.

The Australian War Memorial and Mount Ainslie

To the east of the city, the massive, domed building perched at the base of Mount Ainslie, at the far end of **Anzac Parade** (its length lined with smaller war memorials), is the **Australian War Memorial** (daily 10am–5pm, school and public holidays from 9am; call ☎ 02/6243 4211 for details of free guided tours). At the same time as commemorating the 102,000 Australian soldiers who lost their lives in seven wars in the last hundred years, most movingly in the Hall of Memory, this is also a military museum, depicting war through miniature battle dioramas and old aircraft. Although it's the most visited museum in Australia, with an average of about a million visitors a year – many of them motivated by patriotism – this mixture makes for slightly uneasy viewing: it's an unquestioningly heroic past that's constructed here, with the Anzac legend as its most illustrious episode. However, the museum does have some intriguing temporary exhibitions – past ones have looked at the Boer War, for example – which do make the point about Australians fighting for interests which were actually remote to them. For something more life-affirming, the picnic grounds in bushland behind the memorial yield the beginning of a walk to the summit of Mount Ainslie – really a large round hill and part of Canberra Nature Park (see p.253) – where a lookout provides a perfect view over the city and the Parliamentary Triangle.

Travelling around Australia you'll notice almost every town – large or small – has a war memorial dedicated to the memory of the Anzacs, the **Australia and New Zealand Army Corps**.

When war erupted in Europe in 1914, Australia was overwhelmed by a wave of pro-British sentiment. On August 5, 1914, one day after Great Britain had declared war against the German empire, the Australian prime minister summed up the feelings of his compatriots: "When the Empire is at war so Australia is at war." On November 1, 1914, a contingent of twenty thousand enthusiastic volunteers – the **Anzacs** – left from the port of Albany in Western Australia to assist the mother country in her struggle.

In Europe, Turkey had entered the war on the German side in October 1914. At the beginning of 1915, military planners in London (Winston Churchill prominent among them) came up with a plan to capture the strategically important Turkish peninsula of the Dardanelles with a surprise attack near **Gallipoli**, thus opening the way to the Black Sea. On April 25, 1915, sixteen thousand Australian soldiers landed at dawn in a small bay flanked by steep cliffs: by nightfall, two thousand men had died in a hail of Turkish bullets from above. The plan, whose one chance of success was surprise, had been signalled by troop and ship movements long in advance; by the time it was carried out, it was already doomed to failure. Nonetheless, Allied soldiers continued to lose their lives for another eight months without ever gaining more than a feeble foothold.

In December, London finally issued the order to withdraw. Eleven thousand Australians and New Zealanders had been killed, along with as many French and three times as many British troops. The Turks lost 86,000 men.

Official Australian historiography continues to mythologize the battle for Gallipoli, elevating it to the level of a national legend on which Australian identity is founded. From this point of view, in the war's baptism of fire, the Anzac soldiers proved themselves heroes who did the new nation proud, their loyalty and bravery evidence of how far Australia had developed. It was "the birth of a nation", and at the same time a loss of innocence, a national rite of passage – never again would Australians so unquestioningly involve themselves in foreign ventures.

Today the legend is as fiercely defended as ever, the focal point of Australian national pride, commemorated each year on April 25, **Anzac Day**. To outsiders, it may seem rather odd that a futile battle in someone else's interests occupies such a central place in the country's conscience, but the ceremony – akin to Britain's Remembrance Day and the USA's Veterans' Day – is a solemn occasion, when one is asked to reflect on the sacrifices made by those who fought in all wars.

ANU and Screensound Australia

The green, spacious **Australian National University** campus (ANU), just west of the city centre in **Acton**, is a pleasant place to wander. The two small **anthropological museums** at the Hope Building on Ellery Crescent are open to the public (Mon–Fri 9am–4pm; free), and there are also the usual student activities, concerts and plays: for information about current and forthcoming events phone the recorded weekly diary on ℡02/6125 0742 or check out the Ⓦ www.anu.edu.au website. Within the grounds of the ANU campus, on McCoy Circuit, **Screensound Australia**, the old National Film and Sound Archive, is the most comprehensive collection of Australian sound and screen recordings in existence, dating back to the 1890s. One of the highlights of a visit here is an interactive exhibition (daily 9am–5pm; $5.50; Ⓦ www.screensound.com.au), where special headphones tune in to the frequency of each display as you pass. A highlight of the exhibits is the yellow car that split in two in the 1986 film *Malcolm* (see "Australian film", p.1166); the scene is replayed on a video screen. A wild-card display of Australian TV ads features some real humdingers from the 1970s, and you can watch fascinating snippets from old newsreels in a small projection room.

Black Mountain and around

The **National Botanic Gardens** (daily 9am–5pm; free guided tours leave from the visitor centre daily at 11am & 2pm), on the flanks of Black Mountain, are well worth a diversion from the city centre – beautiful in themselves and an excellent introduction to Australian flora. About six thousand species of native plants have been planted here in ecological niches, including an example of Sydney Basin flora, some mallee shrubland, and rainforest species growing in a shady, watered gully. There are hundreds of different types of eucalypts, banksias and proteaceas, as well as tree ferns and even an Aboriginal trail. The main entrance is on Clunies Ross Street, beyond the university area, and there's a **visitor information centre** (daily 9.30am–4.30pm) with leaflets for self-guided tours, displays and videos, and a small bookshop; nearby there's a pleasant coffee shop (same hours).

While you're here, you should take the opportunity to drive up to Black Mountain, which rises about 200m above Canberra. On clear days, the panoramic view of Canberra and across the ACT from the 58-metre-high viewing platform at the **Black Mountain Telstra Tower** (daily 9am–10pm; $3.30) is magnificent. The tower also has a café and a revolving restaurant (advance booking recommended on ☎02/6248 6162) for families, serving smorgasbord. Both gardens and tower are on the route of Action bus #904, which also goes to the Zoo aquarium (see p.250).

North of Black Mountain, the **Australian Institute of Sport** (AIS), on Leverrier Crescent in Bruce (tours with an AIS athlete Mon–Fri 10.20am, 11.30am & 2.30pm, school holidays, Sat & Sun 10am, 11.30am, 1pm & 2.30pm; 1hr 30min; $10.80; ⓦ www.ausport.gov.au; bus #431), is a manifestation of Australia's craze for sport. The ultramodern, multimillion-dollar complex was established in 1981 with the aim of churning out world-class athletes, and a visit is particularly relevant in the wake of the Sydney 2000 Olympics. The Sportex interactive sports exhibition gives you the chance to test your sporting prowess, and there's a café and a shop selling souvenirs and sports clothing – just in case you decide to take advantage of the facilities (at an extra charge): a heated pool, spa and sauna, and indoor and outdoor tennis courts.

Canberra Nature Park

The bush hills and ridges which intersperse Canberra's suburbs make up the **Canberra Nature Park**, which has many walking tracks to explore. You can pick up maps and guides from the ACT Government Information Shop Front, Saraton Building, East Row, Civic, or call the park headquarters for more information on ☎02/6207 2090. The park actually comprises many sites, one of the most accessible being the Bruce/O'Connor Ridge section, across Belconnen Way from the Black Mountain area of the park; from here, several walking tracks head through bushland, including one that runs right behind the well-positioned youth hostel.

Eating and drinking

All cuisines imaginable are represented somewhere in Canberra and the surrounding suburbs, and if you have the time it's well worth getting out of the centre to explore some of them. Woolley Street in **Dickson** is the best suburban street to head for, crammed as it is with a variety of Asian restaurants and supermarkets. The well-off areas of **Manuka** and **Kingston**, near New Parliament House, have gourmet café–delis and fine restaurants. **Civic** itself is well served with places to eat, especially in the pedestrian mall around Garema Place. In addition to the restaurants listed here, Canberra's many clubs (see "Entertainment and nightlife", opposite) also serve very inexpensive meals in a typical Aussie atmosphere. **Cafés** are plentiful around the centre, with a particular concentration on Bunda Street, near the cinemas. On the ground level of the City Market shopping mall, on the corner of Bunda Street and Ainslie Avenue, there's an excellent **food court**, with cafes and specialist stores serving a wide variety of cuisines, as well as a large **supermarket**. Healthy vegetarian ingredients can be bought from Mount Creek Wholefoods, 14 Barker Street, Griffith. Most local buses go from the City Bus Interchange to the suburbs listed below (see "City transport", p.244, for details).

Cafés and food courts

Ali Baba, cnr Petrie Plaza and Bunda St. A simple Lebanese takeaway with outside tables. Daily to 10pm, very late Fri & Sat.

ANU Union, Union Crescent, Acton. The students' union has a restaurant, a café and a super-cheap bistro specializing in Asian food. BYO. Mon–Fri lunch and dinner.

The Blue Olive, 56 Alinga St. Home-baked speciality breads and cakes, toasted Turkish sandwiches and ice-cold beer from the in-house bottle shop. Daily 7am–late.

The Café, Barrine Drive, west of the Commonwealth Avenue Bridge, next to Mr Spokes Bike Hire. In a lovely spot by the lake. Daily from 9am.

Café Essen, Garema Arcade. A much-loved gourmet coffee house with enormous, cheap and unusual brunches for health freaks and carbo-junkies alike. Live music at the weekend. Daily from 7.30am.

Caffe della Piazza, 19 Garema Place. A lively, people-watching place spilling out into the square, with sidewalk tables. Award-winning Italian coffee, *focaccia*, pizza and pasta. Licensed.

Gus' Café, Bunda St, next to Center Cinema. Canberra's best café serves inexpensive light meals, and fresh soups with lots of choice for vegetarians. Tables outside under vines and a huge tree; magazines and newspapers to read. Popular with students and an arty crowd. Daily 7.30am–10.30pm, later at the weekend.

Iridium, cnr Northborne Ave and London Circuit. This is a beautifully designed space with interesting breakfast and dinner choices, and an all-day menu featuring the scrumptious artistry of its very own pastry chef. Perfect for post-club munchies. Mon–Thurs 7am–midnight, Fri–Sun 24hr.

Red Belly Black Café, Mount Stromlo observatory (☎02/6287 1518). Great BBQs, light lunches and delicious coffee in this out-of-town location underneath the stars.

Zydeco, 173 City Walk. This airy café/restaurant offers a comprehensive breakfast menu, great coffee, and an Australian twist to the omnipresent *focaccia*. Tables outside, too. Mon–Sat 10am–late, Sun noon–6pm.

Restaurants

Anarkali Pakistani Restaurant, cnr London Circuit and Akuna St (☎02/6247 6135). An excellent, affordable curry house. Licensed. Closed Sat & Sun lunch.

Bernadette's Café Restaurant, Ainslie Shops, Wakefield Gardens, Ainslie (☎02/6248 5018). A friendly, sunny BYO vegetarian café with a pleasant terrace, in an unassuming suburb about ten-minutes' walk from the main tourist office. The menu features huge *focaccia* sandwiches, pizzas (with vegan alternatives) and salads, as well as home baking to die for. Booking advised at night. Tues–Fri 11am–10pm, Sat & Sun 9am–10pm.

The Chairman and Yip, 108 Bunda St (☎02/6248 7109). A stylish, good-humoured Chinese restaurant, much more congenial than most of its Civic neighbours. The walls are adorned with Mao paraphernalia and a "workers lunch" costs $12.50. Sun–Thurs 11.30am–11pm, Fri & Sat 11.30am–midnight.

Delicateating, O'Connor Shopping Centre, Macpherson St. Trendy, delicatessen-style place tending towards Italian cuisine, and conveniently located near the youth hostel. Mellow yellow walls and tables outside. BYO. Mon–Fri 10am–10pm, Sat & Sun 9am–10pm.

Fringe Benefits Brasserie, 54 Marcus Clarke St (☎02/6247 4042). Stylish restaurant with an extensive wine cellar. Licensed. Closed Sun.

Gundaroo Pub Restaurant, Cork St, Gundaroo. Features "typical Outback Aussie atmosphere" with dishes such as kangaroo-tail soup, roast and three veg, or damper and billy tea.

Kingsland Vegetarian Restaurant, Shop 5, Dickson Plaza, 28 Challis St, Dickson (ⓣ 02/6262 9350). Earthy, reasonably priced veggie cuisine situated near the visitor information centre. Mon–Fri & Sun 11am–2.30pm & 5–10pm, Sat 5–10pm.

Little Saigon, cnr Alinga St and Northbourne Ave (ⓣ 02/6230 5003). Large, busy, cheap and tasty Vietnamese restaurant, with $5 lunchtime specials. Advisable to book on weekends. Daily 9am–3pm & 5–10.30pm.

Mama's Café and Bar, 7 Garema Place. Decent, usually crowded, Italian restaurant with outside tables. Daily 10am–late.

Montezumas, 197 London Circuit (next to *Canberra City Backpackers*). Loud, accommodating and popular, with live entertainment Fri–Sun.

Licensed. Mon–Sat 5pm–late, also open for lunch Wed–Fri.

Ottoman Cuisine, First floor, Shop 8, Franklin St, Manuka (ⓣ 02/6239 6754). An excellent Turkish restaurant that's a little more expensive than the Sydney equivalent, but worth it. Particularly delicious seafood. Licensed & BYO. Closed Sun.

Three Mothers Thai, Petrie Plaza off Garema Place (ⓣ 02/6249 8900). A modern, trendy brasserie-style Thai, very reasonably priced and with speedy service. BYO. Mon–Fri 11.30am–2pm & 5–10pm, Sat & Sun 5–10pm.

Tilley's, 96 Wattle St, Lyneham. Wonderful platefuls of comfort food – salads, big melts and special carrot cake – in a gorgeous, candlelit locale.

Tosolini's, cnr Franklin and Furneaux streets, Manuka (ⓣ 02/6232 6600). Very popular, award-winning eatery in the most glitzy of neighbourhoods. Sunday brunch on the terrace is a must. Tues–Sun noon–3pm & 6–10.30pm, plus weekend breakfast 8.30–11.30am.

Entertainment and nightlife

Despite the eerie quiet that invades Civic after working hours, there's quite a vibrant and even experimental entertainment scene in Canberra. For current events, the daily *Canberra Times* is your best bet: the most extensive **listings** are published every Thursday in a cultural and entertainment supplement, *Good Times*. For details of bands and clubs, pick up a copy of *BMA*, a free monthly music magazine. The visitor information centre and most hotels also distribute the quarterly booklet *Canberra What's On*, which lists major cultural events. Up-to-date **information** on all local venues and alternative events can be found at the ⓦ www.canberratribe.com website, or by calling the "Today and Tonight" events hotline on ⓣ 02/6257 4347.

Nightclubs and pubs

There are several chart-oriented **nightclubs** in Canberra, including *Pandora's*, on the corner of Mort and Alinga streets, with two floors of dance music, disco and easy rock; and *Insomnia*, above *ICBM* on the corner of Northbourne Avenue and East Row, where the city's public servants let their hair down.

In the centre, the best **pub** for a drink is the tiny *Phoenix Pub*, 23 East Row, which attracts a grungey crowd and has feral live bands. Frequented by locals and tourists alike is the large Irish theme pub *P. J. O'Reilly's*, at the corner of West Row and Alinga Street, which also has a reasonable restaurant and snack menu (daily 11am–10pm). Similarly popular, and rather less forced, are *King O'Malleys* at 131 City Walk, with outside tables, nightly live music (see ⓦ www.kingomalleys.com.au for details) and a hearty bill of fare; and *Filthy McFaddens* on Jardine Street in Kingston. Another good Kingston pub is *Maddie's Bar*, in the *Kingston Hotel*, 73 Canberra Ave; it's popular with resident travellers and is open Wednesday to Saturday until 4am.

Clustered around Garema Place in the city centre are several bars and dance venues, including the legendary *Gypsy Bar*, situated underneath the *City Walk Motel*, a relaxed and friendly club with an eclectic live music schedule, from African dance bands to regular goth nights (see ⓦ www.gypsy.com.au for details; entry $8); and *Heaven*, the best location for house and techno, popular with a predominantly, though not exclusively, gay crowd (entry $5–10). Gay partying with a sense of community happens at the member-owned and operated *Meridian Club*, 34 Mort St, Braddon (closed Mon; ⓦhttp://meridian.webone.com.au).

Live music

The *ANU Bar* on Childers Street at the ANU campus in Acton, entertaining six thousand or so students, is invariably the best place for **rock bands** of all sorts, with live performances at least a couple of times a week during term time (ⓣ02/6249 5010 or ⓦwww.anu.edu.au/events for details), while the *Canberra Workers Club* (ⓣ02/6248 0399) hosts big touring bands, with cheap drinks until midnight.

However, the music you're most likely to hear in Canberra is **jazz**. *Déjà Vu*, the upstairs bar at the *Canberra Casino*, 21 Binara St (ⓣ02/6257 7074), regularly hosts big-name jazz bands. For something more intimate, jazz can be heard on Sunday night from 7pm at the gay-friendly *Tilleys*, an ambient café/bar/gallery in Lyneham at 96 Wattle St (ⓣ02/6247 7753); more mainstream jazz is played on Thursdays and Sundays at *All Bar Nun*, near the YHA in O'Connor, and at the *Wig & Pen* on Alinga Street on Saturday nights.

Weekends see **folk and blues** at the *Pot Belly Bar*, Weedon Close, Belconnen; there's nightly **hardcore rock** and ear-splitting **metal** at *Rockape* in the Northside Fitness Centre, 2 Dickson Place, Dickson (ⓣ02/6257 8195, ⓦwww.rockape.net), and anything from **world music** to **jungle** at the self-consciously cool *Mombasa*, 128 Bunda St. The *Canberra Yacht Club*, Lotus Bay, Coronation Drive, Yarralumla, has more middle-of-the-road lounge-style entertainment on Friday night, featuring a singer and guitarist. **Classical music** performances are staged sporadically at the Canberra Theatre Centre on Civic Square (ⓣ02/6257 1077), and regularly at the Canberra School of Music, Llewellyn Hall (ⓣ02/6249 5700).

Theatre and cinema

The main **drama** venue in the capital is the impressive Canberra Theatre Centre on Civic Square (ⓣ02/6257 1077). In addition to a broad range of plays, its several theatres also host concerts, dance performances and readings – it's always worth finding out what's going on here. Other, less mainstream, options include the Street Theatre (ⓣ02/6247 1223, ⓦwww.thestreet.org.au) on the corner of Childers Street and University Avenue, and a number of active independent theatre groups based at the Gorman House Community Arts Centre on Ainslie Avenue, Braddon (ⓣ02/6249 0448 for information and bookings). The Skylark Puppet & Mask Theatre is based at Strickland Crescent, Deakin (ⓣ02/6285 1121). *Tilleys* in Lyneham (see "Live music", above) also hosts cabaret programmes, as does the *School of the Arts Cafe*, 108 Monaro St, Queanbeyan (ⓣ02/6297 6857), worth checking out for its new plays by fringe theatre groups, as well as its live music, bush poetry and comedy acts – all from Thursday to Saturday.

As for **cinemas**, the Center Cinema on Bunda Street (ⓣ02/6249 7979; cheap day Tues and after 6pm Sun) is probably the best of the regular commercial choices, with a well-considered programme and interesting Saturday late shows at 11pm, while the Electric Shadows Cinema, Akuna Street (ⓣ02/6247 5060; cheap day Wed), shows the best in world cinema, and has a bookshop and café-bar.

Clubs

Numerous **clubs**, most of which admit visitors, are one of the features of Canberra life. They often serve inexpensive meals, and may also organize live music, film evenings, parties or comedy shows – all in the hope of luring visitors to gamble their money away on the one-armed bandits. One of the biggest is the *Canberra Workers Club* on Childers Street (☏ 02/6248 0399): it boasts a bistro serving meals every day, regular discos, and darts and pool as well as pokies. The *Canberra Tradesmen's Union Club*, 2 Badham St, Dickson (☏ 02/6248 0999), has a sauna, gym and squash courts, an observatory with an astronomical officer on duty (dusk until about 12.30am), and a Bicycle Museum (daily 9am–midnight); you can even dine in a restored tram, or have your hair cut in a 1920s-style barber shop. The attractions are all free, but children have to leave by 8pm, when the sinful poker machines rev up. The *Canberra Labor Club*, Chandler Street, Belconnen (☏ 02/6251 5522), serves meals daily and offers bingo as well as occasional disco or rock nights.

Listings

Airlines Ansett, Jolimont Centre, 65 Northbourne Ave (☏ 02/6249 7715, reservations ☏ 13 1300); Qantas Travel Centre, Jolimont Centre, 65 Northbourne Ave (☏ 13 1313).

American Express 185 City Walk, cnr Petrie Plaza (☏ 02/6247 2333).

Banks The city branches of the bigger banks are open Mon–Thurs 9.30am–4pm, Fri until 5pm: ANZ, 19 London Circuit; Commonwealth Bank, cnr London Circuit and Ainslie Ave; National Australia Bank, cnr London Circuit and Ainslie Ave; Westpac, cnr Alinga and Mort streets.

Bike rental Canberra Bike Rental (☏ 02/6241 2216, 24hr phone booking); The Gecko Gang (☏ 02/6254 8047); Wombat Mountain Bikes (☏ 02/6285 4058, after hours ☏ 02/6288 2753; $40 per day). A pleasurable bicycle path goes all the way around Lake Burley Griffin: to enjoy it, contact Mr Spokes Bike Hire (☏ 02/6257 1188; $9.90 per hour), right on the water at Barrine Drive, Acton.

Books Smiths Alternative Bookshop (☏ 02/6247 4459) is the antithesis of all things Canberrian, stocking interesting fiction and cultural theory, as well as radical and left-leaning publications.

Buses For local bus information phone Action timetable information (Mon–Sat 6am–11pm, Sun 8am–5.30pm, ☏ 13 1710), check out their website (ⓦ www.action.act.gov.au) or call at the kiosk at the City Bus Interchange, 11 East Row. Long-distance services, including state-owned Countrylink and V/Line, use the Jolimont Centre, 65 Northbourne Ave, as their terminal. You can buy tickets direct here from the Countrylink Travel Centre (☏ 02/6257 1576 or 13 2232); Countrylink to Eden and Cootamundra, V/Line to Wodonga and Sale); Greyhound Pioneer (Canberra terminal ☏ 02/6257 4424 or free call 1800 801 294) and Murrays Coaches (☏ 13 2251; to Sydney, Wollongong, Batemans Bay and the Snowy Mountains). Travellers Maps and Guides (closed Sun) at the Jolimont Centre is an authorized travel agent selling bus tickets for the remaining bus companies: McCafferty's (☏ 13 1499; to Sydney and Melbourne); Capital Coaches (☏ 02/6292 9412; west and northwest to Orange, Dubbo, Bathurst, Young and Cowra); Rendell Coaches (☏ 02/6884 4199 or free call 1800 023 328; to Dubbo); Sid Fogg's (☏ 02/4928 1088 or free call 1800 045 952; to Newcastle) and Transborder Express (☏ 02/6241 0033; to Yass).

Car rental Inexpensive deals are available from Network Car & Truck Rentals (☏ 02/6251 6626 or free call 1800 077 977); Rent-a-Dent (☏ 02/6280 0320), which also rents campervans; and Rumbles Rent-a-Car (☏ 02/6280 7444). Others, mostly clustered on Lonsdale St in Braddon, with additional locations at the airport, are Avis (☏ 02/6249 6088, airport ☏ 02/6249 1601 or free call 1800 225 533); Budget (☏ 02/6257 2200, airport ☏ 02/6257 1305 or 1300/362 848); Hertz (☏ 02/6257 4877, airport ☏ 02/6249 6211 or 13 3039); and Thrifty (☏ 02/6247 7422 or 1300/367 227).

Embassies and high commissions There are over 70 in Canberra (all the following are in Yarralumla, unless otherwise stated): Canada, Commonwealth Ave (☏ 02/6273 3844); Germany, 119 Empire Court (☏ 02/6270 1911); Indonesia, 8 Darwin Ave (☏ 02/6273 3222); Ireland, 20 Arkana St (☏ 02/6273 3022); Malaysia, 7 Perth Ave (☏ 02/6273 1543); Netherlands, 120 Empire Circuit (☏ 02/6273 3111); New Zealand, Commonwealth Ave (☏ 02/6273 3611); Norway,

17 Hunter St ($\oplus$02/6273 3444); Papua New Guinea, Forster Crescent ($\oplus$02/6273 3322); Singapore, 17 Forster St ($\oplus$02/6273 3944); Sweden, 5 Turrana St ($\oplus$02/6273 3033); Switzerland, 7 Melbourne Ave, Forrest ($\oplus$02/6273 3977); Thailand, 111 Empire Circuit ($\oplus$02/6273 1149); UK, Commonwealth Ave ($\oplus$02/6270 6666); US, 21 Moonah Place ($\oplus$02/6270 5000).

Emergency $\oplus$000 for fire, police or ambulance.

Environmental contacts The Environment Centre, Kingsley St, Acton ($\oplus$02/6247 3064, $\otimes$www.spirit.net.au/envoz), is a library and archive on environmental topics as well as a book and gift shop (Mon–Fri 9am–5pm). The Wilderness Society Shop, 16 Garema Place ($\oplus$02/6249 8011), is a book and gift shop with information about the local environment.

Festivals The big event of the year is the Canberra Festival – the anniversary of the city's foundation – celebrated with concerts, theatre, exhibitions, street parades and fireworks for ten days from the beginning of March. It's followed in late March by Word Fest, a writers' festival held at ANU (programme available from January; details on $\oplus$02/6249 7068). The Royal Canberra Show is an agricultural fair lasting three days over the last weekend in February, while the Floriade is a spring festival marked by floral displays, theatre and music, from mid-September to mid-October. Even more popular, though less feted by the tourist board, is the annual Summernats Car Festival in January (details on $\oplus$02/6241 8111 or at $\otimes$www.summernats.com.au), when revheads convene in Exhibition Park to compare modified street machines and compete at the world's only purpose-built burnout facility.

Galleries Good private galleries include the Chapman Gallery, 31 Captain Cook Crescent, Manuka (Wed–Sun 11am–6pm; $\oplus$02/6295 2550), specializing in Aboriginal art; and the Beaver Galleries, 81 Denison St, Deakin (Wed–Sun 10.30am–5pm; $\oplus$02/6282 5294), for paintings, sculpture, jewellery and furniture.

Gay and lesbian Canberra Gayline $\oplus$02/6247 2726 (nightly 6–10pm); Gay Contact $\oplus$02/6257 2855 (same hours); Gaywaves Radio Mondays 92.9 FM.

Golf Royal Canberra Golf Club, Westbourne Woods, Yarralumla ($\oplus$02/6273 3622).

Horse riding Brindabella Valley Trails, 19 Sabine Close, Garran ($\oplus$02/6281 6682), offers riding in the Brindabella Ranges close to Kosciuszko National Park.

Hospitals John James Memorial Hospital, Strickland Crescent, Deakin ($\oplus$02/6281 8100).

Internet access *Cafe Cactus*, Centre Cinema Building (opposite *Cafe Essen*), Bunda St, Civic (Mon–Fri 8am–late, Sat & Sun 9.30am–late); *Internet Lounge*, Level 1, City Walk Arcade (Mon–Fri 9am–5pm).

Markets Gorman House Arts and Crafts Market, Gorman House Arts Centre, Ainslie Ave, Braddon (Sat 10am–4pm; bus #302, #303 or #385), is a community market where items such as pottery, hand-painted T-shirts, bric-a-brac and secondhand clothes are sold; Belconnen Markets, Lathlain St (Wed–Sun 8am–6.30pm), is a large fresh-food market featuring an organic grocery, seafood and poultry outlets, organic veggies, home-made jams, health foods, a naturopath and several cafes. There's also an open-air bric-a-brac market in the piazza here at weekends.

Nature reserves Information on ACT parks and reserves from Canberra Nature Park (north $\oplus$02/6207 2113, or south $\oplus$02/6207 2096) and Environment ACT ($\oplus$02/6207 9777, $\otimes$www.act.gov.au/environ). For Namadgi National Park, which takes up virtually the whole southern half of the ACT, and nearby national parks in NSW, contact the Australian National Parks and Wildlife Service, 153 Emu Bank, Belconnen ($\oplus$02/6250 0200).

NRMA (National Roads and Motorists Association), 92 Northbourne Ave, Braddon, or Belconnen Mall, Belconnen ($\oplus$13 2132). Publishes a very useful map of Canberra and the ACT, free to members. Touring and accommodation enquiries $\oplus$1300/131 122.

Police $\oplus$02/256 7777.

Post office Alinga St, Canberra, ACT 2600 (Mon–Fri 9am–5pm; $\oplus$02/6209 1680).

Rape Crisis Centre 59 Majura Ave, Dickson (24hr; $\oplus$02/6247 2525).

Scenic flights Canberra Flight Centre ($\oplus$02/6257 6331) charges from about $60 per person for 30–55 min.

Shopping Shopping hours are Mon–Thurs 9am–5.30pm, Fri 9am–9pm, Sat 9am–noon. Shops in the Canberra Centre are open daily. In the city centre the shopping focus is on Bunda St, with department stores such as David Jones and Grace Bros, and a comprehensive Target. The shops and supermarket at City Market, on the corner of Bunda St and Ainslie Ave, are also open daily. There are late-opening supermarkets in the shopping centres of the satellite towns.

Taxis Aerial Taxis ($\oplus$02/6285 9222; credit cards accepted); Queanbeyan Taxi Co-operative, Queanbeyan ($\oplus$02/6297 3000). There is a taxi rank on Bunda St outside the Center Cinema.

Tours and cruises Murrays, the Jolimont Centre, 67 Northbourne Ave ($\oplus$13 2251), has half- or full-day bus tours around Canberra and to the Snowy Mountains; Bunyip Bush Safaris (℡ 02/6255 1472), arranges trips for small groups to the Snowy Mountains and further afield to the national parks of southeast Australia for reasonable rates; Canberra's Top Secret Tour (℡ 02/6297 8585, ⓦ www.topsecret.canberra.net.au) is a self-drive spy tour for budding James Bonds, on which you discover the scenes of Canberra's secret intelligence organizations and political intrigue; Harley Rides 'r' Us (℡ 02/6231 7231 or free call 1800 242 753), offers sightseeing trips in and around Canberra from the back of a Harley-Davidson from $55; Wild Things Tours (℡ 02/6254 6303, ⓦ www.wildthingtours.com) runs six-hour tours into Namadgi National Park for guaranteed Eastern Grey kangaroo-spotting and indigenous rock art ($80, including light lunch, park entrance, pick-ups and drop-offs); Australia Capital Tours (℡ 02/6284 7160) offers 90min cruises twice daily ($15) in the Central Basin of Lake Burley Griffin, with additional evening cruises in summer; and Dawn Drifters (℡ 02/6285 4450, ⓦ www.dawndrifters.com.au) will fly you over the city in a balloon (Mon–Fri $190, weekends & holidays $240) , and then feed you breakfast when safely aground.

Trains The Xplorer train links Canberra and Sydney (3 daily; 4hr) via Queanbeyan, Bungendore, Goulburn, Bundanoon, Moss Vale, Bowral and Mittagong. Ticket sales and information at the Countrylink Travel Centre, Jolimont Centre, 67 Northbourne Ave (℡ 02/6257 1576), and at the train station in Kingston (℡ 02/6239 7039).

Travel agents Canberra Flight Centre, City Walk Arcade, 2 Mort St, Civic (Mon–Sat 9am–5pm; ℡ 02/6247 8199); STA Travel, 13–15 Garema Place, Civic (Mon–Sat 9am–5pm; ℡ 02/6247 8633).

Women Women's Information and Referral Centre, 6th Floor, FAI Insurance Building, 197 London Circuit (Mon–Fri 9am–5pm; ℡ 02/6205 1075 or 6205 1076, ⓦ www.act.gov.au/womensinfo).

Around Canberra

The residents of Canberra live with nature right on their doorstep: the numerous **picnic grounds** and **bushwalking trails** in the state reserves and national parks are only about half an hour's drive from the city centre. Be warned, though, that at the height of summer, when there is a high risk of bushfires, a total fire ban is declared and all the nature reserves and national parks are closed (call ℡ 02/6207 8600 to check). Bushland aside, the environs of the capital can also lay claim to historic **homesteads and villages**, private zoos, a former gold-mining town and a few **wineries**, some of them across the border in New South Wales.

South

Just 4km south from Canberra's New Parliament House is the private, open-range **Mugga Lane Zoo** (Mon–Fri 9am–4pm, Sat & Sun 9am–5pm; $7.50), at Mugga Lane, off Hindmarsh Drive, Symonston. Here you can see kangaroos, wallabies and wombats, as well as dingoes and emus. Leaving the city further behind, the Tharwa Road follows the course of the **Murrumbidgee River** as it approaches Tharwa. Thirty-two kilometres from Canberra, at the southern end of the Tuggeranong Valley, the convict-built **Lanyon Homestead** (Tues–Sun 10am–4pm, grounds open to 5pm; $6.50, admission to grounds free) dates back to the earliest European settlement of the region. Thoroughly refurbished by the National Trust, it now houses a small display outlining the history of the area before Canberra existed, but the real reasons to come are the house itself and the **Sidney Nolan Gallery** (same hours as homestead; $3.50) next door, where works by the famous Australian painter are on permanent display alongside changing exhibitions of contemporary Australian art. There's no public transport out here.

Beyond the Lanyon Homestead and Tharwa, old cottages on the Naas Road, overlooking the river, house the galleries and antique shops of the **Cuppacumbalong Craft Centre** (Wed–Sun & holidays 11am–5pm). Nearby, a small, licensed café serves hearty meals and local cider, and there's also a spot nearby where you can swim in the river.

Namadgi National Park

Namadgi National Park occupies almost half of the ACT, largely made up of wilderness areas in the west and southwest. Its mountain ranges and high plains, rising to 1900m, have a far more severe climate than low-lying Canberra and give rise to the Cotter River and many smaller streams. In the northwest, the Corin Road leads to Corin Dam, while in the south the partly surfaced Bobyan Road cuts right through the national park, emerging beneath the Snowy Mountains in the south (the park abuts the Kosciuszko National Park along the state border). There are picnic grounds and bush campsites by the Orroral River and near Mount Clear in the south.

The **Namadgi Visitors Information Centre**, 3km south of Tharwa on the Naas Road (Mon–Fri 9am–4pm, Sat, Sun & holidays 9am–4.30pm; ☎02/6207 2900 or in emergency call ranger on ☎02/6281 5878), has displays and videos about the park, and also provides guided tours on request as well as detailed information on bushwalking tracks and emergency shelters in the remote areas.

West: Tidbinbilla Nature Reserve and Cotter Reserve

The small **Tidbinbilla Nature Reserve**, to the southwest of the city (daily 9am–6pm, later during daylight saving; $8.50 per car; ⓦwww.act.gov.au/env-iron/tidbin.html), is an enjoyable place with relatively easy walks, and some wheelchair-accessible paths. In the area around the park entrance and **information centre** (Mon–Fri 11am–3pm, Sat & Sun 9am–6pm; ☎02/6205 1233) kangaroos and wallabies roam in spacious bush enclosures, and you can also see koalas and lots of birds. Picnic grounds are dotted all along the sealed road that leads through the reserve, and on long weekends and during the school holidays it's a busy place, especially popular with families. The **Canberra Space Centre** on Discovery Drive in Tidbinbilla (visitors centre open daily 9am–5pm, summer to 8pm; free; ⓦwww.cdscc.nasa.gov) sounds like every child's dream, though in fact the displays of spacecraft and highly sensitive communications equipment are not as exciting as you might have hoped. Operated in conjunction with NASA, the purpose of the station is to pick up even the most obscure signals from outer space; there are only two others in the world with the same range as Tidbinbilla – one near Madrid, the other in Goldstone, California.

Southwest of here, Corin Road turns off the Tidbinbilla Road towards the **Corin Forest** (Sat, Sun & holidays 10am–5pm, Mon–Fri during school holidays 10am–4pm; ⓦwww.corin.com.au) and reservoir, a popular recreation spot in the hills, with many walking trails, year-round bobsledding, picnic grounds and barbecue facilities. In winter you can ski on artificial snow and during school holidays special activities are organized for children.

Cotter Reserve

The **Cotter Reserve**, near the Cotter Dam, 22km west of the city, is another popular spot for short weekend outings. Here, around an artificial lake that was the original reservoir built to serve the new capital, you'll find picnic grounds, a restaurant and a **campsite** (℡02/6288 4930). The **Murrumbidgee River** nearby is suitable for swimming. On the way to the Cotter Reserve you pass the **Mount Stromlo Observatory** (visitors gallery open daily 9.30am–4.30pm; guided tour $5.40; ℡02/6249 0232), about 16km from Canberra. The giant silver dome houses the telescopes of the ANU's Department of Astronomy; inside the complex, there are photographic displays and textual information on various aspects of astronomy, and you can see some of the viewing equipment – enquire at the above number for viewing nights. Note that there is no public transport to the observatory.

North

Leaving Canberra by the Barton Highway to the north, the first place of interest is **GINNINDERA**, approximately 9km out. It's a rather consciously touristy village with a few arts and crafts shops and *The Green Herring* restaurant in a log hut. Just before Ginnindera, on Gold Creek Road, the **National Dinosaur Museum** (daily 10am–5pm; $8.50; Ⓦ www.nationaldinosaurmuseum.com.au) is not a big, government-run museum as the name might suggest, but rather a private collection of replica skeletons and some bones and fossils. Other local tourist attractions include **Cockington Green** (daily 9.30am–4.30pm; $11.50; Ⓦ www.cockington-green.com.au), a miniature model English village; and the **Artgems Gallery** (daily 10am–5pm) in the village, with exhibits of paintings, gems (especially opals and crystals), and local arts and crafts. **HALL**, 3km north of Ginnindera, is a similar village with a few shops and a restaurant, and another Artgems Gallery.

More or less opposite the turn-off for Hall, the Wallaroo Road heads west towards the New South Wales border. Not far down the road, at Woodgrove Close, is Brindabella Hill Wines (℡02/6230 2583), where you can sample some of the local "cool climate" vintages. There are more **wineries** around **MURRUMBATEMAN**, north along the Barton Highway into NSW between Canberra and the large country town of Yass (see p.357); full lists are available from the tourist office.

The Federal Highway

Northeast of Canberra, the Federal Highway crosses into NSW shortly after leaving the city. The first of the sights along this way is the **Bywong Gold Mining Town** (daily 9.30am–4.30pm; tours 11am, 1pm & 3pm; $8; Ⓦ www.bywonggold.citysearch.com.au), where a brief goldrush at the end of the nineteenth century has left shafts and some old mine workings. The gold-diggers' camp has been reconstructed with some serious attention to historic detail, and it's well worth stopping in if you're passing by; you can also try your hand at panning, and there are picnic and barbecue areas. The mining village is on Bungendore Road, further down which lies the attractive village of **BUN-GENDORE**, with a pottery, woodturner, café and shops arranged around the village green. Heading on, you can circle back round to Canberra via Queanbeyan, or strike east, a scenic drive that takes you through **BRAID-WOOD** – which has more antiques and crafts shops, and a fine old hotel – towards the coast at Batemans Bay (see p.272).

Southern NSW

There are two quite separate parts to the southern half of New South Wales, just as there are to the state as a whole: the coast, and the mountains and hinterland beyond them. The **south coast**, with its green dairylands, is delightful in a quiet sort of way – an area for fishing or surfing or relaxing on the beaches, with no huge resorts or commercial developments. Inland, the **Snowy Mountains** constitute the Dividing Range's highest peaks; they have Australia's best skiing and, in summer, some fine bushwalking. Beyond the mountains, the southwest is dull farming country – you're better off crossing to the riverlands of Victoria, or driving straight through.

The direct route from Sydney to Melbourne is via the inland **Hume Highway**, from which you can easily detour to Canberra or the Snowy

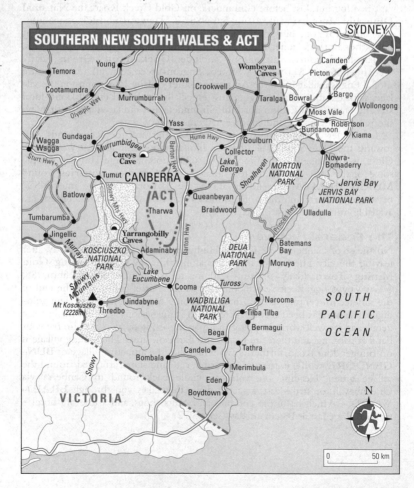

Mountains. There's a four-lane freeway from Sydney to Moss Vale, and the rest of the way it's a normal two-lane road with occasional overtaking lanes, but very winding between Yass and Albury. It is also very busy, with heavy truck traffic, and most of the time quite boring – a potentially lethal combination. It takes roughly twelve hours to drive straight through from Sydney to Melbourne, which is fine if you're sharing the driving, but otherwise allow two days.

The coastal route, the **Princes Highway**, is slightly longer but much more attractive in terms of scenery. Give yourself two or more days if you want to appreciate the surf, the sandy beaches, and the mountains, valleys and forests that back this beautiful stretch of the coast.

Most **buses** run via the Hume Highway, usually with a detour to Canberra; the **train** follows largely the same route.

The Snowy Mountains

The **Snowy Mountains** are just one section of the alpine highlands that spread across the southeast corner of the Australian continent. The Australian Alps sprawl from Mount Buller, Mount Bogong and Mount Beauty in northeast Victoria via the Crackenback Range in New South Wales to the township of Cooma; though it's a continuous massif, only the New South Wales section is strictly known as the Snowy Mountains. **Mount Kosciuszko**, at 2228m the highest mountain in mainland Australia, is located close to the Victorian border in the far southeast. It was named in 1840 by the Polish-born explorer Paul Strzelecki after the Polish freedom fighter General Tadeusz Kosciuszko, and, although Strzelecki stressed he was "in a foreign country and on a foreign ground", he couldn't resist giving it its name "amongst a free people who appreciate freedom". The **Kosciuszko National Park** which surrounds the peak includes most of the Snowy Mountains region, and almost everything of interest. To the north and east of **Cooma** – the main approach to the range – the treeless, brownish-yellow **Monaro High Plain** is sheep country famous for the quality of its Merino wool.

Compared to the high mountain ranges of other continents, the "roof of Australia" is relatively low and, despite the name, the flattened mountaintops lie below the line of permanent snow. After heavy snowfalls in winter, however (roughly from the end of June to the beginning of Oct), winter-sports fans from all over southeast Australia congregate at the **ski resorts** in the Mount Kosciuszko area – Perisher Blue Resort, Thredbo, Mount Selwyn and Charlotte Pass. It's not the most exciting skiing in the world – there are few challenging runs – and prices are hiked up to ridiculous levels as the resorts attempt to make their living during a very short season. Selwyn, a family resort, which is generally half the price of other resorts in the region, is one cheap alternative. Only the most fanatical European winter-sports enthusiast would come here especially to ski, but if you're passing it can be an enjoyable diversion. This is also an ideal area for cross-country skiing, an increasingly popular pursuit. In **summer** it's a different story: price levels return to normal, the towns and resorts are not quite so crowded, even sleepy, and there are fabulous walks and mountain scenery to be enjoyed. Perisher and Selwyn almost completely close down, but Thredbo operates ski-lifts throughout the year, transporting hikers and sightseers to mountaintops from where they can embark on short or extended bushwalks across the wildflower-covered high country. There are also plenty of opportunities for horse riding, mountain biking and trout fishing or white-water rafting in the crystal-clear mountain streams.

Skiing in the Snowy Mountains

The easiest option is to arrange a **ski package** departing from Sydney – always check exactly what's included in the price. Recommended operators include Kosciuszko Accommodation Centre (℡02/6456 2022 or free call 1800 026 385), who can put together a low-season basic weekend package including transport by bus, national park entry, ski rental, lift and lessons, and two-nights' accommodation, dinner and breakfast for around $300; similar deals can be arranged through Alpine World (see below).

A one-day **ski-lift pass** starts from about $44 at Selwyn, $71 at Charlotte Pass and $73 at Thredbo and Perisher Blue, and beginners' one-day group lessons cost around $90. Resorts are generally pretty child-friendly, particularly at Charlotte Pass where the homely and old-fashioned *Kosciuszko Chalet* (free call ℡1800 026 369) offers free childcare throughout the ski season; Paddy Pallin at Jindabyne (℡02/6456 2922 or free call 1800 623 459) has several cross-country skiing sessions, including an easy three-hour introduction aimed at family groups.

Another good source of information on the latest deals is Inski, a popular ski shop with its own attached ski travel agency, Alpine World, at 46 York St, Sydney (℡02/9290 2688 or 1300/138 311, ℠www.alpineworld.com.au).

The system of roads which made possible the existence of the townships and ski resorts was established by the **Snowy Mountains Hydroelectric Scheme**, which was begun in the 1950s. Many postwar immigrants from middle and southern Europe found their first jobs on the "Snowy"; some lost their lives here. Twenty-five years and about $800 million later, in 1974 the project was completed: seven power stations now utilize the waters of the Upper Murrumbidgee, Tumut and Snowy rivers to generate electricity and provide New South Wales, the ACT and Victoria with power. The scheme's generating capacity is about eighteen percent of the total for southeast Australia, while the water of the redirected rivers is used for irrigation right across New South Wales, Victoria and South Australia.

Getting around

The most important of the area's roads is the **Snowy Mountains Highway**, which leads straight across the mountain ranges and through the national park from Cooma to Tumut and Gundagai. If you want to see more of the alpine scenery, the fully-sealed **Alpine Way** offers a spectacular circuit, turning off the highway at Kiandra in the heart of the park and heading via Khancoban and Geehi to Thredbo. In winter, check road conditions before driving anywhere, even on the Snowy Mountains Highway; on the Alpine Way and on Kosciuszko Road (after Sawpit Creek) **snow chains** must be carried between June and October, and the roads might be closed altogether.

Bus services are far more frequent in winter than in summer – a **rental car** is strongly recommended for summer sojourns. Greyhound (℡13 2030) has a daily service between Sydney, Canberra, Cooma, Jindabyne, Perisher Valley and Thredbo, with additional services in the winter. Summit coaches (℡02/6294 1236) operate four times a week from Canberra, and then twice a week to Albury along the Alpine Way. Backpacker busline Autopia Tours operate a year-round Melbourne–Sydney route (℡02/9326 5536 or free call 1800 000 507, ℠www.netspace.net.au/~autopia; $170) via the Alpine Way, picking up and dropping off in Jindabyne. Additional winter-only bus services include Adaminaby Bus Service (℡02/6454 2318) between Cooma, Adaminaby and Mount Selwyn ski resort. Perisher Blue Skitube (free call

🕾 1800 654 681; see p.266 for more details) is a **railway** specially designed for skiers, but it also operates for bushwalkers in the summer months, linking the ski areas of Bullocks Flat, Perisher Valley and Mount Blue Cow. Countrylink (🕾 13 2829) have a daily train from Sydney, with a coach connection in Cooma.

Cooma

Because of its location at the intersection of two highways – the Monaro Highway south from Canberra and the Snowy Mountains Highway from the coast to the high peaks – **COOMA** is the obvious base for trips into the Snowy Mountains. Although it functions mainly as a service centre for skiers, it's also an attractive place in its own right, with a number of fine old buildings, notably on Lambie and Vale streets – the visitors centre (see below) has a brochure detailing buildings of interest.

The town has really come into its own since the 1950s, when it took on the mantle of administrative centre for the hydroelectric scheme. Many of the migrants who worked on the "Snowy", as it's known – particularly those who arrived from central Europe – ended up settling here, making it a fairly cosmopolitan town. If you're interested in the history of the project and the technical details, check out the **visitors centre** of the Snowy Mountains Authority, on the Monaro Highway in North Cooma (Mon–Fri 8am–5pm, Sat & Sun during school holidays 8am–1pm; free call 🕾 1800 623 776 for details of guided visits to various power stations, 🌐 www.snowyhydro.com.au). That's about all there is to Cooma, except for **Llama World**, 19km out of town on the Adaminaby Road (Fri–Sun 10am–4pm, daily during school holidays; $11; 🌐 www.lamaworld.com.au), where llamas, alpacas and guanacos are bred. Llamas aside, the Snowy Mountains are traditionally regarded as prime **horse-riding** country. The long-established Yarramba Trail Riding at Berridale, 34km southwest of Cooma (🕾 02/6453 7204), offers escorted rides at $25 per hour or full-day picnic rides ($75), as well as extended camping safaris ($180 for two days).

Practicalities

The helpful **Cooma Visitors Centre**, 119 Sharp St (daily: June–Oct 7am–6pm; Nov–May 9am–5pm; 🕾 02/6450 1742 or free call 1800 636 525, 🌐 www.visitcooma.com.au), has detailed information on Kosciuszko National Park, plus farmstays, horse riding and fishing safaris, and offers a free accommodation booking service. Pick up a copy of the free monthly *Snowy Times*, which has detailed resort information and maps, plus listings of skiing prices and packages. Harvey World Travel, 96 Sharp St (🕾 02/6452 4677), is a helpful **travel agency** which can book flights out, provide details of bus services and arrange local tours; **car rental** is available from Thrifty, 60 Sharp St (🕾 02/6452 5300).

Accommodation can be hard to come by in the ski season, when everything, especially the motels, is booked up pretty early, but the rest of the year you shouldn't have too many problems. Good options include the inexpensive and central *Royal Hotel*, on the corner of Lambie and Sharp streets (🕾 02/6552 2132; ❸): built in 1858, it has loads of character – many of the rooms have French windows opening onto the huge balcony. The family-run *Bunkhouse Motel*, 28 Soho St (🕾 02/6452 2983; rooms ❸, dorms ❶), is a guesthouse-style backpackers' with dorms and lots of en-suite singles. The good-value *Swiss Motel*, 34 Massie St (🕾 02/6452 1950; ❸), also has holiday apartments on offer

(⑤) – there are plenty of other motels nearby, and a great value B&B, the *Alpine Country Guesthouse* (☎02/6452 1414; ❸), just next door. *Snowtels Caravan Park*, Snowy Mountains Highway (☎02/6452 1828; apartments ❹–❺, cabins ❸–❹, on-site vans ❸), with a tennis court and communal kitchen, is probably the best of the campsites.

Cooma's not really a foodie sort of town. The best place to **eat** is the licensed *Sharp Food*, 122 Sharp St, a lovely cosy place with outdoor dining in a pleasant courtyard out the back, serving delicious soups and sandwiches. More banal fare can be found at *Grumpys*, 112 Sharp St, and inexpensive **pub meals** are available at the bistro of the *Australian Hotel*, across the road at no. 137.

Kosciuszko National Park and around

The largest national park in New South Wales, **Kosciuszko National Park** extends 200km north to south, from Tumut to the Victorian border, encompassing an area of some 6500 square kilometres. The scenery includes almost all of the high country, with ten peaks above 2100m, forested valleys and a treeless plateau with glacial lakes, as well as the headwaters of Australia's biggest river system, the Murray–Murrumbidgee. The main centres are the lakeside resort of Jindabyne, just outside the eastern boundary of the park, and the ski resort of Thredbo, 30km further west along the scenic Alpine Way, actually in the national park. Perisher and Mount Blue Cow can be reached via the Skitube from Bullocks Flat, roughly midway between Jindabyne and Thredbo.

If you're driving through, there's a **fee** of $15 per car per day – so if you plan to stay more than a day or two and especially if other national parks are on your itinerary, the annual national park pass ($80) may be a good investment (see p.240 for details). Arriving by bus, you'll still have to fork out a one-off payment of $6. Note that **parking** is heavily restricted throughout the park, and can reach crisis point in Thredbo – if you've come by car it might be worth paying extra for accommodation with space to park.

The **National Parks and Wildlife Service** has its headquarters in Jindabyne (daily: summer 8am–6pm, winter 7am–7pm; ☎02/6450 5600, Ⓦwww.npws.nsw.gov.au), a $5.4 million complex featuring red-gum interiors and including a tourist information office, cinema, café and bus station. It offers a comprehensive service, with leaflets about walking trails in the national park, activities such as ranger-guided tours, details of campsites, as well as maps for sale and a display on the natural features of the park. There are also NPWS **ranger stations** at Perisher Valley (☎02/6457 5214; winter only), Khancoban (☎02/6076 9373) and Tumut (☎02/6947 1849).

Bushwalking in the park

Some of the country's most interesting and beautiful **bushwalking tracks** pass through the area. One of the most accessible of these is the walking trail around **Mount Kosciuszko**. The **chair-lift** from Thredbo (see opposite) will take you up to Crackenback station on the edge of the plateau; the actual summit is about 6km from here, though it seems barely higher than the surrounding country, or you can walk 2km to **Mount Kosciuszko Lookout** for panoramic views. Another good way up to the high country is to take the **Skitube** from Bullocks Flat on the Alpine Way, a funicular railway that leads uphill and through a tunnel to Perisher Valley and Mount Blue Cow (which has a bistro and art gallery), where more fine trails await. Even if you plan only a brief walk of an hour or so, bear in mind that the weather up here is very fickle, and pack a sweater and some rain protection.

Jindabyne and Thredbo

A resort town at the man-made lake of the same name, **JINDABYNE**, 63km west of Cooma, is the jumping-off point for the ski resorts of Thredbo, a further 30km west, and Guthega, or up the Kosciuszko Road to Smiggin Holes and Perisher Valley (these two are also accessible by the Skitube – ☏ 02/6456 2010 or free call 1800 654 681 to check times; $17–25 return). Jindabyne itself is entirely new, having been relocated when the Snowy Mountains Scheme dammed the Snowy River and drowned the first settlement, and the lake is now its main attraction: there's good fishing, and in summer you can also swim and sail – most equipment is available to rent in the town. The **Snowy Region Visitors Centre** is within the NPWS headquarters here (daily: summer 8.30am–5pm; winter 8am–5.30pm; ☏ 02/6456 2444).

From Jindabyne, the Alpine Way continues into the national park and up to **THREDBO**, a compact and attractive village, squeezed into a narrow valley beside the road and the Crackenback River, with alpine-style houses huddled against the mountainside. In winter it offers the best and most expensive skiing in Australia, but unlike the other resorts, it is also reasonably lively in summer and – with its Crackenback **chair-lift** (daily 8.30am–4pm; $20 return) giving easy access to the high country – makes a good base for bushwalking and other explorations. The **Thredbo Resort Centre** (☏ 02/6459 4198 or free call 1800 020 589) can advise on chair-lift timetables and provide other tourist information. There are several annual events in the Thredbo calendar. Musical highlights include the three-day Thredbo **Blues Festival** in mid-January, the three-day **Global Music Festival** in March and the four-day **Jazz Festival** in early May.

Yarrangobilly Caves and Kiandra

The **Yarrangobilly Caves**, a system of about sixty limestone caves at the edge of a rocky plateau surrounded by unspoiled bushland, are one of the few specific sights in the park; they're 6.5km off the Snowy Mountains Highway near Kiandra, 113km north of Cooma and 70km south of Tumut. There are several guided tours daily to the **North Glory**, **Jersey** and **Jillabenan Caves** (the last is wheelchair-accessible; all $11; ☏ 02/6454 9597 for tour times). A fourth cave, the **Glory Hole Cave** (daily 10am–4pm; $6.60), can be explored on a self-guided tour. From walking trails along the edge of the rock plateau there are panoramic views of the Yarrangobilly Gorge, and a steep trail leads from the Glory Hole car park to a thermal pool at the bottom of the gorge near the Yarrangobilly River. The spring-fed pool, which you can swim in (for free), has a year-round constant temperature of 27°C.

KIANDRA itself is a ghost town, but the detailed interpretive boards of the Heritage Trail will help you find your way through the remaining ruins on this desolate, windswept spot – the extensive plains in the northern part of the park are too cold for any trees to survive. It's hard to believe that fifteen thousand prospectors camped here during the goldrush of 1860; the short-term rush left behind a town of about three hundred people who eked out a living mining and grazing.

Accommodation

In winter, **rooms** are at a premium – despite the plethora of holiday apartments and motels, accommodation is almost impossible to come by without a reservation. In summer, the situation is less dire, and you should have little difficulty finding somewhere in one of the resorts, or at motels on the fringes of the park – such as at Tumut in the north or even back in Cooma (see p.265).

Most accommodation in Thredbo can be **booked** through the Thredbo Resort Centre (see p.267) or Thredbo Accommodation Services (free call ℡1800 801 982); the Snowy River Information Centre in Jindabyne (℡02/6456 2444) also handles accommodation bookings, and there is extensive information and a booking service online at Ⓦwww.thredbo.com.au. Note that prices given below are for high season (winter), and that prices can drop dramatically in summer.

Alpine Inn, Alpine Way, Khancoban (℡02/6076 9471). The *Alpine Inn* offers motel-style accommodation attached to a great pub and restaurant. ❹

Banjo Patterson Inn, Kosciuscko Rd, Jindabyne (℡02/6546 2372, Ⓔbanjopaterson@ski.com.au). Newly refurbished en-suite rooms with disabled access, balconies, cable TV and fridges. The inn itself has open fires, a laundry, bistro and communal cooking facilities. ❺

Fishermen's Lodge, Alpine Way, Khancoban (℡02/6076 9471). Under the same management as the *Alpine Inn*, this lodge caters to backpackers with inexpensive single rooms, plus activities such as horse riding and white-water rafting; they also rent out fishing gear, boats and canoes. ❶

Kasees Mountain Lodge and Apartments, Banjo Drive, Thredbo (℡02/6457 6370). One of several lodges and motels along Banjo Drive, this one is particularly cosy and boasts a pool, sauna, log fires and bargain summer rates (❺). ❽

Kosciuszko Mountain Retreat, Sawpit Creek, near the park headquarters (℡02/6456 2224 or free call 1800 064 224). Tent sites, and cabins and chalets sleeping six, set among a forest of snow gums. Advance booking recommended, especially in winter when prices rise. Chalets ❻, cabins ❹

Nettin Chalet, 24 Nettin Circuit, Jindabyne (℡02/6456 2692, Ⓕ6456 1115). Motel-style units, all with private balconies boasting lake and mountain views. Facilities include a bistro, bar, spa and sauna. Two-night minimum booking in winter includes Thredbo lift pass. ❽

Riverglade Caravan Park, Snowy Mountains Highway, Tumut (℡02/6947 2528). Camping and cabins by the river, with kiosk and BBQ. Cabins ❹

Snowline Caravan Park, junction of Alpine Way and Kosciuszko Rd, Jindabyne (℡02/6456 2099). Camping or cabins, and good facilities, including spa, sauna, café-restaurant and boat rental. Backpacker bunks ❶, cabins ❸–❻

Snowy Mountain Backpackers, 7–8 Gippsland St, Jindabyne (℡02/6456 1500 or free call 1800 333 468, Ⓦwww.snowybackpackers.com.au). This brand-new, friendly, purpose-built hostel is a backpacker haven: facilities include an internet lounge, a good café with tasty food, massage, laundry, a tour booking desk and fantastic kitchens and common areas. Full disabled access. Rooms ❹, dorms ❷

Snowy Valley Motel, Kosciuszko Rd, 9km east of Jindabyne (℡02/6456 7138 or 6456 7180). Motel with indoor swimming pool and sauna, as well as meals for residents and non-residents. Lots of big family rooms sleeping five – ask about backpackers' specials in these. ❹–❽

Thredbo Alpine Hotel, Friday Drive, Thredbo (free call ℡1800 026 333, Ⓕ02/6459 4201). Large luxury hotel complex in the centre of the village, close to the chairlift. Wine bars and the resort's only nightclub. ❼

Thredbo YHA Lodge, 8 Jack Adams Pass, Thredbo (℡02/6457 6376, Ⓕ6457 6043; Ⓔthredbo@yhansw.org.au). A modern hostel, with reception open 7–10am and 4.30–9pm. Between June and September, bookings must be made in writing through the YHA head office in Sydney (℡02/9261 1111). Dorms ❸–❹

The South Coast

The south coast of New South Wales is relatively quiet and relaxed, its numerous bays, coastal lakes and inlets interspersed with unspoiled, sandy beaches, small fishing villages and seaside resorts. During the summer months, especially from Christmas to the end of January, a lot of holiday-makers escape here from the "big smoke" up north, or come up from Victoria: the towns can get busy then, especially the **Shoalhaven area** around **Nowra** and **Batemans Bay**, and **Merimbula**. But don't expect glamorous resort hotels and entertainment Queensland-style – it's all rather low-key and family-oriented. There are a few wildlife and amusement parks to keep the children happy, and plenty of opportunities for traditional outdoor pursuits. (One of the region's highlights is the awesome **Pebbly Beach**, 20km from **Ulladulla**, where a tame kangaroo colony lives right on the sand dunes.) Exposed parts on this stretch of the coast are battered by powerful waves that are perfect for **surfing**, while the calmer waters of the numerous coastal lakes, bays and inlets are suited for **swimming**, windsurfing, sailing or paddling your own canoe. There's great **fishing** too, in the rivers and lakes, as well as the inevitable deep-sea season, when game-fishers set out to tussle with marlin. Away from the ocean there's some superb, rugged scenery and great bushwalking and horse riding in the forest-clad, mountainous hinterland. When summer holidays are over, even the bigger towns revert back to an unassuming, laid-back lifestyle, and the weather is mild enough to enjoy them pretty much year round.

Most of the way down the coast, the **Princes Highway** runs a few kilometres inland. Away from the towns, apparently obscure turn-offs from the highway often lead to beautiful and secluded beaches – it's worth taking some time to make your own discoveries. Heading towards **Canberra** there are three main routes from the coast: through Kangaroo Valley (see p.232), continuing via Moss Vale (or Bundanoon) and Goulburn; the Capital Highway from Batemans Bay; or the Snowy Mountains Highway from Bega via Cooma.

Transport links from Sydney, Canberra and Melbourne to the south coast include Greyhound Pioneer's daily Sydney–Canberra route via the coast as well as a daily Canberra–Nowra service; the daily Sydney–Eden route offered by Pioneer Motor Services (℡ 02/4421 7722 or free call 1800 816 234); Countrylink services (℡ 13 2232) from Canberra to Eden daily; Murray's (℡ 13 2251) daily route from Canberra to Narooma with several stops including Batemans Bay and Moruya, and from Canberra to Sydney via Batemans Bay, Ulladulla and Nowra; and Southern Highlands–South Coast express, between Sydney and Narooma via Mittagong and Kangaroo Valley. From Melbourne, the Sapphire Coast Express (free call ℡ 1800 812 135) runs on Tuesday and Friday to Batemans Bay, stopping at Eden, Merimbula and Bega.

Nowra-Bomaderry

Straddling the wide Shoalhaven River, the twin town of **NOWRA–BOMADERRY** is the centre of the Shoalhaven holiday region: Bomaderry is situated north of the river, Nowra south. The river here is great for sailing, windsurfing and boating in general, while the coast, 13km away, is dotted with popular holiday settlements and numerous beaches. **Shoalhaven Heads** north of the river mouth, **Greenwell Point** in the south, **Huskisson** at Jervis Bay (see p.270) and **Sussex Inlet** are all easily accessible on good roads, although public transport doesn't run this far. Possible inland trips include a one-hour tour to the top of nearby Mount Coolangatta with Australian Bushmobile Tours (℡ 02/4423 0495; $10).

For further information on the beaches and how to get to them, and on local accommodation, stop first at the **Shoalhaven Tourist Centre**, 245 Princes Highway, in Bomaderry (daily 9am–5pm; ℡ 02/4421 0778 or free call 1800 024 261, Ⓦ www.shoalhaven.nsw.gov.au). **Accommodation** includes an abundance of motels, and an ever-increasing choice of guesthouses, hostels and boutique B&B's. Rooms at *Armstrong's White House*, 30 Junction St (℡ 02/4421 2084, Ⓕ 4423 6876; ❹), share bathrooms but they're reasonably priced, or you could bag one of the beds in the four-person dorms at the old-fashioned, welcoming *M & M's Guesthouse* at 1A Scenic Drive (℡ 02/4422 8006; rooms ❹, dorms ❷ including breakfast). One of the better motels, the *Riverhaven Motel*, is next door, on a riverfront landscaped property but only one block from the shops, by the bridge (☎02/4421 2044, ℱ4421 2121; ❹); facilities include a kitchen and swimming pool. You can camp at the central, riverside *Shoalhaven Caravan Village*, Terrara Road, Nowra (☎02/4423 0770, ℰeddytim@hotmail.com; cabins ❸–❹), with its own pool and tennis courts and bikes available to rent. There's not much by way of **restaurants** or **nightlife** in Nowra, but it does have one alternative hangout, the *Tea Club*, 46 Berry St (☎02/4422 0900; closed Sun & Mon), a veggie café with a bohemian feel, exhibitions and artworks for sale, drumming workshops (Thurs) and alternative show nights (Sat). They also run monthly poetry and philosophy evenings (call for details). If you need a seafood fix without the showtime thrills, the Co-op next to Shoalhaven River Bridge sells oysters caught by Jimmy Wildes, the reigning world oyster-opening champion.

Jervis Bay

Just southeast of Nowra, the sheltered waters of **Jervis Bay** (pronounced "Jarvis"), by a political quirk, are technically part of the ACT, in order to provide Canberra with access to the sea. The beautiful coast of the **Jervis Bay National Park**, at the southeast arm of the bay, is very popular, with its rugged cliffs facing the pounding ocean and tranquil beaches of dazzling white sand and clear water within the confines of the bay, while inland heaths, wetlands and forests offer strolls and bushwalks; details are available from the **visitor centre** (☎02/4443 0977) as you enter the park. There are a couple of **campsites** (bookings essential in summer on ☎02/4443 0977): the more secluded and small *Cave Beach* on Wreck Bay is the most sought-after site, despite its cold showers; the larger, more expensive *Greenpatch*, on a creek by Jervis Bay, has the benefit of hot showers, and cars can be parked at each tent site. Holiday-unit accommodation is available on Ellmoos Road, right next to the beach, at *Kullindi* (☎ & ℱ 02/4441 2897; ❻, two-night minimum), and at *Lumeah* (☎02/4441 2018, ℱ4441 0021, ℰlumeah@beaconquest.com.au; $1110 per week sleeping four people).

The **Wreck Bay Aboriginal Community**, which has land in the middle section of the park, organizes a summer cultural interpretation programme, Wreck Bay Walkabouts (bookings and information on ☎02/4442 1166), which covers diet and medicines, archeology and wildlife; plus there's the recommended Barry's Bushtucker Tours (☎02/4442 1168). **Jervis Bay Botanic Gardens** (Mon–Fri 8am–4pm, Sun & holidays 10am–5pm; free), on Cave Beach Road, is an annexe of Canberra's Australian National Botanic Gardens and has specimens of plants from around Australia, including a pleasantly cool rainforest gully. Heading south from Sydney to Jervis Bay, 10km south of Nowra, down the turn-off for Huskisson takes you to **Marayong Park Emu Farm**, 132 Jervis Bay Rd (Wed–Sun 10am–4pm; guided tours and emu feeding sessions 10.30am, 11.30am, 1.30pm & 2.30pm; ☎02/4447 8505).

On the western shores of Jervis Bay, 21km southeast of Nowra, **HUSKISSON** is an old town that's a popular tourist spot, with several beachside campsites: the council-run *Huskisson Beach Tourist Resort*, Beach Street (☎02/4441 5142 or free call 1800 676 433, ℰhuskybeach@shoalhaven.nsw.gov.au; cabins ❹–❽), has a playground and tennis courts; or try *Huskisson White Sands Tourist Park*, corner of Nowra and Beach streets (☎ & ℱ 02/4441 6025; cabins ❼–❽). A friendly B&B is *Huskinsson B&B*, 12 Tomerong St (☎02/4441 7551; ❻). For a wonderful splurge of guilt-free hedonism, however, the only option is *Paperbark Camp* (T 02/4441 6066 or 4441 7299, W www.paperbarkcamp.com.au; full-board in tents ❻, or B&B in lodge ❺), a luxury ecotourist resort modelled on permanent tented camps in South Africa. Accommodation is in beautiful en-suite tents with huge beds, private verandahs and solar powered lighting, and modern bush tucker is provided for meals; there are often great weekend and midweek offers available. The focus of the town is the beachfront *Huskisson Hotel*, which has a good bistro and plenty of pool-playing opportunities. **Sealife**-watching tours are available all year, and there's an eighty percent success rate of seeing whales and other marine life with Dolphin Watch Cruises, 74 Owen St (tours depart 10am weekends & holidays, daily during NSW school holidays; $20; T 02/4441 6311 or free call 1800 246 010, W www.dolphinwatch .com.au). Huskisson is also a good base for **diving** into the pristine waters of Jervis Bay: contact ProDive at 64 Owen St (T 02/4441 5255) for details of one-off dives ($80 including tank and weight) and four-day packages ($385). The cheapest way to see the water, though, is to hire a small boat from Husky-Hire-a-Boat at 625 Woolamia Rd (T 02/4441 6200).

Ulladulla

In the 1930s many Italian fishermen settled in the small fishing village of **ULLADULLA**, and they're still a strong influence on the atmosphere of this tranquil outpost: the traditional Blessing of the Fleet continues to be celebrated every Easter at the harbour breakwater. It's a beautiful area, dominated by the sandstone plateau of the **Morton National Park**, rising steeply to the west of town. Mostly this is an inaccessible barrier, but there's a good bushwalk to the top of the 719-metre-high **Pigeon House Mountain** in the Budawang Range; the walk there and back takes about four hours and is accessed from the Princes Highway, via a turn-off 8km south of Ulladulla. Along the coast in both directions are attractive river mouths, beaches and lakes: among those worth visiting are pretty **Lake Conjola**, 10km to the north; **Lake Burrill**, 5km to the south; and **Lake Tabourie**, 13km to the south – all are popular with fishermen, canoeists and campers. Around Ulladulla there are also some quaint country towns worth visiting. **Mollymook**, 3km to the north, has some sensational surfing sites and hiking trails and a few kilometres further on there's lots to see and do in the village of **Milton**, home to numerous antique shops, craft shops and cafés. This region provides a relaxing weekend escape from Sydney or a worthwhile stopover en route to or from Melbourne, but you really need your own transport to appreciate the area and to get off the main roads onto some of the scenic drives.

   Tourist information is available from the Civic Centre on the highway (Mon–Fri 10am–5pm, Sat & Sun 9am–5pm; T 02/4455 1269). They can advise you on **accommodation**, and the local Chamber of Commerce also operates a central reservations hotline (T 02/4454 4434). Places to stay include the *Quiet Garden Motel* on a rocky promontory at 2 Burrill St (T 02/4455 1757, F 4454 3090; ❺); the elegant *Ulladulla Guesthouse*, near the harbour at the corner of Burrill and South streets (T 02/4455 1796, F 5545 4660, W www.guesthouse.com.au; ❽), which has a spa and sauna and excellent-value singles; and the *VIP/South Coast Backpackers*, 63 Princes Highway (T 02/4454 0500; rooms ❸, dorms ❶), a small, renovated hostel which can provide lifts to Pigeon House Mountain, Jervis Bay or Murramarang National Park, and also have bikes and canoes for hire. The *Beach Haven Holiday Resort*, on Princes Highway in Ulladulla South (T 02/4455 2110 or 4455 1712; holiday apartments ❹–❻, cabins ❹, on-site vans ❷–❸), boasts a beachfront location, complete with swimming pools, spa and tennis courts. There's also a council-run caravan park on South Street, close to the beach: *Ulladulla Headland Tourist Park* (℡02/4455 2457; six-person cabins ❻; tent site ❶).

In terms of **activities**, there's swimming at the free seawater pool by the wharf, or open-water scuba courses run by Ulladulla Divers Supplies, Watson Street (℡02/4455 5303). The local Budamurra Aboriginal community has also constructed an interesting cultural trail, the Coomee Nulunga (℡02/4455 5883, ⓦwww.budamurra.asn.au); access is via Deering Street, opposite the Lighthouse Oval car park. The track meanders through eucalypts and heath flowers to a viewing platform over the ocean, and then on to a secluded beach. Guided tours ($10) are offered by the Budamurra people, and include tips on boomerang throwing, didgeridoo playing and fire making, as well as some bush tucker.

There are a couple of good Italian places to **eat** in the town, including *Tory's Seafood*, 30 Watson St, by the wharf (daily for dinner plus Sun lunch; ℡02/4454 0888). *Cookaburra's*, 10 Watson St (closed Thurs; ℡02/4454 1443) is an ambient, BYO restaurant with waterfront views serving innovative Asian and Cajun-inspired seafood and poultry dishes, while the *Harbourside Restaurant*, 84 Princes Highway (℡02/4455 3377) specializes in modern Australian cuisine and fresh seafood open daily and is licensed and BYO. The *Ulladulla Guesthouse* has a Provençal-style BYO restaurant, *Elizans*, and there's also a modern noodle bar, *Soba*, in the Pavilion Centre on Green Street (℡02/4454 3565).

Batemans Bay and around

BATEMANS BAY, at the mouth of the Clyde River and the end of the highway from Canberra, is a favourite escape for the landlocked residents of the capital, just 152km away. It's not the most exciting place on the coast, but since it's a fair-sized resort, there's plenty to do. Around Batemans Bay itself you can take a **cruise** on the Clyde River with one of several companies, including Clyde Princess (℡02/4478 1005; $20 for 3hr), Blue Dolphin Cruises (℡02/4472 4220; $25 for 2hr), or Merinda Cruises (℡02/4472 4052), departing daily from the wharf at 11.30am for a three-hour tour ($22) including a lunch stopover upriver in the historic township of **Nelligen** with arts and crafts and a nice café. Redfin Charters (℡02/4472 4319) organize half-day fishing charters ($75) and whale-watching trips in season ($60 for 2hr). Alternatively, you can board one of the little trains that run through the woodlands of the **Birdland Animal Park**, 55 Beach Rd (daily 9am–5pm; $9), for a closer look at the birds and native animals – the wombat display is among the best in the country.

In the **Murramarang National Park** (ranger ℡02/4478 6006), a small coastal strip just north of town, there are campsites at **Pretty Beach**, **Pebbly Beach** and **Durras Beach** – popular not only with campers but also with kangaroos, which come here at dawn or dusk to frolic on the beach. Rumour has it that they even enjoy body surfing. You can stay at *Murramarang Resort* (℡02/4478 6355, ⒺMurra@batemansbay.com; cabins and on-site vans ❹), where there's bike and canoe rental available, plus organized geology walks, lake rides and fishing cruises, or at **Pebbly Beach** where there's a basic campsite (℡02/4478 6006).

From **MOGO**, 10km to the south, you can visit the open-air **Old Mogo Town** museum (Fri–Sun 10am–4pm, Mon–Thurs 9am–5pm during school holidays; $12; ℡02/4474 2123, ⓦwww.oldmogotown.com.au), a reconstruction of a mid-nineteenth-century goldrush town near an old gold mine. The best time to come is Sunday morning when there's a bric-a-brac **market** held here. Twenty-five kilometres south of Batemans Bay, just before **Moruya**, a small, unsealed road turns off the highway to the west, heading through a pretty valley and then up over hills at the edge of the remote **Deua National Park** to the former goldrush town of **Araluen** where, between 1868 and 1872, about fifteen thousand prospectors congregated in the hope of striking it lucky.

Batemans Bay Tourist Information is on Princes Highway, at the corner of Beach Road (daily 9am–5pm; ℡ 02/4472 6900 or free call 1800 802 528). As you'd expect of a resort, **accommodation** consists mainly of motels and a wide range of holiday units; most of the latter require a minimum week's booking during peak summer times. However, there are also two hostels: *Shady Willows Holiday Park* (℡ & Ⓕ 02/4472 4972; cabins ❸–❻, dorms ❶), is close to town (but not the beach), with a YHA hostel section attached, while *Beach Road Backpackers*, at 92 Beach Rd (℡ 02/4472 3644; dorms ❶), is a small independent place; the owner here will book tours and cruises. Otherwise, try *Bay Surfside Holiday Flats*, 7km out of town at 662 Beach Rd (℡ 02/4471 1275; ❹–❻), whose units sleep up to six and have all mod cons. There's **camping** at eight caravan parks including the *Coachhouse Marina Resort*, by the beach on Beach Road 1km south of town (℡ 02/4472 4392; cabins ❹–❼, on-site vans ❸–❻), with a pool and tennis court; or the excellent *River Breeze Caravan Park* (℡ 02/4474 2370, Ⓦ www.riverbreeze.com.au; four-person cabins ❹, bunkroom bed ❶), a five-minute walk from the coach stop on the Princes Highway in Moruya. *Mogendoura Farm*, on Hawdons Road, 8km west of Moruya on the Moruya River (℡ 02/4474 2057, Ⓦ www.southcoast.com.au/mogendoura; ❺–❻), offers week-long cottage **farmstays** with horse riding, canoeing and bushwalking opportunities; occasionally overnight stays are also possible.

There's a range of **restaurants** in Batemans Bay, mainly with fish and seafood-based menus. Cheap and healthy luncheon fare – mugs of coffee and home-made savouries and cake – can be found at the *Good Food Cafe* on 45 Orient St. *Rafters*, 28 Beach Rd has a relaxing, intimate atmosphere, with à la carte dining and vegetarian options. On the promenade, *Seagulls* serves rather overpriced seafood and steaks, but the sweeping waterfront views make it worth the extra expense (closed Tues; ℡ 02/4472 0253), while the trendy and popular *Starfish Deli* also has a marine panorama with a modern menu, including a variety of wood-fired pizzas and many veggie dishes. *Jameson's on the Pier* offers fine dining on fresh fish and is set on its own jetty opposite the promenade, jutting out over the river.

Narooma and around

A small but expanding fishing village surrounded by beautiful beaches, bays and coastal lakes, **NAROOMA** lies at the heart of an area famous for its succulent **mud oysters**. You can canoe and windsurf on the **Wagonga Inlet** or sail to **Montague Island** – an offshore sanctuary for sea birds, seals and penguins. If you actually want to disembark at the island, you'll have to join a tour organized by the NPWS in Narooma (tours daily: winter 3.30pm; summer 6.30pm, though 9.30am tours are sometimes available; 3hr; $66; ℡ 02/4476 2888, Ⓕ 4476 2757), since it's a protected wildlife reserve. Southern right and humpback **whales** have begun to reappear in the bay between September and November, and tour operators also organize whale-watching tours in the event of any sightings; you can book at the **Narooma Tourist Information Centre** on the highway (daily 9am–5pm; ℡ 02/4476 2881 or free call 1800

240 003, ⓦwww.naturecoast-tourism.com.au). Non-landing **cruises** cost $45–55 for a two- to three-hour trip, including a visit to Montague Island to see the seal colonies. The visitors centre can also book you on a scenic cruise aboard the *Wagonga Princess* (ⓣ02/4476 2665) a century-old pine ferry which winds its way in and out of secluded bays on the river, stopping off for a guided rainforest walk and oyster-tasting session ($22 for a 3hr tour). **Diving** can be found off Montague Island all year, organized by Ocean Hut, 123 Princes Highway (ⓣ02/4476 2278), costing $55 for one dive and $65 for two (Jan–April grey nurse sharks and tropical fish; Aug–Dec mainly seal-spotting).

In Narooma there's a newly renovated YHA **hostel**, *Bluewater Lodge*, 8 Princes Highway (ⓣ02/4476 4440, ⓕ4476 5444, ⓔnaroomayha@narooma.com; rooms ❸, dorms ❶). Accommodation is in well-equipped wooden cabins, surrounded on three sides by lakes and bay; there is also a very reasonable internet lounge, cheap bike and canoe rental and free fishing gear. Steve, the everhelpful owner, will happily dispense advice and book local tours for his guests. Good **motels** and resorts include *Forsters Bay Lodge Motel*, Forsters Bay Road (ⓣ & ⓕ 02/4476 2319; ❹); *Tree Motel*, 213 Princes Highway (ⓣ02/4476 4233; ❺), which has air-conditioned suites, a pool and barbecue; and the beachside *Island View Beach Resort*, on the highway 3km south of town (ⓣ02/4476 4600 or free call 1800 641 590, ⓦwww.islandview.com.au; cabins ❺–❽). *Pub Hill Farm*, Scenic Drive, 8km west of Narooma (ⓣ02/4476 3177, ⓕ4476 3153, ⓔpubhillfarm@sci.net.au; ❺), is a farm-style B&B which has four en-suite rooms (including one private, garden room with log fire – ❻), and offers a baby-sitting service. The beautifully located *Clark Bay Farm* (ⓣ02/4476 1640, ⓔamethyst@sci.net.au; ❻–❼) offers disabled-access accommodation sleeping up to six, with electronically activated doors and beds.

Local favourites for **dining** include *Restaurant at Lynch's* on Princes Highway (ⓣ02/4476 3022), serving excellent contemporary Australian cuisine and local oysters; and the acclaimed fusion restaurant *Iguana* (ⓣ02/4476 3396), inopportunely located in the shopping plaza on the south side of town. There are several **bistros** at the Marina on Riverside Drive at Forsters Bay, including the award-winning *Simply Seafood* (lunch Tues–Sun, dinner Tues–Sat; ⓣ02/4476 2403), and the less pricey *Quarterdeck* next door. *Rockwall Restaurant* on Campbell Street has à la carte seafood specials, costing around $15 for main courses (closed Sun & Mon; ⓣ02/4476 2040). *Casey's Cafe* at the top of the town's hill, on the corner of Canty and Wagonga streets (ⓣ02/4476 1241) is a bright, cheery establishment, serving healthy, hearty food with many veggie options and the best coffee in town. For something more special, you could try the oyster bar overlooking Forsters Bay in the Narooma Oyster Supplies shop on Riverside Drive (ⓣ02/4476 1256).

Narooma's **nightlife** doesn't extend much beyond the vast *Golf Club* on Ballingalla Street (daily 10am–10pm), with pool tables and poker machines, serving the latest drink in town. If you're in need of a film fix, there is a delightfully preserved, National Trust classified Kinema picture theatre worth visiting – an original cinema from 1926 screening modern movies on Friday and Saturday evenings and Sunday matinees (daily showings except Mon during school holidays and the Dec/Jan holiday season).

A thriving local **Koorie** community run their own Umbarra Aboriginal Cultural Centre (ⓣ02/4473 7232, ⓕ4473 7169, ⓔumbarra@acr.net.au) at **Wallaga Lake**, 25km south of Narooma. They operate daily tours to local sacred sites, including Gulaga (Mount Dromedary), with hands-on activities such as painting with ochres, building bark huts and sampling bush tucker and traditional medicine. (As some of their tours traverse Aboriginal lands, special

Burnum Burnum: Aboriginal activist

Wallaga Lake is the birthplace of one of Australia's most important Aboriginal fig-
ureheads, the elder named **Burnum Burnum**, an ancestral name meaning great
warrior. He is best known for his flamboyant political stunts, which included plant-
ing the Aboriginal flag at Dover to claim England as Aboriginal territory in
Australia's bicentennial year, 1988, highlighting the dispossession of his native country. He was born under a sacred tree by Wallaga Lake in January 1936. His mother
died soon afterwards and he was taken by the Aborigines Protection Board and
placed in a mission at Bomaderry, constituting one of the "stolen generation" of
indigenous children removed from their families in this period. After graduating in
law and playing professional rugby union for New South Wales, he became a
prominent political activist in the 1970s. He was involved in various environmental and indigenous protests, including erecting the "tent embassy" outside the
Federal Parliament in Canberra (see p.249), and standing twice, unsuccessfully, for
the senate. Burnum Burnum died in August 1997 and his ashes were scattered near
the tree where he was born.

permits are required for external visitors planning on visiting these areas independently.) They also have a cruise with commentary on Wallaga Lake, one of
the largest saltwater lakes on the Australian coast. The lake's black duck is the
sacred totem for the local indigenous people. Entry to the centre is free; activities and tours range from $6.25 to $45.

Tilba Tilba

Continuing south, take a break in the picturesque mountain villages of **TILBA
TILBA** and **CENTRAL TILBA**, 17km south of Narooma, where time seems
to have stood still – and various craft shops and workshops are ready and willing to exploit the olde worlde ambience. It's an area famous for its cheeses, and
is also a little-known wine-growing region: Central Tilba's hundred-year-old
ABC Cheese Factory is open for visits and free tastings (daily 9am–5pm); and
you can follow this up with some wine tasting at **Tilba Valley Winery**, signposted off the Princes Highway, 5km north of town (Mon–Sat 10am–5pm, Sun
11am–5pm). Situated on Corunna Lake, the working family vineyard and winery is an idyllic spot for a ploughman's lunch on the terrace or a picnic on the
grounds, overlooking a lake. Try the unusual local mead made at the winery.

The *Dromedary Hotel*, on Bates Street in Central Tilba (☎02/4473 7223,
℉4473 7229; ❹), is a quaint, historic pub with open fires and super-cheap singles; counter **meals** are served and there's **B&B** accommodation. The nearby
Rose & Sparrow Cafe offers cream teas and light meals but is self-consciously
twee. If you're feeling energetic you can follow the walking trail which starts
from Pam's Store in Tilba Tilba and leads through a forest to the summit of
Mount Dromedary, at almost 800m. The hike there and back is about 11km,
and you should allow five to six hours – or go for the lazy option, with a **horse**
from Mount Dromedary Trail Rides (☎02/4473 7290, or book through the
Narooma Tourist Information Centre – see p.273).

Bermagui

There's a delightful scenic detour along the coast: turn off the highway just
after Tilba Tilba and after 8km you reach **BERMAGUI**, on both the Bermagui
River and sheltered Horseshoe Bay. Bermagui attracts quite a few **game-fish-
ing** fanatics, thanks to its associations with Zane Grey, the American writer of

Westerns and a legendary marlin fisherman. There are several big-game fishing tournaments annually, and charter boats offer trips to catch black marlin, yellow-fin tuna and other big fish. In addition to several **motels**, there's the pleasant old *Bermagui Hotel*, Lamont Street (℡02/6493 4206; ❸), which serves good meals; *Elite Holiday Flats*, 84 Murrah St (℡02/6493 4274; ❻), which only takes weekly bookings; or the central *Zane Grey Caravan Park* on Lamont Street (℡02/6493 4382; cabins ❹–❻). There are two **Bermagui Information Centres**, one as you come into town in the BP Service Station at 8 Coluga St (daily 7am–7pm; ℡02/6493 4174); the other on Lamont Street by the *Bermagui Hotel* (daily lunch & dinner; ℡02/6493 3054). **Eating choices** include a Thai restaurant and a pizzeria, but *Roly's Wharf Restaurant* (℡02/6493 4328) is the best place to try Bermagui's legendary fish catches.

Further south, unsealed tracks branch off the coast road to **Mimosa Rocks National Park**, where there are opportunities for bushwalking and swimming. There are NPWS **campsites** at Middle Beach, Picnic Point and Argannu Beach (℡02/6476 2888 for details and bookings).

Bega and around

Lush green meadows, munching cows, wide valleys and mountains in the background – you could almost mistake this pastoral scenery for somewhere in the foothills of the Swiss Alps. Certainly the area around **BEGA** is prime dairy country: at the **Bega Cheese Factory & Heritage Centre**, Lagoon Street, North Bega (daily 9am–5pm; ⓦwww.begacheese.com.au), you can watch the famous local cheese being made, and try a few samples. Scenery and cheese apart, there's no great reason to come here, but it's a convenient stopover, handy for the junction of the Princes Highway with the Snowy Mountains Highway. In town, the **Historical Museum**, on the corner of Bega and Auckland streets (Mon–Fri 10.30am–4pm, holidays also Sat 10am–noon), has regional memorabilia and photos. For more on local attractions, including the Grevillea Winery, check out the **Bega Tourist Information Centre**, 91 Gipps St (Mon–Fri 9am–4pm; ℡02/6492 2045, ⓔbegatic@acr.net.au).

The small, pleasant and very friendly *Bega YHA* on Kirkland Crescent (℡02/6492 3103; reception 4–8.30pm; rooms ❷, dorms ❶) is built from mud bricks. Less earthy accommodation can be found at the *Grand Hotel*, 236 Carp St (℡02/6492 1122; ❸), which has motel-style pub **rooms**, as well as counter **meals** during the week. Even more salubrious is the *Prickled Pear*, a beautifully restored and comfortably furnished three-room 1870s guesthouse on the main street (℡02/6492 1393, ℻6492 0030, ⓦwww.ausac.com/ppear; ❻). Campers can head for *Bega Caravan Park* on the Princes Highway (℡02/6492 2303; cabins and units ❹, on-site vans ❸).

Candelo and Tathra

CANDELO, reached by a country road off the highway 11km south of Bega, is a pretty village where you can browse in the galleries and craft shops, have a cream tea at one of the tearooms, or a drink in the preserved *Candelo Hotel* on Sharp Street, which also has good counter meals. A good **accommodation** choice should you decide to stay is *Bumblebrook Farm* on Kemps Lane, 4km northwest of Candelo (℡02/6493 2238, ℻6493 2299, ⓦwww.snsw.world-tourism.com.au/BumblebrookFarmstay; ❺), which is comprised of self-contained units, although you can also dine in the homestead.

Heading on from Bega, an alternative route to Merimbula takes you along the coast road via the small holiday and fishing village of **TATHRA**.

Accommodation ranges from the motel-style units at the *Tathra Hotel Motel* on Bega Street (☎02/6494 1101; ❹–❺), to the *Tabja Rural Retreat* on Barrabooka Road (☎02/6494 0166, ⓦwww.tanjaruralretreat.com.au; ❼), an artist-owned B&B with an emphasis on good food and relaxation. Alternatively, try the timber cottages at *Kianinny Park Cabins* on the Snowy Mountains Highway, 2km west of town (☎02/6494 1990 or free call 1800 064 225, ⓦwww.ker.com.au; ❼–❽), a family place with a saltwater pool; at peak times, only weekly bookings are accepted. **Tourist information** is dispensed at the helpful Tathra Wharf Trading Post right on the wharf (usually daily 9am–5pm; ☎02/6494 4062), an all-purpose place which also rents out fishing, diving and surfing gear, and has a decent café; there's a **maritime museum** upstairs (daily 8am–5pm; $1.50).

Just to the south, coastal **Bournda National Park** features stunning beaches, brackish lagoons and freshwater lakes: there are NPWS **campsites** at Hobart Beach on the southern end of Wallagoot Lake (book well ahead from Dec to Easter; ☎02/6494 1209 or 6496 1434).

Merimbula

The pretty township of **MERIMBULA** attracts a lot of holiday-makers from Victoria because of its accessibility, year-round temperate climate and good beaches. Between tanning sessions, you can cruise Merimbula Lake (actually the wide mouth of the Merimbula River) and Pambula Lake with several different companies for around $20 for two hours: Sinbad Cruises (book at the tourist centre) are recommended for their interesting commentary on Aboriginal history and oyster cultivation, while Merimbula Marina (☎02/6495 1686) offer $30 dolphin cruises. There are also whale-watching tours (Sept to early Dec) costing $50 for four hours. Cruises and boat rental can both be arranged at the **Merimbula Tourist Information Booking Service** on Beach Street (daily 9am–4pm, school holidays until 5pm; ☎02/6495 1129, Ⓕ6495 4264, ⓦwww.merimbula–tourism.com.au); they also have information on lots of other activities in the area, including 4WD forest tours, scenic flights, diving and horse riding. If the Sinbad cruise kindles an interest in the Aboriginal culture of the area, look up Umburra Cultural Tours (☎02/4473 7232), run by the local land council based at Wallaga Lake and led by Koorie guides (for more details, see the Narooma section on p.274).

By **bus**, you can get to Merimbula from Canberra with Countrylink, from Sydney or Melbourne with Greyhound Pioneer (daily except Sat), and from Sydney or Eden with Pioneer Motor Service. Hazelton (☎13 1713) **flies** to Merimbula from Sydney at least twice daily and Kendell Airlines (free call ☎1800 338 894) flies twice daily from Melbourne.

There are several places to **eat** out, including the renowned *Waterfront Cafe*, on the promenade by the tourist office, which has a seafood and snack menu (daily: March–Dec 8am–5pm; Jan–Feb 8am–midnight; ☎02/6495 2211). Also on the promenade, the *Lakeside Cafe* is open for lunch and dinner serving assorted fish dishes and some veggie options, and the *Lakeview Hotel* on Market Street has a bistro open for lunch and dinner. *Wheelers*, across the road from the Golf Club on the south side of town (☎02/6495 6330), serves excellent local oysters. Merimbula has several good Asian restaurants, particularly *Bahn Thai* at 17 Merimbula Drive (☎02/6495 4555), open daily for dinner. Opposite each other in the shopping centre on Princes Highway, try *Saigon Palace* (☎02/6495 3255) for Vietnamese cuisine, or *Pedro's* for Mexican meals.

Accommodation

Though there are dozens of **motels** (❹–❻, depending on the season) and **holiday apartments**, all of them can be heavily booked during the summer holidays, when many holiday apartments accept only weekly bookings with rates starting at around $220. There's a free **phone booking service** run by the local Chamber of Commerce (free call ☏1800 150 457) covering all grades of accommodation. The places listed below may have space at short notice.

Mandeni Resort, Sapphire Coast Drive, 7km north (☏02/6495 9644 or free call 1800 358 354, ℱ6495 9668, ⓦwww.mandeni.com.au). Fully equipped timber cottages in a bushland setting, sleeping a maximum of six. Facilities include tennis courts, two swimming pools, a golf course and many walking trails. Nightly rates available on request. Weekly rate per cottage ❸–❼

Merimbula Beach Cabins, Short Point, Merimbula (☏02/6495 1216, ℱ6495 4206, ⓔjaybee@acr.net.au). Bushland cabins by the beach, with half-court tennis, laundry and BBQ. Weekly rate per cabin ❷–❺

South Haven Caravan Park, Elizabeth St, between Merimbula Lake and the beach (☏02/6495 1304). Sauna, heated pool, tennis and squash courts. Cabins ❸–❹

Wandarrah YHA Lodge, 8 Marine Parade (☏02/6495 3503, ℱ6495 3163). A modern, purpose-built youth hostel close to both the beach and lake. Facilities include two lounges, internet access and a BBQ area. Generous free breakfast, lots of organized activities and outings (including free canoe hire), friendly, knowledgeable staff and free pick-up from bus or plane. $2 discount per night for three-nights' stay or more. Rooms ❸, dorms ❶

Woodbine Park Holiday Cabins, Sapphire Coast Drive, 7km north (☏ & ℱ 02/6495 9333). Award-winning wooden cabins in a bushland setting, sleeping a maximum of six. Swimming pool, tennis court and golf course. Weekly rate per cabin ❷–❼

Eden – and heading inland

EDEN, on Twofold Bay, is pretty much the last seaside stop before the Princes Highway heads inland towards Victoria. As well as the bus services mentioned on p.269, Eden can be reached from Bega and Merimbula daily on Edwards Bus Services (☏02/5496 1422), from Bermagui daily on Bega Valley Coaches (☏02/6492 2418), and from Tathra on weekdays with the Bega Tathra Service (☏02/6492 1991). In 1818 the first whaling station on the Australian mainland was established at Eden, and **whaling** remained a major industry until the 1920s. For information on the local area, call in at the **Eden Visitor Information Centre** on the highway (daily: summer 9am–5pm; winter 9am–4pm; ☏ & ℱ 02/6496 1953 or free call ☏1800 633 012, ⓔinfo@sapphirecoast.com.au).

Today Eden is touristy in a quiet sort of way, with good fishing, and there are plenty of reminders of the old days, the best of which is the **Killer Whale Museum** on Imlay Street (Mon–Sat 9am–5pm, until 4pm in winter, Sun 10am–4pm; $5; ⓦwww.acr.net.au/kwmuseum); as well as whaling, it looks at the fishing and timber industries which still contribute to Eden's livelihood. At the information centre you can also book **cruises** on Twofold Bay and further out to sea – with luck, penguins, dolphins and, in winter, even whales might be sighted. Cat Balou (☏02/6490 2027, ⓦwww.acr.net.au/~catbalou) offer excellent year-round dolphin-spotting cruises ($25 for 2hr 30min, or $17 for 1hr 30min), and seasonal whale-watching trips ($50 for 4hr); student discounts are available. There's more on the important and controversial timber industry at the **Harris Daishowa Chipmill**, which gobbles up thousands of eucalypts from the surrounding forests and transforms them into woodchips for export to Japan. The **visitors centre** at Edrom Road (daily 8am–5pm; free guided mill tour Thurs 10.30am, book in advance on ☏02/6496 0222) presents an exhibition and slide show about the local timber industry, past and present – no prizes for guessing whose side they're on in the forestry debate.

The forests themselves may seem a more attractive option, and as you head south you become increasingly surrounded by the vast temperate rainforests that characterize southeastern Australia. Roads lead off the highway in both directions into the magnificent **Ben Boyd National Park** (NPWS Eden office ℡02/6495 5000), which hugs the coast to the north and south of Eden, offering good camping, walking and beaches. Inland, the summit of **Mount Imlay** can be reached by a three-kilometre walking track which starts at the picnic grounds at Burrawang Forest Road, 14km south of Eden. The steep, strenuous ascent is rewarded by a panoramic view over the coast and across the dense forests of the hinterland onto the Monaro plain. Camping and park passes can be obtained from the visitors centre in Eden. At **BOYDTOWN**, 9km south of Eden, take a look at the mock-Tudor **Seahorse Inn**, which nowadays houses a small museum of local history as well as tearooms, a restaurant and a hotel (see below).

Accommodation

Australasia Hotel, Imlay St (℡02/6496 1600). Budget, basic accommodation in an old pub, catering mostly to backpackers; counter meals available. Rooms ❸, dorms ❶

Bayview Motor Inn, Princes Highway (℡02/6496 1242, ℻6496 1273). Deluxe motel with room service, swimming pool and spa. ❻

Crown & Anchor Inn, 239 Imlay St (℡02/6496 1017, ℻6496 3878, ℠www.acr.net.au/~crownanchor). A much talked-about Eden sleep-haven, offering gourmet breakfasts, sea views, and complimentary port by the open fire. Ten percent discounts for stays of three nights or more. ❻

Fountain Caravan Park, Princes Highway (℡02/6496 1798). Decent site with swimming pool and camp kitchen. Cabins ❺, on-site vans ❷–❺

Seahorse Inn, just off the Princes Highway in Boydtown (℡02/6496 1361, ℻6496 1394, ℠www.seahorse.com.au). A mock-Tudor inn offering B&B, with a tennis court, tearooms and restaurant. ❺

Twofold Beach Resort, 7km south of Eden (℡02/6496 1752, ℠www.ausac.com/twofold). Beachside location with pool and hospitable management. Cabins and on-site vans ❹

Wonboyn Lake Resort, 40km south of Eden (℡02/6496 9162, ℻6496 9100, ℠www.wonboynlakeresort.com.au). A scenic location off the beaten track at Lake Wonboyn. Swimming pool, spa, shop, boat-ramp, canoe and boat rental; beach nearby. Cottages ❺

Northern NSW

Northern New South Wales may have nothing to match the majesty of the Snowy Mountains, as the Dividing Range falls away to the lower slopes that protect the **New England Plateau**, but the World Heritage–listed temperate and subtropical areas of the range's northeast end harbour sixteen pockets of rainforest which more than compete in terms of natural beauty. In many ways the north is more varied than the south, offering a taste of everything: big resorts and empty beaches on the coast, with alternative-lifestyle villages and communes in the hinterland beyond; lovely parks and forests on the steep slopes behind the coast; and further inland quietly attractive agricultural country, dotted with interesting old towns.

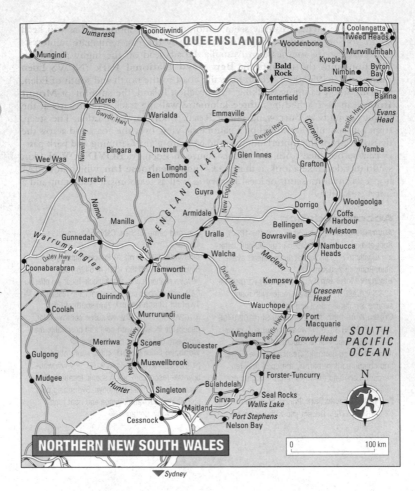

NORTHERN NEW SOUTH WALES

| 0 | | 100 km |

▼ Sydney

The roads are generally in fairly good condition, but the busy **Pacific Highway** is not the best of them. Though it's gradually being upgraded and widened, with the addition of much-needed overtaking lanes, sections of this winding coastal road are still alarmingly narrow considering the weight of traffic and the big trucks that use it; bus services on the highway almost invariably run late. The inland route on the **New England Highway** via Muswellbrook, Tamworth and Armidale is a faster alternative if you're heading straight for Brisbane – plenty of buses go this way too.

The North Coast

The coast from Sydney north to the Queensland border is more densely populated and much more touristy than the southern coast. Popular holiday destinations are strung up the coast north from Newcastle (see p.201). **Port Stephens**, **Port Macquarie**, **Coffs Harbour** and the twin city of **Tweed Heads**–Coolangatta, straddling the state line, attract local tourists as well as overseas visitors. The subtropical part of the coast, from Coffs Harbour north, is much the most attractive: since the 1970s the area around **Lismore**, **Byron Bay** and **Murwillumbah** has been a favoured destination for people from the southern cities seeking an "alternative" lifestyle. This movement has left in its wake not only disillusioned hippie farmers (as well as a few who've survived with their illusions intact) but also a firmly established artistic and alternative scene.

As in the south, the **coastline** consists of myriad inlets, bays and coastal lakes, interspersed by white, sandy beaches and rocky promontories. Parallel to the coast, the rocky plateaus of the **Great Dividing Range** rise up from the plain; so steep is the eastern edge of this range that it defied even the efforts of the early foresters, so that to this day the hills remain densely wooded. A handful of townships still depend on the timber industry, but most **forest** areas are now protected as either national parks or state forests. From the highlands, numerous streams tumble down from the escarpment in mighty waterfalls, and once on the coastal plain they flow together to form short, very wide and fast-flowing rivers. In the fertile river valleys the predominant agricultural activity is cattle breeding, while in the north subtropical and tropical agriculture takes over, especially the cultivation of bananas.

In essence, the further you go, the better this coast gets – the northeast corner is one of the most scenic areas in the state, its remote country roads well worth exploring. If the bigger coastal resorts are too touristy for your liking, there's no shortage of quiet, even lonely, beaches as you head further up, along with small fishing villages and sleepy hamlets inland that are virtually undiscovered. For bushwalkers there are vast areas of totally remote, rugged, wild terrain to explore in the national parks of the Great Dividing Range.

Getting up the north coast is easy, with frequent **train** and **bus** services between Sydney and Brisbane stopping en route. There are also some excellent one-way tours from Sydney to Byron Bay (see box on pp.192–193). Kirklands (℡02/9281 2233) runs between Brisbane and Lismore via Surfers Paradise (see p.421), Tweed Heeds, Murwillumbah, Brunswick Heads, Byron Bay, Lennox Heads and Ballina.

Port Stephens and the lakes

Just north of Newcastle, the wide bay of **Port Stephens**, which extends inland for some 25km, offers calm waters and numerous coves ideal for swimming, water sports and fishing, while the ocean side has good surf and wide, sandy beaches. In January thousands of families arrive to take their annual holiday in the "Blue Water Paradise", as the area has been dubbed. Port Stephens is actually the collective name for the main township of **NELSON BAY**, perched at the tip of the southern arm of the bay, together with the quieter settlements of Shoal Bay, Soldiers Point, Fingal Bay, Boat Harbour and Anna Bay. Although Nelson Bay is highly developed and filled with high-rises, you can still enjoy the simple pleasure of **dolphin-watching** in the quiet waters here. Most dolphin cruises, which give you the opportunity to swim with the dolphins, leave from **Tea Gardens** on the northern arm of the bay (see p.283 for details of operators). There are also opportunities to go on bush walks to spot **koalas** in the wild at **Tilligery Habitat**, 14 Tilligery Plaza, on the Tilligery Peninsula (Mon–Sat 9.30am–4pm, Sun

10am–2pm; daily guided tours at 10.30am and 2pm; $11; ☎02/4982 4441).
The smaller beaches around the bay offer various other activities; naturalists
should head for the nudist beach Samurai, which played host to a very popular Nude Olympics in 2000.

Myall Lakes National Park and around

From Port Stephens the Pacific Highway continues north for about 40km to
Bulahdelah, a small town surrounded by bush-covered hills and rocky outcrops. From here, Myall Way heads via a toll ferry (daily 8am–6pm) to more
deserted spots along the lakeshore, the most popular being **Mungo Brush**,
where an easy walking track (30min return) heads through the littoral rainforest – a variant adapted to salty and harsh seafront conditions, with a low
canopy. A more challenging 21-kilometre walking track leads from here to
Hawks Nest, on Port Stephens Bay and the Myall River, linked by a bridge
across the river to Tea Gardens.

Just after Bulahdelah, you turn east on the Lakes Highway towards the
coast, past Myall Lake and Lake Wallis to the holiday town of
Forster–Tuncurry. At Bungwahl a turn-off leads down mostly unsealed roads
to **SEAL ROCKS**, a remote fishing village and the only settlement in the
Myall Lakes National Park. Its national park status means it's unspoilt, and
the small beach is truly beautiful with crystal-clear waters marooned between
two headlands. Seal Rocks' seasonal agglomerations of nurse sharks make it
one of the best dive sites in New South Wales; contact Forster Dive Centre
(see opposite) to arrange a trip. **Sugar Loaf Point Lighthouse**, built in
1875, is a ten-minute stroll away; the grounds (Tues & Thurs 10am–noon &
1–3pm) offer a fantastic view along the coast, and the lookout below leads
down to a deserted, rocky beach with a view of the 4WD track that extends
through the national park.

North of Seal Rocks, the tiny **Booti Booti National Park** is located
between Cape Hawke and Charlotte Head. The park encompasses many
beaches, oceanside forests and – on the western boundary – Wallis Lake, an
excellent boating and fishing spot. There's also a secluded camping site on the
coastline near Seal Rocks. Ten kilometres further north, a bridge connects the
twin cities **FORSTER–TUNCURRY** on the spit of land that separates
Lake Wallis from the ocean. The lake is very pretty, surrounded by trees and
with bush-covered **Corrie Island** at its centre. Forster is famous for its **oysters**, and for its playful resident **dolphins**. The lake itself is superb for fishing
and swimming – you can rent houseboats as well as dinghies, canoes and
windsurfers. The abundant seafood made the spot attractive to the local
Aboriginal people, the Wallamba, and their descendants can take you on a tour
of significant sites.

Practicalities

Port Stephens, Forster–Tuncurry and Myall Lakes National Park are not the
easiest places to reach on public **transport**. Long-distance Sydney–Brisbane
buses, such as Greyhound Pioneer, tend to stop only at Raymond Terrace or
Karuah on the Pacific Highway (a few stop at Bulahdelah). However, there are
reasonably good connections to Newcastle and Sydney with Port Stephens
Buses (☎02/4982 2940, ⊛www.psbuses.nelsonbay.com), which stop daily at
Nelson Bay, Shoal Bay and Fingal Bay, from where local buses run to Boat
Harbour, Anna Bay and Soldiers Point. In addition, Great Lakes Coaches
(☎02/4983 1560) run weekdays only from Newcastle to Tea Gardens, Hawks
Nest, Bulahdelah, Forster and on to Taree.

Both the **Port Stephens Visitors Centre** at Victoria Parade in Nelson Bay (Mon–Fri 9am–5pm, Sat & Sun 9am–4pm; ℡02/4981 1579 or free call 1800 808 900, Ⓦwww.portstephens.org.au) and the well-organized **Great Lakes Visitors Centre** at Little Street in Forster (daily 9am–5pm; ℡02/6554 8799, Ⓦwww.greatlakes.org.au), can provide you with stacks of information and can book accommodation and tours. The **NPWS** office is on Teramby Road in Nelson Bay (℡02/4984 8200). **Dolphin-watching** jaunts are organized by Dawson's Scenic Cruises (℡02/4982 0444; 2hr; $16) at Nelson Bay; Dolphin Watch Cruises (℡02/6554 7478; 2hr 30min; $30) at Forster; and Myall River Charter Cruises (℡02/4997 1084) at Tea Gardens (daily 10am; 3hr; $18) and Nelson Bay (Wed & Sun 11am; 2hr; $14). Much more satisfying than a motor cruise, however, are the environmentally-aware dolphin- and whale-watching trips ($20/$43 respectively) aboard *Imagine*, a fifteen-metre catamaran moored at Nelson Bay (℡02/4981 1381, Ⓦwww.imagineportstephens.com.au). General two-hour **cruises** on Wallis Lake, Forster, are run by Amaroo Scenic Lake Cruises, opposite the post office (℡0419 333 445). Forster Dive Centre at 15 Little St in Forster (℡02/6555 4477) arranges **diving trips** at Seal Rocks.

A good place to **eat** in Forster–Tuncurry is the *Lakeside Tavern*, near the K-Mart shopping village, which serves fresh, good-value seafood, while *Merret's Restaurant* (℡02/4984 2555) in Peppers Anchorage, just outside Kallaroo, is well worth the detour for its award-winning modern cuisine. As for **accommodation**, there are scores of motels and even more holiday apartments to choose from in the area, though they may insist on weekly bookings during the holiday season. If you want to stay within the national park itself, **camping** is the way to go. **Houseboats** are also an option: try Myall Lakes Houseboats, 90 Crawford St, Bulahdelah (℡02/4997 4221), or Tea Gardens Houseboats, Marine Drive, Tea Gardens (℡02/4997 0555); weekly rates range from $550 to more than $2000, weekends from $390 to $1160.

Accommodation

Forster Dolphin Lodge (YHA), 43 Head St, Forster (℡ & Ⓕ 02/6555 8155, Ⓔdolphin_lodge@hotmail.com). Just two minutes from the beach and the ocean baths, this lodge/hostel has plenty of doubles, as well as dorms. Facilities include communal kitchens, a BBQ area and laundry. Free use of bikes, fishing gear and surf- and boogie-boards. Rooms ❸, dorms ❶
Halifax Holiday Park, Beach Rd, Little Beach, 2km east of central Nelson Bay (℡02/4981 1522). A well-outfitted beachside campsite with camp kitchen, BBQs and kiosk. Cabins ❸–❻
Myall Shores, Bombah Point, 16km east of Bulahdelah in the Myall Lakes National Park (℡02/4997 4495). Campsite with restaurant, shop and boat-ramp, plus bushwalks, 4WD tours and cruises on offer. Cabins ❹–❺, bungalows ❸–❹
Samurai Beach Bungalows, Frost Rd, cnr Robert Connell Close, Anna Bay (℡02/4982 1921 or 0409 327 502). A gorgeous backpackers' hostel in an idyllic bushland setting; cabins are arranged around an undercover "bush" kitchen. Free use of boards and bikes, plus campfires, surfing excursions to nearby beaches and other social activities. Port Stephens Buses from Sydney or Newcastle stop outside. Rooms ❸, dorms ❶
Seal Rocks Camping Reserve, Seal Rocks (℡02/4997 6164). Small site just across from the beach; all sites unpowered. Bookings essential during school holidays. On-site vans ❸
Smuggler's Cove Holiday Village, 45 The Lakes Way, 2km south of Forster (℡02/6554 6666). Lakeside campsite with camp kitchen, pool and children's playground. Cabins ❷–❻
Thurlow Lodge, Thurlow Ave, Nelson Bay (℡02/4981 1577). Central self-catering units sleeping up to six, with a communal swimming pool. $250–750 per week.
YHA Shoal Bay/Shoal Bay Motel, 61 Shoal Bay Rd, Shoal Bay (℡02/4981 1744, Ⓔshoalbaymotel@bigpond.com). Beachfront motel with sauna and spa that also runs a small YHA section – nonmembers welcome. Advance booking recommended. Motel rooms ❺, YHA rooms ❸, dorms ❶–❷

A detour inland: Barrington Tops

There's equally attractive scenery inland, and the drive from Forster via Nabiac, Krambach and Gloucester to the World Heritage-listed **Barrington Tops National Park** ($7.50 entry per car) makes an enjoyable day-trip. On the way up to the country town of Gloucester it's gently hilly farming country; from here, unsealed roads lead to various scenic spots in the national park – the Barrington Road towards Scone (see p.318), or the Gloucester Tops road to the park's southwestern section. You can also approach it via the Hunter Valley from Maitland via Dungog. The closest you'll get to the park with public transport is on the train from Sydney or Newcastle to Dungog or Gloucester; the *Barrington Guest House* (see below) does free pick-ups from Dungog.

The Barrington Tops themselves are two high, cliff-ringed plateaus, Barrington and Gloucester, that rise steeply from the surrounding valleys. The changes in altitude within the park are so great – the highest points are Mount Barrington (1555m) and Polblue Mountain (1577m) – that within a few minutes you can pass from areas of subtropical rainforest to warm and cool temperate rainforest, and then to high, windswept plateaus covered with snow gums, meadows and subalpine bog. Up on the plateau, snow is common from the end of April to early October, while heavy fogs and rains are possible at virtually any time.

The **Great Lakes Visitors Centre** in Forster (see p.283) can help with specific routes or organized 4WD tours into the national park; one company running tours is All Around Oz Tours (℡02/6553 5977 or free call 1800 633 772, ⑩www.allaroundoztours.com.au), which has pick-ups from Forster, Taree and Sydney. There are plenty of picnic grounds and scenic **lookouts** in the park, plus several **campsites**, some of which are accessible only by 4WD. The main camping area, reached by car, is in the Gloucester River area, with barbecues, toilet (but no shower) and water ($5 per site). You don't need to book, but for more information contact the NPWS in Raymond Terrace (℡02/4987 3108). A good camping alternative, with hot showers, is *Riverwood Downs*, just outside the park in the Monkerai Valley, 30km south of Gloucester (℡02/4994 7112; ❷). The closest **accommodation** to the park is the expensive *Barrington Guest House* in Salisbury, about 40km from Dungog (℡02/4995 3212, ⑩www.barrington-g-house.com.au; ❸), which charges between $75 and $115 per person (shared bathroom or en suite), including meals and activities ranging from kangaroo feeding to spotlight bushwalking. Horse riding incurs a $20 per hour surcharge. A cheaper alternative is *Barringtons Country Retreat* on Chichester Road, 23km north of Dungog (℡02/4995 9269, ℻4995 9279; cabins ❹, lodge ❺), which has a pool, spa and horse riding on offer (meals or self-catering available).

The Manning Valley: Taree and around

TAREE, on the Pacific Highway north of Forster–Tuncurry, is a quiet riverside town and the main centre of the fertile, scenic Manning Valley. Served by trains and buses from Sydney and Brisbane, it's a pleasant alternative to the touristy hustle and bustle of Port Macquarie, the next stop north (see below), and especially good as a base for some gentle exploration of the hills, forests and deserted beaches.

The very helpful **Manning Valley Visitor Information Centre**, on the old Pacific Highway in Taree North (daily 9am–5pm; ℡02/6552 1900 or free call 1800 801 522, ⑩www.retreat-to-nature.com), has detailed leaflets describing forest drives, most of which lead to the high plateau where waterfalls abound. Taree's main attraction, its **river cruises**, are organized by Manning River Marina and Boat Hire (3hr; $15; ☎02/6553 2683). There's the usual abundance of **motels** along the highway, including the wheelchair-friendly *Pacific Motel*, 500m north of town (☎02/6552 1977; ❹), which has air-conditioned rooms and a swimming pool. Cheaper options include the *Royal Bar* (☎02/6552 1242; ❶) with counter food and music on weekends, and the *Exchange Hotel* on Victoria Street (❶), which is close to the river for boating. *Fotheringham's Hotel* at 236 Victoria St (☎02/6552 1153; ❷) is a pleasant old pub and restaurant, with all rooms newly decorated but no en suites; and the *Twilight Caravan Park*, Pacific Highway, 3km north of town (☎02/6552 2857; cabins ❸, on-site vans ❷) has a saltwater pool, barbecues and kiosk. If you want to stay aboard a **houseboat**, contact Manning River Holidays Afloat (☎02/6552 6271) who have moored and moving boats available for rent.

Along the route from Taree to Port Macquarie, there are a number of worthwhile detours. One of the most impressive waterfalls on the whole coast is the 160-metre-high **Ellenborough Falls**, about an hour's drive northwest of Taree beyond Wingham on the Bulga Forest Drive – unsealed much of the way. From the main Pacific Highway at Moorland, a road turns off to the small **Crowdy Bay National Park**, situated between Crowdy Head and the lofty Diamond Head, whose landscape includes heathlands, swamp, lagoons, woodlands, forests and sand dunes, all enlivened by prolific birdlife. Back on the Pacific Highway, there is a convenient gateway tourist office fuelling drivers with free tea and coffee at **Kew**, between Taree and Port Macquarie; turn right at the *Kew Hotel* for the more interesting route that hugs the coast.

Port Macquarie

PORT MACQUARIE, at the mouth of the Hastings River, was established in 1821 as a place of secondary punishment for convicts who had committed offences after arrival in New South Wales, as well as for hardened criminals from Britain. By the late 1820s, however, the spread of population meant that this was no longer an isolated outpost, so the penal settlement was closed and the area was opened up to free settlers. The convicts who were still considered incorrigible were sent off either to Moreton Bay in the Brisbane area, or to remote Norfolk Island (see p.335).

As with many other northern coastal ports, the **harbour** was unreliable and its approaches difficult, so for more than a century the town failed to live up to its early promise of commercial success. Prosperity and expansion finally came only with the tourism boom, which started in the early 1970s and shows no signs of abating; with a population of about forty thousand, Port Macquarie is now one of the fastest-growing towns on the north coast of New South Wales, particularly popular with older people from the southern cities who want to spend their retirement years in a sunny place with what the CSIRO meteorologists have declared "Australia's best year-round climate". If you approach from the south, you'll see the town's featureless **suburbs** sprawling along the beaches, encroaching further on the bush. Once visitors have reached the town itself, however, there are obvious scenic attractions – long, sandy beaches that start right in town and extend far along the coast, and forests and mountains in the hinterland – as well as plenty laid on in and around the town itself: amusement parks, mini-zoos, nature parks, cruises on the Hastings River and connecting waterways, horse riding and, above all, water sports and fishing.

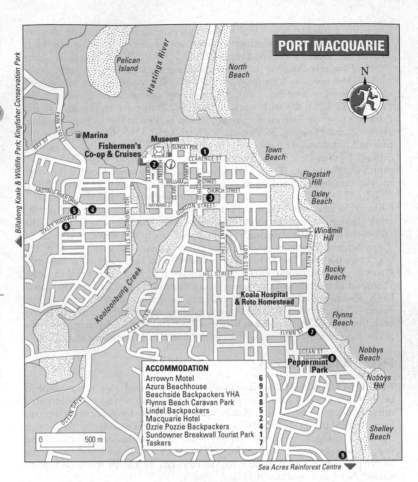

ACCOMMODATION

Arrowyn Motel	6
Azura Beachhouse	9
Beachside Backpackers YHA	3
Flynns Beach Caravan Park	8
Lindel Backpackers	5
Macquarie Hotel	2
Ozzie Pozzie Backpackers	4
Sundowner Breakwall Tourist Park	1
Taskers	7

Arrival and information

As a popular resort, Port Macquarie is well served by transport from Sydney, Tamworth (see p.320) and Brisbane, although not all **buses** make the detour from the Pacific Highway, so check carefully. Buses drop you off outside the tourist information office. **Trains** stop in Wauchope, 22km west, from where there's a Countrylink bus connection with Port Macquarie Bus (☎02/6583 2161). You can also **fly** into Port Macquarie from Sydney with Eastern Australian (☎13 1313). Horton Street is the main downtown street, running north to the Hastings River. The helpful and friendly **tourist information office** (Mon–Fri 8.30am–5pm, Sat & Sun 9am–4pm; ☎02/6581 8010, accommodation and tour bookings free call ☎1800 025 935, ⓦwww.portmacquar-ieinfo.com.au), on Clarence Street paralleling the river, will also mind your bags free of charge if you've time to kill. The town's attractions and beaches are far flung, and transport isn't the best. You can get around town on Port Macquarie Bus Service (☎02/6583 2161), which has five different routes running mainly in the daytime Monday to Friday, with some services on Saturday. Only bus #334 to Wauchope runs daily. Waits are long between buses (often an hour or more), so a timetable – available from the tourist information office – is vital. Otherwise the best option is **cycling** (see "Listings", p.289).

Accommodation

With sixty motels and holiday apartments in town, you're not going to be hard-pressed to find somewhere to stay; the cheaper, older motels are mostly found on Gordon Street, with the average double going for $60.

Arrowyn Motel, 170 Gordon St (℡02/6583 1633, ℻6583 3040). Simple, inexpensive motel with a communal kitchen/dining area and outside BBQ. Within walking distance of the river and Main Beach. ⑤

Azura Beach House, 109 Pacific Drive (℡02/6582 2700, ⓦwww.azura.com.au). A great guesthouse near the beach with modern, elegant rooms designed to blend with private rainforest views, balconies, a guest lounge, comfy library and heated pool. Complimentary travel transfers. B&B ⑦

Beachside Backpackers YHA, 40 Church St (℡ & ℻ 02/6583 5512, ⓔportmaqyha@hotmail.com). Central, family-run, friendly YHA hostel, with kitchen/TV/video room and BBQ on the patio. Free pick-up from the bus terminal. Small gym area; free bikes, boogie- and surfboards, with free surf lessons every morning. Dorms ①, rooms ③

Flynns Beach Caravan Park, 22 Ocean St, 2.5km from the centre (℡02/6583 5754). A good camping option for people with no transport, as they will pick up travellers from the bus terminal. On-site vans ③, cabins ④–⑤

Lindel Backpackers, Hastings River Drive, cnr Gordon St (℡ & ℻ 02/6583 1791 or free call 1800 688 882, ⓔlindel@midcoast.com.au). Pleasant hostel in an 1888 Victorian Gothic building. Clean, friendly and family-run, with a BBQ area and swimming pool, plus free use of bikes, surfboards and fishing gear. Book in advance for free pick-up service from the bus terminal; free

trips by shuttle-bus to the koala hospital and beaches. Rooms ③, dorms ①

Macquarie Hotel, Clarence St, opposite the post office (℡02/6583 1011, ℻6583 5822, ⓦwww.pubstay.com.au). Clean, good-value rooms with or without bath, in a pub overlooking the river; some cheap singles available. Good beer garden and bistro. ④

Ozzie Pozzie Backpackers, 36 Waugh St (℡02/6583 8133 or free call 1800 620 020, ⓦwww.nomadsworld.com). The best hostel in Port Stephens, and one of the friendliest in New South Wales. Boons include free pick-ups and drop-offs, free use of bikes and boogie boards, comfortable dorms, separate video and games rooms and free chilli (Wed) and $6 pizza (Mon). Rooms ③, dorms ①

Rainbow Beach Holiday Village, Beach St, Bonny Hills, about 23km south (℡02/6585 5655 or free call 1800 045 520). Spacious, beachside camping complex in a bushland setting, with solar-heated pool, playground, BBQ and shop. On-site vans ③, cabins ④, cottages ⑤

Sundowner Breakwall Tourist Park, right on the riverfront (℡02/6583 2755 or free call 1800 636 452, ⓦwww.sundowner.net.au). Park offering shops, amenities, free internet access for guests and a palm-fringed pool. Cottages ④–⑧, cabins ④–⑤

Taskers, 14 Flynn St, opposite Flynns Beach (℡02/6583 1520). Nice, shady complex with pool, children's playground and BBQ. Cabins ⑤–⑦

The Town and around

Port Macquarie has a history of destroying reminders of its past. The only surviving remnants are **St Thomas' Church** (1824–28) on Hay Street; the **courthouse** on Clarence Street (Mon–Fri 10am–3pm; free), built in 1869 and refurbished accordingly; the **Historical Museum** opposite (Mon–Sat 9.30am–4.30pm, Sun 1–4.30pm; $2), which has an extensive and well-presented collection of documents and memorabilia dealing with the history of the Hastings River area; and there's also a **Maritime Museum** at 6 William St (Mon–Sat 11am–3pm; $2), with model ships, nautical paintings and artefacts. The 1890s **Pilots Boatshed Museum** at Town Wharf (Tues–Sat 10am–2pm; $1) also has a small collection covering the history of maritime and river wrecks. Several **river cruises** leave from the **Fishermen's Co-op** at the beach end of Clarence Street (see "Listings", p.289). The river foreshore provides a pleasant place for a peaceful sunset stroll and you can watch the pelican colony begging for tiddlers from the local anglers.

Perhaps the best of the attractions is the **Kooloonbung Creek Nature Reserve**, a large bushland reserve remarkably close to the town centre. From the entrance at the corner of Horton and Gordon streets, you step onto trails among casuarinas, mangroves and eucalypts, or sweat through a small patch of rainforest, and it's amazingly easy to believe that you're lost in the wilderness of the Australian bush, rather than minutes from the main road. The eastern part of the nature reserve is accessible to wheelchairs, and at the **old cemetery** near the main entrance a few graves of pioneer settlers have been preserved.

On the ocean-facing side of town, Port Macquarie's three flagged, patrolled **beaches** are Town Beach, Flynn's and Lighthouse. The **Sea Acres Rainforest Centre** (daily 9am–4.30pm; free guided walks at regular intervals; $9), south of the town on Pacific Drive, is impressive, conveying an urgent environmental message about the fast-disappearing coastal rainforest of New South Wales which you can learn about in the ecology display room and enviro-theatre. The centre comprises three different types of rainforest, which can be inspected at close quarters from a boardwalk (again wheelchair-accessible).

Back towards the town centre, on Lord Street, **Roto** is a fine nineteenth-century homestead, with Australia's oldest **koala hospital** in its grounds (both open daily 9am–5pm; free, donations welcome; check feeding times on ☎02/6584 1522). Run and financed by volunteers, the hospital takes in disease-stricken koalas, as well as the inevitable road casualties.

If you've not had your fill of cuddly animals, the **Billabong Koala & Wildlife Park**, 233 Oxley Highway (daily 9.30am–4.30pm; $8.50), advertises cute kangaroos that can be hand-fed and koalas that can be patted and embraced. There's also the **Kingfisher Conservation Park**, on Kingfisher Road (daily 9am–5pm; $9), home to over four hundred animals, some of which are threatened by extinction. **Peppermint Park**, corner of Pacific Drive and Ocean Street (Tues–Sun 10am–5pm, daily during school holidays; $14.90), is a typical amusement park, with giant waterslides, a mini-golf course and a roller-skating rink.

Eating, drinking and nightlife

As you'd expect in a resort of this size, there are plenty of places to **eat**, particularly fast-food outlets: not surprisingly, seafood and fish predominate and the local oysters really must be tried. *Macquarie Seafoods*, centrally located on the corner of Clarence and Short streets, is the best place for takeaway fish and chips. You can also buy fresh fish and seafood from the **Fishermen's Co-op** at the end of Clarence Street in the town wharf area and cook it yourself. *Scampi's*, at the Marina on Park Street, just west of the town centre (BYO; nightly dinner plus lunch in summer; ☎02/6583 7200), is one of the most enjoyable of several seafood restaurants, while *Coolenberg* (☎02/6584 3770), at the corner of Lake Road and Hill Street, is an award-winning modern Australian establishment in a historic building just out of town. *Toro's Mexican Cantina* at 22 Murray St (☎02/6583 4340) has build-your-own burritos and tacos in the evenings, while *Spicy Kruthai* on the corner of Clarence and Hay streets (☎02/6583 9043) has reasonably priced Thai seafood and stir-fries. On the waterfront at 74 Clarence St, *Crays Seafood Restaurant* is a pricey establishment with decent lunchtime deals, while the *Macquarie Hotel* has a reasonably priced bistro. The Port Central Shopping Centre, behind the tourist information office on Clarence Street, has a good-value food court on the second floor; choices include fresh, healthy fare from the *Pure and Natural Food Co*, and excellent coffee and cakes at *The Coffee Club* – both open daily. The

Cosmopolitan Caffe, on the corner of Clarence and Short streets, is a sidewalk café with an extensive list of flavoured coffees plus lunchtime nachos and sandwiches, while nearby *Cafe 66* at 66 Clarence St (℡02/6583 7885) has pasta and *focaccia* at lunchtime and a patio popular with evening diners.

The space-age *RSL Club* at 1 Bay St (℡02/6825 2300) has a cocktail bar, an auditorium and **live music** at the weekends, when it's open for 24-hour drinking (and, regrettably, for its pokies). More central and tackier (but good-naturedly so) is *Finnians Irish Tavern* at 97 Gordon St; they also have live music at the weekend, and serve decent grub. Opposite the tourist information office, on the corner of Clarence and Horton streets, is a good **drinking** spot with a riverfront location and lots of different bars; bands play here Wednesday and Saturday. The attached nightclub has varied entertainment from Wednesday to Sunday night. Other nightclubs are *TC's*, on William Street, popular with the 18–25 set; and *Down Under*, on Short Street next to Coles supermarket, a tiny underground place for the over-thirties.

There are also a few **wineries** in the area: Cassegrain Winery, on the Hastings River on Fernbank Creek Road off the Pacific Highway south of town (daily 9am–5pm; ℡02/6583 7777), has a particularly pleasant restaurant on a verandah overlooking the vineyards.

Listings

Airlines Ansett Australia (℡13 1300) have daily flights to/from Sydney. Eastern Australia (℡13 1313) supplies daily Sydney services.

Bike rental Port Push Bikes, 155 Horton St (℡02/6583 4540).

Boat rental Settlement Point Boatshed (℡02/6563 6300) next to the Settlement Point Ferry, rent out tin boats for around $25 per day; they also rent out party boats, complete with BBQ, beer cooler and toilet, to groups.

Buses Long-distance buses on the Sydney–Brisbane route stop outside the tourist information office. Kings Bus Service (℡02/6562 4724) runs between Port Macquarie and Tamworth via Kempsey, Macksville, Nambucca Heads, Urunga, Coffs Harbour, Bellingen, Dorrigo, Armidale, Uralla and Walcha three times a week. As well as running around town, Port Macquarie Bus Service (℡02/6583 2161) also serves Wauchope and Kempsey.

Camel safaris Port Macquarie Camel Safaris (bookings through the tourist information office or call ℡02/6583 7650; $12 for 20min, $22 per hour).

Car rental Avis (℡02/6584 9555); Budget, William St (℡02/6583 5144); Economical Rent-a-Car, 190 Oxley St (℡02/6581 1020); Hertz, 73 Hastings River Drive (℡02/6583 6599); and Thrifty at the airport (℡02/6584 2122).

Cruises Cruises depart from the Clarence St Wharf: MV *Port Venture* cruises up the Hastings River (Tues & Thurs 10.30am & 2pm; 2hr; $15; ℡02/6584 5425); Pelican River Cruises departs from the Fishermen's Co-op Wharf to the ever-glades in Limeburners Creek National Park and an oyster farm for tastings (Mon–Fri 10am; 2hr $15; 5hr $30; ℡02/6583 7558 or 0418 652 171); and the Waterbus Everglade Tours offer a dolphin-spotting cruise (daily 10am & 2pm; 2hr 30min; $22; ℡02/6582 5009 or free call 1800 025 935) among others.

Hospital Port Macquarie Hospital, Wright's Rd (℡02/6581 2000).

Internet access *Felglow Internet Cafe* at 4–16 Clarence St has cheap cakes and coffee (Mon–Fri 9am–6pm, Sat 9am–5pm), but the town library (Mon–Fri 9.30am–6pm, Sat 9am–noon) is much cheaper.

Police ℡02/6583 0199.

Post office Port Macquarie Post Office, Clarence St, NSW 2444.

Surfing The Paradise Surf Centre at 49 Horton St (℡02/6583 6062) sells surfboards and gear. Round House Surfing (℡0417 479 972) charge $25 for a two-hour lesson.

Taxis Port Macquarie Taxicabs (℡02/6581 0081); Wauchope Radio Taxicabs (℡02/6585 2100). There is a taxi rank on Horton St.

Trains The XPT links Wauchope and Sydney (3 daily; 6hr).

Water sports Several companies operate parasailing, fishing charters and jet-ski tours on the river and ocean, including Watersports World (℡02/6583 9777), Port Water Sports (℡0412 234 509) and Sea Quest (℡02/6583 3463).

Heading inland: Wauchope

Surrounded by forest, the pretty little village of **WAUCHOPE** (pronounced War-hope), 22km west of Port Macquarie, makes an enjoyable contrast to the coast. Through working exhibits, the open-air museum of **Timbertown**, 3km from the village on the Oxley Highway (daily 9.30am–3.30pm; free), depicts life as it must have been in the isolated timber settlements 150 years ago. Timber logs are pulled over muddy roads to saw-pits, where they are cut and shaped, the bakery bakes and sells bread fresh from the oven, and many other aspects of Victorian life are re-enacted. North of Wauchope, the **Wilson River Rainforest Reserve**'s picnic grounds are a popular destination for day-trips from Port Macquarie. Another feature of Wauchope is the large separatist lesbian community that lives in the vicinity – something strangely absent from the tourist literature. For more on Wauchope, see the ⓦ www.emeraldheart-land.org.au website.

Basic pub **accommodation** and counter meals can be had at the *Hastings Hotel*, on the corner of High and Cameron streets (ⓣ 02/6585 2003; ➋), and there are slightly fancier rooms at the *Wauchope Motel* (ⓣ 02/6585 1933; ➍). The delightful *Mount Seaview Retreat*, on the Oxley Highway towards Tamworth (ⓣ 02/6587 7155 or free call 1800 818 804, ⓕ 6587 7195, ⓦ www.mtseaviewretreat.com.au; resort ➍–➎, lodge ➋, bunkhouse ➊, linen $5 or BYO), a cattle station on the Hastings River, offers farmstays and campsites as well as rooms; there's a bar, restaurant and tennis court, and the resort organizes very popular cross-country **horse-riding** (also available for non guests; $22 per trail ride) and **rainforest 4WD safaris** ($27–71). You can also swim in the river here. They will pick up guests from Wauchope train station or Port Macquarie airport.

You can get to Wauchope daily with the Port Macquarie Bus Service (ⓣ 02/6583 2161); on weekdays the 9.20am service goes directly to Timbertown, returning at 2.30pm (around $6).

The coast north to Nambucca Heads

The coastline between Port Macquarie and Nambucca Heads, 115km north, has some magic spots. **KEMPSEY**, a large service town on the Macleay River, 49km from Port Macquarie, is home to a prominent Aboriginal population, the **Dunghutti** people. The first white settlers moved into the region five years after the explorer John Oxley entered the Macleay River area in 1818. Between 1830 and 1850 the Dunghutti put up resistance to the settlers, and several Aboriginal massacres resulted. By the 1850s resistance was so widespread that native police were called in to stop the fighting. In the following decade Aboriginal reserves were established, and a degree of self-determination existed from the 1890s when several Aboriginal farms were set up, but the people were pushed off the farms after World War I. The Dunghutti were still holding traditional ceremonies as late as the 1940s. Their ability to demonstrate continuous links with their land led in 1996 to a successful claim for Native Title for a portion of land at **CRESCENT HEAD**, 21km northeast from Kempsey along a good sealed road, although they held title only temporarily and have since received compensation for the loss of their native title rights to property developers in the area. The agreement was the first recognition of native title by an Australian government on the mainland and the first time that an Australian government negotiated an agreement with indigenous people to acquire their land. There are some wonderful waterfront **campsites** here: *Crescent Head Tourist Park* (☏02/6566 0261), which also has some very pleasant verandah-fronted wooden chalets (❸–❻); and *Delicate Nobby Camping Ground* (☏02/6566 0144), which is in extensive but secluded bushland, ten-minutes' drive from the township. Meandering back and then away from the Pacific Highway, you come to the coastal **Hat Head National Park** and the small town of **SOUTH WEST ROCKS**, perched on a picturesque headland. Three kilometres east on **Trial Bay**, the **Arakoon State Recreation Area** has as its centrepiece **Trial Bay Gaol** (daily 9am–5pm; $3.30). Classified as a public works prison in which prisoners could learn a trade, the jail was considered progressive when it was established in 1886. Built from local granite, it's certainly an impressive construction – the massive outer walls surround an extensive complex of buildings and are supported by high buttresses with four watchtowers. The prison was closed in 1903, but reopened during World War I when it was used as an internment camp for over five hundred internees, including some Buddhist monks from Ceylon, though most of those held here were German.

Nambucca Heads

About 100km away, via the Pacific Highway, the casual resort town of **NAMBUCCA HEADS** makes a good base for trips to the rivers, mountains and forests of the hinterland; it's also a great place to break the long haul from Sydney to Brisbane – whether you're travelling by car, bus or train (the train station is on Bowra St, about 3km from the centre). From the headlands near the town centre there are fantastic views of the mouth of Nambucca River, and of the seemingly endless sweep of sandy beaches that stretch both north and south from here. There's fishing, windsurfing and canoeing available to take advantage of the gentler waters at the river mouth, and some excellent surf on the ocean beaches. From vantage points at **Scotts Head**, a popular surfing spot, whales can sometimes be sighted during their southern migration (Aug–Oct).

For information on these and other activities around town (including white-water rafting and horse riding), call in at the **visitor information centre** on the Pacific Highway at the southern entrance to town (daily 9am–5pm; ☏02/6568 6954, ⓦwww.here.com.au). You can book **accommodation** here; motels and apartments are generally better value here than in Port Macquarie or Coffs Harbour. Perhaps the cosiest place of all to stay is *Beilby's Beach House* at 1 Ocean St (☏02/6568 6466, ⓦwww.midcoast.com.au/~beilbys; ❹), a great, homely B&B with a pool, good-value rooms and a great location overlooking the dramatic coastline, just a ten-minute walk from the shops. Alternatively, try the renovated family-run *Scotts Guesthouse*, 4 Wellington Drive (☏02/6568 6386, ⒻD6569 4169, ⓦhttp://nnsw.worldtourism.com .au/ScottsHeadBB; en-suite B&B ❹–❺), or the attractively located *White Albatross Holiday Centre*, Wellington Drive (☏02/6568 6468; cabins ❸, on-site vans ❷), with a tennis court, tavern, café and children's playground. The cheapest option is the pleasant *Nambucca Backpackers*, 3 Newman St (☏ & Ⓕ 02/6568 6360 or free call 1800 630 633; rooms ❸, dorms ❶), a small, cosy, family-run hostel with free use of boogie-boards, snorkelling and fishing gear, and free pick-up from the bus terminal or train station. A good place to **eat** is *Johnny's Pizza*, in the town centre on Kent Street, serving delicious gourmet hot dogs, salad sandwiches and pizzas, while *Nirvana Sawadee*, next door to the tourist office, is a traditional Thai restaurant that makes good use of fresh local seafood. The coolest place in town is the licensed *V–Wall Tavern* on Wellington

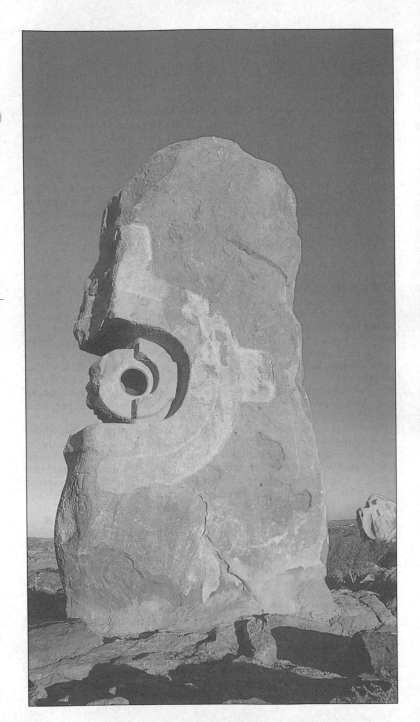

Drive (☎02/6568 6344), which serves great coffee and gourmet city café fare. Singapore–Malay and Chinese dishes are on offer at *Ken Leong's* at the *Nambucca League's Club* by Coronation Park (☎02/6568 7415).

Nambucca Heads is on the main Sydney–Brisbane bus and train routes; Kings Bus Service (☎02/6562 4724) runs to Port Macquarie or Tamworth and back three times a week. **Local buses** leave from Bowra Street outside the police station: Newman's Coaches (☎02/6568 1296) operates Monday to Friday only between Nambucca Heads and Coffs Harbour via Bowraville; Jessups Bus Service (☎02/6653 4552) goes on schooldays only to Coffs Harbour via Urunga and Bellingen; and Joyce's (☎02/6655 6330) goes to Urunga, again on schooldays only.

Heading inland from Nambucca, it's about half an hour's drive to the picturesque former timber town of **BOWRAVILLE**, where you can rest up in the old pub, now renovated to its former glory, and browse in a few arts-and-crafts shops and the jumble of Gleeson's Second Hand Store. *The Phoenix Gallery & Tea Rooms* is a pleasant refreshment stop. From here, you can travel on unsealed forest roads to the small, alternative town of Bellingen (see below), although it's more easily reached on the sealed road which turns off the Pacific Highway after Urunga.

The Bellinger River and around

URUNGA, 20km north from Nambucca Heads, is a pleasant beachside spot where the Bellinger and Kalang rivers meet the sea. From here you can walk right along the beach to nearby **MYLESTOM** (the turn-off is 7km further down the highway), which occupies a stunningly beautiful spot on the wide Bellinger River. You can take advantage of its riverside setting at the **Alma Doepel Reserve**'s sheltered, sandy river beach, which has changing rooms and showers. Two-minutes' walk to the east is a gorgeous sweep of surf beach – often gloriously deserted – which is patrolled on summer weekends and school holidays. You can walk along the beach to **Bundagen**, an alternative, environmentally friendly community that welcomes visitors and hosts frequent music and spoken-word evenings.

A great **place to stay** in Mylestom is the haphazard *Riverside Lodge*, on River Street facing Tuckers Island (☎02/6655 4245; rooms ❷, dorms ❶). Although there's no transport here, Sandy, the friendly owner, will pick guests up from Urunga or Coffs Harbour. The lodge has the comfortable, relaxed feel of an Indonesian guesthouse; all the rooms are well furnished with desks, lamps and armchairs. You can use the lodge's boat and kayaks, ride one of their bicycles through Bongil Bongil Floral Reserve, or take a special-interest tour (dance, storytelling, bushcraft) with a guide from the indigenous Gambarri Cultural Tours (☎02/6655 4195, ⓦwww.midcoast.com.au/~devaprivy). Other **facilities** in Mylestom are limited: a post office with supplies and EFTPOS, a decent Chinese **restaurant**, and a swanky riverfront brasserie called *Beaches* (with a handy bottle shop).

Bellingen

Just after Urunga, the turn-off west heads through the verdant Bellinger River valley for 12km to **BELLINGEN**, a gorgeous, relaxed little town with a strong alternative bent, full of arts-and-crafts outlets and workshops, cafés and thriving small businesses. Just before town, the **Old Butter Factory** (☎02/6655 9599), a renovated dairy, holds a complex of several craft shops where you can check out the work of local artisans, plus a chilled-out café and a massage and float tank centre ($45 for a 2hr combo pamper). In town there's a **Historical Museum** at Hyde Street (Mon & Wed–Fri 10am–noon, Tues 10am–3pm, or by appointment on ℡02/6655 0289; $2.20) containing local memorabilia which charts the development of the district from 1860. Also on Hyde Street, The Yellow Shed (daily 9am–5pm) is a crafts outlet worth a peek, although it sells some of the Old Butter Factory products at an inflated price. Bellingen also has an interesting monthly **market**, held on the third Saturday of the month (7am–2pm) in Bellingen Park, with buskers, crafts and organic food stalls. There's more shopping at the **Hammond and Wheatley Emporium** on Hyde Street, a glorious old restored department store with an Aladdin's cave of locally-produced jewellery, artefacts and artworks. Each year Bellingen hosts a lively **jazz festival** (℡02/6655 9345, ℻6655 1053, ⓦwww.midcoast.com.au /belljazz) over the third weekend in August, followed by the newly launched three-day Global Festival of world music over the October long weekend. For a cooling break from crafts and culture, you can swim in the waterholes of the Bellinger and Never Never rivers.

More **information** on the town and surrounding area is available at Traveland on Hyde St (℡02/6653 3500), which has details of rafting, bush-walking and other tours, and acts as an agent for Countrylink. The creekfront *Bellingen YHA Backpackers*, 2 Short St (℡02/6655 1116, ℻6655 1358, ⓔbelloyha@midcoast.com.au; rooms ❸, dorms ❶), is one of the best **hostels** around, a beautiful two-storey building with a huge balcony facing a rainfor-est island full of jacaranda trees that come alive at dusk with the stirrings of fruit bats; you can even sleep outdoors under a gazebo, or camp out the back if you prefer. Free pick-ups from Urunga railway station are available, as are weekly trips to Bundagen (see p.293) and lifts to Dorrigo for $10. They also offer canoes and bikes for rent, plus BBQs and frequent shenanigans round the campfire. Otherwise, there's the gay-friendly *Rivendell Bed and Breakfast*, cen-trally located at 10 Hyde St (℡ & ℻ 02/6655 0060, ⓦwww.midcoast.com /~rivendell; ❻) with a pool and breakfast included. The *Bellinger Valley Inn* (℡02/6655 1599, ℻6655 1824; ❻–❼) is also in a green expanse on the way to Dorrigo, but only 1km out of town, with room service, a swimming pool, spa, playground and barbecue. You can **camp** at the *Bellingen Caravan Park* on Dowle Street, North Bellingen (℡02/6655 1338).

The town is full of great **cafés**. *Lodge 241*, an art gallery-cum-café on Short Street serves some of the best coffee in town and delicious, wholesome lunch-es. The light and airy *Carriageway Cafe*, 75 Hyde St, serves wholesome and affordable city fare – melts, burgers and gourmet sandwiches, plus dinner at the weekend; at the back, a polished wooden staircase heads upstairs to an art gallery. On Church Street, the spacious *Cool Creek Cafe* (closed Tues & Wed) has a folksy ambience and an extensive veggie menu, as well as live music and poetry readings. Next door on one side you'll find the early-opening *Swiss Patisserie & Bakery*, on the other *The Good Food Shop*, a real find for wholefood picnic supplies; it also serves good lunches. Finally, there's *McNally House* on Hyde Street (Tues–Sat eve only; ℡02/6655 0344), a BYO restaurant in a cute cottage, with a distinctly European menu, and *Bare Nature* (daily except Wed; ℡02/6655 1551), which serves pizza, pasta and crepes, and a champagne brunch on Sunday mornings. The town has only one **pub**: the animated her-itage-listed *Federal Hotel* on Hyde Street, with live music (usually free) from Thursday to Sunday.

Interstate **buses** do not detour into Bellingen; the nearest drop-off point is Urunga or Coffs Harbour, from where Jessups Bus Service (℡02/6653 4552) runs here on schooldays. You can also reach Bellingen on Kings Bus Service

(☎02/6562 4724), which operates three times a week between Port Macquarie and Tamworth.

Inland to Dorrigo

The Dorrigo Road from Bellingen follows the beautiful Bellinger River, with bewitching green hills in the distance and fat cows grazing in lush riverside fields, passing through **THORA**, and its roadhouse with the pleasant *River Bend Cafe* attached. Beyond Thora, the scenic road winds ever more steeply through the **Dorrigo National Park**, a startlingly beautiful rainforest remnant of an area that was once similarly heavily forested; however, the lure of the valuable Australian cedar – "red gold" – left most of the plateau cleared by the 1920s. The ultramodern **Dorrigo Rainforest Centre** (daily 9am–5pm; ☎02/6657 2309) has a detailed interpretive display that goes through this sorry saga, with some insights into the life of the north coast Aboriginal people, and some examples of red cedar furniture. The *Canopy Cafe* here, with wonderful views, serves light lunches and afternoon teas until 4pm. Starting at the visitor centre, the **Skywalk** is easily the most spectacular of the walks and the least strenuous, a wooden walkway stretching out high over the rainforest canopy, enabling you to look down on the forest and out over the surrounding landscape and distant hills. The walkway is open 24 hours, to allow observance of the forest's nocturnal creatures. Other trails will take you to some of the park's best features, including a number of beautiful waterfalls; try the Wonga Walk, a 5.8-kilometre stroll through the rainforest past two waterfalls, or there are comprehensive information boards and leaflets at the centre.

DORRIGO itself is an old settlement on the eastern edge of the New England Plateau, a small country town with artistic leanings and an old-fashioned air typified by the kitsch 1950s Formica fittings of *Nick's Cafe* on Hickory Street, which serves scones and pots of tea. There's plenty of **accommodation** here: the wide-verandahed *Hotel Dorrigo* (☎02/6657 2016, ☞6557 2059; ❶–❸) has basic hotel and fancier motel-style rooms, as well as dorm accommodation, while *Dorrigo Mountain Resort*, 1 Bellingen Rd (☎02/6657 2564), close to the national park, has camping and a range of cabins (❷–❹). There are also plenty of farmstays in the area; get full details from the **tourist information** service at 36 Hickory St (daily 10am–4pm; ☎02/6657 2486).

The only way to get to Dorrigo on **public transport** is with Kings Bus Service (☎02/6562 4724), which runs three times a week between Port Macquarie and Tamworth; you can catch it from Bellingen. The bus follows the road west from Dorrigo cutting cross-country, past several more national parks, towards Armidale (see p.321).

Coffs Harbour

Back on the main coastal highway, **COFFS HARBOUR** – or "Coffs" – divides neatly into two separate parts. One half is a modern town snuggled close to the hills near the Pacific Highway – this is the centre of town, with the shopping mall, post office and all other facilities. The other part is the jetty area around the train station and the man-made harbour. For years the dramatic coastline managed to hold at bay the suburban sprawl, but retirement homes, holiday apartments, hotels and motels are gradually encroaching on the area's natural beauty. There is still a lot to admire, though: at this point on the coast the mountains and hills of the Great Dividing Range fall almost directly into the South Pacific Ocean, and glorious white, sandy **beaches** stretch endlessly, from the town shores of Boambee Beach and Jetty Beach through Park Beach

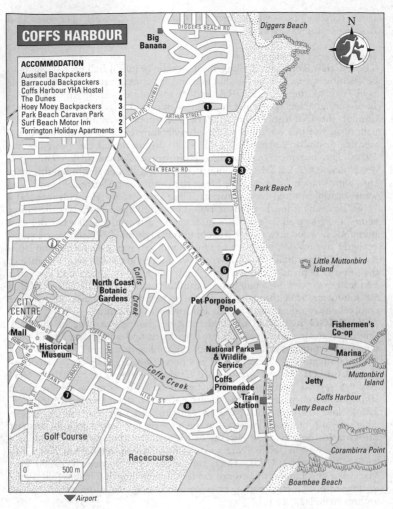

and Diggers Beach, up to northern strands such as Emerald (see p.299). There are several small islands offshore with fringing coral reefs designated as marine reserves; the plethora of fish around these makes diving a popular activity. In summer, the cool, rainforest-clad mountains with crystal-clear creeks and tumbling torrents offer a welcome respite from the heat and humidity of the coast.

Arrival and information

All long-distance buses stop at the new **bus station**, on the corner of Maclean Street and the Pacific Highway; the **train** station (☎02/6651 2757) is by the harbour. You can also fly into Coffs with Eastern Australian and Ansett (both bookable through Qantas on ☎13 1313); the airport is about 5km south and you can rent a car at one of the airport desks, take a **taxi** into town (about $7), or, if you've booked accommodation, you can probably arrange to be picked up. Given the split of Coffs into two halves, the distances you have to cover are considerable, and the **local bus service**, which runs between the town centre, Coffs Jetty and Park Beach (Kings Buses; ☎02/6652 2877; timetables from the visitor information centre), is barely adequate, so you may find yourself having to take taxis. Alternatively, you could rent a bike or car – see "Listings" on p.300 for details. To get to the beaches north of Coffs, take Ryan's Bus Service, which goes to Woolgoolga via Sapphire, Moonee Beach and Emerald Beach (☎02/6652 3201; Mon–Fri 7 daily, Sat 2 daily).

The City Centre Mall, right in the centre off Grafton Street (as the Pacific Highway is called in town), is very much the heart of Coffs, and most facilities and much of the accommodation are nearby. Unfortunately, the **visitor information centre** (daily 9am–5pm; ☎02/6652 1522, ⊛www.visitcoffsharbour.com) is not exactly centrally situated, positioned as it is for drivers' convenience on the corner of Marcia Street and Woolgoolga Road (the Pacific Highway) on the north side of town. The National Parks and Wildlife Service (☎02/6651 9522) has an office in the GIO building at 24 Moonee St, and a branch at the jetty on Orlando Street, providing information on the marine reserve and rangers tours of Muttonbird Island. State Forests also has an information centre and shop at 130 W High St (☎02/6652 0111) with camping maps available covering the mid-north coast region.

Accommodation

Coffs has everything from international resort hotels down to caravan parks. During the summer and Easter holidays the place is packed, and weekly **bookings** are preferred or even compulsory. As trains and buses from Sydney arrive in the late evening, it's wise to book in advance in any case, especially as the **hostels** will pick you up if notified. The cheapest **motels** are on the south side of town; **resorts** sometimes have bargain off-season rates, too. The visitor information centre has a free-call **reservations** line ☎1800 025 650.

Aussitel Backpackers, 312 High St (☎02/6651 1871, ℗6651 5335). Large, well-equipped hostel with a clean communal kitchen and heated pool; free use of bikes, surf- and boogie-boards and canoes, and lots of activities including an inexpensive dive course. Free pick-up from the bus terminal and train station. Rooms ❸, dorms ❶

Barracuda Backpackers, 19 Arthur St (☎02/6651 3514, ⊛www.barracudabackpackers.com). Another popular hostel, affiliated to the Nomads network and situated near bars, restaurants and a cinema complex. Facilities include internet access, free linen, a laundry and a pool. Heaps of organized activities, free pick-ups and drop-offs and free use of fishing gear, as well as surf and boogie boards. Three-night deals available. Rooms ❸, dorms ❶

Coffs Harbour YHA Hostel, 110 Albany St (☎ & ℗ 02/6652 6462). Friendly, active hostel, handy for the town centre with lifts every morning to the beach and other attractions. Kiosk with basic foodstuffs, garden with a pool, BBQ, plus bike rental, free surf- and boogie-boards and fishing gear. Surf lessons and special-rate dive courses arranged. Free pick-up from bus terminal, train station and airport. Rooms ❸, dorms ❶

The Dunes, 28 Fitzgerald St, off Ocean Parade (☎02/6652 4522 or free call 1800 023 851, ⊛www.dunes.com.au). A luxurious complex of one-, two- and three-bedroom serviced apartments near Park Beach, with a heated pool, tennis courts, spa and sauna. Good internet specials often available. ❻

Hoey Moey Backpackers, Ocean Parade (☎02/6652 3833, ℮hoey@hoeymoey.com.au). This converted old VIP/Backpackers pub has the best location in town, fronting on to the activity-centred Park Beach. More of a party hostel than a relaxing place to stay, dorms are cramped but features include a BBQ area, pool competitions with free pizza, free beer on arrival and frequent live music. Surf- and boogie-boards and mountain bikes are free. Rooms ❸, dorms ❶

Moonee Beach Caravan Park, 12km north off the Pacific Highway (☎02/6653 6552). Magic camping spot in bush surroundings, with beach, estuary and headlands to explore. Cabins ❸–❹, on-site vans ❷–❸

Park Beach Caravan Park, Ocean Parade (☎02/6652 3204, ⊛www.parkbeachcaravanpark.com.au). Huge, well-run beachfront campsite, with BBQ facilities and children's playground. Cabins ❺, on-site vans ❷

Surf Beach Motor Inn, 25 Ocean Parade
(☎ 02/6652 1872, ℱ 6652 1498,
ⓦ www.pb.uss.net.au/surfbeach). Good-value
motel with pool. ④–⑦
Torrington Holiday Apartments, 27 Boultwood

St (☎ 02/6652 7546, ℱ 6652 8505,
ⓦ www.pb.uss.net.au/torrington). On a quiet street
close to Park Beach. Fully self-contained apartments ideal for families, with a playground, swimming pool, spa and sauna. ④

The Town

The small **Historical Museum**, at 191 High St (Tues–Thurs & Sun
1.30–4pm; $2), has a collection of relics and tools owned by early pioneers and
cedar-getters, as well as local Aboriginal artefacts of the **Gumbaingirr**, whose
boundaries extended from the Nambucca River north to the Clarence River,
and inland to the foothills of the Great Dividing Range. From the museum, it's
only a short distance to the magnificent **North Coast Botanic Gardens**,
with an entrance on Hardacre Street, just off High Street (daily 9am–5pm).
These delightfully tranquil subtropical gardens are located on a triangle of land
surrounded on two sides by **Coffs Creek** and feature a mangrove boardwalk
and a slice of rainforest. A charming **creek walk** and **cycle trail** begin just
near the town centre at Rotary Park on Coffs Street and head 5.4km to
Muttonbird Island (see below); the final thirty minutes are along the northern
breakwater – detailed maps are available from the visitor information centre.
The new development of **Coffs Promenade**, along the creek towards Coffs
Jetty, contains crafts and speciality shops as well as an ice-cream parlour, a café
and restaurant, the last two with outdoor tables overlooking the tranquil, tree-
lined creek. You can rent bikes here (see "Listings" on p.300), as well as canoes
($15 half-day, $30 full day).

The **Fishermen's Co-op**, on the northern breakwater of the harbour,
sells fresh fish; the wharf here is also the departure point for most of Coffs'
cruises (see p.300). Beyond the boat-filled marina is **Muttonbird Island
Nature Reserve**, high enough to offer fantastic views of Coffs Harbour
and the southern and northern beaches. There's plenty of birdlife too, with
an interpretive walk describing the lifestyle of the oily, migratory birds who
come here to nest in summer. The best time to come is at sunset, when you
can watch the muttonbirds return to their nests. You can sometimes see dolphins frolicking close to the island. If you want to see domesticated dolphins
(and seals) being put through their paces, visit the misleadingly named **Pet
Porpoise Pool**, between Coffs Jetty and Park Beach (performances
10.30am & 2.15pm; 1hr 30min; $15.50), which seems stuck in a 1970s time
warp; there's also a small aquarium with sharks, other marine animals and a
reef tank.

Banana plantations indicate that at Coffs you're entering a subtropical climatic zone. The cultural influence of nearby Queensland becomes apparent,
too, in tourist attractions such as the **Big Banana** (daily 9am–5pm), a huge,
bright-yellow concrete banana, 3km north of Coffs on the Pacific Highway,
advertising a "horticultural theme park". It's free to walk through the banana
and look at displays dealing with early pioneer life in the district and Coffs
Harbour's $70-million-a-year banana industry. There are monorail tours of
the plantation (1hr 30min; $11), which show you packing sheds and hydro-
ponics glasshouses, as well as a space station and an Aboriginal Dreamtime
Cave. A newer attraction is a toboggan ride ($4.40), which whizzes 720m
down through the steep hillside plantations. For the complete banana experience, stop in at the milk bar, which serves bananas in every conceivable
way.

Around Coffs Harbour

An hour's drive inland from Coffs, on Bushmans Range Road at Lowanna, 42km northwest, is **George's Gold Mine** (Wed–Sun 10am–5pm, daily during school holidays; $8.50), where you can take a tour of a gold mine and look at the old stamper battery that was used to crush the ore. There are also picnic grounds, barbecues and walking trails through the rainforest.

To the north of Coffs is a string of fantastic sandy beaches. **Sapphire Beach**, 9km north, has an **environment centre** (daily 10am–5pm) with a relaxing café. **Moonee Beach Reserve**, 3km further, is in beautiful bush surroundings with a winding creek that has safe swimming – but beware of strong currents at its mouth. The reserve has plenty of shade, picnic tables and barbecues, making it a great spot for picnics. There's a caravan park here (see "Accommodation", p.297), and little else except for a small shop which sells supplies, good fish and chips and hamburgers. About 8km further on, the relatively unspoilt **Emerald Beach** is popular with surfers; it's very picturesque, with a small island offshore.

At **WOOLGOOLGA**, another 10km or so north on the Pacific Highway, a gleaming white **temple** is evidence of the large Sikh population which settled here in the early 1970s. Woolgoolga is also a popular seaside holiday resort, with excellent surfing on the ocean beach, while the calmer waters of **Woolgoolga Lake** to the north offer swimming and boating opportunities. Eight kilometres north of Woolgoolga, **Corindi Beach** is the site of the **Yarrawarra Aboriginal Cultural Centre** (phone for opening hours and to book guided walks on ☎02/6649 2669), which provides a focus and employment for the **Gumbaingirr** people in the area. There's an arts and crafts shop, bush-tucker café, and a native bush-tucker medicine nursery with plants for sale. After Corindi Beach, the road turns inland towards Grafton (see p.301); for more beaches, take the first turn off the Pacific Highway and follow a short road northeast for 6km to reach the coast again at **Red Rock** and the beginning of the **Yuraygir National Park** (detailed on p.302).

Eating, drinking and nightlife

For **coffee** and gourmet **snacks** and cakes, head to the creek for the *Up the Creek Cafe*, on the Promenade, or in town at the Mall end, to *Icehouse Cafe & Ice-creamery* at 181 High St (closed Sun). Good city fodder – *focaccia*, large breakfasts and decent cups of coffee – can be found at *Zigges on the Mall*, in the City Centre Arcade.

For more extensive **eating** try High Street, particularly at either end – around the City Centre Mall and nearby Grafton Street, and down in the block or so before Coffs Jetty. At the ocean end of High Street, on the corner of Camperdown Street, the *Pier Hotel* has a bistro with good, inexpensive counter meals (daily 7–9am, noon–2pm & 6–9pm), while the *Tahruah Thai Kitchen*, 360 High St (☎02/6651 5992), is recommended for its spicy stir-fries. *Tandoori Oven*, nearby at no. 384 (☎02/6652 2279), has tasteful, marine-inspired decor and a menu to match, along with good-value vegetarian thalis. *Tequila* at no. 24 (☎02/6652 1279) serves Mexican food and margaritas while *Maria's*, no. 368, is an Italian BYO with pasta, pizza and seafood chowders. For French-style cuisine, try *Peter's Peppermill* at no. 372 (closed Sun & Mon; ☎02/6652 5855), with specialities such as barramundi in Chardonnay sauce. Chinese food is available at the *Golden Crown* at no. 374 (Tues–Sat eve only; ☎02/6651 6787), which serves a large selection of seafood stir-fries. Innovative, international food with a hefty price-tag can be found at *Passionfish Brasserie*, 384 High St (closed Sun & Mon; ☎02/6652 1423). Down at the Marina, the *Tide & Pilot*

Brasserie (☎ 02/6651 6888) has excellent, though expensive, seafood specials with waterfront views, while the *Fisherman's Co-op* does $5 fish & chips to die for, but closes at 5pm.

Nightlife in Coffs is lively in summer, but very mainstream. There are generally **live bands** playing cover versions at some venue around town from Wednesday to Sunday, usually with free entry. On Friday and Saturday nights the *RSL Club*, on the corner of Vernon Street and the Pacific Highway, has two live bands, free entry and very cheap drinks until 2am. The *Plantation Hotel*, 88 Grafton St, puts on live music once or twice a week. For a more sedate drink, the *Greenhouse Tavern*, on the corner of Bray Street and the Pacific Highway, lets you sip in a reasonable approximation of tropical rainforest surroundings in its gazebo – they also serve tasty, good-value food. For a contemplative drink overlooking the ocean, the verandah at the yacht club bar in the marina is hard to beat.

Listings

Bike rental Promenade Leisure Hire, Coffs Promenade, Coffs Creek, 321 High St (☎ 02/6651 1032), charges $9 per hour; call for cheap daily specials.

Buses Besides the interstate services, there's Jessups Bus Service (☎ 02/6653 4551) to Bellingen, Urunga and Nambucca Heads; Watsons City Link (☎ 02/6654 1063) to Grafton via Red Rock and Woolgoolga (5–8 services Mon–Fri); and Sawtell Coaches (☎ 02/6653 3344) to Sawtell, 6km south. Kings Coaches (☎ 02/6652 2877) offer air-con tours to Bellingen, Dorrigo and Nambucca Heads.

Canoeing Wild Water Adventures (☎ 02/6653 3500) organizes full-day canoeing trips on the Bellinger River for $90 including gourmet lunch.

Car rental Choice Auto Rentals (☎ 02/6651 5221); Coffs Harbour Rent-a-Car (☎ 02/6652 5022); Hertz (☎ 02/6651 1899); Thrifty (☎ 02/6652 8622).

Cinemas Coffs Cinema, Bray St (☎ 02/6651 6444).

Cruises Pacific Explorer (☎ 02/6652 7225) runs whale-watching cruises on a sailing vessel June–Nov; regular cruises during summer.

Diving The Solitary Islands Marine Reserve, five islands and several islets north of Coffs, is the largest marine reserve in NSW; the mingling of tropical and temperate waters means that there's a huge variety of sealife, described in a range of excellent leaflets, available from the visitor information centre or the Fisheries office (☎ 02/6652 3977). Jetty Dive Centre, 398 High St, at the harbour (☎ 02/6651 1611), offers dives for beginners and advanced divers at the coral reefs around South Solitary Island, costing from $137 for two dives, as does Divers Depot (☎ 02/6652 2033) at the Marina and Pacific Blue Dive Centre (☎ 02/6652 2759) at the Promenade. All hostels arrange inexpensive snorkelling expeditions and scuba courses.

Horse riding Valery Trails, 20km southwest of Coffs (☎ 02/6653 4301): turn off the Pacific Highway at Bonville. Closer to Coffs, Bushland Trails (☎ 02/6649 4491, ⓦ www.bushlandtrails.com.au) offer horse rides and overnight treks from $22 per hour, $50 per half-day.

Hospital High St, near *Aussitel Backpackers* (☎ 02/6652 2866).

Internet access *Happy Planet* (closed Sun), is just down from Woolworths on Park Ave.

Laundry Marina Laundrette (daily 8am–8pm) at the jetty has the best views whilst you wait for your whites.

Markets Sunday-morning markets are held at the Jetty Village Shopping Centre, on Coffs Jetty (8am–2pm), and in the Big W car park, cnr Castle and Vernon streets (same hours).

Police ☎ 02/6652 0299.

Post office In the arcade off the Grafton Street Mall, NSW 2450.

Sky Diving Coffs Sky Divers (☎ 02/6651 1167, ⓦ www.coffsskydivers.com.au) offer single dives from $84 and tandem from $299.

Surfing East Coast Surf School, based at Diggers Beach (☎ 02/6651 5515), is an excellent place to learn to surf in small groups. Introductory two-hour lesson ($22) or three classes ($45); includes surfboard and wetsuit. Write for details of their excellent-value three-day surf camps: PO Box 6336, Coffs Harbour, NSW 2450.

Taxi ☎ 13 1008.

Tours 4WD Adventure Safaris (☎ 02/6655 9477) does half- and full-day tours including George's Gold Mine ($80) and a twilight glow-worm trek including dinner ($65), plus canoeing and horse riding; Mountain Trails 4WD Tours (☎ 02/6658

3333) operates recommended half- and full-day 4WD adventures along remote tracks to banana plantations, waterfalls and the rainforest, weekend trips to Dorrigo and mountain country, and wildlife tours at night; Gambaarri Tours (⊤02/6655 4195) runs Aboriginal cultural tours with a local guide to Red Rock and the Yarrawarra Cultural Centre, plus other tours from Nambucca Heads and Bellingen (all $45, including bush tucker).

Travel agent Kelly Travel, cnr High and Moonee streets (⊤02/6651 2747, ℮ kellytravel@key.net.au), is a discount flight agent for Qantas and STA Travel.

White-water rafting Coffs Harbour is one of the few places on the east coast where you can go rafting, though after a dry winter the rivers can be low. The best outfit is WOW (⊤02/6654 4066; around $139 per day).

Grafton and around

Between Woolgoolga and Ballina the Pacific Highway runs inland, and the unspoilt coast between the two towns consists of a series of national parks to which access is gained by a few intermittent side roads. **GRAFTON**, an 83-kilometre drive along the Pacific Highway from Coffs Harbour, is a peaceful district capital on a bend of the wide **Clarence River**, which almost encircles the city and occasionally floods it. The "Big River" is the largest river system on the north coast and, with its tributaries, drains a vast area of northern New South Wales. An afternoon sitting on the balcony of the *Crown Hotel*, sipping a beer and watching the majestic river roll by, is truly well spent. Northeast of Grafton, the river widens as it approaches the ocean and branches out into a network of waterways and channels. There are more than a hundred river islands, on many of which sugar cane is grown.

Grafton is proud of its wide, tree-lined streets and has the air of a genteel, old-fashioned town. In spring, when the jacaranda and flame trees are ablaze with purple, mauve and red blossoms, they even have a **Jacaranda Festival** to celebrate them (last week of Oct and first week of Nov). Out of festival time this is a quiet place, where the main attraction is cruising on the river or visiting some of the historic buildings preserved by the National Trust. **Schaeffer House**, 192 Fitzroy St (Tues–Thurs, Sun 1–4pm; $2), has a collection of beautiful china, glassware and period furniture donated to the Trust over the years; on the same street at no. 158 is the **Grafton Regional Gallery** (Tues–Sun 10am–4pm; donation), which has a pretty garden café.

Practicalities

Call in at the **Clarence River Tourism Association**, on the Pacific Highway at the corner of Spring Street, South Grafton (daily 9am–5pm; ⊤02/6642 4677, ⓦ www.tropicalnsw.com.au), which can give you information on scenic drives, river cruises and the national parks that surround Grafton; there's also a centrally located NPWS office at 50 Victoria St (⊤02/6640 3910), in the State Office Block. **Long-distance buses** stop near the tourist office, and Harvey World Travel, 54 Prince St (⊤02/6640 3910), can provide timetables and make reservations. Ryans (⊤02/6654 1063 or 6652 3201), a **local bus** service, leaves from the city centre in the direction of Coffs Harbour via Red Rock and Woolgoolga (Mon–Fri), and the Grafton–Yamba Bus Service (⊤02/6646 2019) runs north to Yamba. There's plenty of **accommodation**: try the *Grafton Hotel*, 97 Fitzroy St (⊤02/6642 2000; ④), a good pub offering beds and counter meals; or the *Crown Hotel-Motel*, 1 Prince St (⊤02/6642 4000; ③–④) for hotel rooms with a river view or ground-level motel units (③–④) – they also have some dorm beds (①). If you want a swimming pool, spa and all the mod-cons, check out the more expensive *Fitzroy Motel*, 27 Fitzroy St (⊤02/6642 4477; ⑤), 500m east of the centre. For **camping**, head for South Grafton to the well-equipped *Glenwood Tourist Park* on Heber Street (⊤02/6642 3466; cabins ③–④). A good place to **eat** is *Crabba Jack's Takeaway*, 79 Fitzroy St, for fresh fish and chips and seafood, or try *Georgie's Cafe* (℡02/6642 6996; closed Sun & Mon), at the *Village Green Hotel* on the corner of Pound and Turf streets

Around Grafton

From Grafton it's 47km **northeast** on the Pacific Highway, paralleling the Clarence River, to **MACLEAN**, a small delta town which proclaims its Scottish heritage with street signs in Gaelic. From the Maclean lookout on Wharf Street, 2km from the centre, panoramic views of the coast, bushland, canefields, river islands and the town itself can be enjoyed – while you are here, sample some of the much-feted local prawns from the Co-Op. A few kilometres further north, you can turn east off the highway in the direction of the twin towns of **YAMBA** and **ILUKA** – increasingly popular holiday spots facing each other across the mouth of the river. Clarence River Ferries shuttles between the two communities (4–5 daily; $3.30; also cruises to river islands; ℡018/664 555). In Yamba, the *VIP/Yamba Pacific Backpackers*, 1 Pilot St (℡02/6646 2466, ℮pachotel@nor.com.au; rooms ❸, dorms ❶), is in a great old pub right on the beach, and offers very cheap singles and twins and live music on Thursday to Sunday nights; ask about lifts to Byron Bay. You can get to Yamba on several daily public transport routes with the Grafton–Yamba Bus Service (℡02/6646 2019) or Kings Brothers (℡02/6642 3111).

A few kilometres south of Yamba is **Yuraygir National Park**, with several basic but attractive NPWS campsites ($5.50 per site payable in advance, details from Grafton NPWS – see overleaf) surrounded by isolated beaches and placid lake systems. North of Iluka, between the town and Bundjalung National Park, the **Iluka Nature Reserve** contains within it a World Heritage-listed **rainforest remnant**, one of sixteen such areas in northern New South Wales. **Bundjalung National Park** itself has a long coastline on the Coral Sea, as well as the sheltered inland waterways of the Esk River; **camping** is available at Woody Head, a spacious, modern site very popular with anglers (bookings advised; ℡02/6646 6134). Just north of Bundjalung, the town of **EVANS HEAD** has a range of accommodation and shops, plus boat rental outlets. The tropical climate begins to make its presence felt here, with sugar cane growing by the roadside.

West from Grafton, the **Gwydir Highway** takes you to Glen Innes, 160km away on the New England Plateau. En route it passes the rugged and densely forested adjoining **national parks** of Gibraltar Range and Walshpool. **Gibraltar Range** is an elevated plateau 1200m above sea level, scattered with huge granite outcrops and intersected by deep gorges, and is famous for its wild-flower displays of Christmas bells and waratahs in late summer. There's a **visitors centre** on the highway at Dandahra Picnic Area and a gravel road leads from here into the park, where you'll find walking tracks, lookout points and waterfalls. **Walshpool National Park** is very remote, a wilderness park on the eastern escarpment of the New England Tableland. Its **rainforest** is worth visiting, and there are picnic facilities, walks and camping at Coombadjha Creek – reached via the Coombadjha Road off the Gwydir Highway, 88km from Grafton.

Ballina

The old port of **BALLINA**, at the mouth of the Richmond River, experienced a short-lived goldrush in the 1880s, but it has few reminders of this era and is now mostly a holiday town, with some pleasant beaches and the opportunity to take river trips to Lismore (see p.313) and other destinations. Neither has it escaped the clutches of the "big things", with the **giant prawn** marking the entrance to town, just off the highway from Grafton. It's a fairly conservative cousin to nearby Byron Bay, although the fact that you're entering New Age territory is obvious by the outskirts of Ballina, where the **Thursday Plantation** (daily 9am–5pm; free), 4km north on Gallans Road, east of the Pacific Highway, was the first commercial **tea tree** plantation, producing the all-healing tea tree oil and its products. One of the highlights of the town is a lively **market**, held on the third Sunday of the month at the town's Fawcett Park.

There's a cycling and walking track from the centre of town along the sea wall to the beach, a twenty-minute walk. In Las Balsas Plaza, on River Street, is a small **maritime museum** (daily 9am–4pm; free), whose exhibits include the *Atzlan*, a balsa raft that made it across the Pacific from Ecuador in 1973 as part of the Thor Heyerdahl-inspired Las Balsas expedition. The **tourist information centre** (Mon–Fri 9am–5pm, Sat & Sun 9am–4pm; ℡02/6686 3484, ℻6686 0136, ⓦwww.ballina.tropicalnsw.com) is in the same plaza, and can book lodging, river cruises and other tours. **Accommodation** includes the lovely *Ballina Manor*, a luxurious B&B at 25 Norton St (℡02/6681 5888; ❼), and the *Ballina Travellers Lodge Motel*, 36 Tamar St (℡02/6686 6737; rooms ❹, dorms ❶), with a pleasant YHA hostel section; it's modern and family-run, with a swimming pool and free use of bicycles, fishing rods, surf- and boogie-boards. *Ballina Central Caravan Park* (℡02/6686 2220; cabins ❷–❸) is situated right by the Richmond River and has disabled access, but if you have a car, the prime spot to pitch a tent is at *Flat Rock Tent Park* (℡02/6686 4848), on the coast road 5km east of Ballina; right on the beach, this unspoilt site is for tents only and there's no electricity, so it's very peaceful – solar-heated hot showers supply a touch of comfort.

Ballina has quite a lively summer **nightlife**: the *Henry Roux Tavern*, on River Street, has a popular café and hosts occasional bands, while the *Australian Hotel*, on the corner of Cherry and River streets, is more sedate, with jazz, piano music and a pleasant beer garden. Backpacker types tend to gravitate towards the nightly craic on offer at *Paddy McGintys* on River Street. For tasty alfresco **food**, try the *Shattered Plate* on Moon Street (℡02/6686 7119; open Mon–Thurs 10am–4pm, Fri 10am–late & Sat 4pm–late). The best place for brunch – with great ocean views and healthy, creative cooking – is *Shellys on the Beach* at Shellys Beach; follow the bridge and sea wall 2km out of town.

Ansett (℡13 1313) fly daily from Sydney to Ballina. By land, the town is connected by the long-distance Kirklands **bus** (℡02/6622 1499) to Brisbane via Lismore, Lennox Head and Evans Head. **Local** services include Blanch's (℡02/6686 2144) to and from the airport east of town, and to Lennox Head, Byron Bay and Mullumbimby. To get around, you can rent a **bike** from Jack Ransom Cycles, 16 Cherry St (℡02/6686 2180); rental **cars** are available from North Coast Rent-a-Car (℡02/6686 9966) or Hertz (℡02/6686 4852).

Lennox Head

The best of the **surf beaches** are those around the small town of **LENNOX HEAD**, 11km north of Ballina, a relaxed resort with a small shopping centre, some good cafés and restaurants and a lively pub. Lennox rates among the top ten **surfing** spots in the world and professionals congregate here for the big waves in May, June and July. Adding to Lennox Head's appeal is the calm, fresh water of **Lake Ainsworth** close to the beach: stained dark by the tea trees around its banks, it's a popular swimming spot for families seeking refuge from the crashing surf, and the soft, practically medicinal water is wonderful for your skin. Lennox Head Sailing (℡02/6687 6010), on the lake, rents out sailboards and can arrange lessons.

Ideally situated between the lake and the beach, *Lennox Head Backpackers*, 2–3 Ross St (☎02/6687 7636; rooms ❸, dorms ❶), is a relaxed place where massage and aromatherapy are available in-house; there's free use of boards and fishing gear, as well as bargain rental of windsurfers and catamarans. Also in a prime position is the *Lake Ainsworth Caravan Park* on Pacific Parade (☎02/6687 7249; cabins ❸–❹). The cheap but excellent pizza, pasta and salad available at *Lenno Head Pizza* on Ballina Street (☎02/6687 7080) is popular with surfies, as is the delicious grub at *Mi Thai* a few shops further down. The *Lennox Point Hotel* serves great modern Australian food in a convivial atmosphere with water views; it also plays host to bands on Thursday, Friday and Saturday nights.

Since Lennox Head is off the Pacific Highway, only one Greyhound **bus** a day makes it out here; Kirklands also stops in town daily, and there are local services to and from Byron Bay (see p.311).

Byron Bay and around

Situated at the end of a long sweeping bay, the township of **BYRON BAY** boasts 30km of almost unbroken sandy beaches. Formerly a working-class coastal town of dilapidated weatherboard cottages, best known for its abattoir, it's now a thriving resort, first discovered by the surfies, then the hippies and more recently by better-heeled travellers – these days Byron is as much of a "must do" on the backpacker circuit as the Whitsundays and Uluru. In summer it can seem like Sydney-by-the-sea, as half of Paddington and Darlinghurst arrive en masse, fleeing the city only to form another urban jungle further up the coast. It's a pity, because what once made the place special – the small-community feel, the free-for-all atmosphere, the barefoot hippies and the herbalists – is fast disappearing. Byron these days is still beautiful and undeniably good fun, but the ever-encroaching chain stores and the profusion of competing tie-dye therapies combine to make it, in summertime at least, about as subversively alternative as MTV.

Arrival and information

If you come by **train**, you'll arrive right in the heart of town on **Jonson Street**, the main thoroughfare. Not all north coast **buses** stop at Byron Bay; however, those that do will also drop you here, or else a little way north near the junction of Jonson and Lawson streets (see "Listings" for details of bus companies and booking agents, on p.311). The closest **airports** are at Ballina, 39km south (from where you can get a bus connection with Kirklands, see p.303), or Coolangatta, 109km north in Queensland; Byron Bay Connection buses link up with both airports (☎02/6685 5980; Ballina from \$22, Coolangatta from \$55).

Check out the helpful **Byron Bay Tourist Information Centre**, staffed by volunteers at 80 Jonson St, next to the train station (daily 9am–5pm; ☎02/6685 8050). You'll be able to pick up an excellent range of printed information here about accommodation (free booking service), eating, national parks, scenic drives, sights, activities and tours. A *Disabled Access Guide* is also available. An alternative for information is the Byron Bus & Backpacker Centre, next to the information centre (daily 7am–8pm; ☎02/6685 5517), which books tours, activities, accommodation, bus tickets, car rental and arranges freight.

Accommodation

There are plenty of places to stay in Byron Bay, but that doesn't mean it's easy to find a bed. During December and January especially, demand for accommodation in all categories far exceeds supply, and it's essential to book well in advance. A1 Accommodation, 69 Jonson St (☎02/6685 7523), will make

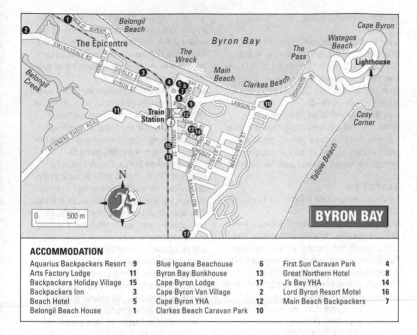

BYRON BAY

ACCOMMODATION

Aquarius Backpackers Resort	9	Blue Iguana Beachouse	6	First Sun Caravan Park	4
Arts Factory Lodge	11	Byron Bay Bunkhouse	13	Great Northern Hotel	8
Backpackers Holiday Village	15	Cape Byron Lodge	17	J's Bay YHA	14
Backpackers Inn	3	Cape Byron Van Village	2	Lord Byron Resort Motel	16
Beach Hotel	5	Cape Byron YHA	12	Main Beach Backpackers	7
Belongil Beach House	1	Clarkes Beach Caravan Park	10		

bookings for all accommodation free of charge. The **hostels** in Byron Bay are among the best in Australia, but prices and stress levels rise dramatically in summer, and choosing the wrong kind of hostel could ruin your stay. If you're part of a group, **holiday apartments** (booked through A1 Accommodation and real estate agents in town) might be a more practical option. If all places in town are full, you may strike it lucky in the surrounding area – either towards **Brunswick Heads**, about 18km further up the coast (see p.308), or in the quiet town of **Mullumbimby** – known for its very potent marijuana – just inland at the foot of Mount Chincogan on the Brunswick River.

Motels, hotels, guesthouses and apartments

Beach Hotel, cnr Jonson and Bay streets (☎02/6685 6402, ⓕ6685 8758). This luxury waterfront hotel is a favourite amongst visiting Aussie celebs. Spacious, tasteful units with patios or balconies. Outdoor heated pool and spa set among greenery. ⑧

Brunswick Hotel, Mullumbimby St, Brunswick Heads (☎02/6685 1236). Bargain accommodation in a restored riverfront pub; counter meals and live music. ③

Byron Bay Beach Club, Bayshore Drive, 3km north (☎02/6685 8000, ⓕ6685 6916, ⓦwww.byronbay.to/beachclub/). Lovely complex of serviced wooden chalets with self-contained

cooking facilities and TV. The resort-style extras include a pool, bar, restaurant, tennis courts and golf course. ⑧

Byron Bay Rainforest Resort, Broken Head Rd, Suffolk Park, 3.5km south, opposite the golf course (☎02/6685 6139, ⓕ6685 8757, ⓦwww.byron-bay.com/rainforestresort). A prize-winning resort designed to be completely accessible to people with disabilities. Private one- or two-room cabins, fully equipped (linen is provided), with verandah and TV, set in a rainforest with easy access to the beach; there's also a swimming pool with ramp. Cheaper weekly rates available. Cabins ⑦–⑧

Byron Sunseeker Motel, 100 Bangalow Rd, 1.5km south (☎02/6685 7369, ⓕ6685 5181, ⓦwww.byron-bay.com/byronsun). Cottage-style motel units with balconies or verandahs. Saltwater pool, playground and BBQ. All units sleep six and

have limited cooking facilities. Close to Tallow
Beach. **❼**

Great Northern Hotel, cnr Jonson and Byron
streets (℡ 02/6685 6454). No-frills pub rooms in
an excellent location on the main street. The noise
from the bands playing below make this place one
for confirmed night owls. Cheap single rates, particularly off-season. **❸ –❹**

Lord Byron Resort Motel, 120 Jonson St
(℡ 02/6685 7444, ℻ 6685 7120). Central location,
with amenities including a swimming pool, spa,
sauna and tennis court. All units air-con. Some
serviced apartments available (with fans only). **❼**

Hostels

Aquarius Backpackers Resort, 161 Lawson St
(℡ 02/6685 7663, ℻ 6685 7439,
℮ aquarius@om.com.au). Newly renovated motel
with self-contained units with kitchenettes. Pool,
BBQ area, café, bar, free use of bikes and boogie-
boards. Internet and currency exchange facilities
are also available. Rooms **❸** , dorms **❷**

Blue Iguana Beachhouse, 14 Bay St (℡ 02/6685
5298). In a lovely old bungalow with a wooden
verandah, this is perfect for lone travellers and
those needing a touch of home. It's small enough
to feel personal – a place to relax, listen to music
and BBQ on the deck among the hibiscus, before
swimming at the beach opposite. Double, twin and
four-share rooms, all en suite. Couples might like
to try sleeping in the honeymoon suite parked outside – a converted double decker bus. Rooms **❹** ,
dorms **❷ –❸**

Byron Bay Bunkhouse, Carlyle St (℡ 02/6685
8311, ⓦ www.nrg.com.au/~byronbay). Large,
rowdy, laid-back hostel with dorms only. Free pancakes, but the place is not for the faint at heart.
Dorms **❶ –❷**

Cape Byron Lodge, 78 Old Bangalow Rd (℡ &℻
02/6685 6445). Has a swimming pool and attractive garden, as well as free breakfast, bikes and
boogie-boards. A 15min walk from town or take
the shuttle bus; a 10min walk to Tallow Beach.
Rooms **❹** , dorms **❷**

Cape Byron YHA Hostel, cnr Middleton and
Byron streets (℡ 02/6685 8788, ℻ 6685 8814).
Large, central hostel which feels more like a resort
hotel, except you have to pay a deposit on crockery. Facilities include a pool and basketball court;
also free pancakes, bikes and boogie-boards, and
two BBQ nights a week. Some rooms en suite.
Rooms **❸ –❹** , dorms **❷**

J's Bay YHA Hostel, 7 Carlyle St (℡ 02/6685
8853 or free call 1800 678 195, ℻ 6685 6766,
℮ jbay@nor.com.au). Bright, airy resort-style hostel with two central courtyards, one with BBQ and

outdoor eating area, the other with heated saltwater pool. Good-value social pizza evenings, and a
weekly pub crawl. Extras include free boards and
bikes and a TV room with videos. Dorms range
from small to immense; many rooms are en suite.
Rooms **❹** , dorms **❷**

Nomads Main Beach Backpackers, cnr Lawson
and Fletcher streets (℡ 02/6685 8695 or free call
1800 150 233). Safe and pleasant old Council
chambers converted to a hostel, complete with
pool, car parking, internet access and secure lockers in every room. Rooms **❹** , dorms **❷**

VIP/Arts Factory Lodge, Skinners Shoot Rd
(℡ 02/6685 7709, ℻ 6685 8534, ⓦ www.artsfac-
tory.com.au). More an experience than an establishment, the Arts Factory attracts those who value
a social scene and sleepless nights over space
and security – most guests either love it immediately or desperately want to leave. The wooden
lodge is situated in a bushland creek setting, with
a choice of dorms, tepees and canvas huts by the
creek; there's also a camping area. Facilities
include pool and free bikes, as well as New Age
workshops and classes. No children allowed.
Advance booking required for pick-ups from train
or bus station, and expect to pay a deposit for
everything. Huts **❸** , dorms **❷**

VIP/Backpackers Holiday Village, 116 Jonson
St (℡ 02/6685 8888 or reservations free call 1800
350 388). One of the most central and long-established hostels, this well-liked place is clean,
friendly and well equipped, with a solar-heated
swimming pool, spa and BBQs. Free bikes, boards
and luggage storage. Rooms **❸ –❹** , dorms **❷**

VIP/Backpackers Inn on the Beach, 29 Shirley
St (℡ 02/6685 8231, ℻ 6685 5708). Arranged
around a central courtyard. Facilities include a
communal kitchen, swimming pool, BBQ and volleyball court. Free bikes and boards. Rooms
❸ –❹ , dorms **❷**

VIP/Belongil Beach House, Childe St
(℡ 02/6685 7868, ℻ 6685 7445). Beautiful complex in the style of a Balinese resort, with spacious, cool, high-ceilinged timber cottages around
a landscaped garden. Single travellers may find it
a little remote. Parking, free bikes and boards
available, plus there's an excellent café, *Switch*,
next door. Apartments **❺** , rooms **❸ –❹** , dorms **❷**

Campsites

Cape Byron Van Village, Ewingsdale Rd, 2km
northwest (℡ 02/6685 7378). Pool and tennis
court; 10min walk to Belongil Beach. Cabins
❹ –❺

Clarkes Beach Caravan Park, off Lighthouse Rd
(℡ 02/6685 6496). Only 1km west of town, and

right on the beach. Cabins ⑤
Ferry Reserve Caravan Park, Pacific Highway, Brunswick Heads (☏02/6685 1872). Pleasant campsite near the river, with a kiosk and BBQ. Cabins ③
First Sun Caravan Park, Lawson St (☏02/6685 6544). Very central, overlooking Main Beach. Cabins ③–⑤
Maca's Camping Ground, Main Arm Rd, near

Mullumbimby (☏02/6684 5211). Campsite in the bush. Communal kitchen and dining room, plus laundry; tents for rent.
Suffolk Park Caravan Park, Alcorn St, Suffolk Park, 5km south (☏02/6685 3353). Good location in a shady setting on Tallow Beach. Cabins ②–⑤
Terrace Caravan Park, The Terrace, Brunswick Heads (☏02/6685 1233). Shady spot by the river, near the beach. Cabins ③–⑤

Alternative and artistic Byron Bay

Byron Bay offers a truly wide variety of alternative therapies, extensive browsing in New Age bookshops, a wealth of crystals, and a future foretold through palmistry and tarot readings – all underlaid with a good dose of capitalism as prices for massages and tarot readings are hiked up during the lucrative summer months. The alternative culture attracts artists and artisans in droves, and galleries and artists' studios abound.

The **Community Centre**, at 69 Jonson St (☏02/6685 6807, @bbcc@mullum.com.au; closed Sun), opposite the train station, is hard to miss with its bright figurative mural, and has great notice boards packed with information on everything from Celtic Shamanism to Tibetan healing workshops. The **Byron Bay Arts School** (☏02/6680 7771), which offers two-hour daily workshops in everything from sushi making to Aboriginal art and surfboard repair, is also run from here – book in the foyer. One of the best New Age emporiums is the **Crystal Temple** at 87 Jonson St, flogging crystals, books, tapes and jewellery. They also have a wide range of alternative therapies on offer. At the rear of the *Belongil Beach House* on Childe Street, the Relax Haven (☏02/6685 8304) has a **float tank** (1hr float $25) and **massage** available (float and massage $40); or the more central Samadhi Flotation Centre, 107 Jonson St (☏02/6685 6905), offers the same, plus classes, workshops and a resident naturopath and homeopath. Quintessence, Shop 8, 11 Fletcher St (☏02/6685 5533), offers aromatherapy massage and reflexology.

The **Byron Bay market**, held on the first Sunday of each month on Butler Street, behind the train station, is the best way to become acquainted with the arts and crafts of the area (if you miss it, there's others at The Channon on the second Sunday, Mullumbimby on the third Saturday, Uki on the third Sunday and one at the showground at Bangalow, 13km southwest, on the fourth Sunday of each month). The **Arts Factory**, on Skinners Shoot Road, has several artists' workshops which you can visit (Tues–Sun 10am–3pm), and the **Byron Craft Market** is held here every Saturday (8.30am–3pm) with a courtesy bus (9.30am–3.30pm) from the community centre on Jonson Street. **The Epicentre**, on Border Street, near Belongil Beach, has several outlets and resident artists and craftspeople, plus a large art gallery showing the work of local artists ($1 donation). Beyond here, northwest of town along Ewingsdale Road, **Byron Bay Industrial Estate**, between Banksia Drive and Acacia Street, has a host of artisans producing everything from leathergoods to hats; the most highly regarded creative talents here are the glassblowers at **Colin Heaney's Hot Glass Studio** (gallery daily 10am–4pm, demonstrations Mon–Fri 9am–3pm). Back in town, one of the best alternative shops is Cat's Recycled Emporium, Shop 1/3, Lawson St, which sells a mixture of clothes and art, most made locally – everything from groovy beach dresses to mobiles made of cutlery. Also check out Love Hemp, Shop 2, Byron Street, devoted entirely to hemp clothing.

Byron Bay is host to an Australian **Writers' Festival** featuring established and budding writers, readings and signings during the last week of July; contact the Northern Rivers Writers' Centre, PO Box II41, Lismore, NSW 2480 (☏02/6622 3599, @6622 7035).

The Town and around

There's plenty of opportunity to soak up local atmosphere – and the often bizarre mix of countercultures as surfie meets soap starlet meets hippie – simply by wandering the streets. Probably the best place to take it all in is on the first Sunday of each month at the **market**, on Butler Street behind the train station, a huge affair containing everything from leather handbags to organic veggies. If you want to explore, one of the first places to visit is the **lighthouse** on the rocky promontory of **Cape Byron**, where there's a small nature reserve (8am–5.30pm). The cape includes the easternmost point of the Australian mainland and is a popular spot to greet the dawn, but don't worry if you're not an early riser – the views from the cape and the lighthouse reserve are fabulous anytime, and there's an excellent circular **walking track** from the lighthouse. With a bit of luck you'll see **dolphins**, who like to sport in the surf off the headland, **humpback whales**, which pass this way heading north to warmer waters in June or July and again on their return south in September or October, and maybe some **sharks**.

Main Beach in town is as good as any to swim from, and usually has relatively gentle surf. One reason why Byron Bay is so popular with surf freaks is because its beaches face in all directions, so there's almost always one with a good swell; however, you can usually find somewhere for a calmer swim.

East of Main Beach, you can always find a spot to yourself on the less sheltered stretch of **Belongil Beach**, from where there's sand virtually all the way to **BRUNSWICK HEADS**, a quieter, more family-oriented resort located between the mouth of the Brunswick River and Simpson's Creek, with a long crescent of beach on the ocean side. The grassy riverfront area is a good spot for children, with several playgrounds and picnic areas. The attractive 1930s-style *Brunswick Hotel* has a popular beer garden facing the river, packed on Sunday afternoon when there's free live music outdoors.

Back in the other direction, Main Beach curves round towards Cape Byron to become **Clarkes Beach**. This and neighbouring **Wategos Beach** – beautifully framed between two rocky spurs – face north, and they usually have the best surfing. On the far side of the cape, **Tallow Beach** extends towards the **Broken Head Nature Reserve**, 6km south of the town centre at Suffolk Park; there's good surf at Tallow just around the cape at Cosy Corner, and also at Broken Head. From the car park here, a short stroll through rainforest leads to the secluded, nudist **Kings Beach**, one of several isolated stretches of sand out this way.

The diversity of marine life in the waters of Byron Bay make it second only to the Great Barrier Reef as a place to **dive** on the east coast. Tropical marine life and creatures from warm temperate seas mingle at the granite outcrop of **Julian Rocks Aquatic Reserve**, 3km offshore; by far the most popular spot here is the **Cod Hole**, an extensive underwater cave inhabited by large moray eels and other fish. Between April and June is the best time to dive, before the plankton bloom (see "Listings" on p.311 for information on dive schools).

Eating

There's a multitude of places selling food in Byron Bay, and the standard is generally pretty high. Lots of alternative **cafés** offer delicious health foods and vegetarian dishes – although they don't usually stay open late, even in summer – and there are plenty of takeaways and fish-and-chip shops, as well as **restaurants** that serve everything from Japanese to Indian. Most have extended opening hours in the peak summer period.

Bay Kebabs, cnr Jonson and Lawson streets. Generous falafel rolls and gourmet kebabs are the thing to have here. Eat sitting on the stools inside, or take away. Daily 10am until late.
The Beach Café, Clarkes Beach (℡ 02/6685 7598). A good place for breakfast after a morning

stroll, open from 7.30am. Serves eclectic dinner choices in the summer.

Byron Thai, 32 Lawson St (☎02/6685 8453). Excellent Thai restaurant with a palm-garden dining area. Loads of choice for vegetarians. Moderate prices. Licensed. Daily from 5.30pm.

The Byronian, 58 Jonson St. This café, frequented by scribbling locals, has a lively atmosphere with lots of chat over good coffee. An attractive front courtyard next to a green park. Early, good-value breakfasts. BYO. Daily 7.30am–4pm.

Café D.O.C., Middleton St. Far from the madding crowds in a local bit of town, this great café is the best in the centre for huge bowls of muesli with fruit and other breakfasty things. Open daily.

Cocomangas, 32 Jonson St (☎02/6685 8493). Philippines-inspired restaurant which turns into a dance spot with theme nights after dark (Mon is 1970s night). There's an impressive wine list. Mon–Sat 5pm–late.

Earth 'n' Sea Pizzas, cnr Lawson and Jonson streets. A favourite place to eat in Byron. Toppings are unusual and imaginative: try "Mullumbimby Madness", with mushrooms, of course. Generous and affordable pasta too, or there's a $10 all-you-can-eat special on Wed nights. BYO and licensed. Daily from 5.30pm.

Fast Eddys Juice Bar, Jonson St. A scrumptious entirely vegetarian sandwich menu, plus delicious smoothies, freshly-squeezed juices and sweet things.

Fins, at the *Beach Hotel*, cnr Jonson and Bay streets (☎02/6685 5029). A hugely popular and very pricey brasserie with an extensive people-watching verandah overlooking the ocean. Mainly fish and vegetarian dishes, with Moroccan and Southern European twists. Booking advised.

Fresh, 7 Johnson St. A recommended and very

funky place to try oriental salads, excellent slices and juices or simply to hang out over a coffee. Evening meals are a delight.

Misaki Byron, 11 Fletcher St (☎02/6685 7966). An excellent Japanese restaurant with minimalist design in a pleasant brick courtyard, serving everything from sushi to noodles. Expensive, but BYO; bookings required. Tues–Sat 6pm–late, plus Wed–Fri 11.30am–2.30pm.

Oh! Delhi, Bay Centre Arcade, upstairs, 6 Lawson St (☎02/6685 6251). Byron's best curry house and takeaway. BYO and licensed. Nightly dinner, with live Indian music and belly-dancing Thurs, Fri & Sat.

The Piggery Supernatural Food, Arts Factory, Skinners Shoot Rd (☎02/6685 5833). Don't be fooled by the name – this is a popular vegetarian place in a vast setting, retaining the open rafters of the building's early days as – ironically – a meat-works. Cheap and candlelit. BYO.

Switch, Childe St, next to *Belongil Beach House*. Another great oceanfront place for breakfast, lunch and dinner, though the sea view is behind beach-front bush. There are outside tables, and frequent avant-garde spoken word, cinema and music nights. BYO. Daily 8am–9pm.

Thai Noodle Bar, 24 Jonson St. Moderately priced fresh noodles wok-fried; you select the fresh ingredients. Also Malaysian-style laksa (noodle soup). Good selection of vegetarian dishes. Small bar-style eating area, but primarily a take-away place. Mon–Sat 10am–6pm.

Toscani's Ristorante, cnr Jonson and Marvell streets (☎02/6685 7320). A sophisticated, multi-award-winning Italian restaurant in an architecturally innovative building. Doubles as a café, with every imaginable kind of Italian coffee. Expensive, though there are coffee and cake specials. Licensed. Live music on Wed. Open noon–midnight; closed Tues.

Entertainment and nightlife

The weekly free community newspaper, *The Byron Shire Echo*, has a comprehensive gig guide. There's plenty of activity in summer: **New Year's Eve** is such a big event that the council has taken to closing the town off – so come early. The huge outdoor **Annual Byron Bay Arts and Music Festival** is normally held for three days in early January but may be moving to February; it takes over Belongil Fields with several stages, a rave field, an all-night cinema, a food fair, market stalls and workshops; to find out exact dates, call the tourist information centre (☎02/6685 5980). Tickets can be bought in advance from independent record outlets around Australia.

Beach Hotel, cnr Jonson and Bay streets (☎02/6685 6402). Owned by John Cornell, who played Paul Hogan's sidekick in a 1970s Australian comedy series, this big and smart pub is superbly sited right opposite Main Beach with a huge terrace beer garden, bistro and restaurant,

and attracts a cross-section of locals. Live music (often free), including jazz sessions on Sunday afternoon.

The Car Park, The Plaza, Jonson St (☎02/6685 6170). Late-night dance club which also hosts laser shows and comedy. Open until 3am.

Tours from Byron Bay

There are many **tours** to the rainforest, waterfalls and national parks in the hinterland around Byron Bay (see "Far North Coast Hinterland", p.312, for details of destinations mentioned). All tours and activities can be booked at Byron Bus & Backpacker Centre, next to the tourist office (daily 7am–7pm; ℡02/6685 5517) who also provide currency exchange and car-rental (from $44/day including 100km mileage) services. Below are listed some of the more specialist and unusual tour operators.

Byron Bay Motorcycle Tours (℡02/6685 6304, ℮rideon@nor.com.au). Whizz around the beaches and hinterland on the back of a Harley-Davidson (1hr for $78, half-day for $214; summer only).

Byron Bay Sea Kayaks (℡02/6685 5830). Dolphin-watching from sea level in two-person boats, leaving at 8.30am & 1.30pm ($40 including breakfast or afternoon tea).

Byron Bay Walking Tours (℡02/6687 1112, ℮walknorth@mullum.com.au). These ten- to fifteen-kilometre hikes change daily, leaving at 8.30am to take in the likes of Nightcap National Park, Minyon Falls and the Angourie coast ($46–88 per person including lunch).

Jim's Alternative Tours (℡02/6685 7720). Tours aimed at presenting a positive, accurate portrayal of the hinterland "back to the land" movement. The tours visit Nimbin and Minyon Falls, with opportunities for swimming ($25). They can also help transport you to the Sunday markets at The Channon ($10) and Bangalow ($5), with more flexible times than other operators.

Mick's Bay to Bush Tours (℡02/6685 6889). The longest-established of Byron Bay's alternative tours, offering the popular Rainbow Trip which takes in Nimbin and Minyon Falls ($30).

Never Never Safaris (℡02/6679 1575 or 07/5539 9110, ℗www.neverneversafaris.com.au). Highly recommended ecotourism from a top-quality operator, with pick-ups in Brisbane, Byron and Murwillumbah. Informative day-trips into the Border Ranges World Heritage rainforest, plus two-day "Wildlife, Winery & Rock" tours; and longer trips to Bald Rock and outback Lightning Ridge.

Nimbin Explorer Tours (℡02/6689 1577). Yet another tour operator doing the Nimbin thing, but this time via Protestor's Falls, with an emphasis on the environment ($30 including lunch).

Rockhoppers Mountain Bike Adventures (℡02/6685 7142). Exhilarating, 24-speed, environmentally-aware mountain biking through rainforest, taking in swimming holes, waterfalls and lookouts. They are licensed by the National Parks and Wildlife service, and the $65 cost includes drinks, snacks and a BBQ lunch.

Chincogan Tavern, Burringbar St, Mullumbimby (℡02/6684 1550). Bands on Friday night.

Great Northern Hotel, Jonson St (℡02/6685 6454). Something for everyone: a front room with pool tables, a typically blokish public bar and *The Backroom*, a large stylish space that doubles as an Italian restaurant and a music venue with big-name Australian bands playing three or four times a week. Open till 1am nightly.

La La Land, Lawson St. If the hair wraps and tie-dye brigade are making you ill, then try this Byron Bay branch of a Melbourne institution; a place for sipping cocktails and wearing black. Sushi, dips and pizza available for "grazing". Daily 7pm–1am.

Pighouse Flicks, Old Piggery, Skinners Shoot Rd (℡02/6685 5828). "The Byron Cinema Experience" shows a hand-picked bill of latest-release films with the emphasis on the quirky and the first-rate, with two to three films nightly and deck chairs or sofas for seating. The price is $10.50 per film with a discount if you eat first at their great vegetarian restaurant.

Listings

Bike rental Many hostels have either free or rentable bikes for guests; otherwise try Let's Go Bikes, 93 Jonson St, opposite Woolworths (℡02/6685 6067; also rollerblades), which charges around $20 a day for a mountain bike. A cycling track runs from Byron to Suffolk Park via Broken Head nature reserve (8km one-way). Hinterland tours are organized by Backcountry Cycling (see box above).

Books Persephone's Window, cnr Byron and

Fletcher streets, has a small but well-chosen selection of quality literature and serves excellent coffee. They will give readers a discount on production of a *Rough Guide*. Second Reading Books on Byron St are good for secondhand bargains.

Buses Booking for McCafferty's, Greyhound, Kirklands and Premier, through Byron Bus & Backpacker Centre, 84 Jonson St (☎02/6685 5517). Kirklands goes daily to Brisbane, and to Ballina (with stops at Murwillumbah and Tweed Heads), also daily to Lismore and Casino; bookings through Cape Byron Travel, 6 Lawson St (☎02/6685 6262). Blanch's Coaches (☎02/6686 2144) runs south to Ballina via Suffolk Park, Bangalow and Lennox Head, and north to Mullimbimby – buy your ticket on the bus.

Car rental Byron Car Rentals (☎02/6685 6345); Byron Odyssey (free call ☎1800 771 244, ☯www.byronodyssey.com.au); Earth Car Rental (☎02/6685 7472); Hertz (☎02/6685 6522).

Diving Most dive schools offer complete scuba-diving courses, together with more affordable one-day courses and daily snorkelling trips (around $30). Byron Bay Dive Centre & Bayside Scuba, cnr Lawson and Fletcher streets (☎02/6685 8333 or free call 1800 243 483), also does a good-value, one-day course for $115 including all equipment; Sundive, Middleton St (☎02/6685 7755), is a small, friendly outfit. If you're already trained, one dive at Julian Rocks, with gear, costs from $75, two dives $105.

Environment Byron Bay Environment Centre, Shop 10, The Plaza (☎02/6685 7066).

Gay and lesbian information Tropical Fruits is a social group for gays and lesbians, holding dance parties every few weeks in halls around the area; the Fruitline (☎02/6622 4353) gives recorded information on upcoming events.

Hang-gliding Tandem take-offs (30min $130) and microlights (15min $70; 30min $135) from Byron's lighthouse point. Call Skylimit (☎02/6684 3711) for aeronautical info.

Horse riding Pegasus (☎02/6687 1446) charge $35 for one hour and $55 for two hours. Combined riding and canoeing trips cost $45 per hour. Seahorses Riding Centre, 9 Boarder St (☎02/6680 8155), offers lessons for $60 per half-day. Rides include beach, rainforest, sunrise and sunset tours ($45).

Hospital ☎02/6685 6200.

Internet access Facilities are available all over town, but *Global Gossip*, by the Information centre on Lawson Street (daily 8am–midnight), has the most reliable connection and the best rates.

Laundries You can use the laundry at most accommodation; otherwise try Byron Dry Cleaners and Laundrette, 42 Jonson St (daily 7am–7pm), with both self-service and service washes available, or the unattended self-service laundry on Marvell St (daily 7am–7pm).

Left luggage Byron Bus & Backpacker Centre, next to the tourist information centre, will mind bags for 24 hours for $3 (daily 7am–6.30pm).

Post office Next door to the Community Centre on Jonson St (postcode NSW 2481).

Surfing Many hostels provide free boards. For surf lessons the best outfits are the professional East Coast Surf School (☎02/6685 5989 or 015/257 243; $290 for a weekend surf camp), with safety-conscious sports science graduates teaching not just technique but how to read the surf; Byron Bay Surf School, at 84 Jonson St (☎02/6685 7536 or free call 1800 707 274, ☯www.byron–bay.com/surf–school), rents out surf gear and also offers 3hr lessons from $33 with free pick-ups daily for classes at 9am, 11am, 1pm and 3pm.

Taxi Byron Taxi & Limousines (☎02/6685 5008). There's a taxi rank on Jonson St, opposite the *Great Northern Hotel*.

Travel agent Byron Bay Travel Centre, Shop 4, 52 Jonson St (☎02/6685 6733), is a general travel agent and STA agent which deals with bus bookings and passes; also sells YHA and VIP membership. Jetset, cnr Jonson and Marvell streets (☎02/6685 6554), can revalidate tickets and book international and domestic flights.

Tweed Heads

From Brunswick Heads, the Pacific Highway heads around 30km inland to Murwillumbah (see p.316) and then a further 30km to the coast at **TWEED HEADS**. Although officially still part of New South Wales, Tweed Heads – the twin city of Coolangatta in Queensland (see p.429) – is for all practical purposes part of the **Gold Coast**. It certainly looks the part: high-rise buildings, concrete apartment blocks and shopping centres vie for space with grandiose club buildings and a roadscape of advertising billboards in gaudy colours. From the shore the jagged skyline of Surfers Paradise can be seen in the distance. In its favour, it does have lots of places to stay (motels are cheaper here than further north), and even more opportunities to eat and drink – not to mention the opportunity to **gamble**, an activity that was once banned in Queensland. **Clubs** and casinos opened up just across the border to cash in: one of the biggest, brightest and longest-established of these is the *Twin Towns RSL Club* (℡ 07/5536 2277) on Wharf Street, whose special offers on cheap food and drink can be a good deal, so long as you don't lose too much in the machines along the way.

One of the few other attractions is the **Minjungbal Aboriginal Cultural Museum**, on Kirkwood Road in South Tweed Heads (daily 10am–4pm; $6), where detailed exhibits and videos illustrate how Aboriginal people lived off this stretch of the coast; near the museum, a signposted boardwalk leads past an old bora ring – a sacred site used in initiation ceremonies. Ironically, the **Captain Cook Memorial Lighthouse** on **Point Danger** celebrates the very event that signalled the demise of Aboriginal culture in these parts: right at the state border, it was erected for the Cook bicentenary celebrations in 1970. Cook gave Point Danger its name after nearly running aground on it, and **Mount Warning** (see p.317) got its name at the same time – as a landmark to help sailors navigate around the point.

Practicalities

The **Tweed Heads Visitors Centre** is at 4 Wharf St (Mon–Fri 9am–5pm, Sat 9am–noon; ℡ 07/5536 4244, free call information line Sat noon–5pm, Sun 10am–4pm ℡ 1800 674 414, Ⓦ www.twintowns.com.au); they also have information on the rest of the Gold Coast. Arriving at Coolangatta airport, **buses** generally make a beeline for the resort strip in Queensland; Kirklands stops at Coolangatta Transit Centre en route between Lismore and Brisbane; Surfside Buslines (℡ 07/5536 7666) runs local services up and down the Gold Coast, and to Murwillumbah.

Should you want to **stay**, there are dozens of motels, caravan parks and holiday apartments strung out along the highway, though there's even more choice over the border and you're probably better off continuing on to Surfers Paradise (see p.421) for the full Gold Coast experience – if that's what you're after. For something less crass, head 20km south down the Coast Road to **Cabarita Beach** near Bogangar where you'll find the *VIP/Emu Park Backpackers Resort* (℡ 02/6676 1190, Ⓦ www.tropicalnsw.com.au/accommodation/emuparklodge; rooms ❸, dorms ❶), a good **hostel** which has internet access, a swap library, laundry, free use of bikes and boards, surfing lessons and trips to Mount Warning; pay for two nights and you get the third free. The village has a pub and several eating places. Back in Tweed Heads itself, it's not hard to find something to **eat**: if the clubs don't appeal, head for oceanfront Marine Parade, where there's everything from takeaway pizza to *Reggae's* (℡ 07/5599 0000) in the modern *Calypso Plaza Resort*.

Far North Coast Hinterland

The beautiful area inland from the far north coast, between artist-filled **Lismore** in the fertile Richmond River valley to the south, and staid **Murwillumbah** in the even lusher valley of the Tweed River near the Queensland border, is known as the **Far North Coast Hinterland**. But pioneers dubbed this region – once covered in **rainforest** that included species of flora extant from the era of the ancient supercontinent of **Gondwanaland**

– the Big Scrub. The hinterland's three national parks, plus several reserves, are World Heritage-listed, protecting pockets of rainforest which the settlers never managed to log, and which protesters helped to save in the first successful anti-logging demonstration in Australia, in 1979.

Mount Warning – Wollumbin or "cloud catcher" to the Bandjalung Aborigines – is what remains of the central magma chamber of a four-thousand-square-kilometre, shield-shaped volcano; from this 1157-metre peak, where the sun's rays first strike Australia, dazzling views reveal the area's geographic features. **Mount Warning National Park** rises in the middle of a massive **caldera** eroded on the eastern side into a huge bowl, where the Tweed River flows to the sea through the mostly agricultural patchwork of the valley floor. The northwest rim section consists of the McPherson and Tweed ranges, in the **Border Ranges National Park**; the southern section is within the **Nightcap National Park**, near countercultural **Nimbin**, and **The Channon** – one of many villages in "the hills" and famous for hosting the largest, most colourful **market** in the area.

Justice Bus Service (☎02/6621 6308) runs daily between Lismore and Murwillumbah via Nimbin. From Byron Bay, there are several tours of the hinterland, and those that stop at Nimbin can be a convenient way to get there (see below).

Lismore and around

On the Bruxner Highway 65km inland from Ballina, **LISMORE** is the principal town of northeast New South Wales and the commercial focus of the fertile Richmond River valley, surrounded by prosperous dairy and farming country. This is one of the most densely populated rural areas in Australia, and has been since the early days of the colony. In the nineteenth century Lismore was an important river port for the **timber** trade, as lumberjacks cut their way through the dense forest of the valley – the so-called Big Scrub – before moving up to the steep slopes of the McPherson Ranges near the Queensland border. Local red cedar, especially, was much sought after. There's still a fair amount of forestry in the region, but these days the economic mainstay is dairy farming and cattle breeding, along with a rapidly growing tropical agriculture sector: bananas, sugar cane, avocados, tropical fruit and macadamia nuts. The Rainbow Region organic market takes place at the Lismore Showground on Tuesdays.

For all the intense agriculture, however, this is not your typical Ocker backwater; the city of 46,000 even has its own **Southern Cross University**, which includes a Koala Hospital on its grounds. Since the alternative-lifestyle seekers discovered the northeast in the 1970s, **cultural life** has flourished and jewellers, potters, painters, graphic artists, sculptors and other arts-and-crafts people who have settled here have established a whole network of shops and galleries where they can sell their work. Every weekend they all come together for the region's **Art and Craft Expo**; at other times the **Regional Art Gallery**, 131 Molesworth St (Tues–Fri 10am–4pm, Sat & Sun 10.30am–2.30pm; free), is the best place to get an overview. The **Historical Museum**, on the same street (Mon–Fri 10am–4pm), houses an interesting, if somewhat motley, collection of pioneer relics and photographic records of the region's history. An annual **Folk Festival** with the best of the local and national bands takes place over the October long weekend (for details, call Jylie Jackson on ☎02/6621 7537).

Practicalities

Lismore is the home base of Kirklands **buses** (☎02/6621 9299 or 1300/367 077), who, along with Premier (☎02/9281 2232) and Greyhound (☎13 2030), stop here on the Sydney–Brisbane route; their terminal is on Molesworth Street. Lismore is also on a branch line of the Sydney–Murwillumbah **train** route; trains from Brisbane call in at Casino, 31km southwest (see p.315), from where there's a connecting bus. You can **fly** from Sydney with Hazelton (℡ 13 1713); if you've booked accommodation, you'll normally be picked up from the airport; there are **car rental** desks here, as well as branches of the usual multinational agencies on Dawson Street. For details of what's going on locally, head for the Lismore **Visitor and Heritage Centre**, at the corner of Molesworth and Ballina streets (daily 9am–4.30pm; ℡ 02/6622 0122, ⓦ www.liscity.nsw.gov.au), where there's also an indoor rainforest display, a cultural gallery with the works of 100 artists and craftspersons and a history exhibit; ask here about **river cruises**.

There's a wide range of **accommodation** choices in the Lismore region, including hostels, hotels, motels, B&Bs and caravan parks, most of which can be booked through the Visitor and Heritage Centre. The friendliest place to stay is the *VIP/Lismore Backpackers*, 14 Ewing St (℡ 02/6621 6118, ⓕ 6622 8090; rooms ❸, dorms ❶), a pleasant **hostel** which will pick you up from the bus, train station or airport, or from Byron Bay by arrangement; they also organize tours to the surrounding national parks, and take WWOOF volunteers. Note that no smoking or drinking is permitted in the hostel. An alternative is the newly renovated *Civic Hotel* at 210 Molesworth St (℡ 02/6621 2537; rooms ❸). A couple of kilometres south of town, the *Lismore Lake Caravan Park*, Bruxner Highway (℡ 02/6621 2585; cabins ❸), has inexpensive campsites, a pool, barbecue, children's playground and small shop.

Lismore isn't a bad place to **eat**, and has a couple of excellent cafés and cosmopolitan restaurants. The favoured haunt of artists is *Caddies Coffee Company*, at 20–24 Carrington St, which has excellent bagels, *panini*, salads and coffee, while retro fans should head for the *Mecca Cafe* in the mall on Magellan Street, for tasty lunchtime snacks. Vegans and juice freaks will love *20,000 Cows Cafe* on Bridge Street, and *Dr Juice*, a vegetarian healthy heaven, just round the corner on Keen Street. If meatballs are more tempting than mushrooms, there are a number of fine Italian establishments, including *Paupiettes* on Ballina Street (℡ 02/6621 6135) for à la carte dining and *Cafe Giardino* on Keen Street (℡ 02/6622 4664). *Thai Lotus* at 207 Ballina St (℡ 02/6622 0062) is also recommended.

The presence of students means there's some **nightlife** in Lismore. Most of the pubs feature live bands throughout the week, and the area is developing a bit of a reputation for its local musical talent: *Maggie Moore's* pub at 29 Molesworth St hosts bands on Thursdays, Fridays and Saturdays, and *Mary Gilhooley's Irish Pub & Restaurant* at the corner of Keen and Woodlark streets is also very popular. There are also a couple of nightclubs: the best music is played at the *Powerhouse* on Molesworth Street. For other diversions, there's a four-screen **cinema** in town, on the corner of Keen and Zadoc streets (℡ 02/6622 4350).

Around Lismore

To explore the country **around Lismore** you really need your own vehicle, though tours do depart from Byron Bay (see p.304). Most Sundays there's a **market** in at least one of the villages, providing a taste of the area's colourful alternative lifestyle – the big ones are in the hilltop village of The Channon on the second Sunday of the month, and in Nimbin on the last (see opposite). The halls in the various towns have dances and live music, and you may be lucky enough to be invited to a legendary hill party involving live bands, fire-eaters and drumming and dancing till dawn – there's usually one happening somewhere every weekend, usually in the same place as the market.

CASINO, around 30km southwest of Lismore, is a small country town on the Richmond River from where route 91 follows the rail lines south towards Grafton, or north through **KYOGLE**, with its Buddhist temple and retreat, into Queensland. One of the most scenic drives in New South Wales is the short round-trip over the mountainous, winding country roads north and northeast of Lismore to Nimbin (see below), The Channon (see below), and Clunes, and then via Eltham and Bexhill, with superb views from the ridges and hilltops. Accessible via Nimbin, with the peak of Mount Nardi (800m) visible 12km beyond the town, is **Nightcap Range National Park**, a World Heritage-listed park with several walking trails from the summit.

Nimbin and around

NIMBIN, site of the famed Aquarius Festival which launched Australian hippie culture in 1973, is understandably more reluctant than most towns to move out of its 1970s time warp; its house facades and shopfronts are painted in lurid, psychedelic designs, its small stores sell health food, incense sticks and patchouli oil, and many of its three hundred locals have stuck to their 1970s dress code too. Yet the range of Nimbin's cafés and restaurants, and the visible switch from marijuana to heroin use, certainly marks it as a place of the 1990s. Many visitors may want to get out of town as quickly as possible, for you'll invariably be offered dope, and probably heroin, as soon as you set foot on the street. While there is not really any great danger, lone travellers may find this particularly threatening (a simple "no thanks" is usually enough to deter them).

Something akin to a "hippie hall of fame", the **Nimbin Museum** at 62 Cullen St (hours as they please but usually daily; ☎02/6689 1123; $2 donation) is certainly worth a visit. It's a weird and wonderful living museum run by hippies, with plenty of local history relating to the Aquarius Festival, Bundjalung Aboriginal culture, and a huge stone phallus in the centre of one room. Ask here about the **Annual Hemp Mardi Gras and Drug Law Reform Festival**, held around May 1; the place is booked up well in advance so be prepared to camp. If you have affinities with the Green movement, the **Nimbin Environmental Centre**, also on Cullen Street, might interest you: they publicize and campaign on environmental issues, and can also arrange visits to the **Permaculture Centre**, a showcase for a system of sustainable agriculture that is gaining ground worldwide but especially in developing countries. The **Hemp Embassy** (Ⓦ www.nrg.com.au/~hemp) down the lane next to the pub is worth a visit too for its display on the uses of hemp; its owners also run the *Hemp Bar* next door, and organize the town's Mardi Gras, held in the first weekend of May.

THE CHANNON, a 26-kilometre drive southwest of Nimbin, is a pretty village on the banks of **Terania Creek** with a well-known monthly market, and a tavern, teahouse, craft shop and art gallery in an old butter factory. A fourteen-kilometre drive along the unsealed Terania Creek Road brings you to **Protestors Falls**, perhaps the Nimbin area's most famous environmental attraction, saved by a 1979 protest that was dubbed a "hippie guerrilla struggle" by a *Rolling Stone* article of the period. The first successful anti-logging campaign in Australia saved this rainforest valley filled with ancient brush box trees. The falls, named after the dispute, are a seven-hundred-metre walk from the picnic area, and the waterhole underneath is perfect for swimming. You are permitted to **camp** for one night only at Terania Creek – but no open fires are allowed; otherwise you can head back to The Channon, where you can stay at the village campsite on the banks of the creek (☎02/6688 6321) or at *Terania Park* (☎02/6688 6121; cabins ❾), a scenic caravan park with cabins and campsites. Terania Creek is near the western edge of **Whian Whian State Forest**; on the forest's southeastern edge (reached via Mullumbimby or Dunoon), further watery delights are provided by the one-hundred-metre cascade of **Minyon Falls**.

Practicalities

There are a number of **places to stay** in and near Nimbin. *Granny's Farm Backpackers & Camping* (T 02/6689 1333; rooms ❷, dorms ❶), very close to town but in a peaceful farm setting, is an easy-going place with log fires in winter and a swimming pool in summer; you can choose to camp or stay in the farm's own tepee. The other hostel option is the equally good *Rainbow Retreat* (T 02/6689 1262, W http://skybusiness.com/rainbowretreat; ❶), a more intimate place in a bush setting by Goolmanger Creek, with a resident platypus and a swimming hole nearby. The friendly owner also runs the Green Frog, a courtesy bus service from Byron (departs from opposite the bus station at 2pm on Mon, Wed & Fri). The very comfortable, beautifully decorated *Grey Gum Lodge*, 2 High St (T & F 02/6689 1713, W www.nrg.com.au/~nimbin/greygum; ❸–❹), is a relaxed guesthouse right in town, with its own excellent restaurant and a saltwater swimming pool. The *Nimbin Motel*, 413 Crofton Rd (T 02/6689 1420; ❷), 4km north of town near Nightcap National Park, also has a small pool.

Nimbin's main strip, Cullen Street, is full of good **places to eat** – though the once-legendary *Rainbow Cafe* closes (and opens up again) every couple of months. The *Nimbin Cafe*, which invites its visitors to come "experience the joint", has lots of tasty munchies – yummy savouries, hot chocolate, coffee and cakes, while *The E–Bar* offers Italian coffee, smoothies and excellent breakfast fare, as well as internet access. Finally, the *Nimbin Trattoria & Pizzeria* serves up generous servings of pizza, pasta and salad nightly from 5pm (BYO).

In terms of **nightlife and entertainment**, Nimbin's only drinking hole is the *Freemason's Hotel* on Cullen Street, which sees plenty of action (the bistro also serves good counter meals). The cultural heart of town is the small Bush Theatre (T 02/6689 1111), located in an old butter factory over the bridge opposite *Granny's Farm* hostel. Movies are shown here at weekends: call or check town notice boards for details.

Murwillumbah and around

The next major stop on the Pacific Highway is **MURWILLUMBAH**, a quiet, inland town on a bend of the Tweed River, a little over 30km north of Byron Bay, which makes a good base for exploring some of the beautiful Tweed Valley and the mountains that extend to the Queensland border.

Murwillumbah is the terminus of the coastal branch **rail** line from Sydney (one train daily in each direction), and almost all buses on the north coast route stop here. The **tourist information** office is located in the **Rainforest Heritage Centre** on Alma Street (Mon–Sat 9am–4.30pm, Sun 9.30am–4pm; T 02/6672 1340), and has information on the immediate area and on several other magnificent national parks in the vicinity. It's worth dropping by the **Tweed River Regional Art Gallery** on Tumbulgum Road, by Nicholls Park on the river (Wed–Sun 10am–5pm; free). It displays the winners of the Doug Moran National Portrait Prize, which originated here, as well as the work of local artists and travelling exhibitions.

The Tweed Valley and the surrounding area close to the Queensland border are among the most beautiful in New South Wales, ringed by mountain ranges that are actually the remains of an extinct volcano. Some twenty million years ago a huge shield **volcano** (a flat, shield-shaped landform rather than a cone-shaped peak) spewed lava through a central vent onto the surrounding plain. Erosion carved out an enormous bowl around the centre of the resultant mass of lava, while the more resistant rocks around the edges stood firm – these are now the **Nightcap**, **Border** and **McPherson ranges**, the outer rim of a vast bowl. Right at its heart is **Mount Warning** (1150m), the original vent of the volcano, whose unmistakeable, twisted profile rises like a sentinel from the Tweed Valley. A well-marked **bushwalking track** leads to the top from a car park just off the national park access road, itself a turn-off from the road to Uki, southwest of town. The path is extremely steep in its final stages (allow at least 4hr there and back) but you're rewarded by a sweeping view over the ranges of the volcanic rim and across the Tweed Valley to the Pacific.

There's a less strenuous, signposted 64-kilometre scenic drive through the **Tweed Valley**, which takes in some of its best features. A patchwork of sugar-cane fields and tropical fruit plantations is testimony to the fertility of the volcanic soil; there's even a tea plantation. Between the villages of Tumbulgum and Duranbah, the **big avocado** lures the wild-at-heart towards **Avocado Adventureland** on Duranbah Road (daily 10am–5pm; free admission, train and bus rides extra), a plantation that grows avocados, macadamia nuts and many kinds of tropical fruit, and has been turned into a miniature theme park where you can ride through the plantation in open-air buses and miniature trains, or cruise around on man-made "tropical canals". There are canoes and aqua-bikes for rent, an animal park and playground, a restaurant and café, as well as a fruit market selling plantation produce. Slightly less commercial are the tours given during the cane-harvesting season at **Condong Sugar Mill**, on the Tweed River about 5km north of Murwillumbah (guided tours July–Nov Tues–Thurs 9am–3pm; $5.50). The turn-off for the **Tree Tops Environment Centre** (daily 10am–5pm; free) is opposite the sugar mill; the centre is the home of Griffith Furniture, which creates beautiful designs from salvaged native timber such as red cedar, using traditional timber-working techniques that you can observe in the workshop. Halfway between Nimbin and Murwillumbah, **UKI** is a pretty little village with views of Mount Warning; there's a small relaxed **market** here on the third Sunday of each month. A stall sells locally grown organic coffee, or you can sample some at the *Uki Trading Post* (daily 9am–5pm).

Practicalities

Places to stay in Murwillumbah include the recently restored *Imperial Hotel* at 115 Main St (℡02/6672 1036; ❸), a grand old building right in the centre of town with good-value singles, an excellent bistro and a guest kitchen. *Mount Warning Murwillumbah Backpackers*, 1 Tumbulgum Rd (℡02/6672 3763; rooms ❸, dorms ❶), is a truly wonderful find – a cosy hostel in an old sea-captain's home leaning over the river, where free ice cream is served every evening at 8pm. The hostel has private access for swimming; you can also rent their bikes or use their canoes or rowing boat for free. Alternatively, make the most of the countryside by staying in rural or **farmstay** accommodation: *Midginbil Hill Holiday Farm* (℡02/6679 7158, ℻6679 7120; lodges ❸, bunkhouses ❶, plus camping), is a cattle station 30km west near Mount Warning, offering activities such as horse riding, canoeing and archery. *Mount Warning Forest Hideaway* on Byrill Creek Road, near Uki (℡02/6679 7277, ⊛www.foresthideaway.com.au; ❺–❻), consists of small, motel-style units each with a double bed and bunks, fridge and cooking facilities, and there's a swimming pool too.

Places to eat include the old-fashioned *Austral Cafe*, an eat-in bakery on Main Street. *Margherita's Cantina*, also on Main Street, serves salads, lunches and breakfast from 7.30am, while the BYO *South of the Border* is a favourite with backpackers for its inexpensive Mexican food (closed Mon & Tues). The *Imperial Hotel* on Main Street serves the best bistro food in town.

The New England Plateau

The **New England Plateau** rises parallel to the coast in the northeast of New South Wales, extending from the northern end of the Hunter Valley to the Queensland border. At the top it's between 1000m and 1400m above sea level, and on the eastern edge an escarpment falls away steeply towards the coast. This eastern rim consists of steep slopes and precipitous cliff faces, deep gorges and thickly forested valleys, and because of its inaccessibility has remained a largely undisturbed wilderness. Streams and rivers from the highlands tumble over the rocks, and numerous mighty waterfalls pour into narrow gorges. On the plateau itself the scene is far more peaceful, as sheep and cattle graze on the undulating highland. Because of the altitude, the **climate** up here is fundamentally different from the subtropical coast, a mere 150km or so away: winters are cold and frosty, with occasional snowfalls, while in summer the fresh, dry air can offer welcome relief after the heat and humidity of the coast. Even during a summer heatwave, when the daytime temperature might reach 30°C, the nights will be pleasantly cool. Perhaps it was this that attracted the mainly Scottish immigrants who – despite the name – transformed the New England highlands into pastures in the nineteenth century.

The **New England Highway**, one of the main links between Brisbane and Sydney, runs north through New England, passing all the major towns – Tamworth, Armidale, Glen Innes and Tenterfield. From any of these, good, sealed roads branch off towards the coast, and it's these minor roads that are especially worth exploring, with turn-offs leading to gorges, waterfalls and scenic lookouts. The area around Glen Innes and Inverell is rich in gemstones, yielding industrial diamonds, zircons and, above all, sapphires. Farms and stations all over the highlands provide **farmstay accommodation**, offering horse riding and other activities.

The area is well serviced by **bus**: Greyhound and McCafferty's have daily services between Sydney or Canberra and Brisbane and between Brisbane and Melbourne, both via New England; Keans Travel (☎02/9281 9366) operates daily between Sydney and Tenterfield via the Upper Hunter Valley; and Kings Bus Service (☎02/6562 4724) runs three times a week between Port Macquarie and Tamworth via Nambucca Heads, Coffs Harbour, Bellingen, Dorrigo, Armidale, Uralla and Walcha. There is also a daily **train** service between Sydney and Armidale via Tamworth.

The Upper Hunter Valley

The upper end of the Hunter Valley is Australia's main horse-breeding and thoroughbred area – indeed it claims to deal in as much horseflesh as anywhere in the world, with at least thirty stud farms. There are cattle- and sheep-breeding stations up here, too, while the fertile soils of the Upper Hunter also yield a harvest of cereals and fruits including, of course, grapes – see the box on p.208 for a sampling of Hunter Valley wineries.

The pretty township of **SCONE** is at the centre of the Hunter Valley horse trade, and you can get further details of the business from the **Scone Visitor**

Information Centre on the corner of Susan and Kelly streets (daily 9am–5pm; ⊤02/6545 1526, ⓔstic@scone.nsw.gov.au), where you'll also find an excellent internet café. The best time to visit, when everything's open, is during **Scone Horse Festival** – ten days in the middle of May – which features local prize specimens in horse shows, rodeos and races, along with more general cultural and artistic events. If you're planning to be in town at this time, be sure to book accommodation way in advance.

Lake Glenbawn, 15km east of Scone, makes a pleasant excursion. The dam holds back the waters of the Upper Hunter, storing up to 750,000 million litres for irrigation purposes. **Recreation facilities** at the reserve here include accommodation and boat rental: the lake is great for water-skiing, canoeing, sailing and fishing. Next to the kiosk, a small **museum** (open by appointment only – ask at the visitor information centre) exhibits relics from early pioneering days in the Hunter Valley. For a fine day-trip you can continue past the dam and climb to the plateau of the Barrington Tops (see p.284) to the national park of the same name, or you can go on towards the coast via Gloucester (about 150km from Scone).

Northeast of Scone is polo country, the haunt of mega-rich Australians such as the media mogul Kerry Packer. If you fancy watching the elitist sport in action, there are polo grounds at **GUNDY** and at **ELLERSTON**. At Gundy, you can have a drink at the classic green-tin-roofed *Linga Longa Hotel*. In between Gundy and Ellerston, **Belltrees** is the family estate of the White family, who gave the world the Nobel prize-winning novelist **Patrick White**. Belltrees Station is a collection of buildings, including the 1832 Semphill Cottage, set among pepper trees; there's even a small school established in 1879. Further along is the White mansion where the family still live, and if you can afford it you can stay at the country house next door, or in the mountain retreat where in later life Patrick White used to escape when he returned home to visit; there are also a couple of cheaper self-contained cottages sleeping four people (country house from $205 per person per night, including breakfast, dinner and tour of the property; mountain retreat $250 per person per night, including all meals and 4WD transfers; cottages $70–110, with a four-night minimum stay; ⊤02/6545 1688 or ⓕ6546 1122, ⓦwww.belltrees.com); polo tuition can be arranged as part of your stay.

Heading on towards the heart of the New England Plateau, you pass **Burning Mountain** about 20km north of Scone, near the village of Wingen. The smoking vents do not indicate volcanic activity but rather a seam of coal burning 30m under the surface: the fire was ignited naturally, perhaps by a lightning strike or spontaneous combustion, over a thousand years ago. The area, protected as a nature reserve, can be reached via a signposted **walking trail** that starts at the picnic grounds at the foot of the hill, just off the New England Highway; pick up the informative NPWS guide to the area's walking tracks from any NPWS office, or order it on ⊤02/6543 3533. Fourteen kilometres north of Wingen, **MURRURUNDI** marks the end of the Upper Hunter Valley. It's a pretty spot, enclosed by the Liverpool Ranges, and the *Cafe Telegraph* here makes a cheerful refreshment stop, with seats outside in the garden with the creek flowing past.

Practicalities

Trains from Sydney (one daily) and Newcastle (two daily) stop at Scone, and Greyhound and McCafferty's **buses** pass through. **Places to stay** in this area are widely scattered. Right in Scone the *Royal Hotel-Motel*, 119 Kelly St (⊤02/6545 1722, ⓕ6545 3245; ❷–❹), offers simple pub accommodation or fancier motel units – it also serves good counter meals. About halfway to Glenbawn Dam, on Segenhoe Road, is a delightful YHA **hostel** (⊤02/6545 2072, ⓔyhascone@hunterlink.com.au; rooms ❸, dorms ❶) in a former school;

you can rent bikes here to explore the countryside. Right at the lake, the *Lake Glenbawn Resort* (☎ 02/6543 7752; ❹–❺) has camping and three-bedroom cottages. In nearby Aberdeen, a recommended B&B is the *Segenhoe* (02/6543 7382, ⓦ www.segenhoebandb.com.au; ❼), a charming sandstone edifice from the early 1800s. If you're hungry for scones in Scone, then head to *Asser House Cafe* on Kelly Street – they also serve excellent coffee and tea. For entertainment, Scone's **Civic Theatre** (☎ 02/6541 1569) is an Art Deco movie palace with displays of memorabilia in the foyer.

Tamworth and around

TAMWORTH is the first city on the New England Plateau proper, a fair-sized place that's proud of its public buildings, parks and gardens. It also likes to refer to itself as the "City of Lights", having been the first in Australia to be fitted with electric street lighting, in 1888. To most Australians, however, Tamworth means **country music** – it's a sort of antipodean Nashville. The twelve-metre-high golden guitar in front of the **Golden Guitar Complex** (daily 9am–5pm; $5.50; ⓦ www.big-golden-guitar.com.au), on the southern edge of town, sums up the town's role as the C&W capital of Australasia. Inside the centre, you'll find waxwork figures of the great Australian country stars such as Chad Morgan, Buddy Williams, Smoky Dawson and his horse Flash, Slim Dusty, Reg Lindsay and Tex Morton. There's also a slightly incongruous collection of gems and minerals from the region – no rhinestones though. Afterwards, the *Longyard Hotel* next door is a handy place to weep in your beer for a while and, once a year, for a week at the end of January, it becomes the focus of the **Tamworth Country Music Festival** when fans from all over the country descend, packing out camping spots. Every pub, club and hall in town hosts music gigs, record launches and bush poetry, culminating in the presentation of the Australian country music awards – further information and bookings from Rural Press Events (☎ 02/6762 2399, ⓦ www.countrymusic.asn.au) or the visitors centre (see below). The final piece of the country puzzle is found at the corner of Brisbane Street and Kable Avenue, where the **Hands of Fame** cornerstone bears the palm-prints of more country greats. A glorious spoof, the Noses of Fame memorial, can be savoured over a beer at the *Tattersalls Hotel* on Peel Street.

Don't give up on Tamworth entirely if country music isn't your thing. The **Powerstation Museum** at 216 Peel St (Tues–Fri 9am–1pm, Sat & Sun by arrangement; free), celebrates those pioneering street lights, and there are numerous art galleries and crafts studios around town: the **Tamworth City Gallery**, housed in the Guy Kable Building on Marius Street (Mon–Fri 10am–5pm, Sat 9–11.30am, Sun 1–4pm; free) has a surprisingly good permanent exhibition. Natural attractions include the **Oxley Lookout and Nature Reserve** at the end of White Street, with panoramic views of the city and the Peel River Valley, and **Lake Keepit**, 56km northwest of the city, where you can rent boats and mess about on the water.

The former gold-mining township of **NUNDLE** lies some 60km southeast of town in the "hills of gold" – people still visit with picks, shovels and sieves in the hope of striking it lucky, and you can join them for a day. You no longer need to buy a fossicking licence but it's still worth dropping by the General Store on Jenkins Street; they'll point you in the right direction to start digging.

Practicalities

The big **Tamworth Visitor Information Centre** (Mon–Fri 8.30am–4.35pm, Sat & Sun 9am–5pm; ☎ 02/6755 4300, ⓦ www.tamworth.nsw.gov.au) is on the corner of Peel Street and Scots Road. Tamworth is well serviced by **bus**: Greyhound and McCafferty's run daily between Sydney or Canberra and Brisbane and between Brisbane and Melbourne. Kings Bus Service (T02/6562 4724) runs three times a week between Port Macquarie and Tamworth via Nambucca Heads, Coffs Harbour, Bellingen, Dorrigo, Armidale, Uralla and Walcha – you can book through the YHA. **Local buses** can get you to Nundle (Peel Valley Coaches T02/6766 4418) and Gunnedah (McPhersons Coaches T02/6767 7190), while Countrylink buses serve Narrabri, Moree, Armidale, Walcha, Inverell and Dubbo. A **train** arrives from Sydney daily en route to Armidale.

Accommodation

As you drive into Tamworth you'll pass a string of **motels** on the New England Highway – the only time you might have trouble finding a room is during the festival, when everything's booked out. An excellent choice is the friendly Tamworth **YHA hostel** at 169 Marius St, opposite the railway station (T02/6761 2600; rooms ❸, dorms ❶), which has internet access, a laundry and two lovely guest lounges; alternatively, the *Tamworth Hotel* on Marius Street, in the centre of town, offers simple pub accommodation and good counter meals (T02/6766 2923; ❸). If, however, you feel like staying somewhere a little more luxurious, the *Flag Inn Powerhouse Boutique*, on the New England Highway 1.5km northeast of the centre (T02/6766 7000, F6766 7748; ❼), has four-star facilities – room service, gym, swimming pool and sauna – but plenty of old-fashioned charm. The closest place for **campers** and caravanners is the *Paradise Caravan Park*, Peel Street (T02/6766 3120; cabins ❹, on-site vans ❷–❸), on the river about five-minutes' walk from the main part of town. Further out, 4km from town but right on the riverfront off the New England Highway, is the award-winning *Austin Tourist Park* (T02/6766 2380; cabins ❸), with a pool and children's playground. In **Nundle** there are rooms and meals on Jenkins Street: at the historic *Peel Inn* (T02/6769 3377, F6769 3307; ❷), where they also organize gold-panning, and at the very special *Jenkins Street Guest House* (T02/6769 3239, Wwww.bart.northnet.com.au/~ghnundle; ❸ full board), where you'll find polished wood floors, fresh flowers in all rooms and an excellent local chef. If you want a taste of Australian country living, *Leconfield* (T02/6769 4328, Wwww.leconfield.com) offer a five-day residential **Jackeroo and Jilleroo school** ($341), where you learn to ride and groom horses, shear and throw fleeces, lassoo, whip crack and go out mustering. They can also arrange pickups from Tamworth YHA.

Entertainment

There is a profusion of good but pricey Sydney-style **cafés** in Tamworth, and two of the best are on Peel Street: the *Old Vic Cafe* (Mon–Sat 9am–5pm, Sun 9am–2.30pm) at no. 261, and at no. 407 the atmospheric *Inland Cafe* (Mon–Wed 7am–6pm, Thurs 7am–6pm & 7–11pm, Sat 7–11pm, Sun 9am–5pm). For larger portions of perfectly good tucker, try the *Tamworth Hotel* on Marius Street; if you're just after a drink though, there's more fun to be had at the *Tudor Hotel* across the road. Outside festival time, you'll be disappointed if you think the town's **clubs and pubs** constantly resound to C&W twangings, but you can catch some acts on Thursday evening at the *Tamworth RSL Club* on Kable Avenue, and on the first Friday and third Sunday of the month in the *Tamworth Hotel*.

Armidale

The university city of **ARMIDALE**, halfway between Sydney and Brisbane, is something of a rarity in Australia, where most universities are based in the state capitals. About four thousand students are enrolled at the **University of New England**, which, together with a couple of famous boarding schools, provides an unexpected academic aspect in a place so far "up country". Armidale is a city of some natural beauty, especially in autumn when, with its church spires and many parks, it is embedded in a sea of red and golden leaves. At around 1000m, the climate is unpredictable and can be decidedly brisk in winter.

Beardy Street, the town centre's pedestrian mall, is flanked by quaint Australian country pubs with wide, iron-lace verandahs, and is an excellent place to start exploring. On the last Sunday of the month the mall comes alive with a 150-stall market complete with buskers, and the mall's cafés open their doors. One of the best ways to get around town is by **bike**: there's a signposted city tour, as well as a bike path to the **university campus**, 5km northwest of the city, where there are two small specialized museums (both free), a kangaroo and deer park, and the historic Booloominbah homestead, built in the 1880s as a fashionable gentlemen's residence and now housing the principal administration office. Back in the city centre, the **New England Regional Art Museum** on Kentucky Street (daily 10.30am–5pm; free) is worth a visit for its two collections of Australian art. Foremost is the Hinton Collection, a group of paintings from the 1880s to the 1940s that includes works by Arthur Streeton and Tom Roberts. The Coventry Collection, focusing on the second half of the twentieth century, also has some important works, among them a wild self-portrait by Brett Whitely. Next door, the arresting modern building with the distinctive ochre-coloured tin roof is the Aboriginal-run **Aboriginal Centre and Keeping Place** (Mon–Fri 9am–4.30pm, Sat & Sun 2–5pm; entrance fees vary), an educational, visual and performing arts centre that aims to foster the renewal and continuity of Aboriginal culture. Artefacts and interpretive material are on permanent display, and special exhibitions are shown. You might also want to visit the Armidale **Folk Museum**, at the corner of Rusden and Faulkner streets (daily 1–4pm; free), which has a collection of artefacts from the New England region and displays on local history, or take a two-hour **free bus tour** of the city with Heritage Trolley Tours (Mon–Fri 10am, Sat & Sun 10.30am, departing from the visitor information centre; free call ✆ 1800 627 736 to book).

Practicalities

Armidale has a helpful **Visitor Information Centre** at 82 Marsh St (Mon–Fri 9am–5pm, Sat 9am–4pm, Sun 10am–4pm; ✆ 02/6772 4655, ⓦ www.new-england.org/armidale). For details of the area's national parks (see pp.324–5), head for the NPWS in the McCarthy Building, 87 Faulkner St (✆ 02/6773 7211). The **bus** terminal is just by the information centre. Plenty of places offer **car rental** if you plan to explore the surrounding countryside, among them Budget (✆ 02/6771 1535) and Realistic Car Rentals (✆ 02/6772 3004). **Bikes** can be rented from Armidale Bicycle Centre, 248 Beardy St (✆ 02/6772 3718). For **taxis**, call Armidale Radio Taxis (✆ 13 1008).

The very pink, recently refurbished *Wicklow Hotel* (✆ 02/6772 2421; rooms ❷–❸, dorms ❶), on the corner of Marsh and Dumaresq streets opposite the bus terminal, offers **accommodation** for weary travellers. Other pubs include the *St Kilda Hotel* (✆ 02/6772 4459; ❷–❸ including breakfast) on the corner of Marsh and Rushden streets, with a guest lounge and full disabled facilities, and the *Royal Hotel* on the corner of Marsh Street (✆ 02/6772 2259; ❸). There are over twenty motels in Armidale: the information centre has the full list with prices. The most central upmarket choice is the *New England Motor Inn*, 100 Dumaresq St (✆ 02/6771 1011; ❺). For a taste of tranquillity, *Glenhope* on Red Gum Lane is an elegant B&B homestead set in a valley 4km northwest from

The Myall Creek massacre

In the first decades of the nineteenth century, when European settlers started to move up to the highlands and to use Aboriginal-occupied land on the plateau as sheep and cattle pasture, many of the local Aborigines fought back. Time and again bloody skirmishes flared up. The **Myall Creek massacre** is one of the few that has found a place in the history of white Australia, while innumerable others were never mentioned in genteel pioneer circles and have subsequently been erased from public memory.

For Aboriginal people, expulsion from the lands of their ancestors amounted to spiritual as well as physical dispossession, and they resisted as best they could: white stockmen staying in huts far away from pioneer townships or homesteads feared for their lives. In 1837 and 1838, Aborigines repeatedly ambushed and killed stockmen near the Gwydir and Namoi rivers. Then, during the absence of the overseer at Myall Creek Station, near present-day Inverell, twelve farm hands organized a raid in retribution, killing 28 Aborigines. In court, the farm hands were acquitted – public opinion saw nothing wrong with their deed, and neither did the jury. The case was later taken up again, however, and seven of the participants in the massacre were sentenced to death on the gallows.

the city (℡02/6772 1940; ❹). Alternatively, try *Poppy's Cottage* (℡02/6775 1277, ⓦ www.new-england.org/armidale; ❻), a private farm cottage just five-minutes' drive from town, with free port and chocolates, a well-stocked bookcase and an optional gourmet three-course dinner ($38 with wine). The cheapest motels are on the edge of the city: the *Armidale Rose Villa* is on the New England Highway 3km north of the centre (℡ & ⓕ 02/6772 3872; ❸). Further out, try *Pembroke Caravan and Leisure Park*, Grafton Street, on the corner of Cooks Road, 2km east of town (℡02/6772 6470, ⓕ6772 9804; cabins ❹–❺, on-site vans ❷), which has a swimming pool and tennis court; or *Highlander Van Village*, 76 Glen Innes Rd, 2km north of town (℡02/6772 4768, ⓔhvv@tpgi.com.au; cabins and units ❸–❹, on-site vans ❷), which has similar facilities.

Good, inexpensive **counter meals** are served at many of the grand old pubs on Beardy Street, including the *New England Hotel* and the *Imperial*. Amongst the town's better **restaurants** are the BYO *Jean Pierre's*, in the Beardy St mall, and the laid-back *Cafe Yannis* (℡02/6771 5810) in the East End mall. The most lauded of all, though, is the excellent *Archie's On the Park* at the *Moore Park Inn* on Uralla Road in South Armidale (℡02/6772 2358), which offers open fires and grandeur. There are several Chinese restaurants in town, including *Mun Hing* and *St Kilda Mandarin* on Beardy Street; *Eagle Boys Pizza* on Rusden Street (℡02/6772 2577 for deliveries) is open until late. The student population contributes to a **café** society of sorts: the light and airy *Cafe Midalé*, 173 Beardy St Mall, serves up Italian-style food – *focaccia*, *panini* and pasta of the day – while *Rumours on the Mall*, further down, offers good, inexpensive meals and sandwiches, plus a decent breakfast served until noon.

For an evening's **entertainment** visit the Belgrave Twin Cinema (℡02/6772 2856), which screens mainstream and alternative films, and has a café open until late.

Around Armidale

Surrounded by national parks and wild mountain scenery, Armidale makes a good base to stop over for a few days and explore, or perhaps try your hand at a spot of fossicking. The **New England National Park**, 85km east on the

Waterfall Way, and the several patchwork sections of the **Oxley Wild Rivers National Park**, exploit the beauty of the eastern edge of the plateau; gorges and spectacular waterfalls abound, although the falls may diminish to a trickle during prolonged dry spells. The most impressive of them are the **Wollomombi Falls**, just over 40km east of Armidale, off the road to Dorrigo; among the highest in Australia, they plunge 225m into a gorge. Nearby are the Chandler Falls, while **Ebor Falls**, a stunning double drop of the Guy Fawkes River in the national park of the same name, can be viewed from platforms just off Waterfall Way, another 40km beyond Wollomombi. Between Wollomombi and Ebor, **Point Lookout** in the New England National Park offers a truly wonderful panoramic view across the forested ranges. The road to the lookout is unsealed gravel, but is usually in reasonable condition, and there are simple **cabins** and bush **campsites** where you can stay overnight: phone the NPWS in Dorrigo (℡02/6657 2309) or Armidale (℡02/6773 7211) for further information – it's essential you book in advance. The rest of the park is virtually inaccessible wilderness.

On the way back to Armidale, you could detour through the goldrush ghost town of **HILLGROVE**, where the old school has been converted into the **Rural Life and Industry museum** (daily 10am–5pm; free) displaying old mining equipment and trying to re-create the lifestyle of the once-prosperous settlement. **URALLA**, 22km south of Armidale, is another old gold town, though in this case it has managed to hang on, with a population of a couple of thousand. The Historic Building Walk will take you past the town's highlights, including **McCrossin's Mill Museum** (daily noon–5pm; $3.50), an old three-storey flour mill on Salisbury Street. Fossicking is still possible at the old Rocky River diggings: enquire at the **Uralla Visitor Information Centre**, New England Highway (daily 9.30am–4.30pm; ℡02/6778 4496, ⊛www.new -england.org/uralla); or you can go on tour with **Uralla Goldfield Tours** (℡02/6772 6828). Gold apart, Uralla's other claim to fame is that **Captain Thunderbolt**, the bushranger who terrorized the New England region in the nineteenth century, was shot dead here in 1870, after a furious battle in the swampy country southeast of Uralla – an event commemorated by the bronze statue of Thunderbolt and his horse on the corner of Bridge and Salisbury streets.

Southeast of Armidale, towards Walcha, **Dangars Lagoon** is a wetland region visited by more than a hundred different kinds of bird; a hide is provided for spotters. **Dangars Falls** and a network of twenty walking tracks and lookouts around **Dangars Gorge** are only 22km from Armidale on a minor road. Beyond these, about 20km east of Walcha, a turn-off from the Oxley Highway leads to **Apsley Gorge** and two more waterfalls in another section of the Oxley Rivers park. In **WALCHA** itself, 65km southwest of Armidale, there are the usual pioneer museums, but more interesting is the **Amaroo Museum and Cultural Centre** on Derby Street (Mon–Fri 9am–5pm), which displays arts and crafts made by local Aboriginal people.

West of Armidale, 27km along the Bundarra Road, is the Mount Yarrowyck Nature Reserve where an **Aboriginal rock-art site** can be accessed via a 3km circuit walk.

Glen Innes and around

GLEN INNES, the next major stop north on the New England Highway, about 100km from Armidale, is another pleasant town in a beautiful setting. Although agriculture is still important up here, you begin to see more and more evidence of the gemfields – sapphires are big business, as, to a lesser extent, is tin mining. In the centre, on Grey Street especially, numerous century-old public buildings and parks have been renovated and spruced up. There's some fine country architecture including a couple of large corner pubs, their verandahs decorated with iron lace. The **Land of the Beardies History House** (Mon–Fri 10am–noon & 2–5pm, Sat & Sun 2–5pm; $4), in the town's first hospital on Ferguson Street, displays pioneer relics, period room settings and a reconstructed slab hut. The name alludes to the two hairy men who settled the area in the nineteenth century, and it's a title the town's proud of, along with the Scottish connections reflected in the name of the town itself and in many of its streets, which are rendered in both English and Gaelic. The local granite **Australian Standing Stones** at Martins Lookout, Watsons Drive, are based on the Ring of Brodgar in Scotland, and are intended to honour the "contribution of the Celtic races to Australia's development"; there's a great picnic and barbecue area with granite seats and tables, echoing the stones themselves. The strongly Celtic nature of Glen Innes is counterbalanced by the town's department store, Kwong Sing & Co, which has been run by the same family of Chinese origin since 1886. While you're in the area, you might also consider a **horseback pub crawl** with Great Aussie Pub Crawls on Horseback (☎02/6732 1599, ⓦwww.northnet.com.au/~pubcrawl); despite the name, this is really a six-day trekking adventure with overnight stops at traditional Aussie pubs, and no drinking is permitted during the five to six hours of riding each day.

In early November, Glen Innes celebrates the **Land of the Beardies Bushfestival**, with everything from a beard-growing contest and shopping-trolley derby to dances, street parades and arts-and-crafts exhibits. More details, including help with rooms, are available from the **Glen Innes & District Visitors Centre**, 52 Church St, as the New England Highway is called when it passes through town (Mon–Fri 9am–5pm, Sat & Sun 10am–3pm; ☎02/6732 2397, ⓦwww.gleninnestourism.com); there's a café, *The Celtic Kitchen*, in the centre serving soda bread and snacks, and the **bus terminal** is also attached. Good **accommodation** options include the air-conditioned *Central Motel*, Meade Street, opposite the post office (☎02/6732 2200, ⓕ6732 1624; ❹); the fancier (though not air-con) *Rest Point Motel* on Church Street, 1km south of the centre (☎02/6732 2255; ❺), with a swimming pool and extensive landscaped grounds; and the well-equipped *Poplar Caravan Park*, 15 Church St (☎02/6732 1514; cabins ❸, on-site vans ❷). For a homely semi-splurge try *Diarmid's B&B* at 15 Torrington St (☎02/6732 5701, ⓦwww.atn.com.au/diarmids; ❺–❻) – a lovely guesthouse with a log fire in the guest lounge and bedrooms decorated in old Scottish and Irish style. Fresh flowers abound, and included in the price are a high tea – with shortbread, apple cake and home-made preserves – and a tour of the Australian standing stones. For sustenance in the town, try the *Tea and Coffee Shop* on Grey Street, a cosy **tearoom** with loads of choice including Dutch pancakes, an array of interesting sandwiches, savoury croissants and hot breakfasts. If it's all getting a bit too olde worlde for you, Grey Street's *Cafe Heritage* is a modern brasserie with a menu to match, or the *One Eighty Nine Coffee Lounge*, at 189 Grey St, has an even more down-to-earth menu, designed to cure even the worst hangover. The best Chinese **restaurant** is *Dragon Court*, at 173 Grey St.

Inverell

The area between Glen Innes and **INVERELL**, 67km to the west, is one huge gemfield. Industrial diamonds, garnets, topaz, zircons and three-quarters of the world's sapphires are mined in the area. Inverell is also known as

"Sapphire City", and at the **Dejon Sapphire Centre**, on the Gwydir Highway, 18km east of town, you can watch the gems being mined, washed, sorted and cut (daily 9am–5pm; mine tours 10.30am & 3pm). The showroom has a display of sapphires in 155 colours, from pale blue and green, to gold, lemon and pink. To try your own luck, you'll need to contact the **tourist office** on Campbell Street (Mon–Fri 9am–4pm, Sat 9am–noon; ☎ 02/6722 1693, ⓦ www.inverell-online.com.au), which can direct you to the designated areas. If you want to **stay** over and wait for that big strike, try the *Australian Hotel* on Byron St (☎ 02/6722 1611; ❸), which has clean rooms with shared facilities, open fires and air conditioning, and serves counter meals; or *Sapphire City Caravan Park* on Moore Street (☎ 02/6722 1830; cabins ❸, on-site vans ❷).

Tenterfield and around

Less than 20km from the Queensland border, **TENTERFIELD** marks the northern end of the New England Plateau. Although only a small town, it has a confirmed place in Australian history, being the birthplace of the Australian Federation, and in 2001 will be playing host to many centennial celebrations. This title was earned when, in 1889, the Prime Minister of New South Wales, Sir Henry Parkes, made his famous Federation speech here, advocating the union of the Australian colonies; twelve years later the Commonwealth of Australia was inaugurated. A small **museum** (Wed–Sun 10am–4pm; $2) in Centenary Cottage recalls the occasion and displays other items of local interest.

As throughout the region, however, the real attractions of Tenterfield lie outside town – undulating pastures and orchards, remnants of stands of eucalypt and rainforests, and rugged granite hills. **Bald Rock**, in a national park of the same name near the Queensland border, about 30km northeast of Tenterfield, is Australia's second-largest monolith, after Uluru (see p.681), but a grey-granite version, 213m high. It can be climbed from its northeast side, and from the summit there are breathtaking panoramic views taking in both states. The excursion to Bald Rock fits in nicely with a visit to 210-metre-high **Boonoo Boonoo Falls**, set in another national park 32km north of Tenterfield. Access is via an unsealed road which can be a bit rough, but it's worth it (as long as you're not in a hire car), and there's a beautiful picnic area. The NPWS occasionally offers tours to both national parks: details are available from the **Tenterfield Visitors Centre**, New England Highway (Mon–Fri 9.30am–5pm, Sat 9.30am–4.30pm, Sun 9.30am–4pm; ☎ 02/6736 1082, ⓦ www.tenterfield.com). Perhaps the best way to climb the rock, however, is with Woollool Woollool Aboriginal Cultural Tours (book on ☎ 02/6736 3209, at ⓦ www.northnet.com.au/~wwact or through visitors centre; $60); these are conducted by trained Aboriginal guides who, as well as escorting you up the monolith, will guide you through rock art sites, the falls and the ghost town of Boonoo Boonoo. The daily tours also include lessons in boomerang throwing, and free pick-ups and drop-offs from most accommodation in town.

Accommodation in Tenterfield includes the very cheap and central *Commercial Hotel*, 288 Rouse St (☎ 02/6736 1027; ❶), which has a beer garden, shared cooking facilities and counter meals. *Tenterfield YHA*, 2 Manners St (☎ 02/6736 1477; rooms ❸, dorms ❶, cabins ❸, on-site vans ❷), is a lovely old wooden country hotel with a huge balcony, surrounded by parklands, and incorporating a caravan park and a small but well-equipped hostel.

Pacific Islands: Lord Howe and Norfolk

Lord Howe Island, 700km northeast of Sydney, and roughly in line with Port Macquarie, is actually a far-flung part of New South Wales, on the world's southernmost coral reef. Its nearest neighbour is **Norfolk Island**, 900km further northeast – an external independent territory of Australia, though geographically closer to New Zealand. The approach to tourism of the two subtropical islands couldn't be more different: Lord Howe is the perfect ecodestination, attracting outdoor types, and is very sophisticated in terms of food and accommodation, while Norfolk Island mostly disregards its natural beauty to concentrate first on its status as a tax haven and a magnet for Australian pensioners who come for its duty-free shopping, and second on its fascinating history as a tough convict settlement and then as the home for many of the descendants of the *Bounty* mutineers after they had left Pitcairn Island.

Getting there

It's not cheap to get to **Lord Howe Island**: you can **fly** with Qantas (☎13 1313) from Sydney daily except Friday, and from Brisbane twice weekly, for about $800 return; flights via Newcastle and Ballina may be available in peak summer months. Note that the Lord Howe Island Board (for information call ☎02/6563 2066, ℉6563 2127) charges a $40 service levy which is included in your airline ticket. It's much easier to go on a **package tour**, but the lowest you can expect to pay for five nights is about $850 in winter, rising to a steep $1600 in summer: try Pacific Unlimited Holidays (☎02/9290 2266, ℉9232 8150, ⓦwww.pacificunlimited.com.au), who also fly to Norfolk; Pinetrees Travel (☎02/9262 6585 or free call 1800 226 142, ⓦwww.pinetrees.com.au); or the Pacific & International Travel Company (☎13 2747, ⓦwww.pitc.com.au), who also organize trips to Norfolk Island from Sydney. Overseas visitors can also fly to Lord Howe as an add-on sector fare on an airpass.

The Qantas-linked Norfolk Jet Express (free call ☎1800 816 947) flies to **Norfolk Island** from Sydney at weekends, while Ansett-partner Flight West (☎1300/130 092, ⓦwww.flightwest.com.au) operates four flights a week from Brisbane and five from Sydney. Note that there's a $25 departure tax from Norfolk. **Packages**, available through Fastbook Pacific Holidays (☎02/9212 5977 or 1300/361 153, ⓦwww.fastbook.com.au) amongst others, offer the best value, costing from $890 for five days; Fastbook also deal with passengers wishing to visit either island independently, and can arrange flights between the two islands with Tasman Australian Airlines. Air New Zealand flies twice weekly **from Auckland and Christchurch** to Norfolk Island, and a code-share agreement with Flight West mean the destination can now be a stop-over between New Zealand and Australia.

Lord Howe Island

I would strongly urge preserving this beautiful island from further intrusions of any kind...

Government Expedition, 1882

On the UNESCO World Heritage list since 1982 because of its rare birds and plant life, and its coral reef in unpolluted and virtually untouched waters, **LORD HOWE ISLAND** is the ultimate destination for ecotourists. The island's preservation was assured by Victorian-era descriptions of "this gem of the sea" when reports were brought back to the Australian mainland regarding the progress of the multiracial settlers who had arrived in the 1830s. Even today only a tenth of the land has been cleared for cultivation or grazing, and two-thirds of the island is designated as **Permanent Park Reserve**. Only 11km long and just under 3km across at its widest point, the crescent-shaped subtropical island is covered with **kentia palm plantations**, which represent the island's only industry other than tourism. With a population of just 300, only 400 visitors are allowed on the island at any one time; to enforce this limit, accommodation has to be booked in advance. There is only one short road and, although some locals have vehicles, people get around mainly by bicycle, boat or on foot.

As you fly in, you have a stunning view of the whole of the volcanic island: the towering summits of rainforest-clad **Mount Gower** and **Mount Lidgbird** at the southern end, the narrow centre with its idyllic lagoon and a **coral reef** extending about six kilometres along the island's west coast, and a group of tiny islets off the coast at the lower northern end of the island providing sanctuary for the prolific **birdlife** – the island's 32 species make this a heaven for ornithologists.

One of the first things you notice about the island is how easy-going and laid-back the local people are: many prefer to go barefoot. The emphasis is on tranquillity and visitors are mostly couples and families – there are no rowdy nightclubs here. Though it's expensive to get to the island, once here you'll find that cruises, bike rental and eating out are all relatively affordable. The island's **climate** is subtropical, with temperatures rising from an average low of 16°C to 19°C in winter, 26°C in the summer, and an annual rainfall of 1650mm. It's cheaper to visit in the winter, though many places are closed and there's usually a lot more rain and wind.

Some history

Although the ship *Supply* discovered Lord Howe Island in 1778 on a journey from Sydney to found a colony on Norfolk Island, the island was not actually settled for another 55 years. These first **settlers**, who arrived in 1833, were three white men, with Maori women and boys, and the group earned their livelihood by providing whaling vessels with provisions. Other settlers arrived in the 1840s, but in 1853 two white men came with three women from the Gilbert Islands, and it is from this small group that many of Lord Howe's present population is descended. In the 1840s and 1850s the island continued to serve as a stopover for **whaling ships** from the US and Britain, with as many as fifty ships a year passing through. In 1882 a government expedition from the mainland recommended that, in order to preserve the island, no one other than the present "happy, industrious" leaseholders and their families be allowed to make permanent settlement.

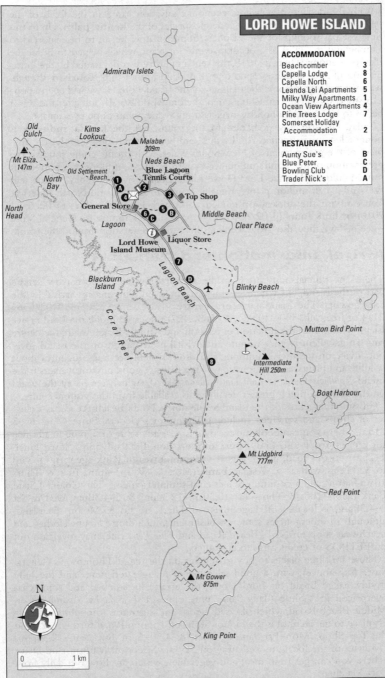

LORD HOWE ISLAND

ACCOMMODATION

Beachcomber	3
Capella Lodge	8
Capella North	6
Leanda Lei Apartments	5
Milky Way Apartments	1
Ocean View Apartments	4
Pine Trees Lodge	7
Somerset Holiday Accommodation	2

RESTAURANTS

Aunty Sue's	B
Blue Peter	C
Bowling Club	D
Trader Nick's	A

Admiralty Islets

Old Gulch

Kims Lookout

▲ Malabar 209m

Mt Eliza 147m

Old Settlement Beach

Neds Beach

Blue Lagoon Tennis Courts

North Bay

North Head

General Store

Lagoon

Lord Howe Island Museum

Blackburn Island

Coral Reef

Top Shop

Middle Beach

Clear Place

Liquor Store

Lagoon Beach

Blinky Beach

Mutton Bird Point

Intermediate Hill 250m

Boat Harbour

▲ Mt Lidgbird 777m

Red Point

▲ Mt Gower 875m

King Point

N

0   1 km

▼ Balls Pyramid (23 km)

2

With the decline of whaling, economic salvation came in the form of the "thatch" palm, one of the four endemic species of the **kentia palm**. Up to this time used as roofing for the islanders' homes, it now began to be exported to Europe and the USA as a decorative interior plant, which helped to boost the island's economy. Then, in 1918, the kentia industry was devastated by the introduction of **rats**, which escaped onto the island from a ship. **Tourism**, though, was eventually to become the mainstay of the island. Lord Howe had been a popular stopover on the cruise-ship circuit before World War II, and after the war it began to be visited by holiday-makers from Sydney, who came by seaplane.

Today, rats still pose a hazard to the palms, but the **kentia industry** is nonetheless in resurgence, run by the Lord Howe Island Board under the auspices of the government of New South Wales, with profits going towards the preservation of the island's unique ecosystem. Seeds are no longer exported but instead cultivated in the Lord Howe Island Board's own **nursery**, which sells two-and-a-half million plants annually, mainly to Europe and North America. You can visit the nursery on guided walks with Ron's Rambles (℡ 02/6563 2010) or Jim's Tours (℡ 02/6563 2263, or book at Thompson's General Store – see below); they also grow seedlings here for regeneration around the island.

Arrival, information and transport

There's no official transport from the **airport**, located in the narrow central part of the island, but wherever you're staying, you'll be met on arrival by the lodge-owner. The island's **visitors centre** (daily 9am–12.30pm; ℡ 02/6563 2114 or free call 1800 240 937, ℱ 6563 2127) is located inside the Lord Howe Island Museum at the junction of Lagoon and Middle Beach roads; the centre runs an excellent twenty-minute audiovisual presentation on the island, gives out advice on weather conditions, and also has plenty of free brochures about wildlife and plants, as well as basic walking maps. A good buy for walkers is the useful *Ramblers Guide to Lord Howe Island* ($7.70), which covers all the walks on the island in much greater detail and is available from the visitors centre.

Crossing the centre of the island to the north, Ned's Beach Road has a cluster of **shops** and **services**, including Thompson's General Store (℡ 02/6563 2155), where you can book most activities – it's advisable to sign up in advance for cruises. You'll also find a **post office** (Mon–Fri 9am–5pm, closed lunch 1–2pm) on this road, which acts as a Commonwealth Bank agent (no fee up to $200), as well as a Westpac **bank** (Mon & Wed 2–4pm, Tues & Thurs 10am–noon) and a community hall-cum-summer cinema. The Colonial State Bank (Mon–Tues & Thurs–Fri 10.30am–12.30pm & 2–4.30pm, Wed & Sat 2–4.30pm) is located off Lagoon Road. There are no ATMs on the island, although in emergencies some establishments, including Larrups clothes and beachwear shop on Ned's Beach Road and *Blue Peter* café, may give cash out on EFTPOS or credit cards to customers.

There are three places to buy **groceries** on the island: Thompson's General Store (see above), with a good selection of refrigerated items and the only freshly baked bread on Lord Howe; the erratically stocked and somewhat overpriced Joy's Shop (daily 9am–7pm), opposite *Leanda Lei Apartments* on Middle Beach Road, which also sells liquor and cigarettes (though the cheapest place to get alcohol is the Liquor Store, off Lagoon Road further east); and the Top Shop (Mon–Fri 9am–12.30pm & 4.30–6pm, Sun 9am–12.30pm), favourite of the locals, tucked away on Skyline Street off Mutton Bird Drive – here you can get fresh meat and vegetables, which are flown in daily from Port Macquarie.

Lord Howe ecology

Seven million years ago a volcanic eruption on the sea floor created Lord Howe Island and its 27 surrounding islets and outcrops – the island's boomerang shape is a mere remnant of the massive shield volcano, mostly eroded away by the sea. While much of the **flora** on the island is similar to that of Australia, New Zealand, New Caledonia and Norfolk Island, the island's relative isolation has led to the evolution of **new species** – of the 241 native plants found here, 105 are endemic, including the important indigenous **kentia palm** (see p.330).

Similarly, until the arrival of settlers, fifteen species of **land birds** (nine of which are now extinct) lived on the island, undisturbed by predators and coexisting with migrating seabirds, skinks, geckos, spiders, snails and the now-extinct giant horned turtle. However, in the eighteenth century Lord Howe became a port of call for ships en route to Norfolk Island, whose hungry crews eradicated the island's stocks of **white gallinule** and **white-throated pigeon**. The small, plump and flightless **woodhen** managed to survive, protected on Mount Gower, and an intensive captive breeding programme in the early 1980s has more than doubled numbers of the species to 66. About one million **seabirds** – fourteen species – nest here annually: as well as being one of the few known breeding grounds of the **providence petrel**, the island also has the world's largest colony of **red-tailed tropic birds** and is the most southerly breeding location of the **sooty tern**, the noddy tern and the masked booby.

The cold waters of the **Tasman Sea**, which surround Lord Howe, host the world's southernmost **coral reef**, a tropical oddity which is sustained by the warm summer currents that sweep in from the Great Barrier Reef. There are about sixty varieties of brilliantly coloured and fantastically shaped coral, and the meeting of warm and cold currents means that a huge variety of both tropical and temperate fish can be spotted by snorkellers in the crystal-clear waters. Some of the most colourful species include the yellow **moon wrasse** and the yellow-and-black **banner fish**. Unique to Lord Howe is the **doubleheader**, with its bizarre, bulbous forehead and fat lips. Beyond the lagoon, the water becomes very deep, with particularly good **diving** in the seas around the **Admiralty Islets**, which have sheer underwater precipices and chasms. The diving season lasts from May to September (for information on dive companies, see p.335).

Transport

The island has only one **road** and relatively few cars. There are no streetlights so you'll need to bring a torch with you, or buy one from Joy's Shop, if you want to venture out at night. There's no regular bus service, but lodge hosts and restaurants will usually pick up and drop off customers. Otherwise, Wilson's (see below) can do pick-ups and drop-offs. The most common ways to get around are by **bicycle**, boat or just plain walking. There are plenty of places to **rent bikes** and most lodges offer them to guests, but the drawback is that they don't have lights either, so if you want to ride at night attach a torch. If your lodge has exhausted its supply, the main outlet is Wilson's Bike Hire, opposite Lagoon Beach (℡02/6563 2045; $5 per day; closed Sat), but be warned that their bikes are basic, with no gears – and there are some steep hills on the island. Both Wilson's and *Leanda Lei Apartments* (℡02/6563 2195) rent **cars** ($50–60 per day) but there are only six of them, so pre-booking is essential.

Accommodation

Since you need to have an accommodation booking before you can buy a flight, package tours are the most convenient option. Most of the accommodation on Lord Howe Island is **self-catering** (otherwise full board is available) and of a good standard, including TV and usually a laundry. All the lodges are very centrally located, with the exception of *Capella Lodge*, where privacy, views and atmosphere more than compensate.

Beachcomber Lodge (ⓣ02/6563 2032, ⓕ6563 2132). Studio apartments including breakfast (some larger suites available with self-catering facilities) in a central location amongst palm-trees. Owned by long-established island family; suitable for couples with kids. ⓑ

Capella Lodge (ⓣ02/6563 2008, ⓕ6563 2180, ⓦwww.lordhowe.com). Towards the southern end of the island, above Salmon Beach and overlooked by Mount Gower and Mount Lidgbird. Nine stylish, breezy rooms with fantastic views, hip *Mambo* furnishings and interior design and large bathrooms. TVs, torches and mountain bikes also provided. Top-class restaurant and cocktail café-bar, with stunning views over the mountains. ⓑ

Capella North (ⓣ02/6563 2113, ⓕ6563 2158). This is run by the same people as *Capella Lodge*. It's simpler but more central than the above, offering artistically designed self-contained units opposite the lagoon. ⓑ

Leanda Lei Apartments (ⓣ02/6563 2195, ⓕ6563 2095). Studio or one- or two-bedroom self-catering apartments in the middle of the island by Lagoon Beach, set in nicely manicured grounds with BBQs. The friendly owners can rent you a bike or a car. ⓑ

Milky Way Apartments (book through Fast Bookings in Sydney on ⓣ02/9958 2799, ⓕ9958 2079). Set amid native forests by Old Settlement Beach at the northern end of the island. One of the best spots, surrounded by bird-filled green forests.

All units have balconies. ⓑ

Ocean View Apartments (ⓣ02/6563 2041, ⓕ6563 2122). Very pleasant, old-fashioned place, with a sunny garden, tennis court, a common room with pool tables and the island's only swimming pool. There *is* a view of the sea at the end of the driveway, but not from the rooms. ⓑ

Pine Trees Lodge (ⓣ02/9262 6585, ⓦwww.pinetrees.com.au). The island's original all-inclusive resort, set in extensive grounds filled with native palms and hundred-year-old Norfolk Island pines. A pleasant, old-fashioned homestead with a guest lounge, verandah, courtyard and tennis court. Units are motel-style, each with a small verandah. The newer, self-catering garden cottages ("Palm Haven"), are better, with courtyards, separate bedrooms and living rooms. The lodge has its own boatshed and deck on Lagoon Beach. Package tours only ($1600 per person per week, including flight, accommodation and all meals). ⓑ

Somerset Holiday Accommodation (ⓣ02/6563 2061, ⓕ6563 2110, ⓦwww.lordhoweisle.com.au). The largest self-contained apartment complex on the island, with kitchenettes, BBQs and private verandahs. ⓑ

Trader Nick's (ⓣ02/6563 2002, ⓕ6563 2022, ⓦwww.lordhowe.com.au). Ten individual suites with private verandahs nestling in among the kentia forest. The rooms are a minimalist's dream: spacious, airy, comfortable and very Zen. The on-site restaurant is by far the island's best. ⓑ

The island

At the island's **northern end**, you can walk, stopping at various lookout points, all the way from Old Settlement Beach on the western side to Ned's Beach on the east. Relaxed, educational half-day **guided walks** are available for around $15 from personable local resident Ron or island biologist Ian Hutton (book at Thompson's Store for both). However, if you simply want to take in the scenery, it's very easy to do it yourself. From the streamside picnic area at **Old Settlement Beach**, it's just over 2km to the summit of **Mount Eliza** (147m). If you want to save time, you can take a boat to **North Bay** with Islander Cruises (see p.335) and begin the walk from there – the return walk will then take only an hour. The summit is the most accessible place to see **sooty terns** in their southernmost breeding grounds. When the colony visits the island between August and March each female lays a single speckled egg on the bare ground, which means that the actual summit has to be closed for the birds' protection. Back at the base, a short five- or ten-minute walk through forest from **North Beach** (good for swimming and snorkelling on

North Reef) leads to **Old Gulch**, a beach of boulders, where at low tide you can rock-hop to the **Herring Pools** at the base of the cliff front and examine the colourful marine life. From **Ned's Beach** (see opposite) the walk to **Malabar Hill** (209m) gives access to one of the world's largest nesting concentrations of **red-tailed tropic birds**, who between September and May make their homes in the crannies of the cliff face below, laying only one egg and looking after the chick for twelve weeks until it can fly. It's fascinating to watch the white-and-red birds' unusual and rather balletic backwards-dancing through the air. From here, you can head along the cliff edge to **Kim's Lookout** (182m), which provides a good view of the settlement and the lagoon beaches and islets at this end of the island, and from where it's just over a kilometre back to Old Settlement Beach (or you can continue on to North Beach and Mount Eliza).

In the **centre of the island** there are other walks to take: from Middle Beach to the Clear Place; from Blinky Beach, the island's main surfing spot, to **Transit Hill** (121m); and from near the airstrip to the summit of **Intermediate Hill** (250m); and two longer walks from the base of Intermediate Hill to **Boat Harbour** or to the base of **Mount Lidgbird** (777m). Less energetic, but no less rewarding, is a trip to the **Lord Howe Historical Museum**, opposite Lagoon Beach on the corner of Middle Beach Road and Lagoon Road, which details the history of the island from its discovery to the present day.

The ultimate view on the island is at its **southern end**, where the lofty summit of **Mount Gower** (875m) gives vistas over the whole island and out to sea towards **Balls Pyramid** (548m), a rocky outcrop 23km from Lord Howe. The mountain is high enough to have a true **mist forest** on its summit, with a profusion of ferns, and tree trunks and rocks covered in mosses. This very strenuous walk can be undertaken only with a licensed **guide** (Jack Shick ☎02/6563 2218; $30; bring your own lunch). The track to the top was blazed by botanists in 1869, who took two days to get there, but they were rewarded with the discovery of a plant seen nowhere else on earth – the **pumpkin tree**, bearing fleshy orange flowers. You can see other rare endemic plants here, such as the island apple and the blue plum, as well as birds such as the providence petrel and the woodhen. On average, the return walk takes eight hours; it's graded medium to hard and you'll need to be fit and have a good pair of walking boots. It's not for the faint-hearted: one section of the walk runs precariously along a narrow cliff face above the sea, and in parts the track is so steep that you must haul yourself up by ropes. To join the walk, you have to be at the Little Island gate on the south of the island by 7.30am: transport there is available for an extra $5.50 round-trip from Whitfield's Tours (☎02/6563 2115), or it's about a half-hour cycle ride from the north of the island.

Slightly less energetic activities are available at the *Blue Lagoon Lodge*'s **tennis courts** on North Beach Road (balls and rackets for hire from Thompson's Store), and the nine-hole **golf course** near *Capella Lodge*, which operates on an honesty system ($15 with your own clubs, $25 with theirs, balls $1); there's a chicken run competition held here on Friday afternoons, and an eighteen-hole competition on Sundays.

Water-based activities

Besides bushwalks, the island has some sensational swimming, snorkelling and diving sites. The water's combined temperate and tropical sealife make local double-headed wrasse, lobsters and angel-fish a common sight. Among the cruises on offer, the **glass-bottom boat cruises** from Lagoon Beach, which take about twenty passengers, are particularly good value at $20 for two hours (book at Thompson's General Store); included are opportunities to snorkel at **Erscotts Hole**, with gear and wet suits provided, and hand-feeding of fish, including a friendly old double-headed wrasse – you also see much more than on other, motorboat excursions. Islander Cruises can take you to North Bay, combining a **snorkelling** excursion around the 1965 wreck of the *Favorite* (where three-stripe butterfly fish have made their home) with bushwalks up to Old Gulch or up to the summit of Mount Eliza (Sept–June 10am–4pm; $28 including morning and afternoon tea, BYO lunch; ℡02/6563 2021).

There's more stunning snorkelling at Sylphs Hole, off Old Settlement Beach, and on the east side of the island at Ned's Beach, where slightly musty snorkelling sets can be rented on an honesty-box system ($2 for 1hr, $4 half-day, $6 full day, $30 per week; wet suit $3 for 30min, $6 for 1hr); sets are also available from most lodges, and Thompson's Store. Every day at 5pm for the last fifteen years, Ned's Beach has been the site of a **fish-feeding** frenzy, when a local man throws fish scraps into the water, attracting a throng of big trevally and reef sharks; the beach is also home to a venerable sea turtle. Stay here until dusk and you can observe **muttonbirds** en masse darkening the sky as they come home to roost. This experience can be a bit frightening, as they fly low through a forest of enormous **banyan trees** whose tangle of aerial roots descends to the ground.

Fishing trips can be arranged with *Lulawai* (℡02/6563 2195; $50 half-day), who guarantee you some fish, which the crew will prepare for you to barbecue later. Thompson's Store provides rods, reels, tackle and bait for those who already know what they're doing. **Sea kayaks** can be rented from Jack & Cindy Shick (℡02/6563 2218), who also arrange kayaking tours. If you're interested in **diving** in the waters around Lord Howe, contact Howea Divers (℡ & ℻ 02/6563 2290), a recommended outfit run by a local. As well as advanced dives and tuition, they offer novices the chance to dive either off boats or from the shore for $80, and they also host sensational dive trips to nearby Ball's Pyramid, the world's tallest monolith. Pro-Dive also has an outlet on the island, with packages bookable through their Sydney central reservations (℡02/9232 5733, ℻ 9232 5788).

Eating and drinking

Bookings are essential at all **eating** places for evening meals. An essential **lunch** or snack stop is the *Blue Peter* (daily 11.30am–6pm), a summer-only café on Lagoon Road, which offers affordable salads, speciality burgers, *focaccia* and daily fish specials. Thompson's General Store also does takeaway fish and beef burgers at lunchtime. The best **restaurants** on the island are *Williams* (at *Trader Nick's*; ℡02/6563 2022) and *White Gallinule* (at *Capella Lodge*; ℡02/6563 2008). Both serve deliciously innovative modern Australian cuisine, with the emphasis on local ingredients and excellent fish dishes. *White Gallinule* offers the best views, and has the advantage of an extensive cocktail list, while *Williams* make their own bread, cakes and pasta and grow their own salads and herbs. Both are open every day in summer for breakfast, lunch and dinner, as well as for coffee and cake during the day. *Aunty Sue's* (℡02/6563 2177) is recommended for their relaxed $15 three-course lunch, generous portions and range of vegetarian options. On Monday nights, they also throw the island's best fish fry – a Lord Howe must involving a smorgasbord of the day's catch with salads and dessert for $33 (advance booking is essential). There's no pub on the island, but the closest thing to a **bar** is the *Bowling Club*, where the locals hang out (daily 4.30–8pm); there's also a very popular disco held here every Friday night (8pm–midnight).

Norfolk Island

Just 8km long and 5km wide, tiny, isolated **NORFOLK ISLAND**, an External Territory of Australia located 1500km due east of Brisbane, nevertheless has had an eventful history, linked with early convict settlements and later with the descendants of Fletcher Christian and other "mutiny-on-the-*Bounty*" rebels and their Tahitian wives who had outgrown Pitcairn Island. It's a beautiful, unique island, forested with grand indigenous pine trees, and with a mild subtropical climate ranging between 11°C and 18°C in the winter and from 19°C to 28°C (with high humidity) in the summer. Nowadays the island's **tax-haven** status makes it a refuge for millionaires, with thirteen of them living on the island including the Australian novelist Colleen McCullough. The island's history is exploited to the full for Norfolk's tourists, who spend a fortune in the numerous duty-free stores; there's a big philatelic industry too.

The island mainly attracts honeymooners or retired Australians and New Zealanders lured by the quiet life and the inexpensive shopping (known collectively as the "newly weds and nearly deads"). Even the most frequent visitors require a passport to visit the island, which has its own government, a nine-member Legislative Assembly, and an administrator appointed by the Australian Governor General. A thirty-day **visitor permit**, extendable to 120 days, is granted automatically on arrival. The island has no income tax, finances being raised from sources such as departure tax ($25) and a road levy included in the price of petrol. There's a $500 fine for working illegally, but finding **work** here through the right channels is not impossible: many of the 1800 residents (who are not entitled to unemployment benefit) hold down two or three jobs, and employment for school-leavers is guaranteed, often in the two tacky sound-and-light shows that tell the story of the mutiny on the *Bounty* and the convict era. Most of the local people remain unaffected by tourism, maintaining their friendly, good-humoured attitude, their ridiculous nicknames and the remnants of their dialect, **Pitcairn**, a mixture of old West Country English and Tahitian (see overleaf).

Much of the land is cleared for cultivation, as islanders have to grow all their own fresh food to keep the island disease-free; cattle roam freely on the green island and are given right of way, creating a positively bucolic atmosphere. Scenic winding roads provide access to the **national park** and the **Botanic Garden** in the northern half of the island, which together cover twenty percent of Norfolk's area. It's here that you get an idea of how the entire island originally looked, as you roam through the best of the remaining subtropical rainforest. Norfolk Island is also an ornithologist's paradise, with nine endemic **landbird** species, including the endangered **Norfolk Island green parrot** with its distinctive chuckling sound. The two small islands immediately south of Norfolk, Nepean and Phillip islands, are important **seabird** nesting sites.

Some history

A violent volcanic eruption three million years ago produced the Norfolk Ridge, extending from New Zealand to New Caledonia (Norfolk Island's closest neighbour, 700km north), with only Norfolk Island and the smaller adjacent and uninhabited **Phillip** and **Nepean islands** remaining above sea level. **Captain Cook** "discovered" the island in 1774, but it's now believed that migrating Polynesian people had lived here for hundreds of years prior to his visit. Cook recommended that the island be secured for the British Crown, seeing value in its vegetation: the tall **Norfolk pines** he thought would make fine ships' masts, with accompanying sails woven from the native **flax**. Norfolk Island was settled in 1788, only six weeks after Sydney, with the idea of establishing a free settlement – of the 23 original settlers, 15 were convicts. However, plans to use the fertile island as a base to grow food for the starving young colony of Australia foundered when, in 1790, a First Fleet ship, the *Sirius*, was wrecked on a reef off the island, highlighting the problem, which still exists today, of its lack of a navigable harbour. This **first settlement** was judged a failure when its wood proved not to be strong enough for masts and it was finally abandoned in 1814. Most of the buildings were destroyed to discourage settlement by other powers, and many free settlers were granted land in New Norfolk in Tasmania (see p.1075).

Norfolk's isolation was one of the major reasons for its **second settlement** (1825–55) – as a **prison** rather than a productive island, described officially as "a place of the extremest punishment short of death". Some of the imposing stone buildings designed by Royal Engineers still stand in **Kingston**, on the southern coast of the island. There were up to two thousand convicts on the island, overseen by sadistic commandants who had virtually unlimited power to run the settlement and inflict punishments as they saw fit. Only under the command of the enlightened reformer Captain Maconochie (1840–44) was there some improvement in prisoners' conditions.

Norfolk Island was again abandoned in 1855, but this time the buildings remained and were used a year later during the **third settlement**, which consisted of 194 Pitcairn Islanders (the entire population of the island), who left behind their overcrowded conditions to establish a new life elsewhere. The new settlers had only eight family surnames among them – five of which (Christian, Quintal, Adams, McKoy and Young) were the names of the original mutineers of the *Bounty*. These names – especially Christian – are still common on the island, and today about one in three islanders can claim descent from the mutineers. The building of an airport during World War II and the arrival of television have helped greatly to reduce Norfolk's linguistic isolation, though these descendants still speak some Pitcairn to each other. Listen for expressions such as "Whataway?" ("How are you?") and "Webout you gwen?" ("Where are you going?"). **Bounty Day**, the day the Pitcairners arrived, is celebrated in Kingston on June 8.

Information, transport and tours

For information and bookings in advance, contact the **Norfolk Island Government Tourist Bureau**, Australian office, PO Box 523, Turramurra, NSW 2074 (T 02/9983 0939, F 9983 0949, W www.norfolkisland.com.au), or consult W www.pi-travel.com/norfolk-island – the most comprehensive of the many island information websites. All tourist facilities are based in the main town of **Burnt Pine**. Here, in the Bicentennial Complex on Taylors Road, you'll find the **Norfolk Island Visitor Information Centre** (T 6723/22147, F 23109), which can book tours and activities, plus the liquor bond store (which sells discounted alcohol on production of your airline ticket), the **post office** and the Communications Centre, where you need to go to make international **phone calls**. There are two **banks** on the main street, Westpac and Commonwealth; the Commonwealth has an ATM.

Transport

There's no public transport on Norfolk Island, so getting around by **car** is much the best option. Many accommodation places offer a car as part of the

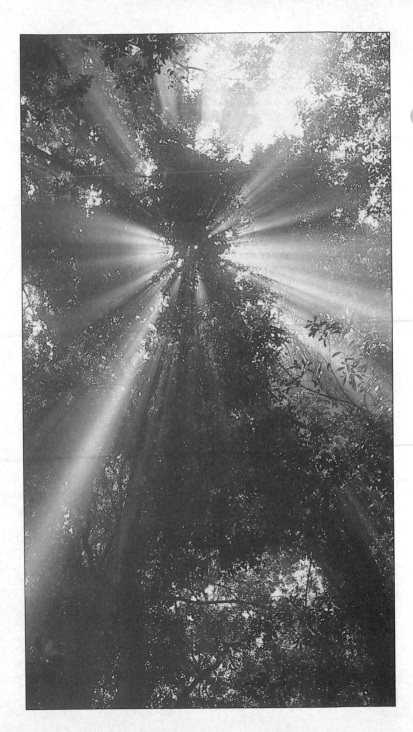

package or give you a big discount on **car rental**. It's very cheap anyway, from just $13 (plus insurance) per day with Norfolk Island Rent-a-Car (☏6723/22656) or Martin's Hire Cars (☏6723/22021). No one's bothered about seat belts or even driving mirrors, and the maximum speed limit is only 50kph (40kph in town). There are also a limited number of **bikes** for rent, which can be arranged through the tourist office, or by calling Bill's Push Bike Hire (☏6723/22551) or Wilson's Hire Service (☏02/6563 2045; $3 per day).

Tours

For **tours**, Jimbo's 4WD Tours ($22; ☏ & ℱ 6723/22990) are a good introduction to the island's ecology, and they also offer cruises around the island; Pinetree Tours (☏6723/22422, ⓦwww.nlk.nf/pinetreetours/), with an office on the main street next to the Commonwealth bank, offers a slew of pricey tours including an extensive introductory half-day bus tour of the island ($18). Bounty Excursions (☏6723/23693, ⓦwww.bountyexcursions.com) cover a range of cultural and historic sites, including a convict ruins tour (Mon 1pm & Thurs 3pm; 3hr; $18) and a panoramic Norfolk Discovery outing (daily except Tues; 3hr; $20). A pleasant way to get around is on **horseback**; try Silky Oaks (☏6723/22291), just down from the Botanic Gardens, which has its own tearoom in a shady, flower-filled garden and offers both daytime and sunset rides around the island, with billy tea and damper.

The island is surrounded by a coral reef and pristine waters, making at least one waterborne tour a must. There are several glass-bottomed **boat cruises** on Emily Bay, including the *Emily Queen* (☏6723/22225) and *Christian's Glaas Bohtam Boet* (☏6523/23258). For fishing trips, ask at the tourist office or call Norfolk Land and Sea (☏6723/23418, ⓦhttp://users.nf/bountydivers/trekking). Bounty Divers at the Village Centre (☏6723/22751, ⓦhttp://users.nf/bountydivers) run PADI courses and have **dive** charters ($79 per dive, including gear). **Snorkelling** and **diving** gear, and **fishing** rods, are all available for rent.

Accommodation

A lot of **accommodation** is in 1970s-style motels, but the island is gradually upgrading its image and now boasts some quaint, faithfully restored five-star cottages. A central online **booking service** is available on the Web at ⓦwww.norfolkaccommodation.com, or call ☏6723/22255.

The two most stunning places to stay are *Christians of Buck Point* (☏6723/22282, ℱ23582, ⓦwww.christians.nf; ❽), a well-renovated historic property sleeping up to six, with floorboards and wooden doors from the original convict quarters in Kingston and car hire included in the price, and *Tintoela of Norfolk* (☏6723/22946, ℱ23376, ℮tintoela@ni.net.nf; ❽), a large, luxury wooden house, and adjacent cottage sleeping up to ten, with panoramic views of Cockpit Valley and the ocean. *Anson Bay Lodge* (☏6723/22897; ❺), a smaller property for two to four people, is attractively priced and located on Bullock's Hut Road. Some of the more attractive **motels** include: *Whispering Pines Luxury Cottages* on Grassy Road (☏6723/22114, ℱ23014, ⓦwww.norfolk-pines-group.nf; ❽), which offers two-bedroom units with garden views over the sea; *Shearwater Luxury Villas* (☏6723/22539, ℱ23359, ⓦwww.shearwater.nf; ❼), with upmarket self-contained accommodation on extensive grounds overlooking the water near Bumbora Reserve; the well-appointed *Crest Apartments*, near Kingston (☏6723/22280, ℱ22977; ❻), which have fully equipped kitchens and excellent views over to Phillip Island; and *Knobbs Apartments* (☏6723/22204, ℱ23204; ❻), in semi-bushland at the base of

Mount Pitt. The *South Pacific Resort* (℡ 6723/23507, ℱ 23508, ⓦ www.south-pacificresort.nlk.nf; ⓐ) is a recommended hotel close to Burnt Pine, with a bar, restaurant and swimming pool set in pleasant green grounds.

The island

At the centre of the island is its only significant settlement, **BURNT PINE**, a fairly modern affair crammed with shops selling everything from Lancôme cosmetics through to Sanyo stereos, all at duty-free prices; most shops are closed on Wednesday and Saturday afternoons and all day Sunday. The island's information centre, banks and post office are all here – see "Information, transport and tours" on p.337.

On the south coast, contrastingly picturesque **KINGSTON** is the sightseeing focus of the island; it's also Norfolk's administrative centre, with the Legislative Assembly meeting in the military barracks, and the old colonial Government House now home to the island's Administrator. There is an excellent view from the **Queen Elizabeth Lookout** (opened by the Queen in 1974, the bicentenary year of the discovery of the island) over the **Kingston and Arthur's Vale Historic Area** and the poignant seafront **cemetery**, containing a number of graves from the brutal second settlement. You can wander freely around the cemetery and the grounds, which have detailed interpretive boards, but it's very expensive to visit the remaining buildings and their museums: you can tour the buildings separately (prices given below) or with a combined ticket ($16) which allows multiple access to all sites spread over several days.

Quality Row bears some of the world's most impressive examples of Georgian **military architecture**, and looking at the buildings now it's difficult to imagine the suffering that took place behind their walls. Here is the place to come for a taste – or a surfeit – of Norfolk Island history; there are four museums housed under the umbrella of the **Norfolk Island Museum** (daily 11am–3pm; ⓦ www.museums.gov.nf), and you can choose to visit the establishments independently ($6) or all together ($18). The **Archeological Museum** where ongoing research is carried out, is located in the basement of the former Commissariat (1835), the upstairs of which was converted by the Pitcairners to All Saints Church. Close by, in the **No. 10 House Museum**, there are examples of Norfolk pine furniture made by convicts. The worthwhile **Social History Museum** is located in the pier store and outlines the story of the island through its three settlements. Perhaps most interesting, though, is the **Maritime Museum**, in what was once the Protestant chapel; various artefacts recovered from the 1790 wreck of the *Sirius* are on display, including its huge anchor, but more compelling is the *Bounty*-related paraphernalia brought here by Pitcairners, including the ship's cannon and even the kettle that was used on Pitcairn Island for everything from fermenting liquor to boiling sea water for salt. Near the museum you can watch cargo being towed ashore to the small jetty – even cars have to come this way, as there are no wharves. The Kingston area is also the site of the sports oval, the golf course and the island's main swimming **beaches**, protected by a small reef: immediately in front of the walls of the ruined barracks, which local people use for shade and wind shelter while picnicking, is **Slaughter Bay**, which has a sandy beach dotted with interestingly gnarled and eroded basalt rock formations; the small bit of coral reef is excellent for **snorkelling**, and at low tide you can take a cruise in a glass-bottomed boat (see "Tours", opposite). Nearby, the more sheltered Emily Bay is a safe swimming area, backed by a large pine forest.

In **Bumbora Reserve**, just west of Kingston, reached by car via Bumbora Road, you can see the natural regrowth of Norfolk pines; from the reserve you can walk down to Bumbora Beach, a shady little beach where you'll find some safe pools for children to swim in at low tide. There's another track down to **Crystal Pool**, which has more swimming and snorkelling.

West of Burnt Pine, along Douglas Drive, you'll find the exquisite **St Barnabas Chapel**, once the property of the Melanesian Mission (Anglican), which relocated gradually here from New Zealand between 1866 and 1921 with the aim of educating Western Pacific people in trades and education. The chapel's rose window was designed by William Morris and some other windows are by Sir Edward Burne-Jones, with the altar carved by Solomon Islanders.

On the **west coast** there's a scenic picnic area with tables and barbecues high over **Anson Bay**, from where it's a satisfying walk down to the beach. Immediately north of here, the **national park** has 8km of walking trails, many of them old logging tracks. Many walks start from **Mount Pitt** (320m), a pleasing drive up a fairly narrow and winding sealed road surrounded by palms and trees – worth it for the panoramic views. The most enjoyable walk from here is the three-kilometre route to the **Captain Cook Memorial** (1hr 45min), which starts as a beautiful grassy path but soon becomes a downward-sloping dirt track with some steps. Just south of the national park, on Pitt Road, the rainforest of the **Botanic Gardens** is worth a tranquil stroll. Here you can observe the forty endemic plant species including the pretty native hibiscus, the native palm, and the island's best-known symbol, the **Norfolk pine**, which can grow as high as 57m with a circumference of up to 11m. Both parks are permanently open, but camping is not allowed in either. The island also has an eco-tourism attraction, **A Walk in the Wild**, at Taylor's Road (daily 2–5pm; free), educating visitors about the fragile, disappearing rainforest and its birdlife.

Eating, drinking and entertainment

Norfolk Island **food** is plain and fresh, with an emphasis on locally caught fish and home-grown seasonal produce. Tahitian influence remains in the tradition of the big fish frys, and in some novel ways of preparing bananas. As most accommodation is self-catering, you'll want to head to the Foodland Supermarket in Burnt Pine (daily to 6pm); most of the products on the shelves are from New Zealand, and the small range of fruit and veg available reflects what is grown on the island – you won't find the variety you would elsewhere. On Sunday afternoon fresh fish is sold at the Kingston pier.

The **clubs** on the island provide good places to eat, drink and mingle with the locals. Facing each other across Burnt Pine's main street are the *Sports and Workers Club* (lunch daily, dinner Mon & Sat 5.30–7pm) and the *Norfolk Island Bowling Club* with a daily bar and food (lunch Sun–Fri, dinner Tues & Thurs, fish frys Wed & Sun). The *Golf Club* in Kingston has a popular bar which also serves meals, while the nearby Royal Engineers Office has a café serving tea and cakes. The only **pub** is the *Brewery*, opposite the airport, with local ales such as "Bee Sting" and "Bligh's Revenge", pool tables and a rough, late-night crowd which can be a bit intimidating for single women.

The best, and most expensive, **restaurants** are locals' favourite *The Garrison* (℡6723/22073), and *Mariah's*, at *Hillcrest Gardens Hotel* on Taylors Road (℡6723/22255), for à la carte dining with spectacular views of Phillip Island. *James' Place* at New Cascade Road in Burnt Pine (℡6723/23039) has innovative, Asian-influenced and vegetarian dishes, while the *South Pacific Resort* has big fish fries, smorgasbord nights, roast carveries and musical shows at various times during the week, while on other nights an ordinary brasserie menu is available from 5.30pm. A superb spot for lunch is the extremely popular *Cafe Pacifica* (☎6723/23210) on Cutters Corn Road, set in a leafy nursery and serving exquisite brunches and afternoon teas.

West of the Great Dividing Range

Western New South Wales is a very different proposition from the other parts of the state. For a start, there's hardly anyone living here. Beyond the Great Dividing Range are a few towns with a pioneer heritage, such as **Bathurst** and **Dubbo**, where there are still small agricultural communities and green fields; beyond them it begins to get increasingly desolate and arid, and even apparently large towns turn out to be tiny communities.

Out beyond the Blue Mountains, the **Great Western Highway** takes you as far as Bathurst; from there the **Mid-Western Highway** goes on to join the **Sturt Highway**, which heads, via Mildura on the Victorian border, to Adelaide. Any route west is eventually obliged to cross the **Newell Highway**, the direct route between Melbourne and Brisbane that cuts straight across the heart of central New South Wales. The most exciting Outback routes head north and west, though, passing through Dubbo, at the junction of the Newell and **Mitchell** highways, and then plunging into real isolation: north to **Lightning Ridge** or **Bourke** and western Queensland, or west on the **Barrier Highway**, right across the state to **Broken Hill**, almost at the South Australian border.

Bathurst, Dubbo and the central west

The central west of New South Wales is much underrated, seldom visited but often passed through. Yet its rich, fertile land lends itself to cherry trees and undulating green hills – providing both seasonal work and ripe picnicking spots for travellers – and the intermittent towns have their own rewards, not least **Mudgee** with its surrounding vineyards. **Dubbo** is the region's major city, and while it's not the most appealing of places, it proves an excellent base from which to start a roadtrip to Broken Hill and the Outback.

Bathurst and around

The gracious city of **BATHURST**, elegantly situated on the western slopes of the Great Dividing Range 209km west of Sydney, is Australia's oldest inland settlement. Its beautifully preserved nineteenth-century architecture makes it worth a weekend visit from Sydney, to browse the antique shops and mellow out in one of the city's many cafés. The settlement was first founded by Governor Macquarie in 1815, but Bathurst remained nothing more than a small convict and military settlement for years, only slowly developing into the main supply centre for the surrounding rich pastoral area. It was the discovery of **gold** nearby at the Lewis Ponds Creek at Ophir in 1851 (see p.346), and more later the same year on the Turon River, that resulted in a goldrush which changed the life of the town and the colony for ever. Soon rich fields of alluvial gold were discovered in every direction and, being the first town over the mountains for those on the way to the goldfields, Bathurst prospered and grew. The population increased dramatically: in 1885 Bathurst was proclaimed a city, and in the late 1890s it was even proposing itself (unsuccessfully) as the site for the capital of the new Commonwealth of Australia.

Although there's still the odd speck of gold and a few gemstones (especially sapphires) in the surrounding area, modern Bathurst has reverted to its role as a community in the centre of some of the richest agricultural land in New South Wales, a pastoral and fruit- and grain-growing district. It's also a tertiary education centre, with many students attending the Mitchell campus of Charles Sturt University. For anyone heading west, it's still the first stop beyond the mountains, and the gateway to the Outback. In October and November, visitors are also drawn to the big annual motor-racing meeting – centred around the famous **F.A.I. 1000** endurance race – at the Mount Panorama Racing Circuit.

The City

Because of its cool climate – proximity to the mountains means it can be cold at night and sometimes snowy in winter – and a scattering of grand nineteenth-century buildings, the town has a very different feel to anywhere on the coast or on the baking plains further west.

Pick up a map from the modern **Bathurst Visitor Information Centre** at 28 William St (daily 9am–5pm; ☏02/6332 1444, ℱ6332 2333, Ⓦwww.bathurstcity.com) to help you find some of the stately mansions scattered around that bear testimony to Bathurst's former wealth; one of their pamphlets outlines an entertaining self-guided walk through the historic city centre. The old **courthouse** on Russell Street, built in 1880, makes a good place to start exploring, and there's also an interesting little **museum** tucked away in the east wing (Tues, Wed, Sat & Sun 10am–4pm or by appointment on ☏02/6332 4755; $2), which displays relics and archives of regional pioneer history along with some interesting Aboriginal artefacts. The **Regional Gallery**, 70 Keppel St (Tues–Sat 1–5pm, Sun 2–5pm; free), is a fine provincial art gallery which has a very good ceramic collection and paintings by Lloyd Rees, as well as regular special and travelling exhibitions. **Machattie Park**, further north up Keppel Street, on the corner of William Street, offers a chance to relax amid landscaped Victorian-era gardens with duck ponds and spreading shady trees; there's also a Fern House, and a Begonia House which has an impressive display from mid-February to Easter. Look out, too, for the **Chifley Home** at 10 Busby St (Tues–Sat 2–4pm, Sun 10am–noon; $2.75), once the residence of Bathurst's most famous son, who was born to a blacksmith and his wife in south Bathurst in 1885, and was Prime Minister of Australia between 1945 and 1949.

Further afield, a drive up to **Mount Panorama** and its famous racing circuit provides, as you might expect, panoramic views of the city: there's the **National Motor-Racing Museum** on Pit Straight (daily 9am–4.30pm; $6.60), at the beginning of the racing circuit, featuring famous racing cars and bikes, along with photographs and memorabilia from the races. **Sir Joseph**

Banks's Nature Park (daily 9am–3.30pm; $3.30) occupies the summit of the hill, enabling native birds and animals, including wallabies, kangaroos and koalas, to enjoy the vistas from a large area of bushland; the visitors centre houses an aquarium and a reptile collection. Not far away, the **Bathurst Goldfields** on Conrod Straight (Mon–Fri 10am–4pm; guided tours $7.15; ⓦ www.bathurstgoldfields.com), a reconstruction of a former gold-mining area, are worth a visit if you're not going to make it to one of the actual gold towns further out. Goldrush mining methods are demonstrated and explained, and you can even take individual lessons in gold-panning. A bit further out, the **Bathurst Sheep and Cattle Drome** on Limekilns Road, 8km northeast of the city, has an educational and entertaining show (daily at 11.30am, extra shows during school holidays; $11, children $6.60) covering everything you always wanted to know about sheepshearing and milking cows.

Practicalities

Accommodation is relatively expensive here, but try the *Park Hotel* at the corner of George and Keppel streets (℡ 02/6331 3399; ④) for comfortable B&B and motel-style units. There are a dozen or more motels along the highway, as well as holiday units at *Rossmore Park Farm Holidays*, at the Bathurst Sheep and Cattle Drome (see above; ℡ 02/6337 3634, Ⓕ 6337 3441, ⓦ http://civ.com.au/rossmore; ⑦ full board), and **camping** at *East Bathurst Holiday Park*, on the highway in Kelso, 5km east (℡ 02/6331 8286, ⓦ www.alaneastholidayparks.com.au; cabins ③). One budget option is the *Family Hotel* on the corner of Bentick and Russell streets (℡ 02/6334 2414; ③), which is clean and cheap and includes breakfast – though be aware that the pub below features topless girls on Thursday and Friday nights. Otherwise the *Edinboro Castle* at 134 William St (℡ 02/6331 5020; ④) has reasonably-priced singles and doubles as does the nearby *Knickerbocker Hotel* at 110 William St (℡ 02/6332 4500; ⑤) which also includes breakfast. For a splurge, the best suites are at the lavish *Royal Hotel* at 108 William St (℡ 02/6332 4920, Ⓕ 6332 3132; ⑦), the town's jewel-in-the-crown heritage building.

There's a variety of **restaurants** in the city centre, including Thai, Indian and modern Australian cuisine. Most of the town's pubs also serve counter meals or have bistros at the back. The *Yoga Tandoori House* at 94 Bentick St (℡ 02/6332 3320; lunch Mon & Wed–Sat, dinner daily) has an extensive selection of curries including many veggie ones. For à la carte dining, try *Lamplighters* at 126 William St (℡ 02/6331 1448; closed Sun) with blackboard specials and old world charm. In a similar vein, *Vines Cottage* at 142 William St (℡ 02/6331 6470; closed Sun) has some more unusual fare, including dishes like kangaroo in port and blackberry sauce. In the *Royal Hotel* building, the *Heritage Royal Coffee House* has superb coffee and cakes, while *Crêpes Royale* serves French-inspired dishes from morning tea to dinner (closed Mon). *Zegelers Cafe* at 52 Keppel St (℡ 02/6332 1565), close to the train station, has good lunches in a leafy courtyard and cosy, candlelight dinners in the evening.

Due to the presence of so many students, Bathurst has a reasonable **nightlife**, centering mainly on the pubs close to the university. Particularly popular is the *Oxford Tavern* on the corner of William and Piper streets, opposite the enormous *Leagues Club*. Friday is club night, featuring guest DJs at the *Site* on George Street ($6 entry).

Around Bathurst

The area **around Bathurst**, heading towards the Mudgee wine country, is dotted with semi-derelict villages and ghost towns dating back to the goldrushes of the nineteenth century. A scenic drive to the north via Peel and Wattle Flat leads to the tiny, picturesque village of **SOFALA**, 35km north of Bathurst on the Turon River, en route to Mudgee. Gold was found in the river here in 1851, just three weeks after the very first gold strikes in Australia, and today the narrow, winding main street still follows the course of the river. A good spot for a drink is the *Sofala Royal Hotel*, a very atmospheric, classic wooden pub with a big balcony; they also offer meals, and **rooms** (℡02/6337 7008; ❹) with a period flavour. There's basic **tent** space at the *Village Camping Area* on Clarke Street (℡02/6337 8206).

From Sofala, a very narrow, bone-rattling unsealed road follows the Turon River towards **HILL END**, an even more important goldrush site located on a plateau above the Turon Valley, 86km from Bathurst. In 1870, Hill End was the largest inland centre in New South Wales, a booming gold-mining town with a population of about twenty thousand, with 53 hotels, plus all the accoutrements of a wealthy settlement. Within ten years, however, gold production had faltered and Hill End had already become a virtual ghost town. It stayed that way until 1967, when the area was proclaimed a historic site and huge efforts were made to restore and preserve the town. You can pick up a leaflet at the NPWS **visitors centre** in the old hospital (daily 9.30am–12.30pm & 1.30–4.30pm; ℡02/6337 8206), where there is also a small museum ($2), and take a self-guided walk around the village, or rent some equipment and try your hand at panning or fossicking. There's an underground **mine tour** daily at 1pm ($4.50) and a gold-panning tour at 11am ($3). You can **stay** in the *Royal Hotel* here (℡02/6337 8261, ℻6337 8393; ❸) and **eat** in the restaurant. There is also a B&B, as well as **camping** areas run by the NPWS.

Another enjoyable excursion, this time to the south, takes in the former gold-mining towns of Rockley, 35km south of Bathurst, and Trunkey Creek, and then continues to the spectacular **Abercrombie Caves**, 72km south of Bathurst in the middle of a large nature reserve. The principal and most impressive cavern, the **Grand Arch** (self-guided tours daily 10am–4pm; $11), is 221m long, about 39m wide at the north and south entrances, and in some places over 30m high – it's said to be the largest natural limestone arch in the southern hemisphere. More than eighty other caves are dotted around the reserve. In one of them, miners constructed a dance floor more than a century ago, and concerts or church services are still held here occasionally. Also within the reserve are old gold mines, and swimming holes in **Grove Creek**, which runs right through the reserve, plunging more than 70m over the Grove Creek Falls at the southern edge. There's a **camping area** on the shore (℡02/6368 8603; cabins ❸), complete with a public fossicking ground.

Mudgee and the wine country

The large, old country town of **MUDGEE**, in the Kamilaroi language meaning "the nest in the hills", is the centre for an often-overlooked wine region about 120km north of Bathurst. The town is set along the lush banks of the Cugewong River, and the countryside appears to have more grazing cows and sheep than vineyards. The wines, once referred to as "Mudgee mud", have improved in the past few years: the Cabernet Sauvignon and Shiraz wines are the tastiest, although the area's Chardonnays are gaining a good reputation. You can reach Mudgee via Hill End, but it's a bumpy unsealed route, and you're better off approaching via Sofala on an 88-kilometre sealed road (except for a small section) – watch out for sheep.

When you arrive, head for the **tourist information centre** at 84 Market St (Mon–Fri 9am–5pm, Sat 9am–3.30pm, Sun 9.30am–2pm; ℡02/6372 1020, www.mudgeewine.com.au) to pick up a copy of the *Mudgee Region Visitors' Guide*, which has detailed winery information and maps. Mudgee's proximity to Sydney means that **accommodation** is booked out at weekends, when it's best to call in advance. Some places worth targeting are the *Federal Hotel* at 34 Inglis St (℗ 02/6372 2150, www.pubstay.com.au; ❸); the central but more upmarket *Wanderlight Motor Inn*, 107 Market St (℗ 02/6372 1088, ℗ 6372 2859; ❺), which has a pool and spa and some units adapted for disabled travellers; and the gay-friendly *Parkview Guest House*, 99 Market St (℗ 02/6372 4477 or free call 1800 621 531; ❼), a quiet, centrally located B&B built in 1859. Other heritage houses worth staying at for the charm factor include *Bleak House*, 7 Lawson St (℗ 02/6372 3030, www.bleakhouse.net; ❼), with private verandahs overlooking the Cugewong River, and the *Lauralla Historic Guesthouse*, Lewis and Mortimer streets (℗ 02/6372 4480, ℗ 6372 3320, www.bedandbreakfast.org.au; ❼) a classic Victorian-style home offering "murder mystery" and wine weekends. **Campers** should head for the *Mudgee Valley Village*, corner of Bell Street and Gulgong Road, 1.5km west of the centre (℗ 02/6372 1236), which has a pool, kiosk and barbecues. With the exception of the award-winning *Grape Vine Restaurant* at *Lauralla Historic Guesthouse*, Mudgee isn't really a town in which to eat out, so your best bet for a **meal** is the pub food at places such as the *Lawson Park Hotel*, a great old country pub on Church Street, which does roasts on Monday and Tuesday and pasta specials on Wednesday night. You could also lunch at one of the wineries such as Poet's Corner (see box below); or try the tearooms (Thurs–Sun 10am–4pm only) attached to the *Parkview Guest House*, for refreshments on the verandah or in the courtyard.

Mudgee wineries – five of the best

Botolabar, Botolabar Lane (Mon–Sat 10am–5pm, Sun 10am–3pm; ℗ 02/6373 3840). An organic winery with self-guided tours (40min). Tastings on a shady terrace; picnic area and BBQs.

Huntingdon Estate Wines, Cassilis Rd (Mon–Fri 9am–5pm, Sat 10am–5pm, Sun 10am–3pm); ℗ 02/6373 3730). A rather bland and functional building producing some of the region's most delicious wines. Particularly recommended are the young Semillions, and the intense, heady Cabernet Sauvignon from 1995. An excellent annual chamber music festival takes place here in November.

Miramar Wines, Henry Lawson Drive (daily 9am–5pm; ℗ 02/6373 3874). Atmospheric tastings among old cobwebbed casks. The well-respected wine maker, Ian MacRae, established the winery in 1977; he's serious about his wines, and specializes in delicious whites.

Pieter Van Gent, Black Springs Rd (Mon–Sat 9am–5pm, Sun 11am–4pm; ℗ 02/6373 3807). Tastings in a delightful setting: beautiful nineteenth-century choir stalls on cool earth floors, overshadowed by huge old barrels salvaged from Penfolds. Try their Pipeclay Port, a tawny port aged in wood, a blend of various vintages. The winemaker is Dutch, and the herbs he uses in his traditional vermouth are specially imported from Holland.

Poet's Corner, Craigmoor Rd (Mon–Sat 10am–4.30pm, Sun 10am–4pm; ℗ 02/6372 2208, www.poetscornerwines.com). Incorporating Craigmoor, Montrose and Poet's Corner wines. The original 1859 cellar, a vast space with a huge open fireplace, has a tin roof held up by tree-trunk beams. Upstairs is an equally characterful, expensive restaurant (daily lunch, Fri & Sat dinner), while outside, views of hills and vineyards are fronted by peaceful lawns fragrant with flowers and a perfect cricket pitch.

Orange, Forbes and Parkes

ORANGE, on the Mitchell Highway en route from Bathurst to Dubbo, is a small city on the eastern slopes of Mount Canabolas; coming from Bathurst, the drive is a pleasant one through undulating countryside, with the valley opening up before you. Orange is a pretty place full of trees, including many European varieties; it claims to have four distinct seasons, and the chilly winter always sees one or two snowfalls. Its major industry is **apple growing**, based in the apple orchards southwest of the town. You can find apple-picking **work** here from late February or early March for a period of about six weeks, while cherry picking takes place from late November to early January; contact the Employment National (℡13 3444). Many growers have rough accommodation on their properties but demand often outstrips supply, so bring a tent. The **Orange Visitors Centre** on Byng Street (daily 9am–5pm; ℡02/6393 8226, ℻6393 8220, Ⓦwww.orange.nsw.gov.au) has information on local attractions, which include the **Ophir diggings**. The first gold field in Australia, established in 1851 and only 30km north of Orange, the site is still much as the diggers left it – beware of open shafts.

Orange prides itself on being rather cosmopolitan, and it has quite a **café** society and some well-regarded **restaurants**. *Scottys on Summer* at 202a Summer St prepare gourmet sandwiches, while the *Union Bank Cafe* at 84 Byng St has a good range of vegetarian dishes and *Cafe 48*, at 48 Sale St (BYO), offer praiseworthy Southeast Asian curries. For something a little more special, *Sloozi's* on Summer Street (℡02/6563 1314; dinner Tues–Sat) serve tasty food in a convivial, casual atmosphere, whilst *Selkines* on Anson Street (℡02/6361 1179, dinner Tues–Sat) offers the opportunity of an expensive foray into modern Australian cuisine. A recommended place both to **stay** and eat is the *Metropolitan Hotel* at 107 Byng St (℡02/6362 1353, ℻6361 3806; ❹–❻), just up from the tourist office. It's a huge old-fashioned country pub built in 1872, with a wooden verandah where you can sit and eat barbecued dishes, hot potatoes, damper and salad. Hotel rooms are clean and nicely decorated, and all have TV but no en-suite facilities, while the more expensive motel suites come with all mod cons. Alternatively, try the *Hotel Canabolas* at 248 Summer St (℡02/6362 2444, Ⓔhotelcanabolas@cww.otec.org.au; ❺), which has live music on Thursday, Friday and Saturday nights. Pickers could consider the two **caravan parks**, both a few kilometres from the centre: to the north, the *Colour City Caravan Park* on Margaret Street (℡02/6362 7254; cabins ❷); and to the east, the *Canabolas Caravan Park*, 166 Bathurst Rd (℡02/6362 7279; cabins ❸).

Forming a triangle, with Orange at the apex, Forbes and Parkes to the west are also important regional towns. **FORBES**, on the Lachlan River, is a graceful old town famous as the stomping ground of the nineteenth-century bushranger **Ben Hall**, who is buried in the Forbes Cemetery. **PARKES**, 33km to the northwest along the Newell Highway, is well known for its **Observatory** which has a 64-metre radio telescope. The observatory's **visitors centre** (daily 8.30am–4.15pm; ℡02/6861 1777, Ⓦwww.parkes.atnf.csiro.au) has a 25-minute audiovisual presentation, The Invisible Universe (daily 8.30am–3.30pm; every 30min; $3). Both towns have fast, reasonable **internet** access: at 195–197 Clannda St in Forbes, and 113–127 Rankin St in Parkes. Just east of Forbes lies the small township of **ELLGOWRA**, where in 1962 Frank Gardiner and his gang pulled off the biggest gold heist in Australian history. They took a total of $3700 in cash and 77kg in gold from a mailcoach – worth an impressive $1.3 million at today's rates.

Cowra

COWRA, on the banks of the Lachlan River, 107km southwest of Bathurst along the Mid-Western Highway, is famous as the location of the **Cowra Breakout** during World War II. The breakout of August 5, 1944 saw the escape of 378 Japanese prisoners of war armed with baseball bats, staves, home-made clubs and sharpened kitchen knives – those who were sick and remained behind hanged or disembowelled themselves, unable to endure the disgrace of capture. It took nine days to recapture all the prisoners, during which four Australian soldiers and 231 Japanese died. The breakout was little known until the publication of Harry Gordon's excellent 1970s account *Die Like the Carp* (republished as *Voyage of Shame*; see "Books", p.1179).

You can see the site of the prisoner-of-war camp, now just ruins and fields, on Sakura Avenue on the northeast edge of town. The graves of the Japanese, who were buried in Cowra, were well cared for by members of the local Returned Servicemen's League, a humanitarian gesture which touched Japanese embassy officials who then broached the idea of an official **Japanese War Cemetery**. Designed by Shigeru Yura, the tranquil burial ground is further north, on Doncaster Drive. The theme of Japanese–Australian friendship and reconciliation continued in Cowra with the establishment of the **Japanese Garden** (daily 8.30am–5pm; $7.70) in 1979 with funding from Japanese and Australian governments and companies. The large garden, designed by the internationally known Ken Nakajima to represent the landscape of Japan, is set on a hill overlooking the town, on a scenic drive running north off Kendal Street, the main thoroughfare. Cherry and other flowering trees blossom and their leaves change colour with the autumn, mirroring the northern hemisphere's change of seasons. It's very peaceful and idyllic here: cooling on a hot day, with the shade and the sound of the stream burbling through the garden. A further anti-war symbol in Cowra is the **World Peace Bell** in Civic Square; and the planting of an avenue of cherry trees connecting the war cemeteries, the POW campsite and the Japanese Garden. The introduction of the **POW Theatre**, at the Cowra Vistors Centre, is another attraction explaining the war years, the breakout and the reconciliation process since then.

For more information on the town, and **accommodation** options if you want to stay, head for the very helpful **Cowra Visitor Information Centre**, at the corner of Grenfell and Boorowa roads on the Mid-Western Highway (daily 9am–5pm; ℡02/6342 4333 or free call 1800 023 082, ⓦ www.cowra.org), near the large riverside park. An interesting alternative to the usual motels and campsitess is the *Woolpack Backpacker's Farmstay* (℡02/6385 8433, ⓦ www.backpackers-farmstay.com.au) at Riverslea Station in nearby Wyangala Waters State Park; their five-day packages cost $370 per person and include your first day's horse riding in serene countryside, with moon parties, candlelight, and a very chilled out vibe thrown in for good measure.

There are lots of **vineyards** in the Cowra area – actually more than in Mudgee – but no wineries; instead, grapes are sent off to large wineries elsewhere to be made into wine. Their origin is often revealed by their names, such as Richmond Grove Cowra Wine. The region is best known for Chardonnay: to taste the product of the local grapes, head for the Quarry Cellar, 5km from Cowra on the Boorowa Road (Tues–Sun 10am–4pm; ℡02/6342 3650); the attached restaurant (lunch Tues–Sun, dinner Fri & Sat) also does Devonshire teas and inexpensive light lunches of pasta and salads. If you're interested in the possibility of some **grape-picking** work, contact the Employment National (℡13 3444).

Young

Seventy kilometres southwest of Cowra along the Olympic Way, the hilly town of **YOUNG** is a good spot to pick up some **cherry-picking** work during the season (approximately six weeks from the first week of Nov). Being monotonous rather than strenuous, the work attracts a genteel crowd and is popular with retired Queenslanders. If you just want to pick your own and have a look at some orchards and packing sheds, there are a number of them on the way into town from Cowra; you could also contact the Employment National on Boorowa Street (℡02/6340 2900). The long weekend in October generally coincides with the time when the **cherry blossoms** are in full bloom – a glorious sight. There's even a Cherry Festival each year, in late November/early December. There are also several vineyards on the slopes of the undulating area, which is becoming known as the Hilltops wine region; one worth visiting is the small, family-run **Woodonga Hill Winery**, 10km north of Young on the Olympic Way (daily 9am–5pm; ℡02/6382 2972).

Young also has some significance as the site of the notorious **Lambing Flat Riots**, described in every Australian history book. A former gold-mining centre known then as Lambing Flats, the town was the site of racist riots against Chinese miners in June 1861. As the gold ran out, European miners resented what they saw as the greater success of the more industrious Chinese. Troops had to be called in when the Chinese were chased violently from the diggings, beaten, their pigtails cut off, and their property destroyed. Carried at the head of the mob was a flag, painted on a tent flysheet, with the Southern Cross in the centre, and "Roll Up, Roll Up, No Chinese" lettered in the manner of a circus flyer. You can see the original flag, and other exhibits relating to the riots, in the **Lambing Flat Folk Museum** (Mon–Sat 10am–4pm, Sun 10.45am–4pm; $2), located on the Olympic Way, just south of Boorowa Street. For more information, including lists of accommodation and where to eat, contact the **Young Visitor Information Centre**, 2 Short St (Mon–Fri 9am–5pm, Sat & Sun 9.30am–4pm; ℡02/6382 3394, ✉tourist@yol.net.au). A recommended **farmstay** outside town is *Old Nubba School House* (℡02/6943 2513; ❹–❺), halfway between Young and Cootamundra on the Olympic Highway; the peaceful self-contained accommodation, a former schoolhouse in the grounds of the friendly family farm, sleeps up to six and breakfast provisions are included.

Dubbo

DUBBO, an Aboriginal word meaning "red earth", is a self-styled "Wild West" country city on the banks of the Macquarie River, 420km northwest of Sydney and about 200km from Bathurst. The regional capital for the west of the state, it supports many agricultural industries and is located at a vital crossroads where the Melbourne–Brisbane **Newell Highway** meets the **Mitchell Highway** and routes west to Bourke or Broken Hill.

As such, it's well used to people passing through, but not staying long. If you do stop, drop by the **Western Plains Zoo** on Obley Road, 5km south of town off the Newell Highway (daily 9am–4pm; $18; keeper talks Sat, Sun & school holidays at 10.30am, 11.30am, 1.30pm, 2pm & 3pm; 2hr zoo walks for an additional $3 Sat & Sun at 6.45am; ⊛www.zoo.nsw.gov.au). The vast, open-range zoo features expansive landscaped habitats, through which many Australian animals are free to roam; other animals from five continents are kept in natural surroundings, separated from the public by moats or creeks rather than fences wherever possible. The zoo is crisscrossed by walking and cycling paths: especially during the hot months, the best idea is to get up early in the morning and set off early – by noon, the temperatures can become unbearable and the animals sometimes slink off out of sight into the shade. There is no public transport to the zoo, so cycling there, and around the zoo itself, is a good option: Wheeler Cycles, 193 Brisbane St (℡02/6882 9899), rents out bikes; electronic carts and bikes can also be rented at the zoo itself ($11 for 4hr bike hire). If you prefer to walk, there's a pleasant cycle track following the river which takes around an hour on foot from the city centre. Otherwise, Langley's Dubbo Day Tours do pricey escorted bus tours (call ℡02/6884 5333 for times and prices) or you can take a taxi (Radio Cabs ℡13 1008).

The state's largest **Livestock Market**, 3km north out of town on the Newell Highway, auctions sheep and cattle every Monday, Thursday and Friday (unloading from 8.30am). It's worth a visit just to see the local farmers decked out authentically in their Akubra hats and Drizabone coats, and to get the authentic smell of country life. The YHA gives lifts to the market to its guests on request.

If you have another hour to spare, head for the **Old Dubbo Gaol** on Macquarie Street in the centre of town (daily 9am–4.30pm; $7). A hundred years ago, this fortress-style building housed some of the most notorious criminals of the west, and today it glories in the details of nineteenth-century prison life, with loving attention to the macabre: the gallows, the hangman's kit and the careers of some of those who were executed here. In the cells, life-size (and convincingly lifelike) animatronic models of convicted criminals tell the stories of their lives and condemned futures.

The **Dubbo Museum** at 234 Macquarie St (daily noon–4.30pm; $5.50) has an extensive and somewhat chequered collection of items of regional history. There are agricultural and transport exhibits, a colonial kitchen, musical instruments, a dentist's surgery and the re-creation of a village square complete with drapery store, bootmaker, barber and blacksmith. Also worth a look-in is the National Trust property **Dundullimal Homestead** (daily 9am–5pm), 2km past the zoo on Obley Road. An 1840s slab house with stone stables, it now houses a craft shop and mini farm, and you can sometimes see the odd jackeroo riding oxen rodeo-style. A visit here is best combined with a "hayride" on a truck and cruise on the Macquarie River, stopping in at the property for afternoon teas. Tours cost from $16, bookable on ℡02/6884 9984 or through the visitors centre.

The Dubbo **Regional Gallery** at 165 Darling St (Tues–Sun 11am–4.30pm) has a kitsch collection of animals represented in art, including, surprisingly, an exceptional painting of a fox by the noted Australian artist Arthur Boyd. They also have a rotating cultural programme, including indigenous works at times.

Practicalities

As it's a crossroads, Dubbo's 24-hour **bus** terminal, at the junction of the Mitchell and Newell highways, is busy with daily connections to Brisbane, Sydney, Melbourne, Adelaide, Canberra, Newcastle and Port Stephens. Just across the railway line is the **train station**, terminal for the XPT to and from Sydney. Countrylink (℡13 2839) buses leave here for Bourke and Lightning Ridge. You can also **fly** to Dubbo with Hazelton (℡13 1713) and Eastern Australia (℡13 1313) from Sydney; Hazelton also flies to Broken Hill and Coolangatta from here, and Air Link (℡02/6884 2435) has other Outback/northwest connections: to Bourke, Brewarrina, Cobar, Coonamble, Lightning Ridge, Nyngan and Walgett. Thrifty (at the train station) rents cars from $50 a day. The helpful **Dubbo Visitors Centre** (daily 9am–5pm; ℡02/6884 1422, Ⓦwww.dubbo.com.au) is set in a riverside park at the corner of Erskine and

Macquarie streets, just off the Newell Highway. As well as giving out good free maps and information, the centre sells discounted "ZooPlusII" tickets.

As you'd expect, there are plenty of **motels**, with the majority on the Mitchell Highway (called Cobar St as it passes through town). A couple of the better-value ones are the *Merino Motel*, 65 Church St, 200m south of the city centre (℡02/6882 4133; ❹), and the budget *Formule 1* (℡02/6882 9211; ❸) on Wyandra Street. Two old **hotels** downtown offer a bit more character: the *Pastoral*, 110 Tabralgar St (℡02/6882 4219; ❸), has a huge verandah and the cheapest rooms in town, or there's the *Castlereagh Hotel*, on the corner of Brisbane and Tabralgar streets (℡02/6882 4877; ❹). The most salubrious pub-hotel in town is the *Amaroo Hotel*, 81 Macquarie St (℡02/6882 3533, ℻6884 2601; ❺), which has renovated rooms and includes a cooked breakfast. *Mayfair Cottage*, 10 Baird St (℡02/6882 5226; ❻), is another good breakfast-included choice, and has a separate guest wing and a pool. The *Dubbo YHA Hostel* at 87 Brisbane St (℡02/6882 0922; rooms ❷, dorms ❶) is a cosy and welcoming family-run hostel with all rooms opening out on to outdoor seating decks. It's located within walking distance of the train station and the city centre, although the owner suggests taking a cab (℡02/6882 1911) if you're arriving at night; the hostel also rent bikes ($6) and sell discounted zoo tickets. **Campsites** include *Dubbo City Caravan Park* on Whylandra Street, 2km west (℡02/6882 4820, ✉ddcp@dubbo.nsw.gov.au; cabins ❸, on-site vans ❷), and *Poplars Caravan Park*, overlooking the river near the city centre on Lower Bultje Street (℡02/6882 4067; cabins ❸, on-site vans ❷).

Dubbo has developed a bit of a **café society**. The self-consciously trendy *Echidna Cafe* at 177 Macquarie St (closed Sun & Mon), serves expensive contemporary Australian cuisine, but you can just drop in for an excellent coffee. The *Grapevine Cafe*, 144 Brisbane St, is more low-key – a relaxing place with a lovely, leafy courtyard, generous portions and breakfast served until noon at the weekend. For fresh bread and cakes, try the *Village Hot Bake* on Darling Street, by the railway station, a bustling bakery on two levels, also serving pies, fries and pizzas. If you crave the usual country-town fare, the *Amaroo Hotel* has the best **bistro** in Dubbo. There are also several **restaurants** at the bottom end of the main shopping area, including the recommended *Darbar* at 215 Macquarie St (℡02/6884 4338), a tandoori house located in an old sandstone basement.

The Northwest

From Dubbo the **Newell Highway**, the main route from Melbourne to Brisbane, continues through the wheat plains of the northwest, their relentless flatness relieved by the ancient eroded mountain ranges of the **Warrumbungles**, near Coonabarabran, and **Mount Kaputar**, near Narrabri, with the **Pillaga Scrub** between the two towns. Clear skies and the lack of large towns with their attendant lights make the area ideal for the **telescopes** that stare into space at both Coonabarabran and Narrabri. The thinly populated northwest has a relatively large percentage of Aborigines, peaking in the largest town of **Moree**. In 1971 Charles Perkins, an Aboriginal activist, led the **Freedom Ride**, a group of thirty people – mostly university students – who bussed through New South Wales on a mission to root out racism in the state. The biggest victory was in Moree itself when the riders, facing hostile townsfolk, broke the race bar by escorting Aboriginal children into the public swimming pool.

The **Namoi Valley** – extending from Gunnedah, just west of Tamworth, to Walgett – with its rich black soil, is **cotton country**. Beyond Walgett, just off the sealed Castlereagh Highway that runs from Dubbo, is **Lightning Ridge**, a scorching-hot opal-mining town relieved by the hot **artesian bore baths** which are a feature of the northwest.

Coonabarabran and the Warrumbungles

COONABARABRAN is a touristy little town on the Castlereagh River, 160km north of Dubbo via the Newell Highway, and 465km northwest of Sydney. People come here to gaze at stars in the clear skies, or for bushwalking and climbing in the spectacular Warrumbungles, an ancient mountain range 35km to the west.

By virtue of its proximity to the **Siding Spring Observatory Complex** (daily 9.30am–4pm; $5.50), perched high above the township on the edge of the Warrumbungle National Park, Coonabarabran considers itself the astronomy capital of Australia. The skies are exceptionally clear out here, due to the dry climate and a lack of pollution and population. The giant 3.9-metre optical telescope (one of the largest in the world) can be viewed close up from an observation gallery, and there's an astronomy exhibition, complemented by hands-on exhibits and a video show. There's no public transport here, but the school bus passes by – ask at the visitors centre (see below). You can't actually view the stars at Siding Spring, but the **Skywatch Observatory** (daily; opening times vary; $7.70, night show $12.10; book before dusk on ☎02/6842 3303; ⊛ www.skywatch.cx) on Timor Road, 2km from town on the way to the Warrumbungles, has night viewing through its modern telescope, plus a planetarium and computer space-simulation programs.

Warrumbungle National Park

The rugged **Warrumbungles** are ancient mountains of volcanic origin with jagged cliffs, rocky pinnacles and crags jutting from the western horizon. The dry western plains and the moister environment of the east coast meet at these ranges, with plant and animal species from both habitats coexisting in the park. Warrumbungle means "crooked mountains" in an Aboriginal language, and the park was in fact bordered by three different language groups – the Kamilaroi, the Weilwan and Kawambarai. Evidence of Aborigines' past visits is common, with stone flakes used to make tools indicating old campsites. The **Warrumbungle National Park** is spectacular, especially in spring when the wild flowers in the sandstone areas are in bloom. The most popular months with visitors are April, September and October: it's really just too hot for walking here in summer, and the cold winters sometimes bring snow. If you do come in the hot months, remember to take plenty of water when you go walking, and something warm for the nights, which get quite cool.

The **visitors centre**, in Coonabarabran at 56 Cassilis St (daily 8.30am–4pm; ☎02/6842 1311), has hands-on displays and detailed maps of walking tracks. The wheelchair-accessible bitumen **Gurianawa Track** makes a short circuit around the centre and overlooks the flats where Eastern Grey Kangaroos gather at dusk. Another good introduction to the park is the short **White Gum Lookout Walk** (1km), with panoramic views over the ranges that are particularly dramatic at sunset. However, the ultimate – for the reasonably fit only – is the 14.5-kilometre **Grand High Tops Trail** along the main ridge and back. The walk begins at the kangaroo-filled Camp Pincham and follows the flat floor of Spirey Creek through open forests full of colourful rosellas and lorikeets, and lizards basking on rocks. As the trail climbs, there are views of the three-hundred-metre-high Belougery Spire, and more scrambling gets you to the foot of the **Breadknife**, the park's most famous feature, thrusting 90m up into the sky. From here the main track heads on to the rocky slabs of the Grand High Tops, with tremendous views of most of the surrounding peaks and with the possibility of spotting a wedge-tailed eagle soaring above. Experienced walkers could carry on to climb Bluff Mountain and then head west for Mount Exmouth (1205m), the park's highest peak; both are great spots from which to watch the sunrise. The Warrumbungles are very popular with **rock climbers**, who are allowed to climb anywhere except the Breadknife; permits are required. There isn't any public transport to the Warrumbungles, so you'll need your own.

Practicalities

Coonabarabran's **Visitor Information Centre** on John Street (daily 9am–5pm; ☎02/6842 1441 or free call 1800 242 881, ⓦwww.lisp.com.au /coonabarabran) has tourist information and can organize special visits to out-of-the-way places, including Aboriginal sites, with Coona Country Tours (from $45 for a half-day trip).

Accommodation in the national park itself is limited to **campsites**, some of which have hot showers, electric barbecues and fireplaces (note that wood is not supplied, and while plenty of places sell it along the way, there's a fine for collecting it in the park), and *Balor Hut*, an eight-bunk hut adjacent to the Breadknife. Bookings aren't necessary for any of the sites, but you may need to book the hut; mattresses are not provided, and bookings and the key are available from the Visitor Information Centre. Anyone planning to stay in the park will need to bring provisions. Between the park and Coonabarabran, the *Warrumbungles Mountain Motel & Cabins* on Timor Road, 19km from town (☎02/6842 1832, ⓕ6842 2944, ⓦwww.warrumbungles.lisp.com.au; rooms ④, cabins ③), is set in bushland on the Castlereagh River. Rooms (BYO linen) have extra bunks and kitchens, so are good for families or small groups; there's also a small saltwater pool and a playing field. Also along Timor Road (16km from town), nestled under Bulleamble Mountain, is the *Tibuc* farm (☎02/6842 1740, ⓦwww.babs.com.au/tibuc; ⑤), where self-contained cabins vary from posh to extremely basic. There are reductions for longer stays and B&B is available; advise upon booking if you're not bringing your own linen. There are plenty of alternatives in town: on John Street you'll find the *All Travellers Motor Inn* (☎02/6842 1133, ⓕ6842 2505; ④–⑥), with air-conditioning and disabled-accessible rooms, or the excellent *Imperial Hotel* (☎02/6842 1023; ②) which has a guest lounge, kitchenette, very reasonable singles and a huge verandah with tables and armchairs for warm spring nights. Along the Newell Highway you'll find the pleasant and well-equipped *Castlereagh Village Holiday Units* (☎02/6842 1706, ⓦwww.skybusiness.com/castlereagh; ③) and on the Oxley, the shady *John Oxley Caravan Park* (☎02/6842 1635; cabins ③, on-site vans ②).

Good **places to eat** in town include the wonderful *Woop Woop*, which has excellent, modern cuisine in a cosy room of exposed brick and iron girders, situated in an alleyway just off John Street. Other establishments are all on John Street itself: the bright and airy *Jolly Cauli*, at no. 30, offers a wide choice of dishes, delicious coffee and home-made cakes, and also serves as the town's internet café. *The Lunch Box* does inexpensive midday meals, the *Imperial Hotel* has the best counter meals, and the *Golden Sea Dragon* serves up reliable Chinese food.

The Namoi Valley: cotton country

On the Oxley Highway, 76km west of the New England city of Tamworth, **GUNNEDAH**, with a population of over eight thousand, is one of the largest towns in the northwest. The town's claim to fame is as the inspiration for the Australian poet Dorothea MacKellar (1885–1968) and her patriotic verse *My Country*, in which she pledged her undying love for what was then – and still is now – a drought-stricken land. The opening stanza is familiar to most Australians, who learnt it by rote at school:

> I love a sunburnt country
> A land of sweeping plains
> Of ragged mountain ranges
> Of drought and flooding rains...

Gunnedah has one of the healthiest **koala populations** in the state, and there is a semi-permanent resident bear in a eucalypt opposite the **information centre** in Anzac Park (Mon–Fri 9am–5pm, Sat & Sun 10am–3pm; ℡ 02/6740 2230, 🖲 www.infogunnedah.com.au). The staff put out a "koala today" sign when he's home, so you'll know if you're in luck; otherwise you still have a high chance of seeing some on the Bindea Walking Track, a 7.4-kilometre walk from the information centre, or a 4.5-kilometre trek through the bush from the car park at Porcupine's Lookout; you'll also see wild kangaroos, and maybe even an echidna, but be careful because the track is quite overgrown and it's easy to get lost. Should you want **to stay** in Gunnedah, try the friendly *Regal Hotel* (℡ 02/6742 2355, 🖲 www.pubstay.com.au; ❷–❸) at 298 Conadilly St, which has a laundry, a guest lounge with an open fire and entertainment on Friday and Saturday nights. The nearest **caravan park** is 1km east of town on Henry Street (℡ 02/6742 1372; cabins and on-site vans ❷). Besides the usual pub bistros you can **eat** in more style at the rather swish *Fiorella's Italian Restaurant* at 378 Conadilly St (℡ 02/6742 5004). *Pantry Creations, Classic Visions Cafe* and *Redgum Outdoor,* all on Conadilly Street, are good for coffee, cake and healthy luncheon fare – *Redgum* also do smoothies.

While Gunnedah does have some cotton crops, **NARRABRI**, 97km northwest via the oddly named communities of Boggabri and Baan Baa, is recognized as the commercial centre of cotton growing. A little smaller than Gunnedah, the town has a prosperous feel. The **tourist information centre**, on Tibbereena Street (Mon–Fri 9am–4pm, Sat & Sun 9am–1pm; ℡ 02/6792 3583), can give you the times to go and see the five linked dishes of the **Australia Telescope** complex (℡ 02/6799 6760), 20km west on the Yarrie Lake Road. Opening times depend on what they're tracking, but the centre is staffed Monday to Friday from 8am to 4pm, entry is free and there are lots of computer models to play with. The other main attraction around Narrabri is **Mount Kaputar National Park**. The drive into the park to the 1524-metre **lookout** – with its panoramic views encompassing the vast Pillaga Scrub, the Warrumbungles and the New England Tablelands – is steep, narrow and partly unsealed (call ℡ 02/6792 1147 to check road conditions). There are eleven marked bushwalking trails in the park, with brochures available from the **NPWS office** in Narrabri at 100 Maitland St (℡ 02/6799 1740), or the **visitors centre** at **Dawsons Spring** campsite and picnic area, although the latter is not permanently staffed. The **camping** facilities at *Dawsons Spring* include hot showers, and there are a couple of cabins sleeping a maximum of six, with bathroom, kitchen and wood stove (reservations via NPWS on ℡ 02/6799 1740; cabins

❹). The most striking geological feature of the park is **Sawn Rocks**, a basalt formation which looks like a series of organ pipes; it's reached via the northern end of the park on the unsealed road heading to Bingara.

If you want to **stay** in Narrabri itself, or **eat** something, the good-value *Tourist Hotel* at 142 Maitland St (℡02/6792 2312; ❷) offers homely and clean rooms, and its restaurant, *Thurlows* (Mon–Sat 9am–3pm & 6–9pm; ℡02/7672 1125), is the most popular in town.

The drive from Narrabri to **WEE WAA**, roughly 40km west, warns of your entry into redneck territory – the roadside glitters with shattered bottles thrown from speeding cars. Wee Waa was where the Namoi cotton industry began in the 1960s, and the large cotton "gins" or processing plants are located here. During the picking and growing season (April–July) free guided tours leave Namoi Co-op (daily 10.30am & 2.30pm; 1hr 30min–3hr 30min), but you'll need your car to get around the various areas. If you can stand the rather raw, dispirited town and the blazing summer heat, there's **cotton-chipping** work here in abundance in December and January; ask at one of the two pubs on Rose Street, the main drag, and someone will send you in the right direction. From Wee Waa you can head west to Walgett and on to Lightning Ridge.

Lightning Ridge

The population of **LIGHTNING RIDGE**, 74km north of **Walgett** on the Castlereagh Highway (the road is fully sealed, but note that there's no place to stop for fuel between the two), is officially 4000 but unofficially it's reckoned to be about 10,000. It's a transient place, where people in their hordes pitch up in town lured by the town's one attraction: opal. Amid this harsh landscape scarred by holes and slag heaps, Lightning Ridge's opal fields are the only place in the world where the extremely valuable **black opal** can consistently be found. This lone enticement is heavily exploited by opal galleries and **mines** you can visit, among them the Big Opal, 3 Mile Rd (daily 9am–5pm; tours 10am & 2pm, $11), which has demonstrations of opal-cutting and guided tours of an underground mine; Spectrum Opal Mines, Bald Hill Road (daily 9am–5pm; $3), a centre displaying solid opals in an underground showroom with a film about opal-mining shown on the hour; and the Walk-in Mine, 1 Bald Hill Rd (daily 9am–4pm; tours $6), which has a mining display and tours to an underground mine. There's even an opal and gem **festival** in late July, which sees the population shoot up by another few thousand souls. The effects of the opal obsession can be seen all over town, in the faces of the residents and the glorious, crazy constructions of the few who do strike it rich; check out the **Bottle House** at 60 Opal St, a bizarrely beautiful cottage and matching dog kennel built entirely from wine bottles set in stone.

There are clearly demarcated fossicking areas where you can try your luck at finding opals – but don't do it anywhere else, or you may stray onto others' claims. Recover afterwards in the 52°C water of the **Hot Artesian Bore Baths** on Pandora Street (open 24hr; free). More cooling is the Olympic Pool on Gem Street (end Sept to Easter daily 10am–8pm), particularly appealing in the scorching heat since parts of the pool are shaded from the sun. The **Goondee Aboriginal Keeping Place** on Pandora Street (call ℡02/6829 2001 for opening times) has Aboriginal artefacts and information on bush tucker.

Practicalities

The **tourist information centre** in Lightning Ridge is in the new Miners Associated building on Morilla Street (℡02/6829 1466 or free call 1800 639

545, Ⓕ 6829 0565, Ⓦ www.lightningridge.net.au) and has opal-buying rooms attached – ask for the useful booklet *Walgett Shire and the Lightning Ridge Opal Fields*, which contains a handy guide to buying opals. The centre can also fill you in on **accommodation** possibilities (all have air-con rooms), which include the *Black Opal Motel* on Opal Street (Ⓣ 02/6829 0518, Ⓕ 6829 0884; ❹–❺), the *Wallangulla Motel*, on the corner of Morella and Agate streets (Ⓣ 02/6829 0542, Ⓔ wgulla@turboweb.com.au; ❹), and *Lightning Ridge Hotel Motel* on Onyx Street (Ⓣ 02/6829 0304, Ⓕ 6829 0306, Ⓦ www.lightning-ridge-hotel-motel.com; ❹), which also has cabins (❸) and van and tent sites (❶). The best place to **camp**, though, is *Crocodile Caravan and Camping Park*, Morilla Street (Ⓣ 02/6829 0437; cabins ❸, vans ❷), which has a pool and spa and air-con cabins. Fossicking backpackers might also like to try the *Tram-o-tel* at 2 Morilla St (Ⓣ 02/6829 0448, ❶), which has basic bunk units and is within 300m of two opal mines. Full **banking** facilities are available at Westpac on Morilla Street, and **internet** facilities at Harrisons secondhand bookstore at 48 Morilla St (Ⓣ 02/6869 0531).

The Hume Highway and the Riverina

The rolling plains of southwestern New South Wales, spreading west from the Great Dividing Range, are bounded by two great rivers: the Murrumbidgee to the north and the Murray to the south, the latter forming the border with the state of Victoria. This area is known as the **Riverina**, a name that conjures up a certain rural romance, suggesting a country Australia little visited by tourists – except those en route to Melbourne along the **Hume Highway**, which cuts a fume-filled swath through the southwest. If you're looking for work on the land, you've a reasonable chance of finding it here. The land the explorer John Oxley described as "uninhabitable and useless to civilized man" began its transformation to fertile fruit bowl when the ambitious **Murrumbidgee Irrigation Scheme** was launched in 1907, and the area around **Griffith** and **Leeton** now produces ninety percent of Australia's rice, most of its citrus fruits and twenty percent of its wine grapes. The capital of the central Riverina is **Wagga Wagga**, Australia's largest inland city. Along the Upper Murray, the main towns are on the Victorian side of the river (and are covered in the Victoria chapter), but you may drop into **Albury** en route to Melbourne on the Hume, or into **Wentworth** as a day-trip from Mildura or on the way to or from Broken Hill on the Silver City Highway. There are several interesting **festivals** in the region, including the Wagga Wagga Jazz Festival in September and the Festival of Griffith, an orgy of Aussie wine, food and culture held every May (Ⓣ 02/6964 1866).

The Hume Highway: Goulburn to Albury

If you want a quick route to Melbourne from Sydney, or vice versa, you'll inevitably end up on the rather tedious **Hume Highway**, which passes through the Southern Highlands, the Riverina and across the Murray River. Over the years the highway has been improved, but though this is one of Australia's main arteries between its two largest cities, it still narrows to one lane either way in parts. Choked with trucks, particularly at night, accidents are not infrequent, so keep your wits about you. While the highway itself may

The Hume and Hovell Walking Track

This long-distance walk starts at **Gunning**, on the Hume Highway 50km east of Goulburn, and runs over 400km southwest **to Albury**, retracing as closely as possible the route taken on foot by the two eponymous explorers in the spring and summer of 1824 on their expedition from Sydney to Port Phillip, the site of what was to become Melbourne. The walk takes about fifteen to twenty days but the layout – a Bicentenary project – allows for half-day, full-day and weekend walks. There are several free leaflets detailing different chunks, available from the Department of Conservation and Land Management in Sydney (☎02/9228 6111), Goulburn (☎02/4823 0665) and Wagga Wagga (☎02/6921 2503); the *Hume and Hovell Walking Track Guidebook* by Harry Hill (Crawford House Press, Bathurst, $19.95) is also useful.

seem dreary, some of the nearby towns are truly and typically Australian; rich in food, wine, flora and fauna and friendly locals, they can be well worth a day or so of your time. Following are the main stopping points along the way in New South Wales (for Sydney to Goulburn, see p.232) and some suggestions for food, accommodation and breaks.

Goulburn and around

Now bypassed by the Hume Highway, **GOULBURN** is still the traditional stop-off point en route to Canberra. It's a large regional centre for the surrounding area, and for a quality **wool industry** which was established in the 1820s. The town, with its wide streets, has a conservative country feel, but boasts city facilities and some large and impressive public buildings. Goulburn's connection to sheep, and one kind in particular, is made obvious to the public with the **Big Merino** (daily 8am–8pm). Another of Australia's unashamedly tacky "big things", the fifteen-metre-high sheep proudly stands next to the Ampol service station on the Old Hume Highway; the first floor has a wool industry display, and on the third level you can look out over the town through the sheep's eyes. Spare a thought for the poor beast as you traverse his insides, though; he was recently emasculated in the name of shop space. To get closer to the real thing, head for the long-established **Pelican Sheep Station** on Braidwood Road, 10km south of town (☎02/4821 4668, ☎4822 1179, ⓦwww.argylecountry.com.au/pelican; bunkhouses ❸, cabins ❹, plus camping), which has been in the same family since 1827. Tours include a shearing demonstration and the chance to see some sheepdogs being put through their paces.

There are several historic places to visit in Goulburn, including the National Trust property **Riversdale**, an 1840 coaching inn on Maud Street (mid-Sept to mid-July Sat, Sun & holidays 10am–4.30pm, at other times by appointment on ☎02/4821 9591), but the most interesting is the **Old Goulburn Brewery** on Bungonia Road (daily tastings from 11am), which has been brewing traditional ales and stouts since 1836. Details of other old properties can be obtained from the **Goulburn Visitors Centre**, next to the very impressive 1887 courthouse and opposite the shady, flower-filled Belmore Park, on Montague Street (daily 9am–5pm; ☎02/4823 0492, ⓦwww.goulbourn.nsw.gov.au); they also have a list of accommodation.

The classic place to **eat** in Goulburn, obligatory when passing through on the way to Canberra, is the *Paragon Cafe*, at 174 Auburn St, open daily for lunch and dinner. A bastion of good, filling food – inexpensive breakfasts, great hamburgers, steaks, fish, veal, pasta and pizza – it's been here for around fifty years and retains its 1940s-era fittings – it's also licensed.

The most intriguing place to **stay** in the area is at the **Gunningbar Yurt Farm**, 20km out of town on Grabben Gullen Road (℡02/4829 2114; $20 as a helper with four-hours' work per day required, but all meals included; or as part of a WWOOF placement, see p.73). A yurt, in its original form, is a Mongolian round leather tent, and the concept was enthusiastically adopted and adapted by Californian New Agers. The ones here are mostly of wood and are portable prefab buildings in the Californian mould – solar-powered, naturally lit and wood-heated. Essentially a sheep property, the "yurt village" has several yurts, each with a different function, providing an educational centre for groups of children to help them become more self-sufficient and environmentally aware. If you want to stay, you must call in advance; if you don't have your own transport, someone can pick you up.

The **Bungonia State Recreation Area**, 25km east of Goulburn, covers a rugged strip of the Southern Tablelands containing some of the deepest **caves** in Australia. The spectacular limestone Bungonia Gorge and the Shoalhaven River are two of its physical attractions.

Yass and the Burrinjuck State Recreation Area

YASS dates back to 1821 when Europeans first entered the area. Prior to this, the area had a high Aboriginal population, who gave the town its name, "yharr", meaning running water. On the outskirts of Yass as you exit the Hume Highway onto the Yass Valley Way from Goulburn (87km away) is the National Trust-owned **Cooma Cottage** (Wed–Mon 10am–4pm; $4.40), the former home of the famous explorer **Hamilton Hume**, set in rolling countryside stocked with sheep. The well-preserved nineteenth-century homestead's architectural interest is outweighed by the excellent interpretive material on Hume and his expeditions. Hume was different from many of his contemporaries in that he was born in Australia – in Parramatta, to free settlers in 1797. His explorations relied on his knowledge of the bush: he befriended Aborigines who taught him their skills and language, which made him infinitely better prepared than those equipped only with romantic notions. His first expedition was at the age of 17, accompanied by his brother and his Aboriginal friend Doual, and the trio discovered prime grazing lands in the Southern Highlands. Three years later he led the Goulburn Plains expedition, and pushing further afield in 1821 he discovered the rich and productive Yass Plains, where he settled in later life. Hume's best-known exploration was when he paired with Hovell, an English sea captain, to head for Port Phillip Bay; you can follow in their footsteps on the Hume and Hovell Walking Track (see box opposite). He also assisted Sturt in tracing the Murray and Darling rivers. The **Tourist Information Centre** (daily 9am–5pm; ℡02/6226 2557, ℱ6226 1509, ℰyasstourism@interact.net.au) has maps outlining a two-kilometre informative walk, and the **Hamilton Hume Museum** (Sat, Sun & school holidays; $2.20) contains displays on what the town looked like back in the 1890s. The old **Tramway** in the centre of town features the smallest platform in Australia (open Sun afternoons only; $3.30).

Continuing along the Hume Highway, 27km south of Yass is a turn-off to the **Burrinjuck Waters State Park**, and from here it's a 25km drive on a sealed road to the bushland park set around Burrinjuck Dam, with camping and picnic areas filled with kangaroos and chirping rosellas (℡02/6227 8114; cottages ⑤, on-site vans, units and tent sites ③). There is a **riverboat cruise** most weekends in summer on the *Lady BJ* (℡02/6227 7270; 2hr; $16) up to the dam and across the main basin. **Wee Jasper** is a picturesque village located on the backwaters of Burrinjuck Dam, with a basic **campsite** (℡02/6227

9626). From here you can visit **Carey's Caves** and see some of Australia's most spectacular limestone rock formations (Fri–Mon 9am–5pm; other times by appointment on ☎02/6227 9622; $9).

Turning off the Hume Highway at **Bowning** brings you to the peaceful village of **Binalong**. Australia's best-known poet, Banjo Patterson, spent much of his childhood here, attending the local school. Binalong railway station was used to transport gold from nearby Lambing Flats (Young), which made it a lucrative area for bushrangers. The grave of the daring bushranger "Flash" Johnny Gilbert, a member of a local outlaw gang is along the side of the road to Harden.

Gundagai and Holbrook

One hundred and four kilometres from Yass, **GUNDAGAI** sits on the southern banks of the Murrumbidgee, at the foot of the rounded bump of Mount Parnassus. The town was once situated on the alluvial flats north of the river, despite warnings from local Aborigines that the area was prone to major flooding, and old Gundagai was the scene of Australia's worst flood disaster in 1852 when 89 people drowned. The relocated Gundagai, on the main route between Sydney and Melbourne (until bypassed by the Hume Highway), became a favoured overnight stopping point, with the bullock wagons which took the pioneers into the interior favouring a camping spot out of town at Five Mile Creek. A large punt was the only means of crossing the Murrumbidgee from 1849 until the Prince Alfred Bridge was erected in 1867; although now closed to traffic, the pretty wooden bridge can still be crossed by pedestrians. Gold was eventually discovered here, and by 1864 Gundagai had become a boom town, preyed upon by the romantically dubbed bushranger **Captain Moonlight** who was eventually captured and tried at the Gundagai courthouse in 1879.

Perhaps this colourful history and the road-much-travelled appeal of Gundagai explains why the town features so often in Australian verse and folk song, finding immortality through a Jack Moses poem, in which "the dog sat on the tuckerbox, nine miles from Gundagai" – and stubbornly refused to help its master pull the bogged bullock team from the creek. Somehow the whole image became elevated from that of a disobedient hound and a fed-up, cursing teamster to a symbol of the pioneer with a faithful hound at his side. As a consequence, a **statue** of the dog was erected at the original five-mile point: it's actually a very pleasant place to take a break from the rigours of the road, with a shady picnic area and undulating fields and hills beyond. Inside the **tourist centre** here, there's a range of cheerfully tacky souvenirs plus the rare opportunity to send a postcard with a special "dog on the tuckerbox" postmark.

In the town itself, the **Gundagai Tourist Information Centre** (Mon–Fri 8am–5pm, Sat & Sun 9am–5pm; ☎02/6944 1341) can help you find somewhere to stay if need be – and also sells a tape of several folk songs featuring Gundagai, including *Along the Road to Gundagai*, from which every Australian remembers only the tuneful snatch "There's a track winding back, to an old-fashioned shack, along the road to Gundagai". Also at the information centre, you can see (for $1) the **miniature Baroque cathedral** by Frank Rusconi, the sculptor who created the statue of the noble dog. The cathedral, a project that required complete patience and precision, took 28 years to build; constructed with absolutely no plans of any sort, it is made from thousands of pieces of twenty different kinds of New South Wales marble. Satisfying more mundane appetites, *Bidgee Cakes*, at 198 Sheridan St, bakes traditional tarts using free-range eggs, and sells lamb sausage rolls plus honey rolls made from local honey.

Sixty-eight kilometres north of Gundagai, **HOLBROOK** is a recommended food break on the drive to Melbourne (or Sydney), with two excellent bakeries on the Hume Highway as it heads through town. The *Holbrook Bakery* dishes out delicious beef and curry pies, and the *Scrummy Buns Bakery* across the road sells more unorthodox pies filled with crocodile, emu, kangaroo and rabbit – plus cappuccino and continental cakes. Perhaps these great bakeries are a legacy of a German past: settled by Germans in the 1860s, Holbrook was called Germantown right up until World War I, when anti-German feeling warranted a name change.

Albury and around

The small city of **ALBURY** on the Murray River is a major stopover point on the route between Sydney and Melbourne, being roughly halfway. It's twinned with Wodonga across the river in Victoria, and although Albury is the major centre, the principal information centre is on the Wodonga side – **Albury Wodonga Visitor Information Centre** on the Hume Highway (daily 9am–5pm; ☎02/6041 3875 or free call 1800 800 743, ⓦwww.wodonga .vic.gov.au). You can also pick up tourist information from the **Albury Regional Museum** (daily 10.30am–4.30pm; free; ☎02/6021 4550) on the Hume Highway in what was once the *Turks' Head Hotel* – opportunistically sited here when the river was crossed by punt; changing exhibitions now focus on the social history of the region. The museum is set in **Noreuil Park**, a peaceful spot looking across to a bush-covered riverbank in Victoria. People lie about under the large gum trees – one of which was marked by the explorer Hovell at the point where he and Hume crossed the Murray – and swim in the river. You can also take to the water with a **cruise** on a replica paddle steamer (mid-Sept to mid-April Wed–Sat, daily during school holidays, 10.30am, 12.30pm & 3pm; $8–9.50; ☎02/6041 5558). Another pleasant place to stretch your legs is in the **Albury Botanical Gardens** at the Dean Street end of Wodonga Place. Established in 1877, the gardens hold some impressive old trees, including a huge 41-metre Queensland kauri pine; palm trees and flowerbeds fill a small grassy park, and the short fern walk is pleasantly cooling. The **Albury Regional Art Centre** is at 546 Dean St (daily 10.30am–4.30pm; free), in the decorative old town hall. The gallery's speciality is photography, but it also has a sizeable collection of Russell Drysdale's sketches and studies for paintings; the Australian artist (1912–1981) lived in the area in the 1920s and married into a local family.

Albury has a good range of places to **stay** for the night, which the tourist office can book for you. There are two **hostels**: the comfortable, activity-based *VIP Albury Backpackers*, near the train station at 452 David St (☎02/6041 1822, Ⓕ6021 6335, Ⓔthecanoeguy@hotmail.com; rooms ❷, dorms ❶), is a slightly shambolic place, reminiscent of a student flat (with the social life to match). The friendly owner rents canoes (half-day $18, full day $25) and arranges overnight **canoe trips** ($55) down the mighty Murray. He can also help line up **fruit-picking and farm work**, as well as get you involved with **conservation volunteers**. The second hostel, the YHA *Albury Motor Village,* 372 Wagga Rd (Hume Highway), Lowington (☎02/6040 2999, Ⓔalbury@yhav-ic.org.au; rooms ❸, dorms ❶), is situated at a caravan park with a pool, but it's 5km out of town. If the hostels don't appeal but you're on a tight budget, one of the best-value central motels is *The New Albury* (☎02/6021 3599, Ⓔmatthewsheridan@hotmail.com; ❸–❹), newly renovated with its own Irish bar, and blissfully situated off the highway at 491 Kiewa St. The most upmarket places to stay are the *Carlton Country Comfort*, on the corner of Dean and

Elizabeth streets (℡02/6021 5366, ⊕6041 2848, ⓔccalbury@dragnet.com.au; ❼), with a swimming pool, sauna, gym, spa and room service; or for a little lost grandeur, you could try *Gondowring B&B* (℡02/6041 4437, ⓌWwww.gundowringbb.com.au; ❼), a restored Federation residence, with full country breakfasts served on the verandah. **Campers** are catered for at *Trek-31 Tourist Park*, 8km north on the highway (℡02/6025 4355, ⓔtrek31@bigpond.com; cabins ❹).

Dean Street is lined with interchangeable, ever-changing cafés and is very much the main street for **food**: if you are ravenous and broke, *The Commercial Club* serves up one of the best deals in Australia, with all the pasta, steak, seafood and salad you can eat for $10. For something a little less functional, the retro *Electra Cafe* on the corner of Dean and Macaley streets serves a variety of internationally-influenced meals on kitsch crockery (Mon–Sat 10am–10pm, Sun 10am–3pm; live music on Tues), while *Cafe L'Espresso*, opposite the cinema, serves excellent coffee and has **internet** access. An alternative way of getting a feed is to visit the **Hume Weir Trout Farm**, a pleasant spot with landscaped gardens and waterfalls off the Riverina Highway (daily 9am–dusk; free; Ⓦwww.humeweirtrout.com.au), where the entry fee includes rods so that you can catch your own freshwater trout; there are barbecues here to cook the fish, although you must pay for the catch by the kilo. Albury is positioned in prime dairy country and you can try (and buy) some of the area's produce at the **Haberfield Dairy**, 470–482 Hovell St (Mon–Fri 10am–5.30pm, Sat 9am–1pm; 02/6021 3455), renowned for its Swiss-style cheeses.

About 10km north of Albury on the Hume Highway, the larger-than-life **Ettamogah Pub** is a parody of an Outback pub, straight out of a sketch by the Aussie cartoonist Maynard, although the precariously askew hotel really does serve drinks. Walk up the slanting staircase to the veering verandah where there are great views of the surrounding countryside. A touristy tin shack in the back flogs souvenirs.

The Murrumbidgee Irrigation Area

Irrigation has transformed the area northwest of Albury, between the Lachlan and the Murrumbidgee rivers, into a fertile valley full of orchards, vineyards and rice paddies, cut through with irrigation canals. The **Murrumbidgee Irrigation Area** (or **MIA**) extends over two thousand square kilometres, a mostly flat and – from ground level at least – featureless landscape that nonetheless is responsible for producing most of Australia's rice, approximately eighty percent of New South Wales's wine grapes, and sixty percent of its citrus fruits. The water for the irrigation area is stored in Burrinjuck and Blowering dams and flows over 400km down the Murrumbidgee River to Berembed Weir, before being diverted into the main canal, which is 155km long and feeds a network of 1450km of supply canals.

Probably the main reason you'll visit this off-the-beaten-track area is to find **work**, which there is in abundance for the intensive fruit-picking season from December to April – plus a considerable picking of Valencia oranges throughout the year as the largest citrus-growing area in Australia. At the peak season there are up to three thousand jobs going begging. The season starts in August with oranges, which are picked right through to March, then onions in November, and stonefruit, prunes and melons from December to March, overlapping with the grape harvest in February and March. Pay is calculated according to the amount picked and, basing yourself in Griffith or Leeton, you'll need your own transport – if only a bicycle – since the orchards are up to 10km outside town. To avoid the possibility of a wasted trip, due to a late season or a poor crop, it's essential to check with Employment National (☎13 3444) before turning up.

Griffith

Citrus orchards line the way into **GRIFFITH**, with a range of low hills in the background. The major centre of the MIA, it's known for its large **Italian population** and their enduring cultural life, despite the fact that some of the families arrived here around the time of World War I. More came in the 1920s, having already tried mining in Broken Hill, and the area attracted post-World War II Italian immigrants as well. Needless to say, a string of excellent Italian cafés and restaurants line the tree-filled main street of Banna Avenue, and the majority of **wineries** are run by Italian families. Designed by Walter Burley Griffin, the landscape architect from Chicago who was responsible for Canberra (see p.241), the city has since grown beyond his plan.

For free maps and information, head for the **Griffith Visitors Centre**, on the corner of Jondaryan and Banna avenues (daily 9am–5pm; ☎02/6962 4145 or free call 1800 681 141, ⓦ www.griffith.nsw.gov.au). During the week, they can arrange for you to hop on a school bus-run (7–9am & 3.30–5pm) to see the surrounding district, its rice paddies, citrus and stonefruit orchards and vineyards, for around a dollar. An even better way to get an overview of the area is to head for **Scenic Hill**, the escarpment that forms the northern boundary of the city. The **Sir Dudley de Chair's Lookout** gives a panoramic view of the horticultural enterprises below. Immediately beneath this rocky outcrop, is the **Hermit's Cave** where Valerio Recetti, an Italian immigrant, lived alone and quite undetected for ten years, working only at night and early in the morning to create his home in the caves. One cave contained a small shrine where you can still see a painted cross. During World War II he was interned in Hay (around 150km to the west of Griffith) – as were most of the local Italians – and in 1952 he returned to Italy, where he died.

Pioneer Park, in an extensive bushland setting 1.5km west of the lookout and 2km from the city centre (daily 9am–4.30pm; $6.60), has 36 buildings re-creating the era of the early MIA. The most interesting part is "Bagtown", a reconstruction of an early makeshift town built in 1910 to meet the needs of the Murrumbidgee Irrigation Area canal workers and pioneer farmers, and so-called because the homes were made of hessian cement bags with corrugated-iron roofs.

There are sixteen **wineries**, many Italian-run, in the area surrounding Griffith. Eleven are open to the public (some by appointment only); all are detailed in the *Griffith Visitors' Guide* booklet available from the visitors centre. The very first winery, McWilliam's, was established in 1913 and holds tastings in a building resembling a wine barrel (Mon–Sat 9am–5pm); there are barbecues in the grounds. Several other wineries have been around for more than fifty years, dating from the post-World War I influx of Italian immigrants. One of these is Rossetto Wines on Rossetto Road, off Leeton Road (Mon–Sat 8.30am–5.30pm). Still run by the same family, it's a down-to-earth, friendly concern known for its muscats and ports.

The *Pioneer Park* has bunkhouse **accommodation** for backpackers and fruit-pickers (☎02/6962 4196; ❶, cheap weekly rates), but it's a long uphill walk out of town, with no public transport. There's also a very basic backpackers, *Griffith International Hostel*, at 112 Binya St (☎02/6964 4236, ⓦ www.griffithinternational.com.au; ❶), but don't expect luxury. Most pickers camp or stay in caravans at the *Griffith Tourist Caravan Park*, 919 Willandra

Ave, 2km south of the centre (℡02/6964 2144, ℗6964 1126; on-site vans ❷); the *Griffith Caravan Park*, on the Leeton Road, 3km east (℡02/6962 3785; ❷); or the cheap and basic campsite at the showground on the edge of town. For a bit more comfort, the popular *Victoria Hotel*, 384 Banna Ave (℡02/6962 1299, ℗6962 1081; ❸, cheap weekly rates), has basic rooms, but there's a TV lounge with tea and coffee provided, a cool, covered courtyard, counter lunches downstairs, live entertainment (Wed–Sat) and quality bistro meals from Tuesday to Saturday.

There's no shortage of good Italian places to **eat and drink** on Banna Avenue, with the pavement tables of the hugely popular *Bassano Cafe* being a good place to sample excellent coffee and delicious *focaccia*; you can also get pasta, home-made *gelati*, pastries and biscuits. The much cheaper bakery-style *Bertoldo's Pasticerria* has budget-priced and filling pasta dishes. For gourmet picnic supplies, *Riverina Grove* on Whybrow Street is a fantastic deli stocking a wide range of regional produce. Casual meals are served at the *Belvedere Restaurant and Pizza*, 494 Banna Ave, while *La Scala*, at no. 455 (℡02/6962 4322; Tues–Sun dinner), is a more upmarket (licensed) and expensive choice. *Romeo & Giulietta Pizza Restaurant*, 40 Mackay Ave (Thurs–Sun dinner), uses a wood-fired oven for its delicious pizzas. For drinking, the town convenes at the *Gemini Hotel* on Banna Avenue, where you can sip a cocktail or down a schooner while listening to live music at the weekends.

Around Griffith

Fifty-nine kilometres southeast of Griffith, **LEETON** is the third-largest town in the MIA, with a quarter of its population of Italian extraction; like Griffith, it was designed by Walter Burley Griffin. For information on the area and details of visiting its **rice mill**, head for the **Leeton Visitor Information Centre** on Yanco Avenue (Mon–Fri 9am–5pm, Sat & Sun 9.30am–12.30pm; ℡02/6953 6481, 🖱www.leeton.nsw.gov.au). There are two **caravan parks**, both 2km southeast: the *Leeton Caravan Park*, on Yanco Avenue (℡ & ℗ 02/6953 3323), caters best for fruit-pickers with basic bunkrooms (❶), but also has on-site vans (❷) and en-suite cabins with TV (❸); while the *Oasis Holiday Park* on Corbie Hill Road (℡ & ℗ 02/6953 3882; cabins and spacious cottage ❸, vans ❷), caters more for tourists with a better range of facilities. The large, tree-filled property at *Gilgal* is also a great spot to pitch a tent, with cheap rates for pickers. Despite the Italian population, Leeton feels less cosmopolitan than Griffith, but you can nevertheless enjoy an Italian **meal** at the *MIA Social Club* on Racecourse Road (daily from 3pm; ℡02/6953 4357).

Twenty-five kilometres northeast of Griffith is the **Cocoparra National Park** in the woodland-covered Cocoparra Range. Enquire about camping and bushwalking at the NPWS office, Yambil Street, Griffith (℡02/6966 8100). Much further away, on the flat plains 185km northwest of Griffith, is **Willandra National Park**, reached via **Hillston** (64km from Griffith) on the unsealed Hillston–Mossgiel Road. The park was created in 1971 from a section of the vast Big Willandra pastoral station, a famous stud merino property which had operated since the 1860s, and now has several temporary wetland areas. As well as enabling you to experience the semi-arid riverine plains country at close quarters, a visit to the 1918 **homestead** gives an insight into station life and the wool industry. Wet weather makes all the roads to Willandra impassable, so check first with the **park office** in Hillston (℡02/6967 8159; this is also the number for **accommodation bookings**, with shared rooms available in shearers' quarters (❶) – and take extra supplies in case you get rained in.

Narrandera

Thirty kilometres southeast of Leeton, at the junction of the Sturt and Newell highways, **NARRANDERA** is a popular overnight stop en route from Adelaide to Sydney, or Melbourne to Brisbane. It's actually a very pleasant place to take a break, set on the Murrumbidgee River with streets lined with tall native and deciduous trees owing to the foresight of the pioneer settlers; its white cedars, which blossom in November, are particularly beautiful.

A good place to cool down is **Lake Talbot**, a willow-surrounded expanse of water flowing from the Murrumbidgee River. Right next to the lake, with just a grassy bank between them, is the splendidly sited Lake Talbot Pool (Nov–April Mon–Fri 6am–9pm daily; adults $2.40, children $1.30). The complex is very family-friendly, with picnic areas and barbecues, various watery slides at 30–90¢ a go, children's pools and an Olympic-sized **swimming** pool. Nearby, a reserve along the river has been declared a **koala regeneration area** for a disease-free colony of koalas; to get there, follow the **Bundidgerry Walking Track** around Lake Talbot and the Murrumbidgee River. Free maps of the track are available at the friendly **Narrandera Tourist Information Centre**, in Narrandera Park on the Newell Highway (daily 9am–5pm; ☎02/6959 1766 or free call 1800 672 392, @tourist.centre@narranderra.nsw.gov.au). Fishing fanatics could try out the lake or river for some Murray cod, yellowbelly or silverbeam; fish abound in the river, and 5km east of Narrandera, off the Sturt Highway, the **John Lake Centre** at the Inland Fisheries Research Station (Mon–Fri 9am–4pm; guided tours 10.30am; ☎02/6959 9021), carries out research into the species of the Murray, Murrumbidgee and Darling rivers.

The best place to **stay** in Narrandera is the *Historic Star Lodge*, on the corner of Whitton and Arthur streets (☎02/6959 1768, ⓕ6959 4164, Ⓦwww.oze-mail.com.au/~historic; ❻), a fine B&B with an award-winning restaurant. Classified by the National Trust, the building retains many of its original 1916 features and is run by a friendly couple. If that's a little beyond your budget, East Street is the main street for hotels and motels, with several classic country hotels, complete with iron-lace balconies, all offering very reasonably priced accommodation. The most appealing of these is the *Murrumbidgee Hotel* at the corner of Audley Street (☎02/6959 2011; ❷), or try the *Mid Town Motor Inn*, situated off the highway on the corner of East and Larmer streets (☎02/6959 2122, ⓕ6959 3271; ❹), which has a swimming pool. Another good spot is the shady *Lake Talbot Caravan Park*, well positioned above the lake and pool (☎02/6959 1302, Ⓔltcp@webfront.net.au; cabins and on-site vans ❸). Aside from the *Historic Star Lodge* (lunch Thurs–Sat, dinner Tues–Sat), the best place for a **good meal** is the reliable Ex-Servicemen's Club opposite the information centre on Bolton Street.

Wagga Wagga

WAGGA WAGGA, known simply as "Wagga" to the locals, is the most populous inland city in Australia with around 58,000 inhabitants, but it still has the appearance of a slow and solid country town. Its curious name comes from the Widadjuri, the largest of the New South Wales Aboriginal peoples: Wagga means crow and its repetition signifies the plural. Set on the Murrumbidgee River just under 100km east of Narrandera, with a beautiful sandy river beach to swim in close to the main street, it is the capital of the Riverina region, with its own **university**, Charles Sturt, boasting a well-regarded wine course and its own on-campus **winery** which is open for tastings and cellar-door sales

(Mon–Fri 11am–5pm, Sat & Sun 11am–4pm; ☎02/6933 2435), an ABC radio station, and a regional theatre.

Wagga's main attractions, though, are on the edge of the city. To the south, about a half-hour hike by foot, are the impressive **Botanic Gardens** at the base of Willans Hill, a huge place with such attractions as a walk-through bird aviary where over three hundred species flit about, a children's petting zoo (aviary and zoo daily 9am–4pm; free), bush trails and picnic areas, specialist gardens of cacti and succulents, and a Chinese-style garden, plus a kiosk café. On the first and third Sunday of each month, a model train takes children around about for 80¢ a ride. There's a **Historical Museum** on Lord Baden Powell Drive, by the Botanic Gardens, with a hotchpotch collection of old farm machinery, printing presses and a display of over 200 door knockers. Further to the south, the artificial **Lake Albert** is a popular spot for water-skiing. Canoe cruises are also available down by the Murrumbidgee River ($12 for 2 hr; ☎02/6926 1777).

Back in the centre, the **Wagga Wagga Regional Art Gallery** on Baylis Street (Mon–Sat 10am–5pm, Sun 2–5pm; free) is home to the National Art Glass collection, a stunning array of contemporary glass pieces, and the Carnegie Print Collection, with over five hundred originals from innovative Australian printmakers from 1940 on; if you're lucky, Sally Robinson's vivid *Kakadu* series might be on display. The adjacent **Museum of the Riverina** (free) keeps the same opening hours and often hosts exhibitions on indigenous artists and local crafts.

On Sunday mornings a bit of life is sparked by the **markets** (7.30am–noon), at the Grace Bros car park on O'Reilly Street, which have secondhand clothes and books, crafts, local produce and cakes on sale. The **Ngungilanna Culture Centre**, 11 Gurwood St (call to check opening hours on ☎02/6921 8982), is also worth checking out: run by the Wagga Advancement Aboriginal Corporation, it sells locally made crafts and clothes, as well as books, cards and paintings from around Australia.

Practicalities

Roughly halfway between Sydney (470km) and Melbourne (435km), Wagga is just off the Sturt Highway, the main route between Adelaide and Sydney. Interstate Greyhound **buses** heading to and from Brisbane, Sydney, Adelaide, Melbourne and Canberra all pass through, stopping at the train station, a little out of town. To **get around**, you can rent bikes from Kidson's Cycles at 107 Fitzmaurice St (☎02/6921 4474), or a car from Avis, on the corner of Edwards and Fitzharding streets (☎02/6921 9977). Baylis Street, the main strip (and Fitzmaurice St, its continuation), extends from the train station to the bridge spanning the Murrumbidgee River.

The **Wagga Wagga Visitors Centre**, on Tarcutta Street, close to the river (daily 9am–5pm; ☎02/6926 9622, ⓦwww.wagga.nsw.gov.au), dispenses free handy driving maps. It doesn't book **accommodation**, but does have information about **farmstays** in the surrounding countryside. In town, the old *Romano's Hotel*, on the corner of Sturt and Fitzmaurice streets (☎02/6921 2013; ❸), has been beautifully renovated; rooms are decorated in late-nineteenth-century style, and some have showers. *The Victoria Hotel*, 55 Baylis St (☎02/6921 5233; ❷), has no-frills pub doubles and reasonable singles, while *The Manor Guesthouse*, 38 Morrow St (☎02/6921 5962; ❺), is a good B&B with excellent weekly rates for singles, next to the beautiful riverfront park. The best-situated **caravan park** is the shady and peaceful *Wagga Beach Tourist Park*, 2 Johnston St (☎02/6931 0603; en-suite cabins ❸–❹), with a free gas

BBQ and a backpackers' room right on the town beach, five-minutes' walk from the main shops.

One of the best places to **eat** is the *Wagga Wagga Winery* (℡ 02/6922 1221), fifteen-minutes' drive out of town on the Oura Road. The wines themselves are mediocre, but the excellent local food and the setting, in an old pine log building with disabled access, a large verandah and a garden area, combine to make a very pleasurable experience. In the town centre, the Baylis/Fitzmaurice strip and its side streets provide fertile eating ground. *Sugars Coffee Lounge* at 16 Forsyth St has fresh and healthy *focaccia* and American-style bagels, as well as excellent coffee and a wide range of breakfast fare. *Romano's Hotel* (see opposite) has a modern and very stylish café/bar that makes a decent espresso and serves breakfast all day, and the slick *Victoria Hotel* at 55 Baylis St has an extensive, quality bistro menu and upstairs balcony open Friday and Saturday nights. For Mexican, try *Montezuma's* cosy wooden cantina at 85 Baylis St (lunch Wed–Fri, dinner Tues–Sun). *The Tourist Hotel* at 97 Fitzmaurice St has a great place to eat out back – *Bernie's Veggie Restaurant* (lunch Wed–Fri, dinner Wed–Sat), serving an array of sumptuous, cheap meals, in an open-fire room with retro decor.

Wagga also has several huge **clubs** providing free courtesy buses. *Wagga RSL*, on the corner of Dobbs and Kincaid streets, also has a Chinese restaurant and Friday-night piano bar, while the *Wagga Leagues Club*, Gurwood Street, has a good brasserie and live entertainment every Saturday. For drinking and dancing, the town's most popular spot is the newly refurbished and ever-lively *Victoria Hotel*, whilst *Maddison's* at 146 Fitzmaurice St (Wed–Sat) is Wagga's venue for bands and irresponsible student shenanigans. The *Black Swan Hotel* (alias "The Muddy Duck") in North Wagga, close to the university, is eternally popular with the student population.

The lower Murray: Albury to Wentworth

Following the **lower Murray River** between Albury (see p.359) and the South Australian border, there's little of interest on the New South Wales side until the old port town of **Wentworth** and its surrounding storehouse of ancient Aboriginal history around **Lake Victoria** and in the remote **Mungo National Park**. The main centres are on the Victorian side of the river, Mildura (see p.1007) and **Echuca** (see p.1013) chief among them, although the NSW riverside towns of **Tocumwal** and **Corowa**, not far from Albury, are pleasant enough.

Corowa and Tocumwal

Following the river, it's 56km from Albury northwest to **COROWA**, across the Murray from Victoria's **Rutherglen wine region** (see p.1034). Blue flags flying all over town proclaim it to be the birthplace of Federation, since the Federation Conference of 1893 was held at Corowa's courthouse. The **Corowa Tourist Information Centre** is in the cream-coloured former train station on John Street (daily 9am–5pm; ℡ 02/6033 3221 or free call 1800 6033 3221). There are stacks of **motels** in town offering very reasonable accommodation, such as the *Murray View* at 193 River St (℡ 02/6033 2144, ℱ 6033 1625; ❹), with a swimming pool, spa and barbecues (some rooms have a private garden courtyard). **Campers** could try the *Ball Park Caravan Park*, by the Murray on Bridge Road (℡ 02/6033 1426; cabins and vans ❸), or the *Lake Talbot Caravan Park* (℡ 02/6959 1302; tent pitches and vans ❸). There are several places on the main street where you can get a **meal**, including the *Star Hotel*, which does a good-value roast of the day; the *Royal Hotel*, which serves up decent counter food; and the *Old Corowa Bakehouse*, a popular café/bakery that opens early.

On the way to Tocumwal, which is just under 80km from Corowa, there's a **boomerang factory** at **BAROOGA** called the Binghi Boomerang, where you can watch boomerangs being made and try them out yourself (call ℡03/5873 4463 for times). **TOCUMWAL** itself ("Toc" to locals) is a small, pleasant river town: its **Foreshore Park**, just behind the main street, is peaceful and shaded by large gum trees, and there's a sandy river beach only ten-minutes' walk away. In front of the park, there's a rather tacky fibreglass model of a huge Murray cod, and alongside is the **Tocumwal Visitor Information Centre** (daily 9am–5pm; ℡03/5874 2131 or free call 1800 677 271), which provides information about the area and can book rides in a glider that flies over the Murray.

Tocumwal has some classic old **country hotels**, most notably the *Tocumwal Hotel* on Deniliquin Street (℡03/5874 2025, Ⓦwww.pubstay.com.au; ❹), a single-storey hotel built in 1861, with self-contained motel units and an iron-lace verandah; rates include breakfast. Next door is Central Store Antiques, which has good tearooms at the back serving scones, jam and cream or reasonably priced sandwiches and light meals. The best place to **camp** is the river-front *Bushlands on the Murray* (℡03/5874 2752, Ⓦwww.murray-net.au/bushlands; cabins ❹), right on the swimming beach.

Wentworth and Lake Victoria

Once a thriving river port, **WENTWORTH** is now a sleepy old town overshadowed by nearby Mildura, 31km back along the Sturt Highway and across the Murray River in Victoria. Located at the junction of the Murray and the Darling, the "two rivers" town was for seventy years the centre of river trade between New South Wales, Victoria and South Australia. The extension of the railway at the turn of the century bypassed Wentworth, however, and at the same time killed off much of the river trade. Nowadays the town makes a pleasant stopover en route to or from Broken Hill, 261km north on the sealed **Silver City Highway**, or a brief excursion from Mildura (in Victoria). Enquire at the **Wentworth Visitor Information Centre**, 28 Darling St (Mon–Fri 10am–4pm, Sat & Sun 10am–3pm; ℡03/5027 3624, Ⓦwww.wentworth.nsw.gov.au/tourism), about river cruises on the MV *Loyalty*, built around 1914 (or direct on ℡03/5027 3224; $14). You could visit the **Old Wentworth Gaol** on Beverly Street (daily 10am–5pm; $5.50), built of handmade bricks in 1879, but the interpretive displays consist of bits of curling cardboard and dejected dummies, making it hardly worth the entrance fee. Opposite, **Pioneer World** (daily 10am–5pm; $4) is a folk museum exhibiting items related to Aboriginal and European history of the area, and very tacky models of large animals. You can also take a tour through citrus groves at **Orange World** in Mourquong, back towards Mildura (daily except Sat 9am–4pm; guided 1hr tractor tours 10.30am & 2.30pm; $6).

The Aboriginal land council in Wentworth organizes visits to significant **Aboriginal sites** around Lake Victoria to the west, and Mungo National Park (see opposite) among the dry salt lakes to the northeast. The tours are run by Harry Nanya Tours at Shop 10, Wentworth Place, Sandych Street (℡03/5027 2076), and are accompanied by accredited Barkindji guides. Ancient Aboriginal graves were recently discovered at **Lake Victoria** – the Barkindji had always spoken of their existence. In April 1994, the partial draining of the eleven-square-kilometre lake revealed skeletons buried side by side and in deep layers; some of the estimated ten thousand graves date back six thousand years, in what is believed to be Australia's largest pre-industrial burial site – surpassing any such finds in Europe, Asia or North and South America. The site also challenges the premise that Aboriginal lifestyles were solely nomadic, suggesting that here at least they lived in semi-permanent dwellings around the lake.

Among the places to **stay** in Wentworth, the luxury apartments at the *Red Gum Lagoon Cottages*, 210 Adams St (℗ 03/5027 2063; ❺), are wonderful, offering free use of canoes and rowboats on the lagoon itself. Another good waterfront choice is the *Willow Bend Caravan Park* on Darling Street (℗ 03/5027 3213; cabins ❸, on-site vans ❷), right near the shops but also at the confluence of the Darling and Murray rivers, where there are plenty of trees – watch out for ferocious possums, though. You can get out on the water by renting a **houseboat** from *Twin Rivers Houseboats* at 1 William St (℗ 03/5027 3626 or free call 1800 037 047; sleeps up to six; $730–1500 per week off-peak, $1055–1750 peak). If you're looking for employment in the area, perhaps the best accommodation option is *Urumba Backpackers* at 81 Darling St (℗ 02/5027 2499, ❶), who can help with finding work.

Mungo National Park

Mungo National Park, in the far southwest of New South Wales, is most easily reached from the river townships of Wentworth (see above) or Mildura (over the Victorian border, about 110km away – see p.1007); organized tours run from both towns. If you want to tackle it on your own, you'll need a 4WD. The park is part of the dried-up **Willandra Lakes System**, a UNESCO World Heritage area in recognition of its Aboriginal legacy and record of past climates preserved in the landscape. The Willandra Lakes contain the longest continuous record of Aboriginal life in Australia, dating back more than forty thousand years. During the Ice Ages, between forty thousand and fifteen thousand years ago, the system formed a vast chain of freshwater lakes strung along Willandra Creek, then the main channel of the Lachlan River, flowing into the Murrumbidgee. The waters teemed with fish, attracting waterbirds and mammals, while Aborigines camped at the shores of the lake to fish and hunt, and buried their dead in the sand dunes. When the lakes started drying out fifteen thousand years ago, Aborigines continued to live near soaks along the old river channel. The park covers most of one of these dry lake beds, and its dominant feature is a great, crescent-shaped dune (a lunette), at the eastern edge of the lake, commonly referred to as the **Walls of China**. Elsewhere, the vegetation consists of saltbush on the lake floors and mallee (a low-growing, scrubby type of eucalypt) on the dune fields. Casuarinas grow on the sand plains, and western grey and red kangaroos can sometimes be seen.

The **visitors centre** (℗ 03/5023 1278), by the southwest entrance to the park, has a very informative display about the geological and Aboriginal history of the national park, and nearby the impressive old **Mungo Woolshed** is open for inspection. From there it's a short drive to the lookout point on the rim of the lake, the former shore, from where you can look across the dry lakebed to the Walls of China. A signposted track takes you on a return trip across the lake floor to the Walls of China, then over the dune and to the northwest part of the park. At sunset, or on nights with a full moon, the scenery takes on an eerie, otherworldly quality.

If you want to **stay** nearby, beds in the former shearers' quarters, or at NPWS campsites in the park, can be booked in advance through the visitors centre. Otherwise, try *Mungo Lodge* on Arumpo Road (℗ 03/5029 7297; ❺), which has motel units and self-contained cottages as well as a licensed restaurant.

Back o' Bourke: the Outback

Once you're past Dubbo, you're really getting away from the populated coast and moving towards the red plains that make western New South Wales the quintessential Australian Outback. The searing summer heat makes touring uncomfortable from December to February, and you'd be well advised to visit at a cooler time of year. **Bourke**, about 370km along the sealed **Mitchell Highway**, is generally considered the turning point; venture further and you're into the land known as "Back o' Bourke" – the back of beyond. The Mitchell passes through **NYNGAN**, at the geographical centre of New South Wales and 133km from Dubbo, where the sealed **Barrier Highway** heads west for 584 sweltering kilometres, through Cobar and Wilcannia, to Broken Hill. Flood-prone Nyngan, on the eastern bank of the Bogan River, is a sizeable (compared to what you'll find beyond), old-fashioned country town where you can refuel and freshen up. There's a small, shady park on Main Street where you can slump at picnic tables, or you can visit *Arnold's Take Away* at 133 Main St – a spacious café where generous pots of tea help to quench thirst and a ceiling fan manages to circulate a bit of air. For more on the area, see the website Ⓦwww.outbacknsw.org.au.

Bourke and around

BOURKE is mainly known for its very remoteness, and this alone is enough to attract tourists; once you've crossed the North Bourke Bridge that spans the **Darling River**, you're officially "out back". If you want to have a drink in the "Back O' Bourke" without pressing too far into the endless, scarcely populated plains all around, try the *North Bourke Hotel*, a shabby, wooden, green-tin-roofed Outback pub where bush poets congregate once a year during the annual **Mateship Festival** weekend normally held in late September (details from the information centre). The lively festival began in 1993 to mark the centenary of the poet **Henry Lawson**'s stay in Bourke during a particularly harsh drought. Discovering mateship in hardship was but a microcosm for the fierce nationalism that arose in 1890s depression and drought-struck Australia. Work was scarce and Lawson often slept out in the town's Central Park, where a plaque is dedicated to him and to two other bush poets who lived in the area at around the same time – Will Ogilvie and **Breaker Morant**, the latter executed during the Boer War. Another famous resident was the well-known ophthalmologist **Fred Hollows**, who began working here in the 1970s with local Aborigines suffering from cataract blindness. As a result of his work the number of cases of incurable blindness among Aboriginal peoples throughout Australia has been halved. Hollows was buried in the town in 1993.

Bourke was a bustling river port from the 1860s to the 1930s, and there are some fine examples of riverboat-era architecture, including the huge reconstructed **wharf** which can be explored – from here a track winds along the magnificent, tree-lined river. A new port with paddle-steamer cruises is promised, but has been "under development" for a number of years. Thanks to irrigation with Darling River water, crops as diverse as cotton, lucerne, citrus, grapes and sorghum are successfully grown here despite the 40°C summer heat, while Bourke is also the commercial centre for a vast sheep- and cattle-breeding area: to the north there are rich grazing lands across the Queensland border around Cunnamulla and Charleville.

With a population of three thousand (approximately twenty-five percent Aboriginal), Bourke acts as a base for regional services and welfare.

Unfortunately, there is sporadic trouble involving alcoholism and aimless young-sters, and after dark the atmosphere can be somewhat disturbing. Visitors are best off drinking in the very pleasant *Port o' Bourke Hotel* (see below), the *Oxley Club* or *Bowling Club*, and avoiding the *Post Office Hotel*. Up-to-date information for visitors can be found at the Council's website – ⓦ www.backobourke.com.

Practicalities

The **information centre** is inside the former train station on Anson Street (daily 9am–5pm; ⓣ02/6872 2280, ⓕ6872 2305, ⓔtourinfo@lisp.com.au). It can pro-vide "**Mud Maps**", roughly drawn maps marking places of interest off the beat-en track in the surrounding area: but bear in mind that these destinations could be as far as 200km away. It can also arrange Back o' Bourke tours (Mon–Sat 9.30am–1pm; 3hr tour covering orchards and vineyards in summer, historical buildings and cotton farms in winter; $10). An ongoing project to seal the roads in this corner of New South Wales has made it much more accessible than in pre-vious times, but many lesser-travelled routes remain little more than dirt tracks.

Countrylink buses arrive here from Dubbo four times weekly, and you can also fly here with Airlink, four times weekly, from Sydney via Dubbo. **Accommodation** in town includes the pleasant *Port o' Bourke Hotel* on Mitchell Street (ⓣ02/6872 2544; ❹), which has air-conditioned rooms, some sharing a bath, some en suite, but all opening out on to a sociable verandah, and the newly refurbished *Bourke Riverside Motel*, 3 Mitchell St (ⓣ02/6872 2539; ❸), boasting deluxe heritage cottages with king-size beds and a communal swimming pool. An ideal way to see how life is lived out here is to stay on an **Outback station**; the information centre has details of those that welcome vis-itors, among them *Comeroo Camel Station* (ⓣ02/6874 7735; self-catering cot-tage $20 per person, full board in homestead $50 per person), a unique experi-ence with artesian hot bores, river waterholes with yabbying and fishing oppor-tunities, and resident buffalo and ostriches. For those interested in **employ-ment** in Bourke – harvesting tomatoes, onions and grapes between November and February and cotton-chipping between December and February – *Kidman's Camp* (ⓣ02/6872 1612 or free call 1800 234 560), 8km north of town on the Darling River, may be able to point you in the right direction.

The *Port o' Bourke Hotel* is the best place in town for **food** and **drink**: their excellent bistro meals (Thurs–Sat) are fresh and healthy, or you can eat count-er meals (lunch daily, dinner Mon, Wed & Thurs) out in the shady beer garden. A palatable alternative is the Chinese food proffered at the *Bowling Club* on the corner of Mitchell and Richard streets, and there's good coffee at *Gecko Cafe* on Oxley Street. **Internet** facilities are available in the library on Mitchell Street (Mon–Fri 9am–5pm), where there is also a reasonable supermarket.

West and north of Bourke

West of Bourke, it's 193km to the small settlement of **WANAARING**, past a reconstruction of **Fort Bourke**, built by Major Mitchell in 1835 as a secure depot to protect his stocks from Aboriginal people, while he explored the Darling River. Near Fort Bourke is the kibbutz-like **Cornerstone Community**, a cotton-farming operation and teaching centre run by Christians; they put a lot of effort into the local community, including running the tourist office, and visitors are welcome.

Northwest, the road runs 215km to **HUNGERFORD**, on the Queensland border, and the **Dingo Fence** (see p.384). The state border bisects Hungerford, which consists of little more than a couple of houses, a post office and a pub but was made famous (amongst Australians) by a Henry Lawson short story of the same name. Make sure you shut the steel dingo-proof fence behind you when you drive through: there's a $1000 fine if you don't. The heart of the town is the corrugated-iron *Royal Mail Hotel* (⊕07/4650 4093; ❸) just near the fence in Queensland: you can buy fuel, bread, milk and meat here, excellent **meals** are served until 9pm, and the friendly owners are happy to give advice. You can also **stay** in the bedrooms running along the front verandah, the caravan or bunkroom in the back, or camp.

Heading directly **north** from Bourke, the sealed Mitchell Highway goes right up to just past Charleville in Queensland (see p.565). **BARRINGUN**, on the border 135km from Bourke, is worth a visit just to have a drink at the remarkably genteel *Tattersalls Hotel*, set amid a flower-scented garden, once frequented by Breaker Morant. The hotel serves only snacks and doesn't have any accommodation. Across the road and closer to the border is the painted tin shed that comprises the *Bush Tucker Inn* (⊕02/6874 7584; ❶), which has **meals**, rooms, fuel and camping space.

South and east of Bourke

Because the empty, featureless plains seem to extend in all directions, the elongated rise of **Mount Gunderbooka** (498m), about 70km **southwest** of Bourke en route to Cobar, likened to a mini-Ayers Rock, is striking. It was also of great cultural significance to the Aboriginal people of the area, with semi-permanent waterholes and caves; several **cave paintings** can be seen; contact the National Parks and Wildlife Services on Mitchell Street in Bourke for details (⊕02/6872 2744).

Twenty-eight kilometres **east** of Bourke, en route to Brewarrina, is a turn-off south to **Mount Oxley**, climbed by the explorers Sturt and Hume in 1829 to herald the white settlement in the area. It's on private property, so you must first pick up a key from the information centre in Bourke. The town of **BRE-WARRINA** (locals call it "Bree"), 100km east of Bourke on the Barwon River, has a large Aboriginal population. The abundant fish stocks in the river made the area a natural fishery for the original population and the **fish traps** – of large, partly submerged boulders – can still be seen in the river. The excellent **Aboriginal Cultural Museum** (Mon–Fri 9am–4.30pm; $6; ⓔbackmac@optusnet.com.au), located near the ancient fisheries in an award-winning, earth-covered building similar to an Aboriginal shelter, explains the history of the area's Ngemba people and offers walkabout **tours**. One of the guides is a teenager whose grandfather recorded over two hundred tapes of his tribe's language, thus saving it for prosperity; these days she is entrusted with educating others in the tongue.

Cobar

Since copper was discovered here in 1869, **COBAR**, just under 160km south of Bourke and the first real stop on the Barrier Highway between Nyngan and Broken Hill, has experienced three mining booms. Today, it's home to the vast **CSA Mine**, said to be the most highly mechanized in Australia, extracting about 850,000 tonnes of copper every year. Earlier booms resulted in a number of impressive public buildings, among them the 1882 **courthouse** and the police station, as well as the *Great Western Hotel* on Marshall Street, whose iron-lace verandahs are said to be the longest in the state. Cobar's most recent industry is **emu farming**: as more and more restaurants serve up bush tucker, the big birds are in demand. Most people only stop here to refuel before the monotonous 250km stretch to Wilcannia, and the town offers little to entice you otherwise. There is, however, a lovely picnic spot in Drummond Park, just off the highway on Linsley Street.

For more about the town, head for the **Cobar Outback Heritage Center** (Mon–Fri 8.30am–5pm, Sat & Sun 9am–5pm; $5.50) on Marshall Street, which is also the local **tourist office** (T02/6836 2448, Wwww.outbackn-sw.org.au/cobar). They can tell you about above-ground tours of the CSA mine (by arrangement on T02/6836 2001; free) and provide "Mud Maps", roughly drawn maps showing places of interest around Cobar that are difficult to reach. Chief of these, and arguably one of the most significant **Aboriginal rock art** locations in New South Wales, is the **Mount Grenfell Historic Site**, a 72-kilometre drive northwest of town. The rocky ridge contains three art sites with over a thousand motifs – human and animal figures, including the emus which you're still likely to see around the site, plus abstract designs and hand stencils. Older layers are visible beneath the more recent pigments, but there's no way to tell exactly how old the art is. The adjacent semi-permanent waterhole explains the significance of the site for the **Wongaibon people**. The NPWS in Cobar, at 19 Barton St (T02/6836 2692), hands out a leaflet detailing the site, with its picnic and barbecue areas, toilets and limited water, plus a five-kilometre signposted return **walk** to the top of the ridge. To reach the site, head west along the Barrier Highway for 40km, then 32km north along a gravel road past Mount Grenfell Homestead to the picnic site.

There are a number of **motels** along the highway in Cobar; two to try – both with air-conditioning and pools – are the *Hi-way Motel* (T02/6836 2000, F6836 1409; ❹) and the *Cross Roads Motel*, at the corner of Bourke and Louth roads (T02/6836 2711; ❹); alternatively, there's the *Cobar Caravan Park* (T & F 02/6836 2425; cabins ❸, on-site vans ❷), or the tourist office can advise on **outback bush stays**, including a recommended one on Trilby Station (T02/6874 7420, F6874 7395, Eliz@lisp.com.au).

Wilcannia and around

The next major town on the Barrier Highway is **WILCANNIA**, 260km west of Cobar. The former "Queen City of the West" was founded in 1864 and towards the twentieth century was a major port on the Darling River, from where produce was transported by paddle steamers and barges down the Darling–Murray river system to Adelaide. Droughts, the advent of the railways and the motor car put an end to the river trade, and today the ruins of the docks and the old lift-up bridge, along with a few impressive public buildings – the post office, police station, courthouse, Catholic convent and Athenaeum Museum (daily 9am–5pm) which houses the **tourist centre** (T08/8091 5909, Ecdsc@outbacknsw.org.au) – are reminders of the once-prosperous era. Nowadays Wilcannia survives as a service centre for a far-flung Outback population, with its banks, shops, motels and service stations, though problems with unemployment and alcoholism combine to make it, while not exactly threatening, perhaps not the most welcoming place to stay.

If you do need somewhere to stop overnight, try the friendly *Wilcannia Motel* (T08/8091 5802; ❺) or *Grahams Motel* (T08/8091 5040; ❹ cash only), both situated on the Barrier Highway. If you want to experience Outback life, head 85km southeast of Wilcannia along the unsealed Cobb Highway to **Yelta Station** (T08/8091 9467, F8091 9444), a sheep and cattle property run by Bill and Chris Elliot. The family take only one set of guests at a time, camping or staying in fully equipped shearers' quarters (❸). You can reach the station by two-wheel drive, unless it's been raining – in which case the road is generally closed.

Heading north or south of Wilcannia you can follow the river along one of Australia's last great 4WD adventures – **The Darling River Run** – 829km of Outback history, heritage and landscape running between Brewarrina and Wentworth. Further information on the run is available from Bourke Information Centre (℡02/6872 2280).

You can travel the Darling River upstream **northwest** of Wilcannia all the way to Bourke (see p.368), just under 300km, on unsealed roads that closely follow the east and west banks with crossings at the settlements of Tilpa and Louth. Station properties dot the riverfront, including Mount Murchinson Station, on the west side of the river 30km north of Wilcannia, said to have once been managed by the son of Charles Dickens. At **TILPA**, 130km north of Wilcannia, there's a classic Outback pub, the 1890s *Tilpa Hotel* (℡02/6837 3928, ✉tilpapub@bigpond.com.au; ❷), where you can find **meals** (the steak sandwiches come highly recommended), **accommodation** and **fuel**, and for a $2 donation towards the Royal Flying Doctor Service, you can immortalize your name on the pub's tin wall. Ninety-three kilometres further on, at **LOUTH**, *Shindy's Inn* sells diesel and petrol and has basic accommodation in miniature cabins (℡02/6874 7416; ❷).

White Cliffs

From Wilcannia, you can branch off the Barrier Highway, heading north along a road partly sealed for 30km, and then graded gravel for the final 67km to the **opal fields** at **WHITE CLIFFS**, 97km away. Besides opals, White Cliffs is famous for the extraordinary summer heat, and for the way in which the miners have avoided it since the 1890s (when about four thousand lived here) – many of the approximately two hundred residents live underground in so-called "dug-outs", where it's cool in summer and warm in winter. There are all sorts of underground attractions, as well as a high-tech attempt to exploit the climate in the form of an experimental solar power station. For the authentic underground experience, there are two places to stay: the original and very friendly *White Cliffs Dug-Out Motel* (℡08/8091 6647 or free call 1800 021 154, ℻8091 6654, ✉underground.motel@telstra.com; ❺), which comes complete with licensed restaurant and outdoor swimming pool; and the only subterranean B&B, *PJs* (℡08/8091 6626, ⓦwww.babs.com.au/nsw/pj.htm; ❻), where you have to share a bathroom and take off your shoes. Cheaper, aboveground options are the *White Cliffs Hotel* (℡08/8091 6606, ℻8091 6782; ❸) and the *Family Inn* at the Post Office (℡ & ℻ 08/8091 6645; ❸). If you can bear the heat, there's also **camping** (with hot showers) at Opal Pioneer Reserve, close to town. **Tourist information** is available on Keraro Road at the White Cliffs General Store (daily 8am–7pm; ℡ & ℻ 08/8091 6611).

There are several **tours** to White Cliffs from Broken Hill (see box p.381); otherwise you'll need your own transport to get here. The only fuel stop between Wilcannia and Broken Hill is at the *Little Topar Hotel*, roughly halfway along the 195-kilometre stretch of the Barrier Highway.

Broken Hill

The ghosts of mining towns that died when the precious minerals ran out are scattered all over Australia. **BROKEN HILL**, on the other hand, celebrated its centenary in 1988, and its famous "**Line of Lode**", one of the world's major lead-silver-zinc ore bodies and the city's *raison d'être*, still has a little life left in

NEW SOUTH WALES AND ACT | Broken Hill

ACCOMMODATION

Black Lion Inn	2
The Imperial	3
Mario's Palace Hotel	7
Mine Host Motel	5
Old Vic B&B	1
Royal Exchange Hotel	6
Theatre Royal Hotel	8
Tourist Lodge	4

it after being mined continuously for over 110 years. Inevitably, Broken Hill revolves around the mines, but in the last decade it has also evolved into a thriving arts centre, thanks to the initiative of the **Brushmen of the Bush**, a painting school founded by local artists Pro Hart, Hugh Schulz, Jack Absalom, John Pickup and the late Eric Minchin. Diverse talents have been attracted to Broken Hill, and their works are displayed in galleries scattered all over town. Some may be a bit on the tacky side, but others are excellent, and it's well worth devoting some time to gallery-browsing. The city was also the memorable location for several scenes of the drag-queens-run-riot-in-the-Outback film *Priscilla Queen of the Desert* which was shot here in 1993.

Almost 1200km west of Sydney and about 500km east of Adelaide, this surprisingly gracious Outback mining town, with a feel and architecture reminiscent of the South Australian capital, and with a population of around 21,000, manages to create a welcome splash of **green** in the harsh desert landscape that surrounds it. Extensive revegetation schemes around Broken Hill have created grasslands that, apart from being visually pleasing, help contain the dust that used to make the residents' lives miserable. It's aided by a reliable water supply – secured for the first time only in 1953 – via a one-hundred-kilometre-long pipeline from the Darling River at Menindee. The city is also a convenient base for touring far northwest New South Wales and nearby areas in South Australia.

Remember to adjust your watch: Broken Hill operates on South Australian **Central Standard Time**, half an hour behind the rest of NSW. All local transport schedules are in CST, but you should always check.

Arrival, information and accommodation

Arriving in Broken Hill by bus or train, you'll be pretty centrally placed. The **bus terminal** (⊤08/8087 2735, or for 24hr reservations ⊤13 2030) is behind the useful **tourist information centre**, at the corner of Bromide and Blende streets (daily 8.30am–5pm; ⊤08/8087 6077, ⊛www.murrayoutback.org.au), where you can pick up a map ($2.20) for a self-guided Heritage Walk along Argent and Blende streets, or get information on the guided walking tour which delves into the city's history (Mon, Wed, Fri & Sat 10am; no tour late Dec to early Feb; 1hr 30min–2hr; donation). The **train station** is on Crystal Street, just a block below Argent Street – though unless you're travelling in style on the Sydney–Perth Indian Pacific, you'll actually come into the city on a Countrylink bus. The **airport** is about 5km south of town; there is no shuttle bus – a taxi costs just under $10 and there are usually a few waiting; alternatively you can arrange to have a hire car waiting (see p.380). In addition to what's on offer at the tourist information centre, you can pick up advice on nearby attractions from the district **NPWS** office at 183 Argent St (Mon–Fri 8am–4.30pm; ⊤08/8088 5933).

Accommodation

Black Lion Inn, 34 Bromide St (⊤08/8087 4801, ⊛theblack@ruralnet.net.au). If the hostel is full this is a good budget option near the bus station. Basic but clean rooms in a separate half of the lively hotel away from the pub noise; ceiling fans but shared bathrooms. Single rates of $20 are comparable to a dorm price. ❷

The Imperial, 88 Oxide St (⊤08/8087 7444). Pricey four-star home-from-home in a beautiful old building with huge verandah. The five rooms have all mod-cons; there's also a kitchenette, a billiard

room, a guest lounge and a garden. ❼
Lake View Caravan Park, 1 Mann St, 3km northeast (⊤ & ⊕ 08/8088 2250). A large site with disabled-access en-suite cabins, a swimming pool and kiosk. Cabins ❸, on-site vans ❷
Mario's Palace Hotel, 227 Argent St (⊤08/8088 1699, ⊕8087 6240). Vast corner pub with one of the largest hotel balconies in NSW, also has to be one of the state's most eccentric. Featured to hilarious effect in *Priscilla, Queen of the Desert*, this place has every available wall and ceiling space covered with murals of Australian bush

scenes plus an outburst of a Botticelli-style Birth of Venus ceiling mural painted by the Italian owner. The rooms are a kitsch lover's dream; the most extreme, with its own mural, was where the drag gang stayed in *Priscilla*. All rooms have air-con, a fridge and a sink and some are en suite. ❸, Priscilla suite ❻

Mine Host Motel, 120 Argent St (☏ 08/8088 4044, ℱ 8088 1313, ℯ minehost@ruralnet.net.au). Modern decor and comfort including air-con; there's also a swimming pool to splash about in. Central location right near the bus station, and close to clubs and pubs. ❻

Old Vic B&B, 230 Oxide St (☏ 08/8087 1169, ℯ jwcooper@pcpro.net.au). A comfortable guest-house in an old bungalow with a wide verandah; a light breakfast is served and all rooms share the bathroom. It's a 15min walk from the centre, though there are a couple of good pubs nearby for eating and drinking opportunities. ❸

Royal Exchange Hotel, 320 Argent St, cnr Chloride St (☏ 08/8087 2308, ℱ 8087 2191). An old pub with some en-suite rooms, but mostly the usual pub accommodation. Breakfast is included. ❸–❹

Scotia Sanctuary halfway between Broken Hill and Wentworth, 163km south along the Silver City Highway, then 30km southwest (☏ 03/5027 1200, ℱ 5027 1294). One of several projects of Earth Sanctuaries, a conservation organization based in South Australia (PO Box 1135, Stirling, SA 5152; ☏ 08/8370 9422, ℱ 8370 8332, ℗ www.esl.com.au), the Scotia Sanctuary protects the rare Mallee fowl in an environment of Mallee sand dunes. There are opportunities to see the birds, as well as other native wildlife and flora, on guided tours (from $15 per person), and you can stay here (providing your own sheets) in the well-equipped homestead (❷) and more basic shearers' quarters (❶), or choose to camp.

Theatre Royal Hotel, 347 Argent St (☏ 08/8087 3318, ℱ 8087 3511). Nineteenth-century drinker's pub with simple rooms, which are air-conditioned and come with TV. Cheap singles and weekly rates available. ❸

Tourist Lodge, 100 Argent St (☏ 08/8088 2086, ℱ 8087 9511, ℗ www3.pcpro.net.au/tlodge/). A rather shabby and institutional guesthouse and YHA-affiliated hostel near the tourist information centre and bus terminal. The budget air-con guesthouse rooms are popular with older Australians and young families; shared kitchen/dining/TV room and common room. YHA section with mostly twin, double or triple accommodation. Solar-heated swimming pool; bike hire. Rooms ❸, dorms ❶

The City

Green it may be, but the huge slag heap towering over the city centre leaves you in no doubt that, above all, this is still a mining town. Even the streets – laid out in a grid – are mostly named after minerals: Argent Street (from the Latin for silver) is Broken Hill's main thoroughfare, with the highest concentration of historic buildings and interest; parallel to either side are Crystal Street, with the train station, and Blende Street, while at right angles across the centre run Bromide, Sulphide, Chloride and Oxide streets. If you want to get an idea of what there is to see in the city centre, stop in at the tourist office for a Heritage Walk map or get information on the walking tour of the town (see opposite). An unexpected sight is the **Afghan Mosque** on the corner of Williams and Buck streets, on the site of the former camel camp where Afghan and Indian camel drivers loaded and unloaded their camel teams; you can visit it on Sunday at 2.30pm.

Public transport in Broken Hill is poor – the tourist office can provide a combined timetable and route map of the Broken Hill Town Bus Service (☏ 08/8087 3311) with four routes operating infrequently within the city only (Mon–Fri 8am–5.15pm; fares start from $1).

Mines and mining museums

One thing you shouldn't miss in Broken Hill is an underground mine tour. You can do it right in town at the disused Delprats mine, behind the railway station, or nearer Silverton at the Daydream Mine. At **Delprats** (tours Mon–Fri 10.30am, Sat 2pm, more during school holidays, arrive 10min before start; 2hr; $26; ☏ 08/8088

The story of Broken Hill began in 1883 when a German-born boundary rider from Mount Gipps Station, Charles Rasp, pegged out a forty-acre lease of a "broken hill" that he believed was tin. A syndicate of seven was formed, founding the **Broken Hill Proprietary** (BHP) to work what turned out to be rich silver, lead and zinc deposits. Broken Hill's mines, dominated by BHP until they withdrew operations in 1939, have contributed greatly to the wealth of Australia: the deposit, more than 7km long and up to 250m wide, is thought originally to have contained more than three hundred million tonnes of sulphide-rich ore. Even now there's said to be ten years left in the "Line of Lode", though only one mining company, **Pasminco**, is currently working it.

In the early years, living and working **conditions** for the miners were atrocious. The climate was harsh, housing was poor and diseases such as typhoid, scarlet fever and dysentery – to say nothing of work-related illnesses such as lead poisoning, and mine accidents – contributed to a death rate almost twice as high as the average in New South Wales. The mine and the growing town rapidly stripped the landscape of timber, leaving the settlement surrounded by a vast, bleak plain. Dust storms were common. Not surprisingly, perhaps, Broken Hill was at the forefront of **trade union** development in Australia, as the miners, many of them recent immigrants, fought to improve their living and working conditions. It was their ability to unite that ultimately won them their battles, above all in the Big Strike of 1919–20, when, after eighteen months of holding out against the police and strikebreakers, major concessions were won from BHP. Not that the trade union movement at Broken Hill should be viewed through too-rosy glasses. The union, which effectively ran the town in conjunction with the mine companies, was also a bastion of racism and male supremacy, though the interpretive boards at the tourist information centre glorify this as "mateship". Non-white persons were not tolerated in town, nor were working women who happened to be married. Even now, these attitudes have not altogether disappeared.

Despite the life left in Broken Hill's mineral deposits, the future is none too certain. With modern mining technology the ore is removed faster, and the numbers employed are lower. Between 1970 and 1975, about 4000 people were employed in the mines. By the early 1980s this number had been reduced to 2500, and less than 700 work there now. The population continues to gradually decrease and every few years another of the city's many pubs closes down.

1604, ⓦwww.delprats.com.au) you don a miner's hat, boots and a heavy belt with batteries for your helmet light, before descending in the miners' cage – jammed with thirty or more people – 130m below the surface. Here, former miners working as guides will take you on a tour through the system of tunnels (stopes), describing and demonstrating how miners used to work in the bad old days, and how the work is done now. The **Daydream Mine** (daily 10am–3.30pm; tours on demand; 1hr; $12.10; ⓦwww.daydreammine.com.au), which operated between 1882 and 1889, is 20km out of Broken Hill on the Silverton Road – turn right at the sign and follow the thirteen-kilometre dirt road; tours here are similar, but half as long and a little tamer. Daydream can be booked through the tourist information centre, but without your own transport, you'll need to go on a bus tour (see box on p.381); Delprats must be booked direct.

If you can't face going underground, it's now possible to take an overground tour of the old **South Mine** which commenced operations in 1888 and closed in 1972. Accessed via Eyre Street in Broken Hill South, the site is being developed for visitors with a $4.6 million Federal Government grant. Ambitious plans include a miners' memorial site and cable car to go right across the old open-cut workings, with the majority of the work to be finished by 2001. For the moment, however, the twice-daily two-hour tours (10am & 2pm) – which concentrate on the old ambulance room and BHP's rather horrific safety record – are rather haphazard and not particularly value-for-money (℡08/8088 6000, Ⓦ www.lineoflode.org.au or the tourist office for details; $11). If you've proven your interest in mining history by making it out to South Mine, you might like to combine it with a visit to the nearby **Photographic Recollections**, also on Eyre Street (Mon–Fri 10am–4.30pm, Sat & Sun 1–4.30pm; $4.40). This privately-run exhibition provides a pictorial history of Broken Hill, with over 600 photographs accompanied by well-researched text which delves into mining, union and social history. The location itself, in the former Central Power Station, tells a story of the city's very Outback past; from the 1930s Broken Hill produced all its power here until as late as 1986 when it finally went on the national grid.

There are three other mining-related attractions in the city. A visit to the bizarre but wonderful **White's Mineral Art Gallery and Mining Museum**, 1 Allendale St (off Silverton Rd; daily 9am–5pm; $4), might well be the next best thing to going underground. The art section is pretty extraordinary, consisting mainly of collages of crushed minerals depicting Broken Hill scenes, and at the back there's a walk-in underground mine, re-created so convincingly that it genuinely looks and feels like the real thing: inside, you're given an entertaining lecture, with videos and models, on the history of Broken Hill and its mines. A shop at the front of the museum sells minerals, opals, jewellery and pottery. The **Railway, Mineral and Train Museum** (daily 10am–3pm; $2), opposite the tourist information centre, features an extensive mineral collection as well as old railway machinery and memorabilia including the fittings from the bedroom of the *Maidens Hotel* in Menindee where the explorers Burke and Wills stayed on their ill-fated expedition (see p.568). Finally, the **Geocentre**, in a nineteenth-century bond store on the corner of Bromide and Crystal streets (Mon–Fri 10am–5pm, Sat & Sun 1–5pm; $3.30; Ⓦ www.pcpro.net.au/~geocentre), looks at Broken Hill's geology, mineralogy and metallurgy. At the back is an example of a tin-miner's shed – you can imagine what the heat must have been like in summer, or experience it yourself if you're foolhardy enough to come out here at that time of year.

Art galleries and sculpture parks

There's not only indoor art in galleries in Broken Hill; the city is full of public murals and outdoor sculpture. Pick up the Broken Hill Art Trail fold-out poster ($2), which has colour photographs and maps, from the **Broken Hill City Art Gallery** (Mon–Fri 10am–5pm, Sat & Sun 1–5pm; $2), in the Entertainment Centre on Chloride Street, where there's an excellent representative collection of artists from Broken Hill. Established in 1904, it's the second-oldest gallery in the state – after the Art Gallery of New South Wales in Sydney – with a small collection of nineteenth- and early twentieth-century paintings. It's the recent work that's interesting, though, including a Sidney Nolan and a great John Olsen, as well as the works of the "Brushmen of the Bush" (though sometimes these might be moved to make way for special exhibitions). One of the highlights of the gallery is the spectacular **Silver Tree**, a 68-centimetre-high figurine, wrought of pure silver from the Broken Hill Mines, depicting five Aborigines, a drover on horseback, kangaroos, emus and sheep gathered under a tree. Also on display are sculptures created by artists who participated in the 1993 Sculpture Symposium at The Living Desert (see below).

The **Pro Hart Gallery**, at 108 Wyman St (Mon–Sat 9am–12.30pm & 1.30–5pm, Sun 1.30–5pm; $4), should also not be missed. Pro Hart is a former Broken Hill miner turned artist and national celebrity who claims that his only artistic influences were the colours and subjects he saw on his family's sheep station where he grew up, which he then turned into illustrations that decorated his correspondence lessons. His trademark humorous Outback scenes depict events such as race meetings or backyard barbecues, all featuring lively figures in a caricature style. The gallery's three cramped levels are said to hold the largest private art collection in Australia, with a truly astounding collection of the artist's own work as well as works by other Australian painters – Tom Roberts, Sidney Nolan and Albert Namatjira among them – although not necessarily their best. A collection of Hart's sculptures are in a lot across the road – you can check them out for free. Hart's daughter Raylee Marie has her studio just next door to her father's gallery, and his sister runs the **Ant Hill Gallery** – the only place in Broken Hill where you can actually buy a Pro Hart – at 24 Bromide St (Mon–Sat 9am–5pm, Sun 1.30–5pm), just opposite tourist information. Also in the centre is the **Art of Broken Hill Gallery**, at 219 Argent St (Mon–Fri 10am–6pm, Sat 10am–1pm, Sun 1–5pm), which, like the Ant Hill Gallery, displays a variety of local artists' works.

Six kilometres out of town, the **Sculpture Symposium** in **The Living Desert Reserve** is the most stunning of Broken Hill's art exhibits, a reserve in the eroded Barrier Ranges desert region that contains a group of sculptures carved from Wilcannia sandstone boulders. The twelve artists involved in their creation were part of a sculpture symposium in 1993 and were drawn from diverse cultures – two from Mexico (including an Aztec Indian), two from Syria, three from Georgia (in the Caucasus), and five Australians, including two Bathurst Islanders – and this is reflected in the variety of their works. The pieces from the Georgian artists are particularly fine: Badri Sulushia's Outback Madonna and Child; Valerian Jiiya's Cubist interpretation; and Jumber Jikiya's horse's head, a tribute to the rare breed of Georgian horses slaughtered under Stalin's orders. Nastra Luna of Mexico badly injured his hands and his piece became a collective effort, depicting a soaring eagle, with the hands of the other sculptors who helped him imprinted in the rock. The Aboriginal artist Badger Bates, from Broken Hill, was inspired by the stone carvings of his ancestors, and his piece shows two rainbow serpents travelling north. The best time to visit the sculptures is at sunset on a clear evening, when the light is magical and the rocks glow crimson, and you can really soak up the atmosphere. It's a pleasant fifteen-minute walk up the hill from the car park to the sculptures; you can also drive right up, but because of unfortunate bouts of vandalism in the past you must first go to the tourist information centre in town, get a key to the gate ($10 deposit) and pay $5.50 per car. A $1.10 information brochure about the sculptures is available from the tourist office.

The Royal Flying Doctor Service and the School of the Air

Broken Hill offers an excellent opportunity to visit two Australian Outback institutions, the **Royal Flying Doctor Service** (RFDS) and the School of the Air. The RFDS, at Broken Hill Airport, offers guided tours (Mon–Fri 9am–noon & 1–5pm, Sat & Sun 10am–noon & 1–4pm; ☏08/8080 1777; it's best to buy your ticket in advance from the tourist office as places are limited; $3.30), with an accompanying video and talk. In the headquarters you'll see the radio room where calls from remote places in New South Wales, South Australia and Queensland are handled before going out to the hangar to see the aircraft. The increasing popularity of the tours is due to the Australian television series *The Flying Doctors*, which is shown worldwide, and since a third of the annual budget of $30 million has to come through fund-raising – the rest of the money is from the State and Federal governments – whatever you spend on the tour and at the souvenir shop here is going to a good cause.

In many ways the **School of the Air** is also indebted to the RFDS: lessons for children in the Outback, in a transmission area of 1.8 million square kilometres, are conducted via RFDS two-way radio. The service was established in 1956 to improve education for children in the isolated Outback, and today visitors listen to the first hour's transmission in a schoolroom surrounded by childrens' artwork (Mon–Fri, term time only 8.30am; book in advance at the tourist centre; $2.20). It's frighteningly like being back at school, with jolly primary-school teachers hosting singalongs; what comes out of the radio is a static squawk, but the children in the far-flung areas seem to enjoy it.

Eating, drinking and nightlife

Broken Hill still has the proverbial **pub** on every corner – most of them serve inexpensive counter meals as well as ice-cold beer on tap. Broken Hill has always been a legendary drinking hole, once having over seventy hotels. Many have been converted to other uses, but at the time of writing there are still more than twenty licensed establishments and a pub crawl is highly recommended. Some places to include for an early drink are the kitsch-crammed *Mario's Palace*, 227 Argent St, which memorably featured in *Priscilla, Queen of the Desert*; the *Rising Sun*, 2 Beryl St (℡08/8087 4856), popular with younger locals on Friday nights when live bands play; the *Black Lion Inn*, 34 Bromide St, good any time (after midnight Tues–Sat but Fri & Sat till 4am) but especially during happy hour at the cocktail bar done out like an underground mine; and the *Mulga Hill Tavern*, on the corner of Oxide and Williams streets.

Another option is to sample the local culture at one of the numerous **clubs**. These make most of their money out of gambling – with snooker tables, darts and endless parades of one-armed bandits – and they're happy to draw their customers in and keep them playing by tempting them with large portions of cheap food, and quite often live entertainment. Best known is the *Barrier Social Democratic Club* (*Demo Club* to the locals) at 214 Argent St (℡08/8088 4477) with $7.10 daily meal specials including a well-assorted salad bar plus great, inexpensive breakfasts (7–9am). You could also try the *Broken Hill Legion Club*, 166–170 Crystal St (℡08/8087 4064); or the *Broken Hill Musicians Club*, 276 Crystal St (℡08/8088 1777), which has inherited Broken Hill's famous **Two Up School**, once an illegal back-lane gambling operation.

Apart from the pubs and clubs, there are several good **cafés and bakeries** on Argent Street where you can get something to eat and drink – restaurants aren't really Broken Hill's style. *Ruby's Coffee Lounge*, at no. 373, near the corner of Oxide Street (closed Sun), places the emphasis on healthy food, with a few vegetarian dishes always on offer and lots of baked goodies. At no. 198, the friendly *Jonathan's Cafe* serves almost exclusively veggie fare, while Cosy *Charlotte's* at no. 317, opposite the post office, is reckoned to serve the town's best cappuccino and has a well-assorted range of cakes, muffins and slices to accompany your foamy brew. *Cafe Alfresco* at no. 343 (closed Sun) is a city-style café with big open doors and wooden floors, but unfortunately the standard of its coffee doesn't match the interior. Their open toasted sandwiches, however, are huge, tasty and cheap; a separate, pricier night-time restaurant menu features grills, pasta and salads. For **grocery** supplies, visit the well-stocked, late-opening IGM behind the police station on Blende Street, or the out-of-town Westside Plaza, Galena Street (open daily) which proffers both an enormous Woolworths (with liquor) and a cheaper Big W supermarket.

Listings

Airlines Hazelton (☎13 1713; flying to Sydney and Dubbo daily except Sat), Kendell (☎13 1300; flying to Adelaide daily) and International Aviation (flying to Sydney and Mildura daily); all can be booked through Traveland at 350 Argent St (☎08/8087 1969).

Bike rental Johnny Windham, 135 Argent St (☎08/8087 3707), rents mainly mountain bikes; $5 per day, $25 per week, plus obligatory helmet $2; closed Sat & Sun. The *Tourist Lodge* hires bikes to guests at similar rates.

Bookshops ABC Centre, 309 Argent St, specializes in local history and the Outback (☎08/8088 1177). For secondhand books, try W Book Exchange, 320 Chloride St, cnr Thomas St (☎08/8087 3383).

Car rental Avis, 121 Rakow St (☎08/8087 7532); Budget, 338 Crystal St (☎13 2727); Hertz, at the tourist information centre (☎08/8087 2719); and Thrifty, 190 Argent St (☎08/8088 1928); all have desks at the airport too. Cheaper deals are available at Holmes' Hire, 475 Argent St (☎08/8087 2210), with older cars from $60 per day and 4WDs from $110.

Cinema Village Silver City Cinema, 41 Oxide St (☎08/8087 4569).

Hospital Broken Hill Base Hospital and Health Services, 176 Thomas St (☎08/8088 0333).

Internet access Bizbyte, 435 Argent St (Mon–Fri 9am–5.30pm, $3/30min); PC Professionals, 387 Argent St (Mon–Fri 9am–5.30pm, Sat 9am–12.30pm; $2.75/30min). There is also free access at the library, on the corner of Blende and Chloride streets, but you have to book.

Laundry Oxide Street Laundrette, 241 Oxide St. Service washes available, with free pick-up and delivery (☎08/8088 2022).

Pharmacy Amcal Chemist, Westside Plaza, Galena St, has an after-hours emergency number (☎08/8088 5639) but the most central pharmacy is Peoples CP Chemist, 323 Argent St.

Post office Cnr Argent and Chloride streets, NSW 2880.

Swimming pool There are two municipal outdoor pools: Alma Pool, Voughtman St, South Broken Hill (mid-Nov to late March daily 9am–6pm; $1); and North Pool, north of the centre on McCulloch St (daily: April–Oct 6–8.30am & 10.30am–6pm; Nov–March 6–8am & 9am–10pm; $2), which is heated in winter.

Taxis Yellow Radio Cabs (☎08/8088 1144). Taxis work out to be very expensive; eg $9 just to get from the centre to the South Mine.

Tours See box opposite.

Excursions from Broken Hill: Silverton

The ghost town of **SILVERTON**, just 25km northwest of Broken Hill on a good road, makes a great day out. Note that there is no fuel available at Silverton. If the scene looks vaguely familiar, you probably have seen it before: parts of *Mad Max II* were shot around here, and the **Silverton Hotel** (daily 8.30am–9.30pm, though they often close earlier) has appeared as the "Gamulla Hotel" in *Razorback*, the "Hotel Australia" in *A Town Like Alice*, and "Juanita's Diner" in *Fiddlers Green* with Don Johnson. It also seems to star in just about every commercial – usually beer-related – that features an Outback scene. The stark impact of the pub, with barren, red earth stretching endlessly to the horizon, has been somewhat diminished by the greening of the desert, but it's still the ultimate Outback image and a must for every photo collection. The pub has its own collection, the lower walls covered with snapshots from the various film shoots, the upper walls piled high with an assortment of beer cans and old bottles. In some ways it feels like a milk bar, with a fridge full of cold soft drinks, a tea urn, and the only available food some limp sandwiches, pies and pasties, rather than the usual counter meals. But in the tradition of all Outback pubs, it has its own in-jokes; you'll find out what all the laughter is about if you ask to "take the test".

There are a big range of tours on offer, from scenic flights to 4WD tours, all of which can be booked from the tourist information centre (see p.374). Most include a pick-up and return service to and from your accommodation.

Air charters and scenic flights
If you have a bit of cash to spare, small aircraft are an excellent way of getting around, covering the enormous distances quickly and in relative comfort.
Crittenden Air, Airport Terminal (℗ 08/8088 5702 or 8087 2930). Tour flights to Tibooburra ($360), White Cliffs ($250), over Lake Eyre and South Australia's Flinders Ranges ($550) as well as several more local scenic tours. Minimum of 4 people or equivalent per person price.

Bus tours
These tend to be overpriced, given that many tours merely provide transport to places that could be more enjoyably visited with a rental car or bike, or even by taxi. Tours are more frequent between early April and the end of November, and have reduced schedules during the hot summer months.
Broken Hill Outback Information and Safari Tours (℗ 08/8087 8574, ⓦ www.bhoutbacktours.com.au). Half-day tours ($40) to Silverton, the Daydream Mine, Delprats Mine, or city art galleries plus the Sculpture Symposium; a day-tour is also offered to Menindee Lakes and Kinchega National Park ($94).
Silver City Tours (℗ 08/8087 3144, ⓦ www.ruralnet.net.au~wincen/). Excursions include Royal Flying Doctor Service ($17), School of the Air ($17), White's Mineral Art Gallery and Mining Museum ($17); half-day tours of city sights ($35), art galleries ($21), sunset Sculpture Symposium ($30), Silverton ($37); day-tours, including lunch, to White Cliffs ($119), Menindee Lakes, Kinchega National Park and Tandou Irrigation Farm ($95), and Mutawintji National Park ($106).

Four-wheel-drive tours
Broken Hill's Outback Tours (℗ 08/8087 7800 or free call 1800 670 120, ⓦ www.outbacktours.net). Amongst these long-haul fully-inclusive tours are a four-day/three-night trip to all three national parks detailed in the following pages ($980), and a six-day excursion to Flinders Ranges. They will happily provide customized tours too.
Corner Country Adventure Tours (℗ 08/8087 5142, ⓦ www.cornercountryadven-ture.com.au). Longer 4WD trips, including a four-day/three-night trip to all three national parks detailed in the following pages ($710), or tailor-made excursions as far afield as the Birdsville Track.
Goanna Safari (℗ 08/8087 6057, ⓦ www.goanna-safari.com.au). Heartily recom-mended tours with a well-informed, uniquely qualified and interesting guide who is never in too much of a rush; maximum four people in the group. One-day tours ($95); to Poolamacca Station, a sheep station 60km north of Broken Hill; Menindee lakes and Kinchega National Park; Mutawintji National Park including the Aboriginal art sites; the Dingo Fence; or closer to home a round-up of the Royal Flying Doctor Service, Silverton, and the Sculpture Symposium. Two-day safari to White Cliffs, staying in a dug-out motel ($340), or extending to three days and including Mutawintji ($510). Tibooburra and Camerons Corner are taken in on another two-day trip (also $340). Short trips out to The Living Desert sculpture site (minimum $10, cheaper depending on numbers) are also available.
Tri-State Safari (℗ 08/8088 2389, ⓦ www.tristate.com.au). Tours ranging from sun-set sculptures and wine ($32), to one-day trips to Muntawinji ($119) and Kinchega ($132) and mammoth Burke and Wills or desert tours, between four and ten days in length.

Taking the **Silverton Heritage Trail**, a two-hour stroll around town marked by white arrows, is a good way to work up a thirst. But it's far too hot to attempt in the summer, and is best undertaken during the cooler months. Along the way it'll take you past the old **Silverton School Craft Centre**, and the 1889 vintage **Silverton Gaol Museum** (daily 9.30am–4.30pm; $2.50), with the usual collection of relics from pioneer days and Outback stations, plus mining equipment. There's a burgeoning art scene here, too, with four galleries to browse through. **Peter Browne's Gallery** (daily 9am–5pm; ⓦwww.out-backgalleries.com.au), in an 1884 house on a hill, is worth a look for its uniquely original decoration and the humorous paintings of bush scenes, koala-shearing, kookaburras boiling the billy, and Browne's trademark emus with huge, saucer-shaped eyes. Also interesting is Albert Woodroffe's and Bronwen Woodroffe-Standley's **Horizon Gallery** (daily 9am–6pm; ⓦwww.brokenhillartists.com), opposite the pub. The husband and wife team paint in a similar style, creating their trademark horizon paintings, mainly in pastels and acrylics – finely detailed works that really capture the sense of space and the seemingly endless skyline.

One of the most enjoyable things to do while in Silverton is to go on a camel tour. The Cannard family who run the **Silverton Camel Farm** (☏08/8088 5316, ⓔmalee@pcpro.net.au) come from a long line of camel trainers and have forty working camels. You can't miss the farm on the way into Silverton, with the shapes of camels looming like desert mirages. You can hop on for fifteen minutes ($5), or trot for an hour along the nearby creek ($20), but the best experience is the sunset trek (2hr; $40), a ride to the Mundi Mundi Plain to look at the setting sun and a return trip under the night stars accompanied by a pack of lively dogs. Longer safaris into the desert are also on offer, from one to three days ($150–300).

Beyond Silverton, the road continues a further 14km to the **Umberumberka reservoir**, Broken Hill's only source of water until the Menindee Lakes Scheme was set up. There's a signposted lookout area which makes a nice picnic spot. A few kilometres further on you reach the **Mundi Mundi Plains Lookout**. Here, the undulating plateau you have been driving across descends gradually to a vast plain, and on clear days you can see in the distance the blurred outline of the northern Flinders Ranges in South Australia. This spot is where, at the end of *Mad Max II*, Mel Gibson tipped the semi-trailer.

If you want to stay in Silverton, your only choice is to **camp** at Penrose Park, where there's a shower, toilets and barbecue; rates are around $3 – ask at the house there or call ☏08/8088 5307.

Kinchega National Park and the Menindee lakes

Flat **Kinchega National Park** is situated among the **Menindee lakes**, near the township of **MENINDEE**, southeast of Broken Hill. There's a sealed road for the 110km to Menindee and the park entrance, and gravel roads thereafter; before you go, visit the Broken Hill NPWS to get information about road conditions (see p.374), or ask at the **Menindee Tourist Information Centre** (Mon–Fri 9am–5pm, Sat & Sun 10am–1pm; ☏08/8091 4274), where a detailed, hand-drawn "Mud Map" of the lakes area, showing areas of interest, is available free of charge. The Menindee lakes are an extensive, natural oasis, feeding the Darling and Murray rivers and, most importantly, supplying water to Broken Hill; they're also a big recreation area, with facilities for camping, powerboating, water-skiing, sailing, swimming and fishing. The waters protected by the Kinchega National Park, **Menindee Lake** and **Cawndilla Lake**, are a haven for **waterbirds**; a common sight are little black cormorants (commonly known as shags), floating in feeding flocks alongside pelicans, with whom they hunt co-operatively. There's an **information** shelter 5km into the park and a normally unmanned visitor information centre about 10km further on near the **Kinchega Woolshed**. Kinchega Station was one of the first pastoral settlements in the area in 1850 and was worked until 1967; you can explore it by following the signposted woolshed **walk**. Accommodation is available in the shearers' sheds here (❶; book at Broken Hill NPWS), or at the thirty river campsites ($5 payable on site) scattered through the river-red-gum woodland along the river – including the site of Burke and Wills' base camp from late October 1860 until late January 1861 (a tree marks the spot). The main camping area, with toilets, is on the shores of Cawndilla Lake, with its sandy beaches and good swimming.

Burke and Wills stayed in Menindee at the *Maidens Hotel*, Yartla Street (☎08/8091 4208, ☎8091 4300; ❷), on their ill-fated trip north in 1860 (see box on p.568). Unfortunately the room in which they stayed is now full of poker machines, but there is some interpretive material in the hotel (the room's fittings are now in the Railway Museum in Broken Hill; see p.377), and the green courtyard's a good place for a drink or a counter meal. Otherwise, you can stay at the *Burke & Wills Motel* opposite (☎08/8091 4313, ☎8091 4406; ❹), or camp in relative comfort at the *Menindee Lakes Caravan Park* on Lakes Shore Road, 5km northwest of town (☎08/8091 4315; on-site vans ❷), which has a kiosk and grocery store. If you don't have transport, you can take a **day-tour** out here from Broken Hill; the best is with Goanna Safari (see box on p.381).

Mutawintji National Park

Mutawintji National Park, 130km northeast of Broken Hill in the Bynguano Ranges, has totally different and perhaps even more fascinating scenery to offer: secluded gorges and quiet waterholes that attract a profusion of wildlife. The main attractions of the park are the ancient galleries of **Aboriginal rock art** in the caves and overhangs; you can only visit these accompanied by an Aboriginal tour guide (Wed & Sat 11am Eastern Standard Time; no bookings required; $15; 2hr; special tours by arrangement on ☎08/8088 7000) – there are no tours in the hot summer months. While on the tour you get to visit the **Mutawintji Cultural Resource Centre**, an amazing multimedia collaboration between indigenous Australians and the NPWS which tells of tribal history and myth in sound and pictures. There's a **camping** area at Homestead Creek, among river red gums at the entrance to Homestead Gorge (camping is payable on site; $6) and a number of **walking trails** (including the short wheelchair-accessible Thakaaltjika Mingkana Walk). Access to and within the park is via unsealed gravel roads, and you'll need to bring extra fuel as none is available here. It's normally fine for 2WD vehicles, but check locally, as the roads can quickly become impassable after even a light rain; bring extra food just in case. The NPWS office in Broken Hill (see p.374) can provide other information. You can also get here from Broken Hill with Goanna Safari; a bushwalk (2hr 30min) is part of their excellent tour (see box p.381).

Corner Country: Tibooburra and the Sturt National Park

A remote Outback settlement in the far northwest corner of New South Wales, 337km from Broken Hill, **TIBOOBURRA** can be reached by normal vehicle on a well-maintained dirt road from Broken Hill – the Silver City

Highway. You can also reach it from Bourke (see p.368), 454km southwest along various unsealed and mostly deserted roads. After rain, roads may become impassable, and it's important to find out about road and weather conditions before you set out; it's also crucial to carry extra food, water, fuel and spare vehicle parts in case you get stranded later on. (Refer to the tourist information office in Broken Hill or Bourke for advice before leaving.) Tibooburra has been settled for over a hundred and ten years: several stone buildings from the 1880s still remain, the result of a flurried goldrush, which add a bit of architectural charm to the tiny township. The nearby granite outcrops – worthy of a sunset stroll – from which the stone was quarried, gave the town its former name of Granites. Outback institutions are well-represented here: there are some classic pubs (the *Family Hotel* and *Tibooburra Hotel* are detailed below), a hospital serviced by the Royal Flying Doctor Service, and a **School of the Air** similar to the one in Broken Hill; visitors can witness the on-air education service on schoolday mornings from 9am ($2). The **NPWS office** in the town (℡08/8091 3308), attached to the old courthouse (with a display about the town's history) provides visitor information, including the latest on the roads and weather, and camping permits for the national park.

In nearby **Sturt National Park**, a network of roads and tracks is maintained by the NPWS to 2WD standard, but check with the rangers at Tibooburra before setting out. The park's 3500 square kilometres are cut in two by the Grey Range: to the west are the rolling red sand dunes of the Strzelecki Desert, and to the east the stone-covered, so-called gibber plains extending for hundreds of kilometres. The area supports a number of red and grey kangaroos, emus and lizards.

At the edge of the park, the border between Queensland, New South Wales and South Australia is delineated by the 1.8-metre-high **Dingo Fence**. This, the world's longest fence (4850km), was originally constructed by the Queensland government to stop the invasion of rabbits from the south; it's now maintained to keep dingoes out of sheep-grazing land. The point where the three states meet is known as **Cameron's Corner** and is marked by a post: it's a popular target for travellers, so much so that there's even a shop here, the wittily named *Corner Store* (℡08/8091 3872). As well as dishing up the ubiquitous meat pies and other typical Aussie fillers, they have fuel and can give you useful road advice.

There are a couple of pleasant **hotels**, with welcome air-conditioning, on Briscoe Street in Tibooburra: the *Family Hotel* (℡08/8091 3314, ℻8091 3430; ❸) is marginally the fancier with a wall mural by the Australian artist Clifton Pugh, while the two-storey *Tibooburra Hotel* (℡08/8091 3310, ℻8091 3406, ⓦwww.pubstay.com.au; $44) vies for attention with its wall full of old hats. Both also serve decent counter meals. *The Granites Caravan Park*, at the corner of Brown and King streets (℡08/8091 3305; cabins ❸, on-site vans ❷), has a refreshing pool.

TRAVEL DETAILS

Most public transport in NSW originates in Sydney, and the main services are outlined in the "Travel Details" at the end of Chapter 1.

Trains

There are nine main train routes departing from Sydney that pass through the region covered in this chapter; all trains connect with Countrylink (ⓦwww.countrylink.nsw.gov.au) buses run by the state rail system to fill in the gaps. Destinations within the area of this chapter are printed below.

- Sydney–**Albury** (2 daily; 7hr 20min), via **Cootamundra** (5hr) and **Wagga Wagga** (6hr).
- Sydney–**Armidale** (1 daily; 8hr 10min), via **Tamworth** (6hr 15min).
- Sydney–**Brisbane** (2 daily; 14hr 10min), with stops including **Taree**, **Coffs Harbour** and **Grafton**.
- Sydney–**Canberra** (1 daily; 4hr 10min), via **Goulburn** (2hr 35min).
- Sydney–**Dubbo** (2 daily; 6hr 30min), via **Bathurst** (3hr 30min).
- Sydney–Melbourne (2 daily; 10hr 20min), with stops at **Cootamundra** and **Wagga Wagga**.

- Sydney–**Moree** (1 daily; 9hr), via **Scone** (4hr 20min), **Gunnedah** (6hr 5min) and **Narrabri** (7hr 15min).
- Sydney–**Murwillumbah** (2 daily; 13hr 45min–14hr), via **Taree** (5hr), **Wauchope** (6hr), **Coffs Harbour** (8hr 30min), **Grafton** (9hr 30min), **Lismore** (11hr 30min) and **Byron Bay** (12hr).
- The NSW leg of the Indian Pacific linking Sydney and Perth via Adelaide takes in **Condoblin** (10hr 35min from Sydney), **Ivanhoe** (13hr 50min), **Menindee** (16hr 10min) and **Broken Hill** (18hr 55min).

Buses

Albury to: Canberra (2 daily; 4hr); Corowa (3 weekly; 1hr); Cowra (1 daily; 4hr); Dubbo (1 daily; 8hr 30min); Echuca (3 weekly; 4hr 15min); Melbourne (3 daily; 4hr); Tamworth (1 daily; 12hr 20min); Yass (2 daily; 3hr 20min).

Armidale to: Brisbane (6 daily; 7hr 45min); Port Macquarie (3 weekly; 6hr 15min); Melbourne (2 daily; 18hr 45min); Sydney (4 daily; 8hr); Tamworth (3 daily; 1hr 45min); Tenterfield (2 daily; 2hr 20min).

Bourke to: Dubbo (3 weekly; 4hr 45min).

Broken Hill to: Adelaide (2 daily; 7hr); Cobar (3 daily; 5hr 20min); Dubbo (5 daily; 9hr 30min); Mildura (3 weekly; 4hr); Sydney (1 daily; 17hr 40min).

Byron Bay to: Ballina (3–8 daily; 35min); Brisbane (10–11 daily; 2hr 15min); Coffs Harbour (6 daily; 3hr 50min); Murwillumbah (4–8 daily; 50min); Port Macquarie (4 daily; 6hr); Surfers Paradise (6–7 daily; 1hr 5min); Sydney (6 daily; 12hr 15min).

Canberra to: Albury (1 daily; 4hr 10min); Bairnsdale (3 weekly; 7hr); Batemans Bay (1–2 daily; 2hr 30min); Bega (1 daily; 3hr 30min); Bombala (3 weekly; 3hr 30min); Cooma (1–2 daily; 1hr 50min); Eden (1 daily; 4hr 20min); Griffith (1 daily; 6hr 35min); Melbourne (6 daily; 8hr 30min); Moruya (1–2 daily; 3hr 25min); Narooma (1–2 daily; 4hr 30min); Nowra (1 daily; 4hr 45min); Wagga Wagga (2 daily; 3hr); Wollongong (1 daily; 3hr 25min).

Coffs Harbour to: Byron Bay (6 daily; 3hr 40min); Grafton (5 daily; 1hr 10min); Nambucca Heads (6 daily; 50min); Tweed Heads (1 daily; 6hr 10min).

Coonabarabran to: Adelaide (3 daily; 12hr); Brisbane (4 daily; 19hr); Canberra (3 daily; 5hr 40min); Melbourne (5 daily; 7hr 30min); Sydney (5–6 daily; 8hr 30min–10hr).

Cootamundra to: Dubbo (1 daily; 4hr 15min); Gundagai (6 weekly; 45min); Tumbarumba (6 weekly; 2hr 45min).

Dubbo to: Albury (1 daily; 9hr); Bathurst (1 daily; 2hr 45min); Bourke (3 weekly; 4hr 45min); Brewarrina (3 weekly; 5hr 45min); Broken Hill (5 daily; 8hr 30min); Canberra (4 weekly; 6hr 10min); Cobar (3 daily; 3hr 30min); Coonabarabran (3–5 daily; 1hr 50min); Cootamundra (3 weekly; 4hr 15min); Cowra (1–2 daily; 3hr 20min); Forbes (2 daily; 2hr 35min); Griffith (2 daily; 4hr 45min); Gunnedah (1 daily; 4hr); Lightning Ridge (1 daily; 4hr 50min); Moree (3 daily; 4hr 20min); Narrandera (1 daily; 5hr 15min); Orange (1 daily; 2hr 40min); Parkes (2 daily; 2hr 10min); Tamworth (3–5 daily; 4hr); Wagga Wagga (2 daily; 6hr).

Griffith to: Canberra (1 daily; 6hr 15min); Cootamundra (1 daily; 2hr 35min); Hay (1 daily; 3hr 50min); Leeton (1–2 daily; 50min); Narrandera (1–2 daily; 1hr 15min); Wagga Wagga (1–2 daily; 2hr 40min).

Lismore to: Ballina (1–3 daily; 45min); Brisbane (3–5 daily; 3hr); Byron Bay (4–6 daily; 1hr 15min); Casino (2 daily; 25min); Murwillumbah (3–5 daily; 2hr); Nimbin (2–3 daily; 25min); Tweed Heads (3–5 daily; 2hr 45min).

Lithgow to: Bathurst (3–6 daily; 1hr); Coonabarabran (6 weekly; 5hr 30min); Cowra (6 weekly; 2hr 40min); Dubbo (6 weekly; 4hr 30min); Mudgee (1 daily; 2hr 30min); Orange (2–5 daily; 1hr 45min–2hr).

Murwillumbah to: Tweed Heads (4–11 daily; 30min).

Port Macquarie to: Armidale (3 weekly; 6hr 15min); Ballina (5 daily; 6hr); Bellingen (3 weekly; 3hr 15min); Brisbane (5 daily; 10hr 30min); Coffs Harbour (5–6 daily; 2hr 40min); Dorrigo (3 weekly;

3hr 50min); Grafton (5 daily; 4hr 10min); Scone (3 weekly; 10hr 20min); Surfers Paradise (5 daily; 9hr); Tamworth (3 weekly; 8hr 30min).
Tamworth to: Armidale (1 daily; 1hr 40min);

Cessnock (1 daily; 4hr); Dorrigo (3 weekly; 4hr 10min); Gunnedah (2 daily; 1hr); Inverell (1 daily; 3hr 40min); Port Macquarie (3 weekly; 8hr 30min); Scone (2 daily; 2hr 15min); Tenterfield (2 daily; 4hr 30min).

Flights

Armidale to: Brisbane (1–2 daily; 1hr 10min); Coolangatta (3 weekly; 50min); Sydney (1–3 daily; 1hr 10min).

Ballina to: Brisbane (1–3 daily; 45min); Sydney (2–5 daily; 1hr 10min).

Broken Hill to: Adelaide (1–4 daily; 1hr 40min); Dubbo (6 weekly; 2hr, Sydney (2–4 daily; 3hr 45min).

Canberra to: Ballina (2–3 daily; 4hr 40min); Dubbo (1–2 daily; 2hr 15min); Grafton (1–2 daily; 2hr 30min); Lismore (1–4 daily; 4hr 10min); Moree (1–2 daily; 3hr 55min); Narrabri (1–2 daily; 3hr 15min); Newcastle (3–4 daily; 2hr 10min); Port Macquarie (3–9 daily; 2hr 25min); Sydney (25–30 daily; 35min); Tamworth (4–8 daily; 2hr 25min).

Coffs Harbour to: Brisbane (2 daily; 45min); Sydney (3–5 daily; 55min).

Dubbo to: Brewarrina (3 weekly; 1hr); Broken Hill (6 weekly; 2hr); Brisbane (2 weekly, 2hr 10min) Cobar

(1–3 a day, Sun–Fri; 1hr); Coolangatta (2 weekly, 1hr 35min); Lightning Ridge (1–2 a day, Mon–Fri; 1hr 40min); Nyngan (4 weekly; 30min); Sydney (3–13 daily; 1hr); Walgett (5 weekly; 1hr 10min).

Lismore to: Brisbane (2–3 daily; 25min); Sydney (5–8 daily; 1hr 50min).

Lord Howe Island to: Brisbane (6 weekly; 2hr); Sydney (6 weekly; 2hr).

Norfolk Island to: Brisbane (6 weekly; 2hr 10min); Sydney (5 weekly; 2hr 30min).

Port Macquarie to: Brisbane (3–6 daily; 1hr); Coffs Harbour (2–3 daily; 25min); Sydney (6 daily; 55min).

Tamworth to: Brisbane (4–12 daily; 2hr 20min); Cobar (8 weekly; 1hr); Melbourne (2–3 daily; 3hr 20min); Mildura (6 weekly; 1hr 30min); Sydney (3–8 daily; 1hr).

Taree to: Port Macquarie (1–2 a day, Mon–Sat; 20min); Sydney (3 daily; 55min).

Southeast Queensland

CHAPTER 3

Highlights

* **Gold Coast nightlife** – The bars, clubs and theme parks of Australia's prime domestic holiday destination provide raucous entertainment around the clock. **p.420**.

* **Lamington National Park** – Packed with beautiful jungle scenery and a huge variety of plants and animals, Lamington National Park is criss-crossed by dozens of enticing forest trails. **p.433**.

* **Glasshouse Mountains** – One of the few really special places on the Sunshine Coast, it's worth climbing at least one of the dramatic pinnacles of the Glasshouse Mountains for the fantastic views. **p.437**.

* **Surf at Noosa** – Catch the waves at exclusive Noosa, popular with surfers since the 1960s. **p.439**.

* **Fraser Island** – The giant dunes of beautiful Fraser Island are best explored on an action-packed 4WD safari. **p.450**.

3

Southeast Queensland

Southeast Queensland consists of an eight-hundred-kilometre stretch between the New South Wales border and Fraser Island containing many of the classic features that lure visitors to Australia's second-largest state. Surf rolls in to long, sandy beaches, backed by vibrant towns in exotic settings; behind them, the land rises a thousand metres or more to lush, rainforest-clad plateaus. It's one of Australia's busiest tourist venues, a factor that will be central to your impressions of the region: some love the hype and pace of it's higher-profile attractions; others loathe it for the same reasons and despair of ever finding an untramped corner.

However, though parts of Southeast Queensland undoubtedly live up to their glitzy reputations, there's far more to the region than its popularity on the "drunken backpackers" trail would suggest. Set down towards the border, the state capital **Brisbane** is an attractive, relaxed city with good work opportunities and a lively social scene, with some very underrated scenery within easy reach – the best of which are the giant, wooded, sand islands of shallow **Moreton Bay**. South of Brisbane, the **Gold Coast** is Australia's prime domestic holiday destination; while its reputation was founded on some of Queensland's best **surf**, this now takes second place to a belt of beachfront high-rises, theme parks, and the host of bars and nightclubs surrounding **Surfers Paradise**. But even here there are quieter corners, such as the often almost empty beaches at the Gold Coast's southernmost town, **Coolangatta**; while just an hour inland, the **Scenic Rim**'s green heights provide the perfect antidote to coastal concretions, with a chain of **national parks** packed with wildlife and endless hiking trails. Heading north of Brisbane, fruit and veg-

---

Accommodation price codes

All the accommodation listed in this book has been categorized into one of eight price bands, as set out below. The rates quoted represent the cheapest available double or twin room in high season – except for category ❶, which indicates per-person rates for a dorm bed, and the categories given for units, cabins and vans, which represent the daily charge for the whole unit.

❶ Under $20	❸ $35–50	❺ $70–90	❼ $115–150
❷ $20–35	❹ $50–70	❻ $90–115	❽ $150 upwards

For more accommodation details, see pp.46–49.

Gladstone & Rockhampton

0   25 km

Rockhampton

Bundaberg

Indian
Head

Hervey
Bay

*Fraser
Island*

Happy Valley

Central Station

Maryborough

Dilli Village

Bruce Highway

Rainbow
Beach

*COOLOOLA
NATIONAL PARK*

N

Gympie

Bruce Highway

Noosa

Tewantin

Kingaroy

Nambour

*Sunshine
Coast*

Maroochydore

Mooloolaba

Caloundra

**Glasshouse
Mountains**

*Bribie
Island*

Roma

Caboolture

*Moreton
Island*

Lake
Wivenhoe

*BRISBANE
FOREST PARK*

*St Helena
Island*

Dalby

Warrego Highway

Cunnamulla

**Mount
Coot-tha**

Brisbane

BRISBANE

*North
Stradbroke
Island*

Toowoomba

Ipswich

Beenleigh

Pacific Hwy

Cunningham Highway

Mount
Tamborine

*South
Stradbroke
Island*

Beaudesert

Surfers Paradise

*Gold
Coast*

Cunnamulla

Cunningham Highway

*LAMINGTON
NATIONAL
PARK*

Coolangatta

Warwick

Scenic Rim

Murwillumbah

Mt Lindesay Hwy

*SPRINGBROOK
NATIONAL PARK*

Stanthorpe

etable plantations behind the gentle **Sunshine Coast** benefit from rich volcanic soils and a subtropical climate. **Noosa** is the hub here, an up-and-coming resort town with more beaches and famous surf. Beyond looms **Fraser Island**, whose surrounding waters host an annual whale migration and where huge forested dunes, freshwater lakes and sculpted coloured sands form the backdrop for exciting safaris in a 4WD.

In a way, Queensland's popularity as a holiday hotspot is surprising, as this is eastern Australia's most **conservative** state, often lampooned – somewhat unfairly – as being slow and regressive. There are, however, very physical and social divisions between the densely settled, city-oriented southeastern corner and the large, rural remainder, which is given over to primary industries such as mining and farming. These divisions date back to when Brisbane was chosen as capital on Queensland's separation from New South Wales in 1859; the city proved an unpopular choice with the northern pioneers, who felt that the government was too far away to understand, or even care about, their needs. These needs centred around the north's sugar plantations and the use of Solomon Islanders for labour, a practice the government equated with **slavery** and finally banned. Ensuing demands for further separation, this time between tropical Queensland and the southeast, never materialized, but the remoteness of northern settlements from the capital led to local self-sufficiency, making Queensland far less centralized than other states.

The darker side of this conservatism has seen Queensland endure more than its fair share of extreme or simply dirty **politics**. During the 1970s and early 1980s, the stranglehold of a strongly conservative National Party government, led by the charismatic Sir **Johannes Bjelke-Petersen** (better known as "Joh"), did nothing to enhance the state's image. Citing issues of law and order to justify granting the police sweeping powers, Joh created a repressive and domineering government, characterized by his own peculiar, slippery oratory. He finally became the victim of his own devices after initiating the Fitzgerald Inquiry – an investigation into government corruption – which implicated his cabinet in a variety of offences and forced him from office. But the following left-wing government was not without controversy, and recent investigations have uncovered high-level electoral fraud by Labor (including one incident when a cat was enrolled to vote); though state Labor leader Peter Beatty escaped untainted from the investigation in 2000 – and was re-elected as Premier with a huge majority in 2001 – several members of his cabinet were forced to resign. The late 1990s were also blighted by the emergence from Southeast Queensland of **Pauline Hanson** and her One Nation Party, whose shallow, racist outbursts have won favour with a fair number of Australians who feel ignored by the main parties and threatened by a slowing economy.

As a major tourist destination, Queensland's south coast seldom presents travel or accommodation problems, and in many places the only trouble is making some sort of choice between the vast array of options. However, during **busy periods** – the Easter and Christmas holidays, and at weekends – there are room shortages and price hikes in all accommodation except hostels. This is most pronounced on the Gold Coast, though you'll find a degree of seasonal inflation right throughout the region. Book in advance whenever possible, and don't be afraid to bargain outside the peak times.

Brisbane and around

By far the largest city in Queensland, **BRISBANE** is not quite what you'd expect from a state capital with almost one-and-a-half million residents. Although there is urban sprawl, and high-rise buildings, slow-moving traffic, crowded streets and the other trappings of a business and trade centre, there's little of the pushiness that usually accompanies them. To urbanites used to a more aggressive approach, the atmosphere is slow, even backward (a reputation the city would be pleased to lose), but to others the languid pace is a welcome change and reflects relaxed rather than regressive attitudes.

In 1823, responding to political pressure to shift the "worst type of felons" away from Sydney and the southeast – the further the better – the New South Wales government sent the Surveyor General **John Oxley** north to find a suitable site for a new prison colony. Sailing into **Moreton Bay**, he encountered three shipwrecked convicts who had been living with Aborigines for several months; they introduced Oxley to a previously unknown river. He explored it briefly, named it "Brisbane" after the governor, and the next year established a convict settlement at Redcliffe on the coast. This was immediately abandoned in favour of better anchorage further upstream, and by the end of 1824 today's city centre had become the site of Brisbane Town.

Twenty years on, a land shortage down south persuaded the government to move out the convicts and free up the Moreton Bay area to settlers. Immigrants on government-assisted passages poured in and Brisbane began to shape up as a busy **port** – an unattractive, awkward settlement of rutted streets and wooden shacks. By far the largest regional settlement of the times, Brisbane was the obvious choice as capital of the new state of Queensland on its formation in 1859, though the city's first substantial buildings were constructed only in the late 1860s, after fire had destroyed the original centre and state bankruptcy was averted by Queensland's first **gold** strikes at Gympie (see p.447). Even so, development was slow and uneven: new townships were founded around the centre at Fortitude Valley, Kangaroo Point and Breakfast Creek, gradually merging into a city.

After World War II, when General Douglas MacArthur used Brisbane as his headquarters to co-ordinate attacks on Japanese forces based throughout the Pacific, Brisbane stagnated, earning a reputation as a dull, underdeveloped backwater – not least thanks to the Bjelke-Petersen regime. As if to remove all trace of his rule, Brisbane underwent a thorough facelift before hosting the 1988 **World Expo**, when eighteen million visitors came to experience "Leisure in the Age of Technology". Not least for locals, who treated it as something of a coming-out party, the Expo provided a real boost after years of tedium and through the 1990s, under the public-spirited mayor **Jim Soorely**, the city became an increasingly busy and pleasant place to spend some time.

Seen from the river or the top of Mount Coot-tha, Brisbane is attractive enough, with the typical features of any Australian city of a comparable age and size: a historic precinct, museums and botanic gardens. There's a confused blur of old and new, crammed in side by side rather than split into distinct districts, while new suburbs are blithely added to the shapeless edges as the need arises. The residents, too, have a spontaneous manner, partly because many are new to the area. In the early 1990s, economic malaise in Australia's southern states resulted in a steady northward migration of people seeking **work** – or at least

Aboriginal Brisbane

John Oxley recorded that the **Brisbane Aborigines** were friendly; they had looked after the shipwrecked convicts and, in the early days, even rounded up and returned runaways from the settlement. In his orders to Oxley on how to deal with the indigenous peoples, Governor Brisbane admitted, though in a roundabout way, that the land belonged to them: "All uncivilized people have wants . . . when treated justly they acquire many comforts by their union with the more civilized. This justifies our occupation of their lands."

But future governors were not so liberal in their views, and things had soured long before the first squatters moved into the Brisbane area and began leaving out "gifts" of poisoned flour and calling in the Native Mounted Police to disperse local Aborigines – a euphemism for exterminating them. Bill Rosser's grim account in *Up Rode the Troopers – The Black Police in Queensland* tells the story through dialogues with the grandson of one of the last tribal members in the Brisbane area, and gives a good idea of how communities were split up and scattered by Queensland's **Protection Act**, which remained in force until the 1970s.

A trace of Brisbane's Aboriginal past is found at the **Nudgee Bora Ring** about 12km north of the centre at Nudgee Waterhole Reserve, at the junction of Nudgee and Childs roads. Last used in 1860, two low mounds where boys were initiated form little more than an icon today, and you'll probably feel that it's not worth the trip. More rewarding are the several **Aboriginal walking trails** at Mount Coot-tha; the City Hall information desk has leaflets on these which explain traditional uses of the area (see Mount Coot-tha, p.414).

finding Queensland a better place to be unemployed – and Brisbane was the obvious first stop. It's still a fairly easy place to find casual, short-term employment, and there's a healthy, unpredictable **social scene**, tempting many travellers to spend longer here than they had planned. As for exploring further afield, you'll find empty beaches and surf on **North Stradbroke Island** and **Moreton Island** – both easy to reach from the city – as well as subtropical woods in **Brisbane Forest Park**, a twenty-minute drive from the centre.

Arrival and information

Brisbane Airport is located 9km northwest of the centre, at the end of Kingsford Smith Drive. You'll find banks (including ATMs) and luggage lockers at both the domestic and the new international terminals. The quickest way to reach Brisbane from either terminal is aboard the new **Airtrain**, which runs four times an hour to the Roma Street Transit Centre (see p.396) and charges $9 one-way ($15 return). For the same price you could take the SkyTrans **bus** (☎07/3236 1000), which delivers direct to central accommodation and the Transit Centre every thirty minutes between 5am and 10.45pm. A **taxi** into the city costs around $30 for the half-hour trip. For the Gold Coast, Airtrain run twice an hour ($20 one-way, $35 return), while buses delivering direct to accommodation include SkyTrans, Airporter (book in advance ☎07/5588 8777), Airport Transit (book in advance ☎1300/655 655) and Active Tours (☎07/5597 0344), who all charge $33 one-way, $54 return.

BRISBANE

FORTITUDE VALLEY

NEW FARM

SPRING HILL

PETRIE TERRACE

Brunswick Street Station

St John's Cathedral

Story Bridge

City Ferry Terminal

Eagle Street Pier

Customs House

Eagle Street Markets

Central Station

Windmill

Wickham Park

Albert Park

Transit Centre

City Hall

William Jolly of Grey Street Bridge

ANZAC SQUARE

KING GEORGE SQUARE

Mall

N

1 & Sunshine Coast

Breakfast Creek & Airport

Ipswich

1 Castlemaine Perkins Brewery & Mount Coot-tha

8

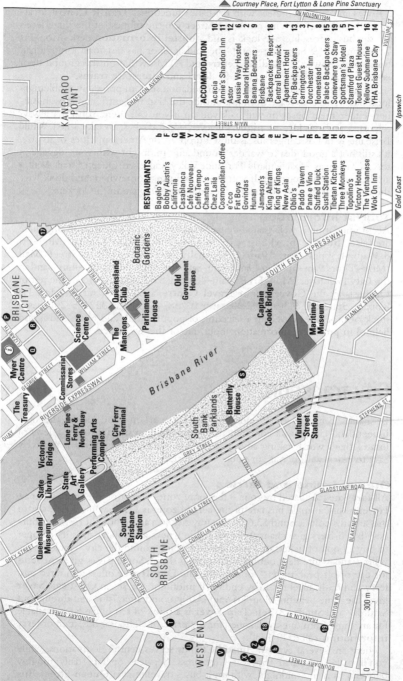

Courtney Place, Fort Lytton & Lone Pine Sanctuary

KANGAROO POINT

SHAFESTON AVENUE

MAIN STREET

VULTURE ST.

▶ Ipswich

▶ Gold Coast

ACCOMMODATION

Acacia	10
Annie's Shandon Inn	11
Astor	12
Aussie Way Hostel	6
Balmoral House	2
Banana Benders	9
Brisbane Backpackers' Resort	18
Central Brunswick Apartment Hotel	4
City Backpackers	13
Carrington's	3
Dorchester Inn	7
Homestead	8
Palace Backpackers	15
Somewhere to Stay	19
Sportsman's Hotel	5
Stamford Plaza	17
Tourist Guest House	1
Yellow Submarine	16
YHA Brisbane City	14

RESTAURANTS

Bagelo's	b
Bobby Austin's	F
California	G
Casablanca	M
Café Nouveau	Y
Caffé Tempo	X
Chantan's	Z
Chez Laila	W
Cosmopolitan Coffee	B
e'cco	a
Fat Boys	J
Govindas	C
Hunan	D
Jameson's	K
King Ahiram	a
King of Kings	E
New Asia	V
Oblio's	T
Paddo Tavern	L
Pane e Vino	R
Stuffed Duck	P
Sushi Station	N
Tibetan Kitchen	H
Three Monkeys	S
Topolino's	I
Victory Hotel	O
The Vietnamese	A
Wok On Inn	U

BRISBANE CITY

The Treasury

Myer Centre

Commissariat Stores

Science Centre

The Mansions

Parliament House

Queensland Club

Old Government House

Botanic Gardens

RIVERSIDE EXPRESSWAY

WILLIAM STREET

GEORGE STREET

ALBERT STREET

EDWARD STREET

MARGARET STREET

MARY STREET

ALICE STREET

ELIZABETH ST.

QUAY

State Library

State Art Gallery

Queensland Museum

Victoria Bridge

Lone Pine Ferry & North Quay

Performing Arts Complex

City Ferry Terminal

Brisbane River

South Bank Parklands

Butterfly House

Captain Cook Bridge

Maritime Museum

SOUTH EAST EXPRESSWAY

STANLEY STREET

STEPHENS ST.

South Brisbane Station

Vulture Street Station

GREY STREET

SOUTH BRISBANE

GREY STREET

PEEL STREET

MELBOURNE STREET

MERIVALE STREET

CORDELIA STREET

RUSSELL STREET

EDMONDSTONE STREET

GLADSTONE ROAD

BLAKENEY ST.

VULTURE STREET

VULTURE STREET

BRIGHTON RD.

FRANKLIN ST.

BOUNDARY STREET

BOUNDARY STREET

WEST END

0   300 m

Buses and trains connect with Brisbane's functional **Transit Centre**, located in the heart of the city on Roma Street. On the highest of the three levels are the bus offices, luggage lockers and a **hostel information** desk (Mon–Fri 7am–6pm, Sat & Sun 8am–5pm). The middle floor has fast-food joints, a bar, toilets and showers, a **medical centre** and ATMs, while on the ground floor is the arrival and departure point for **local** and **interstate trains**.

During the day, reaching your accommodation seldom poses any problems as local buses and taxis leave from just outside the Transit Centre, and most hosteliers either meet buses or will pick you up if you call them. You can't always rely on a pick-up **late at night**, however, when it's best to take a taxi. While Brisbane is not as dangerous as most European or American cities of its size, it's still not a good idea to wander around after midnight with your luggage in tow; some areas – particularly Fortitude Valley, and even Queen Street Mall – are best avoided altogether. If you simply must get somewhere and don't have the cab fare, it's worth considering leaving your luggage in the lockers.

Tourist information

Accommodation is well-geared up to providing general information, and there are also **booths** providing city information at the airport (Mon–Fri 8.30am–4.30pm, Sat 10am–1pm), halfway down Queen Street Mall (Mon–Thurs 9am–5pm, Fri 9am–7pm, Sat 9am–4pm, Sun 10am–4pm), and in the City Hall foyer (Mon–Fri 8.30am–4.30pm, Sat 10am–1pm). For the rest of Queensland, the **Government Travel Centre**, at 243 Edward St (Mon–Fri 8.30am–5pm, Sat 9.30am–12.30pm; ☏ 07/3874 2800, ℻ 3221 5320), has a stock of brochures covering a selection of popular trails and tours, and is also helpful in providing information about out-of-the-way places.

City transport

Brisbane's centre is small and possible to cover on foot, but as the only Queensland city with a comprehensive **transport system**, it offers a level of luxury that's worth taking advantage of. Anywhere further afield is relatively easy to reach with private or public transport.

Buses, trains and ferries

All **fares** are calculated by zone – the more zones you cross, the more you pay. For example, a single bus fare in the central zone is $1.60, while a ride out to the suburbs costs around $3.60. One-way tickets can be bought on your journey (bus drivers give change); for several journeys and longer stays it's cheaper to buy a book of tickets or a **pass** from agencies around the city – look for the yellow-and-white flags outside participating shops. Some passes give discounts for day or off-peak travel - for example, the **Day Rover** offers unlimited bus, ferry and train travel for a day, ending at midnight, for $8; an **Off-Peak Saver** gives the same benefits Mon–Fri 9am–3.30pm and after 7pm, and throughout Saturday and Sunday. A **Ten-Trip Saver** is a book of ten single fares, available for anything from one to all zones, for the price of eight. For bus, train or ferry **information** call ☏ 13 1230.

There are several types of **buses**: Citybus serves central destinations, while you'll make suburban trips on Cityxpress. Services operate daily roughly between 6am and midnight, with most buses travelling via **Queen Street Bus**

Station (below the Myer Centre), where platforms are named after native animals (platypus, koala, etc) and where there's an **information office** open Monday to Friday from 8.30am to 5pm; there are no regular night-time bus services. There's also a special **City Sights** bus, which tours a preset route through the centre with a guide from 9am–5pm daily – look for the specially marked stops. Tickets cost $18 and are valid all day, and also allow unlimited use of bus and ferry services.

The electric **Citytrain** network provides a faster service than the buses, but it's not as frequent or comprehensive, and has at times come under criticism from residents for unreliable service. Trains through central Brisbane run every few minutes, but for the more distant suburbs you may have to wait an hour. The last trains leave **Central Station** on Ann Street at about 11.45pm – timetables are available from ticket offices. Buy **tickets and passes** at most stations.

Revamped in 1996, Brisbane's **ferries** are a quick way of getting across the city. Running every 10–30 minutes between 5.50am and 10.30pm, there are a couple of easy cross-river connections, but the Inner City and City Cat services are the most useful, the latter running at a bracing 27 knots between the University of Queensland campus in the southwest to Bretts Wharf, up towards the airport on Kingsford Smith Drive. **Fares** start at around $1.60 for a single crossing, and most bus passes are also valid. The central departure points for Inner City and City Cat are from South Bank Parklands, Eagle Street Pier and North Quay, next to Victoria Bridge.

Taxis, cars and bikes

During the week, Brisbane's public transport is closed down by midnight, so you may well need a **taxi** if you're out on the town. After dark they tend to cruise round the clubs and hotels; during the day Roma Street is a good place to find one. To call a taxi, try B&W Cabs (☎13 1008), or Yellow Cabs (☎13 1924).

Driving is not much fun until you get your bearings. Unfortunately, signs just *at* junctions, rather than well before them, are typical not only of Brisbane but of all of Queensland, and you'd be well advised to get some sort of street directory as soon as possible. Once familiar with the city, there are no great problems, although **parking** is expensive and in short supply in the centre. For details of car rental agencies, see "Listings", p.412.

Cyclists have a good number of bike routes from which to choose. Maps are available from some information sources (see opposite), libraries and city council offices. A few hostels loan bikes, but they can be easily rented elsewhere – again, see "Listings".

Accommodation

Usually beds are scarce only during major rugby league events and the Brisbane Show (the "Ekka") in August. The most expensive places are in the city centre, though there are also some first-rate motel deals here, with hostels spread around Petrie Terrace, Fortitude Valley and over the river in South Brisbane. If you're staying for a while, ask about **weekly rates**, which might amount to one free night in seven; for stays of a month or more contact *Brisbane City Apartments* (free call☎ 1800 627 538) who rent out one-bedroom apartments for $240 per week that actually sleep three. Prices at more upmarket places may also drop at weekends and outside peak season, due to the scarcity of business customers and competition from the Gold Coast.

Brisbane's **backpackers' hostels** are pretty dependable, with most offering doubles as well as the usual dormitory beds. Many have entertainment, cheap meals, internet facilities, bikes for rent or loan, pools and courtesy buses on arrival (and sometimes departure), and can arrange work connections.

Camping only saves a dollar or two on the price of a hostel bed at around $15 a tent, and you still have to travel into town. The *Alpha Motel/Caravan Park*, 1434 Gympie Rd, Aspley (☎07/3263 4011; bus #55 or #182 from the corner of Queen and Creek streets, or from Adelaide Street outside City Hall), is about 10km north on the main highway. If this is full, try *Acres* next door or *Caravan Village*, 763 Zillmere Rd, about 500m further on. These are the most centrally located van parks and have at least a regular bus service.

City centre and Petrie Terrace

Considering their convenient locations, the following all offer very decent value for money. Petrie Terrace is a ten-minute walk from the Transit Centre – or take bus #144 from opposite the Transit Centre to stop no. 5.

Acacia, 413 Upper Edward St (☎07/3832 1663, ⓕ 3832 2591, ⓔ yale_inn@hotmail.com). Pleasant and central motel-like B&B with shared and en-suite rooms. ❸–❹

Annie's Shandon Inn, 405 Upper Edward St (☎07/3831 8684, ⓕ 3831 3073). A nice, cosy family-run B&B with single, double, and en-suite rooms just a five-minute walk from the city centre. Singles ❸, doubles ❹

Astor, 193 Wickham Terrace (☎07/3831 9522, ⓕ 3831 7360, ⓔ theastor@optus.net.au). Boutique hotel in a smart, renovated nineteenth-century colonial building with a range of en=suite rooms and fully serviced apartments. Doubles ❹, suites ❺, two-bedroom apartments ❼

Aussie Way Hostel, 34 Cricket St (☎07/3369 0711, ⓕ 3252 5172). Renovated nineteenth-century town house with quiet ambience, large pool, verandahs, balcony and period decor. ❶

Banana Benders, 118 Petrie Terrace (☎07/3367 1157, ⓕ 3368 1047, ⓦ www.backpackersaustralia.com.au). A small, friendly hostel with a homely, easy=going feel. There's a small kitchen and BBQ area, casual TV and video lounge, deck-space for dining, and free entry to local public pool. Bunk room ❶, doubles ❸

Carrington's, Gregory Terrace, Spring Hill (☎07/3315 2630, ⓦ www.carringtons.com.au). Men=only gay bed and breakfast in freshly restored 1880s Queenslander. ❹

Dorchester Inn, 484 Upper Edward St (☎07/3831 2967, ⓕ 3832 2932, ⓔ dorchesterinn@bigpond.com.au). Comfortable, self-contained one- to four-bed serviced apartments. ❺

City Backpackers, 380 Upper Roma St (☎07/3211 3221, bookings only free call ☎1800 062 572). One

of Brisbane's biggest hostels, this busy and well-run place has clean, new facilities, fair-sized rooms, own bar with budget meal deals and BBQ nights, and swimming pool. En-suite doubles ❸, dorms ❶

Palace Backpackers, cnr Ann and Edward streets (☎07/3211 2433 or free call 1800 676 340, ⓕ 3211 2466). Huge hostel, purpose-built in 1911 but completely revamped (except for the ancient lift). Bang in the centre of town – which means that there's no parking space – with a restaurant and rowdy *Down Under Bar*, whose noise prompts some travellers to move elsewhere for some sleep. Poky singles, high-ceilinged and spacious doubles, and three- to nine-bed dorms. Rooms ❷–❸, dorms ❶

Sportsmans Hotel, 130 Leichhardt St, Spring Hill (☎07/3831 2892). Gay-friendly pub with rooms; predominantly male clientele but both sexes welcome. ❸

Stamford Plaza, Edward St (☎07/3221 1999 or free call 1800 773 700, ⓕ 3221 6895, ⓦ www.stamford.com.au). Top-notch hotel with a grand mix of colonial and modern buildings overlooking the river and Botanic Gardens. ❽

Yellow Submarine, 66 Quay St (☎07/3211 3424). Small, comfortable hostel in a refurbished 1860s building. Full kitchen facilities, laundry, BBQ and pool. Friendly owners put on boat trips around the bay and free BBQs, ensuring a sociable atmosphere, and the staff have good work connections. ❶–❸

YHA Brisbane City, 392 Upper Roma St (☎07/3236 1680, ⓕ 3236 0647, ⓔ travel@yhaqld.org). Sterile but with excellent facilities, including a first-rate budget canteen (open to nonguests). There's a $3-per-night surcharge for nonmembers. Doubles & twins ❸, dorms ❶

Fortitude Valley and New Farm

The Valley's streets are well placed for clubs but can be seedy late at night, although New Farm is quiet enough. Most buses travelling up Adelaide Street pass through the Valley, or you can take the train to Brunswick Street Station. For New Farm, take a bus (#177, #178, #167 or #168) from Adelaide Street.

Balmoral House, 33 Amelia St, Fortitude Valley (T 07/3252 1397, F 3253 5892). A very quiet, secure and clean hostel, handy for Chinatown and Brunswick St; not for partying. ❶ –❸

Central Brunswick Apartment Hotel, 455 Brunswick St, Fortitude Valley (T 07/3852 1411 or free call 1800 622 686, F 3852 1015, E brunswick@strand.com.au). Gay-friendly accommodation in a sparkling new building. Rooms are very comfortable, all with own bath, TV etc, and some apartment-style with kitchen facilities. Shared amenities include spa and gym. ❻ –❼

Homestead, 57 Annie St, New Farm (free call T 1800 658 344). A large house converted to a hostel, with a pool shaped like a shamrock and plenty of outdoor space. Free use of bikes, trips to Mt Coot-tha, and bus to Stradbroke Island. Tends towards a party atmosphere. ❶ –❸

Tourist Guest House, 555 Gregory Terrace, Fortitude Valley (T 07/3252 4171, F 3252 2704, E tourist_guest_house@yahoo.com.au). Another of Brisbane's converted Queenslanders, this is a clean, quiet place with parking space, bar, laundry, and kitchen. Rooms ❸ , dorms ❶

South of the river and Manly

Brisbane Backpackers' Resort, 110 Vulture St (T 07/3844 9956, reservations free call T 1800 626 452, F 3844 9295, E bbr@bo22.aone.net.au). Massive, soulless hostel complex with round-the-clock reception, video surveillance and all facilities, including a licensed travel agent. Booking is essential, and be clear about what you're getting: some low-rate rooms are in a dilapidated old house across the road. Courtesy bus into town and free pick-up. Rooms ❸ , dorms ❶

Moreton Bay Lodge, 44 Cambridge Parade, Manly Harbour Village, Manly (T 07/3396 3020, F 3396 1355, E backpackerbay@hotmail.com). Small, well-furnished place out at Manly, on Moreton Bay, a thirty-minute train ride from central Brisbane. Just a stone's throw from Manly harbour, and well geared up to sailing and island trips; there are plenty of shops and places to eat nearby too. Free pick-up from town, or a five-minute walk from Manly train station. ❶

Somewhere to Stay, 45 Brighton Rd (T 07/3846 4584 or free call 1800 812 398, W www.somewheretostay.com.au). Reasonable facilities, but nonchalant staff; building and furnishings are showing distinct signs of wear. Pay the extra and get a room with a view over Brisbane's skyline rather than one of the basic dorms. Courtesy bus into town and free pick-up. ❶ –❸

The City

The city is focused around the meandering loops of the **Brisbane River**, with the triangular wedge of the business centre on the north bank surrounded by community-oriented suburbs. At its heart are the busy, upmarket commercial and administrative precincts around **Queen Street** and **George Street**, an area of glass towers, cafés and century-old sandstone facades that extends to the **Botanic Gardens** on the river. Radiating **north**, the polish gives way to less conservative shops, accommodation and eateries around Spring Hill, Fortitude Valley and New Farm, and the aspiring suburbs of Petrie Terrace and Paddington. To the **west** is a blaze of riverside homes at Milton and Toowong and the fringes of Mount Coot-tha and Brisbane Forest Park. **Across the river**, the major landmarks are the Cultural Centre and the Convention Centre, and South Bank Parklands, which stretch to Kangaroo Point. Beyond are the open, bustling streets of **South Brisbane** and the **West End**, more relaxed than their northern counterparts.

Downtown

Queen Street is Brisbane's oldest thoroughfare, its southern section between George and Edward streets now a pedestrian mall with the **Myer Centre** – a multistoreyed shopping complex – as its focus. Most of the stores inside are on the chic side but you can, for kicks, ride the glass elevators or buy designer Outback accessories and fluffy koalas. It's also worth investigating the food centres on the Queen Street level, crammed at midday with office workers having lunch. There's a huge variety of classy fast-food outlets, from Asian takeaways to Greek kebab shops, at slightly higher prices than the local hotel food. Outside, the **mall** is always busy with people running errands, window shopping or just socializing. There's usually some kind of entertainment, too: either informal efforts – acrobats, buskers and the occasional soap-box orator – or more organized events such as Aboriginal and Torres Strait Islander dancing or jazz sessions on the small stage about halfway down the street.

City Hall, the Observatory and the business district

North from the mall along Albert Street, you arrive at **City Hall**, facing King George Square: in front of the fountains are bronze sculptures of swaggies, native wildlife and what look like large pieces of futuristic circuitry. A stately building ruined by an ugly clock tower, there's a reflection of former policies in the triangular sculpture over the portico, which depicts the Aboriginal way of life "dying out before the approach of the white man". The **City Art Gallery** (daily 10am–5pm; free) inside has a smattering of paintings, pottery and glassware, though it's worth checking to see if there are any temporary exhibitions of work by Australian artists, or if there are any screenings at the tiny cinema. The clock tower is open, too, if you want a view of the city centre (Mon–Fri 8am–5pm; free); access is through the City Hall foyer.

Further up Albert Street is Wickham Park and the grey cone of Brisbane's oldest building, a **windmill** known locally as the **Observatory**, built by convicts in 1829 to grind corn for the early settlement. The original wooden sails were too heavy to turn but found use as a gallows until being pulled off in 1850, and all grinding was done by a treadmill – severe punishment for the convicts who had to work it. After the convict era the building became a signal station and now stands empty, held together with a cement glaze and firmly locked.

East of here lies Brisbane's **business district**, which was heavily developed in the 1990s and left with a legacy of glassy high-rises sprouting alongside the restaurants and shops of the **Riverside Centre**; the few surviving old buildings are hidden among the modern ones. The copper-domed **Customs House** (free tours Sun 10am–4pm) at the north end of Queen Street, built in 1889, harbours a small collection of Chinese antiques and hosts free concerts given by the Queensland University Orchestra every month, while rustic **All Saints' Church** on the corner of Wickham Terrace, and neo-Gothic **St John's Cathedral** on Ann Street, have some elegant stained-glass windows. Sunday morning is made lively by the **Eagle Street Markets** between the river and the road – too trendy for bargains, but not bad for jewellery and leatherwork, clothing and $20 massages.

The historic precinct

The area between Queen Street and the Botanic Gardens contains some of Brisbane's finest architecture, dating from the earliest days of settlement until the late nineteenth century. Between Elizabeth and Queen streets, occupying an entire block, is the former **Treasury** with its classical facade. Built in the 1890s, its grandeur reflects the wealth of Queensland's gold mines (though by this point most were on the decline) and was a slap in the face to New South Wales, which had spitefully withdrawn all financial support from the fledgling state on separation some forty years previously, leaving it bankrupt. With a twist typical of a state torn between conservatism and tourism, the building is now – appropriately enough – Brisbane's **casino**.

South along William Street, the **Commissariat Stores** is contemporary with the windmill, though in considerably better shape. Originally a granary, it is now a museum (Tues–Fri 11am–2pm; $5) and headquarters of the Royal Historical Society of Queensland; the knowledgeable staff pep up an otherwise dusty collection of relics dating back to convict times. Brisbane's **Science Centre** (daily 10am–5pm; $8), whose entrance is one block over on George Street, is more interesting to visit. A hands-on approach makes it great fun, especially for children, and very therapeutic if you like to prod and dismantle exhibits instead of merely peering at them through a protective glass case. Favourites include the various optical illusions – try the "swinging bridge", guaranteed to induce nausea though it remains stock-still – and the "Thongophone", a set of giant pan pipes played by whacking the top with a flip-flop. It's all good rainy-day material.

Further south along George Street you pass **Harris Terrace** and **The Mansions**, two of the city centre's last surviving rows of Victorian-era terraced houses, the latter guarded by stone cats on the parapet corners. Nearby, on the corner of George and Alice streets, the **Queensland Club** was founded in 1859, just four days before the separation of Queensland from New South Wales. Heavy walls, columns and spacious balconies evoke a tropical version of a traditional London club; entrance and membership – still barred to women – are by invitation only. Diagonally opposite, **Parliament House** was built to a design by Charles Tiffin in 1868 and presents an appealingly compromised French Renaissance style which incorporates shuttered north windows, shaded colonnades and a high, arched roof to allow for the tropical climate. You can see the grand interior on an hour-long **guided tour** (Mon–Fri: 9.30am, 11.15am & 3.15pm when Parliament not in session; 10.30am & 2.30pm when it is; free) and there's access to the chambers when there's no debate in progress.

South of Parliament House, George Street becomes a lane along the western side of the Botanic Gardens. Here you'll find **Old Government House** (variable hours; donation), the official residence of Queensland's governors and premiers between 1862 and 1910. Another of Tiffin's designs, the building is being comprehensively restored to its stately turn-of-the-century condition, beginning with the ground floor; work has started on the main dining room, drawing room and entrance hall. The National Trust offices are in the upper storey.

The Botanic Gardens

Bordered by Alice Street, George Street and the river, Brisbane's **Botanic Gardens** overlook the cliffs of Kangaroo Point and, while more of a park than a botanic garden, provide a generous arrangement of flowers, shrubs, bamboo thickets and greenery that offers an escape from the claustrophobia of the city. Once a vegetable patch cultivated by convicts, formal gardens were laid out in 1855 by Walter Hill, who experimented with local and imported plants to see which would grow well in Queensland's then untried climate. Some of his more successful efforts are the oversized **bunya pines** around the Edward Street entrance at the east end of Alice Street, planted in 1860, and a residual patch of the **rainforest** that once blanketed the area, at the southern end of the park. Mangroves along the river, accessible by a boardwalk, are another native species more recently protected. You can spend summer evenings here at the open-air **stage** listening to classical music recitals. During the day, cyclists flock to the park, as it's at one end of a popular cycling and jogging track that follows the north bank of the river south to St Lucia and the University of Queensland. Free **guided tours** (11am & 1pm Tues–Sun) leave from the rotunda 100m inside the gardens' main entrance, halfway along Alice Street.

The northern suburbs

North of the river, just beyond Brisbane's business district, are several former suburbs which have been absorbed by the city sprawl: Paddington and Petrie Terrace to the west, Spring Hill and Fortitude Valley to the north, and New Farm to the east. Houses in these areas are popular with Brisbane's aspiring professional class, and while office buildings and one-way streets are beginning to encroach, there's also an older character reflected in the high-set **Queenslander**-style houses (see box, below) still standing around Spring Hill and Petrie Terrace.

The Castlemaine Perkins Brewery

Just down the hill from Petrie Terrace, the **Castlemaine Perkins Brewery**, Milton Rd, Milton (☎ 07/3361 7597), has been making Queensland's own beer since 1878, and had no real competition until Powers came on the scene in the 1980s. Their famous yellow-and-red **XXXX** emblem is almost part of the Queensland landscape: splashed across T-shirts and the roofs of Outback hotels, or on labels on countless discarded bottles and cans that litter everywhere from roadsides to the depths of the Barrier Reef. For enthusiasts, the brewery opens its gates for **tours** (Mon–Wed 11am, 1.30pm, 4.30pm & 7pm; $6), which incorporate a brief rundown on the brewing process and then about thirty minutes during which you watch filmed eulogies and swill beer. Booking ahead by phone between 9 and 11am is essential, because you won't get past the security guards unless your name is on the list.

Fortitude Valley

While the other areas are mainly residential, **Fortitude Valley**'s tangled mix of shops, restaurants, bars and clubs is blossoming into Brisbane's unofficial centre of artistic, gastronomic and alcoholic pursuits. An eclectic mix of the gay, the groovy and the grubby, the Valley is now in stage two of inner-city gentrification, which sees the urban-poor make way for hipsters, artists and students. Stage three – the arrival of yuppies and inflated real estate prices – is probably

---

Queenslander houses

There can hardly be a more typical image of rural Queensland than a high-set **"Queenslander"** surrounded by green fields of sugar cane. A response to the northern climate, these houses come in all shapes and styles but the basic design is a wooden box on piles with a verandah or balcony – the idea being to have a cool flow of air underneath the house to reduce the humidity inside. Traditional colours, now more commonly seen in cities where it's becoming popular to renovate them, are cream, red or green, while older buildings may have corrugated-iron awnings, red "bull-nosed" roofs and wooden latticework on porches and eaves. In Brisbane they're generally low-set, but tend to be raised further off the ground as you move up into the tropics – the exception to the rule is at Redcliffe, 12km north of Brisbane, where the pole houses have supports 10m high to compensate for a steep hill.

a few years away, so in the meantime you can enjoy an evening out among Brisbane's young, fun and adventurous. In less than a kilometre, the main thoroughfare of **Brunswick Street** has a dozen nightclubs, an Irish pub, a compact **Chinatown** complete with the usual busy restaurants and stores, and a burgeoning European **street-café scene**. It's best at weekends; on Saturday there's a secondhand **market** in the mall and the cafés are buzzing. After dark the Valley's streets can still be somewhat menacing, with an element of drug-related petty crime. Although there are usually crowds around until very late, if you've any distance to go on your own after the pubs close, take a taxi.

Breakfast Creek

Named by John Oxley, who tucked into a morning meal here in 1823 on his voyage of exploration upstream, **Breakfast Creek** has shops and a hotel marking an acute traffic bottleneck where the road bridges the creek between the upper reaches of Fortitude Valley and the route to the airport. A pretty, if noisy, spot, looking out over usually placid water to inactive wharves, the real estate in nearby Hamilton and Ascot is becoming quite exclusive. If you're out this way – perhaps going to the airport or heading north – consider looking around **Newstead House**, Brisbane's oldest residence. A low, solid brick-and-stone building with a slate roof, it was constructed as a private home in 1845 by convict labour, and became the Government House twelve years later. Enlarged by the governor, the house was the focus of social gatherings, and on the nights that balls were held armed police protected the house from attacks by Aborigines. Restored and now open as a **museum** (Mon–Fri 10am–4pm, Sun 2–5pm; $5), the house and grounds are remarkably quiet. As you stand surrounded by century-old furniture, taking in the views across the creek from one of the elegant windows, it's easy to forget how close you are to the city. The house is off Breakfast Creek Road just south of the bridge; to get there by public transport, take bus #117, #190 or #160 to stop 12.

South Brisbane

Across the river from the city centre, the **Cultural Centre** and its environs – comprising the state museum, library, gallery, performing arts complex, convention centre and South Bank Parklands – is Brisbane's most obvious tourist attraction. Immediately south of Victoria Bridge (itself a continuation of Queen St), it's easily reached by train to South Brisbane Station, while plenty of buses from all parts of the city stop outside the station on Melbourne Street.

Beyond here, the **West End** is South Brisbane's answer to Fortitude Valley, with Boundary Street a similar ethnic mix – Asian, Greek and Italian – but a more genteel atmosphere. There are no sights here as such, but it's worth a visit for the cluster of Asian stores and continental delicatessens, and for an escalating number of inexpensive restaurants and cafés around the hub at Boundary Road and Vulture Street, popular with students from the University of Queensland across the river at St Lucia; see pp.407–408 for details.

Queensland Museum

The Queensland Museum (daily 9.30am–5pm; free, except for special exhibitions) is essentially a natural history museum, but it benefits from a bias towards unorthodox methods of presentation. Wedge-tailed eagles hover overhead, koalas climb the walls and, in the foyer, there's the unsettling experience of walking underneath full-scale models of a family of humpbacked whales suspended from the ceiling. There's an overview of the state's marine environment and western Queensland's fossil beds, including a reconstruction of Queensland's own Muttaburrasaurus and a section of the Lark Quarry **dinosaur trackways**. Above swings a furry pterodactyl, reflecting recent theories that Australia was subject to a cold climate during the era of the dinosaurs. Upstairs, the more recently extinct **megafauna** from the Darling Downs, just west of Brisbane, unexpectedly come to life – a breathing, twitching model of a marsupial lion lounging on a rock at the top of the escalators catches everyone by surprise. Rock hounds and prospective gem hunters will also be interested in the museum's **mineral collection** – dozens of multi-coloured rocks from around the state together with information on identifying them in the field.

Ethnographic displays mostly relate to traditional life in New Guinea and Melanesia, with the glaring omission – apart from a handful of tools and a small section on the rainforest tribes from the north – of anything on Queensland's Aboriginal and Torres Strait Islander history. The displays are rounded off by miscellaneous items, including bits and pieces from aviation history and an eclectic collection of period furniture.

State Art Gallery and Library

Queensland's **State Art Gallery** (daily 10am–5pm; free, except for special exhibitions) provides a large, airy space for its wide-ranging collection, which includes a sizeable exhibition of twentieth-century painters. As well as works by visionaries such as Brett Whitely, Arthur Boyd and Sidney Nolan, there are some unusual (and very European) watercolour landscapes by **Aboriginal artists** Walter Ebataringa and Albert Namatjira (for more on the latter, see p.672) alongside a few functional tribal items – dilly bags, headwear and shields – labelled as "art" but somehow out of place here. One of the most interesting pieces in the gallery is a nineteenth-century stained-glass window depicting a kangaroo hunt – an Australian theme executed in a very European medium. Other Australian works include the romantic paintings of Tom Roberts and the Impressionistic canvases of Frederick McGubbin. Sculpture is scattered throughout the gallery in a somewhat offhand manner, and there's a small collection of high-quality **glass** hidden away in the back.

Next door, the **State Library** (Mon–Thurs 10am–8pm, Fri–Sun 10am–5pm) is best known for its **John Oxley Library** (closed Sat) up on level four, which records every aspect of Queensland's past in endless books, journals and photographs. Level three is devoted to music and art; they lend scores and there's even a piano room available for practice. Film buffs should head to level two to sample the video collection and check out the cinema's programme, while there's **free internet access** via terminals on levels two, three and four – limited, not surprisingly, to one hour a day and booked up several days in advance (for bookings call ☎ 07/3840 7785).

The South Bank Parklands

The **South Bank Parklands** are a resoundingly successful contrivance, conceived with little rhyme or reason other than that *something* had to be done with the 1988 Expo site. Weekend crowds come to stroll along the river under the shady trees or to sit on the lawns, watch street performers and stuff their faces full of candy floss and hot dogs – blissfully unconcerned that everything, including the sand "beach" around the pool, bamboo-flanked streams, and subtropical undergrowth is imported (although it's authentic enough to attract large, sunbathing water dragons). Bands play most Saturday nights on the outdoor stage, or at the *Plough Inn*, a restored, century-old pub in the reconstructed, cobbled high street; other attractions include exhibits at the **Maritime Museum** (daily 9.30am–4.30pm; $5.50), including a ninety-year-old Torres Strait pearling lugger and the World War II frigate *Diamantina*, on show in the dry dock.

Along the river

The sluggish, meandering **Brisbane River** is four hundred million years old, one of the world's most ancient waterways. It flows from above Lake Wivenhoe – 55km inland – past farmland, into quiet suburbs and through the city before emptying 150km downstream into Moreton Bay, behind Fisherman Island. Once an essential trade and transport link with the rest of Australia and the world, it now seems to do little but separate the main part of the city from South Brisbane; though it's superficially active around the city centre, with ferries and dredgers keeping it navigable, most of the old wharves and shipyards now lie derelict or buried under parkland.

If the locals seem to have forgotten the river, it has a habit of reasserting its presence through **flooding**. In February 1893 cyclonic rains swelled the flow through downtown Brisbane, carrying off Victoria Bridge and scores of buildings: eyewitness accounts stated that "Debris of all descriptions – whole houses, trees, cattle and homes – went floating past". This has since been repeated many times, notably in January 1974 when rains from **Cyclone Wanda** completely swamped the centre, swelling the river to a width of 3km at one stage. Despite reminders of this in brass plaques marking the depths of the worst floods at **Naldham House Polo Club** (1 Eagle St, near the markets), some of Brisbane's poshest real estate flanks the river, with waterfront mansions at Yeerongpilly, Graceville and Chelmer. They're all banking on protection from artificial Lake Wivenhoe, completed in 1984, which should act as a buffer against future floods.

Of the various ways to explore the river, the easiest is simply to take a return ride on the City Cat – such a popular, if unofficial, sightseeing trip that the service can be severely overcrowded during holidays. More stylish are the oddly-named *Club Crocodile River Queens*, three-tiered Mississippi-style **paddleboats** decked out in timber and brass, which leave daily from Eagle Street pier; it's a favourite Sunday excursion (several times daily from 12.15pm; $22–49, depending on level of refreshments), and there are additional evening cruises with full meals (Mon–Sat 7.30pm, Sun 6.30pm; $45 buffet or $60 for seafood); for bookings call ☎07/3221 1300.

Fort Lytton National Park

Surrounded by the pipes and chimneys of the Ampol oil refinery at Wynnum, **Fort Lytton National Park** (Sun–Fri 10am–4pm, museum open Sun only; $5 entry to fort and museum) is a product of the colonial struggles around the Pacific Rim at the end of the nineteenth century. Only a few days away from French forces on Nouméa (New Caledonia), Queensland felt threatened by competing European empires and developed a string of coastal defences during the 1880s. Brisbane received the best of these: by 1900, the river mouth at Fort Lytton bristled with artillery and a barrage of floating mines. However, the defences were never put to the test and modern warfare made them obsolete. The fort was downgraded to a secondary line of defence after World War I and abandoned altogether in 1945.

As a piece of military history, the buildings look the part: austere concrete bunkers dug into slopes and capped in grass, gun ports trained on the river and an underground tunnel for checking the mines running down to the water. The best time to visit is the first Sunday of each month when the historical museum is open. The **Brisbane Garrison Battery** dresses up in period costume and fires the massive gun at Easter, and again on the Queen's birthday. The fort is at the end of Lytton Road, west of Wynnum at the mouth of Brisbane River; there's no public transport.

Lone Pine Sanctuary

Lone Pine Sanctuary on Jesmond Road, Fig Tree Pocket (daily 8am–5pm; $15), has been a popular day-trip upstream since first opening its gates in 1927. Here you can see a large number of native fauna in their natural state which, in the case of the sanctuary's hundred-odd **koalas**, means being asleep for eighteen hours a day. At close quarters they're revealed as grey cushions wedged into convenient forks in the trees, occasionally waking up for long enough to chew eucalyptus leaves and blink myopically at the crowds. In nearby cages you'll find other slumbering animals: Tasmanian devils, fruit bats, blue-tongued lizards and dingoes. Indeed, about the only lively creatures you'll see are birds and a colony of hyperactive sugar gliders in the nocturnal house. Alternatively, head for the outdoor paddock where tolerant wallabies and kangaroos allow themselves to be petted, fed and occasionally roughed up by visitors.

The best way to reach Lone Pine is to take a ninety-minute **river cruise** past Brisbane's waterfront suburbs with Mirimar Cruises (daily departures 10am from Queens Wharf Rd beside Victoria Bridge; return 2.50pm; $22, not including entry to Lone Pine). Free pick-up from your central accommodation is usually possible (for bookings call ☎07/3221 0300).

Eating

Brisbane has no gastronomic tradition to exploit, but there's a good variety of bars and restaurants all over the city, with a trend towards "Modern Australian" (creative use of local produce, influenced by Asia and the Mediterranean), and a fashionable café society in Fortitude Valley and the West End.

Counter meals and unlimited buffets at hotels are the cheapest route to a full stomach – aim for lunch at around noon and dinner between 5pm and 6pm – or try one of the scores of **cafés** in the centre catering to office workers. The city's **restaurants** open from around 11am to 2pm for lunch, and from 6 to 10pm or later for evening meals; many are closed for one day a week (often Monday).

City centre

Café the Hague, Myer Centre, Level A (next to cinema complex). Dutch-style coffee house, way above the fast-food joints opposite. Try the *poffertjes* – sweet pancakes – and a gourmet coffee for breakfast.

e'cco, 100 Boundary St (☎ 07/3831 8344). Boasts an impressive awards list that includes Australia's "Restaurant of the Year" for 1997 – so you'll have to book, sometimes days ahead. Surprisingly good value, with local favourite "steamed mussels" $15, and most mains around $22. Open for lunch Tues–Fri, dinner Tues–Sat.

Govindas, Elizabeth St. Hare Krishna-run vegetarian food bar, with a $7.50 all-you-can-eat menu. Open for lunch Mon–Sat 11.30am–2.30pm, dinner Fri 5.30–7.30pm; there's a $4 banquet every Sunday (5–7pm), but you'll have to sit through a lot of chanting before you actually get to eat.

Jameson's, 475 Adelaide St (☎ 07/3831 7633).

Ostensibly a wine bar, Jameson's reputation rivals that of *e'cco*. Billed as "Modern Australian", the menu features dishes such as woodside goat's cheese, snail and parsley soufflé, and breast of wood pigeon, all complemented by wine from what is reputed to be Brisbane's most satisfying and extensive cellar. It's one of the only places open late in the city (till 3am) on the weekend and has nightly entertainment (from jazz to hip-hop). Restaurant bookings essential; lunch Mon–Fri, dinner Mon–Sat.

Pane e Vino, cnr Charlotte and Albert streets. Smart Italian café-restaurant with pavement tables, catering mainly to nearby office executives. Pastas from $12, main courses (lots of fish, chicken and lamb) around $21.

Stuffed Duck, 153 Elizabeth St, opposite *McDonald's*. Strange restaurant-bar, worth a visit just to read the menu – the "Wobbly Duck that goes moo" is a steak, "sea ducks" are oysters, and "Duck in orange sauce" is just that. There's a happy hour Friday and Saturday nights 9.30–10.30pm, followed by DJ ambience, and a Wednesday Wine Appreciation Night from 6pm. Lunchtime specials all around $10; evening mains $15–22.

Sushi Station, 142 Elizabeth St, next to *McDonald's*. One in a chain of Japanese sushi bars where the selection of dishes parades around the tables on the back of a model train, featuring low-priced soups, rice, fish, seaweed and green-tea ice cream.

Topolino's, 124 Leichhardt St. Cavernous budget Italian restaurant with huge pizzas, small but surprisingly filling pasta favourites and very average salads. Pasta dishes under $11; pizzas $7–19 depending on size and topping.

Victory Hotel, 127 Edward St. Nice beer garden with braziers taking the chill off in winter. The bistro meals are popular with the local business folk.

Petrie Terrace

Casablanca, 52 Petrie Terrace. Inexpensive brasserie and café serving the young and pretentious. Tapas is served at the bar for around $10, and the food is excellent and mouthwateringly spicy, with genuine leanings towards North African cuisine. Taped Brazilian music or live bands provide atmosphere and there's an "open" jam (mostly jazz/funk) on Monday nights.

Paddo Tavern, 186 Given Terrace. Respectable pub lunches served every day for only $1.95, leaving you with enough money for a beer or two.

Fortitude Valley

Bobby Austin's, 360 Brunswick St ☎ 07/3252 2511). "Modern Australian" fare such as kangaroo

tenderloin served on a courgette cake alongside more conventional lamb shanks braised with thyme and garlic. Main courses around the $20 mark; open Tues–Fri 5.30pm–late, Sat & Sun 3pm–late.

California, 376 Brunswick St. Perfectly preserved 1950s diner, with original coffee cups, Formica-covered tables and hulking jukebox. Only two (men) have managed the *California*'s legendary "truckie's breakfast" of five eggs, steak, liver, bacon, sausage and tomato: otherwise, a regular cooked breakfast is $9. Daily 7am–2pm.

Cosmopolitan Coffee, 322 Brunswick Street Mall. Relaxed place, something of an institution with Brisbane's café society – and better than the surrounding competition.

Fat Boys, 321 Brunswick Street Mall. The place for an early-morning "heart-starter" after a night out in the Valley, with very good, cheap coffee. Most people opt for the $5 cooked breakfast while reading a newspaper, or just rest their hangover on a streetfront table. At other times, try a gourmet pizza, or the soup-with-sourdough will warm you up for only $5.50. Mon–Wed 6am–midnight, Thurs–Sun 24hr.

Hunan, Duncan St (halfway up Chinatown Mall, on the left). Stick to the "chef's suggestions" on the menu and you'll enjoy Brisbane's most authentic Chinese cuisine – though be warned, Hunanese cooking can use copious amounts of chilli and garlic. Try steamed beef in lotus leaf, fish in bamboo, or Mao's sliced pork – apparently a favourite dish of the late Chairman. Big portions; mains $12–17.

King of Kings, 169 Wickham St. A busy place, popular with the local Chinese community and fast becoming a Valley institution thanks to its fine late morning *yum cha* selection. Come prepared to queue at weekend lunchtimes. Open every day for lunch and dinner.

Tibetan Kitchen, 454 Brunswick St. It's hard to resist any place that advertises "traditional Tibetan, Sherpa, Nepalese foods", but the food here, including the Valley's best samosas ($4.90 for four), is tasty and cheap, and served in a very attractive setting. Mains $10–14. Open daily for dinner only.

The Vietnamese Restaurant, 194 Wickham St. With an interior every bit as plain and unassuming as the name over the door, this is no-frills, genuine Vietnamese cuisine. Mains around $9; open daily for lunch and dinner.

South Brisbane

Bagelo's, cnr Boundary and Vulture streets. Basically a fast-food joint and café, which does interesting things with every type of bagel from

spinach-feta to cinnamon-raisin (all baked on-site and very fresh), plus sandwich combos. Open daily.
Café Nouveau, 185 Boundary St. Friendly, with Mediterranean-style salads, pasta and seafood for $14–16, and a pleasant courtyard in the back; excellent cakes, too. Open daily 7.30am–late.
Caffé Tempo, 181 Boundary St (☎07/3846 3161). Not sophisticated cuisine, but great Italian-style home cooking, with fresh salads and fine seafood pasta. Most expensive dish is $14.50, and they stay open until the last customer leaves.
Chantan, Boundary St, nr junction with Vulture. Greek BYO with basic furnishings but excellent food – the meze are a good standby, as is lamb kleftiko and eggplant risotto. "Early Bird" menu between 5 and 7pm with various specials under $6, otherwise mains are $15–20.
Chez Laila, on the Boardwalk, Southbank Parklands. Airy, open-plan restaurant and bar with fine river views and Lebanese cuisine. Upmarket falafel, kebabs and kibbi, along with side dishes of stuffed vine leaves, hummus, and baba ghanouj (grilled aubergine and tahini puree). Mains around $15.
King Ahiram, 88 Vulture St. A long-running Lebanese takeaway and restaurant; not worth crossing town for, but good for kebabs and sticky

Mediterranean desserts if you're in the area.
New Asia, 153 Boundary St (☎07/3846 3569). Forget flashier Vietnamese restaurants in the neighbourhood: this is the best – prawns grilled on sugar cane, deep-fried quail, rice-noodle dishes – all for less than $8 a dish.
Oblio's Café, cnr Melbourne and Boundary streets. Popular newcomer to the West End's restaurants, sporting minimalist decor and Mediterranean colours inside, but open front gives feeling of pavement dining. Food is Mediterranean/eclectic – tapas, antipasta, risottos, polenta and Moroccan lamb alongside Asian noodles and spiced quail. Mains around $20.
Three Monkeys Coffee Shop, 58 Mollison St. Decorated with a funky assortment of African oddments; serves average coffee, awesome cakes, and effortlessly achieves the sort of bohemian atmosphere most coffee shops merely aspire to. Greek-influenced menu with plenty of vegetarian/lentil options, and nothing over $10. Open daily 9.30am–midnight.
Wok On Inn, 94 Boundary St. All kinds of fresh, tasty soups, and noodles in combination with veggies, chicken, beef or prawns; $8–12 for anything on the menu. Open 7 days.

Nightlife and entertainment

The city's entertainment horizons consist of an ever-fluctuating range of clubs, and a sound, if unadventurous, arts scene. The best cross-section of attractions are north of the river in **Petrie Terrace** – upmarket yet subdued – and in **Fortitude Valley**, which throbs with the nightclub crowd. **South Brisbane** and the **West End** are more down-to-earth.

Pubs, clubs and live music

Brisbane nights were once a byword for boredom: the few places that offered after-dark entertainment were either illegal or lifeless and closed early, and locals headed to the coast for their weekends. Things have changed, however, and Brisbane has seen a recent explosion of home-grown musical talent, with bands such as Savage Garden, Regurgitator, Custard and Powderfinger putting the city firmly on the Australian pop-culture map. On Friday and Saturday evening the centre is crowded, but the big push is out to the clubs, bars and restaurants (many with quality entertainment) of a reinvented and revamped Fortitude Valley. Live music venues, however, are on the decline and tend to open and close in the blinking of an eye; places listed below might be here to stay, but check with music stores such as Rocking Horse, 101 Adelaide St, or weekly free magazines for up-to-the-minute reviews and **listings**: *RM* and *Time Off* for rock and live bands, and *The Scene* for dance. The **webzine** ⓦ www.brisbanetribe.com covers the same, plus restaurants and **gay venues**. There's no standard charge for club entry, and many places offer free nights and special deals.

Gay and lesbian Brisbane

Despite its name, Queensland has long had a reputation for repressive attitudes towards gays and lesbians. However, whereas in 1985 you could virtually be arrested on suspicion of being gay, homosexuality has since been **decriminalized** and anti-discrimination legislation is in force. Today, Brisbane's gays and lesbians are revelling in a loud and energetic scene which gets better every year. In June the Pride Collective hosts the annual **Pride Festival**, a diverse event, with a street march, fair, art exhibitions, a film festival, sports events, general exhibitionism and a dance party – the **Queen's Birthday Ball**. At the **Sleaze Ball** in November there's another opportunity to indulge.

The gay scene is largely clustered around the suburbs of Spring Hill, Fortitude Valley, New Valley, New Farm and Paddington. For up-to-the-moment **information**, listen to Queer Radio, station ZZZ 102.1FM (Wed 6–9pm) or pick up a copy of *BrotherSister* or *Queensland Pride* from gay nightclubs, street distributors and some coffee shops.

For gay-friendly **accommodation**, try *Central Brunswick Apartment Hotel*, *Carrington's*, or the *Sportsmans Hotel* (see "Accommodation" listings, pp.398–399); **nightlife** focuses on *The Beat, Options, The Wickham Hotel, Sportsmans Hotel* and the *Cockatoo Club*) – all listed under "Pubs, Clubs and Live Music".

Support groups and information

AIDS Gladstone Road Medical Centre, 38 Gladstone Rd, Highgate Hill (℡ 07/3844 9599), medical services and counselling; Queensland AIDS Council, 32 Peel St, South Brisbane (℡ 07/3844 1990, ✉ info@quac.org.au); QUIVAA, 191 Brunswick St, Fortitude Valley (℡ 07/3252 5390), needle exchange and safe-sex gear.

Books Women's Bookshop, 15 Gladstone Rd, Highgate Hill (℡ 07/3844 6650), stocks the latest lesbian titles. Red Books, opposite the *Empire Hotel* on Ann Street, Fortitude Valley, has a big range of gay and lesbian titles, plus seats for you to sit down and browse.

Counselling and information Gay (℡ 07/3891 7377), lesbian (℡ 07/3891 7388); daily 7am–10pm; free call for both ℡ 1800 249 377.

The Pride Collective Organizers of the Pride Festival – contact them through ⓦ www.pridebrisbane.org.au.

Queensland Pride PO Box 8151, Woolloongabba, QLD 4102 (℡ 07/3392 2922). Free monthly publication covering Brisbane and the rest of the state.

Travel The website Pinkstay (ⓦ www.pinkstay.com) gives Australia-wide and international accommodation listings with detailed reviews, plus forthcoming events, work options, and links to other gay sites.

City centre

Down Under Bar, at *Palace Backpackers*, cnr Ann and Edward streets. Hugely popular and often overtly sexist get-drunk-throw-up-and-fall-down venue for travellers.

Jameson's, 475 Adelaide St. Restaurant with nightly entertainment in the bar varying from live jazz and Wednesday's "songwriters night" to DJ's playing hip-hop and acid jazz on Friday and Saturday.

Orient Hotel, cnr Queen and Ann streets. Just a regular pub, but a good bet for some local music talent, as it's a place that supports young Brisbane bands.

Petrie Terrace

Paddo Tavern, 186 Given Terrace. Band and disco on Friday night with a crowded beer garden early on in the evening.

Viva, 183 Given Terrace. A gathering of beautiful people, pricey drinks, and regular big-name live bands; closed Mon.

Spring Hill

Options, at the *Spring Hill Hotel*, cnr Leichhardt and Little Edward streets. Two-level gay and lesbian nightclub with bar, dance floor, coffee shop and cabaret stage. Events include drag shows, karaoke, strip nights and sausage sizzles. Young crowd, with women's nights every Friday, when

Drinks for women: the Regatta Hotel

Though Australian pubs tend towards being all-male enclaves, women were once legally barred to "protect" them from the corrupting influence of foul language. On April 1, 1965, Merle Thornton (mother of the actress Sigrid Thornton) and her friend Rosalie Bogner chained themselves to the footrail of the **Regatta Hotel** bar at Toowong in protest; the movement they inspired led to the granting of "the right to drink alongside men" in the mid-1970s. The pink-and-white colonial hotel is now a trendy place for a drink after work on Friday. It's on the west bank of the river along Coronation Drive, about 2km from the city centre towards St Lucia.

there's a $5 cover charge, and free entry on Sundays for cheap drinks, free wine and a floor show. Closed Mon & Tues.

Sportsmans Hotel, 130 Leichhardt St. Gay, lesbian and straight crowds fill the two floors; pool tables, pinball, bottle shop and bistro.

Fortitude Valley and New Farm

Arena, 201 Brunswick St. Long-established venue hosting popular DJ's and dance parties as well as local and international touring bands.

The Beat, 677 Ann St. Small, crowded and sweaty, with a beer garden outside where you can recharge your batteries on bar food. $10 cover charge is a bit off-putting, but one of the best techno/dance venues in town, and open until 5am. Upstairs is the *Cockatoo Club*, a stridently gay venue featuring both indoor and outdoor bars, with a penchant for 1980s music. Open Wed–Sun.

Dooley's, cnr Brunswick and McLachlan streets. Rowdy, popular Irish pub hosting bands of variable quality; territorial male behaviour is the norm in the big pool-hall upstairs, and the police seem to get called in on a regular basis.

The Healer, 27 Warner St. A renovated ninety-year-old church, which has remained true to its origins by putting the stage at one end and the bar at the other, with rows of seats in between; feels just right for its menu of quality live blues, soul, and R&B.

Heaven, 25 Warner St. Right next to *The Healer*, and yet another converted church; musicians swear by it as a quality live venue that supports

Brisbane bands.

Queen's Arms Hotel, 64 James St, New Farm. Tuesday night Comedy Club, bands Thursday, Saturday and Sunday, and DJ mix Friday and Saturday. Closed Mon.

The Press Club, in the *Empire Hotel*, cnr Brunswick and Ann streets. "Members only" club (whatever that means); if you make it past the door gorillas, you'll find leather lounges, big "pouf" cushions to rest your feet on and a huge glam/industrial fan as the centrepiece, all of it enveloped in a relaxed and funky dance beat. Rather a "fabulous" crowd, out to see and be seen, with drinks prices to match. Closed Mon.

Ric's Bar, 321 Brunswick St. Narrow, crowded place – getting to the bar takes some effort – very popular with the young, slightly affluent crowd. Nightly mix of live Aussie bands downstairs and DJ-driven techno upstairs at the Upbar.

210 Wickham Street (The Tube), Wickham St. DJs play a variety of the latest dance tracks.

Waterloo Hotel, cnr Ann St and Commercial Rd. manages to attract some big-name Australian touring bands, but almost always has good local talent Friday and Saturday nights.

The Wickham Hotel, cnr Wickham and Alden streets. Reputedly Queensland's most popular gay pub. Men only nights on Thursday, women only Friday and Sunday, but DJ's every night, with cabaret and drag shows as a regular feature.

Zoo, 711 Ann St. A hectic night out with dub or local bands, and Sunday swing sessions; Wed–Sun 5pm–late.

Film and theatre

Compared with the rest of the state, which tends to get only mainstream commercial successes, Brisbane has a varied programme of films. The Dendy, 346 George St (℡07/3211 3244), Palace Centro, 39 James St, Fortitude Valley (℡07/3852 4488), Schonell, University of Queensland, St Lucia (℡07/3321 7690) and Village Twin, on corner of Brunswick and Annie streets (℡07/3358 2021), all show contemporary and vintage foreign-language and "offbeat" films. Even the multiscreen Hoyts cinema (℡07/3229 5544), under the Myer

Centre, and the luxurious Regent (℡07/3229 5544) further down the mall, are worth checking for unexpected offerings, as is the State Library (℡07/3840 7811). In August the **Brisbane International Film Festival** is in town with a bundle of goodies from around the world shown over a week – contact one of the cinemas for details.

Big **theatrical productions** are staged at the **Performing Arts Complex** (℡13 6246) on the South Bank in the Concert Hall, Optus Playhouse (home of the Queensland Theatre Company), Cremorne, or Lyric theatres; look out for lower-key lunchtime performances, workshops and foyer exhibitions. The University of Queensland's Cement Box Theatre, over the river at their St Lucia campus (℡07/3377 2240), offers more down-to-earth repertory fare, and there's also a new venue in town at the **Powerhouse**, on the river next to New Farm Park in eastern Brisbane. A former power station, this once derelict building opened in May 2001 as a centre for the performing arts, including the long-established La Boite Theatre and Vulcana Womens' Circus. Contact information outlets for performance details.

Activities

Queensland's sporting obsession revolves around **rugby league**, though the Brisbane Broncos have lost their edge a little since their glory days in the early 1990s. Their stomping ground is at the ANZ Stadium, west of the city, and the event of the year is the State of Origin series in May or June. **Cricket** matches are played at "The Gabba", Vulture St, and the Queensland Reds **rugby union** team play at Ballymore oval. Tickets are usually easy to get at the games.

For something more hands on, you can spend the day **rock-climbing** outside the city for $48 with the Spicy Tomato Tour Company (℡0414 866 286, ⓦwww.spicytomato.com.au), who lay on an evening of free beer afterwards. For **sailing**, A B Sea Sailing School, a thirty-minute train ride from the city at Manly (℡07/3396 3994), runs one- to eight-day certified training courses aboard their cruise/racer *Red Rizla*, while Bay Dolphin (℡07/3207 9620)

Tours from Brisbane

Most **tours** from Brisbane are pretty straightforward day-trips by bus to take in the highlights of Lamington, Mount Tamborine, the Sunshine Coast or Gold Coast, but there are a few more adventurous options. Allstate Scenic Tours (℡07/3285 1777) have been running day-trips to Green Mountain at Lamington National Park for years (Sun–Fri, $44), and you can arrange with them to be dropped off on one day and picked up another. Australian Day Tours (℡07/3236 4155) have a dozen or so day-tours to the Sunshine Coast, Gold Coast theme parks, or Lamington and Mount Tamborine for $50–80; Backtracks (℡07/5573 5693) go to Lamington and Springbrook national parks from around $50; Coachliner (℡07/3236 1239) go to Mount Tamborine, Green Mountain or the Sunshine Coast ($45–90); while Far Horizons (℡07/3284 5475) operate day-trips to Lamington, the Glasshouse Mountains, or hinterland cattle stations from around $60.

If you want a bit more depth to your trips, or to visit more distant regions, try Araucaria Ecotours (℡07/5544 1283), who offer three days of spotting wildlife around the remote Mount Barney National Park (see p.436; prices by arrangement); the highly recommended Rob's Rainforest Explorer (℡07/3357 7061 or 019 496 607) for day-trips to various parts of the Scenic Rim or Glasshouse Mountains, featuring plenty of wildlife, rainforests, bush tucker and swimming holes ($48); or Sunrover (℡07/3203 4241), for three- to six-day 4WD safaris to Moreton Island, Carnarvon Gorge or Fraser Island.

offers a full-day sailing between the mainland and North Stradbroke Island for $75. **Surfing** trips are covered by Dust Tours (free call ℡1800 111 262, ⓦwww.surftours.com.au), who offer all-inclusive Weekend Wipeouts ($199) and four-day surf safaris ($299) for everyone from complete novices upwards.

Finally, for some plain Aussie weirdness, head west of town to the Australian Woolshed at 148 Samford Rd, Ferny Hills (℡07/3351 5366), where you can watch a highly polished performance including **trained sheep** (a rarity in itself), a shearing demonstration, morning tea and sheepdogs putting startled flocks through their paces. Shows start at 8am, 9.30am, 11am, 1pm & 2.30pm, and entry is $15.

Listings

Airlines Air New Zealand, 133 Mary St (℡07/3853 8340; reservations ℡13 2467); Air Niugini, 99 Creek St (℡1300/361 380); Air Vanuatu, Floor 5, 293 Queen St (℡07/3221 2566); Ansett, 743 Ann St, Fortitude Valley (℡13 1300); British Airways, 247 Adelaide St (℡07/3232 3123); Cathay Pacific, 400 Queen St (℡13 1747); Flight West, Pandanus Ave, Eagle Farm (℡13 2392); Garuda, 288 Edward St (℡1300/365 331); Gulf Air, 217 George St (℡07/3407 7188); Japan Airlines, Level 14, 1 Waterfront Place, Eagle St (℡07/3229 9916); KLM, 141 Queen St (℡07/3229 5811); Korean Air, 400 Queen St (℡07/3226 6000); Malaysia Airlines, 17th Floor, 80 Albert St (℡13 2627); Qantas, 247 Adelaide St (℡13 1313); Royal Brunei, 9/25 Mary St (℡07/3221 7757); Singapore, 344 Queen St (℡13 1011); Thai International, 145 Eagle St (℡07/3215 4777); United, 400 Queen St (℡13 1777); Virgin Blue, Level 7, Centenary Square, 100 Wickham St, Fortitude Valley (℡07/3295 3000 or 13 6789).

Banks Queensland banking hours are Mon–Fri 9.30am–4pm; major branches in the centre are around Queen and Edward streets.

Bike rental and repairs Brisbane Bike Sales, 87 Albert St (℡07/3229 2433); open daily and late Fri night; bikes with helmets from $20 per day, $60 per week. Hotel Cycle Hire (℡0408 003 198) charge $38 a day or $99 a week, but deliver to your accommodation and offer a free emergency repair service within 10km of the city centre.

Bookshops American Book Store, 173 Elizabeth St (℡07/3221 7838), has a broad selection; Angus and Robertsons, Queen Street Mall, is a good standard bookshop; Women's Bookshop, 15 Gladstone Rd, Highgate Hill (℡07/3844 6650), stocks the latest lesbian titles. Bent Books, at the crossroads with Boundary Rd and Vulture St (℡07/3846 5004), is an independent bookshop with a gay bias.

Buses All ticket desks are on the third floor of the Transit Centre, Roma St. Coachtrans (to the Gold and Sunshine coasts; ℡07/3236 4165); Crisp's (to Toowoomba, Warwick, Stanthorpe, Goondiwindi and Tenterfield; ℡07/3236 5266); Greyhound Pioneer (Queensland and interstate; ℡07/3258 1670); Kirkland's (to the Gold Coast, Byron Bay and Lismore; ℡1300/367 077); McCafferty's (Queensland and interstate; ℡07/3236 3035); Premier (all highway destinations to Sydney and Cairns; ℡13 3410); Whites (to Toowoomba and the Gold Coast, including theme parks; ℡07/3245 1308).

Bushwalking Brisbane Bushwalkers Club, 116 Alderley Ave, Alderley (℡07/3856 4050), 8km west of the centre by train.

Camping supplies K2, 140 Wickham St, Fortitude Valley (℡07/3854 1340); Kathmandu, 144 Wickham St (℡07/3252 8054); and Mountain Designs, 120 Wickham St (℡07/3216 1866), for top-quality camping gear and information.

Car rental You'll pay around $40 for a single day's rental; longer terms work out from $25 a day. Shop around and read rental conditions before signing. Most places will deliver; minimum age is 21. Aircond Car Rentals, 53 Montpelier Rd, Bowen Hills (℡07/3216 0303); Coast to Coast, for campervans from $40 a day (free call ℡1800 246 869); Compass (free call ℡1800 640 191); Integra, for campervans and one-way rentals to Melbourne, Sydney or Cairns (free call ℡1800 067 414); Network, 398 St Pauls Terrace, Fortitude Valley (℡07/3252 1599); NQ Australia, 24 Violet St, Eagle Farm (℡07/3268 5800), for campervans; Thrifty, 325 Wickham St, Fortitude Valley (℡07/3252 5994).

Consulates Britain, 1 Eagle St (℡07/3223 3200); Japan, 12 Creek St (℡07/3221 5188); Papua New Guinea, Level 1, 99 Creek St (℡07/3221 7915); Philippines, 126 Wickham St, Fortitude Valley (℡07/3252 8215); Thailand, 87 Annerley Rd (℡07/3846 7771).

Disabled travellers The Disability Information and Awareness Line (DIAL) maintains a database of accessible accommodation and other facilities throughout Queensland (☏07/3224 8444, or outside Brisbane free call ☏1800 177 120, ✉dial@fsaia.qld.gov.au).

Diving The nearest dive sites to Brisbane are off North Stradbroke and Moreton islands; details are on pp.417–420. Nautilus Scuba, 504 Lutwyche Rd (☏07/3857 1440), can cater to all your needs.

Flights Possum Air Tours (☏07/3397 0033, ⓦwww.possumairtours.com.au) depart daily at 5.45am for a spin over the city followed by a champagne breakfast. $214 per person, includes pick-up and return to accommodation.

Hospitals/medical centres Roma Street Medical Centre, Level 2, Transit Centre (Mon–Fri 8am–5.30pm, free dental consultations Tues; ☏07/3236 2988); Royal Brisbane, Herston Rd, Herston (☏07/3253 8111; buses #126, #144 or #172 from outside City Hall); and Travellers' Medical Service, Level 5, 247 Aldelaide St (Mon–Fri 7.30am–7pm, Sat 8am–5pm, Sun 10am–4pm; ☏07/3211 3611, Ⓕ3221 3771), for general services, vaccinations and women's health.

Internet access Most hostels have terminals where you can log on from around $4 an hour, or there are slightly more expensive internet places just up from Central Station and *Palace Backpackers* on Edward St (see p.398), as well as the Backpackers Travel Centre at 138 Albert St.

Left luggage At the airport, Transit Centre and in the basement of the Myer Centre; $4–7 per day per locker.

Maps The Royal Automobile Club of Queensland's series, free to members, or $5.50 each from the RACQ centre at 261 Queen St, covers everything from major highways to almost invisible 4WD-only tracks; and World Wide, 187 George St, stocks a comprehensive range of maps, atlases and travel guides for Queensland and beyond.

Markets Eagle Street (Sun until 3pm) and Brunswick Street Mall (Sat until 4pm) for bits and pieces; South Bank Parklands (Fri night, Sat & Sun until around 4pm) for clothing, arts and crafts and a family atmosphere; while the Riverside Centre (Sun only) is more "arty" than the rest.

National Parks and Wildlife Service (Naturally Queensland) 160 Ann St (☏07/3227 8187). Plenty of fluffy toys, brochures, books and general information about the state's national parks.

Pharmacies Transit Centre Pharmacy (daily 7am–5pm); and Day & Night Pharmacy, Queen Street Mall (Mon–Sat 8am–9pm, Sun 10am–5pm).

Police Queensland Police Headquarters is opposite the Transit Centre on Roma St (☏07/3364 6464).

Post office GPO, 261 Queen St (☏07/3405 1202); bring photo ID to collect poste restante. Mon–Fri 7am–6pm.

RACQ 261 Queen St (breakdown service ☏13 1111).

Telephones International payphones are located in the arcade beside the GPO at 261 Queen St; cheap international rates are also available through the internet places near *Palace Backpackers* on Edward St, and the Backpackers Travel Centre at 138 Albert St.

Trains Queensland and interstate trains leave from the Transit Centre's ground floor; the ticket office and information centre there is open Mon–Sat 5.45am–6.30pm, with variable hours on Sun. For rail information call ☏13 2232.

Travel agents Discounted air fares and other travel arrangements are available from: Flight Centre, 181 George St (☏07/3229 0150); cnr Creek and Queen streets (☏07/3227 1777); STA, 111 Adelaide St (☏07/3221 5722); Trailfinders, 91 Elizabeth St (☏07/3229 0887). There's also the Backpackers Travel Centre at 138 Albert St (☏07/3221 2225), and a YHA office opposite the Transit Centre at 154 Roma St open Mon–Fri 8.30am–5pm, Sat 9am–3pm (☏07/3236 1680).

Women travellers Contact Women's Infolink, 56 Mary St (free call ☏1800 177 577).

Work Popular with job-hunters, Brisbane offers fairly good employment prospects, if you're not too choosy. Regular employment agencies may actively discourage travellers, though several hostels now run very effective ad hoc agencies, or try Backpacker Employment Services, on the top floor of the Transit Centre in Roma St (Mon–Fri 9am–3pm; ☏07/3236 4899, Ⓕ3236 0899, ⓦwww.backpackersaustralia.com).

Outer Brisbane and Moreton Bay

With the grossly hyped Gold Coast and Hinterland for competition, it's not surprising that few people bother with the country immediately surrounding Brisbane. Only 5km to the west, the city is hemmed in by **Mount Coot-tha**'s botanic gardens and the foothills of **Brisbane Forest Park**, which covers the green, wet heights of the D'Aguilar Range and stretches to the edge of **Lake Wivenhoe**.

In the opposite direction, coastal suburbs provide access to the shallow waters of **Moreton Bay**, famous throughout Australia as the home of the unfortunately named Moreton Bay Bug, which is actually a small, delicious lobster-like crustacean. While Brisbane is hardly noted for its beach life, with muddy shorelines attracting mangroves rather than sun worshippers, the largest of the bay's islands, **Moreton** and **North Stradbroke**, are generously endowed with sand, and are just the right distance from the city to make their beaches accessible but seldom crowded. The island of **St Helena** is not somewhere you'd visit for sun and surf, but its prison ruins recall the convict era and are an interesting daytrip. In the bay itself, look for dolphins, **dugong** (sea cows) and humpbacked **whales**, which pass by in winter en route to their calving grounds up north.

For organized **transport and tours** into the area, check the following individual accounts, as well as the box on p.411.

Mount Coot-tha

The lower slopes of **Mount Coot-tha** are the setting for Brisbane's second **Botanic Gardens**, a popular place for a Sunday picnic located on Sir Samuel Griffith Drive (Mon–Sat 8am–5pm; free; bus #471 from Adelaide St runs hourly 9.15am–3.15pm). Careful landscaping and the use of enclosures create varying climates – dry pine and eucalypt groves, a cool subtropical rainforest complete with waterfalls and streams, and the elegant **Japanese Gardens**. In summer, the **tropical plant dome** seems an unnecessary feature in an already sweltering climate; inside, the floor is almost completely occupied by a pond – stocked with tropical lotus lillies and fish – and is overshadowed by tropical greenery dripping with moisture.

The other dome in the gardens does duty as a **planetarium** (call ☎07/3403 2578 for current entry fee and timetable of events). While the foyer display is dry and dated, the show itself, which you view lying back under the dome's ceiling, is an interesting observation of the key features of Brisbane's night sky.

After visiting the Botanic Gardens most people head up the road to the **summit** for panoramas of the city and, on a good day, the Moreton Bay islands. **Walking tracks** from here make for moderate hikes of an hour or two through dry gum woodland, and include several **Aboriginal trails** – the best of which branches off the Slaughter Falls track and points out plants and their uses as food, artefacts and hunting poisons. Pamphlets on the tracks are available from the Botanic Gardens library (Tues–Fri 9.30am–4.30pm, Sat 10am–noon) and the information desk in the foyer of Brisbane's City Hall.

Brisbane Forest Park

If your plans don't include seeing any other forests in the southeast, take advantage of **Brisbane Forest Park**'s proximity to the city. Covering approximately 280 square-kilometres to the west of Brisbane, the park contains substantial tracts of virgin forest, and is well stocked with wildlife, pretty lookouts and easy walking tracks. A day is ample time to look around, or you could make the park the first stage of a scenic circuit from Brisbane via Lake Wivenhoe and Toowoomba.

Highway 31 runs from the city centre right through the park, with a half-dozen places to stop off and explore along the way. First of these is **Bellbird Grove** (4km into the park), containing another of the city's Aboriginal trails with an outdoor museum of bark huts and information on traditional plant uses.

Around 12km along is **Boombana**'s one-kilometre rainforest circuit of moss-covered logs and towering buttressed trees, with the tiny township of **MOUNT NEBO** just beyond. From here it's a long run through gum woodland to similarly-sized **MOUNT GLORIOUS**, and then you're at **Maiala National Park** (30km into the park), a fascinating tract of subtropical forest similar to Lamington's, where palms, figs and other giant trees compete for light, vines tangle up the forest floor and gullies guide fast-flowing creeks. Both townships sport **tearooms** and self-catering **accommodation** (see "Practicalities" below).

There's plenty of **wildlife** to be encountered along the park's many kilometres of **walking tracks**. Catbirds snarl at each other in the rainforest, while dark-blue male **satin bowerbirds** woo females with an elaborate tunnel made from grass and decorated with blue objects – seeds and flowers are the natural choice, though given the opportunity the birds are happy to raid picnic tables and dustbins for blue plastic clothespegs, straws, and even Bushell's teabags, which have a blue paper label attached to the string (Queensland dairies changed the colour of their plastic bottle-lids when it was suggested that bowerbirds might throttle themselves on them). At night, you'll see wallabies on verges, glider possums around flowering trees in open woodland, echidnas scraping through leaf litter for ants, and possibly the bandy-bandy, a timid snake boldly striped in black and white, which forms vertical hoops with its body when frightened.

Lake Wivenhoe was created in the late 1970s to stop the Brisbane River flooding the city – the last of a series of floods struck in 1974. Its southern end is just visible from an outlook on the western edge of the **D'Aguilar Range**, about 10km west of Maiala, that gives a sweeping view down wooded hills to the drier country of the southwest. A road links the park with the Brisbane Valley Highway and if you're heading west, you can get to Toowoomba (see p.556) via the Wivenhoe Dam (140km) – a slower-paced, far more scenic route than the alternative Warrego Highway.

Practicalities

In general, spring (Sept–Oct) is the best time to visit Brisbane Forest Park; animals are active, many plants are in flower and rain is infrequent. It can be cold and damp at night in winter, while **fire bans** can close sections of the park during prolonged dry spells (most frequently in Nov).

The park entrance and headquarters are at **Walkabout Creek Freshwater Study Centre** (Mon–Fri 8.30am–4.30pm, Sat & Sun 9am–5pm; ☎07/3300 4855), about 12km west of the city via The Gap. You can reach Walkabout Creek **by bus** from the Myer Centre #385 (hourly Mon–Fri 9am–5pm, Sat & Sun 9am–4pm). Coming **by car** – the only way to explore more of the park unless you walk – follow College Road west onto Route 31, and stay on it until you reach Walkabout Creek.

Walkabout Creek makes a good first stop for free maps, information, details of **bushwalking tours** and, if you want to **camp rough** (there are no formal campsites), a permit. The Study Centre itself (daily 9am–4.30pm; $3.50) is an idealized creek system where lungfish, turtles, snakes and frogs coexist with few of the stresses they'd encounter living this close together in the wild. Everything is well labelled and it's unlikely you'll ever get better views of crayfish mincing over the gravel at the bottom of the stream or water dragons sunning themselves on rocks. The centre also has a noisy walk-through aviary, as well as a collection of platypuses and a nocturnal house, and there's a smattering of wildlife in the surrounding gum forest.

Accommodation in the park needs to be booked in advance. At Mount Nebo, the *Railway Carriage* (☎07/3289 8120) offers a night in a restored 1930s

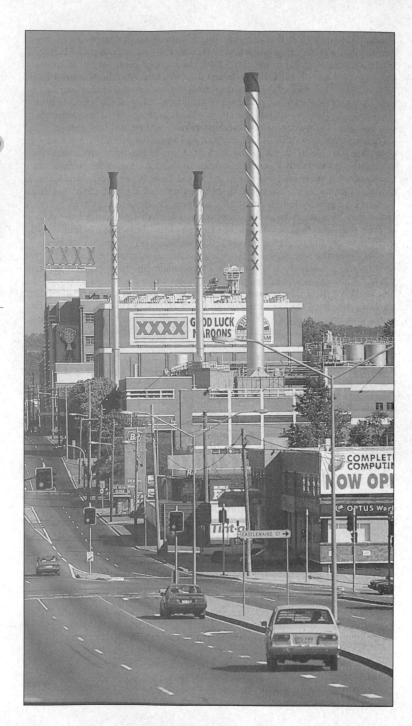

sleeper car, with bed, kitchen and en-suite (④), or a similarly equipped but more conventional chalet (④). At Mount Glorious, *Mt Glorious Getaways* (☎ 07/3289 0172, ⓦ www.mtgloriousgetaways.com.au) have several nicely designed and fully furnished self-catering cottages (⑤).

St Helena Island

Small, low and triangular, **St Helena Island** sits 8km from the mouth of the Brisbane River. Once the hunting ground of local tribes, the island took its name after an aborigine known as Napoleon was dumped here in 1828 after he became too troublesome for the jail at Dunwich on North Stradbroke Island. Forty years later, the spectre of overcrowding in mainland prisons prompted the government to turn St Helena Island into a penal settlement, and after clearing rainforest for timber and to prevent escapes, gardens were planted and houses built from coral blocks and clay. In some respects it was a model system: prisoners were taught a trade and were even paid for their labour, and there were only three escapes in 65 years. The government found it particularly useful for political troublemakers, such as the leaders of the 1891 shearers' strike and, with more justice, a couple of slave-trading "Blackbirder" captains.

A **tour** of the prison island, endearingly tagged the "Hell Hole of the South Pacific" during its working life, leaves you thankful you missed out on the "good old days". A clue to why there were so few escapes is provided by the rusty swimming enclosure at the jetty, which was constructed to protect warders from the sharks whose presence was actively encouraged around the island. Evidence of the prisoners' industry and self-sufficiency is still to be seen in the stone houses, as well as in the remains of a sugar mill, paddocks, wells and an ingenious lime kiln built into the shoreline. The Deputy Superintendent's house has been turned into a bare **museum** (reached from the jetty on a mini-tramway), displaying a ball and chain lying in a corner and photographs from the prison era. Outside, the gardens that once produced prize-winning olive oil are now sparse, and the two cemeteries have been desecrated: many headstones were carried off as souvenir coffee tables, the corpses dug up and sold as medical specimens. The remaining stones comprise simple concrete crosses stamped with a number for the prisoners, or inscribed marble tablets for the warders and their children. The last inmate left in 1933.

Cat-o'-Nine-Tails (☎ 07/3396 3994) offers **day-trips** ($48 including lunch; Mon–Fri departing 9.30am and returning 2.15pm, Sat & Sun departing 11am and returning at 4pm) and **night-tours** ($95 includes three-course meal; departs Saturday 6.30pm), the latter including a theatrical sound-and-light show on the island. Boats leave around 15km east of the city from the public jetty in the suburb of **Manly**, a ten-minute walk from Manly train station; advance bookings are essential.

Moreton Island

A 38km long, narrow band of stabilized, partly wooded sand dunes 20km east off Brisbane, **Moreton Island**'s faultless beaches are distinctly underpopulated for much of the year – making it perfect for a day or two of surfing, fishing or camping. Most people cross to mid-point **Tangalooma Resort** on the daily **ferry** (departs 10am, leaves the island 3pm; $35 return) which leaves from the terminal 8km from the city at the end of Holt Street, off Kingsford Smith Drive at Pinkenba. From mid-June to late October, they also run **whale-watching** tours ($85). A **courtesy bus** to the ferry terminal leaves daily at 9am from the McCafferty's coach bay on the third floor of the Roma Street Transit Centre.

To take your own vehicle to the island, whose sand tracks are 4WD-only, contact the *Combie Trader* **vehicle barge** (℗07/3203 6399 for timetables and departure point), which crosses to the tiny settlement of **Bulwer** on the island's north – it costs at least $150 return. The rules of the road are the same as on the mainland; check tide times before driving on the beach, and be aware that pedestrians may not hear you above the sound of the surf. Alternatively, Sunrover Expeditions (℗07/3203 4241) run excellent **tours** from Brisbane lasting from one to three days ($120–300 per person).

If you're planning to stay a while, note that **supplies** on the island are expensive and limited to Bulwer and southern **Kooringal**, so you need to be self-sufficient and have enough water if you are camping. There are no banks. And before you go in the sea, remember that the beaches aren't patrolled and there are no shark nets. The worst times to visit are at Christmas and Easter, when up to a thousand vehicles crowd onto the island all at once.

The island has designated **campsites** at Tangalooma and Ben-Ewa (3km towards Bulwer) on the west coast, and Blue Lagoon and Eagers Creek on the east side; you can also **camp** anywhere along beaches except where there are signs asking you not to. Permits are available from barge operators or on site for $3.85 per person per night.

Around the island

TANGALOOMA, midway along the island's west coast, is fronted by a set of wrecks, deliberately sunk to create an artificial harbour but now swamped in sand – a fine **snorkelling** site at high tide. Nearby is *Tangalooma Resort*, which has parts of a former whaling station incorporated into its buildings. Pleasantly shaded and busy at weekends and holidays, it's the only place on the island that has a restaurant and serves cold drinks – respectable dress required. There's also a national parks **campsite** here (with water, showers and toilets), which gets as crowded as anywhere on the island. A three-kilometre track heads south from Tangalooma to the **Desert**, where the dunes are a great place to try sand-tobogganing.

With your own vehicle, or if you don't mind hiking, take the ten-kilometre track from Tangalooma across to Moreton's more attractive **eastern side**; generally less crowded, the beach also has good surf. You end up at Eagers Creek, where there's another campsite and a five-kilometre return trip up sandy **Mount Tempest**'s 280-metre peak – an exhausting climb. Head 10km north up the beach, and you'll find **Blue Lagoon**, the largest of the island's freshwater lakes, only 500m from the beach and adjacent to the smaller, picturesque **Honeyeater Lake**. Blessed with shady trees, the dunes behind the beach make an ideal place to camp, and the site is supplied with water, showers and toilets. **Dolphins** come in close to shore – a practice that Moreton's Aborigines turned to their advantage by using them to chase fish into the shallows. Writing in the 1870s about his life in Brisbane, Tom Petrie reported that the Ngugi men would beat the surf with their spears, and:

> By and by, as in response, porpoises would be seen as they rose to the surface making for the shore and in front of them schools of tailor fish. It may seem wonderful, but they were apparently driving the fish towards the land. When they came near, [they] would run out into the surf, and with their spears would jab down here and there at the fish, at times even getting two on one spear, so plentiful were they.

Moreton's **northern end** is about 9km wide, covered in ferns, grasstrees, paperbark and banksias around the shore, and dense scrub inland. The landing point here is **BULWER**, a cluster of weatherboard "weekenders" and a **store** stocking fuel and beer and providing basic **accommodation** in six-person units (℡07/3203 6399 or 3408 2202; ❺). The beach is the only "road" south to Tangalooma, while vehicle tracks cut across to Honeyeater Lake and to the island's northeastern corner, **North Point**, where adjacent dunes form near-vertical cliffs, and fresh water, brown with tannin, seeps out into lagoons. Around from North Point, rocky **Cape Moreton** is capped by a red-and-white lighthouse, built between 1857 and 1928 and still operating. There's a museum in the house below and fine views down the east coast from adjacent cliffs.

The **south end** of the island mostly consists of exposed dunes, some covered in scrub and others forming white "blows", which are destabilized, shifting hills that slowly roll over forests. Right at Moreton's southern tip, **KOORINGAL** is a sleepy version of Bulwer and has a store offering fuel, supplies and drinks from their bar (daily 8am–midnight), as well as holiday units that sleep up to six (℡07/3409 0298 or 3409 0105; ❻–❼). From Kooringal, diversions include the twelve-kilometre return trip to **Big and Little Sandhills** via Toompani beach and eerie, long-dead stands of trees in the wake of the dunes. Take plenty of water.

There's decent **diving** around the deepest points of Tangalooma's wrecks, but **Curtain Reef** is superior: an artificial conglomeration of barges, tugs, cars and tyres encrusted with shells, it attracts all types of marine life including sharks, dolphins, groupers and huge rays. Contact *Tangalooma Resort* for seasonal details, transport and rental gear, or see "Diving" in the Brisbane "Listings", p.413.

North Stradbroke Island

North Stradbroke Island is, at 40km long, the largest and most established of the bay's islands, with sealed roads and the fully serviced townships of Dunwich, Amity and Point Lookout. Ninety percent of "Straddie" is given over to mining **rutile** (titanium oxide); and the majority of the 3200 residents are employees of Consolidated Rutile Ltd. The mine sites south of Amity, and in the central west and south, are far from exhausted but their future is precarious, thanks to an oversupply on the world market. Other industries focus on timber, a by-product of preparing land for mining, and, increasingly, tourism.

Transport to the island leaves from Toondah Harbour at Cleveland, with Stradbroke Ferries (℡07/3286 2666) crossing to Dunwich eleven times daily (return fares $15 per person by water-taxi; $75 per car by barge); bus connection from Brisbane's Transit Centre to the ferry costs $9 return. Also, watch out for good-value package deals from various sources, such as the free **courtesy bus** (not including ferry fare) from Brisbane run on Monday, Wednesday and Friday by *Stradbroke Island Guesthouse* – call them first to book.

To get **around the island**, the Dunwich–Point Lookout **bus** connects with all water taxis and costs $8.60 return, and various operators offer 4WD **safaris** to the east beach and interior – Beach Island Tours (℡07/3409 8098) and Straddie Kingfisher Tours (℡07/3409 9502) both come recommended. Some roads on Stradbroke are open to mining vehicles only, so drivers should look out for the signs. Off-roading through the centre is ill-advised: quite apart from the damage caused to the dune systems, the sand is very soft and having your vehicle pulled out will be very expensive.

Dunwich to Main Beach

Unless you need to fuel up or visit the bank, there's little to keep you at **DUN-WICH**, Straddie's ferry port. Two sealed roads head out of town, east through the island's centre towards **Main Beach**, or north to Amity and Point Lookout.

The road through the centre passes two **lakes**, the second and smaller of which, Blue Lake, is a national park and source of fresh water for the island's wildlife, which is most plentiful early in the morning. Beyond Blue Lake you have to cross the **Eighteen Mile Swamp** to reach Main Beach and, though there's a causeway, the rest of the route is for 4WDs only. You can **camp** behind the beach anywhere south of the causeway (north of it is mining company land), but be prepared for the mosquitoes that swarm around the mangroves; the southernmost point, looking over to South Stradbroke Island (see p.427), is an angling and wildlife mecca, with birdlife and kangaroos lounging around on the beaches.

The Top End

Heading north from Dunwich, it's 10km to where the road forks left to Amity and right to Point Lookout: **AMITY** is a sleepy place built around a jetty, while **POINT LOOKOUT** is where most visitors end up if they don't want to camp. Nineteen kilometres from Dunwich, Point Lookout spreads out around Stradbroke's single rock headland, overlooking a string of beaches. Stretched out along the road are a pub, takeaway pizza place, a store, some cafés and various types of **accommodation**. Top of the range are *Anchorage Village Resort* (℡07/3409 8266; ❽), a comfortable, motel-like option, and *Samarinda* (℡07/3409 8785; ❺–❼), with motel rooms and two-bedroom units. At the other end of the scale, *Stradbroke Island Guesthouse* (℡07/3409 8888, ℻3409 8588, ✉straddieguesthouse@redland.net.au; ❶) has dorm beds, plus free loans of surfboards, bikes and fishing gear; they also organize 4WD-, walking- and trail-riding trips. *Stradbroke Tourist Park* (℡07/3409 8127; four- to six-person cabins ❹, camping ❶) is the best of the local **caravan parks**, or you can camp on the foreshore west of Rocky Point's beach access road.

The **beaches** here are good. **Flinders** runs west of Amity; **Home** and **Cylinder** between here and Cylinder Headland are both patrolled and, therefore, crowded during holiday weekends. If you don't mind swimming in unwatched waters, head for **Deadman's Beach** or **Frenchman's Bay**. On the headland above, there are fine views and the chance to see loggerhead turtles and dolphins; from the walking track around North Gorge down to Main Beach you might see whales – if you have binoculars. Offshore, Stradbroke's **dive sites** around Flat and Shag rocks are renowned for groups of grey nurse sharks, moray eels and summertime manta rays. Stradbroke Island Scuba Centre (℡07/3409 8888, ℻3409 8588) discount their five-day dive course through the hostels.

The Gold Coast

Beneath a jagged skyline shaped by countless high-rise beachfront apartments, the **Gold Coast** is Australia's Miami Beach or Costa del Sol, a striking contrast to Brisbane, only an hour away. Aggressively superficial, it's not the place to go if you're seeking peace and quiet: the endless succession of nightclubs, bars and theme parks provide raucous, relentless entertainment. It can be enjoyable for a couple of days – perhaps as a weekend break from Brisbane –

but there's little variation on the beach and nightclub scene and if you're concerned that this will leave you jaded, bored or broke you would be better off avoiding this corner of the state altogether.

The coast forms a virtually unbroken beach 40km long, from **South Stradbroke Island** past **Surfers Paradise** and **Burleigh Heads** to the New South Wales border at **Coolangatta**. Surfers Paradise has the highest concentration of people and skyscrapers; as you head south through the strip of motels and shops the pace slows (relatively) and it's easier to find some unoccupied sand. The beaches are still touted as the main attraction, though they've become a backdrop to more commercial interests, and they swarm with bathers and board-riders all year round. **Surfing** blossomed here in the 1930s and still pulls in veterans and novices; Coolangatta, Burleigh Heads and South Stradbroke have the best waves and definitely the more serious surfies, but you'll find rideable swell all the way along the coast.

With around three hundred days of sunshine each year there's little "off-season" as such. **Rain** can, however, fall at any time during the year, including midwinter – when it's usually dry in the rest of the state – but even if the crowds do thin out a little, they reappear in time for the Gold Coast **Indy car race** in October, and then continue to swell, peaking over Christmas and New Year. The end of the school year in mid-November also brings on the phenomenon of **Schoolies Week**, when thousands of high-school leavers ditch exam rooms and flock to Surfers for a few days' of hard partying, causing a budget accommodation crisis.

Getting there and around

From Brisbane, Coachtrans runs frequently from the Transit Centre ($15), taking about ninety minutes to get to Surfers Paradise, and slightly over two hours to Coolangatta. Their Airporter service (book in advance ☎07/5588 8777; $33 one-way/$54 return), Airport Transit (book in advance ☎1300/655 655) and Active Tours (☎07/5597 0344; $33/54) also meet arrivals at Brisbane's domestic and international terminals, and deliver direct to Gold Coast accommodation. Coachtrans also organise **theme park transfers** (☎07/3236 1000) from central Brisbane accommodation to Carrumbin Sanctuary, Dreamworld, Movie World, Wet 'n' Wild and Sea World. **Driving** from Brisbane, head down Vulture Street onto the **Gold Coast Highway**, where there's a detour at **Beenleigh** to Queensland's oldest rum distillery at the *Beenleigh Tavern* (tours at 11am, noon, 1pm & 2pm; ☎07/3287 2488); it started in 1860 as a pirate business on the Albert River.

Coming up **from New South Wales**, the coastal highway enters Queensland at Coolangatta, where you'll also find the **Gold Coast Airport**. Airport Transit **shuttle buses** (book in advance on ☎1300/655 655) run to all points between the airport and Surfers Paradise for $11 one-way, $16.50 return.

The Gold Coast Highway from Tweed Heads-Coolangatta to Surfers Paradise, and all the theme parks, are covered by a 24-hour **bus** service run by Surfside Shuttle and Surfside Buses. The whole journey costs around $7, but you can buy **day passes** allowing unlimited use from $13. Otherwise you'll need to take a **taxi** or **rent** a vehicle; there are more details in accounts of the individual resorts.

Surfers Paradise

Spiritually, if not geographically, **SURFERS PARADISE** is at the heart of the Gold Coast, the place where its aims and aspirations are most evident. For the residents, this involves making money by providing services and entertainment for tourists; visitors reciprocate by parting with their cash. All around and irrespective of what you're doing – shopping for clothes, sitting on the beach, partying in one of the frenetic nightclubs or even finding a bed – the pace is brash and glib. Don't come here expecting to be allowed to relax; subtlety is nonexistent and you'll find that enjoying Surfers depends largely on how much it bothers you having the party mood rammed down your throat.

Surfers' beaches have been attracting tourists for over a century, though the town only started developing along commercial lines during the 1950s when the first multistoreyed **beachfront apartments** were built. The demand for views over the ocean led to ever-higher towers which began to encroach on the dunes (not to mention shading them from mid-afternoon); together with the sheer volume of people attracted here, this soon caused serious **erosion** problems along the entire coast. Attempts to stabilize the foreshore with retaining walls, groynes and sand pumping from offshore have had little long-term success. But none of this really matters. Though Surfers Paradise is a firm tribute to the successful marketing of the ideal Aussie lifestyle as an eternal beach party, most people no longer come here for the beaches but simply because everyone else does.

Arrival, information and security

Surfers' **bus station** (6am–10pm) is on Beach Road on the corner of the highway, one street down from Cavill Avenue. Here you'll find **luggage lockers**, **bus company desks** and an **accommodation information** counter. If the hostel you want isn't listed, call them for a **free pick-up**, and don't be surprised if, while walking around with your luggage, hostel minibuses stop for you as they pass. The **tourist information office** is on Cavill Avenue (Mon–Fri 8am–5pm, Sat 9am–5pm, Sun 9am–3.30pm; ☎07/5538 4419).

Security is worth bearing in mind. Many people migrate to Surfers in search of an easier life, only to find themselves homeless and hard up. Others come to prey deliberately on tourists. Don't leave vehicles unlocked at any time, don't take valuables onto the beach, and don't wander alone at night; muggings are common, especially around nightclubs – so take advantage of the courtesy

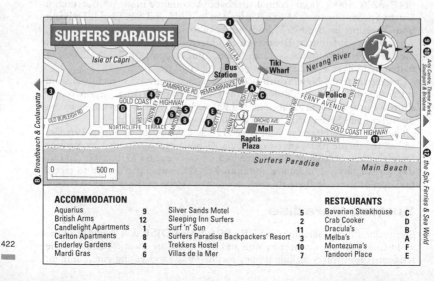

ACCOMMODATION					RESTAURANTS	
Aquarius	9	Silver Sands Motel	5		Bavarian Steakhouse	C
British Arms	12	Sleeping Inn Surfers	2		Crab Cooker	D
Candlelight Apartments	1	Surf 'n' Sun	11		Dracula's	B
Carlton Apartments	8	Surfers Paradise Backpackers' Resort	3		Melba's	A
Enderley Gardens	4	Trekkers Hostel	10		Montezuma's	F
Mardi Gras	6	Villas de la Mer	7		Tandoori Place	E

B, Broadbeach & Coolangatta

Arts Centre, Theme Parks, Southport & Brisbane

the Spit, Ferries & Sea World

buses run by hostels. The situation definitely gets worse around Schoolies Week in November, and Christmas and Easter.

Accommodation

You need to **book** all **accommodation** in advance, and be prepared for slightly above-average room rates everywhere. Typically quiet early on, the **hostels** come to life late in the day and you won't be left in peace until you've signed up for trips to nightclubs, parties and beach events. Most have struck deals with various clubs for cheap entry and drinks, and all have much the same facilities – internet at $5 an hour, pool, dormitories, kitchen, TV and loans of surfboards. Many places don't encourage long stays, but it may be worth asking about weekly rates. **Motels and apartments**, on the other hand, often insist on a minimum three-day stay – during quieter times bargaining may get you a reduced rate. Peak-season motel rates range from $55 to a few hundred dollars a night; during off-season and midweek, rooms are considerably cheaper. Expect to pay more for ocean views. There are simply too many possibilities to give a comprehensive list; those below are central and good value. If you want to **camp**, you'll have to head south to the quieter sections of the Gold Coast.

Aquarius, 44 Queen St, Southport (☎07/5527 1300 or free call 1800 229 955). A new hostel with tiny TV lounge on each floor, pool, communal kitchen, with free basic breakfast; small four- and six-bed dorms. ❷

British Arms, 70 Seaworld Drive (☎07/5571 1776 or free call 1800 680 269, ⓦwww.britisharms.com.au). A YHA property, close to Sea World about 5km north of the centre. Good facilities, plus a lively English bar and grill serving up pub fare, occasional entertainment, and a range of beers till late. Doubles and twins ❹, dorms ❷

Candlelight Holiday Apartments, 22–24 Leonard St (☎07/5538 1277, ⓔcanlight@bigpond.com). Very pleasant, self-contained one-bedroom units in a quiet street close to the bus station; very helpful and friendly owners. ❺

Carlton Apartments, cnr Northcliffe Terrace and Clifford St (☎07/5538 5877). Self-contained two-person units in a seven-storey building on the beach. ❻

Enderley Gardens, 38 Enderley Ave (☎07/5570 1511, ⓕ5592 3878, ⓔenderley@strand.co.au). Self-contained units, one block away from the

Surfing the Gold Coast

As locals will tell you, the Gold Coast has some of the best surfing beaches in the world. And in terms of consistency this might be true – on any given day there will be rideable surf somewhere along the coast – with 200-metre-long sand-bottom point breaks and rideable waves peaking at about four metres in prime conditions. The area is known for its barrels, particularly during the summer cyclone season when the winds shift around to the north; in winter the swell is smaller but more reliable, making it easier to learn to surf. A rule of thumb for finding the best surf is to follow the wind: north when the wind blows from the north, south when it comes from the south. Generally, you'll find the best swell along the southern beaches, and on South Stradbroke Island. While sharks might worry you, more commonplace hostility is likely to come from the local surfies who form tight-knit cliques with very protective attitudes towards their patches.

For expert tuition, tours, or advice anywhere on the Gold Coast, contact locally based Walking on Water (☎07/5534 1886 or 0418 780 311, ⓦwww.walkingonwater.com) or Surfaris (free call ☎1800 634 951, ⓦwww.surfaris.com). On the subject of sharks and general safety, all beaches as far north as Surfers are patrolled; look for the signs. Sea temperatures range between 26°C in summer and 17°C in winter, so a 2–3mm wetsuit is adequate. Hard-core surfies come for Christmas and the cyclone season, though spring is really the busiest time. Competitions or events are held somewhere along the coast on most weekends, advertised through local surf shops.

beach, ten minutes from the heart of Surfers; facilities include pool, spa and tennis court. **7**

Mardi Gras, 28 Hamilton Ave (☎ 07/5592 5888 or free call 1800 801 230). Secure, purpose-built hostel, with safe car park; facilities include a small kitchen and a bar, but there's no pool and the place feels a bit sterile. Tiny doubles **4**, four-bed dorms **2**

Silver Sands Motel, 2985 Gold Coast Highway (☎ 07/5538 6041). Low-rise and pleasant, despite a location on the main highway. One hundred metres from the beach, plus there's a pool. **6**

Sleeping Inn Surfers, 26 Whelan St (☎ 07/5592 4455 or free call 1800 817 832, ✉ sleepinginn@hotmail.com). Close to bus station; nicely furnished, quality budget accommodation in self-contained units, all with TV and free in-house videos. Rooms **4**, dorms **2**

Surf 'n' Sun, 3323 Gold Coast Highway (☎ 07/5592 2363, or free call 1800 678 194). Noisy party hostel, with cramped rooms and ordinary facilities, but it's close to the beach and centre. Twins **3**, five-bed dorms **2**

Surfers Paradise Backpackers' Resort, 2837 Gold Coast Highway (☎ 07/5592 4677, or free call 1800 282 800, ⊛ www.surfersparadisebackpackers.com.au). Purpose-built, sparklingly clean and efficient, with spacious rooms; the price per bed covers everything, including use of washing machines. They also book surfing lessons at $25 per person. Rooms **3**, dorms **2**

Trekkers Hostel, 22 White St, Southport (☎ 07/5591 5616, or free call 1800 100 004, ⊛ www.users.omcs.com.au/trekkers). Beautifully restored old house 3km from the centre; comfortable, and with heaps of deals and trips. Staff are particularly friendly and welcoming, and their weekly BBQ is cheap and good fun. Price includes a basic breakfast, with cheap meals at the nearby RSL club. **2**

Villas de la Mer, cnr Markwell Ave and Northcliffe Terrace (☎ 07/5592 6644, ℻ 5592 6324). Attractive apartments in a three-storey security complex, with ocean views from upper levels. Rooms are simple but modern and well furnished. Two- and three-bedroom apartments. **7**–**8**

The City and theme parks

Downtown Surfers Paradise is a thin ribbon of partially reclaimed land between the ocean and the **Nerang River** which – as the Broadwater – flows north, parallel with the beach, past **the Spit** and South Stradbroke Island into the choked channels at the bottom end of Moreton Bay. Reclaimed land in the river forms islands whose names reflect the fantasies of their founders – Isle of Capri, Sorrento, Miami Keys – and which have become much-sought-after real estate.

From its dingiest club to its best restaurant, Surfers exudes entertainment, and at times – most notoriously at New Year and Christmas – you can spend 24 hours a day out on the town. Another thing you'll spend is money; the only free venue is the beach and with such a variety of distractions it can be financial suicide venturing out too early in the day. The city is full of tourists staggering around at noon, with terrible hangovers and empty wallets, complaining how expensive their holiday has become. The area around **Cavill Avenue** is a bustle of activity from early morning – when the first surfers head down to the beach and the shops open – to after midnight, when there's a constant exchange of bodies between **Orchid Avenue**'s bars and nightclubs. If you spend any length of time in town, you'll get to know the district intimately. The block between the sea and Orchid Avenue is a **mall**, given over to snack bars, coffee houses and shopping arcades; you can pick up a cheap T-shirt or play a game of chess at one of the outdoor tables. **Raptis Plaza** here is a collection of exotic eateries overlooked by a replica of Michelangelo's *David*, with an **indoor rock climbing** wall tucked away in the Plaza's basement.

Across the Esplanade, the **beach** is all you could want as a place to recover from your night out. In early afternoon, the sun moves behind the apartment buildings, but you can escape the shadows by moving up to Main Beach. If you're feeling energetic, seek out a game of volleyball or head for the surf: the swell here is good in a northerly wind, but most of the time it's better for boogie-boards. North of Main Beach, **the Spit**'s attractions include the world's first "Versace hotel" – a six-star edifice fitted out with all things Versace – and **Sea World** (daily 10am–5pm; ☎ 07/5588 2205; $49.80, family rates; access on the Surfside Bus from the highway), the longest running of the Gold Coast's theme parks. Besides various stomach-churning rides, the park features immaculately trained dolphins and killer whales, and helps rehabilitate stranded wild dolphins for later release.

The other theme parks are north out of town, all located on Surfside and Gold Coast Shuttle bus routes. **Dreamworld** (daily 10am–5pm; info ☎ 07/5588 1111; $49.80, family rates), on the Pacific Highway at Coomera, 17km north of Surfers Paradise, has a violent double-loop roller coaster and a fairground atmosphere, as well as a collection of hand-reared tigers in a large enclosure; this may be as close as they'll get to the wild, but at least they're protected from poachers. **Movie World** (daily 10am–5pm; info ☎ 07/5573 8485; $49.80, family rates), also on the Pacific Highway, 14km north of Surfers, is a slice of Hollywood featuring studio tours, and western and stunt shows. Near Movie World, **Wet 'n' Wild** (daily 10am–4.30pm or later; ☎ 07/5573 2255; $28.20) has a series of pools linked by vicious water slides – the back-breaking "twister" and the 25-metre-tall, high-speed slide alone are worth the entrance fee.

Eating

Some of the beachfront resorts offer bargain all-you-can-eat **breakfasts**, while during the rest of the day there's always something to eat at the **cafés** and **snack bars** along Cavill Avenue and the Esplanade. **Restaurants** are geared towards the exotic, although some offer early-bird specials in the evening before a certain hour. More and more people are heading to convenient takeaway and burger joints out of Surfers to eat – south to the area around Broadbeach Mall, or north to Tedder Avenue, in Southport, where there's usually a Porsche or two parked along the trendy café strip. For supplies, there's a **supermarket** downstairs in the Paradise Centre (on Cavill Ave mall) and a 24-hour Night Owl store on the highway near Trickett Street.

Bavarian Steakhouse, cnr Gold Coast Highway and Cavill Ave (☎ 07/5531 7150). Wood-panelled theme restaurant on several floors, where you can wolf down steins of beer and plates of beef while staff dressed in leather and lace pump away on Bavarian brass instruments. Good fun if you're in the mood, and fair value; about $19 for steak, salad and fries.

Crab Cooker, cnr Gold Coast Highway and Thornton St (☎ 07/5538 6884). Nondescript decor but otherwise excellent Australian-style fresh seafood restaurant where a plate of prawns, bugs and fish costs around $26, a "Paradise Platter" spread of seafood and tropical fruit for two is $80, and their famous mud crabs start at $40. Lunch from noon, dinner from 5.30pm.

Dracula's, 1 Hooker Blvd, Broadbeach (☎ 07/5575 1000). Gothic cabaret restaurant open Tues–Sat from 6pm; $49.50 per head ($58 on Sat); advance booking and payment essential.

Melbas, 46 Cavill Ave (☎ 07/5592 6922). New and ambitious café-restaurant attached to the night-club of the same name, with a mix of Mediterranean-style light meals and snacks served, unusually for Surfers, at pavement tables. Their chicken and avocado fettucine, turkey bagel, and Cajun fish salad are all good, and their prices are low, with nothing over $12.50. Opens at 7am for breakfast.

Montezuma's, 8 Trickett St, under the Aloha Tower (☎ 07/5538 4748). A cramped Mexican restaurant hung with luridly-coloured, papier-mache fiesta dolls, but the food's fresh and spicy. $18 will fill you up; open for lunch and dinner.

Sumo, Raptis Plaza. Tiny Japanese takeaway known for its fair prices and large portions, from seafood tempura ($10.45) down to humble buck-wheat noodle soup ($5.50).

Tandoori Place, 7–9 Trickett St (☎ 07/5592 1004). Fast-food ambience, but actually better than first impressions would suggest; their sweet curries are engagingly different, and they have a limited vegetarian menu. Their three-person "Recession Banquet" for $20.95 per head is an excellent deal, otherwise most main dishes are around $15.

Entertainment

Find out **what's on** through accommodation or by word of mouth; the free weekly magazines *Today Tonight Tomorrow* and *Wot's On* are simply business directories. For those desperate for an injection of culture amid all the brash goings-on, check out the programme at the **Arts Centre**, 135 Bundall Rd (℡07/5581 6900), where there's a theatre, gallery, restaurant and bar. You'll find **cinema** complexes on the corner of Clifford Street and Gold Coast Highway (℡07/5575 3355), as well as inside Pacific Fair Shopping Centre, Mermaid Beach (℡07/5575 3355), and Australia Fair shopping centre, Southport (℡07/5531 2200).

Realistically, though, it's Surfers' **clubs** that provide most of the nightlife. Initially, particularly if you're staying at a hostel or have picked up a **free pass** somewhere, your choice will most likely be influenced by the various deals on entry and drinks. The places listed below have been around for a while and have a dependable reputation; none is especially chauvinistic, though places do change. Opening times are from around 6pm until 3am or later.

Benson's, 22 Orchid Ave. Boasts one of the few surviving dance floors that lights up, *Saturday Night Fever*-style. Mostly "alternative" music, very little dance/techno. Closed Mon & Tues.

Berlin Bar, on a lane off Orchid Ave. A bit discreet and stylish for Surfers, with a more civilized scene than you find elsewhere; well-heeled 20–35 crowd being slinky and sexy to Seventies disco and funk tunes. Pricey drinks, no cover charge.

Cocktails and Dreams, Orchid Ave. Seventies nights on Tuesday from 8pm; nightly rhythm and blues at the *Bourbon Bar*; cheap drinks and extended happy hours. Closed Wed.

Melbas, 46 Cavill Ave. Big, new, and relatively upmarket nightclub, with nightly happy hour until 10pm.

Palladium, 7–9 Trickett St (℡07/5570 2100). Surfers' live music mainstay, often attracting major Australian touring bands. There's also a packed

and sweaty nightclub here Friday and Saturday nights.

The Party, at *The Mark*, Orchid Ave. Live rock bands Fri & Sun (often with a $5 cover charge); DJs for the rest of the week.

Penthouse, Orchid Ave. Four floors comprise main dance floor, "R&B room", pool tables and a piano bar. $5 cover charge, generally waived for "back-packers".

Rose and Crown, Raptis Plaza, Cavill Ave. Surfers' "local" pub; entertainment varies from decent local bands to DJs and strip shows (male and female).

Shooters, right beside *Cocktails and Dreams*. Crowds heading for more serious dance spots start out here for a game of pool and a few drinks.

Surfers Beergarden, Cavill Ave, opposite Orchid Ave. Live music with local and interstate band talent on Thursday and Saturday nights.

Listings

Airlines Offices are near Cavill Ave: Ansett, 13–19 Beach Rd (℡13 1300); and Qantas, 3047 Gold Coast Highway (℡13 1313).

Banks and exchange Banks and ATMs are located right throughout Surfers, with most main branches around the Cavill Ave–highway intersection. There are also several bureaux de change in Cavill and Orchid avenues, giving pretty much the same rates.

Boat and jet-ski rental Tiki Village Boat Hire at the river end of Cavill Ave (℡07/5538 0022), and Captain Barb-E, Ferny Ave (℡07/5531 6176) – the latter has self-drive launches from $11 per hour (based on daily rental).

Bungey jumps Banzai Bungey, Palm Ave (℡07/5526 7611); $85 for fourteen storeys of freefall and recoil.

Bookshops Hooked on Books, Paradise Centre, Cavill Ave.

Buses Coachtrans to Brisbane (℡07/5588 8777); Greyhound Pioneer (℡07/5531 6677); Kirkland's to Byron Bay and Lismore (free call ℡1300 367 077); McCafferty's (℡07/5538 2700); Premier to all points between Sydney and Cairns (℡13 3410).

Car rental Competition keeps prices low, but advertised prices are often for long rentals, and exclude insurance and mileage charges: Ariel (℡07/5538 2111), from $29 a day; Betta Rent-a-Car, 108 Ferny Ave (℡07/5538 5559), from $35 a day; Kanga Car and Moped (℡07/5527 6088), old model cars from $19 a day; Red Back Rentals, inside the bus station, Beach Rd (℡07/5592 1655), from $30 a day; Rent-a-Jeep (℡07/5538 6900), 4WDs from $69; Thrifty (℡07/5538 6511)

Gold Coast tours and cruises

Some hostels organize **tours** to the Scenic Rim, or try the following for day-trips to the **Hinterland** (Lamington, Natural Bridge, Mount Tamborine and Binna Burra), **Sunshine Coast** (Noosa, The Big Pineapple or Mooloolaba) and Brisbane. Most offer free pick-ups. Auswild (☏0417 005 184), after-dark wildlife-spotting tours to the hinterland; Backtracks (☏07/5573 5693), to Lamington and Springbrook national parks; Bushwacker Ecotours (☏07/5525 1653, Ⓦ www.bushwacker-ecotours.com.au), to hinterland national parks; Coachliner (☏07/5534 9977); Coachtrans (☏1300/361 788); Mountain Coach Company (☏07/5524 4249); Pacific Tours (☏07/5596 0350); Scenic Hinterland Tours (☏07/5545 2030 or 5531 5536). Mountain Trek Adventures (☏07/5536 1700) run 4WD day-tours around the Hinterland.

The following explore the Nerang River and seafront on 1hr–half-day **cruises**. Aquabus (☏07/5539 0222), a unique amphibious bus, departs several times daily from Orchid Avenue for a 75min trip ($35); Island Queen (☏07/5557 8800) has free accommodation pick-up and return, meals available, and 2hr and evening cruises; Jungle Queen (☏019 645 690) offers 2hr and evening dinner cruises in a forty-year-old ex-Daintree River ferry; St Elmo's (☏404 466 909) is a high-speed, outboard-driven hull seating 8, used for everything from 20-minute river spins ($28) to hour-long trawls after dolphins or whales ($83); Tall Ship (☏07/5532 2444), 2hr calm-water cruises ($31.90) to day-trips to South Stradbroke ($99). See below for more on trips to South Stradbroke Island.

from $39 a day.
Hospitals and medical centres Gold Coast Hospital, Nerang St, Southport (☏07/5571 8211); Gold Coast Medical Centre, Paradise Centre, Hanlan St (☏07/5538 8099)
Pharmacy Galleria Shopping Plaza, cnr Elkhorn Ave and Gold Coast Highway (7am–midnight).

Post office The main post office is in the Paradise Centre, Cavill Ave.
Surf rental Surfworld, Paradise Centre, off Cavill Ave (☏07/5538 4825). Typical prices are $25 a day for board rental, plus credit-card deposit. For tuition see Surfing the Gold Coast box, p.423.
Taxis ☏13 1008.

South Stradbroke Island

South Stradbroke Island is a twenty-kilometre-long, narrow strip of sand, separated from North Stradbroke Island by the 1896 cyclone and, as apartment buildings edge closer, doomed to become an extension of the Gold Coast. For now, though, Stradbroke's relatively isolated and quiet beaches offer something of an escape from the mainland, though most day-trippers come over simply to get plastered in the bar at **South Stradbroke Island Resort** (☏07/5577 3311; rooms ❺, cabins ❼). Alternatively, the new **Couran Cove Resort** (☏07/5597 9000, Ⓦ www.couran.com; cabins and rooms ❽) offers a much more exclusive atmosphere, and doesn't welcome day-guests. There's also fine **surf** to enjoy along the southeast shore (though local surfies are notoriously protective), along with **fishing** in the Jumpinpin Channel between here and North Stradbroke.

Day-cruises to the resort cost around $66 including lunch, with evening booze cruises about $55; operators include Island Queen (see box above) and Jetaway (tickets and departure details from The Hut information booth, corner of Ferny and Cavill avenues; ☏07/5538 3400). A cheaper alternative ($22) is the **resort ferry** (10.30am–4.30pm; Runaway Bay Marina, 5km north of Surfers on Bayview St, but no public transport).

Surfers Paradise to Currumbin

The central section of the Gold Coast lacks any real focus. Haphazardly developed and visually unattractive, it exists very much in the shadow of Surfers Paradise, but can't match its intensity. The highway is just a continuous maze of crowded, multi-lane traffic systems and drab buildings which lose momentum the further south you drive, but once you leave the road there are fine beaches, two **wildlife sanctuaries** and – unbelievable amid all the commotion and noise – Burleigh Heads' tiny **national park** which preserves the coast's original environment.

Burleigh Heads

Around 7km south of Surfers, **BURLEIGH HEADS** consists of a traffic bottleneck where the highway dodges between the **beach** and a rounded headland; there's very good **surf** here but the rocks make it rough for novices. Fifty years ago, before the bitumen and paving took over, this was all dense eucalypt and vine forest, the last fragment of which survives as **Burleigh Head national park**. Entrance is on foot from the car park on the Esplanade, or turn sharply at the lights below the hill just south of the headland for the **visitors information centre** (daily 9am–4pm; ☎07/5535 3032).

 Geologically, Burleigh Heads stems from the prehistoric eruptions of the Mount Warning volcano (p.317), 30km to the southwest. Lava surfaced through vents, cooling to tall hexagonal basalt columns, now mostly tumbled and covered in vines. Rainforest colonized the richer volcanic soils, while stands of red gum grew in weaker sandy loam; along the eastern seafront there's a patch of exposed heathland bordered by groups of pandanus, and a beach along the mouth of Tallebudgera Creek. This diversity is amazing considering the minimal space, but urban encroachment has seriously affected the wildlife. **Butterflies** and **birds** are the most obvious inhabitants – on the heathland look out for the fairy wren's telltale black and red plumage – but the gums also support a small **koala** population (though, notoriously sensitive to disturbance, they often make themselves scarce). The area's natural resources once attracted Yugumbir **Aborigines**, indicated by a few mounds of half-buried shells up on the headland, whose history is brought to life on a "Kaila" tour – book through the park visitors centre, or phone ☎07/5528 9744.

 More of the same awaits you 2km inland at **David Fleay Wildlife Park**, West Burleigh Rd (daily 9am–5pm; $12; take the Surfside Bus). The late David Fleay was the first person to persuade platypus to breed in captivity and the park has a special section devoted to this curious animal, along with tree kangaroos, koalas, plenty of birds and smaller animals, and crocs. The **free guided tours** are worthwhile; take advantage of their night spotlight and daily Aboriginal talk.

Currumbin Beach and Sanctuary

A further 6km past Burleigh Heads, **CURRUMBIN BEACH** is a nice, relatively undeveloped stretch of coast between Elephant Rock and Currumbin Point, and with a breeze there are usually some decent rollers to ride. Just to the north, **PALM BEACH** is more sheltered. *Vikings*, in the surf club building below Elephant Rock, serves Chinese food, or you can fill up on regular pub fare at the *Palm Beach Surf Club*.

 Currumbin Sanctuary, on Tomewin Street (daily 8am–5pm; $18; night tours by arrangement ☎07/5534 1266), was started in 1946 by Alex Griffiths, who foresaw the decline of the coastal environment and developed the seventy-acre park as a wildlife refuge. Forest, lake and grassland fairly bustle with native fauna. There are the usual feeding times and tame kangaroos but the park's strongest point is the beautiful natural surroundings, best experienced from the **elevated walkways** through the forest, where you'll see koalas, tree kangaroos and birds at eye-level.

Coolangatta

On the Queensland–New South Wales border 10km south of Currumbin, **COOLANGATTA** merges seamlessly with Tweed Heads (in New South Wales; see p.311) along Boundary Road. With no signs marking the border and little to tell the two towns apart – other than the sudden proliferation of "Adult Shops" in New South Wales – you'll probably make the crossing between states without realizing it. Unless it's New Year, when everyone takes advantage of the one-hour time difference between the states to celebrate twice, most travellers bypass Coolangatta completely; in doing so, they miss some of the best surf, least crowded beaches and the only place along the Gold Coast which can boast a real "local" community.

Coolangatta is set out one block back from the beach along **Griffith Street**, where you'll find banks, shops and very little in the way of high-density development. Even the motel towers on Point Danger are well spaced, and the general ambience is very small seaside town. **Marine Parade** fronts the shore, the view north over sand and sea ending with the jagged teeth of the skyscrapers on the horizon at Surfers Paradise.

Straddling the border at Point Danger, the **Captain Cook Memorial Lighthouse** forms a shrine where pillars enclose a large bronze globe detailing Cook's peregrinations around the southern hemisphere (see also p.1145). Twenty-five metres below, surfers in their colourful wet suits make the most of Flagstaff Beach's swell – at weekends this area is very crowded.

Coolangatta's daytime action is in the **surf**, the best being between Point Danger and Kirra Point (the latter nominated by world surfing champion Kelly Slater as his favourite break), or at Flagstaff, across the state border in Tweed Heads – exactly where depends on the wind. Greenmount, effectively Coolangatta's town beach, is fairly reliable and is a good beach for beginners; Snapper Rocks and Point Danger further down the peninsula are for the more dedicated. For sun worshippers, Coolangatta beach, just north of Greenmount, is fine if you're staying nearby, but the six-kilometre stretch of sand further up, beyond Kirra Point, is wider and less crowded. **Surfing supplies and rentals** are available from Pipedream, Griffith Street (℡07/5599 1164), the best place for gear and information about local conditions and competitions, and from Coolangatta Surf, Griffith Street (℡07/5361 1239), and Mount Woodgee, 122 Griffith St (℡07/5536 5937). Surfboard and ski rental is around $20 a day plus credit card deposit. All shops have decent secondhand boards for sale, though local boards tend to be too thin and lightweight to use elsewhere. You might also find a bargain in one of the pawnbroker's shops on Griffith Street. For **tuition**, see the Surfing the Gold Coast box on p.423.

Cook Island and Nine Mile Reef are the main **dive sites**, with two shipwrecks nearby. Of interest are nurse sharks, turtles, canyons and scattered groups of reef fish. Kirra Dive Centre, on the corner of Creek and South streets, Kirra (℡07/5536 6622), and Blue Juice Dive, 127 Griffith St (℡07/5536 6277), charge around $65 plus equipment for two local dives.

Practicalities

Griffith Street (the Gold Coast Highway) and the parallel, seafront Marine Parade run south for about a kilometre from the edge of town to the border, with a handful of short streets connecting them. At the border, Griffith Street kinks sharply inland as it enters Tweed Heads, while Boundary Street continues south (uphill) to Point Danger.

The long-distance **bus depot** is actually 150m over the border in Tweed Heads, just off the highway at Golden Gateway Travel, 29 Bay St (Mon–Sat 7.30am–5.30pm, New South Wales time; ☎07/5536 1700) – there's no station as such, and if Golden Gateway is closed, you just get set down on the pavement. The Gold Coast **airport** (flight information on ☎13 1300) is 3km north of Coolangatta, from where Airport Transit **shuttle buses** (book in advance on ☎1300/655 655) run to Coolangatta and all points to Surfers Paradise for $11 one-way and $16.50 return. Coolangatta's helpful **information centre** (Mon–Sat 8am–5pm, Sun 10am–2pm; ☎07/5536 7765) is on the corner of Warner and Griffith streets, about halfway down Griffith towards the border. **Taxis** can be booked on ☎13 1008 while **car rental** is available through Thrifty (☎07/5536 6954), at the Gold Coast Airport, with prices starting at $35.

Accommodation
Accommodation is strung out along the highway at Bilinga and Kirra, while the more expensive places are in the apartment buildings overlooking the sea on Marine Parade and Point Danger. For **camping**, try *Kirra Tourist Park*, Charlotte Street, Kirra (☎07/5581 7744).

Calypso Plaza, 87–105 Griffith St (☎07/5599 0000 or free call 1800 062 189). Sparkling new and expensive resort hotel, with suites and two-bedroom penthouse apartments, right across from Greenmount Beach. **❼**
Kirra Beach Hotel, across from the beach at Kirra Point (☎07/5536 3311). Ideal location for boardriders. Some rooms are quite spacious, and all have bath, TV & fridge; cheap meals available in the pub bistro. Singles **❷**, doubles **❸**
On the Beach, 118 Marine Parade, Greenmount Beach (☎07/5536 3624). Single or double rooms in self-contained apartments. Tidy and well placed for the town and the beach. **❹**–**❻**
Sunset Strip Budget Resort, 199 Boundary St (☎07/5599 5517). Good facilities, including family rooms, huge kitchen and living areas (with three TVs), 20m pool and sun deck; singles **❷**, doubles **❸**, triples **❹**, but no dorms.
YHA, 3km up the coast at 230 Coolangatta Rd/Gold Coast Highway, Bilinga, near the airport (☎07/5536 7644). Helpful management and nicely located for the quieter beaches, though a bit far from Coolangatta itself. **❷**

Eating, drinking and nightlife
If you're doing your own cooking, there's a 24-hour **convenience store** inside the Beach House complex beside the *Coolangatta Hotel*, and bigger **supermarkets** across the border at the main shopping centre on Wharf Street, in Tweed Heads (for further information on Tweed Heads, see p.311). There are plenty of **snack bars** along Griffith Street; check out *Orbansen's Milk Bar*, at no. 23, for its genuine 1950s decor, which includes a jukebox selector at each table. As for **restaurants**, *Little Malaya Restaurant*, right at the northern end of Marine Parade near the *Coolangatta Sands Hotel*, does an unforgettable crispy-fried whole fish in sour chilli sauce for $23 (enough for two), while the Surf Lifesaving Club down near the border at Greenmount Beach has good-value burgers, salads, sandwiches and cold drinks.

Coolangatta's **nightlife** centres around the pubs – you'll have to rely on posters to find out what's on. Best are sessions at the *Coolangatta Sands Hotel's* fairly relaxed bar (corner of Griffith and McLean streets) and the *Coolangatta Hotel's* nightclub (corner of Griffith and Warner streets), which has live music and pool competitions.

The Hinterland and Scenic Rim

One hundred and twenty kilometres inland from the coast's jangling excesses, the **Scenic Rim** forms a barrier between the coastal flatlands and the pastoral Darling Downs, encompassing a series of mountainous **national parks**. Here you'll find Queensland's largest expanse of subtropical rainforest and – the main attraction – the **Lamington Plateau**, packed with powerfully beautiful scenery, animals and birds. Whether you're a day-tripper, veteran hiker or just fancy camping in the same spot for a few days, it's not to be missed. Closest to the coast, **Springbrook**'s waterfalls and undeveloped pockets at **Mount Tamborine** make easy day-trips and are thus the most-visited destinations, while tough tracks at the region's extremes in the **Main Range** remain the prerogative of experienced bushwalkers.

The Eastern and Central Rim

The **Mount Tamborine–Lamington** area is covered with a network of graded, well-trodden paths, so you don't have to be particularly skilled at **bushwalking** to enjoy the experience. Come prepared, though – tackling the longer or steeper routes requires some degree of **fitness**; test your endurance on shorter walks first. **Paths** are often well marked but sometimes narrow and slippery with little fencing along cliffs and waterfalls, so **footwear** should have a good grip and, ideally, be waterproof. Rain is a year-round possibility; the most comfortable weather conditions occur between June and November, though everything looks its best in the middle of the wet season with waterfalls in full flood and the greenery shockingly intense. If you do visit during the Wet (Jan–March), you'll have to endure rain, deep and fast-flowing rivers, occasionally closed paths and an unwelcome abundance of insects.

Accommodation is largely limited to resorts and campsites, so if you're on a tight budget you'll need a tent. Nights in winter (July–Sept) are always cool enough to warrant a sleeping bag and pullover, though after-dark temperatures can drop even in midsummer. Campsites have water and **stores** nearby, but you'll save money by bringing your own supplies. A **fuel stove** is a good idea – collecting firewood in national parks is forbidden, although there are often barbecues with wood supplied. **Access** to the area is easy enough in itself but because of local geography there are few interconnecting roads, making backtracking unavoidable if you want to visit more than one place. If you can, get hold of a vehicle – only Lamington and Mount Tamborine have a regular bus service – and make sure you take a good **road atlas** along, as signposts to the parks are few and far between. **Tours** visit most locations – see accounts below and also the boxes on p.411 and p.427.

Mount Tamborine

Mount Tamborine's nine fragmentary national parks offer a pleasant introduction to many of the key features of the Hinterland. If you're **driving**, consult a map and aim for North Tamborine township: from Brisbane (75km), leave the Pacific Highway at Beenleigh; from the coast (45km) turn inland at Nerang or Oxenford. There's a daily Coachliner **bus** service from Surfers Paradise (℡07/3236 1239; $27.50), but nothing from Brisbane.

The mountain top is moderately cleared and settled, with remaining patches of forest concentrated around the adjoining compact settlements of **NORTH TAMBORINE** and **EAGLE HEIGHTS**, along with smaller **MOUNT TAMBORINE** 5km south – all quiet, upmarket escapes from lowland suburbia. North Tamborine's services include a general store, garage and **information** centre (more reliable than the frequently unattended National Parks office on the Knoll road); Eagle Heights has a post office, but no banks. From North Tamborine it's between four and six kilometres to the most distant **parks**: Cedar Creek in the north and Lepidozamia Grove south. Cosy **accommodation** is on hand at *The Polish Place*, 333 Main Western Rd, North Tamborine (℡07/5545 1603; self-contained chalet ❽); *Maz's on the Mountain*, 25 Eagle Heights Rd (℡07/5545 1766; suites with four-poster beds, plus pool and surrounding forest; ❺), North Tamborine; and *Tambourine Mountain Bed and Breakfast*, Witherby Crescent, Eagle Heights, which offers sweeping views off the mountain (℡07/5545 3595; ❻).

Once the haunt of the Wangeriburra aborigines, Mount Tamborine's forests were targeted by the timber industry in the late nineteenth century until locals succeeded in getting the area declared as Queensland's first national park in 1908. This event is commemorated by a roadside monument 1km south of North Tamborine, where a three-kilometre track slaloms down to **Witches Falls** through open scrub and rainforest. It's an easy walk, but is more rewarding for the views from the mountain than for the falls themselves, which are only a trickle that disappears over a narrow ledge below the lookout.

The most significant feature of Mount Tamborine's parks is their diversity of native forest types. There's a stand of primitive, slow-growing cycads (see box on p.503) at **Lepidozamia Grove** near Mount Tamborine township, and a piccabean palm forest at **Palm Grove**, near Eagle Heights, which creates a limpid, eerie gloom. Hidden 20m up in the canopy are elusive **wompoo pigeons**, often heard but seldom seen – despite their vivid purple-and-green plumage and onomatopoeic call. Closer to North Tamborine, about 1km north, walking tracks at **Joalah** follow Cedar Creek downstream through woodland to a rock pool; look out for giant epiphytic ferns in the canopy and the **Albert lyrebird**, with its fantastically shaped tail and liquid song. For a break from the heat, the refreshingly cold water of **Cedar Creek Falls**, to the north, tumbles into a wide pool – take your swimming gear. Of the other parks, **MacDonald** at Eagle Heights has a very short walk through typical subtropical rainforest; North Tamborine's environmental park has a stand of **flooded gums**; and there are views to the northwest from **the Knoll**'s picnic tables.

Springbrook National Park

Close to the coast along the New South Wales border, **Springbrook**'s three parks feature abundant waterfalls and swimming holes; though grouped together, access to each section is by a different road. **Mount Cougal** is at the end of a road 21km west of Currumbin. Rainforest flanks the upper reaches of Currumbin Creek, and a path follows the stream to an abandoned sawmill, past pools and pretty cascades. For higher drama and a short, moderately demanding walk, head for **Purling Brook Falls**, a 30km drive from Burleigh Heads via Mudgeeraba. There's a campsite outside the forest, near the top of the falls, with a store about 4km back along the main road. The 109m falls are very impressive after rain has swollen the flow; a four-kilometre track zigzags down the escarpment and into the rainforest at the base of the falls before curving underneath the waterfall (expect a soaking from the spray) and going back up the other side. In the plunge pool at the foot of the falls, the force of the water is enough to push you under; **swimming** is more relaxed in a couple of pools downstream, picturesquely encircled by lianas and red cedar. A ten-kilometre drive beyond the falls brings you to **Best of All Lookout** and a broad vista south to Mount Warning from the very edge of the Rim; on the lookout road, *Springbrook Mountain Lodge* **youth hostel** (T07/5533 5366, Wwww.spring-brook@yhaqld.org; dorms ❶, doubles ❸, cabins ❹) has a fair claim to being the first place in Australia to see the sun each day; note that you should phone ahead for $10 transfer from the Gold Coast, and bring all your own supplies.

At **Natural Bridge** a collapsed cave ceiling beneath the riverbed has created a subterranean waterfall. An exciting but very dangerous leap down the falls will take you into the cave: several people have been killed trying it, and the recommended method is simply to walk in through the mouth, 50m downstream. From the back of the cave the forest outside frames the waterfall and blue plunge pool, surreally lit from above; **glow worms** illuminate the ceiling at night. The park is 49km from Burleigh Heads or Southport via Nerang and about 27km from Purling Brook. For a different tour of the area, Numinbah Valley Adventure Trails is highly recommended for half-day **horseback** rides from the base near Nerang to otherwise inaccessible volcanic caves (pick-up from Surfers accommodation extra; book on T07/5533 4137; $49.50).

Lamington National Park

The Lamington Plateau occupies the northwestern rim of a vast caldera centred on Mount Warning, 15km away in New South Wales. This is **Lamington National Park**, an enthralling world of rainforest-flanked rivers, open heathland and ancient eucalypt woods, and its position on a **crossover zone** between subtropical and temperate climes has made it home to a staggering variety of plants, animals and birds, some forming isolated populations of species found nowhere else.

There are two possible bases: **Binna Burra** on the drier northern edge, and at **Green Mountain** (also known as *O'Reilly's Guesthouse*) in the thick of the forest. Routes come in from Canungra to Green Mountain (37km) and from Beechmont to Binna Burra (10km) – these are narrow, twisting roads cutting through patches of forest and cleared grazing land. From the Gold Coast, turn off at Nerang – roads to both Binna Burra and Green Mountain diverge from here; from Brisbane, leave the highway at Beenleigh – you pass through Canungra to reach Beechmont this way.

Buses run from the Gold Coast or Brisbane, although groups will find it's cheaper to hire a car. When you buy your bus ticket, make it clear whether you want to return the same day or another day: it's also possible to walk between Binna Burra and Green Mountain (see overleaf for details), so you might want to arrange to be dropped at one end and collected at the other. Green Mountain can be reached daily from Surfers Paradise with Mountain Coach Company ($39 return, call first to arrange pick-up; T07/5524 4249) and from Brisbane's Transit Centre with Allstate Scenic Tours ($44 return; no Sat service;

①1300/30 700). Binna Burra's only bus is the *Mountain Lodge*'s Gold Coast service (free call ①1800 074 260 for details).

Once here, Lamington has to be explored **on foot**: most of the tracks described below are clearly signposted and **free maps** are available from local NPWS ranger stations. If you're experienced and want to head off along less-defined paths, contact the rangers first for advice.

Binna Burra

It's some time since guests had to walk the last few kilometres through the steep forest to **BINNA BURRA** with their luggage on a horse. Today, upmarket *Mountain Lodge* (lodge ①07/5533 3622; bookings free call ①1800 074 260; **❼**) has cosy wooden cabins and log fires. The only alternative is the **campsite** (①07/5533 3622) up the road, where you use your own gear or rent one of their on-site tents. Facilities include hot showers and a tearoom aimed at day-trippers, but bread and some basic provisions are also sold. Don't leave food unattended at the campsite – it's infested with brazen scrub turkeys. Hikers can bush camp between February and November; for details contact the **park ranger** (8am–4pm; ①07/5533 3584) at the station, 1.5km before the lodge.

Both lodge and campsite overlook the Numinbah Valley from woodland on the crown of Mount Roberts, and **walking** anywhere always leaves you with an uphill return journey. The lethargic can simply wander 500m between the campsite and the lodge at **night** with a torch to be rewarded by the sight of groups of wallabies grazing on the verges; commotion in the trees betrays the presence of brushtail possums foraging for flowers and leaves. Try the lodge's unique **senses trail**: blind-folded and following a rope you become aware that there's more to the forest than just a blaze of green – you sense a drop in temperature under the canopy, feel the textures of bark and leaves, and receive wafts of scent from the forest floor.

Of the longer walks, try the easy five-kilometre **Caves Circuit**, which follows the edge of the Coomera Valley past the white, wind-sculpted **Talangai Caves** to remains of Aboriginal camps, strands of *psilotum nudum*, a rootless precursor of the ferns, and a hillside of strangler figs and red cedar. Plunging into another forest below the campsite, the harder **Ballunji Falls** track is a typical compromise between access and terrain, with occasional vertical drops to test sure-footedness. Features on the way include views of **Egg Rock** from Bellbird Lookout, at its most mysterious when shrouded in dawn mists, and a stand of majestic forty-metre-tall box brush trees. Dedicated walkers can extend the track out to **Ships Stern**, an arduous and dry 21-kilometre return (allow a minimum of 8hr) with some wonderful views off the escarpment. **Dave's Creek Circuit** is similar but about half as long, crossing bands of rain-forest and sclerophyll before emerging onto heathland. Look for tiny clumps of red sundew plants along the track, which supplement their nitrogen intake by trapping insects in sticky globules of nectar.

Other longer tracks can be joined together, allowing you to spend days hiking without ever returning to base. Most popular of these is the **Border Track**; a relatively easy 21-kilometre/nine-hour (one-way) path through rainforest linking Binna Burra with Green Mountain. If you need road transport between the two, the lodge usually runs a free weekly service to *O'Reilly's* for its guests, and will often take others for a fee if there's room – departures depend on demand, so all arrangements have to be made on site.

Green Mountain

Green Mountain's forests are emphatically the best of the entire Scenic Rim. With so much to dazzle the senses here the initial experience is confused, but gradually the various types of plants and trees become familiar, as do the distinct layers between the rainforest floor and canopy. Random rustles and trills resolve into wallabies thumping around tree roots, scrub turkeys scratching up leaf litter and a whipbird's cracking call; it's easy to become lost in the environment's complex structure.

The road from Canungra to **Green Mountain** ends at *O'Reilly's Guesthouse* (℡07/5544 0644, ℻5544 0638, Ⓦwww.oreillys.com.au; ❽), a splendid and comfortable place opened in 1926 – bookings are advised at weekends and during holiday periods. The guesthouse has a limited store (with EFTPOS facilities) and a moderately priced restaurant for meals and snacks throughout the day. There's also an exposed NPWS **campsite** with showers; call the **ranger's office** (Mon, Wed & Fri 1–3.30pm, staffed part-time by volunteers on weekends; ℡07/5544 0634) for essential advance booking. If you can't get in here, about 7km down the road the rustic *Mt Cainbable Cabins* (no phone; ❼) offers bed and breakfast in four-person cabins, or try the *Canungra Motel* (℡07/5543 5155; ❹) at the bottom of the range.

The **birdlife** near the guesthouse is prolific and distracting: you can't miss the chattering swarms of crimson rosellas mingling with visitors on the lawn, and determined twitchers can clock up over fifty species without even reaching the forest – most spectacular is the black-and-gold **regent bowerbird**. But it's worth pushing on to the **treetop walk** just beyond the clearing, where a suspended walkway swings 15m above ground level. At the halfway anchor point you scale a narrow ladder to vertigo-inducing mesh platforms 30m up the trunk of a strangler fig to see the canopy at eye level. Soaking up the increased sunlight at this height above the forest floor, tree branches become miniature gardens of mosses, ferns and orchids. By night the walkway is the preserve of possums, leaf-tailed geckoes and weird stalking insects.

If you manage only one day-walk at Lamington, make it the exceptional five-hour **Blue Pool/Canungra Creek track** (15km), which features all the jungle trimmings: fantastic trees, river crossings and countless opportunities to fall off slippery rocks and get soaked. The first hour is dry enough as you tramp downhill past some huge red cedars to Blue Pool, a deep, placid waterhole where **platypuses** are sometimes seen on winter mornings; this makes a good walk in itself. After a dip, head upstream along Canungra Creek; the path traverses the river a few times (there are no bridges, but occasionally a fallen tree conveniently spans the water) – look for yellow or red **arrows** painted on rocks that indicate where to cross. Seasonally, the creek can be almost dried up; if the water is more than knee-deep, you shouldn't attempt a crossing and will need to retrace your steps. Follow the creek as far as Elabana Falls and another swimming hole, or bypass the falls; either way, the path climbs back to the guesthouse.

Another excellent trail (17.5km) takes six hours via **Box Creek Falls** to the eastern escarpment at **Toolona Lookout**, on the Border Track to Binna Burra; rewards are a half-dozen waterfalls, dramatic views into New South Wales, and encounters with clumps of moss-covered **Antarctic beech** trees, a strange Gondwanan relict also found in South America. For seasoned, well-equipped walkers, there's a chance to delve into local history by way of an overnight hike to the **Stinson Wreck**. In February 1937 a plane bound for Sydney crashed into dense forest and the survivors were only located due to the incredible efforts of Bernard O'Reilly who, on his own, hiked from the plane to Green Mountain and returned with a rescue party. Nearby is **Westray's grave**, the burial place of one of the passengers who died looking for help, but it's difficult to reach. Today most of the wreck has been carted off by souvenir hunters or covered by jungle, but the guesthouse and park rangers can give you advice on the walk and may be able to put you in touch with bushwalkers who've been there.

The Western Rim

In contrast to the obvious charms of the Eastern Rim, the drier **Western Rim** is mainly given over to open eucalypt woods, with the steep peaks covered in heath. With few facilities, it's a place for serious bushwalkers; on weekends you're likely to meet other hikers at the campsites, but the best way to explore is with a **bushwalking club** (see Brisbane "Listings", p.412). Even "easy" routes are fairly demanding, with few neat paths or signposts – so come equipped, don't walk alone, and carry plenty of water. Access is along the Cunningham and Mount Lindesay highways from Boonah or Beaudesert in the east and Warwick from the west; there's no public transport.

Mount Barney, Main Range and Mount Mistake

Mount Barney's multiple peaks – the taller of which is a respectable 1359m above sea level – form an extremely rough region along the New South Wales border, 45km southwest of Beaudesert. From wherever you're approaching, aim for Rathdowney and then take Barney View Road past Bigriggen to **Yellowpinch**. You can also get here with Araucaria Ecotours (℡07/5544 1283), who run three-day wildlife-spotting trips from Brisbane from $198. You can stay south of Rathdowney at *Mt Barney Lodge*, an excellent old homestead at the foot of Mount Barney with camping, cabin and house **accommodation** (℡07/5544 3233; campsites with hot showers $7 per person, cabins ❺; 2- to 8-person house $220 per weekend). The nearest supplies and alternative camping are at Rathdowney and Bigriggen.

From the car park 5km from Yellowpinch there's a distinct, hour-long track to the **Lower Portals**, a pool on Barney Creek flanked by vertical cliffs. The only other marked hike (though even for this you might need a topographic map) is the misleadingly named "tourist trail" along the south ridge to the saddle between **Mount Barney**'s peaks: be prepared for an exhausting seven-hour return trip from Yellowpinch. Experienced walkers, with permits and advice from the NPWS about current conditions (write to PO Box 121, Boonah; ℡07/5463 5041), could camp in the saddle at **Rum Jungle** and climb the peaks in the morning; the eastern peak is the easier of the two and has the better views across to Mount Lindesay's tor, poking above wooded slopes.

Main Range's precipitous terrain and sharp, progressively higher peaks are most directly accessible along the Cunningham Highway at **Cunningham's Gap**, between Brisbane and Warwick, about 90km from Boonah. Here you'll find some of the easier trails: tracks through rainforest along West Gap Creek and ascents of Bare Rock and Mount Mitchell, which you could complete in a couple of hours or a day, depending on your inclination. There's an NPWS **campsite** at the Gap (℡07/4666 1133); call in advance to check on conditions. **Mount Mistake** is an undeveloped park on the junction of three mountain ranges which form the northernmost extent of the Scenic Rim. Walking is said to be tricky but well worth the effort; if you're tempted, contact the NPWS on ℡07/4666 1133.

The Sunshine Coast

The **Sunshine Coast**, stretching north of Brisbane to **Noosa**, is a more pedestrian version of the Gold Coast, where largely domestic tourist development is tempered by, and sometimes combined with, agriculture. Much local character is due to the lack of death taxes in Queensland – something which, together with the pleasant climate, attracts retirees from all over Australia. The towns tend to be bland places, lively enough at Christmas, but out of season you may be hard pushed to find much to do after dark. Even so, the beaches and surf are good, improving in character as you go further north and providing an excuse to linger for a few days. And though you'll find the Hinterland far tamer than it is down south, it still has some arresting landscapes and scattered hamlets rife with Devonshire cream teas and weekend markets.

Without your own **transport**, the easiest way through the area is by **bus** – Sunshine Coast Sunbus (℡07/5492 8700) is the local alternative to the national operators – or on a **tour** from Brisbane or the Gold Coast. Brisbane's expanding **Citytrain** network can also take you into the region, with stops at the Glasshouse Mountains, Woombye, Nambour and Eumundi, from where there's a connecting bus to Noosa. There's also the Sunshine Coast **airport** just north of Maroochydore, serving Brisbane, Sydney and Melbourne. For the intrepid, Adventures Sunshine Coast (℡07/5444 8824) organizes day-trips **climbing** in the Glasshouse Mountains, **bushwalking** the Obi Obi gorge in the Blackall Range, or **canoeing** the Mooloolah River south of Maroochydore ($95 per person, including lunch and pick-up from lodgings along the coast).

Caboolture, the Glasshouse Mountains and Mooloolaba

Caboolture marks the start of the Sunshine Coast, 40km north of Brisbane. There's no reason to stop here, but 10km north are the **Glasshouse Mountains**: nine dramatic, isolated pinnacles, visible from as far away as Brisbane. Catching sight of them from the sea, Captain Cook named them after their shape and "elevation", a resemblance that's obscure today. You can reach them along the old highway 16km north from Caboolture or off the new one 10km north of Beerburrum; Sunbus stops at the Glasshouse Mountains turn-off; and the Citytrain from Brisbane stops at Beerburrum and Glass House Mountains townships. **Accommodation** and camping in the area is at *Log Cabin Caravan Park* (℡07/5496 9338; cabins ❸), south of Glass House Mountains township at the foot of Mount Tibrogargan.

To the Kabi Aborigines, the mountains are the petrified forms of a family fleeing the incoming tide; their names for the peaks – Tibrogargan, Tibberoowuccum and Beerwah, for instance – are far more evocative than Cook's. The peaks themselves vary enormously: some are rounded and fairly easy to scale, while a couple have vertical faces and sharp spires requiring competent climbing skills. It's worth conquering at least one of the easier peaks; the views are superb and the mountains are one of the few really special places on the Sunshine Coast. **Beerburrum**, overlooking the township of the same name, and **Ngungun**, near Glass House Mountains township, are two of the easiest to climb, with well-used tracks; the latter's views and scenery outclass some of the tougher peaks and it will take you only two hours there and back, though the lower parts of the track are steep and slippery. **Tibberoowuccum** must be climbed from the northwest, though otherwise the only special equipment you'll need is a map; ask at the *Log Cabin Caravan Park* for directions. The taller mountains – Tibrogargan and Beerwah (the highest at 556m) – are at best tricky, and Coonowrin should be attempted only by experienced climbers after contacting the NPWS, 61 Bunya Rd, Maleny (℡ 07/5494 3983), for more information.

Mooloolaba and around

Thirty kilometres north of the Glasshouse Mountains, Maroochydore, Alexandra Headland and Mooloolaba are gradually filling the foreshore between the Mooloolah and Maroochy rivers with an amoeba-like blob of high-rise units. But for once there are things to do to fill in time between sun-bathing sessions.

Southernmost is **MOOLOOLABA**, where the kitsch, touristy **Mooloolaba Wharf** and the pedestrianized seafront Esplanade, thick with boutique shops and restaurants, are the central focus. Nearby, on Parkyn Parade, **Underwater World** (daily 9am–6pm, last entry at 5pm; $21.50) has superb saltwater and freshwater tanks where barramundi – fish revered by Queensland anglers for their taste and legendary fighting spirit – and sharks, turtles and inoffensive freshwater crocodiles stare blankly at you through huge windows. For the real thing, Scuba World (℡ 07/5444 8595), just around the corner on Parkyn Parade, can train you or take you **diving** to local sandstone terrain, where you'll find nudibranch, soft corals and bottom-dwelling sharks, or up to **Wolf Rocks** – one of the best dive sites in Southeast Queensland – for bigger game. Sixty-minute **canal cruises** ($10), taking in some rather opulent waterfront real estate, operate from the wharf three times a day.

For budget **accommodation** in Mooloolaba, head to *Mooloolaba Beach Backpackers*, about 250m back from the waterfront at 75 Brisbane Rd (℡ 07/5444 3399, ⓦ www.mooloolababackpackers.com.au; ❶), a new, well-run place which organizes tours of the Sunshine Coast region (including abseiling in the Glasshouse Mountains and surfing tuition). Most of the other accommodation options are 3km north of Mooloolaba, past **Alexandra Headland**, at **MAROOCHYDORE**. At the bottom end of the market, try *Cotton Tree Caravan Park* on Cotton Tree Parade, Maroochydore (❶–❸); for hostels there are *Suncoast Backpackers Lodge* at 50 Parker St, Maroochydore (℡ 07/5443 7544, ⓔ vip_suncoast@hotmail.com; ❶), and the YHA close to the Maroochy River on Schirrmann Drive (℡ 07/5443 3151, ⓔ gharris_yha@hotmail.com; ❶), both of which offer a free pick-up from Maroochydore, free loans of surfboards, bikes and fishing gear, and trips to hinterland towns and the Sunshine Coast Brewery for tours and tasting. **Motels** include *Sunshine Motor Inn*, 122 Alexandra Parade, Alexandra Headland (℡ 07/5443 6899; ❹), and *Blue Waters Motel*, 64 Sixth Ave, Maroochydore (℡ 07/5443 6700; ❻), both with spacious rooms, sea views and easy access to the beach. **Eating** options are everywhere, though *Mooloolaba Surf Club*'s smart café, bar and restaurant on the Esplanade (daily noon–2pm & 6pm–late, Sun from 8am) is worth a visit for views out over the surf, and *Karakas* at no. 59, has fiery Mexican cooking and **live music** through the week. *Mooloolaba Hotel*, also on the Esplanade, hosts rock bands every Friday and Saturday, and opens its doors as a **nightclub** on Sundays;

the *Alexandra Hotel*, on the highway at Alexandra Headland, is another venue for big-name bands.

Nambour to Noosa

Bisected by tramways from surrounding sugar plantations, **NAMBOUR** sits inland from Maroochydore in the centre of the Sunshine Coast's farming community. Five kilometres south between the highway and **Woombye** lurks the Sunshine Plantation (daily 9am–5pm; free except rides; ☎07/5442 1333) overshadowed by its renowned, ridiculous **Big Pineapple**; activities include trips around the plantation on a cane train and, of course, climbing the fibreglass fruit. Woombye is a stop on Brisbane's Citytrain network, or Sunshine Coast Coaches can bring you here from Nambour.

A two-hour circuit drive from Nambour into the **Hinterland** along the Blackall Range takes you into a rural English-like idyll quite unexpected in subtropical Queensland. Fields are dotted with herds of pied dairy cattle, and "villages" such as **WOODFORD** – with its annual **folk festival** over Christmas and New Year – **MONTVILLE** and **MAPLETON** are thick with potteries and tearooms and occasional long views over rolling green hills to the coast. After rain it's worth stretching your legs to reach a couple of respectably sized **waterfalls** up here: **Kondalilla**, 3km from Montville, with swimming holes along **Obi Obi Creek**; and **Mapleton Falls**, just west of Mapleton, where the river plunges over basalt cliffs.

Approaching from Nambour along the highway, you can reach Noosa by turning coastwards at **EUMUNDI**, a tiny town also on the Citytrain line best known for its Saturday **market**, reputed to be the biggest and best in Australia, and as the original home of Eumundi Beer (now shifted elsewhere). An appealing place to overnight here is *Taylor's Damn Fine B & B* (☎07/5442 8685; ❽), an old Queenslander home filled with an extraordinary array of European "kitsch" and collectables – one separate guestroom is a beautifully renovated railway caboose. Otherwise, the turn-off for **Cooroy** sees you entering Noosa along the river via **Tewantin**. Approaching from Maroochydore up the coastal road, the journey is half as long, passing unevenly spaced townships; coming this way, *Coolum Beach Budget Accommodation* at 1862 David Low Way, Coolum (☎07/5471 6666; dorms ❶, doubles ❸), is a very clean and well laid out place to pull up for a couple of days of beach life.

Noosa

The exclusive end of the Sunshine Coast and an established celebrity "des-res" area, **NOOSA** is dominated by an enviably beautiful headland, defined by the mouth of the placid Noosa River and a strip of beach to the south. Popular since surfers first came in the 1960s to ride fierce waves around the headland, the setting compensates for any neon and concrete in town. It's also a starting point for trips to Cooloola National Park and Fraser Island directly north (see p.450), attractions that tend to overshadow Noosa's own sand, pleasant river scenery and tiny national park.

"Noosa" is a loose term covering three merging satellite settlements: **NOOSAVILLE** and the town centre at **NOOSA HEADS**, which between them stretch 7km west along the river from the headland to **Tewantin** – a distinct township in its own right with access to the wilds of Cooloola – and the discreet suburb of **SUNSHINE BEACH** on the headland's south side. You'll find the best sand and surf at **Noosa Beach**, which runs parallel to chic

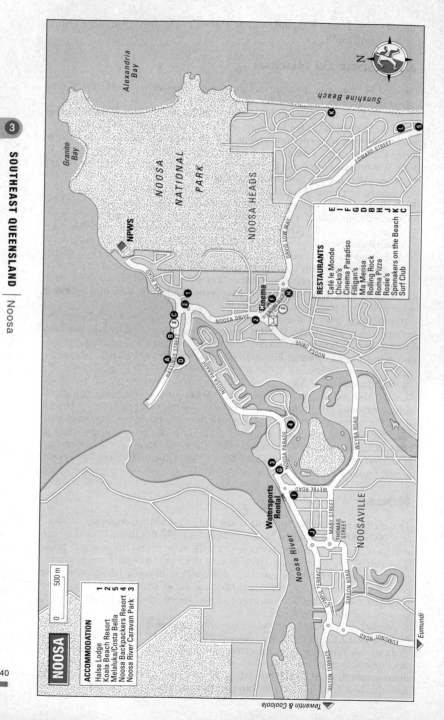

NOOSA

ACCOMMODATION
Halse Lodge — 1
Koala Beach Resort — 2
Melaluka/Costa Bella — 5
Noosa Backpackers Resort — 4
Noosa River Caravan Park — 3

RESTAURANTS
Café le Monde — E
Chicko's — I
Cinema Paradiso — F
Filligan's — G
Ma Mensa — D
Rolling Rock — B
Roma Pizza — H
Rosie's — J
Spinnakers on the Beach — K
Surf Club — C

Hastings Street at Noosa Heads, and at the longer, less crowded **Sunshine Beach**; both are patrolled. All three suburbs are connected by a bus service (Sunbus), which goes by every twenty minutes or so between 5am and 9pm, with service extended to midnight at weekends. Sunshine Beach Road at Noosa Heads is the main street, with banks, restaurants, shops and a supermarket; Noosaville has stores along the river and a sizeable shopping centre, and there are more shops at Sunshine Beach.

More natural attractions can be found around the Noosa River and in the modest national park. The **Noosa River** deposits low, muddy islands as it passes Tewantin and Noosaville, emptying into the sea at Laguna Bay, where there's a splendid, 500m-long white-sand **beach** with views north up the coast to Cooloola National Park (see p.444) off the roundabout at Hastings Street. In the late afternoon, half of Noosa promenades further west along Gympie Terrace as the sinking sun colours a gentle tableau: mangroves on the opposite shore, pelicans eyeing anglers for scraps and landing clumsily midstream, and everything from cruise boats to windsurfers and kayaks out on the water. With a spare day you can **cruise** or **canoe** (if you're energetic and start early enough) upstream to shallow lakes **Cooroibah** and **Cootharaba** (see p.445), or just paddle around, fish at the river mouth or rent a **jet ski** and have fun getting soaked (see box below for rental outlets). If you just want to take a quick ride along the river and don't want to fork out for a tour, hop on the Noosa **ferry**, which runs 6 times daily (10am–6pm) from the Sheraton Noosa Jetty off Hastings Street to Tewantin; it costs $10 for the hour-long return journey.

Noosa's small **national park** is worth a look for its mix of mature rainforest, coastal heath and fine beaches – **Granite Bay** and **Alexandria Bay** ("swimwear optional") have good sand pounded by unpatrolled surf – all reached along graded paths. These start from the picnic area at the end of Park Road (a continuation of Hastings St), where you'll probably see **koalas** in gum trees above the car park.

SOUTHEAST QUEENSLAND | Noosa

Noosa activities

Noosa's original reason to be was the surf, and if you know what you're doing you'll find all the necessary gear at Surf World, 34 Sunshine Beach Rd, Noosa Heads (☎07/5447 3538). If the only surfing you've ever done is on the Net, find out what the real thing is like with Learn to Surf (☎0418 787 577) or Wavesense (☎07/5474 9076) – they can be hard to get hold of, but are worth the effort.

Cruising the Noosa River is a more sedate way to pass time in the area. Blue Laguna (☎07/5449 0799) and Noosa River Cruises, Gympie Terrace, Noosaville (☎07/5449 7362), have day-tours on the river and lakes for around $58. To get as far as Lake Cootharaba, Everglades Express (☎07/5449 9422) and Everglades Waterbus, Harbour Town Complex, Tewantin (☎07/5447 1838), have half-day cruises upriver for around $49 – full-day tours for $95 add a 4WD run along Rainbow Beach.

For water sports, Pelican Boat Hire, on the river bank at Gympie Terrace (☎07/5449 7239), has canoes and surf skis at $9 for the first hour ($4.50 per hour after that); Pro Ski (☎07/5449 7740), in the same place, has waterskiing at $72 for 30min, $110 for 1hr, including instruction for novices, and jet skis at $55 for 30min. Kingfisher Boat Hire (☎07/5449 9353), at the Harbour Town Complex in Tewantin, rents out fishing boats with fuel, rods, bait pumps, crab pots, ice boxes and the rest, for around $18 an hour. If it's diving you're after, Scuba Addict, cnr Project Avenue and Venture Drive, Noosaville (☎07/5449 8503), and Noosa Blue Water Dive, Gympie Terrace, Noosaville (☎07/5447 1300), offer all levels of training, gear hire, shore dives and regular trips out to the legendary Wolf Rock.

Information and accommodation

Noosa's several **information** offices – most of them in Noosa Heads on David Low Way – seem to consider customers a profound nuisance. Try your accommodation, or the sole friendly office, on the roundabout in Hastings Street.

Hostels have courtesy buses for beach, town and nightclubs, and all accommodation will help organize activities and tours, from surfing lessons to Cooloola and Fraser Island trips. **Motels** are concentrated along the river between Noosa Heads and Noosaville; some offer weekly rates which might add up to a free night, but prices double during school holidays. A group of four staying a week or two may get better value – and a slice of luxury – by checking with rental agents about deals on furnished apartments outside holiday periods.

Gagaju Call ahead for directions or pick-up (℡07/5474 3522 or 1300/302 271). This is an authentic bush camp near Noosa, with a dozen bunk-beds and space for campers. Created as an eco-friendly "bush experience", everything is built from recycled timber. Canoes and camping equipment, advice on hikes and canoe trips, and fireside bush-poetry readings are among the attractions. Their 3-day canoe trip is highly recommended as an independent adventure experience. ❶

Halse Lodge (YHA), 17 Noosa Drive, Noosa Heads (free call ℡1800 242 567, Ⓦwww.halselodge.com.au). Giant, sprawling, immaculate 1888 Queenslander building in large grounds close to Noosa Beach; definitely not for partying. Often full despite quantity of rooms, so book in advance. Rooms ❸, dorms ❷

Koala Beach Resort, 44 Noosa Drive, Noosa Heads (℡07/5447 3355 or free call 1800 357 457, Ⓦwww.koalaresort.com.au). Central budget accommodation in dorms and motel units.

Nowhere near the beach, and not especially clean, but a party atmosphere and pool, restaurant and bar might compensate. ❶

Melaluka/Costa Bella, 7 Selene St, Sunshine Beach (free call ℡1800 003 663, Ⓦwww.melaluka.com.au). Two levels of comfort: *Melaluka* has comfortable, hostel-like facilities in a low-set building, while *Costa Bella* is a new, well-appointed high-rise development with excellent, self-contained apartment accommodation – one of the best deals in town. Dorms ❶, units ❷

Noosa Backpackers Resort, William St, Noosaville (℡07/5449 8151 or free call 1800 626 673, Ⓦwww.noosabackpackers.com.au). A small, well-appointed hostel with tours, pool, canoe-, bike- and board-rental. A decent breakfast included, and budget meals on offer from 6pm every night. ❶

Noosa River Caravan Park, Russell St, Noosaville (℡07/5449 7050). Large campsite and van park with splendid river views, but with no cabins or on-site vans. Tent sites ❶

Eating, drinking and nightlife

Noosa's three communities – surfers, retirees and tourists – seldom share the same enthusiasms; evenings tend to be spent with your own crowd. This doesn't seem to affect the nightlife, though, and eating out in particular is pursued as a serious pastime. Hastings Street has long been the place to dine and be seen in Noosa, but soaring rents have seen some excellent eateries relocate to Noosaville, where you'll now find lots of casual diners checking out the places clustered along Gympie Terrace and Thomas Street.

Café le Monde, Hastings St, Noosa Heads (℡07/5449 2366). Slightly snobbish street atmosphere and a mainly international menu – try the *le Monde* salad at $13.50. Open 7am for cappuccino; happy hour Mon–Fri 4–6pm; live music evenings except Mon & Wed.

Chicko's, 281 Gympie Terrace, Noosaville. Unquestionably *the* place for fish and chips; open daily 9am–8pm.

Cinema Paradiso, Sunshine Beach Rd, next to the cinema, Noosa Heads. Outdoor eating and good-

sized portions of sirloin, rack of lamb and salads from around $13; check out the $17 meal-and-film deal.

Filligan's, 9 Russell St, Noosaville (℡07/5449 8811). Fish and a variety of other tasty dishes with a slight Asian influence (around main courses around $17–22). With an appealingly casual, holiday ambience it's extremely popular, so book ahead. Open for lunch and dinner every day.

Ma Mensa, Hastings St. Obligatory Italian bistro with outdoor tables, inexpensive for location. Very fine steamed mussels and lamb shanks (around $16); also specializes in pasta dishes ($12).

Noosa Heads Surf Club, on the beach, Hastings St, Noosa Heads. Bar and inexpensive bistro with great views over the beach. Open 11am–midnight.

Rolling Rock, Hastings St, Noosa Heads. A busy, sweaty club featuring discos and bands every night.

Roma Pizza, 36 David Low Way, Noosa Heads. Good-value takeaway pizzeria, plus a trattoria-style restaurant featuring used chianti-bottle decorations and inexpensive pizza and pasta meals.

Rosie's, Gympie Terrace, near the corner of Albert St, Noosaville (℡07/5449 7888). Tiny and intimate BYO place, with a new menu every week. Popular with locals; mains around $17.

Spinnakers on the Beach, *Sunshine Beach Surf Club* (℡07/5474 5177). Recently refurbished surf club, with a bar, restaurant and unbeatable views. Seafood, steaks, pasta and salad – big servings, all in the $10–15 range.

Listings

Banks Located along Sunshine Beach Rd, Noosa Heads.

Bike rental Koala Bike Hire (℡07/5474 2733), and Mammoth Cycles (℡07/5474 3322) rent mountain bikes from $20 a day, including delivery to your accommodation.

Buses There's no actual bus station for long-distance buses. Drop-off and pick-up points are at the junction of Noosa Parade and Noosa Drive.

Camping supplies and rental Outdoor Store, 28 Sunshine Beach Rd, Noosa Heads (℡07/5447 2688), has all you'll need for Fraser Island and Cooloola.

Car rental Allterrain, 91 Noosa Drive, Noosa Heads (℡07/5449 0877), Sunrover Rentals, at the marina in Tewantin (℡07/5449 7833), and

Sunshine 4WD (℡07/5447 3702), next to the Noosa post office, have five-seater 4WDs from $155 per day plus deposit. For a conventional runaround vehicle, try Virgin (℡07/5474 5777) or Henry's (℡07/5447 3777).

Cinema Sunshine Beach Rd, Noosa Heads (℡07/5449 2255).

NPWS Park Rd, at Noosa National Park's picnic area (℡07/5447 3243).

Pharmacy Noosa Heads Day and Night Pharmacy, Hastings St. Daily until 9pm.

Police 48 Hastings St (℡07/5474 5255 or 5447 5888).

Post office Noosa Drive, Sunshine Beach Rd end (Mon–Fri 9am–5pm, Sat 9am–12.30pm).

Taxis ℡13 1008.

The Cooloola Coast and Fraser Island

Halfway between Brisbane and the tropics, the **Cooloola Coast** and **Fraser Island** between them cover over 190km of the coastline north from Noosa, forming a world of giant dunes, forests, coloured sands and freshwater lakes where fishing and four-wheel driving take precedence over the more usual beach activities. But it doesn't have to be a macho tangle with the elements: for once it's relatively easy and inexpensive to hire tents and a 4WD and set off to explore in some comfort.

Europeans were initially unimpressed with this part of the coast, but abundant fresh water, seafood and plants must have supported a very healthy **Aboriginal population**; campfires along the beach allowed Matthew Flinders to navigate Fraser Island at night in 1802. Flinders labelled the region as "the **Great Sandy Peninsula**" on his maps, though he suspected that Fraser Island was in fact separated from the mainland. The Queensland government declared the area an Aboriginal reserve in the early 1860s but, with the discovery of **gold** at **Gympie** in 1867, Europeans flocked into the region in their thousands. This influx, and the economic boom that went with it, saved the fledgling Queensland from bankruptcy, but brought the usual racial conflicts, and the reserve gradually became little more than a holding pen for tribal survivors from all over the state. They were devastated by disease, and the last few were relocated to other reserves around Queensland at the start of the twentieth century so the area could be opened up for recreation.

Sand mining and **logging** are other incendiary topics here and there's a predictable split between conservationists and those people who count on local industries for their livelihood. **Forestry** is a particularly bitter issue; the inland town of Maryborough was built on timber felling, and logging bans have aroused fury at what is seen as a sell-out to the Green movement. Locals, too, once drawn to the area for its natural appeal, now feel crowded out by regulations made to protect the coast from overuse by 4WDs and by drunken campers leaving piles of garbage behind them. While it's unlikely that any of this will have a negative impact on a brief visit, a balance between protection and "development" – a word with almost religious connotations in Queensland – is far from being established.

Orientation and access

The first thing to decide is where to start. Cooloolah comprises two regions: the inland region around **Cooroibah and Cootharaba lakes**, and the **beach** running north for 40km towards the lower end of Fraser Island and the small township of **Rainbow Beach**. The lakes and the southern end of the beach can be accessed directly from Teewantin, on the river 7km west of Noosa. Unless you drive up the beach from here – for which you'll need a 4WD – Rainbow Beach and northern Cooloola can only be reached 75km off Highway 1 from the inland town of Gympie, itself around 60km from Noosa. **Access to Fraser Island** is by ferry from Rainbow Beach (Inskip Point) in the south, or from the town of **Hervey Bay** in the north, 90km beyond Gympie.

Tours around the area run from Noosa, Rainbow Beach and Hervey Bay, though given the grand scale of the region they're inevitably rushed. The wildlife and overall serenity of the area are elusive, to say the least, unless you get away from the more popular places, camp for the night and explore early on in the day. Assembling a group and hiring a 4WD is one way to do this, with hostels in Hervey Bay well experienced in arranging this type of tour for Fraser Island. Another is simply **walking**, an alternative ignored by almost all visitors, but one which allows unequalled access and intimacy with the region.

Unless you're on a tour, you'll definitely need **maps**, with many available from local garages and newsagents. Relevant sheets on national parks, available from the NPWS, supplement these. **Drivers** need **tide timetables**, as most beaches are only reliably negotiable at low tide. Rain won't ruin your stay – in fact it makes driving on sand far easier and enhances the colours – though in rough conditions services to Fraser might be cancelled, leaving you stranded.

The Cooloola Coast

The southern end of the **Cooloola Coast** is dominated by features of the Noosa River which pools into lakes **Cootharaba** and **Cooroibah** as it nears Tewantin, while stands of commercial timber and dry sclerophyll woodland cover the interior, rising to dunes along the beach stabilized by scrubby heath. The beach runs straight north from Tewantin to **Double Island Point** and then curves west to Rainbow Beach township, where it's backed by vertical, coloured-sand cliffs whose weathered contours and tones constantly change with the shifting sun. Below, the windswept strip of sand separating land from sea becomes a 4WD highway at low tide, with brightly coloured flashes of canvas marking where the cliffs are low enough to form a protective foreshore suitable for camping. Most of the beach and interior north of Cootharaba is **national park**, as is the lake's shoreline.

Before you head in, note that **four-wheel drive** is essential for the beach, and the access roads leading to it – see Noosa "Listings", p.443 for car rental. Conventional vehicles can manage the lake road from Tewantin in the south, and Rainbow Beach from Gympie in the north – both of which are good places to use as bases for day-walks if you don't have the right vehicle. **Hiking**, you'll find the easiest path along the beach, but it makes things more interesting if you head inland at some stage. For the well equipped, walking tracks head upstream from Elanda Point, past the top of Lake Cootharaba and along the forty-kilometre **Cooloola Wilderness Trail**, or towards the coast – contact the NPWS first for maps and an idea of conditions.

The lakes

Cooroibah and its larger and more northerly neighbour **Cootharaba** are joined by a winding six-kilometre stretch of the Noosa River. Placid, and fringed with paperbarks and reedbeds, the lakes look their best at dawn before there's any traffic; they're saltwater and average just 1m in depth, subject to tides. At Cootharaba's top end, Kin Kin Creek and the Noosa River spill lazily into the lake through thickets of mangroves, hibiscus and ti-trees – the so-called **Everglades**. A boardwalk from **Kinaba's information centre** at the northern end of the lake leads to a hide where you can spy on birdlife, and there's more on nearby **Fig Tree Lake**. The picnic area here is a former corroboree ground, which featured in the saga of Eliza Fraser (see p.450).

Beyond here, there's a footpath – or it's an easy paddle – on up the **Narrows** to **Harry Spring's Hut**. A campsite on the edge of the forest here is a gateway to Cooloola's interior: about another 8km upstream are navigable by canoe, and walking tracks mark the start of the Cooloola Wilderness Trail, a three-day hike up to the road at Rainbow Beach. Shorter trails also head across the river from here – you'll have to swim – and through forested dunes to the beach; an exhausting day-trip.

To reach the lakes from Tewantin, turn off the main road onto Werin Street at the school – there is a sign, but it's easy to miss – then turn left again and follow the signposts. The 20km-long road follows the western side of the lakes to Kinaba, with turn-offs along the way to **Boreen Point** and **Elanda Point** townships, both on Cootharaba. **Accommodation** is at **campsites** in either, or there's bush camping at *Harry Spring's Hut* (see above); at Boreen Point, *Lakeside Lodge* (☎07/5485 3127; ④) has comfortable doubles. **Supplies** are available at Boreen Point – where there's fuel, a general store, hotel and telephones – or at Elanda Point's small general store. The township's campsites also **rent canoes** or flat-bottomed tinnies, or you can link up with a river tour from Noosaville (see box p.441).

The coast

To reach the southern end of the beach from Tewantin, catch the vehicle **ferry** from the top of Moorindil Street (daily 6am–10pm or later; cars $4 one-way;

pedestrians free), which lands you about five-minutes' drive from the sea. There's **accommodation** 2km along near Lake Cooroibah's otherwise inaccessible eastern shore at *Lake Cooroibah Holiday Park*, PO Box 220, Tewantin (℡ 07/5447 1225 or 5447 1706); family-oriented, and with every activity from horse riding to canoeing and tennis, they offer camping ($7.50 per person) and caravans (❹), as well as suites and cottages for up to eight people (❻–❽), plus all the associated facilities.

Otherwise, press on to the beach. The powdery foredunes at the end of the road look too small to worry about, but even in a 4WD you won't be the first to get stuck driving through them; a basic **campsite** here has fine views of Noosa, but this close to town things can get busy. From here you have a straight, 40km-run of uninterrupted sand, backed by steep, forested dunes to play with. Just make sure you know what the local **tides** are doing, and remember that steep dunes means that there are no exits off the beach until you reach the **campsite** at **Freshwater Creek** (where there's a boggy patch of quicksand to be avoided), 30km along. For most of the way there's little to look out for in particular, though **coloured sands** are a feature of the region – particularly the northern end of the beach – caused by minerals leaching down the cliffs from above leaving broad bands of orange, red and white. There's also the **shipwreck** of the *Cherry Venture*, grounded just north of Freshwater Creek in 1973 and now eroded down to a rusting frame and funnel.

From Freshwater Creek you can reach Rainbow Beach by either negotiating a rutted, scarred track which runs up off the beach and inland through gum woodland to the township; or by carrying on up the beach, around it's northern extremity at **Double Island Point** – when **Fraser Island** first fills the horizon – and then turning west along the sand for the final 5km or so.

RAINBOW BEACH itself is a small, slowly developing township and access point for Fraser's southern reaches at the end of the sealed road to Gympie and the highway; there's a post office, service station, hotel and shops, and **accommodation** at *Rainbow Beach Holiday Village* (℡ 07/5486 3222; ❶–❹), with tents, on-site vans, one-bedroom villas and two-bedroom chalets; *Rainbow Beach Hotel* (℡ 07/5486 3125; ❹) has motel rooms; and both *The Rocks* (℡ 07/5486 3711; ❷) and *Rainbow Beach Backpackers* (℡ 07/5486 3288; ❶), at *Rainbows Restaurant*, offer budget beds. Accommodation can line up Fraser Island **safaris** from Rainbow Beach lasting one to three days, or contact Sun Safari Tours (℡ 07/5486 3154, ⓦ www.fraser-is.com), who run day-trips to Central Station and Lake Birrabeen ($72). For **4WD hire**, Safari (℡ 07/5486 3485) offer five-seater off-roaders from about $100 per day, and can sort out packages including all vehicle permits for Fraser Island – for more on which, see p.451.

Heading on, Gympie and the highway are 80km away; if you don't have your own transport, there's a very slow local **bus** to Gympie (Mon–Fri 7.30am & 3.45pm, returning 6am & 1.30pm). The Fraser Island **ferry** leaves Inskip Point, 10km north of Rainbow Beach, for the fifteen-minute crossing to Hook Point on the island's south coast (daily 7am–4.30pm; $70 return per vehicle, $12 for foot passengers; ℡ 07/5486 3227): drivers should note that this is a very difficult landing and should only be attempted if you have sound 4WD experience. You'll also need a **permit** for the island from the NPWS on the Rainbow Beach road (daily 7am–4pm; ℡ 07/5486 3160; see p.451 for more about Fraser Island permits and practicalities), and your own transport to Inskip Point.

Hervey Bay

Back on the highway and heading north, it's a couple of hours to Hervey Bay past **GYMPIE** and **MARYBOROUGH**, historic gold and timber communities and now healthy market towns with handsome stone and wooden period buildings in their centres testifying to their wealthy past. **HERVEY BAY**, a rapidly expanding sprawl of coastal suburbs, has no such pretentions, and the only reason to visit is to join the throng crossing to Fraser Island – or to venture into the bay to spot **whales** in the spring. **Pialba** is the centre, with shops strung along the Esplanade as it runs 7km from here east through **Scarness** and **Torquay** to **Urangan** harbour and **marina**; barges and tours to Fraser Island leave from here and from River Heads, 17km south. **Approaching** Hervey Bay from the south, turn off at Maryborough; from the north, leave the highway at Howard. The **bus station** is at **Bay Central** shopping complex, just off the main road into town about 1km from Pialba; the **airport** is about 5km south of Urangan off Booral Road, on the way to River Heads. Hervey Bay has a fairly decent **local bus service**, circuiting around town from Bay Central between about 6am and 6pm, though you'll need a **taxi** for the airport (☎13 1008; $10–15). Almost every place to stay provides information and makes bookings, but you'll get more reliable, pressure-free help from the **tourist information** office right next to the bus station (Mon–Fri 6am–5.30pm, Sat–Sun 6.30am–1pm; ☎07/4124 8244).

Whale-watching from Hervey Bay

Humpbacked whales are among the most exciting of marine creatures to encounter: growing to 16m long and 36 tonnes, they make their presence known from a distance by their habit of "breaching" – making spectacular, crashing leaps out of the water – and expelling jets of spray as they exhale. Prior to 1952 an estimated ten thousand whales made the annual journey between the Antarctic and tropics to breed and give birth in shallow coastal waters; a decade later whaling had reduced the population to just two hundred animals. Now protected, their numbers are increasing and you're fairly likely to see one if you put out to sea between Brisbane and the Whitsundays during the **whale-watching season** In Hervey Bay, this lasts only from late July until October, however; the whales follow the coast, and because Fraser Island leans outwards they're deflected away from Hervey Bay coming up from the south, but get funnelled into its constricted waters when returning. The town makes the most of their visit with an August **Whale Festival** and operators are always searching for new gimmicks to promote **day-cruises** and **flights** In perfect conditions you'll see whales breach, swim directly under the boat and raise their heads out of the water, close enough to touch. You might also, of course, see nothing at all. Whether all this voyeurism disturbs the animals is unclear, but they seem at least tolerant of the attention paid to them.

For **flights**, try Air Fraser Island (☎07/4125 3600); the cost is from $55 per person (depending on the number of passengers) for a thirty-minute buzz. **Cruises** last for a morning or a full day, costing upwards of $65–80 per person, and are booked through an agent; some get very crowded – check the boat size and how many will be going. *Princess II* (the cheapest vessel), *Tasman Venture II*, *Hombre*, *Whalesong* and *Volante III* all come recommended, while *Spirit of Hervey Bay* (the most expensive) has the bonus of being a glass-bottomed vessel. For the added pleasure of sailing out to the whales, make arrangements with the yacht *Stefanie* through your booking agents, or free call ☎1800 650 776.

Watersports enthusiasts with time to kill might want to take advantage of Torquay Beach Hire, on the Esplanade at Torquay, which has it all – from surf skis to windsurfers and outboard-driven tinnies for a day's **fishing**. More sedentary folk could indulge in a beach bonfire, while nature lovers can search out **echidna** in the vegetation strip between the Esplanade and beach, or visit **Natureworld** ($12.50), about 2km back from Pialba on the way to the highway, whose stars include freshwater crocs, snakes, wombats and koalas.

Accommodation

Accommodation is packed during the whale-watching season (July–Oct) and at Christmas and Easter (when motel prices can double). Most places will pick you up from the bus station, and all can organize tours to Fraser, with the hostels specializing in putting together budget self-drive packages. If you're **camping**, the best van parks are on the Esplanade at Torquay ($15 per tent), and the huge *Pialba Caravan Park* on the corner of Main Street and the Esplanade on the foreshore in Pialba (℡ 07/4128 1399; $15 per tent).

Bay Bed & Breakfast, 180 Cypress St, Urangan (℡ 07/4125 6919). Hugely friendly, home-style accommodation with excellent rooms and discounted weekly rates. ❺

Bayview Motel, 399 Esplanade, Torquay (℡ 07/4128 1134). Not much to look at from outside, but the rooms are spotless and the friendly owners can't do enough for you. Rooms ❸

Beaches, 195 Torquay Rd, Torquay (℡ 07/4124 1322, ⓦ www.beaches.com.au). Busy party hostel with lively bar/bistro and cheerful staff, one street back from the Esplanade. ❶

Beachside Motor Inn, 298 Esplanade, Scarness (℡ 07/4124 1999). Comfortable motel units with beach views. ❺

Boomerang Beach House, 335 Esplanade, Scarness (℡ 07/4124 3970). Quiet, tidy rooms. Nothing fancy but good value. Four-person rooms ❹

Colonial Backpackers Resort (YHA), cnr Pulgul St and Boat Harbour Drive, near Urangan Harbour, Urangan (℡ 07/4125 1844 or free call 1800 818 280). Tidy, comfortable and well run, though even double rooms are pretty bare, and you have to leave deposits for everything except the bed. Spacious grounds, with a bar, pool and restaurant, plus tame wildlife, might compensate. Rooms ❹, dorms ❷

Friendly Hostel, 182 Torquay Rd, Scarness (℡ 07/4124 4107). Very homely, secure guesthouse, with small dorms and nice, family atmosphere. Rooms ❷, dorms ❶

Koala Backpackers, 408 Esplanade, Torquay (℡ 07/4125 3601 or free call 1800 354 535, ⓦ www.koalaresort.com.au). Recently renovated rooms, large grounds, and party atmosphere; close to the shops. Rooms ❸, dorms ❶

Oceanic Palms, 50 King St, Urangan (℡ & ℻ 07/4128 9562). Quiet, small and welcoming bed and breakfast, with a pool and orchid-laden garden. Doubles with or without bathroom ❺ –❻

Palace, 184 Torquay Rd, Scarness (℡ 07/4124 5331 or free call 1800 063 168, ⓔ island@palace-backpackers.com.au). Excellent, purpose-built hostel with its own fleet of 4WDs; all units are roomy and come complete with kitchen and TV, and there's a pool too. Rooms ❸, dorms ❶

Playa Concha, 475 Esplanade, Torquay (℡ 07/4125 1544, ℻ 4125 3413). Comfortable, beachfront motel surrounded by palms and ferns, with a mix of single and double rooms and serviced apartments sleeping up to six people. Doubles ❺, six-person apartment ❼

Woolshed, 181 Torquay Rd, Scarness (℡ 07/4124 0677). Unusual place, with dorms done up in corrigated iron and timber, and hung with Outback iconography. There's a bit of a garden and plenty of off-road parking, and it's all much more roomy than appears from the road. Rooms ❷, dorms ❶

Eating

Apart from **snack bars** and fast-food joints in Pialba, most of the places to eat and spend the evening are along the Esplanade at Torquay.

Beachside Hotel, cnr the Esplanade and Queens St, Scarness. Great bar with open front for sea views.

Black Dog Café, cnr the Esplanade and Denman Camp Rd, Scarness. An odd name for what is actually a small, smart restaurant with heavy Asian leanings – mostly Japanese. *Udon* soup, sushi, and beef teriyaki, sit strangely alongside Cajun fish and Caesar salad. Good value, with mains at $11–15.

Curried Away, 174 Boat Harbour Drive, Pialba (☏07/4124 1577). Half-a-dozen tables, 1960s musak, and takeaway ambience, but the food – genuine Sri Lankan curries – will get your mouth watering. Medium portions of rutu chicken, vegetable samosas, *dhal*, raita and chutney – enough for two – will set you back $22; most mains are around $10. Dine in, take away or have it delivered for free.

Dolly's, 410 Esplanade, Torquay, right next to *Koala's* (☏07/4125 5633). Adorned with 1950s iconography, there's a DJ or live music every night and a range of smorgasbord and all-you-can-eat deals.

Gringo's, 449 Esplanade, Torquay. Good Mexican menu of enchiladas, chilli con carne and nachos, spiced to individual tolerances and with bean fillings as an alternative to meat. Main courses $17. Open daily from 5.30pm.

Le Café, near cnr of the Esplanade and Queens St, Scarness. Inexpensive, cheerful service, with the best coffee in town, and budget "backpackers' specials" such as shepherds pie for around $6. Open 7.30am–2pm & 5–8.30pm.

O'Reileys, 446 Esplanade, Torquay. Savoury pizza, pasta and crepes, but best for fruit pancakes and cream. From $10.

Sails, cnr Fraser St and the Esplanade, Torquay (☏07/4125 5170). Moderately upmarket Mediterranean/Asian influenced dishes, and a good place to splash out a little. Good choices are the Singapore noodles, seafood risotto, or seafood marinara, at around $15–18; some decent vegetarian options too, along with good old Aussie steaks. Alternatively, just plump for their tapas platter and a cocktail. Open for lunch Thurs & Fri, and from 6pm Mon–Sat.

Listings

Airport Air Fraser Island (☏07/4125 3600); Flight West (☏07/4125 4011); Sunstate (☏07/4125 3488) for flights to Fraser and Brisbane. For Lady Elliot island, contact the resort direct (see p.466).

Banks Most banks are in Pialba, with a few scattered along the Esplanade at Torquay.

Bicycles Rayz Pushbike Hire (☏0417 644 814) rents out bikes at $12 a day, with free delivery and pick-up.

Camping equipment Some 4WD operators also rent camping equipment.

Car rental Nifty, 463 Esplanade (free call ☏1800 627 583), has decent runarounds from $29 a day. For 4WDs expect around $90 per day for two-seaters such as a Suzuki, $155 per day for an eight-seater Toyota Landcruiser, including insurance. Aussie Trax, 56 Boat Harbour Drive, Pialba (☏07/4124 4433, ☏4124 4965, ☜www.aussie-trax.com) is probably the most clued-up, longest-running operator in Hervey Bay and puts together

Tours and cruises from Hervey Bay

Not surprisingly, all **tours** from Hervey Bay involve **Fraser Island**; day-trips start around $65, overnight camping trips at about $150. Top Tours (☏07/4125 3933 or free call 1800 624 677) is a little pricey at $82–119 depending on the itinerary, but gives the best one-day tour, with BBQ lunch, new vehicles and first-rate guides – it also seems to work out of phase with rival tours' schedules, so you don't keep bumping into busloads of other visitors. Alternatively, Fraser Venture Tours (☏07/4125 4444) scores slightly higher for its overnight trips with accommodation at Eurong ($165). Otherwise try Wilderness Adventure (☏07/4120 3333, ☏4120 3326), a two-day tour including accommodation at *Kingfisher Bay Resort* ($198); and Sand Island Safaris (free call ☏1800 246 911) for three-days-worth covering most of the island (including accommodation at *Eurong Beach Resort*, $250).

Cruises include Stefanie Yacht Charters (free call ☏1800 650 776, ☜www.stefanie-charters.com.au), who spend 2 days or longer cruising around Fraser's western side, with the chance to see dolphin year-round, do some kayaking and land on the island. The cost is dependent on the number of passengers and the exact itinerary. Outside the whale season, Whalesong (☏07/4125 6222, ☜www.whalesong.com.au) spend four hours around the bay looking for dolphins, turtles and – with real luck – dugong (manatees) at $70 per person. Alternatively, Krystal Clear (☏07/4124 0066) allow four–five hours for snorkelling, coral viewing, and a BBQ lunch on a small sand island in the bay for $56. For **whale-watching** operators see box on p.447.

good value all-inclusive packages; Bay 4WD Centre, 54 Boat Harbour Drive, Pialba (☎07/4128 2981, ℻4124 2723); Heritage Island Explorers, 104 Boat Harbour Drive, Pialba (☎07/4124 3770). For information abour 4WD rental for Fraser Island, see box on p.452.

Diving Diver's Mecca, 403 Esplanade, Torquay (☎07/4125 1626 or free call 1800 351 626, ℮diversmecca@optus.com.au), and Wizzer Diving, at the Urangan marina (☎07/4128 9033, ℻4125 6766, ℮wizzer@atcom.net.au), both offer training and exploration of local sites after turtles, groupers, sea snakes and other marine life.

Internet access Several hostels can oblige, as can the tourist information near the bus station at

Pialba's Bay Central shopping complex ($4 an hour).

Laundry Cnr Esplanade and Frank St, behind *Dot's Food Bar*, Scarness; 7am–7pm.

Pharmacy Day and Night Pharmacy, 418 Esplanade, Torquay (daily 8.30am–8pm).

Police 146 Torquay Rd, Scarness (☎07/4128 5333).

Post office On the Esplanade, Torquay.

Taxi ☎13 1008.

Vehicle lock-up Fraser Coast Secure Vehicle Storage, 629 Esplanade, Urangan (☎ & ℻ 07/4125 2783, ℗www.users.bigpond.com/parkingsafe). Somewhere to leave your vehicle safe and sound if you're heading over to Fraser or Lady Elliot for a while.

Fraser Island

With a length of 123km, **Fraser Island** is the world's largest sand island, but this dry fact does little to prepare you for the experience. Accumulated from sediments swept north from New South Wales over the last two million years, the scenery ranges from silent forests and beaches sculpted by wind and surf, to crystal-clear streams and dark, tannin-stained lakes. The east coast forms a ninety-kilometre razor-edge from which Fraser's tremendous scale can be absorbed as you travel its length; with the sea as a constant, the dunes along the edge seem to evolve before your eyes – in places low and soft, elsewhere hard and worn into intriguing canyons. By contrast, slow progress through the forests of the island's interior creates more subtle impressions of age and permanence – a primal world predating European settlement – brought into question only when the view opens suddenly onto a lake or a bald blow.

The idyllic mood, however, is sobered by a number of factors, most alarming of which is the volume of traffic tearing along the beach and main tracks. The foredunes are trampled and littered with camping detritus, too, and the island has become the epitome of Queensland's environmental conflicts, with conservationists, tour operators, foresters and Aboriginal groups vying for control of resources – at present, Fraser's north end is a World Heritage-listed national park, with the rest in private hands.

To the Kabi Aborigines, Fraser Island is **Gurri** (or K'gari), a beautiful woman so taken with the earth that she stayed behind after creation, her eyes becoming lakes that mirrored the sky and teemed with wildlife so that she wouldn't be lonely. The story behind the European name is far less enchanting. In 1836, survivors of the wreck of the *Stirling Castle*, including Captain Fraser and his wife Eliza, landed at Waddy Point. Though runaway convicts had already been welcomed into Kabi life, the castaways suffered "dreadful slavery, cruel toil and excruciating tortures", and after the captain's death Eliza was presented as a prize during a corroboree at Lake Cootharaba two months later. She was rescued at this dramatic point by former convict John Graham, who had lived with the Kabi and was part of a search party alerted by three other survivors from the *Stirling Castle*. The exact details of Eliza's captivity remain obscure as she produced several conflicting accounts, but her role as an "anti-Crusoe" inspired the work of novelist Patrick White and artist Sidney Nolan.

Practicalities

There are several ways to **get to Fraser**. If you're just after a quick day-trip and don't want to find yourself too far from civilization, take the **fast ferry** from Urangan marina to *Kingfisher Bay Resort* on the island's west side ($35 includes return fare, lunch and brief ranger-guided walk; at least five trips daily between 6.45am and 6.30pm, with return ferries departing from Kingfisher Bay 7.40am–8pm).

For more serious explorations, you'll be crossing on one of three **barges**, which leave from Urangan Harbour, River Heads or Inskip Point (see p.446 for the latter), and you need to make arrangements for these in advance. The **Urangan Harbour to Moon Point** (central west coast) barge leaves at 8.30am and 3.30pm, returning at 9.30am and 4.30pm. The Moon Point landing is very difficult, however – unless you have sound 4WD experience, leave from River Heads. The **River Heads to Wanggoolba Creek** barge (access to **Central Station**) departs daily at 9am, 10.15am and 3.30pm, returning at 9.30am, 2.30pm and 4pm. Unless on an organized tour, you need a **barge ticket** (returns are $70 for vehicle and driver, plus $4 for passengers; pedestrians pay $12 each way), **vehicle permit** for the island if driving ($35), plus you'll have to pay **camping fees** in advance for national park sites if you're planning to camp ($3.85 per person a night). All these can be obtained where you rent your vehicle – and are usually covered in package deals – or from barge offices at Urangan and River Heads. It's essential to **prebook** barge services (℡07/4125 4444, ℻4125 4000). Note that you can use return tickets only on the same barge; if you're planning a different exit from the island, you'll have to buy two one-way tickets. Pack insect repellent.

Getting around

Driving requires a **four-wheel-drive vehicle**. The east beach serves as the main highway, with roads running inland to popular spots. Other tracks, always slower than the beach, crisscross the interior; main tracks are often rough from heavy use, and minor roads tend to be in better shape. General advice is to **lower your tyre pressures** to around 12psi to increase traction on the sand, but this isn't generally necessary (if you get bogged, however, try it first before panicking). Rain and high tides harden sand surfaces, making driving easier. Most **accidents** involve collisions on blind corners, rolling in soft sand (avoid hard braking or making sudden turns – you don't have to be going very fast for your front wheels to dig in, turning you over), and trying to cross apparently insignificant creeks on the beach at 60kph – 4WDs are not invincible. Don't drive your vehicle into the surf; you'll probably get stuck and, even if you don't, this much saltwater exposure will rust out the bodywork within days. Noise from the surf means that pedestrians can't hear vehicles on the beach and won't be aware of your presence until you barrel through from behind, so give them a wide berth. Road rules are the same as those on the mainland.

Walking is the best way to see the island. There's only one **established circuit**, and even that is very underused, running from Central Station south past lakes Birrabeen and Boomanjin, then up the coast and back to Central Station via lakes Wabby and McKenzie; highlights are circumnavigating the lakes, chance encounters with goannas and dingoes, and the energetic burst up **Wongi Blow** for sweeping views out to sea. A good three-day hike that by each sundown renders you all but unconscious after all that walking across sand, it requires no special skills beyond endurance and the ability to set up camp before you pass out.

Renting a 4WD for Fraser Island

Fraser Island is simply too large and varied to appreciate fully on a day-trip, and with competition in Hervey Bay keeping prices to a minimum it's a great opportunity to learn to handle a 4WD. See the Hervey Bay Listings, p.449, for some recommended outfits, but from whomever you rent your vehicle, the company should take the time to protect both it and you with a full briefing on the island and driving practicalities.

Conditions include a minimum driver age of 21 and a $500 bond, payable in plastic or cash – note that advertised prices are normally for renting the vehicle only, so tents, food, fuel, and **ferry** and **vehicle permit** for the island are extra, available separately or as part of a **package**. To help cut costs, you'll want to form a **group** of between five and eight, and the easiest way to arrange this is by staying at one of the hostels; they'll organize numbers and provide everything except food and fuel – a three-day, two-night trip works out to about $125 a person. A popular option at present is to pay a little bit extra for a "You Drive, We Guide" tour, where the rental agency or hostel provide a guide to accompany your group and point you in the right direction.

Essentials and accommodation

Accommodation needs to be booked in advance. Top of the range is the plush *Kingfisher Bay Resort* (℡07/4120 3333 or free call 1800 072 555, ℻4127 9333; ➑) on the west coast; the more down-to-earth *Fraser Island Retreat* at Happy Valley on the east coast (℡07/4127 9144, ✉fraser@cyberalink.com.au; doubles, triples and quads ➒) provides comfortable cabins and good food; while *Yidney Rocks Cabins* (℡07/4127 9167; ➏), just to the south, has basic self-contained, three-bedroom units aimed at fishing groups renting on a weekly basis. Further south, *Eurong Beach Resort* (℡07/4127 9122, ℻4127 9178; ➎) has average motel-style rooms, while *Dilli Village* (℡07/4127 9130; ➌) has self-contained, four-bed bunkhouses.

With a permit, you can camp anywhere along the eastern foreshore, or if you need facilities, use the national park **campsites** at **Wathumba** on the west coast, or at **Lake Allom**, **Dundubara** and **Waddy Point** (the last two can be booked through most NPWS offices in the region) on the east. Elsewhere there are sites at **Central Station**, **Lake Boomanjin** and **Lake McKenzie** (which is often full by noon). There are privately run campsites at *Cathedral Beach Resort* (℡07/4127 9177) and the nicer *Dilli Village* (see above).

For **supplies**, the east coast settlements of **HAPPY VALLEY** and **EURONG** have stores, telephones, bars and fuel; there's another store at *Cathedral Beach Resort* but no shops or restaurant at Dilli. You'll save money by bringing whatever you need with you – and make sure you take the empties home.

Around Central Station

Most people get their bearings by making their first stop at **Central Station**, an old logging depot with campsite, telephone and information hut under some monstrous bunya pines in the middle of the island, directly east of River Heads on the mainland. You'll certainly see **dingoes** here; *don't* feed them, and keep your distance, as the expectation of hand-outs makes them aggressive. As there have never been domestic dogs on the island, Fraser's dingoes are considered to be Australia's purest strain.

From the station, take a stroll along **Wanggoolba Creek**, a magical, sandy-bottomed stream so clear that it's hard at first to see the water as it runs across the forest floor. Apart from encounters with swimming dingoes or slender pythons drowsing on a branch, it's a botanic walk past some prehistoric *angiopteris* ferns to **Pile Valley**, where **satinay trees** humble you to insignificance as they reach 60m to the sky. They produce a very dense timber, durable enough to be used as sidings on the Suez Canal – and are consequently in such demand that the trees on Fraser have almost been logged out.

There are several **lakes** around Central Station, all close enough to walk to and all along main roads. Nine kilometres north (track distance), **McKenzie** is the most popular on the island, and often very crowded: ringed by white sand with clear, tea-coloured water reflecting a blue sky, it's a wonderful place to spend the day. To the south, **Birrabeen** (8km) is mostly hemmed in by trees, while **Boomanjin** (16km) is open and geologically "perched" in a basin above the island's water table. There's a fine campsite and communal fireplace here, attended by tame goannas.

East Beach

Seventy-Five Mile Beach on the east coast is one of the busiest strips of sand you'll ever encounter. Vehicles hurtle along, pedestrians and anglers hug the surf, and tents dot the foredunes; this is what beckons the crowds over from the mainland. Sights along the way include **sand** in all its different forms: **Hammerstone Blow**, 6km north of Eurong, is slowly engulfing **Lake Wabby**, a small but deep patch of blue below the dunes – another century and it will be gone. At **Rainbow Gorge**, about 5km south of Happy Valley, a short trail runs between two blows, through a hot, silent desert landscape where sandblasted trees emerge denuded by their ordeal. Incredibly, a dismal spring seeps water into the valley where the sand swallows it up; "upstream" are the gorge's stubby, eroded red fingers. A path leads in, but if you went you'd only be contributing to the vandalization of the brittle structure.

Six kilometres north of Happy Valley you cross picturesque **Eli Creek**, where water splashes briskly between briefly verdant banks before spilling into the sea. Sand-filtered, it's the nicest swimming spot on the island, though icy-cold. Back on the beach, another 4km brings you to the *Maheno*, wrecked in 1935 and now a skeleton almost consumed by the elements. More striking are the coloured cliffs known as the **Cathedrals**, which run from the wreck north to Indian Head.

The interior, west coast and far north

Fraser's **wooded centre**, a real contrast to the busy coast and popular southern lakes, gets relatively few visitors. It encloses **Yidney Scrub**, the only major stand of **rainforest** left on the island, and although the name doesn't conjure up a very appealing image, the trees are majestic and include towering **kauri pines**. There's a circuit through Yidney from Happy Valley, taking in **Boomerang** and **Allom** lakes on the long way back to the beach near the *Maheno*. You can camp at Allom, a small lake surrounded by pines and cycads, and completely different in character from its flashy southern cousins. Further north, another road heads in from Dundabara township to **Bowarrady**, a not particularly exciting body of water famed for turtles who pester you for bread – if you can't imagine being pestered by a turtle, try refusing to hand it over.

The island's **west coast** is a mix of mangrove swamp and treacherously soft beaches, both largely inaccessible to vehicles. Rough tracks cross the island via Lake Bowarraddy and Happy Valley to where the Urangan barge lands at **Moon Point**, though there's a better road to *Kingfisher Bay Resort* from the

Central Station area. Similarly, most of Fraser's **far north** is inaccessible, with the east coast around **Indian Head** as far north as you can reliably get. The bubbling saltwater pools just north of Indian Head at the **Aquarium** are great fun, and there are some good views from the head itself – often of **sharks** cruising through the shallow surf below.

TRAVEL DETAILS

Trains

Main train routes out of Brisbane follow the Queensland coast north, covered at least daily by the Sunlander and Queenslander to Cairns, the Spirit of the Tropics to Townsville, and the new, high-speed tilt train, along with the slightly slower Spirit of Capricorn, to Rockhampton. Southbound interstate services to Sydney also run daily. For Outback destinations from Brisbane, there's the Westlander, which heads inland twice a week to Toowoomba, Roma, and Charleville, and the Spirit of the Outback, another twice-weekly service via Rockhampton to Emerald and Longreach. For the twice-weekly Inlander to Charters Towers and Mount Isa, change at Townsville. All tickets – especially for sleepers – need to be booked as far in advance as possible.

Brisbane to: Ayr (6 weekly; 22hr 30min); Beenleigh (every 20min; 55min); Bowen (6 weekly; 21hr); Bundaberg (at least 1 daily; 4–6hr); Caboolture (every 20min; 1hr); Cairns (4 weekly; 31hr); Charleville (2 weekly; 16hr 25min); Cleveland, for Stradbroke Island (8 daily; 50min); Emerald (2 weekly; 15hr 15min); Eumundi (2 daily; 2hr 10min); Gladstone (at least 1 daily; 6–8hr); Glasshouse Mountains (every 2hr; 1hr 15min); Gympie (2 daily; 3hr); Ingham (4 weekly; 26hr 30min); Longreach (2 weekly; 24hr); Mackay (6 weekly; 16hr 30min); Maryborough (at least 1 daily; 3hr 45min–5hr); Proserpine (6 weekly; 19hr); Rockhampton (at least 1 daily; 7–12hr); Roma (2 weekly; 10hr 30min); Sydney (1 daily; 14hr); Toowoomba (2 weekly; 3hr 45min); Townsville (6 weekly; 24hr); Tully (4 weekly; 27hr 30min); Woombye (1 daily; 3hr).

Buses

The three main regional long-distance bus operators in Queensland are Greyhound-Pioneer, McCafferty's and Premier.

Brisbane to: Airlie Beach (7 daily; 18hr); Ayr (8 daily; 21hr 30min); Beenleigh (8 daily; 40min); Bowen (8 daily; 19hr 30min); Bundaberg (5 daily; 6hr); Burleigh Heads (8 daily; 1hr 50min); Byron Bay (12 daily; 1hr 30min); Cairns (7 daily; 28hr 30min); Cardwell (7 daily; 24hr); Charleville (1 daily; 11hr); Childers (7 daily; 7hr); Coolangatta (8 daily; 2hr 10min); Gladstone (5 daily; 11hr); Gympie (10 daily; 4hr); Hervey Bay-Pialba (10 daily; 4hr 40min); Ingham (7 daily; 23hr 30min); Innisfail (7 daily; 27hr); Lamington National Park (1 daily; 3hr); Longreach (1 daily; 17hr); Mackay (8 daily; 15hr 30min); Maroochydore (5 daily; 2hr 5min); Maryborough (11 daily; 4hr); Mission Beach (5 daily; 26hr 25min); Mount Isa (1 daily; 25hr); Nambour (9 daily; 1hr 30min); Noosa Heads (7 daily; 2hr 50min); Rockhampton (7 daily; 12hr); Roma (2 daily; 7hr 45min); Surfers Paradise (every 30min; 1hr 30min); Sydney (10 daily; 16hr); Toowoomba (8 daily; 2hr 15min); Townsville (8 daily; 21hr 30min); Tully (7 daily; 25hr 30min); Winton (1 daily; 19hr). **Hervey Bay** to: Airlie Beach (6 daily; 12hr 20min); Brisbane (8 daily; 4hr 40min); Bundaberg (5 daily; 1hr 40min); Cairns (6 daily; 22hr); Mackay (7 daily; 10hr); Mission Beach (5 daily; 20hr 30min); Noosa (5 daily; 3hr 15min); Rockhampton (7 daily; 5hr 30min); Townsville (7 daily; 16hr 25min). **Noosa** to: Airlie Beach (4 daily; 15hr 50min); Brisbane (6 daily; 2hr 50min); Bundaberg (1 daily; 5hr); Cairns (2 daily; 25hr 45min); Hervey Bay (7 daily; 3hr 10min); Mackay (4 daily; 13hr 20min); Maroochydore (4 daily; 35min); Mission Beach (2 daily; 24hr); Rockhampton (4 daily; 9hr) Townsville (4 daily; 20hr). **Surfers Paradise** to: Brisbane (every 30min; 1hr 30min); Burleigh Heads (every 10min; 30min); Coolangatta (every 10min; 1hr); Lamington National Park (2 daily; 1hr 30min); Sydney (8 daily; 15hr 30min); Tamborine Mountain (1 daily; 1hr); Toowoomba (2 daily; 3hr 30min).

Ferries

Brisbane to: Moreton Island (1 daily; 2hr); North Stradbroke Island (11 daily; 30min); St Helena (3 or more weekly; 2hr).
Hervey Bay to: Fraser Island (8 daily; 30min–1hr).

Rainbow Beach/Inskip Point to: Fraser Island (daily, on demand; 45min).
Surfers Paradise to: South Stradbroke Island (3 or more daily; 30min).

Flights

The following are direct flights only.

Brisbane to: Adelaide (many daily; 3hr 30min); Alice Springs (3 daily; 4hr 30min); Bundaberg (4 daily; 50min); Cairns (many daily; 2hr 10min); Canberra (many daily; 2hr); Charleville (1 daily; 2hr); Darwin (2 daily; 3hr 40min); Emerald (2 daily; 1hr 40min); Gladstone (4 daily; 1hr 15min); Gold Coast-Coolangatta (1 daily; 25min); Hervey Bay (4 daily; 1hr 15min); Hobart (many daily; 3hr 50min); Longreach (1 daily; 3hr); Mackay (9 daily; 3hr); Maroochydore-Sunshine Coast (many daily; 30min); Melbourne (many daily; 2hr 25min); Mount Isa (2 daily; 4hr); Norfolk Island (4 weekly; 3hr 45min); Perth (many daily; 5hr); Proserpine (2 daily; 1hr 50min); Rockhampton (4 daily; 1hr 5min); Roma (1 daily; 1hr 10min); Sydney (many daily; 1hr 35min); Townsville (6 daily, 1hr 50min).

Gold Coast-Coolangatta to: Adelaide (many daily; 3hr 35min); Brisbane (1 daily; 25min); Canberra (12 daily; 2hr 40min); Melbourne (many daily; 3hr 35min); Sydney (many daily; 1hr 15min).

Hervey Bay to: Brisbane (2 daily; 1hr 15min); Lady Elliot Island (2 daily; 35min).

Sunshine Coast-Maroochydore to: Brisbane (many daily; 30min); Melbourne (1 daily; 3hr); Sydney (1 daily; 1hr 45min).

Tropical Queensland

CHAPTER 4

Highlights

✳ **Great Barrier Reef** – Scuba diving is the best way to make the most of one of the most beautiful coral complexes in the world. **p.464**.

✳ **The Whitsundays** – Lying just off the Great Barrier Reef, the rainforested peaks and long white beaches of the Whitsunday Islands offer some of the best diving and snorkelling in the world. **p.488**.

✳ **The Sanctuary at Mission Beach** – Wake up surrounded by rainforest in the stilt cabins of this outstanding eco-friendly retreat. **p.510**.

✳ **Atherton Tablelands** – The magnificent rainforest of the Atherton Tablelands is brimming with wildlife. **p.524**.

✳ **Four-wheel-driving on Cape York** – The Cape York Peninsula has some of the most challenging 4WD territory in Australia – watch out for crocs on creek crossings. **p.536**.

✳ **Aboriginal Dance Festival at Laura** – In odd-numbered years, the sleepy town of Laura comes alive for two days in June for the fantastic Aboriginal Dance Festival. **p.540**.

Tropical Queensland and the Reef

The move towards, and into, Queensland's **tropical coast** is more obvious than simply passing the Tropic of Capricorn marker at **Rockhampton**. North of Hervey Bay the landscape begins to brown as the temperature rises, and though there's still an ever-narrowing farming strip hugging the coast, the Great Dividing Range edges coastwards as it progresses north, dry at first but gradually acquiring a green sward which culminates in the steamy, rainforest-draped scenery around **Cairns**. Along the way are scores of beaches, archipelagos of **islands** and regularly spaced cities, including **Townsville**, north Queensland's largest. There is also a wealth of **national parks**, some – such as **Hinchinbrook Island** – with superb walking trails, and others where you might encounter rare or unusual wildlife. Several places along the way are well set up for those with work visas to recharge their bank balances by **fruit and vegetable picking**; the most organized spots for this are the towns of Bundaberg, Bowen, Ayr and Innisfail. Moving north of Cairns, rainforested ranges ultimately cede to the savannah of the huge, triangular **Cape York Peninsula**, a sparsely populated setting for what is widely regarded as the most rugged 4WD adventure in the country.

Offshore, the onset of the tropics is marked by the appearance of the **Great Barrier Reef**, among the most beautiful and extensive coral complexes in the world. The reef, which begins to make its presence felt round the level of Bundaberg, drastically changes the nature of the coastline by blocking incoming surf and producing currents that deflect ocean-borne sand far out to sea.

Accommodation price codes

All the accommodation listed in this book has been categorized into one of eight price bands, as set out below. The rates quoted represent the cheapest available double or twin room in high season – except for category ❶, which indicates per-person rates for a dorm bed, and the categories given for units, cabins and vans, which represent the daily charge for the whole unit.

❶ Under $20   ❸ $35–50   ❺ $70–90   ❼ $115–150
❷ $20–35   ❹ $50–70   ❻ $90–115   ❽ $150 upwards

For more accommodation details, see pp.46–49.

Torres Strait

PAPUA
NEW GUINEA

0   250 km

Thursday Is
Prince of   Cape York
Wales Is
Bamaga

SOUTH
PACIFIC
OCEAN

Weipa

Coen

Cape
York
Peninsula

Lizard Is

Cooktown

CORAL
SEA

Laura
Lakeland

Cape
Tribulation

Daintree   Mossman
Port Douglas
Atherton   Green Is
Tablelands   Fitzroy Is

Great Barrier Reef

Cairns

Normanton   Innisfail

Paronella Park   Mission Beach

Tully   Hinchinbrook Is
Bruce   Cardwell
Hwy   Ingham
Wallaman   Magnetic Is
Falls
Paluma   Townsville

Ayr

Charters
Towers   Bowen

The
Whitsundays

Flinders Highway   Proserpine   Airlie Beach

EUNGELLA   Mackay
NATIONAL
PARK

GREAT DIVIDING RANGE

Winton

Yeppoon
Great Keppel Is
Emerald
Rockhampton
Capricorn Highway   Heron Is

Gladstone   Lady Elliot Is

Agnes Water & 1770

Bundaberg

Childers

Mt Isa

As a result, most **islands** north of Fraser are **continental**, formed when the peaks of ranges were drowned by rising waters at the end of the last Ice Age, creating abrupt coastlines and coral rubble beaches entirely different in character from the southeast's sandy formations. On the reef's outer edge, however, small isolated sand islands (**cays**) form, which tend to become encircled by fringing coral reef – these are particularly a feature of the southern reef. Further north, the cays thin out, while the main body of the reef thickens into thousands of individual shoals as it ventures nearer the coast. Whether cay or continental, many of these islands are close enough to ports for a day-trip, but for a real change of pace, try camping on one for a week or splashing out on a comfortable resort. **Divers** are well catered for, but novices needn't miss out on the best of the coral, which is within snorkelling range of the surface.

Access is along the **Bruce Highway** to Cairns, which is then briefly replaced by the **Cook Highway**, until notions of "main roads" begin to fall apart north of Mossman. Beyond here lie the jungles of the **Daintree**, the outpost of **Cooktown** and the beginnings of seasonal roads, humble tracks and the savannah wilderness of the Cape York Peninsula. Frequent **bus** and **train** services stop at all centres between Bundaberg and Cairns, but ideally you'll either be **driving** or willing to hitch to those places that the travel brochures have overlooked. Among the region's peculiar hazards are the slow, endless **sugar cane trains** that cross roads during the crushing season (roughly June–Dec); crossings are often (but not always) marked by flashing red lights.

Winters are dry and pleasant, but the summer climate (Dec–April) can be oppressively humid, with unpredictable **cyclones** bringing torrential rain and devastating storms, making roads on Cape York impassable and frequently even severing the coastal highway. To avoid the worst of the **crowds** at key places such as the Cairns region or the Whitsunday Islands, come as soon as the wet season is over (late April).

The Southern Reef

Outside the tropics, the Barrier Reef is represented by the **Capricorn** and **Bunker** groups, a string of cays about 80km offshore from the ports of **Bundaberg** and **Gladstone**. Fundamentally different in character from towns further south in Queensland, these places are primarily farming and residential centres; you'll notice a change in the climate, which gets increasingly dry as you near the tropics. Bundaberg lies 50km off the Bruce Highway from Childers (south) or Gin Gin (north), and is a popular place to find short-term **farm work** picking fruit and vegetables; Gladstone is 20km off the highway about 170km north of Gin Gin. Both are on the train line.

You enter the region through the pretty, one-horse town of **CHILDERS**, formerly another favoured stop on the crop-picking trail, but tragically blighted by the terrible **fire** which burned down the old *Palace Backpackers* in 2000, killing fifteen. There's talk of rebuilding and reopening the *Palace*, but at the time of writing this was a long way off.

Bundaberg and offshore

Surrounded by canefields and fruit farms, **BUNDABERG** is famous for its **rum**, though the town is otherwise a humdrum place whose value as a jumping-off point for trips to Lady Elliot and Lady Musgrave **islands** is scarcely advertised. The adjacent coast is, however, an important place for **marine turtles**, who mass in huge numbers every summer to lay their eggs on the beaches; and those wanting **work** are virtually guaranteed seasonal employment (mostly Feb–Nov) picking avocadoes, tomatoes, snow peas and zucchini on farms in the area.

The Town and around

"Bundie" is synonymous with dark rum throughout Australia and if you believe their advertising pitch, Bundaberg's **rum distillery** on Whittered Street, about 2km east of the town centre along Bourbong Street (tours Mon–Fri 10am–3pm, Sat & Sun 10am–2pm; $5.50), accounts for half the rum consumed in Australia each year. Fans relish the opportunity to wallow in the overpowering pungency of raw molasses on a tour of the distilling process. The tour ends, of course, with a **free sample** but you probably won't need to drink much after inhaling the fumes in the vat sheds, where cameras are prohibited in case a flash ignites the vapour.

Flying 1270km from Sydney to Bundaberg in 1921, **Bert Hinkler** set a world record for continuous flight in a light aircraft – his flimsy wire and canvas *Baby Avro*, demonstrating its potential as transport for remote areas and leading to the formation of Qantas the following year. In 1983, the house where Hinkler lived at the time of his death in Southampton, England, was rescued from demolition and transported to Bundaberg as a shrine to his feat. Today **Hinkler House** (daily 10am–4pm; $3) sits in the **Botanic Gardens** 4km from the centre over the Burnett Bridge towards Gin Gin, sharing its desirable surroundings with a Sugar Museum, Historical Museum and a steam train (all $3). Outside the house, landscaped gardens flank ponds where Hinkler was supposedly inspired to design aircraft by watching ibises in flight.

Mon Repos Beach and the turtle rookery

Mon Repos Beach is 15km east of Bundaberg, reached by following the Burnett Heads road and looking out for the faded Mon Repos signposts at the junction as you near the beach. Once the site of a French telegraph link to New Caledonia, today its reputation rests on being Australia's most accessible **loggerhead turtle rookery**. From October to March, female loggerheads clamber laboriously up the beaches after dark, excavate a pit with their hind flippers in the sand above the high-tide mark, and lay about a hundred parchment-shelled eggs. During the eight-week incubation period, the ambient temperature of the surrounding sand will determine the sex of the entire clutch; 28.5°C is the change-over point between male and female. On hatching, the endearing, rubbery-brown youngsters stay buried in the nest until after dark, when they dig themselves out en masse and head for the sea. In season, about a dozen turtles lay each night, and watching the young leave the nest and race towards the water is both comical and touching – your chances of seeing both laying and hatching in one evening are best during January. The loggerhead's future doesn't look too bright at present: since 1980 Mon Repos' rookery population has halved, most likely due to net-trawling offshore. The NPWS run nightly **guided tours** ($4) from November to March; most accommodation places can book you on a tour and transport package ($30), or enquire about local buses at the tourist information office (see below).

Practicalities

Bundaberg lies south of the **Burnett River**, with the coast and quiet satellite suburbs – Bargara, Innes Park, Elliot Heads – about 15km to the east. Bourbong Street, the main thoroughfare, parallels the river: several banks line the street, the post office is at no. 157b, and there's internet access at the Bundaberg E-mail Centre at no. 200. The **bus terminal** is on Targo Street, and the **train station** (⊕ 07/4153 9724, bookings ⊕ 13 2232) is 500m west on McLean Street; both streets cross Bourbong. The **airport**, for departures to Lady Elliot amongst other places, is 4km from the centre on the Childers Road. The **tourist information office** (Mon–Fri 8.30am–4.45pm, Sat–Sun 10am–1pm; ⊕ 07/4153 9289) is at 186 Bourbong St.

Salty's, at 208 Bourbong St (⊕ 07/4151 6422, Ⓕ 4152 4938, Ⓦ www.saltys.net), offers probably the cheapest four-day **dive course** in Australia ($169), though this uses shore dives with poor visibility and few fish; for $580 you get trained boat diving around the Bunker Group reefs and Lady Musgrave island (qualified divers get the same trip for $495 plus equipment rental). Bundaberg Coach Tours (⊕ 07/4153 1037 or free call 1800 815 714) run **day-tours** featuring the rum distillery and other sights twice a week ($60), seasonal turtle-watching night tours to Mon Repos ($18), and twice-weekly day-tours to Agnes Water and 1770 ($60). Detours (⊕ 07/4159 3883) take smaller groups on request to 1770, Agnes Water and Deepwater National Park for $90, though only three hours or so is actually spent on site.

Central **accommodation** options include basic beds and inexpensive meals at the *Grand Hotel* on 89 Bourbong St (⊕ 07/4151 2441;❸); the *Backpackers & Travellers Lodge*, opposite the bus terminal on Targo Street (⊕ 07/4152 2080; ❶), a clean but usually full hostel; and the rough-and-ready *City Centre Backpackers*, at 216 Bourbong St near the train station (⊕ 07/4151 3501, Ⓔ ccbackpackers@interworx.com.au; ❶). Both hostels specialize in finding seasonal farm work for travellers and most residents are there to work. For a **motel**, drive west of the station down Bourbong and take your pick. The closest **campsite** is *Finemore Caravan Park* on Quay Street (⊕ 07/4151 3663;

cabins ❸). At Mon Repos Beach, the first-rate beachfront *Turtle Sands Caravan Park* (☎07/4159 2340) is right next to the turtle rookery and comes with an aspiring **restaurant**, cabins (❸) and tent sites. Everywhere will be full over the Christmas holidays, and the hostels are reluctant to take advance bookings except in the quieter months from January to March.

The Great Barrier Reef

The Great Barrier Reef is to Australia what rolling savannahs and game parks are to Africa, and is equally subject to the corniest of representations. "Another world" is the commonest cliché, which, while being completely true, doesn't begin to describe the feeling of donning mask and fins and coming face to face with extraordinary animals, shapes and colours. There's so little relationship to life above the surface that distinctions normally taken for granted – such as that between animal, plant and plain rock – seem blurred, while the respective roles of observer and observed are constantly challenged by shoals of curious fish following you about.

Beginning with Lady Elliot Island, out from Bundaberg, and extending 2300km north to New Guinea, the Barrier Reef follows the outer edge of Australia's continental plate, running closer to land as it moves north: while it's 300km to the main body from Gladstone, Cairns is barely 50km distant from the reef. Far from being a continuous, unified structure, the nature of the reef also changes along its length: cays (low sand islands) are a particular feature of the southern reef; the middle sections comprise intricate mazes of alternately packed and scattered coral formations; continental islands everywhere become ringed by fringing reefs; and northern sections form long ribbons. All of it, however, was built by one animal: the tiny coral polyp. Simple organisms, related to sea anemones, polyps huddle together like building blocks into modular colonies – corals – which form the framework of the reef's ecology by providing food, shelter and hunting grounds for larger, more mobile species. Around their walls and canyons flow a bewildering assortment of creatures: large rays and turtles "fly" effortlessly by, fish dodge between caves and coral branches, snails sift the sand for edibles, and brightly coloured nudibranchs dance above rocks.

The reef is administered by the Marine Parks Authority, which battles against – or at least gauges – the effects of overfishing, pollution and tourism. Underfunding, and the lengthy study time required to find long-term solutions for the reef's protection, mean that little has been achieved. The most obvious signs of damage at popular locations – broken and dead coral – are due to the volume of visitors, caused by people bumping against outcrops. A popular villain, the polyp-eating crown of thorns starfish, also causes severe destruction during cyclic plagues. Don't let this put you off going – damage is restricted to only a handful of sites, and overall the reef is still healthy. But it's clear that the reef needs to be treated with respect if it is to retain its natural wonder. In order to minimize damage, visitors should take care not to stand on shallow reefs when snorkelling, and always avoid touching coral; even if you don't break off branches, you'll certainly crush the delicate polyps.

Diving and other ways of seeing the reef

Scuba diving is the best way to come to grips with the reef, and dive courses are on offer right along the coast. Five days is the minimum needed to safely cover the course work – three-days' pool and theory, two days at sea – and secure you the all-important C-card. The quality of training and the price you pay vary. Cheaper courses use island reefs or shore diving, instead of taking you to the main reef – though this isn't always a bad thing, as some of these sites are good. More importantly, ask about student-to-instructor ratios, as drawing attention to any problems you may have is hard if your instructor has ten other students to worry about as well. In tourist centres such as Airlie Beach or Cairns, businesses are geared to processing as many students in as short a time as possible; for a more relaxed atmosphere, you

The cafés and hotels along Bourbong Street are about the only places in town that provide good **food** and after-dark entertainment; the *Grand Hotel* (see p.463) and the *Old Bridge Steakhouse*, over the bridge on Perry Street, are both geared towards grills; or try the good-value counter meals at the *Old Bundy Tavern*, at the junction of Quay and Tantitha streets.

may be better off learning away from these places and diving them once you are qualified. Another consideration is whether you ever plan to dive again: if this seems unlikely, resort dives (a single dive with an instructor) will set you back only $50 or so, and they're usually available on day-trips to the reef and island resorts.

While the extra weight is a drag between dives, qualified divers can save on rental costs by bringing some gear along; tanks and weightbelts are covered in dive packages but anything else is extra. You need an alternative air source, timer, C-card and log book to dive in Queensland (the last is often ignored but some places insist, especially for deep or night-time dives).

Snorkelling is a good alternative to diving: you can pick up the basics in five minutes and with a little practice the only thing you sacrifice is the extended dive time that a tank allows. If you think you'll do a fair amount, buy your own mask and snorkel – they're not dramatically expensive – as rental gear nearly always leaks. Look for a silicone rubber and toughened glass mask and ask the shop staff to show you how to find a good fit. If getting wet just isn't for you, try glass-bottomed boats or "subs", which can still turn up everything from sharks to oysters.

Reef hazards

Stories of shark attacks, savage octopuses and giant clams all make good press, but are mostly the stuff of fiction and exaggeration. However, there are a few things at the reef capable of putting a dampener on your holiday, and it makes sense to be careful. The best protection is simply to look and not touch, as nothing is actively out to harm you.

Coral and shell cuts become badly infected if not treated immediately by removing any fragments and dousing with antiseptic. Some corals can also give you a nasty sting, but this is more a warning to keep away in future than something to worry about seriously. Animals to avoid tend to be small. Shore divers might encounter dangerous jellyfish (see warning on p.32), but those found at the reef aren't life-threatening, though they can cause nausea and raise a painful weal – wear a protective Lycra "stinger suit" or full wetsuit with hood. Conical cone shells are home to a fish-eating snail armed with a poisonous barb which has caused fatalities. Don't pick them up: there is no "safe" end to hold them. Similarly, the shy, small, blue-ringed octopus has a fatal bite and should never be handled. Stonefish are camouflaged so that they're almost impossible to distinguish from a rock or lump of coral. They spend their days immobile, protected from attack by a series of poisonous spines along their back. If you tread on one, you'll end up in hospital – an excellent argument against reef-walking. Of the larger animals, rays are timid, flattened fish with a sharp spine capable of causing deep wounds – don't swim close over sandy floors where they hide. At the reef, the most commonly encountered sharks are the black-tip and white-tip varieties, and the bottom-dwelling, aptly named carpet shark, or wobbegong – all of these are inoffensive unless hassled.

Reef tax

The Marine Parks Authority levy a reef tax (currently $4 per person per day) to help fund monitoring and management of human impact on the reef. On most tours and boat trips, you will be required to pay reef-tax in addition to the cost of the tour. You may feel a little annoyed at having to fork out the extra money, especially if you've already paid quite a lot for your trip, but this is simply a "user-pays" system to help ensure that the reef is maintained for everyone to experience and enjoy.

Moving on, trains and long-distance buses – Greyhound Pioneer (ⓣ 13 2030), McCafferty's (ⓣ 13 1499) and Premier (ⓣ 13 3410) – head up the coast to Gladstone and down to Childers and beyond; for **Agnes Water** and **1770**, Barbour's Buses (ⓣ 07/4974 9030) run a twice-weekly afternoon service from the post office on Barolin Street ($20 return, $15 one-way).

Lady Elliot Island

The southern outpost of the Great Barrier Reef, **Lady Elliot Island** is a two-kilometre-square patch of casuarina and pandanus trees stabilizing a bed of coral rubble, sand, and – in common with all the southern cays – a thick layer of **guano**, courtesy of the generations of birds which have roosted here. The elegant **lighthouse** on Elliot's west side was built in 1866 after an extraordinary number of wrecks on the reef; on average, one vessel a year still manages to come to grief here. Wailing shearwaters (muttonbirds) and the occasional suicide of lighthouse staff didn't endear Lady Elliot to early visitors, but now a low-key **resort** and excellent reef have turned the island into a popular escape.

Shearwaters aside, there's a good deal of **birdlife** on the island; residents include thousands of black noddies and bridled terns, along with much larger frigatebirds and a few rare red-tailed tropicbirds – a white, gull-like bird with a red beak and wire-like tail. Both loggerhead and green **turtles** nest on the beaches too, and in a good summer there are scores laying their eggs here each night. The main reason to come to Lady Elliot, however, is to go **diving and snorkelling**: the best spots for diving are out from the lighthouse, but check on daily currents with the dive staff before getting wet. The Blowhole is a favourite with divers, with a descent into a cavern (make sure you see the "gnomefish" here), and there's also the 1999 wreck of the yacht *Severence* to explore. You've a good chance of encountering harmless leopard sharks, rays, barracuda, turtles and gigantic **manta rays** wherever you go. Dives cost $38.50 per person ($49.50 for night dives), plus gear rental.

Lady Elliot can only be reached **by air** on daily flights from Hervey Bay or Bundaberg (day-return $199, including use of resort facilities, snorkelling gear and glass-bottom boat; resort guests $159; book through the resort). **Accommodation** on the island is with the comfortable *Lady Elliot Island Resort* (free call ⓣ 1800 072 200, Ⓦ www.ladyelliot.com.au; ❼ – ❽), who have basic four-person tented cabins as well as motel-like, self-contained suites with ocean views. Breakfast and dinner (but not lunch or flights) are included in the rates; or enquire about discounted longer-term packages – but if you're not interested in under-water activities, a day or two is ample time to see everything and unwind.

Lady Musgrave Island

Lady Musgrave Island is another tiny, low island, this time covered in soft-leaved pisonia trees which host the usual throng of roosting birdlife, ringed by a coral wall which forms a large turquoise lagoon. **Diving** the inside of the lagoon here is safe but pretty tame (though snorkelling is good) – the outside wall is more exciting. Relatively easy, inexpensive access means that Lady Musgrave is the best of the southern cays on which to **camp** – there is no resort on the island, nor any facilities – though the island itself is **off-limits** during the tern nesting season (Oct–April).

From Bundaberg, MV *Lady Musgrave* departs from the Port Marina, about thirty-minutes' drive from town (Mon–Thurs & Sat 8.30am; $125 single or day-return), taking three hours to reach the island. The booking office is at the marina (ⓣ 07/4159 4519, Ⓦ www.lmcruises.com.au) and the staff can organize a bus pick-up from your accommodation ($9). The island is also visited on Salty's dive trips (see Bundberg "Practicalities", p.463). Alternatively, you can reach Lady Musgrave **from 1770** (see below) with the MV *Spirit of 1770* (℡07/4974 9077, Ⓦwww.great-barrier-reef.net), which departs four times a week from 1770's marina and zips over to the island in just over an hour – it costs $110 return for a day-trip, or $110 each way if you're camping (in which case you'll need camping permits from the Gladstone NPWS – see overleaf). Campers can arrange with either ferry to bring fresh provisions during long stays – for practical details see the "Island camping" box overleaf.

Agnes Water and 1770

On the coast 100km north of Bundaberg along the Rosedale road (or an additional 65km from the highway via **Miriam Vale**), the tiny settlements of **AGNES WATER** and nearby **1770** mark where Captain Cook first set foot ashore in Queensland on May 24, 1770. It's a pretty area, and one of the few undeveloped places along the Queensland coast that can be reached without a 4WD. If you don't have your own transport, you can take a twice-weekly afternoon **bus from Bundaberg** from outside the Barolin Street post office ($20 return). Nearby attractions include the mangrove, fan palm and paperbark wetlands at **Eurimbula National Park**, and the coast at Agnes Water, which has Queensland's northernmost official **surfing beaches** – though with the reef's lower reaches offshore, don't expect too much from the waves. 1770 is also the closest point on the mainland to the southern cays, from where there is regular transport to two Barrier Reef islands.

Agnes Water itself consists of a service station, a few stores at Endeavour Plaza, and the *Agnes Water Tavern*, set a few hundred metres back from the sea, while 1770 is even smaller, occupying the foreshore of a narrow promontory some 6km north. In 1770, the *Captain Cook Holiday Village* (℡07/4974 9219) has **rooms** and dorms (❶–❸), a store, bar and bistro; while more budget beds are on hand at *1770 Backpackers* (℡07/4974 9849; ❶). For Eurimbula, head 10.5km back towards Miriam Vale from Agnes Water, where you'll see the track and national park sign to the north of the road. Bring all supplies with you, so you can **bushcamp** about 15km inside the park in the dunes behind **Bustard Beach** – ask at the Agnes Water service station for directions. You'll need high clearance or 4WD for the park.

The most interesting of local **tour** options is with 1770 Environmental Tours aboard *The Larc* (℡07/4974 9422), an **amphibious bus** that spends the day exploring the coastline and reaches of the otherwise impenetrable Deepwater National Park, south of Agnes Water. Heading **back to Bundaberg**, the bus leaves early in the morning, twice a week, from Agnes Waters' Endeavour Plaza.

Gladstone and nearby islands

GLADSTONE is a busy port, and also the site of the Boyne Island processing plant which refines aluminium from ore mined at Weipa on the Cape York

Island camping

Campers intending to stay over on undeveloped southern reef cays need to organize camping permits and transport well in advance, particularly for the Easter and September holiday periods, and to contact the boat operator a few days before departure to check on weather conditions – rough seas can suspend services to the islands. Note, too, that Lady Musgrave, Northwest and Masthead islands are **closed to camping** during the tern nesting season, between mid-October and mid-April. **Camping permits** cost $3.85 per person per night, and are only issued by the Gladstone NPWS (see below). You need to be entirely self-sufficient: take food, at least five litres of water per person per day, a fuel stove (wood fires are prohibited), waterproof tents and sand pegs, shovels, first-aid kit, a radio (for weather forecasts), spare batteries, garbage bags and emergency rations for at least two extra days.

Peninsula. Glaringly hot, there's no reason to stop here unless you're trying to reach the reef. If you're planning to camp on any of the southern cays, Gladstone is where you need to make arrangements through the **NPWS office**, at 136 Goondoon St (Mon–Fri 8.30am–5pm; ☎ 07/4972 6055); if booking by post, mail the office at PO Box 5065, Gladstone.

The main strip is Goondoon Street, where there's a "mall" – just the usual high-street shops, post office and banks – and a couple of hotels and motels. You'll find a helpful **information centre** (Mon–Fri 8.30am–5pm, Sat–Sun 9am–5pm) inside the ferry terminal at the **marina**, about 2km north of the centre on Bryan Jordan Drive. A casual, basic **hostel** is hidden away at 12 Rollo St (☎ 07/4972 5744, ℉ 4972 4266; ❶); to get there, go to the marina end of Goondoon Street, turn left and it's three streets down past a small real estate agent, or give them a call and they'll pick you up when you arrive. *Gladstone Reef Hotel*, 38 Goondoon St (☎ 07/4972 1000; ❻), has ordinary **motel** rooms and good views from a rooftop pool. **Cafés** in the mall range from *Munchies* at 46 Goondoon St, a cheap and cheerful Mexican place with budget lunches during the week, to *Swaggy's* at no. 52, where you can spoil yourself with native cuisine – emu, crocodile, kangaroo – at gourmet prices.

Diving can be arranged through Gladstone Diving at Last Wave Watersports, 16 Goondoon St (☎ 07/4972 9185). They take qualified divers out on day-trips to Lamont reef ($155 plus $30 gear hire for two dives), and for the weekend to Llewellyn and Fitzroy reefs south of Heron (Fri–Sun; $350 plus gear for 6–8 dives) – both good value. Their seven-day dive courses cost $495 and are actually conducted at Great Keppel Island up near Rockhampton (for more on which see p.475).

Masthead and Northwest islands

Remote both in feel and location, **Masthead** and **Northwest** islands remain virtually undisturbed, with limited numbers of campers permitted at any one time. Both cays are around 500m long and 100m wide, with a good covering of pisonias; as the usual crowd of seabirds and turtles nest here, both are also closed during the nesting season (Oct–April). Even at other times, the ruckus generated can be quite disturbing, but in the right frame of mind this all becomes part of the experience. Don't overlook the reef's **snorkelling** or **fishing** if you have the gear, though bear in mind that certain sections of reef are protected zones where fishing is prohibited – check first with the NPWS in Gladstone.

The only way to reach Northwest and Masthead from Gladstone is by **charter boat**, and at $3000 minimum, you'll need to get a group together for it to be financially viable: operators include Gladstone Star (℡ 07/4979 2506), Robert Poulsson (℡ 07/4972 5166) and Curtis Endeavour (℡ 07/4972 6990), or contact the NPWS for leads on other boats. Check the "Island camping" box, opposite, for practical details.

Heron Island

Famous for its diving, **Heron Island** escaped the depredations of guano hunters in the early twentieth century, though a turtle-canning factory operated on the island for several years. Small enough to walk around in an hour, half the cay is occupied by a comfortable **resort** and **research station**, the rest covered in groves of pandanus, coconuts and shady pisonias, whose sticky seeds are unwittingly spread between islands on the backs of birds. Patches of long grass hide ground-dwelling **rails** (moorhen-like birds) which rocket from underfoot. **Herons** also stalk around the coral tops at low tide, fishing the pools – they're typically white, but a black form also frequents the area.

You can literally walk off the beach and into the reef's maze of coral, or swim along the shallow walls looking for action. The eastern edges of the lagoon are good for snorkelling at any time, but **diving** must be arranged through the resort (see "Practicalities" below), which charges $54 for a standard dive, and $65 to venture out at night; equipment is extra. Dive **packages** save a few dollars if you're staying long enough to take advantage of them, and you can make two dives daily for free during June.

A drift along the wall facing Wistari reef to Heron Bommie covers about everything you're likely to encounter. The coral isn't that good but the amount of life is astonishing: tiny boxfish hide under ledges; turtles, cowries, wobbegong, reef sharks, moray eels, butterfly cod and octopuses secrete themselves among the coral; manta rays soar majestically, and larger reef fish gape vacantly as you drift past. The Bommie itself makes first-rate **snorkelling**, with an interesting swim-through if your lungs are up to it, while the Tenements along the reef's northern edge are good for bigger game – including sharks.

Practicalities

There is a price to pay for all this natural wonder, namely no day-trips and no camping. The P&O-owned **resort** (reservations ℡ 13 2469; island reception ℡ 07/4972 9055; ❽) is excellent but its rates, coupled with the ferry charge ($165) place it well outside the budget bracket. Last-minute **stand-by packages** offered by travel agents in Gladstone are worth looking into, but don't expect miracles – try Traveland, 124 Goondoon St (℡ 07/4972 2288). **Ferries** leave from Gladstone Marina daily at 11am, except at Christmas; there's a **car lockup** here ($9 a day) operated by the tackle shop (8am–5pm).

The Tropics: Rockhampton to Cape York

Rockhampton marks the start of the tropics, but with the exception of the Mackay region, it's not until you're well past the line and north of **Townsville** that the tropical greenery associated with north Queensland finally appears. Then it comes in a rush, and by the time you've reached **Cairns** there's no doubt that the area deserves its reputation: coastal ranges covered in rainforest and cloud descend right to the sea. **Islands** along the way lure you with good beaches, hiking tracks and opportunities for snorkelling and diving: the **Keppels** near Rockhampton, the **Whitsundays** off Airlie Beach, **Magnetic Island** opposite Townsville, and **Hinchinbrook** and **Dunk** further north. Cairns itself serves as a base for exploring highland rainforest on the **Atherton Tablelands** and coastal jungles in the **Daintree**, and for trips onto the **Cape York Peninsula** and, of course, out to the most accessible sections of the **Great Barrier Reef**.

Rockhampton

Straddling the Tropic of Capricorn, 100km north of Gladstone, **ROCKHAMP-TON** was founded after a false goldrush in 1858 left hundreds of miners stranded at a depot 40km inland on the banks of the sluggish **Fitzroy River**; their rough camp below **Mount Archer** was adopted by local stockmen as a convenient port. The iron trelliswork and sandstone buildings fronting the river recall the balmy 1890s, when money was pouring into the city from central Queensland's prosperous cattle industry and the gold and copper mines 40km west at **Mount Morgan**. Today, however, despite hosting a large university campus, Rockhampton feels a bit despondent: the mines have closed (though before they did, they managed to fund the fledgling BP company), the beef industry is down in the dumps and the summers, unrelieved by coastal breezes, are appallingly humid. Bearing this in mind, the city is best seen as a springboard for the adjacent Capricorn Coast (see p.473), but with half a day to spare it's worth catching the Aboriginal version of history at the **Dreamtime Centre**; and there are a group of **limestone caves** to the north to poke around in.

The City and around

It doesn't take long to look around the city. The **Tropic Marker**, 3km south of the river at Rockhampton's southern entrance, is just a spire informing you of your position at 23° 26' 30" S. And, apart from a riverside stroll to take in the turn-of-the-twentieth-century architecture or the brown-stained boulders in mid-stream that gave the city its name, there's very little to detain you.

About 5km north of town on the Bruce Highway, the **Dreamtime Cultural Centre** (daily 10am–3.30pm; tours with an Aboriginal guide from

10.30am; $14) offers a good introduction to central Queensland's Aboriginal heritage. Inside, chronological and Dreamtime histories are intermingled, with a broad dissection of the archeology and mythology of Carnarvon Gorge (see p.562). Outside, surrounded by woodland, gunyahs (shelters of bark and branches) and stencil art, you'll find an unlikely walk-through dugong, and the original stone rings of a **bora ground** which marked the main camp of the Darumbal, whose territory reached from the Keppel Bay coastline inland to Mount Morgan. The tour also introduces plant usage, plus boomerang, dance and didgeridoo skills – audience participation is definitely encouraged.

The Caves

The limestone hills 25km north of Rockhampton are riddled with an interesting **cave** system discovered in the 1880s. The caves have few classic stalagmites and stalactites, which need continuous dripping water to form; instead, there are tree roots encased in stone after forcing their way down through rocks, "cave corals" and "frozen waterfalls" – minerals deposited by evaporation after annual floods. The **ghost bat** (Australia's only carnivorous species) and the **little bent-winged bat** – both now endangered – seasonally use the caves for roosts, and you might catch the odd group huddled together on the ceilings, eyes peering down at you over leaf-shaped noses.

There are three sets of caverns open to the public, all reached by turning off the Bruce Highway at **The Caves** township: cross the rail line and bear left, and **Etna Caves National Park** is straight on past a council depot and around to the right; for **Cammoo** and **Olsen's**, turn right after the hotel and follow the billboards. Etna caves are undeveloped but none too extensive; between February and June you can explore on your own (6am to 8pm; take a torch and durable shoes), or between November and February you can go on a **bat**

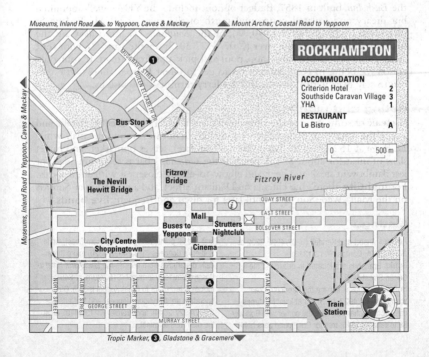

Museums, Inland Road ⮝ to Yeppoon, Caves & Mackay ⮝ Mount Archer, Coastal Road to Yeppoon

ROCKHAMPTON

ACCOMMODATION
Criterion Hotel 2
Southside Caravan Village 3
YHA 1
RESTAURANT
Le Bistro A

0 — 500 m

MUSGRAVE STREET
QUEEN ELIZABETH DR

Bus Stop ★

Museums, Inland Road to Yeppoon, Caves & Mackay

The Nevill Hewitt Bridge

Fitzroy Bridge

Fitzroy River

❷
Mall
Buses to Yeppoon ★
Strutters Nightclub
QUAY STREET
EAST STREET
BOLSOVER STREET
ⓘ

City Centre Shoppingtown

Cinema

NORTH STREET
ALBERT STREET
GEORGE STREET
ARCHER STREET
FITZROY STREET
DENHAM STREET
MURRAY STREET
STANLEY STREET

Ⓐ

Train Station

Tropic Marker, ❸, Gladstone & Gracemere ⮟

tour (four evenings a week; $7) with the NPWS – contact them for details (see opposite). Cammoo (daily 8.30am–5.30pm; self-guided tour $8) and Olsen's (daily 9am–4pm; guided tour $15, caving tour $40) are both impressive – Olsen's is just that bit better – with plenty of spotlights and coloured gel illuminating their interiors. **Bus tours** to Olsen's leave at 9.30am on Monday, Wednesday and Friday from the Arcade Carpark, near the *Leichhardt Hotel* on Bolsover Street (book first on ℡07/4934 2883; $25).

Practicalities

Rockhampton is divided by the Fitzroy River, with all services clustered directly south of the **Fitzroy Bridge** along Quay Street and East Street Mall; the Bruce Highway runs right through town past two pairs of fibreglass bulls (repeatedly "de-balled" by pranksters). **Buses** stop just north of the bridge on the highway; the **train** station is 1km south of the centre on Murray Street; and the **airport** is 4km to the west at the end of Hunter Street. **Tourist information** is available from the booth on the highway at the Tropic Marker, or at the more central **information centre** in the old customs house on Quay Street (Mon–Fri 8.30am–4.30pm, Sat–Sun 9am–4pm; ℡07/4922 5339). Recent reports of nasty incidents involving gangs of Aboriginal teenagers are unfortunately too numerous to ignore; there's no need for paranoia, but do follow local advice and don't walk alone at night.

Accommodation

The pick of the **accommodation** choices are the good-value suites overlooking the river at the historic *Criterion Hotel* on Quay Street (℡07/4922 1225, ℻4922 1226; ❸), which occupies the site of Rockhampton's first pub, the *Bush Inn*, built in 1857. Budget options include the YHA's well-appointed but dreary and isolated compound north of the river at 60 MacFarlane St (℡07/4927 5288, ℻4922 6040; ❶); or the *Southside Caravan Village* on the highway 2km south of the river (℡07/4927 3013; on-site vans ❸), with **tent sites**, cramped on-site vans, shop, pool and pick-ups from town. If your only reason for being in Rockhampton is to get to Great Keppel, there's little reason to stay over with Yeppoon and the ferry terminals so close by.

Eating and nightlife

A **steak** of some kind is the obvious choice in Australia's "Beef Capital", and any of the hotels can oblige. There's a smattering of cafés around the mall, while *Le Bistro* at 152 Quay St (Mon–Sat 6.30pm–late), serves upmarket (and huge) slabs of meat for about $22. A perch at the *Criterion's* bar is recommended for less flamboyant steak and beer, and elbow-to-elbow closeness with a few locals. For **nightlife**, there's the cinema on Denham Street, and a nightclub at *Strutters* on the Mall (Wed–Sun 8pm until late) for disco and frequent **live bands**.

Listings

Airlines Ansett and Kendell (℡07/4922 2202 or ℡13 1300); Qantas (℡13 1313).

Banks Branches are located in or around the Queen Street Mall.

Buses Local buses service the Capricorn Coast: Young's (℡07/4922 3813) run at least five times daily from Denham St, near the corner with Bolsover St, to Yeppoon ($15; free for Greyhound pass hold-ers) and all points along the Capricorn Coast; while Rothery's Coaches (℡07/4922 4320) make three daily departures from outside the *Leichhardt Hotel* to Rosslyn Bay ferry terminal ($15 return, or $45 including ferry fare to Great Keppel Island). Other operators are Greyhound Pioneer and McCafferty's (℡07/4927 2844), and Premier (℡13 3410), all at the main bus terminal.

Camping equipment Campco's, cnr William and Kent streets (☎07/4922 2366).

Car rental Network, cnr George and Archer streets (free call ☎1800 077 977); Rockhampton Car Rentals, south on the Bruce Highway (☎07/4922 7802); Thrifty, 47 Fitzroy St (☎07/4927 8755).

Diving Capricorn Reef Diving, 189 Musgrave St, North Rockhampton (☎07/4922 7720), gives certification courses from around $450 and offers dive courses around the Keppels. Qualified divers can organize trips to the Bunker and Capricorn groups.

Farmstays *Myella Farm*, The Eather Family, Myella, Barabala, Qld 4702 (☎07/4998 1290, ☎4998 1104, ⓦwww.users.bigpond.com/myella), and *Kroombit-Lochenbar*, Valentine Plains Rd,

Biloela (☎07/4992 2186, ⓦwww.kroombit.com.au), are a couple of hours out of town and offer accommodation, meals and participation in farm life from $198 for 3 days.

Hospital Base Hospital, Canning St, South Rockhampton (☎07/4920 6211).

NPWS A helpful office situated 5km out of town on the Yeppoon–Rockhampton road (☎07/4936 0511).

Pharmacy CQ Pharmacy, 150 Alma St (daily 8am–10pm; ☎07/4922 1621).

Police 212 Quay St (☎07/4938 4880).

Post office East St Mall.

Shopping City Centre Plaza on Bolsover St.

Taxi ☎07/4922 7111.

Trains Murray St (☎07/4932 0211).

The Capricorn Coast

Views from volcanic outcrops overlooking the **Capricorn Coast**, east of Rockhampton, stretch across graziers' estates and pineapple plantations to exposed headlands, estuarine mudflats and the **Keppel Islands** 20km offshore. The coastal townships of **Yeppoon** and **Emu Park**, settled by cattle barons in the 1860s, were soon adopted by Rockhampton's elite as places to beat the summer heat. Despite some modern development, the coast retains a pleasantly dated holiday atmosphere, with **Great Keppel Island** as the main draw.

Rockhampton to Yeppoon

First stop on the road to Yeppoon is about 25km from Rockhampton at **Koorana Crocodile Farm** (tours daily at 1pm; $15), where estuarine crocs are bred (*koorana* means "giving birth") to supply the leather industry and restaurants. If this doesn't bother you, the tours are interesting – despite a certain amount of showmanship involved in the feeding and meeting of Koorana's "stars". Some of the crocs are penned individually, but most are viewed en masse from the safety of protected boardwalks, raised over the mudflats and ponds where the reptiles bask. With luck you might see babies hatching, bleating as they squeeze themselves out of tiny eggs.

The **sea** appears suddenly at **EMU PARK**, a breezy hillside covered by scattered "Queenslander" houses, where the wind howls mournful tunes through the wires of the **Singing Ship**, a peculiar monument to Captain Cook. Budget **beds** in a smart one-hundred-year-old building are offered at *Emu House*, 88 Pattison St (☎07/4939 6111, ⓔemu-house@hotmail.com; dorms ❶, rooms and cabins ❷) – they also offer discount packages to Great Keppel and other islands, and can collect from Rockhampton. One place to note between here and Yeppoon is **Rosslyn Bay**, where the cliffs have been weathered into hexagonal columns behind the **island ferry terminal and marina** (for details of getting to the islands, see p.475). Further on, **COOEE BAY** is virtually a suburb of Yeppoon, with an annual "Cooee Competition" when competitors give their tonsils a good airing from Wreck Point.

473

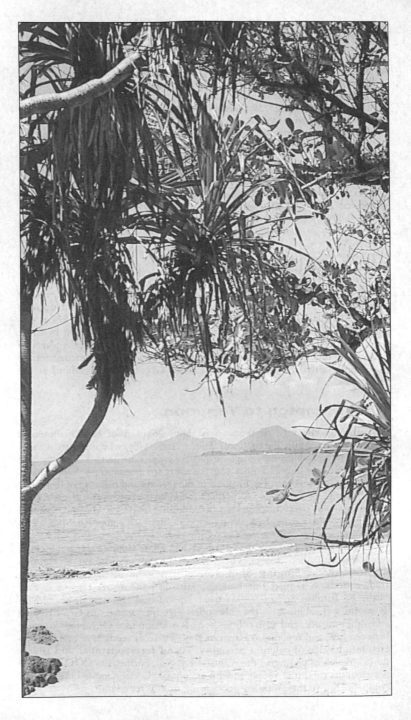

Yeppoon

YEPPOON's quiet handful of streets faces the Keppel Islands over a blustery expanse of sand and sea. All services are on James Street, at right angles to seafront **Anzac Parade**. For **accommodation**, *Tropical Nites Motel*, 34 Anzac Parade (☎07/4939 1914; ❹), has small, self-contained rooms, while friendly *Yeppoon Backpackers*, 30 Queen St (☎07/4939 8080; ❶), has four-bed dorms and an attractive pool area, and operates a daily courtesy bus to Rockhampton to meet evening arrivals; call ahead to check exact times. The *Strand Hotel* (☎07/4939 1301; ❸), on the corner of Anzac Parade and James Street, offers basic, four-bed units, while the *Blue Dolphin Caravan Park* (☎07/4939 3140), at 74 Whitman St, is relatively sheltered.

Kelly's Bar & Grill, next to the *Tropical Nites Motel*, claims to serve the best steaks in town, while a few doors down, *Pass da Pasta*, in a sprucer setting, is popular for its range of pastas, grills and salads. The **Keppel Bay Sailing Club** occupies two separate premises on opposite corners of Anzac Parade: the original building is still a good venue for a beer along with views of the islands, while the ritzy newer section has a poker-machine-filled restaurant that offers budget all-you-can-eat lunch and dinner. Otherwise there's a legion of cafés to choose from along James Street, with weekend entertainment at the *Strand Hotel* or at *Bonkers Nightclub*, one road back from Anzac Parade on Hill Street.

The Keppel Islands

The eighteen **Keppel Islands** boast white sand so fine that it squeaks when you walk through it, and the sea is an invitingly clear blue – just right for a few days of indolence. Most of the islands are national parks and, with the exception of North and Great Keppel, are very small. Easy access, coupled with a resort and associated facilities, has made **Great Keppel** the most popular, but there are also reefs to snorkel and isolated camping spots on the other islands.

All **access** is from **ROSSLYN BAY**, just off the main road about 8km south of Yeppoon on the coastal route to Rockhampton, with departures from both the **ferry terminal** (☎07/4933 6744), and the nearby new **marina** (☎07/4933 6244). For **Great Keppel**, *Keppel Kat* and *Freedom Flyer* run a total of seven daily return services from the ferry terminal (last leaves Great Keppel at 4.30pm), plus a late service on Fridays; both charge $27 return. The marina is the place to find transport to **other islands**, or **cruises** beyond there; *Reef Chief* and *Euphoria* are among boats running charter trips (around $75 per person return, depending on passenger numbers). The ferry terminal and marina both have exposed **free parking**, though for protection from salt spray, leave your car undercover at Great Keppel Island Security Car Park ($7.50 a day), opposite the Rosslyn Bay junction on the main road.

Great Keppel

Arriving at **Great Keppel**, the ferry leaves you on a spit directly in front of the budget **accommodation** choices; most offer good **packages** or **stand-by rates** if you ask for them. *Great Keppel Cabins and Camping* (☎07/4933 6744, ℻4933 6429) occupies sheltered, sandy woodland behind Putney Beach, with beds in a pre-fab tent village (❶) or self-contained cabins for up to six (❾). The YHA-run *Backpackers Village* (☎07/4927 5288, ℻4922 6040; ❶) is yet another tent village; facilities are basic, and the place feels a bit stark and military. *Great Keppel Island Holidays* (☎07/4939 8655, ℻4939 8755; dorms ❶, cabins ❷) is a spruce, very friendly place with a first-rate kitchen, and accommodation in self-contained cabins, tents or dorms.

Along the beach, *Keppel Lodge* (☎ 07/4939 4251, ℻ 4939 8251; ❺) is a pleasant, motel-like affair; further down you come to the modern and comfortable *Great Keppel Island Resort* (☎ 07/4939 5044 or free call 1800 245 658; ❽). Its *Wreck Bar* is the island's after-dark social focus; by day, the resort cultivates a family atmosphere and there's a pool for day-trippers. For food, *Keppel Haven* has a **restaurant** and occasional barbecues, and there's a tearoom at the *Shell House* on Fisherman's Beach. There is also a late-opening **pizza shack** – much frequented after the bar closes.

The main **beaches**, Putney and Fisherman's, are remarkably pleasant considering the number of people lounging on them at any one time, but the effort of a half-hour walk will reward you with some more secluded spots. Reached on a woodland path past the resort, **Long Beach** attracts sun-worshippers, while snorkellers make the short haul over sand dunes at the western end to shallow coral on **Monkey Beach**. Shell mounds on Monkey Beach were left by Woppaburra Aborigines, who were enslaved and forcibly removed to Fraser Island by early settlers.

Other Keppels

Emu House in Emu Park (see p.473) can set up trips to other islands, or contact the marina and enquire about boat charters (see p.475). None have **provisions** or reliable **drinking water**, so take your own. NPWS camping **permits** can be picked up at the Rockhampton (see p.473) or Rosslyn Bay offices. If you want to **scuba dive** around the islands, or simply get certified, contact Keppel Island Dive Centre, near the YHA on Great Keppel (☎ 07/4939 5022).

North Keppel is an undeveloped version of Great Keppel. There's an NPWS campsite on the west side of the island, behind the dunes at Considine Bay, with a sporadic supply of tank water, showers and toilets; take precautions against sandflies, which are abundant in sheltered spots here, and note that wood fires are banned. A walking track from the group of cabins at the southern end of Considine Beach leads to the reef at Maisy Bay.

Middle Island is lightly wooded, with an NPWS camping area and **underwater observatory** complete with scenic Taiwanese junk. It's only a short hop from Great Keppel, and ferries run trips daily for about $10 return. **Humpy Island**, also off Great Keppel, is popular for fishing and has the best snorkelling reef of all the islands. The hump doesn't do much to protect it from the south-easterlies, which are the main problem with camping here; facilities are similar to those on North Keppel.

Mackay and around

Some 360km north of Rockhampton along a famously unexciting stretch of the Bruce Highway, the fertile **Pioneer Valley** makes the **MACKAY** area a pleasant break from the otherwise dry country between Bundaberg and Townsville. Despite encounters with aggressive Juipera Aborigines, John Mackay was impressed enough to settle the valley in 1861, and within four years the city was founded and the first **sugar cane plantations** were established, attracting the migrant communities common to north Queensland – it's not unusual to hear English, Pidgin and Maltese spoken within earshot of each other in town. Sugar and servicing **mining** operations centred inland on the **Bowen Basin coalfields** and remain the core industries today, though both are suffering uncertain futures: various viruses are ravaging crops and the mines are gradually following new coal seams south and out of the region.

Only mildly geared up for tourism, Mackay provides some welcome relief from the east coast "backpackers pub crawl", and with its proximity to unspoilt beaches, plus the delights of **Eungella and Cape Hillsborough national parks**, this is not an area you'll want to miss.

Practicalities

Mackay's centre straddles the crossroads of Victoria Street and Sydney Street, with the **bus station** a short walk away on Milton Street. Both **trains** (station on Connors Road, 3km south off Milton Street along Boundary Road or Paradise Street) and **planes** arrive south of town; a taxi will set you back around $8 into town and $25 to Bucasia (for some beachfront accommodation). The **tourist information** centre (☏07/4952 2677) is poorly located 3km south of town along the Nebo Road (Bruce Highway), but you can get help with bookings from accommodation or the bus station.

Accommodation

Nebo Road is a virtual landing strip of neon motel signs; rooms range from $35 to $105, with comfort and facilities according to price. For sun and sand, take the highway towards Townsville and then turn off and follow the signs for **Bucasia**. If you're going on one of Reeforest Tours' trips to Cape Hillsborough or Eungella national parks (see pp.479 and 480), bear in mind that Reeforest can arrange cheap en-suite motel accommodation at the *Metropolitan Hotel* in Mackay for $18 per person per night; bookings on free call ☏1800 500 353.

Bobby Dazzlers, upstairs at the *Mackay Central Hotel*, 64 West St (℡ 07/4957 7286). Smack in the centre of town, with pleasant rooms all recently repainted and carpeted. Doubles and twins, with TV and shared bathrooms, and a huge communal balcony right over Mackay's downtown action. Can get noisy on weekends. **③**

Bucasia Caravan Park, Bucasia Esplanade, Bucasia (℡ 07/4954 6375). Beachfront camping and units with nice island views. Few amenities, although there is a nearby store. Cabins **③**

Central Caravan Park, 15 Malcomson St (℡ 07/4957 6141). Closest park (1km) to the centre of town, though not terribly well kept. Vans and caravans **③ – ④**

Larrikin Lodge/YHA, 32 Peel St (℡ 07/4951 3728, ✉ larrikin@mackay.net.au). Low-set, comfortable Queenslander house with a laid-back atmosphere, two-minutes' walk from the bus station; also run their own bus to Eungella and Cape Hillsborough. Phone ahead to arrange check-in outside the office opening hours (7–10am & 5–10pm). Rooms **③**, dorms **①**

Paradise Lodge Motel, 19 Peel St (℡ 07/4951 3644, ℻ 4953 1341). Right behind the bus station. Friendly owners, comfortable rooms with TV, but no pool. **③ – ④**

Eating

Mackay has plenty of good, cheap **places to eat**. There are snack bars all around the centre, or try one of the places below for a restaurant meal. Several downtown pubs all offer lunch specials – around $3 for a full meal – as do a couple of the restaurants.

Angelo's, 27 Sydney St. Mediterranean cooking and genuine wood-fired pizzas.

Coco's Bar & Grill (at the *Austral Hotel*), Victoria St (bus station end). A carnivore's dream, with marinated grilled steaks in 600g, 800g and 1kg servings for $15–20.

Meeting House, 53 Sydney St (℡ 07/4953 5835). Singaporean-Chinese cooking in all its splendour: fixed-price lunches for $6.60 (try the laksa – a colossal bowl of noodles, seafood and spicy coconut soup); and à la carte dinners – around $15 – featuring unforgettable five-spice squid and whole fried fish. Very popular, so book or get in early; closed Mon evenings.

Sorbello's, 168 Victoria St. Good choice for pastas and typical Italian dishes for around $20 per person. Lunch specials Mon–Fri; open for dinner daily.

Toong Tong Thai, 10 Sydney St. Long-established Thai restaurant and takeaway with impeccable food, authentically hot and spicy if requested. Around $20 a head for a full meal.

Woody Pear, 7 Wood St (℡ 07/4957 4942). Modern/Mediterranean, with an ex-London chef and fantastic seafood dishes. Lunchtime specials menu, otherwise mains are $18 and up.

Listings

Airlines Ansett, 113 Victoria St (℡ 07/4957 4566 or ℡ 13 1300); Qantas, 105 Victoria St (℡ 07/4957 4999 or ℡ 13 1313).

Banks Branches of all major banks are located around the intersection of Sydney and Victoria streets.

Bus terminal Milton St for all buses (℡ 07/4951 3088).

Camping equipment Mackay Camping World, 54 Gregory St.

Car rental Cut Rate Rentals, 105 Alfred St (℡ 07/4953 1616), are best, with 200km free for each day of rental – just enough to get you to Eungella National Park and back.

Cinema Multiscreen on Gordon St (℡ 07/4957 3515).

Diving Mackay Adventure Divers, 153 Victoria St (℡ 07/4953 1431, ℻ 4951 1472, ✉ mad@mackay.net.au) make visits to the *Llewellyn*, a seventy-five-year-old wreck submerged in 30m of water. They also run trips to local island reefs at weekends, offer regular certification courses and organize regular outings to the famous Hardline – the very edge of the Barrier Reef.

Hospital Mackay Base Hospital, Bridge Rd (℡ 07/4968 6000).

NPWS Cnr Wood and River streets (℡ 07/4951 8788).

Pharmacy Day and Night Pharmacy, 65 Sydney St (daily 8am–9pm; ℡ 07/4957 3360).

Police Sydney St (℡ 07/4968 3444).

Post office Sydney St.

Shopping Canelands Shoppingtown, across the road from the bus station, has everything you'll need.

Taxi ℡ 13 1008.

Train station Boddington St (℡ 07/4951 7211).

Sugar cane on the Tropical Coast

Sugar cane, grown in an almost continuous belt between Bundaberg and Mossman, north of Cairns, is the tropical coast's economic pillar of strength. Introduced in the 1860s, the crop subtly undermined the racial ideals of British colonialists when farmers, planning a system along the lines of the southern United States, employed **Solomon Islanders** – Kanakas – to work the plantations. Though only indentured for a few years, and theoretically given wages and passage home when their term expired, Kanakas on plantations suffered greatly from unfamiliar diseases, while the recruiting methods used by "**Blackbirder**" traders were at best dubious and often slipped into wholesale kidnapping. Growing white unemployment and nationalism through the 1880s eventually forced the government to ban blackbirding and repatriate the islanders. Those allowed to stay were joined over the next fifty years by immigrants from Italy and Malta, who mostly settled in the far north and today form large communities scattered between Mackay and Cairns.

After cane has been planted in November, the land is quickly covered by a blanket of dusky green. Before cutting, seven months later, the fields are traditionally **fired** to burn off leaves and maximize sugar content – though the practice is dying out. Cane fires often take place at dusk and are as photogenic as they are brief; the best way to be at the right place at the right time is to ask at a mill. Cut cane is then transported to the mills along a rambling rail network.

The **mills** are incredible buildings, abandoned for half the year, with giant pipes and machinery looming out of makeshift walls. Cane is juiced for raw sugar or molasses, as the market dictates; crushed fibre becomes fuel for the boilers that sustain the process; and ash is returned to the fields as fertilizer. During operations the mills belch out steam around the clock and acquire a strange organic quality when they're lit up at night. You can get to grips with Mackay's **sugar industry** at **Polstone Cane Farm** (tours May–Dec Mon, Wed & Fri 1.30pm; $15; ☏ 07/4959 7298), where you get a rundown from a tractor-towed wagon; contact them for directions or to arrange a pick-up. **Farleigh Mill** (☏ 07/4953 8400; $15), north of Mackay, is open for tours during the crushing season (June–Nov Mon–Fri 1pm), and lay on a very popular evening tour (Wed 7pm).

Cape Hillsborough National Park

Cape Hillsborough, about an hour's drive north of Mackay, is the site of a pretty beachfront national park with tame wildlife. Your best chance for a tour is to contact the *Larrikin Lodge* in Mackay (see opposite) or Reeforest Tours (☏ 07/4953 1000); if you're driving, head towards Townsville and take the signposted Seaforth Road from **The Leap**. This takes its name from events of 1866, when a settler was killed by Aborigines and the police drove an Aboriginal woman over the cliff during reprisals. The woman turned out to be holding a baby in her arms which miraculously survived and was adopted by a local family. *The Leap*, one of Mackay's oldest hotels, is right underneath, and you can contest the details of the story over a cold beer if you're interested. From here the road passes the inevitable canefields on the way to Mount Jukes, before descending to coastal flats and turning off to Cape Hillsborough a couple of kilometres before **Seaforth** township.

The national park

The main area of the national park is set around a flat, broad, two-kilometre beach bounded by the wooded cliffs of Cape Hillsborough to the north and

Andrews Point to the south; the shallow bay is good for swimming outside the stinger season. Local fauna include bush turkeys, pretty-face wallabies and some butch **kangaroos** – they're often on the beach in the early morning, males flexing muscles and chasing does in a parody of the stereotypical Aussie male. There's a **ranger station** here, with a small rundown on local history and geology, but it's often closed. Hidden in bushland at the end of the road, *The Cape* (℡07/4959 0152; ❹) has cabins, an expensive and limited **store** (which closes at 6pm) and a restaurant.

Five hundred metres back up the road towards Mackay there's an excellent two-kilometre-long trail which follows a boardwalk through coastal **mangroves** (bring instect repellent), and then snakes up to a ridge for views out over the area from open gum woodland peppered with grevillias, cycads (see box on p.503) and grasstrees – the latter identified by their tall, spear-like flower spike. There's also a huge **midden** up here, the remains of Aboriginal shellfish feasts, plus plenty of reptiles sunning themselves around the edges of the path. Another good walk heads out 2km past *The Cape* to **Hidden Valley**, a patch of cool, shady forest on a rocky beach where you'll find more – much smaller – middens and the outline of an **Aboriginal fish trap**; keep you eyes peeled for dolphins, turtles and pelicans out in the bay.

Eungella National Park

At the end of the bitumen, 80km west of Mackay, magical rainforest and rivers would make **EUNGELLA NATIONAL PARK** (pronounced "young-g'lla") worth the journey even if you weren't almost guaranteed to see **platypuses**. There are two separate sections: lowland swimming holes at **Finch Hatton Gorge** and highland forest at **Broken River**. Finch Hatton's rainforest is authentically tropical, while Broken River's plants are more closely allied with subtropical forests; isolation has produced several unique species, including the Mackay tulip oak, the Eungella honeyeater and the much-discussed but probably extinct **gastric brooding frog**, known for incubating its young in its stomach.

Day-trips to both sections of the park can be arranged with Reeforest Tours from Mackay (℡07/4953 1000; $65) or Airlie Beach (℡07/4948 2455; $99), or hop aboard *Larrikin Lodge*'s bus (see p.478; $68); with prior arrangement, either operator might be able to take you up on one day and bring you back another. Otherwise, rent a car from Mackay (see "Listings" on p.478), head south down the Nebo Road/Bruce Highway to the city limits and follow the signs.

Finch Hatton Gorge

The Eungella road passes through prime cane country as it runs the length of the **Pioneer Valley**; 35km along, call in at **Illawong Fauna Park** (daily 8am–5pm; $11) for a close look at a big slice of the local wildlife, from crocodiles and dingoes to koalas and the bizarre tawny frogmouth. Feeding time is 2.15pm, there's a pool to cool off in and tickets are valid for unlimited entry all day.

Some 60km from Mackay, signposts just before Finch Hatton township mark the turn-off to **Finch Hatton Gorge**, 12km from the main road across several **fords** – access depends on the season, though generally it's negotiable by all vehicles. Immediately across the first creek, *Platypus Bush Camp* (℡07/4958 3204; bunk-beds ❶, or camping at $5.50 per person), provides **accommodation**: mattress, pillow, amenities and kitchen are supplied, and the rest (including food) is up to you. This is the most authentic rainforest experience you can have anywhere in Queensland: you'll see an astonishing array of bird- and animal-life (including the elusive platypus), sit by a fire under the stars, shower in the rainforest amidst fairy-like fireflies, and be lulled to sleep by a gurgling creek.

About another kilometre and three creeks further you'll find *Finch Hatton Gorge Cabins* (℗07/4958 3281; six-person cabins with showers, toilets and shared barbecue area ❺) and a small **tearoom**, and then the road ends at a picnic area, with walking tracks leading off into the forest. The gorge winds down the side of Mount Dalrymple as a rocky creek pocked with swimming holes and overshadowed by a hot jungle of palms, vines and creepers. **Araluen Falls** (1.5km from the picnic area), a beautiful, if icy, swimming hole and cascade, is the perfect place to spend a summer's day; further up (3km from picnic area) is an even more attractive version at the **Wheel of Fire Falls**, where you can sit up to your neck in the water while the canopy rises around you.

Eungella township and Broken River

Back on the main road past Finch Hatton township, you climb the range road, once a nightmare track with crumbling edges until cyclone Aivu dropped 120cm of rain in one afternoon in 1989 and the hillside collapsed into the valley. Repair works have widened the road, and though still steep it is now well surfaced. Take an immediate left at the top of the slope and stop for a drink at *Eungella Chalet* (℗07/4958 4509; twins and doubles with shared bath ❷–❸, suites ❺, five-person cabins ❼), whose back lawn beer garden and swimming pool sit just metres away from a 700m drop into the forest, with a fantastic panorama down the valley. They've also installed a hang-glider ramp next to the pool that's used for the sporadically staged **North Queensland Hang-gliding Championships** (ask locally for dates). Around the corner, a general store, chip-shop and couple of cafés form the rest of **EUNGELLA** township (the *Hideaway Café*, with its surprisingly international menu and superb apple strudel, is the best place for lunch), while 5km further, through patches of forest and dairy pasture, is **Broken River**. There's **accommodation** here at the *Broken River Mountain Retreat* (℗07/4958 4528; doubles ❺, four-person self-contained cabins with fireplaces ❻), or across the river at the NPWS campsite (hot showers and barbecues). Book in advance and pick up free maps at the **ranger's office** (daily 8–9am, 11.30am–12.30pm & 3.30–4.30pm; ℗07/4958 4552). Next door is a **kiosk** open daily for snacks and minimal supplies. Be prepared for **rain** – Eungella translates as "Land of Cloud".

Crowded during holidays and weekends, at other times the forest is quiet and cool, its interior chock full of wildlife and unusual plants. The best vantage points for **platypus watching** are upstream from the road bridge on the purpose-built platform, or from the bridge itself. Normally fairly timid creatures, here they've become quite tolerant of people, and you can often find them right through the day. Wander around the picnic area after dark with a torch to see other **wildlife**: feathertail gliders, bettong, possums, grey kangaroos and owlet nightjars. Down by the river you're more likely to come across frogs, cane toads and platypuses in the evening, while squirrel gliders are sometimes seen in the huge gum trees up along the main road, and pythons use the warm verges to energize before a night's hunting.

The real star of Broken River, though, is the **forest** itself, whose ancient trees with buttressed roots and immensely high canopies conceal a floor of rich rotting timber, ferns, palms and vines. Local **cabbage palms**, with their straight trunks and crown of large, fringed leaves, along with huge, scaly-barked **Mackay cedar** and **tulip oaks**, are all endemic; many other shrubs and trees here are otherwise only found further south, indicating that Eungella may have been once part of far more extensive forests. It can be difficult to see animals in the undergrowth but the sun-splashed paths along riverbanks attract goannas and snakes, and you'll certainly hear plenty of birds. The best two **walking tracks** are either following the river upstream to Crediton, and then returning along the road (16km); or heading through the forest and down to the *Eungella Chalet* (13km return). If you're not that dedicated, there's also an easy fortyminute circuit from the picnic grounds upstream to **Crystal Cascades**.

On to Whitsunday

PROSERPINE, 123km north of Mackay, is an everyday sugar town on the turn-off from the Bruce Highway to Whitsunday, and a major transit point for the Whitsunday region. **Trains** are met by Whitsunday Transit's buses (℡ 1300/655 449), which run about five times a day to Whitsunday. The main long-distance **bus** lines also have services which detour daily to Airlie. The **airport** is 10km south of town; call Whitsunday Transit 24 hours in advance to arrange a transfer to or from Proserpine or Whitsunday. Late arrivals can be put up at the *Proserpine Motor Lodge*, 184 Main St (℡ 07/4945 1788; ❹), or the van park on Jupp Street.

Twenty kilometres east off the highway, **WHITSUNDAY** is the cover-all name for **Cannonvale**, **Airlie Beach** and **Shutehaven** (Shute Harbour), thinly sprawling communities that as recently as the early 1980s were known only to a handful of weekend campers and yachties. Mass tourism then discovered the **Whitsunday Islands** (see p.486) and the area boomed, but even now nobody comes to Whitsunday to spend time in town; it's just a place to be while deciding which island to visit. Airlie Beach and Cannonvale are the service centres; Shutehaven, from where island ferries generally leave, is 10km on from Airlie, past Cape Conway National Park. Other cruise and dive boats leave from **Abel Point Marina** between Airlie and Cannonvale. Whitsunday Transit runs a daily bus from the Wildlife Park (see below) through Cannonvale to Airlie and Shutehaven roughly once an hour from around 6am to 10pm.

Cannonvale, Airlie Beach and Shutehaven

Coming from Proserpine, Whitsunday's first community is **CANNONVALE**, a centreless scattering of modern buildings fringing the highway for about a kilometre or so, overlooked by luxury homes set higher up on the wooded slopes of the Conway Range. Just around the headland past **Abel Point Marina** – where most of the yachts and dive boats depart from – **AIRLIE BEACH** is nestled between the sea and pine forests, with just about everything crammed into one short stretch of **Shute Harbour Road** and the hundred-metre-long **Esplanade**. Despite the name, Airlie Beach has only a couple of gritty stretches of sand, which get covered at high tide – though an artificial beach, with imported sand, is in the making.

The main preoccupation in Whitsunday is organizing a **cruise**, but you can also rent **watersports** gear from the kiosk on the beach at Airlie; spend the day exploring the coastline in a **kayak** with Salty Dog Sea Kayaking Adventures (℡ 07/4946 1388, ⓔ Saltydog@mackay.net.au; $75); or hop on the courtesy bus to the **Wildlife Park** (daily 9am–4.30pm; $15), a small zoo 7km towards Proserpine, which has an excellent reptile collection. You can explore the hills behind Cannonvale on **horseback** with Brandy Creek Trail Rides (℡ 07/4946 1121), 2km past the Wildlife Park, who pick you up from your accommodation and for $49 offer a half-day horseback ride following Brandy Creek through meadow and rainforest. If you don't want to ride, Fawlty Tours (☎07/4948 0999) runs a similar excursion by bus, including a forest walk and barbecue lunch for $42; while Proserpine River Eco Tours (☎07/4946 5111) spend a half-day ($48) cruising the **Proserpine River**, where you'll get to see plenty of birds and, if you're very lucky, crocodiles.

Conway National Park comprises a mostly inaccessible stretch of mountains and mangroves facing the islands, but there's a small picnic area on the roadside about 7km from Airlie on Shute Harbour Road, from where an easy walking track climbs **Mount Rooper** to an observation platform giving views of the islands' white peaks jutting out of the unbelievably blue sea. A final 3km on, **SHUTEHAVEN** (Shute Harbour) is a cluster of houses overlooking the islands from wooded hills above Coral Point; it's one of Australia's busiest harbours, and most of the island ferries and bareboat charters depart from here. Those with cars will find limited **parking space** here; undercover facilities are available behind the Shell garage ($11 a day), which also rents tinnies for fishing; there's an open-air grid at the harbour itself ($7.70 a day); and a free (but unguarded) area up the hill from the Shell garage overlooking the harbour.

The Reef

The Barrier Reef starts about 50km northeast of Airlie, further out than at Cairns but not so heavily touristed. If you fancy a very easy couple of hours' of snorkelling or diving, head for the pontoon at **Hardy reef** with Fantasea Reefworld (☎07/4946 5111, ⓦ www.fantasea.com.au; $141 plus dive gear). **Bait reef** is a popular spot visited by Reefjet (☎07/4948 1212, ⓦ www.reefjet.com.au; $99 plus dive gear), with patchy coral gardens, shells, maori wrasse and morays; bommies (isolated coral outcrops) on the outer edge make for good drift diving, and manta rays are occasionally seen too. The best sites – which are only visited by live-aboard dive boats (see "Listings", p.485) – are **Elizabeth**, **Seagull** and **Fairey**; Elizabeth and Seagull have great visibility, swarms of mackerel, trevally, humpheaded wrasse, sharks, and juvenile reef fish hiding in the coral, while Fairey's strong currents make for exhilarating drift dives. Don't discount the fringing reefs around the islands either – see the island accounts for details of these.

Before heading out to the reef, make sure you catch **Reef Discovery**, a slide show and talk about the reef and its inhabitants given by local divers. Shows are held four times a week at 5.30pm ($10) in the Reef Discovery building, towards the Shutehaven end of Shute Harbour Road; times are posted on the door.

Practicalities

Arriving, Airlie's **long-distance bus terminal** keeps moving around but is presently at the eastern end of town, past the *Airlie Beach Hotel*. While accommodation and other agents offer limitless **information**, your best option for an unbiased opinion is Destination Whitsunday, at the corner of Shute Harbour Road and the Esplanade, above an ice-cream shop (☎07/4948 0999, ⓔ dw@sonshinetravel.com.au).

Unless you're in town during the September **Whitsunday Fun Race**, Christmas or New Year, you'll have little trouble finding **accommodation**. All places act as tour agents, offering reductions or free nights if you book through them, although competition is ruthlessly cutthroat and some eject guests found making bookings through other agents. Hostels are all cramped, but pool, kitchen and room fridges are standard amenities.

Airlie's **restaurants** are as ubiquitous as its accommodation, with a string of places along the Esplanade or Shute Harbour Road. For self-caterers, there's a **supermarket** near the bridge.

Accommodation

Motels and resorts often offer **discounted rates** of ten to twenty percent during the low season. For a **campsite** or cabins, try *Airlie Cove Van Park*, 3km towards Shutehaven on Shute Harbour Road (℗07/4946 6727; cabins ❸).

Airlie Beach Hotel, on the Esplanade, Airlie (℗07/4964 1999, Ⓦ www.airliebeachhotel.com.au). A recent facelift has turned this former seedy motel into one of the smartest places to stay in Airlie. Older motel rooms ❺, new hotel rooms ❼

Airlie Waterfront Backpackers, near the *Airlie Beach Hotel*, Airlie (℗07/4948 1300, Ⓔ awbpack@airlie.net.au). Self-contained apartments with private rooms and shared facilities, plus dorms, above a boutique shopping complex; the loft here has great views over the bay. Dorms ❷, rooms ❹

Airlie Waterfront Bed and Breakfast, cnr Broadwater and Mazlin streets, Airlie (℗07/4946 7631, Ⓔ awbb@mackay.net.au). One- or two-bedroom serviced apartments in a modern timber high-set house with sweeping bay views; rooms are comfortably furnished. ❺

Backpackers By The Bay, 12 Hermitage Drive, Airlie (℗07/4946 7267, Ⓔ bythebay@whitsunday.net.au). Small, comfortably renovated place that's quieter than those in the centre of town and has nice bay views. Dorms ❶, rooms ❸

Beaches, 362 Shute Harbour Rd, Airlie (℗07/4946 6244 or free call 1800 636 630). Brash backpackers' hostel, with plenty of bunks and double rooms available. Dorms ❶, rooms ❸

Bush Village Budget Resort, 2 St Martins Rd, Cannonvale (℗07/4946 6177 or free call 1800 809 256). Verging onto bushland at the foot of a hill, this is relatively quiet. The owners rescue injured and orphaned animals, so you'll often find tiny kangaroos and wallabies in their care. Facilities include a kitchen and pool, and prices include breakfast. Dorms ❶, rooms ❸

Club Habitat/YHA, 394 Shute Harbour Rd, Airlie (℗07/4946 6312, Ⓔ clubhabitat@yhaqlg.org). Tidy dorms and doubles, generally busy and somewhat crowded. Dorms ❶, rooms ❸

Coral Point Lodge, 54 Harbour Ave, Shute Harbour (℗07/4946 9500, Ⓕ 4946 9469). A bit hard to find – turn up the hill immediately after the Shell garage and keep going to the end – but worth it for what are the best views of any of the Whitsundays' accommodation. Good café-restaurant here too, even if you're not staying. ❺

Coral Sea Resort, 25 Oceanview Ave, at the Cannonvale end of Airlie (℗07/4946 6458, Ⓦ www.coralsearesort.com). Airlie's newest, most exclusive accommodation; rooms are all very smart, some with ocean views, and there's a private jetty and popular bar and pool area too. ❽

Koalas, Shute Harbour Rd, right beside *Wanderers* resort, Airlie (℗07/4946 6001 or free call 1800 800 421). Basic six-bed dorms, each with bathroom and TV. Facilities include a communal kitchen, volleyball court and large pool, in pleasant landscaped grounds; you can also camp here. Dorms ❶, rooms ❸

Magnums, by the bridge on Shute Harbour Rd, Airlie (℗07/4946 6266 or free call 1800 624 634). Tidy self-contained cabins, pleasantly sheltered lawns, comprehensive booking service and a loud bar next door. Dorms plus dinner ❶, rooms ❸

Reef Oceania Village Resort ("Reef O's"), 147 Shute Harbour Rd, Cannonvale (℗07/4946 6137 or free call 1800 800 795). Probably the cheapest beds in all of Australia, with 4-, 6- and 8-bed units, some with kitchen and air-con. Price includes an excellent breakfast and a regular shuttle-bus to town (6am–midnight). There's a pool, inexpensive bar/bistro with live music, and a poorly-equipped communal kitchen. ❶

Whitehaven Holiday Units, 285 Shute Harbour Rd, Airlie (℗07/4946 5710, Ⓕ 4946 5711). Extraordinarily quiet, given its central location. Rooms are simply furnished and face out to sea. ❺

Whitsunday Wanderers Resort, Shute Harbour Rd, Airlie, at the Cannonvale end (℗07/4946 6446, reservations only free call 1800 075 069). Huge grounds with a generous assortment of leisure facilities – including three pools and two spas – to help while away the day. ❼

Eating and entertainment

You'll find a variety of places to **eat** in the area, though the majority of restaurants, as well as the liveliest nightclubs, are in Airlie. Many of the smaller cafés open early and offer cheap breakfast specials.

Airlie Beach Hotel, on the Esplanade, Airlie. Smartly renovated, incorporating *Mangrove Jack's Café* and *Capers* restaurant with a tropics-style menu and wood-fired pizzas. Ambience entirely ruined by the poker machines and TAB betting window at rear of pub.

Café Mykonos, near the *Airlie Beach Hotel* on Shute Harbour Rd, Airlie. Cheap and cheerful kebabs, souvlakia, dolmades and salads, with nothing over $7. Basically a takeaway, but there are a few tables and chairs if the nearby beach doesn't appeal.

Chatz, Shutehaven end of Shute Harbour Rd, Airlie. Bar and brasserie serving mammoth helpings of grilled and basted meats for around $12. Top-value lunchtime burger for $7.50.

The Courtyard, 301 Shute Harbour Rd, across from *Chatz*. Award-winning BYO restaurant with seasonal menu (around $30 per person). Highly rated by locals. Dinner only (Tues–Sun).

Hog's Breath Café, Shute Harbour Rd, Airlie. The original of this chain of Tex-Mex grill restaurants, still serving good grub. Main courses around $18.

KC's, 50 Shute Harbour Rd, Airlie. Blowout on chargrilled steak and seafood in noisy comfort; stays open until 3am and often has live bands. Around $20–30 for a full meal.

Morocco's, Shute Harbour Rd, next to *Wanderers Resort*. Cheerful place with a huge video screen, superb view from the terrace and excellent lunch specials. Coral trout recommended for dinner, and the Mediterranean salad for lunch. Open daily 7am–midnight.

Paddy Shenanigan's, next door to *Tricks Nightclub* (see below). Popular place to down a few and set the mood before heading next door.

Panache, Shute Harbour Rd, up past the bus terminal, Airlie. Yet more pasta and fish and beef grills, dressed up in a pricey "European" à la carte-style menu. Main courses around $20.

Tricks Nightclub, Cannonvale end of Shute Harbour Rd. Nightly grind 10pm–late.

Listings

Airlines Ansett, 46 Main St, Proserpine (☎ 07/4945 1433 or ☎ 13 1300); Flight West (☎ 1300/130 092); Island Air (☎ 07/4946 9933); Qantas-Sunstate (☎ 07/4945 1613 or ☎ 13 1313).

Airports Long-distance flights use Proserpine; local flights to or around the islands depart from Whitsunday Airport, about halfway between Airlie and Shutehaven.

Banks NAB and Commonwealth in Airlie; ANZ and Westpac in Cannonvale.

Boat charters Unless you know exactly what you want, bookings are best made through an agent. Bareboat charters should be undertaken by experienced sailors only: average wind velocity in the Whitsundays is twenty-five knots, which means serious sailing. Five-person yachts start around $350 a day, though you can add another $100 during holiday seasons. Australian Bareboat Charters (☎ 07/4946 9381, ✉ ABCcharters@bareboat.com.au) and Whitsunday Rent-a-Yacht (☎ 07/4946 9512, ✉ rentayacht@bareboat.com) have been going for years and are thoroughly reliable; or try Queensland Yacht Charters (☎ 07/4946 7400).

Car and scooter rental Airlie Beach Budget Autos, Begley St, Airlie (☎ 07/4948 0300); Thrifty, 406 Shute Harbour Rd, Airlie (☎ 07/4946 7727); Tropic Car Hire, 283 Shute Harbour Rd, Airlie (☎ 07/4946 5216).

Diving All dive shops offer training (around $535) and organize live-aboard outings for qualified divers – three days and three nights work out to about $490 for ten dives. Weather, tides and currents will determine the most promising sites on any given day, but check first on how long is spent at the reef – often a couple of dives will be around an island. Island cruises and day-trips can often accommodate divers too – see the box on pp.488–489. Dive shops include: Oceania Dive, 257 Shute Harbour Rd (☎ 07/4946 6032, ⓦ www.oceaniadive.com), who have an excellent vessel; Kelly Dive, 1 Esplanade, Airlie (☎ 07/4946 6122, ⓦ www.kellydive.com.au), who often visit little-dived reefs such as Ross and Hewitt; and Reef Dive, in the centre of town, across from *McDonald's* (☎ 07/4946 6508, ⓦ www.reefdive.com.au).

Doctor Shute Harbour Rd, Airlie (24hr ☎ 07/4948 0900; daily 8am–8pm).

Flea market By the creek, for local produce and souvenirs. Sat 8am–noon.

Flights Island resort transfers aside, various flights are available – from a spin in a helicopter over the bay (10min; $85), to a seaplane trip out to the reef and Whitehaven Beach (4hr; $235). The two operators are Flying the Whitsundays/Heli-Reef Whitsunday (☎ 07/4946 9102, ⓕ 4946 9949), and Air Whitsunday (☎ 07/4946 9111, ⓦ www.greatbarrierreef@bigpond.com).

NPWS Shute Harbour Rd, 3km out towards Shute

on the left of the road (Mon–Fri 9am–5pm, Sat 9am–1pm; ☎07/4946 7022). Island camping permits and a small environmental display. **Pharmacy** Airlie Pharmacy, opposite *Magnums* (daily 8am–6pm).

Police Shute Harbour Rd, Cannonvale (☎07/4948 8888).
Post office In the centre of town, right behind *McDonald's*.
Taxi ☎13 1008.

The Whitsundays

The **Whitsunday Islands** look just like the mountain peaks they once were before rising sea levels cut them off from the mainland six thousand years ago. They were seasonally inhabited by the Ngaro Aborigines when Captain Cook sailed through in 1770; he proceeded to name the area after the day he arrived, and various locations after sponsors of expeditions. Today, dense green pine forests and roughly contoured coastlines give the islands instant appeal, and the surrounding seas bustle with yachts and cruisers. Resorts first opened in the 1930s and now number eight, but the majority of islands are still undeveloped and controlled by the NPWS, who maintain campsites on thirteen of them. Resorts aside, the few islands left in private hands are mainly uninhabited and largely the domain of local yachties. Those covered below all have regular connections to the mainland.

Underlying all the hype, there are two ways to explore the Whitsundays – staying on the islands or cruising around them. **Staying** allows you to choose between camping and resort facilities, with snorkelling, bushwalks and beach sports to pass the time. **Cruises** spend one or more days around the islands, perhaps putting ashore at times (check this if it's the islands themselves you want to see) or indulging in diving and snorkelling. Don't miss the chance to do some **whale-watching** if you're here between June and September, when humpbacks (for more on which see p.447) arrive from their Antarctic wintering grounds to give birth and raise their calves before heading south again.

If you're **camping**, you first need to arrange transport, then obtain **permits** from the Whitsunday NPWS office (see "Listings", p.485; $3.85 per person a night). Take everything you'll need with you, especially insect repellent, a fuel stove and **drinking water** – ferrying supplies for long stays can be arranged with cruise boats. **Resorts** sometimes have a higher profile than the islands they're built on; though staying is often beyond budget means, stand-by deals can slash prices and polite bargaining is always worth a try. Most, in any case, allow day-trippers the use of their facilities.

The resort islands all offer relatively expensive return **ferry transfers** to and from the mainland. If you'd like to see more than one island, or plan to camp away from a resort, it's cheaper to choose some sort of a **cruise** – for details, see the box on pp.488–489. Once you've arranged everything else, check your **departure points**; most cruises and dive boats leave from Abel Point Marina, while resort ferries and island transfers tend to use Shutehaven – both stops on the Whitsunday Transit bus (see p.482).

Whitsunday Island

The largest island in the group, NPWS-run **Whitsunday Island** is also one of the most enjoyable, with tropical forests, short walking tracks and the brilliant Whitehaven Beach, darling of every tour boat. On the west side, **Cid Harbour**

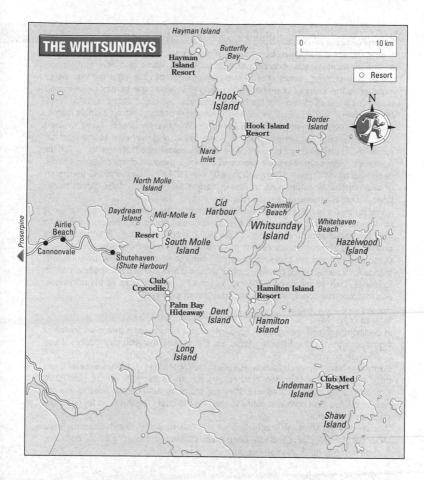

Hayman Island

Hayman
Island
Resort

Butterfly
Bay

0   10 km

○ Resort

Hook
Island

Hook Island
Resort

Border
Island

N

Nara
Inlet

North Molle
Island

Daydream
Island

Mid-Molle Is

Cid
Harbour

Sawmill
Beach

Airlie
Beach

Resort

South Molle
Island

Whitsunday
Island

Whitehaven
Beach

Hazelwood
Island

Cannonvale

Shutehaven
(Shute Harbour)

Club
Crocodile

Palm Bay
Hideaway

Dent
Island

Hamilton Island
Resort

Hamilton
Island

Long
Island

Lindeman
Island

Club Med
Resort

Shaw
Island

Proserpine

has three **campsites** above coral and pebble beaches. Dugong Beach is the nicest, sheltered under the protective arms and buttressed roots of rainforest trees, and reached by a twenty-minute walk along narrow hill paths from Sawmill Beach, where you'll probably be dropped off if you arrive on a cruise boat; there are no regular ferry services.

On the east side, isolated **Whitehaven** is easily the finest beach in all the islands. Long, white and still clean despite the numbers of day-trippers and campers, it's a beautiful spot as long as you can handle the lack of distractions. The campsite is above the tide line, with minimal shelter provided by whispering casuarinas. Snorkellers should head down to the far end of the beach facing Hazelwood Island.

Hook Island

Directly north of Whitsunday and pretty similar in appearance, **Hook Island** is the second largest in the group. A daily **ferry** ($27.50) runs to the low-key backpackers resort and the campsite at the island's southern end; there are also

Island transfers are offered by a couple of companies, who whisk you over to your choice of resort islands according to their schedules; some also offer multi-island deals. Day-cruises usually take in two or more islands, and offer the chance to experience the thrills of boomnetting – sitting in a large rope hammock stretched above the water at the front of the boat so that you can catch the full soaking force of the waves – and do some snorkelling; others may concentrate on a single theme, such as whale-watching, fishing or lazing on Whitehaven Beach. Long cruises cover much the same territory but at a slower pace, and may give sailing lessons. Experienced groups might consider a bareboat charter (see "Listings" on p.485 for operators). Some operators will drop and collect campers if given advance notice, or contact Island Camping Connection (☎07/4946 5255), who charge $45 (minimum of two people) for return runs to beach campsites at North Molle, South Molle, Long Island, Planton and Tancred islands.

The list below is not exhaustive; word of mouth is the best method of finding out about who is still in business, what the current deals are and if operators live up to their advertisements. Things to check for include: how much time is actually spent cruising and at the destination, how many others will be on the cruise, and the size of the vessel. There are scores of beautiful boats, so you'll be swayed by your preference for a performance racing yacht, or a fun trip and lots of deck space on which to lounge. Bear in mind that a cheerful (or jaded) crew can make all the difference, and that weather conditions can affect destinations offered.

Island transfers
In addition to the following services, some island resorts have their own ferries or flights for guests. The following fares are for day-returns; you pay double if you come back on a different day.

Fantasea-Blue Ferries, at Shute Harbour (☎07/4946 5111). Ferries several times daily to resorts on Hamilton ($40 return), South Molle ($20 return), and *Club Crocodile Long Island* ($20 return). Their six-trip pass ($84) can be used by several people at once, and comes in useful for halving the cost of return fares for overnight stays on the islands.

Whitsunday All Over, at Shute Harbour (☎07/4946 9499). Daily ferries to South Molle ($20 return), *Club Crocodile Long Island* ($45 return including lunch) and Long Island *Palm Bay* ($20), plus several inter-island ferries.

Day-trips: Sailing
Cost $55–65.

Illusions (☎07/4946 5255). Catamaran trip includes snorkelling and boomnetting; live music on board every Sun.

Maxi Ragamuffin (☎07/4946 7777, ⊛www.maxiaction.com.au). 25-metre-long racer to Blue Pearl Bay (Mon, Tues, Wed & Sat) and Whitehaven Beach (Thurs & Sun).

Nari (☎07/4946 5755). Refurbished fifteen-metre-long yacht; snorkelling and good deals on scuba diving.

two NPWS sites at **Curlew Beach** and **Stonehaven Beach**, both sheltered, pretty and accessible only with your own vessel or by prior arrangement with a tour operator. The **resort** has no frills but offers doubles and shared-cabin accommodation (☎07/4946 9380, ⊛www.hookislandresort.com.au; ❷–❺) with fine views over the channel to Whitsunday, a bar, free gas barbecues, a small store and a cafeteria serving meals and snacks. **Campers** utilizing their beachfront sites ($13 per person) can use resort facilities.

Day trips: powered vessels

Cost $60–75.

Jetstream (℗07/4946 7777, ⓦwww.maxiaction.com.au). Fast, open-sided speed-boat, spending a couple of hours' worth of R&R at Whitehaven before zipping up to suitable diving and snorkelling sites around Hook Island.

Ocean Rafting (℗07/4946 6848, ⓦwww.oceanrafting.com). Inflatable-hull "raft" which gives you a snorkelling trip, island walk and sprawl on a beach, all in one day. Highly recommended for a thorough taste of the islands.

Reef Express (℗07/4946 6266, ⒺExpress@whitsunday.net.au). Crowded but friendly and fast trip to Whitehaven Beach and Manta Ray Bay, the latter with excellent snorkelling.

Whitehaven Express (℗07/4946 6922, ⒺLinpac@mackay.net.au). Whitsunday Island, stopping for scenery at Hill Inlet, before a snorkel and beach BBQ at Whitehaven.

Longer trips

Cost $250–400 for two-night, three-day outings; departure time is around 9am from Abel Point Marina, returning on day three about 4pm. The basic itinerary is to visit Hook Island via Nara Inlet, then move round to Whitehaven Beach on Whitsunday.

Anaconda (℗07/4946 5299, ⓦwww.airliebeach.com). *Anaconda II* is a 25-metre-long maxi, concentrating on visiting Whitsunday; *Anaconda III* is the largest yacht in the Whitsundays, and fantastically comfortable; it heads to Whitehaven and then the reef.

Derwent Hunter (℗07/4946 6665, Ⓕ4946 7902). 90ft schooner built in 1945 and totally refitted after years spent as a research vessel, a film set and dubious activities in the South China Seas.

Mollo (℗07/4948 1511, ⓦwww.mollocharters.com). Small catamaran with a highly experienced owner who has been sailing the Whitsundays for decades. Not really a party boat.

Prosail (℗07/4946 5433, ⓦwww.prosail.com.au). Wide-ranging group of yachts – including *Gretel*, winner of the 1983 America's Cup race and still proudly flying the green-and-gold boxing kangaroo – with a variety of safe anchorages for most weather conditions.

Providence V (℗07/4946 6057 or free call 1800 677 119). Very stylish wooden replica of a nineteenth-century topsail schooner, where there's the chance to help the crew sail and steer.

Southern Cross Sailing Adventures (℗07/4946 4999, ⓦwww.soxsail.com.au). Whole stable of racing yachts, including *Siska*, a 25-metre-long ocean maxi yacht, winner of races between the UK and Australia; *Southern Cross*, a high-speed, 21-metre-long America's Cup challenger; and *The Card*, a 26-metre-long Whitbread Round-the-World racer.

Tallarook (℗07/4946 4777). At least four comfortable yachts cruising the usual selections of islands; *Tallarook II* has one of the best menus of any of the cruise boats.

Cruises often pull into **Nara Inlet** for a look at the **Aboriginal paintings** on the roof of a small cave above a tiny shingle beach. Though not dramatic in scale or design, the art is significant for its net patterns – though the connection here seems obvious – which are otherwise found only at central highland sites such as Carnarvon Gorge (see p.562). On the rocks below the cave are some more recent graffiti, left by boat crews over the last thirty years.

Snorkelling on the reef directly in front of the resort is a must; snorkelling gear and surf skis are free (with deposit) to guests. The water is cloudy on large tides, but the coral outcrops are all in fairly good condition and there's plenty of life around, from flatworms to morays and parrotfish. Other opportunities to spy on marine life include the **underwater observatory** (daily 2–4pm; $7) near the resort. Day-cruises run from Airlie to the snorkelling spots and visit the top-rate fringing coral at **Manta Ray Bay**, **Langford Reef** and **Butterfly Bay** on the northern and northeastern tips of the island.

Hayman Island

The extremely high price of accommodation at the **Hayman Island** resort (T 07/4940 1244, W www.hayman.com.au; ➒), pales into insignificance when compared with the building costs, which topped $300 million. Guests indulge in lush rooms with extravagant and genuine Baroque and Renaissance furnishings, and staff move about through underground tunnels so that they don't get in the way. Not surprisingly, day-trippers aren't allowed anywhere near the place, although cruises and some dive trips stop off for a look at the coral off **Blue Pearl Bay**, on the island's west coast.

The Molles and nearby islands

South Molle Island was a source of **stone** for Ngaro Aborigines, a unique material for tools that have been found on other islands and may help in mapping trade routes. The slightly shabby **resort** (free call T 1800 075 080; ➐) in the north of the island offers heaps of extras – such as guided walks, and all sports and facilities – along with stand-by rates. Walking tracks from behind the golf course lead to gum trees and rainforest, encompassing vistas of the islands from the top of Spion Kop and Mount Jeffreys, and some quiet beaches at the south end. There are also daily **ferries** from Shute Harbour ($20 return) if you just want a day out.

South Molle's resort can sometimes organize a lift to the campsite on uninhabited **North Molle Island**, only 2km away, or contact Island Camping Connection (see box on p.488); the beach here is made up of rough coral fragments, but the snorkelling is fairly good. There are another couple of campsites on **Mid-Molle Island**, joined to South Molle by a low-tide causeway about half a kilometre from the resort.

Daydream Island is little more than a tiny wooded rise between South Molle and the mainland, with a narrow beach running the length of the east side and coral to snorkel over at the north end. The **resort** (T 07/4948 8488; ➐) offers fine food and hospitality, but its regimental lines dominate views of the island from the sea and detract from an otherwise very pretty scene. At present, day-trippers are not allowed on the island, though this could change in the near future.

Tiny **Planton**, **Tancred** and **Denman islands** are just offshore from South Molle – with no facilities and limited camping at NPWS sites, they're about as isolated as you'll get in the Whitsundays. All three are surrounded by reef, but be careful of strong currents. Again, Island Camping Connection or cruise boats bound for Whitsunday Island may drop you off here.

Long Island

Long Island is exactly that, being not much more than a narrow, ten-kilometre ribbon almost within reach of the mainland forests. There are a few worthwhile hikes through the rainforest to **Sandy Bay** (where there's an NPWS **campsite**) or up **Humpy Point**, as well as two low-profile **resorts** at the north end of the island. *Club Crocodile Long Island* (℡07/4946 9555, Ⓦwww.clubcroc.com.au; packages including meals and transfers ❼–❽) at **Happy Bay**, and *Palm Bay Hideaway* (℡07/4946 9233, Ⓔpalmbay@whitsunday.net.au; units or canvas cabins ❺), half a kilometre south at the island's waist, have similar attractions (a disco, parasailing, water-skiing and a dozen other sports), but the latter's emphasis is more on peace and quiet. Ferries run daily from Shute Harbour to both ($20 return).

Hamilton and Lindeman islands

The apartment buildings dominating the view on **Hamilton Island** are the Gold Coast revisited, and it's interesting to speculate about what will happen to them during the next big cyclone. An enormous colony of fruit bats live in the trees behind the waterfront and, apart from the flocks of cockatoos, seem to be the only native wildlife here.

The island is privately owned, and its businesses operate under a lease: development includes a quaint colonial waterfront with hotel, bakery and various other stores, the *Hamilton Island Resort* (free call ℡1800 075 110; ❾), a small zoo, and so many restaurants, pools, gift shops and sports facilities that the original character of the island has long since vanished. The twin towers of the resort loom over the beach complex, and give the best view of the whole area from one of the external glass lifts taken up to penthouse level. Inside the **beach complex** you'll find one of the pricier places to eat, and lots of signs in Japanese. There's a daily ferry service from Shute Harbour ($40 return).

Lindeman Island suffered as a victim of feral goats, though their eradication has seen native plants making a comeback in a small melaleuca swamp and on the wooded northeast side. **Mount Oldfield** offers panoramic views, while other walking tracks lead to swimming beaches on the north shore. The *Club Med* resort (free call ℡1800 801 823; ❾), Australia's first, has all the services you'd expect.

Bowen and the route to Townsville

BOWEN, a quiet seafront settlement 60km north of Proserpine, was once under consideration as the site of the state capital, but it floundered after Townsville's foundation. Today, stark first impressions created by the sterile bulk of the saltworks on the highway are offset by a certain small-town charm and some pretty beaches just off to the north. The other attraction is the prospect of seasonal **farm work**: Bowen's mangoes and tomatoes are spoken of in reverential tones, and there's a large floating population of itinerant pickers in town between April and January. All three backpackers' hostels (see below) can help with finding work, though nothing's guaranteed.

The town centre overlooks **Edgecumbe Bay**, at the harbour end of **Herbert Street**, where you'll find the usual range of services and a couple of old colonial exteriors on the **Grand View Hotel** and the Harbour Office; **buses** stop outside Barrier Reef Travel (℡07/4786 2222). Budget **accommodation** – which should be booked in advance – consists of *Bowen Backpackers* (℡07/4786 3433; ❶) on Herbert Street; *Barnacles* (℡07/4786

4400; ❶), around the corner on Gordon Street; and *Trinity's at the Beach* (℡07/4786 4199; ❶), located near the beaches (see below) at 93 Horseshoe Bay Rd – they offer pick-ups from the centre. There's nothing particularly inspiring about any of these, which act as a base for workers; if you don't plan to work, you're unlikely to stay long. Mid-range options include *Castle Motor Lodge*, 6 Don St (℡07/4786 1322; ❹), about the closest to the centre of town. You can **eat** at the *Club Hotel* across from the post office and the late-night **pizza shop** down by the harbour, or stock up at Magees Supermarket on Williams Street and at numerous fruit and vegetable stalls.

Bowen's attractive **beaches** are a couple of kilometres north of the town centre. The best is **Horseshoe Bay**: small, and hemmed in by some sizeable boulders, with good waters for a swim or snorkel. *Horseshoe Bay Resort* (℡07/4786 2564; units ❺) makes an excellent base, two-minutes' walk from the sea, or you could simply borrow snorkelling gear and a bicycle from one of the hostels and make a day of it.

With your own transport, it might be worth skipping Bowen in favour of the **ranch-style** *Bogie River Bush House* (℡07/4785 3407, ⓦ www.bogiebushhouse.com.au), about 60km west of town towards Collinsville. This is a splendid retreat, with a range of accommodation from full-board rooms (❽) through to backpacker dorms (❶); there's a pool, you can go horse riding or fishing, and they also organize **farm work**.

The Burdekin River, Ayr and Mount Elliot

Further on up the highway, 115km past Bowen, are the towns of **Home Hill** and **Ayr**, separated by a mill, a few kilometres of canefields and the iron framework of the **Burdekin River Bridge**. The river, one of the north's most famous landmarks, is still liable to flood during severe wet seasons, despite having to fight its way across three weirs and a dam. On the northern side, **AYR** is a compact farming town which is becoming another popular stop on the **farm work** trail. The highway – which runs through town as Queen Street – is where you'll find the **bus stop** and all essential services, as well as two **workers' hostels** which can find you employment picking and packing capsicums, amongst other things – *Wilmington House* (℡07/4783 5837; phone in advance for pick-up; ❶) is definitely the better option.

North of Ayr, **Mount Elliot** looms on the horizon, the only accessible section of the fragmented **Bowling Green Bay National Park**; turn off from the highway when you see the signs for **ALLIGATOR CREEK**, about 55km from Ayr. There's a NPWS **ranger station** and **campsite** (℡07/4778 8203), in a valley at the end of the road (open 6am–6pm only), from where the creek widens into a chain of rock pools and deeper channels. The pools become more private the further you get from camp and though swimmers might attract cruising eels and nibbles from freshwater shrimp, it's pretty idyllic.

Townsville

Hot and stuffy **TOWNSVILLE** sprawls around a broad spit of land between the isolated hump of Castle Hill and swampy Ross Creek. While cynics describe its two biggest attractions as **Magnetic Island** (just offshore) and Cairns, Townsville has undergone some tasteful development in recent years,

TOWNSVILLE

0   500 m

N

Townsville Common ►

◄ Airport

◄ Ingham & Cardwell

► Charters Towers, Bowen & ⑨

Cleveland Bay

Ross Creek

Thiess Dr

Lennon Drive

Leslie St

Magnetic Island Vehicle Ferry

Reef HQ & Museum of Tropical Queensland

Maritime Museum

Breakwater Terminal

Tobruk Pool

Flinders St East Terminal

Bus Station

Dean Street

Oxley Street

The Strand

Leichhardt St

Denham St

Stokes St

Wills Street

Walker Street

Stanley Street

Stanton Street

Flinders Mall

Sturt Street

Train Station

Hospital

Gregory St

Queen St

Eyre Street

Mitchell Street

Warburton Street

Gregory Street

West Street

Castle Hill

Goat Track

Lookout

National Trust Houses

Military Museum

Saltwater Pool

Isley Street

Howitt Street

Primrose Street

Bundock Street

Heatley Parade

Mckinley Street

Durbo Street

Ingham Road

Hugh St

Percy Street

Boundary Street

Sixth Ave

Hubert Street

Nelson Street

Bell Street

Allen Street

Perkins Street

Tully Street

Morey Street

Davidson Street

Cannan Street

Archer Street

Moreland St

Saunders St

Plume St

Palmer St

Wickham St

Flinders St East

ACCOMMODATION

Civic Guesthouse   7
Globetrotters   5
Great Northern Hotel   8
Reef Lodge   3
Rowes Bay Caravan Park   1
Sun City Caravan Park   9
Townsville Centre   4
Transit Centre Hostel   6
Yongala Motel   2

RESTAURANTS

The Balcony   C
Blue Jeans Cuisine   F
Café Flores   E
Café Nova   H
Covers   B
Gauguin   A
Reef Thai   G
Tim's Surf & Turf   D

and does have its moments – above all in the muggy, salty evening air and old pile houses on the surrounding hills, which distinguish it as the coast's first really tropical city.

Townsville was founded in 1864 by John Melton Black and **Robert Towns**, entrepreneurs who felt that a settlement was needed for northern stockmen who couldn't reach Bowen when the Burdekin River was in flood. Despite an inferior harbour, the town soon outstripped Bowen in terms of both size and prosperity, its growth accelerated by **gold** finds inland at Ravenswood and Charters Towers (for more on which see pp.580–583). Today, it's the gateway to the far north and transit point for routes west to Mount Isa and the Northern Territory; it's also an important military centre, seat of a university and home to substantial Torres Strait Islander and Aboriginal communities.

Arrival and information

Townsville's roughly triangular city centre is hemmed in by Cleveland Bay on the north, Ross Creek to the south and Castle Hill to the west. Oriented northeast and parallel with Ross Creek, **Flinders Street** is the main drag, sectioned into a downtown pedestrian **mall** before running its last five hundred metres as **Flinders Street East**. The **airport** is 5km northwest; a **shuttle bus** ($6) meets most flights, stopping at points around town – phone in advance on ☏07/4775 5544. Long-distance buses stop at the **Transit Centre** on the south side of Ross Creek on Palmer Street, while the **train station** is on the north side of the creek on Flinders Street.

Public **transport** serves the suburbs rather than the sights, though much of what there is to see is central; some hostels have bikes available. A very helpful **information** booth, with a separate counter handling (and booking) diving, cruises and tours, is located in Flinders Street Mall (daily 9am–5pm).

Accommodation

Lodgings are concentrated around the city centre and near the Transit Centre, but hostels and caravan parks might collect you from further afield if you call ahead.

Civic Guesthouse, 262 Walker St (☏07/4771 5381, ⓦ www.backpackersinn.com.au). Clean and helpful, if not wonderfully modern, with a well-equipped kitchen, pool table and table tennis. Ask about deals on dive courses with Diving Dreams (located next door), and don't miss the sunset bus-ride up to Castle Hill lookout, or the weekly trip to Alligator Creek. Dorms ❶, rooms ❸

Globetrotters, Palmer St, just down from the bus station (☏07/4771 3242, ⓔ globetrotters@ultra.net.au). Small, peaceful hostel with pool and simple rooms; almost always full. ❶

Great Northern Hotel, cnr Flinders and Blackwood streets (☏07/4771 6191). Old "Queenslander" pub; downstairs bar has lots of character, and serves huge meals from $7. Rooms have fan or air-con and shared bath. ❷–❸

Reef Lodge, 4–6 Wickham St (☏07/4721 1112). The cheapest place in town, but cramped and with ordinary facilities. ❶

Rowes Bay Caravan Park, Heatleys Parade (☏07/4771 3576). Off The Strand, 3km north of the centre towards Pallarenda, overlooking Magnetic Island across the bay; take bus #7 from the mall. Very popular cabins and campsites, so worth booking in advance. Cabins ❷–❸

Sun City Caravan Park, 119 Bowen Rd (☏07/4775 7733, ⓕ 4725 1407). Family-style, self-contained units and holiday cabins with kitchen and TV, located on Ross Creek. Also tent sites, each with toilet, shower and laundry. Units and on-site vans ❸

Townsville Centra, Flinders Street Mall (☏07/4772 2477, ⓦ www.centra.com.au). Resembles a giant sugar-shaker; comfortable and bland business venue. ❻

Transit Centre Hostel, Palmer St, above the bus station (☏07/4721 2322). Minimum space, comfort and security; only worth it if you arrive late at night. ❶

Yongala Motel, 11 Fryer St (☏07/4772 4633). A

The City and around

Funded by inland gold mines during the late nineteenth century, some of Townsville's architecture is quite imposing. A stroll through the mall and along Flinders Street East, among the unimaginative assortment of pharmacies, newsagents and banks, will reveal a good number of stylishly solid stone facades and iron wraparound balconies on buildings that were formerly shops and warehouses. In the mall itself, the Perc Tucker Art Gallery (Mon–Thurs, Sat & Sun 10am–5pm, Fri 10am–6pm; free) is one such building, now featuring travelling exhibitions of mainly antique art. More offbeat, modern work by local artists is on view at the Umbrella Gallery, 222 Sturt St (Mon–Fri 10am–4pm). On Sunday the mall hosts **Cotters Market** (8.30am–2pm), which has good local produce.

The Strand runs northwest along Cleveland Bay, lined with more old houses and fig trees. The waterfront strip has been relandscaped in recent years, and the palms, fountains, lawn and strip of sand make it a nice place to sit and admire Magnetic Island and the bay; an increasing number of cafés and restaurants are springing up here too. About half an hour's walk away, **Kissing Point**, at the far end, is a grassy headland, with a stretch of sand and accompanying enclosed **saltwater pool** below – very welcome during the scorching stinger season.

An obvious target if you're after clear views of the region, **Castle Hill** looms over the city centre. There's a road to the top from Stanley Street; on foot go along Gregory Street to Stanton Terrace and join a walking path of sorts that climbs to the lookout for vistas over the city to the distant Hervey Range and Magnetic Island.

The Reef HQ and Museum of Tropical Queensland

The **Reef HQ**, on Flinders Street East (daily 9.30am–5pm; aquarium $14.80, Omnimax theatre $12), houses a terrific aquarium and the **Omnimax theatre** (hourly shows), which projects films with a popular science theme onto a domed ceiling to create an overwhelming, wraparound image. The colossal live tanks in the **aqaurium** contain immaculate re-creations of the reef, where you can watch schools of fish drifting over coral, clown fish hiding inside anemones' tentacles and myopic turtles cruising past. Equally absorbing is a stroll beneath the glass tunnel which houses sharks and other predators, as well as a partial replica of the famous *Yongala* wreck (see p.497). Between the main tanks are smaller ones for oddities: sea snakes, deep-sea nautiluses, baby turtles and lobster. Upstairs, videos about the reef are shown, and you can handle some inoffensive invertebrates – tiny clams, sea slugs and starfish.

Next door to Reef HQ, an innovative building houses the superb **Museum of Tropical Queensland** (daily 9am–5pm; $9), which showcases the Queensland Museum's marine archeology collection. The centrepiece is a full-sized, cut-away replica – figurehead and all – of the front third of the **Pandora**, a British frigate tied up in the tale of the **Bounty mutiny**, which sank on the outer reef in 1791 (see box opposite for the full tale). Accompanying artefacts salvaged off the wreck since its discovery in 1977 include water jars and bottles, tankards owned by the crew, and the surgeon's pocket watch, with glass face and finely chased gold and silver mountings. Dioramas re-create life on board, with views into the cramped captain's cabin, and a dramatic reconstruction of the sinking; and a life-sized blueprint of the *Pandora*'s upper deck is mapped out on the carpet. Other sections of the museum cover Outback

In 1788, the British Admiralty vessel *Bounty* sailed from England to Tahiti, with a mission to collect **breadfruit** seedlings intended to provide a cheap source of food for Britain's plantation slaves in the West Indies. But the stay in Tahiti's mellow climate proved so much better than life on board the *Bounty* that on the return journey in April 1789 the crew **mutinied**, led by the officer **Fletcher Christian**. Along with eighteen crew who refused to join in the mutiny, **Captain William Bligh** was set adrift in a longboat far out in the Pacific, while the mutineers returned to Tahiti, intending to settle there.

Things didn't go as planned, however. After an incredible feat of navigation over 3600 nautical miles of open sea, in June Bligh and all but one of his companions reached the Portuguese colony of Timor, emaciated but still alive, from where Bligh lost no time in catching a vessel back to England, arriving there in March 1790. His report on the mutiny immediately saw the Admiralty dispatch the frigate *Pandora* off to Tahiti under the cold-hearted **Captain Edwards**, with instructions to bring back the mutineers to stand trial in London.

Meanwhile in Tahiti, Christian and seven of the mutiny's ringleaders – knowing that sooner or later the Admiralty would try to find them – had, along with a group of Tahitians, taken the *Bounty* and sailed off into the Pacific. Fourteen of the *Bounty*'s crew stayed behind on Tahiti, however, and when the *Pandora* arrived there in March 1791, they were rounded up, clapped in chains and incarcerated in the ship's brig, a 3m-long wooden cell known as "Pandora's Box".

Having spent a fruitless few months island-hopping in search of the *Bounty*, Captain Edwards headed up the east coast of Australia where, on the night of August 29, the *Pandora* hit a northern section of the Great Barrier Reef. As waves began to break up the vessel on the following day, Edwards ordered the longboats to be loaded with supplies and abandoned the ship, leaving his prisoners still locked up on board; it was only thanks to one of the crew that ten of them managed to scramble out as the *Pandora* slid beneath the waves.

In a minor replay of Bligh's voyage, the *Pandora*'s survivors took three weeks to make it to Timor in their longboats, and arrived back in England the following year. Edwards was castigated for the heartless treatment of his prisoners, but otherwise held blameless for the wreck. The ten surviving mutineers were court-martialled: four were acquitted; three hanged; and three had their death sentences commuted. Captain Bligh was later made Governor of New South Wales, where he suffered another mutiny known as the "Rum Rebellion" (see "History", p.1146). And the *Bounty*'s whole project proved a failure; when breadfruit trees were eventually introduced to the West Indies, the slaves refused to eat them.

Seventeen years later, the American vessel *Topaz* stopped mid-Pacific at the isolated rocky fastness of **Pitcairn Island** and, to the amazement of its crew, found it settled by a small colony of English-speaking people. These turned out to be the descendants of the *Bounty* mutineers, along with the last survivor, the elderly **John Adams** (also known as Alexander Smith). Adams told the *Topaz*'s crew that having settled Pitcairn and burned the *Bounty*, Christian and the mutineers had fought with the Tahitian men over the women, and in the fighting all but Adams and three mutineers had been killed. The others had later died, leaving only Adams, the women, and the mutineers' children on the island. After Adams' death, Pitcairn's population eventually outgrew the island and were moved to **Norfolk Island** in the 1850s (see p.336).

Queensland's extensive **fossil finds** (including several life-sized dinosaur models), and touch on Aboriginal and Torres Strait Islander history.

The Maritime Museum

You'll find more about shipwrecks at the **Maritime Museum** (Mon–Fri 10am–4pm, Sat–Sun 1–4pm; $3), across Ross Creek near the Transit Centre on Palmer Street. Less lavish than the Museum of Tropical Queensland's displays, material here focuses on local shipwrecks. Most attention is given to the story of the **Yongala**, a 100m-long passenger liner which went down with all hands during a cyclone in 1911, and was finally located intact in shallow waters in 1958; exhibits here are a must for scuba divers planning to dive the wreck (see p.498). Other wrecks covered include the Blackbirder vessel *Foam*, and the *Gothenburg*, a gold-miners' transport which sank near Bowen in 1875; ghoulish salvagers recovered the captain's safe and, assuming that corpses loaded with bullion had been eaten by sharks, began to fish for them, spurred on by the prospect of recovering gold from the carcasses.

Townsville Common Environmental Park and Billabong Sanctuary

The **Townsville Common Environmental Park** (daily 7.30am–7.30pm; free) is 6.5km north of the centre, on the coast at Pallarenda. The **Bohle River** pools into wetlands below the **Many Peaks Range**, a habitat perfect for wildfowl including the brolga, the stately symbol of northern marshes. Less popular – with rice farmers anyway – are huge flocks of magpie geese that visit after rains and are a familiar sight over the city. You need a vehicle to reach the park, but once there you can get about on foot, although a car or bike makes short work of the less interesting tracks between lagoons. Camouflaged **hides** at Long Swamp and Pink Lily Lagoon let you clock up a few of the hundred or more bird species: egrets stalk frogs around waterlilies, ibises and spoonbills strain the water for edibles and geese honk at each other, undisturbed by the low-flying airport traffic. Bring binoculars.

Seventeen kilometres south of Townsville on the highway, **Billabong Sanctuary** (daily 8am–5pm; $19.80; call in advance about transfers from town or the airport ☎07/4778 8344) is a well-kept collection of penned and wild Australian fauna laid out around a large waterhole. Amongst the free-ranging wildlife you'll find wallabies and flocks of demanding whistling ducks on the prowl for handouts; things you'll probably be happier to know are caged include saltwater crocs, cassowaries (bred for release into the wild), dingoes, wedge-tailed eagles and snakes. A swimming pool and accompanying snack bar make the Sanctuary a fine place to spend a few hours, and there's also the chance to tour the grounds with an Aboriginal guide and get an introduction to bush foods.

Eating, drinking and entertainment

There are plenty of good **eating** options in Townsville. For evening entertainment, many of the town's hotels have regular **live music**, for which you might have to pay a cover charge; check *This Month in Townsville*, the local free magazine, for listings.

Cafés and restaurants

The Balcony, Flinders Street Mall. Mediterranean-style salads and grills; also good coffee and cakes and a great view over the mall from upper-storey balcony tables. Mains $10–18.

Blue Jeans Cuisine, 1 Palmer St. "Casual" cuisine in this upmarket bar-restaurant with a menu featuring barramundi, Moroccan chicken and designer pizzas. Mains from $20.

Café Flores, Palmer St. Upmarket and expensive, with bizarre and somewhat overworked – if interesting – concoctions, including peanut-crusted lemongrass chicken and roast duckling in blueberry sauce. Expect to pay upwards of $40 per person for a full meal.

Café Nova, Flinders St, near the station. A student venue, with generous helpings and meals for under $12. Serves huge and tasty salads. Tues–Fri 10.30am–midnight, Sat & Sun 6pm–midnight.

Covers, upstairs at 209 Flinders St East (☎ 07/4721 4630). A cocktail bar and restaurant that's primarily somewhere to go to be seen. The menu features ordinary grills ($25), and there's a café downstairs. Tues–Sun from 6pm.

Gauguin, on the Strand. One of the new restaurant-cafés springing up in the area – right on the seafront with outside tables and a bar. Good for anything from a coffee or beer to succulent chargrilled steak or lamb kebabs and salad. Happy hour daily from 5pm to 6pm, with live local bands on Sun evenings. Mains around $15.

Reef Thai, Flinders St. Seafood green curry, satays and the mysterious "crying tiger" (try it and find out). Mains around $11. Daily 5.30–10pm.

Tim's Surf & Turf, by the bridge, Flinders St. Open-air, riverside restaurant and bar strung along the embankment. Good-value steaks, mango

chicken, oysters and seafood (nothing over $18), and the best views in Townsville.

Yongala Restaurant, 11 Fryer St (☎ 07/4772 4633), next to the motel. Historic, authentically furnished surroundings where you can enjoy live music and good, Greek-influenced food. Appropriately, the building's architect was on the *Yongala* when it sank.

Pubs, bars and clubs

Bank, Flinders St East. A sometimes heavy nightclub sporting Corinthian columns, spiked iron railings and bars on the windows.

Exchange Hotel, Flinders St East. Run-down pub, but a real locals' watering-hole; occasionally has live bands.

JD's Sports Bar & Grill, Flinders St. Newly decked out in timber, television sets and sports memorabilia; a JD's barstool is the ideal perch for watching big sports events.

Mad Cow, Flinders St East. Pool tables and dancing to "Top 40" – packed on weekends.

Molly Malones, Flinders St East. Standard Irish bar with stout on tap, happy hour Mon–Fri 5–6pm, live bands Wed & Sat, and Irish dancing on Sun evenings.

Shamrock Hotel, Palmer St. Very busy hotel opposite the Transit Centre, with cheap meals and a happy hour 6.30–7.30pm; good choice for pool-players.

Listings

Airlines Ansett (☎ 13 1300); Qantas (☎ 13 1313).

Banks All located on Flinders Street Mall.

Bookshops Mary Who?, 155 Stanley St, has a fine range of everything.

Buses Greyhound Pioneer (☎ 07/4772 5100); McCafferty's (☎ 07/4772 5100); Premier (☎ 13 3410).

Car and scooter rental Independent, 25 Yeatman St (☎ 07/4772 6850), have basic models from $28 a day; Meteor, 333 Ingham Rd (☎ 07/4779 4422), and Can Do, 194 Flinders St East (☎ 07/4721 4766), offer deals on one-way rental to Cairns; Thrifty, cnr Ingham Rd and Hugh St (☎ 07/4772 5558), charge from around $40 a day; Townsville Car and Scooter Rentals, 12 Palmer St (☎ 07/4772 1093), start at $28 per day for a car and $7.15 for a scooter.

Diving and reef trips The pontoon at Kelso Reef is the day-trip destination of Pure Pleasure Cruises (☎ 07/4721 3555), whose fast catamaran leaves five times a week from the Barrier Reef HQ jetty, picking up from Magnetic Island en route ($122).

Diving and snorkelling gear is also available on board. Townsville's best dive destination is the coral-encrusted *Yongala*, in 15–30m of water some distance offshore; this is a fabulous dive, particularly at night. Tricky anchorage means that dives can only be made in good weather. Also be aware that the *Yongala* is a demanding site – deep, with strong currents and startlingly big fish; best not to go unless you are an advanced diver with at least twenty dives. Operators include: the Dive Bell, just south past Palmer St at 16 Dean St (☎ 07/4721 1155), who are geared towards locals rather than tourists; Diving Dreams, 252–256 Walker St (☎ 07/4771 2500); Pro Dive, in the Reef HQ complex, Flinders St (☎ 07/4721 1760); and Blue Adrenalin, 390 Flinders St Mall (☎ 07/4721 3001). All the above also offer regular courses from around $490 (including training and reef diving); qualified divers are looking at $425 plus gear hire for a three-day reef-and-*Yongala* package.

Hospital Townsville General Hospital, Eyre St (☎ 07/4781 9211).

Internet access Internet Den, Alexandra House Arcade, opposite *McDonald's* off Flinders Street Mall (daily 9am–10pm).
Left luggage At the Transit Centre and airport.
NPWS Information on regional parks at the Reef HQ (Mon–Sat 9am–5pm; ℡07/4721 2399).
Pharmacy Amcal, Flinders Street Mall.
Police 30 Stanley St (℡07/4760 7777).
Post office Flinders Street Mall, cnr Denham St.

Swimming Tobruk Swimming Pool, The Strand, in the parkland on the north side of the road, about 1km west of the junction with Wickham St.
Taxi Stand at Flinders Street Mall (℡13 1008).
Tours Birds & Bush Tours (℡07/4721 6489, ⓦwww.ultra.net.au/~bbt) run small, personalized 4WD day-tours to Paluma, the Hervey Ranges and the Town Common for around $100.

Magnetic Island

Another island named by Captain Cook in 1770 – after his compass played up as he sailed past – **Magnetic Island** is a beautiful triangular granite core about 12km from Townsville. There's a lot to be said for a trip: lounging on a beach, swimming over coral, bouncing around in a moke from one roadside lookout to another, and enjoying the sea breeze and the island's vivid colours. Small enough to drive around in half a day, but large enough to harbour several small settlements, Magnetic Island's accommodation and transfer costs are considerably lower than for many of Queensland's other islands, and if you've ever wanted to spot a **koala** in the wild, this could be your chance – they're often seen wedged into gum trees up in the northeast corner of the island.

Seen from the sea, **Mount Cook** hovers above eucalypt woods variegated with patches of darker green vine forest. The north and east coasts are pinched into shallow sandy bays punctuated by granite headlands and coral reefs, while the western part of the island is flatter and edged with mangroves. A little less than half the island is designated a **national park**, with the settlements of **Picnic Bay**, **Nelly Bay**, **Arcadia** and **Horseshoe Bay** – idyllic suburbs of Townsville – dotted here and there along the east coast. Although prices are higher than on the mainland, there's no need to bring any supplies with you.

Arrival, island transport and diving

Ferries leave from the Flinders Street East terminal and the Breakwater terminal for Picnic Bay at the island's southernmost point at least ten times daily, with extra departures at weekends ($15.70 return); pick up a **timetable** from any information booth. There's no need to book – just buy a ticket at the jetty and hop on board. Some Townsville accommodations sell discounted fares, and island hostels frequently offer deals which include ferry transfers and a few night's accommodation. The **car ferry** (℡07/4772 5422; $112.20 return for a car and up to six passengers; pedestrians $13.20 return), runs to Geoffrey Bay, Arcadia, at least three times daily from Ross Street, about a ten-minute walk east along Palmer Street from the Transit Centre.

The island has 35km of road, including a dirt track to West Point and a sealed stretch between Picnic and Horseshoe bays. Magnetic Island Bus Service (℡07/4778 5130) meets all ferries and runs from Picnic Bay to Horseshoe Bay more or less hourly between 7.40am and 7.20pm; their **day pass** ($11) allows unlimited travel. The alternatives are to call accommodation in advance for a pick-up, or make use of Moke Magnetic at Picnic Bay mall (℡07/4778 5377), who rent out **mini-mokes**. Mokes are great fun and cost $44 a day (plus mileage); rental conditions stipulate a minimum driver age of 21 and that you stick to sealed roads. Various places on the island, including accommodation, hire out **bicycles** for about $14 a day, and Road Runner, in the mall at Picnic Bay, have **scooters** from $28 a day. For a **tour**, plump for a day out in a 4WD with Tropicana (T 07/4758 1800; $125); the cost seems steep but you get very well fed and looked after, plus you'll see just about all of the island's beaches and bays. You can, of course, simply **walk** your way around the network of trails, or spend a day **sailing** to hard-to-reach beaches and bays with Island Girl (T 07/4778 5505; $60) or Jazza (T 07/4778 5530; $55), both including lunch and afternoon tea.

Relatively murky waters don't make Magnetic Island the most dramatic place to learn to **scuba dive**, but with easy shore access it is very cheap here – certification courses start at $175 – and on a good day there's some fair coral, a couple of small shipwrecks and decent fish life. The two operators are Magnetic Island Dive Centre on Picnic Bay Mall (T 07/4758 1399), a relative newcomer to the island; and the long-established Pleasure Divers, next to *Arcadia Resort* at Arcadia (T 07/4778 5788).

Accommodation

Magnetic Island's busiest location is **Picnic Bay**, though that's not saying very much. **Nelly Bay** and **Arcadia** are even more relaxed, but the nicest beaches are to be found up around **Horseshoe Bay**. Most lodgings rent out snorkelling gear, bikes, beach gear and watersports equipment, can make tour bookings and might pick you up if you call in advance.

Picnic Bay and Nelly Bay

Dunoon, The Esplanade, Picnic Bay (T 07/4778 5161, W www.dunoon.au.com). Huge pool and shady palm garden surround fairly simple, fully-furnished one- and two-bedroom apartments, some of which have sea views. **6**

Hideaway, 32 Picnic St, Picnic Bay (T 07/4778 5110). Right next to Picnic Bay's hotel, with a small pool and the choice of twin or double rooms only, though you can pay per bed. **1**

Magnetic Island Tropical Resort, Yates St, Nelly Bay (T 07/4778 5955, F 4778 5601). Exceptionally clean and comfortable chalet-style cabins each with bathroom, in a lovely bush setting. Good-value evening bistro, pool, kitchen, BBQ, plus lots of friendly birdlife. Dorms **1**, cabins **3**–**4**

Palm View Chalets, 114 Sooning St, Nelly Bay (T 07/4778 5596). Totally self-contained and very private A-frame units surrounded by palms and views; advance booking essential. **4**

Surf Side Palms, 15 Esplanade, Nelly Bay (T 07/4778 5855). Self-contained beachfront units; very quiet and relaxing. **5**

Travellers Backpacker Resort (*Picnic Bay Hotel*), The Esplanade, Picnic Bay (T 07/4778 5166). Comfortable units and pristine four- to six-bed dorms, each with bathroom. Large pool, beer garden, kitchen and BBQ. Dorms **1**, units **3**

Arcadia and Horseshoe Bay

Arcadia Hotel Resort, 7 Marine Parade, Arcadia (T 07/4778 5177). Neat, motel-style units around a pool, plus a bar that aspires to be the island's only nightclub. Organizes dive trips, with equipment. **5**

Beaches Bed & Breakfast, 39 Marine Parade, Arcadia (T 07/4778 5303, E beaches@tpgi.com.au). Small, quiet timber guesthouse with very hospitable owners, a pool, gardens and just two rooms, right across the road from the beach. **5**

Foresthaven Backpackers, 11 Cook Rd, Arcadia (T 07/4778 5153). The only quiet budget venue on the island; low-key and slightly shabby, but also a cheap, friendly spot to chill out for a couple of days. Dorms **1**, self-contained cabins **4**

Geoff's Place, 40 Horseshoe Bay Rd, Horseshoe Bay (T 07/4778 5577, E geoffsplace@beyond.net.au). Shaded, busy and frequently crowded hostel, with chaotic atmosphere, pool, bar and restaurant and reasonable facilities. The owner feeds hundreds of wild lorikeets every afternoon. **1**

Maggie's Beach House, Pacific Drive, Horseshoe Bay (T 07/4778 5114, W www.maggiesbeachhouse.com.au). Large, purpose-built backpackers' complex overlooking the sea, with its own pool, budget restaurant, internet facilities and noisy bar.

Rooms are decent and the place is well run, but this sort of high-density party accommodation misses the whole point of Magnetic Island. Dorms ❶, rooms ❸
Magnetic North Apartments, 2 Endeavour Rd, Arcadia (☎07/4778 5647, ✉ magneticnorth@iprimus.com.au). Large apartments sleeping up to six; nothing flash, but good value. ❺

Marshall's, 3 Endeavor Rd, Arcadia (☎07/4778 5112). Family atmosphere in this very friendly bed and breakfast with quiet garden; facilities are nothing extravagant but owners more than make up for it. Three-day discounts are available. ❸–❹
Sails, 13 Pacific Drive, Horseshoe Bay (☎07/4778 5117). Modern, self-contained apartments with all mod-cons, including pool and outdoor BBQ area. ❺

The island

After the thirty-minute crossing, the first thing to strike you as you step ashore at **PICNIC BAY** is the shade, a welcome contrast to Townsville's parched environment. Picnic Bay is quiet, and an unnecessary pedestrian mall fortunately fails to dispel the languid atmosphere. Services include an unhelpful **information** booth (Mon–Fri 8am–4.30pm, Sat & Sun 8am–1pm), a **bank**, **post office** and Dee Jay's **store** (with EFTPOS facilities). There's also an **internet café** in the mall charging $6.60 an hour for access. For somewhere to **eat** there's *Gossip's Café*; huge portions at *Andy's Chinese*; and *Relax-Ay-Voo Restaurant*'s grills and salads. Like everywhere else to eat on the island, they all close by 8pm.

Picnic Bay's **beach** has a swimming enclosure and is pretty enough, but most people head off after sorting out transport. The island's often-unattended NPWS office (☎07/4778 5378) – where you'll need to check in before climbing Mount Cook – is at the end of Granite Street; this is also the starting point of a **walking track** (8km round-trip) out to West Point, a small, assertively private community. The "main" road is closed to rental cars as it ends in a blaze of loose, powdery sand, and the only reason to head out this way is to birdwatch in the mangroves and dry-season lagoons.

Nelly Bay, Arcadia and the Forts

On the east coast, north of Picnic Bay, **NELLY BAY** is simply a sprawl of houses fronted by a good beach with a little reef some way out. Two streets back is a shopping complex with a supermarket, Mexican restaurant and coffee shop, and just around the corner is an **aquarium** (daily 9am–5pm; $3), which has tanks of giant clams and a few reef fish – all part of a research project and only open to the public as an afterthought. Bushwalkers with permission from Picnic Bay's NPWS office can follow the difficult trail up **Mount Cook** from the end of Mandalay Avenue. Forest blocks the view, but take a pen and you can add your name to the list in the metal cylinder left there for the purpose.

A little further along the coast, **ARCADIA** surrounds **Geoffrey Bay** and counts the good-value *Bannister's Seafood Restaurant* among its attractions – their fish and chips are one of the culinary highlights of the island. **Alma Bay** is a perfect swimming beach hemmed in by cliffs and boulders, and there's good snorkelling over the coral, just offshore. **Diving** here (through the *Arcadia Hotel Resort*) is marred by low visibility, but there are plenty of fish and brain coral, and a disintegrating **shipwreck**. A walking track from the end of Cook Road leads towards Mount Cook and the track to Nelly Bay, or up to Sphinx Lookout for sea views. At dawn or dusk you might see the diminutive island **rock wallaby** on an outcrop or boulder near Arcadia's jetty.

North of Arcadia the road forks, with the right branch leading to **Radical Bay** – impassable to conventional vehicles – and the main road carrying on to

Horseshoe. Leave your car at the junction and continue uphill on foot to **the Forts**, built during World War II to protect Townsville from attack by the Japanese. The walking track climbs gently for about 1.5km through gum-tree scenery to **gun emplacements** (now just deserted blockhouses) set one above the other among granite boulders and pine trees. Best views are from the slit windows at the command centre, right at the pinnacle of the hill. The woods below the Forts are the best place to see **koalas**, introduced to the island in 1930. They sleep during the day, so tracking them down involves plenty of wandering around – although if you hear ferocious pig-like grunts and squeals, then some lively koalas are not far away.

Horseshoe Bay and Radical Bay

The road ends in the north at **HORSESHOE BAY** on the island's longest beach, with a cluster of shops at its eastern end. Water World here has **jet skis**, **paragliding equipment**, **surf skis** and **boats** for rent. Other diversions include wandering around the **Magnetic Mango** fruit plantation, where there's also a café with all kinds of fruit-laden delicacies, or going on a trail ride with **Bluey's Horseshoe Ranch** ($48 for the popular beach ride, $66 for a half-day ride; advance bookings only on ☏07/4778 5109). Walking tracks lead over the headland to Radical Bay by way of tiny **Balding Bay**, arguably the nicest on the island; you can spend a perfect day here snorkelling the coral gardens just offshore and cooking on the hotplate provided. **Radical Bay** itself is small but pretty, half a kilometre of sandy beach sandwiched between two huge, pine-swathed granite fists.

Townsville to Cairns

The character of the coast gradually begins to change beyond Townsville: just an hour to the north the arid landscape that has prevailed since Bundaberg transforms into dark green plateaus shrouded in cloud. There's superlative scenery at **Wallaman Falls**, inland from Ingham, and also near Cairns as the slopes of the coastal mountains rise up to front the **Bellenden Ker Range**. Forests here once formed a continuous belt almost to Cooktown but logging has thinned them to a disjointed necklace of plantations and national parks. Even so, it seems that almost every side-track off the highway leads to a water-hole or falls surrounded by natural jungle – this is where it really pays to have your own vehicle. There is also a handful of **islands**, including the wilds of **Hinchinbrook**, as well as the **Mission Beach** area between Tully and Innisfail, where you might find regular work on fruit plantations or further opportunities to slump on the sand.

Paluma and Jourama Falls

The change in climate starts some 60km north of Townsville, where the Mount Spec road turns west off the highway and climbs a crooked 21km into the hills to **Paluma** township. Halfway there, a solid stone bridge spans **Little Crystal Creek**, which you might want to follow as it cascades into swimming holes overshadowed by rainforest – beware of slippery rocks and potentially strong currents. Look out too for large, metallic-blue Ulysses butterflies bobbing around the canopy.

> ## Cycads
>
> Cycads are extremely slow-growing, fire-resistant plants found throughout the tropics with tough, palm-like fronds – relics of the age of dinosaurs. Female plants produce bright orange seed cones which, in Australia, attract emus to eat them and thereby distribute the seeds. Despite being highly toxic to humans – almost every early Australian explorer made themselves violently ill trying them – these seeds were a staple of Aborigines, who detoxified flour made from the nuts by prolonged washing. They also applied "fire-stick farming" techniques, encouraging groves to grow and seed by annual burning.

PALUMA itself is a handful of weatherboard cottages in amongst the rainforest at the top of the range. A couple of walking tracks from 500m to 2km in length take you into the gloom; look out for chowchillas, plump little birds with a dark body and white front which forage by kicking the leaf litter sideways; you'll also hear whipbirds and the snarls of the elusive **Victoria riflebird**, a gorgeous black-and-blue bird of paradise. To get a good glimpse of these head for *Ivy Cottage Tearooms* (daily except Mon 10am–4pm), whose garden and birdtable is the riflebird's favourite afternoon haunt; their Devonshire cream teas aren't bad either. *Ivy Cottage* also offers bed-and-breakfast **accommodation** (℡07/4770 8533; ❺) in the house attached to the tearoom; alternatives include self-contained cabins at *Misthaven Units* (℡07/4771 5964; ❹), and two cottages for rent (℡07/4723 1925; weekend ❺).

Past Paluma the range descends west, leaving the dark, wet coastal forest for open gum woodland. *Hidden Valley Cabins* (℡07/4770 8088; ❷–❹), 24km beyond Paluma on a dirt road, provides everything you'll need: spa, pool, beer, meals and packed lunches. Nearby is **the Gorge**, a lively section of river with falls, rapids and pools – drive down in a 4WD or walk the last kilometre.

Back on the coastal highway heading north, you pass *Frosty Mango* roadhouse (daily 8am–6pm), whose exotic fresh cakes and ice creams are made from locally grown fruit, before encountering more aquatic fun at **Jourama Falls**, 30km from the Paluma road. After turning west off the highway, the five-kilometre unsurfaced road to Jourama ends at a very pleasant NPWS **campsite** (contact Ingham NPWS for booking details) set amongst gum and wattle bushland peppered with huge **cycads**. From here an hour-long walking track follows chains across the rocky riverbed to more swimming holes surrounded by gigantic granite boulders and cliffs, finally winding up at the falls themselves – which are impressive in full flood but fairly insignificant by the end of the dry season.

Ingham and around

INGHAM, 110km north of Townsville and home to Australia's largest Italian community, is well placed for trips inland to **Lumholtz National Park** – which contains Australia's **highest waterfall** – and gives access twenty-five kilometres coastwards to the tiny port of **Lucinda**, southern terminus for Hinchinbrook Island (p.505). The road through the centre is Lannercost Street, on which you'll find everything you need; interstate **buses** stop opposite the theatre ten times daily. You can pick up information on the area at the well-informed **Hinchinbrook Visitor Centre** (Mon–Fri 8.45am–5pm, Sat & Sun 9.30am–2pm; ⓦwww.hinchinbrooknq.com), on the corner where the highway from Townsville meets Lannercost Street; the **NPWS office**, which issues permits and information about local parks and Hinchinbrook Island, is at 49

Cassady St (PO Box 1293; Mon–Fri 9am–4.30pm; ☎07/4776 1700).
Accommodation prospects include *Palm Tree Caravan Park* (☎07/4776 2403;
cabins ❸) and *Motel Ingham* (☎07/4776 2355; ❹) on the highway at the south
entrance to town, or the dubious comforts of a cheap dorm bed at the *Royal
Hotel* (☎07/4776 2024; ❶) on Lannercost Street. For the various sections of
Lumholtz National Park, turn west on the road to **Trebonne** (lucidly marked
"This road is not Route 1"); for Lucinda, follow the signs for Forest Beach and
Halifax from the town centre.

Lumholtz National Park

Several disconnected areas of wilds west of Ingham together form **Lumholtz
National Park**, named after the nineteenth-century Danish ethnographer
Karl Lumholtz, who passed through in the 1880s. The road from Ingham
divides at Trebonne, with separate routes from here to either Mount Fox or
Wallaman Falls.

For **Mount Fox**, stay on the sealed road for 55km as it crosses cattle country to the base of this extinct volcano cone. A rocky, loose path climbs to the
crater rim through scanty forest; it's hot work, so start early. With prior permission, you can **camp** at the nearby township's cricket crounds – either ask
at the school, or call ☎07/4777 5117. The **Wallaman Falls** track initially follows the same road, but soon leaves the bitumen, on a signposted turning to
the right, for a dusty forty-kilometre run up the tight and twisting range; heavy
rain makes it impassable. Tunnelling through thick rainforest along the ridge,
the road emerges at an NPWS **campsite** before reaching the falls lookout. The
falls – Australia's highest at 305m – are spectacular, leaping in a thin ribbon over
the sheer cliffs of the plateau opposite and appearing to vaporize by the time
they reach the gorge floor. A walk down to the base dispels this impression, as
the mist turns out to be from the force of water hitting the plunge pool; platypuses are sometimes seen further downstream on Stony Creek.

Cardwell

There's very little to **CARDWELL** – just a quiet string of shops on one side of
the highway, and the sea on the other – but it's somehow attractive, not least
because Hinchinbrook Island hovers just offshore, so close that it almost seems
to be part of the mainland. In recent years, Cardwell has become a bit of an environmental battleground, with the recently completed **marina** 1.5km south of
town built in a "protected" mangrove zone and **dugong** sanctuary. Future plans
to add a resort aim to double tourism in the region, but the resulting increase in
marine traffic and the uncontrolled access to Hinchinbrook could be disastrous
for this fragile area. The numbers of once-common dugongs (sea cows), and the
sea-grass beds on which they feed, have already declined drastically.

Cardwell spreads for about 2km along the highway, with banks, the post
office, supermarket, hotel and the BP service station near or south of the **jetty**,
itself about halfway along. **Buses** pull up beside the post office and service station at the "Transit Centre" – actually just an open-sided bus shelter. Buy
onward tickets at the **travel agent** next to the post office. The best of the
accommodation is north of the jetty at *Kookaburra Holiday Park*, 175 Bruce
Highway (☎07/4066 8648, ⓦ www.kookaburra@znet.net.au; ❶–❹), which
has everything from motel rooms to tent sites and a self-contained backpackers' block, and free use of bikes and fishing gear; and *Cardwell Beachfront Motel*,
1 Scott St (☎07/4066 8776; ❹), which nearly faces the sea. For **food**, head to
DA's Supermarket if you're self-catering, or *Cardwell Muddies* at the northern

end of town (look for the giant fibreglass mud crab), a **restaurant–bar** with a happy hour (4–6pm), giant video screen and dance area, endless cocktails, and a mix of grills, seafood, salads and open sandwiches.

Just north of the jetty, the NPWS-run **Rainforest and Reef Centre** (Mon–Fri 8am–4.30pm, Sat–Sun 8am–noon; free; ⊤07/4066 8601) issues island permits, and has a walk-through rainforest and mangrove display. If you want to see some wildlife, contact Dugong & Island Cruises (⊤07/4066 8555), who spend half a day looking for dugong in the Hinchinbrook channel ($55), or an evening chasing crocodiles ($40).

Hinchinbrook Island

Across the channel from Cardwell, **Hinchinbrook Island** looms huge and green, with mangroves rising to forest along the mountain range that runs along the island's spine and peaks at **Mount Bowen**. The drier east side, hidden behind the mountains, has long beaches separated by headlands and the occasional sluggish creek. This was Giramay Aboriginal land, and though early Europeans reported the people as friendly, attitudes later changed and nineteenth-century "dispersals" had the same effect here as elsewhere. The island was never subsequently occupied; apart from an insular resort, Hinchinbrook remains much as it was two hundred years ago.

Bushwalkers explored as best they could until the NPWS joined the vague paths along the **east coast** into a 32-kilometre track during the 1980s. If you are moderately fit and have the slightest interest in hiking, this **Thorsborne Trail** is a must. More adventurous, unmarked routes scale Mount Straloch – site of a USAF B24 **plane wreck** from World War II – and Mount Bowen from the east coast; you'll need permission and advice from the NPWS in Cardwell (see above) to tackle these.

The Thorsborne Trail

The 32-kilometre **Thorsborne Trail** is manageable in two days, though at that pace you won't see much. **Trailheads** are at Ramsay Bay in the north and George Point in the south, and the route is marked with orange triangles (north to south), or yellow triangles (south to north).

Boats from Cardwell take you through the mangroves of Missionary Bay in the north to a boardwalk that crosses to the eastern side of the island at **Ramsay Bay**. The walk from here to **Nina Bay**, which takes a couple of hours, is along a fantastic stretch of coast with rainforest sweeping right down to the sand and Mount Bowen and Nina Peak as a backdrop. If long bushwalks don't appeal, spend a few days camped on the forest's edge at Nina instead; a creek at the southern end provides drinking water and Nina Peak can be climbed in an hour or so. Otherwise, continue beyond a small cliff at the southern end of Nina, and walk for another two hours or so through a pine forest to **Little Ramsay Bay** (drinking water from Warrawilla Creek), which is about as far as you're likely to get on the first day.

Moving on, you rock-hop over boulders at the far end of the beach before crossing another creek (at low tide, as it gets fairly deep) and entering the forest beyond. From here to the next camp at **Zoe Bay** takes about five hours, following creek beds through lowland casuarina woods and rainforest, before exiting onto the beach near Cypress Pine waterhole. A clearing and pit toilets at the southern end of Zoe Bay marks the campsite, and water bottles can be filled just beyond. This is one of those places where you'll be very glad you brought insect repellent.

Next day, take the path to the base of **Zoe Falls** – the waterhole here is fabulous – then struggle straight up beside them to the cliff top, from where there are great vistas. Across the river, forest and heathland alternate: the hardest part is crossing **Diamantina Creek** – a fast-flowing river with huge, slippery granite boulders. **Mulligan Falls**, not much further on, is the last source of fresh water, with several rock ledges for sunbathing above a pool full of curious fish. Zoe to Mulligan takes around four hours, and from here to George Point is only a couple more if you push it, but the falls are a better place to camp and give you the chance to backtrack a little to take a look at the beachside lagoon at **Sunken Reef Bay**.

The last leg to **George Point** is the least interesting: rainforest replaces the highland trees around the falls as the path crosses a final creek before arriving at unattractive **Mulligan Bay**. The campsite at George Point has a table and fireplace in the shelter of a coconut grove but there's no fresh water and nothing to see except Lucinda's sugar terminal, and little to do except wait for your ferry.

Practicalities

The usual procedure for the Thorsborne Trail is to start in the north at Missionary Bay and walk south to George Point, opposite Lucinda. **Camping permits** ($3.85 per person per night) are available from Cardwell's NPWS, who also hand out trail **maps** and practical details. Be aware that, as visitor numbers to the island are restricted, the trail is usually booked solid: for the Christmas and Easter holidays, aim to book three or four months in advance; otherwise, a month should be enough. Since different **transport** operators service the north and south ends of the island, you'll need to make two separate bookings if you're planning to enter and exit off separate ends. Hinchinbrook's **north** is served by Hinchinbrook Island Ferries (℡07/4066 8270, ⓦwww.hinchinbrookferries.com.au) from Cardwell's marina, who run daily from June until October; and three times a week from November until January, and also through April and May. There are no ferries during February or March. The journey costs $59 one way. For the **south**, contact Bill Pearce/Hinchinbrook Wilderness Safaris in Lucinda (℡07/4777 8307), who charge $44 one way, or $59 for a pick up from the island plus a bus back to Cardwell. Both operators also offer return fares for their ends of the island; contact them for prices.

Optimum conditions are during winter (June–Oct) but it rains frequently all year. Essentials include water-resistant footwear, pack and tent, a lightweight raincoat and insect repellent. Although streams with **drinking water** are fairly evenly distributed, they might be dry by the end of winter, or only flowing further upstream from the beach – take care to collect from flowing sources only. Wood fires are prohibited, so bring a fuel stove. Accommodation and booking agents in Cardwell rent out limited **camping gear**. White-tailed rats and marsupial mice will gnaw through tents to reach food; the NPWS have installed metal food stores at campsites, though hanging anything edible from a branch may foil their attempts. Snakes are also common, if seldom encountered, and you should beware of crocodiles in lowland creek systems.

Aside from camping, the island's northern tip boasts a luxurious **resort** (℡07/4066 8585, ⓦwww.hinchinbrookresort.com.au; ❸), whose charming units are connected by wooden walkways; it's a real treat, if your budget will allow for $320 per person a night. If you'd prefer to spend your time **cruising**, there are a number of options from Cardwell. Hinchinbrook Island Ferries run **day-trips** ($85) to Hinchinbrook or the reef around **Brook** and **Gould** islands – you can camp on the latter. **Bareboats** from Hinchinbrook Rent a Yacht (℡07/4066 8007) work out around $90 per person per day for a group.

Edmund Kennedy National Park, Murray Falls and Tully

In May 1848, the **Edmund Kennedy expedition** landed just a few kilometres north of where Cardwell was later to be founded, and set off to walk to Cape York. Thick vegetation forced them to abandon their one hundred sheep and three carts, and, harassed by local tribes, the party gradually ran out of food; by December, Kennedy had left the others while he raced the last 100km with his Aboriginal companion, **Jackey-Jackey Galmarra**. Kennedy was killed by Jadhaigana Aborigines while negotiating a river within sight of the cape; Jackey managed to reach the waiting schooner *Ariel*, which set off down the coast to find only two of the other expedition members still alive. **Edmund Kennedy National Park**, off the highway 22km from Cardwell, marks the spot where the doomed expedition struck inland, and you have to ponder the wisdom of trying to manoeuvre carts through the paperbark and mangrove thickets – romantically described by Kennedy's informant as "wooded hills and green valleys". There are boardwalks and trails here, and views across to Dunk and Hinchinbrook islands from the beach.

The road to **Murray Falls**, off the highway 10km north, heads 20km inland past banana plantations to the edge of the Cardwell Range and the falls themselves. There are two free **camping areas** here and tracks through the forest to permanent swimming holes and lookouts across the bowl of the valley. The nearest source of supplies is the store on the approach road, some distance from the falls.

Forty-five kilometres north of Cardwell, **TULLY** lies to the left of the highway on Mount Tyson's foothills, its 450-centimetre annual rainfall the highest in Australia. Settled by Chinese, who pioneered banana plantations here at the beginning of the twentieth century, it's nothing special today: cultivated lawns and flowerbeds back onto roaring jungle at the end of Brannigan Street, a constant reminder of the colonists' struggle to keep chaos at bay. Though most people drive the extra thirty minutes coastwards to Mission Beach (see below), there's **accommodation** here at *Green Way Caravan Park* (℡07/4068 2055; cabins ❸); while both *Tully Backpackers* at 19 Richardson St (℡07/4068 2820; ❶) and *The Savoy*, 4 Plumb St (℡07/4068 2400; ❶), also have **farm work** connections.

Mission Beach and Dunk Island

After branching east off the Bruce Highway a couple of kilometres past Tully, the coastal road runs 18km through canefields and patches of rainforest to where four peaceful hamlets collectively known as **Mission Beach** are strung out along a fourteen-kilometre-long stretch of sand. The area owes its name to the former **Hull River Mission**, destroyed by a savage cyclone in 1918; aside from the lure of the beach, forests here are a reliable place to spot **cassowaries**, a blue-headed and bone-crested rainforest version of the emu, whose survival is being threatened as their habitat is carved up. Many larger trees rely on the cassowary to eat their fruit and distribute their seeds, meaning that the very makeup of the forest hinges on its presence. Unlike the emu, the cassowary is not at all timid: if you see one, remain quiet and keep a safe distance.

Right down at the bottom end of the beach, **SOUTH MISSION** is a quiet, mostly residential spot. Signposted off the main road on Mission Drive is a

MISSION BEACH

N

GARNERS BEACH

HULL ROAD

❶

BINGIL BAY ROAD

❷

BUTLER ROAD

CULTEN STREET

BINGIL BAY

ALEXANDER DRIVE

Clump Point
Jetty

ALEXANDER DRIVE

BAMBOO CRE

❸   FERRER WALK   ❹

BOYETT ROAD

❺

CAMPBELL ST

ROYAL PALM DRIVE

SEAVIEW STREET

PORTER PROMENADE

DONKIN LANE

PACIFIC ST

CONCH STREET

i **Visitor
Information
Centre**

❻

**MISSION
BEACH**

Tam O'Shanter Walking Track

MISSION BEACH-TULLY ROAD

**TAM
O'SHANTER
STATE
FOREST**

ACCOMMODATION

Coconut Village Caravan Park	10
Eco Village Hideaway	4
Holiday Village	5
Licuala Lodge	7
Mackays	6
Mission Beach Backpackers	8
Perrier Walk Guesthouse	3
Sanctuary	1
Scotty's Beachhouse	9
Treehouse	2

Tam O'Shanter Walking Track

MISSION CIRCLE

MISSION BEACH-TULLY ROAD

❼

COOLA STREET

❽

WONGALING BEACH ROAD

❾

**Water Taxi ★
to Dunk Island**

BANFIELD PARADE

**TAM
O'SHANTER
STATE
FOREST**

**WONGALING
BEACH**

WEBB STREET

Tully & Highway

MISSION BEACH-TULLY ROAD

KOOL ROAD

NORTH ROAD

SOUTH MISSION BEACH ROAD

REID ROAD

MISSION DRIVE

**Hull River
Mission
(site of)** ◆

❿

CAMMOO ST

SEAFARER STREET

KENNEDY ESPLANADE

**SOUTH
MISSION
BEACH**

Hull River

JACKY JACKY STREET

Kennedy
Walking Track

Not to scale

monument to the original site of the Hull River Mission; after the cyclone, the mission was relocated to safer surroundings on Palm Island. At the end of beachfront Kennedy Esplanade, the **Kennedy Walking Track** weaves through coastal swamp and forest for a couple of hours to the spot where Edmund Kennedy originally landed near the mouth of the Hull River; it's a good place to spot coastal birdlife and, most likely, crocodiles.

Heading 4km north of South Mission takes you to **WONGALING BEACH**, a slowly expanding settlement based around a shopping centre and Mission's only **pub**; and a further 4km lands you at **MISSION BEACH** itself, a cluster of shops, boutiques, restaurants, banks, and a post office on Porter Promenade. Inland between the two, a six-kilometre-long walking track weaves through **Tam O'Shanter State Forest**, a dense maze of muddy creeks, vine thickets and stands of **licula palms** (identified by their frilly, saucer-shaped leaves). If you don't see cassowaries here – sometimes leading their knee-high, striped chicks through the undergrowth – you're very unlucky. Continuing 6km north of Mission township past **Clump Point** – a black basalt outcrop with views south down the beach sitting above **Clump Point Jetty** – the road winds through sleepy **BINGIL BAY** and then heads back to the highway.

Mission Beach practicalities

Long-distance buses set down outside the post office at Mission Beach, from where your accommodation might collect you if forewarned. Alternatively, a **local bus** (⊕07/4068 5468) plies between South Mission and Bingil Bay roughly eight times daily between 8.30am and 8.30pm (restricted service Sat); for a **taxi** call ⊕07/4068 8155.

The **Visitor Information Centre** (Mon–Sat 9am–5pm, Sun 9am–1pm) is just north of Mission Beach township along Porter Promenade. Behind the centre, the **Environmental Information Centre** (daily 10am–5pm) run a display explaining local habitat, along with a nursery growing seeds collected from cassowary droppings, with the aim of safeguarding the food supply for future generations of this giant bird. There are **stores** and **places to eat** at all four hamlets, though only Mission Beach has a comprehensive range.

Away from obvious attractions, there are also a couple of **tours** worth looking out for. Bush 'n' Beach (⊕07/4068 7893) organize **horse riding** on the beach, and also offer beginners' courses from $88. Skydive Mission (⊕07/4052 1822, ⊚www.jumpthebeach.com) can take you to 8000ft for **freefall** fun ($228), and also offer skydive/**white-water rafting** packages ($335). If it's riverine wildlife you're after, River Rat (⊕07/4088 6078) spend a day exploring the local coast in a flat-bottomed punt ($38); you ought to clock up sea eagles and crocs at the very least. Finally, Sunbird (⊕07/4068 8229, ⊜sunbird@znet.net.au) organize jungle **night walks** ($25), along with highly recommended **sea kayaking** day-trips across to Dunk Island ($80) – you can also do this for the same price with Coral Sea Kayaking (⊕07/4068 9154, ⊚www.coralseakayaking.com).

Accommodation

Places to stay are fairly evenly distributed along the coast and cover everything from camping to resorts. All can provide information and book you on to tours of the area. **Campsites** include the tidy *Coconut Village Caravan Park* at South Mission (⊕07/4068 8129; units ❷), and *Hideaway Holiday Village* at Mission Beach (⊕07/4068 7104; cabins ❸).

Eco Village, Clump Point (⊕07/4068 7534, ⊚www.ecovillage.com.au). Smart, motel-like accommodation set just back from the beach amongst pandanus, native nutmeg trees and tropical gardens. Luxury rooms have jacuzzi and private pool. ❻

Licuala Lodge, 11 Mission Circle, Mission Beach (⊕07/4068 8194, ⊚www.licualalodge.com.au). A tropical-style bed-and-breakfast with airy wooden verandahs and traditional, high-ceilinged interior; the landscaped garden and pool are worth a stay in themselves, and the huge breakfast will keep

you going all day. ❻

Mackays, 7 Porter Promenade, Mission Beach (⊕07/4068 7212, ⊚www.mackaysmission-beach.com). Standard Australian resort complex, with comfortable modern units arranged around gardens and a pool. ❻

Mission Beach Backpackers, 28 Wongaling Beach Rd, Wongaling (⊕07/4068 8317, ⊚www.missionbeachbackpackers.com). Large open dorms and more-private double rooms, good kitchen and lawn – all close to shops, the beach and the area's only pub. Dorms ❶, rooms ❸

Perrier Walk Guesthouse, Perrier Walk, Mission Beach (℗ 07/4068 7141, ⓦ www.perrierwalk.nq.au). Vivid tropical architecture, with a mix of Thai, Indonesian and Mexican elements in the guesthouse design and decor; friendly and very comfortable too, with pleasant gardens. Each room has its own verandah and outdoor shower. ❺

Sanctuary, Holt Rd, Bingil Bay (℗ 07/4088 6064, ⓦ www.sanctuaryatmission.com). An outstanding eco-friendly operation set in 50 acres of thick rainforest. There's abundant wildlife – including cassowary and the endangered striped possum – and a 700m walking track down to a tiny, private beach. Cabins are on stilts at tree-level and sided in fine-meshed netting, so you wake up surrounded by forest; there's a bar and an excellent-value restaurant. Even with your own transport, you need to call in advance to arrange a pick-up. ❸

Scotty's Beachhouse, 167 Reid Rd, Wongaling (℗ 07/4068 8676, ⓔ scottys@znet.net.au). A popular budget party place right across from the beach at Wongaling, with bunkhouses, a pool and a fine restaurant offering cheap meals. ❶

Treehouse, Bingil Bay (℗ 07/4068 7137, ⓔ missionbeach@yhaqld.org). Large, open-sided pole-frame backpacker haunt with a pool surrounded by forest, though distant from beaches; also tends to be overcrowded and in need of a clean. Dorms ❶, rooms ❸

Dunk Island and the Reef

In 1898 Edmund Banfield, a Townsville journalist who had been given only weeks to live, waded ashore on **Dunk Island**. He spent his remaining years – twenty-five of them – as Dunk's first European resident, crediting his unanticipated longevity to the relaxed island life. A tiny version of Hinchinbrook, Dunk attracts far more visitors to its resort and camping grounds. While there is a reasonably satisfying track over and around the island, it's more the kind of place where you make the most of the beach – as Banfield discovered.

Vessels from the Mission Beach area put ashore on or near the jetty, next to a beach rental shop and **canteen** selling sandwiches and hot meals; there's no store on the island. On the far side is the shady NPWS **campsite** (℗ 07/4068 8199 for permits and details), with toilets, showers and drinking water. Five minutes along the track is the **resort** (℗ 07/4068 8199; ❺), a low-key affair well hidden by vegetation. The best places to relax are either on **Brammo Bay**, in front of the resort, or **Pallon Beach**, behind the campsite. Note that the beaches are narrow at high tide and the island is close enough to the coast to attract box jellyfish in season, but you can always retreat to the resort pool.

Before falling victim to incipient lethargy, head into the interior past the resort and Banfield's grave for a circuit of the island's west. The full 9km up **Mount Cootaloo**, down to **Palm Valley** and back along the coast is a three-hour rainforest trek, best tackled clockwise from the resort. You'll see green pigeons and yellow-footed scrubfowl foraging in leaf litter, vines, trunkless palms and, from the peak, a vivid blue sea dotted with hunchbacked islands.

Dunk Island ferries

All the ferries detailed below run daily and cost $26 return.

Dunk Island Express, Wongaling Beach (℗ 07/4068 8310, ⓔ dunktaxi@znet.net.au). Departs 8am (not Sat & Sun), 9.30am, 11am, 12.30pm, 2.30pm & 4.30pm; last boat leaves Dunk 5pm. Free car lock-up available.

Dunk Island Ferry & Cruises, Clump Point Jetty (℗ 07/4068 7211). Departs 8.45am & 10.30am; can also provide a coach pick-up from Cairns or Innisfail.

Quick Cat, Clump Point Jetty (℗ 07/4068 7289). Departs 10am; after dropping passengers at Dunk, continues out to Beaver Cay on the Barrier Reef for coral viewing, snorkelling and diving ($134; two dives $88 extra).

Ferries to Dunk cost $26 (see box opposite for details of operators), though occasional price wars between operators might save a few dollars; book directly or through your accommodation. The island is 5km – barely fifteen minutes – offshore, but even so the tiny water taxis are not really suitable if you have much luggage. **Camping gear** can be rented from the complex next to the post office in Mission Beach; you can also leave surplus equipment with them.

Some distance northeast of Dunk is **Beaver Cay**, the local section of the Barrier Reef, with a sand island and some very pretty coral gardens that make for easy snorkelling or diving. In addition to *Quick Cat* (see box opposite), Friendship Cruises (℡07/4068 7262) at Clump Point Jetty run their old pilot vessel daily to Beaver for a very reasonable $66, which includes a pick-up and lunch (two dives $65 extra). More serious aquanauts should contact Mission Beach Dive Charters, near the post office in Mission Beach (℡07/4068 7277), who offer **diving certification courses** ($225) and explore some of the regions less-known reefs, as well as occasional forays to the **wreck** of the *Lady Bowen*, a converted paddle steamer that went to the bottom in 1894; day-trips (two dives and lunch) cost $125 plus gear hire.

Paronella Park, Innisfail and the Bellenden Ker Range

Back on the highway around 25km north of Tully, tiny **Silkwood** marks the turning inland for the 23km run through canefields to **Paronella Park** (daily 9am–5pm; $13; ℡07/4065 3225). This extraordinary estate was laid out by **José Paronella**, a Spanish immigrant who settled here in 1929 and constructed florid staircases, a **castle**, water features and avenues of exotic kauri pines in amongst the forests. Left to moulder for twenty years, the park was reclaimed from the jungle and restored through the late 1990s, and now forms a splendidly romantic theme park, with half-ruined buildings artfully part-covered in undergrowth, lush gardens and arrays of tinkling fountains – all gravity-fed from the adjacent Mena Creek. A former walk-through aquarium has become the roost of endangered little bent-winged bats, and native vegetation includes a bamboo forest and dozens of *angiopteris* ferns, rare elsewhere. You need a good couple of hours to do the place justice, and it's possible to **camp** here and explore after dark – phone ahead for details. There's a **restaurant** on-site, or you can eat across Mena Creek at the old pub.

The Paronella Park road and highway converge again 25km on at **INNIS-FAIL**, a busy town on the Johnstone River which has seen better times but remains a good spot to look for **work** picking bananas in season: the run-down *Backpackers Innisfail*, near the bright pink Catholic church on Rankin Street (℡07/4061 2284; ❶), can help if you stay with them. Otherwise, seek accommodation at the much smarter *Codge Lodge* nearby (℡07/4061 8055; dorms ❶, rooms ❸). Innisfail is anyway worth a quick look as a reminder that modern Australia was in no way built by the British alone: there's a huge **Italian community** here, represented by the handful of delicatessens displaying herb sausages and fresh pasta along the central Edith Street. The tiny red **Chinese Joss House** (and huge longan tree next to it) was first established in the 1880s by migrant workers from southern China, who cleared scrub and ran market gardens; and many of Innisfail's banana plantations have been bought up recently by **Hmong** immigrants from Vietnam.

Just beyond town, the Palmerston Highway turns off across the bottom end of the Atherton Tablelands, and at about the same point you begin to see the **Bellenden Ker Range**, which dominates the remaining 80km to Cairns. This coastal aspect of the tablelands includes Queensland's highest mountain, **Bartle Frere**. While the two-day return climb through **Wooroonooran National Park** to the 1600-metre summit is within the reach of any fit, well-prepared bushwalker, you should contact the park ranger (℡07/4067 6304) or the Cairns NPWS in advance (see "Listings" p.520) for accurate information about the route. To reach the start of the track, leave the highway 19km north of Ingham at one-house Pawngilly and continue for 8km, past Bartle Frere township, to **Josephine Falls**. Even without going any further, the falls – wonderfully enclosed jungle waterslides – are worth the trip. Marked with orange triangles, the climb to the peak passes through rainforest, over large granite boulders and out onto moorland with wind-stunted vegetation. Much of the summit is blinded by scrub and usually cloaked in rain, but there are great views of the tablelands and coast during the ascent.

Further along the highway, there's a detour at **Babinda** township – dwarfed by a huge sugar mill – to another waterhole at **the Boulders**, where an arm of Babinda Creek forms a wide pool before spilling down a collection of house-sized granite slabs. Cool and relatively shallow, the waterhole is an excellent place to swim and do acrobatics from a rope swing, but belies a more sinister reputation. Legend has it that an Aboriginal girl was raped here and in reprisal she cursed the pool against men; several deaths have been caused by subtle undertows dragging people over the falls – be very careful. You can also **camp** here for free.

Nearing the end of the range is **Gordonvale**, the place where the notorious **cane toad** was first introduced to Australia (see box below). From here, the tortuous **Gillies Highway** climbs from the coast to lakes Barrine and Eacham on the Atherton Tableland (for more on these see pp.529–530). Marking the turn-off is **Walsh's Pyramid**, a natural formation which really does look like an overgrown version of its Egyptian counterpart. From here, the last section of the Bruce Highway carries you – in thirty minutes – through the suburbs of Edmonton and White Rock to Cairns.

Cane toads

Native to South America, the huge, charismatically ugly cane toad was recruited in 1932 to combat a plague of greyback beetles, whose larvae were wreaking havoc with Queensland's sugar cane. The industry was desperate – beetles cut production by ninety percent in plague years – and resorted to seeding tadpoles in waterholes around Gordonvale. They thrived, but it soon became clear that toads couldn't reach the adult insects (who never landed on the ground), and they didn't burrow after the grubs. Instead they bred whenever possible, ate anything they could swallow, and killed potential predators with poisonous secretions from their neck glands. Native wildlife suffered: birds learned to eat non-toxic parts, but snake populations have been seriously affected. Judging from the quantity of flattened carcasses on summer roads (running them over is an unofficial sport), there must be millions lurking in the canefields, and they're gradually spreading into New South Wales and the Northern Territory – Kakadu is expecting its first arrivals in the immediate future. Given enough time, they seem certain to infiltrate most of the country.

The toad's outlaw character has generated a cult following, with its warty features and nature the subject of songs, toad races, T-shirt designs, a brand of beer and the award-winning film *Cane Toads: An Unnatural History* – worth seeing if you come across it on video. The record for the largest specimen goes to a 1.8kg monster found in Mackay in 1988.

Cairns

CAIRNS was pegged out over the site of a sea-slug fishing camp when gold was found to the north in 1876, though it was the Atherton Tablelands' tin and timber resources that established the town and kept it ahead of its nearby rival, Port Douglas (see p.532). The harbour is the focus of the north's fish and prawn concerns, and tourism began modestly when **marlin fishing** became popular after World War II. But with the "discovery" of the **reef** in the 1970s and the appeal of the local climate, tourism snowballed, and high-profile development has now replaced what everyone originally came to Cairns to enjoy: a beautiful, unspoiled, lazy **tropical atmosphere**.

For many visitors primed by hype, the city falls far short of expectations. However, if you can accept the tourist industry's shocking glibness and the fact that you're unlikely to escape the crowds, you'll find a great deal on offer and easy access to the surrounding area – the Atherton Tablelands, Cape York and, naturally, the Great Barrier Reef and islands. Used as a base to explore these regions, Cairns can be fun, as long as you accept its limitations.

Arrival and information

Downtown Cairns is the grid of streets behind the Esplanade, overlooking the harbour and Trinity Bay. **Buses** arrive at the end of the Esplanade at **Trinity Wharf Transit Centre**, while the **train station** is 750m away under the **Cairns Central** development between Bunda Street and McLeod Street

CAIRNS

ACCOMMODATION

The Balinese	4	Gone Walkabout	16
Bellview	9	Grey Whale Anchor Inn	5
Cairns' Girls Hostel	6	Hides Hotel	15
Caravella's 77	8	Inn the Tropics	7
Castaways	2	Lake Central	10
City Caravan Park	3	Leo's	14
Dreamtime		Outrigger Cairns Resort	12
Travellers Rest	18	Ryan's Rest	17
Floriana	1	Tropic Days	20
Gecko's	19	Up Top Down Under	21
Global Palace	13	YHA on the Esplanade	11

(the bus terminal may also eventually move here from Trinity Wharf). If you're staying in a hostel, you'll usually be picked up at the Transit Centre, and possibly from the train and airport if you give advance notice. The **airport** is about 7km north, along the Cook Highway. A **taxi** from the airport into Cairns costs $11; a **shuttle bus** ($5.50) connects with most flights and delivers to all central accommodation. Sunbus, the **local bus** service, is based at the **Transit Mall** on City Place (Lake St), and serves several beaches north as far as Ellis Beach; passes are available for a day, week or month and you can get free **timetables** from the driver. You may also be able to **rent bikes** at your accommodation, or check out the rental outfits in "Listings" on p.519. If you're after a secondhand car, or want to sell one, head for the Esplanade, scene of an informal trade amongst backpackers; backpackers' cars are also advertised on the **notice board** in an arcade beside the museum at City Place.

Unofficial **tourist information centres** abound, each promoting its favourite tours, though accommodation and many businesses in Cairns can offer much the same. If you want to browse through piles of tour brochures or need less biased advice, head to the information office just outside the Transit Centre on Wharf Street (Mon–Sat 7.30am–6pm, Sun 8.30am–6pm). Cairns also has several contact points geared to helping out **backpackers** with accommodation, travel bookings, notice boards and **work**; two close to each other at City Place on Shields Street are Backpackers World/World Wide Workers (℡07/4041 0999, ⓦwww.worldwideworkers.com) and Travellers Contact Point (℡07/4041 4677, ⓔcairns@travellers.com.au); both also offer cheap phone and internet deals.

Accommodation

Most of Cairns' luxury high-rise lodgings overlook the bay along the lower end of the Esplanade. This also used to be the core of the city's backpacker scene, and, though some long-established venues such as *Caravella's* 77 and the *Bellview* remain, they're relatively expensive and **budget accommodation** is spreading elsewhere. In particular, the area west of the station is a focus for a number of smaller, owner-operated hostels, of which *Dreamtime*, *Gone Walkabout* and *Tropic Days* are the pick. Large, noisy, party hostels are on the decline, though if that's what you're after, the Esplanade long-termers and brand new *Global Palace* can help out.

Expect seasonal **price fluctuations** everywhere; **book ahead** but beware of committing yourself to a special deal on a longer stay until you've seen the room – you probably won't be able to get a refund. All hostels have kitchens, most have a courtesy bus service, laundry and a pool. There is often scope for haggling over hostel prices, especially when it's quieter (Oct–April) but bear in mind that competition means slim profits are made on beds: you're only of value while you're still booking tours through the hostel. The nearest **campsite** to the centre is the **City Caravan Park**, at 14 Little St (℡07/4051 1467).

Hotels, motels and guesthouses

The Balinese, 215 Lake St (℡07/4051 9922, ⓕ4051 9822). Stylish motel with carved wooden doors, bamboo blinds and lots of tiling, plus an owner-manager who can't do enough for guests. There's a small pool, satellite TV, inclusive breakfast and free airport pick-up-delivery at any time of the day or night. ⑤

Floriana, 183 Esplanade (℡07/4051 7886, ⓦwww.cairnsinfo.com/floriana). Amiable guesthouse with sea views and Art Deco decor in the reception. Rooms overlooking the Esplanade are good, as are the self-contained "flats"; the cheaper rooms have no windows and get pretty stuffy. Rooms ③–④, flats ④

Grey Whale Anchor Inn, 19 Gatton St
(☎ 07/4051 9249). Fully self-contained, spacious rooms in an older, quiet house, with very friendly owners. ❹

Hides Hotel, cnr Lake and Shields streets
(☎ 07/4051 1266). One of the oldest hotels in town (and formerly the roughest), now under the Flag banner. Higher-priced rooms have been totally revamped, but cheaper ones are still fairly basic pub rooms, though with original high ceilings and fittings. ❺–❼

Lake Central, 137–139 Lake St (☎ 07/4051 4933, �🌐 www.rydges.com). Modern and smart self-contained units with pool; good downtown location. ❼

Lillybank, 75 Kamerunga Rd, Stratford
(☎ 07/4055 1123, 🖷 4058 1990). Very pleasant B&B accommodation off the highway 8km north of the centre. ❹–❺

Outrigger Cairns Resort, 53–57 Esplanade
(☎ 07/4046 4141, �🌐 www.outrigger.com.au). Plush new high-rise hotel with Roman-style atrium in the lobby, in a prime location close to the casino, restaurants, shops and new beach. ❽

Hostels

Bellview, 85 Esplanade (☎ 07/4031 4377, 🖷 4031 2850). The best organized hostel on the Esplanade, with motel-like facilities and a range of rooms. Dorms ❷, rooms ❹

Cairns' Girls Hostel, 147 Lake St (☎ 07/4051 2016, �🌐 www.girlshostel.webprovider.com). Renovated 1930s Queenslander, now a secure, cool and quiet place to stay with relaxed management and low prices. Can be hard to locate; look for the adjacent laundry. ❶

Caravella's 77, 77 Esplanade (☎ 07/4051 2159). Typical Esplanade hostel; a very busy place, with small dorms and a warren of dark corridors and passages. ❷

Castaways, 207 Sheridan St (☎ 07/4051 1238, ⌐ www.castaways.com.au). Welcoming hostel, about twenty-minutes' walk from the centre, with good facilities including many double and twin rooms and small dorms. ❶–❸

Dreamtime Travellers Rest, 4 Terminus St, behind the train station (☎ 07/4031 6753, ⌐ www.dreamtimetravel.com.au). Small, friendly hostel with hyperactively keen owner about ten-minutes' walk from the centre. They run day-tours

of Tableland highlights, plus offer tour/accommodation packages with their sister hostel at Yungaburra (see p.529). Dorms ❶, rooms ❸

Gecko's, 187 Bunda St (☎ 07 4031 1344, 🖷 4051 5150). New, fairly large hostel with wooden floors and dated furnishings in restored 1920s house; developing into a bit of a party venue. Some rooms get quite hot, though air-conditioning is planned. Dorms ❶, rooms ❸

Global Palace, at City Place, Lake St (☎ 07/4031 7921, 🖷 4031 3231). Brand new, enormous backpacker joint slap in the centre of town, and destined to draw much of the Esplanade traffic to its doors. Seamlessly organized with good facilities, but also expensive. ❷

Gone Walkabout, 274 Draper St (☎ 07/4051 6160). One of the longest-running hostels in Cairns, with staff who go out of their way to help, and an extremely well-informed owner. Some rooms are a little threadbare, but it's kept spotlessly clean; there's also a spa pool and small garden. ❶

Inn The Tropics, 141 Sheridan St (☎ 07/4031 1088, ⌐ www.cairns.net.au/~innthetropics). Comfortable, upmarket hostel with pool, kitchen, BBQ area and self-contained rooms on the main road out of town. ❸

Leo's, 100 Sheridan St (☎ 07/4051 1264, 🖷 4031 6281). Clean and orderly rooms in an old-style pub converted to a backpackers; wooden balcony, small pool and garden. Dorms ❶, rooms ❸–❹

Ryan's Rest, 18 Terminus St (☎ 07/4051 4734). Another quiet and comfortable budget option west of the train station, in a converted old Queenslander house. ❶

Tropic Days, 28 Bunting St (☎ 07/4041 1521, 🖂 tropicdays@iig.com.au). Though a little bit out of town, this is one of the best hostels in Cairns, with a big pool, nice gardens, good rooms and highly sociable atmosphere. Dorms ❶, doubles ❸

Up Top Down Under, 164 Spence St (☎ 07/4051 3636). Quite a way from the centre, but otherwise the best of Cairns' bigger hostels. Cheap meals, helpful staff, a huge pool and enough space to relax. ❶

YHA on the Esplanade, 93 Esplanade
(☎ 07/4031 1919, ⌐ www.esplanade@yhaqld.org). Crowded, animated hostel, but expensive (especially for non-YHA members), and pushy with tour bookings. ❷

The City

Cairns' strength is in doing, not seeing: there are few monuments, natural or otherwise. This is partly because the Cape York goldfields were too far away and profits were channelled through Cooktown, and partly because Cairns was remote, lacking a rail link with Townsville until 1924; people came here to exploit resources, not to settle. Your best introduction to the region's heritage is at the **Cairns Historical Museum**, at the junction of Shields and Lake streets (Mon–Sat 10am–3pm; $4), which uses photos and some interesting exhibits to cover maritime history, the Tjapukai and Bama Aborigines from the tablelands, and Chinese involvement in the city and Palmer goldfields.

At **City Place**, the **pedestrian mall** around the museum, you'll find Cairns' souvenir-shopping centre, with a rash of cafés, and shops selling didgeridoos, T-shirts, paintings and cuddly koalas. Local performers do their best at the small **sound shell** here from time to time, and there are often more professional offerings in the evenings. Between Grafton and Sheridan Streets, towards Spence Street, **Rusty's Bazaar markets** (Fri evening, Sat & Sun morning) sell a great range of local produce from crafts to herbs, fruit and veg, coffee and fish. Moving from the mall area down towards Trinity Wharf, the shops become more upmarket, though they're still selling essentially the same things; an increasing number of signs target the many Japanese visitors. **Trinity Wharf** itself is a dormant collection of offices and **cruise terminals**, but you might find solace in the bar above the bus station, which overlooks the yachts and trawlers moored in Trinity Inlet. The *Barrier Reef Hotel*, opposite, is the last of the original rough-and-ready bars, recently given a face-lift; if you're after local colour, this is where you'll find it.

The glass-domed **casino** faces **The Pier**, a flashy shopping complex, where many tour and cruise operators have booking offices ready to tempt you with brochures and videos of their activities. An **aquarium** (daily 8am–8pm; $12.50) here has regular feeding shows and big tanks full of hulking reef fish such as maori wrasse, sharks and potato cod, but somehow lacks punch.

Through the day and into the night, the **Esplanade** is packed with people cruising between accommodation, shops and restaurants. Grabbing an early-morning coffee here, you'll witness a quintessentially Australian scene: fig trees framing the waterfront, a couple of trawlers and seaplanes bobbing at anchor in the harbour, and drunks languishing on the benches. Joggers jog, and others promenade along the edge at low tide and watch birds feeding in the shallows – there's an identification chart in the park. Though originally fringed in mangroves and mud flats, developers have, after years of wrangles, created an **artificial beach** down near the Pier; at present the sand is in place but grassed over while it stabilizes and settles. Many locals consider the whole project a waste of money, but when the turf is peeled off at some point in 2002, Cairns will finally have its own beach. The **night market** (daily 5pm–late), which runs right through from the Esplanade to Abbott Street, has a mix of fast-food courts, trendy tack and good-quality souvenirs, and a good location near plenty of bars.

Just around the corner from the Esplanade on Shields Street, **Cairns Regional Art Gallery** (Mon–Fri 10am–6pm, Sat & Sun 1–6pm; $6.60) is worth a look if Cairns' crasser commercial side is beginning to grate; exhibitions include both local artists' work and travelling shows. While you're down this way, drop into **Gallery Tikowi** next door – though actually a shop, it's virtually a museum of New Guinea and eastern Indonesian crafts and well worth a visit.

Heading out of the centre, the city's natural attractions include the **Botanic Gardens** (Mon–Fri 8.30am–5.30pm; free) and the adjacent **Mount Whitfield Environmental Park** on Collins Avenue, off the highway near the airport (bus #7 from the City Place transit mall, or a dull forty-minute walk). Ringed by suburbia, the rainforest is dense enough for wallabies, and a raised board-walk track through the wonderfully cool and tranquil atmosphere makes a fine escape from the city. Also worth a look are the **mangrove walks** on the airport road, which, from boardwalks and hides, give you a chance to see the different varieties of mangrove trees, mudskippers and red-clawed, asymmetric fiddler crabs. Take some repellent or else give the flies a free lunch.

Eating and nightlife

Cairns has no shortage of places to **eat**. Least expensive are the takeaways between the Esplanade's hostels serving Chinese food, falafel, kebabs and pasta. Some open early while others, such as *La Pizza* on the corner of Aplin Street, never close, switching from fast food during the day and evening to coffee and croissants at dawn. The night market also houses a fast-food plaza, with a choice ranging from fish and chips to pizza or sushi. If you want to eat in, any of the restaurants listed below offer good value; alternatively, you can stock up at the **supermarkets** on Abbott Street or in Cairns Central.

Openly **drinking** on the streets is illegal in Cairns, but the pub and club culture thrives undaunted. **Clubs** open around 6pm, most charging $5 entry for bar and disco entertainment, or more if there's a band playing; some will collect you from your hostel and throw in a free or discounted meal. Many **pubs** also feature **live music** once a week, and some home-grown talent such as Women in Docs have recently made the national music scene – reviews and details are in Cairns' free weekly **listings magazine**, *Barfly*. Try not to make yourself an obvious target for **pickpockets** and bag-snatchers who work the nightclubs, though the steady reports of rapes and muggings are more worrying – take advantage of the **Home and Dry Bus** which leaves from outside *PJ O'Briens* on Shields Street on the hour between 11pm and 4am, and delivers to all the city's backpackers for just $1.

Cafés and restaurants

Barnacle Bill, 65 Esplanade (☏07/4051 2241). Popular seafood restaurant, where you choose your lobster and Moreton Bay bugs from the live tank. Food is good, but it's the Esplanade location which really pulls in the crowds. Main courses for around $25. Open daily from 5pm.

Cock & Bull, 6 Grove St, cnr Grafton St. Keg Guinness, good-quality and huge counter meals ($12–17) and a pleasant garden atmosphere.

Curry Bowl, in the arcade between Grafton and Lake streets, just south of Shields St. Very ordinary looking fast-food counter, but portions of Sri Lankan *dahls* and curries are large, cheap and pretty authentic. Mostly vegetarian too.

Dundees, Spence St. Popular upmarket grill restaurant, with leanings towards native fauna – kangaroo, emu, crocodile – and seafood. Best dishes are the kangaroo satay, and seafood platter (includes crays and mud crab). Mains around $25.

Fetta's, Abbott St. Very reasonably priced Greek restaurant with particularly good seafood. Most main dishes around $20; vegetable dishes from $16.

Gypsy Dees, 41a Shields St (☏07/4051 5530). A mixture of Oriental and European main courses from $19, backed by a bar and live music.

Havannahs, Bunda St. Cheap, cheerful and tasty evening meals; mains – such as spicy chicken salsa or meat grills served with rice or chips – are only $8. Singer-songwriter night every Tues, when anyone can get up and air their vocal chords.

La Fettuccina, 43 Shields St (☏07/4031 5959). Excellent home-made pasta from $15; very popular, so get in early or book at table.

Matsuri, next to the night-market entrance on Abbott St. Best place for sushi, noodle soups or other Japanese light meals in an authentic environment – popular with Japanese tourists. Nothing over $12.

Mozart Pastry, 42 Spence St. Top-notch patisserie with crisp strudels, rich cakes and fine coffee.

Rattle and Hum, Esplanade. Smart bar and grill serving huge platters of steak and seafood while Sade warbles out of the jukebox. Neon-lit pool tables are popular too. Mains $17 or less.

Red Ochre, 43 Shields St (☏07/4051 0100). Long-running restaurant with Outback decor and a menu revolving around truly Australian ingredients. Their emu or kangaroo dishes are the best in town, and the green salad with lemon aspen and macadamia nut dressing is not to be missed. $25 and up.

Sports Bar-Nightclub-Café, Spence St. Bar with light, good-value meals, and plenty of satellite sport channels playing on the video screen. $10 lunchtime specials include pasta or chicken, or barramundi dishes; stays open until 5am.

Underdog, cnr Spence and Sheridan streets. Noisy pub whose *Tuckerbox* beer garden bistro caters mostly to an evening backpacker crowd, with similar atmosphere and intent as the *Woolshed*, including discount meals and voucher deals.

Windows, upstairs at the Pier. After a night out, settle your stomach with a $10 all-you-can-eat-breakfast here from 7am. Fixed-price lunches and seafood dinners too.

Woolshed, 22 Shields St. Budget/backpackers' diner, with huge and inexpensive meals, beer by the jug and party fever. Hostels give out vouchers for various discount meal deals here; it's worth "upgrading" these for a couple more dollars and getting a full-blown feed.

Nightlife

Casa De Meze, cnr Aplin St and the Esplanade. Open nightly, but best to come for Sun afternoon jam sessions of Latin and jazz spilling out of the bar.

Club Nu Trix, 53 Spence St (⊤07/4057 8075). Gay club. Wed–Sun 9pm–late.

Johno's, cnr Abbott and Aplin streets. Traditional backpackers' haunt, with a huge video screen and a youngish clientele. Live music most nights too; it's worth catching the legendary Johno and the house band.

P.J.O'Brien's, City Place, next to Hides, Shields St. Irish bar with mix of local and tourist custom – a popular place to meet and warm up before later club sessions. Best on Fri, Sat, and Sun nights.

Playpen, cnr Lake and Hartley streets. Nightclub and disco, with action on most nights.

XS, 10 Shields St (⊤07/4051 6887). Cairns' newest gay bar. Daily noon–2am.

Activities

In addition to the tours covered in the box opposite, several operators offer more activity-led excursions. The Adventure Company (⊤07/4051 4777) spends two days **bushwalking** in the jungle around the foothills of Bartle Frere ($225); while Jungle Tours (⊤07/4031 1110 or free call 1800 817 234), has two- to six-day rainforest and bush trekking adventures in the Daintree and Chillagoe areas. **Bicycle tours** around the Atherton Tablelands are on offer with Bandicoot Bike Hire & Tours (⊤07/4055 0155), or adrenaline junkies can get stuck into some moderate to extreme off-road biking around Cairns and Cape Tribulation ($69–130) with Dan's Mountain Biking (⊤07/4033 0128). For something a little tamer, Mulgrave River Horse Adventures (⊤07/4056 3000) organizes three- to six-hour **trail rides** in the bushland and forest around Gordonvale ($69–120; pick-up from Cairns available).

Finally, for the really brave, Rock Wallaby (⊤07/4054 7902) run half- to three-day **abseiling** and rap-jumping trips to the Barron Gorge and other rock faces around Cairns ($55–495), while Skydive Cairns (free call ⊤1800 444 568) offer tandem **parachuting** thrills for $228, or solo skydive tuition and jump for just $550 – the most frightening thing you can ever do. The best place to **bungee-jump** in Queensland is from a purpose-built platform surrounded by rainforest in the hills off the coastal highway 5km beyond Smithfield (see p.520), just north of Cairns. With airborne time, including rebounds, at only a matter of seconds, it's the climb up to the tower and steeling yourself to take the plunge into what looks like a fishpond that gets the adrenaline going. Contact A.J. Hackett to make bookings (⊤07/4057 7188); the first jump costs $99, but it gets cheaper thereafter, or with various deals. For even more action, there's **white-water rafting** in the Barron Gorge (see p.520) – wild fun despite being a conveyor-belt business: as you pick yourself out of the river, the raft is dragged back for the next busload. Agents include Raging Thunder (⊤07/4030 7990, ⓦwww.ragingthunder.com.au) and Foaming Fury (⊤07/4031 3460, ⓦwww.foamingfury.com.au), who also cover the less crowded Johnstone and Russel rivers.

For **diving**, see box on pp.522–523.

Tours from Cairns

Before exploring locally or around the Atherton Tablelands, Port Douglas and Cape Tribulation, bear in mind that the cheapest day-tours will set you back $65 per person, while car rental comes as low as $50 for the day – though you'll miss out on a tour guide's local knowledge. For Cape York beyond Cooktown, you'll need a tour or your own vehicle. For the Atherton Tablelands the Daintree and Cape Tribulation (and possibly Cooktown), the following come highly recommended: Tropical Horizons (☏07/4058 1244); the backpacker-oriented Jungle Tours (☏07/4032 5600); Queensland Adventure Safaris (☏07/4041 2418, ⍟www.qastours.com); and Uncle Brian (☏07/4050 0615); also worth trying are Trek North Safaris (☏07/4051 4328, ⍟www.treknorth.com.au); the exhaustingly full-on Eco-Mania (☏07/4031 6171); long-running Wait-a-While Spotlighting Tours (☏07/4033 1153, ⍟www.waitawhile.com) for night wildlife hunts; the well-informed Wilderness Challenge (☏07/4055 6504, ⍟www.wilderness-challenge.com.au); Australian Wilderness Safaris (☏07/4098 1766); Northern Exposure (☏07/4051 5111); and Tropics Explorer (☏07/4055 4555). For Cape York, the following organize trips to the tip by 4WD, boat and plane, and enjoy reliable reputations: OZtours (☏07/4055 9535, ⍟www.oztours.com.au); Billy Tea Bush Safaris (☏07/4032 0077, ⍟www.billytea.com.au); and Kamp-Out Safaris (☏07/4031 4862, ⍟www.heritagetours.com.au). Wilderness Challenge (☏07/4055 6504, ⍟www.wilderness-challenge.com.au), visit the Daintree Cape Tribulation and Mossman Gorge, and also go to Cooktown and the Aboriginal rock art sites around Laura.

Listings

Airlines Air New Zealand (☏13 2476); Air Niugini, 4 Shields St (☏13 1380); Ansett (☏13 1300); Cape York Air Services, airport (☏07/4035 9399); Flight West (☏13 2392); Garuda, *Hilton Hotel*, Wharf St (☏07/4031 2288); JAL, 15 Lake St (☏07/4031 2285); Malaysia, 15 Lake St (☏13 2727); Qantas (☏13 1313); Singapore, 15 Lake St (☏07/4031 7538); Transtate (☏13 1528).

Banks and exchange Banks are scattered throughout the city centre, mostly around the intersection of Shields and Abbott streets and in Cairns Central. Some hostels on the Esplanade also offer bureau de change facilities, though rates are lower than at the banks.

Bike and motorbike rentals Bandicoot Bicycle Hire & Tours, 59 Sheridan St (☏07/4055 0155); Jolly Frog, 147 Sheridan St (☏07/4031 2379).

Books and maps Walkers Bookshop, 96 Lake St (☏07/4051 2410) for general needs; for second-hand, try the excellent Exchange Book Shop, 78 Grafton St. The Croc Shop, City Place, also produces a good road map of Cape York.

Buses Coral Coaches, Transit Centre (☏07/4031 7577) for routes to Cooktown, the Atherton Tablelands, Normanton, Karumba, Cloncurry and Mount Isa; Greyhound Pioneer, Transit Centre (☏07/4051 5899); McCafferty's, Transit Centre (☏07/4051 5899); Premier, Transit Centre (☏13

3410); White Car Coaches, next to the *Underdog*, Spence St (☏07/4051 9533), for the Atherton Tablelands.

Camping equipment Adventure Equipment, 133 Grafton St (☏07/4031 2669), stock and hire out all types of outdoor gear and even kayaks; City Place Disposals, cnr Shields and Grafton streets; Geo Pickers, 108 Mulgrave Rd, cnr Draper St; Wolfies Disposals, 56 McLeod St, for basic equipment and secondhand gear.

Car rental All of the following offer discounts on long rentals; on a day-by-day basis, you're looking at around $50–55 for a four-person runaround. A1 Car Rental, 141 Lake St (☏07/4031 1326); All Day, 151 Lake St (☏07/4031 3348); Billabong, 132 Sheridan St (☏07/4051 4299); Britz, 411 Sheridan St (☏07/4032 2611), for 4WDs, motorhomes and campervans; Cruising, 196 Sheridan St (☏07/4041 4666); Thrifty, 40 Aplin St and at the airport (☏07/4051 8099).

Cinemas Multi-screens, 108 Grafton St (☏07/4051 1222), and in Cairns Central.

Farmstays *Mount Mulligan Station* (☏07/4094 8360). Budget accommodation west of the Tablelands; from $89 for two nights, including courtesy bus from Cairns. *Springmount Station* (☏07/4093 4493), concentrates on horse riding, with two-day camp-outs or farmstay accommodation for around $200.

Hospital Base Hospital, northern end of the Esplanade (℡ 07/4050 6333) or if you have insurance, Calvary Private Hospital (℡ 07/4052 5200); 24hr Medical Centre, cnr Grafton and Florence streets (℡ 07/4052 1119).

Internet access If your accommodation isn't connected, try the travellers' information centres at City Place ($4–5 per hour), or the Tourist Information Centre near Trinity Wharf ($3 per hour).

Left luggage At the airport, train and bus stations; also Tropical Paradise Travel, 29 Spence St ($4 a day).

NPWS In the Government Offices at 10–12 McLeod St (Mon–Fri 8.30am–4.30pm; ℡ 07/4052 3096). Not very helpful with practical information, but they have plenty of brochures.

Pharmacy Cairns Day and Night Pharmacy and Medical Centre, 29b Shields St (daily 8am–9pm; ℡ 07/4051 2466).

Police 5 Sheridan St (℡ 07/4030 7000).

Post office 13 Grafton St; and upstairs in Orchid Plaza off the Transit Mall, Lake St.

Shopping Tourist-oriented shops are concentrated close to the Esplanade and around City Place and Lake St, where Aboriginal art galleries have sprung up in profusion, though little is truly local – didgeridoos on sale here might have been made in Indonesia. Moving down Shields St the shops become more general, preparing you for what's on offer at the modern air-conditioned shopping complex in the Cairns Central development. Many shops don't open Sat or Sun.

Taxis Black and White Cars ℡ 13 1008. Main cab rank on Lake St, west of City Place.

Trains Bunda St, under Cairns Central (℡ 13 2232). Trains head south down the coast to Brisbane, up to Kuranda on the Atherton Tablelands (p.526), and west to Forsyth in the Gulf (p.596).

Travel agents For budget travel and tours try Flight Centre, 24 Spence St (℡ 07/4052 1077); STA, 9 Shields St (℡ 07/4031 4199); Trailfinders, next to *Hides Hotel*, Shields St (℡ 07/4041 1199); Tropical Paradise Travel, 44 Spence St (℡ 07/4051 9533).

Work You may be able to work a passage on barges going to Cape York; check "General Notices" in the *Cairns Post* for openings. For more regular employment try the backpacker contact points listed in the Cairns' "Arrival" section, p.514.

Yacht club 4 Esplanade (℡ 07/4031 2750). Worth contacting for hitching/crewing north to Cape York and the Torres Strait, south to the Whitsundays and beyond, and even to New Guinea and the Pacific.

Around Cairns

There's a fair amount to see and do **around Cairns**, most of it reached by turning off the highway north of town. Take one of the various roads west to **Redlynch**, and follow the signs to **Crystal Cascades** (Wongalee Falls), a narrow forest gorge gushing with rapids, small waterfalls and swimming opportunities less than 15km from the city. It's somewhere to picnic rather than explore; you should leave nothing valuable in your car, and heed warnings about the large, pale-green, heart-shaped leaves of the **stinging tree** (also known locally as "Dead man's itch"), common on the sides of the paths here; the stories may seem apocryphal but if stung you'll believe them all. Backtracking through Kamerunga, you can drive into the **Barron Gorge** as far as the **power station** (free tours; details ℡ 07/4051 2213) and then walk through the forests to **Kuranda** (see p.526).

About 10km north of Cairns, the township of **Smithfield** marks the starting point for the Kennedy Highway's ascent to Kuranda on the Atherton Tablelands. Shortly before, a large complex on the roadside houses both the Kuranda Skyrail **cable-car terminus** (see p.526) and the **Tjapukai Aboriginal Centre** (daily 9am–5pm; $27). The centre's hefty admission price isn't bad value, as it includes entry to boomerang and didgeridoo displays, a fine museum, and three separate theatre shows featuring Dreamtime tales and dancing; it's not eye-opening stuff, but is a good introduction to Aboriginal culture.

Cairns' variously developed **beaches** start 20km north of town (with regular Sunbus connections from the Transit Mall): **Palm Cove** has a full-scale resort, while **Trinity** and **Yorkeys Knob** attract campers and day-tripper crowds with a van park, shops and watersports gear for rent. If you want to escape for a few days, however, get out to **Ellis Beach**, thirty minutes north on the way to Port Douglas, the last stop on Sunbus. You couldn't ask for a finer place to camp, with tent sites and cabin accommodation at *Ellis Beach Caravan Park* (℡07/4055 3538; cabins ❸).

The Reef and diving

Seeing the **Great Barrier Reef**, either on a cruise or as a diver, is what attracts many visitors to Cairns, and there are so many ways to do this that making a choice can be almost impossible. Broadly speaking, the reef can be classified into three **regions** – inner, outer and island – each somewhat different in character. The **inner reef**, a sheltered section between the outer walls and Cairns, is flat and fairly shallow, a good place for novices. The **outer reef** borders the open sea, so has more dramatic appeal, in the shape of walls, canyons, deeper water and bigger fish. **Island reefs** are generally a blend of inner and outer sites, but have very easy access – again, ideal if you're unsure of your limits.

All regions are visited on **day-cruises**, with vessels ranging from old trawlers to racing yachts and high-speed cruisers. If you want to stay longer, check into an island **resort** or take an extended **dive trip**. One way to choose the right boat is simply to check out the **price**: small, cramped tubs are the cheapest while roomy, faster catamarans are the most expensive. To narrow things down further, find out which serves the best food. Generally, if you've seen the reef or dived before, consider going cheaply; if this is going to be your only visit, pay the extra. Before going, or even if you're not, take in the superb two-hour **Reef Teach** slide show in Cairns at the Bolands Centre, 14 Spence St (Mon–Sat 6.15pm; $13; ⓦ www.reefteach.com.au), at which eccentric marine biologist Paddy Colwell gives more essential background than the dive schools and tour operators have time to impart.

You might be a little taken aback by the state of the Reef's **coral**: the sheer number of visitors has had a visibly detrimental effect on Cairns' inner reef; further afield, the outer reaches are in better condition, though popular sites are beginning to suffer. From a wider perspective, things are not as bleak as they may first appear: since only a limited number of sites are open to the public, these are inevitably going to be sacrificed in order to minimize the impact on the entire structure. In any case, you'll still see abundant wildlife, ranging from squid to sharks; only seasoned divers are likely to be disappointed.

Dive sites

The dozen or more **inner reef** sites are much of a muchness. Concentrated day-tripping means that you'll probably be sharing the experience with several other boatloads of people, with scores of divers in the water at once. On a good day, snorkelling over shallow outcrops is enjoyable; going deeper, the coral shows more damage but there's plenty of patchily distributed marine life. **Michaelmas Cay**, a small, vegetated crescent of sand, is worth a visit: over thirty thousand sooty, common and crested terns roost on the island, while giant clams, sweetlips and reef sharks can be found in the surrounding waters. Nearby **Hastings Reef** has better coral, resident moray eel and maori wrasse, and plenty of starfish and snails in the sand beneath. The two are often included in dive- or reef-trip packages, providing shallow, easy, fun diving. Another one-time favourite, **Norman Reef**, has very clear water, but has been badly hit recently by crown of thorns starfish – some parts are still healthy, others completely sterile.

One of the cheaper options for diving the **outer reef** is to take an **overnight trip** (sleep on board) to nearby sections such as **Moore** or **Arlington reefs**,

which take between ninety minutes and two hours to reach – rather general-
ized terrain, but the advantages over a simple day-excursion are that you get

Reef trips and dive schools

The Reef Cruises and Diving categories below are not mutually exclusive – most outfits offer diving, snorkelling or just plain sailing – but are based on main interests. Prices
can come down by as much as thirty percent during the low seasons (Feb–April & Nov),
depending on how busy operators are, and stand-bys on live-aboard boats can save
even more. On trips longer than a day, you generally sleep on board. All dive schools run
reef trips in their own boats, primarily to take students on their certification dives –
experienced divers may want to avoid these, as you tend to get babied a bit.

The Queensland government has been issuing warnings about "expenses only"
boat trips offered to backpackers by dubious characters in pubs and clubs followed
by sexual harassment once out at sea. If in doubt, find out from any booking office
in town if you are dealing with an authorized, registered operator.

Reef cruises

SAIL BOATS

Day-trips $55–110; three days (two nights) $420–550

Falla (☎07/4031 3488). Ancient wooden pearling lugger from the Torres Strait, now
restored to original condition for top-value day-trips to the inner reef, including
snorkelling and storytelling.

Ocean Free, Silver Sails Cruises Ltd, PO Box 1045 (☎07/4041 1118). Day-trips to
the reef around Green Island aboard a nineteen-metre rigged schooner.

Passions of Paradise (☎07/4050 0676). Roomy sail catamaran (very stable), cruising out to Paradise Reef and Upolu Cay.

Santa Maria, PO Box 5957 (☎07/4031 0558). Replica nineteenth-century twenty-
metre rigged schooner to Thetford and Sudbury reefs.

POWERBOATS

$90–150 (day-trips only)

Frankland Islands Cruises (☎07/4031 3355). Along the mangrove-fringed
Mulgrave River to the Frankland Islands, a group of sand cays, for underwater pursuits; coral here is fair.

Great Adventures, from Trinity Wharf (☎07/4044 9944). Large, fast catamaran via
Green Island to their private reef pontoon.

Reef Magic, from the Marlin Jetty (☎07/4031 1588). High-speed catamaran to
Thetford or Moore reefs for snorkelling and glass-bottom boat trips.

Sea Quest, from the Pier (☎07/4031 2223). Very comfortable and speedy vessel to
Norman Reef.

Sunlover Cruises, Trinity Wharf (☎07/4050 1333, ⓦwww.sunlover.com.au). Fast
catamaran to Moore and Arlington reefs and Fitzroy Island; also packages including
reef trip and overnight stay on Fitzroy.

Diving

DAY-TRIPS

$60–145; diving upwards of $50 for two dives, including gear rental.

Compass, 73 Esplanade (☎07/4031 7217, ⓦwww.reeftrip.com). Good selection of
reefs, and a broad, stable budget vessel for windy weather. Departs 8am, giving you
five hours at the reef; price includes snorkel gear and a glass-bottomed boat trip.

Noah's Ark (☎07/4050 0677). Real budget diving at Michaelmas Cay and Hastings
Reef; great value but don't expect any comforts.

Seastar II, 262 Amuller St (☎07/4033 0333). Long-established family-run business
with permits for some of the best sections of Hastings Reef and Michaelmas Cay.

longer in the water plus the opportunity for night dives. **Longer trips** venture further from Cairns into two areas: a circuit north to the Cod Hole and

Top value full-day trip allows a good long time in the water.
Tusa Dive, cnr the Esplanade and Aplin St (℡ 07/4031 1248, ⊛ www.tusadive.com). Purpose-built vessel with a maximum of 28 passengers; a roving permit means each trip could go to any of ten separate reefs.

LIVE-ABOARDS
Live-aboard trips cater to more serious divers, last from three days upwards and cover the best of the reefs; you'll make savings of up to thirty percent with **stand-by rates**, if offered, which only become available 48 hours or so before departure and have to be booked direct with the operator. All costs below include berth, meals and dives, but not gear rental. Remember that weather conditions can affect the destinations offered.
Aquarius 3 (℡ 07/4051 6449, ⊛ www.aquarius3.dtedemo.com.au). Six days exploring the Ribbon Reefs and Cod Hole (June–Aug), or Coral Sea sites – including Bougainville Reef (Sept–April); good value at $990.
Coral Sea Diving Company (℡ 07/4041 2044, ⊛ www.rumrunner.com.au). Slow boat to Holmes Reef for shark feeding, then taking in wall dives, pinnacles, drifts and undersea freshwater springs. Four days (three nights), with around ten dives, from $880 per person.
Kangaroo Explorer (℡ 07/4032 4000, ⊛ www.kangaroocruises.com.au). Eight-day, 23-dive package between Cairns and Thursday Island, diving a string of reefs and several wrecks – including the *Quetta* (see Thursday Island account on p.545). Only runs six or so times per year; phone first for prices and dates.
Mike Ball, 143 Lake St (℡ 07/4031 5484, ⊛ www.mikeball.com). Luxury diving with one of Queenslands' best-equipped and longest-running operations; venues include Cod Hole and Ribbons, Coral Sea sites, plus the *Yongala* near Townsville (see p.497) and even New Guinea. From $970.
Nimrod Explorer, 46 Spence St (℡ 07/4031 5566, ⊛ www.explorerventures.com). Motorized catamaran with basic or plush cabins; four- to seven-day Cod Hole and Coral Sea trips where you fly out and cruise back cost $935–1870.
Taka II (Underwater Camera Centre), 131 Lake St (℡ 07/4051 8722, ⊛ www.taka.com.au). Refurbished trawler with fair facilities, including photographic equipment rental and E-6 processing on board. Four days at the Cod Hole and Ribbon reefs $875; five days including Coral Sea sites $985.

DIVE SCHOOLS
As always, ask around about what each dive school offers, though training standards are pretty uniform these days. You'll pay around $280 for a budget Open Water Certification course, diving lesser reefs for your training and returning to Cairns each night; and $450–590 for a four- or five-day course using better sites and staying on a live-aboard at the reef for a couple of days doing your certification. The following schools are long-established and have a sound reputation; certification dives are either made north at Norman, Hastings and Saxon reefs, or south at Flynn, Moore and Tetford.
CDC, 121 Abbott St (℡ 07/4051 0294, ⊛ www.cairnsdive.com.au).
Deep Sea Divers Den, 319 Draper St (℡ 07/4031 2223).
Down Under Dive, 287 Draper St (07/4052 8300, ⊛ www.downunderdive.com.au).
Pro-Dive, cnr Abbott and Shields streets (℡ 07/4031 5255, ⊛ www.prodive-cairns.com.au).
Tusa Dive, cnr the Esplanade and Aplin St (℡ 07/4031 1248, ⊛ www.tusadive.com). Also offers Nitrox and rebreather certification courses to divers with Advanced OW/OW2 qualifications.

Ribbon reefs, or straight out into the Coral Sea. The **Cod Hole**, near Lizard Island (see p.539), has no coral but is justifiably famous for mobs of giant potato cod which rise from the depths to receive hand-outs; currents here are strong but having these monsters come close enough to cuddle is awesome. **The Ribbons** are a two-hundred-kilometre string with some relatively pristine locations and good visibility, as are **Coral Sea** sites; these are isolated reefs some distance out from the main structure and surrounded by open water teeming with seasonal bundles of pelagic species including mantas, whales, turtles and sharks. The most visited Coral Sea site is **Holmes Reef**, but try to get out to **Bougainville Reef**, whose walls drop almost vertically for a kilometre from the surface and are home to everything from brightly coloured anthias fish to fast and powerful silvertip sharks.

Green Island and Fitzroy Island

Heart-shaped, tiny and sandy, **Green Island** is the easiest of any of the Barrier Reef's coral cays to reach, making it a near-essential, if expensive, day-trip from Cairns. This, combined with the island's size, means that it can be difficult to escape other visitors, but you only need to put on some fins, visit the **underwater observatory** ($5; free admission with some ferry tickets) or go for a cruise in a glass-bottomed boat to see plentiful coral, fish and turtles. The five-star rooms at the **Green Island Resort** (⊤07/4031 3300, Ⓦwww.greenislandresort.com.au; ❽) attract long-term guests, and there's a restaurant and pool open to day-trippers, plus plenty of sand to laze on. Daily **ferries** include *The Big Cat* (⊤07/4051 0444, Ⓦwww.bigcat-cruises.com.au; $49) from the Pier Marketplace; and Great Adventures (⊤07/4044 9944; $44) from Trinity Wharf. Both leave Cairns around 9am and return about 5pm, and run **courtesy buses** which will collect you from your accommodation.

Fitzroy Island is a continental island, not a cay like Green Island, and sports a YHA-run **resort** (⊤07/4051 9588, Ⓦwww.fitzroyislandresort.com.au; bunkhouse ❷ per person, cabins ❻) set in forest near the shore, from where you can dive on the island's reef. There's also a council-run **campground** here, which charges $11 per tent per night. Fitzroy is actually quite large and, away from the resort, there are some good walks through highland greenery where you can escape the sunbathing hordes. Sunlover from Trinity Wharf (⊤07/4050 1333, Ⓦwww.sunlover.com.au) and Great Adventures (see above) operate daily **ferries** to the island from Cairns (55min each way; $36), and also offer overnight package deals.

The Atherton Tablelands

The **Atherton Tablelands**, the highlands behind Cairns, are named after **John Atherton**, who made the tin deposits at **Herberton** accessible by opening a route to the coast in 1877. Dense forest covered these highlands before the majority was cleared and given over to dairy cattle, tobacco and grain. The remaining pockets of forest are magnificent, but it's the understated beauty that draws most visitors today, and though **Kuranda** and its markets pull in busloads from the coast, there are several quieter **national parks** brimming with rare species. You could spend days here, driving or hiking through rainforest to crater lakes and endless small waterfalls, or simply camp out for a night and search for wildlife with a torch. For a contrast, consider a side trip west to the mining town of **Chillagoe**, whose dust, limestone caves and Aboriginal art place it firmly in the Outback.

Drivers can reach the tablelands on the **Palmerston Highway** from Innisfail, the twisty **Gillies Highway** from Gordonvale, or the **Kennedy Highway** from Smithfield to Kuranda. Two stylish and unforgettable ways to ride up to the tablelands are by **train** from Cairns to Kuranda, which winds through gorges and rainforest; and in the green gondolas of the **Kuranda Skyrail cable car**, with a fantastic 7km (40min) aerial view of the canopy between Smithfield and Kuranda – either method costs $30 one-way or $45 return, and a "Skyrail up & train back" package is $59. Numerous **tours** run from Cairns (see box on p.519). For point-to-point **buses** to the tableland towns, White Car Coaches (from Tropical Paradise Travel, 48 Spence St, Cairns; ☎07/4051 9533) make at least one run daily from Cairns and back to Kuranda, Mareeba, Atherton, Yungaburra, Malanda, Herberton and Ravenshoe. Ideally, however, you really need your own transport to explore at leisure.

Kuranda

A constant stream of visitors arriving from the coast has turned **KURANDA** into a stereotypical resort village – something, ironically, this once atavistic community was keen to escape. But despite expanding development and heavy market-day tourism, it's hard not to like the place. **Buses**, and the highway, stop at the top of town, **trains** and the Skyrail **cable car** 500m down the hill, with essential services – post office, store (EFTPOS), bank, cafés – laid out between them along Coondoo Street. **Cafés** are legion, though pricey; *Annabel's Pie Shop*, across from the main markets, has excellent pasties and pies; and if you're staying the night, *Billy's* at the *Middle Pub* (halfway down Coondoo) does tasty charcoal grill and salad fare.

This accessible from Cairns, Kuranda is not a place where many people stay overnight – it's virtually a ghost town after the markets close – and there's little **accommodation**. Just up from the cable-car terminus and orchid-shrouded **train station**, you'll find the quiet and slowly mouldering *Kuranda Backpackers' Hostel*, 6 Arara St (☎07/4093 7355, ✉kurandabackpack@ozemail.com.au; ❶), with a plentiful supply of bunks, large grounds (where you can camp), kitchen and laundry. Around the corner is *The Bottom Pub and Motel* (☎07/4093 7206; ❹), whose bar has more than a little atmosphere on Friday nights.

While some stalls operate every day, the **markets** that attract so many tourists operate 8.30am–3pm on Wednesday, Friday and Sunday. Don't expect bargains – the market is a commercial affair hawking crafts, fruit and clothes, set around a fake plane wreck and "rainforest pool", with an overflow of stalls across the road. Nearby, forest fauna can be seen close up at the **Butterfly Sanctuary** (daily 10am–3pm; $11.50), a mix of streams and "feed trees" where giant ulysses and birdwing butterflies are the most obvious of the dozen local species protected by the breeding programme. **Birdworld**, behind the markets (daily

Wet tropics and World Heritage

Queensland's **wet tropics** – the coastal belt from the Paluma Range, near Townsville, to the Daintree north of Cairns – has been nominated under UNESCO **World Heritage** listing as containing one of the oldest surviving tracts of **rainforest** anywhere on earth. Whether this listing has benefited the region is questionable, however; logging has slowed, but the tourist industry has vigorously exploited the area's status as an untouched wilderness, constantly pushing for more development so that a greater number of visitors can be accommodated. The clearing of mangroves for a marina and resort at Cardwell is a worst-case example; Kuranda's Skyrail project was one of the few cases designed to lessen the ultimate impact (another highway – with more buses – was the alternative). Given the profits to be made, development is inevitable, but it's sadly ironic that a scheme designed to promote the region's unique beauty may accelerate its destruction.

9am–4pm; $10), is a superb aviary with realistically arranged vegetation and nothing between you and a host of native and exotic rarities such as ecclectus parrots. The **Noctarium**, at the upper end of Coondoo Street (daily 10am–3pm; $9.90), has a collection of glider possums, wallabies and bats. Tucked away down a backstreet, the **Aviary** (daily 10am–3.30pm; $11) is partly a replay of Birdworld with purely Australian species, but they also have a collection of snakes and frogs, and a freshwater crocodile.

Around Kuranda

Kuranda sits at the top of the **Barron Gorge**, spectacular in the wet season when the river rages down the falls, but otherwise tamed by a hydroelectric dam upstream. Cross the rail bridge next to the station and take a path leading down to the river, where 45-minute **cruises** ($10) depart five times a day; the cruise operators often rent out canoes too. On foot, a newly prepared **walking track** descends to cold swimming spots along the railway and river from the lookout at the end of Barron Falls Road, 2km from town. Other trails follow the road beyond the falls to **Wright's Lookout**, then continue to dense forest along **Surprise Creek** and to the **Power Station**. Closer to town, there's another forest walk from the Noctarium to Jumrum Creek (about 1hr) and, opposite the BP garage at the top of Coondoo Street, a huge colony of **flying foxes** to see, hear and smell.

Mareeba

West of Kuranda, rainforest quickly gives way to dry woodland and **tobacco** plantations, quite a change from the coast's greenery. **Davies Creek** is at the end of a track branching off the road after 25km; paths lead from a campsite to where falls pour over a granite rock face to a pool surrounded by boulders and scrub.

The main road continues to **MAREEBA**, a quiet place and the tablelands' oldest town, founded in the 1900s after the area was opened up for tobacco farming. With the tobacco industry now under attack, local farmers face an uncertain future, but Mareeba's birdlife will benefit from the industry's demise: crop spraying has both poisoned birds and killed off any insects on which they feed. The newly-opened **Mareeba Wetlands**, a pocket of grass-fringed lagoons 13km northwest of town via Biboohra (Wed–Sun 8.30am–4pm; ☎07/4093 2514), tries to redress the balance, attracting seasonal flocks of brolgas, jabiru storks and black cockatoos, along with resident wallabies and goannas; book ranger-led **guided tours** in advance. Another spot to spend a few hours is at **Granite Gorge**, 14km southwest of town off the Dimbulah road; the last kilometre is a dirt track and entrance costs $2. At the gorge, a small river flows between a mass of house-sized granite boulders, creating plenty of swimming holes and opportunities for short hikes.

Back in Mareeba, Byrnes Street has all the shops and banks, while the **motels** and pleasant *Tropical Tablelands Caravan Park* (☎07/4092 1158) are along the highway as you enter town from the south, as is the **information** centre and small museum (daily 8am–4pm; $4), marked by a memorial to **James Venture Mulligan**, the veteran prospector who discovered the Palmer River Goldfields (see p.540). After dark you can tangle with the farming fraternity in one of the hotels, or at *Jimmy D's Night Club* (Thurs–Sat 7pm–3am) on Byrnes Street. **Leaving**, Atherton is 30km south, while the **Peninsula Developmental Road** heads north to Mount Molloy. The AMPOL service station at the north end of town marks the start of the Chillagoe road.

West to Chillagoe

The 150-kilometre road to Chillagoe mysteriously alternates between corrugated gravel and isolated sections of bitumen, but poses no real problem during the dry season. Look for graffiti on boulders (**Top Cat Pass** is a gem) and enticing adverts for the *Almaden Hotel*, whose cool, mirrored, well-supplied bar and beer garden are an incredible oasis in ramshackle, dilapidated **ALMADEN**. From here until Chillagoe's inactive smelter chimney appears from behind an outcrop of rock, the road passes blocks of cut marble awaiting shipment to Italy.

CHILLAGOE dates from 1887, when enough copper ore was found to keep a smelter running until the 1950s; now a gold mine 16km west at **Mungana** seems to keep the place ticking over. Red dust, a service station, oversized hotels and general store complete the picture. The **NPWS office** (℡07/4094 7163) is in the post office down the main street, and can arrange **tours** of Chillagoe's caves (see below; daily 9am & 1.30pm) – though check well in advance as the tours may be closed during the wet season and numbers are limited. It can also arrange **camping**: there are two campsites (tank water and pit toilets), one close to town, the other 7km out near the caves themselves. If you need more luxury, the *Chillagoe Lodge Motel*, 7 King St (℡07/4094 7106; ⑤), has a pool, TV and a sheltered garden, and serves meals.

The caves

Chillagoe's **caves** are ancient coral reefs, hollowed out by rain and broken up into fluted masses half-buried in the scrub. Guides can take you through some, while others are open to solo exploration with instructions from the ranger. The caverns are varied by **limestone sculptures** deposited by evaporation and, unusually for the location, some large **stalagmites**; the best formations are at **Royal Arch**, **Donna** and **Trezkinn**. Wildlife here includes grey swiftlets and agile pythons, which somehow manage to catch bats on the wing. A **footpath** leads through grassland between the caves, where you'll find echidnas, kangaroos, black cockatoos and frogmouths, the last odd birds whose name fits them perfectly. Given that this is some of the best snake country, solid shoes and trousers ought to be worn. **Balancing Rock** offers panoramic views, with the town hidden by low trees, while obscure **Aboriginal paintings and engravings** have been found near **the Arches**, west at Mungana. Past here, the road continues 500km to Normanton, Karumba and tracks up western Cape York – but it doesn't improve and there's no fuel or help along the way.

Atherton

Thirty kilometres south of Mareeba and centrally placed for forays to most of the tablelands' attractions, **ATHERTON** is the largest highlands town, with a variety of businesses and accommodation. Banks, shops and early-opening **cafés** – *Chatterbox* is best - are along Main Street, with a supermarket right at the south end past the post office. **Buses** stop at the junction of Main and Vernon streets. **Accommodation** includes the heavily tiled and hospitable *Atherton Travellers Lodge*, 37 Alice St, off Vernon Street (℡07/4091 3552, ✉athertonbackpack@hotmail.com; ❶), who specialize in finding **farm work** picking potatoes, pumpkins and various fruit; and the very pleasant *Blue Gum Bed & Breakfast*, at 36 Twelfth Ave (℡07/4091 5149; ⑤), a modern timber home. There are green and spacious campsites at the *Woodlands Tourist Park*, just at the edge of town on Herberton Road (℡07/4091 1407). **Leaving**

Atherton, roads head north to Mareeba, south to Ravenshoe and Herberton, and east to Yungaburra.

The main distraction in Atherton is to catch the authentically grubby 1920s **steam train to Herberton**, which leaves from Platypus Park, just south of town (Wed, Sat, Sun & holidays 10.30am; $27.50 return); along the way you get to look at tunnels, forest and the pretty Carrington Falls, and then have an hour or so to look around Herberton (see overleaf) before the return trip. Another place to clock up local birdlife is **Hasties Swamp**, a big waterhole and associated wetland surrounded by cattle pasture and gum woodland, about 5km south of town. While nothing astounding, it's a peaceful place populated by magpie geese, swamphens and assorted marsh tiggets.

Yungaburra and around

Just 13km east of Atherton at the start of the Gillies Highway to Gordonvale, the self-conciously pretty village of **YUNGABURRA** makes another good base, and consists of the old wooden *Lake Eacham Hotel*, a store and a handful of **places to stay** and eat. Run by the *Dreamtime* hostel in Cairns, the pine-and-slate *On the Wallaby Hostel*, 37 Eacham Rd (☏07/4050 0650; ❶–❸), is very clued up on the area and also organizes canoe and wildlife-spotting trips. The upmarket cottages at *Eden Park* (☏07/4095 3355, ⓦwww.edenhouse.com.au; ❼) are another good bet, or for something special, treat yourself to a weekend at the romantic *Mt Quinkan Crater Retreat*, on the Peeramon Road about 8km southeast of Yungaburra (☏07/4095 2255, ⓦwww.mtquinkan.com.au; ❽); self-contained wooden units with spa baths are all built on tall poles looking into an extinct volcano crater. **Eating**, there's always the hotel for a quick feed, or try bratwurst and *rosti* at *Nick's Swiss Italian Restaurant* (daily except Wed for lunch and dinner, with bands on Sat). *Eden House* has an expensive "Australian Contemporary" menu; or there's similarly pricey, eclectic gourmet treats – from Tuscan lamb to kangaroo pie – at the *Burra Inn*.

Before heading further afield after wildlife, visit the **platypus viewing platform** above a stream just on the edge of Yungaburra; it's best in the early morning and late afternoon, when the crowds have dispersed. Another good place for wildlife spotting is the **Curtain Fig Tree**, an enormous parasitic strangler fig just a couple of kilometres southwest on a minor road; while common enough in rainforest, one this size is extraordinary, with the base all overhung by a stringy mass of aerial roots drooping off the higher branches. Come here in the late afternoon or early morning to see **tree kangaroos** hopping along the branches, or well after dark to catch rare green ringtail possums.

Lakes Tinaroo, Eacham and Barrine

Northeast from Atherton and north of Yungaburra, **Lake Tinaroo** is a convoluted reservoir formed by pooling the Barron River's headwaters. An unsurfaced, dry-weather road runs 25km around from the dam out from Atherton to the Gillies Highway 15km east of Yungaburra, passing **campsites** on the north shore before cutting deep into native forests. It's worth stopping along the way for the short walks to bright-green **Mobo Crater** and the **Cathedral Fig**, another giant tree some 50m tall and 43m around the base, with the thick mass of tendrils supporting the crown all fused together like melted wax.

Only a few kilometres east of Yungaburra at the start of the Gillies Highway, Barrine and Eacham are **maars**, or crater lakes – blue, still circles surrounded by thick rainforest. **Lake Eacham** has an easy 4km trail around its shores bringing you across birds and insects foraging on the forest floor, along with inoffensive **amethystine pythons** – Australia's largest snake – sunning themselves around down by the water. Some 5km further east on a dirt road, **Red Cedar** is another forest giant, a valuable timber tree somehow overlooked by nineteenth-century timber getters; the tree's support roots are thicker than an average tree, and its straight, 35-metre-high trunk is two metres in diameter. For its part, **Lake Barrine** is relatively developed, with a **tearoom** overlooking the water serving good cream teas and canteen-style meals, and a **cruise boat** (daily at 10.15am, 2pm & 3.15pm; $10) which spends an hour circuiting the lake. To get away from the crowds, head for the two enormous **kauri pines** which mark the start of an underused and pretty muddy six-kilometre **walking track** around the lake; keep your eyes peeled for spiky-headed water dragons, and hordes of **musky rat-kangaroos**, which look exactly as you'd expect them to.

The Southern Tablelands: to Ravenshoe and beyond

The Kennedy Highway continues 80km down from Atherton to **Ravenshoe**, the highlands' southernmost town, past **the Crater** at Mount Hypipamee, a 56-metre vertical rift formed by volcanic gases blowing through fractured granite that's now filled with deep, weed-covered water. **Picnic tables** are on the site, as are ridiculously tame Lewins honeyeaters, but camping is prohibited. An alternative road from Atherton – and the **train** (see overleaf) – circles west via **HERBERTON**, a quaint, one-time timber town without a modern building in sight and huge Sunday lunchtime barbecues at the *Royal Hotel*'s beer garden. Just south of town, the **Historic Village** (daily 10am–4pm; $10) is a meticulous but lifeless collection of about thirty pioneer buildings relocated from elsewhere: a schoolroom, bishop's residence, hotel, Chinese relics, bottle dump – you name it.

RAVENSHOE, apart from endless explanations for its name, is mainly notable for the *Tully Falls Hotel*, Queensland's highest pub, and **Millstream Falls**, Australia's broadest waterfall, 5km away. Northeast, the road back to Atherton takes you past a blustery hillside sprouting an array of twenty long-stemmed **windmills**, part of a new wind-generator power scheme. Southwest, the road drops off the tablelands past **Innot Hot Springs** – with its huge anthills and steamy upwellings behind the *Hot Springs Hotel* – and the township of **Mount Garnet**, to the start of the Gulf Developmental Road (see p.593).

Malanda, Millaa Millaa and the Palmerston Highway

About 25km southeast of Atherton, the **dairy** at **MALANDA** provides milk and cheese for the whole of Queensland's far north, plus most of the Northern Territory and even New Guinea. There's a roadside swimming hole and short rainforest walk starting about 1km back towards Atherton at **Malanda Falls Environmental Park**; the display at the **information centre** here (daily 10am–4pm; $1) gives a run-down on the tableland's geology and its Aboriginal and settler history. For somewhere **to stay**, *Platypus Forest Lodge*, 8km east of town at 12 Topaz Rd (☎07/4096 5926; ❹), has motel-like rooms, meals by arrangement and outdoor hot tubs on a large, forest-fringed lawn.

From Malanda, you can descend to the coastal highway south of Cairns via **Millaa Millaa** and the **Palmerston Highway**. Before you do, there's a **waterfall circuit** starting 2km east of Millaa Millaa, where a fifteen-kilometre road passes three small tumbles and swimming holes; best is **Elinjaa**, with its curtain cave. The highway itself was named after **Christie Palmerston**, a

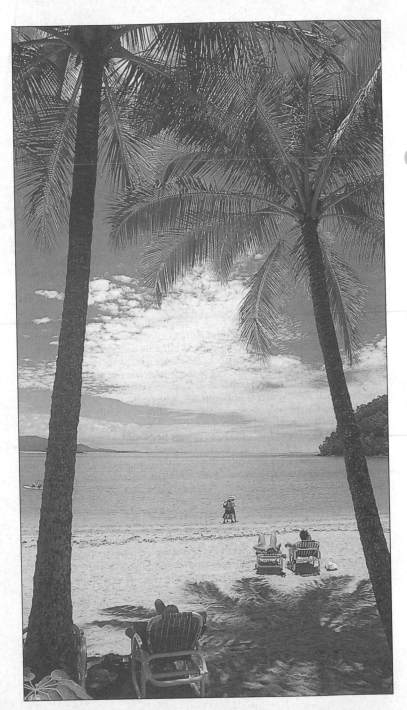

fugitive who hid with Aborigines on the tablelands in the 1870s. The **Palmerston section** of Wooroonooran National Park, which includes the Bellenden Ker Range (see p.511), occupies a huge area north of the highway and is worth a stopover to explore the most extensive, undisturbed spread of Atherton's rainforest – though you'll need some protection from summer flies. There's a NPWS **campsite** ($3.85 per person per night) about 27km from Millaa Millaa, from where the best of the walking tracks lead to mossy **Tchupala Falls** and the impressive **Nandroya Falls**, while the highway descends 40km past the park to Innisfail.

Heading north: Cairns to Cape Tribulation

The Daintree and Cape Tribulation, tamed fringes of the Cape York Peninsula, are only a couple of hours' drive north of Cairns on the **Cook Highway**. The highway initially runs in sight of the sea to **Port Douglas** and **Mossman**, a beautiful drive past isolated beaches where hang-gliders patrol the headlands. North of Mossman is the road to **the Daintree**, Australia's largest and the world's oldest surviving stretch of tropical rainforest. World Heritage listing hasn't saved it from development: roads are being surfaced, land has been sub-divided, and there's an ever-increasing number of services in place, undermining the wild and remote brochure image. While this disappoints some visitors, the majestic forest still descends thick and dark right to the sea, and you can explore paths through the jungle, watch for wildlife, or just rest on the beach. The government has recently allocated funds to restore the land so there is some hope that developments will stop where they are now.

Tours from Cairns will show you the sights, but you really need longer to take in the rich scenery and atmosphere. For once it's not essential to have a vehicle: Coral Coaches (℡07/4031 7577) runs frequent **buses** through the day to Port Douglas and Mossman, and at least two daily services between Cairns and Cape Tribulation, all of which allow multiple stopovers. The smaller and faster Airport Shuttle (℡07/4099 5950, bookings essential) also run to Port Douglas and Cape Tribulation three times a day.

Port Douglas and Mossman

Massive development in recent years has seen the once pretty fishing village of **PORT DOUGLAS**, an hour north of Cairns, turned into an upmarket tourist attraction, with a main street full of boutiques, shopping malls and holidaying hordes. However, the town does have a huge **beach**, along with plenty of distractions to keep you busy for a day or two, and it's getting to be as good a place as Cairns to pick up a regional tour or dive trip to the reef – though prices are steeper.

All services are on five-hundred-metre-long Macrossan Street, which runs between Four Mile Beach and Anzac Park. As in Cairns, a prolific number of businesses offer tourist information – the **Port Douglas Tourist Information Centre** at no. 23 (daily 8.30am–5.30pm; ℡07/4099 5599) can sort out everything from Aboriginal-guided tours of Mossman Gorge to sailing trips and buses to the Daintree. Top of the **accommodation** options is the huge *Mirage Resort* (℡07/4099 5888; ⓦwww.mirageresort.com.au; ❺) off Davidson Street on the way into town, which hosted former US president Bill Clinton during his 1996 visit. Less flamboyant lodgings include *4 Mile Beach Caravan Park* on Reef Street (℡07/4098 5281; cabins ❸); the very pleasant *Port O'Call Lodge/YHA* on Port Street (℡07/4099 5422; ❷), with its *Shoestrings Restaurant* and free transfer from Cairns' YHA; the new and laid-back *Dougies Backpackers* at 111 Davidson St (℡07/4099 6200; ❷), with bar, restaurant and pool; the very central *Coconut Grove Motel* at 58 Macrossan St (℡07/4099 5124; ❷) which, despite the name, is another backpacker-oriented place; and *Mango Tree Apartments*, 91 Davidson St (℡07/4099 5677; ❺), with self-contained units just back from Four Mile Beach.

Places to eat abound along Macrossan Street: the *Central Hotel* has live bands on Wednesday and at weekends, while the *Court House Hotel* has boozers and dogs sprawled across the ample verandah, and lunch specials and a barbecue menu in the garden. Between the two, *Iron Bar* has rough-cut timber furniture and a mid-range "surf & turf" menu, while *Mango Jam Café* across the road is open from noon to 2am for wood-fired pizza, and the nearby *Star of Siam* has first-rate, moderately-priced Thai fare. At *Catalina*, around the corner on Wharf Street (Tues–Sun 6.30pm–late; ℡07/4099 5287), it's worth paying the high prices for delicacies such as coral trout grilled in banana leaves; the restaurant is in a beautiful setting with a verandah shaded by two ancient mango trees.

Between the end of Macrossan Street and the sea, **Anzac Park** is the scene of a Sunday-morning **produce market**, good for fruit, vegetables and souvenirs. Near the park's jetty you'll find the whitewashed timber church of **St Mary's by the Sea**, built after the 1911 cyclone carried off the previous structure. Behind, at **Ben Cropp's Shipwreck Museum** (daily 9am–5pm; $5.50), bronze cannon, teapots and the results of twenty years salvaging are piled around a continuously playing video of Ben's exploits.

Out to sea, local **dive sites** include the **Low Isles**, **Chinaman**, **Tongue** and **Opal reefs**, all decent enough, though in much the same condition as popular reefs off Cairns. Quicksilver, based at Marina Mirage attached to the *Mirage Resort* (℡07/4099 5500, ⓦwww.quicksilver-cruises.com), also runs a sailing boat to the Low Isles ($105), while its high-speed catamaran will whisk you to the **Agincourt Reef** for the day ($150). For around the same price, Poseidon Cruises, 34 Macrossan St (℡07/4099 4772, ⓦwww.poseidon-cruises.com.au), and Silverblue (℡07/4099 4544, ⓦwww.silverblue.com.au), take smaller boats for day-trips to less touristed sections; and serious divers should contact Undersea Explorer (℡07/4099 5911, ⓦwww.undersea.com.au), who make exploratory trips up the ribbons and into the Coral Sea – contact them for current prices and destinations.

Mossman

MOSSMAN, 14km past Port Douglas, is a quiet town which has hardly changed in the last thirty years; rail lines between the canefields and mill still run along the main street. Ten minutes inland, **Mossman Gorge** looks like all rainforest rivers should; the boulder-strewn flow is good for messing around in on a quiet day but attracts streams of tour buses and car break-ins in peak season. Kuku Yalangi, the local community, put together the Aboriginal **walking trail** here and conduct tours of the gorge explaining history and plant usage – phone them on ℡07/4098 2595 for details. If you want to stay somewhere plush in the area, book in at the exclusive *Silky Oaks Lodge* (free call ℡1800 737 678, ⓦwww.poresorts.com.au; ❼), 12km from town through the canefields; there's not much rainforest here, but you get very well looked after.

Continuing north, the road splits left to Daintree township or right for the Daintree Ferry to Cape Tribulation. Backtracking southeast lets you leave the highway and climb to Mount Molloy and the Peninsula Developmental Road – the easier, inland route to Cooktown.

The Daintree

If you detour off the Mossman–Cape Tribulation road to take in riverside **DAINTREE** township, you'll find that the former timber camp is just somewhere to organize a half-day **crocodile tour** with the Daintree Wildlife Safari (℡ 07/4098 6125; $35) or a one-hour drift with Daintree River Cruise Centre (℡ 07/4098 6115; $11). Experienced 4WD hands can also test their mettle on the **CREB Track** from here to Cooktown; erroneously marked as a proper road on some maps, you'll need tyre chains for steep, slippery gradients, and some practice at manouvering over large granite boulders.

Most people skip all this and instead follow the road to the **Daintree River Ferry** (continuously 6am–midnight; pedestrians $1, vehicles $8) and the start of the mostly sealed 35-kilometre Cape Tribulation road. The river crossing can be very busy, with the cable ferry taking a dozen cars and tour coaches every fifteen minutes or so; wait in the *Big Croc Café*, or take a two-hour **cruise** with *River Train* or *Crocodile Express*, which prowl through the local mangroves looking for crocodiles and snakes.

Across the river, a seven-kilometre side road ends at the quiet *Club Daintree* (℡ 07/4090 7500; ❶–❺) at **Cape Kimberley**, with cabins, campsite, restaurant-bar and plenty of walking tracks. Sticking on the main road after the ferry, it's 8km through rainforest over the convoluted range to the **Jindalba Environmental Centre** (daily 8.30am–5pm; $11), which features a five-level, 27-metre-high **tower** with identification charts for the plants and birds you're likely to see at each stage – the top also provides a fabulous view over the canopy. Trails head off into the forest from the car park beneath. Just up the road, **FLORAVILLE**'s **café** hands out local advice and doubles as a Commonwealth Bank agent; past here, a six-kilometre side road from the airstrip heads straight to the coast at **Cow Bay**. There's **budget accommodation** available 2km or so along in the jungle-clad cabins of *Crocodylus Village/YHA* (℡ 07/4098 9166; ❷); rooms are showing their age, but meals are good and inexpensive, and they arrange night walks, and offshore trips to Snapper Island and the local reef – the **beach** at Cow Bay is also excellent.

Back on the Cape Tribulation road and past an unexpected tea plantation, there's further accommodation up against the forest wall around 8km from Floraville at *Deep Forest Lodge* (℡ 07/4098 9162; ❻), who have well-furnished, self-contained cabins; and, inland off the main road, in "boutique cabins" at *Heritage Lodge* (℡ 07/4098 9138, ✉ hertiage@c130.aone.net.au; ❽), which also sports a fancy restaurant and local walking trails along **Cooper Creek**. The next stop is 4km on at sandy **Thornton Beach**, where you'll find a licensed kiosk and the *Café on Sea*; then it's another few kilometres to where concrete paths and boardwalks follow the creek through a mixture of forest to mangroves at the river mouth on the **Marrdja Botanical Walk** at **Noah Beach**. Look for spiky lawyer cane, lianas twisted into corkscrew shapes where they once surrounded a tree, and the spherical pods of the **cannonball mangrove** – dried and dismembered, they were used as puzzles by Aboriginal peoples, the object being to fit the irregular segments back together. The NPWS has a **campsite** here in woodland behind the beach; it's big but prone to be muddy and is closed during the wet season.

Just up the road is the exclusive beachfront *Coconut Beach Resort* (☏07/4098 0033, ⓦwww.coconutbeach.com.au; ⑧), with an extensive array of facilities including a huge A-frame restaurant requiring "smart tropical dress"; and its sister lodge, the *Ferntree Rainforest Resort* (☏07/4098 0000, ⓦwww.ferntree.com; ❼), set back in the forest. Plants close in again a couple of kilometres beyond at **Dubuji Boardwalk**, a 1.2-kilometre-long replay of Marrdja, though with a greater variety of forests. Aside from fan palms, rainforest cycads and vines, look out for the very odd peppermint stick insect, which hides in pandanus leaves alongside the path; they're a strange blue-green colour, and squirt out a mint-scented spray when disturbed.

Cape Tribulation

Cape Tribulation ("Cape Trib") – a forty-minute drive from the ferry crossing – was named when Captain Cook's vessel hit a reef offshore in June 1770. The cleared area below **Mount Sorrow** has a café, store, a boardwalk onto the beach and a **Bat House** (daily approximately 10.30am–3.30pm; $2), worth a visit to handle tame orphaned flying foxes. **Beds** are available at the often noisy and overcrowded *PK's* **hostel** (☏07/4098 0040; dorms ❷, rooms ❹), who also run the adjacent *Jungle Lodge* at similar prices. Alternatively, there's the eco-friendly *Jungle Treehouse* (☏07/4099 5651, ⓦwww.jungletreehousecapetrib.com.au; ❺), a bed-and-breakfast set 200m up in the hills; and the new and friendly *Cape Trib Beach House*, 2.5km north of the Bat House (☏07/4098 0030, ⓦwww.capetribbeach.com.au; dorms ❷, cabins ❺), who have limited camping space as well as beds. All can organize horse riding, sea-kayaking and guided forest walks.

The area is best explored on foot – for the simple pleasure of walking through the forest with the sea breaking on a beach not five minutes distant. A **path** runs out to the cape, where you may see brilliantly coloured pittas (small, tailless birds with a buff chest, green back and black and rust heads) bouncing around in the leaf litter, or even a crocodile sunning itself on the beach. One way to penetrate the undergrowth away from the paths is to follow small creeks: **Emmagen**, about 6km north, runs halfway up Mount Sorrow and is recommended for its safe swimming holes.

The Bloomfield Track

The scene of vicious confrontations in 1984 between construction crews and environmentalists who tried unsuccessfully to stop this alternative road to Cooktown being built through virgin forest, the **Bloomfield Track** is completely impassable after rain and otherwise requires a 4WD. Spanning 80km from Cape Tribulation to where the track joins the Cooktown Road at **Black Mountain**, the exciting section with drastic gradients lies below the halfway mark of the tidal **Bloomfield River**, which has to be crossed at low water. Beyond **Wujal Wujal** Aboriginal community on the north side, the road flattens out to run past *Bloomfield Cabins and Camping* (☏07/4060 8207, ⓦwww.bloomfieldcabins.com; ❺), who have plentiful camping space and three basic cabins; and *Home Rule Rainforest Lodge* at **ROSSVILLE** (☏07/4060 3925; ❸), which offers kitchen facilities and inexpensive meals. Alternatively, you could fork out for the reclusive *Bloomfield River Lodge* (☏07/4035 9166, ⓦwww.bloomfieldlodge.com.au; ❽), though at a minimum of two nights at $586 per person – including transport from Cairns – it's not for everyone. Moving on, it's not far now to the more down-to-earth *Lions Den* pub at **Helenvale** near Black Mountain (see p.538), about thirty minutes from Cooktown.

The Cape York Peninsula and Torres Strait Islands

The **Cape York Peninsula** points north towards the **Torres Strait** and New Guinea, and tackling the rugged tracks and hectic river crossings on the "Trip To The Tip" is an adventure in itself – besides being a means to reach Australia's northernmost point and the communities at **Bamaga** and **Thursday Island**, so far removed from southern attitudes that they could easily be in another country. But it's not all four-wheel driving across the savannah: during the dry season the historic settlement of **Cooktown**, the wetlands at **Lakefield National Park** and **Laura**'s Aboriginal heritage are only a day's journey from Cairns in any decent vehicle. Given longer you might get as far as **Weipa**, but don't go further than this without off-road transport; while some have managed to reach The Tip in family sedans, most who try fail miserably.

With thousands making the overland journey between May and October, a **breakdown** won't leave you stranded, but the cost of repairs will make you regret it. **Bikers** should travel in groups and have off-roading experience. Those without their own vehicle can take Coral Coaches' thrice weekly **bus** from Cairns to Cooktown, or overland **tours** right to the tip; see box on p.519. From Cairns, it's also possible to **cruise** up to Thursday Island, calling in at islands on the way with Kangaroo Explorer, PO Box 7110, Cairns (℡07/4032 4000, Ⓦwww.kangaroocruises.com.au; one-way economy berths from $1895); or aboard the *Sea Swift* passenger **ferry** (℡07/4035 1234, Ⓦwww.seaswift.com.au; one-way $325). You can also **fly** to various places on the Cape from Cairns, or join Cape York Air (℡07/4035 9399, Ⓦwww.capeyorkair.com.au), for a one-day return run up to Thursday Island with the postman.

You'll find a few roadhouses and motels along the way, but north of Weipa **accommodation** on the Cape is mostly limited to camping, and it's inevitable if you head right to The Tip that one night at least will be spent in the bush. Settlements also supply meals and provisions, but there won't be much on offer so take all you can carry. Don't turn bush campsites into rubbish dumps: take a pack of bin liners and remove all your garbage. **Estuarine crocodiles** are present throughout the Cape: read the warning under "Wildlife dangers" in Basics. There are few **banks**, so take enough cash to carry you between points – some roadhouses accept plastic. In Cairns, the RACQ can help with advice on road conditions and **maps**; other maps from Pinevale Publications (try bookshops), Croc Shop at 10 Shields St, and the NPWS fill in local and historical information. Vehicles heading to The Tip should carry a **first-aid kit**, a comprehensive tool kit and spares, extra fuel, and a tarpaulin for creek crossings. A winch, and equipment for removing, patching and inflating tyres may also come in handy.

Mossman to Cape York

Not as pretty as the coastal Bloomfield track but considerably easier, the 260-kilometre inland road to Cooktown and points north leaves the Cook

Highway just before Mossman and climbs to the drier scrub at **MOUNT CARBINE**, a former tungsten mine whose roadhouse and *Wolfram Hotel* (②), with simple but clean rooms, fulfil all functions. The descent of the far side of the range an hour later is rough, a foretaste of the Cape's incredibly dusty byways, but almost all this road is now sealed. **LAKELAND**'s café, hotel and fuel stop marks the junction for routes north along the **Peninsula Developmental Road** to Laura (p.540), but the way to Cooktown lies east,

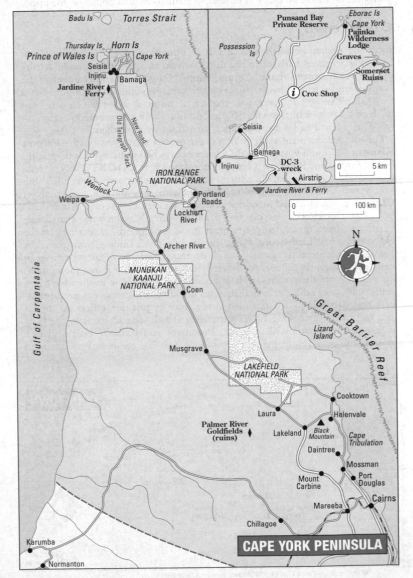

past the **Annan River Gorge** and the mysterious **Black Mountain**, two huge dark piles of lichen-covered granite boulders near the road. Aborigines reckon the formation to be the result of a building competition between two rivals fighting over a girl, and tell stories of people wandering into the eerie, whistling caverns, never to return.

At this point it's worth a four-kilometre detour south along the **Bloomfield Track** to the *Lions Den* at **HELENVALE**. The *Den* is an old-style pub playing up for tourists during the day but one hundred percent authentic at night, from the iron sheeting and beam decor to those nasty exhibits in glass bottles on the piano.

Cooktown

After the *Endeavour* nearly sank at Cape Tribulation in 1770, Captain Cook landed at a natural harbour to the north, where he spent two months repairing the vessel, observing the "Genius, Temper, Disposition and Number of the Natives" and – legend has it – naming the kangaroo after an Aboriginal word for "I don't know". Tempers wore thin on occasion, as when the crew refused to share a catch of turtles with Aborigines, and Cook commented perceptively: "They seem'd to set no value upon any thing we gave them."

The site lay dormant until gold was discovered southwest on the **Palmer River** in 1873, and within months a harbour was being surveyed at the mouth of the Endeavour River for a tented camp known as **COOKTOWN**. A wild success while gold lasted, the settlement once boasted a main street alive with hotels and a busy port doing brisk trade with Asia through thousands of **Chinese** prospectors and merchants. But the reserves were soon exhausted and by 1910 Cooktown was on the decline. Today, Cooktown's main drag, Charlotte Street, is neat but pretty quiet, good for random wandering past the old wharves and **Endeavour Park**, the site of Cook's landing, now graced by a statue of the great navigator. A kiosk on the waterfront organizes two-hour **cruises** through the Endeavour River's mangroves ($22). Among monuments on the lawn are the remains of defences sent from Brisbane in the nineteenth century to ward off a threatened Russian invasion: one cannon, three cannonballs and two rifles – accompanied at the time by just one officer. At the far end of town, 500m along Endeavour Valley Road, separate areas in the half-wild **cemetery** for Jewish, Chinese, Protestant and Catholic burials gives a glimpse of how cosmopolitan the town once was. The cemetery's most famous resident is **Mary Watson** of Lizard Island (see overleaf), whose grave near the entrance is decorated with seashells and a pietá painting.

The best **views** of the town and river are from the top floor of the old Sisters of Mercy Convent, now a **regional museum** (daily 9.30am–4pm; $5.50) with a bit of everything: artefacts jettisoned from *Endeavour*, exhaustive local history, a reconstructed joss house, a rundown on pearling around Thursday Island, and the history of the "hopelessly insolvent" Cooktown–Laura railway. Not far away on the corner of Helen and Walker streets, the **Marine Museum** (daily 8.30am–5.30pm; $5.50) details the 1899 cyclones Mahina and Nachon, which collided north of Cooktown sinking 76 vessels and killing 350 people.

There are more views of the district from the red-and-white corrugated-iron cone of **Grassy Hill Lighthouse**, reached on a concrete track from the end of Hope Street. **Mount Cook** is a rather tougher proposition, a two-hour return hike through thick forest on meagre paths – follow orange triangles from the nondescript starting point that you'll find beyond Ida Street (pick up free maps for this from the Council Offices next to the post office, open Mon–Fri 9am–4.30pm). At the end of Walker Street, the **Botanic Gardens**, founded by Chinese and recently re-established, merge into original paperbark woodland, with a track running to **Finch Beach** on Cherry Tree Bay. Although it is sometimes rated as a safe swimming beach, you should heed the home-made warning signs in pidgin: "Dispela Stap Hia" and a picture of a croc.

Practicalities

The June **Discovery Festival** is a predictably thorough piss-up, but even then **accommodation** shouldn't be too difficult to find. If you're **camping**, the *Tropical Breeze* site near the cemetery is handy for town, but the *Peninsula Van Park* (℡07/4069 5107) has the nicer location, in forest below Mount Cook. *Pam's Place*, Charlotte Street (℡07/4069 5166; ❶), is a hostel with inexpensive beds and spacious cooking facilities; while the lavish *Sovereign Resort* on Charlotte Street (℡07/4069 5400; ❼), with a pool and café-bar-restaurant, and the *River of Gold Motel*, corner of Hope and Walker streets (℡07/4069 5222; ❺), are surprisingly sophisticated alternatives. A few kilometres out of town on a secluded hillside, *Milkwood Lodge* (℡07/4069 5007, ⓦwww.milkwood-lodge.com; ❺) offers self-contained cabins with verandah views out over the valley. Numerous cafés and hotels supply **food and drink**; a **supermarket** and grocer are the last source of fresh provisions before Weipa, and the ATM at the **bank** here is the only one on the Cape. For all **information**, including vehicle rentals or local **tours**, head to Cooktown Travel Centre on Charlotte Street (Mon–Fri 8am–6pm, Sat 8am–noon, Sun 3–5pm; ℡07/4069 5446).

Heading **back to Cairns**, Cooktown Travel take bookings for Coral Coaches and Transtate Airlines and arrange a bus to the airport ($7), which is 10km from town. Those continuing **up the Cape** have two options: vehicles other than 4WDs have to head southwest to Lakeland for Laura and points north; stronger sets of wheels can reach Lakefield National Park more directly by heading towards Hope Vale community and then taking the Battlecamp Road. The **last fuel** this way until Musgrave is about 33km from Cooktown at *Endeavour Falls Tourist Park* (℡07/4069 5431; self-contained units ❹), a nice spot in itself with a neighbouring waterfall, forest and croc-free swimming hole.

Lizard Island

A granite rise covered in stunted trees and heath, **Lizard Island** is one of the most isolated resorts in Australia, 90km north of Cooktown, and within sight of the outer reef. Divers rave about the fringing coral reefs here but, even so, reaching Lizard is an expensive business: options are limited to a daily **flight** on Qantas from Cairns or Cape Air Transport from Cooktown, or a lift hitched through Cairns Yacht Club (see "Listings", p.520). Those unable to afford the **lodge** (℡07/4060 3999; ❽) can use the NPWS **camping area** (permits from Cairns; see p.520) down on Watson Beach. The lodge won't help out with *anything* except in real emergencies, and, as gas cylinders can't be carried on the plane, charcoal beads are the recommended fuel for fires.

Shell middens show that Lizard was regularly visited by Aboriginal peoples, but the island was uninhabited when **Robert Watson** built a cottage and started a sea-slug processing operation here in the 1870s, accompanied by his wife **Mary** and two Chinese servants. Aborigines attacked the house while Robert was at sea in October 1881, killing one of the Chinese and forcing Mary, her baby and Ah Sam to flee in a water tank; they paddled west for five days before dying of thirst. Her painfully matter-of-fact diary is kept at Brisbane's John Oxley Library, while the tank is on display at the Museum of Tropical Queensland in Townsville.

Quinkan Country: Laura and the Palmer River

Back on the Peninsula Road, 60km north of Lakeland, **LAURA**'s store-cum-post office, roadhouse and *Quinkan Hotel* (℡07/4060 3255; ❻) support the two-day **Aboriginal Dance Festival**, an electrifying assertion of Aboriginal identity, held in June of odd-numbered years. At any time of year you can visit the sandstone caves and ridges at **Split Rock**, 13km south of town, where a steep track leads to a two-hour gallery circuit. Paintings depict animals and startling spirit figures associated with sorcery: spidery, frightening Quinkan with pendulous earlobes, and dumpy Anurra, often with their legs twisted upwards. Other sites show scenes from post-Contact life, depicting horses, rifles and clothed figures; some caves were probably in use until the 1930s. You can find out more through the *Ang-Gnarra Aboriginal Corporation Caravan Park* (℡07/4060 3200) or from Trezise Bush Service/Quinkan Tours (℡07/4060 3236), which has a camp west in the scrub at Jowalbinna, about an hour's drive from Laura (4WD only; for reservations call ℡07/4051 4777, ⓦwww.adventures.com).

Sites along the **Palmer River**, 80km (8hr) southwest of Laura along a terrible 4WD track, recall the gigantic 1873 goldrush. Mining life was volatile: Aborigines waged guerrilla warfare, and race riots erupted between whites and the Chinese – who at one time outnumbered the entire European population of Queensland and infuriated whites by doggedly extracting gold from "exhausted" claims. The settlements at Maytown and German Bar were abandoned once the gold had gone and today there's virtually nothing left except atmosphere; the Cairns NPWS (see p.520) stocks **maps** and permits.

Lakefield National Park

Ideally you'd take at least a week to absorb **Lakefield National Park**'s fifty thousand square kilometres of savannah and riverine flats, drifting between the 21 **campsites**. But even a single night spent here will give you a feel for the Cape's most accessible wilderness area. Apart from the **Old Laura Homestead** – built between 1892 and 1940 and standing abandoned in the scrub on the Laura River – the park's pleasures revolve around outdoor pursuits, fishing and exploring lagoons for wildlife. Lakefield's **crocodile-conser-**

vation programme means you might see both fresh- and saltwater types; birdlife is plentiful and plenty of kangaroos put in an appearance. "**Magnetic**" **anthills** are a common landmark: the ants build flattened towers aligned north–south to prevent overheating in the noonday sun.

Vehicles other than 4WDs can sometimes manage the rough 170-kilometre track through the park between Laura township and *Musgrave Roadhouse*, but only if there hasn't been any rain for a good while. High clearance is essential for other routes, including the Battle Camp road to Cooktown. **Ranger stations** (☎07/4060 3271) are located along the road at New Laura, at the southern end of the park, 50km from Laura township; Lakefield (central, 80km) and Bizant (north, 100km). Popular places to camp and watch wildlife are **Horseshoe Lagoon** beyond Old Laura, **12 Mile Hole** near New Laura (4WD only), **Kalpowar Crossing** (near Lakefield, with showers and toilets) and **Hann Crossing**, in the north of the park.

Laura to Iron Range and Weipa

Following the main road, the 300km that stretches between Laura and Archer River passes in a haze of dust, jolts and roadhouses supplying fuel, food, beds and drink. First on the list is **MUSGRAVE** (135km from Laura; ☎07/4060 3229 for road condition check), a converted homestead where the track from Lakefield National Park joins the road; there's **accommodation** about 10km in towards the park at *Lotus Bird Lodge* (☎07/4059 0773, ✉lotusbird@iig .com.au; ❻), whose spacious wooden cottages are surrounded by much the same scenery as you'll find in the national park. Back on the road north, the next two hours are a wild roller-coaster ride – look out for "Dip" signs warning of monster gullies – down to **COEN**'s *(S)Exchange Hotel*, 107km from Musgrave. Coen's Ambrust General Store handles **camping**, provisions, fuel, post office business and EFTPOS. The *Homestead Guest House*, on Regent Street, has beds (☎07/4060 1157; ❷) and can provide meals, while you can have any car problems fixed at Clark's workshop.

Some 25km further north, a 4WD track west heads into the dry woodland and rainforest of the **Mungkan Kaanju National Park**; the ranger station lies 75km along at Rokeby station (☎07/4060 3256), with camping at undeveloped bush sites. Back on the main road north, its 45km from the park turn-off to the **Archer River Roadhouse** (☎07/4060 3266), which has a camp site and **accommodation** in units (❸), as well as the last reliable **fuel** on the main road before Bamaga, 400km away. Beyond are routes east to Iron Range (155km) and west to Weipa (190km) – covered below.

Iron Range

There's nothing in Australia quite like the magnificent jungle at **Iron Range National Park**, a leftover from the Ice Age link to New Guinea, which hides fauna found nowhere else on the continent – the nocturnal **green python** and brilliant blue-and-red **eclectus parrot** are the best-known species. Four hours bouncing along a 4WD track from the main road should bring you to a clearing where the army simulated a nuclear strike in the 1960s – fortunately using tons of conventional explosives instead of the real thing. Turning right at the junction here takes you past the **ranger station** (☎07/4060 7170) to **LOCKHART RIVER**, an Aboriginal mission and fishing beach; supplies and fuel are sold here during weekday trading hours. The road left passes two **bush campsites** near the Claudie River and Gordon's Creek crossings before winding up at **PORTLAND ROADS**' few houses and public telephones, overlooking a monument to Edmund Kennedy (see p.507) and the remains of a harbour used by US forces in World War II. There's further camping a few kilometres back towards the junction at **Chilli Beach**, a perpetually blustery, tropical setting backed by coconut palms. There are no stores or any public services at Portland Roads.

Next day, you have the chance to experience something unique on the mainland – **sunrise** and **sunset** over different seas – by taking **Frenchman's Road** to Weipa. This starts 30km back from the Lockhart/Portland junction, crosses the difficult **Pascoe** and **Wenlock** rivers, and emerges on the Peninsula Developmental Road, 2km north of **Batavia Downs**. Head through Batavia and cross more creeks, which look worse than they are, to the main Weipa road; the trip coast to coast might take six to eight hours.

Weipa

Those without a 4WD will have to give Iron Range a miss, but can still reach **WEIPA**, a town of red clay and yellow mining trucks dealing in kaolin and **bauxite**. The area was one of the first in Australia to be described by Europeans: Willem Janz encountered "savage, cruel blacks" here in 1606, a report later reiterated by Jan Carstensz who found nothing of interest and sailed off to chart the Gulf of Carpentaria. Apart from a mission built at **Mappoon** in the nineteenth century, little changed until aluminium ore was first mined in the 1950s and Comalco built the town and began mining.

All traffic in Weipa gives way to the gargantuan mine vehicles and stays out of the restricted areas. The town comprises mostly company housing, but it does offer long-forgotten luxuries: you can pick up spares for your vehicle at the **auto wreckers** and service station on the way into town; and there's a **supermarket** and post office just in front of *Weipa Camping Ground* (T07/4069 7871), a large **campsite** featuring hot showers and a laundry, where you can unwind and swap tales about the rigours of the trip; fishing trips and **mine tours** can be arranged at the campsite office. The **Albatross Hotel** (T07/4069 7314; ④–⑥) up the road has rooms and bungalows, is licensed and looks out over the western sea. Hardened **bikers** should try to catch the August **Croc Run**, Australia's richest and most challenging endurance race which weaves its way through mangroves and creeks.

Around town, the library's **Cape York Collection** contains a unique collection of books and documents relating to the area, while the **Uningan Nature Reserve**, situated on the Mission River, preserves sixteen-metre-high **middens** composed entirely of shells left over from Aboriginal meals – some have been dated to sixteen hundred years ago. Driving is the only way to get here, and guidebooks are available from the campsite. Keep an eye out for crocs while walking around the reserve.

Leaving, there's a barge to Normanton (see p.596) in the Gulf once a week, and there are occasional services to Thursday Island – contact Gulf Freight Services (T07/4069 7309 or free call 1800 640 079). Note that there is **no fuel** between Weipa and Bamaga (340km).

North of the Wenlock

The seasonally deep, fast-flowing **Wenlock River**, an hour north of the Weipa junction on the main road, marks the start of the most challenging part of the journey north, with road conditions changing every wet season. Formerly requiring some skill and a bit of luck to cross safely, the Wenlock River itself may soon be tamed by a **causeway**. Routes divide 42km further on, where

Crossing creeks by 4WD

While Cape York's crocs make the standard 4WD procedure of walking creek crossings before driving them potentially dangerous, wherever possible you should make some effort to gauge the waters' depth and find the best route. *Never* blindly follow others across. Make sure all rescue gear – shovel, winch, rope, etc – is easy to reach, outside the vehicle. Electrics on petrol engines need to be waterproofed. On deep crossings, block off air inlets to prevent water entering the engine, slacken off the fan belt and cover the radiator grille with a tarpaulin; this diverts water around the engine as long as the vehicle is moving. Select an appropriate gear (changing it in midstream will let water into the clutch) and drive through at walking speed; clear the opposite embankment before stopping again. In deep water, there's a chance the vehicle might float slightly, and so get pushed off-track by the current – though there's not much you can do about this. If you stall, switch off the ignition *immediately*, exit through windows, disconnect the battery (a short might restart the engine) and winch out. Don't restart the vehicle until you've made sure that water hasn't been sucked in through the air filter – which will destroy the engine. If you have severe problems, recovery will be very expensive; see "Basics", pp.40–44.

die-hards follow the **Old Telegraph Track**, which has all the interesting scenery and creek crossings; those less certain of their abilities take the longer **New Road** to the east, consisting of 200km of loose gravel and bulldust. The Telegraph Track's lines were dismantled in the wake of satellite communications, and many of the poles have been robbed of their ceramic caps by souvenir hunters. The first travellers of the year build simple rafts and log bridges to cross the creeks; as tracks dry and traffic increases, jarring corrugations and potholes are more likely to pose a problem, constituting a serious test of vehicle strength. There are some fine **creeks** on this route: Bertie's potholes are large enough to submerge an entire vehicle; Gunshot's three-metre vertical clay banks are a real test of skill (use low range first, and keep your foot off the brake); and the north exit at Cockatoo is deceptively sandy. Dozens wipe out on Gunshot every season; for the cautious there's a 24-kilometre detour via open scrub at **Heathlands** to the north side.

The two routes rejoin briefly after 75km, then the New Road diverges left 54km to the **Jardine River Ferry** ($80 return, including use of the Injinu campsite at Bamaga), while the Telegraph Track ploughs on past beautiful clear green water and basalt **waterfalls** (both with safe swimming holes) to Nolans Brook – often necessitating a brief submarine dip – and the hundred-metre-wide **Jardine River**. This spot was once the only crossing point on the Jardine, but the river's width makes the crossing extremely testing, and the likelihood of crocodiles adds to the risks. However, it *is* worth the trip to camp (assuming you have enough fuel) before heading back to the ferry. From there, the last hour to Bamaga passes the remains of a **DC-3** that crashed just short of the airstrip in 1945.

Bamaga

BAMAGA, a community of stilt houses and banana palms founded by Saibai islanders in 1946, owes nothing to suburban values. Around the intersection you'll find a workshop and service station selling **fuel** (Mon–Fri 9am–5pm, Sat 9am–12.30pm, Sun 1.30–3pm), a Commonwealth Bank (Mon–Fri 9.30am–3pm; bank books only), airline offices, a hotel and a **shopping centre** (fresh veggies, National Australia Bank agent, telephones, café and post office). For **accommodation**, turn left at the junction to **Injinu campsite**

(Cowall Creek), or right past the shopping centre to the coast at **SEISIA** (Red Island Point). You can stay here at the Seisia *Village Resort* (☎07/4069 3243; units ❹), under palms near the jetty, and take advantage of showers, laundry facilities, a canteen and fishing safaris. Other services in Seisia include a roadhouse, tackle shop, taxi (☎07/4069 3333) and 4WD rental.

Cape York and Somerset

To make local contacts, stay around Bamaga. To keep with the overland crowd head 16km north to the Croc Shop's information hut, then bear left for 11km to the idyllic beach at **Punsand Bay Private Reserve** (☎07/4069 1722; ❷–❹), a just reward for the trials of the journey, with prefab tents, camping, meals, basic provisions, and a limited repairs service but no fuel. Around here you might spot the rare **palm cockatoo**, a huge, crested black parrot with a curved bill.

You could spend a day recuperating on the beach, or return to the Croc Shop and take the 17km road past the Somerset fork to its end at another **campsite** (shower, water and kiosk) and the luxurious, Aboriginal-owned *Pajinka Lodge* (☎07/4069 2100, bookings free call ☎1800 802 968; ❼). Follow the footpath through vine forest onto a wild, barren headland and down to a turbulent sea opposite the lighthouse on **Eborac Island**. A sign concreted into an oil drum marks the **tip of mainland Australia** and the end of the journey.

Somerset

Established on government orders in 1864 to balance the French naval station in New Caledonia, **Somerset** was founded by John Jardine, who was succeeded by his son Frank the following year. Frank became a legend on the Cape and tales of his exploits assume larger-than-life proportions (fearless pioneer to some, brutal colonial to others). Though envisaged as a second Singapore, Somerset never amounted to more than a military outpost under constant attack from termites and local tribes. In 1877, after the pearling trade in the Torres Strait erupted into lawlessness, the settlement was abandoned in favour of a seat of government closer to the problem at Thursday Island.

Today, Somerset is a large paddock with only a few cannon, machine parts and mango trees as signs of former habitation; the buildings succumbed to white ants or were moved long ago. Frank and his wife Sana are buried on the beach directly below (standing up, say locals), next to a Chinese cemetery and traces of a jetty into the Adolphus Channel. Exploration of the dense undergrowth above the beach to the left might uncover remains of a **sentry post** and a cave with stick-figure paintings, presumably Aboriginal. Past Somerset, a track continues onto another beach before circling back towards the Croc Shop.

The Torres Strait

Beyond Cape York, barely 200km of sea separates Australia from New Guinea: the **Torres Strait** is an obstacle-strewn stretch named after Luís Vaez de Torres, who navigated the waters in 1606. Prior to European contact, the Strait's islands had developed trade links with Australia and highland New Guinea, which supplied outrigger canoes – no suitable trees grow in the Strait

– in exchange for oyster and trochus shell, and heads. Warfare between islands pervaded all aspects of life, and the eastern cult of Malo required human jaws as tribute.

The early nineteenth century saw the first trade with Europeans, who soon discovered the Strait's rich pearl beds and occupied the islands as bases for the industry, decimating the Islanders through violence and disease. Then on July 1, 1871, the **London Missionary Society** landed on Darnley Island. Once Islanders realized that the mission protected them from the more piratical whites, they converted to Christianity at a speed that amazed even the missionaries. The advent of Christianity (known here as the **Coming of the Light**) stabilized communities but also heralded the end of traditional life, as cults were undermined and wages and stores replaced the barter network. Another influential group were **South Sea Island** teachers, who brought their own dance styles and crops, and gradually intermarried with the locals.

The church created **island councils**, but Queensland held the real power with its **segregation laws**, which prevented emigration to the mainland. The only job in the Strait was pearling (for mother-of-pearl), and white boat-owners would have lost their labour pool if Islanders went south. Until World War II the islands made the best of it, but army service overseas gave returning recruits a better understanding of what they deserved from the government, and pressure removed some barriers to migration. The advent of plastics led to the collapse of the mother-of-pearl industry, and the unemployment that followed forced the government to drop all protectionist policies, with the result that by the mid-1970s half the Strait's former population was living on the mainland. The remainder formed a movement to establish an **Islander Nation**, which bore its first fruit on June 3, 1992, when the **Mabo Decision** acknowledged the Merriam as traditional owners of Murray Island, thereby setting a precedent for mainland Aboriginal claims and sending shock waves through the establishment.

Ferries cross regularly between Cape York and Thursday Island, the Strait's administrative centre – which, even on a brief visit, offers a fascinating glimpse into an all-but-forgotten corner of Australia. In theory, travel beyond Thursday (except to neighbouring islands) is forbidden to casual travellers, but the rules are occasionally relaxed.

Thursday Island

A three-square-kilometre speck within sight of the mainland, between Prince of Wales, Hammond and Horn islands, **Thursday Island** wears a few aliases: coined "Sink of the Pacific" for the variety of peoples who passed through in pearling days, the local tag is *Waiben* or (very loosely) "Thirsty Island" – once a reference to the availability of drinking water and now a laconic aside on the quantity of beer consumed. The hotel clock with no hands hints at the pace of life and it's only for events like Christmas, when wall-to-wall aluminium punts from neighbouring islands make the harbour look like a maritime supermarket car park, that things liven up. Other chances to catch Thursday in carnival spirit are during the Coming of the Light festivities on July 1, and for the full-bore Island of Origin rugby league matches later in the same month – in one season 25 players were hospitalized, and one killed.

In town there are traces of the old **Chinatown** district around Milman Street, and a reminder of Queensland's worst shipping disaster in the **Quetta Memorial Church**, way down Douglas Street, built after the ship hit an uncharted rock in the Adolphus Channel in 1890 and went down with virtually all the Europeans on board. The Aplin Road **cemetery**, where two of the victims are buried, has tiled Islander tombs and depressing numbers of **Japanese** graves, each marked by a short pillar and kanji inscription. All died pearl diving. As a by-product of the industry, Japanese crews had accurately mapped the Strait before World War II and it's no coincidence that the airstrip was bombed when hostilities were declared in 1942; fortifications are still in place on Thursday's east coast. Bunkers and naval cannon at the **Old Fort** on the opposite side date from the 1890s.

Practicalities

There are **ferries** to Thursday Island every weekday morning from Cape York (2hr), Punsand Bay (1hr 30min) and Seisia (1hr 15min); prices are $77 each way. Passing **Possession Island** on the way over, you come within sight of a plaque commemorating James Cook's landing here on August 22, 1770, when he planted the flag for George III and Great Britain. Then it's into the shallow channel between Horn Island (see below) and **Prince of Wales Island**, the Strait's largest island, stocked with deer and settled by an overflow population unable to afford Thursday's exorbitant land premiums.

The wharf on Thursday sits below the colonial-style **Customs House**, a minute from the town centre on **Douglas Street**. Here you'll find a **post office** with payphones, the National Australia **bank**, cafés and two of the island's **hotels**: the *Torres* just beats the neighbouring *Royal* as Australia's northernmost bar. Facing the water on **Victoria Parade**, the *Federal* (℡07/4069 1569; ⑤) is fractionally quieter as **lodgings** on a busy night, while on Douglas Street, *Mura Mudh* (℡07/4069 2050; ①) is a good-value hostel run by Thursday Islanders. Other facilities include *Café Gallery*, and a **pharmacy** and **laundry** on Douglas Street. Peddell's Buses (℡07/4069 1551) meets incoming ferries for a ninety-minute **tour** of the island ($17.50).

Other islands

Though you generally need permission from the local council, it's possible that you may be privately invited to other islands in the Strait. While some are within outboard range – "one drum trips" – you're looking at $400 or more each way to charter a five-seater plane to anywhere more distant. Torres Strait Tours on Thursday Island (free call ℡1800 420 666, ℻07/4069 1408) can arrange water taxis and island transfers if needed.

Just a few minutes from Thursday's wharf by water taxi ($15), **Horn Island** is another small chunk of land surrounded by mangroves and coral, the site of an open-cut gold mine and the regional **airport** (with regular flights to and from Cairns). The main reason to trip across is to visit the **pearling museum**, run by an ex-diver and stocked with his memorabilia – including an old-fashioned bronze dive helmet. He also owns Horn's sole place to **stay** or **eat**, the *Gateway Torres Strait Resort* (℡07/4069 2222, ⓦwww.gtsr.com.au; ⑤).

Somewhere that requires minimum planning is uninhabited **Coconut Island**, a thirty-minute flight northeast of Horn, which has self-contained cabins for $90 a night. Far to the east, **Murray Island** (Mer) is enticing for its remoteness and importance in island history. To the north are **Badu**, centre of the Strait's burgeoning crayfish industry, and **Saibai**, a low deltaic island just 16km from the New Guinea mainland. This is the only place in Australia where you can see another country, but regular trading across the Strait has recently included "grass-for-guns" exchanges, and New Guinea is not the place to be caught without a visa.

TRAVEL DETAILS

Trains

Ayr to: Bowen (6 weekly; 2hr); Bundaberg (6 weekly; 16hr); Cairns (4 weekly; 9hr); Gladstone (6 weekly; 13hr); Ingham (4 weekly; 3hr 30min); Innisfail (4 weekly; 6hr 45min); Mackay (6 weekly; 5hr); Proserpine, for Airlie Beach (6 weekly; 2hr 40min); Rockhampton (6 weekly; 11hr); Townsville (6 weekly; 1hr 30min); Tully, for Mission Beach (4 weekly; 5hr 30min).

Bowen to: Ayr (6 weekly; 2hr); Bundaberg (6 weekly; 14hr); Cairns (4 weekly; 11hr); Gladstone (6 weekly; 11hr); Ingham (4 weekly; 5hr); Innisfail (4 weekly; 9hr 30min); Mackay (6 weekly; 3hr); Proserpine, for Airlie Beach (6 weekly; 2hr); Rockhampton (6 weekly; 8hr 20min); Townsville (6 weekly; 3hr); Tully, for Mission Beach (4 weekly; 7hr).

Bundaberg to: Ayr (6 weekly; 16hr); Bowen (6 weekly; 14hr); Cairns (4 weekly; 25hr); Gladstone (6 weekly; 2hr 30min); Ingham (4 weekly; 18hr); Innisfail (4 weekly; 21hr); Mackay (6 weekly; 11hr); Proserpine, for Airlie Beach (6 weekly; 13hr 30min); Rockhampton (6 weekly; 4hr 30min); Townsville (6 weekly; 17hr); Tully, for Mission Beach (4 weekly; 20hr).

Cairns to: Ayr (4 weekly; 9hr); Bowen (4 weekly; 11hr); Bundaberg (4 weekly; 25hr); Forsayth (1 weekly; 11hr 15min); Gladstone (4 weekly; 22hr); Ingham (4 weekly; 5hr); Innisfail (4 weekly; 2hr); Kuranda (1–2 daily; 1hr); Mackay (4 weekly; 13hr 20min); Proserpine, for Airlie Beach (4 weekly; 11hr 30min); Rockhampton (4 weekly; 19hr); Townsville (4 weekly; 4hr 40min); Tully, for Mission Beach (4 weekly; 3hr 15min).

Gladstone to: Ayr (6 weekly; 13hr); Bowen (6 weekly; 11hr); Bundaberg (6 weekly; 2hr 30min); Cairns (4 weekly; 22hr); Ingham (4 weekly; 16hr); Innisfail (4 weekly; 19hr); Mackay (6 weekly; 8hr); Proserpine, for Airlie Beach (6 weekly; 10hr); Rockhampton (6 weekly; 1hr 30min); Townsville (6 weekly; 14hr); Tully, for Mission Beach (4 weekly; 18hr).

Ingham to: Ayr (4 weekly; 3hr 30min); Bowen (4 weekly; 5hr); Bundaberg (4 weekly; 18hr); Cairns (4 weekly; 5hr); Gladstone (4 weekly; 16hr); Innisfail (4 weekly; 3hr); Mackay (4 weekly; 9hr); Proserpine, for Airlie Beach (4 weekly; 7hr); Rockhampton (4 weekly; 15hr); Townsville (4 weekly; 2hr); Tully, for Mission Beach (4 weekly; 2hr).

Innisfail to: Ayr (4 weekly; 6hr 45min); Bowen (4 weekly; 9hr 30min); Bundaberg (4 weekly; 21hr); Cairns (4 weekly; 2hr); Gladstone (4 weekly; 19hr); Ingham (4 weekly; 3hr); Mackay (4 weekly; 12hr); Proserpine, for Airlie Beach (4 weekly; 9hr 30min); Rockhampton (4 weekly; 18hr); Townsville (4 weekly; 5hr); Tully, for Mission Beach (4 weekly; 1hr 15min).

Mackay to: Ayr (6 weekly; 5hr); Bowen (6 weekly; 3hr); Bundaberg (6 weekly; 11hr); Cairns (4 weekly; 13hr 20min); Gladstone (6 weekly; 8hr); Ingham (4 weekly; 9hr); Innisfail (4 weekly; 12hr); Proserpine, for Airlie Beach (4 weekly; 2hr 30min); Rockhampton (6 weekly; 5hr 30min); Townsville (6 weekly; 7hr); Tully, for Mission Beach (4 weekly; 10hr 30min).

Proserpine to: Ayr (6 weekly; 2hr 40min); Bowen (6 weekly; 2hr); Bundaberg (6 weekly; 13hr 30min); Cairns (4 weekly; 11hr 30min); Gladstone (6 weekly; 10hr); Ingham (4 weekly; 7hr); Innisfail (4 weekly; 9hr 30min); Mackay (6 weekly; 2hr 30min); Rockhampton (6 weekly; 7hr 40min); Townsville (6 weekly; 4hr 40min); Tully, for Mission Beach (4 weekly; 8hr).

Rockhampton to: Ayr (6 weekly; 11hr); Bowen (6 weekly; 8hr 20min); Bundaberg (6 weekly; 4hr 30min); Cairns (4 weekly; 19hr); Gladstone (6 weekly; 1hr 30min); Ingham (4 weekly; 15hr); Innisfail (4 weekly; 18hr); Longreach (2 weekly; 12hr 30min); Mackay (6 weekly; 5hr 30min); Proserpine, for Airlie Beach (6 weekly; 7hr 40min); Townsville (6 weekly; 12hr); Tully, for Mission Beach (4 weekly; 16hr).

Townsville to: Ayr (6 weekly; 1hr 30min); Bowen (6 weekly; 3hr); Bundaberg (6 weekly; 17hr); Cairns (6 weekly; 4hr 40min); Gladstone (6 weekly; 14hr); Ingham (4 weekly; 2hr); Innisfail (4 weekly; 5hr); Mackay (6 weekly; 7hr); Mount Isa (2 weekly; 19hr); Proserpine, for Airlie Beach (6 weekly; 4hr 40min); Rockhampton (6 weekly; 12hr); Tully, for Mission Beach (4 weekly; 4hr).

Tully to: Ayr (4 weekly; 5hr 30min); Bowen (4 weekly; 7hr); Bundaberg (4 weekly; 20hr); Cairns (4 weekly; 3hr 15min); Gladstone (4 weekly; 18hr); Ingham (4 weekly; 2hr); Innisfail (4 weekly; 1hr 15min); Mackay (4 weekly; 10hr 30min); Proserpine, for Airlie Beach (4 weekly; 8hr); Rockhampton (4 weekly; 16hr); Townsville (4 weekly; 4hr).

Buses

Airlie Beach to: Ayr (7 daily; 2hr 20min); Bowen (7 daily; 1hr); Bundaberg (7 daily; 11hr 30min); Cairns (7 daily; 9hr 45min); Gladstone (7 daily; 10hr); Ingham (7 daily; 6hr); Innisfail (7 daily; 8hr 30min); Mackay (7 daily; 3hr); Mission Beach (5 daily; 8hr); Rockhampton (7 daily; 8hr 30min); Townsville (7 daily; 3hr 30min).

Ayr to: Airlie Beach (7 daily; 2hr 20min); Bowen (8 daily; 1hr 20min); Bundaberg (8 daily; 15hr); Cairns (8 daily; 7hr 30min); Gladstone (8 daily; 12hr); Ingham (8 daily; 3hr); Innisfail (8 daily; 6hr); Mackay (8 daily; 5hr); Mission Beach (5 daily; 5hr 30min); Rockhampton (8 daily; 10hr); Townsville (8 daily; 1hr).

Bowen to: Airlie Beach (7 daily; 1hr); Ayr (8 daily; 1hr 20min); Bundaberg (8 daily; 13hr 30min); Cairns (8 daily; 9hr); Gladstone (8 daily; 11hr); Ingham (8 daily; 5hr); Innisfail (8 daily; 8hr); Mackay (8 daily; 4hr); Mission Beach (5 daily; 7hr); Rockhampton (8 daily; 10hr); Townsville (8 daily; 3hr).

Bundaberg to: Airlie Beach (7 daily; 11hr 30min); Agnes Water/1770 (2 weekly; 2hr); Ayr (8 daily; 15hr); Bowen (8 daily; 13hr 30min); Cairns (8 daily; 21hr); Gladstone (8 daily; 3hr); Ingham (8 daily; 18hr); Innisfail (8 daily; 21hr); Mackay (8 daily; 9hr); Mission Beach (5 daily; 19hr); Rockhampton (8 daily; 4hr); Townsville (8 daily; 14hr 30min).

Cairns to: Airlie Beach (6 daily; 9hr 45min); Atherton (1 daily; 1hr 45min); Ayr (8 daily; 7hr 30min); Bowen (8 daily; 9hr); Bundaberg (8 daily; 21hr); Cape Tribulation (3 daily; 4hr); Cooktown (2–5 weekly; 8hr); Gladstone (8 daily; 19hr 30min); Herberton (1 daily; 2hr); Ingham (8 daily; 3hr 15min); Innisfail (8 daily; 1hr); Karumba (3 weekly; 12hr); Kuranda (1 daily; 35min); Mackay (8 daily; 12hr); Malanda (1 daily; 40min); Mareeba (1 daily; 1hr 10min); Mission Beach (5 daily; 1hr 55min); Mossman (8 daily; 1hr 45min); Port Douglas (8 daily; 1hr 45min); Ravenshoe (1 daily; 2hr 30min); Rockhampton (8 daily; 17hr); Townsville (8 daily; 4hr 45min); Undara (3 weekly; 5hr); Yungaburra (1 daily; 2hr 15min).

Gladstone to: Airlie Beach (7 daily; 10hr); Ayr (8 daily; 12hr); Bowen (8 daily; 11hr); Bundaberg (8 daily; 3hr); Cairns (8 daily; 19hr 30min); Ingham (8 daily; 15hr); Innisfail (8 daily; 17hr); Mackay (8

daily; 6hr); Mission Beach (5 daily; 16hr); Rockhampton (8 daily; 1hr 15min); Townsville (8 daily; 13hr).

Ingham to: Airlie Beach (7 daily; 6hr); Ayr (8 daily; 3hr); Bowen (8 daily; 5hr); Bundaberg (8 daily; 18hr); Cairns (8 daily; 3hr 15min); Gladstone (8 daily; 15hr); Innisfail (8 daily; 3hr); Mackay (8 daily; 9hr); Mission Beach (5 daily; 2hr); Rockhampton (8 daily; 10hr); Townsville (8 daily; 1hr 30min).

Innisfail to: Airlie Beach (7 daily; 8hr 30min); Ayr (8 daily; 6hr); Bowen (8 daily; 8hr); Bundaberg (8 daily; 21hr); Cairns (8 daily; 1hr); Gladstone (8 daily; 17hr); Ingham (8 daily; 3hr); Mackay (8 daily; 11hr); Mission Beach (5 daily; 2hr 45min); Rockhampton (8 daily; 16hr); Townsville (8 daily; 3hr 45min).

Mackay to: Airlie Beach (7 daily; 3hr); Ayr (8 daily; 5hr); Bowen (8 daily; 4hr); Bundaberg (8 daily; 9hr); Cairns (8 daily; 12hr); Gladstone (8 daily; 6hr); Ingham (8 daily; 9hr); Mackay (8 daily; 11hr); Mission Beach (5 daily; 23hr); Rockhampton (8 daily; 4hr); Townsville (8 daily; 5hr 15min).

Mission Beach to: Airlie Beach (5 daily; 8hr); Ayr (5 daily; 5hr 30min); Bowen (5 daily; 7hr); Bundaberg (5 daily; 19hr); Cairns (5 daily; 1hr 55min); Gladstone (5 daily; 16hr); Ingham (5 daily; 2hr); Innisfail (5 daily; 2hr 45min); Mackay (5 daily; 23hr); Rockhampton (5 daily; 15hr); Townsville (5 daily; 4hr).

Rockhampton to: Airlie Beach (7 daily; 8hr 30min); Ayr (8 daily; 10hr); Bowen (8 daily; 10hr); Bundaberg (8 daily; 4hr); Cairns (8 daily; 17hr); Gladstone (8 daily; 1hr 15min); Ingham (8 daily; 10hr); Innisfail (8 daily; 16hr); Longreach (3 weekly; 9hr); Mackay (8 daily; 4hr); Mission Beach (5 daily; 15hr); Mount Morgan (14 weekly; 2hr); Townsville (8 daily; 9hr 30min); Yeppoon (3 daily; 1hr 30min).

Townsville to: Airlie Beach (7 daily; 3hr 30min); Ayr (8 daily; 1hr); Bowen (8 daily; 3hr); Bundaberg (8 daily; 14hr 30min); Cairns (8 daily; 4hr 45min); Charters Towers (3 daily; 1hr 30min); Gladstone (8 daily; 13hr); Ingham (8 daily; 1hr 30min); Innisfail (8 daily; 3hr 45min); Mackay (8 daily; 5hr 15min); Mission Beach (5 daily; 4hr); Mount Isa (3 daily; 11hr 30min); Rockhampton (8 daily; 9hr 30min).

Ferries

Airlie Beach/Shute Harbour to: Daydream Island (1–2 daily; 45min); Hamilton Island (1–3 daily; 1hr); Hook Island (1–2 daily; 1hr 30min); Lindeman Island (2 daily; 1hr 30min); South Molle Island (2 daily; 45min); Whitsunday Island (1 daily; 2hr).
Cairns to: Thursday Island (2 weekly; 36hr).
Cape York to: Thursday Island (Mon–Fri 3 daily; 1hr 15min–2hr).

Cardwell to: Hinchinbrook Island (2 daily; 1–2hr).
Mission Beach to: Dunk Island (10 or more daily; 15min).
Rosslyn Bay to: Great Keppel Island (4–5 daily; 45min–1hr).
Townsville to: Magnetic Island (10 or more daily; 45min).
Weipa to: Normanton (1 weekly; 24hr).

Flights

Bundaberg to: Brisbane (3 daily; 1hr); Cairns (1 daily; 50min); Gladstone (1 weekly; 35min); Lady Elliot (daily; 45min); Mackay (1 daily; 2hr); Rockhampton (1 daily; 50min).
Cairns to: Bamaga (1 daily; 1hr 45min); Bundaberg (3–5 daily; 3hr 30min); Cooktown (1 daily; 45min); Dunk Island (1 daily; 45min); Lizard Island (2 daily; 1hr); Mackay (2 daily; 2hr 45min); Proserpine (6 weekly; 2hr); Rockhampton (2 daily; 3hr); Thursday Island/Horn Island (1–2 daily; 2hr); Townsville (2 daily; 1hr); Weipa (1 daily; 1hr 15min).

Gladstone to: Bundaberg (1 weekly; 35min); Rockhampton (5 weekly; 25min).
Mackay to: Cairns (2 daily; 2hr 45min); Rockhampton (2 daily; 45min); Townsville (4 daily; 1hr).
Rockhampton to: Cairns (2 daily; 3hr); Gladstone (5 weekly; 25min); Great Keppel Island (3 daily; 25min); Mackay (2 daily; 45min); Townsville (2 daily; 1hr 50min).
Townsville to: Cairns (2 daily; 1hr); Mackay (4 daily; 1hr); Rockhampton (2 daily; 1hr 50min).

TROPICAL QUEENSLAND | Travel details

Outback Queensland

CHAPTER 5

Highlights

* **Artesian hot spa at Mitchell** – The hot springs in single-street Mitchell make an enjoyable wallow on a cold winter's morning. **p.561**.

* **Carnarvon Gorge** – Reach fantastic Aboriginal art sites with a hike through the verdant Carnarvon Gorge. **p.562**.

* **Birdsville Races** – The population of this dusty little township swells during the infamous annual Birdsville Races, a weekend of horseracing and free-flowing beer. **p.568**.

* **Crayfish Derby at Winton** – The winner nets $1500 and the runner up gets to eat all the competitors at the biennial Australian Crayfish Derby, held in September in the archetypal frontier town of Winton. **p.577**.

* **Lawn Hill Gorge** – Taking to the water is a wonderful way to explore the lush Lawn Hill Gorge, a spectacular Outback oasis. **p.592**.

* **Undara Lava Tubes** – Explore the massive contorted lava tubes at Undara, formed by a volcanic eruption 190,000 years ago. **p.594**.

Outback Queensland

Outback Queensland, the west of the state, is thinly populated by tenacious farming communities swinging precariously between famine and survival, and seems hard to reconcile with the lushness of the wet tropics. The population is concentrated in the relatively fertile highlands along the **Great Dividing Range**, running low behind the coast; on the far side, featureless plains slide over a hot horizon into the fringes of South Australia and the Northern Territory. Almost untouched by overseas visitors, the only places attracting tourists in any numbers are the **Stockman's Hall of Fame** at Longreach, the oases of **Carnarvon Gorge** in the Central Highlands, and the northwest's **Lawn Hill Gorge**. But elsewhere the opportunities for exploration are immense, with **precious stones**, **fossils**, **waterholes** and **Aboriginal art** in abundance.

Choosing where to go is often determined by the most convenient starting point. **Main roads** and **trains** head west from the coast at Brisbane, Rockhampton and Townsville; interstate **bus** services from Townsville are good, but otherwise the highways are only partially covered. If you're **driving**, your vehicle must be sound and you should carry essential spares, as even main centres often lack replacements.

Unless you're experienced and well equipped, you'll find that western **summers** effectively prohibit travel, with searing temperatures and violent flash floods that can isolate regions (especially in the Channel Country on the far side of the Great Dividing Range) for days or weeks on end. Consequently, many tour companies, information offices and motels simply shut up shop between November and March, or at least during January and February. On the other hand, water revives dormant seeds and fast-growing desert flowers, which cover the ground to the horizon in good years. At other times, expect hot days and cool nights, plenty of dust and sparse landscapes.

Accommodation price codes

All the accommodation listed in this book has been categorized into one of eight price bands, as set out below. The rates quoted represent the cheapest available double or twin room in high season – except for category ❶, which indicates per-person rates for a dorm bed, and the categories given for units, cabins and vans, which represent the daily charge for the whole unit.

❶ Under $20	❸ $35–50	❺ $70–90	❼ $115–150
❷ $20–35	❹ $50–70	❻ $90–115	❽ $150 upwards

For more accommodation details, see pp.46–49.

Brisbane to Cooper Creek and Birdsville

The thousand-plus-kilometre haul from the coast's comforts to Queensland's remote southwestern corner dumps you tired and dusty on the South Australian border, with some exciting routes down the Birdsville and Strzelecki tracks or through the hostile red barrier of the Simpson Desert yet to come (see Chapter Eight, "South Australia", on p.779). There are two ultimate targets: the outpost of **Birdsville**, with its annual horse races, and the Dig Tree at Nappa Merrie on **Cooper Creek**, monument to the Burke and Wills tragedy (see box, p.568). The highway scenery is as bleak as you'd expect: after crossing the fertile disc of the **Darling Downs**, the country withers and dries, marooning communities in isolation and hardship. Detour north through Queensland's **Central Highlands**, however, and you'll find a landscape peppered with forested sandstone gorges and **Aboriginal sites** at **Carnarvon National Park** – worth the journey even if you don't go any further.

The most practical route into the area from Brisbane is on the **Warrego Highway**, through Toowoomba, Roma and Charleville towards Quilpie. Roma is the jumping-off point for the highlands; from Quilpie there are largely unsurfaced roads to Birdsville and the Dig Tree. The twice weekly Westlander **train** runs in this direction to Charleville, as do daily **buses** en route from Brisbane to Mount Isa.

Running parallel to the Warrego to the south, the **Cunningham Highway** crosses the Downs between Warwick and Goondiwindi (the limit of the **bus** service in this direction), then heads out to Cunnamulla. West of Cunnamulla you're on your own, heading across oil-, gas- and opal-fields towards the Dig Tree; 4WD is preferable **beyond the bitumen** and is generally essential for reaching the Dig Tree.

The Darling Downs

The **Darling Downs**, a broad spread of prime agricultural land opened up by the explorer **Ludwig Leichhardt** in the 1840s, sprawl westwards from the back of the Great Dividing Range behind Brisbane down to the state's southern boundaries. The Warrego Highway climbs a steep escarpment to **Toowoomba** and the Northern Downs, while the Cunningham Highway cuts through Cunningham's Gap to **Warwick** and the south. Highway towns west of Toowoomba – Dalby, Miles and Chinchilla – are unadorned farming centres, and it's more the scenery along the Downs' fringes, particularly at the **Bunya Mountains** and **Girraween**, that warrants a visit. But even as you tear across the Central Downs without stopping, you'll notice that the flat grasslands are clear evidence of Aboriginal custodial practices: created by controlled burning designed to clear woodland and increase grazing land for game, they perfectly suited European pastoral needs. The Downs are relatively fertile and stud farms, dairy, cotton, wool and cereal farming have all been successfully tried at one time or another. Even unwanted plants thrive. During the 1920s millions of acres were infested by **prickly pear**, a South American cactus finally brought to heel by the tiny *cactoblastis* moth in 1930 – a success story of biological control in Queensland to match the later failure of the introduction of the cane toad (see box on p.512).

Toowoomba

TOOWOOMBA is a stately but staid university city perched on the edge of a six-hundred-metre escarpment, a promising setting that it can't quite live up to. To be fair, though, Toowoomba's side streets and numerous gardens are pleasant, the stylish houses and blaze of late nineteenth-century sandstone architecture along central Main and Ruthven streets – all recently renovated – a reminder of its former business wealth. There's a September **flower festival** during which the **tourist office** on James Street/Warrego Highway (daily 8.30am–5pm; ☎07/4639 3797) hands out lists of exhibition gardens to visit. At other times the main attraction is the **Cobb and Co. Museum**, near the Botanic Gardens at 27 Lindsay St (daily 10am–4pm; $4.40), recalling days when these intrepid coaches bounced across the Outback delivering mail and passengers between the 1860s and 1924. Amongst the exhibits are coaches (including one emblazoned with a Royal Mail badge), two-wheeled sulkys and a two-tier omnibus from Brisbane, and there's also a working **smithy** out the back. If you've any spare time, **Picnic Point** at the top of Tourist Road 2.5km east of the centre, is a pleasant spot on a warm day, offering a café, bar and restaurant as well as picnic space, all with splendid views of the escarpment.

Downtown Toowoomba is a compact area based around **Ruthven Street** and **Margaret Street**; many of the city's shops, restaurants, banks and a post office are within 100m of the intersection of the two streets. The **bus station** is on Neil Street (☎07/4690 9888 for all companies), which runs parallel to Ruthven; while the **train station** is 500m north on Railway Street. **Accommodation** prospects include the *Jolly Swagman Caravan Park*, 47 Kitchener Rd (☎07/4632 8735; cabins ❹), about 1km southeast of the centre; *Range Motel*, on Tourist Road (☎07/4632 3133; ❸), near the plateau's edge and with fine views; and the more central *Burke and Wills Hotel*, 554 Ruthven St (☎07/4632 2433; ❺). **Moving on** from Toowoomba, the **New England Highway** runs north to Kingaroy, plied by Polleys Coaches, and south to Warwick and Stanthorpe (Greyhound-Pioneer and Crisps). Goondiwindi is three hours southwest with McCafferty's, who also follow the Warrego Highway west across the Central Downs.

Around Kingaroy: the Northern Downs

KINGAROY is a small town in the heart of peanut country, on the very fringes of the Downs, a couple of hours' drive from Toowoomba and Dalby to the south or Gympie on the coast. A cluster of castle-like **peanut silos** in the middle of town aptly symbolize the fame Kingaroy owes to **Johannes Bjelke-Petersen**, who farmed nuts here before taking Queensland under his thumb in 1968. His equally charismatic wife Flo made it onto postcards featuring her pumpkin scone recipe, and with a dam, bridge, road and sportsground named after him, not to mention his ominous catch phrase "Don't you worry about that" still on everyone's lips, Joh is in no danger of obscurity. To get in touch with what Kingaroy is all about, take the free fifty-minute **tour** at Kingaroy Toasted Peanuts (Mon–Fri 10.30am), 1km south of the centre on Kingaroy Street, where the scent of roasting is so seductive that you'll want to head back to the

Peanut Van outside Lions Park between the factory and town, which sells roasted nuts by the kilo. The last couple of years has also seen a rash of **wineries** springing up around Kingaroy, most open for **tasting** – and of course, buying – Tuesday to Sunday, with guided tours twice daily. Stuart Range Estates, just northeast of the centre at the end of William Street (℡ 07/4162 3711), has definite potential, though at present the wine is still a little green.

For **information** – including a wineries map – Kingaroy's **tourist office** (Mon–Fri 9am–4.30pm; ℡ 07/4162 3199) is right under the peanut silos on Haly Street, immediately north of the town centre. *Kingaroy Caravans*, 1km south near the peanut factory on Walter Road (℡ 07/4162 1808; cabins ❸) is a friendly **place to stay**, while the central *Club Hotel* (℡ 07/4162 2204; ❷) offers beds, cheapish meals and occasional live music. Polleys Coaches leaves daily from Kingaroy to Gympie and Toowoomba, while drivers can also take the Bunya Highway to Dalby.

The Bunya Mountains

Southwest of Kingaroy, there's a sixty-kilometre section of twisting road along the crumpled **Bunya Mountains** before you reach **Dalby** (p.560), back on the Warrego Highway. Among general greenery and clusters of unlikely flowers, you'll find enormous **bunya pines**, which once covered large tracts of southern Queensland. Every few years tribal boundaries were overlooked as clans gathered to gorge on the pine seeds. Assisted by loops of vine, the Aborigines scaled the trees and threw down the cones, which gave up their thumb-sized nuts to be eaten raw or roasted. On his trip across the Downs in 1844, the indefatigable **Ludwig Leichhardt** (see p.1146) witnessed such a feast and persuaded the government to make the area an Aboriginal reserve, free from logging or settlement. The decree was revoked in 1860 and today the Bunya Mountains contain the last significant stand of pines, along with orange-flowering **silky oaks** and stands of **grass trees**, with their three-metre-high, spear-like flower heads.

Two NPWS-run sites along the road at Burton's Well and Westcott make for good bush **camping**, with another wallaby-infested site at the hamlet of **Dandabah**, where you'll also find the **ranger's office** (daily 9am–4pm; ℡ 07/4668 3127; advance booking essential during holiday periods). Less frugal accommodation is also on hand at *Rice's Log Cabins* (℡ 07/4668 3133; ❺), and the elegant *Bunya Mountain Lodge Guest House* (℡ 07/4668 3134; ❻). Note that the mountains are generally several degrees cooler than the plains below, and it gets cold in winter. **Walking tracks** between the three campsites lead through the forest to orchid-covered lookouts and waterfalls; satin bowerbirds (see p.415) and paradise riflebirds, with their deep blue-black plumage and long curved beaks, are fairly common here.

The Granite Belt

The southeastern edge of the Darling Downs along the New South Wales border, known as Queensland's **Granite Belt**, regularly records the state's coldest temperatures – on a winter's night it drops well below freezing here. Heading south from Toowoomba, you pass through the one-horse town of **NOBBY**, whose former resident **Steele Rudd** created archetypal Australian country characters in his "Dad and Dave" tales – commemorated at the *Nobby Hotel* in paintings and farm bric-a-brac.

Around 85km south of Toowoomba, **WARWICK** makes a fine base for exploring the region, and is known state-wide for it's **cheese**, though you can't tour the factory. Services are centred around Grafton and Palmerin streets, where sandstone buildings date back to the time when Warwick graziers competed fiercely with Toowoomba's merchants to establish the Downs' premier settlement. The October **rodeo** is about the only time you might experience trouble finding **accommodation**: try *Warwick Tourist Caravan Park*, 18 Palmer Ave, north of town on the highway (℡07/4661 8335; cabins ❸), or *Centre Point Motel*, 32 Albion St (℡ & ℉ 07/4661 3488; ❹). Alternatively, ask at the **tourist office and art gallery** halfway down Albion Street (Mon–Fri 9am–5.30pm, weekends variable; ℡07/4661 3122).

The **Condamine River**, unimpressive where it flows through town, is part of Australia's longest river system. Originating on the highlands east of Warwick, it joins the Murray/Darling before emptying into the ocean near Adelaide. At **Queen Mary Falls**, 43km from Warwick beyond Killarney, a tributary exits the forest in a plunge off the top of the plateau. A 2km-long track climbs to the escarpment at the head of the falls from the road, with a kiosk, **accommodation** and lunches provided by *Queen Mary Falls Tourist Park* (℡07/4664 7150; cabins ❺); you need your own transport to get here.

Moving on from Warwick, the **New England Highway** (served by Crisps Coaches and Greyhound-Pioneer) runs south to Stanthorpe then over the border to Tenterfield. The Cunningham Highway continues 200km west to **Goondiwindi** and the banks of the Macintyre River, which marks the state border with New South Wales.

Stanthorpe and Girraween National Park

Sixty kilometres south of Warwick along the New England Highway, **STANTHORPE** is a small town full of retiree bungalows, known for the **fruit stalls** and small-scale **wineries** that throng the region. Heritage Wines (℡07/4685 2197), 15km north on the New England Highway – worth a visit alone for its huge, antique-laden reception room – and Ballandean Estate, the region's oldest vineyard, 20km southwest of town (℡07/4684 1226); both produce excellent wines and are open daily. If you need to **stay** in Stanthorpe, *Top of Town Accommodation*, on the highway 2km north of town (℡07/4681 4888; tents or dorms ❶, cabins ❹) is a campsite-style operation with huge grounds and good **work connections** for fruit pickers; *Stannum Lodge Motor Inn* (℡07/4681 2000; ❺) on Wallangarra Road is a central motel; while *Acacia Cottages* (℡07/4696 4557; five-person cottage $250 per weekend only) is a countryside retreat 15km east of town.

The surrounding hills are granite, exposed as fantastic monoliths at **Girraween National Park**, 30km south down the New England Highway. There's an NPWS **campsite** and rangers office here (℡07/4684 5157) with showers and toilets – and the chance of seeing small, shy, active sugar gliders just after dark. Listen for claws clattering over bark and then shine your torch overhead to catch a glowing set of eyes in the spotlight.

With more energy than skill, you can climb several of the giant hills with little risk, as long as rain hasn't made them dangerously slippery. **Castle Rock** (2hr return) is entertaining: initially a gentle incline past lichen-covered boulders in the forest, the track follows a dotted white line into a fissure – look up and you'll see loose rocks balanced above you – before emerging onto a thin ledge above the campsite. Follow this around to the north side and clamber to the very top for superb views of the Pyramids, Sphinx and Mount Norman poking rudely out of the woods. **The Sphinx** and **Turtle Rock** are another thirty minutes from the base of Castle. Sphinx is a broad pillar topped by a boulder, while Turtle's more conventional shape means a scramble, with no handholds on the final stretch. But pat yourself on the back if you make it to the top of the

5

completely bald **South Pyramid** (2hr return) without resorting to hands and knees. Take a well-earned rest at the top and look across to the unscaleable North Pyramid from below **Balancing Rock**, an oval boulder teetering so precariously on its narrow end that you can see underneath to where the support is surely only a few years away from collapse. **Mount Norman**, the park's 1267-metre apex, lies an hour beyond Castle Rock and should only be attempted by experienced climbers; check details with the ranger at Girraween.

Goondiwindi and St George

Before European settlers put weirs on the Macintyre River in the **GOONDI-WINDI** area (pronounced "Gundawindee"), right on the New South Wales border, it was little more than a string of waterholes and lagoons, attracting a lot of birdlife and inspiring the Aboriginal name Goonawinna – "birds' resting place". The irrigation weirs now supply the huge demands of the local cotton and wheat industries, but this hasn't dented the varied birdlife, despite the constant stream of road train transports rumbling through at all hours.

Goondiwindi is best known in Australia for the racehorse Gunsynd, alias the **Goondiwindi Grey**, who won over half of his races through the early 1970s. There's a monument to him at the southern end of McLean Street, close to where the **Macintyre River** marks the state boundary. Nearby, also on McLean Street, the **Old Customs House Museum** (daily except Tues 10am–4pm; $2) has an eclectic gathering of anything old, from preserved snakes to steam engines. It predates the rest of the town and even the wood-paved bridge over the river.

The main road east–west through town is Marshall Street, with shops, **banks**, a post office and most services nearby. You'll find a **tourist information centre** with brochures galore and **internet** facilities just around the corner on Bowen Street (daily 9am–5pm; ℡ 07/4671 2653). Cheap and central **accommodation** can be found at *Devon's Caravan Park*, near the information centre at 3 DeLacy St (℡ 07/4671 1383; cabins ❸), and the *Border Motel*, 126 Marshall St (℡ 07/4671 1688; ❺); be aware that during the November **cotton chipping** season places to stay are in very short supply. **Eat** at the *Victoria Hotel* on Marshall Street, whose $10 counter meals feature a half-kilo steak buried under a mountain of vegetables.

Two hundred kilometres further west on the Barwon Highway, **ST GEORGE** sits on the banks of the Balonne River and is the administrative centre for the tranquil shire of Balonne. From St George, roads leave in almost every direction, and on your way through the shire every town offers a taste of farming history, wildlife and a relaxed atmosphere. **Information** on the region is available from the Council Offices under the clock tower in the town centre (Mon–Fri 9am–4.45pm; ℡ 07/4625 3222), and you can **stay** at the *Australian Hotel* (℡ 07/4625 5000; ❶–❹) on the river bank. At the back of the Balonne Sports Store, a few doors down from the Council Offices, the proprietor has combined the woodcarving skills of his native Greece with the Aboriginal tradition of emu egg-carving and the wonders of electric lighting to produce a unique display of carved, illuminated **emu eggs** (daily 9am–5pm; $2).

The Central Downs and around

To break the unexciting journey west across the Downs from Toowoomba to Dalby, call in at **Jondaryan Woolshed** (daily 9am–4pm; $10), 3km south of the highway from Jondaryan and about 45km from Toowoomba, to look around the collection of old buildings – all relocated from elsewhere, with the exception of the shed itself. Exhibits worth a closer look include a document, dating from 1880, which itemizes some of the schoolmistress's tasks – including splinting broken legs, wallpapering buildings to keep out snakes and being able to fight off swaggies trying to sleep in the schoolhouse. Make sure you catch one of the **tours** (Mon–Fri 1pm, Sat, Sun & holidays 10.30am & 1.30pm) when the smithy is working, and you can watch sheep shearers at work beneath the vast emptiness of the handcrafted woolshed roof, lit by a bare bulb – a very surreal tableau.

The next stops over the following 200km are **Dalby**, **Chinchilla** and **Miles**, rural centres devoid of specific attractions but with the usual complement of van park and motel accommodation. If you have your own transport, however, two **national parks**, Expedition Range and Isla Gorge, north from Miles off the Leichhardt Highway, are worth investigating: you need to be self-sufficient, competent at orientation and bushwalking – and to contact the ranger first (PO Box 175, Taroom, QLD 4420; ☎07/4627 3358). The massive **Expedition Range** is centred on Robinson Gorge, west of **Taroom** (itself 125km north of Miles) along a ninety-kilometre road that becomes a rough track 20km before the campsite. Rock formations, Aboriginal art and waterfalls lie in tributary canyons, and a couple of the northern gorges are said to have some fine plant fossils, but, even with survey maps, navigation is tricky. Easier to reach, but with the same provisos on getting around, **Isla Gorge** is a small, triangular park right on the highway, 54km north of Taroom. Climb up to the lookout for orientation before descending down the dangerously loose slopes into a maze of offshoot gorges, which you could spend days exploring.

Roma and Mitchell

ROMA, 140km west of Miles, was founded by settlers eager to occupy country made available by the opening up of the Darling Downs in 1862. Once considered for a fantasy rail junction to link the east coast with the Gulf of Carpentaria, the town thrives on farming, supplemented by the **oil** and **gas fields** which have been exploited intermittently since the 1900s. There's not much for visitors to do here, but Roma is a useful place to stock up before heading north to **Carnarvon National Park** (see p.561).

Roma is a typical inland town: tidy, with streets lined with **bottle** trees (not only bottle-shaped but also full of sugary water for emergency stock-watering), and a slightly dated air lent by the iron decorations and wraparound balconies of its hotels. It also has a reputation for **cattle markets** – one day-long event saw over $1.6 million change hands; and every Easter there is a **rodeo and carnival**. Romavilla Winery has been producing prize-winning **wine** since 1863 – if you want to buy, it's about a kilometre north of town on the Carnarvon Road, at Quintin Street (Mon–Fri 8am–5pm, Sat 9am–noon & 2–4pm; ☎07/4622 1822). For history buffs, Roma was also the venue for the 1871 trial of the audacious **Captain Starlight** (also known as Harry Redford), who stole a thousand head of cattle off a nearby property and drove them down through the South Australian deserts to Adelaide for sale. An unusual white bull in the herd was recognized and Redford arrested, but his pioneering of a new stock route won such popular approval that the judge refused to convict him.

The Warrego Highway runs through Roma as Bowen Street, and it's here on the eastern side of town you're greeted by the **Big Rig**, a drilling tower left as a monument to the oil boom of the 1920s, and beside it the **information centre** (daily 9am–5pm; ☎07/4622 4355). A landscaped bend in the river behind makes a good picnic spot if you just want a rest; for supplies, most of the town's shops, banks and businesses are one block north of Bowen on parallel **McDowall Street**. Roma's **accommodation** choices include *Motel Carnarvon*, 18 Northern Rd (℡07/4622 1599 or free call 1800 621 155; ❹), and the *Starlight Motor Inn* (℡07/4622 2666; ❺), which both offer standard motel beds; the *Big Rig Caravan Park*, 4 McDowell St (℡07/4622 2538), near the Big Rig, has welcome hot showers available during sub-zero winter nights. **Restaurants** in Roma are fairly basic, though *Deano's*, at 77 Quintin St, does good steaks.

The **train station** is one block south of the highway on Station Street at the corner of Charles Street (℡07/4622 9411), and the **bus terminal** is on Bowen Street by the BP roadhouse near the Big Rig. The **airport** is a small strip a few kilometres outside town. Tickets for all these can also be obtained from Maranoa Travel, 71 Arthur St (℡07/4622 1416). Heading north, the **Carnarvon Developmental Road** (take Quintin St from the town centre) gives access to Carnarvon National Park (see p.561); otherwise the next stops west along the highway are Mitchell and Charleville.

Mitchell

MITCHELL is a delightful, single-street town right on the western rim of the downs beside the Maranoa River, 88km west of Roma on the Warrego Highway. As at Roma, Mitchell has its local outlaw legend; the protagonists this time were the two **Keniff Brothers**, who raided the district for cattle and horses in the early 1900s. After killing a policeman during one arrest attempt they were finally ambushed south of town and dragged off for trial in Brisbane; unlike Captain Starlight, they were sentenced to death, though one brother had this commuted to a prison term.

All this aside, there are two reasons to stop at Mitchell: either to follow the 200km-long track north to Mount Moffat in Carnarvon National Park (p.564); or to make use of the town's **hot artesian springs**, which have been thoughtfully channelled into an open-air **swimming pool and spa** (Mon–Fri 9am–4pm, Sat 9am–noon, Sun 10am–noon; $5.50) in the grounds of the old Kenniff Courthouse – good, steamy fun on a cold winter's morning. The courthouse itself now houses an **information centre** (daily 8am–7pm; ℡07/4623 1133), the *Healthy Byte Café*, an **internet** terminal and a weekend cinema; and you can stay for free for two nights ($5.50 a night thereafter) at the council-run **campsite** back across the Maranoa. The information centre can also arrange hour-long **river cruises** ($8.80), or 4WD day **tours** to Mount Moffat ($88 per person, minimum of four).

Moving on, all transport and the Warrego Highway continue a further 180km west to Charleville; the **train station** is 500m from the courthouse at the western side of town, and the main-street newsagent doubles as the **bus** agent.

Carnarvon National Park

North of Roma and Mitchell, Queensland's Central Highlands consist of a broad band of weathered sandstone plateaus along the Great Dividing Range, thickly wooded and spectacularly sculpted into sheer cliffs and pinnacles. It's an extraordinarily primeval landscape, and one still visibly central to Aboriginal culture, as poor pasture left the highlands relatively unscathed by European colonization. Covering a huge slice of the region, **Carnarvon National Park** includes **Carnarvon Gorge**, **Mount Moffatt** and other remoter sections further west.

Most people head for Carnarvon Gorge, where you'll find the main facilities, the highest concentration of **Aboriginal art** and arguably the best scenery. For the more adventurous, Mount Moffatt can usually be reached in a non-4WD vehicle, but requires high clearance – and often 4WD – to get around once there.

As there is **no public transport** to the park, you'll need your own vehicle: **access** to Carnarvon Gorge is from Roma or Emerald (p.571); and to Mount Moffat from Roma or Mitchell. All these roads involve some stretches of dirt, making them impassable after heavy rain (most likely Nov–May). Always carry extra rations in case you get stranded for a while and, unless you're desperately short of supplies, stay put in wet weather – you'll only churn the road up and make it harder for others to use. Note too, that it is not possible to drive directly between the Gorge and Mount Moffat sections (though you can hike). Summer **temperatures** often reach 40°C, while winter nights will be below freezing. Gathering firewood is prohibited inside the park, so stop on the way in or bring a gas stove. The **NPWS district headquarters** are in Emerald (☏07/4982 4555), and regional offices are detailed below.

Carnarvon Gorge

To reach Carnarvon Gorge **from Roma**, head 199km north along the Carnarvon Developmental Road, past **Injune**, then 45km west to the park headquarters. **From Emerald**, it's 230km south along the Gregory/Dawson highways through Springsure and Rolleston. Driving in, the **Consuelo Tableland** stands out magnificently above dark forests as the road crosses the plains below, rising gradually to the foothills on the park's edge before terminating at the mouth of the gorge. The future of the **ranger station** here is uncertain (daily 8am–5pm; ☏07/4984 4505), but at present it has a payphone, an orientation model of the gorge, **free maps** and a library on the highlands and its wildlife.

Accommodation – best booked well in advance – is available either 2km back down the road at *Oasis Lodge* (free call ☏1800 644 150, ⓦwww.fortland.com.au; ⓼), where comfortable rooms are surrounded by a neat lawn and respectably sized cycad palms; or a further 2km away at the creekside *Takarakka* (☏07/4984 4535, ⓔtakarakka@telstra.easymail.com.au; ❶–❸), which has canvas-sided "cabins" and a big **campsite**. The lodge also has a bar and a **store** selling basics, fuel and LP gas refills. If both these are full, *Warremba Farmstay and Camping* (☏07/4626 7175; ❶–❺), 57km east of the gorge off the Carnarvon Developmental Road, has all-weather access, homestay **accommodation** and a campsite with hot showers, toilets, and big kitchen area.

Along the gorge

Carnarvon Creek's journey between the vertical faces of the gorge has created some magical scenery, where low cloud often blends with the cliffs, making them look infinitely tall. A three-kilometre trail heads downstream from near the *Lodge*, crossing the creek a few times by means of stepping stones and fallen trees. If you're not prepared to get wet, you can't get past the frigid **swimming hole** here. **Baloon Cave**, in woodland behind the lodge, shelters some stencil art of hands and boomerangs – easy to reach if unimpressive compared with other sites in the park. Before setting off to find them, climb **Boolimba Bluff** from the campsite for a rare chance to see the gorge system from above; it's a tiring climb but the views from the "Roof of Queensland" make the three-kilometre track worth the effort.

The day-walk (19km return) **into the gorge** takes some beating, with intriguing side gorges: best are the **Moss Garden** (3.5km), a vibrant green car-

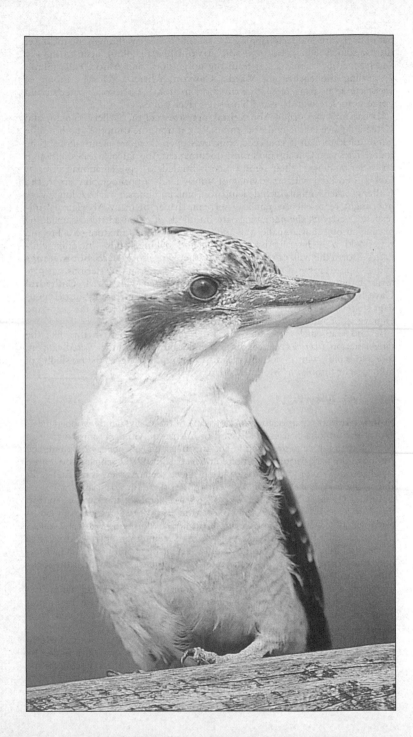

pet of liverworts and ferns lapping up a spring as it seeps through the rockface; the awesomely quiet, claustrophobic **Amphitheatre** (4km), open to the sky and reached by a long ladder from the gorge floor; and **Alijon Falls** (5km), concealing the enchanting **Wards Canyon**, where a remnant group of *angiopteris* ferns hang close to extinction in front of a second waterfall and gorge, complete with bats and blood-red river stones.

Carnarvon's two major **Aboriginal art sites** are the Gallery (5.6km) and Cathedral Cave (at the end of the trail, 9.3km from the campsite), both on the gorge track, though if you keep your eyes open there are plenty more to be found. These are Queensland's most documented Aboriginal art sites, although an understanding of their significance is limited to representational terms. A rockface covered with engravings of vulvas lends a pornographic air to **the Gallery**; other symbols include kangaroo, emu and human tracks. A long, wavy line might represent the rainbow serpent, shaper of many Aboriginal landscapes. Overlaying the engravings are hundreds of coloured stencils, made by placing an object against the wall and spraying it with a mixture of ochre and water held in the mouth. Always personal and striking, hands – including children's – form the bulk of the designs, but there are also artefacts, **boomerangs** and complex crosses formed by four arms. Goannas and mysterious net patterns at the near end of the wall have been painted with a stick. **Cathedral Cave** is larger, with an even greater range of designs, including seashell pendant stencils – proof that trade networks reached from here to the sea – and engravings of animal tracks and nests of emu eggs.

Beyond Cathedral Cave, there's a **bush campsite** (though this, like the ranger station, may close in the future) and a number of little-visited canyons to explore plus, with advice and permission from the rangers, the possibility of hiking right through to Mount Moffatt.

Mount Moffatt

Mount Moffatt is part of an open landscape of ridges and lightly wooded grassland at the top of a plateau to the west of Carnarvon Gorge. From Roma, it's a 248-kilometre drive to the campsite via **Injune**; from Mitchell it's 220km direct. Although the park perimeter can often be reached in 2WD vehicles, you'll need to rely on a 4WD or walking to get around once there. As there is **no fuel** available in the park, make sure you have enough for the return trip; last supplies are at Injune (150km) or Mitchell. The access road ends at the **ranger station** (☎07/4626 3581) where you can collect your map of the area, plan any bushwalking and book a site. The **campground** here has drinking water and toilets.

Mount Moffatt's attractions are spread out, so seeing them involves driving to an area and then walking around. More or less in the vicinity of the ranger station, **the Chimneys** area has some interesting pinnacles. Alcoves in the rockface here once housed bark burial cylinders – look for the stencil of an entire body, arms spread-eagled. **Marlong Arch**, 6km west of the ranger station, is a sandstone arch decorated with handprints and engravings. Five kilometres northeast, a trail leads to **Kookaburra Cave**, named after a weathered, bird-shaped hand stencil.

Further afield, consultation with the ranger might get you access to **Marlong Plain** (10km from the station), a pretty expanse of blue grass surrounded by peaks, and **Kenniff Cave** (20km), Mount Moffatt's richest site. A hideout for the Kenniff brothers around 1900 (see p.561), the cave had been used long before this, and excavations here in 1960 were the first to reveal that Aboriginal occupation of Australia predated the last Ice Age. Art in the cave includes stencils of feet, artefacts and a painted human figure. If you're still in doubt as to the area's significance in Aboriginal culture, visit the **ochre mine** and **bora ring** at **West Branch Camp**. Ochre was used ceremonially in stencilling and body-painting, and mines were a source of trade for tribes who controlled them, while a bora ground was central to male initiation ceremonies. For pure scenery, head east 15km north of the ranger station and follow the track (4WD or on foot) about 7km to the **Mahogany Forest**, a stand of giant stringybark trees. **Mount Moffatt** itself and pink-walled **Devils Canyon**, in the park's southeast, are more difficult to reach – you need to carry reliable maps and have bushwalking skills.

Charleville to Cooper Creek and Birdsville

The last place of any size on the journey west from Roma is **CHARLEVILLE**, terminus for the **train** and a compact, busy country town with broad streets, shaded pavements and some solid buildings constructed when the town was a droving centre and staging post for Cobb & Co. It's well known as a victim of contradictory weather – in November 1947 a typical hot summer afternoon was interrupted for twenty minutes as the temperature plummeted and a blast of massive hailstones stripped trees, smashed windows and roofs and killed pets and poultry. In 1990 the town centre was inundated by five-metre-deep floodwaters from the **Warrego River** – a dramatic end to years of drought. At the turn of the twentieth century, attempts were made to end another dry spell with **Stiger Vortex Guns**, giant conical contraptions supposed to seed rainclouds. During trials, two of the six guns exploded and the meteorologist who recommended them was run out of town. Only two have survived: one is in the Queensland Museum in Brisbane and the other is outside the Scout Hut on Sturt Street, heading south towards Cunnamulla.

Around town, the NPWS complex and **fauna park**, at Park Street on the Roma road (Mon–Fri 9am–4pm; free), is dedicated to studying and breeding populations of rare local fauna such as the absurdly cute **bilby** (for more on which see Currawinya National Park, overleaf) and the graceful yellow-footed rock wallaby, both of which are on show. The **Historic House** on Galatea Street (Mon–Sat 9am–3.30pm; $4.50), originally a bank, is now a museum with some rooms decorated in period style and showing some elegant architectural touches. **Anglers** can try their luck along the river where the prize catch is large Murray cod, though perch and freshwater catfish are more likely.

All services are clustered around the Wills/Galatea junction on the Quilpie side of town; you can draw **cash** on bank cards at the BP service station opposite the post office. The **tourist information centre** (Mon–Fri 9am–5pm; ☎07/4654 3057), just south of town on the Cunnamulla Road, also organizes stargazing sessions at the Skywatch Observatory – there are two powerful telescopes and an astronomy chart to guide you. Motel **rooms** can be found at the *Charleville Motel* on King Street (☎07/4654 1566; ❹), or *Corones Hotel* on Wills Street (☎07/4654 1022; bed in the hotel $30, motel doubles ❹). To **camp**, head for *Cobb & Co. Caravan Park* off Alfred Street (☎07/4654 1053), a pleasant spot, with hot water, barbecues and a small shop (6am–8pm). There are the usual coffee shops, and generous **meals** at the *Corones Hotel*, whose dining rooms have been lavishly refurbished to original 1900s condition.

Curved **throwing sticks** were once found throughout the world. Several were discovered in Tutankhamen's tomb, Hopi Indians once used them and a 23,000-year-old example made from mammoth ivory was recently found in Poland. Since that time the invention of the bow and arrow superseded what Aborigines call a **boomerang** or *karli*, although they seem to be the only people to have invented returning boomerangs; they were originally used as children's toys but were then modified into decoys for hunting wildfowl. The non-returning types depicted in Carnarvon Gorge show how sophisticated they became as hunting weapons. Usually made from tough acacia wood, some are hooked like a pick, while others are designed to cartwheel along the ground to break the legs of game. Thus immobilized, one animal would be killed while another could be easily tracked to meet the same fate. Besides hunting, the boomerang was also used for digging, levering or cutting, as well as for **musical** or **ceremonial instruments**. At Carnarvon Gorge the long, gently curved boomerangs stencilled on the walls in pairs are not repetitions but portraits of two weapons with identical flight paths; if the first missed through a gust of wind, for instance, the user could immediately throw the second, correcting his aim for the conditions. For the definitive book on the subject, check out Philip Jones' nicely illustrated *Boomerang: Behind an Australian Icon* (Wakefield Press).

Moving on from Charleville, roads head north to Blackall and Longreach (covered by Brisbane–Mount Isa buses), south to Cunnamulla and New South Wales, and further west to Quilpie. The **bus stop** is next to *Corones Hotel* on Wills Street, with two services daily in each direction; the **train station** is 200m south at the end of Wills Street, with two trains a week heading back to Brisbane. **Flights** to Brisbane leave from the tiny strip outside town. All transport bookings can be made with Western Travel Service, 37 Wills St (℡07/4654 1260).

Cunnamulla and Currawinya National Park

CUNNAMULLA, a nondescript handful of service stations and motels 200km south of Charleville on the Mitchell Highway, is a trucking stop on the long run down the Mitchell Highway to **Bourke** in New South Wales (see p.368). There is a helpful **information centre** (daily 9am–3pm; ℡07/4655 1416) in the old schoolhouse at the end of Jane Street. West towards Thargomindah, 160km from Cunnamulla, are the **Yowah Opal Fields** where shallow deposits yield much-sought-after Yowah Nuts – opalized ironstone nodules. You'll need a Miner's Right ($14.50 from the Mining Office at Cunnamulla's council offices) to start your own diggings. Beware of unfenced vertical shafts, which are practically invisible until you're on your way down: always look where you're going and never step backwards. Yowah has bore water, fuel and a **caravan park** (℡07/4655 4953; cabins ❷).

Two hundred kilometres southwest of Cunnamulla on minor roads, **Currawinya National Park** features lakes, wetlands and associated wildlife in contrast to the semi-arid land more typical of the region. One animal to benefit is the highly endangered **bilby**, which, with its long ears and nose, looks like a cross between a rabbit and a bandicoot. Feral cats, rabbits, and grazing cattle have brought the bilby close to extinction, but a recently completed **fence** at Currawinya will keep all these pests out, allowing the new bilby population – reintroduced from the NPWS fauna centre in Charleville – to prosper. You can **camp** at Currawinya, but check on road conditions and practicalities with the NPWS ranger first (☎07/4655 4001). Past Currawinya is the tiny border town of **Hungerford**, and from there it's a 200km run southeast on a largely unsealed road to Bourke (see p.368).

Quilpie and the road to the Dig Tree

QUILPIE is a dusty farming community 200km west of Charleville. Amenities include a baker, butcher, fuel depot, **caravan park** and **beds** at the *Quilpie Motor Inn* (☎07/4656 1277; ❺). The *Imperial Hotel* serves evening meals between 6 and 7.30pm, and there are a couple of cafés in town which close at about 5.30pm.

As there are few signposts, a **map** is essential if you plan to drive from Quilpie to the Dig Tree at Nappa Merrie, 50km from Innamincka in South Australia. Last place to get **fuel** on the 490-kilometre, largely unsealed route lies an hour west of Quilpie at **EROMANGA**. From here you're heading across the stony plains above the huge gas and oil reserves of the Cooper Basin, past the cattle stations of Durham Downs and Karmona, lonely "nodding donkeys" and unaccountably healthy-looking droughtmaster cattle, to the Dig Tree on **Cooper Creek**.

The site of Burke and Wills' stockade (see box, overleaf), **Depot Camp 65** is a beautiful shaded river bank alive with pelicans and parrots, and it's hard to believe that anyone could have starved to death nearby. **The Dig Tree** is still standing and protected by a walkway, but the three original blaze marks reading "BLXV, DIG 3FT NW, DEC 6 60-APR 21 61" have been cemented over to keep the tree alive. Burke's face was carved into the tree on the right by John Dickins in 1898, and is still clearly visible.

Pressing on, you'll be relieved to know that Innamincka's pub is only 50km away at the top of the **Strzelecki Track** in South Australia (see p.876). If you've made it this far you shouldn't have much trouble with the road.

Quilpie to Birdsville

The long road from Quilpie to Birdsville is a relatively easy journey, manageable in good conditions without a 4WD, though depth markers along the road give an idea of how saturated this **Channel Country** becomes after rain. First stop is **WINDORAH**, a limp settlement of a dozen buildings offering fuel, a post office and an amazingly well-provisioned store. The *Western Star Hotel* (☎07/4656 3166; ❺) is hard to pass by for a cold drink and a look at its collection of old photos; they have tidy air-conditioned rooms and might let you camp out the back.

Ruins of the **John Costello hotel** lie 80km further on towards Betoota, opposite a windmill. Tired of riding 30km every morning to round up his stockmen from the bar, the manager of a nearby station had the local liquor licence transferred from the *JC* to his homestead in the 1950s. He pulled the roof off the hotel for good measure, and there's now little left beyond the foundations and some posts.

BETOOTA, 220km from Windorah, is also on the verge of crumbling back into the dust, its tiny, century-old adobe hotel opening only once a year for the races and gymkhana. Even then they don't provide beds but there's plenty of room to pitch a tent along the river banks behind. Beyond Betoota the country turns into a rocky, silent plain, with circling crows and wedge-tailed eagles the only signs of life, and it's hard to imagine what the occasional fenceline or grid is keeping apart. Look for **red sand dunes**, distant outposts of the Simpson Desert. Driving can be hazardous here – you'll pass plenty of wrecks and shredded tyres – but with care (and luck), the Diamantina River and Birdsville are just three hours away.

Birdsville and beyond

Famous for the **horse races** on the first weekend in September, when thousands of beer-swilling spectators pack out the dusty little settlement, at other times **BIRDSVILLE** promises to be something of an anticlimax, a handful of buildings where only the hotel and roadhouses seem to be doing business. But unless you've flown in, you'll very probably be glad simply to have arrived intact. The **caravan park** (℡07/4656 3214) comprises a large patch of scrub by the creek with an amenities block, or you can camp for free along the artesian overflow where huge flocks of raucous corellas seem to justify the township's name – though it's actually a corruption of "Burt's Ville", after the first storekeeper. Given the lack of alternatives, don't be surprised to find the comfy **accommodation** at the *Birdsville Hotel* full (℡07/4656 3244, ⓔPeg@arcom.au; ❺); during race weekend, all beds are reserved for the bar staff anyway, so you have to camp. **Provisions** and snacks can be bought from the general store. If you're organizing your own food, prepare the next day's meals after dark when the flies have settled down. You owe yourself at least one drink in the hotel's mighty bar; order by 5.30pm if you want a full **evening meal** – the "$15, seven-course takeaway" is a pie and a six-pack.

The Burke and Wills saga

In 1860, the government of Victoria, then Australia's richest state, decided to sponsor a lavish expedition to make the first south–north crossing of the continent to the Gulf of Carpentaria. Eighteen men, twenty camels (shipped, along with their handlers, from Asia) and over twenty tons of provisions started out from Melbourne in August, led by **Robert O'Hara Burke** and **William John Wills**. Problems had already begun by the time the party reached **Cooper Creek** in December: Burke had impatiently left the bulk of the expedition and supplies lagging behind and raced ahead with a handful of men to establish a base camp on Cooper Creek. Having built a stockade, Burke and Wills started north, along with two other members of their team (Gray and King), six camels, a couple of horses and food for three months. Four men remained at camp, led by William Brahe, waiting for the rest of the expedition to catch up. In fact, most of the supplies and camels were dithering halfway between Cooper Creek and Melbourne, unsure of what to do next.

As Burke and Wills failed to keep a regular diary, few details of the "rush to the Gulf" are known. They were seen by Kalkadoon Aborigines following the Corella River into the Gulf, where they found that vast salt marshes lay between them and the sea. Disappointed, they left the banks of the Bynoe (near present-day Normanton) on February 11, 1861, and headed back south. Their progress slowed by the wet season, they killed and ate the pack animals as their food ran out. Gray died after being beaten by Burke for stealing flour; remorse was heightened when they staggered into the Cooper Creek stockade on April 21 to find that, having already waited an extra month for them to return, Brahe had decamped that morning. Too weak to follow him, they found supplies buried under a tree marked "Dig", but failed to change the sign when they moved on, which meant that when the first rescue teams arrived on the scene, they assumed the explorers had never returned from the Gulf. Trying to walk south, the three reached the Innamincka area, where Aborigines fed them fish and nardoo (water fern) seeds, but by the time a rescue party tracked them down in September only King was still alive. The full, sad tale of their trek is expertly told by Alan Moorehead in his classic work *Cooper Creek*, a book well worth tracking down in your library.

The **Wirrarri Information Centre** on Billabong Boulevard (Mon–Fri 9am–4pm; ☎07/4656 3300, ℮wirrarri@hotmail.com) will give you the low-down on the state of the various Outback tracks if you're planning to use them, or ask at the pale blue **police station** (☎07/4656 3220), across from the hotel on the far side of the **airstrip**. Monuments at the airstrip name the various expeditions that have passed through the area, including the Simpson Desert traverse by Ted Coulson and an Aborigine named Peter in 1936. The Information Centre can direct you to another tree blazed by Burke and Wills across the Diamantina, otherwise hard to locate among the scrub, or to attractions in town such as the **old hospital**; originally built as a hotel and now just a stone shell, it operated as the original Australian Inland Mission between 1923 and 1927. The **Birdsville Working Museum**, as its name suggests, is more than just a collection of old stuff; all the exhibits, from petrol pumps and farm machinery to a complete blacksmith's shop are fully restored and regularly operated.

Outside Birdsville there's a stand of slow-growing, old and very rare **Waddi trees**, 14km north on the Bedourie road. They're about 5m tall and resemble sparse conifers wrapped in prickly feather boas with warped, circular seed pods; the wind blowing through the needles makes an eerie noise like the roar of a distant fire. For something more dramatic, head out 33km to **Big Red** at the start of the Simpson Desert crossing. Simpson's largest dune may seem unimpressive from below, but your opinion will change radically if you walk up or try to plant a 4WD on the top. If you're having a hard time getting up the long western face, there is a less steep track immediately on the right, which has a couple of quick turns near the summit. Two-wheel-drive vehicles can often reach the base (check with the police before setting off) and it's worth it to see the dunes, flood plains and stony gibber country on the way.

North of Birdsville, the next substantial settlement, Mount Isa (see p.585), is a lonely 700km further on, with fuel available about every 200km. Those heading west across the Simpson Desert to Dalhousie Springs in South Australia need a **Desert Parks Pass** ($80) from the Birdsville NPWS office on Jardine Street (☎07/4656 3272). Feasible in any sound vehicle during a dry winter, the 520-kilometre **Birdsville Track** heads from the racecourse down to Marree in South Australia – see pp.878–882 for details of this and the Simpson Desert crossing.

Rockhampton to Winton

Heading west from Rockhampton, the **Capricorn** and **Landsborough** highways run through the heart of central Queensland to Winton and, ultimately, Mount Isa. There's a lot to see here: just a couple of hours from the coast, there's magical scenery atop the forested, sandstone plateau of the **Blackdown Tablelands**; while the town of **Emerald** offers the chance of seasonal farm work, as well as a gateway to Carnarvon Gorge and the Gemfield's **sapphire mines**. Continuing inland, both **Barcaldine** and **Longreach** are historically important towns, the latter hosting the archetypal Outback museum in the **Stockman's Hall of Fame**. For its part, **Winton** sits surrounded by a timeless, harsh orange landscape, unexpectedly imprinted with a dramatic set of dinosaur footprints at **Lark Quarry**.

Buses connect Rockhampton with Winton, and all main-town settlements west of Barcaldine are also on the Brisbane–Mount Isa bus run. Alternatively, you can catch the twice-weekly Spirit of the Outback **train** from Rockhampton as far as Longreach.

Into the Northern Highlands

As you move inland the coastal humidity is left behind and the gently undulating landscape becomes baked instead of steamed. Passing the white rubble moonscape atop **Mount Hay**, where you can stay at the van park and fossick for agates, the road loops over low hills before adopting a pattern that becomes ever more familiar: straight for miles and then an unexpected bend. Bottle trees, with their bulbous, thick grey trunks and spindly, thinly leaved branches, herald the drier climate. Gradually, the deep-blue platform of the **Blackdown Tablelands** emerges from the horizon, and, by the time you reach **DINGO**, dominates the landscape. Dingo is somewhere to stock up: there's a hotel, van park, fuel station and store, and a bronze monument to the town's namesake.

The Blackdown Tablelands

Floating 600m above the heat haze, the **Blackdown Tablelands'** gum forests, waterfalls and escarpments are a delight, a scenic refuge from the dry, flat lands below. A corrugated, unsealed twenty-kilometre **access road** is signposted on the highway 11km from Dingo. National Park campsite bookings can be made through the NPWS in Rockhampton or Emerald, or with the local **ranger** (via Dingo, QLD 4702; ☎07/4986 1964). Outside school holidays you could well have the place to yourself. There's no public transport into the park, but call in advance and catch the McCafferty's bus to Dingo, and **Namoi Hills Cattle Station** (☎07/4935 9121, ⓕ 4935 9234; ❶), set at the base of the tablelands, will pick you up at the drop-off point on the highway. They offer accommodation-and-meal packages, run tours round the station and onto the tablelands and regularly cater to the tour-bus crowd – phone ahead and check which days are booked if you want peace and quiet.

The access road from the highway runs flat through open scrub to the base of the range; the climb is steep, twisting and slippery, as "pea gravel" puts in an appearance. Views over a haze of eucalypt woodland are generally blocked by the thicker forest at the top of the plateau, but at **Horseshoe Lookout** there's a fabulous view north and, after rain, **Two Mile Falls** rockets over the edge of the cliffs. From here the road widens and runs past **Mimosa Creek campground** ($3.85 per person per night), dead-ending at the **Rainbow Falls** car park. The campground is excellent, shaded by massive stringybark trees with tank water, tables, toilets, fire pits and a creek to bathe in. At night the air fills with the sharp scent of woodsmoke, and the occasional dingo howls in the distance; with a torch, you might see **greater gliders** or the more active brush-tail possum. Watch out for pied currawongs (crows) that raid unattended tables, tents and cars for anything, edible or not. Temperatures can reach 40°C on summer days, and drop below zero on winter nights.

Walks in the park include the short trip to **Officers Pocket**, a moist amphitheatre of ferns and palms with the facing cliffs picked out yellow and white in the late afternoon; a **circuit track** along Mimosa Creek, past remains of cattle pens and stock huts, to some beautifully clear **ochre stencils** made by Gungaloo Aborigines a century ago; and the park's finest scenery at **Rainbow Falls**, 6km past the campsite. At its glorious best around dawn, this track leads from the car park through an eerie gum forest to the top of the gorge, then follows around to where the creek seeps down steps into the greenery. From the edge you can spy on birds in the rainforest beneath; explosive thumps from below signal rock wallabies tearing across ledges hardly big enough for a mouse. A long staircase descends into a cool world of spring-fed gardens, ending on a large shelf about halfway into the gorge where Rainbow Falls sprays from above into a wide, clear pool. It may be pretty, but the water's paralyzingly cold; for a warmer dip, climb back up the stairs and follow the path to the top of the falls, where the creek runs in full sun and the bed has handy, bath-sized holes to sit in.

Emerald and around

The road west of Dingo crosses the lower reaches of the **Bowen Basin coalfields** at **Blackwater**, then moves into **cotton country**, signalled by fluffy white tailings along the roadside around **YAMALA**, where there's a **cotton gin** to tour (by appointment ☎07/4982 3888).

    EMERALD is a misleadingly named place. This close to the Gemfield towns of Sapphire and Rubyvale, you'd think its origins could be traced to precious stones, but in fact the area was named Emerald Downs by a surveyor who saw its rich green after heavy rains. A dormitory town for the **Bowen Basin coal mines** to the north, and set at the junction of routes north to Mackay and south to the Central Highlands, Emerald is a busy place at the heart of a soundly productive district: the rich soil supports sunflowers, citrus trees, grape vines, lychees and rockmelons, all of which attract swarms of seasonal **fruit-pickers**. Despite being around a hundred years old, the town appears quite modern due to rebuilding after a series of disastrous fires in the 1950s.

    Most essential services are on the Capricorn Highway, here called **Clermont Street**, where the main feature is the pristine **station**, built in 1901 and restored in 1986. One road back from this is Egerton Street, where 250-million-year-old **fossil tree trunks** outside the town hall are preserved in great detail, right down to the texture of the bark. The **tourist information** booth at the west end of Clermont Street (Mon–Sat 9am–5pm, Sun 10am–2pm; ☎07/4982 4142) has leaflets on local attractions; at the other end is McCafferty's **bus station** (☎07/4982 2755). **Accommodation** is plentiful, though during the April harvest or November cotton chipping season there may be very little room available: the *Central Inn*, near the station on Clermont Street (☎07/4982 0800, ⓦwww.centralinn.com.au; ❸), has a big kitchen, simply furnished rooms, and offers good advice for either farm work or visiting the Gemfields; the *Meteor Motel*, corner of Opal and Egerton streets (☎07/4982 1166; ❹), has a pool and a good steak restaurant; and the *Explorers Inn Motel* (☎07/4982 2822; ❹–❺) is in a quiet spot at the edge of town – it's newer than the rest with comfortable, well-appointed rooms and a saltwater pool.

Ten kilometres south of Emerald, **Lake Maraboon** has been created by the **Fairbairn Dam** as the region's main water supply. Drought conditions over much of the last decade meant water levels dropped, but they have now recovered along with the popularity of water sports, fishing and bird-watching. All modern amenities and accommodation are provided by the *Lake Maraboon Holiday Village* (⊤ 07/4982 3677, ⊕ 4982 1932; ❹), including fuel, a restaurant and a grassed camping area, which is pleasantly situated among trees by the lake.

From Emerald you can reach **Carnarvon Gorge** (see p.562), 200km or so south through the town of **SPRINGSURE**, set below the dramatic orange cliffs of **Mount Zamia**, also known as Virgin Rock – though weathering since it was named means you can barely see a likeness of the Madonna and Child. From the moment this district was settled, Aborigines put up a strong resistance. At **Rainworth Fort** (Fri–Wed 9am–5pm; $3) settlers built a squat stockade of basalt blocks and corrugated iron for protection after "**the Wills Massacre**" when, on October 17, 1861, Aboriginal forces stormed Cullin-la-ringo station and killed nineteen people in apparent retaliation for the slaughter of a dozen Aborigines by a local squatter. White response was savage, spurred on by vigilantes and a contingent of Native Troopers; newspapers reported that "a great massacre has been made among the blacks of the Nogoa River". The fort and later structures of **Cairdbeign School and Homestead** are 10km southwest of Springsure and house a few relics of the period. Springsure and **Rolleston** (the last stop before Carnarvon Gorge) both have a choice of hotel, motel or caravan park, plus fuel.

The Gemfields

The country an hour west of Emerald is sparse and always hot, the scrub interrupted only by ugly cleared patches covered in rubble from mining operations. This wasteland masks one of the richest **sapphire fields** in the world and, with hard work, the chances of finding some are good – though you're unlikely to get rich. The easiest fields to reach are the **Anakie Fields**, with facilities at Anakie, Sapphire and Rubyvale. Anakie township is off the highway about 45km from Emerald; Sapphire is 9km north of Anakie, and Rubyvale a further 8km. Though well worked, the Anakie Fields are the best place for the newcomer to pick up tips; old hands proceed directly to **the Willows**, 27km west of Anakie along the Capricorn Highway.

ANAKIE ("permanent water") has no gemfields itself, but gave its name to those at Sapphire and Rubyvale. Unusually pretty, it comprises a van park (⊤ & ⊕ 07/4985 4142; cabins ❷–❸) with hot showers by the waterhole and a small shop open every day, backing onto a pub, post office and store. The **information centre** near the highway has fuel, licences, rough maps and advice.

In contrast, the country around **SAPPHIRE** looks like a war zone. You'll find a post office and houses scattered along the road and an elbow of Retreat Creek, where the first gems were found. *Sunrise Cabins* (⊤ 07/4985 4281; ❷–❸) are across the road from the medical centre, in sight of the creek, and *Blue Gem Caravan Park* (⊤ 07/4985 4162) has a **store** and fast food, or try a meal at *Kesorn's Thai & Chinese* next door. Towards Rubyvale is **Pat's Gem Park** (⊤ 07/4985 4544) with a café, jewellery and craft displays and fossicking lessons for beginners; and **Forever Mine** (⊤ 07/4985 4616), who charge a seemingly steep $50 to fossick, though for this you get a tractor-scoop (about four buckets of wash) to pick through.

Gem mining

Gems were first discovered in 1870 near **Anakie** but until Thai buyers came onto the scene a century later operations were low-key, and even today there are still solo fossickers making a living from their claims. Formed by prehistoric volcanic actions and later dispersed along waterways and covered by sediment, the **zircons**, **rubies** and, especially, **sapphires** found here lie in a layer of gravel above the clay base of ancient riverbeds. This layer can be up to 15m down, so gullies and dry rivers, where nature has already done some of the excavation for you, are good places to start.

Looking for surface gems, or **specking**, is best after rain, when a trained eye can see the stones sparkle in the mud. It's erratic but certainly easier than the alternative – **fossicking** – which requires a pick, shovel, sieve, washtub full of water and a canvas sack before even starting (this gear can be rented at all the fields). Cut and polished, local zircons are pale yellow, sapphires pale green or yellow to deep blue, and rubies are light pink, but when they're covered in mud it's hard to tell them from gravel, which is where the washing comes in: wet gems glitter like fragments of coloured glass.

You have to be extremely enthusiastic to spend a summer on the fields; the mercury climbs steadily to 42°C, topsoil erodes and everything becomes filmed in dust. The first rains bring floods as the sunbaked ground sheds water, and if you're here then you'll be treated to the sight of locals specking in the rain, dressed in Akubras and Drizabones and shuffling around like mobile mushrooms. Conditions are best as soon after the wet season as possible (around May), when the ground is soft and fresh pickings have been uncovered – not surprisingly, this is also the busiest period.

If this all seems like too much hard work, try a **Gem Park** such as Pat's (see p.572), where they've done all the digging for you and supply all the necessary gear for about $5. All you have to do is sieve the wash, flip it onto the canvas and check it for stones. There's an art to sieving and flipping, but you're pretty sure to find something, since park owners lace the wash with rejects. Gem parks will also value and cut stones for you. Another break from the business end of a pick is to pay $5, take a **mine tour** and see if the professionals fare any better. In some ways they do – the chilled air 5m down is wonderful – but the main difference is one of scale rather than method or intent.

You need a **fossicker's licence**, available from shops and gem parks, which allows digging in areas set aside for the purpose or on no-man's-land. The $7.25 licence is valid for two months and gives you no rights at all other than to keep what you find and to camp at fossick grounds. To stake a claim and keep others away you need a **Miner's Right** from the field officer in Emerald (Department of Minerals and Energy, Clerana Centre, Clermont St; ☏07/4982 4011); this also carries obligations to restore the land to its original state and maintain it for two years after quitting the site.

RUBYVALE has several shops, service stations and a few **mines** to look around: tour groups tend to visit Miner's Heritage (open daily; $5 per person), but equally interesting is Bobby Dazzler (daily; $5) on the hill as you approach town. The ground beneath each new development here has to be mined first; outdoor tennis courts and the surfaced road were built only after years of wrangling over whether the ground had given up all its treasures. Rubyvale also seems to be the place to pick up on apocryphal stories, such as the one about the largest star sapphire ever found being used as a doorstop. You'll also hear plenty more during the annual **August Gemfest** which includes, in odd-numbered years, a **Wheelbarrow Race** when, in imitation of the first pioneering miners, all comers push their one-wheeled transport laden with pick and shovel up the eighteen-kilometre track from Anakie to Rubyvale, pausing only at Sapphire to take on board a bucket of dirt. There's a good **van park** in Rubyvale (Ⓣ 07/4985 4118; cabins ❸) with camp sites and cabins, and the *New Royal Hotel* nearby is a smart stone and timber building, with a mighty fireplace and $7 meal specials.

The **Willows Gemfield** is still in the making, part mining camp, part township. The immaculate *Willows Caravan Park* (Ⓣ & Ⓕ 07/4985 5128; cabins ❷) is well shaded, has wangled a liquor licence and acts as a bank agent as well as supplying fuel and digging equipment. The gemfields are just down the track from the park.

Over the Range to Winton

Vistas from the rounded sandstone boulders at the top of the Great Dividing Range west of the tiny railway stop of **Alpha** reveal a dead-flat country beyond; rivers flow to the Gulf of Carpentaria or towards the great dry lakes of South Australia, while unsealed roads run north to Clermont and south to Charleville. You'll notice an increase in temperature; flies appear from nowhere, tumbleweeds pile up on fences and trees never seem closer than the horizon. In terms of numbers, sheep are the dominant mammal in these parts, though there are some cattle and even a few people out here. Down below, **JERICHO** is somewhere to freshen up and, if you're passing through on a Saturday night, to catch a **drive-in movie**.

Barcaldine and Blackall

The only place of any size on the way to Longreach is **BARCALDINE**, 300km from Emerald, an unassuming grid of quiet streets belying an important niche in Australian history. It was near here during the 1885 drought that geologists first tapped Queensland's artesian water, revolutionizing Outback development. The town further secured its place in history during the 1891 **shearing strike** which, though a failure itself, ultimately led to the **formation of the Labor Party**. On the highway, outside the station which became the focus of the dispute, is a granite monument – sculpted to resemble the tips of a pair of shears – to shearers arrested during the strike. Right next to it, the sagging silver trunk of the **Tree of Knowledge** struggles gamely to improve on its 160 years. Sadly, this ghost gum, where shearers rallied a century ago, looks to be on the way out.

The **Australian Workers' Heritage Museum** (Mon–Sat 9am–5pm, Sun 10am–5pm; $7) is unmissable underneath a yellow and blue marquee on Ash Street. With an expanding collection of displays concentrating on the history of the workers' movement after the shearers' strike, as well as videos, artefacts and plenty of sepia-tinted photos covering themes including Outback women and Aboriginal stockmen, the museum rounds out Longreach's Stockman's Hall of Fame (see p.576). On the highway in the old *Shakespear Hotel*, the **information centre** (Mon–Fri 8.30am–4.30pm; Ⓣ 07/4651 1724) will direct you to other attractions such as the self-styled **Mad Mick's Funny Farm** (open most mornings April–Sept or by arrangement on Ⓣ 07/4651 1172; adults $7.70, children $4.40), which has been restored to its turn-of-the-twentieth-century condition and is inhabited by friendly, hand-reared animals; admission includes a ride in a Ford Model-T and tea and damper.

Banks and other services are mostly on Box Street, which runs south off the highway. **Accommodation** options include the *Ironbark Inn* (℡07/4651 2311; ❺), *Barcaldine Motel* (℡07/4651 1244; ❹) and *Homestead Van Park* (℡07/4651 1308), all on Box Street. Across the road from the Tree of Knowledge, the shaded verandahs of the *Artesian Hotel* provide a reminder of the value of a reliable watering hole, and you can also get a drink and a meal at the adjacent *Commercial* or *Union* hotels.

Blackall

One hour south of Barcaldine on the Landsborough Highway (and covered by Brisbane–Mount Isa **buses**), a sign at **BLACKALL** welcomes you to Merino Country. It was near here in 1892 that Jackie Howe fleeced 321 sheep in under eight hours using hand shears, a still-unbroken record. If you want to visit a **sheep station** to see modern shearers in action, it can be arranged by the **tourist office** just off Shamrock Street on Short Street (daily 9am–noon & 1–5pm; ℡07/4657 4637). There's more on the industry at the steam-driven **woolscour**, built in 1908 and in operation for seventy years; it has been restored recently and runs daily from April to November, with guides on hand to show you around (8am–4pm; $5.50).

In town, you could also track down the famous **black stump**, a surveying point used in pinpointing Queensland's borders in the nineteenth century and now the butt of many jokes; the original stump has been replaced by a more interesting fossilized one. Around 100km southwest of Blackall, **Idalia National Park** preserves one of Queensland's last population of yellow-footed rock wallabies in the wild – more easily seen at the fauna park in Charleville if you're heading that way (see p.565). For details of access to Idalia, and possible guided **night tours** of the park, contact the ranger on ℡07/4657 5033.

Blackall town sits on the banks of the often dry (but occasionally five-metre-deep) **Barcoo River**; 200m-long Shamrock Street, shaded by palms and bottle trees, is the main road on which you'll find banks, supplies and a few places to **eat** – if your dress is reasonably smart you can savour good food at the *Blackall Club*. The most central **place to stay** is the brand-new *Accacia Motor Inn* (℡07/4657 6022; ❺), and at *Blackall Caravan Park* (℡07/4657 4816; on-site vans ❷) on Hart Lane you can yarn with other travellers around a huge campfire and be fed pot roasts, billy tea and damper for an extra fee. Long-distance **bus** tickets are available from Blackall Travel (℡07/4657 4422).

Longreach

LONGREACH, 110km west of Barcaldine and right on the Tropic of Capricorn, is different from other western towns: it's doing more than surviving. This is mainly due to the Stockman's Hall of Fame, an ambitious museum which pulls in busloads of tourists. Yet even before the museum, Longreach was an enterprising settlement with a firm place in history. Ever since the discovery of artesian water it has been a stronghold of cattle- and sheep-farming, but it really took off as the original headquarters of **Qantas** – their first hangar still stands at the airport, and there are plans to open it up as a museum.

Qantas

There's always been contention between Longreach and Winton as to which was the birthplace of Qantas (the Queensland and Northern Territories Aerial Service), but the first joy-flights and taxi service flew from Longreach in 1921, pioneered by Hudson Fysh and Paul McGuiness. Their idea – that an airline could play an important role by carrying mail and passengers, dropping supplies to remote districts and providing an emergency link into the Outback – inspired other projects such as the Flying Doctor Service. Though the company's headquarters moved to Brisbane in 1930, Qantas maintained their offices at Longreach until after World War II – during which time US Flying Fortresses were stationed here – by which time both the company and its planes had outgrown the town.

The Stockman's Hall of Fame

On the highway 2km from the town centre, **The Stockman's Hall of Fame** (daily 9am–5pm; $18.70) is a masterpiece, not just in architectural design – a blend of aircraft hangar and cathedral – but in being an encyclopedia of the Outback right in its heart. Since opening in 1988 its success has silenced critics who underestimated the Outback's widespread appeal. A minor complaint might be that the displays themselves are fairly ordinary, but once you're here the Hall of Fame has achieved its dual aim of bringing people out west and providing background to the development of a vast portion of Australia.

Inside the museum, the Outback is romanticized through videos, slide shows, photographs and exhibits – but this is not just another local museum where anything more than five years old is shown for its own sake. History starts in the Dreamtime and moves on, via a directory of those on the First Fleet, to early explorers and pioneers (including a large section on women in the Outback), ending with personal accounts of life in the bush. Among more day-to-day features are some offbeat selections; if you thought barbed wire was just something to get stuck on, then check out the collection here, with over a hundred types – from the old hook design to modern razor wire. You'd be hard pushed not to find something of interest, be it boxing kangaroos, rodeos, bark huts or tall stories. The library and exhibitions by Outback artists (displayed in the art gallery) are also worth a browse.

Practicalities

Longreach is a more active version of Barcaldine, with plenty of spruce old buildings. The main drag is south off the highway along Eagle Street, where you'll find hotels, cafés, **banks**, a cinema and the first well-stocked **supermarket** in a long while. The **airport** is off the highway between town and the Hall of Fame; **trains** terminate at the station at the junction of Galah Street and the highway; and buses set down on Eagle Street at Longreach Outback Travel, who can also arrange all tickets (☎07/4658 1776). The **tourist office** (April–Oct Mon–Fri 9am–5pm & Sat–Sun 9am–1pm; Nov–March Mon–Fri 9am–5pm; ☎07/4658 3555) is in a replica of Qantas' original office on the corner of Eagle and Duck Street, opposite the **post office**, and can advise on **tours** around nearby sheep stations or waterway **cruises**.

There are two **campsites**: *Gunnadoo Van Park*, on Thrush Road looking across to the Hall of Fame (☎07/4658 1781), and *Longreach Caravan Park* on Ibis Street (☎07/4658 1770). *Hallview Lodge*, 81 Wompoo St (☎07/4658 3777; ❸–❹), is a friendly **B&B**; or you can indulge in **motel** comforts at the *Albert*

Park Motel, Hudson Fysh Drive (℡07/4658 2411, ℻4658 3181; ⑤), or *Longreach Motor Inn*, Galah Street (℡07/4658 2322; ⑥). For **meals**, the *Indian Gourmet Express* on Eagle Street is an unexpected find, a tiny takeaway offering Hyderabad byriani, Goan fish curry, chicken tikka, or samosas for well under $10 a serving. The *Longreach RSL Club* also welcomes visitors; you can dine in their inexpensive restaurant, or just settle into a chair in the lounge-bar. Of Eagle Street's half-dozen **hotels**, try the *Lyceum* for counter food, or *Starlight's* for nightlife.

Winton and beyond

Scenery doesn't come blander than on the 173-kilometre-long Longreach–Winton stretch: your only worry as a driver is to keep your foot down and stay awake as the car cruises the empty Mitchell Plains. At the far end, **WINTON** is a real frontier town: dust devils blow tumbleweeds down the streets, and the main change over the last fifty years is that 4WDs have superseded the horse as a means of getting around. As Queensland's largest cattle-trucking depot, Winton has a constant stream of road trains rumbling through it, and conversations in hotel bars tend to revolve around problems of stock management. Winton has its share of history, too: Qantas held its first meeting here in 1920 and **Waltzing Matilda**, that evergreen ballad, premiered at the *North Gregory Hotel* (see box, overleaf). The surrounding countryside is an eerie world of windswept plains and eroded **jump-ups** – flat-topped hills layered in orange, grey and red dust – complete with **opal deposits** at Opalton and a stunning set of **dinosaur footprints** at Lark Quarry.

All **services** (bank, post office and service station with EFTPOS and cash-withdrawal facilities) are around Elderslie Street. If there's a film on, treat yourself to a session in the open-air **cinema**, complete with canvas seats and original projector, at the corner of Elderslie and Cobb streets; the café here stays open until after dark. A few doors down, next to the *North Gregory Hotel*, the immense wooden **Corfield & Fitzmaurice** building (Mon–Fri 9am–5pm, Sat 9am–12.30pm; $5) opened as a store in 1916 and now houses a vast collection of rocks and fossils from around the world, along with a life-size diorama of the Lark Quarry dinosaurs – garbage bins around town are also shaped as dinosaur feet.

Further down Elderslie Street, opposite a tepid swimming pool and bronze statue of the jolly swagman, the **Waltzing Matilda Centre** (daily 8.30am–5pm; $14; ℡07/4657 1466) has some unusual items, including an indoor billabong, a fine display of Aboriginal artefacts featuring an entire tree with a boomerang half-carved out of its trunk, and a bottle collection covering everything from poisons to schnapps. The centre also doubles as an **information office** and sorts out **bus** tickets and **tours** to local sights – check with them about road conditions before visiting Opalton or Lark Quarry. For some really ludicrous fun, the **Australian Crayfish Derby**, part of the **Outback Festival** held in September in odd-numbered years, has to be worth a look; the owner of the winning crustacean nets $1500, and the runner up gets to eat all the competitors. In April the **Waltzing Matilda Festival** involves a rodeo and arts events attracting bush poets to compete with "Banjo" Paterson.

Waltzing Matilda

In April 1995, Winton celebrated the centenary of the first public performance of "Banjo" Paterson's ballad **Waltzing Matilda** at the *North Gregory Hotel*, and stirred up a century of gossip and rumour. Legend has it that Christina MacPherson told Paterson the tale of a sheep-rustling swagman while he was staying with her family at nearby Dagwood Station. Christina wrote the music to the ballad, a collaboration which so incensed Paterson's fiancée, Sarah Riley, that she broke off their engagement. While a straightforward "translation" of the poem is easy enough – "Waltzing Matilda" was contemporary slang for tramping (carrying a bedroll or swag from place to place), "jumbuck" for a sheep, and "squatters" refers to landowners – there is some contention as to what the poem actually describes. The most obvious interpretation is of a poor tramp, hounded to death by the law, but first drafts of the poem suggest that Paterson – generally known as a romantic rather than social commentator – originally wrote the piece about the arrest of a union leader during the shearers' strike, and later toned it down. Either version would account for the popularity of the poem, which was once proposed as the national anthem – Australians readily identify with an underdog who dares to confront the system.

Winton's **accommodation** prospects include the *Matilda Country Tourist Park*, about 700km from Elderslie where the Landsborough Highway kinks into town (☎07/4657 1607); the nearby neat and trim *Banjo Motel* on Manuka Street (☎07/4657 1213; ❹); and the *North Gregory Hotel* (free call ☎1800 801 611; ❸–❹), which has en-suite and shared-bath rooms as well as some basic budget beds in the old shearers' quarters (❶). The *North Gregory* is also one of the best places **to eat** in town, with an early-opening café opposite. **Leaving**, there are two **buses** daily in each direction along the Landsborough Highway towards Mount Isa and Brisbane; the Winton Newsagency on Elderslie Street is the pick-up point and sells tickets.

Lark Quarry

It takes about two hours to drive the 120km south from Winton to **Lark Quarry**, dodging kamikaze kangaroos and patches of bulldust, and once you've arrived there's no doubt that this is the rough heart of the Outback. Nor is it surprising to find **dinosaur remains** here: the place looks prehistoric, swarming with flies and surrounded by stubby hills where stunted trees and tufts of grass tussle with rocks for space. A hundred million years ago this was a shrinking waterhole across which a carnivorous dinosaur chased a group of various turkey-sized herbivores through the mud to a rockface where it caught and killed one as the others fled back past it. Over three thousand **footprints** have been found recording these few seconds of action, excavated in the 1970s and now protected by an awning and walkway around them. Indentations left by small, amazingly sharp, three-clawed feet – some very light as the prey panicked and ran on tiptoe – stream in all directions, while those left by the larger predator go only one way. Paths lead around to other, buried tracks where the chase ended.

Opalton and Carisbrooke

The Opalton track (130km) from Winton follows the Jundah road for a short way before bearing left. Ten kilometres past Bladensburg Station turn-off is a track on the left to **Skull Waterhole**, named after the "dispersal" of the Goa Aborigines by the Native Mounted Police. Despite this sad history it's an interesting spot, as the water attracts kangaroos, budgerigars and ring-necked parrots, and there are also some **caves** to poke around in.

OPALTON is a multicultural shanty town, with Yugoslav and Czech miners, as well as deserters from Coober Pedy in South Australia, reworking century-old diggings with Chinese and Korean finance. You need to be entirely self-sufficient here: the only modern feature is a solar-powered telephone and there isn't any drinking water. During the summer there won't be any miners either – hotels in Winton are easily preferable to Opalton's 40°C-plus temperatures. Fossicking zones have been established where you can pick over old tailings for scraps. There is a **camping and caravan area**, "washing water", and a small **store** that's open most days from 10am to 2pm – they don't sell fuel, however.

If you don't have your own transport, it's worth seeing the area on a **day-tour** from Winton to **Carisbrooke Station**, 85km southwest of Winton (by arrangement, minimum of four passengers; $105; ☎07/4657 3984), where you can also spend the night in renovated shearer's quarters (❷). The trip includes visits to an opal mine and to caves covered in Aboriginal paintings – some abstract, others recognizable outlines of boomerangs and club-like nulla-nullas.

Onwards to McInlay and Boulia

Heading **on from Winton**, the main route follows the Landsborough Highway 340km northwest to Cloncurry on the Townsville–Mount Isa road. Heading this way, the **Combo Waterhole** near **Kynuna** (165km) provided the inspiration for "Banjo" Paterson's classic poem "Waltzing Matilda" (see box, opposite). It's a fairly typical muddy soak, decorated by trees and beer cans, and with some solid stone weirs built at the turn of the twentieth century by Chinese labourers. Kynuna's low-slung *Blue Heeler Hotel* (☎07/4746 8650; ❹) is also worth a stop, not least for its ice-cold beer; it's possible to camp here too. The other feature on the journey is the *Walkabout Creek Hotel* at **McKINLAY**, 75km past Kynuna, which you might recognize as the rowdy Outback pub in the film *Crocodile Dundee*. The whole building was moved 400m recently, in order to make it more visible to passing tourists.

It's also possible to head due west of Winton along the **Kennedy Developmental Road** to Boulia, around 350km away. The journey is a continuation of the Winton landscape, with fuel available every 150km and the chance to see the enigmatic **Min Min Light**, an unexplained glowing oval reputedly seen bobbing around the bush at night; in case you miss it, thoughtful townspeople have erected a larger-than-life Min Min model. **BOULIA** consists of a hotel (☎07/4746 3144), van park and roadhouse; if you need a reason to visit, make it the annual **camel races** in July, when the town gets lively and inordinate quantities of beer are consumed. At quieter times of the year, drop in to the **Fossil Museum** (Mon–Fri 9am–4pm; $5) displaying regional finds, and the **Min Min Encounter Centre** (Mon–Fri 9am–4pm; $11), a cross between a museum and sound-and-light show. Boulia's **information office** is here too (daily 9am–5pm; ☎07/4746 3386), along with *Encounter's Café*, which claims to serve the Outback's best cappuccino – there's certainly no competition for a good many miles around.

From Boulia, Mount Isa is 300km north on bitumen, and Birdsville is 400km south on a mostly reasonable road. If you're really enjoying the ride, Alice Springs is 800km west on the often-used Plenty or less-frequented Donahue "highways" – both of them long stretches of dust and gravel. There's fuel every 250km or so, and track conditions improve once you're over the border into the Northern Territory.

Townsville to Lawn Hill

All the major settlements along the Townsville to Lawn Hill route are **mining towns**, spaced so far apart that precise names are redundant: **Mount Isa** becomes "the Isa", **Cloncurry** "the Curry", **Charters Towers** "the Towers", as if nowhere else existed. Scattered across the vast tracts between are geological treasures waiting to be discovered, as well as traces of those who've tried before, and with a 4WD or careful manoeuvring there's plenty to see as you head interstate. Most people never stop to find out, grimly tearing along as fast as possible between Townsville and Three Ways along the **Flinders/Barkly Highway**. It's a shame, because even if time is limited and you're relying on public transport, Charters Towers' century-old feel and Mount Isa's strange setting are worth a stopover. With the freedom of your own vehicle, there's untramped bush at the **Great Basalt Wall** and **Porcupine Gorge** and the spectacular oasis of **Lawn Hill Gorge**, all a lifetime away from the coast's often banal spirit. With the highway forming the main link between Queensland and the Northern Territory, the major **bus lines** have at least daily services interstate, or there's the twice-weekly Inlander **train** between Townsville and Mount Isa.

Gold Country

There's little scenic variation over the two-hour journey from the coast to the heights of the inland range at the community of **Mingela**, but dry scrub at the top once covered seams of ore which had the streets of both Charters Towers and Ravenswood bustling with lucky-strike miners. Those times are long gone – though gold is still extracted from old tailings or sporadically panned from the creek beds – and the towns have survived at opposite extremes: connected by road and rail to Townsville, Charters Towers became a busy rural centre, while Ravenswood, half an hour south of Mingela, was just too far off the track and wasted to a shadow. Detours (℡07/4721 5977) runs day-trips from Townsville to one or the other for about $45.

Ravenswood

As wind blows dust and dried grass around the streets between mine shafts and lonely old buildings, **RAVENSWOOD** fulfils ideas of what a ghost town should look like. Gold was discovered here in 1868 and within two years there were solid brick houses, a frenetic atmosphere and seven hundred miners on Elphinstone Creek working seams of gold, silver and lead ore: "every building in the main street was either a public house and dance house or public house and general store".

The main attraction is to wander between the restored buildings, trying to imagine how the others must have looked; the curator of the **Court House Museum** (daily except Tues 10am–3pm) gives entertaining tours of the museum, town and – with sufficient notice – current mining efforts (℡07/4770 2047 to book). Built in 1879, the Post Office today doubles as the town's **store** and fuel supply. Unsurprisingly, the two most complete survivals are **hotels**, though how they both keep going with a scattered population of barely a hundred souls is anybody's guess. You'll probably end up in one as the day heats up; the *Railway* (☎07/4770 2131; ❺) seems to be the more popular, but though the *Imperial* (☎07/4770 2131; ❹) looks the worse for wear it has original wood panelling, mirrors and swing doors on the bar; **accommodation** and counter meals are available at either.

Charters Towers and around

Once Queensland's second-largest city, and often referred to in its heyday simply as "the World", **CHARTERS TOWERS** is a showcase of colonial era architecture. An Aboriginal boy named **Jupiter Mosman** found gold here in 1871 and within twelve months three thousand prospectors had stripped the landscape of trees and covered it with shafts, chimneys and crushing mills. At first, little money was reinvested – the cemetery is a sad record of cholera and typhoid outbreaks from poor sanitation – but by 1900, despite diminishing returns, Charters Towers had become a prosperous centre. There's been minimal change since then and the population, now mainly sustained by cattle farming, has shrunk to about a third of what it was in its prime. Good times to visit are for the May Day weekend **Country Music Festival**, and the Easter **Rodeo**.

Just about every building on Gill and Mosman streets catches the eye: a brightly painted police station, the classical elegance of the post office, and the shaded country arcades outside the stores. The courtyard and glass roof at the former Stock Exchange and Assayer's Office now front some quiet shops and a lifeless **mining museum** (daily 9am–4pm; $3). Next door, the solid facade of the **town hall** betrays its original purpose as a bank, which stored gold bars smelted locally; and the next bank along is now a grand facade for The World Theatre and Cinemas. Just down Mosman Street is the **Zara Clark Museum** (daily 10am–3pm; $3), housing an absorbing jumble of everything from old wagons to a set of silver tongs for eating frogs' legs. Further along the road there's plenty of shade under giant fig trees at **Lissner Park**, whose Boer War memorial recalls stories of **Breaker Morant**, a local poet executed by the British after shooting a prisoner.

The **Venus Gold Battery**, 5km out of town down Gill Street (tours daily 10am & 2pm; $3), is a fascinating illustration of the monumental efforts needed to separate gold from rock. Abandoned in 1972 after a century of operations, the battery is a huge, gloomy temple to the past, its machinery lying silent and piecemeal around the place. The intention is to restore it to full working order, presumably without re-creating the actual conditions – it was a hideous place, a sweatbox filled with noxious fumes and noise. Ore was ground to a powder in one of the seven massive crushers, mixed with water and passed over a mercury screen. Any gold formed an amalgam and adhered to the mercury, which was then heated in a crucible to leave a pitted nugget and later re-melted with flux to absorb any impurities. Sludge from the mercury screens was soaked in cyanide to leach out more gold, and then the cyanide was neutralized with sulphur and piled up outside. These mounds are now being reprocessed using modern methods to extract the last vestiges of the precious metal.

Practicalities

The main streets are Gill and Mosman, where you'll find everything from supermarkets to banks; **trains** stop at the far end of Gill Street, **buses** halfway along by the Caltex service station. For **accommodation**, the *Mexican Tourist Park*, at the corner of Church and Mexican streets (☎07/4787 1161; on-site vans and cabins ②–③) on the site of the once-busy Mexican Mine, is shaded and central. In tune with the local atmosphere is *York Street B&B* at 58 York St (☎07/4787 1028; ②–⑤), a nicely restored old timber building with wide verandahs and a pool. The *Park Motel*, on the corner of Mosman and Deane streets (☎07/4787 1022; ⑤), is also central and comfortable. For **food**, your best bet is to try the hotel dining rooms. There's a Sunday morning **market** in the Stock Exchange building. The helpful **information centre** (daily 9am–5pm; ☎07/4752 0314), on Mosman, facing down Gill Street, has rough maps and advice on **gold-panning** tours in the area, while Gold Nugget Scenic Tours packs the town sights into three hours (Mon–Sat; $22; ☎07/4787 4115) and makes longer excursions by arrangement.

The Great Basalt Wall

About thirty minutes north of Charters Towers, the Gregory Developmental Road crosses the eastern side of a hundred-kilometre-long **lava flow** known with some justification as the **Great Basalt Wall**. Central sections form an impenetrable band of black boulders, riddled with gullies and caves; aerial surveys show dense vegetation weighed down beneath rubber vines, hiding colonies of fruit bats and hundreds of unconnected saline waterholes. Compasses don't work properly around basalt and those who've entered the maze are not short on tales about promptly getting lost and wandering around for hours.

You can get an impression of what it's like on the fringes of the wall, at Big Bend and Red Falls. **Big Bend**, 33km north of the Towers and then 2km east, is best reached in a high-clearance vehicle, though it's not far to walk from the main road. This is where the Burdekin River was diverted as lava edged into it, forming a concave cliff and swimming spot at **Echo Hole**. The flows covered an ancient coral reef and you can still pick out some shapes in the limestone rocks where the lava has worn away. At **Red Falls**, 40km along the Developmental Road and then 44km west down a dry-season track, the river runs at right angles to the lava flow; water pours into an Olympic-sized swimming hole and then down a sandy creekbed lined with paperbark trees and overlooked by a bush **campsite**. Walking about 200m further upstream to swim at Silent Hole, you'll see that the riverbed is pocked by the frozen impressions of burst bubbles where gases erupted through the solidifying rock.

Dalrymple National Park
Dalrymple National Park, 46km north of Charters Towers and then 2.5km on a track, marks the site of the now-vanished **Dalrymple Township**, founded in 1864 as the first official inland settlement in northern Australia. A gold-mining town, finds were rich enough to support five hotels during Dalrymple's very brief heyday; having been completely demolished by a flood in 1870, today the remains include only the traces of pavements, foundations, and gravesites.

Dinosaur country

HUGHENDEN, 245km west of Charters Towers along the highway, looks big compared with some of the places you pass on the way here. A dozen wide streets, a supermarket, a couple of **hotels** and banks all conspire to make you feel that you've arrived somewhere. The *Grand Hotel* on Gray Street (⊤07/4741 1588; ❷–❸) offers filling meals and budget beds, but the *Rest Easi Motel* ⊤07/4741 1633; ❺) is quieter; you can also camp here. *Pete's Country Kitchen*, the café before the tracks on the other side of town, has good burgers. Opposite is the service station-cum-**bus stop** and a newsagent selling yesterday's papers. There are two places to spend time: the swimming pool on Resolution Street and the **Dinosaur Museum** and **information centre** on Gray Street, just past the hotel (daily 9am–5pm; $2; ⊤07/4741 1021). The display here focuses on the swamp-dwelling Muttaburrasaurus, bones of which were found south of town in 1963 and assembled into a ten-metre-long skeleton after souvenir hunters handed over pieces to the Queensland Museum in Brisbane. Though this family of dinosaurs were formerly believed to be vegetarian, Muttaburrasaurus' needle-like teeth have prompted a rethink about their possible diet.

Porcupine Gorge is 70km north of Hughenden along the partially surfaced Kennedy Developmental Road, accessible only if you have your own vehicle (although you can usually scrape by without a 4WD). A deep gash completely invisible among the drab brown scrub until you're virtually in it, it's best seen at the start of the dry season (May–July) before the **Flinders River** stops flowing, when good **swimming holes**, beautifully coloured cliffs and flowering bottlebrush and banksia trees reward the effort of getting here. A **campsite** at the top of the gorge has limited cold water, toilets and nothing else. Look for wallabies on the walk into the gorge, which leads down steps and becomes an increasingly steep, rough path carpeted in loose stones. The white riverbed has been moulded by water into soft, elongated forms, curving into a pool below the orange, yellow and white bands of **Pyramid Rock**. This is the bush at its best: sandstone glowing in the afternoon sun against a deep-blue sky, with animal calls echoing along the gorge as the shadow of the gorge wall creeps over distant woods.

Richmond
More on the regional fossil record is on show 115km west along the highway at **RICHMOND**, whose own **Fossil Museum** (daily 8.30am–4.45pm; $8) displays the petrified remains of hundred-million-year-old fish, long-necked

elasmosaurs, and models of a kronosaur excavated in the 1920s by a team from Harvard University and now on show in the USA. Pride of the collection are a complete skeleton of a seal-like pliosaur – the most intact vertebrate fossil ever found in Australia – and the *minmi* ankylosaur, with its armour-plated hide.

Not many people hang around in Richmond, though it's by no means an unpleasant place – just very small. A roadside **park** makes a good spot to stretch you legs, with an original Cobb & Co **coach** (see p.556) and views out across the Flinders River. There's **accommodation** at the *Richmond Caravan Park* (℡07/4741 3772; ❶–❸), which has tent sites, "backpacker" rooms with a communal kitchen, and cabins; or *Entriken's Pioneer Motel* (℡07/4741 3188; ❹–❺). The museum **café** is the only one in town; otherwise head to the Ampol service station on the Hughenden side of town for a feed.

Cloncurry to Mount Isa

CLONCURRY, 390km west of Hughenden, is caught between two landscapes, where the flat eastern plains rise to a rough and rocky plateau. Besides being the place where Australia's highest temperature (53.1°C) was recorded, Cloncurry offers glimpses into the mining history that permeates the whole stretch west to the larger and less personal settlement of Mount Isa. Copper was discovered here in 1867 but as the town lacked a rail link to the coast until 1908, profits were eroded by the necessity of transporting the ore by camel to Normanton. This meant that Cloncurry never reflected the quality of its mines: there are no traces of a wealthy past because there never was one. Even the current resurgence in mining hasn't had much effect on Cloncurry; miners are flown in from the coast to the mines, work their two-week shifts, then head home again, all without spending more than a couple of hours in town.

Buildings at the **Mary Kathleen Memorial Park Museum** (Mon–Fri 7am–4pm, Sat & Sun 9am–3pm; $5) were salvaged from Mary Kathleen, a short-lived uranium mining town between Cloncurry and Mount Isa (see p.585). The museum is primarily of geological interest, a comprehensive catalogue of local ores, fossils and gemstones arranged in long cases, though Aboriginal tools and Burke's water bottle add some historical depth. The office gives out information on old mining camps and fossicking details if you feel inspired to try your luck hunting for garnets, copper and Maltese crosses (hard, reddish-brown staurolite crystals paired at right angles).

A positive side to Cloncurry's isolation is that it inspired the formation of the **Royal Flying Doctor Service**. Over on the corner of King and Daintree streets, **John Flynn Place** (Mon–Fri 7am–4pm, Sat & Sun 9am–3pm; $7) is a monument to the man who pioneered the use of radio and plane to provide a "mantle of safety over the Outback". The exhibition explains how ideas progressed with technology, from pedal-powered radios to assistance from the young Qantas, resulting in the opening in Cloncurry of the first Flying Doctor base in 1928. A very different aspect of Cloncurry's past is also evident in the two foreign **cemeteries** on the outskirts of town. To the south of the highway, before you cross the creek on the way to Mount Isa, a hundred overgrown plots recall a brief nineteenth-century goldrush when the harsh conditions took a terrible toll on **Chinese prospectors**; equally neglected are the unnamed graves of **Afghans** at the north end of Henry Street, all aligned with Mecca. Afghans were vital to Cloncurry's survival before the coming of the railway, organizing camel trains which carried the ore to Normanton whence it was shipped to Europe – a role now largely forgotten.

Cloncurry practicalities

Cloncurry's **services** are clustered along the highway and a block to the north on Scarr Street. Draw money from the bank or via Lee's Supermarket's EFT-POS facilities. The best of Cloncurry's six **bars** – serving good meals as well – is the *Wagon Wheel* **motel** (℡07/4742 1866; ⑤), on Ramsay Street; a public house has occupied this same site since 1867. The best place to **camp** is on the Hughenden side of town at the new *Gilbert Park Tourist Village* (℡07/4742 2300; cabins ④), which also has decent cabins.

  Moving on, the highway, buses and trains continue west for 118km to Mount Isa, while the **Burke Developmental Road** heads 380km north to Normanton (see p.596) via the one-pub settlement of **Quamby** (which also has races and an underwear-throwing competition in May), and the **Burke and Wills Roadhouse**. Aside from being a welcome break in the journey, with fuel pumps and a bar and canteen selling drinks, sandwiches and burgers, the roadhouse also marks the turning west on a sealed road to **Gregory Downs**, gateway to the oasis of Lawn Hill Gorge (p.592).

Mary Kathleen

The rough country between Cloncurry and Mount Isa is evidence of ancient upheavals which shattered the landscape and created the region's extensive mineral deposits. While the highway continues safely to Mount Isa past the **Burke and Wills monument** and the **Kalkadoon/Mitakoodi tribal boundary** at Corella Creek, forays into the bush will uncover remains of less fortunate mining settlements. About halfway to Mount Isa, a short and steadily crumbling road north to **MARY KATHLEEN** is marked with a small plaque. By all accounts, **uranium** was found here by accident when a car broke down; while waiting for help the driver and his friends tried fossicking and found ore. The two-street town was built in 1956 and completely dismantled in 1982 when export restrictions halted mining. Since then, once-manicured lawns have run riot, and an occasional bougainvillea and an unkempt row of casuarinas tangling along the access road are the only signs that there were gardens here; in a few years it will all have gone. About a kilometre past the old town the road becomes a dirt track and splits; a kilometre along the right fork a bumpy uphill track leads to the terraces of the open-cast **mine**, now reminiscent of a flooded Greek amphitheatre. On a cloudy day you can be sure that the alarming blue-green colour of the water is not simply a reflection of the sky. Locals maintain it's safe to swim here, and some even claim health benefits.

Mount Isa and around

As the only place of consequence for 700km in any direction, the smokestacks, concrete paving and sterile hills at **MOUNT ISA** assume oasis-like qualities on arrival, despite being undeniably ugly. Though the novelty might have worn off by the time you've had a cold drink, the city has a few points to savour before heading on. There's evidence of the area's **Aboriginal heritage**, a couple of unusual **museums**, tours of the mines themselves, Australia's largest **rodeo** every August and, not least, the fascinating situation and the community it has fostered.

School of Distance Education, Warrigal Waterhole & Cloncurry

N

MOUNT ISA

Rotary Lookout

Kalkadoon Tribal Council

Riversleigh & Fossils Interpretive Centre

MARIAN STREET

PAMELA STREET

Shopping Complex

Frank Aston Museum

ACCOMMODATION

Burke and Wills Resort	2
Moondarra Caravan Park	1
Mount Isa Van Park	3
Traveller's Haven	4

RESTAURANTS

Los Toros	C
Mount Isa Hotel	B
Red Lantern	D
Sweet Oasis	A
The Tavern	E

Buffalo Club

GRACE STREET

CAMOOWEAL STREET

MARIAN STREET

ISA STREET

MARY STREET

MILES STREET

WEST STREET

Civic Centre & Library

Leichhardt River

Royal Flying Doctor Base

Mining Museum

Campbell's Coach Terminal

CAMOOWEAL ROAD

Train Station

250 m

0

Airport, Lake Moondara & Camooweal

The Irish Club & Dajarra

The Tent House

MIM

The largest city in the world in terms of surface area – its administrative boundaries stretch as far as Cloncurry – Mount Isa sits astride a wealth of zinc, silver, lead and copper, and owes its existence to these reserves and the need for a staging post for interstate travellers. The city's founding father was **John Miles**, who discovered ore in 1923, established **Mount Isa Mines** (MIM) the next year and began commercial mining in 1925. Originally a settlement of canvas and scrap wood, the city enjoyed a forty-year boom under the benevolent hegemony of MIM until the late 1980s saw a decline in profits. New mining developments such as the new Hilton Mine, north of the city, keep business ticking over, but mines further afield, as at Cloncurry, tend to be staffed by workers who live on the east coast and fly in for their shifts, staying on site until they take their money home, completely bypassing The Isa.

Arrival, information and accommodation

With its two huge chimneys illuminated at night – the Rotary lookout on Hilary Street gives a good view – **MIM** is the city's major landmark, west of the often dry **Leichhardt River**. The Barkly Highway runs through town as Marian and Grace streets, with the city centre immediately south between Simpson and West streets; it then crosses the river and joins the Camooweal Road in front of MIM. All **buses** pull in across the river at Campbell's Coach Terminal; **trains** terminate at the station below MIM; and the **airport** is 7km to the north, where taxis meet arrivals. The **tourist information office** (daily 8.30am–5pm; ☎07/4749 1555) is in the Riversleigh Fossils Interpretive Centre on Marian Street, and can make all tour bookings.

Accommodation

Motel accommodation can be found at the *Burke and Wills Resort*, on the corner of Grace and Camooweal (☎07/4743 8000 or free call 1800 679 178; ❻), where somewhat twee rooms decorated in "period" style cluster around a courtyard. Cheaper beds, mostly two to a room, are on offer at *Traveller's Haven*, on the corner of Spence and Pamela streets (☎07/4743 0313; ❶), with a free pick-up from bus or train stations. For **camping**, *Mount Isa Van Park*, on the eastern side of town at 112 Marian St (☎07/4743 3252; cabins ❹), has a few too many rules but is very tidy, while *Moondarra Caravan Park*, 4km from the city off the Camooweal Road (☎07/4743 9780), is plain and tranquil, close to a creek that draws plenty of local birdlife.

The City

Having passed so much mining heritage consigned to history on the way here from the coast, there's novelty value in exploring Mount Isa's active mines. The **surface tour** ($17.60) includes a stint looking at videos and pieces of machinery at the **John Middlin Mining Display** on Church Street (daily 9am–4pm; $5) and a bus ride around surface operations. **Underground tours** ($60), from which women were once barred as harbingers of bad luck, descend to see subterranean mining, crushing and the workshops; book through the tourist office (see above) and expect a waiting list of up to a month in the tourist season between April and September. Near the centre of town, displays at the **Frank Aston Museum** on Shackleton Street (daily 9am–4pm; $6) are partly outdoors and partly underground in a tunnel full of antiquated mining memorabilia. A staircase rises up through a mineshaft to a walkway above the museum, graced by old cars and mining trucks which look dated in MIM's shadow.

MIM

The **Mount Isa Mines** complex is a land of trundling yellow mine trucks, mountains of slag, intense activity and miles of noisy vibrating pipelines. Above all this the two chimneys trail Mount Isa's signature across the sky, marking the copper mine to the south and separate silver, lead and zinc deposits. Ore is mined almost 2km down by a workforce of twelve hundred; roughly crushed, and hoisted to the surface before undergoing a second crushing, grinding and washing in flotation tanks, to separate ore from waste rock. Zinc is sold as it is, copper is smelted into ingots and transported to Townsville for refining while four-tonne ingots of lead/silver mix are sent to England for the few ounces of silver to be separated. Power for the mines and the entire region comes from MIM's own plant; surplus is sold to the state grid.

The scale of the process will be brought home to you if you stand under one of the mountains of tailings awaiting future treatment – next to which are humble mounds of green copper ore, bought off a local miner and representing maybe a year's effort – or look down into the depths of the open-cut mine, worked simply for rubble to fill in old shafts. At the edge of the mine the last ridge of the original Mount Isa, and site of the first finds seventy years ago, has been left as a memorial.

Mount Isa's geological wonders are not confined to minerals, however. Over 400km northwest, the lime-saturated waters of the Gregory River at Riversleigh Station (see p.591) have been encapsulating a fossil record since Australia was a teeming tropical forest. Paleontologists working there since the 1980s have discovered an incredible record of marsupial and mammalian evolution and environmental change between ten thousand and twenty million years ago, all magnificently displayed at the **Riversleigh Fossils Interpretive Centre** on Marian Street (Mon–Fri 8.30am–4.30pm, Sat & Sun 9am–2pm; $9). Imaginative, life-sized dioramas and an informative video re-create the region at a time when it was a lush wetlands populated by ancestral platypus and koalas, giant snakes and emus, carnivorous kangaroos and the enigmatic "thingadonta". You can also visit the **laboratory** out the back, where fossils are being prepared by soaking boulders collected at Riversleigh in weak acid, dissolving the rock but leaving bones, beaks and teeth intact. It's all essential viewing, particularly if you're planning to head out to Riversleigh itself.

Over the river and left down Camooweal Road is the **Royal Flying Doctor Base** (Mon–Sat 9am–3pm; $2). Ten minutes further south on the corner of Third and Fourth avenues, the National Trust **Tent House** is the last survivor of the city's earliest architecture – a canvas hut with a roof. The **School of Distance Education** (tours at 10am and 11am on school days) is by the Kalkadoon State High School at Abel Smith Parade on the Cloncurry side of town.

Eating and drinking

Mount Isa's hotels and clubs are the main source of **meals**, though *Red Lantern Chinese*, on the corner of Simpson and Isa streets, is pretty good, if a little expensive. *Los Toros Mexican*, 19 Camooweal Rd, is a friendly family restaurant and serves **real ale** brewed on the premises in Australia's smallest registered brewery. The city boasts members of over fifty nationalities, many of whom have their own clubs with restaurants. You'll have to befriend a few locals to find these, but you'll almost definitely end up at the *Irish Club*, on Buckley Avenue 2km south of the centre, where everyone converges for weekend bands and inexpensive food. Closer to the centre the upstairs grill at the bulky *Mount Isa Hotel*, on the corner of Marian and Miles streets, is reliable, and *The Tavern* on Isa Street has excellent-value lunches; look out for other hotels' all-you-can-eat specials or try one of the fast-food outlets on Simpson Street, where you'll also find the flashy *Buffalo Club* ("The Buffs"), which hosts an **Oktoberfest**, and a shopping complex for **provisions**. For somewhere to unwind, try *Sweet Oasis* café on Miles Street.

Listings

Airlines Air Mount Isa (☏ 07/4743 2844); Ansett, 8 Miles St (☏ 07/4749 0240); Flight West, 14 Miles St (☏ 07/4743 9333); North Western Air (☏ 07/4743 7720).

Bus station For all enquiries, contact Campbell's Coach Terminal (☏ 07/4743 2006 or free call 1800 242 329). Services include Greyhound-Pioneer and McCafferty's to Townsville, Tennant Creek and Brisbane; Coral Coaches to Normanton, Karumba and Cairns; and Campbell's Coaches for local trips.

Car rental Avis, Marian St (☏ 07/4743 3733) and at the airport; Four Wheel Drive Hire Service, Simpson St (☏ 07/4743 6306, ⊛ www.4wdhire .com.au); Thrifty (☏ 07/4743 2911).

Cinema Cnr Marian and West streets.

Hospital 30 Camooweal St (☏ 07/4744 4444).

Internet access At the newsagent at 25 Miles St.

Pharmacy Corner Pharmacy, cnr Marian and Miles streets.

Police 7 Isa St (☏ 07/4744 1111).

Post office For poste restante, Isa St (☏ 07/4743 2454); there is another office in Simpson St opposite the shopping complex.

Taxi ☏ 07/4743 2333.

Tours Campbell's (☏ 07/4743 2006 or free call 1800 242 329) runs day-tours to local mines and Aboriginal sites for around $30, as well as three-day safaris to Lawn Hill Gorge between May and October ($220). Book through the bus station, tourist information office or your accommodation. Bob's Look About Trips (☏ 07/4743 9523) has a more personalized range of tours of the city and environs for small groups, while Air Mount Isa (☏ 07/4743 2844) organizes day-trips to Lawn Hill.

Trains For information and bookings, call ☏ 07/4744 1202. There are two services each week back to Townsville.

Kalkadoon country

The scrub around Mount Isa is thick with abandoned mines, waterholes and Aboriginal sites. Either take a **tour** (see above and below) or, if you're doing your own driving, check at the tourist office for latest news on road conditions.

The city marks the centre of the territory of the **Kalkadoons**, a tribe often compared with the Zulus for their fierce opposition to white invasion in the nineteenth century. After hounding squatters for ten years with guerrilla tactics, they were all but exterminated in a pitched battle with an army of local settlers and Native Mounted Police near Kajabbi in 1884. Kalkadoon bones littered the region for years, but their stand gained them respect for their organized resistance to Europeans.

Numerous sites around Mount Isa attest to the Kalkadoons' abilities as prolific toolmakers and painters, and it's worth paying the token entry fee to visit their **Tribal Council office** (Mon–Fri 9am–5pm; $1; ☏ 07/4749 3838), next to the Riversleigh Centre on Marian Street, and talk to the staff; they also organize four-hour **cultural tours** ($55) with an Aboriginal guide, taking in local art sites and explaining bush tucker and medicine. Bear in mind that, although it's against the law to alter Aboriginal sites in any way, many local sites have been vandalized and you might find the council evasive.

Warrigal Waterhole, Poison Hole and Lake Moondarra

You need high clearance or great care to reach **Warrigal Waterhole**: drive 7km towards Cloncurry from the Tribal Council office on Marian Street, turn south through the gate and bear left along a very rough track to reach a parking area 3.4km later, from where you walk past "ripple rocks" to the waterhole. One red figure with strange hair outlined in yellow on the left seems to have escaped damage; not so other figures and symbols, which have melted to ochre smears. The waterhole itself is hemmed in by sheltering rocks, which makes for a cool retreat from the sun.

A flooded open-cut mine, **Poison Hole**'s name comes from the surreal appearance of the water, coloured green by copper, but it's actually safe to swim in. Tracks there change each year, but the hole is about ten minutes from the highway, and the turn-off should be roughly 25km back towards Cloncurry; look for signs spray-painted on the road. **Lake Moondarra**, 20km along on a good road (follow the signs from the highway heading towards Camooweal), is less offensively toned, and packed out at weekends with windsurfers and boats. During the week it is nearly deserted and other animals are attracted to the water – goannas, wallabies and flocks of pelicans. By the dam at the north end of the lake, the neat and tidy **Warrina Park** is the unlikely home of peacocks.

Camooweal and Lawn Hill

West of Mount Isa, the **Barkly Highway** continues to Camooweal and the Northern Territory, with an unsealed road, a little over halfway to the state border, heading north off it leading to **Gregory Downs**, **Lawn Hill National Park** and **Burketown**. If you're making for Lawn Hill, ensure you have a **campsite** booked (see p.592 for details) and check the latest **road conditions** – the route via Riversleigh is sometimes 4WD-only or closed, while the Gregory Downs road is fine for most cars if it's dry. Wherever you're driving, fuel up; it's two hundred monotonous kilometres to Camooweal and the fringes of the black-soil **Barkly Tablelands**, and at least twice that to Lawn Hill.

Camooweal and the Caves

There's no way to avoid **CAMOOWEAL** but you might wish there were; the township's atmosphere of lazy aggression is exacerbated by a total lack of charm. The highway from Mount Isa forms the main street, built in 1944 by American servicemen whose names are painted on a rock at the edge of town. You'll find a roadhouse, mechanic, general store (and Westpac agent), post office and hotel – a risky place for a last drink in Queensland. The store's old decor is worth a peek, and murals at the *Camooweal Roadhouse* (℡07/4748 2155; cabins ❹) should raise a chuckle; around the back are cabins and a **campsite** with thick grass to raise a tent over. Otherwise, move on.

The best features of the surrounding area are dolomite sinks known as **the Caves**; drive 8km down the Urandangie road south of Camooweal, then turn left and follow the dirt track for about thirty minutes. There's an NPWS **campsite** here with toilets and a fence to keep out marauding cattle. Flocks of gibbering green budgerigars congregate around the creek and, if you can put up with their racket, it's preferable to a night in town. The park's nine **caves** are intriguing terraces, spiralling down 10m before tapering to vertical shafts. The district is riddled with them; one is a roost for **ghost bats**, and another has become famous for its coolabah trees. Caused by tunnels into the water table collapsing at the surface, the shafts continue straight down for anything between 18m and 75m before levelling out into an uncharted system. Instability makes approaching the mouths dangerous, so don't even think about exploring underground.

Heading on from Camooweal there's another track north to Lawn Hill, while 200km south beyond the Caves is **Urandangie** and a 650-kilometre, 4WD "short cut" across to Alice Springs. West, it's a mere ten-minutes' drive to the cattle grid separating Queensland from the Northern Territory's time zone and better roads. Next fuel is at the Barkly Homestead, 275km away.

Gregory Downs and Lawn Hill National Park

Hidden from the rest of the world by the Constance Range and a hot ocean of bleached grass, the red sandstone walls and splash of tropical greenery at **Lawn Hill National Park** seem outrageously extravagant. There's little warning: within moments a land which barely supports scattered herds of cattle is exchanged for palm forests and creeks teeming with wildlife. There are two places to aim for: **Riversleigh Fossil Site** and **Lawn Hill Gorge**, connected to each other by a 70km track; most people base themselves at the gorge, which has the easiest access and the best facilities and scenery, though a trip to Riversleigh is definitely worth it.

For Lawn Hill Gorge, routes from Cloncurry, the Barkly Highway, Camooweal and Burketown all converge at **GREGORY DOWNS**, whose pub provides cold drinks, fuel, mechanical repairs, and a wild **canoe race** down the Gregory River on the May Day weekend. From here, the gorge is 76km west along a decent gravel road via the controversial **Century Zinc mine**, where work was halted when local Aborigines claimed traditional ownership of the region; after several years of negotiations they finally accepted a substantial payment for use of the land and the mine reopened. While the situation has exacerbated the frustration felt by mining companies and farmers over the legal ambiguities surrounding the 1992 Mabo Decision (see Contexts, p.1152), it's evidence that the wishes of Aboriginal communities are now being taken far more seriously.

For Riversleigh, follow the Gregory Downs road for about 120km from either the Barkly Highway or Camooweal, then take a 35km track to Riversleigh; this can be a rough road, and at times the track onwards from Riversleigh to Lawn Hill is 4WD only.

Riversleigh Fossil Site

The track from Gregory Downs road to Riversleigh crosses the **Gregory River** three times around **Riversleigh Station**, which is why you might need a 4WD on this route. The crossings are a foretaste of Lawn Hill – sudden patches of shady green and cool air in an otherwise hostile landscape – and you can **camp** from April until the end of October at *Campbell's Riversleigh Camp* (satellite phone ☏014 511 6441), where you'll also find on-site double tents (❸), hot showers, toilets and a barbecue area; they also hire out canoes ($5.50 per hour) and organize various **guided tours** ($33–66).

Like Lawn Hill, Riversleigh was once cloaked in rainforest supporting many ancestral forms of Australian fauna. The **fossil finds** here cover a period from twenty million to just ten thousand years ago, a staggering range for a single site and one which details the transitional period from Australia's climatic heyday to its current parched state. Riversleigh may ultimately produce a fossil record of evolutionary change for an entire ecosystem, but don't expect to see much *in situ* as the fossils are trapped in limestone boulders which have to be blasted out and treated with acid to release their contents (see p.588). A roadside shelter houses a map of the landscape with fossil sites indicated on a rock outcrop nearby where, with some diligence, you can find bones and teeth protruding from the stones.

Lawn Hill Gorge

When **Lawn Hill Creek** started carving its forty-metre-deep gorge, the region was still a tropical wetland but, as the climate began to dry out, vegetation retreated to a handful of moist, isolated pockets. Animals were drawn to creeks and waterholes and people followed the game – middens and art detail an Aboriginal culture at least seventeen thousand years old. The NPWS **campsite** (tank water, showers, toilets) occupies a tamed edge of the creek at the mouth of the gorge and is booked solid between Easter and October (bookings on ☏07/4748 5572). An alternative campsite is at the pleasant **Adels Grove** (☏07/4748 5502), a Savannah Guides post 5km from the gorge and run by Barry Kubala, an expert on the gorge's vegetation.

Canoes ($5 per person per hour) let you explore the gorge from the inside. An easy hour's paddle over calm green water takes you from the NPWS campsite between the stark, vertical cliffs of the Middle Gorge to **Indari falls**, an excellent swimming spot with a ramp to carry your gear down. Beyond here the creek relaxes, alternating between calm ponds and slack channels choked with vegetation before slowing to a trickle under the rockfaces of the Upper Gorge. Saltwater crocs are absent from the gorge, but you'll certainly see plenty of **birds** – egrets, bitterns and kites all put in an appearance. Freshwater crocodiles are unlikely to show: since visitor numbers have increased, this timid reptile has retreated to quieter spots, although you might see a "freshie" at dusk in the **Lower Gorge** – a sluggish tract edged in waterlilies and forest where goannas lounge during the day and rare **purple-crowned fairy wrens** forage in pandanus leaves.

In the creek itself are turtles, shockingly large catfish, and sharp-eyed **archer fish** that spit jets of water at insects above the surface. Just how isolated all this is becomes clear from the flat top of the **Island Stack**, a twenty-minute walk from the camp. A pre-dawn hike up the steep sides gives you a commanding view of the sun creeping into the gorge, highlighting orange walls against green palm-tops which hug the river through a flat, undernourished country. The rocks along the banks of the Lower Gorge are daubed with designs relating to the Dingo Dreaming, while fuel drums, tins and middens inside an overhang demonstrate that Lawn Hill has only recently been abandoned by **Aborigines**. This fact was rammed home when a group of fifty people from local communities staged a month-long sit-in at the park in October 1994, demanding joint management – something they'd been promised three years previously. The case is still being milled through the legal system, but it's possible that Aboriginal tour guides may soon be on hand to show you around.

The Gulf of Carpentaria

The great savannahs and intricate river systems of western Cape York and the **Gulf of Carpentaria** were described in 1623 by the Dutch explorer Jan Carstensz as being full of hostile tribes – not surprising, since he'd already kidnapped two men and chased the rest off with musket fire. The Gulf was ignored for centuries thereafter, except by Indonesians gathering sea-slugs to sell to the Chinese, but interest in its potential was stirred in 1841 by **John Lort Stokes**, a lieutenant on the *Beagle* (which had been graced by a young Charles Darwin on an earlier voyage) who absurdly described the coast as "Plains of Promise":

> A vast boundless plain lay before us, here and there dotted with woodland isles. . . I could discover the rudiments of future prosperity and ample justification of the name which I had bestowed upon them.

It took Burke and Wills' awful 1861 trek (see box on p.568) to discover that the "woodland isles" were deficient in nutrients and that the black soil became a quagmire during the wet season. Too awkward to develop, the Gulf hung in limbo as settlements sprang up, staggered on for a while, then disappeared; even today few places could be described as thriving communities. Not that this should put you off visiting: with few real destinations but plenty to see, the Gulf is a perfect destination for those who just like to travel. On the way, and only half a day's drive from Cairns, the awesome lava tubes at **Undara** shouldn't be missed, while further afield there are **gemstones** to be fossicked, the coast's birdlife and exciting **barramundi** fishing to enjoy, and the Gulf's sheer remoteness to savour.

Two sealed roads head through the region to Normanton and Karumba: the **Gulf Developmental Road**, which starts southwest of Ravenshoe on the Atherton Tablelands, and the **Burke Developmental Road** from Mount Isa; both routes are covered by Coral Coaches (℡07/4031 7577), which run three

Gulf Trains

Two unconnected, anachronistic railways still operate in the Gulf region, mostly as tourist attractions. For advance bookings on either, call in to the relevant stations, or contact Queensland Rail (℡13 2232).

The Savannahlander runs every Wednesday morning from Cairns to Almaden on the Chillagoe Road (p.528), where it overnights before continuing south to Forsayth, arriving Thursday afternoon. Friday morning it leaves Forsayth for Mount Surprise (where you can catch the connecting Coral Coach bus on to Undara and Cairns if you've had enough), arriving back in Cairns on Saturday evening. You spend the snails-pace journey being hauled over rickety bridges in carriages with corrugated-iron ceilings and wooden dunnies – a pastiche of Outback iconography. The trip costs $93.50 each way; you'll need to bring extra for hotel accommodation and meals.

The Gulflander runs once a week each way along an isolated stretch of line between Croydon and Normanton, a journey that takes a mere four hours (departs Croydon Thurs 8.30am, departs Normanton Wed 8.30am; $38.50 each way). You can reach both Croydon and Normanton on Coral Coaches, who pass through both towns three times a week in each direction on their Cairns–Karumba run.

times a week from Cairns, stopping at all major settlements. The Mareeba–Normanton "road", via Chillagoe, is a shattering, unserviced, five-hundred-kilometre track best tackled by well-equipped off-road transport only – as are all the Gulf's remoter stretches. In the **wet season**, flying is the sole option for *any* travel. **Safaris** run from Cairns (see box p.519) if you don't have the right vehicle, or you could get at least part of the way around on the Gulf's two rustic **railways** (see box, overleaf).

Most visitors to the Gulf need to be reasonably self-sufficient, as there are few banks and accommodation is largely in campsites (no hostels) or pricey hotels. For **information** before you go, contact Gulf Savannah Tourism at 74 Abbott St, Cairns (℡07/4031 1631, Ⓦ www.gulf-savannah.com.au), who have heaps of brochures and advice, though they don't make bookings. Once in the region, you'll find the local NPWS are joined by the **Savannah Guides**, a private ranger organization recently voted the best of its type in the world, which runs campsites with guides to show you around. On a more alarming note, you might also come face to face with the Gulf's two **crocodile** species – take care.

Undara Lava Tubes

The **Undara Lava Tubes** are astounding, massive tunnels running in broken chambers for up to 35km from the side of the volcano's low cone. It wasn't until 1989 that the majority of the caves were located and mapped and Undara declared an area of scientific interest, currently run by the Savannah Guides but NPWS-owned. Undara is on **Yarramulla Station**, ten minutes south off the Gulf Developmental Road, 130km from Ravenshoe; the Coral Coaches **bus** calls in here three times a week on their Cairns–Karumba run. **Accommodation**, bar and restaurant at the *Lava Lodge* (℡07/4097 1411, Ⓦ www.undara.com.au; cabins ❺, tent village ❶, camping also available) are in eleven restored railway carriages brought over from Mareeba and set up among a thin wattle forest – an eccentric but comfortable idea.

Because the tunnels are hard to enter – and some host a virulent lung fungus – you must take a **tour**. Although not cheap ($33 for a 2hr introduction, $63.80 for a half-day, $93.50 full-day), these are good value considering that, as well as the chance to explore the tubes, you get an intimate rundown on local geology, flora, fauna and history from a member of the Collins family, who've lived on the station for more than a century. There are also some good short **walks** up to lookout points in the low hills above the *Lodge*, and plenty of insect and reptile nightlife.

Tubes and caves

When the Undara volcano erupted 190,000 years ago, the liquid lava followed rivers and gullies as it snaked northwest towards the Gulf. Away from the cone, the surface of these lava rivers hardened, forming insulating tubes which kept the lava beneath liquid and allowed it to run until the tubes were drained. These were then covered by later accumulations, and they'd still be unexplored if hot gases hadn't popped holes in the tube ceilings which eventually collapsed, creating a way in.

The edge of the flow is marked by darker soil and healthier vegetation; at cave mouths this becomes rampant, successfully concealing the entrances and making your first view of the tubes something of a shock – what looks like a bush at ground level turns out to be the top of a giant fig tree growing from the cave floor. The caves are decked in rubble and remnant pockets of thick prehistoric vegetation quite out of place among the dry scrub on the surface. **Tool sites** around the cave mouths show that Aborigines knew of their existence, though there's no evidence that they ever ventured in.

Once **inside**, the scale of the 52 tubes is overpowering. Up to 19m high and 900m long, their glazed walls bear evidence of the terrible forces that created them: coil patterns and ledges formed by cooling lava, whirlpools where lava forged its way through rock from other flows, and "stalactites" made when solidifying lava dribbled from the ceiling. Some end in **lakes**, while others are blocked by lava plugs. Animal tracks in the dust indicate the regular passage of kangaroos, snakes and invertebrates, and seasonally you'll encounter twittering colonies of bats clinging to the ceiling, but the overall scale of the tubes tends to deaden any sounds or signs of life.

Mount Surprise and around

MOUNT SURPRISE, 40km from Undara, takes its name from the shock of the local Aborigines when they first saw whites. Aside from being a stop for the Savannahlander train on its weekly return leg to Cairns (see box on p.593), there's little more here than the *Bedrock Caravan Park* (℡07/4062 3193; cabins ❸), a gem shop/service station (℡07/4062 3153) and **hotel** (℡07/4062 3118; ❸). The main attraction lies a bumpy 40km north at **O'Briens Creek Topaz Field** (check in Mount Surprise on road conditions), where you can **camp** at a waterhole known as The Oasis, and then organize fossicking with Pete and Pam at *Diggers Rest* (℡07/4062 5241; a few snacks available), who also hire out all the gear you'll need and can point you in the right direction. You might find a handful of topaz in a couple of hours, and while it's not very valuable, there's pleasure in the hunt – and it's beautiful when cut.

Beyond Mount Surprise the main road crosses the **Wall**, where expanding gases in a blocked subterranean lava tube forced the ground above it up 20m into a long ridge. The same gaseous expulsion also seems to have cracked open a much deeper seam at **Ambo Springs** on Tallaroo Station. Formed by water 3km down becoming heated and forcing its way to the surface, the clear blue, sulphurous pools gradually accumulate a crusty grey collar around their vent from dissolved lime, which eventually closes the outflow – until the build-up of pressure explodes through to create a new spring. The water emerges at 92°C, but there are some cooler spas that are more comfortable for soaking in. Tallaroo Station itself is open to the public (Easter–Oct daily until 4pm; $9; ℡07/4662 1221).

South of the main road near Ambo, there's a 40km detour down to **EINASLEIGH**, an ordinary handful of weatherboard and iron houses, made memorable by the huge, delicious evening meals served at the *Central Hotel* (℡07/4062 5222; ❹), and summer dips in **Einasleigh Creek**'s deep basalt gorge. If you don't have your own vehicle (and you might need 4WD after rain), the Savannahlander train also passes this way.

Georgetown, Forsayth and around

Back on the main road about 90km west of Mount Surprise, **GEORGE-TOWN** is a similarly-scaled, tidy town, home to the *Midaway Caravan Park* (℡07/4062 1219), and the rather plusher *Latara Resort Motel* (℡07/4062 1190; ❺), along with a couple of shops and hotels (*Wenaru* has the best meals) and *Teresa's Museum and Coffee Shop*, which houses a mass of local trinkets. The area around Georgetown has a reputation as somewhere to fossick for **gold**

nuggets, and you can get information on likely places to try from the Shire Offices (Mon–Fri 9am–5pm; ℡07/4062 1233).

Forty kilometres south off the highway down a decent gravel road is **FOR-SAYTH**, terminus for the Savannahlander train and home to the *Goldfields Hotel* (℡07/4062 5374; ➍ including dinner); it's also the last place to stock up before heading bush to two unusual locations. Two hours south in a 4WD through the scrub, the basic **camp** at **Agate Creek** (Easter–Oct; ℡07/4062 5335) caters to agate hunters who scour the creek banks after each wet season and rate this the best site in the world for these semiprecious stones. This may be a matter of opinion but the colours, ranging from honey through to delicate blue, justify the time spent grubbing around with a pick looking for them. **Cobbold Gorge**, at Robinhood Station (access to area permitted April–Oct only), 50km south of Forsayth on a passable dirt road, is a recently discovered and starkly attractive oasis inhabited by freshwater crocs and crayfish and surrounded by baking hot sandstone country. You can **camp** here at *Cobbold Camping Village* (℡07/4062 5470; to arrange a pick up from Georgetown or Forsayth call ℡07/4062 5386), who also organize **tours**, including a 4WD trip around the station and a scout up the kilometre-long gorge in a motorized punt – an excellent way to experience a very remote corner of the Outback.

Croydon

CROYDON, 150km west of Georgetown along the main road, was the site of Queensland's last major **goldrush** after two station hands found nuggets in a fence-post hole in 1885. For a brief period the region received the attention it had always craved: within five years the railway was built and lucky miners whooped it up at Croydon's 36 hotels, but by 1900 chaotic management had brought operations to a close. Today, most buildings predate 1920; the *Club Hotel* (last of the 36), the general store and the restored old courthouse all have their original fittings and offer directions to other scattered relics. There's also plenty of atmosphere, and if you're tempted to stay, the *Club Hotel* (℡07/4745 6184; ➎) has **beds** and there's a **van park** on the Georgetown side.

Moving on, buses and the main road plough on to Normanton, 154km west, as does the Gulflander **train** (see box on p.593); which leaves Croydon on Thursday mornings from the station on Helen Street. When the rails and sleepers were unloaded at Normanton's wharves in the nineteenth century they were meant to form the first stage of a line to Cloncurry, but this was redirected to Croydon when gold was found. At the height of the gold rush the service carried 200 passengers a week.

Normanton

Founded on the banks of the Norman River in 1868, **NORMANTON** was the Gulf's main port, connected to the Croydon goldfield by rail and Cloncurry's copper mines by camel train, and today the town has an air of faded splendour. The train still runs once a week to Croydon (see above) and also makes day-trips (June–Sept; $25) to a local waterhole for tea and damper. Set in gritty, flat country, Normanton's fortunes declined along with regional mineral deposits, and today there's only a collection of stores and service stations, a **bank** and **post office**, with shop awnings and a handful of trees providing scant shade. A worthy survivor of former times is the **Burns Philp Store**, whose timber shell, built in the 1880s, covers almost an acre; it's still in use as a general store and they haven't yet got around to installing air-conditioning.

Fishing for barramundi (check out Norman River Cruises; ☎07/4745 1347) is beginning to brighten the area's prospects, celebrated by the *Gulfland Motel* (☎07/4745 1290; ●) under the sign of the "Big Barra" at the south entrance to the town; the motel has a thick lawn and pleasant **rooms**. The *Normanton Van Park* (☎07/4745 1121) provides access to a shower block and the dubious choice of which bit of gravel to camp on. Normanton's **hotels** rate a mention, especially the luridly painted *Purple Pub*, and the *Albion* with its corrugated iron and wooden fittings – both are pretty frenetic watering holes. When you've had enough boozing, Karumba and routes on to western Cape York lie north, and Cloncurry is 400km south via the *Burke and Wills Roadhouse* (p.585) – both covered by Coral Coaches. To the west is the fuelless, 220-kilometre Burketown road, with features along the way including the site of Burke and Wills' northernmost camp near the Bynoe River, and the often difficult **Leichhardt River** crossing where the pocket-sized **Leichhardt Falls** contrasts with the aridity of the surrounding sand dunes, deposited each year when the river is in spate.

Karumba and the Gulf

Reached from Normanton across 70km of cracked, burning saltpan patrolled by saurus cranes and jabiru storks, **KARUMBA**'s tidy gardens are ridiculously suburban and camouflage the remote setting – betrayed the moment you buy a newspaper and realize that it's two days old. Once an airforce base for Catalina flying boats moving between Brisbane and Singapore, today the town is overlooked by huge **sheds** storing slurry from the Century Zinc Mine near Lawn Hill Gorge (p.591); the slurry is fed through pipes to Karumba, then shipped overseas for refining. Mostly, however, the town survives on prawn trawling and fishing; declining stocks of barramundi in the Gulf have inspired the **Barramundi Farm**, 2km from town along the river (daily 8.30–10.30am & 2.30–5pm; $3), which raises fish for release into the wild. One thing that you'll probably register is that there are no Aborigines in town; they shun the area, as many died in a tribal battle nearby.

The centre of town is a 250-metre stretch of Yappar Street, which runs along the Norman River's south bank. Coral Coach **buses** pull up outside the *Karumba Café* here, with services heading on to Mount Isa or back to Cairns three times a week. Luxuries include a **store**, Westpac **bank** (Tues & Thurs only) and a **post office**. *Sunset Park* is a good, central **campsite** (☎07/4745 9277), while *Matilda's End* (☎07/4745 9368; ●) has tidy units. You can also stay at the *Karumba Lodge* (☎07/4745 9121; ●), which started life as the airforce mess; the ramp that runs alongside the lodge down to the river was where the Catalina aircraft berthed. The *Lodge* has two **bars**: the infamous *Animal Bar* – which you should probably avoid unless you're extremely serious about drinking and occasional bouts of hand-to-hand combat – and the *Suave Bar*. For a more relaxing time and the chance to spot crocodile and birds, or catch something for the pot, contact Ferryman Cruises (☎07/4745 9155) or Katherine MII Fishing Charters (☎07/4745 9445). If you have your own tackle, Gulf Hire Boats (☎07/4745 9148) rents out four-metre-long tinnies from $55 for a half-day.

The Wellesleys and western Cape York
Gulf Freight Services on Yappar Street (☎07/4745 9333 or free call 1800 640 079) operates a weekly barge from Karumba to **Weipa** (see p.542 for more on Weipa itself). The journey takes around thirty hours, leaving on Friday and returning Tuesday. A one-way trip costs $235 including meals and cabin; prices for vehicles, which must be containerized, start at $420. Erratic services also go to the **Wellesley Group**, which comprises two dozen windswept islands north

of Burketown with excellent fishing around fragmented coral rubble. Never settled by whites, today they are Aboriginal communities with expensive but basic **resorts** on **Mornington Island** (⊕07/4745 7277; ❼) and **Sweers Island** (⊕07/4748 5544; ❼), catering to serious fishermen. Transfers ($160 per person, minimum of four) can be booked with Karumba Air Services on Yappar Street (free call ⊕1800 300 121), who can also fly you to Lawn Hill for the day ($250 per person, minimum of four).

Off-road drivers after wildlife might be tempted by superb **wetlands** on the western edge of the Cape York Peninsula, accessed from the Normanton–Karumba road off a 4WD-only, 500km track which ultimately takes you to Chillagoe (see p.528). Detouring north from it, you'll find the coast thick with creeks, waterholes and animals. **Dorunda Station** (food, drink and limited fuel supplies; ⊕07/4745 3477; units ❺), about 180km up the road, is a working cattle property which arranges hunting safaris with cameras or .303s – targets are pigs, fish, birds and crocodiles. There's more of the same even further north at **Mitchell and Alice Rivers National Park**, via the Aboriginal community of **Kowanyama**. You'll need to take all supplies for this, an NPWS permit and permission from the community (contact Cairns NPWS on ⊕07/4052 3096 for details).

Burketown and on to The Territory

Set on the Albert River some 230km west of Normanton, **BURKETOWN** balances on the dusty frontier between grassland and the Gulf's thirty-kilometre-deep, unfriendly coastal flats. Styled Queensland's "Barramundi Capital" after the delicious sports fish, it has a huge road maintenance depot employing most of its 235 inhabitants. Despite lukewarm fame for providing background to Nevil Shute's *A Town Like Alice*, there's little beyond the historic *Burketown Pub* (⊕07/4745 5104; units ❺), a hot artesian spring, a store, a couple of **fuel pumps** and a post office which also acts as the **tourist information** office and agent for day-flights to the Wellesley Islands (Mon–Fri 9am–5pm; ⊕07/4745 5111). The store runs a **campsite** but to engage in barra fishing, you'll need your own boat and fishing gear. To rent these, head for **Escott Lodge** (⊕07/4748 5577, ⓦwww.escott-lodge.com; units ❺), 16km west, where you can also go riding or mustering, or tour one of the Gulf's precarious cattle stations. There's a **restaurant** and **bar** at the lodge but no store.

The Hells Gate Track

The best road from Burketown heads south for about 120km to **Gregory Downs Hotel** and routes to Lawn Hill and Cloncurry (see p.584). If you're serious about **fishing** and have a 4WD, however, head 170km west from Burketown via *Tirranna Roadhouse* (food and fuel facilities) and the Aboriginal community at **Doomadgee**, to the **Hells Gate Roadhouse** (⊕07/4745 8258), 50km from the Northern Territory. Fishing information and guided tours can be obtained from the Savannah Guides here, or you could try **Massacre Inlet**, reached from **Wollogorang Station** (⊕08/8975 9944; ❻) just on The Territory border; they will supply you with a $12 fishing permit as well as camping, motel rooms, meals, beer and the last fuel before Borroloola. Giant anthills, pandanus-frilled waterholes and irregular tides are the rewards – and the area is stacked with wildlife, including **saltwater crocs**.

The road on from Hells Gate improves inside The Territory and once there you shouldn't have any trouble reaching Borroloola (see p.649), 266km down the track.

TRAVEL DETAILS

Trains

Barcaldine to: Emerald (2 weekly; 6hr); Longreach (2 weekly; 2hr); Rockhampton (2 weekly; 10hr).

Cairns to: Almaden (1 weekly; 6hr 30min); Forsayth (1 weekly; 2 days).

Charleville to: Brisbane (2 weekly; 17hr); Mitchell (2 weekly; 3hr 30min); Roma (2 weekly; 5hr); Toowoomba (2 weekly; 12hr).

Charters Towers to: Cloncurry (2 weekly; 11hr 30min); Hughenden (2 weekly; 5hr); Mount Isa (2 weekly; 20hr); Richmond (2 weekly; 7hr); Townsville (2 weekly; 2hr 30min).

Cloncurry to: Charters Towers (2 weekly; 11hr 30min); Hughenden (2 weekly; 8hr); Mount Isa (2 weekly; 4hr); Richmond (2 weekly; 5hr 30min); Townsville (2 weekly; 15hr).

Croydon to: Normanton (1 weekly; 4hr).

Emerald to: Barcaldine (2 weekly; 6hr); Longreach (2 weekly; 8hr); Rockhampton (2 weekly; 4hr 30min).

Forsayth to: Cairns (1 weekly; 2 days); Mount Surprise (1 weekly; 5hr 15min).

Hughenden to: Charters Towers (2 weekly; 5hr); Cloncurry (2 weekly; 8hr); Mount Isa (2 weekly; 11hr); Richmond (2 weekly; 2hr 10min); Townsville (2 weekly; 6hr).

Longreach to: Barcaldine (2 weekly; 2hr); Emerald (2 weekly; 8hr); Rockhampton (2 weekly; 12hr 30min).

Mitchell to: Brisbane (2 weekly; 14hr); Charleville (2 weekly; 4hr); Roma (2 weekly; 2hr); Toowoomba (2 weekly; 10hr).

Mount Isa to: Charters Towers (2 weekly; 15hr 30min); Cloncurry (2 weekly; 4hr 15min); Hughenden (2 weekly; 11hr); Richmond (2 weekly; 9hr); Townsville (2 weekly; 19hr).

Mount Surprise to: Cairns (1 weekly; 11hr).

Normanton to: Croydon (1 weekly; 4hr).

Richmond to: Charters Towers (2 weekly; 7hr); Cloncurry (2 weekly; 5hr 30min); Hughenden (2 weekly; 2hr 10min); Mount Isa (2 weekly; 9hr); Townsville (2 weekly; 9hr).

Roma to: Brisbane (2 weekly; 10hr 20min); Charleville (2 weekly; 5hr 10min); Mitchell (2 weekly; 2hr); Toowoomba (2 weekly; 11hr 40min).

Toowoomba to: Brisbane (2 weekly; 3hr 30min); Charleville (2 weekly; 12hr 30min); Mitchell (2 weekly; 10hr); Roma (2 weekly; 6hr 40min).

Buses

Barcaldine to: Anakie (2 weekly; 4hr); Blackall (1 daily; 1hr 15min); Brisbane (1 daily; 17hr); Chaleville (1 daily; 6hr); Cloncurry (1 daily; 8hr); Dingo (2 weekly; 6hr); Emerald (2 weekly; 4hr); Longreach (2 weekly; 2hr); Mitchell (1 daily; 13hr); Mount Isa (1 daily; 10hr); Rockhampton (2 weekly; 8hr); Roma (1 daily; 8hr); Toowoomba (1 daily; 13hr); Winton (1 daily; 6hr).

Charleville to: Barcaldine (1 daily; 6hr); Blackall (1 daily; 4hr 10min); Brisbane (2 daily; 10hr 40min); Cloncurry (1 daily; 13hr 30min); Longreach (1 daily; 6hr 30min); Mount Isa (2 daily; 15hr); Roma (2 daily; 3hr 40min); Toowoomba (2 daily; 8hr); Winton (1 daily; 9hr).

Charters Towers to: Camooweal (2 daily; 13hr); Cloncurry (2 daily; 8hr); Hughenden (2 daily; 3hr); Mount Isa (2 daily; 10hr); Richmond (2 daily; 5hr); Townsville (2 daily; 1hr 40min).

Cloncurry to: Camooweal (2 daily; 4hr 30min); Hughenden (2 daily; 5hr); Mount Isa (2 daily; 1hr 30min); Richmond (2 daily; 3hr 40min); Townsville (2 daily; 10hr).

Croydon to: Cairns (3 weekly; 10hr); Georgetown (3 weekly; 2hr 15min); Karumba (3 weekly; 3hr); Mount Surprise (3 weekly; 3hr 20min); Normanton (3 weekly; 2hr); Undara (3 weekly; 3hr 50min).

Emerald to: Anakie (2 weekly; 35min); Barcaldine (2 weekly; 3hr 40min); Dingo (1 daily; 1hr 35min); Longreach (2 weekly; 5hr 30min); Rockhampton (1 daily; 3hr 30min).

Georgetown to: Cairns (3 weekly; 6hr); Croydon (3 weekly; 2hr); Karumba (3 weekly; 5hr); Mount Surprise (3 weekly; 1hr); Normanton (3 weekly; 4hr); Undara (3 weekly; 1hr 35min).

Goondiwindi to: Brisbane (2 daily; 5hr); Toowoomba (2 daily; 3hr); Warwick (1 daily; 2hr 30min).

Karumba to: Cairns (3 weekly; 12hr); Croydon (3 weekly; 3hr 15min); Georgetown (3 weekly; 6hr); Mount Isa (3 weekly; 7hr 30min); Mount Surprise (3 weekly; 7hr); Normanton (3 weekly; 5hr); Undara (3 weekly; 7hr).

Longreach to: Anakie (2 weekly; 5hr); Barcaldine (1 daily; 1hr); Blackall (1 daily; 3hr 15min); Brisbane (1 daily; 16hr 10min); Charleville (1 daily; 6hr 30min); Cloncurry (1 daily; 6hr 30min); Dingo

(2 weekly; 7hr 30min); Emerald (2 weekly; 5hr 30min); Mitchell (1 daily; 8hr); Mount Isa (1 daily; 7hr 50min); Rockhampton (2 weekly; 9hr 30min); Roma (1 daily; 10hr 25min); Toowoomba (1 daily; 14hr); Winton (1 daily; 2hr).

Mitchell to: Barcaldine (1 daily; 7hr); Blackall (1 daily; 5hr); Brisbane (2 daily; 9hr); Charleville (1 daily; 2hr 10min); Cloncurry (1 daily; 15hr); Longreach (1 daily; 8hr); Mount Isa (1 daily; 16hr); Roma (2 daily; 1hr); Toowoomba (2 daily; 6hr); Winton (1 daily; 11hr).

Mount Isa to: Barcaldine (1 daily; 9hr); Blackall (1 daily; 11hr 10min); Brisbane (1 daily; 25hr 20min); Camooweal (2 daily; 2hr 10min); Charleville (1 daily; 14hr 40min); Charters Towers (2 daily; 9hr 50min); Cloncurry (2 daily; 2hr 35min); Hughenden (2 daily; 7hr); Karumba (1 weekly; 7hr 30min); Longreach (1 daily; 8hr); Mitchell (1 daily; 16hr); Richmond (2 daily; 6hr); Roma (1 daily; 18hr 20min); Toowoomba (1 daily; 23hr); Townsville (2 daily; 12hr); Winton (1 daily; 6hr).

Mount Surprise to: Cairns (3 weekly; 5hr); Croydon (3 weekly; 3hr); Georgetown (3 weekly; 1hr 30min); Karumba (3 weekly; 7hr); Normanton (3 weekly; 6hr); Undara (3 weekly; 30min).

Normanton to: Cairns (3 weekly; 10hr); Croydon (3 weekly; 2hr); Georgetown (3 weekly; 4hr); Karumba (3 weekly; 1hr); Mount Surprise (3 weekly; 5hr); Undara (3 weekly; 5hr 30min).

Richmond to: Charters Towers (2 daily; 5hr); Cloncurry (2 daily; 3hr); Hughenden (2 daily; 2hr); Mount Isa (2 daily; 4hr 30min); Townsville (2 daily; 7hr).

Flights

Charleville to: Brisbane (1 daily; 2hr).
Emerald to: Brisbane (2 daily; 2hr); Cairns (1–2 daily; 6hr 40min); Mackay (5 weekly; 5hr); Maroochydore (1 daily; 4hr 35min); Rockhampton (1–2 daily except Sun; 4hr); Townsville (1 daily except Sat; 4hr).
Longreach to: Brisbane (1 daily; 2hr 25min); Roma (5 weekly; 2hr).
Mount Isa to: Brisbane (1–2 daily; 2hr 15min);

Roma to: Barcaldine (1 daily; 8hr); Blackall (1 daily; 7hr); Brisbane (2 daily; 7hr); Charleville (1 daily; 3hr 30min); Cloncurry (1 daily; 16hr 20min); Longreach (1 daily; 10hr); Mitchel (2 daily; 1hr); Mount Isa (1 daily; 18hr); Toowoomba (2 daily; 4hr 30min); Winton (1 daily; 12hr).

Stanthorpe to: Brisbane (1 daily; 5hr); Toowoomba (2 daily; 2hr 30min); Warwick (2 daily; 40min).

Toowoomba to: Barcaldine (1 daily; 13hr); Blackall (1 daily; 12hr); Brisbane (8 daily; 1hr 50min); Charleville (1 daily; 8hr); Cloncurry (1 daily; 21hr 30min); Goondiwindi (2 daily; 3hr); Kingaroy (1 daily except Fri; 3hr); Longreach (1 daily; 14hr 30min); Mitchell (2 daily; 6hr); Mount Isa (1 daily; 23hr); Rockhampton (1 daily; 12hr 45min); Roma (2 daily; 5hr); Stanthorpe (2 daily; 2hr 30min); Surfers Paradise (2 daily; 3hr); Warwick (2 daily; 3hr); Winton (2 daily; 16hr 30min).

Undara to: Cairns (3 weekly; 4hr); Croydon (3 weekly; 4hr); Georgetown (3 weekly; 2hr); Karumba (3 weekly; 6hr); Mount Surprise (3 weekly; 30min); Normanton (3 weekly; 5hr).

Warwick to: Brisbane (2 daily; 3hr); Goondiwindi (1 daily; 2hr 30min); Stanthorpe (2 daily; 40min); Toowoomba (2 daily; 3hr).

Winton to: Barcaldine (1 daily; 3hr); Blackall (1 daily; 5hr 15min); Brisbane (1 daily; 19hr 25min); Charleville (1 daily; 9hr 20min); Cloncurry (1 daily; 4hr 30min); Longreach (1 daily; 2hr); Mitchell (1 daily; 11hr); Mount Isa (1 daily; 6hr); Roma (1 daily; 12hr 25min); Toowoomba (1 daily; 17hr).

Burketown (1 weekly; 1hr 35min); Cairns (1–2 daily; 5hr 20min); Mackay (1 daily except Sun; 8hr); Mornington Island (5 weekly; 1hr 50min); Rockhampton (1–2 daily; 4hr); Townsville (1–3 daily; 2hr).
Roma to: Brisbane (1–2 daily; 1hr 10min); Longreach (4 weekly; 2hr).
Winton to: Townsville (2 weekly; 1hr 25min).

Northern Territory

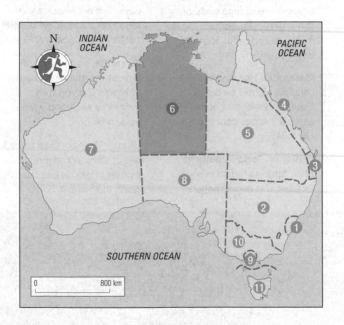

CHAPTER 6

Highlights

* **Kakadu National Park** – The rainforest, woodlands, swamps and wetlands of unspoilt Kakadu are a haven for Australian wildlife. p.623.

* **Arnhemland** – Step back in time into this vast wilderness – Australia before the Europeans arrived. p.631.

* **Katherine Gorge** – A cruise beneath the orange walls of this spectacular gorge makes a wonderful, leisurely day-trip. p.641.

* **Mataranka Hot Springs** – A candlelit night-time dip in Mataranka's idyllic palm-shaded thermal pool is blissful. p.646.

* **Henley on Todd Regatta in Alice Springs** – Held every October, this hugely popular event sees crowds cheering on bottomless boat races down the dry riverbed. p.663.

* **Hot-air ballooning around Alice** – Start the day with a champagne breakfast and a dawn flight over Alice in a hot-air balloon. p.665.

* **Chambers Pillar** – Used as a landmark by early overlanders, this enormous sandstone pillar lies in the desert 165km from Alice. p.676.

* **Kings Canyon** – Cool off amidst the stunning scenery of King's Canyon with a swim in a secluded waterhole. p.677.

* **Uluru** – The Aboriginal sacred site of Uluru, otherwise known as Ayers Rock, is emphatically worth the hype. p.679.

6

Northern Territory

Far in the north of Australia lies a little-known land, a vast half-finished sort of region, wherein Nature has been apparently practising how to make better places. This is the Northern Territory of South Australia . . . The decline and fall of the British Empire will date from the day that Britannia starts to monkey with the Northern Territory.

A.B. ("Banjo") Paterson, 1898

This rather ominous prophecy by the bush balladeer "Banjo" Paterson, author of "Waltzing Matilda", is still the way many Australians view the frontier lands of the **Northern Territory**, usually known as "The Territory", or simply "NT". Even the name conjures up a distant, untamed province and, to an extent, this is so: just over one percent of Australians (170,000) live in an area covering nearly twenty percent of the continent. Until recently this tiny population and lack of economic autonomy explained why The Territory never achieved full statehood. There was talk that by the new millennium the NT would have become the **seventh Australian state** (with a few strings still held by the federal government) but provincial politics has put this in the same basket as Australia becoming a republic. Incidents like the failed euthanasia bill (quickly quashed by Canberra) and extremes like mandatory sentencing (a fortnight in jail for a first offence, two months for a second, and so on), which has been linked in the press with some Aboriginal deaths in custody, give liberals the impression that some Territorian necks are redder than Ayers Rock at sunset.

Territorians relish this tough, maverick image, as well as the extremes of climate, distance and isolation that mould their temperaments. In this utmost corner of the country, drifters get washed up, fugitives cower and failed entrepreneurs pursue another abortive venture or become politicians. That great Australian institution of the "character" is in his element here, propping up the bars and bolstering the mythology of The Territory's recent lawless frontier history in what Xavier Herbert once described as the "Land of Ratbags". His classic 1938 novel, *Capricornia*, remains a scathing allegorical saga of the early Territorian years, based on Herbert's experience in 1930s Darwin.

Accommodation price codes

All the accommodation listed in this book has been categorized into one of eight price bands, as set out below. The rates quoted represent the cheapest available double or twin room in high season – except for category ❶, which indicates per-person rates for a dorm bed, and the categories given for units, cabins and vans, which represent the daily charge for the whole unit.

❶ Under $20   ❸ $35–50   ❺ $70–90   ❼ $115–150
❷ $20–35   ❹ $50–70   ❻ $90–115   ❽ $150 upwards

For more accommodation details, see pp.46–49.

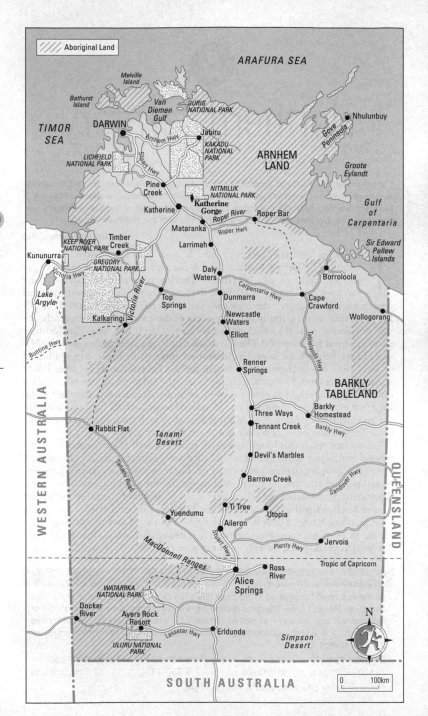

Aboriginal Land

ARAFURA SEA

Melville Island

Bathurst Island

Van Diemen Gulf

GURIG NATIONAL PARK

Nhulunbuy

TIMOR SEA

DARWIN

Jabiru

KAKADU NATIONAL PARK

ARNHEM LAND

Gove Peninsula

Groote Eylandt

LICHFIELD NATIONAL PARK

Arnhem Hwy

Stuart Hwy

Pine Creek

NITMILUK NATIONAL PARK

Katherine

Katherine Gorge

Roper River

Roper Bar

Gulf of Carpentaria

KEEP RIVER NATIONAL PARK

Timber Creek

Mataranka

Roper Hwy

Sir Edward Pellew Islands

Kununurra

Larrimah

GREGORY NATIONAL PARK

Victoria Hwy

Daly Waters

Carpentaria Hwy

Borroloola

Lake Argyle

Victoria River

Top Springs

Dunmarra

Cape Crawford

Wollogorang

Kalkaringi

Newcastle Waters

Elliott

Tablelands Hwy

Buntine Hwy

Renner Springs

BARKLY TABLELAND

WESTERN AUSTRALIA

Rabbit Flat

Tanami Desert

Three Ways

Barkly Homestead

Tennant Creek

Barkly Hwy

Tanami Road

Devil's Marbles

Barrow Creek

Sandover Hwy

QUEENSLAND

Yuendumu

Ti Tree

Aileron

Utopia

Stuart Hwy

Plenty Hwy

Jervois

MacDonnell Ranges

Tropic of Capricorn

WATARRKA NATIONAL PARK

Alice Springs

Ross River

Docker River

Ayers Rock Resort

Lasseter Hwy

Erldunda

Simpson Desert

N

ULURU NATIONAL PARK

SOUTH AUSTRALIA

0   100km

Within The Territory's boundaries there's evidence of the most recent colonial presence set among the oldest-occupied Aboriginal sites in Australia. **Darwin**, The Territory's capital, is a prospering tropical town – a year-round temperature in the low thirties compelling a laid-back lifestyle. Travellers the world over flock here to explore the **Top End** (as tropical NT is known), primarily **Kakadu National Park's** prolific wildlife and the Aboriginal art sites. Adjacent **Arnhemland**, to the east, is Aboriginal Land, too – and out of bounds to casual visitors, although a few tours are now beginning to visit this never-colonized wilderness of scattered communities. Heading south, you arrive at **Katherine**, where nearby gorges within the **Nitmiluk National Park** are the town's principal attraction. At Katherine, the **Victoria Highway** heads west, past the Gregory National Park to Western Australia, while to the south, just beyond the thermal resort of **Mataranka**, a road winds east along the palm-fringed Roper River to the Gulf Country. Here, **Borroloola**, a briefly thriving and lawless outpost, once on the Gulf stock route from northern Queensland, has since been bypassed into oblivion.

By the time you reach **Tennant Creek** you're out of the interminable light woodland and passing pastoral tablelands on the way to the central deserts surrounding **Alice Springs**. By no means the dusty Outback town many expect, Alice makes an excellent base to explore the natural wonders of the region, of which that famous monolith, **Ayers Rock** – or **Uluru** – 450km to the southwest, is but one of many. This is one of the finest areas to begin to learn about the Aborigines of the western desert, among the last to come into contact with European settlers.

Aborigines in the Northern Territory

Nearly a quarter of The Territory's inhabitants are Aborigines, a far higher proportion than anywhere else in Australia. Most modern maps show that over one-third of The Territory is **"Aboriginal Land"**, commercially unviable and returned to nominal Aboriginal control following lengthy land claims. This uniquely Territorian demography is the result of the formerly sympathetic federal government's co-operation with the politically powerful Land Councils within the NT, established following the Land Rights Act of 1976. Since that time, one of the most notable victories has been the return of the national park surrounding Uluru (Ayers Rock) to its traditional custodians in 1986. Excepting the national parks, Aboriginal lands are out of bounds to visitors without a permit or invitation, although some roads which cross them are exempt.

While the overwhelming majority of non-Aboriginal people tend to live in the two major urban centres of Darwin and Alice Springs, most Aborigines live in remote Outback communities, or **outstations**, in self-imposed isolation from modern white society. This is worth remembering before you judge the depressing spectacle of the Aboriginal underclass staggering around Katherine, Tennant Creek and Alice Springs. Estranged from their own "dry" communities, while at the same time alienated from the affluent white society that surrounds them, these people are the casualties of the catastrophic clash of white and Aboriginal culture which, in The Territory, is still within living memory. As Bill Harney, the first ranger at Ayers Rock, observed 35 years ago: "The traveller only sees the ones on the roadway, for should he want to visit one of the Aboriginal Reserves he has to go through a wall of red tape. Thus is the best side of Aboriginal life hidden and the worst exposed to our view." The same is true today.

The chasm between the two vastly different cultures is actually far greater than most visitors realize. The failure of assimilation – the naive policy of the

1950s and 1960s – added to mutual cultural (rather than racial) ignorance makes any meaningful contact for the short-term visitor unlikely. Weary suspicion of patronizing white curiosity, as well as an entirely different strategy in social dealings, render most exchanges awkward and superficial.

Despite the scandal of the "Third World" standards of living, Aboriginal **culture** is thriving. Political clout has encouraged self-determination and a renaissance of cultural pride in the face of overwhelming white control has enabled a self-expression in lifestyle, spirituality and – most obviously to the visitor – arts, crafts and tours. Gradually, progressive outstations are inviting responsible tour operators to visit their settlements, or else are setting up their own operations, so allowing you to experience something of their former way of life – for it must be remembered that even in The Territory no Aborigines live in or off the bush as they once did. Nevertheless, for those interested in getting to the heart of the enigmatic Australian wilderness, the Northern Territory personifies the remote and mythologized Outback, offering enriching and memorable travel: an introduction to a land that has sustained a fascinating and sophisticated culture for at least sixty thousand years.

Darwin and the Top End

Darwin, The Territory's capital, lies midway along Australia's convoluted northern coast. Most tourists end up spending no more time here than it takes to visit nearby **Kakadu** and **Litchfield national parks**, continue their Australian circuit or fly on to Indonesia. Until recently the city had little appeal to short-term visitors, but things have changed and Darwin is beginning to mature into a worthwhile destination in itself.

Darwin and around

Establishing a European settlement on Australia's remote northern shores was never going to be easy. It took four abortive attempts over a period of 45 years before **DARWIN** (originally called Palmerston) was surveyed in 1869 by the new South Australian state keen to exploit its recently acquired "northern territory". The early colonists' aim was to pre-empt foreign occupation and create a trading post, a "new Singapore", for the British Empire.

Things got off to a good start with the arrival in 1872 of the **Overland Telegraph Line** (OTL), following the route pioneered by explorer **John McDouall Stuart** in 1862, that finally linked Australia with the rest of the world. **Gold** was discovered at Pine Creek while pylons were being erected for the OTL, prompting the inevitable goldrush, and the construction of a southbound railway. After the goldrush subsided, a cyclone flattened the depressed

Top End weather

There is a certain amount of misunderstanding about the tropical climate of the Top End, usually summed up as the hot and humid "Dry" and the hotter and very humid "Wet". Give or take a couple of weeks either way, this is the pattern: the Dry begins in April when rains stop and humidity decreases – although this always remains high in the tropics, whatever the season. It may take a couple of months for vehicular access to be restored to all far-flung tracks, but the bush never looks greener, while engorged waterfalls pound the base of the escarpments. From now until October skies are generally cloud-free with daily temperatures reliably peaking in the low thirties, though August nights might cool down to 10°C – sheer agony for seasoned Top Enders but bliss for unacclimatized tourists.

From October until the end of the year temperatures and humidity begin to rise – the dreaded Build Up. Clouds accumulate to discharge brief showers, and it's a time of year when the weak-willed or insufficiently drunk can go "troppo" as the unbearable tensions of heat and humidity push them over the edge. Around November promising storms can still be frustratingly dry but often give rise to spectacular lightning shows; Darwin is the world's most lightning-prone city. While rain showers become longer and more frequent towards Christmas – the onset of the Wet – access on sealed roads is rarely a problem.

Only when the actual monsoon commences at the turn of the year do the daily afternoon storms quickly rejuvenate and then saturate the land. This daily cycle lasts for at least three months and is much more tolerable than you might expect, with a daily thunderous downpour cooling things off from the mid- to the low-thirties. Along with Queensland's Cape York, Darwin's proximity to the equator gives it a true monsoon. Two hundred kilometres south the rains are much less heavy, though a Wet is experienced along the coast as far southwest as Derby, WA and Townsville on the north Queensland coast.

Cyclones, sometimes just a week apart, occur most commonly at either end of the Wet and can dump 30cm of rain in as many hours, with winds of 100kph and gusts twice that speed. Frequent updates on the erratic path and intensity of these tropical depressions are given on national and state radio, so that most people are fully prepared if and when the storm actually hits. Some fizzle out or head back out to sea; others can intensify and zigzag across the land, as nearly every community between Exmouth, WA (1996) and Darwin (1974) has found to its cost.

town in 1897, but by 1911, when Darwin adopted its present name, the rough-and-ready frontier outpost had grown into a small government centre, servicing the mines and properties of the Top End. In 1942, just five years after a second cyclone had razed the town, repeated **Japanese air raids** destroyed Darwin yet again – this time at a human cost of hundreds of lives (a fact concealed for years from the jittery nation). The fear of invasion, and an urgent need to get troops to the war zone, led to the swift construction of the Stuart Highway, the first reliable land link between Darwin and the rest of the country.

Three decades of guarded postwar prosperity followed until Christmas Day, 1974, when **Cyclone Tracy** devastated Darwin. For many residents this trauma was the last straw and having been evacuated they never returned. Indeed, the myth of Darwinian resilience is just that: the town has always accommodated a transient, easy-going population, happy to "give it a go" for a couple of years and then move on. The surrounding land is agriculturally unviable and Top End beef (an industry hampered by disease-eradication programmes and foreign competition) is among the poorest in Australia; most beef is exported as live cattle to Asia.

Palmerston and Alice Springs ▽

But since the mid-Nineties Darwin has been making a concerted effort to take itself seriously as Australia's commercial "gateway" into Asia. With the help of the tourist boom, kicked off by Kakadu's exposure in the film *Crocodile Dundee*, as well as some thoughtful refurbishments in Mitchell Street and the Mall, Darwin has shaken off the bland feel of a company town armoured against the climate. A spate of cool new outdoor eateries now allow you to appreciate the tropical ambience so that where once the city centre had all the life of a weekend car park, now it can be as lively as any other Australian capital. The NT government has even started work on an Alice to Darwin rail link, but many locals will believe it when they see it despite promises for completion within the next few years.

Day-trips from Darwin include the popular national parks, Kakadu and Litchfield (see pp.623 & 634) as well as the Aboriginal-owned Bathurst and Melville islands (see p.621), which are a thirty-minute flight from town. They are Australia's largest islands after Tasmania and are well worth more than just a flying visit, if you can afford it. Also worth a visit are Crocodylus Park (see p.617) and the Territory Wildlife Park (see p.634).

Arrival and information

All flights arrive at **Darwin Airport**, 12km northeast of the city centre. A **shuttle bus** service (☎08/8981 5066 or free call 1800 358 945; $7.50) meets international flights and drops you off at all major hotels or delivers you to the central **Transit Centre** behind 69 Mitchell St; a **taxi** (☎13 1008) to town from the airport costs about $16. Given the proximity of Indonesia, Darwin is the cheapest place from which to leave Australian soil (see "Listings", p.620, for details).

Renting and buying a vehicle: some tips

The hit-and-run pace and variable guide quality of many Kakadu tours has made the renting of a car or campervan big business in Darwin. The advantages of driving yourself are obvious and with a group of three or four you can end up paying less than with a tour. At the bottom end of the trade, a car can cost as little as $25 a day plus a typical surcharge rate of 25¢ for each kilometre. Alternatively you can pay up to $35 with 100 free kilometres – handy for a day round town – or around $70 a day with unlimited kilometres. The older the cars the company offers, the lower their charges.

Seemingly special deals for the standard Kakadu/Litchfield run (eg $200 for three days with 1000km free) are commonly offered, but note that this trip will easily clock up 1200km and clued-in operators price accordingly. As mentioned overleaf, it's an open secret in the trade that all cars booked though the DRTA come with unlimited kilometres, no matter what the actual rental company may be charging itself. It's a good offer that most operators stick to and which could work only in a small town such as Darwin.

It's important to understand the limitations of your insurance and where you can drive conventional cars. Basically, with one or two clearly defined exceptions, you cannot take your $25-a-day sedan on unsealed roads, and any underbody, roof, windscreen and water damage is down to you. Your insurance obligations are something that not all companies spell out, but be assured that if you damage their car you end up paying. An additional premium of a few dollars a day can reduce this liability to a few hundred dollars. Local operators know too well that European drivers are unused to the vagaries of driving on cambered dirt roads and that sliding off into the bushes or hitting a tree are common accidents. If you get tempted to take to the dirt, remember that even with the windows shut and air-con on recycle, fine dust will leave a clear message of where you've been. Bear in mind, though, that whatever you drive and whatever you pay in surcharges, most rental vehicles – even 4WDs – are uninsured off the bitumen. If you have an accident here, you pay dearly. It's a way of ensuring that people take it easy on the dirt roads or don't leave the highway at all.

Wherever you go from Darwin distances are long. The Territory has Australia's highest death rate on the roads: a combination of drunkenness, fatigue and the dangers of wandering stock and wild animals. New laws and speed traps are desperately trying to reduce this, but avoid trying to pack in a Katherine and Kakadu run in a couple of days, take it easy if driving top-heavy 4WDs on dirt roads and avoid driving at night in rural areas.

Self-contained campervan rentals have boomed across Australia over the last few years and in Darwin they are available from $90 a day with unlimited kilometres, although most companies specify a few days minimum rental. The smallest models can get crowded with more than two people, but the savings in accommodation and the independence offered make them a great way to see the parks or even the whole country. Like ordinary cars, campervans must stick to sealed roads unless you opt for the 4WD models.

Many visitors assume a 4WD will allow them to really see Kakadu but it's not essential. Built to take a beating, a Toyota Land Cruiser will cost around $150 a day and use twice as much fuel as an ordinary car, although the only road in Kakadu where you need a 4WD is the Jim Jim/Twin Falls track (see p.630), which involves crossing Jim Jim Creek. Several vehicles have been lost here over the years and even in a "four-wheeler" some companies may still exclude this track so make sure you ask.

If you're prepared to leave Twin Falls off your itinerary, it's a bit cheaper (if less fun) to rent a so-called off-road vehicle, such as the chunky 2WD twin-cab utes supplied by Territory Thrifty Rental Cars. Nifty Car Rental, on Mitchell Street, are sympathetic to the demands of Rough Guide readers if you explain exactly where you want to go.

If you're looking to buy a vehicle, hostel notice boards are an excellent starting-point, or check to see if the semi-squatted lot on Mitchell Street behind the Night Markets has any prospective sellers parked up.

On the other hand, Darwin is a long way from anywhere in Australia – the bus journey from Cairns takes a gruelling day and a half, including changes, and coming direct from Sydney, Melbourne or Perth, you'd do much better to fly. **Interstate buses** arrive behind the Transit Centre, where you can make reservations for onward journeys. After years of political chitchat and endless red tape, work finally began in early 2000 on the **Alice to Darwin rail** link. The implications of this are not yet clear but it is hoped that the line will open up the centre and provide a viable alternative to road or air transport.

Five-minutes' walk up Mitchell Street, the **Darwin Regional Tourism Association** (daily 9am–5pm; ℡08/8981 4300, ✉info@drta.com.au) is the official tourist information outlet and has a **Parks and Wildlife Commission (P&WC)** desk with plenty of material on national parks throughout NT. It's also worth noting that local rental cars booked through the DRTA come with unlimited kilometres (see box overleaf). All around town you'll find several other independent tourist information offices, all competing for their slice of the cake; shop around before you shell out a couple of hundred dollars on a tour. The free booklets *This Week In Darwin* and *Darwin and the Top End Today*, which can be picked up all around town, are mostly rose-tinted advertorials, but are handy for **maps**, including bus routes (see below). A five-hundred-metre radius around Smith Street Mall encompasses Darwin's city centre, catering for most of your needs; there are few attractions in the sea of suburbs spreading towards the north and the east. Also worth checking out is the Northern Territory Holiday Centre **website** at ⓦwww.ntholidays.com.au.

City transport

The city's inexpensive **bus service** (maximum fare $2.20 for all three zones; pay the driver) can deliver you to most corners of Darwin. Services operate daily from around 7am to 8pm, with some routes running until after 11pm on Friday and Saturday. "Multirider" tickets are also available, giving you ten trips for $17.50. Another alternative is the "Tourcard" which gives unlimited travel for seven days for $25. One-day cards cost $5. The **bus terminal** (℡08/8924 7666) is on Harry Chan Avenue, at the bottom of Cavenagh Street, plus there's also a major interchange in the shopping centre at Casuarina, in the northern suburbs. Buses leave the city for the suburbs along Cavenagh Street and come back in along Mitchell and Smith streets. They head out as far as Palmerston, Howard Springs and, on weekdays, Humpty Doo, 50km from town on the Kakadu road.

Most hostels and some hotels rent out **bicycles** for $15 a day. Although Darwin is flat, it's also hot and humid, so East Point Reserve, 8km from the centre, is about as far as you'd want to ride for fun. Along Mitchell and Smith streets, a few local **car rental** outfits do battle, with prices starting at around $25 a day, plus a kilometre fee (see box, overleaf and "Listings", p.621, for more). **Taxis** work out at about a dollar a kilometre and there are plenty cruising around: either hail one on the street or give them a call on ℡13 1008.

Accommodation

Darwin has plenty of **accommodation**, from luxury hotels to hostels galore, and most of it is conveniently central. During the wet season (Jan–March) prices in the upmarket establishments can take a dive, with half-price weekend packages frequently available. In the hostels it seems the price has settled at around $15 a bed, but brief price wars can flare up at any time of the year.

Hotels, motels and apartments

Most **hotels** and **motels** are right in the city centre, with the more prestigious examples found along the Esplanade offering views of the bay. If you're looking for self-catering accommodation, there are several **apartment–hotels** in the centre, but for the most part they're further out.

Air Raid City Lodge 35 Cavenagh St (T 08/8981 9214, F 8981 6024). Survivor of Cyclone Tracy, the windowless singles and doubles can be dingy but the bright "family" room suits a group. Communal kitchen and TV in every room. Ten percent discount for Rough Guide readers. ④–⑤

Atrium Novotel, 100 Esplanade (T 08/8941 0755, F 8981 9025, E novotel@topend.com.au). Upmarket hotel along the Esplanade with a foliage-draped atrium and all the comforts and service you'd expect, as well as a sea view. ⑧

City Gardens Apartments, 93 Woods St (T 08/8941 2888, F 8981 2934, W www.citygardensapts.com.au). Centrally located family units with a pool. Two-minutes' walk from Frogshollow Park, five minutes from town. ⑧

Darwin Central Hotel, Knuckley St (T 08/8944 9000, F 8944 9100, W www.allseasons.com.au).

Excellent All Seasons luxury hotel right by the Mall with spacious rooms, several restaurants and bars, and friendly and knowledgeable staff. ⑧

Palms Motel, 100 McMinn St (T 08/8981 4188, F 8981 4415, W www.palmsmotel.citysearch.com.au). Good-sized rooms, pool and off-street parking make this one of Darwin's better-value motels. ⑤

Top End Hotel, cnr Mitchell and Daly streets (T 08/8981 6511 or free call 1800 626 151, F 8981 1253). Well-kept motel-style rooms in Darwin's "party pub", complete with garden and pool. ⑧

Value Inn, 50 Mitchell St (T 08/8981 4733, F 8981 4730). Set price, no-frills motel with small en-suite rooms (TV, air-con and fridge) that sleep up to three – a real squeeze but a good deal and there's a pool too. ④

Hostels

The situation for backpackers' **hostels** in Darwin has improved in recent years with the opening of the *YHA* and *Chilli's Backpackers* next door to each other and introducing "East Coast" standards to the Top End. Note that some establishments offer a free pick-up on the airport shuttle if you book with them in advance and also that some places charge a dollar or two extra for beds in air-conditioned rooms or run the air conditioning only at night.

Banyan View Lodge, 119 Mitchell St (T 08/8981 8644 or free call 1800 249 124, F 8981 6104, E bookings@travel-ys.com). Quiet with well-kept twin rooms with fans and fridge and big recreational rooms. Rooms ⑧, dorms ❶

Chilli's Backpackers, 69a Mitchell St (T 08/8949 9722 or free call 1800 351 313, F 8941 9835). The old YHA half knocked down and cleverly redesigned with airy decks to eat, chat or sunbake by the pool, internet café and travel shop. Doubles ④, dorms ❷

CWA Hostel, 3 Packard Place (T & F 8941 3305). Not a backpackers' place but a small, shady house in its own grounds for women, couples and families only. Rooms ④, dorms ❶

Elke's, 112 Mitchell St (T 08/8981 8399 or free call 1800 808 365, F 8981 2834, W www.elkesbackpackers.com.au). Friendly old house at the quiet end of Mitchell St, with a shady pool and free pick-ups from airport: and a good tour desk. Rooms ⑧, dorms ❶

Frogshollow Backpackers, 27 Lindsay St (T 08/8941 2600 or free call 1800 068 686, F 8941 0758, E frogs@octa4.net..au). Attractive,

tropical building opposite a large park, with friendly new owners who are big on cleanliness. Rooms ⑧, dorms ❶

Gecko Lodge, 146 Mitchell St (T 08/8981 5569 or free call 1800 811 250, F 8981 3680, W www.ozemail.com.au/austour/). At the far end of Mitchell St, a small, friendly hostel with a pool. Free breakfast pancakes and Tuesday sausage sizzle. Airport pick-ups and nightly lifts uptown. Rooms ⑧, dorms ❶

Globetrotters, 97 Mitchell St (T 08/8981 5385, F 8981 9096, W www.globetrotters.com.au). Ex-motel with a pool and licensed bar that shows live European football on TV and holds music jam sessions, making up for shabby rooms. Rooms ⑤, dorms ❶

Melaleuka Lodge, 52 Mitchell St (T 08/8941 3395 or free call 1800 623 543, F 8941 3368, W www.darwin-backpackers.com.au). Well-run, popular and well-equipped warren of rooms and courtyards right opposite the Transit Centre. Air-con in all rooms. Rooms ④, dorms ❷

Whoop Whoop Backpackers, 151 Mitchell St (T 08/8941 1295 or free call 1800 808 151,

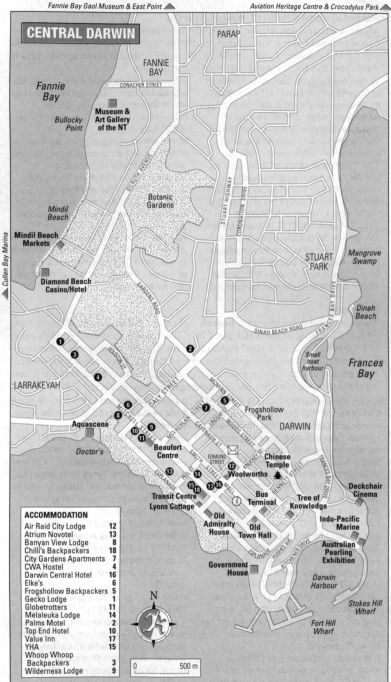

CENTRAL DARWIN

PARAP

FANNIE
BAY

*Fannie
Bay*

CONACHER STREET

Museum &
Art Gallery
of the NT

*Bullocky
Point*

Botanic
Gardens

*Mindil
Beach*

Mindil Beach
Markets

STUART
PARK

*Mangrove
Swamp*

Diamond Beach
Casino/Hotel

GILRUTH AVENUE

GARDENS ROAD

STUART HIGHWAY

CORONATION DRIVE

*Dinah
Beach*

DINAH BEACH ROAD

FRANCES BAY DRIVE

*Small
boat
harbour*

*Frances
Bay*

▲ *Cullen Bay Marina*

LARRAKEYAH

HOUSTON ST

DALY STREET

MITCHELL STREET

MCLACHLAN STREET

CAVENAGH ST

SMITH STREET

MCMINN STREET

LINDSAY ST

WOODS STREET

Frogshollow
Park

DARWIN

Aquascene

Doctor's

ESPLANADE

Beaufort
Centre

EDMUND
STREET

PEEL ST

SMITH STREET MALL

KNUCKEY ST

BENNETT STREET

FRANCES BAY DRIVE

Chinese
Temple

Woolworths

Deckchair
Cinema

Transit Centre
Lyons Cottage

Bus
Terminal

Tree of
Knowledge

Indo-Pacific
Marine

Old
Admiralty
House

Old
Town Hall

HUGHES AVE

KITCHENER DRIVE

Australian
Pearling
Exhibition

Government
House

*Darwin
Harbour*

*Stokes Hill
Wharf*

*Fort Hill
Wharf*

ESPLANADE

ACCOMMODATION

Air Raid City Lodge	12
Atrium Novotel	13
Banyan View Lodge	8
Chilli's Backpackers	18
City Gardens Apartments	7
CWA Hostel	4
Darwin Central Hotel	16
Elke's	6
Frogshollow Backpackers	5
Gecko Lodge	1
Globetrotters	11
Melaleuka Lodge	14
Palms Motel	2
Top End Hotel	10
Value Inn	17
YHA	15
Whoop Whoop Backpackers	3
Wilderness Lodge	9

N

0   500 m

ⓕ 8942 0719, ⓔ whoopwhoop@ozemail.com.au). Friendly, comfortably converted house featuring a pool, free meal vouchers, good-size doubles, tour-booking service and lifts uptown. Pool promised for 2001. Rooms ❹, dorms ❶

Wilderness Lodge, 88 Mitchell St (ⓣ 08/8941 8363 or free call 1800 068 886, ⓕ 8941 3360, ⓦ www.wildlodge.com.au). Breezy outdoor feel

with pool, BBQ, pick-ups and air-con dorms. Rooms ❹, dorms ❶

YHA, 69 Mitchell St (ⓣ 08/8981 3995, ⓕ 8981 6674). Refurbished modern, clean and thoughtfully designed hostel resort right by the Transit Centre. Breezy dining area overlooks the pool. Rooms ❸, dorms ❶

Camping and caravan parks

The following **camping** and **caravan parks** are both along the Stuart Highway in Winnellie, between 7km and 14km from the centre. Comments by visitors at the DRTA have not been kind to Darwin's caravan parks and Winnellie itself is a rather godforsaken light-industrial suburb, lying along the southern edge of the airport. Many of Darwin's caravan parks are pitched at long-term stays or touring retirees. Buses #5 and #8 run here from the central bus terminal. From the airport it's only a five-minute taxi ride.

Overlander Caravan Park, cnr Stuart Highway and McMillans Rd, Berrimah (ⓣ 08/8984 3025). Plenty of shade and lawns and close to shops. On-site vans ❸

Shady Glen Caravan Park, cnr Farrell Crescent and Stuart Highway (ⓣ 08/8984 3330). Pool and kiosk with tent sites. On-site vans ❹

The City

Present-day Darwin projects north from the end of a stubby peninsula where a settlement was originally established in 1869 on the lands of the Larrakeyah Aborigines. Over the years, the suburbs have spread across the flat, mangrove-fringed headland, but for the visitor most of the points of interest lie between the city and East Point, 8km to the north. Tropical vegetation apart, it's by no means a good-looking city: huge tides create a warm, sludge-filled sea devoid of waves, while repeated destruction from cyclones, air raids and termites has left any surviving colonial architecture discreet and intermittent.

Short of renting a car or a bike, the **Tour Tub** (daily 9am–4pm; day-ticket $25 ⓣ 08/8981 5233) is a fun way to see most of the places detailed below over a day. Departing on the hour from Smith Street Mall, opposite Woolworth's, the minibus trundles along its route allowing you to hop on and off as you please.

The Wharf Precinct

Slow but sure development is refashioning **Stokes Hill Wharf** at the southern end of town into a thriving new tourist precinct. Souvenir shops and alfresco cafés have sprung up along the pier which comes to life every evening. Well worth a visit is the live coral display at **Indo-Pacific Marine** (daily: April–Oct 10am–5pm; Nov–March 9am–1pm; $15.40; ⓣ 08/8981 1294). In the right frame of mind, you could spend hours observing these marine environments, and the regular informative talks will set you straight about corals – the Timor Sea north of Darwin is one of the world's richest and most diverse coral environments, obscured by an overabundance of tidal silt. The night tours are something else and include dinner, with wine (bookings essential). In the same building, the **Australian Pearling Exhibition** (Mon–Fri 10am–5pm, Sat & Sun 10am–5.30pm; $6) is a similarly imaginative display, entertainingly describing Darwin's part in northern Australia's pearling exploits.

Round the other side of the harbour, a stairway up the cliff just past the Oil Storage Tunnels (on the Tour Tub itinerary, but about as interesting as they sound) leads up to a viewing point and to **Government House**, built in 1883 after the original residence was devoured by white ants. Rarely open to the public, it's nevertheless a good example of an elegant, though much restored, tropical building.

The City Centre

There are more old buildings on nearby Smith Street. The **Old Town Hall** (1883) was practically demolished by Cyclone Tracy, but its ruins occasionally host outdoor performances by the theatre group based in the stone building, **Brown's Mart**, opposite. In the park behind Brown's Mart is a huge banyan tree known as the **Tree of Knowledge**, while nearby stands the ornate **Chinese Temple** (Mon–Fri 8am–4pm, Sat & Sun 8am–3pm) on Woods Street, near the corner of Bennett Street. Another post-cyclone restoration, using the altar and statues from the 1887 original, this still serves Darwin's Chinese population – considerably diminished since the early days of white settlement, when Chinese labourers were responsible for building virtually everything, including the former railway down to Pine Creek.

From the temple take a walk through the city's commercial heart: the restyled **Smith Street Mall** or known just as the **Mall** these days. The new look was at the cost of a few trees but there's a **walk-through fountain** which tempts passers-by with a quick plunge and your willpower will be much depleted after a good session at the **Hotel Victoria** – as the erstwhile *Vic*, it was once Darwin's answer to a Wild West saloon and some clients are still having trouble adjusting to the city's pub-gentrification programme. All along and off the Mall several art galleries and gift shops entice you to buy Aboriginal crafts or Australiana. From here, a left turn down Knuckey Street leads to the Esplanade, where two more buildings await inspection. On the left corner is the former **Admiralty House** (Mon–Sat 10am–5pm; free), a tropical-style house elevated on stilts that has survived cyclones and air raids. Opposite, **Lyons Cottage** (daily 10am–5pm; free), a stone bungalow, also dates from the 1920s, with displays of early Territorian history and the Overland Telegraph Line (OTL) in particular. For a diversion step round to the **Mitchell Street Tourist Precinct**. Formerly a backpackers' ghetto, it has been redefined with the help of a few outdoor bars and cafés, night markets and occasional entertainment into somewhere to linger rather than loiter.

A pleasant walk along the lawns of the **Esplanade** leads to Daly Street, which marks the very end of the Stuart Highway. From here it's a straight 1500-kilometre run to Alice Springs with only about half a dozen traffic lights on the way. Otherwise, a left turn down Doctor's Gully leads to the ever-popular **Aquascene** (call ☏08/8981 7837 for tide-dependent opening hours; $5), where at high tide scores of catfish, mullet and metre-long milkfish come in to be hand-fed on stale bread (supplied free).

Cullen Bay Marina and the Fannie Bay museums

Walking north down the full length of Smith Street will bring you to a small roundabout and a sign leading down to **Cullen Bay Marina**. Like most marina's around the world there's not much to do here except observe "yachties" fiddling with their boats, envy those who can afford to live here, poke around the "speciality" shops, and enjoy a waterside meal or a drink. Apart from taking one of the harbour cruises or the jet shuttle over the harbour to Mandurah's deserted beaches (☏08/8981 7600) that about sums up Cullen Bay, but it's well worth at least one visit just to mingle in the reflected light of the sails and deliberate on your dream vessel.

From the centre it's a two-kilometre walk north to the **Botanic Gardens** (daily 7am–7pm; free), Darwin's main park, housing a large collection of palms as well as a separate Plant Display House (daily 7.30am–4pm). A further kilometre north brings you to the excellent **Museum and Art Gallery of the NT** (Mon–Fri 9am–5pm, Sat & Sun 10am–5pm; free) on Conacher Street, overlooking Fannie Bay. An excellent museum and art gallery, it's particularly notable for its Southeast Asian perspective, in pleasing contrast to the usual focus on recent white achievements. With an absorbing display of Aboriginal art by the Tiwi people of Bathurst and Melville islands as well as Top End bark paintings and the familiar pointillist style of the Central deserts, there's just enough here to keep your attention without seeing dots yourself. Elsewhere the stuffed remains of "Sweetheart", a five-metre-long rogue crocodile with a taste for outboard engines, are particularly alarming, while the massive boat shed is a mariners' paradise, with boats as diverse as pearling luggers, Indonesian *praus*, Polynesian outriggers and the simplest of bark canoes.

There's also an imaginatively designed exhibition commemorating Darwin's destruction by **Cyclone Tracy**. By 3am on Christmas Day, 1974 – a day that most Darwinians who lived through the cyclone would like to forget – the worst was thought to be over as winds that had raged since midnight began to abate. Instead, the becalmed eye of the storm was passing over the part-ruined city, only to return with even greater fury from the opposite direction. Lampposts were bent flat along the ground, houses were ripped from their piers, and at the Yacht Club mangled remains of boats filled the car park. Mercifully, a low tide meant that only 66 people lost their lives, but Tracy marked the end of old Darwin, psychologically as well as architecturally.

Fannie Bay Gaol Museum (daily 10am–5pm; free; bus #4 or #6), further north along the bay, 5km from the city centre, served as Darwin's prison for nearly a hundred years until 1979. Displayed alongside the grim prisoners' quarters is an old train, a reminder of the thorny issue of Darwin's rail link with the rest of the country. This has been promised by successive campaigning prime ministers and with Darwin's current boom has yet again been resurrected.

On to East Point

Right by the Gaol Museum, the main route (and buses #4 and #6) curves right, while East Point Road continues straight up to the **East Point Reserve**, an area of largely natural bushland that's home to around two thousand wallabies. After a kilometre you pass **Lake Alexander**, a recreational saltwater lake suitable for year-round swimming and, nearby, a **mangrove boardwalk** takes you into the tidal environment.

The road ends 3km from the former prison at the **Military Museum** (daily 9.30am–5pm; $5) and **gun turrets**. Most visitors – and quite a few Australians – are unaware that Darwin was repeatedly bombed by the Japanese in 1942; at the time, news of both the air raids and the thirty thousand enemy troops massed on Timor, awaiting the order to invade, was suppressed. The museum commemorates these events with a short video and some rather staid displays of uniforms, medals and other wartime memorabilia, while in the grounds a collection of neglected World War II guns, aircraft engines and associated hardware quietly rusts away. At the top of East Point, the guns themselves were never actually fired and the huge barrels were eventually sold ten years later as scrap to – ironically – the Japanese. East Point is also an ideal spot to watch the striking hues of Darwin's multichrome sunsets; if driving, watch out for roadside wallabies on the way back.

Aviation Heritage Centre, Crocodylus Park and Charles Darwin National Park

Set in a hangar off the Stuart Highway, on the southeastern edge of the airport, the non-profit **Aviation Heritage Centre** (daily 9am–5pm; $11; bus #5 or #8) is easily dominated by the huge bulk of a B52 bomber on loan from the US Air Force. The museum offers an alternative history to Southeast Asia and the Top End through the engaging story of civil and military aviation in the region.

Further down the Stuart Highway, and taking a left at the Berrimah traffic lights, leads you to the crocodile research facility and farm of **Crocodylus Park** (daily 9am–5pm; tours 10am, noon, 2pm; $18; bus #5) in McMillans Road. No visit to Australia is complete without a close look at these prehistoric-looking beasts and in the croc-filled lagoon you can get within kissing distance of a three-metre man eater should one happen to doze off right by the fence. These usually dormant reptiles are coaxed into action during daily feeding sessions which coincide with tours led by excellent guides, and there's an absorbing museum giving you the lowdown on the world of crocs.

Returning along Tiger Brennan Drive you can pay a visit to the new **Charles Darwin National Park**, designated to protect an area of natural bushland against a rash of surrounding development. Along with views onto the city and a few wartime storage hangars, **mangroves** is what it's all about down here. Although not much to look at, mangroves provide a crucial and biodiverse coastal habitat. Nearly eighty percent of the world's many species are found in tropical NT. The trees' salt-tolerant root systems inhibit coastal erosion, filter the water and provide shelter to everything from mud crabs and crocs to pesky sandflies which can waltz through mosquito nets five abreast. Altogether the park's a nice spot for a picnic, a walk or a traffic-free cycle: just don't forget some repellent for the insects.

Darwin's beaches

Several factors exclude Darwin from being the beach resort you might have hoped for. A high tidal range, the fierce tropical sun, sheets of mangroves and the seasonal but deadly menace of stinging box jellyfish (from Oct to May) – which rules out swimming in the sea at the hottest time of year – mean that, despite its few beaches, you're rarely pushed for a spot to roll out your towel. Traps in the harbour regularly capture *most* of the crocodiles. **Fannie Bay**'s beaches (bus #4 or #6) are closest to the town centre and have a kiosk and water craft rental. However, the **Casuarina Coastal Reserve** (bus #4 or #10; 40min), capping the northern suburbs, has the city's least unattractive sandy stretches, including a "free beach" for nudists. A good place to splash about is **Lee Point**, mainly used by sunset dog walkers and found at the end of Lee Point Road, directly north of the airport.

Eating

There have been big improvements in the ambience of Darwin's restaurants in the last few years, and they've finally realized that whatever you're eating, sitting in an open-air tropical environment with a few palms flapping about is far more agreeable than inside an air-con box. For a city of this size, there's a wide selection of good-quality options for every budget – certainly enough to keep your taste buds busy. Adventurous carnivores can tackle exotic meats such as **kangaroo**, **buffalo**, **camel** and **crocodile**, though they're often more memorable running about in the bush than on a plate. Ironically, the climate makes it likely that **seafood** will have been frozen, and so might as well be from Cape Cod as from the Timor Sea. That said, anglers are drawn to the Top End hoping to catch **barramundi**, a bland tasting and overrated "fighting fish"; **snapper** (aka Red Emperor) is much more flavoursome.

City centre and the wharf area

Café Bella, 9–11 Cavenagh St. Alfresco resto with Italian dishes from early till late.

Cafe Uno, Mitchell St. Pleasant Mediterranean-style menu with pasta and *focaccia* from $8. Groovy cocktail bar at the back.

Capri, 37 Knuckey St. City-centre coffee bar serving good-value big brekkies and meals with a Mediterranean theme.

Coyotes Cantina, Transit Centre, Mitchell St. Mexican dishes on an elevated deck overlooking Mitchell St. Moderately-priced, though discount "backpacker" nights are also advertised.

Crustacean's, Stokes Hill Wharf (℗08/8981 8658). At the end of the pier, offering swish steak and fish from $21.

Delicious Blue, 84 Mitchell St. Airy inside and outside tables with $5 breakfast from 7.30am and Asian-influenced meals from $9.

Fisherman's Wharf, Frances Bay Rd. A long-time Darwinians' select getaway for cheap seafood and chips.

Lemongrass, Stokes Hill Wharf. Thai-style fish and chips – the more interesting of many cheap options on the wharf.

The Mental Lentil, Mitchell St Transit Centre. Hole-in-the-wall veggie and vegan paradise offering cheap curries, burgers and ice cream.

Roma, Cavenagh St. This classic, Italian-inspired coffee bar serving tasty meals and breakfasts is an old favourite with Darwinites.

Cullen Bay, Fannie Bay and East Point

Bay Seafood Cafe, Marine Blvd, Cullen Bay. Inexpensive large portions of seafood and chips.

Cornucopia, MAGONT Complex, Conacher St (℗08/8981 7791). Sunset views from the terrace and a contemporary Australian menu. Moderate prices.

Dos Amigos, Marine Blvd, Cullen Bay. Huge serves of authentic and moderately priced Tex-Mex food with good bar and outdoor tables.

Pee Wees at the Point, East Point Rd. Tucked away in the trees on a grassy terrace overlooking the bay serving up steak and seafood at around $20 plus.

YOTS, Shop 4, 54 Marine Blvd, Cullen Bay. One of a dozen or so restaurants in the marina, this one has a varied and reasonably priced seafood menu and pleasant location. Ideal for a post-cruise evening meal.

Drinking, nightlife and entertainment

Darwin's thirst for alcohol used to be legendary, with statistics for **beer** consumption averaging out at around 230 litres per year for every man, woman and child. Eliminating the largely teetotal children and moderate women drinkers, that meant each grown man knocked back nearly a pair of "slabs" (24-can cartons) each week – fifty percent more than in the rest of Australia, although to be fair, consumption of soft drinks is also well above the national average. In recent years, consumption has eased off considerably, as the NT government, embarrassed by this boozy image, instigated a "Drink Less Live More" campaign, imploring moderation and reducing the price of "lite", low-alcohol beer. They've got their work cut out however as beer-drinking is still considered a prerequisite or indeed the main way of having a good night out in Darwin.

Pubs and bars

Many **pubs** have transformed their functional frontier-town interiors into something more conducive to the new-found clientele of public servants and tourists. The atmosphere that may once have been at home in the Wild West is long gone, in the centre of Darwin at least. The *Hotel Victoria*, on the mall, is the looser venue in Dawin's CBD, but even this place is calming down in its old age.

Don't turn down any invitations to the "members only" *Yacht Club* in Fannie Bay, a fine spot to watch the sun set over the Timor Sea. Next to the Transit Centre the Guinness-serving *Shenanigan's* brought "Oirishness" to the Territory and has struck the right chord with both locals and visitors. Now there's also *Kitty O'Shea's* at the top of Mitchell Street creating the same sort of hooley but serving food as well. Over the road, *Rourk'es Drift* features a bit of wood and brass and calls itself a "British Pub", it's actually something much more continental but not bad for all that.

Clubs and live music

Like Darwin's transient population, things change quickly on the city's **club scene**, if it can be called that, which is centred on Mitchell Street, with several options stretching up to the *Top End Hotel*; just walk along it and see what takes your fancy. The **casino** (see below) hosts several diversions, including *Crystals*, a straightforward disco, while karaoke crooning takes off in the early hours at the *Sweethearts Bar*. On Sunday afternoon "Jazz on the Lawn", behind the casino, is strictly middle of the road.

Theatre, cinemas and the casino

For **theatrical performances**, see what Brown's Mart Community Arts (℡ 08/8998 5522) is up to, or check out the programme at the Performing Arts Centre (℡ 08/8198 1222) on Mitchell Street, which hosts top acts and shows from all over the country and even international ones. The five-screen **cinema**, Cinema Darwin, just over the road, has cheap tickets on Tuesday, but the air-con can give frostbite; for an alternative to mainstream films, see what's on at the outdoor Deckchair Cinema, on Frances Bay near Stokes Hill Wharf (closed Nov–March).

Down on East Point Road the **casino** (near Mindil Beach; open nightly) is a sawn-off pyramid designed to withstand 350kph winds – and filled with a variety of distractions designed to remove your money just as fast. Don't be put off by the jet-setting image of European casinos; the Australian's love of **gambling** means that anyone can fit in comfortably as long as they're presentable.

Events and festivals

The Dry season sees an upsurge in popular activity as the city shakes off the languor of the Wet. As well as agricultural shows, rodeos and racing, August's **Festival of Darwin** sees bands, plays, parades and all sorts of happenings around the city, and is well worth catching. Late July is the time for the famous **Beer Can Regatta** in Fannie Bay – wacky boat races in sea craft made entirely from beer cans. A genuine manifestation of Territorian eccentricity, this inevitably involves drunken revelries, and there have been attempts by the "Drink Less Live More" brigade to make the event more family-oriented. Also in August, there is more nuttiness during the barefoot **Mud Crab Tying Competition**, a speed event that can cost you your digits.

Markets

Every Thursday night from 5.30pm (May–Oct only) **Mindil Beach Markets** attracts thousands of locals who park, unpack their eskies and garden furniture, and settle in for the sunset. A mouthwatering array of sizzling food stalls from all corners of the earth (but mostly Asia) torments your nostrils, and New Age remedies, handicrafts and teeming humanity round off Darwin's one unmissable event. It's a three-kilometre walk from town through the Botanic Gardens, or a short ride on a #4 or #6 bus from the city centre. Alternatively, call Tour Tub (℡08/8981 5233) or Galaxy Tours (℡08/8932 6222) for a pick-up. **Parap**'s Saturday morning market, on Parap Road (bus #6), or **Rapid Creek market**, off Trower Road on Sunday (bus #6 or #10), are good year-round substitutes, with a smaller food selection, old books and knick-knacks. There is also the recently developed **Night Markets** which have spiced up Mitchell Street.

Listings

Airlines Ansett Airlines, 46 The Mall (℡13 1300), has inexpensive, one-way backpackers' fares to Kununurra and Broome. Garuda (℡08/8981 6422) and Merpati (℡08/8941 1030) have flights to Bali and Kupang, in Timor, both departing four times a week, while Malaysian Airlines (℡08/8941 2323)

Tours from Darwin to the Top End

For the visitor, Darwin itself isn't really a destination of enduring interest compared to the surrounding countryside. Kakadu is the obvious draw, and for many is the primary reason for visiting the Top End, but Litchfield Park is nearer, croc-free and a fun day out. While Litchfield remains a popular day-trip, many Kakadu tour operators are now offering two- and three-day tours, providing a less hurried way of enjoying the park. Below are some recommended tour operators in the Top End not mentioned elsewhere in the text. Prices fluctuate but generally expect to pay $110 a day. Most of these tours include the $15 Kakadu park entry fee.

Darwin's harbour may not be the world's most picturesque inlet but there are a number of ways of making it an enjoyable experience. At Stokes Hill Wharf a sea plane and helicopter stand by, waiting to fly you over the city while down at the Fishing Boat Harbour off Frances Bay Road a hovercraft offers the same thing at a lower altitude. But the best options are either the yacht, catamaran or pearl lugger based at Cullen Bay Marina. A sunset cruise brings you back in time to enjoy an evening meal by the waterfront and in the meantime you'll get an amusing commentary as well as drinks and snacks for your two-hour trip.

Blue Banana (℡08/8945 6800). Hop-on, hop-off, stay-as-long-as-you-like bus, pitched at backpackers, doing a circuit between Darwin, Katherine and Kakadu. Travel pass valid for three months.

Coo-ee Tours (℡08/8981 6116). Enjoyable twelve-hour waterfall hop through Litchfield and Reynolds River with a dinkum Aussie family.

Darwin Day Tours (℡08/8947 4060). Day- and half-day tours (essentially a bus service plus a cuppa) to the croc farm and Territory Wildife Park.

Kakadu Adventure Safaris (℡08/8947 2677). Two or three full days in a packed 4WD for the fun-hearted and budget-minded; a longer tour includes Twin Falls.

Kakadu Dreams (℡08/8981 3266). Low-cost, fun, activity tours in another packed 4WD.

Keetleys (℡08/8947 2472). Established tour operator for those who prefer not to rough it too much. One-day Litchfield and Katherine tours or two-day Kakadu tours for $300.

Travel North (℡08/8972 3989) Variety of well-organized trips south to Katherine and into Kakadu.

Wild Thing (℡0409 956 892). All-out one- and two-day action and adventure in Litchfield: waterfalls, etc.

Wilderness 4WD Adventures (℡08/8941 2161). Competitively priced two- to five-day tours through Kakadu and Litchfield. Plenty of fun and action with the longer tours always a better deal in the long run.

Willis Walkabouts (℡08/8985 2134). Bushwalking in the Top End, Kimberley and the Centre for committed walkers.

flies to Singapore twice a week. Qantas (☎13 1313) flies pretty much everywhere too, including Dili.

Banks All major banks are located in or near Smith Street Mall.

Bookshops Readback Book Exchange in Darwin Plaza off The Mall (Mon–Fri 9am–5pm, Sat 9.30am–1.30pm) offers a good selection of secondhand books including used travel guides. Also try Dusty Covers, Chin Arcade, 29 Cavenagh St (Mon–Fri 10.30am–5pm) for rare Australian first editions.

Buses Greyhound Pioneer, Transit Centre, 69 Mitchell St (☎08/8941 6433) and McCafferty's, corner of Peel and Smith streets (☎08/8941 0911), for journeys within the Territory and out of state. Bus passes can also be purchased at both places, which for longer stays are much better value than ordinary tickets.

Camping equipment The NT General Store, 42 Cavenagh St, has everything you need for going out into the bush, from a new pair of blunnies to mozzie nets, eskies and billies.

Car rental Advance, 86 Mitchell St (☎08/8981 2112), has a wide range of vehicles from $25 a day; Network, 90 Mitchell St (☎08/8924 0000), also has mokes from $25 a day, plus charge per km. Territory Thrifty Rental Cars, 64 Stuart Highway (☎08/8981 8400), is out of town but has a big fleet of vehicles.

Car trouble AANT, 79–81 Smith St (☎08/8981 0611). Vehicle breakdown service, road maps and information. For roadside service call ☎08/8941 0611.

Consulates Indonesia, 18 Harry Chan Ave (Mon–Fri 9am–1pm & 2–5pm; ☎08/8941 0488).

Hospital Royal Darwin Hospital, Rocklands Drive, Casuarina (☎08/8922 8888).

Internet access The State Library in the Parliament Building gives you half an hour of emailing or an hour of surfing free per day. Territory Internet Services on Knuckey St, near the mall, is the cheapest ($4 per hour) in town while the central Global Gossip on Mitchell St, near the Tourist Precinct, is the busiest.

Pharmacy 46 Smith St Mall (9am–9pm; ☎08/8981 9202).

Police The main police station is at West Lane, behind Knuckey St (☎08/8981 1866).

Post office 48 Cavenagh St, cnr Edmunds St. Open on Saturday morning and with a well-organized poste restante service.

Secondhand stuff City Secondhand and Pawnbrokers, 6 Harriet Place (where Daly crosses Smith St), has some useful used gear such as cameras, bikes, eskies, tools and hats.

Swimming The nearest decent-sized pool is at Ross Smith Ave, Parap (☎08/8981 2662); take bus #6 or #10 from the city centre. Or try Lake Alexander at East Point.

Vaccinations Contact the Travel and Immunization Service, 43 Cavenagh St (☎08/8981 7492), for vaccination service if you're heading for Asia.

Bathurst and Melville islands

Around six thousand years ago, rising sea levels created **Bathurst and Melville islands**, 80km north of Darwin. Home of the **Tiwi** Aborigines, the islands are often collectively known as the Tiwi Islands. Differing significantly from mainland Aborigines, with whom they had limited contact until the nineteenth century, the Tiwi people's hostility towards all intruders hastened the failure of **Fort Dundas**, Britain's first north Australian outpost (on Melville Island), which lasted just five years until 1829. The Tiwi word for white men, *murantani* or "hot, red face", probably originates from this time.

In just two generations, since a Belgian missionary cautiously established the present-day town of **NGUIU**, on Bathurst, the Tiwi have moved from a hunter-gatherer lifestyle to a commodity-based economy with remarkable ease. Running their own tours and manufacturing their own crafts and garments, they are now seen as an offshore model for successful Aboriginal self-determination.

The **Tiwi Land Council** (☎08/8947 1838) issues permits for visitors to the islands, but doesn't allow individual tourism. Without an invitation, **tours** are the only way to see the islands. Tiwi Tours (☎08/8947 4090, ©aussieadventure@attglobal.net) offers small-group tours of the islands, from $260 for a day-trip, including return flight and permit. It's a bit of a shopping trip, inspecting Tiwi art and craft outlets such as Bima Wear's showroom, but lunch at Taracumbie Waterfall and a visit to an overgrown burial ground, where lopsided crosses mingle with carved *pukamani* burial poles, add some flavour – as does the thirty-minute flight over Van Diemen Gulf. At $460 the **overnight tours** are much more worthwhile. You'll get a chance to go food-gathering with local Tiwi, either offshore or through the bush, making it a refreshingly spontaneous encounter. For more information call in at Aussie Adventure Holidays, on the corner of Smith and Knuckey streets.

The Arnhem Highway to Kakadu

The **Arnhem Highway**, which runs east towards Kakadu, parts company with the main southbound Stuart Highway 10km after Howard Springs. Eleven kilometres from the turning, the small settlement of **HUMPTY DOO** (bus #19 from Palmerston, a suburb of Darwin) has a **pub** renowned for its Sunday sessions; adjacent is the *Hard Croc Café* roadhouse where the "boxing croc" – a giant parody of the "boxing kangaroo", Australia's famous sporting flag – is worth a photo stop. Down the road a bit is **Grahame Gow's Reptile World** (daily 10am–5pm; $10), which displays an array of deadly, and deadly-looking, reptiles. Australia contains over 75 percent of the world's venomous snakes and most of them, as well as pythons and other reptiles, are represented here. Grahame Gow, a world authority on snakes, has been bitten enough times to be thought immune to snake venom.

A few kilometres further on is the turn-off to **Fogg Dam Conservation Reserve**. Originally established in the late 1950s as an experimental rice- and cotton-growing area which was to have transformed The Territory's economy, for various "operational" reasons the whole scheme was a flop. Since then the dam has become successful as a bird sanctuary: early morning or twilight are the best times for spotting jacanas, egrets and geese, as well as pythons who feed on the water rats, goannas and wallabies. There's also a 3.6-kilometre signposted boardwalk through the adjacent woodland and another leading into the lagoon itself. During the Dry, rangers lead night-time walks along the dam.

Back on the highway you'll spot the distinctive observation platform of the **Windows on the Wetlands Visitors Centre** (daily 7.30am–7.30pm), which overlooks the Adelaide River flood plain from the top of Beatrice Hill. On the top floor you can look out onto the flood plain through binoculars, play with interactive displays describing the surrounding ecology and get the full story on the Fogg Dam fiasco.

Adelaide River Crossing

Seeing crocodiles in their natural habitat is one of the Top End's undoubted highlights and at the **Adelaide River Crossing**, 64km east of Darwin, you can sign up for the so-called **jumping crocodile cruise**. The familiar appeal "Don't Risk Your Life", posted along northern Australian waterways and shorelines, took on greater significance when in August 1998 part of the Adelaide River Bridge sank into the mud. The temporary closing of the Arnhem Highway soon had a devastating effect on passing trade east of the river, and while divers prepared to inspect the bridge's foundations, the *NT News'* cartoonist Wicking drew a pair of bug-eyed crocs offering "jumping human cruises".

The *Adelaide River Queen* ($22 for a 90min cruise; up to four times daily; check times and availability of seats in advance on ℡08/8988 8144) cruises involve enticing the river's numerous salties with bits of boney offal, making the business of snapping stunning photographs straightforward and safe. All the crocs have individual personalities, such as the sprightly Mr Reliable or the generally languid nine-hundred-kilogram Hannibal. Sea eagles sometimes swoop in and snatch morsels from the crocs' maw and, whatever your thoughts on the methods or wisdom of encouraging crocodiles to jump 2m out of the water, they are an amazing spectacle.

The Mary River Wetlands

Continuing along the Arnhem Highway, 12km past the *Bark Hut Inn,* the **Old Darwin Road** (also known as the Jim Jim Rd) leads southeast into Kakadu. Another 6km further on, the unsealed Point Stuart Road turns north into the **Mary River Wetlands**, ending at the point where Stuart actually reached the sea in 1862. It's an opportunity for those with their own vehicle to explore a wetlands environment no less impressive for not being in Kakadu – indeed as Kakadu's wetlands are largely inaccessible it's your best option. Accommodation is offered at *Wildman River Wilderness Lodge* (℡08/8978 8912, ℱ8978 8907, ℮wildman.lodge@octa4.net.au; cabins ❼), a tidy resort around 15km off the Point Stuart Road with camping or small air-con cabins and a nice bar/restaurant area with a pool. From here you can take fishing tours out to the **Rock Hole**, a lush billabong similar to the better-known Yellow Waters near Cooinda; for details call the Darwin Regional Tourism Association (℡08/8991 4000). Another 25km up the road is *Point Stuart Wilderness Lodge* (℡08/8981 7263, ℱ8981 9058, ℮nttours@adventuretours.com.au; units ❺, dorms ❷), which can be a less expensive place to spend the night, with a pool, boat tours, gear rental and, with advance notice, meals available.

Directly south of the *Bark Hut Inn* on the Arnhem Highway, a track leads 2km to the *Annabaroo Billabong* (℡ & ℱ 08/8978 8971; ❶), a rustic collection of airy bush cabins and campsites spread out among the light woodland and including the original, century-old bark hut used by buffalo hunters. It's a lovely, peaceful spot where you can swim and canoe in the billabong, and there's also a small shop and a bar.

Kakadu National Park

A hundred and fifty kilometres east of Darwin you reach the western boundary of **KAKADU NATIONAL PARK**, a unique area of largely unspoilt wilderness. On UNESCO's World Heritage List, it was brought to worldwide attention when used as a backdrop in the film *Crocodile Dundee*. The park derives its name from the Gagudju language group of Aborigines, who number among the area's traditional custodians; the Gagudju Association, the Aboriginal traditional owners, and the federal government now jointly manage the park, with the assistance of the Australian National Conservation Agency (ANCA). Many of the traditional owners also claim a royalty from the **uranium** mined in Kakadu: along the eastern border with Arnhemland lies fifteen percent of the world's known reserves, and the Ranger Uranium Mine near Jabiru yields around $10 million a year for the association. Indeed, the

NORTHERN TERRITORY | Kakadu National Park

Crocodiles

Two distinct types of crocodile inhabit the Top End. Bashful Johnston or freshwater crocodiles ("freshies") grow up to 3m in length, and are almost exclusively fish eaters, living in freshwater rivers and billabongs. Unique to Australia, and distinguishable by their narrow snouts and neat rows of spiky teeth, they look relatively benign and are considered harmless to man. Some swimming areas in Kakadu are known to harbour freshies.

Estuarine, or saltwater crocodiles ("salties"), can inhabit both salt and fresh water and are the world's biggest reptiles. Once fully mature (up to 6m long and 1000kg in weight), they have no natural predators other than each other and have been known to "take" (the approved euphemism) buffaloes trapped in the mud – although fishermen and swimmers are a much less desired snack. Their broad, powerful snouts and gnarled jawline comprise a fascinating and gruesome sight that has changed little since the time of the dinosaurs 160 million years ago – only then salties were four times bigger than they are now. They are opportunistic hunters, catching their prey in sudden, short bursts of speed and then resuming their customary inactivity for days if not weeks at a time. Apart from the jumping crocs at Adelaide River, most you'll see are inactive, sunning themselves in the mud or cooling off underwater.

Aborigines have lived alongside crocodiles, and eaten them or their eggs, for thousands of years, but in the early twentieth century crocodiles were hunted close to extinction – either for sport, as vermin, or for their skin. Legislation reversed this trend in the mid-1960s though with current conservation, farming and elimination of rogue crocs, it's unlikely the Top End will ever see the really huge five-metre-plus crocs ever again.

The absence of warning signs does not guarantee safe swimming (the signs are persistently stolen as souvenirs), nor does the *apparent* absence of salties. Hard enough to spot even when they're above water, crocodiles can lie submerged for hours. In short, unless you're sure it's safe, don't swim. If you're camping, don't prepare fresh meat by the water's edge, and don't collect water from the same place every day. Fatalities are surprisingly rare but all attacks make the front page of the *NT News*. Grisly stories are part of every tour guide's repertoire and are firmly entrenched in Territorian folklore.

environmental debate over the proposed mining in the late 1970s was instrumental in the establishment of the park, though controversy erupted again in 1998 over the proposed mining of a new site at **Jabiluka**. Located close to Ubirr, one of the park's most beautiful spots, anti-nuclear graffiti appeared all over Darwin as protesters occupied the site. The situation is still unresolved.

The park's 20,000 square kilometres encompass the entire catchment area of the **South Alligator River**, misnamed by an early British explorer after the river's prolific crocodile population. In its short run to the sea, the river passes through, and creates, a number of varied topographical features. Ravines in the southern sandstone escarpment, itself topped with plateau **heathlands**, shelter scattered pockets of monsoonal **rainforest**, while downstream the more commonly seen **eucalypt woodlands** merge into the paperbark **swamps** and tidal **wetlands** of the coastal fringe.

Within these varied habitats an extraordinary diversity of flora and fauna thrives. Included are 1600 different **plants**, over 10,000 species of **insect**, half The Territory's species of **frog**, a quarter of Australia's **freshwater fish** and over 75 different **reptiles** – some, such as the freshwater (or Johnston) crocodile, unique to Kakadu. A third of Australia's **birds** can also be found in Kakadu, including the elegant Jabiru stork, the similarly large brolga, with its curious courting dance, lily-hopping jacanas, white-breasted sea eagles, which build lifelong nests from heavy sticks, as well as galahs and magpie geese by the thousand. **Mammals** include kangaroos, wallabies, wallaroos, 26 bat species, and dingoes – a barkless and incorrigibly wild dog introduced to the continent by Aborigines some five thousand years ago.

With so many interdependent ecosystems, maintaining the park's natural balance has become a full-time job. The **water buffalo**, brought in from Timor early in the nineteenth century and one of ten **feral species** found in the park, proliferated so successfully that its wallowing behaviour soon turned the fragile wetlands into saltwater mudbaths. However, concerted bovine eradication in the Top End has left other problems in its wake, not least the aptly named **salvinia molesta weed**. With no buffaloes to eat it, the exotic weed has invaded vast areas of the wetlands, creating a thick, sunlight- and oxygen-depleting mat that chokes all other plant and fish life.

The other ever-present danger is **fire**. Burning off has long been recognized as a technique of land management by Aborigines who lit small, controllable fires as an aid to hunting and to stimulate new plant growth. Today, rangers imitate age-old Aboriginal practice, burning off the drying speargrass during June to preclude bushfires at the end of the Dry, when the desiccated countryside could be devastated by an early electrical storm. Finally, the disastrous effect that Queensland's poison-army of **cane toads** (see p.512) might have on Kakadu's precious ecology doesn't even bear thinking about.

Ancient rock art

Up to five thousand **Aboriginal art sites** cover the walls of Kakadu's caves and sheltered outcrops, ranging from thirty to over twenty thousand years in age. Most of them are inaccessible to visitors, and many are still of spiritual significance to the three hundred or so Gagudju and other language groups who live in the park. The paintings include a variety of styles, from hand prints to detailed cross-hatched depictions of animals and fish from the rich **Estuarine period** of six thousand years ago. At this time, rising sea levels submerged the land bridge by which Aborigines crossed into Australia. It is not unusual to see paintings from successive eras on one wall: **Contact period** images of seventeenth-century Maccassan fishing *praus* and larger European schooners might be superimposed over depictions of ancient and bizarre spirit-beings. Though partially understood at best, Kakadu's rock art provides a fascinating record of a culture that, as recent excavations at Jinmium on the NT/WA coastal border suggest, might have inhabited the Top End for over 100,000 years.

Visiting the park

It must be stressed that Australia's largest national park is a difficult place to appreciate in one short visit. Access to the park's diverse features is limited, and those expecting to find the air a-flutter with colourful birds and the bush humming with wildlife will be disappointed. Furthermore, at the most popular times of year for visitors, Kakadu is much drier than might be imagined, and most of the wildlife is active only during the early morning, in the evening or at night. The danger from crocodiles and of inadvertent desecration of sacred Aboriginal sites, as well as the harsh terrain, means that the wetlands and especially the escarpment country are best appreciated from a small aircraft, something which can be arranged in Jabiru (see p.628) or through the *Gagudju*

Lodge in Cooinda (☎08/8979 2411), with thirty-minute scenic flights from $75.

Although Kakadu's Aborigines distinguish six **seasons** throughout the year, to most people it's either the Wet, with up to 1600mm (just over five feet) of torrential rainfall between December and March, or the Dry, an almost complete drought.

The **dry-season months** of June, July and August are the most popular times to visit the park, with acceptable humidity and temperatures and fairly conspicuous wildlife. Towards the end of the Dry, birdlife congregates around the diminishing waterholes, while November's rising temperatures and epic electrical storms – known as the Build Up – herald the onset of the Wet. To see Kakadu during the **Wet** or the early Dry is, some say, to see it at its best: water is everywhere and, while some sights are inaccessible and the wildlife dispersed, the land demonstrates the kind of verdant splendour that people often expect, but fail to find, in the most visited months.

Getting there

The **Arnhem Highway** leaves the Stuart Highway 43km south of Darwin, following which it's a fairly dull 210-kilometre drive to the Park HQ near Jabiru (see below). On the way you'll pass the **park entrance station**, where you pay the $16-per-person entrance fee; tickets are valid for two weeks, and you can leave and re-enter the park as many times as you like during this period. From Jabiru the sealed **Kakadu Highway** heads southwest through to Pine Creek on the Stuart Highway (an alternative entry point into the park if approaching from the south), passing Cooinda, which is pretty much at the heart of the park. Along this road you'll encounter many of Kakadu's best features.

The **Old Darwin Road** (or **Jim Jim Rd**), unsealed, but usually passable for robust 2WD-cars in dry conditions, is a good alternative to slogging the full length of the Arnhem Highway. It starts 12km east of the **Bark Hut Inn** on the Arnhem Highway and joins the Kakadu Highway near Cooinda, 100km further on. Entering the park this way you should pay at the Cooinda resort, or at the Park HQ near Jabiru; for both, see below.

Without your own transport you'll have to rely on a **tour** (see box, p.620 for some recommended Darwin-based operators). There are **buses** into the park: Greyhound Pioneer operates daily between Darwin, Jabiru and Cooinda, and the Kakadu Parklink (free call ☎1800 089 113) runs between the main accommodation centres of the Frontier Kakadu Village, Jabiru and Cooinda. But make no mistake, those trying to see the park using only their bus passes will end up frustrated. You're probably going to be in Kakadu only once, so do it properly: rent a car or join a tour. **Car rental** can be arranged through The Territory Thrifty office at the *Gagudju Crocodile Hotel* in Jabiru (☎08/8979 2552). The **map** you're given when you enter the park is handy, but details only the most popular areas; for the whole picture get yourself a copy of the HEMA 1:400,000 *Kakadu National Park* map ($5.95).

The Park Headquarters and Bowali Visitors Centre

At the eastern edge of the park, 250km from Darwin, near the junction of the Arnhem and Kakadu highways, you arrive at the **Park Headquarters and Bowali Visitors Centre** (daily 8am–5pm; ☎08/8938 1120). The visitors centre is a masterpiece of thoughtful and relevant landscaping and design and should not be missed. Here you can get an official *Visitors' Guide* that suggests how to make the most of your visit, while for further information, *Park Notes*, covering all aspects of the park, are available at the desk. A *What's On* pamphlet has details of the informative ranger-led walks at many of the sites covered below, and the programme of evening slide shows at the caravan parks and resorts.

An innovative walk-through exhibition takes you through a condensed Kakadu habitat, passing across underfloor snakes and under a croc's belly. There's also a range of **videos**, shown near the main desk. A café and gift shop round off the facilities.

Accommodation

Within Kakadu there are resorts near the **South Alligator River** and at **Cooinda**, and a hotel and caravan park at **Jabiru**. There are also seventeen camping areas scattered all over the park, some accessible only along deliberately unmaintained tracks requiring 4WDs and all ranging from basic sites, which are free, to better-equipped caravan parks at **Mardugal** near Cooinda, **Muirella Park** near Nourlangie Rock, **Merl** at Ubirr and at **Gunlom**. In the Dry season, booking ahead at the Park HQ is advisable.

Aurora Kakadu Lodge and Caravan Park, Jabiru (☎ 08/8979 2422, ⓕ 8979 2254, ⓔ klodge@aurora-resorts.com.au). Caravan park (camping available) surrounding a grassed pool and bar area, with plain, four-bed, air-con rooms, shared facilities and basic kitchen (extra charge for linen). Close to Jabiru and Park HQ. Rooms ❻, dorms ❷
Aurora Kakadu Resort, Arnhem Highway, 2.5km west of South Alligator Bridge (☎ 08/8979 0166, ⓕ 8979 0147, ⓔ kresort@aurora.com.au). Attractively landscaped resort with café, restaurant, and pool area visited by birds and wallabies. Has its own Gungarre nature trail on the doorstep. Motel rooms with camping available. Rooms ❽
Gagudju Cooinda Lodge, Cooinda (☎ 08/8979 0145, ⓕ 8979 0148, ⓦ www.sphc.com.au). Well-positioned resort near Yellow Waters and Warradjan Cultural Centre; good campsite, decidedly afterthought air-con cabins and motel units

with a totally inadequate BBQ area, which makes the $15 all-the-veggies-you-can-eat bistro obligatory unless you have your own cooking gear. Motel units ❽, cabins ❷
Gagudju Crocodile Hotel, Jabiru (☎ 08/8979 2800, ⓕ 8979 2707, ⓦ www.sphc.com.au). Overpriced crocodile-shaped hotel popular with coach parties. ❽
Kakadu Hostel, next to the Border Store near Ubirr (☎ 08/8979 2232). An old lodge past its prime but with all facilities; the cheapest bed in Kakadu but popular with mosquitoes too. Open all year subject to access. ❶–❸
Mary River Roadhouse, Kakadu Highway, Pine Creek (☎ 08/8975 4564, ⓕ 8975 4730). At the far end of the park, but handy if arriving from the south, with a range of simple rooms. Its reputation has improved with new ownership – it is now owned and run by the local Jawoyn people. ❷–❺

Around the park

If your visit to Kakadu is short, seeing **Ubirr** or **Nourlangie Rock**, taking a **cruise** at Guluyambi or Yellow Waters and checking out the Bowali Visitors Centre or Warradjan Cultural Centre will give you a taste of the park, and can just about be fitted into a long day. However, you can easily spend a week visiting all the spots detailed below, ideally followed by a return visit six months later to observe the seasonal changes. All the following places are reached off the **Kakadu Highway** which runs southwest from Jabiru out of the park, joining the Stuart Highway at Pine Creek. Unless indicated, all roads below are sealed and so accessible to rental cars.

Jabiru and the Ranger Uranium Mine

JABIRU, a couple of kilometres east of the Park HQ, is a company town, originally built to serve Kakadu's uranium-mining leases before the park was established. There are four mine leases in the park (and another in Arnhemland) but only one or possibly two are operating at present. As a result, Jabiru is less than

One of Kakadu's biggest disappointments is the lack of long-distance marked trails. A leaflet at the Park HQ lists twenty marked trails in the park, but most are short nature trails, such as the six-kilometre Rockholes Walk near Ubirr. Only the twelve-kilometre Barrk Walk – a six-hour trek through Nourlangie Rock's back-country – offers any challenge. Although the trail is marked and gets you into the bush without the need for skilled navigation, it still should not be undertaken lightly. In the often-overlooked southwest of the park near Gunlom, the Yurmikmik area on the edge of the escarpment offers a similar challenge in the unmarked Motor Car Creek Walk (11km) and Motor Car and Kurrundie Creek Circle Walk (14km; overnight stop recommended). Ask for the *Yurmikmik Park Notes* at the visitors centre. You're more than likely to have the faint track to yourself.

Experienced bushwalkers can apply to Park HQ with proposed itineraries, which need to be approved before a permit is given. Willis Walkabouts (℡08/8985 2134) in Darwin organizes extended bushwalks up in the escarpment country. For something less strenuous, The Darwin Bushwalking Club (℡08/8985 1484) organizes weekend walks in the Top End and welcomes visitors.

6

half full of mineworkers and park employees. There is a **tourist information centre** (℡08/8979 2548), a small **supermarket**, a takeaway, bakery, post office and Westpac bank, all found in the **shopping plaza**. You'll also find a **Health and Dental Clinic** (℡08/8979 2018) and a swimming pool (daily 9am–7pm; $2).

Kakadu Air (℡08/8979 2411) operates out of the airport at Jabiru East (as the original town site 6km east of Jabiru is known), offering one-hour **scenic flights** along the escarpment and wetlands from $75. From Kakadu Air's office you can also take a one-hour tour of **Ranger Uranium Mine** (daily at 9.15am, 10.30am, 1.30pm & 2.30pm; $20). However, the mine is nothing more than a pit, pipelines and mysterious-looking buildings where the ore is processed, while the tour itself is largely a public-relations litany designed to assuage visitors' misgivings. Australia's only other productive uranium mines are in South Australia and across the park boundary in Arnhemland.

Ubirr and the Guluyambi Cruise

The rock-galleries at **Ubirr**, 43km north of the Park HQ, illustrate the rich food resources of the wetlands. Fish, lizards, marsupials and the now-extinct Tasmanian tiger or thylacine are depicted, as well as stick-like Mimi spirits, mischievous beings said to inhabit cracks in the rock. The **Lookout** offers one of the park's most beautiful views across the East Alligator River to the rocky outcrops of Arnhemland and should not be missed, while the six-kilometre return **Rockholes Walk** along the East Alligator River is one of the few longish walks in the park – a good way to escape the crowds.

Right by the start of the Rockholes Walk you can take a ninety-minute **Guluyambi Cruise** (℡08/8979 2411; $30) along the East Alligator River. A local Aboriginal guide takes you upstream to view the towering escarpment and rock paintings while demonstrating some canny bush trickery and he even gives you a chance to set foot, albeit briefly, on Arnhemland. The dramatic scenery makes it an enjoyable, if not superior, alternative to the better-known Yellow Waters option at Cooinda and one of the most informative guided tours in the region.

Nourlangie Rock Area

Nourlangie Rock, Kakadu's most accessible and therefore most visited site, is 31km south of the Park HQ. It includes the **Anbangbang Rock Shelter**, where the dry ground preserves evidence of occupation stretching back twenty thousand years; dimples on boulders show where ochre was ground and then mixed with blood for painting. The **Anbangbang Gallery**, nearby, depicts the dramatic figures of Nabulwinjbulwinj, Namarrgon (the Lightning Man) and his wife Barrkinj. Unusually vivid, they were in fact repainted (a traditional and sometimes ritual practice) between 1963 and 1964 over similar but faded designs. The **Lookout** over the Arnhemland escarpment, to the home of Namarrgon, is also the beginning of the twelve-kilometre **Barrk Walk** (see box overleaf). Other places in the Nourlangie Rock area, all signposted, and marked in the *Visitors' Guide*, include **Nanguluwur**, a less popular but fascinating art site 1.5km from the Nourlangie car park, which includes images from the Contact period when Aborigines first encountered explorers and settlers. **Nawulandja Lookout** looks onto the imposing hulk of Nourlangie Rock itself, which looms over **Anbangbang Billabong**, one of the locations used in the film *Crocodile Dundee*. During the Dry, a two-and-a-half-kilometre track circumvents the billabong. **Gubara** or Burdulba Springs, an unsealed 13km off the Nourlangie road, is a string of small pools along a palm-shaded creek, itself a hot forty-minute walk from the car park.

Jim Jim Falls and Twin Falls

Although over 100km south of Park HQ, at the end of a tricky 4WD-only track, these two falls are definitely worth visiting; allow two hours for the sixty-kilometre drive from the Kakadu Highway or get an operator like Kakadu Gorge and Waterfall Tours to take you there (℡ 08/8979 0111; around $150). **Jim Jim Falls** tip 215m straight off the edge of the escarpment and are best caught in the early Dry, as soon as the road reopens – they often stop flowing later and will certainly look less impressive. A rocky, one-kilometre trail leads alongside the large pool to the base of the falls.

Twin Falls is a rough ten-kilometre drive from Jim Jim, including the crossing of Jim Jim Creek, which genuinely does require a 4WD and not just high clearance although they have lately added a firm concrete base under the sands. From the car park it's a short walk and then a swim up the monsoon-forested gorge for another kilometre – an airbed and waterproof containers help here. This little bit of adventure is rewarded by the sight of Twin Falls cascading into a pool edged by an idyllic sandy beach, a beautiful and recently very popular spot to while away the day. The sure-footed can scramble to the top of the falls via the overgrown gully to the right – a difficult climb capped with a view you won't forget in a hurry, but note that fatal accidents have occurred here. Both falls quickly become inaccessible after the first big rains.

Yellow Waters and the Warradjan Aboriginal Cultural Centre

As Jim Jim Creek begins meandering into the flood plains close to the Cooinda resort, 50km southwest of Jabiru, it forms the inland lagoon of **Yellow Waters**. From the car park here, a short walk leads along the edge of the billabong, from where popular **cruises** (five daily; book in advance on ℡ 08/8979 0145) weave through the lushly vegetated waterways. The early morning cruise (2hr; $31) catches the lagoon and wildlife at their best: heat-of-the-day tours are thirty minutes shorter and a few dollars cheaper.

The turtle-shaped **Warradjan Aboriginal Cultural Centre** (daily 9am–5pm), on the Cooinda access road, offers unusually designed interpretive displays on the culture and lore of the local Aborigines, together with an arts and crafts shop. Interesting though it is, it has to be said that the display is not particularly effective at communicating its message and, unless you have some previous understanding of Aboriginal culture, you've forgotten much of what you've seen soon after leaving.

Barramundie Gorge, Gunlom and other beauty spots

Robust cars can manage the twelve-kilometre corrugated track from the Kakadu Highway to **Barramundie Gorge** (also known as Maguk), the best of Kakadu's few swimming holes, 57km southwest of Cooinda. From the car park, a path leads along the creek to the large pool, possibly still the home of a harassed freshie; for its sake rather than yours, keep away from the left bank. The top of the waterfall and more rock pools can be reached by clambering up the tree roots to the right of the falls.

Gunlom (also known as Waterfall Creek) is another *Crocodile Dundee* location, on an unsealed road 36km off the Kakadu Highway, close to the park's southwestern exit. Although the falls don't flow all year, it's a lovely paperbark-shaded swimming spot, and as you can camp here comfortably it's well worth the diversion if entering or leaving via Pine Creek. The steep path at the top of the falls reveals still more pools for an inviting dip.

A right turn at the junction that leads to Gunlom follows on through Koolpin Creek to a locked gate and **Koolpin Gorge**. The key is available from the Southern Entry Station (℡08/8975 4859) on the Pine Creek road where you must leave a $50 deposit. The track to the gorge is definitely for 4WDs, ending just before the actual gorge which begins 1km upstream and continues deep into the escarpment. You can camp here or follow the escarpment on foot to the northwest for 3km to the narrow chasm of **Freezing Gorge** which, you'll be pleased to discover, lives up to its name. Five kilometres past the locked gate is **Gutatba**, a picnic site on the South Alligator River. Also known as Coronation Hill, this is the site of a former uranium mine. To local Jawoyn Aborigines this area is traditionally "Sickness Country", suggesting that even in its natural state uranium proved harmful to human health.

Arnhemland

Individual tourist access into Aboriginal-owned **ARNHEMLAND**, a vast wilderness east of Kakadu, is virtually impossible. By and large, the three thousand Aborigines who live in this remote region, where supplies come in by sea or air, want to be left alone – as they have been for over forty thousand years. In 1963 the Yirrkala of northwestern Arnhemland appealed against the proposed mining of bauxite on their land. It was the first such protest of its kind, and included the presentation of sacred artefacts as well as a petition in the form of a bark painting to the government in Canberra. Although unsuccessful on this occasion, their actions brought the issue of Aboriginal land rights to the public eye and paved the way for subsequent successful land claims.

The **Northern Land Council** (Darwin ℡08/8920 5100; Jabiru ℡08/8979 2410) issues free permits to drive the 4WD Central Arnhem Road but only allows a maximum of fifteen tourist vehicles in at any one time. The only major settlement is **NHULUNBUY**, in the northeast corner, a mining town of no appeal to tourists, and with only basic and overpriced facilities. Nevertheless, Arnhemland is beginning to open up, and not just at exclusive prices. Most visitors are fishermen heading up to **Smith Point**, an approved destination for which permits are booked up months in advance. Birds, Bees, and Things, based in Nhulunbuy (℡ 08/8987 1814, ✉ bbtt@octa4.net.au), run half-day and longer **tours** that focus on flora, fauna and local culture, but can also incorporate fishing. *Walkabout Lodge* in Nhulunbuy has good rooms and also organizes fishing tours (℡ 08/8987 1777, ℻ 8987 2322, ✉ walkaboutlodge@octa4 .net.au). Billy Can Tours (℡ 08/8981 2560) drives you out and flies you back for a three-day tour costing $485 twin share. Davidson's Arnhemland Safaris (℡ 08/8979 2411) is another established operator offering tours in the Mount Borradaile area for around $300 a day plus flights. Lord's Kakadu (℡ 08/8979 2970, ✉ lords@topend.com.au) offers a day-hop into Arnhemland from the Border Store.

The Cobourg Peninsula

The **Cobourg Peninsula** – encompassing the **Gurig National Park** and **Cobourg Marine Park** – is a largely inaccessible headland clinging to northwestern Arnhemland by a slender isthmus. Although you have to drive through Arnhemland to get there, the peninsula is not part of the Aboriginal-owned reserve. With the failure of Fort Dundas on nearby Melville Island, the British tried again to establish a foothold, first at **Raffles Bay** and later at **Port Essington** (from 1838 to 1849), where the explorer Ludwig Leichhardt arrived in 1844 after his epic overland trek from Moreton Bay in Queensland. Port Essington was abandoned after eleven years due to malarial epidemics, harassment by Aborigines and Indonesian pirates, and – more tellingly – the peninsula's severe climatic extremes, being hotter and wetter than anywhere else in The Territory.

On the peninsula is **Seven Spirit Bay** (℡ 08/8979 0277), an exclusive low-key "eco-resort" reached by boat or light aircraft offering five-star service and cuisine, with various activities at your disposal. At over $200 per person per night for twin-share "habitats" (minimum, and flights are extra), it's the place to politely ignore film stars trying to get away from it all. Alternatively, you can visit this area under your own steam with a 4WD. It's about 260km from the Border Store in Kakadu to **Smith Point** (camping and s/c chalets, ℡ 08/8979 0263), on the other side of the inlet from *Seven Spirit Bay*. You can get fuel and check in with the ranger at the Gurig Store at **Black Point** (daily 3–5pm; ℡ 08/8979 0263). For more information ask at the Parks and Wildlife Commission (P&WC) desk in the Darwin Regional Tourist Association office on Mitchell Street (daily 9am–5pm; ℡ 08/8989 5511).

Along the Stuart Highway

From Darwin the **Stuart Highway** passes early mining and pastoral outposts and is bordered intermittently by overgrown, but still commemorated, airstrips dating from World War II. Along its length are a number of attractions which can be visited either as excursions from Darwin or as diversions on the journey to Katherine, 320km to the south.

Darwin Crocodile Farm

South of the Arnhem Highway turn-off, 40km from Darwin, is the **Darwin Crocodile Farm** (daily 10am–4pm; $12) where crocodiles are both studied and bred for their skins and meat as they are at Crocodylus Park near Darwin (see p.617). The lucky ones get scarred at an early age, rendering themselves unsuitable for conversion into $3000 handbags and become breeding stock. Rogue crocs that harass local communities, as well as the sixty odd caught annually in the traps around Darwin Harbour, are also relocated here. If you haven't been to Crocodylus Park in Darwin, this is a good place to learn the difference between salties, freshies and American alligators. Besides, nowhere

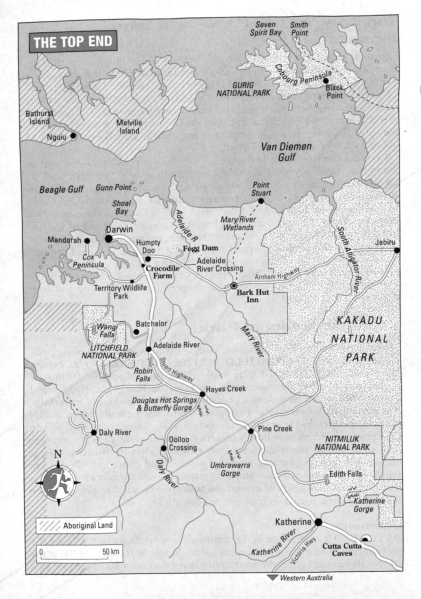

else could you get as close to such a monster as Burt, the five-metre star of *Crocodile Dundee*, and live to tell the tale.

Souvenirs (including photo opportunities to cradle baby salties) and croc burgers are available at the shop, and **guided tours** set off on the hour, when some of the eight thousand crocodiles and alligators also get fed. It's worth trying to catch the main feeding time (Mon–Fri 2pm, Sat & Sun noon & 2pm), since it's one of the few occasions when the crocs actually move. Darwin Day Tours (℡08/8947 4060) can bring you here four times a week for $30, including entry fee.

Territory Wildlife Park – and termite mounds

Eight kilometres further south down the highway, the turning west to the Cox Peninsula leads to the four-square-kilometre **Territory Wildlife Park** (daily 8.30am–6pm, last admission 4pm; $18), where you can spend a happy couple of hours wandering through a variety of Territorian habitats, which include walk-in aviaries, nocturnal houses and walk-through aquariums. The entry fee – worth every cent – includes free rides on the circulating train, which saves trudging along the four-kilometre roadway. Darwin Day Tours (℡08/8947 4060) do daily runs out from Darwin.

Twenty kilometres west before the Cox Peninsula road veers north to Mandorah there's a turning onto the corrugated northern approach track to Litchfield National Park (see below). Crossing through the usually dry Finniss River, this track passes fields of **termite mounds**, both fluted "cathedral" mounds, up to 4m high, and so-called "magnetic" or "meridian" mounds. Not often seen in the same vicinity, both designs accomplish their aim of regulating the internal temperature. Magnetic mounds are unusual things: made of digested grass, they're always aligned along a polar axis, and were once thought to be in tune with the earth's magnetic field. In fact, they are arranged so as to present a knife edge to the midday sun, thus maintaining the habitat at a termite-preferred 30°C; you can feel the temperature difference by touching either side of the mound.

Litchfield National Park

"Kaka-don't, Litchfield-do" is an over-simplified quip expressing many people's preference for **LITCHFIELD NATIONAL PARK** over its better-known neighbour. Situated 100km south of Darwin, and roughly 16km west of the Stuart Highway, it encompasses the **Tabletop Range**, a spring-fringed plateau from which issue several permanent and easily accessible **waterfalls**. The whole park is a popular and enjoyable destination, generally free of restrictions, long drives and intangible expectations. It is also crocodile-free, so you can splash around to your heart's content – a much more attractive prospect than some of the sterile dammed lakes closer to Darwin. **Bushwalking** is encouraged: walkers planning extended hikes should contact the P&WC in Batchelor (see opposite) for camping permits, as well as information about trails and maps. For details of **organized tours**, which are the only way to see the park without your own transport, see box p.620.

Batchelor

BATCHELOR – 8km west of the highway – was originally built to serve the postwar rush to mine uranium at nearby Rum Jungle. In the early 1970s, when large-scale mining ceased, the townsfolk managed to resist Rum Jungle's closure. The establishment of the national park in the 1980s gave the town a new lease of life, though don't expect much; just about the only sight of note is a replica of the Gothic **Karlstein Castle**, next to the police station, built by a homesick Czech immigrant. The local **P&WC** (℡08/8976 0282) gives out information on Litchfield National Park. There are a couple of **caravan parks** around Batchelor, but **camping** in the park is generally more appealing (some of the best sites are detailed in the text below). For those who don't want to rough it, try the *Rum Jungle Motor Inn* (℡08/8976 0123, ℻8976 0230; ❻), on Rum Jungle Road, a comfortable **motel** with a decent restaurant, or the *Jungle Drum Bungalows* (℡08/8976 0555, ℻8976 0599, ✉jungledrumbungalows@bigpond .com; ❺) which has cabin-style rooms.

Into the park

There's no admission fee to enter the park, and no visitors centre either, so get all the information you need from the P&WC at the DRTA in Darwin or in Batchelor. Heading into the park from Batchelor you'll pass black-soil plains dotted with grey, tombstone-like termite mounds. **Buley Rock Holes**, down a right turn, 38km from Batchelor, are nothing more than a couple of rock pools, but a five-kilometre trail follows the creek from here to **Florence Falls**. A high lookout surveys the twenty-metre falls, which can be reached along a path leading from the car park down to the plunge pool. There's not much room to spread out picnics, but the water is beautifully cool, and a 4WD track leads back to the Batchelor road. **Camping** is permitted at both the rock holes and the falls.

The **Lost City**, off the main road through the park, 6km after the Florence Falls turn-off, is a jumble of unusually weathered sandstone columns. These are interesting enough in themselves, but getting to them is the real highlight, as they're at the end of an increasingly difficult, eight-kilometre 4WD track which should not be visited in rented vehicles unless you know how to drive over steep rock steps without damage. The rarely used track, which continues on to Blyth Homestead and Sandy Creek (see below for more on these – and an easier way of getting to them), gets trickier still after the Lost City. Back on the main road through the park, the pool below **Tolmer Falls** is closed to the public, to grant the rare orange horseshoe bat some seclusion. However, the long, slender falls can be appreciated from a fine lookout (signposted off the main road). A two-kilometre path leads from here to an area of pools and minor cascades at the top of the falls, which are swimmable in the Wet, before heading back to the car park.

From the highway a track leads south to **Blyth Homestead** and **Sandy Creek** (or Tjaynera Falls). The abandoned homestead adds some token historic interest to the park, while Sandy Creek (accessible by 4WD only) is a series of falls and a pool surrounded by rainforest, with a **campsite** less than 2km away. From Sandy Creek, the 4WD track continues (with several steep creek crossings) to the Reynolds River – back in crocodile country – and halfway between Daly River (see p.636) and the Stuart Highway.

Green Ant Creek is a new destination carved out of the bush. From the car park a stiff one-hour return walk leads to the top of **Tjaetaba Falls**, with a pool to cool off in right on the lip of the cascade.

The park's most popular waterfall, with easy access to tree-shaded lawns and a large pool, is **Wangi Falls**, 55km east of Batchelor. There is a sun-warmed natural spa pool near the base of the left-hand cascade, once a sacred site for Aboriginal women and forbidden to men. Strangely enough, several men, including some trying to save drowning women, have perished at Wangi; trilingual signs now warn of the danger, and the pool closes in the Wet when abnormal **undertows** develop. A trail leads through a rainforest boardwalk (the initial section of which is wheelchair-accessible), up over the falls and down the other side via a **lookout** – a good way to work off lunch. Wangi tends to get overcrowded at weekends and in school holidays, since it has the best-equipped **campsite** in the park.

A corrugated dirt road leads north from Wangi out of the park, past *Pethericks Rain Forest* (waterfalls and quiet **camping**) and across the Finniss River (where "Sweetheart" the crocodile once roamed before falling prey to the taxidermist at the museum in Darwin) and on to the Territory Wildlife Park.

Adelaide River and the Daly River Region

Established during the construction of the Overland Telegraph Line, the town of **ADELAIDE RIVER** was the supply head for Darwin's defence during World War II and consequently suffered sporadic Japanese bombing after 1942. Today the town, 110km south of Darwin, provides little more than a lunch-stop along the Stuart Highway. You may, however, want to visit the town's **war cemetery** where many of the victims of the air raids are buried. Officially, 243 people died as a result of the eighteen months of Japanese bombing, which began in February 1942, but it is thought that the actual death toll may have been up to four times as high. Enquire at the *Mobil Roadhouse* for **camping** space, or try the *Adelaide River Inn* (☎08/8976 7047; rooms ❺, dorms ❶), which also provides counter meals and has a **restaurant**.

Just south of town, the old highway forks west along a rolling 75-kilometre **scenic drive** before rejoining the main road at *Hayes Creek* roadhouse. After the first 17km you'll come to the turn-off for **Robin Falls**, a pretty little cascade reached after a ten-minute scramble up the creek bed from the car park, while a further 17km marks the turn-off for Daly River.

The Daly River Region

A quiet backwater, 120km southwest of Adelaide River, the **Daly River Region** is best known as an excellent fishing spot. Apart from a twenty-kilometre section, the road is sealed all the way from the highway to the police station at **DALY RIVER** – beyond that it's dirt in all directions. It wasn't always so pleasant: in 1884, four copper miners were killed by local Aborigines. The *Northern Territory News* was apoplectic with indignation, but calmed down enough to reassure its readers that "the right class of men are now on the tracks of the Daly River natives, but we do not expect to hear many particulars of their chase; the less said the better". Two years of punitive "bush riding" followed until the Wilwonga Aborigines were all but wiped out.

There are no banks or shops here, but you'll find **accommodation** spread out along both sides of the river. The pick of the crop is *Mango Farm* (☎08/8978 2464, ℱ8978 2331), signposted a few kilometres over the causeway and offering cabins (❺), safari tents with full linen (❷) and a ten-person unit (❼) as well as a pool, small bistro, dinghy rental, river cruises and "24-hour power", something to boast about in these parts. Its most outstanding feature, however, is the stand of mature **mango trees** which arch over the whole compound like the vaulting of a Gothic cathedral; in season you'll be woken repeatedly by the thud of mangoes dropping onto the tin roofs. Another good place to stay is the *Woolianna Tourist Park* (☎08/8978 2478, ℱ8978 2634; cabins ❺), on the other side of the river about 30km downstream, with more boats to rent, a pool and **camping**, while the main attraction at the *Daly River Roadside Inn* (☎08/8978 2418; ❹), in what might be called the "town centre", is a four-metre-long pet saltie called Boris.

Douglas Hot Springs and Butterfly Gorge

Back on the scenic route from Adelaide River, a turn-off leads 35km south-west to **Tjuwaliyn Hot Springs**, where water bubbles at 40°C out of the sandy creek bed – very agreeable, but often crowded during school holidays. **Camping** costs just $3.50, but you'll need to collect your firewood on the way in, as the nearby woods have been picked clean. From the springs, a 4WD track leads another 17km to the secluded **Butterfly Gorge**. When you can drive no further, follow the creek upstream on foot, past massive paperbarks and over rocky outcrops to the beautiful, orange-walled gorge and sandy beach. Here you can swim in several rock pools.

Pine Creek and around

Site of The Territory's first goldrush, the small town of **PINE CREEK**, 230km from Darwin, has retained its colonial appearance, making it an unusually appealing stop along the highway. Gold was discovered while digging holes for the Overland Telegraph Line pylons in 1871, and fools rushed in, hoping to pan their way to fortune. Unfortunately the gold was in the rock, not the riverbeds, requiring laborious crushing with heavy stamp batteries – which, for most prospectors, was too much like hard work for unpredictable returns. The subsequent labour shortage was solved by importing cheap Chinese labour, which kept the progressively poorer-quality ore coming for a couple of years until fears of Asian dominance (the Chinese workers outnumbered Europeans eight-to-one by this time) led to their being banned from The Territory in 1888, a shot in the foot for gold production. A modern gold mine now goes at it hammer and tongs, as new technology extracts the remaining deposits. If you're lured by the prospect of easy pickings, Gun Alley Gold Mining Tours (℡08/8976 1221) can give you a chance to try some gold-panning.

Around the town, the various time-worn buildings, such as the 1889 **Old Playford Hotel** and **Old Bakery**, may lead you to contemplate the crucial role of corrugated iron, or "galvo", in the pioneering colonial process. The **Miners Park**, at the northern end of town, displays the crude mining hardware from a hundred years ago and there's a **museum** (Mon–Fri 1–5pm; $2) on Railway Terrace, near the police station, and an old locomotive on the old train station itself. For accommodation there's a **caravan park** with camping, or the *Pine Creek Diggers Rest Motel* (℡08/8976 1442, ℻8976 1458; ❾) on Main Street. **Places to eat** amount to the pub and the *Hard Rock Café*, presumably an ore-crushing pun, next to it. Ah Toys general store on Main Terrace is still run by the descendants of its original Chinese owner.

From Pine Creek it's 200km along the sealed **Kakadu Highway** to Jabiru, in the heart of Kakadu National Park, passing the majority of the park's highlights on the way (described in the Kakadu section, pp.623–631). South of town, on the way to Katherine, there are a couple of other diversions within a short drive of the Stuart Highway.

Umbrawarra Gorge and Edith Falls

At **Umbrawarra Gorge**, 22km southwest of Pine Creek along a corrugated track with several dry creek crossings, you can camp for $2.50 and walk up the shaded gorge which has pools throughout the year, but **Edith Falls**, halfway to Katherine, 20km east of the highway, is more impressive. The falls, just within Nitmiluk National Park, drop to a large, forest-encircled pool in three stages, around which an adventurous five-kilometre loop **walk** has been completed. There's **camping** at Edith Falls, for a $2.50 fee. It's also possible to walk to

Katherine Gorge from here, along a 66-kilometre trail (see "Nitmiluk National Park", p.641).

Katherine to Alice

An obligatory stopover (at least for a couple of days) for visitors to the Top End, **Katherine** is a small but rapidly growing regional centre on the southern banks of the Katherine River. It's just 30km from **Katherine Gorge**, the town's primary tourist attraction and itself part of the larger **Nitmiluk National Park**.

West of Katherine, the **Victoria Highway** leads for 500km west to the WA border, passing Timber Creek and the entrance to the 4WD tracks of the **Gregory National Park** on the way. South of town, a dip in **Mataranka**'s thermal pool and a couple of "bush pubs" are the highlights of the 670km to **Tennant Creek**, unless you take the former droving route via **Borroloola** and the Gulf of Carpentaria, to northern Queensland, still a rough track but passable to sturdy cars in the Dry. South of Tennant Creek, only the rotund boulders of the **Devil's Marbles** brighten the string of roadhouses along the Stuart Highway, which stretches for just over 500km to Alice Springs.

Katherine

Traditionally home of the Jawoyn and Dagoman people, the **Katherine River** area must have been a sight for explorer John McDouall Stuart's sore eyes as he struggled north in 1862. Having reached here, he named the river after a benefactor's daughter, Catherine, and within ten years the completion of the Overland Telegraph Line (OTL) encouraged European settlement, as drovers and prospectors converged on the first reliable water north of Alice Springs. In 1926 the railway from Darwin finally spanned the river and "Kath-rhyne", as the die-hard locals still call the town of **KATHERINE**, became established on its present site. It's essentially a "one-street" town, with Tennant Creek the only other place of consequence in the 1500 kilometres between Darwin and Alice.

Arrival, information and getting around

All buses arrive at the **Transit Centre**, at 6 Katherine Terrace (daily 7.30am–6.30pm; ☎08/8972 1044), next to the 24-hour *BP Roadhouse*. Katherine is a busy interchange for buses, with at least one daily arrival or departure for Darwin, Kununurra (WA) and Alice Springs. Just over the road you'll find the modern **tourist information centre** (Mon–Fri 8.30am–5.30pm, Sat & Sun 10am–3pm; ☎08/8972 2650, ℱ8972 2969, ℮krta@nt-tech.com.au), which produces a free guide to the region and can book all your accomodation, tours and cruises (see p.641). For more detailed information on Nitmiluk, Gregory and Keep River national parks call in at the **Parks and Wildlife Commission** on Giles Street, just over 1km from town, past O'Shea Terrace (℡08/8973 8770). There are **email** facilities at the Katherine Art Gallery at 12 Katherine Terrace. The **airport** is 8km south of town; a **taxi** to Katherine will cost about $15 (℡08/8972 1777 or 8972 1999).

To **rent a car** call Territory Thrifty (℡08/8972 3183), Hertz Rent-A-Car (℡08/8971 1111) or Delta Car Rentals (℡13 1390). **Bikes** can be rented from most accommodation.

Accommodation

Thanks to the immense popularity of Katherine Gorge, there's plenty of choice for places to stay in town. The tourist information centre provides a list and current prices of all the town's accommodation; the best options and all the hostels are detailed below.

Motels

All Seasons Frontier Katherine, Stuart Highway (℡08/8972 1744, ℻8972 2790, ✉fkath@afh.allseasons.com.au). Good-value resort just out of town, with pool, bar and restaurant. ❻

Beagle Motor Inn, 2 Fourth St (℡08/8972 3998, ℻8972 3725). The best choice for a cheap motel in town. ❹

Paraway Motel, cnr O'Shea and First streets (℡08/8972 2644, ℻8972 2720). The most comfortable motel in the town centre. ❺

Hostels

Kookaburra Lodge, cnr Lindsay and Third streets (℡08/8971 0257 or free call 1800 808 211, ℻8971 1567, 🌐www.inspirit.com.au/kookaburra). Well-converted motel units in spacious grounds with eight-bed air-con dorms and twins, making this currently Katherine's best backpackers' choice by far. Also ping pong, pool and Transit Centre drop-offs. Rooms ❸, dorms ❶

Palm Court Backpackers, cnr Giles and Third streets (℡08/8972 2722, ℻8972 1443, 🌐www.travelnorth.com.au). Old motel with tiny pool and packed eight-bed dorms plus four-bed dorms and twins, all with own bathroom, mini-fridge, and lame air-con. Rooms ❸, dorms ❶

Victoria Lodge, 21 Victoria Highway (℡08/8972 3464, ℻8971 1738). In between the above two places in standards, with eight- and four-bed dorms, plus twins. Rooms ❸, dorms ❶

Caravan parks

Katherine Low Level, Shadforth Rd (℡08/8972 3962). Close to the Low Level Nature Reserve, with plenty of shady, grassed sites. Cabins ❺

Knotts Crossing Resort, 4km down Giles Rd. Well-appointed resort with all sorts of cabins and units, motel rooms and camping. Cabins ❺

Nitmiluk Gorge Caravan Park, Nitmiluk National Park (℡08/8972 3150, 🌐www.travelnorth.com.au). Right by the gorges but 30km from Katherine. Makes a good base for exploring the park on foot.

The Town and around

The Stuart Highway becomes **Katherine Terrace**, the main street, as it passes through town. Along it lie most of the shops and services, including a big Woolworths, as well as a surprising number of galleries proferring anything from traditional Aboriginal to modern art, giving Katherine a compact – and unexpectedly busy – feel. The **Railway Museum** (Mon–Fri 1–3pm; $2), housed in the old station on Railway Terrace, isn't really worth the bother. If you want the full story on the town head 3km up Giles Street to the **Katherine Museum** (Mon–Fri 10am–4pm, Sun 2–5pm; $5), just before the old town site at Knotts Crossing, where a few original OTL pylons still remain upright. Inside are displays relating to Katherine's colonial history, including early medical instruments and a biplane from the time when the building did duty as a Flying Doctor base.

As you cross the road bridge into Katherine from the north you'll pass a height scale on the redundant rail bridge alongside. The scale ends at 18 metres above the river but by the evening of January 26, 1998, following an Australia Day few in the town will forget, the engorged Katherine river peaked at a record twenty and a half metres.

This staggering volume of water was the result of two cyclones dumping their load over southern Arnhemland – a Wet season of rain in a few days – and was exacerbated by a king tide from the Timor Sea which backed up the water inland. Just about every business in town was under 2m of water, four lives were lost and a crocodile was spotted cruising lazily past the semi-submerged Woolworths. Within two days the waters dropped away as quickly as they had risen and the evacuated townsfolk returned to their ruined homes and businesses to begin the clean-up. Knee-high silt was shovelled out of shops and motel rooms, while the stench of rotting food and drowned cattle enveloped the town. And yet, with voluntary help from other communities and government aid, the town was on its feet within just a couple of weeks.

The 1990s saw successive record Wet's in the Top End – partly the consequence of La Niña, El Niño's less well-known and deluge-bringing counterpart.

Three kilometres down Victoria Highway are some decidedly **warm springs** first right after the *Red Gum Caravan Park*. From here, it's just a short walk to the **Low Level Nature Park**, a pleasant spot for a stroll, swim or canoe along the pandanus-fringed river, seasonal floods permitting. **Springvale Homestead**, at the end of Shadforth Road, 8km west of the town centre, is a tourist resort based around the oldest homestead in The Territory, built in 1884. The station was at one time run by Ted Ronan, a writer of the wry and romantic school, who helped mythologize the Outback with novels such as *Vision Splendid*. There are free, half-hourly tours of the homestead (May–Oct daily 10am & 2pm); you can eat here, too (see below).

Cutta Cutta Caves, 27km south of town, offer guided tours (hourly 9–11am & 1–3pm; closed at the height of the Wet; $9.50; ☎08/8972 1940) of the Limestone Cave and Cutta Cutta. These caves display extraordinary subterranean karst features as diverse as they are delicate. Cutta Cutta is the more visually impressive and is also the home of the rare orange horseshoe bat and rather alarming stalactite-climbing brown snakes.

Eating, drinking and nightlife

With the gradual improvement in tourist services it is no longer mandatory to go to a hotel to get a good feed, but don't discount this possibility. This is just as well, because the pubs' front **bars** are rough and sometimes rowdy places.

Restaurants and cafés

Buchanan's, *Paraway Motel*, cnr O'Shea and First streets (☎08/8972 2644). Sharing the honours, with *Seasons*, as the best restaurant in town. Around $22 a head.

Croc Room, *Beagle Motor Inn*, 2 Fourth St (☎08/8972 3998). Serves up its namesake, baked, at moderate prices.

Jade Café, Katherine Terrace. One of the few lunch spots in town, serving wholesome snacks.

Mekhong Thai, cnr Katherine Terrace and Victoria Highway. Authentic Thai cuisine using home-grown herbs.

Seasons, *All Seasons Frontier Motel*, Stuart Highway, 3km south of town. Eat your heart out from a droolsome à la carte menu of steak and seafood for $20–25 a meal. **Springvale Homestead**, Shadforth Rd

(☎ 08/8972 1044). "Bush kitchen" meals coincide with other activities, such as croc-spotting cruises along the Katherine River.

Tours from Katherine

Campbells Trail Rides (☎ 08/8972 1394) and **Brumby Tracks** (☎ 08/8972 1425) both offer horse rides from a few hours to a few days.
Gecko Canoe Tours (☎ 1300/361 055). Three- to twelve-day canoeing trips for around $140 per day. Suitable for beginners and in many ways far more satisfying than the rather crowded Katherine Gorge.
Manyallaluk (☎ 08/8975 4724). One of the best Aboriginal culture tours in The Territory for $120 ($99 self-drive).

Nitmiluk National Park

The central attraction of the **Nitmiluk National Park** is the magnificent twelve-kilometre **Katherine Gorge**, carved by the Katherine River through the Arnhemland plateau. Often described as thirteen gorges, it is in fact one continuous cleft, turning left and right along fault lines and separated during the Dry season by rock bars. The spectacle of the river, hemmed in by orange cliffs, makes for a wonderful **cruise** or canoe trip and, unlike Kakadu, Nitmiluk also welcomes bushwalkers along its many marked **trails**.

Travel North (free call ☎ 1800 089 103) operates **shuttle buses** along the sealed road between Katherine and the gorge for $17 return. The all-new **Park Visitors Centre** (daily 8am–7pm) has interpretive displays on the park's features from the local Jawoyn Aborigines' perspective (they own the park), and provides maps and further information on the trails, including the *Guide to Nitmiluk National Park* ($4.95) with topographical walking maps. It also includes a restaurant, gallery and a model of the gorge system which puts it all in perspective. As you sit on the terrace overlooking the river below, consider that in the catastrophic floods of January 1998 you would have been under a metre of water.

Bushwalks include the 66-kilometre **hike to Edith Falls**, in the park's northwestern corner, for which you'll need at least three days, a minimum of two people and a $50 returnable deposit. Away from the gorge itself, the terrain is rough and very dry; be sure to wear sturdy footwear and a hat, and carry plenty of water. As a safety precaution, all walkers must **register** ($1; overnight stays $20 refundable deposit) with the rangers at the visitors centre: those on day-hikes must check in again by 6pm.

Exploring Katherine Gorge

Buses from Katherine terminate at the new canoe ramp and jetty designed to save canoeists tangling with the cruise boats heading **up the gorge**. Tickets for cruises are sold at the visitors centre. They've also sorted out safe swimming access, too, and you'll be pleased to know that saltwater crocs are virtually unknown in the gorge. While waiting for a cruise, you might want to take the steep, four-hundred-metre walk leading from the jetty to a superb clifftop **lookout** up the river (no need to register for this short walk).

Cruises ply the gorge in a series of boats. Travel North (free call ☎ 1800 089 103) offer somewhat rushed two-hour cruises to the second gorge for

$33, a four-hour cruise to the third gorge (the limit during the Wet season, when a more powerful jet boat is brought in) for $47, and an eight-hour "safari", which includes some rock-hopping that demands secure footwear, for around $82. The relaxed "safari" cruise includes a barbecue lunch, refreshments, plenty of time for swimming and a peep at the sixth gorge; it gets away from the rather busy downstream sections and is highly recommended. There are also exhilarating **helicopter flights** up the gorge (for a minimum of two at $82.50 per person for 15min or $137.50 for 25min; ℡08/8972 1253).

Canoeing up the gorge is an option for the more energetic, but don't expect to paddle up to the "thirteenth" in a day; canoeing is hard work for unaccustomed arms and shoulders, especially against the breeze which wafts down the gorge but is a definite alternative to the sedate cruises. Nitmiluk Tours (free call ℡1800 089 103) rents solo canoes for $38 a day, $27 per half-day – add about fifty percent for two-person canoes (easier to control and a shared load for beginners). Waterproof containers are provided. The rental period is 8.30am–4.45pm; overnight trips cost a bit less than an extra day's rental. Alternatively, put your own canoe on the river, for a small fee payable at the visitors centre. Expect long sections of canoe-carrying over boulders and successively shorter sections of water as you progress up the gorges. Those determined to reach the thirteenth gorge (which, scenically speaking, is not really worthwhile) will find it easier to leave the canoe at the fifth and swim/walk the last couple of kilometres.

The first permissible overnight **campsite** is Smith's Rock in the fourth gorge (or anywhere upstream from there) – this is regarded as a fair day's paddling and portaging. The best time to canoe the gorge is early in the Dry season, when small waterfalls run off cliff walls and the water level is still high enough to reduce the length of the walking sections.

The Victoria Highway to Western Australia

The **Victoria Highway** stretches for 510km southwest of Katherine to Kununurra in Western Australia. After an initial, dull 125km a narrow sealed road leads south off the highway down to a bleak roadhouse at **TOP SPRINGS** where there's camping and fuel. From here, a dirt road heads west past the legendary **Victoria River Downs** (VRD) station through to Jasper Gorge, rejoining the Victoria Highway east of Timber Creek. Once the country's biggest cattle station, known colloquially as the "Big Run", Victoria River Downs was established in the great droving days of the 1880s, and, like many "unmanageable" properties, is now owned by a business consortium better able to weather the currently depressed market. It still operates over a massive, semi-arid area, with the "homestead" more like a small township, incorporating a post office and shop. The station is also the base of Australia's biggest **heli-mustering** outfit, which pursues the daredevil practice of mustering widely dispersed stock with single-seater helicopters.

From Top Springs, the **Buchanan Highway** (in fact just a dirt road) continues south and west through Wave Hill to **Halls Creek** (WA), a stretch of

6

nearly 700km that should not be undertaken lightly. Wave Hill is notable as the site of the Aboriginal stockmen's strike in 1966, which led to the first successful land claim and the birth of the Aboriginal **Land Rights Movement**.

Back on the Victoria Highway, the road narrows as it enters a picturesque spur of the Gregory National Park (see overleaf). The *Victoria River Wayside Inn* (**4**), at the Victoria River crossing, boasts "the cheapest caravan park in Australia" and twin-share **motel** rooms. It also books **river cruises** (daily April–Oct; $30) on the Victoria River.

End of the line for the big runs

The iconography of the Australian cattle industry is etched deep in the nation's psyche. The romance of the gritty station owner in a crumpled Akubra, his kids educated from the remote homestead by the School of the Air, while triple-trailer roadtrains drag tornadoes of dust across the plains, creates a stirring idea of the modern-day pioneer battling against the elemental Outback.

Australia remains the world's largest exporter of beef, but in recent years shrewd business interests from the USA and Japan (the latter Australia's biggest overseas market) have bought into the trade – lock, stock and barrel – including everything from stations to abattoirs, packers and shipping companies. This has enabled them to control the price of beef and drive marginal stations over the edge into bankruptcy.

Indeed, it could be said that the days of old-fashioned station dynasties are coming to an end. With cattle fetching only half the prices they did a few years ago, the extravagance of maintaining thousand-kilometre fences and mustering over a vast area with helicopters has been put to the test. Despite the glory associated with the great drovers such as Nat Buchanan and the Duracks, the semi-arid interior and tropical Top End of the Northern Territory produce less beef than New South Wales. Western Australia's Kimberley region similarly glorifies in its great stations, but it's the worst land in the country, cut with seasonal torrents, and with boulder-strewn plains prone to fires and flooding. Many stations haven't mustered for years, leaving their stock to run feral; you'll come across some huge and essentially wild bulls in the Kimberley.

It's far simpler to keep the beasts in enclosed and well-watered paddocks munching decent grass rather than leave them roaming the semi-desert for years. Slow to respond to the dominance of overseas interests in its country's livestock, the Australian Cattleman's Association has squandered its members' money on ill-conceived schemes of automated abattoirs rather than attempting to secure the protection of its industry.

Only slowly are consumer's eyes being opened to "non-traditional" meats. Kangaroos, now a plague in Australia, have meat leaner than anything a cow can produce, and it tastes virtually the same. Meanwhile, Ian Conway, the half-Aboriginal owner of Kings Creek station near Ayers Rock, raises camels, descendants of those introduced as beasts of burden from Afghanistan in the nineteenth century and which were released to roam free with the advent of rail and roads. They are detested by cattle owners, who shoot them on sight; a thirsty mob can drain a tank and run through bovine fences with impunity. Yet one of Conway's disease-free camels can fetch ten times the price of a cow when sold to a private zoo in America or a racing cartel in Oman. When the station gets low on stock they simply drive out into the Gibson Desert for more, capitalizing on a resource which prospers in the Australian desert rather than turning it into a dust bowl.

Timber Creek

Although little more than a pair of roadhouses/bars with adjacent campsites, **TIMBER CREEK** makes a welcome break on the long run to Kununurra, 300km west of Katherine. Lying on the Victoria River, a century ago it was known as the "Depot", when the inland port supplied the vast pastoral properties being established throughout the region. But this remote outpost was soon the scene of bitter disputes between the Aborigines and the new landowners. In 1885 a police station was set up at Timber Creek, staffed by two policemen and a black tracker whose task was to patrol an area the size of Tasmania. Diana Bell's harrowing book, *Hidden Histories*, describes the ruthless pastoral occupation of the area from an Aboriginal perspective.

The **museum** (ask around for times and the key; $2) is housed in an early police station, west of the town. It's a familiar display of miscellaneous pioneering relics, retrieved from the surrounding undergrowth and used to illustrate a pithy historical commentary about the region. On a different note, the town has the easternmost examples of the curious, bottle-trunked **boab trees**, similar to Africa's baobabs and according to Aboriginal mythology a once-arrogant tree turned upside down to teach it a lesson in humility. Behind one such tree, a twin-trunked boab on the south side of the highway 4km west of town, lies the miserable **grave** of Tom Lawler (or Lander). He was not the first disillusioned inhabitant of Timber Creek to seek solace in alcohol, and in 1906 got a bullet through his brains, but he is one of the few to get a marked grave. Another boab, **Gregory's Bottle Tree**, on the banks of the Victoria River, was inscribed by the explorer, Gregory, in 1856. A short distance upstream, his ship ran aground and he was forced to make repairs here, giving Timber Creek its name.

Practicalities

Tourist information is dispensed by the ever-spry Max from his office situated between the two pubs (℡08/8975 0850). He will doubtless insist that you undertake his morning boat tour ($35) along the Victoria River, an indefatigable performance of bushcraft, legend and history straight out of vaudeville, which is interrupted at your peril.

Accommodation can be found at the grandly named *Timber Creek Hotel* (℡08/8975 0772; ❹), incorporating the *Circle 'F' Caravan Park* and Fogarty's Store, which has camping, cabins and motel rooms. The *Wayside Inn* (℡08/8975 0732; ❹) also has camping and cabins, with shared bathrooms. The *Shell Roadhouse* here is open 24 hours.

Eating entails sampling the customary frozen/microwaved roadhouse fare, while the two pubs have all the character of a gym changing-room. During all-nighters at the graffiti-covered *Wayside Inn*, a chummy game of darts gives way to belly-sliding head first off the beer-oiled bar. You might as well enjoy it – it's a sobering 225km to the next pub.

Gregory National Park

GREGORY NATIONAL PARK, The Territory's second-largest park, is entered off the Victoria Highway, 11km east of Timber Creek. Carved out from various pastoral leases, the park exhibits sandstone escarpments and limestone hills covered in light woodland. Because of its remoteness and rough terrain, it's best explored in a suitable **4WD vehicle**, and it's a good idea to call at the **P&WC** office in Timber Creek (turn right just before Watch Creek, west of town; ℡08/8975 0888) to study the large map and get information about conditions.

A **permit** is required for the two 4WD tracks (see below), available at the office or from the Park Ranger at **Bullita Outstation** (⊕08/8975 0833; see below).

Conventional cars can get as far as **Limestone Gorge**, on a corrugated road 60km south of the entrance. Here you'll find a 25-minute marked walking trail looping up onto the surrounding escarpment, a croc-free billabong and a **campsite**. There's no point in 2WDs going on to the stockyards at Bullita, 6km south of the Limestone Gorge turn-off, unless you want to see the ranger. However, self-sufficient drivers in 4WDs should register here before starting the **Bullita Stockroute**, 90km of scenic limestone outcrops and river crossings, which loops back northwards and involves a full day's driving. **Camping** is permitted at designated spots along the way.

Alternatively, 4WDs can choose to leave the park further south, along the **Humbert River Track** – allow at least six hours for the 112km to the park's eastern boundary, from where you head east along station roads. For another route continue circuitously south to the **Buntine Highway** and Kalkarindi via the **Broadarrow** or **Wickham tracks**. Allow three days from Bullita: the ranger will explain the way (Wickham Ranger Station ⊕08/8975 0600). Some sections of this route have some very slow, rocky sections and the tricky Humbert River crossing will challenge the inexperienced even in the Dry. Both the Limestone Gorge and this route are **one-way** only from Bullita, and are closed from December to March.

Keep River National Park and the WA border

West of Timber Creek, the land flattens out into the evocatively named **Whirlwind Plains**, where the East and West Baines rivers frequently cut the Victoria Highway in the Wet. **KEEP RIVER NATIONAL PARK** lies just before the Western Australia border, 185km from Timber Creek. Accessible to all vehicles, it's an easily explored area of dissected sandstone ridges, shallow gorges and Aboriginal art sites, the best of which is **Nganalam**, 24km from the park entrance. Marked trails start from the two **campsites** in the park, and the ranger station (⊕08/9167 8827), 3km from the highway, supplies details on longer walks and other attractions.

By now you can hardly have failed to get the message that Western Australia does not want any infested Territorian livestock, produce or honey, or even boxes which have carried those products. The intensively irrigated agricultural area around Kununurra is hoping to remain free from pests found elsewhere in Australia, so eat up your fruit and veg before the border or throw it away. Note, too, that Western Australia is an hour and thirty minutes behind The Territory.

At the **border**, Kununurra (see p.774) is just 40km away.

South to Alice

The 1100km from Katherine, south down the **"Track"** (as the Stuart Highway is known) to Alice Springs, are regarded as something of a no-man's-land for travellers. A flat, arid plain rolls from the Top End's big rivers to the waterholes of the Red Centre. The white population in this region is sparse, and consists largely of individuals who are either unusually tenacious, transient or slowly going "troppo". West of the Track, the vast Aboriginal lands of the Warlpiri and neighbouring groups just about occupy the entire **Tanami Desert**, while to the east are the grasslands of the **Barkly Tableland**, a declining pastoral region extending north to the seldom-visited coast of the **Gulf of Carpentaria**. **Tennant Creek**, just over halfway, can be an expectedly anti-climactic break to a bus journey, and even car drivers tend to press on down the Track before something breaks or wears out. The landscape as seen from the Stuart Highway encourages a kind of agoraphobic urgency (or just plain boredom), while the mind churns repetitively over such imponderables as "just how many anthills *are* there in the Northern Territory?"

Mataranka and the Roper River Region

MATARANKA – just over 100km from Katherine – is a small town, the capital of the tediously hyped "Never Never" country named after Jeannie Gunn's 1908 novel of a pioneering woman's life, *We of the Never Never*, set and later filmed in the region. Site of despised Administrator John Gilruth's planned Northern Territory capital, and of failed experimental stations in the early Federation years, today the town is practically eclipsed by the nearby **Mataranka Homestead** resort, which lures in buses and passing tourists (see below). South of town the **Elsey National Park** leads to the often-overlooked freshwater wetlands of the **Roper River**.

There's not much to the town itself. Outside the *Stockyard Gallery* you can feed a dollar into the statue of **The Fizzer** to hear the tale of the punctual postman, Henry Peckham of "Never Never" fame, who was tragically drowned in action. Tom Coles' account of his escapades in the Top End between the wars, *Hell West and Crooked*, describes the hair-raising river crossings with pack horses while delivering mail in the Wet season. Invariably the post would be delivered with barely a smudge.

All **accommodation**, along with the supermarket, roadhouses, museum, café and craft shop, is lined up along **Roper Terrace**, the main highway. Both the Shell and Mobil roadhouses have on-site cabins and at the town **pub**, the *Old Elsey Hotel* (℡08/8975 4512; ❹), you'll find motel rooms. The *Territory Manor*, on Martins Road (℡ & ℻ 08/8975 4516; ❺), is a plush motel set in its own landscaped grounds, catering for bus tours: it also boasts a caravan park (with camping) as well as the town's only licensed **restaurant**.

Mataranka Homestead

Mataranka Homestead, 6km from town (℡08/8975 4544, ℻8975 4580, ⓦ www.travelnorth.com.au; rooms ❸, cabins ❺, dorms ❶), was established by Gilruth to raise sheep and horses and is now a popular holiday resort offering an array of recreational activities, including (expensive) bike and canoe rental and horse riding. A replica of the **Elsey Homestead**, used in the 1981 film of *We of the Never Never*, is open for daily tours. The original "Old Elsey Homestead" site and cemetery are south of town, just past the Roper Highway turn-off – of interest only to Jeannie Gunn devotees.

The resort has a bar and bistro, and free nightly entertainment (April–Sept only) as well as a tour-booking service. Accommodation includes self-catering cabins, motel rooms, and three-bed en-suite rooms with air-con. There is also a youth hostel (advance booking recommended) and a campsite. Overland **buses** stop at the homestead, which is signposted to the south of Mataranka.

The **thermal pool**, actually in Elsey National Park (see p.648), but seemingly part of the resort, is the main attraction – it's free, always open, and the water is a pleasant 34°C. A soak in the palm-shaded, pale blue water is divine, with early mornings or candlelit night-time dips less crowded.

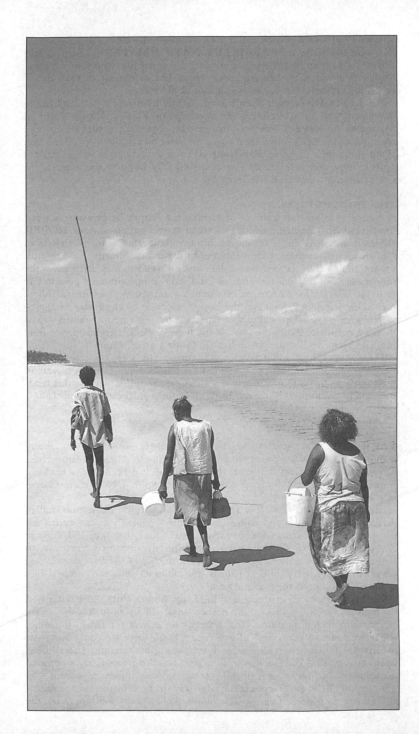

Elsey National Park and the Roper River

A twelve-kilometre road into **ELSEY NATIONAL PARK** (turn off just before the *Homestead*) leads to a more secluded **campsite** with less of a holiday-camp atmosphere, offering canoe rental and swimming in the (almost croc-free) upper Roper River, as well as a small kiosk.

The **Roper River** itself is difficult to visit independently, since it's barely developed, yet it's as scenic as the wetlands of Kakadu. Brolga Tours in Mataranka (☎08/8975 4538) is your best bet, operating **cruises** along the river from May to October. Their four-hour river tour (around $70) leads you along the river's so-called **Pandanus Avenue** and through some "African Queen"-type channels into the beautiful **Red Lily Lagoon**, the most extensive freshwater wetland in The Territory.

The Roper Highway

A couple of kilometres south of Mataranka, the **Roper Highway** leads east for 185km (the bitumen ends after 140km) to the remote store at **ROPER BAR**. It was here in 1844, during his five-thousand-kilometre trek from Queensland, that naturalist-cum-explorer **Ludwig Leichhardt** dined on fruit bat and built a "bar" (a ford) across the Roper River. You may drive across the slippery bar, but beyond is Aboriginal Land – off-limits without a permit. The store provides the local Aboriginal community and visiting barramundi fishermen with pricey fuel, food and the biggest selection of cheap toys and gobstoppers for 200km. Up behind the store are some self-catering **cabins** (❷) or there's a **campsite** 2km back towards the highway. If you go boating or fishing here, take care because you're back in "saltie waters" again.

If you've got this far, you'll have seen the turn-off to Borroloola, 380km away (see opposite). Corrugated enough to test the calmest temperaments, this rarely used route to the Gulf of Carpentaria and Queensland (where the dirt roads deteriorate still further) is passable in the Dry for regular cars in good shape.

Down the Track to Three Ways

LARRIMAH, 72km south of Mataranka, was where the old Darwin railway terminated until 1976 when it closed for good, due to a lack of maintenance following Cyclone Tracy. Up until then, Larrimah had been a busy road-rail terminus, receiving goods brought up from Alice Springs. Now it's just a fuel stop on the highway.

The *Larrimah Hotel* and *Wayside Inn* comprise a typical **bush pub**, full of eccentricity, old bottles and half-melted Spitfire engines; you can **camp** for free but there's a $2 charge for showers. Over the road, the *Green Park Caravan Site*, part of the *Shell Roadhouse*, has a pool (the five-metre croc gets one to himself) and camping plus a café and shop. At the *Top of The Town*, Angela also offers camping as well as budget **rooms** (❶), cabins (❸) and "the cheapest slabs in town". You'll need them round here.

Another 89km south brings you to the **Daly Waters Pub**, situated 3km off the highway. Having held a "gallon licence" since 1893, it positively drips with memorabilia including money and women's underwear pinned to the walls: you're welcome to contribute. If you need a break there are cheap and basic **rooms** (❸). During the 1930s, when Qantas's Singapore flights refuelled here, world-class aviators used to pop in for a pint, and these days tourists come to marvel at the quaintness of it all and buy the famously offbeat tea towels.

Just beyond here, the **Carpentaria Highway** (technically the circumnational Highway 1) heads off east to Borroloola, 414km away (see opposite); the turn-off is at the *Highway Inn Roadhouse* (open 24hr). There's a second turn-off, further down the Track, just before *Dunmarra Roadhouse*, where the **Buchanan Highway** heads west to *Top Springs Roadhouse* (185km) and ultimately Halls Creek in Western Australia (see p.772) along almost 800km of unsealed road suitable for sound vehicles only. Dunmarra's drive-through drudgery was livened up a couple of years ago when it received a bizarre shower of fish, although the hoped-for cloud of chips never materialized.

Back on the Track, **Newcastle Waters** can't seem to make up its mind whether it's an historic droving township wanting to encourage tourists or a semi-abandoned ghost town. Right up to the 1950s, when road trains replaced the great cattle drives, it was the junction (hence the *Junction Hotel*) of the Barkly and Murranji stock routes. However, it's of little interest today except to nostalgic drovers.

ELLIOTT is little more than a string of roadhouses with cheap **camping** at the *Mobil Roadhouse* and slightly better facilities at the *Midland Caravan Park* (also the local post office). The *BP Roadhouse* (❸) and the *Elliott Hotel* (☎08/8969 2018; ❸) both offer simple **rooms**. There are a few shops serving the Jingili Aboriginal communities at either end of town, but apart from filling up with fuel or a counter meal at the pub, there's no earthly reason to stop.

As you leave town to the south, the trees which have blocked the horizon for days recede into shrubs and soon disappear altogether as you approach the deserts of Central Australia. **RENNER SPRINGS** is a roadhouse (rooms ❸–❹) built after World War II from bits of ex-army junk and recently done up; you can camp here, and eat the same sort of food you were probably offered at the last roadhouse.

On the way to the roadhouse at **THREE WAYS** (open 24hr) watch out for the turn-off to a rocky profile of Churchill's Head and also the **Attack Creek Memorial** – where explorer Stuart was repelled by Aborigines on one of his expeditions. At Three Ways, the **Barkly Highway** heads east to Camooweal, Mount Isa and eventually Townsville, all in Queensland; it's 210km on to the *Barkly Homestead* (6am–1am; ☎08/8964 4549), a roadhouse with all the usual services. From Three Ways, Tennant Creek (see p.651) is just 26km down the road.

Borroloola and the Gulf Country

Situated on the croc-infested **MacArthur River**, which drains the predominantly flat Gulf Savannah lands, **BORROLOOLA** has a colourful history which reads like an exaggerated version of the familiar boom, bust and dribble pattern of so many Outback towns. The explorers Leichhardt and Gregory came this way in the mid-nineteenth century, reporting good pasture, and the cattle followed in droves. By the early 1880s, when Tennant Creek and Katherine were still just shacks on the Overland Telegraph Line, the settlement was a wild outpost that even the missionaries avoided. Ships that supplied the OTL in the early 1870s now came upriver with provisions for the hard-living drovers, who were helping stock the pastoral leases right across the north of Australia.

Borroloola was proclaimed, or "gazetted", in 1885 and a new police station was established in an attempt to control the town's lawless urges. Although well watered, the **Great Coast Route** which Borroloola serviced fell victim to the bovine disease of Red Water Fever, after which the southern stock route (today's Barkly Highway) became the favoured droving route. By the turn of 1900, just a handful of whites remained in "The 'Loo" and, with their frenzied passing, the four local Aboriginal groups have reclaimed the town and surrounding land, which now serves their communities and outstations.

The classics library and hermits of Borroloola

There are a number of more or less unlikely explanations for Borroloola's improbable **classics library**, including that which starts with a bored policeman's request for reading matter to New York's Carnegie Foundation. In truth, it was a gradual acquisition of nearly two thousand literary classics by the town's MacArthur Institute at the beginning of the twentieth century. Termites tucked into the library, a cyclone destroyed the remains and only a handful of books survived, many in "private collections", gathering what must be enormous overdue fees.

In 1963 a boyish David Attenborough made a TV documentary about three **hermits** who had chosen to retreat to the 'Loo. Jack Mulholland came across as a slightly jaded recluse when pressed about "loneliness and . . . women", and the reputedly aristocratic "Mad Fiddler" was too deranged to face the camera, but **Roger Jose** was, and looked like, the real thing. Having devoured the library ahead of the ants, he lived in a water tank with his Aboriginal wife and was a humane if eccentric "bush philosopher" who once observed that "a man's riches are the fewness of his needs". He is buried at the end of the airstrip in Borroloola.

The only original building to have survived the punch-ups, white ants and cyclones is the **Old Police Station**, now a museum. The key is available from *MacArthur Caravan Park* on Robinson Road – or at least they'll know who has it – and a donation of $2 is welcome. With Borroloola's exceptional white history (see box above), the museum couldn't fail to be fascinating. Read, for example, E. Gaunt's hair-raising account of "The Birth of Borroloola", recalling the sporadic insanity of the early days; it seems the toxic home brew known as "Come Hither", whose label showed a red-eyed Lucifer beckoning malevolently, was to blame. Not surprisingly, the coverage of local Aboriginal history is lightweight.

Practicalities

Although on Aboriginal land, no permit is required to visit the town, which sees a few intrepid tourists and fishermen. Borroloola is mainly on the itinerary of those taking the coast route from Queensland to Darwin or travelling on to Western Australia.

There's plenty of light **air traffic** to and from the town, mostly from Katherine, which otherwise is over 700km away to the northwest by sealed road. Skyport makes mail runs three times a week; the Bulk Discount Store supermarket (T 08/8975 8775) is their agent in Borroloola, and it will cost you about $240 one-way.

By road, Borroloola is easily accessible along the **Carpentaria Highway**, via the *Heartbreak Hotel* at Cape Crawford (see opposite), set at the junction where the single-width **Tablelands Highway** comes up from the main Queensland road. Depending on who you ask, the **dirt road** to **Wollogorang** (a roadhouse with access to coastal inlets) and Hells Gate (Queensland) is either terrible or not bad, but it's bound to be an adventure; the Queensland gulf towns are by no means renowned for their sobriety. The dirt road up to Roper Bar is good until Nathan River, where the corrugations will turn your brain into a froth for about 100km.

Borroloola's isolation makes it an **expensive** place to visit, with little fresh food available and prices (except for fuel) up to thirty percent higher than those you'll find in Katherine. Most facilities are on Robinson Road including a **tourist information centre** at the council offices on the corner of

Broad Street (Mon–Fri 8am–4pm; ℡08/8975 8799). As for **accommodation**, the *MacArthur River Caravan Park* has cabins and on-site vans as well as camping space (cabins ❷–❺, on-site vans ❶). This is also the home of Croc Spot Tours (℡08/8975 8734), which can run you up and down the river, or out to islands to go fishing, for about $100 a day. The town's **pub**, the *Borroloola Inn* (℡08/8975 8766, ℻8975 8773; ❹), has "quiet" and "rowdy" bars and a grassed pool area popular with cane toads on the march for Kakadu. The MacArthur River is renowned for its massive crocodiles, but you can camp for free by the boat ramps along the river, providing you have your own "shower and toilet facilities" and are familiar with croc-etiquette (see box on p.625). There is also a **post office** in town, and a couple of fast-food joints.

The Savannah-Gulf Country

The inviting coast and islands of the **Savannah-Gulf Country** are presently off-limits to independent tourists, hidden away on largely defunct cattle properties or on Aboriginal land. However, because of disastrous over-grazing and a disease-eradication programme which has decimated the herds, station owners right across the north are looking towards tourism to save them, either developing "dude ranches" that take paying guests or exploiting unusual natural features.

The *Heartbreak Hotel* at **Cape Crawford** (℡08/8975 9928, ℻8975 9993) – a bougainvillea-draped roadhouse, 113km southwest of Borroloola – offers helicopter rides to one of the many "**Lost Cities**" (unusual sandstone formations) hereabouts, as well as 4WD tours with Savannah Guides to the water-holes of the Bukalara Ranges. The **Caranbirini Conservation Reserve**, 46km southwest of "the 'Loo" is one of their destinations: more weird rock formations and a bird-filled lagoon.

Just offshore, northwest of Borroloola, are the **Sir Edward Pellew Islands**, mostly owned by the Mara Aborigines or the subject of land claims in progress. However, the P&WC has acquired **North Island**, creating the **BARRANYI NATIONAL PARK** and turning it into a simple island retreat where you can escape into your own world for a few days – providing you can actually get there. Borroloola's Croc Spot Tours (℡08/8975 8734 or 8975 8721) will give you up-to-date information on how to get there by air or sea.

Tennant Creek

Visitors expect to be disappointed by **TENNANT CREEK**, lying 26km south of Three Ways and the butt of much "nether regions of the Universe" humour. Its appeal to tourists is not immediately apparent, but hang around and you'll discover an unpretentious Outback town, defying stagnation and hoping for prosperity.

John McDouall Stuart came through in the early 1860s, followed by the Overland Telegraph Line ten years later. Pastoralists and prospectors came from the south and east, and in 1933 Tennant Creek was the site of the last major **goldrush** in Australia. This was the time of gritty "gougers", such as Jack Noble and partner Bill Weaber (with one eye *between* them), who defied the Depression by pegging some of the town's most productive claims. Modern methods of gold retrieval have caused a revival in recent years, although tenacity and luck still have much to do with striking it rich. Recently, the near-exhausted Peko mine was assessed one more time and then sold for a song; its new owners drilled a little bit deeper and struck payable gold.

Arrival, information and accommodation

Tennant Creek is 504km from Alice and 664km from Katherine. The **airport** is about 3km from the centre, at the end of Davidson Street; for a **taxi** into town from the airport, call ☎08/8962 1061 or your chosen accommodation may pick you up. On Paterson Street (the town's main street – essentially the Stuart Highway) you'll find the Transit Centre where interstate **buses** pull in – some buses come through at 3.30am, which doesn't exactly encourage stopovers, although the hostel (see "Accommodation", below) tries to meet all buses; look out for the yellow van.

The visitors centre, **Battery Hill Regional Centre** (daily 9am–5pm, Sat 9am–noon during the Wet; ☎08/8962 3388, ⓔ tcrta@topend.com.au), is at an old mine site 1.5km east along Peko Road. Once here you might as well take the sixty-minute **tour** of the site (at least two daily; $13), which includes an entertaining stroll through a specially built show mine and a chance to appreciate the din of the old stamp battery itself. If staying overnight, expect free frogs in the bathrooms.

Accommodation

El Dorado, Paterson St North (☎08/8962 2402, ⓕ 8962 3034). One of the town's better motels, with a licensed restaurant and nice pool area. ❺

Outback Caravan Park, Peko Rd (☎08/8962 2459). Shady and comfortable caravan park with shop and pool. On-site vans ❸, cabins ❹

Safari Backpackers, Davidson St (☎08/8962 2207, ⓕ 8962 3188). Clean new block with four-bed dorms, doubles, kitchen, TV and functional air-con. Rooms ❶–❸, dorms ❶

Safari Lodge Motel, Davidson St (☎08/8962 2207). Comfortable motel rooms right in town with *Fernanda's* (see opposite) right next door. ❹

TC Caravan Park, next to the Shell service station, Paterson St (☎08/8962 2325). Good deals for camping with a backpackers' bunkhouse, and roomy cabins. Bunkhouse ❷, cabins ❸

Tennant Creek Tourist's Rest, Leichhardt St (☎08/8962 2719). The characterful former youth hostel, hopefully still hanging on with an ageing row of two- and three-bed rooms with rattly air-con, a pool and an authentic "Tennant" feel. Rooms ❸, dorms ❶

The Town and around

With one or two free days on your hands, the limited prospects of Tennant Creek are spread before you. In town, the **museum** (daily 3.30–5.30pm; $2), across the road from the Memorial Club, minutely details the history of Tennant Creek, using a chronological time scale starting from the year 0 "AS" (After Stuart) and displaying plenty of pioneering relics. On the other side of Anzac Hill, check out the Ngalipanyangu Cultural Centre Aboriginal Arts and Crafts Gallery (Mon–Fri 8.30am–5pm) on Davidson Street, where you'll find a small selection of local dot **paintings and crafts** which are much cheaper than in Alice Springs – this is a place to buy as well as look.

That's about it unless you've got your own vehicle or want to **rent a bike** (see "Listings", opposite), in which case head up Peko Road, past the swimming pool, to the visitors centre and the **tour** mentioned above. Back in town there's also a paved cycle and walking trail out to the **Mary Ann Dam Recreation Area**, 5km north of town, with picnic space, birdlife and swimming in the rather dank reservoir.

Perhaps the best way to spend your time in town is by taking a **tour** ($28–50) of the various abandoned mine sites east of town. Norm's Gold and Scenic Tours (☎08/8962 2719) is highly recommended, giving you the lowdown on gold mining and making the whole business appear more interesting than you might expect. They also do fossicking tours; don't be surprised if you come home with a little nugget. Ten Ant Tours' (☎08/8962 2358) sunset rides to the

Devil's Pebbles (16km northwest of town) shouldn't be confused with trips to the much more impressive Devil's Marbles (see p.654) on the road to Alice Springs. On the way to the Pebbles, you pass one of four surviving **telegraph stations**, recently restored as an historic exhibit (☎08/8962 3388 for opening times). If you've come down the Track and not seen an OTL station yet, here's your chance.

Restaurants

Tennant Creek's **eating** opportunities are slowly catching up with the rest of the world. The better places are listed below. Besides these, there are functional restaurants in the *El Dorado* and *Bluestone* motels.

Fernanda's, 1 Noble St (☎08/8962 3999). Mediterranean flavour and the best seafood in Tennant Creek. Have a look at a map to find the nearest beach to see just how big a claim this could be.
Memorial Club, Schmidt St. At the "Memo" you can sign in and get a decent counter meal to eat in (or take away) for around $10 plus a quiet place for a drink afterwards. Meals noon–2pm & 6pm until late.
Tennant Creek Hotel, Paterson St. Good restaurant attached to one of the town's more tranquil pubs.

Drinking and nightlife

Dedicated drinkers are well looked after, as the town boasts around thirteen licences and two **pubs**. The fortnightly "Thirsty Thursday" sees takeaway sales banned in an effort to curb excessive waste of welfare cheques (issued on Thurs). Like a lot of pubs in Outback towns, front bars can become intimidating arenas of flying bottles and vitriol, while the carpeted back bars are for games of pool and benign socializing. Pubs are generally open from 10am to midnight.

The *Goldfields*, on Paterson Street, has a cleared front bar where you can get a good swing at your neighbour without breaking any of the fittings; the back bar is the place to take your mum for a sherry. Over the road, the *Tennant Creek Hotel* has tried to revamp its old mining image with a blues-proof (punch-ups, not John Lee Hooker) front bar and a tamer back bar for a quiet drink, and *The Shaft*, the town's only **disco** (Thurs–Sat 11pm–3am), enabling licensed drinking into the night. *Jackson's Bar* is where the legendary beer cart got mired on the way to the original settlement near the telegraph station, sixty years ago. The beer cart wouldn't budge, so the settlement relocated around it, drank it dry and the rest is history.

If you just want a quiet drink don't forget the "Memo" (see above) or "Sporties" clubs (the latter on Ambrose Street); at either you can easily sign in as a guest and enjoy the tame if somewhat suburban atmosphere.

Listings

Airlines Air North (free call ☎ 1800 627 474) has daily flights to Darwin and Alice Springs. Tickets can be bought or changed at the newsagent, 54 Paterson St (☎08/8962 2211), just up from the Transit Centre.
Bike rental Bridgestone Tyre Centre, 52 Paterson St (Mon–Sat 8am–5pm; ☎08/8962 2361).
Book exchange Holly's, opposite the swimming pool on Peko Rd.
Bus tickets Tickets can be bought or changed at the Paterson St newsagent (see above).
Car rental *Outback Caravan Park*, Peko Rd (☎ 08/8962 2459), for Hertz; or Ten Ant Tours,

Transit Centre, Paterson St (☎08/8962 2358).
Hospital Leichhardt St (☎08/8962 4399).
Internet access *Switch*, next to the Transit Centre.
Pharmacy 50 Paterson St (after hours ☎08/8962 2093).
Police Paterson St, next to the post office (☎08/8962 4444).
Post office Cnr Memorial Drive and Paterson St.
Supermarket The Food Barn, opposite the post office (daily 8am–6pm).
Swimming pool Peko Rd (Sept & Oct 11am–6pm; Nov–May 6–7.30am & 11am–7.30pm; $1).

Towards Alice and the Centre

The 500km from Tennant Creek to Alice are no more enthralling than the 500km that's gone before, and the places en route, detailed below, are easily visited only by those with their own transport or by especially determined bus travellers.

The **Devil's Marbles**, just over 100km south of Tennant Creek, are a genuine geological oddity, a scattering of huge rounded boulders thought by the local Warumungu Aborigines to be the eggs of the Rainbow Serpent; they're well worth a look, as they're only 2km off the highway. You'll find a spacious camping area and car park with toilets, barbecues and shaded tables, but no water and little firewood. A **helicopter** stands by, offering ten-minute flights for $35 (℡08/8964 1936; minimum of three people required) and Norm's and Ten Ant Tours do day-trips down here from Tennant, if there are enough people. A short drive from the Marbles is the comfortable old roadhouse/pub of **WAUCHOPE** (pronounced "walkup"). **WYCLIFFE WELL**, a little further south, has a good foreign beer selection, a nice park and lake round the back, an alien spaceship in the forecourt, camping and rooms (❹). Several UFOs have been seen around here in recent years.

BARROW CREEK, 60km further on, is one of the oldest roadhouses on the Track, originally a telegraph station, and remembered as the site of the **Barrow Creek Massacre** in 1874. It's never quite clear to whom the word "massacre" applied – the two dead and several wounded during an attack on the two-year-old station by the local Kaitej, or those who perished in the two-months' "speedy and severe" retribution demanded by the *Northern Territory News*. The pub itself (℡08/8956 9753) has walls daubed in coarse humour, as well as old-fashioned rooms (❹) and cheaper cabins (❷–❸) out back.

At **TI TREE**, an Aboriginal community close to the middle of the continent, the Aaki Gallery sells keenly priced artefacts and paintings produced by local Anmatjera. After another 43km, the **AILERON** roadhouse (❺) has the last fuel before Alice and also sells Aboriginal art; in a shrewd marketing ploy, the first beer in the bar is free to backpackers staying overnight.

The Plenty Highway and Tanami Road

Heading towards Alice, the land finally begins to crumple as you near the MacDonnell Ranges. The **Plenty** and **Sandover highways**, which run off the Stuart Highway 66km south of Aileron, head northeast towards Queensland through the scenic Harts and Jervois ranges. Both are passable to sound, well-equipped conventional cars – the Plenty is generally the busier and better maintained. If you're heading down to Birdsville or Winton (Queensland) this way, the Donahue Highway short cut down to Boulia isn't half as bad as maps suggest.

Twenty kilometres north of Alice, the **Tanami Road** leads over 1000km northwest to Halls Creek in Western Australia. Again, the track is easily passable in a 2WD up to the NT/WA border where things can get a little rough and sandy. The longest section without fuel is the 322km from Yuendumu to **Rabbit Flat** roadhouse (closed Tues–Thurs), with the next section to Billiluna station nearly as long at 292km. You can also pop into the art gallery at the desert outstation of **Balgo Hills** (sometimes fuel), 31km south of the Tanami, whose garish and splodgy school of dot paintings is highly distinctive; the turn-off is about 88km on the WA side of the track.

Before embarking on either route, it's worth checking out the condition of the tracks; phone RACQ (for Queensland sections ℡07/3219 0900,

Emergency Services in Alice Springs ℡08/8922 3232 or Main Roads Dept WA ℡08/9168 6007); you can also read daily **print-outs** of the track conditions at the tourist information office in Alice Springs (daily 9am–6pm; ℡08/8952 5800). While they shouldn't be considered a time-saving short cut, the Plenty and Tanami tracks are both perfectly feasible in a tough, well-equipped 2WD vehicle, and certainly give a taste of the real Outback you'll never get on the tarmac highway.

Alice and the Centre

A land such as this, with its great loneliness, its dearth of life, and its enshrouding atmosphere of awe and mystery, has a voice of its own, distinctly different from that of the ordinary Australian bush.

Ernest Favenc, *Voices in the Desert*, 1905

Set in what is just about the geographical centre of the continent, **Alice Springs** has a population of just 25,000, yet is still the largest settlement of the Australian interior. A clean, modern and compact town in the midst of the MacDonnell Ranges, it makes an excellent base from which to plan trips into the surrounding countryside.

The **Red Centre**, a marketing term coined to describe the area to the south, west and east of Alice Springs, is an historically rich and scenically spectacular region. It includes the lands inhabited by the "Anangu", the more easily pronounceable name for the Aborigines from the Uluru region. The Aborigines around here were fortunate in being among the last to come into contact with white settlers. As a result of this and the necessary strictness of desert nomads' laws, they and their fascinating but arcane culture have survived relatively unscathed. Here, as much as anywhere in Australia, some Aborigines are living the life of their choice on their traditional homelands, and dealing with the neighbouring white culture on their own terms.

Ayers Rock – known to the Anangu as **Uluru** – is Australia's most famous and most visited natural spectacle, and still the primary reason why most people come to the Red Centre. At first sight, even jaded "seen-it-all" cynics will find it hard to take their eyes away from its awesome bulk. But there's much more here than just the Rock, and it's rare in Outback Australia to find such a large region crammed with worthwhile and accessible places of interest. The **West MacDonnells**, a series of rugged ridges cut at intervals by slender chasms or enormous gorges, start right on Alice's doorstep. In the other direction, the **Eastern MacDonnells** are less visited but no less appealing, with the remote tracks of the **Simpson Desert** to the south attracting the intrepid. To the west, **Palm Valley**, now linked to **Kings Canyon** via a good dirt road, can add a few days to a trip which, including the Rock, makes for probably the most memorable tour in the Outback. While most of these places certainly don't need a 4WD vehicle to get to, there are a few enjoyable and easy off-road tracks that can be fun in a rented 4WD; they're detailed in the box on pp.674–675.

When to go

The aridity of the Centre results in extremes of temperature that are best avoided, if at all possible. In the midwinter months of July and August the air is lovely and clear although **freezing nights**, especially around Uluru, are not uncommon. But there's no escaping the **summer heat**: in December and January the temperature may have already reached 40°C by 10am and doesn't drop below 30°C all night. Autumn (April–June) and Spring (Sept & Oct) are ideal times to explore the region in comfort.

Rain is a rare and wonderful thing in the Centre. In Alice, most houses don't have gutters: they would rarely be needed and, in any case, would be unable to cope with the deluge when it comes. Whenever you visit, a sudden storm may temporarily transform the desert into a garden of exquisite flowers as well as cut off access along even the main roads.

Out here a **wide-brimmed hat** is not so much a fashion accessory as a life saver, keeping your head and face in permanent shadow. All but the shortest of walks will also require a **water bottle** and loose, long-sleeved clothing plus lashings of **sun block** on any exposed skin. Australia's many venomous but rarely seen snakes and, more relevantly, rocky tracks and the carpet of prickly spinifex grass that covers one-fifth of the continent, make a pair of **covered shoes or boots** the final elementary precaution to safe and comfortable enjoyment of the Centre.

Alice Springs and around

Most visitors are surprised by the modern appearance of **ALICE SPRINGS**. The bright, clear desert air gives the Outback town a charge you don't find in the languid, tropical north. In Alice, the shopping centre is in the busy town centre and not in some peripheral suburb, and so allusions to Nevil Shute's fly-blown *A Town Like Alice*, or even Robyn Davidson's ockersome observations in *Tracks*, have long been obsolete.

The area has been inhabited for at least thirty thousand years by Aranda Aborigines, who moved between the waterhole of Alice Springs (Tjanerilji) and other reliable water sources in the MacDonnell Ranges. But, as elsewhere in The Territory, it was only the Overland Telegraph Line's arrival in the 1870s that led to a permanent settlement here. Following **John McDouall Stuart's** exploratory journeys through the area in the early 1860s, it was the visionary **Charles Todd**, then South Australia's Superintendent of Telegraphs, who saw the need to link Australia with the rest of the empire. The town's river and its tributary carry his name, and the spring that of his wife, Alice.

With repeater stations needed every 250km from Adelaide to Darwin to boost the OTL signal, the site just north of today's town, with its permanent "spring" (actually a billabong on the Todd River), was ideal as a place to erect the necessary buildings. When a spurious ruby rush led to the discovery of gold at Arltunga in the Eastern MacDonnells, **Stuart Town** (the town's seldom-used official name in its early years) became a jumping-off point for the long slog to the riches out east. Arltunga's goldrush fizzled out under desperate conditions, but the township of Stuart remained, a collection of shanty dwellings serving a stream of pastoralists, prospectors and missionaries.

In 1929 the **railway line** from Adelaide finally reached Stuart Town. Journeys that had once taken weeks by camel from Oodnadatta could now be under-

ACCOMMODATION

Alice Lodge	1
Alice Tourist Apartments	12
Desert Rose Inn	3
Diplomat Hotel	6
Elke's	9
Frontier Oasis Motel	10
Melanka Backpackers Resort	7
Ossies Homestead	2
Outback Motor Lodge	15
Pioneer YHA	4
Swagman's Rest	13
Territory Inn	5
Toddy's Backpackers	8
Vista Hotel	11
White Gum Holiday Inn	14

CENTRAL ALICE SPRINGS

Pedestrianised street

Train Station

N

Anzac Hill

Anzac Oval

WILLS TERRACE

Alice Plaza

Old Courthouse

"Sails"

PARSONS STREET

Stuart Town Gaol

The Residency

Mall

Adelaide House

Yeperenye Shopping Centre

McCafferty's Bus Terminal

GREGORY TERRACE

Panorama Guth

STOTT TERRACE

Greyhound Pioneer Bus Terminal

Olive Pink Botanical Reserve

RFDS Visitors' Centre

Hospital

0   250m

Todd River (usually dry)

STUART HIGHWAY

RAILWAY TERRACE

BATH STREET

HARTLEY STREET

TODD STREET

GEORGE CRES

GEORGE CRES

LARAPINTA DRIVE

STUART TERRACE

Alice Springs Desert Park & West MacDonnell Ranges

NORTHERN TERRITORY | Alice Springs and around

taken in just a few days and by 1933, when the town officially took the name Alice Springs, the population had mushroomed to nearly five hundred Europeans. In 1942 the bombing and subsequent evacuation of Darwin saw Alice Springs become The Territory's administrative headquarters and a busy military base, supplying the war zone in the north. After the hostilities ceased, some of the wartime population stayed on and Alice's fortunes continued to grow slowly. In the meantime, wealthy tourists began to visit the mysterious monolith in the desert, southwest of town – for thousands of years a store of sites sacred to the Anangu.

With the reconstruction of the notoriously unreliable rail link from Adelaide and a new, tar-sealed, Stuart Highway completed in the mid-1980s, Alice has only recently attained its present size and unexpected modernity. A **tourist boom** at that time, helped in no small measure by the massive publicity surrounding Azaria Chamberlain's reputed canine abduction at the Rock (as portrayed in the movie *A Cry in the Dark*), has waned a little in recent years, but Alice still remains the undisputed "capital" of the Outback. Even so, the population remains tiny: within a thousand-kilometre radius of "The Alice", as it's affectionately known, there are fewer than forty thousand inhabitants. The town has embraced tourism wholeheartedly and although the continuing improvements of the on-site *Ayers Rock Resort* has affected trade, Alice still seems set to succeed, primarily because both the town and surrounding area have much to offer, even without the obligatory visit to the Rock.

Arrival, information and transport

The **airport** is 14km south of town. The airport shuttle (☎08/8953 0310) meets incoming flights and costs $9.90 or $16.50 return, while a taxi (☎08/8952 1877) will be about $25. Greyhound Pioneer **buses** arrive at the

Coles Complex on West Stott Street; McCafferty's buses outside their office on Gregory Terrace, opposite the tourist office. Some of the keener hostels send minibuses to meet incoming buses (as well as some incoming flights). Alice's **train station** – open only when trains are due to arrive – is on George Crescent on the west side of the Stuart Highway, just off Larapinta Drive, about a fifteen-minute walk (or $4 taxi ride) from the town centre.

The **tourist information office** (daily 9am–6pm; ☎08/8952 5800, ⦿www.centralaustraliantourism.com) is in Gregory Terrace at the river end by the library and council offices. Besides all the usual stuff there's also a helpful Parks and Wildlife Commission desk (☎08/8951 5210), providing information on their parks and other services in Central Australia.

Transport

The centre occupies a compact area between the Stuart Highway and Leichhardt Terrace, along the dry Todd River, bordered to the north and south by Wills Terrace and Stott Terrace respectively. Bisecting this rectangle is **Todd Mall**, once the main street, now a relaxing pedestrian thoroughfare lined with alfresco cafés, galleries and souvenir outlets.

The town's sights are scattered, but you can still get around them all in a couple of days on foot. An alternative is to use the green and yellow **Alice Wanderer** (☎08/8952 2111; day-ticket $22), a "hop on, hop off" bus service with commentary, visiting most of the places of interest every seventy minutes. The Yeperenye Shopping Centre, around the corner from the tourist office, on Hartley Street, is the terminus for the **suburban bus** network. This is tailored for shoppers and schoolchildren, which means you'll have to plan your ride around a timetable (available from the tourist office or the Council Offices on Gregory Terrace) rather than just turning up at a bus stop and waiting; of the four main routes, **#1 West** and **#4 South** are the most useful. Otherwise your best bet is to rent a **car** (see "Listings", p.664), or a **bicycle** from any of the hostels, for around $12 a day. There's an enjoyable seventeen-kilometre **paved cycle track** through the bush to Simpson's Gap, starting at Flynn's Grave, 7km along Larapinta Drive, west of the town centre.

Accommodation

There's plenty of choice of accommodation in Alice, most places (except the campsites) are either in the central area or along **Todd Street** and its continuation, **Gap Road** – a fifteen-minute walk from the centre, despite what people may claim. Booking ahead is advisable during the winter school holidays (June & July) or during special events. Note that the price codes given for self-contained apartments are for a unit sleeping between four and six people; they often work out a better deal all round than a motel and are certainly more spacious.

Motels

Desert Rose Inn, 15 Railway Terrace (☎08/8952 1411 or free call 1800 896 116, ⓕ 8952 3232, ⓔ desertroseinn@octa4.net.au). Good-value budget motel in town, with cooking facilities in the rooms, a BBQ area and off-street parking. ❹

Diplomat Hotel, 15 Gregory Terrace (☎08/8952 8977, ⓕ 8953 0225, ⓔ fort.diplomat@bigpond.com.au). Right in town, a large four-star motel popular with big bus tours. ❻–❽

Frontier Oasis Motel, 10 Gap Rd (☎08/8952 1444, ⓕ 8952 3776, ⓔ foasis@allseasons.com.au). Nicely laid-out motel with landscaped pool area, comfortable rooms and a fine restaurant/bar. ❼

Territory Inn, Leichhardt Terrace (☎08/8950 6666 or free call 1800 089 644, ⓕ 8952 7829, ⓔ tti@aurora-resorts.com.au). Large motel backing onto Todd Mall and about as central as they get. ❼

Vista Hotel, Stephens Rd (☎08/8952 6100 or free call 1800 810 644, ⓕ 8952 1988). Well-equipped, modern four-star hotel tucked under the MacDonnell Ranges with a pool, tennis courts and a good restaurant. **❼**

Self-contained apartments

Alice Tourist Apartments, cnr Gnoilya St and Gap Rd (☎08/8952 2788 or free call 1800 806 142, ⓕ8953 2950). Large, well-equipped apartments at the far end of Gap Rd. **❺**

Outback Motor Lodge, South Terrace (☎08/8952 3888 or free call 1800 896 133, ⓕ8953 2166, ⓔoml@asaccom.mtx.net.au). Among the best deals in this category, with more room than many more expensive motels. **❺**

Swagman's Rest, 67–69 Gap Rd (☎08/8953 1333 or free call 1800 089 612, ⓕ8953 0404). Another good-value, self-contained option on Gap Rd. **❺**

White Gum Holiday Inn, 17 Gap Rd (☎08/8952 5144 or free call 1800 896 131, ⓕ8953 2092). Nearest self-contained apartments to town centre. **❹**

Hostels

Alice Lodge, 4 Mueller St (☎08/8953 1975 or free call 1800 351 1925). Often-overlooked converted house in a quiet, residential area on the east side of the river, with no parking problems. Long-stay deals, nice garden and pool. Converted caravans are a good option. Rooms **❸**, dorms **❶**

Elke's, 39 Gap Rd (☎08/8952 8134 or free call 1800 633 354, ⓕ8952 8143). Former self-contained apartments with various-sized air-con rooms from twins to eights, each sharing a bathroom and small kitchen with TV. Nice pool area and free breakfasts make up for the lack of a good communal area. Rooms **❹**, dorms **❶**

Melanka Backpackers Resort, 94 Todd St (☎08/8952 4744 or free call 1800 896 110, ⓕ8952 2890, ⓦwww.melanka.com.au). Huge complex of central but ageing motel buildings pop-ular with unfussy young backpackers. Has a popular bar, *Skippy's*, and a cafeteria with cheap meals, a pool and even beach volleyball. Avoid the four-bed dorms unless you're a sardine; the eights have more room. Rooms **❸**, dorms **❶**

Ossies Homestead, 18 Warburton St (☎08/8952 2308 or free call 1800 628 211, ⓕ8953 2211, ⓔossies@ossies.com.au). Small and friendly hostel in quiet residential street no further than the Gap Rd options, with pet 'roo, pool, bikes and horse rides too. Mixed dorms plus some four- and twin-bed rooms. Rooms **❷**, dorms **❶**

Pioneer YHA, Todd River end of Parsons St (☎08/8952 8855, ⓕ8952 4144, ⓔalicepioneer@yhant.org.au). The most central location by far, just half a minute from the "Sails" awning (though parking can be a problem). Mostly four-bed air-con dorms, plus a pool and a clean and spacious kitchen. Dorms **❷**

Toddy's Backpackers, 41 Gap Rd (☎08/8952 1322, ⓕ8952 1767). Popular large (but friendly) resort next to *Elke's* and with very cheap mixed, eight-bed dorms, smaller dorms and "de luxe" double rooms with bath, fridge and TV. Bargain evening meals with bar, BBQs and occasional entertainment, pool, bikes, tour information and bookings. Rooms **❸**, dorms **❶**

Campsites and caravan parks

Macdonnell Range Holiday Park, Palm Place (☎08/8952 6111). Camping and cabins in a leafy setting with all mod-cons and aiport pick-ups. Cabins **❸**

Stuart Tourist Park, opposite Araluen Centre, Larapinta Drive (☎08/8952 2547). Most central caravan park with regular camping and powered sites. On-site vans **❸**

Wintersun Caravan Park, Stuart Highway, 3km north of town (☎08/8952 4080). Regular camping and powered sites. On-site vans **❸**

The Town

Start your tour of town by nipping up to **Anzac Hill** (off Wills Terrace) for a great view over Alice to the Heavitree Ranges beyond. In town, on Parsons Street is the **Old Courthouse** (daily 10am–2pm; $2), former residence of the governor of southern NT; it now displays the National Pioneer Women's Hall of Fame. Across the street, though barely worth the effort, is the **Residency** and the **Stuart Town Gaol**, the latter Alice's oldest building, dating from 1909.

From the "Sails" awning, a short stroll down the mall will take you past **Adelaide House** (March–Nov Mon–Fri 10am–4pm, Sun 10am–noon; $3), an ingenious convection-cooled building designed by the Reverend John Flynn, founder of the Royal Flying Doctor Service (RFDS). Adelaide House was the first hospital in Central Australia, and also the site of Flynn and Alf Treager's innovative radio experiments using portable, pedal-generated electricity. Inside you'll come across early medical and RFDS memorabilia. If you want to find out more about the RFDS, head down Hartley Street to the **RFDS Visitors Centre** (March–Nov Mon–Sat 9am–4pm, Sun 1–4pm; $5.25) on Stuart Terrace, which has half-hourly tours including a film describing the work of this unique medical organization, still subsidized by charitable donations.

Next door to Adelaide House is the **John Flynn Memorial Church** and, at 65 Hartley St, you'll find **Panorama Guth** (Mon–Sat 9am–5pm, Sun 2–5pm; $5), a museum and art gallery displaying Henk Guth's eminently forgettable landscapes, as well as original Albert Namatjira watercolours (see box p.672 for more on Namatjira's life and the Hermannsburg school of painting he initiated). Much more curious is the collection of rare Aboriginal artefacts found here, including some sacred and totemic objects (*tjuringas*) that you'll rarely see elsewhere. The panorama, from which the gallery takes its name, is a novel if unremarkable painting, 60m in circumference, showing the area around Alice, but the gallery below is a wonderfully comfy and congenial place to snooze through the regional home movies on show.

When you've had enough of artefacts and memorabilia, pack a lunch and cycle out to the **Olive Pink Botanical Reserve** (daily 10am–6pm; donation), just across the causeway on Tuncks Road. Olive Pink, whose life story is about to be made into a film, was a passionate defender of Aboriginal rights long before the issue became fashionable. Like Ted Strehlow (see opposite) she practised a kind of fanatical "inverted eugenics", working solely for the welfare and preservation of "full blood" tribal Aborigines and their lore, while dismissing those of mixed blood as a lost cause. She also found time to collect native flora from the surrounding lands, all of which can be seen neatly labelled along pathways winding up through the reserve. Displays in the **visitors centre** (daily 10am–4pm) explain the various strategies the plants use to survive in the desert.

The Telegraph Station and School of the Air

The old **Telegraph Station** (daily 8am–5pm, picnic grounds until 9pm; $6) is tucked in the hills just to the north of town. Fully restored and accessible along a three-kilometre riverside walk from Wills Terrace (or off the Stuart Highway, 4km north of town), the historic reserve – situated right by the pool from which the town derives its name – faithfully re-creates the settlement's earliest years. There are free and informative thirty-minute **tours** (April–Oct 8.30am–4.30pm; Nov–March 10am–3pm) further detailing pioneering life at the telegraph station. All in all, it's a pleasant place to while away a quiet afternoon, with the surrounding picnic area giving a taste of the Outback on the edge of a city. The station is also the starting point of the **Larapinta Trail** bushwalk to Standley Chasm in the Western MacDonnells (see p.667).

On the other side of the Stuart Highway is the **School of the Air** (Mon–Sat 8.30am–4.30pm, Sun 1.30–4.30pm; closed during school holidays; $3.50), at 80 Head St. Explanatory sessions are offered every thirty minutes on this famous Outback institution, through which children living on remote stations are taught over the radio. It's mostly visited by overseas schoolchildren and teachers, though visiting British royalty have taken a nodding interest at various times, too. From town, take bus #3 and alight at stop 5 or 11.

Along Larapinta Drive to the Alice Springs Desert Park

Larapinta Drive heads out through the western suburbs past the **Alice Springs Cultural Precinct** (daily 10am–5pm; $7), some 2km from the town, to the new Alice Springs Desert Park, one of the town's premier attractions.

The walk to the Precinct isn't too bad, but check out the bus service heading this way if you're continuing to the park.

The precinct has brought together some of Alice's more interesting attractions. The **Araluen Centre for Arts and Entertainment**, for example, is the focal point for the performing arts in the region with a 500-seat theatre, cinema, and art galleries that always have something on that is worth checking out. **The Central Australian Aviation Museum**, located in the Old Connellan Hangar, houses many of the aircraft that pioneered travel in the Outback and has a special memorial to the "Coffee Royale Incident" of 1929, in which rescuers searching for missing aviator and national hero Charles Kingsford-Smith crashed and perished in the northern Tanami desert. Kingsford-Smith, was accused of cynically staging the crash for publicity purposes, though this was never proved; the memorial poignantly displays the wreckage of the long-lost *Kookaburra* used in the search.

The **Museum of Central Australia** contains local fauna, including the largest bird that ever lived, an impressive display of locally found meteorites and an exhibition on the life and works of **Ted Strehlow**, son of a Hermannsburg missionary and Aranda initiate, who devoted his life to studying these Aborigines. Betraying their trust in later years, Strehlow disclosed his ceremonial knowledge and sacred objects to his second wife, Kathleen, and a battle now seethes for the return of the material that the late Strehlow collected. Many of the *tjuringas* are locked "for safe keeping" in the centre's vault; some are so sacred that they should only ever be seen by initiated Aranda men. For a taste of Strehlow's work, his sixty-page article *Central Australian Religion*, published in 1964, is available at the Arunta Bookshop (see "Listings", p.664); it's a good taster before getting stuck into his weightier *Aranda Traditions* (1947), whose ideas were taken up in the well-known works of Claude Lévi-Strauss.

Around the corner on Memorial Drive is the **Alice Springs Memorial Cemetery**, includes the graves of pioneer aviator Eddie Connellan, artist Albert Namatjira and the reburied remains of the legendary, luckless prospector Harold Lasseter, after whom the town's casino is rather ironically named.

Alice's latest attraction is the **Alice Springs Desert Park** (daily 7.30am–6pm; $18) phase one of which opened in March 1997. Set right beneath the ranges topped by Mount Gillen, the park is an example of a thoughtful and imaginative design displaying various natural environments of The Territory. Allow yourself at least two hours to fully appreciate the centre's ecology. Shown on the hour, the twenty-minute **film** is actually a little overportentous, and the real highlight, after you've wandered through various **aviaries** and creek, sand-dune and woodland habitats, is the large **nocturnal house** where The Territory's varied, but rarely seen, fauna can be seen scurrying around in moonlit action. The park succeeds in blurring the boundary between the surrounding bush and the fenced interior – there's as much birdlife darting about outside the aviaries as in. Not to be missed.

Eating

For a town with the population of a couple of New York precincts, the **eating opportunities** in Alice aren't at all bad. And some places can turn a meal into an event, such as the dinners served on the old Ghan train once or twice a week (℡08/8955 5047); evenings at *The Winery* (℡08/8955 5133); or a ride out into the bush to crack whips and throw boomerangs, while the damper bakes, with the *Camp Oven Kitchen* (℡08/8953 1411). Alternatively, start the day with a gourmet **champagne breakfast**, having just watched the sunrise from a thousand metres up in a hot-air balloon (see "Tours from Alice" box, p.665).

Otherwise, Todd Mall is lined with **cafés** providing outdoor seating, and the **pubs** (see "Drinking, nightlife and entertainment", below) supply counter meals for well under $10. Besides the places listed below, some of the **hotels** have good restaurants; a queue of chattering locals is always a good sign.

Cafés and snack bars

Alice Plaza, Todd Mall. Food halls with Asian- and Italian-inspired lunches.

Bar Doppio Mediterranean, Fan Arcade, Todd Mall. Mouthwatering concoctions of trans-Adriatic and Asian dishes with pitta or rice.

Red Rock Café, Todd Mall, south end. Good breakfast spot for croissants and early morning people-watching.

Swinger's, Gregory Terrace, opposite the Environment Centre. A distinctly "arty/green" feel, serving imaginative snacks and meals.

Restaurants

Al Fresco, Todd Mall, next to the cinema. Delicious pasta and salad dishes with movie-and-meal deals on Monday night.

Dingos, Stott Terrace. Distinctive old building with a "bush meat", seafood and veggie menu.

Madigans, Alice Springs Desert Park, Larapinta Drive. Top quality bush tucker with a great setting (noon–3pm & 6.30pm–late).

Malathi's Restaurant, 51 Bath St. Possibly the world's first Irish–Indian restuarant with a bar that is a popular alternative to the town's more raucous pubs.

Oscars, Todd Mall Cinema Complex. A classy Italian restaurant offering surprisingly good-value and large portions, mostly under $15.

Overlander Steakhouse, 72 Hartley St (☏ 08/8952 2159). For the spirit *and* taste of the Outback; the "Drover's Blowout" gives you all your favourite Aussie fauna on a plate. Popular tourist spot, often featured on lifestyle and travel TV shows.

Red Ochre Grill, Todd Mall. Creative native Australian with some imaginative vege options. Breakfast from 6.30am and dinner until 9.30pm from $16.

Scotty's Tavern and **Alice's Restaurant**, Todd Mall. Bar and restaurant serving typical Territorian food (including emu).

Sultan's, cnr Gregory Terrace and Hartley St. Good-value traditional Turkish food with BYO wine.

Drinking, nightlife and entertainment

Like the surrounding desert, night-time Alice initially appears lifeless. However, something can be found going on somewhere most nights, particularly in the latter half of the week. The fortnightly freebie, *Pulse*, or Alice's daily *Centralian Advocate*, carry details of what's going on.

The *Todd Tavern*, at the top of Todd Mall, is the town's landmark **drinking** spot, complete with "unofficial" segregated bars. Thursday night at *Bojangles* on Todd Street is all action and *The Stuart Arms*, right by the "Sails", also features **live bands** most nights. The latter pub also houses *Legends*, the town's most popular **nightclub**; if you want to get past the bouncers, then collars and covered shoes are "the go". There's **jazz and blues** at *Scotty's* and at *The Winery* on Sunday afternoon from 1pm. *Sean's Irish Sibin* at *Malathi's Restaurant* (see above) is a quieter option, while homesick Brits can head for the *Firkin and Hound*, on Hartley Street, a British theme pub that shows just what can be done with a multilevel car park and a little imagination. If nothing else tempts you, there's always the **cinema** at the top of Todd Mall, with cheap nights on Tuesday. Check the programme at the **Araluen Arts Centre** (☏ 08/8952 5022) on Larapinta Drive: you'll usually find a worthwhile play, film or concert. And if you're feeling lucky, *Lasseters Hotel Casino* on Barrett Drive can accommodate you – but again, not in thongs and a tatty singlet.

Events

More energetic activities tend to occur in the cooler months, starting with April's **Heritage Week** celebrating Alice's history, followed by the **Bangtail Muster** on the first Monday in May, a colourful and irreverent parade of silliness. The **Camel Cup races** in mid-July are Australia's biggest camel race meeting, ending in a huge fireworks display. The string of **rodeos** along the Track hits Alice in late August, while the town's most famous event, the wacky **Henley-on-Todd Regatta** kicks off in early October. Bottomless boats are run down the dry riverbed; needless to say, the event is heavily insured against the Todd actually flowing. On the last Sunday in November there is the **Corkwood Festival**, a celebration of art, music and dance, with food and craft stalls in Todd Mall. There's also a rather uninspiring **market** every Sunday in the mall.

Shopping for Aboriginal art

Alice has become the country's foremost centre for the art and crafts produced by Aboriginal people, and Todd Mall is full of galleries selling a vast range of

Buying and playing a didgeridoo

Didgeridoos, the simple wooden instruments whose eerie sound perfectly evokes the mysteries of Aboriginal Australia, have become phenomenally popular souvenirs in the last couple of years, with many vendors offering to pack and ship them to your home for free (expect a three-month delivery time to Europe). Authentic didges are created by termite-hollowed branches of trees and are considered to be indigenous to the Katherine region (where they can also be cheaper to buy). Minuscule, bamboo and even painted fibreglass didges have found their way onto the market, but a real didge is a natural tube of wood with a rough interior. Painted versions haven't got any symbolic meaning; plain ones look less tacky and are less expensive. Branches being what they are, every didge is different but if you're considering playing it rather than hanging it over the fireplace, aim for one around 1.3m in length with a 30–40mm diameter mouthpiece. Beeswax is often used to bring an oversize didge's mouthpiece down to an operable size, but a didge with a body of the right diameter and without wax can feel nicer to use. The bend doesn't affect the sound but the length and wall thickness (ideally around 10mm) does – avoid cumbersome, thick-walled items which get in the way of your face and sound flat.

You'll be surprised that making the right sound instead of an embarrassing raspberry will take only a few minutes of persistence; the key is to hum while letting your pressed lips flap, or vibrate, with the right pressure behind them – it's easier using the side of your mouth. The tricky bit – beyond the ability of most initiates – is to master circular breathing; this entails refilling your lungs through your nose while maintaining the sound with air expelled from your cheeks. A good way to get your head round this concept is to blow or "squirt" bubbles into a glass of water with a straw, while simultaneously inhaling through the nose. Unless you get the hang of circular breathing you'll be limited to making the same lung's worth of droning again and again.

Most outlets that sell didges also sell tapes and CDs and inexpensive "how to" booklets which offer hints on the mysteries of circular breathing and how to emit advanced sounds using your vocal chords.

The Sounds of Starlight show in Todd Mall (Nov–April Tues–Sat 7pm; $15) features Alice didge impressario Andrew Landford and friends and gives you a good chance to hear what can be done with a didge as well as being an entertaining night out. You'll also be given a free lesson afterwards, if you want.

And finally, remember that there is nothing magical about a didgeridoo; it's your lips that make the sound, which resonates through the tube – any tube. A length of grey 40mm PVC pipe from Mitre 10 may not have the same kudos but produces a similar sound at around $4 a metre.

high-quality work. Most common are the **dot paintings**, canvas depictions of the temporary sand paintings formerly used to pass on sacred knowledge during ceremonies of the Central Desert tribes. The modern manifestation of this school of art originated in the early 1970s at Papunya, northwest of Alice, under the encouragement of a local teacher, Geoff Bardon. What was intended as a kind of constructive graffiti for youngsters was taken up by the elders. Clifford Possum and Billy Stockman were among the earliest of the Papunya artists to find fame, and their paintings are free of the clumsy flashiness of some contemporary work. There are half a dozen lavish books offering a compilation of Central Desert art, the best of which is *Songlines and Dreamings* by Patrick Corbally Stourton (Lund Humphries) – you'll find it in Alice's bookshops.

While it's more difficult to recommended a single **gallery**, you'd do well starting your search at the Original Dreamtime Gallery, 63 Todd Mall, the Aboriginal Art and Culture Centre, 86 Todd St (it's still just a gallery despite the name) or Gallery Gondwana, 43 Todd Mall; all are attractive galleries full of good-quality work with the latter displaying some lovely Indonesian artefacts too. Less fancy in appearance but loaded with quality unframed canvases is the Aboriginal-owned Papunya Tula Artists, at 78 Todd St, and the similar Warumpi Arts round the corner on Gregory Terrace; you certainly won't save money by buying direct – usually the opposite – but you might feel happier about who benefits from the proceeds. Another place offering mediocre but inexpensive paintings and didgeridoos is The House of Oz, opposite *Melanka Backpackers Resort*, but in the end it's just a matter of spending half a day or more looking for what you want at a price that you find acceptable. The more you spend, the more chance there is of making a deal, with free overseas postage and insurance usually offered at the bigger places. If you're heading north, the galleries in Aileron, Ti Tree (see p.654) and Tennant Creek (p.652) have a much smaller range of Aboriginal art on sale, but often at less than half the price of that in Alice's galleries.

Listings

Airlines Ansett (☎08/8950 4115); Qantas (☎08/8950 5211). Both in Todd Street Mall near the "Sails", where you'll also find Flight Centre for discount flights (☎13 1600).

Banks All major banks are located on Todd Mall.

Bookshops Arunta Bookshop, Todd St, is very good for local history plus Aboriginal art and culture. Bookworm, Colacag Plaza (in the block between Gregory and Stott terraces), buys and sells secondhand books.

Camping supplies Alice Springs Disposals, Reg Harris Lane, off Todd Mall. See also "Secondhand Stuff" opposite.

Car rental Advance Car Rentals (☎08/8953 3700) have good deals, as do Boomerang Rentals (☎08/8955 5171). CC Rentals (☎08/8952 1405 or free call 1800 652 133), at 78 Todd St opposite the council offices, has mopeds, mokes and Suzuki 4WD jeeps, as well as special deals, as does Territory Thrifty (☎08/8952 9999), on the corner of Hartley St and Stott Terrace. They offer larger and much more comfortable Land Cruiser 4WDs with twin fuel tanks, plus an easily erected roof tent and a bundle of camping gear for just $25 extra per day. Britz Rentals Australia (☎08/8952 8814) uses more basic Land Cruisers converted into campers which have the advantage of built-in equipment which doesn't rattle around. Maui (free call ☎1800 363 800) offers identical campers, and Thrifty, at 92 Todd St (☎08/8952 2400), has bargain-priced 2WDs.

Fuel 24hr service and marginally cheaper fuel at the Shell truckstop on the North Stuart Highway.

Hospital Gap Rd (☎08/8951 7777).

Internet access There are two internet cafés in town: Outback Email, inside the Outback Travel Shop, on the corner of Gregory and Todd St, or at *Melanka* backpackers (see p.659).

Maps The Map Shop, 21 Gregory Terrace (☎08/8951 5393), for detailed maps of the Centre.

Pharmacies On Todd Mall and in the Yeperenye Shopping Centre.

Police Parsons St (☎08/8951 8888).

Post office Hartley St (☎08/8952 1020).

Trains The Ghan leaves Alice Springs each

Tours from Alice

A large number of professional **tour operators** offer adventurous, cultural or historic tours throughout the area – some recommended operators are listed below. Just about every hostel and hotel offers a tour-booking service, but if you feel you need more advice, ask at the official tourist information office on Hartley Street on the corner of Gregory Terrace (see "Arrival, information and transport", p.658). Alice Springs Tour Professionals, cnr Todd Street and Gregory Terrace (☎08/8953 0666, ✉astp@ozemail.com.au) act as a one-stop shop for many different tour companies.
Austour (free call ☎1800 335 009) Day-trips to Uluru for $180 – but you'll regret such a short visit. Also offers Eastern and Western MacDonnell tours.
Ballooning Downunder (☎08/8952 8816), **Outback Ballooning** (☎08/8952 8723) and **Spinifex** (☎08/8953 4800). Alice is Australia's ballooning capital and any of these will take you up, up and away – and back down to a champagne breakfast (around $170 for five hours). Don't wear your best clothes, as all hands are needed to pack up the dusty balloon.
Frontier Camel Tours (☎08/8953 0444). Short camel rides down the Todd River, two-and-a-half-day West Mac jaunts from *Glen Helen Lodge*, and five-day Simpson Desert treks.
Ooramina Bush Camp (☎08/8953 0170). One hour south of Alice offering horse rides and cattle station tours (from $160).
Ossie's Outback Horse Treks (☎08/8952 2308). Day, sunset and overnight rides up the Todd River's east bank from $60. Beginners welcome; discounts for YHA/VIP members.
Outback Experience (☎08/8955 2666). The best operator currently running trips to Chambers Pillar ($135) and other places in the northern Simpson.
Outback Mail Flights (☎08/8953 5000). Join the air-mail delivery service on their three weekly runs up to Rabbit Flat northwest of Alice; northeast to the Utopia region or southeast to Mount Dare station on the edge of the Simpson. It's an interesting alternative to standard scenic flights for around $220.
Rockayer (☎08/8956 2345) and **Yarringka Air** (☎08/8956 7873). Flights to the Rock and back in a day for around $300.
Rod Steinert (via AAT Kings, free call ☎1800 334 009). Several Aboriginal culture tours in the Alice area, including the excellent, half-day Dreamtime tour ($79). While the apparently solemn "corroboree" will bore or embarrass you, the rest of the tour is unusually informative, educational and provocative.
Sahara Outback Tours (☎08/8953 0881). Offers two-, three- and five-day camping tours through the West MacDonnells, to Kings Canyon and Uluru. As is often the case, the longer tours are much the best value.

Tuesday and Friday at 2pm and arrives in Adelaide at 10am the next day, with the return leg to Alice departing Adelaide on Monday and Thursday at 2pm and arriving at 10am. Coach class (no bed or meals) costs $170 ($136 from Port Augusta); first class costs over three times as much, with a sleeper and meals included; with "holiday class" you get a four-berth sleeper for around $351, but no meals. Change at Port Augusta to connect with the Indian Pacific line.

Sights south of Alice

Several sites of interest are located beyond **Heavitree Gap**, a couple of kilometres south of town. The first three described below are within range of the #4 bus, which terminates at the **Old Timers Folk Museum** (April–Nov daily 2–4pm; $2), just off the Stuart Highway, yet another display of pioneering memorabilia. The remainder are easily reached by bike, or on the Alice Wanderer bus route.

Head first for the **Pitchi Ritchi Aboriginal Cultural Experience** (daily 9am–2pm; $15), out on Palm Circuit, which, in addition to being a collection of fairly crude, bush-gnarled relics, is also an animal sanctuary. The work of Leo Corbett, who once staked a bogus gold-mining claim on Heavitree Gap (Pitchi Ritchi means "gap in the range") to prevent it being quarried and widened, the sanctuary also features the peculiar Aboriginal-inspired sculptures of William Ricketts, which further enhance the place's eccentric feel. While here you're offered a mug of billy tea and damper and given the opportunity to crack whips, throw boomerangs and play a didgeridoo while the resident "bushie" plies you with yarns and Aboriginal lore.

Next door, the **Mecca Date Garden** (Mon–Fri 9am–5pm, Sat 9am–1pm; free) was Australia's first commercial date farm, set up in the 1950s. Dates themselves are believed to be the first plant to be cultivated by man, and the farm now produces around 3000kg of the fruit a year from trees introduced in the nineteenth century by Afghan cameleers. You are offered a free sample on arrival. Tours of the farm – basically rows of date palms with an informative commentary – start on the hour.

A farm of a very different sort is just a couple of kilometres down the Ross Highway. The **Frontier Camel Farm** (daily 9am–5pm; $9) offers short rides on camels, plus a museum of camels and cameleering as well as the **Arid Australian Reptiles Display**, a creepy round-up of the Centre's snakes and lizards. Introductory camel talks are given at 10.30am and 2pm (the Alice Wanderer bus coincides with these), and the Camel Farm also organizes longer tours in the region.

Back down the Stuart Highway just before the airport, about 10km south of town, the **Ghan Preservation Society** (daily 9am–5pm; $12) at MacDonnell Siding features a converted old train station housing a **museum** of Alice Springs' early rail years and is also involved in the refurbishment of old Ghan locomotives and rolling stock, which are used for **train rides** (☏08/8955 5047) along a short section of track. The next door **National Transport Hall of Fame** (9am–5pm; $5) features a collection of old cars, trucks and motorbikes, including a cute red Fiat Tipo, something called the "Mulga Express" (not your average touring Kingswood) as well as the original 8WD road train that used to slog up to Darwin during the 1930s at a hot and noisy 30kph.

Ghan .... but not forgotten

The legendary unreliability of the old Ghan rail service must have had the Afghan cameleers, whose services it replaced and in whose honour it was named, chuckling in their graves. The poorly surveyed line, which was laid directly onto the sand with little regard for contours and floodways, buckled, subsided and was frequently completely washed away by flash floods. Indeed, it was not terribly uncommon for the track to be washed out either side of the stranded train, requiring parachute drops of essential supplies to sustain the passengers while the line was relaid and bedded-in. Consequently, late arrivals were common – trains arriving up to three months late were recorded.

In 1980, the new line from Port Augusta, rerouted and constructed from "continuous", welded rails, reached Alice ahead of schedule, with trains now carrying twice the number of passengers in half the time. With its arrival, the fifty-year-long era of the notorious Ghan passed into history. The millions of redundant timber sleepers from the old line have been put to a variety of uses all over central Australia, propping up bars and cattle yards or fabricated into restaurant tables. They can still be found in the bush out along the old Ghan route or bought inexpensively at the Ghan Preservation Society (see above), making an authentic, if cumbersome, souvenir of the Centre's first rail link.

The MacDonnell Ranges

The **MacDonnell Ranges** are among the longest of the parallel ridge systems that corrugate the Centre's landscape. Their east–west axis, passing right through Alice Springs, is broken in many places by gaps carved through the ranges during better-watered epochs. It is these striking ruptures, along with the grandeur and colours of the rugged landscape – particularly west of Alice – which make a few days spent in the MacDonnells so worthwhile. The expansive **West MacDonnells National Park** is best appreciated with at least one overnight stay at any of the campsites mentioned below, while the often-overlooked **Eastern MacDonnells** have a more compact, intimate feel; a better bet if your time is limited. Both ranges can be visited as part of a tour (see box on p.665) or with your own vehicle. Although some tracks are unsealed, 4WD vehicles are mostly unnecessary. However, because most rental companies prefer you not to drive conventional cars on corrugated tracks, you may end up renting one. If you do, then make the most of its all-terrain capabilities; check out the box on pp.674–675.

A better way to get in touch with the West Macs is to do part of the **Larapinta Trail**, a long-distance footpath along the West MacDonnell ridge, starting at the telegraph station north of town (see p.660) and ending 220km to the west at Mount Sonder. The walk is divided into around a dozen sections with water tanks situated no more than a day's walk apart. So far, only some sections of the trail have been completed; call or visit the Parks & Wildlife Commission (℡08/8951 5210) in Alice's tourist information office for latest details and maps.

The West MacDonnells and Finke Gorge national parks

The **route** described below follows an anticlockwise loop out along Larapinta Drive and then Namatjira Drive to *Glen Helen Lodge*, from where a 110-kilometre dirt road brings you round to the turn-off for Palm Valley (4WD vehicles only), Hermannsburg and back to Alice – a total distance of 370km. The track passes through **Aboriginal land** on its return section, but no permit is required (unless stated), providing you keep to the road and camp at designated sites.

Leaving Alice along Larapinta Drive, you reach **John Flynn's Grave**, just past the Desert Park, 7km from town. Situated beneath Mount Gillen, a granite boulder set on a plinth marks the spot where John Flynn, founder of the RFDS, had his ashes interred in 1951. Originally one of the Devil's Marbles (see p.654), the boulder was recently claimed back by the Aborigines of that area, an example of the ridiculous excess of some land claims following the Mabo Decision (see p.1152). A little further is a turning to **Simpsons Gap** (gates open daily 8am–8pm), the nearest and most popular of the West Macs' gaps, where a white, sandy riverbed lined with red and ghost gums leads up to a small pool. Agile rock wallabies live on the cliffs and there's a **visitors centre** and barbecues, as well as a seventeen-kilometre cycle track leading back to town. The first stage of the **Larapinta Trail** ends here – a tough day's walk from the telegraph station in Alice.

Further along Larapinta Drive are the **Twin Ghost Gums**, immortalized in Albert Namatjira's definitive painting of the Centralian landscape, and just after the famed gums is a turn-off north to the tourist trap of **Standley**

Chasm (daily 7.30am–6pm; $4), 50km from Alice. Situated on Iwupataka Aboriginal Land, this is another popular spot, where a walk up the cycad palm-lined riverbed leads to a narrow chasm formed by the erosion of softer rock that once lay between the red-quartzite walls. Around noon both the eighty-metre-high walls are briefly lit by the overhead sun. There is also a café with a terrace and a souvenir shop; black-footed rock-wallabies are fed here daily at 9.30am.

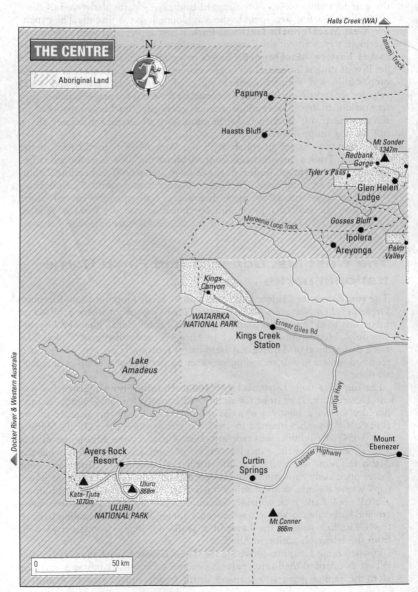

Along Namatjira Drive

Another 6km along Larapinta Drive, **Namatjira Drive** turns north amid the West MacDonnell Ranges; continuing on Larapinta brings you to Hermannsburg and Palm Valley (see p.671). Along Namatjira Drive, a scenic 42km ahead is **Ellery Big Hole** (barbecues, toilets and camping; $1), the deepest – and thus most permanent – waterhole in the area, and at times the coldest. Nevertheless, caught between the brief ebb and flow of visiting bus tours,

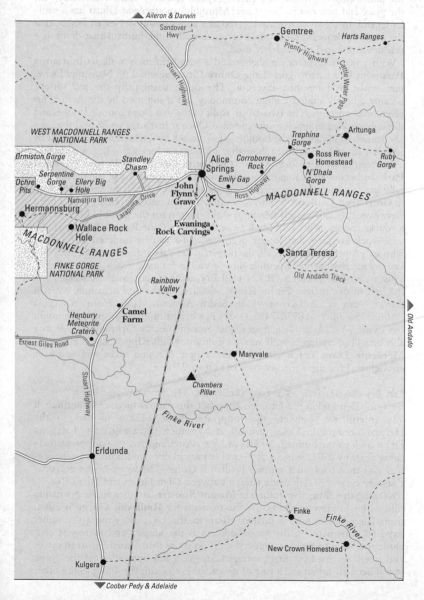

it's a pleasant spot, and your stealth may be rewarded by glimpses of wildlife quenching their thirst. Eleven kilometres to the west is **Serpentine Gorge** (toilets but no camping): the only way to appreciate this gorge is to swim across the small pool which sometimes blocks the entrance to the gorge (or climb over the ridge to the right). Few bother to exert themselves, but rock hopping upstream brings you to a flooded chasm. Like many concealed and perennial pools in Central Australia, its Aboriginal custodians have nurtured a myth about the pool being the home of a fierce serpent, and even today reluctantly visit the place and never enter the water; Mutujulu waterhole at Uluru has a similar legend. In this way the myth acted as a superstitious device to ensure that the pool – a droughtproof source of water vital to the humans that drank it – was never polluted or carelessly used.

With a new interpretation shelter and a wonderful new walk to **Inarlanga Pass** (actually a narrow gorge), the **Ochre Pits**, signposted off Namatjira Drive, now make an interesting diversion. The ochre, particularly the red variety, became a highly valued trading commodity and is still used by the Aranda for ceremonial purposes. The **two-hour walk** to the pass along rounded ridges and through wooded valleys is most enjoyable. Once at Inarlanga you'll find the egg-like kernels of cycads on the boulder-strewn creek bed, which is itself framed by acutely twisted beds of rock; altogether a lovely spot lacking only a waterhole.

Fourteen kilometres further west, **Ormiston Gorge** and **Pound National Park** (barbecues and camping) are also worth the effort. One of the most scenically spectacular and easily accessible spots in the West Macs, the short ascent up to **Gum Tree Lookout** (the walk continues down into the gorge) gives a great view over the 250-metre-high gorge walls rising from the pools below – home to ducks and even the odd black swan. The three-hour **Pound Walk** includes some rock-hopping, and longer overnight walks can be undertaken by those who are properly prepared – ask the rangers at the Park Information Centre, who also organize occasional free slide show evenings for campers.

Just west of Ormiston is **GLEN HELEN**, another perennial waterhole along the bed of the ancient **Finke River**, which – on the rare occasions when it flows – can reach Lake Eyre in South Australia. *Glen Helen Homestead* (☏ 08/8956 7489, ℻ 8956 7495; ❷–❽) is a beautiful place to spend the night out in the West Macs. Helicopter flights over the nearby Ormiston Gorge may also be still operating here. If you're heading towards Kings Canyon along the **Mereenie Loop Track**, get your permit here ($2) and make sure you have enough fuel for the entire journey of at least 250km.

On to Redbank Gorge, Gosses Bluff and Ipolera

Beyond Glen Helen the bitumen ends, but the natural spectacles continue. If you intend to complete the loop, it's about 111km of dirt to the Hermannsburg/Palm Valley turn-off, and another 30km east along Larapinta Drive back to the bitumen leading to Alice. Providing you stay on the road, it's easily done by 2WD vehicles at a sensible pace in dry conditions, but most regular cars turn back after visiting Redbank Gorge. The worst of the corrugations are on the 37-kilometre stretch between Glen Helen and Tyler's Pass.

Keeping the distinctive outline of **Mount Sonder** (another classic Namatjira silhouette) in view to the north, the turn-off for **Redbank Gorge** is 20km from Glen Helen, with a further 10km to the car park, passing the rather exposed **campsite** on the way. Redbank is the longest and narrowest cleft along the MacDonnells, its slippery walls no more than a metre apart in places and rarely warmed by direct sunlight. To get a full impression of the gorge you'll need an airbed and a pair of sports shoes to swim the 400m to the other end, which involves crossing seventeen freezing pools and some awkward scrambling.

Seventeen kilometres from the Redbank turn-off, you keep straight on for **Tyler's Pass**, passing the Haasts Bluff and Papunya turn-off to your right. The road becomes fairly rough until you're over the pass, from where a steep ascent to the radio mast gives a superb view of **Gosses Bluff**, about 30km to the south by road. Day-visits to the interior of this extraordinary and oddly played-down feature are now possible with a permit from the Central Lands Council in Alice Springs (31–33 Stuart Highway; ℡08/8951 6320). You can actually drive into the five-kilo-metre-wide crater, known to the Western Aranda as *Tnorula*, though the majority of the interior is a fenced-off sacred site. When you consider the magnitude of this comet impact 140 million years ago, it makes you wonder whether this might not have been the climate-shifting explosion which caused the extinction of the dinosaurs around the same time (give or take 20 million years). The interpretive dis-plays don't speculate quite so daringly, instead explaining how the crater is actually the frayed relic of a dome created by rebounding rock strata. An easier way to appre-ciate the wonder of it all is to scramble up to the rim; there's no path and it's prob-ably not allowed, but from this vantage point the impact which created the two-hundred-metre-high circular ridge is made a little more comprehensible.

South of the bluff, along a perfectly smooth, sandy track, you reach the Hermannsburg–Kings Canyon road: the Mereenie Loop. Turning west leads to the Aboriginal community of **IPOLERA**, set up by the visionary Hermann Malbunka as a Utopian outstation away from the deteriorating Hermannsburg of the early 1980s. This model community offers camping as well as gender-segregated **tours** (Feb–Nov Mon, Wed & Fri 10am; $25; ℡08/8956 7466) focusing on local Aboriginal culture. You are requested to respect the privacy of Ipolera's residents and also not to bring in or consume alcohol here.

Finke Gorge National Park

The popularity of **FINKE GORGE NATIONAL PARK** is founded on its pre-historic cycads and unique red cabbage palms which have survived in the park's sheltered **Palm Valley** for over ten thousand years. Despite the difficult 4WD road leading to the valley it's on every tour's itinerary, though it doesn't quite live up to the hype. The pleasant forty-minute loop walk is the valley's highlight; visiting the rest of the park requires a 4WD vehicle and seems discouraged, as does the route along the Finke riverbed from Hermannsburg (see box on pp.674–675). On the way in or out of the valley, you can climb up to the once-sacred **Initiation Rock**, giving a fine view over the **Amphitheatre**, a cirque of sandstone cliffs. The park has barbecues, toilets, solar-heated showers and camping.

HERMANNSBURG, until recently a Lutheran Mission, is the oldest Aboriginal community in the Centre, dating from the 1870s. Unusually, visi-tors are able to visit the town, or more particularly the **Historic Precinct** (daily 9am–4pm; $4.50) which features the original mission buildings convert-ed into tearooms and an art gallery (tours $3.50). Bob will rattle off his spiel on the history of the mission and the life and work of Albert Namatjira who was born here (see box, overleaf), although his observation about the "totemic faces" concealed in Namatjira's paintings should be taken with a pinch of salt. There is also a supermarket and fuel (cash only), but no accommodation.

Back towards Alice Springs, passing the **Albert Namatjira Memorial**, you reach the small community of **WALLACE ROCKHOLE**, offering sixty-minute tours (℡08/8956 7415; $5) of the nearby Aboriginal petroglyphs as well as a shop, fuel and camping. The same rules and courtesies apply as for Ipolera (see above). From here, it's 117km of bitumen back to Alice Springs.

Born on the Hermannsburg Lutheran mission in 1902, Albert, who added his father's name to appease Eurocentric propriety, was the first of the Hermannsburg mission's much-copied school of landscape watercolourists. Although without much previous painting experience, Namatjira assisted Rex Battarbee on his painting expeditions through the Central Australian deserts in the 1930s. His talent soon became obvious to Battarbee, who later became Namatjira's agent. Like all NT Aborigines at that time, Namatjira was forbidden to buy alcohol, stay overnight in Alice Springs or leave The Territory without permission, but at the insistence of southern do-gooders – and against his wishes – he was the first Aborigine to be awarded Australian citizenship, in 1956. This meant he could travel without limitations, but needed a permit to visit his own family on Aboriginal reserves, while the house in Alice he longed for was denied him for fear of the "entourage" he might have attracted. Following the success of his first exhibition in the south, which sold out in three days, he became a reluctant celebrity, compelled to pay taxes on his relatively huge earnings which were further depleted by the "share-it-all" kinship laws that still hamper successful Aboriginal artists today. A shy and modest man, much respected for his earnestness and generosity, he died in 1959 following a sordid conviction and short imprisonment for supplying alcohol to fellow Aborigines.

Critics could never make up their minds about his work, but his popular appeal was undoubted: exhibitions in the southern cities, which he rarely attended, persistently sold out within hours of opening, and today his paintings remain among the most valuable examples of Australia's artistic preoccupation with its landscape. If you'd like to buy prints of Albert Namatjira's work, the cheapest place in Alice is the Museum of Central Australia's shop in Alice Plaza, and not in Hermannsburg, as claimed.

The Eastern MacDonnells

Heading out of Alice through the **Heavitree Gap** and along the Ross Highway, you soon reach **Emily Gap**, Alice's nearest waterhole, 10km from town. This is one of the most significant Aranda sacred sites, the start of the Caterpillar Dreaming trail. There are engravings on the far side of the soupy pool, and plenty of darting birds and irksome flies; camping or open fires are not permitted. **Jessie Gap**, a little further east, is similar in appearance, but usually dry and of limited appeal. **Corroborree Rock** (camping), 45km east of Alice, is an unusual, fin-like outcrop of limestone with an altar-like platform and a crevice whose polished appearance suggests that, if not Aranda initiates, then plenty of tourists have squeezed through in a rite of passage. Known as *Antanangantana* to the Aranda, it was once a repository for sacred *tjuringa* objects.

John Hayes Rockhole and Trephina Gorge

John Hayes Rockhole and Trephina Gorge, by far the most satisfying of the accessible destinations in the Eastern MacDonnells, are just 80km from Alice. Both offer superb scenery and a selection of enjoyable walks, and there's a four-hour ridge walk linking the two. **John Hayes Rockhole** (limited camping space), reached along a rocky four-kilometre track requiring a high-clearance vehicle, is a series of pools linked by (usually dry) waterfalls along a canyon. The ninety-minute "Chain of Pools" walk takes you to the top of the gorge and down through the pools – an ideal way to get hot, but with plenty of opportunities to cool off. Alternatively, the lower pools are accessible from the car park.

Trephina Gorge, perhaps the most impressive spot in the eastern part of the range, is a beautiful, sheer-sided sandy gorge whose rich red walls support slender, white-barked ghost gums and a pool. There is a pleasant **campsite** and the "Gorge" and "Panorama" walks (both taking about 30min) are well worth the effort.

Ross River Homestead and Arltunga Historical Reserve

Five kilometres beyond Trephina Gorge, the Ross Highway peters out into two tracks: 8km to the southeast (90km east of Alice Springs) is the **Ross River Homestead**, an Outback resort (℗08/8956 9711 or free call 1800 241 711, ℗8956 9823; cabins ❼, bunkhouse ❷, camping also available), which offers "dude ranch" activities such as camel, horse and wagon rides, boomerang throwing, whip cracking and billy tea with damper. It's a comfortable, if relatively busy, base for a few days' stay in the Eastern MacDonnells, and has a popular bar, pool and restaurant.

The other track, a 35-kilometre corrugated dirt road heading east, leads to **ARLTUNGA**, the site of Central Australia's first goldrush. The road here may be long overdue for a grading, but a whole heap of money has been spent on restoring the ghost town and providing it with a fancy **visitors centre** (daily 8am–5pm; ℗08/8951 5210). All the place needs now is some visitors. Arltunga's story began in the 1890s, in the midst of the country's first economic depression, when gold was discovered by the miners originally drawn to the garnets at Ruby Gorge (see below). Over the next fifteen years they regularly pushed barrows the 600km from Oodnadatta railhead to grope in desperate conditions for pitiful returns. Arltunga was never a particularly rich field and remains an abandoned testament to pioneering optimism. On the way here you pass the somewhat overnamed *Arltunga Hotel & Bush Resort* (℗08/8956 9797; ❸), which offers camping, basic rooms and a pub that was once known as "The Loneliest in the Scrub".

Ruby and Glen Annie gorges

From Arltunga it's a fairly rough 4WD out to Ruby and Glen Annie gorges, both of them beautiful and wild places. Back in 1885 the explorer Lindsay discovered "rubies" while in the process of digging for water, thereby initiating the customary rush for what turned out to be worthless garnets. Crossing the sandy Hale riverbed leads into **Ruby Gorge** and then **Glen Annie Gorges** (no facilities except camping). At the end of the day, even with the flies handing over to the mozzies, it's one of the most tranquil places you'll find in Central Australia.

South to Uluru: the Stuart Highway and Kings Canyon

Kings Canyon is 320km southwest of Alice Springs, of which the hundred-kilometre section from the Stuart Highway turn-off towards Stockyard Homestead/Wallara is unsealed. From Stockyard, it's bitumen all the way to the

While most us have little need to own a heavy, fuel-guzzling 4WD, renting one for a few days of off-road driving is fun and can get you to some beautiful corners of the central deserts visited only by other intrepid "four wheelers". Below are some **4WD-only** routes close to Alice, which will give you a chance to fiddle with the transmission levers and which could all be linked into a leisurely and memorable week in the dirt. Remember that 4WD vehicles are not invincible: when driven carelessly they can easily get stuck, become uncontrollable or damaged. They can also make a mess of the terrain if driven away from main tracks; avoid wheel spins and tearing up vegetated ground which takes years to recover. Finally, make sure the outfit you're renting from understands and approves your proposed 4WD itinerary and, *at the very least*, read the advice and carry the gear recommended in "Basics", pp.40–44. Ask at Alice's tourist office for the *4x4 Tracks and Unsealed Roads of Central Australia* leaflet, which details other routes in the area. For recommended 4WD rentals agents see the "Listings" for Alice. One problem with renting is that you're never supplied with any essential recovery gear; even a second spare tyre has to be prised out of the rental companies and yet they encourage you to take your vehicle off road. Although most of the rental cars are in good shape, it is in your own interest to make sure you are appropriately equipped, especially for travelling in remote areas.

Finke River Route

With a day to spare and minimal experience with a 4WD, following the Finke riverbed from Hermannsburg down to the Ernest Giles Road offers an adventurous alternative to the highway. Rewards include stark gorge scenery, a reliable waterhole and the likelihood that you'll have it all to yourself. Before you set off, seek out the ranger at Palm Valley (☎08/8956 7401) who'll fill you in on the state of the track and provide a handy map that clarifies all the junctions. When on the route follow the small signs for "Kings Canyon".

The hundred-kilometre track starts immediately south of Hermannsburg and after 10km of corrugated road, you descend into the riverbed. From now on it's slow driving along a pair of sandy or pebbly ruts – you must deflate your tyres to at least 25psi/1.7bar and keep in the ruts to minimize the risk of getting stuck. The sole designated campsite is at Boggy Hole, much nicer than it sounds and around two hours (28.5km) from Hermannsburg. The campsite looks out from beneath river red gums to permanent reed-fringed waterholes, best seen at dawn as the sunlight creeps across the gorge and the ponds are alive with birdlife.

Beyond Boggy Hole, the track crisscrosses rather than follows the riverbed before the roller-coaster ride to the Giles Road across some low dunes thinly wooded with desert oaks – beware of oncoming traffic on blind crests. Boggy Hole to the Giles

Watarrka National Park which envelopes Kings Canyon. You can also get to Kings Canyon the back way along the **Mereenie Loop Track** from Hermannsburg, a distance of around 260km. You'll need a $2 **permit** from Alice's tourist information, *Glen Helen Lodge* or reception at the *Kings Canyon* resort (if you're returning to Alice via the Mereenie). If you're heading straight down the Track there's an increasingly barren run of nearly 700km to Coober Pedy (itself no oasis) in South Australia.

Most **tours** of two days or more departing from Alice include Kings Canyon on their see-it-all itineraries, providing the easiest and cheapest way to enjoy the canyon. There are daily McCafferty's and Greyhound Pioneer bus services from Alice Springs to Kings Canyon, or from Ayers Rock Resort with AAT Kings.

Road is 65km, so allow three hours. If you fancy taking the direct route to the Ernest Giles Road from the Tempe Downs station track, keep straight over the dunes just after a salt pan instead of turning sharply east; subsequent dunes can be avoided but the Palmer River crossing can be very sandy and may require further tyre deflation. Back on the road, keep speeds down until you can reflate your tyres.

Arltunga to Ruby Gap
The same sensible precautions are required for this route; make sure you're well equipped and see the ranger at the Arltunga Visitors Centre (℡08/8951 8211), 101km east of Alice, for the latest track conditions. It's a very scenic if bumpy 53-kilometre drive (allow two hours) through the ranges and including some steep creek crossings until you reach the sandy riverbed of the Hale and the Ruby Gap Nature Park. From here keep to the sandy ruts and inch carefully over the rocks for 7km to Glen Annie Gorge, a dead end with maroon red cliffs, bright green reeds and off-white sand.

Cattlewater Pass and the Harts Ranges
A less difficult track heads north from Arltunga past Claraville station and up over the Harts Ranges through the Cattlewater Pass to the Plenty Highway, 67km or three hours from Arltunga. It's a worthwhile and no less scenic way of returning to Alice from Ruby Gap via a different route and you're bound to see some hopping marsupials along the way. Once you reach the Plenty Highway it's an easy dirt road via Gemtree to the Stuart Highway and Alice, 150km away.

The Finke and Old Andado Tracks
More ambitious than the above and a satisfying 750-kilometre loop into the fringes of the Simpson Desert are the Finke and Old Andado tracks whose routes diverge at Alice's airport and rejoin at Mount Dare station just over the South Australian border. At Alice airport the westerly Finke branch follows the route of the old Ghan railway past Ewaninga rock carvings and Maryvale (fuel), where you can take an 88-kilometre return diversion to Chambers Pillar (more on these three places below and overleaf). After Maryvale it's a straight run to Finke (fuel) with the sandy or corrugated track being fun and mostly 2WD. On the way you'll pass stands of desert oak, shrubs and claypans and you might even see some feral camels. Just as things seem to be getting too easy the track sometimes gets sandier soon after Charlotte Waters towards Mount Dare, where you can buy fuel, provisions and a beer at the bar. Heading back to Alice (433km, no fuel) towards Old Andado, the track can again be sandy, but from the old homestead the going gets much easier as you cross the low ranges bringing you past the Santa Teresa community and the road back to the airport. For an outline of the Simpson crossing itself, from Mount Dare to Birdsville, see p.881.

The Old South Road and the northern Simpson Desert

Just 14km out of Alice, shortly after the airport turn-off, a sign indicates "Chambers Pillar (4WD)". This is the **Old South Road**, which follows the abandoned course of the Ghan and original Overland Telegraph Line to Adelaide, 1550km away; these days the sandy and corrugated route has become one arm of a loop which takes adventuresome four-wheel-drivers through the northern Simpson Desert past Finke settlement and Old Andado homestead (see box, above).

Ordinary cars can easily manage to cover the 35km to **Ewaninga Rock Carvings**, a jumble of rocks by a small claypan (a dried-up pool) littered with

Neolithic chippings. Their meaning, like that of other petroglyphs in the area, remains unknown but their age, estimated at 35,000 years, suggests that they certainly predate occupation of the Centre by today's Aborigines. A full-size cast of the mysterious engravings can be found at the Museum of Central Australia in Alice (see p.661).

Heading into the northern fringes of the **Simpson Desert**, past the windswept community at **MARYVALE** (shop and fuel), you'll need a 4WD vehicle to get across the Charlotte Ranges and subsequent dunes on the way to **Chambers Pillar** (toilets, barbecues and camping), an historic dead-end, 165km from Alice. Named by Stuart after one of his benefactors (who has natural features named after him and his family all the way to the Timor Sea), the eighty-metre-high sandstone pillar was used as a landmark by early overlanders heading up from the railhead at Oodnadatta, in South Australia. The plinth is carved with their names, and with those of many others, and can be seen after scrambling up the pillar's base. After many futile warning notices, a visitors' book was found to be the most expedient way of averting illegal, modern additions to the pillar. If you don't fancy renting your own vehicle, Outback Experience in Alice (℡08/8953 2666) has interesting full-day tours to this area.

The Stuart Highway to Kings Canyon

Around 76km from Alice, the turn off the Stuart Highway to **Rainbow Valley** (barbecues and camping, but no water or firewood) is easy to miss – turn left just before the yellow sign indicating "Jim's Place 14km". A twenty-kilometre dirt track, the very last bit of which may be sandy, leads to the "valley", actually a much-photographed outcrop set behind claypans which are said to produce rainbows following rain. More commonly, sunset catches the red-stained walls spectacularly and it's a wild place to spend the night, best followed in the morning by a climb up the crag.

Noel Fullerton's Camel Farm (daily 7am–5pm; ℡08/8956 0925) lies another few kilometres down the main highway. One of Australia's most experienced cameleers, Fullerton exports some of the Centre's huge population of feral camels back to their Arabian homelands, where a fit racer is worth about $5000. Popular photo-opportunity rides cost $3, and longer camel safaris can also be arranged.

Beyond the Camel Farm you reach the Ernest Giles Road, where you turn off right for Kings Canyon; note that the first hundred kilometres are unsealed. Not far along this road there's another turn-off, to **Henbury Meteorite Craters**. The extra-terrestrial shower that caused these twelve depressions, 2–180m in diameter, may have occurred in the last twenty thousand years, given that the Anangu have several names for the place, one of which translates as "sun walk fire devil rock". A walk with interpretive signs winds among the faintly visible craters, long since picked clean of any unearthly fragments. It's a rather bleak, treeless area for camping, but there are barbecues and toilets.

The Ernest Giles Road heads west, sandy at times but a lot of fun if you're in the mood, joining the sealed Luritja Highway linking Ayers Rock Resort to Kings Canyon. The bitumen road continues west, past **Kings Creek station** (℡08/8956 7474, ℻8956 7468) 35km from the canyon. Unlike most other pastoral properties in Australia, Kings Creek has taken to rounding up and selling the feral camels which other station owners regard as vermin (see box p.643). Ninety-minute **tours** of the four-thousand-square-kilometre property are available ($11) as well as camel rides around the paddock ($5). You'll also find a well-equipped campsite, pool, fuel and a shop.

Watarrka National Park (Kings Canyon)

As you cross the boundary of the **WATARRKA NATIONAL PARK**, you'll see the **ranger station** (☎ 08/8956 7460), which has a relief model of the park and its environs, but is not really a visitors centre and you may well have to coax the rangers into imparting their knowledge. Just on from here is the turning to **Kathleen Springs**, an easy twenty-minute stroll to a sacred Aboriginal waterhole once used to corral livestock and now a good place to catch sight of colourful birdlife.

Another few minutes down the road is **Kings Canyon** itself. The big attraction here is the superb three-hour horseshoe **walk** from the car park up and around the canyon's rim: undertaken in a clockwise direction, it starts with a steep ascent as the well-marked trail leads through the **Lost City**, a maze of domes resembling giant petrified cowpats stacked at random. Don't miss the exposed **lookouts** onto the two-hundred-metre-high southern wall before you cross the **Garden of Eden**, a palm-filled cleft bridged by an impressive array of staircases. On the far side there's an easily missed detour downstream to the waterhole where you can **cool off**, and, a bit further on, a dramatic lookout from the very throat of the canyon. From the car park another less strenuous and undemanding walk leads into the canyon itself, while a new two-day trail east to Kathleen Springs may be completed by now.

There are now some long overdue improvements in facilities but no **camping** at Kings Canyon itself, although you can camp elsewhere in the park with a ranger's permit. Ten kilometres past the canyon, the *Kings Canyon Resort* (☎ 08/8956 7442, ⊕ 8956 7410, @ reservations@ayersrockresort.com.au) is a small **resort** with a neat, grassy campsite, a bunkhouse with four-bed rooms (②) and a bare kitchen. Away from the rabble, the much more expensive *Lodge* (③) offers a pool and great views. The café (6am–10pm), by the service station and shop (daily 7am–7pm), serves meals for about $12; otherwise try the $30 buffet at *Carmichaels Restaurant* at the *Lodge*. Lilla Tours (☎ 08/8956 7417), run by local Keith Aitken, give a personal and insightful look at the region though Aboriginal eyes. A **shuttle bus** ($10) operates daily from the resort reception to the canyon.

Uluru–Kata Tjuta National Park and Ayers Rock Resort

Uluru–Kata Tjuta National Park encompasses **Uluru** (the Anangu name for **Ayers Rock**) and **Kata Tjuta** (or the **Olgas**). The park is the most visited single site in Australia and if you're wondering whether all the hype is worth it, then the answer is, emphatically, yes. The Rock, its textures, colours and not least its elemental presence, is without question one of the world's natural wonders. Overt commercialization has been controlled within the park and other tourists can be avoided, especially if you choose not to undertake the climb.

Kata Tjuta (meaning "many heads") lies 45km west from the park entry station. A cluster of rounded domes divided by narrow chasms and valleys, it is geologically quite distinct from Uluru. Public access is largely limited to the "Valley of the Winds" walk, partly because the eastern area is still a sacred site to the Anangu men. None of the domes, including Mount Olga, actually 200m higher than Uluru, is safe to climb.

You can't camp, let alone so much as pick a flower in the park, nor can you go anywhere other than Uluru and Kata Tjuta or the Cultural Centre. Instead the **Ayers Rock Resort**, part of the settlement of Yulara, just outside the park, takes care of all tourists' needs.

Getting there

It's 210km from Alice to **ERLDUNDA**, a busy roadhouse (camping and cabins; ❹) on the Stuart Highway, from where the **Lasseter Highway** heads to Ayers Rock Resort, 247km to the west. After 56km is *Mount Ebenezer Roadhouse* and later the turning for the **Luritja Highway**, which leads up to the Kings Canyon road.

The next thing to catch your eye will be the flat-topped mesa of **Mount Conner**, sometimes mistaken for Uluru by the myopically over-keen. *Curtin Springs Station* (☎08/8956 2906), 11km west of Mount Conner, is a roadhouse and bar offering the last inexpensive accommodation (camping free with $1 charge for showers; rooms ❸–❹) before Ayers Rock Resort. There's also a shop, fuel, bar and a collection of colourful parrots out back. You-know-what is now only 80km away.

Ayers Rock Resort (Yulara)

Like any purpose-built settlement, **AYERS ROCK RESORT** (aka Yulara), built at a cost of $250 million, possesses a certain prefabricated sterility, but it's not the eyesore it could have been. A few years ago a private company took over the management of the resort from the NT government, which somehow managed to keep losing money at a place just about everyone *has* to visit on the way to the Rock. Liberal renaming and more relevant improvements have succeeded in burying Yulara's notorious reputation once and for all.

All the town's facilities branch off a central ring road called Yulara Drive around which a **free bus** circulates 10.30am–2.30pm and 6.30pm–midnight. Within this ring is a duned area crisscrossed with tracks and the Imalung Lookout, scanning the Rock and Kata Tjuta on the horizon. In the **Shopping Square**, off Yulara Drive, you'll find a post office (Mon–Fri 9am–6.30pm, Sat & Sun 10am–2pm), supermarket (daily 8.30am–9pm), newsagent, baker and an ANZ **bank** (Mon–Thurs 9.30am–4.30pm, Fri 9.30am–5pm) with a 24-hour cashpoint. The nearby **amphitheatre** hosts evening entertainment including "tribal" dancing (Tues–Sun).

Near the Imalung Lookout there's an **Observatory** (☎08/8956 2563), which takes advantage of the exceptionally clear skies in the desert to scan the sun by day and stars by night. Tours, costing $20, include pick-ups and drop-offs and start at 8.30pm and 10.15pm.

Practicalities

Buses will either drop you off at your chosen accommodation, where you'll be given a town map, or at the Shopping Square which is the hub of the resort. All incoming **flights** to Connellan Airport, 6km from town, are met by a free shuttle bus – **taxis** (☎08/8955 2152) cost about $5. The **Uluru–Kata Tjuta Cultural Centre** (daily 7am–6pm; ☎08/8956 3138) is located within the park while the **visitors centre** (☎08/8957 7377 daily 8.30am–5pm) on Yulara Drive is a good place to start providing absorbing visual displays on the geology, nature and Anangu connections with Uluru – well worth an hour's browse.

Uluru National Park tours from Ayers Rock Resort

Air North (☎ 08/8945 2999) and **Ayers Rock Helicopter** (☎ 08/8956 2077). Thirty-minute scenic flights from $65 and fifteen-minute helicopter flights around the Rock from $95 with longer options as far as Kings Canyon available.

Anangu Tours (☎ 08/8956 2123, ✉ lbanangu@bigpond.com) Variety of tours led by local Aboriginal guide; sunset and sunrise tours cost from $79.

Austour (free call ☎ 1800 335 009). Bus tours to the park, sunrise, the climb and sunset suppers from $70.

Sounds of Silence (☎ 08/8957 7888) Sip champagne while the sun sets over the Olgas and Ayers Rock and then tuck into a gourmet BBQ with a tour of the night sky, from $105.

Uluru Experience (☎ 08/8956 2563). Personalized walking tours around Uluru and Kata Tjuta with local experts from $35. See their free sixty-minute slide show at the auditorium, next to the visitors centre, daily at 2pm.

Accommodation

Wherever you stay, **book ahead** unless camping. All accomodation is run by the Ayers Rock Resort (free call ☎ 1800 139 889, ✉ reservations@ayersrockresorts) so if they can't help you, not many others will be able to. All these places are situated off Yulara Drive, no more than ten-minutes' walk from the Shopping Square.

Ayers Rock Campground (☎ 08/8957 7888, ☏ 8956 2260). Electric BBQs, small shop, swimming pool and well-kept grassy sites for tents. Air-con cabins ❼

Desert Gardens Hotel (☎ 08/8957 7888, ☏ 8957 7716). Four-star hotel offering quality rooms and a pool. ❽

Emu Walk Apartments (check-in at *Desert Gardens Hotel*; ☎ 08/8956 7888, ☏ 8956 7742). Oddly designed but well-equipped self-contained apartments with one or two bedrooms (sleeping 4–6). Close to shops and pub. ❽

Outback Pioneer Lodge (☎ 08/8957 7888,

☏ 8957 7615). Modern place for backpackers and self-caterers with kitchen facilities, a takeaway kiosk and the pricier *Rocks Bistro* by the grassy pool area. En-suite motel rooms, twenty-bed dorms and four-person cabins with fridge and tea/coffee-making facilities. Rooms and cabins ❼ , dorms ❷

Sails in the Desert Hotel (☎ 08/8957 7888, ☏ 8957 7475). Luxury-class hotel with rates starting around $365. ❽

Spinifex Lodge (☎ 08/8957 7888; ☏ 8957 7755). One-bedroom units (sleeping up to four), with a basic kitchenette but shared bathrooms, near the Shopping Square. ❼

Eating and drinking

Geckos, Shopping Square. Continental-style restaurant serving wood-fired pizzas, pastas, seafood and steak, all from around $15–25. Open 10am–10pm.

Outback Pioneer Lodge, Yulara Drive. The kiosk (6.30am–9pm) here has various offerings, including fish and chips for $7, but the best deal is the hotel's cook-your-own BBQ (6.30–9.30pm) for around $6–10 including salad. The *Bough House*

Restaurant also has an Outback-style buffet for around $28 a head.

Quick Bites, Shopping Square. Open 9am–6pm. Good-quality sandwich bar.

Sails in the Desert Hotel. The *Kunia Room* here is a top-notch à la carte restaurant – perfect for a splurge, or if someone else is paying. Or try the less expensive *Rockpool* for Thai and Western dishes.

Uluru-Kata Tjuta National Park

Even with our bus tours and our fully automatic cameras and our cries of "Oh, wow!", we still couldn't belittle it. I had come expecting nothing much, but by the power of the thing itself I had, like some ancient tribesman wandering through the desert and confronting the phenomenon [sunset on Uluru], been turned into a worshipper. Nobody was more surprised than I.

Geoff Nicholson, *Day Trips to the Desert*

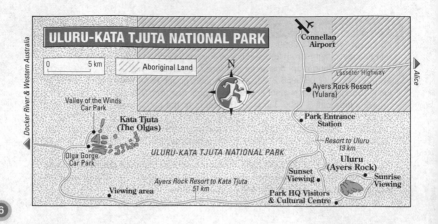

The entry fee for **ULURU–KATA TJUTA NATIONAL PARK** (daily: from one hour before dawn to one hour after dusk; $15, under 16s free) permits unlimited access for up to five days. Besides the two major sites of Uluru and Kata Tjuta, the park also protects over 500 species of plants, 24 native mammals and no less than 72 species of reptiles – for this reason access off the sealed roads, away from the two sites, is forbidden.

The **Uluru–Kata Tjuta Cultural Centre** (daily: April–Oct 7.30am–5.30pm; Nov–March 7am–6pm; ☎08/8956 3138), situated on the access road 1km before the Rock, opened in 1995, on the tenth anniversary of the handing back of Uluru to its traditional owners. The centre also houses a café, souvenir shop and gallery, and all together you'd want to allow yourself two hours to fully appreciate the place. As in the Kakadu equivalent at Cooinda, the strikingly innovative design doesn't conceal the fact that you're getting a very sanitized coverage of Aboriginal life. You pass an exposition of the dramatic mythical events at the dawn of creation, an uninspiring film of an *inma* (ceremony) and end with a display of men's and women's artefacts. In the next hall you can play with buttons to learn the right pronunciation of words such as "Anangu" or "Uluru". You leave saturated with the usual "Dreamtime myths, caring for the land" and the ever-present "bushtucker" know-how, while interesting if sensitive questions such as how significant, if at all, are age-old spiritual values to contemporary Aboriginal people are not considered. There are free, ninety-minute **tours** of the cultural centre (Mon–Wed 3.15pm). The free ranger-guided **Mala Walk** (daily: April–Oct 10am; Nov–March 9am; 90min) takes you from the centre to the base of the Rock and is a good introduction to Anangu perceptions and beliefs. Anangu Tours (☎08/8956 2123; from $65) offers a chance to explore the park with Aboriginal guides.

Otherwise, leaflets are available at the information desk on the park's geology, flora and fauna, as well as informative *Park Notes* on various topics and issues. The *Tour Operator's Workbook* ($35) is the definitive handbook to the park, with as comprehensible an explanation of Anangu culture as you'll find here. Around the back, the outdoor Maruku Gallery (daily 8.30am–5.30pm) displays arts and crafts from local artisans, and at the shop consider buying yourself the *Triumph of the Nomads* video, based on Geoffrey Blainey's incisive book. Both recount how the Aborigines were skilful masters rather than helpless victims of their environment.

Uluru

The first European to set eyes on the Rock was the explorer Ernest Giles, in 1872, but it was another explorer, William Gosse, who followed his Afghan guide up and so completed the first recorded ascent by a European a year later, naming it **Ayers Rock** after a South Australian politician. With white settlement of the Centre came relocation of its occupants from their traditional lands, merely to make way for pastoralists' stock to overgraze the fragile desert environment.

In 1958 the national park was excised from what was then the Petermann Aboriginal Reserve but subsequently returned, with much flourish, to the Yankunytjatjara and Pitjantjatjara groups in 1985, following a ten-year battle. Reclaimed, and renamed, as **Uluru**, the site was initially not much changed under Aboriginal ownership, since the park was simultaneously leased back to the ANCA and tourism continued unaffected. But since that time the traditional owners' influence has manifested itself with characteristic subtlety, gently guiding the park's development. The owners get twenty percent of your park entry fee as well as a $75,000 yearly royalty.

Anangu mythology

Uluru, Kata Tjuta and the surrounding desert are bound to a culture whose holistic cosmology sees the People – *anangu* – as having the Land and the Law – *tjukurpa* – as their central tenet of belief. A little confusingly, *tjukurpa* can also refer to the Time of Creation or "Dreamtime". The Anangu are thought to have occupied this area for around twenty thousand years and *Uluru* is the name of a waterhole near the summit. Like all religious mythology (and traditional fairy tales for that matter), the *tjukurpa* seeks to provide its adherents with a connection with the past, and a code of strict rules by which to live and behave correctly.

While Uluru is a key intersection along many "dreaming trails" (or Songlines, as Bruce Chatwin's book of that title described them) – principally those of the **Mala** (hare wallaby), **Liru** (poisonous snake), **Kuniya** (python) and **Kurpany** (monster dog) – it is not the shrine some imagine; a muddy waterhole 200km away may be as significant. Uluru is important to the Anangu as a reliable source of water and food and as one of many landmarks along the trails created by the Anangu's Dreamtime ancestors.

Geology

The reason Uluru rises so dramatically from the surrounding land is because it is a **monolith** – that is, a single piece of rock. With few cracks to be exploited by weathering, and the layers of very hard, coarse-grained **sandstone** tilted to a near-vertical plane, the Rock successfully resists the denudation of the landscape surrounding it. If one can visualize the layers of rock, then Uluru is like a cut loaf, its strata pushed up to near-vertical slices so that from one side you look at the flat ends while elsewhere the separate layers are clearly evident as eroded grooves – the pronounced fluting effect along the Rock's southeast and northwest flanks. Brief, but spectacular, waterfalls stream down these channels following storms. In places, the surface of the monolith has peeled or worn away, producing bizarre features and many caves, mostly out of bounds. The striking orangey-red hue, enhanced by the rising and setting sun, is merely skin deep, the result of oxidation ("rusting") of iron in the normally grey rock.

Up and around Uluru

It takes less than an hour to **climb** to the summit of Uluru, but make no mistake, it will be the greatest exertion you will undertake during your visit to Australia. An Anangu sign at the base requests you not to undertake the climb (only Mala men used to do so) but seventy percent of visitors to the Rock persist in attempting to conquer the summit. Probably a third give up and, on average, one climber a year dies, either from a heart attack, straying off the track or chasing windborne lens caps into oblivion. Gasping up the chained section you'll see why – for about fifteen minutes it's a very hard slog and if you slip or collapse you'll roll straight back down to the car park. Each accident and death is seen by its traditonal owners as a distressing spiritual revenge. With a firmly attached hat, some water, secure footwear and frequent rests, you'll safely attain the summit, often a windy spot, especially in the morning. If you're at all unfit or nervous about heights and exposed places, *do not* attempt the climb.

Far less strenuous and more acceptable to Aboriginal beliefs is the nine-kilometre **walk around the Rock**, which takes an easy three hours. It offers a closer look at Uluru's Anangu sites (though note that some of the sacred sites are closed to "uninitiates" – heed any warning notices) and the extraordinary textural variations. While the walk may not be a triumphant achievement, it can be more rewarding and is certainly more in keeping with the spirit of the place. For incorrigible couch potatoes, the twenty-minute walk from the base of the climb to **Mutitjulu**, a secluded pool, low-grade art site and scene of epic ancestral clashes marked by gashes in the rock, is recommended.

Kata Tjuta and on to WA

The "many heads", as **Kata Tjuta** – or the **Olgas** – translates from the local Aboriginal language, are situated 51km from the resort or Uluru. This remarkable formation may have once been a monolith ten times the size of Uluru, but has since been carved by eons of weathering into 36 "monstrous domes", to use Giles' words, each smooth, rounded mass divided by slender chasms or broader valleys. The composition of Kata Tjuta, very different from Uluru's fine-grained rock, can be clearly seen in the massive, sometimes sheared, boulders set in a conglomerate of sandstone cement. Access to this fascinating maze is limited to just two walks, in part because of earlier problems with over-ambitious tourists. Furthermore, the east of Kata Tjuta is a site sacred to Anangu men and is not accessible to the public.

The first of the permitted walks, the **Olga Gorge Walk**, is a rather pointless one-kilometre stroll into the dead-end chasm flanking Mount Olga (which, at 546m, is the highest point in the massif). Better by far is the **Valley of the Winds Walk**, a seven-kilometre loop trail which takes about two hours, or the five-kilometre "there and back" walk to a **pass** between two domes. This is as much as you can see of Kata Tjuta's interior without a permit. It's worth knowing that the large tour buses tend to visit the Rock in the early morning and Kata Tjuta in the afternoon. By reversing this trend you can avoid the worst of the crowds and enjoy this magical place in reasonable solitude.

From Kata Tjuta a track leads to the WA border at Docker River and from there along the **Warburton Road** to Laverton, north of Kalgoorlie (see p.736). The need for permits required to cross Aboriginal land in NT and WA has eased up in recent years (no one ever checked anyway) and now this short cut between the Centre and southern WA is seeing much more traffic. A 4WD is not necessary but the usual precautions for driving on the dirt should be taken, spare fuel, tyres and water, especially in summer. For more details of facilities along the Warburton Road, see p.736.

TRAVEL DETAILS

Trains

Alice Springs to: Adelaide (Tues & Fri; 20hr); Port Augusta (Tues & Fri; 17hr; change for Sydney or Perth).

Buses

Alice Springs to: Adelaide (3–4 weekly; 27hr); Darwin (1 daily; 19hr); Katherine (1 daily; 15hr; change here for WA); Tennant Creek/Three Ways Roadhouse (1 daily; 6hr–6hr 30min; change at Three Ways for Queensland destinations).

Darwin to: Alice Springs (1 daily; 19hr); Katherine (2 daily; 4hr; change for WA); Tennant Creek/Three Ways Roadhouse (2 daily; 13hr–13hr 30min).

Katherine to: Alice Springs (1 daily; 15hr); Darwin (2–3 daily; 4hr); Kununurra (2 daily; 6hr 30min); Tennant Creek/Three Ways Roadhouse (2–3 daily; 9hr 30min).

Tennant Creek to: Alice Springs (1 daily; 6hr); Darwin (2 daily; 13hr); Katherine (2–3 daily; 13hr); Townsville (1 daily; 12hr).

Domestic flights

Alice Springs to: Darwin (1–2 daily; 2hr).

Darwin to: Alice Springs (1–2 daily; 2hr); Brisbane (1–2 daily; 4hr); Broome (1 daily; 2hr); Cairns (1 daily; 3hr); Perth (1 daily; 4hr 30min).

International flights

Darwin to: Denpasar, Bali (3 weekly); Kuala Lumpur, Malaysia (1 direct weekly, or change at Singapore); Kupang and Dili, East Timor (4 weekly); Singapore (5–6 weekly).

Western Australia

CHAPTER 7   # Highlights

✳ **Cottesloe Beach**, Perth – Fish and chips and a cold beer at sunset on Perth's Cottesloe Beach make a perfect end to the day. p.706.

✳ **Tall Timber Country** – Climb the world's tallest fire-look-out tree, paddle down the gentle Blackwood River or drive through magnificent karri forests in WA's Tall Timber Country. p.717.

✳ **Monkey Mia** – Dolphins have been coming in nearly every day to meet people at Monkey Mia for the past thirty years. p.746.

✳ **Ningaloo Reef** – Running down the North West Cape, the spectacular Ningaloo Reef is considered by some to be superior to its more famous cousin in Queensland. p.748.

✳ **Karijini National Park** – The legendary Dave's Gorge Tours' "Miracle Mile" is described by FHM magazine as "one of the hundred things a man must do in his life". p.758.

✳ **The Kimberley** – Often described as Australia's last frontier, the desolate and beautiful Kimberley region is the closest you'll get to the Australian Wild West. p.768.

Western Australia

Western Australia (WA) covers a third of the Australian continent; nearly the size of India, yet with less than half a percent of that country's population. Always revelling in its isolation from the more populous eastern states, WA is, like them, primarily a suburban state: three-quarters of its 1.7 million inhabitants live within 100km of Perth and almost all the rest live in communities strung along the coastline.

Perth itself retains the leisure-oriented vitality of a young city, while the port of **Fremantle** resonates with a largely European charm. South of Perth, the **Margaret River Region**'s wooded hills and trickling streams support the state's foremost wine-growing and holiday-making area. To the southeast, the giant **eucalypt forests** around Pemberton further soften a land fed by heavy winter rains; the state's intensively farmed **wheat belt** stretches to the east, an interminable man-made prairie. Along the Southern Ocean's storm-washed coastline, **Albany** is the primary settlement, a rejuvenated resort with the dramatic granite peaks of the **Stirling Ranges** just visible from its hilltop lookouts. To the east, past Esperance on the edge of the Great Australian Bight, the deserted monotony of the **Nullarbor Plain** extends to South Australia, while inland the Eastern Goldfields' **Kalgoorlie** is the sole survivor of the century-old mineral boom on which WA's prosperity was originally built.

While the temperate southwest of WA has been relatively tamed by colonization, the north of the state is where you'll discover the raw appeal of the **bush**. The virtually unpopulated eastern deserts are blanketed with spinifex and sparse communities of Aborigines, while the west coast's winds abate once you venture into the tropics north of **Shark Bay**, home of the amicable dolphins at **Monkey Mia**. From here, the mineral-rich **Pilbara** region fills the state's northwest shoulder with the often-overlooked gorges of the **Hamersley Ranges** at its core. Visitors are also discovering the submarine spectacle of the

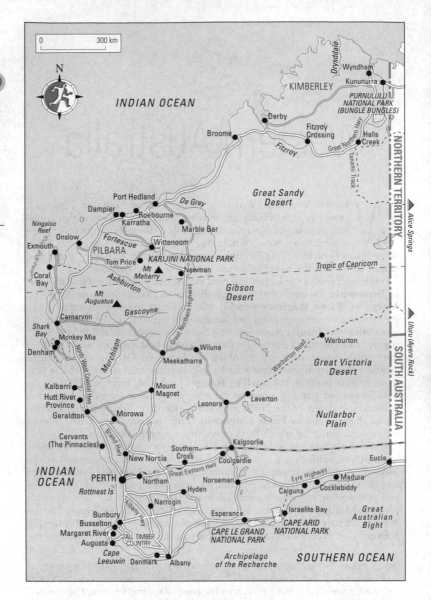

Ningaloo Reef, lapping the North West Cape's beaches – some consider it superior to Queensland's Barrier Reef.

Northeast of the Pilbara, **Broome**, once the world's pearling capital, is indeed a jewel in the cyclone-swept coastline of the rugged Northwest, and an ideal preliminary to the **Kimberley**'s wilderness and hard-won cattle country. Generally cut off by floods in the wet season, the Kimberley is regarded as Australia's last frontier, its convoluted and inaccessible coasts washed by enor-

mous tides and inhabited only by isolated Aboriginal communities and crocodiles. On the way to the Northern Territory border, the surreal enigma of the
Bungle Bungle massif is one of WA's greatest natural wonders, carefully protected by minimal development.

If you hope to explore any significant part of the state's million-and-a-half
square kilometres, and in particular the remote and fascinating Northwest, your
own vehicle is essential, although you'll get to the most interesting places by
combining buses with local **tours**. Either way, WA offers an essential mix of
Outback grandeur, albeit more dispersed than elsewhere, and it's beginning to
attract tourists from the more popular "Eastern States", as the rest of Australia
is known in these parts.

WA's **climate** is a seasonal mix of temperate, arid and tropical. **Winters** are
cool in the south and very wet in the southwest corner, while in the tropics
the temperature sits around 32°C but with no rain and tolerable humidity: this
is the dry season. Come the **summer**, the enervating "Wet" (from Dec to
March) washes out the north while the rest of the state, particularly inland
areas, crackles in the mid-40s heat. The southern coast is the only retreat for
the heatstruck, although the temperate west coast is cooled by dependable
afternoon sea breezes – in Perth known as the "Fremantle Doctor".

Some history

Aborigines had lived in most areas of WA for thousands of years by the time
the seventeenth-century traders of the **Dutch East India Company**, and
possibly the **Portuguese** before them, began bumping into the west coast on
their way to the East Indies. A Dutch mariner, **Dirk Hartog**, was among the
first of these when, in 1616, he left an inscribed pewter plate on the island off
Shark Bay which now bears his name. Recent evidence was also found hereabouts to suggest that the **French** claimed the whole continent just a few years
before Cook. For the next two hundred years, however, impressions of WA's
barren and waterless fringes remained – commercially at least – uninspiring to
European colonists.

France's subsequent interest in Australia's southwest corner at the beginning
of the nineteenth century, which left a legacy of attractively named coastal features, led the **British** hastily to claim the unknown western part of the continent in 1826. Fredrickstown (Albany) was established on the south coast in that
year and the Swan River Colony, today's Perth, two years later. The **new
colony**, initially rejecting convict labour and so struggling desperately in its
early years, had the familiar effect on an Aboriginal population that was at best
misunderstood and at worst annihilated. Aborigines and their lands were
cleared for agriculture: these days black faces are not seen as regularly south of
Perth as in the north.

Economic problems continued until stalwart explorers in the mid-nineteenth
century opened up the country's interior, leading to the goldrushes of the
1890s which propelled the colony into autonomous statehood in less than a
decade. This **autonomy**, and growing antipathy towards the eastern states, led
to a move to secede from the Federation in the depressed 1930s, when WA felt
the rest of the country was dragging it down. But following World War II the
whole of white Australia, and especially WA, began to thrive, making money
from wool and, later, from huge mineral discoveries that to this day form the
basis of the state's wealth. In fact, so prosperous is the state that at present its
wealth accounts for a quarter of the nation's economy. Meanwhile, many of
WA's forty thousand Aborigines continue to live in comparatively squalid and
remote communities, as if in another country, though in the wake of the Mabo

and Wik rulings (see p.1152), lawyers supposedly representing them have put vast areas of the state under land claim, creating a situation destined to stagnate in the courts for years to come.

Perth and the South

South of the **Great Eastern Highway**, which joins Perth to Kalgoorlie, is the most climatically benign portion of Western Australia, supporting intensive agriculture and seaside towns, and with all points well-connected to **Perth**, the modern face of the state's wealth. East of the state capital, the **Darling Ranges** offer a number of appealing day-trip destinations, while south of Perth, the **Margaret River Region**'s uniquely mellow landscape is especially attractive, supporting orchards, wineries and numerous homey holiday hideaways in the giant karri forests around **Pemberton**. Both **Albany** and **Esperance** are engaging resort towns on the Southern Ocean's rugged coastline, where sea breezes take the edge off the summertime heat. They make ideal bases for exploration of their adjacent national parks, while the dreary **Wheatlands**, north of the coast, is a region to pass through rather than head for. **Kalgoorlie**, at the heart of the once-thriving **Eastern Goldfields**, is a colourful caricature of an Outback mining town and certainly deserves a stop as you travel east.

Perth

Try as you might, and contrary to expectations, it's hard to get excited about **PERTH**, although its lack of urban grime creates a favourable first impression. Western Australia's modern capital of 1.3 million people has a reputation for sunshine, youthfulness and an easy-going lifestyle – after work, people often go sailing or swimming. It is perhaps because of this complacency that Perth lacks the substance and charisma, and the tension, of diverse wealth and ethnicity, that make a really great city something more than just a group of modern skyscrapers.

In the 1980s mineral prosperity and a spate of cocky, self-made wheeler-dealers (now largely bankrupt or disgraced) created a mini-boom for Perth. Wealth begat growth, recognition and an exciting, "upwardly mobile" tag; suddenly Perth, separated from everywhere else by thousands of kilometres of desert or ocean, was the place to be. But the many glass towers that rose on the city's skyline in the 1980s are still only half full, mocking the callow values of that era's transient prosperity. Although upbeat campaigns have managed to attract some people back into the city centre outside office hours, apart from shopping and some museums and galleries, the centre has little to offer tourists bar the buzzing restaurant and club district of **Northbridge**. If you're looking for action, imitate the locals and head for the hills, the beaches, the western sub-

CENTRAL PERTH

ACCOMMODATION

Britannia International YHA	10
Brownlea Holiday Apartments	1
Chateau Commodore	18
City Backpackers HQ	8
City Waters Lodge	24
Coolibah Lodge	4
Court Hotel	11
Exclusive Backpackers	23
Grand Central Backpackers	15
Globe Backpackers	13
Hay Street Backpackers	19
Kings Park Motel	14
Miss Maud Swedish Hotel	17
Mountway Holiday Units	16
Hotel Northbridge	3
Northbridge YHA	9
Ozi Inn	6
Royal Hotel and	
Wentworth Plaza Hotel	12
Shiralee	5
Sullivans Hotel	20
Terrace Hotel	21
12.01 East	22
Underground Backpackers	7
The Witch's Hat	2

Albany Highway

Herrison Island

Swan River

WACA Oval

CAUSEWAY

East Perth Rail & Bus Terminal

JEWELL STREET

Limit of Free Transit Zone

Claisebrook Station

SMITH STREET
LORD STREET

WITTENOOM STREET

Perth Mint

BENNETT STREET

EAST PERTH

HILL ST

PIER STREET

STIRLING STREET

BEAUFORT STREET

McIver Station

Royal Perth Hospital

VICTORIA SQUARE

ADELAIDE TERRACE

TERRACE ROAD

RIVERSIDE DRIVE

Perth Train Station

WELLINGTON STREET

VICTORIA AVE

Queens Gardens

WILLIAM STREET

NEWCASTLE STREET

LAKE STREET

FRANCIS STREET

MILLIGAN STREET

Perth Cultural Centre

HORSESHOE BRIDGE

PARKER STREET

CITY CENTRE (Malls)

Town Hall

Government House

Stirling Gardens

BARRACK STREET

TERRACE ROAD

Concert Hall

Swan River

0   500 m

NORTHBRIDGE

Entertainment Centre

Wellington St. Bus Station

ROE STREET

JAMES STREET

FITZGERALD STREET

MURRAY STREET

KING STREET

HAY STREET

MILL ST

ST GEORGES TERRACE

Barrack St Jetty

City Busport

N

Undercover Pass

Limit of Free Transit Zone

City West Station

THOMAS STREET

WELLINGTON STREET

MURRAY STREET

HAY STREET

HARVEST TCE

WEST PERTH

Parliament House

MOUNTS BAY ROAD

KINGS PARK RD

FRASER AVENUE

Kings Park

Narrows Bridge

Mill Point, Old Mill & Zoo

urbs of Leederville, Subiaco, Claremont and Cottesloe, or cruise on down to the port of Fremantle, 20km from Perth.

Arrival and information

Perth's **international airport** is 16km east of the city centre and the **domestic** one a few kilometres closer. **Shuttle buses** (international $11, domestic $8.80; ℡ 08/9479 4131) meet arrivals at both airports and take you directly to your accommodation in the city; poorly signposted but directly opposite the Qantas domestic terminal, you can also catch a green Transperth bus #200, #201, #202, #208 and #209 to the city, at least every forty minutes ($2.70). Otherwise, a trip by **taxi** to or from the international airport will take thirty minutes and cost around $20 (call ℡ 08/9333 3333 or 9444 4444), or a bit less and a bit quicker from the domestic terminal. An airport shuttle runs to **Fremantle** ($15 one-way, $24 for two; ℡ 08/9383 4115) once an hour. Interstate **trains**, **buses** and Westrail country buses arrive at the **East Perth Rail and Bus Terminal**, three train stops from the central Transperth suburban train and bus station on Wellington Street.

The main **tourist office** (Mon–Fri 8.30am–6.30pm, Sat 9am–1pm; ℡ 1300/361 351 or free call 1800 812 808) is just across the road from the Transperth station, in Forrest Chase precinct, and has numerous free city guides and maps, tour information and statewide promotional videos. The **Travellers' Club Tour and Information Centre** (Mon–Fri 9am–5.30pm, Sat 10am–4pm; ℡ 08/9226 0660, ℻ 9226 0661, ℗ www.travellersclub.com.au) just round the corner at 499 Wellington St offers a specific information service for backpackers and budget travellers as well as providing **emailing** facilities. See p.697 for listings magazines.

City transport

Transperth is the city's excellent and inexpensive **suburban transport** network, with frequent trains to Fremantle and the northern, eastern and southern suburbs of Joondalup, Midland and Armadale, and a fleet of buses filling the gaps in between. The city centre has two **bus stations**, one at Wellington Street, next to the central **train station**, and, for services south of the river, the City Busport ten-minutes' walk south at the bottom of Mill Street. There are Transperth **information offices** with helpful staff at both bus stations (Mon–Fri 7.30am–5.30pm, Sat 8am–1pm; ℡ 13 2213) and also in the city centre at Plaza Arcade, Hay Street Level (Mon–Fri 8am–5.30pm, Sat 8am–5pm, Sun noon–5pm).

Outside the FTZ (see box opposite), Perth is divided into eight concentric zones – zones 1 and 2 ($2.70) are the most useful to visitors, incorporating Fremantle, the northern beaches and Midland. **Tickets** are available from bus conductors or vending machines at all (mostly unstaffed) stations; they are valid for up to two hours' (some for 90min) unlimited travel within the specified zones on Transperth buses, trains and the ferry to South Perth from Barrack Street jetty. Day-passes ($6.90) and ten-trip MultiRiders ($22.95) are also available from certain newsagents.

The tourist-oriented **Perth Tram** (daily 8am–5.10pm; day-ticket $15; ℡ 08/9322 2006), running every ninety minutes and most conveniently caught at Barrack Street jetty, allows you to jump off at points of interest and reboard a later tram.

Perth's web of **bicycle** lanes, which spread from the city out to the suburbs, can also make bike rental (see p.699 for rental agents) a pleasant and viable option; Bikewest (℡ 08/9216 8000) can provide more information.

Free transport in central Perth: the FTZ

Both of Perth's central bus stations, as well as the local train stations one stop on either side of the main train station, are within the Free Transit Zone, or FTZ. Most buses passing through the FTZ offer free travel within it, as do the snazzy "CAT" (Central Area Transit) buses serving the city centre. You can board the buses at special CAT stops to take you along two circular CAT routes; press a button and a voice tells you when the next bus is due. The Blue CAT runs north–south from Barrack Street jetty up to Aberdeen Street and then down William Street back to the river, while the Red CAT runs east–west along George Terrace and back along Wellington Street. Both routes run from Monday to Thursday 7am–6pm, Friday 7am–1am, Saturday 8.30am–1am and Sunday 10am–5pm, with intervals of fifteen minutes at the most. Timetables are available from Transperth offices.

Accommodation

There's a full range of **accommodation** around the centre of Perth, all of it – from backpackers' hostels to hotels and apartments – inexpensive, presentable and conveniently close to, or even right in, the city centre. Self-contained apartments can be great value for groups of four or more. The nearest campsites are 7km from the city. Booking ahead for motels and apartments is advisable in summer if you want to stay at the first place on your list.

Hotels and motels

Chateau Commodore, cnr Victoria Ave and Hay St (☏ 08/9325 0461, ℻ 9221 2448). Right in the centre of town, with parking, restaurant, bar and pool. ❻
Court Hotel, 50 Beaufort St (☏ 08/9328 5292). Central gay and lesbian accommodation over a very lively pub. ❸
Kings Park Motel, 255 Thomas St, Subiaco (☏ 08/9381 0000 or free call 1800 655 362, ℻ 9381 4159). Good-value modern motel, five minutes from the city, on the edge of Kings Park. Restaurant and spas in some rooms. ❺
Miss Maud Swedish Hotel, 97 Murray St (☏ 08/9325 3900, ℻ 9221 3225, ℮ missmaud@missmaud.com.au). A pleasant variety of rooms, an interior with a Swedish/Alpine flavour and a popular buffet breakfast included. ❼
Hotel Northbridge, 210 Lake St (☏ 08/9328 5254, ℻ 9227 7494, ℮ hotelnb@delron.com.au). Excellent refurbished old-style hotel for those on a budget as well as good value four-star alternatives

with a spa in every room. Off-street parking and three-bar pub below. ❸–❼
Royal Hotel cnr Wellington and William streets (☏ & ℻ 08/9324 1510, ℮ wentpert@fc-hotels.com.au). One of central Perth's bargains, a tidy grand-era hotel (mostly shared facilities) with some big rooms better and cheaper than the Wentworth next door. ❹
Sullivans Hotel, 166 Mounts Bay Rd (☏ 08/9321 8022, ℻ 9321 2443). Excellent, family-run hotel at the foot of Kings Park and just inside the FTZ. Offers pool, free bikes and great breakfasts. ❻
Terrace Hotel, 195 Adelaide Terrace (☏ 08/9492 7777). Superior motel right in the city centre. ❼
Wentworth Plaza, cnr Wellington and William streets (☏ 08/9481 1000, ℻ 9321 2443, ℮ wentpert@fc-hotels.com.au) Plusher version of its sister, the Royal (above) with same central location, mix of en-suite and basin-only rooms plus 24hr reception and lifts. ❻

Self-contained apartments

Brownlea Holiday Apartments, 166 Palmerston St (☏ 08/9227 1710, ℻ 9328 4840, ℮ brownlea@iinet.net.au). Just north of the centre with a spa, pool and bargain rates. ❺
City Waters Lodge, 118 Terrace Rd (☏ 08/9325 1556, ℻ 9221 2794,

℮ perth@citywaters.com.au). Small one- and two-bedroom apartments close to the river and ten-minutes' walk from the centre. ❺
Mountway Holiday Units, 36 Mount St (☏ 08/9321 8307, ℻ 9324 2147). Budget units between the city centre and Kings Park. ❹

Hostels

Perth offers a wide selection of **hostels** and with new ones opening every year the market is becoming competitive. Just about all of them are converted from older buildings located around Northbridge – don't expect the purpose-built palaces you get out East. The selection below includes the more popular and reliable establishments; most offer bike rental, tour bookings, email and employment contacts. Note that on-street parking is a hassle in the very centre of Northbridge. In all the hostels listed below, dorms fall in the ❶ category, and twins or doubles are ❸, however, some hostels can offer bargains especially with longer stays.

Northbridge and City Centre

Britannia International YHA, 253 William St (☎08/9328 6121, ⑤9227 9784, ⓔbritannia@yhawa.com.au). In the heart of Northbridge and a stone's throw from the clubs and cafés, and with a handy 24hr reception allowing you to take full advantage of these. No smoking.

City Backpackers HQ, 158 Aberdeen St (☎08/9328 6667 or free call 1800 247 444, ⑤9328 8813). Roomier than most hostels, with eight-bed dorms and off-street parking.

Globe Backpackers, 497 Wellington St (☎08/9321 4080, ⓔglobebak@iinet.net.au). Old hotel converted for the budget traveller, where the central location makes up for the disinterested staff.

Grand Central Backpackers, 379 Wellington St (☎08/9421 1123, ⑤9421 1650, ⓔgrandcentralbp@hotmail.com). Converted former YMCA, one minute from train station. Doubles with en suite. Free city-centre parking, plus the cheapest email in town.

Northbridge YHA, 46 Francis St (☎ & ⑤ 08/9328 7794, ⓔyhanb@hotmail.com). Good layout with a shady courtyard and plenty going on. A few twins, but mostly six- and eight-bed dorms.

Ozi Inn, 282 Newcastle St (☎08/9328 1222, ⑤08/9328 1172, ⓦwww.oziinn.com). Recently upgraded converted large house with knowledgeable owners offering a warm welcome. Best bargain for longer stays.

Underground Backpackers, 268 Newcastle St, (☎08/9228 3755, ⑤9228 3744, ⓔunderground@electrolley.com.au). Retains its friendliness even with megahostel status. Swimming pool, free breakfast, bar, internet café, air-conditioned rooms, videos.

North of Northbridge

Coolibah Lodge, 194 Brisbane St (☎08/9328 9958, ⑤08/9227 6231, ⓔmail@coolibahlodge.com.au). Well-kept renovated rambling house in a quiet location with BBQ and shady garden.

Shiralee, 107 Brisbane St (☎08/9227 7448, ⑤9227 7446, ⓔshiralee@global.net.au). Small, long-established, hostel with winter log fires and summer air-con. Four-bed dorms and rooms.

The Witch's Hat, 148 Palmerston St (☎08/9228 4228 or free call 1800 818 358, ⓔwitchs_hat@hotmail.com). Small doubles, "real beds" and away from the throng.

East of the Centre

Exclusive Backpackers, 158 Adelaide Terrace (☎08/9221 9991, ⑤9362 5872). Attractive jarrah wood interior and balcony offering a touch of class and large bunkless dorms. Off-street parking and a nice café next door to supplement the inadequate kitchen. Five-bed dorms and comfortable twins or doubles.

Hay Street Backpackers, 266–268 Hay St (☎ & ⑤ 08/9221 9880). Well-looked-after, converted house with a spacious kitchen, small pool and parking. Four- to six-bed dorms with air-con and new twins and doubles in the back.

12:01 East, 195 Hay St (☎08/9221 1666, ⑤9221 1662). Large communal areas and kitchen near WACA cricket ground but 30min walk from Northbridge action. Four-bed dorms and some twins and doubles.

Caravan parks

Central, 38 Central Ave, 7km east of Perth (☎08/9277 5696). Located in Redcliffe, by the domestic airport. Closest good caravan park to the city centre. Cabins ❸

Scarborough Starhaven, 18 Pearl Parade (☎08/9341 1770). Situated in a popular beach suburb, a 30min bus ride from the centre. On-site vans ❸

The City

The compact and walkable **central area** of Perth, from Wellington Street down to St Georges Terrace, and bounded vaguely by Hill Street to the east and Milligan Street to the west, is an easy to negotiate grid. Much of your time will be spent exploring the links between **Hay Street** and **Murray Street**, both of which are pedestrianized between William and Barrack streets and linked by numerous, glittering arcades: the mock-Tudor **London Court** and its idealized "Olde English" imagery is much photographed. William Street runs north over the railway at **Horseshoe Bridge** and on into lively Northbridge, while Barrack Street runs south down to the ferry **jetty** on Perth Water, a lagoon on the **Swan River** formed by the bridged **Narrows** and popular with windsurfers, sailors and jet-skiers. From the jetty a Transperth ferry regularly crosses the Narrows to Mends Street jetty on the south shore, while tourist ferries ply the river upstream to the Swan Valley wineries and downstream to Fremantle and Rottnest Island (see box on p.699). Generally speaking, the best way to **sightsee** in Perth is simply to wander idly and window-shop.

Museums and Old Perth

Situated just over the tracks in Northbridge, at the end of James Street, the **Perth Cultural Centre** comprises the **Art Gallery of Western Australia** (daily 10am–5pm; free) and the state **museum** (daily 9.30am–5pm, closed Good Friday; free), as well as the state library. The gallery's constantly changing displays include Aboriginal art, and other contemporary and classic works by Western Australian artists. There's always something worth seeing, the air-con is blissful in summer, and free guided tours (Tues–Sun 1pm; free) provide good information about the work displayed. The museum, part of the same complex, is housed in a collection of old and new buildings. It includes a floor devoted to Aboriginal culture, plus exhibitions of vintage cars, stuffed marsupials, a 25-metre whale skeleton, meteorites, a diorama of a swamp, and a reconstruction of an old jail.

Perth's old buildings, popular with many sightseeing tours, are colonial survivors on the endangered list while the city fathers remain obsessed with continual renewal and development, where even modern soaring skyscrapers, barely twenty years old, are not safe from demolition in the name of progress. In a westward sweep from the manicured perfection of **Queens Gardens**, at the east end of Hay Street, start with the **Perth Mint** (Mon–Fri 9am–4pm, Sat & Sun 9am–1pm), on the corner of Hill and Hay streets. Operating from its original 1899 base, Australia's principal specialist mint still trades in precious metals in bar or coin form and displays some large-scale replicas of gold nuggets and alluring 400-ounce ingots. Visitors can also take a tour ($5) to observe minting operations in the refurbished foundry.

Further down are the **Stirling Gardens**, on the corner of St Georges Terrace and Pier Street, with their "Ore Obelisk" sculpture symbolizing WA's mineral diversity, and the ornate Gothic extravagance of the 1860s **Government House**. The **Old Courthouse** (Tues & Thurs 10am–2.30pm; free), the colony's oldest surviving building, is also in the gardens and houses the less than electrifying **Francis Burt Law Museum**, while other sights in the area include the **Deanery** on the corner of Pier Street, the **Cloisters** – now an office – and the **Old Perth Boys' School**, at 139 St Georges Terrace, now a café and wine bar. Barely discernible at the far end of the terrace is the **Barracks Archway**, the remains of an 1860s' structure not really worth closer inspection unless you're heading up that way to Kings Park. Easily missed on the corner of Hay and Barrack streets is the neo-Jacobean facade of the **Town Hall**, dating from the 1870s.

The **Old Mill** (daily 10am–4pm; $3; Transperth ferry from Barrack Street jetty), situated at Mill Point, south of the Narrows and in the shadow of the Kwinana Freeway bridge, is an early building that has managed to retain its charm. A quaint, fairy-tale relic, the mill ground the colony's first flour and now houses a collection of pioneering bull-carts and period artefacts in its own attractive grounds.

Perth Zoo and Kings Park

Perth Zoo (daily 9am–5pm; $13.20), on Labouchere Road a short walk from the Old Mill (see above), is a hundred-year-old park where animals are not confined to small cages, in keeping with the trend away from traditional zoos. There is enough indigenous and exotic wildlife here to make a great afternoon out.

Perhaps the city's best attraction is the mostly-wild, five-square-kilometre expanse of **Kings Park**, a two-kilometre walk west of the centre down Mount Street, turning off at the end of St Georges Terrace (or take bus #33 or #5 from St Georges Terrace, free FTZ). Created with great foresight in 1872, the park remains Perth's premier recreational area (other than the river), enlivened by various flora and fauna, and no visit would be complete without a wander around. Although the park is small enough to enjoy on foot, you can rent **bicycles** from Koala Cycle Hire (Mon–Fri 9.30am–4pm, Sat & Sun 9.30am–6pm) in the main car park on the park's east side, where there's a fine, tree-framed view over the city. There's a trail leading through the native bushland, a botanic and an aromatic garden, playgrounds, picnic areas and free guided tours from the **information centre** (daily 9.30am–3.30pm; ☎08/9480 3600) by the car park, which also provides maps of the park.

Eating and drinking

To eat well and inexpensively in Perth, stick to **Italian** and **Asian** places. Both dominate the **food courts**, where you can easily get a decent meal for as little as $6. In Northbridge there are the Asian *Shang Hai* and *Pavilion* on James Street, while in the city you'll find the *Metro* and the cosmopolitan *Carillon* off Hay Street Mall. At the other end of the scale, some of the better seafood restaurants may cost you $30 or more per head – still great value. **Northbridge**, especially around James and Lake streets, is the heart of Perth's café and restaurant scene, with over forty establishments crammed into a square kilometre. Except for Sunday and Monday Northbridge is very busy in the evenings, as people wander from place to place, eating (it is also the city's focus for late-night dining), drinking and enjoying themselves.

Cafés, snack bars and inexpensive restaurants

Café Universal, 251 William St, south of Francis St. Trendier cappuccinos, beers and street life than anywhere else, with Italian dishes if you're hungry.

Fast Eddys Café, cnr Murray and Milligan streets. Local BYO institution, open 24hr and offering burgers and breakfasts. Takeaway also available.

Hans Café Noodle Bar, cnr Francis and William streets. Cheap Southeast Asian in a central location. From $5.

Hare Krishna Food for Life, 200 William St. Vegetarian dishes including an all-you-can-eat for $5.50.

Plaka Shiskebab, 83 James St. Late-night hot spot with kebabs and pool tables.

Seoul Korean, 253a William St. Two-course lunches for around $6 and evening meals for twice that in a low-key oriental setting. Daily noon–1pm & 6pm til late.

Sri Melaka Nyonya, 313 William St. Best of the

budget Malay places, with "home-style" cooked food. Vege specials. Tues–Sat from noon.

The Street Café, 78 Lake St. Serves smooth cappuccinos and cheap, tasty pasta every day. Opens early.

Villa Italia, cnr Aberdeen and William streets. Jazzy Italian café with $8.50 lunch specials.

Restaurants

Costa Brava, 137 James St. Authentic Spanish and seafood dishes. Lunch Wed–Fri, dinner daily.

Dusit Thai, 233 James St. Authentic Thai place (cheaper than others in Perth), on the edge of Northbridge, with main courses for around $7. Closed Mon.

Emperor's Court, 66 Lake St (☎ 08/9328 3881). Sumptuous decor and fine Szechuan, Beijing and Cantonese dishes. Nightly karaoke in the cocktail bar. Lunch Mon–Fri, dinner nightly.

Fishy Affair, 132 James St (☎ 08/9328 6636). Treat yourself to the seafood platter. Lunch Mon–Fri, dinner nightly.

Il Padrino, 198 William St. Huge, wood-fired pizzas and lunch-time specials. Closed Wed and weekend lunch times.

Mamma Maria's, 105 Aberdeen St (☎ 08/9328 4532). Long-established and sometimes hectic pasta house; try the grilled chicken. Lunch Mon–Fri, dinner nightly.

Royal India, 1134 Hay St West (☎ 08/9324 1368). Elegant, upmarket restaurant specializing in tandoori dishes. Lunch Mon–Fri, dinner nightly from 6pm.

Woodpeckers Woodfired Pizza, 372 Hay St, Subiaco (☎ 08/9388 1122). Gourmet pizza and pasta. Seven days, from 6pm.

Entertainment and nightlife

As with food, **Northbridge** is the focal point of after-dark action, with plenty of **pubs**, **bars** and teeming **dance clubs** concealed in improbable buildings. In view of Perth's famed isolation, a night in Northbridge is the hottest spot for thousands of kilometres in any direction but there are also some lively bars in the city and inner suburbs. Many pubs and bars feature **free beer**, happy hours and other value-added incentives to get loaded and let the good times roll. Perth's nightlife centres around alcohol and the city has attempted to curb intoxicated revellers and promote responsible behaviour, to little avail.

The free weekly music and gig guides, *X-Press Magazine* and *Hype* have **listings** for all the places below, as well as many others. Alternatively, check out the entertainment section of Thursday's *West Australian* newspaper. For the lowdown on the **gay and lesbian scene**, see the box overleaf.

Pubs and bars with music

Aberdeen Hotel, 84 Aberdeen St. Ever-popular meeting place in Northbridge, with a long-established gay night on Sundays.

Brass Monkey, cnr William and James streets. Enduringly popular pub with a good atmosphere in the heart of Northbridge. Live entertainment and a range of local beers.

Fuel @ PICA, James St Cultural Centre. A young arty crowd, drinking imported beer.

Leederville Hotel, Oxford St, Leederville. The Sunday sessions are all the rage but you need to be smartly dressed. Mainstream bands and DJs.

Moon & Sixpence, 300 Murray St. Popular English theme pub in city centre.

Northbridge Hotel, 198 Brisbane St. Quiet piano lounge and restaurant which does good breakfasts. Rowdier public bar with internet facilities.

Queens, 520 Beaufort St, Mt Lawley. One of Perth's best bars, with a great atmosphere, locally-brewed beers and a good restaurant.

Spirit Sound Bar, Murray St. Popular pre-club meeting place with DJs on weekends.

Subiaco Hotel, cnr Rokeby and Hay streets. Mixed and unpretentious crowds, popular Thursdays and weekends.

Clubs

Amplifier, rear of 393 Murray St. Late-night bar with bands and DJs from Thursday nights. Pinball, pool and giant bottles of beer.

Connections, 81 James St. Perth's established gay and lesbian nightspot offers the best dance music for all sexual preferences. Closed Mon.

DC's, 105 Francis St. *DC's* attracts a young crowd with dance and hardcore techno and good DJs.

Men only on Wed. Closed Mon.

The Globe, 393 Murray St. Live international alt-rock acts and DJs for an otherwise mainstream crowd.

Grosvenor, cnr Hill and Hay streets. Indie, rock, pop and grunge at your service in the front and back rooms and not a cover band in sight. Dark and dingy. Pub hours.

Hip-E-Club, cnr Anzac Rd and Oxford St, Leederville. Very popular retro-psychedelia plus backpackers' nights.

The Loft, 104 Murray St. Eighties retro Sundays and a variety of popular local DJs.

Cinemas, theatres and live music

Most of Perth's mainstream movie **cinemas** are located in the arcades off Hay and Murray streets in the city centre. Tuesday nights are cheap, with matinees also discounted at some places. Art-house cinemas close to the centre include Cinema Paradiso, in James Street's Galleria complex; the lovely, Deco-style Astor, on the corner of Beaufort and Walcott streets; and, a little further out, the award-winning Luna on Oxford Street, Leederville, a fifteen-minute walk west of Northbridge. One cinematic experience that shouldn't be missed, especially if you've never seen an IMAX film, is a visit to the Omni Theatre in the City West Complex on Sutherland Street, West Perth. A huge, wrapround screen turns what would otherwise be fairly ordinary documentaries into sensory roller-coaster rides.

Any out-of-the-ordinary **shows** that visit Perth tend to set the city astir and are advertised and patronized heavily. The *Burswood Resort and Casino* (℡08/9362 7777), just over the Causeway, southeast of the centre, is a do-it-all leisure complex comprising a five-star hotel, numerous restaurants and a huge dome hosting all sorts of sporting and show-business events. Otherwise the Perth Concert Hall on St Georges Terrace (℡08/9325 9944), Her Majesty's Theatre (℡08/9322 2929) on the corner of King and Hay streets, or the Perth Entertainment Centre on Wellington Street next to the bus station are likely venues for the city's main concerts and plays. International bands such as Travis, Coldplay and PJ Harvey play at the monolithic and somewhat suburban Metropolis Club by the railway at 146 Roe St.

Gay and lesbian Perth

Perth has a robust, self-sufficient and extremely friendly gay and lesbian scene. The heart of the action is **Northbridge**, but neighbouring North Perth, Highgate and Mount Lawley all have more than their share of gay residents, while lesbians seem to opt for a relaxed lifestyle down in Fremantle. As usual, the quickest way to plug into the scene is to pick up the community paper: in Perth it's the *Westside Observer* (WSO) and *Women Out West* (WOW), both free at gigs or available for $1 at the Arcane Bookshop, 212 William St, Northbridge (Mon–Fri 10am–5.30pm, Sat 10am–5pm; ℡08/9328 5073), which has plenty of other gay, lesbian and feminist literature.

October heats up with **Perth Pride**, celebrated with the usual array of fun and games, including a night march and dance party. Also in October, lesbians march to **Reclaim The Night**. Every November competitors get set to "go for glory" at the **Western Australia Gay Olympics**. At other times of year, outdoor organizations such as GAGS and Team Perth (see below) can put you in touch with other pink athletes.

The main **community organizations** for gays and lesbians in Perth are the Gay Activities Group Services (GAGS), PO Box 8234, Perth 6000, which is responsible for the Gay Olympics and other sporting events; the Gay Outdoor Group, PO Box 263, Cottesloe, Perth 6011 (℡08/9270 7181); Team Perth, PO Box 3234, Stirling St, Perth 6849; and Wednesday Women (℡08/9328 9044), a lesbian social group.

For gay- and lesbian-friendly **accommodation**, try the *Court Hotel* (see p.693) or the beachside *Swanbourne Guest House* (see p.707). **Night-time venues** include *Connections*, *Court Hotel*, and the *Red Lion* at the *Aberdeen Hotel* on Sundays (see p.697).

River cruises and tours from Perth

As well as commercial ferry operators, all based at Barrack Street jetty and offering cruises up and down the Swan River from as little as $10 to Fremantle or $70 for a full day upriver, bus and 4WD tours leave daily in all directions from Perth. Popular day-tours include the curious Pinnacles, near Cervantes (see p.739); Wave Rock, near Hyden (see p.726); and the wineries of the Upper Swan Valley (see p.708) and the Margaret River Region (see p.713). Longer excursions can be taken to see the dolphins at Monkey Mia or to make a more thorough appraisal of WA's diverse Southwest region. Booking for all tours can be made at your hostel or hotel; at YHA Travel, 236 William St, Northbridge (☎08/9227 5122); the tourist office in Forrest Chase (☎08/9483 1111); or the Travellers' Club and Tour Information Centre round the corner at 499 Wellington St (☎08/9226 0660).

River cruises

Boat Torque (☎08/9221 5844). A full range of tours on plush vessels upriver to Tranby House and to the Swan Valley for wine-tasting (half-day and full-day). From $20.

Captain Cook Cruises (☎08/9325 3341). Daily half- and full-day runs to Fremantle, with the option of a three-hour stopover. From $15.

Golden Sun Cruises (☎08/9325 9166). Cruises upriver to visit the National Trust property at Tranby House, faintly historic Guildford, and a day-cruise and bus tour around the Swan Valley wineries. Also downriver cruises to Fremantle. From $10.

Oceanic Cruises (Perth ☎08/9325 1191, Fremantle ☎08/9430 5127). Cruises to Fremantle, Rottnest Island and upriver. From $20.

Tours

Pinnacles Tours and Travel Centre, 16 Irwin St, cnr Hay St (☎08/9221 5411). One-day tours to the Pinnacles (4WD option), Wave Rock and Margaret River, plus longer runs as far afield as Coral Bay (5 days), together with seasonal whale-watching and wildflower tours. From $90.

Planet Perth Tours (☎08/9276 5295). Fun days out around Perth visiting wildlife parks, the Darling Ranges and the beach to view the sunset. From $20.

Redback Safaris, YHA Travel (☎08/9227 5122). One-day tours specializing in the Pinnacles, with a small 4WD van to indulge in a spot of dune-riding on the way back.

Travelabout, YHA Travel (☎08/9227 5122). One of WA's leading tour companies offering a full range of professionally run all-adventure tours, from one-day excursions to the Pinnacles to one-month trips up to the Kimberley and Kakadu National Park (NT) and back by way of Ayers Rock (NT). Around $80 a day.

Western Travel Bug, YHA Travel (☎08/9561 5236). Popular bargain-priced tours of the Southwest (though not all basic costs are covered), offering plenty of activities and a lively atmosphere. Five-day Southwest tour around $365; seven-day Southwest tour including Wave Rock $525.

Listings

Airlines (domestic) Ansett (☎13 1300); Qantas (☎13 1313); Rottnest Airtaxi (free call ☎1800 500 006); Skywest (☎08/9334 2288 or free call 1800 244 833).

Airlines (international) Air New Zealand (☎08/9325 1099); British Airways (☎08/9425 7711); Garuda (☎08/9481 0963); Malaysian Airlines (☎13 2627); Qantas (☎13 1313); Singapore Airlines (☎13 1011); United Airlines (☎13 1777).

Airport shuttle buses Airport–City Shuttle (☎08/9479 4131).

Bicycle rental About Bike Hire, Barrack Street jetty (☎08/9221 2665), has bikes for riverside cycling from $15 a day, or try the hostels. Secondhand bikes from WA Bicycle Disposals, 278 Hay St, East Perth (☎08/9325 1176), from around $80. They also offer an informal rental and buy-back service, plus local and regional cycling maps.

Buses Greyhound Pioneer (☏13 2030), for inter-state services; Integrity Coach Lines (☏08/9226 1399 or free call 1800 226 339) head north up the coast to Exmouth three times a week; South West Coach Lines (☏08/9322 5173), for daily services to the Margaret River Region as far as Augusta; Westliner (☏08/9250 2838), for twice-weekly serv-ices to Kalgoorlie, Leinster and Laverton; Westrail (☏131053), for daily services south and east of Perth and, less frequently, north to Kalbarri and Meekatharra. All have offices at the Wellington Street Bus Station, but interstate and Westrail country buses come and go from the East Perth Terminal.

Car rental Perth's car-rental companies are among the cheapest in the country and while the "$25 per day" deals should be scrutinized careful-ly, a week's rental is the best way of exploring rel-atively compact areas such as the Southwest at your own pace. Outlets include Atlas Rent-a-Car (☏08/9277 8311); City Centre Car Rentals (☏08/9322 1887); Myaree Rent-a-Car (☏08/9330 8848); and Network Rent-a-Car, 259 William St, Northbridge (☏08/9227 8810).

Disabled travellers ACROD, Unit 9, 189 Royal St, East Perth (☏08/9222 2961), provides information for disabled visitors to WA. For information about accessible accommodation, call the Para Quad Association (☏08/9381 0173), or use the fairly reliable *RACWA Touring Guide* (see below).

Hospitals Royal Perth, Victoria Square (☏08/9224 2244); King Edward, Bagot Rd, Subiaco (☏08/9340 2222), for women; Fremantle, Alma St (☏08/9321 3333).

Internet access The city library (see below) has several somewhat clunky computers free for surf-ing up to an hour a day. There are a number of internet cafés on Barrack St and William St, between Murray St and Wellington St. The cheap-est in town is at *Grand Central Backpackers*, 379 Wellington St.

Library Perth Cultural Centre, James St. An attrac-tive and air-conditioned place to sit and read the newspapers and surf the Net.

Maps Perth Map Centre, 1st floor, 884 Hay St (☏08/9322 5733), has a full range of topographic and touring maps.

Motoring associations RACWA, 228 Adelaide Terrace (☏08/9421 4444), offers a complete range of services, as well as maps.

Police 2 Adelaide Terrace (☏08/9222 1111).

Post office Forrest Chase, opposite the train sta-tion, with a mail collection service.

Around Perth

While Perth may not be all it's cracked up to be, the area around the city offers some compensation. The port of **Fremantle**, at the mouth of the Swan River, should not be overlooked, nor should a day-trip to **Rottnest Island**, an eighty-minute ferry ride from the city or half that from Fremantle. Perth's **beaches** form a near-unbroken line north of Fremantle, just a short train or bus ride from the centre, while with your own vehicle you can escape to the **national parks** northeast of Perth, atop the **Darling Ranges**, which parallel the coast. Patchily forested hills, just half an hour's drive east of the city, they offer a network of cool, scenic drives and marked walking trails among the jar-rah woodlands. After Fremantle, Rottnest Island and the beaches, the best of the local trips are detailed on p.699, described in a clockwise arc starting to the north of the city.

Fremantle

Although long since merged into the metropolitan area's suburban sprawl, Perth's port of **FREMANTLE** – "Freo" – retains an identity and charm all of its own. Much of the convict-built dock dates from the 1890s, though spruced up for the 1987 Americas Cup yacht race and an eagerly anticipated tourist boom that never quite materialized. The formerly rough and run-down port town is now quite presentable, but the jazzed-up image takes a knock as an unmistakeable ovine pong settles over the whole town when a stream of "baa-ing" road trains load up Arabia-bound sheep freighters.

Freo's relaxed, Mediterranean ambience attracts hordes of weekenders to its famed artsy markets (worth planning your visit around) and "cappuccino strip", as the café-lined **South Terrace** is known. It's worth noting that in the heat of summer Fremantle is often a breezy 5°C cooler than Perth, a mere 25 minutes away by train. **Trains** leave regularly from Perth for the nineteen-kilometre run down to Fremantle Station, located at the top end of Market Street, five-minutes' walk north of the town centre. **Buses** (routes #102–#106 and

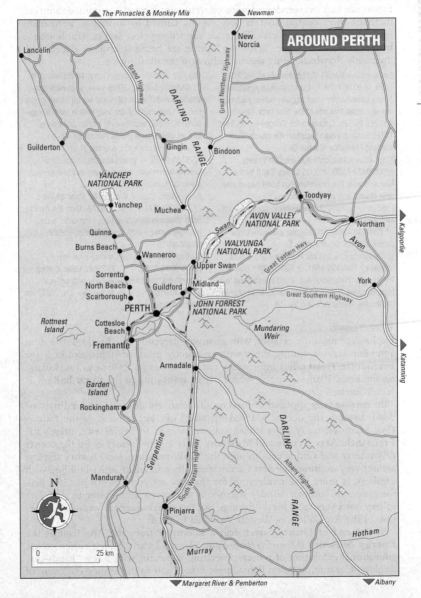

AROUND PERTH

▲ The Pinnacles & Monkey Mia

▲ Newman

Lancelin

New Norcia

Guilderton

Gingin

Bindoon

DARLING RANGE

Brand Highway

Great Northern Highway

YANCHEP NATIONAL PARK

Yanchep

Muchea

Toodyay

AVON VALLEY NATIONAL PARK

Swan

Northam

Avon

Quinns

Burns Beach

Wanneroo

WALYUNGA NATIONAL PARK

Great Eastern Hwy

Sorrento

North Beach

Scarborough

Upper Swan

Guildford

Midland

York

Great Southern Highway

PERTH

JOHN FORREST NATIONAL PARK

Rottnest Island

Cottesloe Beach

Fremantle

Mundaring Weir

DARLING RANGE

Garden Island

Armadale

Rockingham

Serpentine

Albany Highway

Mandurah

Pinjarra

South Western Highway

Hotham

N

Murray

0   25 km

▼ Margaret River & Pemberton

▼ Albany

#151 from Perth's City Busport) also stop here; local **taxis** can be called on ☏08/9335 3944. For **ferries** to and from Perth, see box on p.699. The **Fremantle CAT** – Fremantle's free transport system – runs roughly every ten minutes, in a loop from the town hall through most of the port area. There's a small **tourist office** in the town hall on St John's Square (Mon–Sat 9am–5pm, Sun noon–4.40pm; ☏08/9431 7878).

Accommodation

Fremantle isn't over-endowed with conveniently located accommodation, but there are three central **hostels** only slightly tainted by lounging "permanent residents" and a caravan park. There are also some pricey but tasteful boutique **hotels** and some of the "grand era" hotels are being splendidly refurbished, their only drawback being shared bathrooms for most rooms.

Backpacker Inn, 11 Packenham St (☏08/9431 7065, ℱ9336 7106, ✉bpinn_freo@hotmail.com). A very good location and big, airy rooms with high ceilings make this one of the best bets. ❶–❸
Coogee Beach, Cockburn Rd, Coogee (☏08/9418 1810). Large caravan resort on the beach, 7km south of Fremantle. Cabins ❸
Fremantle Hotel, cnr High and Cliff streets (☏08/9430 4300, ℱ9335 2636). Right by the Round House, this unpretentious hotel has rooms with shared and en-suite facilities. ❺
Fremantle Village Caravan Park, cnr Cockburn and Rockingham roads, South Fremantle (☏08/9430 4866). The nearest campsite to the centre of town. On-site vans ❸
His Majesty's Hotel, cnr Phillimore and Mouat streets (☏08/9336 4681, ℱ9336 4691). One of Freo's many Federation-era hotels refurbished to a high standard. Nearly all large rooms have shared bathrooms. Restaurant and bar. ❹

Old Fire Station Backpackers, 18 Phillimore St (☏08/9430 5454, ℱ9319 1494, ⓦwww.firestation.fdns.net). Big on rules and big on security. Just two minutes south of the train station, with a huge common room, women-only lounge and dorms, and an inexpensive Indian restaurant. ❶–❸
Pirates Backpackers, 5 Essex St (☏ & ℱ 08/9335 6635, ⓦwww.planetbackpack.com). Central hostel with mixed dorms and popular with a young crowd. ❶–❸
Rosemoore B&B, 2 Winifred St, Mosman Park (☏08/9384 8214, ℱ9385 6373). Over the river in posh Mosman Park 5km from Fremantle, a country-style cottage with private access and full breakfast. ❺
Tradewinds Hotel, 59 Canning Highway (☏08/9339 8188, ℱ9339 2266). Good-looking, Federal-era hotel with well-equipped, self-contained apartments, close to the river and 2km from the centre. ❼

The Town

Exploring Fremantle on foot, with plenty of streetside café breaks, is the most agreeable way of visiting the town's compactly grouped sights, although the **Fremantle Tram** offers informative commentaries on its various tours (daily, on the hour, 10am–4pm; $8), which depart from outside the **town hall** on St John's Square.

By starting your appraisal of Freo on the relatively dull east side and moving down towards the ocean, you end up, worn out but satisfied, at the Fishing Boat Harbour, ready for a sunset seafood dinner. To begin with, there's the **Fremantle Arts Centre** and **Museum** (daily 10am–5pm; free) on the corner of Finnerty and Ord streets, though the small museum's local history displays are not very exciting. The Arts Centre itself, albeit in an attractive building with a gallery, is more of a rendezvous for the arty set and a venue for live performances on summer Sunday afternoons than a rewarding place to visit. The gallery has a variety of local offerings, but they can't compare with the collection of the Art Gallery of Western Australia in Perth.

At the end of Quarry Street, half a kilometre from the Arts Centre, the **Energy Museum** (Mon–Fri 9am–5pm; $3), at 12 Parry St, is a rather stodgy, educational exhibition of power-generating apparatus with a few "hands-on" displays. Continuing down Parry Street brings you to the hillside enclosure of

FREMANTLE

Stirling & Canning Highways & Perth

N

ACCOMMODATION

Backpacker Inn	3
Fremantle Hotel	5
Fremantle Village Caravan Park	7
His Majesty's Hotel	4
Old Fire Station Backpackers	2
Pirate's Backpackers	6
Tradewinds Hotel	1

Rous Head Harbour (Northport)

Fremantle Harbour

Victoria Quay

Energy Museum

Fremantle Museum & Arts Centre

Fremantle Station

B Shed

E Shed markets

Fremantle Art Gallery

Town Hall

Fremantle Prison

Round House

West Australian Maritime Museum

Fremantle Markets

Oval

Bather's Beach

Lombardos

Hospital

Crocodile Park

0   250 m

Fishing Boat Harbour

ST JOHN'S SQUARE

Fremantle Prison (daily 10am–6pm; \$11), whose entrance is in The Terrace. Built by convicts in 1855, soon after the struggling colony found it couldn't do without their labour, it's now one of the biggest tourist jails in a country full of these grim reminders of its modern origins. The high admission charge is offset by free tours of the prison buildings, guided by ex-wardens: the building was only decommissioned as late as 1991.

Things look up from here on in. If it's a Friday, Saturday or Sunday, **Fremantle Markets** (Fri 10am–9pm, Sat & Sun 10am–5pm), on the corner of Henderson Street and South Terrace, will be open and a hub of activity. A real local market where people actually buy things, it's well worth a browse for some fresh food, unusual souvenirs from the many arts and crafts stalls, or cosmic clothes and accessories. Moving down **South Terrace**, Fremantle's main street, you can revive your aching feet with some refreshment in one of the many inviting, alfresco **cafés** that give the town its vaguely European atmosphere.

Suitably re-caffeinated, you now head into the **"West End"**, as the old shipping office and freight district of Freo is known. As South Terrace curves to the right, you can turn left down Bannister Street to the **Bannister Street Craftworks** at no. 8 (daily 11am–5.30pm), where you can watch local wood, glass and ceramic artisans engaged in their craft.

The **West Australian Maritime Museum** on Cliff Street (Mon–Sun 9.30am–5pm; donation) is one of Fremantle's highlights. Pride of place goes to the Batavia display, the Dutch East Indiaman wrecked off present-day Geraldton over 360 years ago. As well as the ship's reconstructed stern, the display includes the stone portico bound for the Company's unfinished fort at Batavia (Jakarta) and numerous corroded artefacts, together with a fascinating video about the extraordinary drama and subsequent salvage of the wreck. The rest of the museum displays exhibits from other Dutch vessels which regularly struck Australia's west coast on their way to the East Indies.

Just north of the museum, past **Bather's Beach**, is the **Round House** (10am–5pm; donation), the state's oldest building and original jail, with fine views across town and out to sea. From here you can take a walk to the end of **South Mole**, where the Swan River meets the ocean, or continue up to the Port Authority Building on **Victoria Quay**. Here there's a statue to C.Y. O'Connor, who masterminded the rebuilding of the docks in the 1890s. Nearby, the **E Shed markets** (Fri 10am–9pm, Sat & Sun 10am–5pm) offer a similar range of stalls and a food hall as found at the better-known Fremantle Markets.

South of the Maritime Museum you pass the grassy **Esplanade**, with its numerous seafood restaurants on **Fishing Boat Harbour** (see "Eating", below).

Eating

Although taken seriously, dining out in Fremantle is pleasantly free of unnecessary formality. **Seafood** restaurants overlook the Swan River or jut out into Fishing Boat Harbour by the Esplanade. In town, South Terrace and its adjacent streets are lined with predominantly **Italian** or **Asian** cafés and restaurants, none of them expensive and all adding to Freo's distinctive ambience. The **Food Halls**, Henderson St (Thurs–Sun noon–9pm), next to the markets, where they serve up an array of global, but mostly Asian "pop foods", make for a good place to experiment with inexpensive Japanese morsels.

Captain Munchies, 2 Beach St. Twenty-four-hour fast-food establishment for those late-night appetites.

Chunagon, 46 Mews Rd, Fishing Boat Harbour (☏ 08/9336 1000). Classy Japanese restaurant which suits those who know their sushi from their sashimi or can afford to learn. Closed Mon.

Cicerello, Fishing Boat Harbour. One of the best fish-and-chip places in town.

George Street Café, 73 George St, East Fremantle. Pleasant, small café, an east-side alternative to the central Freo coffee "strip".

Gino's, 1 South Terrace. Best streetside café on the strip. Enduringly popular and unpretentious, serving great coffee and inexpensive food.

Kailis, Mews Rd, Fishing Boat Harbour. Fast and inexpensive seafood cafeteria and takeaway, right on the waterfront.

Left Bank Bar & Café, 15 Riverside Rd, East Fremantle. Trendy riverside venue with brimming subs, or for around $20 you can eat in the upstairs restaurant, which has great views.

Mexican Kitchen, 19 South Terrace. Classic, wholesome Mexican dishes at around $15, with half-price nachos on Tuesday night.

Old Papa's, 17 South Terrace. Local legendary Italian café, very popular with locals, serving up cheap meals.

Pigeon Restaurant, 4 Market St. Vietnamese place with all dishes under $10.

Sails, 47 Mews Rd, Fishing Boat Harbour (☏ 08/9430 5050). Elegant, upmarket, harbourside seafood specialities for around $25 per person.

Drinking and entertainment

Like the town itself, entertainment in Fremantle is generally a laid-back, easy-going affair – a jazzy or folksy scene, as opposed to Northbridge's techno venues. The *Sail & Anchor* on South Terrace is the town's main watering hole, serving a variety of "boutique" **beers** (this upmarket home-brew trend originated in Fremantle). The *Left Bank Bar & Café*, on Riverside Road in East Freo, is a good-looking and popular spot, usually packed on sunny weekends. Bars with **live music** include *Rosie O'Grady's* on William Street; *The Bar* at *Lombardos* on the harbour; and the spruced-up *Orient Hotel* on the High Street. The *Metropolis*, 52 South Terrace, is Fremantle's gigantic **nightclub**, offering a choice of bars and dance floors while the *Fly By Night*, at the prison end of Queen Street, is a musicians' co-op airing local **folk** talent and makes an enjoyable, smoke-free change from pub venues.

For **performing arts**, check out the *Fremantle Herald* or Thursday's *West Australian*. Local troupes, such as the innovative Deck Chair Theatre based at 3 Packenham St (℡ 08/9336 2372), or Spare Parts Theatre, 1 Short St (℡ 08/9335 5044), are worth seeing, or head for the Arts Centre, Ord Street, on a Sunday afternoon in summer. Fremantle has four **cinemas**, on Essex Street, William Street, Collie Street and Adelaide Street, all with cut-price tickets on Tuesday and for some matinees.

Rottnest Island

Eighteen kilometres offshore, west of Fremantle, **Rottnest Island** was so named by seventeenth-century Dutch mariners who mistook its unique, indigenous **quokkas**, beaver-like marsupials, for rats. Today, following an ignominious period as a brutal Aboriginal penal colony in the nineteenth century, Rottnest is a popular holiday destination, easily accessible from Perth or Fremantle by ferry and, at the very least, makes for a fun day out.

The island, colloquially abbreviated to "Rotto", is 11km long and less than half as wide, with one settlement, the main resort, stretching along the sheltered Thompson Bay on the east side. West of the settlement, a low heathland of salt lakes meets a coastline of clear, scalloped bays, small beaches and offshore reefs ending at the "West End", as the seaward "tail" of the island is known. Although well attuned to the demands of its 400,000 annual visitors, Rotto gets packed out during school summer holidays, especially around New Year when accommodation can be hard to find. Motorized traffic on the island is virtually non-existent, a real treat which makes **cycling** from bay to sparkling bay the best way to appreciate Rotto. Besides riding around the island, you can take a **train ride** up to Oliver Hill (five trips daily, allow 2hr; $12), or get underwater with the Dive Shop (daily 7.30am–6pm; ℡ 08/9292 5111), which organizes **dive trips** and rents out everything from a snorkel and fins to a full scuba rig. The diving and snorkelling off Rotto's beautiful coves are unlike anywhere on the adjacent mainland and a couple of days spent here, especially midweek, when it's less busy, are well worth the excursion from Perth.

Practicalities

There are no fewer than four **ferry** operators that service Rotto from a variety of points in Fremantle and Perth. After a brief price war, prices have stabilized at around $25 day-return from Freo and $35 from Perth. The trip from Perth takes about eighty minutes, half as long from Fremantle. You can also **fly** to Rotto in twenty minutes from Jandakot airport (about 20km south of Perth) with the Rottnest Airbus (℡ 08/9478 1322). Rottnest Airport is a fifteen-minute walk from the settlement.

Ferries arrive at the jetty in Thompson Bay right in front of the island's **information office** (Mon–Sat 8.30am–5pm, Sun 10am–4.30pm; ☏08/9372 9752, ⓦwww.rottnest.gov.au), which has maps and bus timetables. The office is also a **post office** with Commonwealth and Westpac bank agencies. Daily two-hour **bus tours** depart from the bus stop behind the information office at varying times throughout the day ($13.20). The more-or-less hourly Bayseeker **bus service** (Oct–April daily 9am–5pm; $5.50 per trip) also takes you to the island's bays as far as the isthmus, Narrow Neck, 3km from the West End. The settlement has a general **store** (daily 9am–5.30pm, with R&I and ANZ teller machine), bakery, takeaway and **bistro**, with **bike** rental (daily 9am–1pm & 2–5pm; $15 per day; ☏08/9372 9722) behind the hotel, a couple of minutes south of the information office.

Accommodation is found along Thompson, Longreach and Geordie bays, all adjacent to each other at the developed northeast end of the island and linked by an hourly bus service (daily 8am–5pm; $2). A small YHA-associate **hostel** (☏08/9372 9780, Ⓕ9292 5154; booking essential; ❶) is located in Kingstown Barracks, at the southeastern end of Thompson Bay, 1km from the shops. **Camping** is available just behind the settlement (☏08/9372 9729): tents and mattresses can be rented (❶) or there are four- and six-bed cabins (❸); note that camping is not permitted elsewhere on the island. The island authority rents out all sorts of bungalows, villas, units and cottages (book ahead on ☏08/9432 9111; four-bed units ❹–❼); rates are substantially lower for subsequent nights, and there's a minimum stay of two nights at weekends. The *Rottnest Lodge Resort* (☏08/9292 5161, Ⓕ9292 5158; ❻) is a prison converted into first-class motel units.

Perth's beaches

Perth's closest **beaches** extend along the Indian Ocean's **Sunset Coast**, 30km of near-unbroken sand and coastal suburbs stretching north of the Swan River and cooled by afternoon sea breezes. There are also **inshore beaches** along the Swan River at Crawley, Nedlands, Peppermint Grove and Mosman Bay on the north shore, and Como, Canning Bridge and Applecross on the south – all are calm and safe for kiddies.

Cottesloe Beach, 7km north of Fremantle, is the most popular city beach, with safe swimming in the lee of a groyne, although in the summer of 2000 a swimmer was taken by a shark. There are ice-cream vendors, cafés and watercraft-rental outlets all just a ten-minute walk from Cottesloe train station. North of here, **Swanbourne Free Beach**, cut off by army land in both directions but accessible from the road, has nude bathing. Further north, the surf and currents are more suited to wave riding and experienced swimmers, with fewer beachside facilities, which tends to reduce crowds.

Scarborough Beach, dominated by the *Rendezvouzs Observation City Hotel*, is as much a holiday resort as a somewhat dowdy beachside suburb with a love of concrete. Popular with surfers and their groupies, the suburb has an easy-going air of "Californian tan-upmanship", plus enough services, inexpensive accommodation and activity to sustain a few days out of central Perth. **Bus #400** leaves from Perth's Wellington Street Bus Station for the forty-minute journey.

Beachside accommodation

The accommodation at Scarborough Beach is mostly self-catering, suited to extended stays. The *Western Beach Lodge* serves backpackers in a converted house at 6 Westborough St (☏08/9245 1624; ❶) or try *Sunset Coast*

Backpackers, 119 Scarborough Beach Rd (☎08/9245 1161; ❶). The *Mandarin Gardens Holiday Resort*, at 20 Wheatcroft St (☎08/9431 5431, Ⓕ9245 1553, Ⓔmandarin@crystal.com.au), has backpacker accommodation (❶) as well as motel rooms (❹), plus it does free pick-ups from the airport. Further south in **Swanbourne**, the excellent and welcoming *Swanbourne Guest House*, 5 Myera St (☎08/9383 1981, Ⓕ9385 4595, Ⓦwww.iinet.net.au/~swan5; ❻), is great for couples, as well as being gay- and lesbian-friendly. The *Cottesloe Beach Chalets*, 6 John St (☎08/9383 5000, Ⓕ9385 4196, Ⓔdavies@git.com.au; ❽) have motel-style apartments sleeping six right by the beach that are suitable for families or small groups.

New Norcia and Toodyay

One of WA's most extraordinary architectural sights is the nineteenth-century monastic community of **NEW NORCIA**, 130km northeast of Perth on the Great Northern Highway. This unexpected collection of Spanish-style buildings, bizarrely out of place in the Australian bush, is part of a community founded by Benedictine monks in 1846. **Dom Rosendo Salvado** established the mission (named after St Benedict's birthplace in Italy) with the aim of converting the local Aborigines to the "twin blessings" of agriculture and Christianity, and to escape persecution back home. Nowadays it's a popular tourist attraction, which tends to compromise the monastic tranquillity its ageing inhabitants seek, and yet pays for the upkeep of their remarkable endowment.

The community has a roadhouse with a restaurant, a **tourist office** (daily 9am–5pm; ☎08/9654 8056) and a **museum and art gallery** (daily 9.30am–5pm; $4.50) describing the Benedictines' motivations in coming here and displaying a fine collection of religious art. The tourist office also runs two-hour tours of town that leave at 11am and 1.30pm ($12.50). The **rooms** in the *New Norcia Hotel* (☎08/9654 8034, Ⓕ9654 8011; ❹) don't quite match the building's grand exterior, but they still offer an old-fashioned treat. The two-kilometre New Norcia **heritage trail** (guide leaflet available from the tourist office or museum; $3.30) begins here and takes you on a circuit past the community's impressive buildings.

The two most ornate buildings, on either side of the cemetery, are **St Gertrude's Residence for Girls** and **St Ildephonsus's for Boys**, the latter with striking Moorish minarets. Both were built by the mission's second abbot, Bishop Torres, at the beginning of the twentieth century. You can also visit the **Flour Mills** and the **Abbey Church** – relatively ordinary by comparison. The **monastery** is still the residence of New Norcia's few remaining monks and is closed to the public, although there's the guesthouse (☎08/9654 8002; ❸ per person for full board) which gives the opportunity to experience true Benedictine hospitality. From here an eight-hundred-metre marked trail leads down to the old wells and Bishop Torres' gazebo-like **Beehouse** by the Moore River; on the way back there are great views of St Ildephonsus's turreted roofline poking through the trees.

Several bus-tour companies offer **day-tours** from Perth to New Norcia, which is otherwise served only three times a week by Westrail's rural bus service.

Toodyay

The charming old town of **TOODYAY**, set among the wooded hills of the Avon Valley, 85km northwest of Perth, makes an agreeable diversion on the way to or from New Norcia. The town was founded in 1836, making it one of the earliest inland settlements of the Swan River Colony, and many buildings survive from that era. The unembellished bulk of **Connors Mill** on the main road, Stirling Terrace, is now an **information centre** and **museum** (Mon–Sat 9am–5pm, Sun 10am–5pm; ☎08/9574 2435; museum $1), featuring, among the usual relics, displays on the exploits of the local bushranger known as "Moondyne Joe". The **Old Newcastle Gaol** on Clinton Street is also a local history museum (Mon–Fri 11am–3pm, Sat 1–4pm, Sun 11am–4pm; $2). Other historic buildings include **St Stephen's Church**, opposite the mill, and the **Mechanics' Institute**, on Stirling Terrace, which features unusual scissor trusses supporting the roof.

These aside, the town is an attractive place for a stroll, with antique and country crafts outlets, a couple of **tearooms**, pleasant parks and riverside walks. The **Avon Valley** and **Walyunga national parks** (CALM fee; see box on p.719) follow the Avon River southwest of town and make a further scenic diversion on the road to Perth.

Guildford and the Swan Valley

North of the town of **GUILDFORD**, a thirty-minute drive from Perth, is the **Upper Swan Valley**, WA's oldest wine-growing region. Set at the foot of the Darling Ranges, it makes for a pleasant day's **wine-tasting**, although the wines produced here cannot match the more recent vintages from the Margaret River Region (see p.713). Guildford itself is a historic town dating back to the earliest years of the colony, with several Federation-era grand hotels to admire and Guildford Village Potters, at 22 Meadow St, acting as the town's **tourist office** (Mon–Fri 10am–3pm, Sat & Sun 10am–4pm; ☎08/9279 9859). If you're heading up the valley, pick up the *Swan Valley Drive – Route 203* guide from here, which details the area's attractions and its dozen or so wineries. And before you leave town (or on your way back), visit the **Halls Museum**, at the back of the *Rose and Crown Hotel* (WA's oldest), at 105 Swan St (Tues–Sun 10am–4.30pm; $4). Proclaiming itself the largest private collection of **diverse memorabilia** in the southern hemisphere, it includes displays of inkwells, corkscrews and evening bags, the like of which you won't find anywhere else.

The Swan Valley Drive

Heading north from Guildford Village Potters, a clearly marked thirty-kilometre drive follows the west side of the river. A turn-off left down Banera Road leads to **Pinelli Wines** on Bennett Road (Mon–Sat 9am–6pm, Sun 10am–5pm), offering two-litre flagons of decent table wine from $15. Back on the West Swan Road, the simply named **Wines** (Mon–Sat 10am–5pm, Sun 11am–4pm) has some of the valley's best wines, but you'll probably be more impressed by their Margaret River selection. (All of WA's wines are rather pricey, while being no better than Australia's eastern equivalents.) Further up Route 203, the **Little River Winery & Café** (daily 10am–5.30pm) is a small, independent winery with some award-winning wines and a pleasant café in which to enjoy them.

Coming down the valley's east side, several more wineries tempt you: **Talijancich Wines'** (Sun–Fri 11am–5pm) rich muscat can be bought rather than tasted, while **Houghton's**, on Dale Road (daily 10am–5pm), is the area's biggest and most diverse producer of wines, with an art gallery and tended lawns on which to contemplate your tastings. The route returns to Guildford and thence to Perth via Midland, passing the Toodyay Road (see above) winding up into the Darling Ranges. Feature Tours (☎08/9479 4131) runs regular **bus tours** through the valley from Perth, as do some of the Swan River **boat cruises**.

Mundaring Weir and around

At the crest of the Darling Ranges, 40km from Perth and 7km south of the town of Mundaring on the Great Eastern Highway, is **Mundaring Weir**, a dam constructed in the 1890s to provide water for the Goldfields Water Scheme. At the time, a desperate water shortage was hampering development of the Eastern Goldfields and the dam was part of the innovative solution devised by the colony's chief engineer, C.Y. O'Connor, who planned to raise the water the 400km up to Kalgoorlie with the aid of a series of pumping stations. Such a radical idea was ridiculed in the press and mocked in parliament – O'Connor struggled constantly to secure funds for his scheme and eventually committed suicide on Fremantle Beach just months before water finally gushed into Kalgoorlie's Mount Charlotte Reservoir in 1903. Today, the Goldfields are still fed by an upgraded version of the pipeline and pumping stations which parallel the Great Eastern Highway to Kalgoorlie.

At the base of the dam wall is the **C.Y. O'Connor Museum** (Mon & Wed–Fri 10.30am–3pm, Sun noon–5pm; $5), housed in the primary steam pumping station. Inside are early versions of the pitch and wood pipeline, at that time the longest in the world, and details of O'Connor's other public works, as well as a biographical video on his achievements.

The **John Forrest National Park** (CALM fee; see box on p.719) lies north of the Great Eastern Highway between Mundaring and Midland, right on the edge of the Darling escarpment and a mere thirty-minutes' drive from Perth. An area of natural bushland with swimming spots, waterfalls, and walking and riding trails, as well as barbecues and a restaurant, it's among the best of the nearby parks.

York

Stranded in the Avon Valley, 97km from Perth via the Great Southern Highway, **YORK** looks like a film set for an Australian western. The town is the state's most complete pioneering settlement, filled with attractive and well-preserved early architecture. The commercial centre of the Avon Valley until the railway – and with it the Great Eastern Highway – bypassed it 30km to the north, York is now an agricultural centre but also plays a historic role as a venerable museum of ornate nineteenth-century public buildings, coaching inns and churches.

The **Old York Gaol & Courthouse** (daily 11am–4pm, $3.30) on Avon Terrace harks back to its pioneer history while the **York Motor Museum** (daily 9am–4pm; $6), opposite the tourist office on Avon Terrace, capitalizes on York's antiquarian charisma with a large collection of vintage and classic vehicles – from a hundred-year-old single-cylinder tricycle to Ossie Cranston's 1936 Ford V8 racer. At the north end of the terrace are the **Sandalwood Yards** where the perfumed wood, once prolific in WA and highly prized in the Orient, was stored during York's heyday. Near here you can take a walk down to the wobbly **suspension bridge** spanning the generally sluggish Avon River and have a look at the 1854 **Holy Trinity Church**, with its modern stained-glass designs by Robert Juniper, one of WA's foremost artists.

Recrossing the river, passing the Shire Offices and old cemetery, a left turn down the southern end of Avon Terrace leads to **Balladong Farm** (daily 10am–5pm; $5), restored by the National Trust. At a time when York was a key inland settlement and jumping-off point for treks into the interior, the farm played a pivotal role in the region, and today it still employs machinery and husbandry techniques from that era. An elevated view of York and the Avon Valley can be enjoyed from **Mount Brown Lookout**, signposted 2km to the east of town.

Practicalities

York's **tourist office** (daily 9am–5pm; ℡08/9641 1301) is at 105 Avon Terrace, the main road on which most of York's fine old buildings are located. A **town map** and information sheet is available here, which locates and briefly describes all of these structures as well as places to stay and eat. York's **hotels** ooze charm, with the *Settlers' House* (℡08/9641 1096; ❼) offering elegantly furnished rooms with breakfast, with a fine restaurant and pleasant daytime café too. The *Imperial Hotel*, 83 Avon Terrace (℡08/9641 1010, ℻9641 2201; ❼), is a restored, century-old hotel also full of old-world charm, while the pricier *Castle Hotel* (℡08/9641 1007; ❼) is even more splendid. The only real budget accommodation is at the *Mount Bakewell Caravan Park* (℡08/9641 1421; on-site vans ❷).

Cafés to enjoy include *Café Bugatti* and *Il Bocconcino* (both on Avon Terrace), as well as the one attached to the *Settlers' House* hotel, while *Yorky's Coffee Carriage* on Glebe Street, by the river, makes for a picturesque stop. **Buses** leave Westrail's East Perth terminal for York up to three times daily (no service on Sat), while some **tours** stop here on the way to or from Wave Rock at Hyden, 250km to the east. The town hosts the **York Jazz Festival** around September, but note that in the summer months, York, like all of inland WA, often sees temperatures of 40°C and gets few visitors.

The Southwest

The region south of Perth and west of the Albany Highway, known as **The Southwest**, is the temperate corner of the continent, where the cool Southern and warm Indian oceans meet. North of **Bunbury**, 180km from Perth, is a knot of industrial installations and satellite towns such as Rockingham and Mandurah, which offer little of interest to the visitor compared to what's ahead.

South of Bunbury things improve greatly. The **Margaret River** Region offers tasteful tourist facilities in a picturesque landscape of dairy farms and wineries – WA's most popular holiday destination. To the southeast is the so-called **Tall Timber Country** and **Pemberton**, a logging town amid the remnants of centuries-old eucalypt forests. Finally, again to the southeast, the **Rainbow Coast**'s sheltered inlets and rocky headlands lead to the historic and fashionable town of **Albany** – described in the section "Albany, the Rainbow Coast and inland", starting on p.720.

South West Coach Lines (in Busselton ℡08/9752 1500; in Perth, at Wellington Street Bus Station, ℡08/9322 5173) offers an alternative to Westrail's provincial bus service as well as ten-day unlimited-travel **bus passes** for around $120, and has introduced a useful circular bus service from Perth via Margaret River and Pemberton. The Easyrider Backpackers' little yellow minibus (℡08/9226 0307; three-month pass $149) runs from Perth to Pemberton every Tuesday, Friday and Sunday, passing all hostels and major highlights, and the following days continues from Pemberton on to Albany. Failing these choices, the best way to get about is with your own **car**,

THE SOUTHWEST

INDIAN OCEAN

N

Wanneroo
Gingin
Bindoon
Gingin
Goomalling
Dowerin

Rottnest Is
PERTH
Fremantle

Rockingham
Mandurah

Bunbury
Capel
Busselton
Cowaramup
Margaret River
Augusta

Cape Naturaliste
Dunsborough
Yallingup
Prevelly Park
Cape Leeuwin

Armadale
Mundaring
Clackline
Northam
Meckering
Cunderdin
York
Beverley

Pinjarra
Dwellingup
Wardona
Harvey

Donnybrook
Balingup
Nannup

Boddington
Brookton
Pingelly
Williams

Collie
Bridgetown
Boyup Brook
Blackwood

Manjimup
Pemberton
Northcliffe
Windy Harbour

D'ENTRECASTEAUX NATIONAL PARK

TALL TIMBER COUNTRY

Wyalkatchem
Trayning
Kellerberrin
Bruce Rock
Quairading
Corrigin
Kondinin
Kulin

Wagin
Arthur River
Darkan

Narrogin
Wickepin

Dumbleyung
Katanning
Cranbrook
Tambellup

Nyabing
Gnowangerup

Walpole
Denmark
Albany

Mount Barker

STIRLING RANGES NATIONAL PARK

PORONGURUP NATIONAL PARK

Jerramungup

Merredin
Narembeen

Hyden (Wave Rock)

Lake Grace

Lake King

Southern Cross

Coolgardie
Kalgoorlie
Boulder

Norseman

Esperance

Ravensthorpe
Hopetoun

Bremer Bay

FITZGERALD RIVER NATIONAL PARK

Lake Leffroy
Lake Cowan
Lake Dundas
Lake Johnston
Lake Tay

SOUTHERN OCEAN

INDIAN OCEAN

SOUTHERN OCEAN

0   100 km

although the area is also ideal for **cycling**, with many logging roads passing through shaded forests. Try to obtain the excellent *Cycling Down South* biking map from the government agency Bikewest in Perth (⊤ 08/9389 0611). Otherwise, the five Streetsmart **touring maps** make informative aids for all travellers in the region.

Bunbury

Described as the capital of the Southwest, **BUNBURY**, the state's second-largest population centre, is a pleasant town, clearly prosperous and content, but not the sort of place you've crossed oceans to see. A day's dallying here on the way south certainly won't give you nightmares, and a chance to commune with the visiting **dolphins** (found around The Cut on Leschenault Inlet) is a lot less regimented, if less predictable, than traipsing all the way up to Monkey Mia (see p.746). Two **boat tours** can take you to the right spot: one from the Dolphin Discovery Centre on the beach off Koombana Drive (daily 9am–2pm; ⊤ 08/9791 3088; $4 admission; tours $15–25), the other with Bunbury Dolphin Tours (⊤ 08/9721 7922; $15) at the *Parade Hotel* on Stirling Street alongside Leschenault Inlet.

Daily **bus services** from Perth (3hr) drop you at the well-stocked **tourist office** (Mon–Sat 9am–5pm, Sun 9.30am–4.30pm; ⊤ 08/9721 7922) in the old train station on Carmody Place. Shuttle buses operate from the new **train station**, 3km from the centre, during the daytime; otherwise **taxis** (⊤ 08/9721 2300) generally meet evening arrivals. The train from Perth takes two hours and costs $20.

Accommodation includes the *Wander Inn* at 16 Clifton St (⊤ 08/9721 3242, ⓔ wanderinnbp@yahoo.com; ❶–❷), a dowdy but well-run backpackers' place with bikes and cheap twin rooms, ten minutes' walk from Koombana Beach. The *YHA* (⊤ 08/9791 2621, ⓕ 9791 4742, ⓔ yhabunbury@hotmail .com; ❶–❸) on Stirling Street is comparatively serene despite some huge dorms. The elegant *Rose Hotel* (⊤ 08/9721 4533; ❺) on Victoria Street boasts a reasonable restaurant and a large range of boutique beers, or there's the lovely Federation-style *The Clifton* (⊤ 08/9721 4300, ⓕ 9791 2726, ⓔ theclifton@tpgi.com.au; ❻) at 2 Molloy St. There are many sidewalk **cafés** and **restaurants** ranged along the colonial frontage of Victoria Street all the way up to *Fast Eddy's*.

Geographe Bay to Cape Naturaliste

South of Bunbury the Bussel Highway curves west around **Geographe Bay** to **BUSSELTON**, named after a prominent pioneering family. The town, sheltered from the ocean's currents and swells, is a popular "bucket and spade" resort where parents can be sure their kids won't be swept away or dashed onto the rocks. There's a **museum** (Mon & Wed–Sun 2–5pm; $4) in the Old Butter Factory, off Peel Terrace, with an exhibit on the ill-fated **Group Settlement Scheme**. During the 1920s, overseas families with little or no farming expertise were induced to settle the Southwest – most failed miserably and ended up rotting in "humpies" such as the one on display. You're unlikely to want to stay with the holidaying masses and better off heading for Dunsborough, but there's **backpackers'** accommodation at 14 Peel Terrace (⊤ 08/9754 2763; ❶) if you get caught out.

After Busselton, the highway turns south towards Margaret River, though continuing west brings you to **DUNSBOROUGH**, 21km from Busselton, a small holiday resort with an excellently located YHA **hostel** (T & F 08/9755 3107, E dunsboroughyha@hotmail.com; ❶-❸). Situated 2km southeast of town (get off the bus at Quindalup), right on the beach, the modern hostel offers bike hire and has a happy, family atmosphere. The *Dunsborough Inn* (T 08/9756 7277, F 9756 7377, E dunsinn@wn.com.au; ❶-❹), on Dunn Bay Road, has good-value self-contained units and motel rooms, as well as dorms. A step up in quality is the *Mercure Inn* (T 08/9756 7711, F 9756 7722, E mercure@netserve.net.au; ❺) which is also the town's only **pub**. *Café Ibis*, across the road from the post office, has interesting if pricey **meals** while *My Thai*, next to the service station, gives Dunsborough's best impersonation of Bangkok. With numerous wrecks and little tidal variation, Geographe Bay is ideal for **diving**, with several places in the main shopping precinct renting equipment and boat charters.

Cape Naturaliste, 14km northwest of the resort, is the less impressive of the two capes which define the Margaret River Region. Its truncated **lighthouse** (Mon & Wed–Sun 9.30am–4.30pm; $3) is open for inspection, and along the way there are turn-offs to secluded beaches with the **Sugarloaf** offering particularly fine views.

Along Caves Road to Margaret River and Cape Leeuwin

South of Dunsborough you head into the **Margaret River Region** proper, characterized by caves, wineries, choice restaurants and snug hideaways all interspersed with more galleries, craft studios and potteries than in the rest of the state put together. Passing **Ngilgi Cave** (see box on p.716) you come to the turn-off for **YALLINGUP**, a small seaside resort with a lovely clean beach and surfers waiting for the big one. Further along Caves Road is the Gunyulgup Gallery (daily 10am–5pm) with a particularly fine selection of pottery, glass, paintings and jarrah furniture by local artisans; down the road another gallery features a lovely restaurant overlooking a lake.

Yallingup Forest Resort (T 08/9755 2550, F 9756 6016; ❼) on Hemsley Road off Caves Road would suit an extended stay in the area, offering large, self-contained chalets with the use of a pool and tennis court. The site also hosts the **Wicked Ale Brewery** (T 08/9755 2848) where chocolate beer is on tap and **Yallingup Camel Safaris** (T 0419 194 998). A couple of kilometres back down Caves Road, from the *Gunyulgup Gallery and Restaurant*, is a crossroads where the *Crayfish Lodge* (T 08/9755 2028, F 9755 2406; ❼) gives the impression you have walked into an English B&B. The right turn leads 3km to **Canal Rocks**, where the waves relentlessly pound the pink-granite outcrops into curious, scalloped forms. Further south are turn-offs to the **Abbey Vale Winery** and **Moonshine Brewery** (daily 10.30am–5pm) and, further on, **Cape Clairault Winery** (daily 10am–5pm), one of the better choices if you fancy some wine-tasting. Those intent on visiting some of the 45 wineries within half as many kilometres should pick up the *Margaret River Regional Vineyard Guide* ($4.35) or the *Regional Map and Guide* (35¢) from the Margaret River **tourist office** (see p.715).

Another turning west off Caves Road leads 4km to **Quininup Beach**, accessible only to high-clearance vehicles and thus rarely crowded, and **Gracetown**, 12km south, on the sheltered Cowaramup Bay. Five kilometres further on, a right turn leads to **Ellenbrook House**, a Bussell homestead dating from 1857 – bare inside but in a lovely, quiet spot by the brook. From here it's a thirty-minute walk up to the luxuriant **Meekadarribee Falls** which, unusually, manage to spiral underneath themselves.

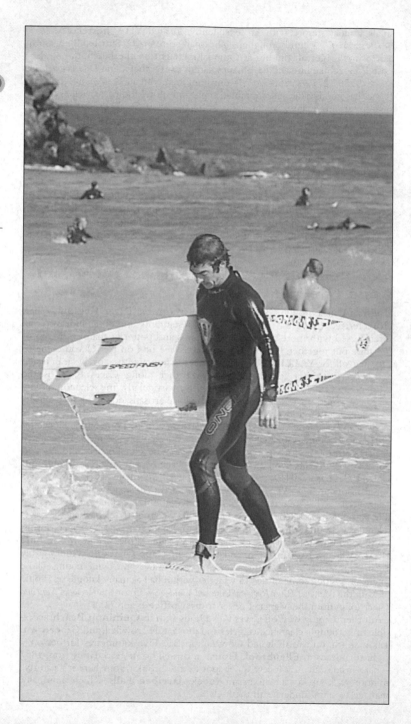

After Ellenbrook you come to the crossroads leading east 5km to Margaret River township (see below), while a right turn takes you to the resort of **PREVELLY PARK**, on the estuary of the Margaret River. The Greek **Chapel of St John** will certainly catch your eye: a memorial to the Preveli Monastery on Crete which sheltered Allied soldiers, Australians among them, in World War II. The turning opposite leads down to the blustery beach where November's annual Margaret River Classic **surfing** championships are held, so long as sponsors continue to support the event. The surf here is legendary among WA boardriders.

Back at the chapel, the road continues down into the **resort**, which has the usual assortment of chalets and caravan parks. Check out the *Café Gnarabup* (Nov–Feb daily 8.30am–sunset), overlooking the sea and offering the mouthwatering aroma of sizzling fish or just coffee and cakes. The modern *Surfpoint Lodge*, on Reidle Drive (ⓣ08/9757 1777, ⓕ9757 1077, ⓦ www.surfpoint.com; ensuite rooms ❸, dorms ❶) is one of WA's best-keep secrets and is a far better idea than heading into Margaret River. Free pick-ups are on offer from Margaret River if you call ahead.

Margaret River

The town of **MARGARET RIVER**, like the eponymous region, has come to symbolize every stress-worn Perthian's dream to escape the rat race, set up a craft boutique or a sylvan getaway, and claim their share of the Good Life. It's a favourite place for a mix of holiday-makers, partying wave-riders, floral-clad muses and the vanguard of fortunate "mappies" (middle-aged professionals) who moved in ahead of the real-estate boom.

Margaret River is not necessarily the best place actually to stay – prices can be high in summer when the town is busy – but it's handy for shopping, eating out and browsing, while its **tourist office** (daily 9am–5pm; ⓣ08/9757 2911, ⓔ amrta@netserv.net.au), on the Bussell Highway, represents the whole region. Westrail and South West Coach Lines **buses** visit daily from Perth; local **taxis** (ⓣ08/9757 3444) are used to being taken along on some serious wine-tasting jaunts. Highly recommended are local Bushtucker Tours (ⓣ08/9757 9084), who run a **cave and canoe tour** ($33) as well as a **winery tour** ($44).

The range of **accommodation** is vast, with over sixty sites in the immediate vicinity, but the woodland settings out of town are the ones to go for; the helpful tourist office has big portfolios full of ideas. The *Inne Town* **backpackers'** (free call ⓣ1800 244 115; ❶–❸), on the main road at the north end of town, is ideally central but that's the only thing going for it. A better idea for budget travellers is *Margaret River Lodge*, 2km out of town on Railway Terrace (ⓣ08/9757 9532, ⓕ9757 2352, ⓦ www.mrlodge.com.au), which also has rooms with en suites (dorms ❶, rooms ❹) or sample backpacker luxury at *Surfpoint Lodge* out on the beach (see above). At the other end of the scale, *Basildene Manor* on Walcliffe Road (ⓣ08/9757 3140, ⓕ9757 3383, ⓦ www.basildene.com.au; ❽), built in 1912, is a re-creation of an English manor listed by the National Trust as a significant Heritage property. Both the *Margaret River* (ⓣ08/9757 2180; on-site vans ❸) and the *Riverview* (ⓣ08/9757 2270; on-site vans ❸) **caravan parks** are just a kilometre out of town.

The whole countryside is dotted with charming restaurants, often attached to **wineries**. In town, the main street has a host of good-quality **restaurants** and **cafés**. Try the *Ark of Iris* café; the sesame burgers and veggie breakfasts at *Café 1 Eleven*; or join the young crowd at *Settlers*, the town's main **pub**, which puts on live music in summer. *Café Fortés* (ⓣ08/9757 3101) is an upmarket restaurant that uses locally grown produce. There's an **internet café** behind the Challenge bank on the Bussell Highway.

Margaret River caves

A band of limestone passing through the cape has created some 350 caves around Margaret River, four of which are open to the public. Most involve guided tours to avoid damage and accidents, with relatively high entrance fees and shuffling crowds rather detracting from the cavernous spectacle. Nevertheless, a visit to the region would be incomplete without seeing at least one. All are humid and include some long, stepped ascents, with temperatures around 17°C. Tours are less frequent from May to August – for more details about all except Ngilgi Cave, enquire at the Margaret River tourist office. The Cave Works Interpretive Centre at Lake Cave (see below) sells a Grand Tour pass for $33, which includes entry to Lake, Jewel and Mammoth caves; it also offers special discount options to visit all the caves except Ngilgi.

Jewel Cave (daily 9.30am–4pm, 7–12 tours per day; 60min; ☏08/9758 4541; $14). The best cave, featuring extraordinary and fragile formations such as five-metre "helictites" (delicate, straw-like formations) protected by breeze-proof doors. Also includes a two-hour tour of Moondyne Cave (daily 2pm; maximum of seven people; $27.50, with equipment supplied), a mildly adventurous and less rushed excursion with some belly crawling, although you won't miss any amazing features by not taking the tour. Enclosed footwear is compulsory (ie no sandals).

Lake Cave (daily 9.30am–4pm, 7–12 tours per day; 45min; $14). A collapsed cavern, overgrown with huge karri trees, is the impressive entrance to the cave where a unique "suspended table" hangs over the subterranean lake. The cave is also the site of the new Cave Works Interpretive Centre (daily 10am–5pm; ☏08/9757 7411; $3), dealing with all things speleological.

Mammoth Cave (daily 9am–4pm, self-guiding; $14). Large cavern and easy access with some bones and fossils of extinct creatures, but it really should be your last choice.

Ngilgi Cave (daily 9.30am–4.30pm; $13). Not visited on the cave tours but with plenty of nooks to explore and delicate features to admire.

Augusta and Cape Leeuwin

Five kilometres southwest of Margaret River, on Boodjidup Road, one of the more interesting attractions vying for your attention is **Eagles Heritage** (daily 10am–5pm; $6), a fascinating collection of birds of prey. Aviaries house huge wedge-tail and white-breasted sea eagles, peregrine falcons and a few owls – a rare menagerie of impressive flying hunters.

Rejoining Caves Road, having passed the turning for the **Leeuwin Winery** (daily 10am–4.30pm) with its art gallery and restaurant, you head south into the silvery-barked **karri forest**. It's a magnificent sight, well worth taking some time to appreciate now if you're not planning to visit Pemberton. Down the road are Mammoth and Lake caves (see box above). If you have visited the latter cave and have noticed the stream that trickles out of its subterranean lake, you can catch up with it at the spring on **Cowup Bay** beach, 4km from the cave entrance along a dirt road, and with a campsite on the way. Back on Caves Road, Boranup Drive takes an off-road detour through the **Boranup Forest**, a great place for biking and riding, while *Boranup Gallery and Chalets* (☏08/9757 7585, 🖷9757 7527; ❼) sells local art and gorgeous **furniture** made from local timbers and offers accommodation in self-contained rammed-earth **chalets** in bushland settings.

South of the forest, the Brockman Highway leads 90km east to Nannup, while continuing 3km south down Caves Road brings you to a turn-off to the old timber port of **Hamelin Bay**, which has a clutch of shipwrecks ideal for snorkellers and scuba divers. There's a beachside **caravan park** (☏08/9758 5540; on-site vans ❸) offering bikes for rent. Passing **Jewel Cave**, the Bussell

Highway takes you 8km further to the small town of **AUGUSTA**, on the estuary of the Blackwood River – Western Australia's oldest settlement after Albany and Perth. Little remains from those days, although the **museum** (daily: June–Sept 10am–noon; Oct–May 9am–5pm; $2), on Blackwood Avenue, retains some old relics and is more absorbing than you might expect. **Buses** visit Augusta once a day, generally in the evening, heading back north early the next morning. For **accommodation**, there are two **motels** on Blackwood Avenue, with the *Augusta Motel* (℡08/9758 1944, ℻9758 1227; ❷–❺) having great river views as well as budget rooms, but the excellent *Sheoak Chalets* (℡08/9758 1958; ❽ for four people min) comes with pet kangaroos. The pristine *Baywatch Manor Resort YHA* (℡08/9758 1290, ℻9758 1291; ❶–❸), also on Blackwood Avenue, offers quality backpackers' accommodation and rents bikes and canoes. The self-contained chalets at *Augusta Homes for Holidays* (❺) is run by the same friendly couple at *Baywatch Manor*. *Doonbanks Caravan Park* (℡08/9758 1517; on-site vans ❸) is up the road, and there are two more caravan parks south of town. You can **eat** at the *Colonial Restaurant* on the main road, or at the *Augusta Moon* Chinese restaurant on Allnutt Terrace.

Cape Leeuwin, 9km south of town, is probably why you've come this far, and it's worth the journey, giving a bleak, windswept "land's end" feel to this continental corner, especially on a mean and moody day. A Dutch captain named the cape after his ship 370 years ago, and Matthew Flinders began the onerous task of mapping Australia's coast right here in 1851. From the top of the still working **lighthouse** (daily 9am–4.30pm; $4.40), built in 1895, you can contemplate your position – halfway between the equator and the coastline of Antarctica. Nearby, an **old water wheel**, originally constructed for the lighthouse builders and now petrified in salt, is a well-known landmark. Naturaliste Charters (℡08/9755 2276) run whale-watching cruises from Augusta from June to August before moving north to Dunsborough until December.

Hikers may want to consider the 140-kilometre Cape Leeuwin to Cape Naturaliste **coastal walk**, though even the less adventurous can tackle its five sections individually. The CALM office in Busselton (℡08/9752 1677) has detailed information on this, while the Cape Leeuwin lighthouse store has maps and friendly advice.

Tall Timber Country

Sandwiched between the popular tourist areas of Margaret River and Albany's Rainbow Coast, the forests of the so-called **Tall Timber Country** are one of WA's greatest sights. Along with the sinuous **Blackwood River** (ideal for sedate canoeing, especially west of Nannup), the highlight of the region is the brooding, primeval majesty of the **karri forests**, known not as much for their arboreal gimmicks – of which the "climb-if-you-dare" **Gloucester Tree** near Pemberton is the best-known – as they are for the raw, elemental nature of the unique forest environment. **Logging** remains this region's primary industry and small towns, each with their own mill, busy themselves with their controversial work, while **Pemberton** is prospering through tourism, with its woodcraft galleries and scenic drives.

Public transport is much improved with the new Augusta–Pemberton link, but you'll get much more out of a visit by renting a car.

The Blackwood River Valley and south

The northern part of the forest country is watered by the **Blackwood River** and divided by scenic roads through jarrah woodlands linking the riverside mill towns. **NANNUP**, on the Vasse and Brockman highways, 60km southeast of Busselton, remains a picturesque town, a cluster of wooden cabins nestling quietly among wooded hills. The **tourist office** (℡08/9756 1211) is located in the old police station on Brockman Street; the *Blackwood Café* nearby is an ideal lunch spot. For **accommodation**, the laid-back *Black Cockatoo Hostel*, 27 Grange Rd (℡08/9756 1035; ❶), is a cosy backpackers' treat, while the upmarket *Lodge* (℡08/9756 1276, ℻9756 1394; ❼), on the hill, will spice up your sex life with lavish comforts. Lost among the jarrah 6km northwest of town, the *Nannup Bush Cabins* (℡ & ℻ 08/9756 1170; ❹) are enchantingly situated hideaways. Blackwood Expeditions (℡08/9756 1209) offers **canoe rental** and **guided tours** on the lower Blackwood River.

From Nannup, a **scenic drive** winds 41km along the river to unremarkable Balingup, while the equally tree-lined Brockman Highway heads east 46km to **BRIDGETOWN**, a busy mill town with a large **tourist centre** (daily 9am–5pm; ℡08/9761 1740) on Hampton Street. Despite some token tea and craft shops, Bridgetown is really a place to get your ute serviced or chainsaw sharpened. By the river, where some pleasant bankside walks begin, the National Trust property of Bridgedale House (10am–4pm; closed Tues & Wed; $3) rents out **canoes**.

Thirty-seven kilometres south of Bridgetown, **MANJIMUP** is the region's commercial centre, handy for shopping and other services but, apart from a visit to the **Timber Park** (daily 9am–5pm), behind the **tourist office** (daily 8.30am–5.30pm; ℡08/9771 1831) on Rose Street (both celebrating the local timber industry), it has little appeal. Graphite Road is a picturesque forest drive heading west 22km to **One Tree Bridge** and, after another couple of kilometres, to the magnificent **Four Aces**, a quartet of huge, 350-year-old karri trees standing in a row. With a detailed map it's possible to spend all day driving around these gravelly, winding logging roads, but should you head south to Pemberton along the tarmac road you'll pass a turn-off to the **Diamond Tree**, where you can climb a fifty-metre lookout tree for free.

Pemberton and around

Small enough to retain its backwoods charm while maintaining the high standard of accommodation, eating and creative outlets that make the Southwest such an attractive destination, **PEMBERTON** is the most central base for touring the area. You'll find the **tourist information** office on Brockman Street (daily 9am–5pm; ℡08/9776 1133), where you can pick up the excellent *Pemberton–Northcliffe* map and guide ($1), as well as information on **horse riding**, **canoe** and **bicycle rental**, and local **tours**. Round the back is the interactive Karri Forest Discovery Centre (daily 9am–5pm; donation), which replicates the forest environment.

On Dickinson Street, Fine Woodcraft, an excellent **craft gallery** and restaurant, displays regional works, with a commendable dearth of wombat tea cosies and similar tack. A fun way of seeing the surrounding forest is to take the **tram** (℡08/9776 1322) between Pemberton and Northcliffe (Tues, Thurs & Sat; 5hr 30min return, including photo stops). If your time is limited, settle for the shorter trip to Warren, which is actually the better half of the ride (2 daily; 1hr 45min return). The tram rattles along the old logging railway, over rustic timber bridges spanning tiny creeks, and visits the local beauty spot, the **Cascades** (also accessible by road) – a thoroughly enjoyable excursion. In summer there's also a **steam train** service up to Lyall Sidings, north of town.

The region's single most popular attraction is the **Gloucester Tree** (CALM fee; see box below), situated on a clearly signposted road 3km southeast of town. At 61m, it's the world's tallest fire-lookout tree and its platform is accessible by climbing a spiral of horizontal stakes. Only a quarter of those who visit the tree actually climb up to the platform – the climb itself is more satisfying than the actual view – and those who do can have their efforts validated by a certificate available at the tourist office in town. The countryside all around is crisscrossed with peaceful walking trails and enchanting forest drives cutting deep into the wonderful karri woodlands. **Beedelup National Park**, on the Vasse Highway 20km west of town, has a short walk to a suspension bridge over **Beedelup Falls**, while the drive through the native karri forests of the **Warren National Park**, 10km southwest of town, will leave you in awe of these huge trees flourishing in their natural environment. If you have time for only one such drive, make it this one.

As for **accommodation**, the basic *YHA* at Pimelea (℡08/9776 1153, ℻9776 1819, ✉yhapemberton@hotmail.com; ➊), 10km northwest of town, has seen some improvements and offers free pick-ups from town as well as bike rental. You could also try *Warren Lodge* (℡08/9776 1105; ➊), a similarly basic ex-millworkers' lodgings right in town by the bus stop. Otherwise, the surrounding countryside abounds in tranquil woodland retreats, such as *Pump Hill Farm Cottages* (℡ & ℻ 08/9776 1379; ➎), 2km west of town, or *Karri Valley Hideaway Cottages* (℡ & ℻ 08/9776 2049; ➎), 20km west. Campers can stay at the town's central **caravan park** (℡08/9776 1300; on-site vans ➌) or at any of the CALM-approved **campsites** in the surrounding forests. There are a couple of cafés in town but for trout or marron (freshwater crayfish), both local delicacies, try the restaurant at the *Eagle Springs Trout Hatchery*, signposted north of town.

Thirty kilometres south of Pemberton, **NORTHCLIFFE** is a small, untouristed logging town of little interest to passing visitors. Southwest of the town is the long spread of coastal heathland and inland dunes comprising the **D'Entrecasteaux National Park**. It's barely accessible, although Southern Forest Adventures in Northcliffe (℡08/9776 1222) offers one- to five-day 4WD tours as well as a weekend package canoeing down to the park and returning by 4WD. **Windy Harbour**, 30km south of Northcliffe, is the only point between Augusta and Walpole where non-4WD vehicles can get to the ocean shore. There is a small break in the limestone cliffs here, allowing access to a couple of exposed white beaches and a basic **campsite**, usually occupied by fishermen.

CALM National Park entry fees

In addition to camping fees CALM now levies an entry fee or "pass" at the most-visited national parks in WA. The prices of the various passes are listed below. Throughout this chapter those CALM parks that require an entry fee have the phrase "CALM fee" placed in parentheses after their names. You can obtain a pass from the entry gate or a CALM office.

Day Pass: $8 per car, $3 per motorbike.

Holiday Pass: $20 per vehicle, allowing entry into all parks for four weeks.

Annual Local Park Pass: $15, giving unlimited access for a year to parks in a given area.

Annual All Parks Pass: $45, allowing entry into all parks for a year.

Albany, the Rainbow Coast and inland

The alternating sheltered bays and rugged headlands of the **Rainbow Coast** around **Albany**, WA's original colonial settlement, have gradually been gentrified by semi-retired pastoral yuppies with cultivated tastes and a yen for alternative lifestyles. As elsewhere in the Southwest, the temperate climate here creates a rural antipodean-English idyll unknown in the rest of WA.

Albany, 410km from Perth, is promoted as a mildly sophisticated holiday destination, while **Denmark**, 54km to the west, is a twee, arty hamlet with **Walpole**'s bays and tingle forests marking the Rainbow Coast's limit. An hour's drive north of Albany lie the wine-making region of **Mount Barker** and the **Porongurup** and **Stirling Ranges national parks**.

Perth's radial **bus services** to the main centres run on a frequent basis, but moving around requires some planning to avoid inconvenient delays. Westrail buses depart from Perth for Albany at least twice daily, either directly down the Albany Highway (6hr) or four times a week via Bunbury and twice weekly via Pemberton (8hr). **Car rental**, or shared lifts, are clearly a better option and **tours**, despite their breathless pace, will at least show you it all, however briefly.

Albany

In 1826, two years before the establishment of the Swan River Colony, the British sent Major Lockyer and a team of hopeful colonists to settle the strategic **Princess Royal Harbour**. It was a pre-emptive response to French exploration of Australia's Southwest, and the small colony, originally called Fredrickstown, was allowed to grow at a natural pace – avoiding the vicissitudes of Swan River Mania that plagued Perth in the 1880s, when thousands of colonists poured into the town. Prior to the building of Fremantle Harbour in the 1890s, **ALBANY** was a key port on the route from England to Botany Bay, a coaling station in the age of steamers. It was also the last of Australia that many Anzacs saw on their way to Gallipoli in 1914.

Now serving the southern wheat and sheep belt, Albany has also become the centre of one of the Southwest's main holiday areas. Factors such as weekend proximity to Perth, moderate summer temperatures, a surfeit of natural splendour and historical kudos all combine to make an agreeable and genuine destination, largely bereft of bogus tourist traps.

Arrival, information and accommodation

Westrail **buses** arrive near the old train station on Lower Stirling Terrace, the location of the **tourist office** (Mon–Fri 8.30am–5.30pm, Sat & Sun 9am–5pm; ℡08/9841 1088 or free call 1800 644 088, ℮ albany@albany.jrc.net.au), which dispenses handy local and regional sketch **maps**. Loves Bus Service (timetables at the tourist office, or call ℡08/9841 1211) offers in-town **public transport**: the #301 route between York Street, the town's main road, and Middleton Beach/Emu Point is particularly useful (Mon–Fri 9am–3pm, Sat 9.15–11am).

Albany offers several **guesthouses** and **B&Bs**, especially along Shirley Terrace near the harbour, as well as the customary range of highway motels and self-contained units found in the Middleton Bay area, 3km east of the centre. In the countryside, farmstays mix with classy cottages and other pastoral hideaways. The tourist office has a detailed photographic portfolio of the town's accommodation options.

Motels, units, hostels and guesthouses

Albany Backpackers, cnr Stirling Terrace and Spencer St (☎08/9841 8848). The energetic owners provide a lively atmosphere and plenty of activities with rooms painted in individual themes. Free breakfast and internet access. ❶–❸

Bayview YHA, 49 Duke St (☎ & ⓕ 08/9842 3388, ⓔyhaalbany@hotmail.com). Good accommodation that's popular with groups. Tours and car hire available, plus there are organized pub crawls. ❶–❹

Coraki Holiday Cottages, Lower King River, 11km east of town (☎08/9844 7068, ⓕ9844 1068, ⓔcoraki@albanyis.com.au). Great-value cottages in their own gardens by Oyster Harbour. ❹–❺

Cruize Inn, 122 Middleton Rd (☎08/9842 9599, ⓕ9842 9588, ⓦwww.skynary.com/albanycruize-inn). Small, modern guesthouse with pianola in the lounge. ❹

Discovery Inn, 9 Middleton Rd (☎08/9842 5535, ⓕ9842 2571). An especially agreeable old guesthouse and restaurant, close to Middleton Beach with breakfast included. ❹

Dog Rock Motel, 303 Middleton Rd (☎08/9841 4422, ⓕ9842 1027). Good-value rooms close to town and the shops, plus there's a restaurant. ❹

Dolphin Lodge, 1 Golf Links Rd, Middleton Beach (☎ & ⓕ 08/9841 6600, ⓔdolphin@omninet.net.au). Inexpensive family units. ❺

Foreshore Apartments, 81 Proudlove Parade, (☎08/9842 8800, ⓕ9842 3522, ⓦwww.foreshoreapartments.com.au). Four-star self-contained apartments in the heart of town. ❻

Norman House, 28 Stirling Terrace (☎ & ⓕ 08/9841 5995). Plusher sort of guesthouse, close to town, with disabled access and bright rooms. ❹

Parkville Guest House, 136 Brunswick Rd (☎ & ⓕ 08/9841 3704). Nice old house with a resident ghost. ❺

Travel Inn, 191 Albany Highway (☎08/9841 4144, ⓕ9841 6215). Albany's best motel, with large comfortable rooms. ❻

Caravan parks

Emu Beach, Emu Point, 7km from the town centre (☎08/9844 1147). Not a bad spot to stay for a few days. Amenities include trampolines and mini-golf. Cabins ❹, on-site vans ❸

Middleton Beach, Flinders Parade, Middleton Beach (☎08/9841 3593). Right on the weekend-posing drag and the sometimes windy beach. Cabins and on-site vans ❸

Mount Melville, 22 Wellington St (☎08/9841 4616). Has a useful camp kitchen and is just 1km from town. Chalets ❹, on-site vans ❸

The Town and around

Albany's attractions are spread between the Foreshore, where the original colonists set up camp, and the beaches around **Middleton Beach** and Emu Point on the still waters of Oyster Harbour. Driving around the harbour brings you after 40km to the nature reserve at Two Peoples Bay, while the features and attractions on the **Torndirrup Peninsula**, 20km from town, along Frenchman's Bay Road, are well worth a look.

On the **Foreshore** there's a replica of the *Amity* (daily 9am–5pm; $2.50), the brig that landed its three-score colonists here on Boxing Day, 1826, after six months at sea. Nearby is the **Old Gaol** (daily 10am–4.30pm; $4), with the usual bare cells and barred doors. The **Albany Residency Museum** (daily 10am–5pm; free) is much more interesting, with meticulous displays of the town's maritime history, a section on Aboriginal bush medicines, an annexe with an obsolete lighthouse lens that was too good to throw away and, upstairs, an educational see-and-touch gallery for children.

Heading towards Middleton Beach, the curious tower on top of **Mount Melville Lookout**, off Serpentine Road, is colloquially known as "the spark plug". One of two lookouts in Albany, this one offers the better seaward vista. From here, backtrack to York Street, turn left and head 2km down Middleton Road to **The Old Farm**, Strawberry Hill (daily 10am–5pm; closed June; $4), tucked behind modern houses in its own enchanting gardens. Reminiscent of an English cottage, the farm (WA's first) provided the colonists with fruit and veg, while the 1836 building here housed visiting Governor Stirling and today offers Devonshire teas and displays of domestic accoutrements.

Middleton Beach itself is dominated by Albany's pride and joy, the prestigious *Esplanade Hotel*, and the town's main beach as well as the more sheltered inlet of **Oyster Harbour**. From the beach, head up Marine Drive and turn right towards **Mount Clarence Lookout**, with its Anzac memorial and, on a clear day, a view as far as the Stirling Ranges, 80km to the north. On the way down you pass **The Forts** (daily 9am–5pm; $4), an impressively restored naval installation dating from the end of the nineteenth century.

Southeast of town, Frenchman Bay Road curls round Princess Royal Harbour to **Whaleworld** (daily 9am–5pm, hourly tours 10am–4pm; $11), the site of Australia's last whaling station until operations finally ceased in 1978. The informative tours begin with a gory video and move on to the crude and sickening whale-dismembering machinery and towering *Cheyne IV* whale chaser, before an upbeat, eco-ending in the skeleton shed.

Returning along the Torndirrup Peninsula, check out the view at **Stony Hill** but give the feeble **blowholes** a miss – they're a washout unless the wind and swell are aligned properly. **The Gap** and **Natural Bridge** are well worth a look, however; there is something mesmeric about watching the Southern Ocean pound into the Gap's boxed walls and rebound, frothing, in all directions, while the Natural Bridge satisfies those who get excited about "freaks of nature". This area has claimed several lives, many by **king waves** that well up imperceptibly onto the shore here; play it safe, and don't walk under the bridge.

Eating

Fortunately, Albany shares the rest of the Southwest's laudable preoccupation with quality eating; several independent **restaurants** fill the gap between fast-food franchises and dreary motel dining rooms in a most appetizing way. The sometimes lively *Earl of Spencer* and *White Star* **pubs** on Spencer Street also have counter meals.

Al Fornetto, York St (☎08/9842 1060). Italian-style steak and seafood, as well as pizzas from $12. Avoid the watery pasta. Daily 6pm–late.

Argyle's, 42 Stirling Terrace. Overlooking the bay, with meals for around $15 and internet access. Wed–Sun 11.30am–late.

Cello's, Church Lane Rd, Kalgan River. Top-quality country restaurant in landscaped grounds 17km east of Albany, also with antiques galleries and bookshop. Thurs–Sun 11am–5pm.

Cravings, Mermaid Ave, Emu Point (☎08/9844 1111). Popular buffet place right by Emu Beach, with good-value seafood and chips next door. Daily 5.30pm–late.

Curry Pot, 30 Spencer St (☎08/9842 9399).

Unpretentious all-you-can-eat curries from $14. 6pm–late.

Dylan's on the Terrace, 82 Stirling Terrace. Burger and pancake dispensary; good for early breakfast. Mon–Sat 7am–midnight, Sun 7am–10pm.

Kookas, 204 Stirling Terrace (☎08/9841 5889). Quaintly restored old house serving gourmet dinners at around $25 per person. Tues–Sat 11.30am–late.

Rookleys, cnr Peels Place and York St. Deli-style café with *focaccia* and half-decent coffee. Mon–Sat 8am–5.30pm.

Shamrock Café, 184 York St. Full "Irish" breakfast from $7, meals from $10. Mon–Sat 8am–8pm.

Listings

Banks Most branches are along York St.
Bus Westrail ☎13 1053.
CALM (Department of Conservation and Land Management), 120 Albany Highway (Mon–Fri 9am–5pm; ☎08/9841 7133). Information and passes to local national parks (see box on p.719).
Car rental Albany Car Rental charges from $36 per day with 150km free (☎08/9841 7077).

Post office Cnr Grey and York streets (☎08/9841 1811).
Taxi ☎08/9844 4444.
Tours and cruises Albany Sailing Academy (☎08/9844 4146) offer half a day's tuition, or you can just lie on deck for $40; longer options are available. Albany Whale Tours (☎0409 107 180) take a catamaran into King George Sound for two

hours from $27.50. Escape Tours (☎08/9844 1945) have day- and half-day tours around the region in a minibus; Bushed (☎08/9842 2127) do adventure activity tours; and Silver Star Cruises (☎08/9841 3333) offer cruises in King George Sound for around $22.

Along the Rainbow Coast

West of Albany, **West Cape Howe National Park** is a coastal wilderness best suited to exploration by 4WD, while **William Bay National Park**, west of Denmark, has many inviting coves accessible to regular vehicles. Just before Walpole, the **Valley of the Giants** is the home of the now-famous **Tree Top Walk** and marks the edge of the giant tree country. Westrail buses run on Monday and Friday between Albany and Perth (via Bunbury; 6hr), but you won't see much along this way – renting a car or arranging a lift is a better bet.

Denmark and William Bay National Park

DENMARK, set on the eponymous river that leads into Wilson Inlet, has been transformed into a cute little town, a great spot to enjoy a pleasant lunch, wander around some galleries, and take a stroll or boat up the river. If you want to get to the coast, give the anaemic Wilson Inlet a miss and head west to **William Bay National Park**, through the hills along **Shadforth Scenic Drive**. Once there, you'll find **Green Pool** to be one of the prettiest spots along the coast, with Madfish Bay and Waterfall Bay also worth a visit.

Denmark's **tourist office** (daily 9am–5pm; ☎08/9848 2055), on the corner of Strickland and Bent streets, can advise you on the array of **places to stay** in the vicinity and has a comprehensive free guide to the area. The pristine *Edinburgh Guest House* (☎08/9848 1477; ❺) is in the centre of town, while on Inlet Drive is *Denmark Waterfront Motel and Cottages* (☎08/9848 1147, ℱ9848 1965, ⓦwww.denmarkwaterfront.com), an idyllic hideaway on the water with budget rooms (❶), motel-style accommodation (❹) and great-value studios (❺). For a **meal**, the natty *Fig Tree Café*, off Strickland Street, and the friendly *Blue Wren* on the main road, are good alternatives to fast food.

The Valley of the Giants' Tree Top Walk and Walpole

About 40km west of Denmark you can turn south to **Peaceful Bay**, a pleasant lunch stop with a **caravan park**, or turn north along Valley of the Giants Road, from where another turn-off leads to a secluded **youth hostel** (☎08/9840 8073; ❶), off Dingo Flats Road. The forest of massive tingle and karri trees that make up the **Valley of the Giants** is now much better known for its **Tree Top Walk** (daily 8am–5pm; $7), an amazingly engineered six-hundred-metre walkway (accessible to wheelchairs), which sways on half a dozen pylons among the crowns of the karris, 40m above the ground. Ironically, the most exciting aspect of the walk is not the scrutiny of the tree canopy – which isn't especially dense, close or teeming with anything more exotic than crows – but rather the fairground thrill of actually treading on the tremulous walkway. To gain a better impression of the surrounding forest, take the **Ancient Kingdom Walkway** (free) which winds through the forest floor.

Back on the coastal highway, you pass through **Nornalup**, remarkable for having no arts-and-crafts outlets. You'd do better to take the track 6km west of town leading to the lovely **Conspicuous Beach**. **WALPOLE**, 10km down the road, is the hub of many scenic drives to more towering forests, oceanic lookouts and sheltered inlets. Light **meals** are served at the *South Coast Café*, or try the *Top Deck Café* next to the Glassblower's Gallery. There are a couple of **caravan parks** on Walpole and Nornalup inlets, but for more creature comforts try *Hideaway Cottage* (℡08/9840 1138; ❹), 10km north of town, or *Che Sara Sara Chalets*, 15km north (℡ & Ⓕ 08/9840 8004; ❺). Backpackers head for the *Tingle All Over YHA* (℡08/9840 1041, ⒺNenquiries@yhawa.com.au; ❶) at the west end of town or the low-key but welcoming Walpole Backpackers on Pier Street (℡08/9840 1244; ❶) which does meal deals with the local pub and tours. Just east beyond Walpole you'll pass the turn-off to **Nuyts Wilderness**, where several walking trails pass through groves of jarrah and karri on to secluded coastal coves where camping is permitted.

From Walpole, the **South Western Highway** begins its scenic run northwest through more colossal forests to Northcliffe (100km) and Pemberton (138km) at the heart of the Tall Timber Country (see p.719).

The Porongurups, the Stirling Ranges and Mount Barker

North of Albany lie the ancient granite highlands of the Porongurups and the majestic thousand-metre-high Stirling Ranges, 40km and 80km from Albany respectively. Both have been designated as **national parks** (CALM fees; see box on p.719) and CALM in Albany provides further information and maps. To the west are the youthful vineyards of **Mount Barker**, whose viticultural potential has barely been exploited and which may one day merge with Margaret River as a homogeneous wine-making region. Several small **wineries** open their cellar doors for tasting and prospective purchases; details are available from the tourist office in Albany.

The Porongurups

The **Porongurups**, said to be the oldest hills in the world, feature a dozen wooded peaks with bald summits and an elevation of over 600m. The fifteen-kilometre-long ridge catches any coastal moisture to support its isle of karri forests, thereby leaving the loftier Stirlings to the north dry and treeless.

Most people are happy to do no more than take the five-minute stroll to the **Tree in a Rock**, a natural oddity near the park's northern entrance, but if you want to get your teeth into a good walk, head up the marked trail to **Devil's Slide** (671m) and, if you're up to it, return via Nancy and Hayward peaks; the full route needs at least half a day, stout footwear, water and a hat. **Balancing Rock**, at the eastern end of the park, can be reached in 45 minutes from the car park, with a cage on the exposed outcrop of Castle Rock providing safe viewing. There's no camping in the park, but half a dozen establishments offer **accommodation** close to the northern entrance, among them hostel accommodation at the *Porongurup Shop & Tearooms* (℡08/9853 1110; ❶) and the nearby *Karribank Lodge* (℡08/9853 1022; ❹), an inexpensive guesthouse.

The Stirling Ranges

Taking the Chester Pass Road north towards the looming **Stirlings**, the distinctive profile of Bluff Knoll will, if you're lucky, reveal itself from the cloud banks which often obscure its summit. Avid hillwalkers could spend a few days "peakbagging" here and come away well satisfied – the mild weather makes the Stirlings WA's best mountain-walking area, although five peaks are over 1000m and sometimes receive winter snow. Less strenuous activities are also catered for: the unsealed 45-kilometre Stirling Range **scenic drive** winds amid the peaks to Red Gum Pass in the west, where you can turn around and go back the same way (with superior views) or continue down to Mount Barker. **Bluff Knoll** (1073m), the park's highest and most popular ascent, has a well-built path involving a three-hour-return slog. The weather can often surprise you from the unseen, southeast side: no matter how hot you may feel in the car park before beginning the climb, take a sweater with you. There are better views looking onto the park's eastern summits from the west: **Talyuberup**, halfway along the scenic drive and around 800m high, is a short, steep ascent to magnificent views, while **Toolbrunup** (1052m) is among the harder climbs in the park, with some exposed scrambling – allow a tough half-day to get there and back. Many other **trails** wander between the peaks and could link up into overnight walks. Before heading off, discuss your plans with the **ranger** (℡08/9827 9230 or 9827 9278) at his residence by the park campsite off Chester Pass Road.

There are basic facilities at the **campsite**, or much better options at the *Stirling Range Chalet and Caravan Park* (℡08/9827 9229; on-site vans ❸, four-bed chalets ❶–❸), just outside the park's northern boundary, opposite the Bluff Knoll turn-off.

Mount Barker

MOUNT BARKER is at the centre of a small wine-growing region and makes a pleasant day out from Albany, driving around the lanes sampling the fruits of the vine. There are six wineries around the town and a couple more near Porongurup. **Plantagenet Wines** (Mon–Fri 9am–5pm, Sat & Sun 10am–4pm), on Albany Highway, is the region's most established, and undertakes bottling for the lesser wineries in the vicinity. The atmosphere is civilized and amiable, with tastings as well as informal behind-the-scenes **tours**. Wine-tasting apart, Mount Barker, on the old mail-coach route between Albany and Perth, is just another country town, although **St Werburgh's Chapel**, built in 1873 on a hillside a few kilometres west of town (get directions from the **tourist office**, 57 Lowood Rd; ℡08/9851 1163) is worth a look – an unexpected relic of Mount Barker's God-fearing pioneers.

The Wheatlands

WA's **Wheatlands**, the wheat belt, is a region of intensive grain agriculture and sheep pastures extending from the southwest coast into the arable areas north of the Great Eastern Highway. The main reasons visitors come here is to see a number of unusual granite rock formations, of which **Wave Rock** near Hyden, 340km from Perth, is the best known. The names of the desolate farming communities often end with the letters "-in", as prolific as the ending "-up" in the Southwest: both are thought to be an Aboriginal suffix meaning "place of water".

Narrogin and Katanning

Many visitors pass through the eastern Wheatbelt on their way down the **Albany Highway** or its parallel alternative, the **Great Southern Highway**, to Albany. The former is a direct route to the Rainbow Coast, with few notable distractions, while the latter emanates from the top of the Avon Valley and winds its way casually south to the confluence of the two highways, 90km north of Albany.

There's not much to stop for along the way. In **NARROGIN**, 192km from Perth, you can visit the **Axe Handle Factory** (℡08/9883 6075 to arrange a visit), which displays a selection of axe handles hand made from local wood – the only place of its kind in WA. Eleven kilometres east of town on the Harrismith Road are **Yilliminning** and **Birdwhistle Rocks**, picnic spots on the way to **Albert Facey's Homestead** (daily 9am–5pm), 39km from Narrogin. The late Albert Facey's autobiography (and subsequent TV mini-series) *A Fortunate Life* is a self-effacing account of his life's few ups and repeated downs, endured with the stoic fatalism of a true Aussie "battler". The homestead conveys those hard times with authentic paraphernalia, as well as a range of locally made crafts. **Overnight stays** in Narrogin are catered for at the *Narrogin Motel*, 56 Williams Rd (T 08/9881 1660; ❹), west of the town centre, the *Albert Facey Motor Inn* (T 08/9881 1899, E aldfacey@treko.net.au; ❹) or at the B&B *Stoke Farm* (T 08/9885 9018, F 9885 9040; ❹) at Highbury, 10km south of Narrogin.

You can hardly fail to notice the seven-metre-high giant merino ram as you drive through **Wagin**, 38km south of Narrogin, which is reason enough to keep going. A further 56km south of Wagin, **KATANNING** is a late nineteenth-century farming centre on the mail route from Albany to Perth. These days the **Old Mill**, on the corner of Clive Street and Austral Terrace, houses the **tourist office** (T 08/9821 2634), although the town is better known for the mosque serving its Muslim community from Christmas Island – an Australian protectorate south of Java. The *Katanning Motel* (T 08/9821 1657; ❹) on Albion Street offers **accommodation**.

Hyden, Wave Rock and around

Perhaps WA's best-known natural oddity is **Wave Rock**, 3km from the tiny farming settlement of **HYDEN**, at the eastern edge of the Wheatlands. At 15m high and 110m long, the formation resembles a breaking wave, an impression enhanced by the vertical water stains running down the overhanging face. While the rock, formed by wind and rain, is certainly unusual, its spell wears off within minutes and it's not worth the commonly undertaken day-trip from Perth unless you enjoy sitting in a bus all day. Even as a diversion south of the Great Eastern Highway (Merredin is 185km away and Southern Cross 178km), its appeal is still dubious. At the base of the rock a marked, twenty-minute trail leads to another outcrop, **Hippo's Yawn**, while 21km from Wave Rock, on the way to Southern Cross, **Bates Cave** features Aboriginal hand paintings.

Hyden has a **tourist information** service (T 08/9880 5182), and you can **spend the night** at the *Wave Rock Caravan Park* (T 08/9880 5022; chalets ❸) 5km east of town. In Hyden itself, try the *Hyden Hotel* on Lynch Street (T 08/9880 5052; ❹).

Esperance and the South Coast

Esperance, 721km southeast of Perth, is at the western end of the **Archipelago of the Recherche**. Both town and archipelago are attractively named after French ships which visited the area in the late eighteenth century and whose persistent nosing around precipitated the hasty colonization of WA by the British. The archipelago is a string of haze-softened granite isles bobbing in the inky blue Southern Ocean, presenting an almost surreal seascape common to coasts washed by cold currents. The mild summer weather (rarely exceeding

30°C), fishing possibilities (especially the local snapper) and surrounding national parks make the town a popular destination for heat-sensitive holiday-makers.

Southeast of Esperance are **Cape Le Grand** and the much less visited **Cape Arid National Park** (both charge CALM fees; see box on p.719) on the edge of the Great Australian Bight, while 130km north of town is the undeveloped Peak Charles National Park – a hill in the middle of nowhere. Back towards Albany, the **Fitzgerald River National Park** offers a wilderness of rare flora. Care should be taken all along this restless coastline, as **king waves** (unexpectedly huge waves indistinguishable in the swell) frequently sweep away fishermen and climbers from exposed, rocky shores.

You can get to Esperance from Kalgoorlie with Westrail's **bus service** (1 daily Mon–Wed, 2 daily Fri; 5hr) or direct from Perth on the *Spirit of Esperance* service (1 daily Mon–Thurs, 2 on Fri; 10hr). Albany, nearly 500km to the east along the South Coast Highway, can only be reached from Esperance direct on Mondays and Thursdays (connecting buses on Tues & Fri). To get from Albany to Esperance, it's best to arrange a **lift** with fellow travellers. Skywest Airlines (free call ☎1800 642 225) **flies** from Perth to Esperance twice daily on weekdays and daily at weekends (1hr 50min).

Esperance and around

The town of **ESPERANCE**, which prospered briefly as a supply port during the heyday of the Eastern Goldfields, was revived after World War II when its poor soils were made fertile with the addition of missing trace elements. Now an established farming and holiday centre, the town lacks the charm promised by its name, but makes an ideal base from which to enjoy a westward exploration of WA's often spectacular and storm-washed southern coast.

Dempster Street is the town's main road and site of the arts-and-crafts vending cabins which comprise the **Museum Village**. Nearby, the actual **museum** (daily 1.30–4.30pm; $3), on James Street, is a surprisingly good repository of local memorabilia – diverse enough momentarily to engage most visitors. It's very proud of its Skylab display: the satellite disintegrated over Esperance in 1979 and NASA was reputedly fined $400 for littering.

Besides a walk along the Norfolk pine-lined Esplanade and a round of mini-golf or go-karting, there's not much else to do in Esperance, so rent a bike or a car and head out along the 36-kilometre **scenic loop** west of town. Travelling clockwise, you'll come first to the **Rotary Lookout** (following a mean climb for cyclists), which overlooks the captivating seascape. You'll spot the **windfarm**, a modest experiment in alternative energy generation, on the way to **Twilight Beach**, an idyllic and sheltered spot, much prettier than the town's more exposed beaches. From here it's more windswept grandeur to **Observation Point Lookout** and a free (nudist) beach, before the road turns inland towards **Pink Lake**, sometimes coloured a lurid shade by salt-tolerant algae, whose marine cousins give the coastline its enchanting turquoise hue.

The approximately one hundred islands of the romantically named Archipelago of the Recherche, known as the **Bay of Isles** around Esperance, are chiefly occupied by colonies of seals, feral goats and multitudes of seabirds. Dolphins may also be seen offshore and southern right whales are commonly observed migrating to the Antarctic in spring. Mackenzies Island Cruises, 71 The Esplanade (☎08/9071 5757), offers daily trips with the possibility of overnight stays on **Woody Island** (summer only), which is equipped with enough facilities to cast yourself away in comfort.

Practicalities

Westrail buses stop in the town centre, with **taxis** available on ℡ 08/9071 1782. The **tourist bureau** (Mon–Fri 8.45am–5pm, Sat & Sun 9am–5pm; ℡ 08/9071 2330), in the Museum Village on Dempster Street, provides detailed town maps and takes care of bookings for local tours and onward travel. The **post office** is on the corner of Dempster and Andrew streets, with a **shopping centre** up Andrew Street, over the roundabout. CALM (℡ 08/9071 3733), at 92 Dempster St, provides information and passes to the national parks around Esperance. **Bicycles** are rented out along The Esplanade from Wilds Jet Ski Hire (Dec–March daily 8.30am–5pm; $12–15 per day; jet ski $1 per min), with a tattier but cheaper selection of cycles at the *Captain Huon Motel*. For inexpensive **car rental**, ask at the YHA or backpackers' accommodation. The Diving Academy, 56 The Esplanade (℡ 08/9071 5111), takes care of **dive** charters and courses, while Vacation Country Tours (℡ 08/9071 2227) offers half-day **tours** to Cape Le Grand, and Safari Wheels (℡ 08/9071 1564) deals with the more active pursuits along the coast. Both hostels (see "Accommodation", below) have 4WDs for making informal runs along the coast if there's enough in-house interest.

Accommodation

There are plenty of **places to stay** around town, although the self-contained units will almost certainly be booked out during school holiday periods; air-con is rarely necessary in Esperance.

All Seasons Holiday Units, 53 The Esplanade (℡ 08/9071 2257). The cheapest units in town and fully equipped; book ahead. Each unit sleeps up to four. ❹

Bayview Motel, 31 Dempster St (℡ 08/9071 1533, ℱ 9071 4544). Motel with some self-contained units. ❹

Blue Waters Lodge YHA, Goldfields Rd (℡ & ℱ 08/9071 1040, ℮ yhaesperance@hotmail.com). Recently renovated hostel facing the bay. Tours, free pick-ups and bikes. ❶ –❸

Captain Huon Motel, 5 The Esplanade (℡ 08/9071 2383, ℱ 9071 2358). Excellent small motel with some self-contained units; bike rental. ❺

Esperance Backpackers, 14 Emily St (℡ 08/9071 4724). The town's livelier hostel, with twenty beds and all mod-cons. Tours and pick-ups are also offered. ❶

Esperance Bay Caravan Park, cnr The Esplanade and Harbour Rd (℡ 08/9071 2237). So close to town you feel like you're camping in someone's garden. Chalets ❸, on-site vans and cabins ❷

Esperance Seafront Caravan Park, Goldfields Rd (℡ 08/9071 1251). The best choice for camping close to the town and beach. On-site vans ❷

Jetty Motel, 1 The Esplanade (℡ 08/9071 5978, ℱ 9071 5540). Well-appointed, two-storey motel with ocean views. ❹

Old Hospital Motel, William St (℡ 08/9071 3587, ℱ 9071 5768). "Boutique" establishment offering an antidote to motel sterility with considered and tasteful decor. ❺

Orleans Bay Caravan Park, Cape Le Grand National Park (℡ 08/9075 0033). Located at Duke of Orleans Bay, reached along a turn-off about 88km from Esperance, this site is ideal for those in search of seclusion. Cabins ❸, on-site vans ❷

Restaurants

Besides the counter lunches at the *Pier* and *Esperance* hotels, there are a couple of interesting **restaurants** to match the mouthwatering seascapes.

The Gray Starling Restaurant, 126 Dempster St (℡ 08/9071 3187). Attractive and relaxing and serving a tasty menu – one of the best eating places in town. Daily, but Wed from 6pm, Sun 11.30am–3pm.

Ollies on the Esplanade, 32 The Esplanade. Coffee house with an all-day menu. Attractive sea views. Daily 7am–8pm.

Peaches Restaurant, *Bay of Isles Motel*, 32 The Esplanade (℡ 08/9071 3999). Top-quality à la carte cuisine for around $20 a meal and with a view to match. Daily 6–9pm.

Spice of Life, Andrew St. The quest for original names for vegetarian cafés continues. Daily 9am–6pm.

Village Café, Museum Village. A convenient little lunch spot for seafood and chips. Daily 9am–5pm.

Cape Le Grand and Cape Arid national parks

A visit to **Cape Le Grand National Park** (CALM fee; see box on p.719) is well worth the expense of renting a car or taking a tour; it's essentially a climb up a hill and a beach-hop – but they're the sort of beaches you want to roll up and take home with you. Once in the park, the climb to the summit of **Frenchman's Peak** (262m) is not as hard as it looks, and well worth the half-hour's exertion in a sturdy pair of shoes. The secret of the distinctive, hooked summit is an unexpected hole that perfectly frames the impressive view out to sea. Just after the Frenchman's Peak turn-off, a track leads to **Hellfire Bay**; sheltered coves don't come any more perfect than this. From here you can take a tough, three-hour walk to **Le Grand Beach** (limited camping; water available) to the northwest or a less demanding two-hour trek to **Thistle Cove**, from where an easier trail leads to the broad arc of **Lucky Bay** (camping and water), with more sheltered swimming and unbelievable colours. **Rossiter Bay**, 6km east, is distinctly unimpressive by comparison and not worth the trip.

If you're still having trouble getting away from it all, keep heading east to **Cape Arid National Park** (CALM fee; see box on p.719). This is best explored in a 4WD, but ordinary cars can make it as far as **Yokinup Bay**, **Thomas River** and **Sandy Bight**, where there's camping; all visitors must bring their own **fresh water**. East of the park is **Israelite Bay**, well worth a visit if you've come this far, with another impossibly blue sea, the remains of an old telegraph station and a track up to Balladonia on the Eyre Highway, which blasts its way through to South Australia (see p.736 for details of this route).

Esperance to Albany

From Esperance, the **South Coastal Highway** leads 479km to Albany with just a couple of small farming settlements along the way; it's a fairly dull day's drive with only the military museum and rabbit-proof fence at Jerramungup to perk you up. If you're not in a hurry, turn south along a network of dirt roads, just after **Stokes Inlet National Park** (CALM fee; see box on p.719), popular with beach fishermen and waterfowl alike, to Hopetoun on the coast. West of here is the mountainous eastern edge of the Fitzgerald River National Park which can be traversed to **Bremer Bay**, a peaceful resort a couple of hours' drive from Albany. The *RAC Bremer Bay–Hopetoun* map covers the area in excellent detail.

RAVENSTHORPE, 186km along the highway west of Esperance, is a farming community that was formerly a mining town. **Accommodation** options here include the good-value *Ravensthorpe Motel* (℡08/9838 1053; ❹), or the caravan park at the east end of town. Grab a **snack** at the *Ravensthorpe Country Kitchen* (daily 9am–8pm) on the main road at the east end of town. There's a good route from here to **HOPETOUN**, with a scenic diversion up Ethel Daw Drive. A picturesque holiday and fishing spot, Hopetoun is most usefully a place to get into the adjacent national park. If you need to stay **overnight**, the best deals are at the *CWA Cottages* (℡08/9838 3128; ❸) on Canning Street or the cushy **caravan park** on Spence Street (on-site vans ❸). Otherwise, pamper yourself at the *Hopetoun Motel* (℡08/9838 3219; ❹) on Veal Street, and tuck in at the rather pleasant *Starboard Café* (7am–2pm & 4–8pm) right in the middle of town.

Just outside Hopetoun, a road leads west, across the causeway separating the ocean from Culham Inlet – where the explorer John Eyre observed Aborigines fishing in 1841 – and up towards **East Mount Barren**. This marks the eastern edge of the **Fitzgerald River National Park**, one of two parks in WA designated by UNESCO as a World Heritage Biosphere. Nearly two thousand species of wild flower are protected in the park, including the curious, flame-like hakae and scores of orchids, seventy of which are found nowhere else in the world. Access is limited due to the presence of the tropical fungus known as dieback, the root-rotting spores of which are easily spread by wheels and boots. Four-wheel-drives can reach the sea at **Quoin Head** and camping for all is provided at **Mylies Beach**, at the foot of East Mount Barren. In the western half of the park, **Point Ann**, 64km south of the **ranger's residence** (℡08/9835 5043) along Quiss Road, is the spot to head for; the magnificent view across the sea alone is worth the corrugations. Think twice before descending the sandy track to the campsite here if you're in a 2WD.

The Eastern Goldfields

Five hundred kilometres east of Perth, at the end of the **Great Eastern Highway**, lie the **Eastern Goldfields**. Just over a century ago, gold was found in what still remains one of the world's richest gold-producing regions. Lack of fresh water made life very hard for the early prospectors, driven by a national economic depression into miserable living conditions, disease and, in most cases, premature graves. Nevertheless, boom towns of thousands, boasting grand public buildings, several hotels and a periphery of hovels, would erupt and collapse in the length of time it took to extract any payable ore.

In 1892 the railway from Perth reached **Southern Cross**, just as big finds turned the rush into a national stampede. This huge influx of people accentuated the water shortage, until the visionary engineer C.Y. O'Connor oversaw the construction of a 556-kilometre **pipeline** from Mundaring Weir (see p.709) to Kalgoorlie in 1903. By this time many of the smaller gold towns were already in decline, but the Goldfields' wealth and boost in population finally gave WA the economic autonomy it sought in its claim to statehood.

In the years preceding the goldrush, the area was briefly one of the world's richest sources of **sandalwood**, an aromatic wood greatly prized throughout Asia. Supplies in the Pacific had become exhausted so that, by 1880, the perfumed wood was WA's second-largest exportable commodity after wool. Exacerbating the inevitable over-cutting came the goldrush's demand for timber to prop up shafts or to fire the pre-pipeline water desalinators. Today the region is a pit-scarred and prematurely desertified landscape, dotted with the scavenged vestiges of past settlements.

The Goldfields are centred around the rich reef of gold adjacent to the twinned towns of **Kalgoorlie–Boulder**, with Kalgoorlie being the thriving, energetic core. This prosperous town's unexpected vitality is accentuated by stagnating or decaying settlements all around it: adjacent Boulder and **Coolgardie** to the west, and the semi-abandoned communities and **ghost towns** in the desert to the north.

Even if you're not planning to pass through the Goldfields, a couple of days based in Kalgoorlie are worth the excursion from Perth – if for nothing else than the novelty of riding on the **Prospector**, the daily rail link between Perth and Kalgoorlie, which stops off at all the towns along the highway. Greyhound Pioneer, Goldfields Express and Westrail **buses** depart with similar regularity (and journey times) and a visit to the Goldfields can be undertaken as part of a two-thousand-kilometre loop along WA's southern coast, making use of Perth's inexpensive car-rental agencies. The *Streetsmart Goldfields Touring Map* is highly recommended, especially if you're thinking of exploring the area north of Kalgoorlie.

The Great Eastern Highway

Heading from Perth to the Goldfields, there's precious little to detain you until you reach Coolgardie. **MECKERING**, 132km east of Perth, was destroyed by an earthquake in 1968 and a gazebo off the main road commemorates the event. **CUNDERDIN**, 24km further east, has a pioneering **museum** (daily 10am–4pm; $2), housed in one of the eight steam pumping stations that once propelled the water to Kalgoorlie at a little over 1.5km per hour. **KELLER-BERRIN**, not far beyond Cunderdin, was one of the earliest settlements along the Great Eastern Highway, and dates from 1861. It also has a **museum** (Mon–Fri 8.30am–5pm; $2), located in a historic building, and inexpensive **rooms** at the *Ampol Roadhouse Motel* (☎08/9045 4007; ❹) on the highway. **MERREDIN** is a bigger wheat and wool town than most, with a **museum** (daily 9am–3pm; $2) housed in an old train station, built from bricks of Kalgoorlie clay that are said to contain gold of mineable grade.

East of Merredin the country becomes drier and, by the time you get to **SOUTHERN CROSS**, 370km from Perth, you have passed through the Wheatbelt. It was here in 1887 that small traces of gold precipitated the country's largest and most fruitful goldrush, and with the arrival of the railway in 1892, the town became a jumping-off point for the greater finds to the east. Nowadays Southern Cross has that moribund feel so familiar to rural settlements with prosperous pasts; the disproportionately wide streets, common to all the goldrush towns, allowed camel trains to turn round. Local goldrush history is recounted in the **Yilgarn History Museum** (Mon–Sat 9am–noon & 1.30–4pm, Sun 1.30–4pm; $1) on Antares Street, while **accommodation** is available at the *Southern Cross Palace Hotel* (☎08/9049 1555, ℱ9049 1509; ❹), near the museum, or the *Southern Cross Caravan Park* (☎08/9049 1212; on-site vans ❸), on the eastern edge of town.

Coolgardie

Rather too tidy and intact to carry the name "ghost mining town", **COOLGARDIE** is more of a museum to itself, a town which, at its peak, had twenty-three hotels, three breweries and six newspapers serving a population ten times greater than its present fifteen hundred. Arthur Bayley increased the pitch of the gold fever when he returned to Southern Cross – then the easternmost extent of the rush – in 1892 with nearly sixteen kilograms of gold. The ensuing wave of prospectors started within hours – ten thousand men rushed out of Southern Cross, culminating in a fourfold increase in WA's population by the end of the century. Recently the abandoned Bayley's Reward mine at the east end of town was just about to open for tourists, when a last-minute check for mineable ore resulted in a change of plans and a resumption of full production.

The Town and around

The imposing **Wardens Court Building** on Bayley Street is a good point from which to start an appraisal of Coolgardie's numerous gold-boom relics. The building houses the **tourist office** (daily 9am–5pm; ☎08/9026 6090) and has one of the most extensive provincial **museums** in WA (daily

9am–5pm; $3.30), filling the grand upper floors with an especially comprehensive collection of bottles. It rewards a prolonged browse, giving you a feel for the dramatic effect the goldrush had on the area.

Outside the museum is an index to the 155 **historic markers** set around the town, and right opposite you can't miss the varied miscellany and just plain old junk comprising **Ben Prior's Open-Air Museum** (Mon–Fri; free). Half a kilometre up Hunt Street, at the end of McKenzie Street, **Warden Finnerty's Residence** (Mon–Wed 1–4pm, Sat & Sun 10am–noon & 1–4pm; $2) is the finely restored 1895 residence of the man whose unenviable job it was to set the ground rules for mining at the height of the rush.

On the way back to Bayley Street, a left down Woodward Street leads to the **Railway Station Museum** (daily 9am–5pm, closed Wed; donation welcome), housed in a station used until 1971, when the railway was rerouted north of town. Featured is the drama of the 1907 Varischetti mine rescue and the story of the once-thriving sandalwood industry.

Other attractions around Coolgardie include the **cemetery**, west of town (the last resting place of explorer Ernest Giles), and the **Coolgardie Camel Farm** (daily during school holidays 10am–4pm, or by appointment; 1hr camel rides $1, day and overnight treks from $20 for a minimum of two people; booking essential on ☎08/9026 6159), a couple of kilometres further west, which describes the crucial role camels played in the years before the arrival of the railway.

Practicalities

Coolgardie is best reached from Perth by the daily Greyhound Pioneer, Goldfields Express or Westliner **bus services**, as the train now stops at Bonnie Vale, 14km north of town, and is actually no quicker. Alternatively, during school term time, you can visit the town from Kalgoorlie with Goldenlines (Mon–Fri departs Kalgoorlie at 7.10am, returns at 4.15pm; $2.75 one-way; ☎08/9021 2655). Kalgoorlie-based Goldrush Tours (☎08/9021 5826; Tues & Sat mornings; $43) also offers half-day tours to Coolgardie. There are no banks, although there is a cash machine in the BP service station on Hunt Street; the **post office** is around the corner. The cheapest **accommodation** in town is the *Goldrush Lodge* (☎ & ℱ 08/9026 6446; ❹), a B&B at 75 Bayley St. For up-to-date comfort try the *Coolgardie Motor Inn* (☎08/9026 6002; ❹) at the east end of Bayley Street. There are two **caravan parks** with on-site vans (❷) just west of town.

When it comes to gourmet restaurants, Coolgardie earns its ghost-town appellation with ease. For light **meals**, try the *Premier Café* (Mon–Sat 7.30am–8pm, Sun 8.30am–7pm), opposite the tourist office. For something more substantial, the *Coolgardie Motor Inn's* restaurant (daily 6–8pm) or the outdoor one at the *Coolgardie Motel* (daily 6–8.30pm; ☎08/9026 6080), opposite Ben Prior's Open-Air Museum on Bayley Street, are the only alternatives to foraging in the bush.

Kalgoorlie–Boulder

Whichever way you approach **KALGOORLIE**, the bustling town now twinned with its shabbier neighbour **Boulder**, it comes as a surprise after hundreds of kilometres of desolation. It possesses the idiosyncratic appeal of similar places such as Coober Pedy (in South Australia) or Las Vegas. All three blithely disregard their isolation and bleak surroundings, so devoted is their attention to the pursuit of earthly riches – which, in Kalgoorlie's case, is **gold**.

In 1893 **Paddy Hannan** (then 53 years old) and his mates, Tom Flannigan and Dan O'Shea, brought renewed meaning to the expression "the luck of the Irish" when a lame horse forced them to camp by the tree which still stands at the top of Egan Street. With their instincts highly attuned after eight months of prospecting around Coolgardie, they soon found gold all around them: as the first on the scene, they enjoyed the unusually easy pickings of surface gold. Ten years later, when the desperately needed water pipeline finally gushed into the Mount Charlotte Reservoir, Kalgoorlie was already established as the heart of WA's rapidly growing mineral-based prosperity, a position it still retains. As sole survivor of the original rush, revitalized by the 1960s nickel boom, Kalgoorlie has benefited from new technology that has largely dispensed with slow and dangerous underground mining. Instead, the fabulously rich **"Golden Mile"** reef east of town – which Boulder was originally built to serve – is being devoured wholesale by machinery and explosives to create the vast, open-cast "Super Pit".

Proud of its history, isolation and continued prosperity, Kalgoorlie is one of the most parochial towns in a country that's full of them. An ongoing gentrification programme means that soon sophistication in "Kal" will no longer be regarded as a fully clothed barmaid, and, if nothing else, the Federation-era **architecture** and history deserve to be appreciated. The city has dramatically grown over the past ten years, but still clings to vestiges of its colourful past. Even in the sniggeringly louche red-light district of Hay Street, only three of the infamous "tin shack" brothels remain in business, and, interestingly enough, they forbid any male ownership or control. But Kal remains a Working Man's Town, a dinky-di testament to the ethos of hard work and hard play that flourished in Australia's Anglo-Celtic heyday. The town is still a good place to find employment if you have engineering-related skills, though expect to work nothing less than twelve hard and dusty hours a day.

Start your tour of the town by taking a walk up to the top of Hannan Street, where the bright red head-frame immediately attracts your attention. This is the impressive entrance to the **Museum of the Goldfields** (daily 10am–4.30pm; free), right next to the spot where Paddy and his crew found their first, auspicious nuggets. Inside is a modern display of Goldfields artefacts and history, with the very stuff that keeps the town going viewable in the basement vault. Aboriginal history and the sandalwood industry are also covered in this excellent introduction to the area, and there's a lookout over the town from the top of the red-head frame. Next door is the **British Arms** pub, now a coffee shop but better known as Australia's narrowest pub.

Hannan Street itself is one of Kalgoorlie's finest sights, with its superbly restored turn-of-the-twentieth-century architecture, imposing public buildings and numerous flamboyant hotel facades. You're welcome to inspect the grandiose interior of the **town hall** (Mon–Fri 9am–4pm; free), with its splendid hall and less impressive art gallery. It's only when you stop to reflect that this is a remote, hundred-year-old town in the West Australian desert that the stunning wealth of the boom years, which still continues, is brought home to you. Outside, a replica of a bronze **statue** of Paddy himself invites you to drink from his chrome-nozzled waterbag – the much vandalized original is inside the town hall.

The **School of Mines Museum** (Mon–Fri 10am–4pm; free), on the corner of Egan and Cassidy streets, perhaps outstrips most visitors' enthusiasm, with its vast display of minerals and replicated nuggets; just over the road, on Maritana Street, is the stop for the Boulder-bound bus.

Boulder and around

BOULDER, 5km south of Kalgoorlie, is much quieter and smaller – a place to visit rather than stay in. One glance down **Burt Street** reveals that it's Kalgoorlie's poorer sister, although this is not an observation to make at the top of your voice in any of the local pubs. It was originally set up as a separate settlement to serve the Golden Mile; Boulder's heyday passed as Kalgoorlie's suburbs slowly expanded towards it.

Boulder has a similar collection of grand old buildings which, as in Kal, have received a face-lift, with the pubs, especially the *Cornwall*, *Grand* and deliciously ramshackle *Metropole*, a delight to look at if not to drink in. One thing worth coming to Boulder for is a ride on the **Golden Mile Loopline**. Departing daily (Mon–Sat 10am & 12.45pm, Sun 3pm; $12; ℡ 08/9093 3055) from the former train station at the top of Burt Street, the "Rattler", as it is known, once delivered workers to their pits and served all shifts round the clock. Now it will take you on a one-hour circuit of the Super Pit. Whether you take a ride or not, the **Super Pit Lookout** is worth a look, if for no other reason than to appreciate the full scale of the operation; the little yellow Haul-Pacs you see below carry two hundred tons at a time and their tyres are as high as the storey of a building.

Just north of town are a couple more attractions without which a visit to Kalgoorlie–Boulder would not be complete. **Hannan's North Tourist Mine** (daily 9.30am–4.30pm; $18, surface only $12; ℡ 08/9091 4074) is an old mine now transformed into a mining theme park. From the gloomy interior of a tent an amusing, video-faced mannequin of the venerable Mr Hannan cheerily regales you with the details of his fortuitous "stroike", while the forty-minute guided underground tours, led by former miners, are probably as long as you'd want to spend down a mine – especially when you're given a brief demonstration of the pneumatic "air leg" drill. Allow about two and a half hours for your visit.

Back on the Menzies Road, follow the "Two Up" signs a short distance to Kalgoorlie's once-clandestine and, since 1983, the country's only legal **Two Up School**, 7km from town. Two Up is, more or less, a game of "heads or tails" played with two pennies. In the decidedly functional "galvo" arena, the deadly serious and utterly absorbed gamblers bet on how the pennies will land – each double tails (or "white cross") result punctuated by the exchange of fistfuls of notes. It sounds simple and you are welcome to join in ($10 minimum stake), but to most outsiders the proceedings are totally baffling. Gambling takes place daily (except on paydays – once every two weeks) and runs from 4pm until dusk, with no alcohol or anyone under eighteen allowed within 100m.

Practicalities

Westliner (free call ℡ 1800 199 649) and Greyhound Pioneer (℡ 08/9021 7100) **buses** now arrive at Forrest Street in Kalgoorlie, opposite the **train station** (Westrail; ℡ 08/9021 2923). **Taxis** (℡ 08/9021 2177) meet incoming trains, which are no quicker than buses, yet more expensive. Kalgoorlie's **tourist office** (Mon–Fri 8.30am–5pm, Sat & Sun 9am–5pm; ℡ 08/9021 1966, Ⓦ www.kalgoorlieandwagoldfields.com.au) is at 250 Hannan St, on Kalgoorlie's main thoroughfare, and gives out informative sketch maps pinpointing Kal's dispersed attractions. The **post office** is just up the road at 204 Hannan St.

A local **bus service** operates between the two towns (Mon–Sat 8am–6pm; $1.40), with timetables available from Kalgoorlie's tourist office or the town hall. **Car rental** is expensive, though Halfpenny Rentals, 544 Hannan St south (℡ 08/9021 1804), is an exception. **Bikes** can be rented at Johnstons Cycles, 78 Boulder Rd (℡ 08/9021 1157). Goldrush Tours (℡ 08/9021 5828) is the main local operator whose daily "Kalgoorlie–Boulder" tour ($30) is recommended.

Accommodation

Although it's unlikely that Kalgoorlie will maintain your interest for more than a couple of days, the town does get busy with holiday-makers in the winter school holidays, when it's best to check room availability in advance. The many splendid-looking hotels along Hannan Street deteriorate alarmingly inside, but they all offer inexpensive rooms with either shared or en-suite facilities.

7

Australia Hotel, 138 Hannan St (℡08/9021 1320, ℻9091 2720, ℮oah@bigpond.com) Four-star hotel with old-time Federation feel. ❻

Cornwall Hotel, 25 Hopkins St, Boulder (℡08/9093 2510, ℮cornwallhotel@bigpond.com). A fabulous-looking old hotel with a dark history and an outdoor restaurant. Shared bathrooms. ❹

Gold Dust Backpackers, 192 Hay St (℡08/9091 3737, ℮golddust@aurum.net.au). Backpackers are now spoilt for choice. Similar to *Goldfields Backpackers* with ten-bed air-con dorms plus local tours. ❶–❸

Golden Village Caravan Park, 406 Hay St (℡08/9021 4162). The caravan park closest to town. On-site vans ❸

Goldfields Backpackers, 166 Hay St (℡08/9091 1482, ℮goldbak@emerge.net.au). A clean, modern, purpose-built hostel that is better than anything Perth has to offer. Air-con rooms, pool, bike rental, help with employment in the area, and free pick-ups. ❶–❸

Hannan's View Motel, 430 Hannan St (℡08/9091 3333, ℮hvm@emerge.net.au). Motel units with pool, cheap breakfasts and some wheel-chair-accessible, self-contained units. ❺

Hay Street Homestay, 164 Hay St (℡08/9091 1482). Once the town's classiest bordello, now a B&B that retains the gilt-taps-and-black-onyx decor but no ceiling mirrors. ❹

Midas Motel, 409 Hannan St (℡08/9021 3088 or free call 1800 813 088, ℻9021 3125). Top-of-the-range motel with nightclub, pool and the excellent *Amalfi* restaurant. ❻

Prospector Holiday Park, Great Eastern Highway, 3km west of town (℡08/9021 2524). Excellent park with pool, playground, kitchen and grassy sites. Cabins ❸, on-site vans ❷

Sandalwood Motel, Lower Hannan St (℡08/9021 4455 ℻9021 3744). Reasonably priced and comfortable motel with air-con, TVs and en-suite bathrooms. ❺

Surrey House, 9 Boulder Rd (℡08/9021 1340). Guesthouse offering cheap breakfasts and a TV room. ❸

York Hotel, 259 Hannan St (℡08/9021 2337). Probably the best-looking facade on Hannan St. Shared bathrooms, but rates include breakfast. ❹

Eating and drinking

An unpretentious Outback town hundreds of kilometres from the nearest fresh tomato isn't the place to look for gourmet delicacies. Instead, treat yourself to a good old **counter meal** for under $10 at any of the pubs, or try *Basil's*, 268 Hannan St, for Italian home-style cooking and something to read, or the *Kalgoorlie Café* (10.30am–3pm & 6pm–1am) on the other side of the road, which has more of a family atmosphere. There's a **food hall** near Coles/K-Mart, and *Health Works*, 75 Hannan St, caters for veggies. Next door is the *Top End Thai* (6pm–late; ℡08/9091 4027), a rare, exotic treat at around $15, and the *Main Reef Bistro*, 32 Dwyer St, for Italian, seafood and buffets.

Twenty years ago Kal's **nightlife** was a riot; scantily clad barmaids ("skimpies") laid on the beer while drink-addled miners threw themselves at the nearest punch-up. Nowadays the appalling scent of yuppification wafts through Kal's once-functional drinking pens, but you'll still need at least a couple of weeks to have a nightly pint at every licensed establishment in Kalgoorlie–Boulder – if you're going to do the complete rounds, ask about the "**Kal pub crawl**" (T-shirts available at the tourist office). These days the roughest of the rough is the *Foundry*, 148 Boulder Rd, with the *De Benares' Tavern*, on Hannan Street, imposing dress regulations for customers *and* staff. Skimpies still serve in most pubs, with the *Exchange* adding the occasional live band and the *Palace* offering a more formal atmosphere. The balcony of the *York* is no longer a launching pad for vomit and beer cans. If you're **in**

Boulder, the transformed *Recreation* or the *Albion & Shamrock* hotels are the ones to visit for a drink, and if you want to have a generally quiet evening, go to the bars in the back.

North of Kalgoorlie–Boulder

North of town a number of isolated communities supporting either small mining operations or rural Aboriginal communities stretch along a sealed road (bar a short section north of Leinster) to Meekatharra, 726km from Kalgoorlie and halfway up the Great Northern Highway. This arid and sparsely populated region offers visitors prime chunks of WA's Outback: dust, heat, flies, treacherous salt lakes, more flies, and towns in varying stages of atrophy. It's worth knowing that most **ghost towns** in this area, especially the ones closer to Kalgoorlie, are mere stumps of long-since ruined buildings, surrounded by decidedly un-ghostly rubbish. The desperate shortage and expense of building materials in the Goldfields ensured that any abandoned structure was quickly scavenged for use elsewhere.

Though it once boasted twelve thousand residents, two breweries and an hourly train to Kalgoorlie, give the rubble remains of **Kanowna** a miss. Instead, the two ghost towns of **BROAD ARROW** and **ORA BANDA** (respectively 38km and 66km from Kalgoorlie) can make a satisfactory nibble into this area, especially if you complete the 185-kilometre loop (100km of corrugated dirt) back to Kalgoorlie via Coolgardie. Broad Arrow is just a couple of dilapidated shacks and a **pub** covered with inane graffiti (to which you are most welcome to contribute) and is popular with weekending Kal–Boulderians looking for a change of pub interiors. The historic *Ora Banda Hotel* (T 08/9024 2059, F 9024 2166; ❸) is built of stone rather than the more usual galvanized iron, and has recently been rebuilt. There's an old stamp battery nearby and the track continues back south to Coolgardie, passing the abandoned townsites of Kintore and Kununalling.

From **Leonora**, where there's a motel (❺), a sealed road also branches northeast to Laverton where the **Warburton Road**, now being touted as "The Great Central Road", a straightforward if desolate track (often confused with the long-unmaintained Gunbarrel Highway) leads 1160km to Yulara, NT (see p.678). You'll need an Aboriginal Land Permit to drive this route, available from the Permit Office of the Aboriginal Land Trust, PO Box 7770, Cloister Square, Perth WA 6850 (T 08/9235 8000, e alt@aad.wa.gov.au). With **fuel** after Laverton at Tjirrikarli (longest stretch, 320km), Warburton, Warakurna and Docker River, this long-useful dirt-road connection between central and western Australia is opening up. The Perth–Goldfields Express (free call T 1800 620 440) runs **buses** as far as **Leinster**, which posesses a motel (❹) and **Laverton**, which also has one (❺), three times a week, stopping on the way at **Menzies**, where there's a hotel (❹), and Leonora.

The Eyre Highway to South Australia

South of Kalgoorlie is the twin-centred, nickel-mining town of **KAMBALDA**, on the shores of salty Lake LeFroy where you can windsurf during the wet season and land yacht during the dry. There's nothing here you haven't already seen in Kalgoorlie, so rejoin the Great Eastern Highway and continue south to Norseman, at the western end of the **Eyre Highway**. The highway is named after the explorer John Eyre, who crossed the southern edge of the continent in 1841, a gruelling five-month trek which cost his companion's life and would have cost his own but for some Aborigines, who helped him locate water. Eyre crawled into Albany on his last legs but set the route for future crossings, the laying down of the telegraph lines and, most recently, the highway.

NORSEMAN was named after a prospector's horse which kicked up a large nugget in 1894 – a real case of lucky horseshoes; a bronze statue of the creature now stands proudly on the corner of Roberts and Ramsay streets. Arrivals from South Australia may be eager to pick up their "I crossed the Eyre Highway" certificate from the **tourist office** (daily 9am–5pm; ℡08/9039 1071) on Roberts Street. There are also public showers and a **swimming pool** next door in which to celebrate further this achievement. You can continue to celebrate with a meal and an overnight stay at the *Norseman Eyre Motel* (℡08/9039 1130 or free call 1800 094 824, Ⓕ9039 1547; ❺) on Princep Street. More modest accommodation is available at the **caravan park** (on-site vans ❸) next to the *Great Western Motel*, or there are budget rooms at *Norseman Guest House & Backpackers Lodge* (℡08/9039 1541; ❶) nearby. If you've **come from the east** and are in a quandary about which route to take to Perth, the inland road, after a stop in Kalgoorlie–Boulder, is fast and fairly dull while the coast road can be made into a week-long scenic dawdle. For the best of both worlds, nip up to Kalgoorlie and then back down and west along the coast.

Following the Eyre Highway, it's about 730km to the South Australian border and another 480km from there to Ceduna, where the bleak **Nullarbor** section ends (see p.865). That still leaves 800km before you reach Adelaide – a solid, two-day drive of legendary monotony. Although the road has been sealed for over twenty years and the longest stretch without fuel is only around 200km, do not underestimate the rigours of the journey in your own vehicle. Carry reserves of fuel and water, take rests every two or three hours and beware of kangaroos and other beasts, especially between dusk and dawn. There are no banks between Norseman and Ceduna, and both towns have a quarantine checkpoint where a large range of prohibited animal and vegetable goods must be discarded.

BALLADONIA, 193km from Norseman, is the first settlement on the way to the border, with the *Balladonia Hotel* (℡08/9039 3453; ❹) and adjacent caravan park your choice for an overnight stop. Then, 200km further, mostly along a 145-kilometre section of dead-straight road, you reach **CAIGUNA**, which has a motel and caravan park (℡08/9039 3459; motel units ❹, on-site vans ❷), and then **COCKLEBIDDY**, another 66km further on (motel ❹). On the coast near here, 16km east of town and 32km south of the highway along a 4WD track, are the remains of an old **telegraph station** that once linked WA with the rest of Australia and which today houses the Eyre Bird Observatory, where you can stay overnight if you book in advance (℡08/9039 3450; ❺, plus $30 for pick-up and return). Overlooking **Twilight Cove** on the Great Australian Bight, this is a great spot to break a Nullarbor crossing. The place to stay in **MADURA**, 92km east of Cocklebiddy, is the *Madura Pass Oasis Motel* (℡08/9039 3464 or 13 1779; ❺), while **MUNDRABILLA**, 116km further on, has a combined motel and campsite, the *Mundrabilla Motor Hotel* (℡08/9039 3465; motel units ❹, cabins ❷).

EUCLA, just 12km from the border, was re-established up on the escarpment after sand dunes exposed by overgrazing engulfed the original settlement by the sea. Only 4km away, the old telegraph and weather station are still visible above the sands, an eerie sight well worth a stroll. From **Eucla National**

Park, the vertical cliffs can be seen extending east for hundreds of kilometres along the coast of South Australia. For accommodation, Eucla has a **caravan park** (on-site vans ➋) and the *Eucla Motor Hotel* (℡08/9039 3468; ➍). Right on the border there's the Border Village (℡08/9039 3474; ➍).

For the South Australian section of this route, see p.864.

From Perth to Kununurra

The 4400-kilometre haul up Western Australia's arching coastline from Perth to Broome, across the Kimberley and on to Darwin in the Northern Territory, is one of Australia's great road journeys. Even without detours it's a huge, transcontinental trek between the country's two most isolated capitals, fringing the barely inhabited wilderness that separates them. From the **WA–NT border** 40km east of Kununurra, it's still another 730km to Darwin. This final stretch, along the Victoria and Stuart highways, which meet at Katherine, is covered on pp.632-645.

If any single trip across Australia benefits from independent mobility, it's this one: a car enables you to explore intimately or linger indefinitely. While some days in WA's **Northwest** will be punctuated by nothing more than road trains, road kills and roadhouses, there are several places where the climate, scenery and ambience will collectively conspire to subdue your road fever for a few days. If you're interested in discovering the wayside attractions, allow at least a fortnight for the journey right through to Darwin; otherwise a week to ten days will let you whizz through the highlights.

The route is sealed all the way, but a glance at any map clearly shows the long distances between roadhouses, let alone settlements. Your vehicle should be in sound condition, particularly the tyres and the cooling system, both of which will be working hard in the heat and dirt-road detours of the Northwest. If you're undertaking the trip between January and March, once you get **north of Exmouth** you can expect **storms**, flooding and even cyclones. Following damage, roads and bridges on Highway 1 are repaired amazingly quickly, but if rain persists, routes can be closed for weeks. A **radio** is a handy aid to keeping track of cyclones, similarly troublesome "rain-bearing depressions" and the status of roads. Unfortunately, beyond Geraldton reception fades a few kilometres outside each settlement; but you can rely on roadhouse staff to know the latest. With forewarning, it's usually possible to gun ahead of a front or find somewhere agreeable to sit out the storm.

If you don't have a car, the rigid schedules and butt-numbing sectors of long-distance **bus** travel require a certain equanimity. Greyhound Pioneer and Integrity Coachlines offer a range of good-value **regional passes** up the coast to Exmouth, Broome and Darwin. It should be noted that by doing the journey *from* Perth, schedules generally match connections to places off the highway with little delay. In the opposite direction, you are travelling "against the flow" of the timetable and can expect long waits on roadhouse forecourts unless heading directly back to Perth.

Up the coast to Broome

Ironically, nowhere along the 2400-kilometre drive along the North West Coastal Highway to Broome will you glimpse vistas of frothing surf breaking temptingly onto golden beaches or taste the salt in the air. The highway takes a more sheltered inland course, with access to the ocean limited by the presence of private land, not to mention the sheer impenetrability of some of the terrain. The myth of beach-camping your way up a deserted coast is unfortunately just that, but there are enough attractions to make up for this deficiency. High points along the route include the spooky **Pinnacles** near Cervantes, the idyllic resort of **Kalbarri**, and the **Shark Bay** Peninsula, with its chummy dolphins. Further north, the **Ningaloo Reef** running down the North West Cape should not be missed, while a detour into the highlands of the **Pilbara** will make **Broome's** serene charm all the more delectable.

The Brand Highway

Travelling the **Brand Highway**, there's an all but obligatory detour to view the remarkable Pinnacles in **Nambung National Park**, 250km from Perth and 70km off the highway. A young crayfishing town, beaten by strong winds in summer, **CERVANTES** is the closest overnight stop. There are two caravan parks here, with campsites and on-site vans (❷), plus *Pinnacles Beach Backpackers*, at 91 Seville St (℡08/9652 7377, ℻9652 7318;❶), which has kitchen facilities, a laundry, TV/video lounge and books tours. For greater comfort, try the *Cervantes Pinnacles Motel* (℡08/9652 7145, ℻9652 7214; ❺). You can eat at the *Tavern* or the *Thirst Point* pizzeria. Minibus **tours** of the park leave daily (1pm plus 9.45am & 4.15pm, depending on demand; $12; ℡08/9652 7041) from the *Pinnacle Country Café*, which is also the **tourist information centre** (daily 8am–6pm), next to the Shell service station. Better still, Happyday Tours (℡08/9652 7244) do **pick-ups** from the Greyhound Pioneer bus on the highway and next morning takes you for a two-hour stroll ($30) through the Pinnacles on the way back to the bus.

Otherwise, in the park (CALM fee; no camping; see box on p.719) there's access to the ocean at **Kangaroo Point** and **Hangover Bay** but the **Pinnacles** are the main attraction: a forest of limestone columns up to four metres high, formed by subsurface erosion and since exhumed from their sandy tombs by the perennial southwesterlies. A three-kilometre loop drive winds among them, but however lazy you're feeling, you'll find it hard not to park and wander around this eerie expanse, sometimes enhanced by a "mist" of fine, windblown sand. Most day-tours from Perth arrive around midday, missing the evening sun's long shadows, which add still further to the Pinnacles' photogenic qualities.

After the Pinnacles there's really very little of interest until you get to the tiny coastal resort of **GREENOUGH**, 400km north of Perth. The **Greenough Historical Hamlet** (daily 9.30am–4.30pm; ℡08/9926 1140; $2.50 including guided tour) is an unusually well-restored nineteenth-century farming community that would make an ideal period-film location. Up the road you'll see Greenough's strange **leaning trees** – some bent almost flat against the ground by the prevailing salt-laden winds – as well as the imposing, three-storey bulk of **Clinch's Mill**, the **Pioneer Cemetery**, and the **Pioneer Museum** (Sat–Thurs 10am–4pm; ℡08/9926 1058; $1.50), recording the area's heritage.

On the west side of the highway (turn off at the *S Bend Caravan Park*), more of Greenough's relics include the *Hampton Arms Inn*, restored into a delightful

guesthouse (℡08/9926 1057, ℻9926 1238; ❹, with breakfast and lunch) and **restaurant** (daily noon–2pm & 7pm–late), which make a welcome rustic change from anodyne motels. The *Greenough Rivermouth Caravan Park* (℡08/9921 5845) is a better-than-average facility offering tent spaces, on-site vans (❸) and cheap fuel. The nearest **backpackers'** (℡08/9927 1581; ❶) is the youth hostel at 32 Waldeck St, Dongara, 40km to the south.

Geraldton

Situated in the middle of the **Batavia Coast**, **GERALDTON** is a crayfishing, mining and pastoral centre whose downtown feels more like a busy Perth suburb than a country town. In fact it's the state's second-largest city and a **windsurfing** haven, currently experiencing a mini-boom.

The **tourist office** is in the Bill Sewell Complex (Mon–Fri 8.30am–5pm, Sat & Sun 9am–4.30pm; ℡08/9921 3999) on Chapman Road, 2km north of town and will happily sort out all accommodation bookings. Greyhound Pioneer and Integrity **buses** arrive here daily and Westrail buses alight at the old train station, just down the road. The modern town has little of interest except for a museum and an extraordinary cathedral. The **Maritime Museum** (Mon–Sat 10am–4pm, Sun 1–5pm; donation) on Marine Terrace, by the yellow submarine (an aborted crayfishing venture), focuses on the fascinating tragedy of the *Batavia* and the many other shipwrecks off the treacherous Batavia Coast, as well as describing the contemporary "treasures" of the crayfishing industry.

St Francis Xavier Cathedral on Cathedral Drive, built over a 25-year period and completed in 1938, was the crowning glory of Monsignor John Hawes' career. He was a qualified architect before taking up the cloth, and there are half a dozen examples of his unique Romanesque-Byzantine architectural style in the vicinity, of which the cathedral is his masterpiece, just as stunning and bold inside as out. There are free tours on Mondays at 10am and Fridays at 2pm. If you're sufficiently impressed, ask about the **John Hawes Heritage Trail** at the tourist office (see above), which leads you around some of his other works.

Of Geraldton's other attractions, the city's **beaches** aren't particularly appealing and are often windy, like much of the west coast. There's the obligatory **Old Gaol**, now a craft centre, next to the Bill Sewell Complex, and a **lighthouse** at Point Moore, while the old **Keepers' Cottage** (Thurs 10am–4pm; donation welcome), off Chapman Road, 5km north of town, is fastidiously maintained in its original state. If you're around for a while, you might want to take the Touch the Wild Safari Tour (℡08/9921 8435; $105 per day), which shows you what the Geraldton region's natural history has to offer.

The Houtman Abrolhos islands

Seventy kilometres off the Geraldton coast is the archipelago of the Houtman Abrolhos, over a hundred sparsely vegetated islands barely above water, surrounded by a maze of reefs and channels.

While these are "desert islands" in the scientific sense, tropical and temperate currents mingle here to create an unusual diversity of marine flora and fauna, offering some of the best diving and snorkelling along the west coast.

Access is limited to tours of various kinds, all of which are based in Geraldton: Abrolhos Adventures (℡08/9921 6416) has a superbly equipped vessel for charter, at a cost of $270 per person for a fully-inclusive weekend dive trip, or you can join the Batavia Coast Diving Academy (℡08/9921 4299) for a weekend dive. Shine Aviation Services (℡08/9923 3600) offers a memorable and great-value seaplane flight including ninety-minutes of snorkelling on the reefs for $165.

Accommodation

Batavia Backpackers, Bill Sewell Complex, Chapman Rd (℡08/9964 3001). Spacious and clean former hospital with wards for dorms. **①**–**③**

Batavia Motor Inne, Fitzgerald St (℡08/9921 3500, ℻9921 1061). Close to the city centre and with restaurant and pool. **⑤**

Foreshore Backpackers, 172 Marine Terrace (℡08/9921 3275, ✉foreshorebp@hotmail.com).

Right in the town centre and close to the harbour. YHA discounts and free pick-ups. **①**–**③**

Mercure Inn, Brand Highway (℡08/9921 2455 or free call 1800 642 244, ℻9921 5830). Customary motel-chain comforts. **⑥**

Sun City Tourist Park, Sunset Beach, 6km north of town (℡08/9938 1655). Geraldton's best caravan park but rather a long way out. On-site vans **③**

Eating and drinking

Geraldton has a fair selection of places to eat, and if you're heading north this will be your last chance to sample a choice of decent food rather than take what you are offered. For **drinks** and **live bands**, the *Geraldton Hotel* on Lester Avenue is the place to go, with the *Freemasons* on Marine Terrace offering a more refined alternative.

Boat Shed, 357 Marine Terrace. Quality seafood from around $20. Daily from 6pm.

Go Health Café, Marine Terrace. Breakfasts and lunches with vegetarian options and big burritos.

Lemon Grass, 18 Snowdon St. The town's best choice for Thai food.

Montego's, Marine Terrace, Dinner seven days with the best views of the bay.

Skeetas, George Rd. Very popular garden restaurant, an ideal place for salad lunches in the sun.

Topollini's, 158 Marine Terrace. Stylish and affordable Italian lunch spot in the town centre.

Hutt River Province and on to Kalbarri

North of Geraldton, the North West Coastal Highway heads through **NORTHAMPTON**, an early lead-mining and pastoral settlement with a good caravan park and budget accommodation at the delightful *Old Convent* (℡08/9934 1692; **①**), next to the church. A few kilometres after Northampton you can turn left to investigate the tiny seaside resort and crayfishing port of **HORROCKS** (25km west), or **PORT GREGORY** (46km northwest, and where the bitumen ends), with the ruins of an aborted convict-hiring depot from the 1850s nearby.

A couple of kilometres after the Horrocks turn-off, the Chilimony Road leads you to one of Australia's strangest tourist attractions, the independent sovereign state of **HUTT RIVER PROVINCE**, a 75-square-kilometre tax-free principality governed by the enigmatic Prince Leonard and his family. In 1970, farmer Leonard Casley seceded his property from the Commonwealth of Australia in disgust at the government of the time, and after two days of "hostilities" – in which no shots were fired – Hutt River gained sovereignty under international law. Today, most of Hutt River's citizens choose to live elsewhere (just thirty are resident in Hutt River itself), but the administrative centre of Hutt River comprises a post office, gift shops and an impressive chapel – a must-see, even more so if guided by local royalty – and there's even basic **accommodation** available through the Minister of Housing (℡08/9936 6035; vans **①**). Visas, which last indefinitely, are available on arrival at the post office where the province's currency, the HRP dollar, can also be exchanged. Prince Leonard often greets visitors personally at the border. For more, see the Hutt River website at ⓦwww.wps.com.au/hutriver/hut1.htm.

Kalbarri

Situated at the mouth of the Murchison River, whose sandbar shelters its beach, **KALBARRI** is the best of the west coast's resorts. Without so much as the cliffs above **Natural Bridge** (at 16km, the furthest from town) gives the impression that you are indeed perched on the edge of a vast continent.

Eleven kilometres east of Kalbarri, a corrugated road turns north for 25km to the **gorge** along the Murchison River, where at a junction you can go a few kilometres further north to **the Loop**, or south to **Z Bend**. It's possible to walk round the Loop (a horseshoe bend in the Murchison River) in rather less than half the six hours suggested by the notice board, but this may be prolonged by the abundance of swimming opportunities, birdlife and the odd, mean-looking feral pig; the walk is best undertaken early in the morning. Z Bend is the most dramatic lookout over the Murchison River far below, accessible down a steep track. Kalbarri Coach Tours (see details on overleaf) does canoe trips a few kilometres downstream from here, and Kalbarri Safari Tours (T 08/9937 1011) offers a day-trek through the Murchison canyons for $35. You can also **abseil** down and climb up Z Bend's cliff; enquire at *Kalbarri Backpackers* – no experience is necessary. Back on the Ajana Road, heading inland for 30km from the Loop turn-off, **Hawks Head** and **Ross Graham Lookout**, both a few kilometres off the road, are less impressive but worth stopping for on the way out of Kalbarri if you're driving.

It is possible to **walk** from Z Bend to the Loop over a couple of days and from Ross Graham Lookout to the Loop in four days, but both are demanding walks and you should speak to the **park ranger** (T 08/9937 1140) first.

Shark Bay

Shark Bay is the name given to the two prongs of land and their corresponding lagoons which comprise Australia's westernmost point, forming a roughly W-shaped coastline. **Denham**, the only settlement, is on the west side of the Peron Peninsula, while at **Monkey Mia Dolphin Resort**, on the sheltered east side of the peninsula, dolphins have been coming in almost daily to meet people for the past thirty years. The shallow, aquamarine waters of Shark Bay have earned it a World Heritage listing as a remarkable **ecological habitat**, a fact that tends to be overshadowed by the visits of the dolphins. It's worth noting that dolphins also "interact", albeit less reliably, at Rockingham and Bunbury south of Perth (see p.712).

To **get there** from Perth, take the Greyhound Pioneer bus, which runs all the way to Monkey Mia twice daily on Monday, Thursday and Saturday (12hr): if you plan to visit, make sure your bus pass includes this excursion. Otherwise Western Airlines flies three times a week and Skywest four times. Shark Bay Taxi Service (T 08/9948 1331) connects with interstate buses at the notoriously hot *Overlander Roadhouse*, which marks the turning off the highway to Shark Bay, charging $25 to Denham and $30 to Monkey Mia.

The roads to Monkey Mia and Steep Point

It's 150km to Monkey Mia from the *Overlander Roadhouse*, a drive that is much like the rest of the coastline in this area – a rather dull one through dense mulga scrub punctuated with some unusual sights along the way. **Hamelin Pool**, 5km off the Denham road, is home to a uniquely accessible colony of **stromatolites**, mats of sediment-trapping algae which are some of the earth's earliest life forms, dating back over three billion years. The examples in Hamelin Pool, flourishing because no potential predator can handle the pool's hypersaline water, are about three thousand years old and look rather like lumps of blackened concrete. The **Old Telegraph Station** (daily 8.30am–5.30pm; $5.50), 2km from the pool, has a display, video and a pet "stromie" in a tank –

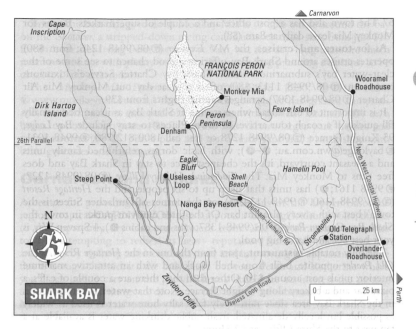

altogether more interesting than the actual colony. There are also some old telecommunications relics and an interesting gift shop and café with a small **camping ground** (℡08/9942 5905; ❶).

Fourteen kilometres further along the Denham road, a turn-off leads to the salt and gypsum mine at Useless Loop, with another branch road, accessible by 4WDs only, leading to **Steep Point** ($20 entry fee; camping allowed), Australia's most westerly mainland extremity. **Dirk Hartog Island**, off the north end of Steep Point, is where the first European is known to have set foot on what is now Australian soil, 150 years before Captain Cook. The Dutch mariner Hartog left a pewter plate inscribed "Anno 1616" on the island.

Continuing towards Denham, you'll pass *Nanga Bay Resort* (℡08/9948 3992, ℻9948 3996, ✉nangabay@wn.com.au; ❶–❺), where there are accommodation units, cabins and dorms; it's a popular fishing spot but otherwise uninspiring. Across the isthmus is **Shell Beach**, composed of millions of tiny shells several metres deep. Where they've consolidated they're cut into blocks for local buildings. Twenty kilometres before Denham, **Eagle Bluff** is an impressive clifftop lookout where dugongs, dolphins and manta rays can be spotted in the clear waters of Freycinet Reach below.

Denham

A small prawning port and holiday resort, **DENHAM** thrives in the lee of Monkey Mia's indefatigable popularity. Between here and Monkey Mia (25km away), **François Peron National Park** (CALM fee; see box on p.719) is fully accessible only in a 4WD vehicle. The CALM office (℡08/9948 1208) on Knight Terrace has more information about the park and other natural features in the Shark Bay area.

The **tourist office** (daily 8am–6pm; ℡08/9948 1253, ✉bayjet@wn.com.au) is on the town's main road at 71 Knight Terrace, and there's another one at no.

known. As for the **hostels**, the *Backpackers Paradise*, near the end of Robinson Street (℡ 08/9941 2966, ℻ 9941 3662; ❶), is the best choice, with a huge kitchen, TV room, ping pong and a garden with pool. There are no fewer than seven **caravan parks** within 5km of town: the *Carnarvon Tourist Centre* (℡ 08/9941 1438; on-site vans ❸), 500m up Robinson Street from the post office, is the most central.

Snacks and counter **lunches** can be had at the *Port* and *Carnarvon* hotels (trouble-free nights switch between one and the other) or at *JR's Lunch Bar*, all on Robinson Street. The *Harbourview Café*, near the Small Boat Harbour south of town, has good but pricey seafood. The best bet in town is the *Tropicana Restaurant and Cocktail Bar* at the *Carnarvon Tavern*, which has excellent-value buffets from $13, or *Tropical Bird Park*, 55 Angelo St (book on ℡ 08/9941 2471), where there are barbecues on Friday and Saturday nights for $8.

Inland to Mount Augustus

East of Carnarvon, a dirt road follows the Gascoyne River inland, past the swimming hole of **Rocky Pool**, to **GASCOYNE JUNCTION**, a moribund, one-pub settlement from the droving days, where the outlaw Ned Kelly (see p.1031) was reputed to have once hidden out. The *Junction Hotel* (℡ & ℻ 08/9943 0504; ❺) is a century-old relic with a small general store and fuel. North, a road leads past the escarpment of the **Kennedy Ranges National Park** which is accessible to regular cars. This is a slightly longer route to **Mount Augustus National Park** (also known as Burringurrah National Park) than continuing to the main access road another 215km away, but is well worth the detour.

Mount Augustus, the world's largest monadnock (a residual hill), is trumpeted as being bigger and older than Uluru (Ayers Rock) in the Northern Territory. While it hardly matches Uluru's elemental majesty, the drive there gives you a good feel for the Outback's dusty isolation and expanse – assuming that's something you've yet to experience. Camping and basic **accommodation** is provided at *Cobra Station Homestead* (℡ 08/9943 0565, ℻ 9943 0992; fuel, shop, closed Sat; cabins ❹), 40km from the hill, or at the *Mount Augustus Outback Resort* (℡ 08/9943 0527, ℻ 9943 3527; fuel, shop; ❹), right at the base, from where a day's hike to the summit can be undertaken. Mount Augustus is 450km from Carnarvon and 350km from Meekatharra on the inland highway. Whichever way you come, it's a long, hot drive on dirt roads, so be sure you and your vehicle are prepared for the trip. West Coast Safaris (see box on p.750) runs four-day tours from Exmouth to this region on demand.

The North West Cape

Six kilometres after the *Minilya Roadhouse* (dorms ❶), whose new owners are working hard to change its perception as the one-time "roadhouse from Hell", a turning splits off to the **North West Cape**. This hot and arid spike of land is notable for the 250-kilometre **Ningaloo Reef** which fringes its western edge, never more than 7km offshore, and is, in places, accessible right off the beach. **Exmouth** is the only settlement on the cape, but without your own transport the resort of **Coral Bay** is not only more convenient and more pleasant, but the easiest place from which to view the reef.

Buses leave from Carnarvon (Mon, Thurs & Sat morning), stopping at Coral Bay on the way to Exmouth before returning to Carnarvon each afternoon. If you're heading further north after an excursion to the cape, you might as well go all the way back to Carnarvon and catch the bus you'd otherwise wait for at *Minilya* – it's certainly more comfortable that way. Ansett flies between Perth and Exmouth (Sun–Fri; 6hr).

Coral Bay

CORAL BAY is a tiny beach resort 12km off the Exmouth road and, school holidays excepted, is a lovely, quiet spot with a tropical-island feel to it. At present the resort is little more than three caravan park/motels, a mini shopping centre and a shop. Lack of fresh **water** has held back large-scale development of the resort. The water comes from a hot and salty bore, making it suitable for cooking and washing but not for drinking; make sure you drink from freshwater taps.

Two glass-bottomed boats operate one-hour **cruises** over the reef in Coral Bay (daily, times depend on the tides): the Sub-Sea Explorer (☏08/9942 5955; $20) is the better of the two and for another $5 you also get an hour's snorkelling off the boat and can keep the gear for the rest of the day. What you'll see is an amazing variety of soft and hard coral that's slowly recovering from cyclone damage in 1996. Sub-Sea also organizes scenic flights.

The *Bayview Coral Bay* **motel** (☏08/9942 5932; ❼) forms a large resort that also offers camping, on-site vans (❹) and various configurations of chalets and cabins (❸), as well as backpackers' accommodation (❶), a small shop and a restaurant. The *Ningaloo Reef Resort* (☏08/9942 5934, ✉whaleshark@bigpond.com; ❻), offers similar options and prices for accommodation and camping, with a bleak backpackers' place (❶), plus a **bar**, restaurant/takeaway and a grassed pool area with a great view over the small bay.

Sex and food on the reef

Sex on the reef is a spectacular yet strangely impersonal affair: around the time of full moon in March or April, the **corals** off Exmouth all spawn simultaneously, releasing huge clouds of sperm and eggs, which are fertilized as they mingle in the waters above the reef. The perpetuation of life on this scale makes it an incredible event to witness – all the better at night because, lit by divers' flashlights instead of filtered sunlight, the **polyps** appear in their true, vivid colours. As a side-effect, the spawning creates a largesse of food that attracts marine animals, notably forty-ton filter-feeding **whale sharks**, the world's largest fish, which migrate annually to the North West Cape region between March and May.

Another phenomenon is triggered by the spawning, as huge shoals of **bait fish** move into the area in search of easy pickings. Similarly motivated groups of whales and sharks herd these shoals into shallow water, trapping them in dense black bands against the shore and then charging in, mouths agape. The waters are so shallow that the larger predators are often in danger of being beached, and have to turn on their sides, bodies half out of the water, to feed.

Dive boats from Exmouth and Coral Bay sometimes run out to witness the spawning, and there are regular (expensive) excursions while the whale sharks are around (see the "Tours and cruises from Exmouth" box, overleaf). Witnessing the coastal feeding frenzy is pretty hit-and-miss – it was first observed as recently as 1992 – and you'll have to ask around to find out the latest. There's no need to get wet, however, as the best vantage points are the clifftops overlooking the action north of Carnarvon (see p.747). Ask at the tourist office there to see the video of the 1992 event.

Exmouth

On the Exmouth road, north of Coral Bay, you pass the part-sealed Bullara–Giralia road to the highway, which cuts 150km out of the journey between Exmouth and the north. A worthwhile overnight stopover along this road is *Giralia Station* (℡08/9942 5937, ✉giralia@aol.com) a working sheep station which offers **caravans** and **camping** (❶), backpacker **rooms** (❷), or boutique private rooms with en-suite bath (❼). Continuing towards Exmouth, two roads lead up onto the Cape Range: the Charles Knife Road climbs precipitously to the top of the range, 311m above sea level. From here it's possible to walk to the head of Shothole Canyon (allow 2hr), which is also accessible off the Exmouth road though this option makes a far less dramatic introduction to the range.

EXMOUTH was built in 1967 to serve the American Naval VLF (very low frequency) Communications Station and has since become a tourist base for visits to the Cape Range National Park and Ningaloo Marine Park (see opposite). The cloud-free atmosphere – so suited to VLF transmissions – and the prolific marine wildlife (including whale sharks in autumn and giant turtles in summer) make the town a popular winter holiday-makers' resort which is set to boom as the wonders of the Ningaloo reef become more widely known. The town's so-called Sunrise Beach is now the site of a marina. To see the reef you need to head up to **Bundegi Beach**, 14km north of Exmouth, opposite the antennae of the naval station.

Buses stop at the shopping centre on Thew Street, where the excellent **tourist office** (Mon–Fri 8.30am–5pm, Sat & Sun 9am–4pm; ℡08/9949 1176, ℻9949 1141, ✉exmouth-tour@nwc.net.au) is located. The **post office** is nearby on Maidstone Crescent, and there's a vast **book exchange** in the secondhand shed opposite the *Exmouth Cape Tourist Village* on Murat Road, 1km south of the town centre. ExCape Hire, on the same road (℡08/9949 1334), rents out everything from light 4WDs and bicycles to beach umbrellas.

Accommodation is available from *Exmouth Base Lodge* (℡08/9949 1474 or free call 1800 241 474, ℻9949 1440, ✉baselodge@nwc.net.au; dorms ❶), the converted US airforce base with a gym, tennis courts, huge swimming pool and all the kinds of facilities dicarded by the US military that you can think of; free pick-ups from the coach stop and a shuttle service between the base and

---

Tours and cruises from Exmouth

Ningaloo Safari Tours (℡08/9949 1550) offer full-day "over the range" tours for $140, or a shorter "round the range" half-day tour for $70. The full-day tour is highly recommended, a 240-kilometre round trip showing you the best of the cape; West Coast Tours also do day-trips to Coral Bay as well as four-day tours to Mount Augustus and the Karijini (Hamersley Range) National Park.

The Ningaloo Coral Explorer (℡08/9949 2424) offers reef-viewing cruises off Bundegi Beach ($15), and the Exmouth Dive Centre (℡08/9949 1201) on Payne Street takes care of dive charters and equipment rental: day-runs out to the Muiron Islands cost around $120 with gear loan, snorkelling half that price. The Village Dive Shop (℡08/9949 1101) at the Exmouth Cape Tourist Village offers broadly the same for a few dollars less. Open-water scuba courses cost around $300, and dives to watch the coral spawning (see box, overleaf) are sometimes available. Exmouth Air Charter (℡08/9949 2492) will take you on scenic flights around the cape for around $100. The tourist office (see above) has an extensive list of other tours along the coast including snorkelling and canoe expeditions.

the town centre are offered. The *Potshot Hotel Resort* (☎08/9949 1200, ℱ9949 1486; ⑤) is the town's upmarket complex with restaurants, a pool and sporting facilities, where you can stay in motel rooms or units. *Excape Backpackers* on Payne St (☎08/9949 1201, ℱ9949 1680; ❶) has four-bed dorms and a swimming pool. The tourist office has a complete accommodation guide and booking service.

When it comes to **eating** there's nothing much to get excited about: *Whalers Café* near the shopping centre has appeal, with the usual takeaways, a baker and two **supermarkets** just over the road. The *Rock Café*, behind the Ampol service station, is worth a try, Mon–Fri 12.30-9.30pm. The *Potshot Hotel Resort* accommodates the town's one **pub**.

Cape Range and Ningaloo

The parks are adjacent land- and sea-conservation areas on the western edge of the North West Cape: to explore them, you really need a vehicle, or you could take one of various tours (see box, opposite). The proximity of the continental shelf to the shore gives the **Ningaloo Marine Park** a stunning variety of marine life: over 500 species of fish and 220 species of coral have been recorded here. **Cape Range National Park** (CALM fee; see box on p.719) is essentially a coastal drive past several bays, lagoons and campsites. For snorkelling, the reef comes closest at the south point of Turquoise Bay where the wind and current tend to drift you north across the bay.

The **Milyering Visitors Centre** (daily 10am–4pm), 52km from Exmouth, is a modern, solar-powered complex with videos and displays on the local ecology, and enthusiastic, helpful staff. Another 30km past various bays and campsites brings you to Cape Range's most accessible highlight, **Yardie Creek**, a steep-walled canyon just a kilometre from the ocean. This is as far south as 2WDs can get in the park but the walk up along the gorge's cliffs is well worth the effort. You can take a one-hour cruise (April–Oct; $22) up the short gorge but there's not much point.

To Dampier and Karratha

Back on the North West Coastal Highway, it's over 500km from Carnarvon to the industrial twin towns of Dampier and Karratha, with nothing but the occasional roadhouse along the way. At *Nanutarra Roadhouse* a road heads east to **Tom Price** and the Pilbara's highlands, and further on a road leads north 80km to the cyclone-battered **ONSLOW** (camping and motel, ⑤), an old coastal settlement bypassed by the highway and most travellers. Between Onslow and Dampier another turn-off leads to Robe River Iron's mine at Pannawonica, a closed town with no facilities for tourists. However, suitable vehicles can take a track starting 20km west of the town, which crosses the Robe River on the way to the Millstream–Chichester National Park (see p.754), a distance of 127km.

The two young towns of **DAMPIER** and **KARRATHA** are a major industrial conurbation and the Northwest's largest population centre. Dampier is the port for Hamersley Iron's mines at Tom Price, Paraburdoo and Marandoo, linked by a 350-kilometre railway. Karratha was established in 1968 when Dampier's boulder-strewn environs were deemed unsuitable for further expansion, growing dramatically when the **North-West Shelf Natural Gas Project** got underway in the early 1980s. The project collects gas from an offshore platform 135km northwest of Dampier, from where it's piped 1500km to Perth or liquefied for export to Japan.

While being well equipped for shopping, vehicle repairs and other services, the two towns hold little of interest to the traveller apart from tours of the industrial installations or as a launchpad for a mission into Karijini (see p.759). For those keen and determined enough, exploration of the prolific **Aboriginal engraving** on the **Burrup Peninsula** (enquire at CALM, see below). Snappy Gum Safaris (☎08/9185 1278) organizes **day-tours** from Karratha/Dampier to the Roebourne, Cossack and Point Samson area, and further afield to Millstream–Chichester National Park (see p.754). There is a host of quality **accommodation** in Karratha but most is pitched at business travellers. The *Mercure Inn* (☎08/9185 1155, ℱ9185 4325; ❼), on Searipple Road has four-star accommodation while the *Karratha Lodge* (☎08/9144 4600; ❹) has budget units. *Karratha Backpackers* (☎08/9144 4904 or 9144 4600; ❶) is at 110 Welland Way – take the second turning right after the Shell service station. For **eating**, *Jasmine Chinese Restaurant* (☎08/9185 2725) on Balmoral Road also has a passable Thai menu and does takeaway. **Internet** facilities are at the town library and *Adrienne's Cafe* in Karratha City Shopping Centre. The Northwest's regional **CALM** office is based in the SGIO Building, Welcome Road, Karratha (☎08/9186 8288), and is a good place to pick up information and maps on all the national parks of northern WA.

In Dampier, the *Mercure Inn* (☎08/9183 1222; ❻) and Peninsula Palms Resort (☎08/9183 1888; ❻) provide an alternative to Karratha's motels.

Roebourne and around

ROEBOURNE, established in 1864 (and once the capital of the Northwest), is the oldest existing settlement between Port Gregory and Darwin. The renovated **Old Gaol** is perhaps the most significant survivor in the small town, nowadays housing the **tourist office** (Mon–Fri 9am–5pm, Sat 9am–4pm; ☎08/9182 1060) and **museum**. In 1982, the Old Gaol was the scene of the first of a spate of Aboriginal "deaths in custody" that tarnished Australia's human rights record throughout the 1980s and early 1990s. Although similarly suspicious deaths had occurred prior to this, these were the first such incidents to garner worldwide publicity and condemnation.

Other nineteenth-century institutional buildings are dotted around the town, with the *Victoria Hotel* (☎08/9182 1001; ❹), on the main street with a **diner**, open from 8am to 8pm and next door there's *Mount Welcome Motel* (☎08/9182 1282, ℱ9182 1046; ❹), and a **caravan park** (☎08/9182 1063; on-site vans ❸) on De Grey Street, at the town's east end but with better options in Karratha there is little reason to stay here.

Cossack and Point Samson

COSSACK, once simply known as "the Landing", was the small seaport which begat the town of Roebourne, and it's well worth a look. All early settlers to the Northwest came through Cossack: pastoralists, pearlers and prospectors heading for the goldfields of the East Pilbara. The original tin and timber buildings used to be chained to the ground so they could weather the occasional cyclones. At the end of the nineteenth century the inlet by the quay began silting up and the harbour was moved to nearby Point Samson until Port Hedland became pre-eminent, and by the 1950s Cossack was all but abandoned, its tram lines to Roebourne long since uprooted for scrap.

This historic "ghost port" has been excellently restored in a matter of only a few years. The **courthouse**, with its museum of the settlement (donation), is the most impressive building, both inside and out, while the **post and telegraph**

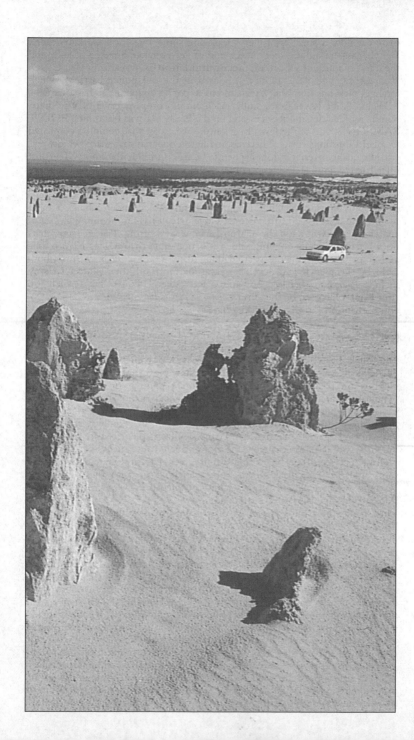

office is now a small art gallery displaying some fine local work. **Settler's Beach**, past the old cemetery at the end of Perseverance Street, is a sandy and sheltered swimming spot. Basic **accommodation** is available at the *Cossack Backpackers* (℡ 08/9182 1190; **①**), housed in the old police barracks, which arranges pick-ups from the Wickham bus stop. The building also has a **café**.

Beyond Robe River Iron's oddly anachronistic company town of **Wickham** (handy for facilities and services, and on the Perth–Darwin bus route), **POINT SAMSON** is one of the few places on the WA coast that could be compared to a British fishing village. The coastline hereabouts has that sharp, windswept, Atlantic quality, even if it does happen to be 320km inside the tropics. The port once had the ignoble distinction of receiving and shipping out the blue asbestos mined at Wittenoom, in the Hamersley Ranges. This may explain the inordinate abundance of car parks for such a tiny settlement, with the potentially cancer-causing dust in the tailings being expediently sealed under lashings of bitumen. Close to town is **Honeymoon Cove**, which has fine swimming.

Gastronomes will relish the **seafood** with a view at the *Trawlers Tavern* first-floor restaurant (daily 6–8pm), which is better value than *Moby's Kitchen* fish-and-chips takeaway on the ground floor (daily 11am–2pm & 5–9pm), both right by the pier. If you develop a taste for the food, then **places to stay** include *Point Samson Lodge*, 56 Samson Rd (℡ 08/9187 1052; **⑥**), which also runs **boat charters**, or the small *Solveig Caravan Park* (℡ 08/9187 1414; **③**), also on Samson Road, next to the *Trawlers Tavern*.

Millstream–Chichester National Park

Not much more than a scenic drive and an oasis of palms and pools along the Fortescue River, the **Millstream–Chichester National Park** (CALM fee; see box on p.719) is worth a visit if you're coming or going from the Hamersley Ranges – note, however, that this entails a three-hundred-kilometre stretch where no fuel's available. Two routes lead into the park from the north: the private road alongside the Dampier–Tom Price railway can be used with an easily gained **permit** from Hamersley Iron's security gate in Dampier (℡ 08/9143 5364). Alternatively, the conventional route breaks off the coastal highway between Roebourne and Whim Creek, passing Pyramid Homestead soon after. Looking back north from the climb up into the **Chichester Ranges** you'll see why the homestead is so named; the view across this ancient Pilbara landscape is stirring and timeless.

Just inside the park, **Python Pool** is a pea-green waterhole backed with black and orange cliffs, and cut by the shriek of birds – worth a photo if not a dip. From this point it's a sixty-kilometre run to **MILLSTREAM**, 150km from Roebourne and 183km from Wittenoom, where an old homestead has been converted into an unusually good **visitors centre** (daily 8am–5pm; ℡ 08/9184 5144). A section describes the rustic bliss of the Yinjibarndi Aborigines of Ngarrari (Millstream), but omits to mention that they were cleared out by pastoralists and today live in the Roebourne area. **Chunderwarriner Pool**, a short walk from the homestead, is a lily-dappled pool surrounded by palm trees. The date palms, introduced by Afghan cameleers, have overrun the indigenous Millstream palm, but this does not detract from the unexpectedly luxuriant scene. Black flying foxes hang from the palms' fronds, and Millstream is also a haven for dragonflies and damselflies: 22 species have been recorded here. Walking trails up to 7km long follow the palm- and paperbark-lined Fortescue River to **Crossing** and **Deep Reach pools**, where you can **camp**.

Port Hedland and on to Broome

You'll find an array of heavy industrial grot at **PORT HEDLAND**. Labelling itself rather clumsily "The Port of Big Ships", it's an iron and salt port of such unrefined ugliness that it's somehow oddly captivating. The old town centre is set on an island surrounded by mangroves and sludge, while South Hedland, on the coastal highway, has only a shopping centre and cheap fuel to distract the passing traveller. If you're travelling by bus north along the coast to Broome (only 600km away) you should get off at Port Hedland if you want to get to Wittenoom's gorges.

The tourist office (see below) runs a ninety-minute town tour on Mondays, Wednesdays, and Fridays at 1.30pm ($11) but one of the most popular diversions is the tour (Mon–Fri 9.30am; $11) of the **BHP loading facility** (also ninety-minute) where ships load up with 250,000 tonnes of iron at a time. Whale- and turtle-watching tours are organized in the wet season (roughly Nov to March) by the tourist office, as well as fishing and diving charters and

The strike that never ended

There can be little doubt that Australia's once-legendary pastoral wealth was accrued at the expense of the Aboriginal people, on whose land and cheap labour it depended. Even John Forrest, WA's turn-of-the-twentieth-century premier, pastoralist and former explorer, conceded that "many of us could not be in the position we are today without native labour on our stations".

By the 1940s Australia was producing a sixth of the world's mutton and a quarter of its wool. In the Northwest, two million sheep grazed vast tracts of meagre land, a marginal enterprise made economical by the employment of black stockmen paid barely $2 a week. The archaic **Native Administration Act** protected the interests of rural industry by hampering mobility and sanctioning low or nonexistent pay for black workers.

Around this time **Don McLeod**, a white prospector still active in Aboriginal rights campaigning today, encouraged **Clancy McKenna** and **Dooley Binbin** to defy their degrading conditions and, after several years of painstaking preparation, eight hundred black workers simultaneously walked off the stations in the Port Hedland/Nullagine region on May 1, 1946. Police were instructed to harass the two camps established near Port Hedland and east of Marble Bar, and arrested McKenna and Binbin for communist subversion. Postwar food coupons were withheld, so the strikers returned to traditional ways of feeding and trading among themselves. Port Hedland was at this time a small town with an "official" (white) population of just 150 and a "mob" of 400 strikers down the road. Jittery police arrested a visiting mediator, Padre Hodge, for being "within five miles of a congregation of natives", adding further support to the strike, coverage of which was largely censored from the national press.

In 1949 things came to a head, and a **station-to-station march** was organized calling all remaining workers to join the strike. Arrest for such defiance was certain, and the strikers cheerfully offered to fill up the jail at Marble Bar and others throughout the Northwest. Only when the Seamen's Union banned the handling of "slave station" wool did the government hastily concede to McLeod's proposals – though they swiftly reneged on the deal. All through the 1950s McLeod employed and assisted the strikers in mining ventures around Marble Bar until the big mining companies began taking an interest in the Pilbara's mineral wealth and pushed them off their claims. The strikers never returned to the stations, demonstrating black assertion long before the 1960s civil rights campaigning in the USA with which the movement is associated in the popular imagination.

that offer discounts if booked though the tourist information centre, and two **caravan parks** (on-site vans ❹), as well as a busy shopping centre.

Marble Bar and Rudall River National Park

From Newman a dirt road leads north for 300km through the scenic East Pilbara to **NULLAGINE** and **MARBLE BAR**, the latter notorious for being Australia's hottest town, in 1923–24 clocking up 160 days over 38°C. This is the sole reason many visitors come to "the Bar", misnamed after a colourful bar of jasper by the Coolingan River 5km south of town. For an overnight stay, there's a **caravan park**, a **motel** (☎08/9176 1166; ❺) and the town's famed, windowless *Ironclad Hotel* (☎08/9176 1066; ❹) – a good place to get some drinking done or, if you're a woman, be stared at.

Rudall River National Park, 300km east of Newman, is an undeveloped national park, designated more for reasons of conservation than recreation, and also the site of some ultra-remote Aboriginal outstations. Accessible only to self-sufficient 4WDs from Newman, Telfer to the north, or off the Canning Stock Route, the park's protective role stands to be severely tested following the discovery of substantial **uranium** deposits just inside the park's boundaries – part of BHP's systematic combing of the WA deserts for the mineral wealth thought to exist there.

Wittenoom and the Karijini (Hamersley Range) National Park

The **Karijini (Hamersley Range) National Park** (CALM fee; see box on p.719) remains one of WA's undiscovered pearls, offering dramatic, time-worn scenery equal to any in Australia. Although it is hampered by its off-highway location and hesitant promotion, due to the controversy surrounding the future of Wittenoom (the park's most convenient base), its main attractions are the **gorges** cut deep into the Pilbara's north-facing escarpment and the singular lack of tourist trappings.

All the points of interest can be briefly visited on a long day's drive or tour, but Wittenoom's bargain accommodation (which is all that's left these days) and pervasive charm make a few days' exploration and relaxation much more rewarding. All the roads in the park are unsealed but usually in good condition; indeed, barring thunderstorms, the park remains accessible throughout the year.

Wittenoom

At each end of **WITTENOOM**, warning signs proclaim the possible health hazard incurred by entering the town as a result of the asbestos mining carried out here from 1937 to 1966, by – among others – the young Rolf Harris. It is estimated that one in ten ex-miners and former inhabitants have died of diseases associated with inhaling asbestos dust.

In its natural state **blue asbestos** is a completely harmless and unusual fibrous mineral, readily found in the Yampire and Upper Wittenoom gorges; it's only the **dust** produced during milling that can be lethal. Unfortunately, tailings from the mine were once used to grade the town's streets, leaving all those resident at the time susceptible to disease and with grounds for compensation. These days, resurfacing has long been completed and, unless you're kicking about in the tailings, the air contains no more harmful particles of asbestos than most urban centres. The emotional overreaction to the "Town of Death" is neatly summed up in the bumper sticker available at the Gem Shop that states "I've been to Wittenoom and lived".

Perhaps because of its tragic history, and certainly due to the intransigence of its remaining 25 inhabitants, the town, which the government wanted razed long ago, possesses an intangible ambience like few other places in WA. In the 1950s it was the biggest settlement in the Northwest but today the empty lots speak of a ghost town not prepared to die. In late 1994 the WA government stepped up the pace by threatening to cut off power and water in late 1996. At the last minute the courts won a reprieve but with Wittenoom missing from most maps (and public telephone boxes being located outside the town limits) its future remains a fight. These extreme tactics have led to speculation that health concerns (or more precisely, fear of subsequent litigation) may not be the only issue at stake. With Wittenoom gone, the way would be clear for the construction of a new resort in the south of the national park or the exploitation of rich iron-ore reserves on Wittenoom's doorstep. Recently some tourist offices have been misinforming visitors, claiming that the town no longer exists or the access road requires 4WD – none of this is true.

Buses stop at the *Munjina/Auski Roadhouse* (T 08/9176 6988; ❼) on the Great Northern Highway, 42km from town. If you call in advance, Dave's Gorge Tours (T 08/9189 7026) will pick you up for $10. As far as services in town go, there's a **post office** at the Gem Shop on Sixth Avenue which also dispenses **tourist information** (daily 8am–6pm; T 08/9189 7096), including detailed **maps** of the national park.

There's plenty of choice for **accommodation** in Wittenoom, none of it fancy but all cheap. *Wittenoom Holiday Homes* (T 08/9189 7096; ❸; ask at the Gem Shop on Sixth Ave) offers complete three-bedroom houses for rent. The *Bungarra Bivouac*, on Fifth Avenue (T 08/9189 7026; ❶), with its distinctive rainbow tree, has seen better days but at $8 is the cheapest backpackers' in WA. The *Wittenoom Guest House*, or "the Convent", on Gregory Street (T 08/9189 7060; ❷), is a lovely and well-kept old building with a screened verandah and mild air-conditioning. The town's café will reopen once the population rises above 30.

Exploring the gorges

The many gorges in **KARIJINI NATIONAL PARK** ($9 per vehicle) offer opportunities for some spectacular views, adventurous walks and, at times, exposed or slippery climbs. Deaths and several accidents have occurred but **rangers** are rarely seen, their headquarters (T 08/9189 8157) being, for some absurd reason, tucked away in the corner of the park on the new road to Newman. Take heed of the "Gorge Risk" warnings and take advantage of tours (or their guides' advice). If you're driving through the park, note that distances can be deceptive: a full tour of all the gorges can involve over 240km.

Just south of Wittenoom itself is **Wittenoom Gorge**, not actually in the park but with a number of pools handy for a cooling dip. At the end of the sealed road which leads up the gorge is the **Settlement**, 11km from town. On the west side of the gorge are the **mine** and the mill, surrounded by the dreaded and dangerous **tailings**. From the Settlement, it's possible to walk up to the dramatic entrance to **Red Gorge** (2hr) and walk and swim (including some long stretches) for another hour up to **Junction Pool** below Oxer's Lookout. From this apparent dead end, the meeting branches of the "Miracle Mile" (see overleaf) tempt the truly intrepid, but unless you've already been initiated, this shouldn't be tackled without a guide. All in all, the above itinerary is a hard day's adventuring.

East of town, 24km towards the *Munjina/Auski Roadhouse*, a turning leads south into the wooded Yampire Gorge and on to the park entry station and stopgap **visitors centre**. Here a right turn continues to the main "Four Gorges" area, and a little further on a left turn leads 10km to **Dales Gorge** (with camping), in which the idyllic Fortescue Falls, Fern Pool and Circular Pool are found. All can be joined up in a superb half-day walk with plenty of water to cool off in along the way.

Kalamina Gorge, on the way to the Four Gorges area, offers good walks along its bed without too much climbing and scrambling, and **Joffre Gorge** is an impressive lookout onto the tiered amphitheatre of Joffre Falls (usually dry) which can be easily reached and crossed along a spinifex-fringed path. There is camping nearby and the road leads on to **Knox Gorge**, which ends in the exhilarating (to say the least) "Knox Slide" featured in Dave's Gorge Tours and a stunning **lookout** down into the pools of Red Gorge.

Back on the main road, a turning north ends at a car park on the spur between **Hancock** and **Weano gorges**. From here, it's a short walk to the exposed **Oxer's Lookout**, surveying a confluence of four gorges that is as impressive as any in WA. Straight ahead is **Red Gorge**, which runs on into Wittenoom Gorge and the Settlement. Also starting from the car park, the "Miracle Mile", with its origins as a 1960s character-building exercise for Perth schoolboys, descends over loose rock into Hancock and returns up Weano Gorge. A thrilling half-day's swimming and climbing, this should only be attempted with someone who knows where the tricky parts are. For the less adventurous, the short walk into Weano Gorge to **Handrail Pool** is recommended. From the Four Gorges the road continues across the roof of the Pilbara to **Mount Bruce**, at 1235m WA's second-highest peak, now climbable along a new six-kilometre track from where you can survey the Marandoo mine, with a sealed road leading to Tom Price. East, a track passes the Rangers Headquarters to Highway 95 and Newman.

With the new roads, it's now quite a detour to visit **Hamersley Gorge**, just outside the northwestern corner of the park, 48km west of Wittenoom and 105km from Tom Price. With its spa-like pool and acutely folded beds of blue-grey and orange rock, it's unlike any of the other gorges and a bit of exploring up- and downstream could easily fill a day here. Just east of the Hamersley Gorge turn-off, the road passes through **Rio Tinto Gorge**, which bears an extraordinary resemblance to a box-canyon film set from 1950s westerns.

Tours of the Pilbara

Dave's Gorge Tours (☎08/9189 7026), in Wittenoom, has become a legend on the backpackers' circuit. All tours cost around $50 a day but "Tour 3" is the one they come and even wait days for, incorporating the "Miracle Mile" and "Knox Slide" – chosen by *FHM* magazine as "one of the hundred things a man must do in his life". If there are enough of you, Dave is also open to many other adventurous tours through the Ranges.

Karijini Day Tours (☎08/9188 1670) is a Tom Price-based company offering a full day's run around all the gorges from $70 (with lunch) and also longer tours.

Newman Eco Tours (☎08/9175 2944) runs 4WD tours to beauty spots around Newman and into Karijini.

Red Rock Abseiling Adventures (☎08/9189 2206) run alternative gorge tours dangling from a rope. No experience is required.

Snappy Gum Safaris (☎08/9185 1278), based in Karratha, runs two- to four-day tours through the Pilbara, including Millstream–Chichester National Park, from $240.

Accommodation

Most of the **hotels** are in the southern part of town, and the **hostels** congregate around Chinatown, with self-contained apartments in between. The tourist office has a comprehensive list of all accommodation in Broome and has a free booking service.

Hotels

Broome Motel, 51 Frederick St (☎08/9192 7775 or free call 1800 683 867, ☏9192 7772). Central location just 5min walk from the airport with self-contained rooms sleeping three. ❻

Eco Beach, Cape Villaret (☎08/9192 4844 or free call 1800 636 414, ☏9192 4845). Situated by an effectively private beach 30km across Roebuck Bay, this network of breezy elevated cabins is an affordable wilderness retreat that you won't want to leave. Bathrooms are shared but with all meals paid for, it'll cost less than most Broome motels. Day-visits from Broome around $60. ❻

Mangrove Hotel, Carnarvon St (☎08/9192 1303 or free call 1800 094 818, ☏9193 5169). Very comfortable and well positioned on a rise overlooking Roebuck Bay. ❼

Mercure Inn–Continental, cnr Weld and Hamersley streets (☎08/9192 1002 or free call 1800 094 822, ☏9192 1715). Plush hotel right on the bay with a good restaurant and pool area. ❽

Palms Resort, Hopton St (☎08/9192 1898 or free call 1800 094 848, ☏9192 2424). Apartments and motel-style rooms in tropical garden setting. Three pools, two restaurants and bars, including the *Beer and Satay Hut*; close to the town beach and Seaview Shopping Centre. ❼

Roebuck Bay Hotel/Motel, Napier Terrace (☎08/9192 1221, ☏08 9192 2390, ✉roey@broome.wa.com.au). Smack bang in the middle of town with a good pool to hang around. Part of the "*Roey*" *Hotel* gives access to bars, restaurants and entertainment. ❻

Tropicana Inn, cnr Saville and Robinson streets (☎08/9192 1204, ☏9192 2583). With restaurant, bar, pool and BBQ, right opposite the Seaview Shopping Centre and close to the town beach. ❼

Hostels and caravan parks

Broome Bird Observatory, Crab Creek Rd (☎08/9193 5600, ☏9192 2063). Secluded nature spot 25km from town on Roebuck Bay with chalets, rooms and camping. Chalets ❺, rooms ❸

Broome's Last Resort, Bagot St (☎08/9193 5000 or free call 1800 801 918, ☏9193 6033, ✉lastresortyha@smartchat.com.au). Deafening rock music as you check in adds up to a sometimes too lively 18–30s feel. Pool, bar, bikes, coin-operated lockers and air-con. Could change under new ownership. Rooms ❸, dorms ❶

Broometime Lodge, 59 Forrest St (☎ & ☏ 08/9193 5067 or free call 1800 804 322). Hostel/motel hybrid with private rooms but a communal atmosphere, suitable for older backpackers able to wash their own dishes and weary of snorers and early morning rucksack rustlers. Big kitchen, small pool, town bus stops at the door. Offers weekly rates. Book ahead. ❹

Cable Beach Backpackers, Lullfitz Drive (☎08/9193 5511 or free call 1800 655 011, ☏9193 5532). A change from the sometimes rowdy central Broome alternatives. Ten minutes from Cable Beach. ❶

Cable Beach Caravan Park, Millington Rd (☎08/9192 2066). Cable Beach's only caravan park, 2km from the beach. Also has a cottage available. ❶–❻

Kimberley Klub, Frederick St, opposite *Broome Motel* (☎08/9192 3233, ☏9192 3530, �🌐www.kimberleyklub.com). Award-winning, purpose-built, "offer-it-all" backpackers' resort about as good as they get. Spacious and breezy layout with volleyball, landscaped pool, email, bikes, coin-op air-con, tours, bar and café. Rooms ❹, dorms ❶

Roebuck Bay Caravan Park, Walcott St (☎08/9192 1366). The best-located caravan park in town, right next to the small town beach and Seaview Shopping Centre. Bike rental available. On-site vans ❸

Roebuck Bay Backpackers, Napier Terrace (☎08/9192 1183, ☏9192 2390, ✉roey@broome.wa.com.au). Some musty rooms (but several with TV) makes this less attractive than others but being part of the rocking *Roebuck Bay Hotel* complex might be a positive. Dorms ❶, doubles ❹

The Town and around

Broome first flourished around the old port area in **Chinatown**, which once accommodated a lively mix of pearl-divers and seamen. This old Asiatic quarter has seen the most concentrated reconstruction of original buildings, with street signs in five languages and payphones topped with jaunty Chinese roofs. Modern boutiques and cafés occupy most of the buildings, but Sun Pictures (see "Nightlife and events" on p.766) on Carnarvon Street, which opened in 1916 (making it as old as Hollywood itself), is one of the oldest "walk-ins" still in use today. During the daytime you can take in the virtually unchanged interior and see photographs showing the segregated seating codes of the old days (tours Mon–Fri 11am & 2pm; $3.30). At the end of the street is the **post office** and the Paspaley Pearls Plaza **shopping centre**. The dilapidated Streeter's Jetty runs into the mangroves off Dampier Terrace; the terrace hosts several **pearl dealers** operating from former warehouses.

A walk down Hamersley Street, past the 1888 courthouse on the corner of Frederick Street, leads to what was the rich end of the old town, where masters and merchants once lived in splendid, airy bungalows such as **Captain Gregory's House**, now a brewery near the junction with Carnarvon Street. Next door, Matso's Store (daily 10am–5pm) displays local artwork and is a cool place for an outdoor lunch.

Next to the old Seaview Shopping Centre (daily 8am–6pm), now without a supermarket, the Customs House houses the local **museum** (May–Nov Mon–Fri 10am–4pm, Sat & Sun 10am–1pm; Dec–April daily 10am–1pm; $3). Naturally focusing on the town's maritime traditions, and with a pleasing "junk shop" appearance, it could easily occupy a couple of hours. Round the back, the old **Pioneer Cemetery** overlooks **Town Beach**, the nearest to the town centre. From the jetty, very low tides reveal the remains of Dutch sea planes bombed by the Japanese in 1942. This is also the best vantage point for observing the "**Staircase to the Moon**", the overrated lunar reflections in the mud flats, which occur for a few nights each month, around the full phase of the moon. Dates and precise times for the "Staircase" can be obtained from the tourist office.

Gantheaume Point and Cable Beach

The outskirts of Broome offer a number of interesting attractions, and a full day could be spent cycling along the following route, which ends at Cable Beach, 6km from town on the ocean side of the peninsula. The town's **bus service** ($2.70, day-passes $8.50) runs daily between the town and Cable Beach, via most of the town's accommodation centres, and finally returns outside the super-swish *Cable Beach Inter-Continental Resort* at 6.15pm. Timetables are available at the tourist office or in the town guide.

Just past the turning for Cable Beach, off Frederick Street, is the old **cemetery** from the pearling years. The Japanese section's enigmatic headstones (refurbished by an anonymous philanthropic countryman) testify to the nine hundred lives lost in the hazardous search for mother-of-pearl. The 1908 cyclone alone cost the lives of over 150 men, five percent of the workforce at that time. The Chinese cemetery next door is less cared for, and the Muslim and Aboriginal graveyards at the back are barely distinguishable.

Continuing down Port Drive for 5km, a right turn onto the nine-kilometre dirt road section leads to **Riddell Beach**. Walk right along the shore, past the outcrops weathered by eons of wind and water, to **Gantheaume Point**, where the dark red-sandstone formations contrast sharply with the pearly-white expanse of Cable Beach stretching north. The old **lighthouse** is now a beacon, but the **pool** built by the former keeper for his disabled wife, Anastasia, remains among the tidal rocks. A cast of some 120-million-year-old **dinosaur footprints** is set in the rocks – the originals are out to sea and only visible at extremely low tides. More dinosaur footprints were found on Aboriginal land north of Cable Beach in 1996, but despite secrecy surrounding their discovery they were bizarrely cut out of the rock and stolen. Casts of the prints can be seen at the *Broomtime Lodge*.

Named after the nineteenth-century telegraph cable which came ashore here, **Cable Beach** extends for an immaculate 22km north of Gantheaume Point. Cars are permitted onto the beach north of the rocks, near the access ramp, but note that several cars a year are caught by up to ten-metre **tides** around Broome's beaches: on Cable Beach's flat sands it can come in very fast. The area north of the rocks is a nudist beach. The *Cable Beach Tea Rooms* overlooking the beach serves some of Broome's best meals, as does the *Diver's Camp Tavern* and bottle shop, on Cable Beach Road. Windsurfers and sailboards are available on the beach during the season.

Broome Crocodile Park and Bird Observatory

Broome is loosely regarded as the very westernmost limit of saltwater **crocodiles**. The **Broome Crocodile Park** (April–Oct Mon–Sat 10am–5pm, Sun 2.30–5pm; Nov–March Sun–Fri 3.30–5pm, closed Sat; guided tours at 3pm; $15), on Cable Beach Road, can show you hundreds of these fascinating beasts at close quarters.

Roebuck Bay, on Broome's eastern flank, is on the flight path for thousands of migratory wading birds – a third of Australia's species have been seen here. The **Broome Bird Observatory** (☏08/9193 5600; free), 25km from town (last 9km is dirt road) welcomes day and overnight visitors (see "Accommodation" on p.763). There are walks through the bushland around the observatory, with tours and courses also offered for those interested in local fauna, feathered or otherwise. **Kimberley Ostrich Farm** (9am–5pm; tours Mon, Wed, Fri & Sun 3pm & 4pm; $5.50; ☏08/9192 1728), 29km out of Broome toward Derby, has ostriches, alpacas and minature horses.

Eating and entertainment

Not surprisingly, the food in Broome is distinctly oriental in flavour. The customary fast-food outlets and a couple of health-food shops are also prominent, while some hotels have their own very reputable restaurants.

Bloom's Café Restaurant (7.30am–late), on Carnarvon Street, is one of the town's best **cafés**, with an airy jarrah interior, great drinks, snacks, meals and vegetarian breakfasts. *Henry's*, has coffee and meals with a view of the corner of Carnarvon and Short streets, while over the road there's the *Shady Lane Cafe*, off Johnny Chi Lane, featuring good lunch choices. Next to the Checkpoint Shell Service Station on Hamersley Street are a couple of **takeaways**: *Noodlefish* does Thai food and their soups are a meal in themselves. A further option, at 12 Napier Terrace, is the *Sheba Lane Garden Restaurant*, specializing in fish dishes. The *Beer & Satay Hut* at the *Palms Resort* (see p.763; entrance on Walcott Street), is a good outdoor alternative to the **pub food** at the *Roebuck Bay Hotel* (see).

For a proper **restaurant** meal, the hard-to-find *Rosita's* (Tues–Sat from 5pm, Sun brunch 8am–2pm; ☏08/9192 7606), tucked away in Jones Place off Dora Street opposite Saville Street, serves Eastern and Western cuisine. For Chinese food, *Chin's*, opposite the Checkpoint Shell Service Station on Hamersley Street, is the least expensive of the good places, though the service and decor aren't up to much. With its verandah, *Murray's*, on Dampier Terrace, is a much better-looking place for Asian and seafood dishes. *Sanga's Thai Food* on Coghlan

Street is good value and also does takeaway. Out at the fancy *Cable Beach Inter-Continental* resort there are no less than five restaurants to tempt you and turn your wallet inside out; the least expensive is *Lord Mac's* which offers ocean views with your burgers, salad and pasta. Closer to town, *Charters*, at the *Mangrove Hotel* on Carnarvon Street is the best of the hotel restaurants and also has views of the ocean.

Nightlife and events

Broome's raging **pub** is the *Roebuck Bay Hotel* on Napier Terrace, with live entertainment, happy hours and garage bands. The least rough of the three bars here is the *Pearlers' Rest*. The *Divers' Camp Tavern* at Cable Beach comes a close second and usually gets the bands after the "*Roey*". Two **nightclubs** are to be found in Chinatown that are open until 2am: the *Nippon Inn* on Dampier Terrace and *Tokyo Joes* round the corner on Napier Terrace, with banks of pool tables. If you prefer **real ale** to tinned lager pay a visit to the Broome Brewery at Matso's Store at the end of Hamersley Street where all sorts of local fermentations await you. But for a uniquely "Broometime" experience, Sun Pictures **walk-in cinema** in Chinatown is a real treat: watch the latest movies while mosquitoes nibble your ankles and the odd light aircraft comes in low across the screen. The *Sunset Bar* at the *Cable Beach Inter-Continental* has pricey **cocktails** but is worth the splurge at dusk.

The tourist office has information on various events, such as the **Broome Fringe Arts Festival**, usually held in early June, a celebration of local artiness and culture. However, the big one is the **Shinju Matsuri**, or Festival of the Pearl, in late August or early September – it lasts over a week and attracts people from all over the country. The town celebrates its ethnic diversity, and the pearl which created it, with the crowning of the Pearl Queen and a beach concert, finishing up with a huge fireworks display. Broome gets packed out for the Shinju, so unless you want to end up camping miles away, book your accommodation in advance. Exact dates for both festivals can be checked with the tourist office.

Listings

Airlines Ansett, Paspaley Pearls Plaza, Chinatown (☎08/9193 6855).

Bicycle rental and repair Broome Bikes, cnr Hamersley and Stewart streets (☎0413 262 363); and Broome Cycle Centre, cnr Hamersley and Frederick streets (☎08/9192 1871).

Bookshop Kimberley Bookshop, 6 Napier Terrace, is the best bookshop between Darwin and Perth; while Magabala Books, 2/28 Saville St, stocks authentic Aboriginal publications, including contemporary and traditional local stories.

Buses Greyhound, Bagot and Broome streets (☎08/9192 1561).

Car rental Besides the big companies, try Broome Car Rentals, who deliver the car to you (☎08/9192 2219, ✉ ptre@bigpond.com), or Woody's, Dampier Terrace (☎08/9192 1791); both do local runabouts and offer some of the cheapest 4WDs in town. Hertz Kimberley Camp Hire, Frederick St (☎08/9193 5354), opposite the

Kimberley Klub, has all you need to rent or buy for an expedition to the Kimberley. Broome Discount Hire Car, McPherson St (☎08/9193 3100) has small cars from $45 per day, while Just Broome (☎08/9193 6636) deliver to your door and start at $29 a day. Ask about one-way rental to Kununurra or Darwin.

Hospital Robinson St (☎08/9192 9222).

Internet access Telecentre, 51 Dampier Terrace, (☎08/9193 7153); and Field Star, Napier Terrace. There are also coin-ops at the aiport, the post office and Paspaley Pearls Plaza.

Medical Centre 30 Barker St (☎08/9192 2022).

Motorbike and scooter rental Roadrunner Motorcycle Hire, 7 Farrell St (☎08/9192 1971).

Police ☎08/9192 1212.

Post office Carnarvon St, WA 6725. Next to Paspaley Pearls Plaza.

Taxi ☎08/9192 1133 or free call 1800 880 330.

Tours Broome Day Tours (free call ☎1800 801

068) organize daily three-hour historic tours, plus trips out to Willie Creek Pearl Farm (see below); Ships of the Desert (☎08/9192 2222) have sunset camel rides along Cable Beach, though Broome Camel Safaris (☎0419 916 101) may be a cheaper option; Broome Aviation (☎08/9192 1369) and King Leopold Air (☎08/9193 7155) offer scenic flights over the region; while Seair Broome (☎08/9192 6208) uses sea-planes. For more unusual jaunts on Harleys, helicopters and hover-crafts, enquire at the tourist office (see p.762). For excursions to the Kimberley, Flak Trak Tours (☎08/9192 1487) have 4WD tours for small groups, including one-day Cape Leveque and four-day West Kimberley/Gibb River Road tours; Over The Top Adventure Tours (☎08/9192 3977, ☎overtop@broome.wt.com.au) offer 1–5-day packages; Australian Adventure Travel (☎08/9248 2355, ⓦwww.safaris.net.au) run four-day West Kimberley tours.

The Dampier Peninsula and Cape Leveque

About 10km outside Broome, just after the turn-off for the Bird Observatory, a road leads north to the Aboriginal Lands of the northern Dampier Peninsula. Continuing down this turn-off you soon come to the **Willie Creek Pearl Farm** but after this you're best off arming yourself with a 4WD campervan, or better still someone else's 4WD, as the 200km **Cape Leveque track** is as rough as they come. If you plan staying at any of the three Aboriginal communities on the Cape, booking in advance is essential.

Willie Creek Pearl Farm and the Western Peninsula

Thirty-five kilometres north from Broome (follow the signs), most of which is along a dirt track and tidal flat, the **Willie Creek Pearl Farm** (9.30am–12.30pm & 1.30–4.30pm: June–Sept daily; Oct–May Mon, Tues, Thurs, Fri & Sun; $25) is housed in a beautiful building on Willie Creek. In the creek, racks of seeded oysters hang for two years at a time, building layers of pearlescent nacre over their implants as they feed from the tidal nutrients. The fact that this process takes half the normal time is what makes the Dampier Peninsula's environs so suitable for pearl cultivation. The mysteries of this fascinating and once highly secretive process are explained by informative **tours** (up to three daily). Bookings are essential and they get stroppy if you just turn up. Broome Day Tours (☎08/9192 1068) offers daily visits to coincide with the guided tours.

Continuing past the Willie Creek turn-off leads to a dead end coastal track with a number of short turn-offs to basic beach campsites (three days maximum stay). Popular with fishermen, they can make for a few tranquil days camping to which you best come fully equipped as there are no facilities whatsoever. The first of these is **Barred Creek**, passing through a sandy section in which most 2WDs get stuck. Take your pick of the cleared spots dotted either side of the creek mouth. A few kilometres up the coast is **Quondong Point** overlooking the low red cliffs and a white rocky beach below. **Price Point**, after another 10km, is often considered the pick of the points. Continue a few hundred metres past the signed turn-off to the point and you'll find a ramp giving easy access to the beach and numerous coves below. Just be sure you know how far the tide is coming up if you spend the night. After Price Point the track continues close to the cliff edge with views to the ocean but in early

1999 was blocked a few kilometres before **Malari** or Coulomb Point as a result of erosion from the preceding Wet. From here it's around 55km back to the Cape Leveque road.

The road to Cape Leveque

By no means a scenic drive and an infamously vehicle-destroying track, the **Cape Leveque** road continues wide and corrugated to the Aboriginal community of **Beagle Bay** (entry $5), 120km from Broome. The highlight here is the **Sacred Heart Church**, built by German missionaries in 1917, a beautiful building with an unusual altar decorated with mother-of-pearl. After Beagle Bay the track gets narrower and sandier and once you've travelled a further 40km you'll reach the turn-off leading, after another 35km, to **Middle Lagoon** (℡08/9192 4002; bookings essential), a lovely white-sand cove with camping, basic shelters (❸) and four-berth cabins (❻). The bay offers sheltered swimming and good snorkelling over the reefs at each point. Up the road another 20km or so is the community of **Lombadina/Djarindjin** (℡08/9192 4936; entry $5), where you'll find dorms (❸), units (❼), fuel and 4WD access to the beach over banks of soft sand (follow the signs). The wide shallow bay before you is again ideal for safe swimming, and with Lombadina's mixed reputation, something you'll likely have to yourself when other places are busy.

A stay at the very popular **Kooljaman** (℡08/9192 4970, ℻9192 4978; beach shelters ❸, cabins ❻, units ❽), where there's fuel, a restaurant and a small kiosk selling basic provisions at the tip of Cape Leveque, is the reason why you've endured the last 220km; as long as the car survived no one leaves here disappointed. Situated right on the "sunrise" beach, the paperbark **cabins** and **beach shelters** (basically shade, a windbreak and a barbie) are the pick of the accommodation – fancier four-berth tent-based accommodation (❽) is up the hill. Come well prepared, however, as Kooljaman is no upmarket wilderness experience.

From Kooljaman you can try fishing, mudcrabbing and bushtucker **tours** (ask a local) with the local Bardi people or follow the very sandy track down to Hunter Creek. You'll find the "sunset" beach on the western side of the point a bit exposed for swimming but usually deserted, and at dusk the low red-sandstone cliffs glow warmly. If you don't fancy driving up to Kooljaman there are tours available from Broome as well as **flights** – an experience in itself. The airstrip is a short walk from all accommodation. Ask at the Broome tourist office for a schedule.

The Kimberley

A highland area between Derby and Kununurra that's about the size of Poland, **The Kimberley** is commonly described as Australia's last frontier. Divided by ranges and seasonally huge rivers, it is a wilderness of marginal cattle stations and small, isolated Aboriginal communities, with a ragged, tide-swept coastline inhabited chiefly by crocodiles. The extreme seasons and harsh terrain make access slow and difficult – for those who live here, light aircraft are a necessity rather than an indulgence.

With the demise of the beef industry (for more on which, see the box on p.643) in a region racked by floods and bushfires, many stations are opening up to adventure tourism, and there is talk of turning the whole area into a vast national park. There is little else here: even the exploitation of minerals known

THE KIMBERLEY

/// Aboriginal Land

TIMOR SEA

Joseph
Bonaparte
Gulf

NORTHERN
TERRITORY

Katherine

Wyndham

Kununurra

Lake Argyle
Dam

Lake
Argyle

Home Valley

Emma Gorge

El Questro

Ellenbrae

Chamberlain

Turkey
Creek
(Warmun)

Ord

Duncan Rd

Buchanan Highway

PURNULULU
NATIONAL PARK
(BUNGLE BUNGLES)

Old
Town

Kalumburu

DRYSDALE RIVER
NATIONAL PARK

Drysdale

Edward

King

Mitchell
Falls

Mitchell

Prince Regent

Manning
Gorge

Mount
Barnett

Adcock
Gorge

Galvans
Gorge

Gibb River

Road

Bell Creek
Gorge

Lennard River

Chamley

Gorge

WINDJANA GORGE
NATIONAL PARK

TUNNEL CREEK
NATIONAL PARK

Mt Wells
983m

Halls
Creek

Tanami Track

GEIKIE GORGE
NATIONAL PARK

Fitzroy
Crossing

Fitzroy

Derby

King
Sound

Cape
Leveque

Lombadina
Mission

Beagle Bay
Mission

Price Point

Broome

Cape
Villaret

Port Hedland

INDIAN OCEAN

N

100 km

0

to exist in the northwest of the region is made barely economical by the climate and isolation, and this alone says a lot about the Kimberley's remoteness. The road between Fitzroy Crossing and Halls Creek was the last section of the circumcontinental Highway 1 to be sealed, in the mid-1980s.

The region, particularly the barely accessible **Drysdale River National Park**, has many examples of the unusual Wandjina-style rock paintings, which depict rows of mouthless beings with owl-like heads, or the slender Bradshaw figures, thought to be much older. **Tours** of the Kimberley operate from Broome, Fitzroy Crossing (see below), Halls Creek (see p.772) and, most conveniently, from Kununurra (see box on p.775), along the **Gibb River Road** and to the popular **Bungle Bungles**. It would take a lifetime to get to know the whole of this immense wilderness, but that in itself is the very essence of the Kimberley's untameable appeal.

Derby to Fitzroy Crossing

Situated 36km north of the coastal highway on a flat spur of land jutting into the mud flats of King Sound, **DERBY** is a mineral exploration base and an administrative centre for local Aboriginal communities. There's precious little reason for tourists to visit the town other than to refuel at the end of a **Gibb River Road** crossing or perhaps take a **scenic flight** over the West Kimberley coastline (from $130; ask at the tourist office). Without your own transport you'll find the spread-out town hard work to navigate.

The **tourist office** (Mon–Fri 8.30am–4.30pm, Sat 8.30–11.30am; ☏08/9191 1426) is on Clarendon Street, where **buses** also arrive. If you're desperate, **places to stay** include the *Spinifex Hotel* (☏08/9191 1233), the town's main **pub** with ultrabasic dorms (❶) and small, budget motel rooms (❹). With your own transport you'll be much more comfortable at the *West Kimberley Lodge* (☏08/9191 1031, ☏9191 1028; ❹), at 17 Sutherland St, a guesthouse with shared facilities; or the *Derby Boab Inn* on Loch Street (☏08/9191 1044, ☏9191 1568; ❹). There's a good **restaurant** at the *Boab*, but for something special (and expensive) try the *Wharf* seafood restaurant, out by the wharf (daily from 6.30pm; closed Jan & Feb), which also does takeaways.

The **Gibb River Road** (see p.776) starts just east of Derby and cuts straight across the Kimberley, rejoining the tarmac near Wyndham 667km further on. If you are heading east and want to see **Windjana Gorge** and **Tunnel Creek**, follow the Gibb River Road for 119km to the Windjana turn-off. From here you rejoin the Great Northern Highway after 123km. This section is no problem in dry weather in a 2WD and is more interesting (and only 30km longer) than following the highway to Fitzroy Crossing, 256km from Derby.

Since the pastoral expansion into the Kimberley in the late nineteenth century, **FITZROY CROSSING** has been a small travellers' rest stop and crucial ford across the still-troublesome Fitzroy River. Today it's little more than a roadhouse and "welfare town" serving the region's Aboriginal communities. In the Dry it's a bleak, dusty place, the river a string of pools, but during a good Wet, when the town is frequently cut off, water laps just under the road bridge and the land is flooded for miles around.

The town itself has nothing of interest; a Friday-night session at the century-old *Crossing Inn* on Skuthorpe Road will give you the most memorable experience of the place. The *Fitzroy River Lodge* (☏08/9191 5141, ☏9191 5142; ❼), on the highway east of the bridge, caters comfortably for passing tours. It has **motel rooms**, bushland lodges (or "canvas accommodation modules") and grassy campsites, as well as a pool, **restaurants** and a bar. *Darlngunaya Backpackers* (℡08/9191 5140; ●) on Russ Road is situated in the old post office, around which the settlement originally grew. If you call up they'll meet your bus, which comes through in the early hours. The *Crossing Inn* (℡08/9191 5080; cabins ●) also has tent sites and the obligatory counter meals, while the neglected *Tarunda Caravan Park*, next to the **supermarket/post office** on Forrest Road, has cheap tent sites and on-site vans (●). The **tourist office** (℡08/9191 5355) is on Flynn Drive, by the roadhouse.

The local CALM office (℡08/9191 5121) organizes the least expensive **tour** of Geikie Gorge National Park for around $20, and also offers other day-tours. There's a five-hour Danggu Heritage Aboriginal cruise (℡08/9191 5355) run by local Aborigines for $75.

The Devonian Reef national parks

During the Devonian Era, 350 million years ago, a large barrier reef grew around the then-submerged Kimberley plateau. The limestone remnants of this reef are today exposed north of Kununurra and in the national parks of **Geikie Gorge**, **Tunnel Creek** and, most spectacularly, **Windjana Gorge**. These three attractions are sometimes erroneously described as the "West Kimberley", but they are just a dramatic and easily accessible fraction of the West Kimberley's many natural spectacles. All three parks are closed and periodically submerged from November to April.

Geikie Gorge National Park

Seventeen kilometres upstream from Fitzroy Crossing, the river has carved out the five-kilometre **Geikie Gorge** through the exposed reef, best seen on the **boat cruises** (April–Nov daily 8am & 3pm; ℡08/9191 5121; $15) lasting one and a half hours. High-water marks on the gorge's walls clearly show how high the river can rise, while below the surface harmless freshwater crocodiles jostle with freshwater-adapted stingrays and sawfish. Walking trails lead along the forested western banks, strategically dotted with picnic sites, barbecues and campsites.

Tunnel Creek and Windjana Gorge national parks

Along the highway, 42km west of Fitzroy Crossing, a well-graded dirt road turns north to follow the Napier Range (as the reef is known here) to **Tunnel Creek National Park** (no camping), 105km from Fitzroy. Here Tunnel Creek has burrowed its way under the range, creating a 750-metre tunnel hung with bats and with who-knows-what in the pools. Although the collapsed roof illuminates the cavern halfway, the wade into progressively deeper and colder water to the other end still takes some nerve – it helps to carry a torch and wear shoes that you don't mind getting soaked.

A hundred years ago the caves were the hideout for a Bunuba Aborigine, Jandamarra (better known as **Pigeon**), and his gang of bushrangers. A police tracker for many years, one day he shot the officer at nearby Lillimoorla police station (now a ruin 2km south of Windjana Gorge) and released all the prisoners. A three-year spree of banditry followed before Pigeon was cornered and killed by fellow trackers in 1897.

The most dramatic remainders of the reef are the towering walls of **Windjana Gorge** (camping allowed), 135km from Fitzroy and 140km from Derby. A walking trail leads through a limestone crevice into a wide gorge splitting the Napier Range, lined with paperbark and Leichhardt trees.

Freshwater crocs share the pools with various birds and can be seen sunning themselves in the afternoons.

Halls Creek

HALLS CREEK, strung out along the highway, has a much livelier appearance than its nearest neighbour, Fitzroy Crossing, 288km to the west. In 1885 WA's first **goldrush** took place in the hills south of town, 17km away, where the mud-brick ruins of the **Old Town** continue to crumble. In less than four years the thousand prospectors succeeded in exhausting the area's potential, before stampeding off to new finds in the Eastern Goldfields.

There's precious little to see in town, but the gold-bearing hills to the southeast offer a few diversions for those with their own transport. **China Wall** is a block-like vein of quartzite looming over a toxic pool, 6km from town, which appears even more impressive from the air. **Caroline Pool**, 15km from town, is a bit muddy for swimming; **Palm Springs** and **Sawtooth Gorge**, a further 30km to the south, are scenically more appealing.

Practicalities

There's an **information centre** (May–Sept daily 8am–5pm; ☎08/9168 6262) off the main road in the middle of town. For **somewhere to stay**, the *Halls Creek Caravan Park* (☎08/9168 6169), Roberta Avenue, has tent sites, grim single cabins (❶) and more spacious on-site vans (❸). The *Shell Roadhouse* (☎08/9168 6060) has twin-share cabins (❹), and the relatively salubrious *Kimberley Hotel* (☎08/9168 6101, ℱ9168 6071), opposite the caravan park, has pokey bunkhouses (❶) and motel units (❺). It's also the only pub and decent **restaurant** in town, although there's a **bakery** on the highway. But for somewhere special head out to *The Lodge* by the Old Town (☎08/9168 8999; ❹), a little oasis overlooking the spinifex-covered ranges, which glow at sunset.

If you fancy flying over the **Bungle Bungles**, call Oasis Air (☎08/9168 6462) or Kingfisher Air (☎08/9168 6162) a day or two in advance. The ninety-minute early-morning flights are the ones to go for, costing around $120. Alternatively, rent a 4WD for between $75 and $125 per day from the *Mobil Roadhouse* (☎08/9168 6164) on the highway. Halls Creek and Bungle Bungle Tours (☎08/9168 6060) offer various **tours**, including a day in the Bungles for around $130.

Outback tracks near Halls Creek

Three long-distance Outback tracks converge near Halls Creek, each giving you a taste of remote Outback dust. The **Tanami Track** is signposted off the highway, 17km west of town, indicating 1040km to Alice Springs. The WA section can be rough and sandy, but after the NT border it's merely corrugated, and it's half the distance of the sealed road. A turning at Carrunya Station leads to **Wolfe Creek Meteorite Crater**, the second biggest in the world, but not worth the 137-kilometre detour from the sealed highway unless you're coming from or going to Alice.

The road south of Halls Creek to the Old Town leads on to the **Buchanan Highway**, an old stock route that joins the Stuart Highway near Dunmarra (NT) – nearly 800km long, it gets even less traffic than the Tanami while lacking some of its flat monotony. Finally, you're unlikely just to drive down the **Canning Stock Route** to Wiluna on a whim. At 1860km (4WD only) it's the world's longest stock route and the ultimate challenge for well-equipped off-roaders.

Purnululu (Bungle Bungles) National Park

The spectacular **Bungle Bungle** massif (officially known as **Purnululu National Park**; closed Jan–April; $11) is one of Australia's greatest natural wonders and a couple of days spent exploring its chasms and gorges is well worth the effort and expense involved. Brought to prominence ten years ago by a film crew documenting the ravages of overgrazing in the area, the Bungles have quickly attracted a mystique matching that of Uluru (Ayers Rock). The delicate nature of the banded rock domes, as well as the difficulty in patrolling the remote park, means that limiting land access to 4WDs saves money, the ecostructure of the park, and tourists' lives.

The **fly-drive tours** available in Halls Creek (see opposite) and Kununurra (see box on p.775), which involve flying to the park's airstrip and then being driven around in a 4WD, offer the best of both worlds, and the half-hour **helicopter flights** ($160) available in the park get right into the gorges and will leave you grinning for hours – if you've ever wanted to fly in a chopper, save your money for the Bungles, you will not be disappointed. Helicopter flights are also available from Turkey Creek (see below) and Kununurra (see overleaf).

From the highway it's a rough 55-kilometre, two-hour, 4WD journey to the **ranger's residence** (℡ 08/9168 7300), where the entry fee must be paid in return for a map. From here you can go to either of the two basic camps in the park. **Kurrajong Camp** is 10km to the north and gives access to **Echidna Chasm**, a one-hour return walk into a slender chasm a thousand metres long and half as high. **Frog Hole** is another, wider chasm with a pool at the end, while **Mini Palms** involves squeezing into yet another narrow gorge to a cave at the end, as part of a walk that takes at least two hours – take plenty of water and a torch. At any point on these walks you can look up and see palms clinging to the rock walls hundreds of metres above you; the scale of the clefts is underlined when you realize the palms can be up to 20m high.

Wilardi Camp (25km from the ranger's residence) is where tour groups stay. From here a track leads on to a cleared patch of ground used as a car park on the south flank of the plateau, site of the striped domes for which the Bungles are best known. The weathered, beehive-like domes have horizontal bands of silica (orange) and lichen (grey), together forming a fragile crust over the powdery interior, and are a most unusual sight. From here a half-hour walk leads into **Cathedral Gorge**, a huge overhanging amphitheatre with a seasonal pool whose rippled reflections flicker across the roof above.

Piccaninny Gorge is a hard, thirty-kilometre return walk for which you'll need large quantities of water. The ground underfoot is soft sand and shade is negligible during the day. Although there is a pool near the end, if you plan to walk up the gorge, leave very early in the morning and turn back long before your water runs out. There is an emergency hand-pump close to the car park.

On to Wyndham

Halfway between Halls Creek and Kununurra is the roadhouse at **TURKEY CREEK** (Warmun), where a helicopter (℡ 08/9169 1300) offers **flights** into the Bungles. A faster, though less exhilarating, enclosed "Jetranger" is used, but it's still a memorable way of seeing the domes.

From Turkey Creek the road continues directly north, passing the **Argyle Diamond Mine** (tours from Kununurra), source of a third of the world's diamonds – although most of them end up in industrial use. The scenery hereabouts takes on a rugged turn as you pass the **Ragged** and **Carr Boyd ranges** to the junction with the Victoria Highway. Kununurra is 46km to the east and Wyndham 51km northwest.

Strung out in three built-up areas along the muddy banks of the Cambridge Gulf, **WYNDHAM** was the port established to serve the brief goldrush at Halls Creek in the 1880s. The town was well positioned to process and export beef from the East Kimberley until the meat works closed in 1985, but with the expansion of the Ord River Irrigation Project (see below), the West Kimberley's only port could be set to thrive again. Until that day the town ticks over quietly, with the **Crocodile Farm** (May–Nov daily 8.30am–4pm; feeding time 11am; $7) and the **Five Rivers Lookout** from the top of the 335-metre Bastion Ranges the only things worth checking out, besides cheap **fuel** at almost urban prices. The **tourist office** (daily 8am–5pm; ☎08/9161 1054) is on O'Donnell Street, and you can **camp** at the *Three Mile Caravan Park* (☎08/9161 1064; on-site vans ❷) on Baker Street or enjoy a bit more luxury at the *Wyndham Community Club* (☎08/9161 1130; ❸) on the highway, 4km from town. The *Wyndham Town Hotel* (☎08/9161 1003; ❺) on O'Donnell Street has **rooms**, backpackers **dorms** plus the town's one **restaurant** – the only choice for food besides the usual takeaways. On the way to Wyndham you'll pass a turn-off to the **Grotto**, where steps lead down to a small flooded gorge.

Kununurra and the Ord River

KUNUNURRA is the Kimberley's youngest town, built in the early 1960s to serve the **Ord River Irrigation Project**, fed by Lake Kununurra. The Diversion Dam Wall, an impressive sight as you come in from the west, created this lake, essentially the bloated Ord River. Fifty kilometres upstream is another dam, known as the Argyle Dam Wall, built in 1971 to ensure a year-round flow to the project, which has created **Lake Argyle**, the world's largest man-made body of water. Despite early problems, the Ord River Irrigation Project has moved on to something called Stage Two, expanding an intensive, yet still barely developed, agricultural area where cotton and sugar cane are set to transform the economy.

Perhaps because of its youth and the surrounding countryside, Kununurra escapes the resigned, rather jaded feel of the older Kimberley towns. Instead, the town has an appealingly relaxed atmosphere, enhanced by the copious amounts of fresh water nearby which lend themselves to recreational use. Besides being an ideal base from which to explore the adjacent Kimberley, the town is also a good place to seek out casual **farming work** from June to November – some of the hostels may be able to help in this respect.

A couple of kilometres from town is Kununurra's own national park, **Hidden Valley**, where a road leads into a narrow valley of "mini-bungles" and terminates with some short trails – you couldn't ask for a better walking area so close to town. Another popular spot is **Ivanhoe Crossing**, 13km north of town on the Ord River. Officially the ford is closed to vehicles and you wouldn't want to try crossing it in anything less than a hefty 4WD. This is croc country and, although locals still fish and bathe by the banks, it's inadvisable, being just the sort of habitual behaviour salties apparently go for. **Valentines Pool**, **Black Rock Falls** and **Middle Springs** are other popular spots in the area, though the water in all three gets pretty soupy towards the end of the Dry.

Triple J Tours (☎08/9168 2682) offers cruises up **Lake Kununurra** to **Argyle Dam** with optional return by bus, a much more enjoyable excursion than you might expect. Big Water Kimberley Canoeing Safaris (ⓣ 08/9169 1257 or free call 1800 641 998) organizes canoeing trips down the Ord River, driving you up to the dam and letting you float back over three days for $110 (plus camping gear). The Zebra Rock Gallery (daily 8am–6pm; free), 6km out of town on Packsaddle Road, has examples of the unusually banded rock found on an island in Lake Argyle, as well as a small wildlife park. In town, Warringarri Aboriginal Arts (Mon–Fri 8.30am–noon & 1–4.30pm; free), on Speargrass Road opposite the **Kelly's Knob** turn-off (a sunset-viewing spot), has displays of locally made arts and crafts which are for sale.

Practicalities

The **tourist bureau** (daily 8am–5pm; ⓣ 08/9168 1177), on Coolibah Drive, has displays and videos on the area's many attractions, and details of all the tours that can take you there. There is a perennially warm **swimming pool** ($2) over the road, and the **post office** is also on Coolibah drive. **Buses** arrive outside the Shire offices, passing through daily for Katherine and Darwin (NT) and Broome.

There are two **hostels** in town. The *Desert Inn* (ⓣ 08/9168 2702; ❶) on Konkerberry Drive, close to the pub and supermarket, has twins, eight-bed air-conditioned dorms and a shaded pool and terrace. *Kununurra Backpackers* (ⓣ 08/9168 1711 or free call 1800 641 998; ❶), 111 Nutwood Crescent, has a small pool, TV room and a section accommodating longer-term workers. Of the town's five **caravan parks**, the *Town* (ⓣ 08/9168 1763), on Bloodwood Drive, is the most central; the *Kona* (ⓣ 08/9168 1031) is by Lake Kununurra, west of town; and *Hidden Valley* (ⓣ 08/9168 1790), a kilometre north of town, has cheap campsites. The *Mercure Inn* (ⓣ 08/9168 1455 or free call 1800 642 244, ⓕ 9168 2622; ❼), on the highway, is the town's best **motel**; you could try the cheaper *Hotel Kununurra* (ⓣ 08/9168 1344 or free call 1800 642 244, ⓕ 9168 1946; ❻) on Messmate Way.

Places to eat include the *Kimberley Craft Café* on Banksia Street, *Valentino's* (daily 5–10pm) on Papuana Street for pizzas, or *Chopsticks Restaurant* (daily 6–9.30pm) at the *Country Club*, next to the *Hotel Kununurra*. *Gulliver's Tavern*, opposite the *Desert Inn*, gets the occasional band in the picking season, when the town gets fairly lively.

Regional tours from Kununurra

Kununurra is in the best position to offer a range of tours to the Bungles as well as the East Kimberley, and many operators are based here. The *Desert Inn* (free call ⓣ 1800 632 533) offers two- to three-day Bungles and five-day Gibb River Road adventures, costing around $130 a day and leaving from both Broome and Kununurra. Kimberley Wilderness Adventure (free call ⓣ 1800 804 005) runs 4WD tours throughout the region for around $140 a day for camping or $200 a day using homestead accommodation. East Kimberley Tours (ⓣ 08/9168 2213) has a whole raft of options from one day in the Bungles to an eleven-day see-it-all tour for over $2000 (including some flights). Belray Diamond Tours (ⓣ 08/9168 1014) visits the diamond mine in a day by road, air or with the Bungles thrown in from $150–285; ask at the tourist office or call Alligator Air (free call ⓣ 1800 632 533) who have two-hour Bungle flights in high-wing aircraft for around $150 (no minimum numbers). Their six-hour Kimberley "The Works" flight ($320) includes a stop on the Mitchell Plateau and is one of the best scenic flights over the Kimberley but needs a minimum of four passengers; call in advance if you're heading for Kununurra.

Lake Argyle

When the **Argyle Dam** was completed in 1972, the Ord River managed to fill **Lake Argyle** in just one wet season; along with the Victoria and the Fitzroy, these three rivers account for a third of Australia's freshwater run-off. The lake itself, which covers an area of nine hundred square kilometres, holds enough water to supply the world's population with a thousand litres each. The fish population has grown over the years to support commercial fishing, as well as providing ample food for the numerous birds that flock here. When the lake was proposed, the Durack family's Argyle Homestead was moved to its present site, 2km from the tourist village (see below), and is now a **museum** (May–Oct daily 8.30am–4.30pm; $2) of early pioneering life in the Kimberley, as described in Mary Durack's droving classic, *Kings in Grass Castles*.

Close to the dam wall, 70km from town, the old construction workers' camp has been turned into *Lake Argyle Tourist Village* (⊤08/9168 7361; ❺), offering camping and cabins. Lake Argyle Cruises runs a half-day trip across the lake to show you wallaby caves, jabirus and other birds, freshwater crocs and **Zebra Rock Island**.

The Gibb River Road

On the way to Wyndham you pass the start of the mostly unsealed **Gibb River Road** with its attendant warning sign. Originally built to transport beef to Wyndham and Derby, it cuts through the heart of the Kimberley, offering just a slice of this vast and rugged expanse. At around 670km to Derby, it's 230km shorter than the Great Northern Highway, but no one uses the "Gibb River" as a short cut. The route's notorious corrugations (as a rule, they're worst in the eastern half) depend a lot on the quality of your suspension but it's rare to get across without something breaking or falling off, and punctures are common. The attractions that make the route interesting – mostly gorges and their pools – are off the road and some are accessible only to robust, high-clearance vehicles, although unless stated a 4WD is not necessary in the places listed below. **Tours** are available from Broome (see p.766) and Kununurra (see box p.775).

If you want to do some serious exploration of the Kimberley's remoter corners, ideally in a 4WD, the two Streetsmart **maps** entitled *West Kimberley* and *East Kimberley* are highly recommended. Distances given in brackets below are to destinations off the Gibb River Road.

Along the Cockburn Range to the Kalumburu Road junction

The scenically impressive 250-kilometre eastern section up to the Kalumburu junction is the roughest part of the road, crossing many ranges and crossed in turn by big rivers, the first of these being the **King River**, 17km from the sealed highway.

The turn-off for the plush mini-resort at **Emma Gorge** (1km; $5 day-use; ⊤ & Ⓕ 08/9169 1777; ❻), part of *El Questro Station*, leads to an "executive" bushcamp with shared facilities and a restaurant, bar and pool. There's a forty-minute walk along Emma Creek to the beautiful, fern-draped **gorge** which is worth the entry fee alone.

Further down the road, *El Questro Station* itself (16km; $5 day-use; ⊤ & Ⓕ 08/9169 1777) is a blend of working cattle station, upmarket dude ranch and private national park. There are all sorts of station activities (at a price), including heli-fishing, gorge cruises, horseback- and camel-riding, use of dirt bikes and bullcatchers (stripped-down, armoured jeeps), but bargain **overnight deals** include some of the above, meals *and* pick-ups from Kununurra. Among the many attractions, the three-hour slog up to **El Questro Gorge** is straight out of an "Indiana Jones" movie. **Accommodation** includes secluded camping (with distant washing facilities), and bungalows with shared kitchens (⑥).

From the *El Questro Station* turn-off, the Cockburn Range's cliffs lead you to the stony **Pentecost River** crossing. Just east of the crossing, the Karunjie Track (4WD only) leads 45km back to Wyndham, crossing the lower King River. Eight kilometres after the Pentecost River crossing is *Home Valley Station* (1km; ☏08/9161 4322, ℻9161 4340; ⑥), another moribund cattle property finding better rewards in adventure tourism; as well as fuel and camping, they offer full-board lodgings. The same family also runs *Jack's Waterhole* ($5 entry fee; ⑥), where there's fuel and camping, by the Durack River. From here until you reach the junction with the road up to Kalumburu (see p.777) it's just wide-open Kimberley countryside recovering from the last bushfire. On the way, **Ellenbrae** station (5km; ☏08/9161 4325) has cheap camping and a lovely open-plan homestead (rooms ⑥) without a rattly air-con unit on-site.

Mount Barnett to Derby

From this point the road west is smoother and, from *Mount Barnett Roadhouse* (May–Oct daily 7am–6pm; ☏08/9191 7007; bungalows ④), which has the **last fuel** until Fitzroy Crossing (352km) or Derby (306km), there are a number of watered gorges and possibly waterfalls that you'll most likely have to yourself. You can camp at the **Manning Gorge** for $5, or take an hour's walk to the multitiered **Upper Manning Gorge** (follow the beer-can markers on the far side of the pool).

Further down the road both **Galvans** (700m) and **Adcock** (5km) gorges are a bit gungy by comparison, but with the improved access track **Bell Creek Gorge** (30km, camping at 20km) is well worth some extra corrugations – the latter is the loveliest gorge along the Gibb River Road. **Lennard River Gorge** (8km; 4WD only), on the other side of the King Leopold Ranges, is a dramatic cleft carved through tiers of tilted rock.

A rock-chiselled profile of Queen Victoria's head is evident as you pass through the gap in the **Napier Range**, and 9km later a turn-off leads southeast to Windjana Gorge National Park (21km; see p.771) and Fitzroy Crossing (165km; see p.770). The last 62km to Derby is a sealed avenue of portly boab trees.

The Northern Kimberley

Though a common destination for four-wheel drivers in the Dry, the Northern Kimberley is a remote part of the region where a self-sufficient 4WD is essential. The main destination here is the beautiful, five-tiered **Mitchell Falls**, 240km off the Gibb River Road. You'll find the **Kalumburu Road** surprisingly smooth, with a store and fuel at *Drysdale River Homestead* (59km; April–Nov daily 8am–noon & 1–5pm; ☏08/9161 4326; units ④), which also has dinner and B&B at $80 per person. The **Drysdale River National Park** is tantalizingly inaccessible by private vehicle but the determined should call Darwin-based Willis Walkabouts (☏08/8985 2134), which operates bushwalking tours that sometimes include the park – access is by light plane, 4WD and helicopter, so it won't be cheap.

Kalumburu (276km; ☏08/9161 4300; $25 entry permit) has the languorous feel of a dispersed African village, where ancient cars lie rusting and palms flap and sway in the tropical breeze; buy your permit on arrival from the community office (if there's anyone there). As well as being able to get (expensive) fuel and basics from the store here, you can visit a mission set up in the nineteenth century by Benedictine monks (tours available). North of town along sandy tracks there are basic campsites at **McGowans Beach** (22km) and **Honeymoon Beach** (26km), the latter situated on a small bay and the better of the two.

TRAVEL DETAILS

Trains

Perth to: Bunbury (2–3 daily; 2hr); Kalgoorlie (1–2 daily; 7hr 30min); Port Augusta, SA (1 daily; 37hr); Sydney (2 weekly; 60hr).

Buses

Dampier–Karratha to: Perth (daily; 21hr); Port Hedland (daily; 4hr).

Kalgoorlie to: Adelaide (1 daily; 36hr); Esperance (3 weekly; 5hr); Leonora (2 weekly; 11hr); Perth (5 weekly; 8hr).

Perth to: Adelaide (1 daily; 35hr); Albany (3 daily; from 6hr); Augusta (6 weekly; 6hr); Broome (daily; 32hr); Bunbury (1–2 daily; 2hr); Carnarvon (daily; 11hr); Dampier–Karratha (5 weekly; 21hr); Darwin (daily; 56hr); Denham (for Monkey Mia; daily; 12hr); Derby (3 weekly; 37hr); Esperance (4 weekly; 10hr); Exmouth (6 weekly; 6hr); Fitzroy Crossing (3 weekly; 40hr); Geraldton (2–4 daily; 6hr); Halls Creek (daily; 44hr); Hyden (for Wave Rock; 2 weekly; 5hr); Kalbarri (daily; 8hr); Kalgoorlie (5 weekly; 8hr); Kununurra (daily; 49hr); Margaret River (3 daily; 5hr); Meekatharra (2 weekly; 10hr); Newman (2 weekly; 13hr); Port Hedland (1 daily; 25hr).

Flights

Perth to: Adelaide (6 daily; 4hr 15min); Alice Springs (5 weekly; 4hr); Ayers Rock Resort (3 weekly; 3hr 45min); Brisbane (3 weekly; 6hr 15min); Broome (1 daily; 2hr 30min); Darwin (1 daily; 6hr 15min); Esperance (2 daily; 1hr 50min); Kalgoorlie (1 daily; 1hr); Kununurra (6 weekly; 3hr 15min); Melbourne (12 daily; 5hr 15min); Sydney (12 daily; 6hr).

8

South Australia

CHAPTER 8

Highlights

✳ **Adelaide Festival of Arts** – The country's best-known and most innovative arts festival. **p.805**.

✳ **Barossa Valley** – A popular day-trip from Adelaide, the Barossa Valley is home to some of Australia's finest wineries. **p.816**.

✳ **Kangaroo Island** – Spectacular scenery and a huge range of wildlife. **p.831**.

✳ **Murray River** – Lined with majestic river red gums, the beautiful Murray River is best explored by renting a houseboat. **p.846**.

✳ **The Nullarbor Plain** – Drive across – or even better, catch a train – and appreciate how vast Australia is. **p.865**.

✳ **Coober Pedy** – Surrounded by desert, the inhabitants of scorching Coober Pedy live underground to escape the heat of summer. **p.867**.

✳ **Wilpena Pound** – The main attraction of the rugged Flinders Ranges National Park is the huge natural basin of Wilpena Pound, with its fantastic bushwalks and great views. **p.874**.

✳ **The Strzelecki, Birdsville and Oodnadatta tracks** – Fill up your tank and head off into the Outback on one of Australia's fabled journeys. **p.876, p.878 & p.878**.

✳ **Lake Eyre** – Surrounded by desert, this massive salt lake has filled up only four times in over a hundred and thirty years. **p.878**.

South Australia

S outh Australia, the driest state of the driest continent, is split into two very distinct halves. The long-settled southern part, watered by the Murray River, and with **Adelaide** as a cosmopolitan centre, has been thoroughly tamed; the northern half, arid and depopulated, most definitely has not.

Most of southern – which is to say southeastern – South Australia lies within three-hours' drive of Adelaide. Food and especially **wine** are among its chief pleasures: this is prime grape-growing and wine-making country. As well as its wineries the **Fleurieu Peninsula**, just south of Adelaide, has a string of fine beaches along the Gulf St Vincent coastline. Cape Jervis, at the peninsula's tip, is the departure point for ferries to sparsely populated **Kangaroo Island**, a fine place to see Australian wildlife at its unfettered best. Facing Adelaide across the Investigator Strait, the **Yorke Peninsula** is primarily an agricultural area, preserving a little copper-mining history and some great fishing. The superb wineries of the **Barossa Valley**, originally settled by German immigrants in the nineteenth century, are only an hour from Adelaide on the **Sturt Highway**, the main road to Sydney. This crosses the Murray River at Blanchetown and follows the fertile **Riverland** region to the New South Wales border. Following the **southeast coast** along the Princes Highway, you can head towards Melbourne via the extensive coastal lagoon system of the Coorong and enjoyable seaside towns such as Robe, exiting the state at **Mount Gambier** with its crater lakes. The inland trawl via the **Dukes Highway** is faster, but far less interesting. Heading north from Adelaide, there are old copper-mining towns to explore at Kapunda and Burra in the area known as the **mid-north**, which also encompasses the **Clare Valley**, a quieter, more down-to-earth wine centre and perhaps the southeast's most enjoyable.

Accommodation price codes

All the accommodation listed in this book has been categorized into one of eight price bands, as set out below. The rates quoted represent the cheapest available double or twin room in high season – except for category ①, which indicates per-person rates for a dorm bed, and the categories given for units, cabins and vans, which represent the daily charge for the whole unit.

① Under $20	③ $35–50	⑤ $70–90	⑦ $115–150
② $20–35	④ $50–70	⑥ $90–115	⑧ $150 upwards

For more accommodation details, see pp.46–49.

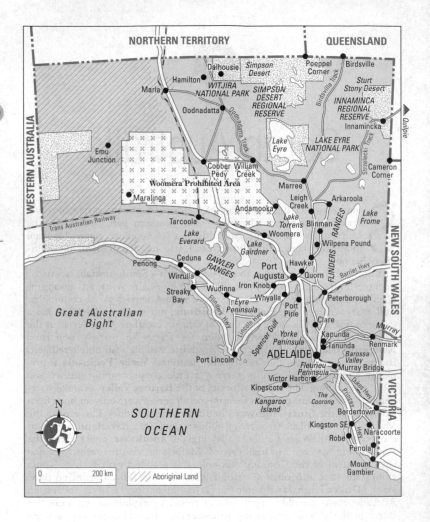

In contrast with the gentle and cultured southeast, the remainder of South Australia – with the exception of the relatively refined **Eyre Peninsula** and its strikingly scenic west coast – is unremittingly harsh desert, a naked country of vast horizons, salt lakes, glazed gibber plains and ancient mountain ranges. Although it's tempting to scud over the forbidding distances, rewards from this introspective and subtle landscape develop slowly and you'll miss its essence by hurrying. For every predictable, monotonous highway there's a dirt alternative, which may be physically draining but enables you to get closer to this precarious environment. The folded red rocks of the central **Flinders Ranges** and **Coober Pedy**'s post-apocalyptic scenery are on most agendas and could be worked into a sizeable circuit, but overall the Outback lacks any real destinations. Making the most of the journey is what counts – the fabled routes to **Oodnadatta**, **Birdsville** and **Innamincka** are still real adventures, and not necessarily 4WD only.

Rail and road routes converge in Adelaide before the long cross-country hauls west to Perth via Port Augusta or north to Alice Springs and Darwin. The Ghan to Alice Springs is one of Australia's great train journeys; as is the Indian Pacific between Perth and Sydney, which passes through Adelaide – though if you hop on the eastbound train here, you'll have missed traversing part of the country, which is really the point of the journey.

Adelaide and the surrounding gulflands, cooled by the Gulf St Vincent, enjoy a Mediterranean **climate** that makes them tremendously fertile. As you head further north the temperature hots up to such an extreme that by Coober Pedy people live underground to escape the searing summer temperatures.

Some history

When South Australia was first settled by Europeans in 1836, it was home to as many as fifty distinct **Aboriginal groups**, with a population estimated at 15,000. Three distinct cultural regions existed: the Western Desert, the Central Lakes, and the Murray and southeast region. It was the people of the comparatively well-watered southeast who felt the full impact of white settlement, those who survived being shunted onto missions controlled by the government. Some Aboriginal people have clung tenaciously to their way of life in the Western Desert, where they have gained title to some of their land, but most now live south of Port Augusta, many in Adelaide.

The coast of South Australia was first **explored** by the Dutch in 1627. In 1792 the French explorer Bruni d'Entrecasteaux sailed along the Great Australian Bight before heading to southern Tasmania, and in 1802 the Englishman Matthew Flinders thoroughly charted the coast. The most important expedition, though – the one which led to the foundation of a colony here – was **Captain Charles Sturt**'s 1830 navigation of the Murray River from its source in New South Wales to its mouth in South Australia.

South Australia was planned from the start: in the idealistic scheme of the English entrepreneur Edward Wakefield, there were to be no convicts – instead free settlers would be sold small units of land (rather than given large free land grants) in a state guaranteeing them civil and religious liberty. The success of the scheme was guaranteed when George Fife Angas formed the **South Australia Company** to finance it. In 1836 **Governor John Hindmarsh** landed at Holdfast Bay, now the Adelaide beachside suburb of Glenelg, with the first settlers; the next year Colonel William Light planned a spacious, attractive city, with broad streets and plenty of parks and squares, some distance inland. By 1839, Angas was assisting persecuted Lutheran communities from the eastern provinces of Prussia to settle in South Australia.

Early problems caused by the harsh, dry climate and financial incompetence (the colony was bankrupt in 1841) were eased by the discovery of substantial reserves of **copper** over the next decade. By 1870 Adelaide's population had almost doubled. The tradition of **libertarianism** in South Australia continued; in 1894 its women were the first in the world to be permitted to stand for parliament and the second in the world to gain the vote (after women in New Zealand). Social improvement through slum clearances began after World War I. Of all the mainland states, the depressions and recessions of the interwar period hit South Australia the hardest. After World War II new migrants came, boosting the output of industry and injecting new life into the state.

The 1970s were the decade of **Don Dunstan**. The flamboyant Labor Premier, who died in January 1999, was an enlightened reformer who had a strong sense of social justice: he abolished capital punishment, outlawed racial discrimination and decriminalized homosexuality. The state has been a duller place since his retirement in 1979, and a poorer one since the recession started to have an effect at the end of the 1980s. Unemployment levels are still high.

Adelaide and the southeast

Adelaide is very much the transport hub of the state, with all routes radiating from the city. There are good **bus** connections throughout the southeast, but more rewarding alternatives are worth considering. Much of the country is flat and great for **cycling**. The principal route is the **Mawson Trail**: 800km specifically planned for cyclists, extending from the Mount Lofty Ranges through the Barossa Valley and traversing the Flinders Ranges to the Outback town of Blinman. **Walkers** can follow a parallel route along the 1500-kilometre **Heysen Trail** starting at Cape Jervis and running up the coast of the Fleurieu Peninsula before heading north over the Mount Lofty Ranges to the Flinders, on the same tracks some of the way. Note that the Heysen trail is closed between December and April – partly due to the high risk of fire and partly as a result of an agreement with private landowners, through whose property some of the trail passes. Further information and maps for the trails are available from Information SA in Adelaide (see p.786).

Adelaide

ADELAIDE is always thought of as a gracious city and an easy place to live; despite a population of around one million and a slick veneer of sophistication, it still has the feel of an overgrown country town. It's a pretty place, laid out on either side of the **Torrens River**, ringed with a green belt of parks and set against the rolling hills of the **Mount Lofty Ranges**. During the hot, dry summer the parklands are kept green by irrigation from the waters of the Murray River on which the city depends; there's always a sense that the rawness of the Outback is waiting to take over.

The traditional way of life of the **Kuarna people**, the original occupants of the Adelaide Plains, had been destroyed within twenty years of the landing of Governor John Hindmarsh at Holdfast Bay in 1836. The Surveyor General for the colony, Colonel William Light, had visionary plans for the new city. After a long struggle with Hindmarsh, who wanted to build on a harbour, Light got his wish for a city on the western side of "the enchanted hills", with a strong connection to the river. In 1823, Light had fondly written of the Sicilian city of Catania: "The two principal streets cross each other at right angles in the square in the direction of north and south and east and west. They are wide and spacious and about a mile long", and this became the basis for the plan of Adelaide. Postwar immigration provided the final element missing from his plan – the human one: Italians now make up the biggest non-Anglo cultural group, and the café society they introduced adds spirit to the city.

In the Mediterranean-style hot, dry summers, alfresco eating and drinking are commonplace and lend the city a vaguely European air, with its wide, well-planned streets and squares transformed with a squint of the eye into boulevards. One of the chief delights of Adelaide is the interest its inhabitants take in **food** and **wine**, with restaurants and cafés as culturally varied as Sydney's and Melbourne's but much cheaper, and South Australian wine monopolizing every cellar. Unlike a European city, though, the centre is virtually deserted in

ACCOMMODATION						
Adelaide Backpackers Inn	23	City Central Motel	8	Kiwi Motel & Lodge	7
Adelaide Caravan Park	2	Crown and Sceptre	22	Metropolitan Hotel	17
Adelaide Central YHA	11	Director's Studios	21	Rucksackers Riders	25
Adelaide City Backpackers	15	The Cumberland	10	Stamford Plaza Adelaide	6
Adelaide Meridien	1	East Park Lodge	20	Strathmore	5
Austral Hotel	9	Franklin Central Apartments	14	Sunnys	16
Backpack Australia Hostel	19	Georgia Mews	12	The Travellers Inn	24
Backpack Oz	18	Greenways Apartments	3		
Cannon Street Lodge	13	Grosvenor Vista	4		

the evening and on Sunday – except for a couple of lively thoroughfares. However, culture is held in high esteem, and the city comes to life every year with a festival: the **Adelaide Festival of Arts** (held on even years) or **Womadelaide** (odd years).

Outwardly conservative, Adelaide nonetheless has the advantage of South Australia's liberal traditions, with a nudist beach, relaxed drug laws and 24-hour hotel licences. It's the free and easy **lifestyle** within an ordered framework that's so appealing; Adelaide may not be an obvious destination in itself, but it's a great place for a relaxed break on your way up to the Northern Territory or across to Western Australia, with only daunting Outback and great distances ahead.

Arrival, information and city transport

Buses from out of town, including the airport bus, will drop you off at the **Central Bus Station**, 101–111 Franklin St, which, compared to bus terminals in other major cities, is very basic. The international **airport**, 7km southwest from the centre, is small, modern and easy to handle; there's a currency exchange and information booth. The domestic terminal is about half a kilometre southwest. Both are serviced by the **airport bus** (Transit Regency Coaches depart hourly between 5.30am & 8.30pm, every 30min Mon–Fri 8am–8pm, with a final departure daily at 9.45pm; $6.60 one-way; to book a return trip call ☎08/8381 5311), which will drop you off at most city accommodation on request; its set route stops at Victoria Square and North Terrace, as well as the bus station. A taxi costs around $15 to either the city or the beachside suburb of Glenelg, 11km from the centre. Arriving by **train** at the Keswick Interstate Terminal, you can also take the airport bus, which stops here en route ($3.30 to city or airport), or walk to the suburban platform and catch a train into Adelaide Train Station on North Terrace. Taxis to the city from the Interstate Terminal charge about $8.

Information

The obvious first stop for information is the **South Australian Travel Centre**, at 18 King William St, between Rundle Mall and North Terrace (Mon–Fri 8.30am–5.30pm, Sat & Sun 9am–2pm; ☎1300/655 276, ⓦwww.southaustralia.com). Staff are very helpful at this large modern office, where masses of general information is displayed, including excellent, free touring guides and maps of Adelaide and the state. However, tour and accommodation bookings are only dealt with via the website or over the telephone on the ☎1300 number above, which you can call for free from the centre. There's also free access to the statewide tourist information website ⓦwww.touristvision.com.au on a terminal in the centre, as well as a freephone to the Passenger Transport InfoLine – you'll need to queue for more specific enquiries. If you arrive by bus, head straight for the **Backpacker Transit and Travel Centre**, a bright pink building opposite the station at 110 Franklin St (daily 8.30am–6pm; ☎08/8410 3000). They can provide free maps, book all domestic tours and rent bikes; there's also a currency exchange, telephone, a good notice board, and **internet access** ($2 for 30min).

The government-run **Information SA**, 77 Grenfell St (Mon, Tues, Thurs & Fri 9am–5pm, Wed 9.30am–5pm; ☎08/8204 1900, ⓦwww.info.sa.gov.au), sells the Department of Sport and Recreation's maps of the Heysen Trail, Mount Lofty walks and South Australian cycle routes (these can also be purchased online); there are also some free maps and brochures, and free internet access for half an hour. On the ground floor of the same building, the **Environment Shop and Information Centre** (same hours; ℡08/8204 1910) has lots of information on national and conservation parks in and around Adelaide and the state. The **City of Adelaide Customer Centre**, a block south on 25 Pirie St (Mon–Fri 8.30am–5.30pm; ℡08/8203 7203, ⓦwww.adelaide.sa.gov.au), has a range of free maps and booklets, including the glossy fold-out *Art in Public Places Walking Guide*, which contains information on art throughout South Australia, and the bimonthly glossy booklet *Adelaide City Scene*, which details all upcoming events and travelling exhibitions in the city. Some of these are also available at the South Australian Travel Centre and the South Australian Museum.

City transport

The city centre is compact enough to walk around, and its flatness makes this an easy option. There are two **free buses** that can help you get around the centre. The **Bee Line** (#99B) is a handy alternative that cuts out a lot of the leg-work – it leaves from Victoria Square (every 5min Mon–Thurs 7.40am–6pm, Fri 7.40am–9.20pm; every 15min Sat 8.30am–5.30pm) and heads up King William Street to North Terrace, then along past the train station down the end of Hindley Street and back to Victoria Square along the same route. The **City Loop Bus** (same times; every 15min) is designed to be accessible for people with disabilities or burdened with prams, with ground-level access ramps; there are thirty stops taking in all the major cultural and commercial centres, beginning at Adelaide Train Station.

To explore further out of the city centre, you'll need to use the integrated **Adelaide Metro** system, which comprises mainly buses but also includes suburban trains and one tramline from the city to Glenelg. Free timetables are available from the **Passenger Transport InfoCentre** on the corner of King William and Currie streets (Mon–Sat 8am–6pm, Sun 10.30am–5.30pm; ℡08/8210 1000 daily 7am–8pm; ⓦwww.adelaidemetro.com.au), where staff can advise on routes and fares, as well as sell tickets, and you can pick up *The Metroguide*, a free information booklet including a handy map of the system. Timetable information and advice are also available via the freephone at the South Australian Travel Centre. Waits at stops – where times are not always displayed – can be long, making it all the more important to pick up the relevant timetables before setting out. However, as part of a drive to improve services and entice Adelaidians away from their preference for cars, Adelaide Metro has made nine of the more popular routes around the city into high-frequency **Go Zones**. These routes guarantee maximum waits of 5–15 minutes between 7.30am and 6.30pm Monday to Friday, and half-an-hour at night and on weekends; stops are distinguished by bright-red information boards.

Adelaide Metro buses and trains run until about 11.30pm, with reduced services at night and on Sunday. **Tickets** come in multi-trip, single-trip and day-trip permutations, and can be used on buses, trains and the tram. You can buy single train tickets from a ticket vending machine on board, as well as from station ticket offices and the Passenger Transport InfoCentre (see above). Single tickets range from $1.10 to $2.90, depending on whether it's peak or off-peak time, or whether a two-hour transfer is required. The day-trip ticket ($5.60) is much easier and better value. Only multi-trip tickets cannot be bought on board buses or the tram but must be purchased, along with other tickets, from the Passenger Transport InfoCentre, train stations, post offices and some newsagents. **Night buses** run by MAC Nightmoves operate on Saturday only; five routes run from city nightspots (pick-up points outside *Heaven* and *The*

Planet nightclubs; midnight to 4am; $6.60) to: Reynella and Noarlunga via Brighton Road and Glenelg; Adelaide Hills via Stirling and Aldgate; Semaphore and Henley Beach; north to Elizabeth; and northeast to Tea Tree Plaza. A nightbus timetable is available from the Passenger Transport InfoCentre.

Four suburban **train** lines run from Adelaide Train Station, a modern complex with shops and cafés on North Terrace. The trains run every five to thirty minutes south to Christie Downs via Brighton, east to Bel Air, north to Gawler via Salisbury and northwest to Port Adelaide via Semaphore, with a branch heading west to Grange. Security guards are present on all trains after 7pm to deter violence. The **tram** to seaside Glenelg (30min) leaves from Victoria Square every fifteen to twenty minutes. The **O-Bahn** is a fast-track bus which runs on concrete rails through scenic Torrens Linear Park, between the city (Grenfell St) and Tea Tree Plaza in Modbury, 12km northeast.

Cycling is a popular and excellent alternative: the flat city area and its wide, multilaned streets make riding a breeze, and there are several good cycling routes – including the **Torrens Linear Park track**, which goes from the sea at Westbeach to the hills at Athelston, weaving along the river. A map of this and other cycling routes is available from Information SA (see p.786), and several other cycling route maps from the City of Adelaide Customer Centre (see overleaf); for bike rental outlets, see "Listings", p.810.

Accommodation

The only time you may have difficulty finding accommodation is during the Arts Festival at the end of February and beginning of March (even years), and Womadelaide in late February (odd years), when you'd be well advised to book ahead. Rooms also fill up quickly at weekends, especially at the more popular **hostels** around the Central Bus Station on Franklin Street and adjacent Waymouth Street. Adelaide has loads of hostels, competing to keep prices low and often throwing in free breakfasts and bed linen; dorm rates are typically $18, while rooms range from $30 to $50. Those on Gilles or Carrington streets in the southwest quarter, about ten-minutes' walk from the city centre, are generally cheaper and will pick up from the bus or train station if you call ahead (several also send minibuses to scout for custom); some hostels will even come to the airport if you call in advance. Otherwise, buses #171 or #172 from Victoria Square stop close to Gilles Street. There are cheap **hotel** rooms on Hindley Street, Adelaide's nightclub area and its tame answer to a red-light district, but some women may find it threatening. The swankiest accommodation is along North Terrace.

The most central **campsite** is the *Adelaide Caravan Park*, Bruton Street, Hackney, on the Torrens River 2km east of the centre (T08/8363 1566, F8362 1989, Wwww.adelaidecaravanpark.com.au; cabins ❸, on-site vans ❸, two-bed holiday units ❺, villas with spas ❻); it's right on the Torrens Linear Park cycling route and can be reached by bus #281 or #282 from North Terrace, or on foot through parkland and along the river. For a beachfront setting, head to *Adelaide Shores Caravan Park*, Military Road, West Beach (T08/8356 7654, Eadelaideshores@senet.com.au; bus #278 from Currie St; cabins ❹–❺, on-site vans ❸), or the *Adelaide Beachfront Tourist Park*, 349 Military Rd, Semaphore (T08/8449 7726 or free call 1800 810 140, F8449 5877; en-suite cabins ❺–❻), which has a swimming pool, recreation room, playground and a free shuttle bus service to West Lakes Mall and Ethelton train station; to stay at either you'll need to be prepared for the summertime hordes.

You could also pitch your tent on the rooftop of *Backpack Australia* (see overleaf) in the centre of the city.

The seaside suburb of **Glenelg** and the nearby beach resorts (see p.791), about half an hour away by public transport, are good alternatives to the city, with plenty of self-catering apartments and one of Adelaide's liveliest hostels.

City centre

Hotels, motels and pubs

Austral Hotel, 205 Rundle St (☎ 08/8223 4660, ℱ 8223 4175, ⓦ www.theaustral.com). Basic rooms in one of Adelaide's best pubs on this "arty" street. Bands or DJs nearly every night, so it can be noisy. ❹

City Central Motel, 23 Hindley St (☎ 08/8231 4049, ℱ 8231 4804). Centrally located budget motel. ❹

Crown and Sceptre, 308 King William St (☎ 08/8212 4159, ℱ 8231 9169). Centrally located pub with inexpensive rooms upstairs on request (shared bathroom). It's currently one of Adelaide's most popular drinking holes, with a young clientele and live music downstairs; good for socializers rather than sleepers. ❷

Director's Studios, 259 Gouger St (☎ 08/8213 2500 or free call 1800 882 601, ℱ 8213 2519, ⓦ www.savillesuites.com.au). Modern hotel aimed at executives, with pleasant, well-furnished self-catering studio apartments and standard rooms. A five-minute walk to Chinatown and the Central Market; very good value. 24hr reception and free parking. ❻–❼

Franklin Central Apartments, 36 Franklin St (☎ 08/8221 7050, ℱ 8210 6333, ⓦ www.ihm.com.au/franklin.html). Fully serviced one-, two- and three-bedroom apartments in a central location ideal for business or extended stays. 24hr reception and valet parking. ❽

Grosvenor Vista, 125 North Terrace (☎ 08/8407 8888 or free call 1800 888 222, ℱ 8407 8866, ⓦ www.grosvenorvistahotel.com.au). Genteel establishment dating from 1918, complete with potted palms in the foyer. Spacious, modern en-suite rooms with air-con. 24hr room service, gym and sauna, bar and bistro and undercover parking. Breakfast included. ❻–❼

Kiwi Motel & Lodge, 262–266 Hindley St (☎ 08/8231 9524, ℱ 8231 2671, ⓔ princesarcade@one.net.au). Motel-cum-hostel in a converted arcade, with spacious rooms – some en suite and with a kitchenette – and quiet four-bed dorms with their own TV. Helpful tour desk, laundry and internet access. Rates include linen and a filling breakfast. Rooms ❸–❹, dorms ❶

Metropolitan Hotel, 46 Grote St (☎ 08/8231 5471, ℱ 8231 0633). Rather tacky locals pub but with basic clean rooms upstairs at bargain prices. Good-value bistro meals. Light breakfast included. ❸

Stamford Plaza Adelaide, 150 North Terrace (☎ 08/8461 1111, ℱ 8231 7572, ⓦ www.stamford.com.au/adelaide/adpla1bar.html). This central, high-rise luxury five-star hotel has all you'd expect: swimming pool, sauna, three restaurants, room service and views of the Festival Centre. Room rates are in excess of $200, though cheaper weekend packages are available. There is also a beachside equivalent, the *Stamford Grand Hotel*, on the foreshore at Glenelg. ❽

Strathmore, 129 North Terrace (☎ 08/8212 6911, ℱ 8231 5475, ⓦ www.strath.com.au). Smart, small hotel in a desirable location. En-suite motel-style rooms are small and have no views, though they come with all mod cons from air-con to room service; free undercover parking. Breakfast included. ❻

Hostels

Adelaide Backpackers Inn, 112 Carrington St (☎ 08/8223 6635 or free call 1800 247 725, ℱ 8232 5464, ⓦ www.tne.net.au/abackinn/). In a converted two-storey ex-pub, this place is shabby, but has a friendly ambience and helpful staff. Reception doubles as a travel agency, selling bus and train tickets. There are six- to twelve-bed dorms here and annexe accommodation across the road with plenty of singles and doubles in a brighter, more modern air-con building. Generous breakfast thrown in. Internet access. Rooms ❹, dorms ❶

Adelaide Central YHA, 135 Waymouth St (☎ 08/8414 3010, ℱ 8414 3015, ⓔ adlcentral@yhasa.org.au). Modern, rather ugly and extremely efficient youth hostel with over 200 beds in a convenient location in the heart of the city – though don't expect a lively atmosphere. Dorms (four- to eight-bed) all have lockers, some doubles are en suite and there are even two family rooms ($80). Well-equipped kitchens, large laundry room, lockers, a comprehensive travel centre and internet access next door. Some off-street parking spaces can be reserved. Rooms ❸–❹, dorms ❶

Adelaide City Backpackers, 239 Franklin St (☎ 08/8212 2668,

Wwww.citybackpackers.com.au). This family-owned hostel is a beautifully restored Victorian house with charm and character throughout. There's a country-style kitchen and breakfast room, small bar and cosy plant-filled courtyard. If you can put up with a ten-bed dorm, or are lucky enough to get one of the immaculate double rooms, this place is the closest you'll get in Adelaide to a home away from home. Courtesy pick-up, free night tour and hearty continental breakfast all included. Rooms ❸, dorms ❶

Backpack Australia Hostel, 128 Grote St (☎08/8231 0639 or free call 1800 804 133, ℱ8410 5881). Friendly, clean and modern, with colourful murals decorating the entrance area, this is one of the more sociable hostels. You can even pitch your tent on the roof terrace, making this the cheapest spot in town. Travel agent service, BBQs, free bikes and an excellent notice board. Light breakfast and linen included. Rooms ❷, dorms ❶

Backpack Oz, 144 Wakefield St, cnr Pulteney St (☎ & ℱ 08/8223 3551, free call ☎1800 633 307, Wwww.backpackoz.com.au). Converted from a nineteenth-century hotel, this low-key hostel has light, spacious rooms and dorms (four-, six- and ten-bed) with sinks, mirrors and ceiling fans; linen and a light breakfast included. Comfortable common room downstairs; laundry and small kitchen. The bar opens summer only. Pick-ups from bus, train and airport available, and tours booked. Rooms ❸, dorms ❶

Cannon Street Lodge, 11 Cannon St, entrance on Franklin St opposite the bus station (☎ & ℱ 08/8410 1218, free call ☎1800 069 731, Wwww.cannonst.com.au). Huge, warehouse-style space with a groovy young feel to it. Very clean and well-run; definitely one of the best. The big foyer has a travel centre, internet access and a funky licensed bar complete with pinball and a pool table; cheap $4.50 meals are served here. While there's lots of noise and action downstairs, it's peaceful upstairs. Free light breakfast includes

percolated coffee; other perks are cheap day-membership at the gym around the corner, under-cover parking and bed linen. Rooms ❸, dorms ❶

The Cumberland, 205 Waymouth St (☎08/8231 3577, ℱ8231 3578). Nomad hostel above a trendy wine bar in a delightful old hotel. The large Victorian rooms are musty smelling and in a state of disrepair, but renovations are planned under new management. Rooms ❸, dorms ❶

East Park Lodge, 341 Angas St (☎08/8223 1228 or free call 1800 643 606, ℱ8223 7772, Wwww.eastpark.com.au). Huge three-storey mansion, with singles and doubles as well as four-bed dorms, all with air-con. It has a peaceful atmosphere and views of the hills from its balconies and rooftop. Outdoors there's a pool to cool off in. Bus and train pick-ups if pre-booked; airport buses drop off here. Limited on-street parking. Tours booked. Free breakfast. Rooms ❸, dorms ❶

Rucksackers Riders, 257 Gilles St (☎08/8232 0823). The small dorms are the cheapest in Adelaide ($14); not surprisingly, there are few facilities and even the pay showers (20¢ for 5min) are a drag. Popular with Japanese cyclists and motorbike riders, hence the name. Rooms ❷, dorms ❶

Sunnys, 139 Franklin St (☎08/8231 2430 or free call 1800 631 391, ℱ8231 0131, Wwww.sunnys.com.au). A friendly place in an old house next to the bus station. Facilities include a pool table, sound system, TV and video; good security too. Six- to eight-bed dorms (bunks) plus one twin and a double, all with ceiling fans. Train, bus and plane tickets sold and tours booked, and plenty of useful information on hand as well as internet access ($2.50 for 30min). Small courtyard out back. Off-street parking. Rates include linen and a pancake breakfast. Rooms ❸, dorms ❶

The Travellers Inn, 118 Carrington St (☎08/8224 0753). Drab and pokey but cheap: this would not be your first choice but at least there's air-con and heating, good security and parking. Licensed travel agent. Rooms ❷, dorms ❶

North Adelaide and Kent Town

Adelaide Meridien, 21 Melbourne St, North Adelaide (☎08/8267 3033, ℱ8239 0275, Wwww.adelaidemeridien.com.au). Located on fashionable Melbourne St, the modern brick building itself is an eyesore and the 1980s-style decor is rather outdated, but creature comforts include a sauna, spa and outdoor pool. Undercover parking is included in the rates. ❽

Georgia Mews, 31–33 Wakefield St, Kent Town (☎08/8362 0600, ℱ8362 1317, Wwww.georgiamews.com.au). Just east of the city centre but still

within walking distance, and close to the restaurants and cafés of The Parade in Norwood. Beautifully decorated, light and spacious one-bedroom apartments, with a shady, flower-filled courtyard, telephone, TV, outside laundry and car parking. Fully self-catering, and supplies for a hearty breakfast included. ❼

Greenways Apartments, 41–45 King William Rd, North Adelaide (☎08/8267 5903, ℱ8267 1790, Wwww.greenways.auz.net). One-, two- and three-bedroom fully furnished self-catering units in an excellent location. ❻

Gay and lesbian-friendly accommodation

The beachfront **Semaphore Hotel**, 17 Semaphore Rd (℡08/8449 4662, ℻8449 4626, ℮cathstarrs@bigpond.com), in Semaphore, a beach suburb about 15km northwest of the centre, is lesbian-run but also welcomes gay male guests and straights. The pleasant pub rooms, sharing bathrooms, are well set up with duvets, clock radios, lamps and sink (❹, weekly rates available) and there's a comfortable common room with a wood combustion stove, pool table, couches and TV. The pub itself is nothing out of the ordinary; it has pokies out front, a pleasant bistro out back serving inexpensive meals with a Thai, Malaysian and Indian slant, and an entertainment venue with live bands and DJs Wed–Sun until 2am. Other, more central gay-friendly establishments include self-catering apartments at **Gurny Lodge**, 190–194 Gover St, North Adelaide (℡ & ℻ 08/8239 2301; ❺), and at **Greenways Apartments** (see opposite); and deluxe hotel rooms at the **Stamford Plaza Adelaide** (see p.789). Parkside Travel (℡08/8274 1222) has an accommodation service, or you can check the ads in *Blaze* (see box on p.807).

Beach suburbs

Glenelg Beach Resort, 1–7 Moseley St, Glenelg (℡ & ℻ 08/8376 0007, free call ℡ 1800 066 422, ℠ www.glenelgbeachresort.com.au). Excellent hostel near the beach. Lots of doubles (with fridge and sink) and some singles and apartments available, as well as five- to six-bed dorms (no bunks). The lively common area downstairs has a bar open to the public, with loud music and activities ranging from bands, karaoke and comedians to pool comps and theme nights. Lots of extras, including internet access, free breakfast, bikes, videos and free weekly tours of the city and the Fleurieu Peninsula. No parking. Rooms ❹, dorms ❶

Glenelg Jetty Hotel, 28 Jetty Rd, Glenelg (℡08/8294 4377, ℻ 8295 4412). Friendly, homely pub accommodation popular with country people visiting the city. Rooms are en suite or with shared bathroom, and there is one self-contained flat. ❺

Glenelg Seaway Apartments, 18 Durham St, Glenelg (℡08/8295 8503). Four basic and slightly run-down apartments in a quiet location close to the beach. Linen supplied. ❹

Meleden Villa, 268 Seaview Rd, Henley Beach (℡08/8235 0577). Good-value B&B one street back from the beach in a lovely old two-storey building with a pool and outdoor terrace. Downstairs rooms share bathroom while upstairs rooms, with balconies and sea views, are en suite. ❹–❺.

Taft Motor Inn, 18 Moseley St, Glenelg (℡08/8376 1233, ℻ 8294 6977, ℠ www.taftmotorinn .citysearch.com). Well-equipped motel units and one- and two-bedroom self-catering apartments near the beach; all have air-con and slightly dreary old-fashioned decor. Good for families, with a playground, garden and swimming pool (and toddler pool); baby-sitting available. 24hr reception. ❻

The City

Adelaide's city centre, south of the river, is a strict grid surrounded by parkland: at the very centre of the grid is **Victoria Square**, and each city quarter has its own smaller square. **North Terrace** is the cultural precinct with all the major museums, the two universities and the state library. **Hindley Street** is the liveliest in town, and the focus of the city's nightlife, while **Rundle Mall**, its continuation, is the main shopping area, and **Rundle Street**, further east, the arty café strip. The other important area lies west of Victoria Square: between Grote and Gouger streets is the lively **Central Market** and the small **Chinatown**. The **Torrens River** flows to the north of North Terrace, with the Botanic Gardens and the Zoo on its south bank. Three main roads cross the river to the distinctive colonial architecture and café culture of **North Adelaide**, with **O'Connell Street** the main drag on this side.

As you wander Adelaide's streets, you're struck by the bourgeois solidity of the structures – a solidity enhanced by the fact that virtually every building, public or domestic, is **stone**: sandstone, bluestone, South Australian freestone or slate. The city's well-preserved **Victorian architecture** is not the over-the-top style built from money made quickly in the 1850s goldrush, as it is in Melbourne. Rather Adelaide, which suffered numerous economic setbacks before establishing a steady mining industry, built up its wealth slowly, and the buildings have a reassuring permanence. There's really only one place to start your tour, and that's tree-lined **North Terrace**, a long heritage streetscape perfect for exploring on foot.

The Botanic Gardens and Ayers House

At the eastern extremity of North Terrace is the main entrance to the **Botanic Gardens** (Mon–Fri 8am–dusk, Sat & Sun 9am–dusk; free guided tours from the kiosk by the main lake Tues, Fri & Sun 10.30am; Ⓦwww.environment.sa .gov.au/botanicgardens). The gardens, opened in 1857, are lovely – with statues and heritage buildings to gaze at, wisteria arbours to wander through and ponds and fountains to dally by – just like a classic English-style garden but with plenty of native trees too. The elegant glass and wrought-iron **Palm House**, completed in 1877, was based on a similar building in Germany. Its role of displaying tropical plant species has been taken over by the stunning **Bicentennial Conservatory** (daily 10am–4pm, summer until 5pm; $3). This, the largest glasshouse in Australia, houses a complete tropical rainforest environment with its own computer-controlled cloud-making system. Make sure you pick up the leaflet *Walk with the Plants*, which gives detailed information about the plants. Other attractions are a fragrant herb garden, a rose garden and **Simpson House**, a pleasantly cool thatched hut containing palms and ferns beside a stream. By the duck-filled main lake, you can sit under shady trees outside the excellent licensed **kiosk** and have a beer or snack. At the northern entrance to the gardens, **North Lodge**, once the caretaker's residence, is now a shop (daily noon–4pm) that sells books on botany and gardening, plus other souvenirs.

Heading away from the gardens on North Terrace, the first notable building you come to is the National Trust-owned **Ayers House** (Tues–Fri 10am–4pm, Sat & Sun 1–4pm; $6). Home to the politician Henry Ayers, who was premier of South Australia seven times between 1855 and 1897, it began as a small brick dwelling in 1845: the fine bluestone mansion you now see is the result of thirty years of extensions. Inside, it's elaborately decorated in late nineteenth-century style, with portraits of the Ayers family.

The universities and the Art Gallery of South Australia

Between Frome Road and Kintore Avenue, a whole block of North Terrace is occupied by the University of Adelaide, and the art gallery, museum and state library. The **University of Adelaide**, the city's oldest, was established in 1874 and began to admit women right from its founding – another example of South Australia's advanced social thinking. The grounds are pleasant to stroll through: along North Terrace are **Bonython Hall**, built in 1936 in a vaguely medieval style, and **Elder Hall**, a turn-of-the-twentieth-century Gothic-Florentine design now occupied by the Conservatorium of Music (concerts Fri 1.10pm; $3; Ⓣ08/8303 5925 for details). The highly decorative Gothic-inspired **Mitchell Building** beside it constituted the entire original university; on the first floor is the **Museum of Classical Archaeology** (Mon–Fri noon–3pm, term time only; free).

Overbearing Victorian busts and statues of the stern and upright founders of Adelaide line the strip between Bonython Hall and Kintore Avenue. But respite is at hand, in the form of the two contemporary abstract sculptures outside the **Art Gallery of South Australia**, established in 1881 (daily 10am–5pm; free; guided tours Mon–Fri 11am & 2pm, Sat & Sun 11am & 3pm; talks 12.45pm most Tuesdays; ⊛ www.artgallery.sa.gov.au). The gallery itself has an impressive collection of **Aboriginal art**, including many non-traditional works with overtly political content; major works by the Western Desert school of Aboriginal artists are on permanent display in Gallery 7. There's a fine selection of **colonial art**, too: it's interesting to trace its development, from the earlier work deriving from European art up to the point where the influence of the Australian light, colours and landscape begins to take over and make the pictures come alive. The collection of **twentieth-century Australian art** has some good stuff – Sidney Nolan, Margaret Preston, Grace Cossington-Smith – but a lot of dross too. There's also a large collection of twentieth-century British art, including paintings by Roger Fry and Vanessa Bell (Virginia Woolf's sister). The gallery also has a good bookshop and coffee shop.

Museums – and the State Library

Next to the art gallery in the **South Australian Museum** (daily 10am–5pm; free; tours Sat & Sun at 2pm; ⊛ www.samuseum.sa.gov.au), a huge whale skeleton can be seen through the unfortunate modern glass frontage. Two matching wings with cupolas enclose a pleasant, palm-filled courtyard. The east wing houses the engrossing **Australian Aboriginal Cultures Gallery** (40min guided tours daily; $10; book at museum shop or on ☏ 08/8207 7370); the world's largest collection of **Aboriginal artefacts**. Amongst the exhibits are a 10,000-year-old boomerang and the *Yanardilyi (Cockatoo Creek) Jukurrpa*, a huge painting by a collection of artists from across the continent recalling four important dreaming stories, Marlu (Kangaroo), Wati-Jarra (Two men), Ngatijirri (Budgerigar) and Pingirri (Meat ant). The west wing focuses on **natural history and geology**. On level 3 there's an extensive collection of minerals from around the world including local malachites, quartz and opals. There's also a permanent exhibition on local geologist **Sir Douglas Mawson** (1852–1958), who was commissioned by the museum to explore much of Australia in the early 1900s and who also undertook the historic Australasian Antarctic Expedition in 1911. Some of the animals he brought back from this expedition are still on display along with others from around Australia. There's even a section on **Australian dinosaurs**, including a skeleton of Diprotodon, the largest marsupial to walk the earth. Don't miss the **Normandy Nugget** at the east wing entrance on the ground floor – its the second largest gold nugget in the world, weighing 26kg.

Next door to the museum, on the corner of Kintore Avenue, the 1884 **State Library** (Mon–Wed & Fri 9.30am–8pm, Thurs 9.30am–5pm, Sat & Sun noon–5pm; ☏ 08/8207 7200, ⊛ www.slsa.sa.gov.au) has everything from archives to a newspaper reading room and free internet access (15min maximum, or book for longer duration); there's also a cosy magazine room with comfortable chairs and hundreds of the latest glossies to leaf through. The building is currently being extensively renovated and disruptions will occur until its completion in mid-2003. The State Library also encompasses the **Bradman Collection** in the adjacent building, The Institute (Mon–Fri 10am–5pm, Sat & Sun noon–5pm; $3; ⊛ www.bradman.sa.com.au). Sir Donald Bradman (1908–2001), the Australian cricket legend, donated his personal collection of cricket memorabilia to the State Library, including his own memoirs of the infamous Bodyline series with England. A large screen shows interviews and footage of his finest moments.

Around the corner on Kintore Avenue is the **Migration Museum** (Mon–Fri 10am–5pm, Sat & Sun 1–5pm; free; Ⓦwww.history.sa.gov.au), which takes you on a journey from port to settlement in the company of South Australia's migrant settlers, through interactive displays and reconstructions. The museum's permanent exhibits have a reputation for innovation: the "White Australia Walk", for example, has a push-button questionnaire giving you the red, green or amber light for immigration under the guidelines of the White Australia policy, which was in force from 1901 to 1958. One writer called it a "museum of grief", no doubt affected by its focus on the grim individual struggles of everyday lives, though it does celebrate cultural diversity too. The museum is housed in a former **Destitute Asylum**, where the city's poor and homeless were hidden away in the nineteenth century; its story forms a part of the permanent exhibition, which shares the museum with continuous special exhibitions.

Government buildings and arts spaces

Continuing west along North Terrace past the **War Memorial**, on the next corner is **Government House**, Adelaide's oldest public building, completed in 1855: every governor except the first has lived here. Across King William Road, two parliament houses, the old and the new, compete for space. The current **Parliament House**, begun in 1889, wasn't finished until 1939 because of a dispute over a dome, and while there's still no dome (and only half a coat of arms), it's a stately building all the same, with a facade of marble columns. Alongside is the modest **Old Parliament House**, built between 1855 and 1876 (closed to the public). On the corner of North Terrace and Morphett Street, the **Lion Arts Centre** is the base for the biennial Adelaide Fringe Festival (see box on p.805) and alternative arts in general – there are theatres, bars, a cinema and galleries. The **Experimental Art Foundation** here functions to educate people about contemporary art and was the first alternative art space in Australia to be government-funded; artists have studios upstairs and the gallery downstairs always has provocative exhibitions (Tues–Fri 11am–5pm, Sat 2–5pm). The bookshop has a notice board where invitations to private views are tacked up, so if you want some free wine and a peek at the (small and incestuous) Adelaide art scene, take a look. Meanwhile, the **Jam Factory Craft and Design Centre** (Mon–Fri 9am–5.30pm, Sat & Sun 10am–5pm, Ⓦwww.jamfactory.com.au) highlights the tenuous nature of the dividing line between art and craft: here beautiful objects made of leather, glass, wood and clay combine aesthetics with utility. The work is for sale and there's always an exhibition in the gallery, while a blue-metal spiral staircase leads to a viewing platform above the **glass-blowing centre** (demonstrations Mon–Fri 9am–4pm, Sat & Sun 10am–4pm). The latest addition to Adelaide's contemporary art scene is the **Light Square Gallery** (Mon–Fri 10am–5pm; free) in the basement of the Roma Mitchell Arts Education Centre on Light Square. Here the focus is on **techno art** and the digital age with international exhibitions alongside student displays.

Along the Torrens River: the Festival Centre and Zoological Gardens

The **Torrens River** meanders between Adelaide and North Adelaide, surrounded by parklands. Between Parliament House and the river is the **Festival Centre**: two geometric constructions of concrete, steel and smoked glass, in a concrete arena scattered with abstract 1970s civic sculpture. The theatre complex was built for the 1973 Adelaide Arts Festival and is still its focus (see box on p.805 for more on the festival itself), but the **theatres** are open all year. An extensive redevelopment programme is due to be completed in mid–2002 to bring the Festival Centre into the twenty-first century. The main auditorium, the Festival Theatre, has the largest stage in the Southern Hemisphere, hosting opera, ballet and various concerts; the foyer displays paintings of the Coorong by Fred Williams and is often the venue for free Sunday afternoon concerts from 2 to 4pm. The smaller Playhouse Theatre is the drama theatre; it has a small commercial gallery, Art Space, in its foyer (Mon–Fri 10am–5pm, Sat 1–5pm). The Space Theatre is often used for cabaret and stand-up comedy, and its foyer hosts free children's workshops and low-cost shows on Saturday in winter (2–4pm). Call ☎ 13 1246 for details of specific events.

A short walk across **Elder Park** is the river with its large fountain and black swans. **Popeye Cruises** to the zoo leave from here (hourly Mon–Fri 1–3pm, every 20min Sat & Sun 11am–5pm; $4 one-way, $7.50 return). You can also rent paddleboats ($8.80 per 30min) from the green shed at **Jolleys Boathouse**, across King William Road. The boathouse is an Adelaide institution, housing a restaurant (see p.803) as well as a kiosk with seats, where you can enjoy the same river views as the restaurant without paying the high prices.

The most pleasant way to get to the **Zoological Gardens**, whose main entrance is on Frome Road (daily 9.30am–5pm; $11, children $8; free guided walks at 11am and 2pm; call ☎ 08/8267 3255 for feeding times and keeper talks), is to follow the river, either by boat (see above) or on a fifteen-minute stroll. Alternatively, walk from the Botanic Gardens through Botanic Park, entering through the children's zoo entrance on Plane Tree Drive, or take bus #272 or #273 from Grenfell or Currie streets. Opened in 1883, the country's second-oldest zoo (after Melbourne's) is as much a botanical garden as anything. There are century-old European and native trees, including a huge Moreton Bay fig, and the grounds are full of picnic tables. The Victorian architecture is well preserved; most of the animal houses have long since been replaced but a few classic examples have survived, such as the **Elephant House**, built in 1900 in the style of an Indian temple. The newest section is the Southeast Asian Rainforest exhibit, whose naturalistic settings are home to sixteen animal species, including the endangered Malaysian tapir. However, Adelaide Zoo is best known for its extensive collection of **native birds**, and there are two large walk-through aviaries.

King William Street and Victoria Square

As the city's main thoroughfare, **King William Street** is lined with imposing civic buildings and always crowded with traffic. Look out for the **Edmund Wright House** at no. 59, whose elaborate Renaissance-style facade (designed by Wright) is one of Adelaide's most flamboyant. You can see inside, too, since it houses the administrative **State History Centre** which sometimes has free travelling exhibitions. On the other side of the street, and a couple of blocks south, the **Town Hall** (1866) is another of Edmund Wright's Italianate designs. The **General Post Office**, on the corner of Franklin Street, is yet another portentous Victorian edifice, this time with a central clock tower: look inside at the main hall with its decorative roof lantern framed by opaque skylights. Opposite, on the corner of Flinders Street, the **Old Treasury Building** retains its beautiful facade although it now houses executive apartments.

Interrupting King William Street, pleasant **Victoria Square** with its fountain is a favourite Aboriginal meeting place, with people sitting on the shady ground and talking. Also around the square are the Catholic **Cathedral of St Francis Xavier** (1856) and the imposing **Supreme Court** on the corner of

Gouger Street. Just to the west, the covered **Central Market** (Tues 7am–5.30pm, Thurs 11am–5.30pm, Fri 7am–9pm, Sat 7am–3pm) has been a beloved feature of Adelaide for over a hundred years; here you can find delectable European and Asian produce in a riot of smelly stalls and lively banter. The market area also has around 250 permanent shops (open Mon–Sat), as well as several good cafés, food stalls and restaurants; sushi and noodle bars are closely packed together, and the theme continues into surrounding Gouger and Grote streets, filled with lively restaurants and cafés.

Rundle Mall and Rundle Street

The main shopping area in the central business district is **Rundle Mall**, where several arcades branch off a busy pedestrian mall. It manages to be bustling yet relaxed at the same time, enhanced by trees, benches, alfresco cafés, fruit and flower stalls, and usually a busker or two to draw a crowd. The two main shopping centres are the Myer Centre, with over 120 specialty stores over five floors and the Adelaide Central Plaza, dominated by the upmarket David Jones Department Store and a fantastic foodmart in the basement. Towards the east end of the Mall is the decorative **Adelaide Arcade** and the Regent Theatre. By night, Rundle Mall is eerily deserted, a strange contrast to Hindley and Rundle streets on either side, which really come to life after dark.

Rundle Street was once the traditional home of Adelaide's wholesale fruit and vegetable market, and later its lively, down-at-heel feel was appropriated by the alternative and arty, and by university students from the nearby campuses on North Terrace. It is now the focus of up-and-coming Adelaide, with over fifty cafés and restaurants, many of them alfresco, several slick wine bars and two of the best pubs in town (*The Austral* and *The Exeter*, see p.806 respectively). Only a few trendy hairdressers, designer stores and record shops break up the party. The disused **Adelaide Fruit and Produce Exchange** (1903) is worth a peek. Built of red brick with curved archways and yellow plaster friezes above of fruit, vegetables and wheat, it's a classically Edwardian building. Nearby, off Vaughan Place, is an IMAX giant-screen cinema (see p.808) that shows mostly international documentaries and cartoons.

Tandanya: the National Aboriginal Cultural Institute

Tandanya, the National Aboriginal Cultural Institute, is situated opposite the classic old market buildings at 253 Grenfell St (daily 10am–5pm; $4; ☎08/8224 3200 for details of exhibitions and events; ⓦwww.tandanya.com.au). The centre is managed and controlled by Aboriginal people, who lobbied for fifteen years for such a space: its major focus is **visual arts**, with temporary exhibitions of national significance and a permanent display of work called the Desert Dream, created by remote Aboriginal communities from the Northern Territory. Displays cover Dreamtime stories, history and contemporary Aboriginal writing, while political paintings confront black deaths in custody and other issues, and explore Aboriginal self-expression and identity. There are even a few scattered sand paintings around the floor representing the mortality of traditional art. The shop is an excellent place to buy Aboriginal products, original paintings, didgeridoos, tapes and books, as well as T-shirts and other souvenirs. There's also a 160-seat theatre for live performances – daily **didgeridoo performances** are held at noon – and a café where you can try some bush tucker (Mon–Fri only).

North Adelaide

North Adelaide, a ten-minute walk from the central area, makes for an enjoyable stroll past stately mansions and small, bluestone cottages, or a good pub

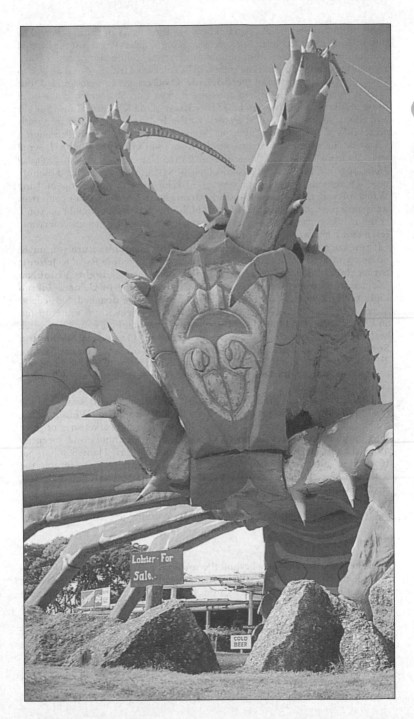

Lobster · For Sale..

COLD BEER

crawl around the many old hotels. There are three ways of getting there. The best walking route to North Adelaide is up King William Road past the Festival Centre (nearly every bus from outside the Festival Centre also goes this way). From Elder Park you cross the pretty 1874 Adelaide Bridge over the river to Cresswell Gardens, home of the **Adelaide Oval** cricket ground (guided tour Tues & Thurs 10am, Sun 2pm, not match days; 2hr; $8), which has a small museum of cricketing memorabilia (Tues 10am–noon & Thurs 10am–1pm; $2) and affords superb views of **St Peter's Cathedral** (daily 9am–5pm; free guided tours Wed 11am & Sun 3pm) on Pennington Terrace opposite Pennington Gardens. The Anglican cathedral was built in 1869 in French Gothic-Revival style; its main entrance is suggestive of Notre-Dame in Paris. The *Cathedral Hotel*, opposite, is Adelaide's second-oldest hotel, built in 1850; it has a humorous "Quasimodo" theme and very good-value meals. At the top of King William Road, the peaceful and shady **Brougham Gardens** boast palm trees set against the backdrop of the Adelaide Hills. If you continue straight up, you'll come to the commercial strip of O'Connell Street, which has an embryonic restaurant scene to rival that of Rundle Street.

If you want to see a wide range of early **colonial architecture** you might do better to head north via Morphett Street and Montefiore Road to **Jeffcott Street** (buses #233 and #253 from King William Street). **Lights Vision**, on Montefiore Hill in Montefiore Park, is a bronze statue of Colonel William Light pointing proudly to the fine views of the city he designed. On Jeffcott Street itself is the neo-Gothic 1890 mansion **Carclew**, with its round turret, and the **Lutheran Theological College**, a fine bluestone and red-brick building with a clock tower and cast-iron decoration. On peaceful **Wellington Square** the pretty 1851 *Wellington Hotel* retains its original wooden balcony. Turning into tree-lined **Gover Street** you'll find rows of simple bluestone cottages; in contrast, **Barton Terrace West**, two blocks west, has grand homes facing the parklands.

The third route from the city to North Adelaide is via Frome Road (past the zoo) to **Melbourne Street** (buses #204 and #209 from King William Street, #272 and #273 from Currie and Grenfell streets), an upmarket strip of good cafés, antique stores, restaurants, designer clothing boutiques and speciality shops. The Banana Room along here at no. 125 (Fri 11am–5.30pm, Sat 10am–5pm, otherwise by appointment on ☎08/8390 1088) is probably the best retro-chic clothes store in Australia, with an immaculate range of designer dresses from the 1920s through to the 1950s; a 1926 Coco Chanel dress is on display. Don't expect bargains – most things are over $100, but it's fascinating to browse, and there is a range of cheaper costume jewellery.

The suburbs

Adelaide spreads a long way beyond the small inner-city enclaves, but few visitors see much of this. Most will at some stage venture down to the sea – a flat stretch of **beaches** west of the city, from Henley via **Glenelg** to Brighton, are sheltered by the Gulf St Vincent and characterized by their long jetties, while **Port Adelaide** further north has some excellent museums to set off its dockside atmosphere – but the inner suburbs remain uncharted territory. Some of them are well worth breaking the mould for, with local character, inexpensive restaurants and out-of-the-ordinary shopping.

NORWOOD, just east of the city, has two interesting streets: Magill Road (bus #106 from Grenfell or Currie streets), with its concentration of antique shops, and The Parade (bus #123 and #124 from Grenfell or Currie streets), a lively shopping strip with some great cafés and pubs and good bookshops. At weekends the small **Orange Lane Market** (Sat & Sun 10am–5pm), at the corner of Edward Street and The Parade, is a sedate place to browse among secondhand and new clothes, books and bric-a-brac, and there are Asian and fry-up food stalls.

In **THEBARTON**, west of the city, the lively **Brickworks Market** (Fri–Sun 9am–5pm; bus #110, #112 or #113 from Grenfell or Currie streets) spreads out from the 1912 Brickworks Kilns at 36 South Rd. There are plaza shops and indoor and outdoor stalls, mostly selling new clothes, and it's always busy with buskers and crowds of people.

Immediately south of the city **Unley Road** (buses #190–198 from King William Street) is known for its antique shops and expensive boutiques. Parallel King William Road at **Hyde Park** (bus #203 from King William Street) is shaded by lots of trees, plants and vine-covered awnings, and has some good cafés to relax in.

Port Adelaide and Torrens Island

The unfortunate early settlers had to wade through mud at Port Misery when they arrived; nowadays **PORT ADELAIDE** takes the strain. Established not far from Port Misery in 1840, by 1870 it was a substantial shipping area with solid stone warehouses, wharves and a host of pubs. The area bounded by Nelson, St Vincent and Todd streets and McLaren Parade is a well-preserved, nineteenth-century streetscape; several ships' chandlers and shipping agents show it's still a living port, a fact confirmed by the many corner pubs (with pretty decorative iron-lace balconies) still in business. The **Port Adelaide Tourist Visitor Information Centre**, near the waterfront on the corner of Commercial Road and St Vincent Street (daily 9am–5pm; ☏08/8447 4788, Ⓦwww.portenf.sa.gov.au) provides up-to-date details of attractions and information about local history.

To get here, take a train from the central station or bus #151 (Mon–Sat, daytime only) or #153 (evenings and Sun) from North Terrace, or #340 from Glenelg (Mon–Fri only); the best day to visit is Sunday or public holiday Monday, when the **Fishermen's Wharf Markets** (9am–5pm) take over a large waterfront warehouse on Queens Wharf and several **cruises** are available on the water. The market (mainly bric-a-brac) adds some life to the waterfront, but the once-varied food stalls now seem to be dominated by purveyors of meat pies and steak sandwiches. Outside is the quaint, red-painted metal **lighthouse** (daily 10am–4pm), dating from 1869, that was originally at the entrance to Port River; it can be climbed and inspected as part of your explorations of the South Australian Maritime Museum (see below), as can the museum's two floating vessels moored 300m away, the steam tug *Yelta* and the coastal trader *Nelcebee*. There are Sunday afternoon trips from the lighthouse with Adelaide Cruises Ltd (☏08/8447 2366) and Port Adelaide River Cruises (☏08/8341 1194).

The pick of Port Adelaide's several museums is the **South Australian Maritime Museum** on Lipson Street (daily 10am–5pm; $8.50, combined ticket with the Port Dock Station Railway Museum $15). Located in the old Bond Store with its massive timber posts and wooden floors, the museum is concerned with the migrants who came through the port and the South Australian **coastal ketch trade**. Starting from the basement, the migration section has faithfully reconstructed three typical steerage or economy cabins from 1840, 1910 and 1950; you can wander through them, lie on a bunk, listen to sails creaking or hear "new Australians" remembering their journey. Level two explores the various ways that South Australia relates to the sea, from seaside scenes with a working penny arcade, to pleasure cruises on the gulf, fishing and making model ships. On the ground floor you can board a real ketch; upstairs is a more traditional collection. Further along Lipson Street, the **Port Dock Station Railway Museum** (daily 10am–5pm; $9; combined ticket with the South Australian Maritime Museum $15) is a trainspotter's delight, with a collection of over twenty steam and diesel locomotives. A free train ride runs on demand.

A few kilometres north of Port Adelaide is **TORRENS ISLAND**. Apart from a lively fresh fish and produce market on Sunday (7am–2pm), its main attraction is its intricate **mangrove forests**, a tranquil habitat rich in marine life that can be explored by foot in the **St Kilda Mangrove Trail** (Mon–Fri 10am–3pm, Sat & Sun 10am–5pm; $6; ☏08/8280 8172), which has an interpretive centre and a 1.7km boardwalk for self-guided tours; or by kayak with Blue Water Sea Kayaking (weekends and school holidays only; $40; booking essential as departures are dependant on tides; ☏08/8295 8812), giving the chance to spot Port River dolphins along the way.

Semaphore to Henley Beach

On the coast just east of Port Adelaide, **SEMAPHORE**, with its picturesque jetty and fine old buildings, was important as the site of Adelaide's signal station from 1856 until the mid-1930s, before becoming a desirable holiday spot. Its current incarnation is as a popular lesbian area (see box on p.807) with several gay and lesbian-run cafés, a pub and a feminist bookshop. These are all on Semaphore Road, a charming street running perpendicular to the beach, with awnings, stained glass on shop and café windows, and an old-fashioned cinema. A Sunday steam train runs from Semaphore Jetty to **Fort Glanville** at 359 Military Rd (Sept–May every third Sun 1–5pm; $5), the only complete example of the many forts built in Australia in the mid-nineteenth century, when fear of Russian invasion reached hysterical heights after the Crimean War. To get to Semaphore by public transport, take a bus to Port Adelaide (see p.799) and then bus #333.

About 8km south of Semaphore, **GRANGE** is a charming beachside suburb, with a row of Victorian terraced houses facing the sands (bus #112 or #135 from Grenfell Street, 30min; Grange line train, 20min) and a popular pier with an upmarket kiosk. The next beach along is atmospheric **HENLEY BEACH** (Mon–Sat bus #137, Sun #130, both from Currie Street, 20min; #286 or #287 from North Terrace, 35min), where the focus is Henley Square opposite the long wooden pier. The square is lined with classic Federation-style buildings housing several popular restaurants and cafés. *Henley on Sea* (see p.804), a waterfront café around the corner, featured as *Moby Dick's* in the film *Shine*. South of here, on the way to Glenelg, **West Beach** (#278 bus from Currie Street; 25min) is a rather soulless spot with a caravan park. It does have a good, long, sandy beach though.

Glenelg and Brighton

The most popular and easily accessible of the city's beaches is at **GLENELG**, immediately south of West Beach, and 11km southwest of the city. The thirty-minute tram ride here from Victoria Square is part of the experience: the beautiful 1929 trams have original fittings – red leather seats and leather hanging straps, and wood-panelled compartments.

Glenelg was the site of the landing of Governor John Hindmarsh and the first colonists on Holdfast Bay; the **Old Gum Tree** where he read the proclamation establishing the government of the colony still stands on McFarlane Street (bus #167 or #168 from Currie or Grenfell streets in the city centre), and there's a re-enactment here every year on Proclamation Day (Dec 28).

Nowadays, Glenelg is busy even off season. **Jetty Road**, the main drag, is crowded with places to eat (for the obligatory seaside fish and chips, *Bay Fish Shop* at no. 27 is the best) and there's lots of accommodation (see p.791). The tram terminates at **Moseley Square**, with its elegant town hall and clock tower. On the opposite corner, the original Victorian *Pier Hotel*, now part of the imposing seafront *Stamford Grand Hotel*, is crowded with drinkers on Sunday, when Glenelg is at its most vibrant. From Moseley Square, the jetty juts out into the bay, and in summer the beach on either side is crowded with people swimming in the calm waters; it's also a popular windsurfing spot year-round. The foreshore is also overlooked by the very tacky **Magic Mountain** (Sun–Thurs 10am–sunset, Fri 10am–11pm, Sat 9am–11pm; free entry, rides by token), a 1970s mistake of a mock-stone monolith housing a predictable beachside funfair. In summer you can speed down waterslides ($7.50 for 30min), while dodgem cars, bumper boats, mini-golf and pinball machines operate all year round. Luckily the deafening noise levels you'll experience if you step inside are reasonably well-contained. Also facing the shore, **Glenelg Tourist Information** (daily 9am–5pm ℡ 08/8294 5833, ⓦ www.holdfast.sa .gov.au) can help with the booking of accommodation, tours and hire cars. When the centre is closed, you can access information on the 24hr touch-screen terminal outside. Next door, Beach Hire (℡ 08/8294 1477) rents out deck chairs, umbrellas, bikes, surf skis, body-boards and snorkel sets. Rollerblading and cycling are other popular activities in Glenelg, with a **bike track** south of the square and mountain and touring bikes to rent from Holdfast Cycles at 726 Anzac Highway (℡ 08/8294 4537; $20 per day).

South of Glenelg, **BRIGHTON** has an old-fashioned, sleepy air, perhaps lent by the stone Arch of Remembrance that's flanked by palm trees and stands in front of the long jetty, the suburb's focal point. Here families and couples wander as joggers, cyclists and skateboarders strut their stuff along the Esplanade. Running inland from the beach, Jetty Road has a string of appealing one- and two-storey buildings shaded with awnings that contain an assortment of art, craft and secondhand stores, and two popular alfresco cafés: *A Cafe Etc* and *Horta's*. Brighton is reached by train from Adelaide (25min) or bus #266 from Grote Street. For beaches further south, see p.825.

Eating and drinking

Adelaide has roughly one restaurant for every thirty people, so not surprisingly **eating out** is a local obsession, and it's incredibly inexpensive here compared to Sydney or Melbourne. Moonta Street, closed to traffic between Gouger and Grote streets, is a small **Chinatown** heralded by Chinese gates which has several Chinese restaurants and supermarkets. An excellent **food plaza** off Moonta Street (daily 11am–4pm, except Fri until 9pm) serves Vietnamese, Indian, Singaporean, Thai and Malaysian food as well as Chinese *yum cha* and Cantonese BBQ. There are over thirty restaurants on **Gouger Street**, many of which are alfresco and at their busiest on Friday night when the nearby Central Market stays open until 9pm. **Café** society is based around Rundle Street in the city, and in North Adelaide on O'Connell Street and the upmarket, decidedly chic Melbourne Street. Finally, eating in **pubs** in Adelaide doesn't just mean the usual steak and salad bar but covers the whole spectrum, from some of the best "contemporary" Australian food in town to bargain specials in several pubs along King William Street.

As for drinking, South Australian **wine** features heavily – which is just as well, since, by general consensus, **tap water** in Adelaide tastes dreadful.

Although it's perfectly safe, there's usually only a small charge for spring water, which is what everybody drinks. And thanks to the state's liberal licensing laws, even most cafés are licensed.

City centre

Cafés and cheap meals

Al Fresco Gelateria & Pasticceria, 260 Rundle St. If you go to only one café in Adelaide, make it this one. Packed every night, the young Italian community have made it their own, and it's *the* place to see and be seen. Great coffee, *biscotti*, delicious *gelati* made on the premises and *focaccia* and calzone to eat. Daily 6.30am–late, which means around 4am at weekends.

Blumsteins, 203 Grenfell St. Organic café near Tandanya with a wood-fired oven for baking excellent bread. Diverse and completely organic menu covers everything from biodynamic yogurts to cooked breakfasts and light vegetarian and meat dishes. They also sell organic fruits and cheeses to take away. Mon–Fri 7am–10pm, Sat 8am–10pm, Sun 8am–5pm.

Cowley's Pie Cart, An Adelaide institution, this mobile pie cart takes up its position each night outside the GPO on Franklin St. It's famous for its pie floaters. Mon–Thurs & Sun 6pm–1am, Fri & Sat 6pm–3.30am.

Eros Ouzeri, 275–277 Rundle St. Greek meze-style dining: choose from a variety of inexpensive snacks to put together a tasty meal. The setting is smart and airy, in a renovated old building with high, pressed-metal ceilings. Sit outside at the attached café for Greek pastries and coffee. Licensed.

Fasta Pasta, 131 Pirie St and 465 Pulteney St. Part of a chain which serves authentic, inexpensive fresh pasta with interesting sauces, ordered informally at the counter. Also at Glenelg and Brighton (see p.804).

Govinda's, 79 Hindley St. Small vegetarian restaurant with Indian sweet cakes and an all-you can-eat lunch for $7. Lunch Mon–Sat 11.30am–3pm, dinner Tues–Sat 5–8pm.

Hawkers Corner, 141 West Terrace, cnr Wright St. Something of an Adelaide cheap eats institution. Chinese, Thai, Malaysian and North Indian stalls. Try the Malay seafood laksa. Unlicensed and no BYO allowed. Tues–Sat 5–10pm, Sun 11.30am–8.30pm.

Jerusalem Sheshkebab House, 131B Hindley St. Dimly lit Lebanese BYO that serves fresh and tasty Middle Eastern dishes. Daily noon until midnight.

Marcellina Pizza Bar, 273 Hindley St (℡08/8211 7560). At the quieter western end, this all-night pizza, steak and pasta bar is always full with the spillout from the area's clubs and pubs; the pizzas are among the best in town. Deliveries too. Sun–Thurs 11.30am–2am, Fri & Sat 11.30am–5am.

Roma's, 200 Hutt St. A recommended deli-style café with gleaming counters and displays packed with cosmopolitan edibles; reasonably priced. Great breakfasts and excellent coffee. Licensed and BYO. Mon–Fri 7.30am–5pm, Sat & Sun 7.30am–6pm.

Ruby's Café, 255B Rundle St. A popular market café in the 1950s; the decor is real here, not retro. But cocktails, an arts notice board and changing exhibitions bring it up to the 1990s, and the famous Sunday breakfast is now served from 9am until 5pm. Otherwise, it's open evenings only (6.30pm–late).

Zuma Caffe, 56 Gouger St. With its back entrance opening onto the Central Market, this place buzzes more than ever during market hours. Locals flock here for the huge breakfasts, big salads, and filo parcels, bruschetta, *focaccia* and quiche baked on the premises. Mon–Thurs 7am–6pm, Fri 7am–10pm, Sat 7am–4am.

Pubs and wine bars

Ambassadors Hotel, 107 King William St. Slightly sleazy pub, but a ridiculously cheap, simple pub lunch ($4.95, weekdays only) put on to attract people to play the pokies here.

Austral Hotel, 205 Rundle St. Excellent inexpensive bistro meals, Malaysian, Thai, Mexican and Italian dishes, and good old Aussie steaks, burgers and seafood. There's also a restaurant with a smaller, pricier menu.

Bull and Bear Ale House, 91 King William St. A snazzy bar in the basement of the State Bank Centre – a cool retreat on a hot day for sticky stockbrokers. Imported ales and sophisticated meals.

Earl of Aberdeen, 316 Pulteney St, Hindmarsh Square (℡08/8223 6433). Gazebo full of greenery serving huge portions of imaginatively cooked pasta, steak, fish and kangaroo. Attentive service.

Universal Wine Bar, 258 Rundle St (℡08/8232 5000). Stylish bar run by a wine maker aiming to educate people about South Australia's wines. Sit at the bar or choose a table; wine by the glass or bottle. The atmosphere is distinctly European, and the small menu of delicious bistro food has a provincial French and Mediterranean slant. Mon–Sat 11.30am–midnight.

Restaurants

Amalfi Pizzeria Ristorante, 29 Frome St (☏ 08/8223 1948). Creative Italian place; upbeat, jazzy and young with a variety of vegetarian dishes, experimental pasta sauces and traditional ones given a hot edge. Crowded, and open very late. Licensed. Closed Sat lunch & Sun.

Garage, 163 Waymouth St (☏ 08/8212 9577). Funky restaurant and bar in a converted garage warehouse with original brick walls. Great breakfasts and a lively lunch menu plus snacks served throughout the evening when the focus turns to socializing, dancing and DJ music. Restaurant Mon–Fri 8am–3pm, otherwise open Tues–Sun 8am till late.

Gaucho's, 91 Gouger St (☏ 08/8231 2299). If you're after red meat, this Argentinian place serves some of the best steaks in town: name your weight. Licensed and BYO. Closed Sat & Sun lunch.

The Grange, *Adelaide Hilton*, 233 Victoria Square (☏ 08/8217 2000). European-style fine-dining restaurant where the top chef brings an Asian angle to already adventurous dishes. Very expensive. Dinner Tues–Sat, closed Dec & Jan.

Irodori, 291 Rundle St (☏ 08/8232 6799). Modern Japanese restaurant specializing in sushi and *teppanyaki*. Some alfresco dining. BYO and licensed. Open daily for lunch and dinner.

Jolleys Boathouse, Jolleys Lane, off Victoria Drive next to City Bridge (☏ 08/8223 2891). Converted boathouse serving mouthwatering but pricey contemporary Australian cuisine. A popular venue for Sunday lunch. Licensed. Closed Sun night.

Noodles, 119 Gouger St (☏ 08/8231 8177). Popular Southeast Asian restaurant serving Thai and Malaysian food. Licensed and BYO. Lunch Tues–Fri, dinner nightly.

The Oyster Bar, 14 East Terrace (☏ 08/8232 5422). Contemporary bar with alfresco dining overlooking the park, just around the corner from busy Rundle St. Oysters $14.50 per dozen. Daily noon–late.

T-chow, 68 Moonta St (☏ 08/8410 1413). Huge, popular Chinese restaurant serving Teochew regional specialities. Well-known for Teochew tender duck, shark's fin soup and green peppercorn chicken. Quick lunch of noodles for $5.

Ying Chow, 114 Gouger St (☏ 08/8211 7998). An unpretentious place, always crowded. Serves Northern Chinese cuisine, including specialities such as aniseed tea duck or scallops cooked with coriander and Chinese thyme. Vegetarians can enjoy delicious dishes such as bean curd with Chinese chutney. Inexpensive. Licensed and BYO. Lunch Fri only, dinner nightly.

North Adelaide, Norwood and Unley

Cafés and cheap meals

Café Paradiso, 150 King William Rd, Hyde Park, near Unley. A long-established Italian favourite; great coffee and *biscotti* and alfresco dining out front. Food ranges from pasta to *fritto misto*. Licensed. Daily 8.30am–11.30pm.

Caffe Buongiorno, 145 The Parade, Norwood. Large, always lively café which reaches a crowded and noisy crescendo on Sunday night. Serves a wide variety of Italian food and drink. Daily 8am–1am or later.

Elephant Walk Coffee Lounge, 76 Melbourne St, North Adelaide. Carved wooden elephants and bamboo dividers make small, private lounge areas; lively but intimate. Daily 8pm–late.

The Oxford Deli Bar, *Oxford Hotel*, 101 O'Connell St, North Adelaide. The *Deli Bar* is good value: order at the counter and eat in the groovy pub. There are plenty of meals around $8, with full marks going to the Oxburger and fries at $7.50.

Red Rock Noodle Bar, 48 Unley Rd, Unley (☏ 08/88357 3888). One of five braches of this stylish quick-meal restaurant. Generous and inexpensive servings of every kind of delicious noodle dish you could think of. The $6 lunch specials are good value. Other locations include 125 The Parade, Norwood and 141 O'Connell St, North Adelaide.

Restaurants

Bacall's, 149 Melbourne St, North Adelaide (☏ 08/8267 2030). Cajun specialist with authentic oven-baked dishes and a lively New Orleans-flavoured atmosphere. Book early if you want one of the few streetside tables. Moderate. BYO and licensed. Tues–Sat 6–10pm.

Kwik Stix, 42 O'Connell St, North Adelaide (☏ 08/8239 2023). Spacious modern Asian restaurant with good-value meals. Excellent chargrilled and sizzling dishes from Laos, Korea and Malaysia are served dinner only. Daily noon–2.30pm and 5–10pm.

The Melting Pot, 160 King William Rd, Hyde Park, near Unley (☏ 08/8373 2044). One of the best modern French restaurants in Adelaide, with fantastic veal, spiced duck and seasonal fish on the menu. And, of course, good wines and champagnes. Lunch Thurs & Fri, dinner Mon–Sat.

Shibata, 131 Melbourne St, North Adelaide (☏ 08/8267 3381). Japanese restaurant specializing in *nabe mono* (one-pot dishes). Moderate. BYO and licensed. Daily 6–11pm.

The Snake Charmer, 60 Unley Rd, Unley (℡08/8272 2624). Upmarket North Indian place. BYO and licensed. Closed Sun.

Beach suburbs

Cafés and cheap meals

Fasta Pasta, 16 Jetty Rd, Glenelg; and 430 Brighton Rd, Brighton. Inexpensive pasta chain.

Henley on Sea, immediately south of Henley Square, opposite the Henley Beach Life Saving Club (℡08/8235 2250). Relaxed café-brasserie with a summery atmosphere and views of the jetty and water. Mellow interior, and shaded tables outside. Used as the location for *Moby Dick's* piano bar in the film *Shine* – unfortunately there's no piano in sight now. Light contemporary dishes with an emphasis on seafood. Licensed. Lunch & dinner daily from 11am; closed Tues.

Horta's, 75–77 Jetty Rd, Brighton. With its pavement tables and fish mosaic out front, this is a pretty licensed beachside place, popular for lunch; dishes range from pasta to Thai. If it's full try the neighbouring *A Cafe Etc* which does great all-day breakfasts and big salads. Closed Mon.

The Lovin' Spoonful, 69A Semaphore Rd, Semaphore. Gay- and lesbian-friendly café/restaurant with rich cakes, light vegetarian meals and Aussie bush tucker on the menu. Quaint courtyard serving cocktails gives this place its identity. Wed–Sat 7am–late, Sun & Mon 7am–5pm; closed Tues.

Sarah's, 85 Dale St, Port Adelaide (℡08/8341 2103). Popular vegetarian restaurant, open for lunch Mon–Fri, dinner Wed–Sat.

Zambracca, 94–98 Melbourne St, North Adelaide (℡08/8239 1345). A lively, licensed bistro crowded with the smart set. Superb moderately-priced Mediterranean food in slick, spacious surroundings. Daily 8am–late.

Stamford Grand Hotel, The Foreshore, Glenelg (℡08/8375 0622). There are several good cafés and places to eat in this hotel, including the excellent café-style *Rickshaw's* restaurant, split in half by an open kitchen so you can watch the chefs at work: one side serves spicy Indian meals, the other a variety of Asian dishes. There's also a more upmarket contemporary restaurant, *The Promenade*, with great sea views.

Restaurants

Durham's Restaurant, 2 Durham St, Glenelg (℡08/8294 8224). A classy menu of classic European-influenced dishes. Modern dining in an 1880s Victorian terrace building featuring open fires, polished floors and high ceilings. Expensive. Open by appointment only.

Estias, Henley Square, Henley Beach (℡08/8353 2875). Fun seaside place for casual dining on Greek meze amongst a playful modern Hellenic-themed decor, with repro classical sculptures and columns supporting the bar. Also more substantial dishes such as moussaka, and daily specials. Licensed and BYO. Closed Mon.

Mama Carmella, 4 Jetty Rd, Glenelg (℡08/8331 2288). Very popular gleaming Italian café-pizzeria established for over twenty years; good for lunch, a late meal or just coffee. Outside tables overlook the square. Daily 8am–late.

Entertainment and nightlife

Adelaide may appear dead at night, but there's actually quite a lot going on – bands, clubs, film and theatre – if you know where to look. The best place to find out **what's on** is *The Guide*, a pull-out weekly with film and theatre listings and reviews in Thursday's *Advertiser*. There's also a thriving **free press**: top of the culture stakes is *The Adelaide Review*, a highbrow monthly covering the visual and performing arts, dance, film, literature, history, wine and food, available from bookshops such as Imprints on Hindley Street, museums, galleries and just about everywhere else. At the more populist end of the scale, *Rip It Up* is a gig listings magazine, out every Thursday, with film, theatre, club and music reviews and interviews, and there's the *db Magazine* in the same vein, published every two weeks on Wednesdays; both can be picked up at Rundle Street record stores such as B# Records, at no. 240 (jazz and world music specialists; ℡08/8223 7258), and Verandah Music at no. 182 (rock, metal and punk specialists; ℡08/8223 6753). Most big music events can be booked through Bass (℡13 1246, ⓦwww.bass.sa.com.au), who have an outlet at Verandah Music, while B# Records sells tickets for underground events around town.

At night, the two spots to head for are **Rundle Street**, which boasts the most fashionable pubs and bars, and the more mainstream and rather sleazy **Hindley Street**, where you'll find several funky clubs and live-music venues east of Morphett Street catering for the nearby university crowd. And, of course, there's the **Adelaide Casino** (Mon–Thurs & Sun 10am–4am, Fri & Sat 10am–6am; neat dress required; ℡08/8218 4111), near the train station. As unpromising as this might sound, it's worth at least one visit: the marble entrance with its dome is stunning and, although this elegance isn't matched by the glitzy gaming rooms, the Austrian crystal chandeliers are jaw-slackening.

The Adelaide Festival of Arts and Womadelaide

The **Adelaide Festival of Arts**, which takes over the city for three weeks at the beginning of March in even-numbered years, is a huge event, attracting an extraordinary range of international and Australian theatre companies, performers, musicians, writers and artists. Around the main festival has grown an avant-garde and experimental **Fringe**, which for many is more exciting than the main event. The official festival began in 1960 and since 1973 has been based at the purpose-built **Festival Centre** (see p.794); there's late-night cabaret here after the evening's events. There are also free outdoor concerts and opera – even films. Other venues around town host **Artists' Week**, exploring the visual arts, and a small film festival. **Writers' Week**, the free literary festival, is held under marquees in the Pioneer Women's Memorial Gardens, across King William Road from Elder Park. The 2002 Festival of Arts runs from 1–17 March (ⓦwww.adelaidefestival .org.au).

The **Fringe Festival** begins with a wild street parade on Rundle Street a week before the mainstream Festival of Arts. Based at the **Lion Arts Centre**, on the corner of North Terrace and Morphett Street, and at venues all over town, it also unleashes buskers en masse onto Rundle Mall. Twenty-four hour licensing laws are taken advantage of, as the Sydney and Melbourne arts scenes join the locals for some serious partying: late through the hot night the Fringe Club has bands, cabaret and comedy, and there are free outdoor shows and activities. The 2002 Fringe Festival runs from 22 February to 17 March (ⓦwww.adelaidefringe.com.au).

Advance programmes for both the main and the fringe festival and further information is available from the offices of Tourism South Australia, or from all Bass outlets.

Womadelaide is an outdoor world music weekend that began in 1992 as part of the Arts Festival. It has now developed its own successful identity, attracts over 30,000 people and is held every alternate (odd-numbered) year to the festival, although organizers are considering making it an annual event. Womadelaide takes place in late February under the trees and night skies of Botanic Park – four stages, two workshop areas, multicultural food stalls and visual arts – and is typically laid back. This is a great event to sample some of Australia's local talent with a broad selection of Aboriginal musicians as well as internationally acclaimed contemporary and traditional artists from around the world. The full weekend (Fri night–Sun night) costs $150, but day and session passes are also available. Bass (℡13 1246, ⓦwww.bass.sa.com.au) are the official store selling Womad tickets in Adelaide. For advance information check out the websites of Womadelaide (ⓦwww.womadelaide.ozemail.com.au) or Advance Tours and Travel (ⓦwww.advancetravel.com.au).

Pubs and bars

Austral Hotel, 205 Rundle St (☎08/8223 4660). More consciously arty and music-oriented than the *Exeter* (see below), the *Austral* is frequented by students for the independent local bands on Fri and Sat nights, and DJs Tues–Thurs & Sun nights. DJs are free, as is most of the music – when there's a cover charge, it's around $4. Fri & Sat open until 3am.

Boltz Bar and Café, 286 Rundle St (☎08/8232 5234). The café downstairs has fabulous food with an international flavour, while the venue room upstairs hosts local and interstate comedians on Thursday nights (10pm–1am cover charge), and the thought-provoking Philosophy Jam on the second Tuesday of the month conducted by two lecturers from Adelaide University (8.30pm; free). Café daily 10am–11pm, Thurs–Sat until 1am.

The Daniel O'Connell, 165 Tynte St, North Adelaide (☎08/8267 4032). Huge Irish pub with a lovely beer garden around the 150-year-old peppertree. Large restaurant, bar meals and live bands – sometimes Irish folk musicians – play on Friday and Saturday nights when the place is heaving.

Exeter Hotel, 246 Rundle St (☎08/8223 2623). This spacious old pub with an iron-lace balcony is a long-established hangout for Adelaide's artists and writers, yet remains totally unpretentious. Good lunches served, and music nightly except Monday; no cover charge.

Rio's, 111 Hindley St. The tackiest bar in town; open 24 hours.

Worldsend, 208 Hindley St (☎08/8231 9137). Multifunctional large pub popular with the nearby university crowd. Two bars, a restaurant, cocktail bar, lounge, beer garden and live music at weekends. Licensed till 4am.

Clubs, comedy and live music

Café Tapas, 242A Rundle St (☎08/8223 7564). Spanish tapas bar (tapas $8.50–16 plus paella and $6 lunch specials) with arty events including flamenco music and dancing on Friday and Saturday, and funky dance sounds for chilling out on Sunday. Closed Sat lunch & Mon.

Cargo Club, 213 Hindley St (☎08/8231 2327). Casual club that features live jazz, spoken word, cabaret, soul, Latin, African and reggae acts and local and international DJs; the decor is a mix of classic cool and 1990s postmodernism, and there's something on most nights.

Church, 9 Synagogue Place, off Rundle St (☎08/8223 4233). This industrial-chic club venue in a converted temple is the enduring focus for Adelaide's rave scene. Local and international DJs. Wed–Sat 9pm–5am.

Crown and Sceptre, 308 King William St (☎08/8212 4159). A Heritage-listed pub with original leadlighting that's been groovified into one of Adelaide's best venues. Sparkly bar stools, cosy couches in the intimate band area and a busy espresso machine make the place really comfortable. Local bands Tues–Fri & Sun (usually free); Saturday is club night (until 5am; around $5), alternating weekly from *Comfy Club* (funk-beat oriented) to jungle and techno. Plays and poetry readings are sometimes held in the lounge.

Enigma, 173 Hindley St (☎08/8212 2313). Hip venue for the alternative university crowd. Small bar spills into the street at weekends and there's either funk or live grunge music upstairs. Wed–Sat till late.

Heaven 2, 1 West Terrace (☎08/8211 8533). Huge dance club. Resident DJs as well as visiting international acts and one-off events. Wed–Sat 9pm–5am.

The Planet, 77 Pirie St (☎08/8359 2797). There's certainly a whole world of entertainment crammed into this place, with a dance club where the best of local and international DJs play, as well as a pool room, cocktail bar, wine bar and several cafés.

Rhino Room, upstairs, 13 Frome St (☎08/8227 1611). Underground club venue with an intimate lounge atmosphere; come casual or get glammed up – no one cares. The regular clientele may make you feel as if you've barged into a private party, though. Comedy and poetry on Wednesdays, local bands Thursdays, funk on Friday and techno DJ on Saturday. Cosy little bar provides a retreat from the performance. Wed–Fri 9pm–1am, Sat & Sun until 3am. Standard charge $5.

Royal Oak, 123 O'Connell St, North Adelaide (☎08/8267 2488). Popular North Adelaide bar and restaurant with arty decor and a young crowd. Live jazz/latin Sunday and Wednesday, local bands Tuesday and Friday.

South Australia was the first state to legalize gay sex and remains one of the most tolerant of lesbian and gay lifestyles. Adelaide has a more modest gay community than Sydney or Melbourne but the scene enjoys a serenity the bigger cities can't match. Apart from the city's more mainstream annual festivals, there are a few strictly gay and lesbian fiestas. The biggest and best is Adelaide's Gay & Lesbian Cultural Festival Feast (℡08/8231 2155), launched in 1997. It runs for three weeks from late October to mid-November, with the Lion Arts Centre on North Terrace as its focus. An official opening party here kicks off the celebrations in carnival style. Festival events over the next 21 days include theatre, music, visual art, literature, dance cabaret, historical walks, a Gay and Lesbian Film Festival at the Mercury Cinema (see p.808), and the year's best dance party, the Adelaide Sleaze. The festival culminates in Picnic in the Park, an outdoor celebration in Elder Park which has been a feature of the Adelaide scene for over a decade; entertainment includes a very camp dog show. Earlier in the year, June's Stonewall Celebrations are less flamboyant, featuring serious talks and exhibitions in a number of venues.

A popular gay hangout is Pulteney 431 Sauna, 431 Pulteney St (Wed–Fri noon–1am, Fri & Sat noon–3am; ℡08/8223 7506), with a spa, sauna, steam room, pool and snack bar.

To find out where the action is, pick up a copy of *Blaze* (see below) or contact the Women's Information Service (see p.812), or check out other possibilities in the listings below.

Publications and bookshops

Blaze, 213 Franklin St (℡08/8211 9199, ⓦwww.blazemedia.com.au). Free from venues and bookshops; you'll definitely find it at Imprints, 80 Hindley St. Blaze also publish the handy free *Lesbian & Gay Adelaide Map*.

Liberation, available from the Women's Information Service (see p.812). A monthly women's newsletter – good for contacts and local happenings.

Murphy Sisters Bookshop, 240 The Parade, Norwood (℡08/8332 7508). Gay/lesbian bookshop with a handy notice board. Wed–Sat only.

Sisters by the Sea Bookshop, 14 Semaphore Rd, Semaphore (℡08/8341 7088). Specializes in lesbian and feminist books, with a choice of more popular fiction titles too, and has a small notice board. Tues–Sun 11am–6pm.

Organizations and support groups

AIDS Council of South Australia (ACSA), 64 Fullarton Rd, Norwood. Education, support and counselling (information line ℡08/8362 1611; outside the city free call ℡1800 888 559).

Clinic 275, 1st Floor, 275 North Terrace (℡08/8226 6025). Free and confidential testing for all STDs (including HIV) and counselling Mon, Thurs & Fri 10am–4.30pm, Tues & Wed noon–7pm. No appointment necessary.

Darling House Gay and Lesbian Community Library, 64 Fullarton Rd, Norwood (℡08/8362 3106). Fiction, non-fiction and newspapers. Mon–Fri 9am–5pm, Sat 2–5pm.

Gay and Lesbian Counselling Service (℡08/8362 3223). Counselling, information and needle exchange. Counselling line daily 7–10pm, plus Sat & Sun 2–5pm.

Gay Men's Health (℡08/8362 1617). Counselling, support and information.

Lesbian Healthline (℡08/8267 4185; outside the city free call ℡1800 182 098). Health advice Mon 3–7pm.

Parkside Travel, 70 Glen Osmond Rd, Parkside (℡08/8274 1222 or free call 1800 888 501). Gay-owned and operated. Hotel reservations, information and travel services.

See also p.791 for gay- and lesbian-friendly places to stay and p.808 for gay and lesbian nightspots.

Eclipse Tavern, 258 Hindley St (☎ 08/8231 9614). Predominantly lesbian bar, though only Friday (5–9pm) is strictly women only. DJs, performances and pool competitions feature. An intimate, relaxed atmosphere. Tues–Sun 9pm–late.
Edinburgh Castle Hotel, 233 Currie St (☎ 08/8410 1211). Friendly gay and lesbian-only venue with a dance floor with DJ Thursday to

Sunday, jukebox, bistro and beer garden with drag shows on Sunday. Mon–Thurs 11am–midnight, Fri 11am–1.30am, Sat 11am–1am, Sun 2pm–1am.
Mars Bar, 122 Gouger St (☎ 08/8231 9639). This Adelaide institution has been around for years. Drag acts and a big, friendly mixed crowd. Wed–Sat 9pm–late.

Film

As well as several city and suburban mainstream film complexes, Adelaide now has four art-house/retro cinemas and an IMAX cinema. The main **discount day** for mainstream cinemas is Tuesday. In the summer, you can watch films outdoors at the **Moonlight Cinema** in the Botanic Gardens; bookshops around town have programmes (or check out ⓦ www.moonlight.com.au), and tickets ($13) are available at the gate from 7.30pm onwards or through Bass (☎ 13 1246, ⓦ www.bass.sa.com.au).

Academy, Hindmarsh Square (☎ 08/8223 5000). Mainstream downtown multiscreen.
Capri, 141 Goodwood Rd, Goodwood (☎ 08/8272 1177). Alternative and arty films complete with pre-show Wurlitzer organ on Tuesday, Friday and Saturday evenings.
Chelsea, 275 Kensington Rd, Kensington Park (☎ 08/8431 5080). The latest releases and a "Crying Room" for parents and babies.
Cinema Nova, 251 Rundle St (☎ 08/8223 6333). A new arts cinema complex with three screens. Despite its modern interior – stainless steel stairway and opaque resin candy-bar counter – there's neither a licensed bar nor even a coffee machine. Monthly "cry baby" sessions for parents with babies. Substantial backpacker discounts (with the relevant card); discount day for everyone is Wednesday.
Glenelg Cinema Centre, 119 Jetty Rd, Glenelg (☎ 08/8294 3366). Three-screen mainstream cinema. Cheap day Tuesday.
Greater Union, 128 Hindley St (☎ 08/8231 5961, ⓦ www.greaterunion.com.au). A large mainstream complex at the heart of the action: $25 special includes a meal at one of five participating restaurants.
Hoyts Regent Cinema, Regent Arcade, 101 Rundle Mall (☎ 1902 263 456, calls charged at

85¢, ⓦ www.hoyts.com.au). Central multiscreen cinema; discount day Tuesday.
IMAX Theatre, Vaughan Place, off Rundle St (☎ 08/8227 0075, ⓦ www.imax.com.au). Largest screen in South Australia showing visually stunning nature-based documentary films. Hourly films every day 10am–10pm; 2D $14.50, 3D $15.50.
Mercury Cinema, Lion Arts Centre, 13 Morphett St (☎ 08/8410 1934, ⓦ www.mrc.org.au). A great art-house cinema showing short and foreign films; the venue for lots of foreign film and video festivals, and for the gay and lesbian film festival Feast.
Odeon Star Cinema, 65 Semaphore Rd, Semaphore (☎ 08/8341 5988). Quaint, local, beachside cinema showing mainstream films.
Palace East End, 274 Rundle St (☎ 08/8232 3434). Opening off the IMAX theatre foyer, but this is a more alternative venue, showing foreign-language, art-house and prestige new releases. Cheap day Monday.
Piccadilly, 181 O'Connell St, North Adelaide (☎ 08/8267 1500). Prestige new releases.
Trak Cinemas, 375 Greenhill Rd, Toorak Gardens (☎ 08/8332 8020). Good alternative cinema with two screens. Cheap day Tuesday. Bus #145 from North Terrace to stop 10.

Theatre and performance

Out of festival time, mainstream theatre, ballet, opera, contemporary dance, comedy and cabaret continue to thrive at the **Festival Centre**, and classical concerts are held at the **Adelaide Town Hall** (usually performed by the Adelaide Symphony Orchestra), and at **Elder Hall** at the Conservatorium of Music on North Terrace. However, more experimental theatre disappointingly all but dries up: the focus of what remains finds its base at the **Lion Arts Centre**, home of the biennial Fringe Festival. Almost anything that's on can be booked through Bass (☎13 1246, ⓦwww.bass.sa.com.au).

Doppio Teatro, based at the Lion Arts Centre (☎08/8231 0070, ⓦwww.doppio-parallelo.on.net). This bilingual company promotes cultural diversity in the arts as well as exploring new media in its performances at various venues around Adelaide.
Festival Centre, King William Rd (☎08/8216 8600). Three major auditoriums and free music events in the foyer (Sun 2–4pm, winter only). See p.794 for more details.
Music House, Lion Arts Centre, cnr Morphett St and North Terrace (☎08/8218 8400). The Lion Theatre is the main venue at the centre, and there's always lots going on here, from interstate performers and jazz bands to comedy line-ups. An irregular programme, so watch out for flyers.
Theatre 62, 145 Burbridge Rd, Hilton (☎08/8234 0838). Two venues under one roof: The Chapel is the smaller experimental space which often has women's performances, while the bigger space (seating three hundred) hosts mostly pantomime and sometimes a theatre-restaurant.

Shopping

You can find most things you'll need in **Rundle Mall** (see p.796), which has three department stores, plus a handy Woolworths at no. 86 with a small supermarket attached. There is another central supermarket, Coles, at 21 Grote St (open daily), next to the Central Market. The large metropolitan shopping centres are at Tea Tree Plaza (northeast), West Lakes (beachside suburbs) and Marion (south).

For **alternative fashion**, Rundle Street, and particularly Miss Gladys Sym Choon at no. 235, is the place to go. For retro clothing visit Mabs, 207 Grenfell St, or The Banana Room (see p.798). For **Aboriginal arts and crafts** try Tandanya (see p.796) or the Otherway Shop at 185 Pirie St. B# Records on Rundle Street (see p.796) and Krypton Discs, 34 Jetty Rd, Glenelg, are both good for **records**.

There are several good **bookshops** around the city: Imprints, 80 Hindley St, is a good highbrow shop; the excellent Unibooks, at Adelaide University, provides an excuse to nose around the university; Angus & Robertsons, 138 Rundle Mall, is a large mainstream store; Europa Books at no. 238 Rundle St, sells foreign-language literature and travel books and guides in English as well as maps; Adelaide Booksellers, 6A Rundle Mall sells good secondhand titles, as does O'Connell's Bookshop at 62 Hindley St, which will also buy or exchange books. For antiquarian books, head for Michael Treloare, 196 North Terrace, and admire his beautiful bookcases. In Norwood, Murphy Sisters Bookshop, 240 The Parade, is a feminist bookshop also specializing in Aboriginal studies.

Markets include Central Market (see p.796), Orange Lane Market (see p.799), Brickworks Market (see p.799), Port Adelaide Market (see p.799) and Torrens Island Fish and Produce Market (see p.800). In a lane tucked away behind the excellent *Universal Wine Bar* (see p.802) on Rundle Street, East End Cellars, 22–26 Vardon St, is an excellent **bottle shop** if you want to buy some choice South Australian wines to take away.

Shopping hours are Monday to Saturday 9am to 5 or 6pm, with late-night shopping until 9pm on Friday in the city and Thursday in the suburbs, plus Sunday trading (11am–5pm) in the city only.

Listings

Airlines (domestic) Airlines of South Australia (☎08/8234 3000 or free call 1800 018 234, ⓦwww.asa.mtx.net) fly to Port Augusta, Leigh Creek, Innamincka, Birdsville, Boulia and Port Lincoln; Ansett (☎13 1300) fly to a range of destinations including Alice Springs and Ayers Rock, and also sell tickets for Kendell Airlines flying to Broken Hill, Ceduna, Mount Gambier, Port Lincoln, Whyalla, Coober Pedy, Olympic Dam and Kangaroo Island; Emu Airways (☎08/8234 3711,

Ⓦwww.emuair.mtx.net) fly to Kangaroo Island.
Airlines (international) Air New Zealand (Ⓣ13
2476); Alitalia (Ⓣ1300/303 747); British Airways
(Ⓣ08/8238 2000); Cathay Pacific (Ⓣ13 1747);
Garuda (Ⓣ1300/365 330); Japan Airlines
(Ⓣ08/8212 2555); Lufthansa (Ⓣ08/8212 6444);
Malaysia Airlines (Ⓣ08/8231 6171); Qantas
(Ⓣ08/8407 2233); Singapore Airlines (Ⓣ08/8203
0800).

Airport bus Transit Regency Coaches (Ⓣ08/8381
5311) has pick-up points at various locations,
including the *Hilton Hotel* on Victoria Square and
the Central Bus Station, but will pick you up at
other city locations if you pre-book; it also services
Keswick Interstate Train Terminal. See p.786 for
airport departure times and prices.

American Express Shop 32, Citi Centre, Rundle
Mall (Mon–Fri 9am–5pm, Sat 9am–noon;
Ⓣ1300/139 060); 120 Jetty Rd, Glenelg (Mon–Fri
9am–5pm, Sat 9am–noon; Ⓣ08/8376 7731).

Banks and foreign exchange All the major
banks are located on King William St. Exchange
services are available at the international airport,
at American Express (see above) and at Thomas
Cook, 45 Grenfell St (Mon–Fri 9am–5pm;
Ⓣ08/8212 3354), 4 Rundle Mall (Mon–Fri
9am–5pm, Sat 10am–4pm, Sun 10am–2pm;
Ⓣ08/8231 6977). If you're desperate beyond
these hours, the casino (see p.805) or international
hotels on North Terrace can help, but obviously the
exchange rates will be poor.

Bikes and bike rental Flinders Camping, 187
Rundle St (Ⓣ08/8359 3344), rents bikes for $15
per day and offers weekly rates; Linear Park
Mountain Bike Hire at Elder Park (Ⓣ08/8223
6271), situated near a section of the River Torrens
Linear Park bike track, hires bikes by the hour or
day at competitive prices; Bicycle SA, 1 Sturt St
(Ⓣ08/8410 1406), is a nonprofit cycling organization providing information and cycling maps and
organizing regular touring trips.

Buses *The State Guide*, available from South
Australian Travel Centre has route maps and
timetables of all South Australia's bus routes. Most
long-distance buses leave from the Central Bus
Station, Franklin St. Greyhound Pioneer (Ⓣ13
2030) has a nationwide service that includes Alice
Springs and Broken Hill in its destinations, while
Firefly Express (Ⓣ08/8231 1488) and McCafferty's
(Ⓣ08/8212 5066, reservations Ⓣ13 1499), run to
Melbourne and Sydney. V-Line (Ⓣ08/8231 7620
or 13 6196, Ⓦwww.vline.vic.gov.au) also run to
Melbourne from Adelaide and Mount Gambier.
State services are dominated by Premier Stateliner
Coach Service (Ⓣ08/8415 5555, Ⓦwww.premier-
stateliner.com.au), which goes to the Riverland,

Whyalla, Port Lincoln, Ceduna, Woomera, Roxby
Downs and Olympic Dam, Wilpena Pound via Port
Augusta, the Yorke and Fleurieu peninsulas and to
Mount Gambier either inland (via Keith,
Bordertown, Naracoorte, Coonawarra and Penola)
or along the coast (via Meningie, Kingston, Robe
and Millicent). Other local operators include the
Barossa–Adelaide Passenger Service (Ⓣ08/8564
3022), which stops at the main towns in the
Barossa Valley en route to Angaston; the Yorke
Peninsula Passenger Service (free call Ⓣ1800 625
099), which runs from Adelaide to Yorketown,
down the east coast via Ardrossan, Port Vincent
and Edithburgh, and down the centre via Maitland
and Minlaton; the Mid North Passenger Service
(Ⓣ08/8826 2346) via the Clare Valley and/or Burra
to Peterborough; and the Murray Bridge Passenger
Service (Ⓣ08/8532 2633) to Pinnaroo via Murray
Bridge and to Murray Bridge via Mannum and
Meningie. Tickets can be purchased at the Central
Bus Station; the Bus Booking Centre at Station
Arcade, 52 Hindley St (Ⓣ08/8212 5200), can
arrange travel on any bus service.

Camping equipment and rental Rundle St is the
place: for rental, try Flinders Camping at no. 187
(Ⓣ08/8223 1913), who can kit you out for the
Flinders Ranges given 24hr notice – they are also
the only place in town that repairs backpacks;
Paddy Pallin at no. 228 sells a range of high quality gear, plus maps; or there's Scout Outdoor
Centre at no. 192.

Canoe rental and tours Try Canoe & Kayak Hire,
29 Angus St, Goodwood (Ⓣ08/8271 6354), which
also offers canoe trips to the Torrens Island mangroves, an area frequented by dolphins.

Car rental Avis (Ⓣ1300/367 227), Hertz (Ⓣ13
3039) and Thrifty (Ⓣ08/8211 8788) have desks at
the airport. Otherwise, try the recommended small
and friendly Access, 121 Currie St (Ⓣ08/8212
5900 or free call 1800 812 580,
Ⓔaccess@tne.net.au), who do free airport deliveries and are one of the few companies which allow
you to take their cars to Kangaroo Island; they also
hire out sports cars. Also try Action (Ⓣ08/8443
8855, Ⓦwww.actioncars-australia.com) or Excel
(Ⓣ08/8234 1666, Ⓦwww.excelrentalcar.com.au).
Older, cheaper cars can be obtained from Cut Price
Car Rentals (Ⓣ08/8443 7788,
Ⓦwww.cutprice.com.au), who also do one-way
rentals and buy backs, or Rent-a-Bug (Ⓣ08/8234
0911). Campervans Australia NQ Rentals, 151
Burbridge Rd, Hilton (Ⓣ08/8443 3002, Ⓕ8443
3656), has two-berth campervans, sometimes on
stand-by deals.

Disabled travellers Disability Information and
Resource Centre, 195 Gilles St (Ⓣ08/8223 7522);

Access Cabs (☎1300/360 940).

Environment and conservation The Conservation Council of South Australia, 120 Wakefield St (☎08/8223 5155), is a good place to find out what's going on; there's a notice board and reference library. The Environment Shop, 77 Grenfell St (☎08/8204 1910, ⓦwww.parks.sa.gov.au) has good free maps of the national parks and other useful brochures. The Wilderness Society has its campaign office at 116 Grote St (☎08/8231 6586) and a shop in Victoria Square Arcade, Victoria Square (☎08/8231 0625).

Hospital Royal Adelaide Hospital, North Terrace (☎08/8222 4000). Dental Hospital, North Terrace (☎08/8222 8222).

Internet access Ngapartji, 211 Rundle St (Mon–Thurs 8.30am–7pm, Fri 8.30am–10.30pm, Sat 10am–10pm, Sun noon–7pm; ☎08/8235 4001) is a snazzy multimedia centre whose Aboriginal name means "community skills brought together". A couple of computer terminals out front can be used for free; the cybercafé inside charges $8 per hour ($4 per 30min, $2 per 15min). There's limited-time free access at the State Library (see p.793; book in advance) and at the Women's Information Service (p.812; women only), and cheap access at Talking Cents, 53 Hindley St ($2 per 30min). Many of the backpackers now have internet access for guests, including *Adelaide YHA*, *Canon St Lodge*, *Backpack Australia*, *Sunny's* and *Glenelg Beach Resort*.

Laundries Adelaide Launderette, 152 Sturt St (daily 7am–8pm; service washes 8am–5pm); Gilles St Laundromat, 316 Gilles St (daily 7am–8pm; unattended), is handy for hostels.

Left luggage Adelaide Train Station has 24hr lockers. Facilities also at the Central Bus Station: Premier Stateliner ($2 per 24hr); Greyhound/McCafferty's (from $6 per 24hr).

Maps The Map Shop, 16A Peel St, between Hindley and Currie streets, has the largest range of local and state maps; if you're a member of an affiliated automobile association overseas, you can get free regional maps and advice on road conditions from the Royal Automobile Association, 41 Hindmarsh Square (☎08/8202 4540, ⓦwww.raa.net).

Medical centre City Centre Medical Clinic, 29 Gilbert Place (☎08/8212 3226).

Motorbike rental Show & Go Motorcycles, 236 Brighton Rd, Somerton Park (☎08/8376 0333).

Newspapers Adelaide's *The Advertiser* is very provincial and doesn't have good coverage of national and international news, but is useful on Thursday for entertainment listings, and Wednesday and Saturday for classifieds; Melbourne's *The Age* is freely available as an alternative. The best place to buy foreign and interstate newspapers is Rundle Arcade Newsagency, off Gawler Place.

Pharmacy Midnight Pharmacy, 13 West Terrace (Mon–Sat 7am–midnight, Sun & public holidays 9am–midnight). In Glenelg try Walker & Stevens Chemmart, cnr Jetty Rd and Gordon St (daily 8.30am–10pm).

Police For emergencies call ☎000.

Post office GPO, 141 King William St, cnr Franklin St (Mon–Fri 8am–6pm, Sat 8.30am–noon); poste restante, Adelaide GPO, SA 5000.

Rape and Sexual Assault Service ☎08/8226 8777 or free call 1800 817 421; after-hours emergency line ☎08/8226 8787.

Swimming pool Adelaide City Swim, 235 Flinders St (Mon 5.30am–8pm, Sat 6am–5pm, Sun 9am–1pm; $6 per hour). Adelaide Aquatic Centre, cnr Jeffcott Rd and Fitzroy Terrace, North Adelaide (daily 5am–10pm; swim $4.95), is an indoor centre with pool, gym, sauna and spa; take bus #231 from North Terrace.

Taxis Adelaide Independent (☎13 2211); Suburban Taxi Service (☎13 1008); Yellow Cabs (☎13 2227). There's a taxi rank on the corner of Pulteney and Rundle streets.

Telephones Rundle Mall has lots of phones, including ones that take credit cards. For peace and quiet, try the Phone Room in the GPO.

Tours The hop-on hop-off Adelaide Explorer City Sights Tour, in a bus dolled up as a tram (☎08/8364 1933; $35; 3hr; departing the Travel Centre, 14 King William St, daily 9am, 10.30am, noon, 1.30pm & 3pm), takes in the city, Glenelg and West Beach. Further afield, the majority of tours from Adelaide head for the Barossa Valley (see p.816), Kangaroo Island (see p.831) and the Fleurieu Peninsula (see p.823). General operators include Gray Line (☎1300/858 687, ⓦwww.grayline.com), for upmarket tours to Cleland Wildlife Park, Adelaide Hills and Hahndorf, the Barossa Valley, McLaren Vale, Clare Valley and Kangaroo Island; Premier Day Tours (☎08/8415 5566, ⓦwww.premierstateliner.com.au), and Adelaide Sightseeing (☎08/8231 4144, ⓦwww.adelaidesightseeing.com.au), which both also range further afield to Murray River, the Coorong and Flinders Ranges. Adelaide is also the home base for the excellent Wayward Bus, 115 Waymouth St (☎08/8410 8833 or free call 1800 882 823, Ⓕ8410 8844, ⓦwww.waywardbus.com.au), which does a good one-way, small-group tour from Adelaide to Melbourne (or vice versa) via the scenic coastal route (three and a half days; $290 includes breakfast, lunch and hostel accommodation). Wayward also runs one-way tours to Alice

Springs taking in the Clare Valley, Flinders Ranges, Oodnadatta Track, Lake Eyre, Coober Pedy, Uluru, Kata Tjuta and Kings Canyon (eight days; $770 all-inclusive); plus a five-day option taking in Coober Pedy, Oodnadatta Track, Lake Eyre, Maree, Wilpena Pound and Flinders Ranges ($460). Heading Bush 4WD Adventures (☎08/8648 6655, ⓦwww.head-bush.mtx.net) does ten-seater camping tours to the Flinders Ranges (three days; $299); while Camp Wild (☎08/8332 6601 or free call 1800 444 321, ⓦwww.campwild.com.au) offers an adventurous 4WD camping tour to Kangaroo Island (two and a half days; $260 all inclusive), and another tour all the way to Alice Springs taking in the Flinders Ranges, Simpson Desert, Uluru, Kings Canyon, Devils Marbles and Kakadu (ten days; $985 all inclusive).

Trains The Great Southern Railway Travel Pty (☎13 2147, ⓦwww.gsr.com.au) produces a glossy brochure with current timetables. The Australian National Travel Centre, Station Arcade, North Terrace (Mon–Fri 8.30am–5.30pm; ☎08/8231 4366), deal with interstate train enquiries and sell tickets; or call in at the Australian Rail Travel Centre, 18–20 Grenfell St (Mon–Fri 8.30am–5.30pm, Sat 9am–1pm; ☎08/8231 4366).

Travel agents Adelaide YHA Travel, 135 Waymouth St (☎08/8414 3000, ⓔtravel@yhsa.org.au); City Centre Travel, 75 King William St (☎08/8221 5044), domestic travel specialists; Flight Centre, 54 King William St (☎08/8211 7246); Jetset, 23 Leigh St, off Hindley St (☎08/8217 8111); Peregrine

Travel, upstairs at 192 Rundle St (☎08/8223 5905); STA Travel, 235 Rundle St (☎08/8223 2426); Thor Adventure Travel, upstairs at 228 Rundle St (☎08/8232 3155).

Vaccinations Travellers Medical and Vaccination Centre, 27–29 Gilbert Place (☎08/8212 7522).

Women's Adelaide The Women's Studies Resource Centre, Station Arcade, 64 Pennington Terrace, North Adelaide (Mon–Fri 9am–5pm, Sun 2–5pm; ☎08/8267 3633), is a good meeting place with library, video, computer and internet facilities; at the same address is Women's Health Statewide (☎08/8267 5366) for over-the-phone health information, contraception information and abortion referrals. The Pregnancy Advisory Centre, 21 Bellmore Terrace in Woodville Park (☎08/8347 4955) offer pregnancy testing, abortion and counselling. The Women's Information Service, Station Arcade, Adelaide Railway Station, 136 North Terrace (Mon–Fri 8am–6pm, Sat 9am–5pm; ☎08/8303 0590), has loads of practical information and very handy free internet access which does not have to be prebooked (women only; max 30min per person).

Work Employment National, 55 Currie St (☎13 3444). Information on work rights is available from the Department of Immigration and Multicultural Affairs (☎13 1881, ⓦwww.immi.gov.au/employers). Unemployment is high in Adelaide itself, but it's a good place to find out about casual fruit-picking work in the Riverland. Hostels can help with finding work, and often provide a source of employment for young travellers.

Around Adelaide

Escaping Adelaide for a day or more is easy and enjoyable, as you can choose from beaches, hills and wine, or any combination thereof. Closest at hand are the **Adelaide Hills**, southeast of the city, which are popular for weekend outings and have numerous small national and conservation parks that are great for walking. To the south, the **Fleurieu Peninsula** extends towards Cape Jervis and has plenty of fine beaches and several small wineries. If wine is your priority, though, head for the **Barossa Valley**, Australia's premier wine-producing region, with over thirty excellent wineries all less than 50km from Adelaide. The valley is easily visited in a day from the city, or on a tour, but it's also a great place to stop over and unwind. The **Yorke Peninsula**, across the gulf from Adelaide, is far less known, though many locals holiday here: as well as beaches, it has the remains of an old copper-mining industry and an excellent national park.

The Adelaide Hills

The beautiful **Adelaide Hills** are the part of the Mount Lofty Ranges closest to the city, just thirty-minutes' drive away, and for the most part accessible by train and the Hills Transit bus service (☎08/8339 1191). Several tours heading for the Fleurieu Peninsula also take in the area (see p.811). Many people live in the hills to take advantage of the cooler air, and there are some grand old summerhouses here. The **Heysen Trail** long-distance walk cuts across the hills, with four quaint YHA hostels along it; most are run on a limited-access basis and the key must first be obtained from the Adelaide office, 135 Waymouth St (☎08/8414 3010). Due to the high fire risk in midsummer, the trail is closed from mid-December to April.

Leaving the city by Glen Osmond Road you soon start to wind steeply up on the way to the South Eastern Freeway, the main road to Melbourne. This was the traditional route to Melbourne – there's an old tollhouse not far out of the city at Urrbrae and several fine old coaching hotels such as the *Crafers Inn*. At **CRAFERS** itself you can leave the freeway for the scenic Summit Road, which runs along the top of the hills, past the western side of the extensive **Mount Lofty Botanic Gardens** (daily 10am–4pm) to the **Mount Lofty Lookout**, the highest point of the range (727m). Hills Transit buses #820, #821 and #822 run from Adelaide bus terminal or Currie Street via Crafers and up Piccadilly Road, from where you can access the eastern side of the Botanic Gardens. The free *Adelaide Hills Monthly* has information about local events and is available from the South Australia Travel Centre in Adelaide (see p.786) and other regional tourist information centres.

The turn-off to **Cleland Wildlife Park** (daily 9.30am–4.30pm; $9.50; Ⓦ www.cleland.sa.gov.au) is the first on the left after the lookout. Here you can cuddle a koala and see other Australian fauna in enclosures. There are several good walking trails through native bush leading from the park into the surrounding Cleland Conservation Area. You can get up here as part of a tour with Gray Line (Ⓣ 1300/858 687, Ⓦ www.grayline.com; $30), Adelaide Sightseeing (Ⓣ 08/8231 4144, Ⓦ www.adelaidesightseeing.com.au; $30) or Premier Day Tours (Ⓣ 08/8415 5566, Ⓦ www.premierstateliner.com.au; $34). Otherwise, take the Hills Transit bus #822.

The **Morialta Conservation Park**, north of here, is most easily reached by taking the #105 bus from Grenfell Street (35min), which goes right into the park along the scenic Morialta Falls Road; from the entrance it's a two-kilometre bushwalk into the park to a lovely waterfall. By car you can approach the park along the equally impressive Norton Summit Road; the *Scenic Hotel*, clinging to the side of the hill at **Norton Summit**, is a great place to stop for a drink. Running off here, Colonial Drive leads to **Fuzzies Farm** (Ⓣ 08/8390 1111, Ⓔ fuzzies@dove.net.au; bookings essential; closed July & Aug), an experiment in co-operative living set on seventeen bush hectares and overseen by the philosophical Fuzzy. You can stay here in four-bed cabins (minimum one-week stay costs $88 including meals) and in return Fuzzy asks for thirty hours of your time helping out with carpentry, building, tending goats, gardening – or anything else that interests you (even the swimming pool has been made by helpers). Holidaying guests can stay in the cottage (❼).

South of Crafers, virtually in the southern suburbs of Adelaide, is **Belair National Park** (daily 8am–sunset; entry fee per car $6). Getting there is half the pleasure – you take a suburban train that winds upwards through tunnels and valleys with views of Adelaide and Gulf St Vincent (35min). From Belair Station, steps lead to the valley and the grassy recreation grounds and kiosk. With its joggers, tennis courts, man-made lake, hedge maze and **Old Government House** (open to visitors on Sun 12.30–4pm), a residence built in 1859 as a summer retreat for the governor, this seems more like a garden than a national park, though there are also some more secluded bush trails through gum forests.

The **Warrawong Sanctuary**, southeast of Belair National Park on Stock Road, reached by Sturt Valley Road, Heather Road and Longwood Road, was set up in the late 1960s as a sustainable conservation model to halt the loss of Australian wildlife: half of all the mammals that have become extinct in the last two centuries have been Australian. Guided **bushwalks** starting at dawn or sunset (Ⓣ 08/8370 9197, Ⓕ 8370 8332, Ⓦ www.esl.com.au/warrawong.htm; $19.50; bookings essential) offer you the opportunity to spot the mostly nocturnal animals in their natural habitat. These include several endangered species

B&B in the Hills

Less than an hour from the city, the Adelaide Hills' many B&Bs in bush surroundings are well worth seeking out for a treat – but they aren't cheap. Some of the best are *Apple Tree Cottage* in Oakbank (T08/8388 4193, F8388 4733, Wwww.ahcc.com.au/apple_tree.html;), a self-contained 1860 cottage beside an idyllic lake from $180 per room per night; and *Allessandro Maandini's Ryokan* in Blackwood (T & F 08/8370 3507, Wwww.ryokan-maandini.com; $150 per person), a stunning, glass-walled Japanese-inspired house offering authentic "Ryokan" (Japanese-style) B&B, four-course Japanese meals ($80 a head) and pick-up service in a Rolls Royce; discounts are available for backpackers in groups of at least three. The South Australia B&B Association (Wwww.sabnb.gov.au) has a useful brochure listing its associated members, available from the South Australian Travel Centre in Adelaide (see p.786).

For **other accommodation** in the hills, try Warrawong Sanctuary (see opposite), *Geoff and Hazels* and *Fuzzies Farm* (both below), or contact the Adelaide Hills Visitors Information Centre in Hahndorf (see below).

such as bettongs and potoroos (both from the marsupial family) as well as the elusive platypus. There's a licensed **restaurant**, and also **accommodation** in air-conditioned, en-suite tent-cabins ($137 per person including dusk and dawn tours, dinner and breakfast). There's no public transport or tours to Warrawong but Hills Transit buses #166 or #193 go to Stirling, where you can get a taxi for the remaining 5km.

ALDGATE, just 3km to the north of Warrawong, is a charming village with an old-fashioned white-washed pub, the *Aldgate Pump House*. Almost opposite the pub, on Kingsland Road, you can stay at *Geoff and Hazels* (T08/8389 8360, Wwww.geoffandhazels.com.au;) including breakfast), a lovely wooden lodge set in the hillside amongst trees. The owners have three guestrooms with a communal kitchen/lounge, laundry and internet access. Geoff will also happily take guests to Warrawong Sanctuary for the dawn or dusk tours. Hills Transit buses #163 and #165 go to Aldgate from Grenfell Street.

Hahndorf

HAHNDORF, 28km from the city, is the most touristy destination in the hills (frequent Hills Transit bus services from Central Bus Station; 40min; T08/8399 1191) and is always crowded at weekends. Founded in 1839, it's Australia's oldest German settlement and still has the look of a nineteenth-century village. The Bavarian-style restaurants and coffee houses, crafts, antique and gift shops are thoroughly commercial, but it's still enjoyable, especially in autumn when the chestnuts and elms lining the main street have turned golden and the German food tastes just right for the season. The **Adelaide Hills Visitors Information Centre**, 41 Main St (daily 9am–5pm; T08/8388 1185 or free call 1800 353 323, Wwww.visitadelaidehills.com.au), has lots of information on B&Bs and other accommodation in the hills (no charge for bookings). It can also provide information about the entire area, though you won't need much help in the village itself: there's basically just one street and all the buildings have blue plaques recounting their history. The **Hahndorf Academy** (Mon–Sat 10am–5pm, Sun noon–5pm; free) is a working artists studio with a small collection of photographs, prints, displays and well-written interpretive boards that shed light on the lives of early German settlers. There are also a few sketches by the town's most famous resident and one of Australia's best-known artists, **Hans Heysen**, who settled here in 1908. There's a more comprehensive collection of Heysen's paintings on display at his old home, **The Cedars**, about 2.5km northwest of the village, off Ambleside Road (daily except Sat 10am–4pm; guided tours 11am, 1pm & 3pm; $7 studio and house; shop and garden free).

For a glass of authentic locally brewed pilsner, head for the lovely wooden bar of the *German Arms Hotel*, which has a log fire and photos of old Hahndorf, a reasonably priced bistro, and a more expensive **restaurant**. There are dozens of other places to eat, all with filling meals for around $8. At the other end of the main street, *Karl's German Coffee House*, in a homestead with verandah dining (closed Mon & Tues), serves marginally lighter meals than the hotel, while *The German Cake Shop*, near the tourist office, just off the main street on Pine Avenue (daily 8.30am–6pm), is a crowded bakery and coffee shop where the speciality is *bienenstich*, a yeast cake topped with honey and almonds, and filled with cream, butter and custard. For a picnic, stock up at Hahndorf Smallgoods, two shops south of tourist information, famous for their home-made wurst; try their excellent café for meaty snacks.

Torrens River Gorge

Further north in the upper valley, the 27-kilometre **Gorge Scenic Drive** beside the Torrens River Gorge is one of the loveliest areas in the Adelaide Hills, but you'll need your own car to get there; take the Gorge Road off the A11 from Adelaide, a few kilometres past the suburb of Cambelltown. Fourteen kilometres along this road is the **Gorge Wildlife Park** (daily 8am–5pm; koala holding 11.30am, 1.30pm & 3.30pm; $7), a private park with mainly native birds and animals housed in walk-through enclosures. A few kilometres past the park, at Cudlee Creek, the Gorge Scenic Drive turns southeast away from the river and passes through picturesque valleys and vineyards to Mount Torrens. If you want to stick with the river, turn north before Cudlee Creek towards the Chain of Ponds where the road connects after a few kilometres to the equally stunning **Torrens Valley Scenic Drive**. **GUMERACHA**, the first town east of here, is home to **The Toy Factory**, 389 Birdwood Rd (daily 9am–5pm; Ⓦ www.thetoyfactory.com.au), which sells wholesale wooden toys, games and puzzles to the public and has a tacky eighteen-metre-high rocking-horse; children (and adults) can climb up it for good views of the countryside. At the eastern end of the Torrens Valley Scenic Drive is **BIRDWOOD**, which is home to the **National Motor Museum** on Shannon Street (daily 9am–5pm; $9) – Australia's largest collection of veteran, vintage and classic cars, trucks and motorcycles.

The Barossa Valley

The **Barossa Valley**, only an hour's drive from Adelaide, produces internationally acclaimed wines and is the largest **premium wine** producer in Australia. Small stone **Lutheran churches** dot the valley, which was settled in the 1840s by German Lutherans fleeing from religious persecution: by 1847 over 2500 German immigrants had arrived and after the 1848 revolution more poured in. The German dialect in the area was strong until World War I, when the spoken language was frowned upon and German place names were changed by an Act of Parliament. The towns, however – most notably Tanunda – remain thoroughly German in character, even without the large doses of oompah tourist hype that they all serve up, and the valley is well worth visiting for the vineyards and wineries, the architecture, and the bakeries and butcher's shops where old German recipes have been handed down through generations. The valley makes a popular **day-trip** from Adelaide, and many of the big commercial wineries are besieged by busloads of tourists intent on a

SELECTED WINERIES

Winery	No.
Bethany Wines	11
Charles Melton	12
Grant Burge Wine	14
Henschke	9
Kies Family Wineries	16
Langmeil	8
Penfolds	3
Peter Lehmann	5
Richmond Grove	6
Rockford Wines	13
St Hallets	10
Saltram	2
Veritas	4
Wolf Blass	1
Yaldara Estate	15
Yalumba Wines	7

day's free drinking. The area seems thoroughly touristy and traffic-laden if you quickly whizz through it; however, the peaceful back roads yield more interest, with a number of small, family-owned wineries to explore. Many provide picnic areas and barbecues, and even children's playgrounds.

The first vines were planted in 1847 at the Orlando vineyards, an estate which is still a big wine producer. There are now over fifty **wineries**, from multinationals to tiny specialists. Because of the variety of soil and climate, the Barossa seems able to produce a wide range of wine types of consistently high quality; the white rieslings are among the best. The region has a typically Mediterranean climate, with dry summers and mild winters; best time to visit is autumn (March–May), when the vines turn russet and golden and the harvest has begun in earnest. Much of the grape-picking is still done by hand and **work** is available from February. This is also the time of the week-long **Vintage Festival**, beginning on Easter Monday in every odd-numbered year (☎08/8563 0600 for more information). Another local celebration is the **International Barossa Music Festival**, held annually for two weeks in early October and featuring mostly chamber music. Its headquarters are at Richmond Grove Winery on Para Road near Tanunda; other wineries act as venues, as do some of the area's pretty Lutheran churches.

Wine tasting tips

Smaller wineries tend to have more charm and intrinsic interest than the larger commercial operators and it's here you'll often get to talk personally to the wine maker. Generally you'll get the best reception if you visit as a pair: wineries have become increasingly distrustful of groups intent on getting drunk for free, and some have begun to charge a nominal tasting fee to discourage this, but it's still rare. You're under no obligation to buy any wine, but coming away with a few of your favourite taste sensations of the day – often only available at the cellar door – and a few fruity adjectives to describe them is part of the fun.

For a novice, wine tasting can be an intimidating experience. On entering the **tasting area** (or cellar door) you'll be shown a list of wines that may be tasted, divided into reds and whites, all of which are printed in the order that the wine maker considers best on the palate. Unless you know what you're doing, it's not acceptable to alter this order, though by all means concentrate on red or white if you prefer. To get the full taste, sniff the wine first to appreciate the aroma or bouquet, and then take a sip, rolling it around on your tongue before swallowing; there's usually a spittoon if you don't want to swallow. Don't be shy about discussing the wines with the person serving – their purpose is to dispense chat and wisdom, and even wine snobs are down-to-earth Australians at heart.

Getting into and around the valley

The principal **route** from Adelaide follows the Main North Road through Elizabeth and Gawler, and then joins the **Barossa Valley Highway** to Lyndoch. A more scenic drive takes you through the Adelaide Hills to Williamstown or Angaston, while from the **Sturt Highway** you can turn into the valley at Nuriootpa.

Getting to the valley by **bus** is also reasonably easy: the Barossa–Adelaide Passenger Service (Mon–Sat 2 daily, Sun 1 daily; ☎08/8564 3022) stops at the main Barossa towns en route to Angaston, or the daily Premier Stateliner (☎08/8415 5555) service to Riverland can drop you at Nuriootpa on request. The exclusive tourist **Barossa Wine Train** runs from Adelaide all the way into Tanunda (Tues, Thurs & Sun 8.50am, returning 5.20pm; $65 return; bookings essential on ☎08/8212 7888, ☻www.barossawinetrain.com.au; tour packages also available). If you're cycling, you might want to consider taking your bike on the standard train to Gawler, 14km from Lyndoch.

Driving is not the ideal way to explore the Barossa, particularly if you want to enjoy tasting wines – once here, you can always rent a bike or take a tour. If you decide you do need a **car** to get around, you can rent one from the Caltex service station, 8 Murray St, Tanunda (☎08/8563 2677; $50 per day). A better way to experience the area is to **cycle**; there's a sealed bike track avoiding the busy highway between Tanunda and Nuriootpa and bike rental (around $10 a day) is available at *Zinfandel's*, 58 Murray St, Tanunda (☎08/8563 2822), *The Bunkhaus*, Barossa Valley Way, Nuriootpa (☎08/8562 2260), and *Barossa Caravan Park*, Barossa Valley Way, Lyndoch (☎08/8524 4262). Alternatively, you can take a two- to five-day **cycling tour** with *Ecotrek* (☎08/8383 7198, ☻www.ecotrek.com.au), with an emphasis on wine tasting, gourmet food and Heritage accommodation. There's also a range of **sightseeing tours** from Adelaide offered by all the big commercial tour operators (see Adelaide "Listings", p.811) For something different, try the small-group day-tour with Groovy Grape Getaways (free call ☎1800 661 177, ☻www.groovygrape.com.au; $46), which stops at Gumeracha's giant rocking horse, the Whispering Wall near Lyndoch, and four large wineries, and includes a barbecue lunch – the emphasis on a free grog-up makes it popular with backpackers. Prime Mini Tours (☎08/8293 4900, Ⓦwww.primeminitours.com; $55) runs a more sedate minibus tour from Adelaide, with a similar itinerary including a three-course sit-down lunch.

Lyndoch and around

"A beautiful place, good land, plenty of grass and its general appearance open with some patches of wood and many kangaroos," reported Colonel William Light in 1837 on first sight of the **LYNDOCH** area; settled in 1839, it's one of the oldest towns in South Australia. Although vineyards were established from the outset, the primary activity was the growing of wheat until 1896, when someone had the bright idea of converting a flour mill into a winery. Today there are ten wineries in the immediate Lyndoch area, from some of the smallest to one of the largest in the Barossa, all still family-owned. **Kies Family Wineries** on Barossa Valley Way, provides free and informal **tourist information** and can book tours and accommodation (daily 10am–4.30pm; ☎08/8524 4110); their wine-tasting cellars are in the same building (same hours).

Eight kilometres south of Lyndoch, off **Yettie Road**, is the **Whispering Wall**, a retaining wall for the **Barossa Reservoir**; it's shaped in such a way that a spoken message can be heard plainly on the opposite side 140m away. To the northeast, four kilometres along the Barossa Valley Way, the village of **ROW-LAND FLAT** is dominated by the **Orlando Winery** complex (Mon–Fri 10am–5pm, Sat & Sun 10am–4pm), the oldest winery in the valley and home of some of Australia's best-known wines, sold under the **Jacob's Creek** label. Johann Gramp planted the first commercial vines at nearby Jacob's Creek in 1847, and forty years later his son expanded the winery and moved it to Rowland Flat.

Four kilometres north of Rowland Flat, the peaceful **Krondorf Road/Hallet Valley** area runs east of the Barossa Valley Way, with three charming wineries, each with its own philosophy of wine making and tasting: Rockford, St Hallets and Charles Melton. Behind St Hallets Winery you can watch skilled coopers at work at the **Keg Factory**, St Hallet Road (Mon–Sat 8am–4.30pm, Sun 10.30am–4.30pm); the huge stainless steel fermentation tanks you'll see around the valley aren't suitable for all wines, many of which still need to be aged in wood to impart flavour.

Parallel to Krondorf Road to the north, Bethany Road runs east off the Barossa Valley Way to **BETHANY**, the first German settlement in the Barossa. The land is still laid out in the eighteenth-century Hufendorf style, with long, narrow farming strips stretching out behind the cottages, and the creek running through each property. Pretty gardens set off the old stone cottages, which remain well cared for. At dusk each Saturday the bell tolls at **Herberge Christi Church**, keeping up a tradition to mark the working-week's end, and Bethany – without even a pub or shop – retains its peaceful, rural village feel. The common where cattle grazed is now the Bethany Reserve, with a picnic spot by the creek.

Tanunda

TANUNDA, the Barossa's most quintessentially German town, announces itself as a tourist destination as you head along the Barossa Valley Way and enter through the Orlando archway that spans **Murray Street**. This tree-lined main street, with several old and beautiful buildings, proclaims its pedigree with German music wafting out of small wooden kegs above the shops. More authentic atmosphere can be found in the narrow streets on the western side of town, towards the river. Here, **Goat Square** was the site of the first town

Barossa wineries

It's hard to choose between so many wineries, as almost all of them are worth a look. However, the twelve below should start you off.

Bethany Wines, Bethany Rd, Bethany. A hillside winery set in an old quarry, with views over Bethany village (see overleaf); five generations of the Schrapel family have grown grapes here. The ports are worth trying, especially the unusual white variety. Mon–Sat 10am–5pm, Sun 1–5pm.

Charles Melton, Krondorf Rd, Tanunda. Small, friendly winery concentrating on a limited range of full-bodied reds that sell out fast. Informal tasting area in a wooden shed, where you sit at a long wooden table, with the door open to the vineyards and a friendly dog at your feet. Daily 11am–5pm.

Grant Burge Wines, Barossa Valley Way, Jacob's Creek. Small, quality winery, established in 1988 to process wine from the area's oldest vineyards. Daily 10am–5pm.

Henschke, Moculta Rd, Keyneton, 14km southeast of Angaston. Fifth-generation wine makers, the Henschke family's wines have won many international prizes. In a peaceful setting off the beaten track where you'll need to ring the bell to rouse the amiable staff and start tasting. Mon–Fri 9am–4.30pm, Sat 9am–noon.

Langmeil Winery, Langmeil Rd, near Tanunda. This was the original Langmeil village, built in the 1840s; the little vineyard you can see from the tasting area was planted in 1846. Prints of nineteenth-century photos on the walls document the local wine industry. With a slow and thoughtful approach to tasting and a small range (four reds, five whites and two tawny ports), you really get to know the wines; the very peppery Grenache is definitely worth trying. This is one of four adjacent wineries on the Para Trail, including Peter Lehmann (below), Richmond Grove and Stanley Brothers. Daily 10am–4.30pm.

Peter Lehmann, Para Rd, near Tanunda. Another pleasant spot for a bit of tasting in a homestead with vine-entwined verandahs surrounded by flowerbeds, gum trees and palms, overlooking a lawn leading down to the Para River; you're welcome to picnic here. A local figure, Lehmann is as much known for his red wines as his art collection. The wine labels feature South Australian artists, whose original paintings are on display. Mon–Fri 9.30am–5pm, Sat & Sun 10.30am–4pm.

Richmond Grove, Para Rd, near Tanunda. Large historic winery sourcing grapes from around the Barossa and from other premier wine-growing areas in Australia – good if you want to compare the different regional characteristics of wine. There's a lovely picnic area alongside the North Para River. Mon–Fri 10am–5pm, Sat & Sun 10.30–4.30pm.

Rockford Wines, Krondorf Rd, Tanunda. No-nonsense approach and big unfussy wines using grapes by wine maker Robert O'Callahan, produced by old-fashioned techniques; good Basket Press Shiraz, and an amazing fizzy Black Shiraz at around $50 a bottle. Tasting in an 1850s stone barn. Mon–Sat 11am–5pm.

St Hallets Winery, Krondorf Rd, Tanunda. Medium-size quality producer. Its star wine is Old Block Shiraz, sourced from vines eighty to a hundred years old, with an intense flavour and a velvety softness. Daily 10am–5pm, lunch Sat & Sun.

Veritas, Langmeil Rd, near Tanunda. Established in the 1950s and known for its Hungarian-style wines, this is a family operation; they control the whole process, from crushing, fermenting and bottling, to labelling, tastings and sales in an unpretentious shed. A good place to come during harvest, around April. Mon–Fri 9am–5pm, Sat & Sun 11am–5pm.

Yaldara Wines, Gomersal Rd, Lyndoch. The ruins of a nineteenth-century flour mill have been transformed into a Baroque-style chateau. Tours (daily 10.15am, 10.45am, 1.15pm, 2.15pm & 3.15pm; $5) focus on the chateau's antiques collection. European-style wines, specializing in sweet and sparkling whites. See p.823 for details of bistro. Mon–Fri 8.30am–5pm, Sat 9am–5pm.

Yalumba Wines, Eden Valley Rd, Angaston. Largest and oldest family-operated Barossa winery, established in 1849. Lovely building and gardens. Mon–Fri 8.30am–5pm, Sat 10am–5pm, Sun noon–5pm.

market and is bordered by the original cottages; during the Vintage Festival (see p.817), the early market is re-enacted. Many **wineries** dot the town, the largest concentration along **Para Road**, beside the Para river: Stanley Brothers, Peter Lehmann, Richmond Grove, Langmeil and Veritas, all of which can be visited by taking a pleasant stroll along the road and the river.

For a good introduction to the wine-making industry, head for the **Barossa Wine and Visitor Centre**, 66–68 Murray St (Mon–Fri 9am–4pm, Sat & Sun 10am–4pm; wine centre daily 10am–4pm; $2; ℡08/8563 0600 or free call 1800 812 662, Ⓦwww.barossa-region.org). The centre tells the history of the Barossa in an original way – on three tiers of cylinders, which you roll to consult. Each group of cylinders represents a different historical period: you spin the top tier for a background on world events, the middle tier for a specific Barossa chronology, and the bottom tier for Australia-wide happenings at the time to examine the Barossa's wine industry in the context of Australian and world history – it's quite engrossing. There are also engaging interpretive displays about wine making, and it's here that you can pick up some additional tips on wine-tasting etiquette. There are also lots of tourist information racks with brochures to thumb through. The low-key **Barossa Valley Historical Museum**, 47 Murray St (Mon–Sat 11am–5pm, Sun 1–5pm; $2), crams local history into a small quaint building which it shares with an antiques shop.

Three kilometres out of town, **Norm's Coolies** at "Breezy Gully" off Gomersal Road (Mon, Wed & Sat 2pm; $8, children $2), could only be in Australia: 28 sheepdogs are put through their paces by Norm and a herd of sheep. **Mengler's Hill Lookout**, east of Tanunda along Basedow Road and then the Mengler's Hill Road Scenic Drive, provides an unmatched view of the valley and its vineyards: there's a **Sculpture Garden** with white marble sculptures on the slopes below, and at night you can see the lights of Adelaide.

Seppeltsfield, off the highway 4km northwest of Tanunda, must be the most spectacular of the wineries (tastings Mon–Fri 10am–5pm, Sat & Sun 11am–5pm). During the Great Depression the Seppelt family paid their workers in food to plant an avenue of date palms from Marananga to Seppeltsfield. On a hill halfway along the palm-lined avenue is the **Seppelt family mausoleum**, resting place of the male members of the family. The estate itself was founded in 1851 when Joseph Seppelt, a wealthy merchant, arrived from Silesia with his workers: he turned to wine making when his tobacco crop failed. Seppelts became the largest winery in the colony, having everything from a port-maturation cellar to a distillery, vinegar factory and brandy bond store. All have been preserved in their original condition, and can be seen on a **tour** (Mon–Fri 11am, 1pm, 2pm & 3pm, Sat & Sun 11.30am, 1.30pm & 2.30pm; $3).

Nuriootpa, Angaston and Springton

Just 7km from Tanunda, **NURIOOTPA** is the valley's commercial centre: as the place where local Aborigines gathered to barter it takes its name from the word for "meeting place". It's not the most attractive of towns, dominated as it is by **Penfolds**, the Barossa's largest winery; it churns out mass-produced wines, not all of which are made from local grapes. The finest building here is **Coulthard House**, a gracious, two-storey edifice commissioned by the area's first settler, William Coulthard. The town grew around his red-gum slab hotel, now the site of the *Vine Inn* community hotel. Together with the community store (where co-op members purchase shares and share in the profits), this finances many developments in the town such as the excellent **swimming centre** in Coulthard Reserve by the shady, gum-lined North Para River.

There's free **internet access** at the Public Library, 10 Murray St (Mon–Fri 9am–5pm, Sat 9am–noon, Sun 2–4pm).

ANGASTON, southeast of Nuriootpa, is a pretty little town situated in the Barossa Ranges, an area of predominantly grazing land, red gums and rolling hills, although a few of the Barossa's oldest wine makers have been here for more than a century. This is the side of the Barossa that attracted the British pioneers, including George Fife Angas, the Scotsman after whom the town is named. The **Collingrove Homestead** (Mon–Fri 1–4.30pm, Sat & Sun 11am–4.30pm; $5; W www.colgrove.mtx.net), 6km from town on Eden Valley Road, was one of his homes. Owned by the National Trust, it's surrounded by lush gardens and offers accommodation (see "Barossa accommodation" below). Angas also lived at nearby Lindsay Park, now the private **Lindsay Park Stud**, Australia's leading racehorse breeding and training complex.

At **SPRINGTON**, 20km south of Angaston, the major attraction is the **Herbig family tree**, a hollowed-out gum tree in which a pioneer German couple began their married life and had two of their sixteen children, living there for five years from 1855. Inevitably, Springton's old buildings have undergone the "boutiquing" process: the blacksmith shop is now a winery, and the old post office has been transformed into an arts and crafts gallery.

Barossa accommodation

There's comfortable accommodation, B&Bs and caravan parks throughout the valley, and you shouldn't have a problem finding somewhere decent to stay. Listed below are some of the better-value places.

Barossa Brauhaus Hotel, 41 Murray St, Angaston (T 08/8564 2014). Good-value basic rooms and cheap singles in a pub first licensed in 1849. Central location. Light breakfast included. **4**

Barossa Gallery, 8 Lyndoch Valley Highway, Lyndoch (T & F 08/8524 5191). Historic homestead in the heart of Lyndoch town. There's a small art gallery next door and cosy open fires for winter. Continental breakfast included. **7**

Bunkhaus Travellers Hostel and Cottage, Barossa Valley Way, 1.5km south of Nuriootpa (T & F 08/8562 2260). A comfortable, friendly, family-run hostel set in vineyards, with a cosy common room for winter, and a swimming pool for summer. Bike rental. Self-contained cottage **3**, dorms **1**

Collingrove Homestead, Eden Valley Rd, 6km from Angaston (T & F 08/8564 2061, W www.colgrove.mtx.net). National Trust-listed B&B accommodation in old servants' quarters, set in English-style gardens. **8**

Hillview Guesthouse, 12 Hill St, Angaston (T 08/8564 2761, F 8564 2508, W www.dove.net.au/~hillview). A former girls' grammar school whose lower storey has been transformed into a gracious guesthouse run by a friendly family. There's a sitting room complete with open fires, a stereo and bar, plus a swimming pool and spa. Each of the two spacious guestrooms has its own bathroom and antique furnishings. Gourmet breakfast is served beside the pool. **8**

Langmeil Cottages, Langmeil Rd, Tanunda (T & F 08/8563 2987, W www.langmeilcottages.com). German-style stone cottage with cooking facilities, peaceful setting and views of the Barossa Ranges; extras include champagne on arrival, breakfast provisions, free use of bicycles, BBQ and heated pool. Laundry facilities too. **7**–**8**

Lawley Farm, Krondorf Rd, south of Tanunda (T & F 08/8563 2141, W www.lawleyfarm.com.au). Restored stone cottages shaded by pepper trees on a quiet road ideal for walking and cycling and within walking distance of the best wineries. Full breakfast in the farmhouse kitchen and a hot spa in the garden. **7**–**8**

Seppeltsfield Holiday Cabins, Seppeltsfield Rd (T 08/8562 8240, F 8562 8563). These well-equipped log cabins, with wood fires, offer some of the best-value accommodation in the valley, set on a rural hillside overlooking the Seppelt winery. Deluxe cabins with spa **6**, standard rooms **4**

Tanunda Caravan and Tourist Park, Murray St, Tanunda (T 08/8563 2784, F 8563 3711, E tanpark@dove.net.au). Set in parkland among beautiful waratah trees. Cabins **3**, on-site vans **2**

Tanunda Hotel, 51 Murray St, Tanunda (T 08/8563 2030 or 8563 2165). Built from local stone and marble in 1845, with Edwardian additions and decor inside. All rooms have TV, air-con, fridge, tea and coffee; some are en suite. **4**

Vine Inn Hotel Motel, 14 Murray St, Nuriootpa

(☎08/8562 2133, ⓕ8562 3236, ⓦwww.vineinn.com.au). Spacious, modern motel-style units with air-con and queen-size beds; continental breakfast included. Spa and heated pool. ❺–❻

Vineyards Motel, cnr Stockwell and Nuriootpa roads, Angaston (☎08/8564 2404, ⓕ8564 2932, ⓦwww.mdt.net.au/~vinmot). Good location opposite the *Vintners Bar and Grill*, just a short walk away from Saltram Winery and its bistro. Modern units; facilities include room service, swimming pool and spa. ❹–❺

Barossa eating and drinking

To go with the wine, and to cater for all the tourists, there are excellent restaurants throughout the valley, as well as plenty of picnic spots and barbecue areas.

Barossa Bistro, 37 Murray St, Angaston (☎08/8564 2361). Casual dining nightly with affordable, filling main courses including some interesting kangaroo dishes; lighter, cheaper meals at lunchtime. Licensed.

Barossa Wurst Haus and Bakery, 86A Murray St, Tanunda. Specializing in traditional Barossa *Mettwurst*, this delicatessen offers cheap but very tasty food. Good cappuccino. Daily 8am–5.30pm.

Harvesters, 29D Murray St, Nuriootpa (☎08/8562 1348). Contemporary spacious café with a nice courtyard serving great cooked breakfasts, home-made soups and a variety of vegetarian dishes. Tues–Sun 9am–5.30pm.

Lyndoch Bakery & Restaurant, Barossa Valley Highway, Lyndoch. Best German bakery in the Barossa. The adjoining licensed restaurant serves moderately priced hearty, traditional dishes. Daily 8.30am–5.30pm.

1918 Bistro and Grill, 94 Murray St, Tanunda (☎08/8563 0405). Fresh food and local ingredients are cooked with a Mediterranean twist. Eat outside on wide, plant-shaded verandahs in this fab old house. Local wines or BYO. Expensive.

The Park Restaurant/Café, 2A Murray St, Tanunda (☎08/8563 3500). A 1840s stone villa set in a park; alfresco eating, or dining by the fire inside if it's cold. Affordable Modern Australian cuisine.

Rendezvous House, 22 Murray St, Angaston (☎08/8564 3533). Friendly organic café and restaurant in an old cottage with a small garden overlooking the pretty main street. Vegetarian and

meat dishes under $10 and plenty of delicious tapas as well. Wed–Sun lunch, Fri–Sun dinner.

Salters, Saltram Winery, Nuriootpa Rd, Angaston (☎08/8564 3355). Elegant bistro attached to a nineteenth-century winery. Choose from the latest contemporary dishes, all fresh and delicious. Full-bodied reds are Saltram's forte and you can try them at the cellar doors before eating. Lunch only.

Vine Court Restaurant, 49 Murray St, Nuriootpa. Serving simple but good Australian dishes and a few German specials, this place has the best-value meals in the valley: three courses for $15. Open daily for lunch and dinner.

Vintners Bar and Grill, cnr Stockwell and Nuriootpa roads, Angaston (☎08/8564 2488). A wine-makers' hangout with Mediterranean-style regional produce on the menu and a suitably impressive wine list; cool, contemporary decor meets old stone walls, fireplaces and wooden beams, and there's a vine-covered courtyard for warm days. Expensive. Tues–Sun lunch, Wed–Sat dinner.

Yaldara, Gomersal Rd, Lyndoch. Affordable prices aimed at families, with a children's menu too; pasta dominates. Also morning and afternoon tea. Daily 10am–4pm.

Zinfandel Tea Rooms, 58 Murray St, Tanunda. Popular place for hot, cooked breakfasts, German and Australian dishes for lunch and a delicious choice of strudels and cakes. You can sit inside the cosy cottage or out on the verandah. Daily 8.30am–6pm.

The Fleurieu Peninsula

The **Fleurieu Peninsula**, thirty minutes south of Adelaide by car, is bounded by Gulf St Vincent to the west and the Southern Ocean to the south, the two connected by the Backstairs Passage at **Cape Jervis** (where the ferry leaves for Kangaroo Island, see p.831). There are fine beaches on both coasts and, inland, more wineries in the rolling **McLaren Vales**. It's pleasantly undeveloped: many of the towns were settled from the 1830s and there's a lot of **colonial architecture**, often housing restaurants and B&Bs. For a round trip, leave the city via the Adelaide Hills and cut down through Mount Barker to well-preserved Strathalbyn and Goolwa, on the south coast, circling round through Victor

Harbor, Willunga and McLaren Vale. The peninsula is a good place to **cycle** – in addition to its roads it has two sealed bike paths: the 24km Encounter Bikeway (see box on p.828) follows the coast from Goolwa to just beyond Victor Harbor; another (shorter) path runs between Willunga and McLaren Vale. For **walkers**, the **Heysen Trail** starts at the southern tip of the peninsula at Cape Jervis and winds its way across the hilly countryside north to the Adelaide Hills and beyond. Although the trail is meant for long-distance walking, there are a number of well-signposted short walks along the way, including the 3.5km Deep Creek Waterfall Trail, just east of Cape Jervis with its wild coastal scenery. The Heysen Trail also passes through the Mount Magnificent Conservation Park, which contains a number of shorter walks offering excellent panoramic views. Fleurieu Bush Walks (℡08/8555 5880, ⓦwww.fleurieubushwalks.com) offer guided walks from Goolwa along the Heysen Trail from Parson's Point to Waitpinga Beach and Newland's Head (Sun 10am–4pm; $72), and can also arrange overnight treks.

If you're relying on **public transport**, try Premier Stateliner (℡08/8415 5555) which makes four daily trips from Adelaide to Goolwa via McLaren Vale, Willunga, Victor Harbor and Port Elliot. There's also a sporadic service provided by the Southern Encounter and The Highlander **steam trains** (occasionally replaced by a diesel locomotive) which chug from Mount Barker to Victor Harbor and Strathalbyn respectively (select Sun June–Nov; call ℡08/8231 4366 for details). If you'd rather take a **tour**, Bee-init Tours (℡08/8332 1401, ⓦwww.users.senet.com.au/~beeinit) offer several half and full-day minibus tours of the peninsula from Adelaide; the most popular includes afternoon wine-tasting in McLaren Vale and an evening observing the Little Penguins at Victor Harbor (6hr; $48).

The McLaren Vales

The seventy wineries of the **McLaren Vales**, in the northwest of the peninsula, are virtually in Adelaide, and the suburban fringes of the city now push right up to **REYNELLA**, where the first vineyards were planted in 1838. Among the earliest was Hardy's Reynella Winery on Reynell Road (Sun–Fri 10am–5pm, Sat 10am–4pm), where the tasting room occupies the original ironstone and brick building set in botanical gardens. There are several other wineries in Reynella but the largest concentration, often in bush settings though only an hour's drive from Adelaide, is around the small town of **McLAREN VALE**, which has about forty wineries, mostly small and family-run. Since the 1960s there's been a trend for grape growers to switch from supplying wine makers to producing their own wine in a bid for independence, and as a result there's a swath of "boutique" wineries here.

McLaren Vale is itself a "boutique" town, with many B&Bs and restaurants catering for the wine-buff weekend crowd. The liveliest time is in October when the **Bushing Festival** celebrates the new wines, and the Bushing King or Queen, the wine maker who has produced the wine judged to be the best of the vintage, is crowned. A big part of the festival is the **craft market** held during the last weekend at Kay's Amery Vineyards (see box, opposite), where there are fifty stalls manned by the artisans themselves, as well as food and entertainment. Information on this, and on the area's wineries, can be found at the **McLaren Vale and Fleurieu Visitor Centre** on Main Road, about 2km from the centre (daily 10am–5pm; ℡08/8323 9944, ⓦwww.visitorcentre.com.au) – it even has its own vineyard with a café and wine bar; you can sample wines here from across the Vale including those wineries without cellar doors. The centre can also book **accommodation**. Among the B&Bs are *McLaren Vale*, 56 Valley View Drive (℡08/8323

McLaren Vale wineries

Listed below are half a dozen favourites from a wide choice of excellent wineries.

Chapel Hill, Chapel Hill Rd, McLaren Vale, adjacent to the Onkaparinga Gorge. A small but very civilized winery in an old stone chapel. Wine maker Pam Dunsford was McLaren Vale's first Bushing Queen; her wines have won several prizes. There are nice views over vineyards. Daily noon–5pm.

D'Arenberg, Osborn Rd, McLaren Vale. A family winery set up in 1928 and long well-known for its prize-winning reds. Tastings daily 10am–5pm. The superb restaurant, *D'Arry's Verandah*, is garnering accolades for its chef and stunning hilltop views over the vineyards (Wed–Sat lunch, Fri & Sat dinner; bookings on ☏08/8323 8710).

Hoffman's, Ingoldby Rd, McLaren Flat. Smallest of the wineries with only three labels to choose from, and these only available through the cellar doors or by mail order. A great place to sit in a peaceful setting and talk about wines with the friendly owners. Daily 11am–5pm.

Kay's Amery Vineyards, Kays Rd, McLaren Vale. A wonderful family winery established in 1890; old photos of the family and the area cover the oak casks containing port. It's renowned for its Block 6 Shiraz from vines planted in 1892, though this wine is a very fast mover and you might be out of luck. There's a picnic area set amid towering gum trees and cottage accommodation with stunning vineyard views (☏08/8323 8201, ✉rckay@picknowl.com.au; ❼). Cellar doors Mon–Fri 9am–5pm, Sat & Sun noon–5pm.

Scarpantoni, Scarpantoni Drive, McLaren Flat. A small prize-winning winery run by an Italian family, with a contemporary cellar door more akin to a city wine bar. Mon–Fri 9am–5pm, Sat & Sun 11am–5pm.

Wira Wira, McMurtie Rd, McLaren Vale. A large classic ironstone building sets the theme here – there's an impressive range of reds, whites and award-winning tawny ports, not forgetting the fortified Shiraz. Daily 9am–5pm.

9351; ❺), within the town's residential area; *Southern Vales*, 13 Chalk Hill Rd (☏08/8323 8144; ❻), a more modern and hotel-like place with vineyard views; and *Samarkand*, Branson Road (☏ & ℻ 08/8323 8756; ❼), a separate wing of a large log cabin on a peaceful property with alpacas. Most **places to eat** are fairly fancy, and many of the wineries also have restaurants attached (for options see box on above); simpler meals can be had at *Koffee n Snax*, an unpretentious coffee shop at 150 Main Rd. The award-winning *Magnum Bistro* in the *Hotel McLaren*, 208 Main Rd (☏08/8323 8208), has delicious main courses, all reasonably priced. Across the road, at no. 201, the stylish *Oscar's* serves pizzas and Mediterranean salads (daily 11am–11pm; BYO). Restaurants include *The Barn*, on the corner of Main and Chalk Hill roads (☏08/8323 8618), where you can dine on moderately priced contemporary cuisine and choose your own local wine from the cellar. On the corner of McMurtie Road, in the direction of Willunga, is the *Salopian Inn* (☏08/8323 8769; lunch daily, dinner weekends only), an atmospheric 1851 stone inn with a seasonally varied menu.

Gulf St Vincent beaches

A series of superb swimming beaches, often known as the **wine coast**, runs along the Gulf St Vincent shore roughly parallel to the McLaren Vales, from **O'Sullivans Beach** down to **Sellicks Beach** They're all easily accessible from Adelaide on public transport: take the train from Adelaide to Noarlunga Centre and bus #750 or #751 to the various beaches. Alternatively, Premier Stateliner (☏08/8415 5555) runs a coach to Victor Harbor which stops at Willunga, or Public Coach Service (☏08/8231 1744) has a daily service from Adelaide to Cape Jervis via Aldinga and Normanville.

PORT NOARLUNGA is the main town, surrounded by steep cliffs and sand hills: its jetty is popular with anglers, and with wetsuit-clad teenagers who dive-bomb from it; at low tide a natural reef is exposed. Lifesavers patrol the local beaches, and you can rent surf and snorkelling gear at Ocean Graffix Surf and Skate Centre, 21 Salt Fleet Point. For the latest **surf report** call T1902/241 018 (75¢ per min). **Moana**, two beaches south, has fairly tame surf that's perfect for novices. The southern end of **Maslins Beach**, south again, broke new ground by becoming Australia's first legal **nude** bathing beach in 1975. The wide, isolated beach is reached by a long, steep walking track down the colourful cliffs from the Tait Road car park, deterring all but the committed. **Port Willunga**, the next stop down, offers interesting diving around the wreck of the *Star of Greece*, and just south is **Aldinga Beach**, reached by the daily Adelaide–Cape Jarvis Public Coach Service. From here there's a connecting bus to **Sellicks Beach** where, if you have your own car, you can drive along 6km of firm sand.

The coastal region south of here is more rugged, although there are some nice secluded beaches as well as the popular Heritage-listed sand dunes at **NORMANVILLE**. You can camp at *Normanville Beach Caravan Park* (T08/8558 2038; en-suite cabins ④–⑤). A few kilometres inland, the **Yankalilla District Visitor Information Centre**, 106 Main Rd (daily 10am–4pm; T08/8558 2999, Wwww.fleurieupeninsula.com.au), has a complete list of other caravan parks and B&Bs along the coast. Cape Jervis is at the end of the Main South Road and ferries depart from here for Kangaroo Island (see p.831).

Victor Harbor

VICTOR HARBOR, on Encounter Bay, was once a popular holiday destination for Adelaidians. In the 1920s there were 65 guesthouses and thousands poured in during the peak season; an uncomfortable four-hour train ride only added to the adventure. Then, as decent roads and the motor car brought it within an hour's drive, fewer people came – it was too close to home. Now, however, thanks to whales, penguins and the re-emergence of train power, Victor Harbor is experiencing a resurgence, evident in a much-redeveloped esplanade centred around a grassy foreshore square with a bronze fountain of a diving whale.

In the 1830s there were three whaling stations here, hunting **southern right whales**. They were so called because they were the "right" ones to kill: slow-moving because of their high oil content, which fortuitously also made them float after their slaughter. They would come to Encounter Bay to mate and breed between June and September, heading close to shore where they became easy targets. After the peak period in the decade of the 1830s, their numbers began to decline: the last one taken here was in 1878, and by 1930 they'd been hunted almost to extinction. Half a century later there were signs of recovery, and in 1991 forty were spotted in the bay and eighty thousand people flocked to see them. Between June and October in 1998, sixteen females stayed in the bay to calf, and a dozen humpback whales were also spotted – it's estimated that almost a hundred thousand visitors came here to watch the whales from the shoreline. Not surprisingly, Victor Harbor has converted a Heritage-listed former railway goods shed on Railway Terrace into the **South Australian Whale Centre** (daily 10am–5pm; $4.50). It has excellent interpretive displays, exhibits and screenings on whaling and on the natural history of whales, dolphins and the marine environment. The centre also acts as a monitoring station, locating and tracking whales, and confirming sightings, most likely in

June, July or August (hotline for information on locations ☎1900/931 223, calls cost 75¢ per min; ⓦwww.webmedia.com.au/whales). To report your own sighting, dial ☎08/8552 5644.

It's not only whales that bring visitors to Victor Harbor, but also **Little Penguins**, who come to nest, roost and moult on **Granite Island**, linked to the Esplanade by a narrow causeway. A couple of hours after dusk they come back from feeding – this is the best time to see them, on one of the **ranger-led penguin walks** run by Granite Island Nature Park (depart daily at dusk; 1hr; $10; booking essential on ☎08/8552 7555, ⓦwww.fleurieu.com.au/tourism). Before exploring the island you can visit the **Penguin Interpretive Centre**, which houses an audiovisual holographic display with a 3D park ranger giving the lowdown on daily penguin life (opens an hour before the start of a walk). You can walk across the 600-metre causeway to the island at any time, or get there on a traditional holiday ride with the Granite Island Horse Tram (daily 10am–4pm, after which a shuttle bus takes over until 8.30pm; $5 return). The Granite Island Nature Park also has a small shark aquarium ($10), just offshore from the Penguin Interpretive Centre, and runs several cruises, including one to the Page Islands to spot the largest **sea-lion colony** in South Australia (minimum twelve people; $75; bookings essential on ☎08/8552 7555).

Other local attractions include two Sunday steam **trains** (sometimes diesel-hauled): the Cockle Train that runs on the otherwise disused line along the coast to Goolwa via Port Elliot and back (every Sun & daily during school holidays; $20 return); and the Southern Encounter from the Adelaide Hills to Goolwa via Victor Harbor (see p.824). If you're travelling with restless children, **Greenhills Adventure Park**, Waggon Road, alongside the Hindmarsh River (daily 10am–5pm, 6pm in summer; $16 adult or child), has activities from canoeing to waterslides and for an extra charge, go-karting, while **Urimburra Wildlife Experience** (daily 9am–6pm; $8, child $4.50), 5km north on Adelaide Road, is an open-range park with native animals from all over the continent.

Practicalities

For further information, head for the volunteer-run Victor Harbor **Tourist Information Centre** next to the causeway (daily 9am–5pm; ☎08/8552 5738, ⓦwww.tourismvictorharbor.com.au); in the same building, the Fleurieu & KI Booking Centre (free call ☎1800 088 552, ⓔgenesis@granite.net.au) can book **accommodation** and tours. The best place to stay is the *Anchorage*, 21 Flinders Parade (☎08/8552 5970, ⓕ8552 1970, ⓦwww.anchorage.mtx.net; ❹–❼), a lovingly restored beachfront guesthouse with en-suite and spa facilities, a good restaurant attached (see below) and an adjoining backpackers hostel (dorms ❶). Alternatives include the *Villa Victor Bed and Breakfast*, 59 Victoria St (☎08/8552 4258; ❺–❻); and the *Family Inn Motel*, 300 Port Elliot Rd (☎08/8552 1941, ⓕ8552 8645; ❹)

Good places to **eat** abound. The super *Cafe Bavaria* at 11 Albert Place is a gleaming venue with delicious fresh-baked German cakes and savouries at reasonable prices (closed Mon). The *Blackfriars Bookshop and Coffee Bar*, 157 Hindmarsh Rd, also has good cakes, coffee and **internet access** ($4 per 30min) If you're after Italian food, head for *Nino Solari's Pizzeria*, nearby at no. 16 (closed Mon), where you can plough into some generous portions of pasta and home-made *gelati*; for seafood, try the *Anchorage Café* on beachfront Flinders Parade, a lively city-style café with an eclectic menu that's good for vegetarians. The best place to **drink** is on the Esplanade at the *Hotel Crown* which serves cheap bar meals, has streetside tables and big-name bands on Thursday and Friday and DJs on Saturday.

The Encounter Bikeway – Victor Harbor to Goolwa

The Encounter Bikeway follows a scenic 24km stretch of coast between Victor Harbor and Goolwa. Parts of the route are on-road and slightly inland, but mostly it follows the coastline and is for **cyclists**, rollerbladers and walkers only. The return trip can be completed comfortably in a day; the most scenic section, and hilliest, is between Dump Beach in Victor Harbor and the town of Port Elliot. **Mountain bikes** can be **hired** from Goolwa Cycle Hire, Ampol Service Station, Cadell Street, Goolwa (T08/8555 1000; $22 per day), or Victor Harbor Cycle, 73 Victoria Street, Victor Harbour (T08/8552 1417; $18 per day); or you can take your pick from a unique selection of brightly painted **tandem bikes**, some side-by-side and some with trailers, from Victor Bike Hire, 12 Flinders Parade, Victor Harbor (T08/8552 4458; from $10 per hour). Unfortunately none offer a drop-off service for one-way journeys, but on Sundays you can take your bike on the Cockle Train (see p.827) between Victor Harbor and Goolwa and cycle back.

Port Elliot

PORT ELLIOT, just 5km east of Victor Harbour, is a pleasant little town with some good **coastal walks** along the cliffs at Freeman Knob and an attractive sandy beach with safe swimming at Horseshoe Bay. Campers can enjoy the beachside setting at *Port Elliot Caravan Park* (T08/8554 2134, F8554 3454, W www.portelliotcaravanpark.com.au; cabins ❹, cottages ❺). A short stroll inland on the main Victor Harbour–Goolwa road, *Arnella by the Sea* (T08/8554 3611; rooms ❹, dorms ❷) is a charming nine-bedroom guesthouse in a National Trust-listed building retaining its original wooden floorboards. You can rent bikes here to explore the coastal Encounter Bikeway (see box above), or learn how to **surf** at nearby Middleton. For experienced surfers, Waitpinga Pass and Chiton offer more thrills. Boards can be rented from Southern Surf, 36 North Terrace (T08/8554 2375). For the latest surf report, call T08/8554 2047.

Goolwa

GOOLWA lies 14km east of Port Elliot, and 12km upstream from the ever-shifting sand bar at the mouth of the Murray River. Boaties love its position adjacent to vast Lake Alexandrina, yet with easy access to the Coorong (see p.838) and the ocean. Although so close to the coast, Goolwa feels like a real river town, and it thrived above all in the days of the Murray paddle-steamer trade, when it was the final offloading port: then a rip-roaring river town

Cruises from Goolwa

Cruises to the mouth of the Murray and as far as **Coorong National Park** (see p.838) leave from the end of the wharf. Spirit of the Coorong Cruises (T08/8555 2203, W www.coorongcruises.com.au) runs three trips: MV *Aroona* heads to the river mouth, passing through the barrages which keep saltwater out of the freshwater system, and into the Coorong wetlands (Tues & Sat; 2hr 45min; $26); the Discovery Cruise goes to the dune-covered Younghusband Peninsula where passengers can alight and walk to the Southern Ocean (Mon & Thurs; 4hr; $53.50 or $98 from Adelaide); the Adventure Cruise is a 30km trip right into the national park (Wed & Sun; 6hr; $70 or $114 from Adelaide). Coorong Cruises (T08/8555 1133) offers a day-long trip which focuses on bird-watching and looks at Aboriginal sites on the Younghusband Peninsula (Oct to end of June Tues, Thurs & Sun; $75).

with over 88 taverns, it had the biggest police station in South Australia. The **railways** brought the good days to an end, and today only a few reminders of boom times remain along Railway Terrace, with its old buildings painted in Federation colours. Steam trains make a comeback on Sundays, however, when the Cockle Train runs along the coast to Victor Harbor and back (every Sun & daily during school holidays; $20 return); and the Southern Encounter operates from the Adelaide Hills to Goolwa via Strathalbyn and Victor Harbor (see p.824). There's also a frequent coach service from Adelaide to Goolwa run by Premier Stateliner (Mon–Fri 5 daily, Sat 2 daily, Sun 1 daily; ☏08/8414 5555).

Overlooking the wharf beside the Hindmarsh bridge is **Signal Point Interpretive Centre** (daily 10am–5pm; $5), an innovatively designed exhibition telling the story of the Murray and its river trade. The centre houses a small souvenir shop and café as well as the helpful **Goolwa Tourist Information Centre** (daily 10am–4pm; ☏08/8555 1144, ⓦwww.alexandria.sa.gov.au), who can book local river tours but not accommodation. The PS *Murray River Queen* (☏08/8555 1733, Ⓕ8555 1990, ⓦwww.fleurieuregion.com/MurrayRiverQueen.htm; ❷–❼), an old paddleship moored at the wharf, has a wide range of **accommodation** from tiny backpacker cabins to stateroom suites. *Goolwa Riverport Motel* (☏08/8555 5033, Ⓕ8555 5022; ❺), on Noble Avenue 3km northeast of Goolwa, has motel units in a quiet setting beside the Lower Murray River, plus a pool, tennis court, bar and inexpensive dining room. The alternative in town is the *Corio Hotel* on Railway Terrace (☏08/8555 2011, Ⓕ8555 1109, Ⓔcorio@dove.net.au; ❹), which is also a popular **eating** place. Campers can head for *Goolwa Camping and Tourist Park*, Kessel Road, just 1km northwest of the centre (☏08/8555 2144; on-site vans ❷).

Strathalbyn

The pretty town of **STRATHALBYN** sits quietly amongst rolling hills about 25km north of Goolwa and an hour's drive south of Adelaide. Settled in 1839 by Scottish immigrants, the historic town is the market centre for the surrounding farming community. Renowned for **antique shops**, Heritage-listed buildings and a serene atmosphere, Strathalbyn comes alive for irregular but well-publicized **horse-racing** meetings and for a few traditional **festivals**: an antiques fair held in the third week of August, and an agricultural show and duck race in October. For a self-guided walking brochure of the town, head to the **Strathalbyn Tourist Information Centre** at the Old Railway Station, on South Terrace (daily 9am–5pm; ☏08/8536 2478). The best of the many **B&Bs** are *Watervilla House*, 2 Mill St (☏ & Ⓕ 08/8536 4099, Ⓔwatervillahouse@triplei.net.au; ❼), a beautiful 1840s cottage overlooking landscaped gardens and the River Angas Park; and the equally charming *Hamilton House*, 23 Commercial Rd (☏08/8536 4275; ❾). *Café Ruffino*, on the High Street, serves excellent home-made pastries and cakes. The only regular **public transport** is from Adelaide – Transit Bus #843 via Adelaide Hills (Mon–Fri only) – or if your timing is right, the Southern Encounter steam train chugs from Mount Barker and Goolwa on selected Sundays (see p.824).

The Yorke Peninsula

The **Yorke Peninsula** was almost the last section of the Australian coastline to be mapped by Matthew Flinders in 1802, and it still seems a bit of an afterthought: flat plains stretch out to the sea, so extensively cleared for farming that only tiny areas of original vegetation remain – in the Innes National Park at the very tip of the peninsula and in a couple of conservation parks. Much is now made of the northern peninsula's **Cornish heritage**, but the miners from Cornwall who flocked to the area when **copper** was discovered in 1859 have left behind little but their names and the ubiquitous Cornish pasty. The three towns of the Copper Triangle or "**Little Cornwall**" – Kadina, Wallaroo and Moonta – make the most of it at the Kernewek Lowender (Cornish Festival), held over the long weekend in May of every odd-numbered year, though in fact the mining boom ended seventy years ago, and they've been plain country towns ever since.

Just two-hours' drive from Adelaide, the peninsula offers a peaceful weekend break as well as good **fishing**. The east coast ports of Ardrossan, Port Vincent and Edithburgh on the Gulf St Vincent were visited first by ketches and schooners, and later by steamers transporting wheat and barley to England. Now the remaining jetties are used by anglers. They're all pleasant to visit, but **EDITHBURGH** offers most facilities: once a substantial salt-production town and grain port, it still has a few fine old buildings and a long jetty. There's a tidal swimming pool set in a rocky cove, and from Troubridge Hill you can see across to the Fleurieu Peninsula and to **Troubridge Island Conservation Park**, with its 1850s iron lighthouse, migrating seabirds and Little Penguin population: guided tours are available (Sept–June only; 2hr; $20; T 08/8852 6290 for bookings and details). **Accommodation** is available in the lighthouse-keeper's cottage, which sleeps up to ten – if you stay here you'll have the whole island to yourself, but it doesn't come cheap (arrange through the tour guide; minimum two-night stay; ❽). In Edithburgh itself, more affordable options include foreshore motel units and comfortable two-bedroom apartments at *The Anchorage Motel and Holiday Units* at 25 O'Halloran Parade (T 08/8852 6262, F 8852 6147; holiday units ❸–❹, rooms ❺) and *Edithburgh Caravan Park* (T 08/8852 6056) further along the foreshore, which has vans (❷) and en-suite cabins (❹–❺). There are also motel units at the back of the *Troubridge Hotel* on Blanche Street (T 08/8852 6013, F 8852 6323; ❹); this faces the 1878 *Edithburgh Hotel* (T 08/8852 6263), which is the best place for **meals** and includes local oysters on its menu. The *Edithburgh Café* on Edith Street (8am–4.30pm, closed Tues) does good simple meals, from baked potatoes to quiche and salad.

At the tip of the peninsula lies the **Innes National Park**, with its contrasting coastline of rough cliffs, sweeps of beach and sand dunes, and its interior of mallee scrub. The park is untouched except for the ruins of the gypsum-mining town of **Inneston**, near **Stenhouse Bay**. The **visitor centre** (T 08/8854 4040) in the park sells entry permits ($6 per car) and **camping** permits ($6–18 per car depending on which campsite you choose) and offers facilities such as hot showers. The main camping area is at **Pondalowie Bay**, which has some of the best surf in the state; there are several other good surfing spots around the park and north towards Corny Point. Other more sheltered coves and bays are good for snorkelling, with shallow reef areas of colourful marine life, while on land you might see emus, western grey kangaroos, pygmy possums and mallee fowl. The NPWS also operate five self-contained lodges around Inneston (T 08/8854 3200, F 8854 3299; ❹–❺); there's a minimum two-night stay.

Premier Stateliner (T 08/8415 5555) has a daily **bus** service from Adelaide to Moonta, via Kadina and Wallaroo. The Yorke Peninsula Passenger Service (T 08/8823 2375) runs from Adelaide to Yorketown, alternating daily between the east coast via Ardrossan, Port Vincent and Edithburgh and the centre via Maitland and Minlaton. There's no transport to the national park itself.

Kangaroo Island

As you head towards **Cape Jervis** along the west coast of the Fleurieu Peninsula, **KANGAROO ISLAND**, only 13km offshore, first appears behind a vale of rolling hills. Once you're on the island, its size and lack of development – there's only one person for every square kilometre – leave a strong impression: this is actually Australia's third-largest island after Tasmania and Melville Island (north of Darwin). The island has 450km of quite spectacular wild coastline, so takes some time to explore. To see all the unusual **geological features** and **wildlife habitats**, you'll need at least three days. Most people visit the major attractions on the south coast – Seal Bay, Little Sahara, Remarkable Rocks and Flinders Chase National Park – and miss the other sights. **Aboriginal people** once lived on the island, their presence evidenced by the discovery of stone tools and other items. Kangaroo Island was once joined to the mainland by a land bridge, but it's a mystery exactly when or why the people left, or if they just died out.

Although the island is promoted as South Australia's premier destination for tourism, it's still very unspoilt and the locals are as friendly as ever; only in the peak holiday period (Christmas to the end of Jan, when most of the accommodation is booked up) does it feel busy. Once out of the few small towns, you won't see many shops or service stations; what you will see are long, straight stretches of road through undulating fields, dense forests of gum or mallee scrub, and the sea. There's often a strong wind off the Southern Ocean, so bring something warm whatever the season, and take care when **swimming**: there are strong rips on many of the beaches. Safe swimming spots include Hog Bay at Eastern Cove and Antechamber Bay both near Penneshaw, Emu Bay, northwest of Kingscote, Stokes Bay, further west and Vivonne Bay on the south side of the island.

Kangaroo Island is possibly the best place in Australia to see an astonishing range of **wildlife**, largely untroubled by disease or natural predators, with a third of the landmass protected in the form of **national or conservation parks**. When Matthew Flinders first sighted the island in 1802, "black substances" seen on shore in the twilight turned out to be **kangaroos**, prolific and easily hunted. Kangaroos still abound, as do wallabies. **Koalas** were introduced at Flinders Chase National Park in 1923 as a conservation measure. They have remained free of *chlamydia*, which is common in the mainland population, and have spread so widely that they are killing off many of the gum trees – calls for culling in the mid-1990s caused national controversy, so fertility control and relocation to other parts of Australia are being tried instead. Other animals found here are echidnas, platypuses, Little penguins, fur seals, sea lions and, in passing, southern right whales; the last three attracted whalers and sealers, many of them American, to make a base on the island after Flinders' discovery. What's more, the island is home to over two hundred kinds of **birds**, as well as snakes.

Wild pigs and feral goats are the successors of those left here by early seafarers, and a pure strain of **Ligurian bees** brought by early settlers has resulted in a honey industry. There are also over a million **sheep** on the island, most of them merino. However, since wool prices have dropped drastically in recent years, farmers have had to find other sources of income and Kangaroo Island is now becoming known for its gourmet foodstuffs. A sheep dairy here makes delicious Continental-style cheeses, but the latest craze is for **marron farming**, with about 140 licensed producers of the freshwater crustacean, a bit like a cross between a lobster and a yabbie. Other diverse new industries include abalone farming, oyster and mussel production, olive-oil pressing and the revival of eucalyptus-oil distilling.

Getting to the island

Kangaroo Island Sealink **ferries** ply across the Backstairs Passage **from Cape Jervis to Penneshaw** – often a rough journey, though mercifully short. Two large vehicle ferries make the journey at least four times daily, and up to seven times during peak holiday periods, taking about forty minutes to cross: buses connect the service with Adelaide twice daily ($64 return, $96 including bus from Adelaide, cars $138, motorbikes $44, bikes $11; ⓣ13 1301, ⓦ www.sealink.com.au). At Penneshaw connecting Sealink buses to American River ($7.50 one-way) and Kingscote ($11) need to be booked in advance.

In addition, it's worth checking out the various cheap **packages** that include accommodation and tours or car rental, often with special backpackers' rates. At one end of the scale, Sealink does a whirlwind $159 one-day coach tour leaving Adelaide at 7am and returning at 10.30pm, but it's pretty exhausting. More leisurely options aimed at independent-minded budget travellers are with Kangaroo Island Wildlife and Scenic Tours (ⓣ08/8553 1284 or free call 1800 686 620) and Kangaroo Island Ferry Connections (ⓣ08/8553 1233 or free call 1800 018 484, ⓦ www.ki-ferryconnections.com.au); both companies offer similar two-day, one-night small-group packages from Adelaide for about $250 per person, staying in the Penneshaw hostels. Camp Wild Adventures (ⓣ08/8332 6615 or free call 1800 444 321, ⓦ www.campwild.com.au) has an excellent, more laid-back two-day 4WD tour from Adelaide, camping overnight in a secluded spot on the southern coast ($260 per person). The Wayward Bus's two-day tour from Adelaide also takes advantage of an overnight stop near the Flinders Chase National Park, giving more time for viewing the spectacular sights here ($265 per person, or $295 to upgrade from dorm to twin or double room; ⓣ08/8410 8833 or free call 1800 882 823, ⓦ www.waywardbus.com.au).

It takes thirty minutes to **fly** to Kingscote on Kangaroo Island from Adelaide and costs about $130 return. The two airlines are Kendell Airlines (ⓣ13 1300, ⓦ www.kendell.com.au; 4 daily) and Emu Airways (ⓣ08/8234 3711, ⓦ www.emuair.mtx.net; 8 daily). **Car rental** companies have offices at Kingscote Airport, and there's a bus to town for about $11 with Airport Shuttle Services (ⓣ08/8553 2390).

Getting around, tours and activities

Once you're on the island, you really need your own transport. As there are only four **car rental** firms, it's best to book to be sure of a vehicle – that way you'll also be met with the vehicle off the ferry or plane. In Kingscote try Budget Rent a Car, Commercial Street (☎08/8553 3133; $92 per day, $495 per week), or Kangaroo Island Rental/Hertz, on the corner of Franklin Street and Telegraph Road (☎08/8553 2390 or free call 1800 088 296, ✉hertzki@kin.net.au; $77 per day, $504 per week or $120 per day for 4WD); Penneshaw Hire run by the *Penneshaw Youth Hostel* (☎08/8553 1284; $80 per day, $150 per two days) rents out new model cars. **Campervan hire** is available from Kangaroo Island Campers, Kingscote (☎08/8553 7195, ℱ8553 7323, ✉kicamp@kin.on.net; $100 per day, minimum two-day rental).

Roads to most major attractions are bitumen-sealed, including the scenic 80km **South Coast Road** from Cygnet River to the Flinders Chase National Park and on to Remarkable Rocks and Admirals Arch. The main drag is the **Playford Highway** from Kingscote through Cygnet River and Parndana to the western tip of the island at Cape Borda, although the last part of the highway along the northern edge of Flinders Chase National Park is not sealed and can be rough. At the eastern end of the highway, sealed roads feed off to the airport, Emu Bay and American River and Penneshaw. Most other roads are constructed of ironstone rubble on red dirt and can be very dangerous; the recommended speed on these roads is 60kph. Driving between dusk and dawn on all roads is best avoided due to the high risk of collision with kangaroos and wallabies. You'll see the carnage of animal remains alongside the road at depressingly short intervals – most being hit by speeding trucks. Cars have far less protection from impact and insurance excesses are often a mandatory $2000 for animal collision. The main roads are all good for **cycling**. For the island's best **mountain bikes**, as well as tandem bikes, go to Rent-a-Bike, 1 Commercial Rd, Kingston (☎08/8553 2349; $27 per day); the *Penneshaw Youth Hostel* (see p.835) also has bikes for hire for $20 per day.

Most people opt for **tours**, which can be made flexible and are good value if bought as part of a package (see opposite). There are several small-group tour companies based on the island: Adventure Charters of Kangaroo Island in Kingscote (☎08/8553 9119, ⓦwww.adventurecharters.com.au), led by an ex-park ranger, offers 4WD tours with an emphasis on fine food, wine and accommodation as well as nature. There are also a couple of **dive** tour operators: Kangaroo Island Diving Safaris (☎08/8559 3255, ℱ8559 3225, ⓦwww.kidivingsafaris.com), based at Telhawk Farm on the north coast, offers diving charters and residential dive courses with special backpackers' rates; and Adventureland Diving, based at *Penneshaw Youth Hostel* (☎08/8553 1233, ✉advhost@kin.on.net), has three-day residential scuba courses and certification ($310 includes hostel accommodation), as well as half-day **snorkelling** at Kangaroo Head ($50) and abseiling at Cape Willoughby ($66).

Information and park entrance fees

With about one-third of the island deemed a national or conservation park area, many of the parks charge entry fees and extras for guided tours. However, a one-year **Island Pass** ($28) covers virtually all these costs (except for camping and the night-time penguin tours from Penneshaw and Kingscote, see p.834 and p.836 respectively), and is worth it if you're here for a while. The entry fees and tour prices quoted in the following accounts apply only if you don't have a pass – add up the cost of what you want to see and work out which is cheaper. Passes can be bought from the parks themselves or from the

NPWS office on Dauncy Street, Kingscote (Mon–Fri 8.45am–5pm; ☎08/8553 2381, ⓦwww.environment.sa.gov.au); this office can also arrange camping permits and cottage accommodation in most of the national parks around the island. Passes can also be purchased from the **Kangaroo Island Gateway Visitor Information Centre**, at the edge of Penneshaw on the main road to Kingscote (Mon–Fri 9am–5pm, Sat & Sun 10am–4pm; ☎08/8553 1185, ⓦwww.tourkangarooisland.com.au), which also has an interpretive display on the island's history, geology and ecology and dispenses free maps.

The island

Coming by boat, you'll arrive at Kangaroo Island's eastern end at the small settlement of **Penneshaw** with its Little penguin colony. **Kingscote**, to the west, is the focus of administration and services, and also has status as an historic town, being South Australia's second colonial settlement, though few vestiges remain. Between Penneshaw and Kingscote, sheltered **American River** is another good base. The airport is situated near **Cygnet River** – a quiet spot inland from Kingscote. From here, the Playford Highway and South Coast Road branch out to traverse the island entering **Flinders Chase National Park** in the north and south respectively. The national park and surrounding wilderness protection area cover the entire western end of the island. The rugged **south coast** provides more wildlife spotting and natural beauty: running west to east, you can visit the aptly named Remarkable Rocks and Admirals Arch, both within the national park; go bushwalking in Hanson Bay; tour the limestone caves of Kelly Hill; camp at Vivonne Bay Conservation Park; play Lawrence of Arabia among the impressive sand dunes of Little Sahara or roam amongst resident sea lions at Seal Bay. The quieter **north coast** has a series of sheltered beaches, including Emu Bay and Stokes Bay, and wild coastal cliff walks around Scotts Cove.

Penneshaw

Most people arrive by ferry at **PENNESHAW**, set on low, penguin-inhabited cliffs. This is a popular base, with comfortable accommodation and plenty of places to eat (see opposite). Penneshaw's crescent of sandy beach at Hog Bay curves from the rocks below the wharf, where the ferries come in, around to a wooded headland. The bay provides safe **swimming** and even a shady shelter on the sand; above, there's a grassy picnic reserve with barbecues and the **Penguin Centre**. A national park guide (daily: April–Sept 7.30pm & 8.30pm; Oct–March 8.30pm & 9.30pm; $6) provides an informative commentary on the **Little penguin** antics from the centre at dusk. This is the time they return from feeding in the unpolluted sea and cross the beach at Hog Bay to their cliffside burrows – a specially lit **boardwalk** provides a rookery viewing area.

Antechamber Bay, the next body of water, 10km by road southeast of Penneshaw, also has good, safe swimming. If you drive or cycle a further 10km along the unsealed dusty road you'll come to **Cape Willoughby Lighthouse**, at the eastern end of the island. Guided tours are offered by the NPWS (daily every 30min 10am–4pm; $6.50), and you can even stay in the sandstone homes of the original keepers (see opposite). You'll find more safe swimming at **American Beach**, southwest from Penneshaw along the scenic road that hugs Eastern Cove.

The **Dudley Peninsula**, on which Penneshaw stands, is attached to the rest of the island by a narrow neck of sand; at the isthmus 511 steps lead up to

Mount Thisby (Prospect Hill), a 99-metre hill of sand with views across to the mainland, to Hungry Beach, Pelican Lagoon and American River on the island's north coast, and in the opposite direction to **Pennington Bay**. Here there are sponge-textured weathered rocks to clamber over, and some good surf, but a dangerous undertow.

Practicalities

Penneshaw's Sealink office is at 7 North Terrace (Mon–Fri 8am–6pm, Sat & Sun 8am–1pm & 3–6pm; ℡08/8553 1122). There's no bank, but the **post office** (Mon–Fri 9am–5pm, Sat 9am–11pm) acts as an agent, and there's EFT-POS at Grimshaw's, the town's **general store** opposite the hotel (daily 8am–7pm, summer until 8pm). Penneshaw has the island's widest range of accommodation: there are two **hostels**, the modern but lively non-YHA *Penneshaw Youth Hostel* (℡08/8553 1284, ℱ8553 1295, ℮advhost@kin.on.net; rooms ❸, dorms ❶), which hires bikes and cars and runs a diving school, and the more spacious and relaxed *Penguin Walk YHA* (℡08/8553 1233, ℱ8553 1190, ⓦwww.ki-ferryconnections.com.au; rooms ❹–❺, dorms ❶); both run their own tours (see p.833). The upmarket alternative is the friendly *Kangaroo Island Seafront Hotel* (℡08/8553 1028, ℱ8553 1204, ⓦwww.seafront.com.au; ❼–❽), set in landscaped gardens with motel-style rooms and fully equipped cabins, plus a heated pool, spa, sauna and tennis court, bar and restaurant. There's **camping** at the small, shady *Penneshaw Caravan Park* on Talinga Avenue, to the left of the Sealink terminal overlooking the beach (℡ & ℱ 08/8553 1075; on-site vans ❸, cabins ❼). You can also stay in the two light-house-keepers' cottages at **Cape Willoughby** (℡08/8559 7235, ℱ8559 7268; BYO linen ❹).

The best **restaurant** in town is the relaxed *Old Post Office Restaurant*, serving vegetarian and home-style meals (licensed; nightly except Tues & Wed). *Penneshaw Pizza*, overlooking the Sealink wharf, serves pasta, while the tin-roofed bungalow of the *Penneshaw Hotel* is a small and friendly place to drink, with a verandah overlooking the water; counter meals include cheap daily specials. *Dolphin Rock Takeaway* (daily 7.30–11am & 5–7.30pm), attached to the *Penneshaw Youth Hostel*, does fast food and a breakfast fry-up and sells a small range of groceries, but you'd be better off going to Grimshaw's; it sells virtually everything and has a takeaway service and seating area in the adjoining *Ruby Joe's Café*.

American River and Cygnet River

Facing Penneshaw across Eastern Cove, **AMERICAN RIVER** is actually a sheltered bay, where many small fishing boats moor, aiming to catch some of its abundant whiting. It's a peaceful place to stay, with a concentration of accommodation along the hilly shoreline and a general store. American River Rendezvous, the kiosk at the wharf (℡08/8553 7150; kayak rental $40 per day), provides a bit of a spectacle here with its raucous **pelican feeding** (daily 4.30pm; free). Boats can be chartered for local **fishing and sailing** from the kiosk or direct from Cooinda Charter Services (℡ & ℱ 08/8553 7063). *Matthew Flinders Terraces* (℡08/8553 7100, ℱ8553 7250, ⓦwww.falconweb.net.au/~matthewflinders; ❼) is a beautifully situated **motel** with pool, spa and a good licensed restaurant (reservations only), or try the *Wanderers Rest* (℡08/8553 7140, ℱ8553 7282, ⓦwww.wanderersrest.com.au; ❽), an upmarket B&B where each room has a patio. Holiday units include the budget *Casuarina Units* (℡08/8553 7020; ❹) and the more expensive *Ulonga Lodge* (℡ & ℱ 08/8553 7171; ❺).

CYGNET RIVER, at the junction of Playford Highway and the road from Penneshaw, boasts one of the best places to stay on the island: *Koala Lodge* (℡ & Ⓕ 08/8553 9006; ❻), set amidst large gum trees, has personalized en-suite units near the river bank.

Kingscote and the north coast

It's a 45-minute drive on a sealed road from Penneshaw to **KINGSCOTE** (60km), the island's main town with banks, shops, public internet access, a hospital, library and the only high school. The coast here has been the scene of several **shipwrecks** – interpretive boards on the foreshore provide details. For more history, you can walk north along the Esplanade to the **Reeves Point Historic Site**, where more interpretive boards provide the only clue to the South Australia Company's first landing of settlers in July 1836, before they headed off to establish nearby Adelaide; with three hundred at its peak, the settlement failed and was folded by 1839. Less than a kilometre up the hill above, on Seaview Road, is **Hope Cottage Folk Museum** (daily 2–4pm, closed July & Aug), the restored 1859 home of a pioneering family. Kingscote has a small colony of **penguins** that were transported from Penneshaw during the building of the boardwalk there; not as impressive as Penneshaw's, they're best seen on the **guided ranger talks** that leave from the Marine Centre underneath the *Ozone Hotel* (April–Sept 7.30pm & 8.30pm; Oct–March 9pm & 9.40pm; $7). There's also **pelican feeding** around the Fisherman's Jetty with a small talk about their habits and habitat (daily 5pm; $2).

Established in 1907, the waterfront *Ozone Hotel* (℡08/8553 2011 or free call 1800 083 133, Ⓕ8553 2249, Ⓦ www.ozonehotel.com; ❻–❼) is a local institution and the best place in town to eat, with a bistro and **restaurant**. Back from the beach on Dauncy Street is the *Queenscliffe Family Hotel* (℡08/8553 2254, Ⓕ8553 2291; ❹), another old pub offering **rooms** and meals; and next door is the *Blue Gum Cafe*, which has a varied city-style menu, with vegetarian dishes and real coffee (closed Sun). Upmarket motel accommodation, with sea views, is found at *Wisteria Lodge*, Cygnet Road (℡08/8553 2707, Ⓕ8553 2200, Ⓦ www.kigateway.kin.on.net/wisteria; ❼). For the budget-conscious there's the *Kangaroo Island Central Backpackers Hostel*, at 21 Murray St (℡08/8553 2787, Ⓕ8553 2694; rooms ❸, dorms ❶); it has large, clean dorms, a kitchen and common room. *Nepean Bay Caravan Park* (℡ & Ⓕ 08/8553 2394; on-site vans ❸, cabins ❹, cottages ❹) at Brownlow Beach, 3km away, is the only place for **campers**.

The **beaches** on the north coast are more sheltered than those on the south. **Emu Bay**, 21km along a sealed road from Kingscote, is a secluded and quiet spot with a clean, sandy beach, a small penguin community, no shops, a few holiday homes and a couple of B&Bs. Wintersun Holiday Units (℡ & Ⓕ 08/8553 5241, Ⓔ dmorris@kin.net.au; ❹–❺) manages several self-contained cottages along the bay and in the nearby hills. About 30km further west, secluded **Stokes Bay** is reached along a dirt road passing through a natural tunnel between overhanging boulders. There's a delightful calm rock pool – a perfect semicircle of rounded black stones which conveniently provides protection from the dangerous rip in the bay. Outside the tunnel, the *Rockpool Cafe* (daily 10am–5.30pm; ℡08/8559 2277) looks after the beachfront **campsites** and also sells milk and bread as well as more exotic fare such as Asian and Italian dishes and lentil burgers; it's sometimes open for dinner by appointment only.

The south coast

Several conservation parks are strung along the exposed south coast. The largest is **Cape Gantheaume**, an area of low mallee scrub supporting prolific birdlife around **Murray Lagoon** – where you'll find the ranger station (daily 8am–5pm) – the largest freshwater lagoon on the island. The adjacent **Seal Bay Conservation Park** is home to almost six hundred **sea lions**, the third-largest breeding population in Australia. They are unusually tolerant of humans and you can walk quietly among the colony on the beach at Seal Bay, accompanied by a national park guide (9am–4.15pm, until 7pm during summer holidays; every 15min in summer, every 45min in winter; $10), or take a stroll on the boardwalk ($6.50).

Vivonne Bay, with its long, sandy beach and bush setting, is a great place to camp. The beachside **campsite** (toilets, water, barbecues) is privately run ($4) and there's a well-stocked store 1km away on the main South Coast Road. It's safe to swim near the jetty or boat ramp or in the Harriet River, but the bay itself has a dangerous undertow. Between Seal Bay and Vivonne Bay, **Little Sahara** is 15km of perfect white-sand dunes rising unexpectedly out of mallee scrub.

The main features of the **Kelly Hill Conservation Park** are the **Kelly Hill Caves**, extensive limestone cave formations (NPWS guided tours daily: June–Aug hourly 10am–3pm; Sept–May hourly 10am–4pm, in summer until 5pm; $5). The tour explores only the largest cave, which is not the usual damp, bat-filled cavern but very dry, with a constant temperature of 16°C. The NPWS runs adventure caving tours of three other caves ($22.50–33.50 depending on the cave; ☎08/8559 7231 for details and booking). The eighteen-kilometre return **Hanson Bay Trail** goes from the caves to the sea, passing freshwater lagoons and dune systems: allow at least eight hours – or longer, if you're tempted to stop for a swim. *Hanson Bay Cabins* (☎08/8553 2603 ℱ8853 2673, ⊛www.esl.com.au; ➐), just west of the Kelly Hill Conservation Park, are situated in a lovely secluded spot surrounded by bushland with excellent walking trails.

Flinders Chase National Park

Flinders Chase National Park, South Australia's largest, occupies the entire western end of the island. It became a park as early as 1919, and in the 1920s and 1930s koalas, platypuses, emus and Cape Barren geese from the Bass Strait islands (see p.1106–1110) were introduced. The land is mainly low-lying mallee forest, with occasional patches of taller sugar gum trees. The **Flinders Chase Visitors Centre** (daily: June–Aug 10am–5pm; Sept–May 9am–5pm; ☎08/8559 7235, ℱ8559 7268, ⊛kiparksaccom@deh.sa.gov.au; park entry fee $13) is surrounded by open grasslands where large numbers of kangaroos and wallabies graze. Koala signs lead to a glade of trees, where you'll see the creatures swaying high up, within binocular range. Follow the **Platypus Waterhole Walk** for 3km to a platypus viewing area, but be warned that to get a glimpse of the creatures requires endless patience. The winding sealed road through the park will take you on to its most spectacular features, the huge and weirdly shaped, rust-coloured **Remarkable Rocks** on Kirkpatrick Point, and the impressive natural formation of **Admirals Arch,** where hundreds of fur seals bask around the rocks. At the northern corner of the park, you can go on a guided tour of the 1858 **Cape Borda Lighthouse** (school holidays seven daily 10am–4pm; winter 4 daily 11am–2pm; rest of the year four/six daily 11am–3.15pm; $6.50).

The main **camping** area is at Rocky River, where there are also two **cottages**, the four-bedroom *Mays Homestead* (➎ en suite) and the one-room *Postmans Cottage* (➌, with use of campsite showers and toilets). There are more cottages at the park's north and south corners, respectively at Cape Borda

(❷–❺) and Cape Du Couedic (❸). Bookings for all cottages are made through the Flinders Chase Visitors Centre (see overleaf). There are several other good places to stay along the South Coast Road just outside the park. *Kangaroo Island Wilderness Resort* (℡ 08/8212 0446 or free call 1800 228 212, ⓦ www.aust-dreaming.com.au; rooms ❽, dorms ❷) has large wood cabins set amidst bush-land, plus an excellent restaurant – at dusk you can watch the nocturnal ani-mals coming out to feed. Nearby, is the *Western KI Caravan Park* (℡ 08/8559 7201, Ⓕ 8559 7298, ⓔ beckwith@kin.on.net; cabins ❻) where you can camp under the tall gum trees and try to spot koala bears. By staying this end of the island you'll see the spectacular coastal sights at their best – particularly Remarkable Rocks which turn deep orange with the setting and rising sun.

The southeast

For most travellers, the southeast – the area between Melbourne and Adelaide – is an area to be passed through as quickly as possible. From Tailem Bend, just beyond Murray Bridge some 85km out of Adelaide, three highways branch out. The **Ouyen Highway** is the quintessential road to nowhere, leading through the sleepy settlements of Lameroo and Pinnaroo to the insignificant town of **Ouyen** in Victoria's Mallee country (see p.1005). The **Dukes Highway** is the fast, boring route to Melbourne via the South Australian mallee scrub and farming towns of **Keith** and **Bordertown**, birthplace of for-mer Prime Minister Bob Hawke, before continuing in Victoria as the Western Highway across the monotonous Wimmera (see p.1005). It is, however, well worth breaking your journey to visit **the Coonawarra** and **Naracoorte**, in between the Dukes Highway and the coastal route: the former is a tiny wine-producing area that makes some of the country's finest red wine; the latter is a fair-size town with a freshwater lagoon system that attracts prolific birdlife, and a conservation park with impressive World Heritage-listed caves.

The **Princes Highway** (Highway 1) is much less direct but far more inter-esting; it follows the extensive coastal lagoon system of **the Coorong** to **Kingston SE**, and then runs a short way inland to the lake craters of **Mount Gambier**, before crossing into Victoria. On this last stretch, another possible route – Southern Ports Highway – sticks closer to the coast, and there's a detour along the Riddoch Highway into the scenic Coonawarra wine region. Premier Stateliner (℡ 08/8415 5555) has two routes between Adelaide and Mount Gambier, one inland via Keith, Bordertown, Naracoorte, Coonawarra and Penola; the other along the coast via Meningie, Kingston SE, Robe and Millicent. If you're coming from Melbourne, V-Line (℡ 08/8231 7620 or 13 6196, ⓦ www.vline.vic.gov.au) has a daily service that terminates at Mount Gambier. The NPWS free newspaper, *The Tatler*, gives practical details relating to the southeastern coastal parks – pick up the latest copy from the Adelaide office (see p.787), or regional offices en route. More information can be found at the regional visitor information website at ⓦ www.thelimestonecoast.com.

Coorong National Park

From Tailem Bend, the Princes Highway skirts Lake Alexandrina and fresh-water Lake Albert, where **MENINGIE** is a popular fishing centre, before passing the edge of the **Coorong National Park**. The coastal saline lagoon system of the Coorong (from the Aboriginal *Karangk* meaning long neck) is separated from the sea for over 100km by the high sand dunes of the **Younghusband Peninsula**: the famous Australian children's film *Storm Boy*, about a boy and his friendship with a pelican, was filmed here. The state's most prolific **pelican breeding ground** is an excellent place to observe these awkward yet graceful birds – at Jacks Point, 3km north of Policemans Point on the Princes Highway, there's a shelter with seating and a telescope focused on the small islands where some birds breed. Without your own **transport**, one way to see the Coorong is to head off in a 4WD with a local naturalist from Coorong Nature Tours (day-trip $133 from Meningie, $185 from Adelaide; longer two- and three-day trips available; ⓣ & ⓕ 08/8574 0037, ⓦwww.lm.net.au/~coorongnat). You can also get to the park on a **cruise** from Goolwa (see box on p.828).

There are several designated camping areas with shelters, barbecues, toilets, running water (but no showers) and marked walking trails. The Coorong is also good for beach **camping**: with a permit (see below) you can camp anywhere along the beach between high and low watermark, but cars must be parked in designated places, and you must bring your own drinking water which can be collected outside the seldom-manned **Salt Creek NPWS ranger station** on the edge of the park about 60km south of Meningie. Elsewhere, **information** and **camping permits** ($5 per car) and maps of the park and campsites can be obtained at the national park **headquarters** at 34 Main St, Meningie (Mon, Wed & Fri 9am–5pm; ⓣ08/8575 1200), the Melaleuca Information Centre, 76 Princes Highway (daily 9am–5pm; ⓣ08/8575 1259), and most petrol stations on the way to the park including Salt Creek's Shell petrol station, which has an outside notice board and a **café** serving delicious grilled Coorong mullet. There are **caravan parks** at Long Point, Parnka Point, Gemini Downs and 42-mile Crossing – the only land access to the Younghusband Peninsula. If you're passing by, park your car at the 42-Mile Crossing information area and walk 1km along a sandy 4WD track for great views of the sand dunes and wild Southern Ocean. The 4WD track runs alongside the beach all the way up the peninsula to Barkers Knoll and down to Kingston SE, with camping along the way. If you want to stay in more comfort, there are plenty of **motels** at Meningie.

Camp Coorong, run by the Ngarrindjeri Lands and Progress Association, is 10km south of Meningie, and 3km from another stretch of the Coorong National Park. This cultural centre attempts to explain the heritage and culture of the Ngarrindjeri Aborigines who were one of the largest groups in South Australia, occupying the land around the Coorong and the lower Murray River and lakes. There's a museum (Mon–Fri 9am–5pm; donation), and you can camp here or stay in the well-outfitted **cabins** (booking required on ⓣ08/8575 1557, ⓕ8575 1448; ❸).

Southern Ports Highway

KINGSTON SE, on Lacepede Bay, is the first town past the Coorong: here the Princes Highway turns inland, while **Southern Ports Highway** continues along the coast before rejoining the main road at Millicent. As the **Big Lobster** signifies, Kingston has an important lobster industry: you can buy them freshly cooked at *Lacepede Seafood* by the jetty (daily 9am–6pm) for around $40 a kilo.

Lobsters apart, you're better off continuing down the coast. **ROBE**, on the south side of Guichen Bay 44km from Kingston, was one of South Australia's first settlements, established as a deep-water port in 1847. After 1857, over sixteen thousand Chinese landed here and walked to the goldfields, 400km or so away, to avoid the poll tax levied in Victoria. As trade declined and the highway bypassed town, Robe managed to maintain both dignity and charm, and during the busy summer period the population of less than eight hundred expands to over eleven thousand. Adelaidians love the place, with its well-preserved nineteenth-century streetscapes, and its beach setting surrounded by lakes and bushland; some even drive the 366km for a weekend. Summer is also the season for crayfishing, Robe's second substantial industry. It's all deliberately low-key: the main thoroughfare of Victoria Street is tree-lined and semi-residential, the shops blending unobtrusively with the houses. **Tourist information** is inside the library on the corner of Smiley and Victoria streets (Mon–Fri 9am–5pm, Sat & Sun 10am–4pm; ℗ 08/8768 2465, Ⓦ www.robe.sa.gov.au); they have walking and driving maps, a Historical Interpretation Centre and free limited-time internet access.

There's a choice of dozens of places to **stay**, most of which double up as places to eat. *Robe Hotel*, Mundy Terrace (℗ 08/8768 2077, Ⓕ 8768 2495; ❹–❺), is an old stone beachfront hotel with modern budget accommodation and en-suite motel-style rooms with views and spa units; the downstairs bars serve good bistro meals – lots of fish and a vegetarian dish of the day. The *Caledonian Inn*, Victoria Street (℗ 08/8768 2029, Ⓕ 8768 2636, Ⓔ caled@seol.net.au; ❹–❼ including breakfast), is a charming, ivy-covered stone building, first licensed in 1858, that would not look out of place in an English village – it offers B&B accommodation upstairs or in homely cottages, and serves excellent food. Also on Victoria Street, *Guichen Bay Motel* (℗ 08/8768 2001; ❺) has good-value, spacious rooms, some with kitchenette, as well as the licensed *Robetown Cottage Restaurant* which has special crayfish dishes in season. *Sea Vu Caravan Park*, 1 Squire Drive (℗ 08/8768 2277; cabins ❹, on-site vans ❸), is family-run and close to town, with a swimming beach just below. The excellent *Bushland Cabins* set in bushland southeast of the centre on Nora Creina Road (℗ 08/8768 2386, Ⓔ bushland@seol.net.au; shared lodge ❶, cabins ❸–❹), offer tent sites, a backpackers' lodge comprising two bedrooms and a kitchen/lounge area with TV, and en-suite cabins with TV, fridge, heaters and ceiling fan; walking trails into the surrounding bush include the 1km clifftop track into Robe. For **meals** outside your accommodation you can treat yourself to excellent Italian coffee, city-style café fare or an all-day breakfast at *Wild Mulberry Cafe*, 46 Victoria St, opposite the Shell garage (summer & Easter daily 8am–9pm, rest of year 8am–5pm). For self-caterers, Foodland Supermarket, opposite the Ampol petrol station, is open daily 7.30am–7.30pm.

Between Robe and **BEACHPORT** are four lakes: for part of the way you can take the Nora Criena Drive through **Little Dip Conservation Park**, 14km of coastal dune systems. The drive provides views of Lake Eliza and Lake St Clair before returning to Southern Ports Highway and the former whaling port of Beachport, which boasts one of the longest jetties in Australia and many lobster-fishing boats at anchor on Rivoli Bay. The tiny town, whose population of four hundred increases tenfold over the Christmas and New Year season, has its own movie house, South Coast Cinema (℗ 08/8375 8455), which shows films on Wednesday, Saturday and Sunday nights.

Beachport has plenty of **accommodation**. *Bompas*, overlooking the bay at 3 Railway Terrace (℗ 08/8735 8333, Ⓕ 8735 8101, Ⓦ www.beachportaustralia .com; ❹–❻), was the town's first licensed hotel in 1879, and is now a pleasing B&B guesthouse with a coffee bar, bistro and **restaurant** downstairs, all sharing a menu featuring Thai, Malay, Italian and Australian dishes. Places to stay on the foreshore include the long-established and well-equipped *Beachport Backpackers* (℗08/8735 8197; dorms ❶, self-contained family apartment ❹; booking advisable), which rents out fishing rods, surf and snorkelling gear, and the *Beachport Caravan Park*, opposite the beach on Beach Road (℗ & ℱ 08/8735 8128; on-site vans ❷, en-suite cottage ❺).

Continuing south on Southern Ports Highway, there are several turn-offs to **Canunda National Park** which has giant sand dunes, several signposted coastal walking trails, an abundance of birdlife and camping facilities ($6 per vehicle honesty box). The best place to explore the park is from **SOUTHEND** – you can pick up leaflets detailing the walks from the **National Park Headquarters** just beyond the town (Mon–Fri 8.30am–5pm; ℗08/8735 6053). One of the park rangers, Cookie, loves the area so much that he takes private 4WD tours into the park on his days off (weekends and public holidays; $95 for two people; by appointment only on ℗08/8735 6132). The only **place to stay** apart from the campsites is the *Southend on Sea Tourist Park* (℗08/8735 6035, ℱ8735 6034; cabins ❹, on-site vans ❷). More accommodation is available in the rather ordinary town of **MILLICENT**, 15km to the south, which also has its own **Visitor Information Centre**, 1 Main St (Mon–Fri 9am–5pm, Sat & Sun 9.30am–4.30pm; ℗08/8733 3205) and access to the park. The Southern Ports Highway rejoins the Princes Highway at Millicent.

Mount Gambier

MOUNT GAMBIER is the southeast's commercial centre; not far from the border with Victoria, the small city sprawls up the slopes of an extinct volcano which has three craters, each with its own lake surrounded by heavily wooded slopes and filled from underground waterways that are perfect for unusual subterranean pursuits (see box below). The **Blue Lake** is the largest of the crater lakes, up to 204m deep and 5km in circumference. From November to March it's a stunning cobalt blue, reverting to duller grey in the colder months. There are lookout spots and a scenic drive around the lake, and guided tours to the surface are offered by Aquifer Tours (Nov–Jan: daily on the hour 9am–5pm; Thurs also 7pm, Feb–Oct: daily on the hour 9am–3pm; 45min; $4). The second largest crater holds **Valley Lake** and a Wildlife Park (daily 7am–dusk; free) where indigenous animals range free amid native flora; there are lookouts, walking trails and boardwalks.

The centrepiece of **the city** is Cave Gardens, a shady park surrounding a deep limestone cavern with steps leading some way down; the stream running into it eventually filters into the Blue Lake. At the rear of the park the municipal offices contain the Civic Centre, library and a small theatre. Fronting thepark is the former Town Hall and the **Riddoch Art Gallery** (Tues–Fri 10am–4pm, Sat 10am–2pm, Sun noon–3pm; free) whose focus is the impressive Rodney Gooch collection of Aboriginal art from Utopia, Central Australia, which includes work by the late Emily Kame Kngwarreye. In the same building, Studio One sells the work of local artists (Mon–Fri 10.30am–4pm).

West of the centre, on Jubilee Highway West, is the extensive complex of underground caverns at **Engelbrecht Cave** (guided tours hourly 11am–3pm; 45min; $5.50), while east of the city, **Umpherston Sinkhole** (open access) is also known as the Sunken Garden, since it contains Victorian-era terraced gardens – they are floodlit at night when possums come out to feed.

8

Subterranean exploration

From **Engelbrecht Cave** you can dive in limestone waterways under the city. However, an open-water PADI classification is not enough to dive these dark and dangerous waters – you need a CDAA (Cave Divers Association of Australia) qualification. Contact the Mount Gambier NPWS office at 11 Helen St (☎ 08/8735 1177, ⓦ www.adelaide.net.au/~ecave) for further information. They can also issue permits for snorkelling at the crystal-clear waters of **Piccaninnie Ponds Conservation Park** or **Ewans Pond Conservation Park**, both south of Mount Gambier near Port Macdonnell. At Piccaninnie Ponds, a deep chasm with white-limestone walls contains clear water that is filtered underground from the Blue Lake – it takes five hundred years to get here.

Practicalities

For more information on Mount Gambier's attractions, head for the excellent **Lady Nelson Victory and Discovery Centre**, on Jubilee Highway East (daily 9am–5pm; exhibition $7.70; ☎ 08/8724 1730, ⓦ www.mountgambiertourism.com.au), where the ecology, geology and history of Mount Gambier are explored from Aboriginal and European perspectives. A ten-minute narration by the ghostly holographic image of missionary Christina Smith, is based on her book *The Booandik Tribe of South Australian Aborigines*. She worked with a local Aboriginal tribe for 35 years, and opened a charitable home in Mount Gambier in 1865, but even though she was sympathetic to the Aboriginal plight, her attempts at conversion only contributed to the destruction of traditional values. Other highlights of the centre are the short wetlands boardwalk and a demonstration of a volcanic eruption complete with steam – quite scary when it booms.

Mount Gambier has heaps of places to **stay**, with motels lining the highway either side of town. *The Jail*, on Margaret Street (☎ 08/8723 0032, ⓕ 8723 2477, ⓦ www.adelaide.net.au/~turnkey; rooms ❸, dorms ❶), was built in the 1860s and is now a Heritage-listed building. The last inmates left in 1995 and you can stay in the original cells behind locked doors (some even have a solitary loo in the corner), or in the simple three-bed dorms. Meals are provided in the large common room, which also has a bar, and there are also laundry facilities, internet access and organized paintball in the large exercise grounds when the Wayward Bus arrives. Central *Jens Hotel*, at 40 Commercial St (☎ 08/8725 0188, ⓕ 8723 9016, ⓔ jens.town.hall.hotel@alhgroup.com.au; ❹), is a classic, wide-balconied old boozer with cheap bar and bistro meals, late opening hours and en-suite accommodation. The best place to **eat** is the licensed *Café Capri Restaurant*, 53 Gray St (Mon–Sat 8.30am–10 or 11pm). Nearby, *Fasta Pasta*, 102 Commercial St (West), is one of a chain serving inexpensive fresh pasta with interesting sauces. There's **internet access** at the Cave Internet Lounge, 15–17 Commercial St ($2.50 per 30min), and – free of charge – at the Mount Gambier Public Library at the end of Watson Terrace (Mon–Fri 9am–4pm).

Heading on to Melbourne from Mount Gambier, V/Line (☎ 13 6196) has a daily service via Portland, Hamilton, Warrnambool, Geelong and Ballarat.

The Coonawarra wine region

Directly north of Mount Gambier, the **Riddoch Highway** heads through the **Coonawarra wine region**, and past some World Heritage-listed caves at Naracoorte, eventually linking up with the Dukes Highway at Keith. With most wineries located on a 90km stretch of highway between **Penola** and

Padthaway, this is one of the easiest wine areas "to do" and it's low key and pretty. The region is renowned for the quality of its reds, which have been compared to those of Bordeaux; they account for about eighty percent of production, with **Cabernet Sauvignon** being the favourite variety, lauded each October at the Cabernet Celebration. The soil and drainage is ideal, classic Terra Rossa over limestone, and the climate is perfect – and as the weather is not really variable from year to year, the wines are consistently good.

Premier Stateliner (℡08/8415 5555) stops daily at Penola and Naracoorte on its Adelaide to Mount Gambier inland service.

Penola

Twenty-two kilometres north of Mount Gambier, **PENOLA**, gateway to the Coonawarra wine region, is a very simple but dignified country town of well-preserved nineteenth-century architecture. For information, head for **Penola Coonawarra Visitor Centre** in the old Mechanics Institute Building (Mon–Fri 9am–5pm, Sat 10am–5pm, Sun 9.30am–4pm), which also houses a display featuring John Riddoch, pioneer of Coonawarra's vineyards, and hands out the free *Historic Penola and Coonawarra* map with details of the region's wineries.

Beside the 1857 Cobb & Co booking office (now a restaurant), St Joseph's Catholic Church looks like something out of an Italian village, a world away from the very modern **Mary MacKillop Interpretative Centre** (daily 10am–4pm; $3.50; ⓦwww.penola.mtx.net.au/~mackillop) next door. Sister Mary MacKillop (1842–1909) was Penola's most famous resident, and Australia's first would-be saint – in 1995 Pope John Paul II pronounced her "Blessed", the last stage before full saint status. MacKillop set up a school, created her own teaching method and, with Father Julian Tennyson Woods, co-founded the Sisters of St Joseph of the Sacred Heart, a charitable teaching order that spread throughout Australia and New Zealand. Dramatic episodes of alleged disobedience and excommunication give her story a certain oomph. There's an inform-

Coonawarra wineries

There are twenty Coonawarra wineries that do tastings, most open Monday to Friday 9am to 5pm, Saturday and Sunday 10am to 4pm (for more information visit the Coonawarra Wine Association website – ⓦwww.coonawarra.org). A few favourites arranged in directional order as if you are driving along the Riddoch Highway from Penola towards Coonawarra Township include **Hollick Wines,** in a tiny restored 1870s slab wood and stone cottage; **Balnaves**, with its innovative award winning architecture; **Leconfield**, with very well-regarded Cabernet Sauvignons and, unusually, a female wine maker; and **Zema Estate**, a small family-run winery with Italian roots and an old-fashioned hands-on process. **Wynns Coonawarra Estate**, west of the Riddoch Highway on Memorial Drive at Coonawarra Township, is the Coonawarra's longest established (1896) and most well-known winery, with wines exported worldwide. Its stone gabled building, with vineyards stretching out in front, is just as depicted on all its wine labels. Continuing back on the Riddoch Highway towards Padthaway, **Brands** are an old family of wine makers who notably make a sell-out Shiraz from the original vineyard planted in 1896, while the down-to-earth Redman family of **Redman** have also been making wine for generations, but only red, focusing exclusively on three varieties: Cabernet Sauvignon, Shiraz and a blend of Cabernet Sauvignon and Merlot. Beyond Redman, the modern winery complex of **Rymill**, attractively located on Clayfield Road, west of the Riddoch Highway, includes a glass-walled tasting area overlooking the winery, and platforms upstairs for viewing the testing lab.

ative display in the centre, lightened up by Barbie-doll look-alike "nuns on the run" and dressed-up dummies in the original school room. Across the fields are the National Trust-listed cottages of **Petticoat Lane**, where many of Mary's poverty-stricken students lived. One of the buildings now houses a craft shop (daily 10am–5pm), while a display in another and an interpretive board in the garden tells the story of the seventeen-member Sharam family. You can also visit Wilson's Cottage (same hours) which doubles as a linen shop.

There are backpacker **rooms** at the comfortable and centrally located *McKay's Trek Inn*, 38 Riddoch St (☎08/8737 2250 or free call 1800 626 844; rooms ❸, dorms ❶), which caters to the Oz Experience crowd a couple of nights a week, and long-stay grape pickers, so it's worth booking ahead. *Penola Caravan Park* on South Terrace (☎08/8737 2381) has good-value on-site vans (❷) and en-suite cabins (❸). The focus of the town is the friendly National Trust-listed *Heywood's Royal Oak Hotel*, 31 Church St (☎08/8737 2322, ℻8737 2825; ❺), with four-poster doubles and some twin rooms. Out of town, on the Riddoch Highway, *Chardonnay Lodge* (☎08/8736 3309, ⓦ www.chardonnaylodge.com.au; ❼) is an upmarket motel complex set amongst lawns and rose gardens, with a swimming pool and an attached café/restaurant.

The best place to **eat** is *Heywood's Royal Oak Hotel*, which has a beautiful beer garden and an excellent bistro. Otherwise, *Sweet Grape*, 48 Church St (daily 8.30am–4.30pm) dishes up affordable café favourites and international dishes. On the Riddoch Highway, *Hermitage Café and Wine Bar*, attached to Wetherall Winery (☎08/8737 2122; daily 11am–9pm; bookings advised for dinner), hand out cheese and crackers with wine, while meals focus on local and organic produce. The vineyard setting is very pleasant, with a little pond for yabbies and a native garden out back, filled with banksias and big gum trees.

Coonawarra Township

There isn't much to what is called **COONAWARRA TOWNSHIP**, a settlement which developed to house and service the adjacent Wynns Coonawarra Estate (see box overleaf), but it does make a good base if you're touring local vineyards. Cottage **accommodation** here includes *Skinner Cottage* (☎08/8736 3304, ℻8736 3016; ❻), a quaint tin-roofed bungalow just around the corner from the old Coonawarra school, now *Nibs Bistro and Grill* (☎08/8736 3006; licensed and BYO; bookings on Sat night recommended), which is a fun place to **eat** – choose from a display of marinated meats and grill them yourself.

Naracoorte Caves

In 1994 the system of limestone caves east of the Riddoch Highway, midway between Penola and Padthaway, were proclaimed a World Heritage Area, now accessible as the **Naracoorte Caves Conservation Park**. The **Wanambi Fossil Centre** (daily 9am–5pm; ☎08/8762 2340) gives an insight into the area and its highly significant **Victoria Fossil Cave** – the chamber, discovered in 1969, revealed fossils of extinct Pleistocene megafauna including giant kangaroos and wombats. Another notable feature is the **Bat Centre**, the only place in the world where you can watch bats in real time with the help of infrared remote control cameras filming inside a cave. You can also watch the small common bent wing bats on **tours** (daily Christmas and early Jan; around 7.30pm).

The caves are spread out over the Conservation Park: **Alexandra Cave** has the prettiest limestone formations (9.30am & 1.30pm; 30min); **Victoria Fossil Cave** is popular for its fossils (10.15am & 2pm; 1hr). A visit to the Bat Centre includes viewing of the more robust **Blanche Cave** (10.30am &

3.30pm; 1hr). You can guide yourself through the **Wet Cave**, named after the very wet chamber at its deepest part, and stay for as long as you please between 9am and 5pm; an automatic lighting system switches on as you walk through. **Admission fees** are $9 for one cave, $16 for two or $28 for all four caves. There are also **adventure caving** tours in several other caves (2hr novice tours $22; 3hr advanced tours $200 per party, maximum six people; overalls can be hired for $5; lights and helmets supplied).

You can **camp** within the park ($18 per car), where facilities include powered sites, hot showers and even a free laundry, or stay in **dorms** at *Wirreanda Bunkhouse* (T08/8762 2340; ①). For more comfortable beds you can stay in rural tranquillity at the *Cave Park Cabins* (T08/8762 0696, F8762 0693; ④), only 1.5km from the caves. There's a basic campsite at nearby **Bool Lagoon Conservation Park** ($15 per car; water and toilets only), which is a magnet for birds; camping permits are issued at the Wanambi Fossil Centre. For **meals**, the licensed *Bent Wing Cafe* at the centre is surprisingly sophisticated, dishing up everything from a Greek salad to chargrilled kangaroo fillets with native plum chutney.

On the highway 12km west of the caves, the town of **NARACOORTE** is a small regional centre with a supermarket (open daily) and several places to eat and stay. *Naracoorte Hotel Motel*, 73 Ormerod St (T08/8762 2400; ③–④) has motel rooms and cheap meal specials; *Naracoorte Backpackers* (T & F 08/8762 3835, W www.nctebackpackers.mtx.net; dorms ①) offers tours to the caves, has bikes for rent and 24hr internet access. At 81 Park Terrace, a ten-minute walk north of town, *Naracoorte Caravan Park* (T08/8762 2128; cabins ③–④) is in a shady spot by a creek, close to a swimming lake.

The Riverland

The **Riverland** is the long irrigated strip on either side of the three-hundred-kilometre meander of the Murray River from Blanchetown to Renmark near the Victorian border. The Canadian Chaffey brothers had already developed successful irrigation settlements in California when they were invited to Australia to look into possibilities for the Murray, establishing an **irrigation colony** at **Renmark** in 1887. The Riverland's deep red-orange alluvial soil – helped by this extensive irrigation – is very fertile, making the area the state's major supplier of oranges, stone fruit and grapes. Fruit stalls along the roadsides add to the impression of a year-long harvest, and if you're after **fruit-picking work** it's an excellent place to start. The Harvest Labour Office on Riverland Drive in Berri (T1300/720 126) can assist in obtaining seasonal work. The area is also Australia's major **wine-producing** region, though the technologically advanced wineries with huge production bases make mainly mass-produced wines for casks and export. Many are open to visitors, but their scale and commercialism make them less enjoyable for a wine-tasting trawl than, say, the McLaren Vales (see p.824).

From Waikerie to Renmark all the **towns** feel pretty much the same, with a raw edge, little charm or sophistication, and an undercurrent of violence most apparent on a drunken Friday night. Time here is best spent on or around the river, with the towns considered as departure points for river cruises, and places to eat and stay. Each town has only one hotel – even Berri and Renmark, with their seven-thousand-strong populations. These huge and mostly graceless

The Murray River

The **Murray River** is Australia's Mississippi – or so the American author Mark Twain declared when he saw it in the early 1900s. It's a fraction of the size of the American river, but in a country of seasonal, intermittent streams it counts as a major river. Like the Mississippi, the Murray helped open up a new continent, first to explorers, later to trade. Fed by melting snow from the Snowy Mountains, and the Murrumbidgee and Darling rivers, the Murray has enough volume to flow through the arid plains, eventually reaching the Southern Ocean southwest of Adelaide near Goolwa (see p.828). Together the Murray and the Darling and its tributaries make up one of the biggest and longest watercourses in the world, giving life to Australia's most important agricultural region, the **Murray-Darling basin**. For much of its length the Murray forms the border between New South Wales and Victoria, slowing its course on reaching South Australia to meander and produce extensive alluvial plains where irrigation areas are now established. Almost half of South Australia's water comes from the Murray: even far-off Woomera in the Outback relies on it.

Historically, the Riverland was densely populated by various **Aboriginal peoples**. They navigated the river in bark canoes, the bark being cut from river red gums in a single perfect piece; many trees along the river still bear the scars. Nets and spears were used to catch fish, duck and emu; mussels were also an important food source. The Ngarrindjeri people's Dreamtime story of the river's creation explains how Ngurunderi (a Dreamtime hero) travelled down the Murray from its confluence with the Darling, looking for his two runaway wives. The Murray was then just a small stream. As Ngurunderi searched, a giant Murray cod surged ahead of him, widening the river with swipes of his tail. Ngurunderi tried to spear the fish, which he chased right through to the ocean: the thrashing cod carved out the pattern of the Murray River during the chase.

The explorers **Hume** and **Hovell** came across the Murray at Albury in 1824. In 1830 **Sturt** and **Mitchell** navigated the Murray and Darling in a whale boat, Sturt naming it after the then Secretary of State for the Colonies (coincidentally *Murrundi* was the Aboriginal name for part of the river). Their exploration opened up the interior and from 1838 the Murray was followed as a **stock route** to South Australia by drovers or "overlanders" taking sheep and cattle to newly established Adelaide. In 1853 the first **paddle steamer** on the Murray, the *Mary Ann*, was launched near Mannum. Goods were transported far inland, opening up new areas for settlement; in return, wool was carried to market. River transport reached its peak in the 1870s,

---

community hotels are a feature of the Riverland: owned and run by the town, their profits are ploughed back into the hotel or channelled into the community, generally into sporting groups.

The **Sturt Highway**, the major route between Adelaide and Sydney, passes straight through the Riverland. Leaving Adelaide, it bypasses Gawler and cuts across the northern end of the Barossa Valley, reaching the Murray at Blanchetown, about 130km from the city. Premier Stateliner runs a twice-daily service along the highway from Adelaide to Renmark via Blanchetown, Waikerie, Barmera and Berri, and also goes daily (except Sat) to Loxton.

Blanchetown to Waikerie

BLANCHETOWN, 130km from Adelaide, is the first Riverland town, and with Lock No. 1 completed here in 1922, is the starting point of the Murray's lock and weir system which helps maintain the river at a constant height between the town and Wentworth in New South Wales (see p.366). Eleven kilometres west of town, **Brookfield Conservation Park**, a gift to South Australia from the Chicago Zoological Society, is home to the endangered **southern**

but by the mid-1930s it was virtually finished – bowing to the superior speed and flexibility of the railways.

Seeing the river

The best way to appreciate the calm brown beauty of the Murray – lined with majestic river red gums and towering cliffs that reveal the area's colourful soils – and its prolific birdlife is to get out on the water. Several old **paddle steamers**, and a variety of other craft still cruise the Murray for pleasure, and you can spend a weekend or more on board the *Murray Princess* (Fri 6.30pm to Sun 2pm; $369 per person; 6-day package for $865 per person also available; ☎08/8569 2511, ⊚www.captain-cook.com.au), based at **Mannum**, one-hour's drive east of Adelaide (or take the Murray Bridge Passenger Service; Mon–Fri daily; ☎08/8532 2633). Other cruises from Mannum include sporadic trips on the restored paddle-steamer *Marion* (book at Mannum Tourist Information Centre, 67 Randell St; ☎08/8569 1303), and regular outings on the MV *Proud Mary* (morning tea cruises Mon 11am; 1hr 15min; 3-, 4- or 6-day cruises also available; ☎08/8231 9472, ⊕8212 1520, or book at Mannum Tourist Information Centre). You'll find details of other cruises in the Riverland town accounts.

Renting a **houseboat** is a relaxing and enjoyable way to see the river. All you need is a driving licence, and the cost is not astronomical if you can get a group of people together and avoid the peak holiday seasons. A week in an eight-berth houseboat out of season should cost around $1000, in a four-berth $750. The South Australian Tourism Commission (☎1300/655 276, ⊚www.southaustralia.com) has pamphlets giving costs and facilities; they can also book for you, or you could contact the Houseboat Hirers Association (☎08/8395 0999, ⊚www.murrayriver .com.au/hbc).

A more hands-on way to explore the wetlands and creek systems is in a canoe. The best place to rent **canoes and kayaks** is Riverland Canoeing Adventures, Alamein Avenue, North Loxton (☎08/8584 1494, ⊚kamajo@riverland.net.au; $25 per day double kayak, $15 per day single kayak, cheaper weekly rates); they can also provide maps and rent out camping equipment. The flat country, short distances between towns and dry climate are perfect for cycling, and **bikes** can be rented at various hostels along the way.

For other Murray River accounts, see Goolwa (p.828), and the Victoria and NSW chapters (pp.1006–1016 and pp.365–367 respectively).

hairy-nosed wombat; the creatures also thrive at nearby *Portee Station* (☎08/8540 5211, ⊕8540 5016, ⊚www.portee.com.au; B&B ❹, or with dinner and tours $240 per person), a two-hundred-square-kilometre sheep-grazing property where, if you can afford it, you can stay in the 1873 riverfront homestead. Tours include an exploration of the river in a small boat to look at the prolific birdlife, and a 4WD station tour where you'll see wombats close up.

A 40km drive from Blanchetown, between Sedan and Swan Reach, is the fascinating **Yookamurra Earth Sanctuary** (☎08/8562 5011, ⊕8562 5023, ⊚www.esl.com.au/yookamurra.htm; ❻), one of several projects of Earth Sanctuaries, a conservation organization based in South Australia. Surrounded by the world's largest feral-proof fence, 14km long, the property is home to some of Australia's most endangered species – including ant-eating numbats and large-eared bilbies – who, protected from feral predators, thrive on the mallee scrubland. Accommodation is half-board in air-conditioned lodges, and the $125 price tag includes dusk and dawn animal-spotting tours.

Following the river from Blanchetown, it's 36km directly north to **MORGAN**, the most attractive of the Riverland towns. At the height of the river trade between 1880 and 1915 Morgan was one of South Australia's busiest river ports, transferring wool from NSW and Victoria onto trains bound for Adelaide at the twelve-metre-high river wharves; although two sections had to be demolished after collapsing in 1994, the rest of the mainly red gum and jarrah wharf remains intact. You can wander through the riverfront park, past the old train station and the stationmaster's building, now a **museum** (Tues 2–4pm, on other days knock on the caretaker's door at the back of the museum or call ☎08/8540 2130), and up onto the wharves overlooking moored houseboats on the river to bushland beyond. The well-preserved nineteenth-century streetscape of Railway Terrace, the main street, sits above the old railway line and wharf; its focus is the huge Landseer shipping warehouse. A couple of shops cash in on the heritage feel here by selling antiques and bric-a-brac. Two old pubs have standard **accommodation**: the *Terminus Hotel* (☎08/8540 2006; ❷) and the *Commercial* (☎08/8540 2107; ❸) sit next to each other, creating a lively riverport feel. You can also stay at *Morgan Riverside Caravan Park* (☎08/8540 2207, ℮morgancp@riverland.net.au; cabins ❸–❹, on-site vans ❷), in a great spot right in town by the river. For **food**, try the pubs or *Morgan Pizza Bar*, 17 Railway Terrace (☎08/8540 2103; Fri–Sun from 5pm only).

From Morgan the river takes a sharp bend east, meandering south to **WAIKERIE**; it's 32km from Morgan to Waikerie on a riverside road, with a free ferry crossing at Cadell. A less attractive drive from Blanchetown bypasses the river loop, reaching Waikerie directly by heading 42km northeast along the Sturt Highway. Waikerie is at the heart of the largest citrus-growing area in Australia; the first thing you notice is **Waikerie Co-op Producers**, a huge complex taking up both sides of a street – the "largest fruit-packing house in the southern hemisphere". A good base for **fruit-picking** work is the *Kingston-on-Murray Backpackers* (☎08/8583 0211 or free call 1800 737 378; rooms ❸, dorms ❶), on the Sturt Highway about 30km east of Waikerie.

Loxton

The Murray makes another large loop away from the Sturt highway, with **LOXTON** at its southernmost reach before twisting back north to Berri (see p.849). Leaving the highway at Kingston-on-Murray, you pass the **Moorook Game Reserve**, a large swamp fringed with river red gums and home to many waterbirds. In Loxton itself, the **Tourist & Art Centre**, at Bookpurnong Terrace (Mon–Fri 9am–5pm, Sat 9.30am–12.30pm, Sun 1–4pm; ☎08/8584 7919, ⓦwww.riverland.net.au/~loxinfo), acts as an agent for Stateliner and can fill you in on local attractions such as the riverside **Loxton Historical Village** (Mon–Fri 10am–4pm, Sat & Sun 10am–5pm; $8), a replica of a turn-of-the-twentieth-century Riverland town. Altogether more compelling is the **Katarapko Game Reserve**, opposite Loxton, where Katarapko Creek and the Murray have cut deep channels and lagoons, creating an island. Access from Loxton is by water only – perfect for canoeing and observing birdlife; to **camp** you need a permit from the NPWS, 28 Vaughan Terrace, Berri (☎08/8595 2111). *Loxton Riverfront Caravan Park*, Packard Bend (☎ & ℉ 08/8584 7862, ℮loxtoncp@sa.ozland.net.au; cabins ❸), is a peaceful spot opposite the game reserve, with canoes for rent ($6.60 per hour, $30 per day).

Back in town, the only **accommodation** option is the rather too glitzy *Loxton Hotel-Motel*, East Terrace (☎08/8584 7266, ⓦwww.loxtonhotel .com.au; ❺), where you can get good bistro **meals** from noon to 2pm and 6 to 8pm only. Alternatively, cheap meals and free **internet access** are available from the friendly and down-to-earth *Loxton Club* at 27 Bookpurnang Terrace.

Barmera

If you haven't followed the river to Loxton, **BARMERA**, on the shores of Lake Bonney, is the next major stopping point along the highway. Its claims to fame are varied and dubious: at **Pelican Point**, on the lake's western shore, there's an official **nudist beach** (and a nearby nudist resort with camping, and one on-site van ❸; ℡08/8588 7366, bookings essential), while every June, over the long weekend, the **South Australian Country Music Awards** are held in the lovely old Bonney Theatre. For more about the music awards, and **tourist information** in general, contact the Barmera Travel Centre, Barwell Avenue (Mon–Fri 9am–5.15pm, Sat 9am–noon; ℡08/8588 2289). The *Barmera Hotel/Motel* (℡08/8588 2111; ❷–❹) is not the most attractive of the big Riverland community hotels. A cut above is the expensive *Barmera Country Club*, on Hawdon Street (℡08/8588 2888, ℱ8588 2785, ⓦwww.countryclubs.com.au/barmera; ❻–❼), overlooking the golf course, with a pool, spa, tennis courts and restaurant. The extensive *Lake Bonney Holiday Park*, on Lakeside Drive, is a scenic alternative (℡08/8588 2234; cottage ❹, cabins ❷–❹). Eating options include the *Pagoda Chinese Restaurant* (℡08/8588 3167; closed Tues & Sun lunch). If you want to get on the water at Barmera, Riverland Leisure Canoe Tours, Thelma Road (℡08/8588 2053), rents out **canoes** for $15 per day or you can take a day or overnight guided tour.

Just under 20km from town towards Morgan, a bend in the river was dubbed Overland Corner from 1838, as it was the crossing point for the overland cattle trade to New South Wales. The restful and delightfully isolated *Overland Corner Hotel* (℡08/8588 7021; ❹ including breakfast), opened in 1859, serves food and drink and has **accommodation**. You can camp and bushwalk in adjacent Herons Bend Reserve, where an eight-kilometre trail (around 3hr) takes you past old Aboriginal campsites. A pamphlet detailing sites on the walk can be purchased from the pub (50¢). Look at the flood level from the incredible 1956 flood, practically up to the roof.

Berri

The **Big Orange** sets the scene in **BERRI**, announcing the fact that this is the town where the trademark orange juice comes from; and accordingly, travellers are mainly drawn here between October and April by the prospect of **fruit-picking work**. You can climb up the Big Orange to the observatory on level three for a good view of the Riverland; for more juice, visit Berrievale Orchards. The river is the main attraction, of course, with scenic river walks above coloured sandstone cliffs, as well as the **Wilabalangaloo Flora and Fauna Reserve** (Mon & Thurs–Sun 10am–4pm, daily during school holidays; $4), a native animal enclosure and a local history museum on the waterfront. For more information on Berri, head for the **tourist office** on 24 Vaughan Terrace (Mon–Fri 9am–5pm, Sat 9–11.30am; ℡08/8582 1655).

In town the *Berri Resort Hotel*, Riverview Drive (℡08/8582 1411, ℱ8582 2140, ⓦwww.ozemail.com.au/~berrihot; motel units ❻, pub rooms ❹), is a huge riverfront pub that grows ever tackier and ritzier – though it's not a bad place to stay, with a swimming pool, tennis courts and good food. The excellent *Berri Backpackers* (℡08/8582 3144; rooms ❶, dorms ❶), out of town towards Barmera on the Sturt Highway opposite the *Berri Club*, is the place to stay if you're fruit-picking, but the place is so popular it's hard to get a bed. The energetic and enterprising owner has laid on such amenities as free bikes, a sauna, swimming pool, gym, tennis, volleyball and basketball courts and two tree houses, one for couples to stay in, the other used as a general chill-out area. For **food**, *Berri Canton Palace*, 1 Worman St (℡08/8582 2818; closed Tues & Sun lunch), is a good Chinese restaurant; and *Dawns Coffee Shop*, 28 Wilson St, serves hearty breakfasts and light lunches (closed Sun). Swan Houseboats (⊤ 08/8582 3663 or free call 1800 083 183, ⓦ www.murrayriver.com.au/swan) rents out **canoes** for those who want to enjoy the river here.

Renmark

RENMARK, on a bend of the Murray 254km from Adelaide, is the last major town before the border with New South Wales. There's not a great deal to see in the town, although **Olivewood**, an interesting National Trust property on the corner of Renmark Avenue and 21st Street (Mon & Thurs–Sun 10am–4pm, Tues 2–4pm; $4), is the former home of the Chaffey brothers. A palm-lined drive leads through a citrus orchard and olive trees to the house, which is a strange hybrid of Canadian log cabin and Australian lean-to. The attached museum is the usual hotchpotch of local memorabilia, unrelated to the Chaffeys or their ambitious irrigation project. The **Chaffey Theatre** on 18th Street (⊤ 08/8586 5462) has an impressive performing arts centre hosting amateur and professional plays, films and concerts. The main attraction of Renmark, however, is the river and its surrounding wetlands.

The riverfront **Renmark Paringa Visitor Centre** on Murray Avenue (Mon–Fri 9am–5pm, Sat 9am–4pm, Sun 10am–4pm; ⊤ 08/8586 6704, ⓦ www.riverland.net.au) can book **river cruises**. The PS *Industry* – one of the few wood-fuelled paddle steamers left on the Murray – is moored outside and cruises once a month (1hr 30min; $15; contact the tourist centre for times and bookings). Daily cruises are run by Renmark River Cruises (⊤ 08/8595 1862, ⓦ www.riverland.net.au/~renriv), who offer both motorized dinghy expeditions through the local backwaters (2hr; $45), and trips aboard the *Big River Rambler* (daily 2pm; 2hr; $23), which leaves from Renmark wharf and heads upstream 7km past colourful river cliffs. The UNESCO-backed **Bookmark Biosphere Reserve**, a few kilometres from Renmark, manages 9000 square kilometres of land north of the River Murray. To explore this region by land or river, Bookmark Guides (⊤ 08/8582 5299, ⨍ 8582 5277, ⓦ www.riverland.net.au/~bbwaters) offers a variety of day and overnight tours from 4WD bush safaris to wine-tasting.

The obvious **place to stay** in Renmark is the landmark *Renmark Hotel/Motel* (⊤ 08/8586 6755, ⓦ www.renmarkhotel.com.au; ④–⑤), overlooking the river. Built in 1897 and given its facade in the 1930s, the hotel has been thoroughly modernized and has a large bistro, gaming rooms, outdoor swimming pool and spa. The *Renmark Riverfront Caravan Park*, on Patey Drive 2km east of town (⊤ 08/8586 6315; en-suite cabins ④, on-site vans ②), has an idyllic setting along 1km of riverfront. Two good **restaurants** are *Ginger Mick's Pizza*, 124 Murray Ave, open late nightly except Sunday; and, for Italian food, *Cafe Toppo e Ristorante*, 179 Murray Ave. You can eat Chinese food at *The Golden Palace*, 114 Renmark Ave (closed Tues & Sun lunch).

The mid-north

The area north of the **Sturt Highway**, bounded by **Port Augusta** (see p.858) and the **south Flinders Ranges**, is a fertile agricultural region known as the **mid-north**. **Kapunda**, only 16km northwest of Nuriootpa, became the country's first mining town when **copper** was discovered in 1842. It can also be reached as a short detour from the **Barrier Highway** en route to Broken Hill in New South Wales, a route that continues through the larger mining town of **Burra**, and then to **Peterborough**, the self-proclaimed "frontier to the Outback". The centre of the mid-north's wine area, **Clare**, is 45km southwest of Burra, on the Main North Road, the alternative route to Port Augusta. The **Heysen Trail** runs through Kapunda, Burra and then, via **Crystal Brook**, into the foothills of the Flinders. Heading north to Port Augusta on **Highway 1** for the Northern Territory or Western Australia, you'll pass through the ugly lead-smelting city of **Port Pirie**, and thence on to the south Flinders Ranges.

Getting around the area by **bus** is problematic: while most of the major towns have transport links to Adelaide, there are virtually no buses between towns, however close they might be. Greyhound Pioneer, on its Adelaide–Broken Hill route, goes via Burra. The Mid North Passenger Service (daily except Mon & Sat; ℡08/8826 2346) from Adelaide takes in Burra, Peterborough and the main Clare Valley settlements, while the Barossa–Adelaide Passenger Service (℡08/8564 3022) has a weekday service from Gawler – which can be reached by train – to Kapunda. All interstate buses to Darwin or Perth take Highway 1 through Port Pirie; if you get off 27km before this, it's only a couple of kilometres walk to Crystal Brook and the Heysen Trail.

Copper-mining towns

In 1841 South Australia was in serious economic trouble; the discovery of **copper** at Kapunda the following year rescued the young colony and put it at the forefront of Australia's mining boom. The early finds were soon overshadowed by those at Burra 65km north: the Burra "**Monster Mine**" was the largest in Australia until 1860, creating fabulous wealth and attracting huge numbers of Cornish miners in particular. The boom ended as suddenly as it began, as resources were exhausted – mining finished at Burra in 1877 and Kapunda in 1878.

Heading to **KAPUNDA** from the Barossa, the landscape changes as vineyards are replaced by crops and grazing sheep. As you come into town, you're greeted by a colossal sculpture of a Cornish miner entitled *Map Kernow* – "son of Cornwall". A place that once had its own daily newspaper, eleven hotels and a busy train station is now a rural service town, pleasantly undeveloped and with many old buildings decorated with locally designed and manufactured iron lacework.

If you have your own transport, you can follow a ten-kilometre **heritage trail** that takes in the ruins of the Kapunda mine, with panoramic views from the mine chimney lookout; details are available from the **Kapunda Information Centre** on Hill Street (Mon–Fri 9am–4pm; ℡08/8566 2902, Ⓦwww.kaptour.mtx.net). On the same street, the **Kapunda Museum** (June–Aug Sat, Sun & holidays 1–4pm; Sept–May daily 1–4pm; $4) occupies the mammoth Romanesque-style former Baptist church. The best time to come to Kapunda is during the **Celtic festival** held on the first weekend before Easter, when Celtic music, bush and folk bands feature at the four pubs.

For **accommodation**, *Ford House*, 80 Main St (℡ & Ⓕ 08/8566 2280; ❺), has colonial-style B&B; and the *Sir John Franklin Hotel*, also on Main Street (℡08/8566 3233, Ⓕ8566 3873; ❹), has simple, clean rooms and is the most popular pub for inexpensive **meals**. Campers are catered for at *Dutton Caravan Park*, 11 Montefiore St (℡08/8566 2094; cabins ❸).

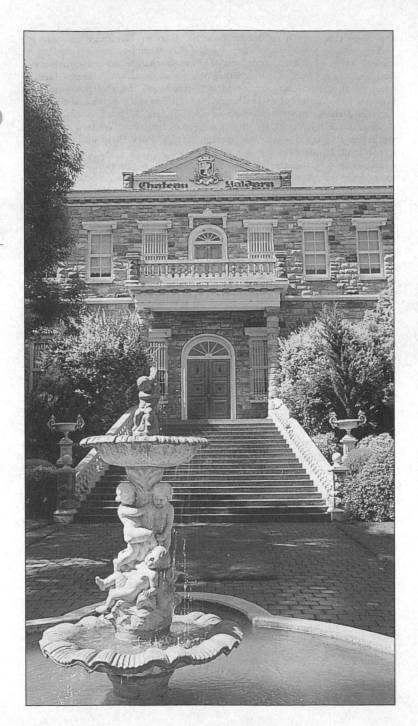

Burra

In 1851 **BURRA** had five thousand residents and was mining five percent of the world's copper; when the mines closed in 1877 it became a service centre for the surrounding farming community. It also takes advantage of its position on the Barrier Highway, using its copper heritage to draw visitors. Plenty of money is spent restoring and beautifying the place, even to the extent of topping up pretty, gum-shaded **Burra Creek** to ensure that it's always flowing. With its well-preserved stone architecture, shady tree-lined streets, great country pubs and upmarket home stores, art and craft and antiques shops, Burra is a popular weekend escape between March and November (before it gets too hot). The creek divides the town grid in two: the mine is in the north, while the southern section has the shopping centre, based around **Market Square**, where you'll also find the **tourist office** (daily 9am–5pm; ☎08/8892 2154, ⓦ www.weblogic.com.au/burra). Its main function is to issue the **Burra Passport Key** to people driving the eleven-kilometre **heritage trail** ($11 per person, plus $5 deposit); the key gives you access to eight sites en route – and for an extra $9 you gain entry to all four museums (see below).

Heading north along Market Street you come to the **Burra Monster Mine** site, where there are extensive remains and interpretive walking trails, as well as the **Morphetts Enginehouse Museum** (Mon–Fri 11am–1pm, Sat & Sun 11am–2pm; $4.50). Continuing north, the **Bon Accord Mine Complex** on Linkson Street (Mon–Fri 1–3pm, Sat & Sun 1–4pm; $4.50) was a short-lived failure compared to its hugely successful neighbour; there's a scale model of the monster mine and a shaft and mining relics on view. Other key-pass places in the northern section of the town are the old **police lock-up and stables**, **Redruth Gaol**, and **Hampton**, a now-deserted private township in the style of an English village. Back in the main part of the town, the pass will allow you entry to the **Unicorn Brewery Cellars** (1873) and the fascinating two remaining **miners' dugouts**: in around 1851 nearly two thousand people lived in homes clawed out of the soft clay along Burra Creek, because of a housing shortage. There are two further **museums**: the **Market Square Museum** (Sat & Sun 1–3pm; $4.50) was a general store, post office and home from 1880 to 1920; and "Malowen Lowarth Cottage", on Kingston Street (Sat 2–4pm, Sun 2.30–4.30pm; $4.50), is one of the **Paxton Square miners' cottages**, decorated in 1850s style.

You can **stay** in other miners' cottages in Paxton Square, all overseen by the office in the former Methodist Chapel at the end of the row (☎08/8892 2622, Ⓕ8892 2555; ❸–❹). There are 32 in all; even so, on weekends from mid-March to October they are booked out by Adelaidians on short winter breaks. The stone cottages are freezing in winter but do have fireplaces (wood is $5 extra) and plenty of blankets (BYO linen or $5 extra); they all have modern kitchens, though breakfast is available at the office. Other accommodation in town includes *Burra View House*, Mount Pleasant Road (☎08/8892 2648, Ⓕ8892 2150; ❻), and the tree-surrounded *Burra Motor Inn*, Market Street (☎08/8892 2777, Ⓕ8892 2707; ❺) with contemporary-styled rooms backing onto the creek, an indoor swimming pool and a well-priced restaurant. All the **hotels** in town also have rooms, and most provide breakfast. Best of the lot is the 1884 *Kooringa Hotel* opposite the Paxton Cottages on Kingston Street (☎08/8892 2013; B&B ❹), which serves excellent food. Less expensive is the down-to-earth *Commercial Hotel*, 22 Commercial Rd (☎08/8892 2010; B&B ❸). If you have a **tent** you could try *Burra Caravan Park*, Bridge Terrace (☎08/8892 2442; on-site vans ❷), in a pretty spot beside the creek, a couple of minutes' walk from the shops. *Price's Bakery*, Commercial Road, serves good coffee, home-made soups, baked goodies and sandwiches with a gourmet slant (daily 9am–4 or 5pm).

The Clare Valley

The wine industry in the **Clare Valley**, west of the Barrier Highway between Kapunda and Burra, was pioneered by Jesuit priests at **Sevenhill** in the 1850s. There's no tourist overkill here: bus trips are not encouraged, and because it's a small area with just over thirty wineries, you can learn a lot about the local styles of wine; the area is recognized especially for its fine Rieslings. Often, too, you'll get personal treatment, with the wine maker presiding at the cellar door. In the cool uplands of the North Mount Lofty Ranges, Clare Valley is really a series of gum-fringed ridges and valleys running roughly 30km north from **Auburn** to the main township of **Clare**, on either side of the Main North Road. Huge sheep runs were established here in the nineteenth century and the area, which is prime merino land, still has an obvious pastoral feel; several stations can be visited. There are also beautiful old villages and some well-preserved mansions on view, plenty of charming B&B accommodation and some superb restaurants attached to wineries. The big event of the year is the **Clare Valley Gourmet Weekend**, held in May at local wineries.

Between Clare and Auburn, the old railway line has been transformed into a 27km cycling path, the **Riesling Trail**; to cycle one way takes about two hours. Mountain **bikes** can be hired from Clare Valley Cycle Hire, 32 Victoria Rd, Clare ($22 per day; ☎08/8842 2782), who will deliver to anywhere in the valley.

Auburn to Watervale

Heading north through the valley, **AUBURN**, 120km from Adelaide, is the first settlement, small and village-like, which began life as a halfway resting point for wagons carrying copper ore from Burra to Port Adelaide. The *Rising Sun Hotel* (☎08/8849 2015, ⓕ8849 2266, ⓔrising@capri.net.au; ❺–❼ including breakfast) is one of many great **pubs** in the valley, first licensed in 1850. It has small bedrooms in the hotel and mews-style accommodation in old stone stables, as well as a very affordable modern Australian menu and an appropriately long wine list. A more luxurious place to stay is *Dennis Cottage* (☎08/8277 8177, ⓦwww.denniscottage.com.au; ❻), which has a spa, as well as paraphernalia associated with C.J. Dennis, the popular poet who was born here in 1876. *Tatehams*, on the Main North Road (☎08/8849 2030, ⓕ8849 2260, ⓔtatehams@capri.net.au; ❼) is a very distinguished dining/guesthouse combination. Nearby are two small **wineries** to visit, with restricted opening hours: **Grossets** (Wed–Sun 10am–5pm) and **Mount Horrocks** (Sat & Sun 10am–5pm).

The next small village is **LEASINGHAM**, where you can camp or stay at *Leasingham Village Caravan & Cabins* (☎08/8843 0136; cabins ❹), a popular place for **grape-pickers** from March to May. An attached restaurant serves simple inexpensive weekend lunches (licensed or BYO; Thurs–Sun lunch & dinner). You can taste wines nearby at **Tim Gramp Wines** (Sat & Sun 10.30am–4.30pm). At **WATERVALE**, 2km north, there are four small wineries: **Crabtree of Watervale**, North Terrace (daily 11am–5pm, occasionally closed midweek), is one of the most enjoyable in the valley.

Mintaro

From Leasingham, you can turn off east to **MINTARO**, a village whose tree-lined streets and cottages are beautifully preserved from the 1850s, when it was a resting place for bullock teams travelling from Burra copper mines. There's no general store or petrol supply here: the emphasis is on upmarket cottage accommodation, popular with Adelaide weekenders. The focus of the village is the *Magpie and Stump Hotel*, which is particularly lively on Sunday afternoons. On a fine day you can sit shaded under the awning or sprawl on the grass. Opposite, at **Reilly's Wines** (daily 10am–5pm), housed in an 1856 Irish bootmaker's building, you can taste vintages produced since 1994 from Watervale grapes; the **restaurant** here serves Italian food, with mains around $15 (reservations ⓣ08/8843 9013; closed dinner Tues, Thurs & Sun), and can book **accommodation** in the nearby *Mintaro Pay Office Cottages* (❻–❼ including breakfast). *Mintaro Mews*, on Burra Street (ⓣ08/8843 9001, ⓕ8843 9002; ❼), has upmarket B&B accommodation (no children) with an indoor heated pool and spa; Saturday nights are package only ($110 per person), including a four-course meal in the atmospheric restaurant (dinner nightly except Wed).

Southeast of the town, the National Trust extols the virtues of the Georgian-style **Martindale Hall** (Mon–Fri 11am–4pm, Sat & Sun noon–4pm; $5; ⓣ08/8843 9088, ⓕ8843 9082, ⓔmarthall@chariot.net.au; B&B ❽), the mansion featured in the 1975 film *Picnic at Hanging Rock*. For $165 per person you can **stay overnight** and enjoy a four-course meal, cooked breakfast and the full run of the place (except the smoking room) – but it's freezing in winter.

Head northwest from Mintaro to get to Sevenhill (see below) via the rolling hills of the Polish Hill River area. About 8km along the route, **Paulett Wines** (daily 10am–5pm) has fabulous views, its verandah overlooking the area and the "river" – a dry creek for eleven months of the year.

Sevenhill and the Spring Gully Conservation Park

The village of **SEVENHILL** has the valley's oldest winery, **Sevenhill Cellars**, on College Road (Mon–Fri 9am–4.30pm, Sat 9am–4pm). This is still run by a religious order and mainly makes sacramental wine, though the brothers have diversified into table wines, sweet sherry and port, doing everything from growing the grapes to bottling. The sandstone building has a tasting room with lots of character and history, and there's an old Catholic church in the grounds. Nearby on College Road, *Thorn Park Country House* (ⓣ08/8843 4304, ⓕ8843 4296, ⓦwww.thornpark.com.au; ❽) is an 1850 stone and slate building in a gorgeous setting; it offers **B&B** and a beautifully indulgent dinner – but at a price ($195 per person; just B&B is $145 per person). *Sevenhill Hotel*, on the Main North Road, is a classic country pub serving popular inexpensive meals daily except Sunday.

To the west of the Main North Road, **Spring Gully Conservation Park** has the last remnant of red stringybark forest in South Australia. There are steep gullies, waterfalls, wildlife and, in spring, lovely wild flowers; free camping is allowed outside the fire-ban season. Nearby, attached to boutique **wineries** signposted from Sevenhill, are two excellent **restaurants** serving gourmet meals from deliciously fresh local produce; both are moderately priced. Eldredge Wines, Spring Gully Road (tastings daily 11am–5pm; lunch Thurs–Sun; restaurant bookings ⓣ08/8842 3086) is located in a small farmhouse fronting a dam; Skillogalee Winery (daily 10am–5pm; ⓣ08/8843 4311 lunch bookings advised) is in a wonderful spot with a backdrop of a clunking windmill, bushclad hill and vineyards, and holds meals and tastings by the fire in the 1850s cottage or on the verandah.

Clare

CLARE itself is a surprisingly ordinary town, with few concessions to the weekend visitors who pour in from Adelaide: it consists primarily of Main

North Road, and everything is closed on Sunday. **Tourist information**, in the town hall at 229 Main North Rd (Mon–Sat 9am–5pm, Sun 10am–4pm; ℡08/8842 2131, ⓦwww.clarevalley.com.au), provides an excellent free visitors' guide and can book accommodation and restaurants.

Wineries around town include Knappstein Wines, 2 Pioneer Ave (Mon–Fri 9am–5pm, Sat 10am–5pm, Sun 11am–4pm), an ivy-covered sandstone building with a verandah and an open log fire in winter; Jim Barry, a friendly, family-run place on the Main North Road (Mon–Fri 9am–5pm, Sat & Sun 11am–4pm); and Leasingham, 7 Dominic St (Mon–Fri 9am–5pm, Sat & Sun 10am–4pm), a large commercial winery established in 1893. There are also stations open for tours and **farmstays**: pick of the bunch is *Bungaree Station* (℡08/8842 2677, Ⓕ8842 3004; cottages B&B ❻, BYO-bedding shearers' quarters ❶), a working merino station 12km north on the Main North Road; one of the oldest and largest properties in the district, it has its own church as well as a swimming pool. *Geralka Rural Farm* (℡08/8845 8081, Ⓕ8845 8073; on-site vans ❷, units ❹), is a sheep and cereal property 25km north of Clare which offers weekend **farm activity tours** aimed at families (Sun & daily during school holidays 1.30pm, or by appointment; 2hr; $8, children $4).

Places to **stay** in Clare itself are all along Main North Road: overlooking the hills, 2.5km south of the centre, is *Clare Valley Motel* at no. 74 (℡08/8842 2799, Ⓕ8842 3121; ❺–❻); the *Clare Central Motel* is at the north end of town at no. 325 (℡08/8842 2277, Ⓕ8842 3563; ❻ including breakfast); both motels have pools. The best of the hotels are the friendly family-run *Bentleys*, 191 Main North Rd (℡08/8842 1700, Ⓕ8842 3474; motel rooms ❹, hotel rooms ❸–❹), which has an atrium bistro; and the *Taminga Hotel* (℡08/8842 2808; ❷), offering basic pub rooms. You can **camp** 4km south of town at *Clare Caravan Park*, on Main North Road (℡08/8842 2724, Ⓔclarpark@rbe.net.au; on-site vans ❷, cabins ❸–❹), with a swimming pool on site.

Besides the pubs, you can **eat** well during the day at *Clare Fine Foods*, 279 Main North Rd (closed Sun), a small deli serving gourmet rolls and sandwiches and dishes such as Caesar salad or pasta; the espresso coffee here is the best in town. The only place for **internet access** is at Caprice Clare ($5 per 30min) in the Village Plaza on the Old North Road.

Port Pirie

From Clare, the Main North Road heads to Jamestown, 65km north. To the west, a road branches off towards Crystal Brook, where there's a hikers' lodge at Bowman Park providing basic overnight shelter for hikers on the Heysen Trail. From here it's not far up Highway 1 to **PORT PIRIE**, the fourth-largest urban centre in South Australia. An ugly industrial city, its skyline is dominated by smelters' chimneys: as the nearest seaport to Broken Hill, the lead and zinc smelting industry here dates back to the discovery of the rich vein of lead-silver-zinc found there in 1883. The **Port Pirie Tourism and Arts Centre** on Mary Elie Street (Mon–Fri 9am–5pm, Sat & Sun 9am–4pm; ℡ & Ⓕ 08/8633 0439, free call ℡1800 000 424) has interpretive brochures and self-guided walking tours of the town if you're interested in **historic buildings** and the smelting industry. If not, there's little else to keep you here. Beyond Port Pirie, Telowie Gorge and Mount Remarkable National Park, in the southern stretches of the Flinders Ranges (see p.871), are within easy reach.

Outback South Australia

All routes in the Outback radiate out from **Port Augusta** and, with few connecting roads, interstate destinations will probably dictate which direction you leave town. Buses cover the highways but elsewhere you'll need to have your own transport or take a safari. To the west, the **Eyre Highway** runs 950km to the border of Western Australia, with desert scenery all the way unless you detour around the coast of the Eyre Peninsula. The rail line west runs further inland, through even more extreme desolation. North, the **Stuart Highway** and **New Ghan rail line** link Port Augusta with the Northern Territory through 890km of progressively drier scenery where regular markers along the roadside record the distance covered, as well as how far there is to go. **Prohibited zones** surround much of the highway, though about the only places you'd want to leave it anyway are at **Woomera** and **Coober Pedy**, both outside military areas and the boundaries of Aboriginal Land.

All other roads north head from Port Augusta along the route taken by the legendary but now defunct **Old Ghan** (see box on p.666) to the country towns of **Quorn** and **Hawker**, where routes diverge: northeast through the **Flinders Ranges** and along the **Strzelecki Track** to **Innamincka**; or due north to **Marree**, at the head of the **Birdsville** and **Oodnadatta tracks**. **Sealed roads** end at Lyndhurst on the way to Marree, and Wilpena Pound in the central Flinders. Check conditions if you plan to go any further – in dry weather 2WD vehicles often make it to Innamincka and Oodnadatta, but none of the north's remoter tracks should be attempted during the searing summer months. **Buses** run the length of the Stuart Highway, between Woomera and Andamooka, and from Port Augusta to Marree and Arkaroola in the northern Flinders.

A **Desert Parks Pass** is required for legal entry into Innamincka Regional Reserve, Lake Eyre National Park, Witjira National Park and the Simpson Desert: $80 per vehicle allows twelve-months' unlimited access and use of campsites, with copies of the detailed NPWS *Desert Parks Handbook* and Westprint Heritage Maps' surveys thrown in. Passes are available from agencies throughout the north, or by post from the Port Augusta NPWS (PO Box 78, Port Augusta 5700; Desert Park Pass free call ☎1800 816 078). To find out about **road conditions** in these regions, call ☎1300/361 033, or check out the Desert Access **website**, ⓦwww.desertaccess.com.au/desertparksbulletin.htm.

Independent travellers share common concerns throughout the north. **Plastic** is often carried in preference to wads of cash; many roadhouses and fuel pumps have EFTPOS facilities. **Water** is vital: with few exceptions, lakes and waterways are dry or highly saline, and most Outback deaths are related to dehydration or heatstroke – bikers seem particularly prone. As always, stay with your vehicle if you break down. Summer **temperatures** are lethally hot, winters pleasant during the day and subzero at night; rain can fall at any time of year, but is most likely to do so between January and May.

RAA **road maps** are good but lack surface detail. If you're spending any time in the north, pick up the excellent Westprint Heritage Maps and the cluttered *Landsmap Outback: Central and South Australia*. The South Australia Tourist Association issues a road map of the Flinders Ranges, but it's inadequate for walking, so **hikers** traversing the Flinders on the Heysen Trail need topographic maps of each section and advice from the nearest NPWS office. Conditions of **minor roads** are so variable that maps seldom do more than indicate the surface type; local police and roadhouses will have current information.

Port Augusta and the west

How you see **Port Augusta** depends on where you've come from. Arriving from the Outback the trees, shops and hotels can be a real thrill, but compared with the southeast, it's pretty tame. However, being a transport bottleneck has saved the town from destitution and plans are afoot to make more of its seaside location. While you're deciding where to head next, there are a few things to see in town and some good **bushwalking** country around **Mount Remarkable**, at the tail end of the Flinders Ranges. The direct route west from Port Augusta, the **Eyre Highway**, begins its daunting journey towards Western Australia across the top of the **Eyre Peninsula**, but going this way you'll see virtually nothing. An alternative route detours around the peninsula's coastline (via the Lincoln and Flinders highways) before rejoining the highway at **Ceduna** on the brink of the **Nullarbor Plain**, while the rail line parallels the coast some 100km inland.

Port Augusta

Unkindly dubbed "Porta Gutter" by Adelaide's smart set, who paint dire pictures of a town rife with petty crime, **PORT AUGUSTA** sits at the tip of the Spencer Gulf and on the edge of everywhere else. Despite the name, the docks closed long ago and more recent employment mainstays such as the power station and railways were drastically scaled down during the 1980s – the former rail buildings have been converted to Employment Service offices.

During summer, you should make the most of the small **swimming beach** at the end of Young Street to escape the dust and heat – the old wooden pile crossing, now a footbridge, and a hundred-year-old jetty, all that remains of the port, make good perches for fishing. The chief source of **information** is the **Wadlata Outback Centre**, at 41 Flinders Terrace (Mon–Fri 9am–5.30pm, Sat & Sun 10am–4pm; $9; ⊤ 08/8641 0793), which is well worth a look in its own right. Audiovisual technology, didgeridoo loudspeakers and a giant model of Akurra, the Dreamtime snake, are deployed to explain Aboriginal bushcraft and Flinders Ranges' creation myths, while geological and mining displays give a scientific perspective; tales of the hardships suffered by the nineteenth-century explorers Eyre, Sturt (and his boat), Stuart and Giles fill in the background.

If you still feel like exploring after Wadlata, drop in to the **Homestead Park Pioneer Museum** on Elsie Street (daily 9am–5pm; $3.50), centred around a log-built sheep station building. The 135-year-old homestead has been moved 100km from Yudnapinna and filled with well-restored period furnishings; in the grounds is enough farm and railway machinery to keep an enthusiast enthralled for several hours, along with animals, birds and a photographic museum in a vintage railway carriage. Nearby, the **School of the Air**, at 59

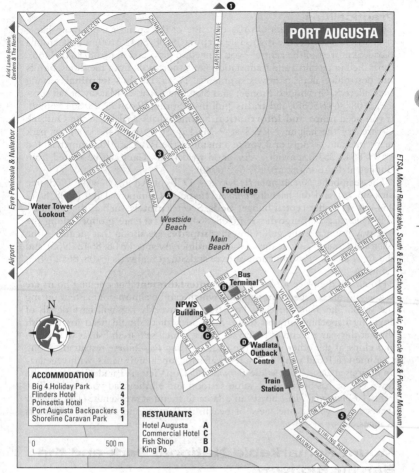

PORT AUGUSTA

Arid Lands Botanic Gardens & The North

Eyre Peninsula & Nullarbor

Airport

Footbridge

Water Tower Lookout

Westside Beach

Main Beach

N

Bus Terminal

NPWS Building

Wadlata Outback Centre

Train Station

ACCOMMODATION

Big 4 Holiday Park	2
Flinders Hotel	4
Poinsettia Hotel	3
Port Augusta Backpackers	5
Shoreline Caravan Park	1

0   500 m

RESTAURANTS

Hotel Augusta	A
Commercial Hotel	C
Fish Shop	B
King Po	D

Power Crescent (10am on school days; $2 for a 30min tour), invites you to listen to a lesson conducted over the airwaves. The interaction is pretty lively and might help explain the better-than-average academic record for students in remote areas who use the school. You could also take a look at the **ETSA** power station (free tours Mon–Fri; ☎08/8642 0737), which produces forty percent of all South Australia's electricity, or watch the sunset illuminate the Flinders mountains from the water tower **lookout** on Mildred Street.

Flanking the north side of town on the Stuart Highway is the new and ambitious **Australian Arid Lands Botanic Garden** (Mon–Fri 9am–5.30pm, Sat & Sun 10am–4pm; free), a showcase and research centre for regional and international desert flora, the slow-growing nature of which means that the garden's full splendour has yet to be realized; however, a closer look will reveal a surprising wealth of species. The rain-gathering, solar-powered information centre, shop and café underline the ideals of the garden as an ongoing ecological project.

Practicalities

The centre of town overlooks the east side of the Spencer Gulf, more like a river where it divides the town. The **airport** (☎ 08/8642 3100) is on Caroona Road, 5km west of the centre – you'll need to get a taxi in (☎ 08/8642 4466). Both the bus terminal and train station are a short walk from the shops, **banks** and post office along narrow Commercial Road. The **bus terminal**, serving McCafferty's, Greyhound Pioneer and Stateliner, is at 21 Mackay St (all services ☎ 08/8642 5055), and **trains** pull in at Stirling Road (☎ 08/8642 6699). If you need **maps and information** beyond what's available at the Outback Centre, try the helpful NPWS at 9 Mackay St (☎ 08/8648 5300) for park maps, info and permits; or if you're a member, the RAA, at 91 Commercial Rd (☎ 08/8642 2576), provides very good road maps. **Cars** can be rented from Budget, at 16 Young St (☎ 08/8642 6040).

The shambolic *Port Augusta Backpackers*, 17 Trent Rd (☎ 08/8641 1063; free pick-up; ❶), and the friendly *Flinders Hotel*, 39 Commercial Rd (☎ 08/8642 2544; ❶–❸), offer central budget **beds**. Several **motels**, such as the comfortable *Poinsettia*, 24 Burgoyne St (☎ 08/8642 2411; ❹), are grouped along the highway just across the gulf. Closest **campsites** are also in that vicinity – the *Shoreline Caravan Park* at the end of Gardiner Avenue (☎ 08/8642 2965) and the *Big 4 Holiday Park*, junction of Eyre and Stuart highways (☎ 08/8642 6455; cabins ❸).

Hotels are the place for **meals and entertainment**, but opening hours are vague and often depend on demand, which can be almost nonexistent during the week. The *Transcontinental*, Port Augusta's weekly rag, will have details of anything happening around town. Seafood addicts should head for the fish shop at the seaward end of Marryatt Street, which sells fresh fish, as well as fish and chips; at the other end of the street is *King Po* Chinese restaurant. Along Commercial Road you'll find a few cafés for lunch and snacks, with vegetarian options at *Basic Foods*, while *Barnacle Bill's*, on Victoria Parade 3km from the town centre, has pretty good-value seafood and all the salad you can eat. The central *Commercial Hotel* boasts an à la carte menu at weekends; *Hotel Augusta* serves meals with a fine view of beach, mangroves and the distant Flinders Ranges.

Mount Remarkable National Park and the Barrier Highway

The Flinders run low in their southern extremes, more heavily timbered than the desert ranges but otherwise similar in formation. **Mount Remarkable National Park** lies in two sections, encircled by a ring road that starts 45km southeast of Port Augusta and runs via Wilmington, Melrose and Port Germein. The larger **western** slice contains Mambray Creek and Mount Cavern, and connecting tracks from them to Alligator Gorge; Mount Remarkable and sections of the Heysen Trail rise to the **east** behind Melrose. If time is short, Alligator Gorge is easy going, while the Mount Cavern circuit is considerably harder – but both make good day-trips from Port Augusta. The only **campsite** with facilities is at Mambray Creek but bush camping is allowed elsewhere with permission from the NPWS (☎ 08/8634 7068); you should also consult them in hot weather, as the park may be completely closed if there is a high risk of fire. Stateliner **buses** go daily to Mambray Creek, and three times weekly to Wilmington and Melrose; *Port Augusta Backpackers* (see above) organize one- to six-day hikes with all fees, maps and transport included.

Alligator Gorge, Melrose and Mount Remarkable

The eleven-kilometre dirt road from Wilmington to **Alligator Gorge** ($3.30 visitor's permit available on entry) ends at a picnic area perched on a spur above two **campsites** at Teal and Eaglehawk dams. Stairs descend the gorge wall, with several walking options once you reach the floor: a three-hour circuit north to the ranger's office past the rippled **Terraces** – remains of a fossilized lake shore; or south along the creek for an hour through a tight red canyon alive with frog calls, moss gardens and echoes. These narrows are sometimes flooded, though usually there are enough stepping stones to avoid wet feet. Longer hikes down to Mambray Creek need maps and approval from the NPWS.

MELROSE is a quiet former copper-mining town with two hotels, a pleasant creekside **caravan park** (☎08/8666 2060; dorms ❶) and a few cottage industries. **B&B** is available at *Bluey Blundstone's Blacksmith Shop* (☎08/8666 2173; ❻), carefully restored to its original 1865 condition. When the proprietor isn't producing decorative wrought-ironwork he serves cakes in a coffee shop at the back of the forge. The caravan park hands out walking maps for historic buildings, old mines and ascents to **Cathedral Rock** in the national park. The unremarkable summit of **Mount Remarkable** can be reached in three hours via the **Heysen Trail**, starting a couple of kilometres north of town from the showground.

Telowie Gorge, Mambray Creek and Mount Cavern

The small and appealing **Telowie Conservation Park** lies to the south off the Port Germein–Murray Town road. A very short path leads between the gorge walls, but, unless you're properly equipped for a long hike over to Wirrabara Forest and the Heysen Trail, you'll get more of a flavour of the area by camping along the creek and looking for rare wallabies at dawn and dusk.

The access track to **Mambray Creek** is east off the highway, halfway between Port Germein and the Wilmington road. Here you'll find a **campsite** (water, toilets) and national park headquarters. Mambray Creek is the start of some serious walks, either into the north part of the park along the **Battery Track** and **Alligator Creek**, or on the tough but shorter Mount Cavern circuit. Follow the path anticlockwise along the Black Range to **Mount Cavern**, which has spectacular views and occasionally attracts wedge-tailed eagles. The descent is down a loose stone slope held together by grasstrees, then entering cool woodland at Mambray Creek Gorge, where you might be able to get close to large groups of **emus**.

The Barrier Highway

The last place of any size east of Mount Remarkable, before the Barrier Highway continues to the border with New South Wales, is **PETERBOROUGH**, once a major rail junction where three different track gauges met. **Steamtown Peterborough** is a preservation society which keeps a few steam trains running on 90km of scenic track between Eurelia and Orroroo; for times (usually only on a few holidays) enquire at the **information centre** in a restored train carriage on Main Street (daily 9am–4pm; ☎08/8651 2708). Small-scale gold prospectors bring their finds to be processed and refined here at the state's only **Gold Battery**, which can be viewed by appointment (☎08/8651 2969). **YUNTA**, 100km further, is a collection of roadhouses and services at the start of a backdoor route into the Flinders; it's 300km of gravel road from here to Arkaroola, 200km to Hawker.

The Eyre Peninsula

Far from the rigours of the true Outback, and long appreciated by Adelaidians as an antidote to city stress, the **Eyre Peninsula**'s broad triangle is protected by the **Gawler Ranges** from the arid climate further north. The area began to be farmed in the 1880s; fishing communities sprang up at regular intervals and iron ore, discovered around 1900, is still mined around **Whyalla**. The detour **around the coast** brings you in contact with imposing scenery and superlative **surfing** and **beach fishing**, especially where the Great Australian Bight's elemental weather hammers into the western shore – a chance to give your senses a workout before dealing with the Nullarbor's deadening horizons. Stateliner **buses** from Port Augusta run either across the top of the Peninsula to Ceduna, or via Whyalla down the east coast to **Port Lincoln** at the southern tip, so you'll need your own transport to tackle the west side. Major **car rental** companies have outlets at both Whyalla and Port Lincoln which, if time is limited, are only fifty minutes by air from Adelaide. Note that locals don't rate Eyre Peninsula **tap water** as worth drinking; bottled water and filters are readily available in supermarkets.

Whyalla and the east coast

First visible an hour from Port Augusta as a smudge of grey over Long Sleep Plain, **WHYALLA**, the state's second most important city and headquarters of its heavy industry despite a present downturn, is not the prettiest of places. One Steel has its massive "long products" **steelworks** here (tours Mon, Wed & Sat 9.30am; 2hr; $8; book through the information centre, see below) and tankers queue offshore to fill up at Santos' oil and gas refinery and distillery. Until it closed in 1978, the **shipyard** produced a few famous vessels, the first being the *Whyalla*, which now guards the northern entrance to town, having been dragged 2km from the sea in a complicated and expensive manoeuvre. The accompanying **information centre** and **maritime museum** (daily 10am–4pm; $5 including ship tour; ☏08/8645 8900) is largely occupied by a huge model of the oil refinery as well as more relevant displays of shipping history. From the southwest, Whyalla presents a much greener visage. You can cuddle a koala or a python at the **Wildlife and Reptile Sanctuary** (daily 10am–dusk; $5), and at the junction of Broadbent Terrace and Playford Avenue an old aerodrome site has been landscaped into a series of ponds to recycle stormwater and, once the trees grow a bit, will provide a pleasant recreational area.

The highway curves through the old town as Darling Terrace; you'll find a **post office**, **banks**, a **bus station** (☏08/8645 9911), hotels and shops around the junction with Forsyth and Patterson streets, all periodically covered in (harmless) red fallout from the steelwork's mysterious pellet plant. **Accommodation** options include the *Foreshore Caravan Park* on Broadbent Terrace (☏08/8645 7474; cabins ❸) and *Derham's Motel* on Watson Terrace (☏08/8645 8877; ❻), both a ten-minute walk from the centre along a surprisingly attractive beach with Hummock Hill to mercifully obscure your view of the steelworks; people and pelicans find good fishing off the jetty. Otherwise, try your luck at one of the hotels: *Spencer* on Forsyth Street (☏08/8645 8411; ❸–❹) has rooms, good food and weekend music. For **food**, seafood at *Spagg's*, 30 Patterson St, makes a welcome change from counter meals; after eating, walk past the rows of fifty-year-old workers' homes to the top of Hummock Hill for a view of the industrial complexes by night.

Beyond Whyalla, the east coast is an unassuming string of sheltered beaches and villages nestled beneath towering grain silos, the sort of places you could drive through without a second glance or else get waylaid beachcombing for a week. **COWELL** is known for its whiting and as the world's largest source of black "nephrite" jade, though not much of it is in evidence as it is largely exported rough. **Arno Bay**, **Port Neil** and the larger **Tumby Bay** all boast clean, quiet beaches and good fishing and a range of accommodation – they will try to entice you with their sundry museums and even a worm farm.

If you venture about 90km inland from Cowell, you can view the patchwork of farmland from **Carappee Hill**, the highest point on the peninsula, but you need to be a very determined bushwalker to penetrate its spiky vegetation – the surrounding Carappee Conservation Park has no official paths, although there is a water supply for campers.

Port Lincoln

A tuna port and resort town built on a hillside above Boston Bay, **PORT LINCOLN** has the busiest atmosphere of anywhere on the peninsula. Its harbour is dotted with trawlers, and the seafront main streets of Tasman Terrace and Liverpool Street are full of eateries and far-from-genteel taverns. There's a **tourist information centre** here too (daily 9am–5pm; ℡ 08/8683 3544 or free call 1800 629 911), between the post office and shopping mall; Stateliner **buses** (℡ 08/8682 1288) terminate a couple of streets away on Darling Terrace.

Porter Bay, until recently a swamp just south of town, has been transformed into a **marina** which has drawn many of the boats and some of the life away from the old town. The development includes a large, modern **leisure centre** (Mon–Fri 6am–9pm, Sat, Sun & holidays 9am–6pm; ℡ 08/8682 3833). Entering town from the north, the Lincoln Highway affords splendid views of Boston Bay and presents you with myriad motel **accommodation**, such as the luxurious *Limani Motel* (℡ 08/8682 2200, ℻ 8682 6602; ❻–❽), as it becomes the beachfront Tasman Terrace and then London Street, at the far end of which lie the terraced tent sites of *Kirton Point Caravan Park* (℡ 08/8682 2537).

Most of Port Lincoln's attractions are underwater. You can get bait and tackle from any service station and **fish** off the town jetty; for heavier game contact Sea Charters (℡ 08/8682 2425), which can also take you on a cruise to **Dangerous Reef** for spotting seals, birdlife and sharks. The seas off Lincoln were once rated as the best place in the world to see **great white sharks** – footage for *Jaws* was filmed here – but trawling and hunting since the mid-1970s have placed this little-understood fish on the endangered species list. If this doesn't put you off **diving** – or if you just need advice on good places to fish, or to arrange a boat charter – contact Got One at 80 Tasman Terrace (℡ 08/8683 0021).

Around Port Lincoln

Lincoln National Park, just south of Port Lincoln, is a rough peninsula of sandy coves, steep cliffs and mallee scrub, which is home to the discreet rock parrot. The NPWS at 75 Liverpool Street (℡ 08/8688 3111) can supply maps and advice on road conditions. Similar scenery 32km south at **Whalers Way** is open to all traffic, once a permit and key have been collected from the information centre in Port Lincoln ($17, plus $3 deposit); the name derives from the whaling station which once operated at Cape Wiles – relics are stacked up around the gate. If you've ever felt the need to be impressed by the sea's power, head for **Cape Carnot**: giant waves and frosty blue surf force through **blowholes** which sigh as they erupt in sync with the swell.

Coffin Bay National Park, an hour's drive west from Port Lincoln, is a landscape of dunes and saltmarsh, mostly only accessible by 4WD. Though parts are open to other types of vehicles, you should consult the NPWS in Port Lincoln before venturing here. You'll be rewarded by isolation, sand sculptures at Sensation and Mullalong beaches, and the quality of the fishing. Semicircular stone walls on the northern shore are **Aboriginal fish traps** – fish were chased in at high tide and then the gaps in the side blocked with nets as the water receded. If you don't have your own 4WD, Great Australian Bight Safaris (℡08/8682 2750) will take you on various day-trips for around $60, as well as on longer camping and fishing adventures.

The picturesque setting of the town of **COFFIN BAY** is worth a look, though perhaps not during school holidays when the caravan park (℡08/8685 4170) and abundant holiday cottages are full to bursting. A stroll along the coastal "Oyster Walk" takes you past the original fishermen's shacks, now mostly summer houses, and reveals a wealth of bird and plant life – a taste of Coffin Bay National Park to the west.

The west coast

To catch the best of the west coast and the townships along the way, you'll need to detour off the main road between Coffin Bay and Ceduna. The region's coastal communities are an unlikely mix of conservative farmers and "alternative" surfies who come to ride the endless succession of strong, hundred-metre-long crests rolling into Waterloo Bay at **ELLISTON**, one of the state's most highly regarded **surf beaches**. Bold **murals** at the Community Hall between the café and campsite address local themes – including a long-suppressed incident when Aboriginal people were driven over the cliffs. South of Venus Bay, rocks have been hollowed by the sea to form the **Talia Caves** but the lengthy beach is more compelling; camping is prohibited but you'd probably get away with sleeping in the car. Turning to the coast about 20km north of Port Kenny, you go past the strangely flared **Murphy's Haystacks**, a group of low granite monoliths that look like giant mushrooms. Push on to **Point Labatt** for a look at mainland Australia's only colony of **fur seals**. Binoculars or a telephoto lens help to distinguish mother seals teaching pups to swim from the torpid, bulkier males basking on the rocks. Then it's back to the highway at **Streaky Bay** – the only place on the west coast that has a real centre – and then to drier country as you approach Ceduna and the Nullarbor.

The Eyre Highway and Gawler Ranges

Taking the **Eyre Highway** directly across the top of the peninsula from Port Augusta ensures an easy, comfortable crossing to Ceduna, speeding past the mines at **Iron Knob** and a dry scrub populated by green ring-necked parrots. Unusual geology appears around Wudinna in the form of isolated granite mounds (inselbergs) of various shapes and sizes. The largest, **Mount Wudinna**, 10km to the northeast, is second only to Uluru (Ayers Rock; see p.679) in monolithic magnitude, and 30km southwest you'll find **Ucontichie Hill** with curved forms including a **wave rock** similar to Hyden's in Western Australia (see p.726).

Iron Knob can be the start of forays along dirt tracks into the **Gawler Ranges**, before rejoining the highway at Wirrulla. While you might not need a 4WD, it's a remote area that requires advance preparation and advice from the NPWS. The ranges are low, rounded volcanic ridges coloured orange by dust, with occasional speckled boulders poking through a thin grass cover; it's worth frightening the sheep and pink Major Mitchell cockatoos by walking up one of the peaks for a closer look. The centrally located *Mount Ive Homestead* (℡08/8648 1817; ❶–❷) has fuel, information and **accommodation** in basic rooms (❷) or camping space, but don't turn up unannounced. The track into the ranges passes **Lake Gairdner**, largest of the Gawler's **salt lakes**, with the ruins of Pondanna Homestead on a lonely plain at its southern end.

High-impact – the Acraman meteorite

In the mid-1980s a band of red earth from 600-million-year-old deposits in the Flinders Ranges was bafflingly identified as coming from the Gawler Ranges, 400km away. Investigations and satellite mapping suggested that 35-kilometre-wide **Lake Acraman** in the Gawler Ranges was an eroded **meteorite crater**, while Lake Gairdner and fragmented saltpans (such as Lake Torrens, see p.867) further east were set in ripples caused by the force of the strike. Estimates suggest that to have created such a crater the meteorite must have been 4km across; the mystery band in the Flinders was dust settling after impact. Though there is fossil evidence of animal life prior to this event – notably the Ediacaran fauna (see p.1159) – recent research indicates that the Acraman meteorite may well have killed it all. It's certainly true that the ancestors of almost all species living today evolved after this impact.

Ceduna and the Nullarbor Plain

Nullarbor may not be strictly correct Latin for "treeless", but it's an apt description of the plain which stretches flat and infertile for over 1200km across the Great Australian Bight. Taking the **train**, or **motorbiking** the rail service track (which requires a backup crew, fuel and provisions dumps), brings you closer to the dead heart than does the **road**, which allows some breaks in the monotony of the journey to scan the sea for southern right whales and visit at least one Aboriginal site.

You know where you are in **CEDUNA**: all the shops from camping store to supermarket are unambiguously named and a large signpost in the centre gives distances to everywhere between Perth and Port Augusta. The place is set to receive a moment of fame on December 4 2002, as it's one of the few settlements in Australia which will be totally blacked out by a major **solar eclipse**. Despite being small enough to walk around in twenty minutes, there's no lack of **caravan parks**, **banks** or **service stations**, with almost every brand of fuel on offer – some places even hand out discount cards for use at their pumps along the way. The *Foreshore Van Park* on South Terrace (☏08/8625 2290; cabins ❸) and the *Community Hotel/Motel* on O'Loughlin Terrace (☏08/8625 2008 or free call 1800 655 300; ❹) are right next to the jetty – you can fish for whiting on the turn of the high tide – and *Ceduna Greenacres Backpackers* is also not far from the sea at 12 Kuhlmann St (☏08/8625 3811; ❶). Before your early morning start – it's a long way to anywhere – call in at the **information centre** on Poynton Street (Mon–Sat 9am–4.30pm; ☏08/8625 2780) and the NPWS on McKenzie Street (☏08/8625 3144) for the latest on the Nullarbor's attractions. Incidentally, it almost never rains on the plain, and there's always a charge for **water**, which has to be distilled from underground reserves – so carry your own.

The plain

From Ceduna to the Western Australian border it's 480km, which you can easily cover in under five hours if you want; Daliesque fridges standing along the highway in the early stages of the drive are actually makeshift mailboxes for remote properties. The last chance to catch some waves is at **Cactus Beach/Point Sinclair** south of **Penong**, though its popularity took a dive after a surfer was killed by a great white here in 2000. Even for non-surfies it's worth the drive through white dunes, green shrubbery and blue lagoons to extraordinary wave formations; there's a **campsite** with firewood but no drinking water) and a basic store (12.30–2pm), while the lized **accommodation** is at the *Penong Hotel* (☎08/8625 1050; ❸). rs from Penong you arrive at **Yalata Community**, settled by the peoples cleared off their ancestral land by the British atomic bomb aralinga in the 1950s. At the roadhouse and **whale watch centre** (☎08/8625 6986) you can obtain permits to cross community borders and reach the **Head of the Bight**, the best place to see whales when they migrate up here between June and October. The Head is a stirring setting, where powdery dunes rise to absurdly melodramatic cliffs over just a couple of kilometres – you can't help feeling that this is how early cartographers must have envisaged the edge of the world. The southern right whales (see p.826) sport idly with their calves in the water below. Twenty minutes away is the **Nullarbor Roadhouse** (☎08/8625 6271; ❸), which has **beds** and a campsite, and is the last place to get fuel before Border Village. The famous triple yellow sign on the highway warning of camels, wombats and kangaroos marks the beginning of the run, which has absolutely no trees. Ironically, rabbits – no longer controlled by farmers now that the area is a national park – have almost crowded out the wombats.

Curiously enough for a land with minimal rainfall, the Nullarbor is undermined by partially flooded limestone **caverns** explored in the 1980s by scuba divers and visited 25,000 years ago by Aborigines looking for water and chalcedony to make tools. From the outside, **Koonalda Cave** (just north of the *Nullarbor Roadhouse*) is a large hole with recently planted fruit trees growing in the mouth; inside, a tremendously deep network of tunnels leads to an underground lake, the shafts grooved by fingers being dragged over their soft walls. Although the patterns are clearly deliberate, their meaning is unknown. The cave is closed off to protect the engravings, but the Ceduna NPWS (see overleaf) might be able to arrange a visit.

Border Village is just another roadhouse (☎08/9039 3474; ❹) with a natty fibreglass kangaroo in the car park – certainly the largest one between here and Antarctica. **Eucla** (see p.737) and the rest of the Nullarbor lie 16km over the border in Western Australia on a noticeably worse road and in a considerably earlier time zone.

The Stuart Highway: Woomera and beyond

WOOMERA, an uncharismatic but well-appointed barracks town two hours north of Port Augusta on the Stuart Highway, has been in the news recently for the harshness of its **detention centre**, which houses political asylum seekers while their cases are being decided. In fact, the whole town was closed to the public until 1982, as it sits at the southeast corner of a five-hundred-kilometre corridor known locally as "the Range" and ominously highlighted on maps as **Woomera Prohibited Area**. Don't expect to find out why at the mostly military **Heritage Centre** (daily 9am–5pm; $5), at the crossroads of Dewrang and Banool avenues. Models, rocket-relics and plenty of pictures detail the European Launcher Development Organisation's (ELDO) unsuccessful efforts to launch satellites here in the 1960s, but the reasons for the creation of the Prohibited Area – weapons-testing and the British-run 1950s **atomic bomb tests**, contaminated dust from which is still being scraped up and vitrified – are not mentioned. For a first-hand account, read Len Beadell's *Outback Highways*, cheerful tales of the bomb tests and the construction of "some sort of rocket range – or something" by the chief engineer. Currently, Australian, UK and US rocket prototypes are once again being tested here in the hope of turning Woomera into a launching centre.

There are two **places** to stay: the *Eldo Hotel* on Kotara Crescent (℗08/8673 7867, ℱ8673 7226; ❷–❹), which also provides **meals** and booze; and the welcoming *Woomera Travellers Village* on Wirruna Avenue (℗08/8673 7800; ❷) – **camping** on the lawn is preferable to the beds in the dreary ex-barracks. The **shopping centre** has banks and other facilities, and next to it is **The Oasis**, a small leisure centre with a café, bar and bowling alley. Greyhound buses travelling on the Stuart Highway don't go into Woomera but will drop you off at the roadhouse at Pimba, 7km away; Stateliner actually call in to the town.

Roxby Downs, Andamooka and Lake Torrens

Instead of returning to the highway, consider carrying on past Woomera to the strangest two companion towns in Australia (a Stateliner **bus** goes from Woomera six nights a week). **ROXBY DOWNS**, 80km away, is completely modern, a service centre built in 1986 for miners working the copper, gold, silver and uranium deposits at the nearby Olympic Dam Mine (tours March–Nov daily 9.45am; 2hr 30min; $35; for bookings call Olympic Dam Tours information office, next to the BP service station on Olympic Way; ℗08/8671 0788). Another thirty minutes on an unsurfaced road, and you come to **ANDAMOOKA**, an **opal**-mining shantytown of block and scrap-iron construction whose red-earth high street becomes a river after it rains. The soil proved to be too loose for the underground homes which became *de rigueur* at Coober Pedy (see p.867) but **mud lean-tos** built in the 1930s are still standing opposite the post office. **Facilities** include fuel, a supermarket, the *Tuckerbox Restaurant* (11am–late), two hotel/motels, two campsites, and the Opal Creek Showroom which distributes maps and advice. If you fancy your luck "noodling", head to **German Gully**, where the local opal is more strongly coloured than Coober Pedy's, but little has been found for years. Olympic Dam Tours (see above) does a three-hour tour for $35.

Lake Torrens, a sickle-shaped salt lake related to the Acraman meteorite (see box on p.865), is another thirty-minute ride in a 4WD – in wet years bird-watchers find it a worthwhile trip to observe the waterfowl. The lake is also renowned in paleontological circles for traces of the 630-million-year-old **Ediacaran fauna**, the earliest-known evidence of animal life, which was first found in Australia and was possibly wiped out by the meteorite. Delicate fossil impressions of jellyfish, sea pens and obscure organisms are preserved in layered rock. The South Australian Museum in Adelaide (see p.793) has an extensive selection, but rarely issues directions to the site, which has been plundered by collectors since its discovery in 1946 by the geologist Reg Sprigg.

Coober Pedy

COOBER PEDY is the most enduring symbol of the harshness of Australia's Outback and the determination of those who live there. It's a place where the

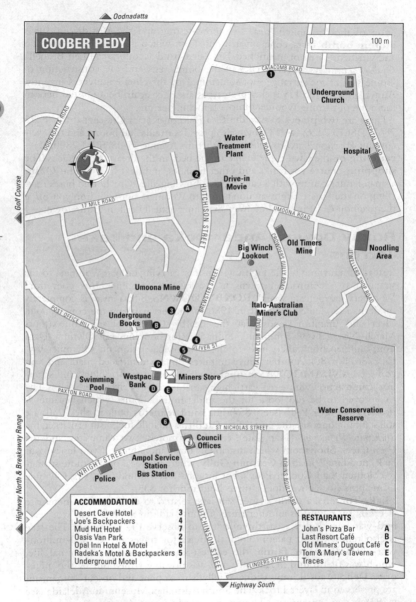

COOBER PEDY

▲ *Oodnadatta*

0   100 m

❶ Underground
Church

Water
Treatment
Plant

Hospital

❷ Drive-in
Movie

N

17 MILE ROAD

HUTCHISON STREET

O'NEIL ROAD

UMOONA ROAD

Big Winch
Lookout

Old Timers
Mine

Noodling
Area

ODNADATTA ROAD

Golf Course

POST OFFICE HILL ROAD

Umoona Mine

BREWSTER STREET

CROWDERS GULLY ROAD

JEWELLERS SHOP ROAD

HOSPITAL ROAD

❸ Ⓐ

Underground
Books Ⓑ

Italo-Australian
Miner's Club

❹ OLIVER ST

❺

ITALIAN CLUB ROAD

Ⓒ

Swimming
Pool

Westpac
Bank

Miners Store

PAXTON ROAD

Ⓓ Ⓔ

Water Conservation
Reserve

❻ ❼

ST NICHOLAS STREET

ℹ Council
Offices

ROBINS BOULEVARD

WRIGHT STREET

Ampol Service
Station
Bus Station

Police

HUTCHINSON STREET

Highway North & Breakaway Range

FLINDERS STREET

ACCOMMODATION

Desert Cave Hotel	3
Joe's Backpackers	4
Mud Hut Hotel	7
Oasis Van Park	2
Opal Inn Hotel & Motel	6
Radeka's Motel & Backpackers	5
Underground Motel	1

RESTAURANTS

John's Pizza Bar	A
Last Resort Café	B
Old Miners' Dugout Café	C
Tom & Mary's Taverna	D
Traces	E

▼ *Highway South*

terrain and temperatures are so extreme that homes – and even churches – have been built underground, yet which has managed to attract thousands of opal prospectors. In a virtually waterless desert 380km from Woomera and considerably further from anywhere else, the most remarkable thing about the town – whose name stems from an Aboriginal phrase meaning "white man's burrow" – is that it exists at all. **Opal** was discovered by William Hutchison on a gold-prospecting expedition to the Stuart Range in February 1915, and the town itself dates from the end of World War I, when returning servicemen headed for the fields to try their luck and used their trench-digging skills to excavate dwellings.

In summer Coober Pedy is seriously depopulated but, if you can handle the intense heat, it's a good time to look for bargain opal purchases – though not to scratch around for them yourself: gem-hunting is better reserved for the "cooler" winter months. At the start of the year, spectacular **dust storms** often enclose the town for hours in an abrasive orange twilight.

The local scenery might be familiar to you if you're a film fan, as it was used to great effect in *Mad Max III* and Wim Wenders' epic *Until The End Of The World*. There's not much to it, just a plain disturbed by conical pink mullock (slag) heaps, with clusters of trucks and home-made contraptions off in the distance, and **warning signs** alerting you to treacherously invisible, unfenced thirty-metre shafts. Be very careful where you tread: even if you have transport, the safest way to explore is to take a tour, examine a map, then go back on your own. Past the diggings, the **Breakaway Range** is a brightly coloured plateau off the highway about 11km north of town, of interest for the views, close-ups of the hostile terrain, and bushwalking through two-hundred-year-old stands of mulga.

Wandering around the dusty streets, it can be hard to tell whether some of the odd machinery lying about is bona fide mining equipment or left-over film props. The **Big Winch Lookout** in the centre gives a grandstand view of the

Finding and buying an opal

Opal is composed of fragile layers of silica and derives its colour from the refraction of light – characteristics that preclude the use of heavy mining machinery, as one false blow would break the matrix and destroy the colour. Deposits are patchy and located by trial and error: the last big strikes at Coober Pedy petered out in the 1970s and, though bits and pieces are still found – including an exceptional opalized fossil skeleton of a pliosaur (the reptilian equivalent of a seal) in 1983 – it's anybody's guess as to the location of other major seams (indeed, there may not be any at all). Because so much depends on luck, you'll hear little about mining technique and more about beating the system. For instance, it's now illegal to mine in town, but there's nothing to prevent "home extensions"; similarly, non-mining friends are often roped in to register claims and sidestep the "one per person" rule. Working another's claim (the "night shift") is a less honourable short cut.

Unless you're serious (in which case you'll have to pay $45 a year to the Mines Department for a Miner's Permit to peg your 50 x 50 metre claim), the easiest way to find something is by noodling over someone's diggings – ask the owner first. An area on the corner of Jewellers Shop and Umoona roads has been set aside as a safe area for tourists to poke about freely without danger of finding open mineshafts. Miners use ultraviolet lamps to separate opal from potch (worthless grey opal), so you're unlikely to find anything stunning – but look out for shell fossils and small chips.

The best time to buy opal is outside the tourist season, but don't expect wild bargains and don't deal through grizzled prospectors in the hotels unless you're very clued in. There are three categories: cabochon, a solid piece; doublet, a thin wafer mounted on a dark background to enhance the colour; and triplet, a doublet with quartz lens. While cabochons are most expensive and triplets least valuable, it takes some experience to price accurately within each category as size, clarity, strength of colour, brightness and personal aesthetics all contribute. With about fifty dealers in town, it's up to you to find the right stone; reputable sources give full written guarantees.

mix of low houses and hills pocked with ventilation shafts. The welded metal "tree" up here was assembled before any real ones grew in the area, though in the last few years there have been some attempts to encourage greenery with recycled waste water.

For more on **mining**, check out one of the several mine displays and museums: try **Old Timers Mine**, Crowders Gully Road (☎08/8672 5555; $4), or **Umoona** on Hutchison Street (☎08/8672 5288; $5). Numerous **tours** are on offer for around $28: they all feature a town drive, a spot of noodling and a visit to an underground home – which you might find embarrassingly like visiting a zoo. Book through your accommodation, or try Radeka's five-hour tour (☎08/8672 5223) which includes a look at the Breakaway Range.

Coober Pedy has lately achieved a bit of a reputation for **violence**, which is perhaps not surprising given its extreme climate and the fact that most people have access to explosives. However, signs warning "no parking unless your car is dynamite-proof" are really for amusement value only and visitors are unlikely to be the object of any discord.

Practicalities

Just about everything you'll need in Coober Pedy lies around the five-hundred-metre strip between the *Opal Inn Hotel* and the water treatment plant on **Hutchison Street** (also known as Main Street) which leads north off the highway. **Buses** drop you off either at the Ampol service station (Greyhound Pioneer and Stateliner; ☎08/8672 5151) or at *Radeka's Motel* (McCafferty's; ☎08/8672 5223). From the **airport** you may be able to get a lift with one of the hostel buses that meet most flights, or make an advance reservation to ensure that someone meets you. *Desert Cave Hotel* (see below) are agents for Territory Rent a Car; book well in advance.

The council offices on Hutchison Street (Mon–Fri 9am–5pm; free call ☎1800 637 076), opposite the Ampol service station, are a mine of local **information**. Underground Books (☎08/8672 5558), on Post Office Hill Road opposite the Mobil service station, is a good alternative source – it stocks packs of local sketch maps which are a useful back-up to road maps. The Miners Store supermarket on Hutchison Street (☎08/8672 5051) is also the **post office** and Commonwealth **bank** agent (there's a Westpac branch opposite). The **hospital** is on Hospital Road, at the north end of town (☎08/8672 5009), and there's a **pharmacy** at the Medical Centre in the middle of Hutchison Street. Everyone shops on Thursday, as fresh meat and veggies arrive in a refrigerated lorry on Wednesday night and are scarce by the weekend. The **swimming pool** at the school on Paxton Road gives a welcome chance to cool down; it's open to the public for a few hours daily.

Accommodation

Coober Pedy relies heavily on tourist income, so finding **lodgings** should be no problem. To some people, the idea of sleeping underground is disturbing but, while not all accommodation is subterranean, it's worth spending at least one night in naturally cooled tunnels for the experience.

Desert Cave Hotel, halfway up Hutchison St (☎08/8672 5688, ⊛www.desertcave.com.au). Offers a choice of below- or above-ground four-star accommodation. There's a swimming pool, and scenic flights, tours and car rental can be arranged. ❼
Joe's Backpackers Hostel and Motel, Oliver St (☎08/8672 5163 or free call 1800 631 758).

Above-ground motel rooms sleep up to three people, backpackers go underground. ❶–❷
Mud Hut Motel, next to council offices (☎08/8672 3003, ⊛www.mudhutmotel.com.au). The bare, rammed-earth construction of this well-furnished motel gives a flavour of the subterranean without losing out on daylight. ❻

Oasis Van Park, opposite the water treatment plant, Hutchison St (☎08/8672 5169). The only place to camp under trees. Cabin rooms ❸

Opal Inn Motel, Hutchison St (☎08/8672 5054). A standard motel block behind the hotel of the same name. ❹

Radeka's Motel and Backpackers Inn, Oliver St (☎08/8672 5223). The best budget option in town. Recently extended with snaking tunnels and alcoves with two to six beds – it can be a long trek upstairs to the well-appointed kitchen and toilets. The new bar and pool table provide evening entertainment. Motel rooms ❺, dorms ❶

Underground Motel, Catacomb Rd (☎08/8672 5324). Clean, tiled rooms with views over the desert from the front porch. ❺

Eating, drinking and entertainment

Restaurants in town are good value and portions are huge – beware of overordering; all those listed below are on the main street. The drive-in **cinema** on Hutchison Street shows a double bill most Saturday nights.

Italo-Australian Miner's Club Big Italian dinners on Italian Club Rd.

John's Pizza Bar Takeaway fast food and coffee.

Last Resort Café Upmarket place with pavement tables, excellent pastries and coffee.

Old Miners' Dugout Café Kangaroo dishes and budget specials.

Tom and Mary's Taverna Souvlakia morning to midnight.

Traces Greek grills, plus dancing. Daily 4pm–late.

Beyond Coober Pedy

The Stuart Highway ploughs another 350km north from Coober Pedy to the border. From **Marla** township (shop, post office and Commonwealth Bank at the roadhouse) you could head east to Oodnadatta across the **Painted Desert** at Arkaringa Hills, a larger version of the Breakaway Range, or 35km west into Aboriginal Land to the state's newest opal strike at Mintabie – seek permission from Marla's police.

If you want to get to **Oodnadatta**, there's also a direct two-hundred-kilometre dirt road from Coober Pedy across the pan of Giddi-Gidna (the **Moon Plain**), covered by the **mail run** which departs from Underground Books (free call ☎1800 069 911) on a roughly twelve-hour triangular route to William Creek and Oodnadatta every Monday at 9am (anticlockwise) and Thursday (clockwise); passengers can join the trip anywhere for $25 each side of the triangle.

Australia's hottest 4WD journey has to be west from Coober Pedy to the **atomic bomb sites** at **Emu Junction**: concrete slabs cap pits where contaminated equipment lies buried, and sand fused into sheets of glass by the blasts covers the ground – the area is still highly radioactive and you'd be advised to pass through quickly. Beyond lies the virgin **Unnamed Conservation Park** and routes across the sand-dunes and Aboriginal Land to the **Warburton Road** in Western Australia (see p.736). The NPWS at 11 McKenzie St in Ceduna (☎08/8625 3144) supplies practical details and permits to 4WD convoys only.

The Flinders Ranges and the northeast

The first stop between Port Augusta and the **Flinders Ranges National Park** is 50km northeast at **QUORN**, whose stone buildings and village atmosphere are a last vestige of the south. Best known for the **Pichi Richi railway**, the sole operational section of the old Ghan, Quorn was a major rail centre until the line was rerouted through Port Augusta in the 1950s. Enthusiasts restored the service twenty years later and started taking passengers on a two-hour return haul to Woolshed Flats through the **Pichi Richi Pass** – whose name has been variously attributed to a medicinal herb or an Aboriginal word for "gorge". Punctuated by a break at Woolshed Flats for a cream tea, it makes a relaxing and mildly scenic journey. Trains run only on a few weekends and holidays April–October; call ahead to check and book (☎08/8658 6598).

There's a **caravan park** in Quorn (☎08/8648 6206; cabins ❹) but a night spent at the *Transcontinental Hotel* (☎08/8648 6076; ❶–❸) is much more congenial, with an easy-going crowd of truckies and drovers from the north for company. A good alternative is the *Andu Lodge* (free call ☎1800 639 9933; rooms ❸, dorms ❶), who have excellent dorm and double rooms, plus run a host of one- to three-day **tours** into the different sections of the Flinders for between $99 and $299.

The main road through town is Railway Terrace where you'll find the post office, civic buildings and hotels which all do good-value **meals** but are quite strict about serving times. First Street and the block between it and Railway Terrace contain a few **art and craft** and secondhand shops to poke about in, with the **tourist information** centre at 3 Seventh St (☎08/8648 6419). If you want to explore some of the country round here, Intrepid Tours, 17 Sixth St (☎08/8648 6277), runs a 4WD tour any day they can fill a vehicle.

There's good local bushwalking off the back road to Hawker along a string of ridges and cliffs, outrunners from the main body of the central Flinders 100km north. Closest to Quorn is **Dutchmans Stern**, a solid day's hike for the reasonably fit from the car park to various lookouts. Less dedicated walkers will find **Warren**, **Buckaringa** and **Middle gorges** an easier proposition; Buckaringa's steep face is the most reliable place in the ranges to see the rare and ravishingly pretty **yellow-footed rock wallaby**, with its bushy, ringed tail and tobacco-yellow paws – climb to the top at around 4pm and sit still until they appear. Closer to Hawker, it's also worth taking in the well-preserved remains of **Kanyaka Homestead**, abandoned after a drought in the 1880s, and **Yourambulla Cave**, which has some unusual charcoal symbols in a high overhang, reached by a ladder. Both are signposted from the road.

Flinders dreaming and geology

The almost tangible spirit of the Flinders Ranges is reflected in the wealth of Adnyamathanha ("hill people") **legends** associated with them. Perhaps more obvious here than anywhere else in Australia is the connection between landscapes and Dreamtime stories, which recount how scenery was created by animal or human action – though, as Dreamtime spirits took several forms, this distinction is often blurred. A central character is **Akurra**, a gigantic maned serpent (or serpents) who guards waterholes and formed the Flinders' contours by wriggling north to drink dry the huge salt lakes Frome and Callabonna.

Ochre paintings are one type of **art** often encountered at sites, but there's a more extensive, older tradition of engraving. Circles generally depict a campsite, with additional lines and rings representing stages in initiation rites.

You may well prefer the Aboriginal legends to the complexities of geology illustrated on boards placed at intervals along the Brachina Gorge track, which explain how movements of the "Adelaide Geosyncline" brought about the changes in scenery over hundreds of millions of years.

HAWKER itself, some 100km from Port Augusta, is somewhere to fuel up, make use of the last banks and shops for a while, have a meal at the *Old Ghan Restaurant* down past the hotel, organize a **flight over the Flinders** through *Hawker Caravan Park* on the Wilpena exit (☎08/8648 4006), and seek **Desert Park Passes** and advice about road conditions from the NPWS office at 60 Elder Terrace (Mon–Fri 8.30am–4pm; ☎08/8648 4244). Decisions have to be made in Hawker about whether to press on into the Flinders and the north-east or continue following the former Ghan line north towards Marree; the bitumen on the latter route extends past the Leigh Creek coalfields to Lyndhurst, start of the Strzelecki Track. Stateliner **buses** pass through Sunday, Wednesday and Friday, continuing to Wilpena, with a connection (Mon & Fri) to Arkaroola in the Northern Flinders. On Sunday, Thursday and Friday the buses return to Port Augusta and Adelaide.

Flinders Ranges National Park

The procession of glowing red mountains at **Flinders Ranges National Park**, folded and crumpled with age, produces some of the Outback's most spectacular and timeless scenery, rising from flat scrub to form abrupt escarpments, gorges and the famous elevated basin of **Wilpena Pound**. The hard contrast between sky and ranges is softened by native cypresses and river red gums, and in spring the plains are burnished by **wild flowers** of all colours. Bushwalkers, photographers and painters flock here in their hundreds, but with a system of graded **walking tracks** ranging from a few minutes' length to several days – not to mention roads of varying quality – the park is busy without being crowded.

WILPENA is a good place to orient yourself: it has a motel, campsite and an expensive store and NPWS **information centre** (daily 8am–6pm) situated at the end of the bitumen and at the start of the main routes into Wilpena Pound. Wilder places further into the park to set up camp for a few days include the national park campsites at **Bunyeroo** and **Brachina Gorge** in the west, **Trezona** and **Oraparinna** in the centre, and **Wilkawillana Gorge** in the extreme northeast, all accessible on unsealed roads. Even the more formal **lodgings** tend to be basic; for a longer stay you might consider renting a holiday cottage, which can be a bargain during the summer – contact Flinders Outback Tourism (☎08/8373 3430).

Back at Wilpena, *Wilpena Pound Motel* (☎08/8648 0004, ⓦ www.wilpena-pound.on.net; ❻) provides comfortable but overpriced **accommodation**: there's a good, surprisingly exotic restaurant, however, and the chalet-like bar makes an atmospheric setting for an après-hike drink. 4WD tours and flights over the Pound can also be arranged here. If you've a tent, the adjacent *Wilpena Campsite* (☎08/8648 0008) is wooded and well-equipped. Otherwise, places to stay lie elsewhere through the park: about 15km back towards Hawker *Rawnsley Park* (☎08/8648 0030; cabins ❹, plus tent spaces) is beautifully located below Rawnsley Bluff, and has its own fuel, store, mountain bike rental, 4WD trips and horse riding; *Willow Springs* (☎08/8648 6282; ❷), 17km north of Wilpena before the Wilkawillana Gorge junction, is a working sheep station with blockhouse dormitories; and *Oraparinna Homestead* (book through the Hawker NPWS; ❸), in the centre of the park off the Blinman Road, 24km north of Wilpena, has self-contained shearers' quarters and cabins. Alternatively, Flinders Ranges Accommodation Booking Service (free call ☎1800 777 880, ⓦ www.frabs.mtx.net) offers a similar range of cabins (❸–❹) in the region.

Most **walking tracks** lead into Wilpena Pound, though you can also pick up the Heysen Trail and follow it north from Wilpena for a couple of days around the ABC Range to **Aroona Ruins** on the northern edge of the park. The Wilpena NPWS offers booklets, maps (sometimes the 1:50,000 topographical series) and the latest information on routes; you're required to log out and back with them on any walk exceeding three hours. Realistically, hiking is restricted to the cooler winter months between May and October, as scant shade and reflective rocks raise summer temperatures above 40°C. Don't underestimate conditions for even short excursions: you'll need good footwear, a hat, sunscreen and **water** – at least half a litre per hour is recommended. **Camping out**, a waterproof tent, groundmat and fuel stove are essential, and note that the **weather** is very changeable; wind-driven rain can be a menace along the ridges and heavy downpours make tracks dangerous.

Wilpena Pound

Wilpena Pound's two major hiking destinations are **St Mary's Peak** on the rim and **Edowie Gorge** inside the Pound, easily tackled individually or joined into an overnight circuit if time allows. For the round-trip, leave the peak until last and head off across the Pound's flat, grassy bowl to the remains of **Hill's Homestead** – further evidence of the region's unsuitability for farming – then follow the track northwest to **Cooinda Camp**, about two hours from the start. Assuming you left early enough, there's time to pitch a tent and spend the rest of the day following the creek upstream past **Malloga Falls** to **Glenora Falls** and views into Edowie Gorge before heading back to Cooinda – there might be places to swim after a rain. Next morning, it's a steep climb to **Tanderra Saddle** below the peak, but not as bad as the last burst to St Mary's summit, which often involves scrambling on all fours. The effort is rewarded by unequalled views west to Lake Torrens and north along the length of the ABC Ranges towards Parachilna; on exceptional mornings the peak stands proud of low cloud inside the Pound. The direct descent from the saddle back to Wilpena campsite is initially steep but shouldn't take more than three hours. Splitting the tracks into separate return walks from Wilpena, allow nine hours for Edowie Gorge, eight hours for a straight ascent of St Mary's, and ten hours for a circuit via St Mary's and Cooinda Camp but omitting Edowie Gorge.

Shorter routes lead up **Mount Ohlssen Bagge** (a not too tiring four hours) and **Wangara Lookout** (2hr) for lower vistas of the Pound floor, and southwest across the Pound to **Bridle Gap** (6hr) following the Heysen Trail's red markers. Things to look out for are euro wallabies, emus and parrots inside the Pound, and cauliflower-shaped fossil **stromatolites** – algal corals – on the Mount Ohlssen Bagge route, similar to those still living at Hamelin Pool in Western Australia (see p.744).

Art sites, more gorges and onwards

Two **Aboriginal galleries** worth seeing are Arkaroo Rock and Sacred Canyon, both a short drive from Wilpena. **Arkaroo** is back off the main road towards Rawnsley Park and involves an hour's walk up the outside of Wilpena Pound to see mesh-protected rockfaces covered in symbols relating to an initiation ceremony and the Pound's formation, some dating back six thousand years. Snake patterns depict St Mary's Peak as the head of a male Akurra coiled round the Pound. To reach **Sacred Canyon**, briefly take the road from Wilpena into the north of the park, past the **Cazneaux Tree** – a river red gum made famous by Harold Cazneaux's prize-winning 1930 photograph *Spirit of Endurance* – before turning right and following a bumpy track to its end. Rockhop up the narrow, shattered gorge to clusters of painted swirls covered in a sooty patina and clearer engraved emu prints and geometric patterns; the best examples are in the vicinity of the second cascade.

The main road through the park heads straight out to Blinman, but there's a detour track to **Bunyeroo** and **Brachina gorges** on the western limits. The gorges make good campsites: you have to walk into Bunyeroo but the track passes through Brachina on its way to the surfaced Hawker–Marree road. If you're pressing directly on to the Northern Flinders, you can avoid Blinman by turning right off the main road about 20km from Wilpena, heading to **Wirrealpa Homestead**.

The Northern Flinders

The Wilpena–Blinman road passes through a low group of hills, thin in timber but still swarming with wallabies, emus and galahs. **BLINMAN** comprises a few houses with well-tended gardens, three fuel pumps, and a hotel (℡08/8648 4867; ❷–❹) with log fires, games room, pool and campsite; the keys to everywhere else in town are kept at the bar. The main track winds west through beautiful Parachilna Gorge, in the middle of which you could stay at **Angorichina**'s *Tourist Village* (dorms ❶, and campsite; ℡08/8648 4842). The track meets the Hawker–Marree road at **Parachilna** where you can sample some great food from a menu featuring almost all the area's wild plants and animals at the *Prairie Hotel* (℡08/8648 4895).

According to the Adnyamathanha, **coal** was made by Yoolayoola the kingfisher man, who built fires at Leigh Creek, halfway between Hawker and Marree. Today 2.6 million tonnes of it are scooped out of the ground annually to be sent by rail and burnt at the ETSA power station in Port Augusta, and it is estimated it will run out in about 25 years. At a car park just off the road you can climb around an old dragline crane and look over the edge of an open-cast mine; there are free **tours** daily (℡08/8675 4210). Coal-workers live in the thoroughly well-planned and modern township of **Leigh Creek South** or at more traditional **Copley**, where it's worth stopping at *Tulloch's Bush Bakery* for a very civilized cappuccino and quandong pie. Fuel and camping sites are available at both towns.

The route into the Northern Flinders lies east, joining up with the direct road from Wilpena and then running north to the **Gammon Ranges National Park** and Arkaroola.

Chambers Gorge and Big Moro

Chambers Gorge and **Big Moro** are remote, little-visited sites on the road to the Gammon Ranges, worth every groan and twang of your vehicle springs for their stark beauty and Aboriginal significance. The ten-kilometre access track east into **Chambers Gorge** (28km after Wirrealpa) is decidedly dodgy after rain when you'll need a 4WD, but at other times 2WD vehicles – with care – should reach a natural campsite at the foot of **Mount Chambers**, within twenty-minutes' walk of the gorge mouth. In a Dreamtime story, Yuduyudulya, the Fairy Wren spirit, threw a boomerang which split Mount Chambers' eastern end and then circled back to form the crown. An indistinct left fork before the gorge leads to a dense gallery of **pecked engravings**; most are circles, though a goanna stands out clearly on the right, facing the main body of art. Chambers Gorge itself is huge and silent, the broad stony entrance guarded by high, perpendicular cliffs and brilliant green waterholes; it would take days to explore it properly.

Big Moro is sacred to the Adnyamathanha as the residence of an Akurra. The creek trickles through a crumbling gorge into two clear green pools; limestone outcrops on the south side conceal miniature caves. The gorge lies west down an exceptionally tortuous fifteen-kilometre 4WD track opposite **Wertaloona Homestead**, 60km from the Mount Chambers junction. Pay attention to any signs and leave the three gates as you found them.

The Gammon Ranges

Arid and bald, the **Gammon Ranges** are the Flinders' last fling, a vicious flurry of compressed folds plunging abruptly onto the northern plains. Balcanoona is the NPWS headquarters for the otherwise undeveloped **Gammon Ranges National Park**, a thick band of sandstone cliffs – check with the Hawker NPWS (see p.873) for current conditions. Two ways to experience the area are either to carry on to Arkaroola (outside the park) or to take the road west across the park through **Italowie Gorge** to Copley on the Hawker–Marree road. The steep red walls of the gorge are home to iga – native orange trees which symbolize the Adnyamathanha as a people. There are **bush campsites** here and shearers' quarters at **Balcanoona** (book through the Hawker NPWS; ❷).

ARKAROOLA (Mount Painter Sanctuary) is a private wildlife sanctuary and resort (☏08/8370 8454 or free call 1800 676 042, ⓦwww.arkaroola.on.net; ❺) and a source of fuel, provisions, meals, rooms and a campsite. Scene of Australia's most recent volcanic activity, the area is a geologist's dream: **Paralana Hot Springs** (two hours away in a 4WD) bubble out radioactive radon gas, and walks into the shattered hills surrounding the resort turn up fossils and semiprecious minerals. According to Aboriginal legend, the springs mark the site where a dreamtime warrior extinguished his firestick after using it to kill a rival. The area is so rugged that conventional mining isn't really a profitable venture – drilling rigs are airlifted in, then ferried around on the lower half of a Chieftain tank – and mining giant CRA Zinc concentrates on mapping uranium and copper deposits in order to show progress and keep their licence. The resort's $85 **Ridgetop Tour** brings you closest to the heart of the scenery: four hair-raising hours in an open 4WD (wear something warm) following precipitous contours to **Sillers Lookout** and views east to the shimmering salt lakes of **Frome** and **Callabonna**. Remains of the hippopotamus-sized marsupial diprotodon have been found at Callabonna; the diprotodon survived well into Aboriginal times, but died out as the climate changed after the last Ice Age.

Arkaroola marks the limit of public transport, running its own connection to meet the Stateliner bus at Hawker on Monday and Friday. Some vehicles (with either high clearance or very careful drivers) can continue directly north to join the **Strzelecki Track** at Mount Hopeless, a little under half the distance to Innamincka. If you're unsure, the track can also be reached via Lyndhurst on the Hawker–Marree road, but this involves a three-hundred-kilometre detour from Arkaroola.

The Strzelecki Track

The 460-kilometre **Strzelecki Track** between Lyndhurst and Innamincka was laid down in 1870 by **Harry Redford**, better known as Captain Starlight, who stole a thousand cattle from a property near Longreach in Queensland and drove them south across the Strzelecki Desert and down to Adelaide (see p.560 for more). Later used for more orthodox purposes, the track had a reputation as one of the roughest stock routes in the country, a serious obstacle for transport. Much of its epic nature has since been flattened, along with the road surface, by companies draining the **Moomba gas and oil fields**, and it's negotiable in any sound vehicle when dry.

Start at Lyndhurst by filling the tank – the next **fuel** is at the other end – and heading off around the northern tip of the Flinders; once past them, the journey becomes flat and pretty dull. At around the 105-kilometre mark you cross the 4850-kilometre-long **Dog Fence** (or Great Dingo Fence), which stretches from the Nullarbor Plain east into New South Wales and is intended to keep dingoes from southern flocks. Although its value is debatable, you do frequently see desiccated canine corpses poisoned by "1080" bait. The road from Arkaroola connects within sight of **Mount Hopeless** (a pathetic rise, appropriately named), and the next place to stop and perhaps camp is at the hot outflow from **Montecollina Bore**, 30km on. From here the scenery improves slightly as the road runs between dunes, and it's hard to resist leaving footprints along one of the pristine red crests.

At **Strzelecki Crossing** there's a choice of routes: you could abandon the track and head east to where Queensland, New South Wales and South Australia meet at **Cameron Corner**, where there's a store with **fuel**, campsite and a small bar (℡08/8091 3872); or you could continue to Innamincka either via Moomba or by following the direct but less-frequented **Old Strzelecki Track**. Cameron's Corner and the old track are 4WD only, and all of the routes are crossed by straight **seismic test lines** which run off to dead ends in the bush – you risk becoming permanently lost if you accidentally follow one, so take care. **Moomba**'s jumble of pipes and lick of flame are sometimes marked as a township on maps but, though visible from the road, the refinery is closed to the public. Within an hour you've crossed into the **Innamincka Regional Reserve** and are approaching Innamincka's charms.

Innamincka

Cooper Creek, which runs through Innamincka, is best known for the misadventures of explorers Burke and Wills, who ended their tragic 1861 expedition by dying here (see box on p.568). **INNAMINCKA** was later founded on much the same spot as a customs house to collect taxes on stock being moved between Queensland and South Australia. Never more than a handful of buildings, it found fame mainly because John Flynn's Flying Doctor Service ran a mission here and because the hotel piled up decades of empties into a legendary 180-metre-long bottle dump before the town was abandoned in 1952. Recreational four-wheel driving has led to a renaissance: the new *Innimincka Hotel* (℡ & ℻ 08/8675 9901; ❺) has weekend barbecues, a video jukebox and impromptu dance sessions on Friday and Saturday nights; the Innamincka Trading Post (℡08/8675 9900) has a couple of comfortable **cabins** (❺), and stocks provisions and fuel; the mission was rebuilt in 1994 as a **museum** (for opening hours ask at the Trading Post); and opposite is a solar-powered telephone and spotless toilet/shower block. Pelicans, parrots and inquisitive dingoes will be your companions if you camp out for free along the creek.

It only takes an hour to look around the museum and hunt for evidence of the bottle dump before you're ready for other distractions: taking a walk, **fishing** for yellowbelly, bream and catfish, swimming in the creek, or renting a canoe from the hotel or the Trading Post. With a vehicle you could strike out 20km west to **Wills' grave** or 8km east to where **Burke** was buried (both bodies were removed to Adelaide in 1862). Another 8km beyond Burke's cairn is **Cullyamurra waterhole**, the largest permanent body of water in central Australia, and a footpath to rock engravings of crosses, rainbow patterns and bird tracks. Four-wheel-drive vehicles can also tackle the 110-kilometre track north to the shallow **Coongie Lakes**, where you can swim and watch the abundant birdlife. An hour's drive east of Innamincka along a rather poor track is Queensland, the **Dig Tree** and a fuelless route to Quilpie (see p.567).

The far north: Marree and beyond

MARREE is a collection of tattered houses which somehow outlived the old Ghan's demise in 1980, leaving carriages to rust on sidings and rails to be used for tethering posts outside the hotel. Although it was first a camel depot, then a staging post for the overland telegraph line, and finally the point where the rail line skirted northwest around **Lake Eyre**, today all traffic comes by road and is bound for the **Birdsville Track** into Queensland or the **Oodnadatta Track**, which follows the former train route to Oodnadatta and beyond into the Northern Territory or Simpson Desert.

Accommodation is limited to the hotel on the main street (℡08/8675 8344; ❹), which is also good for lunch or dinner, and the caravan park run by the *Oasis Café* (℡08/8675 8352; cabins ❹), a fairly well-stocked shop, fuel and fast-food outlet which was originally the telegraph relay station. The General Store (℡08/8675 8360), across the railway track towards Oodnadatta, doubles as a Commonwealth Bank agent and post office with fuel and EFTPOS. If it's open, visit the Arabana Community Centre, where friendly staff explain how each type of boomerang is used.

Lake Eyre

Lake Eyre is a massive salt lake caught between the Simpson and Strzelecki deserts in a region where the annual evaporation rate is thirty times greater than the rainfall. Most years a little water trickles into the lake from its million-square-kilometre catchment area, which extends well into central Queensland and the Northern Territory, but floods have filled the basin only four times since white settlement of the region – most dramatically in 1974, when the lake expanded to a length of 140km. A hypnotic, glaring **salt crust** usually covers the southern bays, creating a mysterious, spiritual landscape whose harsh surrounds are paved by shiny gibber stones and walled by red dunes – the crust was thick enough in 1964 to be used as a range for Donald Campbell's successful crack at the world land-speed record. Some **wildlife** also manages to get by in the incredible emptiness. The resident Lake Eyre dragon is a diminutive, spotted grey lizard often seen skimming over the crust, and the rare flooding attracts dense flocks of birds, wakes the plump water-holding frog from hibernation and causes the plants to burst into colour.

While you can **fly** over the lake (make bookings through the *Oasis Café* in Marree), only 4WDs can reach the shore 95km north of Marree, though the track to the campsite at a gum-shaded waterhole, just over halfway at **Muloorina Homestead**, is good. Timber at the lake is sparse and protected, which means that there's little shade and no firewood. There's no one to help you if something goes wrong, so don't drive on the lake's crust – should you fall through, it's impossible to extricate your vehicle from the grey slush below.

The Birdsville Track

Assuming there's been no rain, the 520-kilometre **Birdsville Track** is no obstacle to careful drivers during the winter: the biggest problem is getting caught in dried wheel ruts and being pulled off the road. Tearing north from Marree, the distant tips of the Flinders Ranges dip below the horizon behind, leaving you on a bare plain with the road as the only feature. Look for the **MV Tom Brennan**, a vessel donated to the area in 1949 to ferry stock around during floods, but now bearing an absurd resemblance to a large grey bathtub. Before the halfway house at Mungeranie Gap, a scenic variation is offered by the **Natterannie Sandhills** (150km), once a severe obstacle but now graded by digging out the soft sand and replacing it with clay. The **Mungeranie roadhouse** (℡08/8675 8317; ❷) provides the only services on the track (fuel, beds and snacks), but seems to be unattended on Sunday when you'll have to slog up the hill to the manager's house. In a 4WD you can head west from the roadhouse to **Kalamurina campsite** near Cowarie Homestead (58km) for the thrill of desert **fishing** on Warburton Creek.

Back on the track, a windmill at **Mirra Mitta bore** (37km from the roadhouse) draws piping-hot water out of the ground beside long-abandoned buildings; the water smells of tar and drains into cooler pools, providing somewhere to camp. By now you're crossing the polished gibber lands of the **Sturt Stony Desert**, and it's worth going for a walk to feel the cold wind and watch the dunes dancing in the heat haze away to the west. The low edge of **Coonchera Dune** to the right of the track (190km from the roadhouse) marks the start of a run along the mudpans between the sandhills; look for desert plants and dingoes. In two more hours you should be pulling up outside the Birdsville pub (see p.568).

The Oodnadatta Track

The road from **Marree to Oodnadatta** is the most interesting of the three famous Outback tracks, mainly because abandoned sidings and fettlers' cottages from the old Ghan provide frequent excuses to get out of the car and explore. Disintegrating sleepers lie by the roadside along some of the route; otherwise, embankments and rickety bridges are all that remain of the line. As with the roads to Birdsville and Innamincka, with care any sound vehicle can drive the route in dry winter weather.

About 100km into the journey, near **Curdimurka ruins**, the road runs within sight of **Lake Eyre South**, giving a flavour of its bigger sister if you can't get out there. In alternate Octobers (even-numbered years) the **Curdimurka Outback Ball** is organized by the Ghan Railway Preservation Society, which maintains a few buildings, relics and 5km of track. Three thousand souls from everywhere between Alice Springs and Sydney pay $70 a head and don their finest threads for a night of mayhem under the stars; eagles and crows pick over the debris for a couple of weeks afterwards. Twenty-five kilometres later, a short track south ends below three conical hills – two of which have hot, bubbling **mound springs** at the top, created when water escaping from the artesian basin deposits heaps of mud and minerals. The perfectly symmetrical **Blanche Cup** looks out across a plain – stripped of every shred of greenery by rabbits and cattle – to **Hamilton Hill**, an extinct spring, while further south the **Bubbler** gurgles a verdant stream into the desert where it evaporates after a couple of hundred metres. Important to the Arabana, these springs were used by Sturt in the 1850s and later by the telegraph and rail depots, but tapping the artesian basin for bore water has greatly reduced their flow.

One of these bores is not far up the road at **Coward Springs**, where a corroded pipe spilling into ponds beside the track has created an artificial environment of grasses and palms behind a **campsite**, with toilet blocks and cabins built from sleepers. The ground can be boggy after rain but it's still a tempting stop; a $2 donation is requested for overnight stays. **WILLIAM CREEK**, 75km further, has a resident population of just ten – and is a source of fuel, camping and relaxation in the **hotel** (☏ 08/8670 7880). Bar, walls and ceiling are heavily decorated with cards and photographs of 4WD disasters, and it is the hangout for stockmen from **Anna Creek Station**, which, covering an area the size of Belgium, is the world's largest cattle property. A solar-powered phone outside faces the battered remains of a Black Arrow **missile** dragged off the Woomera Range, just a few minutes' drive away. Off-road drivers can take a seventy-kilometre track from here to Lake Eyre's western shore; in the other direction is a more passable road to Coober Pedy with almost nothing to see on the way except for **Lake Cadibarrawirracanna**, a salt lake with permanent water and consequent birdlife, at the halfway mark.

After William Creek the track gets rougher, crossing sand dunes and then moving into stony country cut by frequent creeks – shallow for most of the year. Hardy mulgas line the banks, their soft yellow blooms giving off a distinctive acrid scent. On the last stretch to Oodnadatta, stay alert for a sight of the extraordinary red and black crescent petals of **Sturt's desert pea**, the state emblem, growing by the roadside.

Oodnadatta

Unless you stay long enough to meet some locals, you'll probably feel that, like Marree, **OODNADATTA** survived the Ghan's closure with little to show for it. A few logically arranged but untidy streets lacking atmosphere or purpose, Oodnadatta was founded as a railhead in 1890, and mail and baggage for further north had to make do with camel trains from here until the line to Alice Springs was completed in 1928. Now that has gone, the town has become a base for the Aranda community – *utnadata* ("mulga blossom") is the Aranda name for a local waterway – and 4WD crews heading into the Simpson Desert. After rain you'll even need a 4WD for the last slippery kilometre into town, past the racecourse. If your visit coincides with the **race weekend** in May, helicopters will be circling the track on the left, trying to dry it out, and the town will be deserted, so stop at the track, buy a pass and join in. With neat clothes and some sort of tie, you'll even get into the "formal" ball afterwards.

Camp at the **Pink Roadhouse** (☏ 08/8670 7822, ✉ Lynne_plate@bigpond.com), unless the relative luxury of a bed at the *Oodnadatta Hotel* appeals (☏ 08/8670 7804; ❹). The roadhouse acts as a store, bank, post office and café, and sells detailed sketch maps of the area. The hotel holds the key to the **Railway Museum** opposite, where you'll find a strangely timeless photographic record of the town – scenes are hard to date because so little seems to have changed. Stock up with provisions and then check in at the **police station** (☏ 08/8670 7805) for a report on the roads and next fuel supplies if you plan to head north towards Dalhousie Springs and the Simpson Desert (4WD only), or west to the Stuart Highway at Coober Pedy or Marla.

Dalhousie Hot Springs and desert crossings

If you don't follow the track out to the Stuart Highway, the area north of Oodnadatta is strictly for four-wheel driving, with **Dalhousie Hot Springs** in the Witjira National Park a worthwhile destination, or the **Simpson Desert** for the ultimate challenges. The route directly north, initially towards Finke and the Northern Territory, is relatively good as far as **Hamilton Homestead** (110km), though Fogarty's Claypan, over halfway, might present a sticky problem. From Hamilton the direct route east to Dalhousie Springs, shown on some maps, is now closed; take the longer route via **Eringa ruins** (160km) and **Bloods Creek bore** on the edge of **Witjira National Park**.

The Simpson Desert crossing

Crossing the approximately 550km of steep north–south dunes through the **Simpson Desert** between Dalhousie in South Australia and Birdsville in Queensland is the ultimate challenge for any off-roader; in June, 4WD groups are joined by bikes attempting to complete the punishing **Simpson Desert Cycling Classic**. In winter a steady stream of vehicles moves from west to east (the easier direction since the dunes' eastern slopes are steeper and harder to climb), but there's no help along the way, so don't underestimate the difficulties. Convoys need to include at least one skilled mechanic and, apart from the usual spares, a long-handled shovel and a strong tow-rope. While keeping weight to a minimum, you'll also need more than adequate food and water (six litres a day per person), and of course fuel – around a hundred litres of diesel if you take the shortest route, or two hundred litres of petrol. **Dune-ascent techniques** start with reducing tyre pressures to around 15psi to increase traction; select the gear and build up revs before starting. Don't attempt a gear change on the way up, and beware of oncoming vehicles on blind dune crests. If you don't make it over, slide down and try again; lighter vehicles may end up towing overburdened trucks. If all else fails, detours bypass many dunes.

The most testing, direct route follows the **French Line**, with the **Rig Road** detouring around the worst section but adding substantial distance (and fuel requirements) to the crossing. The enjoyment is mostly in the driving, though there's more than sand to look at: trees and shrubs grow in stabilized areas and at dusk you'll find dune crests patrolled by reptiles, birds, small mammals and insects. Photographers take advantage of clear skies at night to make time exposures of the stars circling the heavens. **Purni Bore**, 70km from Dalhousie, is another uncapped spout (though this may change with growing concerns over diminished ground water) where birdlife and reeds fringe a 27°C pool; camping facilities here include a shower and toilet. A post battling to stay above shifting sand at **Poeppel Corner** (269km) marks the junction of Queensland, South Australia and the Northern Territory; salt lakes here vary in their water content and sometimes have to be skirted around. After the corner the dunes become higher but further apart, separated by claypans covered in mulga and grassland; you'll have to negotiate some of **Eyre Creek**'s channels too, which can be very muddy. **Big Red**, the last dune, is also the tallest; once over this it's a clear 41-kilometre run to Birdsville.

Note: A large area of the Simpson Desert outside the Witjira National Park and the Simpson Desert Conservation Park is now a Regional Reserve under the control of the NPWS, from whom you should seek advice and a **Desert Parks Pass** before setting out. Contact the NPWS at Port Augusta (free call ☎1800 816 078), Hawker (☎08/8648 4244) or Birdsville (☎07/4656 3272).

From there you can detour 30km north to **Mount Dare Homestead** (fuel, accommodation, food and provisions; ☎08/8670 7835, ✉braithwaite10@hotmail.com; ❶–❺). In winter the homestead is busy with groups of 4WDs arriving from or departing for the desert crossing; it's at least 550km to the next fuel stop at Birdsville in Queensland. From the homestead it's a rough and bleak drive to Dalhousie Hot Springs.

The explorer Giles passed through this way in the 1870s, before the artesian basin had been extensively tapped by pastoralists, and described the scene:

> The ground we had been traversing abruptly disappeared, and we found ourselves on the brink of limestone cliffs. . . From the foot of these stretched an almost illimitable expanse of – welcome sight – waving green reeds, with large pools of water at intervals, and dotted with island cones topped with reeds or acacia bushes.

Though reeds and water are less lavishly distributed today, Giles' account still rings true. The collection of over one-hundred **mound springs** form Arabian-like oases, an impression enhanced by the green circle of date palms clustered around many of the pools. The largest spring, next to the **campsite** (which has showers and toilets), is cool enough to swim in and hot enough to unkink your back. What survives of the vegetation simmers with birdlife: budgerigars, galahs and the eye-catching purple, blue and red fairy wren. As nothing flows into the springs, the presence of **fish** – some, like the Dalhousie hardyhead, unique to the system – has prompted a variety of improbable explanations. One theory is that fish eggs were swept up in dust storms and later fell with rain at Dalhousie, but it's more likely that fish were brought in during an ancient deluge or that the population survives from when the area was an inland sea.

While the main springs area is flat and trampled by years of abuse from campers and cars – please stay on the marked paths here to avoid causing further erosion – trudging out to other groups over the salt and samphire-bush flats armed with a packed lunch and camera gives you an idea of what Giles was describing, and a good overview of the region from the top of well-formed, overgrown mounds. More views can be had from the stony hills to the west, and from **Dalhousie Homestead**, 16km south of the springs along the Pedirka road. The homestead was abandoned after the Ghan line was laid down, and today the stone walls, undermined by rabbit burrows, are gradually falling apart in the extreme climate.

TRAVEL DETAILS

Trains

Adelaide to: Alice Springs (Ghan, 2 weekly; 20hr); Melbourne (Ghan, 1 weekly, 10hr 20min; Overlander, 4 weekly; 10hr 30min); Perth (Indian Pacific, 2 weekly; 38hr); Peterborough (Indian Pacific, 2 week-ly; 4hr); Port Augusta (Ghan, 2 weekly; 4hr); Sydney (Ghan, 1 weekly, 23hr; Indian Pacific, 2 weekly; 26hr). For all trains contact Great Southern Railway (☎13 2147, 🖥www.gsr.com.au).

Buses

Adelaide to: Alice Springs (2–3 daily; 18hr 30min); Ayers Rock Resort (1 daily; 20hr); Barossa Valley (2–3 daily; 1hr 30min); Broken Hill (1 daily; 7hr); Ceduna (2 daily; 12hr); Clare (1 daily except Mon & Sat; 2hr 15min); Coober Pedy (4–5 daily; 10hr 30min); Goolwa (2–4 daily; 1hr 55min); Loxton (1 daily except Sat; 3hr 30min); Mannum (1 daily except Sat & Sun; 2hr 10min); McLaren Vale (4 daily; 50min); Melbourne (6 daily; 9hr 30min–14hr); Mount Gambier (2–4 daily; 6hr); Perth (1 daily; 34hr); Port Augusta (6–8 daily; 6hr); Port Lincoln (1–2 daily; 10hr); Renmark (2 daily; 4hr); Sydney (3 daily; 21–24hr); Victor Harbor (4 daily; 1hr 30min); Whyalla (4–6 daily; 5hr); Woomera (1–2 daily; 6hr); Yorke Peninsula (1–2 daily; 3–4hr).
Ceduna to: Adelaide (2 daily; 9hr 30min); Kalgoorlie (6 weekly; 26hr); Penong (6 weekly; 50min); Perth (6 weekly; 47hr); Port Augusta (2 daily; 5hr); Port Pirie (2 daily; 5hr 30min).

Coober Pedy to: Adelaide (at least 1 daily; 11hr); Alice Springs (at least 1 daily; 7hr); Oodnadatta (2 weekly; 5hr); Port Augusta (at least 1 daily; 6hr 10min).
Port Augusta to: Adelaide (at least 3 daily; 4hr 15min); Alice Springs (at least 1 daily; 14hr); Arkaroola (2 weekly; 7hr); Blinman (2 weekly; 3hr 15min); Ceduna (2 daily; 5hr); Coober Pedy (at least 1 daily; 6hr 10min); Hawker (3 weekly; 1hr 30min); Mambray Creek (for Mount Remarkable; several daily; 1hr); Marla (at least 1 daily; 10hr); Marree (2 weekly; 5hr); Melrose (2 weekly; 1hr); Port Lincoln (1–2 daily; 4hr 30min); Quorn (3 weekly; 40min); Roxby Downs (5 weekly; 3hr); Wilmington (2 weekly; 45min); Whyalla (1–2 daily; 50min); Wilpena Pound (3 weekly; 2hr 15min); Woomera (5 weekly; 2hr).
Port Lincoln to: Adelaide (1–2 daily; 10hr); Port Augusta (1–2 daily; 4hr 30min); Whyalla (1–2 daily; 3hr 30min).

Flights

Adelaide to: Alice Springs (2 daily; 2hr); Ayers Rock Resort (2 daily via Alice; 3hr 45min); Brisbane (5–9 daily; 4hr); Broken Hill (1–2 daily; 1hr 40min); Cairns (1 daily; 4hr); Canberra (3 daily; 3hr 10min); Ceduna (1 daily except Sat; 1hr 30min); Coober Pedy (1 daily; 1hr 30min); Darwin (2 daily; 5hr); Kangaroo Island (12 daily; 30min); Leigh Creek (1 daily Mon–Fri; 2hr), Melbourne (11 daily; 1hr); Perth (3 daily; 5hr); Port Augusta (2–3 daily Mon–Fri; 1hr); Port Lincoln (5–7 daily; 30min); Sydney (9 daily; 2hr 10min); Whyalla (1–3 daily; 45min); Woomera (1 daily Tues, Wed & Thurs; 2hr).

Ceduna to: Adelaide (8 weekly; 1hr 20min).

Coober Pedy to: Adelaide (1 daily; 2hr).

Port Lincoln to: Adelaide (6 daily; 45min).

The **Channel Mail Run** is a weekend in a light aircraft taking in 47 stops between Port Augusta and Boulia in southwestern Queensland – check latest prices at ⓦ www.asa.mtx.net/mailrun.htm, or contact Port Augusta Airport (☏ 08/8642 3100).

Melbourne and around

CHAPTER 9 # Highlights

* **Chinatown** – The low-rise, narrow streets of Melbourne's Chinatown haven't changed much since the nineteenth century when a goldrush brought every corner of the world to this cosmopolitan city. **p.905**.

* **Aussie Rules match at the MCG** – Join the cheering Melbourne crowds for an action-packed "footy" game at the MCG. **p.909**.

* **Roller blading in St Kilda** – The beachside suburb of St Kilda is an ideal place for roller blading, especially along the palm-lined boulevard. **p.918**.

* **Seal Rocks** – Sail out to Seal Rocks, part of Phillip Island Reserve, to see the largest known colony of Australian fur seals. **p.947**.

* **Yarra Valley** – Victoria's answer to South Australia's Barossa Valley boasts pretty scenery and some great wineries. **p.950**.

* **Healesville Sanctuary** – Beautifully situated wildlife sanctuary for injured and orphaned animals. **p.951**.

* **Puffing Billy through the Dandenongs** – Enjoy the quaint villages and shady forests of the Dandenong Range with a ride on the old Puffing Billy steam train. **p.952**.

9

Melbourne and around

M ost overseas visitors' impressions of a typical Aussie city are shaped by
their perception of Sydney, with its splendid harbour and exciting
energy. Unlike its kinetic northern neighbour, Australia's second city
is bound to disappoint at first glance. **Melbourne**'s location on rather
flat terrain beside a muddy river is no match for Sydney's brilliant sunsets or
stunning, smack-in-the-mouth harbour setting.

However, any initial disappointment is likely to give way to feelings of pleasant
contentment and growing curiosity once you've begun to explore the city's
streets, hidden arcades and alleyways, rested in the soothing greenery of its parks,
and ventured into vibrant and unique inner suburbs. There's a lot here that makes
Melbourne the most "English" or "European" of all Australian cities: a reasonably
cool climate (although January and February are prone to barbaric hot spells
when temperatures can climb into the forties), stately public buildings, Victorian
mansions, leafy avenues and decorative parklands. Last, but certainly not least,
Melbourne has a lively passion for eating and drinking well, a predilection for
style and elegance, and a vivid interest in intellectual debate and the arts.

Its atmosphere has been deeply influenced by migrants who arrived in waves
from southern and eastern Europe and Southeast Asia following World War II,
bringing with them cultures that have become part of the fabric of the city. In
summer, the relaxed, universal outdoor Australian way of life asserts itself with
backyard barbecue parties, riverside picnics and days on the beach. Sports too
are important – people from all walks of life show a keen interest, and, uniquely in Melbourne, "footy" (**Australian Rules Football**) has been elevated to
almost religious status.

Accommodation price codes

All the accommodation listed in this book has been categorized into one of eight price
bands, as set out below. The rates quoted represent the cheapest available double or
twin room in high season – except for category ❶, which indicates per-person rates
for a dorm bed, and the categories given for units, cabins and vans, which represent
the daily charge for the whole unit.

❶ Under $20	❸ $35–50	❺ $70–90	❼ $115–150
❷ $20–35	❹ $50–70	❻ $90–115	❽ $150 upwards

For more accommodation details, see pp.46–49.

Like its home state Victoria, Melbourne can be compared to a mosaic, and there's a challenge to every visitor to go out and experience as many facets of the city as possible. Outside the centre, this means exploring the **suburbs**, each one a little urban centre in its own right. Beaches, cafés, promenades and boutiques fringe the coast, south of the centre, while inland Victorian mansions, Vietnamese, Jewish, Greek and Italian communities, museums, art galleries and parks each make their distinct mark on the city. All are easily reached from the centre in a tram or bus, and many make great bases, offering exciting nightlife and a refreshing mix of flamboyance, seediness, industrial activity and residential tranquillity.

Owing to Melbourne's central location at the middle of Victoria's coastline excursions further out are also feasible by day-trip. The ranges in the east and northeast are covered by forests of towering eucalypts and patches of cool temperate rainforest. Closest to Melbourne are the **Dandenong Ranges**, partly suburban with quaint villages, partly covered by protected eucalypt forest. The scenic **Yarra Valley** in the northeast, Victoria's answer to South Australia's Barossa Valley, is one of many wine regions around Melbourne. To the south, huge Port Phillip Bay is encircled by the arms of the Bellarine and Mornington peninsulas. **Mornington Peninsula** offers more opportunity for wine-tasting, and in addition to bucolic scenery there are beaches galore, the windswept ones at the ocean coast popular with surfers, while the placid waters of the bay are good for swimming and messing about in boats. While **Geelong** and most of the Bellarine Peninsula are not quite so captivating, Queenscliff near the narrow entrance to Port Phillip Bay, with its beautiful, refurbished grand hotels from the Victorian era is enjoying something of a comeback as a stylish (and expensive) weekend getaway.

Melbourne

MELBOURNE is Australia's second-largest city, with a population of around three million – about half a million less than Sydney. Rivalry between the two cities – in every sphere from cricket to business – is on an almost childish level. In purely monetary terms, Sydney is now clearly in the ascendancy, having stolen a march on Melbourne as the nation's financial centre. The state government, led by Steve Bracks of the Labor Party, has continued the work of former premier Jeff Kennett, who tried and mostly succeeded in lifting the economy out of the doldrums in the 1990s, mainly by severe cutbacks or privatization of public services and of previously state-run utilities boards. While Kennett's fiscal puritanism definitely scored points by reducing public debt and improving the credit rating of the state, critics were quick to counter that outsourcing or privatizing public services did not necessarily translate into greater efficiency and even more importantly that Victoria's economic growth has been achieved at a very high social cost – wealth is now more unevenly distributed, with increasing numbers of homeless people and drug addicts on the streets. In 1999, Kennett surprisingly lost the "unloseable election" to rank outsider Bracks, largely because his government neglected rural Victoria – Kennett once memorably described Melbourne as the vital heart of the state and rural towns as the "toenails" – but also because Kennett's election campaign focused almost entirely on his autocratic style of leadership, which proved a big turn-off for voters. Since seizing the reins of power, Steve Bracks has enjoyed a remarkably high standing in the polls, and his style is more inclusive and less confrontational than his predecessor. He has also concentrated his party's efforts on improving the key areas of health and education, as well as providing greater funding for rural areas.

However, Melburninans never tire of pointing out, in all modesty, that they have the incredible fortune to inhabit "one of the world's most liveable cities". Melbourne may lack a truly stunning natural setting or "in-your-face" sights, but with its subtle charms it is a city that grows on you, one that is undeniably a very pleasant place to live, and enjoyable to visit too. Magnificent landscaped gardens and parks in the English style provide green spaces near the centre, while beneath the skyscrapers of the **Central Business District** (CBD), an understorey of solid, Victorian-era facades ranged along tree-lined boulevards present the city on a more human scale. The air of approachability is further enhanced by the numerous arcades, lanes and alleyways in which are hidden some of the country's best cafés, pubs and speciality shops.

An extensive and ambitious redevelopment programme, begun during Kennett's tenure, continues apace and has markedly changed the feel of the city – if only by the sheer magnitude of the projects. This new Melbourne for the millennium has meant a host of public buildings, as well as the new **Federation Square** by the Yarra just south of the CBD, were completed in 2001 to celebrate the centenary of the Australian federation, and the redevelopment of the **Docklands** precinct west of the CBD is planned for the next decade. From this area of unused docks and rotting old warehouses a brand new city will rise, complete with hotels, office and apartment buildings, department stores, marinas and other leisure facilities. This, if nothing else, will at long last put Ava Gardner's much cited – but erroneously so – remark from 1959 to rest. She came here to film *On the Beach* and reputedly summed up her impression: "It's a story about the end of the world, and Melbourne sure is the right place to film it." A great line, but in fact the celebrated swipe was coined by Melbourne journalist Neil Jillet.

Actually, change came to Melbourne way before the Nineties. Large-scale immigration since World War II has, in a sense, brought the world to Melbourne, shaking up the formerly self-absorbed, parochial WASP mindset for good. Whole villages have come here from Lebanon, Turkey, Vietnam and all over Europe, most especially from Greece, furnishing the well-worn statistic that Melbourne is the third-largest Greek city behind Athens and Thessaloniki. The **European** influence is perhaps most obvious in winter, as trams rattle past warm cafés and bookshops, and promenaders dress stylishly against the chill. Not surprisingly, the immigrant blend has transformed the city into a foodie mecca, where tucking into a different cuisine each night – or new hybrids of East, West and South – is one of the great treats. **Sport** too, especially Australian Rules Football, is almost a religion here. The Melbourne Cup in November is a public holiday celebrated with gusto, and the city's collection of fine sporting venues are well used. Melbourne's strong claim to being the nation's **cultural capital** is well-founded: laced with a healthy dash of counterculture, Melbourne's artistic life flourishes, culminating in the highbrow Melbourne Festival in the last two weeks in October, and its slightly more offbeat (and shoestring) cousin, the Fringe Festival. The city also takes pride in its leading role in Australian literary life, based around the Writers' Festival in August. Throughout the year, there are heavyweight seasons of classical music and theatre, a wacky array of small galleries, and enough art-house movies to last a lifetime.

Arrival and information

Melbourne's **Tullamarine Airport** is 22km northwest of the city on the Tullamarine Freeway; the Skybus service (from the airport every 30min between 6.40am and 11.40pm, then hourly until 6.40am; $11; ✆ 03/9662 9275) will take you to the Melbourne Transit Centre (Greyhound Pioneer Bus Terminal), the Spencer Street Railway Station and Bus Terminal, Town Hall and Exhibition Street (the night services between 12.40am and 4.40am run to the Town Hall only). On weekdays (7.40am–4.10pm), Saturday (8.10am–12.40pm) and Sunday (1.40–5.30pm), the bus driver will drop you off at most city hotels on request. A **taxi** from the airport costs around $30 to the city centre, $40 to St Kilda.

Greyhound Pioneer buses arrive at the **Melbourne Transit Centre** on the north side of the city centre at 58 Franklin St, whereas McCafferty's, Firefly and V/Line use the **Spencer Street Bus Terminal** on the west side. **Spencer Street Railway Station** nearby handles country and interstate trains. Some hostels pick up from these terminals, as well as from the Tasmanian ferry terminal.

About 4km southwest of the city centre, the **ferry terminal** is served by the #109 tram to Collins Street in the CBD. Skybus also runs a service to ferries to Tasmania which dock at Station Pier in Port Melbourne, departing from Melbourne Transit Centre at 3.45pm, and from Spencer Street Railway Station and Bus Terminal, bus bay #45, at 4pm ($4.40); *Spirit of Tasmania* sails year round (departures Mon, Wed and Fri evenings), while *Devil Cat* operates between December and April (daily departures during peak season, four per week at other times).

Information

The **Victoria Visitor Information Centre** is housed in the Town Hall on Swanston Street, corner of Little Collins Street (Mon–Fri 9am–6pm, Sat & Sun 9am–5pm; ℡03/9658 9955 or 13 2842; transport, tour and accommodation **telephone-booking service** is available through AUSRES: Mon–Fri 9am–6pm, Sat, Sun & public holidays 9am–5pm; ℡03/9650 1522). There are free pamphlets galore although some, such as the *Golden Mile Heritage Walk* ($2) describing **self-guided walking tours** to many of Melbourne's older attractions, attract a small charge. Next to the information centre is the **City Experience Centre** (Mon–Fri 9am–6pm, Sat, Sun & public holidays 9am–5pm), which has up-to-date information on Melbourne, in particular on events and activities around town, provided by helpful staff, or from videos, touch-screens and permanent displays. Of special interest is the Centre's free **Greeter Service** (℡03/9658 9955, ℻9650 6168, ✉greeter@melbourne .vic.gov.au), whereby visitors are matched up for two to four hours with local volunteers according to language and interests, which gives you an unparalleled insider's viewpoint, though you need to book at least three days in advance. **Information Victoria**, at 356 Collins St (Mon–Fri 8.30am–5.30pm; ℡1300/366 356), has free maps and brochures, as well as a notice board of city events and a shop selling the city's largest range of local maps, while **Victoria Tourism** (daily 8am–6pm; ℡13 2842, ⊛www.visitvictoria.com) is a phone-only service providing information on attractions, accommodation and upcoming events.

Around the city are two volunteer-staffed **Visitor Information Booths**, in the middle of Bourke Street Mall (Mon–Thurs 9am–5pm, Fri 9am–7pm, Sat 10am–4pm, Sun 11am–4pm) and Flinders Street Station (same opening times except Fri until 5pm). An interactive touch-screen terminal, where you can look up anything from a cab phone number to a Chinese restaurant, is located on Collins Street outside the Sportsgirl Centre (between Swanston and Elizabeth streets).

Alternative sources of information include the **NRE Information Centre**, 8 Nicholson St, East Melbourne, run by the Department of Natural Resources and Environment (Mon–Fri 9am–5.30pm; ℡03/9637 8080, ⊛www.nre.vic .gov.au); and **Parks Victoria** (telephone information service only ℡13 1963, ⊛www.parkweb.vic.gov.au). Both dispense information about national parks and conservation areas in Victoria. Another good resource is the **National Trust** office, Tasma Terrace, 6 Parliament Place (Mon–Fri 9am–5pm;

CENTRAL MELBOURNE

GRATTAN STREET

PELHAM STREET

ELIZABETH STREET

LEICESTER STREET

BOUVERIE STREET

SWANSTON STREET

CARDIGAN STREET

LYGON STREET

QUEENSBERRY STREET

ERROL STREET

LEVESON STREET

CHETWYND STREET

HOWARD STREET

CAPEL STREET

PEEL STREET

VICTORIA STREET

KING STREET

Queen Victoria Market

QUEEN STREET

Melbourne Transit Centre

FRANKLIN STREET

City Baths

Old Melbourne Gaol

FRANKLIN ST

Flagstaff Gardens

LATROBE STREET

Melbourne Central Station

State Library

SWANSTON STREET WALK

Flagstaff Station

LITTLE LONSDALE STREET

LONSDALE STREET

HARDWARE ST

Law Courts

WILLIAM STREET

QUEEN STREET

ELIZABETH STREET

RACV

Victoria Visitor Information Centre

LITTLE BOURKE STREET

BOURKE STREET (MALL)

ROYAL ARCADE

BLOCK ARCADE

Melbourne Town Hall

CITY SQUARE

Spencer Street Bus Terminal

Pedestrian Bridge

Colonial Stadium

Colonial Stadium

SPENCER STREET

KING STREET

Information Victoria

LITTLE COLLINS STREET

BANK PL

COLLINS STREET

FLINDERS LANE

Young and Jackson's

Stock Exchange

Immigration Museum and Hellenic Antiquities Museum

FLINDERS STREET

Flinders Street Station

Spencer Street Station

N

Rialto Towers (Observation Deck)

Melbourne Aquarium

Yarra River

SOUTHBANK

Southgate Centre

Victorian Arts Centre

World Trade Centre

SOUTHBANK

Polly Woodside Maritime Museum

Melbourne Exhibition Centre

Crown Casino Complex

- - - Tram routes

Pedestrianised street

(34), CUB Malthouse & Australian Centre for Contemporary Art

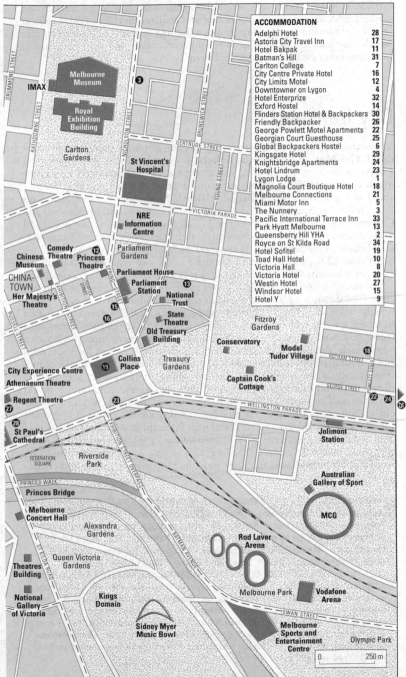

ACCOMMODATION

Adelphi Hotel	28
Astoria City Travel Inn	17
Hotel Bakpak	11
Batman's Hill	31
Carlton College	7
City Centre Private Hotel	16
City Limits Motel	12
Downtowner on Lygon	4
Hotel Enterprize	32
Exford Hostel	14
Flinders Station Hotel & Backpackers	30
Friendly Backpacker	26
George Powlett Motel Apartments	22
Georgian Court Guesthouse	25
Global Backpackers Hostel	6
Kingsgate Hotel	29
Knightsbridge Apartments	24
Hotel Lindrum	23
Lygon Lodge	1
Magnolia Court Boutique Hotel	18
Melbourne Connections	21
Miami Motor Inn	5
The Nunnery	3
Pacific International Terrace Inn	33
Park Hyatt Melbourne	13
Queensberry Hill YHA	2
Royce on St Kilda Road	34
Hotel Sofitel	19
Toad Hall Hotel	10
Victoria Hall	8
Victoria Hotel	20
Westin Hotel	27
Windsor Hotel	15
Hotel Y	9

Shrine of Remembrance, Royal Botanic Gardens, Government House & Observatory Gate

ⓣ03/9654 4711), which sells several historical walking-tour guides. *Melway,* available from all newsagents, is the best **street directory**. The Friday edition of *The Age* contains an excellent pull-out **listings** section, "EG", detailing the week's entertainment as well as fairs and markets, art and craft exhibitions, sport, and other events in and around town.

City transport

Melbourne's efficient public transport system of trams, trains and buses is called **The Met**, and a range of **tickets** is available. Unless you're going on a day-trip to the outer suburbs, you can get anywhere you need to go, including St Kilda and Williamstown, on a zone 1 ticket. A ticket covering zones 1 and 2 will get you as far as Brighton Beach, Sandringham and Carrum on Port Phillip Bay, Springvale and Glen Waverley in the southeast, Alamein and Canterbury in the east, and to the end of all Met train lines in the north and west. Zone 3 includes the "far east" and "far south-east" – Frankston, Cranbourne, Ferntree Gully, Ringwood and Lilydale. An ordinary zone 1 ticket costs $2.60, a short hop $1.90; these tickets are valid for two hours, or all night if bought after 7pm. A day-ticket ($5 for zone 1; $8 for zones 1 and 2; $10.80 for zones 1, 2 and 3) is better value if you're making a few trips in zone 1, or if you are planning a trip to the outer suburbs. For longer stays, a weekly ticket ($21.70) is an even better bargain. The Metcard automated ticketing system, which operates on all services in the metropolitan area, means you need to validate your ticket by machine every time you board a new vehicle. Vending machines on board trams supply tickets for short trips and two hours; these and day-tickets are also available from vending machines at train stations, buses (a limited selection only), the City Met Shop at 103 Elizabeth St and other selected shops (most newsagents, some milk bars and pharmacies). The supposedly smooth-running system has its hiccups, such as out-of-order coin machines, fare dodgers, and ticket inspectors riding trams and blocking station exits in an attempt to catch them. Melbourne's beloved tram conductors, who were officially phased out in 1998, reappeared in 2001, with one hundred "connies" selling tickets (more expensive than those bought at newsagents and the like), providing travel information and checking for fare evasion.

Melbourne's vintage trams

Some of the trams traversing Melbourne's streets on a daily basis are vintage wooden ones. None is quite as old as the system, which dates from 1885, but a few from the 1930s are still in use. Vintage **City Circle trams** (free) run in a loop along Flinders Street, Spring Street, Latrobe Street and Spencer Street (every 20min: Mon–Fri 10am–3pm, Sat & Sun 10am–6pm). The **Colonial Tramcar Restaurant** (ⓣ03/9696 4000) is a converted 1927 tram offering traditional silver- and white-linen restaurant service as you trundle around Melbourne. Operating daily, the restaurant (non-smoking) offers a three-course early dinner (5.45–7.15pm; $66) and a five-course dinner ($104.50 Fri & Sat, $93.50 other nights), plus a four-course lunch (Sun 1–3pm and other days subject to demand; $71.50). All drinks are included. Make reservations as early as possible – Friday and Saturday evenings can be booked up two months in advance.

Driving in Melbourne requires some care, mainly because of the trams. You can overtake a tram only on the left and must stop and wait behind it while passengers get on and off, as they step directly into the road (there's no need to stop if there's a central pedestrian island). A peculiar rule has developed to accommodate trams at major intersections in the city centre: when turning right, you pull over to the left-hand lane and wait for the lights to change to amber before turning – a so-called "hook turn". Signs overhead indicate when this rule applies.

Cyclists should also watch out for tram lines – tyres can easily get wedged in them. This apart, Melbourne is perfect for cycling and you'll be in good company as it's a popular way of getting around. The friendly staff at Bicycle Victoria, 19 O'Connell St, North Melbourne (Mon–Fri 8.45am–5.15pm; ☎ 03/9328 3000), assist with practical information and hand out *The Great Rides Wall Planner* listing their organized bike rides in Victoria and interstate; cycle enthusiasts might also want to buy a copy of the booklet *Discovering Victoria's Bike Paths* ($18.95), available at Bicycle Victoria or at newsagents. See "Listings", p.937, for **bike rental**.

Services operate Monday to Saturday from 5am until midnight, and Sunday from 8am until 11pm, supplemented in the early hours of Saturday and Sunday by **NightRider buses** (every 60min 12.30–4.30am; $5), which head from the City Square (in front of the new *Westin Hotel* – see p.897) on Swanston Street to the outer suburbs, more or less in the same direction as the suburban train routes. Each bus has an onboard mobile phone, on which the driver can book a taxi to meet you at a bus stop (free call), or you can call a friend ($1) to meet you. For further information, call the **Met Transport Information Centre** (daily 6am–midnight; ☎ 13 1638; for a range of public transport information including timetables and disability services, visit ⓦ www.victrip.com.au).

Trams

Melbourne's **trams** give the city a distinctive character and provide a pleasant, environmentally friendly way of getting around: the **City Circle** (see box opposite) is particularly convenient, and free. Trams run down the centre of the road, and stops are signposted (the "Central Melbourne" map on pp.892–893 shows the main routes in the centre); they often have central islands where you can wait, but if not, take care crossing the road. It can be uncomfortable waiting in the middle of a busy road, especially for a woman alone at night – you may feel less vulnerable waiting on the footpath, where there's often a shelter anyway. Some trams can be boarded only at the front; others also have access via middle and rear doors. A fleet of modern, low-floor, European-style trams was introduced in 2001, providing improved access for people with disabilities.

Trains

Trains are the fastest way to reach distant suburbs. An underground loop system feeding into seventeen suburban lines connects the city centre's five train **stations**: **Spencer Street**, which also serves as the station for interstate and country trains; **Flagstaff** on the corner of Latrobe and William streets; **Melbourne Central** on the corner of Swanston and Latrobe streets; **Parliament** on Spring Street; and **Flinders Street**. The last is the main suburban station, with its clocks detailing the times of all train departures ("under the clocks" is a traditional Melbourne meeting place). Bikes can be carried free, except during peak periods (Mon–Fri 7–9.30am & 4–6pm), when an extra adult concession fee has to be paid. Surfboards can also be brought on board, for which an extra adult concession fee is payable.

Buses

Regular **buses** often run on the same routes as trams as well as filling gaps where no train or tram lines run, but they are likely to be the least useful mode of public transport for visitors. However, the **City Explorer** might be the easy answer to sightseeing headaches – and footaches. The red double-decker (ⓣ03/9650 7000, ⓕ9650 7033; every 60min 10am–4pm), tickets for which should be bought on-board (day-ticket $24.50, two-day ticket $38.50) does circuits of the city, starting from Melbourne Town Hall and running past the Rialto Observation Deck and the Polly Woodside Maritime Museum to the Arts Centre south of the CBD, then back up the eastern side of the city to Lygon Street, the Zoo, Queen Victoria Market and Melbourne Central. Passengers can stay on the bus and use it as a sightseeing tour, or jump off and reboard later. The same company also runs very inexpensive night tours, shopping tours, tours of the city including sites and meals, and half- and full-day sightseeing tours going out to Melbourne's suburbs.

Accommodation

When looking for somewhere to stay in Melbourne, the most obvious areas to head for are the **city centre** (and the adjoining suburbs of **North Melbourne**, **Carlton**, **Fitzroy** and **East Melbourne**) and down by the sea around **St Kilda**. Some of the cheap accommodation areas on the fringes of the city centre are fairly dead at night, though they are within easy reach of all the action. St Kilda is very lively, if a bit rough around the edges, with an abundance of hostels and inexpensive hotels and motels. **Richmond**, **South Melbourne** and **South Yarra** offer a good compromise, handy for both the centre and St Kilda's nightlife, and with enough tasty eating options of their own to keep you going (see map of "Melbourne Suburbs" on p.915).

The most exclusive **hotels** are downtown (particularly around Collins Street) and the leisure precincts of Southgate and the Crown Casino, while there's a collection of large and recently revamped hotels around Spencer Street Station. Melbourne has plenty of **backpacker accommodation**, ranging from fairly basic, even scruffy places to salubrious Victorian-era mansions with dorms attached. Hostel beds can go as low as $16 (in winter), though the average for a dorm bed is around $20. **Campsite** cabins and vans are an alternative worth considering for those with their own transport (see p.901). An excellent resource for budget accommodation in Melbourne is ⓦwww.yha.com, while ⓦwww.wotif.com is where you can book last-minute, **discounted accommodation** in the city.

City centre

Hotels and motels

Adelphi Hotel, 187 Flinders Lane (ⓣ03/9650 7555, ⓕ9650 2710, ⓔinfo@adelphi.com.au). This stylish hotel has a striking exterior and a sparse, ultramodern interior design that extends to the large guestrooms, all topped with a huge pool on the roof. ❽

Astoria City Travel Inn, 288 Spencer St (ⓣ03/9670 6801, ⓕ9670 3034, ⓔastoria@pow- ernet.com.au). Pleasant motel three blocks north of Spencer Street Station with spacious and bright units. In-house amenities include a saltwater pool and laundry. ❻

Batman's Hill, 66 Spencer St (ⓣ03/9614 6344 or free call 1800 335 308, ⓕ9614 1189, ⓦwww.batmanshill.com). An elegant Edwardian exterior belies a functional and modern interior. A wide range of facilities includes bars, a restaurant and 24hr room service, and it's handy for Spencer Street Station and the Casino Entertainment Complex just south of the river. ⑧

City Limits Motel, 20 Little Bourke St (☎03/9662 2544 or free call 1800 808 651, ⓕ9662 2287; ⓦwww.citylimits.com.au). Motel-style units with en suite and the usual mod-cons on a quiet street just around the corner from Parliament station. Rates include breakfast. ⑥–⑦

Hotel Enterprize, 44 Spencer St (☎03/9629 6991 or free call 1800 033 451, ⓕ9614 7963, ⓔentrpriz@ozemail.com.au). Solid hotel in central location opposite Spencer Street Station. Good, no-frills singles and doubles (en suites available). Room service and undercover parking ($5 per day) available. ⑥–⑦

Kingsgate Hotel, 131 King St (☎03/9629 4171 or 1300/734 171, ⓕ9629 7110, ⓦwww.kingsgatehotel.com.au). Huge, renovated old private hotel. En-suite rooms with colour TV, heating, air-con and telephone are good value; there are also inexpensive no-frills budget rooms with shared facilities, a few rooms for small groups or families (up to four beds), a laundry and a pleasant TV lounge, but no kitchen facilities. Bar and café on premises. Cheap breakfast available. ④–⑤

Hotel Lindrum, 26 Flinders St (☎03/9668 1111, ⓕ9668 1199, ⓦwww.hotellindrum.com.au). Intimate five-storey boutique hotel named after the legendary Australian billiards player Walter Lindrum. The lobby has large comfy chairs, an open fireplace and books, and instead of a formal reception you register at the front bar. Apart from a billiard table and lots of Lindrum memorabilia, you'll find a back bar with a selection of wines and cigars, and rooms complete with huge beds, fax, CD player and complimentary in-house movies. ⑧

Miami Motor Inn, 13 Hawke St, off the north end of King St (☎03/9329 8499 or free call 1800 132 333, ⓕ9328 1820, ⓦwww.themiami.com.au). Renovated en-suite rooms with TV, wardrobe and ceiling fan as well as simple, clean, standard rooms with shared facilities – good-value rates include a cooked breakfast. TV lounge, pool table, laundry and free off-street parking; no kitchen. ④–⑥

Pacific International Terrace Inn, 16 Spencer St (☎03/9621 3333 or free call 1800 816 168, ⓕ9621 1922, ⓦwww.pacifichotels.com.au). Popular with business people, this very pleasant, well-maintained hotel constitutes good value, offering B&B, en-suite rooms, elegant breakfast room, bar, restaurant and other facilities. ⑧

Park Hyatt Melbourne, 1 Parliament Square, off Parliament Place (☎03/9224 1234, ⓕ9224 1200,

ⓦhttp://melbourne.hyatt.com). This opulent bunker for business travellers and Melbourne's junior moguls has deluxe rooms and suites with lush trimmings, such as open fireplaces and spa baths with TV. The service, naturally, is first class. ⑧

Royce on St Kilda Road, 379 St Kilda Rd (☎03/9677 9900, ⓕ9677 9922, ⓔreservations@roycehotels.com.au). This luxury boutique establishment is usefully positioned within walking distance of the CBD, Royal Botanic Gardens, Shrine of Remembrance and Arts Centre. There's a variety of room types available, from mezzanines with a ground-level lounge to deluxe spa rooms and rooms with balconies. All have the usual trimmings, plus there are dataport connections and ISDN. ⑧

Hotel Sofitel, 25 Collins St (☎03/9653 0000, ⓕ9650 4261, ⓦwww.sofitelmelbourne.com.au). I.M. Pei-designed hotel with marvellous views across Melbourne and surrounds. Gloriously comfortable rooms, which begin on the 36th floor, as well as a good spread of cafés and restaurants, including the airy and reasonably cheap *Cafe La* (see p.921) and *Le Restaurant* (see p.922), a formal dining place with sensational vistas. ⑧

Victoria Hotel, 215 Little Collins St (☎03/9653 0441 or free call 1800 331 147, ⓕ9650 9678, ⓦwww.victoriahotel.com.au). Huge, old, but refurbished hotel in an unbeatable central location, with its own café and bar; all rooms – with or without their own bathrooms – have telephones, heating, tea and coffee-making facilities. Undercover parking available ($6 per day). ⑥–⑧

Westin Hotel, 205 Collins St (☎03/9635 2222, ⓕ9635 2333, ⓦwww.westin.com.au). Plonked squarely on the City Square, the monstrously huge and hideous exterior of this new 260-room hotel hides surprisingly glamorous interiors and rooms noticeable for their understated elegance. ⑧

Windsor Hotel, 103 Spring St (☎03/9633 6000 or free call 1800 033 100, ⓕ9633 6001, ⓦwww.thewindsor.com.au). This opulent Victorian-era hotel, a landmark opposite Parliament House, is classified by the National Trust. ⑧

Hostels and budget accommodation

Hotel Bakpak, 167 Franklin St (☎03/9329 7525 or free call 1800 645 200, ⓕ9326 7667, ⓦwww.bak-pak.com). A happening place with lots of activity and information. Hundreds of beds in a converted former school building brightened up with colour co-ordinated paintwork, carpets and polished timber. Standard facilities plus in-house employment agency, travel shop, small gym, basement bar, internet café, cinema and a rooftop terrace with a tiny pool and great views of the city, and dorms with four to twelve beds (separate men's and women's dorms available on request), fans and lockers; doubles are spartan. Rooms ❹, dorms ❶–❷

City Centre Private Hotel, 22 Little Collins St (T 03/9654 5401, F 9650 7256). Good position on a quiet street 100m from Parliament Station. Inexpensive doubles, singles and a few dorms (mainly four beds, usually separate for males/females), all sharing bathrooms. Most rooms have fridges; other facilities include heating, basic kitchens, a TV lounge, laundry and car parking. Rooms ❸–❹, dorms ❶

Exford Hotel, 199 Russell St (T 03/9663 2697, F 9663 2248, W www.exfordhotel.com.au). In an extremely central position above a refurbished pub, this hostel is secure and clean, with friendly and helpful staff. Usual amenities, plus a tiny sun deck with BBQ. Two- to four bed dorms, (separate for women on request). Twins and doubles are good value. Rooms ❹, dorms ❶–❷

Flinders Station Hotel & Backpackers, 35 Elizabeth St (T 03/9620 5100, F 9620 5101, W www.flindersbackpackers.com.au). Reasonably well-organized hostel in a former office building, centrally located a few hundred metres from Flinders Street Station. Basic twins and doubles, and two en-suite doubles for wheelchair users. Dorms have lockers and are mainly four-bed, though a few have up to ten beds (separate men's and women's dorms available on request). Rooms ❹–❺, dorms ❶–❷

Friendly Backpacker, 197 King St (T 03/9670 1111 or free call 1800 671 115, F 9670 9911, E friendlybackpacker@optusnet.com.au). New hostel in refurbished office building lives up to its name and is clean and secure: bright rooms (with air-con and heating) are used as dorms (mainly four beds; some women-only); each floor has a

cosy sitting area with TV. Good kitchen and common room in the basement. Dorms ❶

The Greenhouse Backpacker, 228 Flinders Lane (T 03/9639 6400, F 9639 6900, E friendlybpacker@optusnet.com.au). Superb location amidst the characterful alleys and laneways of Melbourne's CBD. Clean and secure singles, doubles and dorms, plus there's a range of free services – from pick-ups and employment assistance to luggage storage and as much tea and coffee as you can drink. Rooms ❸–❹, dorms ❷

Melbourne Connections, 205 King St (T 03/9642 4464, F 9642 0643, E marspike@bigpond.com). Convenient though hard-to-find location close to Spencer Street Station and Victoria Market. Rooms and dorms are clean; facilities include laundry, kitchen and lounge with satellite TV. Rooms ❸, dorms ❶

Toad Hall Hotel, 441 Elizabeth St (T 03/9600 9010, F 9600 9013, W www.toadhall-hotel.com.au). Excellent choice close to Melbourne Transit Centre: friendly, cosy, secure and clean, with good facilities. Pleasant courtyard out the back; off-street car parking available ($6 per day). Rooms ❹, dorms ❷

Victoria Hall, 380 Russell St (T 03/9662 3888, F 9639 0101, W www.victoriahall.com.au). Centrally located international student accommodation, but accepts budget travellers from the end of November until the end of February. Great value twins and singles. Rooms ❹

Hotel Y, 489 Elizabeth St (T 03/9329 5188, F 9329 1469, or call central YWCA reservations on free call T 1800 249 124, W www.ywca.net). Close to Melbourne Transit Centre and Victoria Market; simple en-suite standard rooms, and deluxe rooms with fridge, telephone, air-con and colour TV. The few dorms are overpriced. Limited kitchen facilities in bright, spacious common room; laundry also available. Rooms ❻–❼, dorms ❷

North Melbourne, Carlton and Fitzroy

Carlton College, 101 Drummond St, Carlton (T 03/9664 0664 or free call 1800 066 551, F 9639 2165, W www.carltoncollege.com.au). Ideally located near the Lygon St cafés and shops, this student accommodation in Italianate terraces turns into a backpackers' hostel from mid-November to the end of February. The small dorms, singles, twins and doubles are simple, but excellent value. Rooms ❷–❸, dorms ❶

Chapman Gardens YHA, 76 Chapman St, North Melbourne (T 03/9328 3595, F 9329 7863, W www.yha.com.au). More intimate than its sister

hostel, the *Queensberry Hill YHA*, but further away from the city centre (3km) – take tram #50, #57 or #59 north from Elizabeth St. Mainly twins, a few singles, doubles and dorms (four beds); car parking available and free use of bicycles. Skybus drops off and picks up 50m from here. Reception for new guests staffed 7.30am–12.30pm & 2–10pm. Rooms ❶

Downtowner on Lygon, 66 Lygon St, Carlton (T 03/9663 5555 or free call 1800 800 130, F 9662 3308, W www.downtowner.com.au). Attractively refurbished rooms with all mod cons (some with spa) in the heart of Carlton. Undercover parking. **7**–**8**

Global Backpackers Hostel, 238 Victoria St, North Melbourne (T 03/9328 3728, F 9329 8966). Small, basic hostel opposite Victoria Market, preferably for people who don't mind loud music as the pub next door features indie and heavy-metal bands. Shared facilities. Rooms **2**–**3**, dorms **1**

Lygon Lodge, 220 Lygon St, Carlton (T 03/9663 6633, F 9663 7297). Good motel in central Carlton; attractive rooms, some with small kitchenette. Undercover car parking. **7**

The Nunnery, 116 Nicholson St, Fitzroy (T 03/9419 8637 or free call 1800 032 635, F 9417 7736; take #96 tram from Bourke St). Half of this ex-convent is an attractive guesthouse, half a not-so-special hostel with rather crammed

dorms. A small courtyard and a tiny rooftop are the only outdoor sitting areas, but the atmosphere is busy and friendly; there's also a big, cosy TV lounge, a kitchen and internet facilities. Two doors away is a great pub, and Brunswick St cafés are within five-minutes' walk. Rooms **4**, dorms **1**–**2**

Queensberry Hill YHA, 78 Howard St, off Victoria St (T 03/9329 8599, F 9326 8427, W www.yha.com.au). Ultramodern, huge hostel – more like a smart hotel – with family rooms, double rooms and dorms (4–8 beds), as well as cafeteria, TV rooms, a huge, well-equipped kitchen and an in-house travel agent. The office is open 7am to 11pm, but access is 24hr. An easy 10min walk from Melbourne Transit Centre; Skybus will drop off here and pick up every half hour. Free use of bicycles. Rooms **4**, dorms **1**–**2**

East Melbourne

George Powlett Motel Apartments, Powlett St, cnr George St, East Melbourne (T 03/9419 9488 or free call 1800 689 948, F 9419 0806, W www.georgepowlett.com.au). Motel-style units off two central courtyards. All mod cons, including parking. Central location. **6**–**7**

Georgian Court Guesthouse, 21–25 George St, East Melbourne (T 03/9419 6353, F 9416 0895). Standard rooms with shared facilities, and en-suite rooms equipped with colour TV, fridge and radio; all are bright, tastefully furnished and serviced daily. Rates include light breakfast. Quiet yet very central location. **5**–**6**

Knightsbridge Apartments, 101 George St, East

Melbourne (T 03/9419 1333, F 9486 0861, W www.knightsbridgeapartments.com.au). Bright, serviced self-catering studio apartments 1km from the centre, on a quiet street running off the east side of Fitzroy Gardens. Laundry and off-street parking. Excellent value. **7**–**8**

Magnolia Court Boutique Hotel, 101 Powlett St, East Melbourne (T 03/9419 4222, F 9416 0841, W www.magnolia-court.com.au). Elegant hotel in a quiet street, but within walking distance of Fitzroy Gardens, the city, the MCG and the Rod Laver Arena in Melbourne Park. Very tastefully furnished rooms with all facilities in two older, lovingly restored buildings and in a motel section. Breakfast available. **7**–**8**

South Melbourne, Richmond, Albert Park and South Yarra

Beach House Hotel, 97 Beaconsfield Parade, Albert Park (T 03/9690 4642, F 9690 4062, E beach.house@alhgroup.com.au). Pub accommodation in renovated, bright and clean rooms with polished floorboards. Front rooms have great views over the beach and Port Phillip Bay, but get a bit of traffic noise. Shared facilities. Next to a tram stop (take #1 or #2 from Swanston St to South Melbourne Beach) and very close to the Tasmanian ferry terminal. **3**–**5**

Central Accommodation, 21 Bromham Place, Richmond (T 03/9427 9826, F 9427 9001). Luxury apartments converted into a small hostel – not spotlessly tidy, but with a homely, very friendly atmosphere. Four- and six-bed dorms (one women-only) plus a few double rooms. Central location close to the main drags of Church St and

Bridge Rd with their great pubs and shops, and within walking distance of MCG and Melbourne Park (15–20min). Owners have good employment contacts in the area. Pick-up from the airport, bus terminals or the Tasmanian ferry. Take tram #75 or #48 from Spencer St or Flinders St to stop no. 18. Dorms **1**

Chapel Street Backpackers, 22 Chapel St, Windsor (T 03/9533 6855 or free call 1800 613 333, F 9533 6866, W www.csbackpackers.com.au). Small and very clean nonsmoking hostel at the southern, quieter end of Chapel St. Some of the dorms (four–eight beds; women-only available) and doubles are en suite. All rates include a continental breakfast. Opposite Windsor Station (Sandringham line). Rooms **4**–**5**, dorms **1**–**2**

The Como, 630 Chapel St, South Yarra
(☎ 03/9824 0400, ℻ 9824 1263, ⓦ www.hotelco-
mo.com.au) Formerly the *Hotel Como*, this upmarket pile has undergone a nip and tuck and several
layers of slap, which should please visiting celebs
who seem to stay here in droves. Rooms are generously spacious, and feature the usual facilities,
not to mention unusually bold colours and CD
players. Special offers abound, such as free bike
rental during winter, while the overhaul has seen
the revamp of the former lounge bar into trendy
SO Bar (Mon–Thurs 4pm–midnight, Fri & Sat
4pm–3am, Sun 4–10pm), where jazz is performed
every Friday night. ❽

The Hatton Hotel, 65 Park St, South Yarra
(☎ 03/9868 4800, ℻ 9868 4899, ⓦ www.hatton
.com.au). Modern boutique hotel with 32 rooms,
each immaculately arranged. ❽

Lords Lodge Backpackers, 204 Punt Rd, cnr
Greville St, South Yarra (☎ 03/9510 5658, ℻ 9533
6663). Small, family-run, nonsmoking hostel in an
old mansion, centrally positioned in a fashionable
area. Singles, doubles and triples, as well as medium-size dorms (some women-only), each with a
fridge and lockers. Owners have good work contacts in and around Prahran. Take tram #3, #5, #6
or #16 from Swanston St and get off at stop no.
26, or take the Sandringham line train to Prahran
Railway Station. Pick-up from airport and bus terminals on request. Rooms ❷–❸, dorms ❶

Middle Park Hotel, 102 Canterbury Rd, cnr
Armstrong St, Middle Park (☎ 03/9690 1882,
℻ 9645 8928). Dorms and simple but pleasant
rooms with shared facilities above refurbished
pub. Take tram #96 from Spencer St. Close to
Aquatic Centre, beach and lots of restaurants and
delis. Rooms ❸, dorms ❶

Nomads Market Inn, 115 Cecil St, South
Melbourne (☎ 03/9690 2220 or free call 1800 689
948, ℻ 9690 2544). Small, clean hostel with lots
of atmosphere, above a pub opposite South
Melbourne Market. Pick-up from bus terminals in
the city, and lots of freebies: BBQs on Sunday,

bicycles, even the first beer. Rooms ❹, dorms ❶

Pint on Punt, 42 Punt Rd, Windsor (☎ 03/9510
4273 or free call 1800 835 000, ℻ 9529 5518,
ⓦ www.pintonpunt.com.au). Hostel above totally
refurbished, British-style pub in central location,
walking distance from Chapel St and St Kilda
nightlife. Clean dorms (four–six beds), twins and
doubles. Common room has hot water for tea/cof-
fee making, microwave and cable TV; cheap pub
dinners available. All rates include continental
breakfast. Reception 7am–2pm and 4–7pm; check
in at other times through the bar. Take train to
Windsor Station (Sandringham line) or tram #3, #5,
#16, #64 or #67 from Swanston St to St Kilda
Junction. Rooms ❸–❹, dorms ❶–❷

Richmond Hill Hotel, 353 Church St (between
Bridge Rd and Swan St), Richmond (☎ 03/9428
6501 or free call 1800 801 618, ℻ 9427 0128,
ⓦ www.richmondhill.com.au). Clean and well-run
ex-YWCA in a refurbished old mansion with very
cosy sitting rooms, large kitchen and a small
courtyard. Dorms (some women-only) and many
pleasant private rooms, as well as some apartments; non-dorm rooms include continental breakfast ($6 otherwise). Tram #75 or #48 from Spencer
St or Flinders St. Rooms ❺–❽, dorms ❷

Victoria Hotel, 123 Beaconsfield Parade, South
Melbourne (☎ 03/9690 3666, ℻ 9699 9570). This
grand hotel, built in 1888, has been restored to its
Victorian splendour. The upstairs accommodation
is in a more modern style, the bright front rooms
have good views of the waterfront but intrusion of
traffic noise. Choose between stylish en-suite doubles and cheaper rooms with shared facilities.
Great house music from some of Melbourne's best
DJs is performed every Sunday from 2pm till late
in the downstairs area. ❹–❼

West End Hotel, 76 Toorak Rd West, South Yarra
(☎ 03/9866 3135). An old-fashioned B&B overlooking a shady park and close to the heart of
exclusive South Yarra. Doubles and singles with
shared facilities. Take tram #8, or the train to
South Yarra. ❹–❺

St Kilda

Coffee Palace, 24 Grey St (☎ 03/9534 5283 or
free call 1800 654 098, ℻ 9534 2005,
ⓔ backpaca@ozemail.com.au). Very busy hostel in
an old, rambling building. Some of the dorms are
women-only, and there are plenty of twins and
doubles with en-suite bathrooms. In-house travel
agent and job agency, lots of activities; tours run in
conjunction with *Enfield House*. Pick-up from the
airport, bus terminals and the ferry. Rooms ❸,
dorms ❶

Enfield House, 2 Enfield St (☎ 03/9534 8159 or
free call 1800 302 121, ℻ 9534 5579,
ⓔ enfield@bakpak.com). A few dorms, a TV lounge
and a reading room have been carved out of a
stately, Victorian-era mansion, with a bewildering
number of very basic dorms and rooms in former
apartments desperately needing renovation and
refurbishment. There's a smallish central kitchen, a
courtyard, good notice boards, employment contacts and lots of activities, including cheap tours to

the Great Ocean Road, Phillip Island, and Ramsay Street – the latter very popular with British backpackers. Prearranged pick-up from the bus terminals. Rates include breakfast. Rooms ④, dorms ②

Leopard House, 27 Grey St (☏ 03/9534 1200). Large, pleasant old house, with lockable dorms, either segregated or mixed, and a good notice board. Friendly atmosphere. Dorms ①

Olembia, 96 Barkly St (☏ 03/9537 1412, ⓕ 9537 1600, ⓦ www.olembia.com.au). Very comfortable nonsmoking guesthouse in fine old building with open fireplaces, a cosy lounge and dining room and a well-equipped kitchen. Singles, twins and doubles are very appealing; the dorms (some women-only) have handbasins and clothes-hanging space. Off-street parking available. Rooms ④, dorms ②

The Prince, 2 Acland St (☏ 03/9536 1111, ⓕ 9536 1100, ⓦ www.theprince.com.au). This boutique hotel housed within The Prince St Kilda complex is one of Melbourne's most elegant places to lay your head. Minimalistic bedrooms include Loewe TVs and DVD players, Bose stereo radios, and a data connection for modem and fax, while the bathrooms are stocked with Aesop products, which you're allowed to take home. Away from your room you can relax in the day spa and relaxation centre, dine in the elegant *Circa* (see p.927) restaurant or the more laid-back *Circ* (see

p.927), drink at *Mink* (see p.931), or dance at the club/band room. ⑧

The Ritz Backpackers, 169 Fitzroy St (☏ 03/9525 3501 or free call 1800 670 364, ⓕ 9525 3863). Friendly hostel above a British-style pub, within range of restaurants, cafés and milk bars. Rooms are simple but spotless, all with shared facilities, and there are two TV lounges, a dining room and a tiny kitchen. Lots of activities and tours run in conjunction with *Enfield House*. Rooms ③, dorms ①

Hotel Tolarno, 42 Fitzroy St (☏ 03/9537 0200, ⓕ 9537 7800, ⓦ www.hoteltolarno.com.au). A boutique hotel in a restored building right in the thick of things, upstairs from the *Tolarno Restaurant and Bar*. Pleasant rooms with polished timber floors and all mod cons are good value. All rooms are en suite. ⑦

Warwick Beachside St Kilda, 363 Beaconsfield Parade (☏ 03/9525 4800 or free call 1800 338 134, ⓕ 9537 1056, ⓦ www.warwickbeachside.com.au). Just around the corner from the cafés and pubs of Fitzroy St, these 1950s-style brick buildings contain one- and two-bedroom units, all with colour TV, direct-dial phones and complete kitchen facilities. Management is not very obliging, but weekly rates are good. ④ –⑥

Camping and caravan parks

There are no **campsites** anywhere close to the centre; the nearest is *Melbourne Holiday Park*, with scenic *Hobsons Bay* not much further on.

Gay and lesbian accommodation

For further accommodation possibilities, other than those listed below, ring **Gay Share** (☏ 03/9691 2290), which arranges house shares for gays and lesbians.

California Motel, 138 Barkers Rd, Hawthorn (☏ 03/9818 0281 or free call 1800 331 166, ⓕ 9819 6845, ⓦ www.californiamotel.com.au). Gay-friendly motel accommodation close to the city, with parking available. Take tram #109 or #42 from Collins St. ⑦ –⑧

Fitzroy Stables, 124 Victoria St, off Brunswick St, Fitzroy (☏ & ⓕ 03/9415 1507). Lovely self-contained unit with a cathedral ceiling, mezzanine bedroom and small kitchen, facing a courtyard with a cottage garden. ⑥ –⑦

Heathville House, 171 Aitken St, Williamstown (☏ & ⓕ 03/9397 5959, ⓔ heath@jeack.com.au). B&B in pretty, restored weatherboard house. Nonsmoking. ⑥ –⑦

Laird Hotel, 149 Gipps St, Abbotsford (☏ 03/9417 2832, ⓕ 03/9417 2109, ⓦ www.lairdhotel.com). Rooms for gay men only. ⑤ –⑥

163 Drummond Street, 163 Drummond St, Carlton (☏ 03/9663 3081, ⓕ 9663 6500, ⓦ www.163drummond.com.au). Non-smoking B&B in two adjacent, two-storey refurbished Victorian mansions. Eleven rooms, with en-suite or shared facilities. ⑦ –⑧

Palm Court B&B, 22 Grattan Place, Richmond (☏ 03/9427 7365 or 0419 777 850). Spacious bedrooms in Victorian mansion at a moderate rate. Nonsmoking. ④ –⑥

Crystal Brook Holiday Centre, cnr Anderson's Creek and Warrandyte roads, East Doncaster (☎03/9844 3637, ⓕ9844 3342). Modern campsite and holiday park with tennis courts and a pool, 21km northeast of the city centre (20min via the Eastern Freeway). On-site vans & cabins ❹–❺

Hobsons Bay Caravan Park, 158 Kororoit Creek Rd, Williamstown (☎03/9397 2395). Thirteen kilo-metres west of the city. Pitch your tent facing St Kilda across Hobsons Bay. Cabins ❹

Melbourne Holiday Park, 265 Elizabeth St, Coburg East (☎03/9354 3533 or free call 1800 802 678, ⓕ9354 4550). Ten kilometres north of the city, the closest spot to camp, with a kitchen and a swimming pool. Bus #526 to the city (day-time only, no service Sun). Cabins ❹–❻

The City

Accessible and approachable, Melbourne has long been known as a city of few sights but plenty of lifestyle, a place to sit and enjoy a coffee or stroll in a park rather than traipse round museums and tourist attractions. However, successive governments have transformed the city, and now high-rise buildings and new developments are popping up like mushrooms. The shift towards the Yarra river that kicked off in the mid-1990s with the waterfront development of Southgate, Crown Casino and Melbourne Exhibition Centre is complement-ed by the new Federation Square opposite Flinders Street Station. CityLink, a network of city bypasses connecting the freeways out of the city, began oper-ation in late 2000, the same year that the brand-new Colonial Stadium and Melbourne Museum opened their doors, and major refurbishment of the National Gallery of Victoria is due to finish in early 2002.

This construction frenzy is to continue unabated with the Dockhands proj-ect. In the next ten to fifteen years an entire new waterfront city will rise from what is at present an urban wasteland. Depending on the outcome (and one's point of view, of course) the Docklands might add an exciting new dimension to the city or create yet another manifestation of shallow, hedonistic material-ism in the vein of the casino. Looking at the artists' impressions of the future slick waterfront city, however, the association of "Gold Coast on the Yarra" does not seem terribly far-fetched.

North of this area of redevelopment, the **Central Business District** (CBD), bounded by Latrobe, Spring, Flinders and Spencer streets, offers some fine pub-lic buildings and lots of shops, with the **Old Melbourne Gaol** exerting a ghoulish fascination and a new museum in the Old Customs House sheds light on Victoria's immigration history. On all sides, save the downtown west, the CBD is surrounded by gardens; few cities have so much green space so close to the centre. To the north a wander through lively, century-old **Queen Victoria Market** will repay both serious shoppers and people-watchers, while the newly built **Melbourne Museum** in the tranquil Carlton Gardens draws on the latest technology to give an insight into Australia's flora, fauna and cul-ture. In the east the CBD rubs up against **Eastern Hill**, with its government buildings and landscaped **Fitzroy Gardens**, from where it's a short walk to the venerable **Melbourne Cricket Ground (MCG)**, a must for sports fans. To the south is the previously much-maligned, muddy **Yarra River**, which is slowly being turned into an attraction. You'll get a rewarding view of the city skyline on a stroll along the riverbanks in front of Southgate and the casino, and a unique look at underwater life at **Melbourne Aquarium** on the oppo-site side of the river, while the best way to appreciate the changing vistas of city and parklands is on a **boat cruise**. South of the river, the **Victorian Arts Centre**, whose highlights are the **Performing Arts Museum** and the

National Gallery of Victoria, forms a cultural strip on one side of St Kilda Road, while on the other Government House and the impressive Shrine of Remembrance front the **Royal Botanic Gardens**, where along with the soothing greenery you'll get a dose of horticultural education.

The CBD

Seen from across the river or from the air, Melbourne's **Central Business District** offers up a spectacular, modern skyline; at ground level, however, what you notice are the florid nineteenth-century facades, grandiose survivors of the great days of the goldrushes and after, when Melbourne consolidated its position as a financial centre. The former **Royal Mint** on William Street near Flagstaff Gardens is one of the finest examples, but the main concentrations are on **Collins Street** and along Spring Street to the east. At the centre of the CBD, trams still jolt through busy **Bourke Street Mall**, so it's not quite a pedestrian haven; **Swanston Street**, bounding the mall to the east, was closed in 1992 to all traffic except trams between Flinders and Latrobe streets, but has since reopened to cars between 7pm–7am. A stone's throw from these central thoroughfares, narrow lanes, squares and arcades with quaint, hole-in-the-wall-type cafés, small restaurants, shops and boutiques add a surprisingly cosy, homely feel to the city.

Collins Street

Collins Street is *the* smart Melbourne address – especially if you're an international banker – becoming increasingly exclusive as you climb the hill from the Spencer Street end. Even here though, things are getting smarter, reflecting the buzz of the successful new developments along the south bank of the Yarra. At the western end of Collins Street the Stock Exchange squares up to the **Rialto Building** opposite, an Italianate Gothic complex built in the 1890s, which houses a luxury hotel, the *Meridien*. The massive **Rialto Towers**, to date Melbourne's tallest structure, is a classic skyscraper, the reflective surface of its twin towers lending the skyline a bit of oomph. On clear days, especially in the evening, a trip in the lift up to the **Rialto Towers Observation Deck** on the 55th floor is a must (Mon–Thurs & Sun 10am–10pm, Fri & Sat 10am–11pm; $9; ⓦ www.ob.deck@rialto.com.au). The admission fee includes the use of high-powered binoculars, and a twenty-minute film at the Rialto Vision Theatre on street level that highlights the best parts of Melbourne and Victoria. Nearby, at 333 Collins St, the former **Commercial Bank of Australia** has a particularly sumptuous interior, with a domed banking chamber and awesome barrel-vaulted vestibule, that you're welcome to admire during business hours.

Further up Collins Street, beyond the worthwhile diversion down William Street to the new museums in the Old Customs House (see overleaf), shops become the focus of attention. The 1890s **Block Arcade**, at nos. 282–284, is Melbourne's grandest shopping centre, its name appropriately taken from the tradition of "doing the block" – promenading around the city's fashionable shopping streets. Restored in 1988, the L-shaped arcade sports a mosaic-tiled floor, ornate columns and mouldings, and a glass-domed roof. **Australia on Collins**, a modern alternative next door, has set its sights firmly on the street's glitzy shopping crown; in the basement it boasts an upmarket food court and adjacent licensed restaurants and bars. Beyond this, on the corner of Collins and Swanston streets, Neoclassical **Melbourne Town Hall** faces the new *Westin Hotel* (see p.897) squatting on **City Square**, a beleaguered space that never achieved the intended purpose of providing Melbourne with a focal point – it's hoped that Federation Square, further south by the Yarra, will achieve this. There is, however, an unmissable landmark on the south side of the square: the splendid **St Paul's Cathedral**, built in the 1880s according to the Gothic-revival design of English architect William Butterfield, who never actually visited Australia. Across from the cathedral on Swanston Street, the restored *Young and Jackson's Hotel* is now protected by the National Trust, not for any intrinsic beauty but as a showcase for a work of art which has become a Melbourne icon: **Chloe**, a full-length nude now reclining upstairs in *Chloe's Bar and Bistro*. Exhibited by the French painter Jules Lefebvre at the Paris Salon of 1875, it was sent to an international exhibition in Melbourne in 1881 and has been here ever since, although it was briefly loaned to the National Gallery of Victoria while the hotel was being refurbished.

Back on Collins Street, the pompous **Athenaeum Theatre** next to the Town Hall is an important ingredient in the rising streetscape leading up past **Scots Church**, whose Gothic-revival design merits a peek, though it's famous mainly as the place where Dame Nellie Melba first sang in the choir. Further up, beyond expensive boutiques and even more expensive souvenir shops, **Collins Place** shopping centre and the towering **Hotel Sofitel** next door dominate the upper part of Collins Street, known as the "Paris end". The (male) toilet of *Le Restaurant* on the 35th floor of the *Sofitel* is known as the "loo with a view", but the **view** from the tables by the window isn't bad, either – though it doesn't come cheap (see "Eating and drinking", p.922). A dreary **arts and crafts market** plies its wares in the atrium of Collins Place on Sunday between 9am and 5pm. Opposite, overshadowed by the *Sofitel* tower, stands one of the last bastions of Australian male chauvinism: the very staid, men-only Melbourne Club.

The Old Customs House: Immigration Museum and Hellenic Antiquities Museum

At the corner of Flinders and William streets, just off the western stretch of Collins Street, the **Immigration Museum** (daily 10am–5pm; $7.70; Ⓦ www.immigration.vic.gov.au) is dedicated to one of the central themes of Australian history. Housed in the beautifully restored **Old Customs House**, it tells personal stories of immigration using voice, music, objects, moving images, light effects and interactive computers to build a very vivid picture; the experiences of being a migrant on a square-rigger in the 1840s, a passenger on a steamship at the turn of the twentieth century or a postwar refugee from Europe are all illustrated with touching effect. Each story is unique because of its personal, cultural, political and historical background, yet shared experiences and common emotions – grief and fear, loneliness and doubt, relief and hope – are evident. In the **Tribute Garden**, the outdoor centrepiece of the museum, a film of water flows over polished granite on which are engraved the names of migrants to Victoria, symbolizing the passage over the seas to reach these far-away shores. The names of all the Koorie people living in Victoria prior to white settlement are listed separately at the entrance to the garden.

The **Hellenic Antiquities Museum** on the second floor of the same building (same hours; admission fee depends on the exhibition; min $7.70) is an exhibition space for antique treasures loaned by the government of Greece, most of them rarely seen outside their homeland. The museum is also the starting point for the Golden Mile Heritage Walk.

Bourke Street and Chinatown

Bourke Street Mall extends west from Swanston Street to Elizabeth Street. Lined with trees and seats but not quite traffic-free, it is in desperate need of an overhaul (removing the trams would be a good start), although this increasingly dishevelled pedestrian centre still has the wonderful Victorian-era **General Post Office** set against department stores and crowded shops. Unfortunately, the GPO is earmarked to become either a shopping mall or twenty-storey hotel as part of the redevelopment; at the time of writing the GPO shop was moving to the corner of Little Bourke and Elizabeth streets. Running off the mall, the lovely **Royal Arcade** is Melbourne's oldest (1839), paved with black and white marble and lit by huge fanlight windows. A clock on which two two-metre giants, Gog and Magog, strike the hours adds a welcome hint of the grotesque. As you climb the hill east of here, Bourke Street keeps up the interest, with several cafés and bars that put out pavement tables at night – including *Pellegrini's*, Melbourne's first espresso bar and still buzzing – as well as late-opening book and record stores.

North of Bourke Street, running parallel, is **Little Bourke Street**, with the majestic **Law Courts** by William Street at the western end, and **Chinatown** in the east between Exhibition and Swanston streets. Australia's oldest continuous Chinese settlement, Melbourne's Chinatown began with a few boarding-houses in the 1850s (when the goldrushes attracted Chinese people in droves, many from the Pearl River Delta near Hong Kong) and grew as the gold began to run out and Chinese fortune-seekers headed back to the city. Today the area still has a low-rise, narrow-laned, nineteenth-century character, and it's packed with Chinese restaurants and stores. The **Chinese Museum** in an old warehouse on Cohen Place (daily 10am–4.30pm; $6.50), is concerned particularly with the Chinese role in the foundation and development of Melbourne. The museum organizes two-hour guided tours of the building and Chinatown ($16.50, or $33 including lunch). Tours require a minimum of four people, and bookings two or three days in advance are preferred (☎03/9662 2888).

State Library, National Gallery of Victoria and Melbourne Central

Still functioning, although it is undergoing renovation, the **State Library** (general opening Mon–Thurs 10am–9pm & Fri–Sun 10am–6pm; ⓦ www.slv.vic .gov.au) dates from 1856, and is the state's largest research and reference library accessible to the public. The Queen's Hall and its centrepiece, the domed reading room, are splendid examples of Victorian architecture. After refurbishment (to be completed by 2003) the venerable old building is going to house state-of-the-art storage facilities and information services. The Museum of Victoria, which for many years shared the block between Swanston and Russell streets with the library, reopened in October after a few years closure a few blocks northeast as **Melbourne Museum**, the largest museum complex in the southern hemisphere, giving a new lease of life to the historic Royal Exhibition Building, which lies adjacent in the Carlton Gardens. A small selection of the museum's collection can be seen at Scienceworks in Spotswood (see p.920). The old museum site, entered from Russell Street, is occupied by select exhibits from the **National Gallery of Victoria**, itself closed for renovation.

Opposite, **Melbourne Central** is an ultramodern shopping complex that has skilfully incorporated an old red-brick shot tower under its pointed glass dome. Among the shops here is the Daimaru department store, which offers a fascinating taste of things Japanese – not least in the food hall.

Old Melbourne Gaol

The **Old Melbourne Gaol** (daily 9.30am–4.30pm; $9.90; ⓦ www.home.vic-net.net.au), on Russell Street, a block north of the State Library, is probably the most worthwhile of all the downtown sights. Certainly it's the most popular,

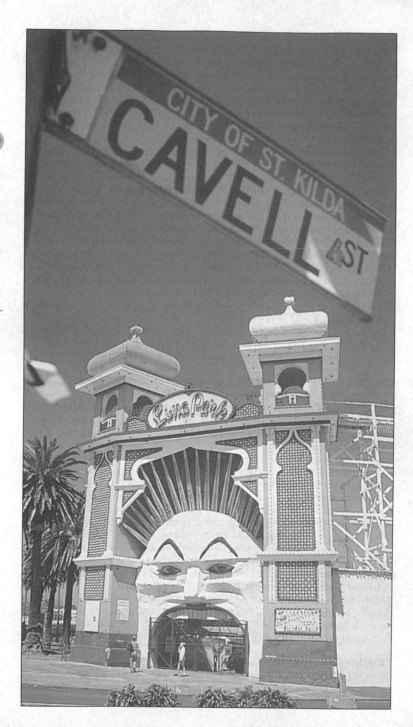

largely because Australian folk hero and bushranger **Ned Kelly** was hanged here in 1880 – the site of his execution, the beam from which he was hung and his death mask are all on display (for more on Ned Kelly's exploits, see p.1031), as is assorted armour from the Kelly Gang. The "Melbourne Gaol Night Tour" (Wed, Fri & Sun: April–Oct 7.30pm, Nov–March 8.30pm; $18.70; advance bookings required on ☎03/9663 7228) uses the spooky atmosphere of the prison to full effect.

The bluestone prison was built in stages from 1841 to 1864 – the goldrushes of the 1850s caused such a surge in lawlessness that it kept having to be expanded. A mix of condemned men, remand and short-sentence prisoners, women and "lunatics" (often, in fact, drunks) were housed here; long-term prisoners languished in hulks moored at Williamstown, or at the Pentridge Stockade. Much has been demolished since the jail was closed in 1923, but the entrance and boundary walls at least survive, and it's worth walking round the building to take a look at the formidable arched brick portal on Franklin Street.

The gruesome collection of death masks on show in the tiny cells bears witness to the nineteenth-century obsession with phrenology, a wobbly branch of science which studied how people's characters were related to the size and shape of their skulls. Accompanying the masks are compelling case histories of the murderers and their victims. Most fascinating are the women: Martha Needle, who poisoned her husband and daughters (among others) with arsenic, and young Martha Knorr, the notorious "baby farmer", who advertised herself as a "kind motherly person, willing to adopt a child". After receiving a few dollars per child, she killed and buried them in her backyard. The jail serves up other macabre memorabilia, including a scaffold still in working order, various nooses, and a triangle where malcontents were strapped to receive lashes by the cat-o'-nine-tails. Perhaps the ultimate rite of passage for visitors is the "Art of Hanging", an interpretive display that's part educational tool and part setting for a medieval snuff movie.

Queen Victoria Market and Melbourne Museum

Opened in the 1870s, **Queen Victoria Market** (Tues & Thurs 6am–2pm, Fri 6am–6pm, Sat 6am–3pm, Sun 9am–4pm; Ⓦ www.qvm.com.au) remains one of the best loved of Melbourne's institutions. Its collection of huge, decorative open-sided sheds and high-roofed halls is fronted along Victoria Street by restored shops, their original awnings held up with decorative iron posts. Although undeniably quaint and tourist-friendly, the market is a boisterous, down-to-earth affair where you can buy practically anything from new and secondhand clothes to fresh fish at bargain prices. Stallholders and shoppers seem just as diverse as the goods on offer: Vietnamese, Italian and Greek greengrocers pile their colourful produce high and vie for your attention, while the huge variety of deliciously smelly cheeses effortlessly draws customers to the old-fashioned deli hall. Saturday morning marks a weekly social ritual as Melbourne's foodies turn out for their groceries; Sunday is for clothing and shoe shopping; while Wednesday night's focus in summer is on live music, jugglers, alfresco eating and drinking, and shopping for jewellery and furniture. The guided Foodies Dream Tour takes in all the culinary delights of the market (10am each market day except Sun; $22 including food sampling), while the Heritage Market Tour acquaints visitors with its history (10.30am each market day except Sun; $16.50 including brunch); bookings essential for both tours, call ☎03/9320 5835.

At the CBD's northeast corner is Carlton Gardens, home to one of Melbourne's most significant historic landmarks – the **Royal Exhibition Building**. Built by David Mitchell (father of Dame Nellie Melba) for the International Exhibition of 1880, this is where Australia's first parliament sat in 1901 (the northern facade and majestic dome have been restored to mark the centenary of Federation in 2001) and where the Victorian State Parliament resided in 1901–27. It was also used as a sporting venue for the 1956 Melbourne Olympics. Buildings originally covered the whole of the park, but only the magnificent Neoclassical Main Hall remains, dwarfed by the mammoth **Melbourne Museum** (daily 10am–6pm; $12; ⑳ www.melbourne.museum.vic.gov.au). Opened in 2000, the state-of-the-art museum is in dramatic contrast to its nineteenth-century neighbour, with its geometric forms, vibrant colours, immense blade-like roof and a greenhouse accommodating a lush fern gully flanked by a canopy of dozens of tall forest trees. The museum, which also houses a 400-seat amphitheatre, touring hall for major exhibitions and museum shop, has been designed with the internet generation in mind – glass-covered display cabinets are few and far between; instead there is a greater emphasis on digital culture and multimedia, with exhibition spaces exploring the way science and technology are shaping the future. Spread over six huge levels, half of which are below ground level, highlights include the **Science and Life Gallery**, which explores the plants and animals inhabiting the southern lands and seas; the **Bunjilaka Aboriginal Centre**, showcasing an extraordinary indigenous collection of Aboriginal culture (curving for 50m at the entrance is "Wurreka", a wall of over seventy zinc panels etched with Aboriginal artefacts, shells, plants and fish); and the **Australia Gallery**, focusing on the history of Melbourne and Victoria, and featuring the legendary racehorse Phar Lap (reputedly Australia's most popular museum exhibit) and the kitchen set from the TV show *Neighbours*. Also of interest is the **Evolution Gallery**, which looks at the earth's history and holds an assortment of dinosaur casts, and the **Children's Museum**, where the exhibition gallery, "Big Box", is built in the shape of a giant, tiled cube painted in brightly coloured squares. One of the most striking exhibits is the **Forest Gallery**, a living, breathing indoor rainforest containing over 8000 plants from more than 120 species, including 25-metre-tall gums, as well as birds, insects, snakes, lizards and fish.

Also part of the museum is the **IMAX Melbourne**, which boasts the world's biggest movie screen. Up to seven different IMAX films (daily on the hour 10am–11pm, plus Fri & Sat midnight & 1am; $16.20, 3D films $17.30; ☏03/9663 5454, ⑳ www.imax.com.au/melbourne) are projected each day; for some you need to don special liquid-crystal glasses for 3D action.

Eastern Hill and the MCG

The **Eastern Hill** area beyond Spring Street has many fine public buildings, centred around **Parliament House**. Erected in stages between 1856 and 1930, the parliament buildings (50min guided tours on non-sitting days Mon–Fri 10am, 11am, noon, 2pm, 3pm & 3.45pm; free) have a theatrical presence, with a facade of giant Doric columns rising from a high flight of steps, and landscaped gardens either side. Just below, the Old Treasury Building from 1857 and adjacent State Government office, facing the beautiful Treasury Gardens, are equally imposing. In the old gold vaults deep in the basement of the **Old Treasury Building** (Mon–Fri 9am–5pm, Sat, Sun & public holidays 10am–4pm; $7.70) an audiovisual presentation, *Built on Gold*, illustrates the impact of the Victorian goldrushes on the fledgling colony. A permanent exhibition on the social and architectural history of Melbourne shares the ground floor with temporary shows.

To the east, the broad acres of **Fitzroy Gardens** run a close second to Carlton Gardens as a getaway from the CBD. Originally laid out in the shape of the Union Jack flag, the park's paths still just about conform to the original pattern, but, in between, the formal style has been fetchingly abandoned. The flowers, statuary and fountains are best appreciated on weekdays, as at the weekend you'll spend most of your time dodging the video cameras of wedding parties. The gardens' much-touted main attraction is really only for kitsch nostalgists: **Captain Cook's Cottage** (daily: winter 9am–5pm; summer 9am–5.30pm; $3.30) was the supposed home of Captain James Cook, the English navigator who explored the southern hemisphere in three great voyages and first "discovered" the east coast of Australia. The cottage was purchased in 1933 by Russell Grimwade, a wealthy Melbourne businessman, who had it shipped over piece by piece from its original location in Whitby, Yorkshire, and presented as a gift to the state of Victoria for its 1934 centenary. The red-brick and creeper-covered cottage with period fittings attempts to re-create the atmosphere of eighteenth-century England, reinforced by worthy displays about the explorer himself. Elsewhere in the gardens, a tacky open-air **model Tudor village** continues the "olde worlde" theme, but you'll probably find the **Conservatory**'s flower displays (daily 9am–5pm; free) more interesting.

The MCG

Yarra Park, home of the hallowed **Melbourne Cricket Ground**, lies across Wellington Parade from the southeastern corner of Fitzroy Gardens – also easily reached by tram along Wellington Parade or train to Jolimont Station. Home to the Melbourne Cricket Club since 1853, the MCG is now a vast and rather ugly slab of concrete, as only the historic members' stand survived the complete reconstruction that made the ground the centrepiece for the 1956 Olympic Games. As well as hosting state and international cricket matches and some of the top Aussie Rules football games, the MCG contains the **Australian Gallery of Sport and Olympic Museum** and the **Australian Cricket Hall of Fame** (daily 9.30am–4.30pm; $17; Ⓦ www.mcg.org.au). One-hour tours of the ground itself (hourly 10am–3pm; no tours on event days) are included in the admission fee; the highlight is the members' pavilion – home of the most traditional and elitist club in Australia – packed with fascinating cricketing memorabilia. The Olympic Museum covers all the Olympiads, and incorporates an audio tour of the museum.

The Yarra River and the south bank

The muddy **Yarra River** is an essential part of Melbourne; it was traditionally home to the docks and is now the focus of lots of leisure activities. In the early days, tidal movements of up to two metres meant frequent flooding, a problem only partly solved by artificially straightening the river and building up its banks – but with the incidental benefit of reserving tracts of low-lying land as recreational space, now pleasingly crisscrossed by paths and cycle tracks.

Four **bridges** cross the river from the CBD: Spencer Street Bridge at the end of Spencer Street; Kings Bridge on King Street; Queens Bridge, not quite at the end of Queen Street; and Princes Bridge, which carries Swanston Street across. There's also a pedestrian bridge from the bank below Flinders Street Station to the Southgate Centre. The best way to see the Yarra is on a **cruise** – see box overleaf.

River cruises on the Yarra

The main central departure points for cruises along the Yarra are Princes Walk and Southgate in the city, and Williamstown at the mouth of the Yarra further west (see p.920). You can choose between short trips and longer journeys towards the sea and the bird colonies at Port Phillip Bay and Herring Island.

Melbourne River Cruises (bookings ☎03/9629 7233; $16.50, or combined up- and downriver cruise $29.70) make half-hourly departures from Princes Walk below the northern end of Princes Bridge. Their Scenic River Garden Cruise (1hr 15min) will take you upriver past affluent South Yarra and industrial Richmond to Herring Island; the Port and Docklands Cruise (also 1hr 15min) runs downriver past the Crown Casino and the Melbourne Exhibition Centre – and then past shipping channels and docks to the Westgate bridge.

Southgate River Tours (bookings ☎03/9682 5711). Trips daily on the hour from 11am up- or downriver. There are also daily departures to Williamstown at 10.45am, 12.45am, 2.45pm and 4.45pm. Both cruises are $19.80 and depart from Berth 4 at Southgate.

Williamstown Bay and River Cruises (for recorded information call ☎03/9506 4144; for bookings ☎03/9397 2255; $10, or $18 return) ply the lower section of the Yarra between Williamstown and Southgate in the west of the city, passing the Crown Casino, the Melbourne Exhibition Centre and the docks. There are daily departures throughout the summer at 11am, 1pm, 3pm & 5pm, returning from Williamstown at noon, 2pm, 4pm & 6pm. Their cruises are pleasantly uncommercial, with no commentary or pressure to buy anything.

On the south side of Princes Bridge you can rent **bikes** to explore the salubrious left bank (see "Listings", p.937); on fine weekends especially, the Yarra comes to life, with people messing about in boats, cycling and strolling, and family groups gathered for barbecues. **Southgate**, immediately west of Princes Bridge, is a highly successful development: once dingy and industrial, it's now an upmarket shopping complex with lots of smart cafés, restaurants, bars and a huge food court with very popular outdoor tables; at lunchtime and weekends it's very hard to find a table, even indoors.

The Crown Casino, Docklands and Colonial Stadium

Providing the unavoidable focal point for the Yarra is the **Crown Casino**, Australia's largest gambling and entertainment venue, stretching across 600m of riverfront west of Southgate between Queens Bridge and Spencer Street Bridge. Next door, the **Melbourne Exhibition Centre** (known locally as "Jeff's Shed", a reference to Jeff Kennett, the former state premier behind its construction) is a whimsical example of the city's dynamic new architectural style: facing the river is an immense, 450-metre-long glass wall, while the street entrance has an awning resembling a ski jump propped up by wafer-thin pylons. The interesting **Polly Woodside Maritime Museum** (daily 10am–4pm; $9.90) is tucked into a small old dock next to the Exhibition Centre. The focus is the *Polly Woodside* itself, a small, barque-rigged sailing ship, built in Belfast in 1885 for the South American coal trade and retired only in 1968, when it was the last deep-water sailing vessel in Australia still afloat.

The squat building facing the Exhibition Centre and the museum across the Yarra is the **World Trade Centre**. Next to it, opposite the Crown Casino on the corner of Queenwharf Road and King Street, is **Melbourne Aquarium** (daily: Jan 9am–9pm; Feb–Dec 9am–6pm; $19; ⓦ www.melbourneaquarium .com.au), a new attraction. Resembling a giant fish-and-chip shop, the aquarium harbours thousands of creatures from the Southern Ocean. Part of it is taken up by the Oceanarium tank, which rests seven metres below the Yarra, holding over two million litres of water and containing 3200 animals from 150 species (there are over 550 species, or 4000 creatures, in the aquarium in total), a sting-ray filled beach with a wave machine and a fish bowl turned inside out where visitors stand in a glass room surrounded by shark-filled water. The curved, four-storey building also comprises a hands-on learning centre where children get a fish-eye view of life underwater, "Ride the Dive" platforms that simulate an underwater roller coaster, lecture halls, an amphitheatre, cafés, shop and a restaurant.

Further downstream is the old dock area, an urban wasteland of warehouses, sheds, empty open spaces and old docks that's now the site of grand-scale commercial, residential and leisure development. Of all the new developments, the **Docklands project** is going to have the biggest impact on the look and feel of Melbourne: in ten to fifteen years an entire new city will stand by the waterfront.

Another of Melbourne's giant sporting venues lies northwest of here on the fringes of the CBD – **Colonial Stadium**. This spanking new 54,000 seater has a giant sliding roof, which makes it an all-weather venue for AFL, cricket, and international soccer and rugby union matches. Concerts by big-time performers such as Barbara Streisand and Ricky Martin are performed at the stadium, while the Channel 7 TV station has set up headquarters there.

Federation Square and the sports grounds

Just across the river from Southgate and opposite Flinders Street Station, the bold **Federation Square** is intended to form a link between the CBD and the river, completing the city's shift of focus; at the time of writing the individual buildings, with their striking facades of geometric panels, are slowly taking shape and should be completed by the end of 2001. Conceived as a tribute to the federation of the nation, the square covers an entire block, comprising Civic Plaza, an open auditorium, an underground tourist and visitor's centre, the Centre for the Moving Image (the headquarters and studios of multicultural TV station SBS), a Cinemedia Centre and **The Atrium**, a covered, 120-metre-long area reaching from Flinders Street almost all the way to the banks of the Yarra. **Civic Plaza** will be partly open towards the river, and partly flanked by a structure designed to accommodate cafés, restaurants, a pub and shops. Alongside Federation Square, the **Museum of Australian Art** will house works by indigenous and non-indigenous Australian artists from the National Gallery of Victoria collection.

The development has, however, been embroiled in controversy over the "**shards**", enormous three-storey glass office blocks, but more specifically the western shard, which was to frame the square's main plaza. If it had been built, it would have partly obscured the views of St Paul's Cathedral, and under pressure from the National Trust, the Heritage Council of Victoria and vocal members of the public, premier Bracks ruled against its development. This, however, was much to the disappointment of the project's architects and their supporters, who believe its axing went against the spirit of the original design and would provide too much open frontage – something that bedevilled the City Square. In the western shard's place will now stand a single-storey building, which will act as an entrance to the visitor's centre.

The parklands east of Federation Square are being redeveloped and extended to form **Riverside Park**, a green link between Federation Square and the Rod Laver Stadium (home of the Australian Open tennis championship), the "Glasshouse", or Melbourne Sports & Entertainment Centre, and Olympic

Park (where the Melbourne Storm rugby league team play their matches). Also within the wide, open spaces is the recently finished **Vodafone Arena**, which can seat up to 10,500 people, and has a retractable roof and moveable seating that allows for fully enclosed or open-air events such as cycling, tennis, basketball and concerts.

Victorian Arts Centre

The **Victorian Arts Centre**, just off St Kilda Road, comprises the National Gallery of Victoria, the Melbourne Concert Hall and the Theatres Building, topped by a hideous spire. The "Arts Tower", as it's sometimes called, is meant to represent the pinnacle of the arts in Melbourne, its curved surfaces supposedly evoking the flowing folds of a ballerina's skirt. Germaine Greer's attempt at explanation was that "stunned by the bad taste of the Sydney Opera House, the Melburnians have clearly decided to fight fire with fire . . .".

There are guided **tours** (Mon–Sat noon & 2.30pm; $10; backstage tour Sun 12.15pm; $13.50; Ⓦ www.artscentre.net.au) of the **Melbourne Concert Hall** and **Theatres Building** – two separate buildings linked to each other and to the National Gallery of Victoria by walk-throughs – which are worth joining mainly to see the collection of art in the various foyers. Tours begin from the souvenir shop, just to the left as you enter the Theatres Building. The highlight of the Arts Centre if you're not seeing a performance, however, is the fun and accessible **Performing Arts Museum** (Mon–Sat 9am–11pm, Sun 10am–5pm; free) on the ground level of the Theatres Building, which covers everything from opera to TV and rock 'n' roll and has wonderful temporary exhibitions, normally on aspects of popular culture. Adjacent to the museum, the small George Adams Gallery (formerly Westpac Gallery) shows temporary exhibitions (same hours; free).

The **National Gallery of Victoria** has always been a more serious contender, with the best collection of Australian art in the country: seventy thousand works, rotated regularly, form its permanent collection. The gallery will be closed for major refurbishment until early 2002, when it will reopen with exhibits from its international collection; the works of Australian artists will be housed in the new **Museum of Australian Art** on Federation Square (see overleaf). Until then, a small part of the exceptional collection can be seen at the old site (see p.905).

The **Australian Centre for Contemporary Art** (Tues–Fri 11am–5pm, Sat & Sun noon–5pm; free), at the time of writing on Dallas Brooks Drive, has consistently challenging exhibitions of contemporary international and Australian art, as well as forums, lectures and performances. In 2001 the gallery will relocate to its new home in Malthouse Plaza, a development next to the CUB Malthouse Theatre complex in Sturt Street further south.

On Sunday between 10am and 6pm the stalls of a good **arts and crafts market** line the pavement outside the Arts Centre, extending onto the footpath under the Princes Bridge.

Kings Domain

Across St Kilda Road from the National Gallery of Victoria, the **Kings Domain** is a grassy open park encompassing the **Sidney Myer Music Bowl**, which serves as the outdoor music arena for the Victorian Arts Centre. South of the Bowl, and behind imposing iron gates with stone pillars and a British coat of arms, you glimpse the flag flying over **Government House**, the ivory mansion of the Governor of Victoria, set in extensive grounds. The National Trust run **guided tours** (Mon, Wed & Sat, times appointed by booking;

①03/9654 4711; closed Dec 16–Jan 25; $11), whose highlight is the state ball-room. This occupies the entire south wing and includes a velvet-hung canopied throne, brocade-covered benches, gilded chairs, ornate plasterwork and three huge crystal chandeliers.

Just south of the Government House grounds, **Latrobe's Cottage** (Mon, Wed, Sat & Sun 11am–4pm; $2.20) has been re-erected as a memorial to Lieutenant-Governor Latrobe, who lived in this tiny house throughout his term of office (1839–54). The whole thing was sent over from England in pre-fabricated form, and as the first governor's residence makes a telling contrast to the later one. Inside are interesting historical displays on Latrobe and the early days of the colony.

The **Shrine of Remembrance**, in formal grounds in the southwestern cor-ner of the Domain, is aligned with St Kilda Road – which describes a gentle arc around it – so that its forbidding mass looms ahead as you enter or leave the city. Completed in 1934, it's a rather Orwellian monument, apparently half Roman temple, half Aztec pyramid, given further chill when a mechanical-sounding voice booms out and calls you in to see the symbolic light inside. The shrine is designed so that at 11am on Remembrance Day (Nov 11) a ray of sunlight strikes the memorial stone inside – an effect that's simulated every half-hour.

Royal Botanic Gardens

The **Royal Botanic Gardens** (daily: April–Oct 7.30am–5.30pm; Nov–March 7.30am–8.30pm; free; ⑩ www.rbgmelb.org.au) contain twelve thousand differ-ent plant species and over fifty thousand individual plants, as well as native wildlife like cockatoos and kookaburras, in an extensive landscaped setting. Melbourne's much-maligned climate is perfect for horticulture: cool enough for temperate trees and flowers to flourish, warm enough for palms and other subtropical species, and wet enough for anything else. The **Visitors Centre** (daily 10am–5pm) on Dallas Brooks Drive is the best place to start your wan-derings, with its displays, maps and brochures.

Highlights include the **herb garden**, comprising part of the medicinal gar-den established in 1880; the **fern gully**, a lovely walk through shady ferns, with cooling mists of water on a hot summer's day; the large ornamental **lake** full of ducks, black swans and eels; and various hothouses where exotic cacti and fascinating plants like the Venus flytrap thrive. The *Terrace Tearooms and Conference Centre* (daily 9.30am–5pm) by the lake serves refreshments and Devonshire teas. On summer evenings, bucolic plays such as *The Wind in the Willows* or *A Midsummer Night's Dream* are often performed in the gardens. Cinema buffs can also swap popcorn for picnic baskets each year from late December to early March when art-house, cult and classic films like *Breakfast at Tiffany's* are projected onto a big outdoor screen at the **Moonlight Cinema** (for information and schedules call ①03/9663 9555 or visit ⑩ www.moon-light.com.au); don't forget to take an extra layer of clothing, a rug and, most importantly, insect repellent.

Guided walks (Sun–Thurs 11am & 2pm; bookings on ①03/9252 2300; $4.40) through the gardens' highlights start at the Visitors Centre. Other guid-ed tours include the Aboriginal Heritage Walk, which explores the traditional uses of plants for foods, medicine, tools and ceremonies (Thurs 11am & sec-ond Sun of month 10.30am; $15.40), and tours to the painstakingly restored **Observatory Gate** complex, a group of Italianate buildings (originally built 1861–63) next door to the Visitors Centre. The observatory performed a wide range of important functions for the fledgling colony of Victoria, providing scientific data essential for the running of businesses from shipping to farming (Night Sky Experience tours from the Visitors Centre include viewing through the telescopes in the Observatory group of buildings (Tues 7.30–9.30pm; $15.40; ☎ 03/9525 2300). Booking is essential for both tours.

Melbourne suburbs

Far more than in the city centre, in Melbourne's **inner suburbs** you'll get a feel for what life here is really all about. Many have quite distinct characters, whether as ethnic enclaves or self-styled artists' communities. What's more, they're all easily reached on a pleasurable tram ride. Day-trips to places further afield around Melbourne are detailed on p.941.

Café society finds its home to the north among the alternative galleries and secondhand shops of **Fitzroy**, and to the south in **St Kilda**, which has a trendy but raucous nightlife, and the added advantage of the beach. On Lygon Street in **Carlton**, which fuelled the Beat Generation with espresso, there are now as many boutiques as bookshops and art centres. Grungy **Richmond**, to the east, can claim both Vietnamese and Greek enclaves, and a diverse music scene in its many pubs, while across the river is the place to shop until you drop: wealthy **South Yarra**, flanked by self-consciously groovy **Prahran** and snobby **Toorak**.

Browsing through markets and shops, cruising across Hobsons Bay, sampling the world's foods and, of course, sipping espresso are the primary attractions of the suburbs. To firm up your itinerary with something more concrete, make for the well-designed **Zoo** in Carlton, or **Scienceworks**, a hugely enjoyable interactive museum in Spotswood. Also of interest is the **Museum of Modern Art at Heide** in Bulleen and, a bit further along in the same direction, Eltham with its artists' colony of **Montsalvat**.

Carlton

Carlton lies just north of the city (tram #1, #3 or #5 from Swanston Street) but, with its university presence and its long-established Italian café scene, it could be a million miles away. **Lygon Street** is the centre of the action, and it was here, in the 1950s, that espresso bars were really introduced to Melbourne; exotic spots such as the *Caffe Sport, La Gina, University Caffe, Don Basilio, La Cacciatora* and *Toto's* (which claims to have introduced pizza to Australia) had an unconventional allure in staid Anglo-Melbourne, and the local intelligentsia soon made the street their second home. Victorian terraced houses provided cheap living, and this became the first of the city's "alternative" suburbs. These days Carlton is no longer particularly bohemian; its residents are older and wealthier, and Lygon Street has gone very definitely upmarket, though the smart fashion shops still jostle with arts centres, bookshops, and excellent ethnic restaurants and cafés like *Tiamo* (see p.924).

Lygon Street itself is the obvious place to explore, but the elegant architecture also spreads eastwards to Drummond Street, and, flanking Carlton Gardens, Rathdowne and Nicholson streets. In the grounds of **Melbourne University** you'll find cheap food and useful notice boards (for accommodation and items for sale) in the Union Building. Running along the western side of the university, Royal Parade gives onto **Royal Park**, with its memorial to

MELBOURNE SUBURBS

BROADMEADOWS

THOMASTOWN

BUNDOORA

Hume Highway

Valley Highway

Latrobe
University

PRESTON

COBURG

Planty Road

HEIDELBERG

Museum of
Modern Art
at Heide

Road

Tullamarine Freeway

ESSENDON

Sydney Road

BRUNSWICK

Yarra
Valley Park

BULLEEN

Thompsons Road

NORTH-
COTE

Bulleen
Park

DONCASTER

ROYAL
PARK

Melbourne
Zoo

Victoria
Park

Flemington
Racecourse

Royal
Park

CLIFTON
HILL

Yarra
Bend

Western Highway

Melbourne
University

FITZROY

KEW

FOOTSCRAY

CARLTON

COLLING-
WOOD

MELBOURNE

RICHMOND

HAWTHORN

CAMBERWELL

BOX
HILL

West Gate Freeway

SOUTH
MELBOURNE

PORT
MELBOURNE

ALBERT
PARK

Albert
Park

SOUTH YARRA

PRAHRAN

TOORAK

Burwood Highway

Tasmanian
Ferry
Terminal

MIDDLE
PARK

WINDSOR

Princes Highway

South East Arterial Freeway

ST
KILDA

Jewish
Museum

Port Phillip Bay

Ripponlea
House

Caulfield
Racecourse

ELWOOD

ELSTERNWICK

CAULFIELD

CHADSTONE

NORTH
BRIGHTON

OAKLEIGH

Monash
University

N

BRIGHTON

Nepean Highway

BENTLEIGH

0   2 km

MOORABBIN

SANDRINGHAM

Frankston and Mornington Peninsula

Essendon Airport & Melbourne Airport

Scienceworks Museum & Planetarium

Eltham

Yarra Valley Wineries, Lillydale & Ringwood

Ferntree Gully & Dandenong Ranges

Dandenong City, Warragul and Gippsland

the explorers Burke and Wills (see box, p.568), and from there it's a short walk
through the park to the Zoo.

Melbourne Zoo

When it opened in 1862, **Melbourne Zoo** (daily 9am–5pm; also Jan & early
March Thurs–Sun & Feb Fri–Sun until 9pm for Twilight Concerts at the Zoo;
$16.40; Mon–Sat tram #55 from William Street, Sun #68 from Elizabeth

Street; ⓦ www.zoo.org.au) was the first in Australia. Some of its original features are still in evidence, including Australian and foreign trees, landscaped gardens, and a few restored Victorian-era cages, but almost all the animals have been rehoused in better, more natural conditions. The Australian area contains a central lake with waterbirds, open enclosures for koalas and other animals, and a bushland setting where you can walk among emus, kangaroos and wallabies. Strolling along the boardwalks of the **Great Flight Aviary** (daily 10.30am–4.30pm) you'll come across areas of rainforest, wetland, and a scrub area with a huge gum tree where many birds nest. The dark **Platypus Habitat** (daily 9.30am–4.30pm) is also worth a look, since the mammals are notoriously difficult to see in the wild – even here there's no guarantee you'll be lucky. Highly enjoyable, too, is the **Butterfly House** (daily 9.30am–4.30pm), a steamy tropical hothouse with hundreds of colourful Australian butterflies flitting about.

Fitzroy and Collingwood

In the 1970s, **Fitzroy** took over from Carlton as the centre for artistic nonconformity; its focus is **Brunswick Street** (tram #11 from Collins St), especially between Gertrude Street, home to Turkish takeaways, and Johnston Street, with its lively Spanish bars and restaurants. Brunswick Street has recently been nominated for inclusion on the historic register of the National Trust. Every year at the beginning of October, the colourful Fringe Parade and a street party on Brunswick Street usher in the **Fringe Festival**, the alternative scene's answer to the highbrow Melbourne Festival. The **International Comedy Festival** (April) and the **Next Wave Festival** (May, even-numbered years), two other notable arts events, also take place mainly in Fitzroy. In the shadow of Housing Commission tower blocks, welfare agencies and charity shops rub shoulders with funky secondhand clothes and junk shops, ethnic supermarkets and restaurants, cafés full of students and equally grungy artists, writers and musicians, and thriving bookshops that stay open late and are often as crowded as the many bars and music pubs. Most of the rough old hotels have been done up to match the prevailing mood: the *Provincial* is a good example, with its distressed paint-job and deli/café/bar inside.

Fitzroy's fringe art leanings are reflected in wacky "street installations" such as mosaic chairs, and sculptures like *Mr Poetry*. The eye-catching wrought-iron gate at the entrance to the Fitzroy Nursery at 390 Brunswick St, with its fairytale motif, sets the theme for the Artists Garden above the nursery, which exhibits sculptures and other decorative items for garden use. Small **galleries** worth looking out for are the New York-style Tolarno Galleries (Tues–Sat 11am–6pm) at 121 Victoria Street, which showcases leading contemporary artworks; 200 Gertrude Street (Tues–Sat 10am–5.30pm), a converted warehouse transformed into a state-funded gallery and studio space for emerging artists; and monthly exhibitions at the Centre for Contemporary Photography, 205 Johnston Street (Wed–Sat 11am–5pm). Fitzroy also boasts its own **arts and crafts market** (third Sun of the month 10am–3.30pm) at the old Fitzroy Town Hall on the corner of Napier and Moor streets. The **Fitzroy Pool**, in the north of the suburb on the corner of Young and Cecil streets, is a summer meeting place where people occasionally swim between posing sessions.

While not as trendy as Brunswick Street, formerly shabby **Smith Street** (tram #86 from Bourke St), which forms the boundary between Fitzroy and **Collingwood** to the east, is catching up. You'll still find many charity shops, ethnic butchers and cheap supermarkets, but New Age bookshops, quirky little cafés and revamped pubs are edging in. Collingwood and the adjacent suburb of Abbotsford have a large **gay** population, with a clutch of gay bars and clubs, particularly on Peel and Glasshouse streets.

Around Prahran

Prahran Council, covering South Yarra, Prahran and, to the east, Toorak and Armadale, oversees an extensive area of **shopping**, both downbeat and upmarket. Chapel Street is the main drag: in South Yarra it extends for a Golden Mile of trendy shopping and *very* chic cafés; heading south beyond Commercial Road through Prahran and Windsor it gradually moves downmarket, until Dandenong Road and the Astor Cinema mark the start of St Kilda. Crossing Chapel Street at right angles in South Yarra, Toorak Road boasts equally ritzy designer boutiques and, if that's possible, becomes even more exclusive east of Grange Road, as it enters Toorak, a suburb synonymous with wealth in Melbourne. Below Toorak, High Street Armadale, between Kooyong and Glenferrie roads, holds a concentration of antique shops. **Trams #5, #6** and **#72** from Swanston Street will get you from the city centre to Chapel Street.

South Yarra and Toorak

Among the boutiques and speciality shops, bistro bars for the beautiful people and cooler-than-thou nightclubs, the **Jam Factory** shopping complex, named after its former incarnation, is worth making a beeline for on the **South Yarra** stretch of Chapel Street. **Como Historic House and Gardens**, overlooking the river from Como Avenue in South Yarra (daily 10am–5pm; $11), is a good example of the town houses built by wealthy nineteenth-century landowners. The elegant white mansion, a mixture of Regency and Italianate architectural styles, has been restored by the National Trust. To reach the house, walk east along Toorak Road from Chapel Street, and then north on Williams Road, or, from the city centre, take tram #8 from Swanston Street.

Toorak has never been short of a bean: when Melbourne was founded, the wealthy chose to build their stately homes here on the high bank of the Yarra, leaving the flood-prone lower ground for the poor. This old money has in recent years been joined by new; many European Jews who worked hard after arriving penniless in Australia celebrated their new wealth by moving to Toorak in the 1950s and 1960s. There's little to see or do in the suburb: the hilly, tree-lined streets are full of huge mansions in extensive private gardens, while so-called Toorak Village is stuffed with wickedly expensive designer boutiques.

Prahran

Beyond Commercial Road in **Prahran** proper, Chapel Street still focuses on fashion, but in a more street-smart vein, becoming progressively more downmarket; as Chapel Street crosses High Street the suburb changes to Windsor and becomes more interestingly ethnic. Landmarks include **Prahran Market** (Tues & Thurs dawn–5pm, Fri & Sat dawn–6pm), round the corner on Commercial Road, an excellent, though fairly expensive, food emporium (fish, meat, fruit, vegetables and delicatessen). **Chapel Street Bazaar**, back on the main drag, has good secondhand clothes, Art Deco jewellery, furniture and bric-a-brac. **Greville Street**, off Chapel Street in the heart of Prahran, is a fantastic pocket of eccentric bohemia – young, brash and full of freewheeling brio. These days, it's taken over from Chapel Street as the corridor of cutting-edge cool, with retro and designer boutiques, music outlets, and bijou nightspots like the *Continental* (see

Things really hot up over the weekend, and every Sunday the small **Greville Street Market** has arts, crafts and secondhand clothes and jewellery on the corner of Gratton Street in Gratton Park (noon–5pm).

South Melbourne and Albert Park

If it's the bay you're heading for, then St Kilda is the obvious destination; the quickest and most interesting way there is on the #96 tram from Bourke or Spencer streets, which runs on a light rail track via South Melbourne and Albert Park, past the Aquatic Centre with its five swimming pools (see "Listings", p.939). Both suburbs are worth checking out in their own right if you have the time. **South Melbourne**'s focus is the **South Melbourne Market** on the corner of Coventry and Cecil streets (Wed 8am–2pm, Fri 8am–6pm, Sat & Sun 8am–4pm), an old-fashioned, value-for-money place where you can browse stalls selling everything from fruit and vegetables to clothes and continental delicacies. Opposite here, a number of cafés and upmarket retail stores line Coventry Street; at no. 399, three portable iron houses (Sun 1–4pm; viewing by appointment on ☎03/9822 4369), prefabricated residences constructed in England and shipped to Melbourne during the goldrush, have been preserved by the National Trust. At the other end of Coventry Street, Clarendon Street is South Melbourne's main shopping precinct, and is a fine example of a nineteenth-century streetscape with original Victorian awnings overhanging numerous cafés, clothing shops and restaurants.

Exclusive **Albert Park** has the feel of a small village, with many lovely old terraced houses and Dundas Place, a shopping centre of mouthwatering delis and bakeries. In the shadow of the St Kilda Road office buildings lies Albert Park itself, the highly controversial site for the **Australian Grand Prix** at the beginning of March, which Melbourne snatched from Adelaide in 1996.

St Kilda and around

The former seaside resort of **St Kilda** has an air of shabby gentility, which enhances its current schizophrenic reputation as a sophisticated yet seedy suburb, largely residential but blessed with a raging nightlife. Running from St Kilda Road down to the Esplanade, **Fitzroy Street** is Melbourne's red-light district – usually pretty tame, though late at night not a comfortable place for women alone – and epitomizes this split personality: it's lined with dozens of thoroughly pretentious cafés and bars from which to gawp at the strip's goings-on. On weekend nights these and others throughout St Kilda are filled to overflowing with a style-conscious but fun crowd. During the day there's a very different feel, especially on **Acland Street** with its wonderful continental cake shops and bakeries. Ogling the mouthwatering window displays is a favourite way of passing the time on Sunday.

Also on Sunday, the **St Kilda Craft Market** (10am–5pm, until about 4pm in winter) lines the waterfront on Upper Esplanade. It's mainly arts and crafts, and not really good enough to justify the hordes of strollers, but going there is part of the ritual that includes taking a look at the beach, feeding your face, ambling into a few shops, listening to a busker, and perhaps calling at the covered market on Albert Street. St Kilda's most famous icon, **Luna Park** (Fri 7–11pm, Sat 11am–11pm, Sun 11am to dusk; ⓦwww.lunapark.com.au) is on the Esplanade, entered through the huge laughing clown's face of "Mr Moon". Despite a couple of new attractions, there's nothing very high-tech about this amusement park built in 1912: the Scenic Railway – the world's oldest operating roller coaster – runs along wooden trestles, the dodgem cars could do with a lick of paint and the Ghost Train wouldn't spook a toddler, but that's half the fun. Wandering around is free, but you pay $4.35 for individual rides. You can sit under the palm trees of **O'Donnell Gardens** next door, or nearby **St Kilda Botanical Gardens**, and eat your Acland Street goodies. The **beachfront** is a popular weekend promenade all year round, with separate cycling and walking paths stretching down to Elwood and Brighton, and a long pier thrusting out into the bay. Near the base of the pier are the **St Kilda Sea Baths**. Redevelopment of the historic site, which dates back to 1931, has dragged on for years, but work on this cement blunder (an heroically bad mix of shopping complex and function centre with a Moorish twist) is now complete, with a seawater pool, food shops, and various health facilities like spa and gym available to the public.

On Saturday, Sunday and public holidays, **boat trips** from the pier across Hobsons Bay to Williamstown (Williamstown Bay and River Cruises; departures hourly between 11.30am and 3.30pm – last departure one-way only; 20min; $6, $10 return; ☎ 03/9397 2255) are rewarded with lovely views of St Kilda and the city. An alternative is a ninety-minute cruise with Penguin Waters Cruises (daytime $23, sunrise and sunset cruise $33; bookings on ☎ 03/9645 0533), with a barbecue lunch or dinner thrown in. On the evening cruises – with a little luck – you'll catch a glimpse of **Little penguins** coming ashore at a certain spot 4km from the mouth of the Yarra. As the exact location is not publicized, you can see them without the crowds that congregate on Phillip Island (see p.946).

If you want to get a bit more serious, call in at one of the bookshops on Acland Street, or check out the local arty community at the Linden Gallery (Tues–Sun 1–6pm), based in a fine Victorian-era mansion at 26 Acland St, where painting, installations and video art are displayed.

Elwood and Elsternwick

The next stop south along the bay, **Elwood**, is a quieter version of St Kilda, still with a faintly alternative air. Ormond Road's original shopfronts conceal a health-food store, an alternative-therapies centre and a couple of cheap vegetarian takeaways, but more-yuppified cafés are slowly edging in. Ormond Esplanade runs past parkland through which occasional paths run down to the beach.

East of Elwood, **Elsternwick** (train to Ripponlea) is a largely Orthodox Jewish area. The original 1918 fittings and facade of Brinsmead Chemist at 73 Glen Eira Rd are protected by the National Trust, as is **Ripponlea House** at 192 Hotham St (daily 10am–5pm; $11), which shows how Melbourne's wealthy elite lived a century or so ago. The 33-room mansion has magnificent gardens, complete with ornamental lake and fernery, and a way-over-the-top interior. The grounds are popular for picnics at weekends, when the tearoom is also open (11am–4pm). Ten- to fifteen-minutes' walk away in East St Kilda, at 26 Alma Road opposite the St Kilda Synagogue, is the **Jewish Museum of Australia** (Tues–Thurs 10am–4pm, Sun 11am–5pm; $7; tram #3 or #67 to stop 32 from Swanston Street in the city or from St Kilda Road). It has four permanent exhibitions: the Australian Jewish History Gallery, documenting Jewish life in Australia since the beginning of colonization 200 years ago; the Timeline of Jewish History, tracing the last four thousand years; and Jewish Year and Belief and Ritual, both dedicated to the religious and ethical foundations of Judaism, with a focus on festivals and customs. Changing exhibitions on a wide range of related topics are another feature of the museum.

Spotswood and Williamstown

Docks and industry dominate the area west of the city centre, reached by suburban train, by the ferry *Williamstown Seeker* (11.10am, 1.10pm & 3.10pm) from the Southbank jetty at the Melbourne Exhibition Centre, or by heading out on the Westgate Freeway across the huge Westgate Bridge. A good reason for visiting **Spotswood**, the first suburb across the Yarra, is **Scienceworks**, at 2 Booker St (daily 10am–4.30pm; $8.80, or $14.30 for combined Scienceworks and Planetarium ticket; ⊛http://scienceworks.museum.vic.gov.au). Inside the Space Age building, set in appropriately desolate wasteland, the displays are ingenious, fun and highly interactive. Part of the exhibition consists of the original Spotswood Pumping Station, an unusually aesthetic early industrial complex with working steam pumps. Also here are some displays from the Melbourne Museum. The **Planetarium** features state-of-the-art digital technology to take visitors on a virtual journey through the galaxy (Sat & Sun 11am, noon, 1pm, 2pm & 3pm, plus Thurs 8pm; $11; bookings essential on ℡03/9392 4819).

On a promontory at the mouth of the Yarra, **Williamstown** is a strange mix of rich and poor, of industry, yachting marinas and working port. Expensive cafés ring Nelson Place, but the down-to-earth *Yacht Club Hotel* here offers the cheapest meal in town – prices have been fixed since the 1970s and it's always packed on Sunday, especially when the **Williamstown Market** is held along the waterfront (third Sun of each month). The most enjoyable way to get to Williamstown is by **boat** from St Kilda (see overleaf), or you can take a trip into the city with Williamstown Bay and River Cruises ($10); for more see box on p.910.

Bulleen and Eltham

Further afield in the northeastern suburbs two attractions – the Museum of Modern Art at Heide in Bulleen and Montsalvat in Eltham – are well worth the trek, or make a day-trip of it and visit them en route to the Yarra Valley wineries and the Healesville Sanctuary (see p.951).

The **Museum of Modern Art at Heide**, on Templestowe Road at Bulleen, was the home of Melbourne art patrons **John and Sunday Reed**, who in the mid-1930s purchased what was then a derelict dairy farm on the banks of the meandering Yarra River. During the following decades the Reeds fostered and nurtured the talents of young unknown artists and thus played a central role in the emergence of Australian art movements such as the Angry Penguins, the Antipodeans and the Annandale Realists. The painters Sidney Nolan, John Perceval, Albert Tucker and Arthur Boyd were all members of the artistic circle at Heide at one time or another. The government of Victoria purchased the property shortly before the Reeds' deaths in 1981, and their former home, itself an attractive specimen of the modernist architecture of the 1960s, is now a gallery housing consistently interesting, changing exhibitions of contemporary Australian art (Tues–Fri 10am–5pm, Sat, Sun & public holidays noon–5pm; $6.60). There's also a good café, and you can ramble through the extensive **gardens**, which feature sculptures and a kitchen garden (no admission fee). The museum is about 14km from the city centre, but only fifteen-minutes' drive via the northeastern freeway, or you could take the suburban train to Heidelberg Station (Eltham line) and from there bus #291 to Templestowe Road (frequent services).

Eltham, a bushy suburb further northeast, about 24km from the city, is known as a centre for arts and crafts. Its reputation was established in 1935 when the charismatic painter and architect **Justus Jorgensen** moved to what was then a separate town and founded **Montsalvat**, a European-style artists' colony. Built with the help of his students and followers, the colony's eclectic design was inspired by medieval European buildings with wonderful quirky results; Jorgensen died before it was completed and it has deliberately been left unfinished. He did, however, live long enough to see his community thrive, and to oversee the completion of the mud-brick Great Hall, whose influence is evident in other mud-brick buildings around Eltham. Today Montsalvat, a two-kilometre walk from Eltham Station, is still operating as a colony of painters, potters and craftspeople, and can be visited daily (9am–5pm; $6.50; ⓦ www.montsalvat.com.au).

Eating and drinking

Melbourne is Australia's premier city for **eating out**. Sydney may be more stylish and Adelaide cheaper, but Melbourne has the best food and the widest choice of it, almost all exceptionally good value. In March each year, the city celebrates its pre-eminence with a **Food and Wine Festival**, in which the distinct ethnic areas host culinary street parties. In the **city centre**, Greek cafés line Lonsdale Street between Swanston and Russell streets, while Little Bourke Street is the home of Chinatown. Lygon Street, in inner-city **Carlton**, is just one of many pockets across the city with a concentration of Italian restaurants. Johnston Street in **Fitzroy** is the Spanish strip, while nearby up-and-coming Smith Street and arty Brunswick Street both have a huge variety of international cuisines and smart cafés. Greek restaurants fill Swan Street in inner-city **Richmond**, and Vietnamese places dominate Victoria Street. Fitzroy and **St Kilda**, another gastronomically mixed bag, are the centres of café society; St Kilda also has great restaurants, bakeries and delis, as does Jewish **Balaclava**.

Most of Melbourne's restaurants are BYO, and even the licensed ones generally allow you to bring your own drink – though check first, and note that a corkage fee ($1–2 per person) often applies. If you're going to be around for a while, *The Age Cheap Eats in Melbourne* and its more upmarket companion, *The Age Good Food Guide*, are worthwhile investments, as is *The Age Good Bar Guide*.

City centre

There are still plenty of old-fashioned **coffee lounges** in the city – the type of place where you can get a milky cappuccino and grilled cheese on toast, with a mini-jukebox at your table – but stylish **cafés** with a more thoughtful decor and much more diverse menus are edging in. In the department stores, both the Myer and David Jones food halls are excellent for upmarket picnic ingredients, while Melbourne Central has several good eating places – the Daimaru food department on the ground floor also sells Japanese food items.

Cafe La, 35th Floor, *Hotel Sofitel*, cnr Collins and Exhibition streets (ⓣ 03/9670 411). Café with the best views in Melbourne, and much more affordable than the exclusive *Le Restaurant* on the same floor. Open daily from 6.30am until about 10pm for breakfast, lunch, dinner and afternoon teas.
Cafe Segovia, 33 Block Place, near Little Collins St (ⓣ 03/9650 2373). Very pleasant, Spanish-style café, serving good coffee and excellent food. Licensed and BYO (wine only). Mon–Fri 7.30am–late, Sat 8am–late, Sun 9am–5pm.

Campari, 25 Hardware St (ⓣ 03/9670 3813). Casual and characterful, this daytime spot pulls in lawyers from the nearby courts with excellent Southern Italian food. Pasta dishes for around $13 and steaks and fish around $16. Breakfast is also available. Licensed and BYO. Mon–Thurs 7am–5.30pm, Fri 7am–8.30pm.
Crossways Food for Life, 123 Swanston St. Dirt-cheap Indian-style vegetarian food prepared by Hare Krishnas. Mon–Sat 11.30am–2.30pm.
Curry Bowl, 250 Elizabeth St (ⓣ 03/9639 0868).

Sri Lankan fast food to eat in or take away. Closed Sun.

Dish, 379 St Kilda Rd (℡ 03/9677 9933). Modern, cavernous restaurant nestled in the heritage-listed *Royce on St Kilda Road* hotel a few minutes from Melbourne's CBD. Food is expensive and mostly satisfactory, and runs from salmon fish cakes, risotto and lamb shanks to vegetable tarts and a reasonable choice of desserts. Licensed. Mon–Fri 6.30am–11pm, Sat 8am–11pm, Sun 8–11am.

ezard at the Adelphi, 187 Flinders Lane (℡ 03/9639 6811). Down a small flight of stairs, this hip, dimly lit place is one of Melbourne's hottest eateries, with a tasty and moderately expensive range of East meets West favourites. Licensed. Mon–Fri noon–11pm, Sat 6–11pm.

Gopals, 139 Swanston St (℡ 03/9650 1578). *Crossways'* sister restaurant – another Hare Krishna-run, very cheap veggie place. Mon noon–3pm, Tues–Fri noon–8.30pm, Sat 5–8.30pm.

Grand Hyatt Foodcourt, 123 Collins St (℡ 03/9653 4549). Spacious, airy place where customers choose cakes, imaginative salads and other dishes from various stalls and bars; Friday night happy hour is popular with the office crowd.

Grossi Florentino, 80 Bourke St (℡ 03/9662 1811). A Melbourne institution, which divides loyalties between the cellar café-grill-restaurant, serving inexpensive, home-style pasta dishes, drinks and good coffee, and the very pricey and elegant Italian–French restaurant upstairs. Licensed. Mon–Sat noon–3pm & 6–11pm, upstairs restaurant closed Sat morning.

Güust Cofetärie, 174 Queen St (℡ 03/9602 4846). Arrive famished to this popular spot, as the East European fare like debrezin sausage is impressive. Bookings essential for lunch. Licensed. Mon–Tues 7am–7pm, Wed–Fri 7am–11pm.

Hopetoun Tea Rooms, Block Arcade, 282 Collins St (℡ 03/9650 2777). Tea, scones and delicious cakes have been served in these elegant surroundings for more than one hundred years, but new-fangled delicacies such as *focaccia* with pesto sauce have now wheedled their way onto the menu. Mon–Thurs 9am–5pm, Fri 9am–6pm, Sat 10am–3pm.

Il Solito Posto, Basement, 113 Collins St (off George Parade) (℡ 03/9654 4466). Charming basement location, casual atmosphere and fine no-fuss Italian food make for one of Melbourne's best dining experiences. Licensed. Mon–Fri 7.30am–11pm, Sat 9am–11pm.

Kappo Okita, 17 Liverpool St (℡ 03/9662 2206). Modest Japanese café with good, inexpensive food, especially sushi and sashimi. Best to reserve for weekend evenings. BYO. Mon–Fri

noon–2.30pm, plus Mon–Thurs 6–10pm, Fri & Sat 6–11pm.

Kenzan, 45 Collins St (℡ 03/9654 8933). Sushi bar renowned for the freshness of its sushi and sashimi; more upmarket than *Kappo Okita*, with slightly cheaper lunches. Licensed. Mon–Fri noon–2.30pm & 6–10pm.

Le Restaurant, 35th Floor, *Hotel Sofitel*, cnr Collins and Exhibition streets (℡ 03/9653 0000). Luxurious restaurant with silver service and fantastic views over Melbourne and Port Phillip Bay. Serves carefully prepared seasonal dishes, together with Australian produce such as barramundi and yabbies. Expect to pay in the region of $70 per person (not including drinks). Tues–Sat from 7pm till late.

Medallion Cafe & Cakes, 209 Lonsdale St (℡ 03/9663 4228). Popular Greek café, once shabby, now with an over-the-top, disco-style interior, but still serving authentic, cheap food. Daily 8am until late (3am Fri & Sat).

Mekong, 241 Swanston St (℡ 03/9663 3288). Small Vietnamese café specializing in *pho* (beef or chicken noodle soup). Excellent-value food (dishes about $5), but packed at lunchtime. Mon–Sat 9am–10pm, Sun 10am–10pm.

Ong International Food Court, basement of the *Welcome Hotel*, 256 Little Bourke St (℡ 03/9662 3416). Authentic Asian food court with stalls selling Chinese, Vietnamese, Malaysian/Singaporean and Thai food. Licensed. Daily 10am–10pm.

Pellegrini's Espresso Bar, 66 Bourke St (℡ 03/9662 1885). Melbourne's first espresso bar, and still an institution. Crowded after work with chat and clatter. Classic 1950s interior and great pasta. Mon–Sat 8am–11.30pm, Sun noon–8pm.

Radii, *Park Hyatt Melbourne*, 1 Parliament Square (℡ 03/9224 1234). Part of the swank *Park Hyatt Melbourne*, this monstrously large and very expensive restaurant seats close to 150 souls. If you can take your eyes off the over-the-top decor (all marble and mirrors), you'll discover enough waiters to serve a small island state, as well as some of the most imaginative Mediterranean-style dishes prepared in the city. Food fit for a king and an ideal place for marriage proposals and assorted special occasions. Licensed. Mon 6–10.30pm, Tues–Sat noon–10.30pm.

Republic, 299 Queen St (℡ 03/9670 2999). Located in the eye-catching Republic Towers apartment block, this dramatic new restaurant serves up contemporary Australian food with a slight Greek-Mediterranean and Japanese twist. The service is excellent and so is the wine list. Reasonably expensive, but a big hit with the business crowd. Licensed. Mon–Fri noon–11pm, Sat 6–11pm.

Satay Inn, 250 Swanston St (☎ 03/9663 4703). Excellent, affordable Malaysian place, close to the big department stores. BYO. Daily 11am–11pm.

Southgate, across the river from Flinders Street Station. With fine views of the river and the city skyline, this centre has developed into a very popular place to dine and drink. The food court is packed during lunch hours and at weekends, and on Friday and Saturday nights advance booking is essential for the restaurants. Some of the best places are *The Blue Train Café* (☎ 03/9696 0111), which attracts a young, hip crowd and serves drinks and tasty and very inexpensive light meals; *E Gusto* (☎ 03/9690 9819), which does "Modern Australian" cuisine with an Italian slant; and the more upmarket *Walter's Wine Bar* (☎ 03/9690 9211) and *Simply French* (☎ 03/9699 9804), the latter serving superb French food – leave some space for the brilliant desserts.

Swiss Rosti Bar, 87 Flinders Lane, between Exhibition and Spring streets (☎ 03/9654 0088). Tasty and well-presented Swiss–German fare which is quite a few notches above the stodge that passes for German food elsewhere, along with a few international dishes. Try *kassler* (pickled pork) with sauerkraut or bratwurst, fried onions and mushrooms, all served with *rosti* (fried grated potatoes), a Swiss specialty. Licensed and moderately priced. Mon–Fri 9am–late.

Syracuse, 23 Bank Place (☎ 03/9670 1777). Come for the mouthwatering tapas (served from 3pm) and the lamb and leek sausages, then top it off with fantastic cheeses, panforte and coffee. Extensive, almost daunting wine list, good selection of cigars and seductive atmosphere. Licensed.

Mon–Fri 7.30am–11pm.

Tsindos, 197 Lonsdale St (☎ 03/9663 3194). All the Greek classics from taramasalata to moussaka and souvlakia at reasonable prices, plus live bouzouki music every night except Sunday. Licensed and BYO. Mon–Fri noon–3pm plus Mon–Thurs & Sun 5–10pm, Fri & Sat 5–11pm.

VIS, 245 Swanston St (☎ 03/9662 9995). Stylish café-restaurant underneath *The Lounge* with food to match – check the blackboard menu for unusual dishes such as prawn and basil ravioli and smoked rack of lamb *harissa*. Licensed. Mon–Fri 10am–late, Sat noon–late.

Waiters Restaurant, 20 Meyers Place, off Bourke St between Exhibition and Spring streets (☎ 03/9650 1508). Long-established Italian place on the first floor above a bar, once a waiters' favourite for its late hours. No frills, simple food and low prices. Licensed and BYO. Mon–Fri, plus Mon–Sat 6pm–midnight.

William Angliss College, Latrobe St (☎ 03/9606 2111). Licensed restaurant with fine food and service. Incredibly cheap, but you're at the mercy of the catering students. Booking essential.

Zukini, 310 Flinders Lane (☎ 03/9620 1900). Designed by local architectural gun Tom Kovacs, this stylish two-level canteen and restaurant is renowned for its mix of chemical-free food and Zen-like decor. If you can decipher the verbose menu, you'll find there's a big emphasis on seasonally fresh produce, plus a selection of meat dishes, a large wine list and superb variety of teas. The canteen menu is also available downstairs in the more formal dining area. Licensed. Mon–Fri 7am–1am, Sat 10am–1am.

Chinatown

Yum cha (elsewhere known as dim sum, a series of small delicacies served from trolleys) is available at lunchtime almost everywhere; on Sunday it's a crowded ritual.

Camy Shanghai Dumpling and Noodle Restaurant, Tattersalls Lane, between Little Bourke and Lonsdale streets, close to Swanston St (☎ 03/9663 8555). An extremely cheap, partly self-service place, dishing up very simple but delicious dumplings and noodles. No alcohol. Mon–Fri 11am–10pm, Sat & Sun 11am–9.30pm.

Chez Phat, 7 Waratah Place (☎ 03/9663 0988). First-floor hideaway with a marvellously lived-in, 1970s atmosphere. Everything on the small but appetizing menu is bright-tasting and well thought out, from baguettes, pizza, polenta and steak to apple pie for dessert. Licensed. Mon–Tues 8am–8pm, Wed–Fri 8am–10.30pm.

Empress of China, 120–122 Little Bourke St (☎ 03/9663 1883). Expensive but good value, with lots of lesser-known dishes on offer. Licensed. Closed Sat lunchtime.

Flower Drum, 17 Market Lane, between Bourke and Little Bourke streets (☎ 03/9662 3655). Among some very good Chinese restaurants, this is simply outstanding: sophisticated Cantonese cuisine, including exquisite seafood and fish, but also expensive – about $110 for two, plus drinks. Licensed. Mon–Sat noon–2pm, plus daily 6–10pm.

King of Kings, 209 Russell St (☎ 03/9663 2895). Simple, inexpensive Hong Kong-style food, including

congee, and lots of dishes with pork and offal. BYO. Lunch and dinner daily; open until 2.30am.
Little Malaysia, 26 Liverpool St (☎ 03/9662 1678). Cheap and good Malaysian hawker fare. Licensed and BYO. Daily 11.30am–3pm & 5.30–11pm.

Shark Fin House, 131 Little Bourke St (☎ 03/9663 1555). Converted warehouse with three storeys devoted to about fifty kinds of *yum cha*, all through the week, night and day. Very busy at lunchtime, especially at weekends. Licensed. Daily 11am–11pm.

Carlton and North Melbourne

As well as an Italian strip of restaurants and cafés on Lygon Street, between Gratton and Elgin streets, Carlton is home to several good Asian restaurants. To the south of Carlton, North Melbourne harbours an excellent Balinese restaurant.

Brunetti, 198–204 Faraday St (☎ 03/9347 2801). A steady stream of customers walks past an array of display cases filled with a mouthwatering selection of chocolates, pastries, biscuits and cakes to get their daily espresso in the café section. Licensed restaurant next door. Cakes and café daily 7am–10pm; restaurant Mon–Fri noon–3pm, Sat from 12.30pm; dinner Mon–Sat 6–10pm.
Jimmy Watson's, 333 Lygon St (☎ 03/9347 3985). Robin Boyd-designed establishment with a good reputation for pub grub in convivial, atmospheric surroundings. Super wine list. Licensed. Mon 10am–6pm, Tues–Sat 10am–9.30pm.
Nyonya, 191 Lygon St (☎ 03/9347 8511). Authentic Nyonya cuisine, a blend of Malaysian and Chinese cooking, at moderate prices. BYO. Daily noon–2.30pm, plus Mon–Fri 5.30–10pm, Sat & Sun 5.30–10.30pm.
Shakahari, 201–203 Faraday St (☎ 03/9347 3848). Excellent, imaginative vegetarian food, influenced by various Asian cuisines, at moderate prices. Licensed and BYO. Mon–Sat noon–2pm &

6–10pm, Sun 6–10pm.
Tiamo 1, 303 Lygon St (☎ 03/9347 5759). One-time beatnik hangout and still popular with students, with layers of browning 1950s posters and a good-value blackboard menu. Next door is its sibling, *Tiamo 2*, which is more upmarket but still excellent value. Licensed and BYO. Mon–Sat 7.30am–11pm, Sun 9.30am–10pm.
Toofey's, 162A Elgin St (☎ 03/9347 9838). Considered to be Melbourne's best seafood restaurant. Extremely fresh fish and seafood are prepared in a light, Mediterranean or Middle Eastern style. About $90 plus drinks for two for dinner. Licensed. Tues–Fri noon–3pm & 6–10pm, Sat & Sun 6–10pm.
Toto's Pizza House, 101 Lygon St (☎ 03/9347 1630). Melbourne's first pizzeria, dating from the 1950s – cheap, cheerful and noisy. Licensed. Daily 11am–11pm.
Warung Agus, 305 Victoria St (☎ 03/9329 1737). Authentic Balinese restaurant with superb, affordable food. BYO. Tues–Sat 6.30–10pm.

Fitzroy and Collingwood

Adjacent Fitzroy and Collingwood probably have the widest choice of cuisines in the city, and are good places to finish off your night on the town, as there's always lots going on. There's a smallish Spanish centre with a few tapas bars on **Johnston Street**, between **Brunswick and Nicholson streets**.

Brunswick Street

Afghan Gallery, 327 Brunswick St (☎ 03/9417 2430). Cheap and authentic food with a decor of Afghan hangings and rugs. Very popular with students. Licensed and BYO. Daily 6–11pm.
Babka Bakery Cafe, 358 Brunswick St (☎ 03/9416 0091). A deservedly popular place, as the bread and cakes, made on the premises, are divine, and dishes from the changing blackboard menu are equally enticing and satisfying. Try Russian blintzes for breakfast or their justly famous "shoo fly buns", currant buns that are eaten with butter. Licensed & BYO. Tues–Sun 7am–7pm.

diningroom 211, 211 Brunswick St (☎ 03/9419 7211). A new addition to the strip serving contemporary Australian cuisine in a space designed to the very inch of its life. Licensed. Tues–Sun 6.30pm til late, plus Wed–Fri noon–3pm, Sat & Sun noon–5pm.
Guernica, 257 Brunswick St (☎ 03/9416 0969). This swish, stylish and invitingly intimate place offers highly original Australian food, yummy desserts and a few drops by the glass. Licensed. Mon–Fri & Sun noon–3pm & 6–10.30pm, Sat 6–10.30pm.
Mario's, 303 Brunswick St (☎ 03/9417 3343). European-style café where you can eat breakfast

(until midnight), lunch and dinner or just have a coffee or a drink. Dauntingly smart staff and decor, but not expensive or dressy. The clientele is an interesting mixture of poseurs, celebrities and scruffs. Mon–Wed & Sun 7am–midnight, Thurs–Sat 7am–1am.

Rhumbaralla's, 342 Brunswick St (℡ 03/9417 5652). The neon sign in the window is one of the street's landmarks, and the inside of this stylish café is just as vibrantly coloured. The place hums to the sound of the ceiling fan, jazz music and conversation. Breakfast until midday – eggs Benedict the favourite – then anything from *focaccia* to steak. Licensed and BYO. Daily 9am–1am.

Shanti, 285 Brunswick St (℡ 03/9416 2170). Serves tandoori dishes as well as Southern Indian specialities cooked in coconut milk rather than cream and yogurt. Lots of vegetarian options and seafood. Moderately priced, the masala dosa is especially good value. Licensed and BYO (wine only). Mon–Fri noon–2pm & 6–10.30pm, Sat & Sun noon–2pm.

Thai Thani, 293 Brunswick St (℡ 03/9419 6463). One of Melbourne's best Thai restaurants, on two crowded levels, with moderate prices. BYO. Daily 6–10.30pm.

The Vegie Bar, 380 Brunswick St (℡ 03/9417 6935). Simple, fresh food cooked to order. Cheap, popular and hip rather than hippie: jazzy soul sounds and poster-covered walls. Licensed and BYO. Daily 10.30am–10pm.

Johnston Street

Carmen Bar, 74 Johnston St (℡ 03/9417 4794). The best value tapas bar in the area, usually full of Spanish people. Live flamenco Thurs–Sat. Tues–Sun 6pm–1am.

Guru da Dhaba, 240 Johnston St (℡ 03/9486 9155). Cheap Indian restaurant specializing in Punjabi cuisine that's always packed – advance bookings are advised. BYO. Daily 5.30–11pm, plus Sat & Sun noon–3pm.

Kahlo's, 36 Johnston St (℡ 03/9417 7810). Smallish, cosy tapas bar. Wed–Sat 6pm–1am.

Smith Street

Cafe Bohemio, 354 Smith St, north of Johnston St (℡ 03/9417 7626). This laid-back place, reminiscent of a student café in the 1970s, seems to be a meeting place for Melbourne's small Hispanic expatriate community. Serves Latin American dishes (recipes from Argentina to Uruguay), often accompanied by live music (jazz, salsa, Brazilian guitar). Licensed & BYO (wine only). Tues–Sat noon–late.

Cafe Coco, 129 Smith St (℡ 03/9417 39370). Cosy spot, where the blackboard menu of inexpensive light meals, excellent cakes and good coffee changes regularly. Licensed and BYO (wine only). Mon–Fri 11am–10.30pm, Sat & Sun 9am–10.30pm.

Gluttony – It's a Sin, 278 Smith St (℡ 03/9419 2949). Good cakes, cooked breakfasts and meals. Popular with locals. Licensed and BYO. Tues–Sat 7am–11pm, Sun 10am–11pm.

Soulfood Cafe, 273 Smith St (℡ 03/9419 2949). Comfortable cafeteria-style vegetarian café with wooden trestle tables, pine walls, and a good notice board at the back. Mon–Fri 8am–6pm, Sat 9am–5pm, Sun 10am–4pm.

Richmond

Swan Street, running from Church Street towards Wattle Park, is home to Melbourne's best Greek restaurants. On the north side of Richmond, **Victoria Street** is lined with Vietnamese supermarkets, clothes shops and dozens of cheap, authentic restaurants.

Fenix, 680–682 Victoria St (℡ 03/9427 8500). Great views over the Yarra, especially in summer on the deck. As for the food, you can dive into steak, fish and steamed pudding, all of it decently priced and well presented. Mon–Fri 9am–11pm, Sat & Sun 8am–11pm.

Salona, 262a Swan St (℡ 03/9429 1460). Long-established Greek restaurant – one of four in this block – serves good, plain and very reasonably priced dishes. Licensed and BYO. Daily noon–11.30pm.

Tho Tho's Bar-Restaurant, 66 Victoria St (℡ 03/9428 2036). Much more upmarket than most of its neighbours, but usually packed and noisy. Inexpensive food, with the lunch specials offering especially good value. Licensed and BYO. Daily 11am–midnight.

Thy Thy 1, upstairs at 142 Victoria St (℡ 03/9429 1104). The most sought-after Vietnamese restaurant on Victoria St, always with a queue to get in. The food is basic but great. BYO. Daily 8am–10pm.

Thy Thy 2, 116 Victoria St (℡ 03/9428 5914). Slightly upmarket from *Thy Thy 1*, but similar and also very popular. BYO. Daily 10am–11pm.

Vao Doi, 120 Victoria St (℡ 03/9428 3264). Another much-frequented Vietnamese place, with set lunch menus for the uninitiated. BYO. Daily 10am–11pm.

VV, 86 Victoria St (☎03/9429 8328). Another upmarket bar and restaurant. This one attracts a

mixed clientele of local Vietnamese, Australians and students from Malaysia, Singapore and Thailand. Inexpensive food. Licensed and BYO. Daily 11am–11pm.

South Yarra, Prahran and Windsor

Caffe e Cucina, 581 Chapel St, South Yarra (☎03/9827 4139). Still one of Melbourne's coolest eating spots, attracting a smart clientele and dishing up fantastic pasta. Licensed. Mon–Sat 7am–midnight.

Candy Bar, 162 Greville St, Prahran (☎03/9529 6566). Funky joint popular for eating, drinking and bopping into the early hours. Sample a range of food from noodles and curries to polenta whilst sitting on comfy sofas and grooving to the music. Licensed. Daily noon–late.

Chinois Deux, 176 Toorak Rd, South Yarra (☎03/9826 3388). Formerly *Chinois*, this icon of fine French food has been rechristened and renovated, not altogether successfully. Two constants remain: the service, which is consistently sublime; and the prices, which are stubbornly upmarket, especially for the wines. Licensed. Lunch Mon–Fri noon–3pm, dinner Mon–Fri 6.30–11pm, Sat & Sun 6–11pm.

Chinta Ria Jazz, 176 Commercial Rd, Prahran (☎03/9510 6520). One of Simon Goh's string of Malaysian eateries – the owner is a dedicated jazz and blues fan. Very moderately priced. BYO. Daily except Wed noon–2.30pm & 6–10/11pm.

The Continental Cafe, 132–134 Greville St, Prahran (☎03/9510 2788). Hugely popular restaurant and nightclub, with waistcoated waiters and

an equally smart, arty clientele. Breakfast all day, very good pasta dishes, and a wide range of wines and liqueurs. Licensed. Mon–Fri 7am–11pm, Sat 8am–11.30pm, Sun 8am–10.30pm.

Falafel House, 196 Toorak Rd, South Yarra (☎03/9827 6236). Middle Eastern takeaway, perfect after pubbing or clubbing. Daily 9am–5am.

Greville Bar, 143 Greville St, Prahran (☎03/9529 4800). Dim and sexy downstairs space with a sophisticated Japanese-style menu, plus an upstairs "dining club" specializing in contemporary Australian cuisine. Licensed. Daily noon–11pm.

Helens Polish Restaurant, 134 Chapel St, Windsor (☎03/9530 2694). Simple, authentic Polish place, open from breakfast to dinner; great cakes and full meals. BYO. Mon–Sat 9am–10pm, Sun 1–10pm.

Tamani Bistro, 156 Toorak Rd, South Yarra (☎03/9866 2575). Dimly lit, crowded Italian cheapie. BYO. Daily 9am–10.30pm.

2BC, 177 Greville St, Prahran (☎03/9529 4922). Mixing Mediterranean, Middle Eastern and Asian influences, the menu sounds the part and mostly delivers, although the tacky marble bar and drab artworks on the wall mar an otherwise pleasant dining experience. Licensed. Mon–Fri noon–3pm, plus Tues–Thurs 6–10.30pm, Fri & Sat 6–11pm.

South Melbourne, Albert Park and Port Melbourne

There's not much of a night-time scene in these suburbs, but cafés and delicatessens dish up a mouthwatering selection of food during the day.

Albert Park Deli, 129 Dundas Place, Albert Park (☎03/9699 9594). Superb delicatessen takeaway, specializing in delicious breads and *arancini* (Italian rice balls). Daily 5am–9pm.

Arkibar, 27 Coventry St, South Melbourne (☎03/9690 6688). Modern café serving good Italian food. Licensed. Mon–Wed 7.30am–4.30pm, Thurs & Fri 7.30am–10pm, Sat 9am–1pm.

Cafe Sweethearts, 263 Coventry St, South Melbourne (☎03/9690 6752). Good for breakfast – numerous (and some very exotic-sounding) varieties of sandwiches and eggs served here. Mon–Fri 7am–3pm, Sat & Sun 8am–3pm.

Coventry Blue, 313 Coventry St (☎03/9682 5844). Café with an alternative feel in a terrace house opposite the South Melbourne market. Cheap vegetarian dishes. BYO. Tues–Thurs 7am–3pm, Fri & Sat 7am–5pm, Sun 8am–5pm.

Montague Hotel, cnr Park and Montague streets, South Melbourne (☎03/9690 9044). Renovated, atmospheric old pub and a good restaurant out the back serving hearty fare.

Montague Park Foodstore, 406 Park St (☎03/9682 9680). Delicious dishes and desserts to take away or eat in. Particularly pleasant in summer when the tables are out on the footpath. Daily 8am–5pm.

Ruby Ruby, 321 Bay St, Port Melbourne (☎03/9645 2810). Popular meeting place for the happening seaside set, this part-bar, part-café is a great place for a meal, snack, wine or coffee. Licensed. Mon–Fri 11am–1am, Sat & Sun 9am–1am.

Sushi Chef, 193 Clarendon St (☎03/9645 5008). Inexpensive sushi bar relying mainly on the takeaway trade, but you can also eat in. Mon–Sat 11am–8pm.

Villagio Continental Delicatessen , Dundas Place, Albert Park (T) 03/9690 3144). Gleaming shop full of all kinds of Italian food, with tables outside where you can eat your selections and drink coffee. Closed Sun.

Vista Bar & Bistro , cnr Bridport and Montague streets, Albert Park (T) 03/9699 7757). An eclectic international mix of dishes and a good selection of wines by the glass. Tues–Fri & Sun noon–3pm, plus Tues–Sun 6–10pm.

St Kilda

Although **Acland Street** is still very popular – especially for late breakfasts and pigging out on cakes – **Fitzroy Street** has taken over as St Kilda's new cool area, especially the block from Grey Street to the waterfront. A new, stylish café or restaurant (with prices to match) opens almost every day, making it incredibly difficult to keep track of the latest developments. Walk past any of them on a warm summer evening and you'll be eyed up and down by the crowds sitting at the outdoor tables. On most evenings it's nearly impossible to find a parking space in the area, even though there's a car park at either end of Fitzroy Street. It's probably better to hail a cab, take public transport or otherwise be prepared for a long hike.

Bala's , 1D Shakespeare Grove, just off Acland St near Luna Park (T) 03/9534 6116). Excellent, cheap Asian takeaway food – lots of things stir-fried in the wok, with ultrafresh ingredients, as well as samosas, curry puffs and lassis. There are a few tables if you want to eat in, but beware – the place is very busy at lunch and dinner time. Mon–Sat 4–10.30pm, Sun noon–10.30pm.

Big Mouth , 201 Barkly St (T) 03/9534 4611). Excellent position at the corner of Barkly and Acland streets makes this a great spot for people-watching. The café downstairs is open for breakfast and light meals from 10am until late, while the upstairs restaurant is open Monday to Friday 5pm–1am, Saturday 11am–late, and Sunday 10.30am till late. Licensed.

Birdcage , 129 Fitzroy St (T) 03/9534 0277). In a corner of the *George Hotel* foyer, this tiny bar-cum-bistro does a great line in Japanese tapas-style, or "Japanesque", as they like to tell it. Choose from sashimi and noodle and rice dishes, which can be scoffed in either banquettes, booths or on stools at the bar. Doesn't take evening bookings. Licensed. Tues–Fri noon–10.30pm, Sat 5–10.30pm, Sun noon–midnight.

Cafe Ninety Seven , 97 Fitzroy St (T) 03/9525 5922). Cosy little café. The back of the courtyard is framed by palm trees and the columned facade of the former French consulate (now a private house). Licensed. Daily 7.30am–midnight.

Cafe Racer , 15 Marine Parade (T) 03/9534 9988). Ocean-facing café that provides excellent coffee and snacks to posses of cyclists and bikers, their Harley Davidsons and Vespas parked at the kerbside. Daily 6am–6pm.

Chinta Blues , 6 Acland St (T) 03/9534 9233). There are two of well-known restaurateur Simon Goh's string of Malaysian eateries in St Kilda – this

one is just around the corner from Fitzroy St and has a breezy, airy feel to it. The other is a small place at 94 Acland St (bookings on (T) 03/9525 4664). Very moderately priced. BYO. Both open Mon–Sat noon–2.30pm & 6–10.30pm, Sun noon–10pm.

Cicciolina , 130 Acland St (T) 03/9525 3333). Lots of tables crammed into a small space. Friendly staff and Italian food with an interesting twist is the formula that keeps this restaurant going from strength to strength. Licensed. Mon–Sat noon–11pm, Sun noon–10pm.

Circa , The Prince St Kilda, 2 Acland St (T) 03/9534 5033). Big on style and big on price, this is one of Melbourne's best spots for fine dining, boasting a magnificently theatrical fit-out, excellent food and wine and top service. More casual dining can be found at *Circ*, its slightly younger offshoot downstairs, where you can breakfast or lunch in a gorgeous courtyard filled with olive trees and massive terracotta urns. Licensed. Tues–Thurs & Sat 6–11.30pm, Fri & Sun noon–3pm & 6–11.30pm.

The Espy Kitchen at the Esplanade Hotel , 11 Upper Esplanade (T) 03/9534 0211). The veggie restaurant at the back is casual and slow, with slapdash decor to match, but the excellent food is worth the wait. Daily noon–3pm & 6–8pm.

Galleon Cafe , 9 Carlisle St (T) 03/9534 8934). Breakfast, served until 4pm, is the big attraction here, especially popular at weekends. There's also a useful notice board. Licensed and BYO. Mon–Fri 9am–11pm, Sat & Sun 8.30am–11pm.

Greasy Joe's , 68 Acland St (T) 03/9525 3755). Good greasy breakfast until 6pm, and a range of burgers both meaty and veggie, which you can eat at pavement tables. Licensed. Daily 7am–1am.

Lip , 133 Fitzroy St (T) 03/9593 6133). Cheapish restaurant serving flavoursome nosh from all points of the globe. Good wine list too, with lots of by-the-glass selections. Licensed. Mon–Thurs & Sun noon–midnight, Fri & Sat noon–1am.

Luxe, 15 Inkerman St (℡03/9534 0255). Divine, perfectly formed restaurant with food, European-bistro in style, that satisfies rather than stupefies. If it seems too busy try the *Luxe Cellar*, a snug bar/café next door, for first-rate wine and nibbles. Licensed. Mon–Thurs 5pm–midnight, Fri–Sun noon–3pm & 5pm–midnight.

The Melbourne Wine Room, cnr Fitzroy and Grey streets (℡03/9525 5599). Located in the *George Hotel*, this swanky restaurant, bar and café is where you can have a drink, dinner or a quick bite with some wine. More than 300 wines on the list. Daily noon–11pm.

One Fitzroy Street (℡03/9593 8800). Hard-to-beat location at the corner of Fitzroy St and The Esplanade, with a café and bar downstairs, and an ultramodern restaurant upstairs sporting a balcony that rewards the higher prices with stupendous views over Port Phillip Bay. Meals in the café cost about $45–60 for two; in the restaurant $100 (not including drinks). Licensed. Daily noon–midnight.

Stokehouse, 30 Jacka Blvd (℡03/9525 5555). Located by the beach and packed in warm weath-er. The restaurant has two sections: downstairs is affordable with lots of unusual pizzas and pastas, fantastic cakes, coffee and wines; upstairs has better views of the bay, but is beyond most budgets. Licensed. Downstairs open Mon–Sat 11am–1am, Sun 10am–1am, upstairs daily noon–midnight.

Termini, 60A Fitzroy St (℡03/9537 3465). Formerly the excellent *Victory Cafe*, *Termini* subscribes to the what-do-they-know-about-food style of dealing with customers. Luckily, they know one end of a pot from another: the main courses, from pasta to pork, are simple and rustic, while desserts, such as rich chocolate *sfomato*, are sensational. The business card – designed like a train ticket – is also a nice touch – as befits the restaurant's location in the old St Kilda Railway Station. Licensed. Tues–Fri 9am–11pm, Sat & Sun 10am–11pm.

Topolinos, 87 Fitzroy St (℡03/9534 4856). A dimly lit, noisy and smoky St Kilda institution, which pumps out pizzas, generous pasta dishes and good cocktails until dawn. Licensed. Mon–Thurs noon–3am, Fri–Sun noon–6am.

Wild Rice, 211 Barkly St (℡03/9534 2849). Vegan macrobiotic café with a lovely courtyard garden. Daily noon–10pm.

Elwood and Balaclava

Elwood's easy-going haunts are similar to St Kilda's, while **Balaclava**, to the east along Carlisle Street, specializes in inexpensive kosher food.

Beach House, 63A Ormond Esplanade, Elwood (℡03/9531 7788). Friendly, if somewhat chaotic café next to the car park at Elwood beach. Very good for breakfast, and *very* crowded on weekends, so book ahead. Licensed. Daily 9am–5.30pm.

Cafe Tarrango, 15 Ormond Rd, Elwood (℡03/9531 7151). Indian-run café, with delicious organic, biodynamic vegetarian food but not much atmosphere. Licensed and BYO. Mon 5–11pm, Tues–Sun 10am–11pm.

Glicks, 330A Carlisle St, Balaclava (℡03/9527 2198). Very friendly spot, renowned for bagels and traditional Jewish savouries: try kreplach, *latkes* or gefilte fish. Mon–Thurs & Sun 6am–9pm, Fri until sunset. Closed Sat.

Jerry's Milk Bar, 345 Barkly St, Elwood (℡03/9531 3078). Cornershop milk bar-cum-café brimming with old-fashioned trappings and locals who come for the delicious soups, pasta and risotto. Daily 7am–6pm.

Turtle Cafe, 34 Glenhuntly Rd, Elwood (℡03/9525 6952). Relaxed old corner café that attracts a faithful crowd. Daily 7am–7pm.

Zartowa, 114 Ormond Rd, Elwood (℡03/9531 1700). More upmarket than the *Turtle*, this popular café-restaurant at the yuppie end of Ormond Rd features a varied à la carte menu of Australian, Mediterranean and Asian-inspired dishes. Lots of focaccias and salads for brunch, plus good coffee. Licensed. Daily 9am–11pm.

Nightlife and entertainment

Melbourne prides itself on being a cultural city with intellectual leanings, so there's a rich arts and music scene and always plenty to do in the evening. To find out **what's on**, check out *The Age* on Friday, when the newspaper publishes a comprehensive entertainment guide, "EG" – much better than the *Sun-*

Herald's Thursday supplement. *Melbourne Events* is a handy, and surprisingly hip, free monthly guide to all sorts of happenings, published by Melbourne Council and available at tourist information outlets. Also check out the free street-press magazines *Beat* and *Inpress*, which you can pick up at most record shops, cinemas and cafés.

Annual festivals further enliven the scene: the **Melbourne International Festival** (ⓦwww.melbournefestival.com.au) in October concentrates on mainstream visual and performing arts, with a sprinkling of good concerts and opera. The much more experimental and innovative **Melbourne Fringe Festival** (ⓦwww.melbournefringe.org.au) happens more or less at the same time, as does the **Melbourne Writers' Festival** (ⓦwww.mwf.com.au). The heavily promoted **Moomba Festival**, held during the first half of March, has events including firework displays and dragon boat races on the banks of the Yarra River in Alexandra Gardens, but is actually rather drab and commercial. Three music festivals take place in the first half of the year: the **Melbourne Jazz Festival** in the last week of January, at venues in the city centre; the **Melbourne Music Festival** in February, one of the largest Australian festivals of contemporary music; and the **Brunswick Music Festival** in the third week of March, concentrating on folk and world music. The **Next Wave Festival**, held over two weeks in the second half of May, celebrates Victoria's young artists, writers and musicians.

Tickets for most venues can be booked through Ticketmaster (☎13 6166, ⓦwww.ticketmaster.com.au) or Ticketek (☎13 2849, ⓦwww.ticketek.com.au); both take credit-card bookings only. You can buy tickets half-price on the day of performance from the Half Tix booth, on the Bourke Street Mall (Mon & Sat 10am–2pm, Tues–Thurs 11am–6pm, Fri 11am–6.30pm; cash only; ☎03/9654 9420).

Bars and pubs

Melbourne's love affair with drinking is reflected in its plethora of excellent **bars and pubs** – from places so obscure and cutting-edge you'll only know they exist by word of mouth to large establishments catering to broader and louder tastes. The push to revive Melbourne's once staid CBD has seen many older watering holes transformed into lively, youth-oriented venues, while cheap bar licences have meant that new spots are popping up each week. In addition, the relaxing of Melbourne's once draconian licensing laws has produced enlightened opening hours, meaning that it's now possible to drink from noon until dawn. The distinction between restaurant, bar, café and nightclub is often blurred, but not at the handful of pub breweries, where a range of beers are made on the premises. A number of drinking places are also listed under "Live music", p.931.

City Centre

Bridie O'Reilly's, 62 Little Collins St. Above-average theme pub, with lots of Irish gewgaws and hearty grub such as stew, steak and Guinness pie. Another *Bridie*'s is in South Yarra (see overleaf).

Charles Dickens Tavern, downstairs, Block Court, 290 Collins St. Comfy place for homesick Brits, with bitter and Guinness on tap, pint glasses, and live soccer and rugby on big-screen TVs.

The Elephant and Wheelbarrow, 96 Bourke St. A popular Friday night spot, this English theme pub has timber booths and a photograph of Big Ben on the wall. The food is simple, wholesome and inexpensive.

Gin Palace, 190 Little Collins St (entry via Russell Place). Glamorous subterranean joint with an upmarket drinks list specializing in cocktails – not cheap, but delicious and generous. Yummy food and good lounge music too.

Glowbar, 422 Queen St. Opposite the Victoria Market, this sci-fi-style bar is flooded with blue neon lighting and attracts a very fashion-savvy crowd.

Hairy Canary, 212 Little Collins St. This modern and stylish bar is a real people-puller, especially later in the week. An extensive menu is available most of the day, with a wide range of local and imported beers, wines by the glass and cocktails.

Khokolat, 43 Hardware Lane. Attracts a laid-back crowd in search of cool retro styling, sophisticated sounds and simple but tempting food.

The Lounge, 243 Swanston St. Genuine all-rounder, attracting an arty-grungy crowd. Bar and nightclub with live music (see "Clubs" on p.932), and good food in the upstairs restaurant – eat alfresco on the terrace.

Meyers Place, 20 Meyers Place (off Bourke St). This swish, dimly lit hole in the wall has proved a massive hit with Melbourne's trendy office workers and is the grooviest place to fall down in town on a Friday night, bar none.

Pugg Mahone, 106–112 Hardware Street. Another Irish theme pub, with a great party atmosphere on Fri & Sat, fuelled by house bands playing a mixture of folk and R&B.

Stork Hotel, 504 Elizabeth St. This phlegmatic watering hole, located in a historic hotel from the goldrush era, features lovely Art Deco fittings, emphysemic regulars and superb artwork on the walls from some of Australia's finest cartoonists, including Melbourne-based Michael Leunig.

Tony Starr's Kitten Club, 267 Little Collins St. Sleek and stylish interior tricked out with slightly Oriental furnishings, conducive to lolling on comfy sofas and ottomans while cradling a cocktail and nibbling on Asian-inspired food from the grill.

Young & Jackson's, cnr Swanston and Flinders streets. Victoria's oldest and most famous boozer has undergone a massive renovation, but it's still as good a place as anywhere to start drinking your way around town.

North Melbourne, Carlton and Fitzroy

Builders Arms, 211 Gertrude St, Fitzroy. Groovy pub with guest DJs on weekends, when it's easily identifiable by the punters queuing to get in. Meals and snacks are available, and the atmosphere is laid-back and unpretentious. The "No Pokies" sign above the door has become a Melbourne landmark.

Gypsy Bar, 334 Brunswick St, Fitzroy. Intimate bar crammed with Brunswick St's finest, especially for jazz on Sunday night. Great coffee and food.

Lemon Tree, 10 Grattan St, Carlton. Upmarket bar that often features live jazz and has a fine beer garden.

Lord Newry, 543 Brunswick St, North Fitzroy. The cosy front bar with an open fire is a good place for conversation. Delicious food is served upstairs, where there might be anything from poetry readings to jazz.

Pumphouse Hotel, 128 Nicholson St, Fitzroy. Pub brewery, very popular with backpackers from the nearby hostel, *The Nunnery*.

Punters Club Hotel, 376 Brunswick St, Fitzroy. Legendary knees-up drinking hole boasting a rough-and-ready band scene each night and obscenely cheap pool tables.

The Redback Brewery, 75 Flemington Rd, North Melbourne. Slick boutique brewery packed out on Friday and Saturday with the striped-shirt brigade. Redback, the house beer, is one of the tastiest around.

Richmond, Prahran and South Yarra

All Nations Hotel, 64 Lennox St, off Swan St, Richmond. Old-style Aussie pub with exceptional bar meals and a relaxing beer garden.

Black Match, 545 Church St, Richmond. Favourite university students' haunt with neo-punk decor.

Bridie O'Reilly's, 462 Chapel St, South Yarra. Irish-themed pub incongruously housed in an old church and saved from terminal tackiness by the pleasant front patio. Has meals and plenty of memorabilia from the Emerald Isle. Can get raucous on weekends, but it's fun if you're desperate for a Guinness or British beer.

Candy Bar, 162 Greville St, Prahran. Roomy bar populated with couches, fireplaces and, at night, Melbourne's twenty-something, party-going dance crowd. Dress up, however, or you may have trouble getting past the fashion police at the door.

Fawkner Club, 52 Toorak Rd, South Yarra. Swanky pub with a great beer garden, though it's hard to get a seat on a sunny day.

Revolver, 229 Chapel St, Prahran. Electronic beat DJs and artists create a cool vibe every night, bands play most weekends, while it's the perfect place on a Saturday afternoon, when DJs spin throbbing reggae and dub sounds. You can grab a snack in the Thai restaurant, lounge around with a drink in the spacious, comfortable main area, or boogie in the back room.

St Kilda

Dog's Bar, 54 Acland St. Chic setting attracting a dedicated clientele. The wine list is terrific although there's a surprisingly small range of beers. Great tucker like bangers and mash, steak, pizza, pasta and chips.

The Esplanade Hotel, 11 Upper Esplanade. Famous for its beachside views, this hotel is the epicentre of St Kilda's drinking scene and shouldn't be missed. Bands play every night and there are inexpensive meals from *The Espy Kitchen* at the rear, plus pool tables and pinball machines.

The George Public Bar, 127 Fitzroy St. Very cool underground bar with an upbeat design. Favoured by locals, it has a large range of beers on tap, plus a pool table and free live music on Saturday afternoons. The service is friendly and the kitchen is open until late each night, serving a wide range of snacks and good-value meals. Table seats outside.

Mink Bar, The Prince St Kilda, 2B Acland St. This subterranean space has back-lit refrigerated shelves stacked high with an astonishing array of Russian, Polish, Swedish, Finnish, Lithuanian and – gulp – Japanese vodka. There are also private booths for intimate tête-à-têtes and a portrait of Karl Marx hanging from the wall. A great place for convivial quaffing and mellowing, it also has film nights (free) most weeks on a big screen.

The Prince St Kilda, 29 Fitzroy St. Defiantly local and no-frills, the downstairs public bar has an air of stubborn resistance in the face of St Kilda's freewheeling gentrification. Frequented in equal parts by colourful local identities and desperadoes, this hotel is not for the faint-hearted.

Veludo Bar, 175 Acland St. Magnet for St Kilda fashion plates, *Veludo* sports a bar downstairs with interesting and cheap food, and a smart restaurant upstairs overlooking Acland St. Spacious and stylish, it really gathers steam on the weekends.

Live music

Melbourne has a thriving **band** scene, in which just about every pub puts on some sort of music – often free – at some time during the week. The pubs listed below are also good places for a drink, and always have at least two bars so you can escape the din if you want to. Grungy Richmond has a big concentration of **music pubs**, with several putting on African and reggae music; Fitzroy and St Kilda are the other areas to head to for a range of live music. Free **listings** magazines such as *Beat*, *Inpress* or *Zebra* are good sources of information about the local music scene, while local FM stations Triple R (102.7) and PBS (106.7) air alternative music and tell you what's on and where.

City centre and the northern suburbs

Bennetts Lane, 25 Bennetts Lane, a small alley off Little Lonsdale St in the CBD, between Exhibition and Russell streets. One of Melbourne's most interesting jazz venues, it has recently been expanded to include a larger back room to complement the original cramped, Fifties-style cellar.

Dan O'Connell's, 225 Canning St, between Rathdowne and Nicholson streets, Fitzroy. Irish music Wed–Sun; no cover charge.

Grace Darling Hotel, 114 Smith St, Collingwood. Pleasant watering hole, which sometimes features live jazz and R&B.

The Punters Club, 376 Brunswick St, Fitzroy. One of the nerve centres of the Melbourne band scene, with well-known independent bands nightly; usually $5. Licensed until 3am.

The Rainbow, 27 St David St, Fitzroy. Mellow atmosphere, interesting crowd and decor in an intimate bar with free music – eclectic jazz, funk and fusion – every night.

The Stage, 1st floor, 231 Smith St, Collingwood. Live bands play African and Latin American music Thurs–Sun from 8 or 10pm. Dance floor and cover charge. Come earlier and have a two-course dinner for an additional $15.

The Tote, 71 Johnston St, Fitzroy. Hardcore thrash.

Richmond and the southern suburbs

Bridge Hotel, 642 Bridge Rd, Richmond. Jazz, reggae and African music.

Continental Cafe, Greville St, Prahran. Smart venue for established and up-and-coming artists.

Corner Hotel, 57 Swan St, Richmond. Alternative independent bands.

The Esplanade Hotel, 11 Upper Esplanade, St Kilda. The "Espy" is the soul of St Kilda and of Melbourne's eclectic band scene (huge bouncers make it look rougher than it actually is). Interesting nightly line-up of free bands in the front bar; small admission charged to see bands in the Gershwin Room.

Molly Bloom's, 39 Bay St, Port Melbourne. Irish music most nights; no cover charge.

The Palace, Lower Esplanade, St Kilda (next to the *Palais*). Entertainment complex with big-name bands in the main room, smaller bands in the pool room, and a club at the rear.

The **Prince St Kilda**, Fitzroy St, St Kilda. Another St Kilda icon, but unlike the *Espy* this one has undergone a facelift to fit in with the smart cafés and restaurants at this end of Fitzroy St. Late-night venue with good bands.

Clubs

Promoters hand out **flyers** for reduced or free admission to a rapidly changing array of clubs on the corner of Bourke and Russell streets, or you can pick up the passes in record shops such as Gaslight, further up Bourke Street. King Street, in the CBD between Collins Street and Flinders Lane, has a handy concentration of clubs. Most clubs have a **cover charge** of between $5 and $10.

The Bull Ring, 95 Johnston St, Fitzroy. The best place to dance to Latin rhythms. The band starts at 10.30pm, the dance-floor show at 11pm.

Carousel, Aughtie Drive, Albert Park. Dance venue playing good acid jazz and funk.

Chasers, 386 Chapel St, South Yarra. Veteran of the Melbourne club scene, with regular focus on accessible house, retro and electronic beats, presented in the spacious main room and two snug lounges.

Club UK, 169 Exhibition St, city centre. Retro and mainstream pop and rock, with an emphasis on the UK scene.

Heat, Mercury Lounge and **Odeon**, Crown Casino Entertainment Complex, south of the Yarra. Clubs on level 3 of the complex, playing mainstream pop from the 1980s onwards; occasional live bands.

Ibiza, 116 Chapel St, Windsor. Dance club popular with the gay/lesbian scene. DJs play house and techno.

Lizard Lounge, *The Union Hotel*, 90 Chapel St, Windsor. Alternative indie club.

The Lounge, 243 Swanston St, city centre. Upstairs club with bands, films, pool, dance floor and a cool-off balcony.

The Metro, 20 Bourke St, city centre. Huge old theatre on three floors with eight bars and three dance floors, all very lavish. Enormous queue of spivved-up kids on Friday night.

Monsoon, Russell St. Upmarket club at the *Grand Hyatt*. *daFunk Club* for R&B, funk and soul.

Viper Room, 373 Chapel St, Prahran. Popular spot with Melbourne's dancing crowd.

Gay and lesbian nightspots

Club 80, 10 Peel St, North Melbourne. Melbourne's largest, sleaziest male cruising bar, with backroom facilities. Cover charge.

Diva Bar, 153 Commercial Rd. Cocktail and dance bar with a mixed crowd.

DT's Hotel, 164 Church St, Richmond. Mixed crowd and popular pool competitions.

The Duke, 374 St Kilda Rd, cnr of Market St, St Kilda. Beer garden and pool competitions attract a mixed crowd.

Glasshouse Hotel, 51 Gipps St, Collingwood. Sociable pub that attracts a mixed bunch.

Laird Hotel, 149 Gipps St, Collingwood. Well-equipped boys' venue, with two bars, DJs, a beer garden and games room. Popular with the leather crowd. Cheap drinks until 10pm.

The Market, 143 Commercial Rd, South Yarra.

Excellent dance club with weekly menu of top-notch drag shows, karaoke nights and talent quests. No cover charge.

Peel Dance Bar, 113 Wellington St, cnr of Peel St, Collingwood. Dance floor, music videos and shows, drawing a large and appreciative crowd of gays and lesbians.

The Prince St Kilda, 29 Fitzroy St, St Kilda. Each Sunday is gay night, *Homosexualle*, and one Friday per month is *Girl Bar*, another gay night.

Star Hotel, 176 Hoddle St, Collingwood. Sociable pub; mixed crowd with a strong Asian clientele.

Trade Bar, 9 Peel St, Collingwood. Gay bar with drag shows.

Xchange Hotel, 119 Commercial Rd, South Yarra. Mainly men.

Melbourne's gay and lesbian scene may not be as upfront as Sydney's, but it's almost as formidable; this is such a diverse city that gays and lesbians seem just two more of the different groups that give the city its easy-going, multifarious feel.

The scene in Melbourne is less ghettoized than in Sydney. That said, Fitzroy, Collingwood and Carlton, north of the river, and St Kilda, South Yarra and Prahran, to the south, boast a strong male presence. Lesbians are everywhere, but Fitzroy, Northcote and Clifton Hill are Melbourne's recognized stomping grounds. There are two gay and lesbian free papers to help you navigate new waters: the *Melbourne Star Observer*, published weekly, and the fortnightly *Brother Sister*.

Big events are mostly organized by the ALSO (Alternative LifeStyle Organisation) Foundation, including one over the Australia Day weekend at the end of January – Red Raw Resurrection. The scene's annual highlight, however, has to be the fabulous Midsumma Festival in late January and early February. Already in its twelfth year, Midsumma (☏ 03/9415 9819, ⊛ www.midsumma.org.au) provides an umbrella for a wide range of sporting, artistic and theatrical events. The Queen's Birthday in June is celebrated at the Winterdaze party, and while the whole city is taking a day off to celebrate Melbourne Show Day in September, the Show Off dance party is the place to be.

Organizations, support groups and bookshops

Melbourne is blessed with a dazzling variety of gay and lesbian organizations, support services and businesses, the most important of which are listed below. Everything else, from gay vets to lesbian psychologists, can be found in the *ALSO Directory*.

AIDS organizations and medical care AIDS Line (☏ 03/9347 6099 or free call 1800 133 392) for phone counselling, referral and information Mon–Fri 9am–10pm, Sat & Sun 11am–2pm & 7–10pm; Gay Men's Health Centre and the Victorian AIDS Council (☏ 03/9865 6700 or free call 1800 134 840), 6 Claremont St, South Yarra; People Living With Aids at the Positive Living Centre (☏ 03/9525 4455), 46 Acland St, St Kilda; Positive Women (☏ 03/9276 6918 or free call 1800 032 017), run by and for women with HIV, through the Melbourne Sexual Health Centre.

ALSO Foundation, 1st floor, 35 Cato St, Prahran (☏ 03/9510 5569, ⊛ www.also.org.au). Organizes events and publishes the *ALSO Directory*, free from community outlets.

Beat Books, 157 Commercial Rd, Prahran (☏ 03/9827 8748). Gay bookshop with a large range of gay magazines, books, sex toys and leather goods.

Gay and Lesbian Switchboard (☏ 03/9510 5488) for counselling, referral and information.

Gay and Lesbian Switchboard Information Service (☏ 0055/12504). Recorded information service (24hr) covering entertainment, as well as social and support groups.

Hares and Hyenas, 135 Commercial Rd, Prahran (☏ 03/9824 0110). Gay and lesbian bookshop.

Women's Information and Referral Exchange (WIRE) (☏ 1300/134 130). Information about lesbian groups, referral to feminist doctors, solicitors, etc.

Cafés and meeting places

Globe Cafe, 218 Chapel St, Prahran (☏ 03/9510 8693). Good choice for a well-deserved treat after a hard morning's browsing on Chapel St.

Jackie O, 204 Barkly St, St Kilda (☏ 03/9537 0377). Comfy, atmospheric surroundings complemented by relaxed service and value-for-money food.

189 Espresso Bar, 189 Acland St, St Kilda (☏ 03/9534 8884). Huge *pides*, pizza, cakes and expertly made coffees, while outside tables make this a good place for crowd surveillance.

Red Orange, 194 Commercial Rd, Prahran (☏ 03/9510 3654). Cosy, inexpensive café in the heart of gay Prahran. Licensed.

See also p.901 for gay and lesbian-friendly places to stay and opposite for gay and lesbian nightspots.

Comedy

Melbourne is the comedy capital of Australia, home of the madcap Doug Anthony All Stars, Wogs Out of Work and comedians from TV shows such as *The Big Gig* and *The Comedy Company*. The highlight of the comedy year is the **Melbourne International Comedy Festival** (℡03/9417 7711, Ⓦwww.comedyfestival.com.au) in April, based at the Town Hall in Swanston Street, with performances at several other venues around town. As well as local and interstate acts, you're likely to see some of the best stand-up comedians from overseas. For irregular performances and other venues, refer to the "EG" (supplement to *The Age* on Fridays).

Armadale Hotel, 1068 High St, Armadale. Monday night comedy from 8.30pm.
Comedy Club, 380 Lygon St, Carlton. Slick, cabaret-style space, which features largely mainstream comedians.

The Esplanade Hotel, 11 Upper Esplanade, St Kilda. Stand-up shows each Tuesday and Sunday from 8pm.
Star & Garter Hotel, 70 Nelson Rd, South Melbourne. Comedy nights each Thursday.

Theatre

Melbourne offers a rich array of **dramatic productions**, from fringe to mainstream, with venues everywhere. Watch out for **outdoor performances** in summer, including alfresco Shakespeare and shows for children in the Royal Botanic Gardens from December until the end of February (℡03/9650 1500 for details; credit-card bookings with Ticketmaster ℡13 6166).

Athenaeum Theatre, 188 Collins St (℡03/9650 1500). One of numerous small Victorian theatre buildings in the city. The venue for guest performances; mainly plays and concerts.
Comedy Theatre, 240 Exhibition St (℡03/9209 9000). Like the Athenaeum – not a comedy venue, as its name might suggest.
CUB Malthouse, 113 Sturt St, South Melbourne (℡03/9685 5111). A renovated malthouse containing two venues: the Beckett Theatre and the larger Merlyn Theatre. The resident company is Playbox, which produces contemporary Australian plays. Guest performances include opera, dance, concerts and readings.
Her Majesty's Theatre, 219 Exhibition St, city centre (℡03/9663 3211). Lavish musicals in a fabulously ornate old theatre.
La Mama, 205 Faraday St, Carlton (℡03/9347 6948). Plays by new writers, as well as poetry and

play readings.
Playhouse Theatre, Victorian Arts Centre, 100 St Kilda Rd (℡03/9281 8000). Mainstream productions, mainly from the Melbourne Theatre Company.
Princess Theatre, 163 Spring St, city centre (℡03/9299 9500). Musicals and mainstream plays make up the programme at this small but lavish old-fashioned theatre.
Regent Theatre, 191 Collins St, near City Square (℡03/9299 9500). This lovingly restored old theatre puts on productions of big-name musicals.
Theatreworks, 14 Acland St, St Kilda (℡03/9534 4879). Puts on ground-breaking new Australian plays.
Universal Theatre, 19 Victoria St, off Brunswick St, Fitzroy (℡03/9419 3777). Venue for productions by smaller local theatre companies and alternative/fringe plays by overseas guests.

Classical music, opera and dance

The **Melbourne Symphony Orchestra** has a season from February to December based at the Melbourne Concert Hall and at the Melbourne Town Hall on Collins Street, while the **State Orchestra of Victoria** performs less regularly at the Concert Hall, often playing works by Australian composers. If you can't afford the ticket prices – expect to pay $40–80 for classical music performances, $60–130 for opera – listen to the Symphony Orchestra concerts broadcast on Tuesday at 7pm on Radio 3MBS (103.5FM).

George Fairfax Studio, Victorian Arts Centre, 100 St Kilda Rd ☎ 03/9281 8000). Modern dance and plays.
Her Majesty's Theatre, 219 Exhibition St, city centre ☎ 03/9663 3211). Occasionally hosts some of the great foreign ballet companies.

Melbourne Concert Hall, Victorian Arts Centre, 100 St Kilda Rd ☎ 03/9281 8000). Big-name concerts.
State Theatre, Victorian Arts Centre, 100 St Kilda Rd ☎ 03/9281 8000). Venue for the Victoria State Opera and the Australian Ballet Company.

Film

The **Melbourne International Film Festival** in July (☎ 03/9417 2011, Ⓦ www.melbournefilmfestival.com.au) has been going for over forty years and is the centrepiece of Melbourne movie life, based at a number of cinemas around Melbourne. Everyday mainstream cinemas are concentrated on Bourke Street, where discount day is usually Tuesday. The casino has a number of cinemas showing blockbuster movies; at the Gold Class Cinema you can eat a three-course dinner while you watch. In summer, watching a film under the stars at the Moonlight Cinema in the Botanic Gardens (see p.913) or at the Cinema at the Bowl (Sidney Myer Music Bowl) nearby can be a real treat (details from local press; bookings through Ticketmaster ☎ 13 6166). And there are always the independent cinemas, listed below, which tend to **discount** on Monday – we've indicated below where this is the case.

Astor Theatre, cnr of Chapel St and Dandenong Rd, St Kilda ☎ 03/9510 1414). Classic double bills and prestige new releases in a beautiful Art Deco cinema. On Saturday night there's a pianist and singer between films.
Brighton Bay Twin Cinemas, 294 Bay St, Brighton ☎ 03/9596 3590). Very comfortable setting for European and art-house films. Cheap day Monday.
Chinatown Cinema, 200 Bourke St, city centre ☎ 03/9662 3465). Screens a variety of Chinese films with English subtitles.
Cinema Europa, Jam Factory, 500 Chapel St, South Yarra ☎ 03/9827 2440). Opulent movie house with three small arthouse cinemas in which Australian short films precede the main event.
Cinema Nova, Lygon Court Plaza, 380 Lygon St, Carlton ☎ 03/9347 5331). Art-house and European films. Come just before the show starts to avoid prolonged exposure to the awful crimson and purple bordello decor. Cheap day Monday.
Cinemedia at Treasury Theatre, 1 Macarthur Place, city centre ☎ 03/9651 1515). Film-buffs cinema. Often shows Australian movies.
Classic, 9 Gordon St, off Glenhuntly Rd, Elsternwick ☎ 03/9523 9739). Art-house and European films; near Elsternwick station.
Como, Gaslight Gardens, cnr of Toorak Rd and Chapel St, South Yarra ☎ 03/9827 7533). Belongs to the same Palace Cinema chain as the George Cinema in St Kilda and the Brighton Bay Twin Cinemas – and shows similar films.
George Cinema, 133–137 Fitzroy St, St Kilda ☎ 03/9534 6922). Has the latest releases, bordering between art-house and mainstream. *Lip*

restaurant (see p.927) in the same complex is ideal for supper or an after-movie coffee.
IMAX Theatre, Melbourne Museum complex, Rathdowne St, Carlton ☎ 03/9663 5454). Part of the new Melbourne Museum complex (see p.908), IMAX has kitsch interiors and awesome technology, including a gigantic screen and film reels so big they require a fork-lift to move them. Shows both 2D and 3D films, usually lasting from 45min to 1hr, mostly documentaries on inaccessible places or anything involving a Tyrannosaurus Rex.
Kino, 45 Collins St, city centre ☎ 03/9650 2100). In the opulent Collins Place atrium, with several cafés and bars in the complex. Stylish, arty new-release films. Cheap tickets on Monday.
Longford Cinema, 59 Toorak Rd, South Yarra ☎ 03/9867 2700). Exclusive release for quality films, somewhere between art-house and mainstream. Late films on Friday and Saturday. Cheap day Monday.
Lumiere, 108 Lonsdale St, city centre ☎ 03/9639 1055). Art-house movies. Cheap day Monday.
Rivoli, Camberwell Rd, Camberwell Junction ☎ 03/9882 1221). Shows first releases of quality films. Two theatres in an Art Deco building.
Trak Cinema, 445 Toorak Rd, Toorak ☎ 03/9827 9333). Art-house and quality mainstream films, often with a focus on European work.
Westgarth Theatre, 89 High St, Northcote ☎ 03/9482 2001). Art Deco period piece, decorated by the planner of Canberra, Walter Burley Griffin. Presents quality mainstream and art-house films, cult classics and late shows. Cheap day Monday.

Shopping

Melbourne's big two **department stores**, David Jones and Myer, are located off the Bourke Street Mall, while Daimaru, on Elizabeth Street, is Japanese-owned, with a very sophisticated feel. **Shopping hours** are generally Monday to Friday 9am to 5.30pm, with late-night shopping on Thursday and Friday evenings; many places also open at the weekend from around noon to 5pm.

Fashion

Chapel Street in South Yarra is the home of interesting upmarket **fashion**, getting younger and less expensive towards Prahran. Greville Street, Prahran, has lots of retro chic, although Brunswick Street in Fitzroy is the best spot for secondhand clothes. Dangerfield (in the city centre at 224 Flinders St, the Sportsgirl Centre on Collins St and Melbourne Central, and in Greville St, Prahran and Brunswick St, Fitzroy) has modern funky clothes, including lots of great hats and jewellery. In Richmond, Bridge Road between Punt Road and Church Street is the discount centre of Melbourne; clothes and shoe shops sell seconds, samples and end-of-season stock – lots of cheap rubbish, but also brand names such as Country Road, Sportsgirl, Jag and Witchery. In the city, Little Bourke Street (from no. 349 upwards) and Hardware Street, round the corner, are the places to go for **travel clothing** and equipment.

Books

Mainstream **bookshops**, all with many branches, are: Angus & Robertson Bookworld on the corner of Bourke and Elizabeth streets and 35 Swanston St, and Bookcity at 205 Swanston St for discounts; Collins Booksellers, 104 Elizabeth St, 86 Bourke St and 401 Swanston St; and Readers Feast at Midtown Plaza at the corner of Bourke and Swanston streets. One of Melbourne's best literary bookshops is Readings, 309 Lygon St, Carlton, with another branch at 153 Toorak Rd, South Yarra, down the road from Black Mask Books at no. 78, which specializes in mystery and crime. In Fitzroy, Brunswick Street has the very good Brunswick St Bookstore, at no. 305, and Grub St Bookshop at no. 379 for secondhand books. In Prahran at the Jam Factory there's the large Border's Books & Music, 500 Chapel St, which also has a pleasant café (both open daily 9am–midnight). St Kilda also has several bookshops, including Chronicles Bookshop, 91 Fitzroy St, and Cosmos Books and Music, 112 Acland St. Map Land, 372 Little Bourke St, specializes in **travel books and maps**. Topographical maps, maps of national parks in Victoria and other publications on Victoria are available at Information Victoria (see p.891).

Music

Gaslight, 85 Bourke St, has a superb range of everything except classical; Thomas's Records nearby at no. 31 is small but very good; Au-go-go, at 2 Somerset Place, sells independent and rare recordings, and displays notices for room shares and what's on. Discurio, 105 Elizabeth St, sells classical music, jazz, blues and folk; while Basement Discs, 24 Block Place, off Little Collins St, also has a great range of jazz and world music. In the southern inner city suburbs Border's Books & Music, at the Jam Factory, South Yarra, has a big CD department, and in Prahran at 128 Greville St, the funky Rhythm and Soul Records is where you'll find the latest funk, electronic, trance and techno grooves.

Markets

Melbourne's best-loved **market** is the venerable Queen Victoria Market (see p.907), though the Sunday Victorian Arts Centre crafts market (see p.912) is also popular, and there are good local markets at Prahran (see p.917), South Melbourne (see p.918) and St Kilda (see p.918). Camberwell Market, Station Street (Sun 7am–3pm; train to Camberwell), is a large flea market with lots of good secondhand clothes, books and records as well as bric-a-brac, and with plenty of food vans and cafés.

Listings

Airlines (domestic) Air New Zealand (T 13 2476); Ansett (T 13 1300); Qantas (T 13 1313); Virgin Blue (T 13 6789).

Airlines (international) Alitalia (T 1300/653 747, F 03/9602 3802); British Airways (T 03/9603 1133, F 9258 3251); Canadian Airlines (T 1300/655 767, F 03/9602 2041); Garuda Indonesia (T 1300/365 330, F 03/9650 1731); Japan Airlines (T 03/9654 2733, F 9650 6820); KLM (T 03/9654 5222 or free call 1800 500 747, F 9650 6771); Lauda Air (free call T 1800 642 438, F 03/9602 2331); Malaysia Airlines (T 13 2627, F 02/9650 9296); Olympic (T 03/9629 5022, F 9629 2220); Qantas (T 13 1313); Singapore Airlines (T 13 1011, F 02/9350 0262); Thai International (T 1300/651 960, F 03/9650 7003); United (T 13 1777, F 02/9292 4551).

Airport bus Skybus (T 03/9662 9275) departs roughly every 30min from bay 30 at Spencer Street Bus Terminal (see also "Arrival and information", p.891).

American Express, 233–239 Collins St (Mon–Fri 8.30am–5.30pm, Sat 9am–noon).

Banks and foreign exchange All major banks can be found on Collins St. Standard banking hours are generally Mon–Fri 9.30am–4pm (Fri until 5pm), although some branches of the Bank of Melbourne, including the one at 142 Elizabeth St, are open on Saturday (9am–noon). Most banks have 24-hour automatic teller machines (ATMs), which accept a variety of cash, credit and debit cards. Thomas Cook is at 257 Collins St (Mon–Fri 8.45am–5.15pm, Sat 9am–5pm); other branches are at 330 Collins St and 261 Bourke St. The Thomas Cook desks at the international and domestic terminals of Tullamarine Airport are open 24hr.

Bike rental Hire a Bicycle, a stall at Princes Bridge (T 03/9758 7811 or 019 429 000; weather permitting Mon–Fri from 11am, Sat & Sun from 10am) has basic bicycles, geared bikes, mountain

bikes and tandems; prices for 1hr range from $8 for a standard bike to $11 for a geared bike, and helmets, locks, maps and backpacks are provided. You can also rent bikes at Fitzroy Cycles Bike Hire, 224 Swanston St, near Little Bourke St (T 03/9419 4397; full day $35). In St Kilda, try the helpful, long-established St Kilda Cycles, 11 Carlisle St (Mon–Fri 9am–6pm, Sat 9am–5pm, Sun 10am–4pm; T 03/9534 3074; full day $20), or the stand next to the cycle path near St Kilda Pier, which rents out bicycles on weekends, and daily during the summer holidays.

Buses Buy last-minute tickets at the bus company offices in the Spencer Street and Franklin Street terminals (V/Line reservations daily 7am–9pm; T 13 6196, W www.vlinepassenger.com.au). Operators include Greyhound Pioneer (T 13 2030; Franklin St terminal reservation desk daily 6.30am–10.30pm; T 03/9663 3299); McCafferty's, Spencer St Coach Terminal (T 13 1499, reservations daily 5am–11.30pm); Firefly, Spencer St Coach Terminal (T 03/9670 7500, reservations daily 7am–8.30pm). For advance bookings, it's easier to go to the Bus Booking Centre (BBC), 24 Grey St, St Kilda (Mon–Sat 10am–6pm, T 03/9534 2003), or Backpackers Travel Centre, Shop 1, 250 Flinders St (Mon–Fri 9am–6pm, Sat 10am–4pm; T 03/9654 8477). They will shop around for you to find the cheapest deals, and they also sell bus passes, and make bookings for tours around Melbourne and one-way to Sydney or Adelaide (see "Tours" below). City bus information is available from the Met Transport Information Centre (T 13 1638).

Car rental Avis, 20 Franklin St (T 03/9663 6366); Budget, 398 Elizabeth St (T 13 2727); Delta, cnr Franklin and Elizabeth streets (T 03/9600 9025 or 13 1390); Hertz, 97 Franklin St (T 03/9663 6244 or 13 3039); National, cnr Queensberry and Peel streets (T 03/9329 5000); Thrifty, 390 Elizabeth St (T 03/9663 5200); all do one-way rentals, subject to availability. Used-car

937

companies with cheaper rates include Rent-A-Bomb, 507 Bridge Rd, Richmond (☏03/9428 0088); and Ugly Duckling, 197 Inkerman St, St Kilda (☏03/9525 4010). Campervans are available from Britz Australia (☏03/9483 1888); Koala Campervan Rentals (☏03/9415 8140); and NQ Australia Campervan Rentals (free call ☏1800/079 529).

Consulates Canada, 1st Floor, 123 Camberwell Rd, Hawthorn East (☏03/9811 9999); France, 492 St Kilda Rd (☏03/9820 0921); Germany, 480 Punt Rd, South Yarra (☏03/9828 6888); Italy, 509 St Kilda Rd (☏03/9867 5744); Norway, Suite 2, 416 High St, Kew (☏03/9853 3122); Sweden, 61 Riggall St, Broadmeadows (☏03/9301 1888); Switzerland, 420 St Kilda Rd (☏03/9867 2266); Thailand, 277 Flinders Lane (☏03/9650 1714); UK, 17th Floor, 90 Collins St (☏03/9650 4155); USA, 553 St Kilda Rd (☏03/9526 5900).

Disabled travellers Disability Information Victoria, 454 Glenferrie Rd, Kooyong (☏1300/650 865); Paraquad Victoria, 208 Wellington St, Collingwood (☏03/9415 1200, ⊛www.paraquad.asn.au). Assistance is available at metropolitan, suburban, country and interstate stations, while relevant information for people with disabilities can be obtained by calling the Met Transport Information Centre (☏13 1638). Buses are progressively being replaced with low-floor wheelchair accessible models; however passengers in wheelchairs still need to contact local bus operators for information. The Melbourne City Council produces a free mobility map of the CBD showing accessible routes and toilets in the city centre, available from the front desk of the Melbourne Town Hall. For wheelchair-accessible taxis, call Central Booking Service (☏1300/364 050).

Diving Underwater Victoria – Dive Industry Victoria Association (free call ☏1800 816 151, ✉inquires@diva.asn.au) has a list of members in the Greater Melbourne area who hire equipment, organize diving trips and offer dive courses.

Emergency ☏000 for fire, police or ambulance.

Employment Backpackers Resource Centre, at Hotel Bakpak (☏03/9329 7525, ☏9326 7667, ⊛www.bakpak.com). Traveller's Contact Point on the ground floor of 29–31 Somerset Place, a lane off Little Bourke St between Elizabeth and Queen streets (☏03/9642 2911; Mon–Fri 8.30am–5.15pm, Sat 10am–4pm).

Environment and conservation Australian Trust for Conservation Volunteers (☏03/9686 5554); NRE Information Centre, 8 Nicholson St, East Melbourne, run by the Department of Natural Resources and Environment (Mon–Fri 9am–5.30pm; ☏03/9637 8080); Parks Victoria

(telephone information service ☏13 1963); Wilderness Society Shop, 247 Flinders Lane (☏03/9639 5455). The Victoria Visitor Information Centre at the Town Hall also has a range of brochures on national parks.

Ferries If you're heading for Tasmania on the Bass Strait there's a choice between *Spirit of Tasmania* (3 per week; 14hr 30min; $131 one-way) and *Devil Cat* (during peak season & Dec 21–January 28, 3 per week; 6hr; $175 one-way); reservations for both ☏13 2010. To get to Station Pier in Port Melbourne take the #109 tram from Collins St in the city. The airport bus Skybus also runs to the pier.

Flat-hunting and sharing Check the Saturday edition of *The Age*, as well as the notice boards of hostels, cafés along Brunswick St in Fitzroy, the *Galleon Café* at 9 Carlisle St, St Kilda, and Readings bookshop, 309 Lygon St, Carlton.

Hospitals and medical centres Alfred Hospital, Commercial Rd, Prahran (☏03/9276 2000); Royal Children's Hospital, Flemington Rd, Parkville (☏03/9345 5522); Royal Melbourne Hospital, Grattan St, Parkville (☏03/9342 7000); and St Vincent's Hospital, Victoria Parade, Fitzroy (☏03/9807 2211). For vaccinations, anti-malaria tablets and first-aid kits contact the Travellers Medical and Vaccination Centre (TMVC), 2nd Floor, 393 Little Bourke St (☏03/9602 5788, ⊛www.tmvc.com.au).

Internet access Some backpacker hostels have internet access for reading email, and some even have an internet café for surfing, such as Backpackers World at *Hotel Bakpak* (see p.897; daily 8am–9pm; about $3 for 30min, $5 per hour). Traveller's Contact Point (see "Employment" above) provides internet access among many other services including mail forwarding, voicemail, luggage storage and travel bookings. There are plenty of cybercafés throughout Melbourne. Most charge around $6–10 per hour online and there's usually an extra charge for printing out emails (around 25¢ for a laser printout). *Cafe Wired*, 363 Clarendon St, South Melbourne (☏03/9686 9911) has internet and computer-related services (Mon–Fri 9am–9pm, Sat noon–6pm); *Outlook Internet Café & Cyber Lounge*, 196 Commercial Rd, Prahran (☏03/9521 4227) is a good café opposite Prahran Market, that also offers services such as scanning and photocopying (Mon–Fri 10am–9pm, Sat & Sun 10am–6pm).

Laundries Most hostels and hotels have their own laundry. Commercial laundries include City Edge Laundrette, 39 Errol St, North Melbourne (daily 6am–11pm); *The Soap Opera Laundry & Cafe*, 128 Bridport St, Albert Park (Mon–Fri 7.30am–9.30pm,

Sat & Sun 8am–9pm), and Blessington Street Launderette, 22 Blessington St, St Kilda (daily 7.30am–9pm).

Left luggage Spencer Street Station has lockers (daily 6am–10pm; $2; emptied nightly); luggage can be left overnight at the cloakroom ($3.50 per item). Flinders Street Station has lockers (8am–8pm; $2). The lockers at the Melbourne Transit Centre on Franklin St are accessible 24hr ($6–10). Travellers Contact Point also stores luggage (see "Employment" opposite).

Library The General Reference and Information Centre at the State Library of Victoria, 328 Swanston St, keeps popular Australian and overseas magazines; the Newspaper Room has foreign papers (Mon–Thurs 10am–9pm, Fri–Sun 10am–6pm).

Motorbikes The northern end of Elizabeth St in the city centre has a string of motorbike shops. Garner's Motorcycles, 179 Peel St, North Melbourne (☏ 03/9326 7326), and Victorian Motorcycles, 606 High St, East Kew (☏ 03/9817 3206), do rentals and may sell secondhand machines with buy-back deals.

Newspapers Melbourne's *The Age* is one of Australia's better papers; the pulpy *Sun-Herald* is the city's only other daily. Foreign newspapers can be perused at the State Library or bought from McGill's Newsagency, 187 Elizabeth St.

Pharmacies Henry Francis Chemists, 286 Little Bourke St, next to Myer department store (Mon–Wed 9am–5.45pm, Thurs 9am–6.30pm, Fri 9am–9pm, Sat 9.30am–5pm, Sun 10am–5pm); Leonard Long, cnr of Williams Rd and High St, Prahran (daily 9am–midnight); Mulqueeny's Pharmacy, cnr Swanston and Collins streets, opposite the Town Hall (Mon–Fri 8am–8pm, Sat 9am–6pm, Sun 11am–6pm).

Police Melbourne City Police Station, 637 Flinders St; ☏ 03/9247 5347; emergency ☏ 000.

Post office The General Post Office at the cnr of Bourke and Elizabeth streets is set to become a hotel. At the time of writing, the new GPO retail shop is moving to 250 Elizabeth St (Mon–Fri 8.15am–5.30pm, Sat 10am–3pm (including the poste restante counter). Other post offices are open Mon–Fri 9am–5pm. For voicemail and mail forwarding, contact Travellers Contact Point. ("see Employment", opposite).

RACV The two RACV outlets in the city are at 360 Bourke St (cnr of Elizabeth St) and 123 Queen St; they have good maps on Melbourne, Victoria and the rest of Australia (free for RACV members and members of affiliated overseas motoring associations; ⊛ www.racv.com.au). They also book accommodation listed in their guides and package

holidays; members get special rates.

Rape and sexual assault CASA House (Centre Against Sexual Assault), 270 Cardigan St, Carlton (☏ 03/9344 2210, after hours ☏ 03/9349 1766, free call ☏ 1800 806 292), provides medical care, support and counselling.

Skiing Skiman, 295 Clarendon St (☏ 03/9696 4955), and AUSKI Ski Hiring & Information Centre, 9–11 Hardware Lane (☏ 03/9670 1412), can advise on skiing conditions at Baw Baw, Buffalo, Mount Hotham, Buller, Falls Creek and at Thredbo in NSW.

Swimming pools City Baths, in a Victorian redbrick building on the cnr of Swanston and Franklin streets (Mon–Fri 6am–10pm, Sat & Sun 8am–6pm; $3.30 for a swim plus $4.40 for use of sauna and spa; ☏ 03/9663 5888), has a 30-metre heated indoor pool for swimming, plus a pool for water-aerobics and a gym. In the state-of-the-art Melbourne Sports & Aquatic Centre, Aughtie Drive, off Albert Park Rd in Albert Park there's a choice between a wave pool, a 50-metre pool, a dive pool, a 25-metre lap pool and a 20-metre multipurpose pool; there are also 10 squash courts (Mon–Fri 6–10pm, 50-metre pool Mon–Fri 5.30–8pm, Sat & Sun 7am–8pm; admission $4.90; ☏ 03/9926 1555). Take tram #96 from Bourke St in the city.

Taxis Taxi rank on Swanston St outside Flinders Street Station, and plenty to flag down. Call Black Cabs Combined (☏ 13 2227); Embassy Taxis (☏ 13 1755); or Silver Top (☏ 13 1008).

Telephones Melbourne is well stocked with public telephones. Some backpacker hostels and shops in the city sell discount phonecards (such as Phoneaway, Unidial, EZI Great Rate Card, One Card and AAPT) which can be used in any payphone for cheap international calls. The official Telstra rate for a call from a public phone to the UK is $2 per minute Mon–Fri, $1.20 Sat & Sun. With one of the phonecards mentioned above, expect to pay about 39–55¢ per minute, plus a small connecting fee (less than $1).

Trains Spencer Street Station has a staffed information desk where you can get hold of all V/Line train (and bus) timetables; buy your ticket at the V/Line Travel Centre opposite or on ☏ 13 6196 (6am–midnight). If you're travelling with a bicycle, come at least thirty minutes earlier to book it on the train. Suburban train information is available from the Met Transport Information Centre (see p.895).

Travel agents Backpackers Travel Centre, Shop 19, Centre Place, 258 Flinders Lane (☏ 03/9654 8477, ⊜ info@backpackerstravel.net.au); Flight Centre, 19 Bourke St, 53 Elizabeth St and many other branches (☏ 13 1600); STA Travel, 273 Little Collins St, 142

Acland St, St Kilda, and other branches (book and pay over the phone ℡1300/360 960; or for nearest branch ℡13 1776); Student Uni Travel, Shop 4, 440 Elizabeth St (℡03/9662 4666); YHA Travel, 83 Hardware Lane (℡03/9670 9611).

Travellers aid centres Lower ground floor, Spencer Street Station (Mon–Fri 7.30am–7.30pm, Sat & Sun 7.30am–11.30am; ℡03/9670 2873), and 2nd Floor, 169 Swanston St (Mon–Fri 9am–5pm, Sat & Sun 11am–4pm; ℡03/9654 2600): both provide nappy-changing facilities, showers (for a fee), toilets, lounge rooms, wheelchairs for rent, assistance for disabled and frail persons, and information. There are also tearooms and lockers ($1) at the Swanston St centre.

Women Queen Victoria's Women's Centre Trust, is in the former Queen Victoria Women's Hospital at Level 1, 210 Lonsdale St (℡03/9663 8799). The beautifully restored, 1890s building houses a Women's Health Library, an Aboriginal Resource Centre, an art gallery, seminar rooms as well as a café and restaurant. Services include classes and seminars, professional consulting (on topics such as health and finance) and notice boards (Mon–Fri 8.30am–5.30pm). The Women's Information and Referral Service (WIRE; Mon–Fri 9.30am–5.30pm; ℡1300/134 130) is a telephone information service run by women for women.

Tours from Melbourne

With Melbourne as a base, a wide variety of **tours** can be made to the interior of Victoria or both east and west along the coast. Popular destinations – both as **day-trips** and **one-way tours** – are to the Grampians, Phillip Island and the Mornington Peninsula, and along the Great Ocean Road. For **longer trips**, you could consider several two- to four-day bushwalking excursions offered by several operators. Listed below are some of the more popular tours.

Autopia Tours (℡03/9326 5536). Long-established tour operator running very popular minibus tours: Great Ocean Road (1 day $54, 2 days $82); Phillip Island (1 day $60); Great Ocean Road–Phillip Island combination (2 days $108); and Great Ocean Road–Grampians combination (3 days $140).

Echidna Walkabout (℡03/9646 8249, ℱ9681 9177, ℮ekidna@netcore.com.au). Tours focusing on native wildlife and local Koorie culture. Day-tours to the Brisbane Ranges and You Yangs, west of Melbourne; longer trips to the Ballarat goldfields, Grampians, Great Ocean Road, remoter parts of East Gippsland and Tasmania. Tours are upmarket, with very small groups and enthusiastic, knowledgeable guides.

Let's Go Bush (℡03/9662 3969, ℱ9894 0411). Two-day tour to the Great Ocean Road departs twice-weekly and includes an overnight stay in a house owned by the tour company ($99).

Oz Experience (℡1300/300 028). Backpacker transport service doing regular runs three times weekly along the south coast to Adelaide and four times weekly going to Sydney; all major sights visited on the way to Adelaide (Great Ocean Road and the Grampians) or Sydney (Phillip Island, the High Country, Canberra and the coast south of Sydney).

Wayward Bus (free call ℡1800 882 823, ℴwww.waywardbus.com.au). Regular runs to the Great Ocean Road (3 days $265) and Kangaroo Island (2 days, $265), as well as longer trips to Adelaide and Alice Springs.

Wild-Life Tours (℡03/9747 1882, ℱ9747 1930, ℮wildlife@eisa.net.au). One-way tours between Melbourne and Adelaide (1–2 days; $80–130) and Melbourne and Sydney (2 days $139–160), as well as round trips from Melbourne (1–3 days $50–130; day-tour departs daily, other tours at least three times a week). Depending on the length of the trip, the tours take in the Great Ocean Road, the Grampians and Phillip Island; longer stopover options are available.

Around Melbourne

There are many possible day-trips out of Melbourne, mainly around the shores of the huge **Port Phillip Bay**, encircled by the arms of the Bellarine and Mornington peninsulas. The **Mornington Peninsula** on the east side is home to some of the city's most popular beaches and surfing spots, packed on summer weekends. **Western Port Bay**, beyond the peninsula, encloses two fascinating islands – little-known **French Island**, much of whose wildlife is protected by a national park, and **Phillip Island**, where the waddling ashore of masses of Little penguins each night is among Australia's biggest tourist attractions. Inland to the east, the **Yarra Valley** and the **Dandenong Range** offer beautiful countryside, wine-tasting and bushwalking. The **Bellarine Peninsula** and the western side of Port Phillip Bay are less exciting, but they do give access to the west coast and the Great Ocean Road.

The Mornington Peninsula

The **Mornington Peninsula** curves right around Port Phillip Bay, culminating in Point Nepean, well to the southwest of Melbourne. The shoreline facing the bay is beach-bum territory, though the well-heeled denizens of the main resorts, **Sorrento** and **Portsea**, might well resent that tag. On the largely straight, ocean-facing coast, **Mornington Peninsula National Park** encompasses some fine seascapes, with several walking trails marked out. Interspersed among the peninsula's bushland, grazing land and orchards are 100 **vineyards** which produce superb, if pricey, Pinot Noir and Shiraz wines, as well as good whites. Wineries are open for **tastings** and cellar-door **sales**, and some also serve food. Among the most notable are Dromana Estate, Harrison's Road, Dromana (☎03/5987 3800), a beautifully located winery where light lunches are served daily; Red Hill Estate, 52 Red Hill–Shoreham Road, Red Hill (☎03/5989 2838), in an equally appealing location, for excellent champagne and light lunches daily; and Main Ridge Estate, William Road, Red Hill (☎03/5989 2686), one of the first vineyards in the area, for Chardonnay and Pinot Noir, it serves lunches every Sunday. For details, refer to the brochure *Wine Regions of Victoria*, available at tourist information centres, or local information magazines.

As well as the beaches, the peninsula's **community markets** selling local produce and crafts attract many city dwellers: most are monthly affairs, so there's usually one every weekend. One of the biggest and best is Red Hill Community Market, held on the first Saturday of every month (7am–1pm; Sept–May), at Red Hill Recreation Reserve, Red Hill Road, 10km east of Dromana.

You can get to the peninsula by **public transport** from Melbourne to Frankston and from there to the main beach resorts and towns along the Nepean Highway on the northern side, but for a sightseeing trip taking in wineries, beaches and Arthur's Seat you need your own vehicle. Take a Met train to Frankston and change there for Stony Point, or connect with a Portsea Passenger Service bus #788 from Frankston to Sorrento ($6.80) and Portsea

($7) (for timetable information, free call ☏1800 115 666). From Sorrento there's a community bus to Dromana via Blairgowrie, Rye and Rosebud (4 daily Mon–Fri) but no transport to Arthur's Seat. V/Line's "Round the Bay" package deal ($39) will give people in a hurry a quick glimpse of both the Mornington and the Bellarine Peninsulas; it comprises the train to Frankston and bus to Sorrento, then a ferry transfer from Sorrento to Queenscliff, and the return trip by bus to Geelong and train to Melbourne. It's best to book this trip a day in advance at V/Line Holidays in Spencer Street Station. For timetable and other information call ☏03/9619 8080.

The western coast

The peninsula essentially starts at suburban **Frankston**, 40km from central Melbourne, and from here on down, the western coast, flanked by the Nepean Highway, is beach after beach, all crowded and traffic-snarled in summer. Twelve kilometres beyond Frankston, the old fishing port of **Mornington** preserves some of its heritage in fine buildings along Mornington Esplanade; every Wednesday there's a produce and craft market on Main Street. **Mount Martha**, 5km on, is another old settlement, the **Briars Historic Park** (homestead daily 11am–4pm, parklands and wetlands 9am–5pm; admission fee for both $5.50), an 1860s homestead, complete with a collection of furniture and memorabilia given to the owner by French Emperor Napoleon, surrounded by lawns and gardens, woodlands and extensive wetlands. At the visitor's centre near the homestead, an audiovisual display gives you an overview on how the affluent upper crust lived in early pioneering days as well as a rundown on the present-day facilities of the park. The 74 acres of **wetlands** are of interest to naturalists, as they are used by more than fifty species of waterbirds, which can be observed at close distance from two bird-hides, accessible from the visitor information centre. There are also two woodland **walkways**, and guided bushwalks are conducted at night on request (except in winter). In summer, there are additional events, such as jazz concerts, astronomical viewing of the night sky, and Heritage Day with actors in period costume.

Inland from Dromana, where seaside development begins in earnest, the granite outcrop of **Arthur's Seat State Park** rises 305m, providing breathtaking views of Port Phillip Bay. A **chairlift** makes the vista more easily accessible, leaving from the picnic area on Arthur's Seat Road, just off the Mornington Peninsula Freeway (Sept to the second Mon in June daily 11am–5pm; rest of the year Sat 11am–5pm, Sun 11am–5.30pm; $8.50 return). Only 500m from the summit is **Arthur's Seat Maze** (daily 10am–6pm; $10), which combines traditional hedge mazes with theme gardens and giant tree sculptures. Beyond, the peninsula arcs and narrows: the sands around Sorrento and Portsea offer a choice between the rugged surf of the ocean ("back" beaches) or the calmer waters of the bay ("front" beaches).

Sorrento

With some of the most expensive real estate outside the Melbourne CBD, **SORRENTO** is the traditional haunt of the city's rich throughout the "season", from Boxing Day to Easter; many move to their second homes here for the duration. Well-heeled outsiders also make it their playground in January and on summer weekends, flocking here to swim, surf and dive at the bay and ocean beaches. Exploring beautiful rock formations and low-tide pools, and swimming with bottlenose dolphins add to the attraction. The smell of money is everywhere – in the wide, tree-lined residential streets, the clifftop mansions boasting million-dollar views, and the town-centre cafés, restaurants, galleries and antique shops, running along Ocean Road down to the beach.

Sullivan Bay, 3km southeast, was in 1803 the site of the first white attempt to settle in what is now Victoria; the settlers struggled here for four months before giving up and moving on to what is now Tasmania. One of the convicts in the expedition was the infamous William Buckley, who escaped, was adopted by the local Aborigines and lived with them for 32 years. When the "wild white man" was seen again by settlers he could scarcely remember how to speak English; his survival against all odds has been immortalized in the phrase "Buckley's chance". A display centre on the site (Sun & school and public holidays 1–4.30pm; free) fleshes out the story of the settlement. For more information call ☎03/5988 0775.

Swimming with dolphins and seals is becoming one of the prime attractions of Port Phillip Bay, so much so that tour operators are obliged to follow a code of practice to ensure they don't adversely affect the animals. Two long-established operators are the environmentally conscious operator Polperro Dolphin Swims (☎03/5988 8437 or 0428 174 160), who take the smallest groups, and Moonraker (☎03/5984 4211 or 0418 591 033). Both depart twice daily during the season (Sept/Oct–May), weather permitting, for a four-hour trip ($70 per swimmer, including wetsuit and snorkelling equipment; $38.50 for sightseers).

Practicalities

Only one of Sorrento's **hotels** provides accommodation: the 1871 limestone *Hotel Sorrento*, 5 Hotham Rd (☎03/5984 2206, Ⓕ5984 3424; ❼–❽), which is very charming and is located in a secluded spot on a hill above the jetty. The equally old *Continental Hotel*, 21 Ocean Beach Rd, now only does food but on weekend nights there's live music and a disco. There are a few **B&B's**, though: nonsmoking *Carmel*, 142 Ocean Beach Rd (☎03/5984 3512, Ⓕ5984 0146; ❼–❽), a charming, sandstone B&B smack in the middle of town; *Tamasha House*, 699 Melbourne Rd (☎03/5984 2413, Ⓕ5984 0452; ❽), a modern house halfway between ocean and bay beaches. For people on a budget, *Sorrento Hostel YHA*, 3 Miranda St (☎ & Ⓕ 03/5984 4323; rooms ❸, dorms ❷), is a modern, comfortable **hostel** with small dorms and a twin room, some with en-suite facilities, and stacks of local information as well as some walks organized to local points of interest. **Caravan parks** tend to be either closed (out of season) or completely booked up and cost twice the normal price: two of the more reasonable are *Nautilus* (☎03/5984 2277; on-site vans ❹) and the *Foreshore Reserve* (☎03/5984 2797), which has tent sites only.

As you might expect, all this glitz needs to be nourished by plenty of fancy **eating places**. More modest options include getting a takeaway to eat on the benches along Ocean Road or on the beach: try the *Sorrento Village Bakehouse*, 29 Ocean Beach Rd. In the moderate price range, *Buckley's Chance*, 174 Ocean Beach Rd, is a relaxed pancake parlour, which also serves burgers and steaks; and the century-old former Sorrento Tearooms on 3278 Nepean Highway now house the *Sandpiper Licensed Restaurant* (daily 10am–5pm), which is open for breakfast, lunch and dinner (international cuisine) and has great views of the bay. The *Continental Hotel*, 21 Ocean Beach Rd, has a good café serving Mediterranean cuisine and Mornington Peninsula wines.

Ferries run across the mouth of the bay from Sorrento to **Queenscliff** on the Bellarine Peninsula. The *Peninsula Searoad Ferry* (☎03/5258 3244) carries passengers and vehicles year-round (about every 2hr 8am–6pm, in summer until 8pm; advanced car bookings recommended). The *Sorrento Passenger Ferry* (℡03/5984 1602; call to check times) departs from Sorrento daily every hour between 9am and 5pm from Boxing Day to Easter as well as during school holidays, calling at Portsea en route.

Portsea and Point Nepean

PORTSEA, just beyond Sorrento, is a mecca for divers, with excellent **dives** of up to 40m off Port Phillip Heads; trips operate from the pier throughout the summer and there are a couple of good dive shops. Portsea Front Beach, on the bay by the pier, is wall-to-wall beautiful people, as is Shelley Beach, which also attracts playful dolphins. On the other shore, Portsea Ocean Beach has excellent surfing, and a hang-gliding pad on a rock formation known as London Bridge. Back on the bay side, the extensive lawns of *Portsea Hotel*, a hugely popular drinking spot which features bands at weekends, overlook the beach.

The tip of the peninsula, with its fortifications, quarantine station and army base, was off-limits to the public for a century until the establishment of the Point Nepean National Park in 1988. It is now part of a patchwork of other national parks sprinkled over the southern end of the peninsula, collectively known as **Mornington Peninsula National Park**. The Point Nepean orientation centre (daily 9am–5pm; ℡03/5984 4276) is 1km west of Portsea. Because of its fragile sandy environment, visitor numbers are limited, so you need to book to visit.

If you're driving, you can leave your car at Gunner's car park which is located 2.5km into the national park and walk to Fort Nepean (8km return; admission fee $6.80). A **bus** (daily every hour from 9.30am–3pm; $12 return) runs the 7km to the fortifications at the point, part of the park, with four optional drop-offs for walks: the first, the **Walter Pisterman Heritage Walk** (1km return; suitable for wheelchairs), leads through coastal vegetation to the Port Phillip Bay shoreline; the second (1km return; steep in sections) leads to the top of Cheviot Hill, where you can look across to Queenscliff, and takes you on to views of **Cheviot Beach** where on December 17, 1967, **Harold Holt**, Australia's prime minister at the time, went for a swim in the rough surf of Bass Strait and disappeared, presumed drowned: his body was never found. The third walk, the **Fort Pearce and Eagle's Nest Heritage Trail** (2km return; suitable for wheelchairs), crosses through defence fortifications that were once inaccessible. A fourth walk takes you around **Fort Nepean**, right at the point. Built at the same time as Fort Queenscliff opposite to protect wealthy post-goldrush Melbourne from an imagined Russian invasion, the fort is essentially a two-storey building below ground. It takes about an hour to explore the tunnels, which lead down to the Engine House at water level. The old **quarantine station** near the point offers guided tours (Sun 2pm; $5).

The rest of Mornington Peninsula National Park, which spreads itself along the ocean coast, is freely open to the public. An enjoyable two-day walk (27km) runs from London Bridge along the coast to **Cape Schanck**, site of an 1859 lighthouse. Here a timber staircase and walkways lead down to the sea along a narrow neck of land, providing magnificent coastal views. The **lighthouse keeper's cottages** has to be the most scenic accommodation on the peninsula (℡03/5988 6184; ❻–❼). Dating back to 1859, they are completely self-contained with a cosy lounge and kitchen, one cottage with four bedrooms, the other with three bedrooms. There's a kiosk in the car park (daily 10am–4pm; in summer longer) and the lighthouse and museum are open daily for tours (every 30min 10am–4pm; $7).

Also worth embarking on in this area is the **Bushrangers Bay Nature Walk** (6km return; 2hr) from the cape to Main Creek, which begins as a leisurely walk along the clifftop, then leads down to a wild beach facing Elephant Rock.

French Island

FRENCH ISLAND, off the eastern side of the Mornington Peninsula, is well off the beaten track. A former prison farm, about two-thirds of the island is a national park with the remaining third used as farm land. The island is renowned for its rich **wildlife**, especially birds of prey, and a flourishing koala colony. Virtually vehicle-free, it's a great place to cycle, and this is encouraged, with all walking tracks open to bikes. In the national park you can either **camp** at the *Fairhaven Campground* or **stay** at the *McLeod Eco Farm and Historic Prison* (⊤ 03/5678 0155, ⓕ 5678 0166; ❹–❺) in former prison cells converted into twins with bunk beds, or in the former officer's quarters with queen-size beds. The very reasonable rate includes three meals using the produce organically grown on the farm, and transfer from and to the ferry jetty 21km away. The farm is surrounded by national park and has 8km of beach frontage. The small *Tortoise Head Guesthouse* near the jetty (⊤ 03/5980 1234, ⓕ 5980 1222; ❻–❼) has rooms with water views. The rate includes accommodation, three sumptuous wholefood meals as well as free use of mountain bikes.

The general store (2.5km from the jetty) has takeaway **food**. Refreshments and Devonshire teas are available at the *Bayview Chicory Kiln Tea Room* (10km from the jetty), which also has a private campsite; both are run by Lois Airs (⊤ 03/5980 1241 or 0412 671 241), a longtime resident and an inexhaustible mine of information about the island. Lois also does afternoon **tours** of the island ($15, includes afternoon tea and entry to the prison site), and if you want to camp at *Fairhaven*, she will transport your luggage there, leaving you free to cycle. A **ferry** service from the French Island Ferries company connects the Mornington Peninsula with French Island and Phillip Island. It leaves at least four times daily from Stony Point on the eastern side of the Mornington Peninsula (from Melbourne, connect with Met train services from Flinders Street Station via Frankston), departing from Tankerton jetty on French Island thirty minutes later for Phillip Island ($15 return, bike $4; ⊤ 03/9585 5730). The Cowes (Phillip Island) cruise company Bay Connections runs a charter service to French Island and to Stony Point on Wednesday and Sunday, during the summer holidays (mid-Dec to Jan) also on Thursday – all services are subject to demand and must be booked 24 hours ahead. The ferry service can be combined with a tour of the island (⊤ 03/5678 5642; ferry service $26 return, ferry and tour of the island $40).

Phillip Island

PHILLIP ISLAND, with its southern edge facing Bass Strait and its northern edge in the calm waters of Western Port Bay, is a hugely popular holiday destination from Melbourne, famous above all for the nightly roosting of hundreds of **Little penguins** at Summerland Beach. Most visitors come only for the **Penguin Parade**, but spending a few days on the island will allow you to explore some dramatic coastline where there is always plenty of **surfing** action (for more information, call the Phillip Island Surf Report on ⊤ 1902/243 082), fine swimming beaches, and a couple of well-organized wildlife parks. **Cowes**, on the sheltered bay side, is the main town and a lively and attractive place to stay. Other, smaller, communities worth a visit are **Rhyll**, to the east, and **Ventnor**, just west of Cowes.

A daily **V/Line bus** to Cowes departs from Melbourne in the afternoon, with an additional evening service on Friday; the bus drivers will usually drop you off where you request in Cowes. There's no public transport when you get there, however, so it can be tricky trying to get to the Penguin Parade, over 10km from Cowes. Planning to stay at the *Amaroo Park YHA* makes sense: their "duck truck" package ($84 including transport to and from Melbourne, up to three-nights' dorm accommodation, island tour and admission to Penguin Parade plus a half-day use of mountain bikes; daily departures) is extremely good value, as is their tour from Cowes to Wilson's Promontory National Park ($45 including meals and entrance fees). If you are short of time, a **day-tour** from Melbourne is a good way of making the most of the island. One of the best is the long-established Autopia Tours (℡03/9326 5536), who pick you up from central Melbourne or St Kilda. Their daily one-day tour (noon–midnight; $60 including entrance fees) takes in the Wildlife Park, Koala Conservation Centre and Penguin Parade, as well as Seal Rocks and the Nobbies. Another tour operator, Oz Experience include Phillip Island in their itinerary on their Melbourne to Sydney run (for more information, see box p.940).

If you're **driving**, head southeast from Melbourne on the Princes Highway to Dandenong, then follow the South Gippsland Highway to Lang Lang and from there the Bass Highway to Anderson where the road heads directly west to San Remo and the bridge across to the island, a drive of approximately three hours in total. The scenic lookout about 3km before San Remo is worth stopping at, for fantastic views of Western Port Bay and the surrounding countryside. **SAN REMO** itself has lots of motels, a picturesque fishing fleet by its wharf and a co-operative selling fresh fish and crayfish. Not surprisingly, you can get delicious fish and chips; the best are served at the building at 121 Main St.

NEWHAVEN, the first settlement you come to after crossing the bridge, has a large **tourist information centre** (daily 9am–5pm, longer in summer; ℡03/5956 7447), where you can pick up a free map and buy tickets for the Penguin Parade, ferry tours and for **Churchill Island** (daily 10am–4pm; $5.40), barely 1km out of town via a rickety bridge. Your admission allows you to look round a historic homestead and cottage in English-style gardens, surrounded by ancient moonah trees, abundant birdlife and an unspoilt coastline.

Apart from the numerous wildlife attractions the island also boasts a winery: **Phillip Island Vineyard and Winery**, on a signposted route on Berrys Beach Road, off Back Beach Road (daily: April–Oct 11am–5pm; Nov–March 11am–7pm), where you can sample their various wines, among them Chardonnay, Sauvignon Blanc, Cabernet Sauvignon and Merlot (tastings $5 per person). There's also a small courtyard café serving cakes and cheese platters, which you can enjoy while overlooking the vineyard and fields.

Phillip Island Reserve and the Penguin Parade

The **Phillip Island Reserve** includes all the public land on the **Summerland Peninsula**, the narrow tip of land at the island's western extremity. The reason for the reserve is the **Little penguin**, smallest of the penguins, which is found only in southern Australian waters and whose largest colony breeds at Summerland Beach (around 2000 penguins in the parade area and 20,000 on the island altogether). The **Penguin Parade** (nightly after dusk; $12.50; ℡03/5956 8300, ⓦwww.penguins.org.au) sounds horribly commercial – and with four thousand visitors a night at the busiest time of the year (immediately after Christmas), it can hardly fail to be. Spectators sit in concrete-stepped stadiums looking down onto a floodlit beach, with taped narration in Japanese, Taiwanese and English. But don't be too hard on it: ecological disaster would ensue if the penguins weren't managed properly, and visitors would still flock here, harming the birds and eroding the sand dunes. As it is, all the money made goes back into research and looking after the penguins, and into facilities such as the excellent **Penguin Parade Visitor Centre** (open from 10am; admission included in the parade ticket): the "Penguin Experience" here is a simulated underwater scene of the hazards of a penguin's life, and there are also interactive displays, videos and even nesting boxes to which penguins have access from the outside, where you can watch the chicks.

The parade itself manages to transcend the setting in any case, as the penguins come pouring onto the beach, waddling comically once they leave their preferred environment. They start arriving soon after dark; fifty minutes later the floodlights are switched off and it's all over, at which time (or before) you can move on to the extensive boardwalks over their burrows, with diffused lighting at regular intervals enabling you to watch their antics for hours after the parade finishes – they're active most of the night. If you want to avoid the worst of the crowds, the quietest time to observe them is during the cold and windy winter (you'll need water- or windproof clothing at any time of year). Remember too that you can see Little penguins close to St Kilda Pier in Melbourne (see p.919) and at many other beaches in southern and southeastern Australia, perhaps not in such large numbers, but with far fewer onlookers.

The Nobbies and Seal Rocks

At the tip of the Summerland Peninsula is **Point Grant**, where **The Nobbies**, two huge rock stacks, are linked to the island at low tide by a wave-cut platform of basalt, affording views across to Cape Schanck on the Mornington Peninsula. From the point a boardwalk leads across spongy greenery – vibrant in summer with purple and yellow flowers – along the rounded clifftops to a lookout over a blowhole. This is a wild spot, with views along the rugged southern coastline towards Cape Woolamai, a granite headland at the eastern end of the island. From September to April you may see muttonbirds (shearwaters) here – they arrive in September to breed and head for the same burrows each year, after an incredible flight from the Bering Strait in the Arctic Circle. Further off Point Grant, **Seal Rocks** are two rocky islets with the largest known colony of Australian fur seals, estimated to number around 16,000. In the breeding season between late October and December the number of seals present on the rocks peaks, but it is possible to see seals here all year round. The antics of the seals in the water and on the rocks are caught on camera and beamed to the **Seal Rocks Sea Life Centre** (daily 10am–dusk; $11) where visitors can watch them live on a big screen. In addition, there are other displays, such as videos of seals, artificial rockpools, and information displays on the amazing long-distance migration of the short-tailed shearwater as well as other seabirds one can see on Phillip Island. Note that at the time of writing the future of the centre was in doubt; check with the Victoria Visitor Information Centre (see p.891) for the latest.

The other attractions are more of the theme park variety: a boat ride along eleven scenes where experiences of George Bass's voyage from Sydney to

Western Port Bay in 1797 are told complete with special effects like a storm scene and a waterfall, and a hologram of a great white shark. The two **cafés** and the upmarket restaurant give panoramic views of the Nobbies and Seal Rocks. During the high season and school holidays there's a free shuttle bus between the Seal Rocks Sea Life Centre and the Penguin Parade Visitor Centre. **Cruises** to Seal Rocks are available from Cowes (see below).

Phillip Island Nature Park and the Koala Conservation Centre

Two further parks complete Phillip Island's rich collection of wildlife attractions. **Phillip Island Nature Park**, on Thompson Avenue just 1km south of Cowes (daily 10am–10.30pm; $12.50), is a shady shelter for Australian animals, most of them enclosed and not all native to Phillip Island. Highlights include the beautiful pure-bred dingoes, Tasmanian devils, fat dozy wombats which you can hold and feed if they're awake (but watch out, they bite), as well as an aviary and a koala reserve. Free to range are emus, Cape Barren geese, wallabies, eastern grey kangaroos and pademelons.

The **Koala Conservation Centre** on Phillip Island Tourist Road between Newhaven and Cowes (daily 10am–5.30pm; $5) is run by Phillip Island Nature Park and aims to keep the koala habitat as natural as possible while still giving people a close view. A treetop boardwalk through a part of the bushland park allows visitors to observe these marsupials at close range. At 4pm the rangers provide fresh gum leaves – a very popular photo opportunity. The centre's purpose is to breed disease-free koalas, as on Phillip Island they're infected with chlamydia. You can learn about koalas in the excellent interpretive centre.

Cowes and Rhyll

In the centre of the north coast, where the sandy bays are sheltered enough for good swimming, **COWES** is Phillip Island's main town. Several good places to eat and stay can be found here on The Esplanade, a lively strip facing the jetty. Based in the old Rotunda, Bay Connections (ⓣ03/5678 5642) offers several **cruises** from the jetty, the best being the trip to Seal Rocks (mid-Oct to end of April at least once daily, in winter less often; 2hr; $42) to watch the Australian fur seals close up. The same company runs day-tours from Cowes to Stony Point to French Island (Wed & Sun, but not in winter; ferry service plus island tour $52). Worth considering as a quieter place to base yourself is **RHYLL**, about 6km to the east of Cowes.

Accommodation

The main reason to come to Cowes or Rhyll is if you're planning to stay on the island. Out of season you should have no trouble, but during the peak Christmas–Easter season accommodation nearly doubles in price and some places require weekly bookings. The Phillip Island Visitor Information centre handles all accommodation bookings for the island; a private agency in Melbourne, Island Retreats (free call ⓣ1800 629 319) can arrange accommodation and packages.

Amaroo Park, cnr Church and Osborne streets, in the centre of Cowes (ⓣ03/5952 2548, ⓕ5952 3620). A budget YHA hostel with a convivial bar and a swimming pool. It also does cheap meals, rents out bikes, organizes various day-trips, has a free bus (Tues & Fri) to and from Melbourne, as well as the "duck truck" transport/accommodation/tour package (see p.946). Rooms ④–⑥, dorms ②

Castle Inn by the Sea, 7–9 Steele St, Cowes (ⓣ03/5952 1228, ⓕ5952 3926). A delightful B&B

in a pleasant location. ⑦–⑧

Coachman Motel, 51 Chapel St, Cowes
(☎03/5952 1098, ℱ5952 1283). This luxurious
town house offers motel units and suites. Facilities
include a heated pool and spa for communal use.
⑤–⑦

The Continental Phillip Island, 5–8 The
Esplanade, Cowes (☎03/5952 2316, ℱ5952
1878). A conveniently central hotel with en-suite
rooms, some with seafront balconies. Also a heated pool and spa. ⑥–⑦

Kaloha Holiday Resort, cnr Chapel and Steele
streets, Cowes (☎03/5952 2179, ℱ5952 2723).
Motel units with cooking facilities, plus cabins,
camping sites and facilities for on-site vans.

Lo
swi
s giving onto a quiet
Narr
(☎03/ 16 Steele St, Cowes
guesth 3670). A delightful
dinners. can arrange gourmet
Penguin
and Back B e **B&B**, cnr of Ventnor
8777). A rura ☎ & ℱ 03/5956
Rothsaye on cean views. ⑦–⑧
(☎ & ℱ 03/59 Roy Court, Cowes
⑦–⑧ , comfortable B&B.
Seahorse Motel,
(☎03/5952 2003, St, Cowes
age, centrally locate An above-aver-

Eating and drinking

Castle Inn by the Sea, 7–9 Steele St, Cowes.
Very good restaurant and bar.

The Clock Cafe, 1 Findlay St, Cowes. Near the
western end of the Esplanade. Small cosy café
with a view of the pier and a small sun deck. Open
daily for breakfast, light lunches and dinner.

Fountain Place, Thompson Ave, Cowes. Café
known for its delicious ice cream.

Isle of Wight Hotel, The Esplanade, Cowes. Hotel
with a good-value bistro offering sea views. Also a

couple of bars, a lively bee
ment at summer weekends d entertain-
The Jetty, The Esplanade, C
2060). An expensive but relaxe 3/5952
cializing in fresh local seafood. at spe-
Praha Coffee House, Thompson A wc A
simple café serving excellent fool p ea coffee.
Taylor's Seafood & Steak Restau 114
Thompson Ave, Cowes. Good seafood steaks
at reasonable prices.

The Yarra Valley and the Dandenongs

Northeast of Melbourne, the **Yarra Valley** stretches out towards the foothills
of the Great Dividing Range, with **Yarra Glen** and **Healesville** as targets
for excursions into the wine country and to the superb forest scenery
beyond. To the east, and still within the suburban limits, the cool, high
Dandenong Range is as pretty as anywhere in Australia, with quaint villages, fine old houses, beautiful flowering gardens and shady forests of eucalypts and tree ferns.

To get to all these destinations and to have a good look round, you really
need your own vehicle. On weekdays it is possible, although not exactly easy,
to explore the Dandenongs by **public transport**. Trains run via Ferntree Gully
to Belgrave at the southern edge of the Dandenongs. Buses from Belgrave follow a complicated schedule – enquire at the Met Transport Information
Centre (☎13 1638) in Melbourne. Healesville comes within the orbit of the
suburban transport system: take a train from Melbourne to Lilydale and then
bus #685 (for a visit to the Healesville Sanctuary, it's best to take the daily bus
departing from Lilydale).

A bus company runs a daily service for V/Line from Melbourne to Eildon
via Healesville and Marysville, the V/Line service to Mansfield passes through
Lilydale and Yarra Glen daily (for further information: V/Line ☎13 6196).
There are local buses from Belgrave to Emerald.

The Ya...y

Just half an ...m Melbourne, many of Victoria's best small **winer-**
ies – abou... of them serving food – lie en route to Healesville, or
you can v...king detours to Warburton or Yarra Glen. The combination of ...id fine food is really taking off in the Valley, in recent
years quit...ry restaurants succeeded in making a name for themselves in ...net circles.

Wine c...s in outer suburbia north of the Maroondah Highway just
before Li...offs are signposted). North of Lilydale, you can check out
wineries...signposted) along or near three routes – the Warburton
Highwa...st, the Maroondah Highway to Healesville, and the Melba
Highwa...north past Yarra Glen. The brochure *Wineries of the Yarra
Valley* ...omplete list of all wineries and a map of their locations. Even
better ...iled booklet *Wine Regions of Victoria* – both are available at
tourist ...ion centres. The recently transformed Yering Station, south of
Yarra C...off the Melba Highway, is dominated by a sweeping wall hewn
from lo..., and has magnificent views along the Yarra Valley, wine-making fac...glass-walled restaurant, performance space and amphitheatre.
The ce...operates from the original brick building; there's also a wine
bar and ...allery. Next door is Yarra Valley's first vineyard, Chateau Yering,
which as ...blished in 1854 and re-established in 1996 as a magnificent luxury hotel – ...*Chateau Yering Historic House Hotel*. For real comfort and luxury, wine a...ine at the hotel's *Café Sweetwater* or elegant *Eleonore's Restaurant*,
then sink ...a four-poster bed in one of the period-style rooms (T03/9237
3333, F ...73300, Wwww.chateau-yering.com.au; ❼–❽).

Equally... nique and beautiful is *De Bortoli Winery & Restaurant* (bookings
advisabl... T03/5965 2271, F5965 2464) whose building, the interior decoration an...the excellent food all betray strong influences of Northern Italy. It is
in an u...beatable location at Pinnacle Lane, off the **Melba Highway** at Dixon's
Creek north of Yarra Glen, with views over gently rolling hills.

On the **Maroondah Highway**, Domaine Chandon, near the town of
Coldstream, is owned by the French champagne house Möet et Chandon, producing fine *méthode champenoise* sparkling wine, which you can sample ($6–8
per glass) in a modern, bright and airy tastings room with brilliant views. Free
guided thirty-minute **tours** depart hourly from 11am to 4pm. *Eyton on Yarra
winery* and restaurant further up towards Healesville, at the corner of
Maroondah Highway and Hill Rd (T03/5962 2119), a relative newcomer on
the gourmet scene, specializes in locally produced food and Pinot Noir, Merlot
and Chardonnay wines. From October–March there are concerts at the *Eyton
on Yarra*-soundshell (Summer Music series).

Off the **Warburton Highway** detours there are four wineries, including
Yarra Burn on Settlement Road at Yarra Junction. The food at the restaurant can
be classified as hearty "Australian country" cuisine (lunches daily; Fri & Sat
dinner); B&B accommodation is available in the homestead.

From Yarra Junction it's not far to **WARBURTON**, a pretty, old-fashioned
town on the Upper Yarra River, and starting point for the **Upper Yarra Track**,
which follows old timber tram and vehicle tracks upstream for over 80km. The
track can be covered as a series of short walks or as a continuous five- to seven-
day trek, finishing in the Baw Baw National Park where it joins the Alpine
Walking Track. For more information contact the NRE Information Centre in
Melbourne (T03/9637 8080) or the telephone information service run by
Parks Victoria (T13 1963).

Apart from many wineries in its vicinity, **YARRA GLEN** also boasts the splendidly restored *Grand Hotel* and, not far away on the Melba Highway, the National Trust **Gulf Station** (Wed–Sun & public holidays 10am–4pm; $6), a collection of ten 1850s slab farm buildings set in a large area of farmland.

Healesville and beyond

HEALESVILLE is a small, pleasant town nestled in the foothills of the Great Dividing Range. Collect information about the region at the **visitor information centre** in the old courthouse building at the southern end of town, just off the Maroondah Highway (daily 10am–5pm). Healesville's main attraction is the renowned **Healesville Sanctuary** (daily 9am–5pm; free guides 10am–3pm if booked in advance; ℡03/5957 2800, 24hr information line ℡1902/240 592 at 50¢ per minute, ⓦwww.zoo.org.au; $16.40).

This is a genuine sanctuary, established over fifty years ago to provide care for injured and orphaned animals, some of which are then returned to the wild; those that stay join the sanctuary's programmes for education and the breeding of endangered species. It's a fascinating place in a beautiful setting, with a stream running through park-like grounds, dense with gum trees and cool ferns, and 3km of paths to follow past picnic and barbecue areas. Many of the animals are in enclosures, but there are paddocks of emus, wallabies and kangaroos you can stroll through. Don't miss the excellent "Animals of the Night" enclosure (10am–4.30pm); other star attractions include the aviaries (9am–4.30pm), a scary Reptile House (Mon–Fri 9am–4.30pm, Sat, Sun & public holidays 9am–5pm) and a Platypus Display Centre (9.30am–4.30pm). The informative "meet the keeper" presentations throughout the day are worth joining: the raptors (birds of prey) at noon and 3pm (weather permitting) are unmissable.

Continuing north on the Maroondah Highway over the Black Spur and Dom Dom Saddle towards Alexandra, the scenery becomes progressively more attractive. Worth a brief stop is the **Maroondah Reservoir Lookout**, just off the highway 3km north of Healesville, with picturesque views across the forest-fringed dam. There are very popular **picnic grounds** and **gardens** in the park on the southwest side of the reservoir. Soon after the reservoir, the highway meanders along bush-clad mountain slopes and enters luxuriant wet eucalypt forest with incredibly tall mountain ash, moss-covered myrtle beech, manna gum, tree ferns, gurgling creeks and waterfalls. The **Fernshaw Reserve and Picnic Ground** is a good place to stop and view the scenery. After the Dom Dom Saddle, 509m above sea level and 16km past Healesville, the highway descends towards Narbethong, where it enters drier country. Three kilometres past Narbethong a turn-off leads to scenic **MARYSVILLE**, 9km off the highway. A worthwhile detour, the village is nestled in the foothills of the Great Dividing Range, with **Lake Mountain** (1400m), a very popular area for cross-country skiing and tobogganing, 20km further west. In summer Marysville makes an excellent base for **bushwalking**, being surrounded by wet mountain ash forests with many creeks and waterfalls. The best-known, **Steavensons Falls**, can be reached from the village by a walking trail or by road and is floodlit at night until 11pm. Just out of Marysville, the unsealed **Lady Talbot Forest Drive** turns off the Lake Mountain road and then winds 46km through the forest, past picnic areas and walking tracks (suitable for conventional vehicles, though after heavy rainfall it's best to check in Marysville for road conditions). Return to Marysville via the Buxton Road, or turn right and head straight north to Buxton where you rejoin the highway. Further up, the Maroondah Highway passes the drier **Cathedral Range State Park**, where to the west of the road the mighty sandstone cliffs of Cathedral

Mountain (845m) seem to rise almost vertically behind the paddocks, over-looking the Acheron Valley.

The Dandenongs

This mountain range, reaching heights of up to 633m, shares with NSW's Blue Mountains the natural phenomenon of a blue haze rising from forests of gum trees. Abundant rain ensures the area stays cool and lush, while fine old hous-es and gardens add to the scenery. Easy bushwalks in the **Dandenong Ranges National Park** start from Ferntree Gully, accessible by train or by car via the Burwood Highway.

Another pleasant way to enjoy the forests and fern gullies is to take a ride on the **Puffing Billy** (for inquiries, bookings, and timetable and fare information, call ☏03/9754 6800 or visit ⊛www.pbr.org.au), which runs for 13km from the Puffing Billy Station in Belgrave to Lakeside ($20.50 return) on Lake Emerald, stopping at Menzies Creek and Emerald: one train a day continues a further 9km from Lake Emerald to Gembrook ($28 return).

The Puffing Billy Station is a short, signposted walk from Belgrave Railway Station (suburban trains). The steam train has run more or less continuously since the early twentieth century, though its operation now depends on dedi-cated volunteers; on total fire ban days, diesel locomotives are used. Timetables vary seasonally but there are generally several services daily until late afternoon; local buses also cover the Belgrave–Emerald route.

Just outside Emerald, man-made **Emerald Lake** has paddle-boats to rent and a swimming pool with waterslide, as well as trails through bushland continu-ing into the nearby state reserve. As for **accommodation**, *Emerald Backpackers*, 49 Emerald Lake Rd (☏03/5968 4086; rooms ❸, dorms ❶), has a country set-ting and a casual party atmosphere; the owners can help long-stay guests find local work. On weekdays and Saturday morning, bus #695 runs from the Belgrave train station to Emerald. *Choo Choos Restaurant and Bar*, at 32 Monbulk Rd in Emerald, is a friendly, reasonably priced oddity, serving **meals** on authentic railway crockery in old railway dining carriages.

Geelong and the Bellarine Peninsula

Heading west towards Geelong – for the Bellarine Peninsula or the Great Ocean Road – it's just a short detour off the Princes Freeway to **WERRIBEE** (or a half-hour train ride from Melbourne; zone 3), where the restored **Mansion at Werribee Park** (daily 10am–5pm; $11; ☏03/9741 2444) is locat-ed on K Road. Built in 1874–77 by Scottish squatters Thomas and Andrew Chirnside, who struck it rich on the back of sheep, the 60-room mansion is the largest private residence built in Victoria. Guides in period costume can show you inside the ornate homestead, or around the tranquil Victorian-era lawns and adjoining Victoria State Rose Garden; alternatively, free lightweight headsets providing a self-guiding commentary are available at the entrance.

Southeast of here is the recently built **Shadowfax Winery**, an impressive box-like structure that offers cellar door sales (Sat & Sun from 10am), glimpses of the wine-making process and gourmet food from the deli. Beyond the Mansion's gardens are the extensive grounds of **Victoria's Open Range Zoo** grassland where animals from Africa, Asia and Australia (giraffes, rhinoceroses, hippopotamuses, monkeys, meerkats and other creatures) roam in large open enclosures. A 50min safari bus takes visitors through the property and is included in the admission price (daily 9am–5pm; bus tours 10.30am–3.40pm; ☎03/9731 9600; $16.40; ⊛ www.zoo.org.au).

Continuing along the freeway, you can detour west again through Little River to the **You Yangs**, small but rugged volcanic peaks which rise sharply out of the surrounding plains and were once used by the local Barrabool tribe as hunting grounds. Scramble to the top of the highest, Flinders Peak (348m), which Matthew Flinders climbed in 1802, and you're rewarded with fine views of Geelong and Port Phillip Bay. The You Yangs, as well as the nearby **Brisbane Ranges**, are excellent places for spotting kangaroos, wallabies, koalas and possums at dusk. Alternatively, you can observe kangaroos, wallabies and emus, as well as numerous waterbirds, in their natural habitat at the little-known **Serendip Sanctuary**, 20km north of Geelong at 100 Windermere Rd, Lara (daily 10am–4pm; ☎03/5282 2570; $5.50). A refuge for threatened birds of the Western Plains of Victoria, this square kilometre of bush-, marsh- and wetlands, was originally part of an extensive sheep property. The sanctuary is renowned for its captive breeding programme of brolgas, magpie geese and Australian bustards, and has been in operation for more than twenty years.

Geelong

GEELONG, en route to the Bellarine Peninsula, is not particularly attractive, being too industrial to appeal as a coastal resort: the fact that the National Wool Museum is the main attraction gives you some idea of the place. You may have heard of the town, however, because it's wealthy – on wool money – and the site of an exclusive boarding school. The Geelong Wool Exchange, a National Trust-listed building at the corner of Brougham and Moorabool streets, houses the **National Wool Museum** (daily 9.30am–5pm; $8). The well set-up exhibition concentrates on the social history surrounding wool, with reconstructions of typical shearers' quarters and a millworker's 1920s cottage. On the top floor of the exchange wool is still auctioned off on thirty days in the year. Many of the best of the town's Victorian buildings are on Little Malop Street, including the elegant **Geelong Art Gallery** (Mon–Fri 10am–5pm, Sat & Sun 1–5pm; $4), which has an extensive collection of paintings by nineteenth-century Australian artists such as Tom Roberts and Frederick McCubbin, plus twentieth-century Australian paintings, sculpture and decorative arts. From Malop Street, Moorabool Street leads down to **Corio Bay**. Neglected for a fair while, Geelong's waterfront has undergone a facelift in recent years, so that the views of shipping traffic and, across the water, of an industrial skyline with hills behind don't seem quite so drab anymore. The promenades, rotunda and fountains on Eastern Beach have been renovated, as has a lovely nineteenth-century carousel featuring over thirty sculpted wooden horses. As well, new waterfront eating places have emerged, notably the large restaurant complex at the end of new **Cunningham Pier**, which comes into its own at night. Nestled among the lawns and trees of Eastern Park around 10min walk from the city centre are Geelong's historic **Botanic Gardens** (Mon–Fri 7.30am–5pm, Sat & Sun 7am–7pm; free). Begun in the late 1850s, the gardens boast rare and endangered plants, fountains, a geranium conservatory, sculptures and the *Tea House* (daily 11am–4pm), where you can take refreshments or collect brochures and other material. Swimming is permitted in a swimming enclosure at Eastern Beach.

On the way to Torquay, **Narana Creations**, an Aboriginal Arts, Crafts and Cultural Centre at 410 Torquay Rd (Surfcoast Highway) in Grovedale is worth a brief stop. Paintings and various arts and crafts are sold here, a native garden with a lake has been added, and sometimes visitors can listen to Dreamtime stories or didgeridoo playing (Mon–Fri 9am–5pm, Sat 10am–4pm; free).

Practicalities

In addition to the **visitor information centre** (daily 9am–5pm; free call ☎1800 620 888) at the Wool Museum, there's a helpful staffed **tourist information stall** (Mon–Sat 9am–5pm) in the Market Square Shopping Centre at the corner of Moorabool and Malop streets. Both provide lots of brochures and free maps. The main **shopping** strip is just a block south of the Wool Museum along Malop Street. Places to **stay** include the *Kangaroo Motel*, The Esplanade South (☎03/5221 4365; ❹), which has reasonably priced units in a central location; the *Lucas Innkeepers Motor Inn*, 9 Aberdeen St (☎03/5221 2177; ❺–❻), just west of the town centre; the reasonably priced *Ardara House B&B*, 4 Aberdeen St (☎03/5229 6024; ❸–❹), and on the other end of the price scale the luxurious air-con *Mercure Hotel Geelong*, corner of Gheringhap and Myers streets (☎03/5221 6844; ❽), which has a restaurant, bar, bistro, sauna and pool.

If you want to **camp**, try the *City Southside Caravan Park* on Barrabool Road, south of the Barwon River at Barwon Valley Park (☎03/5243 3788; cabins ❸–❹), and the nearby *Billabong Caravan Park* (☎03/5243 6225; cabins ❸). For **food**, there's plenty of choice, especially along the foreshore where there is the *Beach House Restaurant* overlooking Eastern Beach, then *Fishermans Pier Restaurant* at the end of Yarra Street, *Sailor's Rest* on Moorabool Street, *Bazil's Café* next to Deakin University and *Smorgy's Restaurant* on Cunningham Pier. Another concentration of eateries is to be found along Malop and Little Malop streets, with fast-food outlets, cafés and the stylish *Cats Bar Café and Restaurant* at 90 Little Malop St. A bit further uphill at 51 McKillop St the Geelong Wintergarden in a former church now houses an antique centre, a nursery, shops and a very pleasant café.

To check out what's going on, pick up a copy of the free **listings magazine** *Forte*, available at CD and record shops, and sometimes also at the visitor information centre. It covers the whole of southwest Victoria; as well as entertainment it has information on surfing, scuba diving and other activities. There's a surprisingly healthy local **band** scene in Geelong; check out *Irish Murphy's*, 30 Aberdeen St, the *Wool Exchange Hotel*, 59 Moorabool St, *The Barwon Club Hotel* at 509 Moorabool St, *Lamby's Bar* downstairs at the Wool Museum, and the *Scottish Chief's Tavern & Restaurant* at 99 Corio St which has its own microbrewery.

To get to the Bellarine Peninsula, take the Bellarine Transit **bus**, which departs from the Busport on Brougham Street (next to the Wool Museum) for Ocean Grove and Barwon Heads, Point Lonsdale via Queenscliff, St Leonards via Portarlington, and Grovedale via Torquay and Jan Juc.

Queenscliff and around

From Geelong, the Bellarine Highway runs 31km southeast to **QUEENSCLIFF** through flat and not particularly scenic grazing country. Queenscliff is essentially a quiet fishing village on Swan Bay – with several quaint cottages on Fishermens Flat – that became a favourite holiday resort for Melbourne's wealthy elite in the nineteenth century, then fell out of favour, and only recently has begun to enjoy something of a revival as a popular place for a weekend away or a Sunday drive. Its position near the narrow entrance to Port Phillip Bay made it strategically important: a **fort** here faces the one at Point Nepean, defending Melbourne against an enemy that never materialized. Now the

home of the Australian Army C[...]
ited on guided tours (Sat, Sun &[...]
daily 11am, 1pm & 3pm; 90min;[...] ollege, the fort can be vis-
 Full details of other things to do[...] n & 3pm; school holidays
centres in Geelong, or enquire at[...]
During school holidays and in su[...] the tourist information
(℡03/5258 3403) rents out a variety o[...] brary on Hesse Street.
a map of the town, a cassette tape and a[...] ff **Historical Tours**
seeing tour at your own pace. You can pick[...]), as well as providing
of Symonds Road, or they will deliver it to[...] you can do a sight-
the map, the ride takes little under two hour[...] r the pier at the end
($24 for 2hr; ℡03/5258 2166; rentals from th[...] ation. If you follow
the coast or further offshore, or diving among[...] s include kayaking
Queenscliff Dive Centre (℡03/5258 1188; $[...] rkin Parade) along
 Among the attractions is the **Queenscliff Ma**[...] rine life with the
Parade (Mon–Fri 10.30am–4.30pm, Sat & Sun 1.[...] y session).
daily 10.30am–4.30pm; ℡03/5258 3440; $4.40), w[...] **eum**, Weerona
many shipwrecks caused by The Rip, a fierce current a[...] chool holidays
Point Lonsdale and Point Nepean. Outside, a tiny fishe[...] ntrates on the
as it would have been in 1870, and there's a shed whe[...] wide between
painted, in naive style, all the ships he'd seen pass throug[...] age is set up
(imaginatively including the *Titanic*). Next door, the M[...] fisherman
Centre has a small aquarium (daily during school holidays[...] 95 to 1947 **iscovery**
times by appointment; ℡03/5258 3344; $3.30), stocked with[...] m, other
it also organizes a lot of activities, mainly during the summer h[...] ine life;
marine biology cruises, rock pool rambles, canoe trips and snor[...] uch as
The **Queenscliff Historical Centre** (daily 2–4pm; donation app[...] ours.
Hesse Street next to the post office, helps put the rest of the town i[...] on
text. Every Sunday, the **Bellarine Peninsula Railway** operates stea[...]
from the old Queenscliff Railway Station to Drysdale, 20km nort[...]
(11.15am & 2.30pm, more often during school holidays; ℡03/5258 2[...]
Ⓦwww.bpr.org.au; $14). Queenscliff Sunday Market is held on the last Sun
of each month from August to May on Symonds Street.

Point Lonsdale and Portarlington

From Queenscliff it's about 5km to peaceful **Point Lonsdale**, whose most noticeable feature is a magnificent 1902 lighthouse, 120m high and visible for 30km out to sea. Below the lighthouse, on the edge of the bluff, is "Buckley's Cave" where William Buckley is thought to have lived at some stage during his thirty-year sojourn with the Aborigines. At **PORTARLINGTON**, which sits on Port Phillip Bay about 14km north of Queenscliff, there's a beautifully preserved steam-powered flour mill, four storeys of solid stone, owned by the National Trust (Wed, Sat & Sun noon–4pm; ℡03/5259 3847; $2.50).

Practicalities

Three grand **Victorian-era hotels** in Queenscliff are popular settings for romantic (but very expensive) breaks: the *Vue Grand*, 46 Hesse St (℡03/5258 1544, Ⓕ5258 3471; ❽), has a Spanish-style exterior and a fabulously ornate Victorian interior with a very expensive restaurant; the clifftop *Ozone Hotel*, 42 Gellibrand St (℡03/5258 1011, Ⓕ5258 3712; ❼), features sea views from two iron-lace decorated verandahs and a gorgeous dining room; while the refined *Mietta's Queenscliff Hotel*, 16 Gellibrand St (℡03/5258 1066, Ⓕ5258 1899; ❽), is perhaps the best of all, and certainly the least intimidating. If it's available, go

wer. **Budget alternatives** include the
for the octago...03/5258 4600, ⓕ5258 3737; rooms ②–⑥,
Queenscliff Inn Y.../5258 1133, ⓕ5258 1152; ④–⑦), which has
dorms ①), a p...hotel rooms, a heated pool and tennis courts.
Motel, 78 Bella...esthouse offering B&B, and *Beacon Resort*
tent sites, cabi...esse St. Among the cafés there are *Mietta's Shop*
Among the ...noon) in the *Queenscliff Hotel*, which does light
*Queenscliff Fis...*and *38 South*, a café at the car ferry terminal with
& Bar (daily ...s of the bay and the Mornington Peninsula. There's
lunches, coff...e-to-expensive price bracket; to name the most out-
a fantastic vi...*Sea*, an excellent seafood restaurant at the foreshore at
a lot more i... & Sun, dinner Fri–Sun; BYO) and the stylish (and
standing: H...he historic *Mietta's Queenscliff Hotel* and the *Vue Grand*,
Princes Pa...ensed and serve lunch and dinner daily.
pricey) re... Queenscliff across the mouth of Port Phillip Bay to
both of w...
Ferries.).
Sorrento

TRAVEL DETAILS

Trains

...delaid...daily; 12hr); Alice
Melbo...kly; 3...); Ballarat (5–10 daily;
Spring (2–4 daily; 2hr); Geelong (9–24 2hr);

daily; 1hr); Perth (2 weekly; 50hr); Sydney via Albury (2 daily; 13hr); Warrnambool (2–3 daily; 3hr 15min).

Buses

...rne to: Adelaide (4 daily; 10hr); Brisbane ...e Gold Coast (4 daily; 25hr); Perth via ...laide (1 daily; 46hr); Sydney via Bega (1 daily;

18hr); Sydney via Canberra (5 daily; 12–14hr); Sydney via Dubbo (1 daily; 20hr).

Ferries

Melbourne to: Devonport, Tasmania (3 weekly; 14hr 30min); between mid-Dec and mid-April also

to Georgetown, Tasmania (4 weekly; 6hr).

Flights

Qantas and Ansett fly from **Melbourne** to: Adelaide (9–12 daily; 1hr 10min); Alice Springs (2 daily; 3hr 30min); Ayers Rock Resort (1–3 daily; 3hr 30min); Brisbane (10–12 daily; 1hr 10min); Cairns (7–11 daily; 3hr 15min direct); Canberra (4–7 daily; 55min); Coolangatta/Gold Coast (6–12 daily; 2hr); Darwin (3 daily; 3–4hr with one stopover); Hobart (4–7 daily; 1hr); Launceston (4 daily; 50min); Mackay (3–4 daily; 4hr 15min with

one stopover); Perth (5–7 daily; 4hr); Rockhampton (6–7 daily; 3hr 30min with one stopover); Sydney (16–24 daily; 1hr 20min); Townsville (3–5 daily; 5hr with one stopover).
Virgin Blue fly from **Melbourne** to: Brisbane (3 daily; 1hr 10min). At the time of writing, Virgin Blue were planning to open new domestic routes; for more information, call ☎13 6789.

Victoria

CHAPTER 10

Highlights

* **Great Ocean Road** – Wait until the sun is down and the crowds are gone and watch the fairy penguins come out to play at the Twelve Apostles. **p.962.**

* **Goldfields** – Mining memorabilia and grandiose architecture grace the old gold towns of Ballarat and Bendigo. **p.980.**

* **Trail riding in the Gippsland bush** – Canter through the wilderness, watched by goannas in the surrounding trees, in Victoria's "high country". **p.1017.**

* **Wilson's Promontory National Park** – There's great bushwalking and fantastic coastal scenery – once you escape the crowds – at Victoria's favourite national park. **p.1018.**

* **Milawa Gourmet trail** – Excellent local produce washed down with great wines from the Brown Brothers winery – all sampled against a backdrop of stunning Alpine scenery. **p.1033.**

* **Victorian Alps** – Perfect for skiing in winter, the Victorian Alps makes ideal bushwalking territory in summer. **p.1035.**

Victoria

A ustralia's second-smallest state, **Victoria** is the most densely populated and industrialized, and has a wide variety of attractions packed into a small area. It may not be a state to tour comprehensively, but Australians, at least, lap up the legends of their history that are thick on the ground: you're never too far from civilization, but everywhere there's a wild past of **gold prospectors** and **bushrangers**. All routes in the state radiate from **Melbourne**, bang in the middle of the coastline on the huge Port Phillip Bay, and no point is much more than seven hours' drive away. Yet all most visitors see of Victoria apart from its cultured capital is the **Great Ocean Road**, a winding 280km of spectacular coastal scenery. Others may venture to the idyllic **Wilsons Promontory National Park** (the "Prom"), a couple of hours away on the coast of the mainly dairy region of **Gippsland**, or to the **Goldfields**, where the nineteenth-century goldrushes left their mark in the grandiose architecture of old mining towns such as **Ballarat** and **Bendigo**.

There is, however, a great deal more to the state. Marking the end of the Great Dividing Range, the massive sandstone ranges of the **Grampians**, with their Aboriginal rock paintings and dazzling array of springtime flora, rise from the monotonous wheatfields of the **Wimmera** region and the wool country of the western district. To the north of the Grampians is the wide, flat region of the **Mallee** – scrub, sand dunes and dry lakes heading to the **Murray River**, where **Mildura** is an irrigated oasis supporting orchards and vineyards. In complete contrast, the **Victorian Alps** in the northeast of the state have several winter **ski slopes**, high country that provides perfect bushwalking and horse-riding territory in summer. In the foothills and plains below, where bushranger **Ned Kelly** once roamed, are some of Victoria's finest **wineries** (wine buffs should pick up a copy of the excellent hundred-page brochure,

---

Accommodation price codes

All the accommodation listed in this book has been categorized into one of eight price bands, as set out below. The rates quoted represent the cheapest available double or twin room in high season – except for category ❶, which indicates per-person rates for a dorm bed, and the categories given for units, cabins and vans, which represent the daily charge for the whole unit.

❶ Under $20	❸ $35–50	❺ $70–90	❼ $115–150
❷ $20–35	❹ $50–70	❻ $90–115	❽ $150 upwards

For more accommodation details, see pp.46–49.

Wine Regions of Victoria, available from the tourist information centre in Melbourne and other towns). Beach culture is alive and well on this **coastline** with some of the best **surfing** in Australia.

The only real drawback is the frequently cursed **climate**. Winter is mild, and the occasional heatwaves in summer are mercifully limited to a few days at most, but the problem is that of unpredictability. Cool, rainy "English" weather can descend in any season, and spring and autumn days can be immoder-

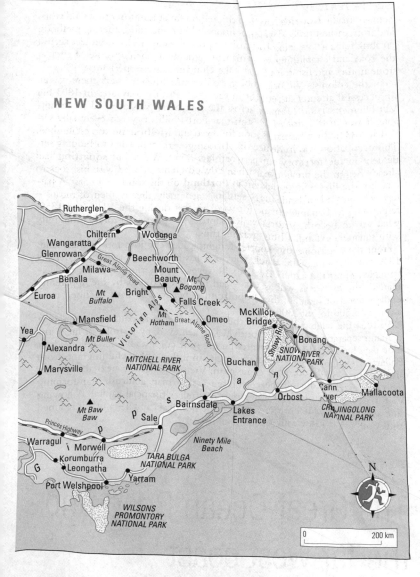

NEW SOUTH WALES

Rutherglen
Chiltern　Wodonga
Wangaratta
Glenrowan　　　Great Alpine Road
　　Milawa　　Beechworth
Benalla　　　　Mount
　　　　　　　　Beauty　Mt
Euroa　Mt　　Bright　　Bogong
　　　Buffalo　　　　Falls Creek
　　Mansfield　Mt　　　　　McKillop
Yea　　　　Hotham Great Alpine Road　Bridge
　　　　　　　Mt Buller　　Omeo
Alexandra
　　　　　　　　　　　　　Buchan　　SNOW　Bonang
Marysville　MITCHELL RIVER　　　　NATIONA　RIVER
　　　　　NATIONAL PARK　　　　　　　　PARK
　　　　　　　　　　　　　　　　　　　　　Cann
　　　　　　　　　s　Bairnsdale　　　　Orbost　iver　Mallacoota
　　Mt Baw　　p　Sale　　Lakes　　　　CR　JINGOLONG
　　Baw　　　　　　　　Entrance　　　NA　NAL PARK
Princes Highway　　p
Warragul　Morwell　　　Ninety Mile
Korumburra　　　　　　Beach
　G　Leongatha　TARA BULGA
Port Welshpool　Yarram　NATIONAL PARK
　　　　　　　　　　　N
　　　WILSONS
　　　PROMONTORY
　　　NATIONAL PARK
　　　　　　　　　0　　　　　　200 km

ately hot. But even this can be turned to advantage: as the local saying goes, if you don't like the weather, just wait ten minutes and it'll change.

Public transport, by road and rail, is with **V/Line** and subsidiary country bus lines. After the restructuring of recent years, however, using one's own vehicle is definitely a more convenient transport option, as train and bus services are fairly infrequent and quite a few places of interest can be reached only with difficulty, if at all.

Some history

Semi-nomadic **Koories** have [...] in this region for at least forty thousand years, and from earliest times develo[...] sophisticated hunting and gathering methods, creating rock art, weaving ba[...], making possum-skin cloaks to protect against the cold, and establishing se[...]ermanent settlements such as those of circular stone houses and fish traps [...]d at Lake Condah in western Victoria.

For the colonists, Victoria[...]d not get off to an auspicious start: there was an unsuccessful attempt at se[...]ment in the **Port Phillip Bay** area in 1803 but Van Diemen's Land (Tasm[...]a) across the Bass Strait was deemed more suitable. It was in fact from [...]nceston that Port Phillip Bay was eventually settled, in 1834; other Tasma[...]ns soon followed and **Melbourne** was established. This occupation was in d[...]ance of a British government edict forbidding settlement in the territory,[...]en part of New South Wales, but **squatting** had already begun the previo[...] year when Edward Henty arrived with his stock to establish the first white [...]tlement in **Portland** on the southwest coast. A pattern was created of lan[...]hungry settlers – generally already men of means – responding to Britain's [...]emand for wool, so that during the 1840s and 1850s what was to become V[...]ctoria evolved into a prosperous pastoral community with squatters extend[...]g huge grazing runs.

From the beginning the [...]oories fought against the invasion of their land: 1836 saw the start of [...]the **Black War**, as it has been called, a bloody guerrilla struggle against the settlers. By 1850, however, the Aborigines had been decimated – by disease as well as war – and felt defeated, too, by the apparently endless flood of invaders; their population is believed to have declined from around 15,500 to just 2300.

By 1851 the white popul[...]ion of the area was large and confident enough to demand separation from [...]ew South Wales, achieved, by a stroke of luck, just nine days before **gold** [...]s discovered in the new colony. The rich goldfields of Ballarat, Bendigo and [...]astlemaine brought an influx of hopeful migrants from around the world. [...]ore gold came from Victoria over the next thirty years than was extracted[...]during the celebrated Californian goldrush, transforming Victoria from a [...]storal backwater into Australia's financial capital. Following federation in 1[...]1, Melbourne was even the political capital – a title it retained until Canber[...] became fully operational in 1927.

The Great Ocean Road and the far west coast

The **Great Ocean Road**, Victoria's famous southwestern coastal route, starts at Torquay, just over 20km south of Geelong, and extends 285km west to Warrnambool. It was built between 1919 and 1932 with the idea of constructing a scenic road of world repute, equalling California's Pacific Coast Highway – and it certainly lives up to its reputation. The road was to be both

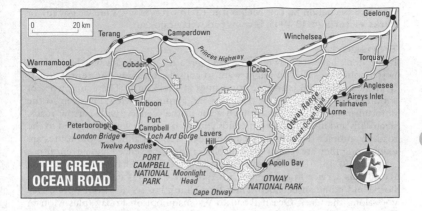

THE GREAT
OCEAN ROAD

a memorial to the soldiers who had died in World War I, and an employment scheme for those who returned. Over three thousand ex-servicemen laboured with picks and shovels, carving the road into cliffs and mountains along Australia's most rugged and densely forested coastline; the task was speeded up with the help of the jobless during the Great Depression. The road hugs the coastline between **Torquay** and **Apollo Bay** and passes through the popular holiday towns of **Anglesea** and **Lorne**, set below the Otway Range. From Apollo Bay the road heads inland, through the towering forests of the **Otway National Park**, before rejoining the coast at Princetown to wind along the shore for the entire length of the **Port Campbell National Park**. This stretch from Moonlight Head to Port Fairy, sometimes referred to as the "Shipwreck Coast", is the most spectacular – over eighty ships have been sunk here, victims of the rough Southern Ocean and dramatic rock formations such as the **Twelve Apostles**, which sit out to sea beyond the rugged cliffs. The often windy and stormy weather enhances the jagged coastline, and even at the height of summer you can't rely on it being sunny here. Information on all the villages and sights on the Great Ocean Road can be found on the area's website, Ⓦ www.greatoceanrd.org.au.

If you're in a hurry to get from Melbourne to Warrnambool, the **Princes Highway** is a much faster route – and a much duller one. The only place you might consider stopping briefly is Colac, where **Lake Colac** and the vast **Lake Corangamite** support a profusion of birdlife, with botanical gardens and a bird sanctuary.

From **Warrnambool**, the small industrial coastal city where the Great Ocean Road ends, the Princes Highway continues along the coast, through quaint seaside **Port Fairy** and industrial **Portland**, before turning inland for the final stretch to the South Australian border. If you're determined to stick to the coast, you can continue along the Portland–Nelson road, with Mount Richmond National Park and Discovery Bay Coastal Park on the coastal side, and Glenelg National Park on the other, to end up at the unspoilt little town of **Nelson** on the peaceful Glenelg River, with the spectacular Princess Margaret Rose Caves nearby.

The **Great Southwest Walk**, a 250-kilometre circuit starting from just outside Portland, going on to the Glenelg River and Nelson, and then back through the two coastal parks to Portland, is magnificent. There are campsites all along the route; for further information, and to obtain maps, contact the NRE Information

Centre, 8 Nicholson St, East Melbourne (☎13 6186, Ⓦwww.nre.vic.gov.au), or **Parks Victoria** (☎13 1963, Ⓦwww.parkweb.vic.gov.au).

Transport

If you don't have your own car or can't get a **lift** (it's always worth checking hostel notice boards), you might want to consider one-way **car rental**, usually available from the big-name companies in Melbourne. There are plenty of parking spots where you can pull over and admire the view, but even so the unfortunate driver will miss out on a lot of the scenery; with narrow roads, steep cliffs and incessant hairpin bends you need to keep your eyes glued to the road. In summer the road is filled with **cyclists**, and although the routes are exhilarating they are really only suitable for the experienced and adventurous.

V/Line (☎13 6196, Ⓦwww.vlinepassenger.com.au) has a "Great Ocean Road" **bus** service from Geelong to Apollo Bay, calling at Torquay, Anglesea, Lorne and points in between. Their Coast Link bus service from Apollo Bay goes along the Great Ocean Road to Warrnambool on Friday (plus Mon in Dec & Jan). There's a **train** service from Melbourne, via Geelong and Colac, to Warrnambool (2–3 daily), with connecting buses to Port Fairy, Portland and Heywood (1–2 daily) and on to Mount Gambier in South Australia (1 daily). From Warrnambool you can also return to Melbourne on the inland road, or go north to Ballarat. There's no public transport to Nelson.

Tours

One-way tours between **Melbourne** and **Adelaide**, via the Great Ocean Road, are a good way to take in the scenery. The backpackers' busline Oz Experience (☎1300/300 028, Ⓦwww.ozexperience.com) covers this route in four days, taking in the Great Ocean Road, the Grampians and the Coonawarra wine region in South Australia ($240 all inclusive), while Wayward Bus (free call ☎1800 882 823, Ⓦwww.waywardbus.com.au) sticks to the coast all the way to the Coorong in South Australia on its three-day tour ($265 all inclusive). With both you can get off the bus and continue your trip a few days later (booking required). The small and friendly Groovy Grape (free call ☎1800 661 177, Ⓦwww.groovygrape.com.au) cover the route in an all-inclusive three-day tour ($245) with overnight stops at the Aboriginal-run *Brambuk Hostel* in the Grampians and Port Campbell.

A few other reliable tour operators do **one- or two-day round-trips** from Melbourne to the Great Ocean Road, some with an extra Grampians option and/or possible transfer to Adelaide – note that prices given below do not include food and accommodation costs. Autopia Tours (☎03/9326 5536 or free call 1800 000 507, Ⓦwww.autopiatours.com.au) does one-day (daily; $54) and two-day tours (Tues & Sat; $82); their three-day tour adds on a visit to the Grampians (Mon, Wed, Fri & Sun; $140 or $150 with connection to Adelaide); there's also a two-day combination of the Great Ocean Road and Phillip Island (Mon, Wed & Fri; $108). Let's Go Bush Tours (☎03/9662 3969) is a smaller, long-established tour operator that offers a two-day tour of the Great Ocean Road where you stay overnight at their own house near Lavers Hill in the Otway Ranges (Wed & Sat, plus extra trip Mon Nov–May; $99 half board). A similar outfit, Eco Platypus Tours (free call ☎1800 819 091), offer a two-day tour including a full day in the Grampians ($99), with a choice of tent or shared accommodation at their own lodge between Warrnambool and the Grampians. Some more recent tour operators on the market include Princetown Tours (☎0407 090 800; two-day tour departs Mon & Sat; $85); Go West (☎03/9828 2008; one-day tour departs daily; $54); and Otway Discovery (☎03/9654 5432 or free call 1800 444 432; one-day hop-on, hop-off tour departs daily; $50).

Torquay

TORQUAY is the centre of **surf culture** on Victoria's "surf coast", which extends from Point Lonsdale, on the Bellarine Peninsula, to Lorne; two local beaches, **Jan Juc** and **Bells Beach**, are solidly entrenched in Australian surfing mythology. If you're not here for the surf, then there's not really a lot happening: in hot weather the place is boisterously alive, but out of season it's somnolent and low-key. The big event here is the Rip Curl Pro & Sun Smart Classic, held at Bells Beach in Easter, which draws national and international contestants and thousands of spectators (call Surf Victoria on ☎ 03/5261 2907 or see ⓦ www.ripcurlpro.com.au for details). Local **buses** run between Geelong and Torquay via Jan Juc – call Bellarine Transit (☎ 03/5223 2111) for the latest information.

As you come into Torquay along the Great Ocean Road (Geelong Rd in town), you'll see the **Surfcity Plaza** shopping centre, by far the best place to rent surf gear. The **Surfworld Museum** (daily 9am–5pm; $6.50; ⓦ www.surfworld.com.au) at the rear of the plaza is devoted to Torquay's main industry – and a prosperous one it is, taking in at least $200 million a year. Surfworld features a wave-making machine, interactive videos that explain how waves are created, and displays about the history of surfing. The museum also functions as the **Torquay Visitor Information Centre**, handing out a few leaflets and brochures. Many of the biggest surfing businesses are based in Torquay, and every surf accessory conceivable is sold here. The biggest and oldest is Rip Curl, 101 Surf Coast Highway (daily 9am–5.30pm), which started making surfboards here in 1969 and now stocks all the major brands, as well as its own boards and gear. Based at the same shopping centre are showcase outlets for other big names, such as Billabong, Piping Hot and Quiksilver. Bargains can sometimes be found at Baines Beach Surf Seconds, around the corner on Baines Street (fourth factory on the right). The **Mary Elliott Pottery**, 80 Surfcoast Highway (open daily), is worth a look; it supplies tourist information as well.

A grassy public reserve shaded by huge Norfolk pines (with electric barbecues and picnic tables) runs along rocky **Fisherman's Beach** and **Front Beach**. The **Surf Beach** (or "back beach"), south of Cosy Corner (a headland separating Front and Surf beaches), is backed by rugged cliffs and takes a full belting from the Southern Ocean; it's patrolled in summer. **Jan Juc**, just south of Surf Beach across Torquay Golf Club, is also patrolled in season and has better swimming and surfing. The **South Coast Walk** to Aireys Inlet via Anglesea begins from here (25km; 8hr); the sector to **Bells Beach** is a one-hour, three-kilometre walk.

Practicalities

Accommodation in Torquay comprises two hostels, a couple of motels, several B&Bs, and a few caravan and camping parks. *Nomads Bells Beach Backpackers* on 51–53 Surfcoast Highway, painted bright blue with beachhouse murals, is hard to miss (☎ 03/5261 7070 or free call 1800 819 883, ⓕ 5261 3879; dorms ❶–❷, rooms ❸–❹), or there's *Amiko's at Torquay*, on Anderson Street in the centre (☎ 03/5261 4732, ⓦ www.amikos.com; rooms ❺, dorms ❷), which is much cosier but has fewer facilities. *The Torquay Hotel*, 36 Bell St (☎ 03/5261 6046, ⓕ 5261 4065; ❻), is very centrally located and serves good bistro fodder, while *Just June's B&B*, 12 Casino Court (☎ 03/5261

3771; ❺), is a homestay option in a modern home on a quiet street at the north end of town. When it comes to **food**, there are a few excellent, typically casual, places designed to satisfy a surfer's hunger: *Micha's Restaurant on the Esplanade*, 23 The Esplanade (☎03/5261 2460; licensed or BYO), is a longtime favourite dinner spot serving Mexican food and cheap drinks – you'll need to book at summer weekends. *Spooners* and *Kuzies*, both in the Plaza, are good for filling fare, and the *Nocturnal Donkey* on Bell Street is popular for munchies late into the night. Good ice cream is sold at *The Great Australian Ice Creamery*, Shop 4, 57 Surfcoast Highway, and *The Scandinavian Ice Cream Company*, 34 Bell St. For **entertainment**, surfies head for the *Torquay Hotel*, 36 Bell St, where live bands play at weekends. At Jan Juc, both *Pabs Tavern* and the *Birdrock Bar* on Stuart Avenue are popular hangouts day and night.

For **surfing lessons**, call the West Coast Surf School in Torquay (☎03/5261 2241), or Go Ride a Wave (☎03/5263 2111), an outdoors activities company based in neighbouring Anglesea. If you feel like taking to the air, turn to **Tiger Moth World Adventure Park**, a family amusement park on the Bellarine Peninsula halfway between Geelong and Queenscliff (daily 10am–5pm; ☎03/5261 5100, ⓦwww.tigermothworld.com), which has lots of fun and sports facilities, most of them water-based. They also do **scenic flights** aboard vintage Tiger Moths.

Anglesea and Aireys Inlet

On the way to Anglesea from Torquay, you can make a short but worthwhile detour to **Addis Point**; turn left just beyond Bells Beach. The road goes right out to the headland where, from the car park, you look down on the waves crashing onto the point. Steps lead down to an even better vantage point, with surf heaving below you and Bells Beach stretching to the northwest.

ANGLESEA itself is a perfectly pleasant place for a holiday, with the Anglesea River running through to the sea, and picnic grounds along its banks. Despite tourist development, the beach has managed to retain its sand dunes and its untouched aspect. Children can swim safely here, as the surf is fairly gentle, but the waves are high and powerful enough for body-surfers to enjoy. Anglesea's main claim to fame is a large population of **kangaroos**, which graze on its golf course. The small *Anglesea Backpackers Hostel* on 40 Noble St (☎03/5263 2664, ⓦwww.angelsea-backpackers.com.au; dorms ❶, rooms ❸), located between the river and the golf course, has small dorms and an en-suite double. Mountain bikes are available to hire ($10 per day), and the owner arranges lots of activities: surfing lessons (2hr; $30, gear included), snorkelling, spotlighting tours at night, horse riding, mountain bike tours in the bush and trips to Torquay. Phone for a pick-up from the bus stop.

From Anglesea the road goes inland for a few kilometres through scrubby bush. Beyond, a pretty white lighthouse with a red cap overlooks the small town of **AIREYS INLET**. There's little more than a general store here (which sells heavily discounted fuel) and the *Aireys Inlet Caravan Park* opposite (☎03/5289 6230 or free call 1800 66 88 66, ⓦwww.aicp.com.au; cabins ❹–❺). *Airey's By the Light*, on the way out of town (☎02/5289 6134, ⓦwww.tourvic.com.au/accommodation/aireys.htm; ❻–❼), offers more upmarket B&B accommodation with private decks and stunning sea views, in keeping with the huge and ritzy houses that jostle for ocean views on the way to Lorne. A little further down the road in **FAIRHAVEN**, the small *Surfcoast Backpackers* (☏ 03/5289 6886 or 0419 351 149; dorms ❷) has very clean en-suite dorms and a cosy kitchen/common room with a piano. The hostel is located in a prime location, 100m away from the main road and the long, sandy Fairhaven Beach, which is patrolled. The owner books horse rides through the bush and along the beaches. Ask the bus driver to stop at the Yarringa Road bus stop – there's a signpost on the Great Ocean Road pointing towards the hostel.

Lorne and around

Picturesquely located at the foot of the heavily forested **Otway Range**, on the banks of the Erskine River, **LORNE** has long been the premier holiday town of the Great Ocean Road. Only two-hours' drive from the city, it's hugely popular with Melbourne weekenders who relish its well-established café society and whiff of 1960s counterculture overlaid on an essentially middle-class 1930s resort. To complete the picture, the **Angahook–Lorne State Park** (see p.969), with its walking tracks, plunging falls and fern gullies, surrounds the town.

About one thousand people live in Lorne, but from Christmas until the end of January twenty thousand more pour in; if you arrive unannounced, you'll have no hope of finding even a camping spot. The **Falls Festival** (ⓦ www.falls-festival.com) on New Year's Eve is celebrated with a big rock concert that attracts droves of teenagers, followed eight days later by the Mountain to Surf Run and one day later by the highlight of the peak season, the **Pier to Pub Swim**. It is the largest blue-water swimming event in the world and attracts as many as two and a half thousand competitors who race the 1200m from Lorne Pier to the main beach. The atmosphere surrounding these events is a lot of fun, but generally Lorne is much more enjoyable when it's less crowded, which means avoiding weekends and the peak summer season.

The main beachfront promenade, Mountjoy Parade, is enlivened by the *Pacific Hotel*, with its 1870s facade, and the modern, very pink, terraced *Cumberland Resort*. Between the street and the beach is a foreshore with trampolines and a pool. The **surf beach** itself is one of the safest in Victoria, protected from the Southern Ocean by two headlands, but in summer it gets very crowded. Ten minutes east of Lorne is the secluded beach of Cathedral Rocks, a very popular **nudist beach**.

Practicalities

Lorne's **tourist office**, at 144 Mountjoy Parade (daily 9am–5pm; ☏ 03/5289 1152), is very helpful and has a good stock of leaflets packed with local information, including several free driving maps and details of walks in the state park. Mocean Surfboards on Mountjoy Parade (daily 9.30am–5.30pm), rents out quality surf- and boogie-boards and wetsuits. Other services, such as banks, a post office and shops, are clustered primarily along Mountjoy Parade and parallel Smith Street.

Accommodation

Lorne has a mix of old guesthouses and modern holiday apartments – often side by side. There's plenty of motel, hotel and self-catering accommodation, but most of it is in the upper price bracket, and in December and January most places rent by the week, with even B&Bs insisting on a three- or four-night minimum stay. If you want to keep costs down (but don't fancy the dorms at the *YHA* or *Great Ocean Road Cottages*), contact the Lorne Foreshore Committee, Ocean Road by Erskine Bridge (℡03/5289 1382), which runs four **caravan parks** (on-site vans ❹) in the vicinity.

The Anchorage, 32 Mountjoy Parade (℡ & ℻ 03/5289 1891). Self-catering accommodation with BBQs, pool and heated spa. ❺

Cumberland Lorne Resort, 150 Mountjoy Parade (℡03/5289 2400 or free call 1800 037 010, ℻5289 2256, ⓦwww.cumberland.com.au). Luxurious but pricey one-bedroom apartments, some with ocean views; lots of facilities, including tennis and squash courts, an indoor pool, spa, sauna, and rental of windsurfers, boogie-boards and bikes. ❽

Erskine House Beachside Resort, Mountjoy Parade (℡03/5289 1209 or free call 1800 629 417, ⓦwww.erskinehouse.com.au) A huge country house with guest lounges and open fires, decorated in Art Deco style. Tennis, badminton and croquet are all available in the magnificent gardens overlooking the ocean. ❻

Great Ocean Road Backpackers YHA, 10 Erskine Ave (℡03/5289 1809, ℻5289 2508, ⓔlorne@yhavic.org.au). Excellent, attractive hostel with wooden verandahs and balconies, in a central location beside the Erskine River. Rooms ❸, dorms ❶

Great Ocean Road Cottages, 3 Erskine Ave (℡03/5289 1070, ℻5289 1380). Well-designed, comfortable, self-catering cottages in a lovely forest setting beside the Erskine River; also some dorm accommodation. Cottages ❺, dorms ❷

Lemonade Creek Cottages, 690 Erskine Falls Rd (℡ & ℻ 03/5289 2600). Self-contained weatherboard cottages with central heating; in a bushland setting, but not far from the beach and town. ❻

Lorne Hotel, 176 Mountjoy Parade (℡03/5289 1409, ℻5289 2200). Very large rooms, some with balconies and sea views, but noisy at weekends. ❺

Ocean Lodge Motel, 6 Armytage St (℡03/5289 1330, ℻5289 1380). Run-of-the-mill, but good-value, motel accommodation. ❺

Pacific Hotel, 268 Mountjoy Parade (℡03/5289 1609, ℻5289 2279). A building whose faded grandeur conceals motel-style accommodation. ❺

Eating and entertainment

There are great places to **eat** and **drink** everywhere in town. *Kosta's* often has music in the evenings, while the *Lorne Hotel* has bands on Friday and Saturday nights, and its public bar, with pool table and pinball machine, is a favourite with the young crowd. The *Lorne Theatre*, 78 Mountjoy Parade (℡03/5289 1272), screens **films** all week during summer.

The Arab, 94 Mountjoy Parade. An original beatnik hangout, which opened two weeks before the Olympic Games in 1956 and has been going strong ever since. It now sports minimalist decor but is still good for daytime snacks and fancier meals at night.

Kafé Kaos, 52 Mountjoy Parade. Huge, delicious, healthier-than-thou sandwiches, salads and wraps with extensive (and much less healthy) breakfast options.

Kosta's, 48 Mountjoy Parade (℡03/5289 1883). A popular, Greek-style bar and eating place, decorated with Surrealist wall paintings. Licensed or BYO.

Lorne Hotel, 176 Mountjoy Parade. Best pub meals in town, and has a dining room overlooking the ocean.

Lorne Pier Seafood Restaurant, on the pier at Point Grey. Excellent seafood. Licensed or BYO.

Mark's, 124 Mountjoy Parade (℡03/5289 2787).

A modern restaurant with a menu featuring a large variety of dishes, from marlin steak to home-made potato gnocchi. Licensed.

Moon's Espresso Bar, 108 Mountjoy Parade. A little taste of city life by the sea, this ultramodern establishment serves excellent coffee and Mediterranean lunches and even has an attached cocktail bar.

Qdos, Allenvale Rd (℡03/5289 1989). Tucked away in the eucalypt-clad hills above Lorne, this art gallery-cum-café serves light lunches, dinners and tasty home-made cakes and coffee in a relaxed atmosphere. Bookings advisable.

Reifs Restaurant & Bar, 84 Mountjoy Parade (℡03/5289 2366). Serves a wide range of dishes, including seafood and vegetarian, with Asian and Mediterranean influences. A large outdoor area overlooks Loutit Bay. Licensed.

Angahook–Lorne State Park

Angahook–Lorne State Park extends along some 50km of coastline, from Aireys Inlet to Kennett River. Pockets of temperate rainforest, towering blue-gum forests, cliffs and waterfalls characterize the Lorne section of the park, south of the Erskine River. The **Erskine Falls**, one of the most popular attractions, drops 30m into a fern-fringed pool – you can reach them along a winding eight-kilometre road (some of it gravel), which ends with a short descent on a very steep but sealed section. From the car park the falls are a few minutes' walk through majestic trees and tall umbrella ferns; another 150m takes you down to the quiet, rocky Erskine River. It's also possible to walk through the bush from Lorne to the falls (7.5km one-way; 4hr), starting from the *Erskine River Caravan Park* and following the river; after 1km you'll pass the Sanctuary, a natural rock amphitheatre, then Splitter Falls and Straw Falls, before reaching Erskine Falls.

Closer to Lorne, **Teddy's Lookout**, in Queens Park, is either a quick drive from the Great Ocean Road (up Otway St, turn left at the roundabout into George St), or a three-kilometre walk. You end up high above the sea, with a view of the St George River below and the Great Ocean Road curving around the cliffs. On the way back to Lorne, the **Qdos Arts centre** (daily 11am–11pm) on Allenvale Road, with an art gallery, sculpture gardens and a very good café-restaurant, merits a visit – just turn left at the roundabout and go up the hill.

Apollo Bay and the Otway Range

After Lorne, wooded hills fall away steeply into the ocean. The road follows the coastline in twisted serpentines, becoming very narrow in places where it was literally gouged out of the rockface, occasionally descending to small bays at the mouths of the Wye and Kennett rivers. On a fine, sunny day the views are glorious, but best admired from one of the many scenic lookout points as you need to drive with care.

APOLLO BAY is in a picturesque setting between pounding surf and gently rounded green hills. **Fishing** – commercial and recreational – is the main activity here. If you're interested in doing a bit yourself, enquire at Apollo Bay Boat Charter (℡ 03/5237 6214), which offers fishing trips and scenic boat cruises. The town has an enjoyably alternative feel – a lot of musicians live here and both local pubs often have music at weekends. The annual **Apollo Bay Music Festival** takes place over a weekend in mid-March and features jazz, rock, blues and country, plus many workshops (information ℡ 03/5237 6761; bookings through Ticketmaster, free call ℡ 1800 136 100). For information on local activities, head for the **Great Ocean Road Visitor Information Centre** on the foreshore at the eastern end of town (daily 9am–5pm; ℡ 03/5237 6529, ℻ 5237 6194), with an informative display on the rainforest and local history. **Flying** is becoming increasingly popular here: the Wingsports Flight Academy (℡ 0419 378 616) offers courses in hang-gliding and paragliding and allows those with no prior experience to fly with a fully qualified pilot along the coast in a powered hang-glider. Twelve Apostles Airtours (℡ 03/5237 7370) does scenic flights to a variety of destinations, including nearby Cape Otway and the Twelve Apostles ($70), and as far afield as King Island, Tasmania ($130); prices are per person and based on a minimum of three passengers. If you're interested in **horse riding**, book a trail ride with Wild Dog Trails (℡ 03/5237 6441; 1hr 30min $28, full day $73); **cycling** enthusiasts can enquire about mountain bike tours run by Otway Expeditions (℡ 0419 007 586; minimum of two people required). A few tour operators offer **eco-tours**, amongst them Otway Eco-Guides (℡ 03/5237 7240 or 5237 9255), who run walking tours through the Otway National Park, and twilight glow-worm tours. For other sightseeing tours (4WD or normal vehicle) enquire at the Visitor Information Centre.

Apollo Bay has a wide variety of **accommodation**. Numerous holiday apartments, cosy B&B cottages, guesthouses and farmstays are to be found in the area, many of them picturesquely located in the hills and valleys surrounding the town. One that's particularly worth seeking out is *Wongarra Heights* on Sunnyside Road, Wongarra (℡ 03/5237 0257; ❻), which offers B&B accommodation on a farm 12km east. Apollo Bay's main street is lined with **motels**, most of them rather drab affairs dating from the 1970s; one of the newer and better ones is *Beachfront Motel & Cottages* at 163 Great Ocean Rd (℡ 03/5237 6437, ℉ 5237 7197; ❼). For budget travellers, there are two **hostels**: the *Surfside YHA*, at the corner of Great Ocean Road and Gambier Street (℡ 03/5237 7263, ℮ apollobay@yhavic.org.au; dorms ❶, rooms ❷–❸), is a small and friendly place in a scenic location on a hill at the western side of town offering free use of surfboards, windsurfing and skin-diving equipment; while just 400m up from the main street, the *Apollo Bay Backpacker Hostel*, 47 Montrose St (℡ 03/5237 7360 or 0419 340 362; ❶–❷), is a small weatherboard house with dorms, cheap singles and doubles, some out the back in an extension to the house. There are several **caravan parks**, the closest to town being the *Waratah Caravan Park* at 7 Noel St (℡ 03/5237 6562; cabins ❹, on-site vans ❸). *The Pisces Caravan Resort*, 2km north of the town centre (℡ 03/5237 6749), also has cabins (❷–❺). For foreshore **camping** in more secluded surroundings, try the *Marengo Camping Reserve* on Marengo Crescent (℡ 03/5237 6162; closed May–Oct), or *Skenes Creek Camping Reserve*, 6km back along the Ocean Road.

In town, the **eating** places are strung along the Great Ocean Road. *Nautigal's*, at no. 58, serves great coffee, sandwiches and cakes; it's also the town's **internet café**. You can eat in the atmospheric *Bay Leaf Gourmet Deli* at no. 131, or choose to take your picnic fodder towards the sea. *Buffs Bistro* at no. 51, serves light snacks, seafood and pasta, while *Sea Grapes Wine Bar*, at the other end of the strip at no. 141, is more upmarket, serves good coffee and is open for breakfast, lunch and dinner. Vegetarians and wholefood junkies will like the *Sandy Feet Café*, a tribute to all things healthy next door at no. 139. The *Apollo Bay Hotel* on Collingwood Street has good seafood, and also cheaper counter and bistro meals. Outside town, *Chris's Beacon Point Restaurant*, 2km up Skenes Creek Road in the hills up the coast above Skenes Creek (℡ 03/5237 6411), is renowned for its Mediterranean cuisine and especially its seafood. The *Tanybryn Tea House and Gallery*, on the corner of Skenes Creek and Wild Dog roads, is also worth the fifteen-minute drive for its well-stocked craft shop, café and fine panorama (10am–5pm; closed July to mid-Sept).

Otway National Park

From Apollo Bay, the Great Ocean Road soon enters **Otway National Park**, curving and bending upwards through temperate rainforest and offering occasional glimpses of cleared hilltops and grazing sheep in the distance. From Maits Rest car park, 17km west of Apollo Bay, you can take an easy stroll through a lovely fern gully, which gives a good idea of the dense rainforest that once covered the entire Otway Ranges. A little further down the road, towards Lavers Hill, there's a turn-off to the **Cape Otway Lighthouse**, 14km along an unsealed road, where there's pleasant accommodation in two renovated cottages, former residences of the lighthouse keepers (T 03/5237 9240; ❼–❽). You can take a guided tour of the grounds and the lighthouse (daily 9am–5pm; $5.50; advance booking necessary), as well as various specialist tours, including a paleontology trip focusing on prehistoric plants and animals, in particular one type of dinosaur unique to this area – the polar dinosaur.

The only **caravan park** actually within the national park is *Bimbi Park* (T 03/5237 9246; on-site vans ❸), about halfway along the road to the lighthouse. The facilities and some of the cabins are quite basic but the setting is gorgeous – on a small farm with paddocks surrounded by bushland – and the caravan park offers excellent **horse-riding** excursions, including a ride to Station Beach ($20 per hour, $60 per day), a three-kilometre-long stretch of sand with freshwater springs and waterfalls.

Back on the Great Ocean Road, you momentarily return to the ocean at **Castle Cove**, a good lookout point across green, undulating dairy country. As you turn inland again, stepped hills rise sharply from the road as it passes turn-offs to **Johanna**, one of Victoria's best-known surf beaches, and winds up towards **LAVERS HILL**, high in the Otway Range. The tiny town is characterized by its fern nursery and two cosy tearooms: the *Gardenside Manor* and the *Blackwood Gully Tea Rooms & Tourist Centre*, both of which serve light snacks and Devonshire teas daily from 10am. The *Otway Junction Motor Inn* (T 03/5237 3295 or free call 1800 138 139) offers more solid meals as well as motel-style accommodation (❻). An alternative, and cheaper, place to stay is the *Lavers Hill Roadhouse* (T 03/5237 3251; ❷–❸), where you have a choice of bunkhouses and on-site vans. Three kilometres out of town is **Melba Gully Conservation Park**, one of the wettest spots in Victoria. It's the location of the Big Tree, a three-hundred-year-old Otway messmate, its base covered in moss; at night glow-worms are a common sight.

From Moonlight Head to Peterborough

The 130-kilometre stretch of coast between lonely, windswept Moonlight Head and Port Fairy is known as the **Shipwreck Coast** – all of it protected within Otway National Park and **Port Campbell National Park**. The **Historic Shipwreck Trail**, which links the sites of dozens of shipwrecks with informative plaques and signed walking paths, also runs between these two points. The stretch from Princetown to Peterborough is the most obviously hazardous to shipping, with its sheer limestone cliffs and massive eroded stacks. Beyond Princetown, the first worthwhile stop is the steep and slippery **Gibsons Steps**, where you walk down to a kelp-covered beach beneath towering cliffs. From here on, the spectacle gets more and more extraordinary, with plenty of convenient stopping points from where you can admire the amazing formations. The most stupendous are the **Twelve Apostles** – gigantic limestone pillars, some rising 65m out of the ocean, which retreat in rows as stark reminders of a wasting coastline (the cliff faces erode at a rate of about 2cm a year). Sunset here (summer around 9pm, winter around 5.45pm) is a popular time for photographers and, unfortunately, crowds. Wait ten minutes or so after dusk, however, when the tourists have jumped back on their coaches and left, and you'll be treated to another fantastic spectacle, as hordes of fairy penguins waddle into shore in their droves.

Next stop is **Loch Ard Gorge**, where a small network of coastal walks gives you the chance to view the fantastic rock formations all around. It was here that the *Loch Ard*, an iron-hulled square rig, hit a reef and foundered while transporting immigrants from England to Melbourne in the spring of 1878. Of fifty-three people on board, only two survived: Eva Carmichael and Tom Pearce, both in their late teens. They were swept into a long gorge that had a narrow entrance, high walls and small beach, and Tom dragged Eva into a cave in the western wall of the gorge before going for help. A walkway leads down to the beach, covered with delicate pink kelp, and you can scramble over craggy rocks to the cave where Eva sheltered, now a nesting site for small birds. The Loch Ard cemetery, where the ship's passengers and crew are buried, is on the clifftop overlooking the gorge. As you drive further, you pass more scenic points, with resonant names such as the Blowhole and the Thundercave, before reaching Port Campbell.

Port Campbell and around

PORT CAMPBELL is a small and companionable settlement on the edge of the Port Campbell National Park. The **Port Campbell Information Centre** on Morris Street (daily 9am–5pm; ☎ 03/5598 6089 or 1300/137 255) has displays and information about the area and its national parks, and can also book accommodation. Ask here too about the self-guided **Port Campbell Discovery Walk** (90min), which will take you along a clifftop to a viewpoint above Two Mile Bay.

Port Campbell **beach** is a small sandy curve, safe for swimming and patrolled in season. The town climbs the hill behind the beach. At 27 Lord St, the Port Campbell Trading Company is a small **art gallery** displaying works by local artists and craftspeople. Opposite, the **Loch Ard Shipwreck Museum** (daily 9am–5pm; $4) has exhibits and videos relating the stories of five of the South West Coast shipping disasters (the *Loch Ard*, *Fiji*, *Schomberg*, *Falls of Halladale* and *Newfield*), as well as artefacts salvaged from some of the wrecks. If you're really fascinated by the wrecks, Port Campbell Boat Charters (☎0500/566 588) offers **diving** to some wreck sites and can hire out snorkelling or diving gear to those who want to go it alone.

Practicalities

Port Campbell's General Store (daily: winter 8am–6pm; summer 7am–7pm) also functions as the post office and newsagent, and has an EFTPOS system that takes every type of card. It's expensive, though, and has limited stock, so if you're planning to stay you'd be advised to shop on the way in Warrnambool or Lorne. The town itself is a pleasant place to while away an evening, and with two hostels in town, **staying** needn't be prohibitive. *Ocean House Backpackers* (free call ☎ 1800 035 093, ℱ 03/5598 6471; dorms ❷) is a brand-new homely place in a lovely old house on the main street. It's run by the more upmarket *Southern Ocean Motor Inn* (ⓦ www.great-ocean-road.com; ❻–❽), which also boasts a café with internet access and a good licensed restaurant, *Napiers* (☎03/5598 6231). There's also a rather commonplace hostel, *Port Campbell YHA*, on Tregea Street (☎ & ℱ 03/5598 6305; rooms ❸, dorms ❶), with four large and grubby dorms, a huge kitchen and a TV lounge with wood-fired heater. *Port O'Call* at 37 Lord St (☎03/5598 6206; ❺) is an attractive, inexpensive motel on the main street, while the *Port Campbell National Park Cabin*

& Camping Park on Tregea Street (T 03/5598 6492, F 5598 6369; ❺) offers beachside cabins.

Places to **eat** include the good-quality bistro at the *Port Campbell Hotel* on Lord Street (daily lunch and dinner), the basic *Great Australian Bite*, on Lord Street opposite the beach; and the no-frills *Port Campbell Take Away Cafe*. For a bit more of a choice, and good coffee, go to cosy *Emma's Tearooms* at 25 Lord St, or the fancy but delicious *Waves* at no. 29, a licensed café/restaurant serving breakfast, lunch and dinner daily (booking advised on T 03/5598 6111).

London Bridge, the Grotto and Timboon

Tourists could once walk across the double-arched rock formation known as **London Bridge**, a short distance west of Port Campbell, to the outer end facing the sea. In mid-January 1990, however, the outer span collapsed and fell into the sea, minutes after two very lucky people had crossed it – they were eventually rescued from the far limestone cliff by helicopter. As fate would have it, the couple were conducting an extra-marital affair, and fled from the waiting media as soon as the helicopter arrived. Another good place to stop, just before Peterborough, is the **Grotto**, where a path leads from the clifftop to a rock pool beneath an archway.

Moving on, you pass through undulating dairy country on the last stretch of the Great Ocean Road from Peterborough, on Curdies Inlet, to Warrnambool. There's little to detain you along the route, although if you're a cheese fan you might consider a detour to **TIMBOON**, 18km inland from Port Campbell: at Timboon Farmhouse Cheese (daily 10am–4pm), on the corner of Ford and Fells roads, you can taste and buy excellent cheese and wine.

Warrnambool and onwards

WARRNAMBOOL seems unable to decide whether it's an industrial city or a charming, seaside agricultural town. Coming into town on the Great Ocean Road you see the more pleasant aspects: the city's lovely coastal setting, with **Allansford Cheeseworld** (Mon–Fri 8.30am–4.30pm, Sat 8.30am–5pm, Sun 10am–5pm) indicating that this is the centre of rich **dairy country**. As well as selling cheese, it has cheese and wine tastings, a café serving teas and light meals, and a museum. However, if you approach Warrnambool from the west along the Princes Highway, you'll pass car lots, motels and an ugly factory belching smoke.

Lady Bay, where Warrnambool is sheltered, was first used by sealers and whalers in the early nineteenth century and was permanently settled from about 1839. **Southern right whales**, hunted almost to extinction, have begun to return in the last few years and have been sighted in the surf off **Logans Beach** between May and October. The bay was never a good port – exposed as it is to unpredictable weather, reefs and shallow water – and between 1836 and 1908 there were 28 shipwrecks here. The well set-up **Flagstaff Hill Maritime Village** on Merri Street (daily 9am–5pm; $12) has displays on these and other shipwrecks along the treacherous coast, paying particular emphasis to the *Loch Ard* disaster (see opposite). The re-created nineteenth-century village is arranged around a fort erected in 1887, a time when, improbably, the fear of Russian invasion was widespread in Australia.

Warrnambool has a bustling downtown, with a major shopping centre on Liebig Street, several galleries and museums, and some fine old churches.

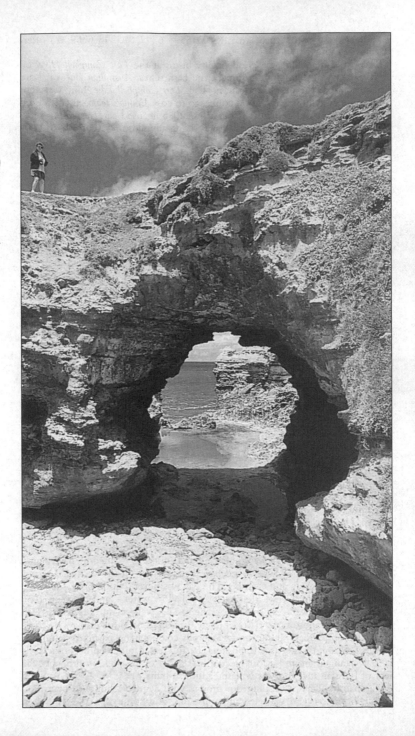

Perhaps the best of the sights is the **Warrnambool Art Gallery** on Liebig Street (daily noon–5pm; $3), a fine provincial gallery with collections of Western District colonial paintings and contemporary Australian prints. The **Botanic Gardens** on Botanic Road, designed in 1877 by William Guilfoyle, then Director of the Melbourne Botanic Gardens, are also worth visiting if you happen to have some spare time. The classically designed, ornamental gardens are filled with winding paths and hills, and provide glimpses of the sea. There's also a fernery, a waterlily pond and a small rotunda.

Practicalities

The well-organized **Warrnambool Visitor Information Centre** (daily 9am–5pm; ℡ 03/5564 7837 or free call 1800 637 725) is at 600 Raglan Parade. For backpacker **accommodation**, the pleasant *Stuffed Backpacker*, operated by Flaherty's Chocolate Shop, 52 Kepler St (℡ & ℻ 03/5562 2459, ⓦ www.stuffed.axs.com.au; dorms ❶, twins ❷), is just around the corner from the busy end of Liebig Street and offers B&B lodgings in a renovated old building with dorms and twin rooms. The *Backpackers Barn* at the *Victoria Hotel* at the corner of Lava and Liebig streets (℡ 03/5562 2073, ℻ 5561 3775; dorms ❶, rooms ❷–❸) is equally centrally located, has dorms and doubles and a fully equipped kitchen. From the clean and friendly *Nomads Warrnambool Beach Backpackers*, at 17 Stanley St (℡ 03/5562 4874; dorms ❶, rooms ❸), you're less than ten-minutes' walk away from the beach. The hostel has doubles and comfy dorms with lockers, and you can phone for a pick-up from the bus stop in town. Moving upmarket, the refurbished *Hotel Warrnambool*, on the corner of Koroit and Kepler streets (℡ 03/5562 2377; ❸–❺), offers good B&B pub accommodation in the town centre, while *Pertobe B&B* at 10 Banyan St (℡ 03/5561 7078; ❺) is in a convenient location between the town centre and the beach. Just south of the roundabout along Pertobe Road and near the fore-shore there are a few more options: *Warrnambool Surfside Holiday Park*, with self-contained one- to three-bedroom cottages and cabins as well as campsites right on the beach (℡ 03/5561 2611; cabins ❹–❻); and *Port Warrnambool Village B&B* (℡ 03/5562 8063; ❼), which has brand-new three-bedroom apartments with direct beach access. In whale-watching season, an excellent choice is the charming *Whale Bay B&B* (℡ 03/5562 2204, ℮ bodycoat@datafast.net.au; ❻), 6km from town at 234 Hopkins Point Rd, just steps away from the beach and whale-watching platform. If none of these places have room, you could try any of the motels that line the Princes Highway at each end of town.

There are plenty of good places to **eat** on Liebig Street. Freshly cooked fish and chips are served at *Seafoods*, at no. 126. The *Victoria Hotel*, on the corner of Liebig and Lava streets, has bar meals and all-you-can-eat pasta, soup and casserole for $9 on Wednesday nights. *Beach Babylon* at no. 72 serves pizza and pasta, while the *Freshwater Cafe* at no. 78 is a renowned modern Australian restaurant (Tues–Fri lunch and dinner, Sat & Sun dinner). On the other side of the road, the funky *Fishtales Café* at no. 63 has an open courtyard, good coffee and is open from 7.45am until late; *Restaurant Malaysia* at no. 69 features inexpensive Southeast Asian cuisine; and *Figsellers Café* at no. 89 is a simple, pleasant joint serving sandwiches, quiches and other snacks from 8.30am. Further up the street there's *The Black Olive Bar Restaurant & Cafe* in the *Hotel Grand* at no. 158 and *Rios Deli* at no. 142 for sandwiches, bagels and cakes. *Rogers Bar* in the *Whalers Inn*, on the corner of Liebig and Timor streets, is a slick, modern-looking place where Warrnambool's young and trendy go to **drink**. It's only rivalled by the basement bar attached to *Café Regal*, itself a cheap but stylish lunch spot near the art gallery on Timor Street.

Internet access is available at the hostels (residents only) and at *Hotspot*, 200 Timor St.

Tower Hill State Game Reserve and Koroit

About 13km west of Warrnambool along the Princes Highway, **Tower Hill State Game Reserve** is located in the crater of a volcano which last erupted about 18,000 years ago. In the nineteenth century pioneer settlers stripped Tower Hill of its trees and used it as grazing land, but since the 1960s it has been reforested and wildlife has gradually returned. If you visit the island in the middle of the crater lake at dusk, you'll encounter **emus, koalas** and loads of **kangaroos** and **wallabies**. The game reserve is open daily from dawn to dusk, but on days of extreme fire danger it may sometimes be closed (call the ranger on ☎03/5565 9202 to check). The **Natural History Centre** (daily 9.30am–12.30pm & 1.30–4.30pm) on the island has displays about the area's geological history and the revegetation programme, while a bird hide nearby enables you to spy on the abundant birdlife. There are also five self-guided short **walks** around the reserve (30min–1hr).

    KOROIT, 7km north, is a tiny, old-fashioned town with Australia's largest concentration of people of Irish descent. The Catholic church is impressive, but the building that really dominates the town is the elegant two-storey **Koroit Hotel** on the main street, run by the same family since 1922. If you cut north from here to the Hamilton Highway you'll know you're getting into wool country when you see sheep walking down the main street of Woolsthorpe.

Port Fairy and Mount Eccles

PORT FAIRY, the next stop along the coast, was once an early port and whaling centre but is now a quaint crayfishing town with a busy jetty, a harbour full of yachts, and over fifty National Trust-listed buildings. Heavy southern breakers roll into the surrounding beaches, and on **Griffiths Island**, poised between the ocean and Port Fairy Bay, there's a **muttonbird** rookery with a specially constructed lookout where between September and April you can watch them roost at dusk. For a historic town, it's also quite a happening place, hosting numerous events: in summer the six-week-long **Moyneyana Festival** focuses on outdoor activities with events such as a raft race on the Moyne River, reaching its climax with the Moyneyana New Year's Eve procession; and at Easter the annual Queenscliff to Port Fairy **yacht race** ends here, with a huge party. The biggest event, however, takes place over the Labour Day long weekend in March, when the huge **Port Fairy Folk Festival** takes over the town, with Australian and overseas acts playing world, roots and acoustic music. Tickets are sold in early November, and usually sell out in less than a day. Up to twenty thousand people pour into town for the festival, and even a tent site is hard to get. For more information and festival bookings call the **visitor information centre**, on Bank Street (daily 9am–5pm; ☎03/5568 2682, ℉5568 2833). The centre also produces an excellent 20¢ map of the Port Fairy Heritage Walk, which takes you on a route around town to admire the many fine buildings. **The History Centre**, in the old courthouse on Gipps Street by the river (Wed, Sat & Sun 2–5pm, daily during holidays; $3), displays costumes, historic photographs, shipwreck relics and other items relating to the town's pioneer history.

Port Fairy practicalities

With its village-like atmosphere and its variety of excellent **accommodation** options, as well as good pubs, tearooms and restaurants, Port Fairy makes a good place to break your journey between Melbourne and Adelaide. The *Port Fairy YHA*, at 8 Cox St (℡03/5568 2468, ℉5568 2302; ❶), is in a lovely old house right in the town centre. More luxurious is the *Seacombe House Motor Inn* at 22 Sackville St (℡03/5568 1082, ⓦwww.seacombehouse.com.au; ❻–❽), one of many National Trust-listed buildings in the town, with gorgeous but pricey modern motel units and historic cottages. There are also a number of B&Bs in quaint colonial cottages, amongst them *The Douglass*, by the river at 85 Gipps St (℡03/55668 1016, ⓦhttp://users.bigpond.com/thedouglass; ❼), the *Merrijig Inn* at 1 Campbell St (℡03/5568 2324; ❻), and *Lough Cottage* at 216 Griffith St (℡03/5568 1583; ❺). Full details of all cottages and B&Bs, and of Port Fairy's six caravan parks, can be obtained from the visitor information centre.

The best **food** in Port Fairy is probably at the *Victoria Hotel* (℡03/5568 2891, ⓦwww.vichotel.com), a beautifully renovated building at 42 Bank St with a highly recommended atmospheric restaurant and a cheaper – but equally good – café (try the brunch for a real treat). Customers can use the **internet** in the hotel reception area for free; at the time of writing the hotel's new and very stylish accommodation (❻) was almost complete. There are other upmarket licensed restaurants at the *Merrijig Inn* and the *Seacombe House Motor Inn* (daily 6am–3pm; bookings required on ℡03/5568 1077). *Rebecca's*, at 70 Sackville St, serves breakfasts and light lunches, cakes and good coffee, and next door at no. 72 there's delicious home-made ice cream. *Culpepper's*, a healthfood shop at 24 Bank St, serves healthy soups and light meals. The best place to **drink** is the *Caledonian Inn* ("The Stump"), on the corner of Bank and James streets – it's the oldest continually licensed pub in Victoria (since 1844).

Mount Eccles National Park

Just over 50km north of Port Fairy is **Mount Eccles National Park**. Mount Eccles (though it hardly deserves to be called a mountain) is an extinct volcano with lava caves, channels and a crater lake set in rugged, stony country; there used to be a quarry here and you can see the various layers of different lava flows where the mountain has been cut. **Lake Surprise** is the delightful crater lake, shimmering blue in summer. Walks – all of which begin from the picnic ground at the end of the entrance road – include a two-kilometre walk around the rim of the crater, or you can descend and walk around the shoreline (with a chance to swim in the lake, which is 21°C in summer); there's also a two-hour walk along a lava canal leading to a lava cave.

Birdlife around the lake includes wedge-tail eagles, kookaburras, tawny frogmouths, dog birds, barn owls and boobooks. The trees are loaded with koalas, seen at any time of the day. There are also eastern grey kangaroos, echidnas, bats, tiger snakes, copperhead snakes and blue-tongued lizards. Mid- to late spring is a good time for wild flowers – from orchids to native geraniums – and wattle. Look out for a tree in the southwest corner of the park that has had an Aboriginal shield cut out of it with a sharpened stone tool. The **visitors centre** (℡03/5576 1338) has an informative display to help you explore the park and learn about the history of the volcano and the area's Aborigines. You can also **camp** here: wood is supplied, and there are toilets and water.

Portland to Nelson

PORTLAND, the last stop on the Victoria coast going west on the Princes Highway, is a large industrial and fishing port. There's a smattering of historic buildings, but they don't add up to form a coherent townscape. Despite the best efforts of the local tourist industry to promote Portland there's nothing in town that would merit an extended stay unless you wanted to explore the local industry. However, the wild coastal scenery to the southwest around Cape Nelson and Cape Bridgewater is well worth a detour.

Huge ships dock in **Portland Bay**, where a vast heap of sandy brown bauxite sits beside the Alcoa smelter, in full view of the Esplanade. **Aluminium** is one of Australia's largest exports, and in 1980 big business was met with **Aboriginal resistance** here, when a legal battle developed over the siting of the smelter on land that had great importance for the Gunditj Mara. There were traces of over sixty Aboriginal campsites and workshop areas on the proposed site, and sacred places including a burial ground. Plans for building the smelter eventually went ahead, but Alcoa was forced to pay the Gunditj Mara $1.5 million in compensation, which was used to buy back land in the area of the Lake Condah mission (see below).

Before the area was permanently settled by whites – it's the oldest settlement in Victoria – there had been conflict between whalers and Aborigines that resulted in massacres and the decimation of an entire tribe. The first **squatters** in Victoria, the Hentys, came to the Portland area in 1834 to pasture sheep on vast landholdings, and they, too, soon came into conflict with the Koories – from 1838 clans began to use their traditional burning-off process in an attempt to drive the Hentys away. During the 1840s a sustained guerrilla war, known as the **Eumeralla War**, was fought against settlers occupying land around Port Fairy, Mount Napier and Lake Condah. In the end it was only the deployment of the Aboriginal **Native Police Corps** in 1842 that finally broke the resistance – and even they took four years.

The seafront Esplanade is lined with fish-and-chip shops and cafés. The **Visitor Information Centre** is located in the **Portland Maritime Discovery Centre** (daily 9am–5pm; ☎ 03/5523 2671 or free call 1800 035 567), and gives out information on the numerous museums and historic buildings around town, which mainly celebrate white settlement. Should you wish to stay, there's haphazard **accommodation** available at *Portland Backpackers*, 14–16 Gawler St (☎ 03/5523 6390; ❶), and at the **Cape Nelson Lightstation** (☎ 03/5523 5100, ⓦ www.lightstation.com.au; rooms ❻, eight-bedroom cottage $290), just outside Portland. The on-site licensed café is open for lunch and dinner daily and hosts regular live events and entertainment.

Along the coast to the southwest, around craggy **Cape Nelson** and stormy **Cape Bridgewater**, the scenery is stunning: caves, freshwater lakes close to the cliff coast, blowholes, a petrified forest of limestone columns where ancient trees used to stand, and the beach at **Bridgewater Bay**, which extends in a wide, sandy arc from one cape to the other. The best way to explore these features is along the walking tracks that start from the Blowholes car park, which is signposted left off the road to Cape Bridgewater. Bring good walking shoes, as the volcanic rocks can be very sharp, and carry food and drink.

Lake Condah Mission

Lake Condah Mission is about 50km northeast of Portland, on the western edge of Mount Eccles National Park. A mission was established in 1867 in this traditional Aboriginal area, with its plentiful game and fish, and surviving Aborigines from the area were brought here but were forbidden to speak their own language or practise their culture. At its height in 1880 there were over twenty buildings of timber and stone. Although the mission was officially closed in 1919, a large community remained until the 1950s, when they were gradually dispossessed as land was given to returned soldiers under the soldier settlement scheme. Perhaps the greatest injustice occurred when several Aboriginal returned soldiers, who had lived on Lake Condah, applied for land, only to be refused. With the money paid in settlement of the Alcoa dispute (see opposite), the land was finally bought back in the 1980s, and the government have since pledged $50,000 towards uncovering some of the original rock art there.

Lower Glenelg National Park and Nelson

From Portland the Princes Highway makes its uneventful way, via Heywood, to Mount Gambier in South Australia. After 120km it crosses the **Glenelg River** (which has its source in the Grampians) at Dartmoor, a popular point to begin a four-day canoeing trip down to the river's mouth at Nelson; ask about canoe hire at the Nelson Parks & Visitor Information Centre (see below). For most of the journey the clear, blue river flows through the unspoilt **Lower Glenelg National Park** in a sixty-kilometre gorge cut through limestone. The spectacular **Princess Margaret Rose Cave** (guided tours hourly Mon–Fri 10am–4.30pm; $6.60; ☎08/8738 4171) lies beside the river as it loops round by the South Australian border and can be reached by canoe, car (unsealed roads from both sides of the border lead to the caves) or on a cruise from Nelson (see below).

NELSON is at the end of the coastal road and virtually on the border, less than 40km from Mount Gambier and well worth an overnight stay. A peaceful, friendly little hamlet, it feels caught in a time warp, and there's little to do but wander along the coast, read on the beach, and **fish** or **canoe** on the Glenelg. South West Canoe Service (☎08/8738 4141) arrange overnight canoe or kayak trips, camping in special riverside camps. Nelson Boat Hire on Kellet Street (daily 8.30am–6pm; ☎08/8738 4048) also rents out canoes and kayaks, and sells bait; you'll need a licence, obtained from the Nelson Kiosk (daily 8am–6pm; ☎08/8738 4220), the local service station or post office. Fishing shelters line the river. Glenelg River Cruises on Old Bridge Road on the opposite bank, operates **cruises** to the Princess Margaret Rose Caves (daily in holidays, otherwise Tues–Thurs, Sat & Sun; departs 1pm; 3hr 30min; $20; ☎08/8738 4191, ⓦ www.glenelgrivercruises.com.au).

The **Nelson Parks & Visitor Information Centre** (daily 9am–5pm; ☎08/8738 4051) is signposted just off Leake Street; it also covers the Discovery Bay Coastal Park, which protects the shoreline almost all the way from Portland to the border. Here you can get camping permits (book in advance in peak season) and information on walks and activities. A gorgeous **place to stay** in Nelson is the *Motel Black Wattle* (☎08/8738 4008, ⓦwww.motelblackwattle.com.au; ❺), situated in a lovely garden setting on the crest of Mount Gambier Road, overlooking the river and ocean. The on-site restaurant serves delicious modern Australian cuisine, with an emphasis on local seafood, and excellent wines. Alternatively, the one-storey *Nelson Hotel* on Kellet Street (☎08/8738 4011; ❸) is a classic and untouristy pub that has budget accommodation and very inexpensive counter meals. Other options include the *Nelson Cottage B&B* on the corner of Kellet and Sturt streets (☎08/8738 4161; ❹), *Nelson Kywong Caravan Park* on North Nelson Road (☎08/8738 4174), which has cheap vans (❷) and cabins (❸), and the four-bunk cabins at the Margaret Rose Caves (☎08/8738 4171; cold water only & BYO linen; cabin ❸).

Central Victoria: the Goldfields

Central Victoria is classic Victoria: a rich pastoral district, chilly and green in winter and parched a brownish yellow in summer, with two grand provincial cities, **Ballarat** and **Bendigo**, whose fine buildings were funded by gold. Nowadays both are major tourist centres on the gold trail. The many surrounding country centres such as **Maryborough** and **Castlemaine**, once prosperous gold towns in their own right, now seem too lowly for their extravagant architecture.

The goldrushes

The Californian goldrushes of the 1840s captured the popular imagination around the world with tales of the huge fortunes to be made gold-prospecting, and it wasn't long until Australia's first goldrush took place – near Bathurst in New South Wales in 1851. Victoria had been a separate colony for only nine days when gold was found at Clunes on July 10, 1851; the goldrush began in earnest when rich deposits were found in Ballarat nine months later. The richest goldfields ever known soon opened at Bendigo, and thousands poured into Victoria from around the world. In the golden decade of the 1850s Victoria's population increased from eighty thousand to half a million, half of whom remained permanently in the state. The British and Irish made up a large proportion of the new population but over forty thousand Chinese came to make their fortune, too, along with experienced American gold-seekers and other nationalities such as Russians, Finns and Filipinos. Ex-convicts and native-born Australians also poured into Victoria, leaving other colonies short of workers; even respectable policemen deserted their posts to become "diggers", and doctors, lawyers and prostitutes crowded into the haphazard new towns in their wake. The goldfields were a great equalizer; all you needed was a shovel and perseverance, and a fortune was as likely yours as the next man's.

In the beginning, the fortune-seekers panned the creeks and rivers searching for **alluvial gold**, constantly moving on at the news of another find. But gold was also deep within the earth, where ancient riverbeds had been buried by volcanoes; in Ballarat in 1852 the first **shafts** were dug, and because the work was unsafe and arduous, the men joined in bands of eight or ten, usually grouped by nationality, working a common claim. For deep mining, diggers stayed in one place for months or years, and the major workings rapidly became stable communities with banks, shops, hotels, churches and theatres, evolving more gradually, on the back of income from gold, into grandiose towns.

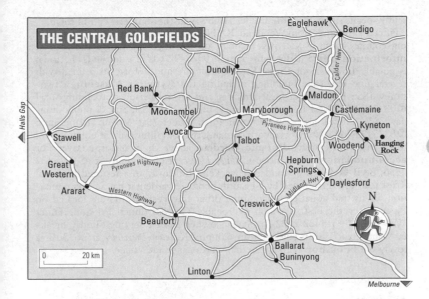

THE CENTRAL GOLDFIELDS

Eaglehawk • Bendigo
Dunolly •
Red Bank •
Moonambel • Maldon •
Maryborough • Castlemaine •
Avoca • Kyneton •
Stawell • Talbot • Woodend • Hanging Rock
Great Western • Pyrenees Highway
Ararat • Western Highway
Clunes • Hepburn Springs • Daylesford
Creswick • Midland Hwy
Beaufort •
0   20 km
Ballarat • Buninyong
Linton •
Halls Gap
Pyrenees Highway
N
Melbourne

There's fairly good **transport** in this direction, with regular V/Line trains and buses to Bendigo, Ballarat and the other major centres, and local buses filling most gaps. If you're driving, the best way to tour the area is to follow the **Goldfields Tourist Route**, whose chocolate-brown signs are marked by a distinctive circled capital G. The route links the major cities and towns – Bendigo, Castlemaine, Ballarat, Ararat and Stawell – with many smaller places in between.

Towards the Goldfields: the Calder Highway

Though you could take the Western Freeway or the train directly to Ballarat, the route **towards Bendigo**, 150km northwest of Melbourne along the Calder Highway, is much more interesting. The railway to Bendigo, which continues to Swan Hill, follows the same route, calling at the main towns. At Diggers Rest, 22km from Melbourne, a short detour to the east will take you to tiny **Organ Pipes National Park**, so designated for its outstanding geological interest. The rock formations here are a series of basalt columns, formed by lava cooling in an ancient riverbed, and rising up to 20m above Jacksons Creek. The park (daily: April–Sept 8.30am–4.30pm; Oct–March 8.30am–6pm) can be explored along walking tracks and has picnic areas with tables. Back on the highway you'll come to **Gisborne**, 50km from Melbourne, developed as a coaching town for travellers on their way to the Bendigo and Castlemaine goldfields; it's dominated by **Mount Macedon**, an extinct thousand-metre volcano.

Fifteen kilometres or so from Gisborn, **WOODEND** is the jumping-off point for **Hanging Rock**, in a reserve 6km northeast (daily dawn–dusk; $7 per car). The rock became famous because of the eerie film *Picnic at Hanging Rock*, about a group of schoolgirls who mysteriously go missing here after a picnic – a story which many people falsely believed to be true, though the rock itself is not at all spooky. You can walk around the base or climb to the summit with its massive boulders and crags in around an hour. Encounters of a more freaky kind can be had at the **Insectarium of Victoria** (daily 10am–4pm; $8), a gruesome collection of oversized cockroaches, spiders, giant snails and other scuttly beasts situated on the Calder Highway at the southern end of town.

Fifteen kilometres from Woodend, **KYNETON** seems like just another boring country town as you pass through on the highway, where the **tourist information office** (daily 9am–5pm; ☎03/5422 6110) is located. The town is notable, however, for **Piper Street**, a picturesque historic strip lined with several fine bluestone buildings, including the **Kyneton Museum**, a two-storey 1855 bank full of local artefacts, and several period outbuildings (call ☎03/5422 1228 for hours, which vary: usually Wed, Sat, Sun & public holidays; $3). There's also a winery on Piper Street (Sat & Sun 10am–6pm; ☎03/5422 7444, Ⓦ www.vincorp.com.au), two old flour mills at either end of town and the expansive **Botanic Gardens** above the Campaspe River. For **accommodation**, the *Kyneton Country House*, at 66 Jennings St (☎03/5422 3556; B&B ❼–❽), is a wonderful weekend hideaway in a restored National Trust mansion surrounded by a beautiful cottage garden; it has a good reputation for its traditional cooking. Some other fine **restaurants** are located on Piper Street, the best of which is probably *Gonellas* (lunch Fri–Sun, dinner Wed–Sun; ☎03/5422 2022), an Italian-owned eaterie serving Sunday breakfasts and great Tuscan cuisine from 6.30pm. *Kyneton Provender* at no. 30 is a lovely old **bookshop** with a café that serves cakes and coffee.

Bendigo

Rich alluvial gold was first discovered in **BENDIGO** in 1851, and once it was exhausted shafts were sunk into a gold-bearing quartz reef. Bendigo became the greatest goldfield of the time, and had the world's deepest mine. Mining continued here until 1954, long after the rest of central Victoria's goldfields were exhausted, so it's a city that has developed over a prosperous century: the nationwide department store Myer began here, as did Australia's first building society in 1858. Although in many ways more magnificent than Ballarat (see p.990), Bendigo is considerably lower key, never having turned itself into a purely tourist town. Its most visited sights are legacies of the mining days – the **Chinese Joss House** and the **Central Deborah Mine**.

At the heart of Bendigo is the vast **Rosalind Park**, and three important religious buildings constructed through money from gold-digging – All Saints Church, St Pauls Cathedral and **Sacred Heart Cathedral**. Local Catholics imported stonemasons from Italy and England, and their craftsmanship can be seen in the design and details of Sacred Heart, begun in 1897 in English Gothic style. The interior has beautiful woodcarvings of the Twelve Apostles, and the crypt is the burial place of local bishops. Wanting to give Bendigo a sophisticated air reminiscent of London, the newly prosperous citizens called its central crossroads **Charing Cross**. Pall Mall runs off to the east, while View Street, with its many fine old buildings, climbs north off Pall Mall. Mitchell Street leads south to the **train station** and High Street (the Calder Highway) is the main exit west out of the city. The other important street is Hargreaves, parallel to Pall Mall one block south, with its impressive town hall and a bland shopping mall.

The City

Many of Bendigo's finest goldrush buildings are along **Pall Mall**, including the law courts (1896) and the ornate Italianate (1887) edifice which now houses the visitor information centre – neither of which would seem out of place in a capital city. The amazingly decorative **Shamrock Hotel** stands opposite, four storeys of gold-boom architecture at its most extreme. **View Street**, climbing the hill beside Rosalind Park, has a few more elaborate goldrush buildings. The **Bendigo Regional Arts Centre** here is a massive Neoclassical pile, joined to the much more homely red-brick fire station which now serves as the Community Arts Centre. The **Art Gallery**, in another beautifully restored nineteenth-century building at no. 42 (daily 10am–5pm; free), has an extensive collection of Australian painting from Bendigo's goldfield days to the present, as well as nineteenth-century British and European art acquired with all that gold. Several antique shops, restaurants, cafés and bars add to the arty feel of the street. The **Queen Elizabeth Oval**, with its old red-brick stadium, backs onto Rosalind Park, and you can watch Aussie Rules football here on winter weekends.

Bridge Street, one of the oldest in Bendigo, was once **Chinatown**, home to the Chinese who came by the thousands in the 1850s and who knew Bendigo as *dai gum san* ("big gold mountain"); when the gold ran out, many turned to market gardening in the area. Until as late as the 1960s old shops sporting faded signs were still in evidence, but now Chinese customs and ways of life are best seen in the **Golden Dragon Museum and Classical Chinese Gardens** (daily 9.30am–5pm; $7), where there is an impressive collection of Chinese processional regalia including what are supposed to be the world's longest and oldest Imperial dragons, Sun Loong and Loong. An exhibition tells the full story of Bendigo's Chinese community since the days of the goldrush, whilst the attached gardens feature a temple to the goddess Kuan Yin. The National Trust-operated **Joss House**, on Finn Street in North Bendigo (daily 10am–5pm; $3), was built by the Chinese in the 1860s and is the oldest Chinese temple still in use in Australia. The route to the shrine passes manmade Lake Weeroona, whose picnic grounds are the setting for the lovely *Boardwalk Restaurant & Café* (daily 7am till late) in an old Chinese teahouse. To get to the Joss House, take bus #7 (approximately hourly Mon–Fri).

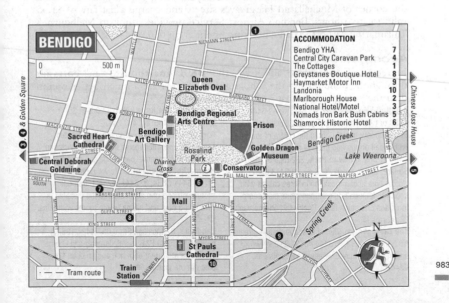

The Central Deborah Goldmine

The Central Deborah Goldmine, at the corner of Violet Street and the Calder Highway (daily 9am–5pm; underground tour $16.50), was the last mine in the Central Goldfields to close. The sixty-minute underground tour is worth taking if you've never been down in a mine; everybody is issued with a reassuring hard hat, complete with torch and generator. You go down to a depth of 60m in a lift, which takes 85 seconds – it would take thirty minutes to reach the bottom of some of the deepest shafts. The further down you go the hotter it gets, but at 60m it's quite warm and airless, dripping with water and muddy underfoot.

Above ground, you're free to wander about and take a look at the engine room with its steam-driven air compressor. You can also see a room set up like a modest miner's house from the 1840s, a model of the mine itself, and a museum installed in the old changing rooms.

Practicalities

Interstate McCafferty's **buses** stop at the Caltex service station, on the corner of High and Oak streets. The **visitor information centre** on Pall Mall (daily 9am–5pm; ℡ 03/5444 4445 or free call 1800 813 153, ⓦ www.bendigo-tourism.com) provides lots of brochures and maps, including the free *Bendigo & Region* booklet, complete with walking map (you'll also find "Heritage Walk" panels outside significant buildings). A good way to get an impression of Bendigo is to take the **Talking Tram Tour**, though the taped commentary can be rather irritating (daily 9.30am–3pm; departures every 1hr, or every 30min Sat & Sun, from the Central Deborah Goldmine; 1hr; $10; combined ticket for the mine and tram tour $23). The tram tour ticket includes entrance to the Bendigo Tram Museum, located on Hargreaves Street at the opposite end of the route. Bendigo had electric trams even before Melbourne, but they ceased operation in 1972. **Buses** (Christians Bus Company ℡ 03/5447 2222) have since replaced trams as a means of everyday transport – they all leave from the corner of Mitchell and Hargreaves streets and charge a flat fare of $1.65 valid for two hours. Bendigo Airport Service provides a link to Melbourne's Tullamarine Airport (3 daily; booking essential on ℡ 03/5447 9006).

Accommodation

In terms of atmosphere and style, the **B&B guesthouses** and **cottages** throughout Bendigo and the whole goldfields area are a much better option than the average, somewhat sterile motel room.

Bendigo YHA, 33 Creek St South (℡ 03/5443 7680 or 0438 437 680, ⓔ buzza@bendigo.net.au) Small, cheery hostel right in the centre of town with small dorms and internet access. ❶

Central City Caravan Park, 362 High St, Golden Square, 2.5km south (℡ & ℻ 03/5443 6937). Hostel-type accommodation in three cabins with separate kitchen and common room, plus camping, vans and cabin units. Cabins ❹, on-site vans ❸, dorms ❶

The Cottages, cnr Niemann and Anderson streets (℡ 03/5441 5613, ℻ 5444 4313). B&B in two small, self-contained weatherboard cottages. ❻–❼

Greystanes Boutique Hotel, 57 Queen St (℡ 03/5442 2466, ℻ 5442 2447, ⓔ greystanes@netcon.net.au) Centrally located, beautifully appointed rooms in an elegant Victorian mansion with separate bar/lounge and open fires. ❼

Haymarket Motor Inn, 5 McIvor Highway (℡ 03/5441 5654, ℻ 5441 5655). Ultramodern motel with one unit accessible to the disabled, a swimming pool and sauna; some rooms with spas. ❺–❻

Landonia, 87 Mollison St (℡ 03/5442 2183). A centrally located B&B in a Federation-style home, with separate guest entrance and an open fireplace in the lounge. ❻

Marlborough House, 115 Wattle St (☎03/5441 4142). B&B in a goldrush-era mansion near the cathedral, with stained-glass windows, marble fireplaces and a canopied balcony. ❼

National Hotel/Motel, 182 High St, 1km south (☎03/5441 5777, ℻5441 5890). Facilities include a pool and spa, as well as a bar and bistro. One suite ❽, units ❹–❻

Nomads Iron Bark Bush Cabins, Watson St (☎03/5448 3344 or free call 1800 737 378,

ⓦwww.nomadsworld.com). Shared accommodation in self-contained cabins in a bushland setting a few kilometres out of town. Free pick-ups and drop-offs, lockers and linen. Horse riding available. ❶

Shamrock Historic Hotel, cnr of Pall Mall and Williamson St (☎03/5443 0333, ℻5442 4494). Fabulous Victorian hotel that has a wide range of accommodation, from budget-priced rooms to executive suites. ❹–❼

Eating, drinking and nightlife

The town offers a fairly good choice when it comes to eating and drinking, and there is plenty of student-influenced nightlife during term time. Entertainment facilities at the LaTrobe University campus are open to all – call ☎03/5444 7478 to find out what's happening. Several pubs have **bands** playing on Friday and Saturday nights, including the *Old Crown Hotel* at 238 Hargreaves St and *The Vine* at 135 King St, which also has an open-stage night on Mondays. Of the **Irish bars** in town, the Celtic-run *Brian Boru* on McIvor Road is by far the best, serving up decent Guinness and real Irish craic without the four-leaved clovers, while the *Shamrock Hotel* may not be Irish but is certainly popular for balcony drinking in the late afternoon. A young crowd congregates at the *Rifle Brigade Hotel* at 137 View St, a brewery pub with great food and beer and a wrought-iron verandah and moves on to the *Eclipse* nightclub at the corner of Hargreaves and Williams streets. Other **nightclubs** include Hargreaves Street's hipper-than-thou techno haven *The Tonic Bar*, and alt rock hangout *The Icon* at 2–4 Howard Place. Thirty-somethings might prefer *Studio 54* on Queen Street, playing three floors of mainstream pop from the last three decades.

Bazzani Bar & Ristorante, Howard Place (☎03/5441 3777). Cosy restaurant at the end of the mall renowned state-wide for the interesting, aesthetic and downright tasty dishes on the menu. Lunch and dinner daily; licensed. Daily 11am–late.

Café Tram, 76 Violet St (☎03/5443 8255). Tourist nonsense with a strange appeal – forget your cynicism and chow down on fine local produce aboard Australia's first café tram. Bookings essential. Dinner Fri & Sat, lunch Sun, afternoon tea Sat & Sun.

Colonial Bank Gallery and Mully's Cafe, 32 Pall Mall. In a grand, historic bank building from the 1880s, with an art gallery upstairs. Good breakfasts, brunches and afternoon teas. Licensed or BYO. Mon–Sat 10am–5pm, Sun from 9am.

Green Olive Delicatessen, 11 Bath Lane. Fantastically cosy Italian-run café with outdoor

seating, serving excellent coffee and desserts as well as gourmet deli fare to go. Open daily.

The Match Bar & Bakehouse, 58 Bull St. Stylish café-restaurant with lots of pasta, *focaccia* and pizza. Dinner daily, lunch daily except Sat.

Shamrock Hotel Café, cnr Pall Mall and Williamson St. This café-restaurant in the lovely, refurbished former public bar serves good breakfasts (home-baked bread) and has interesting, mainly Modern Australian cuisine for lunch and dinner. Open daily.

Whirakee Restaurant and Wine Bar, 17 View Point, at the beginning of View St, just opposite the fountain (☎03/5441 5557). Outstanding Modern Australian cuisine, with an excellent wine list featuring local wines. Casual dining available lunchtimes and early evening. Lunch Wed–Fri, dinner Tues–Sat.

Castlemaine and around

CASTLEMAINE is at the centre of the area once known as the Mount Alexander Goldfields. Between 1851 and 1861, when its gullies were among the richest in the world, 105,000kg of gold were found here (more modest quantities are still found at Wattle Gully mine at nearby Chewton, the oldest working gold mine in Australia). Castlemaine became the headquarters of the Government Camp for the area in 1852, and its impressive buildings were all built during the following ten years. With no deep mines to sustain it, however, Castlemaine has developed little since then.

The town's finest building is the **Old Castlemaine Market** on Mostyn Street, a wonderfully over-the-top piece of Neoclassical architecture. The **Theatre Royal** on Hargraves Street, one of the oldest theatres in Australia, is also quite magnificent; it's said that when the famous Lola Montez performed here, miners threw nuggets of gold at her in appreciation. It's now a **cinema** (T03/5472 1196) incorporating a cabaret-style section and a licensed bistro downstairs, and more traditional movie-house seating upstairs. Theatre groups and live bands sometimes perform here, and there's even a sporadic disco.

Another unusual attraction, a short distance from the centre, is **Buda**, at 42 Hunter St (Wed–Sun noon–5pm, Mon & Tues by apppointment only; call for prices T03/5472 1032), a gracious nineteenth-century home and garden originally built in 1861 by a retired Baptist missionary in the style of an Indian villa. It was added to by its subsequent owner Ernest Leviny, a Hungarian silversmith, in the 1890s. The house and gardens give an insight into the good life enjoyed in the goldrush days, and much work by Leviny and his family is on display, including lampshades, carved woodhangings and embroidery made by his daughters, as well as early photography and the family's art and silverware collection. The **Castlemaine Art Gallery and Museum** on Lyttleton Street (Mon–Fri 10am–5pm, Sat & Sun noon–5pm; $3) is also worth a visit. Established in 1913 in a classic Art Deco building, the gallery specializes in Australian photographs and paintings, featuring many works by the Heidelberg School, notably Frederick McCubbin and Tom Roberts. Partly because of the big **Castlemaine State Festival** (info@castlemainefes.net.au), which takes place over ten days in March and April in odd-numbered years, this is quite an arty place, and there are several other galleries around town. In odd-numbered years lots of gardens in the Castlemaine district open their doors to visitors during the **Festival of Gardens**, which takes place during the Melbourne Cup week in November.

If you're here on a Saturday, trek the 2km out along the Melbourne Road to **Wesley Hill Market**, a giant flea market selling local produce and crafts (7.30am–noon). Another tourist attraction is the **Dingo Farm** (daily, but call to confirm times and prices on T03/5470 5711) between Castlemaine and Chewton, where around one hundred dingoes are kept in fenced-in enclosures on bushland; signs along the Pyrenees Highway will direct you there.

Practicalities

The very helpful **Castlemaine Visitor Information Centre** is in the Market Building at Mostyn Street (daily 9am–5pm; T03/5470 6200 or free call 1800 171 888, Wwww.mountalexander.vic.gov.au/tourism) and can arrange accommodation in the area. Places **to stay** include *Campbell Street Lodge* in a historic building at 33 Campbell St (T03/5472 2377; ⑤), which has motel-style rooms in a National Trust-listed house; and the *Old Castlemaine Gaol* on Bowden Street (T03/5470 5311; F5470 5097; ⑦), converted into an unexpectedly cosy guesthouse, with beds in former prison cells and a restaurant/wine bar (Wed–Sun). Two centrally located B&B's are the very popular late-Victorian *Clevedan Manor*, 260 Barker St (T03/5472 5212; ⑥), and the *Coach and Rose*, 68 Mostyn St (T03/5472 4850; ⑥). The *Botanic Gardens Caravan Park*

(☎03/5472 1125; vans **②**–**③**) is ideally situated between the botanic gardens and the open-air swimming pool (Dec–March only).

Food in Castlemaine is excellent, with a wide variety of places to choose from. The best café is *Saff's* at 64 Mostyn St (breakfast and lunch daily, dinner Thurs–Sat; ☎03/5470 6722), which serves up great breakfasts, smoothies and other feelgood fodder, and hosts special night-time events, including recitals and poetry readings, as well as live jazz most Sunday afternoons. Otherwise, the popular *Togs Place Café* (dinner Sat & Sun; ☎03/5470 5090) at 58 Lyttleton St provides good food in a peaceful atmosphere, and has a courtyard where you can sit out in summer. The licensed *Globe Restaurant*, 81 Forest St (☎03/5470 5171), is another pleasant place with a courtyard and an attached cheaper bistro, both serving a seasonally varied menu of local fare. Or go for cheap pub meals at the local hangout, the *Criterion Hotel* at 163 Barker St, which has pool tables and bands at weekends, or the *Cumberland Hotel* on the corner of Barker and Lyttleton streets.

Maldon

MALDON, closely surrounded by low hills, is a tiny, peaceful town of tearooms, antique shops and B&Bs. In 1965 the National Trust declared it the best-preserved gold-era settlement in Victoria. Gold was found here in 1853 and the rich, deep alluvial reefs were mined until 1926, almost rivalling Bendigo for longevity. The main shopping street largely preserves its original appearance, with single-storey shopfronts shaded by awnings and decorated with iron-lace work. It's a popular weekend getaway where you can simply relax and unwind.

It's best to come here in your own vehicle, as **public transport** from Melbourne operates only on weekdays, and to a very limited timetable; take a train from Melbourne (Mon–Fri 8.35am & 3.50pm) to Castlemaine where you catch the connecting Castlemaine V/Line service to Maldon. Return buses leave from Maldon post office to connect with trains back to Melbourne (Mon–Fri 9am & 4.40pm). On Sundays and holidays you can take a ride on a tourist **steam train** (or diesel locomotive on days of total fire ban) from Maldon to Castlemaine (11.30am, 1pm & 2.30pm; $8; ⊛www.castlemaine .net.au/~vgr).

Apart from the town's architecture, there are a few other points of interest: the **Maldon Museum**, in the Old Shire Hall on High Street (daily 1.30–4pm; $2), is a typical pioneer memorabilia museum, and you can also take an underground tour at the stunning candlelit **Carman's Tunnel Goldmine**, off Parkin's Reef Road, 3km south of town (Sat, Sun, school & public holidays every 30min 1.30–4pm; 30min; $4). To find out about other activities, check with the **Maldon Visitor Information Centre** in front of the museum (daily 9am–5pm; ☎03/5475 2569, ⊛www.maldon.org.au).

An excellent place to **stay**, if you're hankering for a little luxury, is *The Barn*, at 242 Barker St (☎ & ⓕ 03/5475 2015; **⑤**–**⑥**), which offers self-catering amongst whitewashed stone walls, an open fire and French windows. *Heritage Cottages*, 25 Adair St (☎03/5475 1094; **⑧**), has a selection of ten historical cottages, most with period furnishings and open fires; there's a minimum stay of two nights. Much cheaper yet still a treat are *Agatha Panthers Cottages*, on Church Street (☎03/5475 1066, ⊛www.apcottages.com.au; **⑤**). In a town where **tearooms** prevail, the best value is *Berryman's*, an old bowling alley at 30 Main St. *McArthur's*, further up at no. 45, is much quainter and has a very pleasant courtyard. Two other good tearooms are *The Gold Rush*, at no. 24, and the *Maldon Cafe*, at no. 52.

Maryborough and around

MARYBOROUGH was relatively late getting on the gold bandwagon – the first find here was in 1853, but it didn't take long to exploit it. The town is now a large, solid and rather dull country place, interesting only for its remnants of architecture far too pompous for this quiet setting. The **train station** is exceptional: when Mark Twain visited Maryborough he described it as a train station with a town attached. The restored building has been converted into a tourist complex, housing the **tourist information centre** (daily 10am–6pm; ☎03/5460 4511), an antiques and collectables emporium, a gallery and exhibition space, and a restaurant and café. The Civic Centre at the heart of town is a classic nineteenth-century square with an elegant post office and gracious town hall and courthouse. If you want to stay, try the *Bull & Mouth Hotel* at 119 High St (☎03/5461 1002; ❸–❹), which has a bistro downstairs serving inexpensive **meals** (Mon–Sat). For B&B accommodation try the *Maryborough Guesthouse* at 44 Goldsmith St (☎03/5460 5808; ❹–❺).

Twenty-one kilometres north of Maryborough is **DUNOLLY**, an attractive town filled with many distinctive old buildings and with kurrajong trees lining the main street. The goldfields here produced more nuggets than any in Australia, including the largest ever found: the 65kg "Welcome Stranger" nugget was found in 1869 by two Cornish miners just 3cm below the surface as they were working around the roots of a tree, and valued at £10,000. Fourteen kilometres south of Maryborough, **TALBOT** is a tiny settlement consisting of little more than a restaurant, a pub and a corner store. It's hard to believe now that the town once had 56 hotels and a population of 33,000. The licensed *Bull and Mouth Restaurant and B&B* (lunch Sun, dinner Thurs–Sun; ☎03/5463 2325), located in an 1859 bluestone hotel on Ballarat Street, serves hearty but sophisticated country fare and also has five timber miners' cottages for rent (❻–❼ including breakfast). **AVOCA**, 26km southwest of Maryborough on the Pyrenees Highway, was another rich source of alluvial gold, and today boasts a collection of nineteenth-century buildings, including a chemist's shop established in 1854 and believed to be the oldest in Victoria. These days, the area around Avoca, known as the **Pyrenees region**, is increasingly known for its **vineyards**. A cluster of them is located in or near Moonambel, a hamlet 17km northwest of Avoca: one to aim for is the *Warrenmang Winery Resort* on Mountain Creek Road (daily 9am–5pm; ☎03/5467 2233, ℱ5467 2309, Ⓦwww.bazzani.com.au/warrenmang), which has a picturesque setting, an excellent restaurant, and offers accommodation in a homestead and timber lodges (full board from $155 per person).

Daylesford and Hepburn Springs

The attractive, hilly country around Daylesford and Hepburn Springs is known as the "spa centre of Australia", with a hundred **mineral springs** within a fifty-kilometre radius. Daylesford grew from the Jim Crow gold diggings of 1851, but the large Swiss–Italian population here quickly realized the value of the water from the mineral springs, which had been bottled since 1850. People have been taking the waters at Hepburn Springs for almost as long – the spa complex was built in 1895. The **Daylesford Visitor Information Centre**, servicing the whole area, is next to the post office on Vincent Street in Daylesford (daily 9am–5pm; ☏03/5348 1339); it has loads of brochures for the many places offering bed and breakfast and a board listing the vacancies at weekends, when places tend to fill up. You can get a **bus** to Hepburn Springs outside the office (Mon–Fri 4 daily). To get to Daylesford from Melbourne, take a **train** to Woodend, then a connecting bus to Daylesford (Mon–Sat 2 daily, Sun 1 daily). You can also take a train from Melbourne to Ballarat (Mon–Fri 1 daily) and then get the connecting bus to Daylesford. There's also a train/bus service from Bendigo (Mon–Thurs 1 daily, Fri 2, Sun 1) via Castlemaine.

Daylesford

The town of **DAYLESFORD**, a popular weekend retreat for Melbournians, has a New Age, alternative atmosphere, with a large gay community and several gay-friendly guesthouses. Its well-preserved Victorian and Edwardian streets rise up the side of Wombat Hill, where you'll find the **Botanical Gardens**, between Hill Street and Central Springs Road, whose lookout tower has panoramic views. Not far away, on the corner of Daly and Hill streets, is the **Convent Gallery** (daily 10am–5pm; $3), a rambling former convent which now has seven galleries selling high-quality arts, crafts and antiques, and a Mediterranean-style café open for lunch and coffee. There's a great Sunday **market** (8am–2pm) just nearby, on the main road to Castlemaine, and another more artsy market, on the third Sunday of each month in Victoria Park. All your **esoteric needs** are effortlessly taken care of at places like the Yasodhara Spiritual Resource Centre, 107 Vincent St, which sells crystals and offers tarot readings and free meditation sessions.

Lake Daylesford, a short distance south from the town centre on Vincent Street, is the location of the Central Springs Reserve, which has several walking tracks and old-fashioned water pumps from which you can drink the water of the mineral springs. The **Lake Daylesford Book Barn** here (open daily) is a picturesquely situated bookshop, with an extensive range of secondhand books. The charming *Boathouse Café* (breakfast and lunch daily, dinner Sat & Sun; ☏03/5348 1387) has lakeside dining, as well as dinghies, canoes and paddle-boats for rent. Alternatively, with your own transport you could head out to **Tuki trout farm** (☏03/5345 6233, ⓦwww.tuki.com.au) in nearby Smeaton, 17km away, where you can catch your own lunch and have it boned and cooked for you while you wait.

Practicalities

You should book well in advance if you want **to stay** in Daylesford at the weekend. The newly opened *Wildwood YHA* is by far the best deal in town, situated in an old house on the Daylesford–Hepburn Springs road, with internet access and a homely kitchen, as well as a great garden area; if you're arriving by bus, phone ahead for a pick up. Otherwise, you could try *The Balconies* at 35 Perrins St (☏03/5348 1322, ⓦwww.spacountry.net.au/balconys; ❻), a rambling mansion with several balconies overlooking the lake and a favourite with gay visitors; *35 Hill Street* (☏03/5348 3878; ❹), an early Victorian brick cottage just below the Botanical Gardens, much-loved for its casual, friendly attitude; *Ambleside* at 15 Leggat St (☏03/5348 2691; ❼–❽), a meticulously renovated Edwardian guesthouse overlooking Lake Daylesford; or the enchanting *Bergamo* (☏03/5348 7572, ⓦwww.daylesford.net.au/bergamo; ❺–❻), two mud and timber cottages situated ten minutes from town at nearby Porcupine Ridge. *Walsh's Daylesford Hotel*, on Burke Square (☏03/5348 2335; ❸–❹), has pleasant pub rooms.

The *Himalaya Bakery* at 73 Vincent St, makes heavy but nutritious dark rye bread and delicious cakes. Less puritan offerings are available at *Sweet Decadence*, 57 Vincent St, where you can have chocolates, **coffee** and cake in the characterful old bar of what was once the *Victoria Hotel*, and at *Frangos & Frangos*, 82 Vincent St, a **café-restaurant** in a restored pub, serving scrumptious breakfasts and Mediterranean-inspired food for lunch and dinner. The *Harvest Café*, at 29 Albert St (Thurs–Mon 9am–9pm), is a friendly, nonconformist haven that has an extensive menu, plus folk and acoustic music on Sunday night, while the *Hill End Café* has delicious lunches and a gallery attached. For a real splurge, try *Lake House* on King Street near the lake, an outstanding but expensive restaurant (daily for coffee, brunch and dinner; ☎03/5348 3329).

Hepburn Springs

HEPBURN SPRINGS is not really a town at all, but a collection of guesthouses and a wonderful Art Deco resort hotel in a green, hilly and peaceful spot only 4km north of Daylesford. From the bus stop, walk through the shady Soldiers Memorial Park to the **Mineral Springs Reserve**, where you can taste three kinds of mineral water from old pumps and take advantage of the facilities at the ultraposh **Hepburn Spa Resort** (Mon–Fri 10am–8pm, Sat 9am–10pm, Sun 9am–8pm; ☎03/5348 2034, ℱ5348 1167, ⓦwww.hepburnspa.com.au). You can spend as long as you like here in the relaxation pool (32°C) and mineral-water spa (38°C; both Mon–Fri $8.80; Sat, Sun & public holidays $11); or you could indulge yourself with twenty minutes in your own aero-spa bath, with essential oils (Mon–Fri $20.90; Sat, Sun & public holidays $25.30). The southern wing has massage, saunas, flotation tanks, and therapy and couch pools. Bookings must be made at least three (preferably six) weeks in advance, especially for weekends.

The Springs Hotel at the corner of Main Road and Tenth Street (☎03/5348 2202; en suite ❹–❺) is a classic 1930s resort with guestrooms, some en suite. There's a good-value buffet lunch in the dining room and a more expensive dinner menu; tasty counter meals are also available in the bar. *Dudley House*, at 101 Main Rd (☎03/5348 3033, ⓦhttp://ren.netconnect.com.au/~dudley; ❼, ❽ at weekends), is a lovely Federation-style weatherboard house with bed and breakfast and a fine restaurant. At the budget end of the scale is the *Continental House*, 9 Lone Pine Ave (☎03/5348 2005; ❷), which has shared twins (bring your own linen), a kitchen (vegetarian only), and a vegetarian café on Saturday night. Another good choice for vegetarian food is the *Cosy Corner Café* at 3 Tenth St (breakfast and snacks daily, lunch and dinner Thurs–Mon).

Ballarat

BALLARAT is a grandiose provincial city that makes a lasting impression from whichever direction you approach it. From the west, you enter via the Western Highway along the **Avenue of Honour**, lined on either side with over 22km of trees and dedicated to soldiers who fought in World War I. It ends at the massive **Arch of Victory**, through which you drive to enter Sturt Street and the city. Coming from the east, you approach the city on the Western Highway (Victoria St), flanked by lawns, trees and colourful flowerbeds. Trains pull in to the elegant 1889 **station**, topped by a domed clock tower.

The Ballarat area was already settled before gold was discovered, and thus preserves a rural life for which the city is the supply centre. Nonetheless, it's gold which has marked the place indelibly: over a quarter of all **gold** found in Victoria came from Ballarat and its fantastically rich reef mines before they were exhausted in 1918. Nowadays, in addition to the more obvious tourist attractions – especially Sovereign Hill – and fine **architecture**, the town is interesting in its own right, with a fairly large student population that lends some cultural presence and gives the city a reasonably active nightlife. Most people don't stay here overnight, however, as it's only little more than an hour's drive from Melbourne.

The City

Sturt and Victoria streets terminate on either side of the Bridge Mall, the central shopping area at the base of quaint **Bakery Hill** with its old shopfronts. Southeast of the city centre, Eureka Street runs off Main Street towards the site of the **Eureka Stockade**, with several museums and antique shops along the way. Main Street becomes Ballarat–Buninyong Road, and six blocks down is crossed by Bradshaw Street, where you'll find Sovereign Hill, the re-created gold town. Northwest of the centre, approached via Sturt Street, are the Botanical Gardens and Lake Wendouree.

ACCOMMODATION

Ansonia	5
Ballarat City Apartments	1
Craigs Royal Hotel	7
Eastern Station Hotel	2
George Hotel	3
Goldfields Caravan Park	8
Irish Murphys	4
Miners Retreat Motel	6
Sovereign Hill Lodge YHA	9

The Eureka Stockade

The **Eureka Rebellion** is one of the most celebrated events of Australian history, regarded as the only act of white armed rebellion the country has seen. It was provoked by conditions in the goldfields, where diggers had to pay exorbitantly for their right to prospect for gold (as much as thirty shillings a month), without receiving in return any right to vote, to have decent roads, transport or police protection, or to have any chance of a permanent right to the land they worked. Checks for licences were ruthless and brutal, and corruption rife. Protest meetings calling on diggers to refuse to pay drew huge crowds at Ballarat, Bendigo and Castlemaine; in response, in November 1853 the government made a small reduction in the fee.

The administration at Ballarat was particularly repressive, and in November 1854 local diggers formed the **Ballarat Reform League**, demanding full civic rights and the abolition of the licence fee, and proclaiming that "the people are the only legitimate source of power". At the end of the month a group of two hundred diggers gathered inside a **stockade** of logs, hastily flung together, and determined to resist further arrests for nonpossession of a licence. They were attacked at dawn on December 3 by police and troops; thirty died inside, and five members of the government forces also lost their lives.

The movement was not a failure, however: the diggers had aroused widespread sympathy, and in 1855 licences were abolished, to be replaced by an annual **Miner's Right** which carried the right to vote and to enclose land. The leader of the rebellion, the Irishman Peter Lalor, eventually became a member of parliament.

The **Eureka Flag**, with its white cross and five white stars on a blue background, has become a symbol of the Left – and indeed of almost any protest movement: shearers raised it in strikes during the 1890s; wharfies used it before World War II in their bid to stop pig-iron being sent to Japan; and today the flag is flown by a growing number of Australians who support the country's transformation to a republic. On a deeper level, all sorts of claims are made for the Eureka Rebellion's pivotal role in forming the Australian nation and psyche. The diggers are held up as a classic example of the Australian (male) ethos of mateship and anti-authoritarianism, while the goldrush in general is credited with overthrowing the hierarchical colonial order, as servants rushed to make their fortune, leaving their masters and mistresses to fend for themselves.

The most complete **nineteenth-century streetscape** is probably along Lydiard Street, which runs from the centre up past the train station; the street has several two-storey terraced shopfronts, with verandahs and decorative iron-lace work, mostly from the period 1862–89. The former **Mining Exchange** (1888) has been recently renovated to its former splendour, and the architecture of Her Majesty's Theatre (1875) also proclaims its goldrush-era heyday. The **Ballarat Fine Art Gallery** at 40 Lydiard St (daily 10.30am–5pm; guided tours Mon–Fri 2pm, Sat & Sun 2.30pm; $4), another superb building, is the oldest provincial art gallery in Australia, established in 1884. Its extensive collection is particularly strong on colonial and Heidelberg School paintings; the original **Eureka Flag** – tatty and ragged – is also on show here (see box, above). Displayed alongside are the watercolours of S.T. Gill, a self-taught artist who painted scenes of goldrush days in Ballarat. In another part of the gallery is a reconstruction of the drawing room of the famous Lindsay family (whose best-known members are the artist Norman and the writer Jack), from nearby Creswick, complete with several of their paintings. Nearby, on Sturt Street, check out the imposing Classical-revival **town hall**, which dominates the centre.

There are still over fifty hotels in Ballarat – survivors of the hundreds that once watered the thirsty diggers. Some of the finest are on Lydiard Street: *Craig's Royal Hotel* at no. 10 and the *George Hotel* at no. 27 are an integral part of Ballarat's architectural heritage. Sadly, during the 1970s, the council forced most of the old pubs to pull down their verandahs on the grounds that they were unsafe, so very few survive in their original form. One that does is attached to the *Golden City Hotel*, 427 Sturt St, which took the council to the Supreme Court to save its magnificent wide verandah with original cast-iron decoration; the hotel is now open at weekends as a bar and is appreciatively packed out in summer.

The Botanical Gardens

The **Botanical Gardens**, laid out in 1858, comprise about half a square kilometre alongside **Lake Wendouree**, just to the northwest of the city centre (#15 bus from Sturt St, by Myer). Begonias grow so well in Ballarat that a **Begonia Festival** runs for ten days in March, and the glasshouse here is used to display them. Otherwise, highlights are the **Avenue of Big Trees**, with a Californian redwood among its monsters, and the classical statuary, donated by rich gold-miners, scattered about the gardens. Pride of place goes to Benzoni's *Flight from Pompeii*, housed in the Statuary Pavilion. Along Prime Minister Avenue you can see a bust of every prime minister of Australia.

Eureka and York streets

As you head towards Eureka Street and the Eureka Stockade (bus #8 from outside the ANZ Bank on Sturt St), take a look at the unique shop facades on Main Street. The site of the Eureka Stockade (see box, opposite) is in Eureka Memorial Park, and the nearby **Eureka Stockade and Interpretation Centre** (daily 9am–5pm; $8.80) gives detailed background information on the Eureka story. On the same street further toward the town centre, **Montrose Cottage** at no. 111 (daily 10am–5pm; $6.50) is the last original miner's cottage in Ballarat – it's furnished in 1850s style and fitted out with a social history display.

Parallel to Eureka Street is York Street, where you'll find the free-range **Ballarat Wildlife Park**, on the corner of Fussell Street (daily 9am–5.30pm; tours Mon–Fri 11am, Sat and Sun 11am & 2pm; $12). Come at feeding time (koalas 2pm, wombats 2.30pm, crocodiles 3pm, tasmanian devils 3.30pm) to see the beasts at their best.

Sovereign Hill and the Gold Museum

The re-created gold-mining township of **Sovereign Hill** is located 1.5km from the city centre, on Bradshaw Street (daily 10am–5pm; $22 also includes admission to the Gold Museum; ☎03/5331 1944, ⊛www.sovereignhill .com.au; bus #9 from outside the ANZ Bank on Sturt St). Seventy buildings and shops here are modelled on those that lined Ballarat's main street in the 1850s, with a cast of characters wandering about in the dress of the period. The township was planned around an actual mine shaft from the 1880s, where guided underground tours are available. There are diggings where you can learn how to pan for gold (and perhaps get a small memento) and a mining museum filled with steam-operated machinery. Sovereign Hill puts on a spectacular outdoor **sound and light show**, "Blood on the Southern Cross" (nightly during school holidays, Mon–Sat rest of the year; 1hr 20min; $26.50, or joint ticket for show and Sovereign Hill $44.50; ⊤03/5333 5777), which makes use of the whole panorama of Sovereign Hill to tell the story of the Eureka Stockade.

Opposite Sovereign Hill, the **Gold Museum** (daily 9.30am–5.20pm; $6.60) offers a good overview of the re-created settlement. It has an outstanding display of real gold, and a large collection of coins are arranged in displays exploring the history and uses of gold. The museum's **Eureka Exhibition** details life on the goldfields and explains the conditions that provoked the Eureka Stockade. Central to the exhibition is a large painting of the rebellion by George Browning, a mid-nineteenth-century artist: it's interesting to see quite a few black faces portrayed in the stockade, which is generally labelled as the only white armed uprising to have taken place in Australia.

Practicalities

The centrally located **Ballarat Visitor Information Centre**, on the corner of Sturt and Albert streets (daily 9am–5pm; ⊤03/5320 5741 or free call 1800 648 450, ⊛www.ballarat.com), has free information and maps of the town and can make accommodation bookings. Regular **buses** can take you anywhere you don't feel like walking – the Ballarat Transit System (⊤03/5331 7777) has a flat two-hour fare of $1.45. Bus routes run from the bus terminal on Curtis Street, at the northern end of Bridge Mall, to Sovereign Hill and Eureka Street, and from Little Bridge Street past the Myer department store on Sturt Street to Lake Wendouree. You can use the system to get as far as Creswick (see opposite), 18km north.

Accommodation
There's an abundance of accommodation in all price ranges in Ballarat, from hostels to grand hotels, so you shouldn't have a problem finding a room to suit. Bear in mind that many places will be more expensive at weekends.

Ansonia, 32 Lydiard St (⊤03/5332 4678, ⓕ5332 4698, ⊛www.small-hotel.com/ansonia). Lovely boutique hotel with restaurant, library and guest lounge in the historic precinct. ❽

Ballarat City Apartments, 225 Lydiard St North (⊤03/5332 6992, ⓔbca@cbl.com.au). Centrally located studios and self-contained suites, all with spas. ❺–❻

Craigs Royal Hotel, 10 Lydiard St South (⊤03/5331 1377 or free call 1800 059 051, ⓕ5331 7103). A grand Victorian-era hotel; ask for the wonderful two-level North Tower suite if your budget will allow it. ❺–❽

Eastern Station Hotel, cnr Humffray St and Scott Parade (⊤03/5338 8722). Reasonably priced comfortable doubles with shared kitchen and bathroom facilities. ❸–❹

George Hotel, 27 Lydiard St (⊤03/5333 4866, ⓕ5333 4818). Three-storey 1850s hotel with colonial-style decor, an inexpensive bistro and rooms, some with four-poster beds. ❸–❹

Goldfields Caravan Park, 108 Clayton St (⊤03/5332 7888). Well located, right next to Sovereign Hill. Good facilities for campers, including a camp kitchen. Cabins ❹, on-site vans ❸

Irish Murphys, 36 Sturt St (⊤03/5331 4091). Bargain rates at this pleasant, central Irish bar, but for heavy sleepers or night owls only. Dorms ❶

Miners Retreat Motel, 602 Eureka St (⊤03/5331 6900, ⓕ5331 6944). Standard motel units, just 100m from the site of the Eureka Stockade; light breakfast included. ❸

Sovereign Hill Lodge YHA, Magpie St (⊤03/5333 3409, ⓕ5333 5861, ⓔballarat@yhavic.org.au). This small hostel – actually a part of Sovereign Hill – has alienating rooms but a pleasant kitchen/dining area and a bar on site. Dorms ❶, rooms ❸, motel rooms ❼

Eating and drinking
You won't starve in Ballarat, nor die for want of a drink, as the city has over fifty pubs. Fast food can be had at *McDonald's* on Bakery Hill and *Pizza Hut* opposite.

The Ansonia, 32 Lydiard St (☎ 03/5332 4678). Restaurant in refurbished building that also houses a swish boutique hotel. The eclectic cuisine betrays influences from the Mediterranean to Southeast Asia. Licensed; open daily for breakfast, lunch and dinner (book for dinner).

Cafe Pazani, 102 Sturt St. Slick Italian café serving expensive food and excellent coffee. Licensed. Tues–Sat 9am–1am, Sun & Mon 9am–5.30pm.

Da Vincis, 29 Sturt St. The best place for pasta in town: a lively atmosphere and generous, good-value servings, plus vegetarian options. Licensed. Open daily.

Europa Café, 411 Sturt St. A pleasant café serving good coffee, cakes and breads, and light meals. Sun–Wed 9am–6pm, Thurs–Sat 9am until late.

Game Keeper's Secret, Humffrey and Mair streets (☎ 03/5332 6000). African-themed restaurant run by South Africans. The place for fun-loving thirty-somethings in search of good, interesting cuisine. Open daily for lunch and dinner.

Golden City Hotel, 427 Sturt St. This historic 1896 hotel packs them in with an all-you-can-eat lunch, and a varied dinner menu. Relaxed bar with espresso machine, pool tables, music videos and locally brewed Ballarat Bitter.

Irish Murphys, 36 Sturt St. Big food at small prices, decent beer and frequent live music with minimal Irish kitsch combine to make this bar one of the most popular in town.

L'Espresso, 417 Sturt St. European-style and understandably hip place for coffee and eclectic breakfasts; "proper" food is good, too, and very moderately priced. Bring a book, a friend, or just eavesdrop. Daily 7.30am–6pm, also Thurs–Sun 6.30pm until late.

Masons at the Gallery, 40 Lydiard St North. A pleasant little café at the Fine Art Gallery, with lots of flowers and imaginative food. Daily 10.30am–4.30pm.

The Pancake Kitchen, 2 Grenville St South. Pancakes on order all day and night in a cosy gold-drush building.

Porter's Restaurant, cnr Mair and Peel streets. An old pub transformed into a stylish bar and restaurant. Lunch Tues–Fri, dinner Mon–Sat.

Rendezvous Cafe, 54 Lydiard St. Coffee and light meals served in a renovated café across from the Regent Multiplex Cinema. Closed Sun.

Tokyo Grill House, 109 Bridge Mall (☎ 03/5333 3945). Specializes in *teppanyaki* cooking, which means it's prepared on hotplates in front of you. Expensive. Open daily for lunch and dinner.

Entertainment and nightlife

The music scene in Ballarat is more lively than you might expect; for up-to-date information about what's on, check *The Courier* on Thursday, or log on to the city's local entertainment Web guide, ⓦ www.ballaratunderground.com.au.

Located in an old church at 120 Dana St, *The Chapel* is the best of the local **clubs**, popular with students, or there's the bustling *21 Arms*, at 21 Armstrong St, which has six bars. There are **live bands** on Friday and Saturday nights at the *Grand Hotel Ballroom*, 120 Lydiard St, while *Sturt Street Blues*, 404 Sturt St (☎ 03/5332 3676), occasionally showcases excellent live jazz and blues. The elaborate Victorian-era Her Majesty's Theatre, at 17 Lydiard St (☎ 03/5333 5800), stages all types of touring productions, and there's a three-screen cinema on the same street at no. 49 (☎ 03/5331 1399).

Around Ballarat

Rich alluvial **gold** was found at **CRESWICK**, 18km north of Ballarat, in 1851, which made it an important mining centre. It's now a quiet little town, where the only reminder of earlier days is the wildly out-of-place Victorian architecture. The *American Hotel* and the *British Hotel* face each other across the main street, a hangover from mining days when miners of different nationalities stuck to their segregated groups. **CLUNES**, just beyond Creswick, to the northwest, was the site of the first worthwhile Victorian goldfield in 1851. The reefs here were too deep for small-scale mining, and the Port Phillip Company took over operations. The only profitable British gold mine in Australia, it was most productive between 1857 and 1881. The main street has many solid old buildings and rows of original shopfronts which are sadly vacant – entrepreneurial attempts to attract the tourist trade with antique and craft shops have foundered. The

Clunes Museum (Sat 10am–4.30pm, Sun & school holidays 11am–4.30pm; $2) details the gold-mining era of the town. *The Club Hotel*, at 34 Fraser St (☎03/5345 3250; ❹), has inexpensive **accommodation**, with a buffet breakfast included, and rustles up cheap rump steaks for lunch and dinner.

Western Victoria and the Mallee

Several roads run west from the goldfields to the South Australian border through the seemingly endless wheatfields of **the Wimmera**. To the west of the farming centre of **Ararat** is the major attraction of the area, **The Grampians (Gariwerd) National Park**, the southwestern tail-end of the Great Dividing Range. Stawell and **Horsham** – the latter regarded as the capital of the Wimmera – are good places to base yourself, but **Halls Gap**, inside the park, is even better. North of Horsham are **Nhill** and **Dimboola**, close to **Little Desert National Park** and, like **Warracknabeal** further north, wheat centres. Beyond here is the least populated part of the state, the wide, flat **Mallee** with its twisted mallee scrub, sand dunes and dry lakes. This region, with several state and national parks, extends from **Wyperfeld National Park** in the south, right up to Mildura's irrigated oasis on the Murray River. South of the Grampians is sheep country; following the Hamilton Highway from Geelong you'll end up at **Hamilton**, the major town and wool capital of the western district, also accessible via **Dunkeld** on the southern edge of the Grampians.

Transport

V/Line has a **bus** service from Ballarat to Hamilton via Dunkeld (Mon–Sat 2 daily, Sun 1 daily; Mon–Fri the morning service continues to Mount Gambier in South Australia), and a bus service from Warrnambool (1 daily Mon–Fri & Sun) V/Line timetables are prone to changes, so call ☎13 6196 to check the current schedule. Interstate buses to Adelaide travel the Western Highway via Ballarat, Ararat, Stawell, Horsham, Dimboola and Nhill. The Grampians Link consists of a **train** service from Melbourne to Ballarat and a connecting bus to Halls Gap, via Ararat and Stawell (1 daily). There's a nightly Overlander train service between Melbourne and Adelaide (departing Melbourne 9.30pm and arriving in Adelaide 10hr later), and a Daylink connection (train from Melbourne to Ballarat, and from there a connecting bus via Horsham and Dimboola to Adelaide).

Hamilton

Three highways converge at **HAMILTON**, where you can see the Grampians from the edge of the main street. It's a civilized little city whose main claim to fame is that it's the "Wool Capital of the World". The only reason you're likely to be here is if you're a traveller passing through, en route from the Goldfields to South Australia, or from the mountains to the coast. There's plenty to distract you, however, and the friendly **Hamilton Visitor Information Centre** on Lonsdale Street (daily 9am–5pm; ☎03/5572 3746 or free call 1800 807 056) can book accommodation if you decide to stay.

The most worthwhile of the town's five museums and galleries is the **Hamilton Art Gallery**, on Brown Street (Mon–Fri 10am–5pm, Sat 10am–noon & 2–5pm, Sun 2–5pm; donation), one of the finest provincial art galleries in the state. Its collection of eighteenth-century watercolours of English pastoral scenes by Paul Sandby is the largest outside Britain; among other gems are ninety engravings by William Hogarth and several pieces of eighteenth-century English furniture. The influence of the rich, local Ansett family (of airline fame) is obvious; many of the excellent contemporary paintings were acquired through the Ansett Hamilton Art Awards.

Also in the town centre, but of marginal interest, is the **Hamilton History Centre** (2–5pm; closed Sat; $1), located in the Mechanics Institute Building at 43 Gray St. East of town, on the Ballarat Road, is the **Sir Reginald Ansett Transport Museum** (daily 10am–4pm; $2), charting the history of the Ansett flight network which began here, while **The Big Woolbales** (daily 9.30am–4pm) on Coleraine Road contain a small exhibition telling you about the wool industry of the Western district; shearing demonstrations can be arranged (☎03/5571 2810). There's also some refreshing greenery in the town centre: the Botanical Gardens are on the corner of French and Thompson streets, just one block from Gray Street, the main thoroughfare, while the banks of the **Grange Burn** are home to the eastern barred bandicoot, the only known population in mainland Australia. Grange Burn flows into man-made **Lake Hamilton**, which has a safe, sandy swimming beach and is filled with trout.

Practicalities

If you want to stay, there's a wide variety of **accommodation**. Budget travellers can stay at the pleasantly-sited *Lake Hamilton Caravan Park* (☎03/5572 3855; cabins ❸) or the *Peppercorn Lodge* (☎03/5571 9046; rooms ❷, dorms ❶, BYO linen), which has backpackers' accommodation and comfortable, heated rooms; the properties are adjacent to each other on Ballarat Road. On the same road at no. 142 is the luxurious *Grange Burn Motor Inn* (☎03/5572 5755; ❼). The relaxed *Grand Central Hotel*, at 141 Gray St (☎03/5572 2899; ❸–❹), is a good place both to eat and sleep: breakfast is included in the price of the motel-style rooms, there's an unpretentious bistro, and bands play here at weekends. The top **eating** spot however is *The Hamilton Strand* at 56 Thompson St (Mon–Sat 11am until late; BYO; ☎03/5911 9111), which serves coffee, cakes and light snacks out the front, and more substantial meals in the rooms behind. The menu features dishes like carpaccio of salmon, seared kangaroo or wildberry torte, and the wine list has lots of wines from the Pyrenees region in Victoria. Alternatively, the pleasant *Gilly's Coffee Shop & Grill*, 106 Gray St, is open from early morning until evening, while *The George Hotel*, at 213 Gray St, serves up lovely pub food and drink in a great atmosphere.

Around Hamilton

Hamilton is situated on the fringe of an extensive volcanic plain that runs across western Victoria and into South Australia. Mount Napier (439m) to the south and Mount Rouse at Penshurst to the east were the sources of most of the lava flow covering the Hamilton area. Byaduk Caves Road, going towards MacArthur, has a very good view of Mount Napier, directly ahead as you drive. Lava flows are still clearly visible here, with black wattle trees flourishing on many of them. The **Byaduk Caves** are actually fern-filled lava tubes; three of the twelve are easy enough to get into, but the others have restricted access – call the ranger at Mount Eccles (☎03/5576 1338) for further information. As you explore, watch out for stinging nettles and rough terrain, with frothy textured lava rocks scattered around, porous and covered in moss.

COLERAINE, 35km west of Hamilton on the Glenelg Highway, is picturesquely sited in the Wannon River Valley, between two tablelands. The **Points Aboretum** here (open 24hr; free) is the nation's official eucalypt collection, and has the largest number of species in the world. At **CASTERTON**, 29km further west on the Glenelg River, the 1843 **Warrock Homestead** (daily 10am–5pm; $5.50) is one of the most interesting in the country: more than thirty buildings are still used by the descendants of the original settlers and are open to visitors. From here it's less than an hour's drive to South Australia and the Coonawarra wine region (see p.844).

Ararat and the Western Highway

ARARAT, some 90km west from Ballarat, is still very much a goldfields town, with an overabundance of grandiose Victorian architecture and a main street laid out to show off the best profiles of the nearby mountains: **Mount Ararat** in the west and the **Pyrenees Range** with **Mount Cole** in the east. The town was founded in 1857, when a group of seven hundred hopeful Chinese, making the slow trudge from the South Australian ports to the central Victorian goldfields, stumbled across a fabulously rich, shallow alluvial goldfield, the **Canton Lead**. As the only town in Australia founded by the Chinese, Ararat has it's own Chinese museum at the site of the old mine entrance, the **Gum San Heritage Museum**. Few other signs of the embryonic Chinese settlement survive, though the new multi million-dollar **Gum San Chinese Heritage Centre** (daily 10am–4pm; call ☎03/5352 2203 for more details and admission prices), an authentic re-creation of a two-storey Chinese pagoda set in traditional Chinese gardens, is due to open in 2001, relating the tale of the founding of the city.

These days Ararat is the commercial centre for a sheep-farming and wine-producing area; **wineries** in the area include the Montara Winery, 3km south along the Chalamabar Road (Mon–Sat 10am–5pm, Sun noon–5pm), and Mount Langi Ghiran on Vine Road north of Buangor (turn north from the Western Highway towards Warrak; Mon–Fri 9am–5pm, Sat & Sun noon–5pm), renowned for its superb white and red wines. Both wineries have reasonable prices.

Next door to the town hall, with its clock tower and fountain, is the **Visitor Information Centre** on High Street (Mon–Fri 9am–5pm; ☎03/5355 0281 or free call 1800 657 158), which provides information on the Grampians and can book accommodation in the area. The **Langi Morgala Museum** nearby (Sat & Sun 1–4pm; $2.20) occupies an old brick building banded with bluestone at the base and around the huge arched windows and doors. Along with the usual pioneering displays, there's an important collection of Aboriginal artefacts.

For **food**, go to Barkly Street, where you'll find a healthfood store, a decent delicatessen and *Vines Café & Bar*, which serves classy sandwiches, good-value meals and wine. Also on Barkly Street are the *Ararat Hotel*, serving bar meals;

10

the *Cafe Dominica*, in a Victorian mansion, which has a coffee shop, bistro and pricey licensed restaurant (open late; closed Mon); and the *Pyrenees Country Kitchen*, an award-winning restaurant.

Great Western and Stawell

Between Ararat and Stawell is the small settlement of **GREAT WESTERN**, the centre of a wine-producing area whose most famous **wineries** are right in town, on the Moyston Road. Seppelt's Great Western (daily 10am–5pm), established in 1865, and Best's Wines at Concongella (daily 9am–5pm), established in 1866, are both renowned for their sparkling méthode champenoise wines. Seppelt's, with its extensive National Trust-classified underground cellars, is the more atmospheric and interesting of the two. A much-respected newcomer on the wine circuit is Garden Gully on the Western Highway (Mon–Fri 10.30am–5.30pm, Sat & Sun 10am–5.30pm), whose sparkling reds and innovative whites have won over ninety awards in recent years.

STAWELL (pronounced "stall") is most famous for the **Stawell Gift**, a foot race offering big prize money that has been held here every Easter since 1877. It's also the closest major town to the Grampians and the departure point for the **bus** to Halls Gap. The helpful **Stawell & Grampian Visitor Information Centre** is at 52 Western Highway (free call ☎1800 246 880); the **Stawell Gift Hall of Fame** on Main Street (Mon–Fri 9–11am or by appointment; $2; ☎03/5358 1326) charts the history of the race itself. The town, with its winding main street, has a pleasant, old-fashioned feel, and it's a much less expensive place to stay than Halls Gap. The many motels along the highway all charge much the same (❹) for similar facilities. More expensive B&Bs and two caravan parks are the only real alternatives: *Walmsley B&B* at 19 Seaby St (☎03/5358 3164; ❹–❻) is reasonably priced, and has a pleasant lounge and a verandah; while the *Stawell Grampians Gate Caravan Park* on Burgh Street (☎03/5358 2376; cabins ❷–❸), is the closest camping area to town.

The Grampians National Park

Rising from the flat plains of western Victoria's wheat and grazing districts, the sandstone ranges of the **Grampians**, with their weirdly formed rocky outcrops and stark ridges, seem doubly spectacular. In addition to their scenic splendour, in the **GRAMPIANS NATIONAL PARK** you'll find a dazzling array of **flora**, with a spring and early summer bonanza of wild flowers; a wealth of **Aboriginal rock art**; an impressive **Aboriginal Living Cultural Centre**; **waterfalls** and **lakes**; and over fifty **bushwalks** along 100km of well-marked tracks. There are also several hundred kilometres of road, from sealed highway to rough track, on which you can make exciting **scenic drives** and **4WD** tours.

HALLS GAP, 26km from Stawell, on the eastern fringes of the Grampians, is the only settlement actually in the national park. Its setting is gorgeous, in the long flat strip of the Fyans Valley surrounded by the soaring bush and rock of the Mount Difficult and Mount William ranges; koalas are frequently seen in the surrounding trees. Packed with accommodation (see p.1003) and other facilities catering to park visitors, this is the obvious place to base yourself, especially if you don't have your own transport. The newsagent in town has an EFTPOS machine and acts as an agent for the ANZ and Commonwealth **banks**.

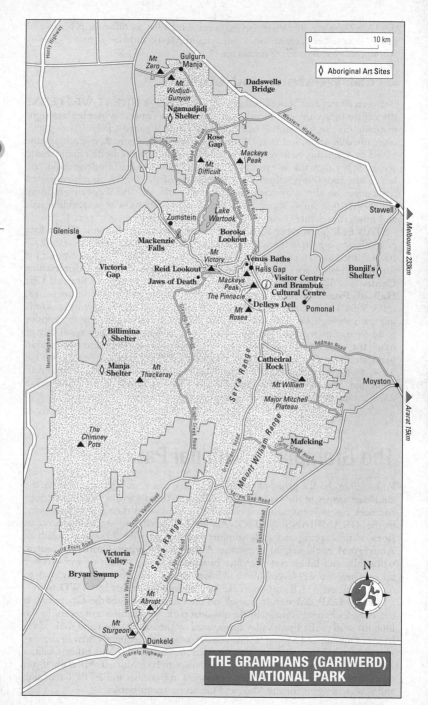

THE GRAMPIANS (GARIWERD)
NATIONAL PARK

Aboriginal Art Sites

0   10 km

Henty Highway

Mt Zero
Gulgurn Manja
Mt Wudjub-Gunyun
Dadswells Bridge
Ngamadjidj Shelter
Rose Gap
Mackeys Peak
Mt Difficult
Western Highway
Stawell
Melbourne 233km
Smith Road
Rose Gap Road
Mount Difficult Road
Mount Zero Road
Zumstein
Lake Wartook
Boroka Lookout
Glenisla
Mackenzie Falls
Venus Baths
Halls Gap
Bunjil's Shelter
Victoria Gap
Mt Victory
Reid Lookout
Jaws of Death
Mackeys Peak
The Pinnacle
Visitor Centre and Brambuk Cultural Centre
Pomonal
Delleys Dell
Mt Rosea
Henty Highway
Billimina Shelter
Glenelg River Road
Serra Range
Redman Road
Cathedral Rock
Manja Shelter
Mt Thackeray
Mt William
Moyston
Major Mitchell Plateau
Grape Creek Road
Ararat 15km
The Chimney Pots
Mafeking
Mount William Range
Jimmy Creek Road
Grampians Road
Moyston Dunkeld Road
Yarram Gap Road
Victoria Valley Road
Serra Range
Victoria Point Road
Victoria Valley
Bryan Swamp
Mount Abrupt Road
Mt Abrupt
Mt Sturgeon
Dunkeld
Glenelg Highway

N

Rock art in the Grampians

It's estimated that **Koorie** Aborigines lived in the area known to them as **Gariwerd** at least five thousand years ago. The area offered such rich food sources that the Koories didn't have to spend all their time hunting and food-gathering, and could therefore devote themselves to religious and cultural activities. Evidence of this survives in rock paintings, which are executed in a linear style, usually in a single colour (either red or white), but sometimes done by handprints or stencils. You can visit some of the rock shelters where Aborigines camped and painted on the sandstone walls, although many more are off-limits. In the northern Grampians one of the best is **Gulgurn Manja** (also known as Flat Rock), 5km south of the Western Highway near the Hollow Mountain campsite; from Flat Rock Road it's a signposted fifteen-minute walk. The name means "hands of young people", as many of the handprints here were done by children. In the southern Grampians is **Billimina** (Glenisla Shelter), a fifteen-minute walk above the Buandik campsite; it's an impressive rock overhang with clearly discernible, quite animated red stick figures. **Guided rock art tours** are organized by the Brambuk cultural centre (see below).

Just over 2km south of Halls Gap along the Grampians Road (also known as the Dunkeld Road or the Dunkeld–Halls Gap Road) is the **National Park Visitor Centre** (daily 9am–4.45pm; ℡03/5356 4381, Ⓦ www.parkweb.vic.gov.au), the best place to start your visit; it has a fascinating display and videos which trace the development of the Grampians over four hundred million years. Here you can buy books, including the excellent *Grampians Touring Guide* (ideal for short walks) and more detailed topographic maps. Although most walking tracks are clearly defined and well signposted, it's a good idea to buy Vicmap, or the walking maps published by the NPWS, and carry a compass if you're planning an overnight trek. Details of bushwalks are posted and there are masses of free leaflets; before beginning an extended walk, call into the visitors centre and register. Some **walks** start from the campsite at Halls Gap, while others branch off the Victory and Grampian roads, making them difficult to get to without a car.

The **best times to come** are in autumn, or in spring and early summer when the waterfalls are in full flow and the wild flowers are blooming (although there'll always be something in flower no matter when you come). Between June and August it rains heavily and can get extremely cold; at that time many tracks are closed to avoid erosion. Summers are very hot, with a scarcity of water and the ever-present threat of bushfires. If you're undertaking extended walks in summer, carry a portable radio to get the latest information on the fire risk: on **total fire ban days** no exposed flames – not even that from a portable gas stove – are allowed.

Brambuk Aboriginal Living Cultural Centre

Located behind the visitors centre, **Brambuk Aboriginal Living Cultural Centre** (daily 10am–4.30pm; ℡03/5356 4452) grew from an idea for a rock-art facsimile centre that would draw the tourist traffic away from the actual art sites, which are very fragile. From that beginning, it developed into a full-blown cultural centre for western Victorian Aboriginal culture – a place where visitors could learn and Koories could find employment, with a management committee composed entirely of Koories. The centre's building, with its undulating red-ochre tin roof, blends in wonderfully with the backdrop of bush and rocky ridge; it was designed in consultation with the five Koorie communities responsible for the centre and incorporates many symbolic features.

A small **exhibition** inside features a poignant photographic history of the area's Aborigines, and there's a visual display of traditional Aboriginal foods and lifestyles, plus a section devoted to Central Australian land rights. Downstairs, a shop sells Aboriginal music, books and souvenirs, while the small **Bushtucker Café** upstairs sells snacks and light meals, with, as its name implies, an emphasis on bushtucker – try possum-tail soup with damper, a rooburger or emu kebab, followed by a "wattlecino" (a cappuccino-style drink made from wattle seeds); for the less adventurous, more familiar fare is available too. Outside, the landscaped grounds are planted with examples of the major plant species found in the park.

There are short **rock art tours** from the centre, as well as half- and full-day walks to other Aboriginal art sites in the national park. All tours are on demand only, must be booked at least a week in advance, and require a minimum of five people.

Bushwalks, scenic drives and tours

The scenery and wildlife of the Grampians is tremendously varied, and the diversity of **vegetation** in the park is enhanced by the fact that this is the meeting place of the ecosystems of the forested areas in the south and east of Victoria and the dry mallee country in the north. It's significantly warmer in the northern Grampians, an area of arid bushland filled with bent and twisted trees and scrubby undergrowth. In the cooler south, the vegetation ranges from stringybark forests and red-gum woodland in the wet Victoria Valley to luxuriant fern gullies such as Delleys Dell in the Wonderland Range. There are also subalpine communities of plants in exposed sites such as Mount William, as well as areas of stunted heaths on the Major Mitchell Plateau.

You can **drive** on roads through the park to major points and then get out and walk. Take care, though, as animals are often killed by drivers, especially on the Grampians Road south of Halls Gap and the Mount Abrupt Road north of Dunkeld. The most popular section for visitors is the **Wonderland Range**, immediately to the west of Halls Gap. From the Halls Gap campsite you can head directly to **Venus Baths** (2km), **Mackeys Peak** (1km) or **The Pinnacle** (10km), the most popular lookout in the Grampians with a narrow rock ledge nearby – the **Nerve Test** – that many try out. **Delleys Dell** is another Wonderland walk (5km), through canopies of tree ferns: start at the Rosea picnic area. The other major features are the Balconies, Mackenzie Falls and Zumstein, all accessible via the Mount Victory Road northwest of Halls Gap. The walk to the **Balconies** (1.6km return), also known as the **Jaws of Death**, begins from the Reid Lookout car park and goes through a stand of lichen-covered tea trees. The weird formation consists of one ledge above another, and if you're brave enough you can stand right on the edge of the lower jaw and be enthralled by splendid views over the forested Victoria Valley. The much-photographed formation can also be seen at a distance from the **Reid Lookout** itself.

At **Zumstein** (5km east of Mount Victory Rd) there's a picnic area and car park where western grey kangaroos stand passively, waiting for food. They're tame enough to pet, but can be a serious nuisance when you get out your food; don't encourage them by feeding them. A three-kilometre walk runs along the Mackenzie River Gorge from here to the base of thundering **Mackenzie Falls**, which you can also reach more directly from the Mount Victoria Road. There's parking above the falls, and it's a short but strenuous walk to the base.

The Major Mitchell Trail

The first Europeans to reach the Grampians were **Major Thomas Mitchell** and his exploration party in 1836. Mitchell was the Surveyor General of New South Wales, and his glowing reports of the explorations subsequently attracted many squatters in the early 1840s. The **Major Mitchell Trail**, a signposted 1700-kilometre "long-distance cultural trail" along backroads and sometimes bush tracks, allows you to follow his route through Victoria, from Mildura along the Murray River to Swan Hill, then south to Horsham, detouring into the Grampians to ascend Mount William, and thence to the coast at Nelson and Portland. Heading back, it runs inland via Hamilton and Dunkeld on the southern edge of the Grampians, through central Victoria via Castlemaine, and then across the northeast part of the state via Benalla and Wangaratta, crossing back into New South Wales at Wodonga. A **handbook** of the walk is sometimes available at the NRE Information Centre or Information Victoria in Melbourne (see p.891), or enquire at the visitor information centres along the trail.

If you're reasonably fit, consider tackling the walk to the peak of **Mount William** (1168m; 3.5km return), the highest point in the park. This starts from the Mount William Road car park, for which you turn off 16km south of Halls Gap. More challenging overnight walks include one to the **Major Mitchell Plateau**, starting from the same car park but involving a difficult five-hundred-metre climb to the plateau; and the **Mount Difficult** walk, which starts from Rose Gap and goes across a large, undulating, rocky plateau.

Tours and activities

A few tour operators banded together to form the **Grampians Central Booking Office** at the Halls Gap newsagency (daily 9.30am–6pm; ☎ 03/5356 4654), which does bookings for all kinds of activities from abseiling, bike riding and bushwalking to spotlight tours and rock climbing. Between September and June the eco-tour operator Echidna Walkabout (☎ 03/9646 8249) does a two- to three-day Grampians tour out of Melbourne, which includes accommodation on a sheep farm, bushwalking, evening spotlight walks, and on the third day the option of exploring the regional Koorie heritage, sometimes with a Koorie guide. At about $400 for two days, the tour is not cheap, but it's thoroughly recommended. Grampians Scenic Flights (Dec–June only) give the definitive overview of the mountain range, with sky-high prices to match; book through the Grampians store (☎ 03/5356 6294).

Accommodation

During school holidays, particularly in January and at Easter, the Grampians are packed, and although Halls Gap has lots of **accommodation** of every kind, you'll need to book in advance. Note that many places will insist on long stays, and prices also rise at weekends. In addition to the Grampians Visitor Information Centre in Stawell, the privately run Grampians Booking Service (free call ☎ 1800 624 991, ℱ 03/5383 6347) also makes accommodation **bookings**.

There's no booking for the **campsites** in the national park – they operate on a first-come, first-served basis, and a permit is required: fill in a form and put your money into the box at the site, or buy one from the visitors centre or from tourist offices in nearby towns. **Bushcamping** is allowed in the park, except in the Wonderland Range and within 100m of a dam, river or creek, or within 50m of a road. Besides the basic park campsites, there are dozens of **caravan parks** in the vicinity. The most convenient, *Halls Gap Caravan Park*

(☎03/5356 4251, ℻5356 4421; cabins ④, on-site vans ③), is right opposite the shopping centre and so a bit noisy, but it's well equipped, and at the start of many walks. *Grampians Gardens Caravan Park* (☎03/5356 4244, cabins and vans ③, motel units ④), 3km out of town at the corner of the Ararat and Stawell Roads, is another good option. At the northern end of the park is *Roses Gap Recreation Centre* (☎03/5359 5264; ③–④), which has cabins, a camp kitchen and sheltered BBQ.

Brambuk Backpackers, Grampians Rd (☎03/5356 4250). Run by the Aboriginal Living Cultural Centre. this hostel is clean, comfortable and friendly, making judicious use of natural space and light. Backpacker busline Groovy Grape stops here. Rooms ③, dorms ①

Grampians Wonderland Cabins, Ellis St, just off the Grampians Tourist Rd on the way to Brambuk (☎ & ℻ 03/5356 4264, ⓦwww.grampians.net.au/wonderland). Beautiful two-bedroom timber cabins in a bushland setting; good for a splurge. ⑦–⑧

Grand Canyon Motel, less than 1km north of Halls Gap on Grampians Rd (☎03/5356 4280, ℻5356 4513). The cheapest motel accommodation in the park. ④–⑤

Hall's Gap YHA, Grampians Rd (☎03/5356 4544, ⓔgrampians@yhavic.org.au). New hostel built according to environmentally friendly principles, recycling waste water and using solar electricity and wood-heating stoves. It's a

huge place with excellent facilities, but a little too functional to be welcoming. Rooms ③, dorms ①–②

Kingsway Holiday Flats, Grampians Rd (☎03/5356 4202). Spartan, but cheap and clean self-catering accommodation, with TV and fully equipped kitchens. ④

Kookaburra Lodge, 14 Heath St (☎03/5356 4395, ℻5356 4490). One of the better motels in town. ⑤–⑥

Mountain Grand, Grampians Rd, Halls Gap (☎03/5356 4232, ℻5356 4254, ⓦwww.mountaingrand.com.au). Elegant, friendly guesthouse with a licensed restaurant and a jazz café and bar downstairs. ⑥–⑧

Tim's Other Place, Grampians Rd (☎03/5356 4288, ⓦwww.timsplace.net). Very cosy, centrally located hostel, though not as well-equipped as the YHA. Bikes available for $10 per day, and internet access is the cheapest in town. Breakfast included. Rooms ③, dorms ①

Eating, drinking and entertainment

There's no shortage of places to **eat** in Halls Gap, yet most visitors don't venture beyond the limited choices at the rather touristy and overpriced Stony Creek Stores complex on the main Grampians road: the *Stony Creek Bakery* (daily 8am–5pm) makes fresh bread daily; the *Cafe Rosea* does good burgers, steak sandwiches, roast meals, pizza and pasta, and is open for breakfast, lunch and dinner; the more expensive, rather sterile *Flying Emu Café* serves cakes, snacks and light meals of rather debatable quality; or you can pick up delicious home-made ice cream at *Coolas*. Away from the stores, the *Halls Gap Tavern*, Lot 5, Dunkeld Road (daily 5pm till late), is a pleasant, moderately priced restaurant and bar, while the *Kookaburra Restaurant* on Grampians Road (lunch, dinner, coffee and cake daily, bookings advisable for dinner on ☎03/5356 4222) comes highly recommended for its inexpensive café-style dishes – mainly pasta and salads – and for its restaurant food, which features venison and home-made ice cream. *Darcy's* at the *Colonial Motor Inn* on Grampians Road (daily from 6.30pm, bookings advisable on ☎03/5356 3440) is a motel restaurant dishing up good food including emu. Both restaurants have local wines on their wine list.

For entertainment, there's Saturday night **jazz** at the *Mountain Grand Guest House* from 10pm; they also have a cocktail bar. An alternative **film festival** comes to town at the beginning of November, and there's a jazz festival in mid-February.

The Wimmera

The Wimmera, dry and hot, relies heavily on irrigation water from the Grampians for its vast wheatfields; before irrigation and the invention of the stump jump plough, the area was little more than mallee scrub, similar to the lands beyond **Warracknabeal**, the northernmost wheat-growing centre.

HORSHAM, capital of the wheatfields, makes a good stop-off point en route to Adelaide; it has an idyllic picnic spot, complete with barbecues, by the Wimmera River. However, there's little else to attract you here, though the Grampians National Park (see p.999) is within striking distance to the southeast, and **Mount Arapiles**, 40km west, is one of the most important **rock-climbing** centres in Australia – if you're interested contact Arapiles Climbing Guides (T03/5387 1284), who can also organize abseiling and bushwalking. The **Horsham Visitor Information Centre**, at 20 O'Callaghan Parade (daily 9am–5pm; T03/4382 1832 or free call 1800 633 218, W www.grampians.org.au), books both accommodation and tours. One central **place to stay** is the *Royal Hotel*, 132 Firebrace St (T03/5382 1255; ❸), a grand old place established in 1881, which has retained many of its original features. *The Fig Tree Cafe*, at 59 Firebrace St, serves coffee and the usual **café** fare, while *Cafe Bagdad* at 48 Wilson St has a very local, slightly arty alternative feel and serves espresso, cakes and ice cream, as well as big portions of cheap soups, salads and *focaccia*. *Café Conexus*, across the road from the cinema at 14–16 Pyment St, has super-cheap **internet** access, hot showers and hearty fodder for weary travellers. Seventeen kilometres out of town towards Natimuk and Mount Arapiles the friendly, small *Tim's Place*, Asplins Road, Quantong (T & F 03/5384 0236; dorm ❶, rooms ❸), has dorm accommodation and three private rooms for prospective rock-climbers and anyone who'd like to break their journey; enjoy a mud bath or simply relax in a hammock with the dogs. Book ahead, as Oz Experience and other backpacker tour operators call in here.

Continuing on the Western Highway, you come to **DIMBOOLA**, deep in the dreary flatlands; it's the sort of place that runs to its own dusty clock, frustratingly closing down for lunch just as interstate buses stop for a break. The *Dimboola Motel* (T03/5389 1177; ❹) and *Dimboola Hotel* (T03/5389 1380; ❹) are both on Horsham Road. **NHILL** and **Kaniva**, further along the highway, are similarly undistinguished. All three towns are within a few kilometres of **Little Desert National Park**, with Nhill being the best starting point if you plan to explore. *Little Desert Lodge* (T03/5391 5232; B&B rooms ❸, dorms ❷), 16km southeast of the town on the Harrow Road, lies on the fringe of the park and runs good 4WD **tours**; it has camping, motel units and bunk rooms for groups. Far from being a desert, the national park has a great variety of plants, with colourful wildflower displays in spring; much of the vegetation is low mallee scrub, among which the now rare mallee fowl can be found. There are three **campsites** within the national park: one on the Kiata South Road 13km from Kiata, east of Nhill, the others are at Horseshoe Bend and Ackle Bend, south of Dimboola (call Parks Victoria for more information on T03/5391 1255).

The Mallee

The Mallee, the most sparsely populated area of Victoria, begins north of Warracknabeal, from where the **Henty Highway** heads up to join the

Sunraysia Highway and forge its way to Mildura, on the border with New South Wales. This is an area worth visiting only in winter, when it's drier and warmer than the rest of Victoria, but not too hot to make bushwalks unbearable. You really need your own transport to see anything; just about the only **public transport** is the small Henty Highway Coach that runs between Horsham and Mildura (departs Horsham BP service station and Mildura train station three times weekly; 4hr; call for prices and times on ℡03/5382 4260), which mainly carries freight. Along the way are small dusty towns such as Brim, Bealah and **HOPETOUN** ("gateway to the Mallee"), whose shops still have their old awnings and apparently their original window displays too.

Fifty kilometres away from Hopetoun is the **Wyperfeld National Park**, which at 3500 square kilometres is Victoria's third largest, with a chain of normally dry lake beds, mallee scrub, river red gum and black box woodlands, and rolling sand plains, with emus, kangaroos and mallee fowl among its wildlife. A sealed road goes to the *Wonga Campground*, where there's a shady camping and picnic area with water and toilets, as well as an **information centre** (daily 9am–4pm; ℡03/5395 7221) where you can find out about the many walks in the park. The **Big Desert Wilderness** is directly west of Wyperfeld but can be reached only by the Nhill–Murrayville track that runs between Broken Bucket, northwest of Nhill, and Murrayville, on the Mallee Highway west of Ouyen; there are no tracks, roads or facilities in the park, just more sand dunes, mallee scrub and lots of wildlife. You'll need a 4WD and considerable dedication to get the most out of it.

Beyond Hopetoun, the Henty Highway merges into the Sunraysia Highway. Heading north on the Sunraysia, you come to the small town of **SPEED** – which could hardly have a less appropriate name; tourist information is available at the general store here. From here the mallee scrub tenaciously clings to the edges of the highway, threatening to invade the red soil of cleared fields on either side, and the equally red dust of the unsealed road. **OUYEN**, the "heart of the Mallee", is another small, undistinguished town where two highways meet. Heading west on the Mallee Highway, the access track to the picturesque **pink salt lakes** of the **Murray–Sunset (Yanga–Nyawi) National Park** leads north from Linga. Continuing north on the Calder Highway from Ouyen, you pass the **Hattah–Kulkyne National Park**, just east of the highway; the park consists of dry mallee scrub, native woodland, and a lakes system lined with gums. Lake Hattah is reached by turning off the highway at Hattah, 34km north of Ouyen, onto the Hattah–Robinvale Road. From Hattah it's less than 70km to Mildura and the Murray River.

The Murray region

From its source close to Mount Kosciuszko high in the Australian Alps, the **Murray River** forms the border between Victoria and New South Wales until it crosses into South Australia (someone got a ruler out for the rest of the border to the coast); although the actual watercourse is in New South Wales, the Victorian bank is far more interesting and more populous. After the entire length was navigated in 1836, the river became the route along which cattle were driven from New South Wales to the newly established town of Adelaide, and later in the century there was a thriving paddle-steamer trade on the lower reaches of the river, based at Wentworth on the New South Wales side (see p.366). In 1864, **Echuca** was linked by railway to Melbourne, stimulating the river trade in the upper reaches, and thus became a major inland port, the furthest extent of the navigable river. At the height of the paddle-steamer era, **Mildura** was still a run-down, rabbit-infested cattle station, but in 1887 the Chaffey brothers instituted irrigation projects that now support dairy farms, vineyards, vegetable farms and citrus orchards throughout northwestern Victoria. Between Mildura and Echuca, **Swan Hill** marks the transition to sheep, cattle and wheat country; the **Pioneer Settlement** here explores the extraordinarily hard lives of the early settlers. Above Echuca the Murray loses much of its magic as it flows through the more settled northeast.

Nowadays **paddle steamers** cruise for leisure, and are the best way to enjoy the river and admire magnificent **river red gums** lining its banks, as well as the huge array of birds and other wildlife that the Murray sustains. Renting a **houseboat** is also a relaxing (if expensive) way to travel.

Mildura

MILDURA has the mirage-like aura of an oasis, its vineyards and orange orchards standing out from a hot, dry landscape. To the southwest is the evocatively named **Sunset Country**, with nothing but gnarled mallee scrub, red sand and pink salt lakes (reached via Linga on the Mallee Highway). Mildura makes a good winter getaway, but summer can be stiflingly hot – the green grape vines in the surrounding countryside and the flowers and towering red gums that line Deakin Avenue, the main thoroughfare, offer some relief, but you'd do best to avoid the area at this time if you can.

Deakin Avenue runs northwest through town to the river, with 7th Street and the train station facing the parklands that run along the river. Like any self-respecting small city, Mildura has a couple of malls, one running parallel to Deakin Avenue between 8th and 9th streets, and another, smaller one out of town at Deakin Avenue and 15th street. The **Mildura Visitor Information and Booking Centre** is situated in the state-of-the-art Alfred Deakin Centre at Deakin Avenue and 12th Street (Mon–Fri 9am–5.30pm, Sat & Sun 9am–5pm; ⓣ03/5021 4424 or free call 1800 039 043, Ⓦwww.milduratourism.com), which also houses a pool and gym, a decent café and a modern library, where you can check your email for free (booking advised). The visitor centre will book accommodation and supply free town maps, and also have particularly good information on the Murray–Sunset (Yanga–Nyawi) and Hattah–Kulkyne national parks.

Down on the river the seventy-year-old **Mildura Weir** system, designed to provide stable pools for irrigation and to enable navigation throughout the year, makes a pleasant place to while away an hour or so. There's a pretty picnic spot by lock 11 (the trickiest), just beyond the art gallery at the arts centre. Alternatively, wander down to the **Mildura Arts Centre**, 199 Cureton Ave (daily 10am–5pm; gallery $3), which consists of a historic home, Rio Vista, the Mildura Regional Art Gallery, a theatre and a sculpture park. **Rio Vista** was built in 1890 for William Chaffey, who lived here with his first and second wives (both called Hattie Schell, the second niece of the first) until he died in 1926. It's a lovely house, though rather ill-suited to the climate, and inside are various displays about the Chaffeys and the development of Mildura. The art gallery's most important piece is *Woman Combing Her Hair at the Bath*, a pastel work by Edgar Degas; it also has some excellent sculpture by Australian artists. Artwork of a less colonial nature can be found at the **Tulkana Kumbi Aboriginal Gallery**, 22 Langtree Ave (Mon–Fri 10.30am–5pm, Sat 11am–5pm; free).

Cruises, tours and activities

The best **short river cruise** is on the PS *Melbourne* (daily 10.50am & 1.50pm; 2hr 10min; $18.50; ☎03/5023 2200), Mildura's only genuinely steam-driven paddle steamer. Built in 1912, it still has its original boiler and engine. The same company runs *Paddleboat Rothbury*, built in 1881 and in its day the fastest steamboat on the river; it's now been converted to diesel and takes people on cruises to local attractions such as the Trentham Estate Winery ($42 including lunch and wine tasting), as well as operating dinner cruises on Thursday nights ($40). *Paddleboat Coonawarra* (☎03/5023 3366 or free call 1800 034 424) has **longer cruises**: four nights for $442–618 (depending on season) or five nights for $716–879. All cruises leave from **Mildura Wharf** at the end of Madden Avenue, west of the train station.

Away from the river, the most outstanding natural attraction is **Mungo National Park** (see p.367), 110km across the border in New South Wales. It's visited by a few tour operators from Mildura, all of whom charge around $60 a head: Junction Tours (☎03/5027 4309 or 0408 596 438, ✉tom@ruralnet.com.au); Mallee Outback Experiences (☎03/5021 1621 or 0418 521 003); and Jumbunna Enterprises (☎0412 581 699, ✉jumbunna@hotmail.com). Koorie tour operators belonging to the Barkindji people also lend their perspective on the park with Harry Nanya Tours, based just over the border in Wentworth (Mon–Sat; ☎03/5027 3697). Like all the others, they also do tours around Mildura, to Wentworth, and to other attractions and national parks in the surrounding area.

Camerons, 72 Lime Ave (☎03/5021 2876 or 0427 793 297, ⓦwww.cameronsmildura.com.au), rents out sports gear and arranges **hot air balloon flights** daily, weather permitting, from $185 per person. Rainy days can be passed at the **Deakin Cinema Complex** at 98 Deakin Ave, while a back-to-nature alternative to the swimming pool on Deakin Avenue is available at the sandy **swimming beach** at Chaffey Bend. There are lifeguards in summer, but take local advice and beware of dangerous currents; people have drowned here.

Practicalities

Mildura is 555km from Melbourne, about as far as you can go in this small state; right on the border of New South Wales, and little over 100km from South Australia, it's ideally located for **onward transport** to either. Buses on the Sturt Highway, the major route between **Adelaide** and **Sydney**, pass through several times daily, with a 3am Greyhound service to Adelaide, a 3am V/Line service to Sydney, and a 4am Countrylink service to Sydney and **Melbourne** via Cootamundra. From Melbourne, there's also a V/Line train–bus connection via Bendigo or Swan Hill at least three times daily (call ☎13 6196 to book). **Broken Hill**, north up Silver City Highway, can be reached by bus via Wentworth (departing Mildura train station Mon, Wed & Fri 9am; 3hr 30min; $49.50; book at the visitor information centre). **Ballarat** is served once a day (except Sat) by V/Line ($54.60), whilst you can get to **Albury**, via Echuca and Rutherglen, on Tuesday, Wednesday, Friday and Sunday ($56). In terms of **local transport**, there are buses to Red Cliffs,

Buronga and across the river to Wentworth (see p.366), as well as a very regular Sunraysia Buslines (☎03/5023 0274) servicing the area from 7th to 15th Streets and the East and West. Alternatively, you can **rent a car** from, among others, Budget at 7th Street and Etiwanda Avenue (☎03/5021 0133).

Mildura has a good reputation as a place to obtain **work** as a fruit-picker; the only guaranteed time is in February, when the grape harvest takes place. Unfortunately, this is also the time when the heat is most intense. If you think you could handle it, come around the end of January, the beginning of the eight-week season. Most of the town's hostels have work contacts with a wide range of employers, and during the harvest season you can also phone the Mildura and District Harvest Labour Office (end of Jan to mid-March; ☎03/5021 1797); alternatively, call Employment National (☎1300/720 126). Some growers have accommodation but normally you'll need your own transport and a tent.

Accommodation

Mildura has lots of reasonably priced accommodation, and an ever-increasing amount of hostels to cater to the hordes of hard-up backpackers that drift here looking for work.

Adventure Houseboats, 16 Sturt Highway, Buronga (☎03/5023 4787, ✉bturner@vic.ozland.net.au). Bed and breakfast with a difference, in a self-contained houseboat with laundry, CD player, TV and BBQ. Sleeps up to six. Two people ⑤

Carncourt Holiday Apartments, 826 15th St (☎03/5023 6311 or free call 1800 066 675). Good, inexpensive choice if you want self-catering; also has an outdoor pool but is quite far out of town. ⑤

Mildura Grand Hotel, 7th St, opposite the train station (☎03/5023 0511, ✆5022 1801, ⊕www.milduragrand.com). Recently restored hotel, complete with guest ballroom, bistro, games room, spa, sauna and outdoor swimming pool. Accommodation ranges from basic to luxurious, with breakfast included. The hotel's chef is very respected and an ABC TV star. ⑥

Nomads Mildura International Backpackers, 5 Cedar Ave (☎03/5021 0133, ✉mildrabp@vic.ozland.net.au). Work-oriented hostel with air-conditioning, recreation area, cable TV and laundry. Twin-share rooms only. ①

Nomads Riviera Backpackers Motel, cnr 7th St and Pine Ave, and **Nomads Northaven Backpackers Motel**, 138 Deakin Ave (☎03/5023 0521, ⊕www.nomadsworld.com). Very central air-conditioned backpacker motels with good facilities and sociable atmospheres, swimming pools, work registries and a work bus service. Aimed at long-term guests. Dorms ①

Riverbend Tourist Park, Chaffey Bend (☎03/5023 6879). Well-equipped site, right on the Murray by the beach. Cabins and on-site vans ③

Riverboat Bungalow 27 Chaffey Ave (☎03/5021 5315 or 5023 0984, ⊕http://users.mildura.net.au/bungalow). This shambolic 1891 house is a work-and-play oriented place with work registry, cable TV and a large backyard near the river. Weekly rates available. Rooms ③, dorms ①

Rosemount House/Mildura YHA, 154 Madden Ave (☎ & ✆ 03/5023 1535, ✉rosemont@rural-net.net.au). Central, family-run old-style guesthouse that doubles as a YHA. Good if basic facilities, breakfast and an outdoor pool. Can arrange work contacts, but is more for casual visitors than workers. Very friendly owners. Weekly rates available. Rooms ①–②

Zippy Koala Backpackers, 206B 8th St (☎03/5021 5793 or 0412 185 150). Central work-oriented hostel, with small dorms, cable TV, air-conditioning, two kitchens, a beer garden and transport to work for guests. Weekly rates available. ①

Eating and drinking

Healthy food abounds in Mildura's cafés and restaurants, most of which are clustered on Langtree Avenue, just south of the mall. If you have your own transport, you can make an enjoyable outing to buy fruit and vegetables from surrounding farms. Otherwise, there are three excellent supermarkets, including a 24-hour Coles, surrounding Langtree Mall.

Hudak's Bakery Café, Langtree Mall, 8th St and Central Plaza. Good continental breads and delicious zucchini slices. Daily from 7am.

Lauretz of Langtree, 30 Langtree Ave. All-you-can-eat pizza, pasta, soup and salad – suitable for big appetites, and only $8.75. Daily from 5pm.

Outlaws, Langtree Ave, opposite *Stefano's*. Big food of the surf, turf and salad variety, with half-price steaks on Wed night meaning you're guaranteed a quality feed for under ten bucks. Outside tables. Open daily.

The Rendezvous, 34 Langtree Ave (℡03/5023 1571). Cheap lunches and other meals served in the bistro. There's also an upmarket restaurant, as well as a bar and courtyard seating. Lunch Mon–Fri, dinner Mon–Sat.

Stefano's Restaurant, at the *Mildura Grand Hotel* (℡03/5023 0511). The restaurant (Mon–Sat 7pm–midnight; booking essential) is tucked away in the hotel's cellar. No menu, but the Northern Italian food is excellent, prepared by Mildura's own national TV chef. The café-wine bar upstairs (daily 10am–midnight or 1am) is cheaper and serves good pasta, wood-fired pizzas, coffee and cakes, while the downstairs bistro proffers surf 'n' turf between noon & 2pm and 6 to 9pm daily (not Sun lunch).

Taco Bills, Langtree Ave. Cheap, substantial Mexican fare in cheery surroundings near the river. All main meals half-price on Tues. Tues–Sun from 6pm.

27 Deakin, 27 Deakin Ave. This gorgeous shrine to food serves eclectic breakfasts and delicious frittatta, salads and soups, as well as excellent coffee and cakes. Gourmet foodie haven/picnic shop inside. Mon–Fri 9am–7pm, Sat & Sun 9am–3pm.

Nightlife

Mildura's nightlife may not be the world's greatest, but there's enough to keep you occupied. Perhaps the best thing to do is to try out one of the **clubs**, where you can be signed in as a visitor; as an incentive to get you to the gambling machines, there's lots of inexpensive food and drink. The *Mildura Workingman's Club*, on Deakin Avenue between 9th and 10th streets, is one of many in town. Established in 1895, the club reputedly has the world's longest bar, 91m long. Another good place for a drink is the vibrantly coloured, youth-oriented *Sandbar* at 43 Langtree Ave (nightly until 1am; light meals until 10pm; happy hour Mon–Fri 5–8pm), which has a courtyard and puts on live music weekly in the summer and at weekends the rest of the year. *Dom's Nightclub*, upstairs from the restaurant of the same name at 32 Langtree Avenue, is open Thursday to Saturday. If all else fails, *Malley's Irish Pub* on Deakin Ave in the centre of town (nightly until 2am) has regular drink promotions and live music Wednesday to Saturday; there's a $5 cover charge after 9.30pm at the weekends.

Around Mildura

The easiest excursion from Mildura is to **RED CLIFFS**, some 15km south, with its vineyards and tree-lined streets. The huge Lindemans Karadoc Winery (daily 10am–4.30pm) is one of the largest **wineries** in Australia, where fifty thousand tonnes of grapes are crushed every year. The range of wines for tasting is extensive, prices are very reasonable and there's a café serving light lunches, coffee and cake (Mon–Fri 10am–3pm).

Across the Murray from Mildura at **BURONGA** (actually in NSW but more readily accessible from the Victorian side of the river), you can rent your own vessel to really get the full experience of the river. Buronga Boatmen Hire Boats, next to the bridge (℡03/5023 5874), rents out **fishing boats** (from $15 per hour) and canoes (from $10 per hour). Or you could phone Aquavilla Houseboats (℡03/5027 2272 or free call 1800 039 094, Ⓦwww.aquavilla.com.au) about renting a **houseboat**: weekly rates range from about $935 to almost $1375 for a luxurious six-berth boat, and if you get a group together it can work out to be quite reasonable – you'll need a driver's licence, and must supply your own food. The nearby *Floating Cafe* (daily 10am–6pm) is a colourful pontoon moored in a lovely spot where there are lots of pelicans and ducks. Also at Buronga is the **Stanley Winer Company** (Mon–Fri 10am–4pm, Sat 10.30am–4pm, Sun noon–4pm; ☎03/5023 4341), the largest cask winery in New South Wales – you can taste the wine here or just pose for photos in front of the big wine cask outside. On a much smaller scale, **Trentham Estate Winery**, 10km down the Sturt Highway in an idyllic setting overlooking the river, has cellar door sales (Mon–Fri 8.30am–5pm, Sat & Sun 9.30am–5pm; (☎03/5024 8888, ⓦwww.trenthamestate.com.au) and an upmarket restaurant (lunch Tues–Sun; bookings on ☎03/5024 8747).

Swan Hill and around

Heading for Swan Hill, you can go south down the Calder Highway, turning east at Hattah onto the Hattah–Robinvale Road and continuing past the Hattah Kulkyne National Park (see p.1006). Alternatively, you can cross the Murray into New South Wales and follow the Sturt Highway, recrossing the river at **ROBINVALE**, a small, rather characterless fruit-growing town, but idyllically situated within a great loop of the river. Wine buffs should make a stop at the **Robinvale Winery**, Sea Lake Road (daily 9am–5.30pm; ☎03/5026 3955, ⓦwww.organicwines.com.au), where a wide range of wines, including some Greek varieties, are biodynamically produced.

Twenty-five kilometres from Swan Hill you reach the highly productive stone-fruit and vegetable-growing area of **NYAH**. Bushcamping (no water or facilities) is allowed in the nearby Nyah and Vinefera **state forests** along the Murray; for full details contact Parks Victoria in Swan Hill (see p.1012). Eight kilometres beyond Nyah is the **Tyntynder Homestead** (open by appointment only on ☎03/5037 6380; $8.25), a classic 1846 bungalow furnished in wealthy squatter style and set amid flowering gardens. Part of the homestead is a museum containing, among other things, a collection of Aboriginal artefacts.

As you approach **SWAN HILL** itself, the landscape changes – this is cattle and sheep country, with wheatfields further north. The Murray here is shallow and tricky to navigate, so there's not much river traffic. Swan Hill is a service centre for the pastoral industry and has a typically solid, conservative atmosphere. Surprisingly, it's quite a multicultural place, having ten percent of Victoria's Aboriginal population, and a large Italian community. The Pioneer Settlement (see below) is undoubtedly Swan Hill's main attraction, but while you're here, you could also visit the **Swan Hill Regional Art Gallery** (Tues–Sun 10am–5pm; $3), which specializes in folk and Aboriginal art, and the **Murray Downs Homestead** (Sat–Thurs 9.30am–noon, daily during school holidays; closed for three weeks in Dec; guided tours at 10am & 11am; $7.50), an impressive Victorian mansion at the heart of a forty-square-kilometre station – it's over the bridge in New South Wales, but barely 1km from town. The town's **swimming pool**, on Monash Drive (Nov–March daily 11am–7pm; $2.50), has several pools and a waterslide.

Pioneer Settlement

Swan Hill's **Pioneer Settlement** (daily 9am–5pm; $16), a reconstruction of a pioneering community at Horseshoe Bend about 1km south of the train station, was the first of its kind in Australia and is still one of the best. The buildings are all authentic, having been transported from various sites near and far.

One of the most interesting is the **Iron House**, an example of a nineteenth-century "kit home", many thousands of which were shipped out from Britain during the housing crisis that accompanied the goldrush – cities and towns in Victoria had whole streets of them, and they were stiflingly hot in summer and freezing cold in winter. This particular example came from South Melbourne, where it was inhabited until 1967.

In the settlement's streets many of the **shops** are functional – the baker, the printer, the haberdashery and the porcelain doll shop – with assistants dressed in vaguely period costume. Generally, though, it's low-key and peaceful: buildings such as the barber's shop and the stock and station agents are open for you to wander around undisturbed. The pharmacy has a large collection of old medicines, with a gruesome dentist's surgery out back; the church is made from old bricks of the original courthouse; and there's even a rather creepy Masonic Lodge, which is still in use. The **Mechanics Institute** has a traditional collection of books and a wonderful working "Stereoscopic Theatre" from 1895: the wooden cylinder has 25 viewfinders, each with a leather seat from which you can admire the 3D scenes. You can go on rides around the settlement in a 1924 Dodge or a horse-drawn carriage. In the evening, the **sound and light show** (nightly from dusk; $10) is strikingly effective.

The settlement is situated on the banks of the Marraboor River, a branch of the Murray. A wooden bridge spans the river to Pental Island, which has an assortment of native flora and fauna. Meanwhile, an old **paddle steamer**, the *Pyap*, cruises from the settlement upriver past Murray Downs every day at 10.30am and 2.30pm (1hr; $10), while the MV *Kookaburra* offers a longer lunchtime cruise (2hr 30min; $28), departing at 12.30pm daily.

Practicalities

The **Swan Hill Visitor Information Centre**, 306 Campbell St (daily 9am–5pm; ☎03/5032 3033 or free call 1800 625 373, ⓦ www.swanhill.vic.gov.au), has a free map of the town giving detailed information on local attractions; it also sells tickets for the Pioneer Settlement, its sound and light show and the MV *Kookaburra* and MV *Pyap* cruises. **Parks Victoria** at 1 McCallum St (Mon–Fri 8.30am–5pm; ☎03/5033 1290) can provide you with information on camping in the nearby Nyah and Vinefera state forests.

There's a strip of **motels**, all with swimming pools, along Campbell Street, where almost all the town's facilities are located. The *Sundowner Swan Hill Resort* at no. 405 (free call ☎1800 034 220, ⑤03/5032 9109; ❻) is the most luxurious, with an indoor and outdoor pool and spa, plus gym and other sports facilities; it's easily located because of its restaurant, *The Silver Slipper*, which has a huge rotating stiletto outside and even tackier decor inside. The *Station Motor Inn* at no. 421 (☎03/5032 2017, ⑤5033 1387; ❸–❹) is older and better value; at no. 182 is the *White Swan Hotel* (☎03/5032 2761; ❸), which has simple rooms with shared facilities as well as more luxurious ones. The *Riverside* at 1 Monash Drive (☎03/5032 1494; cabins ❹–❺, on-site vans ❸) is a good, centrally located **caravan park** right on the riverfront.

The large Italian population in Swan Hill has had a beneficial effect on the **food**: *Bartalotta's Hot Bread Kitchen*, 178 Campbell St, is excellent, as is *Quo Vadis*, an authentic pizzeria on Campbell Street serving pasta and ribs as well as pizza. *Café 202*, at 202 Beveridge St, serves tasty lunch-time options and good, strong coffee. *Teller's Restaurant & Bar* at no. 225 is a slick-looking, city-style brasserie in an old bank, open daily for lunch and dinner.

Swan Hill to Gunbower Island

From Swan Hill the Murray Valley Highway heads southeast, away from the river, and follows the rail line past a series of about fifty freshwater lakes. At the first of these, **Lake Boga**, 16km from Swan Hill, Lake Boga Jet Ski Hire and Parasailing rents out jet skis and offers parasailing. Also by the lake – follow the signs – is Best's at St. Andrew's Winery, a large, commercial **winery**, the oldest in the Swan Hill region, and the sister winery to Best's Cocongella at Great Western (Mon–Sat 10am–5pm, also Sun noon–4pm during holidays; tours Mon–Fri 11am & 3pm; ☎03/5037 2154). The lakes peter out at **Kerang**, a sizeable town in a citrus-growing area on the Loddon River. Nearby **Lake Reedy** is one of the largest ibis-breeding grounds in Australia and has a public-viewing hide; the birds are widespread in the area, though, so you probably won't have any trouble seeing some.

From Kerang, the Murray Valley Highway continues east to Cohuna, in a rich dairy-farming area, and from there towards **Gunbower Island**, a further 23km. The "island", encircled by the Murray River and Gunbower Creek, is a state forest of huge red gums and Gunnawarra wetlands, with 160 species of birds and a lot of wildlife. It's most easily approached from Cohuna (follow the signs on the Kerang–Koondrook road); details of walks and camping can be obtained from the Kerang office of Parks Victoria (☎03/5450 3951).

Echuca and around

ECHUCA, a lively and progressive place, is the most easily accessible river town from Melbourne – it's only three hours or so by bus or car, making it a popular weekend getaway. Echuca became the largest inland port in Australia after the railway line connected it with Melbourne in 1864. When the **missions** began to close in the 1930s, many Aboriginal families, especially Yorta Yorta people from Cummeragunga mission, and Wemba Wemba from Moonacullah mission, migrated to the Echuca area. Since they weren't made welcome in the towns, the migrants were forced to live on the fringes in badly constructed, flood-prone housing, just close enough to be able to get to work and school. Women commonly worked in the canneries and hospitals, and the men packed fruit, sheared sheep and did other labouring jobs.

Nowadays, **Port of Echuca**, with its massive wharves and collection of old buildings, is a major tourist attraction, and several cruises ply along the river from here. The town itself, however, is not too touristy, and has retained much of its charm. There are two principal streets: High Street, the former main street, leads to Murray Esplanade and the wharf, and is the centre of tourist activity, with lots of cafés and boutiquey shops; Hare Street, the present-day main street, is lined with more commercial buildings.

Port of Echuca

To enter the old wharf area, dubbed the **Historic Wharf** (daily 9am–5pm), you'll need to pay a $10 entrance fee, which also allows entry to the *Star Hotel* and the *Bridge Hotel*. Alternatively, you can combine a tour with a cruise on the *Pevensey* or the *Alexander Arbuthnot* (see overleaf) for $20. The **Star Hotel** was first licensed in 1867 and is a typical pioneer pub, a tiny one-storey building with a tin roof and verandah. As the river trade declined, the *Star* was delicensed (in 1897), along with many of the other 79 hotels in town. Drinking on the premises became illegal, so the loyal clientele dug a tunnel to the street through which they could escape at the first hint of a police raid – you can examine this, along with the cellar and a small museum.

The magnificent red-gum **wharf** was nearly a mile long in its prime and is still fairly extensive. Three landing platforms at different levels allowed unloading, even during times of flooding, and there are wonderful views from the top, high over a bend in the river. Goods were transferred from train to steamer via this top level, and old train carriages sit on sidings here, piled high with trunks of red gum. You can wander below to the other levels, through a network of thick river-red-gum piles standing 12m high. At the lowest level, several **old boats** are moored, including the *Pevensey*, a 1911 steam-driven cargo boat which you can wander aboard; **cruises** are available on either the *Pevensey* or the similar *Alexander Arbuthnot* daily (☎ 03/5482 4248; $15). In the wharf cargo shed there's a scale model of the working port and a ten-minute narrated audiovisual presentation.

Back outside the wharf complex, along Murray Esplanade opposite Hopwood Gardens, is the **Bridge Hotel**, opened in 1858 but delicensed in 1916. It was built by the founder of Echuca, Henry Hopwood, an ex-convict who also started a punt service across the Murray; the story goes that if the pub wasn't doing well he'd close the ferry down for a few hours, leaving prospective passengers with little else to do but drink. Other attractions in the area include the **Red Gum Works** (daily 9am–5pm; free), housed in a large loading shed which is wonderfully scented by the wood as it's transformed from tree-trunk to souvenir; there's also a steam-operated sawmill and a blacksmith at work. The **World in Wax Museum**, 630 High St (daily 9am–5pm; $8.80), displays sixty wax figures of "world-renowned personalities", with Australia rather unimaginatively represented by Paul Hogan and Dame Nellie Melba.

River cruises

A wide choice of **cruises** are on offer, departing from berths just beyond the old wharf, best approached from High Street. One-hour port cruises are available on the PS *Pride of the Murray* (daily 9.45am, 11am, 12.15pm, 1.30pm, 2.30pm & 3.45pm; $12.50; ☎ 03/5482 5244) and the PS *Canberra* (daily 10am, 11.30am, 12.45pm, 2pm & 3.15pm; $12.50; ☎ 03/5482 2711). The PS *Emmylou*, a wood-fired paddle steamer, has slightly longer cruises (daily 10.30am, 11.30am, 1pm, 2.30pm & 3.30pm; 1hr $15, or 1hr 30min $18; ☎ 03/5482 2237, ⓦ www.emmylou.com.au), while the MV *Mary Ann* does lunch and dinner cruises ($28/$44; call ☎ 03/5480 2200 for days and times). Kingsfisher Wetland Cruises offer a two hour eco-cruise through Barmah forest, the largest red gum forest in the world (see p.1016).

Practicalities

The **tourist information centre**, 2 Heygarth St (daily 8am–5pm; ☎ 03/5480 7555 or free call 1800 804 446, ⓦ www.echucamoama.com), sells tickets to the port complex and for cruises, books accommodation and is an agent for V/Line and Countrylink **bus** tickets. There are up to six **trains** a day between Melbourne and Echuca, and two daily connections with Sydney.

Budget accommodation is offered by *Echuca Gardens YHA*, 103 Mitchell St (☎ 03/5480 6522 between 8–9.30am & 5–8pm, ⓔ echuca@yhavic.org.au;

dorms ❶, rooms ❻–❼), a beautifully restored small wooden hostel set in tranquil gardens right on the edge of the Banyule Forest; the owners also offer country-style B&B accommodation. From here, it's a ten-minute walk through red gums to sandy river beaches where it's safe to swim on the inner bends. Those looking for work might try the somewhat institutional *Nomads Oasis Backpackers*, 410–424 High St (℡03/5480 7866, ✉nomads@river.net.au; dorms ❶, rooms ❸), which has air-conditioned dormitories and twins/doubles, a small kitchen and a courtyard. The owner has outdoor employment contacts and can provide transport to places of work. Moving upmarket, the *Steam Packet Inn*, on the corner of Leslie Street and Murray Esplanade (℡03/5482 3411; ❺), is a National Trust-listed **motel** in the heart of the old port area, while the *Echuca Hotel*, 571 High St (℡03/5482 1087; ❹), the town's first pub, still has some of its original features and offers simple accommodation in large pleasant rooms; it also offers motel units at the associated *Campaspe Lodge* (units ❺). Upmarket **B&B** accommodation can be found in several pretty, historic homes: one of the nicest is *The River Gallery Inn*, 578 High St (℡ & ℻ 03/5480 6902, ✉inn@echuca.net.au; ❽), where all the self-contained rooms have open fireplaces, and some have spas. The *Echuca Caravan Park*, Crofton St, Victoria Park (℡03/5482 2157, ✉hughd@mccmedia.com.au; cabins ❸–❺, on-site vans ❸), is a well-equipped **caravan park** right on the riverfront. There is even a thriving **nudist resort**, the *River Valley Nudist Resort* (℡03/5482 6650, 🌐www.rivervalley.com.au; ❹), near Echuca in a bushland setting along the Goulburn River. Enquire at the tourist office about the many **houseboats** available to rent in the area.

With hungry Melburnians to feed, there's no shortage of decent **eating places**. *Sutton's* on Hare Street is an old-fashioned bakery, and *Top of the Town* on the High Street near the swimming pool does good-quality, freshly cooked fish and chips. *Drovers Bakehouse* on 513 High St near the Campaspe River sells a variety of breads baked in a wood-fired oven and has a sun deck which is a good spot for breakfast or lunch. *The Bridge Hotel* has a coffee shop, bar and a restaurant in the historic port area, and serves good coffee, cakes and desserts, light lunches and mainly traditional Aussie dishes in the restaurant. For excellent Italian food go to *Giorgio's on the Port*, 527 High St, which is open daily for dinner; or try *Fiori*, 554 High St. *Oscar W's* boasts a wonderful setting next to the old Echuca Wharf and serves food to match (daily 10am until late; book for dinner on ℡03/5482 5133). *Ogilvie's Bar & Restaurant* at the *Philadelphia Motor Inn*, 30 Ogilvie Ave (℡03/5482 5700) also has a very good reputation. On the other end of the price scale, the *American Hotel*, on the corner of Hare and Heygarth streets, does good, plain counter meals.

Nightlife is better than you might expect; the small and friendly *American Hotel* is a good place to start with a drink. The *Harvest Hotel*, 183 Hare St, draws a youngish crowd and plays host to live bands at weekends, while *Radcliffes* has live jazz on Sunday afternoons. There's a **Jazz, Food and Wine Weekend** in mid-February. **Campaspe Multiarts Centre** is a brand new multimedia extravaganza due to open in 2001, boasting three cinema screens and an auditorium.

Around Echuca

Thirty kilometres southeast of Echuca, Kyabram's main attraction is **Kyabram Fauna Park** (daily 9.30am–5.30pm or 8.30pm in summer; $8.50), a community-owned wildlife park divided into grassland for free-ranging kangaroos, wallabies, emus and other animals, and a huge wetland area. You can wander around the grassland area and through several aviaries; a two-storey observation tower affords views of the more than eighty species of native birdlife on the water. Diamond pythons, tiger snakes, crocodiles and other not-so-pleasant creatures can be viewed from a safe distance at the Reptile House.

BARMAH, some 30km upstream on the Murray, is most easily reached by crossing into NSW at Echuca and heading north on the Cobb Highway, then turning east. This small river town is associated with red-gum milling, and with sleeper cutting in the early railway days. The *Barmah Caravan Park* (☎03/5869 3225; ❶–❸) has a great site on the banks of the river among red gums, with a small, sandy beach for swimming. **Barmah State Park**, 10km out of town, has Australia's largest stands of **river red gum**, some of them 40m tall and five hundred years old. The forest runs along the Murray for over 100km and stands in an extensive flood plain: **canoeing** among the trees at flood time (July–Nov) is a magical experience; you can arrange transport and rent canoes from Echuca Boat and Canoe Hire (☎03/5480 6208, ⓦwww.echucaboatcanoehire.com). During the wet season more than two hundred species of waterbird come here, and there's plenty of other wildlife; you might even see brumbies (wild horses). When it's dry you can use several well-established walking tracks: the place was of special significance to the Yorta Yorta Aborigines and you can still see fish traps, middens and scars on trees where the bark was used for canoes. During the **Barmah Cattle Muster** every April, two thousand head of cattle that are grazed in the forest are mustered in a frenzied, exciting atmosphere.

Yorta Yorta culture and lore are explained in the park's **Dharnya Centre** (daily 10.30am–4pm; ☎03/5869 3353), which also has archeological information and artefacts. A **cruise** in the MV *Kingfisher* leaves from here (Mon, Wed, Thurs, Sat & Sun, plus other days during busy times; 2hr; $18; booking essential on ☎03/5840 1839) – a flat-bottomed boat that glides over Barmah Lake and through stands of red gum. Bushcamping is permitted in the park; contact Parks Victoria (☎13 1963) for details.

Gippsland

GIPPSLAND stretches southeast of Melbourne from Western Port Bay to the New South Wales border, between the Great Dividing Range and Bass Strait. Green and well watered, it's been the centre of Victoria's dairy industry since the 1880s. **South Gippsland** is also, in contrast, the site of vast brown-coal deposits between Moe and Traralgon in the Latrobe Valley, where power stations generate most of the state's electricity, while offshore, Bass Strait wells exploit natural gas and crude oil reserves, with several gas-processing and oil-stabilizing plants disfiguring the coastline. South Gippsland also has Victoria's most popular national park, **Wilsons Promontory**, or "The Prom", a hook-shaped landmass jutting out into the strait, with some superb scenery and fascinating bushwalks. In the east, around the **Gippsland Lakes** and **Ninety Mile Beach**, the region is less industrialized; and just beyond Orbost–Marlo the unspoilt coastline of the **Croajingolong National Park** – with its rocky capes, high sand dunes and endless sandy beaches – stretches to the New South Wales border.

Transport

V/Line **trains** run from Melbourne to Sale, basically following the Princes Highway through South Gippsland. From Sale, **buses** leave for Orbost, stopping at Lakes Entrance. The Sapphire Coast Link is a daily train–bus connection between Melbourne and Narooma on the south coast of New South Wales: take the train to Sale, then a connecting bus along the Princes Highway via Lakes Entrance, Orbost, Cann River and Genoa. Similarly, the Capital Link train/bus service heads to Canberra via Sale on Monday and Thursday mornings, returning Tuesday and Friday afternoons. Bookings for all the above should be made through V/Line (☎13 6196, ⓦwww.vlinepassenger.com.au). There's also a daily Greyhound Pioneer service along the coast from Melbourne to Sydney, but it's not very convenient if you want to get off at stops in East Gippsland: the bus leaves Melbourne at 10pm and gets to Lakes Entrance and Cann River in the small hours of the morning. Having your own **car** is vastly preferable, as you need to get off the highway to really experience the region's diverse highlights and to get to the unspoilt bush campsites on the coast. The Princes Highway itself is a very boring drive, particularly the stretch from the Latrobe Valley to Bairnsdale, but after Orbost the highway becomes more scenic as it goes through the tall, dense eucalypt forests of Far East Gippsland. If you don't have a car, or don't want to spend much money, you might want to consider travelling on Oz Experience, the backpacker bus line that covers the Sydney–Melbourne route via the very scenic high country and Gippsland.

Tours and activities

The north part of Gippsland, in the foothills and mountains of the Great Dividing Range, is Victoria's "high country" – and it's ideally suited for a lot of **outdoor activities**. In the past, local operators have been a bit slow in exploiting the area's appeal, but the scene is gradually changing. At present, there are a few good **trail-ride** outfits, including Walhalla Mountain Saddle Safaris based in Erica, in the hills north of Moe, Latrobe Valley (☎03/5165 3365; not suitable for beginners), and Snowy Range Horseback Tours in Heyfield (☎03/5148 3268). There are also some companies that organize **white-water rafting**, among them Snowy River Expeditions, located in Gelantipy (☎03/5155 0220), and Detours, in Buchan (☎03/5155 9464); both also organize a host of other activities like rock climbing, abseiling, caving and **bushwalking**. Adventurama in Melbourne (☎03/9682 1771 or free call 1800 801 464) take people on the Thomson River near Moe, the Mitta Mitta River near Omeo, and the Snowy River near Gippsland, they also run flexible camping trips with or without guided bushwalks to Wilsons Promontory. Bunyip Tours (☎03/9600 9207, ⓔmrbunyip@hotmail.com.au) also do inexpensive, nature-oriented camping trips to the Prom in association with Parks Victoria. The comprehensive, very relaxed and informative trips offered by the ecotour operator Echidna Walkabout (☎03/9646 8249, ⓔekidna@netcore.com.au) are at the other end of the price scale, but well worth the expense. They offer four- or six-day trips to the coastal Croajingolong National Park and the remote mountainous Errinundra National Park in the hinterland of Far East Gippsland – they take care of transporting the gear and provisions, setting up camp and cooking. Most tour companies don't operate during the winter months.

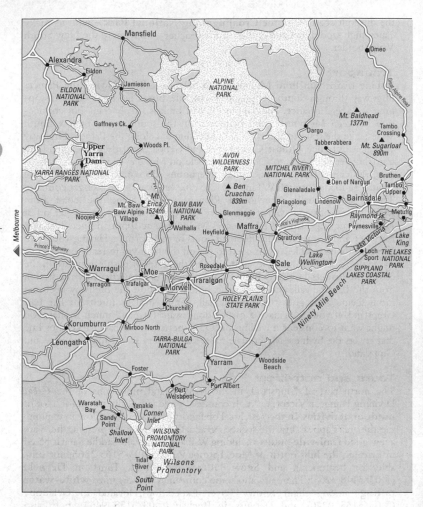

◀ Melbourne

Wilsons Promontory and Tarra Bulga

WILSONS PROMONTORY, the most southerly part of the Australian mainland, was once joined by a land bridge to Tasmania. Its barbed hook juts out into Bass Strait, with a rocky coastline interspersed with sheltered sandy bays and coves; the coastal scenery is made even more stunning by the backdrop of granite ranges. It's understandably Victoria's most popular **national park**. Though the main campsite gets totally packed in summer, there are plenty of walking tracks and opportunities for bushcamping; the park's big enough to allow you to escape the crowds, with about 130km of coastal scenery, and inland areas covered with tall forests, heathlands and salt marshes. You can swim at several of the beaches and even **surf**: Wilsons Prom Surf School, based at

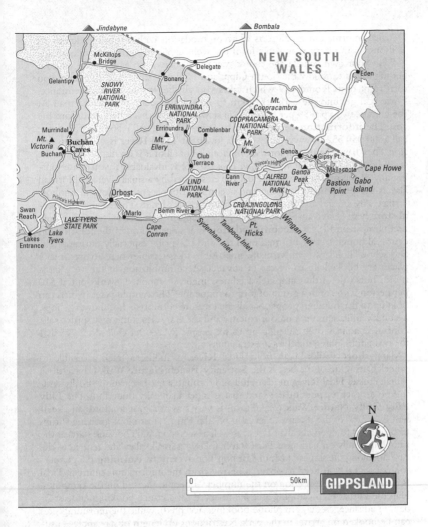

Jindabyne Bombala

NEW SOUTH WALES

McKillops Bridge
Delegate
Gelantipy
Bonang
Eden

SNOWY RIVER NATIONAL PARK

Mt. Coopracambra

ERRINUNDRA NATIONAL PARK

COOPRACAMBRA NATIONAL PARK

Murrindal
Errinundra
Comblenbar
Mt. Victoria
Mt. Ellery
Mt. Kaye
Buchan Caves
Buchan
Genoa
Gipsy Pt.

Club Terrace
Prince's Highway
Mallacoota
Cape Howe

Orbost
Cann River
Genoa Peak
Bastion Point
Gabo Island

LIND NATIONAL PARK

Prince's Highway
Swan Reach
Marlo
Bemm River
ALFRED NATIONAL PARK

Lakes Entrance
LAKE TYERS STATE PARK
Lake Tyers
Cape Conran
CROAJINGOLONG NATIONAL PARK
Pt. Hicks
Wingan Inlet

Sydenham Inlet
Tamboon Inlet

N

0   50km   **GIPPSLAND**

Tidal River, operates courses for all ages and abilities, with all equipment provided (⊤03/5680 8512).

There's no public **transport** to Wilsons Promontory; the nearest you can get to it is with the evening V/Line bus from Dandenong, which will take you as far as **FOSTER** on the South Gippsland Highway. Here you can stay overnight at the intimate and idiosyncratic *Foster Backpackers Hostel*, either in small dorms in a cosy house (①), or in a self-contained cottage on the same grounds ($50 sleeps 3–4); check in at the office on 17 Pioneer St (⊤03/5682 2614). The hostel runs a transport service to Tidal River in the national park (daily; $40 per one-way busload), and rents out camping equipment; it also has a car available to rent for $40 per day. If you're coming from Phillip Island, *Amaroo Park Backpackers* in Cowes (⊤03/5952 2548) has a good, inexpensive **tour**. For other tour operators offering camping and bushwalking trips from Melbourne, see box p.940.

Detailed information on all sorts of accommodation within touring vicinity to Wilsons Promontory is available from the website ⓦwww.promaccom.com.au.

With your own vehicle, the easiest way to get here from Melbourne without getting lost is to follow the South Gippsland Highway to Meeniyan, where you turn right onto Route 189 which takes you all the way to the park entrance. Once you get into the park, it's 30km to Tidal River on a good sealed road. At the entrance you pay $9 per car – if you stay overnight, this is deducted from the cost. The **information centre** (daily 8.30am–4.30pm; ℡03/5680 9555 or free call 1800 350 552, ⓦwww.parkweb.vic.gov.au) at **Tidal River** is an obvious first stop. They have plenty of information, though not all of it is on display, so ask: the small booklet *Discovering the Prom on Foot* ($7.95) is invaluable if you're attempting any of the overnight walks. Tidal River, situated by a small river on Norman Bay, is the park's main camping and accommodation centre; colourful rainbow lorikeets fly around and land to be fed from people's hands. There's also a **general store** here (daily 9am–7pm), with a pricey supermarket section, takeaway food, fuel pumps and LP gas. **Accommodation** is arranged through the information centre, although from Christmas until the end of April – especially during public and school holidays – it's virtually impossible to get somewhere to stay; many places are booked up to a year in advance. Accommodation in the very basic motor huts (use of the campsite's facilities; linen not supplied) works out at $10 per person if you're in a group of four to six people. The camping area, which can hold up to five hundred people, has all the creature comforts – hot showers, shops, a laundry and a summer outdoor cinema, and there are also some very spruce self-contained holiday units sleeping up to six people (May–Oct ❻ & Nov–April ❼ for two adults, plus $16.50 each extra adult).

Many **short walks** begin from Tidal River, including a track accessible to wheelchairs. One of the best is the **Squeaky Beach Nature Walk** (1hr return), which crosses Tidal River, heads uphill and through a tea-tree canopy, finally ending on a beach of pure quartz sand that is indeed squeaky underfoot. The **Lilly Pilly Gully Nature Walk** (3hr return) is very rewarding, as it affords an excellent overview of the diverse vegetation of "the Prom", from low-growing shrubs to heathland to open eucalypt forest, as well as scenic views. The walk starts at the Lilly Pilly Gully car park near Tidal River, follows a small valley and returns to the car park along the slopes of Mount Bishop. For **overnight camping** ($5 per person per night), you need to obtain a permit from the information centre at Tidal River, as there is a restriction on the number of people allowed on the campsites. Half the sites at each camping area are reserved for advance bookings (at least 21 days in advance; credit-card phone bookings accepted), while the remaining sites can be booked on arrival in the park. Restrictions on length of stay apply – usually only one or two nights. The tracks in the southern section of the park are well defined and not too difficult; the campsites here have pit toilets and fresh water. The most popular walk here is the two- to three-day (36km) Sealers Cove–Refuge Cove–Waterloo Bay route, beginning and ending at the Mount Oberon car park. Crowds are much thinner in the remote north of the park, where there are no facilities and limited fresh water: this is the province of experienced, properly equipped bushwalkers. However, during summer holidays and at long weekends between November and the end of April all tracks become extremely busy, so book well in advance or show up early.

Tarra Bulga National Park

Another good national park can be reached from Yarram, 50km beyond Foster on the South Gippsland Highway. **Tarra Bulga National Park**, in the heart of the Strzelecki Ranges, is dominated by forests of mountain ash and myrtle beech with a lower canopy of ferns – a cool green environment alive with colourful lyrebirds, crimson rosellas and yellow-breasted robins among the rich birdlife. The **visitors information centre** (Sat & Sun, daily in summer and Easter holidays, usually 10am–4pm; ℡03/5196 6166) at Balook on the Grand Ridge Road, between the two separate sections of the park, has information about walks. The Grand Ridge Road (mostly unsealed) winds along the top of the Strzelecki Ranges through fern gullies and towering trees, affording gorgeous views of South Gippsland. The *Tarra Bulga Guest House* (℡03/5196 6141; ❼), on a beef and lamb property on Grand Ridge Road just 50m from the visitors centre, has every amenity, including a library and games room.

The Gippsland Lakes region

The **Gippsland Lakes**, Australia's largest system of inland waterways, are fed by the waters of the Mitchell, Nicholson and Tambo rivers, and are separated from the sea by Ninety Mile Beach. East of Yarram, the beach stretches long and straight towards **Lakes Entrance**, the tacky focal point of the area and one of Victoria's most popular holiday spots, with the foothills of the high country within easy reach to the north.

SALE, at the junction of the South Gippsland Highway and the Princes Highway, is a good point from which to head off to explore the coastal park and Ninety Mile Beach. From Seaspray, 35km south, a coastal road hugs the shore for 20km to Golden Beach, from where a scenic drive heads through the Gippsland Lakes Coastal Park to Loch Sport; here you're faced with the enviable dilemma of lakes on one side, and ocean beaches with good surfing on the other. An unsealed road then continues on to Sperm Whale Head in the Lakes National Park. Sale's **tourist information centre** (daily 9am–5pm; free call ℡1800 677 520, ⓦwww.sale3850.com.au), on the Princes Highway, can provide you with all the details. They can also give you information about the **Bataluk Cultural Trail**, which starts in Sale and links sites of cultural and spiritual significance to the Gunai people, the original inhabitants of the Gippsland coast. The first stop on the trail, the **Rahmayuck Aboriginal Corporation** at 117 Foster St in Sale, sells arts and crafts, paintings and T-shirts (Mon–Fri 9am–5pm).

BAIRNSDALE is the next major town on the highway east of Sale and serves as another departure point for the lakes to the south. The efficient staff at the **tourist office** on Main Street (daily 9am–5pm; ℡03/5152 3444) will provide all the local information you'll need. The well set-up exhibition at the **Krowathunkoolong Keeping Place**, parallel to the Princes Highway at 37–53 Dalmahoy St (Mon–Fri 9am–5pm; $4), explains the history of the Gunai people. Bairnsdale Air Charter (℡03/5152 4617) arranges cheap **scenic flights** from the Bairnsdale Aerodrome over the extensive waterways of the Gippsland Lakes (10min; from $25 per person; minimum two people).

A beautiful place **to stay** nearby is *café espas* on Raymond Island (℡03/5156 0983, ⓦwww.espas.com.au; dorms ❷), a short ferry ride away across the McMillan Straits from **PAYNESVILLE**, 16km south of Bairnsdale. The Raymond Island Ferry runs every half-hour throughout the day (Mon–Thurs 7am–10.30pm, Fri & Sat 7am–midnight, Sun 8am–10.30pm; $3 return; ℡03/5150 9100); *café espas* can also arrange pick-ups from Bairnsdale train station. Alteratively, try the *Grand Terminus Hotel* at 98 McLeod St in Bairnsdale

(☎ 03/5152 3444; ❸). *Espas* do excellent all-day **food**, or try the delicious bush tucker served at *Wallaby Rise Camp Food* (☎ 03/5158 0376), just outside Sale.

Forty-five kilometres northwest of Bairnsdale is another site on the Bataluk Cultural Trail, the **Den of Nargun** in the **Mitchell River National Park**. According to a Gunai legend, the small cave here was inhabited by a large female creature, a *nargun*, who would abduct people who wandered off on their own. As the Den of Nargun was a special place for Gunai women and may have been used for initiation ceremonies, the story served the purpose of keeping unauthorized people away. The cave is located in a small, beautiful valley; follow the loop track from the park picnic area via a lookout to the Mitchell River (30min), then take the track along Woolshed Creek to the cave and climb up the steep path back to the starting point (40min).

Lakes Entrance and Metung

The sandy barrier between the Gippsland Lakes and the sea was formed about six thousand years ago; when first seen by white men in the 1840s the outlet to the sea was a seasonal, intermittent gap, unsuitable for reliable trade. In 1889 the present stable entrance was opened 6km east of the old one: the artificial entrance effectively cuts off the town's access to the length of **Ninety Mile Beach**, and means that it's no longer really ninety miles either.

As you might expect from the area's popularity, **LAKES ENTRANCE** is a big, rather tawdry, tourist town, with loads of motels at either end of town as you enter from the highway. There are all sorts of attractions aimed at keeping holidaying children happy – from Fun Park to minigolf – on the Esplanade, which fronts onto an arm of Lake King. The **Griffiths Sea Shell Museum** at 125 Esplanade (daily 10am–5pm; $4), with its rather off-putting 1950s-style facade, has a huge collection of shells and marine life, as well as an aquarium containing an intriguing assortment of fish from the Gippsland Lakes. Lakes Entrance is also a big **fishing port**: the Fishermans Cooperative Wharf has a viewing platform where you can watch the catch being unloaded, as well as a tantalizing fish shop.

Beaches are obviously the big attraction here. Lakes Entrance Surf Beach, a substantial stretch of white sand patrolled in season by surf lifesavers, can be reached via a footbridge across the lake to Hummocks Reserve. Of the many **lake cruises** on offer, one of the most popular is the trip from the *Club Hotel* jetty at the western end of town, up North Arm to the Wyanga Park Winery – the most famous local winery – on the fringe of the Colquhoun Forest, in the winery's own boat, *The Corque* (daily lunch cruise $35, Thurs, Fri & Sat dinner cruise $50, Sun brunch cruise $28; book at Lakes Entrance Tourist Information, or through the winery on ☎ 03/5155 1508). The winery also run a non-landing morning tea cruise (Mon–Sat 9am; $18). Other lake activities include environmentally friendly, electrically-powered cruises on Lake Tyers, just east of Lakes Entrance, with MB *Rubeena* (boats leave from Fisherman's Landing; from $17; ☎ 03/5155 1283), **parasailing** with Parasailing Victoria (☎ 03/5155 3032) and three-hour **fishing** trips, including morning or afternoon tea, with Mulloway Fishing Charters (☎ 0427 943 154). Those who prefer less watery pursuits could try the excellent Lakes Entrance Wilderness Trail Rides, offering **horseback treks** for all levels through bushland replete with all sorts of wildlife ($25 per hour, call for longer or overnight rates; ☎ 03/5156 3288).

Practicalities

Lakes Entrance Tourist Information (daily 9am–5pm; free call ☎ 1800 637 060), on the Esplanade, provides local advice and tickets for cruises on the lakes, and can also book accommodation, a useful service in summer when the place gets very crowded. The two town **hostels** are both excellent. *Riviera Backpackers YHA*, at 5 Clarkes Rd in the east end of town just 50m from the Greyhound Pioneer bus stop (℡03/5155 2444, ℻5155 4558, ✉riviera@net-tech.com.au; rooms ❷, dorms ❶), is a friendly place situated close to a beautiful stretch of lake. It has 24-hour reception, dorms and rooms in refurbished former holiday units, a large kitchen/common room with internet access and library, a laundry and a small pool with spa. They also rent out bikes. *VIP/Silver Sands Backpackers* on Myers Street (℡03/5155 2343, ℻5155 3134, ✉ssands@b150.aone.net.au; rooms ❷, dorms ❶), part of a small, well-maintained caravan and camping park in a quiet location a block behind the Esplanade, has en-suite cabins and facilities for on-site vans, plus a camp kitchen, barbecue area, laundry, table tennis and pool with spa.

Most of the **motels** are as tacky as their names suggest: probably the best of the lot are the *Coastal Waters Motel* on the Esplanade (℡03/5155 1792; ❼), which has its own heated saltwater pool, and the *Sand Bar Motel*, almost next door at 637 Princes Highway (℡03/5155 2567; ❹–❺), also with a heated pool and a common spa. Better, and usually cheaper, options are **cabins** or **cottages**. *Lazy Acre Log Cabins*, 35 Roadknight St (℡03/5155 1323, ℻5155 1212, ✉lazy-acre@net-tech.com.au; ❺–❼), is a good bet, with a pool, BBQ, adventure playground, spa and facilities for the disabled; or try the cottages at *Kalimna Woods*, some with spas and log fires (℡03/5155 1957; ❻). *Deja Vu* is a rather special **B&B** in a pleasant location out of town at 17 Clara St (℡03/5155 4330, ℻5155 3718, ❾www.dejavu.com.au; ❼–❽), with spacious en-suite units overlooking the waterway of North Arm.

Places to **eat** in Lakes Entrance include *Egidios Wood Oven*, 573 Esplanade, for good Italian food; the upmarket *Skippers Winebar and Restaurant* (℡03/5155 3551) at no. 481; *Caffe 567*, at no. 567 for delicious coffee and Italian-style ice cream; and *Fish-a-Fare*, at no. 509, an excellent fish-and-chip shop. Backpackers' favourite *Tres Amigos Mexican* serves super-cheap stodge at no. 521, while the best (and the most expensive) meal in town can be found on *The Nautilus* (℡03/5155 1400), a floating restaurant specializing in local seafood. In addition to wine tasting, the popular *Henry's Winery Cafe* at Wyanga Park Winery, 3km from town near North Arm (follow the signposts), also serves cakes and Devonshire teas, cheese platters and other meals; wines are available by the glass at cellar door prices (daily lunch and snacks noon–3.30pm, Thurs–Sat dinner from 6pm; bookings preferred on ℡03/5155 1508).

Metung

If the commercialism of Lakes Entrance turns you off, head for the more refined charms of **METUNG**, a pretty, upmarket boating and holidaying village just 10km west along the shoreline. To get there, take the highway towards Bairnsdale, then turn south on a side road at Swan Reach.

A typically civilized **accommodation** option in Metung is *Maeburn Cottages*, 33 Mairburn Rd (℡03/5156 2736; ❺–❻), where you stay in three- to four-person cabins (BYO linen). *McMillans of Metung*, at 155 Metung Rd, comprises motel units and very comfortable, fully equipped cottages of different sizes in a garden setting, with a solar-heated pool, tennis court and a private jetty (℡03/5156 2283; motel ❻, cottage ❼, extra adults $25). *The Moorings at Metung*, 28 Main Rd (℡03/5156 2750, ❾www.themoorings.com.au; ❼), are very grand cottages with sun decks and BBQs overlooking Bancroft Bay; their bistro menu offers everything from champagne brunch to coffee and cake. Cheaper is the *Metung Hotel* (℡03/5156 2206; ❹), which also offers bistro meals. The pleasant BYO *Little Mariners Café* at 57 Metung Rd serves breakfast, light **meals** and local seafood daily; while *Marrillee at Metung* on the same road at no. 50 (℡03/5156 2121) is pricier, licensed and specializes in local wines and fish. Both offer alfresco dining.

Buchan and the Snowy River Loop

Nowa Nowa is the inauspiciously named town where you turn north off the Princes Highway for Buchan, in the foothills of the Victorian Alps, and take a satisfying loop through the Snowy River National Park. The small town of **BUCHAN** boasts over six hundred **caves**, the most famous of which – the Royal Cave and the Fairy Cave – can be seen on **guided tours** (daily: April–Sept 11am, 1pm & 3pm; Oct–March 10am, 11.15am, 1pm, 2.15pm & 3.30pm; $11; booking advised on ℡03/5155 9264). In the extensive park surrounding the caves there's an icy, spring-fed swimming pool, a playground, walking tracks, and a campsite, plus lots of wildlife.

The delightfully idiosyncratic *Holloways Colonial Tea Rooms and B&B* (℡03/5155 9329; ●), tucked away in a valley near Buchan South, serves excellent Devonshire teas, light lunches and hearty dinners – call for bookings and directions. In Buchan itself, on the north bank of the Buchan River, is the wonderful independent backpackers' **hostel** *Buchan Lodge* (℡ & ℻ 03/5155 9421; ●), where people have been known to come for a night and stay half a year. Dorms are in a wooden home with log fire and resident dog, and facilities include a volleyball court, country-style kitchen, BBQ garden and laundry. The owner, Dick, will happily advise about local activities, including caving, trail riding and rafting, and the village itself boasts the lovely *Willow Café*, serving all manner of drinks, grub and live music to a friendly, welcoming crowd.

The road continues north from Buchan through hilly country, following the Murrindal River and slowly winding its way up to the plateau of the Australian Alps. The sealed road ends at Wulgumerang, just before the *Seldom Seen Roadhouse*, where you can get fuel and supplies, and the turn-off to McKillops Bridge. You can continue straight up to Jindabyne in the Snowy Mountains of New South Wales – a spectacular drive – but about two-thirds of the road is unsealed and can be rough; check road conditions before setting out.

Snowy River National Park

Turning right at Wulgumerang, about 55km north of Buchan, enables you to make a scenic arc through the northern end and around the eastern fringe of the **Snowy River National Park**, following the unsealed road towards Bonang (check road conditions in advance, as this is an unsealed road that can deteriorate badly in adverse weather conditions). **Little River Falls** are well worth a stop on this stretch: a short walk leads from the car park past snow gums to a lookout with breathtaking views of Little River Gorge and the falls. The view from the second lookout from the top of the northeastern cliff face of **Little River Gorge** is equally stunning (about 10min from the car park).

Further on, you descend to the valley of the Snowy River, which you cross at **McKillops Bridge**, set in the landscape that inspired "Banjo" Paterson's famous ballad, "The Man from Snowy River". The river's sandy banks are a favourite swimming spot, and also the place to set out on a **rafting** trip

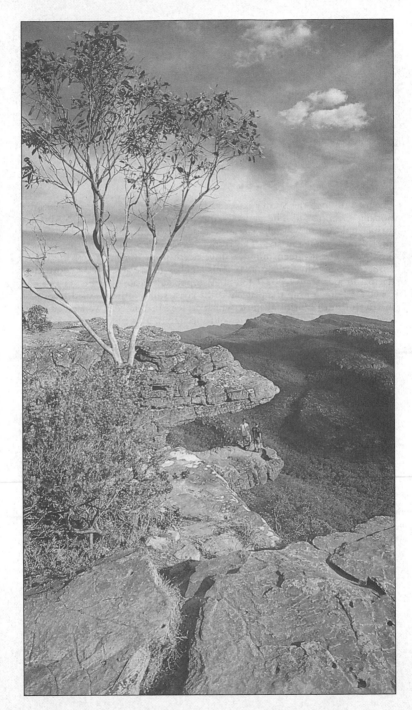

through deep gorges, caves, raging rapids and tranquil pools; Snowy River Expeditions in Buchan (☏03/5155 0220) offers good-value expeditions. If you want to play at being "the man from Snowy River", contact Snowy Mountain Rider Tours (same ☏) to arrange **horse riding** or an overnight camping trip; in addition they organize rafting, **abseiling** and **rock-climbing** adventures. The operators also run the *Karoonda Park YHA* (☏03/5155 0220, ℗5155 0308, ℮gelantipy@yhavic.org.au; dorms ❶, rooms ❸), a small country hostel situated in a beef and sheep farm in Gelantipy. The manager can arrange transfers from *Riviera Backpackers YHA* (see p.1023), 100km south. Oz Experience buses pass through Gelantipy, and the Wayward Bus stops here overnight on its Mountains and Rivers tour from Melbourne to Sydney.

Bonang to Orbost

The road through the Snowy River National Park continues until it meets the Bonang–Orbost road. The general store (☏02/6458 0265) at **BONANG**, a former goldrush town, sells takeaway food, groceries and fuel and has some information about the area. The rustic *Delegate River Tavern*, on the Monaro high plains about fifteen-minutes' drive north from Bonang across the NSW border, is open daily for counter **meals** and has good-value B&B **accommodation** in log cabins (☏02/6458 8009, ℮pub@delegate-river.net; ❸).

The road down from the plateau to the coast, still mostly unsealed, leads past the **Errinundra National Park**, which protects magnificent wetland eucalypt forests containing giant, centuries-old specimens, as well as Victoria's largest surviving stand of **rainforest**. At **Errinundra Saddle**, in the heart of the park, there's a delightful picnic area and a self-guided boardwalk through the forest (about 40min). Take special care while driving, for all roads in the area are heavily used by logging trucks.

The road from Bonang eventually leads to the old-fashioned town of **ORBOST**, on the Princes Highway where it crosses the Snowy River. There's a tranquil picnic spot opposite the *Snowy River Orbost Camp Park*, on the corner of Lochiel and Nicholson streets (☏03/5154 1097; on-site vans ❷), with huge gums lining one bank and cows roaming the paddocks on the other. The **Orbost Visitors Centre** on Lochiel Street (daily 9am–5pm; ☏03/5154 2424) books accommodation and tours.

Croajingolong National Park

From Orbost to **CANN RIVER** the Princes Highway continues well inland, not to reach the coast again until Eden, across the border in New South Wales. The **Parks Victoria ranger office**, on the Princes Highway in Cann River (Mon–Fri 9am–noon & 12.30–3.30pm; ☏03/5158 6351), provides information on the **Croajingolong National Park**, which begins southeast of the town at Sydenham Inlet and continues for 100km along the coast to the state border. Within the park, foothills cloaked in warm temperate rainforest drop down to the unspoilt "Wilderness Coast"; recommended is the two-hour hike to Genoa Peak, which rewards sore legs with stupendous views over the forest and bay. There are several scenic camping spots in the park, which are very popular in summer and allocated way in advance by a ballot system. You can also stay in the lighthouse-keeper's cottage of *Point Hicks Lighthouse* at Point Hicks (☏03/5158

4268; sleeps eight ➍). If you want to break your journey, Cann River itself offers very good-value accommodation at three motels – the cheapest being the *Cann River Motel* on the Princes Highway (℡03/5158 6255; ➌ including breakfast) – and at the *Cann River Caravan Park* at the junction of Princes and Cann Valley highways (℡03/5158 6369; ➋), which has on-site vans for rent.

Mallacoota and around

MALLACOOTA is a stylish holiday resort surrounded by Croajingolong National Park, on the lake system of the **Mallacoota Inlet**. It's approached via Genoa, 47km east from Cann River along the Princes Highway. About 10km from Genoa, a turn-off to the left leads to **Gipsy Point**, an idyllic spot near the confluence of the Genoa and Wallagaraugh rivers on the upper reaches of the Mallacoota Inlet; it's a fine place to spend a blissful day or two.

There is no tourist office in Mallacoota, but the people at the *Mallacoota Camp Park* (see below) will do their best to help any visitors with enquiries. **Activities** in the area range from 4WD tours to guided walks and kayaking on the lakes and rivers of Croajingolong National Park and the ocean offshore. Rankins Hire Cruises (℡03/5158 0555) are a top-class operation arranging leisurely **cruises** via Bottom Lake and Top Lake and Wallagaraugh River up to the New South Wales border, or you can explore on your own by renting a boat or canoe from Buckland's Jetty Boat Hire (℡03/5158 0660). The **Parks Victoria** office, on the corner of Allan and Buckland drives (daily 9.30am–3.30pm; ℡03/5158 0219, ⓦwww.parkweb.vic.gov.au), has details of secluded camping spots and local bushwalks.

During the summer Mallacoota, although seemingly remote, teems with avid holiday-makers. Mallacoota's small population of just over a thousand trebles again for the Easter **Festival of the Great Southern Ocean**, which includes all sorts of music, theatre and comedy, a community market, and fascinating sand sculptures.

Practicalities

Several **accommodation** options are located outside Mallacoota (and away from the summer crowds): try the friendly B&B *Mareeba Lodge*, 59 Mirrabooka Rd (℡03/5158 0378, ⓕ5158 0050, ⓦwww.mallacoota.net/mareeba; ➍–➎), or the cosy mud-brick apartments at *Adobe Flats*, 17 Karbeethong Ave, Karbeethong, 4km northwest of town (℡03/5158 0329, ⓦwww.mallacoota.com/adobe; BYO linen; ➍), which boast beautiful views of Bottom Lake and are located in an area teeming with birdlife. In Mallacoota itself, just behind the *Mallacoota Hotel* is the subdued but serviceable YHA hostel, *Mallacoota Lodge* (℡03/5158 0455, ⓕ5158 0453; units ➋, dorms ➊), which has accommodation in renovated motel units. Alternatively, you can pitch your tent at *Mallacoota Camp Park*, right on the shores of the lake (℡03/5158 0300, ⓔcamppark@vicnet.net.au; sites ➊–➋).

Choices for **food** are very limited. The deli next to the newsagent on Allan Drive serves brunch, light meals and good coffee, while the *Tide Restaurant & Cocktail Bar* on Maurice Avenue is probably the best place in town for dinner. Otherwise, counter meals are served at the *Mallacoota Hotel* nearby. Other distractions include **bands** at the *Mallacoota Hotel* every night in January, and a summer cinema at the Mallacoota Community Centre, Allen Drive. There's an **ATM** machine at 58 Maurice Ave, another in the supermarket, and a small Commonwealth Bank branch inside the post office next door. Additionally, EFTPOS facilities are available at the Mobil service station and the supermarket.

Gipsy Point, about 20km northwest, has another good accommodation option: the friendly *Gipsy Point Motel & Apartments*, set in a garden by the Wallagaraugh River (℡03/5158 8200 or free call 1800 688 200, Ⓕ5158 8308; ❹–❻), has attractive en-suite rooms or new apartments, and serves counter meals. The *Gipsy Point Lodge*, nearby on McDonald Street, has B&B rooms and cottages (free call ℡1800 063 556, Ⓕ03/5158 8205, www.gipsypoint.com; rooms ❼, cottages ❺), and arranges bird-watching and bushwalking excursions; note that there's a two-night minimum stay.

The Northeast

The **Hume Highway**, the direct route between Melbourne and Sydney, cuts straight through Victoria's northeast – an area that has become known as **Ned Kelly country**. **Euroa**, **Benalla** and **Glenrowan** (where the outlaw was finally seized after a bloody shoot-out) all have traces of the masked bushranger's activities, with Glenrowan wholeheartedly cashing in on his fame. West of the Hume, **Rutherglen**, right up against the state border, is Victoria's oldest established wine-producing region. There are also vineyards in the rich fruit-growing region of the **Goulburn Valley**, north along the Goulburn Valley Highway from **Seymour**. **Bushwalking** in the Alpine region is most easily organized through an outdoor tour operator such as Bogong Jack Adventures (℡08/8383 7198, Ⓕ8383 7377).

V/Line runs several **train and bus routes** through the northeast. The Melbourne–Albury train service goes via Seymour, Euroa, Benalla, Glenrowan, Wangaratta, Chiltern and Wodonga (at least 4 daily). There are also trains and buses from Melbourne to Shepparton, with connections to Cobram and Tocumwal in NSW (2–3 daily). Buses depart from Albury to Bendigo via Wangaratta and Benalla (1 daily). Bus services to Rutherglen are rather limited: from Albury (4 weekly in the morning). From Melbourne, there's a train to Wangaratta and then a connecting bus (3 weekly in late afternoon).

The Goulburn Valley

The **Goulburn River** rises at Lake Eildon and flows through Seymour, Nagambie and Shepparton to join the Murray just east of Echuca. The rich plains of the Goulburn Valley yield much **fruit**, and there's an important fruit-canning industry based at Shepparton, as well as several **wineries**.

Seymour is the first major stop on the Hume Highway out of Melbourne; an important train interchange, it's an uninspiring place for the visitor. The Goulburn Valley Highway begins here, heading north to **NAGAMBIE** on the shores of the man-made Lake Nagambie. The town itself is uninteresting, but two prominent **wineries** nearby add some welcome flavour. **Chateau Tahbilk**

(Mon–Sat 9am–5pm, Sun 11am–5pm, ☏03/5794 2555, ⊛www.tahbilk.com.au), 6km southwest, is the oldest continually operating winery and vineyard in Victoria; it opened in 1860, and the Shiraz and Marsanne are still made from the old vines that have seen more than 130 harvests. The whitewashed buildings have been well preserved and there are extensive grounds to explore. In complete contrast is the ultramodern **Mitchelton Winery** (daily 10am–5pm; ☏03/5736 2222, ⊛www.mitchelton.com.au), 14km southwest of Nagambie in Mitchellstown, off the Goulburn Valley Highway: its distinctive sixty-metre observation tower features on the Mitchelton label. The extensive riverside grounds have a pool and barbecues, which draw the crowds on Sunday. At the *Mitchelton Restaurant & Winebar*, overlooking the river, the wines from the winery are matched with outstanding food, using regional produce (daily 10.30am–3pm). **Goulburn River Cruises** ply the Goulburn River between Chateau Tahbilk and the Mitchelton Winery (summer only; ☏03/5794 2877, ⊜ijjr@mcmedia.com.au; or book through Victoria Winery Tours on ☏03/9621 2089, ⊛www.winetours.com.au/others). The **Nagambie Lakes Visitor Information Centre**, at 145 High St (daily 9am–5pm; ☏03/5794 2647 or free call 1800 444 647), also deals with bookings for V/Line – or get your tickets at the newsagent at 310 High St. As few people stopover in town, **accommodation** is very inexpensive: try the *Nagambie Goulburn Valley Highway Motel*, 143 High St (☏03/5794 2681; ❸–❹), or the *Nagambie Caravan Park* next door (☏03/5794 2681; on-site vans ❷).

The small city of **SHEPPARTON** is the operations centre for the SPC and Ardmona canned fruit companies, with peaches, pears, apples and plums tinned and exported worldwide; with its pleasant riverside picnic spots, it also makes a good place to stop for a while on the way to Echuca. The **Shepparton Visitor Information Centre** is located beside Victoria Park Lake in the south of town, at 534 Wyndham St on the Goulburn Valley Highway (daily 9am–5pm; ☏03/5831 4400 or free call 1800 808 839, ⊛www.shepparton.vic.gov.au). A good place **to stay** for budget travellers is the *River Road Holiday Camp* (☏03/5823 1656; dorms ❶–❷, motel units ❸) which has small dorms, a pool and tennis courts; during the harvest season from December to March there's a transport service to the farms.

The Hume Highway and Kelly Country

Forty-seven kilometres beyond Seymour, **EUROA** is a small, friendly town with many fine red-brick buildings. The **Euroa Visitor Information Centre** is located on the Hume Highway (daily 9am–5pm; ☏03/5795 3677 or 1300/134 610). Binney Street has a pleasant, old-fashioned feel, with the colourful and airy *Blue Dorset Deli* serving fresh coffee, gourmet sandwiches and other goods. For **accommodation**, try the *Euroa Caravan Park*, Kirkland Avenue (☏03/5795 2160; on-site vans ❷–❸), which sits by the creek among huge gum trees; or the *Castle Creek Motel*, on the Old Hume Highway (☏03/5795 2506; ❹), which has inexpensive units, a pool, large garden and laundry.

BENALLA, 45km northeast of Euroa on the Hume Highway, is a civilized town on the lake of the same name, formed by the Broken River which runs through town and occasionally floods it. There's a rose festival held here every November, which transforms the town's picnic spots and gardens. The helpful **Benalla Visitor Information Centre**, 14 Mair St (daily 9am–5pm;

☏03/5762 1749, ⓦhttp://users.hdc.com.au/~benallavic), has lots of pamphlets and information on the region, and can also book accommodation. In the same building, the **Costume and Pioneer Museum** ($3) displays a collection of women's dresses from the 1930s but more fittingly has a range of Ned Kelly relics, including the green silk cummerbund he was awarded as a child for saving a friend from drowning, and which he proudly wore when captured. The renovated **Benalla Art Gallery**, in a lovely setting across the lake (daily 10am–5pm; free), has a fine collection of early twentieth-century and contemporary Australian art. Benalla is Australia's main centre for **gliding** and is home to the biggest gliding club in the southern hemisphere; contact the Gliding Club of Victoria (☏03/5762 1058, ⓔgliding@benalla.net.au) to find out about flights.

If you want **to stay**, there's a new hostel, the well-equipped *Trekker's Rest* (☏03/5762 3535, ⓦwww.trekkersrest.com.au; dorms ❶–❷, rooms ❸), 1km out of town on the Kilfeera Road. For something to **eat** during the day, try *Hides Bakery* at 111 Bridge St, which prepares excellent vegetarian pies, salads and sandwiches and serves good coffee; in the evening two good choices are the very reasonable *Brigall's Caffe-Ristorante* on Bridge Street, for interesting wood-fired pizza; and the excellent contemporary Australian cuisine at *Raffetys*, 92 Nunn St (lunch Mon–Fri, dinner Mon–Sat; ☏03/5762 4066).

Glenrowan and Kelly's last stand

GLENROWAN, 29km on from Benalla, was the site of the **Kelly Gang's last stand**. You're never allowed to forget it: a gigantic effigy of Ned Kelly, in full iron-armour regalia, greets you as you enter town, and there are lots of other tawdry attractions along the highway, such as the **Last Stand Show** (daily 9.30am–4.30pm and Sat nights; 40min; $16), a "computerized animated theatre" using dummies shuffling around on cue to dramatize the story of the siege – your money's better spent elsewhere. The last stand itself took place in Siege Street near the train station. Along the rail lines north of town, a small stone monument marks the spot where Kelly forced railworkers to rip up a section of the track, to try to derail the trainful of troopers he had lured to the town – though visitors are asked to stay away as the site is dangerous. Overlooking the town to the west is Mount Glenrowan, which the bushrangers used as a lookout.

More interesting and far better value than the Last Stand Show is **Kate's Cottage and Ned Kelly Memorial** (daily 9am–5.30pm; $2.50), a replica of the Kelly home. With its bare earth floor, bark roof and newspaper-lined walls, it speaks volumes of the deprivation that drove the family towards crime. An evocative audiotape narrates Ned's story from childhood and is interspersed with folk songs inspired by his life. The original homestead, 9km west along Kelly Gap Road, is now nothing more than rubble and a brick chimney.

Wangaratta

The small city of **WANGARATTA**, at the junction of the Ovens and King rivers, 16km from Glenrowan, is a convenient overnight stop between Sydney and Melbourne, but there are few reasons to linger unless you're here for the famous four-day **Wangaratta Festival of Jazz** (☏03/5722 1666, ⓦwww.wangarattajazz.org.au). Beginning on the Friday prior to the Melbourne Cup (usually the last weekend in Oct), this is one of the pre-

The Ned Kelly story

Even before Ned Kelly became widely known, folklore and ballads were popularizing the free-ranging bush outlaws as potent symbols of freedom and resistance to authority. By the time he was 11, **Ned Kelly**, son of an alcoholic rustler and a mother who sold illicit liquor, was already in constant trouble with the police, who considered the whole family troublemakers; constables in the area were instructed to "endeavour, whenever the Kellys commit any paltry crime, to bring them to justice . . . the object [is] to take their prestige away from them".

Ned became the accomplice of the established bushranger **Harry Power**, and by his mid-teens had a string of warrants to his name. Ned's brother, Dan, was also wanted by the police and, hearing that he had turned up at his mother's, a policeman set out, drunk and without a warrant, to arrest him. A scuffle ensued and the unsteady constable fell to the floor, hitting his head and allowing Dan to escape. The following day warrants were issued for the arrest of Ned (who was in New South Wales at the time) and Dan for attempted murder; their mother was sentenced to three-years' imprisonment.

From this point on, the **Kelly gang**'s crime spree accelerated and, following the death of three constables in a shoot-out at Stringybark Creek, the biggest manhunt in Australia's history began, with a £1000 reward offered for the gang's apprehension. On December 9, 1878 they robbed the bank at Euroa, taking £2000, before moving on to Jerilderie in New South Wales, where another bank was robbed and Kelly penned the famous **Jerilderie Letter**, describing the "big, ugly, fat-necked, wombat-headed, big-bellied, magpie-legged, narrow-hipped, splay-footed sons of Irish bailiffs or English landlords which is better known as Officers of Justice or Victoria Police" who had forced him onto the wrong side of the law.

After a year on the run, the gang formulated a grand plan: they executed Aaron Sherritt, a police informer, in Sebastopol, thus attracting a trainbound posse from nearby Beechworth; this train was intended to be derailed at Glenrowan with as much bloodshed as possible before the gang moved on to rob the bank at Benalla and barter hostages for the release of Kelly's mother. In the event, having already sabotaged the tracks, the gang commandeered the *Glenrowan Inn* and, in a moment of drunken candour, Kelly detailed his ambush to a schoolteacher who escaped, managing to save the special train. As the armed troopers approached the inn, the gang donned the homemade **iron armour** that has since become their motif. In the ensuing gunfight Kelly's comrades were either killed or they committed suicide as the inn was torched, while Ned himself was taken alive, tried by the same judge who had incarcerated his mother, and sentenced to hang.

Public sympathies lay strongly with Ned Kelly, and a crowd of five thousand gathered outside Melbourne Gaol on November 11, 1880 for his execution, believing that the 25-year-old bushranger would "die game". True to form, his last words are said to have been **"Such is life."**

mier jazz events in the country, attracting national stars and international legends. Much of the city's accommodation is booked out two years in advance, so reserve ahead if you're planning to attend. The highway on either side of "Wang" is lined with motels, and the staff at **Wangaratta Tourist Information**, on the corner of Handley Street and Tone Road (daily 9am–5pm; ☏03/5721 5711 or free call 1800 801 065, Ⓦwww.wangaratta .vic.gov.au), can book local tours and accommodation and give out stacks of leaflets about the area. The **Wangaratta Arts Centre** on Ovens Street is a fine old red-brick building containing a gallery (daily noon–5pm; free; ☏03/5722 0865) which has a changing programme of exhibitions and hosts occasional music recitals on Sunday afternoon.

There is a vast range of **accommodation**. Good choices include the *Wangaratta Central Motel*, 11 Ely St, next to Merriwa Park (☎03/5721 2188; ❹); the *Billabong Motel*, 12 Chisholm St (☎03/5721 2353; ❸), with good-value singles; and the modern *Hermitage Motor Inn,* corner of Mackay and Cusack streets (☎03/5721 7444, ℱ5722 1812; ❺), which has a pool. In terms of **food**, *Scribbler's Cafe*, at 66 Reid St, serves good cakes and lunchtime fodder, while *Coffee.com*, at 74 Ovens St, has similar fare and internet access. Dinner is predominantly an Italian affair: the renowned *Café Martini* at the *Bull's Head Hotel*, 87 Murphy St, has great but pricey wood-fired pizza, while *D'Amico's* at the corner of Vincent and Greta roads has overcooked alternatives. For something a little more special, the bistro at the *Vine Hotel* on Detour Road serves excellent local food and wine in a congenial setting (☎03/5721 2605).

V/Line operates a daily **bus service** from Wangaratta to Bright via Beechworth, and a bus service three times a week to Rutherglen and once to Yarrawonga.

Beechworth

Thirty-five kilometres east of Wangaratta, off the Ovens Highway (also known as as the Great Alpine Road), is **BEECHWORTH**, once the centre of the rich **Ovens gold-mining region**. Sited picturesquely in the foothills of the Victorian Alps, the entire town has been acknowledged by the National Trust as being of historic significance, and the surrounding area has been designated a **historic park** by the Department of Conservation and Natural Resources. The **visitors information centre** is located in the fine old shire office on Ford Street (daily 9am–5pm; ☎03/5728 3233 or 1300/366 321, ⓦ www.beechworth.com/bworthinfo), and can book accommodation as well as provide you with pamphlets on places of interest, including the Gorge Scenic Drive (see below). They also have **internet** access.

As is true in so many other towns in the northeast, Beechworth is rich in **Ned Kelly** history. The **government buildings** on Ford Street house the imposing HM Training Prison, where he and his mother were incarcerated before the 1880 trial, and the **courthouse** (daily 9am–5pm; $2.50) where the fatal trial was held. Opposite, underneath the town hall, is the grim cell where he was imprisoned as a teenager (daily 10am–4pm; free). Other sights of interest in town include the **Burke Museum** on Loch Street (daily 10am–3.30pm; $5.50), which displays relics of the goldrush and tells the story of the Chinese miners who flocked here. The museum is dedicated to the explorer Robert O'Hara Burke, one-time Superintendent of Police in Beechworth, who perished with William John Wills on their historic journey from Melbourne to the Gulf of Carpentaria (see box on p.568). On Last Street the century-old **Murray Brewery Cellars** (daily 10am–4pm; free) is well worth a visit, not only for its free tastings and sales, but also for its National Trust display of twenty beautifully restored old carriages, including a Cobb & Co stagecoach.

The five-kilometre, one-way route of the **Gorge Scenic Drive** begins at Sydney Road and ends at Bridge Street, along the western edge of the town. It includes the famous Spring and Reid creeks, which supported eight thousand diggers in 1852, and an old storehouse for blasting powder known as the powder magazine, as well as natural features such as Flat Rock, Telegraph Rock and Woolshed Falls.

Practicalities

There's a very good choice of B&B **accommodation** in Beechworth: try *Rose Cottage*, 42 Camp St (☎03/5728 1069, ⓦ www.hotkey.net.au/~rose–cot; ❻), or

The Milawa Gourmet Region

The high country area of Victoria – and in particular the small town of MILAWA – is renowned amongst foodies for the excellent quality of its locally produced food and wine, so much so that it has been dubbed the Milawa Gourmet Region, and even the most urban of Melburnians have been known to make the two-hour trip just to stock up on dinner party supplies.

If it's a tipple of something special you're after, try a tour of the Brown Brothers Winery (daily 9am–5pm; ☎ 03/5720 5547, ⓦ www.brownbrothers.com.au), situated about 2km from Milawa; there's also a great café-restaurant here, the *Epicurean Centre* (daily 11am–3pm), which specializes in complementing Brown Brothers wines with unusual local foods. Back in the town, there's the Milawa Cheese Factory (daily 9am–5pm) on Factory Road, where you will find award-winning cheeses and another excellent café. At the crossroads nearby, Milawa Mustards (10am–5pm, closed Wed) offer seventeen home-made seed varieties, while Walkabout Apiary (daily 9am–4.30pm) on the Snow Road has a wide array of sticky, sweet honeys that put commercial brands to shame.

Milawa is situated around 15km southeast of Wangaratta on the Snow Road, which heads off east from the Hume Highway towards the Victorian Alps. Grapevine Getaways (☎ 02/6023 2599, ⓦ www.grapevinegetaways.com.au) operate a Milawa Meander tour, leaving Albury/Wodonga at 10am and returning about 4.30pm (Thurs–Sun only). The $60 price includes transport, all tastings and a two-course gourmet lunch, and includes visits to the Brown Brothers Winery, Milawa Cheese Factory and Milawa Mustards.

the *Apple Tree Cottage* on Frederick Street (☎ 03/5728 1044, ⓔ appletre@hotkey .net.au; ❻). Another good-value place is *The Old Priory*, on Priory Lane (a continuation of Loch St), almost at the corner of Church Street (☎ 03/5728 1024, ⓕ 5728 2035; ❹–❺), a historic B&B with very reasonably priced singles. If you want peace and quiet, it's best to come at the weekend, when the school groups have gone. The *Empire Hotel*, on Camp Street (☎ 03/5728 1030; ❹), and *Tanswells Commercial Hotel*, 30 Ford St (☎ 03/5728 1480; ❹), are historic pubs that also offer B&B accommodation. The latter has been continuously licensed since 1853 and has pleasant bars and bistro food.

The *Beechworth Bakery*, 27 Camp St (daily 6am–7pm) is famous all over Australia for its delicious pies, bread, cakes and pastries, and on sunny days you can have breakfast on the balcony. A good place for dinner is *Gigis*, 69 Ford St (☎ 03/5728 2575), though if you really want to splurge, head across the road to the *Bank Restaurant*, in the Bank of Australia building at 86 Ford St (licensed; ☎ 03/5728 2223). Depending on the day, dinners will either be formal and candlelit (Thurs–Sat) or a simpler, more rustic affair (Mon–Wed & Sun).

V/Line has a **bus service** from Wangaratta to Beechworth, and further on to Bright (2–3 daily Mon–Fri, 1 daily Sat & Sun), and Beechworth Buslines (☎ 03/5722 1843 or 0419 622 522) has a service twice daily (Mon–Fri) from Beechworth to Albury and Wodonga.

Chiltern

CHILTERN, a sleepy former gold-mining centre with a well-preserved, mid-nineteenth-century streetscape, lies just off the Hume Highway about 40km from Wangaratta. The setting – with a bit of recent architectural licence on Conness Street – has been used in several period films. Although no longer licensed, the **Star Hotel** is still set up with the original bar and taps, an authentic background to a rather more ordinary souvenir and craft shop. For $2 you can gain access to the back (Fri–Wed) to look at a **monster vine**: planted in 1867 and reputedly Australia's largest, it once produced a single yield of over 6kg of grapes. The 1866 **Athenaeum** (Sat, Sun & public holidays 10am–4pm; $2.20) is now a local history museum that features a collection of paintings by the obsessive local artist Alfred Eustace, who would use any available medium to paint on: paper, cardboard, even large gum leaves. **Dows Pharmacy Museum**, also on Conness Street (Sat, Sun & public holidays 1–4pm; $2.20), has an extensive collection of old pharmaceutical equipment. Chiltern's most interesting attraction, however, is the National Trust-owned **Lake View Homestead** (Sat, Sun & school holidays 1–4pm; $2.20), on the shores of Lake Anderson, near the train station. Built in 1870, it was for a short period the home of the writer Ethel Florence Lindesay (1870–1946), who, under the pseudonym **Henry Handel Richardson**, immortalized the house in the novel *Ultima Thule*, the last book in *The Fortunes of Richard Mahoney* trilogy. For **refreshment**, stop in at the *Mulberry Tree Restaurant and Tearooms* on Conness Street.

Rutherglen

RUTHERGLEN, 18km west of Chiltern and 32km west of Wodonga on the Murray River Highway, is at the heart of Victoria's oldest wine-producing region, renowned for its excellent fortified wines, Rutherglen Muscat and Tokay. Fifteen **wineries** are situated in the area, most of them third- or fourth-generation establishments with cellars full of character. The landscape is rather disappointing, consisting largely of flat paddocks of cattle and sheep where you'd expect undulating vineyards. In fact, wine making has always been just one of a range of farming activities in this area, where diversification remains the key to survival. The weather partly accounts for the quality of Rutherglen's fortified wines: the long, mild autumns allow the grapes to stay on the vines for longer, producing higher levels of sugar in the fruit. All the wineries are open for free **tastings** and cellar door sales Monday to Saturday from 10am to 5pm – Sunday hours differ from place to place.

The **tourist information centre**, at 13–21 Drummond St (daily 9am–5pm; ☏ 02/6032 9166), has stacks of brochures, including the informative *Rutherglen Touring Guide* and map published by the wine makers of Rutherglen. Besides selling local wines, the Vintage Cellar, 84 Main St (☏ 02/6032 9784), also rents out bicycles. On the Queen's Birthday weekend in June the town hosts the **Winery Walkabout** – one of Australia's biggest wine-tasting festivals, when the new season's releases are presented to the public. Another festive event, the **Tastes of Rutherglen**, is held over the Victorian Labour Day weekend in mid-March, and sees some of the best local restaurants guest-staring at the wineries.

Rutherglen is a popular weekend getaway from Melbourne, so **accommodation** can be hard to find at that time; during the week you'll have no problem. The focus of the small town is the excellent, National Trust-listed *Victoria Hotel*, 90 Main St (☏ 02/6032 9610, ☎ 6032 8128; ❸–❹), where you can both eat and sleep well. On the walls of the bar is a framed cover of the June 28, 1880 *Melbourne Herald* chronicling the capture of the Kelly Gang, which makes for fascinating reading. Alternatively, a good-value B&B is *Country Cottage Accommodation* (☏ 02/6032 8328; ❺), or there's the *Walkabout Motel* (☏ 02/6032 9572, ☎ 6032 8187; ❹–❺), both on the Murray Valley Highway. The wineries all offer delicious, if expensive, gourmet **food**.

The Snowfields and the High Country

The **Victorian Alps**, the southern extension of the Great Dividing Range, bear little resemblance to their European counterparts; they're too gentle, too rounded, and above all too low to offer really great **skiing**. Nonetheless in July and August there is usually plenty of snow, and the resorts are packed out. Most people come here for the downhill skiing, though the **cross-country skiing**, which is rapidly growing in popularity, is excellent: **Lake Mountain**, 21km from Marysville, is the region's premier cross-country destination. **Snowboarding** was first encouraged at Mount Hotham and is now firmly established almost everywhere. **Falls Creek**, **Mount Hotham** and **Mount Buller** are the largest and most commercial skiing areas, particularly the last which is within easy reach of Melbourne; smaller resorts such as **Mount Baw Baw** are more suited to beginners. While you wouldn't come to Victoria especially to ski, you might as well give it a go if you're here at the right time of year, though be warned that accommodation is very pricey.

In summer, when the wild flowers are in bloom, the alps are ideal **bushwalking** territory, with most of the high mountains (and the ski resorts) contained within the vast **Alpine National Park**. The most famous of the walks is the four-hundred-kilometre **Alpine Trail**, which begins in Baw Baw National Park, near Walhalla in Gippsland, and follows the ridges all the way to Mount Kosciuszko in the Snowy Mountains of New South Wales. If you are doing any serious bushwalking, you'll need to be properly equipped. Even in summer it can be very cold up here, especially at night, and the weather can change suddenly and unexpectedly; it's often also surprisingly hard to find water. **Mansfield** and **Bright** are good bases for exploration of the alps and great places to unwind. In summer the ski resorts can be ugly and only half the facilities are open, but there are often great bargains to be had on rooms.

If you're **driving**, you'll need snow chains in winter (they're compulsory in many parts), and you should heed local advice before venturing off the main roads.

Mansfield and Merrijig

MANSFIELD is located at the junction of the Maroondah and Midland highways, just a few kilometres north of Lake Eildon, 140km east of Seymour and 63km south of Benalla. As the main approach to Mount Buller, it's a lively place with good pubs, restaurants and a cinema. The annual highlight is the **Mountain Country Festival** in early November, which begins the weekend prior to the Melbourne Cup in Nov; activities include a picnic race known as the "Melbourne Cup of the bush". At the end of April hundreds of hot-air-balloon pilots flock here for the three-day **Mansfield Balloon Festival**.

V/Line has a year-round **bus** service from Melbourne to Mansfield (1–2 daily; 3hr). The helpful **Mansfield Visitor Information Centre** on the Maroondah Highway (daily 9am–5pm; ☎03/5775 1464 or free call 1800 060 686 for accommodation bookings, Ⓦwww.mansfield-mtbuller.com.au), has complete information on all sights and **activities**, including skiing and walks in the surrounding country. Out of the snow season you have a choice of horse riding, hiking, climbing, abseiling, hang-gliding, rafting, canoeing or 4WD tours. Among the many local outfits are Stirling Experience (☎03/5775 3541; Ⓦwww.stirling.com.au), for 4WD tours around Mount Buller and Mount Stirling (see p.1036); Stoney's Bluff and Beyond Trail Rides (☎03/5775 2212, Ⓦwww.stoneys.com.au), for great trail rides; and Mountain Adventure Safaris

(☎ 03/5777 3759 or free call 1800 642 234), for rafting, canoeing, abseiling and other activities.

The *Alzburg Inn Resort*, 39 Malcolm St (☎ 03/5775 2367 or free call 1800 033 023, Ⓦ www.alzburg.com.au; rooms ❸, self-contained units ❹), is a popular **hotel** for skiers, while the neat and friendly *Mansfield Traveller's Lodge*, at 112 High St (☎ 03/5775 1800, Ⓕ 5775 1589; motel rooms ❹, dorms ❶), has a backpacker wing and organizes all sorts of activities, particularly hang-gliding. The managers also have good work contacts for fruit-picking in summer and for the Mount Buller ski resort in winter. The area around Mansfield is renowned for **luxurious B&Bs**, the most famous of which is the very expensive *Howqua Dale Gourmet Retreat*, south of town near Howqua (☎ 03/5777 3503, Ⓕ 5777 3896; two nights $770, three nights $1155 all inclusive), which is run by two chefs and is renowned for its outstanding food; aspiring chefs might be tempted to attend one of their weekend cooking courses ($880 per person). On a more modest scale, *Willawong Bed & Breakfast Gallery* at 12 Mt Buller Rd, Merrijig (☎ 03/5777 5750, Ⓦ www.willawongbnb.com.au; ❻), offers European-style accommodation in a gorgeous, wooden house set in a lovely garden at the foot of the Alps, or there are four cottages with private spas at *Alpine Country Cottages*, 5 The Parade, Mansfield (☎ 03/5775 1694, Ⓕ 5775 1586, Ⓦ www.alpinecc.com.au; ❼ –❽).

In winter, Mansfield–Buller Bus Lines run frequent bus services for skiing from Mansfield to Mount Buller in conjunction with the V/Line bus service from Melbourne to Mansfield (☎ 03/5775 2606). In summer there are two services a day with Mansfield–Buller Bus Lines from Mansfield to Mount Buller via Merrijig (booking essential on ☎ 0417 307 504).

Merrijig

The small town of **MERRIJIG**, a little under halfway to Mount Buller from Mansfield, is largely responsible for the great number of **riding** outfits in the area. The breathtaking high-country scenery nearby was used as the location for the film *The Man from Snowy River*, and visitors have been trying to live out their fantasies ever since. If you want to combine riding with lodge **accommodation**, try *Merrijig Lodge and Trail Rides*, Mount Buller Road (☎ 03/5777 5590; dorms ❶, rooms ❻ –❽).

Mount Buller and Mount Stirling

To reach **MOUNT BULLER ALPINE VILLAGE**, 48km from Mansfield, you ascend gradually upwards on Summit Road, a smooth, sealed road. With 7000 beds, 24 modern ski lifts and 80km of runs, it has the greatest capacity of any Australian ski resort. In **winter**, during the ski season, the Central Reservation Service books **accommodation** and dispenses information about all things skiing (☎ 03/9809 0291 or free call 1800 039 049; in summer, call the Mansfield Visitor Information Centre on ☎ 03/5775 1464 or free call 1800 060 686, Ⓦ www.mtbuller.com.au). The *ABOM Hotel & Bistro*, on Summit Road on Mount Buller (☎ 03/5777 6091 or free call 1800 810 200; ❽), is the hub of the Alpine Village when it is open in winter. There are great views from here, and further up, on the **summit** of Mount Buller, there's an even more spectacular panorama west to Lake Eildon, north to farmlands and east to Falls Creek and Mount Hotham. The huge *Arlberg Hotel*, 53 Summit Rd (☎ 03/5777 6298 or free call 1800 032 380; summer ❺, winter ❽), provides entertainment in ski season, and has everything from fast food to an expensive restaurant; alongside its rooms it also has some six-person self-contained apartments (summer $185, winter $660). More reasonably-priced, although still excellent, is the B&B *Duck*

Inn (☎ 03/5777 6326; summer ❼, winter ❼–❽). In winter the truly budget-conscious can stay at the *YHA Lodge*, on The Avenue right in the centre of the Village (☎ 03/5777 6181, ✉ mountbuller@yhavic.org.au; open June–Sept; dorms ❸–❹), which has self-catering facilities; advance booking (available from March 1) is essential. The self-catering *ABV Lodge* (☎ 03/9848 3309; summer ❷, winter ❹) has dorm beds in bunk rooms and is open all year round; there's a two-night minimum stay at weekends.

Mount Stirling, a few kilometres northeast, has more than 60km of maintained trails and is a good place for **cross-country skiing**. The only facility here is Mount Stirling Alpine Resort, a large complex at Telephone Box Junction, 9km from the turn-off left at Mirindah along Mount Stirling Road (☎ 03/5777 6441, ⓦ www.stirling.au.com); within the complex there's a visitor centre and a ski school (☎ 03/5777 6441), and ski rental is also available. As it's a day-resort, there's no accommodation in the complex itself, but the owners do have bunkroom and loft dormitories on a nearby farm, *Wairere Lodge* (☎ 03/5777 3541, ⓦ www.stirling.au.com; ❶), about 45 minutes from the mountain; in summer (Oct–June) there's a minimum booking of four people allowed ($20 per person); in winter, you'll have to hire out the whole place (sleeps 24; $300 first night, $220 thereafter). All roads beyond Telephone Box

Skiing practicalities

The official start of the ski season is the Queen's Birthday long weekend in June (though there may not be enough snow cover until Aug), lasting through to October. Day-trip or weekend packages are the best way to go, and are far cheaper than trying to do it yourself. The best value for money are the day-trips organized by the *Alzburg Inn* at Mansfield (free call ☎ 1800 033 023, ⓦ www.alzburg.com.au), as they leave Melbourne at 4am in the morning and arrive at Mount Buller at about 9am, giving the opportunity for a full day's skiing ($110–120, including a lift pass and beginner's ski lesson). It's also worth checking out the area around Hardware Street in Melbourne, where such companies as Ski Haus at no. 17 (☎ 03/9670 2855), Auski at no. 9 (☎ 03/9670 1412), Mountain Designs at 377 Little Bourke St (☎ 03/9670 3354) and Paddy Palin (☎ 03/9670 4845) at 360 Little Bourke St, can advise on skiing conditions at the resorts, and sell or rent equipment. In South Melbourne at 295 Clarendon St, Ski Man (☎ 03/9696 4955) also sells and rents out equipment.

The Alpine Resorts Commission (☎ 03/9895 6900) administers the resorts and during the ski season it charges an entry fee of $17.50–20 per car, depending on resort. For weather and snow conditions, call the Snow Reports Line (☎ 1902/240 523); accommodation bookings are organized by Alpine Reservations Australia (☎ 03/9455 1277), or phone the central reservation hotlines of each mountain resort. The free *Australian Alpine News* is good for facts and is available at the Visitor Information Centre in Melbourne as well as in the Alpine region. As a rough guide to costs, a ski pass at Mount Buller is $55–65 per day, ski school $55 (limited pass) or $99 (full pass) per day, and full equipment rental $55 per day.

During the season Mansfield–Mount Buller Bus Lines, 133 High St, Mansfield (☎ 03/5775 2606), operates a ski transport service to Mount Buller; and Stirling Experience (☎ 03/5777 6441) runs a daily service from Mansfield and Merrijig to Mount Stirling (prebooking essential; price depends on number of people). In Bright, Adina Ski Hire, 15 Ireland St (☎ 03/5755 1177), and Bright Ski Centre, 22 Ireland St (☎ 03/5755 1093), rent out skiing and snowboarding equipment, offer package deals including off-mountain accommodation and transport to Mount Hotham, and have up-to-date snow reports and information on road conditions. There's no transport to Mount Buffalo.

Junction are open only from the beginning of November until the beginning of June, weather permitting. The fifty-kilometre **Circuit Road** from Telephone Box Junction circumnavigates Mount Stirling, and a 4WD access track from this road leads to **Craig's Hut**, which was used as a film set for *The Man from Snowy River*. As sections of Circuit Road are very rough for 2WD vehicles even in good weather conditions, you'll really need a 4WD for this route. In summer, Stirling Experience (℡ 03/5775 3541) does 4WD **tours** to Craig's Hut and other destinations around the Mount Buller–Mount Stirling area.

Bright

BRIGHT is at the centre of the picturesque Ovens Valley, between Mount Buffalo and Mount Beauty about 75km southeast of Wangaratta on the Ovens Highway. It began life as a gold-mining town in the 1850s and today still has a faintly elegant air, with tall European trees lining the main street and filling the parks. A clear stream flows through Centennial Park, opposite the tourist information centre, and in autumn the glorious colours of the changing leaves make for a very un-Australian scene.

As the ski fields of Mount Hotham, Mount Buffalo and Falls Creek are less than an hour's drive away, the town is popular as a **ski base** in winter. In summer **outdoor activities** are on offer – such as paragliding, hang-gliding, bushwalking, horse riding and cycling. Alpine Paragliding, 6 Ireland St (℡ 03/5755 1753), organizes tandem flights for novices, and introductory and full courses leading to a licence. You could also take to the air in a powered hang-glider from Bright Micro-Light Centre (℡ 03/5750 1555) or with the Eagle School of Hang-Gliding (℡ 03/5750 1174 or 0428 570 168), who also do very enjoyable instructor-accompanied tandem flights. Or enjoy a bird's-eye view of the gorgeous mountain scenery from a small plane with Holiday Air Adventures (℡ 03/5753 5250). Freeburgh Trail Rides, on Harrietville Road in Freeburgh, about 4km north of Bright (℡ 03/5755 1370), do very good short horseback rides for beginners; they also have longer rides and can arrange overnight safaris with bushcamping.

For a change of pace, visit Boynton's of Bright, a **winery** 10km northwest of Bright at Porepunkah, on the northeast slopes of the Ovens River Valley, which specializes in cool-climate wines (daily 10am–5pm; ℡ 03/5756 2356). There's a café here, open from 11am to 4pm on summer weekends, and a picnic area on its lawns, with spectacular views of Mount Buffalo. Alternatively, head south to nearby **WANDILIGONG**, a beautiful village that's entirely owned by the National Trust, where you'll find the *Wandiligong Café* and **maze** (Wed–Sun 10am–5pm). The maze itself is a lot of fun but the café, serving salads, freshly squeezed juices and home-made treats, and set in a tranquil garden at the end of a 6km bushwalk from Bright, is a truly wonderful find.

Practicalities

V/Line operates a **bus** service to Bright from Wangaratta (daily except Sat; 1hr 15min). To **get around**, you can rent a mountain bike from the Sports Centre, 47 Gavan St (℡ 03/5755 1339) or Cyclepath, 9 Camp St (℡ 03/5750 1442) – both outfits also arrange biking tours. The **tourist information centre**, at 119 Gavan St (daily 9am–5pm; ℡ 03/5755 2275, ⓦ www.home.aone.net.au/bright), has complete information on what's happening around town and also books accommodation particularly helpful in the busy winter season. There's also an excellent internet café in the same building.

One of the best budget **places to stay** is the *Bright Hikers Hostel* at 4 Ireland St (℡ 03/5750 1244, ⓕ 5750 1246, ⓦ http://brightbackpackers.netc.net.au; rooms ❸, dorms ❶), right in the centre of town. Its wide range of facilities includes a games room and an internet lounge. The excellent *Ellenvale Holiday Units*, east of town at 68 Delany Ave (℡ 03/5755 1582; ❹–❺), has a solar-heated pool and spa, tennis court and barbecues. Also good-value, and with similar facilities, are the *Mystic Valley Cottages*, 9 Mystic Lane, 2km southeast on the way to Wandiligong (℡ 03/5750 1502; $350–800 per week), situated on a hill overlooking the beautiful Wandiligong Valley. A great B&B option is *Knox Farm* (℡ 0417 367 494; ❼), five minutes from Bright in the Wandiligong Valley, which has just one fantastic room – self-contained, with a spa and a wooden balcony with beautiful mountain views. *Buckland Valley Retreat* (℡ 03/5756 2656; ❻), out of town on the Buckland Valley Road, offers meals, meditation and massage in a gorgeous bush setting. The best-value **motels** in Bright are the centrally located *Elm Lodge Holiday Motel*, 2 Wood St (free call ℡ 1800 245 845, ℻ 03/5755 2206; ❸–❹), and the charming century-old *Alpine Hotel*, 7 Anderson St (℡ 03/5755 1366; ❸). The latter is the focal point of town, with a rowdy bar, good-value bistro meals and excellent breakfasts; the back bar has **bands** on Friday night, and outside there's a sunny beer garden.

Other good **places to eat** are the *Liquid Am-Bar Restaurant Cafe*, opposite the *Alpine Hotel*, which (besides the amber fluid alluded to in its name) also serves good coffee; the *Riverdeck Café* at the tourist information centre, which sells great deli sandwiches; and the *Bright Bakery* at 80 Gavan St. Two cheap, casual family restaurants are *Tin Dog Pizza* at 94 Gavan St, and the *Cosy Kangaroo* across the street. For a treat head to *Poplar's Restaurant*, at 4/7 Star Rd (open daily for dinner; licensed and BYO; ℡ 03/5755 1655), or *Simone's*, at the *Ovens Valley Motor Inn*, at the corner of Ovens Highway and Ashwood Avenue (open daily for dinner; licensed; ℡ 03/5755 2022), which ranks as one of the top Italian restaurants in Victoria. Its offshoot is the equally reputable *Cafe Bacco* at 2D Anderson St (Wed–Sun lunch and dinner; ℡ 03/5750 1711).

Mount Hotham and around

Heading southeast out of Bright on the Alpine Tourist Road, it's 18km to **HAR-RIETVILLE**, tucked just below Mount Hotham and Mount Feathertop. Originally a gold-mining town, it's now a pretty little village of wide, tree-lined streets, and is also a popular skiing base: there are outlets to rent skis and chains, a seasonal shuttle bus service up to the resorts, and several places to stay and eat. Beyond Harrietville, it's a steep ascent to **Mount Hotham** in the Alpine National Park, the "powder snow capital of Australia". Because this is the state's highest ski area, the snow here can be marginally less sticky than elsewhere. **Dinner Plain**, a resort 8km from the summit and about 1500m above sea level, has much more of a cosy, alpine village feel – complete with architect-designed timber houses that are meant to resemble cattlemen's mountain huts – than the somewhat unsightly Hotham "village". **Cross-country trails** lead from Hotham to Dinner Plain. Hotham is also considered the home of Victorian **snowboarding**, with special facilities, rental and lessons available. During the ski season tractor-driven carts ferry you around the village and to the start of cross-country trails and skiing areas (all day until late; free), and helicopter shuttle flights in winter link Mount Hotham with Falls Creek, only a few minutes away by air. A few lodges and pubs stay open in summer, including the *General Hotel*, which has a bar, bistro, bottle shop and fantastic mountain views. Hotham is set to expand and become a lively all-year **resort**: plans are underway to expand the airstrip at Horsehair Plain, 20km south, into a fully fledged airport capable of handling seventy-seater jet planes.

A few centres handle bookings for the mainly lodge-style **accommodation**: for Mount Hotham there's the Mount Hotham Ski Company (℡ 03/5759

4444) or Mt Hotham Alpine Accommodation Services (☎03/5759 3636 or free call 1800 246 462); for Dinner Plain try the Mount Hotham Falls Creek Reservation Centre (free call ☎1800 354 555) or Dinner Plain Central Reservations (free call ☎1800 670 019).

Falls Creek

Thirty kilometres east of Bright, in the Upper Kiewa Valley, the town of **Mount Beauty** lies at the base of the state's highest peak, **Mount Bogong** (1986m). **FALLS CREEK**, 32km further along, on the edge of the Bogong High Plains, has a much more villagey feel than its sister resort at Mount Hotham. It also has probably Victoria's **best skiing**, with the largest snow-making system in Victoria to supplement any shortage of the real stuff, a wide variety of downhill pistes, and good cross-country trails. A park for **snowboarders** has been established, too, in the Vertigo Valley near the Scott's Chair ski lift. For **accommodation** bookings and information, contact Falls Creek Central Reservations (free call ☎1800 033 079), or ask at the **Mount Beauty Visitor Information Centre** (daily 9am–5pm, ☎03/5754 4531 or free call 1800 808 277, ⓦ www.mtbeauty.com) on the Bogong High Plains Road in the town. The budget-conscious would do best to stay in Mount Beauty and travel to Falls Creek for their skiing: enquire about packages at the Mount Beauty Accommodation Service (☎03/5754 1267 or free call 1800 636 239). Accommodation options in the valley include *Mountain Creek Lodge* in Tawonga (☎03/5754 4247, Ⓕ 5754 4860; motel units ❺–❻, dorms ❷), and the wonderful *Brae View* in Mount Beauty (☎03/5754 4746, ⓦ www.braeview.com.au; ❻–❽).

Many of the pubs, restaurants and lodges in Falls Creek stay open in **summer**: some of the best are *The Cock 'n' Bull*, a pleasant old-English-style pub on the corner of Christie and Slalom streets, *The Man*, a cosy pub on Telemark Street, and the *Winterhaven Restaurant* on Slalom Street. There's a wide variety of summer **activities** from which to choose: Falls Creek Trail Rides (☎03/5758 3655 or 0419 244 773), operating from December to the end of April, has day-rides on the Bogong High Plains for around $80 per day as well as shorter trips, and Dinner Plain Trail Rides (☎03/5159 6661, ⓦ www.horsetreks.com) offers fully-inclusive overnight horse treks from $160 per day. Halleys Comet Quad Chairlift (☎03/5758 3280) takes bushwalkers to the top of Frying Pan Spur (Dec 26–Jan 26/27 daily 11am–3pm, Labour Day & Easter weekend same hours; $11); and nature lovers can join Jill from the Australian Alpine Nursery on one of her Alpine Nature Rambles (☎03/5758 3492, ⓦ www.rambles.com.au/rambles; $100–120 per walk for a minimum of four people). From December until the end of April, Bogong Horseback Adventures (☎03/5754 4849, Ⓕ 5754 4181, ⓦ www.bogonghorse.com.au), based on a farm at Tawonga near Mount Beauty, organizes five- to twelve-night **packhorse tours** across the high plains ($1530–2900 per person), traversing country that is otherwise only accessible to the most experienced and hardy bushwalkers; the rest of the year they run all-inclusive food, wine and riding weekends through the Kiewa Valley and the lower levels of the Alpine National Park (from $429 per person). As for **festivals**, the entire village of Falls Creek, plus visitors, get together to celebrate the Food, Wine & Wildflower Weekend in mid-January.

Mount Buffalo National Park

Six kilometres northwest of Bright, back along the Ovens Highway, you can turn off into **Mount Buffalo National Park** ($9 per car in summer, $12.50

in winter), which encompasses a huge plateau around Mount Buffalo. **Skiing** here is for beginners to intermediates – and it's a gorgeous place to learn, among surreal-looking snow-covered gum trees. Relatively inexpensive packages, including accommodation at the *Mount Buffalo Chalet* (see below), ski lessons and other fees, can be arranged through Mount Buffalo Reservations (free call ⓉUP1800 037 038). The *Mount Buffalo Lodge*, a tiny resort at the ski slopes of the Cresta Valley (Ⓣ03/5755 1988) has motel units (summer ❻, winter ❼), lodge rooms (❻) and bunkhouse dorm beds (summer ❷, winter ❸) – all subject to a two-night minimum stay. There are also kitchen facilities, a bistro and restaurant.

The park looks at its best in **summer**, though, when there are wild flowers and waterfalls, and it's a great place for walking, water sports and other outdoor activities. Among the main attractions is *Mount Buffalo Chalet* (Ⓣ03/5755 1500, Ⓕ5755 1892, Ⓦwww.mtbuffalochalet.com.au; ❽ full board), about a forty-minute drive on a sealed road from the Ovens Highway turn-off. Built by the Victorian government in 1910, it's very Australian in appearance, with a bottle-green tin roof, but is European in feel, surrounded by flowers and magnificent views. You can play croquet on the lawn, and there's a sauna, billiard room, games room and tennis court, plus horse riding (summer only), and canoes and mountain bikes for rent. The *Chalet Café* (daily 9.30am–4.30pm) is a no-frills, no-views cafeteria; if you want to have a proper meal, reserve a place in the main dining room. On the way to the chalet, you'll pass **Lake Catani**, where there's the only **camping** in the park (Nov–April; booking essential on Ⓣ03/5755 1466, or through Parks Victoria on Ⓣ13 1963), as well as swimming, canoeing, kayaking and trout-fishing; the chalet rents out equipment. **Bent's Lookout**, opposite the chalet, has tremendous views over the Ovens Valley, with small stone cabins doing duty as winter picnic areas. There's a **hang-gliding ramp** near here: if you're experienced and want to leap into the void, contact one of the operators in or near Bright (see p.1038). Beyond the chalet a sealed, not too steep road continues to Mount Buffalo itself (1721m).

Mount Baw Baw

The ski village at **MOUNT BAW BAW**, near the edge of the Baw Baw National Park, is considerably south of all the resorts and is, strictly speaking, in Gippsland. It's a quiet little place, commanding magnificent views south over much of Gippsland and consisting mainly of **private lodges** (reservations on free call Ⓣ1800 629 578). Otherwise, try the *Cascades Apartments* (Ⓣ03/9764 9939 or free call 1800 229 229, Ⓦwww.bawbaw.net.au). There are nine ski lifts here, and a lift day-pass costs about $50, a much more reasonable price than at other resorts. As at Mount Buffalo, the ski runs are mainly for beginners and intermediates. In addition to **downhill skiing**, you can ski **cross-country** on 9km of groomed trails.

Getting to the resort is a major problem. There's **no public transport** to the mountain, and the closest town is Noojee, 48km west. The road between the town and the resort is narrow, steep and winding. To make matters worse, there are lots of logging trucks thundering along, so take care. For more on Mount Baw Baw, see the **website** Ⓦwww.bawbawr.com.au.

TRAVEL DETAILS

V/Line monopolizes transport within Victoria, with a comprehensive combination of **train** and **bus** services; Melbourne, Ballarat and Geelong are the main interchanges. Following are the main V/Line Victorian services; local buses are detailed in the text. Timetables are subject to frequent change – call V/Line on Ⓣ13 6196 or consult Ⓦwww.vlinepassenger.com for the latest information.

Trains

Melbourne to: Albury (3 daily; 3hr 25min) via Euroa (1hr 30min), Benalla (2hr) and Wangaratta (2hr 30min); Ballarat (6–11 daily; 1hr 30min); Bendigo (5–9 daily; 2hr) via Castlemaine (1hr 35min); Echuca (2 daily; 3hr 20min) via Bendigo (2hr); Geelong (9–24 daily; 1hr); Sale (1–3 Mon–Sat; 2hr 35min); Shepparton (1–2 daily; 2hr 10min); Swan Hill (2 daily; 4hr 10min) via Castlemaine (1hr 35min) and Bendigo (2hr); Warrnambool (1–3 daily; 3hr 15min) via Geelong (1hr) and Colac (1hr 50min).

Buses

Apollo Bay to: Geelong (2–3 daily; 2hr 30min); Lorne (1–2 daily; 55min); Warrnambool (1 weekly; 3hr 20min) via Twelve Apostles (1hr 25min), Port Campbell (1hr 55min); Torquay (1–2 daily; 2hr).

Ballarat to: Bendigo (5 weekly; 2hr); Castlemaine (2 weekly; 1hr 45min); Daylesford (6 weekly; 1hr); Hamilton via Dunkeld (1–2 daily; 2hr 15min); Horsham (6 weekly; 2hr 55min); Maryborough (1 weekly; 1hr); Mildura (6 weekly; 7hr 50min); Warrnambool (5 weekly; 2hr 40min).

Beechworth to: Bright (1–2 daily; 1hr); Wangaratta (1–3 daily; 30min).

Bendigo to: Echuca (3–5 daily; 1hr 20min); Geelong (5 weekly; 4hr); Horsham (daily; 3hr 15min); Swan Hill (1–3 daily; 2hr 20min).

Bright to: Beechworth (1–2 daily; 1hr); Wangaratta (1–3 daily; 1hr 25min).

Castlemaine to: Ballarat (6 weekly; 1hr 45min); Maryborough (1–4 daily; 55min).

Cowes to: Melbourne (1–4 daily; 3hr 15min).

Echuca to: Albury (4 weekly; 4hr 55min); Bendigo (2–3 daily; 1hr 20min); Melbourne (4–6 daily; 3hr); Rutherglen (4 weekly; 4hr 5min); Shepparton (4 weekly; 1hr 50min); Swan Hill (daily; 1hr 55min).

Foster (closest to Wilson's Promontory NP) to: Melbourne (daily; 2hr 40min).

Geelong to: Apollo Bay (2–4 daily; 2hr 55min); Ballarat (2–4 daily; 1hr 20min); **Bendigo** (5 weekly; 4hr); Lorne (2–4 daily; 1hr 50min); Maryborough (1 weekly; 2hr 30min); Mildura (1 weekly; 9hr); Torquay (2–4 daily; 45min).

Halls Gap (Grampians) to: Stawell (daily; 35min).

Hamilton to: Ballarat (1–2 daily; 2hr 15min); Warrnambool (1–2 daily; 1hr 30min).

Horsham to: Ararat (6 weekly; 1hr 35min); Ballarat (6 weekly; 1hr 50min); Stawell (6 weekly; 1hr 10min).

Lakes Entrance to: Bairnsdale (1–4 daily; 35min); Canberra (2 weekly; 6hr 15min); Cann River (daily; 1hr 45min); Orbost (daily; 45min); Sale (1–3 daily; 1hr 40min).

Mansfield to: Melbourne (6 weekly, during snow season 7 weekly; 3hr); Mount Buller (snow season only;1–3 daily; 1hr).

Maryborough to: Ballarat (6 weekly; 1hr); Castlemaine (1–4 daily; 55min).

Mildura to: Ballarat (6 weekly; 7hr 50min); Geelong (1 weekly; 9hr); Swan Hill (1–2 daily; 2hr 30min).

Mount Beauty to: Melbourne (1 weekly; 5hr 30min).

Mount Buller to: Mansfield (snow season only; 1 daily; 1hr).

Portland to: Mount Gambier (1–2 daily; 1hr 30min); Port Fairy (1–2 daily; 1hr); Warrnambool (1–2 daily; 1hr 30min).

Sale to: Bairnsdale (1–3 daily; 1hr); Canberra (2 weekly; 7hr 40min); Cann River (daily; 3hr 10min); Lakes Entrance (1–3 daily; 1hr 40min); Orbost (daily; 2hr).

Shepparton to: Melbourne (1–2 daily; 3hr).

Stawell to: Ballarat (daily; 1hr 40min); Halls Gap (Grampians; daily; 35min); Horsham (6 weekly; 1hr 10min).

Swan Hill to: Albury (daily; 6hr 20min); Bendigo (1–3 daily; 3hr); Echuca (daily; 1hr 55min); Mildura (1–2 daily; 2hr 30min).

Wangaratta to: Beechworth (1–2 daily; 30min); Bendigo (3 weekly; 4hr 25min); Bright (1–3 daily; 1hr 25min); Mount Beauty (2 weekly; 1hr 30min); Rutherglen (6 weekly; 50min).

Warrnambool to: Apollo Bay (1–2 weekly; 3hr 20min); Ballarat (5 weekly; 2hr 40min); Casterton (7 weekly; 2hr 25min); Hamilton (6 weekly; 1hr 30min); Mount Gambier (1–2 daily; 3hr); Port Fairy (1–3 daily; 40min); Portland (1–2 daily; 1hr 30min).

Flights

Albury to: Melbourne (2–8 daily; 50min).
Mildura to: Melbourne (3–8 daily; 1hr 10min).

Portland to: Melbourne (1–3 daily; 40min).

Tasmania

CHAPTER 11

Highlights

✳ **Salamanca Market** – Lined with old stone warehouses and characterful old pubs, Hobart's Salamanca Place comes alive for its colourful open-air Saturday market. **p.1061**.

✳ **Port Arthur** – The infamous old penal settlement is the biggest draw on the wild, scenic Tasman Peninsula. **p.1079**.

✳ **Freycinet National Park** – The hike to exquisite Wine Glass Bay is one of the finest walks in the glorious Freycinet National Park. **p.1084**.

✳ **Arthur River cruise** – See the largest tract of temperate rainforest found anywhere in the world on the five-hour Arthur River cruise. **p.1122**.

✳ **Gordon River cruise** – A cruise up the dark, brown Gordon River is the best way to get a glimpse of the World Heritage-listed wilderness. **p.1128**.

✳ **Cradle Mountain–Lake St Clair National Park** – Famed for its gruelling Overland Track bushwalk, Cradle Mountain/Lake St Clair National Park is one of the most glaciated areas in Australia, with many lakes and tarns. **p.1131**.

✳ **Franklin River** – Raft one of Australia's most dangerous rivers – or see it safely from above on a seaplane flight. **p.1135**.

Tasmania

here's an otherworldly quality to **Tasmania**, with its gothic landscape of rain clouds and brooding mountains. This was a prison island whose name, Van Diemen's Land, was so redolent with horror that when convict transport ended in 1852 it was immediately changed. Yet the island has another, friendlier side to it too, with distances comprehensible to a European traveller – it's roughly the size of Ireland – and resonant echoes of England: cream teas, old-fashioned B&Bs and amiable, homespun people. In winter, when the grass is green, the gentle and cultivated midlands, with their rolling hills, dry stone walls and old stone villages, are reminiscent of England's West Country. Town names, too, invariably invoke the British Isles – Perth, Swansea, Brighton and Somerset among them. It's a "mainlander's" joke that Tasmania is twenty years behind the rest of Australia, and it's true that in some ways it is very old-fashioned, a trait that is by turn charming and frustrating. However, things are changing fast: with a new arts festival and a literary festival, the island is keen to promote itself as a cultural centre, and most towns now have internet access (see p.1052) thanks to federal government funding.

Tasmania is the closest point in Australia to the Antarctic Circle, and the **west coast** is wild, wet and savage, bearing the full brunt of the Roaring Forties. Inland, the **southwest** has wild rivers, impassable temperate rainforests, buttongrass plains, and glacially carved mountains and tarns that have been linked to create a vast **World Heritage Area**. This region – crossed only by the Lyell Highway – extends from the South West National Park, through the Franklin Lower Gordon Wild Rivers National Park, and across to the Cradle Mountain–Lake St Clair National Park, providing some of the world's best wilderness walking and rafting. It's the stage for frequent and dramatic conflicts between conservationists and the logging and mining communities, but is still one of the cleanest places on earth, and a wilderness walk, where you can

Accommodation price codes

All the accommodation listed in this book has been categorized into one of eight price bands, as set out below. The rates quoted represent the cheapest available double or twin room in high season – except for category ❶, which indicates per-person rates for a dorm bed, and the categories given for units, cabins and vans, which represent the daily charge for the whole unit.

❶ Under $20   ❸ $35–50   ❺ $70–90   ❼ $115–150
❷ $20–35   ❹ $50–70   ❻ $90–115   ❽ $150 upwards

For more accommodation details, see pp.46–49.

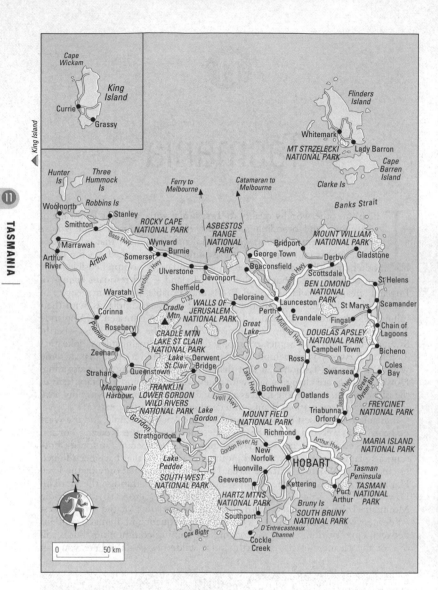

breathe the fresh air and drink freely from tannin-stained streams, is a genuinely bucolic experience.

A north–south axis divides the settled areas, with the two major cities, **Hobart**, the capital, in the south, and **Launceston** in the north. The **north-west coast**, facing the mainland across Bass Strait, is the most densely populated region, the site of Tasmania's two other cities, **Devonport** (where the Bass Strait ferry docks) and **Burnie**, and several other large, conservative towns. Tasmania's **central plateau**, with its thousands of lakes, is sparsely populated, though full of weekender fishing shacks. The sheltered, mostly flat **east**

coast is the place to go for sun and watersports activities; it has plenty of deserted beaches, safe for swimming, set against a backdrop of bush-clad hills.

Don't expect boiling hot **weather** in Tasmania. It rarely gets above 25°C, even at the height of summer, and the weather is notoriously changeable, particularly in the uplands, where it can sleet and snow at any time of year; the most stable month is February. However, with the ozone layer thinning every year the UV rays are particularly strong and in the middle of a summer day can burn unprotected skin in fifteen minutes. Wear plenty of sun screen and a hat. Winter is a bitterly cold time to visit unless you choose the more temperate east coast; wilderness walks are best left to the most experienced and well-equipped at this time of year.

Some history

The Dutch navigator **Abel Tasman** sighted the west coast of the island in 1642. Landing a party on its east coast, he named it **Van Diemen's Land** in honour of the Governor of the Dutch East Indies. Early maps show it connected to the mainland, and several eighteenth-century French and British navigators, including William Bligh and James Cook, who claimed it for the British, did not prove otherwise. It was not until 1798 that Matthew Flinders circumnavigated the island, and his discovery of the **Bass Strait** reduced the journey to Sydney by a week. In 1803, after the French had been observed nosing around the island's southern waters, it was decided to establish a second **colony** in Australia. (The first had been established at Sydney Cove in 1788.) Lieutenant David Bowen was dispatched to Van Diemen's Land, settling with a group of convicts on the banks of the Derwent River at Risdon Cove. In the same year, Lieutenant-Colonel John Collins set out from England with another group to settle the Port Phillip district of what would become Victoria; after a few months they gave up and crossed the Bass Strait to join Bowen's group. **Hobart Town** was founded in 1804 and the first **penal settlement** opened at Macquarie Harbour in 1821, followed by Maria Island and Port Arthur; they were mainly for those who had committed further offences while still prisoners on the mainland. Van Diemen's Land, with its harsh conditions and repressive, violent regime, became part of British folklore as a place of terror, a prison-island hell. Collins was Lieutenant-Governor of Van Diemen's Land until his death in 1810, but it is Lieutenant-Governor **George Arthur** (1824–36) who has the most prominent position in the island's history. His ideas were an influence on the prison settlement at Port Arthur and he was in charge at the time of the **Black Line** (see box, overleaf), the organized white militia used against the indigenous Aboriginal population.

Tasmania did not experience the postwar industrialization that transformed the mainland. A small, isolated and neglected state, it even missed out on postwar immigration and consequently remains predominantly Anglo-Saxon in character, with an insular, often conservative, population. Its **natural resources** include forests – covering forty percent of the island – and water, and the mountainous terrain and fast-flowing rivers meant that hydroelectricity schemes began early here, under the auspices of the huge Hydro Electricity Commission (HEC). The flooding of **Lake Pedder** in 1972 led to the formation of the **Wilderness Society**, a conservation organization whose successful **Franklin Blockade** in 1982 managed to save one of the last wild rivers. Controversy over these issues still divides the state into "Greens" and a pro-logging, pro-dam working class worried about their jobs. By voting for the **Tasmanian Greens** in 1989, enough ordinary Tasmanians showed that they didn't want Tasmania's natural assets destroyed, and the party held the balance

The attempted genocide of the Aboriginal peoples of Tasmania is one of the most tragic episodes of modern history. Ironically, if it were not for American and British sealers and whalers who had operated from the shores of Van Diemen's Land since 1793, abducting Aboriginal women and taking them to the Furneaux Islands in the Bass Strait as their slaves and mistresses, the Tasmanian Aborigines would have disappeared without trace. Until recently, it was stated in school books that the last Aboriginal Tasmanian was **Truganini**, who died at Oyster Cove, south of Hobart, in 1876. However, a strong Aboriginal movement has grown up in Tasmania in the last twenty years, with over six thousand descendants proclaiming their heritage and pushing for land rights.

The **Aboriginal people of Tasmania** appear to have been racially distinct from those of the mainland, although their beliefs and rituals were similar. About twelve thousand years ago, the thawing of the last Ice Age brought rising ocean levels, which separated these people from the mainland and caused their genetic isolation; it's thought that on the mainland new cultures probably entered ten thousand years ago. This isolation was also evident in **cultural development**: they couldn't make fire but kept alight smouldering fire sticks; their weapons were simpler – they didn't have boomerangs; and although seafood was a main source of food, eating scaly fish was taboo. In **appearance**, the men were startling, wearing their hair in long ringlets smeared with grease and red ochre, while women wore theirs closely shaved. To keep out the cold, they coated their bodies with a mixture of animal fat, ochre and charcoal; women often wore a kangaroo-skin cloak. Men decorated their bodies with linear scar patterns on their abdomens, arms and shoulders. Their **art** consisted of rock carvings of geometric designs, still to be seen in areas on the west and northwest coasts.

When the first **white settlement** was established in the early years of the nineteenth century there were reckoned to be about five thousand Aboriginal people in Tasmania, divided into nine main tribes. A tribe consisted of bands of forty to fifty people who lived in adjoining territory, shared the same language and culture, socialized, intermarried and – crucially – fought wars against other tribes. They also traded such items as stone tools, ochre and shell necklaces, and bands moved peaceably across neighbouring tribes' territory along well-defined routes at different times of the year to share resources: the inland Big River tribe, for example, would journey to the coast for sealing. Once they realized the white settlers were not going to "share" their resources in this traditional exchange economy but were instead stealing the land, the nomadic people displayed a determination to defend it – by force, if necessary. Confrontation was inevitable, and by the 1820s the white population was in a frenzy of fear – though for every settler who died, twenty Aborigines met a similar fate. In 1828 Governor Arthur declared martial law, expelling all Aboriginal people from the settled districts and giving settlers what was, in practice, a licence to shoot on sight. Alarmed by these events, the British government planned to round up the remaining Aborigines and confine them to **Bruny Island**, south of Hobart Town. In 1830 a mass militia of three thousand settlers formed an armed human barrier, the **Black Line**, which was to sweep across the island, clearing Aborigines before them, in preparation for "resettlement".

The line failed; but unfortunately the final tactic was "divide and rule", in which the Aboriginal people themselves, with their superb tracking skills, were enlisted to help ensnare their tribal enemies. The 135 Aborigines who survived the Black Line were moved in 1834 to a makeshift settlement on exposed and barren **Flinders Island** . Within four years most of these people died of disease, or as a result of harsh conditions. In 1837 the 47 survivors were transferred to their final settlement at Oyster Cove, where – no longer a threat – they were often dressed up and paraded on official engagements. The skeleton of the last survivor, "Queen" Truganini (see p.1059 and p.1074), originally from Bruny Island, was displayed in the Tasmanian Museum until 1976, when her remains were finally cremated and scattered in the D'Entrecasteaux Channel, according to her final wishes.

of power in the state's parliament until 1992; in early 1996 the Greens again held the balance of power, with a Liberal state government. Before the 1998 state elections, the two major opposing parties, Labor and Liberal, conspired together to change the electoral structure, voting to reduce the number of members in the Lower House from 25 to 15, purposefully making it more difficult for the Greens to win seats. The Labour government was voted in, and the sole Green Member of Parliament in the Lower House has little chance of exercising any influence. The Tasmanian Green party is represented federally by one senator, the Tasmanian environmental activist **Dr Bob Brown**.

Recent campaigns have been aimed at stopping old-growth logging in particularly sensitive areas, and ending **woodchipping** (pulping trees for paper) for export to Japan; currently some ninety percent of the wood taken from Tasmania's forests ends up this way, with Tasmania the only state in Australia that woodchips **rainforests**. It's claimed that the state government is subsidizing the industry, selling woodchips off at a third of the going rate to keep Tasmanians employed. At the time of writing a new campaign had begun to stop a woodchip-fuelled power station being built just south of Hobart. Another high-profile issue is genetically engineered (GE) farming. After much campaigning, the Tasmanian Government has defied the rest of Australia and announced a one-year moratorium on **GE crops**. The majority of the Tasmanian people want this moratorium extended indefinitely and many would like to see Tasmania market itself as a clean, green, organic state.

Tasmanian practicalities

Although it's small in Australian terms, make sure you give yourself enough **time** to see Tasmania; if you want to see only its cities you need no more than a few days, but to get a flavour of the countryside – the great outdoors is the real reason to come here – a couple of weeks or longer is necessary. **Tasmanian Travel Centres** (Ⓦ www.tastravel.com.au) in the major cities (see box, below) can provide **information** and also book all transport, tours and accommodation; their free information paper, *Travelways* (also available online at Ⓦ www.travelways.com.au), is extremely useful, filled with detailed, reliable and comprehensive information on accommodation, attractions, bus timetables, car rental, adventure tours and national parks. The free magazine *Tasmanian Adventures*, available from information centres in Tasmania (also online at Ⓦ www.tasmanianadventures.com.au), is an excellent source of information on **tours** ranging from "mild" to "wild". For extremely helpful directories of businesses and services across Tasmania, try Tasmania Online (Ⓦ www.tas.gov.au), and for general tourist information check out the goverment-run site Ⓦ www.tourism.tas.gov.au.

Tasmanian Travel Centres in Australia

Adelaide 1 King William St, SA 5000 (information and reservations ☏ 08/8400 5506, ℱ 8400 5588).

Brisbane 239 George St, QLD 4000 (information ☏ 07/3405 4106, reservations ☏ 07/3405 4133, ℱ 3405 4140).

Melbourne 259 Collins St, VIC 3000 (information and reservations ☏ 03/9206 7901, ℱ 9206 7947).

Sydney 60 Carrington St, NSW 2000 (information and reservations ☏ 02/9202 2004, ℱ 9202 2055).

If you plan to be in Melbourne, or have a car you want to take over, a good way to get to Tasmania is across the Bass Strait on the TT Line *Spirit of Tasmania* **ferry** from Port Melbourne to Devonport (departing Port Melbourne Mon 7.30pm, Wed & Fri 6pm, arriving Devonport 8.30am; departing Devonport Tues & Thurs 6pm, Sat 4pm; ⊤ 13 2010, ⓦ www.tt-line.com.au). If a fourteen-hour overnight trip doesn't worry you too much, this is the best way to travel. There are restaurants, bars and entertainment, and every passenger has a bed: there's a hostel section ($152 one-way), as well as private cabins ranging from basic to luxury suites ($184–354 per person one-way); in low season prices can drop by around twenty percent. You'll need to **book in advance** in summer, especially if you want to take a vehicle. Whatever standard of accommodation you choose, you'll pay between $40 and $55 extra to take a car across, and $27 for a bicycle. There is also a summer-only **high speed catamaran**, the *Devil Cat*, which takes six hours to cross between Port Melbourne and George Town (Jan–April departing Port Melbourne Tues, Thurs & Sat 8.30am; departing George Town Wed, Fri & Sun 2pm; one-way passenger $175; vehicles as per *Spirit of Tasmania*), but prepare for a rough ride. Cheaper Apex return fares (21-day advance purchase) are available on both boats, and packages, including on-ground travel passes or accommodation and tours, are also worth looking into.

Several airlines **fly** from the mainland to Tasmania, as well as to King and Flinders islands. You can fly with **Qantas** from all the major cities, usually changing planes in Melbourne; it's always cheaper to fly to Launceston direct from Melbourne, and you'll save money if you book well in advance, with an economy return at $428 and an Apex return at $267. Other return fares are Melbourne–Hobart $525/$300 and Sydney–Hobart $756/$411 ($668/$377 to Launceston). Look out for special offers that can reduce prices further. There are also several Tasmanian- and Victorian-based airlines worth checking out. The major player is **Kendell Airlines** (free call ⊤ 1800 338 894), a subsidiary of Ansett, who as well as connecting both Melbourne and Sydney to Launceston and Hobart, also fly from Melbourne to Devonport (return $470), Wynyard (Burnie Airport; return $441) and King Island (return $338). All Kendell flights operate from Ansett Australia terminals, who provide reservation services and some ground handling at major capital city airports. **RegionAir** (free call ⊤ 1800 818 455, ⓦ www.regionair.com) flies from Moorabbin, just outside Melbourne, to Launceston ($420 return) and Flinders Island ($349 return); they are the only carrier flying to Flinders Island in a jet. **Island Airlines** (free call ⊤ 1800 645 875) offers the same two routes – from Melbourne to Launceston ($210 one-way) and Flinders Island ($175 one-way). At the time of writing **Virgin Airlines** was also planning to extend its Virgin Blue services to Tasmania.

Fly-drive packages, which include accommodation, can be particularly good value: ask at travel agents about the availability of special deals. There are no **international flights** to Tasmania.

Accommodation

Compared to the mainland, Tasmania has few **motels**, other than those in and around the main towns, and not as many caravan parks, but plenty of high-quality **hotel (pub)** accommodation (usually serving breakfast) and British-style **B&Bs**. Consequently, you should try to plan ahead, as you won't just happen upon a cheap motel or cabin, and in peak periods only the most expensive B&B accommodation or the most simple hostel beds may be vacant. Outside peak season, however, most places offer stand-by rates which are often substantially lower than their advertised prices. **YHA hostels** tend to be basic

⑪

and old-fashioned, offering mainly dorm beds, but they're gradually being modernized – the good news is that prices start from as low as $9, and you'll find them off the beaten track. In the major tourist areas **backpackers' hostels** have sprung up, with plenty of twin and double rooms; prices start from about $12, reaching up to $16 in summer. **Campers** will find lots of free sites, often with the minimal facilities of a pit toilet and tap water, as well as an abundance of good spots (often with fees attached) in the national parks.

Getting around

Six local **bus companies** and one charter service reach most destinations on the island, the main two companies being Tasmanian Redline Coaches and Tassie Link. You cannot use a mainland bus pass with either of these, and services are limited, often not running at weekends, especially on the east and west coasts; in winter and spring services are even further reduced. The largest operator, **Tasmanian Redline Coaches** (℡03/6231 3233 or 1300/360 000), offers frequent scheduled services between Hobart and Launceston via the east coast or direct via the Midland Highway, from Devonport to Hobart via Deloraine and Launceston, and along the northwest coast from Devonport to Burnie and on to Smithton. **Tassie Link** (℡03/6272 7300, Ⓦwww.tigerline.com.au) specializes in bushwalkers' transport, getting you to some of the more remote destinations all over the state in their minibuses: scheduled services run from Hobart to Queenstown via Lake St Clair, with a connecting service to Strahan; Queenstown to Launceston via Cradle Mountain and Devonport; from Hobart up the east coast as far as St Helens; and from Launceston east to Bicheno. Tassie Link also run "Wilderness" services (minimum of four people) and separate tours. "Wilderness" services include routes running west from Hobart to Mount Field National Park and Scotts Peak or south to Cockle Creek via Huonville and Lune River, and from Launceston to the Walls of Jerusalem National Park and to Cradle Mountain via Deloraine and Devonport. Their **fares** are rather high, considering the short distances – for example, Strahan to Launceston is $55 one-way, and Hobart to Mount Field is $22. Fares on Redline are government-regulated: for example, $23 for the trip from Hobart to Launceston, and $38 from Hobart to Devonport. **Hobart Coaches** (℡03/6234 4077) head north out of Hobart to Richmond and New Norfolk, and south to Woodbridge, Cygnet, Geeveston and Dover. Several smaller local operators on the east coast, such as **Bicheno Coach Service** (Coles Bay–Bicheno; ℡03/6257 0293), **Peakes Coaches** (St Marys–Swansea; ℡03/6372 5390) and **Sun Coast** (Derby–St Helens; ℡03/6376 3458), help to fill in the gaps. **Maxwell's Charter Bus** (℡03/6492 1431) provides a service based on a minimum of four passengers from Devonport and Launceston to and around the Cradle Mountain–Lake St Clair area.

Buying a local **bus pass** is one way of cutting costs: Tassie Link (Ⓦwww.tigerline.com.au) offer a **Tassie Wilderness Pass** which covers a range of time spans and journeys (from $150 for seven-days' travel within a 10-day period, to $250 for 21-days' travel within a 30-day period), and combines its scheduled and "Wilderness" services, getting you to all the major bush-walking areas and giving you discounts off their tours. You'll also reach the main cities and towns, though very indirectly. Also, it's worth investing in YHA or VIP membership before coming to Tasmania, which will give you substantial savings on all bus tickets and tours (see Basics, p.48).

Renting a car is a sensible option, considering the vagaries of the transport system, particularly if you can get a group together. Local operators offer reasonable weekly rates, starting from about $300 for a budget car or $720 for a top-of-the-range model, including basic insurance; as Tasmania is such a small island kilometres are usually unlimited, and you don't need a lot of petrol. Though distances seem short compared to the mainland, roads are often winding and mostly two-laned – there are few freeways, except some short stretches on the outskirts of large cities – so **driving** can be slow and tiring. At dusk and night-time you have to be especially careful of animals darting in front of your car, as evidenced by the high number of dead native animals you'll see by the roadsides. However, there are few cars on the road, so you should be able to relax a bit and enjoy the scenery. The lack of traffic also makes **cycling** an attractive option, especially in summer, and on the flatter midlands and east coast routes; otherwise, there are plenty of gruelling hills to keep you in shape. Several operators in Hobart, Launceston and Devonport rent bikes for touring (see the respective accounts).

You could also choose to go on a **tour of the island** with a small-group outfit aimed at independent-minded travellers. Under Down Under Tours (T 03/6369 5555 or free call 1800 064 726, W www.vision.net.au/~under_downunder) offer a five-day tour (departing Devonport or Launceston Thurs & Sun; $395 including breakfast and lunch but not accommodation) which does a loop of the island and includes plenty of bushwalking and some wildlife spotting. They also offer a two-day tour (departing Devonport or Launceston Tues & Thurs; $199) of the northwest, which includes the Arthur River cruise. The tours can also be combined ($575).

National parks and bushwalking

All **national parks** in Tasmania charge daily (24hr) **entry fees**, often on an honour system, of $3.30 per pedestrian or cyclist, $9.90 per vehicle: if you plan to go bush for long periods, then a two-month holiday pass (person, cyclist or motorcyclist $13.20, car $33) or an annual pass (car $19.80 for one park, $46.20 for all parks) might be better value. Tasmania's wilderness has always attracted thousands of **bushwalkers**, and many of the tracks have become churned-up and are gradually being boardwalked; keeping to set paths to avoid further erosion is just one of the national park's minimum-impact guidelines, available in a leaflet from the **Tasmania Parks and Wildlife Service**, 134 Macquarie St, Hobart (T 03/6233 6191, W www.parks.tas.gov.au), which also supplies detailed maps. To get leaflets before your trip, you can write to GPO Box 44A, Hobart, TAS 7001. It must be emphasized that walking in the wilderness can be dangerous if you're ill-prepared: you should never go by yourself and you should always register your plans with a park ranger or inform others of your intentions. The free *Bushwalking Trip Planner for Tasmania's World Heritage Area* gives you information about the clothing and equipment you'll need in these parks, where the weather can change rapidly – even on a warm summer day hail, sleet or snow can suddenly descend in the highlands, and walkers who have disregarded warnings have died of hypothermia. As a minimum, you'll need wet-weather gear, thermal clothing, walking boots, a sturdy tent, warm sleeping bag, a fuel cooking stove, maps and a compass (which you should know how to use). Gear can be rented from outdoor shops in Hobart, Launceston and Devonport.

Internet access

Its easy to find internet access in Tasmania, as most towns now have an Online Access Centre; check W www.tco.asn.au for locations. This website also gives access to local town sites, often useful sources of information on local attractions and businesses. The centres provide email, internet access and word processing facilities for $5 per half-hour, with a volunteer to help you out if needed. Phone ahead to book a session.

Hobart and the east

From Lake St Clair in central Tasmania, the **Derwent River** flows past **Mount Field National Park**, Tasmania's oldest and most popular national park, through well-preserved **New Norfolk**, and towards **Hobart**, Tasmania's capital. Here, the river estuary widens to form a fine harbour before flowing into the waters of **Storm Bay** and out to the Tasman Sea. Hobart is Australia's most southerly city, battered by winter winds roaring in from the Antarctic, while the coastline around it is so jagged it looks as if someone has poured acid on a map of the area. The hook-shaped **South Arm**, at the entrance to Storm Bay, is echoed on a larger scale by the **Tasman Peninsula**, with its infamous convict settlement at **Port Arthur**. To the south, the two tenuously connected halves of **Bruny Island** protect the waters of the **D'Entrecasteaux Channel**. On the mainland opposite Bruny Island is the fertile and cultivated **Huon Valley**, but as you head further south the coastline becomes increasingly wild: there are caves and thermal springs, the **Hartz Mountain National Park** inland, and the **Picton River**, where there's good rafting. The last settlement in this direction is **Cockle Creek**, the starting point for the South Coast Track which takes you towards the South West National Park (see p.1136), the great mass of wilderness forming Tasmania's southwest corner.

North of Hobart, the **east coast** of Tasmania is the tamest and most temperate part of the island, providing a popular cycling route past numerous sandy and deserted beaches and some lovely national parks. The **Tasman Highway** follows this coastline from Hobart to Launceston, heading inland through the northeast at **St Helens**, the east coast's largest town. The northeast corner is virtually unpopulated, and the **Mount William National Park** here is a haven for the Forrester kangaroo. Inland are some old tin-mining towns, and superb rainforest remnants and mountain scenery at **Weldborough Pass**, beyond which you pass through rich agricultural and forestry country to Launceston.

Hobart

HOBART is small but beautifully sited, and approaching it from any direction is exhilarating: speeding across the expressway on the Tasman Bridge over the wide expanse of the Derwent River, or swooping down the Southern Outlet with hills, harbour, docks and houses spread out below. The green- and red-tin-roofed timber houses climb up the lower slopes of Mount Wellington, snow-topped for two or three months of the year, and look down on the expansive harbour. It's a city focused on the water: the centre is only a few minutes' walk from the waterfront, where fresh seafood can be bought directly from fishing boats in Sullivans Cove, and yachties hang out at old dockside pubs or head for fish and chips served from the punts moored in Constitution Dock. South of Constitution Dock is Salamanca Place, a well-preserved streetscape of waterfront stone warehouses which is the site of a famous Saturday market, a Hobart highlight. Yacht races and regattas are held throughout the year, while at weekends the water is alive with boats; you can choose any type of craft for a harbour cruise – perfect in the summer when it's dry and not too hot. In winter, though, the wind roars in from the Antarctic and temperatures drop to 5°C and below.

Australia's second-oldest city after Sydney, Hobart has managed to escape the clutches of developers, and its early architectural heritage is remarkably well preserved – more so than any other antipodean city. In 1803 **Lieutenant John Bowen** led a party of 24 convicts from Sydney to settle on the eastern shores of the Derwent River at Risdon Cove. A year later **Lieutenant-Colonel David Collins** arrived, with about three hundred convicts, a contingent of marines to guard over them, and thirty or more free settlers including women and children, and founded Hobart Town on Sullivans Cove, 10km below the

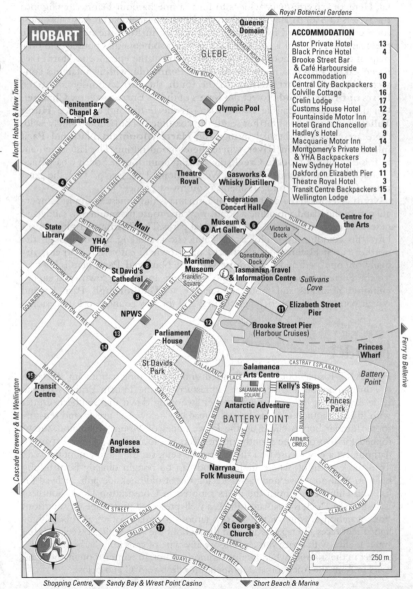

ACCOMMODATION

Astor Private Hotel	13
Black Prince Hotel	4
Brooke Street Bar & Café Harbourside Accommodation	10
Central City Backpackers	8
Colville Cottage	16
Crelin Lodge	17
Customs House Hotel	12
Fountainside Motor Inn	2
Hotel Grand Chancellor	6
Hadley's Hotel	9
Macquarie Motor Inn	14
Montgomery's Private Hotel & YHA Backpackers	7
New Sydney Hotel	5
Oakford on Elizabeth Pier	11
Theatre Royal Hotel	3
Transit Centre Backpackers	15
Wellington Lodge	1

original settlement and on the opposite shore. Collins went on to serve as Lieutenant-Governor of the colony for ten years. For the first two years, food was scarce, and settlers had to hunt local game, creating an early culture based on guns that was later to have terrible effects on the Aboriginal population. The fine deep-water port helped make the town prosperous, and a merchant class became wealthy through whaling, shipbuilding and the transport of crops and wool. The period between the late 1820s and the 1840s was a golden age for building, with the government architect **John Lee Archer** and the convict **James Blackburn** responsible for some of Hobart's finest buildings. There's a wealth of colonial Georgian **architecture**, with more than ninety buildings classified by the National Trust, sixty of which are on Macquarie and Davey streets. **Battery Point**, a village of workers' cottages and grand houses set in narrow, irregular streets, has hardly changed in the last 150 years.

Arrival, information and transport

Hobart **airport** is 26km northeast of the city at Cambridge (flight information ☏ 13 1515). Tasmanian Redline Coaches runs an airport **shuttle bus** to the city ($8; bookings on ☏ 0419 383 462 or 382 240), dropping off at central accommodation, as well as the *Adelphi Court YHA* in New Town; a **taxi** costs around $22. If you come by Redline or Tassie Link **bus**, you'll disembark at the **Transit Centre**, 199 Collins St (Mon, Tues, Thurs & Fri 7am–6pm, Wed 8am–6pm, Sat 9am–3pm, Sun 9am–6.15pm), where there are showers ($5) and left-luggage facilities ($1.10 per item), and even hostel accommodation upstairs (see p.1057). If you're arriving by **car**, be aware that most of the streets are one-way. There's plenty of cheap metered **parking** available on the streets, plus several council-run car parks charging around $1 per hour ($8.50 for 24hr).

Information

The first stop for general information is the **Tasmanian Travel & Information Centre** at 20 Davey St, corner of Elizabeth Street (Mon–Fri 8.30am–5.15pm, Sat & Sun 9am–4pm; ☏ 03/6230 8233, ⓦ www.tourism.tas.gov.au), though it functions mainly as a travel, car hire and accommodation booking agency. The **National Trust Shop**, in the Penitentiary Chapel at the corner of Brisbane and Campbell streets (Mon–Fri 10am–2.30pm; ☏ 03/6231 0911), has inexpensive architectural guides detailing the bewildering range of listed buildings. On a more alternative note, the **Tasmanian Environment Centre**, 102 Bathurst St (Mon–Fri 9am–5pm; ☏ 03/6234 5566, ⓦ www/tased.edu.au/tasonline/tech), is a relaxed resource space with lots of books and information on Tasmania and notice boards featuring environmental events, rooms to let and items for sale. Organizations such as Bicycle Tasmania (tours of Hobart and Tasmania are free to members) and the Hobart Walking Club (visitors can join their walks free of charge) use this as their base, and the centre operates its own programme of walks and talks throughout the year. For **bushwalking information** and a full range of Tasmaps, head for the Service Tasmania Shop at 134 Macquarie St (Mon–Fri 9am–4.45pm; ☏ 03/6233 3382); upstairs, the Parks and Wildlife Service (Mon–Fri 9am–5pm; ☏ 03/6230 8011, ⓦ www.parks.tas.gov.au) has information sheets and can refer you to a parks officer for advice; other general and bushwalking maps are stocked at the Tasmanian Map Centre, 96 Elizabeth St (☏ 03/6231 9043).

City transport

Hobart's public transport system, the **Hobart Metro** (timetable and fares ☏ 13 2201, ⓔ infoline@metrotas.com.au), is useful for getting to less central accommodation and some more distant points of interest. You can pre-purchase Metro Tens (a pack of ten discounted tickets) and get timetables from the Metroshop, inside the GPO on Elizabeth Street; the area outside – Elizabeth Street, Franklin Square and Macquarie Street – acts as the bus interchange. The handy yellow-painted **Busy Bee bus** does a circuit from Franklin Square through Battery Point and up Sandy Bay Road to the casino and back again. Single **tickets**, available from the driver, are valid for ninety minutes and cost from $1.30 (for a one- or two-zone journey); off-peak day-rover passes are $3.10. Busy Bee buses run until around 11pm from Monday to Thursday, until midnight on Friday and Saturday, and until about 10.30pm on Sunday, when there are only a few services. The *Southern Cross Wanderer*, a private **ferry**, runs to Bellerive, on the eastern shore, from Brooke Street Pier (ⓣ 03/6223 1914 for times); the weekday peak-hour service ($3 one-way) is direct, while the weekend service stops en-route at the casino at Sandy Bay ($5 one-way; $3 to casino only). You can hail a **taxi** on the street, or there are taxi stands around the city, with the major one outside the Town Hall on Elizabeth Street (for phone numbers, see "Listings" p.1068).

For **cruises**, see the box on p.1060; and for city **tours**, see "Listings", p.1068.

Accommodation

There's plenty of **accommodation** in Hobart, but during the peak season in January, when the yachties hit town, prices can shoot up and inexpensive places are hard to find. City and dockside **hotels** are the best option for clean, affordable private accommodation, and there's always a bed at one of Hobart's several **hostels**. Battery Point is full of (sometimes pricey) **B&Bs**, and the area has several good **self-catering** holiday apartments, with costs comparable to a motel. Most **motels** are situated in Sandy Bay, about 3km south of the centre, or along the Brooker Highway, but B&Bs and guesthouses tend to offer better value.

Hotels and motels

Argyle Motor Lodge, cnr Lewis and Argyle streets, North Hobart (ⓣ 03/6234 2488, ⓕ 6234 2292, ⓔ ArgyleMotorLodge@bigpond.com). Situated in a quiet area twenty-minutes' walk from the city centre. Some self-catering units also available. ⓺

Black Prince Hotel, 145 Elizabeth St (ⓣ 03/6234 3501, ⓕ 6234 3502). Centrally located hotel offering budget motel-style rooms, breakfast included. ⓸

Brooke Street Bar & Cafe Harbourside Accommodation, 19 Morrison St, above the trendy *Brooke Street Bar* (ⓣ 03/6234 6254, ⓕ 6224 3657, ⓦ www.view.com.au/Brookest). Great location on Sullivans Cove; inexpensive pub-style rooms, all clean and well-furnished, some with TV, some en suite. ⓸

Customs House Hotel, cnr Murray and Morrison streets, opposite Watermans Dock (ⓣ 03/6234 6645, ⓕ 6223 8750, ⓦ www.view.com.au/customs/index.html). Old-style waterfront hotel next to Parliament House with great views, though rooms at the front get pub noise on Fri nights. Rates include access to kitchenette, which has breakfast provisions. ⓹

Fountainside Motor Inn, cnr Liverpool St and Brooker Ave (ⓣ 03/6234 2911, ⓕ 6231 0710, ⓦ www.bestwestern.com). Multistorey motel set on a noisy intersection, but with room service and a 24hr coffee shop. ⓹

Hotel Grand Chancellor, 1 Davey St (ⓣ 03/6235 4535, ⓕ 6223 8175, ⓦ www.hgchobart.com.au). Hobart's most upmarket hotel, the five-star *Grand Chancellor's* facilities include two restaurants, two bars and a health club. ⓼

Hadley's Hotel, 34 Murray St (ⓣ 03/6223 4355 or free call 1800 131 689, ⓕ 6224 0303, ⓔ hadleys@bigpond.com.au). National Trust-listed hotel close to the waterfront, with an old-fashioned feel but modern facilities; restaurant, café, bistro and bar are all in-house. Room service, 24hr reception, and free parking. ⓻

Macquarie Motor Inn, 167 Macquarie St (ⓣ 03/6234 4422, ⓕ 6234 4273, ⓦ www.oakford.com/html/cities/hobart/). Very central high-rise, friendlier than it looks; under-15s stay for free. Facilities include a pool, sauna and spa. ⓺

Oakford on Elizabeth Pier, Elizabeth St Pier (ⓣ 03/6220 6600, ⓕ 6244 1277, ⓦ www.oakford.com). Waterfront apartment hotel – gorgeous one-bedroom and family studio apartments are split level, spacious and flooded with light. Some have walk-out balconies, all have kitchen and laundry, and there's a gym and sauna. **❽**

Theatre Royal Hotel, 31 Campbell St (℡ 03/6234 6925, ℻ 6231 1773). A basic hotel, but in a great position across from the Theatre Royal, with plain but presentable rooms; some singles available, and light breakfast included. Excellent bar and bistro downstairs. **❹**

Wrest Point Hotel–Casino, 410 Sandy Bay Rd, Sandy Bay (℡ 03/6225 0112, ℻ 6225 3909, ⓦ www.wrestpoint.com.au). Upmarket four-star hotel with riverside rooms. Heated indoor pool, sauna and 24hr room service. As well as the luxury tower, there's a cheaper motel section. **❼–❾**

B&Bs and guesthouses

Astor Private Hotel, 157 Macquarie St (℡ 03/6234 6611, ℻ 6231 4053, ⓦ www.astorprivatehotel.com.au/). Central, old-fashioned, family-run guesthouse; rates include breakfast. **❺**

Colville Cottage, 32 Mona St, Battery Point (℡ 03/6223 6968, ℻ 6224 0500, ⓦ www.colville.com.au). Peaceful Victorian weatherboard B&B, with en-suite rooms and a pleasant garden. **❼**

The Lodge on Elizabeth, 249 Elizabeth St, cnr Warwick St (℡ 03/6231 3830, ℻ 6234 2566, ⓦ www.view.com.au/lodge/index.html). Delightful guesthouse in an elegant National Trust-listed 1829 mansion; guest lounge with fireplace, games and complimentary port. All rooms en suite. **❼**

Wellington Lodge, 7 Scott St, Glebe (℡ 03/6231 0614, ℻ 6234 1551, ⓔ wellodge@telstra.easymail.com.au). A weatherboard B&B classified by the National Trust, close to Queens Domain park and the city centre. All rooms are en suite and nonsmoking. **❻**

Hostels and budget accommodation

Adelphi Court YHA, 17 Stoke St, New Town (℡ 03/6228 4829, ℻ 6278 2047). Modern, motel-like hostel and guesthouse arranged around a courtyard, on a quiet suburban street. Cramped kitchen facilities, but catered breakfasts in the dining room. There's a large TV/games room (closes early) and a small kiosk. The hostel books tours, does pick-ups, rents bikes and camping equipment, and has plenty of parking. A long way from the city centre, but 10min walk to the Elizabeth St restaurant strip in North Hobart. Take bus #15 or #16 from Argyle St to Stoke St, or #25–42, #100 or #105–128 from Elizabeth St, to stop no. 13, then walk. Rooms **❹**, dorms **❶**

Central City Backpackers, 2nd Floor, Imperial Mansions, 138 Collins St, entrance through the Imperial Arcade (℡ 03/6224 2404 or free call 1800 811 507, ℻ 6224 2316, ⓦ www.centralbackpackers.com.au). One of Hobart's best hostels, in the spacious quarters of a once grand hotel. The management is friendly and efficient, and the hostel is popular – so book ahead. Six- or four-bed dorms, singles, twins or doubles available, all heated; linen and bedding hire $5 extra. Facilities include a well set-up kitchen, pleasant dining area, TV and games rooms, storage room and a licensed bar downstairs. No parking. Rooms **❷–❸**, dorms **❶**

Jane Franklin Hall, 6 Elboden St, South Hobart (℡ 03/6223 2000, ⓦ www.utas.edu.au/docs/jane.franklin.hall/). Student rooms available in the holidays; many single rooms. Excellent facilities include a kitchen, free laundry, TV lounge, gym and pool. B&B **❷**

Montgomery's Private Hotel & YHA Backpackers, 9 Argyle St (℡ 03/6231 2660, ℻ 6231 4817, ⓔ engel@southcom.com.au). Popular new hostel with a great friendly atmosphere, centrally located in a renovated old warehouse building. Excellent facilities dining room/kitchen with TV, bus and tour booking facilities and bike rental ($8 half-day, $16 full day). Rooms **❺**, dorms **❷**

New Sydney Hotel, 87 Bathurst St (℡ 03/6234 4516, ℻ 6236 9965, ⓦ www.view.com.au/newsydney/index.html). Clean and central backpacker accommodation above a pub, with kitchen facilities and guest lounge – and noisy bands playing downstairs six nights. Always lively, though, and you can get budget meals in the pub. **❶**

Transit Centre Backpackers, 199 Collins St, above the Transit Centre (℡ & ℻ 03/6231 2400). Modern, central, well-equipped and spacious, but lacking in atmosphere. Dorms **❶**

Caravan parks and self-catering apartments

Crelin Lodge, 1 Crelin St, Battery Point (℡ & ℻ 03/6223 1777). Pleasant units with up to five beds, in a great spot. **❻**

Graham Court Apartments, 15 Pirie St, New Town (℡ 03/6278 1333, ℻ 6278 1087, ⓔ grahamcourt@vision.net.au). Comfortable, well equipped, one-to-three-bedroom self-contained apartments, conveniently located near the city centre. **❺**

Sandy Bay Caravan Park, 1 Peel St, Sandy Bay (℡ 03/6225 1264, ⓦ www.ozemail.com.au~islandcp/). The closest caravan park to the city centre (3km), on a densely occupied site in a salubrious suburb. Full range of facilities, including playground and camp kitchen. Cabins ❹, on-site vans ❸

Treasure Island Caravan Park, 671 Main Rd, Berriedale (☎ 03/6249 2379). Large park 14km from town, with a kitchen and pool. Cabins ❹, on-site vans ❸

The City

Hobart is small and easy to find your way around, with the streets arranged in a grid pattern running southeast towards **Sullivans Cove**. You can walk anywhere in the city centre, which is mostly flat, although surrounded by some steep hills. The civic centre is **Franklin Square**, bounded by **Macquarie** and **Davey** streets, which between them have a concentration of listed buildings. The main shopping area is **Elizabeth Street Mall**, roughly in the centre of the **CBD** (the City Business District); Elizabeth Street slopes down from **North Hobart**, known for its many fine restaurants, to the Elizabeth Street Pier on **Franklin Wharf**. Here, at the harbour, fishing boats and yachts are moored, and cruises leave from Brooke Street Pier. **Salamanca Place**, with its row of Georgian warehouses, is on the waterfront on the south side of the cove; a steep climb up Kelly's Steps brings you to **Battery Point**, to the south. Following the Derwent River around from Battery Point, you reach salubrious **Sandy Bay**, with its casino and Royal Yacht Club. To the north of the centre are the parklands of the **Queens Domain**, with the **Royal Botanical Gardens** along the waterfront; from the Domain, the **Tasman Bridge** crosses the river to the residential eastern shore.

There are relatively few sights in Hobart other than the streets themselves, but these are enough to keep you wandering around for hours, stopping at a few museums and parks along the way. While walking through the city, it's worth glancing up occasionally to observe the **street signs**; the streets are often named after important local figures and the signs have portraits and biographies of them. Around the docks area, and in Battery Point, there are also interpretive boards pointing out historic and architectural features.

Franklin Square and the Tasmanian Museum and Art Gallery

Starting from **Franklin Square**, you can walk south past many of the fine old buildings on Davey Street to **St Davids Park**, originally the graveyard of St Davids Cathedral (at the corner of Murray and Macquarie streets) but converted to a park in the early twentieth century. It's a quiet spot containing some important monuments, among them a huge memorial to the first governor, David Collins. Other gravestones have been removed and set into two undulating sandstone walls at the bottom of the park.

Just north of Franklin Square is the excellent **Tasmanian Museum and Art Gallery** at 40 Macquarie St (daily 10am–5pm; free but charge for some special exhibitions; free guided tours Wed–Sun 2.30pm; ⓦ www.tmag.tas.gov.au). The collection is, as the building's name suggests, a mixed bag. Much space is devoted to exploring Tasmania's tragic history, dwelling on penal cruelty, near genocide and the extinction of animal species. As you enter, there's a collection of photographs of the **Tasmanian tiger** (thylacine), thought to have been extinct since 1936 – including a 1920s photo of a proud-looking family posing with their Tasmanian tiger rug spread out before them. The peculiar, flesh-eating, dog-like marsupial, which had a rigid tail, stripes and a backwards-opening pouch, was hunted out of existence by farming families who were fearful for their stock – although unconfirmed sightings of them still occur from time to time. A stuffed example is part of the unexciting taxidermy exhibition in the adjoining room, though the life-size reconstructions of the **megafauna**, giant marsupials that once roamed Australia, on the same level, are far more riveting. On the next level above, an **Aboriginal room** displays cultural artefacts of the island's indigenous people, including some examples of the kind of exquisite shell necklaces that would have adorned "Queen" Truganini, reputed to be the last Aboriginal Tasmanian (see box on p.1048). The display gives a comprehensive account of the Aboriginal people, from their tragic near-extermination to recent events involving land rights campaigns. Particularly poignant is the recording of the voice of **Fanny Cochrane** (1834–1905) singing traditional songs; it is she who was probably the last full-blooded Aboriginal Tasmanian rather than Truganini as the myth relates. The **art gallery** section has a display of colonial art featuring several 1830s and 1840s portraits of the well-known "final" Aborigines, including Manalargenna and Truganini, as well as superb landscape paintings of Tasmania by the nineteenth-century Tasmanian **W.C. Piguenit**. There's also an excellent section on **convicts**: if you can't get to Port Arthur, Richmond Gaol or any of the other convict ruins, this display will convince you of the brutality of the regime.

The **Maritime Museum** (daily 10am–5pm; $6.60) is in the red-brick Carnegie Building opposite the museum on the corner of Argyle and Davey streets. There are memorabilia, photographs and exhibits dominated by models of boats – the most impressive being a third-scale model of an open whaling boat – but the small, modest museum struggles to do justice to Tasmania's maritime history.

West of Franklin Square

There are several worthwhile sights along the straight streets that run west of Franklin Square, particularly Murray and Campbell streets. Three blocks west of the square, on Murray Street, the **State Library** (Mon–Thurs 9.30am–6pm, Fri 9.30am–8pm, Sat 9.30am–12.30pm) holds the **Allport Library and Museum of Fine Arts** (Mon–Fri 9.30am–5pm; free), a private collection of eighteenth- and nineteenth-century furnishings, ceramics, silver and glass, paintings, prints and rare books relating to Australia and the Pacific.

The **Theatre Royal**, on Campbell Street at the corner of Sackville Street (bookings ☎03/6233 2026, ✉ throyalhob@peg.pegasus.oz.au), is Australia's oldest surviving theatre, built in 1837. It has an intimate interior decorated in Regency style, best seen while attending a performance (see p.1067); otherwise, the staff might let you in for a peek. Further up, at the corner of Brisbane Street, the **Penitentiary Chapel and Criminal Courts** (daily tours except Aug 10am, 11.30am, 1pm & 2.30pm; $6.60; bookings essential on ☎0417 361 392) comprise a complex of early buildings with two courtrooms, underground tunnels and cells. There's also a rather spooky ghost tour (nightly 8pm; $8.80).

The Waterfront

The focus of **Sullivans Cove** is busy **Franklin Wharf**, the first commercial centre of Hobart, where merchants erected large warehouses as the colony grew wealthier. In the 1830s Hobart was one of the world's great whaling centres, and to cater for the growing volume of shipping, the New Wharf – **Princes Wharf** – was built, featuring a row of handsome sandstone warehouses on Salamanca Place. As the new wharf became the focus of port activity, the old wharf developed into an industrial centre of flour mills and factories. Part of the the Henry Jones Jam Factory, between Victoria and Macquarie docks on Hunter Street, is now the **Centre for the Arts**, the University of Tasmania's art school. Beyond the original facade in a courtyard there are several large pieces of sculpture and the high-tech new face of the art school. Inside, the **Sir James Plimsoll Gallery** (daily noon–5pm when there is an exhibition; free; ☎03/6266 4300 for details of exhibitions) has several shows a year featuring the work of contemporary Australian artists. The rest of the old jam factory is to be redeveloped and extended into a complex made up of a luxury hotel, restaurant, bar and shops – an indication of the direction the area is now taking. Beyond this, is the renovated old **Gasworks** on Macquarie Street in the former red-light slum district of **Old Wapping**. Its restored stone buildings are attractive enough, but the slick shops, restaurants and enterprises within – many are part of chains – try too hard to attract tourists; one of these is a **whisky distillery** and adjoining museum (daily 9am–7pm; $5.50 including tasting). Opposite is the new **Federation Concert Hall** (bookings free call ☎1800 001 190), attached to the *Hotel Grand Chancellor* and home to the Tasmanian Symphony Orchestra. The brass-clad building is oval shaped, in keeping with the original gas cylinder in the old gasworks, and its accoustics are supposedly the best in Australia.

The old docks along Franklin Wharf are also thriving: at **Victoria Dock** lobster boats are moored, at **Constitution Dock** boats sell fresh and cooked seafood, and alongside is the Mures Fish Centre, a two-level complex of restaurants and cafés (see "Eating and drinking", p.1064). The stylish new development on Elizabeth Street Pier has a slew of trendy bars, eateries and luxury hotel apartments. From Brooke Street Pier and Watermans Dock, any number of **cruises** depart (see box, below), while Murray Street Pier has been jazzed up with several restaurants. In summer, huge international cruise ships berth at the harbour, creating a rather glamorous backdrop to the waterfront pubs. Just behind the Travel and Information Centre on the corner of Davey and Elizabeth streets, is **Mawson's Place**, completed in January 2001. Named after the Antarctic explorer Sir Douglas Mawson (see opposite), this public space uses wooden benches, glass screens and light towers to evoke a strong maritime theme sympathetic to its dockside location. In the square the **Waterside Pavilion** retains the dimensions and facade of the original 1930's building, but the interior is a light, minimalist modern space designed for use as a display area.

Harbour cruises

Cruise Company, Brooke Street Pier (☎03/6234 9294). Fast catamaran cruises. The best trip on the Derwent is their "Iron Pot Cruise" to the river mouth and across to the top of Bruny Island (summer only Sat 2pm; 2hr; $22). The Cadbury's Cruise heads upriver to the chocolate factory at Claremont; it's essential to book in advance as chocaholics treat this as a pilgrimage (Mon–Fri 10am; 4hr; $36.50).

Fell's Historic Ferries, Franklin Wharf Pier (☎03/6223 5893). A range of particularly good-value harbour cruises on the MV *Emmalisa*, all of which include meals of some kind ($11–35).

Lady Nelson, Elizabeth Street Pier (☎03/6234 3348). This replica of the brig in which Matthew Flinders made his exploratory journeys is a sail-training vessel, but also offers bargain summer-only weekend pleasure trips (Sat & Sun 11am, 1pm & 3pm; 1hr 30min; $5). When the ship leaves Hobart at the end of summer for longer journeys on the eastern seaboard, you can join as a paying passenger (about $125 per day).

MV Cartela, Brooke Street Pier (☎03/6223 1914). An eighty-year-old boat that used to bring apples from the Huon. Offers a range of daytime cruises (daily 10am, 12.10pm & 2.30pm; 2hr; $14–31), as well as dinner cruises (Mon, Wed, Thurs & Sat 6pm; 2hr 30min; $36 all-inclusive).

⑪

TASMANIA | Hobart

On **Salamanca Place** the old warehouses, shipping offices and storerooms are now full of arts-and-crafts galleries, speciality shops and cafés, interspersed with characterful waterfront pubs. Salamanca Place comes alive for the open-air **Salamanca Market** (Sat 8am–3pm), an event with an alternative feel and wonderful local food, including produce grown and sold by the Hmong people from Laos, Hobart's most distinctive immigrant group. Several of the narrow lanes and arcades in the area are worth exploring, as is the **Salamanca Arts Centre** (℡ 03/6234 8414, Ⓦ www.salarts.org.au), a former jam-canning factory that's now home to a diverse range of arts-based organizations, from the Tasmanian Writers' Centre to the Terrapin Puppet Theatre. Downstairs, the Peacock Theatre is the performance venue, and there are several galleries (daily 10am–5pm); upstairs, emerging contemporary artists show at the Long Gallery, and there are smaller displays in Side Space (same hours). Outside the theatre, the *Foyer Café* doubles as an installation venue and a large notice board has news of alternative events around town. The Arts Centre also houses studios and offices as well as several shops, including a very browseable secondhand bookshop.

Through the Arts Centre, Woobies Lane leads to **Salamanca Square**, a large public square filled with cafés, boutiques and small shops that was once an old quarry. Here you'll find **Antarctic Adventure** (daily 10am–5pm; $16; Ⓦ www.antarctic.com.au), an overpriced tourist attraction which cashes in on Hobart's obvious links with the Antarctic. Australia has the oldest continuously operating Antarctic station, Mawson, established in 1954, and has considerable claims under the Antarctic Treaty. Organizations based in Hobart include the Australian Antarctic Division and the Australian National Research Expedition (ANARE); the latter was the brainchild of the legendary Australian explorer, **Sir Douglas Mawson**, who led an Australian expedition from 1911 to 1914. Part theme park, part museum, the centre has everything from a "cold experience" room and a mock Antarctic field camp to a planetarium, but a free visit to the foyer exhibition at the Antarctic Division Headquarters at Kingston (see p.1070) is more informative and compelling in its authenticity.

You can take a **guided walk** (daily 10am; 2hr; $17; booking essential on ℡ 03/6230 8233) that explores Sullivans Cove and Salamanca Place, starting from outside the Travel and Information Centre (see p.1055); if this doesn't appeal, excellent interpretive boards are found all around the waterfront.

Battery Point

Kelly's Steps lead up from Salamanca Place to **Battery Point**, a district with an enduring village atmosphere. With the building of the new wharf in the 1830s, a working-class community grew up behind Salamanca Place, transforming what had been farmland into a residential area; it takes its name from the battery of guns that were once sited on present-day **Princes Park**, protecting the harbour below. The newly developing area was first home to small cottages for waterfront workmen and, later, fine merchants' houses: the old pubs, with names such as the *Shipwrights Arms* and *Whalers Return,* leave no doubt about the nature of the population. Narrow streets, closely packed cottages, the flower-filled green of **Arthurs Circus** and the "corner-store" nature of the shops (such as the delightful Bahr's Chocolate Shop, 95 Hampden Rd), enhance the nineteenth-century village feel.

There's a particular concentration of early buildings on De Witt and Cromwell streets. **St George's Church**, on Cromwell Street, is the joint work of John Lee Archer (responsible for the nave, completed in 1838) and James Blackburn (the tower, added in 1847), the early colony's two best-known architects. **Hampden Road** has more fine nineteenth-century mansions, including one at no. 103 known as **Narryna** (Tues–Fri 10.30am–5pm, Sat & Sun 2–5pm; $5), furnished with period antiques. Inside, the **Van Diemen's Land Folk Museum** has a display of entertaining miscellany, while at the back there's a blacksmiths, a vehicle shed housing old traps, and a coach house filled with brewery equipment.

If you want to become really acquainted with the history and architecture of the area, take the **Battery Point Walking Tour** (Sat 9.30am–12.30pm, departing from the Wishing Well, Franklin Square; $10 including morning tea; bookings on ✆03/6223 7570), led by admirably knowledgeable National Trust volunteers.

Around the harbour

The estuary of the **Derwent River** is the deepest (and second-busiest) natural port in Australia. Heading upstream, the scenery becomes increasingly industrial, with a huge zinc-processing plant and, in a more unspoilt setting at Claremont, the **Cadbury's Factory**. Tours of the factory include as much chocolate as you can eat and are understandably popular (Mon–Fri 9am, 9.30am, 10.30am & 1pm; 2hr; $11; booking essential on ✆03/6249 0333); from the city centre, take bus #37 direct to the factory. Alternatively, you can take a cruise there (see box on p.1060), or go on a guided coach tour with Tiger Line (Mon–Fri 9.30am; 3hr; $29; ✆03/6272 6611).

The eastern side of the river is more residential, and looking across you'll see swelling, bush-clad hills with a modest line of homes below. The **Tasman Bridge** connects the eastern shore with the city: it was put out of action for over two years from January 1975, when the 20,000-tonne tanker *Lake Illawarra*, heading for the zinc-smelting works, crashed into it and destroyed two pylons. The ship is still at the bottom of the river, with its cargo of zinc concentrate, as are the bodies of seven crew members and five people in four cars.

The **Kangaroo Bluff Battery** at Bellerive, on the eastern shore – along with its counterparts at Sandy Bay (Alexandra Battery) and Battery Point (Mona Street Battery) – was erected in response to a Russian scare in the late nineteenth century, but it never saw active service. **Bellerive**, which you can reach by ferry from Brooke Street Pier (see box p.1060), has a long, sandy beach at the Esplanade; some swim from it, although the water is somewhat polluted. There's cleaner water and surf beaches across the promontory from Bellerive at **Opossum Bay** (bus #296 from the city centre; no service Sun); while **Seven Mile Beach**, on Frederick Henry Bay, offers calmer swimming (bus #292 or #293). Ten kilometres north of Bellerive is **Risdon Cove**, site of the first European settlement of Van Diemen's Land; interpretive boards explain its early history. To get there, take bus #267, #269 or #270 from the city centre.

Queens Domain

The **Queens Domain**, just north of the city centre, looks attractively green on the map but is considerably less inviting in reality: a sparse, bush-covered hill traversed by walking and jogging tracks but positioned between two very busy highways. At the base of the hill on the Derwent, where the trees suddenly become lush and green, are the **Royal Botanical Gardens** (daily 8am–4.45pm), a formal collection of flower displays and orderly trees. Pick up a leaflet outlining the features of the garden at any entrance, or from the **information centre** (Mon–Fri 9am–noon & 1–4.30pm) at the main entrance on the west side of the park. It's easy enough to walk to the Domain, following Davey Street or Liverpool Street from the city centre, but the gardens are quite far inside the grounds: from the city centre to the gardens should take you about thirty minutes. Bus #17 or any bus to Eastern Shore (including #285, #287, #289 and #293) will drop you at Government House, in the centre of the Domain near the gardens, but there's no transport back. A more interesting way of getting to the gardens is to cruise on the MV *Cartela* from Brooke Street Pier (see box on p.1060).

Sandy Bay

Leafy, well-heeled **Sandy Bay**, a suburb south of Battery Point, is home to a rather luxurious shopping centre, the Royal Yacht Club, and the **Wrest Point Casino** on Sandy Bay Road. An ugly 1970s high-rise, the casino strives hard to be glamorous, but a rather downmarket tone is set by groups of slacks-clad pensioners and swarms of tour groups wearing name tags. More glamorous is the annual weekend **Sandy Bay Regatta** in January, when yachts are moored all around Sandy Bay's marinas, the river is filled with boats, and a funfair is held on the waterfront. At weekends throughout the year, too, there are hundreds of yachts on the water. Several buses go to Sandy Bay from the city centre, among them #56 and #60, and the yellow Busy Bee bus also runs here on a regular circuit from Franklin Square; you can reach Sandy Bay over water from Brooke Street Pier on the MV *Cartela* ($3 one-way; see box on p.1060).

Inland to Mount Wellington and Mount Nelson

Heading inland, the route south and west towards Mount Wellington takes you through South Hobart, on to Cascade Road and past the pretty **Cascade Gardens**. Here, at 140 Cascade Road, the magnificent seven-storey **Cascade Brewery** is the oldest in Australia, still using traditional methods and taking advantage of the pure spring water that cascades – of course – down Mount Wellington. There's a traditional north–south divide between beer drinkers in Tasmania: in Launceston and the north you drink Boags, in Hobart you drink Cascade, although in fact the two breweries merged in 1922. **Tours** run Monday to Friday only (9.30am & 1pm; 2hr; $8.25; bookings essential on ℡ 03/6221 8300), and at a fairly gruelling pace, but you're rewarded with a couple of (light) beers at the workers' bar, and a bottle of Premium Lager at the end of the tour in the brewer's original residence. The small museum of brewing paraphernalia includes a few childhood pictures of the Hollywood actor Errol Flynn, who was brought up in the Cascades area. Buses #48 and #49 go right to the brewery.

In any image of Hobart, **Mount Wellington** (1270m) is always looming in the background, sometimes snow-covered. Access is up a winding road lined with houses as far as **Fern Tree**, where a tavern offers teas and meals at the bottom of the walking track up the mountain (2hr up, 1hr down); the thick bush begins to thin out as you ascend, and by the time you've reached the top it's bare and rocky. Pure, drinkable water cascades from rocks as you climb, and halfway up, just after the first lookout, there's a grassy picnic area with barbecues, toilets and information boards. At the top, the stone **Pinnacle Observatory Shelter** (daily 8am–6pm) has details of the magnificent panorama spread before you – from here it's surprising how empty the land around Hobart really is, nothing but uninhabited bush and grass plains. In summer, the Hobart Metro sometimes runs special **buses** right up to the summit of Mount Wellington from Franklin Square (information on ℡ 13 2201); at other times, you can get halfway up on bus #48 or #49 to Fern Tree. The Mount Wellington Shuttle Bus Service runs to the summit year-round, leaving from the Visitor Information Centre at 20 Davey St, or picking up from accommodation (3 daily; $19.80; ☎0417 341 804). Brake Out Cycling Tours has a tour that includes a visit to the summit, and then a twenty-kilometre downhill mountain-bike ride to Salamanca Place (year-round, subject to demand; $40; ☎03/6239 1080, ⓦwww.view.com.au/brakeout).

The views are also terrific from the Old Signal Station on **Mount Nelson** (340m) above Sandy Bay. The station was established in 1811 to announce the appearance of ships in Storm Bay and the D'Entrecasteaux Channel; the signalman's residence has been converted into tearooms (daily 9.30am–4.30pm), from where you get a panorama of the city below. To get to Mount Nelson, take bus #57 or #58.

Eating and drinking

Hobart's steadfastly Anglo-Saxon fare can't compare with the mainland cities' ethnically eclectic range of cuisines, but its food is becoming more cosmopolitan; the greatest diversity of restaurants and cafés is found along the Elizabeth Street strip in North Hobart. Superlative **seafood** can be had throughout the city, but especially in the restaurants down by the docks. Fishing boats moor at Victoria Dock and sell their catch direct to the public. The food stalls at Saturday's Salamanca Market are excellent – particularly those run by the Hmong from Laos.

Bar Celona, 23 Salamanca Square. Trendy Spanish style café/bar; licensed. Daily 9am–midnight.

Da Angelo Ristorante, 47 Hampden Rd, Battery Point (☎03/6223 7011). A great village spot for a more upmarket Italian meal plus gourmet pizzas; tasty food, generous portions and good service. Licensed. Dinner nightly.

Fish Frenzy, Elizabeth Street Pier. A stylish modern fish café – order your food at the counter and find a seat. The food is cheap and terrific, the staff are friendly and it's licensed. Open daily for lunch and dinner.

Jackman & McGross, 57–59 Hampden Rd, Battery Point. Stylish eat-in bakery that fits in with the upmarket village atmosphere of Battery Point. Excellent pastries and baked savouries, and gourmet baguettes and rolls. Mon–Fri 7.30am–6pm, Sat 7.30am–5pm.

Kaos Cafe, 237 Elizabeth St, North Hobart. Trendy, gay-friendly coffee spot, with groovy music and magazines to read. Focaccias, real fruit muffins and cakes plus delicious all-day breakfast. BYO. Mon noon–8pm, Tues–Fri noon–midnight, Sat 10am–10pm.

La Cuisine, 85 Bathurst St, and the Trafalgar Centre at 110 Collins St. Two café-patisseries serving great cappuccino and excellent pastries, plus mounds of healthy salad. Mon–Fri 9am–6pm, Sat 9.30am–1.30pm.

Machine, 12 Salamanca Square. This quirky combination 1950s retro café-laundry with outside seating is a good cheap place to come for a coffee and join the city's young trendies (often with babies in tow). Mon–Sat 8am–6pm, Sun 9am–6pm.

Mako, Constitution Dock. Takeaway seafood from a boat moored in the dock; cheap and reasonable fish and chips. Daily 10am–8pm.

Marti Zucco, 364 Elizabeth St, North Hobart (☎03/6234 9611). Italian restaurant serving imaginative dishes, including fish, schnitzels and thick-crust pizzas. Large and very popular, with a casual atmosphere; licensed and BYO. Lunch Thurs–Sat, dinner daily from 5.30pm.

Mit Zitrone, 333 Elizabeth St, North Hobart (☎03/6234 8113). Chic award-winning café-restaurant, very much in the Melbourne style, with an innovative, cosmopolitan menu. If the delicious main dishes are out of your range (around $18), there's a cake selection and excellent coffee. BYO. Mon–Sat 10am till late.

Mummy's Coffee Shop, 38 Waterloo Crescent, Battery Point. Trendy café; it's best feature is its range of delicious cakes, but there are also main meals from the Contemporary Australian menu. Licensed and open late. Mon–Thurs & Sun until midnight, Fri & Sat until 2am.

Mures Fish Centre, Victoria Dock. Set among yachts and fishing boats, this two-level food centre (open daily) houses three restaurants, a fishmonger, a bakery (great scallop pies) and a café. Mures Upper Deck (☎03/6231 1999) is an upmarket restaurant which has lovely harbour views; Mures Lower Deck (☎03/6231 2121) has bistro food, with cheaper prices; Orizuru (☎03/6231 1790; closed Sun) serves authentic sushi – their salmon is delicious.

Orient Express, 147A Little Collins St. Good, cheap servings of Malaysian, Indian and Thai food;

there's a small eat-in area, but the emphasis is on takeaways. Closed Sat & Sun.

Palette's Studio Café, 14 Davey St. A handy spot to recharge, right near the Travel and Information Centre and the Tasmanian Museum and Art Gallery, and located below an artist's studio. Mon–Fri 10am–4pm.

Renown Milkbar, 337 Elizabeth St, North Hobart. A Hobart institution whose windows are full of imported chocolates. Good for a coffee or snack after a movie at the nearby cinema. Daily 9am–10.30pm.

Retro Café, 31 Salamanca Place. Relaxed, light and airy place serving the best espresso in town, plus amazingly frothy cappuccinos and wonderful breakfasts. A good place to find out what's on – notices and flyers cover one wall. Outside tables popular on market day (Sat). Mon–Sat 8am–6pm, Sun 8.30am–6pm.

Shipwright's Arms Hotel, cnr Colville and Trumpeter streets, Battery Point. Old pub, popular with the yachtie crowd. Dishes up a legendary fresh seafood platter.

Sisco's on the Pier, Murray Street Pier (☎ 03/6223 2059). Waterfront Spanish–Mediterranean restaurant guarantees a fine, though pricey, feast. Licensed.

Vanadol's, 353 Elizabeth St, North Hobart (☎ 03/6234 9307). Popular, casual place serving Thai, Indonesian and Malaysian food. Very affordable; BYO. Booking advised. Open Tues–Sun from 6pm.

Zanskar Café, 39 Barrack St. Laid-back place for serious vegetarians and vegans, serving delicious food. There's a warm community atmosphere and plenty of useful notice boards, while the feel is spacious with a gallery level, and clean wood decor. Mon–Fri 9am–9pm.

Entertainment and nightlife

Nightlife – what there is of it – is focused around the waterfront. The focal point is *Knopwood's Retreat* (see below), which attracts a large crowd on Friday and Saturday night, and has a popular nightclub upstairs. The more conservative *Wrest Point Casino*, at 410 Sandy Bay Rd in Sandy Bay, is open late every night for gambling, drinking and dancing (☎ 03/6225 0112; casino Fri & Sat 2pm–3am, Sun–Thurs 2pm–2am; *Regine's* nightclub Wed–Sun 10pm–4am).

If you want to know **what's on**, Thursday's *Mercury* has a "gig guide", (ⓦ www.tasguide.com.au) and you could also check its Friday and Saturday entertainment section or *W-Hole Magazine*, a do-it-yourself monthly with a gig guide and reviews. As for **live music**, Tasmania is too small to attract many bands, so the ones that play the pubs are mainly local. The few big events that do occur attract an extraordinarily varied audience, as everybody goes to everything. For more interesting gigs, keep an eye on what's happening at the University of Tasmania campus at Sandy Bay (☎ 03/6220 2861). **Concerts** are staged by the Tasmanian Symphony Orchestra at the Federation Concert Hall (see p.1060) and by the Tasmanian Conservatorium of Music at the Conservatorium (5–7 Sandy Bay Rd; ☎ 03/6226 7306); the Conservatorium also perform at churches around town (free or $3–5). You'll find traditional and touring **theatre** at the Theatre Royal, and more contemporary local shows at the Peacock Theatre in Salamanca Place; in February and March there's a season of outdoor Shakespeare in the Royal Botanical Gardens. Most **tickets** can be booked via Centretainment, at 132 Liverpool St (☎ 03/6234 5998); guides and calendars can be picked up at *Kaos* and other cafés.

Bars, clubs and live music

Bavarian Tavern, 281 Liverpool St (☎ 03/6234 7977). Known to locals as the "Bav Tav", this fun down-to-earth venue has bands, jamming sessions, dancing and cheap meals.

Brooke Street Bar and Café, 19 Morrison St, cnr Brooke St. Waterfront pub, with large windows letting in lots of light onto the wacky beachbar-style

interior. Outside tables too. Open until 2am Sat & Sun.

Carbon, 11 Franklin Wharf. Hobarts newest, trendiest club. Open Wed, Fri & Sat 11pm–late. Entry $5–9.

Juice Niteclub, 7 Watchorn St (☎ 03/6234 5165). Barn-like bar, lively and packed on Fri and Sat night.

Knopwood's Retreat, 39 Salamanca Place. Pub

Gay and lesbian Hobart

Acts of male homosexuality were still a criminal offence in Tasmania until 1997. Founded in 1988, the **Tasmanian Gay and Lesbian Rights Group** (TGLRG) put persistent pressure on the government. Led by spokesperson **Rodney Croome**, their rally cry "We're here, we're queer, and we're not going to the mainland" certainly shook up conservative Tasmania; thousands signed the petition to urge the reform of the law. Backlash across Tasmania included the infamous anti-gay rally in Ulverstone on the northwest coast in 1988. The Federal Government and the UN Human Rights Committee also pressed for change, and Tasmania's anti-gay upper house finally cracked, changing the law on May 1, 1997.

The TGLRG office is at 82 Hampden Rd, Battery Point (☏03/6224 3556), and there's a Gay and Lesbian Community Centre (GLC) in North Hobart (PO Box 152, North Hobart, TAS 7002; ☏0419 565 452). GLC publish a monthly newsletter, *CentreLines* ($1), which is sold from the TGLRG stall at Salamanca Market and details events and occasional dance parties round town. The only **gay and lesbian club** is tame but enjoyable: *La Cage*, 73 Collins St (Thurs–Sat from 11pm; ☏03/6231 5882). *T-42°* and *Syrup* are popular alternatives. The **Gay Information Line** (☏03/6234 8179) is a five-minute recorded message that provides pointers for gay and lesbian visitors, details of events and meeting places and numbers for further information; there's also a specifically **Lesbian Line** (Thurs 6–10pm; ☏03/6231 4228).

that's a favourite with students, yachties and just about everyone else, with a relaxed coffee parlour/bar feel; plenty of magazines and newspapers, plus outside tables. Open until midnight on Fri, when the pavement outside is packed. Closed Sun.

The New Sydney Hotel, 87 Bathurst St (☏03/6234 4516). Hobart's Irish pub, featuring live music nightly except Mon – from traditional Irish to blues and folk.

Republic Bar & Café, 299 Elizabeth St (☏03/6234 6954). Laid-back lounge atmosphere, funky decor and free music, usually blues and jazz, five nights a week. Good meals too – with lots of seafood on the menu.

Rockerfeller's Café & Bar, 11 Morrison St (☏03/6234 3490). Cocktails, live jazz Sun nights and a Contemporary Australian menu. Lunch Mon–Fri, dinner daily.

St Ives Hotel, 86 Sandy Bay Rd, Sandy Bay (☏03/6323 3655). "Boutique" hotel that has its own brewery. Popular club nights on Fri and Sat. The excellent bottle shop at the back has a good range of Tasmanian wines.

Syrup, above *Knopwood's*, 39 Salamanca Place (☏03/6224 8249). The second floor of this trendy club doubles as a restaurant until 11.30pm; at midnight the nightclub takes over. Thurs & Sat there's techno, house, drum'n'bass on one floor, 1980s retro on another; Fri it's live disco and funk; and Wed is a 1960s theme night with go-go girls and visuals. Open till 6am on Fri & Sat; $5–7.

T-42°, Elizabeth Street Pier (☏03/6224 7742). Stylish lounge bar, upmarket but not snobby. Half

the place is an eating area serving well-priced modern meals at lunch and dinner, or you can come in for a coffee or cake in the afternoon. Good choice of wines available by the glass. Daily 11.30am–1.30am.

Temple Place, 121 Macquarie St (☏03/6223 2883). Sophisticated jazz venue, with restaurant, cocktail bar and cigar lounge. Open nightly and Sun afternoons.

Theatre Royal Hotel, 31 Campbell St (☏03/6234 6925). Despite the trendily upmarket renovations, the public bar is as down-to-earth as ever. People spill in here after the theatre. Recommended bistro too. Open until midnight; closed Sun.

Film, theatre, concerts and cabaret

AFI State Cinema, 375 Elizabeth St, North Hobart (☏03/6234 6318). Art-house and foreign films; reduced ticket prices Wed night. Licensed bar.

Federation Concert Hall, 1 Davey St (bookings free call ☏1800 001 190) Home to the Tasmanian Symphony Orchestra, with concerts on a regular basis.

Playhouse Theatre, 106 Bathurst St (☏03/6234 1536). Home to an amateur theatrical society that regularly puts on plays. Premises are also rented out to travelling shows.

Salamanca Arts Centre, 77 Salamanca Place (☏03/6234 8414). Base of several performance companies, including the Terrapin Puppet Theatre, which puts on touring shows – including a puppet picnic at the end of December in St Davids Park.

Puppeteers are welcome to come in and look around. The theatre venue here is the Peacock Theatre which specializes in contemporary works, performed by various local theatre companies. **Theatre Royal**, 29 Campbell St (℡ 03/6233 2299). This lovely old place (see p.1059) is not too expensive or stuffy, offering a broad spectrum of entertainment from comedy nights to serious drama. The ancillary Backspace is smaller and more experimental – often hosting very entertaining Theatresports on Fri nights.
Village Cinema Centre, 181 Collins St (℡ 03/6234 7288). Seven screens showing mainstream new releases; discount day is Tues.

Festivals and events

Hobart's premier event is the last part of the **Sydney–Hobart yacht race** (see also p.182). The two hundred or so yachts, which leave Sydney on December 26, arrive in Hobart around December 29, making for a lively New Year's Eve waterfront party. **Taste of Tasmania** (Dec 28–Jan 5), a festival promoting Tasmanian food, wine and beer, is held at Princes Wharf to coincide with the arrival of the boats; stalls sell samples of Tasmanian products at around $5 a plate, and there's lots of entertainment.

The week-long **Hobart Fringe Festival** at the beginning of February has visual arts and performance components; check cafés for flyers. The new **10 Days on the Island** festival is Tasmania's first international arts festival, held biannually in March/April in venues around Tasmania (℡ 1300/136 784, Ⓦ www.tendaysontheisland.org); a celebration of island cultures, it combines the best of local arts with the best from island cultures throughout the world. Also held in different locations around Tasmania is the **Tasmanian Writer's Festival**, held each August and featuring readings and talks from local and international writers (℡ 03/6224 0029, Ⓦ www.fearless.net.au/taswriters). In late February the six-day outdoor **Forest Festival** held near the Huon River features environmental talks and workshops, market stalls, local and interstate bands, circus performance and DJs; ask at the *Zanskar Café* (p.1065) for details. The whole city shuts down on October 24 during the **Royal Hobart Show** (Oct 23–26), an agricultural festival. The **Australian Wooden Boat Festival** is held in November in even-numbered years, marked by a host of boats moored around the docks; activities include theatrical and musical performances, and there's even a School of Wooden Boat Building offering courses to visitors (℡ 03/6266 3486).

Listings

Airlines Kendell (℡ 13 1300); Par Avion, Cambridge Airport (℡ 03/6248 5390); Qantas (℡ 13 1313) or their travel centre at 77 Elizabeth Street Mall (℡ 03/6237 4900); RegionAir (free call ℡ 1800 818 455); TasAir, Cambridge Airport (℡ 03/6248 5577).
American Express, 74A Liverpool St (℡ 03/6234 3711).
Banks Branches of all major banks on Elizabeth St.
Bike rental and tours Cycling Adventures Tasmania (℡ 0412 913 148) has mountain bikes to rent outside the *Machine* café on Salamanca Square. They also offer cycling tours of the city centre. Brake Out Cycling Tours (℡ 03/6239 1080) offer a Mount Wellington descent tour (see p.1064), plus fully equipped mountain bikes for touring, with cheaper long-term rates.

Bookshops Ellison and Hawker Bookshop, 90 Liverpool St, is the best in Hobart, with an excellent travel section upstairs. Fullers Bookshop, 140 Collins St, and Hobart Bookshop, 22 Salamanca Square, are also good. For a fine range of secondhand books, try Rapid Eye Books, 36–38 Sandy Bay Rd, Battery Point.
Bus companies Tasmanian Redline Coaches (℡ 1300/360 000) and Tassie Link (℡ 03/6272 7300), both based at the Hobart Transit Centre, 199 Collins St. Hobart Coaches, 4 Liverpool St (℡ 03/6233 9466).
Campervan rental Tasmanian Campervan Hire (Hobart airport; ℡ 03/6248 9623 or free call 1800 807 119), from $95 per day, minimum five-day hire.
Car rental Auto Rent Hertz, 122 Harrington St (℡ 03/6237 1111, ℻ 6234 1955), has rates from

$67 per day, also campervans; Avis, at the airport (☎03/6248 5424), has similar rates; Lo-Cost Auto Rent, 225 Liverpool St (☎03/6231 0550 or free call 1800 647 060), has rentals from $55 per day; Advance Car Rentals (☎03/6224 0822) also have 4WDs, from $105 per day; Marquee Car Rentals, 248 Argyle St (☎03/6231 3820), offers very cheap weekly rates; Rent-A-Bug, 105 Murray St (☎03/6231 0678 or 6231 0300), has VW Beetles from $45 per day.

Disabled travellers The Aged and Disability Care Information Centre, 181 Elizabeth St (☎03/6234 7448, ✉adcis@tassie.net.au), is an excellent source of information, providing free mobility maps of Hobart. Maxi Taxis (☎03/6234 8061) has specially adapted vehicles.

Diving Southern Tas Divers, 212 Elizabeth St (☎03/6234 7243), organizes dive charters and rents out equipment; The Dive Shop, 42 Bathurst St (☎03/6234 3428), runs PADI certification courses; Sport and Dive, 109 Elizabeth St (☎03/6234 3798), arranges fishing charters and rents out dive gear.

Environment If you want to find out about, and volunteer for, any environmental conservation programmes, the Wilderness Society's campaign office is at 130 Davey St (☎03/6224 1550) and its shop is at 33 Salamanca Place (☎03/6234 9370). The Australian Trust for Conservation Volunteers has an office at the Salamanca Arts Centre, Salamanca Place (☎03/6224 4911).

Hospitals Royal Hobart Hospital, 48 Liverpool St (☎03/6222 8308).

Internet access There's free access at the Service Tasmania Shop at 134 Macquarie St (Mon–Fri 9am–4.45pm; max 30min; bookings on ☎03/6233 3382), and at the State Library (see p.1059). *Drifters Cafe* is at Salamanca Place (Mon–Fri 10am–6pm, Sat 10am–5.30pm, Sun 11am–5.30pm; $5 per 30min).

Laundrette *Machine*, 12 Salamanca Square, is a combined café/laundry (see p.1064).

Newspapers Ellison and Hawker Newsagency, 92 Elizabeth St, is the island's only outlet for foreign newspapers.

Outdoors and sport Jolly Swagman, 107 Elizabeth St, is a good outlet for renting camping gear; Paddy Pallin, 76 Elizabeth St, has quality outdoor equipment to buy and rent, and provides bushwalking information; Gowshawk Gear, 55 Liverpool St sells secondhand, samples and discounted outdoor gear and will buy your used stuff.

Pharmacy Macquarie Pharmacy, 180 Macquarie St (daily 8am–10pm); North Hobart Pharmacy, 360–362 Elizabeth St (daily 8am–10pm).

Post office GPO, cnr Elizabeth and Macquarie streets (Mon–Fri 8am–6pm). Poste restante: Hobart GPO, TAS 7000.

Taxis City Cabs Co-op (☎03/6234 3633); Combined Services (☎13 2227). Maxi taxis (☎03/6234 8061) for disabled-friendly taxis.

Tours Tiger Line (☎03/6272 6611) runs large-group bus tours: their Mount Wellington and Hobart Great Sights Tour covers the city, the dock area, Battery Point, Mount Wellington and the Royal Botanical Gardens (Tues, Thurs & Sat 2pm; 3hr 30min; $29). Tiger Line also offers day-trips to Port Arthur, Richmond, the Huon Valley, Bruny Island, and the Derwent Valley. The other big tour operator, Experience Tasmania (☎03/6234 3336), has a wide range of city tours; their *Hobart Explorer*, a bus dolled up as a tram, does a three-hour sightseeing tour (daily: Jan–April 10am & 2pm; May–Dec 10am), plus trips to Mount Field National Park. More satisfying are Tassie Link's small-group day-tours (☎03/6272 7300) to Port Arthur (Tues, Thurs, Fri & Sun; $57–65) and Mount Field National Park (daily; $84). The best tour to Bruny Island is with Bruny Island Ventures (book through Tiger Line), which does a small-group day-tour led by a knowledgeable guide (departing Hobart Mon, Wed, Fri & Sun 8.30am, returning 5.30pm; $105 including meals). City Sites Under Lights do evening tours of Hobart (daily April–Sept 7pm, Oct–March 8pm; $40; ☎03/6235 4353). The Bottom Bits Bus (free call ☎1800 777 103, ⊛www.bottombitsbus.com) offer a range of really excellent small-group tours from Hobart (all $69), including Port Arthur and the Tasman Peninsula, Bruny Island and Mount Field National Park.

Women There are women's information services at the Office of the Status of Women, 3rd Floor, Franklin Square Building, Macquarie St (☎03/6234 2166), and the Hobart Women's Health Centre, 326 Elizabeth St, North Hobart (☎03/6231 3212).

YHA Tasmania, Head Office, 28 Criterion St (Mon–Fri 9am–5pm; ☎03/6234 9617, ⊛www.yha.com.au).

Around Hobart

South of Hobart is picturesque channel, orchard and island country. The D'Entrecasteaux Channel region and the Huon Valley form Tasmania's premier fruit-growing district, which once exported millions of apples to England; since the UK joined the European Community, however, two-thirds of the apple orchards have been abandoned. The region is also heavily forested, and around **Geeveston** magnificent forests are still logged. **Hartz Mountains National Park** and the **Picton River** are easily accessible to the west of Geeveston. As you head down the coast, caves, thermal springs and an operational railway are all accessible en route to **Cockle Creek**, the southernmost point you can drive to in Australia, with foot access along a track into the South West National Park. Offshore, across the D'Entrecasteaux Channel, **Bruny Island** – Truganini's birthplace – has deserted beaches and coastal bushwalks. To the north, you can head inland to New Norfolk and on to **Mount Field National Park**, while to the east lies historic **Richmond**, and, on the Tasman Peninsula, the old penal settlement at **Port Arthur**.

South: the D'Entrecasteaux Channel, Huon Valley and beyond

The **Channel Highway** hugs the coastline south from Hobart and makes a lovely drive around the shores of the **Huon Peninsula**, circling back beside the Huon River to Huonville: heading to Huonville directly, it's a much shorter 37km on

AROUND HOBART

the Huon Highway. The first community on the Channel Highway is
KINGSTON (Metro bus #60 from the Hobart bus interchange), a leafy resi-
dential suburb with a wide, sandy beach; there are more good beaches, such as
Blackmans Bay, on the little promontory below Kingston. Good cafés on Beach
Road include *Echo Café* and there's excellent curry at *Goa*. Just south of Kingston,
Australia's **Antarctic Headquarters** (Mon–Fri 9am–5pm; free) will fill you in
on Antarctic exploration and stock you up with cheap food at the decent canteen.
Further south at **SNUG**, the *Snug Beach Caravan Park*, 34 Beach Rd (ⓣ & ⓕ
03/6267 9138; cabins ❹–❺; on-site vans ❸), has grassy campsites right on the
beach, and an excellent campers' kitchen. At **KETTERING**, a thriving fishing
port, there's an attractive marina full of boats; it's from here that you catch the ferry
for Bruny Island. The *Oyster Cove Inn* (ⓣ03/6267 4446; B&B ❹–❺) is right on
the water, not far from the ferry terminal, and has good views from its restaurant,
which specializes in seafood and local produce. More upmarket is *Herons Rise
Vineyard* on Saddle Road (ⓣ036267 4199, ⓦwww.heronsrise.com.au; ❻–❼),
which has luxury self-contained cabins gazing across the marina. Inside the visitors centre at the ferry terminal, the *Mermaid Cafe* has good food and excellent
coffee (daily 9am–5pm; licensed). Roaring 40s Ocean Kayaking, based at the
marina (ⓣ03/6267 5000), has **sea kayaks** for rent (from $15 per hour, $45 per
day), and also organizes day-trips (Mon–Fri; $110) and longer tours. At the pret-
ty village of **WOODBRIDGE**, 4km further south, there are a couple more
places to stay: the *Woodbridge Hotel* (ⓣ03/6267 4604, ⓕ6267 4828; B&B ❺) has
great rooms and moderately priced food (lunch daily, dinner Thurs–Sat), or there's
the *Old Woodbridge Rectory* (ⓣ03/6267 4742; ⓦwww.rectory.alltasmanian.com;
B&B ❼), an attractive B&B with disabled access. You can get to Kettering and
Woodbridge with Hobart Coaches on weekdays (4 daily).

On the other side of the peninsula, **CYGNET**, at the centre of a major fruit-
growing region, is a likely spot to look for **fruit-picking work** in the harvest
season of March and April. *Balfes Hill YHA*, at 340 Craddoc Rd (ⓣ03/6295
1551, ⓕ6295 0875; ❶), has all the necessary contacts; the manager here also
offers day-trips to surrounding sights ($15). The hostel is 4km from Cygnet,
but will pick you up if you call in advance. In town, the laid-back *Red Velvet
Lounge Cafe* (open daily) has a great atmosphere, affordable **meals** and an in-
house healthfood shop. **Talune Wildlife Park**, 6km southeast of Cygnet, just
off the Woodbridge Hill Road (daily 9.30am–5pm; $8.50;
ⓦwww.talune.com.au), has a wide range of native marsupials (you can pat a
wombat and a koala), birds and farm animals, as well as an excellent platypus
display. You can stay here in one of their self-contained cabins (❺). Tassie Link
runs an evening service from Hobart to Cygnet (Mon–Fri 5.15pm).

HUONVILLE, on the Huon River, is a commercial centre, the focus of the
region's apple industry. You can arrange to take a **jet-boat ride** through the rapids
(35min; $48) or rent a pedal boat (30min; $12) at the kiosk on the Esplanade
(ⓣ03/6264 1838). At **GROVE**, 6km towards Hobart on the Huon Highway, is
the **Huon Valley Apple and Heritage Museum** (daily 9am–5pm; $4.50),
which celebrates the local produce; the museum is surprisingly interesting, with
hundreds of varieties of apples, assorted apple paraphernalia from what was once
a huge export industry, and plenty of things to taste. For more substantial eats, try
the *Apple Valley Teahouse* just outside Huonville on the way to Grove.

Southwest beyond Huonville, the road follows the west bank of the Huon to
FRANKLIN, a handsome riverside community with several fine old buildings. You can stay in the swanky *Franklin Lodge* (ⓣ03/6266 3506; ❼), have a
good-value meal at the *Franklin Tavern* or stop off at the *Franklin Tea Gardens*, a
popular and affordable café with great home-made food. **PORT HUON**,

about 10km further along, was once a bustling, apple-exporting port but is now a quiet, recreational fishing area. The hub of activity here is *Kermandie Lodge*, on the highway (Ⓣ03/6297 1110, Ⓕ6297 1710; ❺–❻). The resort has a variety of places to eat and runs day-cruises on the Huon River to the Atlantic salmon farms (daily 2pm; 1hr; $18; minimum six people; bookings on Ⓣ03/6297 1052). The council-run riverfront Sports Club has every facility, including a heated swimming pool, gym, spa, sauna and squash courts.

Tassie Link runs through Grove, Huonville, Franklin and Port Huon en route to Geeveston and Dover (Mon–Fri 6 daily, Sat & Sun 1 daily).

Geeveston and around

GEEVESTON, 8km from Port Huon, is a sleepy but solid town at the centre of the Southern Forest, a traditional logging centre, with two huge upright logs acting as an entrance to the town. Confrontation between conservationists and the timber industry here led to the so-called "Battle of Farmhouse Creek" in 1986, a dispute won by the conservationists, after which some of the forests were awarded World Heritage listing. The Forestry Commission was awarded millions of dollars in compensation, to be used on special forestry projects, one of which is the **Forest and Heritage Centre** in the town hall on Church Street (daily 10am–4.30pm; $4). Displays explain how the Southern forests grow and look at the history of logging in the area – including the Farmhouse Creek dispute. There's also a gallery of local woodwork and a woodturner in residence (lessons are available if you're keen). After visiting the centre, drive along Arve Road, where several boardwalks have been constructed through magnificent swamp gum and eucalypt forests – they're detailed on the free leaflet that's handed out.

Twenty-four kilometres southwest along Arve Road is the rugged **Hartz Mountains National Park**, with its glacial lakes, rainforests and alpine moorlands; a day-walk map is available from the Forest and Heritage Centre. From Arve Road, a stony, unsealed track winds up for 12km, with several stopping-off points; at the end of the track it's a couple of minutes' walk to Waratah Lookout, with great views over the Huon Valley and the Southern forests. Another walk (4km) heads off to the sometimes snowcapped Hartz Peak (1255m); most of the walk is boardwalked, but parts are wet and boggy underfoot and there's the potential for fog to settle and icy winds and snow to sweep in at any time – recommended for well-prepared walkers only.

The **Picton River** skirts the Hartz Mountains from its source deep in the South West National Park and continues towards the **Tahune Reserve**, at the junction with the Huon River, just north of Hartz Mountain National Park. With its bouncy rapids, intermittent gentle sections and magnificent wilderness scenery, it's a popular, short (and affordable) **rafting** alternative to the Franklin River. Rafting Tasmania (Ⓣ03/6227 9516) runs year-round day-trips from Hobart for around $125.

Dover and around

DOVER, 21km from Geeveston, is a scenic fishing village on a large bay – **Port Esperance**. Though it's not especially friendly, it's very pretty, with trees everywhere, and lush hills surrounding the village, backed by the clear, virtually triangular, outline of **Adamsons Peak** (1226m), snowcapped in winter. Boats moor off a picturesque jetty in the bay, where two tiny tree-covered islets are silhouetted against the sky at dusk. Between November and May you can arrange **cruises** around the bay on the vintage 1880 cutter *Olive May*, locally crafted from Huon pine, with the Southwest Passage Cruising Co (daily 10.30am; 2hr; $35; longer cruises and charters are also available; Ⓣ03/6298 1062).

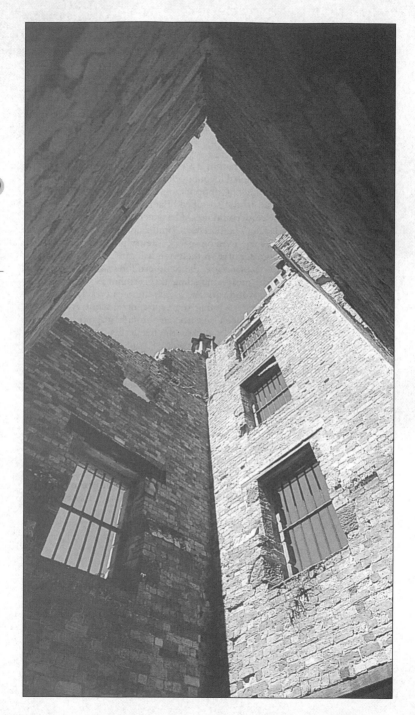

The hub of Dover is the *Dover Hotel*, on the Huon Highway (☎03/6298 1210, ⓕ6298 1504; motel units ❹, rooms ❹, dorms ❶), which has an old-fashioned dining room overlooking the water, and a backpackers' lodge at the back beside an apple orchard and rolling fields. The *Dover Beachside Caravan Park* on Kent Beach Road (☎03/6298 1301; cabins ❹, on-site vans ❷) is also scenically sited near the jetty, beside a creek. Back up towards Geeveston, the picturesque waterfront cottage *Huon Charm* (☎03/6297 6314, ⓦwww.tassie.net.au/huoncharm; ❻) is a more secluded alternative; it's 12km north near Police Point. Although you can find fuel and supplies 20km south of Dover at **Southport** (the last place to get either), you're better off stocking up in Dover itself, where there's more choice and better value.

Thirty-one kilometres from Dover are the Hastings Caves, in the foothills of Adamsons Peak, with the **Thermal Springs State Reserve** en route. The springs (daily 10am–4pm, in Jan until 6pm; $4.40; ⓦwww.dpiwe.tas.gov.au) are in a lush setting, and there are several walks in the grounds, though the pool itself is very disappointing – small, shallow and tepid (ranging from 20°C to 30°C). At the time of writing a new visitors centre (also housing a café and some self-contained accommodation) was under construction in the reserve; call ☎03/6298 3209 for more information. **Hastings Caves**, a few kilometres further on from the springs, are more worthwhile: Newdegate Cave, the best, is open daily for tours (11am, 1pm, 2pm & 3pm, with extra tours Oct–March; 45min; $13); it's always wet and cold inside, so bring something warm to wear. Also on offer are **adventure tours** of King George V Cave (6hr including BBQ and swim; $135), and a Caves, Formation and Wildlife Tour (3hr; $69); tours are run on demand and need to be booked a week ahead – phone ☎1300/368 550 for availability.

Other attractions in the immediate area include the **Ida Bay Bush Tram**, the most southerly railway in Australia (1hr 20min; $12; ☎03/6223 5893 for details of services). This vintage, narrow-gauge bush railway, in operation since 1914, runs 16km along the southern edge of Southport to the beautiful beach at Deep Hole Bay, where trains pause for twenty minutes before returning. You can stay a few kilometres away at **LUNE RIVER** in the rambling weatherboard *Lune River Youth Hostel* (☎03/6298 3163, ⓔluneriver@trump.net.au; ❶), which has a reputation as an outdoor activities centre; it organizes glow-worm cave tours (3hr; $33), rents out mountain bikes and has a full-moon feast every month with pizzas baked in a mud-brick oven. If you notify the hostel in advance, they can pick you up from Dover for a small charge, and they also do pick-ups and drop-offs at Cockle Creek for the South Coast Track (especially useful in the off-season months May–Oct when they can connect you with buses terminating at Dover). **Lune River** itself isn't a town but rather a collection of houses and a post office, with a river that's popular with gem fossickers.

Tassie Link has a weekday service from Hobart to Dover (3–4 daily); their "Wilderness" service to Cockle Creek stops en route at Lune River (Nov–April Mon, Wed & Fri).

Cockle Creek

Beyond Lune River and Ida Bay, the unsurfaced Cockle Creek Road takes you past picturesque sheltered bays and scenic coastal forests, where wild flowers bloom in summer, on the lovely, unspoilt **Recherche Bay** (pronounced "research" by locals). There are lots of camping spots along the shore, and some people love the area so much that they live here semi-permanently in shacks and old buses – mainly fishing-obsessed retirees after the abundant crayfish, cockles and fish in the bay. Pit toilets and water are the only facilities. The pleasant and easy Fishers Bay Walk takes you around the coast (4km round-trip), but by far the most popular walk here is the muddy but boardwalked first part of the **South Coast Track** to the beach at South Cape Bay and back (4hr); the entire length of the track is for the very experienced only, but this portion gives you a small taste (see p.1139 for details of the whole walk).

Bruny Island

For beautiful lonely beaches and superb bushwalking, one of the best places in Tasmania is **Bruny Island**. Almost two distinct islands joined by a narrow isthmus (where you can sometimes see Little penguins from a specially constructed viewing platform), it's roughly 71km from end to end and has a population of only four hundred. The cost of taking a car across on the ferry deters casual visitors, so the island is never very full. The ferry from Kettering goes to substantially rural North Bruny, although most of the settlements, and places to stay and eat, are on South Bruny – the more scenic half, with its state forests and reserves.

North Bruny

The **ferry from Kettering** (see p.1070) sails at least nine times daily (7.15am–6.30pm, later on Fri; 20min; ☏03/6267 4494 for times, or consult Friday's *Mercury* in Hobart; $21 per car return or $23 public holidays, bikes $3, foot passengers free). The **Bruny D'Entrecasteaux Visitor Centre** at the Kettering ferry terminal (daily 9am–5pm; ☏03/6267 4494, Ⓦwww.tasmania-holiday.com) books accommodation on the island, much of which is in self-catering cottages and must be arranged in advance. The centre can also supply you with **information** on the island, including a free map. You'll need a car to get around: there's no transport – and no town – at Roberts Point, where the ferry docks on the north of the island. Renting a bike in Hobart or seeing the island on foot are the only alternatives. Hobart Coaches operates services from Hobart to Kettering that connect with a couple of the ferries, or you could come on the excellent small group day-tour from Hobart with Bruny Island Ventures ($105; book through Tiger Line on ☏03/6272 6611).

The main settlement on **North Bruny** is **DENNES POINT** at the northern extreme of the island, which has a general store, a jetty and an upmarket holiday unit, *Kelly's Lookout*, on Bull Bay Road (☏03/6260 6466, Ⓔkellys lookout@hotmail.com; ❽). En route, in the secluded settlement of **Barnes Bay**, pretty Shelter Cove was the first "Black station" to be established for the forced resettlement of Aboriginal people (see box p.1048). Camel Tracks Tasmania, based at Barnes Bay, offers **camel treks** around the island (daily on demand; 10min $7; 2hr 30min $50 including morning tea; 7hr $100 including gourmet lunch; bookings on ☏03/6260 6335).

South Bruny

At the northern end of the isthmus connecting the two islands, a small monument to **Truganini** (the "last" Tasmanian Aborigine, who was born here) stands atop the tallest sand dune (reached by a high wooden stairway), offering superb views of the southern part of the island, where three former reserves have been turned into **South Bruny National Park** (for permits, see p.1052). You can see the Fluted Cape State Reserve region to the east of Adventure Bay; here, a steep climb to the top of the Cape (2hr 30min return) offers still better views. The Labillardiere State Reserve area occupies the western "hook" of South Bruny Island; a winding, bumpy road leads to the **Cape Bruny Lighthouse**, built in 1836 and manned until 1996; beyond this a seven-hour walking trail explores the peninsula. East of the hook, across **Cloudy Bay** is the final chunk of the national park. You can do a spot of bushcamping here (pit toilet only, no water), and at Neck Beach about 1.5km from the isthmus viewing point (pit toilet, water, shelter with barbecue).

ADVENTURE BAY is the main centre on the east coast; its waters are safe for swimming, and there's a general store and the **Bligh Museum of Pacific Discovery** (daily 10am–3pm; $3). Bruny Island has always been linked with early explorers, for whom it provided a safe refuge after the arduous journey across the Southern Ocean, and the museum displays maps, documents, paintings and artefacts relating to landings there. The *Penguin Tea Rooms* (daily 10am–5pm) serves freshly baked food, while the best place to stay is the helpful *Lumeah YHA Hostel*, in a charming homestead on Quiet Corner, off Main Road (T & F 03/6293 1265; rooms ❸, dorms ❶); the managers can advise on walks and take people to view the penguins. You can **camp** next to the beach at the *Captain Cook Caravan Park* (T03/6293 1128; on-site vans ❷) or at the better *Adventure Bay Holiday Village* (T03/6293 1270; on-site vans ❷, cabins ❹–❺), both on Adventure Bay Road. Just north of town, the *Hothouse Cafe* (open daily for breakfast, lunch & dinner; bookings essential after 5.30pm) offers exotic dining in a hothouse amongst peacocks and parrots, surrounded by an abundant vegetable garden, with panoramic views across the Neck Beach and all the way to Mount Wellington.

ALONNAH, Bruny's main settlement, is on the D'Entrecasteaux Channel coast. As well as a general store here, you'll find the *Hotel Bruny*, on Bruny Main Road (T03/6293 1148; motel-style units ❺), which also does good-value counter meals (except Sun), and has the island's only bottle shop. Five kilometres south at **LUNAWANNA**, the Mangana Store (daily 8am–8pm) sells petrol, groceries and great veggie-, fish- and hamburgers, and has details of *Bruny Island Explorer Cottages* on Light House Road (T03/6293 1271; linen supplied ❾); the bakery next to the store bakes **pizzas** (Sat only). You can also stay at *Sea Rise Cottage* (T03/6293 1255; ❻), a self-contained weatherboard cottage facing the water. From Lunnawanna, it's a scenic drive south to **Cloudy Bay**, with its great sweep of surf beach; there's secluded accommodation here in the self-catering beachfront *Cloudy Bay Cabin* (T03/6293 1171; ❻), powered by solar energy and gas. You can also stay just north of Cloudy Bay in the comfortable self-contained cottage at *Inala* (T03/6293 1217; W www.inalabruny.com.au; ❻), which also serves as the base for Inala Nature Tours. These nature-based guided tours – from half-day to extended trips – are run by a qualified biologist and are customized to suit the interests and size of the group. A typical tour will take in Adventure Bay, Cloudy Bay and Cape Bruny.

Bruny Island Charters do excellent and very popular all-day **wildlife cruises** which explore the south, around Fluted Cape, following the spectacular cliff line, to a seal colony; if you're lucky you'll see dolphins and maybe even a southern right whale, as well as the abundant birdlife in the area (Oct–April daily except Sat; pick up from Hobart 8.30am, from Adventure Bay 10.30am; 6hr; $150 including lunch; T03/6234 3336, F6234 3166, W www.brunycharters.com). They also offer a shorter cruise (Oct–April Mon–Fri 8am, Sat 9am, 11am, 1pm & 3pm; $55).

New Norfolk and Mount Field National Park

Heading inland from Hobart through the Derwent Valley towards Mount Field National Park, the A10 hugs the Derwent River for the 50km to the well-preserved colonial buildings of **NEW NORFOLK**. It was to here that the original settlers of Norfolk Island (see p.335) were moved between 1806 and 1814. The sizeable town has been at the centre of the hop-growing industry for 150 years, and there are still oast houses in the surrounding hop fields. The broad stretch of the Derwent here is clean, beautiful and swimmable, disturbed only by thrillseekers in jet boats: Devil Jet run high-speed rides through the rapids (daily 9am–4pm; 30min, $44; ℡03/6261 3460), leaving from behind the *Bush Inn* at 49 Montagu St, the main road. This inn claims to be Australia's oldest continuously licensed **hotel** (℡03/6261 2011; B&B ❹), and with its stained wooden floorboards, huge stone fireplaces and a small ballroom with chandeliers and piano, it's a lovely place to stay; as is the antique-furnished *Old Colony Inn*, a simple, whitewashed building on the same street at no. 21 (℡03/6261 2731; B&B ❺). From New Norfolk, you can visit the **Salmon Ponds** (daily 9am–5pm; $5.50), 18km west on the Glenora Road in Plenty; established in 1864, this is Australia's oldest trout hatchery, set in beautiful formal gardens, with six display ponds and a restaurant.

Hobart Coaches has five **buses** on weekdays from Hobart to New Norfolk and three on Saturday. Tassie Link also runs to New Norfolk (4 weekly) on their scheduled year-round service to Queenstown, and on a "Wilderness" service (daily Jan–April, 2 weekly May–Nov).

Mount Field National Park

It's 37km through pretty rolling countryside full of hop fields from New Norfolk to **Mount Field National Park**, a high alpine area with tarns created by glacial activity where, in winter, there's enough snow to create a small ski field. At the base, the magnificent stands of **mountain ash** known locally as swamp gum (the tallest species of eucalypt and the tallest hardwood in the world), along with the many **waterfalls**, help make this Tasmania's most popular park. Most people come here to see the impressive **Russell Falls**, which cascades in two levels. It's close to the park entrance and can be reached on an easy, well-graded thirty-minute circuit walk. Longer walks continue on to **Horseshoe Falls** (1hr) and **Lady Barron Falls** (3hr return). The best short walk is the **Tall Trees Track** (1hr 30min), where huge swamp gums dominate; the largest date back to the early nineteenth century.

To get away from the tour-group mob, several shorter walks leave from various spots along the Lake Dobson Road, which leads high up to **Lake Dobson**, 16km into the park in the area of the alpine moorlands and glacial lakes. From the lake car park, you can go on plenty of longer walks, including treks along the tarn shelf that take several days, with huts to stay in along the way. The walk to **Twilight Tarn**, with its historic hut, is one of the most rewarding (4hr return), or you can continue on for the full tarn shelf circuit (6hr return). A shorter option is the **Pandani Grove Nature Walk** (with an accompanying leaflet available from the ranger station – see below), a forty-minute circuit of the lake, including a section of tall **pandanis** – the striking heath plant which, with its crown of long fronds, looks like a semi-tropical palm. You'll need your own transport to reach these higher walks, or you could come with the friendly **Close to Nature Tours**, based at the Possum Shed, Westerway (℡03/6288 1477, ✉closetonature@bigpond.com.au); they offer a Waterfalls, Walks and Wildlife Tour (Tues, Thurs & Sat 8am–5.30pm; pick-up from Hobart; $120 including meals), as well as a torch-lit Nocturnal Wildlife Tour (Wed & Fri summer 3pm, winter 2pm; pick up from Hobart; $120 including meals). Tassie Link also operate day-tours from Hobart, visiting the Salmon Ponds (see above) en route and allowing five hours to explore the park (Mon & Wed 9am–5.30pm; $84 including meals).

For information on the walks, to register for overnight hikes and to talk to the ranger, drop in to the **Mount Field Ranger Station** at the entrance to the park (Mon–Fri 9am–4.30pm; ℡03/6288 1149, @www.dpiwe.tas.gov.au), a new complex also housing a café, shop and interpretive centre. An excellent range of free pamphlets detail the natural environment alongside several of the walks in the park. There's also information here about walks in the South West National Park, several of which can be started from Scotts Peak Road, which runs off the Gordon River Road to the west of Mount Field (see p.1136). If you want to **stay** in the vicinity, head for the tiny settlement of **NATIONAL PARK** on Maydena Road, a ten-minute walk from the park, where there's basic ground-floor **pub** accommodation at the friendly *National Park Hotel* (℡03/6288 1103; ❹ including breakfast), and dorms at the easy-going *National Park Youth Hostel* opposite (℡03/6288 1369; ❶); there's plenty of interaction between the two, including pool tournaments, and the pub **meals** are also popular with travellers. The pub has an EFTPOS facility, but the nearest fuel is 7km further on at Westaway. Just outside the entrance to the park are spacious 1950s style self-contained units at *Russell Falls Holiday Cottages* (℡03/6288 1198; ❹); while within the park itself, there's a well-equipped **campsite** near the entrance.

Nearby **Junee Cave State Reserve** is prime platypus-spotting territory; to get there head 11km southwest to Maydena, then right onto the narrow, winding Junee Road for 3.5km. A ten-minute walk from the reserve entrance through lush rainforest will bring you to **Junee Cave**, popular with cave divers. In Maydena you can stay at the friendly *Tyenna Valley Lodge* (℡03/6288 2293, @www.ozemail.com.au/~tvlodge; twin-share ❷, B&B rooms ❹, self-contained cabins ❻), who also offer personalized 4WD ecotours of the surrounding area, as well as pick-ups and drop-offs for bushwalking. The characterful, licensed *Cockatoo Cafe* next door serves delicious organic **meals**. Out of town, you can see the world's tallest Christmas Tree (77m) in the **Styx forest**, a large remnant of old-growth forest that's suffered damage from logging activities. A campaign is currently underway to protect 15,000 hectares of this forest as the Styx Valley of the Giants National Park; contact the Wilderness Society for details and information on guided and self-drive tours (℡03/6224 1550, @www.wilderness.org.au/tasmania).

Richmond

RICHMOND, on the Coal River about 25km north of Hobart and surrounded by undulating countryside, is one of the oldest and best-preserved towns in Australia. Settlers received land grants in the area not long after the fledgling colony had been set up in 1803, and in 1824 Lieutenant Governor Sorell founded the town, on the route between Hobart and the east coast. Soon, traffic to the new penal settlement at Port Arthur began to pass through, and Richmond's strategic location made it an important military post and convict station; by the 1830s it was the third-largest town in Tasmania. In 1872, however, the **Sorell Causeway** was opened, bypassing Richmond, which became a rural community with little incentive for change or development. Most of the approximately fifty buildings – plain and functional stone dwellings – date from the 1830s and 1840s, and many are now used as galleries, craft shops, cafés, restaurants and guesthouses. Attractions along Bridge Street include the wooden **Richmond Maze** (daily 10am–5pm; $3.50) and the **Old Hobart Town Model Village** (daily 9.30am–5.30pm; $7.50), a large-scale outdoor model of Hobart in the 1820s.

Richmond's most authentic attraction, however, is the sandstone, slate-roofed **Richmond Gaol** (daily 9am–5pm; $4.50), an intact example of an early prison. The prison's function was mostly to house prisoners in transit or those awaiting trial, and to accommodate convict road gangs working in the district; the east wing was designed to hold female convicts, who could not be accommodated at Port Arthur. Informative signs explain the various features of the jail, which now seems incongruously pretty, set around a leafy central square. Richmond also has the distinction of having both Australia's oldest Roman Catholic Church – that of **St John**, which dates in part from 1837 – and its oldest bridge. **Richmond Bridge** was constructed in 1823 under harsh conditions using convict labour; legend says that it's haunted by the ghost of the brutal flagellator, George Grover, who was beaten to death by the convicts and thrown into the river during its construction.

Practicalities

Hobart Coaches runs three **bus** services a day from Hobart (Mon–Fri only) and Tassie Link also drop off on their Hobart to Swansea service (2 daily Mon–Fri only). One of the nicest **places to stay** is *Prospect House* (℡ 03/6260 2207, ℻ 6260 2551, ⓦ www.Prospect-House.com.au; ❼), a Georgian country mansion set in extensive landscaped grounds, with its own licensed restaurant; it's on your left as you come into town on Cambridge Road. Further out, 6km from Richmond along Prossers Road, is *Richmond Country Bed and Breakfast* (℡ 03/6260 4238, ℻ 6260 4423; ❺), a comfortable, reasonably priced, non-smoking homestead in a quiet rural setting. The cheapest place to stay is the *Richmond Cabin and Tourist Park*, on Middle Tea Tree Road on the outskirts of town (℡ 03/6260 2192; cabins ❹, on-site vans ❸), which provides shady grounds for camping and has an indoor heated pool.

For **food**, walk along Bridge Street, where you'll find the pretty *Richmond Arms Hotel*, which serves upmarket pub meals; the *Richmond Bakery* on Edward Street, just off Bridge Street, has a Swiss baker who makes delicious pastries; and there's an upmarket brasserie in the *Richmond Food & Wine Centre*, 27 Bridge St (daily 10am–6pm, Fri & Sat until 8pm), where the emphasis is on quality Tasmanian produce.

The Forestier and Tasman peninsulas

The fastest route from Hobart to the **Tasman Peninsula** heads northeast along the Tasman Highway and then across the **Sorell Causeway** to the small town of **Sorell**, your last chance for shopping and banking; on the huge expanse of Pittwater, windsurfers are out in force on a sunny day. From Sorell, the Arthur Highway heads 34km southeast to **Dunalley** (fuel available), where a bridge crosses the narrow isthmus to the **Forestier Peninsula**. The bridge regularly opens to let boats through, which can cause delays. Once across, it's a further 42km to the infamous **Eaglehawk Neck**, the narrow point connecting the two peninsulas, once guarded by vicious dogs that in effect turned the Tasman Peninsula into a kind of prison island.

Port Arthur, at the very bottom of the Tasman Peninsula, is the major attraction, but the hardly developed **peninsula** has several good **bushwalks**, and some impressive rock formations on the rough ocean side. Some of the finest coastal features are around Eaglehawk Neck: just to the north, there's the **Tessellated Pavement**, onto which you can climb down at low tide; and to the south, off the highway, a fierce **blowhole**, the huge **Tasman Arch**, and the **Devils Kitchen**, a sheer rock cleft into which the sea surges. The **Tasman Trail** is an exhilarating sixteen-kilometre coastal walk starting from the Devils Kitchen and ending at **Fortescue Bay**, which has a good camping area (otherwise, the bay is 12km down a dirt road east off the Arthur Highway). South of Port Arthur, several walking tracks begin from **Remarkable Cave**: to Crescent Bay (5hr return), Mount Brown (5hr return) and Maingon Blowhole (3hr return). Much of this area has recently been declared the **Tasman National Park**; you can get information and advice from the ranger (☎03/6250 3497, ⓦwww.parks.tas.gov.au) or from the Officers Mess, a privately owned shop with an information centre at Eaglehawk Neck. Otherwise, to get details on the walking trails, look for a copy of *Tasman Tracks*, by Shirley and Peter Storey, in a Hobart bookshop.

Eaglehawk Neck Backpackers (☎03/6250 3248; ❶), at 687 Old Jetty Rd, 1km west of the Arthur Highway on the Forestier Peninsula side of Eaglehawk Neck, is the perfect **place to stay** to explore these areas – friendly, nonsmoking and green (in both senses of the word). Bunks are in two spacious, self-contained cabins; bikes are loaned (for a small donation) and there are canoes too. Also in the area is the *Wunnamurra Waterfront Bed and Breakfast* (☎ & Ⓕ 03/6250 3145; ❻), which offers more luxury in its en-suite rooms. For something to **eat**, try the French-run *Eaglehawk Cafe Restaurant*, on the Arthur Highway near the turn-off to the blowhole (open daily for breakfast, lunch and dinner; licensed; ☎03/6250 3331), in a two-storey house overlooking Norfolk Bay; the food is tasty and reasonably priced, utilizing local produce with a menu ranging from vegetarian to traditional meat dishes, plus coffee and cakes. The nearby Eaglehawk Dive Centre (☎03/6250 3566) offers **dive-boat charters** (equipment included) at low rates to caves, shipwrecks, kelp forests and nearby seal colonies with an underwater visibility of 15–30m. Southwest of Eaglehawk Neck, in the middle of the Tasman Peninsula at the small settlement of **KOONYA**, *Seaview Lodge* (☎ & Ⓕ 03/6250 2766; ❶) makes another excellent base for bushwalking. The friendly managers have their own minibus and will pick you up from Port Arthur or Eaglehawk Neck, take you to the start of walking trails and give tours of the area.

Port Arthur

The most unceasing labour is to be extracted from the convicts . . . and the most harassing vigilance over them is to be observed.

Governor Arthur

PORT ARTHUR was chosen as the site for a **prison settlement** in September 1830, as a place of secondary punishment for convicts who had committed serious crimes in New South Wales or Van Diemen's Land itself, men who were seen to have no redeeming features and were treated accordingly. The first 150 convicts worked like slaves to establish a timber industry in the wooded surroundings of the "natural penitentiary" of the Tasman Peninsula, with narrow Eaglehawk Neck guarded by dogs. The regime was never a subtle one: **Governor George Arthur**, responsible for all the convicts in Van Diemen's Land, believed that a convict's "whole fate should be . . . the very last degree of misery consistent with humanity". Gradually, Port Arthur became a self-supporting industrial centre: the timber industry grew into shipbuilding, there was brickmaking and shoemaking, wheat-growing, and even a flour mill. There was also a separate prison for boys – "the thiefs prison" – at Point Puer, where the inmates were taught trades. From the 1840s until transport of convicts ceased in 1853, the penal settlement grew steadily, the early timber constructions being replaced by brick and stone buildings. The lives of the labouring convicts contrasted sharply with those of the prison officers and their families, who had their ornamental gardens, drama club, library and cricket fields. The years after transport ended were in many ways more horrific than those that preceded them, as physical beatings were replaced by psychological punishment. In 1852 the **Model Prison**, based on the spoked-wheel design of Pentonville Prison in London, opened. Here, prisoners could be kept in tiny cells in complete isolation and absolute silence; they were referred to by numbers rather than names, and wore hoods whenever they left their cells. The prison continued to operate until 1877, by now incorporating its own **mental asylum** full of ex-convicts, as well as a geriatric home for ex-convict paupers. The excellent **interpretive centre**, housed in the new visitors centre (daily 9am–5pm), provides much more detail on the prison's sad history through artefacts and texts.

In 1870 Port Arthur was popularized by Marcus Clarke's romantic tragedy, *For the Term of his Natural Life*. The public became fascinated by its buildings and the tragedy behind them, and soon after the prison closed, guided tours were offered by the same crumbling men who had been wrecked by the regime. In the 1890s the town around the prison was devastated by bushfires that left most buildings in ruins. A major conservation and restoration project began in the 1970s and today the **Port Arthur Historic Site** covers a huge area (office and most buildings daily 8.30am–dusk; $19.80 for a 24hr pass, including 40min guided tour and 20min harbour cruise in summer; $9.90 for a pass after 4pm; information office ☎ 03/6251 2310 or free call 1800 659 191); you're allowed to wander around the grounds until about 11pm. For an extra $8.80 you can also take a trip on the MV *Bundeena* across the bay to the **Isle of the Dead**, Port Arthur's cemetery from 1833 to 1877, where you can view the resting places of 1100 convicts, asylum inmates, paupers and free men.

The Port Arthur Historic Site houses more than sixty buildings, some of which – like the poignant **prison chapel** – are furnished and restored. Others, like the ivy-covered **church**, are picturesque ruins set in a landscape of green lawns, shady trees and paths sloping down to the cove. The beautiful setting makes it look more like a serene, old-world university campus than a prison, and indeed, the benign feeling of the place seems to have a capacity to absorb tragedy: another horrific chapter in Port Arthur's history occurred in April 1996, when the massacre of 35 tourists and local people by a lone gunman made international headlines. The café where most of the people were killed has been partially dismantled and a memorial has been built – a garden and reflecting pool laid out around the remaining walls. The simple wooden cross on the waterfront which stands in remembrance will now remain permanently. Visitors are requested to act sensitively and not ask the staff about the tragedy.

If you're staying overnight in Port Arthur (see below for accommodation), join the nightly lantern-lit **Historic Ghost Tour** (1hr 30min; $14.30; bookings on ☎ 03/6251 2310), which features lovingly researched and hauntingly retold tales of the settlement's past as you wander through the ruins.

Practicalities

If you don't have your own transport, and want to get to Port Arthur from Hobart on a **regular bus**, you'll have to stay overnight. Tassie Link run just one afternoon service on weekdays only, stopping en route at Eaglehawk Neck and other places on the Tasman and Forestier peninsulas. However, there are plenty of **bus tours** that take in some of the Tasman Peninsula sights along the way. Tiger Line offer a good one-day "Convict Capers" tour (ask for tour 17B; daily except Sat 9am; $50; ☎ 03/6272 6611), and Experience Tasmania has a similar trip (ask for tour 3; Mon, Wed, Fri & Sun; $50; ☎ 03/6234 3336).

There are various **places to stay** on the outskirts of Port Arthur. The *Port Arthur Motor Inn*, on Remarkable Cave Road (☎ 03/6250 2101, ℱ 6250 2417;

❻), is just off the site, overlooking the ruined church; it's a pleasant place, with a bar open to the public – the only place nearby to drink – and reasonable counter meals. Just across the road is the *Roseview Youth Hostel* on Champ Street (☎03/6250 2311; booking essential Jan & Feb; rooms ❹, dorms ❶). The spacious *Port Arthur Villas* (☎03/6250 2239, ℱ6250 2589; ❺–❻), just across Remarkable Cave Road from the site, has the amenities of a motel and kitchens in the units.

Within the Port Arthur Historic Site, you can **eat** at the *Port Arthur Cafe* (daily 9am–5pm), or for à la carte at *Felons Restaurant*, both in the visitors centre. Otherwise there's the *Frances Langford Tea Rooms* in the restored 1930s policemen's quarters, and the *Museum Tea Rooms*.

The east coast: the Tasman Highway

For much of its length along the sunny **east coast**, the **Tasman Highway** gently rises and falls through grazing land and bush-covered hills. In summer there's something of an unspoilt Mediterranean feel about this coast, with its long white beaches, blue water stretching to a cloudless sky, scenic backdrop of hills, and a thriving local fishing industry. Because the east coast is sheltered from the prevailing westerly winds and is washed by warm offshore currents, it has one of the most temperate climates in Australia. This, and the mainly safe swimming beaches, mean that it's a popular destination for Tasmanian families in the school holidays – prices go up and accommodation is scarce from Christmas to the middle of February. Even so, it's still relatively undeveloped and peaceful; there are four national parks, which include a whole island – **Maria Island** – and an entire peninsula – the glorious **Freycinet National Park**.

The east coast is also Tasmania's best **cycling route**: it's relatively flat, and the winter climate is mild enough to tackle it in colder months, too. Distances between towns are reasonable, there's a string of youth hostels so you don't need to camp, and there are few cars. **St Helens** is the largest town on the east coast, with a population of just over a thousand; situated on **Georges Bay**, it makes a good base to explore the northeast corner and **Mount William National Park**. The oldest town, **Swansea**, lies sheltered in **Great Oyster Bay**, facing the Freycinet Peninsula. To the north, **Bicheno** is a small fishing town with fantastic diving, and it's a convenient place from which to visit both the Freycinet National Park (and its tiny settlement of **Coles Bay**) and the **Douglas Apsley National Park** inland. The highway detours inland at **St Marys**, although there's a more recently built road that allows you to follow the coast and enjoy spectacular views without having to tackle any hills.

Because the east coast is not heavily populated, **banking facilities** are rather inadequate, with no ATMs. Only St Helens and Scottsdale have banks (both Westpac), while small settlements have post offices that are also Commonwealth Bank agents. EFTPOS facilities are widely available in shops and service stations, but it's important to make sure you always have enough cash.

Transport services don't run to daily schedules either – another good reason to cycle. From Hobart, Tasmanian Redline Coaches has one service to Bicheno via Swansea (1 daily except Sat), two Sunday Launceston-bound services, which stop at Swansea, Bicheno, St Helens and St Marys, and a weekday service to St Helens and St Marys. From Launceston, Redline goes to Derby via Scottsdale (1–2 daily except Sat), to Bicheno and Swansea (1 daily except Sat), and to St Helens via St Marys (1 daily except Sat). Tassie Link has scheduled year-round services up the east coast from Hobart to St Helens (1 daily Mon, Wed, Fri & Sun). Four local bus companies also operate: Suncoast (2 daily Mon–Fri in summer; ⊤ 03/6376 3488) runs between St Helens and Scottsdale; Peakes (1 daily Mon–Fri; ⊤ 03/6372 5390) takes you from Bicheno to Derby; Broadby's (⊤ 03/6376 3488) operate the postal bus between Derby, St Helen's and St Marys; and the Coles Bay–Bicheno Coach Service (⊤ 03/6257 0293) takes you to Freycinet National Park (daily, though out of season you often need to book). If you don't fancy getting stuck somewhere for a couple of days, check timetables carefully.

Maria Island National Park

As the Tasman Highway meets the sea at **ORFORD**, a small holiday resort on the estuary of the Prosser River, you get your first views across to **Maria Island**. The entire island, 15km off the east coast, is a national park, uninhabited save for its ranger. Its wide tracks are ideal for mountain-biking, an activity encouraged here – because no other vehicles are allowed, you can ride in perfect safety. The island's coastal road has no gradient, but inland there are a few hills to climb. **Birdlife** is prolific, with over 130 species; it's the only national park containing all eleven of the state's endemic bird species. The old airstrip is covered with Cape Barren geese, which you'll see if you walk to the **fossil cliffs**, a twenty-minute stroll from Darlington.

The ferry lands at **DARLINGTON**, where the structures of the former **penal settlement** still stand, including the commissariat store with its visitor information boards, the convict barn, the cemetery, the mill house and the penitentiary. The last of these is now a **bunkhouse** (❶); units have wood stoves and bunks with mattresses, but you'll need to bring your own cooking equipment and bedding. The units are always in demand and are often booked up six months in advance, so call the ranger (see below) before turning up. The **campsite** here (small fee) is the island's best, with a public phone, toilets, fireplaces, cold water taps and tank water for drinking. As there is little water elsewhere on the island, free-range camping is best done at **Frenchs Farm** or **Encampment Cove**, two campsites with a rainwater supply and fireplaces; the latter, on Shoal Bay, is the more picturesque.

You can take many short **walks** on the island, as well as longer bushwalks; free pamphlets are available from the ranger's office at Darlington (Mon–Fri 4.15–5pm; ⊤ 03/6257 1420). With a couple of days to spare, you can walk past the narrow isthmus to the rarely visited **southern end** of the island, which has unspoilt forests and secluded beaches. As there's no water here, be sure to bring supplies with you.

Getting there: Triabunna

Ferries leave for the island from the *Eastcoaster Resort* at Louisville, halfway between Orford and **TRIABUNNA** (reached by Tassie Link and Redline from Hobart). The *Eastcoaster Express* (⊤ 03/6257 1589), a fast catamaran taking only twenty minutes, leaves the resort daily at 10.30am, 1pm and 3.30pm, returning from Maria Island at 11am, 1.30pm and 4pm, with extra trips between December 26 and January 28 (day-trips $17, campers $20, bikes and kayaks $3).

The **Visitor Information Centre** on the Esplanade in Triabunna (daily 10am–4pm; ⊤ 03/6257 4090, ℱ 6257 3675) is staffed by helpful volunteers and has information on the island. A good base for day-trips to the island is the friendly and relaxing *Triabunna YHA* on Spencer Street, 1km west of Triabunna

(☎03/6257 3439; ❶), where you're welcome to pick your own organic fruit and vegetables (in season). **Horse riding** is available with Woodstock Trail Rides (☎03/6257 3186; $20 per hour), while East Coast Ecotours (☎03 6257 1114, ℻6257 1534) offer **boat trips** to local seal colonies; if you're lucky you'll see dolphins, whales and sea eagles along the way.

Swansea

From Triabunna it's a fairly uneventful drive north to **SWANSEA**, overlooking **Great Oyster Bay**, with views across to the Freycinet Peninsula. If you're lucky, you might see dolphins frolicking in the bay from Franklin Street, the main street that runs along the waterfront. One of Tasmania's oldest settlements, Swansea is an administrative centre, fishing port and seaside resort, with well-preserved architecture dating from the 1830s to the 1880s. The focus of town has always been **Morris's General Store**, on Franklin Street, run by seven generations of the family since 1868. Further evidence of Swansea's past can be found at the **Community Centre** (Mon–Sat 9am–5pm; $3), also on Franklin Street, a former school now housing a miscellaneous collection including a billiard table built from a single log of blackwood ($2 for a game), and at the restored **Swansea Bark Mill & East Coast Museum**, 96 Tasman Highway (daily 9am–5pm; $5), once used to produce leather tanning agents from native blackwattle bark.

Accommodation options include the comfortable *Swansea YHA*, at 5 Franklin St (☎03/6257 8367; ❶), with a piano in the common room; and the *Swansea Motor Inn*, at 1 Franklin St (☎03/6257 8102, ℻6257 8397; ❹–❻), a fine old hotel with a pricier red-brick motel addition and a bistro. *Freycinet Waters*, at 16 Franklin St (☎03/6257 8080, ℻6257 8075, ⓦwww.freycinetwaters.com.au; ❻), is a light, refreshingly uncluttered seaside B&B in the old post office building; each en-suite room has its own private verandah overlooking the bay. Other B&B options include the *Oyster Bay Guest House* at 10 Franklin St (☎ & ℻ 03/6257 8110; ❻–❼), and *Meredith House*, 15 Noyes St (☎03/6257 8119, ℻6257 8123; en suite ❼), an antique-filled guesthouse on a hill overlooking the bay. On the waterfront are two **caravan parks** with excellent facilities: *Swansea Holiday Park* on Shaw Street, opposite the Old Bark Mill (☎03/6257 8177; cabins ❹), and the friendly *Kenmore Caravan Park*, 2 Bridge St (☎03/6257 8148; cabins ❺, on-site vans ❸).

As for **food**, Swansea has a wide choice. The *Shy Albatross Restaurant* (daily from 6pm; licensed), downstairs at the *Oyster Bay Guest House*, serves reasonably priced Italian food and local seafood. There's a very smart, award-winning restaurant specializing in seafood and game in the atmospheric 1846 *Schouten House*, 1 Waterloo Rd (☎03/6257 8564), with alfresco dining in summer. The *Left Bank Coffee & Food Bar*, behind the red door on the main street (closed Tues), has a great atmosphere, outdoor dining, excellent coffee and fresh, simple food. A prime spot for dolphin-watching is *Just Maggies*, a relaxed café at 26 Franklin St (daily 9am–5pm), while *Kabuki By the Sea* (open daily for morning and afternoon tea and lunch; May–Nov Fri & Sat dinner, Dec–April Tues–Sat dinner; bookings essential on ☎03/6257 8588) is a fine Japanese-style restaurant 12km south on the Tasman Highway with stunning views; it also has some Japanese-style guest cottages (❺–❽).

The Freycinet Peninsula

Heading for Coles Bay and **Freycinet National Park**, you turn off the Tasman Highway 33km north of Swansea, following the Coles Bay Road. After about 8km, turn left down a side road (3km unsealed) to the **Friendly**

Beaches, a new addition to the national park, taking in a length of unspoilt shoreline backed by eucalypt forest. If you're **cycling**, you can cut 40km from your journey by riding along Nine Mile Beach Road, at the end of which a ferry will take you across the Swan River to **SWANICK**, about 6km north-west of Coles Bay. The ferry (about $10; no service May–Sept) must be booked by calling the night before (☎ 03/6257 0239).

COLES BAY, on the north edge of the Freycinet National Park, is a sheltered inlet with fishing boats moored in the deep-blue water, all set against the striking backdrop of **The Hazards**, three pink-granite peaks – Amos, Dove and Mayson – rising straight from the sea. Since the 1930s the hamlet of Coles Bay has been the base for the park, and for fishing and recreation. As a result, there are numerous fishing shacks and **holiday houses** available to rent: call *Freycinet Holiday Homes* (☎ 03/6257 0218; ❺). Just 3.5km west of Coles Bay, *The Edge of the Bay* (☎ 03/6257 0102, ℉ 6257 0437, ⓦ www.edgeofthebay.com.au; suites ❻, cottages ❼) has secluded self-catering cottages set in bushland, or elegant Japanese-style suites with water views; there's a minimum two-night stay. The *Iluka Holiday Centre*, on the Esplanade 1km from the general store (☎ 03/6257 0115, ℉ 6257 0384, ⓦ www.ilukaholidaycentre.com.au; units ❹–❻, on-site vans ❹, dorms ❶), has a wide variety of accommodation, including a **YHA hostel** section. Attached is a small supermarket, an eat-in bakery selling pastries, *focaccia*, pizza and decent cappuccino (daily 8am–7pm), plus a restaurant and tavern. The *Coles Bay Caravan Park*, 4km further west on Coles Bay Road (☎ 03/6257 0100; dorms ❶), is in a bush setting, with beach access and backpackers' accommodation (twin-share rooms, fully equipped kitchen, dining room and own amenities); the rate includes return transport to the walking track at Wine Glass Bay. **Supplies** of all sorts are available at Coles Bay Trading on Garnet Avenue (daily 8am–6pm, to 7pm in summer; ☎ 03/6257 0109); this also serves as the post office, service station and tourist **information** centre. Next door you can get a seafood dinner at *Madge Malloy's* (closed Sun & Mon nights; licensed; ☎ 03/6257 0399).

Redline and Tassie Link drop off 31km away from Coles Bay, at the turn-off on the Tasman Highway. Here you'll have to wait for the Coles Bay–Bicheno Coach Service (up to three daily, although at off-peak times you may have to book; ☎ 03/6257 0293), which can take you right to the start of the walking tracks – the only other alternative is to walk.

Freycinet National Park

The **national park office** (daily 9am–5pm; ☎ 03/6257 0107) is just 1km from Coles Bay, and sells maps and booklets on day-walks. Opposite, the national park **campsite**, with water and toilets but no showers, is in a sheltered location among bush and dunes behind Richardsons Beach; it's packed in holiday season, when you'll need to book ahead through the park office. At other times of year you can just walk into the park and camp for free. At the other end of Richardsons Beach, *Freycinet Lodge* (☎ 03/6257 0101, ℉ 6257 0278, ⓦ www.freycinetlodge .com.au; ❽–❾) has luxurious wooden cabins spread through bushland and offers guided bushwalks; there's a bistro and a more upmarket restaurant overlooking the bay, both open all day, and a tennis court. You can also stay at the basic *Coles Bay YHA* (no hot water) in the park itself, but only if you've booked in advance through the Hobart YHA office (see p.1068; ❶); a ballot system applies during the summer months as it's very popular.

Tracks into the park begin at the **Walking Track Car Park**, a further 4km from the office. **Water** is scarce, so you must carry all you'll need, although the ranger can advise if there are any streams where the water is safe to drink. The shorter walks are well marked and not too difficult: exquisite **Wine Glass Bay**, with its perfect curve of white beach, is where most walkers head (1hr one–way). The **peninsula circuit** is a wonderful walk (10hr), best done over two days; it makes a good practice run for the big southwest hikes. There's a **campsite** at **Cooks Beach**, with a pit toilet, water tank, and a rough hut where you can stay; the beach has a lot of marsupials who'll pester you for food, so wrap it up tight.

    Schouten Island, off the tip of the peninsula, was included within the national park in 1967: it's perfect for really secluded camping, as you're quite likely to have it all to yourself. Freycinet Sea Charters, in Coles Bay (T03/6257 0355 or 0417 355 524, Wwww.freycinetseacharters.com), will drop you off there for around $110 per person return, or you could spend a little more for a day-trip with them which could take in a walk on the island and a visit to a nearby seal colony; Keno Sea Fisheries, also in Coles Bay (T03/6257 0344), offer charter trips as well. There are campsites with pit toilet, a hut and two water tanks at **Moreys Bay**, and the creek at **Crocketts Bay** has reliable upstream water. Although there are no proper tracks on the island, walking is easy.

    Freycinet Adventures (T03/6257 0500, F6257 0447, Wwww.tasadventures.com/freycinetadventures) offer **sea kayaking tours** on Coles Bay (half-day $75, full day $130), which can be extended to include overnight camping in the national park (three-day trip $560); they also run **abseiling** and **rock-climbing** trips (half-day abseiling $75; full day rock-climbing $100). A couple of operators offer **4WD tours** of the park: All Four Adventures (T03/6257 0500 or 0428 272 787), and Naturally Freycinet (T03/6257 0093 or 0419 570 293, Ebiccoa@vision.net.au).

Bicheno

Halfway up the east coast, **BICHENO** (pronounced "bish-eno"), sheltered in **Waubs Bay**, is a busy crayfishing and abalone port. The same conditions that make Bicheno ideal for fishing also make it a perfect spot for **diving**. The usually clear waters are rich with a variety of marine life, and there's a **marine reserve** on the eastern side of **Governor Island**, with spectacular large caves and extraordinary vertical rockfaces with swim-throughs and drop-offs. The Bicheno Dive Centre, 4 Tasman Highway (T03/6375 1138), offers dive courses and rents out gear. Information on other activities around Bicheno is available from the **Bicheno Information Centre** on the Tasman Highway (daily 9am–5.30pm; T03/6375 1333), which arranges diving, horse riding, cycling, and a wide variety of local tours, the most popular being the evening tours to a local **penguin** rookery (nightly; $15) and a one-hour glass-bottom boat tour of the marine reserve ($15). Opposite the information centre, the French-owned Le Frog's Corner shop is the base for the tour operator Le Frog Trike Rides (T03/6375 1777 or 0407 511 454), which runs a range of motorbike tours; amongst the offerings is a day-trip ($200) complete with wine and frog's legs sampling and a visit to a local oyster farm. The **Sea Life Centre** (daily 9am–5pm; $5), on the Tasman Highway, has a rather dingy aquarium but an excellent seafood restaurant (daily 9am–9pm; reserve for dinner on T03/6375 1311).

    Bicheno makes a pleasant stopover, as it has plenty of **accommodation**. You can camp at the *East Cost Caravan Park* at 4 Champ St (T03/6375 1999, F6375 1956; on-site vans ❸, cabins ❺); or stay at the well-equipped *Bicheno Backpackers Hostel*, 11 Morrison St (T03/6375 1651, ❶). For something really special, head for the *Bicheno Hideaway* at 179 Harveys Farm Rd (T03/6375 1312, F6375 1700; ❼), 3km south of Bicheno, where uniquely designed oceanfront self-contained chalets are set on six acres of natural bushland teeming with wildlife. Other options include the central *Beachfront Family Resort*, near the information office on the Tasman Highway (℡03/6375 1111, ℻6375 1130; ❻), which has a pool and bikes to rent; and the *Bicheno Gaol*, on the corner of James and Burgess streets (℡03/6375 1430; ❼–❽), which offers cottage accommodation in the old prison and its converted stables. **Food**, too, is excellent in Bicheno. The formal *Cyrano French Restaurant*, at 77 Burgess St (daily from 6.30pm; ℡03/6375 1137), is in the classic French vein, while the *Long Boat Tavern*, on the Tasman Highway, has the best counter meals. The *Blue House Mobile Kitchen* is a food van that sets up each evening next door to the information centre; it offers reasonably priced, BYO alfresco dining and is a very popular meeting place. For a good all-day breakfast and real coffee try the *Freycinet Bakery* at 45 Foster St (daily 8am–4pm), or head for *Mary Harvey's Kitchen* in the gardens of the *Bicheno Gaol*, where you can sample some gourmet Tasmanian products (daily 10.30am–5pm).

To get to Freycinet National Park by **bus** from Bicheno, take the Coles Bay–Bicheno Coach Service (℡03/6357 0293), which leaves from the *Night Owl* takeaway at 52 Burgess St.

The Douglas Apsley National Park and the Elephant Pass

Just 4km north of Bicheno on the Tasman Highway there's a turn-off to the **Douglas Apsley National Park**. Proclaimed in 1990, it's the location of the state's only remaining large dry sclerophyll forest. Because of the temperate weather of the east coast, the park's two-day walk, the **Leeaberra Track** – undertaken north to south – is a good one at any time of the year. Although facilities are being improved, this is a low-maintenance, untouristy park, so be prepared for basic bushcamping. You can buy the *Douglas Apsley* map and *Notes* ($9) from the Land Information Bureau, 134 Macquarie St, Hobart, or from the information centre at Bicheno (see overleaf). Tassie Link can arrange bushwalkers' transfers to the park.

Thirty kilometres north of Bicheno, just past Chain of Lagoons, the coastal Tasman Highway continues north to St Helens; turn off to the left for a spectacular climb with views of the surrounding coastline on a detour inland to **St Marys**, 17km away. You can stop at the dramatic Elephant Pass for pancakes at the overrated *Mount Elephant Pancake Barn* (daily 8am–6pm; cash only); next door the Blueberry Cottage Craft Shop and Gardens sells a range of tasty home-made products, including lavender jelly and onion marmalade.

St Marys and St Helens

From Elephant Pass the road heads on to **ST MARYS**, a picturesque little town surrounded by state forest and waterfalls. The place has a quiet, old-fashioned feel to it, plus a slight alternative edge, and there are some fine bushwalks in the area. The nicest place to stay is *Seaview Farm* (℡03/6372 2341; en-suite rooms ❸, dorms ❶), in an idyllic setting 8km uphill from St Marys on German Town Road. Meals aren't provided, so bring provisions; you can arrange a pick-up in advance if you don't have your own transport.

Heading downhill back to the coast, you'll arrive at **ST HELENS**, the largest town on the east coast and the last before the Tasman Highway turns west and inland. It's situated on **Georges Bay**, a long, narrow bay with two encircling arms, and although both the town and bay are fairly dull, the surrounding coastline has plenty of interest. Local **information** is available from the St

Helens History Room, at 55 Cecilia St opposite the post office (Mon–Fri 9am–4pm & Sat 9am–noon, plus Sun 10am–2pm in summer; $2; ☎03/6376 1744), which provides maps and gives information about walks as well as details of the area's mining history.

The southern arm of Georges Bay is the site of **St Helens Point Recreation Area**, where there's a large lagoon – Diana's Basin – which the highway skirts as it enters town. On the ocean side the **Peron sand dunes** stretch for several kilometres, and at the point there's good surfing at **Beer Barrel Beach**. **Binalong Bay**, 10km north of Georges Bay, has a beach of bright sugary sand and is an easy bike ride away, with only a couple of small climbs. It's another popular surf spot (with a strong current, so beware); there's safer swimming in the large lagoon tucked behind, where people boat and waterski. You can **camp** here, as well as further along at the **Bay of Fires Coastal Reserve**.

To get to the southern half of **Mount William National Park** take the road running inland north for 54km from St Helens to the pink-granite tower of the Eddystone Lighthouse. The northern end of the park is reached via Gladstone, by taking an unsealed track to **Great Musselroe Bay**, where there's a free basic **campsite**. There are no real tracks within the park itself, but plenty of beach and headland walking, and lots of Forrester kangaroos. The excellent **Bay of Fires Walk** (☎03/6331 2006, ℻6331 5526, ⓦwww.bayoffires.com.au; four days $1150) is a four-day guided coastal walk through Mount William National Park; packs and waterproof jackets are provided and accommodation is in luxury "eco-tents" and a superbly designed ecolodge 40m above the sea with stunning views up and down the coast.

St Helens practicalities

There's a good range of **accommodation** to choose from in town. The *St Helens YHA*, at 5 Cameron St (☎03/6376 1661; ❶), is clean and friendly; or there are a number of bed and breakfast places: best value is *Artnor Lodge* at 71 Cecilia St (☎03/6376 1234; ❺), or you could try the salubrious *Warrawee Guest House* (☎03/6376 1987, ℻6376 1012; ❺–❼) on the Tasman Highway. The *Bayside Inn*, at 2 Cecilia St (☎03/6376 1466; ❹–❻), is a modern hotel/motel with a restaurant, pool and drive-in bottle shop; or there's the cheaper *Anchor Wheel Motel* at 59 Tully St (☎03/6376 1358; ❹), which also has its own restaurant. For self-contained accommodation, best value is the spacious, well-equipped *Kellraine Units* (☎ & ℻ 03/6376 1169; ❸). *Tidal Water*, facing Georges Bay at 2 Jason St (☎03/6376 1100; dinner only, closed Sun) is an award-winning **restaurant** serving Asian-influenced contemporary cuisine. For all-day breakfasts, excellent coffee and a great menu featuring local organic produce, head for the stylish *Milk Bar Cafe* at 57B Cecilia St (Mon–Fri 9am–5pm, Sat 9am–3pm, Sun 11am–3pm). Next door is the reasonably priced *Wok Stop* (lunch Mon–Fri, dinner Mon–Sat). St Helens' bank is Westpac at 41 Cecilia St.

St Helens to Scottsdale: the Tasman Highway

From St Helens, the **Tasman Highway** cuts across the northeast highlands towards Launceston, 170km away. This is mostly dairy country, although there's the odd patch of surviving rainforest and the remnants of a tin-mining industry, based around the **Blue Tier**, a mountain that experienced a mining boom in the 1870s. Many **ghost towns** were left after the mines finally closed in the 1950s. Twenty-six kilometres out of St Helens is the turn-off south for **PYEN-GANA** (1km) and St Columba Falls (a further 4km). In Pyengana it's worth touring **Healey's Pyengana Cheese Factory** (daily 9am–5pm; free), where you can watch the stuff being made (except Fri & Sat) and buy all the ingredients for a picnic at the falls. Further along, you come to *St Columba Falls Hotel* (℡03/6373 6121; ❸) – the "Pub in the Paddock" – which looks like a farmhouse; it's a real country local, serving huge steaks (meals daily). At the end of the road (the last bit on dirt) is the **Columba Falls State Reserve**, an area of cool, temperate rainforest. The short walk to the viewing platform at the base of **St Columba Falls** is easy, passing through a forest of manferns and under a canopy of sassafras and myrtle. At 110m, the falls are the highest in Tasmania, pouring with tremendous force over the cliffs – they're truly thunderous in winter, when the viewing platform is shrouded in mist. From the falls it is possible to do a 25-kilometre scenic drive, continuing along the recently completed Mount Victoria road to Ringarooman and then on to Scottsdale. On the way it's worth stopping in the **Mount Victoria Forest Reserve** and taking the short walk to **Ralph's Falls**, the highest single-drop falls in Tasmania.

Back on the main road approaching the Blue Tier, **Goshen** is the first of the ghost towns, little more than an old school and the ruins of the *Oxford Arms Inn*. A little further on is the turn-off for **Goulds Country**, with the remaining buildings – all wooden – of what was once a town. The **Weldborough Pass** (595m) is probably the most beautiful part of the drive, with views across the valleys to the sea; it's worth taking the twenty-minute walk through the **Weldborough Pass Scenic Reserve**, predominately myrtle forest with manferns and occasional tall blackwoods. **WELDBOROUGH** itself, once the centre of a Chinese mining community, now consists of the *Weldborough Hotel* (℡ & ℻ 03/6354 2223; B&B ❸), where you can get a **meal** (Mon–Sat) and a basic pub **room** for the night; there's also a campsite with showers at the back. **DERBY**, on the Ringarooma River, was made prosperous by the profitable **Briseis Tin Mine** that operated in the town between 1876 and 1952. The **Derby Tin Mine Centre** (daily: June–Aug 10am–4pm; Sept–May 10am–5pm; $4) is now the only sign of development in a town that's been closing down since the 1950s: it has some interesting relics connected with the Chinese miners and examples of gemstones fossicked in the area.

SCOTTSDALE, 99km from St Helens, is a large, pleasantly situated town servicing the agricultural and forestry industries of the northeast. Though it's none too exciting itself, it has good facilities (including banks and supermarkets) and there are some beautiful areas to visit nearby. The friendly *Bellows*, at 65 King St (℡03/6352 2263 or 0419 570 887, ✉pepper@microtech.com.au; rooms ❹, dorms ❷), has excellent backpackers' accommodation, and also runs Pepper Bush Peaks 4WD Adventure Tours, a range of **tours** which take you off-road to visit magnificent waterfalls, old-growth forests – including the tallest white gum trees in the world – and lookouts, as well as giving you the opportunity to catch your own fish or sample the largest freshwater crayfish in the world (tours range from $80 to $189). Redline runs here from Launceston daily except Saturday.

Twenty-one kilometres northwest, the fishing town and holiday spot of **BRIDPORT** has a couple of places to stay: the *Bridport Caravan Park* (℡03/6356 1227; ❶), which feels like just a bush camp yet with all the amenities, stretches for about a kilometre along Anderson Bay; or you could try the *Bridport Seaside Lodge* at 47 Main St (℡ & ℻ 03/6356 1585; rooms ❷, dorms ❶), a modern purpose-built hostel. The **beaches** in the area are lovely, especially the wide, sandy expanse where the Bird River flows among sand dunes and into the sea. *Bridport Seafoods* (daily 10am–7pm), attached to the fish-processing plant on Main Street, does excellent sit-down meals.

North and central Tasmania and the Bass Strait

The **north** of Tasmania is rich and settled agricultural country, and the fertile soil of the **Tamar Valley** in particular made this a prosperous area during the early colonial period. **Launceston** quickly grew as a port and city, 30km inland at the confluence of the Tamar and the North and South Esk rivers; gracious early houses and well-preserved villages are still found around the area. Also settled early, due to its fine and open land, was the mostly flat, gently undulating **midlands** area between Launceston and Hobart; the **Midland Highway** more or less follows the old coaching route between the two cities. With its stone walls, hedgerows, haystacks and small villages and towns, this rural stretch from the Tamar Valley to Hobart is softly appealing but not particularly exciting. In contrast, the area around **Deloraine**, 45km west of Launceston, is spectacular: the early colonial town is surrounded by rich farmland and dramatically located in hilly country below the crest of the **Great Western Tiers** – a mecca for bushwalkers. From Deloraine, the **Lake Highway** heads steeply south up over the Western Tiers and on to the **Central Plateau**, a sparsely populated lake-filled region dominated by the **Great Lake** and its shambolic fishing shacks.

Lying off the northern coast, in Bass Strait, are two islands worth visiting for their bushwalks and historic associations: **Flinders Island** in the northeast, largest of the Furneaux Islands, and **King Island** to the far northwest, part of the Hunter Island group. Both are reached by plane only, with flights from Victoria or Tasmania.

Launceston and around

LAUNCESTON is dominated by the **Tamar River**, and approaching from the north along the Tamar Highway, zooming through haystack-filled countryside, it's a lovely sight, with grand Victorian houses nestling on hills above the banks. Approaching from the south on the dreary Southern Outlet, however, gives a perhaps more accurate picture of a dull but worthy provincial town. It's Tasmania's second-largest city, with a population of around 68,000, but despite its much-vaunted English look – especially in its many formal parks and gardens – only the surrounding countryside of the **Tamar Valley** (see p.1100) really makes a visit worthwhile.

As the third-oldest city in Australia, first settled in 1804, Launceston has hung on to disappointingly little of its elegant colonial Georgian architecture. Existing examples are mainly utilitarian structures such as merchant warehouses and mills, now converted into museums, galleries or tourist attractions. What the city does have in abundance, however, are many fine examples of colonial **Victorian architecture**: the 1870s and 1880s were prosperous times for Launceston, years of mineral exploration spurred on by the mainland goldrush. There was a boom in construction and a number of massive, dignified public

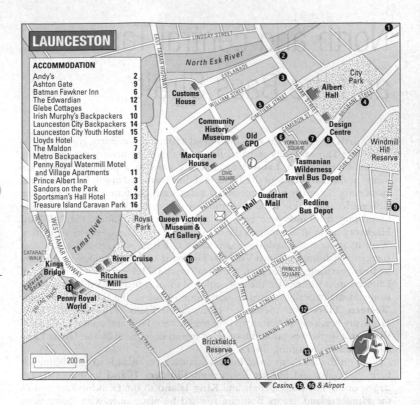

LAUNCESTON

ACCOMMODATION

Andy's	2
Ashton Gate	9
Batman Fawkner Inn	6
The Edwardian	12
Glebe Cottages	1
Irish Murphy's Backpackers	10
Launceston City Backpackers	14
Launceston City Youth Hostel	15
Lloyds Hotel	5
The Maldon	7
Metro Backpackers	8
Penny Royal Watermill Motel and Village Apartments	11
Prince Albert Inn	3
Sandors on the Park	4
Sportsman's Hall Hotel	13
Treasure Island Caravan Park	16

▼ *Casino,* ⑮, ⑯ *& Airport*

buildings date from this period – though, unfortunately, in most cases the often florid facades were simply attached to Georgian structures.

Launceston's real attractions, though, are its natural assets. It's situated at the confluence of the narrow **North Esk** and **South Esk rivers**, with the breathtaking Cataract gorge only fifteen-minutes' walk from the centre, where the South Esk has carved its way through rock to reach the Tamar. Yachts and outboard motors ply the 50km of river, while beyond the western suburbs bushcovered hills fold back into the distance to **Ben Lomond**, an hour's drive away, and popular with Launceston's residents for winter skiing.

Arrival, information and transport

There are direct **flights** from Melbourne, Moorabban and Hobart to **Launceston Airport**, near the town of Evandale, 20km south of the city. The **Airport Shuttle Bus** (℡ 0500/512 009) meets most flights and drops off at your accommodation for $10. A **taxi** costs about $20, or you could **rent a car** – the main car companies have desks at the airport.

Long-distance **buses** arrive in the city centre: Tasmanian Redline Coaches, at 18 Charles St (℡ 03/6336 1444), will also drop you off at accommodation as far out as the *Treasure Island Caravan Park*; Tassie Link (℡ 03/6272 7300) will drop you at the Information Centre (see opposite). There's no problem with **parking** in the city centre – if the short-term metered parking is full, there are loads of **car parks** around, charging $1.10 an hour ($7 per day). Most streets operate on a **one-way system** and the length of Cameron Street is interrupted by Civic Square, and Brisbane Street by the Mall.

Information

For **information**, your first stop should be the **Tasmanian Travel and Information Centre**, on the corner of St John and Paterson streets (Mon–Fri 9am–5pm, Sat 9am–3pm, Sun 9am–noon; ☎03/6336 3133, ⓦwww.gateway-tas.com.au), which can arrange car hire and book accommodation and travel tickets. As well as picking up street and regional **maps** here, grab a copy of the free weekly newspaper, *Launceston Week*, which has some listings. The Wilderness Society Shop, at 174 Charles St, opposite Princes Square (Mon–Fri 9.30am–5.30pm, Sat 10am–1pm; ☎03/6334 2499), is a good source of information about wilderness issues and the environment. You can sign up here for the summer walks programme – weekends and day-walks – that takes you into areas under threat by logging.

City transport

Launceston is very compact and most accommodation is within walking distance of the city centre, although **public transport** (the MTT) is useful for a couple of scattered attractions and some outlying accommodation (buses run until 6.15pm Mon–Thurs, 10pm Fri & Sat; very restricted services on Sun). The **MTT bus interchange** (fare and timetable information on ☎13 2201), where all buses arrive and depart, is on St John Street, on either side of the **Brisbane Street Mall**. Single fares are inexpensive, but it may be worth buying a Day Rover ($3.40) for unlimited travel between 9am and 4.30pm and then again after 6pm; you can buy these on board buses. Ten-trip tickets cost from $10.40 and you can buy these at Teagues Newsagency, opposite the post office.

Accommodation

Accommodation in Launceston is very good value, and rates don't tend to hike up in the busy period from December to February; most places have parking available, too. There's a concentration of **motels** along Brisbane Street and an abundance of **B&B's** and self-catering accommodation around the city, though **hostel** beds can be scarce in summer.

Hotels, motels, B&Bs and self-catering

Ashton Gate, 32 High St (☎03/6331 6180, ⓕ6334 2232). Classified by the National Trust, this weatherboard B&B has been taking guests for over forty years. Bedrooms are large and light; all are en suite, with TV and hot drinks. ❼

Batman Fawkner Inn, 35–39 Cameron St (☎03/6331 7222, ⓕ6331 7158). Established in 1822, and offering bargain, single en-suite rooms with TV and phone ($38); larger, more attractive rooms have similar facilities. Light breakfast included. ❺

The Edwardian, 227 Charles St (☎ & ⓕ 03/6334 7771). A lovely, two-storey red-brick Edwardian house near Princes Square, with self-contained self-catering suites, the largest with four rooms.

Breakfast provisions provided. Handy for the supermarket. No children. ❼

Glebe Cottages, 14A Cimitiere St (☎0500 500 581, ⓕ03/6334 0934, ⓦwww.glebecottages.com.au). Good-value and spacious self-contained cottages, in a convenient location near City Park. ❻

Lloyds Hotel, 23 George St (☎03/6331 4966, ⓕ6331 5589). Solid, rather drab old-fashioned hotel with en-suite rooms. The dining room downstairs does economical meals and there's hot drinks and TV in the lounge. Closed on Sun. ❹

The Maldon, 32 Brisbane St (☎03/6331 3211, ⓕ6334 4641). Elegant Victorian-era B&B, featuring iron-lace verandahs, chandeliers, engraved glass and a carved wooden staircase; en-suite rooms have modern facilities. ❺

Penny Royal Watermill Motel and Village Apartments, 145–147 Paterson St (☏ 03/6331 6699, ⅇ 6334 4282, ⅇ pennyroyal@vision.net.au). Built in 1840, this motel has a comfortable old-world charm, while the more modern self-contained apartments are spacious and reasonably priced. A short walk to the Gorge and Cliff Grounds and close to the city centre. ⓥ

Prince Albert Inn, cnr William and Tamar streets (☏ 03/6331 7633, ⅇ 6334 1579). Refurbished nineteenth-century inn near City Park, with spacious en-suite rooms furnished in Heritage style. The dining room, where you have breakfast, is full of stuffed animals, while old photographs and colonial prints cover the walls. Nonsmokers only. ⓺–ⓥ

Sandors on the Park, 3 Brisbane St (☏ 03/6331 2055, ⅇ 6334 3910). The best of a bunch of motels on this strip overlooking City Park – but not the most expensive – just a short walk from the centre. Friendly professional service; guest laundry. Its bistro-style *Monkey Bar Café* opens noon–10.30pm. ⓹

Sportsman's Hall Hotel, 252 Charles St (☏ 03/6331 3968, ⅇ 6334 4227). Pleasant pub with well-furnished, comfortable rooms (shared bathrooms). Breakfast included. There's an excellent, café-style bistro downstairs serving up very reasonably priced meals. ⓷

Hostels and caravan parks

Andy's, 1 Tamar St, by the bridge. Renovated former pub with the *Malle Grill Restaurant* downstairs, and *Andy's* backpacker accommodation upstairs. Very clean and well run with common

room with TV, a balcony, and a small well-equipped kitchen. Rooms ⓷, dorms (BYO linen) ⓵

Irish Murphy's Backpackers, 211 Brisbane St (☏ 03/6331 4440, ⅇ 6334 5503). Hostel accommodation above a lively, centrally located pub. Facilities include TV lounge and a fully equipped kitchen. Rooms ⓷, dorms ⓵

Launceston City Backpackers, 103 Canning St (☏ 03/6334 2327). A good hostel, with young managers and a friendly atmosphere. Nicely decorated, clean and well equipped. Book ahead in summer. Rooms ⓶, dorms ⓵

Launceston City Youth Hostel, 36 Thistle St, South Launceston (☏ 03/6344 9779). A rather gloomy institutional place, with loads of rules and regulations and a midnight curfew. However, you can rent bikes and camping gear, and the manager is very knowledgeable about bushwalking. Despite the name, this is not a YHA hostel. Take bus #21 or #24 and get off at Wellington St (stop 8); Redline buses also drop-off here. ⓵

Metro Backpackers, 16 Brisbane St (☏ 03/6334 4505, ⅇ metrolaunceston@hotmail.com). New YHA hostel in a 1930s Art Deco building. Great facilities, including a pool table, internet access, satellite TV and a BBQ rooftop area. They also operate as a tourist information centre. Rooms ⓷, dorms ⓵

Treasure Island Caravan Park, 94 Glen Dhu St, South Launceston, 2km south of the centre (☏ 03/6344 2600). A small park, sloping up a hillside and looking right over a freeway. It's noisy, the ground is hard and uneven, and it's crowded in summer – but there's nowhere else to camp in Launceston. Public transport as for *Launceston City Youth Hostel* (see above). Cabins ⓸

The City

The **Brisbane Street Mall** marks the centre of the city, which is arranged in a typical grid pattern around it. **Brisbane Street**, with the mall as its focus, is the main shopping precinct; heading east along the street, two other pedestrian shopping areas branch off it: **Quadrant Mall** and **Yorktown Square**. The city is small and easy to get around, but if you want some background information, join Launceston Historic Walks (departs Mon–Fri 9.45am; 1hr 15min; $11; bookings ☏ 03/6331 3679) outside the travel and information centre on Paterson Street.

City Park and the old wharf area

City Park (daily 8am–5pm), with its entrance of impressive wrought-iron gates on Tamar Street, is a real treasure. Established in the 1820s, the impression of a formally organized, very English park is reinforced by the **John Hart Conservatory**, full of flowers and ferns, and by the wrought-iron drinking fountain erected here for Queen Victoria's Diamond Jubilee in 1897. Referred to by the locals as "Monkey Park", it's the closest thing Launceston has to a zoo: its Japanese macaques (over twenty of them), romp around their small, moat-surrounded island. The **City Park Train** (11am–4.30pm) whizzes children and adults twice around the park for around a dollar a ride.

Within City Park, on the corner of Tamar and Brisbane streets, is the **Design Centre of Tasmania** (Mon–Fri 10am–6pm, Sat 10am–1pm, Sun 2–5pm; free), established in 1976 to support and encourage Tasmanian designers. In a state that's always been perceived by the mainland as lagging behind, it's a source of pride that Tasmanian designers helped furnish the New Parliament House in Canberra; "Furniture Focus", a permanent display of contemporary, innovative furniture made from native Tasmanian woods, includes some of their work. Pieces are regularly sold and shipped overseas; prices are beyond the range of most visitors, but the centre is also one of the best places to buy more portable **craft** items, such as woodwork, leatherwork and jewellery.

Backing onto City Park, near the corner of Tamar and Cimitiere streets, is **Albert Hall**, a grand building in the ornate High Victorian style, built for the Tasmanian Industrial Exhibition of 1891. You can go up the steps and look inside at the Great Hall (restored to its original state) and at the Brindley water-powered organ, imported from England in 1861 and the only one of its kind in the world.

Further along Tamar Street, on the corner of William Street, the elaborate Victorian facade of the three-storey **Prince Albert Inn** hides the original Georgian facade. The 1855 building was once a tavern frequented by the sailors from the clippers that berthed at the **Old Launceston Wharves**, 100m away. The wharves on the North Esk River have disappeared, but the massive Neoclassical **Customs House** is still there on the Esplanade, west of the Tamar Street Bridge. The **old wharf area**, around William Street and the Esplanade, has several other interesting old industrial buildings, including the **Esk Brewery Oast House** (1881) and the **Monds and Afflek Mill** (1860). A multimillion-dollar redevelopment of this complex of old railway yards, reached by the Tamar Street Bridge across the river, has transformed it into a convention and entertainment centre, the **Inveresk Centre**. From November 2001, part of this site will also serve as the new location for the Queen Victoria Museum's Art Gallery (see overleaf).

St John Street and around

If you go south from the Customs House down St John Street, you'll come to the **Community History Museum**, on the corner of Cimitiere Street (Mon–Sat 10am–4pm, Sun 2–4pm; $1), housed in the old Johnston and Wilmot store, built in 1842. With its bare rafters, old wooden floors and staircases and rough, wooden pillars supporting the ceiling, it has changed little in 150 years. The building once housed the old Maritime Museum, and some artefacts relating to whaling and sealing still remain here. A little further on at the corner of Cameron Street, the rather grand, Queen Anne-style, red-brick structure is the now-defunct **General Post Office**, built in 1889. Opposite, the grand white building, with its giant colonnade of nine Corinthian columns, is the **town hall**, erected in 1864.

Shady, grassy **Civic Square**, closed to traffic, does convey a tidy spirit of civic-mindedness. Here, **Macquarie House** was built as a warehouse in 1830 for Henry Reed, a wealthy merchant. These days it's the home of the **Tasmanian Wood Design Collection** (Mon–Fri 10am–1pm; $2.20), which showcases Tasmanian wood pieces of some of the state's superb designers, wood-workers and furniture-makers. **Cameron Street** was one of the first streets laid out after the city's settlement in 1806, and the stretch from Civic

Square to Wellington Street is an almost perfectly preserved nineteenth-century streetscape, including the imposing Supreme Court building and, opposite, a row of fine Victorian red-brick terraced houses adorned with beautiful wrought-iron work.

South of Civic Square is the main shopping thoroughfare, the pedestrianized **Brisbane Street Mall**, a modest precinct taking up one small city block. Just off here is the arc of the **Quadrant Mall**, bounded by Brisbane and St John streets, with several lanes and an arcade off it. Gourlay's Sweet Shop here is a Launceston institution, lined with row upon row of glass jars full of imported and local sweets – for something really local, try the leatherwood honey drops. **Yorktown Square**, designed to re-create the atmosphere of the nineteenth century, can be reached by cobbled lanes off Cameron, George and Brisbane streets; here, you'll find cafés and restaurants – most with outdoor tables – ranged around the square. On Sunday a "village market" (9am–2pm), selling mainly crafts, is held here. Nearly opposite the George Street entrance to the square is The Old Umbrella Shop at no. 60 (Mon–Fri 9am–5pm, Sat 9am–noon; ☎03/6331 9248), a **National Trust information centre** housed in a rare example of a mid-Victorian shop, built in the 1860s and lined with Tasmanian blackwood.

Five blocks south of the old General Post Office, bounded by Frederick and Elizabeth streets, is the peaceful **Princes Square**, a park since 1859, having served as both brickfields and a parade ground.

The Queen Victoria Museum and Art Gallery

The **Queen Victoria Museum and Art Gallery** on Wellington Street (Mon–Sat 10am–5pm, Sun 2–5pm; free) was opened in 1891 to mark half a century of Queen Victoria's reign. Its most valued possession is the Chinese joss house from Weldborough (see p.1088), constructed in the 1870s by Chinese workers introduced to the east-coast tin mines to provide cheap labour. Elsewhere, there's a history of mining in Tasmania, displays of stuffed animals, accounts of the geology of Launceston and the local area, a **Planetarium** (Tues–Fri 3pm, Sat 2pm & 3pm; $3.30), and the "Discovery Plus" room, containing such items as microscopes and specimen trays, as well as a display of live spiders and puzzles to play with. Upstairs, the **Art Gallery** – containing some gothic and wild Tasmanian landscapes by the nineteenth-century painter W.C. Piguenit – is due to be transferred to a new site at the railway yards development across the river (see overleaf) in November 2001. The *Queen Vic Café* downstairs is one of the best in Launceston.

Royal Park to Ritchies Mill Arts Centre

Behind the museum, and across Bathurst Street, **Royal Park** has extensive formal parklands running down to the Tamar River; there's even a croquet lawn here, if you were in any doubt about its English character. Between Royal Park and Cataract Gorge is a concentrated tourist area. **Ritchies Mill Arts Centre**, at 2 Bridge Rd on the Tamar River, has been converted from a nineteenth-century flour mill and millers' cottage and now contains two galleries and an alfresco café (see p.1097).

Opposite Ritchies Mill, **Penny Royal World** (daily 9.30am–4pm; $19.50, children $9.50) is a sort of historical funfair, developed on the site of an old bluestone quarry and based around an 1840 ironstone water mill and farmhouse – transferred to the site – and a replica of an 1825 wooden corn mill. The standard entrance fee includes a cruise on the **paddle steamer** *Lady Stelfox*, departing from the landing stage behind the Arts Centre. It's much the best attraction of the centre, but you can also buy separate tickets; the forty-minute cruise heads along the Tamar and into the mouth of Cataract Gorge (daily 10.10am, 11.10am, 12.20pm, 1.10pm, 2.10pm & 3.10pm; $6.50), allowing a close-up view of the Launceston Yacht Club, as well as the wealthy suburb of **Trevallyn**, filled with classic Victorian mansions strung along the tree-covered hillside. On the return leg, you cruise close to the western side of the Tamar, before briefly entering the natural beauty of Cataract Gorge (see below). A longer trip with Tamar River Cruises, departing from the same landing stage, goes into the mouth of Cataract Gorge and continues north up the Tamar as far as the Rosevear vineyards (see p.1100; Mon–Sat 10am, Sun 11am; 4hr; $50 including lunch; bookings ☎03/6334 9900); there's also a shorter, less pricey afternoon cruise (summer Tues, Wed & Thurs 3pm; winter Mon & Fri 2pm; 2hr 30min; $26).

Cataract Gorge and beyond

Few cities have such a magnificent natural feature within fifteen-minutes' walk of the centre as does Launceston. For a beautiful view of **Cataract Gorge**, turn left out of Penny Royal World and walk to the decorative wrought-iron **Kings Bridge**, fabricated in Manchester and transported to Launceston in 1863, which has a span of 60m. From the bridge the cliffs rise almost vertically from the smooth water of the South Esk River as it empties into the Tamar. The natural spectacle is even more dramatic when floodlit after dusk.

There are two walking routes along the gorge. The **Zig Zag track** (25min one-way), on the Penny Royal World side of the bridge, is the more strenuous, a rock-stepped path shrouded by bush but satisfyingly secluded. It runs steeply along the top of the gorge, from Kings Bridge to the **First Basin**, a large, deep canyon worn away by the river and filled with water. If you cross the Kings Bridge, you can choose to take the easier but busier **Cataract Walk** (40min one-way), which begins by the small tollhouse; it's an easy stroll, suitable for prams or wheelchairs, and offers spectacular views of the gorge. From the trail, particularly at weekends and during summer, you'll see people canoeing, abseiling or even jumping off the cliffs into the water; contact Tas Expeditions if you're interested in having a go at abseiling yourself (Wed & Sat; half-day $75, full day $130; ☎03/6334 3477).

The Cataract Walk leads to the gardens of the **Cliff Grounds**, on the shady northern side of the gorge – genteel, English-style gardens with parading peacocks, they make for a startling contrast with the gorge's wild beauty. The garden's native and exotic plants are artfully arranged around a lovely 1896 rotunda, which contains an interpretive centre detailing the history and botany of the gorge. The *Gorge Restaurant* (closed Mon; ☎03/6331 3330) in the grounds has stunning views over the First Basin. Less expensive Devonshire teas are served from the kiosk at the back of the restaurant. If you enter the grounds from the First Basin end (where there's a car park; or take bus #51), you'll find an enormous, unattractive **swimming pool**, built mainly to discourage people from swimming in the basin itself, where some have died. However, people still continue to swim there, despite prominent signs warning them of the dangers of hypothermia; diving is not recommended, as there are submerged rocks and logs.

To get across the First Basin to the Cliff Grounds, you can take the **Launceston Basin Chair Lift** (daily 9am–4.30pm weather permitting; $6.60), which takes an exhilarating six minutes to cover 457m – it's supposed to have the longest single span (308m) of any chair lift in the world. The views are wonderful, but if you're afraid of heights you might want to cross on foot via the **Basin Walk** directly underneath, although this route is impassable when the river is in flood. The other alternative, the narrow **Alexandra Suspension Bridge**, is fairly alarming, too. Called the "swinging bridge" by locals, it's even shakier when crowded with joggers.

There are several other walks and lookouts in the grounds, all well signposted. It's even possible to undertake longer bushwalks: for example, a track starts from the Alexandra Suspension Bridge and follows the river through unspoilt bush to the narrower **Second Basin** and the disused **Duck Reach Power Station** (90min return). From the station you could continue a bit further to reach the large **Trevallyn State Recreation Area** (daily 8am–dusk; no camping), on the South Esk River, and the **Trevallyn Dam**, 6km west of the city centre. To reach the area by road, go via the suburb of Trevallyn, following Reatta Road. There's an **information centre** at **Aquatic Point** in the recreation area, where there are a children's playground, toilets and barbecues. The rest of the reserve consists of open eucalypt forest, with marked bushwalks and nature trails that you'll share with horse-riders. In summer, canoes and windsurfers can sometimes be rented; enquire at the information centre.

The Waverly Woollen Mills and Franklin House

The city's three woollen mills are all open for inspection, though easily the most interesting is **Waverly Woollen Mills** (Mon–Fri 9am–4pm; tours $4), on Waverly Road, 5km west of the city centre; take bus #34 or #38 from the city to the Waverly Road turn-off, and from there it's a 500m walk. Established in 1874, it's the oldest woollen mill in Australia, and much of the cloth is still manufactured on old-fashioned machinery.

Franklin House, at 413 Hobart Rd, 6km towards Hobart on the Midland Highway (daily 9am–5pm; $7.70; bus #21 from the city), was built in 1838 for Britton Jones, a prosperous local brewer. Furnished as an early Victorian home, it became a leading school for boys four years after it was built, a role it retained for half a century. Beautifully furnished and restored by the National Trust, its most outstanding feature is the woodwork of the interior, made entirely of unusual cedarwood from New South Wales.

Eating

Eating out in Launceston is a predominantly Anglo-Saxon affair, with **pubs** in particular offering decent meals. However, there are also a few excellent **cafés** and the odd ethnic place.

Arpar's Thai Restaurant, cnr Charles and Paterson streets (℡03/6331 2786). Thai restaurant with a good reputation. Licensed and BYO. Daily lunch & dinner.

Calabrisella, 56 Wellington St (℡03/6331 1958). A real find – a crowded, noisy, atmospheric and affordable Italian restaurant. BYO. Dinner nightly except Tues.

Cucina Simpatica, cnr Margaret and Frederick streets, opposite Brickfields Reserve (℡03/6334 3177). Launceston's hip café, with a colourful Mediterranean feel; a good place to relax with a coffee and newspaper. Becomes a restaurant in the evening, with an eclectic, "contemporary" menu: delicious food (though pricey and small portions) and an emphasis on fresh Tasmanian pro-

duce. Licensed or BYO. Tues–Sun 10am until late.

Fee & Me, 190 Charles St (℡03/6331 3195) Award-winning restaurant serving up regional cuisine with an international flavour. Licensed. Mon–Sat from 7pm.

Gourmet on Brisbane, 86 Brisbane St. A big, bright delicatessen doubling as a crowded café. Mon–Sat 8 or 9am–6pm.

Hari's Curry, 152 York St (℡03/6331 6466). Very cheap, well-recommended Indian place. BYO. Closed for lunch Sat & Sun.

Konditorei Manfredi, 106 George St (℡03/6334 2490; dinner bookings recommended). German cakes and pastries accompanied by delicious coffee; there's also a full menu of contemporary meals served on the smart upper level with its polished wood floors, plus a bar and outside courtyard. Licensed. Mon–Fri 8.30am–4.30pm, Sat 8.30am–4pm.

Metz Cafe Bar, 119 St John St, cnr York St. Cosmopolitan combination of café and wine bar with music videos playing day or night. Typical café fare plus wood-fired pizzas and all-day breakfasts. Licensed. Daily 8am–midnight, Fri & Sat until 3am, Sun until 2am.

Montezuma's, 63 Brisbane St (T 03/6331 8999). Typical Mexican restaurant, with pricey main courses, but you can fill up on the taco and nachos starters. Good-value margaritas. Daily from 6pm, plus lunch Mon–Fri.

Narracoopaz, 76 St John St. Contemporary-feeling vegetarian café serving fresh juices and cakes, gourmet pizzas, Italian bread sandwiches and continental salads. Airy interior with art on the walls, and outdoor tables too.

O'Keefe's Hotel, 124 George St. People crowd into the lounge bar for pub meals claimed to be the best in Tasmania: from a warm wallaby salad to a Thai red curry, plus a traditional roast of the day and a large range of fresh seafood.

Pepper Berry, 91 George St (T 03/6334 4589). Great café with an eclectic menu. Local produce is used as much as possible, and they even cure their own trout. Try the damper baked here, served with

native jams. Vegan, vegetarian and other diets catered for. Mains around $15. Licensed or BYO. Mon–Tues 8.30am–5pm, Wed–Sat 8.30am until late.

Satay House, Innocent St, Kingscourt Shopping Centre, behind Roelf Voss Supermarket, Kings Meadows (T 03/6344 5955). You'll have to venture into suburban Launceston (bus #21) for this authentic, family-run Indonesian restaurant, but it's worth it. The chef uses her grandmother's recipes. BYO. Dinner Mon–Sat.

Shrimps, 72 George St, cnr Paterson St (T 03/6334 0584). A Launceston institution, serving the best seafood in town. Formal, but not stuffy, and with an imaginative menu. Expensive. Licensed. Closed Sun & lunch Sat.

Stillwater River Cafe, Restaurant and Wine Bar, Ritchies Mill Arts Centre, Paterson St (T 03/6331 4153). Very popular riverside café/restaurant with a great atmosphere. During the day it's an alfresco café, with generous all-day breakfasts and board specials. At night it becomes a fine-dining establishment. Licensed or BYO. Daily 10am to late (book for dinner).

Tairyo Japanese Restaurant and Sushi Bar, Yorktown Square (T 03/6334 2620). Serves all the Japanese dishes: *ramen*, sushi, tempura, *bento*. Licensed (sake) or BYO. Dinner nightly, plus lunch Tues–Fri.

Entertainment and nightlife

The *Examiner*, based in Launceston, is the newspaper for the north of Tasmania – Thursday's edition contains an entertainment section. However, there's never very much going on in this quiet city, and there's no particularly lively area. The **Princess Theatre**, 57 Brisbane St (T 03/6323 3666), stages regular drama, opera and concerts, usually touring from interstate. Behind the theatre is the Earl Arts Centre, 10 Earl St, which has fringe theatre productions, while the **Silverdome**, out of town on the Bass Highway at Prospect (T 03/6344 9999), is the venue for big entertainment events, exhibitions and sports events. The only **cinema**, the Village 4 at 163 Brisbane St (T 03/6331 5066), has four screens showing mainstream films.

Pubs, clubs and venues

Batman Fawkner Inn, 35–39 Cameron St (T 03/6331 7222). Stylishly decorated old hotel on the weekend pub route. Young crowd and a popular pool table. Interstate bands play once or twice a month.

Country Club Casino, Country Club Ave, Prospect Vale, 9km out of town off the Bass Highway (T 03/6335 5777). From the outside it looks as exclusive as its name suggests, but it's not really – just don't wear sandshoes or T-shirts after 7.30pm. Live music Thurs–Sat in the *Lanai Bar*. Sun buffet lunch in the brasserie, with lots of

seafood, prawns and oysters ($23.50 a head). Bus #61, #64 or #65; if you want to stay late, you'll have to take a taxi back (around $14). Daily noon–1am, Fri & Sat until 4am.

Irish Murphy's, 211 Brisbane St. Lively Irish pub with Guinness on tap, live music Wed–Sun, and pub meals.

K-OS, 107 Brisbane St. Large airy upstairs space with groovy lounge decor, but a rather dull atmosphere. Pumping music is replaced on Fri & Sat nights by stints of an acoustic duo playing covers. Even so, it's Launceston's most happening bar, best enjoyed from the narrow balcony. Doubles as a café. Mon & Tues 11am–10pm, Wed–Sat (with DJs) 11am–3am.

Royal Oak Hotel, 14 Brisbane St. Popular, genial watering hole, with live music Thurs to Sat nights. Crowded bistro serves Greek dishes as well as

counter meals. Mon–Sat until midnight, Sun until 10pm.

Star Bar Café, 113 Charles St. Sophisticated bar with slick, modern decor; brasserie-style Mediterranean food available.

Listings

Banks and foreign exchange Commonwealth Bank, 97 Brisbane St; Thomas Cook, 85 George St, cnr Brisbane St.

Bike rental Rent-A-Cycle Tasmania, from *Launceston City Youth Hostel* (see p.1092). Bikes from $70 per week, mountain bikes from $110.

Camping equipment The best place to rent gear is from *Launceston City Youth Hostel* (see p.1092). Another good option is Allgoods, with two stores at 71–79 York St and 60 Elizabeth St. Paddy Pallin, 110 George St, focuses on the top end of the market and also rents gear and sells fuel, a wide range of freeze-dried foods, guidebooks and maps.

Car rental Advance Car Rentals, 32 Cameron St (☏03/6391 8000 or free call 1800 030 118), has rates from $83 with a $20 surcharge for one-day rental. They also hire out 4WDs, from $105 per day. Auto Rent Hertz, 58 Paterson St (☏03/6335 1111), charges from $67 per day, and has campervans; Economy Car Rentals, 27 William St (☏03/6334 3299), has cars from $62 per day; Lo-Cost Auto Rent, 152 Cimitiere St (☏03/6334 3437), has rates from $55 per day; Ryan's Minicar Rentals (☏03/6344 3600) has old Leyland minis from $27 per day.

Hospital Launceston General, Charles St (☏03/6332 7111).

Internet access Free access at the Service Tasmania Centre, next door to the main library in Civic Square.

Left luggage Redline, 18 Charles St, charges $1.10 per item for 24hr (☏03/6336 1444).

Motorbike rental Tasmanian Motorcycle Hire, 17 Coachmans Rd, Evandale (☏03/6391 9139; from $70 per day, helmets $7.50).

Parking Plaza Quadrant Car Park, entrance on 94 York St, near the corner of George St (Mon–Fri 7am–6.30pm, Sat 7.30am–5.15pm), charges

$7.70 per day, $15.70 per 24hr. It also has cheaper long-term rates if you want to leave your vehicle here while you go on the Overland Track.

Pharmacy Todd's Centre Pharmacy, 84 Brisbane St (daily 9am–10pm; ☏03/6331 7777).

Post office 170 Brisbane St, Launceston, TAS 7250.

Swimming The Launceston Swimming Centre, Windmill Hill Reserve (☏03/6337 1282), has an outdoor 50m pool, a diving pool, children's pool and waterslides. Aquarius Roman Baths, 127–133 George St (☏03/6331 2255), are a very popular, self-indulgent complex of therapeutic warm, hot and cold baths, sauna, steam rooms, gym, massage and solarium; admission to baths and saunas $20 (or $33 per couple).

Taxis There's a taxi rank on George St between Brisbane and Paterson streets, and one on St John St outside Princes Square. Central Cabs (☏13 008); Taxis Combined (☏03/6331 5555).

Tours Tigerline Coaches (☏03/6272 6611 or 1300/653 633) has a programme of tours: Launceston city sights (half-day; $39); Tamar Valley wine tour (half-day; $49); Sea Horse World at Beauty Point (half-day; $55); and a summer-only fairy penguin twilight tour ($49). Their Cradle Mountain tour ($68) doesn't give enough time at the park (no more than 2hr). Tiger Wilderness Tours (☏03/6326 6515) operates a similar programme of tours: Evandale and the market (Sun 9am–1pm; $45); Tamar Valley (half-day; $48); Mole Creek caves and the wildlife park ($49); Freycinet National Park (full-day; $75); and an evening tour to see the fairy penguins ($38). Launceston Wilderness Walks (☏03/6334 3477) offer cycle tours (half-day $55; full day $99), as well as walking tours of Cradle Mountain (3 days; $495) and Freycinet National Park (3 days; $495).

Around Launceston

Before launching yourself into the beauty of the Tamar Valley, there are several local destinations worth visiting **around Launceston**, most notably the well-preserved town of **Evandale**, just 20km from the city. If you're here in winter, you might consider joining the ski crowd who descend upon **Ben Lomond National Park**, southeast of Launceston; out of season, this is fine bushwalking country.

Entally House

Entally House (daily 10am–12.30pm & 1–5pm; $6) at **HADSPEN**, 18km west of Launceston on the Bass Highway, is the oldest National Trust-owned property in Australia. A large homestead, built in 1819 by Thomas Haycock Reibey, it would have remained a classic, colonial Georgian cottage if not for the later addition of a second storey, reached by climbing rickety stairs. The extensive grounds, running down to the river, are a perfect picnic setting and you don't have to pay to wander through them.

Evandale

Twenty kilometres southeast of Launceston is **EVANDALE**, a National Trust-classified town from the 1830s, where the principal attractions are the Sunday market and various places serving good food. At the **Evandale Tourism and History Centre**, on High Street (daily 11am–3pm; ☎03/6391 8128), pick up a *Heritage Walk* brochure ($2.20). When it's closed, consult the map opposite the Ingleside Bakery, also on High Street, that points out notable features – many of the old buildings bear descriptive plaques. **Solomon House** (1836), on the corner of High and Russell streets, is a whitewashed two-storey brick building with a green tin roof, which operated as Clarendon Stores for about 130 years. The bakehouse at the rear once supplied the early settlers, though now it's an excellent tearoom. Another good place for refreshment is the *Dalmeny Bookcafé & Gallery* at 14 Russell St (closed Mon & Tues). The **Clarendon Arms Hotel**, on Russell Street (☎03/6391 8181; ➍), was built in 1847 on the site of the former convict station. Its interior walls are covered in murals depicting the early history of Tasmania; one shows the infamous bushranger Matthew Brady and his gang, and there are also portraits of the Aborigines King Billy and Truganini.

Further down Russell Street is the **Evandale Market** (Sun 10am–2pm), which attracts large crowds to its 140 stalls. A lot of local vegetable-growers – particularly those who grow organically – bring their produce here. You'll also find a flea market, and some food stalls that are rather exotic for Tasmania. Once a year, running over three days in late February, Evandale hosts the **National Penny Farthing Championships** as part of its Village Fair; the races using the old bikes are quite a sight. There's no public transport to Evandale.

Ben Lomond National Park

The plateau of the **Ben Lomond Range**, over 1300m high and 84 square kilometres in area, lies entirely within **Ben Lomond National Park**, 50km southeast of Launceston. A small ski village sits below **Legges Tor** (1572m), the second-highest point in Tasmania, and can be reached in an hour from Launceston (or 30min from Evandale); above it the bumpy outline of the range's steep cliffs dominates the horizon. The **ski season** runs from mid-July to the end of September, and although **accommodation** is limited, the region's accessibility means there's no real need to stay. If you're determined, try the *Ben Lomond Creek Inn* (☎03/6372 2444; rooms ➏ half-board, bunk rooms ➋), which is usually booked out at weekends. Meals are available here, or there's fast food from the ski resort kiosk.

An all-day pass on the **ski lifts** costs around $33. Some ski rental is available on the mountain but there's a better range at Launceston Sports Centre, 88a George St (☎03/6331 4777), which can also advise on ski packages. If you're driving, be warned that the final 20km to the ski village is unsealed and the last leg, **Jacobs Ladder**, is very steep, with several hairpin bends, sheer drops and no safety barriers. You must carry wheel chains, which can be rented from the snowline. Outside the ski season, all services cease and the businesses close down, but **bushwalkers** are lured by the magnificent scenery and the alpine vegetation. There's a 12.5km track from Carr Villa, on the slopes of Ben Lomond, to Legges Tor. Bush **camping** is permitted anywhere in the national park, but Carr Villa is an informal camping area with a pit toilet. For more information, contact the ranger (℡03/6390 6279).

The Tamar Valley

To the north of Launceston is the beautiful **Tamar Valley**, where – for 64km – the tidal waters wind through orchards, vineyards, forested hills and grazing land. Only the Batman Bridge, near Deviot, and the APPM Wood Mill and Bell Bay Power Station, near George Town at the river's mouth, spoil the idyllic pre-industrial scenery.

West of the Tamar

The West Tamar Highway follows the line of the Tamar River from Launceston to Beauty Point, passing through the absurdly tacky **Grindlewald Swiss Village**. Further along, **Brady's Lookout State Reserve** provides magnificent views of the Tamar Valley and Ben Lomond; you can see as far as Low Head, 34km away. Rather than head straight along the highway, you can detour for a stretch through **ROSEVEARS**, on a picturesque sweep of road along the riverbanks that's popular with cyclists. Along the way, stop at the **St Matthias Vineyard** (daily 10am–5pm) for some wine tasting, Tasmanian cheeses and great views. In the village itself there's the **Waterbird Haven Trust** (daily 9am–dusk; $4), extending for half a kilometre along the waterfront, and the **Rosevears Tavern** (1831), where you can have a drink. A few kilometres west of Rosevears is **Notley Gorge State Reserve**, a beautiful fern gorge with a number of walking tracks, reached by turning west off the highway at Legana. **Beaconsfield**, back on the highway, was once at the centre of Tasmania's former **gold-mining** area, and the mining ruins are still visible.

East of the Tamar: George Town and Low Head

Leaving Launceston and heading north along the East Tamar Highway, it's only a few minutes before you're zooming through scenic countryside, passing through Dilston where cows graze in paddocks at the base of bush-covered hills. After Hillwood, you're headed for the port of **GEORGE TOWN**, the third-oldest town in Australia, where Colonel Paterson landed in 1804 to begin settlement of northern Tasmania. It may be your first point of call in Tasmania if you've chosen to take the **high-speed Devil Cat catamaran** from Melbourne, which docks at Adelaide Street, with the town centre opposite, across York Cove. The **George Town Visitor Information Centre**, on Main Road (daily 10am–4pm; ℡03/6382 1700), is about 1.5km northeast of the terminal on the way to Launceston.

Despite its history, George Town isn't particularly old or interesting, with only one colonial building to look at, **The Grove**, an elegant stone Georgian mansion at 25 Cimitiere St (daily 10am–5pm; $4). More appealing is **LOW HEAD**, 5km north, with 24 National Trust-listed buildings, whitewashed cottages and rambling houses, all set amid extensive parkland. The original convict-built **Pilot Station** now houses a **museum** (daily 9am–9pm; $3), which has a display of maritime memorabilia. There's also a **Little penguin colony** at Low Head; guided tours are offered each evening at sunset (1hr 30min; $8; bookings on ☎0418 361 860). Cruises to a nearby **fur seal** colony are also on offer with Seal and Sea Adventure Tours (daily 8am–1pm; $75–100; bookings ☎03/6382 3452).

If you need a **place to stay**, there are several choices in George Town. *Gray's Hotel*, at 77 Macquarie St (☎03/6382 2655; ❺), is the oldest pub in town but has few discernible traces of its early nineteenth-century heritage. The *Pier Hotel*, at 5 Elizabeth St (☎03/6382 1300; ❹–❼), is a pretty wooden hotel on the waterfront with rooms upstairs in the old part, modern motel rooms on the waterfront, and self-catering units; the **food** here is very good, with an extensive menu including pasta and Asian curries. Opposite, at 4 Elizabeth St, is the *Travellers YHA Hostel* (☎03/6382 3261; rooms ❸, dorms ❶) in a pretty 1870 home, with a clean and modern interior. An alternative to eating at the pubs is the *George Town Deli*, at 68 Macquarie St (closed Sat & Sun), which sells health-foods and deli items and serves light lunches.

In Low Head, you can stay in heritage cottage accommodation at the Pilot Station (see opposite; ☎ & ⓕ 03/6382 1143; ❺), and at *Belfont Cottages*, at 178 Low Head Rd (☎03/6382 1841; ❼, with breakfast provisions supplied). You can **camp** at *Low Head Caravan Park*, 136 Low Head Rd (☎03/6382 1573; vans ❸, cabins ❹).

Around George Town

Heading **east** of George Town, a pleasant day can be spent exploring the **vineyards** around the **Pipers River area**, which produce distinctly flavoured, crisp, fresh wines. The *Tasmanian Wine Route* brochure, available from the information centre in Launceston (p.1091), covers fifteen vineyards in the Tamar Valley and Pipers Brook area. At **Ninth Island Winery** at Pipers River, 2km off the B82 on a sealed road (turn south just before the service station at Pipers River), a Swiss couple make European-style wines – the climate here is supposedly similiar to that of the Loire Valley. There are tastings and a restaurant in the original weatherboard farmhouse (tastings daily 10am–5pm; restaurant noon–3pm; ☎03/6382 7122). The friendly, small-scale **Delamere Vineyard**, on Bridport Road at Pipers Brook (daily 10am–5pm; ☎03/6382 7190), also has tastings, while **Pipers Brook Vineyard** (daily 10am–5pm), 2km off the B82, about 10km from Pipers River, is a well-established winery in a modern complex, with self-guided tours. It also has a café and vine-covered courtyard. Tiger Wilderness Tours (☎03/6326 6515) and Tigerline Coaches (☎03/6272 6611 or 1300/653633) both run half-day **wine tours** to the Pipers River area from Launceston for around $50.

The Midland Highway

The **Midland Highway** is a fast three-hour route between Hobart and Launceston, more or less following the old coaching road, although you'll have to detour if you want to visit some of the towns on the way. Tasmanian Redline Coaches have several daily **bus** services between Hobart and Launceston, stopping at the major midland towns.

Campbell Town and Ross

Beyond **Campbell Town** – a rather plain community originally settled by Scots – you drive south through sheep-grazing countryside, eventually turning off the highway to **ROSS**, 2km east. Also settled by Scots, this has a very secluded, rural feel. As you walk through the grounds of St Johns Church of England, just one of the town's three pretty churches, you have views of the Macquarie River, spanned by the sandstone **Ross Bridge**, designed by John Lee Archer and built by convicts in 1836; the intricate stone carvings on its three arches earned the convict stonemason a free pardon. There's a fairly melancholy walk in the other direction from the church, down to the original Ross burial ground and past the site of the **Female Factory**, actually a prison, where women convicts were held before being sent to properties as assigned servants. You can **stay** in several of the old cottages dotted about town: *Colonial Cottages of Ross* (℡03/6381 5354, ℻6381 5408; ❼, including breakfast provisions) have four to pick from. The old sandstone *Man O'Ross Hotel* on Church Street (℡03/6381 5240, ℻6381 5423; ❺ including breakfast) has several intimate rooms in which to eat or drink, and basic accommodation upstairs. The Tasmanian Wool Centre on Church Street (daily 9am–5pm; ℡03/6381 5466) acts as an **information centre** and also houses a wool exhibition and history museum (entry by donation). Internet access here costs $2.20 for half an hour.

Oatlands

Back on the Midland Highway, it's 88km south from Ross to **OATLANDS**, which has Australia's greatest concentration of colonial **Georgian buildings**: 140 in two square kilometres, most built by convicts. Many are now occupied by antique and bric-a-brac shops, B&Bs and guesthouses. The most striking building is the **Callington Mill** and its outbuildings; the partly restored **windmill** was built in 1837 and remained in operation until 1892. From the top there are fine views of the town and the surrounding countryside; unfortunately the mill is presently closed to the public but there are plans to open it again soon. Probably the best way to see the town is to go on one of Peter Fielding's guided **heritage walks** (℡03/6254 1135); he has keys to several other buildings, including the Old Gaol and courthouse. He also runs a spooky evening **ghost tour** which commences outside the mill (9pm during daylight savings, 8pm rest of year; $8).

For **food**, *Oatlands Roadhouse*, on High Street as you come into the town on the Midland Highway, sells the usual fast food plus tasty Lebanese dishes. *Blossom's Tea Rooms*, 116 High St (℡03/6254 1516), serves light lunches, and dinner is available by arrangement. Good **places to stay** are *Oatlands Lodge*, a colonial-style B&B in the centre of town at 92 High St (℡03/6254 1444, ℻6254 1492; ❻), and, further out, the tiny, homely *Oatlands Youth Hostel*, at 9 Wellington St (℡03/6254 1320; ❶), a popular overnight stop for cyclists on their way through the midlands.

The Western Tiers and Central Plateau

Deloraine, on the **Meander River**, is nestled in a valley of rich farmland dominated by **Quamby Bluff** (1256m) and the **Western Tiers**, where the Central Plateau drops abruptly to the surrounding plains. On the Bass Highway, it's roughly equidistant from Devonport (51km) and Launceston (48km). From Deloraine the **Lake Highway** begins, rising up over the Western Tiers to the Central Plateau, with its thousands of lakes. To the west of Deloraine are the extensive **cave systems** around **Mole Creek**, while **Walls of Jerusalem National Park** is accessed from **Western Creek**, 32km southwest of Deloraine.

Deloraine and around

DELORAINE is a delightful hilly town, often shrouded in mist, even on summer mornings, and divided into two parts by the bubbling **Meander River**. Although the area was settled by Europeans in the 1830s, Deloraine didn't really begin to develop until after 1846, and today it's a National Trust-classified town. **West Parade** follows the river, facing the park; at no. 17 is the Georgian **Bonney's Inn** (1830), the town's oldest remaining building (now a B&B; see overleaf). At the next block, Westbury Place rises up steeply from West Parade; if you climb the hill you'll reach **St Marks Church** (1860), with its tall spire. At the top of the hill there's a scenic **lookout** that gives a panoramic view over the town and the Western Tiers to the south. Deloraine has a café culture, plenty of secondhand and antique shops, and a small, alternative arts-and-crafts scene, witnessed regularly at the **market** on the first Saturday of every month across the river opposite the *Apex Caravan Park*, and at the annual **Tasmanian Craft Fair**, a huge event held over four days in early November (contact the information centre for details – see below).

Close to prime **bushwalking** areas in the Western Tiers, Deloraine is an established base for walkers. Popular tracks are the short walk to **Allum Cliffs**, overlooking the Mersey River Gorge (40min return), signposted on the road between Mole Creek and Chudleigh; a difficult walk to **Quamby Bluff**, renowned for its myrtle rainforest (6.5km; 6hr; beginning at Brodies Road, off the Lake Highway); the track to **Liffey Falls** (8km; 3hr; beginning at the picnic ground 5km west of the tiny community of Liffey), and the day-walk to **Meander Falls** through the Meander Forest Reserve, about 25km south of Deloraine, reached via the small settlement of Meander and Meander Falls Road (10km; 6–7hr; beginning from the picnic ground). There's a walker registration and information booth at the Meander Falls car park. A free leaflet issued by Forestry Tasmania, *Visiting the Great Western Tiers*, has a map of the Meander Forest Reserve and tracks; you can pick it up from the Deloraine information centre (see below). If you're not confident to walk on your own, Taswalks lead personalized guided walks ($330 per day per group for small groups; ☎03/6363 6112, ⊛www.microtech.com.au/taswalks); or Tiger Wilderness Tours (based in Launceston; ☎03/6326 6515) offer bushwalking tours of the Meander Valley (6hr 30min; $60) and Liffey Falls (5hr 30min; $55).

The western end of the Great Western Tiers overlooks **MOLE CREEK**, 24km southwest of Deloraine, where you'll find the slightly shabby **Trowunna Wildlife Park** (daily 9am–5pm; $12.50, children $6). You can buy delicious local honey at Mole Creek from **Stephen's Leatherwood Honey Factory** (Mon–Fri 8am–5pm). About 20km west of Mole Creek, are two rather spectacular underground caves: **Marakoopa Cave**, with huge caverns, streams, pools and glow-worms (daily 10am, 11.15am, 1pm, 2.30pm & 4pm; 50–80min); and the smaller but more richly decorative **King Solomons Cave**, with stalactites and stalagmites (daily 10.30am, 11.30am, 12.30pm, 2pm, 3pm & 4pm; 40–60min); admission is $8.80 for each cave, or $13.20 for both. From the caves, you could take a winding route to Cradle Valley (see p.1131).

Practicalities

In Deloraine itself there's a volunteer-run **Visitor Information Centre** at 98 Emu Bay Rd (Mon–Fri 9.30am–4pm, Sat 1–3.30pm, Sun 2–4pm; ☎03/6362 3471), with maps and details on walking times and conditions; the centre is housed in an old inn with an attached folk museum ($2). Among several operators leading **outdoor activities** in the area are Central Highlands Trail Rides, Brodies Road, Golden Valley (℡ 03/6369 5298), who have three-hour horse-rides around Quamby Bluff ($60) or a six-hour ride to Jackys Marsh, with its tall eucalypt forests ($120 including lunch); overnight camping trips to the top of the Central Plateau can also be arranged ($120). Cradle Wilderness 4x4 Tours (℡ 03/6363 1173) operate from Mole Creek and offer a range of half-day tours around the area ($65). You can also head up to the lakes of the Central Plateau with the Tasmanian Fly Fishing School, based in Deloraine (℡ 03/6362 3441). Finally, Wild Caves Tours (℡ 03/6367 8142), based at Mole Creek, offers excellent $65 half-day and $135 full-day caving tours of the Mole Creek caves, underground streams and subterranean systems.

For budget **accommodation**, head for the *Highview Lodge YHA Hostel*, at 8 Blake St (℡ 03/6362 2996; ❶), which is well-run and very clean, and rents out bikes. Set on a hill commanding unparalleled views of Quamby Bluff, the hostel is well signposted from the information centre – about a ten-minute walk – or Tigerline Coaches can drop you off. Another cheap option is the *Bush Inn*, at no. 7 Bass Highway (℡ 03/6362 2365; ❶), which has good-value meals, a pool table and bands at weekends. A good motel on the outskirts of town is *Mountain View Country Inn*, 144 Emu Bay Rd (℡ 03/6362 2633, ℻ 6362 3233; ❻) – though it's on the main road, the row of units afford great views of the Western Tiers. *Bonney's Farm*, off Weetah Road, 4km northwest of Deloraine (℡ 03/6362 2122, ℻ 6362 3566; ❺), has a guesthouse (B&B) and self-contained two- or three-bed units. In the centre of town, the big old *Deloraine Hotel*, faces the river on the corner of Emu Bay Road (℡ 03/6362 2022; B&B ❹). Virtually next door, old-fashioned *Bonney's Inn*, 17 West Parade (℡ & ℻ 03/6362 2974, ⓦ www.bonneys-inn.com; B&B ❼–❽), has spacious suites suitable for families. For something very special, however, head for *Calstock*, on the Lake Highway just outside Deloraine (℡ 03/6362 2642 ℻ 6362 2335, ⓦ www.calstock.net; B&B ❽); this exquisite guesthouse is run by a French couple who provide guests with French country-style meals created from local organic ingredients. **Camping** is available at the riverside *Apex Caravan Park*, 51 West Parade (℡ 03/6362 2345). There are also several places to stay in **Mole Creek**, ranging from an excellent campsite (℡ 03/6363 1150) to the congenial *Mole Creek Guest House* (℡ 03/6363 1399; B&B ❻) with its own restaurant and tourist information.

In Deloraine there are plenty of informal **places to eat** on the main street, Emu Bay Road. The best is the *Delicatessen Coffee Shop* at no. 36 (Mon–Fri 9am–5pm, Sat 9am–2pm), a combination of deli counter and tearoom. It's popular with locals, who enjoy the cakes and freshly baked baguettes with gourmet fillings; the most expensive dish is $8. The *Emu Bay Brasserie* at no. 21 (Tues–Sat 9am–2.30pm & dinner from 6pm; licensed; ℡ 03/6362 2067) has a casual café atmosphere but serves upmarket meals. The best place in town for pub meals is the *Deloraine Hotel* (see above); you can eat in the dining room away from the noisy pokie machines.

The two major **bus** companies both make regular stops in Deloraine. Tasmanian Redline Coaches on its Launceston–Devonport service (2 daily), and its Launceston–Deloraine service (5 daily Mon–Fri, 2 daily Sat & Sun) which continues on to Mole Creek once daily on weekdays; and Tassie Link on its Launceston–Cradle Mountain service (May–Nov 1 daily Tues, Thurs, Sat; Dec–April 1 daily). The depot for Redline is the video shop by the roundabout at 29 West Church St (℡ 03/6362 2046); Tassie Link are based at *Sullivans Restaurant*, at 17 West Parade.

Walls of Jerusalem National Park

The **Walls of Jerusalem National Park** is on the western side of the Central Plateau, a series of five mountain peaks which enclose a central basin, an isolated area noted for its lakes, pencil pines and the biblical names of its various features. The best time to visit is late spring through to April; people have died of exposure here, so make sure you're well prepared. You'll need the *Walls of Jerusalem National Park Map and Notes* ($9), which has walking notes on the reverse, available from the Service Tasmania Shop in Hobart (see p.1055).

The Walls of Jerusalem is the only national park that you can't drive into, so the walk begins outside the park boundaries. From King Solomons Cave (see p.1103), head south, following the Mersey River and the unsealed road east of Lake Rowallan; the car park is at Howells Bluff. You walk through wilderness into the park, which is isolated and lacking even basic facilities, without a ranger (although rangers do patrol). However, the track is well kept, with boardwalks laid down over boggy areas, and there's plenty of clean water to drink from the streams and lakes. There are a few small leaky huts but these are really for emergencies only – bring your own tent. If you just want to walk into the park to the central basin (through **Herods Gate**, with views of Barn Bluff and Cradle Mountain to the northwest), set up camp and then walk back, it's a fourteen-kilometre return hike, which takes seven or eight hours altogether, going at a steady pace over two days. The walk begins with a steep climb then levels out on the plateau. There are numerous routes to the various peaks and lakes – from **Damascus Gate** you get stunning views of Cradle Mountain–Lake St Clair National Park immediately west – and an experienced, well-equipped walker (preferably accompanied) could spend a couple of days here. If you can afford the prices, you can always go on an **organized walk**: Craclair Walking Holidays (T & F 03/6424 7833) has a five-day walk for $875, while Ausprey Tours (T & F 03/6330 2612) offers a two-day version for $210, organized from Hobart or Launceston. Tassie Link can bring you to the beginning of the walk into the park on their service from Launceston, via Deloraine, Mole Creek and Marakoopa Cave (2–3 times weekly), while Maxwell's (T & F 03/6492 1431) goes there on demand from Devonport ($160 1–4 people; $40 per person 5 or more people) and Launceston ($220 1–4 people; $55 per person 5 or more people).

The Central Plateau

At its northern and eastern edges, the **Central Plateau** is rimmed by the long crest of the Great Western Tiers (1440m). At over a thousand metres above sea level, the plateau is often covered in frost and subject to sleet and snowstorms in winter. The **Great Lake** lies on the plateau about 8km from the escarpment, and only 40km from Deloraine, along the Lake Highway that continues to **BOTHWELL**, the plateau's only town, ending at Melton Mowbray, where it joins the Midland Highway. On the unsealed C178, which runs west off the Lake Highway 15km north of Bothwell, you can visit a disused power station, **Waddamana** (daily 10am–4pm; free) and its museum. The major lakes can be reached from roads leading off the Lake Highway. To the west, between Cradle Mountain–Lake St Clair National Park and below the Walls of Jerusalem National Park, is the inaccessible "Land of Three Thousand Lakes".

The Central Plateau has few inhabitants – the permanent population is only around eight hundred – but it's full of **fishing shacks**, and on a fine weekend the population sometimes swells to 25,000. It's also the base for the **Hydro Electricity Commission** (HEC): the countless high-altitude lakes are used as water storage for the generation of electricity. Temporary HEC villages are set up for hydroelectrical workers, and once abandoned they're often transformed into lodge-style accommodation. One is the *Bronte Park Highland Village* (T03/6289 1126, F6289 1109; cabins ❺, lodge ❺, hostel ❷), which also has a campsite and a very basic hostel section, EFTPOS facilities, plus a dining room and bar, a store selling groceries and fuel, and is ideally situated for **Lake St Clair** (25km) and **Lake Big Jim**, popular trout-fishing spots. If you want to try your hand at fishing, Ausprey Tours (T03/6330 2612) offers **fly-fishing tuition** (1–5 days), trout fishing day-tours from Launceston or extended camping treks to fish in the Western Lakes. To reach the *Bronte Park Highland Village*, take the bone-shattering Marlborough Highway (B11), which runs southwest off the Lake Highway as it curves around the bottom of the lake to Miena. Tassie Link drops off at the *Bronte Park* turn-off on the Lyell Highway on their Hobart–Queenstown scheduled service (1 daily Tues, Thurs, Fri & Sun; Dec–Easter an extra service runs on Mon, Wed, Fri & Sat); call in advance to be met.

The Bass Strait Islands

Located in the rough waters of the Bass Strait, battered by the Roaring Forties, are two groups of islands: the Hunter group, dominated by **King Island** off the northwest tip of Tasmania, and the Furneaux group, the largest of which is **Flinders Island**, lying just beyond the northeast corner of the state. In the nineteenth century sealers roamed the Bass Strait, but the two main islands now consist of low-key rural communities, while several tall lighthouses, and many shipwrecks offshore are testimony to the turbulence of the sea at King Island.

Of the two islands, Flinders is the more rewarding to visit as a destination in its own right. The best-case scenario is to visit either island as a **stopover** en route from Victoria to Tasmania with one of the airlines below: it will cost around $110 one-way from Melbourne to King Island and the same price from King Island to Devonport; Melbourne to Flinders one-way is more expensive, at around $150, and then it will cost around $115 from Flinders Island to Launceston. However, **packages**, which often include the Tasmanian mainland, are the best deals – call the airlines below to find out about current deals. To King Island, Kendell Airlines (free call T1800 338 894) fly from Melbourne; King Island Airlines (T03/9580 3777) fly from Moorabbin, on the outskirts of Melbourne; and TasAir (free call T1800 062 900) fly from Burnie or Devonport. To Flinders Island, Island Airlines (free call T1800 645 875) fly from Launceston and Melbourne; while RegionAir (free call T1800 818 455) fly from Launceston to both Flinders Island and King Island.

King Island

The smaller, more heavily populated **King Island** is chiefly known for its rich dairy produce, with crayfish and kelp as secondary industries; green, low and windswept, it can't offer anything like Flinders Island's dramatic landscape, nor its history, though it did witness around sixty **shipwrecks** between 1801 and 1995. There are several working lighthouses – **Cape Wickham Lighthouse** in the north is one of the tallest in the southern hemisphere – and many of the wreck sites can be dived with King Island Dive Charters (T03/6461 1133, F6461 1293; day-trip $154; three-day package including accommodation, diving and on-board lunches $458).

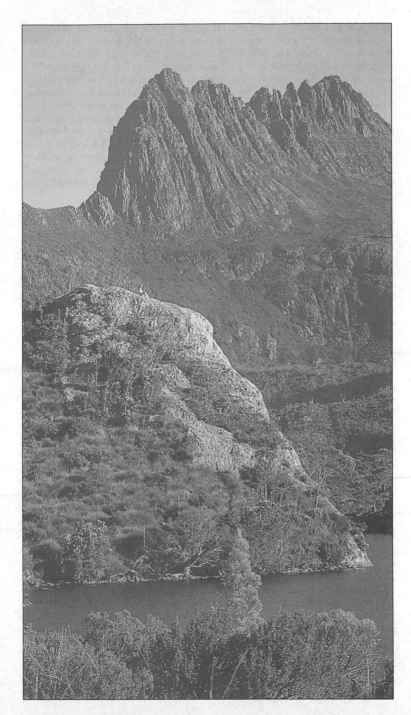

The island's main town is **CURRIE**, which has a simple museum (Mon–Fri 1–4pm). The bleak former tungsten mining village of **GRASSY** is on the eastern side of the island. The best thing about King Island is the food, with free-range lamb and pork and local beef and wallaby, as well as seafood and delicious creamy milk, which you can drink unpasteurized while on the island – a rare treat. Indeed, top of the list of things to do on the island is a visit to the **King Island Dairy** (Mon–Fri 9am–4.30pm, Sun 12.30–4pm; free), 8km north of Currie, for free tastings of the rich local dairy produce; the brie and the thick cream in particular have legendary gourmet status around Australia. The island's **kelp factory** is near Currie's golf course; the bull kelp is gathered from the surrounding shores and left to dry outside the factory on racks – you'll see it as you pass by. After drying the kelp is milled into granules and shipped to Scotland to be processed into alginates, used as a gelling agent in products like toothpaste and ice cream.

Practicalities

King Island Coach Tours, based in Currie at 95 Main St (free call ☎1800 647 702), do prebooked airport transfers to Currie, which is less than 10km away ($5, or $16.50 if you are the only passenger), and transfers to Naracoopa to Grassy. Alternatively, your accommodation may pick you up. For getting around, you'll need to **rent a car** at the airport – two outfits are Cheapa Island Car Rentals (☎03/6462 1603) and Grassy Car Rentals (☎03/6461 1278) – or a **mountain bike** from The Trend, on 26 Edward St, Currie ($15 per day), who also provide **tourist information** (daily 9am–6.30pm; ☎03/6462 1360). King Island Coach Tours run various **day-tours**; the best is the short evening tour to see the **Little penguin** community at Grassy (Tues & Thurs; $27.50). There are also bushwalking and wildlife tours available.

The most obvious **places to stay** are around Currie. The cheapest option is to **camp** at *Bass Caravan Park* (☎03/6462 1260; on-site vans ❹, cabins ❻) on North Road, 2km from town. Right in the centre, *Parers Hotel* (☎03/6462 1633; ❻), has en-suite motel-style rooms, while there are immaculate units near the golf course at *Wave Watcher Holiday Units*, 18 Beach Rd (☎03/6462 1517; ❼). Nearby, the rooms at *Boomerang By the Sea* (free call ☎1800 221 288, ℱ03/6462 1607; ❻) have stunning sea views – even better from the motel's glass-walled **restaurant**. Back in town, *Parers* serves excellent meals in its bistro and *King Island Bakery* makes delicious pies; *Nautilus Coffee Lounge* is Currie's best café. If you're self-catering, there's a supermarket (open daily) and a bottle shop. Currie also has a Westpac bank with an ATM machine.

Flinders Island

With a population of just under one thousand, **FLINDERS ISLAND** is nonetheless the largest of 52 named islands which make up the Furneaux group, first mapped by Tobias Furneaux in 1770. The islands became a base for seal hunters, who slaughtered seals in their tens of thousands and, so legend goes, lured many ships to their demise for a spot of piracy. These rough men provided a vital link in the continuing survival of the Tasmanian Aboriginal people, ironically by stealing women to work for them on the islands. When sealing ended, the communities survived by **muttonbird harvesting**, a seasonal industry which continues today (with land rights claims in 1995 giving title to several outlying islands).

Flinders Island itself played a large part in the attempted genocide of the Tasmanian Aboriginal people; between 1831 and 1834 the remnants of the

Tasmanian tribes were persuaded or forced to accept relocation here. Settled at windswept **Wybalenna** on the west coast of the island, the Aborigines were without adequate food and shelter, and were forcibly Christianized, as their culture was expunged and their numbers dwindled. All that remains of the period of enforced Aboriginal settlement is the **chapel**, built in 1838 at Wybalenna, and the cemetery where only the white graves bear headstones. Of the 135 tribespeople who were sent here, only 47 were still alive when the settlement was abandoned in 1847 and moved to Oyster Cove, near Hobart. The chapel has been restored by the National Trust, but the Aboriginal people of Flinders Island succeeded with their land rights claim on Wybalenna, which was handed over in early 1999, and it is now up to them to decide how they'll run it.

For more history, it's just a few kilometres northwest to the **Emita Museum** (Sat & Sun: summer 1–5pm; rest of year 1–4pm; $2), where there's a display of shell necklaces made by the Aboriginal people of nearby Cape Barren, plus exhibits relating to sealing and shipwrecks. In the grounds there's a replica of a **muttonbirding shed**, with magazines covering the walls and a dirt floor lined with tussock grass. Most professional muttonbirders are Aboriginal, and with Flinders Island Adventures (℡03/6359 4507) you can experience the extraordinary sight and sound of hundreds of thousands of birds flying to the nesting islands each evening at dusk (tours Oct–March only; $28 per person). Enquire on the same number for several other tour options, including cruises to the outer islands, fishing and diving trips and 4WD tours – all available as full- or half-day trips.

History aside, isolated Flinders Island is very much a mecca for **bushwalkers**. Only about half of the island is cultivated, and you can walk its entire length in about six days on the partially signposted north–south **Flinders Trail**, a route designed to provide a sampling of the various terrains. The best-known walk, however, is to the distinctive summit of **Mount Strzelecki**, in the **Strzelecki National Park** in the south. The climb to the top starts about 10km south of Whitemark, signposted on Trousers Point Road – look out for a brown national park sign. Though navigation is easy, it's a strenuous walk – about 5km return (3–5hr). The wind can be fierce at the summit, and mists roll in, so take something wind- and waterproof. **Trousers Point** itself, also near the park, is a good introduction to the delights of the island's deserted beaches. The site, with its fine, white sand and rust-coloured rock formations, is particularly spectacular, with Mount Strzelecki rising up behind the granite headland; there's a free camping area here, with water available.

The **Flinders Island Ecology Trail** is a circuit designed to be followed in a car, with five stopping-points where interpretive material is provided. **Walkers Lookout**, in the Darling Range, is a good starting point, offering the best panorama of Flinders and the surrounding islands, with signs pointing out all the landmarks; the other four points on the route highlight bird habitats. You can see the endemic protected **Cape Barren goose** everywhere – even in people's paddocks – and likewise the island's wombats.

Practicalities

There are two main bases on the island: **WHITEMARK**, the administrative centre on the west coast, and **LADY BARRON** in the south, the main fishing area and deep-water port; both places have shops, fuel and accommodation. The post office in Whitemark houses the island's only **bank** – Westpac (Mon–Thurs noon–3pm, Fri noon–3pm & 4–5pm) – with EFTPOS, but no ATM facilities. As there's no public transport, the best option is to **rent a car** and arrange to pick it up at the airport on arrival. Prices are quite reasonable: from around $60–70 per day with Flinders Island Car Rentals (℡03/6359

2168, ⓕ 6359 2293), Flinders Island Transport Services (ⓣ 03/6359 2060) or Bowman Lees Car Hire (ⓣ 03/6359 2388).

For information on **activities** such as cruises, scuba diving, fishing and scenic flights, or just for general enquiries, you can contact the secretary of the Flinders Island Tourist Committee, Whitemark, Flinders Island, TAS 7255 (ⓣ 03/6359 4507, ⓔ jamesluddington@bigpond.com); the *Flinders Island Visitors Guide*, a free brochure with map, can be picked up at Tasmanian travel centres (see box on p.1049) before you arrive on the island. The General Store in Whitemark also publishes a free leaflet full of useful contacts. You can book accommodation, car rental, air travel and some tours through Flinders Island Holidays, based in Hobart (free call ⓣ 1800 818 826, ⓔ flindersholidays@bigpond .com).

There's a **campsite** with water and showers (ⓣ 03/6359 8560) at Killiecrankie Bay in the northwest of the island – where you can also fossick for topaz – or you can camp for free at the coastal reserves, or on any crown land as long as it's 500m from the road: designated sites are at Allports Beach, Lillies Beach, North East River and Trousers Point, and all have toilets and fireplaces, though only the last has water. In Whitemark you can **stay** at the *Flinders Island Interstate Hotel* in the centre of town (ⓣ 03/6359 2114, ⓕ 6359 2250; B&B ④–⑤), which has some en-suite rooms and serves meals (except Sun); it also offers showers and laundry facilities to nonresidents. *Sweet Surprises Coffee Shop* is a decent place for a daytime snack (closed Sun); or try the *Flinders Island Sports Club* at the end of the Esplanade for a reasonable meal in pleasant surroundings. Lady Barron is a far nicer place to stay than Whitemark, however. The *Flinders Island Lodge* (ⓣ 03/6359 3521 or free call 1800 818 826, ⓕ 6359 3618; ⑤ including breakfast), attached to the *Furneaux Tavern* and overlooking the picturesque Furneaux Sound, has spacious and attractive motel units; **meals** are served here in the *Shearwater Restaurant*. You could also try the self-catering accommodation at *Yaringa Cottages* (ⓣ 03/6359 4522; ⑤), or the excellent cabins with beautiful views at *Partridge Farm*, a ten-minute drive from Lady Barron at the end of the road to Badger Corner (ⓣ & ⓕ 03/6359 3554; ⑦); note that the latter discourages children.

The West

Except for the rich beef, dairy and vegetable-growing land along the northwest coast, the western half of Tasmania is an untamed area. The wild **west coast**, densely forested and battered by the rough Southern Ocean and the Roaring Forties, its shores strewn with huge dead trees washed down from the southwest's many rivers, would probably still be uninhabited if it weren't for the **logging** and **mining** industries. This part of the island is very densely populated (by Tasmanian standards), and the **Bass Highway**, which skirts the northwest coast, passes through two unattractive industrial cities, **Devonport** and **Burnie**. **Rocky Cape National Park** and the town of **Stanley** (originally built by the Van Diemen's Land Company – VDL – which still owns the northwest corner of the state) are the most interesting places for visitors.

Just south of Stanley the highway turns inland to **Smithton**, marking the beginning of a thickly forested region and a logging heartland. The Bass Highway ends at the tiny settlement of **Marrawah**, on the west coast (popular with surfers), where it meets the **Western Explorer** road, which runs south to sleepy **Arthur River** and then through the Arthur Pieman Protected area to **Corinna**, where the road heads east via Savage River and Waratah onto the A10 (Murchison Highway). Alternatively, you can continue southwards, taking a barge across the Pieman River (daily 9am–7pm; $11 car, $5.50 bike; ☎03/6446 1170) and then heading on to Zeehan (on the C249) and **Strahan** (on the B27), on the vast **Macquarie Harbour**. To reach Strahan on sealed roads, you have to go back to Marrawah and then to Somerset on the northwest coast, from where the Murchison Highway heads south through a copper- and lead-mining backwater. On the way you pass **Queenstown**, which has been subject to an ecological disaster; its surrounding rainforest has been destroyed, and in its place are bare and chalky hills.

Strahan sits on the edge of the **southwest wilderness**, an area of rugged coastlines, wild rivers, open plains, thick rainforest and spectacular peaks – the wettest part of Australia after the tropical lowlands of north Queensland. It's mostly inaccessible, except to very experienced and well-prepared bushwalkers, but **cruises** leave from Strahan to go up the **Gordon River**, offering a glimpse of its magnificent scenery. Some years ago, a plan to dam the Gordon River below the point where it joins the **Franklin River** put Strahan at the centre of a struggle between environmentalists and the state government. Eventually the federal government stepped in, and, following a landmark High Court ruling in 1983, the whole of the southwest – including the **South West National Park**, the **Franklin Lower Gordon Wild Rivers National Park** and the adjoining heavily glaciated **Cradle Mountain–Lake St Clair National Park** – became a vast, protected **World Heritage Area**, occupying twenty percent of the land area of the state. From Queenstown, en route east to Hobart, the **Lyell Highway** provides limited access to the mainly inaccessible Franklin Lower Gordon park, and to Lake St Clair at **Derwent Bridge**.

It's worth finding a copy of the excellent and comprehensive booklet, *Tasmania's West Coast*, from a tourist office before you head west.

The northwest coast

A succession of Tasmania's larger towns dot the conservative, agricultural **northwest coast**, including the cities of **Devonport** and **Burnie**, and the smaller community of older **Stanley**, on a peninsula jutting into the Bass Strait. The **Bass Highway**, which connects them, becomes spectacularly beautiful beyond Wynyard, passing Table Cape, Boat Harbour Beach and Rocky Cape National Park, though it skirts the very northwest tip (privately owned by the Van Diemen's Land Company). At the end of the highway is **Marrawah**, from where you can head to Arthur River for a cruise. Tasmanian Redline Coaches (☎03/6331 3233) run daily services from Devonport to Burnie, and from Burnie to Smithton, stopping at all towns along the Bass Highway; there is no public transport to Marrawah or Arthur River.

Devonport and around

The industrial port of **DEVONPORT**, which in 1959 replaced Launceston as the terminal of the **Bass Strait ferry**, the *Spirit of Tasmania*, is not the most

▲ Ferry to Melbourne

DEVONPORT

Bass Strait

Mersey Bluff

Tiagarra

◄ Coles Beach

BEACH RD

BLUFF ROAD

NORTH STREET

JAMES STREET

GEORGE STREET

NICHOLLS STREET

MADDEN STREET

PARKER STREET

OLDAKER STREET

BEST STREET

STEWART STREET

STEELE STREET

TASMAN STREET

CHARLES STREET

MIDDLE ROAD

GUNN STREET

WILLIAM STREET

FENTON STREET

VICTORIA PARADE

FORBES STREET

MCFIE STREET

FORMBY ROAD

Maritime Museum

❶

❸ **Redline Depot**

❹ 🛈

Backpackers Inn

❺

Art Gallery

❻

❼

◄ Don River Railway

N

River Ferry

Ferry Terminal

Mersey River

EAST DEVONPORT

BROOKE STREET

CHURCH STREET

THOMAS STREET

MURRAY STREET

STEPHEN STREET

DOUGLAS STREET

JOHN STREET

TARLETON STREET

WRIGHT STREET

ESPLANADE

❷

Airport ►

BASS HIGHWAY

▼ ❽ & Home Hill

0   500 m

ACCOMMODATION

Abel Tasman Caravan Park	2
Alexander Hotel	5
Gateway Motor Inn	4
MacFie Manor	7
Macwright House YHA	8
Molly Malone's	3
River View Lodge	1
Tasman House Backpackers	6

inspiring first point of contact with Tasmania. As the ship makes its slow progress up the Mersey River, you might almost think you're arriving at a 1950s English seaport, but for the tin-roofed weatherboard bungalows, the brittle quality of the light, the bush-covered hills to the east and a *McDonald's* on the waterfront. As a jumping-off point for Cradle Mountain, the Overland Track and the rugged west coast, Devonport has developed a significant tourism infrastructure – car-rental companies, bus companies, camping stores and backpacking information – and though it's hardly a destination in itself, it makes a good **base** for trips into the surrounding countryside.

Arrival and information

Up to nine hundred people arrive in Devonport at 8.30am each Tuesday, Thursday and Saturday morning on the *Spirit of Tasmania* **Bass Strait ferry** (☎13 2010), which docks at the terminal in East Devonport, just across the Mersey River from the city centre. As the boat has its own tourist information and booking centre, a small interpretive centre and even national park rangers dispensing advice in summer, you might well have made all your arrangements on board before arriving. If not, there are company representatives in the terminal, and you can buy bus passes and tickets here. Most passengers head immediately for the waiting Tasmanian Redline Coaches **express buses** (Mon, Wed & Fri 10.30am, Tues & Thurs 9.10am) to Launceston ($15.70) and Hobart ($38.10). Other bus routes leave from the depots in town (see p.1115). If you decide to stay, you can get to the city centre by walking north for a short distance to the bottom of Murray Street, where the ferry *Torquay* crosses the river (every 15–30min Mon–Fri 8am–6pm, Sat 8.30am–5pm, no service Sun; $2, bikes 50¢).

Southern Australia Airlines, Kendell and Aus-Air fly from the mainland into **Devonport Airport**, 10km east of the city. Taxis into Devonport cost about $12, and Fox Coaches (☎0418 142 692; $5) operate a shuttle bus connecting with all flights, dropping and picking up as far out as the youth hostel. It also picks up at the **Tasmanian Travel and Information Centre**, at 5 Best St (daily 9am–5pm; Sat & Sun information only; ☎03/6424 4466, ✉ttic@dcc.tas.gov.au). Staff here can book accommodation, tours and travel, and sell all types of bus passes. For maps, bushwalking tips and local knowledge of the area visit the **Backpackers Barn**, 10–12 Edward St (daily 9am–6pm; ☎03/6424 3628), which specializes in the planning of itineraries, runs tours and rents equipment for bushwalkers and backpackers; it also offers travellers a day-room, showers ($2) and lockers ($1 per day). The excellent Allgoods, at 10 Rooke St (closed Sun), rents out gear too.

Accommodation

Devonport has plenty of **accommodation**, mainly intended for ferry passengers. Hotels, motels and B&Bs take advantage of the summer trade to raise their prices.

Abel Tasman Caravan Park, 6 Wright St, East Devonport (☎03/6427 8794). Campsites on East Devonport Beach, just a short walk from the ferry terminal. Cabins ❹, on-site vans ❷

Alexander Hotel, 78 Formby Rd (☎03/6424 2252, ✉6424 1046). Neat, well-furnished shared-bath rooms, all with sinks and some with views of the port. TV room, plus tea and coffee room; light breakfast served in the dining room. ❹

Gateway Motor Inn, 16 Fenton St (☎03/6424 4922, ✉6424 7720). Devonport's best hotel, a quiet, centrally located, three-storey hotel offering views over the port and river mouth. Rooms are spacious, tastefully decorated, and all have baths. Also a bar, restaurant and room service. ❼

MacFie Manor, 44 MacFie St (☎03/6424 1719). A rambling, two-storey turn-of-the-twentieth-

century B&B that has distant views of the water from its wrought-iron balcony. ❻

Macwright House YHA, 115 Middle Rd (☎03/6424 5696, ✉6424 9952). A large, barracks-like hostel with loads of rules and regulations, and no doubles – all rooms have metal bunks. More than half an hour's walk from the city centre and not close to any shops, but the local Mersey Bus will get you from the city on weekdays. On the plus side, there's access to a heated pool next door and a big garden. Dorms ❶

Molly Malone's, 34 Best St (☎03/6424 1898). Convenient backpackers' accommodation, with comfortable rooms well away from the noise of the bar which has live bands Thurs–Sat. Good facilities and security. Dorms ❶

River View Lodge, 18 Victoria Parade (☎03/6424

7357). A waterfront guesthouse with a convivial atmosphere. Serves generous cooked breakfasts. All rooms share bathroom. ④–⑤

Tasman House Backpackers, 169 Steele St, entrance off Tasman St (℡ 03/6423 2335, ℱ 6423 2340). A highly recommended, very cheap and secure hostel in a large, former nurs-

es' residence. Mostly well-furnished twins, with a couple of en-suite doubles and some dorms. Facilities include a TV room, kitchen and notice board. Affordable licensed tours run on demand to places such as Cradle Mountain. Fifteen-minutes' walk from the city centre, but free pick-ups on request. Dorms ①

The City

Central Devonport is bounded by the Mersey to the east; Formby Road runs alongside it, while Stewart Street, at right angles, is dominated by a view of the bulky *Spirit of Tasmania*, when it's in port, and sometimes other colourful freighters. The **Devonport Art Gallery** at 45 Stewart St (Mon–Sat 10am–5pm, Sun 2–5pm; free), is a converted church with changing exhibitions and a small permanent collection of Tasmanian ceramics. The city centre is a **shopping** focus for departing tourists in need of last-minute souvenirs, and Stewart Street is full of gift shops selling tasteful wooden items, ceramics and jewellery. There's more shopping in the **Rooke Street Mall**, where most of the big-name chain stores are located.

South of the city centre, at 77 Middle Rd, is **Home Hill** (Tues–Thurs, Sat & Sun 2–4pm; $7.70), the National Trust-administered former home of Sir Joseph Lyons – premier of Tasmania (1923–29) and prime minister of Australia (1932–39) – and his wife, Dame Enid Lyons, who became a federal minister after her husband's death. The **Tasmanian Maritime and Folk Museum**, north of the city centre at 47 Victoria Parade, near the river's mouth (Tues–Sun 1–4pm; $1), has an extensive display of model ships ranging from sailing vessels to modern passenger ferries. The only really compelling place to visit, though, is the **Tiagarra Tasmanian Aboriginal Culture and Art Centre** (daily 9am–5pm; $3.30), located at the dramatic **Mersey Bluff** 1.5km north-west of the Maritime and Folk Museum, near the end of Bluff Road. The centre has preserved around 270 Aboriginal rock engravings (11 of which are on show), and a **Display Centre** provides generalized (and rather rushed) taped background information on how the Tasmanian Aborigines lived.

The **Don River Railway** runs excursions from Don Recreation Ground along the Don River to the popular surfing spot of **Coles Beach** (hourly 10am–4pm; 30min; $7 return). On Sunday, public holidays and from Christmas to the end of January the carriages are pulled by steam locomotives; otherwise, diesel power is used.

Eating, drinking and nightlife

Alexander Hotel, 78 Formby Rd (℡ 03/6424 2252). Refurbished riverfront pub, popular with the young crowd. A good jukebox in the lounge bar, from where you can gaze out at the ships; excellent bistro menu.

Banjo's, Rooke Street Mall. One of a Tasmanian chain of eat-in bakeries. The best budget choice, offering inexpensive fresh-baked goods and unlimited cups of tea and coffee. Great place for an early breakfast. Daily 6am–6pm.

Chinese Garden, 33 King St (℡ 03/6424 4148). A popular Cantonese restaurant serving lunch and

dinner daily. Licensed.

The Old Rectory, 71 Wright St, East Devonport (℡ 03/6427 8037). Located in a heritage church building with an old English garden. There's a day-time alfresco menu, while evening menus specialize in game and local seafood. Licensed. Lunch Thurs–Sun, dinner Wed–Sun.

Spurs Canteena, 18 King St. A bar with Wild West decor and atmosphere; also a bistro and attached nightclub. Wed–Sun 4pm–late.

Taco Villa, Kempling St (℡ 03/6424 6762). Good Mexican food. BYO. Tues–Sun dinner only.

Listings

Bookshop Angus & Robertson Bookworld, on Stewart St.

Buses Tasmanian Redline Coaches and Tassie Link both have ticket desks at the ferry terminal. Redline also have a depot in town at 9 Edward St (☎03/6424 5100), where you can buy tickets, wait for your bus and leave luggage ($1 per item), while Tassie Link (☎03/6334 4442) services leave from the tourist office at 5 Best St. The Backpackers Barn, next door at 10–12 Edward St, acts as a collecting point for Maxwell's Coaches transport service to Cradle Mountain, Frenchmans Cap and Walls of Jerusalem (☎03/6492 8093; service on demand; price according to number of passengers).

Car rental Firms located at the airport and ferry terminal include Autorent-Hertz (☎03/6424 1013),

Avis Tasmania (☎03/6427 9797) and Budget (☎03/6427 0650); among cheaper alternatives are Lo-Cost Auto Rent, 23 King St (☎03/6424 9922; from $55 per day, 4WDs from $105 per day), and the popular Rent-A-Bug, Murray St, near the ferry terminal, East Devonport (☎03/6427 9304; VW Beetles from $44.80 per day).

Cinema Village Cinema One, 9 Stewart St (☎03/6424 4622). No screenings Mon & Thurs. Cheap day Tues.

Post office Cnr Stewart St and Formby Rd, TAS 7310.

Taxi ☎03/6424 1431.

Tours Tassie Link (☎03/6272 7300) offer a day-tour to Cradle Mountain ($52), while The Backpackers Barn (see p.1113) do cheaper small-group day-trips.

Around Devonport

East of Devonport there are some particularly rewarding spots on the **Rubicon River estuary**, where you'll find the seaside resort of **PORT SORELL**, roughly 19km from Devonport and across the river from the Asbestos Range National Park (see below). You can **stay** here at *Heron on Earth Organic Farm* (☎03/6248 6144; ❷–❹), which rents out canoes for you to paddle across to the national park. More luxurious accommodation is provided 4km northeast at **HAWLEY BEACH**, at the well-regarded *Hawley House* (☎03/6428 6221; B&B ❼–❽), which has a fine restaurant and a rooftop bathtub for soaking under the stars. From Hawley Beach there's a ten-kilometre return walk to Point Sorell.

To reach the western edge of the **Asbestos Range National Park**, on the east side of the Rubicon River estuary, it's a meandering, forty-kilometre drive from Devonport. The remote park is worth the trip – particularly at dusk – for the chance to spot some wildlife. Introduced **Forrester kangaroos** come down to feed at **Bakers Beach** at that time, and it's the best place in Tasmania to see **wombats**. The park is renowned for its occasional spectacular storms, accompanied by strong winds roaring along the beach. There's a self-registering **campsite** here, for which you pay a small fee (ranger ☎03/6428 6277), and the beach is good for swimming, and for oyster-hunting from the rocks at low tide. You'll need your own transport to get out here.

SHEFFIELD, 30km **south of Devonport**, is a popular stop en route to Cradle Mountain, and is situated near the base of **Mount Roland** (1231m) among farmland made fertile by red volcanic soils. The town's economy was ailing when the community decided to reinvent itself through the medium of visual art; since the mid-1980s 25 **murals** in various styles, showing the history of the town, have been painted, and there are other murals in the district. Tourism has increased as a result, though at the time of writing the murals were at the centre of a bitter copyright dispute and may be painted over. The **Diversity Murals Theatrette**, at 34 Main St (Mon–Fri 8.30am–5.30pm, Sat 10am–5.30pm, Sun 1–5pm; donation), screens images of the murals and fills you in on the history of the project. Sheffield is also noted for being the home of the notoriously right-wing former premier of Queensland, Johannes ("Joh") Bjelke-Petersen (see p.391), who now lives here part of the year in semi-retirement with his wife Flo. Together they have opened *Flo's Country Kitchen*, and if you're curious you can sample her supposedly "world-famous pumpkin scones". Sixteen kilometres southwest of Sheffield, at **GOWRIE PARK** at the base of Mount Roland, you can **stay** at *Mt Roland Accommodation* (☎ 03/6491 1385, ⓕ 6491 1848; ❶), which has bunk-style sleeping quarters and is a good base for walks up and around the summit. The adjacent *Weindorfers Restaurant* (☎ 03/6491 1385) is recommended for its delicious meals cooked with fresh Tasmanian produce. You can get to Gowrie Park and Sheffield with Tassie Link on their scheduled Queenstown to Launceston service via Cradle Mountain (for details see p.1131).

Ulverstone to Burnie

Tasmanian Redline buses follow the unremarkable coast from Devonport west to industrial Burnie, stopping at Ulverstone and Penguin. **ULVERSTONE**, 20km west of Devonport where the **Leven River** flows into the sea, is a popular family holiday centre, with unpolluted **beaches** and plenty of activities to occupy children, including the **Ulverstone Waterslide** (Dec–Feb 10am–7pm; $3.50). **Accommodation** possibilities include B&B in the pleasant, two-storey *Ocean View Guesthouse* at 1 Victoria St (☎ & ⓕ 03/6425 5401; ❻), and the splendid 1903 red-brick *Furners Hotel* at 42 Reibey St (☎ 03/6425 1488, ⓕ 6425 5933; B&B ❺), the latter complete with carved blackwood staircase and an excellent **bistro**; or try the waterfront *Ulverstone Caravan Park*, 1km east of the centre (☎ 03/6425 2624; cabins and units ❸, on-site vans ❷). You can pick up free maps and information from the **Ulverstone Visitor Information Centre**, behind the post office (Mon–Fri 9am–3.30pm, Sat & Sun 10am–3pm; ☎ 03/6425 2839).

In the picturesque hop-growing countryside south of Ulverstone, the **Gunns Plains Caves** (hourly tours daily 10am–4pm; 50min; $6) are worth visiting for their remarkable limestone formations which, when lit from behind, glow a succulent red. A permanent stream feeds an underground lake, and platypuses and possums enjoy the cool temperatures. You'll need your own transport to get here.

The best route west from Ulverstone follows the old Bass Highway along the coastline, passing the Three Sisters and Goat Islands bird sanctuaries, and Penguin Point where Little penguins roost. **PENGUIN** itself, 12km along the highway, is a neatly tended town with three safe swimming beaches. Tacky blue-and-white penguin-shaped garbage bins line the main street, culminating in the two-metre-high "big penguin" in the foreshore park. Five kilometres outside town, there are walking trails in the **Dial Range State Forest**.

BURNIE, on Emu Bay 15km west of Penguin, is an ugly industrial and paper-manufacturing centre that's undergone something of a transformation in recent years. Situated amid rich farmland and beautiful rocky coves, tourism is being actively developed in the town and Burnie port is attracting passenger ships for the first time in decades. The **Tasmanian Travel and Information Centre** at the Civic Square precinct, off Little Alexander Street (Mon–Fri 9am–5pm; ☎ 03/6434 6111), can direct you towards the many worthwhile places to visit, both in and around the town. Just 1km from the centre is **Fernglade**, a unique river reserve with wild platypus, easy to spot at any time of the day. Conservationist William Walker (☎ & ⓕ 03/6435 7205, ✉ wagwalker@bigpond.com) runs personalized nature-based scenic and cultural interpretive tours, visiting Fernglade and other local points of interest, and specializing in day-walks with local gourmet food. It's also worth stopping at Lactos, a prize-winning speciality **cheese factory** 3km from Burnie on the Old Surry Road (tastings

Mon–Fri 9am–5pm, Sat & Sun 10am–4pm; free); here you can sample and buy blends and variations of European cheeses – "red square" is one of the best. Back in town, the Civic Centre on Wilmot Street is home to both the **Pioneer Village Museum**, with its reconstructed turn-of-the-twentieth-century street (Mon–Fri 9am–5pm, Sat & Sun 1.30–4.30pm; $6), and the **Burnie Regional Art Gallery** (Tues–Fri 10.30am–5pm, Sat & Sun 1.30–4.30pm; free). To get an idea of the region's industrial base, you could visit the AMCOR paper mill (tours Mon–Fri 2pm; free; call ☎03/6430 7777 for bookings and directions).

There's plenty of **accommodation**, should you decide to stay in Burnie. The cheapest hotel is the very basic *Regent Hotel*, 26 North Terrace (☎03/6431 1933; rooms ❸, dorms ❷), and the least expensive motel is the *Ocean View Motel*, 253 Bass Highway, at Cooee on the pleasant, non-industrial side of town towards Wynyard (☎03/6431 1925; motel ❺, cabins ❹, and on-site vans ❸), with an attached campground and caravan park. For more character, the *Glen Osborne House*, at 9 Aileen Crescent (☎03/6431 9866, ☎6431 4354; ❻), is a stylish Victorian-era B&B with en-suite rooms and a lovely garden of lawns, roses and fruit trees. As well as a *McDonald's* on Mount Street and a *Pizza Hut* nearby, there's the *Rialto Gallery*, a popular and affordable Italian restaurant at 46 Wilmot St (BYO; ☎03/6431 7718). The Tasmanian Redline Coaches depot is at 117 Wilson St (☎03/6431 3233).

Wynyard and around

WYNYARD, another 19km along the old Bass Highway from Burnie, snuggles into the lush pasturelands between the **Inglis River** and the sea. Most of the action in the town centres on the wharf area off Goldie Street – the main street that parallels the river – with its fishing boats and fresh fish shop, but the adjacent coastline has much to entice visitors. At **Fossil Bluff**, an easy three-kilometre walk along the Bicentennial Track from the riverfront park in front of the tourist information office (see overleaf), layers of sedimentary rock containing fossilized seashells can easily be examined at low tide, and the beach itself has good views of the 170-metre seaface of **Table Cape**. A drive up to Table Cape will reward you with magnificent views of the coast and hinterland, particularly pretty when the cape's **tulip fields** are in bloom around October. Back in town, there are a few junk/antique shops to browse in.

Eleven kilometres west of town, a turn-off from the Bass Highway winds down to **Boat Harbour Beach**, the prettiest on the northwest coast, with pale-blue water, white sand and very gentle waves. It's perfect for **diving**, too; equipment can be rented from the Scuba Centre at 62 Bass Highway in Wynyard (☎03/6442 2247), which also organizes excursions. The milk bar on the beach is the place to ask about camping nearby, and it also rents **boogie-boards** and **wave skis**. You could choose to **stay** in the luxurious *Boat Harbour Beach Resort* (☎03/6445 1107, ☎6445 1027; ❻), which has a restaurant, indoor heated pool and spa, but you can enjoy the area just as much by camping at the caravan park (☎03/6445 1253; cabins ❺, on-site vans ❸), or sleeping in the spacious dorms at the *Boat Harbour Backpackers*, up the hill on Strawberry Lane (☎03/6445 1273; rooms ❸, dorms ❶). Nearby **Sisters Beach** is another attractive beach.

Rocky Cape National Park

Stretching for a mere 12km along the coast, from Sisters Beach to Rocky Cape, are the rugged hills and cliffs of **Rocky Cape National Park**, Tasmania's smallest national park, created in 1967 for the purpose of preserving some remarkable **Aboriginal archeological finds**. The mainly quartzite hills are pockmarked with caves, of which the two major ones, North Cave and South Cave, contain huge shell middens, bones and stone tools dating back as far as eight thousand years, when the sea was several fathoms below its current level.

Although North Cave can be visited – it's a fifteen-minute walk there and back from the road, reached by driving 5km into the park and taking the left fork at the lighthouse – most people prefer just to walk along the various easy tracks. It takes seven hours to traverse the whole length of the park; there's no water (bring your own), no toilets and camping is not allowed. Rocky pools, safe swimming beaches and picnic areas are scattered along the route, while in spring and summer there's a profusion of wild flowers on the scrubby heathland, including some unique native orchids. At dusk you may see wallabies, echidnas and various species of bird.

Practicalities

Wynyard may well be the first place you see in Tasmania, since "Burnie" **airport** is actually just 800m from the town centre. There are daily flights to and from Melbourne with Kendell and Southern Australian; tickets can be booked through Wynyard Travel Service at 84 Goldie St (☎03/6442 2391). You can **rent a car** at the airport with Autorent-Hertz (☎03/6442 4444), Avis (☎03/6442 2512) or Budget (☎03/6442 1777). MTT **public transport buses** connect Wynyard with Burnie, departing from 38 Jackson St. Tasmanian Redline Coaches call at Gale's Auto Service, 28 Saunders St (☎03/6442 2205), en route from Burnie to Smithton via the turn-offs to Table Cape, Boat Harbour Beach, Rocky Cape and Stanley (though some do go into Stanley itself); there are two services Monday to Friday.

Helpful volunteers at **Wynyard Tourist Information**, in front of the riverfront park on the corner of Goldie and Hogg streets (April–Sept Mon–Fri 10am–4pm, Sat noon–3pm; Oct–March Mon–Fri 9am–4pm, Sat & Sun 1–4pm; ☎03/6442 4143), have information on local activities and **accommodation**. *Wynyard Caravan Park*, at 30B Old Bass Highway (☎03/6442 1998; cabins ➍, on-site vans ➌, dorms ➊), has camping space and dorms for backpackers. Rates at the homely *Federal Hotel*, at 82 Goldie St (☎03/6442 2056, ℻ 6442 1545; ➍), include a cooked breakfast. The *Inglis River Hotel-Motel*, 4 Goldie St (☎03/6442 2344; ➌), offers the best value of the few motels, while the *Alexandria*, on Table Cape Road (☎03/6442 4411; ➏), is a classy B&B. For **places to eat**, try the pubs for cheap fare. *Gumnut Restaurant*, at 43 Jackson St (closed Sat lunch, all Sun, and Mon dinner; BYO and licensed; ☎03/6442 1177), is an expensive à la carte restaurant, and *YT's Fish Place*, on the Wharf, is one of the best places for fresh fish (daily 9.30am–6.30pm).

Stanley

The tiny fishing village of **STANLEY**, 6km off the Bass Highway (A2) and 32km west of Rocky Cape, was the first settlement in northwest Tasmania, being the original 1826 headquarters of the **Van Diemen's Land Company** (see box, opposite). It occupies a scenic setting on a small, foot-shaped peninsula, right at the base of an unusual rock formation – **The Nut**, described by Matthew Flinders as a "cliffy round lump in form resembling a Christmas cake" – that rises directly out of the ocean to a height of nearly 150m. **Circular Head**, as it's officially called (the name also for the surrounding municipality), is thought to be a volcanic plug, with the softer sediments around it having eroded away.

The Van Diemen's Land Company

> . . . how is it that an absentee owner across the world got this magnificent and empty country without having paid one glass bead?

Cassandra Pybus

The **Van Diemen's Land Company (VDL)** was the brainchild of a group of prominent and well-connected private individuals, who in 1824 managed to obtain by Royal Charter 250,000 acres of the mainly thickly forested, unexplored northwest corner of Tasmania. Their plan was to create their own source of cheap wool in the colonies, which could be relied upon even if Europe was subject to political upheaval; the *Tranmere* arrived at Circular Head in 1826, with the personnel, livestock, supplies and equipment to create the township of Stanley.

The first flocks were grazed at Woolnorth on Cape Grim, a plateau of tussock grass and trees that might have been made for the purpose but, in fact, was prime Aboriginal hunting land. When hunting parties began to take sheep, whites killed Aborigines in retaliation, and a vindictive cycle of killings began. The most tragic incident (a version of events denied by Woolnorth) was supposed to have occurred around 1826 or 1827: a group of Aboriginal men, seeking revenge for the rape of their women, speared a shepherd and killed one hundred sheep. These deaths were ruthlessly avenged when a group of thirty unarmed Aborigines, hunting for muttonbirds near the same spot, were killed by shepherds and their bodies thrown over a cliff (now euphemistically called "Suicide Bay"). Ultimately, the Aboriginal people of the northwest were systematically hunted down, the last one being captured near the Arthur River in 1842.

In the 1840s the company changed its emphasis from wool production to the sale and lease of its land, and it now holds just a fifth of its original land. However it is still registered on the London Stock Exchange, and is the only remaining company in the world operating under a Royal Charter; its major shareholder is now a New Zealand public company based in Dunedin.

Although it's still possible to do the strenuous ten-minute walk up the grassy Nut itself, you can get to the top more comfortably by means of an exhilarating **chair lift**, reached via the ramp opposite the post office (daily 9.30am–5pm, weather permitting; call ☎03/6458 1286 to check; $7 return). A short walk around the windy **Nut State Reserve** at the top affords views over the town and port, and southeast as far as Table Cape. Directly below is the exquisitely deserted **Godfrey's Beach**, with its calm and translucent blue waters.

Stanley's main street, **Church Street**, runs below the foot of the Nut, and its restaurants and crafts shops are high enough above the beach, wharves and the rest of the town to command excellent views. On the foreshore area is Stanley Artworks, an art gallery housed in the slate-roofed **Van Diemen's Land Company Store**, designed in 1844 by John Lee Archer, whose work can be seen notably in Hobart (see p.1055). From the nearby **port area**, at low tide, you can see the remnants of a 1923 **shipwreck**, a victim of the "furies" of the Bass Strait. Two kilometres north of the town, the headquarters of the Van Diemen's Land Company are now restored as the **Highfield Historic Site** (daily 10am–4pm; $5.50), from where there are superb views over Half Moon Bay.

Practicalities

For **information** and **internet access**, visit The Booking Centre on Church Street (daily: June–Aug 10am–5pm; Sept–May 9am–6pm; ☎03/6458 2305, Ⓦ www.bookings.tassie.net.au). Wilderness to West Coast Tours (☎ & Ⓕ 03/6458 2038, Ⓦ www.tassie.net.au~batkins) are based in Stanley and offer a variety of **tours**, including a platypus-viewing tour (summer evenings only; 2hr; $22); a penguin tour ($10); trout fishing (half-day $95); and a wilderness 4WD tour which explores the northwest tip of Tasmania, taking you through farm country, temperate rainforest, gum forests and button-grass plains (half-day $85, full day $140) – book by phone, on the website or through The Booking Centre. Stanley Seal Cruises will take you to view the rare Australian fur seal, weather permitting (☎03/6458 1312; 6hr; $25).

In keeping with its historic ambience, Stanley has several "colonial" **B&Bs**, which are actually self-contained cottages with breakfast provisions supplied, such as *Touchwood Cottage*, at 33 Church St (☎ & ℻ 03/6458 1348; ❼), and *Bayside Colonial Cottage* at 44 Alexander Terrace, which rises above Church Street (☎03/6458 1209; ❻). As you come into town, you'll see the signpost for the *Stanley Motel*, 1km along Dovecote Road (☎03/6458 1300, ℻6458 1448; ❻–❼), which has spacious, well-appointed units (some self-catering), plus one for disabled guests; facilities include a bar, and a restaurant open to the public. From the motel you have the best views of the Nut, across the green fields of the Dovecote Estate. For budget travellers, simple rooms are available at the sprawling, three-storey *Union Hotel* on Church Street (☎03/6458 1161; ❸), or the *Stanley YHA*, at the caravan park on Wharf Road opposite Marine Park (☎03/6458 1266; cabins ❹, dorms ❶). The BP service station, near Marine Park, serves as Stanley's Tasmanian Redline Coaches depot (☎03/6458 1263).

Probably the best place to **eat** in Stanley is *Hurseys Seafoods*, next to Marine Park, considered to be one of the best fish-and-chip shops in Tasmania. Inside are huge holding tanks from which you select live fish and crayfish; as well as around twenty kinds of fish, they have freshly cooked local muttonbirds – not to everyone's taste, as they're very oily. Among other options are *Stanleys on the Bay*, a seafood and steak restaurant on the foreshore; the *Dovecote Restaurant*, at the *Stanley Motel* (see above); and the *Union Hotel* on Church Street, serving fresh seafood in its lounge bar. Also on Church Street, the relaxed *Stranded Whale Coffee Shop* (daily 9am–4pm, plus Fri night; bookings preferred on ☎03/6458 1202) has walls covered with photographs depicting various attempts to rescue pygmy right whales, which occasionally get stranded on the beaches around Stanley.

Woolnorth and Smithton

Until recently, the only way to see Tasmania's rugged northwest tip, which remains under the control of the Van Diemen's Land Company, was by tour. Now, however, it's possible to stay at **WOOLNORTH**, the original VDL cattle and sheep property, in a variety of accommodation: the old shearers' quarters, self-contained cabins or the 1970s-built Directors Lodge (☎ & ℻ 03/6452 1493, �🌐 www.woolnorthtours.com.au; lodge ❽, cabins ❼–❽, shearers' quarters ❹). Alternatively you can stay nearby in the unattractive logging town of **SMITHTON**, at the mouth of the Duck River 22km west of Stanley, and visit Woolnorth on a full-day **tour** (daily; $82.50 including morning tea and lunch in the Directors Lodge; bookings as for Woolnorth accommodation); tours also take in **Cape Grim**, where the air is reputed to be the cleanest in the world – it's the site of one of only six baseline air-monitoring stations. A couple of kilometres east of Cape Grim, you can stand at the point where Bass Strait meets the Southern Ocean and walk along the spectacular, rugged coastline.

What Smithton lacks in aesthetics is made up for by its usefulness as a service centre, with supermarkets, fuel and banking facilities. The *Bridge Hotel-Motel* on Montague Road (☎03/6452 1389, �🌐 www.view.com.au/bridge; ❸–❺) has a range of accommodation options, a reasonably priced restaurant and counter **meals**. Six kilometres north of Smithton on the Mella Road, the **Lacrum Dairy** offers tours (Nov–June daily 3.30–5.30pm; $7.50), which include afternoon tea with Tasmanian cheeses. South of Smithton there are ten **forestry reserves**, ranging from rainforests to blackwood swamps and giant eucalypt forests; all are accessible from a circular route, via Kanunnah Bridge and Taytea Bridge on the C218 (90km return). The Forestry Commission, at the corner of Nelson and Smith streets (☎03/6452 1317), can provide maps and route information. The most rewarding reserves are the **Julius River Forest Reserve** and the **Milkshakes Hills Forest Reserve**.

From Smithton or Woolnorth, it's possible to visit the tiny and remote **Three Hummock Island**, 20km north of Woolnorth. The island's range of terrains, from rainforest to white-sand beaches and open heathland, provide a range of walks and opportunities to see some of the island's abundant wildlife – including muttonbirds, fairy penguins, Cape Barren geese and Forrester kangaroos. Three Hummock Island Escape offer **tours** of the island (☎ & ⓕ 03/6452 1554, ⓦ www.tasmanianadventures.com.au; half-day $55, full day $99); or if you're tempted to stay longer, they can also arrange **accommodation** (❻ full-board, self-catering ❸; mountain bikes and sea kayaks available for hire). Note that there are no shops on the island, so if you plan to stay in the self-catering accommodation, take all your supplies with you. There are two forms of **transport** to the island, both pretty exciting: you can fly from Smithton with Becker Aviation (up to three people, $110 return per person), or travel from Woolnorth in an amphibious army vehicle ($110 return) – book through Three Hummock Island Escape.

Marrawah

From Smithton the Bass Highway cuts across the northwest corner to the rich farming settlement of **MARRAWAH** on the west coast. Thirty kilometres along the way, a 1500-metre trail leads through a swamp at the grumpily named **Dismal Swamp Nature Reserve**. Marrawah itself has a small store, and the *Marrawah Tavern* serves plain but filling meals. **Greenpoint Beach**, which has been voted one of the three best **surfing** beaches in Australia, is 2km from Marrawah and has a small **camping area** as well as the stylish *Ann Bay Cabins* (☎03/6457 1361; ❻), decorated by artists. There's also excellent, spacious self-contained **accommodation** at *Glendonald Cottage* on the Arthur River Road, 3km south of Marrawah (☎03/6457 1191, ⓦ www.redpa.tco.asn.au/glenking/; ❺); the owner, Geoff King, is a passionate conservationist who is working to regenerate the coastal land and preserve its Aboriginal sites. Geoff knows a lot about natural, local and Aboriginal history and runs bird and wildlife tours, as well as fascinating nocturnal viewings of Tasmanian devils in the wild. The curve of Ann Bay here is shrouded by the hump of Mount Cameron West to the north. Three kilometres north of this bluff, at the end of a long exposed beach, is the most complex **Aboriginal art** site in Tasmania: rock carvings of geometric or nonfigurative forms cover slabs of rock at the base of a cliff.

Arthur River and the Arthur Pieman Protected Area

Just over 20km south of Marrawah, the scattering of holiday homes at **ARTHUR RIVER** marks the start of one of the Tasmanian coast's last great **wilderness areas**, where mighty trees that have been washed down the Arthur River have crashed and battered against the windswept shoreline. At one time the entire west coast looked like this, but the progressive damming of its rivers has left the **Arthur Pieman Protected Area** as a unique reminder, complete with a spectacular array of birdlife, such as black cockatoos, Tasmanian rosellas, orange-breasted parrots, black jays, wedge-tail eagles, pied heron and azure kingfishers. Trees on the steep banks of the river include myrtle, sassafras, celery-top pines, laurels and giant tree ferns. It's dangerous to swim in the protected area, due to extremely wild conditions and occasional freak waves – even walking along the beach, where you have to pick your way over scattered bits of lumber, can be an obstacle course. It's therefore essential to get the latest information on conditions from the base office of the Department of Parks and Wildlife on Arthur River Road (daily 9am–5pm; ☏03/6457 1225).

The small **shop** on Gardiner Street is the only source of supplies in Arthur River; attached is *Arthur River Holiday Units* (☏03/6457 1288; ❹–❺). *Ocean View Holiday Cottage* (☏03/6452 1278; ❺) and the excellent *Sunset Holiday Villas* (☏03/6457 1197; ❺) are on the same street. **Camping** at Arthur River is a truly pleasurable experience, with facilities that range from a fully serviced caravan park near the base office, to secluded areas among shady trees in the dips and hollows behind the dunes, equipped merely with water taps.

If you want to get out on the river, take a **cruise** (see below) or contact Arthur River Canoe Hire (☏03/6457 1312), which has canoes and boats available for rent (one-person canoes $8 per hour or $33 per day, two-person canoes $10 or $44, boats for overnight camping $12 or $55).

The Arthur River Cruise

Perhaps the biggest attraction of the entire northwest coast is the five-hour **Arthur River Cruise** on the MV *George Robinson* (daily 10am, returning 3pm; no trips June–Aug; $50; reservations ☏03/6457 1158, ⓦ www.tasmanianadventures.com.au), which sails 14km upriver to the confluence of the Arthur and Frankland rivers at Turks Landing. En route you cruise past a white-breasted sea eagle's nest, see a pair of enormous sea eagles being fed and experience the transition from coastal scrub woodland to the edge of the Tarkine – the largest tract of temperate rainforest found anywhere in the world. After a barbecue lunch in a clearing, there's an optional bushwalk. Alternatively, AR Reflections River Cruises offer a slightly shorter – and not so appealing – cruise, from which you return early for a barbecue lunch in the operator's back garden (daily 10.30am–2.30pm; $53; reservations ☏03/6457 1288, ⓦ www.wwt.com.au/arthurriver.ahu.htm).

The Western Explorer route

It is now possible to drive from Arthur River all the way south to Zeehan on the controversial **Western Explorer**, the "tourist road" crossing the wild **Tarkine area** on the west coast. Ignoring the protests of conservationists, the road was constructed hastily and finished in January 1996. A year before, an incredibly vast and ancient Huon pine was found in the area, as big as a city block and thought to date from around 8000 BC. Conservationists are apprehensive that "the road to nowhere", as they've called it, is being used as a cover to open up the area (currently state forest) to logging, thereby degrading it and reducing the likelihood of World Heritage listing in the future. If you choose to drive this route, pick up the *Western Explorer, Travel Guide* – issued by the Department of Infrastructure and available in information centres – and remember that the road is rough and Marrawah is the last fuel stop before Zeehan.

The A10 route to the west coast

From Somerset, a suburb of Burnie on the shores of Emu Bay, the A10 (called the Murchison Highway between here and the Zeehan turn-off) heads to **Queenstown**, in the heart of Tasmania's west-coast mining area. This major route to the west coast is relatively recent; prior to 1932 the coast was accessible only by sea. Following the highway, after 10km you pass **YOLLA**, a picturesque little town surrounded by rich farming country; there are a couple of places here to fill up with fuel. A few kilometres past the Tewkesbury turn-off, the rural landscape ends and the road rises and winds through temperate rainforest to the **Hellyer Gorge State Reserve**. You can take a walk through spicy ferns and dense myrtle forest to the Hellyer River and back on a wide and easy track (20min return). Once through the reserve, you're confronted with the shocking spectacle of a landscape ravaged by logging. By the time you reach the B23 turn-off west to Waratah, on the way to the Pieman River, the forest is beginning to reassert itself.

West to Waratah and the Pieman River

Tiny, windswept **WARATAH**, set in mountain heathland 8km off the A10, reached its peak in the early twentieth century after thirty years of tin-mining at **Mount Bischoff**, when it was linked to Burnie by the **Emu Bay Railway**, built to facilitate access to the silver fields of Zeehan and Rosebery. Though the mine closed in 1935, Waratah is still a miners' town, with recent mining developments at the Que River. Little more than a scattered collection of scruffy weatherboard cottages, it's a pretty soulless place, but you can stop off for a **meal** at the big old two-storey pub on the hill, a relic of former boom times. Beyond Waratah, the last fuel stop on the road is the former mining town of **Savage River**, 45km along the B23.

The beautiful, unspoilt **Pieman River**, within the **Pieman River State Reserve**, is reached from the old gold-mining settlement of **CORINNA** on an unsealed road (C247) 26km south of Savage River. It's hard to believe that 2500 people once occupied what's now just a few shacks surrounded by dense bush. Corinna even had its own port, despite the difficulties of getting through the narrow **Pieman Heads** from the coastline. The river here is too dangerous for swimming, with an average drop of nearly 20m from the banks, and very cold water. The reserve used to be a logging area and it still holds one of the biggest stands of remaining Huon pine – saved because the water here was too deep to allow a dam to be built.

You can take a **cruise** on the river, all the way to the west coast, with MV *Arcadia II* (daily 10.30am; 4hr; $36 including morning tea; ☎ 03/6446 1170). The boat was built in Hobart (from Huon pine) as a luxury pleasure cruiser, but during World War II saw active service off the Philippines and has since been put to other uses. From its deck you can see Huon pine, leatherwood and pandanus ferns among the **temperate rainforest** of the river's north bank; the drier southern bank has mainly brown stringybark eucalypts. The trip allows you an hour and a half to wander on your own along the west coast; by the landing are several intriguing **holiday shacks**, ramshackle affairs with tin verandahs variously propped up by raw tree posts and an old bus. A wide sandy path leads to a beach between two outcrops of jagged orange sedimentary rock, where the dark-blue sea is tinged by the tannin-stained river water.

The affable brothers who run the cruise virtually run Corinna too. They open the **kiosk** daily whenever they have time, but bring food along if you intend to use the **campsite** (no showers) or the *Getaway Resort* (**⑤**, BYO linen), both also operated by the brothers. From the car park there's a walking track leading to a huge 600-year-old **manfern**, one of only four of such antiquity known to exist in Tasmania.

You can take a **barge** across the Pieman River from here (daily 9am–7pm; $11 car, $5.50 bike; ☎03/6446 1170) and continue on the C249 to Zeehan, and then on the B27 to Strahan.

South to Zeehan

Back on the A10, there's no fuel until you reach the small settlement of **TULLAH**, another 40km south of Waratah, where you'll find a pub, tearooms and cottage accommodation. Fourteen kilometres further on is the comparatively large town of **ROSEBERY**, a good place to stock up on supplies, with **banking** facilities at the ANZ bank (Mon, Tues & Fri 9am–noon, Wed 2–4pm). You can stay in comfortable backpacker **accommodation** at *Mount Black Lodge* on Hospital Road (☎03/6473 1039; **①**). From here, it's 23km to the turn-off to **ZEEHAN**, 6km southwest off the A10. The town became prosperous from the silver-lead mines which opened in the 1880s, and at its height boasted a population of eight thousand. However, the mines had already begun to fail by 1908, and the town was not to see a revival until the 1970s, when the Renison Bell tin mines were opened. Several boom-period buildings are still standing, including the elaborate facade of the **Gaiety Theatre**, once the largest theatre in Australia. The **West Coast Pioneer Memorial Museum** on Main Street (daily 8.30am–5pm; $5.50) has displays on mining history. **Accommodation** is expensive: the *Heemskirk Motor Inn* (☎03/6471 6107; **⑥**) charges $112 for a double, and even basic pub rooms at the *Hotel Cecil* on Main Street (☎03/6471 6221; **④**) are steep; however, you can get decent counter **meals** here. An alternative is the *Mount Zeehan Retreat Bed and Breakfast*, which provides evening meals on request (☎03/6471 6424; B&B **⑤**). By far the cheapest option is the friendly **caravan park**, nicely situated 1km from the centre on Hurst Street (☎03/6471 6633; cabins **④**, on-site vans **③**). The ANZ **bank** has restricted opening hours (Mon & Tues 2–4pm, Wed 9.30am–noon, Thurs 9.30am–4pm & Fri 2–4pm), but there's an ATM at Vickers General Store on the main street (Mon–Fri 6am–6pm, Sat 7.30am–5pm & Sun 9am–5pm).

From Zeehan it's possible to go straight to Strahan (47km) on a sealed road (B27), bypassing Queenstown and visiting the Henty Dunes (see p.1129) en route; or you could head back to the A10 (called the Zeehan Highway until Queenstown) and reach Strahan via Queenstown, another 32km along the highway.

Queenstown

QUEENSTOWN is worth a visit, but not for the normal reasons. Its infamous **"lunar landscape"** is chilling evidence of the devastation that single-minded commercial exploitation can wreak in such a sensitive environment. If you approach the town from Strahan you're confronted by the hideously ugly **Mount Lyell Copper Mine**; from Hobart, the road winds down to the town around bare, reddish-brown rock.

The Abt Railway

Queenstown, whose infamous "lunar landscape" was touted by the Tasmanian tourist board as a major attraction in the 1970s, is currently putting itself back on the tourist map for very different reasons, with the opening of the $25 million **Abt Railway** development. The original Abt railway was completed in 1896 to connect the Mount Lyell Mining Company with the port of Teepookana, and in 1899 the line was extended to Regatta Point in Strahan. The railway closed in 1963, when it became more economical to transport by road, but years of lobbying finally led to the federal government financing its redevelopment.

When the railway is fully completed in January 2002, renovated steam trains – each carriage designed using a different Tasmanian wood – will travel the 35km from **Queenstown to Strahan** on restored 1896 rack and pinion track, passing en route some of Tasmania's most scenic wilderness – crossing bridges spanning wild rivers, and climbing over 200m up a 1:16 gradient. On the way it will pass historic settlements such as Lynchford Station, where passengers can alight for some gold panning, and Rinadeena. At the time of writing, the eleven-kilometre stretch between Queenstown and Rinadeena was already up and running (☎ 03/6471 1700, ⓕ 6471 2415; Lynchford return $17.50, Rinadeena return $28).

Queenstown has been a mining centre since 1883, when gold was discovered at Mount Lyell, and it looks like a typical mining-town, with its wide streets, two-storey hotels and identical, pokey tin-roofed weatherboard houses. In 1893 the **Mount Lyell Mining and Railway Company** was formed and began to mine copper at Mount Lyell, which it has continued to do ever since. The weird-looking mountains here, chalky white and almost totally devoid of vegetation, are the result of a lethal combination of tree-felling, sulphur, fire and rainfall. Since the smelters closed in 1969 there has been some regrowth on the lower slopes, but it's estimated that the damage already done has had an impact that will last some four or five hundred years. In late 1994 the Mount Lyell mine closed down, but the lease was taken over by Copper Mines of Tasmania, who foresee another ten years of operation with the remaining ore. Tailings from the mine are now dumped into a multimillion-dollar dam instead of the town's **Queen River**, where aquatic life is beginning to return. The Queen eventually flows into the King River, however, and the moonscaped banks of the **King River** delta near Strahan attest to the lasting and wide-ranging environmental damage of the past century.

There are tours of the **Mount Lyell Mine** (daily: May–Sept 9.15am & 4pm; Oct–April 9.15am & 4.30pm; 1hr 30min; $13.20); it's hard to stifle a lingering cynicism, even though the plans for reforestation are explained. Bookings and departures are from Lyell Tours, at the *Empire Hotel* (☎ 03/6471 2388), which also provides **tourist information**.

Next door to the mine is the **Parks and Wildlife Service office** (☎ 03/6471 2511), the base for the Franklin Lower Gordon Wild Rivers National Park and the place to pick up the department's rafting and bush-walking guidelines. While in town, you could also check out the old photographic displays in the **Galley Museum** (Mon–Fri 10am–5pm, Sat & Sun 1–5pm; $2), housed in the old *Imperial Hotel*. There's also a rather joyless **chair lift** just outside town on the Lyell Highway (daily April–Sept 9am–5pm; Oct–March 9am–6pm; $8), to help you get an even better view of those frightening hills.

If you're **staying** in Queenstown, try the *Empire Hotel*, at 2 Orr St (☎ 03/6471 1699, ⓕ 6471 1788; ❷–❸), a lovely, old-fashioned building noted for its blackwood staircase; it has a good range of reasonably priced rooms, including several budget singles, plus good-value meals. *Mountain View Holiday Lodge*, at 1 Penghana Rd (Ⓣ03/6471 1163, Ⓕ6471 1306; motel units ❹, dorms ❶), has been converted from the mine's single-men's lodgings. For something special, *Penghana*, on The Esplanade at no. 32, provides B&B-style accommodation in an imposing stately mansion set in rainforest overlooking Queenstown (Ⓣ03/6471 2560, Ⓕ6471 1535, B&B ❻). There are **banking** facilities in Queenstown at the Trust Bank, but no ATMs. From Queenstown you can drive to Strahan on the B24 (40km), which starts as a steep, winding road through bare hills, or you continue along the A10 (called the Lyell Highway from Queenstown to Hobart) 86km east to the first fuel at Derwent Bridge, surrounded by the World Heritage Area (see Franklin Lower Gordon Wild Rivers National Park, p.1134, and Cradle Mountain–Lake St Clair National Park, p.1131).

Strahan and around

STRAHAN is easy-going, relaxed and even progressive. The only town and port on the west coast, it sits in the huge **Macquarie Harbour**, site of **Sarah Island**, a harsh secondary convict settlement in use between 1822 and 1830, which can be visited on a Gordon River cruise (see box p.1128). The entrance to Macquarie Harbour, named **Hells Gates** by arriving convicts, is only 80m wide. **Huon pine**, perfect for shipbuilding, grows abundantly in the area – logging and boatbuilding became the convicts' trade. After 1830 the timber continued to attract loggers, but it wasn't until 1882 that Strahan began life as a port for the nearby copper and lead fields. Although it was Tasmania's third-largest port in 1900, its unreliability led to its closure by 1970 and the population dwindled to three hundred. It's now a small **fishing village** for abalone, crayfish and shark, and commercial fish farming of rainbow trout and Atlantic salmon, though the main industry is tourism. The basing of the **Franklin Blockade** campaign here in 1982 shook up the town and brought the Australian media here for two months. **Cruises** on the **Gordon River** had already been running before this event, but the declaration of a **World Heritage Area** has meant that busloads of tourists now regularly descend upon Strahan to see the river, creating a hectic atmosphere for a short time, after which the town rapidly reverts to its usual peaceful state. You would be mad to come all this way and not take a cruise; though they may seem expensive, it's the best way to get to see the wilderness, and well worth the money.

Transport and services

The place to make enquiries and bookings for Tassie Link **bus** services is the visitor centre (see p.1130). There's a scheduled service from Launceston and Devonport via Cradle Mountain (Mon, Tues, Thurs & Sat), connecting with a Queenstown to Strahan service. A service from Strahan to Queenstown departs five times a week (Tues, Wed, Thurs, Fri & Sun), connecting with the service to Hobart via Lake St Clair. There are no ATMs in Strahan. The Strahan General Store (Mon–Fri 7.30am–7pm, Sat & Sun 8am–6pm) has EFTPOS facilities and is an ANZ **bank** agent, while at the far end of The Esplanade, the old **Customs House** contains the **post office**, which also acts as a Commonwealth Bank agent. Next door is the **Parks and Wildlife Service** District office (daily 8am–5pm; Ⓣ03/6471 7122), where you can buy park passes.

If you want to **shop** for food, the Strahan General Store on The Esplanade houses a small supermarket selling a decent range, including fresh vegetables. There's also a supermarket on Reid Street and Banjo's Bakery on The Esplanade.

Accommodation

If you've got your own transport to get there, you can **camp** for free at Ocean Beach and Henty Dunes (see p.1129); there are no facilities, but free hot showers can be had in town in the toilet block opposite the post office. **Accommodation** is expensive and gets booked up in the summer; to be safe, **book ahead** or bring a tent – otherwise you might have to head back to Zeehan or Queenstown. *Strahan Village* has virtually overtaken the town – with pub and motel accommodation and several restaurants along The Esplanade, and a rather impersonal reception/booking office (℡ 03/6471 7160) in a corner building. Another accommodation booking agency is run by Strahan Central (℡ 03/6471 7612), who book for the YHA and several B&Bs. The Strahan Visitor Centre (see below) has a free accommodation hotline – you call and book a room yourself from the list provided.

Franklin Manor, The Esplanade (℡ 03/6471 7311, ℻ 6471 7267, ⓦ www.franklinmanor.com.au). Sedate and elegant two-storey weatherboard B&B, surrounded by trees and flowers. The interior is attractively decorated and lovingly maintained; classical music plays in the guest lounge, always filled with fresh flowers, and there's a classy restaurant. ❽

Gordon Gateway Chalet, Grining St, Regatta Point (℡ 03/6471 7165). Peaceful harbourfront spot looking across to the town and its fishing boats. Spacious rooms with kitchenettes. ❻

Hamers Hotel, The Esplanade (℡ 03/6471 7191, ℻ 6471 7389). A renovated 1930s hotel with clean, modern rooms with washbasins, colour TV and sea views; light breakfast included. Also stylish modern motel units attached to the ground floor of the pub. The café-style lounge bar serves seafood and good salads. ❺

Ormiston House, The Esplanade (℡ 03/6471 7077, ℻ 6471 7007, ⓦ www.ormistonhouse.com.au). This magnificent 1899 stately house was originally the home of Frederick Ormiston, the founder of Strahan; now it's a five-star guesthouse and restaurant. B&B ❽

Risby Cove, The Esplanade (℡ 03/6471 7572, ℻ 6471 7582, ⓦ www.risbycove.com.au). This old sawmill has been fully renovated, using corrugated iron and Huon pine salvaged from the harbour, and now houses upmarket accommodation suites, a restaurant/café, a gallery and theatre. ❼ –❽

Strahan Caravan & Tourist Park, The Esplanade (℡ 03/6471 7239). Good-value camping and cabins near the foreshore. Cabins ❸ –❻, on-site vans ❸

Strahan Colonial Cottages, Reid St (℡ 03/6471 7612) Three beautifully renovated and well-equipped cottages, one a renovated church. ❽

Strahan Village Motor Inn, Jolly St (℡ 03/6471 7160, ℻ 6471 7372). Motel complex on a hill overlooking the town, with some wheelchair-accessible units; the restaurant/bar has sea views. ❻ –❼

Strahan Wilderness Lodge & Bayview Cottages, Ocean Beach Rd (℡ & ℻ 03/6471 7142). The best-value place in Strahan, set in spacious grounds crisscrossed by walking tracks, just out of town. Old homestead B&B, plus private self-catering cottages. B&B ❹, cottages ❺

Strahan YHA, Harvey St (℡ & ℻ 03/6471 7255). Located in two separate buildings beside a bush-lined stream with its own resident platypus, this modern hostel has spacious but slightly neglected common kitchens, eating areas, and lounge. There are well cared-for timber bedroom cabins with made-up double or twin beds, and sharing the hostel bathroom and kitchen. Buses drop off here. Cabins ❸, dorms ❶

The Town

Your first stop should be the innovative wooden and iron **Strahan Visitor Centre**, on The Esplanade (daily: summer 10am–8pm; winter 11am–6pm; 24hr ticket $3.30; ℡ 03/6471 7622, ⓔ strahan@tasvisinfo.com.au), whose exterior design aims to echo the area's boatbuilding and timber industries. The interior features a waterfall, and a huge glass wall providing views of the harbour. The centre sets out its exhibits in a provocative and challenging way, under seven main themes: the Aborigines, convicts, logging, ecology, economy, wilderness and conflict – all making a satisfyingly radical departure from the usual displays in a local museum. If you don't want to see the exhibition you can enter the foyer free of charge to pick up leaflets and information and take advantage of the **internet access**. Outside, an **amphitheatre** is the early evening venue for an entertaining two-man show, *The Ship That Never Was*, which retells – in slapstick vein, with plenty of audience participation – the true story of an 1834 convict escape from Sarah Island (daily 5.30pm plus 8.30pm performance in Jan; $11).

Cruising the Gordon River

The **Gordon River** is deep, its waters dark from the tannin leaching out of but-tongrass plains – even the tap water in Strahan is brown (though perfectly fine to drink). Cruise boats used to travel as far as Sir John Falls, 30km upriver, but the speed at which the boats had to go was causing the river banks to erode. Boats now travel only the 14km to **Heritage Landing**, where there's a chance to see a section of real **rainforest**: a boardwalk above the rainforest floor allows you to get close without disturbing anything. Trunks and branches of ancient myrtles and Huon pines provide homes for mosses, lichens and liverworts on their bark, and ferns and fungi grow from the trunks – even the dead trees support some forms of life, however lowly. The wet and swampy conditions are ideal for **Huon pines**, a threatened tree species found only in Tasmania: they're the second-oldest living things on earth after the bristlecone pines of western North America, with some trees found to be more than ten thousand years old. The massive pines, which may reach a height of 40m, can grow from seed but more often regenerate vegetatively, putting down roots where fallen branches touch the soil. The vast tree at the landing, reckoned to be around 2000 years old, split in two during 1997 – one half fell to the ground – but the trunk won't rot for up to one hundred years as it contains methyl eugenol oil which slows fungal growth. The oil content of the wood helps explain why it was so highly sought after as one of the few green Tasmanian timbers that floats: Huon pine logs were floated down to the boom camp and there fashioned into huge rafts to be rowed across Macquarie Harbour. The **boom camp** is still set up, and anyone can stay for free – all you need to bring is bedding and food – and you need to rent a kayak (from Hell's Gate Wilderness Tours; see p.1130) to be dropped off near the mooring by the *Wanderer II*.

Two operators offer **river cruises**; both visit Sarah Island and make a thirty-minute stop at Heritage Landing. To make the most of the experience, turn up early to bag a good seat and bring water- and windproof gear so you can brave the prow of the boat – much the most exhilarating spot when you whizz through Macquarie Heads (Hells Gates). The larger operator, **Gordon River Cruises** (half-day cruise departs 9am, returns 2pm, $50 including morning tea; full-day cruise Nov–April departs 9am, returns 3.30pm, $68 including smorgasbord lunch; ☏03/6471 7187), has two boats and is located on the waterfront in a spacious complex, where there's a photographic display of Strahan's history. Their full-day cruise stops for an hour at Sarah Island to allow you to wander around the ruins of the prison settlement. **World Heritage Cruises**, the smaller friendlier company, also has two boats (the *Wanderer II and III*), and offers a slightly cheaper cruise, also with a one-hour guided tour of Sarah Island (departs daily 9am, returns about 3.30pm; $55; snacks and $9 buffet lunch available on board; licensed; ☏03/6471 7174, ⊛www.worldheritagecruises .com.au). They also offer a shorter cruise in summer (Oct–April), departing at 9am and returning about 2pm ($50).

Adjacent to the visitor centre is the **Strahan Woodworks**, in a large, corrugated-iron shed (daily 8am–5pm), selling well-designed and crafted woodwork; you're also welcome to roam around Morrison's Saw Mill next door, and watch the Tasmanian timbers being processed. Also worth a visit is the **Forestry Tasmania Office** (Mon–Fri 9am–noon & 1–5pm; ℡03/6471 7176), which has leaflets describing the trees in the area, as well as information on the Teepookana Forest Reserve (see below). You should also check out the amazing window display of a Huon pine log transforming itself into the bow of a boat.

The **Strahan Historic Foreshore Walkway** is a pleasant gravel track following the shore of the harbour around to **Regatta Point** and its 1899 **train station**. Once used by the Mount Lyell Railway and Mining Company to transport ore to the port, it is currently being renovated and from January 2002 will be in use again for the newly opened **Abt Railway** (see box on p.1125). En route you pass the **People's Park**, from where you can take the rainforest walk to **Hogarth Falls** (40min; 2km return).

Eating and drinking

Strahan's best **restaurant** is the dining room of the stylish *Franklin Manor*, across from the centre of town on The Esplanade (℡03/6471 7311). The cheaper, less formal *Hamers Hotel*, also on The Esplanade, is the focus of the town's social life; it has a fine bistro which serves up a varied selection of seafood, and is always a lively place for a **drink**. For snacks, there's *Banjo's* bakery on The Esplanade, or the *Strahan Central Café*, just off The Esplanade on Harold Street – a young, city-style and funky café with waterviews, an outdoor deck and excellent coffee. Alternatively, the general store on Innes Street serves cheap breakfasts and takeaways.

Around Strahan

Six kilometres east of town, **Ocean Beach** is, at 30km, the longest beach in Tasmania. In the early 1990s – and again in 1998 – dozens of **pilot whales** from Antarctica were stranded here: unfortunately, attempts to rescue them were unsuccessful and their skeletons, half-buried in the sand, can still be seen. Come at dusk to observe the marvellous sunsets and to watch – from November to February – the migratory **muttonbirds** roost. It's an eleven-kilometre drive on a gravel road, south off the road to Ocean Beach, to **Macquarie Heads** (Hells Gates). The extensive **Henty Dunes**, 12km north of town on the Zeehan Road (B27), are also worth seeing; you can **camp** at the picnic area.

To get around, you can rent ten-speed **mountain bikes** at the Strahan Visitor Centre (half-day $15, full day $25). If you don't have your own car, Strahan 4x4 Wilderness (℡03/6471 7646) offer a variety of land-based tours, including **4WD trips** to Macquarie Heads via Ocean Beach and Henty Sand Dunes (2hr 30min; $50), and sunset tours to Ocean Beach (2hr 30min; $40). Their best trip is to the ghost town of **Teepookana**, an old railway port, and the surrounding Huon pine forest reserve on the King River (2hr 30min; $40). 4Wheelers (℡03/6471 7622 or 0419 508 175) offer popular guided four-wheel motorbike tours of Henty Sand Dunes (40min; $33; bookings essential). You can also go **horse riding** on Ocean Beach with Strahan Trail Rides (℡03/6471 7426).

In addition to the Gordon River cruises (see box, opposite) there's a wide choice of water-based tours. West Coast Yacht Charters, on The Esplanade (℡03/6471 7422 or 0419 300 994, ⒲www.tasadventures.com/wcyc), runs

TASMANIA | Strahan and around

evening **crayfish dinner sails** on Macquarie Harbour on a 20m ketch, *Stormbreaker* (daily 6–8.30pm except May–Aug; $55 including dinner), plus morning fishing trips (on demand 9am–noon; $45) and longer cruises (one night $275, two nights $360); you can even stay on board the ketch for a waterborne B&B experience (**⑤**). With Wild Rivers Jet (50min; $46; ☎03/6471 7174) you can explore the **King River**, which, like the Gordon, flows into Macquarie Harbour, just south of Strahan. Hells Gate Wilderness Tours (☎03/6471 7576) offer **sea kayak tours** on the Gordon River and the Henty River, and also hire out kayaks so you can explore Macquarie Harbour by yourself (half-day $40, full day $50). Strahan Marine Charters (☎0418 135 983) offer private fishing (3hr; $55) or sightseeing tours (3hr 30min; $55) for up to twelve people; or you can hire the whole boat (1hr; $132; minimum four people).

Wilderness Air, on Strahan Wharf, runs spectacular **seaplane flights** over Macquarie Harbour and the wilderness area (daily from 9am; 1hr 20min; $125; bookings essential on ☎03/6471 7280), which grant you the unforgettable image of the smooth dark ribbon of the pristine Gordon River easing through dense forest (see also box p.1135). The seaplanes make a dramatic landing at **Sir John Falls Landing**, further upriver than the cruise boats can reach – the highlight of the trip. Wilderness Air also has longer flights for viewing the rugged scenery around Frenchmans Cap. There are also **helicopter flights** with Seeair Adventure Charters (☎03/6471 7718) over Hells Gates and Macquarie Harbour ($75; 15min), and the Teepookana Forest ($120; 1hr).

The World Heritage Area

If we can revise our attitudes towards the land under our feet; if we can accept a role of steward, and depart from the role of conqueror; if we can accept the view that man and nature are inseparable parts of the unified whole – then Tasmania can be a shining beacon in a dull, uniform, and largely artificial world.

Olegas Truchanas, conservationist, 1971

It's the lure of the **wilderness** that attracts a certain type of traveller to Tasmania, to commune with nature at its most unspoilt. The state's vast wilderness areas of the South West National Park, Franklin Lower Gordon Wild Rivers National Park and the adjacent Cradle Mountain–Lake St Clair National Park make up the **World Heritage Area**, recognized by UNESCO.

The future of the parks could have been very different had it not been for the bitterly fought battle waged by the environmentalists in the 1980s. In 1972 the flooding of the beautiful and unique **Lake Pedder** led to the formation, in 1976, of the **Wilderness Society**, which began a relentless campaign against the next plan for the southwest by the Hydro Electricity Commission (HEC), which was to build a huge dam on the Lower Gordon River that would efface Tasmania's last wild river, the Franklin. Pro-HEC forces included the then Tasmanian Premier Robin Gray. Years of protests and campaigns ensued, but in 1981 the whole southwest area was proposed for the World Heritage list. The **Franklin Blockade**, organized by the Wilderness Society and led by **Dr Bob Brown**, began on December 14, 1982, the day the southwest officially joined the list – a fact the Tasmanian government was choosing to ignore.

For two months, blockaders from all over Australia travelled upriver from their base in Strahan to put themselves in front of the bulldozers at the site, in nonviolent protest. The **blockade** attracted international attention, notably when the British botanist David Bellamy joined in the protest and was among the twelve hundred or so arrested for trespassing. During the course of the campaign, the Labor government of Bob Hawke was voted in, and in March 1983, following a trailblazing High Court ruling, the federal government forbade further work by the HEC. Though the blockade itself had failed to stop the preparatory work on the dam, it had changed, or at least challenged, the opinion of many Australians. Particularly on Tasmania's west coast, communities and families were split over the Franklin issue; local people who supported the "Greenie" protesters faced a lot of antagonism within the community, and resentment grew towards the mainlanders, who were regarded as denying potential employment to Tasmanians. Recent Wilderness Society campaigns have only added to these tensions.

Cradle Mountain–Lake St Clair National Park

This must be a national park for the people for all time. It is magnificent, and people must know about it and enjoy it.

Gustave Weindorfer, botanist and mountaineer, 1910

Cradle Mountain–Lake St Clair National Park is Tasmania's best known, its northern **Cradle Mountain** end easily accessible from Devonport, Deloraine or Launceston, and its southern **Lake St Clair** end from Derwent Bridge on the Lyell Highway between Queenstown and Hobart. A popular route from Devonport is via Sheffield (see p.1115) on the B14, then the C132 via Wilmot, and for the final stretch to Cradle Valley, the C136. One of the most glaciated areas in Australia, with many lakes and tarns, the park covers some of Tasmania's highest land, with craggy mountain peaks such as **Mount Ossa** (1617m), the state's highest point. At its northern end, **Dove Lake**, backed by the jagged outline of Cradle Mountain, is one of the state's most breathtaking sights, and at the park's southern end, Lake St Clair is the country's deepest freshwater lake at over 200m, occupying a basin gouged out by two glaciers. Between Cradle Mountain and Lake St Clair, the eighty-kilometre **Overland Track**, attracting walkers from all over the world, is the best way to take in the stunning scenery – spread over five or more mud- and leech-filled days of physical, albeit exhilarating, exhaustion. However, you can do just part of the walk, or make several other satisfying day-walks around Cradle Mountain or Lake St Clair (see overleaf).

Transport to the park

Tassie Link services both ends of the national park on two year-round **scheduled routes**, while "Wilderness" services provide more frequent transport in the summer. A service from Launceston and Devonport to Queenstown goes via Cradle Mountain (Tues, Thurs & Sat; connecting with a Queenstown to Strahan service), while the Queenstown–Hobart service takes the Lyell Highway to Lake St Clair (Tues, Thurs, Sat & Sun). A Launceston to Cradle Mountain "Wilderness" service runs via Deloraine and Devonport (mid-April to Nov Tues, Thurs, Sat & Sun; Dec to mid-April daily). A Hobart to Lake St Clair "Wilderness" service via Mount Field National Park runs daily (except Sun) in both directions December–April. You can also try Maxwell's Coaches charter service (☎03/6492 1431), which connects Devonport and Launceston to Lake St Clair ($65), and Launceston and Devonport to Cradle Mountain ($65).

In summer hundreds flock here to walk the Overland Track, probably Australia's greatest extended bushwalk: 80km, unbroken by roads and passing through buttongrass plains, fields of wild flowers, and forests of deciduous beech, Tasmanian myrtle, pandanus and King Billy pine, with side-walks leading to views of waterfalls and lakes and starting points for climbs of the various mountain peaks. Much of the track is boardwalked, but you'll still end up thigh-deep in mud. There are eight basic stove-heated huts (not for cooking – bring your own stove) along the route, with composting toilets, but there's no guarantee there'll be space, so you should carry a good tent; a warm sleeping bag is essential even in the heated huts in summer.

The direct walk generally takes six days – five, if you catch a boat from Narcissus Hut across Lake St Clair; if you want to go on some of the side-walks, allow eight to ten days. On average, most walkers go for six to eight days. You should take enough food and fuel, plus extra supplies in case you have an accident or bad weather sets in; there's always plenty of unpolluted fresh water to drink from streams. Around 4500 people walk the track each year; most people come between November and April, but the best time is during February and March when the weather has stabilized, though it's bound to rain at some point, and may even snow. The track is at its most crowded from Christmas to the end of January. Most people walk north to south, which is more downhill than up, but you can register at either end in the national park office (see below), where you receive an obligatory briefing and have your gear checked to make sure it's sufficient; if you haven't already got some sort of park pass, you'll have to purchase one. The office sells last-minute camping gear and supplies: fuel stoves, meths, water bottles, trowels, warm hats and gloves. The Cradle Mountain–Lake St Clair National Park map and notes ($4.40) is an essential purchase, and the Overland Track Walkers Notebook ($9.90) is a handy reference. Once you end up at Derwent Bridge, exhausted and covered in mud, you can use the hot showers at the campsite, for which there's a small charge.

The logistics of doing a one-way walk are smoothed by a couple of operators: Maxwell's Coaches can do transfers to get you back to your car, while Tassie Link has special Overland Track fares which include transfers from Launceston to Cradle Mountain, and then back from Lake St Clair to Launceston ($95) or Hobart ($66). They can provide baggage transfer for an extra charge. Guided tours are available, the best offered by Craclair Walking Holidays (Oct–April; eight days $1135, ten days $1430; ☎ & ⓕ 03/6424 7833); you'll still have to camp and carry a six-kilo pack, however. The easiest option is to go on a guided walk staying along the track at Cradle Huts, private lodges with hot showers, beds and delicious meals (☎03/6331 2006, ⓕ6331 5525, ⓦwww.cradlehuts.com.au; six days $1595 full board departing and returning Launceston).

Cradle Mountain

At **Cradle Mountain**, the impressive modern **Cradle Mountain Visitor Centre** (daily 8am–5pm, later in summer; ☎03/6492 1133) provides information on the many day-walks available in this area of the park, and acts as a registration point for the Overland Track; it's worth buying the *Cradle Mountain Day Walk Map* ($4.05) for more information. You can start here with a gentle ten-minute boardwalk circuit through rainforest and overlooking **Pencil Pine Falls**, ideal for wheelchairs or strollers. There's also the "Enchanted Walk" which follows the creek through rainforest to *Cradle Mountain Lodge* (1km one-way; 20min). Five kilometres into the park from the visitor centre, **Waldheim** ("Forest Home" in German), is the King Billy pine chalet built by the Austrian-Australian **Gustave Weindorfer** in 1912, and now a museum (open 24hr; free) devoted to the man who loved this wilderness area and helped to have it declared a national park. From **Lake Dove car park**, 2.5km on from Waldheim, you can take the Dove Lake circuit (2–3hr), an easy all-weather walk around the shore of the lake, or a popular, but steep and strenuous, day-walk from here to the summit of **Cradle Mountain** (6hr return; get advice from the ranger first). If you're feeling lazy, you can opt for a **scenic flight** (weather permitting) over the area with Seaair (☏ 03/6492 1132; from $95 for 25min; helicopter from $90 for 20min; minimum four people), who are based by the *Cradle Wilderness Cafe* (see below).

Just on the edge of the national park, and within walking distance of the visitor centre, *Cradle Mountain Lodge* (☏ 03/6492 1303, ⓕ 6492 1309, ⓦ www.poresorts.com; cabins ❽) is the focus for **accommodation**, eating and drinking. Scattered through the bush around the lodge are 96 luxurious serviced timber cabins, all with log fires, kitchenettes and bathrooms. At the lodge itself, guest facilities include lounges, a sauna – with a window providing bush views – a massage room ($38.50 for 30min) and free movies shown each night. Nonguests can book in to eat at the classy **restaurant** (the buffet-style breakfast is well worth the cost – $13.50 continental, $17.50 full buffet), or drop in to eat or drink at the tavern **bar**. You can hire **bicycles** from the lodge and there's a **general store** selling expensive groceries. *Cradle Mountain Tourist Park* (☏ 03/6492 1395, ⓕ 6492 1438, ⓦ www.cosycabins.com/cradle), 2km back along Cradle Mountain Road, has a **campsite**, two hostel-style heated **bunkhouses** (❷; bedding $6) sharing kitchen, toilet and washing facilities with the campers, and some basic huts (❶) plus well set-up cabins sleeping up to six (❺), complete with TV and air-conditioning. The campsite has a small **shop** and is linked to the lodge in summer by a shuttle bus. A bit further on, 1.5km from the park entrance, there's more accommodation at *Cradle Mountain Highlander Cabins* (☏ 03/6492 1116, ⓕ 6492 1188; ❼–❽). The new *Cradle Mountain Wilderness Village* next door has a more antiseptic feel (☏ 03/6492 1018, ⓕ 6492 1076, ⓦ www.cradlevillage.com.au; ❽). Nearby, the licensed fast-food/bistro-style *Cradle Wilderness Cafe* also sells petrol and diesel (daily 8.30am–8pm, 10.30pm in summer). In the park itself, there are eight basic self-catering huts (❹–❺) at Waldheim (see above), which sleep four to eight people with generator electricity, pot-bellied stoves, no fridge or power points, and a shared amenities block – these are looked after by the National Park Visitor Centre.

Lake St Clair and Derwent Bridge

You can register to walk the Overland Track in the opposite direction at the ranger station at **CYNTHIA BAY** on **Lake St Clair** (daily 8am–5pm; ☏ 03/6289 1115), which houses an informative interpretive centre and an attractive bistro restaurant with views over the lake. Short and long **walks** around Lake St Clair are detailed on a board in the centre. You can go on a **cruise** on the MV *Idaclair*, which will drop you off at Narcissus Hut to begin the Overland Track from the southern end, or walk back to the centre (5–6 hours); alternatively, get off at Echo Point and return on a three-hour bushwalk (summer: Cynthia Bay 9am, 12.30pm & 3pm; Narcissus Hut 9.30am, 1pm & 3.30pm; in winter the ferry runs on demand; round-trip 1hr 30min; $20 one-way, $25 return). Tickets (bookings essential) are sold at the restaurant, where you can also rent dinghies with outboard motors, canoes, kayaks and bicycles.

The restaurant also takes bookings for **accommodation**. *Lakeside St Clair Wilderness Holidays* (☏ 03/6289 1137, ⓕ 6289 1250; ❼–❽) has several expensive lodges, and a backpackers' lodge (❷). Compared to Cradle Mountain, the **campsite** here is poor – there's no kitchen and there's a 50¢ fee to use the showers. For supplies (and takeaway alcohol), you have to go to **DERWENT**

BRIDGE, 5km away on the Lyell Highway, served by Maxwell's Coaches (☎03/6289 1125), whose shuttle service ($6) runs on demand. At Derwent Bridge you can stay in luxurious, self-catering units sleeping four to eight at *Derwent Bridge Chalets* (☎03/6289 1000, ℉6289 1230, ⓦwww.troutwalks.com.au; B&B ❼–❽), where you'll be greeted by a welcoming fire, complimentary port and a friendly, considerate host. The focus of the small community is the *Derwent Bridge Hotel* (☎03/6289 1144, ℉6289 1173; ❺–❻), where you can stay in old-fashioned lodge-style accommodation or very basic hostel rooms (❷; no kitchen) out back; there's excellent **food** and drink here too. Derwent Bridge is close to **Lake King William**, equivalent in size to Lake St Clair and popular with anglers.

Franklin Lower Gordon Wild Rivers National Park

The **Franklin Lower Gordon Wild Rivers National Park** was declared in June 1980 and by 1982 had been included with the adjoining parks on the World Heritage List. The park exists for its own sake more than anything, most of it being virtually inaccessible. You can cruise up the Gordon, or fly over it, but the really adventurous can explore by **rafting the Franklin** (see box opposite) and walking the **Frenchmans Cap Track**, both accessible from the **Lyell Highway**, which extends from Strahan to Hobart and runs through the park between Queenstown and Derwent Bridge. There are also plenty of short **walks** leading from the highway to rainforest, rivers and lookouts.

The **Franklin River** is one of the great rivers of Australia, and the only major wild river system in Tasmania that's not been dammed. It flows for 120km from the Cheyne Range to the majestic **Gordon River**, from an altitude of 1400m down to almost sea level. Swollen by the storms of the Roaring Forties and fed by many other rivers, it can at times become a raging torrent as it passes through ancient heaths, deep gorges and rainforests. The discovery in 1981 of stone tools in the **Kutikina Cave** on the lower Franklin has proved that during the last Ice Age southwest Tasmania was the most southerly point of human occupation on earth.

A **seaplane** from Strahan flies over the national park (see p.1130), and from it you can see the confluence of the two rivers – the planned site of the ill-fated dam – surrounded by thick forest, much of it impenetrable and probably never traversed by humans. The Gordon appears wide and slow compared to the narrow, winding Franklin.

Along the Lyell Highway

Heading east from Queenstown, the Lyell Highway enters the Franklin Lower Gordon Wild Rivers National Park, reaching Nelson River bridge after 4km, from where **Nelson Falls** is an easy twenty-minute-return walk through temperate rainforest. From here, the road begins to wind and rise up to **Collingwood River**, the starting point for raft or canoe trips down the Franklin (see box opposite), with some basic camping facilities.

In fine weather, the white-quartzite dome of Frenchmans Cap, looking a little like snow, can be seen from the highway. For a more spectacular viewpoint that takes in the Franklin River Valley, **Donaghy's Hill Wilderness Lookout Walk** begins further along the highway on the right. Walk from the parking area along the old road to the top of the hill, where a sign marks the beginning of the forty-minute-return track. Further along the highway, the **walking track to Frenchmans Cap** (see p.1136) begins with a fifteen-minute stroll

Rafting on the Franklin

One of the most rugged and inaccessible areas left on earth, the surrounds of the Franklin River can't really be seen on foot – there are few tracks through this twisted, tangled and wet rainforest. Rafting is the only way to explore the river and even this is possible only between December and early April. The Franklin is reached by rafting down the Collingwood River from the Lyell Highway, 49km west of Derwent Bridge. The full trip takes eight to fourteen days, ending at the Gordon River, where rafters head finally to Strahan by yacht from Heritage Landing or by seaplane from Sir John Falls Camp.

One of the most dangerous Australian rivers to raft, with average rapids of grades 3 to 4 – and up to grade 6 in places – the Franklin requires an expedition leader with great skill and experience (though even guides have died in the rapids). It's also very remote, and in the event of an accident help can be days away. However, this haunting isolation is part of the attraction for most visitors. The weather, too, can be harsh – and the water is cold. It's inadvisable to attempt the trip independently unless everyone in the party has white-water experience and the group leader has made a previous Franklin River trip; groups are required to have at least two rafts and to stay in contact with the ranger at Queenstown. Bear in mind that there's nowhere to rent rafting equipment in Tasmania. The tour operators don't require you to be experienced – just fit, with lots of stamina and courage. Prices are high, but this is an experience of a lifetime, with the seaplane flight back to Strahan included in the price. The one Tasmanian-based licensed operator is Rafting Tasmania (T 03/6239 1080, F 6239 1090, W www.tasmanianadventures.com.au/raftingtas). The others are based in Melbourne: Peregrine Adventures (T 03/9662 2800, F 9663 8618) and Sydney: World Expeditions (T 02/9264 3366, F 9261 1974). For the shorter four-day trip from Propsting Gorge to the Gordon, expect to pay around $950; for the full ten-day trip from the Collingwood to the Gordon prices start at $1650.

The sketchy *Franklin River Rafting Notesheets* are available free from the Queenstown Ranger Station, PO Box 21, Queenstown, TAS 7467 (T 03/6471 2511) or you can download a copy from the internet (W www.parks.tas.gov.au). There are campsites all along the Franklin, but most have room for only two or three tents.

The route

From the Collingwood River, it takes about three days to raft to the Frenchmans Cap Track. This is the Upper Franklin, alpine country with vegetation adapted to survive snow and icy winds. Watch out for two endemic pines, the Huon pine and celery top pine. There are lots of intermediate rapids along this stretch and a deep quartzite ravine and large still pool at Irenabyss.

The Middle Franklin is a mixture of pools, deep ravines and wild rapids as the river makes a fifty-kilometre detour around Frenchmans Cap. Dramatic limestone cliffs overhang the Lower Franklin, which involves a tranquil paddle through dense myrtle beech forests with flowering leatherwoods overhead. The best raftable white water is here at Newlands Cascades. It's a short distance to Kutikina Caves and Deena-reena; only rafters can gain access to these Aboriginal caves.

to the suspension bridge over the river. Continuing on the Lyell, you have another opportunity to see the Franklin on a ten-minute **Nature Trail**, at a point where the river is tranquil, as it flows around large boulders; there's also a longer 25-minute circuit. At the start of the trail there's a picnic area and a wooden shelter with an **interpretive board** about the river. Beyond this point, open buttongrass plains take over, huge uninhabited expanses fringed with trees. This is **Wombat Glen**, which looks as though it's been cleared into grazing country until you step out into it and discover its bog-like nature.

At the foot of **Mount Arrowsmith**, the highway begins to ascend, winding around the mountain's southern side above the U-shaped glacial Surprise Valley. The **Surprise Valley Lookout** offers a good view of the valley and, across to the southwest, another excellent aspect of Frenchmans Cap. Continuing down, you come to King William Saddle, another fine lookout point with views of the **King William Range** to the south and **Mount Rufus** to the north.

The Frenchmans Cap Track

The most prominent mountain peak in the Franklin Lower Gordon Wild Rivers National Park is the white-quartzite dome of **Frenchmans Cap** (1443m). Its southeast face has a sheer five-hundred-metre cliff and from its summit there are uninterrupted views of Mount Ossa in the Cradle Mountain–Lake St Clair National Park, Federation Peak, Macquarie Harbour and, on a fine day, the whole of the southwest wilderness. It takes three to five days to do the 54-kilometre return trip to the summit, best done between December and March, though you'll be in the company of another nine hundred or so people. Frenchmans Cap is much more demanding than the relatively straightforward Overland Track, as it has some very steep extended climbs and sections of mud, and should be attempted only by skilled bushwalkers – preferably with experience of other Tasmanian walks. The weather is temperamental: it rains frequently, and it can snow even in summer. Beyond Barron Pass, the track is above 900m and at any time of the year is subject to high winds, mist, rain, hail and snowfalls.

The track begins at the Lyell Highway, 55km from Queenstown, served by Tassie Link's scheduled Hobart–Queenstown service (℡03/6334 4442; 1 daily Tues, Thurs, Fri & Sun), or you can charter Maxwell's Coaches (℡03/6492 1431) for $65 from Devonport or Launceston or $60 from Lake St Clair. A fifteen-minute walk from the road brings you to the suspension bridge across the river for the start of the walk. Record your plans in the registration book here and again in the logbook at the two **huts** at Lake Vera and Lake Tahune that provide basic accommodation (though this is usually full and you must bring tents and stoves with you); Frenchmans Cap is a proclaimed "Fuel Stove Only Area". There are composting toilets at both huts and plenty of camping spots along the way; water along the track is safe to drink. From the Franklin River to Lake Vera the well-defined track crosses plains and foothills, then becomes steep and rough as it climbs to Barron Pass – where there are magnificent views – becoming easier again on the way to Lake Tahune, close to the cliffs of Frenchmans Cap. From here it's a steep one-kilometre walk to the summit, before returning the same way.

For further **information**, get the free *Frenchmans Cap Track Bushwalker Notes* from Service Tasmania, 134 Macquarie St, Hobart 7000; you can also buy the *Frenchmans Cap Map and Notes* ($9) there; or contact the Queenstown Ranger Station (℡03/6471 2511). If you don't feel equipped to tackle the walk independently, contact Craclair Walking Holidays (℡ & Ⅎ 03/6424 7833), which organizes seven-day guided treks ($1195).

The South West National Park

Tasmania's **southwest** is an area of contrast: arrow-sharp, crested ranges of white quartzite cut across buttongrass plains. The isolation, rough terrain and unpredictable weather, even in summer – the southwest has more than two hundred days of rain a year – means that this is an area for experienced bush-walkers only. Being able to use a compass and read a map are important, but so is a tolerance for trudging through deep mud and swampy buttongrass while heavily laden with supplies and plagued by leeches.

The map *South Coast Walks* ($9) covers the southern gateways to the World Heritage Area: Cockle Creek through Port Davey to Scotts Peak, as well as Moonlight Ridge and South West Cape, including notes on track conditions, weather and campsites. For the rest of the area you'll need to purchase Tasmap topographic **maps**; and for detailed information refer to John Chapman's *South West Tasmania*, published by Lonely Planet.

Two airlines operate **flights** into the national park from Cambridge aero-drome, 15km from Hobart. **Par Avion** (☎03/6248 5390, ℻6248 5117, ⓦwww.paravion.com.au) runs eighty percent of flights to the southwest, with a daily service to Melaleuca, weather permitting ($138 one-way); you can register your walk at the airstrip. They also offer a combined scenic flight and cruise on Melaleuca Inlet (4hr; $140) or Bathurst Harbour (full-day; $240 including lunch). **TasAir** (☎03/6248 5088) flies to Melaleuca or Cox Bight (both $135 one-way), which can cut out the trudge from Melaleuca, and also offers joyrides over the whole of the World Heritage Area for $176 (2hr 30min includes a landing and refreshment at Cox Bight). If you're plan-ning an extended walk, you can arrange for either airline to drop food sup-plies for you (around $4 per kilo). Aerotechnology (☎03/6248 5490) oper-ates a **Wilderness Camp** ($814 for two nights, including flight, camp accommodation and meals); they also have a boat, the MV *Southern Explorer*, based on Bathurst Harbour with on-board accommodation, which cruises the harbour, Port Davey and the Davey River (two days and two nights from $1155).

Unless you're flying in, or beginning a walk at **Cockle Creek** (see p.1073), south of Hobart, access to the South West National Park is via the **Strathgordon Road**, which passes to the south of Mount Field National Park. The ranger for this (northern) end of South West National Park is based at Mount Field, and you should drop in or call (☎03/6288 1283) to ask about conditions and to check that you're adequately prepared. The good sealed road heads through state forest and the South West Conservation Area, where the amazing craggy landforms of the **Frankland Range** loom above and signposts helpfully point out the names of the features, and past the drowned **Lake Pedder** (see box opposite) and the **Gordon Dam's power station** (under-ground tours daily: May–Oct 11am; Nov–April 10am & 2pm; 40min; $5). The Gordon Dam lookout is breathtaking, and if you're after a thrill you can **abseil** down it with Aardvark Adventures (☎0408 127 714), who run day-tours from Hobart ($165 per person including lunch).

You can **stay** at Lake Pedder at the faded, musty *Lake Pedder Chalet* (☎03/6280 1166, ⓦwww.webimage.com.au/lakepedderchalet; ➎–➑), which originally served as a staff house for the HEC. There's a bar and a very basic overpriced restaurant here. Alternatively there are a number of free **campsites** in the area: just down the road on the shore of Lake Pedder, *Ted's Beach* has a sheltered kitchen area, electric barbecues, water and toilets; or there are two more campgrounds at Scotts Peak at the southern end of Lake Pedder, where the Port Davey walk begins (see p.1139). Tassie Link runs a "Wilderness" service to Scotts Peak and to Condominium Creek from Hobart, via Mount Field (Dec–April Tues, Thurs & Sat; no service May–Nov).

Pedder 2000: the resurrection of Lake Pedder

To Dr Bob Brown, Tasmania's foremost Green activist, and now Senator, Lake Pedder "was one of the most gently beautiful places on the planet". The glacial lake, in the Frankland Range in Tasmania's southwest, had an area of 9.7 square kilometres until 1972, when it and the surrounding valleys were flooded as part of a huge hydroelectric scheme, creating a reservoir covering a massive 240 square kilometres and reached by the Lake Gordon Road via Maydena. Before then, the lake was so inaccessible that it could only be visited by light aircraft, which used to land on the perfect sand of the lake beach.

Pedder 2000 is a visionary campaign spearheaded by the Wilderness Society in 1995, the aim of which is to drain the current Lake Pedder and restore it to its former glory. In late 1994 a scientist revealed that, beneath the water, the sandy beach remained; and in 1995 divers filmed underwater, revealing the still-visible impressions of tyre tracks from the light aircraft that once landed there. Most politicians are opposed to the idea, belligerently declaring that a "large and smelly puddle" would be the only result. Certain scientists and conservationists, however, do consider it possible for the lake to revert to its former state, even though it might take twenty or thirty years. For more information and to provide support, the Pedder 2000 head office is at 130 Davey St, Hobart, TAS 7000 (☎ 03/6257 5292), or check out their website which includes essays, submissions and even poems (ⓦ www.neptune.he.net/~pedder/).

Western Arthurs Traverse and Federation Peak

The most spectacular bushwalk in Tasmania, only 20km in length and 5km in width, **Western Arthurs Traverse** contains 25 major peaks and 30 lakes. The last glacial period gouged into this range, leaving sharp quartzite ridges, craggy towers and impressive cliffs, and carving cirque valleys that are now filled by dark, tannin-stained lakes, surrounded by contrasting buttongrass plains. Violent storms, mists and continuous rain can plague the route in summer since it's in the direct path of the Roaring Forties. Crossing these ranges makes for a superb but difficult walk. Though there's no man-made track, the route, starting at Scotts Peak Road, is not difficult to follow; it involves scrambling over roots and branches and making short descents and ascents into gullies and cliff lines, and you'll need to use a rope at some point. The whole walk takes between nine and twelve days, and camping areas are limited.

The **Eastern Arthur Range** is the location of the major goal for intrepid southwest walkers – **Federation Peak**, often considered the most challenging in Australia, with its steep, almost perfectly triangular outline rising starkly above the surrounding rugged peaks and ridges. It was named by a surveyor in 1901, the year of Federation, when most of the major landmarks in the southwest were still unvisited; in fact, the peak was not successfully scaled until 1949, its thick scrub, forests and cliffs having kept walkers at bay. Although the walk is now easier since the terrain has been "broken in", each year many walkers are turned back by the worst weather in Tasmania, and one person has died tackling the route. All the ascents are extremely difficult, and most parties take between seven and ten days to reach the peak and return; minor rock climbing is required to get to the summit. The walk begins at the same point as the Port Davey Track (see opposite).

Mount Anne Circuit

The highest peak in the southwest, **Mount Anne** (1423m) is part of a small range capped with red dolerite – a contrast to the surrounding white quartzite.

Views from the summit are spectacular in fine weather, but even in summer the route is very exposed and prone to bad weather. It's suitable only for experienced walkers carrying a safety rope. The three- to four-day walk begins 20km along Scotts Peak Road at Condominium Creek (where there are basic camping facilities) and ends 9km south at Red Tape Creek; a car shuttle might be advisable, or you can arrange with Tassie Link (☏03/6272 7300) to be picked up and dropped off from Hobart.

Port Davey Track

Going straight through the heart of the World Heritage Area, from Scotts Peak Dam south to Melaleuca (where you fly out; see p.1137), is the 54km **Port Davey Track**, a wet, muddy four- to five-day trek over buttongrass plains, with views of rugged mountain ranges along the way. Only around 200 people walk the track each year. It's less interesting than some of the other walks in the area and most groups combine it with the **South Coast Track** (see below) for a ten- to sixteen-day wilderness experience, which requires a drop-off of food supplies. This combined walk is often called the **South West Track**. Contact Tassie Link if you want to arrange drop-offs.

South Coast Track

The **South Coast Track** is known for its magnificent **beaches** and spectacular coastal scenery of Aboriginal **middens**, rainforest and buttongrass ridges. At 80km, it's one of the longest tracks in the South West National Park – a five- to ten-day moderate to difficult walk, usually done from Melaleuca east to Cockle Creek. Since the route is mostly along the coast, the climate is milder than in many parts of the World Heritage Area; however, you'll still need wet-weather gear as it tends to rain frequently. Though the track is regularly maintained, you do need to plough through sections of mud and across the exposed Ironbound Range (900m), which should be attempted only in fine weather. There are no huts along the way, except at the Melaleuca airstrip. Around 2000 people do the walk each year, seventy-five percent of them between December and March. The best **approach** is to fly direct to Cox Bight with TasAir, cutting out the boring buttongrass plains walk from Melaleuca, then head for Cockle Creek. Alternatively, you can begin at Cockle Creek and fly out at Melaleuca with TasAir or Par Avion, or arrange for extra food supplies to be flown in at Melaleuca and continue along the Port Davey Track across the water, using the rowboats provided.

Tasmanian Expeditions (☏03/6334 3477, ℱ6334 3463, ⓦwww.tasmanian-expeditions.com.au) runs an extended **organized walk** of the South Coast Track (Nov–March; $1380). You need to be very fit for the nine-day trip, as each party member (maximum of ten) carries a share of the food and tents, a weight of 18–20kg.

South West Cape

The granite South West Cape juts out for 3km into the wild Southern Ocean. **Walking** is fairly easy here, though the rough unmarked tracks across open countryside require sound navigation, and some high windy ridges have to be crossed. All routes start and end at Melaleuca or Cox Bight but there are a variety of ways to the cape and beyond, taking in different beaches and bays. Depending on which you choose, a simple route will take from three to seven days, and the full circuit between six and nine. Because of the growing popularity of the walks, they may be overcrowded in the summer months.

TRAVEL DETAILS

BETWEEN TASMANIA AND THE MAINLAND STATES

Ferries

Spirit of Tasmania Bass Strait ferry from Port Melbourne to Devonport (Mon 7.30pm, Wed & Fri 6pm; returning Tues & Thurs 6pm, Sat 4pm; journey time 14hr 30min).

Devil Cat Bass Strait high-speed catamaran from Port Melbourne to George Town (Jan–April: departing Port Melbourne Tues, Thurs, Sat & Sun 8.30am; returning Mon Wed, Fri & Sun 2pm; journey time 6hr).

Flights

Mainly through Sydney's Mascot or Melbourne's Tullamarine airports, with smaller companies operating from Moorabbin airport, on the fringes of Melbourne. The smaller airlines change frequently in Tasmania, as do their scheduled flights, so check for changes.

Flinders Island to: Launceston (2–4 daily; 45min); Melbourne (Tullamarine 4 weekly, Moorabbin 5 weekly; 50min).

King Island to: Burnie (3 daily Mon–Fri, 2 daily Sat & Sun; 45min); Devonport (4 daily Mon–Fri, 2 daily Sat & Sun; 45min); Melbourne (Tullamarine 1 daily, Moorabbin 2 daily; 45min).

Melbourne to: Burnie (4 daily; 1hr); Devonport (4 daily; 1hr); Flinders Island (Tullamarine 4 weekly, Moorabbin 5 weekly; 50min); Hobart (8 daily; 1hr); King Island (Tullamarine 1 daily, Moorabbin 2 daily; 45min); Launceston (8 daily; 1hr).

Sydney to: Hobart (4–6 daily; 2hr 20min); Launceston (1–2 daily; 2hr 35min).

Traralgon to: Flinders Island (4 weekly; 45min); Launceston (4 weekly; 1hr).

TRANSPORT ON THE ISLAND

Buses

We have only included scheduled services in this list. Extra "Wilderness" services, which need a minimum of four people to depart, are provided by Tasmanian Wilderness Travel to all bushwalking destinations, and some operate in the summer only. These are all detailed in the text of the *Guide*.

Burnie to: Smithton via the northwest coast (1–3 daily Mon–Sat, 1 daily Sun; 1hr 30min).

Deloraine to: Devonport (3 daily; 40min); Hobart (2–4 daily; 4hr); Launceston (3–5 daily; 45min).

Devonport to: Burnie (3–6 daily; 50min); Cradle Mountain (3 weekly; 2hr 15min); Deloraine (3 daily; 40min); Hobart (2–4 daily; 5hr 30min); Launceston (3–5 daily; 1hr 30min); Queenstown (3 weekly; 7hr).

Hobart to: Bicheno (3–6 weekly; 4hr); Burnie (3–6 daily; 4hr 45min); Deloraine (2–4 daily; 4hr); Devonport (2–4 daily; 5hr 30min); Dover (2 daily Mon–Fri; 55min); Geeveston (5 daily except Sat; 55min); Kettering (Mon–Fri 4 daily; 40min); Lake St Clair (4 weekly; 3hr); Launceston (3–7 daily; 2hr 30min); New Norfolk (1–7 daily; 30min); Port Arthur (Mon–Fri 2 daily; 2hr); Queenstown via New Norfolk, Lake St Clair and Frenchmans Cap with connections to Strahan (4 weekly; 7hr 45min); Richmond (Mon–Fri 4 daily; 30min); St Helens (1–2 daily except Sat; 3hr); St Marys (1–2 daily except Sat; 3hr); Swansea (1–2 daily except Sat; 2hr 30min–3hr 30min).

Launceston to: Bicheno (3 daily except Sat; 2hr 40min); Burnie (3–6 daily; 3hr); Cradle Mountain (3 weekly; 4hr); Deloraine (3–5 daily; 45min); Derby (1–2 daily except Sat; 2hr 40min); Devonport (3–5 daily; 1hr 30min); Hobart (3–7 daily; 2hr 30min); Mole Creek (1 daily Mon–Fri; 1hr 30min); St Helens via St Marys (1 daily except Sat; 2hr 45min).

contexts

contexts

A history

The first European settlers saw Australia as *terra nullius* – empty land – on the principle that Aborigines didn't "use" the country in an agricultural sense, a belief which remained uncontested in law until 1992. However, decades of archeological work, the reports of early settlers and oral tradition have established a minimum date of forty thousand years for human occupation, and evidence that Aboriginal peoples shaped, controlled and used their environment as surely as any farmer. Even so, it's difficult for visitors to form a unified idea of pre-colonial times, as two centuries of European rule shattered traditional Aboriginal life, and evidence of those earlier times mostly consists of cryptic art sites and legends – though if you're lucky enough to get beyond the tourist image, you'll realize that Aboriginal culture, though being redefined, is far from confined to the past. The very simplified outline of Aboriginal history below is intended mainly as a background to accounts given in the *Guide*, followed by a fuller description of the years since European colonization.

From Gondwana to the Dreamtime

After the break-up of the supercontinent **Gondwana** into India, Africa, South America, Australasia and Antarctica, Australia moved away from the South Pole, reaching its current geographical location about fifteen million years ago. Though the mainland was periodically joined to New Guinea and Tasmania, there was never a land link with the rest of Asia, and the country developed a unique fauna – most notably the marsupials, or pouched mammals, but also a whole range of giant animals, the megafauna – which flourished, along with widespread rainforests, until about fifty thousand years ago. Subsequent Ice Ages dried out the climate, and though some of the megafauna survived into Aboriginal times, by six thousand years ago the seas had stabilized at their present levels and Australia's environment was much as it appears today: an arid centre with a relatively fertile eastern seaboard.

Humans had been in Australia long before then, of course, most likely taking advantage of low sea levels to cross the Timor Trough into northern Australia, or island-hop from Indonesia onto what is now the Cape York Peninsula via New Guinea. Exactly when this happened, how many times it happened and what the colonists did next are debatable. There's no direct evidence for either distinct or continuous migrations from Asia, but since the earliest dated sites are found in the south of Australia, it seems reasonable that human occupation goes back further than scientists' current forty-thousand-year estimates. The oldest known remains from central Australia are only 22,000 years old, so it's also fairly plausible that initial colonization occurred around the coast, followed by later exploration of the interior – though it's just as likely that corrosive rainforests, which covered the centre until about twenty thousand years ago, obliterated all trace of earlier human habitation. The presence of the dingo and disappearance of the **thylacine** (Tasmanian tiger) on the mainland but not (until recently) in Tasmania indicates that there was a further influx of people and **dogs** more recently than twelve thousand years ago, after Tasmania had become an island. The earliest inhabitants used crude **stone implements**, gradually replaced by a more refined technology based around lighter tools, **boomerangs**, and the use of core stones to flake "blanks" which were then fashioned into spearheads, knives and scrapers. As only certain types of stone were suitable for the process, tribes living away from quarries had to trade with those living near them. **Trade networks** for rock, **ochre** (a red clay used for ceremonial purposes) and other products – shells and even wood for canoes – eventually reached from New Guinea to the heart of the continent, following river systems away from the coast. **Rock art**, preserved in an ancient engraved tradition and more recent painted styles, seems to indicate that cultural links also travelled along these trade routes – similar symbols and styles are found in widely separated regions.

It's probable that the disappearance of the megafauna was accelerated by Aboriginal hunting, but the most dramatic change wrought by the original Australians was the controlled use of **fire** to clear areas of forest. Burning promoted new growth and encouraged game, indirectly expanding grassland and favouring certain plants – cycads, grasstrees, banksias and eucalypts – which evolved fire-reliant seeds and growth patterns. But while the Aborigines modified the environment for their own ends, their belief that land, wildlife and people were an interdependent whole engendered a sympathy for the natural processes, and maintained a balance between population and natural resources. Tribes were organized and related according to complex kinship systems, reflected in the three hundred different **languages** known to exist at that time. Legends about the mythical **Dreamtime**, when creative forces shaped the landscape, provided verbal maps of tribal territory and linked natural features to the actions of these Dreamtime ancestors, who often had both human and animal forms. This spiritual and practical attachment to tribal areas was expedient in terms of use of resources, but was the weak point in maintaining a culture after white dispossession: separated from the lands they related to, legends lost their meaning – and the people their sense of identity.

The first Europeans

Prior to the sixteenth century, the only regular visitors to Australia were the **Malays**, who established seasonal camps while fishing the northern coasts for trepang, a sea slug, to sell to the Chinese. In Europe, the globe had been carved up between Spain and Portugal in 1494 under the auspices of Pope Alexander VI at the **Treaty of Tordesillas**, and all maritime nations subsequently kept their nautical charts secret to protect their discoveries. Therefore it's likely, but not certain, that the inquisitive **Portuguese** knew of **Terra Australis**, the Great Southern Land, soon after founding their colony in East Timor in 1516.

But while contemporary politics later confused the issue of "discovery", various nations were making forays into the area: the **Dutch** in 1605 and 1623, who were appalled by the harsh climate and inhabitants of Outback Queensland, and the **Spanish** in 1606, looking for plunder, and pagans to convert to Catholicism. Guided by the Portuguese **Luis Vaes de Torres**, they blithely navigated the strait between New Guinea and Cape York as if they knew it was there. Torres probably did; there's evidence that the Portuguese had **mapped** a large portion of Australia's northern coastline as early as 1536.

Later in the seventeenth century the Dutch navigators **Dirk Hartog**, **Van Diemen** and **Abel Tasman** added to maps of the east and northern coasts, but eventually discarded "New Holland" as a barren, worthless country. British interests were first stirred in 1697 by **William Dampier**, a buccaneer who wrote popular accounts of his visit to Western Australia, but it wasn't until the British captured the Spanish port of Manila in the Philippines in 1762 that detailed maps of Australia's coast fell into their hands; it took them only six more years to assemble an expedition to locate the continent. Sailing in 1768 on the *Endeavour*, Captain **James Cook** headed to Tahiti (where scientists observed the movements of the planet Venus), then proceeded to map New Zealand's coastline before sailing west in 1770 to search for the Great Southern Land – unsure whether this was New Holland or an as yet undiscovered landmass.

The British sighted the continent in April of 1770 and sailed north from Cape Everard to **Botany Bay**, where Cook commented on the Aborigines' initial indifference to seeing the *Endeavour*. When a party of forty sailors attempted to land, however, two Aborigines attacked them with spears and had to be driven off by musket fire. Continuing on up the Queensland coast, they passed Moreton Bay and Fraser Island before entering the treacherous passages of the Great Barrier Reef where, on June 11, the *Endeavour* ran aground off Cape Tribulation. Cook managed to beach the ship safely at the mouth of the Endeavour River (present-day Cooktown), where the expedition set up camp while the ship was repaired.

Contact between Aborigines and whites during the following six weeks was tinged with a mistrust that never quite erupted into a serious confrontation, and Cook took the opportunity to make notes in which he tempered romanticism for the "noble savage" with the sharp observation that European and Aboriginal values were mutually incomprehensible. The expedition was intrigued by some of the wildlife but otherwise unimpressed with the country, and were glad to sail onwards on August 5. With imposing skill, Cook successfully managed to navigate the rest of the reef, finally claiming Australia's eastern seaboard – which he named **New South Wales** – on August 21 in the name of King George III, at Possession Island in the Torres Strait, before sailing off to Timor.

Convicts

The expedition's reports still didn't arouse much enthusiasm in London, where echoes resounded of the Portuguese and Dutch opinions of the previous century. The outcome of the **American War of Independence** in 1783, however, saw Britain deprived of anywhere to transport convicted criminals; they were temporarily housed in prison ships or "hulks", moored around the country, while the government tried to solve the problem. Sir **Joseph Banks**, botanist on the *Endeavour*, advocated Botany Bay as an ideal location for a **penal colony** that could soon become self-sufficient. The government agreed (perhaps also inspired by the political advantages of gaining a foothold in the Pacific), and in 1787 the **First Fleet**, packed with over 700 convicts, set sail for Australia on eleven ships under the command of Captain **Arthur Phillip**. Reaching Botany Bay in January 1788, Phillip deemed it unsuitable for his purposes and instead founded the settlement at **Sydney Cove**, on Port Jackson's fine natural harbour.

Early years at Sydney were not promising: the colonists suffered erratic weather and starvation, Aboriginal hostility, soil which was too hard to plough and timber which was so tough it dented their axes. In 1790, supplies ran so low that a third of the population had to be transferred to a new colony on **Norfolk Island**, 1500 kilometres east. Even so, in the same year Britain dispatched a second fleet with 1000 convicts – 267 of whom died en route. To ease the situation, Phillip granted packages of farmland to marines and former convicts before he returned to Britain in 1792. The first **free settlers** arrived the following year, while war with France reduced the numbers of convicts being transported to the colony, allowing a period of consolidation.

Meanwhile, **John Macarthur** manipulated the temporary governor into allowing his **New South Wales Corps**, which had replaced the marines as the governor's strong arm, to exercise considerable power in the colony. This was temporarily curtailed in 1800 by **Philip King**, who slowed an illicit rum trade, encouraged new settlements, and speeded production by allowing convicts to work for wages. Macarthur was forced out of the corps into the wool industry, importing Australia's first **sheep** from South Africa; but he continued to stir up trouble, which culminated in the **Rum Rebellion** of 1808, when merchant and pastoral factions, supported by the military, ousted Governor **William Bligh** of "Mutiny on the Bounty" fame. Britain finally took notice of the colony's anarchic state and appointed the firm-handed Colonel **Lachlan Macquarie**, backed by the 73rd Regiment, as Bligh's replacement in 1810. Macquarie settled the various disputes – Macarthur had fled to Britain a year earlier – and brought the colony eleven years of disciplined progress.

Labelled the "Father of Australia" for his vision of a country that could rise above its convict origins, Macquarie implemented enlightened policies towards former convicts or **emancipists**, enrolling them in public offices. He also attempted to educate, rather than exterminate, Aboriginal people, and was the driving force behind New South Wales becoming a productive, self-sufficient colony. But he offended the landowner **squatters**, who were concerned that emancipists were being granted too many favours, and also those who regarded the colony's prime purpose as a place of punishment. In fact, conditions had improved so much that by 1819 New South Wales had become the major destination for voluntary emigrants from Britain.

In 1821 Macquarie was replaced as governor, and his successor, Sir Thomas Brisbane, was instructed to segregate, not integrate, convicts. To this end, New South Wales officially graduated from being a penal settlement to a new British Colony in 1823, and convicts were used to colonize newly explored regions – Western Australia, Tasmania and Queensland – as far away from Sydney's free settlers as possible.

Explorers

Matthew Flinders had already circumnavigated the mainland in 1803 (suggesting the name "**Australia**") in his leaky vessel, *Investigator*, and with the colony firmly established, expeditions began pushing inland from Sydney. In 1823 John Oxley, the Surveyor General, having previously explored newly discovered pastoral land west of the Blue Mountains, chose the **Brisbane River** (in Queensland) as the site of a new penal colony; this opened up the fertile Darling Downs to future settlement. Meanwhile, townships were being founded elsewhere around the coast, leading to the creation of **separate states** to add to that of Van Diemen's Land (Tasmania), settled in 1803 to ward off French exploration: Albany (1827) and Fremantle on the west coast (1829), the Yarra River (Melbourne, Victoria) in 1835, and Adelaide (South Australia) in 1836.

But it was the possibilities of the **interior** – which some maintained concealed a vast inland sea – that captured the imagination of the government and squatters. Setting out from Adelaide in 1844, **Charles Sturt** was the first to attempt to cross the centre. Forced to camp for six months at a desert waterhole, where the heat melted the lead in his pencils and unthreaded screws from equipment, he managed to reach the aptly named Sturt's Stony Desert before scurvy forced him back to Adelaide. At the same time, **Ludwig Leichhardt**, a Prussian doctor, had more luck in his crossing between the Darling Downs and Port Essington (near Darwin), which he accomplished in fourteen months. Unlike

Sturt, Leichhardt found plenty of potential farmland and returned a hero; however, he vanished in 1848 while again attempting to cross the continent. In the same year the ill-fated **Kennedy** expedition barely managed the trek from Tully to Cape York in northern Queensland, but with the loss of most of the party – Kennedy included – as a result of poor planning, starvation and attack by Aborigines. Similarly, **Burke and Wills**' successful 1860 south-to-north traverse between Melbourne and the Gulf of Carpentaria in Queensland was marred by the death of the expedition leaders (see box on p.568 for the full story of their trek). Finally, Australia's centre was located by **John MacDouall Stuart** in 1860, who subsequently managed a safe return journey from Adelaide to the north coast the following year. Hopes of finding an inland sea were quashed, and the harsh reality of a dry, largely infertile interior began to dawn on developers.

Aboriginal response

European advances had been repulsed from the very first year of the colony's foundation, when Governor Phillip sadly reported that "the natives now attack any straggler they meet unarmed". Forced off their traditional hunting grounds, which were taken by the settlers for agriculture or grazing, the Aborigines began stealing crops and spearing cattle. Response from the whites was brutal; a relatively liberal Lieutenant-Governor George Arthur ordered a sweep of Tasmania in 1830 to round up all Aboriginal people and herd them into **reserves**, a symbolic attempt to clear "the uncivilized" from the paths of progress (see box on p.1048). More direct action, such as the **Myall Creek Massacre** in 1838 (see box on p.323), when 28 Aborigines were roped together and butchered by graziers, created public outcry, but similar "**dispersals**" became commonplace wherever indigenous people resisted white intrusion. More insidious methods, such as poisoning waterholes or lacing gifts of flour with arsenic, were also employed by pastoralists angered over stock losses.

Aboriginal peoples were not a single, unified society, and Europeans exploited existing divisions by creating the notorious **Native Mounted Police**, an Aboriginal force that aided and abetted the extermination of rival groups. By the 1890s, citing a perversion of Darwinian theory which held that Aboriginal people were less evolved than whites and so doomed to extinction, most states had followed Tasmania's example of "**protectionism**", relocating survivors into reserves which were frequently far from traditional lands: in Queensland, for instance, Rockhampton Aborigines were moved to Fraser Island, 500km away.

Gold

The discovery of **gold** in 1851 by Edward Hargraves, fresh from the Californian fields, had a dramatic bearing on Australia's future. The first major strikes in New South Wales and Victoria saw an immediate rush of hopeful miners from Sydney and Melbourne and, once the news spread overseas, from the USA and Britain. The British government, realizing the absurdity of spending taxes on shipping criminals to a land of gold when there were plenty of people willing to pay for their passage, finally **ended transportation** in 1853. Gold also opened up Australia's interior far more thoroughly than explorers had done; as returns petered out in one area, prospectors moved on into uncharted regions to find more. Western Australia and Queensland (which was saved from bankruptcy by gold in 1867) experienced booms up until 1900 and, while mining initially followed in the path of pastoral expansion, rushes began to attract settlements and markets into previously uncultivated regions.

A new "level society", based on a work-and-mateship ethic, evolved on the goldfields, where education had little bearing on an ability to endure hard work and spartan living conditions. Yet the **diggers** were all too aware of their poor social and political rights in other arenas. At the end of 1854, frustrations over mining licences erupted at **Eureka** (see box on p.992), near Ballarat in Victoria, where workers built a stockade and ended up being charged by mounted police. In the aftermath, rights, including the vote, were granted to miners. The Victorian goldfields also saw **racial tensions** directed against a new minority – the Chinese – who first arrived there during the 1850s. Disheartened by diminishing returns and infuriated by the Chinese ability to find gold in abandoned claims, diggers stormed a Chinese camp at **Lambing Flat** in 1861. Troops had to be sent in to stop the riots, but the ringleaders were acquitted by an all-white jury. Throughout the country, goldfields became centres of **nationalism** (despite the fact that the Chinese improved life by running stores and market gardens in mining towns), peaking in Queensland in the 1880s where the flames were fanned by the importation of **Solomon Islanders** to work on sugar plantations. Ostensibly to prevent slavery, but politically driven by recession and growing white unemployment, the government forced the repatriation of Islanders, taxed the Chinese out of the country, and passed the 1901 Immigration Act – also known as the **White Australia policy** – greatly restricting non-European immigration.

Federation and war

Central government was first mooted in 1842, but new states were not keen to return to being controlled by New South Wales, lose interstate customs duties, or share the new-found mineral wealth which had consolidated separation in the first place. But by the end of the century they began to see advantages to **federation**, not least as a way to control indentured labour and present a united front against French, German and Russian expansion in the Pacific. A decade of wrangling by the states, to ensure equal representation irrespective of population, saw the formation of a High Court and a two-tier parliamentary system consisting of a House of Representatives and Senate, presided over by a Prime Minister. Each state would have its own premier, and Britain would be represented by a Governor-General. Approved by Queen Victoria shortly before her death, the **Commonwealth of Australia** came into being on January 1, 1901.

It's notable that the Immigration Act (see above) was the first piece of legislation to be passed by the new parliament, and reflected the nationalist drive behind federation. Though the intent was to create an Australia largely of European – and preferably British – descent, the policy also sowed the seeds for Australian independence from the "Mother Country". The first pull away came as early as 1912, when the **Commonwealth Bank** opened; Australia was trying to become less financially reliant on Britain. A negative aspect of the White Australia policy was that Aboriginal people were not included in the national census, or even allowed to vote until 1967. On the progressive side, the new government gave **women** the vote in 1902, and the Australian Labor Party, which had grown out of the Depression and union battles with the government during the 1890s, established the concept of a **minimum wage** in 1907.

Defence had also been a moving force behind federation. But, even forewarned by the war between Japan and Russia in 1904, Australia was largely unprepared for the outbreak of hostilities in Europe a decade later, owning little more than a navy made up from secondhand British ships. Promising to support Britain to "the last man and the last shilling", there was a patriotic rush to enlist in the army, and an opportunistic occupation of German New Guinea by Australian forces.

Surprisingly, the issue of compulsory conscription raised by Prime Minister **Billy Hughes** was twice defeated in referendums during World War I.

From the Australian perspective, the most important stage of the war occurred when Turkey sided with Germany in 1915. **Winston Churchill** formulated a plan to defend British shipping in the Dardanelles by occupying the **Gallipoli Peninsula**, and diverted Australian infantry bound for Europe. Between April and December 1915, wave after wave of Australian troops were mown down below Turkish gun emplacements as they attempted to take control of the peninsula. By the end of the year it became clear that Gallipoli was not going to fall, and the survivors were "evacuated" to fight on the Western Front. The long-term effect of the slaughter was the first serious questioning of Anglo-Australian relations: should Australia have committed and sacrificed so much to help a distant country further its European policies? Conversely, Gallipoli, as Australia's debut on the world stage, still remains a symbol of national identity and pride.

1918–39

After World War I, the Nationalist Party joined forces with the **Country Party** to assume government under the paternalistic and fiercely antisocialist guidance of **Earle Page** and **Stanley Bruce**. The Country Party was formed due to the widening divisions between a growing urban population and farmers, who felt isolated and unrepresented politically. Under the coalition, pastoral industries were subsidized by overseas borrowing, allowing them to compete internationally, and technology began to close the gap between the city and the Outback: radio and aviation developments saw the birth of **Qantas** – the Queensland and Northern Territory Aerial Service – and the **Royal Flying Doctor Service** in Queensland's remote west. In the cities, work started on the Sydney Harbour Bridge, and the new Commonwealth capital, **Canberra**, was completed.

On the social front, the USA stopped mass immigration in 1921, deflecting a flood of people from depressed **Southern Europe** to Australia – which the government countered by encouraging British immigrants with assisted passages. While progressive in some areas – for example, proposing a dole for the unemployed, sick, pensioners and mothers – the government overreacted to opposition, as exemplified by the **seamen and dockers' strike** of 1928. Citing the arch-villain "communism" as behind the dispute, they attempted to stretch the scope of the Immigration Act to allow action to be taken against disturbances that were politically motivated. However, the implications that the law could be altered against anyone who disagreed with the government contributed to the downfall of Bruce and Page the following year. The themes of their rule – differences between rural and urban societies, questions of Australian identity, union disputes, and the effects of heavy borrowing to create artificially high living standards, unsupported by Australia's actual capabilities – are still current issues.

As the **Great Depression** set in during the early 1930s, Australia faced collapsing economic and political systems, with all the parties divided; pressed for a loan, the Bank of England forced a restructuring of the Australian economy. Adding to national embarrassment, politics and sports became blurred during the 1932 "**Bodyline**" cricket series: the loan was virtually made conditional on Australian cricket authorities dropping their allegations that British bowlers were deliberately trying to injure Australian batsmen during the tour.

Meanwhile, worries about communism were succeeded by the rise of fascism, as Mussolini and Hitler took power in Europe and Japanese forces invaded Manchuria – the **Tanaka memorial** in 1927 actually cited Australia as one of Japan's future conquests. Although displaying a certain ambivalence to fascism, Australia assisted the immigration of refugees from central Europe, and after a prolonged union battle, halted iron exports to Japan. When Prime Minister Joseph Lyons died in office, **Robert Menzies**, a firm supporter of British notions of civilization, was elected to the post in time to side with Britain as hostilities were declared against Hitler in September 1939.

World War II and after

As happened in World War I, Australia developed its identity in World War II through participation in global affairs, but this time without Britain's help. Menzies' United Australia Party barely lasted long enough to form diplomatic ties with the USA – in case Germany overran Europe – before internal divisions saw the government crumble, replaced by **John Curtin** and his Labor Party in 1941.

Curtin, concerned about Australia's vulnerability after the Japanese attack on Pearl Harbor, made the radical decision of shifting the country's commitment in the war from defending Britain and Europe to fighting off an invasion of Australia from Asia. After the **fall of Singapore** in 1942 and the capture of twenty thousand Australian troops, Curtin succeeded in ordering the immediate recall of Australians fighting in the Middle East, despite opposition from Churchill, who wanted them for the Burma campaign. In February the Japanese unexpectedly bombed Darwin, launched submarine raids against Sydney and Newcastle, and invaded New Guinea. Feeling abandoned by Britain, Curtin appealed to the USA, who quickly adopted Australia as a base for co-ordinating Pacific operations under General **Douglas MacArthur**. Meanwhile, Australian troops in New Guinea halted Japanese advances along the **Kokoda trail** at Milne Bay, while the Australian and US navies slowed down the Japanese fleet in the **Battle of the Coral Sea** – which, thanks to modern cannon, was notable as the first naval engagement in which the two sides never even saw each other.

Australia came out of World War II realizing that – politically as well as geographically – the country was closer to Asia than Europe, that it could not count on Britain to help in a crisis (Churchill had been ready to sacrifice Australian territory to protect British interests elsewhere), and that it was able to form political alliances independently of the mother country. From this point on, Australia began to look to the USA and the Pacific, as well as Britain, for direction. Another consequence of the war was that immigration was speeded up, fuelled by Australia's recent vulnerability. Under the slogan "Populate or Perish", the government reintroduced assisted passages from Britain – the "ten-pound-poms" – also accepting substantial numbers of European refugees; even Torres Strait Islanders, previously banned from settling on the mainland, were allowed to move onto Cape York in northern Queensland.

With international right-wing extremism laid low by the war, the old bogey of **communism** returned. When North Korea, backed by the Chinese, invaded the south in 1950, Australia, led by a revitalized Menzies and his new Liberal Party, was the first country after the USA to commit troops to counter communist forces. Menzies also sent soldiers and pilots to Malaysia, where communist rebels had been fighting the British colonial administration almost since the end of World War II, under the anti-communist SEATO (Southeast Asia Treaty Organization) banner. At home, he opened up central Australia to British **atomic bomb tests** in the 1950s, because – echoing the beliefs of the first European colonists – "nobody lived there". A number of Aborigines were moved off to reserves; others – along with British troops involved in the tests – suffered the effects of fallout and had their traditional lands rendered uninhabitable for the foreseeable future. Wrangles with the British government over compensation and the clearing of the test sites at **Maralinga** and **Emu Junction** were finally settled in 1993.

Menzies was still in control when the USA became involved in **Vietnam**, and with conflict in Malaysia all but over, Australia volunteered "advisers" to Vietnamese republican forces in 1962. Once fighting became entrenched, the government introduced conscription and, bowing to the wishes of the American president **Lyndon B. Johnson**, sent a battalion of soldiers into the fray in 1965, events that immediately split the country. Menzies quit politics the following year, succeeded by his protégé **Harold Holt**, who, rallying under the catchphrase "All the way with LBJ", willingly increased Australia's participation in the Vietnamese conflict. But as the war dragged on, world opinion shifted to seeing the matter as a civil struggle rather than as a fight between western and communist ideologies, and in 1970 the government began scaling down its involvement. In the meantime, Aboriginal people were finally granted **civil rights** in 1967, and Holt mysteriously disappeared while swimming in the sea off the coast of Victoria, leaving the Liberals in turmoil and paving the way for a Labor win under **Gough Whitlam** in 1972.

Whitlam's three years in office had far-reaching effects: he ended national service and participation in Vietnam, granted independence to **Papua New Guinea**, and instituted free health care and higher education systems. In doing so, however, he alienated the mostly conservative Senate, and when the government attempted to finance mining interests with an illicit overseas loan in 1975, the opposition prevented the Senate from functioning. In an unprecedented move, the Governor-General **John Kerr** (until then, a largely decorative representative of the Crown overseeing Australian affairs) dismissed the government – a move that shocked many into questioning the validity of Britain's ultimate hold on Australia – and called an election, which Labor lost. By contrast, the following eight years were uneventful, culminating in the return of Labor in 1983 under the charismatic Bob Hawke, a former trade union leader. Labor's subsequent thirteen years and record four terms in office, which produced surprisingly little lasting legislation, were suddenly brought to a close by the arrogant antics of Hawke's successor and former treasurer, **Paul Keating**. He was already widely unpopular for his scornful rhetoric and general lack of concern for the country's woes – particularly the effects of a massive foreign debt and crippling drought in eastern Australia – when news of a secret military agreement with Indonesia created a public backlash, resulting in a landslide victory for the **Liberal–National coalition**, led by **John Howard**, in 1996.

Current events

Formerly considered an ineffectual character, Howard has shown consummate – though often unpopular – political skills. One of his first actions was to cut government costs by announcing a reduction of the civil service, replacing the redundant departments with private enterprise. His stand against automatic firearms in the wake of the Port Arthur Massacre in 1996 (see p.1080) also reduced his feeble image, after he pushed through his legislation despite stiff opposition from gun lobbies and several state premiers. Indeed, Howard's political position was so secure by 1998 that the coalition managed to be **re-elected** on what some considered a suicidal platform of **tax reform** through the implementation of a **GST**, or Goods and Service Tax. Since its introduction in 2000, however, Howard's political position has begun to look increasingly shaky: a GST-inspired rise in fuel costs has driven many farmers – traditional National Party supporters – to bankruptcy; businesses are also reeling under the effects of the tax; while consumers are having to pay more for what they buy. Not surprisingly, the Liberal-National coalition was soundly trounced in state elections in Western Australia and Queensland in 2001, leading to uncharacteristic back-pedalling from Howard on a range of issues as a Federal election looms.

Overseas, Australia is becoming more dedicated to its role as part of Asia, rather than Europe or the United States. Although it was the first country to back the USA during the 1992 Gulf War, continual bickering over trade agreements with the USA has since seen a cooling in relations. An Asian bias makes good economic sense, but has led to an often appallingly conciliatory attitude; as early as 1975 Australia didn't protest against the annexation of East Timor by Indonesia (though Australia was quick to offer help when Indonesia finally withdrew from the country in 1999), and the response to regional human rights abuses has been pitifully weak. Nor, with its European heritage, is Australia accepted as "Asian" by other nations in the area, and Malaysia seems to harbour particular antipathy towards it, as shown by its continual vetoing of Australia's attempts to join ASEAN, the regional trading bloc. The rough-hewn right-wing outbursts by former chip-shop owner **Pauline Hanson** and the rise of her **One Nation** party, which has capitalized on widespread dissatisfaction with the major political groups, have likewise done nothing to enhance Australian credibility overseas. In addition, Australia's **currency** is in a downward spiral, as its export strength in primary production has been undermined by the recent collapse of Southeast Asian economies, especially Japan's.

There have been some advances, though, under both Labor and the coalition, in the field of **Aboriginal rights**. An ineffective inquiry into Aboriginal deaths in custody was overshadowed in June 1992 when the High Court handed down the landmark **Mabo Decision**, legally overturning the concept of terra nullius. The Mabo claim, set around Murray Island (Mer) in the Torres Strait, acknowledged the Merriam as traditional landowners and sparked furious debate as to interpretation. Nor was there any less of a reaction when Mabo itself was forced into the background in December 1996 by the **Wik Decision**, which stated that native title and pastoral leases could coexist over the same area. In an effort to test the implications of these rulings, Aboriginal groups across the country have since laid claim to everything from Brisbane city centre to cattle properties and Outback national parks, creating panic amongst developers, farmers and state governments, and something of a public backlash against Aborigines – providing further fuel for One Nation and contributing to Australia's racist image.

While Mabo and Wik are gradually beginning to have an effect – such as in the handing back of the **Silver Plains** property on Queensland's Cape York to its traditional owners in 2000 – few similar land claims are likely to succeed. A **Native Title Tribunal** has been set up to consider each case, but, given former resettlement policies, claimants have an uphill struggle as they need to prove constant association with the land in question since white occupation. Nonetheless, a growing perception that Aboriginal people will eventually be re-enfranchised has seen mining companies and farmers ignoring the political and legal wrangles by making private land-use agreements with local communities. In this sense, Mabo and Wik have finally confirmed that Aboriginal people have land rights, even if it takes years formally to establish exactly what these are.

Australia's indigenous peoples

White Australians and the international community have grouped Australia's indigenous peoples under the term Aborigines since the British invaded in 1788. At the recent insistence of these indigenous groups, Australians are coming to recognize many separate surviving indigenous cultures and lament the loss of others by deliberate or accidental genocide since invasion. Today these surviving cultures include highly urbanized Koorie communities in Sydney and Melbourne, semi-nomadic groups such as the Pitjantjatjaras and Warlpiris living a relatively traditional lifestyle in the central and western deserts, and the seafaring Merriam and Tiwi peoples of the small islands north of the mainland. If there is any thread linking these groups, it is the cultural revival experienced over the last twenty years. Under the banner of national political movements, all of these groups have renewed their commitment to organizing their social world according to extensive kin networks, to re-establishing close religious and legal relationships to the land, and to maintaining and revitalizing their cultures and languages.

Colonization

To understand the magnitude of the progress towards revival made in Australia, it is necessary to understand how dreadful the impact of colonization has been. The estimated 750,000 indigenous inhabitants of Australia in 1788 were unilaterally dispossessed of their lands and livelihoods by the British colonists who failed to recognize them as inhabitants and owners. Australia was annexed to the British Empire on the basis that it was terra nullius, or uninhabited wasteland. This legal fiction persisted until the High Court judged in the 1992 **Mabo** case that native title to land still existed in Australia unless it had been extinguished by statute or by some use of the land that was inconsistent with the continuation of native use and ownership. The **Wik Decision** of 1996 went a step further, acknowledging that native title continues to exist on pastoral leases, though with the proviso that "pastoral interest will prevail over native title rights, wherever the two conflict". (For more on the Mabo and Wik decisions, see "A History", opposite.)

Upon deciding that the country was unoccupied, successive waves of new settlers hastened to make it so. Violent conflicts between indigenous and recently arrived Australians resulted in the decimation of Aboriginal groups. The most widely-known of these conflicts was the **unofficial war** waged against Tasmania's Aboriginal peoples, which resulted in the near-destruction of indigenous Tasmanians (see also box on p.1048). Grisly souvenirs of this war, including skeletons and preserved body parts, still shame the collections of museums throughout the world. Historians estimate that twenty thousand Aborigines may have died in these mostly unrecorded battles. Measuring the impact of colonization on the indigenous population has been hampered by a lack of information about conditions prior to colonization, as well as the failure of successive governments to record indigenous people as part of the population until quite recently.

Disease has also been a powerful, if unintentional, weapon in the war against indigenous Australians, and has proved more effective than shooting or poisoning. Australia's geographical isolation ensured that there were very few communicable diseases on the continent prior to the arrival of Europeans, and successive generations of indigenous Australians had developed resistance to these. The arrival of colonists and their diseases posed an almost insurmountable immunological challenge. Whole populations were wiped out by smallpox and malaria epidemics, and the diaries of officers of the First Fleet record the rapid destruction from smallpox of the Aboriginal camps in the Sydney hinterland within four years of the establishment of the colony of New South Wales. Those who didn't die fled the area, unwittingly infecting neighbouring groups as they went. When Governor Hunter made the first exploratory expedition to western New South Wales in the 1820s, he recorded evidence of prior smallpox epidemics among Aboriginal groups who had not previously come into contact with European settlers. As recently as the 1950s desert peoples were severely affected by outbreaks of influenza and measles. The lack of immunity to these introduced diseases was exacerbated by the trauma of dispossession, the lack of availability of traditional food and water supplies, and the unhygienic results of being required to wear European-style clothing.

The **interruption of traditional food and water supplies** became progressively worse through the nineteenth and twentieth centuries as the pastoral industry expanded in rural Australia, and vast areas were stripped of vegetation to provide for grazing land. Grazing animals competed with local animals for food, fouled established water sources, and their hard hooves damaged the integrity of surface soil, contributing to substantial erosion and salinity problems. Other European animals, originally introduced to make the countryside seem more like "home", rapidly multiplied and have now become ubiquitous throughout Australia. Cats and foxes, both vicious predators, have been blamed for the near extinction of small to medium-size mammal species throughout arid Australia. Rabbit populations have expanded to fill the niche the mammals vacated, and their destructive grazing habits have contributed to the increasing desertification of Australia's arid rangelands. Aboriginal tribespeople in Central Australia have witnessed this ecological disaster within the last sixty years, and have lamented the loss of many animal species that sustained them in the past.

Australia's Aboriginal peoples have also been subjected to various forms of **incarceration**, ranging from prisons to apartheid-style reserves. Much of this systematic incarceration was instigated between 1890 and 1950 as an official policy of **protection**, in response to the devastating impact of colonization. Missionaries and other well-meaning people believed that Aborigines were a dying race, and that it was a Christian duty to "soothe the dying". Parliamentary records of the time reveal a harsher mentality. Aborigines were often viewed as a weak and degenerate people, little better than animals, who exposed white settlers to physical and moral disease. To "protect" the Aborigines and settlers from each other, various state governments enacted legislation for the protection of Aborigines, appointed official **Protectors of Aborigines**, established reserves in rural areas and removed Aboriginal people to them. In some parts of Australia these reserves were established on traditional lands, allowing people to continue to live relatively undisturbed. In other parts of the country, notably Queensland, people were forcibly removed from their home areas and relocated in reserves throughout the state. Families were brutally broken up and the ties with the land and religion shattered. The so-called protectors had virtual life and death powers over those they allegedly protected. In Queensland, for example, Aboriginal people required permits to marry and to move from one reserve to another. They were forced into indentured labour, and their wages collected and banked on their behalf by the State government. If they fell ill with a notifiable disease, they could be arbitrarily removed from home and family to a lock hospital, including the notorious Fantome Island, off the coast from Townsville. This treatment persisted in some areas until the late 1960s. Aboriginal people are still ridiculously over-represented in Australia's prison population, a situation which led to a **Royal Commission into Aboriginal Deaths in Custody**, which reported to the Federal Parliament in 1991. It called for wide-ranging changes in police and judicial practice, and substantial changes to social programmes aimed at improving the lot of Aboriginal peoples in the areas of justice, health, education, economics and empowerment. Although there has been considerable government lip-service to the recommendations of the Royal Commission, this has not resulted in any substantial change to incarceration rates.

Also since the 1920s, Aboriginal children had been legally removed from their black mothers and given into the care of state institutions and white foster parents as part of a policy of **assimilation**. The practice began in Victoria in 1886 and continued until remarkably recently (1969). This period of "taking the children away" still haunts the lives of many Aboriginal Australians who have lost contact with their natal families and their culture. The policy was the subject of a major government inquiry in 1997, bringing the issue to wider attention for the first time. The trauma suffered by the people now known as the **Stolen Generation** has received considerable media attention since the release of the report of the inquiry, and led to calls for a national **apology** to Aboriginal people. Prime Minister John Howard has consistently refused to acknowledge that the Australian people have anything for which to apologize, but his government has made funding available for link-up and counselling services for those who were affected. He has been publicly criticized for his stance by a number of influential Australians, and many people have expressed their personal regrets to the Aboriginal community. The Lord Mayor of Brisbane, Jim Soorley, won national praise when he led a **National Sorry Day** by formally apologizing to Aborigines on behalf of the people of Brisbane in 1998. Many ordinary Australians have joined the popular movement to apologize by buying brightly coloured plastic hands to "plant" in public events known as the **Sea of Hands**, where thousands of the hands are temporarily installed in parks in most State Capitals. The events are seen as a way of expressing personal sorrow to Aboriginal people, as well as castigating the Federal Government for their lack of offical response.

The result of two centuries of brutal mistreatment is that, by almost every statistical indicator, the Aboriginal population is highly **disadvantaged** in both absolute terms and compared to non-Aboriginal groups.

Revitalization

The **revitalization** of Aboriginal peoples effectively began in 1967, when a constitutional referendum recognized indigenous Australians as voting citizens, and gave the federal government the power to legislate for Aboriginal people. Prior to this referendum, Aboriginal people had the status of wards of each of the States – the Letters Patent, documents which established the States, often referred to them, amongst the flora and fauna, as things to be protected and preserved. The referendum ushered in a new era of **self-determination** for Aboriginal people, evidenced by the establishment of the first Ministry for Aboriginal Affairs in the Whitlam Labor Government of 1972–75. After more than a hundred years of agitation, **land rights** were accorded to Aboriginal groups in the Northern Territory in 1976 under federal legislation. Since then, other states have legislated to vest title over various pieces of state-owned land to their traditional Aboriginal owners. All the mainland states and territories have now made provisions for Aboriginal land rights. Various representative bodies were set up by successive federal governments throughout the 1970s and 1980s, culminating in the **Aboriginal and Torres Strait Islanders Commission** (ATSIC), established in 1990. This statutory authority gives elected Aboriginal representatives effective control over many of the federal funding programmes directed at Aboriginal organizations and communities. Since the late 1980s, substantial funds have been directed towards training for employment.

Along with ownership of land and control over funding have come opportunities for economic self-sufficiency and expansion previously unavailable to Aboriginal groups. In many parts of the country, this has allowed Aborigines to buy the cattle stations on which they worked without wages for many years. In central Australia, Aboriginal enterprises include TV and radio stations, transport companies, small airlines, publishing companies, tourist businesses and joint-venture mining operations.

Co-operative agreements with the Australian Nature Conservation Agency have led to Aboriginal ownership and joint management of two of Australia's most important conservation reserves, **Uluru–Kata Tjuta** and **Kakadu** national parks in the Northern Territory. These arrangements recognize that Aboriginal owners retain an enormous understanding about the ecology of their traditional lands that can be of great assistance in the development of land-management plans. The Uluru Fauna Survey, a joint scientific survey between Pitjantjatjara and Yankunytjatjara landowners and the scientific research authority, CSIRO, represents a landmark in the application of indigenous knowledge to solving conservation problems. In the wake of the Mabo Decision, other state and territory governments are looking at the Uluru model of co-operative park management as a way of accommodating Aboriginal land interests, while providing for more effective conservation strategies.

Citizenship and its problems

Despite these successes, Australia's indigenous peoples are still struggling against considerable disadvantages. Along with citizenship in 1967 came the right to purchase and consume **alcohol**, which has proved disastrous. Alcohol is heavily implicated in the destructive downward spiral often observed by visitors to Outback towns in Australia (and some inner cities). The negative repercussions are evident in sickness and death, violence and despair, exclusion from education and meaningful employment, as well as families and communities in disarray. The vast overrepresentation of Aboriginal people in the criminal justice system is directly attributable to the mediation of alcohol: large numbers of Aboriginal people are apprehended by police and held in police cells owing to drunkenness, even where public drunkenness is no longer a criminal offence.

Until recent years, government response to Aboriginal drinking has typically been racist. Statutes such as the notorious **two-kilometre law** in Alice Springs, which made it an offence to consume alcohol in a public place within 2km of licensed premises, were directed specifically at getting Aboriginal drinkers out of sight of visitors to the town centre. In recent times, most governments have begun moving away from racist and draconian measures and towards providing Aboriginal communities and families with the legislative supports to limit drinking within their towns and homes, and have invested money in sobering-up shelters and alcohol **rehabilitation** programmes.

On the **positive** side, many families and communities are confronting the problems that alcohol is causing. This is possible because although some Aboriginal people equate drinking rights with racial equality, most have a negative view of alcohol abuse. A large proportion of Aborigines, particularly women, abstain altogether. Furthermore, Aboriginal people themselves are beginning to put pressure on problem drinkers to limit their drinking, and are now able to implement new laws to reduce the damage that alcohol is doing to their families and communities.

A **case study** illustrates these efforts. Imanpa is a small Pitjantjatjara community between Alice Springs and the tourist mecca, Uluru (Ayers Rock). Seeing their community racked by alcohol-related violence and death, Imanpa residents looked at ways to limit availability of alcohol to residents. With neighbouring communities, they successfully lobbied the Northern Territory Liquor Commission to limit the amount of takeaway alcohol that could be purchased at highway roadhouses to six cans of beer. They reached co-operative agreements with the licensees of these roadhouses that they would not serve takeaway alcohol to anybody travelling to, or living on, Aboriginal communities. Imanpa drinkers can still travel the three hundred kilometres to Alice Springs to purchase alcohol, and the community is looking at the possibility of pressuring government to reduce the number of takeaway outlets in Alice Springs: with approximately seventy outlets for a population of twenty thousand, Alice Springs has the highest per capita availability of alcohol in the world. The people of Imanpa are also supporting the efforts of their neighbours in the Mutitjulu community near Ayers Rock Resort. At the resort, habitual drinkers persist in persuading well-meaning tourists to buy alcohol on their behalf. The community is working with the resort to try to educate the tourists out of being tricked or intimidated in this way, and to stress the benefits of limited alcohol supply for the community's future.

Poor health continues to reduce substantially the life expectancy of Aborigines. In 1989 the first comprehensive National Aboriginal Health Strategy was put in place. More effective and widespread health education, more access to better-quality housing, greater health services specifically aimed at Aborigines and better immunization programmes are all parts of the strategy. As with most areas of social service, health services for Aboriginal peoples have been the province of white professionals until very recently; an essential focus of the new strategy is to empower Aboriginal people by giving resources to them directly.

The future

Improvements in health and education have led to a **revival of interest** in their own culture for many Aboriginal people. **Languages** that have fallen into disuse are being relearned. **Ceremonies** and **art forms** that have been forgotten are being revived through research and reconstruction. Links with land and family that have been torn apart are being reforged. The benefits of this revitalization flow on to visitors to Aboriginal Australia. **Aboriginal tour companies** are introducing visitors to the ancient law, cultural history and culinary possibilities of the land. Aboriginal dance theatres are staging new productions of great originality and imagination, and are reinterpreting ancient **dance** forms for modern audiences. Aboriginal **authors and poets** are publishing major new works that present unique and indigenous viewpoints. Aboriginal **painters and sculptors**, using a mix of traditional and modern techniques and forms, are producing vivid and exciting works of art. Aboriginal

national parks are introducing visitors to an ancient and alternative view of the natural landscape. There has never been a time when these most ancient of cultures have been more accessible to visitors.

Despite this, Aboriginal people remain at a considerable **disadvantage**, exacerbated by the halving of the Aboriginal welfare budget by the incumbent Liberal government in 1996, and the uncertainty caused by the **Mabo and Wik decisions** which potentially put over three-quarters of the country (including virtually all of Western Australia) under land claim. In early 1999 the Australian government was censured twice about its Aboriginal policies by key international bodies. The World Heritage Committee of UNESCO threatened to place Kakadu National Park on the World Heritage Under Threat list if the government proceeds with plans to open a second uranium mine within the park against the wishes of the traditional owners of the land. The government's Wik legislation, which attempts to effectively extinguish Native Title on pastoral leases, received sharp criticism from the United Nations Committee on Elimination of Racial Discrimination, which judge that the provisions of the legislation are inconsistent with the International Convention to which Australia is a signatory. The continuing adversarial stance of the current government ensures that Aboriginal protests continue. The high-profile performance of champion runner **Kathy Freeman**, both on the track and at the opening ceremony, brought Aboriginal issues to the fore at the **2000 Sydney Olympics**, but there was a sad irony – or bare-faced cynicism – in marketing the colourful side of Aboriginal culture to the world through the Olympics, when most Aboriginal people continue to live in desperate poverty with their fundamental legal rights under attack.

Wildlife

Despite forty thousand years of human pressure and manipulation, accelerated in the last two centuries by the effects of introduced species, Australia's ecology and wildlife remain among the most distinctive on earth. Nonetheless, it's also some of the most endangered: in the last two hundred years, more native mammals have become extinct here than on any other continent, and land clearing – particularly in Queensland – kills an estimated 7.5 million birds a year, bringing several species to the edge of extinction.

Australians love to tell stories about the **dangers** that the bush holds for the inexperienced (see the "Health" section of Basics, p.31, for general advice on coping with hazardous wildlife). In reality, fearsome "drop bears" lurking in gums, fallen tree trunks that turn out to be giant snakes, bloodthirsty wild pigs and other rampaging terrors are mostly confined to hotel bars, the product of suburban paranoia laced with a surprising naivety about the Great Outdoors. Apart from a couple of avoidable exceptions, there's little to fear from Australia's wildlife, and if you spend any time in the bush at any stage you'll undoubtedly end up far better informed than the yarn-spinners.

Marsupials and monotremes

In the years after the demise of the dinosaurs, Australia split away from the rest of the world, and the animals here evolved along different lines to anywhere else: as placental mammals gained the ascendency in South America, Africa, Europe and Asia, it was the **marsupials** and **monotremes** – pouched and egg-laying mammals – which took over in Australia, alongside the megafauna (see box, below).

Marsupials and monotremes may not be exclusive to Australia (they're also found in New Guinea and South America), but it's here that they reached their greatest diversity and numbers. **Marsupials** are mammals that give birth to a partially formed embryo which itself then develops in a **pouch** on the mother; this allows a higher breeding rate in good years. Easiest to find because they actively seek out people, **ringtail** and **brushtail possums** are common in

Australia in the past

Australia has a **fossil record** which makes up in range what it lacks in quantity. Imprints of invertebrates from South Australia's **Ediacaran fauna**, dated to over 600 million years, are the oldest evidence of animal life in the world. On a larger scale, footprints and remains of several **dinosaur** species have been uncovered, and **opalized marine fossils** are unique to the country. Perhaps most intriguing is evidence of the **megafauna** – giant wildlife which included the twenty-metre-long constricting snake montypythonides, flightless birds bigger than an ostrich, a rhino-sized wombat, carnivorous kangaroos, and thylacaleo, a marsupial lion – which flourished until about thirty thousand years ago, overlapping with Aboriginal occupation. Climatic changes were probably responsible for their demise, but humans definitely wiped out the **thylacine**, a dog-like marsupial with an oversized head, which vanished from the mainland after the introduction of dingoes but survived in Tasmania until 1936 – the year it received government protection.

suburbs and campsites, often hard to avoid if they think there's a chance of getting some food. With a little persistence, you should encounter one of the several species of related **glider possums** on the edges of forests at dusk. **Kangaroos** and **wallabies** are the Australian answer to deer and antelopes, and range from tiny, solitary rainforest species to the gregarious two-metre-tall red kangaroo of the central plains – watching these creatures bouncing effortlessly across the landscape is an extraordinary sight. The arboreal, eucalyptus-chewing **koalas** and tubby, ground-dwelling **wombats** are smaller, less active and more sensitive to disturbance, and this has made them more elusive, and has placed them on the endangered list as their habitat is cleared. Carnivorous marsupials are mostly shrew-sized today (though a lion equivalent probably survived into Aboriginal times, and fossils of meat-eating kangaroos have been found); two of the largest are spotted native cats or **quolls**, and Tasmania's indigenous **Tasmanian devil**, a terrier-sized scavenger.

Platypuses and echidnas are the only **monotremes**, **egg-laying mammals** that suckle their young through specialized pores. Once considered a stage in the evolution of placental mammals, they're now recognized as a specialized branch of the family. Neither is particularly rare, but being nocturnal, shy and, in the case of the platypus, aquatic makes them difficult to find. Ant-eating **echidnas** resemble a long-nosed, thick-spined hedgehog or small porcupine, and are found countrywide; **platypuses** are confined to the eastern ranges and look like a blend of duck and otter, having a grey, rubbery bill, webbed feet, short fur, and a poison spur on males. This combination seemed too implausible to nineteenth-century biologists, who initially denounced stuffed specimens as a hoax assembled from pieces of other animals.

Introduced fauna

Of the **introduced mammals**, **dingoes** are descended from dogs, introduced to Australia by Aboriginal people in the last twelve thousand years. To keep them away from flocks, graziers built the world's longest fence, which stretched from South Australia into northwest Queensland and down again to New South Wales. **Camels** have also become acclimatized to Australia since their introduction in the 1840s, and thrive in the central deserts – Australia is the only place where dromedaries still occur in the wild, and they are regularly exported to the Middle East. The blight that **hoofed mammals** – horses, cows, sheep and goats – have perpetrated on Australia's fragile fauna is horrendous. Much of the country has been prematurely desertified by their eating habits, abrasive hooves and demand for water; once extracted from below ground, it is not replenished, which alters the mineral balance and kills remaining plant life. The damage caused by **rabbits** is equally all-pervasive, especially in the semi-desert areas where their cyclic population explosions can strip every shred of plant life from fragile dune systems. However, a recently engineered virus has massively reduced their numbers. Feral **cats**, which hunt for sport as well as necessity, are currently seen as the greatest threat to the indigenous fauna, primarily small marsupials and birds.

Reptiles, birds, bats and marine life

Reptiles come in all shapes and sizes. In the tropical parts of the country, the pale lizards you see wriggling across the ceiling on Velcro-like pads are **geckos**, and you'll find fatter, sluggish **skinks** – such as the stumpy blue-tongued lizard – everywhere. Other widespread species are **frill-necked lizards**, known for fanning out their necks and running on their hind legs when frightened; and the ubiquitous **goanna** family, which includes the monstrous perentie, third-largest lizard in the world. In central Australia, look out for the extraordinary **thorny devil** or moloch, an animal that seems part rock, part rosebush.

Crocodiles are confined to the tropics and come in two types. The shy, inoffensive **freshwater crocodile** grows to around 3m in length and feeds on fish and frogs. The larger, bulkier, and misleadingly named saltwater or **estuarine crocodile** can grow to 7m, ranges far inland (often in freshwater), and is the only Australian animal that constitutes an active threat to humans. Highly evolved predators, they should be given a very wide berth (see box on p.625 for specific precautions to take while in crocodile country). Despite their bad press, **snakes** are generally timid and pose far less of a problem, even though Australia has everything from constricting pythons through to three-quarters of the world's most venomous species.

With a climate that extends from temperate zones well into the tropics, Australia's **birdlife** is prolific and varied. Little **penguins** and **albatrosses** live along the south coast, while **riflebirds**, related to New Guinea's birds of paradise, and the **cassowary**, a colourful version of the ostrich, live in the tropical rainforests. The drabber **emu** prefers drier plains further west. Among the birds of prey, the countrywide **wedge-tail eagle** and the **white-breasted sea eagle** of the northern wetlands are most impressive in their size. Both share their environment with the stately grey **brolga**, an Australian crane, and the even larger **jabiru stork**, with its chisel beak and pied plumage. **Parrots**, arguably the country's most spectacular birds, come in over forty varieties, and no matter if they're flocks of green budgerigars, outrageously coloured rainbow lorikeets or white sulphur-crested cockatoos, they'll deafen you with their noisy song. Equally raucous are **kookaburras**, giant kingfishers found near permanent water. The quieter **tawny frogmouth**, an incredibly camouflaged cousin of the nightjar, has one of the most disgruntled expressions ever seen on a bird.

Huge colonies of **bats**, in orange, ghost and horseshoe varieties, congregate in caves or fill entire trees all over Australia. The **fruit bat**, or flying fox, is especially common in the tropics, where evenings can be spent watching colonies of the one-metre-winged monsters heading out from their daytime roosts on feeding expeditions.

In addition to what you'll see on the Barrier Reef (covered in the chapter on Tropical Queensland), **whales**, **turtles**, **dolphins**, **seals** and **dugongs** (sea cows) are part of the country's marine life, with humpbacked and southern right whales recently making a welcome return to the coasts after being hunted close to extinction.

Flora

Australia's most distinctive and widespread **trees** are those which developed a **dependence on fire**. Some, like the seemingly limitless varieties of **eucalypts** or gum trees, need extreme heat to burst open button-shaped pods and release their seeds, encouraging fires by annually shedding bark and leaves to deposit a thick layer of tinder on the forest floor. Other shrubs with similar habits are **banksias**, **grevillias** and **bottlebrushes** with their distinctive bushy flowers and spiky seed pods, while those prehistoric survivors, palm-like **cycads** and **grasstrees**, similarly depend on regular conflagrations to promote new growth. Aborigines possibly enhanced these fire-reliant traits by organizing controlled burn-offs.

Despite the country's extensive arid regions, there is no native equivalent to the cactus, although the dry, spiky **spinifex**, or porcupine grass, the succulent samphire with its curiously jointed stem, and the aptly named **saltbush**, come closest in their ability to survive extreme temperatures. After a rain, smaller desert plants rush to bloom and seed, covering the ground in a spectacular blanket of colour, a phenomenon for which Australia's Outback regions are well known.

On a larger scale, the Outback is dotted with stands of hardy **mulgas** and **wattles**, which superficially resemble scrawny eucalypts but have different leaf structures, as well as scattered groups of bloated, spindly-branched **bottle trees**, whose sweet, pulpy, moisture-laden cores can be used as emergency stock feed in drought conditions. The similar but far larger **boab**, found in the Kimberley and northeastern Northern Territory, is thought to be an invader from East Africa. **Mallee scrub** is unique to the southeastern Outback, where clearing of these tangled, bush-sized eucalypts for grazing has endangered both scrub and those animals who rely on it – the mound-building **mallee fowl** being the best known.

Mangrove swamps, found along the tropical and subtropical coasts, are tidal zones of thick grey mud and mangrove trees, whose interlocked, aerial roots make an effective barrier to exploration. They've suffered extensive clearing for development, and it wasn't until recently that their importance to the estuarine life-cycle won them limited government protection – though Aboriginal people have always found them a rich source of animal and plant products.

Rainforest once covered much of the continent, although today it survives in only a small portion of its former abundance. Nevertheless, you'll find pockets everywhere, from Tasmania's richly verdant wilderness to the monsoonal examples of northern Queensland and the Top End in the Northern Territory. Trees grow to gigantic heights, as they compete with each other for light, supporting themselves in the poor soil with aerial or buttressed roots. The extraordinary **banyan** and **Moreton Bay fig** trees are fine examples of the two types. They support a superabundance of plant species, with tangled **vines** in the lower reaches and **orchids**, **elkhorns** and other epiphytes using larger plants as roosts. **Palms** and **tree ferns**, with their giant, delicately curled fronds, are found in more open forest where there's regular water.

Some forest types illustrate the extent of Australia's prehistoric flora. **Antarctic beech** or nothafagus, found south of Brisbane as well as in South America, along with native pines and **kauri** from Queensland, which also occur in New Zealand (the similarly-named Western Australian **karri** is also huge but unrelated), are all relict evidence of the prehistoric supercontinent Gondwana. Other "living fossils" include primitive marine **stromatolites** – algae corals – still found around Shark Bay, Western Australia, or in fossilized form in the central deserts.

As long as you don't eat them or fall onto the pricklier versions, most Australian plants are harmless – though in rainforests you'd want to avoid entanglement with spiky **lawyer cane** or wait-awhile vine (though it doesn't look like it, this is a climbing palm). However, watch out for the large, pale-green, heart-shaped leaves of the **stinging tree**, a scraggly "regrowth" plant found on the margins of cleared tropical rainforest. Even a casual brush delivers an agonizing and prolonged sting; if you're planning on bushwalking in the tropics, learn to recognize and avoid this plant.

Australian film

No visitor to Australia these days will be unaware of the popularity and respect
for the Australian film industry since the early 1970s. It is generally agreed
(with deference to a 1900 Salvation Army promo, *Stations of the Cross*) that
The Story of the Kelly Gang, made by Charles Tait in 1906, was the world's
first feature-length film. Australians' well-known antagonism towards figures of
authority soon led to a hugely popular series of bushranger movies, eventually
to be banned in 1912 by the New South Wales police on the grounds that their
unsympathetic portrayal in these pictures was corrupting youngsters.

This **early heyday** of Australian film-making predated that of Hollywood and
persisted with the production of various World War I morale boosters, despite the
creation of a distribution duopoly (known as the "combine") which showed little interest in independent Australian films outside its control. With the ending
of the war and its many cinematic testaments to the heroic disaster of Gallipoli,
Australian silent cinema reached a creative peak. **Raymond Longford** was
Australia's Spielberg of Silents at this time, and his 1919 production of *The
Sentimental Bloke* and its sequel, Ginger Mick, a year later, were popular and
notably naturalist dramas about a woman's taming of her larrikin husband's pro-
clivities. Along with the already established contempt for authority, Longford's
films featured a distrust of sophistication and formality and, even then, the myth-
ic spell of "the bush" began to make its mark on Australian productions.

Hollywood domination

The combine gradually squeezed the life from Australian cinema, which continued to decline as the powerful Hollywood studios got into their stride and
entered the Golden Age of Talkies. In 1933 the mildly reformed wild boy from
Tasmania, **Errol Flynn**, starred in his first feature film, *In the Wake of the Bounty*,
directed by **Charles Chauvel**, a leading figure in Australian film-making until
the late 1950s.

During World War II there was a return to newsreels and documentaries, with
the legendary cameraman, Damien Parer, earning **Australia's first Oscar** for
his account of the fighting in New Guinea (Kokoda Front Line, 1942).
Following the war, however, Hollywood's global domination of cinema was
unassailed, and Australian cinema just about perished. Nevertheless, **Chips
Rafferty** turned up as Australia's answer to John Wayne, appearing in an unremarkable series of formula films, such as the scenically superb epic of bovine
migration, *The Overlanders* (1946).

In the 1950s the British Ealing Studios and the American MGM set up production companies in Australia, turning out the odd Outback drama which
was watered-down for international consumption (but not success). This era
produced few notable Australian films other than Cecil Holmes' return to the
bushranger format in *Captain Thunderbolt* (1953), and his similarly leftist study
of mateship, *Three In One* (1957). Chauvel's remarkable *Jedda, the Uncivilized*
(1955) was more unusual in that it tackled the tricky issue of an Aboriginal
girl's white upbringing, sexual temptation and subsequent abduction back to
tribal life, where a tragic death inevitably awaited her. If there is one subject

Australian cinema still has difficulty in dealing with (the New Wave having finally come to grips with women as individuals), it is that of the Aborigines.

Australia was by now nothing more than an exotic, marsupial-speckled location for "**kangaroo westerns**" and other dramas where British and American actors could exercise their skills. In 1959 Stanley Kramer directed *On the Beach*, Nevil Shute's post-Holocaust drama, with Ava Gardner, Gregory Peck and Fred Astaire tiptoeing through the fallout. A year later Fred Zinnemann directed Deborah Kerr and Robert Mitchum in *The Sundowners*, an affectionate classic of Outback itinerant labour.

The New Wave

The birth of the **New Wave** was a response to the burgeoning counterculture of the late 1960s. Among the many notable reforms of Gough Whitlam's Labor government was support for the long-neglected arts. Film-makers in particular were given a shot in the arm with the introduction of extremely generous grants to more than cover the cost of production. While in its early years this financial support helped produce some of the crassest male-fantasy "sex romps" ever seen (Tim Burstall's 1973 *Alvin Purple* and Terry Bourke's *Plugg* are matchlessly dire), the opening of the **Australian Film School** in 1973 allowed genuine talents such as Gillian Armstrong, Bruce Beresford and Paul Cox to flourish.

Two years later, the **Australian Film Commission** evolved from previous similar organizations to help produce and market Australian films, and although the grants have been regularly reduced ever since, their introduction kick-started the moribund industry so that there presently exists a diverse pool of directors and technicians to keep things going.

Peter Weir's unsettlingly eerie *Picnic at Hanging Rock* (1975) remains an early jewel, and the decade ended with further acclaim for his *Gallipoli*, Phillip Noyce's extraordinary *Newsfront* and Gillian Armstrong's first feature, *My Brilliant Career*. Auspicious futures were launched for Armstrong, and actors Sam Neill, Judy Davis and Mel Gibson, whose post-apocalyptic *Mad Max* trilogy saw a gradual stylistic evolution to suit the huge American market.

With the international box office success of *Crocodile Dundee* in 1985, Australia briefly became a fashionable destination. Indeed, Kakadu National Park owes as much to Peter Faiman's fish-out-of-water fairy tale for its present popularity as does Uluru (Ayers Rock) to the famous Dingo Baby case; *Evil Angels* (released in the UK under the title *A Cry in the Dark*) saw Meryl Streep miscast as Lindy Chamberlain in Fred Schepisi's 1987 version of those events.

Contemporary Australian cinema is perhaps most exceptional for establishing a number of **women directors** and **producers** and providing a handful of strong women's roles. Inevitably, only the mainstream hits, such as the uplifting *Strictly Ballroom* and *Death in Brunswick*, have achieved world overseas release, while many equally fine "small" films remain largely unseen. It is these quirky, uniquely Australian films of which the rejuvenated industry can be most proud. The prestige of numerous and consistent awards at the Cannes Film Festival and others proves that Australia's long-established cinematographic heritage has, more than any other art form, helped rid the country of its former philistine reputation. Confident and uncompromising films such as *Malcolm, Celia, Sweetie* and *The Year My Voice Broke* are just a few that complement their better-known siblings, with 1994 seeing a media-led "renaissance" in Australian film. Stephan Elliot's sartorially outrageous *Adventures of Priscilla, Queen of the Desert* was the country's biggest box-office success up to that time and won international acclaim, while P.J. Hogan's wonderful *Muriel's Wedding* perfectly encapsulated the indigenous film-making idiom and proved that Australia still could make financially viable and idiosyncratic films.

Recent developments

More recently, Australian film critics have grown weary of the trend in making "quirky, offbeat romances", such as Shirley Barratt's *Love Serenade* and Emma Crogan's 1996 Cannes hit *Love and Other Catastrophes*, although few would have much to complain about with Scott Hicks' globally acclaimed *Shine*. Another worthy and uniquely Australian film released in 1996 was Nick Parsons' extraordinary *Dead Heart*. Describing the decomposing relationships, as well as the clash of white and tribal law, on an outstation near Alice Springs, the film sensitively and honestly portrays many aspects of contemporary Aboriginal life (deaths in custody, illicit grog runs, "payback", drunkenness and even sorcery).

While the Liberal government has slashed film funding to the Australian Film Commission and Film Finance Corporation, major actors such as Russell Crowe (*L.A. Confidential* and, of course, *Gladiator*), Nicole Kidman (*Eyes Wide Shut*, *To Die For*, *Portrait of a Lady*), Rachel Griffiths (*Divorcing Jack*), Cate Blanchett (*Elizabeth*) and Geoffrey Rush (*Shine* and *Quills*) now work mostly overseas where the pay, recognition and opportunities are much greater. In 1998 box office receipts hit a record A$629.2 million yet Australian films made up only two percent of that – and almost all lost money.

However, a low Australian dollar, skilled crews and Sydney's new Fox Studios have attracted major productions such as *Dark City*, *The Matrix*, *Mission Impossible II* and *Star Wars Episode II* to Australia. Melbourne's developing docklands project includes a Paramount-backed studio which will also boost the Australian film industry's facilities, skillbase and reputation.

Hot spots for film buffs and soap groupies

The majestic scenery of the Northern Territory has featured in many films. **Kakadu National Park** provided the setting for many of the scenes in *Crocodile Dundee*: familiar spots are possibly Anbangbang Billabong (see p.630) and Waterfall Creek (see p.631). *We of the Never Never* was set in the **Mataranka** region, which, predictably, has been rechristened "Never Never" country (see pp.646); some costumes worn in the film are on display in the Old Courthouse and Residency in **Alice Springs** (see p.659).

Desolation and Outback grandeur have a stranglehold on the science-fiction and post-apocalyptic genres. Locations for *Mad Max II* include the **Silverton** area of New South Wales (see p.380); as his parting shot, Mel Gibson upscuttled the semi-trailer on the nearby **Mundi Mundi Plains**. In South Australia, the pockmarked scenery of **Coober Pedy** (see p.867) has found favour with many film-makers, including Wim Wenders, who made his epic *Until the End of the World* here, while the lunar-like landscape was also an invaluable element in creating the atmosphere of *Mad Max III*. And *that* Outback pub in *Crocodile Dundee* was none other than the *Walkabout Hotel*, at **McKinlay** in Queensland.

More lush surroundings have also caught the imagination: in Victoria the eponymous **Hanging Rock** (see p.981), which featured in *Picnic at Hanging Rock*, is within striking distance of **Woodend**.

Inevitably, the **Sydney area** has its fair share of hallowed ground for TV addicts. *Skippy, the Bush Kangaroo*, or at least the son of Skippy, is the star of **Waratah Park** (see p.194). The soapy teenage angst and surfie bonhomie of *Home and Away* revolves around **Palm Beach** in Sydney's northern beaches (see p.155), with the **Barrenjoey Lighthouse** and headland regularly in shot.

Films to watch out for

While you'd be lucky to catch all the recommendations below on the big screen (although keep an eye on the programmes of art-house, or repertory, cinemas in the major cities), many of the titles can be found in video rental stores.

Humour, black comedy and satire

The Adventures of Priscilla, Queen of the Desert (Stephan Elliot, 1994). A queer romp across the Outback, prying into some musty corners of Australian social life along the way.

Babakiueria (Julian Pringler, 1988). A culture-reversing spoof beginning with Aborigines invading Australia during a roadside barbie and continuing with an anthropological-style study of white Australia. Rare, but well worth the search.

The Castle (Rob Sitch, 1997). Family's struggle to defend their home in the face of a trinity of suburban horrors: toxic waste dumps, overhead power lines and airport developers.

Death in Brunswick (John Ruane, 1990). A black comedy about the misfortunes of a hapless dishwasher who becomes embroiled in a gangland killing.

Malcolm (Nadia Tass, 1985). A charming, offbeat comedy about a slow-witted tram driver in Melbourne.

Muriel's Wedding (P.J. Hogan, 1994). Kleptomanic frump Muriel wastes away in an Abba-and-confetti dreamworld until ex-schoolchum Rhonda masterminds Muriel's escape from her awful family and ghastly seaside suburb of Porpoise Spit. Great performances.

Adolescent and misfit romance

Flirting (John Duigan, 1989). This sequel to *The Year My Voice Broke* follows a young boy's adventures in boarding school. Superior coming-of-age film.

Lonely Hearts (Paul Cox, 1981). Following the death of his mother, 50-year-old Peter buys a new toupee and joins a dating agency. A sensitive portrayal of the ensuing, at times awkward, relationship. Other Paul Cox features worth looking out for include *Man of Flowers*, *My First Wife* and *Cactus*.

Strictly Ballroom (Baz Luhrmann, 1991). Mismatched dancers who, together, dare to defy the prescribed routines. A feel-good hit at Cannes and the box office.

Urban dysfunctionals

The Boys (Rowan Woods, 1998). This tense drama follows Brett, played by rising star, David Wenham (*Sea Change*) as an ex-prisoner who terrorizes his dysfunctional family and coerces his unemployed brothers into a violent crime.

Careful, He Might Hear You (Carl Shultz, 1982). An absorbing tug-of-love drama set in 1930s Sydney.

The Devil's Playground (Fred Schepisi, 1975). Burgeoning sexuality oozes between pupils and their tutors in a Catholic seminary.

Head On (Ana Kokkinos, 1998). Unemployed Ari (Alex Dimitriades) escapes living with his strict Greek parents by spending a hectic 24-hours

nightclubbing, drug taking and graph-
ically exploring his homosexuality.
The Last Days of Chez Nous
(Gillian Armstrong, 1991). A middle-
aged woman slowly loses her grip
on her marriage and family.
Romper Stomper (Geoffrey Wright,
1991). A bleak and pointless account
of the violent disintegration of a gang
of Melbourne skinheads, notable only
as Russell Crowe's big-screen debut.
Sweetie (Jane Campion, 1988). Part
black comedy, part bleakly disturbing
portrait of a bizarre suburban family.

Ockerdom

**The Adventures of Barry
McKenzie** (Bruce Beresford, 1972).
Ultra-ocker comes to England to
teach the "pommie sheilas about real
men". Ironically, Humphries' satire
got beer-spurting ovations from the
very people he despised and also set
Beresford back a couple of years.
Crocodile Dundee (Peter Faiman,
1985). The acceptable side of genial,
dinky-di ockerdom saw Paul Hogan
sell Australian bush mystique to the
mainstream. Enjoyable once, but
don't bother with the sequels.
Wake in Fright aka **Outback** (Ted
Kotcheff, 1970). A horrifying gem in
its uncut, 114min version; a real
Deliverance Down Under. A coast-
bound teacher blows his fare in
Outback Hicksville and slowly
degenerates into a brutal, beer-
sodden nightmare.

Gritty and defiant women

Celia (Ann Turner, 1988). A wonderful
allegory that mixes a 1950s rabbit-
eradication programme with a
communist witch-hunt. Stubborn
Celia is determined to keep her bunny.
Dance Me To My Song (Rolf De
Heer, 1998). A unique and moving
film written by and starring cerebral
palsy sufferer, Heather Rose as she is
abused by her carer and falls in love.
The Getting of Wisdom (Bruce
Beresford, 1977). Spirited Laura rejects
the polite sensibilities and snobbery of
an Edwardian boarding school.
My Brilliant Career (Gillian
Armstrong, 1978). An early feminist
questions and defies the expectations
of 1890s Victoria.
Puberty Blues (Bruce Beresford,
1981). Two teenage beach girls refuse
to accept their pushchair-and-
shopping-trolley destiny.
We of the Never Never (Igor
Auzins, 1981). A good-looking
version of Jeannie Gunn's autobio-
graphical classic of turn-of-the-
twentieth-century station life in the
Top End.

Men in rugged circumstances

The Dish (Rob Sitch, 2000). Light-
hearted take on how Australia saved
NASA during the broadcasting of
the 1969 moon landing – and an
aside on how the country's techno-
logical skills are always overlooked.
Gallipoli (Peter Weir, 1980). A
deservedly classic buddy movie in
which a young Mel Gibson strikingly evokes the Anzacs' cheery idealism
and the tragedy of their slaughter.
The Last of the Knucklemen
(Tim Burstall, 1978). Tensions build
up in a remote Outback mine and
explode in bare-fisted punch-ups.
The Man from Snowy River
(George Miller, 1981). Men, horses
and the land from A.B. ("Banjo")

Paterson's seminal and dearly loved poem caught the overseas' imagination. A modern kangaroo western. **Plains of Heaven** (Ian Pringle, 1982). A spookily atmospheric story of two weathermen in a remote meteorological station slowly losing their minds.
Sunday Too Far Away (Ken Hannam, 1973). A simple tale of macho shearers' rivalries in Outback South Australia.

Outback nightmares

Evil Angels (*A Cry in the Dark*) (Fred Schepisi, 1987). A dramatic retelling of the Azaria Chamberlain story; dingoes will never seem quite the same again.
Picnic at Hanging Rock (Peter Weir, 1975). A richly layered tale about the disappearance of a party of schoolgirls and its traumatic aftermath.
Razorback (Russell Mulcahy, 1984). Dark comedy exploiting urban paranoia of the Outback and featuring a remote township, a gigantic, psychotic wild pig, and some bloodthirsty nutters who run the local abattoir.
Walkabout (Nicolas Roeg, 1971). Following their deranged father's suicide during a bush picnic, two children wander through the wilderness until an Aboriginal boy guides them back to civilization.

About Aborigines

The Chant of Jimmie Blacksmith (Fred Schepisi, 1977). Set in the 1800s, when a half-caste boy is forced onto the wrong side of the law. Based on the book by Thomas Keneally.
Dead Heart (Brian Brown, 1996). A long-overdue and regrettably overlooked thriller, set on an Aboriginal community near Alice Springs. Bravely gets its teeth into some juicy political and social issues.
The Fringe Dwellers (Bruce Beresford, 1985). An aspiring daughter persuades her family to move from the bush into a suburban white neighbourhood, with expected results.
Jedda, the Uncivilized (Charles Chauvel, 1955). An orphaned Aboriginal girl brought up by a "civilized" white family cannot resist her "tribal" urges when she is semivoluntarily abducted by a black outlaw.
Manganinnie (John Honey, 1980). Set during the time of the "black drives" of 1830s Tasmania, a young Aboriginal girl gets separated from her family and meets a white girl in similar straits.

Portents of doom

Cane Toads: an Unnatural History (Mark Lewis, 1988). A very eccentric, original and amusing documentary about the mixed feelings Queensland's poisonous amphibians arouse and the real threat they may pose to Australia's ecology.
The Last Wave (Peter Weir, 1977). An eerie chiller about a lawyer defending an Aborigine accused of murder – and the powerful, elemental forces his people control.
Mad Max II (George Miller, 1981). The best of the trilogy, set in a near future where loner Max protects an oil-producing community from fuel-starved crazies. Great machinery and stunts.

Australian music

For a geographically isolated, sparsely inhabited island with a tiny market for its own recorded music, Australia has, with ever-more assurance, shouldered its way in to occupy a distinguished place in the international pop music hierarchy. In contrast with its forty-year rock music heritage, the country's Aboriginal music boasts a creative presence of thousands of years. With a strong influence on contemporary Australian music, its importance in the ongoing reconciliation between black and white Australia can hardly be overstated.

Rock music

The story of Australian contemporary music closely parallels that of Britain and the US – rock'n'roll arrived in the 1950s, and each decade since has offered up its own revolutionary shift in the popular music landscape. Given the ubiquitous nature of Western popular culture, this is hardly surprising. Less predictable, however, has been the impact of Australian music on the world music scene, beginning in the 1970s with AC/DC, continuing in the 1980s with Midnight Oil and INXS, through to the more recent multimillion record sellers silverchair and Natalie Imbruglia.

The early years

Australia's very first rock star emerged in 1957 in the form of a lean, throaty, stage-strutting powerhouse named **Johnny O'Keefe**. All snake-hips and sex appeal, "The Wild One", as he became known, was one of the few early rock performers who could very nearly out-Elvis Elvis. Concert footage of his live performances is largely taken up by shots of women screaming, passing out and being carried from concert venues by sweaty police and exhausted security. O'Keefe discovered early on that all the big players in the industry – performers, managers, promoters and record companies – were expert manipulators, and he quickly set about becoming one himself: legend has it that he bullied his way into his first recording contract by calling a press conference and announcing that the deal was done, guessing correctly that the publicity would leave the record company no option but to sign him.

Johnny O'Keefe was, to Australians, the embodiment of the defiant new brand of music that was then sweeping the world. He was to become synonymous with 1960s TV programmes that showcased Australian rock'n'roll talent, even as his own recording efforts were gradually swamped by the peace-love-hair movement of the time. O'Keefe remained a presence on television and radio until his death of a heart-attack in 1978, aged just 43. In keeping with the requirements of rock God-dom, his last years were characterized by a series of breakdowns, bouts of depression and problems with alcohol. His rendition of the classic crowd-anthem **"Shout"** (1959) remains, to this day, an integral part of early rock-'n'roll's global legacy (video footage of O'Keefe performing live also constitutes the opening sequence of the ABC's late-night music video programme, *Rage*).

Surviving the Sixties

In company with the rest of the world, Australian music rode out the 1960s hanging onto the coat-tails of the massive British rock invasion. Overwhelmed by the omnipresent Beatles and Rolling Stones, Australia was to produce little ground-breaking rock music, beyond the efforts of Billy Thorpe and the Aztecs, The Easybeats and Russell Morris, each of whom left behind a signature song forever embedded in the Australian psyche, and still played on commercial radio today: "Most People I Know (Think that I'm Crazy)" – Billy Thorpe and the Aztecs (1968); "Friday on My Mind" – The Easybeats (1966); "The Real Thing" – Russell Morris (1969).

The Seekers, however, were operating well clear of the crowded rock music mainstream, creating their own musical niche by building three-part harmonies around chords strummed on acoustic guitars, the two male voices cushioning the pristine power of lead vocalist Judith Durham. Songs like "If I Had a Hammer" (1965) might sound like hippie anthems today, but The Seekers' brand of idealism appealed to millions of record-buyers, and a successful recent comeback tour showed that their popularity has barely waned.

It was in 1967, however, that millions of Australians witnessed the decade's most significant music industry event – and not a single one of them even knew it. A young man named **Johnny Farnham** had appeared on television, performing a cute but innocuous ditty entitled "Sadie (the Cleaning Lady)" (1967). Good-looking and with a superb voice, as well as charming beyond his years, Farnham endeared himself immediately to Australian audiences; it was a promising debut, but nobody could have predicted how far he'd go. His name shortened these days to John, Farnham is now into his fifth decade as a performer, and continues to shift with apparently effortless ease between roles as rock star, stage-musical lead and TV personality. From 1982–86 he was a popular frontman for the hugely successful Little River Band (having replaced Glen Shorrock), but it was in 1987 that his career peaked, with the release of his album *Whispering Jack*, which sold millions of copies worldwide, driven, appropriately enough, by the success of the single "You're the Voice" (1987).

Livin' in the Seventies

Having emerged from the shadows of the 1960s, Australian music began to find a voice of its own in the mid-1970s. For no obvious reason, **Glam Rock** was a phenomenon Australian bands not only embraced, but excelled at. Sherbet and **Skyhooks** pulled off the satin-jumpsuits-and-crazy-make-up combo with singular style. The "Mighty Hooks" were at all times the cheekier and sexier of the two. Singer "Shirley" Strachan famously performed in only a pair of tight satin trousers with a large, bright-red hand painted over the crotch; the other band-members were equally indulgent of their penchants for self-expression. There was no sacrifice of substance for style, however, with the band recording several of Australia's finest and most enduring pop songs, including such irresistible numbers as "You Just Like Me 'cause I'm Good in Bed" (1974), "Horror Movie" (1974), "Ego (Is Not a Dirty Word)" (1975), and "Women in Uniform" (1978).

Sherbet seemed almost serious by comparison, doing without the make-up and looking as though they only wore the satin pants, silly shoes and poncy scarves because that was what fashion dictated. It was a highly accomplished band no matter what they were wearing, and led by virtuoso pop vocalist Daryl Braithwaite, they recorded several standout tracks, including "Child's Play" (1976), "Howzat"

(1976), "High Rolling" (1977) and "Summer Love" (1975). Although both bands flirted with overseas success, touring the US (and subsequently expressing bitterness at not having cracked the big time), history has conferred upon them the honour of having kicked open the rock music establishment's door, on behalf of an Australian music fraternity that had simply been waiting around for someone to show them "we're just as good as those bands from overseas".

Proof perhaps of the depth of talent concentrated in these two bands is the continued presence of individual members in Australian music and media today. Trivia buffs will find the following Skyhooks alumni alive and well: Graeme "Shirley" Strachan – former lead singer, now a popular television presenter; Red Symons was until recently the villain on television's *Hey Hey it's Saturday*; and Greg Macainsh is in high demand still, as a bass-player and songwriter. Stalwarts of Sherbet have likewise soldiered on: Daryl Braithwaite, the lead singer, is now a successful solo performer; Harvey James, one of the first Australian guitar-heroes, graduated to session musician and guitar-ace-for-hire; and Garth Porter, former keyboardist, who has gone on to assume the unlikely mantle of producer/guru for many of Australia's top country music performers.

But even as Glam Rock was fading from cool to kitsch, a clannish group of young Scottish immigrants were beginning to play their own version of Chuck Berry-inspired blues-rock, only three times as loud and with heavily distorted guitars. **AC/DC** not only had the skills, the songs and the "muscle" to back it all up, they also boasted two figures who were destined to become universal icons of rock'n'roll rebellion: guitarist Angus Young's delinquent schoolboy persona had to share the adulation of wannabe rock rebels with singer Bon Scott, who was possessed not only of a genuine, self-destructive, live-hard-die-young ethos, but also sported the most mischievous grin ever seen in tandem with a microphone. It's unlikely anyone besides Bon could have delivered songs such as "Highway to Hell" (1979), "Whole Lotta Rosie" (1978), and "Dirty Deeds...Done Dirt Cheap" (1976) with the required sass to make them acceptable in a 1970s commercial market.

True to form, Bon died a rock star's death in London in 1980, poisoned by alcohol in the back seat of a car. It was, ironically, smack in the middle of a golden age for Australian music, when, during the period 1977–83, bands Men at Work, Midnight Oil, Cold Chisel, INXS, Air Supply and Little River Band were lining up right alongside AC/DC to take the pop music world by storm.

Oz music grows up

Even as AC/DC managed – in the space of a year following Bon's death – to recruit a new singer (Brian Johnston), settle permanently into life in Britain, and record the most acclaimed and successful heavy rock album of all time, "Back in Black" (1980), bands back in Australia suddenly found that the world was interested in them, too. **Little River Band**'s sound was so West Coast USA that commercial success in North America had long seemed inevitable; **Air Supply**, meanwhile, had the sort of stranglehold on the American easy listening love-song market to which Michael Bolton was perhaps, even then, beginning to aspire. More surprising was the impact made by **Men at Work**, a band whose well-crafted songs were invariably, if unfashionably, punctuated by arresting melodies played on a flute, and whose style came to be described as "white reggae". They announced their arrival in 1981 with the ska-ish "Who Can it Be Now?", followed by "The Land Down Under", both of which bombarded radio airwaves and shifted by the million.

During this period, Midnight Oil, Cold Chisel and INXS stayed closer to home, recognizing perhaps that their styles were less easily translatable from an Australian to a global audience. It is surely no coincidence that among these bands (all highly-accomplished, and equally revered at home) the least identifiably "Australian" act – **INXS** – was the first to experience worldwide fame and fortune, when in 1987 their album *Kick* plundered the US charts. (This wave of success held tragic implications for singer Michael Hutchence; he would struggle to make the transition from rock star to rock superstar, suffering depression until his death by suicide in late 1997.) Of the other two, most needs to be said about the band that had the biggest impact at home, and the least impact abroad – Cold Chisel. If the period three years either side of 1980 was to be remembered as the grand era of Oz "pub rock", then Chisel was the band that owned it, lock, stock and smoking barrel.

From Chisel to The Church

Formed in Adelaide in 1975, **Cold Chisel** was, like every great band from the Rolling Stones to U2, the sum of its parts. Steve Prestwich (drums) and Phil Small (bass) made a compact and classy rhythm team, variously casting light and shadow about the more illustrious members of the group. Ian Moss's blues-rock guitar virtuosity and awesome soul voice made him a natural star on any stage, in lethal combination with lead singer Jimmy Barnes, Australia's self-styled wild man of rock and working-class hero. A great band must have great songs, and these were duly delivered by the immensely tall and serious man at the piano, Don Walker, arguably Australia's greatest songwriter.

Among hundreds of examples of **Don Walker**'s craftsmanship in capturing the times/places/people/events that make meaning for Australians, "Khe Sanh" (1978) (Walker's treatise on the Australian experience of surviving the war in Vietnam), remains a work without peer, while "Star Hotel" (1980) captures, in three verses and a chorus, the mood and events of September 19, 1979, when, in the working-class steel-town of Newcastle, police came to close down the city's main pub-rock venue, *The Star Hotel*, only to find themselves confronted by an angry crowd spoiling for a fight. Police cars were overturned and set alight in the course of a civil disturbance that echoed convict rebellions of two centuries earlier. The hotel was finally closed down, but the punters had made their point – and Chisel weren't going to let the police forget it.

Cold Chisel not only recorded the boozy summer nights, the trips up the coast, the girls, the fights, the pubs, the streets, the cities and towns, they sang it all back to the faithful in sweaty pubs and heaving stadiums night after night. When they called it a day in 1984, Chisel were Australia's greatest ever rock band, bar none. "Mossy" and "Barnesy" went on to fame and fortune as solo performers, but the band's long-awaited return did not come until 1998, when they released their first studio album in fourteen years "The Last Wave of Summer"; it remains to be seen whether they can be anything like as great again.

During this period, **Midnight Oil** by no means played second banana to Cold Chisel; rather, they had a different agenda, and their commitment and energy in delivering it live were never in question. Always highly political (lead singer Peter Garrett narrowly missed out on a Senate seat and he was leader of Australia's Nuclear Disarmament Party), "the Oils" brought aboriginal land rights into the forum of pop culture, even as their uncompromising album *Diesel and Dust* (1987) brought them worldwide success. Twenty-year veterans with twelve albums to their credit (and bracketed by critics with Queen and U2 as the most powerful live act in the world), Midnight Oil remain establishment cage-rattlers par excellence.

Among the distinguished musicians of the 1970s and 1980s, two songwriters stand (alongside Don Walker) above the rest as chroniclers of their culture and environment: **Richard Clapton** and **Paul Kelly**. Clapton's 1977 album *Goodbye Tiger* is unmatched as a celebration of the very fact of life in Australia – riding the city tram, searching for the perfect wave, soaking up the streetscapes of Oxford Street and King's Cross. Paul Kelly is a more contemporary presence, and his songs go unerringly to the heart of the matter: "Have You Ever Seen Sydney From a 727 at Night?" (1985), "From St Kilda to King's Cross" (1985) and "Adelaide" (1985) capture their respective subjects better than any photograph, while his ode to "Bradman" (1987) – written in homage to Australia's greatest Test cricket batsman Sir Donald Bradman – The Don, is the stuff of a true bard, a composition in verse honouring the glorious return from battle of a people's champion.

But in order to appreciate the depth and diversity of Australian music as it reached **maturity**, one needs to take a stroll out to the fringes. With a well-established canon of "major" Australian bands now in place, others were finding looser creative environments in which to operate. The Triffids, The Birthday Party (with star alumnus Nick Cave), The Church and the Go-Betweens seemed tied to weirder and more eclectic influences (such as The Velvet Underground, David Bowie and Bob Dylan) than their "mainstream" counterparts. Although musically diverse, they held several characteristics in common: their songs seemed more poetic, or just more sensitive to light-and-shade; they were also far less commercially successful in Australia, and all made a big impact in Britain and Europe. Among all of these, The Church alone continue to record and tour from various bases in Europe, while Nick Cave remains intent upon perfecting the art of the murder ballad; his album "Murder Ballads" (1996) features a duet with Kylie Minogue. Australia could boast, too, a white-hot outfit schooled in the nasty traditions of 1970s British punk: The Saints. Although known for their Sex Pistols-ish two-minute thrash exercises, The Saints were nevertheless real musicians, and survivors Chris Bailey and Ed Kuepper continue to record and perform songs of the highest quality.

The Nineties and beyond...

Strangest perhaps of all the facets of Australia's music industry has been its propensity for throwing up TV **soap stars** who mutated into rock stars (of sorts). At last count there were no less than four ex-*Neighbours* cast members at large within the music industry: Kylie Minogue, Danii Minogue, Jason Donovan and Natalie Imbruglia. Australians have never known what to make of this, but the latest of the batch, Natalie Imbruglia, made her mark in 1998 with a superb pop album *Left of the Middle*, so there, at least, is some evidence of genuine musical accomplishment.

The roaring success of these soap-star singers goes some way to explaining the listlessness that afflicted the music community during the late 1980s to early 1990s. It seemed the moment **Jason Donovan** and **Kylie Minogue** were formally adopted by an adoring British public, Australian musicians breathed a collective sigh of relief, and got straight back to work. You Am I, The Whitlams, The Cruel Sea and Skunkhour had always been likely to show the way by writing and recording with passion and originality. By the mid-1990s, quality Australian bands were once again jostling for position in local and overseas markets, this time led by three scruffy-looking fifteen-year-old schoolboys.

In 1994, Newcastle high-school trio Innocent Criminals sent a demo tape to radio Triple J in response to a band competition, the prize for which was use of the station's recording facilities. The song, "Tomorrow", had the Seattle grunge sound all over it, and an awesome rock vocal performance from singer/guitarist Daniel Johns. He didn't sound like a fifteen-year-old, although the band's written entry should have given some kind of clue; their "twenty-five-words-or-less" were written in green felt marker-pen on yellow cardboard: "We're not rap or hip-hop, we're rock and we love to play". "Tomorrow" arrived atop the Australian singles charts where it stayed for several weeks, and with the band renamed **silverchair**, their 1995 album *Frogstomp* took them into league – and onto a stage – with grunge giants like Pearl Jam and Soundgarden, even as the three "boys" were negotiating their last year of high school.

At the start of the new millennium, the feeling is that Australian music has the stuff to tackle it head-on. From rock outfits Powderfinger, Grinspoon and The Superjesus and the thrashier Spiderbait, Jebediah and The Living End, to the stylish and witty The Whitlams, the dance-pop of Savage Garden, and the rock/techno crossover work of Regurgitator, the array of talent is dizzying. Tune in as the next great era of Australian music unfolds.

Aboriginal music

Aboriginal music is an increasingly powerful and invigorating seam in the fabric of world music. Its instruments and rhythms have a strong influence in contemporary Australian music, and there's probably no better example of the musical crossing of cultural boundaries, than in the story of Australia's most recognizable instrument, the didgeridoo. Known also as a yidaki, or simply a "didge", this hollowed-out tree branch, when blown into, produces a resonant hum, punctuated by imitations of animal and bird noises. Its sound is evocative, to many, of the Australian landscape.

The big surprise for many visitors to Australia is the sheer **diversity** of Aboriginal music. From the big rock sound of the Warumpi Band to the heartfelt guitar ballads of Archie Roach, the cruisey island reggae of newcomers Saltwater, and the echoes of an ancient culture in the work of Nabarlek (who sing mostly in their own language) there is no way of pigeonholing the music. And while there's no problem seeing Aboriginal bands, doing everything from metal to hip-hop and performing in all parts of the country, there's really no better way to immerse yourself than by attending an indigenous music festival.

Festivals

Biggest of all the festivals is the **Barunga Sports & Cultural Festival**, which showcases up to forty bands, along with sports events, spear-throwing and didge-playing competitions. It's held at Barunga Community, 80km south of Katherine in the NT, over the first weekend in June (campsites with facilities are available). Also in the Top End, the **Millingimbi Cultural Festival** is purely a music event and, being harder to get to than Barunga, gets fewer white visitors. Dates for this one are hard to nail down, although it's always held sometime mid-year, on Millingimbi Island in the Crocodile archipelago. There are flights from Darwin, otherwise you need permission from the Northern Land Council (Darwin Head Office ☏08/8920 5100) to drive across Arnhemland to Ramingining to catch a barge. Traditional music and dance are featured, along with gospel bands and lots of Arnhemland rock.

The festival held every odd-numbered year at **Laura**, in far north Queensland, attracts high profile performers like the Warumpi Band and Christine Anu, plus all the local Murri bands. Held in either May or June (it varies from year to year), there are usually quite a few backpackers and hippies about, as well as the local Murri community. It's roughly two-hours' drive (on sealed roads) north from Cairns to Laura, a small town 60km west of Cooktown. Otherwise, another intriguing possibility on the west coast just might be the **"Stompin' Ground"** festival. First staged in Broome, Western Australia, in 1992, and then again in 1998, it drew on the strong and highly independent Aboriginal communities of the Kimberley region, attracting singers, dancers and bands into the incomparable beauty of Western Australia's far north. Although it is not really an "established" event, it could be well worth checking out. (Radio Triple J is a good source for music festival info, and they broadcast Australia wide.)

Even if you find yourself stranded in the Big Smoke, you need not miss out; if you're in **Sydney** over summer, there's no better place to be on the Australia Day holiday (January 26) than at "Survival", Waverley Park, Bondi. This festival began as a highly political event, deliberately juxtaposed with the Australia Day festivities which mark the arrival of the first fleet of "white invaders". It continues as a celebration of the survival of indigenous people and cultures in the face of white oppression, and draws many of the biggest names in indigenous music.

Artists

Most of the **bands** mentioned above have work available on CD, while other outstanding artists whose albums are widely available include Yothu Yindi, No Fixed Address, Tiddas, Kev Carmody and Coloured Stone. Compilation albums are worth looking into also, particularly those that cover a wide range of styles: "Meinmuk – Music from the Top End" (1996) is a Radio Triple J compilation of songs by 24 different Arnhemland bands, covering rock, reggae, gospel and metal; "Demarru Hits" is another good one, available through CAAMA (Central Australian Aboriginal Media Association) in Alice Springs, and some music retailers.

Cameron Wilson

Books

Australian writing came into its own in the 1890s, when a strong nationalistic movement leading up to eventual federation in 1901 produced writers such as Henry Lawson and the balladeer A.B. "Banjo" Paterson, who romanticized the bush and glorified the mateship ethos, while outstanding women writers, such as Miles Franklin and Barbara Baynton, gave a feminine slant to the bush tale and set the trend for a strong female authorship. In the twentieth century, Australian novelists have come to be recognized in the international arena, Patrick White having been awarded a Nobel Prize in 1973, and Peter Carey the Booker Prize in 1988. More recently, writers who have made a name for themselves within Australia, such as David Malouf and Tim Winton, have begun to arouse curiosity further afield.

These days, Australian writing is flourishing: as in the USA, the **short story** thrives in Australia, with popular magazines such as *Australian Short Stories* and literary journals such as *Meanjin*, *Southerly*, *Westerly* and *Heat* providing a forum and exposure for short fiction, essays, reviews and new and established writers. Eagerly read anthologies, with an emphasis on women's writing and multiculturalism, are constantly being published; for a taste of the latest, the annual *Picador New Writing* is worth seeking. The big prizes in Australian fiction include the Vogel Prize for the best unpublished novel written by an author under the age of 35, and the country's most coveted literary prize, the Miles Franklin Award.

You'll be surprised at the range of titles available in Australian **bookshops**, though be prepared to pay more than you would at home. A good website to check is that of Gleebooks (@ www.gleebooks.com.au), one of Australia's best literary booksellers, with a whole host of recent reviews; specific titles can be ordered via email (@ books@gleebooks.com.au) and posted out. We've given the publishers of each book, where available, in the United Kingdom (UK), the United States (US), and Australia (Aus) where applicable; obviously, most Australian-interest books are more widely available in Australia. O/p signifies an out-of-print – but still highly recommended – book which you will probably be able to find in a library. University Press is abbreviated as UP.

Travel and travel guides

Bill Bryson *Down Under* (Black Swan UK; Doubleday US). Characteristically dry humour in this outsider's view of national character, though Australians will find Bryson relies overmuch on stereotypes.

Bruce Chatwin *Songlines* (Picador UK; Penguin US; Vintage Aus). A semifictional account of an exploration into Aboriginal nomadism and mythology that turns out to be one of the more readable expositions of this complex subject, though often pretentious.

Sean Condon *Sean and David's Long Drive* (Lonely Planet). Australia's answer to Kerouac's *On the Road*, with humour in overdrive: Melbourne-based Condon and his friend David are fully fledged city dwellers when they set off on a tour around their own country, to come face to face with the dangers of crocs, tour guides and fellow travellers.

Robyn Davidson *Tracks* (Picador UK; Random US). A compelling account of a young woman's journey across the Australian desert, accompanied only by four camels and a dog. Davidson manages to break out of the heroic-traveller mould to write with compassion and honesty of the people she meets in the Outback and the doubts, dangers and loneliness she faces on her way. A classic of its kind.

Neal Drinnan (ed) *The Rough Guide to Gay & Lesbian Australia* (Rough Guides Ltd UK, Aus). Well-reviewed and comprehensive manual listing gay-friendly hotels, bookshops, bars, cafés, restaurants and beaches, plus info on support groups and specialist travel services, and the lowdown on gay and lesbian events countrywide.

Howard Jacobson *In the Land of Oz* (Penguin UK, Aus o/p). Jacobson focuses his lucidly sarcastic observations on a round-Australia trip that gets rather too close to some home truths for most Australians' tastes.

⭐ **Mark McCrum** *No Worries* (Phoenix UK). Knowing nothing of the country except the usual clichés, McCrum arrives in 1990s Australia and makes his way around by plane, train, thumb and Greyhound, meeting a surprising cast of characters along the way. As he travels, the stereotypes give way to an insightful picture of modern Australia.

Ruth Park *Ruth Park's Sydney* (Duffy & Snelgrove, Aus). Prolific novelist Park's 1973 guide to the city was fully revised and expanded in 1999. A perfect walking companion, full of personal insights, anecdotes and literary quotations.

Alice Thomson *The Singing Line* (Chatto & Windus, Aus). The great-great-granddaughter of Alice Todd, the woman after whom Alice Springs was named, retraces her ancestor's journey to central Australia. Nice change from the usual male-centric view of the early pioneers.

Autobiography and biography

Julia Blackburn *Daisy Bates in the Desert* (Minerva UK; Random US). For almost thirty years from 1913, Daisy Bates was Kabbarli, "the white-skinned grandmother", to the Aboriginal people with whom she lived in the desert. Blackburn's beautifully written biography interweaves fiction with fact to conjure up the life of one of Australia's most eccentric and misunderstood women.

Jill Ker Conway *The Road from Coorain* (Minerva UK; Vintage US). Conway's childhood, on a drought-stricken Outback station during the 1940s, is movingly told, as is her battle to establish herself as a young historian in sexist, provincial 1950s Australia.

⭐ **Albert Facey** *A Fortunate Life* (Viking UK o/p; Viking

Penguin US o/p; Penguin Aus). A hugely popular autobiography of a battler, tracing his progress from a bush orphanage to Gallipoli, through the Depression, another war and beyond.

Eddie Mabo and Noel Loos *Edward Koiko Mabo: His Life and Struggle for Land Rights* (University of Queensland Press Aus). Mabo spent much of his life fighting for the autonomy of Torres Strait Islanders and in the process overthrew the concept of *terra nullius*, making his name a household word in Australia. Long interviews with the late black hero form the basis of this book and affectionately reveal the man behind the name.

David Malouf *12 Edmondstone Street* (Chatto UK; Vintage Aus). An evocative autobiography-in-snatches of one of Australia's finest literary novelists, describing, in loving detail, the eponymous house in Brisbane where Malouf was born, life in the Tuscan village where he lives for part of each year, and his first visit to India.

Hazel Rowley *Christina Stead: a Biography* (Minerva Aus). Stead (1902–83) has been acclaimed as Australia's greatest novelist. After spending years in Paris, London and New York with her American hus-band, she returned to Australia in her old age.

Daryl Tonkin and Carolyn Landon *Jackson's Track* (Penguin Aus). Ghostwritten autobiography of Tonkin, a bushman who fell in love with an Aboriginal woman, Euphemia Mullet, who worked on his timber-milling property in East Gippsland in the 1930s. The cross-cultural couple overcame prejudices to create their own life and family, living amongst a wider Aboriginal community at Jackson's Track.

Society and culture

Richard Baker *Land is Life: From Bush to Town – the Story of the Yanyuwa People* (Allen & Unwin Aus). The Yanyuwa people inhabited the Gulf of Carpentaria before the Europeans arrived, but most now live in the town of Booloola, 1600km southeast of Darwin. Historian Baker, assigned a "skin" in the Yanyuwa kinship system, gathered the people's oral history and produced this fascinating story told from the Yanyuwa point of view and time.

★ **Geoffrey Blainey** *Triumph of the Nomads* (Macmillan UK o/p; Overlook Press US; Sun Aus). A fascinating account portraying Aboriginal people as masters and not victims of their environment. One of the best books on the subject.

Frank Brennan *Sharing the Country* (Penguin Aus). Both lawyer and Jesuit priest, and a former Aboriginal Affairs advisor to Australia's Catholic Church, Brennan sets out his legal and social solutions for reconciliation between black and white Australians.

Monica Furlong *Flight of the Kingfisher: a Journey Among Kukatja Aborigines* (Flamingo UK; HarperCollins Aus). Furlong lived among the Aboriginal people of the Great Sandy Desert; this is her account of Kukatja perceptions and spiritual beliefs.

Roslynn Haynes *Seeking the Centre: The Australian Desert in Literature, Art and Film* (Cambridge UP UK, Aus). The geographical and metaphorical impact of the desert on Australian culture is explored in this illustrated book, as is the connection Aboriginal people have with the desert.

David Headon *North of the Ten Commandments* (Hodder & Stoughton UK, Aus o/p). An anthology of Northern Territory writings from all perspectives and sources – an excellent literary souvenir for anyone who falls for the charms of Australia's "one percent" territory.

Donald Horne *The Lucky Country* (Angus & Robertson UK o/p; Penguin Aus). Although over twenty years old, this seminal analysis of Australian society, written in 1976, has yet to be matched and is still often quoted.

Paul Sheehan *Among the Barbarians: the Dividing of Australia* (Random House Aus). *Sydney Morning Herald* journalist Sheehan asserts that while Australia has achieved a brilliant social transformation in the 1990s, it runs the risk of being torn apart on race issues. While the book is certainly cleverly written, its many critics have labelled it a badly researched, preachy tract. A second edition was completely revised after the November 1998 general election.

History and politics

Patsy Adam-Smith *The Anzacs* (Penguin Aus). Gleaned from diaries, letters and interviews, this is a classic account of Australia's involvement in World War I, with a special focus on the campaign that has become part of the Australian legend, Gallipoli, where thousands of "Anzacs" lost their lives.

Robyn Annear *Nothing But Gold* (Penguin Aus). With an eye for interestingly obscure details and managing to convey a sense of irony without becoming cynical, this is a wonderfully readable account of the gold rushes of the nineteenth century, a period in Australia's history which perhaps did more than any other to shape the country's national character.

Len Beadell *Outback Highways* (Weldon Aus). Extracts from Len Beadell's half-dozen books, cheerfully recounting his life in the central Australian deserts as a surveyor, and his involvement in the construction of Woomera and the atomic bomb test sites.

⭐ **John Birmingham** *Leviathan: the unauthorised biography of Sydney* (Knopf/Random House Aus). This Birmingham 1999 tome casts a contemporary eye at the dark side of Sydney's history, from nauseating accounts of Rocks' slum life and the 1900 plague outbreak, through the 1970s traumas of Vietnamese boat people, now Sydney residents, to scandals of police corruption.

Michael Cannon *Black Land White Land: Who Killed the Koories?* (Minerva Aus). An account of the violent 1840s in New South Wales, as colonists and pioneers moving inland clashed with the local Aboriginal tribes.

Paul Carter *The Road to Botany Bay* (Faber & Faber UK o/p; University of Chicago Press US). A fascinating and original analysis of "discovery" as cultural imperialism, and the metaphysics of exploration.

Manning Clark *A Short History of Australia* (Penguin Aus). A condensed version of this leading historian's multivolumed tome, focusing on dreary successions of political administrations over two centuries, and cynically concluding with the "Age of Ruins".

David Day *Claiming A Continent: A History of Australia* (Angus & Robertson Aus). The freshest general and easily readable history available, concluding in 1996. Day looks at Australia's history from a contemporary point of view, with the possession, dispossession and ownership of the land – and thus issues of race – central to his narrative. Excellent recommended reading of recent texts at the end of each chapter.

Bruce Elder *Blood on the Wattle: Massacres and Maltreatment of Aboriginal Australians Since 1788* (New Holland Aus). A heart-rending account of the horrors inflicted on the continent's indigenous peoples, covering infamous nineteenth century massacres as well as more recent mid-twentieth-century scandals of the "Stolen Generation" children.

Tim Flannery (ed) *Watkin Trench 1788* (Text Publishing Aus). One of the most vivid accounts of early Sydney was written by a twenty-something captain of the marines, Watkin Trench, who arrived with the First Fleet. Trench's humanity and youthful curiosity shine through the pages of "A Narrative of the Expedition to Botany Bay" and "A Complete Account of the Settlement of Port Jackson", and the characters who peopled the early settlement, like the Aboriginal Bennelong, come alive.

Harry Gordon *Voyage from Shame: the Cowra Breakout and Afterwards* (University of Queensland Press

Aus). Excellent account of the breakout of Japanese prisoners of war from a camp in New South Wales during World War II.

★ **Robert Hughes** *The Fatal Shore* (Harvill Press UK; Random US; Pan Aus). A minutely detailed epic of the origins of transportation and the brutal beginnings of white Australia.

Alan Moorehead *Coopers Creek* (Penguin UK; Grove Atlantic US o/p). An historian's dramatic retelling of the ill-fated Burke and Wills expedition, which set out in 1860 to make the first south-to-north crossing of the continent. A classic of exploration.

Cassandra Pybus *Community of Thieves* (Minerva Aus). Attempting to reconcile past and future, fourth-generation Tasmanian Pybus provides a deeply felt account of the near-annihilation of the island's Aboriginal people.

Henry Reynolds *The Other Side of the Frontier* and *The Law of the Land* (both Penguin Aus). A revisionist historian demonstrates that Aboriginal resistance to colonial invasion was both considerable and organized. His latest book, *The Whispering in Our Hearts* (Allen & Unwin Aus), is a history of those settler Australians who, troubled by the treatment of Aboriginal people, spoke out and took political action.

Portia Robinson *The Women of Botany Bay* (Macquarie Aus). After ten years of painstaking research into the records of every woman transported from Britain and Ireland between 1787 and 1828, as well as the wives of convicts who settled in Australia, Robinson is able to tell us, with conviction and passion, just who the women of Botany Bay really were.

Eric Rolls *Sojourners and Citizens*: *Flowers and the Wide Sea* (both University of Queensland Press Aus). The first and second volumes of Rolls' fascinatingly detailed history of the Chinese in Australia.

Ann Summers *Damned Whores and God's Police* (McPhee Gribble Aus). Stereotypical images of women in Australian society are explored in this ground-breaking reappraisal of Australian history from a feminist point of view, updated in 1994.

Ecology and environment

★ **Tim Flannery** *The Future Eaters* (Reed Books Aus). Palaeontologist Flannery here poses that as the first human beings migrated down to Australasia, the Aborigines, Maoris and other Polynesian peoples changed the region's flora and fauna in startling ways, and began consuming the resources needed for their own future; the Europeans made an even greater impact on the environment, continuing this "future eating" of natural resources.

Josephine Flood *The Riches of Ancient Australia* (University of Queensland Press Aus). An indispensable and lavish guide to Australia's most famous landforms and sites. The same author's *Archaeology of the Dreamtime* (HarperCollins Aus) provides background on the development of Aboriginal society.

Drew Hutton and Libby Connors *A History of the Australian Environmental Movement* (Cambridge UP UK, Aus). Written by a husband and wife team, Queensland academics and prominent in Green politics, this well-balanced book charts the progress of conservation attempts from 1860 to modern protests.

Peter Latz *Bushfires and Bushtucker*: *Aboriginal Plant Use in Central Australia* (IAD Press Aus). Handbook with photos, published by an Aboriginal-owned press.

Tim Murray (ed) *Archeology of Australia* (Allen & Unwin Aus). The last thirty years have seen many ground-breaking discoveries in Australian archeology, with three sites in particular of great significance: Kakadu in the Northern Territory, Lake Mungo in NSW, and South West Tasmania; a range of specialists contribute essays on the subject.

Mary White *The Greening of Gondwana* (Reed Aus). Classic work on the evolution of Australia's flora and geography.

Contemporary fiction

Thea Astley *The Multiple Effects of Rainshadow* (Penguin Aus). On an Aboriginal island reserve in 1930, a white woman dies in childbirth, and her husband goes on a shotgun and dynamite rampage. The novel traces the effects over the years on eight characters who witnessed the violent events, ultimately exploring the brutality and racism in Australian life.

Murray Bail *Eucalyptus* (Harvill UK). This beautifully written novel has a fairytale-like plot: NSW farmer, Holland, has planted nearly every type of eucalyptus tree on his land. When his extraordinarily beautiful daughter Ellen is old enough to marry, he sets up a challenge for her legion of potential suitors, to name each tree.

John Birmingham *The Tasmanian Babes Fiasco* (Duffy & Snelgrove Aus). This hilarious cult classic, about flat-share hell in contemporary Brisbane, is Birmingham's first novel, and a follow up to *He Died With A Felafel In His Hand* (Duffy & Snelgrove Aus), a collection of squalid and very funny tales emerging from experiences with the 89 people who the dissolute author had the misfortune of sharing house with in the 1980s.

Anson Cameron *Tin Toys* (Picador Aus). The Aboriginal "Stolen Generation" issue explored through the tale of Hunter Carolyn, an unintentional artist who can change skin colour at will.

⭐ **Peter Carey** *Bliss* (Faber & Faber UK; Random US; University of Queensland Press Aus). Carey's first and best novel is the story of a Sydney ad executive who drops out to New Age New South Wales. Other novels by Carey to look out for include the Booker Prize-winning *Oscar and Lucinda* (Faber & Faber UK; HarperCollins US; UQP Aus), and his new opus *The True History of the Kelly Gang* (UQP Aus). Also worth a read are his bizarre short stories, *The Fat Man in History* (Faber & Faber UK; UQP Aus), with which he launched his career.

Peter Corris *The Empty Beach* (Unwin UK, Aus). Australia's answer to Raymond Chandler. Corris's hard-boiled novel is set in a glittering but seedy Sydney, where a soft-centred private eye investigates murder and exploitation in an old people's home.

Robert Drewe *The Savage Crows* (Picador Aus). This first novel, from one of Australia's best writers, is among his most powerful. A writer, whose own life is falling apart in a cockroach-ridden contemporary Sydney, sets out to discover the grim truth behind Tasmania's "final solution".

Delia Falconer *The Service of Clouds* (Picador Aus). Poetically written novel set in 1907 in the Blue Mountains outside Sydney. Narrator, pharmacy assistant Eureka Jones falls in love with Harry Kitchings, "a man who takes pictures of clouds".

Richard Flanagan *Death of a River Guide* and *The Sound of One Hand Clapping* (both Picador Aus). Thoughtful writings about landscape, place, migration and the significance of history in these two novels, both set in Tasmania. In *Death of a River*

Guide, the novel's narrator, Aljaz Cosini, goes over his life and that of his family and forebears as he lies drowning. His second novel, *The Sound of One Hand Clapping*, follows 38-year-old Sonya Buloh as she returns to Tasmania to confront her alcoholic father and her past.

David Foster *Moonlite* (Pan UK o/p; Viking Penguin US o/p; Vintage Aus). Amusing social satire set in the Australian goldfields in the nineteenth century. Also look out for his postmodernist *The Glade Within the Grove* (Random House Aus), about an eccentric postman who discovers an unpublished manuscript.

Helen Garner *Postcards from Surfers* (Bloomsbury UK; Penguin Aus). Recommended short stories by one of Australia's finest women writers. Her first novel, *Monkey Grip* (McPhee Gribble Aus), is a classic 1970s tale of obsession, love and heroin in inner-city Melbourne.

Kate Grenville *Lillian's Story* (Picador UK; Harcourt Brace & Co US; Allen & Unwin Aus). The tragicomic tale of Lillian Singer is loosely based on the life of Bea Miles, the eccentric, Shakespeare-spouting, taxi-hijacking Sydney bag lady.

Janette Turner Hospital *Oyster* (Virago UK; Knopf, Vintage Aus). Disquieting novel set in the literally off the map, opal-mining, one-pub Queensland town of Inner Maroo, whose inhabitants are either rough-as-guts mining people, or religious fundamentalists.

David Ireland *City of Women* (Penguin Aus). Ireland creates weird visions of Sydney and here the setting is a futuristic, violent place from which men have been banished. Also keep an eye peeled for his first novel, *The Glass Canoe* (Penguin Aus, o/p), and *Archimedes and the Seagle* (Penguin UK, Aus), the latter a delightful philosophical discussion between a dog and a bird as they roam The Domain and Woolloomooloo.

Linda Jaivin *Eat Me* (Chatto UK; Broadway BDD US; Text Publishing Aus). A successful first novel billed as an "erotic feast"; opens with a memorable fruit-squeezing scene (and this is only the shopping) as three trendy Sydney women (fashion editor, academic and writer) swap stories of sexual exploits.

Elizabeth Jolley *Woman in a Lampshade* (Penguin UK o/p, Aus). This is an excellent collection of short stories to introduce you to Jolley's original and quirky work, which thrives on black humour. *The Sugar Mother* (Penguin Aus) examines what happens to a faithful husband when his wife goes on sabbatical and a young woman and her mother turn up on his doorstep demanding shelter.

Douglas Kennedy *The Dead Heart* (Abacus UK). A best-selling comic thriller recently made into a film; an itinerant American journalist gets abducted by man-eating hillbillies in Outback Australia.

Julia Leigh *Hunting* (Penguin Aus). Intriguing first novel about the rediscovery and subsequent hunt of the Tasmanian tiger; a bit obvious in places – a faceless biotech company after thylacine DNA plays the bad guy – but nicely written.

David Malouf *The Conversations at Curlow Creek* (Vintage UK; Pantheon US; Random Aus). One of Australia's most important contemporary writers charts the developing relationship between two Irishmen the night before a hanging; one is the officer appointed to supervise the execution and the other the outlaw facing his death. Also look for Malouf's new *Dream Stuff* (Chatto & Windus Aus), a collection of short stories which far outshines much of his output over the last decade.

Christos Tsiolkas *Loaded* (Random House Aus). A gritty debut novel set in suburban Melbourne: caught between the traditional Greek world of his family and his emerging gay identity, 19-year-old Ari is unemployed and self-destructing in his milieu of drugs, clubs and anonymous sex. The 1998 film *Head On* was based on the novel.

Australian classics

Barbara Baynton *Bush Studies* (Collins/Angus & Robertson UK; HarperCollins US; Angus & Robertson Aus). A collection of nineteenth-century bush stories written from the female perspective.
Rolf Boldrewood *Robbery Under Arms* (Currency Press UK; HarperCollins Aus). The story of Captain Starlight, a notorious bushranger and rustler around the Queensland borders.
Marcus Clarke *For the Term of his Natural Life* (Penguin & Oxford UP UK; HarperCollins US; Angus & Robertson Aus). Written in 1870 in somewhat overblown prose, this romantic tragedy is based on actual events in Tasmania's once notorious prison settlement.
Miles Franklin *My Brilliant Career* (Virago UK; St Martin's Press US o/p; Imprint Aus). A novel about a spirited young girl in turn-of-the-twentieth-century Victoria who refuses to conform.
May Gibbs *Snugglepot and Cuddlepie* (Angus & Robertson Aus hb, Bluegum Aus pb). A timeless children's favourite: the illustrated adventures of two little creatures who live inside gumnuts.
Barbara Hanrahan *The Scent of Eucalyptus* (Trafalgar US; University of Queensland Press Aus). This first novel by the late South Australian writer captures the essence of Adelaide in the 1960s.
Xavier Herbert *Capricornia* (Imprint Aus). An indignant and allegorical saga of the brutal and haphazard settlement of the land of Capricornia (tropical Northern Territory thinly disguised).

Tim Winton *Cloudstreet* (Picador UK; Graywolf US; Penguin Aus). A wonderful, faintly magical saga about the mixed fortunes of two families who end up sharing a house in post-war Perth.

George Johnston *My Brother Jack* (Chivers US o/p; Imprint Aus). The first in a disturbing trilogy set in Melbourne suburbia between the wars, which develops into a semifictional attempt to dissipate the guilt Johnston felt at being disillusioned with, and finally leaving, his native land.
Thomas Keneally *The Chant of Jimmie Blacksmith* (Penguin UK, Aus; Viking Penguin US o/p). A prize-winning novel which delves deep into the psyche of an Aboriginal outlaw, tracing his inexorable descent into murder and crime. Sickening, brutal and compelling.
Henry Lawson Ballads, poems and stories from Australia's best-loved chroniclers come in a wide array of collections. A few to seek out are: *Henry Lawson Bush Ballads* (Angus & Robertson Aus), *Henry Lawson Favourites* (Penguin Aus) and *While the Billy Boils – Poetry* (Penguin Aus).
Norman Lindsay *The Magic Pudding* (Angus & Robertson Aus). A whimsical tale of some very strange men and their grumpy, flavour-changing and endless pudding; a children's classic with very adult humour.
Ruth Park *The Harp in the South* (Penguin Aus). First published in 1948, this first book in a trilogy is a well-loved tale of inner-Sydney slum life in 1940s Surry Hills. The spirited Darcy family's battle against poverty provides memorable characters.
A.B. ("Banjo") Paterson Australia's most famous bush balladeer, author of "Waltzing Matilda" and "The Man from Snowy River", who helped romanticize the bush's

mystique. Some of the many titles published include *Banjo Paterson's Favourites* (Faber & Faber UK) and *Man From Snowy River and Other Verses* (Angus & Robertson Aus).

Henry Handel Richardson *The Getting of Wisdom* (Virago UK; Mercury House Inc US; Minerva Aus). A gangly country girl's experience of a snobby boarding school in turn-of-the-twentieth-century Melbourne; like Miles Franklin (see overleaf), Richardson was actually a female writer.

Nevil Shute *A Town Like Alice* (Mandarin UK, Aus). A wartime romance which tells of a woman's bravery, endurance and enterprise, both in the Malayan jungle and in the Australian Outback where she strives to create the town of the title.

Christina Stead *For Love Alone* (Virago UK; Harcourt Brace & Co US o/p; Imprint Aus). Set largely around Sydney Harbour, where the late author grew up, this novel follows the obsessive Teresa Hawkins, a poor but artistic girl from a large, unconventional family, who scrounges and saves to head for London and love.

Randolph Stow *The Merry-go-round in the Sea* (Penguin Aus). An endearing tale of a young boy growing up in rural Western Australia during World War II.

Kylie Tennant *Ride on Stranger* (Imprint Aus). First published in 1943, this is a humorous portrait of Sydney between the two world wars, seen through the eyes of newcomer Shannon Hicks.

Patrick White Considered dense and symbolic – even visionary (though some claim misogynistic) – White's novels can be heavy going, but try and plough through *Voss*, *A Fringe of Leaves* or *The Twyborn Affair* (all Penguin), the last a contemporary exploration of ambiguous sexuality.

Poetry and anthologies

Phillip Adams and Patrice Newell *The Penguin Book of Australian Jokes* (Penguin Aus). An excellent introduction to the Australian sense of humour, divided into twenty sections close to the nation's heart, among them "A Sporting Chance", "The Work Ethic" and "History and the Yarts". You'll probably need a local to explain a lot of the references.

Don Anderson (ed) *65–95 Contemporary Classics* (Vintage Aus). One of the country's most eminent literary critics chooses the best of recent Australian short writing, from Glenda Adams to Tim Winton.

Carmel Bird (ed) *The Penguin Century of Australian Stories* (Penguin Aus). 130 years of short-story writing, from Henry Lawson to Helen Garner and beyond. Ideal interstate bus companion.

Les Murray *Subhuman Redneck Poems* (Carcanet Press UK; FS&G US; Duffy & Snelgrove Aus). A collection by the outspoken, larger than life and internationally recognized Australian poet, who lives on a farm in the New South Wales bush.

Dale Spender (ed) *The Penguin Anthology of Australian Women's Writing* (Penguin UK o/p, Aus). A brick-sized book containing all the best of Australian women's writing, from Elizabeth Macarthur to Germaine Greer.

John Tranter and Philip Mead (eds) *The Penguin Book of Modern Australian Poetry* (Penguin Aus). Poetry has a popular and active appeal Down Under; the twentieth century's best are collected in this anthology.

Aboriginal writing

Faith Bandler *Welour, My Brother* (Wild & Wooley Aus o/p). A novel by a well-known black activist describing a boy's early life in Queensland, and the tensions of a racially mixed community.

John Muk Muk Burke *Bridge of Triangles* (University of Queensland Press Aus). Powerful, landscape-driven images in this tale of a mixed-race child growing up unable to associate with either side of his heritage, but refusing to accept the downward spiral into despair and alcoholism adopted by those around him.

Evelyn Crawford *Over My Tracks* (Penguin Aus). Told to Chris Walsh, this oral autobiography is the story of a formidable woman, from her 1930s childhood among the red sandhills of Yantabulla, through her Outback struggles as a mother of fourteen children, to her tireless work, late in life, with Aboriginal students, combating prejudice with education.

Nene Gare *The Fringe Dwellers* (Sun Aus o/p). A story of an Aboriginal family on the edge of town and society.

Ruby Langford *Don't Take Your Love to Town* (Penguin Aus). An autobiography demonstrating a black woman's courage and humour in the face of tragedy and poverty lived out in northern New South Wales and the inner city of Sydney.

Sally Morgan *My Place* (Virago UK; Little Brown US; Fremantle Arts Centre Press Aus). A widely acclaimed and best-selling account of a Western Australian woman's discovery of her black roots.

David Mowaljarlai and Jutta Malnic *Yorro Yorro* (Magabala Books Aus). Starry-eyed photographer Malnic's musings while recording sacred Wandjina sites in the west Kimberley and, more interestingly, Mowaljarlai's account of his upbringing and Ngarinyin tribal lore.

Mudrooroo *Wildcat Falling* (Angus & Robertson Aus). The first novel by an Aboriginal writer to be published (in 1965), this is the story of a black teenage delinquent coming of age in the 1950s. *Doctor Wooreddy's Prescription for Enduring the Ending of the World* (Hyland House Aus) details the attempted annihilation of the Tasmanian Aborigines. Mudrooroo's three latest novels – *The Kwinkan* (1995), *The Undying* (1998) and *Underground* (1999) – are part of his magic-realist Master of Ghost Dreaming series.

Oodgeroo Noonuccal *My People* (Jacaranda Wiley Aus). A collection of verse by an established campaigning poet (previously known as Kath Walker).

Paddy Roe *Gularabulu* (Fremantle Arts Centre Press Aus). Stories from the west Kimberley, both traditional myths and tales of a much more recent origin.

Kim Scott *Benang* (FACP Aus). Infuriated at reading the words of A.O. Neville, Protector of Aborigines in Western Australia in the 1930s, who planned to "breed out" Aborigines from Australia, author Scott wrote this powerful tale of Nyoongar history using Neville's own themes to overturn his elitist arguments.

Sam Watson *The Kadaitcha Song* (Viking Penguin US o/p; Penguin Aus). A brutal, fast-paced thriller; a modern parable of warring good and evil, mixed with ancient sorcery.

Archie Weller *The Day of the Dog* (Allen & Unwin Aus). Weller's violent first novel came out in an angry burst after being released, at 23, from incarceration in Broome jail. The protagonist, in a similiar situation, is pressured back into a criminal world by his Aboriginal peers and by police harassment. Searing pace and forceful writing. His second novel, *Land of the Golden*

Clouds (Allen & Unwin Aus), is an epic science fiction fantasy, set 3000 years in the future, which portrays an Australia devastated by a nuclear holocaust and populated by warring tribes.

Specialist and wildlife guides

Jack Absalom *Safe Outback Travel* (Five Mile Press Aus). A new edition of the bible for Outback driving and camping, full of sensible precautions and handy tips for preparation and repair.

Jean-Paul Bruneteau *Tukka: Real Australian Food* (Angus & Robertson Aus). The chef, who arrived in Australia in 1967 as a child from France, is passionate about the use and understanding of native Australian foods. This is more than just a cookbook, being a wide-ranging combination of well-researched history and botany as well.

The Great Barrier Reef (Reader's Digest UK). A complete rundown on the Reef, lucid and lavishly illustrated. Available in coffee-table format and in a slighter, more portable, edited edition.

Leigh Hemmings *Great Australian Bike Rides* (Mountaineer Books UK, US; Simon & Schuster Aus). A detailed illustrated guide, with gradient profiles and maps plus sections on packing and maintenance.

Tim Low *Bush Tucker: Australia's Wild Food Harvest* (HarperCollins Aus) and *Wild Food Plants of Australia* (Angus & Robertson UK). Guides to the bountiful supply of bushtucker that was once the mainstay of the Aboriginal diet; the latter is pocket-sized and contains clear photographs of over 180 plants, describing their uses.

Mark Shields and Huon Hooke *The Penguin Good Australian Wine Guide* (Penguin Aus). Released every year in Australia, this is a handy book for a wine buff to buy on the ground, with the best wines and prices detailed to help navigate you around the bottle shop.

Peter and Pat Slater *Field Guide to Australian Birds* (Weldon Aus). Pocket-sized, and the easiest to use of the many available guides to Australian birds.

Tyrone Thomas Regional bushwalking guides (Hill of Content Aus). A series of ten local guides (often updated), which make excellent trail companions.

Mark Warren *Atlas of Australian Surfing* (HarperCollins Aus). A comprehensive guide to riding the best of Australia's waves.

Australian English

The colourful variant of Australian English, or strine (which is how "Australian" is pronounced with a very heavy Australian accent), has its origins in the archaic cockney and Irish of the colony's early convicts as well as the adoption of words from the many Aboriginal languages. For such a vast country, the accent barely varies to the untutored ear; from Tasmania to the northwest you'll find little variation in the national drawl, with its curious, interrogative ending to sentences – although Queenslanders are noted for their slow delivery. One of the most consistent tendencies of strine is to abbreviate words and then stick an "-o" or, more commonly, an "-ie" on the end: as in "bring your cozzie to the barbie this arvo" (bring your swimming costume to the barbecue this afternoon). This informality extends to the frequent use of "bloody", "bugger" and "bastard", the latter two used affectionately. Attempting to abuse someone by calling them a bastard will most likely end up in an offer of a beer. There's also an endearing tendency to genderize inanimate objects as, for example, "she's buggered, mate" (your inanimate object is beyond repair) or "do 'im up nice and tight" (be certain that your inanimate object is well affixed).

The popularity of dire Australian TV soap operas has seen strine spread overseas, much as Americanisms have pervaded the English-speaking world. Popular strinisms such as "hang a U-ey" (make a U-turn) and the versatile and agreeable "no worries" are now commonly used outside Australia.

The country has its own excellent Macquarie Dictionary, the latest edition of which is the ultimate authority on the current state of Australian English. What follows is our own essential list.

Akubra Wide-brimmed felt hat; a brand name.

Anzac Australia and New Zealand Army Corps; every town has a memorial to Anzac casualties from both World Wars.

Arvo Afternoon.

Back o' Bourke Outback.

Banana bender Resident of Queensland.

Barbie Barbecue.

Battler Someone who struggles to make a living, as in "little Aussie battler".

Beg yours? Excuse me, say again?

Beaut! or **you beauty!** Exclamation of delight.

Beyond the Black Stump Outback; back of beyond.

Billabong Waterhole in dry riverbed.

Billy Cooking pot.

Bitumen Sealed road as opposed to dirt road.

Blowies Blow flies.

Bludger Someone who does not pull their weight, or a scrounger – as in "dole bludger".

Blue Fight; also a red-haired person.

Blundstones Leather, elastic-sided workmen's boots, now also a fashion item in some circles. Often shortened to "blundies".

Bonzer Good, a good thing.

Bottle shop Off-licence or liquor store.

Brumby Feral horse.

Buckley's No chance; as in "hasn't got a Buckley's".

Bugs Moreton Bay bug – type of crayfish indigenous to southern Queensland.

Bunyip Monster of Aboriginal legend; bogeyman.

Burl Give it a go; as in "give it a burl".

Bush Unsettled country area.

Bushranger Runaway convict; nineteenth-century outlaw.

Bushwhacker Someone lacking in social graces, a hick.

BYO Bring your own. Restaurant which allows you to bring your own alcohol.

Chook Chicken.

Chunder Vomit.

Cocky Small farmer, cow cocky, dairy farmer.

To come the raw prawn To try and deceive or make a fool of someone.

Coo-eee! Aboriginal long-distance greeting, now widely adopted as a kind of "yoo hoo!"

Corroboree Aboriginal ceremony.

Cozzies Bathers, swimmers, togs; swimming costume.

Crim Criminal.

Crook Sick or broken.

Crow eater Resident of South Australia.

Cut lunch Sandwiches.

Dag Nerd

Daggy Unattractive.

Daks or **strides** Trousers/pants.

Dam A man-made body of water or reservoir; not just the dam itself.

Damper Soda bread cooked in a pot on embers.

Dekko To look at; as in "take a dekko at this".

Deli Delicatessen, corner shop or sandwich bar.

Derro Derelict or destitute person.

Didgeridoo Droning musical instrument made from a termite-hollowed branch.

Digger Old-timer, especially an old soldier.

Dill Idiot.

Dilly bag Aboriginal carry-all made of bark, or woven or rigged twine.

Dinkum True, genuine, honest.

Disposal store Store that sells used army and navy equipment, plus camping gear.

Dob in To tell on someone; as in "she dobbed him in".

Drizabone Voluminous waxed cotton raincoat, originally designed for horse riding.

Drongo Fool.

Drover Cowboy or station hand.

Dunny Outside pit toilet.

Esky Portable, insulated box to keep food or beer cold.

Fair dinkum or **Dinky di** Honestly, truly.

Fossick To search for gold or gems in abandoned diggings.

Galah Noisy or garrulous person.

Galvo Corrugated iron.

Garbo Garbage or refuse collector.

G'day Hello, hi.

Gibber Rock or boulder.

Give away To give up or resign; as in "I used to be a garbo but I gave it away".

Grog Alcoholic drink, usually beer.

Gub, Gubbah Aboriginal terms for a white person.

Gutless wonder Coward.

Hoon A yob, delinquent.

Humpy Temporary shelter used by Aborigines and early pioneers.

Jackeroo Male station hand.

Jilleroo Female station hand.

Joey Baby kangaroo still in the pouch (also, less familiarly, a baby koala).

Koorie Collective name for Aboriginal people from southeastern Australia.

Larrikin Mischievous youth.

Lay by Practice of putting a deposit on goods until they can be fully paid for.

Lollies Sweets or candy.

Manchester Linen goods.

Mate A sworn friend, as essential as beer to the Australian stereotype.

Mexicans Residents of New South Wales and Victoria.

Milk bar Corner shop, and often a small café.

Moleskins Strong cotton trousers worn by bushmen.

Never Never Outback, wilderness.

New Australian Recent immigrants; often a euphemism for Australians of non-British descent.

No worries That's OK; It doesn't matter; Don't mention it.

Ocker Uncultivated Australian male.

Op shop Short for "Opportunity Shop"; a charity shop (UK) or thrift store (USA).

Outback Remote, unsettled regions of Australia.

Paddock Field.

Panel van Van with no rear windows and front seating only.

Pashing Kissing or snogging, often in the back of a panel van.

Perve To leer or act as a voyeur; as in "What are you perving at?"

Piss Beer.

Piss head Drunkard.
Pissed Drunk.
Pokies One-armed bandits; gambling machines.
Pommie or **Pom** Person of English descent – not necessarily abusive.
Rapt Very pleased, delighted.
Ratbag An eccentric person; also a term of mild abuse.
Ratshit or **Shithouse** How you feel after a night on the piss.
Rego Vehicle registration document.
Ridji Didge The real thing or genuine article.
Ripper! Rather old-fashioned exclamation of enthusiasm.
Rollies Roll-up cigarettes.
Root Vulgar term for sexual congress.
Rooted To be very tired or to be beyond repair; as in "she's rooted, mate" – your [car] is irreparable.
Ropable Furious to the point of requiring restraint.
Rouseabout An unskilled labourer in a shearing-shed.
Sandgroper Resident of Western Australia.
She'll be right or **She'll be apples** Everything will work out fine.
Shoot through To pass through or leave hurriedly.
Shout To pay for someone, or to buy a round of drinks; as in "it's your shout, mate".
Sickie To take a day off work due to (sometimes alleged) illness; as in "to pull a sickie".
Singlet Sleeveless cotton vest. The archetypal Australian singlet, in navy, is produced by Bonds.
Skivvy Polo neck.
Slab 24-can carton of beer.
Smoko Tea break.
Snag Sausage.

Speedo Famous Australian brand of athletic swimming costume; speedos (or sluggos) commonly refers to men's swimming briefs, as opposed to swimming trunks.
Spunk Attractive or sexy person of either gender; as in "what a spunk!" Can also be used as an adjective: spunky.
Squatter Historical term for early settlers who took up public land as their own.
Station Very large pastoral property or ranch.
Sticky beak Nosy person, or to be nosy; as in "let's have a sticky beak".
Stockman Cowboy or station hand.
Stubby Small bottle of beer.
Swag Large bedroll, or one's belongings.
Tall poppy Someone who excels or is eminent. "Cutting down tall poppies" is to bring overachievers back to earth – a national pastime.
Thongs Flip-flops or sandals.
Throw a wobbly Lose your temper.
Tinnie Can of beer, or a small aluminium boat.
Ute Short for "utility" vehicle; pick-up truck.
Wacko! Exclamation of enthusiasm.
Walkabout Temporary migration undertaken by Aborigines; also has the wider meaning of a journey.
Gone walkabout To go missing.
Warm fuzzies Feeling of contentment.
Waxhead Surfer.
Weatherboard Wooden house.
Whinger Someone who complains – allegedly common among Poms.
Wog Derogatory description for those of Mediterranean descent.
Wowser Killjoy.
Yabber To talk or chat.
Yabbie Freshwater crayfish.
Yakka Work, as in "hard yakka".
Yobbo Uncouth person.

index

and small print

Index

Map entries are in colour

INDEX

INDEX

N

INDEX

Twenty Years of Rough Guides

In the summer of 1981, Mark Ellingham, Rough Guides' founder, knocked out the first guide on a typewriter, with a group of friends. Mark had been travelling in Greece after university, and couldn't find a guidebook that really answered his needs. There were heavyweight cultural guides on the one hand – good on museums and classical sites but not on beaches and tavernas – and on the other hand student manuals that were so caught up with how to save money that they lost sight of the country's significance beyond its role as a place for a cool vacation. None of the guides began to address Greece as a country, with its natural and human environment, its politics and its contemporary life.

Having no urgent reason to return home, Mark decided to write his own guide. It was a guide to Greece that tried to combine some erudition and insight with a thoroughly practical approach to travellers' needs. Scrupulously researched listings of places to stay, eat and drink were matched by careful attention to detail on everything from Homer to Greek music, from classical sites to national parks and from nude beaches to monasteries. Back in London, Mark and his friends got their Rough Guide accepted by a farsighted commissioning editor at the publisher Routledge and it came out in 1982.

The Rough Guide to Greece was a student scheme that became a publishing phenomenon. The immediate success of the book – shortlisted for the Thomas Cook award – spawned a series that rapidly covered dozens of countries. The Rough Guides found a ready market among backpackers and budget travellers, but soon acquired a much broader readership that included older and less impecunious visitors. Readers relished the guides' wit and inquisitiveness as much as the enthusiastic, critical approach that acknowledges everyone wants value for money – but not at any price.

Rough Guides soon began supplementing the "rougher" information – the hostel and low-budget listings – with the kind of detail that independent-minded travellers on any budget might expect. These days, the guides – distributed worldwide by the Penguin group – include recommendations spanning the range from shoestring to luxury, and cover more than 200 destinations around the globe. Our growing team of authors, many of whom come to Rough Guides initially as outstandingly good letter-writers telling us about their travels, are spread all over the world, particularly in Europe, the USA and Australia. As well as the travel guides, Rough Guides publishes a series of dictionary phrasebooks covering two dozen major languages, an acclaimed series of music guides running the gamut from Classical to World Music, a series of music CDs in association with World Music Network, and a range of reference books on topics as diverse as the Internet, Pregnancy and Unexplained Phenomena. Visit www.roughguides.com to see what's cooking.

Rough Guide Credits

Text editors: Claire Saunders and Geoff Howard
Series editor: Mark Ellingham
Editorial: Martin Dunford, Jonathan Buckley, Jo Mead, Kate Berens, Ann-Marie Shaw, Paul Gray, Helena Smith, Judith Bamber, Orla Duane, Olivia Eccleshall, Ruth Blackmore, Gavin Thomas, Alexander Mark Rogers, Polly Thomas, Joe Staines, Richard Lim, Duncan Clark, Peter Buckley, Lucy Ratcliffe, Clifton Wilkinson, Alison Murchie, Matthew Teller (UK); Andrew Rosenberg, Stephen Timblin, Yuki Takagaki, Richard Koss (US)
Production: Susanne Hillen, Andy Hilliard, Link Hall, Helen Prior, Julia Bovis, Michelle Draycott, Katie Pringle, Mike Hancock, Zoë Nobes, Rachel Holmes, Andy Turner

Cartography: Melissa Baker, Maxine Repath, Ed Wright, Katie Lloyd-Jones
Picture research: Louise Boulton, Sharon Martins
Online: Kelly Cross, Anja Mutic-Blessing, Jennifer Gold, Audra Epstein, Suzanne Welles (US)
Finance: John Fisher, Gary Singh, Edward Downey, Mark Hall, Tim Bill
Marketing & Publicity: Richard Trillo, Niki Smith, David Wearn, Chloë Roberts, Birgit Hartmann, Claire Southern (UK); Simon Carloss, David Wechsler, Kathleen Rushforth (US)
Administration: Tania Hummel, Demelza Dallow, Julie Sanderson

Publishing Information

This fifth edition published October 2001 by
Rough Guides Ltd,
62–70 Shorts Gardens, London WC2H 9AH
4th Floor, 345 Hudson St, New York, NY 10014
Reprinted May 2002

Distributed by the Penguin Group
Penguin Books Ltd,
80 The Strand, London WC2R ORL
Penguin Putnam, Inc.
375 Hudson Street, NY 10014, USA
Penguin Books Australia Ltd,
487 Maroondah Highway, PO Box 257,
Ringwood, Victoria 3134, Australia
Penguin Books Canada Ltd,
10 Alcorn Avenue, Toronto, Ontario,
Canada M4V 1E4
Penguin Books (NZ) Ltd,
182–190 Wairau Road, Auckland 10,
New Zealand
Typeset in Bembo and Helvetica to an
original design by Henry Iles.

Printed in Italy by LegoPrint S.p.A
© Margo Daly, Anne Dehne, David Leffman
and Chris Scott 2001

1216pp – Includes index
A catalogue record for this book is available
from the British Library

ISBN 1-85828-723-5

The publishers and authors have done their
best to ensure the accuracy and currency of
all the information in **The Rough Guide to
Australia**, however, they can accept no
responsibility for any loss, injury, or
inconvenience sustained by any traveller as a
result of information or advice contained in
the guide.

Help us update

We've gone to a lot of effort to ensure that
the fifth edition of **The Rough Guide to
Australia** is accurate and up-to-date.
However, things change – places get
"discovered", opening hours are notoriously
fickle, restaurants and rooms raise prices or
lower standards. If you feel we've got it
wrong or left something out, we'd like to
know, and if you can remember the address,
the price, the time, the phone number, so
much the better.

We'll credit all contributions, and send a
copy of the next edition (or any other
Rough Guide if you prefer) for the best
letters. Everyone who writes to us and isn't
already a subscriber will receive a copy of
our full-colour twice-yearly newsletter.
Please mark letters: "**Rough Guide
Australia Update**" and send to: Rough
Guides, 62–70 Shorts Gardens, London
WC2H 9AH, or Rough Guides, 4th Floor,
345 Hudson St, New York, NY 10014. Or
send an email to:
mail@roughguides.co.uk or
mail@roughguides.com

Acknowledgements

Margo Daly Thanks as ever to my family, for their help and support, especially Mum, Janine and Mike, and to Lila, my happy little research companion. For super organization, patience, good humour and calm, a big thank you to our editor, Claire Saunders.

David Leffman For my father-in-law Jim Shand, the former Sergeant Bilko of Manus Island, who came along to Cape York in the passenger seat and spent eight hours a day for two weeks telling me tall tales and true of a very misspent youth, without once repeating himself. They don't make them like you any more matey. Thanks too to everyone who helped out along the way with accommodation, conversation, and – Paul – alcohol. And a tip of the hat to the cassowary and tree kangaroos that finally put in appearances; Mark, Deb and MAD for good times blowing bubbles; and the owners of the yacht *Severence* for unintentionally providing a great dive site.

Nicky Agate Thanks to Peter Burke for the wheels, Richard McCleod and Silke Kerwick for the beds, Rob & Lois Nixon for the fine wine and labradors and Peter & Kathy at Ocean Yachtsmaster for defying the weather and insisting I had fun. Also to Claire Saunders for being the most patient editor

known to woman, and to my parents for remaining calm in times of mental disarray – cheers.

Matthew Hall Thanks to Rolf Dülks at YHA Australia, Jeff Baker for playing Mal, Mike and Mal for inspiration, Dave at Wittenoom, HRH Prince Leonard, the staff at Darwin Central, and Susan.

Ian Osborn Thanks to David Beard in Adelaide, the staff at Adelaide Central YHA and Kangaroo Island Sealink Ferries.

Stephen Townshend Thanks to Annalisa Giuduci, whose wherewithal and local knowledge greatly helped.

Rosie Waitt and Tim Dub Thanks to Delia Nicholls of Tourism Tasmania, all those too-many-to-list Tasmanians who made us feel welcome, and Margo Daly for an opportunity, some advice and being Margo.

In addition, the editor would like to thank all those involved in producing this book, in particular Link Hall for expert and unruffled typesetting and layout, Ed Wright for some lovely maps, Sharon Martins for fabulous picture research, Russell Walton for proofreading, Ruth Blackmore for extra Basics research and Kate Berens for overseeing it all so brilliantly.

Readers' letters

Our thanks to everyone who has contributed letters, comments, accounts and suggestions over the years, and especially to this 2001 edition. In particular: John Abbott, Katy and Greg Adams, Irene Allan, Lise Andreasen, Justin Atkin, P.D. Authers, Alison Bate, Lynne Bateman, Giles Bearder, Meabh Ni Bhuinneain, Mark Blakemore, Mrs C. de Bone, Michael Bowman, Jenni & Harley Boyd, William Brace, Carol Brown, Alastair Burt, Alexander Buttle, Sue Byron-Swire, Lyn & Graham Campbell, Shelby Campbell, Stephen Churches, Alex Cobley, Ruth Cohen, Nicole Collins, Alex Comerford, Helen Cowan, Tommy Cradock, John R. Dean, Joe DiGeorgio, Adam Dimech, Sarah Dunn, Mark Edwards, Nolle Egan, Phillip Ellis, Sue Emmott, Amanda Evans, Lucy Feather, Gwenda Gedye-High, Cordelia Griffiths, Dennis Gullan, Ben Gunn, Alistair Hamilton, Gary Hardy, Kate Harpwood, Jean Harris, Sheila Harry, Barb & Rob Haughey, Vicky Hill, Willie Holohan, Bronwen Holden, David Holzer, Claire & Geoff Hurlock, Janet & Steve Hutchinson, Robert Hutchinson, Odile Jackson, Uta Jankowiak, Lucy King, Brendan Kirwan, Kristi & Geoff Layton, Gerry van der Lee, Martin Lewis, R.M.J. Lombardi, Katrina Long, Jo Mason, Stella Marshall, Karlie May, Michael Miles, Jason Miller, Louise Misford, Vera De Moor, Di Murphy, Nana Nehrbaß, Michelle O'Connor, Andrew Phillips, Jebby Phillips, Michael Raskop, Carol Reed, Sophie Riddington, Chrissy Riley, Jeffrey V. Robson, Shelley Russell, Paola Sassi, Peter Schinkel, Robert Sessions, Ron Simmonds, Helena Smith, Vanessa Smith-Holburn, Angela Squires, Jane Stevens, Russell & Debbie Stone, Paul Timblick, Darren Tomlinson, Annette Turner, Micheal Weatherhead, Alan Weiley, Julian Wellings, Louise Whitley, Helen Wiseman, Adrian Wood.

Photo credits

The ideas expressed in this code were developed by and for independent travellers.

Learn About The Country You're Visiting

Start enjoying your travels before you leave by tapping into as many sources of information as you can.

The Cost Of Your Holiday

Think about where your money goes - be fair and realistic about how cheaply you travel. Try and put money into local peoples' hands; drink local beer or fruit juice rather than imported brands and stay in locally owned accommodation. Haggle with humour and not aggressively. Pay what something is worth to you and remember how wealthy you are compared to local people.

Embrace The Local Culture

Open your mind to new cultures and traditions - it will transform your experience. Think carefully about what's appropriate in terms of your clothes and the way you behave. You'll earn respect and be more readily welcomed by local people. Respect local laws and attitudes towards drugs and alcohol that vary in different countries and communities. Think about the impact you could have on them.

Exploring The World – The Travellers' Code

Being sensitive to these ideas means getting more out of your travels - and giving more back to the people you meet and the places you visit.

Minimise Your Environmental Impact

Think about what happens to your rubbish - take biodegradable products and a water filter bottle. Be sensitive to limited resources like water, fuel and electricity. Help preserve local wildlife and habitats by respecting local rules and regulations, such as sticking to footpaths and not standing on coral.

Don't Rely On Guidebooks

Use your guidebook as a starting point, not the only source of information. Talk to local people, then discover your own adventure!

Be Discreet With Photography

Don't treat people as part of the landscape, they may not want their picture taken. Ask first and respect their wishes.

We work with people the world over to promote tourism that benefits their communities, but we can only carry on our work with the support of people like you. For membership details or to find out how to make your travels work for local people and the environment, visit our website.

www.tourismconcern.org.uk

TourismConcern
Campaigning for Ethical and Fairly Traded Tourism

Will you have enough stories to tell your grandchildren?

©2000 Yahoo! Inc.

Yahoo! Travel